GENEALOGICAL, BURIAL, AND SERVICE DATA FOR REVOLUTIONARY WAR PATRIOTS BURIED IN VIRGINIA

SECOND EDITION

MYRON E. LYMAN, SR.,
Compiler and Editor

With
Dr Kenneth L. Hawkins,
Debra L. Mills (DAR), Laura E. Ross

Northumberland
Historical Press
NHP

Northumberland Historical Press

ISBN: 978-1-957928-17-3
Library of Congress Number: 2021950251

Printed in the United States of America

CONTENTS

DEDICATION

To the patriots of the Revolutionary War for their sacrifices to achieve this nation's independence and thus provide its citizens with the liberties and freedoms we all enjoy today.

To the descendants of the patriots identified within this publication and to the chapters within the Virginia Society, Sons of the American Revolution that hopefully will take the initiative to place suitable gravestones and Revolutionary War markers on these identified burial sites, for these are memorials to their struggles and sufferings in the pursuit of our liberty and visitors to these burial sites will know that they have been remembered and honored in ceremonies and have not been forgotten.

To the members of the Virginia Society, Sons of the American Revolution and to members of other SAR divisions that assisted in making this publication possible.

To all the VASSAR presidents and executive councils that for several years have enthusiastically supported this endeavor by approving annual budgets to cover expenses.

ACKNOWLEDGEMENTS 2016 PUBLICATION

For many years the presidents and their executive councils of the Virginia Society, Sons of the American Revolution have all voted favorably to budget the funding needed to make this publication possible. I thank them dearly for doing so.

Special thanks is given to compatriot John Abbott of the Colonel Fielding Chapter, VASSAR for merging the JLARC (Joint Legislative Audit and Review Commission) of the Virginia General Assembly's Special Report: *Preservation of Revolutionary War Gravesites*, containing over 2200 veteran gravesites in Virginia into the spreadsheet of veteran and patriot graves maintained by VASSAR's Revolutionary War Graves Committee.

I thank my three assistant editors for their very important contributions to make this publication possible. The late Craig M. Kilby reviewed many marriage and pension sources that added genealogical information to the publication. Laura Ross posted the spreadsheet with all the additional information found, provided a lot of editing time, and prepared Appendix F, the Index of non-patriot names. Karen Hart converted the spreadsheet to the text format, prepared Appendix A and B and used her skills in finalizing a camera ready copy for the publisher.***

Thanks goes to the VASSAR chapter graves chairmen that provided me numerous graves registry forms which furnished information on many of the patriots.
The Virginia Society, War of the War of1812 in the Commonwealth of Virginia provided a large amount of cemetery books and other burial sources that were used to identify patriot burials. This contribution saved VASSAR, and me the expense of procuring these sources.

And thanks is given to several members of VASSAR who provided me valuable details about their patriot ancestors that are used in this report.
Myron E. Lyman, Sr.
Compiler/Editor
August 2016

ACKNOWLEDGEMENTS SECOND EDITION

For this edition the thanks goes to Laura Ross again for editing patriot paragraphs and adding GPS readings in Appendix B; to Dr Kenneth L Hawkins for preparing Appendix F and reviewing Appendix A; and to Debra Mills for obtaining SAR patriot numbers from NSSAR's Patriot Research System(PRS) for some of the patriots.
Much material regarding patriot burials in Virginia was submitted to me from many VASSAR members. Especially useful were their submissions to up-date the PRS.

Myron E. Lyman, Sr.
Compiler/Editor
September 2021

PREFACE 2016 PUBLICATION

This project of identifying the burial places of Revolutionary War patriots in Virginia commenced in late 2001 when the Joint Legislative Audit and Review Commission (JLARC) of the Virginia General Assembly published its special report, *Preservation of Revolutionary War Veteran Gravesites,* House Document No. 42. It listed more than 2200 veteran graves in Virginia. The committee listed 127 sources to support its findings. The main supporting ones were reports from the National Society, Sons of the American Revolution (NSSAR), 1993 and 2000 Revolutionary Graves Registers and the National Society Daughters of the American Revolution, (NSDAR) Senate Documents 1900-1974 and their reports from NSDAR Historian General. The JLARC also received numerous reports from city/county historical societies throughout Virginia.

This publication did not include patriots, defined by the NSSAR and NSDAR as those individuals that performed public service during the war period at the city, county or state level or were supporting the cause by providing material or financial support. Basically the latter was determined if they submitted a claim for the value of the goods or service provided or if it was taken from them by military units.

A project for many years by NSSAR was for state chapters and SAR members to send in graves registration forms for Revolutionary War veteran and patriot burials they found in cemeteries in cities and counties supported by their chapter. These were collected by a state chairman and after retaining a file copy were forwarded to the NSSAR chairman. Since 2001, the Virginia state chairman was William (Bill) Simpson until I, the compiler of this publication, took over the files from him in 2005.

As compiler, I merged these graves registrations which contained both veterans and patriots into the listings of those veterans identified in the JLARC report. This publication as of August 2016 contains 4164 veteran and patriot burials in Virginia and each individual is called a patriot. I felt it was necessary to provide some genealogical information in the publication, but it was also necessary to limit how much it contained as for some patriots a whole page or more could be easily written. Thus, I set the parameters that it would contain only the names and birth and death dates and places of the patriot's parents and the names of his spouses and her parent's birth and death dates and include as well a very brief summary of his major noteworthy accomplishments after the war was over. To this end, a review of some obituaries, estate records and marriage records was deemed necessary and conducted. The various sources used for this additional information are listed in Appendix E.

Soon after the project began I realized that funding was necessary to procure the necessary service and burial sources and to record the detailed information on spreadsheets. Fortunately, the War of 1812 Society in Virginia, in order to produce their book on War of 1812 burials in Virginia in which I was also the compiler, had purchased cemetery source material such as books, computer disks, etc., which contained Revolutionary War veteran service and burial data. This saved a great expense for VASSAR. To speed up the finalization of the project, a data input person was hired.

It was Craig M. Kilby (now deceased), of Lancaster County, Virginia, who had assisted me with the War of 1812 publication. In addition to being a data input person, he also provided some professional genealogical services and editing. Also hired for data input, editing and preparing a by-name index was Laura E Ross. And for conversion of the spreadsheet to paragraphs, formatting the entries, and preparing the final product, Karen Hart was employed.

Like any work of this magnitude, there are no doubt some errors and omissions. With more extensive research, up-dates for content, additions, deletions and corrections will be identified. These should be saved for future revisions. In other words this is a basic start to a more complete and finalized version to be publicized by the society in the future. For example I did not have the time or resources to obtain militia records from all court records at each city/county in Virginia. The society is encouraged to obtain these and to review the sources I have used in Appendix C and D and to find additional source material. To gather more information about each patriot the Society Graves Chairman warmly welcomes any and all up-dates.

Myron E. Lyman, Sr.
Compiler/Editor

PREFACE SECOND EDITION

This second edition is adding 736 new patriots bringing the total to 4900. Hundreds of the existing patriot write-ups have been expanded with new burial information; additional genealogical data on parents of the patriot, his spouses and her parents; and whether the patriot is on NSSAR's PRS. Also each patriot paragraph now indicates whether his gravesite has a grave marker and if so what type is. Also many DAR Ancestor numbers have been added. Appendix B now lists 169 new cemeteries where patriots are buried.

The illustrations now include almost all of the plaques and monuments in Virginia cemeteries where three or more patriots are buried or memorialized. In Appendix B that lists cemeteries where patriots are buried, hundreds of GPS readings have been added. All of the appendices have been up-dated with new data.

Myron E. Lyman, Sr.
Compiler/Editor

INTRODUCTION

This publication includes known burials in all Virginia Counties and Independent Cities, including the City of Alexandria which belonged to the District of Columbia during the war period. It does not include counties now in West Virginia.

EXPLANATION OF ENTRIES IN THE MAIN TEXT (pages 1-378) AND APPENDIX G:

Name, Birth, and Death

Each entry begins with surname of the patriot, followed by his first name(s), his birth date if known, place of birth if known, date of death if known, and place of death if it differs from the burial place. The many alternate spellings for some surnames are not given. Generally the spellings on the gravestones are used.

For birth years, many are derived from the age at death. Some are denoted with a "c" for "circa" before the year (e.g., b c1756). The same applies to years of death. For the most part, dates are derived from the gravestones, census records, death notices, probate records, pension and bounty land records or family records.

Rank and Service Unit ("RU" in the text)

After the name of the veteran and his birth and death information is his rank and unit. The highest rank obtained during the war period is used if known. In many instances the patriot may have obtained a higher rank after the war period which is reflected on gravestones or in other sources. This is sometimes explained further under (VI) Other Veteran Information. Some job titles like Adjutant, Aide de Camp, Quartermaster, Musician, Fifer, Drummer, Engineer and the like are used in lieu of an actual rank such as Sergeant or Lieutenant. In many cases the veteran was also a patriot by performing public service or contributing to the cause, thus his military rank is followed by the word Patriot.

Service units are a more complex matter. Only major unit assignments are generally given and the details of every assignment and when and where they served are normally not given to make the publication less voluminous. The service source code(s) (SS) in the text and the titles they refer to in Appendix C are what they are derived from. The unit assignment of the highest rank received during the war period if identified is used. In many instances the patriot may have obtained a higher rank after the war period which is reflected on gravestones or other sources

The reader should consider that many veterans served or volunteered in counties adjacent to the one in which they resided. Also, that many had service in other counties or independent cities of Virginia or in other states from which they eventually settled and were buried. Many veteran burials are not listed in this publication for this reason as further research would be needed to detect their migration to where they are buried. A sincere attempt has been made by the compiler to list the correct service. The Virginia Society, Sons of the American Revolution thus is not responsible for any errors in identifying the correct service, for listing service for those that did not have it or for not listing the burial at all. Consideration by the reader should be given to see if the service identified belongs to another person of the same name. In some instances the service selected may be for his father, son, uncle, nephew or cousin. The age of the veteran during the war period is therefore considered when making this distinction. Generally a person under the age of twenty would not attain a rank hre are many cases where only the gravestone or a death notice provided the service of the veteran.

Cemetery Name, GPS, General Location, & County/Independent City ("CEM" in the text)

These are presented in the order given above. These are self-explanatory, though it should be noted that many family cemeteries and even church graveyards may go by different names from one source to another. Further searching on the internet may provide missing GPS readings. Locations and directions may vary as well. A place name and it location known by one name in the 1930s when the Works Progress Administration volunteers did its cemetery surveys may well be different than its current name. This is especially true of urban areas. With respect to family cemeteries, the names are apt to go by many names over the course of years and the person or persons who "named" it in a publication. For example, the Thornton-Forbes-Washington cemetery in Fredericksburg was known in 1963 as "Little Falls Burying Ground." The location of course had not moved, but the name was changed.

Names of burial grounds are not the only thing subject to change. For example, the modern location of a site may well have been in Princess Anne County in the 1930s, but is now part of Virginia Beach. Appendix A gives the explanation of county formations and Independent Cities status, and from what jurisdiction they were taken, and when. Last, in terms of exact location, many of our sources were vague or even silent on the matter including those in the JLARC Report. If not known at all, the veteran is not included in this publication despite the fact the veteran may have been buried in a certain county.

A list of counties and independent cities and the cemeteries and graveyards located therein is given in Appendix B. If the GPS reading is not for the cemetery it may be preceded with GS for the gravestone. Appendix B has additional GPS readings.

Gravestones ("GS" in the text)

Items in this section are marked "Y", "N" and U" for "Yes," No," and "Unknown." This was one of the more vexing problems with this project. A stone that may have existed in 1890, or 1937, or even as late as 2011 when an earthquake destroyed many stones in Blandford Cemetery in Petersburg, may not exist today. Many times, stones were moved to another location while the body was not, or vice versa. St. John's, Shockoe Hill and Hollywood Cemeteries in Richmond are good examples. Not unheard of either is more than one stone for the same person in two different places (and in one case, the same cemetery.) Re-internments are listed where the gravestone is placed, however it does not mean the body is at this location. Some cemeteries have memorialized gravestones of persons buried at other locations. If the patriot is listed as being on a plaque or monument in the cemetery it is indicated here.

For this reason, the reader is advised to consult Appendix D which gives the sources for burials, and discussed in more detail below. Further, there are many web sites available to ascertain more up-to-date research. Many of these sites were used in the research process. But like all things, even they are ephemeral and what was here today may be gone tomorrow.

Spousal Information ("SP" in the text)

The spouse information given here comes from a variety of sources as given Appendix E. In many cases, the tombstones themselves may be the only evidence of a marriage, or even multiple marriages for both spouses. This is perhaps one of the greatest contributions to genealogy this book offers. Nevertheless, other sources for marriages were also used such as marriage notices and death notices.

When known, vital statistics (birth and death, and places, date and place of marriage, and names of parents are given, as well other biographical information about the spouse. If the reader does not find the marriage in one of the published sources in Appendix E, the information came from either the gravestone(s) itself or research provided by contributors. Every effort has been made to confirm the marriage data, though there are no doubt errors in some conclusions.

Other Veteran Information ("VI" in the text)

This section provides biographical information such as names of parents, public service, occupation, cause of death, additional military service, major noteworthy accomplishments after the war was over and other anecdotal information. The reader is encouraged to search for more biographical information. A list of the children of the soldier and his decent from ancestors is generally not given otherwise each paragraph might become voluminous. In most cases, the source for this information is given in the text. Otherwise, see Appendix E.

Some men who also served in the War of 1812, are identified, though a detailed explanation of this service is not included. A thorough search for War of 1812 service was not conducted for each patriot thus many more patriots may have had this service

Information regarding pensions and bounty land warrants (BLW) are given in this portion of the text to include when received and who received it and the identifying numbers. If the individual is not listed it does not mean he did not receive one as a complete search of records at NARA and in libraries and court records was not conducted. The reader is encouraged to procure the actual pension and bounty land records from NARA as they may contain additional information about his service and family. Copies of the records may be obtained by mail using NATF form 80 and addressed to NARA References Services Branch, General Services Administration, Washington, D.C., 20408. The reader is encouraged to procure the actual records from NARA as they may contain additional information about his service and family. More information regarding bounty land may be available from the Bureau of Land Management for the state in which was awarded. Many veterans moved and took advantage of their bounty land warrants thus will not be buried in Virginia. However in many cases they simply sold their rights to them and remained in Virginia.

Pensions ("P" in the text)

Y (yes), N (no), or unk (unknown) is given. If Y, see VI (Other Veteran Information) for details.

Bounty Land Warrants ("BLW" in the text)

Y (yes), N (no), or unk (unknown) is given. If Y, see VI (Other Veteran Information) for details.

Registered with NSSAR ("RG" in the text)

An entry of Y (yes) indicates a grave registry form has been submitted though the compiler and forwarded to NSSAR. It should be noted that the NSSAR data base has been updated with the over 2200 Virginia graves in the JLARC report so if JLARC is listed as a burial code (BS) in the text it is considered previously registered with NSSAR and any further inputs on the name should be considered an up-date. Also the same applies that if an SAR ancestor number is listed as a service source (SS) in the text it has been previously registered with NSSAR. SAR members should check NSSAR's Patriot Grave Index to see if a grave has been previously registered at http://patriot.sar.org/fmi/iwp/cgi?-db=Grave%20Registry&-loadframes.

SAR/DAR grave markers ("MK" in the text)

A Y means yes.The type of marker (SAR-DAR),   plaque or monument is indicated here.

Photo ("PH" in the text)

This section is marked "Y" for yes and "N" for no, and indicates whether the Society or a contributor provided a photograph of the gravestone. The compiler has a file on these. The reader is encouraged to search the internet cemetery sites for photographs as they are abundant but these sources are not included in this section because of possible copyrights infringements.

Service Source ("SS" in the text)

The sources for these codes are listed in Appendix C and described in detail there.

Burial Source ("BS" in the text)

The sources for these codes are listed in Appendix D and described in detail there.

Other Sources (Appendix E), Appendix F & G: Miscellaneous Notes

Personal emails, correspondence and research notes are maintained by the compiler. At the bottom of each page of the text are some general abbreviations used. The following pages show others used in the text. The By-Name index is at Appendix F. These include names other than the veteran and unit commanders listed in the text.

A sincere effort has been made to avoid errors in this publication. Errata will be found in Appendix G for additional information that arrived after the original typeset was created. The Society greatly appreciates any corrections or additions.

LIST OF ABBREVIATIONS WITHIN THE TEXT

This list does not include standard state postal code abbreviations. Unless otherwise noted, all locales are in Virginia.

abt	about
Apr	April
acct(s)	account(s)
appl	applied or application
Att	attached or attachment
Aug	August
b	born
bef	before
bet	between
Bk	book
BLW	Bounty Land Warrant
BS	Burial Source
btw	between
bur	buried
c	circa, e.g. c1796 is circa 1796
ca	circa
Capt	Captain
Cem	Cemetery
cert	certificate
C.H. or CH	Court House
Ch	Church
cnr	corner
Co	County or Company
Cos	Counties
Col	Colonel
Cont	Continental
Ct or CT	Court
d	died
DAR	Daughters of the American Revolution Society
daug	daughter
DC	District of Columbia
Dec	December
det	detached or detachment
Doc	Document
d/o	daughter of
Dr	Doctor or Drive
E	East
Enl	Enlisted or Enlistment
Ens	Ensign
ent	entered
ES	East side
Esq	Esquire
Ext	Extension
Feb	February
fr	from

LIST OF ABBREVIATIONS WITHIN THE TEXT
(Continued)

Ft	Fort
GPS	Global position system
gr	grave
GS	Gravestone
H.R.	House Resolution (US Congress)
incl	includes
Inf	Infantry
info	information
Inv	Inventory of estate
Jan	January
jct	junction
Jr	Junior
Jul	July
Jun	June
Lib	Library
LNR	Last Known Residence
Lt	Lieutenant or Light
Lt Col	Lieutenant Colonel
LVA	Library of Virginia
Maj	Major
Mar	March
mar	married
mi	mile(s)
mo(s)	month(s)
Mt	Mount
N	No or North
NARA	National Archives and Records Administration
NE	North East
Nov	November
nr	near
NS	North side
NSDAR	National Society DAR
NSSAR	National Society SAR
NW	North West
obit	obituary
Oct	October
Pen	Pension
p	page
pg	page
PO	Post Office
Recd	Received
Reg	Regiment, Registered, or Regular
Rej	Rejected
Rep	Representative

LIST OF ABBREVIATIONS WITHIN THE TEXT
(Continued)

Rev	Reverend or Revolutionary
Rev War	Revolutionary War
Rd	Road
Rt(s)	Route(s)
RW	Revolutionary War
S	South
SAR	Sons of the American Revolution Society
SE	South East
Sep	September
Sec	Section
serv	service or served in
Soc	Society
sol	soldier
Sr	Senior
St	Street or stone
SS	South side or Service Source
sub	substituted
SW	South West
TS	Tombstone
Twp	Township
U	Unknown
Unk	Unknown
UMC	United Methodist Church
US	United States
USD	United States Daughters of 1812
VASSAR	Virginia Society SAR
V.A.	Veterans Administration
vic	vicinity
vol	volume or volunteered
VMR	Virginia Militia Regiment
W	West
WS	West side
WPA	Works Progress Administration
Y	Yes
yr(s)	year(s)

LIST OF ILLUSTRATIONS

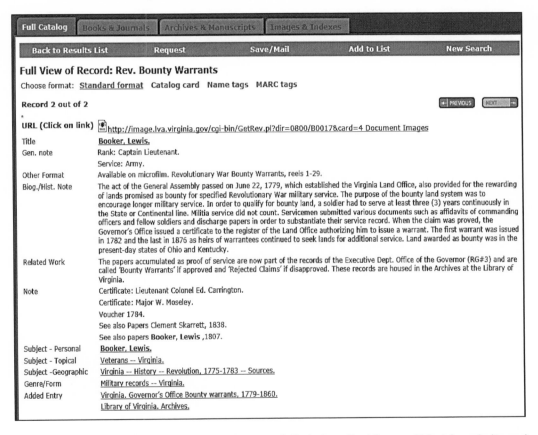

NAME Blakemore, George

AGENCY OF PAYMENT Richmond, Va

DATE OF ACT 1832

DATE OF PAYMENT 3rd qr 1851 (act 6 Apr.) Oct. 1849

DATE OF DEATH July 25, 1833

**FINAL PAYMENT VOUCHER RECEIVED FROM
THE GENERAL ACCOUNTING OFFICE**

GENERAL SERVICES ADMINISTRATION   GSA DC 70-7035   GSA DEC 69 FORM 7068

Above is a sample Revolutionary War image of a Pension Final Payment Voucher that shows a death date. The image is available on the Fold3 website and at the National Archives.

Full Catalog	Books & Journals	Archives & Manuscripts	Images & Indexes

Back to Results List	Request	Save/Mail	Add to List	New Search

Full View of Record: Rev. Bounty Warrants

Choose format: Standard format   Catalog card   Name tags   MARC tags

Record 2 out of 2   PREVIOUS   NEXT

URL (Click on link) http://image.lva.virginia.gov/cgi-bin/GetRev.pl?dir=0800/B0017&card=4 Document Images

Title	Booker, Lewis.
Gen. note	Rank: Captain Lieutenant.
	Service: Army.
Other Format	Available on microfilm. Revolutionary War Bounty Warrants, reels 1-29.
Biog./Hist. Note	The act of the General Assembly passed on June 22, 1779, which established the Virginia Land Office, also provided for the rewarding of lands promised as bounty for specified Revolutionary War military service. The purpose of the bounty land system was to encourage longer military service. In order to qualify for bounty land, a soldier had to serve at least three (3) years continuously in the State or Continental line. Militia service did not count. Servicemen submitted various documents such as affidavits of commanding officers and fellow soldiers and discharge papers in order to substantiate their service record. When the claim was proved, the Governor's Office issued a certificate to the register of the Land Office authorizing him to issue a warrant. The first warrant was issued in 1782 and the last in 1876 as heirs of warrantees continued to seek lands for additional service. Land awarded as bounty was in the present-day states of Ohio and Kentucky.
Related Work	The papers accumulated as proof of service are now part of the records of the Executive Dept. Office of the Governor (RG#3) and are called 'Bounty Warrants' if approved and 'Rejected Claims' if disapproved. These records are housed in the Archives at the Library of Virginia.
Note	Certificate: Lieutenant Colonel Ed. Carrington.
	Certificate: Major W. Moseley.
	Voucher 1784.
	See also Papers Clement Skarrett, 1838.
	See also papers Booker, Lewis ,1807.
Subject - Personal	Booker, Lewis.
Subject - Topical	Veterans -- Virginia.
Subject -Geographic	Virginia -- History -- Revolution, 1775-1783 -- Sources.
Genre/Form	Military records -- Virginia.
Added Entry	Virginia. Governor's Office Bounty warrants, 1779-1860.
	Library of Virginia. Archives.

This above record of a BLW (Bounty Land Warrant) file is from the Library of Virginia website and is derived from microfilm images. To procure the record, open Images and Indexes in the upper margin of the Full Catalog page and scroll to Revolutionary War Bounty Warrants. Then insert a surname and select the given name. The record above shows the information for Lewis Booker. Then click the URL to see the microfilm image (see next illustration).

This image of a BLW (Bounty Land Warrant) microfilm file from the Library of Virginia website obtained as shown on the previous illustration provides valuable service information of the veteran. Note that he received this in 1807 for service performed from Jan 1776 to Jan 1784.

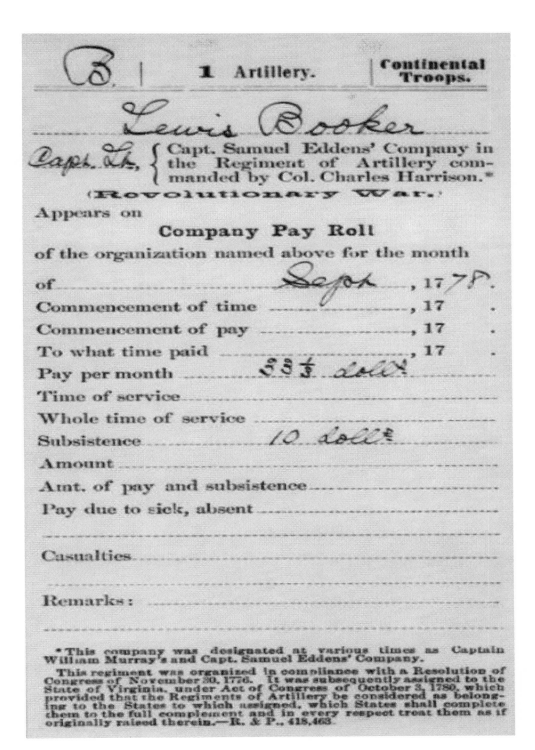

B. | **1 Artillery.** | **Continental Troops.**

Lewis Booker

Capt. Lt, { Capt. Samuel Eddens' Company in the Regiment of Artillery commanded by Col. Charles Harrison.*

(Revolutionary War.)

Appears on

Company Pay Roll

of the organization named above for the month

of .... *Sept* ......, 17 *7 8*.

Commencement of time ...., 17 .

Commencement of pay ...., 17 .

To what time paid ...., 17 .

Pay per month .... *$33 ⅓ doll?*

Time of service ....

Whole time of service ....

Subsistence .... *10 doll?*

Amount ....

Amt. of pay and subsistence ....

Pay due to sick, absent ....

Casualties ....

Remarks : ....

* This company was designated at various times as Captain William Murray's and Capt. Samuel Eddens' Company.

This regiment was organized in compliance with a Resolution of Congress of November 30, 1776. It was subsequently assigned to the State of Virginia, under Act of Congress of October 3, 1780, which provided that the Regiments of Artillery be considered as belonging to the States to which assigned, which States shall complete them to the full complement and in every respect treat them as if originally raised therein.—R. & P., 418,463.

This image of a Revolutionary War service record is available at the Fold3 website and at the National Archives.

REVOLUTIONARY WAR PATRIOTS BURIED IN VIRGINIA

AARON, Abraham Sr; b 1734; d 1816 **RU:** Patriot, Gave supplies and fixed guns **CEM:** Easley Family; GPS unk; Callands; Pittsylvania **GS:** Y **SP:** No info **VI:** No further data **P:** N **BLW:** N **RG:** Y **MK:** N **PH:** unk **SS:** DAR A000005; G pg 434; AS; SAR P-100007 **BS:** AS.

ABBOTT, Joseph; b 1762; d 1819 **RU:** Private, Served in an undetermined unit of the Virginia Cont Line long enough to be eligible for a pension and bounty land. **CEM:** Shockoe Hill; GPS 37.55190, -77.43170; 4th & Hospital Sts; Richmond City **GS:** Y **SP:** No info **VI:** No further data **P:** Unk **BLW:** unk **RG:** N **MK:** N **PH:** unk **SS:** C pg 220; E pg 1; AP Fold3 service index card CZ pg 14; **BS:** 179 #478.

ABENDSCHON (OBENSHAIN), Samuel; b 13 Jan 1754, PA; d Jul 1824 **RU:** Lieutenant/Patriot, Signed Oath of Allegiance, Berks Co, PA **CEM:** Abendschon Family; GPS unk; Nr Mill Creek Baptist; Botetourt **GS:** N **SP:** Phebe Daler **VI:** No further data **P:** unk **BLW:** unk **RG:** Y **MK:** unk **PH:** N **SS:** DAR A000227; J-NSSAR 2000 Reg; DD; SAR P-100251 **BS:** JLARC 2, 76.

ABERNATHY, John D Jr; b c1746; d Jun 1816 or 22 Nov 1824 **RU:** Soldier/Patriot, Military service not identified. Gave material aid to cause **CEM:** Flournoy; GPS unk; Rt 58; Brunswick **GS:** U **SP:** 1) Mar (c1768) Mary Brown 2) Mar (c1785) Mildred Harwell 3) Mar (25 Apr 1814 Brunswick) Molly King **VI:** No further data **P:** unk **BLW:** unk **RG:** Y **MK:** N **PH:** unk **SS:** D Vol 1 pg 161-2; AL Ct lists pg 5, 6; G pg 88, 90; SAR P-100283 **BS:** AS SAR regis.

ABERNATHY, John Sr; b 26 Mar 1723, Prince George Co; d 17 Feb 1812 **RU:** Patriot, Gave brandy and oats to cause **CEM:** Abernathy Family; GPS 36.50420, -77.88047; 400 yds W of Preswood Rd, Rt 646, 1.2 mi N of Linerty Rd, Rt 634; Brunswick **GS:** N **SP:** Lucy (-----) (c1728-7 Feb 1812) **VI:** Son of Robert A III & Mary (Harwell) Abernathy **P:** N **BLW:** N **RG:** Y **MK:** unk **PH:** unk **SS:** DAR A000241; SAR P-100284; D Vol 1 pg 154, 157 **BS:** 196.

ABNEY, John I; b 1739 Albemarle Co, d 1785 **RU:** Patriot, Gave material aid to cause in Augusta Co **CEM:** Abney Family; GPS Not determined; Springfield Lane, Fisherville; Augusta **GS:** Unk **SP:** Isabella Bodby **VI:** Son of Paul Abney (1699-1786) and Isabella (-----) **P:** N **BLW:** N **RG:** Y **MK:** N **PH:** N **SS:** AL Ct Bk pg 4 Augusta Co; SAR Graves Report submitted Aug 2019 **BS:** 196.

ABSHIRE, Abraham; b 1755, Franklin Co; d 28 Jul 1842 **RU:** Soldier, Served in Cont Army, Specifics in Sec of War Report, 1835, Pen, Vol 2, Lib VA **CEM:** Abshire; GPS unk; Boones Mill; Franklin **GS:** U **SP:** Susannah Vinson (1767-1845) **VI:** Received VA pen 6 Apr 1842 **P:** Y **BLW:** unk **RG:** Y **MK:** unk **PH:** unk **SS:** DAR A000293; E pg 2; C pg 14 ; AZ pg 234; CA; SAR P-100338 **BS:** 196.

ABYVON, George; b unk; d Bef 21 Oct 1793 **RU:** Patriot, Provided supplies of 66 rations during the war **CEM:** St Paul's Episcopal; GPS 36.84733, -76.28554; 201 St Paul's Blvd; Norfolk City **GS:** Y **SP:** Mariam (-----) Abyvon (__- bet 20 Nov 1794 & 23 Feb 1795) **VI:** Five-time Mayor of Norfolk (1754, 1767, 1771, 1776 & 1779). **P:** N **BLW:** N **RG:** N **MK:** Y SAR plaque; DAR 02 Dec 2012 **PH:** Y **SS:** CB Oath as Mayor; AK **BS:** 178-8 Jan 11.

ABYVON (ABYNON), Marrim (Miriam Manim Marrim Meriam Marsam); b unk; d bet 20 Nov 1794 to 23 Feb 1795 **RU:** Patriot, Provided supplies of 3 gallons of rum **CEM:** St Paul's Episcopal; GPS 36.84733, -76.28554; 201 St Paul's Blvd; Norfolk City **GS:** Y **SP:** George Abyvon **VI:** No further data **P:** N **BLW:** N **RG:** N **MK:** Y SAR plaque **PH:** unk **SS:** CB Gave to cause **BS:** 178-8 Jan 11.

ACKISS, John; b c1740; d aft 28 Jan1797 **RU:** Patriot, Was member of the Princess Anne Co Ct 28 July 1775 **CEM:** Old Baptist Meeting House; GPS 36.61001, -76.03494; Vic 664 Princess Anne Rd, Creeds; Virginia Beach City **GS:** Y **SP:** No info **VI:** No further data **P:** N **BLW:** N **RG:** Y **MK:** unk **PH:** unk **SS:** DAR A000321; CO pg 46; SAR P-101070 **BS:** 196 (Note FAG is incorrect burial place is unk).

ACKISS, John; b unk; d 1775 **RU:** Patriot, Gave provisions to Prince Anne Co Militia **CEM:** Skirmish at Kempsville Monument; GPS unk; Pleasant Hall; Virginia Beach City **GS:** U **SP:** No info **VI:** No further data **P:** N **BLW:** N **RG:** N **MK:** unk **PH:** unk **SS:** G pg 433 **BS:** JLARC 120.

ADAM, Paul; b unk; d 1781 **RU:** Seaman, Served on "Ville de Parisa". Died from Yorktown battle **CEM:** French Memorial; GPS 36.81944, -79.39933; Yorktown; York **GS:** U **SP:** No info **VI:** No further data **P:** unk **BLW:** unk **RG:** Y **MK:** unk **PH:** unk **SS:** J-Yorktown Historian; SAR P-101150 **BS:** JLARC 1,74.

ADAMS, Jacob; b unk; d 20 Oct 1807 **RU:** Soldier, Served in 7th Cont Line in Col John Gibson's Detachment, Capt Benjamin Bigg's Co, 1780 & 1781. Was in Battle of Guilford CH **CEM:** Adams-

RU=Rank/Unit	CEM=Cemetery	GS=Gravestone	SP=Spousal Information
VI=Other Veteran Info	P=Pension	BLW=Bounty/Land Warrant	RG=Registered Grave
MK=SAR/DAR Marker	PH=Photo	SS=Service Source	BS=Burial Source

1

Graves-Pilson Families; GPS unk; .5 mi south of Rt 717, N side of Goblintown Creek nr Fairystone Park; Patrick **GS:** U **SP:** Mary Peake (___-1809) **VI:** BLW issued 24 Jun 1783 for 200 acres **P:** unk **BLW:** Y **RG:** Y **MK:** unk **PH:** unk **SS:** A pg 284; E pg 3; F pg 3; SAR P-101298 **BS:** JLARC 30; 196.

ADAMS, James; b 3 Sep 1765, Fauquier Co, d 14 Dec 1849, Delaplane Fauquier Co **RU:** Corporal, first was a private in Armand's Corps, then promoted to corporal in Virginia's Continental Line **CEM:** Sharon; GPS 38,9692,-77.7308; loc vic jct E Federal and S Jay Sts, Middleburg; Loudoun **GS:** Unk **SP:** 1) Mar (1801) Elizabeth Brandt (1775-1840), 2) Abigail (-----) (1787-1822) **VI:** No further data **P:** N **BLW:** N **RG:** N **MK:** N **PH:** N **SS:** C Sec I, pg 115, Sec III, pg 387; Bio form submitted PRS **BS:** 196.

ADAMS, James Sr; b 1729, Goochland Co; d 15 Mar 1789 **RU:** Patriot, Gave material aid to cause **CEM:** Adams; GPS unk; Bybee; Fluvanna **GS:** U **SP:** Mar (1751) Cecily Ford, d/o William & (-----) Ford Sr. **VI:** Son of Capt Robert Sr (1689-1740) & Mourning (Lewis) (1694-1765) Adams. During the Indian Wars, James served in the VA militia under command of John Smith, taking part in Cherokee Expedition in 1760. From 1771-73, served as Justice of Peace in Albemarle Co **P:** N **BLW:** N **RG:** N **MK:** unk **PH:** unk **SS:** DAR A000542; Al Ct Bk pg 29 Fluvanna Co **BS:** 196.

ADAMS, Jesse; b NY; d 7 Nov 1781 **RU:** Soldier, Served in 2d NY Line. D Yorktown battle **CEM:** Yorktown Victory Monument Tablet; GPS 38.28350, -78.54150; Yorktown; York **GS:** U **SP:** No info **VI:** Died in Williamsburg **P:** unk **BLW:** unk **RG:** Y **MK:** unk **PH:** unk **SS:** J-Yorktown Historian; SAR P-101331 **BS:** JLARC 74.

ADAMS, John; b 21 Oct 1761, d 20 Jun 1837 **RU:** Private, Capt Porterfield's Co, Col Morgan's Rifle Regt, as of 30 Nov 1778 **CEM:** New Providence Presbyterian Church; GPS 37.95130, -79.30250 1208 New Providence Rd, Raphine; Rockbridge **GS:** Yes **SP:** 1) Jane Hutchinson (Apr 1767-1 Dec 1805), 2) Mclihenny **VI:** No further data **P:** Unk **BLW:** Unk **RG:** Y **MK:** N **PH:** N **SS:** A Part 2, Officers & Privates pg 260; E pg 3; SAR Bio Rpt submitted Aug 2019 **BS:** 196.

ADAMS, Nipper (Napier); b c1732, Prince George Co; d 1820 **RU:** Patriot, Performed public duty. Also gave material aid to cause **CEM:** Adams Family; GPS unk; See county property records for location of family; Halifax **GS:** U **SP:** 1) Lucy McEndree (McKendriee) (1735-1791) 2) Obedience Atkins (c1750-bef 1795) **VI:** Son of John & (-----) Adams (1705-1769) **P:** N **BLW:** N **RG:** Y **MK:** unk **PH:** unk **SS:** DAR A000698; Al Ct Bk pg 12 Halifax Co; CA SAR P-331517 **BS:** 197.

ADAMS, Richard, Jr; b 26 Nov 1760, King & Queen Co, d 9 Jan 1817 **RU:** 1st Lt; Rec'd in this rank; Henrico Co Militia 1 Oct 1781 **CEM:** Hollywood; GPS: 37.53560, -77.45720; 412 S Cherry St; Richmond City **GS:** Yes, lg monument with family names **SP:** 1) Elizabeth Southall Randolph of Chatsworth, widow of Peter Skipsworth Randolph, 2) Sarah Travers (Daniel) Hay, widow of Charles Hay & d/o Travers Daniel & Frances Moncure **VI:** Son of Richard Adams, Sr (1726-1800) & Elizabeth Griffin (1728-1800) Re-interried fr cem loc Richmond at NE corner 23rd St and Marshall St. He built the Adams-Chump house in Richmond **P:** N **BLW:** N **RG:** N **MK:** N **PH:** N **SS:** E pg 1; AZ pg 208 **BS:** 196.

ADAMS, Richard, Sr; b 17 May 1726, New Kent Co, d 2 Aug 1800 **RU:** Patriot performed public service 1775 Henrico Co Commissioner's Committee; represented Henrico Co at 1775 VA Convention; and served as a member of the VA state Senate 1779-1782 **CEM:** Hollywood; GPS: 37.53560, -77.45720; 412 S Cherry St; Richmond City **GS:** Yes **SP:** Mar (10 Apr 1775) Elizabeth Griffin (1728-1800), d/o Leroy Griffin & Mary Anne Bernard **VI:** Son of Ebenezer Adams (1695-13 Jun 1734) and Tabitha Cocke (1698-1760) **P:** N **BLW:** N **RG:** Y **MK:** N **PH:** N **SS:** CD; DAR A000518; SAR P-101546 **BS:** 196.

ADAMS, Robert "Old Robin"; b 1727, Henrico Co; d 1785 **RU:** Patriot, 1780 was member of Vigilance Committee that helped clear the region of outlaws and Tories. Also gave material aid to cause **CEM:** Mt Zion United Methodist; GPS unk; 5662 Red House Rd, Rustburg; Campbell **GS:** N **SP:** Mar 15 Oct 1748 to Penelope Flournoy Lynch (1734-1785) d/o Charles & Sarah (Clark) Lynch of Albemarle Co **VI:** Son of Capt Robert Adams Sr (1689-1740) & Mourning Lewis (1694-1765). One of the first Justices of Bedford Co **P:** N **BLW:** N **RG:** Y **MK:** N **PH:** N **SS:** DAR A000533; AL Ct Bk pg 27; SAR P-101553 **BS:** 196.

ADAMS, Robert Jr; b 1754 or 1750; d 1789 or 1790 **RU:** Captain, Appt Capt 24 Feb 1778 Bedford Militia. In Sep 1778 marched to Chiswell's Lead Mines on New River. In the Fall of 1780 led a Co to Peterburg **CEM:** Ward; GPS 37.05492, -79.43637; Hurt; Pittsylvania **GS:** Y **SP:** Mary (-----) **VI:** No further data **P:** unk **BLW:** unk **RG:** Y **MK:** unk **PH:** unk **SS:** DAR A000553; E pg 3; SAR P-101745 **BS:** 174, JLARC 1, 4, 36, 66, 75 ,96.

RU=Rank/Unit	CEM=Cemetery	GS=Gravestone	SP=Spousal Information
VI=Other Veteran Info	P=Pension	BLW=Bounty/Land Warrant	RG=Registered Grave
MK=SAR/DAR Marker	PH=Photo	SS=Service Source	BS=Burial Source

ADAMS, Thomas; b 1695, Pr George Co; d 1783 **RU**: Patriot, paid personal property tax, Southampton Co, 1782 considered to be partially for Rev War expenses **CEM**: Old Adams Grove; GPS not determined; loc left side of U.S. 58 East in a field nr jct with Rt 651, Adams Grove; Southampton **GS**: Unk **SP**: 1) Anne (-----), 2) Susannah Weathers **VI**: Son of Thomas Adams, Sr (1667-9 Oct 1772, Prince George Co) **P**: N **BLW**: N **RG**: N **MK**: N **PH**: N **SS**: DV, Southampton Co personal property tax listing, 1783, image 02 **BS**: 196.

ADAMS, Thomas Bowler; b 18 Sep1759, d 28 Nov 1794 **RU**; Private Probably the Thomas Adams that served in Capt Henry Young's Co, Col William Russell's 5th VA Regt shown on a payroll of Jan 1779 and served in the Cont Line for 3 years **CEM**: Hollywood; GPS: 37.53560,-77.45720; 412 S Cherry St; Richmond City **GS**: Unk **SP**: mar (30 Jan 1790) Sarah Morrison (__-13 May 1794) **VI**: Son of Richard Adams (1726-1800) & Elizabeth Griffin (1728-1800) **P**: Unk **BLW**: Unk **RG**: N **MK**: N **PH**: N **SS**: CN pg 24, AP Fold3 Payrolls **BS**: 196.

ADAMS, William; b 3 Nov 1723, Stafford Co, d 4 Sep 1809 Fairfax Co **RU**: Patriot Processioner of Truro Parish in 1775, Service recorded in source CZ, War, vol 5, p 27 **CEM**: Old Burying Ground; GPS unk; Directions in Senate Doc DAR annual report 1955 vol 4 serial 11912; Arlington **GS**: N **SP**: Ann Lawyer (1732-1788) of Stafford Co **VI**: Before war period was a Colonel in Fairfax Co Militia and a sheriff in 1768 and a justice in 1770 **P**: unk **BLW**: unk **RG**: Y **MK**: unk **PH**: N **SS**: SAR P-101658; CZ pg 15; EK pg 20 **BS**: JLARC 1, 76.

ADAMS, William; b 1746; d 1823 **RU**: Soldier, Performed personal service, specifics fr DAR not given **CEM**: Back Creek Quaker, aka Gainesboro United Methodist; GPS 39.27861, -78.25694; 166 Siler Ln, Gainesboro; Frederick **GS**: Y **SP**: No info **VI**: No further data **P**: unk **BLW**: unk **RG**: Y **MK**: Y SAR **PH**: Y **SS**: DAR A000783; B; SAR P-101668 **BS**: 196.

ADDISON, John; b unk; d after 1786 **RU**: Colonel, Served in a MD Flying Camp,1776 under BG Benjamin Biggs, 3rd Bn, 7th Cont Line **CEM**: Addison Family; GPS unk; Homeplace Oxen Hill on the Potomac River opposite Mt Vernon; Fairfax **GS**: U **SP**: No info **VI**: Wounded in duel with Maj Joseph Marbury 12 Oct 1786 **P**: unk **BLW**: unk **RG**: Y **MK**: N **PH**: unk **SS**: A pg 238; SAR P-101740 **BS**: JLARC 63.

ADKINS, William; b 21 Sep 1760; d 22 Oct 1748 **RU**: Private, Served in Capt Reuben Vaughan's Co, Mecklenburg Militia 1779 **CEM**: William Atkins Family; GPS unk; Rt 649 nr Cooper's Store, Callands; Pittsylvania **GS**: U **SP**: Mar (1780) Mary Hartman **VI**: No further data **P**: unk **BLW**: unk **RG**: N **MK**: unk **PH**: unk **SS**: DB pg 11 **BS**: 196.

AGEE, Jacob; b 1756; d May 1838 **RU**: Soldier, Ent serv 1778, Buckingham Co. Served in VA Line **CEM**: Greenfield; GPS unk; On Rocky Creek nr Penlan; Buckingham **GS**: U **SP**: Elizabeth Garrett **VI**: Appl pen10 Sep 1832 Buckingham Co. Pen commenced 4 Mar 1831, $50 yr. S6470 **P**: Y **BLW**: N **RG**: Y **MK**: N **PH**: unk **SS**: DAR A000848; E pg 4; AG pg 758; CG pg 19; SAR P-101813 **BS**: JLARC 4, 59.

ADKINS, William Vortimer; b 21 Jul 1721, Henrico Co, d 21 Feb 1784 **RU**: Patriot, paid personal property tax 1782, in Pittsylvania Co, considered a partial payment of Rev War expenses **CEM**: Atkins-Owens (AKA Adkins-Lunsford); GPS not determined loc on his plantation nr Chatham; Pittsylvania **GS**: Unk **SP**: Lydia Lunsford Owens (1724, Henrico Co-1782) **VI**: Son of William Adkins (1689-___) & Elizabeth Parker (1695-___). Will dated 22 Jan 1784, probated 15 Mar 1784 **P**: N **BLW**: N **RG** N **MK**: N **PH**: N **SS**: DV image 04.pdf Pittsylvania Co **BS**: 196.

AGEE, James; b 1725; d 1820 **RU**: Patriot, Gave material aid to cause **CEM**: Agee Family; GPS unk; Nr Dillwyn; Buckingham **GS**: Y **SP**: 1) Elizabeth Ford, 2) mar (before 1747/8) Mary Ford d/o James & (-----) Ford **VI**: No further data **P**: N **BLW**: N **RG**: Y **MK**: N **PH**: unk **SS**: DAR A000832; AL Ct Bk pg 1, 46 Buckingham Co; SAR P-101815 **BS**: AS.

AGNES, Jean; b unk; d 1781 **RU**: Seaman, Served on "Hector." Died from Yorktown battle **CEM**: French Memorial; GPS 36.81944, -79.39933; Yorktown; York **GS**: U **SP**: No info **VI**: No further data **P**: unk **BLW**: unk **RG**: Y **MK**: unk **PH**: unk **SS**: J-Yorktown Historian; SAR P-101821; **BS**: JLARC 1, 74.

AIMONT, Jean; b unk; d 1781 **RU**: Soldier, Served in Regt d'Agenais,and died from Yorktown battle **CEM**: French Memorial; GPS 36.81944, -79.39933; Yorktown; York **GS**: U **SP**: No info **VI**: No further

RU=Rank/Unit	CEM=Cemetery	GS=Gravestone	SP=Spousal Information
VI=Other Veteran Info	P=Pension	BLW=Bounty/Land Warrant	RG=Registered Grave
MK=SAR/DAR Marker	PH=Photo	SS=Service Source	BS=Burial Source

3

data **P:** unk **BLW:** unk **RG:** Y **MK:** unk **PH:** unk **SS:** J-Yorktown Historian; SAR P-101883 **BS:** JLARC 1,74.

AKERS, William; b c1730; d 31 Mar 1810 **RU:** Patriot, Gave material aid to the cause **CEM:** First Concord Presbyterian; GPS unk; Hwy 460 E fr Lynchburg City; Appomattox **GS:** Y **SP:** Mar (17 Mar 1798 Campbell Co) Polly Hardway, d/o Charles & (-----) Hardway. Also mar to Elizabeth Martye. Order unk. **VI:** No further data **P:** N **BLW:** N **RG:** N **MK:** unk **PH:** unk **SS:** AL Ct Bk 3 Campbell Co **BS:** 196.

ALAIN, Georges; b unk; d 1781 **RU:** Seaman, Served on "Magnanime" and died from Yorktown battle **CEM:** French Memorial; GPS 36.81944, -79.39933; Yorktown; York **GS:** U **SP:** No info **VI:** No further data **P:** unk **BLW:** unk **RG:** Y **MK:** unk **PH:** unk **SS:** J-Yorktown Historian; SAR P-101940 **BS:** JLARC 1, 74.

ALARDIOT, Antoine; b unk; d 1781 **RU:** Seaman, Served on "Auguste". Died from Yorktown battle **CEM:** French Memorial; GPS 36.81944, -79.39933; Yorktown; York **GS:** U **SP:** No info **VI:** No further data **P:** unk **BLW:** unk **RG:** Y **MK:** unk **PH:** unk **SS:** J-Yorktown Historian; SAR P-101943 **BS:** JLARC 1, 74.

ALBERT, Jacob Allen; b 1757; d 1856 **RU:** Private, Served in 12th Cont Line **CEM:** Dowdy-Webb; GPS unk; Nr Pembroke; Giles **GS:** U **SP:** No info **VI:** No further data **P:** unk **BLW:** unk **RG:** Y **MK:** unk **PH:** unk **SS:** DAR A000947; SAR P-101984; E pg 5 **BS:** JLARC 3.

ALBRIGHT, Frederick; b Feb 1761, NC; d 28 Aug 1824 **RU:** Private, Served in Capt Thomas Pry's Co, Col Moses Hazen's Regt 1778 **CEM:** McDowell; GPS 37.86860, -79.31080; Nr jct Rts 11 and 712, Fairfield; Rockbridge **GS:** Y **SP:** No info **VI:** No further data **P:** N **BLW:** N **RG:** N **MK:** N **PH:** unk **SS:** AP Roll **BS:** 154 Rockledge; 196.

ALDRIDGE, James; b 1760; d unk **RU:** Private, Served in Capt Thomas Catlett's Co, 2d VA Regt Cont Line for 3 yrs **CEM:** Aldridge Family; GPS unk; Off Rt 607, 2 mi E of Rt 654; Prince George **GS:** N **SP:** No info **VI:** No further data **P:** unk **BLW:** Y **RG:** N **MK:** unk **PH:** N **SS:** DAR A001090; C pg 388; E pg 6; AP Payroll **BS:** 111.

ALDRIDGE, John; b 1764; d 1832 **RU:** Private, served as drummer in Capt James Hook's 7th Co, Col William Russell's 13th Va Regt Oct 1777-Apr 1778; served also in 9th Cont Line **CEM:** Goose Creek; GPS 39.11250, -77.69527, GS 39.11292,-77.69576; Rt 722, Lincoln; Loudoun **GS:** Y **SP:** Harriet West (1765-1857) **VI:** prob son of Jacob Aldridge & Elizabeth Welsh **P:** unk **BLW:** unk **RG:** Y **MK:** N **PH:** Y **SS:** C Sec III pg 389; E pg 6: SAR bio rpt submitted 28 Feb 21 **BS:** 25 pg 54; 196.

ALESHIRE, John Conrad; b 23 Dec 1755, Shenandoah Co; d 17 Dec 1811 **RU:** Private, Served in Capts Rowsch or Denton, or Prince, Cols Bowmans & Church Regts. Was at siege of Yorktown **CEM:** Aleshire Family; GPS unk; E of Rt 616, 8 mi S of Luray, in back of canning factory; Page **GS:** Y **SP:** No info **VI:** Pen #S17816 dated 27 Aug 1832 **P:** Y **BLW:** unk **RG:** N **MK:** unk **PH:** unk **SS:** DAR A001119; CI-Pension file **BS:** 120.

ALEXANDER, Andrew; b Rockbridge Co; d unk **RU:** Soldier, Served in Augusta Co Militia in Capt Long's Co 1778, Capt Kennry's Co 1779, Capt Rankin's Co 1780, and Capt Finley's Co 1782 **CEM:** Stonewall Jackson Memorial; GPS 37.78128, -79.44604; 314 S Main St; Lexington City **GS:** U **SP:** Mar (1800 Rockbridge Co) Isabelle Paxton, d/o William & Eleanor (-----) Hays **VI:** Son of William & Nancy (-----) Alexander **P:** unk **BLW:** unk **RG:** N **MK:** unk **PH:** unk **SS:** E pg 6; N pg 1065 **BS:** JLARC 79.

ALEXANDER, Archibald; b 4 Feb 1708, Ireland; d 1 Feb 1780 **RU:** Patriot, Specific service indicated in Journal VA House of Delegates 1835-6, Doc 6, pg 75. Public service as High Sheriff & Justice, Augusta Co **CEM:** Tinkling Spring Presbyterian; GPS 38.08472, -78.98278; 30 Tinkling Spring Dr, Fishersville; Augusta **GS:** N **SP:** 1) Mar (1734 Rockbridge Co) Margaret Parks; 2) Mar (1757 Rockbridge Co) Jane McClure **VI:** Might be discrepant burial site reported for the same person **P:** unk **BLW:** unk **RG:** Y **MK:** N **PH:** N **SS:** DAR A001134; AD pg 242; CZ pg 16; SAR P-102271 **BS:** JLARC 63.

ALEXANDER, Archibald; b unk, North Ireland; d c1780 **RU:** Patriot, Performed civil service **CEM:** Muse, aka Irvine Family, aka Timber Grove, aka Timber Ridge Presbyterian; GPS unk; 9 mi N of Lexington off Rt 11, SW of jct Rts 11 & 716, 73 Sam Huston Way, Buffalo District; Rockbridge **GS:** N **SP:** No info **VI:**

RU=Rank/Unit	CEM=Cemetery	GS=Gravestone	SP=Spousal Information
VI=Other Veteran Info	P=Pension	BLW=Bounty/Land Warrant	RG=Registered Grave
MK=SAR/DAR Marker	PH=Photo	SS=Service Source	BS=Burial Source

4

Might be discrepant burial site reported for the same person. GS was there but now missing **P:** unk **BLW:** unk **RG:** Y **MK:** unk **PH:** N **SS:** SAR P-102271 **BS:** JLARC 2 ,63;196.

ALEXANDER, Charles Sr; b 20 Jul 1737; d 20 Jul 1806 **RU:** Patriot, Gave wood to Minutemen in Alexandria. He signed the Fairfax Co Resolves in Jul 1774 and was appointed a member of the Committee of Safety **CEM:** Pohick Episcopal; GPS 38.42546, -77.11598; 9301 Richmond Hwy, Lorton; Fairfax **GS:** Y **SP:** Mar (1771) Frances Brown, d/o Reverend Richard Brown & Helen Baily **VI:** Son of John Alexander (1711-1775) & Susanna Pearson (1717-1788). He was the Fairfax Commissioner for state aid in 1780 and president of the Fairfax Board of Overseers of the Poor in 1797 **P:** N **BLW:** N **RG:** Y **MK:** Y SAR plaque **PH:** unk **SS:** DAR A001140; G pg 432; SAR P-102280 **BS:** 20 pg 51.

ALEXANDER, David; b 1754 d 21 Mar 1815 **RU:** Patriot, gave material aid to cause in Surry Co **CEM:** Blandford; GPS 37.22433, -38604; 319 Crater Rd; Petersburg **GS:** Unk **SP:** No spousal info **VI:** No further data **P:** N **BLW:** N **RG:** N **MK:** N **PH:** N **SS:** AL Ct Bk pg 7 **BS:** 196.

ALEXANDER, Gabriel; b 1738; d 6 Mar 1801 **RU:** Private, Served in Capt Baskins & Longs Cos, Augusta Co Militia **CEM:** Tinkling Spring Presbyterian; GPS 38.08472, -78.98278; 30 Tinkling Spring Dr, Fishersville; Augusta **GS:** U **SP:** Jane Black **VI:** No further data **P:** N **BLW:** N **RG:** Y **MK:** unk **PH:** unk **SS:** E pg 7; DAR A134708; SAR P-102203 **BS:** 208 pg 458.

ALEXANDER, George Dent; b 12 Dec 1774; d Jan 1780, Philadelphia RU: Surgeon, appt Feb 1777, Col William Grayson" Regt, Cont Line; Ret 1779 CEM:Rev War Court House Plaque;GPS;not determined; 4110 Chain Bridge Rd; Fairfax GS: Memorialized on plaque 2017 by Geo Washington Chapter, VASSAR SP: No info VI: Died in service P: N BLW: Y 9000 acres RG: N MK: N PH: N SS: E pg 7;N pg 14; EP sources: BS: None.

ALEXANDER, John; b 1763; d 24 Oct 1828 **RU:** Private, Served in Capt Joseph McCutchen's Co, Augusta Co Militia **CEM:** Stonewall Jackson Memorial; GPS 37.78128, -79.44604; 314 S Main St; Lexington City **GS:** U **SP:** Elizabeth Barnes, d/o Richard & (-----) Barnes **VI:** No further data **P:** unk **BLW:** unk **RG:** N **MK:** unk **PH:** unk **SS:** E pg 7 **BS:** 196.

ALEXANDER, John; b 1757, d 1831 **RU:** Sergeant, Lees Legion 27 Jul 1793 (pen List) and/or as private as Forage Master. Also person this name as private in Capt Beale's Co, Col John Gibson's (9th VA Regt 1779 and 13th VA Regt as well. Also same-named person as private in 8th Cont line **CEM:** Alexander family; GPS not determined; Alexander's Corner: Hanover **GS:** Unk **SP:** No spousal info **VI:** Pen cert date 27 Feb 1793 # S692, **P:** N **BLW:** N **RG:** Y **MK:** N **PH:** N **SS:** E pg 21; F pg 4: DP pg 162; SAR bio rpt submitted Aug 2019 **BS:** 196.

ALEXANDER, Robert; c1740, d 1793, Fairfax Co **RU:** Patriot; paid personal property tax 1782 in Fairfax Co which provided funds for Rev War expenses **CEM:** Alexander Family; GPS **38.3372970, -77.1329490**; loc 12181 Caledon Rd on Cedar Grove farm; King George **GS:** N **SP:** Marianne Trueman **VI:** Son of Robert Alexander (___-1795) & Marianne Stoddard (___-1788) **P:** N **BLW:** N **RG:** N **MK:** N **PH:** N **SS:** DV Fairfax Co 1782, image 03.pdf **BS:** 196.

ALEXANDER, Robert; b Nov 1746, **Rockbridge Co**; d 20 Nov 1820 **RU:** Captain, Oath as Capt 27 Jun 1779. Bedford Co Militia **CEM:** Alexander-Adams; GPS unk; Rt 652, Gladys; Campbell **GS:** Y **SP:** Mar (10 Mar 1774, Bedford Co) Ann Austin (1758-1846) **VI:** Son of Robert Alexander, Sr (1710, Co Donegal, IRE-18 Nov 1783 & Ester Beard (1724-1779) **(P:** unk **BLW:** unk **RG:** Y **MK:** N **PH:** unk **SS:** DAR A001240; SAR P-102402 **BS:** JLARC 1, 2, 36; 196.

ALEXANDER, Susanna Pearson; b 29 Dec 1717, Stafford Co, d 6 Oct 1788, Stafford Co **RU:** Patriot. Gave material aid to cause in King George Co **CEM:** Pohick Episcopal Church; GPS: 38.70888, -77.19369; jct Rts 1 & 611, Lorton; Fairfax **GS:** Yes; **SP:** John Alexander (1711-1763) **VI:** Remains reinterred from Preston Plantation in 1922 with her husband. Allegedly she shot Chief Long Tom in self-defense. **P:** N **BLW:** N **RG:** N **MK:** Y SAR Plaque **PH:** N **SS:** **BS:** 196.

ALEXANDER, William; b 1741; d 1811 **RU:** Lieutenant Colonel, Specific Serv indicated Prince William Co, Petitions 17 Oct 1776 **CEM:** Bethel Luthern; GPS 36.46856, -77.30823; 8712 Plantation Ln; Manassas City **GS:** Y **SP:** No info **VI:** No further data **P:** unk **BLW:** unk **RG:** Y **MK:** N **PH:** unk **SS:** AY Muster Roll; CZ pg 16; SAR bio rpt submitted May 2020; **BS:** 190 pg 12.

RU=Rank/Unit	CEM=Cemetery	GS=Gravestone	SP=Spousal Information
VI=Other Veteran Info	P=Pension	BLW=Bounty/Land Warrant	RG=Registered Grave
MK=SAR/DAR Marker	PH=Photo	SS=Service Source	BS=Burial Source

5

ALEXANDER, William; b 3 Mar 1744, Effingham, Prince William Co; d 3 Apr 1814 **RU:** Lieutenant Colonel, Was in charge of Prince William Co Militia **CEM:** Effingham Plantation; GPS 38.639883, -77.521500; 1 mi E of Adan, 14325 Trotter's Ridge Place, Nokesville; Prince William **GS:** U **SP:** Mar (18 Apr 1765) Sigismunda Mary Massie, d/o Sigismunde & Mary (Stewart) Massie **VI:** Son of Phillip M & Sarah (Hooe) Alexander. County Justice 1765-1790. SAR marker **P:** unk **BLW:** unk **RG:** Y **MK:** Y SAR granite **PH:** Y **SS:** DAR A001271; SAR P-100407; E pg 7 **BS:** JLARC 1, 2, 76; 04 CWG Chap Oct 2014.

ALEXANDER, William; b 1738, Chester Co, PA; d 1796 **RU:** Private, Served in Capt Dickey's Co, Augusta Co Militia 1782 **CEM:** Stonewall Jackson Memorial; GPS 37.78128, -79.44604; 314 S Main St; Lexington City **GS:** Y **SP:** Agnes Ann Reid (1740-11 Oct 1825) d/o Andrew & Sarah (-----) Reid **VI:** Son of Archibald (4 Feb 1818 Ireland-1780 Rockbridge Co) & (-----) Alexander **P:** unk **BLW:** unk **RG:** N **MK:** unk **PH:** unk **SS:** DAR A001269; E pg 8 **BS:** JLARC 2, 63, 76; 196.

ALLAMONG (ALLEMONG, Jacob; b 1754, Northampton, PA, d 8 Mar 1808 **RU:** Patriot Served as a wagon master Cont Line and by giving material aid to cause Frederick Co **CEM** Heironimus Family: GPS 39.332, -78.327; off Rt 522 N, turn on Redland Rd, Rt 701, turn left on Old Mill Ln pass two houses, cem behind house behind red gate; Frederick **GS:** Yes **SP:** Mar (c1780) Elizabeth Rinker, d/o Casper Rinker & Maria Shultz **VI:** Son of Johann Alleman (1730-1790) & Elizabeth Barbara Hundsicker (1730-1780). He was a shoemaker **P:** N **BLW:** N **RG:** Y **MK:** N **PH:** N **SS:** AL Ct Bk II, pg 168, Frederick Co; SAR P-100532 **BS:** 196; 221 Frederick Cemeteries.

ALLARD, Andre; b unk; d 1781 **RU:** Soldier, Served in Regt d'Agenais and died from Yorktown battle **CEM:** French Memorial; GPS 36.81944, -79.39933; Yorktown; York **GS:** U **SP:** No info **VI:** No further data **P:** unk **BLW:** unk **RG:** Y **MK:** unk **PH:** unk **SS:** J-Yorktown Historian; SAR P-100493 **BS:** JLARC 1, 74.

ALLEGRE, Daniel; b 31 Mar 1743, Goochland Co.; d 22 Dec 1814 **RU:** Patriot, gave material aid to cause **CEM:** Allegre Tavern; GPS 37.986606, -78.315263; 860 White Hall Rd, Keswick; Fluvanna **GS:** Unk **SP:** Mar (c1760) Susannah Tisdale (1763-1799) **VI:** Son of Giles Allegre (10 Aug 1685, France-22 Aug 1774) & Judith M Cox (1708, Cumberland Co-4 Jul 1782) **P:** N **BLW:** N **RG:** N **MK:** N **PH:** N **SS:** DAR A134003 **BS:** 196.

ALLEGREE, William; b 1764; d 17 Apr 1833 **RU:** Private, Served in Clarks, IL Regt, State line, Col Joseph Crockett's Regt **CEM:** St John's Episcopal; GPS 37.53183, -77.41958; 2401 E Broad St; Richmond City **GS:** Y **SP:** No info **VI:** No further data **P:** unk **BLW:** unk **RG:** N **MK:** N **PH:** unk **SS:** C Sec III pg 324 **BS:** 28 pg 415.

ALLEN, Benjamin; b 12 Sep 1748; d 1808 **RU:** 2d Lieutenant, took oath 25 Aug 1777, Cumberland Co Militia **CEM:** Allen Family; GPS 37.430776, -78.276281; loc on unnamed rd off Putney Rd 3 mi NW of jct with Norwood Ln, Allendale Farm ;Cumberland **GS:** Unk **SP:** Elizabeth Allen (18 Apr 175_, Hanover Co-1795) **VI:** Son of James Allen (1699-1771) & Anne Anderson (1706-1765) **P:** N **BLW:** N **RG:** N **MK:** N **PH:** N **SS:** E pg 8 **BS:** 196.

ALLEN, Charles; b 1754,Cumberland Co; d 5 Feb 1814 **RU:** Lieutenant, Served in Prince Edward Co Militia in 1777. Perhaps served in 9th Cont Line **CEM:** Lakeview; GPS 37.07091, -78.01143; 8th St, Blackstone; Nottoway **GS:** U **SP:** Mar (24 Apr 1777 Prince Edward) Elizabeth Chambers **VI:** No further data **P:** unk **BLW:** unk **RG:** N **MK:** unk **PH:** unk **SS:** DAR A001405; E pg 9 **BS:** 196 cem search.

ALLEN, Charles; b 1746, Hanover Co; d 8 Feb 1816 **RU:** Lieutenant Colonel, Served in Prince Edward's Co Militia and 9th Cont Line **CEM:** Allen-Watkins Family; GPS unk; Farmville; Prince Edward **GS:** N **SP:** Mary Venable (__-1824) **VI:** No further data **P:** unk **BLW:** unk **RG:** Y **MK:** unk **PH:** N **SS:** DAR A001403; E pg 9; G pg 505; SAR P-100611 **BS:** JLARC 1,76.

ALLEN, Hugh; b 4 Sep 1745, Botetourt Co; d 1816 **RU:** Second Lieutenant, Served in Capt Pryor's Co Militia. Specific serv indicated in Lib VA Auditors Accts 1779-80, pg 207 **CEM:** Allen-Carper; GPS unk; Rt 43 nr Eagle Rock; Botetourt **GS:** Y **SP:** Anna Hunter & Jane Anderson **VI:** No further data **P:** unk **BLW:** unk **RG:** Y **MK:** N **PH:** unk **SS:** DAR A001573; E pg 9; CZ pg 17; SAR P-102496 **BS:** 04.

ALLEN, James, b 1716, Ireland, d 1810 **RU:** Lieutenant, in Capt George Mathews's Co fr Augusta County in battle at Poit Pleasant Oct 1774 **CEM:** Augusta Stone Presbyterian; GPS 38.23926,

---

RU=Rank/Unit	CEM=Cemetery	GS=Gravestone	SP=Spousal Information
VI=Other Veteran Info	P=Pension	BLW=Bounty/Land Warrant	RG=Registered Grave
MK=SAR/DAR Marker	PH=Photo	SS=Service Source	BS=Burial Source

6

-78.97356; 28 Old Stone Church Ln, Ft Defiance; Augusta **GS:** Y **Govt SP** Margaret Anderson, d/o John Anderson **VI:** Son of William Allen.of Ireland. Obtained rank of Captain perhaps after war period **P:** Unk **BLW:** Unk **RG:** Y **MK:** Y SAR plaque **PH:** unk **SS:** DAR A001614; SAR P-100747; Z pg 106 **BS:** 196.

ALLEN, James; b 1733; d 10 May 1810 **RU:** Private, Served in Capt Samuel McDowell's Co, Augusta Co Militia. Was in the battle at Pt Pleasant, October 1774 **CEM:** Augusta Stone Presbyterian; GPS 38.23926, -78.97356, GS 38.1411,-78.5815; 28 Old Stone Church Ln, Ft Defiance; Augusta **GS:** Y **SP:** Margaret Anderson **VI:** Govt stone **P:** unk **BLW:** unk **RG:** Y **MK:** Y SAR plaque **PH:** unk **SS:** DAR A001614; E pg 9; Z pg 104; SAR P- 100747; **BS:** JLARC 1, 2, 8, 23, 62, 63; 196.

ALLEN, James; b 6 Dec 1762; d 26 Sep 1844 **RU:** Private, Served in Botetourt Co Militia **CEM:** Allen Family; GPS unk; 5.5 mi S of Buchanan; Botetourt **GS:** Y **SP:** Jane Steele (__-1826 **VI:** Son of Robert Allen & Mary (Walkinshaw (__-1818) **P:** unk **BLW:** unk **RG:** N **MK:** N **PH:** unk **SS:** AZ pg 103 **BS:** 115 pg 3; 196.

ALLEN, James (1716-1810). See Appendix G Addenda

ALLEN, James Jr; b 7 Jul 1724, Hanover Co; d 20 Oct 1793 **RU:** Patriot, Gave material aid to cause and had patriotic public service as member of Prince Edward Co Committee of Safety, Jun & Nov 1775 **CEM:** Allen Family; GPS unk; Vic Farmville; Prince Edward **GS:** N **SP:** Elizabeth Sims **VI:** No further data **P:** N **BLW:** N **RG:** Y **MK:** N **PH:** N **SS:** DAR A001616; AK; AL Ct Bk pg 12 Prince Edward Co; SAR P-100748 **BS:** 04.

ALLEN, James Anderson; b 10 Sep 1748, Hanover Co; d 8 Feb 1816 **RU:** Lt Colonel, recommended this rank at Aug Ct, 1783, Prince Edward Co **CEM:** Col Charles Allen Famley GPS not determined; Farmville: Prince Edward Co; **GS:** Y obelisk **SP:** Mary Anne Venable (1752-4 Feb 1824) **VI:** Son of James Allen (1699-1771) & Anne Anderson (1706-1765) **P:** N **BLW:** N **RG:** N **MK:** N **PH:** N **SS:** G pg 305 **BS:** 196.

ALLEN, John; b 1732, Ireland; d 1794 **RU:** Major/Patriot, Served in Frederick Co Militia. Gave material aid to the cause **CEM:** Opequon Presbyterian; GPS 39.13938, -78.19494; 217 Opequon Church Ln; Winchester City **GS:** N **SP:** Ann Pollock (later renamed Polk) (1743 Carlisle, Cumberland Co, PA-8 Feb 1805 Shelby Co. KY) d/o Thomas and Ann (-----) Pollock **VI:** Son of Robert (1695-1769) & Deborah (Montgomery) (1700-1740) Allen **P:** N **BLW:** N **RG:** Y **MK:** N **PH:** N **SS:** DAR A001674; AL Ct Bk pg 4; SAR P-102572 **BS:** 59 pg 8.

ALLEN, John; b 17 Aug 1759, Botetourt Co; d 30 May 1828 **RU:** Private, Served in Capt Pryor's Co Militia **CEM:** Allen-Carper; GPS unk; Rt 43 nr Eagle Rock; Botetourt **GS:** Y **SP:** Rebecca Poague **VI:** No further data **P:** unk **BLW:** unk **RG:** N **MK:** N **PH:** unk **SS:** DAR A001675 E pg 9 **BS:** 04.

ALLEN, Joseph; b unk; d 1781 **RU:** Soldier, Served fr MA, and died as result of Yorktown battle **CEM:** Yorktown Victory Monument Tablet; GPS 38.28350, -78.54150; Yorktown; York **GS:** U **SP:** No info **VI:** No further data **P:** unk **BLW:** unk **RG:** Y **MK:** unk **PH:** unk **SS:** J-Yorktown Historian; SAR P-102632 **BS:** JLARC 74.

ALLEN, Malcolm; b c1710, Kilbirnie, County Ayr, Scotland; d 15 Feb 1792 **RU:** Patriot, Provided supplies/served on Petit and Grand Juries **CEM:** Allen-Carper; GPS unk; Rt 43 nr Eagle Rock; Botetourt **GS:** Y **SP:** Mary (Unreadable) **VI:** No further data **P:** N **BLW:** N **RG:** N **MK:** N **PH:** unk **SS:** AK Mar 2007 **BS:** 04.

ALLEN, Moses; b 9 Oct 1750, Botetourt Co; d 1812 **RU:** Private, Served in Capt Pryor's Co Militia **CEM:** Allen Family; GPS unk; Off Craig Creek, nr Oriskany; Craig **GS:** Y **SP:** Lydia (-----) **VI:** No further data **P:** unk **BLW:** unk **RG:** N **MK:** N **PH:** unk **SS:** AK Mar 2007 **BS:** 04.

ALLEN, Robert; b 1736, Ireland; d 15 Nov 1791 **RU:** Patriot, Gave material aid to cause **CEM:** Opequon Presbyterian; GPS 39.13938, -78.19494; 217 Opequon Church Ln; Winchester City **GS:** U **SP:** Martha (-----) (1748-1794) **VI:** Son of Robert (1695-1769) & Deborah (Montgomery) (1700-1740) Allen **P:** N **BLW:** N **RG:** Y **MK:** unk **PH:** unk **SS:** DAR A001802; D Vol 2 pg 38; SAR P-102777 **BS:** 196.

RU=Rank/Unit	CEM=Cemetery	GS=Gravestone	SP=Spousal Information
VI=Other Veteran Info	P=Pension	BLW=Bounty/Land Warrant	RG=Registered Grave
MK=SAR/DAR Marker	PH=Photo	SS=Service Source	BS=Burial Source

7

ALLEN, Robert; b 26 Nov 1748, Botetourt Co; d 1778 **RU**: Private, Served in Capt Pryor's Co Militia **CEM**: Allen-Carper; GPS unk; Rt 43 nr Eagle Rock; Botetourt **GS**: Y **SP**: Jane Hill **VI**: No further data **P**: unk **BLW**: unk **RG**: Y **MK**: N **PH**: unk **SS**: AK Mar 2007; SAR P-102780 **BS**: 04.

ALLEN, Robert; b 1736, Ireland; d 15 Nov 1791 **RU**: Private, Gave material aid to cause **CEM**: Opequon Presbyterian; GPS 39.13938, -78.19494; 217 Opequon Church Ln; Winchester City **GS**: U **SP**: Martha Allen (1748-1794) **VI**: Son of Robert (1695-1769) & Deborah (Montgomery) (1700-1740) Allen. Died in Kernstown, Frederick Co **P**: unk **BLW**: unk **RG**: Y **MK**: unk **PH**: unk **SS**: AL Bt Bk pg 22 Frederick Co; DAR A001802; SAR P-102777 **BS**: JLARC 2, 76.

ALLEN, Robert; b 1731; d 1778 **RU**: Private/Patriot, Served in Capt Anderson's Co, Augusta Co Militia. In 1778, was exempted because of his age. Gave material aid to cause **CEM**: Allen Marker; GPS unk; E Waynesboro at Winchester Heights, lot 4, Elkin Ave; Waynesboro City **GS**: Y **SP**: No info **VI**: No further data **P**: unk **BLW**: unk **RG**: N **MK**: N **PH**: unk **SS**: E pg 10; AL Cert Augusta Co **BS**: 142 Allen Marker.

ALLEN, Thomas; b 39 Aug 1734, Ireland; d 15 Jul 1822 **RU**: Patriot, Gave material aid to cause **CEM**: Millar Family; GPS unk; W Main St at Randolph Macon Academy Campus, Front Royal; Warren **GS**: Y **SP**: Mar (24 Feb 1747) Abigail Millar Montgomery (1747-1823) **VI**: Son of Robert (1695-1769) & (-----) Allen. Died in Shenandoah Co **P**: N **BLW**: N **RG**: Y **MK**: Y SAR Granite **PH**: unk **SS**: C pg 593; D pg 4; AL Ct Bk pg 3, 5, 7, 9 Shenandoah Co; DAR A001862; SAR P100672 **BS**: 50, pg 36; 196.

ALLISON, Robert; b 1745; d Jun 1801 **RU**: Patriot, Signed legislative petition 25 Oct 1779 to establish a naval port in Alexandria **CEM**: Old Presbyterian Meeting House; GPS 38.48528, -77.23532; 323 S Fairfax St; Alexandria City **GS**: N **SP**: No info **VI**: Bur 11 Jun 1801, age 56. Name listed on SAR plaque in cemetery **P**: N **BLW**: N **RG**: N **MK**: Y SAR plaque **PH**: N **SS**: CJ Vol 2 series 2 pg 291-3 **BS**: JLARC 1, 76; 23 pg 99; 196.

ALLMAND, Harrison; b 8 Aug 1757, Nansemond Co; d 16 Apr 1822 **RU**: Patriot, Provided supplies for the "publick service" in Nansemond Co VA "for State, a gun lost…and a horse" **CEM**: St Paul's Episcopal; GPS 36.84733, -76.28554; 201 St Paul's Blvd; Norfolk City **GS**: Y **SP**: 1) Mar (1785) Louisa Keele 2) Mar (1803) Mary Thomas Walker 3) Lucy Campbell **VI**: Original owner of "Archer-Allmand House" in Norfolk, first son of Aaron & Ann (-----) Allmand **P**: N **BLW**: N **RG**: N **MK**: Y SAR plaque **PH**: unk **SS**: CB Gave to cause **BS**: 178-Jan 11.

ALSOP, Benjamin (NMI); b 17 Mar 1758, Spottsylvania Co; d 20 Dec 1832 **RU**: Major, Was Minuteman and served in Washington's army at Trenton, Princeton, Brandywine (where wounded), Germantown, Ft Mifflin, Valley Forge; returned to VA. Was in Gates army in Carolinas in Regt of Brig Gen Edward Stevens. Joined LaFayette's army and discharged Williamsburg end of Sep 1781 **CEM**: Alsop; GPS unk; Lake View Estates subdivision in small grove; Snow Hill; Spotsylvania **GS**: Y **SP**: 1) Frances Boswell (___-6 Jan 1799) 2) Mary Rogers (aunt of George Rogers Clark) (___- 6 Mar 1830) **VI**: Soldier's father d 1776 to 1778. Appl pen 7 Sep 1832 Spotsylvania Co. S9269 **P**: Y **BLW**: unk **RG**: Y **MK**: Y SAR **PH**: unk **SS**: SAR P-103048; AZ pg 235; CG pg 48 **BS**: JLARC 1, 2 ,4, 76, 91.

ALTIZER, ALTHAUSEN, Emery Emera; b 1736, Bingen, Germany; d Sep 1819 **RU**: Soldier, Served at Yorktown and in Rockbridge Militia 18 mos **CEM**: Oakley-Altizer; GPS unk; Chestnut Ridge, Riner; Montgomery **GS**: Y **SP**: 76 lists (1762) mar (Jul 1773 Hagerstown MD, but lived in Berkley Co VA) Mary Petzer (c1759-___) **VI**: Widow appl 5 Oct 1840 Montgomery Co. W4720 **P**: Y **BLW**: unk **RG**: Y **MK**: N **PH**: unk **SS**: DAR A002076; SAR P-330624; CG pg 48 **BS**: JLARC 1, 2, 4, 76.

AMBLER, Jacquelin; b 1742; d 1797 **RU**: Patriot, Served as a Commissioner of the VA Navy Board in 1779 **CEM**: Jamestown Church; GPS unk; 3827 Ironbound Rd, Williamsburg; Williamsburg City **GS**: U **SP**: No info **VI**: No further data **P**: N **BLW**: N **RG**: Y **MK**: unk **PH**: unk **SS**: CE pg 150; SAR P-103184; **BS**: 196.

AMBLER, John Esq; b 25 Sep 1762, Jamestown; d 6 Apr 1836 **RU**: Patriot, Provided provisions to cause **CEM**: Shockoe Hill; GPS 37.55190, -77.43170; 4th & Hospital Sts; Richmond City **GS**: Y **SP**: 1) Mar (31 May 1783 Henrico Co) Frances Armistead d/o Gill & (-----) Amistead 2) Mar (19 May 1791 Henrico Co) Lucy Marshall (sister of John) 3) Catherine Bush (Norton) **VI**: Son of Edward & (-----) Ambler **P**: N **BLW**: N **RG**: Y **MK**: Y SAR **PH**: unk **SS**: D Vol 2 pg 472; AK; SAR P-103198 **BS**: 04, Sep 07.

RU=Rank/Unit	CEM=Cemetery	GS=Gravestone	SP=Spousal Information
VI=Other Veteran Info	P=Pension	BLW=Bounty/Land Warrant	RG=Registered Grave
MK=SAR/DAR Marker	PH=Photo	SS=Service Source	BS=Burial Source

AMES, Isaac; b c1724; d 1818 **RU:** Corporal, Served in MA **CEM:** St John's Episcopal; GPS 37.53183, -77.41958; 2401 E Broad St; Richmond City **GS:** Y **SP:** No info **VI:** No further data **P:** unk **BLW:** unk **RG:** N **MK:** N **PH:** unk **SS:** AJ Vol I pg 218 **BS:** 28, pg 414.

AMIRAUD, Philippe; b unk; d 1781 **RU:** Seaman, Served on "Duc de Bourgogne" and died from Yorktown battle **CEM:** French Memorial; GPS 36.81944, -79.39933; Yorktown; York **GS:** U **SP:** No info **VI:** No further data **P:** unk **BLW:** unk **RG:** Y **MK:** unk **PH:** unk **SS:** J-Yorktown Historian; SAR P-103324; **BS:** JLARC 1, 74.

AMISS (AMIS), Joseph; b 1710; d 1801 **RU:** Patriot, Gave material aid to cause **CEM:** Cem name unk; GPS unk; Amissville; Rappahannock **GS:** Y **SP:** Constant Jones **VI:** No further data **P:** N **BLW:** N **RG:** Y **MK:** N **PH:** unk **SS:** AL Ct bk I pg 34; SAR P-103331 **BS:** AS, SAR Rpt.

AMISS (AMIS), Levi; b 1756; d 1780 **RU:** Seaman, Served on the "Diligence" Galley **CEM:** Cem name unk; GPS unk; Amissville; Rappahannock **GS:** Y **SP:** No info **VI:** No further data **P:** unk **BLW:** unk **RG:** Y **MK:** N **PH:** unk **SS:** L pg 140; SAR P-103333 **BS:** AS, DAR Rpt.

ANDERSON, Alexander; b 1762, Augusta Co; d 25 Dec 1825 **RU:** Private/Patriot, Served in Capt John McKitrick's Co 1782 and in Capt Rankin's Co, Augusta Co Militia **CEM:** Schutterle Community; GPS 38.22030, -79.10470; Off Rt 728 SE of Rt 732, Franks Mill; Augusta **GS:** Y **SP:** 1) Esthet Kirkland (1766-1810) 2) Esther Crosby (1788 PA-18 Dec 1867) d/o George (1765-1846) & Susanna (Evans) (1767-1813) Crosby **VI:** Son of William (___-1794) & Margaret (Clendenin) (1743-1805) Anderson. Also served in War of 1812 **P:** unk **BLW:** unk **RG:** Y **MK:** unk **PH:** unk **SS:** E pg 14; SAR P-103412 **BS:** 196.

ANDERSON, Andrew; b 1750; d 1783 **RU:** Captain, Co Commander Augusta Co Militia 1783 **CEM:** Augusta Stone Presbyterian; GPS 38.23926, -78.97356; 28 Old Stone Church Ln, Ft Defiance; Augusta **GS:** N **SP:** 1) (-----) 2) Martha Crawford **VI:** No further data **P:** unk **BLW:** unk **RG:** N **MK:** Y SAR plaque **PH:** N **SS:** E pg 14 **BS:** JLARC 62.**SEE APPENDIX G**

ANDERSON, Daniel; b 1749; d 25 Jan 1813 **RU:** Sergeant, Served in 4th, 8th & 12th Cont Lines & Western Battalion VA Troops **CEM:** Blandford; GPS 37.22433, -77.38604; 319 S Crater Rd; Petersburg City **GS:** U **SP:** No info **VI:** Merchant in Petersburg. A child as his heir received pen of $8 per mo, Act of 1838, last payment 06 Nov 1840. 200 acres BLW issued 20 Jun 1783 **P:** Y **BLW:** Y **RG:** Y **MK:** Y SAR Monument **PH:** unk **SS:** E pg 14; SAR P-335465 **BS:** 213 pg 38.

ANDERSON, David; b 15 Jul 1756, Cumberland Co; d 18 Jun 1812 **RU:** Private, Served in Prince Edward Co Militia & Baylor's Regt **CEM:** Blandford; GPS 37.22433, -77.38604; 319 S Crater Rd; Petersburg City **GS:** U **SP:** No info **VI:** Was Chamberlain in town of Petersburg. Founder of the Corporation of Petersburg **P:** unk **BLW:** unk **RG:** Y **MK:** Y SAR monument **PH:** unk **SS:** E pg 14; SAR P-336111 **BS:** 213 pg 38.

ANDERSON, David Jr; b Sep 1745, Albermarle Co VA; d 15 Mar 1795 **RU:** Captain, Vol as Minute Man Jun 1776 in Chesterfield Co; Ent serv Chesterfield Co May 1777, in Capt Cadwallader's Co of Dragoons serving 13 mos. In Mar 1781 was wagoner & collector of provisions for Army at Yorktown **CEM:** Anderson; GPS unk; Nr South Anna River, Rt 642; Louisa **GS:** U **SP:** Mar (21 Sep 1785, Prince Edward Co) Lucy Horsley (c1768-aft 10 Dec 1843 Prince Edward Co) **VI:** Chamberlain in town of Petersburg and founder of the Corporation of Petersburg. Widow pension, #SW5625 **P:** Y **BLW:** unk **RG:** Y **MK:** N **PH:** unk **SS:** DAR A203412; E pg 14; AZ pg 53-54; DD; SAR P-336436 **BS:** 04 May 07; 80 vol 1, pg 472; 13 pg 38.

ANDERSON, Edmund; b 1 Apr 1763; d 19 Apr 1810 **RU:** Private?, Service information not determined **CEM:** Locust Hill; GPS unk; Off Rt 676 N of Rt 250, Ivy; Albemarle **GS:** Y **SP:** Jane Meriwether Lewis (31 Mar 1770-15 Mar 1845) d/o William (1748-1779) & Lucy (Meriwether) (1752-1837) Lewis **VI:** No further data **P:** unk **BLW:** unk **RG:** N **MK:** N **PH:** unk **SS:** AW pg 3 **BS:** 67 vol 4 pg 105; 196.

ANDERSON, Elijah; b 1758, Culpeper Co; d Dec 1837 **RU:** Private, Served in Capt John Ball's Co, commanded by Col Elias Edmonds. Served 2 mos & 10 days 1782 in Fauquier Co Militia. **CEM:** Elijah Anderson; GPS 38.45380, -77.5833; 27 Shurgen Ln, Amissvile; (Site visit Jul 2017 indicates address is incorrect); Rappahannock **GS:** Y **SP:** 1) Frances Williams 2) Miriam Anderson 3) Mary Priest **VI:** Son of

---

RU=Rank/Unit   CEM=Cemetery   GS=Gravestone   SP=Spousal Information
VI=Other Veteran Info   P=Pension   BLW=Bounty/Land Warrant   RG=Registered Grave
MK=SAR/DAR Marker   PH=Photo   SS=Service Source   BS=Burial Source

9

James & (-----) Anderson. GS replaced by family in 1999. Only stone in middle of pasture **P:** unk **BLW:** unk **RG:** Y **MK:** unk **PH:** Y **SS:** N pg 1247-1248; SAR P-333324 **BS:** 196.

ANDERSON, George; b 1745; d 1828 **RU:** Second Lieutenant, Specific service recorded source Lib VA, Archives, War, vol 4, p 79 **CEM:** Schutterle Community; GPS 38.22030, -79.10470; Off Rt 728 SE of Rt 732, Franks Mill; Augusta **GS:** N **SP:** Jane Presberry & JaneTucker **VI:** No further data **P:** unk **BLW:** unk **RG:** Y **MK:** N **PH:** N **SS:** CZ pg 19; SAR P-103465 **BS:** JLARC 2, 76.

ANDERSON, George; b 1758; d 29 Jun 1814 **RU:** Sergeant, Served in Capt Moffett's Co Augusta Co Militia 1777 & in Capt Trimbel's Co 1781 **CEM:** Schutterle Community; GPS 38.22030, -79.10470; Off Rt 728 SE of Rt 732, Franks Mill; Augusta **GS:** Y **SP:** Mar (12 Feb 1789) Mary Breeden (___-1 Sep 1853) **VI:** Widow appl pen 26 Dec 1846 Augusta Co. Also pen to widow 12 Nov 1814 at $5.50 per mo. W5627. Govt stone says served in Moffat's Co of VA Militia **P:** Y **BLW:** unk **RG:** Y **MK:** N **PH:** unk **SS:** E pg 14; CG pg 55; SAR P-103470 **BS:** JLARC 1 ,2, 3, 62; 196; 196.

ANDERSON, Jacob; b 1756, NJ; d 1825 **RU:** Captain, promoted in Capt Osburne's Co of Militia, Specific service recorded Lib VA, Archives, Report Sec of War 1835, pen vol 2, pg 173 **CEM:** Anderson-Hash; GPS 36.66593, -81.33110; Flatridge & Old Bridle Creek Rd; Grayson **GS:** y **SP:** Mar (before 1779) Susannah Buchanan (1760-1820) **VI:** Pen list of 1820, VA **P:** Y **BLW:** unk **RG:** Y **MK:** Plaque **PH:** unk **SS:** H; AG pg 555; AZ pg 235; CZ pg 19; DAR A002400; SAR P-103493 **BS:** 04, e-mail 04/07.

ANDERSON, James; b 24 Jan 1739, Gloucester Co; d 8 Sep 1798 **RU:** Captain, At age 21 was Lt in Capt Robert McKenzie's Co. Was Capt in Gloucester Co Militia. Was chief armourer for colony 1776-1782. Was prisoner on parole 11 Jun 1781 **CEM:** Bruton Parish Church; GPS 37.27127, -76.70248; 331 W Duke of Gloucester St; Williamsburg City **GS:** U **SP:** Hannah Tyler **VI:** No further data **P:** unk **BLW:** Y **RG:** Y **MK:** unk **PH:** unk **SS:** G pg 362, 437, 433, 475, 507, 574; EE pg 4; SAR P-103529 **BS:** 196.

ANDERSON, James; b 1714, New Kent Co; d 1782 **RU:** Patriot, Gave material aid to cause **CEM:** James Anderson Family; GPS unk; Reeds; Cumberland **GS:** U **SP:** Elizabeth Baker (1737-1792) **VI:** No further data **P:** N **BLW:** N **RG:** N **MK:** unk **PH:** unk **SS:** D pg 5; AL Ct Bk pg 1, 5, 68 Cumberland Co **BS:** 196.

ANDERSON, James; b 1739, Augusta Co d 1815 Greenbrier Co, WVA **RU:** Soldier, Capt David Bell, Augusta Co Militia **CEM:** Old Presbyterian Meeting House; GPS 38.48528, -77.23532; 323 S Fairfax St; Alexandria City **GS:** N **SP:** Elizabeth Light **(14 Jun 1760, PA-1815) VI:** Data from SAR approved application-d in 1815 in Greenbrier Co, WVA, why only memorialized in Alexandria? **P:** unk **BLW:** unk **RG:** Y **MK:** unk **PH:** N **SS:** J-NSSAR 1993 Reg; SAR P-103499 **BS:** JLARC 1, 5.

ANDERSON, John; b 1707, Ireland; d 1786 **RU:** Patriot, Appraised beef and gave material aid to cause **CEM:** Augusta Stone Presbyterian; GPS 38.23925, -78.97356; 28 Old Stone Church Ln, Ft Defiance; Augusta **GS:** N **SP:** No info **VI:** No further data **P:** unk **BLW:** unk **RG:** N **MK:** unk **PH:** unk **SS:** AL Cert Augusta Co **BS:** 196.

ANDERSON, Joseph Edward Sr; b 27 Feb 1746; d 23 Jan 1825 **RU:** Sergeant, Served in Clark's Illinois Regt or 11th VA Regt. Patriot, Furnished 18 gallons of whiskey to cause **CEM:** Anderson Family; GPS 39.85160, -77.52350; "Springfield Farm," Rt 608 nr Morgan Spring Run, Webbtown; Clarke **GS:** N **SP:** Hannah D. Blue (26 Mar 1754, Wilmington, DE-28 Dec 1843, Berryville, Clarke Co) **VI:** Son of Bartholomew Anderson (1710-1754) & Phebe (-----) (1718-1799). On Pen list of 1820, VA. GS missing--it said "Sacred to the memory of JOSEPH ANDERSON who departed this life Jan. 23 1825, aged 78 yrs, 10 mos. And 27 day" **P:** Y **BLW:** unk **RG:** N **MK:** N **PH:** N **SS:** E pg 15; AG pg 555 **BS:** 58 pg 1; 196.

ANDERSON, Matthew (Mathew); b 6 Dec 1745; d 21 Dec 1806 **RU:** Private/patriot, Served in Capt Charles Dabney's Co, Col Dabney's Legion of Calvary for 3 yrs. Gave material aid to cause **CEM:** Ware Episcopal; GPS 37.42275, -76.50789; 7825 John Clayton Mem Hwy; Gloucester **GS:** Y **SP:** Mary (-----) (27 Aug 1749-12 Jun 1820) **VI:** Recd BLW 100 acres,14 Mar 1783. Bur at Exchange Cemetery, thus memorialized here **P:** N **BLW:** Y **RG:**Y **MK:** N **PH:** unk **SS:** A pg 291; N pg 1255-6; AL Ct Bk pg ii 16 Gloucester Co; SAR P-103596 **BS:** 65 Gloucester; 207; 213 pg 100-1.

RU=Rank/Unit	CEM=Cemetery	GS=Gravestone	SP=Spousal Information
VI=Other Veteran Info	P=Pension	BLW=Bounty/Land Warrant	RG=Registered Grave
MK=SAR/DAR Marker	PH=Photo	SS=Service Source	BS=Burial Source

ANDERSON,, Matthew; b 1 Sep 1761, Hanover Co; d 15 Jul 1826 **RU**: Patriot/Private, in Capt Winston's Co, 14th VA Regt, discharged 9 Aug 1777, for medical reasons. As patriot gave material aid to cause in Louisa Co **CEM**: Anderson Family; GPS not determined; loc off Crewsville Rd (Rt 661) .2 mi S on private rd; Inez; Louisa **GS**: U **SP**: Mar (6 Jan 1783) Martha Tanner (4 Aug 1767-11 Nov 1829) **VI**: Son of Thomas Anderson (10 Feb 1733-20 Sep 1794) & Frances Harrod Jones (11 May 1733-19 Feb 1799) **P**: N **BLW**: Y **RG**:Y **MK**: N **PH**: unk **SS**: E pg 16; Lib VA misc reel 612; A L Ct Bk III, pg 14; SAR P-332282 **BS** 196.

ANDERSON, Nathaniel; b 1761, d 21 Apr 1834 **RU**: Seaman VA State Navy **CEM**: German Lutheran Church; GPS 39.183399,-78.160698; loc 305 East Boscawen St, Winchester City **GS**: Y **SP**: Mary Friedley (1761-4 Jan 1835) VI: No further data **P**: N **BLW**:N **RG**:N **MK**: N **PH**: N **SS**:G pg 784 **BS**: 196.

ANDERSON, Nelson; b 1726, Hanover Co; d 28 Aug 1820 **RU**: Captain, Commanded a company in Bedford Co Militia **CEM**: Anderson Family; GPS 37.38970, -79.39045; 2370 Cifax Rd, Goode; Bedford **GS**: N **SP**: Frances Jackson (1741 Louisa Co-13 Mar 1818) d/o Thomas Jackson & Ann (Mills) Jackson **VI**: No further data **P**: unk **BLW**: unk **RG**: Y **MK**: N **PH**: N **SS**: AK Bedford Hist Soc; SAR P-103600 **BS**: 04, Sep 07.

ANDERSON, Robert; b 1712; d 1792 **RU**: Patriot, Gave material aid to cause **CEM**: Goldmine farm; GPS unk; Rt 271, Rockville; Hanover **GS**: Y **SP**: No info **VI**: No further data **P**: N **BLW**: N **RG**: N **MK**: N **PH**: unk **SS**: AL Cert Issued **BS**: 31 pg 3. **SEE APPENDIX G**

ANDERSON, Robert; b 1739; d 22 Jul 1825 **RU**: Private/Patriot, Gave material aid to the cause **CEM**: Fincastle Presbyterian; GPS 37.50017, -79.87558; 108 E Back St, Fincastle; Botetourt **GS**: N **SP**: Mar 1) Margaret Neely, 2) Mary (-----) **VI**: Name is on the SAR plaque at this cemetery **P**: unk **BLW**: unk **RG**: Y **MK**: SAR & Plaque **PH**: N **SS**: AL Ct Bk pg 8, 9; AR pg 20; SAR P-103629; Reg **BS**: 196 JLARC 1, 2, 76; 196. **ANDERSON, Samuel See Appendix G Addenda**

ANDERSON, Thomas, Sr; b 10 Feb 1733, Northumberland, Eng; d 20 Sep 1794 **RU**: Lieutenant, appt Lt Louisa Co, 9 Apr 1781, appt Quartermaster Louisa Co 1782 **CEM**: Anderson Family; GPS not determined; loc on his property "Laurel Branch" along Little River nr Caroline Co line; Hanover **GS**: Unk **SP**: Mar 29 Mar 1754, Gloucester Co, Frances Harrod Jones (11 May1799-19 Feb 1799), d/o Elizabeth Cary **VI**: Arrived as a Naval Architect fr Eng. Will proved 4 Dec 1794, Gloucester Co **P**: N **BLW**: N **RG**: N **MK**: N **PH**: unk **SS**: E pg 16 **BS** 196.

ANDERSON, Thomas; b 1754, Cumberland Co; d 14 Oct 1804 **RU**: Soldier, Served in Capt John Mountjoy's Co, 10th VA Regt and Capt William Gillison's Co 6th VA Regt May 1779 **CEM**: James Anderson Family; GPS unk; Reeds; Cumberland **GS**: U **SP**: Sarah Weldon Anderson (1760-1814) Same last name. **VI**: Son of James (1714-1882) & Elizabeth (Baker) (1737-1792) Anderson **P**: unk **BLW**: unk **RG**: N **MK**: unk **PH**: unk **SS**: E pg 16; Cl: Muster Roll **BS**: 196.

ANDERSON, Thomas; b 1761; d 28 Mar 1824 **RU**: Soldier, Served in 6th and 10th Cont Line **CEM**: Stonewall Jackson Memorial; GPS 37.78128, -79.44604; 314 S Main St; Lexington City **GS**: U **SP**: No info **VI**: No further data **P**: unk **BLW**: unk **RG**: N **MK**: unk **PH**: unk **SS**: E pg 16 **BS**: 196.

ANDERSON, William; b 1720, Ireland, d 1794 **RU**: Patriot, Gave material aid to cause **CEM**: Augusta Stone Presbyterian Church; GPS 38.23926, -78.97356; 28 Old Stone Church Ln, Fort Defiance; Augusta **GS**: U **SP**: Mar 1) Mary Margaret Reid (1720 Ireland-10 Apr 1743), 2) Elizabeth Campbell (1725-1804) **VI**: No further data **P**: N **BLW**: N **RG**: N **MK**: unk **PH**: unk **SS**: AL Cert Augusta Co **BS**: 196.

ANDERSON, William; b 2 Jun 1764, DE; d 13 Sep 1839 **RU**: Private/Patriot, Served at 16 yrs old with Gen Green. Gave material aid to cause **CEM**: Fincastle Presbyterian; GPS 37.50017, -79.87558; 108 E Back St, Fincastle; Botetourt **GS**: Y **SP**: Anne Thomas **VI**: Served in the House of Delegates. Name on SAR plaque at cemetery **P**: unk **BLW**: unk **RG**: Y **MK**:Y SAR plaque **PH**: unk **SS**: AL Ct Bk pg 6, 31, 32; AR pg 20; SAR P-103698 **BS**: JLARC 1, 2, 76; 196.

ANDES, Andrew; b 10 Feb 1749; d 21 May 1821 **RU**: Patriot, Lib of VA Public Service Claim. Gave material aid to the cause **CEM**: Mt Olivet Church of Brethern; GPS unk; 2977 Pineville Rd,

RU=Rank/Unit	CEM=Cemetery	GS=Gravestone	SP=Spousal Information
VI=Other Veteran Info	P=Pension	BLW=Bounty/Land Warrant	RG=Registered Grave
MK=SAR/DAR Marker	PH=Photo	SS=Service Source	BS=Burial Source

11

McGayesville; Rockingham **GS:** Y **SP:** Barbara Bear (Baer) **VI:** No further data **P:** N **BLW:** N **RG:** Y **MK:** N **PH:** unk **SS:** AK; AL Ct bk 1 pg 12; SAR P-332403 **BS:** 4-Oct-06.

ANDRE, Jean; b unk; d 1781 **RU:** Seaman, Served on "Auguste" and died from Yorktown battle **CEM:** French Memorial; GPS 36.81944, -79.39933; Yorktown; York **GS:** U **SP:** No info **VI:** No further data **P:** unk **BLW:** unk **RG:** N **MK:** unk **PH:** unk **SS:** J-Yorktown Historian **BS:** JLARC 1, 74.

ANDREE, John G; b unk; d 1811 **RU:** Private, Specific service recorded Lib VA, Archives, Rejected Claims for BLW **CEM:** Shockoe Hill; GPS 37.55190, -77.43170; 4th & Hospital Sts; Richmond City **GS:** Y **SP:** No info **VI:** No further data **P:** unk **BLW:** N **RG:** N **MK:** N **PH:** unk **SS:** E pg 16; CZ pg 21 **BS:** 179 #1361.

ANDREW, Seth; b unk; d 1781 **RU:** Soldier, Served fr MA, and died as result of Yorktown battle **CEM:** Yorktown Victory Monument Tablet; GPS 38.28350, -78.54150; Yorktown; York **GS:** U **SP:** No info **VI:** No further data **P:** unk **BLW:** unk **RG:** unk **MK:** unk **PH:** unk **SS:** J-Yorktown Historian; SAR P-103738 **BS:** JLARC 74.

ANDREWS, Benjamin; b 1699; d 1799 **RU:** Patriot, Gave material aid to the cause **CEM:** Andrews Family; GPS unk; Thomas Andrews Plantation, Appomattox River; Henrico **GS:** N **SP:** Ann Vodin (1722-____) **VI:** Son of Thomas (1663-1731) & Elizabeth (Thomas) (1664-___) Thomas. Died in Chesterfield Co **P:** N **BLW:** N **RG:** N **MK:** unk **PH:** N **SS:** AL Ct Bk pg 11 Prince George Co **BS:** 196.

ANDREWS, Benjamin; b 1755; d 11 Jul 1803 **RU:** Sergeant, Served in Co Militia. Served several tours; in last tour marched prisoners fr Yorktown to Winchester, Oct 1781 **CEM:** William A. Andrews 1400 acres; GPS 36.78894, -78.13494; South Hill; Mecklenburg **GS:** U **SP:** Elizabeth (Betsy) Dodd (c1751-after 16 Mar 1843) **VI:** Son of Abraham (1725-1799) & (-----) Andrews. Widow appl pen age 92 on 16 Mar 1843 **P:** Y **BLW:** unk **RG:** N **MK:** unk **PH:** unk **SS:** K Vol 1 pg 19 **BS:** 196.

ANDREWS, Bullard; b 20 Jul 1745, Chesterfield Co; d 7 Dec 1828 **RU:** Patriot, Paid the 1783 personal property tax in Chesterfield Co in 1783 which is considered to support the cause by partially providing funds with payment **CEM:** Thomas Andrews Plantation; GPS unk; On the Appomattox River; Henrico **GS:** Y **SP:** Sally (-----) **VI:** Son of Benjamin (1699-1799) & Ann (Vodin) (1722-___) Andrews **P:** N **BLW:** N **RG:** N **MK:** N **PH:** N **SS:** www.southernfern.com/gjt/en-434.htm shows Personal Property tax 1783 **BS:** 196.

ANDREWS, Isham; b 1747; d 3 Oct 1845 **RU:** Private ent serv 1780 in Capt George Peagram Co in Col Ralph Faulker's Regt serving 3 yrs **CEM:** Andrews Family; GPS 37.270020,-77.466500; loc S of Matoaca Rd nr jct with Woodpecker rd, Matoaca; Chesterfield **GS:** Unk **SP** Mar 1) Rebecca May Norman(1745-1774), Mar 2) 3 Feb 1786, Mary Purkinson rec'd pen W5620 in 1747 **VI:** Nothing further: **P:** Widow **BLW:** N **RG:** N **MK:** N **PH:** N **SS:** K vol I pg 20; AZ pg 234 **BS;** 196.

ANDREWS, Robert; b 24 Apr 1761; d 14 Feb 1803 **RU:** Private, Served in 6th VA Regt **CEM:** Thomas Parker Family; GPS unk; Rt 180 nr Pungoteague; Accomack **GS:** Y **SP:** No info **VI:** No further data **P:** unk **BLW:** unk **RG:** N **MK:** N **PH:** unk **SS:** AP 6th VA Regt **BS:** 178 Th. Parker.

ANDREWS (ANDREW), Thomas; b 12 Dec 1761, Cumberland Co; d 31 Aug 1853 **RU:** Corporal, Served in VA Line in 1st Light Dragoons **CEM:** Andrews Family; GPS unk; Evington; Bedford **GS:** U **SP:** Tabitha Lee(1765-1832) **VI:** Son of Mark Andrews (1724-1775) & Avey Garnett (1731-1768); Appl for pen 25 Feb 1833 Bedford Co S6506, rec'd at age 72 **P:** Y **BLW:** unk **RG:** Y **MK:** N **PH:** unk **SS:** E pg 17; CG pg 64; SAR P-103947 **BS:** JLARC 4, 36, 66.

ANDREWS, Varney Sr; b 25 Jul 1760 Mecklenburg Co; d 1848 **RU:** Soldier, Vol summer 1776/77, in Capt Peter Rogers' Co, Col Morgans VA Regt, and marched to Gwyn's Island then Barron Point on Potomac. Served six mos as private, four mos as drummer. Served a mo, summer of 1777/78 in Capt Anthony Street's Co, VA Militia. Enl Feb 1781, served 2 mos as private in Capt Claybourn's Co, Col Munford's VA Regt. Was in Battle of Guilford CH. Served 3 enlistments in Rev Army, two of them under Gen Nathaniel Green **CEM:** William A. Andrews 1400 acres; GPS 36.78894, -78.13494; South Hill; Mecklenburg **GS:** Y **SP:** 1) Lucy Green (1765-___) 2) Amey Thweatt (1765-___) **VI:** Son of William A (1726-1772) & Ann Brooks (Varney) (1730-1772) Andrews. Pen claim, S 11992, based upon the service

RU=Rank/Unit   CEM=Cemetery   GS=Gravestone   SP=Spousal Information
VI=Other Veteran Info   P=Pension   BLW=Bounty/Land Warrant   RG=Registered Grave
MK=SAR/DAR Marker   PH=Photo   SS=Service Source   BS=Burial Source

12

of Varney Andrews in the War of the Revolution **P:** Y **BLW:** unk **RG:** Y **MK:** unk **PH:** unk **SS:** K Vol 1 pg 20; AZ pg 234; SAR P-103952 **BS:** 196.

ANDREWS, William; b 26 Aug 1733; d 4 Apr 1777 **RU:** Seaman, Enlisted 1777 with serv in Galley "Accomack" commanded by Capt William Underhill until 1780. Served onboard ship with William Andrews. Discharged at Chincoteague **CEM:** Thomas Parker Family; GPS unk; Rt 180 nr Pungoteague; Accomack **GS:** Y **SP:** No info **VI:** Appl pen 3 Jun 1824 Accomack Co. Rejected for pension. Was 63 on 3 Jun 1834 **P:** N **BLW:** unk **RG:** N **MK:** N **PH:** unk **SS:** N pg 1267; CG pg 65 **BS:** 178 Th. Parker.

ANDREWS, William A; b 1750, Mecklenburg Co; d 1779 **RU:** Private, Served in Capt Robert Ballard's Co, 1st VA Regt, Cont Line **CEM:** Andrews Family; GPS 36.78894, -78.13494; Whittles Mill Rd, South Hill; Mecklenburg **GS:** U **SP:** No info **VI:** Son of Willam A. (1726-1772) & Ann Brooks (Varney) (1730-1772) Andrews. Died in service; enlisted for three yrs. Service source cites Petition 05 Dec 1785. Lib of VA **P:** unk **BLW:** unk **RG:** N **MK:** unk **PH:** unk **SS:** DB pg 15 **BS:** 196.

ANDUTEAU, Jacques; b unk; d 1781 **RU:** Seaman, Served on "Auguste" and died from Yorktown battle **CEM:** French Memorial; GPS 36.81944, -79.39933; Yorktown; York **GS:** U **SP:** No info **VI:** No further data **P:** unk **BLW:** unk **RG:** Y **MK:** unk **PH:** unk **SS:** J-Yorktown Historian; SAR P-104010 **BS:** JLARC 1, 74.

ANGEVAISE, Nicolas; b unk; d 1781 **RU:** Soldier, Served in Regt d'Agenais and died from Yorktown battle **CEM:** French Memorial; GPS 36.81944, -79.39933; Yorktown; York **GS:** U **SP:** No info **VI:** No further data **P:** unk **BLW:** unk **RG:** N **MK:** unk **PH:** unk **SS:** J-Yorktown Historian **BS:** JLARC 1, 74.

ANGIBAUD, Joseph; b unk; d 1781 **RU:** Seaman, Served on "Solitaire" and died from Yorktown battle **CEM:** French Memorial; GPS 36.81944, -79.39933; Yorktown; York **GS:** U **SP:** No info **VI:** No further data **P:** unk **BLW:** unk **RG:** Y **MK:** unk **PH:** unk **SS:** J-Yorktown Historian; SAR P-104065 **BS:** JLARC 1, 74.

ANGLE (ANGELL), Peter; b 22 Apr 1754, Germany; d 25 Feb 1821 **RU:** Private, Served in Capt Baltzel's Co, Lt Col Weltner's Regt & German Regt **CEM:** Angle Family; GPS 37.06940, -79.86310; Rt 699; Franklin **GS:** Y **SP:** Elizabeth Jane Miller (4 Mar 1758 Germany-18 Apr 1827) **VI:** Died in Wirtz, Franklin Co **P:** unk **BLW:** unk **RG:** Y **MK:** N **PH:** unk **SS:** DAR A002811; E pg 17; CI PA Archives 5th Series Vol III pg 769; SAR P-104071 **BS:** 82 pg 15; 196.

ANGLIN, Philip II or Jr; b 20 Dec 1742, Albemarle Co; d c1837 **RU:** Soldier/Patriot, Served in VA Line. Ent serv Pittsylvania Co (later Henry Co). Fought Tories in battle of Flowers Gap, NC. Supplied food to Guilford Hospital after Battle of Guilford CH **CEM:** Anglin Plantation; GPS unk; Nr Patrick Co line; Henry **GS:** U **SP:** No info **VI:** Appl 9 Apr 1834 Henry Co R225. Will probated 13 Feb 1837 **P:** Y **BLW:** unk **RG:** Y **MK:** unk **PH:** unk **SS:** J-NSSAR 1993 Reg; CG pg 68; SAR P-104078 **BS:** JLARC 1.

ANIBEL, William; b unk; d 1781 **RU:** Soldier, Served fr MA,and died as result of Yorktown battle **CEM:** Yorktown Victory Monument Tablet; GPS 38.28350, -78.54150; Yorktown; York **GS:** U **SP:** No info **VI:** No further data **P:** unk **BLW:** unk **RG:** Y **MK:** unk **PH:** unk **SS:** J-Yorktown Historian; SAR P-104086 **BS:** JLARC 74.

ANIEER, William; b unk; d unk **RU:** Soldier, Served in French unit not specified and died from Yorktown battle **CEM:** Yorktown Victory Monument Tablet; GPS 38.28350, -78.54150; Yorktown; York **GS:** U **SP:** No info **VI:** No further data **P:** unk **BLW:** unk **RG:** N **MK:** unk **PH:** unk **SS:** http://freepages.genealogy.rootsweb.ancestry.com/~wvmystica/Yorktown_Victory_Monument_Tablet_-_American.html **BS:** Cem monument.

ANSLEY, William; b 1756; d 28 Jun 1798 **RU:** Private, Served in1st Light Dragoons **CEM:** Old Stone Methodist; GPS 39.11725, -77.56609; 168 W Cornwall St, Leesburg; Loudoun **GS:** U **SP:** Mar (1779) Nancy Ann Hereford (1766-1792) d/o John (1725-1793) & Margaret (Ammon) (1735-1809) Hereford **VI:** No further data **P:** unk **BLW:** unk **RG:** Y **MK:** unk **PH:** unk **SS:** E pg 18; SAR P-104127 **BS:** JLARC 1, 32; 196.

ANTHONY, John; b 1749; d 1822 **RU:** Private, Served in 6th Cont Line & 10TH VA West's Co **CEM:** Walnut Hill; GPS unk; Anthony home on Otter River, Evington; Campbell **GS:** U **SP:** Susan Austin **VI:**

RU=Rank/Unit	CEM=Cemetery	GS=Gravestone	SP=Spousal Information
VI=Other Veteran Info	P=Pension	BLW=Bounty/Land Warrant	RG=Registered Grave
MK=SAR/DAR Marker	PH=Photo	SS=Service Source	BS=Burial Source

13

No further data **P:** unk **BLW:** unk **RG:** Y **MK:** N **PH:** unk **SS:** DAR A002884; AR Vol 1 pg 23; E pg 18; SAR P-104167 **BS:** JLARC 1, 2, 66, 75.

ARBOGAST, Michael; b 1734, Baden-Wurttemberg, Germany; d 27 Aug 1812 **RU:** Private, Served in Capt Hull's Co, Augusta Co Militia **CEM:** Arbogast Family; GPS unk; Wimer Mountain Rd, Blue Grass; Highland **GS:** Y **SP:** Mar (1759 Pendleton Co, WV) Mary Elizabeth Samuels-Amanapas **VI:** Son of Michael (1694-1743) & Catherine (Konigin) (1695-aft 1736) Arbogast **P:** unk **BLW:** unk **RG:** unk **MK:** unk **PH:** unk **SS:** DAR A002973; J- DAR Hatcher; E pg 19; AR pg 24; SAR P-104293 **BS:** JLARC 2; 196.

ARBUCKLE, Mathew; b c1749; d 22 May 1783 **RU:** Captain, Led Gen Lewis's army through the dense mountain forest to Point Pleasant and later marched a Co over same Rt to build and garrison Ft Randolf **CEM:** George Revercomb property; GPS unk; McClintic by Jackson River; Bath **GS:** U **SP: Jane Lockhart & Frances Lawrence VI:** This stone probably moved (or lost) in the 1970s for the Gathright Dam project **P:** unk **BLW:** unk **RG:** Y **MK:** N **PH:** unk **SS:** DAR A002976; E pg 19; AK; SAR P-104298 **BS:** 04, AZ, pg 33.

ARCHER, Benjamin; b 1751; d 1792 **RU:** Sergeant, Capt William Machen's Co,VA 9th Cont Line at Pittsburg Oct 1775; served for 3 yrs in addition to service at Point Pleasant Oct 1774 **CEM:** Old Cemetery; GPS not determined; lots 76 & 77, Town of Stephensburg' Frederick **GS:** Unk **SP:** No further info **VI:** BLW # 6175 issued to only living heir, son Jeremiah. **P:** N **BLW:** Y heirs **RG:** N **MK:** N **PH:** N **SS:** E pg 19; C Sect III, pg 391; N pg 1266;Z pg 30 **BS:** 196.

ARCHER, John; b 30 Sep 1746; d 3 Mar 1812 **RU:** Major, Served as Maj in Amelia Co Militia 1778 **CEM:** Archer, Red Lodge; GPS unk; Red Lodge Rd; Amelia **GS:** Y **SP:** 1) Elizabeth Bur 2) Anne Hall 3) Mar (24 Apr 1788) Elizabeth Eggleston (bond) (____-Mar 1826) **VI:** Son of William & Elizabeth (-----) Archer **P:** unk **BLW:** unk **RG:** N **MK:** unk **PH:** Y **SS:** E pg 19; CD **BS:** 196.

ARELL, David; b unk; d 1792 **RU:** Captain, Appt Capt of Inf 7 Oct 1776. Capt of Co in 3rd VA Regt of Foot, 28 Sep 1776 fr Pittsylvania Co. Resigned 14 Feb 1778 **CEM:** Old Presbyterian Meeting House; GPS 38.48528, -77.23532; 323 S Fairfax St; Alexandria City **GS:** N **SP:** Phebe Moore **VI:** Will dated 15 Aug, proved 17 Apr 1796 (WB F, pg 79). Awarded BLW of 400 acres 12 Apr 1778 **P:** unk **BLW:** Y **RG:** Y **MK:** Y SAR plaque **PH:** N **SS:** DAR A003021; J-NSSAR 1993 Reg; BX pg 18; CE pg 40; AE Virginia Genealogical Society Quarterlies: Vol 2 pg 368; SAR P-104369 **BS:** JLARC 1; 23 pg 99; 196.

ARELL, H (Henry); b 1719; d Jul 1796 **RU:** Patriot, Gave material aid to cause **CEM:** Old Presbyterian Meeting House; GPS 38.48528, -77.23532; 323 S Fairfax St; Alexandria City **GS:** N **SP:** No info **VI:** Died of consumption in Fairfax Co. Bur 13 Jul 1796, age 77 **P:** unk **BLW:** unk **RG:** N **MK:** Y SAR plaque **PH:** N **SS:** AL Cert issued **BS:** 110, pg 118; 23 pg 99.

ARELL, Samuel; b unk; d 1795 **RU:** Lieutenant/Patriot, Served in Marines 13 Nov 1776. Recommended for Capt 13 Dec 1776. Signed a legislative petition 25 Oct 1779 to establish a naval port in Alexandria **CEM:** Old Presbyterian Meeting House; GPS 38.48528, -77.23532; 323 S Fairfax St; Alexandria City **GS:** N **SP:** Dorothy Craverly **VI:** Died in Fairfax Co. Will dated 1 Nov 1794, proved 20 Dec 1795 (WB G, pg 130). Name listed on cemetery SAR plaque **P:** unk **BLW:** unk **RG:** Y **MK:** Y SAR plaque **PH:** N **SS:** AK; J-NSSAR 1993 Reg; CJ Vol 2 series 2 pg 291-3 **BS:** JLARC 1; 23 pg 99; 196.

ALLEMONG, Jacob; b 1754, Northampton, PA, d 8 Mar 1808 **RU:** Patriot, Gave material aid to cause, Frederick Co. Also wagon master **CEM:** Hieronymus family, GPS 39.332, -78.327; loc behind fence & red gate Old Mill Ln, Whitacre Farm, Whitacre; Frederick **GS:** Y **SP:** Elizabeth Rinker (6 Nov 1761-1848) **VI:** No further data **P:** N **BLW:** N **RG:** Y **MK:** N **PH:** no **SS:** D; AL Comm Bk II, pg 168 Frederick Co; DAR #A001319; SAR P-100532 **BS:** 221 Frederick Cemeteries.

ARGENBRIGHT (ARGENTINE), Augustus (Augustine); b 13 Jun 1755, Shenandoah Co; d 1833 **RU:** Soldier, Served in Capt Smith's Co, Augusta Co Militia **CEM:** Trinity Episcopal; GPS 38.14917, -79.07521; 214 Beverley St; Staunton City **GS:** U **SP:** Anna Hanger (28 Oct 1756 Woodstock, Shenandoah Co-1836) d/o Frederick (1726-1799) & Eva Margaretha (Mayer) (___-1818) Hanger **VI:** Was a blacksmith during Rev War. Recd Pension 1832 **P:** Y **BLW:** unk **RG:** Y **MK:** unk **PH:** unk **SS:** E pg 20; SAR P-104376 **BS:** JLARC 2, 62, 63, 76; 196.

RU=Rank/Unit
VI=Other Veteran Info
MK=SAR/DAR Marker

CEM=Cemetery
P=Pension
PH=Photo

GS=Gravestone
BLW=Bounty/Land Warrant
SS=Service Source

SP=Spousal Information
RG=Registered Grave
BS=Burial Source

14

ARISMENDY, Jean; b unk; d 1781 **RU:** Seaman, Served on "Ville de Paris" and died from Yorktown battle **CEM:** French Memorial; GPS 36.81944, -79.39933; Yorktown; York **GS:** U **SP:** No info **VI:** No further data **P:** unk **BLW:** unk **RG:** Y **MK:** unk **PH:** unk **SS:** J-Yorktown Historian; SAR P-104381 **BS:** JLARC 1, 74.

ARMENTROUT, Frederick: b 16 Oct 1759, PA, d 22 Dec 1838; **RU:** Patriot, Gave material aid to cause, Rockingham Co **CEM:** Armentrout family, GPS unk; Potts Creek; Alleghany **GS:** Y **SP:** No info **VI:** No further data **P:** N **BLW:** N **RG:** N **MK:** Y SAR **PH:** no **SS:** D vol 1 **BS:** 196.

ARMENTROUT, Frederick, b Dec 1764, Augusta Co, d Jun 1855 **RU:** Private, Served in Rockingham Co Militia **CEM:** Old Peaked Mountain Church; GPS 38.3712,-78.7340; loc Rt 996 behind Brown Memorial United Church, McGaheysville; Rockingham **GS:** N **SP:** Mar 2 Feb 1795, Barbara Monger (20 Oct 1773-29 Mar 1847) **VI:** No further data **P:** N **BLW:** N **RG:** Y **MK:** Y SAR **PH:** N **SS:** DAR A003032; SAR P-104390 **BS:** SAR PRS.

ARMENTROUT, George; b c1760-1763, Germany; d 1805 **RU:** Private, Served in Rockingham Co Militia 24 Apr 1780 **CEM:** Old Peaked Mountain; GPS 38.37113, -78.73416; 9843 Town Hall Rd, McGaheysville; Rockingham **GS:** U **SP:** Nancy Kiser **VI:** Died in McGaheysville **P:** unk **BLW:** unk **RG:** Y **MK:** Y SAR **PH:** unk **SS:** SAR P-104391 **BS:** JLARC 76.

ARMENTROUT, Henry; b 1755 VA or 1755; Berks Co, PA; d 16 Jun or 9 Jul 1806 **RU:** Private/Patriot, Performed public service in Rockingham Co **CEM:** Old Peaked Mountain; GPS 38.37113, -78.73416; 9843 Town Hall Rd, McGaheysville; Rockingham **GS:** U **SP:** Mar (20 Oct 1786, Rockingham Co) Elizabeth Argenbright **VI:** Son of Johan Phillip & Elizabeth (Reith) Armentrout. Died in McGaheysville or Rockingham Co **P:** unk **BLW:** unk **RG:** Y **MK:** Y DAR plaque **PH:** unk **SS:** DAR A096347; SAR P-104392; DE Bk I pg 152, 209 **BS:** JLARC 76.

ARMENTROUT, John Henry; b 1722, Germany; d 1789 **RU:** Patriot, Gave material aid to cause **CEM:** Old Peaked Mountain; GPS 38.37113, -78.73416; 9843 Town Hall Rd, McGaheysville; Rockingham **GS:** U **SP:** Mary Catherine Hedrick **VI:** Died in McGaheysville **P:** N **BLW:** N **RG:** Y **MK:** Y DAR plaque **PH:** unk **SS:** DAR A00303***; SAR P-104393 DD **BS:** JLARC 76.

ARMENTROUT, Peter; b 17 Sep 1751, Rockingham Co; d 9 Jan 1824 **RU:** Private, Served in Capt Daniel's Co, Augusta Militia **CEM:** Bethel Cemetery; GPS 38.47592, -78.75641; 3061 Armentrout Path, Keezletown; Rockingham **GS:** Y **SP:** 1) Catherine Ergebrecht 2) Margaret (Margreta) Wolf (Wolfe) **VI:** No further data **P:** unk **BLW:** unk **RG:** Y **MK:** Y SAR **PH:** unk **SS:** DAR A003039; AK; SAR P-104395 **BS:** 04, JLARC 2, 76.

ARMENTROUT (ERMENTRAUDT), Philip; b 26 Oct 1747, Lancaster (now Berks) Co, PA; d 1 Jul 1836 **RU:** Private, Served in Capt Daniel's Co, Augusta Militia **CEM:** Bethel Cemetery; GPS 38.47592, -78.75641; 3061 Armentrout Path, Keezletown; Rockingham **GS:** Y **SP:** Margaret Cool **VI:** No further data **P:** unk **BLW:** unk **RG:** Y **MK:** Y SAR **PH:** unk **SS:** AK; J- DAR Hatcher; SAR P-104396; **BS:** 04, JLARC 2.

ARMSTRONG, John; b 1730; d unk **RU:** Captain, Specific service recorded Lib VA, Archives, Auditors Acct 1779, pg 165 **CEM:** Armstrong Family; GPS unk; Stonewall District; Highland **GS:** Y **SP:** No info **VI:** No further data **P:** unk **BLW:** unk **RG:** N **MK:** N **PH:** unk **SS:** AS; CZ pg 23 **BS:** AS.

ARMSTRONG, John; b c1759, Augusta Co (Highland Co now); d c1821 **RU:** Private, Served in Capt Kirk's Co, Augusta Co, Militia 1783 **CEM:** Armstrong Family; GPS unk; N of McDowell; Highland **GS:** N **SP:** Agnes Ervine (Erwin) **VI:** No further data **P:** unk **BLW:** unk **RG:** Y **MK:** N **PH:** N **SS:** DAR A003140; E pg 21; SAR P-105522 **BS:** 04.

ARMSTRONG, William; b 12 Dec 1759; d 29 Oct 1853 **RU:** Private, Served in Capt Kinkead's Co 1778; Capt Long's Co 1779 and 1782 of Augusta Co Militia. Was at battle of Guilford CH **CEM:** Old Lebanon; GPS 38.08090, -79.37545; Off Rt 42, Craigsville; Augusta **GS:** Y **SP:** 1) Mar (26 Mar 1793) Margaret Jameson 2) Mar (Apr 1809) Margaret Kirkpatrick **VI:** Appl pen 26 Oct 1832 Augusta Co. S8032. Died in Pendleton Co (Highland now). Grave has DAR marker. Son of Archibald Armstrong who was 2nd Lt of 97th VMR. **P:** Y **BLW:** unk **RG:** Y **MK:** Y SAR & DAR **PH:** unk **SS:** DAR A107191; E pg 22; BT; CG pg 78 SAR P-104584 **BS:** JLARC 2, 76; 196.

RU=Rank/Unit	CEM=Cemetery	GS=Gravestone	SP=Spousal Information
VI=Other Veteran Info	P=Pension	BLW=Bounty/Land Warrant	RG=Registered Grave
MK=SAR/DAR Marker	PH=Photo	SS=Service Source	BS=Burial Source

ARNOLD, William; b 1727; d Jan 1813 **RU:** Patriot, Provided a horse for cause **CEM:** Willow Hill; GPS unk; Jct Kennedy Dr and Van Buren Dr, Presidential Lake subdivision; King George **GS:** Y **SP:** Jemima Clift **VI:** Name on monument in cem **P:** N **BLW:** N **RG:** N **MK:** unk **PH:** unk **SS:** DAR A003335; AL Cert Caroline Co; DD**BS:** 196.

ARTEAU, Andre; b unk; d 1781 **RU:** Seaman, Served on "Auguste" and died from Yorktown battle **CEM:** French Memorial; GPS 36.81944, -79.39933; Yorktown; York **GS:** U **SP:** No info **VI:** No further data **P:** unk **BLW:** unk **RG:** Y **MK:** unk **PH:** unk **SS:** J-Yorktown Historian; SAR P-104847 **BS:** JLARC 1, 74.

ARTHUR, Thomas Sr; b 1740; d Nov 1805 **RU:** Private/Patriot, Served in VA Line and Bedford Co Militia. Served over 3 yrs **CEM:** Rural; GPS unk; See property records for homeplace; Bedford **GS:** U **SP:** Mar (29 Nov 1782 Bedford Co (bond)) Sally Dixon **VI:** Widow appl pen 15 Jun 1843 Bedford Co. Widow Sally appl for ½ pay W5636. Brother, John Arthur also served Rev War **P:** Y **BLW:** unk **RG:** N **MK:** N **PH:** unk **SS:** E pg 23; AS; CG pg 82 **BS:** AS.

ARTHUR, William; b 1731(DAR 1717); d 7 Aug 1783 **RU:** Patriot, gave material aid to cause,Bedford Co **CEM:** Findowire; GPS 38.033059,-78.311131; 728 Campbell Rd (Rt 600); Albemarle **GS:** Unk **SP:** Ann Murray (1717-4 Nov 1781) VI: No further data **P:** N **BLW:** N **RG:** Y **MK:** N **PH:** N **SS:** DAR A201140; D vol I, pg 115; SAR P-104869 **BS:** 196.

ASBURY (ASHBURY), Joseph; b 1759, Paris; d 1815 **RU:** Private, Enlisted age 16, 29 May 1778. Served in Lee's Legion **CEM:** Paris Community; GPS unk; Paris; Fauquier **GS:** N **SP:** Hannah Neale Talbott **VI:** No further data **P:** unk **BLW:** unk **RG:** Y **MK:** N **PH:** N **SS:** DAR A003380; E pg 23; H; AK SAR P-104887 **BS:** 04; 18 pg 77.

ASH, Francis; b 1759; d 27 Apr 1828 **RU:** Second Lieutenant, Served in VA Line. Lived in Fauquier Co during service in Fauquier Co Militia. Took oath as 2nd Lt 1779 **CEM:** Ash-Blackmore; GPS unk; Delaplane; Fauquier **GS:** N **SP:** Mar 1) (20 Dec 1774 (bond) Fauquier Co) Ann Adams, d/o John & (----) Adams 2) mar (12 Feb 1789) Elizabeth "Betsy" Hand (c1772-__) **VI:** Son of George & (-----) Ash. Widow appl 4 Apr 1850 Frederick Co. R274 **P:** Y **BLW:** unk **RG:** Y **MK:** N **PH:** N **SS:** DAR A204974; E pg 24; CG pg 83; Fauquier Co Marriages pg 6; SAR P-104894 **BS:** 19 pg 235.

ASH, George; b 1732; d 1807 **RU:** Patriot, Gave material aid to cause **CEM:** Ash-Blackmore; GPS unk; Delaplane; Fauquier **GS:** Y **SP:** Mar (19 Jun 1812 (bond) Fauquier Co) Sarah Ash **VI:** No further data **P:** N **BLW:** N **RG:** N **MK:** N **PH:** unk **SS:** DAR A205705; D Fauquier pg 1; AL Ct Bk pg 1; Fauquier Co Marriages pg 6 **BS:** 18 pg 2.

ASHBY, John; b 1 Apr 1740, east bank Shenandoah River; d 4 Apr 1815 **RU:** Major, Served in 3rd VA Regt. Wounded at Germantown 1776. Resigned 30 Oct 1777, but later was Maj in Fauquier Co Militia 1780-81 **CEM:** Ashby Family, Belmont; GPS unk; Greenland Farm, nr Rt 724, Delaplane; Fauquier **GS:** U **SP:** Mar (22 Feb 1766 Fauquier Co) Mary Turner fr Charles Co, MD **VI:** Wounded and placed on Invalid list 1781. Inquiry made 21 Apr 1837 Norfolk. R12159, VA 1/2 Pay. Died at "Belmont" Greenland Farm **P:** Y **BLW:** Y **RG:** Y **MK:** unk **PH:** unk **SS:** DAR A003415; E pg 24; BY pg 302; CG pg 83; Fauquier Co Marriages pg 6; SAR P-104930 **BS:** JLARC 1, 4,16, 76.

ASHFORD, George; b unk; d 4 Sep 1777 **RU:** Private, serv Capt Thomas Triplett's Co, Col William Grayson' Regt Cont Line **CEM:** Rev War Court House Plaque; GPS; not determined; 4110 Chain Bridge Rd; Fairfax **GS:** Memorialized on plaque 2017 by Geo Washington Chapter, VASSAR **SP** No info **VI:** Died in service **P:** N **BLW:** N **RG:** N **MK:** N **PH:** N **SS:** AP Fold 3 muster roll; EP sources: **BS:** None.

ASHLEY, Warren; b 1756, New Kent Co; d 25 Feb 1829 **RU:** Midshipman, Served in VA Navy **CEM:** Cedar Grove; GPS 36.85798,-76.283160; 238 E Princess Anne Rd; Norfolk **GS:** Y **SP:** No info **VI:** Served in Merchant service as Master **P:** unk **BLW:** unk **RG:** Y **MK:** unk **PH:** Y **SS:** L pg 67; CD; SAR Bio rpt sumitted Jul 2020 **BS:** 196.

ASHLIN, John; b 30 Jul 1762; Goochland d 12 Feb 1823 **RU:** Patriot, Gave material aid to cause **CEM:** Ashlin Family AKA-Ashlin Rivanna Hall; GPS 37.790797, -78.189389; loc 1.3 mi S of end Rt 606 (Rivanna Mills *Ln*), Columbia: Fluvanna **GS:** Y **SP:** No info **VI:** No further data **P:** N **BLW:** N **RG:** N **MK:** N **PH:** unk **SS:** AL Ct bk pg 1, 15 **BS:** 66 pg 4; 196.

RU=Rank/Unit	CEM=Cemetery	GS=Gravestone	SP=Spousal Information
VI=Other Veteran Info	P=Pension	BLW=Bounty/Land Warrant	RG=Registered Grave
MK=SAR/DAR Marker	PH=Photo	SS=Service Source	BS=Burial Source

16

ASHMORE, William; b 1748; d 1834 **RU:** Patriot, Gave material aid to cause **CEM:** Lane Family; GPS unk; Cement Rd; Prince William **GS:** Y **SP:** Mary Edwards **VI:** No further data **P:** N **BLW:** N **RG:** Y **MK:** N **PH:** unk **SS:** DAR Ancestor #A003508; B; I; H; AL Ct Bk pg 1 Fauquier Co; SAR P-105058 **BS:** 15 pg 16.

ASHTON, Henry Alexander; b 1747; d 1806 **RU:** Patriot, Gave material aid to cause **CEM:** Mt Mariah Plantation; GPS unk; Rt 619, 10 mi NE of King George; King George **GS:** Y **SP:** Mary Dent **VI:** Son of Henry & Jane (-----) Alexander **P:** N **BLW:** N **RG:** N **MK:** N **PH:** unk **SS:** AL Ct Bk pg 2 **BS:** 163 Mt Mariah.

ASLIN, Samuel; b unk; d bef 1826 **RU:** Patriot, Gave material aid to cause **CEM:** Eastern State Hospital; GPS 37.25560, -76.71030; S Henry Street; Williamsburg City **GS:** N **SP:** No info **VI:** No further data **P:** N **BLW:** N **RG:** N **MK:** N **PH:** N **SS:** AL Lists pg 7 **BS:** 65, Williamsburg.

ASSELIN, Claude; b unk; d 1781 **RU:** Soldier, Served in Regt de Touraine and died from Yorktown battle **CEM:** French Memorial; GPS 36.81944, -79.39933; Yorktown; York **GS:** U **SP:** No info **VI:** No further data **P:** unk **BLW:** unk **RG:** Y **MK:** unk **PH:** unk **SS:** J-Yorktown Historian; SAR P-105106 **BS:** JLARC 1, 74.

ATHEAN, Claude; b unk; d 1781 **RU:** Seaman, Served on "Saint-Esprit" and died from Yorktown battle **CEM:** French Memorial; GPS 36.81944, -79.39933; Yorktown; York **GS:** U **SP:** No info **VI:** No further data **P:** unk **BLW:** unk **RG:** Y **MK:** unk **PH:** unk **SS:** J-Yorktown Historian; SAR P-105133 **BS:** JLARC 74, 76.

ATHEY, Benjamin; b Unk; d 9 Dec 1778 **RU:** Private, serv 3 yrs, Capt Thomas Triplett's Co, Col William Grayson' Regt Cont Line **CEM:** Rev War Court House Plaque; GPS; not determined; 4110 Chain Bridge Rd; Fairfax **GS:** Memorialized on plaque 2017 by Geo Washington Chapter, VASSAR **SP** No info **VI:** Died in service **P:** N **BLW:** Y #3295 100 acres issued to heirs 29 Jun 1784 **RG:** N **MK:** N **PH:** N **SS:** C pg 389; E pg 4; F pg 4; AP Fold 3 muster roll; EP sources: **BS:** None.

ATKINSON, George; b 1755; d 1755 **RU:** Private, Served in Capt Persifor Frazer's Co, Col Anthony Wayne's PA Bn 1776 **CEM:** Blackburn-Atkinson; GPS 38.36878, -77.16685; Rippon Lodge off Rt 638, Woodbridge; Prince William **GS:** Y **SP:** No info **VI:** No further data **P:** unk **BLW:** unk **RG:** Y **MK:** unk **PH:** unk **SS:** A pg 199; DAR A207575; SAR P-334277 **BS:** 190 name of cemetery.

AUBIN, Jean; b unk; d 1781 **RU:** Seaman, Served on "Destin" and died from Yorktown battle **CEM:** French Memorial; GPS 36.81944, -79.39933; Yorktown; York **GS:** U **SP:** No info **VI:** No further data **P:** unk **BLW:** unk **RG:** Y **MK:** unk **PH:** unk **SS:** J-Yorktown Historian; SAR P-105428 **BS:** JLARC 1, 74.

AUDIGER, Henri; b unk; d 1781 **RU:** Soldier, Served in Regt de Gatinaisand died from Yorktown battle **CEM:** French Memorial; GPS 36.81944, -79.39933; Yorktown; York **GS:** U **SP:** No info **VI:** No further data **P:** unk **BLW:** unk **RG:** Y **MK:** unk **PH:** unk **SS:** J-Yorktown Historian; SAR P-105435 **BS:** JLARC 1, 74.

AUDIOT, Jean; b unk; d 1781 **RU:** Seaman, Served on "Hector" and died from Yorktown battle **CEM:** French Memorial; GPS 36.81944, -79.39933; Yorktown; York **GS:** U **SP:** No info **VI:** No further data **P:** unk **BLW:** unk **RG:** Y **MK:** unk **PH:** unk **SS:** J-Yorktown Historian SAR P-105436 **BS:** JLARC 1, 74.

AUGE, Jean; b unk; d 1781 **RU:** Seaman, Served on "Caton" and died from Yorktown battle **CEM:** French Memorial; GPS 36.81944, -79.39933; Yorktown; York **GS:** U **SP:** No info **VI:** No further data **P:** unk **BLW:** unk **RG:** Y **MK:** unk **PH:** unk **SS:** J-Yorktown Historian; SAR P-105440 **BS:** JLARC 1, 74.

AUGER, Etienne; b unk; d 1781 **RU:** Soldier, Served in Regt de Gatinais and died from Yorktown battle **CEM:** French Memorial; GPS 36.81944, -79.39933; Yorktown; York **GS:** U **SP:** No info **VI:** No further data **P:** unk **BLW:** unk **RG:** Y **MK:** unk **PH:** unk **SS:** J-Yorktown Historian; SAR P-105443 **BS:** JLARC 1, 74.

AUGER, Pierre; b unk; d 1781 **RU:** Seaman, Served on "Languedocand" died from Yorktown battle **CEM:** French Memorial; GPS 36.81944, -79.39933; Yorktown; York **GS:** U **SP:** No info **VI:** No further data **P:** unk **BLW:** unk **RG:** Y **MK:** unk **PH:** unk **SS:** J-Yorktown Historian; SAR P-105445 **BS:** JLARC 1, 74.

RU=Rank/Unit	CEM=Cemetery	GS=Gravestone	SP=Spousal Information
VI=Other Veteran Info	P=Pension	BLW=Bounty/Land Warrant	RG=Registered Grave
MK=SAR/DAR Marker	PH=Photo	SS=Service Source	BS=Burial Source

AULD, Hugh Sr; b 23 May 1745, Talbot Co, MD; d 7 Dec 1813 **RU:** First Lieutenant, Served in Talbot Co MD Militia in 1780 **CEM:** Arlington National; GPS 38.88377, -77.06535; Jefferson Davis Hwy Rt 110; Arlington **GS:** Y **SP:** Frances Harrison **VI:** Died and originally bur in Claiborne MD. Interred in Arlington on 11 Apr 1935. Father of Hugh, Jr also bur here and who had War of 1812 service **P:** unk **BLW:** unk **RG:** Y **MK:** Y SAR **PH:** unk **SS:** DAR A003752; CF; AS; SAR P-105463 **BS:** 203;196.

AUVRAY, Louis; b unk; d 1781 **RU:** Seaman, Served on "Hercule" and died from Yorktown battle **CEM:** French Memorial; GPS 36.81944, -79.39933; Yorktown; York **GS:** U **SP:** No info **VI:** No further data **P:** unk **BLW:** unk **RG:** Y **MK:** unk **PH:** unk **SS:** J-Yorktown Historian; SAR P-105630 **BS:** JLARC 1, 74.

AVARY, Wiliam; b Abt 1746; d Oct 1794 **RU:** Patriot, Signed Oath of Allegience **CEM:** Avary Family; GPS unk; Avary Church Rd; Amelia **GS:** N **SP:** Hannah Clay (___-1822 Amelia Co) d/o Charles (___-1792) & (-----) Clay **VI:** Son of George & Elizabeth (-----) Avary **P:** N **BLW:** N **RG:** N **MK:** unk **PH:** N **SS:** CQ **BS:** 32 - Kilby. (**AVERY**, William Haley **SEE APPENDIX G**)

AXLINE, John; b 19 Sep 1739, Prince William Co; d 19 Feb 1833 **RU:** Patriot, Gave material aid to cause **CEM:** New Jerusalem Lutheran; GPS 39.25736, -77.63891; 12942, GS 39.257277, -77.639162; Lutheran Church Rd, Lovettsville; Loudoun **GS:** U **SP:** Christena Martz **VI:** No further data **P:** N **BLW:** N **RG:** Y **MK:** SAR granite **PH:** unk **SS:** DAR A004044; SAR P-105862; D Vol 2 pg 599 **BS:** JLARC 76; 196.

AYERS, John, b 14 Nov 1755; d 7 Nov 1849 **RU:** Private, served in Capt William McMachen's Co at Pittsburgh, PA Oct 1775 **CEM:** Ayers-Wingert-Wilson; GPS not determined; loc on Byrd Farm Rt 608, 2 mi E of jct Rt 737, Moneta; Bedford **GS:** N **SP:** Nancy Cundiff (30 Mar 1754, Pr George Co-1 May 1832 **VI:** No further data **P:** N **BLW:** N **RG:** N **MK:** N **PH:** N **SS:** N pg 1266, cites Lib VA Archives **GS:** 196.

AYLETT, William; b 1743; d 1781 **RU:** Patriot/Colonel, Was Burgess for King William Co at assemblies of 1772-1774 & 1775-1776 and member of Conventions of 1774-1775-1776. Resigned fr the Convention to accept commission as Deputy Commissary General in VA. Died in Battle of Yorktown, fr a fever he contracted (malaria?) **CEM:** Fairfield Plantation; GPS 37.760697, -77.102705 Aylett; King William **GS:** U **SP:** Mar (1766) Mary Macon, d/o Col James & Elizabeth (Moore) Macon of Kennington (___-1787) 2nd husband was Callohill Minnis. **VI:** Died in Yorktown, York Co. His heirs recd BLW on 6666 acres in 1809 **P:** unk **BLW:** Y **RG:** Y **MK:** unk **PH:** unk **SS:** DAR A004153; BX pg 24; SAR P-105993 **BS:** 196.

AYLOR, Abraham; b 1750, d 1810 **RU:** Private served in Culpeper Minute Men Battalion Sep-Dec 1775 and 1st VA Regt in Lt James Meriwether's Co at Valley Forge **CEM:** Henry Aylor; GPS 38.483508 -78.203544; loc 2012 Novum Rd, Novum; Madison **GS:** Unk **SP:** Mar 19 Oct 1801, Mary Shearer **VI::** Son of Georg Henry Oehler (1718-1806) & Anna Margaret Thomas (1718-1807) **P:** N **BLW:** N **RG:** Y **MK:** N **PH:** N **SS:** DV; CI rolls; SAR P-334962 **BS:** 196.

AYLOR, Henry, Jr; b 1745, Orange Co, d 28 May 1812 **RU:** Patriot, Gave material aid to cause **CEM:** Henry Aylor ; GPS 38.483508, -78.203544; loc 2012 Novum Rd, Novum; Madison **GS:** Unk **SP:** Barbara Carpenter (1753-1836), d/o Anna Barbara Weaver (1730-1808) **VI:** Son of Georg Henry Oehler (1718-1806) & Anna Margaret Thomas (1718-1807) **P:** N **BLW:** N **RG:** Y **MK:** N **PH:** N **SS:** D vol 1, pgs 276, 277; DAR A004157; SAR P-105994 **BS:** 196.

AYLOR, Jacob; b 7 Feb 1749, Culpeper Co; d 24 Oct 1839 **RU:** Private/Patriot, served in Capts Abraham Buford and Henry Hill's Co, Culpeper Minutemen Battalion; at battle at Great Bridge, later Cont Line as patriot, Gave material aid to cause **CEM:** Aylor Family; GPS unk; 2012 Noven Rd, Novum; Madison **GS:** N **SP:** Frances Sparks (1766-___) **VI:** Appl pen 11 Jun 1833 Madison Co. S8040 **P:** Y **BLW:** unk **RG:** Y **MK:** N **PH:** N **SS:** DAR A204668; E pg 29; **K vol, pg 36**; CG pg 101; DV; SAR P-334961 **BS:** 169, Aylor.

AYRES, William; b unk; d Aug 1791 **RU:** Private, Served in Capt George Jenkin's Co, PA Militia, May & Jun 1777 **CEM:** Old Christ Church Episcopal; GPS 38.80625, -77.04718; 118 N Washington St; Alexandria City **GS:** N **SP:** No info **VI:** Burial permit.

BACON, Samuel; b c1734; d 22 Jul 1794 **RU:** Patriot, Submitted claim for losses suffered during burning of Norfolk **CEM:** St Paul's Episcopal; GPS 36.84733, -76.28554; 201 St Paul's Blvd; Norfolk City **GS:** Y **SP:** Mar (8 Apr 1758 Norfolk Co) Mary Ann Dale **VI:** No further data **P:** N **BLW:** N **RG:** Y **MK:** Y SAR plaque **PH:** unk **SS:** CB Friend Amer Cause; SAR P-106530 **BS:** 178 - Jan 8 2011.

RU=Rank/Unit	CEM=Cemetery	GS=Gravestone	SP=Spousal Information
VI=Other Veteran Info	P=Pension	BLW=Bounty/Land Warrant	RG=Registered Grave
MK=SAR/DAR Marker	PH=Photo	SS=Service Source	BS=Burial Source

18

BAGBY, John; b 1728, Hanover Co; d 13 Jul 1789 **RU**: Captain/Patriot, Commanded a company in Louisa Co Militia. Gave material aid to cause **CEM**: Mt Air/Pleasant View; GPS unk; Overton Fork, Rt 723 Bohannon Rd nr Lake Anna; Louisa **GS**: U **SP**: Theadosia Morris (1735-1792) d/o William & (-----) Morris **VI**: No further data **P**: N **BLW**: N **RG**: unk **MK**: unk **PH**: unk **SS**: DAR A004527; Al Ct Bk pg 30 Louisa Co **BS**: 196.

BAGBY, Richard; b 7 Mar 1759; d 23 Apr 1818 **RU**: Patriot Performed public serv for capuring a deserter and paid the personal property taxconsidered a supply tax for Rev War expenses 1782 in King & Queen Co **CEM**: Society Hill; GPS not determined; loc Stevensville: King & Queen **GS**: N: **SP**: Susannah Jeffries (9 Nov 1765-28 Mar 1832) **VI**: No further data **P**: N **BLW**: N **RG**: N **MK**: N **PH**: N **SS**: G pg 440; DV 1782 pers prop tax image 09 PDF **BS**: 196.

BAGGAGE, Jean; b unk; d 1781 **RU**: Soldier, Served in Agenois Bn and died from Yorktown battle **CEM**: French Memorial; GPS 36.81944, -79.39933; Yorktown; York **GS**: U **SP**: No info **VI**: No further data **P**: unk **BLW**: unk **RG**: Y **MK**: unk **PH**: unk **SS**: J-Yorktown Historian; SAR P-106547 **BS**: JLARC 1, 74.

BAGOUS, Michel; b unk; d 1781 **RU**: Seaman, Served on "Saint-Esprit" and died from Yorktown battle **CEM**: French Memorial; GPS 36.81944, -79.39933; Yorktown; York **GS**: U **SP**: No info **VI**: No further data **P**: unk **BLW**: unk **RG**: Y **MK**: unk **PH**: unk **SS**: J-Yorktown Historian; SAR P-106594 **BS**: JLARC 1, 74.

BAGWELL, Isaiah; b 13 Sep 1760, Accomack Co; d 8 Oct 1839 **RU**: Seaman, Served in 9th Cont Line; VA Sea Service **CEM**: Mt Holly; GPS 37.70485, -75.74185; Hill St, Onancock; Accomack **GS**: Y **SP**: Mar Accomack Co 2 Jan 1790 (bond) to Christina Newton; d 11 Jul 1819 (TS at Mt Holly) **VI**: Son of Josiah and Sarah Bagwell (tombstone) Appl pen 4 Sep 1832 Accomack Co. S6550. Child recd final payment **P**: Y **BLW**: unk **RG**:Y **MK**: unk **PH**: Y **SS**: DAR A004566; E pg 30; CG pg 112; SAR P-106597 **BS**: JLARC 4, 5; 209.

BAILEY, Ansel Anselm Ansolem Anselem; b 16 Feb 1758; d Aft 1843 **RU**: Soldier, Served in New Kent Co Militia and 1st VA Regt, & 6th Cont Line **CEM**: Shockoe Hill; GPS 37.55190, -77.43170; 4th & Hospital Sts; Richmond City **GS**: Govt **SP**: Susannah (-----) (c1792-___) **VI**: Entered service in 1776 fr New Kent where also pensioned in 1820. Appl pen 9 Jul 1818 New Kent Co. S37702 **P**: Y **BLW**: unk **RG**: Y **MK**: Y SAR headstone marker; Monument in Cem lists name **PH**: unk **SS**: E pg 30-31; CG pg 112; SAR P-106617 **BS**: JLARC 4,104.

BAILEY, Benjamin; b 1755; d 1813 **RU**: Second Lieutenant, Served in Montgomery Co Militia. Sworn in as 1st Lt at Montgomery Co on 13 May 1788 (after the war) **CEM**: Bailey Family; GPS 37.37075, -77.77635; Matoaca; Chesterfield **GS**: U **SP**: Ann Wilkins (or Watkins) **VI**: No further data **P**: unk **BLW**: unk **RG**: Y **MK**: N **PH**: unk **SS**: DAR A004591; AS cites DAR Report; SAR P-106627 **BS**: 196.

BAILEY, John; b unk; d 29 Aug 1824 **RU**: Captain, Commanded a Co in Brigadier Gen George Rogers Clark's Illinois Regt 1781 **CEM**: Presbyterian Church; GPS 37.40206, -79.13848; 2020 Grace St; Lynchburg City **GS**: Y **SP**: No info **VI**: 4000 acres BLW recd 3 Mar 1784 **P**: **BLW**: Y **RG**: Y **MK**: unk **PH**: unk **SS**: C pg 89; N pg 1243; SAR P-106745 **BS**: 196.

BAILEY, Richard; b 1748; d 1818 **RU**: Private, Served in 15th Cont Line **CEM**: Leatherwood Farm; GPS unk; Rt 460, Bluefield; Tazewell **GS**: Y **SP**: Annie Belcher **VI**: No further data **P**: unk **BLW**: unk **RG**: Y **MK**: N **PH**: unk **SS**: DAR A004746; E pg 31; H; AK Mar 2008; SAR P-106813 **BS**: 4.

BAILLIE (BAILIE), Robert; b 1744; d 1804 **RU**: Second Lieutenant, Served in Capt Joseph Warley's Co, 3rd SC Regt, Aug 1779 **CEM**: Old Presbyterian Meeting House; GPS 38.48528, -77.23532; 323 S Fairfax St; Alexandria City **GS**: N **SP**: No info **VI**: Bur 19 Aug 1804, age 60 yrs. Name listed on SAR cemetery plaque **P**: unk **BLW**: unk **RG**: Y **MK**: Y SAR plaque **PH**: N **SS**: AP roll SC Regt; SAR P-106900; AK **BS**: JLARC 1; 23 pg 99; 196.

BAIN, William; b 12 Aug 1764; d 26 Nov 1815 **RU**: Private, Served in Northampton Co Militia **CEM**: Maria Robins House; GPS unk; 1 mi N of center of Eastville; Northampton **GS**: Y **SP**: 1) Mar (31 Aug 1785) Judith Stevenson 2) Mar (16 Jul 1793) Susanna (Sukey) Dunton **VI**: No further data **P**: unk **BLW**: unk **RG**: N **MK**: N **PH**: unk **SS**: E pg 32 **BS**: 42 pg 5.

RU=Rank/Unit	CEM=Cemetery	GS=Gravestone	SP=Spousal Information
VI=Other Veteran Info	P=Pension	BLW=Bounty/Land Warrant	RG=Registered Grave
MK=SAR/DAR Marker	PH=Photo	SS=Service Source	BS=Burial Source

19

BAKER, Andrew II; b 1749, Grayson Co; d 24 Sep 1815 **RU:** Private, Served in Capt Isaac Riddle's Co **CEM:** Robert Clark Family, aka Thompson-Whitehead-Wilder; GPS 36.61376, -83.15651; Jct Rts 612 & 615, Jonesville; Lee **GS:** Y **SP:** Elizabeth Avant (12 Sep 1752 Brunswick Co-1844 Lee Co) **VI:** Son of Andrew W. (1702)-1781) & Mary Agnes (Bolling) (1702-1776) Baker. Rev. Died in Jonesville, Lee Co **P:** unk **BLW:** unk **RG:** Y **MK:** Y SAR **PH:** unk **SS:** DAR A004862; B; DD cites Hist of KY Vol I pg 13; SAR P-107013 **BS:** 04.

BAKER, Henry; b 10 Jun 1731, Rheinland-Pfatz, Germany; d 17 Mar 1809 **RU:** Private/Patriot, Served in Capt Linchfield Sharp's Co, Shenandoah Co 1781 and Col Eliza Edmondson Regt 2-5 Oct 1781. Gave Frederick County provisions to Dunmore Co Militia, 31 Oct 1775 **CEM:** Mt Hebron; GPS 39.10916, -78.09497; 305 E Boscawen St; Winchester City **GS:** Y **SP:** Mary Ann Elizabeth Fink (1733-1806) **VI:** Newer GS added with "Revolutionary Patriot" at bottom, Founder of Old Lutheran Church **P:** N **BLW:** N **RG:** Y **MK:** Y SAR monument **PH:** Y **SS:** DAR A004941; SAR P-107116; AL Ct Bk pg 29, 30; N pg 1265; Z pg 81 **BS:** 50 pg 43; 65, Frederick; JLARC 76.

BAKER, Henry Sr; b 1763; d 27 Dec 1837 **RU:** Patriot, Signed a legislative petition **CEM:** Baker-Ferry Family; GPS unk; East of Rt 779, Daleville; Botetourt **GS:** Y **SP:** No info **VI:** No further data **P:** N **BLW:** N **RG:** N **MK:** N **PH:** unk **SS:** DAR A004942; N pg 1265 **BS:** 115 pg 67.

BAKER, Hilary (Hillary) Jr; b 1746; d 1798 **RU:** Patriot, Was Clerk of Ct Henrico Co. Check DAR Senate doc 1954 serial 11831, vol 4 for military service **CEM:** Shockoe Hill; GPS 37.55190, -77.43170; 4th & Hospital Sts; Richmond City **GS:** U **SP:** Anna Maria Kreider **VI:** Clerk for militia **P:** unk **BLW:** unk **RG:** Y **MK:** unk **PH:** unk **SS:** DAR A004943; SAR P-107411; J- DAR Hatcher; S NSSAR P-107411 **BS:** JLARC 2.

BAKER, Isaac; b 1726; d 1793 **RU:** Private, Served in Capt Joseph Bowman's Co, lower Dunmore Co (now Shenandoah) Militia **CEM:** Baker Family, aka Spring Creek; GPS unk; N Jct with 647 Bristol-Abingdon Rd; Washington **GS:** U **SP:** No info **VI:** DAR marker **P:** unk **BLW:** unk **RG:** Y **MK:** Y SAR **PH:** unk **SS:** J- DAR Hatcher; AR Vol 1 pg 41; SAR P-107130 **BS:** JLARC 2; 78 pg 286.

BAKER, John Sr; b 15 Sep 1754; d 15 May 1830 **RU:** Private, Served in Capt Thomas Snead's Co, Col Fleming's Regt, Cont Line Nov & Dec 1776 **CEM:** Friedens United Church of Christ; GPS 38.34848, -78.87653; 3960 Friedens Church Rd; Rockingham **GS:** Y **SP:** Anna Whitmer (4 Jun 1761-17 May 1838) **VI:** No further data **P:** unk **BLW:** unk **RG:** Y **MK:** N **PH:** unk **SS:** AP roll; SAR P-107191 **BS:** 191 Frieden's.

BAKER, Joseph; b 1762; d 1833 **RU:** Ensign, Served in Capt Joseph Bowman's Co Dunmore Co **CEM:** Baker Tomb; GPS unk; Albin; Frederick **GS:** Y **SP:** No info **VI:** No further data **P:** unk **BLW:** unk **RG:** N **MK:** N **PH:** unk **SS:** C pg 601 **BS:** 59 pg 18.

BAKER, Martin; b 20 Feb 1751; d 12 Apr 1844 **RU:** Private Capt Henry Pauling's Co fr Botetourt Co in the battle at Point Pleasant, Oct 1774 **CEM:** Baker-Smith Thompson Familes; GPS 38.516080, -78.724390; War Spring Ln nr jct with Mountain Valley Rd, Oakwood: Rockingham **GS:** Y **SP:** No spousal info **VI:** No further data **P:** N **BLW:** N **RG:**N **MK:** N **PH:** N **SS:** Z pg 134.

BAKER, Michael, b 16 Oct 1752; d 6 Dec 1803 **RU:** Captain, Enlisted, served first in Capt Alexander Machir's Company in Strasburg's 15th District, Dunmore Co. As Lieutenant took oath in Capt John Fitzwater's Company, Rockingham Co on 24 Sep 1781 to rank of captain **CEM:** Baker Family; GPS not determined; Haley Good Farm. Fulks Run; Rockingham **GS:** Unk **SP:** No spousal data **VI:** Son of Ludwig Baker (1721-___); burial source AR lists the cem as loc in Brock's Gap, Rockingham Co **P:** N **BLW:** N **RG:** Y **MK:** N **PH:** N **SS:** C pg 605; D Augusta Co; E pg 33; AZ pg 229; SAR P-107263 **BS:** : JLARC 2, 4, 64; 51; 196; AR pg 42.

BAKER, Philip Peter; b 26 Feb 1759, d 2 May 1837 **RU:** Private, Ent serv 1779, Capt Joseph Bowman's Company, Shenandoah Co Militia, serv 3 yrs **CEM:** St Stephens; GPS 39.01580; -78.41310; Rt 623 at jct Back Rd; Shenandoah **GS:** Y **SP:** Mar 28 Dec 1784, Elizabeth Dorthea Volkner (6 May 1765-1842), recd pen **VI:** Pen 1836, Shenandoah Co **P:** Y both **BLW:** N **RG:** Y **MK** N **PH:** N **SS:** K vol 1, pg 41; N vol 1, pg 1251; Bio Rpt Submitted to NSSAR Aug 2019 **BS:** 196.

BAKER, William Henry; b Winchester; d 1837 **RU:** Private, Served in Capt Garnell's Co 1778 **CEM:** Mt Hebron; GPS 39.10916, -78.09497; 305 E Boscawen St; Winchester City **GS:** Y **SP:** Catherine Miller fr

RU=Rank/Unit	CEM=Cemetery	GS=Gravestone	SP=Spousal Information
VI=Other Veteran Info	P=Pension	BLW=Bounty/Land Warrant	RG=Registered Grave
MK=SAR/DAR Marker	PH=Photo	SS=Service Source	BS=Burial Source

20

Fredericktown, MD **VI:** Son of Henry and Ann E (-----) Baker **P:** unk **BLW:** unk **RG:** Y **MK:** Y SAR monument **PH:** Y **SS:** J-NSSAR 2000 Reg; S SAR P-107404; AP Payroll **BS:** JLARC 76; 196.

BALDWIN, Cornelius Dr; b 1751 or 1754; d 1826 or 1827 **RU:** Surgeon, Served in 8th Cont Line May 1777. Was prisoner Charleston 12 May 1780. Served in 1st Cont Line 1 Jan 1781 to close of war **CEM:** Mt Hebron; GPS 39.10916, -78.09497; 305 E Boscawen St; Winchester City **GS:** Y **SP:** 1) Mar (16 Oct 1783) Mary Briscoe, 2) Mar (28 Nov 1809) Nellie Conway Hite 3) Mar (31 Aug 1819) Susan Pritchard **VI:** Originally bur in a Presbyterian cemetery next to German Reformed Church cemetery in Mt Hebron. Moved 1912 with 71 other people **P:** unk **BLW:** Y **RG:** Y **MK:** Y SAR monument **PH:** Y **SS:** DAR A005221; E pg 34; BY pg 361; SAR P-107524 **BS:** JLARC 3, 76.

BALES, Jonathan; b 22 Mar 1761, Hunting, York Co PA; d 1826 or 20 Apr 1837 **RU:** Private, Served in Capt Dobb's Co, York Co PA **CEM:** Jonathan Bales Family; GPS unk; Rt 682 vic Ewing; Lee **GS:** Y **SP:** Mar (10 Mar 1784 York Co, PA) Elizabeth McGuire Turner (20 Apr 1764-1830) **VI:** Dec 1794 made Constable, Botetourt Co. Moved to Lee Co 1814. Died in Martin's Creek, Lee Co **P:** unk **BLW:** unk **RG:** N **MK:** N **PH:** unk **SS:** DAR A207527; AK Nov 06 **BS:** 04, Nov 06.

BALL, Burgess; b 28 Jul 1749, "Bewdley" Lancaster Co; d 7 Mar 1800 **RU:** Lieutenant Colonel, Served in 9th VA Regt. Was as Lt Col, Commandant in VA Line. Was Aide-de-Camp to Gen George Washington. Was captured at Charleston SC May 1780 while serving in 1st VA Regt of Foot **CEM:** Ball Burial Ground; GPS 39.14404, -77.5469; Off Rt 15 nr North Spring Behavioral Healthcare; Loudoun **GS:** Y **SP:** 1) Mar (2 Jul 1770) Mary Chicheste; 2) Frances Ann (Thornton) Washington d/o Charles & Mildred Thornton **VI:** Son of Jeduthun & Elizabeth (Burgess) Ball. BLW issued 28 May 1789 #252-500-28 May 1789. R126. According to Source K was a Col and died in Leesburg **P:** Y **BLW:** Y **RG:** Y **MK:** Y SAR **PH:** unk **SS:** DAR A005389; E pg 858; K pg 42; CG pg 134; CE pg 29; SAR P-107803 **BS:** JLARC 1, 32, 76; 196.

BALL, David; b 1735, St Stephens, Northumberland Co; d 1826 **RU:** Captain/Patriot, obtained rank of Lieutenant in the Northumberland County Militia in 1777 and to the rank of Captain by Royal Commission. As a patriot he gave material aid to cause **CEM:** Ball Family; GPS 37.45912, -76.19536; Cress Field, Bay View on Balls Neck; Northumberland **GS:** Y **SP:** Mar 1860, Hannah Haynie (c1740-1745, Heathsville – c1788-1790) **VI:** Son of Capt George & Ann (Taylor) Ball **P:** unk **BLW:** unk **RG:** Y **MK:** N **PH:** Y **SS:** DAR A005397; E pg 35; AL Comm Bk IV pg 112 Northumberland; AK; SAR P-107803 **BS:** 200; 04.

BALL, David; b unk; d May 1840 **RU:** Ensign, Served in Campbell's Regt **CEM:** Shockoe Hill; GPS 37.55190, -77.43170; 4th & Hospital Sts; Richmond City **GS:** Y **SP:** No info **VI:** On 1813 bur list in cem **P:** Y **BLW:** U **RG:** N **MK:** N **PH:** N **SS:** E pg 35; BX pg 30 **BS:** 196.

BALL, George; b 2 May 1752, Glencarlyn, Arlington Co; d 24 Dec 1825 **RU:** Corporal/Patriot, Paid supply tax, Fairfax Co 1783 **CEM:** Ball Family; GPS unk; Rt 684 vic Ewing; Lee **GS:** Y **SP:** Elizabeth Tunnell (1744 Fairfax Co, VA-19 Mar 1835) **VI:** Son of Moses & Nancy Ann (Brashears) Ball **P:** unk **BLW:** unk **RG:** N **MK:** N **PH:** unk **SS:** DAR A005418; AK Nov 06; DV Fairfax Co 1783 **BS:** 04, Nov 06; 196.

BALL, James; b 20 Feb 1755; d 18 Dec 1825 **RU:** Lieutenant Colonel, Was Capt VA Militia 15 Oct 1778. Promoted to Lt Col 18 Apr 1782 **CEM:** St Mary's White Chapel Episcopal; GPS 37.44782, -76.33181; 5940 White Chapel Rd, Lively; Lancaster **GS:** U **SP:** m. c1776 Fanny Downman, b. 4 May 1758 Westham, Essex Co, England, d. 23 Jan 1821; d/o Rawleigh & Frances (Ball) Downman of Morattico **VI:** Son of Col James & Lettice (Lee) Ball Lived at "Bewdley" where he d after his son William Lee Ball in 1824. Was member of Congress. Purchased "Ditchley in Northumberland Co ca1792 **P:** unk **BLW:** unk **RG:** Y **MK:** Y SAR **PH:** unk **SS:** DAR A005438; SAR P-107858; AK **BS:** JLARC 1; 200; 04; 47 Vol XI.

BALL, James; b 31 Dec 1718; d 24 Aug 1789 **RU:** Patriot, elected 6 Feb 1775 as member of Lancaster Co Committee of Safety. After 1776 made Chief Justice of Ct. Also Lancaster's Commissioner of the Provision's Law that dispensed public service claims. Gave 86 # bacon to cause **CEM:** St Mary's Whitechapel Episcopal; GPS 37.44782, -76.33181; 5940 White Chapel Rd, Lively; Lancaster **GS:** Y **SP:** 1) Margaret Burgess d/o Charles & Frances (Fox) Burgess; 2) Mildred Smith d/o Philip & Mary

---

RU=Rank/Unit   CEM=Cemetery   GS=Gravestone   SP=Spousal Information
VI=Other Veteran Info   P=Pension   BLW=Bounty/Land Warrant   RG=Registered Grave
MK=SAR/DAR Marker   PH=Photo   SS=Service Source   BS=Burial Source

21

(Mathews) Smith; 3) Mar (1752) Lattice/Lettuce Lee (c1731 - 17 Nov 1811) d/o Richard & Judith (Steptoe) Lee of Ditchley **VI:** Son of Col James & Mary (Conway) Ball **P:** N **BLW:** N **RG:** Y **MK:** Y SAR **PH:** unk **SS:** DAR A005436;SAR P-107984; D pg 8; E pg 35; AK **BS:** JLARC 1, 2, 42, 76; 200; 04; 47 Vol XI.

BALL, John; b 1742, Stafford Co; d 1806 **RU:** Captain/Patriot, Recommended for Capt 29 Oct 1779 in Fauquier Co Militia. Provided material aid to cause **CEM:** Ball-Shumate; GPS 38.66382, -77.79851; On a knoll W & slightly S of Rts 15, 29, & 17 where it crosses Licking Run Stream; Fauquier **GS:** Y **SP:** Sarah Ellen Payne **VI:** Son of William & (-----) Ball. Father was first cousin of Washington's mother, Mary Ball **P:** unk **BLW:** unk **RG:** Y **MK:** Y SAR granite **PH:** unk **SS:** DAR A005455; AS; AV; SAR P-107872; SAR applic **BS:** 83, Inv #68.

BALL, John; b 25 Jul 1746; d Dec 1814 **RU:** Ensign, Served in 6th VA Regt, 26 Feb 1776 **CEM:** Old Ball Burying Ground; GPS unk; 3427 Washington Blvd, behind American Legion Bldg; Arlington **GS:** Y **SP:** Mar Mary Ann Thrift, d/o Jeremiah Thrift and Ann Trammell, (19 Sep 1750 Fairfax Co- 10 Oct 1804), Arlington **VI:** Son of Moses Ball (2 May 1717-3 Sep 1792) & Nancy Brashears (1729-1745). Name appears on large monument with 55 family names **P:** unk **BLW:** unk **RG:** Y **MK:** unk **PH:** unk **SS:** DAR A005456; E pg 79; SAR P-107872; **BS:** JLARC 1, 51; 69 pg 58, 60; 196.

BALL, John; b 1756, Augusta Co; d 28 Oct 1809 **RU:** Private?, Served in Capt Samuel Eson's Co 1782 **CEM:** Cliffton Neff Farm; GPS unk; Ewing; Lee **GS:** Y **SP:** Mary Polly Yeary **VI:** No further data **P:** unk **BLW:** unk **RG:** Y **MK:** Y **PH:** unk **SS:** DAR A005458; B; DF pg 122-124; SAR P-107879 **BS:** 04; 196.

BALL, Moses; b 2 May 1717, Stafford Co; d 3 Sep 1792 **RU:** Patriot, Gave material aid to the cause **CEM:** Ball-Carlin Family; GPS unk; 300 S Kensington St; Arlington **GS:** Y **SP:** Mar (23 Jun 1745, Pr Geoge Co, MD) Ann Nancy Brashears (26 Sep 1729-30 Nov 1816) d/o Rober Cager & Charity (Dowell) Brashears **VI:** Son of John (1670-1722) & Winifred (Williams) (1690-1751) Ball **P:** N **BLW:** N **RG:** Y **MK:** unk **PH:** unk **SS:** DAR A210367; AL Ct Bk TBA; SAR P-107907 BS **BS:** 196.

BALL, Spencer; b 6 Aug 1762; Northumberland Co d 28 Feb 1832 **RU:** Seaman, Served in VA State Navy **CEM:** Ball Family; GPS 38.80945, -77.50895; Manassas Battlefield, off Vandor Ln across fr Strayer University; Manassas City **GS:** U **SP:** Elizabeth Landon Carter (1768-1842) **VI:** Son of James (a RW soldier) & (-----) Ball. Died in Prince William Co **P:** unk **BLW:** unk **RG:** Y **MK:** unk **PH:** unk **SS:** C pg 330; SAR P-107927 **BS:** JLARC 95.

BALL, William; b 1759; d 2 or 7 Jul 1829 **RU: Private,** Served as trumpeter in Capt Cadwalladre Co, Col Washington's 3rd Regt Light Dragoons which later was called 1st VA Regt **CEM:** Mt Hebron; GPS 39.10916, -78.09497; 305 E Boscawen St; Winchester City **GS:** U **SP:** Mar (27 Mar 1785 Winchester) Elizabeth Riley (c1768-5 May 1855) **VI:**. Sol appl pen 24 Jun 1828 Frederick Co, a res of Winchester. Widow appl pen 26 Jul 1838 Frederick Co. Pensioned 1828. W3376, BLW #s 356-60-55 & 356-100-22 Sep 1807 **P:** Y **BLW:** Y **RG:** Y **MK:** Y SAR & DAR monument as Capt **PH:** unk **SS:** E pg 858; K pg 42; CG pg 136; EE pg 10; DAR A005508; SAR P-134827 **BS:** JLARC 4 ,47.

BALL, William; b 1738, Northumberland Co, d 25 Dec 1807 **RU:** 2d Lieutenant, recommended this rank 27 Nov 1780, Fauquier Co Militia **CEM:** Ball Family; GPS Not determined; Elk Run; Fauquier **GS:** No **SP:** Hannah Smith; **VI:** Son of Edward Ball (1701-1742) & Sarah Owens (1706-1751) **P:** N **BLW:** N **RG:** Y **MK:** N **PH:** N **SS:** AZ pg 199; DAR A005507; SAR P-107947; **BS:** SAR P-107947 Application & Bio.

BALLARD, Barclay; b 1752, Caroline Co, d 4 May 1814 **RU:** : Patriot, Supported cause by paying supply tax included in his personal property tax in 1782, Bedford Co **CEM:** South River Meeting House; GPS 37.3724590,-79.1919420; loc 5810 Fort Ave (Rt 460); Lynchburg City **GS:** Unk SP: (13 Aug 1755, Amelia Co-17 Jul 1824) **VI:** Son of William Ballard (8 Sep1714-29 Apr 1794) & Mary Sarah Byrum (1710, Essex Co-1765) **P:** N **BLW:** N **RG:** N **MK:** N **PH:** N **SS:** DV 1782 image 03, .05 pdf **BS:** 196.

BALLARD, Edward; b unk; d aft 19 Oct 1781 **RU:** Lieutenant, Was Navy pilot during the war fr enlistment in 1776 and served until after Yorktown in Oct 1781 **CEM:** Lincoln Memorial; GPS 36.80830, -76.32810; Jct Kirby St and Deep Creek Blvd; Portsmouth City **GS:** U **SP:** No info **VI:** No further data **P:** unk **BLW:** Y **RG:** N **MK:** unk **PH:** unk **SS:** EE pg 10 **BS:** 196.

BALLARD, James; b 4 Jun 1763; d 1 Feb 1856 **RU:** Corporal, Served in VA Line. Ent serv Spotsylvania Co in Clark's Illinois Regt. Served in Capt Roberts & Maj Slaughter's Co, Col Crocket's Regt, Gen

RU=Rank/Unit	CEM=Cemetery	GS=Gravestone	SP=Spousal Information
VI=Other Veteran Info	P=Pension	BLW=Bounty/Land Warrant	RG=Registered Grave
MK=SAR/DAR Marker	PH=Photo	SS=Service Source	BS=Burial Source

22

George Rogers Clarke's Brigade **CEM:** Ballard Family; GPS unk; Nr Catherine Furnace see property records for home place location; Spotsylvania **GS:** U **SP:** Isabelle Montague (1755-25 Dec 1841) d/o Clement & Ann (Bartlett) Montague **VI:** Appl pen 3 Sep 1832 Spotsylvania Co. S6584, Sol appl for BLW in 1855. BLW #36509-160-55 **P:** Y **BLW:** Y **RG:** Y **MK:** unk **PH:** unk **SS:** DAR A005528; E pg 36; CG pg 137; SAR P-107977 **BS:** JLARC 1, 4, 76.

BALLARD, Proctor; b 1760; d 1820 **RU:** Sergeant, Clark's Illinois Regt at Falls of Ohio River, 1781 **CEM:** Old Bardstown City; GPS unk; Bardstown; Nelson **GS:** U **SP:** No info **VI:** No further data **P:** unk **BLW:** Y **RG:** Y **MK:** unk **PH:** unk **SS:** J-NSSAR 1993 Reg; E pg 36; EE pg 10 **BS:** JLARC 1.

BALLARD, William Jr; b 8 Sep 1715, York Co; d 1794 **RU:** Patriot, Gave material aid to cause **CEM:** South River Meeting House; GPS 37.37246, -79.19194; 5810 Fort Ave; Lynchburg City **GS:** U **SP:** 1) Mary Sarah Byrum (1710-1765) 2) Mar (25 Aug 1768) Rachel (Clark) Morrman (1714-1792) **VI:** Son of William (1684-1754) & Philadelphia Ludwell (Lee) (1682-___) Ballard. Died in Bedford Co **P:** N **BLW:** N **RG:** unk **MK:** unk **PH:** unk **SS:** DAR A005554; D pg 11; AL Ct Bk pg 10 Bedford Co; SAR P-108018 **BS:** 196.

BALSLEY (BALSEY), Christian; b 1 May 1756, Berks Co, PA; d 22 Jun 1837 **RU:** Ensign, Ent serv Reading, PA in PA Line **CEM:** Shenandoah Methodist; GPS 38.98160, -78.95773; 1919 Howardsville Turnpike, Sherando; Augusta **GS:** Y **SP:** Ann Elizabeth Koiner/Keinadt (1749-___) **VI:** Sol appl pen 3 Sep 1832 Augusta Co. Widow appl 5 Oct 1842 Augusta Co. W7231. Cenotaph monument at Sherando Methodist Church. Son of Peter Baltzly **P:** Y **BLW:** unk **RG:** N **MK:** unk **PH:** unk **SS:** CG pg 139 **BS:** JLARC 2, 4, 62, 63.

BANISTER (BANNISTER), John Monroe; b 26 Dec 1734, Prince George Co; d 30 Sep 1788 **RU:** Lieutenant Colonel/Patriot, Served as Maj & Lt Col of VA Militia. Was in Battle of Petersburg 1781. Gave material aid to cause. Was Cont Congressman. In 1778 was signer and framer of Articles of Confederation. Was Delegate fr Virginia and member of Virginia House of Burgesses 1765-1775. Was member of conventions of 1775 & 1776. Was in VA House of delegates in 1776, 1777, & 1781-83 **CEM:** Blandford; GPS 37.22433, -77.38604; 319 S Crater Rd; Petersburg City **GS:** U **SP:** Mar (26 Feb 1779) Anne Blair (4 May 1746-23 Apr 1813) **VI:** Died in Battersea, Dinwiddie Co. Memorialized in the cemetery as reinterred fr family cemetery at Battersea Estate. Was Col in Colonial War period **P:** N **BLW:** unk **RG:** Y **MK:** Y SAR monument & DAR GS **PH:** Y **SS:** DAR A005765; J-NSSAR 1993 Reg, J- DAR Hatcher; AL Ct Bk pg 4, 22, 26, 32, 39 Dinwiddie Co; AR Vol I pg 94; SAR P-108247; **BS:** JLARC 1, 2; 80 vol 1 pg 47; 196.

BANKHEAD, James; b unk; d 1788 **RU:** Patriot, Gave material aid to the cause **CEM:** Dishman Fam; GPS unk; Forest Glen; Westmoreland **GS:** Y **SP:** 1) Mar (20 Aug 1738) Elinor Monroe d/o Spence & Cheistian (Tyler) Monroe 2) Mar (bet 8 Aug 1754 & 24 Sep 1764) Caty Vault d/o Dr. Robert & (-----) Vault of Washington Parish, Westmoreland Co. **VI:** Was member of Caroline Co Committee of Safety 1775-1776; 1812. Widow appl pen 21 Mar 1837 Clarke Co. Son John W Baylor appl pen 18 Feb 1802 Caroline Co. W5966, Awarded 10,000 acres BLW #114-500. Name is on family monument **P:** N **BLW:** N **RG:** Y **MK:** N **PH:** unk **SS:** AL Ct Bk; SAR P-108260 **BS:** 189 pg 55.

BANKS, John; b 25 Nov 1757; d 30 Aug 1850 **RU:** Sergeant, Ent serv Albemarle Co. Served in Cont Line. Disabled in service fr log falling on back **CEM:** Pine Creek Primitive Baptist; GPS 36.94622, -80.27357; Spangler Mill Rd Rt 682; Floyd **GS:** U **SP:** 1) Mary (-----) 2) Deborah (-----) **VI:** Awarded L300 gratuity 13 Nov 1780 **P:** unk **BLW:** unk **RG:** Y **MK:** unk **PH:** unk **SS:** DAR A005715; BX pg 31; SAR P-108295 **BS:** JLARC 4, 29, 30, 43.

BANNER, John; b c1750, NC, d 1810 Russell Co **RU:** Private NC unit not identified. USDAR cites NC Rev War Soldiers pay vouchers #7637, S115.66 and SAR Gr Reg cites NC Treasurer & Comptrollers Papers, S115.59 **CEM:** Bickley family; GPS: 36.8853753, -82.2776371; abt 1 mi fr jct Rts 683 & 695 on Rt 695, Castleton; Russell **GS:** Yes; **SP:** Mar c1772, Catherine (___) (1752-___) **VI:** No further information **P:** N **BLW:** N **RG:** Y **MK:** N **PH:** Y **SS:** AK May 2017 DAR A005750; SAR P-239537, SAR applic; **BS:** 04.

BAORTON, Robert; b unk; d 1781 **RU:** Soldier, Served fr NY, and died as result of Yorktown battle **CEM:** Yorktown Victory Monument Tablet; GPS 38.28350, -78.54150; Yorktown; York **GS:** U **SP:** No

RU=Rank/Unit	CEM=Cemetery	GS=Gravestone	SP=Spousal Information
VI=Other Veteran Info	P=Pension	BLW=Bounty/Land Warrant	RG=Registered Grave
MK=SAR/DAR Marker	PH=Photo	SS=Service Source	BS=Burial Source

23

info **VI:** No further data **P:** unk **BLW:** unk **RG:** Y **MK:** unk **PH:** unk **SS:** J-Yorktown Historian; SAR P-108413 **BS:** JLARC 74.

BAR (BAER), John, b Apr 1729, PA; d 25 Jun 1791 **RU:** Patriot, Overseer of Roads and gave material aid to cause **CEM:** Rader Lutheran Church; GPS 38.650733, -78.780550; 17072 Raders Church Rd, Timberville; Rockingham **GS:** Y **SP:** Cathrina Elizabeth Miller (1734-1816) **VI:** Son of Jacob Baer (Barr) and Barbara (___) **P:** N **BLW:** N **RG:** Y **MK:** N **PH:** N **SS:** D vol 3, pgs 830, 836; SAR P-332710 cites Levinson, Rockingham Co Minute Bk, Part 1778-1781, pg 8; DAR A207246 **BS:** 196.

BARBARAN, Francois; b unk; d 1781 **RU:** Seaman, Served on "Citoyenand" died from Yorktown battle **CEM:** French Memorial; GPS 36.81944, -79.39933; Yorktown; York **GS:** U **SP:** No info **VI:** No further data **P:** unk **BLW:** unk **RG:** N **MK:** unk **PH:** unk **SS:** J-Yorktown Historian **BS:** JLARC 1, 74.

BARBATON, Joseph; b unk; d 1781 **RU:** Soldier, Served in Boubonnais Bn and died from Yorktown battle **CEM:** French Memorial; GPS 36.81944, -79.39933; Yorktown; York **GS:** U **SP:** No info **VI:** No further data **P:** unk **BLW:** unk **RG:** Y **MK:** unk **PH:** unk **SS:** J-Yorktown Historian; SAR P-108423; **BS:** JLARC 1, 74.

BARCLAY, Hugh; b 1729; d 1806 **RU:** Patriot, Gave material aid to cause **CEM:** High Bridge Presbyterian; GPS 37.62420, -79.58610; 67 High Bridge Rd, Natural Bridge; Rockbridge **GS:** N **SP:** 1) Mary Culbertson 2) Martha Smith **VI:** No further data **P:** N **BLW:** N **RG:** Y **MK:** unk **PH:** N **SS:** DAR A005929; Florida SAR; AL Ct Bk Rockbridge Co pg 2, 4, 7; BY; SAR P-108609 **BS:** SAR Application.

BARCY, (-----); b unk; d 1781 **RU:** Soldier, Served in Touraine Bn and died from Yorktown battle **CEM:** French Memorial; GPS 36.81944, -79.39933; Yorktown; York **GS:** U **SP:** No info **VI:** No further data **P:** unk **BLW:** unk **RG:** N **MK:** unk **PH:** unk **SS:** J-Yorktown Historian **BS:** JLARC 1, 74.

BARDOU, Michel; b unk; d 1781 **RU:** Soldier, Served in Gatinais Bn and died from Yorktown battle **CEM:** French Memorial; GPS 36.81944, -79.39933; Yorktown; York **GS:** U **SP:** No info **VI:** Source 74 lists first name as Michel **P:** unk **BLW:** unk **RG:** Y **MK:** unk **PH:** unk **SS:** J-Yorktown Historian; SAR P-108637 **BS:** JLARC 1, 74.

BARGER, Jacob; b 26 Oct 1745, Rockingham Co; d 24 Aug 1794 **RU:** Private, Served under the direct command of Washington **CEM:** Trinity Lutheran; GPS 38.17201, -78.86820; 2564 Rockfish Rd, Crimora; Augusta **GS:** Y **SP:** Mar (abt 1745) Elizabeth Hedrick **VI:** Son of Casper (1708-1715) & (-----) Barger **P:** unk **BLW:** unk **RG:** Y **MK:** unk **PH:** unk **SS:** S, SAR P-108669 **BS:** JLARC 1, 4, 8, 62, 63, 76; 196.

BARGER, Philip; b 1741; d 1803 **RU:** Private, Served in Montgomery Co Militia 1779 **CEM:** Barger Family; GPS unk; Blacksburg; Montgomery **GS:** Y **SP:** 1) Eve Clements 2) Barba Eve (-----) 3) Barbara May **VI:** No further data **P:** unk **BLW:** unk **RG:** Y **MK:** N **PH:** unk **SS:** AS NSSAR e-mail; DH pg 10, 45; SAR P-108673 **BS:** See SS AS.

BARKER, Charles C; b 10 May 1763, Hanover Co, d 29 Aug 1841 **RU:** Private, Washington Co Militia **CEM:** Livingston Family; GPS not determined; chain link fence surrounds cem; Mendota; Washington **GS:** Yes Govt **SP:** Mar 17 Mar 1791,Washington Co; Frances Nevils Chiles (_-aft 1813) **VI:** Son of John Barker, Sr (1732-1796) & Martha Snead (1725, Hanover Co-unk) **P:** N **BLW:** Unk **RG:** Y **MK:** N **PH:** N **SS:** DL pg 855; DAR A006051, SAR P-108715 **BS:** 196.

BARKER, Edward; b 1755; d 30 May 1845 **RU:** Soldier, Served in VA Line. Ent serv King William Co & Buckingham Co **CEM:** Jackson Lewis; GPS unk; Taylors Valley; Washington **GS:** U **SP:** Mar (nr close of war, 1783?) Elizabeth (-----) (c1763-Jun 1848) **VI:** Sol appl pen 22 Aug 1833 Smyth Co. Widow appl 23 May 1848 Washington Co. R469 **P:** Y **BLW:** unk **RG:** Y **MK:** unk **PH:** unk **SS:** SAR P-108736; CG pg 149; SAR P-108737 **BS:** JLARC 4, 34; 196.

BARKER, John; b 1732 St Pauls Parrish, Hanover Co, d aft 1796 **RU:** Private, Capt James Gray's Co, Col Daniel Morgan's 11th & 15th, VA Regt 30 Nov 1778 **CEM:** Livingston Family; GPS not determined; chain link fence surrounds cem; Mendota; Washington **GS:** No **SP:** Mar 1759, St Pauls Parrish, Hanover Co, Martha Snead (1725-unk) **VI:** No further data) **P:** N **BLW:** N **RG:** Y **MK:** N **PH:** N **SS:** A Part II; E pg 39; SAR P-108774; **BS:** 196

BARKER, Nathaniel; b 1750 or 1751, Charles Co, MD; d 13 Jul 1833 **RU:** Soldier, Served in VA Line. Ent serv Loudoun Co (later Fairfax Co) **CEM:** Frying Pan Meeting House; GPS 38.56240, -77.24480;

RU=Rank/Unit	CEM=Cemetery	GS=Gravestone	SP=Spousal Information
VI=Other Veteran Info	P=Pension	BLW=Bounty/Land Warrant	RG=Registered Grave
MK=SAR/DAR Marker	PH=Photo	SS=Service Source	BS=Burial Source

24

2615 Centreville Rd, Herndon; Fairfax **GS:** N **SP:** Mar (1 Nov 1771) Letitia or Letty or Lettiia Elsey or Elzey or Ellzey (c1756-___) **VI:** Sol pen 11 Dec 1832 Fairfax Co. Widow appl 21 Aug 1838. Pensioned in 1832. W5774 **P:** Y **BLW:** unk **RG:** Y **MK:** N **PH:** N **SS:** CG pg 151; SAR P-108804 **BS:** JLARC 4,14, 28.

BARKSDALE, Beverly; b 1756, Prince Edward Co; d Apr 1822 **RU:** Patriot, Hauled military supplies and gave material aid to cause, Pittsylvania Co **CEM:** Barksdale Family; GPS unk; End of Rt 689 at Depot, Cedar View, South Boston; Halifax **GS:** N **SP:** Mar (1 Jan 180-1) Judith Womack (1782-1830) d/o Charles (1738-1822) & Elizabeth Agnes (Williams) (1740-1800) Womack **VI:** Son of Thomas (1720-1788) & Judith (Beverly) Barksdale. Died in South Boston, Halifax Co **P:** N **BLW:** N **RG:** Y **MK:** N **PH:** N **SS:** DAR A006162; AL Ct Bk pg 32; AS; SAR P-108917 **BS:** 196; 80 vol 1 pg 51; 215.

BARKSDALE, Peter; b 1757; d 1825 **RU:** Captain, Disabled in not identified service **CEM:** Barksdale Family; GPS unk; End of Rt 689 at Depot, Cedar View, South Boston; Halifax **GS:** U **SP:** Mar (11 Jan 1781, Halifax Co) Elizabeth Watlington, d/o Armistead & Susannah (Coleman) Watlington **VI:** Son of Nathaniel & Mourning (Dickerson) Barksdale. Awarded L90 gratuity 4 Nov 1779 **P:** unk **BLW:** unk **RG:** Y **MK:** unk **PH:** unk **SS:** DAR A006172; J-NSSAR 1993 Reg, J- DAR Hatcher; BX pg 34; SAR P-108912 **BS:** JLARC 1, 2; 215.

BARKSDALE, Thomas Henry; b 1710; d aft 14 Feb 1788 **RU:** Major/Patriot, Signed Oath of Allegiance **CEM:** Barksdale Family; GPS unk; Camden Parish; Henry **GS:** Y **SP:** Judith Beverly **VI:** No further data **P:** unk **BLW:** unk **RG:** Y **MK:** N **PH:** unk **SS:** DAR A132797; AS, SAR regis; DG pg 304; SAR P-108915 **BS:** SAR regis.

BARLOW, Jesse; b 20 Sep 1740; d 1779 **RU:** Private/Patriot, Signed Oath of Allegiance Isle of Wight Co **CEM:** St Luke's Church; GPS 36.93940, -76.58670; 14477 Benns Church Blvd, Smithfield; Isle of Wight **GS:** Y **SP:** Lucy Wills **VI:** No further data **P:** unk **BLW:** unk **RG:** Y **MK:** N **PH:** Y **SS:** DAR A006196; B; DD; SAR P-108948 **BS:** Photo 2009.

BARNETT, Ambrose; b 23 Nov 1763; d 23 Dec 1830 **RU:** Ensign, Fauquier Co Militia as took oath 24 Mar 1780 **CEM:** Green Hill; GBS 39.1581001; -77.9768982; loc 428 N Buckmarsh St, Berryville; Clarke **GS:** Yes, area I, lot 841 **SP:** Margaret "Peggy" Helm (26 Jan 1763-7 Apr 1815) **VI:** No further data **P:** N **BLW:** N **RG:** N **MK:** N **PH:** N **SS:** E pg 41; **BS:** 196.

BARNUM, Zeanas; b unk; d 1781 **RU:** Captain, Served fr CT and died as result of Yorktown battle **CEM:** Yorktown Victory Monument Tablet; GPS 38.28350, -78.54150; Yorktown; York **GS:** U **SP:** No info **VI:** No further data **P:** unk **BLW:** unk **RG:** Y **MK:** unk **PH:** Y **SS:** J-Yorktown Historian; SAR P-109516 **BS:** JLARC 74.

BARON, Bernard; b unk; d 1781 **RU:** Seaman, Served on "Palmierand" died from Yorktown battle **CEM:** French Memorial; GPS 36.81944, -79.39933; Yorktown; York **GS:** U **SP:** No info **VI:** No further data **P:** unk **BLW:** unk **RG:** Y **MK:** unk **PH:** unk **SS:** J-Yorktown Historian; SAR P-109523 **BS:** JLARC 1, 74.

BARRAT (BARRET), John; b 19 May 1748; d 9 Jun 1830 **RU:** Private, Served in Richmond Co Militia **CEM:** Hermitage; GPS unk; Cedar Hill Rd, Pendleton; Louisa **GS:** Y **SP:** Mary Strachan (1748 Scotland-19 Sep 1825) d/o Dr Peter & (-----) Strachan **VI:** Was merchant and Mayor of Richmond **P:** unk **BLW:** unk **RG:** Y **MK:** N **PH:** unk **SS:** E pg 43; SAR P-330036 **BS:** 149; 196.

BARRETT, John; b unk; d 19 Oct 1781 **RU:** Soldier, Served fr NY, and died as result of Yorktown battle **CEM:** Yorktown Victory Monument Tablet; GPS 38.28350, -78.54150; Yorktown; York **GS:** U **SP:** No info **VI:** No further data **P:** unk **BLW:** unk **RG:** Y **MK:** unk **PH:** unk **SS:** J-Yorktown Historian; SAR P-109648 **BS:** JLARC 74.

BARRON, James; b 15 Sep 1768; d 21 Apr 1851 **RU:** Midshipman, Had VA Sea Service & USN Service. Was Aide to Com of VA Navy (father). Became Commodore & Commander in Chief of VA State Navy **CEM:** Trinity Episcopal; GPS 36.83459, -76.30105; 500 Court St; Portsmouth City **GS:** U **SP:** 1) Elizabeth Mosley 2) Mary Ann Wilson **VI:** Killed Stephen Decator in 1820 duel. Sol appl pen 14 Jan 1834 Washington DC. Widow appl pen 27 Dec 1853 Norfolk Co. W12264 & VA 1/2 Pay **P:** Y **BLW:** unk **RG:** Y **MK:** Y SAR plaque **PH:** Y **SS:** CG pg 169; SAR P-336619 **SBS:** JLARC 4,127.

RU=Rank/Unit	CEM=Cemetery	GS=Gravestone	SP=Spousal Information
VI=Other Veteran Info	P=Pension	BLW=Bounty/Land Warrant	RG=Registered Grave
MK=SAR/DAR Marker	PH=Photo	SS=Service Source	BS=Burial Source

BARRON, James: b 1740, d 1787 **RU**: Commodore VA Navy and Commander VA Navy in Revolution. As Captain in command of "Liberty" he captured British ship "Oxford" and in command of ship "Patriot: captured British ship "Fanny" **CEM**: St Johns Episcopal Church: GPS 37.0266360, -76.3469110; 100 Queens Way, Hampton **GS**: Unk **SP**: Jane Cowper **VI;** Son of Samuel Barron. Recd pension W12264 for VA half pay **P**: Y **BLW**: N **RG**: Y **MK**: N **PH**: **SS**: N pg 11; AP Serv Index Card; BE pg 65; SAR P-109744 **BS**:196.

BARTHELEMY, Louis; b unk; d 1781 **RU**: Seaman, Served on "Saint-Esprit" and died from Yorktown battle **CEM**: French Memorial; GPS 36.81944, -79.39933; Yorktown; York **GS**: U **SP**: No info **VI**: No further data **P**: unk **BLW**: unk **RG**: Y **MK**: unk **PH**: unk **SS**: J-Yorktown Historian; SAR P-109923 **BS**: JLARC 1, 74.

BARTLEMAN, William; b 1767, Isle of Lewis, Ross Shire, Scotland; d 21 Dec 1742 **RU**: Soldier, Service information not determined **CEM**: Presbyterian Church; GPS 38.80015, -77.05791; Wilkes St & Hamilton Ln; Alexandria City **GS**: Y **SP**: Mar (by 1802) Margaret (-----) **VI**: Died age 77. Merchant of Alexandria **P**: unk **BLW**: unk **RG**: Y **MK**: Y SAR plaque **PH**: unk **SS**: J-NSSAR 1993 Reg; SAR P-110000 **BS**: JLARC 1; 23 pg 12.

BARTON, Elisha; b 1757, Fauquier Co; d 1842 **RU**: Corporal, Ent serv Fauquier Co. Served in Bedford Co Militia, 1776 and VA Line **CEM**: McManaway family; GPS unk; Chamblissburg; Bedford **GS**: N **SP**: Rebecca McManaway **VI**: Enlisted 1781, pensioned in Bedford 1834. Appl pen 26 Mar 1834 Bedford Co. S19198 **P**: Y **BLW**: unk **RG**:Y **MK**: N **PH**: N **SS**: DAR A007098; J- DAR Hatcher; E pg 45; CG pg 177; SAR P-110236 **BS**: JLARC 2.

BARTON, Richard; b 1751; d aft Jun 1837 **RU**: Private, Recd pension Chesterfield Co for militia service. Serv specifics in pension records not determined **CEM**: Hollywood; GPS 37.53560, -77.45720; 412 S Cherry St; Richmond City **GS**: U **SP**: No info **VI**: Member VA Legislature 1834-1835 **P**: Y **BLW**: unk **RG**: N **MK**: N **PH**: unk **SS**: E pg 45 **BS**: 180.

BARTON, Seth; b 29 Jul 1755, Bristol Co, RI; d 29 Dec 1813 **RU**: Lieutenant, Served in Capt Thomas Carlyle's Co, Col Robert Elliott's Regt of Artillery 1778 **CEM**: St George's Episcopal; GPS unk; 905 Princess Anne; Fredericksburg City **GS**: U **SP**: 1) Sarah Emerson Maxwell 2) Mary Chen **VI**: Shipping merchant in Fredericksburg **P**: unk **BLW**: unk **RG**: Y **MK**: unk **PH**: unk **SS**: DAR A007123; BY SAR Application; SAR P-119282 **BS**: JLARC 2, 76; 196.

BASKERVILLE, William; b 12 May 1756; d 6 Nov 1814 **RU**: Captain/Patriot, Served in 2nd Lt Cont Line 1776. Commissioned capt 8 Jul 1778 in Mecklenburg Co Militia. Served as Deputy Clerk Mecklenburg Co, 9 Jul 1781 **CEM**: St James Episcopal; GPS 36.66626, -78.38683; Boydton; Mecklenburg **GS**: U **SP**: Mar (22 Jan 1786, NC) Mary Eaton (1763-1842) **VI**: Son of George (1741-1777) & Martha (Minge) (1720-1802) Baskerville **P**: unk **BLW**: unk **RG**: Y **MK**: unk **PH**: unk **SS**: DAR A007170; J-NSSAR 2000 Reg; CZ pg 36 Lib VA War files Vol 4 pg 28; DB pg 20; SAR P-110355 **BS**: JLARC 76.

BASKETT, William, b Oct !741, Goochland Co; d 39 Apr 1815 **RU**: 2d LT/ Patriot, Capt Richardson's Co, Fluvanna Co Militia; gave material aid to cause **CEM**: Baskett Family; GPS not determined; loc Rt 631(Dogwood Drive) across East Fork Kent Branch stream on logging rd on top of knoll 400 ft fr rd, Wilmington; Fluanna **GS**: Unk **SP**: Mary Pace (13 Sep1744, Goochland-21 Apr 1815), d/o John L Pace (1722-1790) & Susannah Houchin (1723-1790) **VI**: Moved to Fluvanna Co 1770, reared in Church of Eng, became Baptist minister **P**: Unk **BLW**: N **RG**: Y **MK**: N **PH**: N **SS**: DAR A00175; SAR P-110358 **BS**: 196.

BASKIN, Charles; b 1741; d 10 Aug 1822 **RU**: Captain, Lt in Capt Thomas Smith's Co, Augusta Co Militia, Aug 1776. As Capt commanded Co in Augusta Co Militia **CEM**: Tinkling Spring Presbyterian; GPS 38.08472, -78.98278; 30 Tinkling Spring Dr, Fishersville; Augusta **GS**: Y **SP**: Mary Craig, b 25 Sep 1746, d 13 Dec 1816 **VI**: DAR marker **P**: unk **BLW**: unk **RG**: N **MK**: Y SAR **PH**: Y **SS**: DAR A007177; E pg 7 **BS**: JLARC 62, 63; 04; 196. . **(BASS**, Joseph **SEE APPENDIX G)**

BASS, William; b 10 May 1763; d 10 May 1839 **RU**: Ensign, Served in 2nd Battilion, Amelia Co, 28 Apr 1778 **CEM**: Bass Family; GPS unk; Bass St, Appomattox River at Exeter Mills; Petersburg City **GS**: N **SP**: Mar (29 Oct 1789 Chesterfield Co) Sarah Judith Shackleford (10 May 1774 Chesterfield Co-___)

RU=Rank/Unit	CEM=Cemetery	GS=Gravestone	SP=Spousal Information
VI=Other Veteran Info	P=Pension	BLW=Bounty/Land Warrant	RG=Registered Grave
MK=SAR/DAR Marker	PH=Photo	SS=Service Source	BS=Burial Source

26

d/o James & Judith (-----) Shackleford **VI**: No further data **P**: unk **BLW**: N **RG**: N **MK**: N **PH**: N **SS**: G pg 7 **BS**: 196

BASSETT, Burwell; b 3 Mar 1734; d 4 Jan 1793 **RU** Patriot Member Comm of Safety and member of Convention **CEM**: Eltham Plantation; GPS not determined; loc vic of burned Eltham house in Eltham; New Kent **GS**: Unk **SP** Mar at Chestnut Grove, 7 May 1757, Anna Marie Dandridge (30 Mar 1739, Halifax Co-17 Dec 1777, Yorktown), d/o John Dandridge (1700-1756) & Frances Jones (1710-1785) **VI**: Son of William Bassett (1709-1744) & Elizabeth Churchill (1710-1779). Held rank of Colonel. Brother-in-law of George Washington **P**: Unk **BLW**: N **RG**: Y **MK**: N **PH**: N **SS**: DAR A007224; SAR P-110420 **BS**: 196.

BASSETT, Burwell; b 18 Mar 1764; d 26 Feb 1841 **RU**:Private, Capt Cokes Troop of Cavalry, VA Militia **CEM**: Eltham Plantation; GPS not determined; loc vic Eltham burned house in Eltham; New Kent **GS**: Unk **SP** mar 1) Elizabeth McCarthy (_, Westmoreland Co-_), d/o Daniel McCarthy (1726, Westmoreland Co-1792 Fairfax Co), Mar 2) Marry (Polly) Hunter (6 May 1776-26 Jul 1866, MO **VI**: Son of Burwell Bassett (3 Mar 1734-4 Jan 1793) & Anna Marie Dandridge (30 Mar 1739, Halifax Co-17 Dec 1777), Yorktown); was an attorney in W#illiamsburg **P**: Unk **BLW**: N **RG**: N **MK**: N **PH**: N **SS** AP Fold 3 ser rec **BS**: 196.

BATTEZ, Pierre; b unk; d 1781 **RU**: Seaman, Served on "Languedoc" and died from Yorktown battle **CEM**: French Memorial; GPS 36.81944, -79.39933; Yorktown; York **GS**: U **SP**: No info **VI**: No further data **P**: unk **BLW**: unk **RG**: Y **MK**: unk **PH**: unk **SS**: J-Yorktown Historian; SAR P-110887 **BS**: JLARC 1, 74.

BATTLES, James; b unk; d 1781 **RU**: Soldier, Served fr MA and died as result of Yorktown battle **CEM**: Yorktown Victory Monument Tablet; GPS 38.28350, -78.54150; Yorktown; York **GS**: U **SP**: No info **VI**: No further data **P**: unk **BLW**: unk **RG**: Y **MK**: unk **PH**: unk **SS**: J-Yorktown Historian; SAR P-110911 **BS**: JLARC 74.

BAYLOR, George; b 1752; d 19 Nov 1784 **RU**: Brevet Brigadier General, Served in Cont Line. Served as aide to Washington as Lt Col 1775-1777; was Col of 3rd Cont Dragoons 9 Jan 1777. Was wounded and taken prisoner at Tappan 28 Sep 1778. Commanded 1st Cont Dragoons 9 Nov 1782 and was Brevet Brig Gen 30 Sep 1783 **CEM**: Baylor Family; GPS unk; Newmarket, Rt 2, 6 mi S of Bowling Green; Caroline **GS**: Y **SP**: Mar (20 May 1778, consent by Mann Page) Lucy Page (c1760-___). She Mar (2) on 24 Jan 1792, to Nathaniel Burwell of James City **VI**: Member of Caroline Co Committee of Safety 1775-1776; 1812. Widow appl 21 Mar 1837 Clarke Co. Son John W. Baylor appl pen 18 Feb 1802 Caroline Co. W5966. Awarded 10,000 acres BLW #114-500. Name is on family monument but burried in NJ **P**: Y **BLW**: Y **RG**: Y **MK**: N **PH**: unk **SS**: DAR A007680; B; E pg 49; CG pg 193; SAR P-111143 **BS**: JLARC 15; 196.

BAYLOR, John; b 1750; d 1808 **RU**: Colonel, Served in 3rd Cont Dragoons **CEM**: Baylor Family; GPS unk; Newmarket, Rt 2, 6 mi S of Bowling Green; Caroline **GS**: Y **SP**: Frances Norton **VI**: Name is on family monument giving service **P**: unk **BLW**: unk **RG**: Y **MK**: N **PH**: unk **SS**: DAR A007685; B; SAR P-111146 **BS**: JLARC 1, 15, 76; 02 pg 2; 196.

BAYLOR, Walker; b 13 Oct 1762, Caroline Co; d 14 Sp 1822 **RU**: Captain, In Jun 177? commissioned Lt in brother George Baylor's Regt. Promoted Capt 1780 **CEM**: Baylor Family; GPS unk; Newmarket, Rt 2, 6 mi S of Bowling Green; Caroline **GS**: Y **SP**: Ann Bledsoe **VI**: Resigned as Capt, thus rank of Maj obtained probably after war. His name is on a family monument here, as "progenenitor of the Baylor family of Texas." Died in Bourbon Co, KY. Memorialized here **P**: unk **BLW**: unk **RG**: Y **MK**: N **PH**: unk **SS**: DAR A007690; B; SAR P-111151 **BS**: 196.

BAYLY, Pierce, Sr: b 12 May 1742, Fairfax Co, d 7 Oct 1800 **RU**: Patriot, served as Justice of the Peace and Deputy Commissioner of the provisions law, Loudoun Co, Also he gave material aid to the cause **CEM**: Bayly Family: GPS: 38.9476400, -77.6136400; Diamond Hill Farm, Braddock Rd, Gilbert's Corner,; Loudoun **GS**:U **SP**: Mar 1772, Mary Payne (23 Feb 1754, Fairfax Co-31 Oct 1826) **VI**: Given name AKA Pearce, Piece, Pirce, Surname AKA Bagly, Bailie, Baily, Bayle, Bayley, Bayie **P**: N **BLW**: N **RG**: Y **MK**: N **PH**: N **SS**: AL Ct Bk pg 1 Cert, Loudoun Co; DAR A004739; SAR P-111154 **BS**: 196.

RU=Rank/Unit	CEM=Cemetery	GS=Gravestone	SP=Spousal Information
VI=Other Veteran Info	P=Pension	BLW=Bounty/Land Warrant	RG=Registered Grave
MK=SAR/DAR Marker	PH=Photo	SS=Service Source	BS=Burial Source

27

BAYNHAM, Richard; b 1751; d 1809 **RU:** Quartermaster, Served in Orange Co Militia **CEM:** Baynham Family; GPS unk; Rt 653, Ruther Glen; Caroline **GS:** N **SP:** No info **VI:** Son of John Baynham (1725-1768) & Johanna (-----) (1727-1807) **P:** unk **BLW:** unk **RG:** N **MK:** N **PH:** N **SS:** E pg 49 **BS:** 02 pg 10.

BEADLES, John; b 1779; d 1824 **RU:** Second Lieutenant, Served in Capt Miller's Co, Orange Co Militia in 1780. Also gave provisions to cause **CEM:** Beadles Family; GPS unk; Btw Green Acres Rd & N side of Green Acres Lake, Greene Hills; Greene **GS:** U **SP:** 1) Elizabeth (-----) 2) Laurina or Lurenna Miller, d/o Robert Jr & Margaret (Peggy) Maupin. **VI:** Perhaps son of Robert Beadles of Orange Co **P:** unk **BLW:** unk **RG:** Y **SAR MK:** Y **PH:** unk **SS:** DAR A007810; E pg 50; SAR P-111305 **BS:** JLARC 113.

BEALE, John; b 1748, Southampton Co; d 1837 **RU:** Private, Served in 5th & 9th Cont Line. Enl Southampton Co In the 5th VA Regt, served as private in Capt C. Anderson's Co, Sep & Oct 1776. Later served in consolidated 1st and 10th VA Regt 1779 **CEM:** St John's Episcopal; GPS 37.53183, -77.41958; 2401 E Broad St; Richmond City **GS:** Y **SP:** Mar (16 May 1815) Julia (-----) (c1782-___) **VI:** Sol appl pen 19 Nov 1832 Southampton Co. Widow appl 15 Aug 1853 Southampton Co. W4893, BLW #8168-160-55 **P:** Y **BLW:** Y **RG:** N **MK:** N **PH:** unk **SS:** E pg 50; CG pg 196 **BS:** 28, pg 421.

BEALE, Reuben; b unk; d 1802 **RU:** Patriot, Gave material aid to the cause **CEM:** Repton Family; GPS unk; Vic Pratts Post Office; Madison **GS:** Y **SP:** No info **VI:** No further data **P:** N **BLW:** N **RG:** N **MK:** N **PH:** unk **SS:** AL Ct Bk pg 63 **BS:** 169 Repton. (**BEALE,** Richard **See APPENDIX G**)

BEALE, Robert; b 30 Jan 1759, Chestnut Hill, N Farnham Parish, Richmond Co; d 1 Sep 1843 **RU:** Major, Enlisted as ensign at age 17. Served in 13th Cont Line. Was in Battles of Trenton, Princeton, Brandywine. Captured by British in Charleston SC, when surrendered. Achieved rank of Capt by end of war **CEM:** Beale Family; GPS unk; Chestnut Hill, E of Ethel; Richmond Co **GS:** U **SP:** Martha Felicia Turberville (1786-1822). D/O George Lee & Elizabeth "Betty" Tayloe (Corbin) Turberville. **VI:** Son of Capt William (1710-1778) & Ann (Harwar) Beale. Was a twin; Rose to rank of Maj in VA Militia; Recd 4666 acres & 555 more acres; Died in Hague, Westmoreland Co **P:** unk **BLW:** Y **RG:** N **MK:** unk **PH:** unk **SS:** E pg 51; DAR A007899 **BS:** 196.

BEALE, William Jr; b 31 Aug 1710; d 26 Jun 1778 **RU:** Patriot, Signer of Leedstown Resolutions **CEM:** Beale Family; GPS unk; Chestnut Hill, E of Ethel; Richmond Co **GS:** U **SP:** Ann Harwar **VI:** No further data **P:** N **BLW:** N **RG:** Y **MK:** N **PH:** N **SS:** DR; SAR P-336279 **BS:** 213 pg 26; 196 **SEE APPENDIX G**

BEAN, Mordecai; b 28 Mar 1740 Chester Co, PA; d 28 Nov 1814 **RU:** Patriot, Gave material aid to cause **CEM:** St John's Lutheran; GPS 36.96500, -81.10110; 405 W Main, Wytheville; Wythe **GS:** U **SP:** Mar (18 Oct 1772) Judith Hammond (11 Apr 1753-4 Dec 1840 Frederick Co) **VI:** No further data **P:** N **BLW:** N **RG:** Y **MK:** unk **PH:** unk **SS:** DAR A008025; D Vol 1 pg 382; S; SAR P-111527 **BS:** JLARC 3.

BEANS, William; b 15 Jul 1752, Solebury, Bucks Co, PA; d'14 Dec 1817 **RU:** Patriot, Gave material aid to cause **CEM:** Goose Creek; GPS 39.11250, -77.69527; Rt 722, Lincoln; Loudoun **GS:** Y **SP:** Hannah Balderston (11 Mar 1751 Solebury, Bucks Co, PA-1 May 1838 Jefferson, Ashabula Co, OH) **VI:** No further data **P:** N **BLW:** N **RG:** N **MK:** N **PH:** unk **SS:** DAR A008046; E pg 51 **BS:** 25 pg 22; 196.

BEAR (BAER), Jacob Jr; b 15 Nov 1724, PA; d 12 Feb 1783 **RU:** Patriot, Gave material aid to cause **CEM:** Bear Family; GPS 38.434770,-78.618160; 2145 Easrside Hwy (Rt 340); Elkton; Rockingham **GS:Y SP:** Anna Mueller SAR indicates mar Istana (___) & Anna Barbara Miller (1726-1791) **VI:** Son of Jagley Jacob Bar (1683-1740) **P:** N **BLW:** N **RG:** Y **MK:** Y SAR **PH:** unk **SS:** AB; AL Ct Bk pg 13; SAR P-106521 **BS:** 04; 196.

BEARD, James; b 1761 Augusta Co; d unk **RU:** Private, Ent serv Rockingham Co in Capt Trimble's Co 1779 & Capt McCutchen's Co 1783 in the Augusta Co Militia **CEM:** Brenneman Mennonite; GPS 38.62620, -78.87588; Brenneman Church Rd; Rockingham **GS:** N **SP:** Mary Chummy, d/o John & (-----) Chummy **VI:** Appl pen 3 Nov 1845 Rockingham Co. R669 **P:** Y **BLW:** unk **RG:** N **MK:** N **PH:** N **SS:** E pg 51; CG pg 201 **BS:** AK Sep 09.

BEATIE, David; b c1744; d 25 Apr 1814 **RU:** Captain, Capt of Militia at Kings Mountain, Oct 1780 **CEM:** Ebbing Spring; GPS unk; N side of middle fork of Holstein River, vic Glade Spring; Washington **GS:** Y **SP:** No info **VI:** No further data **P:** unk **BLW:** unk **RG:** N **MK:** N **PH:** unk **SS:** N pg 1241 **BS:** 78 pg 174.

RU=Rank/Unit CEM=Cemetery GS=Gravestone SP=Spousal Information
VI=Other Veteran Info P=Pension BLW=Bounty/Land Warrant RG=Registered Grave
MK=SAR/DAR Marker PH=Photo SS=Service Source BS=Burial Source

28

BEATTY, Henry; b 23 Sep 1760, Frederick Co; MD; d 23 Apr 1840 **RU:** Private, Served in MD & VA Lines. Ent serv Frederick Co MD 1776, then moved to Frederick Co VA. Ent serv again 1780 and 1781; Was horseman for General John Smith **CEM:** Mt Hebron; GPS 39.10916, -78.09497; 305 E Boscawen St; Winchester City **GS:** U **SP:** Sara Hening (___-1824) **VI:** Obtained rank of Lt Col in War of 1812 and awarded a sword by US Congress; He owned a saddle shop in Winchester after the war and was an elder in the Presbyterian church; Pensioned for Rev War serv 1833, R193; appl 4 pen Mar 1834 Frederick Co. S19203 **P:** Y **BLW:** unk **RG:** Y **MK** Y SAR monument **PH:** unk **SS:** K pg 61; CG pg 204; SAR P-111754 **BS:** JLARC 2, 47, 76.

BEATTY (OR BEATTIE), William; b 4 Apr 1760 Rockbridge Co; d 4 Apr 1880 **RU:** Private, Served under Gen Campbell **CEM:** Glade Spring Presbyterian; GPS 36.76720, -81.78720; 33234 Lee Hwy, Glade Spring; Washington **GS:** U **SP:** Mary Allison **VI:** No further data **P:** unk **BLW:** unk **RG:** N **MK:** unk **PH:** unk **SS:** DD **BS:** JLARC 2, 76.

BEAUJEARD, Francois; b unk; d 1781 **RU:** Seaman, Served on "Hector" and died from Yorktown battle **CEM:** French Memorial; GPS 36.81944, -79.39933; Yorktown; York **GS:** U **SP:** No info **VI:** No further data **P:** unk **BLW:** unk **RG:** Y **MK:** unk **PH:** unk **SS:** J-Yorktown Historian; SAR P-111810 **BS:** JLARC 1, 74.

BEAUMARTIN, Jean; b unk; d 1781 **RU:** Seaman, Served on "Duc de Bourgogne" and died from Yorktown battle **CEM:** French Memorial; GPS 36.81944, -79.39933; Yorktown; York **GS:** U **SP:** No info **VI:** No further data **P:** unk **BLW:** unk **RG:** Y **MK:** unk **PH:** unk **SS:** J-Yorktown Historia; SAR P-111815 **BS:** JLARC 1, 74.

BEAVER (BEAVERS), John Sr; b 1747, Prince William Co VA; d 2 Aug 1839 **RU:** Private, Served in1st N Regt VA Line **CEM:** Beaver Family; GPS 38.66118, -77.47324; 13380 Bristol Rd, Nokesville; Prince William **GS:** Y Gov't **SP:** No info **VI:** No further data **P:** unk **BLW:** unk **RG:** N **MK:** Y SAR **PH:** Y **SS:** AK; AP roll **BS:** 04; 32, Oct 10. **BECK, Jesse See appendix G**

BEDEL, Etienne; b unk; d 1781 **RU:** Soldier, Served in Boubonnais Bn and died from Yorktown battle **CEM:** French Memorial; GPS 36.81944, -79.39933; Yorktown; York **GS:** U **SP:** No info **VI:** No further data **P:** unk **BLW:** unk **RG:** Y **MK:** unk **PH:** unk **SS:** J-Yorktown Historian; SAR P-112075 **BS:** JLARC 1, 74.

BEDEL, Jacques; b unk; d 1781 **RU:** Soldier, Served in Gatinais Bn and died from Yorktown battle **CEM:** French Memorial; GPS 36.81944, -79.39933; Yorktown; York **GS:** U **SP:** No info **VI:** No further data **P:** unk **BLW:** unk **RG:** Y **MK:** unk **PH:** unk **SS:** J-Yorktown Historian; SAR P-112076 **BS:** JLARC 1, 74.

BEDEL, Jean; b unk; d 1781 **RU:** Seaman, Served on "Saint-Esprit" and died from Yorktown battle **CEM:** French Memorial; GPS 36.81944, -79.39933; Yorktown; York **GS:** U **SP:** No info **VI:** No further data **P:** unk **BLW:** unk **RG:** Y **MK:** unk **PH:** unk **SS:** J-Yorktown Historian; SAR P-112077 **BS:** JLARC 1, 74.

BEDESQUE, Vincent; b unk; d 1781 **RU:** Seaman, Served on "Magnanime" and died from Yorktown battle **CEM:** French Memorial; GPS 36.81944, -79.39933; Yorktown; York **GS:** U **SP:** No info **VI:** No further data **P:** unk **BLW:** unk **RG:** Y **MK:** unk **PH:** unk **SS:** J-Yorktown Historian; SAR P-112103 **BS:** JLARC 1, 74.

BEDFORD, Thomas Sr; b 16 May 1725, Gloucester Co; d Mar 1785 **RU:** Patriot, Was Justice of Charlotte Co Ct in 1779 **CEM:** Locust Grove; GPS unk; Drakes Branch; Charlotte **GS:** Y **SP:** Mary Lignon Coleman [source?] Memorial stone says his wife was Druscilla (-----) **VI:** Memorial marker in cemetery **P:** N **BLW:** N **RG:** Y **MK:** N **PH:** unk **SS:** AL Ct bk pg 1, 3, 18, 24; AS SAR appl; SAR P-112115 **BS:** 196.

BEERY, Abraham; b 1736, Springettesburg, Lancaster Co, PA, d 26 May 1799 **RU:** Patriot, Supported cause by paying supply tax included in his personal property tax in 1781, Rockingham Co **CEM:** Cross Keys; GPS: 38.35817, -78.84124; on Rt 679 nr jct w Rt 276; Rockingham **GS:** Yes **SP:** Mar c1760, Edom, Rockingham Co, Elizabeth Gochenauer (1733-1800) **VI:** No further data **P:** N **BLW:** N **RG:** N **MK:** N **PH:** Y **SS:** DAR A009563 cites PA Archives 3d series, vol 21,pg 424 **BS:** 196.

RU=Rank/Unit	CEM=Cemetery	GS=Gravestone	SP=Spousal Information
VI=Other Veteran Info	P=Pension	BLW=Bounty/Land Warrant	RG=Registered Grave
MK=SAR/DAR Marker	PH=Photo	SS=Service Source	BS=Burial Source

BEERY, Abraham; b 1762, York Co, PA, d 1815 **RU**: Patriot, Supported cause by paying supply tax included in his personal property tax in 1783, Shrewsbury, York Co, PA **CEM**: Lindale Mennonite Church; GPS: 38.53581, -78.84925; 6225 Jesse Bennett Hwy, Linville; Rockingham **GS**: Unk **SP**: Barbara Good (1763-1857) **VI**: Son of Abraham Beery (1736, Lancaster Co, PA-26 Apr 1799) and Elizabeth Gochenauer **P**: N **BLW**: Y **RG**: N **MK**: N **PH**: N **SS**: CI-PA Archives, series 3, vol XXI, Provincial, pg 707 **BS**: 04; 196.

BEGA, Nicolas; b unk; d 1781 **RU**: Soldier, Served in Gatinais Bn and died from Yorktown battle **CEM**: French Memorial; GPS 36.81944, -79.39933; Yorktown; York **GS**: U **SP**: No info **VI**: No further data **P**: unk **BLW**: unk **RG**: Y **MK**: unk **PH**: unk **SS**: J-Yorktown Historian; SAR P-112385 **BS**: JLARC 1, 74.

BEGAIN, Francois; b unk; d 1781 **RU**: Seaman, Served on "Caton" and died from Yorktown battle **CEM**: French Memorial; GPS 36.81944, -79.39933; Yorktown; York **GS**: U **SP**: No info **VI**: No further data **P**: unk **BLW**: unk **RG**: Y **MK**: unk **PH**: unk **SS**: J-Yorktown Historian; SAR P-112386 **BS**: JLARC 1, 74.

BEHER, Pierre; b unk; d 1781 **RU**: Soldier, Served in Beaujolais Bn and died from Yorktown battle **CEM**: French Memorial; GPS 36.81944, -79.39933; Yorktown; York **GS**: U **SP**: No info **VI**: No further data **P**: unk **BLW**: unk **RG**: Y **MK**: unk **PH**: unk **SS**: J-Yorktown Historian; SAR P-112392 **BS**: JLARC 1, 74.

BELANGER, Vincent; b unk; d 1781 **RU**: Soldier, Served in Auxonne Bn and died from Yorktown battle **CEM**: French Memorial; GPS 36.81944, -79.39933; Yorktown; York **GS**: U **SP**: No info **VI**: No further data **P**: unk **BLW**: unk **RG**: Y **MK**: unk **PH**: unk **SS**: J-Yorktown Historian **BS**: JLARC 1, 74.

BELFIELD, John; b 23 Jun 1725; d unk **RU**: Major, Ent serv as Lt in 1st Cont Dragoons, 18 Jun 1776. Promoted to Capt 15 Mar 1777 and to Maj 3rd Cont Dragoons in 1781 **CEM**: Belfield Family; GPS 38.02316, -76.48842; 2804 County Bridge Rd, Warsaw; Richmond Co **GS**: Y **SP**: Mar (5 Apr 1744) (-----) **VI**: Son of Capt Thomas Wright & Mary Meriwether (Colson) Belfield. Member of the Society of the Cincinatti. Recd Pen & 1/2 pay as well. BLW #5397, 5333 acres for 3 yrs service & 888 more acres for 7 yrs service and 370 more acres for 5 mos longer than 7 yrs **P**: Y **BLW**: Y **RG**: Y **MK**: Y SAR **PH**: unk **SS**: A pg 414; G pg 88,146, 313, 395, 612; K pg 65; SAR P-112501 **BS**: 32.

BELFIELD, Sydnor; b unk; d unk **RU**: Second Lieutenant, Served in Capt Beckwith's Co, Richmond Co Militia. Received rank of 2nd Lt Jun 1781 **CEM**: Belfield Family; GPS 38.02316,-76.48842; 2804 County Bridge Rd, Warsaw; Richmond Co **GS**: Y **SP**: Mar (28 Nov 1782) Ann Young, d/o Col William & Elizabeth (Smith) Young **VI**: Son of John & Ruth (Sydnor) Belfield **P**: unk **BLW**: unk **RG**: Y **MK**: Y SAR Granite **PH**: unk; SAR P-335910 **SS**: E pg 66 **BS**: 32.

BELFIELD, Thomas Wright; b 18 Feb 1745; d 20 Oct 1803 **RU**: Captain, Commanded Co in Richmond Co Militia **CEM**: Belfield Family; GPS 38.02316, -76.48842; 2804 County Bridge Rd, Warsaw; Richmond Co **GS**: Y **SP**: Mar (25 Oct 1780) Ann Harwar Beale **VI**: Son of John & Ruth (Sydnor) Belfield **P**: unk **BLW**: unk **RG**: Y **MK**: Y SAR **PH**: unk **SS**: G pg 314; SAR P-335911 **BS**: 32.

BELL, David; b 1722; d 1780 **RU**: Captain, Commanded a Co in the Augusta Co Militia fr 1776 to 1779. Provided a deserter fr Cont Army to Augusta Co Militia **CEM**: Augusta Stone Presbyterian; GPS 38.23926, -78.97356, GS 38.1411,-78.5815; 28 Old Stone Church Ln, Ft Defiance; Augusta **GS**: Y **SP**: Florence Henderson **VI**: No further data **P**: unk **BLW**: unk **RG**: Y **MK**: unk **PH**: unk **SS**: B; D pg 110, Augusta Co; DAR A008695; SAR P-335946 **BS**: JLARC 1, 2, 8, 23, 62, 63; 196.

BELL, David; b 1765; d 1 Feb 1845 **RU**: Captain, Served in Augusta Co Militia 1777-1779 **CEM**: Mossy Creek Presbyterian; GPS 38.35331, -79.04914; 372 Kyles Mill Rd, Mt Solon; Augusta **GS**: N **SP**: Mary Christian, who survived him **VI**: Son of James Bell (1740-1782) & Agnes Hogshead. Helped quell the Whiskey Rebellion **P**: unk **BLW**: unk **RG**: Y **MK**: N **PH**: N **SS**: S; SAR P-112563 **BS**: JLARC 63; 196.

BELL, George; b c1760; d 21 Apr 1834 **RU**: Corporal, Served in 9th Cont Line **CEM**: Red Bank Church; GPS unk; Jct Rts 600 & 617; Northampton **GS**: Y **SP**: Betsey (-----) (1783-24 Apr 1855) **VI**: Died age 87y 9m 16d **P**: unk **BLW**: unk **RG**: Y **MK**: N **PH**: unk **SS**: E pg 55; SAR P-112579 **BS**: 42 pg 7.

BELL, George; b unk; d 1778 **RU**: Patriot, Gave material aid to the cause **CEM**: Pleasant Valley; GPS unk; Mechanicsville; Hanover **GS**: Y **SP**: No info **VI**: Body moved fr Richmond and reinterred **P**: N **BLW**: N **RG**: N **MK**: N **PH**: unk **SS**: AL Ct Bk It I pg 44 **BS**: 31 vol I pg 40.

RU=Rank/Unit	CEM=Cemetery	GS=Gravestone	SP=Spousal Information
VI=Other Veteran Info	P=Pension	BLW=Bounty/Land Warrant	RG=Registered Grave
MK=SAR/DAR Marker	PH=Photo	SS=Service Source	BS=Burial Source

30

BELL, James; b 1748; d 6 Dec 1820 **RU:** Captain, Commanded a company in Col Samuel Lewis Regt **CEM:** Fincastle Presbyterian; GPS 37.50017, -79.87558; 108 E Back St, Fincastle; Botetourt **GS:** U **SP:** No info **VI:** No further data **P:** unk **BLW:** unk **RG:** Y **MK:** unk **PH:** unk **SS:** AZ pg 102; S; SAR P-112596 **BS:** JLARC 2, 60.

BELL, James; b unk, Ireland; d Feb 1782 **RU:** Patriot, Gave material aid to cause **CEM:** Mossy Creek Presbyterian; GPS 38.35331, -79.04914; 372 Kyles Mill Rd, Mt Solon; Augusta **GS:** N **SP:** Agnes Hogshead (Hogsett). Widow after 1782 **VI:** Died in Mt Solon, Augusta Co **P:** N **BLW:** N **RG:** Y **MK:** N **PH:** N **SS:** AL Lists III pg 7; SAR P-112598 **BS:** 196.

BELL, John; b 4 Sep 1755; d 17 Oct 1842 **RU:** Captain, Served in Augusta Co Militia. Took oath as Capt 1780 **CEM:** Mossy Creek Presbyterian; GPS 38.35331, -79.04914; 372 Kyles Mill Rd, Mt Solon; Augusta **GS:** Y **SP:** Mar (1) the widow Young; (2) Esther (-----) ; (3) Elizabeth (-----) **VI:** Son of James Bell (1740-1782) & Agnes Hogshead. Appl pen 22 Dec 1834 Augusta Co S16650. Grave has DAR marker **P:** Y **BLW:** unk **RG:** N **MK:** Y SAR plaque **PH:** Y **SS:** B; E pg 55; CG pg 222; BT **BS:** JLARC 2,62,63; 196.

BELL, Joseph; b c1746; d 1833 **RU:** Private, Specific service not determined in JLARC report **CEM:** Augusta Stone Presbyterian; GPS 38.23926, -78.97356; 28 Old Stone Church Ln, Ft Defiance; Augusta **GS:** Y **SP:** Rebecca Worrell **VI:** No further data **P:** unk **BLW:** unk **RG:** unk **MK:** Y SAR plaque **PH:** unk **SS:** JLARC Report; BY **BS:** JLARC 8, 23.

BELL, Joseph Jr; b Feb 1755; d 13 Sep 1833 **RU:** Captain, Drafted in 1776; served under Capt John Lyle, Col Russell's Regt in battle against Cherokees. Drafted again in 1777, and served under Capt Thomas Smith and other commanders; part of General Lafayette's Army at Yorktown. Took oath as Capt 15 Aug 1780- 18 Sep 1781, Augusta Co Militia **CEM:** Augusta Stone Presbyterian; GPS 38.23926, -78.97356, GS 38.1411,-78.5819; 28 Old Stone Church Ln, Ft Defiance; Augusta **GS:** Y **SP:** No info **VI:** Still lived on farm where he was b at time of pen application. Appl pen 30 Aug 1832 Augusta Co S6608; R207; Govt stone reads 1755-1833 **P:** Y **BLW:** unk **RG:** Y **MK:** Y SAR plaque **PH:** unk **SS:** B; E pg 56; K Vol 1 pg 66; AZ pg 104-5, 18; SAR P-112659 **BS:** JLARC 8, 23. **SEE APPENDIX G**

BELL, Joseph Sr; 25 May 1742; d 4 Mar 1823 **RU:** Soldier, Specific service recorded Lib VA, Archives, Sec of War 1835, pen, vol 2, pg 112 **CEM:** Augusta Stone Presbyterian; GPS 38.23926, -78.97356, GS 38.1411,-78.5819; 28 Old Stone Church Ln, Ft Defiance; Augusta **GS:** Y **SP:** Mar Elizabeth Henderson, d/o William & Susannah (-----) Henderson; b 24 Jul 1746, d 13 Sep 1833 **VI:** Died age 80 **P:** unk **BLW:** unk **RG:** N **MK:** Y SAR plaque **PH:** unk **SS:** CZ pg 41; SAR P-112750 cites Creel, Selected VA Rev War Recs, vol 2 pg. 48, 49 and County Ct Orders; **BS:** JLARC 4, 8, 23, 62, 63, 76; 196; 197.

BELL, Nathaniel (Nathan); b 11 Apr 1744, Hanover Co; d 1 Oct 1807 **RU:** Patriot, Sold 20 bushels of corn to the Cont Army 1781-1782 and furnished provisions for Ann Austin, wife of William Austin continental soldier in the 1st Regt **CEM:** Hollywood; GPS 37.53560, -77.45720; 412 S Cherry St; Richmond City **GS:** Y **SP:** 1) Sarah (-----) 2) Ann Butler Moore **VI:** Died in Pleasant Level, Hanover Co **P:** unk **BLW:** unk **RG:** N **MK:** Y SAR **PH:** unk **SS:** E pg 56 **BS:** 31 vol 1 pg 40.

BELL, Robert; b 25 Dec 1758; d Jul 1841 **RU:** Private, Enl Montgomery Co in Capt Aaron Skaggs, Col Preston's Regt **CEM:** Bell Family, Dunkards Bottom; GPS 37.05702, -80.62087; Claytor Lake State Park, Dublin; Pulaski **GS:** U **SP:** Keziah Farmer (1759 Montgomery Co-1836) **VI:** Pen filed 5 Aug 1833 age 74 **P:** Y **BLW:** unk **RG:** Y **MK:** unk **PH:** unk **SS:** E pg 554; G pg 222; DZ pg 64; SAR P-112686 **BS:** 196.

BELL, Robert; b 1753, Scotland; d 10 Aug 1817 **RU:** Sergeant, Probably the one this name that was Sergeant in 9th Cont Line **CEM:** Shockoe Hill; GPS 37.55190, -77.43170; 4th & Hospital Sts; Richmond City **GS:** Y **SP:** 1) Mar (4 Mar 1791, Louisa Co) Sarah Smith 2) Mar (21 Jun 1792 Louisia Co) Sarah Honson **VI:** Saddler in Richmond many yrs **P:** unk **BLW:** unk **RG:** N **MK:** N **PH:** unk **SS:** E pg 56 **BS:** 179 pg 141.

BELL, Samuel; b Feb 1759; d 15 May 1838 **RU:** Major, Ent serv Augusta Co, in VA Line. Was wounded and captured **CEM:** Hebron Presbyterian; GPS 38.14140, -79.15500; 423 Hebron Rd; Staunton City **GS:** N **SP:** Mar 1) Nancy (---) b 31 Oct 1757, d 07 Feb 1794, 2) unk 3) on 7 Dec 1815 to Rebecca Hayes, b. 6 Feb 1779, d 31 Jul 1855 **VI:** In 1834, Sol was still living on plantation where he was born.

RU=Rank/Unit	CEM=Cemetery	GS=Gravestone	SP=Spousal Information
VI=Other Veteran Info	P=Pension	BLW=Bounty/Land Warrant	RG=Registered Grave
MK=SAR/DAR Marker	PH=Photo	SS=Service Source	BS=Burial Source

Sol appl pen 28 Jul 1834 Augusta Co. Widow appl 5 Jul 1854 Augusta Co. W12267, BLW #26094-160-55; R207 **P:** Y **BLW:** Y **RG:** Y **MK:** unk **PH:** N **SS:** E pg 56; CG pg 222; K Vol 1 pg 66; SAR P-122692 **BS:** JLARC 4, 8, 62, 63; 196.

BELL, Samuel; b 1724, Northern Ireland; d 1803 **RU:** Patriot, Gave material aid to cause **CEM:** Samuel Bell Family; GPS 38.22770, -78.89085; Nr NW jct Craigshop Rd & Rt 608 toward Middle River; Augusta **GS:** N **SP:** Mar (1) Margaret (-----) ;(2) Jane (-----) **VI:** Said to be the son of William Bell (1685-1757), immigrant fr Northern Ireland **P:** N **BLW:** N **RG:** N **MK:** N **PH:** N **SS:** AL Cert list 1 pg 7 Augusta Co **BS:** 196.

BELL, William (1764-1833). See Appendix G Addenda

BELL, William; b 1744; d 22 Aug 1833 **RU:** Private, Served in 1779 in Capt Simpson's and Capt Long's companies and in 1781 in Capt Given's Co, Augusta Co Militia **CEM:** Augusta Stone Presbyterian; GPS 38.23926, -78.97356, GS 38.1411,-78.5819; 28 Old Stone Church Ln, Ft Defiance; Augusta **GS:** U **SP:** 1) Mrs. Robert Bell (1769-1811) 2) Margaret Allen (22 Feb 1767-25 Jan 1844) **VI:** He may be the person with this name that had other service as well. He achieved the rank of major after the war period. **P:** unk **BLW:** unk **RG:** Y **MK:** Y SAR plaque **PH:** unk **SS:** E pg 56; SAR P-112730 **BS:** JLARC 8, 23, 62; 196.

BELL, William; b c1745; d 1804 **RU:** Surgeon, Served 11 Sep 1776 on "Caswell" Gallery, VA State Navy **CEM:** Fatherly Farm; GPS unk; Wierwood; Northampton **GS:** Y **SP:** Mar Elizabeth (-----), b c1745, d. 1802. Bur at Fatherly Farm **VI:** No further data **P:** unk **BLW:** unk **RG:** N **MK:** N **PH:** unk **SS:** C pg 4, 5 **BS:** 42 pg 8.

BELLEDENT, Pierre; b 1744; d 1781 **RU:** Soldier, Served in Soissonnais Bn and died from Yorktown battle **CEM:** French Memorial; GPS 36.81944, -79.39933; Yorktown; York **GS:** U **SP:** No info **VI:** No further data **P:** unk **BLW:** unk **RG:** Y **MK:** unk **PH:** unk **SS:** J-Yorktown Historian; SAR P-112770 **BS:** JLARC 1, 74.

BELSE, Frederic; b 12 Feb 1751, Germany, d 19 Jan 1831 **RU:** Patriot, Supported cause by paying supply tax included in his personal property tax in 1783, Loudoun Co **CEM:** New Jerusalem Lutheran Church; GPS 39.25736,-77.63891; 12942 Lutheran Church Rd, Lovettsville; Loudoun **GS:** Yes **SP:** Catherine Shoemaker **VI:** No further data **P:** N **BLW:** N **RG:** N **MK:** N **PH:** N **SS:** DV Loudoun Co, list 1783A, image 4 pdf **BS:** 196.

BENEDUM, Peter; b Bef 1755, Germany ; d 1857 **RU:** Private, Served in Capt Wendell Weaver's 7th Co, 2nd Battalion, Lancaster Co PA Militia **CEM:** Benedum Family; GPS unk; Leesburg; Loudoun **GS:** Y **SP:** 1) Mary Ann Kurtz 2) Catherine Yantis **VI:** No further data **P:** unk **BLW:** unk **RG:** Y **MK:** N **PH:** unk **SS:** AS SAR applic; CI PA Archives 5th Serv Vol 7 pg 182; DAR A122915, SAR P-P113053 **BS:** SAR Appl.

BENN, George; b c1762; d 24 Nov 1815 **RU:** First Lieutenant, Served in Isle of Wight Co Militia **CEM:** Benns United Methodist; GPS 36.56170, -76.35100; 1457 Benns Church Blvd, Smithfield; Isle of Wight **GS:** Y **SP:** No info **VI:** Gave the land on which Benn's Church was built. Was called Major in 1802. Originally bur in Benn family cemetery **P:** unk **BLW:** unk **RG:** Y **MK:** N **PH:** unk **SS:** G pg 192-193; SAR P-335627 **BS:** 153 Geo Benn; 196.

BENNETT, Charles; b 1720; d by 1818 **RU:** Patriot, Gave material aid to cause **CEM:** Old Christ Church Episcopal; GPS 38.80625, -77.04718; 118 N Washington St; Alexandria City **GS:** N **SP:** No info **VI:** No further data **P:** N **BLW:** N **RG:** N **MK:** N **PH:** N **SS:** AL Comm Bk III **BS:** 110 pg 95.

BENNETT, John; b 24 Apr 1763, Fauquier Co, d 26 Oct `1845 **RU:** Private, Served in Lee's legion for 3 yrs, thus qualifying for BLW **CEM:** Bennett-Lewis; GPS: 36.68523,-79.29350; off Rt 715 toward Grassy Branch, Keeling; Pittsylvania **GS:** No, however family records indicate yes **SP:** Mar 12 Mar 1795, Pittsylvania Co, Mary Lewis (c1760-21 Apr 1851) **VI:** Recd BLW 17 Feb 1792. Held rank of Major in War of 1812 as staff officer, Pittsylvania Co Militia **P:** N **BLW:** Y **RG:** N **MK:** N **PH:** N **SS:** C pg 199; K vol 1, pg 67 **BS:** 196

BENNETT, Jordan; b 1759; d 4 Oct 1822 **RU:** Private, Ent serv fr VA. Lost a leg at Battle of Builford CH **CEM:** Bennett Family; GPS unk; See county property records for location; Mecklenburg **GS:** U **SP:** Mar (17 Dec 1795 Mecklenburg Co) Ann "Nancy" Murfey/Murphey (c1776-___) **VI:** Son of Joseph Bennet,

RU=Rank/Unit	CEM=Cemetery	GS=Gravestone	SP=Spousal Information
VI=Other Veteran Info	P=Pension	BLW=Bounty/Land Warrant	RG=Registered Grave
MK=SAR/DAR Marker	PH=Photo	SS=Service Source	BS=Burial Source

32

Sr. Widow appl 22 Apr 1852 Meckelburg Co. W2713, BLW #31446-160-55. R219 **P:** Y **BLW:** Y **RG:** Y **MK:** unk **PH:** unk **SS:** CG pg 238; K Vol 1 pg 67-8; SAR P-113336; **BS:** JLARC 2, 76.

BENNETT, William; b unk, Middlesex Co; d Oct 1781 **RU:** Lieutenant, Was at siege of Yorktown. Was killed in battle there **CEM:** Unidentified; GPS unk; Nr or on Battlefield; York **GS:** U **SP:** Not mar **VI:** Died in Yorktown. Gen George Washington attended his funeral. His name is not on Victory monument. Sister Catherine Williams appl for BLW **P:** unk **BLW:** Y **RG:** N **MK:** unk **PH:** unk **SS:** EE pg 16 **BS:** Land Grant Claim.

BENNINGTON, Job; b 13 Feb 1758; d 24Jul 1823 **RU:** Matross, Served in PA Cont Line. Enl in PA 1777 **CEM:** Bennington-Gaylor; GPS unk; Waterloo Rd; Rockbridge **GS:** N **SP:** No info **VI:** Appl 5 May 1823 Rockbridge Co. S37753. R221 **P:** Y **BLW:** unk **RG:** Y **MK:** N **PH:** N **SS:** M pg 734; CG pg 240; K Vol 1 pg 68; SAR P-113469 **BS:** 04, May 06. **SEE APPENDIX G**

BENSON, James Sr; b 3 Mar 1735; d 30 Oct 1797 **RU:** Patriot, Gave material aid to cause **CEM:** Benson Family; GPS unk; Nr Jct Cattail Rd Rt 690 & Whites Crossing Rd Rt 690; Accomack **GS:** Y **SP:** No info **VI:** No further data **P:** N **BLW:** N **RG:** N **MK:** N **PH:** unk **SS:** AL Comm Bk I-26 **BS:** 38 pg 45.

BENSON, Robert; b 1744; d 15 Jul 1799 **RU:** Patriot, Performed public service with Cont Congress 1774-1789, as witness. Was Secretary to NY Provincial Congress Feb 1776 **CEM:** Trinity Episcopal; GPS 36.83459, -76.30105; 500 Court St; Portsmouth City **GS:** U **SP:** No info **VI:** No further data **P:** unk **BLW:** unk **RG:** Y **MK:** Y SAR plaque **PH:** unk **SS:** NY State Historical Society; SAR P-336637 **BS:** 57; 196.

BENSON, William (Willis) Lee; b unk; d 1815 **RU:** Quartermaster Sergeant, Enl in Capt William Jameson's Co. Later transferred to Capt Dandridge's Co, 2d VA Regt of Calvary **CEM:** Sanford Family; GPS unk; #1 Rocky Pen area; Stafford **GS:** U **SP:** No info **VI:** No further data **P:** unk **BLW:** unk **RG:** Y **MK:** unk **PH:** unk **SS:** E pg 69; EE pg 17; SAR P-113554 **BS:** 196.

BENTER, William; b unk; d by 7 Jan 17781 **RU:** Private, Capt Thomas Triplett's Co, Col William Grayson' Regt Cont Line **CEM:** Rev War Court House Plaque; GPS; not determined; 4110 Chain Bridge Rd; Fairfax **GS:** Memorialized on plaque 2017 by Geo Washington Chapter, VASSAR **SP** No info **VI:** Died in service **P:** N **BLW:** N **RG:** N **MK:** N **PH:** N **SS** Fold 3 muster roll ;EP sources: **BS:** None.

BENTON, Calab; b CT d 26 Dec 1781 **RU:** Private, Served in CT Cont Troops and died as result of Yorktown battle **CEM:** Yorktown Victory Monument Tablet; GPS 38.28350, -78.54150; Yorktown; York **GS:** U **SP:** No info **VI:** No further data **P:** unk **BLW:** unk **RG:** Y **MK:** unk **PH:** unk **SS:** J-Yorktown Historian; DY pg 342; SAR P-113647 **BS:** JLARC 74.

BERGER, Jacob; b 21 Dec 1765, Germany; d 25 Jan 1837 **RU:** Wagoner, Was Chief Wagoner in his unit **CEM:** Bergers; GPS 36.95748, -79.48408; Nr Siloan Church nr Rt 605; Pittsylvania **GS:** Y **SP:** Mar (27 Jan 1800 Pittsylvania Co) Catey Nowlin **VI:** No further data **P:** unk **BLW:** unk **RG:** Y **MK:** unk **PH:** unk **SS:** S; DAR A017187; SAR P-113757 **BS:** 174, JLARC 76, 96.

BERGER, Jacques; b unk; d 1781 **RU:** Soldier, Served in Brie Bn and died from Yorktown battle **CEM:** French Memorial; GPS 36.81944, -79.39933; Yorktown; York **GS:** U **SP:** No info **VI:** No further data **P:** unk **BLW:** unk **RG:** Y **MK:** unk **PH:** unk **SS:** J-Yorktown Historian; SAR P-113759 **BS:** JLARC 1, 74.

BERKELEY, Edmund; b 5 Dec 1730; d 1802 **RU:** Vestryman, Gave material aid to Army May 1782 **CEM:** Christ Church; GPS 37.60968, -76.54643; Rt 33 2 mi E of Saluda; Middlesex **GS:** U **SP:** 1) Mar (6 Nov 1757) Judith Randolph (1738-___) d/o William & Maria Judith (Page) Randolph 2) Mar (1768) Mary Burwell d/o Carter & (-----) Burwell of the Grove, James City Co. **VI:** No further data **P:** unk **BLW:** unk **RG:** N **MK:** N **PH:** unk **SS:** G pg 202 **BS:** 84 pg 198.

BERKELEY, Nelson; b 16 May 1733, Northumberland Co; d 24 Jan 1794 **RU:** Patriot, Member Committee of Safety **CEM:** Airwell; GPS unk; Rt 738; Hanover **GS:** Y **SP:** Elizabeth Wormley **VI:** No further data **P:** N **BLW:** N **RG:** N **MK:** N **PH:** unk **SS:** DD **BS:** 31 vol 1 pg 2.

BERNAN, Julien; b unk; d 1781 **RU:** Seaman, Served on "Diademe" and died from Yorktown battle **CEM:** French Memorial; GPS 36.81944, -79.39933; Yorktown; York **GS:** U **SP:** No info **VI:** No further data **P:** unk **BLW:** unk **RG:** Y **MK:** unk **PH:** unk **SS:** J-Yorktown Historia; SAR P-113802 **BS:** JLARC 1, 74.

RU=Rank/Unit	CEM=Cemetery	GS=Gravestone	SP=Spousal Information
VI=Other Veteran Info	P=Pension	BLW=Bounty/Land Warrant	RG=Registered Grave
MK=SAR/DAR Marker	PH=Photo	SS=Service Source	BS=Burial Source

BERNARD, John, Jr; b 16 Nov 1736, Manakin, Goochland Co; d 15 Jan 1824 **RU**:Patriot, gave provisions to Buckingham Co Militia 15 Sep 1777 **CEM**: Milton Valley; GPS 39.139999, -77.979202; loc on Josephine St, Berryville; Clarke **GS**: Unk **SP**: Mar 6 Mar 1760, Elizabeth Barnett (14 Apr 1743, Goochland Co-30 Aug 1822, Milton, Albemarle Co) **VI**: Son of John Barnard, Sr & Mary Abney (1714-1761); a Huguenot **P**: N **BLW**: N **RG**: Y **MK**: N **PH**: unk **SS**:G pg 440; SAR P-113806; DAR A009543 **BS**: 196.

BERNARD, Peter; 14 Jul 1747, Fluvanna Co d 1 Oct 1818 **RU**: Captain, commanded a company Apr 1779 in the 2d VA Regt, resigned 24 Aug 1779 **CEM**: Bernard Family; GPS 37.005955, -79.701788; loc on Old Salem School Rd (Rt 662), Union Hall; Franklin **GS**: Unk **SP**:Agnes Witt Key (1752-1811), d/o John W Key & Agnes Witt **VI**: Son of Mary Abney (1714-1761); a Huguenot **P**: N **BLW**: N **RG**: Y **MK**: N **PH**: unk **SS**: E pg 60; SAR P-113810 **BS**: 196.

BERNARD, Walter; b 1758, Frederick Co MD; d 5 Feb 1841 **RU**: Major, Served in VA Line. Ent serv Loudoun Co 1776 or 1777 for first enl. In 1778 moved to Henry Co (now Franklin Co) **CEM**: Tanyard-Bernard-Hill; GPS unk; Rocky Mount; Franklin **GS**: U **SP**: Ruth Hill **VI**: Baptized at Rock Creek Church. Appl pen 3 Sep 1832 Franklin (then Henry) Co. S6634. R225 **P**: Y **BLW**: unk **RG**: Y **MK**: unk **PH**: unk **SS**: J-NSSAR 2000 Reg; CG pg 245; K Vol 1 pg 70; SAR P-113814 **BS**: JLARC 1, 2, 18, 76.

BERRY, Benjamin; b 16 Aug 1724; d Sep 1810 **RU**: Patriot, Supplied 375 lbs of beef to cause **CEM**: Grace Episcopal; GPS 39.15220, -77.98060; 110 N Church St, Berryville; Clarke **GS**: Y **SP**: No info **VI**: Son of Henry Berry of King George Co. Settled in what is now Clarke Co prior to Rev. In 1798 platted and sold the land for Berrytown **P**: N **BLW**: N **RG**: N **MK**: Y SAR **PH**: Y **SS**: AL Ct Bk pg 19 **BS**: 58 pg 34; 196.

BERRY, Benjamin; b 1758; near Monmouth CH, Monmouth, NJ; d 14 Dec 1834 **RU**: Private, Served in NJ & VA Lines. Drafted age 16 Shrewsbury NJ. In 1776 moved to VA & drafted Rockingham Co 1780. Served 13 mos NJ Troops in Capts Walton's and Hunn's Cos. Served in Rockingham Co Militia in Capt Harrison's VA Co and in Capt Baxter's Co, Col Halle's Virginia Regt **CEM**: Old Peaked Mountain; GPS 38.37113, -78.73416; 9843 Town Hall Rd, McGaheysville; Rockingham **GS**: U **SP**: 1) Sarah Matthews 2) Johanna (-----) **VI**: Moved to VA in fall of 1778. Appl pen 2 Aug 1832 Rockingham Co age 74, S6627. R226 **P**: Y **BLW**: unk **RG**: Y **MK**: unk **PH**: unk **SS**: E pg 60; CG pg 246; K Vol 1 pg 70; SAR P-113846 **BS**: JLARC 4, 61, 76.

BERRY, Charles; b 1725; d 1789 **RU**: Patriot, Gave 350# flour in Aug 1780 to cause **CEM**: New Providence Presbyterian; GPS 37.95170, -79.30250; 1208 New Providence Rd, Raphine; Rockbridge **GS**: U **SP**: Mary Cunningham **VI**: Held rank of Col, probably obtained before RW because over military age for war service **P**: N **BLW**: N **RG**: Y **MK**: unk **PH**: unk **SS**: AL Cert 3 Augusta Co; SAR P-113853 **BS**: JLARC 79; 196.

BERRY, David; b unk; d 1810 **RU**: Corporal, Served in US Army. Specific service recorded Lib VA, Archives, Bounty Land Warrants, War, vol 4,1784, pgs 96, 98 **CEM**: Leesburg Presbyterian; GPS 39.11611, -77.56722; 207 W Market St, Leesburg; Loudoun **GS**: Y **SP**: No info **VI**: No further data **P**: unk **BLW**: Y **RG**: N **MK**: N **PH**: unk **SS**: C Sec II pg 222; CZ pg 44 **BS**: 25 pg 27.

BERRY, John; b 1743 County Antrim, Ireland; d 1786 **RU**: Lieutenant, Served in Washington Co Militia. Fought at Battle of Kings Mountain. Served in 7th VA Regt 1780-1783 **CEM**: Green Spring Presbyterian; GPS 36.63670, -81.99560; 2007 Green Spring Ch Rd, Abingdon; Washington **GS**: N **SP**: Sarah Jane Campbell (10 Apr 1743 Washington Co-27 Sep 1833) **VI**: Grave stone missing 1991 **P**: N **BLW**: N **RG**: Y **MK**: unk **PH**: N **SS**: E pg 60; CI: Muster roll; SAR P-113893 **BS**: 78, sec II pg 122; 196.

BERRY, John; b 10 Jun 1765; d 11 Nov 1831 **RU**: Private, Served in Capt Vance's Co, Augusta Co Militia **CEM**: Airy Knoll; GPS unk; E of Rt 252 abt .4 mi N of Rt 620, S of Newport; Augusta **GS**: Y **SP**: Mar (19 Oct 1797) Eleanor Jamison (21 Sep 1768-26 Aug 1959) **VI**: Son of Charles (1725-1789) & (----) Berry **P**: N **BLW**: N **RG**: N **MK**: N **PH**: N **SS**: E pg 60 **BS**: 196.

BERRY, John; b 1735; d 1798 **RU**: Private, Specific service recorded Lib VA, Archives, Report Sec of War, Pen, Vol 2, pg 21 **CEM**: Old Peaked Mountain; GPS 38.37113, -78.73416; 9843 Town Hall Rd, McGaheysville; Rockingham **GS**: U **SP**: Susannah Smith **VI**: No further data **P**: unk **BLW**: unk **RG**: Y **MK**: Y DAR plaque **PH**: unk **SS**: J-NSSAR 2000 Reg; CZ pg 44; SAR P-113892 **BS**: JLARC 76.

RU=Rank/Unit	CEM=Cemetery	GS=Gravestone	SP=Spousal Information
VI=Other Veteran Info	P=Pension	BLW=Bounty/Land Warrant	RG=Registered Grave
MK=SAR/DAR Marker	PH=Photo	SS=Service Source	BS=Burial Source

BERRY (BEERY), Abraham; b c1736, Lancaster Co, PA; d 25 May 1799 **RU:** Patriot, Paid supply tax 1781 in PA **CEM:** Union Church; GPS unk; Rt 679 Battlefield Rd; Rockingham **GS:** Y **SP:** 1) Elizabeth Gochenour 2) Barbara Goode **VI:** No further data **P:** unk **BLW:** unk **RG:** Y **MK:** N **PH:** unk **SS:** AK Sep 09; Cl PA Archives 3d Serv Vol 21 pg 424; SAR P-333080 **BS:** AK Sep 09.

BERRYHILL, John; b 1728; d 28 Dec 1817 **RU:** Patriot, Gave material aid to cause **CEM:** Stonewall Jackson Memorial; GPS 37.78128, -79.44604; 314 S Main St; Lexington City **GS:** Y **SP:** Mar (___ Augusta Co) Rachel Moffatt (1727-28 Sep 1812) d/o James (1700-1764) & (-----) Moffett **VI:** Son of John (1687 London, England-1751 Mecklenburg Co) & (-----) Berryhill **P:** N **BLW:** N **RG:** N **MK:** unk **PH:** unk **SS:** AL Ct Bk pg 4 Rockbridge Co **BS:** 196.

BERTHELOT, Francois; b unk; d 1781 **RU:** Seaman, Served on "Northumberland" and died from Yorktown battle **CEM:** French Memorial; GPS 36.81944, -79.39933; Yorktown; York **GS:** U **SP:** No info **VI:** No further data **P:** unk **BLW:** unk **RG:** Y **MK:** unk **PH:** unk **SS:** J-Yorktown Historian; SAR P-113996 **BS:** JLARC 1, 74.

BERTIN, Jean; b unk; d 1781 **RU:** Seaman, Served on "Hercule" and died from Yorktown battle **CEM:** French Memorial; GPS 36.81944, -79.39933; Yorktown; York **GS:** U **SP:** No info **VI:** No further data **P:** unk **BLW:** unk **RG:** Y **MK:** unk **PH:** unk **SS:** J-Yorktown Historian; SAR P-114003 **BS:** JLARC 1, 74.

BESARD, Jean; b unk; d 1781 **RU:** Soldier, Served in Boubonnais Bn and died from Yorktown battle **CEM:** French Memorial; GPS 36.81944, -79.39933; Yorktown; York **GS:** U **SP:** No info **VI:** No further data **P:** unk **BLW:** unk **RG:** Y **MK:** unk **PH:** unk **SS:** J-Yorktown Historian; SAR P-114016 **BS:** JLARC 1, 74.

BESCOND, Jean; b unk; d 1781 **RU:** Seaman, Served on "Saint-Esprit" and died from Yorktown battle **CEM:** French Memorial; GPS 36.81944, -79.39933; Yorktown; York **GS:** U **SP:** No info **VI:** No further data **P:** unk **BLW:** unk **RG:** Y **MK:** unk **PH:** unk **SS:** J-Yorktown Historian; SAR P-114019 **BS:** JLARC 1, 74.

BESSARD, Claude; b unk; d 1781 **RU:** Seaman, Served on "Magnanime" and died from Yorktown battle **CEM:** French Memorial; GPS 36.81944, -79.39933; Yorktown; York **GS:** U **SP:** No info **VI:** No further data **P:** unk **BLW:** unk **RG:** Y **MK:** unk **PH:** unk **SS:** J-Yorktown Historian; SAR P-114028; **BS:** JLARC 1, 74.

BETTS, Spencer; b 6 Apr 1759, Northumberland Co; d 2 Nov 1837 **RU:** Soldier, Serv in VA Troops under Gen Greene at battle of Guilford CH **CEM:** Betts Family at Snow Hill; GPS 36.35465, -78.57311; 2091 Snow Hill Rd, Cluster Springs; Halifax **GS:** Y **SP:** Nancy Fowlkes **VI:** Was Deacon of Baptist Church 49 yrs **P:** unk **BLW:** unk **RG:** Y **MK:** unk **PH:** unk **SS:** B; DAR A009779; SAR P-114150 **BS:** JLARC 1, 2, 4; 101; 196.

BEVEL, Abel; b unk; d 1781 **RU:** Seaman, Served on "Citoyen" and died from Yorktown battle **CEM:** French Memorial; GPS 36.81944, -79.39933; Yorktown; York **GS:** U **SP:** No info **VI:** No further data **P:** unk **BLW:** unk **RG:** Y **MK:** unk **PH:** unk **SS:** J-Yorktown Historian; SAR P-114185 **BS:** JLARC 1, 74.

BEZE, Antoine; b unk; d 1781 **RU:** Soldier, Served in Gatinais Bn and died from Yorktown battle **CEM:** French Memorial; GPS 36.81944, -79.39933; Yorktown; York **GS:** U **SP:** No info **VI:** No further data **P:** unk **BLW:** unk **RG:** Y **MK:** unk **PH:** unk **SS:** J-Yorktown Historian; SAR P-114258 **BS:** JLARC 1, 74.

BIBLE, Adam Jr; b c1759; d 2 Feb 1826 **RU:** Patriot/Private, Served in VA 8th Cont Line. Was volunteer in Augusta Co 1775. Entered service fr Augusta Co again in 1778; furnished a bullock to the cause **CEM:** Bible Family; GPS 38.897200, -78.144400; Dull Hunt Rd at Fulks Run; Rockingham **GS:** U **SP:** Mar (Sep 1783 or Sep 1785 Rockingham Co) Magdalene or Madelean Shoemaker (c1764-___) d/o George & (-----) Shoemaker **VI:** Widow appl pen 30 May 1839 Rockingham Co. W18596. R233 **P:** unk **BLW:** unk **RG:** Y **MK:** Y **PH:** Y **SS:** E pg 63; CG pg 255; K Vol 1 pg 73; DAR A132793; SAR P-114271; **BS:** 32 Hutchens 08.

BIBLE, Johann.Adam b 2 Jan 1728, Kenigsback, Prussa; d 2 Apr 1795 **RU:**Patriot, gave material aid to cause **CEM:** Bible Family; GPS 38.897200, -78.144400; Dull Hunt Rd at Fulks Run; Rockingham **GS:** Y Govt **SP:** Maria Eva Marcaretha Muller (c1735-aft 1795) **VI:** Govt Gr Stone indicates was in Capt

RU=Rank/Unit	CEM=Cemetery	GS=Gravestone	SP=Spousal Information
VI=Other Veteran Info	P=Pension	BLW=Bounty/Land Warrant	RG=Registered Grave
MK=SAR/DAR Marker	PH=Photo	SS=Service Source	BS=Burial Source

35

Skidmores Co, Rev War but would be Col War instead as over mil age **P:** N **BLW:** N **RG:** Y **MK:** N **PH:** N **SS:** D vol 3, pg 829; DAR A 132793; SAR P-114271 **BS:** 196.

BICKLEY, Charles William; b 27 Jul 1753, Amherst Co; d 1 Jun 1839 **RU:** Private, Served in VA Line. Ent serv Russell Co 1775. Served as a guard, a driver, or a laborer in building a road over the Cumberland Mountain to KY during the Rev War period **CEM:** Bickley Family; GPS 36.88530, -82.27780; Rt 615 across rd fr Rt 640, Castlewood; Russell **GS:** U **SP:** Mary Halter **VI:** Son of John James (1713-1793) & (-----) Bickley. Sol appl pen 8 Sep 1836 Russell City age 83. Five of 7 children granted final payment 22 Apr 1840. S10091. Source 22 has picture of the gravesite. R234 **P:** unk **BLW:** unk **RG:** Y **MK:** unk **PH:** Y **SS:** K Vol 1 pg 73; N pg 1272; CG pg 256; DAR A009884; SAR P-114315 **BS:** JLARC 2, 22; 196.

BICKLEY, John; b 1761; d 31 Aug 1834 **RU:** Soldier, Served in Russell Co Militia abt 1780 **CEM:** Bickley Family; GPS 36.88530, -82.27780; Rt 615 across fr Rt 640, Castlewood; Russell **GS:** Y **SP:** No info **VI:** Son of John James (1713-1793) & (-----) Bickley **P:** unk **BLW:** unk **RG:** N **MK:** N **PH:** unk **SS:** BK WPA Report **BS:** 158 Bickley; 196.

BICKLEY, John James; b 7 Dec 1713, d 16 Sep 1793 **RU:** Patriot, Supported cause by paying supply tax included in his personal property tax in 1782, Amherst County **CEM:** Amherst Cemetery; GPS: 37.59640, -79.03670; off Rt Bus 29, betw jct with Rt 1108 and 1136; Amherst **GS:** No **SP:** Mar 1) 18 Apr 1736, Mary Hurt (1713-1762), d/o James Hurt and Ann Stewart, Mar 2) Susannah Harding Ellis (1722-Mar 1817) **VI:** Grave moved fr Ellis family graveyard to Amherst Cem **P:** N **BLW:** N **RG:** Y **MK:** N **PH:** Y **SS:** DV image 10.pdf , 1782; DAR A009886; SAR P114518 **BS:** 196

BICKLEY, Sebastian; b c1759; d aft 1839 **RU:** Soldier, Exact serv not determined but he & brother Charles entered service Russell Co 1775 **CEM:** Bickley Family; GPS 36.88530, -82.27780; Rt 615 across fr Rt 640, Castlewood; Russell **GS:** U **SP:** No info **VI:** Son of John James (1713-1793) & (-----) Bickley **P:** unk **BLW:** unk **RG:** N **MK:** N **PH:** unk **SS:** BK WPA Report **BS:** 158 Bickley; 196.

BIDEAU, Ange; b unk; d 1781 **RU:** Seaman, Served on "Hercule" and died from Yorktown battle **CEM:** French Memorial; GPS 36.81944, -79.39933; Yorktown; York **GS:** U **SP:** No info **VI:** No further data **P:** unk **BLW:** unk **RG:** N **MK:** unk **PH:** unk **SS:** J-Yorktown Historian **BS:** JLARC 1, 74.

BIDOT, Jean; b unk; d 1781 **RU:** Soldier, Served in Touraine Bn and died from Yorktown battle **CEM:** French Memorial; GPS 36.81944, -79.39933; Yorktown; York **GS:** U **SP:** No info **VI:** No further data **P:** unk **BLW:** unk **RG:** Y **MK:** unk **PH:** unk **SS:** J-Yorktown Historian; SAR P-114379 **BS:** JLARC 1, 74.

BILISOLY, Antonio Sylvester; b 17 Dec 1758; d 6 Oct 1845 **RU:** Seaman, Was Corsican sailing master who fought with Compte de Grasse **CEM:** Cedar Grove; GPS 36.57204, -80.02599; 301 Fort Lane Rd; Portsmouth City **GS:** U **SP:** Marie Adelaide Accinelli **VI:** Source 2 says slab was moved to Cedar Grove Cem **P:** unk **BLW:** unk **RG:** Y **MK:** Y SAR **PH:** unk **SS:** JLARC Appendix B-3 pg 10; SAR P-114629 **BS:** JLARC 2, 39, Appendix B-3 lot 20.

BILLEBOUX, Oliver; b unk; d 1781 **RU:** Seaman, Served on "Caton" and died from Yorktown battle **CEM:** French Memorial; GPS 36.81944, -79.39933; Yorktown; York **GS:** U **SP:** No info **VI:** No further data **P:** unk **BLW:** unk **RG:** Y **MK:** unk **PH:** unk **SS:** J-Yorktown Historian; SAR P-114657 **BS:** JLARC 1, 74.

BILLUPS, Joseph, Sr; b 1723, Gloucester Co; d 1780 **RU:** Patriot, Gave material aid to cause, and paid personal property tax, a Rev War supply tax,1783, Gloucester Co **CEM:** Old Billups; GPS unk; Rt 643, Moon; Mathews **GS:** U **SP:** No info **VI:** Son of Joseph (1697-1790) & Margaret (Lilly) (1700-1770) Billups **P:** N **BLW:** N **RG:** N **MK:** unk **PH:** unk **SS:** Al Ct bk pg ii, 9, Gloucester Co; DV A1783 image 04 pdf **BS:** 196.

BILLUPS, Joseph Jr; b 29 Sep 1760; d 5 Apr 1815 **RU:** Sergeant, Served in Capt Henry Young's Co, 7th Cont line **CEM:** Old Billups; GPS unk; Rt 643, Moon; Mathews **GS:** Y **SP:** Mar 14 Feb 1784, Joice Respass (1 Nov 1766-14 Mar 1847) **VI:** No further data **P:** unk **BLW:** Y **RG:** Y **MK:** unk **PH:** unk **SS:** E pg 64; C pg 224; CD; CZ pg 46; SAR P-114798 **BS:** JLARC 2, 76; 107.

BINNS, Charles; b 7 Mar 1763; d 5 Mar 1837 **RU:** First Lieutenant, Specific service recorded Lib VA, Archives, Auditors Acct vol XVIII, pg 558 **CEM:** Rokeby; GPS unk; Nr Leesburg; Loudoun **GS:** Y **SP:**

RU=Rank/Unit	CEM=Cemetery	GS=Gravestone	SP=Spousal Information
VI=Other Veteran Info	P=Pension	BLW=Bounty/Land Warrant	RG=Registered Grave
MK=SAR/DAR Marker	PH=Photo	SS=Service Source	BS=Burial Source

36

Hannah (----) **VI:** Son of Charles Binns, Sr. Was clerk of Fairfax Co bef Loudoun Co was formed. His vault at home at Rokeby stored the US records during the War of 1812 **P:** unk **BLW:** unk **RG:** Y **MK:** N **PH:** Y **SS:** E pg 64; CZ pg 46; SAR P-11490*** **BS:** SAR registration.

BIRCHETT, Drury; b 23 Jul 1762, d 10 Dec 1836 **RU:** Patriot, Gave material aid to cause **CEM:** Birchett Family, GPS unk; Rt 603, 1.6 mi East fr jct with Rt 460; Prince George **GS:** Y **SP:** Catherine (__) **VI:** Was Capt in War of 1812 **P:** N **BLW:** N **RG:** N **MK:** N **PH:** N **SS:** AL Comm Bk IV, pg 361, Prince George Co **BS:** 111.

BIRD, John; b 1729, d 1819 **RU:** Lieutenant/ Patriot, served in Lt Col James Robertson Regt under Col William Christain at battle of Kings Mountain. As patriot furnished supplies to cause **CEM:** Green Hill Methodist Church; GPS 38.32137, -79.702727; 6745 Mill Gap Rd; Highland **GS:** Y, inscribed "Died at age 90 while plowing" **SP:** mar 2) Anna Margaret Sussanna Wenderoth (Wintrow) (1742, Prince George Co, MD-Unk) d/o Johnnes Casper Wenderoth & Anna Margaretha Strep **VI:** Perhaps came from Germany, settled bef 1780, Big Back Creek Valley nr Valley Center **P:** N **BLW:** N **RG:** N **MK:** N **PH:** N **SS:** DAR A010329; D vol I, pgs 19.95,97, 99 **BS:** 196 cites Morton, Owen F, "Hist of Highland Co, VA": pgs 195, 240, 250, 264-267, 330-331, 354-355.

BIRD, William; b unk; d 1795 **RU:** Patriot, Signed a Legislative Petition in Alexandria **CEM:** Old Christ Church Episcopal; GPS 38.80625, -77.04718; 118 N Washington St; Alexandria City **GS:** N **SP:** No info **VI:** Burial permit issued 12 Apr 1795 **P:** N **BLW:** N **RG:** N **MK:** N **PH:** N **SS:** BB; S-Alexandria **BS:** 20 pg 145.

BIS, Georges; b unk; d 1781 **RU:** Seaman, Served on "Languedoc" and died from Yorktown battle **CEM:** French Memorial; GPS 36.81944, -79.39933; Yorktown; York **GS:** U **SP:** No info **VI:** No further data **P:** unk **BLW:** unk **RG:** Y **MK:** unk **PH:** unk **SS:** J-Yorktown Historian; SAR P-115022 **BS:** JLARC 1, 74.

BISHOP, Billy, b unk, d unk **RU:** Body Guard, A slave that was a body guard to a Revolutionary War officer **CEM:** Belle Air: GPS; GPS 37.20490, -77.34000; vic Belle Air, Rt 5, New Hope; Charles City **GS:** No **SP:** No spousal info **VI:** No further data **P:** N **BLW:** N **RG:** Y **MK:** N **PH:** N **SS:** SAR P-115069 **BS:** JLARC 110; SAR Patriot Search.

BISHOP, Henry; b Apr 1757, Holland; d 2 Jun 1839 **RU:** Private, Served in Capt Daniel Trigg's Co, 13 Sep 1777, Montgomery Co Militia **CEM:** Wright Family; GPS 36.97658, -80.21693; Pizarro off Rt 668; Floyd **GS:** U **SP:** Mar (23 May 1785, Montgomery Co) Frances Simpkins (1768, Floyd Co-29 May 1850) **VI:** Pen # SW5823. Memorialized by DAR plaque in cem **P:** Y **BLW:** unk **RG:** N **MK:** Y SAR **PH:** unk **SS:** DAR A010438 **BS:** 196 for John Mitchell.

BISHOP, James, b 1760, d 2 Feb 1845 **RU:** Private, in militia 9 Apr 1777served under captains Peter Goodwyn, John Burwell; R. Jones, William Measly, Baker Pegram in Col Jones Regt totaling 15 months and had other service in VA **CEM:** Bishop Family; GPS 36.988178,-77.588814; beyond a dam off Courthouse Rd vic jct Sapony Church Rd and Mealy Branch; Dinwiddie **GS:** No; **SP** No spousal info **VI:** Filed for pension 30 Aug 1832 age 72 **P:** Y **BLW:** N **RG:** Y **MK:** N **PH:** N **SS: Fold3 Pensions; G pg 754** SAR P-328286; **BS:** 196.

BISHOP, Jeremiah, b 1754, d I Apr 1836 **RU:** Private, Enlisted in militia 9 Apr 1776 serving 3 mos in Captain Edward Walker's Company, Col Francis Eppes Regt stationed in Hampton. He enlisted again and served 5 tours of 3 mos each **CEM:** Bishop Family; GPS 36.988178,-77.588814; beyond a dam off Courthouse Rd vic jct Sapony Church Rd and Mealy Branch; Dinwiddie **GS:** No; **SP** No spousal info **VI:** Filed for pension 30 Aug 1832 age 79, FS.6636 **P:** Y **BLW:** N **RG:** N **MK:** N **PH:** N **SS:** Fold 3 Pensions; G pg 754 **BS:** 196.

BISHOP, Joseph; b 30 Apr 1715, Stamford, Fairfield Co, CT; d 1799 **RU:** Patriot, Supported cause by paying supply tax included in his personal property tax in 1783 in Washington Co **CEM** Saint Clair Bottom Primitive Baptist Church; GPS: 36.76098,-81.64556; vic jct Rts 660 and 600; Smyth **GS:** Yes, Govt- shows Indian War service **SP:** Sarah Boughton (1719- 1798) **VI:** Son of Stephen Bishop (1684-1731) **P:** N **BLW:** N **RG:** N **MK:** N **PH:** N **SS:** DV image 07.pdf, Washington Co **BS:** 196.

BISHOP, Levi; b 4 Feb 1750, Westchester Co, NY, d 6 Jun 1818 **RU:** Private, Col Brinckerhoff's Co and Regt, NY State Troops **CEM:** St Clair Bottom Primitive Baptist Church; GPS 36.76098, -81.64556; jct Rts 600 & 660, Chilhowie; Smyth **GS:** Yes **SP:** Rachel (-----) (1781-1856) **VI:** Son of Joseph Bishop

---

RU=Rank/Unit   CEM=Cemetery   GS=Gravestone   SP=Spousal Information
VI=Other Veteran Info   P=Pension   BLW=Bounty/Land Warrant   RG=Registered Grave
MK=SAR/DAR Marker   PH=Photo   SS=Service Source   BS=Burial Source

37

(1715-1799) and Sarah Boughton (1719-1798). Styled "Captain"; SAR indicates Lieutenant VA service **P**: N **BLW**: N **RG**: Y **MK**: N **PH**: N **SS**: DY, on CD pg 323; SAR P-335342; **BS**: 196.

BISHOP, John; b 15 Nov 1764; d 25 Sep 1837 **RU**: Private, Served in Capt Daniel Triggs Co, 13 Sep 1777 **CEM**: St Clair Bottom Primitive Baptist; GPS 36.76098, -81.64556; Jct Rts 600 & 660, Chilhowie; Smyth **GS**: Y **SP**: Rhoda (-----) (17 Jun 1745-26 Sep 1817) **VI**: May be person memorialized on DAR plaque in Wright Fam cem in Floyd Co **P**: unk **BLW**: unk **RG**: N **MK**: Plaque **PH**: unk **SS**: G pg 214 **BS**: 196.

BISHOP, John; b 1747; d 1822 **RU**: Soldier, Served in Capt Jason Waits Co **CEM**: Bishop Family; GPS 36.62640, -77.95580; Rt 644, Brunswick; Brunswick **GS**: N **SP**: Mar on 10 Jan 1793 (bond) to Elizabeth Jones, d/o John Jones **VI**: Son of Mathnay Bishop per his marriage bond **P**: unk **BLW**: unk **RG**: N **MK**: U **PH**: N **SS**: A pg 147 **BS**: 196.

BISHOP, Mathew; b 1747; d 1810 **RU**: Private / Patriot, Served in Capt David Beatie's Co at battle of Kings Mountain. Also gave supplies to cause **CEM**: Bishop Family; GPS 36.62640, -77.95580; Rt 644, Brunswick; Brunswick **GS**: N **SP**: Martha (-----) (1750-1828) **VI**: Pension to widow commencing 16 Jul 1814 at $48 per yr **P**: Y **BLW**: unk **RG**: Y **MK**: U **PH**: N **SS**: N pg 1241; AG pg 254, SAR P-115151 **BS**: 196.

BLACK, Benjamin; b unk; d 1789 **RU**: Private, Specific service recorded Lib VA, Archives **CEM**: Old Christ Church Episcopal; GPS 38.80625, -77.04718; 118 N Washington St; Alexandria City **GS**: N **SP**: no info **VI**: Burial permit issued 2 Jun 1789 to Andrew Wales **P**: unk **BLW**: unk **RG**: N **MK**: N **PH**: N **SS**: A pg 191; E pg 66; CZ pg 45 **BS**: 20 pg 145.

BLACK, David; b 1762; d Jan 1831 **RU**: Captain, Gr St inscription gives rank but service not determined **CEM**: Presbyterian Church; GPS 38.80015, -77.05791; Wilkes St & Hamilton Ln; Alexandria City **GS**: Y **SP**: No info **VI**: Death notice in Alexandria Gazette, 5 Jan 1831, pg 3 **P**: unk **BLW**: unk **RG**: N **MK**: N **PH**: unk **SS**: B **BS**: 23 pg 14.

BLACK, John; b 27 Jul 1766; d 10 Jun 1839 **RU**: Private, Served in Capt Buchanan's Co, Augusta Co Militia in 1778, 1779 & 1780 **CEM**: Mossy Creek Presbyterian; GPS 38.35331, -79.04914; 372 Kyles Mill Rd, Mt Solon; Augusta **GS**: Y **SP**: Mar (1) on 20 Sep 1790 to Alice Boyd. b 4 Aug 1767, d 22 Aug 1811 Rockingham Co; (2) on 25 Mar 1756 to Mary Hogshead, b 25 Mar 1756, d 2 Apr 1850 **VI**: No further data **P**: unk **BLW**: unk **RG**: N **MK**: N **PH**: unk **SS**: **BS**: JLARC 62, 63; 196.

BLACK, John; b 21 Dec 1755, Albemarle Co; d 14 Jul 1849 **RU**: Private/Overseer of Roads/Patriot, Served in Capt Buchanan's Co, Augusta Co Militia. Also provided wagon with horses and other items to Col White of Lt Dragoons **CEM**: Blacksburg; GPS unk; Nr Blacksburg; Montgomery **GS**: Y **SP**: 1) Jane Alexander 2) Mary Breeden **VI**: Son of Rev Samuel & (-----) Black. Virginia Tech built on his 200 acres. John Black log cabin on campus (moved for dorm) and lived in by professor. Died in Blacksburg, Montgomery Co **P**: unk **BLW**: unk **RG**: Y **MK**: unk **PH**: Y **SS**: J-NSSAR 2000 Reg; D pg 6 Augusta Co; SAR P-115459 **BS**: JLARC 76.

BLACK, Jonathan; b 1755, Henrico Co; d 6 Jan 1813 **RU** Served in the PA Militia: **CEM**: Norcross-Parrish; GPS 37.874378, -78.336683; 4514 Ruritan Lake Rd (Rt 619, Cunningham; Fluvanna) **GS** Y Family stone **SP**: Mar 1775, Judith Farris Harlow (1755-1813) **VI**: No futher data **P**: N **BLW**: N **RG**: N **MK**: N **PH**: N **SS**: AP fold 3 rolls **BS**: 245.

BLACKBURN, Samuel; b 2 Jun 1759; d 2 Mar 1835 **RU**: General/Patriot, Served in VA unit that was paid at Ft Pitt. Served in Battle of Guilford CH. Gave 11 yds linen 26 Aug 1782 **CEM**: Trinity Episcopal; GPS 38.14917, -79.07521; 214 Beverley St; Staunton City **GS**: Y **SP**: Mar (Augusta Co) Ann or Anne Mathews (___-1840), d/o GA Governor George & (-----) Mathews. Later mar (-----) Blackburn. **VI**: Son of Benjamin & Mary (-----) Blackburn. Taught at Washington Academy in Wilkes Co. GA. Member of GA state legislature until 1759. Represented Bath Co in VA legislature for several terms. Died in Bath Co. In will, liberated 44 slaves, so they'd move to Liberia (42 did) **P**: unk **BLW**: unk **RG**: Y **MK**: unk **PH**: Y **SS**: CY pg 100; CZ pg 47; SAR P-115536 **BS**: JLARC 62, 63.

BLACKBURN, Thomas; b 1742; d 1807 **RU**: Lieutenant Colonel, Served as commander 2nd VA Regiment 20 Dec 1776. Wounded at Germantown Dec 1777 **CEM**: Blackburn-Atkinson; GPS

RU=Rank/Unit	CEM=Cemetery	GS=Gravestone	SP=Spousal Information
VI=Other Veteran Info	P=Pension	BLW=Bounty/Land Warrant	RG=Registered Grave
MK=SAR/DAR Marker	PH=Photo	SS=Service Source	BS=Burial Source

38

38.368780, -77.166850; Rippon Lodge off Rt 638, Woodbridge; Prince William **GS**: U **SP**: Christian Scott **VI**: Owned Rippon Lodge **P**: unk **BLW**: unk **RG**: Y **MK**: Y **SAR PH**: unk **SS**: CZ pg 47; SAR-P115539 **BS**: JLARC 2, 76, 95.

BLACKWELL, David; b 1762 or 24 Aug 1764 (pen says 24 Aug 1765 nr New Castle in Hanover City); d 30 Dec 1837 **RU**: Private, Ent serv in 1779 in Hanover Co. Served at Yorktown, Oct 1781 **CEM**: Blackwell Family; GPS unk; Spring Grove; Hanover **GS**: Y **SP**: No info **VI**: Sol appl pen 23 Oct 1832 Hanover City age 68. S6666. R 256 **P**: Y **BLW**: unk **RG**: Y **MK**: N **PH**: unk **SS**: G pg 766; K Vol 1 pg 78; CG pg 282; SAR P-115668 **BS**: AS, SAR regis.

BLACKWELL, John Gard; b 1755, Northumberland Co, d 23 Jun 1823 **RU**: Lt Col Commanded Fauquier Co Militia having taken oath in 1778 **CEM**: Blackwell family: GPS not determined; probably as his father Joseph buried there a part of Joseph Blackwell Cem loc on first farm past Bethel United Methodist Ch; Fauquier **GS**: No **SP**: Mar Jun 1745, Lucy Steptoe, (1720 Northumberland Co-26 Apr 1787) d/o John Steptoe & Elizabeth Eustace **VI**: No further data **P**: N **BLW**: N **RG**: Y **MK**: N **PH**: N **SS**: E pg 67; SAR P-115677 **BS**: 196.

BLACKWELL, Joseph Jr; b 1752, Northumberland Co; d 20 Jun 1826 or Oct 1836 **RU**: Lieutenant-Quartermaster, Served in 3rd VA Regt, Cont Line. Appt quartermaster 1780 **CEM**: Blackwell Family; GPS unk; The Meadows, E of Rt 628 at the first farm past Bethel United Methodist Church; Fauquier **GS**: Y **SP**: Mar (Dec 1784) Ann Eustace Hull (1761-1840) d/o Isaac & Agatha (-----) Eustace. Her first husband was RW vet Edwin Hull (___-1780) She drew pensions for both husbands. **VI**: Son of Joseph & Lucy (Steptoe) Blackwell. Wife recd pension Fauquier Co. Govt. grave stone. R 256 **P**: Y **BLW**: Y **RG**: Y **MK**: N **PH**: unk **SS**: B; K Vol 1 pg 78; N ps 636-7; SAR P-115683 **BS**: 19 pg 8; 196.

BLACKWELL, Joseph Sr; b 9 Jul 1715, Northumberland Co; d 30 May 1787 **RU**: Patriot, Gave material aid to cause Fauquier Co **CEM**: Blackwell Family; GPS unk; The Meadows, E of Rt 628 at the first farm past Bethel United Methodist Church; Fauquier **GS**: U **SP**: Mar (Jun 1745) Lucy Steptoe (1720-26 Apr 1787) **VI**: Son of Samuel & Margery (Downing Hudnall) Blackwell **P**: N **BLW**: N **RG**: Y **MK**: unk **PH**: unk **SS**: AL Ct Bk pg 1, 21; SAR P-115701 **BS**: 196. **SEE APPENDIX G**

BLACKWELL, William; b 16 Aug 1736, Northumberland Co; d 1780 **RU**: Captain, Served in 11th VA Rgmt **CEM**: Roseland; GPS 37.51131, -76.16576; Reedville; Northumberland **GS**: U **SP**: No info **VI**: Son of Samuel & Elizabeth (Steptoe) Blackwell. Recd 4000 acres BLW. Grave relocated fr "Poplar Farm" Rt 360 near Intermediate Sch **P**: unk **BLW**: Y **RG**: Y **MK**: Y **SAR PH**: unk **SS**: E pg 68; AK; SAR P-115700 **BS**: JLARC 4; 42; 200; 04.

BLAIR, John, Durbarrow; b 15 Oct 1759, Chester Co, PA; d 10 Jan 1823 **RU**: Private?, Served in Clark's III Regt **CEM**: Shockoe Hill; GPS 37.55190, -77.43170; 4th & Hospital Sts; Richmond City **GS**: Y loc Range 13, Sec 8 **SP**: mar 4 Mar 1785, Mary Winston (1763-1831) **VI**: Son of John (1720-1771) & Elizabeth (Durbarrow) Blair; graduated Princeton 1775 **P**: unk **BLW**: unk **RG**: Y **MK**: N **PH**: Y **SS**: E pg 68; SAR P-115782 **BS**: 179 pg 135; 196.

BLAIR, John Jr; b 17 Apr 1732; d 31 Aug 1800 **RU**: Patriot, Helped author VA Constitution 1776 and signer of it; elected 1778 to General Ct; served House of Burgesses 1766-1770 **CEM**: Bruton Parish Church; GPS 37.27127, -76.70248; 331 W Duke of Gloucester St; Williamsburg City **GS**: Y **SP**: Jean Balfour (1736-1792) **VI**: Son of John Blair (1687-1771) & Mary Munro (1708-__); Signer, Declaration of Independence **P**: N **BLW**: N **RG**: Y **MK**: N **PH**: N **SS**: G pg 777; SAR P-115770 **BS**: 26 pg 115; 168; 196.

BLAIR, Thomas; b 1750, Scotland; d 1805 **RU**: Private, Served in Capt O'Hara's Independent Co. **CEM**: Blair; GPS unk; Cliffview; Carroll **GS**: U **SP**: No info, has child **VI**: No further data **P**: unk **BLW**: unk **RG**: N **MK**: unk **PH**: unk **SS**: Cl **BS**: 196.

BLAIR, William; b 5 Jul 1741; d Aft 1798 **RU**: Private, Served in Capt Cunningham's Co, Augusta Co Militia **CEM**: Bethel Presbyterian; GPS 38.04257, -79.17283; 563 Bethel Green Rd, Middlebrook; Augusta **GS**: N **SP**: 1) Mary Logan 2) Elizabeth Fulton **VI**: Son of Alexander Blair & Jane Preston Scott **P**: unk **BLW**: unk **RG**: Y **MK**: unk **PH**: N **SS**: E pg 68: SAR P -115811 **BS**: 196.

BLAIR, William E**See APPENDIX G**

RU=Rank/Unit	CEM=Cemetery	GS=Gravestone	SP=Spousal Information
VI=Other Veteran Info	P=Pension	BLW=Bounty/Land Warrant	RG=Registered Grave
MK=SAR/DAR Marker	PH=Photo	SS=Service Source	BS=Burial Source

BLAKEMORE, George; b 23 May 1759; d 25 Jul 1833 **RU:** Lieutenant, Served in 2nd VA Regt 19 Dec 1776. Resigned 5 Apr 1782. Served in Mid Atlantic & Southern theaters. Was at Germantown where 15 yr old brother Thomas was killed. Was sick at Valley Forge. Captured by British in SC (under Gen Green). Was on British prison ship 13 mos. Was at Yorktown at Cornwallis surrender. **CEM:** Blakemore Family; GPS 39.17245, -77.99008; Blakemore Ln, off Rt 7, Berryville; Clarke **GS:** Y **SP:** No info **VI:** Son of Thomas & (-----) Blakemore Sr. Brother to Thomas Blakemore Jr who was killed at Germantown and bur by George (still there). Met Gen Lafayette during Battle of Monmouth, served on his staff, & was life-long friend with him. Died in Frederick Co. Sol appl pen 26 Nov 1832 Frederick Co. S6665 BLW 1795. R 261 **P:** Y **BLW:** Y **RG:** Y **MK:** Y SAR Granite **PH:** Y **SS:** E pg 69; K Vol 1 pg 80; CG pg 289; SAR P-116022 **BS:** 58 pg 4; 196.

BLAKEMORE, Thomas Sr.; b 1718; d 1808 **RU:** Patriot, Gave 144 lbs of mutton to cause **CEM:** Blakemore Family; GPS 39.10216, -77.59246; Byrd Farm vic Rt 7, Moreland; Clarke **GS:** Y **SP:** Ann Gibbs Neville **VI:** No further data **P:** N **BLW:** N **RG:** Y **MK:** Y SAR Granite **PH:** Y **SS:** AL Ct bk pg 37; SAR P-116026 **BS:** 58 pg 4.

BLANCHET, Louis; b unk; d 1781 **RU:** Seaman, Served on "Saint-Esprit" and died from Yorktown battle **CEM:** French Memorial; GPS 36.81944, -79.39933; Yorktown; York **GS:** U **SP:** No info **VI:** No further data **P:** unk **BLW:** unk **RG:** Y **MK:** unk **PH:** unk **SS:** J-Yorktown Historian; SAR P-116207 **BS:** JLARC 1, 74.

BLAND; Edward; b 16 Dec 1746, d 5 Feb 1795 **RU:** Captain/Patriot Gave material aid to cause in Prince George Co, Commanded a militia company **CEM:** Jordan Point Plantation; GPS: not determined; Jordan Point Manor; Prince George **SP:** Elizabeth Cocke **GS:** Yes **VI:** Son of Richard Bland (1710-1776) and Anne Poythress (13 Dec1712-9 Apr 1758) **P:** N **BLW:** N **RG:** N **MK:** N **PH:** N **SS:** AL Ct Bk pg 1, Comm Bk IV pg 248 **BS:** 196. **(BLAND,** John **See APPENDIX G)**

BLAND, Richard Jr; b 6 May 1710; d 26 Oct 1776 **RU:** Colonel, Was Paymaster, Southampton District Bn Mar 1776 and was Col of a Minuteman Bn Nov 1775 **CEM:** Bland Family; GPS unk; 2 mi E of Hopewell on Rt 10, 1.2 mi N on Rt 36, then 10 ft E; Prince George **GS:** U **SP:** 1) Anne Poythress 2) Martha Macon 3) Elizabeth Blank **VI:** US Continental Congressman, Member of VA House of Burgesses 1742-1775 and a member of the VA Committee of Correspondence in 1773. In 1774, elected a member of First Continental Congress, serving until 1775. Reelected to second First Continental Congress. Elected to VA House of Delegates in 1776, serving until his death **P:** unk **BLW:** unk **RG:** Y **MK:** unk **PH:** unk **SS:** J-NSSAR 2000 Reg; CE pg 22; SAR P-116215 **BS:** JLARC 1, 2, 76, 101; 196.

BLAND, Richard III; b 1731, d 1788 **RU:** Captain/Patriot Captain Virginia militia, Gave material aid to cause **CEM:** Jordan Point Plantation: GPS: Jordan Point Manor. Prince George **GS:** Unk **SP:** Mary Bolling (28 Jul 1744-9 Sep 1803) **VI:** Son of Richard Bland (1710-1776) and Anne Poythress (13 Dec 1712-9 Apr 1758) **P:** N **BLW:** N **RG:** N **MK:** N **PH:** N **SS:** AL Ct Bk Cert Prince George Co **BS:** 196.

BLAND. Richard, IV; b 23 Jul 1762, d 26 Mar 1806 **RU:** Private/Patriot Served in Capt Robert Bolling's Troop of Calvary 1780-1781. Gave material aid to **cause CEM:** Jordan Point Plantation: GPS: Jordan Point Manor. Prince George **GS:** No **SP:** Susannah Poythress (1769-1839) **VI:** Son of Richard Bland II (1731-1788) & Mary Bolling (1744-1803) d/o John Kennon Bolling & Mary Elizabeth Bland **P:** N **BLW:** N **RG:** N **MK:** N **PH:** N **SS:** AL Ct Bk Cert List I, pgs 1,6 **BS:** 196.

BLAND, Theoderick; b 19 Dec 1719, prob Williamsburg, d 16 Jul 1783, Springfield Plantation, Amelia Co, **RU:** Patriot Gave material aid to cause, Prince George Co **CEM:** Jordan Point Plantation: GPS: Jordan Point Manor. Prince George **GS:** Unk **SP:** No spousal info **VI:** Son of Richard Bland (1665-1720) and Elizabeth Randolph (1680-1720). With other members of family, offered slaves for sale to replace gunpowder seized by Lord Dunmore in 1776. In 1758 was Colonel of Prince George Co Militia. Titled Major **P:** N **BLW:** N **RG:** N **MK:** N **PH:** N **SS:** AL Ct Bk p 7, Comm Bk, IV pg 361 **BS:** 196.

BLANDELET, Jean; b unk; d 1781 **RU:** Seaman, Served on "Languedoc" and died from Yorktown battle **CEM:** French Memorial; GPS 36.81944, -79.39933; Yorktown; York **GS:** U **SP:** No info **VI:** No further data **P:** unk **BLW:** unk **RG:** Y **MK:** unk **PH:** unk **SS:** J-Yorktown Historian; SAR P-116217 **BS:** JLARC 1, 74.

RU=Rank/Unit	CEM=Cemetery	GS=Gravestone	SP=Spousal Information
VI=Other Veteran Info	P=Pension	BLW=Bounty/Land Warrant	RG=Registered Grave
MK=SAR/DAR Marker	PH=Photo	SS=Service Source	BS=Burial Source

40

BLANKENBAKER, Michael; b c1730, Orange Co; d 21 Jun 1790 **RU:** Patriot, Gave material aid to cause **CEM:** Cem name unk; GPS unk; Hebron Valley; Madison **GS:** N **SP:** Mar (1745 Orange Co) Elizabeth Barbara Garr (11 Feb 1730 Germany-aft 21 Jun 1790) d/o Andrew & (-----) Garr **VI:** Son of John Nicolas & (-----) Blankenbaker (immigrant). Died in Culpeper Co (now Madison) **P:** N **BLW:** N **RG:** Y **MK:** N **PH:** N **SS:** DAR A011152; D Vol 1 pg 274; K Vol 1; SAR P-116243 **BS:** 04.

BLANKENBECKLER (BLANKENBAKER), Zachariah Jr; b 25 Mar 1752; d 1824, Wythe Co **RU:** Private, Served in Capt Lowe's Co VA Militia **CEM:** Morgan; GPS unk; Rye Valley; Smyth **GS:** Y **SP:** Elizabeth (-----) **VI:** Son of Zachariah Sr. (___-1781) & Elizabeth (Weaver) Blankenbaker There is a stone to his honor & he is said to be bur there **P:** unk **BLW:** unk **RG:** Y **MK:** unk **PH:** unk **SS:** SAR P-116251 **BS:** JLARC 114.

BLANKENSHIP, Abraham Sr; b 1759, Chesterfield Co; d 8 Mar 1845 **RU:** Private, Ent serv Chesterfield Co **CEM:** Blankenship Family; GPS unk; Nr Montvale; Bedford **GS:** N **SP:** Mar (1781 Chesterfield Co) Susan Wiatt **VI:** Moved to Bedford Co in 1784 where he had militia service after Rev War. Sol appl pen 7 Jan 1830 Bedford Co age 72. Pensioned in 1883 Bedford Co. Widow pensioned in Franklin Co at age 87. W10425. R266. Govt stone says he was a private in Capt Gilmore 5th Virginia Regiment **P:** Y **BLW:** unk **RG:** N **MK:** N **PH:** unk **SS:** E pg 68; K Vol 1 pg 82; CG pg 295 **BS:** 4.

BLANKENSHIP, Hudson; b 1737, Chesterfield Co; d Bef 11 Jan 1813 **RU:** Patriot, Gave material aid to the cause **CEM:** Blankenship-Oldham; GPS unk; Winfall; Campbell **GS:** N **SP:** Mar Edith Wilkinson, d 1826 **VI:** Son of John Blakenship (1697-1754) & Elizabeth Hudson (1704-1789) **P:** N **BLW:** N **RG:** Y **MK:** N **PH:** N **SS:** AL Ct Bk pg 19 Campbell Co; SAR P-333568 **BS:** 196.

BLANKENSHIP, James W; b unk; d 18__ **RU:** Private?, Served in 14th Cont Line **CEM:** St John's Episcopal; GPS 37.53183, -77.41958; 2401 E Broad St; Richmond City **GS:** Y **SP:** No info **VI:** No further data **P:** unk **BLW:** unk **RG:** N **MK:** N **PH:** unk **SS:** E pg 696 **BS:** 28 pg 424.

BLEUTAU, Henri; b unk; d 1781 **RU:** Seaman, Served on "Palmier" and died from Yorktown battle **CEM:** French Memorial; GPS 36.81944, -79.39933; Yorktown; York **GS:** U **SP:** No info **VI:** No further data **P:** unk **BLW:** unk **RG:** Y **MK:** unk **PH:** unk **SS:** J-Yorktown Historian; SAR P-116397 **BS:** JLARC 1, 74.

BLEVEL, Guillaume; b unk; d 1781 **RU:** Seaman, Served on "Diademe" and died from Yorktown battle **CEM:** French Memorial; GPS 36.81944, -79.39933; Yorktown; York **GS:** U **SP:** No info **VI:** No further data **P:** unk **BLW:** unk **RG:** Y **MK:** unk **PH:** unk **SS:** J-Yorktown Historian; SAR P-116398 **BS:** JLARC 1, 74.

BLEVENET, Paul; b unk; d 1781 **RU:** Seaman, Served on "Citoyen" and died from Yorktown battle **CEM:** French Memorial; GPS 36.81944, -79.39933; Yorktown; York **GS:** U **SP:** No info **VI:** No further data **P:** unk **BLW:** unk **RG:** N **MK:** unk **PH:** unk **SS:** J-Yorktown Historian **BS:** JLARC 1, 74.

BLONDEL, Pierre; b unk; d 1781 **RU:** Seaman, Served on "Ville de Paris" and died from Yorktown battle **CEM:** French Memorial; GPS 36.81944, -79.39933; Yorktown; York **GS:** U **SP:** No info **VI:** No further data **P:** unk **BLW:** unk **RG:** Y **MK:** unk **PH:** unk **SS:** J-Yorktown Historian; SAR P-116623 **BS:** JLARC 1, 74.

BLONDELLE, Nicolas; b unk; d 1781 **RU:** Soldier, Served in Soissonnais Bn and died from Yorktown battle **CEM:** French Memorial; GPS 36.81944, -79.39933; Yorktown; York **GS:** U **SP:** No info **VI:** No further data **P:** unk **BLW:** unk **RG:** Y **MK:** unk **PH:** unk **SS:** J-Yorktown Historian; SAR P-116624 **BS:** JLARC 1, 74.

BLOW, Richard; b 17 Nov 1746; d 3 Feb 1833 **RU:** Captain 1780 Mate, Neptune; Lt. in Militia, Specific service recorded Lib VA, Archives, Auditors Acct vol XVIII, pg 573 **CEM:** Cedar Grove; GPS 36.57204, -80.02599; 301 Fort Lane Rd; Portsmouth City **GS:** Y **SP:** Frances Phripp Wright **VI:** No further data **P:** unk **BLW:** unk **RG:** Y **MK:** Y SAR **PH:** unk **SS:** E pg 71; CZ pg 49; SAR P-116780 **BS:** 27 pg 99.

BLUNT, Washer; b 1738; d 30 Oct 1806 **RU:** Patriot, Signed Legislative Petition in Fairfax Co **CEM:** Old Presbyterian Meeting House; GPS 38.48528, -77.23532; 323 S Fairfax St; Alexandria City **GS:** N **SP:** No info **VI:** Superintendant of Alms House, died of decay age 69 (Alexandria Gazette, 31 Oct 1806, pg 3) **P:** N **BLW:** N **RG:** N **MK:** N **PH:** N **SS:** BB **BS:** 23 pg 99.

RU=Rank/Unit	CEM=Cemetery	GS=Gravestone	SP=Spousal Information
VI=Other Veteran Info	P=Pension	BLW=Bounty/Land Warrant	RG=Registered Grave
MK=SAR/DAR Marker	PH=Photo	SS=Service Source	BS=Burial Source

BLY, John; b 1757; d 7 Jul 1821 **RU:** Lieutenant, Was received as Lt 1782 in Shenndoah Co Militia. Also was in the 8th Cont line as Sergeant **CEM:** Boehm; GPS unk; Nr Clary; Shenandoah **GS:** U **SP:** Mar 1) Esther Keller, 2) Barbara Bean (c1775-___) **VI:** Sol appl pen 25 My 1818 Shenandoah Co age 64. S37780 **P:** Y **BLW:** unk **RG:** Y **MK:** unk **PH:** unk **SS:** J-NSSAR 1993 Reg, J- DAR Hatcher; E pg 72; CG pg 307; SAR P-116838 **BS:** JLARC 1,c 2.

BOATWRIGHT, Daniel; b 13 Apr 1739; d 26 Mar 1797 **RU:** Patriot, Gave material aid to cause **CEM:** Burnt Chimney; GPS unk; Cat Taile Branch; Cumberland **GS:** U **SP:** Jane Bridgewater Martin (1737-1798) d/o (-----) & Jane (Bridgewater) (1715-1778) Martin **VI:** No further data **P:** N **BLW:** N **RG:** Y **MK:** unk **PH:** unk **SS:** AL Ct Bk pg 6; SAR P-116934 **BS:** 196.

BOATWRIGHT, Reuben; b 21 Mar 1762, Cumberland Co; d unk **RU:** Private, Wounded by a bomb at Yorktown **CEM:** Boatwright Family; GPS unk; Nr Mt Zion Church, 6277 Cartersville Rd, New Canton; Buckingham **GS:** U **SP:** Mar (8 Jun 1796, Prince Edward Co) Jerusha/Lucy Penick (2 Apr 1767-___) d/o Squire William & (-----) Penick of Prince Edward Co **VI:** No further data **P:** unk **BLW:** unk **RG:**Y **MK:** N **PH:** unk **SS:** SAR P-116936 **BS:** JLARC 59.

BOAZ, Thomas; b 27 Sep 1731; d 13 Sep 1791 **RU:** Patriot, Provided supplies for the troops **CEM:** Boaze Family; GPS 36.71055, -79.55003; 1148 County Rd 945, Dry Fork; Pittsylvania **GS:** Y **SP:** Mar (27 Aug 1804 Pittsylvania Co) Lucy Davis; also Agness **VI:** Son of Thomas Boaz, b c1714, d 15 Aug 1780, Buckingham Co, Virginia, and Elinor Archdeacon-Cody, b 1718, Thomastown, Co. Kilkenny, Ireland, d 25 Sep 1787, Buckingham Co. Very rough stone **P:** unk **BLW:** unk **RG:** Y **MK:** unk **PH:** unk **SS:** AL Ct Bk pg 24, 41 Pittsylvania Co; SAR P-116943 **BS:** 196.

BOBBITT, John; b 1742; d 1816 **RU:** Second Lieutenant, Served in 4th VA Regt and in Pittsylvania Co Militia **CEM:** North End; GPS 36.77234, -80.73866; 101 Beaver Dam Rd, Hillsville; Carroll **GS:** Y **SP:** Sarah Gibson **VI:** Inscription illegible **P:** unk **BLW:** unk **RG:** Y **MK** Y SAR **PH:** unk **SS:** SAR P-116950 **BS:** JLARC 43.

BOBBITT, John; b 1751, d 6 Jun 1822 **RU:** Sergeant; in Infantry unit in 4th Cont Line **CEM:** Bobbitt's Forge; GPS; 36.94639, -77.39972; Stoney Creek; Sussex **GS:** Unk **SP:** Frances Mitchell **VI:** No further data data **P:** N **BLW:** N **RG:** Y **MK:** N **PH:** N **SS:** E pg 72; SAR P-337063 **BS:** 196.

BOBBITT, Robert; b 1744; d 1817 **RU:** Captain, Served in Montgomery Co Militia **CEM:** Bobbitt Family; GPS 36.47841, -80.40554; Rt 682 E of Rt 52, Hillsville; Carroll **GS:** N **SP:** No info **VI:** Montgomery Co Circuit Records, pg 164 is indicated also as source of service **P:** unk **BLW:** unk **RG:** N **MK:** N **PH:** N **SS:** E pg 72; **BS:** 04 Jun 04.

BOBBITT, William Sr; b 1744, Prince George Co; d 1817 **RU:** Captain, Commanded a Co Carroll Co Militia 14 Mar 1778. Served in 6th Regt, VA Line **CEM:** Bobbitt Family; GPS 36.47841, -80.40554; Rt 682 E of Rt 52, Hillsville; Carroll **GS:** Y **SP:** Nancy Ann McKenzie (___-1807) **VI:** Modern headstone identifies Bobbett's wife & children bur in family plot. R797 **P:** unk **BLW:** unk **RG:** Y **MK:** N **PH:** unk **SS:** S; DAR A0116630; SAR P-116955 **BS:** JLARC 43; 68; 196.

BOCQ, Jean; b unk; d 1781 **RU:** Seaman, Served on "Marseillais" and died from Yorktown battle **CEM:** French Memorial; GPS 36.81944, -79.39933; Yorktown; York **GS:** U **SP:** No info **VI:** No further data **P:** unk **BLW:** unk **RG:** Y **MK:** unk **PH:** unk **SS:** J-Yorktown Historian; SAR P-116975 **BS:** JLARC 1, 74.

BODEVER, Bernard; b unk; d 1781 **RU:** Seaman, Served on "Ville de Paris" and died from Yorktown battle **CEM:** French Memorial; GPS 36.81944, -79.39933; Yorktown; York **GS:** U **SP:** No info **VI:** No further data **P:** unk **BLW:** unk **RG:** Y **MK:** unk **PH:** unk **SS:** J-Yorktown Historian; SAR P-116987 **BS:** JLARC 1, 74.

BOGER (BOGAR), Michael; b 1 Apr 1762, d 26 Mar 1822 **RU:** Patriot, as patriot supported cause by paying supply tax included in his personal property tax in 1783, Loudoun Co **CEM:** New Jerusalem Lutheran Church; GPS 39.25736,-77.63891; 12942 Lutheran Church Rd, Lovettsville; Loudoun **GS:** Yes **SP:** Mar 13 Apr 1785, Mary Elizabeth Brennerin (27 Jul 1764-13 Dec 1843) **VI:** No further data **P:** N **BLW:** N **RG:** N **MK:** N **PH:** N **SS:** DV Loudoun Co, list 1783A, image 4 pdf **BS:** 196.

BOHEU, Chretien; b unk; d 1781 **RU:** Seaman, Served on "Auguste" and died from Yorktown battle **CEM:** French Memorial; GPS 36.81944, -79.39933; Yorktown; York **GS:** U **SP:** No info **VI:** No further

---

RU=Rank/Unit	CEM=Cemetery	GS=Gravestone	SP=Spousal Information
VI=Other Veteran Info	P=Pension	BLW=Bounty/Land Warrant	RG=Registered Grave
MK=SAR/DAR Marker	PH=Photo	SS=Service Source	BS=Burial Source

data **P:** unk **BLW:** unk **RG:** Y **MK:** unk **PH:** unk **SS:** J-Yorktown Historian; SAR P-117160 **BS:** JLARC 1, 74.

BOISSARD, Michel; b unk; d 1781 **RU:** Soldier, Served in Soissonnais Bn and died from Yorktown battle **CEM:** French Memorial; GPS 36.81944, -79.39933; Yorktown; York **GS:** U **SP:** No info **VI:** No further data **P:** unk **BLW:** unk **RG:** Y **MK:** unk **PH:** unk **SS:** J-Yorktown Historian **BS:** JLARC 1, 74.

BOISSEAU, Pierre; b unk; d 1781 **RU:** Soldier, Served in Touraine Bn and died from Yorktown battle **CEM:** French Memorial; GPS 36.81944, -79.39933; Yorktown; York **GS:** U **SP:** No info **VI:** No further data **P:** unk **BLW:** unk **RG:** Y **MK:** unk **PH:** unk **SS:** J-Yorktown Historian; SAR P-117196 **BS:** JLARC 1, 74.

BOLAR, John; b 1733; d 3 Apr 1818 **RU:** Captain, Commanded a company 8 Apr 1779 Botetourt Co Militia **CEM:** Warm Springs; GPS 38.05030, -79.78110; Rt 220 Sam Snead Hwy, Warm Springs; Bath **GS:** Y **SP:** Mar (abt 1768) Margaret Thornton (c1815-16 Jan 1815) **VI:** One of Dickenson's Rangers in French & Indian War, was at battle of Guildford CH. Justice of Bath Co 1769-1777, Sheriff in 1792. Property was "Walnut Grove." GS moved to Warm Spring in the 1970s for the Gathright Dam project **P:** unk **BLW:** unk **RG:** N **MK:** N **PH:** unk **SS:** AZ pg 191 **BS:** 159 Bolar; 196.

BOLES, William; b unk; d 1832 **RU:** Private, Served in 3rd & 4th Cont Line **CEM:** King Family; GPS unk; Rt 658 Brent Point Rd; Stafford **GS:** Y **SP:** No info **VI:** No further data **P:** unk **BLW:** unk **RG:** N **MK:** N **PH:** unk **SS:** E pg 74 **BS:** 03 pg 262.

BOLLING, Robert; b 3 Mar 1759, Petersburg, Dinwiddie Co; d 26 Jan 1839 **RU:** Captain, Volunteered 1788 in Hanover Co in Capt Thomas Nelson's Co Troop of Cavalry. In 1780 served as capt and raised a troop of cavalry in area south of James River in Col Bannister's unit of Dinwiddie Co. His Co served under Col Parker in General Muhlenberg's Brigade in Battle of Petersburg **CEM:** Blandford; GPS 37.22433, -77.38604; 319 S Crater Rd; Petersburg City **GS:** U **SP:** 1) Mary Burton (c1763- 3 Aug 1787) 2) Catharine Stith (c1776-9 Aug 1795) 3) Anna Dade, (c1778-18 Mar 1846) 4) Sally Washington **VI:** Son of Robert (1730-1775) & Mary (Marshall) (1737-1814) Bolling. British General Philips d at Petersburg home of first wife, Mary and she and four daughters were made prisoners. Sol appl pen 20 Sep 1832 Petersburg age 73. S6689 Will dated 7 Sep 1789, probated 21 Feb 1791. Wardell indicates he d c1790 Dinwiddie Co. Widow had BLW in 1817 and d Aug 1832) Children appl for pen 1850. R282 **P:** Y **BLW:** Y **RG:** Y **MK:** Plaque **PH:** unk **SS:** J- DAR Hatcher; E pg 74; G pg 864; K Vol 1 pg 87; AZ pg 129, 130; CG pg 315; SAR P-117267 **BS:** JLARC 2, 128; 80 vol 1, pg 94; 128; 196.

BOLLING, Robert, Sr; b 12 Jun 1730, Prince George Co, d 24 Feb 1775 **RU:** Captain, Commanded a company in the Dinwiddie Co Militia, 1775. **CEM:** Blandford; GPS 37.22433, -77.38604; 319 S Crater Rd; Petersburg City **GS:** Y plot Ward A-06, Bolling Mausoleum Square 199/208 **SP:** Mary Marshal Tabb (1737-1814) **VI:** Son of Robert Bolling (1682-1747) **P:** N **BLW:** N **RG:** N **MK:** Y SAR monument **PH:** N **SS:** E pg 74 **BS:**196.

BOLLING, Thomas; b 7 Jul 1735; d 7 Aug 1804 **RU:** Major/Patriot, Promoted to major rank Chesterfield Co Militia, 4 Jan 1777; Gave material aid to cause **CEM:** Cobbs Family; GPS unk; Bolling Family property, Enon; Chesterfield **GS:** N **SP:** Elizabeth Gay (1738-7 Aug 1804) **VI:** Son of John (1700-1775) & Mary Elizabeth (Blair) (1708-1775) Bolling. GS destroyed during Civil War **P:** N **BLW:** N **RG:** Y **MK:** unk **PH:** unk **SS:** E pg 74; AL Ct Bk pg 10; SAR P-117273 **BS:** 196.

BONET, Guillaume; b unk; d 1781 **RU:** Seaman, Served on "Marseillais" and died from Yorktown battle **CEM:** French Memorial; GPS 36.81944, -79.39933; Yorktown; York **GS:** U **SP:** No info **VI:** No further data **P:** unk **BLW:** unk **RG:** Y **MK:** unk **PH:** unk **SS:** J-Yorktown Historian; SAR P-117450 **BS:** JLARC 1, 74.

BONGAR, Francois; b unk; d 1781 **RU:** Seaman, Served on "Hector" and died from Yorktown battle **CEM:** French Memorial; GPS 36.81944, -79.39933; Yorktown; York **GS:** U **SP:** No info **VI:** No further data **P:** unk **BLW:** unk **RG:** Y **MK:** unk **PH:** unk **SS:** J-Yorktown Historian; SAR P-117460 **BS:** JLARC 1, 74.

RU=Rank/Unit	CEM=Cemetery	GS=Gravestone	SP=Spousal Information
VI=Other Veteran Info	P=Pension	BLW=Bounty/Land Warrant	RG=Registered Grave
MK=SAR/DAR Marker	PH=Photo	SS=Service Source	BS=Burial Source

43

BONNET, Jean; b unk; d 1781 **RU:** Seaman, Served on "Palmier" and died from Yorktown battle **CEM:** French Memorial; GPS 36.81944, -79.39933; Yorktown; York **GS:** U **SP:** No info **VI:** No further data **P:** unk **BLW:** unk **RG:** Y **MK:** unk **PH:** unk **SS:** J-Yorktown Historian; SAR P-117532 **BS:** JLARC 1, 74.

BOOKER, E Nash; b unk; d 1838 **RU:** Captain?, An Edmond Booker took oath as officer of Ameila Co Ct, 25 Jul 1776. May not be the same person **CEM:** Booker Family; GPS unk; Rt 641 outside Cumberland CH; Cumberland **GS:** Y **SP:** No info **VI:** No further data **P:** unk **BLW:** unk **RG:** N **MK:** N **PH:** unk **SS:** G pg 4 **BS:** 60, Booker; 196.

BOOKER, Edward; b 1761; d 1800 **RU:** Private, Capt Everard Meades Co, March 1777, Col Alexander Spottswoond's 2d VA Regt **CEM:** Booker Family; GPS unk; Rt 641 outside Cumberland CH; Cumberland **GS:** N **SP:** Edith Cobb Anderson **VI:** No further data **P:** unk **BLW:** unk **RG:** Y **MK:** N **PH:** N **SS:** A pg 271; SAR P-117601 **BS:** 32, e-mail 07; 196.

BOOKER, Edmund; b 17 Jun 1760, d 24 Sep 1795 **RU:** Captain, Amelia County Militia **CEM:** Pride Family; GPS: Not obtained, property of Wayne Keene, 1949 (Deed Bk 99, pg 298); Amelia **GS:** Unk **SP:** Mar 28 Jun 1781, Amelia Co, Mary Pride (c1763-___) **VI:** Son of Edmund Booker and Edith Marot Cobbs **P:** N **BLW:** N **RG:** N **MK:** N **PH:** N **SS:** AL Ct Bk II, pg 63; G pg 14 **BS:** 196

BOOKER, Edmund, b 17 Sep 1719, d 1795 **RU:** Lt Col, Amelia County Militia, took oath 25 May 1780 **CEM:** Booker Family; GPS not determined; Grub Hill Church Rd on Winterham Plantation; Amelia **GS:** No **SP:** Mary Hyde Clements (22 Oct 1765-10 Jul 1847) **VI:** No further data **P:** N **BLW:** N **RG:** N **MK:** N **PH:** N **SS:** E pg 78 **BS:** 196

BOOKER, George; b 1721; d Bet 13 Oct & 22 Dec 1791 **RU:** Patriot, Gave material aid to cause in Amelia Co **CEM:** Booker; GPS unk; Rt 612; Amelia **GS:** Y **SP:** Mar (12 Oct 1745, Amelia Co (bond) Sarah Cobbs d/o Col Samuel & (-----) Cobbs **VI:** Will dated 13 Oct 1791, recorded 22 Dec 1791 **P:** N **BLW:** N **RG:** N **MK:** unk **PH:** unk **SS:** AL Ct Bk 1 pg 53 **BS:** 196.

BOOKER, George; b c1747, Amelia Co VA; d 1816 **RU:** Patriot, Provided goods and services to Patriot forces. Was member Elizabeth City/Hampton Town Committee of Safety **CEM:** Sherwood Cemetery; GPS 37.07384, -76.34973; Langley Air Force Base; Hampton City **GS:** Y **SP:** 1) Mary Moore 2) Ann Hollier **VI:** No further data **P:** N **BLW:** N **RG:** N **MK:** Y SAR granite **PH:** Y **SS:** G pg 436-7; AK **BS:** 04; 41 pg 184; 196.

BOOKER, John; b unk; d 1842 **RU:** Private, Specific service recorded Lib VA, Archives, Council Journals 1783, pg 183 **CEM:** Sherwood Cemetery; GPS 37.07384, -76.34973; Langley Air Force Base; Hampton City **GS:** N **SP:** No info **VI:** Listed on cem plaque **P:** unk **BLW:** unk **RG:** N **MK:** Y **PH:** N **SS:** N pg 1250-1; CZ pg 52 **BS:** 41 pg 184; 196.

BOOKER, Lewis; b 21 May 1754; d 23 Dec 1814 **RU:** Captain, Ent serv fr Essex Co 1777. Lt in VA Line, per pen info. Served in Lt Col Edward Carrington's Regt and in the 1st Cont Artillery. Retired 1783 **CEM:** St Paul's Episcopal; GPS 37.82921, -76.96836; 7924 Richmond-Tappahannock Hwy, Millers Tavern; Essex **GS:** Y **SP:** Mar Judith Dudley, b 1 Jan 1765, d 6 Oct 1817 **VI:** Awarded 4666 acres BLW #8-200-12 May 1803, issued to Joseph Mourse. Bur at "Laurel Cove." Memorial stone in St Paul's Episcopal Church **P:** Y **BLW:** Y **RG:** Y **MK:** N **PH:** Y **SS:** DAR A012066; \ E pg 76, 839; K Vol 1 pg 90; CG pg 322; SAR P-117607 **BS:** JLARC 2, 65; 196; 210 pg 291.

BOOKER, Richardson (Richerson); b 1754; d 27 Oct 1806 **RU:** Sergeant, Served in 5th, 11th and 15th Cont Line for 3 yrs **CEM:** Booker Family; GPS unk; Grub Hill Church Rd, check property records for location of plantation; Amelia **GS:** U **SP:** No info **VI:** Son of Richard (1720-1764) & Martha (Brunskill) Booker **P:** unk **BLW:** Y **RG:** N **MK:** unk **PH:** unk **SS:** C pg 394; E pg 76 **BS:** 196.

BOOTH, Beverly; b 7 Jan 1753, Nottaway Parrish, Southampton Co; d 22 Nov 1833 **RU:** Private, Ent serv Southampton Co Oct 1776 in Col Benjamin Blunt's Regt, Mar 1777-May 1778, then in 1779 in Capt Joyner's Co, Col Parkers Regt until abt March 1781. Was in Battle at Petersburg in Capt Nello's Co 1781. Discharged after the Cornwallis surrender Oct 1871 at Yorktown **CEM:** Roger's Family; GPS unk; Off Rt 40, Booth Fork; Surry **GS:** Y **SP:** 1) Mar (1771) Elizabeth Cocke 2) Mar (21 Jan or 4 Feb 1819) Mary Presson Cornwall (____-2 Jul 1855) of Surry Co. Was widowed at age 73 in Surry Co. **VI:** Son of Robert & Sarah (Bailey) Booth IV. 27 Jun 1814 - Collector of the Surry Co. Levy; 15 Aug 1815 - Sheriff -

RU=Rank/Unit	CEM=Cemetery	GS=Gravestone	SP=Spousal Information
VI=Other Veteran Info	P=Pension	BLW=Bounty/Land Warrant	RG=Registered Grave
MK=SAR/DAR Marker	PH=Photo	SS=Service Source	BS=Burial Source

44

Surry Co. Sol appl pen 24 Sep 1832 Surry Co age 80 in 1832 when titled "Rev". Died in Southampton Co. Widow appl pen 24 Jul 1844 Surry Co. W25267. Widow appl again 28 Mar 1855. BLW #28655-160-55. R289 **P:** Y **BLW:** Y **RG:** Y **MK:** N **PH:** unk **SS:** E pg 77; K Vol 1 pg 91; CG pg 323; SAR P-117718 **BS:** 133 Booth Fam.

BOOTH, George; b 11 Apr 1727, England; d 28 Sep 1804 **RU:** Corporal, Served in 9th Cont Line, 3 yrs service **CEM:** Wright Family; GPS 36.97658, -80.21693; Pizarro off Rt 668; Floyd **GS:** Y **SP:** Permelia Carroll (Sep 1735 Gloucester Co-aft 1813 Montgomery Co) **VI:** Memorialized by DAR plaque in cem. BLW issued 5 May 1791 **P:** unk **BLW:** Y **RG:** Y **MK:** Y SAR **PH:** unk **SS:** F pg 14; SAR P-117738 **BS:** 196 for John Mitchell.

BOOTH, George W; b 1768; d 1808 **RU:** Patriot, Gave material aid to cause **CEM:** Toddbury; GPS unk; On North River; Gloucester **GS:** Y **SP:** Mahala (-----) **VI:** No further data **P:** N **BLW:** N **RG:** Y **MK:** N **PH:** unk **SS:** AL Ct Bk 1; SAR P-117764 **BS:** 100 pg 93.

BOOTH James; b 17 Apr 1763, d 31 Jul 1821 **RU:** Private served in the VA State line for 3 yrs receiving a BLW of 200 acres 2 May1783 **CEM:** Booth: for loc contact Thomas Balch Library, Leesburg, Loudoun Co as listed as a cem on database **GS:** U **SP:** Mar 1784, Frances (Fanny) (___) (23 Jun 1768-26 Jan 1840) **VI:** No further data **P:** N **BLW:** Y **RG:** Y **MK:** N **PH:** N **SS:** A pg 326, 405; C pg 326; F pg 6; DAR A012188; SAR P-117751; Lib VA Cert for BLW LO536 **BS:** 222.

BOOTH, John; b 1737, Amelia Co; d 17 Dec 1807 **RU:** Patriot, Gave material aid to cause **CEM:** Booth Family; GPS unk; Rt 666 Nr Smith Mountain Lake; Franklin **GS:** U **SP:** Mary Smith **VI:** No further data **P:** N **BLW:** N **RG:** Y **MK:** unk **PH:** unk **SS:** DD; SAR P-117764 **BS:** JLARC 2, 76.

BOOTH, William E **See APPENDIX G**

BOOTHE, George; b 1737; d 1813 **RU:** Corporal, Served in US Army, Specific service recorded Lib VA, Archives, Bounty Land Warrants **CEM:** Boothe Family; GPS unk; Little River, Christiansburg; Montgomery **GS:** U **SP:** No info **VI:** No further data **P:** unk **BLW:** Y **RG:** Y **MK:** unk **PH:** unk **SS:** J- DAR Hatcher; CZ pg 53; CU; SAR P-117795 **BS:** JLARC 2. **(BOOTH, William See APPENDIX G**

BOSWELL, John Iverson; b 5 Apr 1761, Gloucester Co; d 3 Mar 1823 **RU:** Sergeant, Served in 1st VA Regt **CEM:** Boswell Family; GPS unk; Off Rt 634, SE of Rebobeth; Lunenburg **GS:** Y **SP:** 1) Mar (16 Feb 1784 Mecklenburg Co) Mary Coleman (28 Feb 1766-14 Jul 1797) 2) Mar (27 Oct 1798 nr Amelia Co) Barbara Walker (22 Jan 1775-13 Jun 1854). Both wives bur here **VI:** Son of Joseph Colgate & Elizabeth (Elliott) Boswell of Amelia Co **P:** unk **BLW:** unk **RG:** Y **MK:** N **PH:** unk **SS:** E pg 78; SAR P-118048 **BS:** 04; 172; 196.

BOUCAULT, Mathieu; b unk; d 1781 **RU:** Seaman, Served on "Palmier" and died from Yorktown battle **CEM:** French Memorial; GPS 36.81944, -79.39933; Yorktown; York **GS:** U **SP:** No info **VI:** No further data **P:** unk **BLW:** unk **RG:** Y **MK:** unk **PH:** unk **SS:** J-Yorktown Historian; SAR P-118151 **BS:** JLARC 1, 74.

BOUILLOT, Benoist; b unk; d 1781 **RU:** Soldier, Served in Agenois Bn and died from Yorktown battle **CEM:** French Memorial; GPS 36.81944, -79.39933; Yorktown; York **GS:** U **SP:** No info **VI:** No further data **P:** unk **BLW:** unk **RG:** Y **MK:** unk **PH:** unk **SS:** J-Yorktown Historian; SAR P-118196 **BS:** JLARC 1, 74.

BOULAIRE, Julien; b unk; d 1781 **RU:** Seaman, Served on "Saint-Esprit" and died from Yorktown battle **CEM:** French Memorial; GPS 36.81944, -79.39933; Yorktown; York **GS:** U **SP:** No info **VI:** No further data **P:** unk **BLW:** unk **RG:** Y **MK:** unk **PH:** unk **SS:** J-Yorktown Historian; SAR P-118197 **BS:** JLARC 1, 74.

BOULANGER, Nicolas; b unk; d 1781 **RU:** Soldier, Served in Santonge Bn and died from Yorktown battle **CEM:** French Memorial; GPS 36.81944, -79.39933; Yorktown; York **GS:** U **SP:** No info **VI:** No further data **P:** unk **BLW:** unk **RG:** Y **MK:** unk **PH:** unk **SS:** J-Yorktown Historian; SAR P-118198 **BS:** JLARC 1, 74.

BOULDIN, Thomas Jr; b 31 Dec 1738, Cecil Co, MD; d 1827 **RU:** Ensign, Served in Charlotte Co Militia **CEM:** Grassy Creek; GPS 36.64716, -79.91943; Nr Horsepasture, Rt 829, Drakes Branch; Henry **GS:** Y **SP:** Mar (12 Jan 1768) Martha Moseley (1742-___) d/o Edmund & Amey (Green) Moseley **VI:** Son of

RU=Rank/Unit	CEM=Cemetery	GS=Gravestone	SP=Spousal Information
VI=Other Veteran Info	P=Pension	BLW=Bounty/Land Warrant	RG=Registered Grave
MK=SAR/DAR Marker	PH=Photo	SS=Service Source	BS=Burial Source

Thomas Sr. (1705-1783) & Anne (Clarke) (1712-___) Bouldin. Govt grave stone **P:** unk **BLW:** unk **RG:** Y **MK:** unk **PH:** unk **SS:** AR pg 98; SAR P-118206 **BS:** 196.

BOULDIN, Thomas Sr; b 15 Jan 1706, Cecil Co, MD; d 1 May 1783 **RU:** Patriot, Gave material aid to cause **CEM:** Golden Hills Estate; GPS unk; Drakes Branch; Charlotte **GS:** U **SP:** Mar (29 Jun 1783 MD) Anne Nancy Wood Clarke (1712 New Castle DE __) d/o Richard & (-----) Clarke **VI:** No **P:** N **BLW:** N **RG:** Y **MK:** unk **PH:** unk **SS:** AL Ct Bk pg 8; SAR P-118208 **BS:** 226.

BOULDIN, Wood; b 4 Jun 1742, Cecil Co, MD; d 13 Mar 1800 **RU:** Major, Ent serv Charlotte Co 1776. Was Maj in the Cont Line and cited for gallantry at Brandywine and Germantown **CEM:** Golden Hills Estate; GPS unk; Drakes Branch; Charlotte **GS:** Y **SP:** Mar (2 or 3 Apr 1777, Charlotte Co) Joanna Tyler (1752-___) Thomas Read signed marriage bond **VI:** Son of Thomas Bouldin (1702-1782) & Ann Wood Clark (1715-1780). Fought at battles of Brandywine and Germantown. Awarded 2666 acres BLW. Widow appl pen 24 Apr 1838 Charlotte Co age 86. W18637. R296 **P:** Y **BLW:** Y **RG:** N **MK:** unk **PH:** unk **SS:** E pg 79; K Vol 1 pg 93; AL pg 79 cites 14th CL as unit; CG pg 333 **BS:** JLARC 1, 76; 186.

BOULDIN (BOUDLIN), Thomas; b 15 Jan 1702; d 2 Jun 1782 **RU:** Ensign/Patriot, Served in militia. Patriot, Gave material aid to cause **CEM:** Golden Hills Estate; GPS unk; Drakes Branch; Charlotte **GS:** Y **SP:** Mar (29 Jan 1733, Cecil Co MD) Ann Wood Clark (1715-1780) **VI:** First sheriff of Lunenburg Co. VA. and Charlotte Co, VA. Born aboard ship in the Chesapeake Bay in move fr MD to VA. Served in French and Indian War. Widow pensioned 1838 age 86 commencing 1 Apr 1814 for $48 per yr **P:** Y **BLW:** unk **RG:** N **MK:** unk **PH:** unk **SS:** AG pg 256; AL Ct book Charlotte pg 8 **BS:** JLARC 102; 196.

BOULWARE, Mark; b 1755; d 15 Mar 1811 **RU:** Private, Served in 2nd Cont Line **CEM:** Greenlawn; GPS 38.07030, -77.33830; Lakewood Rd, Bowling Green; Caroline **GS:** Y **SP:** Milly (-----) (___-1790) 2) Agatha Saunders (___-1836) **VI:** Govt stone gives rank as private. Memorialized on cenotaph **P:** unk **BLW:** unk **RG:** Y **MK:** N **PH:** unk **SS:** E pg 79; SAR P-118221 **BS:** JLARC 2, 76; 196.

BOUQUET, Marcel; b unk; d 1781 **RU:** Seaman, Served on "Languedoc" and died from Yorktown battle **CEM:** French Memorial; GPS 36.81944, -79.39933; Yorktown; York **GS:** U **SP:** No info **VI:** No further data **P:** unk **BLW:** unk **RG:** Y **MK:** unk **PH:** unk **SS:** J-Yorktown Historian; SAR P-118234 **BS:** JLARC 1, 74.

BOURDER, Jean; b unk; d 1781 **RU:** Soldier, Served in Santonge Bn and died from Yorktown battle **CEM:** French Memorial; GPS 36.81944, -79.39933; Yorktown; York **GS:** U **SP:** No info **VI:** No further data **P:** unk **BLW:** unk **RG:** Y **MK:** unk **PH:** unk **SS:** J-Yorktown Historian; SAR P-118236 **BS:** JLARC 1, 74.

BOURDIN, Nicolas; b unk; d 1781 **RU:** Soldier, Served in Agenois Bn and died from Yorktown battle **CEM:** French Memorial; GPS 36.81944, -79.39933; Yorktown; York **GS:** U **SP:** No info **VI:** No further data **P:** unk **BLW:** unk **RG:** Y **MK:** unk **PH:** unk **SS:** J-Yorktown Historian; SAR P-118240 **BS:** JLARC 1, 74.

BOURGAIN, Jean; b unk; d 1781 **RU:** Seaman, Served on "Hercule" and died from Yorktown battle **CEM:** French Memorial; GPS 36.81944, -79.39933; Yorktown; York **GS:** U **SP:** No info **VI:** No further data **P:** unk **BLW:** unk **RG:** Y **MK:** unk **PH:** unk **SS:** J-Yorktown Historian; SAR P-118243 **BS:** JLARC 1, 74.

BOURHIS, Francois; b unk; d 1781 **RU:** Seaman, Served on "Hector" and died from Yorktown battle **CEM:** French Memorial; GPS 36.81944, -79.39933; Yorktown; York **GS:** U **SP:** No info **VI:** No further data **P:** unk **BLW:** unk **RG:** Y **MK:** unk **PH:** unk **SS:** J-Yorktown Historian; SAR P-118251 **BS:** JLARC 1, 74.

BOURHIS, Gregoire; b unk; d 1781 **RU:** Seaman, Served on "Auguste" and died from Yorktown battle **CEM:** French Memorial; GPS 36.81944, -79.39933; Yorktown; York **GS:** U **SP:** No info **VI:** No further data **P:** unk **BLW:** unk **RG:** Y **MK:** unk **PH:** unk **SS:** J-Yorktown Historian; SAR P-118252 **BS:** JLARC 1, 74.

BOURIGEOT, Francois; b unk; d 1781 **RU:** Seaman, Served on "Sceptre" and died from Yorktown battle **CEM:** French Memorial; GPS 36.81944, -79.39933; Yorktown; York **GS:** U **SP:** no info **VI:** No

---

RU=Rank/Unit	CEM=Cemetery	GS=Gravestone	SP=Spousal Information
VI=Other Veteran Info	P=Pension	BLW=Bounty/Land Warrant	RG=Registered Grave
MK=SAR/DAR Marker	PH=Photo	SS=Service Source	BS=Burial Source

46

further data **P:** unk **BLW:** unk **RG:** Y **MK:** unk **PH:** unk **SS:** J-Yorktown Historian; SAR P-118253 **BS:** JLARC 1, 74.

BOURNE, William, Sr: 23 Aug 1743, Louisa Co, d 8 Jun 1836 **RU:** Patriot, Supported cause by paying supply tax included in his personal property tax in 1783, Louisa County **CEM:** William Bourne Family; GPS: 36, 71840, -81.05082; on spur off Rt 651, Lonesome Oak Rd, Spring Valley; Grayson **GS:** Yes **SP:** Rosamond Jones (14 Feb, 1750, Louisa Co-16 Mar 1821) **VI:** Son of Stephen Bourne (1710-___) and Hannah (-----). A leader in forming Grayson Co. Was Clerk of Court. He and son William, Jr owned Point Hope Furnace and Forge **P:** N **BLW:** N **RG:** Y **MK:** N **PH:** Y **SS:** DV image 04.pdf; SAR P-118301 **BS:** 196.

BOUSH, William Sr; b 1739; d 1834 **RU:** Patriot, Gave material aid to cause **CEM:** Lynnhaven House; GPS unk; Shore Dr; Virginia Beach City **GS:** Y **SP:** Mary (-----) (1764-1822) **VI:** DAR plaque **P:** N **BLW:** N **RG:** Y **MK:** Y SAR **PH:** unk **SS:** AS & AL ComBk; SAR P-118315 **BS:** 80,vol1, pg 99; 212 pg 236.

BOUTWELL, John T; b unk; d unk **RU:** First Lieutenant, Appt 1st Lt in Capt Stern's Co, Caroline Co Militia Feb 1778 **CEM:** Boutwell-Smith Family; GPS unk; Rt 17, 3.1 mi S of Port Royal; Caroline **GS:** Y **SP:** No info **VI:** No further data **P:** unk **BLW:** unk **RG:** N **MK:** N **PH:** unk **SS:** E pg 80 **BS:** 98.

BOUTWELL, William; b 1734, Port Royal, Richmond Co; d 7 Jul 1803 **RU:** Patriot, Gave material aid to cause **CEM:** Boutwell-Smith Family; GPS unk; Rt 17, 3.1 mi S of Port Royal; Caroline **GS:** Y **SP:** No info **VI:** No further data **P:** N **BLW:** N **RG:** N **MK:** N **PH:** unk **SS:** Caroline Co Rec; Al Ct Bk II ps 1, 3, 4, 18, 25, Caroline Co **BS:** 98.

BOWEN, Arthur; b 17 Jan 1744, Augusta Co; d 1816 **RU:** Captain, Commanded a co in Washington Co Militia. Promoted to Capt 27 Mar 1781 **CEM:** Aspenvale; GPS 36.81420, -81.64000; Rts 641 & 642, Seven Mile Ford; Smyth **GS:** Y **SP:** Mary McMurray (1746-1816) **VI:** Son of John (1696-1761) & Lillian (McIlhaney) (1709-1780) Bowen **P:** unk **BLW:** unk **RG:** Y **MK:** N **PH:** unk **SS:** E pg 80; AS, DAR Rpt; SAR P-118425 **BS:** 196.

BOWEN, Arthur; b 23 Aug 1760, Botetourt Co, d 1826 **RU:** Captain, Washington Co Militia, promoted to Captain 22 Mar 1781 **CEM:** Sunset; GPS: 37.12390,-80.40420; So Francis St, just N of I-81, Christiansburg; Montgomery **GS:** Unk **SP:** No spousal info **VI:** No further data **P:** N **BLW:** N **RG:** N **MK:** N **PH:** N **SS:** E pg 80; AZ pg 233 **BS:** 196

BOWEN, Ephraim; b 12 Feb 1731, Prince George Co, d 1792 **RU:** Patriot, Supported cause by paying supply tax included in his personal property tax in 1783, Albemarle Co **CEM:** Bowen Farnily; GPS: 37.96460,-78.60810; vic jct Townley Lane and Red Hill Depot Rd; Albemarle **GS:** Unk **SP:** Ann (Anne) (-----) (1736-1818) **VI:** Son of Robert Bowen (1704, Prince George Co-1789, Lunenburg Co) **P:** N **BLW:** N **RG:** N **MK:** N **PH:** Y **SS:** DV image 04.pdf **BS:** 196.

BOWEN, John Pratt; b 1754; d 1858? **RU:** Private, Served in 8th Cont Line, Was Quartermaster Dec 1778 and prisoner at Charleston 12 May 1780. Commissioned Lt 8 Feb 1781 but apparently disabled as he drew half-pay. Resigned Jan 1783 **CEM:** Pratt Family, aka Glebe; GPS 38.29934, -77.34450; 1374 White Oak; Stafford **GS:** U **SP:** Elizabeth (-----) **VI:** Plaque on cem wall indicates Rev War soldier. Pen S6761 King George Co, BLW 3222 acres **P:** Y **BLW:** Y **RG:** Y **MK:** unk **PH:** Y **SS:** A pg 414; E pg 80; CZ pg 55; SAR P-334533 **BS:** 196.

BOWEN, Micajah; b 8 Aug 1753, Meherrin, Lunenburg Co; d 24 Dec 1845 **RU:** Soldier, Ent serv Albemarle Co 1781. Albemarle Militia **CEM:** Bowen Farm; GPS unk; Red Hill; Albemarle **GS:** N **SP:** Fannie (-----) **VI:** Son of Ephraim Bowen & Anne (-----). Sol appl pen 5 Nov 1833 Albemarle Co age 80. S29643. Children recd final payment 12 Jul 1854. R300 **P:** Y **BLW:** unk **RG:** Y **MK:** unk **PH:** N **SS:** E pg 81; K Vol 1 pg 94; CG pg 338; SAR P-118489 **BS:** JLARC 2, 4, 76; 196.

BOWEN, Rees; b 1750, Augusta Co; d 7 Oct 1780 **RU:** Ensign, Served in VA Militia under Cols William Campbell, Isaac Shelby and Benjamin Cleveland. Killed in Battle at Kings Mountain **CEM:** Bowen Family; GPS unk; Cove Creek; Tazewell **GS:** Y **SP:** Mar (c1756) Louisa Smith (c1740-16 Feb 1834) **VI:** Son of John (1710 PA-19 May 1761) & Lilly (McIlhaney) (1705 Ireland-20 Jun 1780) Bowen. D in Kings Mountain, SC. Govt GS. SAR marker **P:** unk **BLW:** unk **RG:** Y **MK:** Y SAR **PH:** unk **SS:** CD; SAR P-118510 **BS:** 196.

RU=Rank/Unit	CEM=Cemetery	GS=Gravestone	SP=Spousal Information
VI=Other Veteran Info	P=Pension	BLW=Bounty/Land Warrant	RG=Registered Grave
MK=SAR/DAR Marker	PH=Photo	SS=Service Source	BS=Burial Source

47

BOWERS, Christian Phillip; b 2 Nov 1736, Birkenau, Hessen Germany; d 9 Sep 1815 **RU:** Private/ Patriot, Capt William Brisben's Co, 1st Bn, Lancaster Co PA Militia. Also gave material aid to cause, VA **CEM:** Solomons Lutheran Church; GPS 38.7367, -78.7364; Solomon Church Rd, Rt 727, nr jct with Rt 42, Forestville, Quicksburg; Shenandoah **GS:** Yes **SP:** Mar Frederick Co, MD 1767, Maria Elizabeth Schindeldecker (1738-15 Mar 1815), d/o Johann Jacob Schindeldecker and Elizabeth Schussler **VI:** Son of Johann Ludwig Sebastian and Anna Catherine Weber. Family moved to Shenandoah Co by 1785 **P:** N **BLW:** N **RG:** N **MK:** N **PH:** Y **SS:** Cl> Fold3, PA Archives 5th Ser, vol &, pgs 50/51; AL Ct Bk pgs 2, 13 Pr Wm Co **BS:** 04, James Wood II, Chap 2018.

BOWIE: John; b Scotland, d 1789 **RU:** Patriot, Gave material aid to cause **CEM:** Hill Family; GPS unk; Port Royal; Caroline **GS:** unk **SP:** Mar 1745, Judith Catlett (___-1798), d/o John Catlett and Mary Grayson **VI:** Emigrated fr Scotland 1742 **P:** N **BLW:** N **RG:** N **MK:** N **PH:** N **SS:** AL Ct Bk pgs 4, 16, 24 Caroline Co **BS:** 196.

BOWIE, William S Sr; b unk; d unk **RU:** Lieutenant, Served in MD Flying Camp in 1776 in 3rd Bn **CEM:** Fairfax City; GPS 38.84690, -77.31330; Main St & Page Ave; Fairfax City **GS:** N **SP:** No info **VI:** No further data **P:** unk **BLW:** unk **RG:** N **MK:** N **PH:** N **SS:** A pg 239 **BS:** 61 vol III pg FX-153.

BOWLES, Knight; b 8 May 1746; d 14 Feb 1820 **RU:** Private/Patriot, Served in Amherst Co Militia. Served at least 3 yrs **CEM:** Lyles Church; GPS 37.84793, -78.20337; Palmyra; Fluvanna **GS:** Y **SP:** 1) Mar (17 Feb 1767) Sarah Curd 2) Mar (24 Dec 1798) Martha Wood (26 Jun 1757-20 Nov 1846) widow of John Ellis **VI:** Son of John & Sarah (Knight) Bowles **P:** unk **BLW:** Y **RG:** N **MK:** N **PH:** unk **SS:** C pg 613; D Vol I pg 80 **BS:** 66, pg 8; 196.

BOWLES, Thomas; b 1761; d Jan 1810 or 7 Dec 1839 **RU:** Sergeant, Ent serv Hanover Co 1776. Served in VA Line **CEM:** Bowles Family; GPS unk; Waterloo, Chickahominy Point; Hanover **GS:** N **SP:** Mar (25 Nov 1793 Stafford Co) Sarah Holman or Ford. Widow moved to Indiana in 1829. **VI:** Sol appl pen 6 Aug 1832 Henrico Co. age 72. Widow appl BLW age 84 in Harrison Co, IN in 1849, which was rejected. She reappl age 93 in 1856 which was granted. Died in Spotsylvania Co. S8079. R304 **P:** Y **BLW:** Y **RG:** Y **MK:** unk **PH:** N **SS:** K Vol 1 pg 95; CG pg 343; SAR P-118691 **BS:** JLARC 76.

BOWLES, Thomas Philip; b 1749; d 1789 **RU:** Lieutenant, Specific service recorded Lib VA, Archives, Report of Sec of War, Vol 2, Pen, pg 148 **CEM:** Bowles Family; GPS unk; Waterloo, Chickahominy Point; Hanover **GS:** N **SP:** No info **VI:** No further data **P:** Y **BLW:** unk **RG:** Y **MK:** unk **PH:** N **SS:** J- DAR Hatcher; CZ pg 55; SAR P-118693 **BS:** JLARC 2.

BOWLES (BOLLS), William; b 1754; d 1823 **RU:** Private?, Served in 3rd, 4th, 8th, & 12th Cont Lines **CEM:** Bowles Family; GPS unk; Waterloo, Chickahominy Point; Hanover **GS:** Y **SP:** Elizabeth Napier (1758-1838) **VI:** No further data **P:** unk **BLW:** unk **RG:** N **MK:** N **PH:** unk **SS:** E pg 82 **BS:** 31 vol 1 pg 49; 196.

BOWLING, James; b 9 Jan 1756, NC; d unk **RU:** Corporal, Served in 5th Cont Line **CEM:** Benjamin Bolling; GPS 37.07721, -82.70543; Sulpher Springs Dr, Flat Gap; Wise **GS:** U **SP:** Sarah Blevins **VI:** Son of Benjamin (1734-1832) & (-----) Bowling **P:** unk **BLW:** unk **RG:** N **MK:** unk **PH:** unk **SS:** E pg 82 **BS:** 196.

BOWLING/BOLLING/BOLING, Jarrett; b 18 Jan 1762, Stafford Co; d 2 Jan 1856 **RU:** Private, Virginia Troops serving 3mos each in Capt Williams 1778; Capt John James 1779 and Capt Sharps Co 1781 and 6 mos in Capt Hardias & Ballard's Co under Maj Welsh. Was in siege of Yorktown **CEM:** Morris Knob Old Home Place; GPS not determined; Tazewell **GS:** Unk **SP:** Mar 1782, Eleanor Garrison (1765-1830) **VI:** Perhaps grandson of Simon Bowling will Stafford Co 1736. Allowed pen Mar 18, 1834 as resident of Tazewell Co claim # s18384 and 160 acres BLW # 26360 in 1855 **P** Y **BLW** Y **RG:** Y **MK:** N **PH:** N **SS:** E gg 82; H; Fold 3 pen file; SAR P-118702 **BS:** 05.

BOWMAN, Benjamin, b 1 Nov 1754; d 29 Sep 1829 **RU:** Private/Patriot: served as a private in an undetermined infantry unit long enough to be eligible for a BLT; as a patriot paid personal property tax, Rockingham Co 1783 **CEM:** Greenmount; GPS GS 38.518456, -78.901417; loc Rt 722; Rockingham **GS:** Y **SP;** Sarah Carherine Shoemaker, mar again Mary M Saun (6 Aug 1777, Shenandoah Co-3 Aug 1849) **VI:** Was an Elder **P** N but eligible **BLW** N but eligible **RG:** Y **MK:** N **PH:** Y **SS:** C pg 199; E pg 82; Rockingham 1783 Tax reel 304; SAR P-349040 **BS:** 04.

RU=Rank/Unit	CEM=Cemetery	GS=Gravestone	SP=Spousal Information
VI=Other Veteran Info	P=Pension	BLW=Bounty/Land Warrant	RG=Registered Grave
MK=SAR/DAR Marker	PH=Photo	SS=Service Source	BS=Burial Source

48

BOWMAN, Isaac Hite; b 24 Apr 1757, d 9 Sep 1826 **RU:** Lieutenant and Quartermaster, Col George Rogers Clarks, Illinois Regt, May 1779 Prisoner by Indians, 17 Nov 1779, sold to trader Apr 1780, carried to New Orleans and to Cuba before escaping and returning **CEM:** Bowman family; GPS 39.00450, -78.32823; loc Fort Bowman Rd, Strasburg; Shenandoah **GS:** Yes **SP:** Mar 1) Elizabeth Gatewood (27 Jan 1764, Essex Co-16 Aug 1794), d/o Phillip Gatewood and Susannah Wright, 2) Mary Jane Chinn (31 Oct 1773-21 Aug 1830) **VI:** Son of George Bowman (10 Feb 1699, Germany and Mary Heydt-Hite (1708-1830). Wounded four times by Indians. Congress granted his son, Isaac his half pay 30 Jun 1754 **P:** No **BLW:** No **RG:** Y **MK:** N **PH:** N **SS:** A pg 395; E pg 82; BX pgs 81, 82; SAR P-118729 **BS:** 196; Gr Reg James Wood II Chap Dec 2016.

BOWMAN, Johann "Jacob"; 2 Dec 1733, Switzerland; d 1794 **RU:** Patriot, as Jacob gave material aid to the cause in Rockinham Co **CEM:** Jacob Bowman Farm; GPS not determined; loc Jacob Baumann (Bowmann) farm, Linville; Rockingham **GS:** N **SP:** Mar 1768, Susannah Rachaelb Milhouse (1750 Lancaster Co, PA-1832, TN), d/o Moritz & Dorethe Meyer Mulhausen/Milhouse **VI:**Son of Johann Jakob Baumann-Bowman & Verena Vreni **P:** N **BLW:** N **RG:** Y **MK:** N **PH:** N **SS:** AL Ct Bk I, pg 11, Comm Bk V pg 107 **BS:** 196.

BOWMAN, John; b 18 Jul 1750; d 7 Mar 1816 **RU:** Private, Served by running supplies in Capt Peter Hull's Co, 2nd Bn, Augusta Co Militia 1779 **CEM:** Rader Lutheran; GPS 38.65073, -78.78055; 17072 Raders Church Rd, Timberville; Rockingham **GS:** Y **SP:** Mary Magdalena Zervus (30 Oct 1755-3 Dec 1835) **VI:** No further data **P:** unk **BLW:** unk **RG:** Y **MK:** Y SAR **PH:** Y **SS:** E pg 26; SAR P-118744 **BS:** 04.

BOWMAN, Peter; b c1762; d 22 Dec 1823 **RU:** Private, Served in Capt Jacob Holeman's Co, Dunmore Co Militia **CEM:** Bowman Family; GPS unk; War Branch, Peaked Mountain Rt 726 abt 1 mi fr jct with Rt 613 on private rd; Rockingham **GS:** Y **SP:** Mary Heatwole (18 Dec 1766 PA-Feb 1833) d/o Mathias & (-----) Heatwole **VI:** Killed in hunting accident **P:** unk **BLW:** unk **RG:** N **MK:** unk **PH:** unk **SS:** C pg 607 **BS:** 196.

BOWMAN, Robert; b 20 Jan 1758; d 15 Jul 1824 **RU:** Lieutenant, Serv in Cont Line in III Regt **CEM:** Bowman-Fariss Family; GPS 36.66541, -80.66541; Blue Ridge Pkwy MM 194, Volunteer Rd W side btw Alpine Court Rd & Boundary Rd; Carroll **GS:** Y **SP:** Mary "Polly" Peck **VI:** Modern era Govt stone **P:** unk **BLW:** unk **RG:** Y **MK:** N **PH:** Y **SS:** E pg 83; B; T 63 pg 578; SAR P-118534 **BS:** 63 pg 578.

BOWYER, Henry; b 1760; d 13 Jun 1832 **RU:** Colonel, Ent serv Botetourt Co 1777. Served as Lt in Cont & VA Line **CEM:** Allen-Lauderdale; GPS unk; Fincastle; Botetourt **GS:** U **SP:** Mar (9 Aug 1792 Boutetourt Co) Agatha Madison (c1774-6 Oct 1847) **VI:** Moved to Boutetourt Co c1763 fr Augusta Co. Pensoned under Act of 1828. Widow appl pen 8 Oct 1838 Botetourt Co. W5859, BLW #283-200-31 Dec 1795. Person w/ same name, and death date is reported for Lexington. R306 **P:** Y **BLW:** Y **RG:** Y **MK:** unk **PH:** unk **SS:** K Vol 1 pg 97; CG pg 345; SAR P-118811 **BS:** JLARC 1, 4, 60.

BOWYER, Henry; b unk; d 1832 **RU:** Lieutenant, Specific service recorded Lib VA, Archives, Auditors Acct 1778-1783, vol VII, pg 219 **CEM:** Stonewall Jackson Memorial; GPS 37.78128, -79.44604; 314 S Main St; Lexington City **GS:** U **SP:** No info **VI:** Person w/ same name, and death date, is reported for Botetourt Co **P:** unk **BLW:** unk **RG:** N **MK:** unk **PH:** unk **SS:** CZ pg 56 **BS:** JLARC 63.

BOWYER, John; b 1763; d 1806 **RU:** Lieutenant, Served in Capt James Gilmore's Co under command of Gen Morgan in SC, 1780 **CEM:** Stonewall Jackson Memorial; GPS 37.78128, -79.44604; 314 S Main St; Lexington City **GS:** U **SP:** 1) Madgalene Woods McDowell Borden 2) Mary (-----) **VI:** Attained rank of Col after War **P:** unk **BLW:** unk **RG:** Y **MK:** unk **PH:** unk **SS:** J-NSSAR 2000 Reg; S, SAR P-118814 **BS:** JLARC 1, 2, 63; 76.

BOXLEY, Joseph I Sr; b c1735, King William Co; d 27 Jun 1787 **RU:** Patriot, Gave material aid to cause **CEM:** Cem name unk; GPS unk; Lousia; Louisa **GS:** N **SP:** Catherine Spiller **VI:** Son of George Boxley **P:** N **BLW:** N **RG:** Y **MK:** Y SAR **PH:** N **SS:** D Vol I pg 625, 638, 645; SAR P-118827 **BS:** 04.

BOWYER, Thomas; b 1727, Spotsylvania Co, d Aug 1805; **RU:** Captain, Commanded Co Lt Col Campbell's 1st VA Regt and was in battles at Ninety Six, and Eutaw Springs. Discharged Jan 1882 **CEM:** Fincastle Presbyterian Church; GPS 37.50017, -79.87558, East Back St, Falls Fincastle; Botetourt **GS:** U **SP:** No info **VI:** Son of Michael Bowyer (1695-1761). Name listed on VASSAR plaque in

---

RU=Rank/Unit	CEM=Cemetery	GS=Gravestone	SP=Spousal Information
VI=Other Veteran Info	P=Pension	BLW=Bounty/Land Warrant	RG=Registered Grave
MK=SAR/DAR Marker	PH=Photo	SS=Service Source	BS=Burial Source

49

cem. Recd BLW #659, 4000 acres, 24 May 1783 **P:** N **BLW:** Y **RG:** N **MK** :Y SAR plaque **PH:** Unk **SS:** DP pg 137 **BS:** 196.

BOYAR (BOYARS), John; b 1757; d 19 Nov 1802 **RU:** Sergeant, Served in Spencer's Regt, Cont Troops **CEM:** Old Christ Church Episcopal; GPS 38.80625, -77.04718; 118 N Washington St; Alexandria City **GS:** Y **SP:** No info **VI:** Cooper, died in his 46th yr **P:** unk **BLW:** unk **RG:** N **MK:** N **PH:** unk **SS:** A pg 188; AP serv record Fold 3 **BS:** 20 pg 136; 196.

BOYD, Alexander; b 16 Aug 1743, Irvine, Scotland; d 11 Aug 1801 **RU:** Patriot, Gave 400# beef to cause 9 Apr 1782 **CEM:** Boyd Family; GPS unk; Behind Health Dept Bldg, Boyton; Mecklenburg **GS:** Y **SP:** No info **VI:** Son of Robert (1688-1786) & Elizabeth (Anderson) (1705-1786) Boyd **P:** N **BLW:** N **RG:** N **MK:** unk **PH:** unk **SS:** DB pg 27 **BS:** 54 pg 177; 196.

BOYD, Francis; b unk; d 1850 **RU:** Private, Served in 7th VA Regt **CEM:** Boydton Presbyterian Church; GPS 36.40101, -78.23127; Boydton; Mecklenburg **GS:** Y **SP:** No info **VI:** No further data **P:** Y **BLW:** unk **RG:** N **MK:** N **PH:** unk **SS:** C pg 395; CU **BS:** 54 pg 26.

BOYD, Robert; b unk; d 1800 **RU:** Private, Served in Capt Thomas Buford's Co, Bedford Co at Point Pleasant 10 Oct 1774 **CEM:** Boyd Family; GPS unk; Hwy 895, end of Rt 875; Mecklenburg **GS:** Y **SP:** 1) Mar (20 Apr 1789) Sarah Anderson Jones d/o of Tignal & (-----) Jones; 2) Mar (11 May 1803) Tabitha Walker **VI:** Son of Alexander & (-----) Boyd. Pen to widow commencing 30 Sep 1814 at $48 per yr. Styled Capt on GS **P:** Y **BLW:** unk **RG:** N **MK:** N **PH:** unk **SS:** N pg 1249; Z pg 125; AG pg 256 **BS:** 54 pg 173.

BOYER, Henry; b 22 Feb 1757; d 7 Mar 1799 **RU:** Lieutenant, Served in a VA Regt in Illinois **CEM:** Old Christ Church Episcopal; GPS 38.80625, -77.04718; 118 N Washington St; Alexandria City **GS:** Y **SP:** Margaret (-----) who m (2) John Myers, RW veteran, barber, who d 17 Mar 1802 **VI:** Carpenter. GS styles him Lt, d age 43 yrs, 7 seven days; death notice in Alexandria Gazette 7 Mar 1799, pg 3 **P:** unk **BLW:** unk **RG:** Y **MK:** N **PH:** unk **SS:** J-NSSAR 1993 Reg; CZ pg 57 **BS:** JLARC 1; 20 pg 136; 196.

BOYER/BOWYER, Thomas; b unk; d 1785 **RU:** Captain, Served in 12th VA Regt of Foot as Cmdr of 10th Co 16 Dec 1776. Served in the 8th VA Regt and sent to Guilford CH Mar 1781 as temporary 3rd VA Regt. Served in Armand's Command **CEM:** Fincastle Presbyterian; GPS 37.50017, -79.87558; 108 E Back St, Fincastle; Botetourt **GS:** N **SP:** No info **VI:** Name is on the cemetery SAR plaque **P:** unk **BLW:** unk **RG:** Y **MK:** Y SAR **PH:** N **SS:** CE pg 58, 68; J-NSSAR 1993 Reg, J- DAR Hatcher; E pg 83; SAR P-119098 **BS:** JLARC 1, 2; 196.

BOYKIN, Simon; b unk; d 1834 **RU:** Captain, Served as Co commander in Southampton Co Militia 13 Oct 1774 extending into 1775 war period **CEM:** Boykin Family; GPS unk; Rt 460, across Blackwater River fr Zuni; Southampton **GS:** U **SP:** No info **VI:** Son of Simon (before 1731-1788) & (-----) Boykin **P:** unk **BLW:** unk **RG:** N **MK:** unk **PH:** unk **SS:** AH pg 34 **BS:** 45 pg 18.

BOYKIN, Simon; b Before 1731; d 16 Jun 1788 **RU:** Patriot, Gave material aid to cause **CEM:** Boykin Family; GPS unk; Rt 460, across Blackwater River fr Zuni; Southampton **GS:** Y **SP:** No info **VI:** Son of William (1680-1731) & (-----) Boykin **P:** N **BLW:** N **RG:** N **MK:** N **PH:** unk **SS:** AL Ct Bk pg 2 Southampton Co **BS:** 53 vol 7 pg 17.

BRACKETT, John I; b 1720; d 1785 **RU:** Patriot, Gave material aid to the cause **CEM:** Rural; GPS unk; See county property record for plantation; Henrico **GS:** Y **SP:** Elizabeth (-----) **VI:** Son of Thomas & Elizabeth (Ashe) Brackett **P:** N **BLW:** N **RG:** Y **MK:** N **PH:** unk **SS:** AL Ct bk pg 5; SAR P-119301 **BS:** AS, SAR registration.

BRADFORD, John; b 1717; d 1789 **RU:** Private, Served in a VA unit in Illinois **CEM:** St Paul's Episcopal; GPS 37.76570, -77.37120; 8050 St Paul's Rd, Hanover; Hanover **GS:** U **SP:** (-----) Timberlake **VI:** No further data **P:** unk **BLW:** unk **RG:** Y **MK:** unk **PH:** unk **SS:** CZ pg 59; SAR P-119452 **BS:** JLARC 2, 76.

BRADFORD, Thomas A; b 6 Mar 1764; d 8 Jul 1818 **RU:** Private, Served in Capt Levern Teakle's Co, 5th VA Regt fr 1778 to 1779 **CEM:** Bradford-Burton; GPS unk; Rt 182 and Rt 605, N fr Quinby; Accomack **GS:** Y **SP:** Mar (12 Oct 1786 (bond) Accomack Co) Alesy P. Bradford (12 Jan 1763-29 Mar 1825) **VI:** No further data **P:** unk **BLW:** unk **RG:** N **MK:** N **PH:** unk **SS:** AP 5th CL **BS:** 145 Burton.

RU=Rank/Unit	CEM=Cemetery	GS=Gravestone	SP=Spousal Information
VI=Other Veteran Info	P=Pension	BLW=Bounty/Land Warrant	RG=Registered Grave
MK=SAR/DAR Marker	PH=Photo	SS=Service Source	BS=Burial Source

BRADLEY, John; b 1748; d 1795 **RU**: Private, Served in Shelby's Co, Fincastle Troops. Was in battles at Long Island, Point Pleasant,and Kings Mountain **CEM**: Sinking Springs; GPS 36.71030, -81.98170; 136 E Main St, Abingdon; Washington **GS**: Y **SP**: Sarah Lillard (1745-1821) **VI**: Source 80 reports stone illegible. DAR marker **P**: unk **BLW**: unk **RG**: Y **MK**: Y **SAR PH**: unk **SS**: J-NSSAR 2000 Reg; S, SAR P-119673 **BS**: JLARC 1, 2, 76; 80.

BRADLEY, William; b By 1758; d Aft 1774 **RU**: Sergeant, Served in Capt McKee's Co of Rockbridge Co at Point Pleasant in 1774. Later a Sgt in 15th VA Cont Line **CEM**: Cleek; GPS 38.19310, -79.73220; Rt 220 Sam Snead Hwy, Warm Springs; Bath **GS**: Y **SP**: No info **VI**: Govt stone says Sergeant, 5th VA Cont Line; R318 **P**: unk **BLW**: unk **RG**: N **MK**: unk **PH**: unk **SS**: B; Z pg 136 **BS**: 196.

BRADLEY, William; b 1759, England; d 5 Feb 1819 **RU**: Sergeant, Served in VA Line and 3rd, 5th, 7th, and 11th Cont Lines **CEM**: Stonewall Jackson Memorial; GPS 37.78128, -79.44604; 314 S Main St; Lexington City **GS**: U **SP**: Mar (12 Mar 1791 Rockbridge Co) Mary Carlock or else wife was Elizabeth Susan (-----) (papers burned in Washington DC Fire) **VI**: Sol shown on list of invalid pensioners living in Rockbridge Co. Disability pen recd Rockbridge Co 1786. He recd pen of $60 per annum fr 13 Ju 1786 & was increased to $96 per annum under act of 24 Apr 1816. Papers destroyed in one of the Washington DC fires in War of 1812 **P**: Y **BLW**: unk **RG**: Y **MK**: unk **PH**: unk **SS**: E pg 86; CG pg 361; K Vol 1 pg 102; SAR P-119754 **BS**: JLARC 4,79.

BRAIDFOOT, John; b Bef 1753, Scotland d 1784, Norfolk **RU**: Chaplain, Specific service recorded Lib VA, Archives, Bounty Land Warrants shows was in US Army as Chaplain. Served with Washington throughout war period **CEM**: Trinity Episcopal; GPS 36.83459, -76.30105; 500 Court St; Portsmouth City **GS**: Y **SP**: Blandinah Moseley **VI**: Believed "bur on the Glebe, and his original grave site lost". BLW 1832. DAR marker **P**: unk **BLW**: Y **RG**: Y **MK** Y **SAR plaque PH**: unk **SS**: E pg 87; S; CU; CZ pg 59; DAR A013648; SAR P-119895 **BS**: JLARC 2, 76, 105,127; 92, stone 6.

BRAITHWAITE, William, Sr; b 1755, London, Eng; d 13 Jul 1831 **RU**:Corporal, entered serv 1778, Fredericktown, MD in Capt Gassaway's Co, MD Line serving also in other units until end of war **CEM**:Heironimus Family; GPS 39.330811, -78.327393; Old Mill Ln, Whitacre; Frederick **GS**: Y Gov't **SP**: Mar May 1786, Catherine Brookover, she rec'd pen # S W5934, age 68 in 1838 **VI**: Rec'd pen age 74 Frederick Co, VA in 1826 # R322 **P**: Y both **BLW**: unk **RG**: Y **MK**: Y SAR, granite **PH**: N **SS**: K vol 1, pg 103; EL pg 533 DAR A013697; SAR P-119970 **BS**: 196.

BRAME, John; b 30 Jun 1746, d 14 Nov 1796 **RU**: Patriot, Gave material aid to cause, Mecklenburg Co **CEM**: Young and Richen Brame Family; GPS: unk; one mi S of Railroad Station, Antlers; Mecklenburg **GS**: Unk **SP**: Mar 1768, Mary Norment **VI**: Son of Richens Brame (1722-1789) and Susannah Chiles (13 Jun 1724-5 Dec 1806) **P**: N **BLW**: N **RG**: Y **MK**: N **PH**: N **SS**: AL Ct Bk pg 15, Comm Bk IV, pg 38, Mecklenburg Co; SAR P-120000 **BS**: 196.

BRAME, Richens; b 2 Dec 1722; d 11 Apr 1789 **RU**: Patriot, Gave material aid to cause **CEM**: Young & Brame Family; GPS unk; 5 mi E of Boydton, 1 mi S of Antlers; Mecklenburg **GS**: N **SP**: Mar (14 Feb 1743) Susannah Chiles (13 Jun 1724 King William Co-5 Dec 1806) **VI**: Moved fr Caroline Co to Mecklenburg Co in 1760 **P**: N **BLW**: N **RG**: Y **MK**: N **PH**: N **SS**: AL Ct Bk pg 1, 17, 20 Mecklenburg Co; SAR P-120001 **BS**: 196.

BRANCH, Olive; b 1758, Chesterfield Co; d 1845 **RU**: Private, Ent serv Bedford Co.Served in Buckingham Co Militia **CEM**: Branch; GPS 37.58250, -78.49000; Rt 631, Manteo; Buckingham **GS**: U **SP**: No info **VI**: Sol appl pen 10 Dec 1832 Buckingham Co age 72. S8101. R323 **P**: Y **BLW**: unk **RG**: Y **MK**: N **PH**: unk **SS**: E pg 88; K Vol 1 pg 104; CG pg 366; SAR P-120030 **BS**: JLARC 4, 44.

BRANHAM, John, Jr; b 1727, Farnham, Richmond Co, d 17 Jan 1785 **RU**: Patriot, gave material aid to the cause in Spotsylvania Co **CEM**: Orange CH Area; GPS not determined; loc area vic Old Courthouse; Orange **GS**: Unk **SP**: Not determined **VI**: Son of John Branham (1690-1761) & Rachel Webb (1705-1782) **P**: N **BLW**: N **RG**: N **MK**: N **PH**: N **SS**: AL Ct Bk pg 30 Spotsylvania Co **BS**: 196.

BRANNER, Casper; b 18 Jun 1724; d 1792 Ger **RU**: Private Capt Holeman's Co 29 May 1775. Gave material aid to cause **CEM** Soloman's Lutheran Ch; GPS 38.744640, -78.642650; Solomans Church Rd, Forestville; Shenandoah **GS**: N **SP**: Mar 17 Dec 1751, PA, Catherine Zirkle(Zerchel)(6 Apr 1733, PA-4

RU=Rank/Unit	CEM=Cemetery	GS=Gravestone	SP=Spousal Information
VI=Other Veteran Info	P=Pension	BLW=Bounty/Land Warrant	RG=Registered Grave
MK=SAR/DAR Marker	PH=Photo	SS=Service Source	BS=Burial Source

51

Jan 1817), d/o Johann Ludwig Zirkle & Marie Eva Bear **VI:** No further info **P:** N **BLW:** N **RG:** Y **MK:**N **PH:** N **SS:**C pgs 607; D vol3, pg 841; DAR A013810; SAR P-120122 **BS:** 196.

BRANNER, John; b 12 Aug 1752; d 20 Apr 1837 **RU**. Private/Pariot, Capt David Rogers Co, Dunmore County Militia, serving again 29 May 1775 in Capt Holman's Co. He gave material aid to cause **CEM:** Soloman's Lutheran Ch; GPS 38.744640, -78.642650; Solomans Church Rd, Forestville; Shenandoah **GS**: Y **SP**: Mar 26 Jul 1773, Catherine Harpine (3 Apr 1753, PA-1 Jan 1817) **VI**: Son of Casper Branner (18 Jun 1724, Germany-1792) & Catherine Zircle(1733-1817) **P:** N **BLW:** N **RG:** Y **MK:**Y DAR SAR **PH:** N **SS:**C pgs 146, 607; D vol3, pg 841; DAR A01381; SAR P-120124 **BS:** 196.

BRASSON, Jean; b unk; d 1781 **RU:** Seaman, Served on "Magnanime" and died from Yorktown battle **CEM:** French Memorial; GPS 36.81944, -79.39933; Yorktown; York **GS:** U **SP:** No info **VI:** No further data **P:** unk **BLW:** unk **RG:** Y **MK:** unk **PH:** unk **SS:** J-Yorktown Historian; SAR P-120198 **BS:** JLARC 1, 74.

BRATTON, James; b 30 Jun 1746, Ireland; d 29 Jun 1828 **RU:** Captain, Commanded a company Augusta Co Militia, 21 Aug 1781 **CEM:** Bratton; GPS 37.99750, -79.56170; Rts 39 & 42 Mountain Valley Rd 4 mi E of Millboro Springs; Bath **GS:** Y **SP:** Mar (abt 1774) Rebecca Hogshead **VI:** Son Robert Bratton and Ann McFarland **P:** unk **BLW:** unk **RG:** Y **MK:** N **PH:** unk **SS:** AZ pg 181; SAR P-327054 **BS:** 159 Bratton; 196.

BRATTON, James; b unk; d 2 Jan 1814 **RU:** Captain, Served in Augusta Co Militia. Commissioned capt 26 Aug 1781 **CEM:** Craig; GPS unk; Christiansburg; Montgomery **GS:** Y **SP:** Elizabeth M. (-----) (___-25 Jul 1806) **VI:** No further data **P:** unk **BLW:** unk **RG:** N **MK:** N **PH:** unk **SS:** E pg 90 **BS:** 04, Jul 06; 123 pg 68; 196.

BRATTON, Robert; b 20 May 1712, Ireland; d Aft 18 Oct 1785 **RU:** Patriot, Gave material aid to cause **CEM:** Bratton Family; GPS unk; Nr Goshen; Augusta **GS:** U **SP:** Anne McFarland Dunlap **VI:** No further data **P:** N **BLW:** N **RG:** Y **MK:** unk **PH:** unk **SS:** D Vol I pg 88, 92-94, 96; SAR P-120229 **BS:** JLARC 2, 76.

BRAWNER, William Henry; b unk; d unk **RU:** Soldier, Obtain SAR application for service **CEM:** Presbyterian Church; GPS 38.80015, -77.05791; Wilkes St & Hamilton Ln; Alexandria City **GS:** U **SP:** no info **VI:** Obtain SAR application for birth and death dates **P:** unk **BLW:** unk **RG:** Y **MK:** unk **PH:** unk **SS:** SAR P-120258; **BS:** JLARC 1.

BRAXTON, Carter; b 10 Sep 1736; d 10 Oct 1797 **RU:** Patriot, Voted for independence, signed the Declaration, and then left Congress to return the next yr. In VA, supported bill to recruit slaves to fight for Rev, to be given freedom in exchange for their service (bill defeated). Gave material aid to cause. Was in Cont Congress and the Congress of the Confederation 1775-1776, 1777-1783 & 1785 **CEM:** Braxton Estate; GPS unk; Chericoke; King George **GS:** Y **SP:** 1) Judith Robinson (1736-1757) 2) Elizabeth Corbin (1745-1814) **VI:** Braxton Co in what is now WV was named for him **P:** N **BLW:** N **RG:** Y **MK:** N **PH:** unk **SS:** N pg 145; SAR P-120261; DAR A03880*** **BS:** 196; 80 vol 1 pg 108.

BRECKENRIDGE, James; b 7 Mar 1763; d 13 May 1833 **RU:** Private, Served in Col Preston's Regt under Gen Green **CEM:** Breckenridge Family; GPS unk; Grove Hill Farm 1 mi NW of Fincastle on Rt 606; Botetourt **GS:** U **SP:** Mar (1 Jan 1791 Richmond) Nancy Ann Cary Selden d/o Cary & (-----) Sheldon **VI:** Son of Col Robert & (-----) Breckenridge. Resided at Grove Hill in Botetourt. US Army Brigadier General, US Congressman, member of State House of Delegates 1789-1824. In 1809 elected as a Federalist to the Eleventh Congress and to the three succeeding Congresses, serving until 1817 **P:** unk **BLW:** unk **RG:** N **MK:** unk **PH:** unk **SS:** N pg 737 **BS:** JLARC 1, 2, 60, 124.

BREEDEN, George; b 1764; d 1847 **RU:** Soldier, Obtain SAR application for service **CEM:** Jones-Van Lear; GPS unk; Rt 613, .3 mi S jct with Rt 742 farm of Alfred Ryder; Augusta **GS:** U **SP:** No info **VI:** No further data **P:** unk **BLW:** unk **RG:** Y **MK:** U **PH:** unk **SS:** SAR P-120439; JLARC 62 **BS:** JLARC 62.

BRENEMAN, Abraham; b 1744; d 1815 **RU:** Private, Served in Capt Jacob Holman's Co, Dunmore Co Militia **CEM:** Lindale Mennonite; GPS unk; Jesse Bennett Way,Linville; Rockingham **GS:** Y **SP:** Marie/Maria Reiff **VI:** No further data **P:** unk **BLW:** unk **RG:** N **MK:** N **PH:** unk **SS:** C pg 607 **BS:** 04, 05 Oct 09.

RU=Rank/Unit	CEM=Cemetery	GS=Gravestone	SP=Spousal Information
VI=Other Veteran Info	P=Pension	BLW=Bounty/Land Warrant	RG=Registered Grave
MK=SAR/DAR Marker	PH=Photo	SS=Service Source	BS=Burial Source

52

BRENT, Richard; b 1757, Aquia Creek off Potomac, Stafford Co; d 30 Dec 1814 **RU:** Seaman, Served in US Navy **CEM:** Richland, aka Brent Family); GPS unk; Rt 637, Aquia; Stafford **GS:** U **SP:** Mar (7 Dec 1795) Rachel Moore **VI:** Was in VA House of Delegates fr Stafford Co 1788, Prince William Co 1793, 1794, 1800, 1801. US Rep to 4th & 5th Congresses 1795-99. 7th Congress 1801-03. State Senator fr 1808-09. US Senator 1809-1814. Died in Washington DC **P:** unk **BLW:** Y **RG:** N **MK:** unk **PH:** unk **SS:** G pg 784 **BS:** 201 pg 1795.

BREWER, Lewis; b 1760, NC d 1839 **RU:** Private, Served in Capt Ballard's Co 20 July 1778 for 9 mos **CEM:** Rudy; GPS unk; Rt 660 near Elk Creek, Independence; Grayson **GS:** U **SP:** No info **VI:** No further data **P:** unk **BLW:** unk **RG:** Y **MK:** unk **PH:** unk **SS:** J-NSSAR 1993 Reg, J- DAR Hatcher; CH Roster of Soldiers fr NC During Rev War; SAR P-120631 **BS:** JLARC 1, 2.

BRIAN, Louis; b unk; d 1781 **RU:** Soldier, Served in Gatinais Bn and died from Yorktown battle **CEM:** French Memorial; GPS 36.81944, -79.39933; Yorktown; York **GS:** U **SP:** No info **VI:** No further data **P:** unk **BLW:** unk **RG:** Y **MK:** unk **PH:** unk **SS:** J-Yorktown Historian; SAR P-120767 **BS:** JLARC 1, 74.

BRICKEY, Peter; b 10 Apr 1761, Westmoreland Co; d 1836 **RU:** Private, Ent serv Botetourt Co Sep 1780 for 6 mos in Capt Saunders & Wm McClanahan's Cos. Was in Battles in NC, Reedy Fork & Guilford CH **CEM:** Brickey Family; GPS unk; See county property records for homeplace; Botetourt **GS:** U **SP:** 1) Mar (Sep 1806) Elizabeth (-----) (___- by 1820) 2) Mar (1820) Elizabeth Dunn **VI:** Pension rejected as served less than 6 mo. Source 76 has his death in 1860. BLW #44.800 (160 acres). Widow had BLW fr Carter Co TN 1855 age 56 R333 **P:** unk **BLW:** Y **RG:** Y **MK:** unk **PH:** unk **SS:** SAR Applic; K Vol 1 pg 108; SAR P-120818 **BS:** JLARC 1, 4, 60, 76.

BRICKEY, Peter: b 1690, d 16 Sep 1786 **RU:** Patriot, gave material aid to cause in Westmoreland Co **CEM:** Bickey Family Farm; GPS: not determined; loc unincorporated community named Latanes vic jct Rts 3 & 721; Westmoreland **GS:** Unk **SP:** Mar c1738, Westmoreland Co, Winifred Lucas (___-1786) **VI:** Son of William (John/Jean) Brickey (20 Dec 1640, France-29 Oct 1718) & Mary Alice Crabbe (1650, France-___) who are also buried on the farm **P:** N **BLW:** N **RG:** Y **MK:** N **PH:** Y **SS:** D vol 3 pgs 906, 908 Westmoreland Co; DAR A009563; SAR P-120816 **BS** 196

BRIDGES, Richard; b 1752; d 1826 **RU:** Sergeant, Served in Gen Nelson's Corps in VA Light Dragoons **CEM:** Cool Spring Farm; GPS unk; 10065 Rozell Rd, Woodford; Caroline **GS:** U **SP:** Anne Johnson Norment **VI:** No further data **P:** unk **BLW:** unk **RG:** Y **MK:** N **PH:** unk **SS:** J-NSSAR 2000 Reg; E pg 93; SAR P-120877 **BS:** JLARC 76.

BRIGGS, David; b 9 May 1730, Scotland; d 3 Dec 1815 **RU:** Patriot, Gave 600# fodder and 3 beeves to cause. Also Trustee in Falmouth during war period **CEM:** Stony Hill; GPS 38.439230, -77.581770; Stony Hill Rd nr Curtis Lake; Stafford **GS:** Y **SP:** Jane McDonald (c1760-6 Jun 1810) **VI:** No further data **P:** N **BLW:** N **RG:** Y **MK:** DAR Plaque **PH:** unk **SS:** D pg 882; SAR P-330111 **BS:** 03 pg 366.

BRIGHT, John; b 8 Apr 1753, Germany; d 8 Oct 1826 **RU:** Private, Served in Capt Tate's Co in Augusta Co Militia **CEM:** Bethel Cemetery; GPS 38.47592, -78.75641; 3061 Armentrout Path, Keezletown; Rockingham **GS:** N **SP:** Ann Fawcett **VI:** No further data **P:** unk **BLW:** unk **RG:** Y **MK:** N **PH:** N **SS:** E pg 93; AK Sep 09; BD; SAR P-121184 **BS:** 196.

BRIZENDINE, William Sr; b 1743, Essex Co; d 1833 **RU:** Private, Ent serv Charlotte Co 1781 **CEM:** Private; GPS unk; Nr Glade Hill; Franklin **GS:** U **SP:** Mary Dupree **VI:** Pension 1832 in Franklin Co, R (reel) 345 **P:** Y **BLW:** unk **RG:** Y **MK:** unk **PH:** unk **SS:** J-NSSAR 2000 Reg; K Vol I pg 111; SAR P-121472 **BS:** JLARC 76.

BROACH, Charles; b 1750, d 16 Sep 1829 **RU:** Matross, Enlisted fr King William County, assigned as Matross, in Capt Drury Ragsdale's Co, Colonel Charles Harrison's First Artillery Regt, Continental Troops, 1777 **CEM:** Shockoe Hill; GPS: 37.55190,- 77.43170; 4th and Hospital St; Richmond City **GS:** Gov't **SP:** Mar 1784, Martha (___) (___-aft 1838). Rec'd Pension 1836 $100 per annum **VI:** Recd pen $8.00 mo **P:** Both **BLW:** N **RG:** Y **MK:** Y Name on monument in cem **PH:** N **SS: A Part II, pgs 241-247**E pg 96; SAR P-336976 **BS:** 196.

BROADWATER, Charles; b 1717; d 20 Mar 1806 **RU:** Colonel/Patriot, Served in Fairfax Co Militia, 1776-1780. Probably applies to Charles Lewis Broadwater. Gave material aid to cause **CEM:** Broadwater Family; GPS 38.88940, -77.2610; Cnr of Tapawingo Rd and Frederick St SW, Vienna;

RU=Rank/Unit	CEM=Cemetery	GS=Gravestone	SP=Spousal Information
VI=Other Veteran Info	P=Pension	BLW=Bounty/Land Warrant	RG=Registered Grave
MK=SAR/DAR Marker	PH=Photo	SS=Service Source	BS=Burial Source

53

Fairfax **GS:** Y **SP:** 1) Ann Amelia Markham or Ann Pierson 2) Sarah Ann Harris **VI:** Burgess fr Fairfax in 1774. Delivered Fairfax Resolves in company of Geo. Washington to Alexandria. Helped establish VA Navy. Member Fairfax Co Committee of Safety. Rep to 1st, 2nd, 3rd, and 4th Convs. Justice of Peace, VA House of Delegates. This may apply to Charles Lewis Broadwater. Stone for Charles Broadwater simply says "Colonial Service" Obit in Alexandria Gazette 21 Mar 1806 pg 3 says he d on the 20th instant **P:** unk **BLW:** unk **RG:** Y **MK:** Y SAR **PH:** unk **SS:** D Fairfax Co; SAR P-121502 **BS:** JLARC 1, 2, 13, 27, 28; 196.

BROADWATER, Charles Lewis; b 1751; d 18 Sep 1841 **RU:** Lieutenant, Ent Serv 1776 Fairfax Co. Was Midshipman, VA State Navy 8 Mar 1776; Lt, 10th Va Regt, 18 Nov 1776. Dismissed 21 Apr 1778. Fairfax Co Militia, 1779 **CEM:** Broadwater Family; GPS 38.88940, -77.2610; Cnr of Tapawingo Rd and Frederick St SW, Vienna; Fairfax **GS:** Y **SP:** Betheland Sebastian (1750-before 1841). Died earlier than husband. **VI:** Son of Charles (1717-1806) & Ann Amelia (Markham) (1708-1796) Broadwater. Pensioned Fairfax Co 1830 age 78. Pen S.8096. R346. Small stone with engraved metal plate reads "Lieut Chas L Broadwater 10 VA Regt Rev War" **P:** Y **BLW:** unk **RG:** Y **MK:** Y SAR **PH:** Y **SS:** K Vol 1 pg 112; SAR P-121504 **BS:** JLARC 1, 2, 4 13, 27, 28, 45; 196.

BROCK, John P; b unk; d unk **RU:** Private, Specific service recorded Lib VA, Archives,War, vol 4, pg 28 **CEM:** Brock Spring; GPS unk; Old Telegraph Rd; Hanover **GS:** N **SP:** No info **VI:** No further data **P:** unk **BLW:** unk **RG:** N **MK:** N **PH:** N **SS:** E pg 96; CZ pg 64 **BS:** 31 vol 1 pg 43.

BROCK, John Sr; b 28 Jun 1753; d 17 Apr 1827 **RU:** First Lieutenant, Appt 1/Lt, 2 Dec 1776. Retired 30 Sep 1778. Served in 10th VA Regt in Capt John Spotswood's Co of Foot **CEM:** Brock Family; GPS 36.71055, -79.55003; 2401 Indian Trail Rd, Keezletown 22832; Rockingham **GS:** Y **SP:** Ann Jones **VI:** No further data **P:** unk **BLW:** unk **RG:** Y **MK:** N **PH:** unk **SS:** E pg 96; SAR P-330276 **BS:** 04.

BROCKENBROUGH, John; b 1750; d 20 Nov 1801 **RU:** Private/Patriot, Served in 4th Cont Line. Gave material aid to the cause **CEM:** Doctor's Hall; GPS unk; Nr jct Rappahannock River & Creek; Richmond Co **GS:** Y **SP:** Sarah Roane (d. 1810) **VI:** Son of Col William & Margaret (Flauntleroy) Brockenbrough. Also was signer of the Westmoreland protest of 1764 against the Stamp Act. After war Judge Gen Ct of VA in 1818 **P:** unk **BLW:** unk **RG:** Y **MK:** N **PH:** unk **SS:** AL Ct Bk pg 6; E pg 99; SAR P-121549 **BS:** 108 pg 556-7.

BROCKENBROUGH, William; b 5 Jun 1715; d 1778 **RU:** Colonel, Mil serv during war period not identified. Was signer of Leedstown Resolutions fr Spotsylvania Co **CEM:** Cem name unk; GPS unk; See property Records for cem loc; Richmond Co **GS:** U **SP:** Mar (25 Nov 1735) Elizabeth Fauntleroy d/o Moore & Margaret (Micou) Fautleroy **VI:** Son of Austin (1685-1717) & Mary (Metcalfe) Brockenbrough **P:** unk **BLW:** unk **RG:** Y **MK:** N **PH:** unk **SS:** E pg 97; BQ; SAR P-121551 **BS:** SAR Applic.

BROCKMAN, Samuel Jr; b 1730; d 1790 **RU:** Lieutenant/Patriot, Recommended 1777 as Lt in Orange Co Militia. Gave material aid to cause **CEM:** Brockman Family; GPS unk; Greenway, Monrovia; Orange **GS:** U **SP:** 1) Rebecca Graves (4 Sep 1735, Spotsylvania Co-___) 2) Mary Woolford **VI:** Son of Samuel Sr (1685, St Marys, MD-___) & Mary Henderson (Collins) (1685, Orange Co-___) Brockman. Died in St Thomas Parish **P:** unk **BLW:** unk **RG:** Y **MK:** unk **PH:** unk **SS:** E pg 97; Al Ct Bk pg 5; SAR P-327246 **BS:** 196.

BROCKMAN, William Sr; b 1718 Newtown, King & Queen Co; d 1809 **RU:** Patriot, Donated 50 bushels of wheat and carted it 8 mi **CEM:** Brockman-Mitchell; GPS unk; Petty's Creek Annex, Stony Point; Albemarle **GS:** Y **SP:** Elizabeth "Betty" Embree Faunteler **VI:** Son of Samuel Brockman (1685-1766) & Mary Madison (d. 1776). In French & Indian War in 1750s, enlisted in VA militia. Lived in Orange Co **P:** N **BLW:** N **RG:** N **MK:** unk **PH:** unk **SS:** AL Ct Book pg 2; Commissioners book: IV pg 180 Certificate 1 Lists pg 15 **BS:** 196.

BRODY, John; b unk; d 1848 **RU:** Soldier, Was black soldier who served as body guard to Capt William Campbell **CEM:** Brody Family; GPS unk; Saltville; Smyth **GS:** U **SP:** No info **VI:** Honored w/ others on monument in front of Smyth Co CH **P:** unk **BLW:** unk **RG:** Y **MK:** unk **PH:** unk **SS:** SAR P-121619 **BS:** JLARC 114.

RU=Rank/Unit	CEM=Cemetery	GS=Gravestone	SP=Spousal Information
VI=Other Veteran Info	P=Pension	BLW=Bounty/Land Warrant	RG=Registered Grave
MK=SAR/DAR Marker	PH=Photo	SS=Service Source	BS=Burial Source

54

BRONOUGH, Thomas; b 1741; d 1794 **RU:** Patriot/Captain, Commanded a company in Fauquier Co Militia 25 May 1778. Gave material aid to the cause **CEM:** Bronough Family; GPS unk; Blue Ridge No Sub Div; Fauquier **GS:** N **SP:** Mar (19 Oct 1790 Fauquier Co) Peggy Kerr, d/o John & Sarah (-----) Kerr **VI:** Justice of Peace, 1787; County Sheriff 1790 **P:** unk **BLW:** unk **RG:** N **MK:** N **PH:** N **SS:** AV; Fauquier Co Marriages pg 23 **BS:** 83, Inv #61.

BROOK, Edmund (Edmond); b 1761; d 2 Jun 1835 **RU:** First Lieutenant, Appt Feb 1781, in 1st Regt of Artillery, Cont Line under Col Charles Harrison until Sept 1781 before Yorktown Battle **CEM:** Cem name unk; GPS unk; Snowville; Pulaski **GS:** Y **SP:** No info **VI:** Source at NARA for a claim for pay under Act of 15 May 1828 **P:** unk **BLW:** unk **RG:** Y **MK:** N **PH:** unk **SS:** A pg 388; SAR P-121730 **BS:** AS, SAR regis, Application 48, 1445, 1514.

BROOKE, Francis Taliaferro; b 27 Aug 1763; d 3 Mar 1851 **RU:** Major, Ent serv Essex Co 1781. With twin John, appointed 1st Lt in Gen Harrison's 1st Cont Regt of Artillery at age 16. Fought in VA campaign. After Battle of Green Springs joined Maj Gen Nathaniel Greene in Southern Dept, not returning to VA until Aug 1782. Was Deputy Quartermaster of Harrison's Brigade and served as Maj under General Greene **CEM:** Brooke Family; GPS unk; Rt 2, 6 mi N Fredericksburg, E side of St Julian house; Spotsylvania **GS:** Y **SP:** 1) Mar (3 Oct 1791 Nottingham) Mary Randolph Spotswood 2) Mar (14 Feb 1804, Fredericksburg Co) Mary Champe Carter, Robert S. Chew, security [Catherine L Knorr Marriages of Fredericksburg, VA 1782-1850 Pine Bluff AR 1954] pg 6 **VI:** Son of Richard & Ann May (Taliaferro) Brooke. Judge of VA Ct of Appeals 1848. Pensioned Georgetown DC, increase 1832 & 1850. Recd pen Spotsylvania Co 1832 and increase in pay under Act of 1850. R350 **P:** Y **BLW:** Y **RG:** Y **MK:** unk **PH:** unk **SS:** BY pg 14; K Vol 1 pg 113; SAR P-121741 **BS:** JLARC 1, 76; 196.

BROOKE, Robert; b 1751, Spotsylvania Co; d 25 Feb 1799 **RU:** Private, Served in Capt Larkin Smith's Calvary Co, 7th Cont Line. Was captured by British at Wesham **CEM:** Masonic Cemetery; GPS 38.30198, -77.46142; 900 Charles St; Fredericksburg City **GS:** U **SP:** Mar (1766) Mary Richie **VI:** Represented Spotsylvania Co in House of Delegates 1791-1794. Governor of VA 1794. Freemason in VA fr 1795-97. Nov 1795 succeeded John Marshall as Grand Master of Grand Lodge of Virginia **P:** unk **BLW:** unk **RG:** N **MK:** unk **PH:** unk **SS:** E pg 98 **BS:** 196.

BROOKS, Elias; b 1759, Essex Co; d 1838 **RU:** Soldier, Ent serv in Chesterfield Co. Served in 3rd Regiment, VA State Line **CEM:** Brooks Family; GPS unk; North of Walmsley Blvd btw Angus and Shackleford roads; Chesterfield **GS:** U **SP:** No info **VI:** Son of Elias & (-----) Brooks, Sr. Pen Chestervield Co 1832, age 73 and last payment 3rd quarter 1838, R 352 **P:** Y **BLW:** unk **RG:** Y **MK:** N **PH:** unk **SS:** K Vol 1 pg 114; SAR P-121833 **BS:** JLARC 4, 35.

BROOKS, John; b 6 Dec1748; d 12 May1840 **RU:** Private, Served in Capt Wm. Bentley's Co, 3rd VA Regt in Dec 1778 **CEM:** Brooks Private; GPS unk; Rt 681 W of Halifax, Cluster Springs; Halifax **GS:** U **SP:** 1) Susanna Lightfoot 2) Sarah Falkner **VI:** No further data **P:** unk **BLW:** unk **RG:** Y **MK:** unk **PH:** unk **SS:** AP Payroll code; Cl-Fold 3 website; SAR P-121895 **BS:** JLARC 1, 76; 215.

BROOKS, John Turpin; b 1755; d 26 Jan 1821 **RU:** Private?, Specific service recorded Lib VA, Archives, Auditors Acct, vol XXXI, pg 361 **CEM:** Presbyterian Church; GPS 38.80015, -77.05791; Wilkes St & Hamilton Ln; Alexandria City **GS:** Y **SP:** No info **VI:** Died age 66. Member Baptist Church **P:** unk **BLW:** unk **RG:** Y **MK:** Y SAR marker & plaque **PH:** unk **SS:** E pg 98; CZ pg 65; SAR P-121885 **BS:** 23 pg 16.

BROOKS, Robert; b 1723; d bef 9 Jun 1806 **RU:** Gave material aid to cause and signed a legislative petition in Mecklenburg Co on 14 May 1777 **CEM:** Frederick & Nelly Jones Family; GPS not determined; for exact loc see county property records; Mecklenburg **GS:** No **SP:** Mar 1741 Abigail Brambly **VI:** No further data **P:** N **BLW:** N **RG:** Y **MK:** N **PH:** N **SS:** D vol 2, pgs 665, 668 Mecklenburg Co; DAR A015067 cites petition date of inhabitants of 14 May 1777 SAR P-121965 **BS:** 196.

BROOKS, William; b 3 Feb 1752; d 24 Jan 1841 **RU:** Private, Ent serv 1777 in Culpeper Co **CEM:** Brooks; GPS unk; Rt 604, .2 mi fr grocery behind silo, Thompson Valley; Tazewell **GS:** U **SP:** Mar (5 Sep 1769) Nancy Anne Locke (1749-after 1843) **VI:** Pen Tazewell Co 1832, Widow pension R (reel) 355 **P:** Y **BLW:** unk **RG:** Y **MK:** unk **PH:** unk **SS:** K Vol I pg 115; SAR P-122020 **BS:** JLARC 1, 2, 89.

RU=Rank/Unit CEM=Cemetery GS=Gravestone SP=Spousal Information
VI=Other Veteran Info P=Pension BLW=Bounty/Land Warrant RG=Registered Grave
MK=SAR/DAR Marker PH=Photo SS=Service Source BS=Burial Source

55

BROSTMAN, Jean; b unk; d 1781 **RU:** Soldier, Served in Gatinais Bn and died from Yorktown battle **CEM:** French Memorial; GPS 36.81944, -79.39933; Yorktown; York **GS:** U **SP:** No info **VI:** No further data **P:** unk **BLW:** unk **RG:** Y **MK:** unk **PH:** unk **SS:** J-Yorktown Historian; SAR P-122062 **BS:** JLARC 1, 74.

BROUGH, Daniel; b 19 Jul 1762; d 26 Dec 1825 **RU:** Patriot, Paid supply tax 1783, Botetourt Co **CEM:** Old Dutch; GPS unk; W side of Rt 11 at Mill Creek, 9 mi S of Buchanan; Botetourt **GS:** U **SP:** Elizabeth (-----) **VI:** No further data **P:** N **BLW:** N **RG:** Y **MK:** N **PH:** unk **SS:** J- DAR Hatcher; DI RG 4, 61, roll #343; SAR P-122083 **BS:** JLARC 2.

BROWN, Bazael (Bazel); b unk; d unk **RU:** Captain, As Pvt serv in 1779 in Capt Abriah Springer's Co 9th VA Regt under Col Gibson; as Cpl serv in Capt James Seal's Co of 9th VA Regt **CEM:** Brown Family 1; GPS unk; Mt Fair nr Charlottesville; Charlottesville City **GS:** N **SP:** No info **VI:** Pen #S9713 **P:** Y **BLW:** unk **RG:** Y **MK:** unk **PH:** N **SS:** J-NSSAR 2000 Reg; AP record; CI fold 3 website; SAR P-122248 **BS:** JLARC 76.

BROWN, Benjamin; b 1751; d 1842 **RU:** Ensign, Served in Henley's Co Cont Line **CEM:** Physics Springs; GPS unk; Buckingham; Buckingham **GS:** U **SP:** Mary Jarman **VI:** No further data **P:** unk **BLW:** unk **RG:** Y **MK:** N **PH:** unk **SS:** AP Record; CI fold 3 website; SAR P-122272 **BS:** JLARC 2, 76.

BROWN, Benjamin; b 1767; d 1806 **RU:** Seaman, Served in 4th Cont Line **CEM:** St John's Episcopal; GPS unk; 100 W Queen's Way; Hampton City **GS:** Y **SP:** No info **VI:** No further data **P:** unk **BLW:** unk **RG:** N **MK:** Y SAR plaque cem wall 2009 **PH:** unk **SS:** C pg 326; E pg 88 **BS:** 89, pg 19.

BROWN, Bernis; b 15 Aug 1752; d 30 Oct 1814 **RU:** Private? Ent serv Albemarle Co **CEM:** Brown Family 2; GPS unk; Rt 810, Brown's Cove; Albemarle **GS:** Y **SP:** Mar (14 Nov 1779, Albemarle Co) Henrietta Rhodes, (26 May 1761-1 Jul 1840 Brown's Cove) **VI:** Widow's pension 1842 age 81. Her pension rejected as he was not in regularly constituted military unit. R 360 **P:** Y **BLW:** unk **RG:** Y **MK:** N **PH:** unk **SS:** K Vol 1 pg 117 SAR P-122288 **BS:** 80 pg 119; 176.

BROWN, Brightberry; b 13 Feb 1762; d 26 Jan 1846 **RU:** Captain, Ent serv Brown's Cove, Albemarle Co 1780 **CEM:** Brightberry Brown Family; GPS 38.20972, -78.67243; 5525 Brown's Gap Turnpike, Brown's Cove; Albemarle **GS:** N **SP:** Mar (10 Jan 1788) Mary Susan "Suca" Madison (21 Jan 1776-14 Aug 1832) **VI:** Pension 1832 R360 **P:** Y **BLW:** unk **RG:** Y **MK:** unk **PH:** N **SS:** J-NSSAR 2000 Reg; K Vol 1 pg 117; DAR 574380 SAR P-122292 **BS:** JLARC 76; 196.

BROWN, Christopher Sr; b 16 Jul 1751, Lancaster Co, PA; d 16 Jul 1816 **RU:** Private, Served in Capt Michael Moyer, 6th Battalion, Lancaster Co PA Militia **CEM:** St John's Lutheran; GPS 36.96500, -81.10110; 405 W Main, Wytheville; Wythe **GS:** Y **SP:** Mar (2 Jun 1772 Whytheville, Wythe Co) Anna Maria Mason (10 Oct 754 Philadelphia-10 May 1822) **VI:** Son of Johan Michael (1724-1785) & Anna Juliana (Karger) (1728-1785) Braun **P:** unk **BLW:** unk **RG:** Y **MK:** unk **PH:** unk **SS:** CI PA Archives, 5th Series Vol 7 pg 560-561; SAR P-122324 **BS:** JLARC 122, 123; 196.

BROWN, Daniel; b 1 Dec 1748, Culpeper Co (then Orange Co); d 14 Jul 1833 **RU:** Captain, Ent serv Culpeper Co 1 Dec 1748. Served as Lt in Capt Burgess Ball's Co, 5th VA Regt, appointed Capt May 1777 **CEM:** Brown; GPS unk; 1 mi NW of Reva on Rt 636, then 2 mi NW to gate; Culpeper **GS:** N **SP:** Mar (25 Dec 1779 Culpeper Co) Elizabeth Hill (age 15 c1764-2 Jan 1852) **VI:** Pen 1832 Culpeper Co. Widow pension 1837 R362 **P:** Y **BLW:** unk **RG:** Y **MK:** unk **PH:** N **SS:** K Vol 1 pg 118; SAR P-122337 **BS:** JLARC 1, 76.

BROWN, Henry; b c1736; d 7 May 1782 **RU:** Patriot, Gave material aid to the cause **CEM:** Trinity Episcopal; GPS 36.83459, -76.30105; 500 Court St; Portsmouth City **GS:** Y **SP:** No info **VI:** Was a mariner in Norfolk Co **P:** N **BLW:** N **RG:** Y **MK:** Y SAR plaque **PH:** unk **SS:** AL Ct Bk pg 30; SAR P-336638 **BS:** 92, stone 42.

BROWN, Henry; b 25 Oct 1759, Prince George Co; d 26 Dec 1849 **RU:** Private, ESF 1779 Bedford Co. Reenlisted 1780 as Orderly Sgt in Capt Robert Adam's Co, Col Lynch's Regt. Reenlisted 1781 in Col Parker's Regt **CEM:** Brown Family-Thompson Valley; GPS unk; New London; Campbell **GS:** U **SP:** Mar (29 Aug 1827 Buckingham Co) Elizabeth L. Jones **VI:** Recd pen 1832 Campbell Co age 72. Widow pen and drew BLW at age 76 in Campbell Co R365. Possible duplicate with Henry Brown in Bedford **P:** Y

RU=Rank/Unit
VI=Other Veteran Info
MK=SAR/DAR Marker

CEM=Cemetery
P=Pension
PH=Photo

GS=Gravestone
BLW=Bounty/Land Warrant
SS=Service Source

SP=Spousal Information
RG=Registered Grave
BS=Burial Source

56

BLW: Y **RG**: Y **MK**: N **PH**: unk **SS**: J-NSSAR 1993 Reg; K Vol 1 pg 118;AZ pg 235; SAR P-122505 **BS**: JLARC 1.

BROWN, Henry; b 10 Aug 1760; d 13 Aug 1841 **RU**: Soldier, Wounded at Guilford CH **CEM**: Brown Family; GPS unk; Off New London Rd Rt 709, Forest; Bedford **GS**: N **SP**: Frances Thompson (6 Jun 1775-14 Aug 1822) **VI**: Opened store in New London with his brother Daniel and was Treasurer of New London Agricultural Society (New London is now in Campbell Co). Was Federal Tax Collector in Bedford 1800-1803, and serveral times Sheriff of Bedford Co **P**: unk **BLW**: unk **RG**: Y **MK**: N **PH**: N **SS**: J- DAR Hatcher; SAR P-122507 **BS**: JLARC 2; 197.

BROWN, Isaac; b England; d 27 Aug 1785 **RU**: Sergeant, Served in Capt Wm Smith's Co, 11th Regt of Foot, commanded by Lt Col John Cropper **CEM**: Brown Family; GPS unk; New Castle; Hanover **GS**: Y **SP**: No info **VI**: No further data **P**: unk **BLW**: unk **RG**: N **MK**: N **PH**: unk **SS**: AL Lists pg 17 **BS**: 101 pg 146.

BROWN, Isaac; b 1760, d bef 19 Aug 1859 **RU**: Sergeant, entered service 1775 Charles City Co, served in Capt Sanford's Co, Col Campbell's Regt **CEM**: Elam Baptist Church; GPS 37.363389, -77.018097; loc 8840 Church Lane, Ruthville; Charles City **GS**: N **SP**: Sarah (___) **VI**: Was age 69 when recd pen in 1829 #S39214 **P**: Y **BLW**: N **RG**: Y **MK**: N **PH**: N **SS**: K vol 1; DAR A203808; SAR P-329293 **BS**: SAR PRS; 196.

BROWN, Isaacher; b 1760; d 1840 **RU**: Private, Ent service 1780 in Upper Dublin Twp, Montgomery Co, PA **CEM**: North Fork Baptist; GPS 39.06014, -77.68509; 38130 North Folk Rd, North Fork; Loudoun **GS**: U **SP**: No info **VI**: Pensioned age 71 Loudoun Co, 1832 R366 **P**: Y **BLW**: unk **RG**: N **MK**: unk **PH**: unk **SS**: K Vol I pg 117 **BS**: JLARC 1, 4, 32.

BROWN, James; b unk; d Sep 1801 **RU**: Private, Served in Capt Young's Co, Augusta Co Militia **CEM**: Samuel Brown Family; GPS unk; 9 mi W of Covington; Covington City **GS**: N **SP**: Agnes (-----), d Jan 1809) **VI**: No further data **P**: unk **BLW**: unk **RG**: N **MK**: N **PH**: N **SS**: E pg 100 **BS**: 160 Sam Brown.

BROWN, John; b 1748; d 29 Apr 1836; **RU**: Patriot, gave material aid to cause, Bedford Co **CEM**: Browns #207; GPS not dertermined; loc Old E Ferry Rd, off Rt 705 in woods on property of a Mining Co, Rustburg; Campbell **GS**: Unk **SP**: Anne Burnley(c1753-unk)) **VI**: No info **P**: N **BLW**: N **RG**: N **MK**: Unk **PH**: Unk **SS**: DAR A015651; AL Comm Bk IV pg 292, Ct Bk pgs 10,32, Bedford Co **BS**: 196.

BROWN, John; b 1749; d 2 Jun 1828 **RU**: Patriot, Gave material aid to cause **CEM**: Goose Creek; GPS 39.11250, -77.69527; Rt 722, Lincoln; Loudoun **GS**: Y **SP**: Martha Bell (1754-1784) **VI**: Son of Henry & Esther (-----) Harris **P**: N **BLW**: N **RG**: N **MK**: unk **PH**: unk **SS**: AL Ct Bk pg 28; Comm Bk II pg 286. Loudoun Co **BS**: 196. (**BROWN**, John **See APPENDIX G**)

BROWN, John; b c1765; d 1867 **RU**: Private, Served in 3rd Regt, VA state line **CEM**: Brown-Osborne; GPS unk; 1168 White Pine Rd; Grayson **GS**: U **SP**: No info **VI**: No further data **P**: unk **BLW**: unk **RG**: N **MK**: N **PH**: unk **SS**: AK Apr 2007 **BS**: 04, Apr 2007.

BROWN, John; b 1759; d Aft 1820 **RU**: Soldier/Patriot, Ent serv 1777, Pittsylvania Co, Served in VA Line. Gave material aid to cause **CEM**: Brown Family; GPS unk; Off Rt 705; Campbell **GS**: U **SP**: Two marriages but do not know the dates/order: 1) Nancy (-----); 2) Mar (19 May 1800, Campbell Co. (bond), bondsman Armistead Dudley) Phillis Dudley **VI**: No further data **P**: Y **BLW**: unk **RG**: Y **MK**: N **PH**: unk **SS**: D Campbell Co; SAR P-122741 **BS**: JLARC 4, 36.

BROWN, John b 5 Oct 1762, Harrisburg, Dauphin Co, PA, d 6 Oct 1826 **RU**: Patriot, Supported cause by paying supply tax included in his personal property tax in 1783 in Augusta Co **CEM**: Thornrose; GPS: 38.15120, -79.08460; 1041 W Beverly St; Staunton City **GS**: Yes **SP**: Frances Peyton (1762, Prince William Co-1851) **VI**: Judge of the Superior Court of Chancery. Reinterred fr Trinity Episcopal Churchyard. Styled as "General" **P**: N **BLW**: N **RG**: N **MK**: N **PH**: N **SS**: DV image 07 pdf **BS**: 196.

BROWN, Jonas; b unk; d 18 Oct 1781 **RU**: Sergeant, Promoted 27 Mar 1778, Capt Charles Graham's 3rd Co, Col Van Cortlandt's 2d Regt, NY Line and died as result of Yorktown battle **CEM**: Yorktown Victory Monument Tablet; GPS 38.28350, -78.54150; Yorktown; York **GS**: U **SP**: No info **VI**: No further data **P**: unk **BLW**: unk **RG**: Y **MK**: unk **PH**: unk **SS**: J-Yorktown Historian; AX pg 188; SAR P-122774 **BS**: JLARC 74.

RU=Rank/Unit	CEM=Cemetery	GS=Gravestone	SP=Spousal Information
VI=Other Veteran Info	P=Pension	BLW=Bounty/Land Warrant	RG=Registered Grave
MK=SAR/DAR Marker	PH=Photo	SS=Service Source	BS=Burial Source

57

BROWN, Low (Lowe); b 1756; d 28 Jan 1841 **RU:** Private, Ent serv Montgomery Co, 1776. Served in IL Regt under Capt George Rogers Clark on the Vincennes Expedition in 1779. Was Spy for Capt James Moore on the Bluestone, Clinch, & New Rivers. Was in Battle of Kings Mountain. **CEM:** Hezekiah Harman; GPS unk; In front of HS off Rts 460 & 19, Tazewell; Tazewell **GS:** Y **SP:** Jane Davidson, d/o John Goolman & (-----) Davidson **VI:** Son of William & Mary (Lowe) Brown, both b in Scotland. Entered service 1774, Montgomery Co for Indian Wars (Lord Dunmore's War). Pensioned Tazewell Co 1832 age 76. Govt grave stone. 1832, R373 **P:** Y **BLW:** unk **RG:** Y **MK:** unk **PH:** unk **SS:** K Vol 1 pg 121; CV pg 218; SAR P-122871 **BS:** JLARC 1, 3, 26, 89; 196.

BROWN, Richard; b 13 Nov 1735; d 27 Dec 1781 **RU:** Patriot, Gave material aid to cause **CEM:** St John's Episcopal; GPS 37.53183, -77.41958; 2401 E Broad St; Richmond City **GS:** Y **SP:** No info **VI:** No further data **P:** unk **BLW:** unk **RG:** N **MK:** N **PH:** unk **SS:** C pg 66; Al Ct Bk pg 59 Chesterfield Co **BS:** 39 pg 99.

BROWN, William; b unk; d 1820 **RU:** Midshipman, Served on ship,"Tempest," 1779 **CEM:** St John's Episcopal; GPS 37.53183, -77.41958; 2401 E Broad St; Richmond City **GS:** Y **SP:** No info **VI:** No further data **P:** unk **BLW:** unk **RG:** N **MK:** N **PH:** unk **SS:** BE pg 71 **BS:** 28 pg 419.

BROWN, William; b 1748 or 1749, East Lothian, Scotland; d 13 Jan 1792 **RU:** Physician, Performed as Surgeon General of Hosp, 13 May 1777 and as Director General of Hosp 21 Jul 1780 **CEM:** Pohick Episcopal; GPS 38.42546, -77.11598; 9301 Richmond Hwy, Lorton; Fairfax **GS:** Y **SP:** Catherine Scott, d/o Rev James & Sarah (Brown) Scott **VI:** Son of Richard & Helen (Bailey) Brown. Graduate University of Edenburgh 1770. Originally bur at Preson in Fairfax Co. Moved to Pohick Church in 1921. BLW 6000 acres. Died in Alexandria City **P:** unk **BLW:** Y **RG:** Y **MK:** Y SAR plaque **PH:** Y **SS:** E pg 102; SAR P-123170 **BS:** JLARC 1, 14, 28.

BROWN, William; b 1757; d 1789 **RU:** Private, Service information not specified in SAR application **CEM:** Brown Family; GPS unk; Eagle hills; Scott **GS:** Y **SP:** No info **VI:** No further data **P:** unk **BLW:** unk **RG:** Y **MK:** N **PH:** unk **SS:** AS SAR applic; SAR P-123210 **BS:** 80 vol 1 pg 124.

BROWNE, William; b 17 Sep 1759; d 15 Nov 1799 **RU:** Patriot, Gave material aid to the cause **CEM:** Four Mile Tree; GPS unk; off Swan's Point Rd; Surry **GS:** Y **SP:** Elizabeth Ruffin (17 May 1771-26 Jul 1799) of Richneck Plantation, d/o William & Lucy (Cocke) Ruffin **VI:** Son of Col William (a Rev War soldier ___-1786) & Sarah (Edwards) Browne. Parentage and wives are fr GS inscriptions **P:** N **BLW:** N **RG:** N **MK:** N **PH:** unk **SS:** AL Ct Bk 1 pg 3 **BS:** 147 pg 60.

BROWNE, William Burrnett; b 7 Oct 1738, Salem, Essex Co, MA; d 6 May 1784 **RU:** Private, Served in Capt Benjamin Ward Jr's Co. Enlisted 11 Jul 1775,and served 6 mo. 5 days at Salem and again 22 Jan 1776, 4 mo 7 days at Salem **CEM:** Elsing Green Plantation; GPS 37.61608, -77.04073; Off Mt Olive Cohoke Rd Rt 632; King William **GS:** Y **SP:** Judith Walker Carter **VI:** Son of William (1709-1763) & Mary (Burnett) Browne (1723-1745) **P:** unk **BLW:** unk **RG:** N **MK:** unk **PH:** unk **SS:** AJ MA Rev War Vol 2 pg 705 **BS:** 196.

BROWNING, Francis; b 25 Nov 1753, Culpeper Co; d 18 Jul 1855 **RU:** Private, Ent serv fr Hillsborough NC. Served in NC Cont Line **CEM:** Thomas Family; GPS unk; Poor Farm Rd, Lebanon; Russell **GS:** Y **SP:** Miss Elizabeth Vermillion. Wife d before him. **VI:** Son of John & Elizabeth (Wimercast) Brown. Resided in Lebanon, Russell Co. Pensioned Russell Co 1832 age 79; was 102 when he died. Govt grave stone & SAR marker. R382 **P:** unk **BLW:** unk **RG:** Y **MK:** Y SAR **PH:** unk **SS:** B Govt stone; K Vol 1 pg 125; SAR P-123365 **BS:** 32 Jul 2010.

BROWNING, John; b 16 Apr 1749; d 25 Sep 1818 **RU:** Private, Served in Capt Charles Browning's Co, Culpeper Co. Was in Culpeper Co Class 56 **CEM:** Browning Family; GPS unk; Nr Salem Baptist Ch; Rappahannock **GS:** U **SP:** Elizabeth Strother **VI:** No further data **P:** unk **BLW:** unk **RG:** Y **MK:** unk **PH:** unk **SS:** DJ: Class 56; SAR P-123375 **BS:** JLARC 2, 76.

BROWNLEY, John Jr; b unk; d 1809 **RU:** Surg Mate, Served in VA Cont Line 1782 **CEM:** Castleman's Farm; GPS unk; Berryville; Frederick **GS:** Y **SP:** No info **VI:** BLW indicates he d in 1778 without issue **P:** unk **BLW:** Y **RG:** N **MK:** N **PH:** unk **SS:** BY pg 331; E pg 103 **BS:** 50 pg 25.

RU=Rank/Unit	CEM=Cemetery	GS=Gravestone	SP=Spousal Information
VI=Other Veteran Info	P=Pension	BLW=Bounty/Land Warrant	RG=Registered Grave
MK=SAR/DAR Marker	PH=Photo	SS=Service Source	BS=Burial Source

BRUCE, Charles; b c1733; d 15 Dec 1791 **RU:** Captain, Commanded a Virginia Co that was paid at Ft Pitt in PA **CEM:** Soldier's Rest Plantation; GPS unk; Rt 620; Orange **GS:** Y **SP:** No info **VI:** Died in Fredericksburg **P:** unk **BLW:** unk **RG:** N **MK:** N **PH:** unk **SS:** E pg 103; CZ pg 68 **BS:** 22 pg 89.

BRUCE, Charles; b unk, Scotland; d 1792 **RU:** Captain/Patriot, Achieved rank of Capt for gallant services. Gave 375# of beef 15 Aug 1781 **CEM:** Fredericksburg National Military Park; GPS unk; Fredericksburg; Fredericksburg City **GS:** U **SP:** 1) Diana Banks 2) Mar (1772) Frances Stubblefield (____-1833) **VI:** Served in French & Indian War under George Washington in 1754. Recd land grant **P:** unk **BLW:** Y **RG:** Y **MK:** unk **PH:** unk **SS:** AL Cert Orange Co; SAR P-123463 **BS:** 196.

BRUCE, James; b 20 Mar 1763 Charlotte Co, d 12 May 1837 **RU:** Patriot Gave material aid to cause **CEM:** Bruce Family West of South Boston, Rt 659 at Berry Hill Plantation; Halifax **GS:** Y **SP:** 1) Sarah Coles (1770-1806), 2) Mar Apr 1819, Elvira Cabell (10 Sep 1783-2 Oct 1853) **VI:** Son of Charles Bruce. Died in Philadelphia, buried there, body brought back to Berry Hill 100 years later and reinterred. He owned country stores, flour mills, a fertilizer-plaster factory, a blackmith shop, lumber mills, a cotton factory, and two taverns. **P:** N **BLW:** N **RG:** N **MK:** unk **PH:** unk **SS:** Al Ct Bk pg 13, 47 **BS:** 196.

BRUCE, John; b 23 Apr 1759; d 10 Jan 1832 **RU:** Sergeant, Served in Capt Smith's Co of Foot, 11th VA Regt Commanded by Col Charles Porterfield, Feb 1778 **CEM:** Dews Family; GPS unk; 13 mi SE of Gretna Rt 677; Pittsylvania **GS:** Y **SP:** Mar (1794 Pittsylvania Co) Lucy Doss **VI:** No further data **P:** unk **BLW:** unk **RG:** N **MK:** N **PH:** unk **SS:** E pg 103; AP record; Cl Fold 3 website **BS:** 156 Dews GY.

BRUGH, Daniel Sr; b 19 Jul 1762 York Co PA; d 26 Dec 1825 **RU:** Private, Served 1782 in Capt O'Blain, 8th Co, 1st Bn, York, PA Militia **CEM:** Simmons-Brugh; GPS unk; Nr Mill Creek Baptist Church; Botetourt **GS:** Y **SP:** Mar (c1784) Elizabeth (-----) (1767-1842) **VI:** Son of Hermanus Brugh (1722-1794) & Catherine Meinhardt (1722-1801). Owned 550 acres with sawmill, grist mill, & tavern in Botetourt Co **P:** unk **BLW:** unk **RG:** N **MK:** N **PH:** unk **SS:** DD cites PA Hist & Mus Comm RG 4.61 Roll #343 **BS:** 123 pg 4; 196.

BRUGH, Hermanus; b 1722, Rheinland-Pfalz, Germany; d 13 Aug 1794 **RU:** Patriot, Overseer of the Poor 1778 **CEM:** Simmons-Brugh; GPS unk; Nr Mill Creek Baptist Church; Botetourt **GS:** Y **SP:** Mar (c1748) Catherine Meinhardt (10 Jun 1722, Germany-1801) **VI:** Arrived in Philadelphia PA aboard the Lydia on 20 Sep 1743.Supervisor of Highways 1761. Owned sawmill & grist mill in Barwick Twp, PA, then moved to Botetourt Co 1791 **P:** N **BLW:** N **RG:** Y **MK:** N **PH:** unk **SS:** H; DAR A015158; SAR P-123523 **BS:** 73 pg 2; 196.

BRULON, Francois; b unk; d 1781 **RU:** Seaman, Served on "Auguste" and died from Yorktown battle **CEM:** French Memorial; GPS 36.81944, -79.39933; Yorktown; York **GS:** U **SP:** No info **VI:** No further data **P:** unk **BLW:** unk **RG:** Y **MK:** unk **PH:** unk **SS:** J-Yorktown Historian; SAR P-123526 **BS:** JLARC 1, 74.

BRUN, Jean; b unk; d 1781 **RU:** Seaman, Served on "Hercule" and died from Yorktown battle **CEM:** French Memorial; GPS 36.81944, -79.39933; Yorktown; York **GS:** U **SP:** No info **VI:** No further data **P:** unk **BLW:** unk **RG:** Y **MK:** unk **PH:** unk **SS:** J-Yorktown Historian; SAR P-123549 **BS:** JLARC 1, 74.

BRUNDIGE, Timothy; b c1754; d 15 Sep 1822 **RU:** Quartermaster, Served in Westchester Co NY Militia in 2d Regt, commanded by Col Thomas Thomas, 22 May 1778 **CEM:** Dumfries Public; GPS 38.34110, -77.19964; 17821 Mine Rd, Dumfries; Prince William **GS:** Y **SP:** No info **VI:** SAR monument **P:** unk **BLW:** unk **RG:** Y **MK:** Y SAR monument **PH:** YSS: AX Vol 1 pg 207, 305; SAR P-335629 **BS:** 94 pg 18.

BRUNET, Jean; b unk; d 1781 **RU:** Soldier, Served in Soissonnais Bn and died from Yorktown battle **CEM:** French Memorial; GPS 36.81944, -79.39933; Yorktown; York **GS:** U **SP:** No info **VI:** No further data **P:** unk **BLW:** unk **RG:** Y **MK:** unk **PH:** unk **SS:** J-Yorktown Historian; SAR P-123582 **BS:** JLARC 1, 74.

BRYAN, John Patterson; b 14 Nov 1746, NJ; d 16 Jan 1803 **RU:** Patriot, Civil service as Judge of Ct of Common Pleas, Somerset Co, NJ **CEM:** Bryan Family; GPS unk; Farmington Country Club, 10th tee; Charlottesville City **GS:** U **SP:** No info **VI:** Died in Charlottesville while collecting donations for NJ College **P:** N **BLW:** N **RG:** N **MK:** unk **PH:** unk **SS:** CD **BS:** 196.

RU=Rank/Unit	CEM=Cemetery	GS=Gravestone	SP=Spousal Information
VI=Other Veteran Info	P=Pension	BLW=Bounty/Land Warrant	RG=Registered Grave
MK=SAR/DAR Marker	PH=Photo	SS=Service Source	BS=Burial Source

59

BRYAN, Thomas; b 1721; d 25 Feb 1793 **RU:** Patriot, Gave material aid to cause **CEM:** Spears Family; GPS unk; N of Edom Rt 42 7.3 mi; Rockingham **GS:** U **SP:** Elizabeth Palmer (1729-1793) **VI:** Son of Cornelius & Rebecca (-----) Bryan **P:** N **BLW:** N **RG:** Y **MK:** unk **PH:** unk **SS:** D Vol III pg 830; SAR P-123753 **BS:** 196.

BRYAN, William Jr; b 1716; d 1796 **RU:** Captain, Was in Dunmore's War in Capt William Campbell's Co fr Fincastle Co 04 Aug 1776 for 3 yrs. Another, same name, was at Point Pleasant, perhaps father & son **CEM:** West Hill; GPS 37.29313, -80.06753; Boon St; Salem City **GS:** U **SP:** Margaret Watson (1724-1804) **VI:** Son of William Sr (1685 Ireland - 1786) & (-----) Bryan. Settled in Salem City in Roanoke Co in

BRYAN, William, b 1716, County Clare, Ire, d 1786 **RU:** Patriot, Supported cause by paying supply tax included in his personal property tax in 1783, Botetourt Co **CEM:** West Hill; GPS: 37.29300, -80.06825; end of Boom St; Salem City **GS:** Yes **SP:** Martha Watson **VI:** No further data **P:** N **BLW:** N **RG:** Y **MK:** N **PH:** N **SS:** DV 1782 & 1783: SAR P-123771 **BS:** 196.

BRYANT, William; b c1765; d 15 Mar 1778 **RU:** Private, Capt Thomas Arrell's Co, 3rd VA Regt **CEM:** Rev War Court House Plaque; GPS not determined; 4110 Chain Bridge Rd; Fairfax **GS:** Memorialized on plaque 2017 by Geo Washington Chapter, VASSAR **SP** No info **VI:** Died in service **P:** N **BLW:** N **RG:** N **MK:** N **PH:** N **SS**; EP sources: **BS:** None.

BRYANT, William; b 1761; d 29 Jun 1848 **RU:** Private, Served in 1st, 3rd, 4th, 6th, 10th Cont Lines **CEM:** Bryant Family; GPS unk; Charity, behind the Heidelbach School; Patrick **GS:** Y **SP:** Mar (2 Jan 1828 Patrick Co) Peggy Lewis **VI:** No further data **P:** unk **BLW:** unk **RG:** N **MK:** unk **PH:** Y **SS:** E pg 105 **BS:** 196.

BRYARLY (BRYERLY), Thomas; b 1721, Ireland; d c1791 **RU:** Patriot, Gave material aid to cause **CEM:** Walnut Grove Plantation; GPS unk; White Post; Frederick **GS:** U **SP:** Mar (1 Feb 1752, Baltimore) Anne Tate **VI:** Son of Robert & Margaret (-----) Bryarly **P:** N **BLW:** N **RG:** Y **MK:** unk **PH:** unk **SS:** SAR P-329364; Al Ct Bk pg 4 **BS:** 196.

BRYSON, Robert; b unk; d 1801 **RU:** Matross, Served in Capt John Dandridge's Co of Artillery, 1st Artillery Regt, under Col John Harrison Dec 1778. Also served in Frederick Co Militia **CEM:** Dumfries Public; GPS 38.34110, -77.19964; 17821 Mine Rd, Dumfries; Prince William **GS:** N **SP:** No info **VI:** SAR monument **P:** unk **BLW:** unk **RG:** Y **MK:** Y SAR monument **PH:** N **SS:** E pg 105; SAR P-335630 **BS:** 96 pg 98.

BUCHANAN, Alexander; b 28 Jan 1763; d 22 Sep 1858 **RU:** Private, Serv in Capt Buchanan's Co **CEM:** Buchanan Family; GPS 36.95610, -81.54470; New Cove, E of Saltville; Smyth **GS:** Y **SP:** No info **VI:** No further data **P:** unk **BLW:** unk **RG:** N **MK:** N **PH:** unk **SS:** G pg 212 **BS:** 97 vol 2 pg 14.

BUCHANAN, Andrew; b 1732; d 1780 **RU:** Brigadier General, Served as Maj commandant of 3rd Bn of Minutemen 1776. Later rose to rank of Brig Gen **CEM:** Buchanan Family; GPS unk; Nr Rockbridge Co line, reported on land probably owned by Ben Jacobs, btw Rts 602 & 681; Augusta **GS:** U **SP:** No info **VI:** No further data **P:** unk **BLW:** unk **RG:** Y **MK:** unk **PH:** unk **SS:** CE pg 25; SAR P-123916 **BS:** JLARC 8, 76.

BUCHANAN, John; b 1724; d 1783 **RU:** Captain, Served in VA Co that was in Illinois campaign **CEM:** Locust Grove; GPS unk; W fr Chatham Hill; Smyth **GS:** U **SP:** No info **VI:** No further data **P:** unk **BLW:** unk **RG:** N **MK:** unk **PH:** unk **SS:** CZ pg 70 **BS:** JLARC 2, 76.

BUCHANAN, John; b Aug 1745, d 19 Nov 1824 **RU:** Lieutenant appointed 1778 in Washington Co Militia **CEM:** Buchanan Family; GPS: 36.84163,-81.75199; Clark Farm Rd, vic jct Dundee Lane; Washington **GS:** Yes **SP:** Anne Ryburn (1761, Scotland-24 Aug 1829) **VI:** No further data **P:** N **BLW:** N **RG:** Y **MK:** N **PH:** N **SS:** E pg 106; SAR BIO RPT submitted Aug 2019 **BS:** 196.

BUCHANAN, John; b 1761, Scotland; d 24 Aug 1829 **RU:** Lieutenant, Served in VA Cont Line. Appt Lt in Washington Co Militia 1778 **CEM:** Buchanan Family; GPS 36.84163, -81.75199; Rt 696, S of Saltville; Washington **GS:** Y **SP:** Anne Ryburn **VI:** BLW indicates he was killed in action, Fincastle Co, Mar 1777 and left no issue **P:** unk **BLW:** Y **RG:** N **MK:** N **PH:** unk **SS:** E pg 106; BY pg 351 **BS:** 78 pg 150; 196.

BUCHER, Philip Peter; b 6 Jun 1751, Opequon River, Frederick Co; d 1841 **RU:** Soldier, Ent serv Frederick Co **CEM:** Bucher; GPS unk; Mountain Falls; Frederick **GS:** U **SP:** Margaret (-----) **VI:**

RU=Rank/Unit	CEM=Cemetery	GS=Gravestone	SP=Spousal Information
VI=Other Veteran Info	P=Pension	BLW=Bounty/Land Warrant	RG=Registered Grave
MK=SAR/DAR Marker	PH=Photo	SS=Service Source	BS=Burial Source

60

Pensioned Frederick Co 1832. R393 **P:** unk **BLW:** unk **RG:** Y **MK:** unk **PH:** unk **SS:** K Vol 1 pg 131; SAR P-123978 **BS:** JLARC 4, 47.

BUCK, Charles Jr; b 28 Oct 1750; d 2 Aug 1823 **RU:** Patriot, Gave material aid to the cause **CEM:** Buckton Family; GPS 38.9749020, -78.2740690; loc 1 mi W of Buckton Station on SR 610, cross the railroad tracks and park on the left next to the river. Walk up the hill between the railroad tracks and the river. Cem icon top of hill, surrounded by a stone & mortar fence; Shenandoah **GS:** Y **SP:** Mar (17 Oct 1799) Polly Price of KY **VI:** Son of Charles Buck I (1710-1771) and Letitia Sorrell (1711-1771). In 1789, he erected a ferry across North Fork Shenandoah River. Was vestryman of Frederick Parish **P:** N **BLW:** N **RG:** Y **MK:** N **PH:** unk **SS:** D vol 3, pg 841; AL Ct Bk pg 1; SAR P-124002 **BS:** 01, pg 32; 155.

BUCK, Thomas; b 10 Jun 1756, d 4 Jun 1842 **RU:** Lieutenant, Commissioned 11 Jan 1776 as a Lieutenant in Dunmore County Militia; as Lieutenant, served as Adjutant to Colonel Joseph Pugh. 5 Sep 1777 he was chosen Captain of a company in the 8th Virginia Regiment. In 1778 he raised a militia company **CEM:** Buck Family; GPS 38.974755, -78.2744174; Bucks Mill Rd (Rt 610) next to river on hill left of RR track; Waterlick; Warren **GS:** U **SP:**1) Ann Richardson (1756-1823), d/o Colonel William Richardson (1712-1768) and Isabella Richardson (1729-1796), 2) Ruhama Heath McKim (1773-1851) **VI:** Son of Charles Buck (1710-1771) and Letitia Sorrell (1711-1771). Drew pen 1833 in Frederick Co #S16672 Commissioned Captain after war period **P:** Y **BLW:** unk **RG:** Y **MK:** SAR granite **PH:** unk **SS:** K Vol 1 pg 131; SAR P-1240986 **BS:** JLARC 4, 47; 196.

BUCKLEY, James Jr; b Feb 1763, Loudoun Co; d 22 Nov 1835 **RU:** Sergeant/Patriot, Served in VA Militia Aug 1780 under Capt Lumpkins. Appt Sergeant of the Guard over deserters Jan 1781 in Capt John Buckley Co. Served Jul 1781 in Capt John Wynn's Co. Gave material aid to cause **CEM:** Buckley Family; GPS 36.955067, -79.141450 Mt Airy, Rt 40; Pittsylvania **GS:** Y **SP:** Mar (4 Sep 1778) Mary Ridgeway **VI:** Pen 1832 in Weakley Co, TN. R396. SAR PRS indicates buried in TN so perhaps memorialized in cem **P:** Y **BLW:** unk **RG:** Y **MK:** unk **PH:** unk **SS:** D Pittsylvania Co; SAR P-124182 **BS:** 174, JLARC 3101.

BUCKLEY, James Sr; b 1719 or 1722; d 6 Oct 1787 **RU:** Patriot, Provided provisions & rations & liquor for 57 militia men on march to join Gen Greene. Also provided beef, corn & pasturage for Cont troops **CEM:** Buckley Family; GPS 36.955067, -79.141450; Mt Airy, Rt 40; Pittsylvania **GS:** Y **SP:** Mar (c1752 Prince William Co) Mary Harris (c1752-25 Apr 1817) d/o Samuel & (-----) Harris **VI:** No further data **P:** N **BLW:** N **RG:** Y **MK:** unk **PH:** unk **SS:** DAR A016753; SAR P-124183; D Vol 3 pg 767-8 **BS:** 174, JLARC 3101.

BUCKLEY, John; b c1754; d 8 Apr 1814 **RU:** Major/Patriot, Was Capt of Co Militia 17 Oct 1780. Spring 1781 led Co of PA Militia to join Gen Lafayette at Hanover Co. Marched unit through Richmond and down to "Mobbins Hill" (Malvern). Led Co to Yorktown 1781. Gave material aid to cause **CEM:** Buckley Family; GPS 36.955067, -79.141450; Mt Airy, Rt 40; Pittsylvania **GS:** Y **SP:** Mar (24 Oct 1786 Pittsylvania Co) Polley Harris **VI:** No further data **P:** unk **BLW:** unk **RG:** Y **MK:** unk **PH:** unk **SS:** D Pittsylvania Co; SAR P-124183 **BS:** 174, JLARC 3, 76, 101.

BUCKNER, Baldwin Mathews, Sr; b 1730, Marlfield Plantation, Gloucester Co; d Nov 1776 **RU:**Soldier, service unit not determined but served long enough to be eligible for a BLW in Va Military District in Ohio after the war period **CEM:** Marlfield Plantation (AKA Buckner Plantation); GPS 37.449276,-76.622386; 3780 Pebble Ln, Marlfield; Gloucester **GS:** Unk **SP:** Mar 1) unk, 2) Dorothy *Buckner*(1730- 8 Dec 1757), daug Col Samuel Buckner & Ann (__) **VI:** Son of Thomas Buckner, Jr (1702-1756) & Sarah Mathews **P:** Unk **BLW:** Y **RG:** N **MK:** N **PH:** Unk **SS:** C Sect IV pg 613 **BS:** 196.

BUCKNER, George; b 1760; d 1828 **RU:** Lieutenant, Specific service may be found as a Lt in the Council Journals at the Lib of VA **CEM:** Buckner-Washington-Burke; GPS unk; Off Rt 2, W on Rt 626 Woodford Rd for 4 mi to gate of "Braynefield"; Caroline **GS:** U **SP:** 1) unk; 2) Mar (c1802) Dorothea Brayne Benger (1 Mar 1765-26 Aug 1839) a widow, d/o John & Elizabeth (Johnson) Benger **VI:** Son of George & Elizabeth (Walker) Buckner. Represented Caroline Co. House of Delegates, 1796-1800 **P:** unk **BLW:** unk **RG:** Y **MK:** N **PH:** unk **SS:** E pg 107; CZ pg 70; SAR P-124252 **BS:** JLARC 15; 02 pg 26.

BUFORD, Henry; b 19 Sep 1751, Culpeper Co; d 31 Dec 1814 **RU:** Captain, Commanded company in Bedford Co Militia **CEM:** Locust Level; GPS 37.23180, -79.43420; Rt 460, nr Montvale; Bedford **GS:** U

RU=Rank/Unit	CEM=Cemetery	GS=Gravestone	SP=Spousal Information
VI=Other Veteran Info	P=Pension	BLW=Bounty/Land Warrant	RG=Registered Grave
MK=SAR/DAR Marker	PH=Photo	SS=Service Source	BS=Burial Source

61

SP: 1) Mar (22 Mar 1771) Mildred Blackburn (___Norfolk-___) d/o William & Elizabeth (-----) Blackburn of Christ Church Parish, Middlesex Co 2) Jane Kent Quirk **VI:** Son of John & Judith (Early) Beauford. Built Beuford's Tavern **P:** unk **BLW:** unk **RG:** Y **MK:** N **PH:** unk **SS:** J-NSSAR 1993 Reg, J- DAR Hatcher; CZ pg 71; SAR P-124430 **BS:** JLARC 1, 2; 196.

BUGG, Sherwood; b 8 Jul 1720 New Kent Co; d 1781, Augusta GA **RU:** Captain.served in Jackson's Legionary Corps, Cont Line,and the Richmond Co, GA Militia. Was captured by British and held on a prizon ship at Savannah, Ga **CEM:** Saint Peter's Episcopal Church; GPS 37.540355,-77.056327, loc at 8400 St Peters Ln, Quinton; New Kent **GS** Y memorial church plaque **SP:**Mar Lunenburg Co, 1745 Elizabeth Hobson (1728-8 Oct 1799, Columbia Co, GA)) **VI** Son of Samuel Bugg (1690-1 May 1759 & Deborah Sherwood (1669-14 Dec 1715). Menorialized in the cem but buried in Augusta, GA **P:** N **BLW** N **RG:** Y **MK:** Church plaque **PH:** N **SS:**; DAR A016730; SAR P-124423 **BS: 196**

BUIS, Louis; b 1751; d 1781 **RU:** Seaman, Served on "Northumberland" and died from Yorktown battle **CEM:** French Memorial; GPS 36.81944, -79.39933; Yorktown; York **GS:** U **SP:** No info **VI:** No further data **P:** unk **BLW:** unk **RG:** Y **MK:** unk **PH:** unk **SS:** J-Yorktown Historian; SAR P-124480 **BS:** JLARC 1, 74.

BULLE, Jean; b 1751; d 1781 **RU:** Soldier, Served in Gatinais Bn and died from Yorktown battle **CEM:** French Memorial; GPS 36.81944, -79.39933; Yorktown; York **GS:** U **SP:** No info **VI:** No further data **P:** unk **BLW:** unk **RG:** Y **MK:** unk **PH:** unk **SS:** J-Yorktown Historian; SAR P-124628 **BS:** JLARC 1, 74.

BULLINGTON, Robert; b 1750; d 18 May 1822 **RU:** 2d Lieutenant, Serv in 5th Cont Line. Appointed 2nd Lt in Capt Charlie Oaks Co 17 Aug 1779 **CEM:** Bullington Family; GPS unk; Nr Sandy River; Pittsylvania **GS:** Y **SP:** Mar (1770) Elizabeth Granger Crenshaw **VI:** Son of John and Sally (Giles) Bullington **P:** unk **BLW:** unk **RG:** Y **MK:** N **PH:** unk **SS:** E pg 108; DAR A016853; SAR P-124649 **BS:** 80 vol 1, pg 131.

BULLOCK, David; b 1761, Hanover Co; d 30 Jul 1838 **RU:** Private, Ent serv Albemarle Co 1779 **CEM:** Bullock Family; GPS unk; Rt 758, Walnut Hill; Louisa **GS:** U **SP:** Mar (12 Feb 1782 Lousia Co) Jane Terry (c1756-___) **VI:** Pen Louisa Co 1832 age 71. Widow pen age 84 in 1840, rejected because she was not a widow at date of pension Act. R403 **P:** Y **BLW:** unk **RG:** Y **MK:** N **PH:** unk **SS:** E pg 108; K Vol 1 pg 133; SAR P-124678 **BS:** 4-May-07.

BUMGARDNER, Christian; b unk; d 1795 **RU:** Lieutenant, Served with Washington at Valley Forge 1778 **CEM:** St John's Reformed UCC; GPS 38.05081, -79.17761; 1515 Arbor Hill Rd, Middlebrook; Augusta **GS:** Y **SP:** Mary Gabbert **VI:** Stone reads "With Washington, Braddock's expedition 1754, Valley Forge 1778, Lieut. 1757, Mary Gabbert his wife" **P:** unk **BLW:** unk **RG:** Y **MK:** N **PH:** unk **SS:** B; SAR P-124730 **BS:** JLARC 9, 62, 63; 196.

BUMGARDNER, Jacob; b 8 Feb 1767; d 25 Aug 1857 **RU:** Soldier/Patriot, Member of Boston Tea Party 1775 and later Augusta Co Militia. **CEM:** Bethel Presbyterian; GPS 38.04257, -79.17283, GS 38.0225,-79.1020; 563 Bethel Green Rd, Middlebrook; Staunton **GS:** Y **SP:** Mary Waddle (25 Jul 1768-4 Dec 1849) **VI:** Son of Christian & (-----) Bumgardner **P:** unk **BLW:** unk **RG:** Y **MK:** unk **PH:** unk **SS:** SAR P-124731; DW pg 218 **BS:** JLARC 62, 63; 196.

BUMPASS, Samuel; b unk; d unk **RU:** Patriot, Signed a Legislative Petition in Hanover Co **CEM:** Still House Spring; GPS unk; Rt 669; Hanover **GS:** Y **SP:** No info **VI:** No further data **P:** N **BLW:** N **RG:** N **MK:** N **PH:** unk **SS:** E pg 109; CZ pg 72 **BS:** 31 vol 1 pg 63.

BURCK, Justus; b unk; d 1781 **RU:** Soldier, Served fr MA, and died as result of Yorktown battle **CEM:** Yorktown Victory Monument Tablet; GPS 38.28350, -78.54150; Yorktown; York **GS:** U **SP:** No info **VI:** No further data **P:** unk **BLW:** unk **RG:** Y **MK:** unk **PH:** unk **SS:** J-Yorktown Historian; SAR P-124996 **BS:** JLARC 74.

BURGESS, John; b c1744, Goochland Co; d 16 Feb 1835 **RU:** Soldier, Ent serv 1775, Fluvanna Co **CEM:** Unmarked grave; GPS unk; Overlooking Hardware River N of Rt 6, Fluvanna **GS:** U **SP:** No info **VI:** Pen Fluvanna Co 1833, age 89 R412 **P:** Y **BLW:** unk **RG:** Y **MK:** unk **PH:** unk **SS:** K Vol 1 pg 136; SAR P-125137 **BS:** JLARC 4, 46.

BURK, John Daly; b unk; d 1808 **RU:** Private, Served in Capt Alexander Smith's Co, Col Daniel Morgan's, 11th VA Regt, 1777 **CEM:** Blandford; GPS 37.22433, -77.38604; 319 S Crater Rd;

RU=Rank/Unit	CEM=Cemetery	GS=Gravestone	SP=Spousal Information
VI=Other Veteran Info	P=Pension	BLW=Bounty/Land Warrant	RG=Registered Grave
MK=SAR/DAR Marker	PH=Photo	SS=Service Source	BS=Burial Source

62

Petersburg City **GS:** Y **SP:** No info; has at least one child **VI:** Perhaps this burial is for his son who was too late to be in Revolution. Was author of History of Virginia, portion regarding Petersburg **P:** unk **BLW:** unk **RG:** N **MK:** N **PH:** unk **SS:** AP record **BS:** 188, nbr 147.

BURK (BURKE), Thomas; b 1741, Orange Co; d 1808 **RU:** Captain, Specific service will be found in the Auditors Accts, Vol XI, pg 40 Lib of VA **CEM:** Horseshoe; GPS 37.30353, -80.63395; Scenic View Dr; Giles **GS:** Y **SP:** Mar 1761, Clara Frazier (1742-1811) **VI:** DAR marker. Govt GS says "Capt Fincastle Co Militia Rev War" **P:** unk **BLW:** unk **RG:** N **MK:** Y **PH:** unk **SS:** CZ pg 73 **BS:** JLARC 1, 2, 26.

BURKE, Richard H; b 1767; d 30 Apr 1817 **RU:** Private, Served in 5th Cont Line **CEM:** Old City; GPS 37.41472, -79.15667; 401 Taylor St; Lynchburg City **GS:** Y **SP:** No info **VI:** No further data **P:** unk **BLW:** unk **RG:** N **MK:** Y SAR plaque **PH:** unk **SS:** E pg 111 **BS:** 162 Methodist.

BURKE, Thomas; b c1764; d 6 Feb 1807 **RU:** Private, Served in 1st & 10th Cont Lines **CEM:** Burke Family; GPS unk; 1 mile N of Burke's Bridge, on Burke's Bridge Rd Rt 654, Bowling Green; Caroline **GS:** U **SP:** Isabelle G. M. (-----) **VI:** No further data **P:** unk **BLW:** unk **RG:** N **MK:** N **PH:** unk **SS:** D pg 225; E pg 112 **BS:** 02 pg 32; 196.

BURKE, Thomas; b 1741, Augusta Co, d 1808 **RU:** Captain/Patriot Company commander in the Montgomery Co (note: **GS** inscription indicates Fincastle Co) Militia, civil service as Constable **CEM:** Horseshoe; GPS: 37.30353, -80.63395; Off Horseshoe Farm Rd on Scenic View Drive, Pembroke; Giles **GS:** Yes, Govt **SP:** Mar 1761, Clara Frazier (1742, Augusta Co-1825), d/o Robert Frazier and Clara Graham **VI:** Will dated 10 Mar 1808, probated Sep 1808 **P:** N **BLW:** N **RG:** Y **MK:** Y-DAR **PH:** N **SS:** DAR A017318; DL pgs 760,766; SAR P-125272 **BS:** 196.

BURKE, William; b 2 Apr 1752; d 18 May 1803 **RU:** Private, Enlisted 1778 6th VA Ret, Cont Line, commanded by Col John Green, served Oct 1781 at Yorktown **CEM:** Burke-Shaw; GPS unk; Rt 688; Fauquier **GS:** Y **SP:** Susannah Sweeny **VI:** Son of Thomas & Jane (-----) Burke. Recd pension in Culpeper Co **P:** Y **BLW:** unk **RG:** Y **MK:** Y SAR **PH:** unk **SS:** E pg 112; SAR P-125273 **BS:** 32, Burke 06.

BURNES (BURNS), John; b unk; d 1791 **RU:** Private, Served in 3rd and 7th VA Regts **CEM:** Old Christ Church Episcopal; GPS 38.80625, -77.04718; 118 N Washington St; Alexandria City **GS:** N **SP:** Mar (----) Burns **VI:** Burial permit issued 1 Feb 1791 to Mrs Burns, widow **P:** unk **BLW:** unk **RG:** N **MK:** N **PH:** N **SS:** E pg 112; CI service record **BS:** 110 pg 91; 20 pg 145.

BURNETT, Williamson; b 1761, Buckingham Co; d 3 Jun 1833 **RU:** Private, Served in Capt Charles Patterson's Co, Col Fleming's Regt, & Buckingham Co Militia **CEM:** Staunton Baptist; GPS 37.06970, -79.58140; 15267 Smith Mountain Lake Pkwy, Huddleston; Bedford **GS:** Y **SP:** Mar (15 Mar 1792 Burmingham Co) Pricilla Carter (c1774-after 1843) **VI:** Widow pen age 65, Bedford Co 1840. R419. Has DAR marker on grave **P:** Y **BLW:** unk **RG:** Y **MK:** Y SAR **PH:** unk **SS:** R 419; K Vol 1 pg 138; DD; SAR P-125490 **BS:** JLARC 3; 196.

BURNLEY, Joel Terrell; b unk; d 1781 **RU:** Soldier, Service unit not determined. Died as result of Yorktown battle **CEM:** Yorktown Victory Monument Tablet; GPS 38.28350, -78.54150; Yorktown; York **GS:** U **SP:** No info **VI:** No further data **P:** unk **BLW:** unk **RG:** Y **MK:** unk **PH:** unk **SS:** J-Yorktown Historian; SAR P-125623 **BS:** JLARC 74.(**BURNSIDE,** John See Appendix G)

BURROWS, William Ward; b 16 Jan 1758, Charleston SC; d 6 Mar 1805 **RU:** Lieutenant Colonel, Aide-de-camp, 4th SC Regt (Artillery). Provided supplies to naval facilities. Gave £10,000 loan to SC and provided militia supplies **CEM:** Arlington National; GPS 38.88377, -77.06535; Jefferson Davis Hwy Rt 110; Arlington **GS:** Y **SP:** Mar (13 Sep 1783 at Kinderton Farm, North Liberties, nr Philadelphia) Mary Bond (24 Aug 1765, Philadelphia-Feb 1803, Washingoton, DC) d/o Dr. Thomas & Ann (Morga) Bond. Originally bur at Old Presbyterian Church in Georgetown. It is not known if she was re-interred with her husband at Arlington National. **VI:** Son of William Burrows (1722-1781) & Mary Ward (1728-1775); first Commandant of the reconstituted Marine Corps (1798-1804). Died in Georgetown, DC. Originally bur by his wife at Old Presbyterian Church in Georgetown, he was reinterred at Arlington on 12 May 1892 in Sec 1, Grave 301B, Western Division **P:** unk **BLW:** unk **RG:** Y **MK:** Y **PH:** unk **SS:** AK J-NSSAR 1993 Reg; SAR P-125992 **BS:** 04; JLARC 1; 196.

RU=Rank/Unit	CEM=Cemetery	GS=Gravestone	SP=Spousal Information
VI=Other Veteran Info	P=Pension	BLW=Bounty/Land Warrant	RG=Registered Grave
MK=SAR/DAR Marker	PH=Photo	SS=Service Source	BS=Burial Source

BURRUS (BURRIS) (BURRUSS), Jacob; b 2 May 1755, (Fr Orange Co), d 1 Oct 1832, Smith Co, TN **RU**: Sergeant/Patriot; Enlisted Spring 1778, Orange Co, Capt Frank Taylors Co, Col Spotswood's 2 VA Regt. Was in battle of Brandywine and siege of Fort Mifflin and transferred to MD Line. Wounded twice and returned to Taylor's Co at Valley Forge, serving two years. Gave material aid to cause while residing in Henry Co after his military serv **CEM**: Martin Family; GPS: 36.7410, -79.7464; nr jct Rts 57 & 710, Leatherwood; Henry **GS**: Yes; **SP**: Mar (bond) 13 Mar 1781, Henry Co, Susannah Martin (1763-1844), d/o Gen Joseph Martin. She recd pen **VI**: Memorialized in Martin Cem with Gr St **P**: Both **BLW**: No **RG**: N **MK**: N **PH**: N **SS**: AL: Ct Bk pg 49, Henry Co; AP Pen file Commissioner's Ltr **BS**: 196.

BURSON, Benjamin; b 6 Aug 1735, North Wales, Montgomery Co, PA, d 22 Dec 1790 **RU**: Patriot, Supported cause by paying supply tax included in his personal property tax in 1783, Loudoun Co **CEM**: South Fork Meeting House; 39.02640, -77.80220; Rt 630, Unison; Loudoun **GS**: Unk **SP**: Hannah Young (15 Jul 1753, Morris Co, NJ- 1810) **VI**: Son of George Burson, Jr (1710-___) and Sarah Cox **P**: N **BLW**: N **RG**: N **MK**: N **PH**: N **SS**: DV Loudoun Co 1783A image 04 pdf **BS**: 196.

BURSON, Joseph; b 22 Jan 1737, Bucks Co, PA, d 19 Feb 1825 **RU**: Patriot paid personal property taxes 1782 and 1783 in Loudoun Co. That tax was partially used to pay for Rev War expenses **CEM**: South Fork Meeting House; 39.02640, -77.80220; Rt 630, Unison; Loudoun **GS**: Unk **SP**: Mary Polly Plaster (18 Oct 1758, Chester Co, PA-9 May 1836) **VI**: Was in colonial war in Fairfax Co **P**: N **BLW**: N **RG**: N **MK**: N **PH**: N **SS**: DV-1782 pdf 06; 1783 04 pdf **BS**:

BURT, John; b unk; d 1781 **RU**: Soldier, Served fr MA, and died as result of Yorktown battle **CEM**: Yorktown Victory Monument Tablet; GPS 38.28350, -78.54150; Yorktown; York **GS**: U **SP**: No info **VI**: No further data **P**: unk **BLW**: unk **RG**: Y **MK**: unk **PH**: unk **SS**: J-Yorktown Historian; SAR P-126046 **BS**: JLARC 74.

BURT, John M; b c1758; d 1811 **RU**: Patriot, Gave material aid to cause **CEM**: St Paul's Episcopal; GPS 36.84733, -76.28554; 201 St Paul's Blvd; Norfolk City **GS**: Y **SP**: No info **VI**: No further data **P**: N **BLW**: N **RG**: N **MK**: N **PH**: unk **SS**: AL Com Bk IV pg 352 **BS**: 87 pg 26.

BURTON, John P; b unk; d 1848 **RU**: Patriot, Gave material aid to cause **CEM**: St John's Episcopal; GPS 37.53183, -77.41958; 2401 E Broad St; Richmond City **GS**: N **SP**: No info **VI**: No further data **P**: N **BLW**: N **RG**: N **MK**: N **PH**: N **SS**: D Vol I pg 237 **BS**: 28 pg 351.

BURTON, May Jr; b 1752; d 13 May 1829 **RU**: Captain, Entered serv 1777, Orange Co **CEM**: Burton Graveyard; GPS 38.16240, -78.20570; NE cnr of Rt 29 N and Rt 609 E; Greene **GS**: Y **SP**: Mar (29 Sep 1776 Greene Co) Sarah Head (___-Sep 1842 Greene Co) **VI**: Son of May & Hannah Medley Burton Sr. Died in "Rock Hill" Madison Co R430 **P**: Y **BLW**: unk **RG**: Y **MK**: Y SAR **PH**: unk **SS**: AK; K Vol 1 pg 141; SAR P-126163 **BS**: 04, JLARC 113.

BURTON, Samuel; b c1755; d 16 Feb 1841 **RU**: Sergeant, Served Capt Payne's Co, Parker's Regt, VA Line **CEM**: Burton Family; GPS 37.424557,-77.919160; 1 mi SW jct Genitoe and Brick Church Ln, property of Roger Epperson; Amherst **GS**: U **SP**: Mar (22 Dec 1800), Susannah Morris **VI**: Pen 1840 in Amelia Co age 85 **P**: Y **BLW**: Y **RG**: Y **MK**: unk **PH**: unk **SS**: C pg 223; E pg 115; G pg 752; SAR P-334630 **BS**: 32.

BURTON, Thomas; b 1741; d 1821 **RU**: Ensign, Qualified as ensign, Accomack Co Militia, 1 Oct 1777 **CEM**: Burton Private; GPS unk; Wachapreague; Accomack **GS**: N **SP**: Sinah Roberts **VI**: No further data **P**: unk **BLW**: unk **RG**: Y **MK**: unk **PH**: N **SS**: E pg 115; SAR P-126176 **BS**: JLARC 1, 76.

BURWELL, Lewis, Jr; b 1737; d 1779 **RU**: Patriot, gave wood to Army, Feb 1776 **CEM**: Fairfield Family; GPS not determined; Wicomico; Gloucester **GS**: Unk **SP**:Judith Page (1745-1777), d/o Mann Page (1716-1780) & Alice Grymes (1724-1746) **VI**: Son of Lewis Burwell (1711-6 May 1756) & Mary Frances Willis (1718-1746); owned Fairfield home with walled cemetery **P**: N **BLW**: N **RG**: N **MK**: N **PH**: N **SS**: G pgs 581, 583 **BS**: 196.

BURWELL, Lewis; b 26 Sep 1745; d 2 Jul 1800 **RU**: Lt Col, was County Lieutenant, collected money to pay for Brunswick Co Militia Battallion, 1776; commanded a regiment in General Nellsons Light Dragoons, 1776 **CEM**: Burwell Family; GPS unk; Stoneland; Mecklenburg **GS**: U **SP**: 1) Mar (24 Mar 1768) Ann Spottswood (___-14 Feb 1789) (grand/o Alex Spotswood, Gov of VA) 2) Mar (13 Nov 1789)

RU=Rank/Unit	CEM=Cemetery	GS=Gravestone	SP=Spousal Information
VI=Other Veteran Info	P=Pension	BLW=Bounty/Land Warrant	RG=Registered Grave
MK=SAR/DAR Marker	PH=Photo	SS=Service Source	BS=Burial Source

64

Elizabeth R Harrison (___-19 Nov 1824) (Cousin of Gen Wm H. Harrison) **VI:** Son of Armistead & Christian (Blair) Burwell. For 14 yrs member of VA legislature. According to letters by researchers, he is actually bur at Stoneland Plantation, but stone was moved to church to prevent vandalism **P:** unk **BLW:** unk **RG:** Y **MK:** unk **PH:** unk **SS:** G pg 441; AP Fold3 service index card; CZ pg 76; DAR A019868 SAR P-126200 **BS:** JLARC 2, 76.

BURWELL, Nathaniel; b 1750, James City Co; d 1801 **RU:** Captain, He commanded a Co in the King William Co Militia **CEM:** Vermont Plantation; GPS unk; W River Rd Rt 600, .5 mi E of Dorrel Rd Rt 628, River Hill; King William **GS:** N **SP:** Mar (28 Nov 1772 Middlesex Co) Susanna Grymes, Surty Phillip Grymes **VI:**. No stones at Vermont Plantation (River Hill) graveyard for members of the Burwell family **P:** unk **BLW:** unk **RG:** N **MK:** Y **PH:** N **SS:** J- DAR Hatcher; E pg 115; **BS:** JLARC 2; 196.

BURWELL, Nathaniel; b 1750; d 29 Mar 1814 **RU:** Colonel/Patriot, Served in 1774 James City Co Committee of Safety. Nov 1776 appt Chief Military Officer of James City Co. Procured full proportion of troops to Cont Army. Was Col James City Co Militia, and aide to Gen Robert Howe. Was prob at invasion of "Tidewater" & Yorktown serving Washington. Supplied wagons & 3972 lbs beef **CEM:** Old Chapel Episcopal; GPS 39.10677, -78.01470; Jct US 340 & Rt 255, Millwood; Clarke **GS:** Y **SP:** 1) Mar (3 Dec 1772, Middlesex Co) Susan Grymes d/o Phillip (1720-1768) & Mary (Randolph) (1729-1768) Grymes 2) Lucy (Page) Baylor (1759-11 Nov 1843) **VI:** Builder of Carter Hall. Also built Morgan Mill in Millwood with Gen Morgan. Died in Carter Hall. Rank of Col on grave stone, Recd BLW 4,666 and 300 acres **P:** unk **BLW:** Y **RG:** Y **MK:** Y SAR granite **PH:** Y **SS:** E pg 115; AK; SAR P-126203 **BS:** JLARC 1, 24, 76; 65 Clarke; 196.

BURWELL, Nathaniel Bacon; b 1759; d Mar 1791 **RU:** Colonel/Patriot, in charge of militia in York Co; performed public service as Commissioner to approve inpressed claims York Co; and gave material aid to the cause there **CEM:** Cheatham Cemetery Annex; GPS 37.282200,-76.591100; loc adjacent to a tee on the golf course, Naval Weapons Station, Yorktown; York **GS:** Unk **SP:** No information **VI:** Son of James Burwell (1737-1775) & Ann Jones (1740-1779). He is probably not the same colonel in charge of the militia in James City Co that also gave material aid to the cause there. **P:** N **BLW:** N **RG:** N **MK:** N **PH:** N **SS:** AL Comm Bk IV, pg 272, Ct Bk II, pgs I,1a, 5 **BS:** 196.

BURWELL, Nathaniel Thacker; b 15 Apr 1750-30 Mar 1802 **RU:**Major, as Captain, commanded a company in Col Charles Harrison's 1st Artillery Regt Cont Line, Sep 1778, promoted to Major **CEM:** Fincastle Presbyterian Church; GPS37.500168,-79.875576; loc E Back St, Fincastle; Botetourt **GS:** Unk **SP:** Martha Armistead Digges (10 Aug 1757, York Co-3 Feb 1848), d/o Dudley Powers Digges (1729-1790) & Martha Burwell (1720-1758) **VI:** Son of Lewis Burwell (1716-1779) & Frances Thacker (1722-1784), Cenotaph on SAR plaque **P:** unk **BLW:** unk **RG:**Y **MK:** Y **PH:** N **SS:** DAR A019993; E pg 859; SAR P-126201 **BS:** 196.

BURWELL, Thomas H N; b unk; d 1841 **RU:** Major, Nominated 13 Sep 1775 for rank of Maj in Gloucester Co Militia **CEM:** Bruton Parish Church; GPS 37.27127, -76.70248; 331 W Duke of Gloucester St; Williamsburg City **GS:** Y **SP:** No info **VI:** No further data **P:** unk **BLW:** unk **RG:** N **MK:** N **PH:** unk **SS:** N pg 562 **BS:** 26 pg 118.

BUSH, Philip; b 12 Oct 1733, Mannheim, Ger; d 8 Dec 1812 **RU:**Patriot performed public service assisting Robert Rutherford, Chairman of the Berkeley District Committee in Winchester on 29 September 1775 to choose officers of Regulars & Minute Men raised in the District; served as a member of the Virginia Committee of Safety on 27 December 1775 for expenses in the Indian treaty; performed as commissary to support the struggling Continental Army **CEM:** Mt Hebron; GPS GS 39.183571,-78-160110; 305 E.Boscawen St; Winchester City **GS** Y **SP:** Mary Catherine Slough (1740-1810) **VI:** Owned a tavern "Golden Buck" in Winchester **P:** N **BLW:** N **RG:** Y **MK:**Y SAR granite **PH:** Y **SS:** SAR P-343706 **BS:** 04

BUSTER, Claudius; b 1763, d 1843 **RU:** Private, Served in Augusta Co Militia **CEM:** Trinity Episcopal; GPS 38.14917, -79.07521; 214 Beverley St; Staunton City **GS:** N **SP:** Elizabeth (-----) **VI:** No further data **P:** unk **BLW:** unk **RG:** N **MK:** N **PH:** N **SS:** E pg 116; SAR P-126409 **BS:** 142 Trinity.

BUSTER, William, b 1729, Crozet, Albemarle Co, d 13 May 1795 **RU:** Private, Capt William Love's Co, Montgomery Co Militia **CEM:** Marvin United Methodist Church (AKA Black Lick Cemetery); GPS

RU=Rank/Unit	CEM=Cemetery	GS=Gravestone	SP=Spousal Information
VI=Other Veteran Info	P=Pension	BLW=Bounty/Land Warrant	RG=Registered Grave
MK=SAR/DAR Marker	PH=Photo	SS=Service Source	BS=Burial Source

36.944351, -81.2437683; 2390 Black Lick Rd; Wythe **GS**: No **SP**: Jane Woods (1735, Goochland-1812, Pulsaki, KY) **VI**: Son of William Buster & Elizabeth Wallace **P**: N **BLW**: N **RG**: Y **MK**: N **PH**: N **SS**: G pg 234 cites Roberts, Ruby Alizer," Montgomery County Revolutionary Heritage"; SAR P-333921 **BS**; 196.

BUTCHER, John; b 1747; d 22 Nov 1811 **RU**: Patriot, Signed Legislative Petition in Alexandria **CEM**: Quaker Burial Ground; GPS 38.80749, -77.04676; 717 Queen St, Kate Walker Barrett Library; Alexandria City **GS**: Y **SP**: No info **VI**: No further data **P**: N **BLW**: N **RG**: Y **MK**: N **PH**: N **SS**: S-Alexandria; SAR P-338237 **BS**: 196.

BUTCHER, Samuel, Sr; b 1730, England, d Feb 1778 **RU**: Lieutenant/Patriot, He gave material aid to cause Frederick Co and paid personal property tax 1782 Loudoun Co considered to be supporting the cause **CEM**: Old Ebenezer Baptist; GPS: ; GPS 39.05824, -77.84142; 20421 Airmont Rd, Bloomfield, Loudoun **GS**: U **SP**: mar prob Hanover Co, 1781, Susannah Lewis (1730, Hanover Co-Sep 1Y01), d/o Abraham Lewis I (c1679-1769) & Mary (Morgan) (1687-1764) **VI**: A colonial war soldier **P**: N **BLW**: N **RG**: Y **MK**: Y SAR plaque **PH**: N **SS**: N pg 1254; Al Ct Bk, pg 30 and Comm Bk II, pg 171; DV image 05.pdf, SAR P-336651 **BS**: 196.

BUTLER, James F; b unk; d 1847 **RU**: Patriot, Gave material aid to cause **CEM**: St John's Episcopal; GPS 37.53183, -77.41958; 2401 E Broad St; Richmond City **GS**: N **SP**: No info **VI**: No further data **P**: N **BLW**: N **RG**: N **MK**: N **PH**: N **SS**: D Vol I pg 309 **BS**: 28 pg 351.

BUTLER, Lawrence (Lance); b 1755; d 4 May 1811 **RU**: Captain, Served in 15th VA, then 11th VA. Captured at Charleston SC, in 1780 and was on parole until end of war. Discharged either 1800 (per pension) or after peace treaty with GB (per ledger) **CEM**: Butler Family; GPS 39.53680, -78.63850; Family farm in SE part of Clarke Co. Named as Dearmont Farm by one source; Clarke **GS**: Y **SP**: No info **VI**: Grave re-found, cleaned, restored 2002. BLW 22 May 1789, R 438 **P**: unk **BLW**: Y **RG**: Y **MK**: N **PH**: Y **SS**: K Vol 1 pg 145; SAR P-126563 **BS**: JLARC 24.

BUTT, Epaphroditus; b 1755. d 23 Aug 1829 **RU**: Soldier, Was in Battle of Great Bridge,1775 **CEM**: Butt Family; GPS unk; Old Brooks Farm, St Julian Creek; Chesapeake City **GS**: U **SP**: Sophia Etheridge **VI**: No further data **P**: unk **BLW**: unk **RG**: Y **MK**: unk **PH**: unk **SS**: J- DAR Hatcher; SAR P-126649 **BS**: JLARC 2.

BYBEE (BYBIE), Pleasant; b 1758; d 1835 **RU**: Soldier, Ent serv 1778 in Capt Pelham's and Ballard's Cos; VA Regt, Served in 1st, 5th, 9th Cont Lines **CEM**: Bybee Family; GPS unk; Nr Rt 633, Troy Neighborhood; Fluvanna **GS**: U **SP**: Mar (3 Sep 1789) Mildred Priddy **VI**: Widow pen Fluvanna Co 1840 age 81 and resided Sherwood, Fluvanna in 1823. He was pen there 1818 at age 60 Fluvanna Co. R443 Drew BLW of 100 acres **P**: Y **BLW**: Y **RG**: N **MK**: unk **PH**: unk **SS**: K Vol 1 pg 147 **BS**: JLARC 4, 18.

BYRD(BIRD), Andrew V; b 30 Nov 1754, Augusta Co; d 30 Nov 1838, Shenandoah Co **RU**: Captain sworn in as Capt 24 May 1779, Rockingham Co Militia **CEM**: Byrd Family; GPS 38.615431,-78.675089; Craney Island Rd,.25 mi NW jct with Smith Creek Rd Tenth Legion; Rockingham **GS**: Y **SP**: Nancy Ann Jones (10 Oct 1755-28 Apr 1834), d/o Eaven Jones & Elizabeth(-----) **VI**: Son of Andrew Bird (1729-1799) & Mary Howard (1732-1784) **P**: Y # 444 **BLW**: N **RG**: Y **MK**: N **PH**: N **SS**:K vol 1, pg 148; AZ pg 229; SAR P-126938 **BS**: 196.

BYRD, Thomas Taylor; b 17 Jan 1752; d 19 Aug 1821 **RU**: Sergeant, Served in 3rd and 4th Cont line **CEM**: Old Chapel Episcopal; GPS 39.106770, -78.01470; Jct US 340 & Rt 255, Millwood; Clarke **GS**: Y **SP**: No info **VI**: Obtained rank of Capt but service not identified for this rank. Recd BLW 7 Jul 1792 R444, however some sources indicate he was a Tory **P**: unk **BLW**: Y **RG**: Y **MK**: N **PH**: unk **SS**: SAR P-126957; E pg 119; AS; CI service record **BS**: O5.

BYRD, William; b 1752; d 31 May 1829 **RU**: Private, Entered serv 1776 in Prince Edward Co **CEM**: Samuel Byrd Family; GPS unk; Old Colonial Rd; Grayson **GS**: N **SP**: No info **VI**: Pen Grayson Co age 65 in 1818, R444 **P**: unk **BLW**: unk **RG**: N **MK**: N **PH**: N **SS**: K pg 149; **BS**: 04, Apr 2007. **SEE APPENDIX G**

CABANNES, Jean; b unk; d 1781 **RU**: Seaman, Served on "Solitaire" and died from Yorktown battle **CEM**: French Memorial; GPS 36.81944, -79.39933; Yorktown; York **GS**: U **SP**: No info **VI**: No further data **P**: unk **BLW**: unk **RG**: Y **MK**: unk **PH**: unk **SS**: J-Yorktown Historian; SAR P-126973 **BS**: JLARC 1, 74.

RU=Rank/Unit	CEM=Cemetery	GS=Gravestone	SP=Spousal Information
VI=Other Veteran Info	P=Pension	BLW=Bounty/Land Warrant	RG=Registered Grave
MK=SAR/DAR Marker	PH=Photo	SS=Service Source	BS=Burial Source

66

CABARE, Francois; b unk; d 1781 **RU:** Seaman, Served on "Marseillais" and died from Yorktown battle **CEM:** French Memorial; GPS 36.81944, -79.39933; Yorktown; York **GS:** U **SP:** No info **VI:** No further data **P:** unk **BLW:** unk **RG:** Y **MK:** unk **PH:** unk **SS:** J-Yorktown Historian; SAR P-126974 **BS:** JLARC 1, 74.

CABEL, Joseph; b 19 Sep 1732, Goochland; d 1 Mar 1798, Buckingham Co **RU:** Colonel, Specific service may be found in the Auditors Accts 1776, 1779 and 1780 at the Lib of VA **CEM:** Bruton Parish Church; GPS 37.27127, -76.70248; 331 W Duke of Gloucester St; Williamsburg City **GS:** U **SP:** Mary Hopkins **VI:** No further data **P:** unk **BLW:** unk **RG:** Y **MK:** unk **PH:** unk **SS:** J-DAR Hatcher; CZ pg 78; DAR A018015; SAR P-126986 **BS:** JLARC 2.

CABELL, John; b 1742, d 12 Jun 1815 **RU:** Captain/Patriot, Served as Lt, Buckinham Co Militia, 1780; was member VA Convention 1776 **CEM:** Greenhill; GPS unk; James River State Park; Buckingham **GS:** U **SP:** Mar (Lynchburg City) Henrian Davies (1781-18 Mar 1843), also Frances Johnson **VI:** No further data **P:** N **BLW:** N **RG:** Y **MK:** N **PH:** unk **SS:** CZ pg 78; X, appendix; DAR A018014; SAR P-126985 **BS:** JLARC 59.

CABELL, Nicholas; b 29 Oct 1750; d 18 Aug 1803 **RU:** Colonel, Raised 2 Co of Minutemen 1775. As Capt commanded a Minute Co at Amherst Co CT House Apr 1776 **CEM:** Warminster; GPS 37.68360, -78.69420; Warminster, Norwood; Nelson **GS:** Y **SP:** Mar (16 Apr 1772) Hannah Carriington (28 Mar 1751-7 Aug 1817) d/o George & Anne (Mayo) Carrington **VI:** Son of Dr. William (1699 England-12 Apr 1774) & Elizabeth (Burks) (1705-1756) Cabell. Served in VA Senate 1785-1801. R445 **P:** Y **BLW:** unk **RG:** Y **MK:** unk **PH:** unk **SS:** DC pg 154, SAR P-126989 **BS:** JLARC 4, 83; 196; 213 pg 346-7.

CABELL, Samuel Jordan; b 15 Dec 1756; d 4 Aug 1818 **RU:** Lieutenant Colonel/Patriot, Served 4 Mar 1776 as Capt of Amherst Volunteers, 6th VA Regt. Appt Maj at Saratoga 1777, Was in Gen George Washington's Cont Army until end of war. Obtained rank of Lt Col in war **CEM:** Cabell Family; GPS unk; Norwood; Nelson **GS:** U **SP:** Sarah Syme (5 Nov 1760-15 May 1814) d/o John (1729-1775) & Mildred Thurston (Meriwether) (1739-1760) Syme **VI:** Son of William (1730-1798) & Margaret Meredith (Jordan) (1742-1812) Cabell. VA State House of Delegates 1785-1792. Elected as Republican to 4th, 5th, 6th, 7th Congresses, serving until 1803. Awarded BLW 6000 acres 30 Sept 1782 and 1000 acres 25 Jun 1783 **P:** unk **BLW:** Y **RG:** Y **MK:** unk **PH:** unk **SS:** C pg 90; D pg 3 Amherst Co; SAR P-126009 **BS:** 196.

CABELL, William Jr; b 1759; d 1842 **RU:** Colonel/Patriot, Served fr NC; gave material aid to cause **CEM:** Amherst; GPS 37.59640, -79.03670; Bus Rt 29, Amherst; Amherst **GS:** U **SP:** Ann "Nancy" Carrington (09 Jun 1760-30 Mar 1838) d/o Paul (1733-1818) and Margaret (Reade) (1734-1766) Carrington **VI:** No further data **P:** unk **BLW:** unk **RG:** Y **MK:** unk **PH:** unk **SS:** J-NSSAR 2000 Reg; D pg 39; SAR P-126997 **BS:** JLARC 76.

CABELL, William Sr; b 13 Mar 1730 d 23 Mar 1798 **RU:** Patriot, Was member Committee of Safety for VA 1775 & 1776 **CEM:** Uhion Hill; GPS 37.64348, -7876087; Wingina; Nelson **GS:** Y **SP:** Margaret Meredith & Sarah Syne d/o Col John & (-----) Syne of Hanover Co. (____-15 May 1814) **VI:** Held rank of Colonel. Was member of Society of Cincinnati **P:** N **BLW:** N **RG:** N **MK:** N **PH:** unk **SS:** E pg 119 **BS:** 103 pg 349.

CABON, Yves; b unk; d 1781 **RU:** Seaman, Served on "Northumberland" and died from Yorktown battle **CEM:** French Memorial; GPS 36.81944, -79.39933; Yorktown; York **GS:** U **SP:** No info **VI:** No further data **P:** unk **BLW:** unk **RG:** Y **MK:** unk **PH:** unk **SS:** J-Yorktown Historian; SAR P-127015 **BS:** JLARC 1, 74.

CADDELL, Samuel; b c1759, Ireland; d 12 Oct 1732 **RU:** Private, Vol in Rockbridge Co,1780, 2nd VA Regt Cont Line. Was in Battles of Guilford, Hobkirk's Hill, Ninety Six and Eutaw **CEM:** Caddall; GPS unk; Thornspring Farm; Pulaski **GS:** Y **SP:** Mar (1791) Nancy Ann Cecil (1769-1841) d/o Benjamin & (-----) Cecil **VI:** Emigrated fr County Down, Ireland in 1774 at abt the age of 16. Was blacksmith by trade. Pen appl 7 Aug 1832, died two mos later. DAR marker **P:** Y **BLW:** unk **RG:** Y **MK:** Y SAR **PH:** unk **SS:** G pg 727; CZ pg 64; SAR P-330239 **BS:** 196.

CAFFEE, William; b c1764; d 1839 **RU:** Private?, Served in Capt Joseph Bowmen's Co **CEM:** Bellamy Methodist Church; GPS 37.40149, -76.58883; 4870 Chestut Fork Rd; Gloucester **GS:** Y **SP:** Martha

RU=Rank/Unit	CEM=Cemetery	GS=Gravestone	SP=Spousal Information
VI=Other Veteran Info	P=Pension	BLW=Bounty/Land Warrant	RG=Registered Grave
MK=SAR/DAR Marker	PH=Photo	SS=Service Source	BS=Burial Source

Robins d/o Thomas & Harriet (Stubbs) Robins **VI:** No further data **P:** unk **BLW:** unk **RG:** N **MK:** N **PH:** unk **SS:** C pg 604 **BS:** 196.

CAHOON, Charles C; b 16 Mar 1747 Duck Creek, DE; d Apr 1834 **RU:** Private?, Ent serv Kent Co, DE **CEM:** Cahoon Family; GPS unk; Glade Creek nr Bedford Co line; Botetourt **GS:** U **SP:** No info **VI:** Moved to VA 1795. Pen age 85, Blade Creek, Botetourt Co 1832 age 85, resided in Blade Creek R447 **P:** Y **BLW:** unk **RG:** N **MK:** N **PH:** unk **SS:** K Vol 1 pg 149-50; DAR A106150; SAR P-127171 **BS:** AS, SAR Appl.

CAILLET, Jean; b unk; d 1781 **RU:** Soldier, Served in Soissonnais Bn and died from Yorktown battle **CEM:** French Memorial; GPS 36.81944, -79.39933; Yorktown; York **GS:** U **SP:** No info **VI:** No further data **P:** unk **BLW:** unk **RG:** Y **MK:** unk **PH:** unk **SS:** J-Yorktown Historian; SAR P-127185 **BS:** JLARC 1, 74.

CAIN, Abel; b unk; d 1781 **RU:** Soldier, Served fr MA and died as result of Yorktown battle **CEM:** Yorktown Victory Monument Tablet; GPS 38.28350, -78.54150; Yorktown; York **GS:** U **SP:** No info **VI:** No further data **P:** unk **BLW:** unk **RG:** unk **MK:** unk **PH:** unk **SS:** J-Yorktown Historian; SAR P-127186 **BS:** JLARC 74.

CALAGHAN, John; b unk; d 1781 **RU:** Private, Served in Col Wynkoop's NY Regt, and died as result of Yorktown battle **CEM:** Yorktown Victory Monument Tablet; GPS 38.28350, -78.54150; Yorktown; York **GS:** U **SP:** No info **VI:** No further data **P:** unk **BLW:** unk **RG:** Y **MK:** unk **PH:** unk **SS:** J-Yorktown Historian; AX pg 219; SAR P-127230 **BS:** JLARC 74.

CALDWELL, John F; b 20 Mar 1715, County Donegal, Ireland; d 1795 **RU:** Patriot, Gave material aid to the cause **CEM:** Cub Creek; GPS 37.03220, -78.75830; Rt 616 Cub Creek Church Rd, Brookneal; Charlotte **GS:** U **SP:** 1) Mar (11 Jun 1737, Lunenburg Co) Margaret Eleanor Ewing (1717-1745) 2) Martha Calhoun (1719-1773) 3) Mar (16 Jun 1746 Lunenburg, VA) Jane Kennedy (1727-1780) **VI:** Son of John (1682-1750) and Mary Margaret (Phillips) (1685-1748) Caldwell. Died in Halifax Co **P:** N **BLW:** N **RG:** N **MK:** N **PH:** unk **SS:** AL Ct Bk pg 7; AL Ct Bk 16 Halifax Co **BS:** 245; 196.

CALL, Daniel; b 1765; d 1840 **RU:** Private, Service not obtained from BLW application **CEM:** Shockoe Hill; GPS 37.55190, -77.43170; 4th & Hospital Sts; Richmond City **GS:** Y **SP:** Lucy Nelson Ambler **VI:** Recd BLW of 667 acres, Was an attorney, Richmond 1808 **P:** unk **BLW:** Y **RG:** N **MK:** N **PH:** unk **SS:** C pg 614 **BS:** 179 pg 167.

CALLAND(S), Samuel; b c1750; d 8 Nov 1808 **RU:** Quartermaster/Patriot, Gave horse for state troops; corn & fodder for Conts **CEM:** Callands Family; GPS 36.85587, -79.62549; NE of Callands; Pittsylvania **GS:** Y **SP:** Elizabeth Smith **VI:** Namesake of "Callands" community in Pittsylvania Co **P:** unk **BLW:** unk **RG:** Y **MK:** N **PH:** unk **SS:** E pg 121; SAR P-127482 **BS:** 174.

CALLAWAY (CALLOWAY), Charles; b 1752; d 1827 **RU:** Captain, Commanded a Co at Yorktown **CEM:** Alta Vista Plantation; GPS unk; Altavista; Pittsylvania **GS:** U **SP:** No info **VI:** No further data **P:** unk **BLW:** unk **RG:** Y **MK:** unk **PH:** unk **SS:** CZ pg 79; DAR A018362; SAR P-127485 **BS:** JLARC 1, 2, 66, 75.

CALLAWAY (CALLOWAY), James; b 31 Dec 1736, Caroline Co; d 1 Nov 1809 **RU:** Colonel/Patriot, Served in Bedford Co Committee of Safety 1774; county Lt **CEM:** Callaway-Steptoe; GPS 37.30560, -79.29470, GS37.1819,-79.1741; Rt 460, New London; Bedford **GS:** Y **SP:** 1) Mar (24 Nov 1756) Sarah P Tate (___-1773) d/o Henry & Elizabeth (Netherlannd) Tate 2) Mar (29 Sep 1777) Elizabeth Early (___-1796) d/o Col Jeremiah (1730-1779) and 1st wife Sarah (Anderson) (1729-1770) Early 3) Mar (1799) Mary Turpin Calland Langhorne, d/o Maj Maurice & Elizabeth (Trotter) Langhorne **VI:** Son of Col William Callaway (1714-1777) & Elizabeth Tilley (1713-1750). House of Burgesses 1766-1769. Bedford Co. Committee of Safety,1774. Treasurer New London Academy. Built 1st iron furnace south of James River which exempted him fr military service **P:** unk **BLW:** unk **RG:** Y **MK:** Y SAR **PH:** Y **SS:** B; CD; DAR A018369; SAR P-127490 **BS:** 196; JLARC App D.

CALLAWAY (CALLOWAY), John; b 1738; d 1820 **RU:** Colonel, Served in Bedford Co Militia and was in a VA unit at the Illinois Dept **CEM:** Otter Oaks; GPS unk; Nr Evington; Campbell **GS:** U **SP:** 1) Tabitha

RU=Rank/Unit   CEM=Cemetery   GS=Gravestone   SP=Spousal Information
VI=Other Veteran Info   P=Pension   BLW=Bounty/Land Warrant   RG=Registered Grave
MK=SAR/DAR Marker   PH=Photo   SS=Service Source   BS=Burial Source

68

Tate 2) Agatha Ward **VI:** Source 90 has burial at Callaway-Hewitt Cem **P:** unk **BLW:** unk **RG:** Y **MK:** N **PH:** unk **SS:** CZ pg 79; DAR A018379; SAR P-127493 **BS:** JLARC 1, 2, 36, 66 ,75, 90.

CALLAWAY (CALLOWAY), William; b 1714, Caroline Co; d 1777 **RU:** LtCol, Commanded Bedford Co Militia by 1777 **CEM:** Callaway-Steptoe; GPS 37.30560, -79.29470 GS37.1822,-79.1741; Rt 460, New London; Bedford **GS:** Y **SP:** 1) Mar (8 Jan 1735) Elizabeth Tilley (1713-1750) 2) Mar (abt 1752) Elizabeth Crawford (___-22 Jan 1827) and also bur here **VI:** Son of Joseph Callaway and Catherine Ann Browning. Commander of militia during the French & Indian War as a Col; has a Govt stone for Rev War service **P:** unk **BLW:** unk **RG:** Y **MK:** N **PH:** unk **SS:** B; E pg 122; SAR P-127505 **BS:** JLARC 1, 2, 36; 196.

CALLAWAY (CALLOWAY), William Jr; b 1748; d 22 Sep 1821 **RU:** Colonel/Patriot, Served in Bedford Co Militia. Gave material aid to cause **CEM:** Callaway-Steptoe; GPS 37.30560, -79.29470; Rt 460, New London; Bedford **GS:** Y **SP:** Anna Bowker (Mar 1751-02 Nov 1734) **VI:** Son of Col William Callaway (1714-1777) and Elizabeth Tilley (1713-1750) who also had Rev War service **P:** unk **BLW:** unk **RG:** Y **MK:** N **PH:** unk **SS:** D Bedford Co; SAR P-127506 **BS:** JLARC 2, 36; 196.

CALLENDER, Eleazer; b 9 Nov 1792, MA; d 1792 **RU:** Captain/Patriot, Was Capt of ship "Dragon" built in Fredericksburg, also ship "Defiance"; Petitioned for a valuable horse lost during War. Gave 68# of bacon to the cause **CEM:** Masonic Cemetery; GPS 38.30198, -77.46142; 900 Charles St; Fredericksburg City **GS:** Y **SP:** No info **VI:** Original member of Society of Cincinatti. Served as overseer of the Poor. Postmaster in Fredericksburg in 1783 **P:** unk **BLW:** unk **RG:** Y **MK:** Y SAR Plaque **PH:** unk **SS:** L pg 57, 160; SAR P-335458 **BS:** 11 pg 23, 24.

CALLENDER, John; b unk; d 2 Oct 1797 **RU:** Major, Service information not determined **CEM:** Old Christ Church Episcopal; GPS 38.80625, -77.04718; 118 N Washington St; Alexandria City **GS:** N **SP:** No info **VI:** Teacher, "an old and respectable officer in the American War," bur with Masonic honors (The Columbian Mirror and Alexandria Gazette, 5 Oct 1797, pg 3) **P:** unk **BLW:** unk **RG:** N **MK:** N **PH:** N **SS:** A pg 417 ref 20 **BS:** 20 pg 136.

CALLINAN, Guillaume; b unk; d 1781 **RU:** Seaman, Served on "Diademe" and died from Yorktown battle **CEM:** French Memorial; GPS 36.81944, -79.39933; Yorktown; York **GS:** U **SP:** No info **VI:** No further data **P:** unk **BLW:** unk **RG:** N **MK:** unk **PH:** unk **SS:** J-Yorktown Historian **BS:** JLARC 1, 74.

CALLISON, James, b 1729, Ireland; d 19 Jun 1789 **RU;** Patriot gave material aid to cause, Augusta Co **CEM:** North Mountain; GPS 38.078916, -79-177977; loc off W side Rt 252, Middle Beck Rd, 7 mi S of Staunton; Augusta **GS:** Unk **SP:** Isabella (-----) **VI:** No further data **P:**N **BLW:** N **RG:** N **MK:** N **PH:** N **SS:** DAR A133039; D vol I pg 93 **BS:** 196.

CALVERT, Christopher, b 26 Sep 1736, Princess Anne Co; d 11 Jul 1789, Southampton Co **RU:** Captain USN superintended the building of Row Galley at So Quay shipyard. Also supplied chains to move cannons **CEM:** St Pauls Episcopal Ch; GPS 36.84733, -76.28554; 201 St Pauls St; Norfolk City **GS:** Unk **SP:** Peggy Boush **VI:** No further data **P:** N **BLW:** N **RG:** Y **MK:** N **PH:** N **SS:** C pg 40; E pg 123; D vol 2 pg 704; DAR A129808; SAR P-127568 cites Morgan, William, *Naval Documents American Rev* 1790, pgs 499, 1101, 1119, 1195 **BS:** SAR PRS.

CALVERT, John Salvage; b c1739; d 16 Jan 1809 **RU:** Captain/Navy, Appt superintendant of the construction of a galley for James River by Committee of Safety. Was commissioned as Capt in Navy and assigned to Galley "Revenge" of Norfolk **CEM:** St Paul's Episcopal; GPS 36.84733, -76.28554; 201 St Paul's Blvd; Norfolk City **GS:** Y **SP:** Margaret "Molly" "Peggy" Walke **VI:** Son of Cornelius & Mary (Saunders) Calvert. BLW indicates he d 1809 Nansemond Co **P:** unk **BLW:** Y **RG:** Y **MK:** Y SAR plaque **PH:** unk **SS:** L pg 160; BY pg 327; CB; SAR P-336119 **BS:** 178 Jan 11.

CALVERT, Thomas; b 1725; d 2 Sep 1785 **RU:** Patriot, Took oath of Councilman 1780 **CEM:** St Paul's Episcopal; GPS 36.84733, -76.28554; 201 St Paul's Blvd; Norfolk City **GS:** Y **SP:** Mary (Thomas) Calvert **VI:** Took Oath of Office as a Common Councilman in 1780, per "The Order Book and Related Papers of the Common Hall of the Borough of Norfolk, 1736-1798" **P:** N **BLW:** N **RG:** N **MK:** Y SAR plaque **PH:** unk **SS:** CB Councilman 1780 **BS:** 178 Jan 11.

RU=Rank/Unit	CEM=Cemetery	GS=Gravestone	SP=Spousal Information
VI=Other Veteran Info	P=Pension	BLW=Bounty/Land Warrant	RG=Registered Grave
MK=SAR/DAR Marker	PH=Photo	SS=Service Source	BS=Burial Source

CAMBERNON, Antoine; b unk; d 1781 **RU:** Seaman, Served on "Citoyen" and died from Yorktown battle **CEM:** French Memorial; GPS 36.81944, -79.39933; Yorktown; York **GS:** U **SP:** No info **VI:** No further data **P:** unk **BLW:** unk **RG:** Y **MK:** unk **PH:** unk **SS:** J-Yorktown Historian; SAR P-127602 **BS:** JLARC 1, 74.

CAMERON, Charles; b 22 Feb 1753; d 14 Jul 1829 **RU:** Colonel, Ent serv 1776, Augusta Co; became Col Commander of Militia, Augusta Co, Aug 1781 **CEM:** Fort Dinwiddie; GPS 38.09228, -79.83140; NE of jct of Dinwiddie Trail & River Rd, Warm Springs; Bath **GS:** U **SP:** Mar on 3 May 1792 to Rachel Primrose Warwick, b 14 Mar 1772, d 6 Dec 1856 at Lexington. Stone at Warm Springs **VI:** Widow pen age 67 in Bath Co in 1839 age 67. Widow recd BLW there 1833. R453 **P:** Y **BLW:** Y **RG:** Y **MK:** N **PH:** unk **SS:** E pg 399; K Vol 1; SAR P-127617 **BS:** 159 Warm Sprs; 196.

CAMPBELL, Aeneas; b 3 Oct 1757; d 15 Oct 1828 **RU:** Captain, Commanded co Washington Co, MD Jul 1776 **CEM:** Campbell-Belt Estate; GPS unk; Rock Hill, Leesburg; Loudoun **GS:** Y **SP:** 1) Sarah Hickman 2) Elizabeth Liza Ann Belt 3) Lydia Cartwright **VI:** He is reported by DAR; d in NC, so.memorialized in this cemetery. DAR Plaque. Heirs were rejected for pension **P:** N **BLW:** unk **RG:** Y **MK:** Y SAR **PH:** unk **SS:** J- DAR Hatcher; DK pg 48; SAR P-127735 **BS:** JLARC 2.

CAMPBELL, Alexander; b unk; d unk **RU:** Private, Served in Capt John Cropper's Co, Col Morgan's Regt **CEM:** Stonewall Jackson Memorial; GPS 37.78128, -79.44604; 314 S Main St; Lexington City **GS:** U **SP:** No info **VI:** No further data **P:** unk **BLW:** unk **RG:** Y **MK:** unk **PH:** unk **SS:** A pg 267; SAR P-127736 **BS:** JLARC 63.

CAMPBELL, Alexander; b 1750, d 26 Jul 1806 **RU:** Lieutenant recommended in Rockbridge Co Militia to Lt 6 Nov 1781 and qualified to this rank 1 Jan 1782 **CEM:** Timber Ridge Presbyterian Church; GPS: 37.84200,-79.35800; vic jct Rts U.S. 1, and Rt 716, Timber Ridge; Rockbridge **GS:** Yes **SP:** Janet Smith (1766, Lancaster Co, PA-1843) **VI:** Son of Dougal Campbell, Jr (1710-1795) and Mary (-----) **P:** N **BLW:** N **RG:** Y **MK:** N **PH:** N **SS:** E pg 124; G pg 321; SAR P-127745 **BS:** 196.

CAMPBELL, Archibald; b 20 Nov 1753; d 17 Jun 1852 **RU:** Lieutenant, Became Lt 15 Jun 1781, served in 4th Cont Line **CEM:** Mt Holly; GPS 37.70485, -75.74185; Hill St, Onancock; Accomack **GS:** Y **SP:** No info **VI:** A founder of Old Friendship Church. Awarded 2666 acres BLW **P:** unk **BLW:** Y **RG:** Y **MK:** N **PH:** unk **SS:** E pg 124; SAR P-127768 **BS:** 37 pg 48.

CAMPBELL, Cammuel Elias Sr; b 1730; d 1793 **RU:** Soldier/Patriot, Gave material aid to cause **CEM:** Lillard Family; GPS unk; Syria; Madison **GS:** U **SP:** Elizabeth Yowell **VI:** No further data **P:** unk **BLW:** unk **RG:** Y **MK:** unk **PH:** unk **SS:** AL Ct bk II pg 14 Culpeper Co; SAR P-128107 **BS:** JLARC 76.

CAMPBELL, Charles; b 1741; d 1826 **RU:** Captain, Promoted May 1778, Rockbridge Co Militia **CEM:** New Providence Presbyterian; GPS 37.95170, -79.30250; 1208 New Providence Rd, Raphine; Rockbridge **GS:** Y **SP:** Mary Ann Downey **VI:** No further data **P:** unk **BLW:** unk **RG:** Y **MK:** N **PH:** unk **SS:** E pg 125; CZ pg 81; SAR P-127781 **BS:** SAR PRS.

CAMPBELL, Elias; b 1730, Spotsylvania Co; d 1793 **RU:** Patriot, Gave material aid to the cause **CEM:** Lillard Family; GPS unk; Syria; Madison **GS:** Y **SP:** Elizabeth Yowell d/o Christopher (1720-1775) & (------) Yowell **VI:** No further data **P:** N **BLW:** N **RG:** Y **MK:** N **PH:** unk **SS:** AL Ct Bk 2 pg 14; DJ V 213, pg 16; DAR A018574; SAR P-127821 **BS:** SAR regis.

CAMPBELL, Francis Lee; b 1760, Scotland; d 15 Oct 1840 **RU:** Captain/Patriot, Served in Lousia Co Militia. Gave material aid to cause **CEM:** Clover Hill; GPS unk; S Anna River, Rt 647; Louisa **GS:** U **SP:** mar 01 Jan 1789, Ann Barnet, b 1772, d 08 Sep 1852, d/o James Barnett, (1772-1808) & Ann (-----), d 1817 **VI:** Died at "Cottage Hill" **P:** unk **BLW:** unk **RG:** Y **MK:** unk **PH:** unk **SS:** AR Vol 1 pg 149; DD; SAR P-127832 **BS:** JLARC 1, 61.

CAMPBELL, Hugh; b c1750, Greenoch, Scotland; d 1791 **RU:** Private, Served in 1st VA State Regt **CEM:** Campbell Family; GPS unk; Lot 44, Tappahannock; Essex **GS:** N **SP:** Sarah Roane (1760s-early 1810) d/o Thomas of Newington & Mary Ann (Hipkins) Roane **VI:** Son of Hugh & (-----) Campbell. Land conveyance by heirs of veteran reserved permanent cemetery on this city lot for Hugh and his descendants **P:** unk **BLW:** unk **RG:** N **MK:** unk **PH:** unk **SS:** E pg 125; CI payroll **BS:** 223 pg 125.

RU=Rank/Unit	CEM=Cemetery	GS=Gravestone	SP=Spousal Information
VI=Other Veteran Info	P=Pension	BLW=Bounty/Land Warrant	RG=Registered Grave
MK=SAR/DAR Marker	PH=Photo	SS=Service Source	BS=Burial Source

CAMPBELL, James; b 1745, Dumfries, Scotland; d 18 Mar 1821 **RU:** Captain-Navy, Recruited in Cont Army fr Somerset Co, MD, 30 July 1781-Dec 1781. Capt of the "Enterprise" during Rev **CEM:** Trinity United Methodist; GPS 38.802235, -77.057375; 2911 Cameron Mills Rd; Alexandria City **GS:** Y **SP:** 1) Leah (-----), (c1744-11 Oct 1803) 2) Kitty Cahale **VI:** D age 76. Styled Capt on GS; obits in the Alexandria Gazette 20 Mar 1821, which styles him also "Capt" **P:** unk **BLW:** unk **RG:** Y **MK:** Y **SAR PH:** Y **SS:** SAR P -127874; AR Vol 1 pg 149 **BS:** JLARC 1, 2; 23 pg 119, 196.

CAMPBELL, James; b c1753; d 5 Jan 1825 **RU:** Patriot, Gave material aid to cause **CEM:** Sinking Springs; GPS 36.71030, -81.98170; 136 E Main St, Abingdon; Washington **GS:** N **SP:** No info **VI:** DAR marker **P:** N **BLW:** N **RG:** Y **MK:** Y **SAR PH:** N **SS:** D Montgomery Co; SAR P-127873 **BS:** JLARC 80; 208 pg 73.

CAMPBELL, James; b c1745; d c1822 **RU:** Private, Served in Capt Samuel McDowell's Co fr Rockbridge Co at Point Pleasant Oct 1774 **CEM:** Campbell-Hobbs; GPS unk; Rt 682, vic Ewing; Lee **GS:** Y **SP:** No info **VI:** Son of James & Mary (Gibbs) Campbell **P:** unk **BLW:** unk **RG:** N **MK:** N **PH:** unk **SS:** Z pg 104; AK Nov 06 **BS:** 04, Nov 06.

CAMPBELL, John; b unk; d unk **RU:** Captain, DAR Senate Documents 1836 serial #10054, vol 5 should provide service info **CEM:** Sauger; GPS unk; Elk Creek; Grayson **GS:** U **SP:** No info **VI:** No further data **P:** unk **BLW:** unk **RG:** N **MK:** unk **PH:** unk **SS:** AR Vol 1 pg 150; DD **BS:** JLARC 2.

CAMPBELL, John; b 1738, Augusta Co; d 1781 **RU:** Captain, Specific service may be found as a Capt in War records, pg 23 at the Lib of VA **CEM:** Rich Valley Presbyterian; GPS 36.90248, -81.62490; 3811 Valley Rd, Saltville; Smyth **GS:** U **SP:** Mar (1767) Mary Martin (1770 or1774-___) **VI:** D at Rich Valley **P:** unk **BLW:** unk **RG:** Y **MK:** unk **PH:** unk **SS:** J-NSSAR 1993 Reg, J- DAR Hatcher; CZ pg 81; SAR P-127926 **BS:** JLARC 1, 2.

CAMPBELL, John; b 23 Apr 1742; d 17 Dec 1825 **RU:** Captain/Patriot, Was in battles at Pt Pleasant, Long Island Flats 20 Jul 1776, Kings Mountain Oct 1780. Gave material aid to cause **CEM:** Sinking Springs; GPS 36.71030, -81.98170; 136 E Main St, Abingdon; Washington **GS:** U **SP:** Mar (10 Jun 1778 Botetourt Co) Elizabeth McDonald (29 may 1753-10 Jul 1827) d/o Edward & Elizabeth (Robinson) McDonald **VI:** Son of David (1703-1790) & Mary (Hamilton) Campbell; County Clerk Washington Co until 1815. Signer of Fincastle Resolutions **P:** unk **BLW:** unk **RG:** Y **MK:** unk **PH:** unk **SS:** D Augusta Co; SAR P-127931 **BS:** JLARC 70, 80,101; 196; 208 pg 73.

CAMPBELL, John; b 1761; d 1793 **RU:** Private, Served in Capt John Roger's Troop of Dragoons 1 Oct 1781. Discharged 1 Jan 1782 **CEM:** Jillard & Weakley; GPS unk; Rt 600 Syria; Madison **GS:** U **SP:** No info **VI:** Son of Elias (___-1794) & Elizabeth (Yowell) Campbell **P:** N **BLW:** N **RG:** N **MK:** unk **PH:** N **SS:** G pg 796 **BS:** 196.

CAMPBELL, Thomas; b 1749; d 1827 **RU:** Sergeant, Served in 4th Cont Line **CEM:** Campbell Family; GPS unk; Nr Irving; Bedford **GS:** Y **SP:** Mary Church **VI:** No further data **P:** unk **BLW:** unk **RG:** Y **MK:** N **PH:** unk **SS:** E pg 126; SAR application; SAR P-128045 **BS:** 80 vol 1 pg 150.

CAMPBELL, William; b 12 Dec 1755; d 23 Oct 1823 **RU:** Captain, Ent serv 1775, 7th Virginia Regt under Capt Gregory Smith **CEM:** Campbell Family; GPS unk; Campbellton near Barboursville; Orange **GS:** U **SP:** Mar (19 Aug 1783 King & Queen Co) Susan/Susanna Pierce (c1765-13 Mar 1852) **VI:** Nephew of Supreme Ct of Appeals Judge Edmond Pendleton. Widow pen Orange Co age 73, 1838. R461. Brothers Joseph & James also served in Revolution **P:** Y **BLW:** Y **RG:** unk **MK:** unk **PH:** unk **SS:** BY pg 7; K Vol 1 pg 158; SAR P-128059 **BS:** JLARC 4.

CAMPBELL, William; b unk; d 1781 **RU:** Captain, Service unit not determined. D as result of Yorktown battle **CEM:** Yorktown Victory Monument Tablet; GPS 38.28350, -78.54150; Yorktown; York **GS:** U **SP:** No info **VI:** No further data **P:** unk **BLW:** unk **RG:** N **MK:** unk **PH:** unk **SS:** J-Yorktown Historian **BS:** JLARC 74.

CAMPBELL, William; b 1745, Augusta Co; d 22 Aug 1781 **RU:** Brigadier General; was hero of Battle of Kings Mountain; was brigade commander **CEM:** Aspenvale; GPS 36.81420, -81.64000; Rts 641 & 642, Seven Mile Ford; Smyth **GS:** U **SP:** Elizabeth Henry (1749-1825), sister of Patrick Henry **VI:** Son of (-----) & Margaret (Buchanan) Campbell. Congratulated by U.S Congress. He d of sickness a few days

RU=Rank/Unit	CEM=Cemetery	GS=Gravestone	SP=Spousal Information
VI=Other Veteran Info	P=Pension	BLW=Bounty/Land Warrant	RG=Registered Grave
MK=SAR/DAR Marker	PH=Photo	SS=Service Source	BS=Burial Source

before Battle of Green Springs dying in Hanover Co. Bur at Rocky Mills, Hanover Co, but in 1823, relatives moved remains to old home of Aspenville on the Holston and laid him to rest next to his mother **P**: unk **BLW**: Y **RG**: Y **MK**: unk **PH**: unk **SS**: BY pg 292; J-NSSAR 1993 Reg; DAR A018793; SAR P-128056 **BS**: JLARC 1; 196.

CAMPBELL, Whittaker, b 1727, d 1814, **RU**: Captain,Patriot Commanded a company in the King And Queen Co, militia As a patriot was an active recruiter and gave material aid to the cause **CEM**: Campbell Family, AKA Woodstock; GPS not determined; loc 1/3 mi S of Bruington Comm Colege, Rt 14 **GS**: Unk **SP**: Mar 1) 1760, Jane Hill, (__1786), 2), (_-Deshazo) **VI**: No further data **P**: N **BLW**: N **RG**: Y **MK**: N **PH**: N **SS**: DAR A018771; D Vol 2 pg 551; CD; CZ vol ! pg 82; SAR 128051 **BS**: 196

CANNADAY, James; b 1750 or 1755, Buckingham Co; d 3 Mar 1817 **RU**: Private, Served in 3rd Cont Line **CEM**: Elsie Jones; GPS unk; Nr Endicott Assembly of God Church, Rt 793; Franklin **GS**: G Govt **SP**: Elizabeth Raikes (1756-1 Sep 1853) **VI**: No further data **P**: unk **BLW**: unk **RG**: Y **MK**: unk **PH**: unk **SS**: E pg 127; SAR P-128206 **BS**: JLARC 20.

CANNELLE, Jean; b unk; d 1781 **RU**: Seaman, Served on "Citoyen"; d from Yorktown battle **CEM**: French Memorial; GPS 36.81944, -79.39933; Yorktown; York **GS**: U **SP**: No info **VI**: No further data **P**: unk **BLW**: unk **RG**: Y **MK**: unk **PH**: unk **SS**: J-Yorktown Historian; P-128208 **BS**: JLARC 1, 74.

CANTON, Antoine; b unk; d 1781 **RU**: Soldier, Served in Bourbonnais Bn; d from Yorktown battle **CEM**: French Memorial; GPS 36.81944, -79.39933; Yorktown; York **GS**: U **SP**: No info **VI**: No further data **P**: unk **BLW**: unk **RG**: Y **MK**: unk **PH**: unk **SS**: J-Yorktown Historian; SAR P-128274 **BS**: JLARC 1, 74.

CANYS, Pierre; b unk; d 1781 **RU**: Soldier, Served in Foix Bn and died from Yorktown battle **CEM**: French Memorial; GPS 36.81944, -79.39933; Yorktown; York **GS**: U **SP**: No info **VI**: No further data **P**: unk **BLW**: unk **RG**: Y **MK**: unk **PH**: unk **SS**: J-Yorktown Historian; SAR P-28298*** **BS**: JLARC 1, 74.

CAPPER, John; b 1720, Ireland; d 1808 **RU**: Patriot, paid personal property tax, Frederick County 1782, considered a supply tax for Rev War expenses **CEM**: Capper Family; GPS not determined; fence of cem loc on WVA line, Rock Even Springs, High View: Fredreick **GS**:Unk **SP**: Alice Fawcett (24 Aug 1736, Chester Co, PA-24 Jun 1791), d/o Joseph Fawcett (1710-1776) & Margary Walsh (1717-1777), **VI**: No further data **P**: N **BLW**: unk **RG**: N **MK**: N **PH**: Unk **SS**: DV Frederick Co, 1782 image 02, pdf **BS**: 196.

CARBONEL, Louis; b unk; d 1781 **RU**: Soldier, Served in Auxonne Bn; d from Yorktown battle **CEM**: French Memorial; GPS 36.81944, -79.39933; Yorktown; York **GS**: U **SP**: No info **VI**: No further data **P**: unk **BLW**: unk **RG**: Y **MK**: unk **PH**: unk **SS**: J-Yorktown Historian; SAR P-128386 **BS**: JLARC 1, 74.

CARDWELL, Robert; b 1746, England; d 18 Feb 1839 **RU**: Private, Served in Bedford & Amherst Co Militias. Served under Capt William Lovin in battle at Yorktown Oct 1781. Had tour guarding prisoners. Served for 3 yrs or more **CEM**: Dixon Family; GPS 37.18420, -79.59310; Off Rt 658, Concord quadrant, nr Rustburg; Campbell **GS**: U **SP**: 1) Elmira (-----) 2) Alice (-----) (1766-Jan 1839) **VI**: Son of Willam John (1737-1773) & Mary (Sikes/Sykes) (1738-1806) Cardwell, Recd pension in Campbell Co **P**: Y **BLW**: unk **RG**: Y **MK**: N **PH**: unk **SS**: E pg 129; SAR P-128412 **BS**: JLARC 4, 21, 36.

CARLETON, (CARLTON) Joseph, Esq; b 1754, Belevedere, England; d 11 May 1812 **RU**: Captain, Ent serv Bedford Co 1776 and 1781 Amherst Co; Paymaster, Cont Army, Pulaski Legion 1779 and Auditor of Accounts in Philadelphia May 1779 **CEM**: Arlington National; GPS 38.88377, -77.06535; Jefferson Davis Hwy Rt 110; Arlington **GS**: Y lot 299, officer sect **SP**: No info **VI**: Secretary, Board of War, 1780-1783. Acting/Assistant Sec War, 1783-1785. D in Washington DC. Orig bur in Old Presbyterian Cem in Washington DC; reinterred Arlington 13 Nov 1907. Pen age 85, Campbell Co R467 **P**: Y **BLW**: unk **RG**: Y **MK**: Y SAR **PH**: unk **SS**: J-NSSAR 1993 Reg; E pg 130; SAR P-128515 **BS**: JLARC 1; 196; 223.

CARLIN, William; b 1732, England; d 1820 **RU**: Patriot; George Washington's tailor **CEM**: Ball-Carlin; GPS unk; 300 S Kensington St; Arlington **GS**: Y **SP**: Elizabeth Ball (___-16 Jul 1869) **VI**: Died in Glencarlyn **P**: N **BLW**: N **RG**: N **MK**: unk **PH**: unk **SS**: Sign in cemetery **BS**: 196.

CARLISLE (CARLILE)(CARLYLE), James; b 1725; d 1802 **RU**: Private, Served in a VA unit in Illinois **CEM**: Clover Creek Church; GPS unk; Clover Creek Rt 678 S of McDowell, 7.7 mi, right hand side; Highland **GS**: U **SP**: No info **VI**: No further data **P**: unk **BLW**: unk **RG**: Y **MK**: Y SAR **PH**: unk **SS**: J-

RU=Rank/Unit	CEM=Cemetery	GS=Gravestone	SP=Spousal Information
VI=Other Veteran Info	P=Pension	BLW=Bounty/Land Warrant	RG=Registered Grave
MK=SAR/DAR Marker	PH=Photo	SS=Service Source	BS=Burial Source

72

NSSAR 1993 Reg, J- DAR Hatcher; CZ pg 84; DAR A019225; SAR P-128548, SAR P-128642 **BS:** JLARC 1, 2.

CARLOCK, Hanchrist; b 1727, Holland; d 1803 **RU:** Private, Col Willam Christian Regt in Cherokee Expedition **CEM:** Carlock Family; GPS unk; Lick Run; Botetourt **GS:** U **SP:** 1) Susan Witmer 2) Sarah Whitman **VI:** No further data **P:** unk **BLW:** unk **RG:** unk **MK:** unk **PH:** unk **SS:** J- DAR Hatcher; BC part 2 pg 1420; DAR A019241; SAR P-128576 **BS:** JLARC 2.

CARLYLE, John; b 1720, Dumfrieshire, Scotland; d Sep 1780 **RU:** Major/Patriot, Signed Legislative Petition 25 Oct 1779 to establish Naval port in Alexandria. Gave material aid to cause **CEM:** Old Presbyterian Meeting House; GPS 38.48528, -77.23532; 323 S Fairfax St; Alexandria City **GS:** Y **SP:** 1) Leah (-----) (c1744-11 Oct 1803 2) Kitty Cahale **VI:** Son of Dr. William Carlysle & Raches Murray. Royal Customs Collector for S Potomac; merchant of Alexandria, President of the Virginia Council. One of the first trustees of Alexandria in 1748, Commissary of VA forces in 1754. Name listed on SAR plaque in cemetery **P:** unk **BLW:** unk **RG:** Y **MK:** Y SAR plaque **PH:** unk **SS:** D Fairfax Co; SAR P-128644 **BS:** JLARC 1, 86; 23 pg 100; 196.

CARLYLE< George William; b c1764, Alexandria, d 8 Sep 1781 **RU:** Cadet, Lt Col Washington's Regt, of Light Dragoons **CEM:**Rev War Court House Plaque;GPS;not determined; 4110 Chain Bridge Rd; Fairfax **GS:** Memorialized on plaque 2017 by Geo Washington Chapter, VASSAR **SP** No info **VI:** Died in service **P:** N **BLW:** N **RG:** N **MK:** N **PH:** N **SS:** EP sources: **BS:** None

CARMACK, John; b 1751, Frederick Co; d 1833 **RU:** Private, Ent serv 1774 Washington Co. Served less than 6 mos, was at battle at Point Pleasant **CEM:** Carmack; GPS unk; Nr Bristol; Washington **GS:** U **SP:** Elizabeth (-----) **VI:** Probably brother of William Carmack. Moved with Father to Washington Co 1773. Appl for pension 1832 there but rejected due to less than 6 mos serv. R471 Military marker. Cem #277A in source 80, Was in House of Reresentatives and Rep US Congress **P:** unk **BLW:** unk **RG:** Y **MK:** Y SAR **PH:** unk **SS:** K Vol 1 pg 164; DAR A019247; SAR P-128653 **BS:** JLARC 4, 2, 34, 76, 80.

CARMACK, William; b 5 Jan 1761, Prob Frederick Co; d 24 Sep 1851 **RU:** Private, Enl Washington Co Jan 1779. Served in Capt James Shelby's Army, Montgomery's VA Regt, George Rogers Clark during the Kaskaska Campaign. Discharged 10 Jul 1780 **CEM:** Brooks; GPS 36.6116, -83.4880; Ewing on Kesterson Rd Rt 690, 3 mi fr town; Lee **GS:** Y **SP:** 1) Elizabeth Walker? 2) Mary Polly (Yeary) Ball **VI:** Probably brother of John Carmack. Military marker. Pen 1832 Lee Co S9139. R471 Marker dated 2 Nov 2012 **P:** Y **BLW:** Y **RG:** Y **MK:** Y SAR **PH:** Y **SS:** AK; K Vol 1 pg 164; DAR A019251; SAR P-019251, SAR P-128652 **BS:** JLARC 4, 2, 34, 80.

CARPENTER, Nathaniel; b 1765, d 12 Mar 1837, Alexandria **RU:** Private, Capt Coleman's Co, VA Line serving long enough by 1781 to be eligible for BLW **CEM:** Old Ebenezer Baptist; GPS; GPS 39.05824, -77.84142; 20421 Airmont Rd, Bloomfield, Loudoun **GS:** U **SP:** No spousal data **VI:** No further data **P:** unk **BLW:** unk **RG:** Y **MK:** Y SAR plaque **PH:** unk **SS:** A pg 229; E pg 131; Fold3 Pay Register 1781; C page 229; SAR P-336668 **BS:** 196.

CARPENTER, Samuel; b 15 Mar 1759; d Bef Oct 1825 **RU:** Private, Served in VA Cont Line Regt, 1st VA Brigade, commanded by BG Peter Muhlenberg, Maj Gen Nathaniel Greene **CEM:** Carpenter Family; GPS unk; on first patent land compiled 1940, VA346; Madison **GS:** N **SP:** 1) Dinah Chrisler 2) Mar (1793) Margaret Blankenbaker **VI:** Son of William (1730-1810) & Mary (Wilhoit) Carpenter. Carpenter name aka Zimmerman, GF VA Germanna Colony settler 1717 **P:** Y **BLW:** Y **RG:** Y **MK:** unk **PH:** unk **SS:** SAR P-129019; C pg 227; AP-pen file W6632 **BS:** 197.

CARPENTER, William, Sr; b c1750, d May 1825 **RU:** Private, Served in a VA; discharged in 1775 at Fort Pitt in Pittsburgh, PA **CEM:** Ebenezer Baptist; GPS 39.05824, -77.84142; 20421 Airmont Rd, Bluemont; Loudoun **GS:** Y **SP:** Amelia Keen (___-Jul 1817) **VI:** No further data **P:** unk **BLW:** unk **RG:** Y **MK:** Y SAR plaque **PH:** unk **SS:** E, pg 131 SAR P-336639 **BS:** 196.

CARPER, Jacob; b 1755; d 30 Mar 1829 **RU:** Soldier/Patriot, Gave material aid to cause **CEM:** Fincastle Presbyterian; GPS 37.50017, -79.87558; 108 E Back St, Fincastle; Botetourt **GS:** N **SP:** 1) Mar (5 Jan 1795 Botetourt Co) Sally Raymer 2) Mar (3 Apr 1814 Botetourt Co) Mary Newell d/o John & (-----) Newell 3) Mar (24 May 1815) Elizabeth Nutter d/o Zadock & (-----) Nutter, 4) Mary Peck **VI:** Name

---

RU=Rank/Unit	CEM=Cemetery	GS=Gravestone	SP=Spousal Information
VI=Other Veteran Info	P=Pension	BLW=Bounty/Land Warrant	RG=Registered Grave
MK=SAR/DAR Marker	PH=Photo	SS=Service Source	BS=Burial Source

is on the SAR plaque **P:** unk **BLW:** unk **RG:** Y **MK:** Y SAR **PH:** N **SS:** J-NSSAR 1993 Reg; D VOL I, PG 137, Botetourt Co; DF pg 129; DAR A019558; SAR P-129088 **BS:** JLARC 1.

CARPER, Nicholas; b 1749, MD; d 1813 **RU:** Soldier; Served in Capt Uriah Springer's Co 9th VA Regt; Guarded jail Oct 1782 under Capt Robinson and served until end of war **CEM:** Fincastle Presbyterian; GPS 37.50017, -79.87558; 108 E Back St, Fincastle; Botetourt **GS:** U **SP:** Elizabeth Shrider **VI:** Was juror and constable Botetourt Co. Recd BLW #1065 **P:** unk **BLW:** unk **RG:** Y **MK:** Y SAR plaque **PH:** unk **SS:** DAR A019560; SAR P-129089; A pg 283 **BS:** 196, JLARC 1, 60.

CARPIER, Gilles; b unk; d 1781 **RU:** Seaman, Served on "Solitaire" and died from Yorktown battle **CEM:** French Memorial; GPS 36.81944, -79.39933; Yorktown; York **GS:** U **SP:** No info **VI:** No further data **P:** unk **BLW:** unk **RG:** Y **MK:** unk **PH:** unk **SS:** J-Yorktown Historian; SAR P-129090 **BS:** JLARC 1, 74.

CARR, Dabney Jr; b 1763; d 16 May 1793 **RU:** Private?, Served in Capt William Phillips Co of volunteer rangers **CEM:** Monticello; GPS 38.00829, -78.45520; 931 Thomas Jefferson Pkwy; Charlottesville City **GS:** Y **SP:** No info **VI:** Was an attorney. Recd 50 acres of bounty land. Conflicting info on burial site-- Monticello website research indicates no burial there for him. **P:** unk **BLW:** Y **RG:** N **MK:** N **PH:** unk **SS:** AH pg 295 **BS:** 80 vol 1 pg 156.

CARR, John; b 28 Aug 1738, County Down, Ireland; d 13 Nov 1807 **RU:** Ensign/Patriot, Served in 1st VA Regt. Gave material aid to cause **CEM:** Union; GPS 39.12046, -77.56239; 323 N King St, Leesburg; Loudoun **GS:** Y **SP:** No info **VI:** No further data **P:** unk **BLW:** unk **RG:** Y **MK:** N **PH:** N **SS:** AL Ct bk pg 3, Loudoun Co; DD; SAR P-129155 **BS:** 211 pg. 171.

CARR, John; b 1746; d 1809 **RU:** Patriot, Gave 600# meal for Albemarle Barracks **CEM:** Carr Family; GPS unk; Stoney Pt Rd Rt 20 near Charlottsville; Charlottesville City **GS:** Y **SP:** Mary Elizabeth (Polly) Downer **VI:** DAR marker by Jack Jouett Chapter, 10 Nov 1939 **P:** N **BLW:** N **RG:** Y **MK:** Y **PH:** unk **SS:** AL Ct Bk pg 4, 24; Albemarle & Slatton, Arbemarle Co Public Claims pg 4; DAR A019613; SAR P-129158, SAR P-129146 **BS:** 80 pg 156; 196.

CARR, John; b 15 Jul 1764, Loudoun Co; d 15 Sep 1804 **RU:** Soldier, Served in 13th VA Regt **CEM:** Fox Family; GPS unk; Waterford S on Hwy 62, Paeonian Springs; Loudoun **GS:** Y **SP:** No info **VI:** Son of Thomas (1733-1796) & Mary (Cummings) (1744-1810) Carr. Broken Gr St **P:** unk **BLW:** unk **RG:** N **MK:** unk **PH:** unk **SS:** Cl 13th VA Regt **BS:** 196.

CARR, John; b 26 Dec 1706, d 17 Jun 1778 **RU:** Patriot, Gave material aid to cause, Louisa Co **CEM:** Topping Castle; GPS: 37.92332, -77.54283; nr S end unmarked rd, loc E of Rt 700 and Jericho Rd (Rt 658), Houston Corner; Caroline **GS:** Unk **SP:** Barbara Overton (20 Apr 1720-1794) **VI:** Son of Thomas Carr (1678-1737) and Mary Dabney (1685-1748), brother-in-law of Thomas Jefferson; member of House of Burgesses (1722-73) **P:** N **BLW:** N **RG:** Y **MK:** N **PH:** N **SS:** AL Ct Bk pg 12 Lousia Co; SAR P-129150 **BS:** 196.

CARR, Peter; b 20 Oct 1740, died 1812 **RU:** Private/Patriot Served in Capt Henry McCabe's Co, Col Dabney's Regt, 1st Militia Brigade, Provided beef and a gun to the cause **CEM:** Union; GPS 39.12046, -77.56237; 323 North King St, Leesburg; Loudoun; **GS:** Y **SP:** Rachel Callwell (--- 12 Mar 1798) **VI:** Son of John Carr (1694-1794). Listed on monument with other family names **P:** N **BLW:** N **RG:** Y **MK:** unk **PH:** unk **SS:** DAR A019628, D vol 2, pg 610, 616; N pg 1267; SAR P-129187 **BS:** 196.

CARR, Thomas Sr; b c1733, Ireland; d 15 Oct 1796 **RU:** Sergeant, Served in Capt William Henderson's Co, Morgan's Riflemen; also served in 9th Cont Line **CEM:** Fox Family; GPS unk; Waterford S on Hwy 62, Paeonian Springs; Loudoun **GS:** Y **SP:** Mary Cummings (1744-1810) **VI:** Son of John Carr. Inscription on stone: died age 63 **P:** unk **BLW:** unk **RG:** Y **MK:** unk **PH:** unk **SS:** J-NSSAR 2000 Reg; E pg 132; DAR A019647; SAR P-129233 **BS:** JLARC 76.

CARRE, Rene; b unk; d 1781 **RU:** Seaman, Served on "Hector"; d from Yorktown battle **CEM:** French Memorial; GPS 36.81944, -79.39933; Yorktown; York **GS:** U **SP:** No info **VI:** No further data **P:** unk **BLW:** unk **RG:** Y **MK:** unk **PH:** unk **SS:** J-Yorktown Historian; SAR P-129238 **BS:** JLARC 1, 74.

CARRINGTON, Clement; b 22 Nov 1762, Lunenburg Co, d 28 Nov 1847 **RU:** Ensign, Lee's Bn Lt Dragoons 1780, wounded at Eutaw Springs 8 Sep 1781. Served to end of war **CEM:** Edgehill Plantation

---

RU=Rank/Unit	CEM=Cemetery	GS=Gravestone	SP=Spousal Information
VI=Other Veteran Info	P=Pension	BLW=Bounty/Land Warrant	RG=Registered Grave
MK=SAR/DAR Marker	PH=Photo	SS=Service Source	BS=Burial Source

(AKA Mulberry Hill); GPS 36.88629, -78.70353; Staunton River Battlefield State Park; 1035 Fort Hill Trail, Randolph; Charlotte **GS**: Y **SP**: Jane Watkins (1755-1839) d/o Col Joel Watkins & and Agnes Morton **VI**: Son of Paul Carrington (5 Mar 1733, Cumberland Co-23 Jun 1818) and Margaret Read (1733-1766), recd pen S 46427, recd BLW 2666 acres **P**: Y **BLW**: Y **REG**: Y **MK**: N **PH**: Y **SS**: C pg 288; E pg 132; DAR A019771; SAR P-129289 **BS**: SAR PRS, 196.

CARRINGTON, Edward; b 11 Feb 1748; d 28 Oct 1810 **RU**: Lt Col/Quartermaster General, Ent serv 1776. Was Capt of Militia Co in Cumberland Co in Dec 1775. Commissioned Lt Col of Artillery, Revolutionary Army 1776; later served as Quartermaster General on staff of Gen Nathanial Greene. Commanded artillery in Battles of Hobkirk's Hill and Yorktown 1781 **CEM**: St John's Episcopal; GPS 37.53183, -77.41958; 2401 E Broad St; Richmond City **GS**: U **SP**: Mar (8 Dec 1792 Henrico Co) Mrs. Eliza J. Brent (c1765-___), widow. Her 2nd husband. d/o (-----) and Jacquelin Amber. **VI**: A Delegate fr VA to the Continental Congress, 1789-1788. Appointed Marshal of Virginia by President Washington 1789. Served as jury foreman during Aaron Burr's trial for treason in 1807. Widow pension 1839 Richmond City 1839, age 74. R480 **P**: unk **BLW**: unk **RG**: Y **MK**: unk **PH**: unk **SS**: J-NSSAR 1993 Reg; CE pg 13; K Vol 1 pg 169; SAR P-129290. **BS**: JLARC 1; 196.

CARRINGTON, George, Sr; b 15 Mar 1711, St Philip, Barbados; d 7 Feb 1785 **RU**: Colonel, Was Col of Militia, 1778-81 **CEM**: Hollywood; GPS 37.53560, -77.45720; 412 S Cherry St; Richmond City **GS**: U **SP**: 1) Alice Adams (c1712-15 Feb 1785) 2) Anne Mayo **VI**: Son of Henningham, Codrington (1675-28 Jan 1744, St Philip, Barados) & (-----) (c1675-18 Jan 1744 at sea) Carrington. D in Cumberland Co He was Chairman of the Cumberland Co., VA Committee of Safety 1775-1776 and was a Co. Lieutenant of Cumberland Co, Militia, which he resigned as Col Jan 22, 1781. **P**: unk **BLW**: N **RG**: Y **MK**: unk **PH**: unk **SS**: J-NSSAR 1993 Reg; K Vol 1 pg 169; DAR A019714; SAR P-12992***, SAR P-129294 **BS**: JLARC 1; 196.

CARRINGTON, George; b 21 Nov 1756, Charlotte Co; d 27 May 1809 **RU**: Lieutenant, Served in Lee's Legion of Lt Dragoons, 1779-1783, and was POW 1782 **CEM**: Oak Hill; GPS unk; South Boston; Halifax **GS**: U **SP**: Sarah Coles Tucker **VI**: Son of Paul (1733-1818) & Margaret (Reade) (1734-1766) Carrington; became Brigadier General after war, member House of Delegates, 1802-3 and state senator. BLW 2666 acres **P**: unk **BLW**: Y **RG**: N **MK**: unk **PH**: unk **SS**: E pg 133; F pg 17 **BS**: 196.

CARRINGTON, George Jr; b 15 Mar 1737; d 7 Nov 1784 **RU**: Major/Patriot, Served in Cumberland Co Militia 1777 to 26 Feb 1781. Performed civil service as county clerk, surveyor & member Committee of Safety **CEM**: Boston Hill Plantation; GPS unk; Cartersville; Cumberland **GS**: N **SP**: Mar (1764) Margaret Bernard **VI**: Son of George (1711-1785) & Anne (Mayo) (1711-1785) Carrington **P**: unk **BLW**: unk **RG**: N **MK**: unk **PH**: N **SS**: E pg 133 **BS**: 196.

CARRINGTON, Paul; b 16 Mar 1733, Cumberland Co; d 23 Jan 1818 **RU**: Patriot, Public service as House of Delegates 1765-1776; Rev Convention 1775, 1776; VA Senate 1776-1778. Judge of High Ct of Appeals, 1779-1809; Gave material aid to the cause **CEM**: Mulberry Hill; GPS 36.88629, -78.70353; Staunton River Battlefield State Park, 1035 Fort Hill Trail, Randolph; Charlotte **GS**: Y **SP**: 1) Margaret Read (___-May 1766) 2) Priscilla Sims (___-1803). Both bur there. **VI**: Son of Col George Carrington (1711-1785) & Ann Mayo (1711-1785) of "Boston Hill," Cumberland Co. King's Attorney for Bedford Co in 1756. Helped form Prince Edward Academy in 1755; d in Halifax Co. Small modern ground stone marks his grave **P**: N **BLW**: N **RG**: Y **MK**: N **PH**: unk **SS**: AL Ct Bk pg 3; DAR A019726; SAR P-129300 **BS**: DAR Rpt; 196.

CARRINGTON, Paul; b 20 Sep 1764, Charlotte Co; d 8 Jan 1816 **RU**: Soldier; in battles at Green Springs & Guilford CH **CEM**: Carrington Family; GPS unk; On Bruce Estate "Berry Hill" W of South Boston, off Co Rd 659, on the "River Rd" E of the house; Halifax **GS**: U **SP**: Mar (24 Aug 1786) Mildred Howell Coles (15 May 1769-14 Apr 1840) d/o Col Walter (1739-1780) and Mildred (Lightfoot) (1752-1799) Coles **VI**: No further data **P**: unk **BLW**: unk **RG**: Y **MK**: unk **PH**: unk **SS**: SAR P-129302 **BS**: JLARC 1, 2, 4, 101.

CARSON, Charles; b c1741, Ireland; d 1815 **RU**: Ensign, Served in 4th Cont Line **CEM**: Sinking Springs; GPS 36.71030, -81.98170; 136 E Main St, Abingdon; Washington **GS**: Y **SP**: Did not marry **VI**: No further data **P**: unk **BLW**: unk **RG**: N **MK**: N **PH**: unk **SS**: E pg 133 **BS**: 78 pg 73.

RU=Rank/Unit	CEM=Cemetery	GS=Gravestone	SP=Spousal Information
VI=Other Veteran Info	P=Pension	BLW=Bounty/Land Warrant	RG=Registered Grave
MK=SAR/DAR Marker	PH=Photo	SS=Service Source	BS=Burial Source

75

CARSON, David; b 1741, Ireland, d 1804 **RU**: Private/Patriot, Served in Col Andrews Bn, York Co PA Militia; served as Deputy Surveyor in Capt Edmonson's Co; fought in Battle of Kings Mountain under Col Campbell. As patriot had public service as Tax Commissioner, Road Viewer, and Juror, and he rendered aid to cause **CEM**: Moore; GPS 36.6514015, -82.1905975; 20585 Haskell Station Road, Bristol; Washington **GS**: Unk **SP**: Elizabeth Dysart (1745-1786, Abington), d/o Col James Dysart **VI**: Son of Samuel Carson (1699-1759) **P**: N **BLW**: N **RG**: Y **MK**: N **PH**: N **SS**: AP-Service record card; DL pgs 1054, 1089, 1090, 1177, 1163; DAR A019819; SAR P-129385 **BS**: 196.

CARSON, James; b c1736; d 19 Jun 1814 **RU**: Patriot, Gave material aid to cause **CEM**: Second Concord Presbyterian; GPS 37.34209, -78.96585; Phoebe Pond Rd Rt 609 E of Concord; Appomattox **GS**: Y **SP**: Mar (c1765 Nelson Co) Mary Ann Helm (23 Oct 1743, Piscataway, Middlesex Co, NJ-18 Feb 1837, Henry Co, TN, d/o Moses & Sarah (Jameson) Helm. Bur at Dinwiddie Cemetery in Henry Co, TN **VI**: Died age 78 **P**: N **BLW**: N **RG**: N **MK**: unk **PH**: unk **SS**: AL Ct Bk pg 13, Campbell Co **BS**: 196.

CARSON, Samuel; b 1744; d 20 Mar 1824 **RU**: Private, Served in Capt Tait's Co Augusta Co VA **CEM**: Old Providence; GPS 37.96151, -79.71000; 1005 Spottswood Rd, Spottswood; Augusta **GS**: Y **SP**: Sarah Gibson (1744-03 Mar 1832) **VI**: Son of Samuel & Janet (-----) Carson. New Govt stone beside original. Name also on SAR cemetery plaque **P**: unk **BLW**: unk **RG**: N **MK**: Y SAR plaque **PH**: unk **SS**: E pg 134 **BS**: 44 pg 59.

CARTER, Charles; b 1 Jan 1732, Shirley Plantation; d 24 Jun 1806 **RU**: Captain/ Patriot;, Served in Charles City Co VA Militia. Allowed Shirley to be used as supply depot towards end of war supplying Lafayette with arms and munitions to defeat Cornwallis at Yorktown Also Member of VA Constitutional Convention of 1776. Member of Committee of Safety. **CEM**: Shirley Plantation; GPS unk; Rt 5 SE of Richmond; Charles City Co **GS**: N **SP**: 1) Mary Walker Carter; 2) Ann Butler Moore **VI**: Son of John Carter (1690-1742) & Elizabeth Hill (1703-1771). Planter and member-elect of the Council of State. SAR marker on grave **P**: unk **BLW**: unk **RG**: Y **MK**: Y SAR **PH**: N **SS**: AK 2011; SAR P-129466 **BS**: 04; 196.

CARTER, Charles; b 1733, King George Co; d 29 Apr 1796 **RU**: Patriot, Specific serv at Lib VA Auditors Acct, 1779, pg 25 **CEM**: Willis Hill, Fredericksburg National Military Park; GPS unk; Marye Heights; Fredericksburg City **GS**: Y **SP**: No info **VI**: Son of Charles Cleve & (-----) Carter. D at Ludlowe Plantation **P**: N **BLW**: N **RG**: N **MK**: N **PH**: unk **SS**: D pg 871, 874; CZ pg 86 **BS**: 196.

CARTER, Edward; b 1726; d 1792 **RU**: Patriot, Specific serv at Lib VA War files vol 4, pg 140 Member of General Assembly of VA **CEM**: Shirley Plantation; GPS unk; Rt 5, James River; Charles City Co **GS**: Y **SP**: Sarah Champe **VI**: House of Delegates **P**: N **BLW**: N **RG**: Y **MK**: N **PH**: unk **SS**: AS SAR applic; CZ pg 86; DAR A019907; SAR P-129490, SAR P-129489 **BS**: 80 vol 1 pg 158.

CARTER, Edward; b 21 Apr 1736; d 13 Aug 1810 **RU**: Soldier, Served in Capt Syme's Co, 10th Cont Line **CEM**: Carter Family; GPS unk; Nr Middleburg; Loudoun **GS**: Y **SP**: No info **VI**: No further data **P**: unk **BLW**: unk **RG**: N **MK**: N **PH**: unk **SS**: E pg 134; AS **BS**: 80 vol 1 pg 158.

CARTER, James; b 16 Sep 1743, Orange Co, NC; d 14 Sep 1812 **RU**: Corporal, Served in Capt Thomas Posey's Co 7th Cont line, Sep 1777 **CEM**: South Fork Meeting House; GPS 39.02640, -77.80220; Rt 630 Unison; Loudoun **GS**: Y **SP**: Mar (31 Aug 1765 Loudoun Co) Hannah Eblin (2 Jan 1746 Chester Co, PA-16 Sep 1798 Loudoun Co) d/o John (1724-1795/7) & Mary (Warner) (___-aft 1795) Eblin **VI**: No further data **P**: unk **BLW**: unk **RG**: N **MK**: unk **PH**: unk **SS**: E pg 134; AP Payroll **BS**: 196.

CARTER, Joseph; b 4 Sep 1736, Fauquier Co; d 16 Aug 1808 **RU**: Private/Patriot, Served in 11th and 15th VA Regt **CEM**: Carter Family; GPS 36.71169, -82.69778; Rt 649, Rye Cove; Scott **GS**: Y **SP**: Elizabeth Presley **VI**: Son of Peter (1706 Lancaster Co-1790 Amherst Co) & Judith (Norris) (1710-1765) Carter. SAR marker. Orig GS broken in half **P**: unk **BLW**: unk **RG**: Y **MK**: Y **PH**: unk **SS**: O; CZ pg 87; DAR A019996 cites he paid personal property tax, Washington Co 1782; SAR P-129616 **BS**: 04; 196.

CARTER, Landon; b 18 Aug 1710 Christ Church, Lancaster Co; d 22 Dec 1778 **RU**: Colonel/Patriot; was Clerk of Committee of Safety 1775 **CEM**: Lower Lunenburg Parish Church; GPS 37.96066, -76.76920; Off N Side Rt 360, Warsaw; Richmond Co **GS**: Y **SP**: 1) Mar (16 Nov 1732) Elizabeth Wormeley (1713-1740) 2) Mar (22 Sep 1742) Maria Horsmanden Byrd (1727-1744) 3) Mar (1746) Elizabeth Beale **VI**: Son of Robert King (1663-1732) and Elizabeth (Landon) (1684-1719) Carter of

RU=Rank/Unit	CEM=Cemetery	GS=Gravestone	SP=Spousal Information
VI=Other Veteran Info	P=Pension	BLW=Bounty/Land Warrant	RG=Registered Grave
MK=SAR/DAR Marker	PH=Photo	SS=Service Source	BS=Burial Source

Corotoman Plantation in Lancaster Co **P:** unk **BLW:** unk **RG:** Y **MK:** N **PH:** unk **SS:** A part 2 pg 275; CJ 1st Series Vol 5 no 4 pg 251; DAR A020013; SAR P-129631 **BS:** 24 pg 2184.

CARTER, Landon; b 16 Jun 1757, d 30 Aug 1820 **RU:** Private; Served in Capt Hawe's (Haw's) Company of Foot in the 2d VA Regt, Cont Line commanded by Col Alexander Spotswood in a payroll dated Jun-Jul period 1777 **CEM:** Carter Family; GPS 37.940,132, -76.781693; loc Sabine Hall Rd at Sabine Hall Plantation, Warsaw, Richmond County **GS:** Yes **SP:** Mar Richmond Co, 3 Feb 1780, C/Katherine Griffin Tayloe (10 Oct 1761-27 Dec 1798) **VI:** Son of Robert Wormsley Carter (1734-12 Dec 1797) and Winifred Travers Beale (1733-1794) Recd pen S41471 **P:** Y **BLW:** N **RG:** N **MK:** N **PH:** N **SS:** E pg 135; Fold3 serv index cards & pen file **BS:** 196.

CARTER, Landon Jr; b Aug 1738, Richmond Co; d 1801 **RU:** Private, Served in Capt Wm Sanford's Co, Col Alexander Spotswood's 2d VA Regt, Cont Line **CEM:** Pittsylvania (Carter); GPS 38.49711, -77.31305; Manassas National Battlefield Park; Manassas City **GS:** U **SP:** Mar (1760) Judith Fauntleroy (1746-c1798) **VI:** Son of Landon Sr (7 Jun 1709-10 Aug 1778) & Elizabeth (Wormley) (1713-31 Jan 1740) Carter. His plantation house was named "Pittsylvania" **P:** unk **BLW:** unk **RG:** N **MK:** unk **PH:** unk **SS:** DAR A020017; A pg 135 **BS:** 190 name of cem.

CARTER, Nicholas; b unk; d 1813 **RU:** Private, Served in 7th, 9th,13th Cont Line **CEM:** Fincastle Presbyterian; GPS 37.50017, -79.97558; 108 E Back St, Fincastle; Botetourt **GS:** U **SP:** No info **VI:** No further data **P:** unk **BLW:** unk **RG:** N **MK:** N **PH:** unk **SS:** E pg 135; BY **BS:** 197.

CARTER, Richard; b unk, Kent, England; d 1 Dec 1806 **RU:** Private, Served in Capt Springer's Co in VA Cont line. Also served in Col John Gibson's 7th Regt Cont Line; enlisted May 1st, 1775 in Capt Jackquil Morgan's Co, at siege of Yorktown. Served in 3rd Virginia Regt also **CEM:** Richard Carter Property; GPS unk; Nr Leesburg; Loudoun **GS:** U **SP:** Mar (1780) Catherine (-----) (___-aft 1817, Loudoun) Co **VI:** No further data **P:** unk **BLW:** unk **RG:** Y **MK:** N **PH:** unk **SS:** DAR A020050; AP roll #1022; AS SAR applic; SAR P-129660, SAR P-129661 **BS:** SAR Appl.

CARTER, Robert; b 1763, d 1807 **RU:** Private, serv 14th VA Regt and VA Cont Line, in Col Posey's Regt and in VA Battalion composed of officers and men of various regts **CEM:** Woodlawn; GPS 37.75635, -77.494343; loc 11310 Hanover Ave, Ashland; Hanover **GS:** Unk **SP:** Kezziah Francis **VI:** Grave moved fr family cem in Hanover Co to Woodlawn cem; son of Jesse Carter and Hannah Baylor **P:** Unk **BLW:** unk **RG:** N **MK:** N **PH:** N **SS:** Fold3 Serv Index Cards **BS:** 196.

CARTER, Robert III; b 1728, Lancaster Co; d 11 Mar 1804 **RU:** Patriot, Gave material aid to the cause. Member of the Council of VA 1758-1776 **CEM:** Nomini Hall Graveyard; GPS unk; Hague; Westmoreland **GS:** N **SP:** Mar (2 Apr 1754 Anapolis MD) Francis Ann Tasker (___1787, d/o Benjamin Tasker of MD **VI:** Son of Robert & Priscilla Bladen Carter. Largest slave owner to give freedom to over 550 slaves in 1791; d in Baltimore. He directed that no GS mark his burial place **P:** N **BLW:** N **RG:** Y **MK:** N **PH:** N **SS:** AL Ct Bk pg 1, 3, 4, 5; DAR A020053; SAR P-129664 **BS:** 121 newspaper.

CARTER, Robert Wormley; b 7 Jun 1734, d 6 Jun 1797 **RU:** Colonel Appointed Richmond County Lieutenant 8 Oct 1776, recd as Col 2 Jun 1777 **CEM:** Lower Nunenburg Parish Church, ruins removed, thus no longer exists; GPS 37.960657, -76.769199; loc in town of Warsaw by water tower on Rt 360; Richmond Co **GS:** N **SP:** Mar 9 Mar 1776, Winifred Travers Beale (1733-1794), d/o William Beale & Ann Harwar **VI:** Son of Landon Carter (7 Jun 1709-10 Aug 1778) & Elizabeth Wormley (1714, Middlesex Co-1740) **P:** N**BLW:** N **RG:** N **MK:** N **PH:** N **SS:** E pg 135 **BS:** 196. **SEE APPENDIX G**

CARTER, Thomas; b 27 Nov 1734; d 15 Jul 1817 **RU:** Gunner/Patriot, Enl Cumberland Co in1st Artillery Regt of Cont Army; Gave material aid to cause **CEM:** Glenrock; GPS 36.80060, -79.44548; E of Rt 824, .5 mi S of Greenbuck Branch; Pittsylvania **GS:** Y **SP:** Mar (10 Jul 1764) Winifred Hobson d/o Adcock & Joanne (Lawson) Hobson **VI:** D in Rye Cove, Scott Co; DAR restoring grave. R 487 **P:** Y **BLW:** unk **RG:** Y **MK:** unk **PH:** unk **SS:** D Mecklenburg Co; SAR P-129692 **BS:** 174, JLARC 82, 96.

CARTER, Thomas; b 24 Mar 1731, Lancaster Co; d 5 Oct 1803 **RU:** Patriot, Gave material aid to the cause **CEM:** Carter; GPS unk; Rye Cove; Scott **GS:** U **SP:** Mary Morgan **VI:** Son of Peter and Judith Norris Carter **P:** N **BLW:** N **RG:** Y **MK:** unk **PH:** unk **SS:** AL Comm Bk IV pg 268 Washington Co; SAR P-126690 **BS:** 196.

RU=Rank/Unit	CEM=Cemetery	GS=Gravestone	SP=Spousal Information
VI=Other Veteran Info	P=Pension	BLW=Bounty/Land Warrant	RG=Registered Grave
MK=SAR/DAR Marker	PH=Photo	SS=Service Source	BS=Burial Source

CARTER, William; b unk; d 2 Jul 1828 **RU:** Lieutenant, Served in Henrico Co Militia **CEM:** Shockoe Hill; GPS 37.55190, -77.43170; 4th & Hospital Sts; Richmond City **GS:** Gov't **SP:** No info **VI:** No further data **P:** unk **BLW:** unk **RG:** Y **MK:**Y monument **PH:** unk **SS:** E pg 135; SAR P-336877 **BS:** 196.

CARTER, William; b c1732; d 12 Jun 1799 **RU:** Surgeon, Served in Col Baylor's Regt of Cavalry. Recd severe cuts, both wrists, at Lenew's Ferry-May 1770. Served as surgeon in Cont Hospital in Williamsburg fr Jul 1776-end of war **CEM:** St John's Episcopal; GPS 37.53183, -77.41958; 2401 E Broad St; Richmond City **GS:** Y **SP:** No info **VI:** Resided in Caroline Co. Appl for pen. GS indicates age 67 at death **P:** Y **BLW:** unk **RG:** Y **MK:** N **PH:** unk **SS:** A pg 388; BX pg 136; SAR P-129712 **BS:** 39 pg 99.(**CARTER**, William See Appendix G)

CARTNELL (CARTMELL, CARTMILL), Nathaniel; b c1753; d Oct 1795 (will proven) **RU:** Patriot; Paid Rev War Supply Tax called Personal Property tax, Frederick Co 1782 **CEM:** St John's Lutheran; GPS 39.15310, -78.36520; 3623 Buck Mountain Rd, Hayfield; Frederick **GS:** Y **SP:** 1) Mar (23 Apr 1807) Sarah Bean 2) Mar (7 Mar 1833) Sarah E. Lupton **VI:** No further data **P:** N **BLW:** N **RG:** Y **MK:** N **PH:** unk **SS:** E pg 135; DV; SAR P-129741 **BS:** 59 pg 55.

CARWILES (CARWILE), Jacob Sr; b 1751, Goochland Co; d 1837 **RU:** Private, Served in Campbell Co Militia **CEM:** Carwile; GPS 37.08470, -78.58020; Rt 708 Seamster Rd, go to end, abt 1 mi walk, Noruna; Campbell **GS:** Y gov't **SP:** Mar (26 Feb 1802, Campbell Co (bond) Martha Scott **VI:** Pen awarded 16 Sep 1833 S127093. Descendents placed Govt marker there in the woods **P:** Y **BLW:** unk **RG:** Y **MK:** N **PH:** unk **SS:** SAR P-129813 **BS:** JLARC 3; 196.

CARY, George; b unk; d 1826 **RU:** Private, Hazen's Regt **CEM:** George Cary Family; GPS unk; 4.5 mi W of Courtland; Southampton **GS:** Y **SP:** No info **VI:** No further data **P:** unk **BLW:** unk **RG:** N **MK:** N **PH:** unk **SS:** AP roll **BS:** 144 Geo Cary.

CARY, John; b 1745; d 1795 **RU:** Captain, Co commander Elizabeth City Co Sep 1775 **CEM:** Peartree Hall; GPS unk; Nr Warwick Hall CH and Tabbs Ln; Newport News City **GS:** U **SP:** 1) Sally Slater 2) Susanna Armistead **VI:** Member, Committee of Safety **P:** unk **BLW:** unk **RG:** Y **MK:** Y SAR **PH:** unk **SS:** J-NSSAR 1993 Reg; CE pg 17; SAR P-129850 **BS:** JLARC 1.

CARY, Mary; b 3 Feb 1733; d May 1781 **RU:** Patriot; Gave material aid to cause in James City County **CEM:** James, Jamestown Fort; GPS: 37.2083850, -76.7786880; Jamestown; James City Co **GS:** Unk **SP:** Widow of Edward Ambler **VI:** No further data **P:** N **BLW:** N **RG:** N **MK:** N **PH:** N **SS:** Al Ct Bk, pg 1, James City Co **BS:** 196.

CARY, Richard; b 1739; d 18 Nov 1789 **RU:** Captain/Patriot, Commanded a co in Warwick Co Militia 1775; was member of Committee of Safety. Represented Warwick Co in VA State Convention 1776. Gave material aid to cause in Elizabeth City **CEM:** Peartree Hall; GPS 37.1189400, -76.5378630; 106 Raymond Dr; Newport News City **GS:** Y **SP:** Mary Cole **VI:** Judge of Central Ct. D in Richmond or Newport News City **P:** unk **BLW:** unk **RG:** Y **MK** Y SAR **PH:** unk **SS:** J-NSSAR 1993 Reg, J- DAR Hatcher; AL Ct Bk pg 7; E pg 136; DAR A020257; SAR P-129875 **BS:** JLARC 1, 2. SAR PRS.

CARY, Richard Jr; b 1760; d 1800 **RU:** Captain; Commanded Co in Warwick Co Militia **CEM:** Peartree Hall; GPS 37.1189400, -76.5378630; 106 Raymond Dr; Newport News City **GS:** N **SP:** No info **VI:** Son of Richard Cary (1739-18 Nov 1789) & Mary Cole **P:** unk **BLW:** unk **RG:** Y **MK:** Y SAR **PH:** N **SS:** E pg 136; CZ pg 88; P-129894 **BS:** SAR Appl. PRS.

CARY, Thomas Jr; b 1720; d 1793 **RU:** Captain, Commanded a Co in Warwick Co Militia **CEM:** Windmill Point; GPS unk; N of jct Warwick River and Lucas Creek and S of Rt 173; Newport News City **GS:** U **SP:** 1) Sally (___) Whitaker 2) Frances Godwyn **VI:** Son of Cary Thomas Sr; d 1782 in York Co **P:** unk **BLW:** unk **RG:** Y **MK:** Y SAR **PH:** unk **SS:** J-NSSAR 1993 Reg; CZ pg 88; DAR A020268; SAR P-129895 **BS:** JLARC 1.

CARY, Wilson Miles; b 1734, Warwick Co; d 1 Dec 1817, Fluvanna Co **RU:** Col, Member of Convention 1776 & House of Delegates, Committee of Safety, 1775-6, pg 40 **CEM:** Cary Family; GPS unk; Carysbrook; Fluvanna **GS:** Y **SP:** 1) Mar (25 May 1758) Sarah Blair d/o Honorable John & (-----) Blair (____-28 Feb 1799) 2) Rebecca Dawson **VI:** No further data **P:** unk **BLW:** unk **RG:** Y **MK:** N **PH:** unk **SS:** E pg 137; CZ pg 88; DAR A020276; SAR P-129892, SAR P-129893 **BS:** SAR Appl.

RU=Rank/Unit	CEM=Cemetery	GS=Gravestone	SP=Spousal Information
VI=Other Veteran Info	P=Pension	BLW=Bounty/Land Warrant	RG=Registered Grave
MK=SAR/DAR Marker	PH=Photo	SS=Service Source	BS=Burial Source

CASSELL, Michael; b 1764; d 1826 **RU:** Patriot, Gave material aid to cause **CEM:** Kimberling; GPS 36.91750, -81.30440; Rt 617, Rural Retreat; Wythe **GS:** U **SP:** Catherine Tobler **VI:** No further data **P:** N **BLW:** N **RG:** N **MK:** unk **PH:** unk **SS:** D Montgomery Co **BS:** JLARC 122, 123.

CASSIN, John; b 1758; d 1822 **RU:** Private, Served in PA military **CEM:** Arlington National; GPS 38.88377, -77.06535; Jefferson Davis Hwy Rt 110; Arlington **GS:** U **SP:** No info **VI:** No further data **P:** unk **BLW:** unk **RG:** Y **MK:** N **PH:** unk **SS:** J-NSSAR 1993 Reg; SAR P-130170 **BS:** JLARC 1.

CATEL, Jean; b unk; d 1781 **RU:** Soldier, Served in Gatinais Bn; d from Yorktown battle **CEM:** French Memorial; GPS 36.81944, -79.39933; Yorktown; York **GS:** U **SP:** No info **VI:** No further data **P:** unk **BLW:** unk **RG:** Y **MK:** unk **PH:** unk **SS:** J-Yorktown Historian; SAR P-130318 **BS:** JLARC 1, 74.

CATHER, Jasper; b 1740, Ulster, Trone, Ireland; d 30 Jul 1812 **RU:** Private/Patriot, Served in Frederick Co Militia, Name appears on supply tax list, Fauquier Co, PA **CEM:** Back Creek Quaker, aka Gainesboro United Methodist; GPS 39.27861, -78.25694; 166 Siler Ln, Gainesboro; Frederick **GS:** U **SP:** 1) Catherine Lawrence 2) Barbara Lawrence 3) Mar (27 Mar 1786 by Christian Streit) Sarah Moore **VI:** Son of Robert and Joanna (Thurloe) Cather **P:** unk **BLW:** unk **RG:** Y **MK:** unk **PH:** unk **SS:** AR Vol 1 pg 162; SAR P-130342 **BS:** JLARC 1, 2, 4, 47; 196.

CAVALIER, Francois; b unk; d 1781 **RU:** Soldier, Served in Foix Bn; d from Yorktown battle **CEM:** French Memorial; GPS 36.81944, -79.39933; Yorktown; York **GS:** U **SP:** No info **VI:** No further data **P:** unk **BLW:** unk **RG:** Y **MK:** unk **PH:** unk **SS:** J-Yorktown Historian; SAR P-130484 **BS:** JLARC 1, 74.

CAVE, Thomas; b 1745; d 7 Dec 1802 **RU:** Patriot, Contributed to cause by paying 1783 VA War support tax **CEM:** Dumfries Public; GPS 38.34110, -77.19964; 17821 Mine Rd, Dumfries; Prince William **GS:** Y Section 10 **SP:** Mary Ann (-----) (1760-04 Feb 1818) **VI:** SAR monument **P:** N **BLW:** N **RG:** Y bn **MK:** Y SAR monument **PH:** unk **SS:** AK CWG 2014 **BS:** 04; 196.

CECIL, John; b 24 Jan 1750, Prince George Co, MD; d 5 Aug 1832 **RU:** Private, Served in Capt Cloyd's Co, Montgomery Co Militia Sep 1777 **CEM:** Cecil Family Farm #2; GPS unk; Neck's Creek, Belspring; Pulaski **GS:** U **SP:** Keziah Witten (19 Feb 1751 Frederick Co, MD-15 May 1837) d/o Thomas & Elizabeth (Cecil) Whitten **VI:** Son of Samuel & Rebecca (White) Cecil **P:** unk **BLW:** unk **RG:** Y **MK:** unk **PH:** unk **SS:** G pg 215; SAR P-130519 **BS:** 196.

CECIL, Samuel Witten Sr; b 23 Mar 1719 Prince George Co, MD; d 28 Mar 1786 **RU:** Private/Patriot, Private in Capt McCorkie's Co, Montgomery Co Militia. Performed public service as Juror and Overseer of Roads, and took oath of allegiance, Montgomery Co **CEM:** Cecil Family; GPS unk; Nr Radford and Dublin; Pulaski **GS:** U **SP:** Rebecca White (1719-16 Mar 1815) **VI:** No further data **P:** N **BLW:** N **RG:** Y **MK:** unk **PH:** unk **SS:** DAR A023627; DL Part 1, pg 703, 734; SAR P-130524 **BS:** 80, vol 1, pg 162; 196.

CHABRIER, Fleury; b unk; d 1781 **RU:** Soldier, Served in Bourbonnais Bn; d from Yorktown battle **CEM:** French Memorial; GPS 36.81944, -79.39933; Yorktown; York **GS:** U **SP:** No info **VI:** No further data **P:** unk **BLW:** unk **RG:** Y **MK:** unk **PH:** unk **SS:** J-Yorktown Historian; SAR P-130549 **BS:** JLARC 1, 74.

CHAMBERLAIN (CHAMBERLAINE), George; b 1755, Warrwick Co; d 10 Jan 1792 **RU:** 2nd Lt/Navy, Served in Henry & Manley Galley. Served on five vessels, two of which (the Pilot Boat "Molly" and the Light Boat "Liberty"), were commanded by him after having escaped imprisonment in England **CEM:** St Paul's Episcopal; GPS 36.84733, -76.28554; 201 St Paul's Blvd; Norfolk City **GS:** N **SP:** 1) Ann Harlow Lucas 2) Fannie Lowry Needham **VI:** No further data **P:** unk **BLW:** unk **RG:** N **MK:** Y SAR plaque **PH:** N **SS:** BE pg 66; CB **BS:** 28.

CHAMBERLAYNE, William; b unk; d 15 Jun 1838 **RU:** Rank not determined, Specific serv at Lib VA, Journal House of Delegates, Oct 1814, pg 114 **CEM:** St John's Episcopal; GPS 37.53183, -77.41958; 2401 E Broad St; Richmond City **GS:** N **SP:** No info **VI:** Became a Brigagier Gen in War of 1812 **P:** unk **BLW:** unk **RG:** N **MK:** N **PH:** N **SS:** E pg 142; CZ pg 91 **BS:** 28 pg 351.

CHAMBERS, John; b 1760; d 1815 **RU:** Captain, Commanded a Co in Buckingham Co; other serv at Lib VA, Auditors Acct, XVIII, pg 177 **CEM:** Chambers Family; GPS unk; Rt 659, 2.75 mi W of Ransons; Buckingham **GS:** N **SP:** Martha Hunt Allen (1763-1805) **VI:** Stone no longer standing. Survey in 1935

RU=Rank/Unit	CEM=Cemetery	GS=Gravestone	SP=Spousal Information
VI=Other Veteran Info	P=Pension	BLW=Bounty/Land Warrant	RG=Registered Grave
MK=SAR/DAR Marker	PH=Photo	SS=Service Source	BS=Burial Source

noted it was very small and made of marble **P:** unk **BLW:** N **RG:** N **MK:** N **PH:** N **SS:** AP roll; CZ pg 91 **BS:** 173.

CHAMBLIN, William; b 21 May 1723, d 12 Oct 1806 **RU:** Patriot; Gave material aid to cause and paid personal property tax, 1783, Loudoun Co **CEM:** Old Ebenezer Baptist; GPS; GPS 39.05824, -77.84142; 20421 Airmont Rd, Bloomfield, Loudoun **GS:** Y **SP:** No spousal data **VI:** No further data **P:** unk **BLW:** unk **RG:** Y **MK:** Y SAR plaque **PH:** unk **SS:** AL Ct Bk pg 25, Comm Bk III, pg 289; : DV 1783 Personal Property Tax List 1783C, image .pdf; SAR P-336640 **BS:** 222

CHAMOIS, Claude; b unk; d 1781 **RU:** Soldier, Served in Gatinais Bn; d from Yorktown battle **CEM:** French Memorial; GPS 36.81944, -79.39933; Yorktown; York **GS:** U **SP:** No info **VI:** No further data **P:** unk **BLW:** unk **RG:** Y **MK:** unk **PH:** unk **SS:** J-Yorktown Historian; SAR P-131026 **BS:** JLARC 1, 74.

CHANCELLOR, John; b c1726; d Aft 1815 **RU:** Patriot, Gave 3 beeves to cause **CEM:** Fairview; GPS unk; Rt 3; Spotsylvania **GS:** Y **SP:** 1) Jane Monroe (1760-1840) 2) Elizabeth Edwards **VI:** No further data **P:** N **BLW:** N **RG** N **MK:** N **PH:** unk **SS:** D pg 805; AL **BS:** 06 pg 81, 82; 04.

CHANDLER, Carter; b c1733; d 16 Aug 1813 **RU:** Private, Ent serv Louisa Co 1780. Sub for brother-in-law Barnett Mitchell **CEM:** Chandler Family; GPS 39.1121, -78.03; Helvestine Farm, Rt 7 vic Rt 633; Clarke **GS:** Y **SP:** No info **VI:** Resident of Spotsylvania Co after war 4 yrs; moved to Frederick Co. Pen. 1835, age 72. R512. BLW granted 1835. Illiterate. GSs were read in 1941, but have since been moved to side of nearby barn and are difficult to read. GPS readings is fr center of cemetery **P:** Y **BLW:** Y **RG:** N **MK:** N **PH:** unk **SS:** AP pension Rec; K Vol 1 pg 186 **BS:** 58 pg 7.

CHANPEAU, Francois; b unk; d 1781 **RU:** Seaman, Served on "Northumberland"; d from Yorktown battle **CEM:** French Memorial; GPS 36.81944, -79.39933; Yorktown; York **GS:** U **SP:** No info **VI:** No further data **P:** unk **BLW:** unk **RG:** Y **MK:** unk **PH:** unk **SS:** J-Yorktown Historian; SAR P-131299 **BS:** JLARC 1, 74.

CHAPIN, Benjamin; b 24 May 1736; d 15 Oct 1781 **RU:** Surgeon, Ent VA Navy, 1777. VA State Navy on Galley "Protector" **CEM:** Old Christ Church Episcopal; GPS 38.80625, -77.04718; 118 N Washington St; Alexandria City **GS:** N **SP:** Mar (1) Leah (-----) (c1744-11 Oct 1803); 2) Kitty Cahale, 3) Margaret Colton **VI:** Was referred to as "Dr. Chapin." Wm R Ashton admin estate in Baltimore MD 1834. Memorialized on plaque at the Fairfax Co Ct House. Heirs rejected for pension 1838. R516 **P:** N **BLW:** unk **RG:** Y **MK:** unk **PH:** N **SS:** J-NSSAR 1993 Reg; K Vol 1 pg 188; EP additional sources DAR A020738; SAR P-131317 **BS:** JLARC 1; 196.

CHAPMAN, Elizabeth; b 13 Jun 1733; Charles Co, MD d 1783 **RU:** Patriot, Provided driver and horses for 40 days (claim filed 1782 under Act of 1780) **CEM:** Summer Hill; GPS:38.709930, -77.209946; Glendale Dr, Fairfax **GS:** N **SP:** John Hunter MD (c1732 or earlier-bef 6 Sep 1826) **VI;** SAR PRS erroneously indicates burial is at Pohick Church **P:** N **BLW:** N **RG:**Y **MK:** N **PH:** N **SS:** R pg 2; SAR P-188498 **BS:** 04.

CHAPMAN, George; b 17 Jul 1749, Pomonkey, Charles Co, MD; d 1814 **RU:** Patriot, Signed petition to House of Delegates urging decrease in import duties to increase commerce, 27 May 1782 **CEM:** Pohick Episcopal; GPS 38.42546, -77.11598; 9301 Richmond Hwy, Lorton; Fairfax **GS:** Y **SP:** Amelia McCrae **VI:** No further data **P:** N **BLW:** N **RG:** Y **MK:**Y SAR Plaque **PH:** unk **SS:** I; BB; DAR A097114; SAR P-131514 **BS:** 20 pg 47; 04.

CHAPMAN, Isaac; b 1764; d 1836 **RU:** Captain, Ent serv 1776 Montgomery Co (Now Giles Co) for Indian War. Ent serv again 1777. Served in 2nd Battalion, 86th Regt **CEM:** Mt Prospect; GPS unk; Rt 634, Old Strother Farm, Ripplemeade; Giles **GS:** U **SP:** Margaret Williams **VI:** Appl pen fr Giles Co 1835 age 71. Pension rejected. R520 **P:** N **BLW:** unk **RG:** Y **MK:** unk **PH:** unk **SS:** K Vol 1 pg 189; SAR P-131525 **BS:** JLARC 2, 26.

CHAPMAN, John; b 18 Jan 1740; d Aft Jun 1813 **RU:** Second Lieutenant, Served in Montgomery Co Militia **CEM:** Mt Prospect; GPS unk; Rt 634, Old Strother Farm, Ripplemeade; Giles **GS:** U **SP:** Sallie Abbott **VI:** No further data **P:** unk **BLW:** unk **RG:** Y **MK:** unk **PH:** unk **SS:** J- DAR Hatcher; E pg 144; SAR P-131151 **BS:** JLARC 2.

RU=Rank/Unit	CEM=Cemetery	GS=Gravestone	SP=Spousal Information
VI=Other Veteran Info	P=Pension	BLW=Bounty/Land Warrant	RG=Registered Grave
MK=SAR/DAR Marker	PH=Photo	SS=Service Source	BS=Burial Source

80

CHAPMAN, John; b 1737, Caroline Pines, Caroline Co; d 10 Oct 1816, Amelia Co **RU:** Patriot gave material aid to cause (beef) in Caroline Co and Amelia Co **CEM:** Mount Prospect; GPS not determined; one mi fr Bobtown and abt 3 mi N fr Keller; Accomack **GS:** Unk **SP:** Mar 1) Ann Whitehead (1740-1795), 2) Oney League **VI:** No further data) **P:** N **BLW:** N **RG:** Y **MK:** N **PH:** N **SS:** AL Ct Bk I pg 59 Amelia Co & Lists I, pg 15 **Caroline Co**; DAR A020914; SAR P-131550 **BS:** 196.

CHAPMAN, Nathan; b 3 May 1761; d 29 Jan 1828 or 1829 **RU:** Private, Enl Capt Beverly Stubblefield's Co, Col Richard Parker's Regt, Cont Line. Taken prisoner at Charleston, SC; exchanged at Williamsburg, Oct 1781 **CEM:** Chapman Family; GPS unk; Goodview; Bedford **GS:** U **SP:** Mar (17 Feb 1791 Franklin Co) Elizabeth "Betsy" Colema **VI:** Widow pen 1839 age 69 Bedford Co, BLW granted 1855. Perhaps he is the person by this name that BLW was issued to Nathaniel Chapman of Bedord Co for service of deceased brother Thomas, his only heir. R521 **P:** Y **BLW:** Y **RG:** Y **MK:** N **PH:** unk **SS:** AR Vol 1 pg 168; K Vol 1 pg 189; SAR P-131590 **BS:** JLARC 2.

CHAPMAN, Thomas; b unk; d unk **RU:** Patriot, Gave material aid to the cause **CEM:** Fairfax City; GPS 38.84690, -77.31330; Main St & Page Ave; Fairfax City **GS:** N **SP:** No info **VI:** No further data **P:** N **BLW:** N **RG: N MK:** N **PH:** N **SS:** AL Ct Bk pg 9 **BS:** 61 vol III pg FX-153.

CHAPPELL, John Sr; b unk; d 1826 **RU:** Ensign/Patriot, Served in Amelia Co Militia. Took oath 26 Oct 1780. Gave material aid to cause **CEM:** Chappell; GPS unk; Fowlkes Bridge Rd, Paineville; Amelia **GS:** N **SP:** Elizabeth (-----) **VI:** Rev War BLW issued **P:** unk **BLW:** Y **RG:** N **MK:** unk **PH:** N **SS:** C pg 200; D pg 46; E pg 144 **BS:** 196.

CHARET, Gilbert; b unk; d 1781 **RU:** Soldier, Served in Gatinais Bn; d from Yorktown battle **CEM:** French Memorial; GPS 36.81944, -79.39933; Yorktown; York **GS:** U **SP:** No info **VI:** No further data **P:** unk **BLW:** unk **RG:** Y **MK:** unk **PH:** unk **SS:** J-Yorktown Historian; SAR P-131687 **BS:** JLARC 1, 74.

CHARLES, Jean; b unk; d 1781 **RU:** Seaman, Served on "Diademe" ; d from Yorktown battle **CEM:** French Memorial; GPS 36.81944, -79.39933; Yorktown; York **GS:** U **SP:** No info **VI:** No further data **P:** unk **BLW:** unk **RG:** Y **MK:** unk **PH:** unk **SS:** J-Yorktown Historian; SAR P-131706 **BS:** JLARC 1, 74.

CHARLES, Pierre L'EnFant; b 1755, d 1825 **RU:** Major, French unit not identified **CEM:** Arlington National; GPS 38.88377, -77.06535; Rt 110 Jefferson Davis Hwy; Arlington County **GS:** Y **SP:** No spousal data **VI:** No further data **P:** N **BLW:** N **RG:** Y **MK:** N **SS:** SAR P-131713 **BS:** 80 vol 1, pg 168.

CHASE, Jonathan; b unk; d 1781 **RU:** Soldier, Served fr MA; d as result of Yorktown battle **CEM:** Yorktown Victory Monument Tablet; GPS 38.28350, -78.54150; Yorktown; York **GS:** U **SP:** No info **VI:** No further data **P:** unk **BLW:** unk **RG:** N **MK:** unk **PH:** unk **SS:** J-Yorktown Historian **BS:** JLARC 74.

CHATILLON, Jacques; b unk; d 1781 **RU:** Soldier, Served in Agenois Bn; d from Yorktown battle **CEM:** French Memorial; GPS 36.81944, -79.39933; Yorktown; York **GS:** U **SP:** No info **VI:** No further data **P:** unk **BLW:** unk **RG:** Y **MK:** unk **PH:** unk **SS:** J-Yorktown Historian; SAR P-131998 **BS:** JLARC 1, 74.

CHATTE, Pierre; b unk; d 1781 **RU:** Seaman, Served on "Hector" ; d rom Yorktown battle **CEM:** French Memorial; GPS 36.81944, -79.39933; Yorktown; York **GS:** U **SP:** No info **VI:** No further data **P:** unk **BLW:** unk **RG:** Y **MK:** unk **PH:** unk **SS:** J-Yorktown Historian; SAR P-132000 **BS:** JLARC 1, 74.

CHAUNIET, Guillaume; b unk; d 1781 **RU:** Seaman, Served on "Hector"; d from Yorktown battle **CEM:** French Memorial; GPS 36.81944, -79.39933; Yorktown; York **GS:** U **SP:** No info **VI:** No further data **P:** unk **BLW:** unk **RG:** Y **MK:** unk **PH:** unk **SS:** J-Yorktown Historian; SAR P-132010 **BS:** JLARC 1 74.

CHAUVIN, Julien; b unk; d 1781 **RU:** Soldier, Served in Santogne Bn; d from Yorktown battle **CEM:** French Memorial; GPS 36.81944, -79.39933; Yorktown; York **GS:** U **SP:** No info **VI:** No further data **P:** unk **BLW:** unk **RG:** Y **MK:** unk **PH:** unk **SS:** J-Yorktown Historian; SAR P-132014 **BS:** JLARC 1, 74.

CHAVAILLARD, Thomas; b unk; d 1781 **RU:** Soldier, Served in Gatinais Bn; d from Yorktown battle **CEM:** French Memorial; GPS 36.81944, -79.39933; Yorktown; York **GS:** U **SP:** No info **VI:** No further data **P:** unk **BLW:** unk **RG:** Y **MK:** unk **PH:** unk **SS:** J-Yorktown Historian; SAR P-132116 **BS:** JLARC 1, 74.

RU=Rank/Unit	CEM=Cemetery	GS=Gravestone	SP=Spousal Information
VI=Other Veteran Info	P=Pension	BLW=Bounty/Land Warrant	RG=Registered Grave
MK=SAR/DAR Marker	PH=Photo	SS=Service Source	BS=Burial Source

81

CHEMITTE, Jean; b unk; d 1781 **RU:** Seaman, Served on "Ville de Paris"; d from Yorktown battle **CEM:** French Memorial; GPS 36.81944, -79.39933; Yorktown; York **GS:** U **SP:** No info **VI:** No further data **P:** unk **BLW:** unk **RG:** Y **MK:** unk **PH:** unk **SS:** J-Yorktown Historian; SAR P-132099 **BS:** JLARC 1, 74.

CHENEY (CHANEY), Abram/Abraham; b 1760; d 25 Dec 1848 **RU:** Private, Ent serv Pittsylvania Co **CEM:** Cheney Family; GPS unk; Nr Keeling; Pittsylvania **GS:** U **SP:** 1) Mary Cheatham 2) Mar (4 Apr 1811) Nancy Donalson **VI:** Widow pen Pittsylvania Co 1853 age 77, drew BLW 1855. She resided 1855 Laurel Grove. He pen Pittsylvania Co 1832, age 72; R 575 **P:** Y **BLW:** Y **RG:** N **MK:** unk **PH:** unk **SS:** J-DAR Hatcher **BS:** JLARC 2; 80 Vol 1, pg 171.SEE APPENDIX G

CHENEY (CHANEY), Jacob; b 1715, Anne Arundel Co, MD, d 21 Sep 1801 **RU:** Patriot, Signed an Oath of Allegiance, 1777, Pittsylvania Co **CEM:** Cheney Burial Grounds AKA Cheney-Farson-Reeves; GPS: Not determined; loc on Reeves Rd, Keeling; Pittsylvania **GS:** Unk **SP:** Sarah Midkiff (1727-1801) **VI:** Son of Charles Cheney (6 Jun 1673-1744) & Elizabeth (------) (____-7 Jun 1718) **P:** N **BLW:** N **RG:** Y **MK:** N **PH:** N **SS:** DAR A201202; SAR P-332803 cites Magazine of Va Gen vol 23; No 1, pg 4 **BS:** SAR PRS; 196.

CHERET, Andre; b unk; d 1781 **RU:** Soldier; Served in Royal Deaux Ponts Bn and died from Yorktown battle **CEM:** French Memorial; GPS 36.81944, -79.39933; Yorktown; York **GS:** U **SP:** No info **VI:** No further data **P:** unk **BLW:** unk **RG:** Y **MK:** unk **PH:** unk **SS:** J-Yorktown Historian; SAR P-132214 **BS:** JLARC 1, 74.

CHEROT, Jean; b unk; d 1781 **RU:** Seaman, Served on "Saint-Esprit" and died from Yorktown battle **CEM:** French Memorial; GPS 36.81944, -79.39933; Yorktown; York **GS:** U **SP:** No info **VI:** No further data **P:** unk **BLW:** unk **RG:** Y **MK:** Y **PH:** unk **SS:** J-Yorktown Historian; SAR P-132216 **BS:** JLARC 1, 74.

CHEVALIER, Joseph; b unk; d 1781 **RU:** Soldier, Served in Gatinais Bn; d from Yorktown battle **CEM:** French Memorial; GPS 36.81944, -79.39933; Yorktown; York **GS:** U **SP:** No info **VI:** No further data **P:** unk **BLW:** unk **RG:** Y **MK:** unk **PH:** unk **SS:** J-Yorktown Historian; SAR P-132314 **BS:** JLARC 1, 74.

CHEVALIER, Paul; b unk; d 1781 **RU:** Soldier, Served in Gatinais Bn; d from Yorktown battle **CEM:** French Memorial; GPS 36.81944, -79.39933; Yorktown; York **GS:** U **SP:** No info **VI:** No further data **P:** unk **BLW:** unk **RG:** Y **MK:** unk **PH:** unk **SS:** J-Yorktown Historian; SAR P-132315 **BS:** JLARC 1, 74.

CHEW, John; b 31 Mar 1749; d 22 May 1838 **RU:** Lieutenant, Ent serv 1776 in Capt Towles Co, Col Lees Legion of Calvary 1780 **CEM:** Ketoctin Baptist; GPS 39.15746, -77.74870; Ketoctin Church Rd, Purcellville; Loudoun **GS:** U **SP:** Margaret (-----) (15 Jun 1762-1 Jan 1837) **VI:** R533 **P:** Unk **BLW:** unk **RG:** N **MK:** SAR Plaque **PH:** unk **SS:** A pg 289 **BS:** JLARC 1, 2, 32; 25 pg 53.

CHEW, John Jr; b c 1753; d 12 Feb 1806 **RU:** Lieutenant/Patriot, Appt Lt 1780; wounded in left arm at Battle of Camden SC 16 Aug 1780; arm amputation. Serv in 2nd Regt under Col George Stubblefield. Provided services, drove cattle, and gave two cattle to cause **CEM:** Masonic Cemetery; GPS 38.30198, -77.46142; 900 Charles St; Fredericksburg City **GS:** Y **SP:** 1) Elizabeth Smith 2) Ann (-----) (c1754-7 Oct 1821) **VI:** Appointed 6 August 1787 clerk of Hustings Ct of Fredericksburg. Recd gratuity and 1/2 pay pension 29 Nov 1781 **P:** Y **BLW:** unk **RG:** Y **MK:** Y SAR plaque **PH:** unk **SS:** J-NSSAR 2000 Reg; BX pg 146; SAR P-132331 **BS:** JLARC 76.

CHEW, Robert Beverly; b 1754; d 30 Dec 1791 **RU:** Lt/Patriot, Served in VA state line. Joined Marines Apr 1776 under Capt Gabriel Jones then transferred to land forces. Served as Lt of Inf in 1777. Was Ct Justice 1777 **CEM:** Masonic Cemetery; GPS 38.30198, -77.46142; 900 Charles St; Fredericksburg City **GS:** Y **SP:** No info **VI:** No further data **P:** unk **BLW:** unk **RG:** Y **MK:** Plaque **PH:** unk **SS:** AL; D pg 869; SAR P-132335 **BS:** 04; 11 pg 30.

CHEW, Rodger; b unk; d 18 Mar 1811 **RU:** Patriot, Furnished equipment & supplies, authorized claims in Fairfax Co VA **CEM:** Old Christ Church Episcopal; GPS 38.80625, -77.04718; 118 N Washington St; Alexandria City **GS:** Y **SP:** No info **VI:** No further data **P:** N **BLW:** N **RG:** N **MK:** N **PH:** unk **SS:** AK; AL Ct bk lt pg 13 **BS:** 04; 20 pg 136; 196.

CHEWNING, Samuel; b 21 Jan 1723, Christ Church Parish, Middlesex Co; d Bef 11 Mar 1816 **RU:** Patriot, Paid personal property taxes (considered Rev War supply Tax), 1783 Caroline Co; Gave

RU=Rank/Unit	CEM=Cemetery	GS=Gravestone	SP=Spousal Information
VI=Other Veteran Info	P=Pension	BLW=Bounty/Land Warrant	RG=Registered Grave
MK=SAR/DAR Marker	PH=Photo	SS=Service Source	BS=Burial Source

material aid to cause **CEM:** Samuel Chewning Estate; GPS unk; See tax map for location; Caroline **GS:** U **SP:** Jennett Nancy Garrett **VI:** No further data **P:** N **BLW:** N **RG:** Y **MK:** unk **PH:** unk **SS:** DAR A021485; AL Ct Bk II pg 6; SAR P-132340 **BS:** 80 vol 1 pg 172.

CHICHESTER, Richard "Hard"; b 1736 Lancaster Co; d 22 Aug 1796 **RU:** Lt Colonel/Patriot, Provided beef, wheat, and pasturage; Performed civil service as Commissioner of Specific Tax; Fairfax Co to provide food and shelter for Army of Gen Lafayatee **CEM:** Mt Air; GPS 38.73340, -77.17533; Newington Rd, Newington; Fairfax **GS:** Y **SP:** 1) Mar (9 Jun 1759, bond in Lancaster Co) Ann Gordon (1743-20 Apr 1766) d/o Col James (1714-1768) & Millicent (Conway) (1727-1747) Gordon; 2) Mar (c1766 Fairfax Co) Sara McCarty (1729-1826 Mt Air, Fairfax Co) d/o Daniel (____-1792) and Sinah (Ball) (1728-1798) McCarty **VI:** Son of Richard Chichester (d 1743) & Ellen Ball (d 1759) her first husband. Justice of Fairfax Co 1776-c1788; Commissioner of the Specific Tax in Fairfax Co 1780-1782. Nicknamed "Hard" by his slaves whom he apparently treated cruelly, When he d, the slaves said he ran out fr under his bed in the form of a red rabbit. In the 1920s, a severe thunderstorm hit his tombstone. When the owner when to investigate, the first three letters of first name were gone, leaving only the name "hard." No stone fragments or footprints in the soggy ground were found to explain it. Styled "Col" when he gave 272 bushels of corn to Lafayette's troops as they passed through Colston on their way to Yorktown **P:** N **BLW:** N **RG:** Y **MK:** Y **SAR PH:** unk **SS:** D Vol II Fairfax; DAR A021491; SAR P-132348 **BS:** 04; 196.

CHILDRESS, Benjamin; b 2 Apr 1764; d 25 Mar 1852 **RU:** Private/Drummer, Ent serv 1780 age 16 in Capt John Christian; Capt James Pamplin Cos & others; and at Yorktown **CEM:** Mt Zion Methodist; GPS 37.80220, -78.59140; Rt 170 off Portress Rd Rt 627, Esmont; Albemarle **GS:** Y **SP:** Anne Key Johnson **VI:** Appl for pen 1850, R535. R1926 **P:** Y **BLW:** unk **RG:** Y **MK:** N **PH:** unk **SS:** AP pension rec; K Vol 1 pg 197; DAR A021516; SAR P-132476 **BS:** JLARC 121; 196.

CHILTON, John; b 29 Aug 1739; d 11 Sep 1777 **RU:** Captain, Served in Culpeper Minute Men Bn, Nov 1775. Promoted to Capt 29 Apr 1776, 3rd VA Regt Cont Line. D in Battle of Brandywine **CEM:** Rockspring; GPS unk; See property records for location; Fauquier **GS:** U **SP:** Mar (10 Apr 1768) Leticia Blackwell (3 Oct 1750-___) **VI:** SAR PRS indicates he is memorialized or buried in Birmingham-Lafayettee Cem in West Chester, PA **P:** unk **BLW:** Y **RG:** Y **MK:** unk **PH:** unk **SS:** C pg 502; E pg 148; SAR P-132544 **BS:** 80 vol 1, pg 173.; 196.

CHILTON (CHELTON), Richard Sr; b c1740; d 15 Aug 1821 **RU:** Patriot, Gave material aid to cause **CEM:** Chilton-Moorman; GPS unk; Off Rt 221; Lynchburg City **GS:** U **SP:** Judith Arms **VI:** No further data **P:** N **BLW:** N **RG:** Y **MK:** unk **PH:** unk **SS:** AL Ct Bk I pg 21, 27, 29 Culpeper Co; SAR P-132647 **BS:** JLARC 36.

CHIPLEY, William; b 1739; d 1811 **RU:** Captain/Patriot, Served in MD. Gave material aid to cause **CEM:** Opequon Presbyterian; GPS 39.13938, -78.19494; 217 Opequon Church Ln; Winchester City **GS:** Y **SP:** 1) Sarah Bill 2) Ann B Ponder **VI:** cCem plaque **P:** unk **BLW:** unk **RG:** Y **MK:** Y **SAR;** DAR plaque **PH:** unk **SS:** J-NSSAR 2000 Reg; D Frederick Co; DAR A021619; SAR P-132556 **BS:** JLARC 76, 04.

CHOWNING, William; b c1740; d unk **RU:** Captain, Appointed Lt in Lancaster Co 21 Aug 1777, and later Capt **CEM:** Chowning Ferry farm; GPS unk; Chownings Ferry Rd; Lancaster **GS:** U **SP:** Mar (28 Dec 1764 (bond) Lancaster Co) (Thomasine) **VI:** No further data **P:** unk **BLW:** unk **RG:** Y **MK:** N **PH:** unk **SS:** E pg 150; SAR P-132686 **BS:** 80 vol 1 pg 174.

CHRISMAN, George; b 1742 or 1745, Frederick Co; d 29 Aug 1816 **RU:** Captain, Commanded a co in Rockingham Co Militia after qualifying 26 Mar 1781 **CEM:** Cooks Creek Presbyterian; GPS 38.47472, -78.92997; 4222 Mt Clinton Pike, Harrisonburg; Harrisonburg City **GS:** Y **SP:** Hannah McDowell **VI:** D in Rockingham Co **P:** unk **BLW:** unk **RG:** Y **MK:** Y **SAR, PH:** unk **SS:** E pg 150; AB; AK; SAR P-132692 **BS:** AK, Sep 09; 04.

CHRISMAN, Henry, b 9 Mar 1748; d 1778 **RU:** Patriot, paid for wagon hire: Old Town Cemetery; GPS not determined; lots 76 & 77, Mulberry St, Town of Stephensburg **GS:** N but burial probably adjacent to wife's GS **SP:** Jane Earl Williams (20 Dec 1753-15 Dec 1834) **VI:** Son of Jacob Chrisman (1706-1778) & Magdalena Hite (1713-1771) **P:** N **BLW:** N **RG:** N **MK:** N **PH:** N **SS:** G pg 596 **BS:** 196.

RU=Rank/Unit	CEM=Cemetery	GS=Gravestone	SP=Spousal Information
VI=Other Veteran Info	P=Pension	BLW=Bounty/Land Warrant	RG=Registered Grave
MK=SAR/DAR Marker	PH=Photo	SS=Service Source	BS=Burial Source

83

CHRISTIAN, James; b 1757; d 1825 **RU:** Corporal, Served in 6th VA Regt; also served 2d Cont line **CEM:** Soldier's Rest; GPS unk; Blanks Crossroads; Charles City Co **GS:** U **SP:** No info **VI:** No further data **P:** unk **BLW:** unk **RG:** N **MK:** N **PH:** unk **SS:** E pg 150; AP roll 6th VA R; CU **BS:** 126 Christian.

CHRISTIAN, Joseph; b 04 Sep 1757 New Kent Co; d 10 Apr 1825 **RU:** Lieutenant, Serv in Charles City Militia; and VA Cont Line **CEM:** Soldier's Rest; GPS unk; Blanks Crossroads; Charles City Co **GS:** U **SP:** Mar (1783) Elizabeth Ashfield Graves (Jul 1761-1821) **VI:** Also known as "Fightin' Joe Christian." BLW recd by heirs #8087SS **P:** unk **BLW:** Y **RG:** Y **MK:** unk **PH:** unk **SS:** DAR A021747; G pg 767; BY pg 285; CZ pg 95; SAR P-132727 **BS:** JLARC 110.

CHRISTIAN (CHRISTAIN), John; b unk; d 1822 **RU:** Soldier/Patriot, Specific serv Lib VA, War files, vol 4, pg 126. Provided wagonage for 32 days and other items to cause **CEM:** Bethel Presbyterian; GPS 38.04257, -79.17283; 563 Bethel Green Rd, Middlebrook; Augusta **GS:** N **SP:** Rachel Brownlee **VI:** No further data **P:** unk **BLW:** unk **RG:** Y **MK:** unk **PH:** N **SS:** D pg 45 Augusta Co; SAR P-132717 **BS:** JLARC 62.

CHRISTOL, Jacques; b unk; d 1781 **RU:** Soldier, Served in Auxonne Bn and died from Yorktown battle **CEM:** French Memorial; GPS 36.81944, -79.39933; Yorktown; York **GS:** U **SP:** No info **VI:** No further data **P:** unk **BLW:** unk **RG:** Y **MK:** unk **PH:** unk **SS:** J-Yorktown Historian; SAR P-132786 **BS:** JLARC 1, 74.

CHRYSTIE, Thomas; b 1753, Edinburgh, Scotland; d 22 Feb 1812 **RU:** Surgeon, Served in Navy and Army **CEM:** Studley; GPS 37.40100, -77.17270; Studley Farm Rd, under tree in front yard of Mr. J.A. Francieni, Jr. residence (as of 1978); Hanover **GS:** U **SP:** No info **VI:** BLW issued 19 Dec 1793, R540 & 1812 **P:** unk **BLW:** Y **RG:** N **MK:** unk **PH:** unk **SS:** K Vol 1 pg 200; CU **BS:** JLARC 71.

CHUMARD, Thomas; b unk; d 1781 **RU:** Soldier, Served fr NJ, and died as result of Yorktown battle **CEM:** Yorktown Victory Monument Tablet; GPS 38.28350, -78.54150; Yorktown; York **GS:** U **SP:** No info **VI:** No further data **P:** unk **BLW:** unk **RG:** Y **MK:** unk **PH:** unk **SS:** J-Yorktown Historian; SAR P-132827 **BS:** JLARC 74.

CHUNN, John Thomas; b 1749; d 8 Apr 1804 **RU:** Major, Commanded a Co in Fauquier Co Militia **CEM:** Chunn Family; GPS unk; Behind Mt Independence on Rt 17, north of Delaplane; Fauquier **GS:** U **SP:** Martha (-----) (22 May 1748-28 Mar 1831) **VI:** No further data **P:** unk **BLW:** unk **RG:** Y **MK:** unk **PH:** unk **SS:** CZ pg 96; SAR P-132830 **BS:** JLARC 16.

CIRCLE (CIRKLE), Peter; b 1741, Montgomery Co, PA; d Sep 1818 **RU:** Private, Served in Dunmore Co Militia, 1776 **CEM:** Locust Bottom; GPS 37.74148, -79.81456; Jct Rts 633 & 696; Pittsylvania **GS:** U **SP:** Fanny Meyer (1750-1818) **VI:** No further data **P:** unk **BLW:** unk **RG:** Y **MK:** Y **PH:** unk **SS:** H source AW; SAR P-133075 **BS:** 04, Jul 06.

CLAIBORNE, Augustine; b 1721, King William Co; d 3 May 1787 **RU:** Col/Patriot, Was Deputy Clerk of Ct and member of Committee of Safety. Gave material aid to cause **CEM:** Claiborne Family; GPS unk; See property Records for home place; Sussex **GS:** U **SP:** Mar (c1742 Petersburg) Mary Herbert (25 Aug 1728-14 Mar 1799) **VI:** No further data **P:** unk **BLW:** unk **RG:** Y **MK:** unk **PH:** unk **SS:** D Vol 3 pg 893; CZ pg 96; SAR P-133135 **BS:** JLARC 2, 76.

CLAIBORNE, Thomas; b 1 Feb 1749; d 1812 **RU:** Captain, Co Commander in Brunswick Co Militia. Served as Col & Commander of same **CEM:** Claiborne Family; GPS unk; Nr jct Rts 713 & 715, Lawrenceville; Brunswick **GS:** N **SP:** No info **VI:** US Congressman 1793-1799, 1801-1805. VA House of Delegates 1783-1788. Brunswick Co Sheriff 1789-1792. State Sen 1790-1792 **P:** unk **BLW:** unk **RG:** unk **MK:** N **PH:** N **SS:** G pg 74 **BS:** 196.

CLAIBORNE, Thomas; b 1740, King William Co; d aft 1783 **RU:** Patriot, Member Norfolk Committee of Safety 1755 and Messenger 3rd VA Convention Jul 1775. Supported cause by paying supply tax included in his personal property tax in 1783 in Essex Co **CEM:** Sweet Hall; GPS: 37.57004, -76.90371; Rt 634 (Sweethall Rd), nr Pamunkey River; King William **GS:** Unk **SP:** Mar 13 Apr 1759, Euphan Sweeny **VI:** Son of Nathaniel Claiborne (1716-1756) and Jane Cole (1720-____). Member House of Burgess. 1768-1769. **P:** N **BLW:** N **RG:** Y **MK:** N **PH:** N **SS:** DV image 03.pdf, Essex Co; DAR A022043; SAR P-133139 **BS:** 196

RU=Rank/Unit	CEM=Cemetery	GS=Gravestone	SP=Spousal Information
VI=Other Veteran Info	P=Pension	BLW=Bounty/Land Warrant	RG=Registered Grave
MK=SAR/DAR Marker	PH=Photo	SS=Service Source	BS=Burial Source

CLAIBORNE, William; b 22 Jul 1743; d 29 Sep 1809 **RU**: Private/Patriot, Specific Serv Lib VA, Auditors Acct, XXV, pg 35. Gave material aid to cause in Sussex, Hanover, New Kent Cos .**CEM**: Claiborne Family; GPS unk; Sweet Hall, Rocky Mount; King William **GS**: U **SP**: Mary Leigh (1750, King William Co-11 Apr 1782, Chesterfield, Co) d/o Ferdinand & Mary (Cole) Leigh **VI**: Also buried or memorialised St John's Episcopal; GPS 37.53183, -77.41958; 2401 E Broad St; Richmond City **P**: unk **BLW**: unk **RG**: Y **MK**: unk **PH**: unk **SS**: AR Vol 1 pg 176; SAR P-133142 **BS**: JLARC 2.

CLAPHAM, Josias; b unk; d 1818 **RU**: Colonel, Served 1777, Loudoun Co Militia; Commissary Officer, Prince William Co Battalion 1775-76 **CEM**: St James Episcopal, Old Cemetery; GPS 39.11555, -77.56250; Church St NE, Leesburg; Loudoun **GS**: Y **SP**: No info **VI**: Rev of P.G. Church. D in Lovettsville, Loudoun Co. Note: the service identified by DAR is likely his father, thus more research needed **P**: unk **BLW**: unk **RG**: N **MK**: N **PH**: unk **SS**: E pg 152; AK **BS**: 25 pg 54, 04.

CLAPP, Earl B; b 1741; d 1837 **RU**: Captain, Specific serv not given in SAR registry **CEM**: Sinking Springs; GPS 36.71030, -81.98170; 136 E Main St, Abingdon; Washington **GS**: U **SP**: No info **VI**: No further data **P**: unk **BLW**: unk **RG**: Y **MK**: unk **PH**: unk **SS**: AR Vol 1 pg 177; DD; SAR P-133205 **BS**: JLARC 2; AR vol 1 pg 177.

CLARK, James; b 1700, King & Queen Co; d 1778 **RU**: Patriot; Gave material aid to cause, Gloucester Co **CEM**: First United Baptist Church; GPS 37.37133, -76.53449; 6188 George Washington Mem Hwy Rt 17; Gloucester **GS**: U **SP**: Mar (1772) Elizabeth Summers **VI**: Son of John (1665-1759) & Elizabeth Ann (Lumpkin) (1667-___) Clark. D in Augusta Co **P**: N **BLW**: N **RG**: N **MK**: unk **PH**: unk **SS**: AL Ct Ck ps ii, 16 **BS**: 196.

CLARK, James; b unk; d 1808 **RU**: Private, Served in Capt George Rice Co, 30 Nov 1778, Col Dan Morgan's 11th & 15th VA Regt; served in Capt John Wilson's Co, Augusta Co Militia **CEM**: Trinity Episcopal; GPS 38.14917, -79.07521; 214 Beverley St; Staunton City **GS**: U **SP**: No info **VI**: No further data **P**: unk **BLW**: Y **RG**: N **MK**: unk **PH**: unk **SS**: A pg 265; CU **BS**: JLARC 2, 8; 196.

CLARK, James; b 1754, Lochgilphead, Scotland; d Dec 1818 **RU**: Sergeant, Served in VA State Regt, 6th Cont Line **CEM**: Glade Spring Presbyterian; GPS 36.76720, -81.78720; 33234 Lee Hwy, Glade Spring; Washington **GS**: U **SP**: Isabella Mary Breckenridge (1764 Scotland-09 Sep 1848) **VI**: No further data **P**: unk **BLW**: unk **RG**: Y **MK**: unk **PH**: unk **SS**: E pg 154; SAR P-133672 **BS**: 196.

CLARK, John; b 26 Dec 1745; d 2 Apr 1819 **RU**: Captain, Commanded Co in Campbell Co **CEM**: Clark Family; GPS 37.29563, -79.21086; Cnr Lawyer's Rd and Missionary Manor; Campbell **GS**: U **SP**: Mar (21 Feb 1767 Albemarle Co) Mary Moore (1 Jan 1748-5 Nov 1830) d/o (-----) & Mary Bullock (1720-1814) **VI**: Son of Micaja & Judith (Adams) Clark; Justice of Campbell Co. One of the original Trustees of the City of Lynchburg City. Member of VA House of Delegates 1785-93). Sheriff of Campbell Co (1818 until death 2 Apr 1819) **P**: unk **BLW**: unk **RG**: N **MK**: unk **PH**: unk **SS**: CD **BS**: 196.

CLARK, John; b 1761; d May 1827 **RU**: Second Lieutenant, Served in Prince Edward Co Militia **CEM**: Clark Family; GPS unk; Bannister Lodge; Halifax **GS**: U **SP**: 1) Marie Sims 2) Pricilla Sims **VI**: No further data **P**: unk **BLW**: unk **RG**: Y **MK**: unk **PH**: unk **SS**: J- DAR Hatcher; G pg 300, 301, 308, 309; SAR P-133799 **BS**: JLARC 2; AR Vol I, pg 180.

CLARK, John Shadrock (Shadrick, Shadrach); b 1759; d 1810 **RU**: Private/Patriot; Gave to cause **CEM**: Unidentified; GPS unk; See prop rec for location; Lunenburg **GS**: U **SP**: Mar (9 Jul 1789 Lunenburg) Rebecca Crymes d/o Thomas & Mary (-----) Crymes **VI**: Son of Ellison (c1695 Henrico Co-1766 Chesterfield Co) and Ann (Blanchecil) (c1762-bef 4 Jan 1771, Chesterfield Co) Clark. Son recd his pen 1841 **P**: Y **BLW**: unk **RG**: Y **MK**: unk **PH**: unk **SS**: J- DAR Hatcher; D Mecklenburg Co; SAR P-133813 **BS**: JLARC 2.

CLARK, Peter; b c1761; d Sep 1821 **RU**: Private?, Served in 10th Cont Line **CEM**: Glade Spring Presbyterian; GPS 36.76720, -81.78720; 33234 Lee Hwy, Glade Spring; Washington **GS**: Y **SP**: Mary Galbreath (1758-13 Apr 1856) **VI**: No further data **P**: N **BLW**: N **RG**: N **MK**: N **PH**: unk **SS**: E pg 153; Cl Serv record **BS**: 78 pg 177; 196.

RU=Rank/Unit	CEM=Cemetery	GS=Gravestone	SP=Spousal Information
VI=Other Veteran Info	P=Pension	BLW=Bounty/Land Warrant	RG=Registered Grave
MK=SAR/DAR Marker	PH=Photo	SS=Service Source	BS=Burial Source

CLARK, Thomas; b 1740; d 1792 **RU**: Patriot, Gave material aid to the cause **CEM**: Clark Plantation; GPS unk; Strawberry Br; Halifax **GS**: Y **SP**: No info **VI**: No further data **P**: N **BLW**: N **RG**: Y **MK**: N **PH**: unk **SS**: AL Ct Bk pg 35; SAR P-134152 **BS**: 80 vol 1 pg 183.

CLARK, Thomas; b unk; d 15 Apr 1778 **RU**: Private Capt Arrell's Co, 3rd VA Regt, Cont Line; died fr wounds fr battle at Brandywine **CEM**:Rev War Court House Plaque;GPS;not determined; 4110 Chain Bridge Rd; Fairfax **GS**: Memorialized on plaque 2017 by Geo Washington Chapter, VASSAR **SP** No info **VI**: Died in service **P**: N **BLW**: N **RG**: N **MK**: N **PH**: N **SS**; AP Fold3 serv rec; EP sources: **BS**: None.

CLARK, William; b 3 Jan 1759; d 2 Apr 1827 **RU**: Colonel, In 1781 led Co fr Halifax Co to Point of Fork on James River to a state arsenal and military stores. Commanded a reconnoitering party at Battle of Guilford CH Remained in service until discharged by Gen Lafayette **CEM**: Clark Family; GPS 36.84823, -79.32198; Pineville nr Chatham; Pittsylvania **GS**: Y **SP**: Jane Hamilton White (20 May 1762-23 Apr 1839) d/o Jeremiah & Esther (Herdon) White **VI**: No further data **P**: unk **BLW**: unk **RG**: unk **MK**: unk **PH**: unk **SS**: AR Vol 1 pg 183; SAR P-134221, SAR P-134223 **BS**: 174, JLARC 2.

CLARKE, Christopher; b 05 Apr 1763, Louisa Co; d Feb 1851 **RU**: Private/Patriot, Military service not identified. Gave material aid to cause **CEM**: Tompkins Family(Burk homestead); GPS unk; Shipman Rt 56, at Burk Homestead; Nelson **GS**: U **SP**: Elizabeth Hope (22 Mar 1778-3 Apr 1873) **VI**: D, bur in Fluvanna Co, however memorial grave stone is in cemetery listed **P**: unk **BLW**: unk **RG**: Y **MK**: unk **PH**: unk **SS**: B; D Albemarle Co; SAR P-134274 **BS**: 196.

CLARKE, Christopher; b unk; d unk **RU**: unk, Service not identified in SAR registry **CEM**: Clarke Family; GPS unk; Nr Woodbridge PO, Woodbridge; Prince William **GS**: U **SP**: No info **VI**: No further data **P**: unk **BLW**: unk **RG**: Y **MK**: unk **PH**: unk **SS**: AR Vol 1 pg 183; SAR P-134272 **BS**: JLARC 2.

CLARKE, James; b unk; d 13 Jan 1808 **RU**: Private, Served in Capt McCutchen's Co Augusta Co VA **CEM**: Trinity Episcopal; GPS 38.14917, -79.07521; 214 Beverley St; Staunton City **GS**: U **SP**: No info **VI**: No further data **P**: unk **BLW**: unk **RG**: Y **MK**: N **PH**: unk **SS**: E pg 154; AK; SAR P-334446 **BS**: 36 pg 154.

CLARKE, John; b 24 Apr 1756; d 17 May 1844 **RU**: Major/Patriot; Promoted to Major from Captain in March 1781 in Prince Edward County. Provided material aid to cause in Amelia County during war period **CEM**: Keswick Plantation; GPS-not determined; nr Chesterfield-Powhatan line on Rt 711 at jct with Derby Ridge Way; Powhatan **GS**: Yes (Note birth date on obelisk states born 1766 which is not possible if promoted to Major in 1781, thus probably born 1756) **SP**: Marianne Sallee, d/of Abraham Sallee (31 October 1700-___) and Magdelaine Amonet **VI**: No further data **P**: N **BLW**: N **RG**: N **MK**: N **PH**: N **SS**: G pg 309; AL Ct Bk I, pg 20 & Certificate **BS**: 196.

CLARKE, William; b 28 Jan 1762; d 12 Sep 1846 **RU**: 1st Lt, Commissioned 28 Sep 1778 Cumberland Co Militia. Also in State Line under George Roger's Clark, Illinois Regt **CEM**: Clarke Family; GPS 37.24354, -77.44655; Ravensbourne Dr, Ettrick; Chesterfield **GS**: Y **SP**: Martha Rowlett (28 Dec 1761-14 Aug 1809) **VI**: Recd BLW 2666 acres 3 Mar 1784 **P**: unk **BLW**: Y **RG**: Y **MK**: unk **PH**: unk **SS**: E pg 155; F pg 18; SAR P-134345 **BS**: 196. (**CLARKE**, William **See APPENDIX G**)

CLARKSON, James; b 1764; d 5 Mar 1836 **RU**: Private, Specific service listed in BLW application **CEM**: Clarkson-Meeks, aka Clarkson #2; GPS unk; 5 mi N of Massies Mill cross Tye River Bridge; Nelson **GS**: Y **SP**: Elizabeth Jacobs (1766-13 Jan 1854) d/o John & Sarah (Crawford) Jacobs **VI**: Authorized BLW, receipt unk **P**: unk **BLW**: Y **RG**: N **MK**: unk **PH**: unk **SS**: C pg 524 **BS**: 196.

CLAY, Charles Green; b 24 Dec 1745, Powhatan Co; d 8 Feb 1820 **RU**: Patriot; Supported cause by paying supply tax included in his personal property tax in 1783, Bedford Co **CEM**: Ivy Hill (AKA: Pettygrove); GPS: not determined; Betw 6th & 7th fairways, Ivy Hill Golf Course; Bedford **GS**: Unk **SP**: Edith Landon Davies (17 Apr 1777, Albemarle Co-1838), d/o Henry Landon Davies and Ann Whiting Clayton **VI**: Son of Charles Clay (1716-1789) and Martha "Patsy" Green (1719-1793). A Reverend who served as priest at St Anne Parish Episcopal Church, Albemarle Co (1769-1784) **P**: N **BLW**: N **RG**: N **MK**: N **PH**: N **SS**: DAR A022835; DV image 06.pdf, Bedford Co **BS**: 196.

CLAY, Eleazer; b 4 Aug 1744, Powhatan Co; d 2 May 1836 **RU**: Patriot, Gave material aid to cause **CEM**: Clay Family; GPS unk; At his homeplace, see property records for directions; Chesterfield **GS**: U **SP**: 1) Jane Apperson (1751-1787) 2) Mar (7 Jan 1789) Elizabeth Swepson Whitehead (____-1825)

RU=Rank/Unit	CEM=Cemetery	GS=Gravestone	SP=Spousal Information
VI=Other Veteran Info	P=Pension	BLW=Bounty/Land Warrant	RG=Registered Grave
MK=SAR/DAR Marker	PH=Photo	SS=Service Source	BS=Burial Source

3) Mar (12 Feb 1826) Phoebe Newby **VI:** Was in Colonial War Mar 1758, Became Reverend 1771 **P:** N **BLW:** N **RG:** Y **MK:** unk **PH:** unk **SS:** AL Ct Bk pg 14 Chesterfield Co; SAR P-329241 **BS:** 196.

CLAY, Matthew; b 25 Mar 1754; d 27 May 1815 **RU:** Captain/Quartermaster, Served in 9th VA Regt, 1776. Transferred to 1st VA Regt 1778 and to 5th VA Regt 1781 **CEM:** Clay Family; GPS unk; Danville; Danville City **GS:** U **SP:** Ann (-----) **VI:** Son of Charles (1716-1789) & Martha "Patsy" (Green) (1719-1798) Clay. VA House of Delegates 1790-94. Elected to Congress as Democratic-Republican, served 8 terms fr 1797-1813 **P:** unk **BLW:** Y **RG:** Y **MK:** unk **PH:** unk **SS:** C pg 331; SAR P-134428 **BS:** 196.

CLAY, Mitchell; b 1735; d 20 Jun 1811 **RU:** Private, served in Capt Michael Woods and George Parris Co Montgomery Co Militia Specific Serv Lib VA, War files, 23, 1778 **CEM:** Birchlawn Burial Park; GPS 39.32610, -80.71080; Wenonah Ave Rt 460, Pearisburg; Giles **GS:** U **SP:** Phoebe Belcher **VI:** No further data **P:** unk **BLW:** unk **RG:** Y **MK:** unk **PH:** unk **SS:** CZ pg 99; BW pg 35, 57; DAR A022860; SAR P-134431 **BS:** JLARC 3, 26.

CLAY, William M Sr; b 1739; d 1811 **RU:** Private, Specific Serv Lib VA, Auditors Acct, XVIII, pg 651 **CEM:** Private Grave; GPS unk; Nr Celanese, Pearisburg; Giles **GS:** U **SP:** No info **VI:** No further data **P:** unk **BLW:** unk **RG:** Y **MK:** unk **PH:** unk **SS:** J- DAR Hatcher; CZ pg 99; SAR P-134449 **BS:** JLARC 2.

CLAYTON, John; b 4 Jun 1756, St James Parish, Eng; d 30 Oct 1825 **RU:** Captain, promoted to Lt Feb 1776, to Capt 24 Apr 1781, Bedford County Militia **CEM:** Rocky Spring Presbyterian Church; GPS 38.179028, -79.404671; 567 Marble Valley Rd (Rt 600), Deerfield; Augusta **GS:** Y **SP:** Mar 2 Jan 1786, Margaret Rice (____ Eng-30 Nov 1823) **VI:** No further data **P:** N **BLW:** N **RG:** N **MK:** N **PH:** N **SS:** DAR A022917; AZ pg 186 **BS:** 196.

CLAYTON, Phillip; b 1702, Essex Co; d 1785 **RU:** Patriot, Let the Culpeper Minutemen Bn use his property for encampment 1775 **CEM:** Catalpa Plantation; GPS unk; His homeplace on mountain nr town see property records for directions; Culpeper **GS:** Y **SP:** Anne Coleman (1703-1785) **VI:** Rank of major obtained in Colonial War in Orange Co. Member Soc of Cincinnati; justice in Orange Co; Vestryman of St Mark's Parish 1741 **P:** N **BLW:** N **RG:** N **MK:** unk **PH:** unk **SS:** DAR A022929; DD **BS:** 196.

CLEACH, Jean; b unk; d 1781 **RU:** Seaman, Served on "Auguste"; d from Yorktown battle **CEM:** French Memorial; GPS 36.81944, -79.39933; Yorktown; York **GS:** U **SP:** No info **VI:** No further data **P:** unk **BLW:** unk **RG:** Y **MK:** unk **PH:** unk **SS:** J-Yorktown Historian; SAR P-134507 **BS:** JLARC 1, 74.

CLEM (KLEIM), John David; b 21 Mar 1754; d 27 May 1824 **RU:** Private, Capt Henry Fister's Co, Lt Col Nicholas Hansgger"s (SP?) Regt, Col George Stricker"s Cont Troops (Payroll fr 1 Dec 1776 to 1 Mar 1777) **CEM:** Dry Run Church; GPS 38.857689, -78.400195; 8398 Fort Valley Rd; Seven Fountains Shenandoah **GS:** N **SP:** Elizabeth Sibert (1760-1823) **VI:** Nothing further **P:** N **BLW:** N **RG:** N **MK:** N **SS:** AP Fold s Payroll **BS:** 196.

CLEMENT, Adam Sr; b 22 Apr 1738, Amelia Co; d 11 Oct 1811 **RU:** Captain/Patriot, Commanded company in Bedford Militia. Provided provisions to cause **CEM:** Oakdale; GPS 37.17076, -79.04768; Mollies Creek Rd, Gladys; Campbell **GS:** N **SP:** Agnes Johnson **VI:** Son of Benjamin Clement (1705-1780) & Susannah Hill (1710-1782) **P:** unk **BLW:** unk **RG:** Y **MK:** N **PH:** N **SS:** D vol I, pg 111; E pg 157; AL Ct Bk 6; DAR A022961; SAR P-134632 **BS:** JLARC 36; 196.

CLEMENT(S), Benjamin, Sr; b c1700, King William Co; d Aft1781 **RU:** Patriot, Made gun powder for Army and made Oath of Alligence, 1777 **CEM:** Clement Hill; GPS 37,100580, -79.300170; Rt 29 N, btw Chatham & Hurt; Pittsylvania **GS:** Y **SP:** Sussanna Hill (Nov 1710-Nov 1788), d/o Col Issac Hill **VI:** Son of William Clement, King William Co **P:** N **BLW:** N **RG:** Y **MK:** N **PH:** unk **SS:** AL Ct Bk, pg 35; DAR A022963; SAR P-134590 **BS:** SAR PRS; 04, 196.

CLEMENTS, William; b unk probably King William Co, d 22 Nov 1791 **RU:** Sergeant, in Capt Taylor's Co, 2d VA Regt and 2d Cont Line, commanded by Lt Col Christian Ferber (SP) on payroll of Sep 1778, indicating he was a omitted August 1778 as casualty **CEM:** Clements family; GPS not determined; loc off Rt 60 on Mount Horeb Rd for 1.4 mi, Willow; Amherst **GS:** N **SP:** Isabella Hilliard (c1749, New Kent Co-1832), d/o Jonathon Hilliard **VI:** Was eligible for BLW **P:** N **BLW:** Unk **RG:** N **MK:** N **PH:** N **SS:** E pg 158; Fold 3 payroll **BS:** 196.

RU=Rank/Unit	CEM=Cemetery	GS=Gravestone	SP=Spousal Information
VI=Other Veteran Info	P=Pension	BLW=Bounty/Land Warrant	RG=Registered Grave
MK=SAR/DAR Marker	PH=Photo	SS=Service Source	BS=Burial Source

87

CLEMENTS, William Right (Wright); b 1733; d 1803 **RU**: Patriot; Gave material aid to cause, King William Co **CEM**: Clements family; GPS not determined; loc off Rt 60 on Mount Horeb Rd for 1.4 mi, Willow; Amherst **GS**: N **SP**: Mary (-----) **VI**: No further data **P**: N **BLW**: N **RG**: Y **MK**: N **PH**: N **SS**: Al Ct Bk, pg 29, King William Co and bk ii, pg 4 Gloucester Co; SAR P-134665 **BS**: 196.

CLOARET, Jean; b unk; d 1781 **RU**: Soldier, Served in Beaujolais Bn; d from Yorktown battle **CEM**: French Memorial; GPS unk; Yorktown; York **GS**: U **SP**: No info **VI**: No further data **P**: unk **BLW**: unk **RG**: Y **MK**: unk **PH**: unk **SS**: J-Yorktown Historian; SAR P-134967 **BS**: JLARC 1, 74.

CLOPTON, John; b 7 Feb 1756, New Kent Co; d 11 Sep 1816 **RU**: 1st Lt;, was an artillary officer in Col Proctor's Artillary Regt **CEM**: St Peter's Episcopal; GPS 37.3224, -77.0324; 8400 St Peters Ln, Quinton; New Kent **GS**: U **SP**: Sarah Bacon d/o Edmund & Elizabeth (Edloe) Bacon **VI**: Son of William & Elizabeth (Ford) Cloyton. D in "Roslin" New Kent Co. **P**: unk **BLW**: unk **RG**: Y **MK**: U **PH**: unk **SS**: E pg 159; AK; DAR A023229; SAR P-134989 **BS**: 04, May 06; 80 vol 1, pg 187; 196.

CLOPTON, Robert; b 20 Feb 1755, New Kent Cod; d 22 Jan 1841 **RU**: Private, Specific Serv Lib VA, Auditors Acct, XVIII, pg 532, vol 2, pg 101 indicates he paid for military service **CEM**: Clopton Family; GPS unk; Slatesville Rd, N of jct US Rt 360; Pittsylvania **GS**: U **SP**: Mar (5 Jan 1781 Hanover Co) Frances Anderson (1765-1837) **VI**: No further data **P**: unk **BLW**: unk **RG**: N **MK**: N **PH**: unk **SS**: AK May 06; CZ pg 101; DAR A202990 **BS**: 04; May 06.

CLOPTON, William; b 2 Feb 1722, New Kent Co; d 3 Aug 1796 **RU**: Captain, Commanded a co in the New Kent Co Militia **CEM**: St Peter's Episcopal; GPS 37.3224, -77.0324; 8400; St Peters Ln, Quinton; New Kent **GS**: U **SP**: 1) Elizabeth Darroll Ford 20 Mar (5 Jan 1781 Hanover Co) Fanny Anderson **VI**: No further data **P**: unk **BLW**: unk **RG**: N **MK**: unk **PH**: unk **SS**: AK; E pg 159 **BS**: 04, May 06, 197.

CLORE. John Peter; b 1747, Madison Co; d Dec 1824 **RU**: Patriot listed in Culpeper Co Classes, 1781 a draft list for training before being activated; Gave material aid to cause **CEM**: Hebron Lutheran Church; GPS 38.4067612, -78.2480774 loc 899 Blankenbaker Rd (Rt 653): Madison **GS**: Unk **SP**: Mary Fray **VI**: Son of Johahn Georg Clore (1716-1751) & Anna Barbara Weaver (1730-1808) German surname originally "Klaar". **P**: N **BLW**: N **RG**: Y **MK**: N **PH**: N **SS**:D vol 1, pgs 270, 277; DJ pg 22 class #72; DAR A023235; SAR P-134993 **BS**: 196.

CLOUD, Daniel; b 8 Feb 1756; d 25 Feb 1815 **RU**: Private, Served in Capt Joseph Bowman's Co of Lower District Dunmore Co Militia and in 8th VA Regt, Cont Line, Capt Rich Campbell's Co 1776-1778, commanded by Col Abraham Bowman **CEM**: Prospect Hill; GPS 38.913303,- 78.198332; 200 W Prospect St, Front Royal; Warren **GS**: Y **SP**: Elizabeth Branson Hampton (28 Feb 1756-17 Sep 1829) **VI**:Son of Henry Cloud and Elizabeth (__). Orig buried in family cemetery at Willow Glen. Gravestone moved 1939 to above loc **P**: Y # VAS 3030 **BLW**: unk **RG**: Y **MK**: Y SAR granite **PH**: unk **SS**: AK; C pg 604;DAR A023277; SAR P135143 **BS**: 59, pg 66; 113; 197.

CLOUD, William; b 17 Sep 1750, Rowan Co, NC, d 8 Feb 1842 **RU**: Lt, first served 1776 under Col William Christian in expedition against Cherokee Indians; commissioned Lt in Henry Co company, was at Yorktown 1781 **CEM**: Penn Farm, GPS: unk; Chum area of Cana; Carroll **GS**: No **SP**: Mar Sep 1838, Grayson Co, Nancy Vaughan (1811-20 Feb 1898), recd pen commencing 3 Feb 1853 and BLW 9 Aug 1856, Also Elizabeth Morgan **VI**: Recd pen Act of 1832. County Justice, Grayson Co 1806-1810; surveyor of roads 1811 **P**: Both **BLW**: Widow **RG**: Y **MK**: N **PH**: N **SS**: K, vol 1, pg 214; AP Pen file; DAR A62390***; SAR P-330180 **BS**: 19.

CLOYD, David; b 1738; d 16 Aug 1789 **RU**: Captain/Patriot, Became capt in Rockbridge Co 8 Mar 1780. Gave material aid to cause **CEM**: High Bridge Presbyterian; GPS 37.62420, -79.58610; 67 High Bridge Rd, Natural Bridge; Rockbridge **GS**: U **SP**: Elizabeth Woods (1753 Albemarle Co-Nov 1796 Rockbridge Co) **VI**: No further data **P**: unk **BLW**: unk **RG**: Y **MK**: unk **PH**: unk **SS**: D Rockbridge Co; SAR P-135113 **BS**: JLARC 79; 196.

CLOYD, Joseph; b 20 Jun 1742; d 31 Aug 1833 **RU**: Major/Patriot, Served in Capt Montgomery Co Militia 1777, and as Maj in Col Preston's Regt in SC in 1781;Member of Committee of Safety, Fincastle Co, 1775-1776 **CEM**: Cloyd; GPS 37.16166, -80.70583; Rt 100 Cleyburne Blvd N of Dublin; Pulaski **GS**: U **SP**: Mary Gordon (1750-____) **VI**: Son of David & (-----) Cloyd. Came to Back Creek around 1772 and was fr the James River area of VA **P**: unk **BLW**: unk **RG**: Y **MK**: unk **PH**: unk **SS**: A pg 207; E pg 159-160; SAR P-135116 **BS**: 196, JLARC 92; 212.

RU=Rank/Unit	CEM=Cemetery	GS=Gravestone	SP=Spousal Information
VI=Other Veteran Info	P=Pension	BLW=Bounty/Land Warrant	RG=Registered Grave
MK=SAR/DAR Marker	PH=Photo	SS=Service Source	BS=Burial Source

COBB, William B, Jr; b1746, Albemarle, Stanley Co, NC; d 1796 **RU**: Private 4th VA Regt serving long enough to be eligible for BLW **CEM**: Unnamed Colonial Era Farm Memorial; GPS 37.529945,-76.627602; loc on Waste Mgt Memorial Hwy, nr jct with G W Memorial Hwy, Owl Trap:Gloucester **GS**: N **SP**: Martha Boone (1747, Birdsboro, Berks Co, PA-1818 Hawkins Co, TN) **VI**: Son of William Benjamin Cobb, Sr (1720, NC-Mar 1803, TN) & Beersheba Whitehead (1730-1793) **P**: Unk **BLW**: Unk **RG**: Y **MK**: N **PH**: Nk **SS**: C pg 231; AP serv Index card; SAR P-135227 **BS**: 196.

COBBS, Charles; b 1736; d Aft 13 Jan 1800 **RU**: Captain, Commanded a Co in Bedford Co Militia 28 Feb 1780 **CEM**: Cobbs Hall; GPS unk; nr Rt 643, Brookneal; Campbell **GS**: U **SP**: 1) 2) Ann Walton 2-probably) Mar (4 Dec 1783 Campbell Co (bond) Martha Bailey, d/o (-----) & Elizabeth (-----) Bailey **VI**: No further data **P**: unk **BLW**: unk **RG**: Y **MK**: N **PH**: unk **SS**: E pg 161; SAR P-135338 **BS**: JLARC 2, 36.

COBBS, Jesse; b unk; d unk **RU**: Seaman or Private, Served in VA state Navy and/or 5th Cont Line **CEM**: Cobbs Hall; GPS unk; nr Rt 643, Brookneal; Campbell **GS**: U **SP**: No info **VI**: Son of Charles Cobbs, Sr (1736-1798) & Ann Walton (1738-unk) **P**: unk **BLW**: unk **RG**: Y **MK**: N **PH**: unk **SS**: C pg 230; E pg 161 **BS**: SAR report; JLARC 36, 04; SAR P-135339 **BS**: 196.

COBBS, John L; b 27 Aug 1763; d 9 Sep 1851 **RU**: Private, Served in Capt James Cobbs, Col Greene's Regt of Militia in Halifax Co. Marched to Williamsburg and placed under Command of Capt Rogers, Col Washington's Regt. Later served at Battle of Guilford CH and at Yorktown, serving 3 yrs **CEM**: St Stevens Episcopal; GPS unk; Jct Rts 663 and 221; Bedford **GS**: U **SP**: No info **VI**: Pen recd 1835 **P**: Y **BLW**: unk **RG**: N **MK**: unk **PH**: unk **SS**: E pg 161; G pg 764; CI statement **BS**: 222, Vol 1, pg 215.

COBBS, John Sr; b 8 Oct 1759; d 6 Apr 1847 **RU**: 2nd Lt; Ent Serv Bedford Co 1779-80 (later Campbell Co) Bedford Co Militia. Served as 2nd Lt in Capt William Craddock's Co 22 Jun 1780 **CEM**: Cobbs Hall; GPS unk; nr Rt 643, Brookneal; Campbell **GS**: U **SP**: Sarah "Sallie" McCoy, b 20 Aug 1762, d 28 Jan 1830 **VI**: Son of Charles Cobb Sr. (1736-1798) & Ann Walton (1738-unk). Member of Baptist Denomination & in his own words "A sinner saved by grace." Sr. Pen 1833, Campbell Co, R588 **P**: Y **BLW**: unk **RG**: Y **MK**: N **PH**: unk **SS**: K Vol 1 pg 216; SAR P-135340 **BS**: JLARC 2, 36; 196.

COBBS, Robert; b 2 Mar 1754, Louisa Co; d 2 Aug 1829 **RU**: Captain, Served in Bedford Co Militia under Charles Lewis, 1779-1780 **CEM**: Cobbs Family; GPS unk; Plain Dealing, Naruna; Campbell **GS**: N **SP**: Mar (19 Nov 1783, Louisa Co) Ann Gizzage Poindexter (1762-1 Feb 1842) **VI**: Widow pen Campbell Co, age 79 in 1841 **P**: Y **BLW**: unk **RG**: Y **MK**: N **PH**: N **SS**: K Vol 1 pg 216; SAR P-135342 **BS**: JLARC 4, 36; 196.

COCHRAN, James; b 15 Feb 1756; d c1820 **RU**: Ensign, Served in Capt Moffet's Co, Augusta Co Militia **CEM**: Union Presbyterian; GPS 39.10916, -78.09497; Churchville; Augusta **GS**: N **SP**: Magdeline Moffett, d/o George Moffett; d 6 Dec 1792 **VI**: No further data **P**: unk **BLW**: unk **RG**: Y **MK**: N **PH**: N **SS**: E pg 161; SAR P-135457 **BS**: JLARC 62, 63.

COCHRAN, Samuel R; b unk; d 1847 **RU**: Sergeant, Served in 1st & 10th Cont lines **CEM**: Upperville Methodist; GPS unk; 11134 Delaplane Grade Rd, Upperville; Loudoun **GS**: Y **SP**: No info **VI**: No further data **P**: unk **BLW**: Y **RG**: N **MK**: N **PH**: unk **SS**: A Part II pg 204 **BS**: 25 pg 57; 04.

COCHRAN, William; b 1739; d 10 Oct 1826 **RU**: Sergeant, Specific Serv Lib VA, war files, vol 4, pg 136 **CEM**: Glebe Burying Ground; GPS 38.10940, -79.22190; Glebe School Rd Rt 876, Swoopes; Augusta **GS**: Y **SP**: 1) Mary Logan, 2) Elizabeth Fulton **VI**: No further data **P**: unk **BLW**: Y **RG**: Y **MK**: N **PH**: unk **SS**: E pg 161; CU; CZ 103; SAR P-135508 **BS**: JLARC 8; 210 pg 395.

COCKBURN, Martin; b c1740; d unk **RU**: Patriot, Paid for collecting goods for use of the country **CEM**: Cockburn Family; GPS unk; "Springfield," Gunston Rd Rt 242, W of Gunston Hall, Mason Neck; Fairfax **GS**: N **SP**: Mar c1763 to Anne Bronaugh **VI**: GS said to have been moved to Pohick Church **P**: N **BLW**: N **RG**: N **MK**: N **PH**: N **SS**: G pg 549 **BS**: 61 vol V, pg MN-16.

COCKE, David; b c1748; d 28 Feb 1828 **RU**: Patriot, Rendered aid as a patriot in the defense of Ft Blackmore, 1777 **CEM**: Cocke Family; GPS unk; Ft Blackmore; Scott **GS**: Y **SP**: Jemima Leach **VI**: No further data **P**: unk **BLW**: unk **RG**: Y **MK**: N **PH**: unk **SS**: O; SAR P-135534 **BS**: 04.

COCKE, John Hartwell; b 25 Nov 1749; d 9 Feb 1791 **RU**: Captain, Commanded co in Surry Co Militia **CEM**: Cocke Family; GPS unk; Mt Pleasant; Surry **GS**: U **SP**: Mar (28 Nov 1773) Elizabeth Kennon (13

RU=Rank/Unit	CEM=Cemetery	GS=Gravestone	SP=Spousal Information
VI=Other Veteran Info	P=Pension	BLW=Bounty/Land Warrant	RG=Registered Grave
MK=SAR/DAR Marker	PH=Photo	SS=Service Source	BS=Burial Source

Jul 1755-10 Jul 1791) **VI**: No further data **P**: unk **BLW**: unk **RG**: Y **MK**: unk **PH**: unk **SS**: DAR A027047; G pg 456; SAR P-135541 **BS**: 224 fr Wm & Mary College Qrtly, vol 15, #2 pg 87.

COCQ, Antoine; b unk; d 1781 **RU**: Soldier, Served in Agenois Bn; d from Yorktown battle **CEM**: French Memorial; GPS 36.81944, -79.39933; Yorktown; York **GS**: U **SP**: No info **VI**: No further data **P**: unk **BLW**: unk **RG**: Y **MK**: unk **PH**: unk **SS**: J-Yorktown Historian; SAR P-135589 **BS**: JLARC 1, 74.

COFER, George; b 1 Sep 1756, Culpeper Co; d 31 Aug 1837 **RU**: Corporal, Served in Capts John Hot 1775, and John Nicholas 177***-1779, 1783 1st VA State Regt **CEM**: St Stephen's Episcopal; GPS 37.37811, -79.30831; 1694 Perrowville Rd, Forest; Bedford **GS**: U **SP**: 1) Frances Dawson 2) Mary (-----) **VI**: Died in St Genevieive, MO **P**: unk **BLW**: unk **RG**: Y **MK**: N **PH**: unk **SS**: E pg 163; DAR A200502; SAR P-135759, SAR P-333623 **BS**: SAR PRS, 04; 196.

COFFER, Thomas W; b 1765; d 1784 **RU**: Patriot, Signed Legislative petition in Fairfax Co indicating public service **CEM**: Truro Parish; GPS unk; "On the middle ridge near Ox Road", the present site of Jerusalem Baptist Church off Rt 123; Fairfax **GS**: N **SP**: No info **VI**: No further data **P**: N **BLW**: N **RG**: N **MK**: N **PH**: N **SS**: BB legislative Pet **BS**: 110 pg 98.

COFFEY, Jean; b unk; d 1781 **RU**: Seaman, Served on "Saint-Esprit"; d Yorktown battle **CEM**: French Memorial; GPS 36.81944, -79.39933; Yorktown; York **GS**: U **SP**: No info **VI**: No further data **P**: unk **BLW**: unk **RG**: Y **MK**: unk **PH**: unk **SS**: J-Yorktown Historian; SAR P-135776 **BS**: JLARC 1, 74.

COFFEY (COFFEE), Edmund; b 1735; d Aft 1808 **RU**: Patriot, Obtain SAR application for service **CEM**: Coffey Family; GPS unk; Rt 789 Cub Creek Rd, Tyro; Nelson **GS**: U **SP**: Matilda (-----). Also Nancy Chena (order unk) **VI**: Will dated 1808 **P**: N **BLW**: N **RG**: Y **MK**: unk **PH**: unk **SS**: SAR P-135771 **BS**: JLARC 83.

COFFMAN, Jacob, Sr; b 8 Jan 1746 Shenandoah Co, d Apr 1796 (probate) **RU**: Private, enlisted 1779 in Rockingham Co Militia **CEM**: Lindale Mennonite Church; GPS: 38.53581, -78.84925; 6225 Jesse Bennett Hwy, Linville; Rockingham **GS**: Yes, but not readable in Coffman Lot **SP**: Elizabeth (___) Holdiman (c1744-1805) **VI**: Service source from SAR application with its source not listed in SAR ancestor file, P-135843 **P**: N **BLW**: N **RG**: Y **MK**: N **PH**: N **SS**: BY; CA; SAR P-135843 **BS**: 196.

COINER, Conrad; b unk; d 1816 **RU**: unk, Service information not shown in SAR registry **CEM**: Mt Zion Methodist; GPS 37.66596, -79.46615; Btw Buffalo & Tinkersville; Rockbridge **GS**: U **SP**: No info **VI**: No further data **P**: unk **BLW**: unk **RG**: Y **MK**: unk **PH**: unk **SS**: AR Vol 1 pg 191; SAR P-135933 **BS**: JLARC 2.

COLAR, Andre; b unk; d 1781 **RU**: Seaman, Served in Touraine Bn; d from Yorktown battle **CEM**: French Memorial; GPS 36.81944, -79.39933; Yorktown; York **GS**: U **SP**: No info **VI**: No further data **P**: unk **BLW**: unk **RG**: Y **MK**: unk **PH**: unk **SS**: J-Yorktown Historian **BS**: JLARC 1, 74.

COLE, Hugh; b 14 Mar 1744, Swansea, Bristol Co, MA; d 29 Jul 1780 **RU**: Second Lieutenant, 8th Co, Third Ulster Co Regt of Militia (western) under Capt Peleg Ramson 9 Aug 1775 **CEM**: St Clair Bottom Primitive Baptist; GPS 36.76098, -81.64556; Jct Rts 600 & 660, Chilhowie; Smyth **GS**: Y **SP**: Mar (c1771) Sarah Bishop (____-after 1780) **VI**: Son of Joseph (1716-1785) & Freelove (Mason) (1720-1785) Cole I. On 10 May 1775, signer of Articles of the Association in New-Paltz, Ulster Co, NY. D Washington Co. New grave marker erected 2004-mistake on stone should say NY militia. **P**: unk **BLW**: unk **RG**: N **MK**: unk **PH**: Y **SS**: CD **BS**: 196.

COLE, Joseph Jr; b Mar 1750, Swansea, MA; d 6 Sep 1826 **RU**: Captain, Ent serv 1777, Charlotte Co. Served in Washington Co Militia under Col William Campbel; in Battle of Kings Mountain **CEM**: St Clair Bottom Primitive Baptist; GPS 36.76098, -81.64556; Jct Rts 600 & 660, Chilhowie; Smyth **GS**: U **SP**: 1) Remember (-----) 2) Margaret Leuper **VI**: No further data **P**: unk **BLW**: unk **RG**: Y **MK**: N **PH**: unk **SS**: AR Vol 1 pg 193; E pg 165; SAR P-136305 **BS**: JLARC 2.

COLE, Joseph L, Sr; b 3 May 1716, Swansea, Bristol Co, MA; d 25 Jun 1785 **RU**: Patriot; Supported cause by paying supply tax included in his personal property tax in 1783 in Washington Co **CEM** Saint Clair Bottom Primitive Baptist Church; GPS: 36.76098, -81.64556; vic jct Rts 660 and 600; Smyth **GS**: Unk **SP**: Freelove Mason (1720-1785) **VI**: Son of Hugh Cole (1683-1753) and Martha Luther (1681-

---

RU=Rank/Unit   CEM=Cemetery   GS=Gravestone   SP=Spousal Information
VI=Other Veteran Info   P=Pension   BLW=Bounty/Land Warrant   RG=Registered Grave
MK=SAR/DAR Marker   PH=Photo   SS=Service Source   BS=Burial Source

90

1765).Titled as Captain **P**: N **BLW**: N **RG**: N **MK**: N **PH**: N **SS**: DV image 05.pdf, Washington Co **BS**: 196.

COLE, William; b 12 Dec 1752, Prince Edward Co; d 14 Oct 1838 **RU**: Buglar/Sergeant; Washington's bugler **CEM**: Cole Family; GPS unk; Off Rt 672, NW of Asbury Church, Asbury nr Halifax; Halifax **GS**: U **SP**: Mar (Jun 1786 Halifax Co) Mourning Hitson (1756-1847) **VI**: Widow pen age 88 Halifax Co, 1844. He pen Halifax Co in 1835. Another W. Cole listed in sources 1+2 (1745-1815) **P**: Y **BLW**: unk **RG**: Y **MK**: unk **PH**: unk **SS**: AR Vol 1 pg 194; DAR Magazine 1974-75; SAR P-136295 **BS**: JLARC 1, 2, 4; 196.

COLE, William; b c 1745; d aft 1815 **RU**: Private, served in 7th, 11th, and 15th Regiments of the Virginia Continental Line in Capt Brady's and Rice's Companies, Col Daniel Morgan's Regt **CEM**: Cole Family; GPS unk; Off Rt 672, NW of Asbury Church, Asbury nr Halifax; Halifax **GS**: Unk **SP**: Mar 1770, Nellie Freeman, b (____-Wales-1830, Charleston, OH) **VI**: No further data **P**: Unk **BLW**: Unk **RG**: Y **MK**: N **PH**: N **SS**: AP #1023 payroll; DAR A024267; SAR P-136294; **BS** SAR PRS

COLEMAN, Daniel; b 7 Jun 1768; d 8 Apr 1860 **RU**: Captain; Express rider for the militia **CEM**: Coleman Family; GPS unk; Off Yeats Store Rd, Java; Pittsylvania **GS**: Y **SP**: Anna Payne Harrison (1 Mar 1778-1 Feb 1858) **VI**: Son of Stephen Coleman (1739-1798), was Lt Col in War of 1812 **P**: unk **BLW**: unk **RG**: Y **MK**: unk **PH**: unk **SS**: AR Vol 1 pg 194; DAR A024289; SAR P-136336 **BS**: 174; 196; JLARC 2.

COLEMAN, Hawes; b 1 Jan 1757, Spotsylvania Co; d 27 Dec 1840 **RU**: Private, Entered serv 1775 Spotsylvania Co **CEM**: Wintergreen; GPS unk; Rt 151 beyond Nellysford; Nelson **GS**: U **SP**: Nancy Anne Harris (21 Jan 1756, Albemarle Co-13 Dec 1809) **VI**: Moved 1789 to Amherst Co (now Nelson Co) Pen 1834, R 607 **P**: Y **BLW**: unk **RG**: Y **MK**: unk **PH**: unk **SS**: K Vol 1 pg 222; SAR P-136348 **BS**: JLARC 4, 83.

COLEMAN, Isaac; b unk; d Aft 1782 **RU**: Private?, SAR registration did not indicate service **CEM**: Coleman Family; GPS unk; Nr Riceville; Pittsylvania **GS**: N **SP**: No info **VI**: No further data **P**: unk **BLW**: unk **RG**: Y **MK**: N **PH**: N **SS**: AS; SAR P-136350 **BS**: SAR regis.

COLEMAN, Julius; b 1743; d 1842 **RU**: 1st Lt/Patriot; Gave material aid to cause **CEM**: Coleman Family; GPS unk; Nr Salem Methodist Church; Buckingham **GS**: U **SP**: Elizabeth (-----) **VI**: No further data **P**: N **BLW**: N **RG**: Y **MK**: N **PH**: unk **SS**: D Caroline Co; SAR P-136394 **BS**: JLARC 59.

COLEMAN, Robert; b c1766; d 1846 **RU**: Private, Entered serv 1780, Specific Serv Lib VA, Report Sec War, Pen , vol 2, pg 120 **CEM**: Coleman Family; GPS unk; Bent Creek; Buckingham **GS**: U **SP**: Elizabeth Burks **VI**: Son of Samuel Coleman. Stepmother Elizabeth Coleman. Sub for father. After RW, lived in Buckingham Co where he pen 1833, age 67. R 608 **P**: Y **BLW**: N **RG**: Y **MK**: N **PH**: unk **SS**: CZ pg 105; K Vol 1 pg 223; SAR P-136415 **BS**: JLARC 4, 59.

COLEMAN, Stephen; b 1739; d Aft 1832 **RU**: Lieutenant, Appt Lt Pittsylvania Co Militia 27 Feb 1777 **CEM**: Coleman Family; GPS unk; Nr Riceville; Pittsylvania **GS**: N **SP**: Mar (3 Sep 1799 Pittsylvania Co) Polly Williams d/o Permeneas & (-----) Williams, Also Sarah Ann Watson **VI**: Was a Justice **P**: unk **BLW**: unk **RG**: Y **MK**: N **PH**: N **SS**: G pg 284; DAR A024355; SAR P-136425 **BS**: SAR Appl.

COLERAN, Jean; b unk; d 1781 **RU**: Soldier, Served in Soissonnais Bn; d Yorktown battle **CEM**: French Memorial; GPS 36.81944, -79.39933; Yorktown; York **GS**: U **SP**: No info **VI**: No further data **P**: unk **BLW**: unk **RG**: Y **MK**: unk **PH**: unk **SS**: J-Yorktown Historian; SAR P-136445 **BS**: JLARC 1, 74.

COLES, Isaac Sr; b 2 Mar 1747, Richmond, Henrico Co; d 3 Jun 1813 **RU**: Colonel/Patriot, Served in Pittsylvania Co Militia. Gave material aid to the cause **CEM**: Coles; GPS 36.54722, -79.16470; 8 mi NE of Chatham. Source 76 has Cem as off SR 690. Source 101 has Rt 685 at Chalk Level. Java; Pittsylvania **GS**: Y **SP**: 1) Elizabeth Lightfoot (____-1781) 2) Mar (2 Jan 1790) Caterine Thompson d/o James & (-----) Coles of NYC **VI**: Son of John (1706-1747) & Mary Ann (Winston) (1721-1758) Coles. After US Constitution ratified in 1789, was among first 10 Virginians to be elected to First Congress. Served as At-Large Representative fr VA in US House of Representatives, fr 1789-1791. Later elected to VA's 6th Congressional District, serving fr 1783-1787. D in Chatham, Pittsylvania Co **P**: unk **BLW**:

RU=Rank/Unit	CEM=Cemetery	GS=Gravestone	SP=Spousal Information
VI=Other Veteran Info	P=Pension	BLW=Bounty/Land Warrant	RG=Registered Grave
MK=SAR/DAR Marker	PH=Photo	SS=Service Source	BS=Burial Source

unk **RG**: Y **MK**: N **PH**: unk **SS**: Al Ct Bk pg 47, 53; CD; SAR P-136448 **BS**: JLARC 76, 101; 118 pg 71; 174; 196.

COLES, John; b 29 Apr 1745, Richmond City; d 5 Feb 1808 **RU**: Colonel County Lt; gave material did to cause; signed the list of names for counties Declaration of Independence 1779 **CEM**:Enniscorthy; GPS 37.873800,-78.585200; loc Green Mountain Rd, Keene:Albemarle; **GS** Y **SP**: Rebecca Elizabeth Tucker (20 Sep 1750-11 Apr 1826), d/o John Tucker & Elizabeth (-----) **VI**: Son of John Coles (1706-1747) & Mary Ann Winston (1721-1758) Co **P**: N **BLW**: N **RG**: Y **MK**: N **PH**: N **SS**: DAR A024373; D pg s 15, 24-27, E pg 167; SAR P-136451 **BS**: 196.

COLES, Walter; b 14 Nov 1739, Hanover Co; d 7 Nov 1780 **RU**: Major/Patriot, Served in Halifax Co Militia. Was Justice of Peace and elected to VA House of Delegates **CEM**: Coles-Carrington; GPS unk; Mildendo Plantation; Halifax **GS**: N **SP**: Mildred Howell Lightfoot (Feb 1752 Charles City Co-1 May 1799, Halifax Co) d/o William (1722-1764) & (-----) Lightfoot **VI**: Son of John (1706-1747) & Mary Ann (Winston) (1721-1758) Coles **P**: unk **BLW**: unk **RG**: N **MK**: unk **PH**: N **SS**: AL Certificate & Lists, Halifax Co **BS**: 196.

COLLIER, Aaron; b 15 Jan 1750, Lee Co; d Jun 1842 **RU**: Soldier, Ent serv 1780 Montgomery Co. Served in Cont Line in William Bobbett's Co **CEM**: Collier Family; GPS 36.78160, -80.59830; Jct Rts 628 & 624, Dugspur; Carroll **GS**: Y **SP**: Elizabeth (-----), d Jul 1830 **VI**: Appl pen but not enough service time-needed 6 mos. Lived in Grayson Co 40 yrs. Appl pen 1835 Lee Co, M804 Roll 611. Newer Govt stone R2111 **P**: Y **BLW**: Y **RG**: Y **MK**: N **PH**: unk **SS**: K Vol 1 pg 225; SAR P-136526 **BS**: JLARC 4, 43; 196.

COLLINS, Benjamin; b unk; d unk **RU**: Private, Specific serv Lib VA, War files, vol 4, pg 127 **CEM**: Old Lick aka First Baptist; GPS 37.28250, -79.93690; Hart Ave bet 2nd & 4th St; Roanoke City **GS**: Y **SP**: No info **VI**: No further data **P**: unk **BLW**: unk **RG**: N **MK**: N **PH**: unk **SS**: CZ pg 106; E pg 168 **BS**: 185.

COLLINS: Jeffrey; b 14 Feb 1756, Gooney Manor, Shenandoah Co, d 24 Oct 1851 **RU**: Private Volunteered Mar 1777 in Captain Michael Rader's Militia Company. In Aug 1777, marched to Fort Pitt and served in Colonel John Gibson's Regt under command of General Edward Hand. Later unit sent to Wheeling (now WVA) to guard against Indians; discharged there. **CEM**: Lewin-Lawson Family: 38.841019, -78.229227; loc Rt 340 S, left at Browntown Rd. Go 5.1 mi to Glen Manor Winery to cem; Shenandoah **GS** Y **SP**: Jemima Arterburn (1766-1831) **VI**: Memorialized in cem. Actual gravesite unk. Recd pen 6 Mar 1833 #9192 **P**: Y **BLW**: N **RG**: Y **MK**: Y SAR granite **PH**: Y **SS**: E pg 168; M- NARA pen file; DD DAR A134930; SAR P-136647 **BS**: 04.

COLLINS, Thomas; b 1758; d 22 Aug 1832 **RU**: Sergeant/Patriot, Served in 1st and 10th Cont Line for 3 yrs. Gave material aid to cause **CEM**: Collins Family; GPS unk; See property records for home place; King & Queen **GS**: U **SP**: No info **VI**: No further data **P**: unk **BLW**: unk **RG**: N **MK**: unk **PH**: unk **SS**: E pg 169; G pg 767; Al Cert King & Queen Co **BS**: 04.

COLONNA, Benjamin; b 10 Feb 1763; d 2 Jul 1851 **RU**: Soldier, Ent serv 1779, Accomack Co, Capt Americus Scarborough's Co Militia **CEM**: Waterfield Farm; GPS unk; 1.4 mi N of Rt 614, W of Rt 617, SE fr Pennyville; Accomack **GS**: N **SP**: Mar (29 Jul 1802) Elizabeth Beach (17 Oct 1784-18 Jan 1848) d/o Reuben & Mary (Wilkins) Beach **VI**: Son of Maj (22 Jul 1736-___) & Joice (Hutchinson) Colona. Appl for pension Accomack Co 1832. R616 **P**: Y **BLW**: unk **RG**: Y **MK**: unk **PH**: N **SS**: R 616; K Vol 1 pg 226; SAR P-136801 **BS**: JLARC 4, 5.

COLQUHOUN, James W; b 11 Dec 1766; d 5 Sep 1815 **RU**: Private, Served in Capt Richard Thomas's Co, 6th VA Regt, commanded by Col William Russell, Sep 1778. Served 3 yrs **CEM**: Dumfries Public; GPS 38.34110, -77.19964; 17821 Mine Rd, Dumfries; Prince William **GS**: Y **SP**: T___ (1775-Sep 1815) **VI**: SAR monument **P**: unk **BLW**: unk **RG**: Y **MK**: Y SAR monument **PH**: Y **SS**: E pg 170; SAR P-335635 **BS**: 245.

COLQUITT, John; b unk; d c18 Jun 1847 **RU**: Private? Served US Army. Specific Serv Lib VA, War files, vol 4, pg 136 **CEM**: St John's Episcopal; GPS 37.53183, -77.41958; 2401 E Broad St; Richmond City **GS**: N **SP**: No info **VI**: His claim for BLW rejected by Gov of VA **P**: unk **BLW**: unk **RG**: N **MK**: N **PH**: N **SS**: CZ pg 107; E pg 170 **BS**: 28, pg 351.

RU=Rank/Unit	CEM=Cemetery	GS=Gravestone	SP=Spousal Information
VI=Other Veteran Info	P=Pension	BLW=Bounty/Land Warrant	RG=Registered Grave
MK=SAR/DAR Marker	PH=Photo	SS=Service Source	BS=Burial Source

COLSON, Thomas; b unk; d unk **RU:** Quartermaster, Served in 7th VA Cont Line **CEM:** Vauxhall Site; GPS unk; Rt 607; Spotsylvania **GS:** Y **SP:** No info **VI:** No further data **P:** unk **BLW:** unk **RG:** N **MK:** N **PH:** unk **SS:** B; E pg 170 **BS:** 09, grid 49, 04.

COLUE, Andre; b unk; d 1781 **RU:** Soldier, Served in Gatinais Bn; d Yorktown battle **CEM:** French Memorial; GPS 36.81944, -79.39933; Yorktown; York **GS:** U **SP:** No info **VI:** No further data **P:** unk **BLW:** unk **RG:** Y **MK:** unk **PH:** unk **SS:** J-Yorktown Historian; SAR P-136878 **BS:** JLARC 1, 74.

COLVIN, Daniel; b 1737, Essex Co; d 1790 **RU:** Soldier, Served in Illinois Regt for 3 yrs. Enl 14 Nov 1779 for 3 yrs or duration of war in Capt Benjamin Roberts Co. Discharged with Slaughter's detachment and Crockett's Regt the last of 1781, pursuant to general orders. Was with George Rogers Clark at Vincennes **CEM:** Masonic Cemetery; GPS 38.48530, -77.99470; 950 N Main, Culpeper; Culpeper **GS:** Y Gov't **SP:** Elizabeth Magdalene Hansberger **VI:** Son of Mason & Levina (Tool) Colvin. Govt stone. **P:** unk **BLW:** unk **RG:** Y **MK:** N **PH:** unk **SS:** J- DAR Hatcher; AK; SAR P-136898 **BS:** JLARC 2, 04; 196.

COLVIN, Mason; b c1760 or 63, Culpeper Co; d 23 Jan 1853 **RU:** Private, Ent serv Culpeper Co 1781. Was in Illinois Regt for 3 yrs serving in Capts Nalle, Waugh, Yancy, Slaughter, and Garnett companies **CEM:** Slate Mills; GPS unk; Vic Woodville; Rappahannock **GS:** U **SP:** Mar (24 Apr 1788 (bond) Elizabeth Hawkins d/o Benjamin & Judith (-----) Hawkins of Culpeper Co **VI:** Appl for pension Culpeper Co 1832, age 72. R617. Was listed as pensioner of Rappahannock Co on 1840 census, age 80 **P:** Y **BLW:** unk **RG:** Y **MK:** N **PH:** unk **SS:** M pg 830; R 617; K Vol 1 pg 227; DAR A024681; SAR P-136914 **BS:** 04.

COMBOT, Bernard; b unk; d 1781 **RU:** Seaman, Served on "Duc De Bourgogne"; d Yorktown battle **CEM:** French Memorial; GPS 36.81944, -79.39933; Yorktown; York **GS:** U **SP:** No info **VI:** No further data **P:** unk **BLW:** unk **RG:** Y **MK:** unk **PH:** unk **SS:** J-Yorktown Historian; SAR P-136948 **BS:** JLARC 1, 74.

COMBRUN, Jean; b unk; d 1781 **RU:** Seaman, Served on "Ville de Paris"; d Yorktown battle **CEM:** French Memorial; GPS 36.81944, -79.39933; Yorktown; York **GS:** U **SP:** No info **VI:** No further data **P:** unk **BLW:** unk **RG:** Y **MK:** unk **PH:** unk **SS:** J-Yorktown Historian; SAR P-136949 **BS:** JLARC 1, 74

COMBS, John; b 1744, d 16 Jan 1849 **RU:** Patriot, Supported cause by paying supply tax included in his personal property tax in 1782 in Loudoun Co **CEM:** North Fork Baptist Church; GPS 39.06014, -77.68509; 38130 North Fork Rd, North Fork; Loudoun **GS** Yes **SP:** No spousal info **VI:** Gravestone erected by grandson **P:** N **BLW:** N **RG:** Y **MK:** N **PH:** N **SS:** DV 1782C image 07.pdf, Loudoun Co; SAR P-183385 **BS:** 222.

COMBS, Robert; b 1753, near Berry Ferry, Shenandoah River, Frederick Co; d 7 Sep 1846 **RU:** Private; Ent Serv Loudoun Co 1775 **CEM:** Combs Family; GPS unk; Hopewell; Fauquier **GS:** N **SP:** Sarah Linton **VI:** Pensioned Fauquier Co in 1832. R618 **P:** Y **BLW:** unk **RG:** N **MK:** N **PH:** N **SS:** K pg 228; H **BS:** 19, pg 46; 04.

COMER, John C; b Jul 1753, Caroline Co; d 1836 **RU:** Soldier, Ent serv Amelia Co 1775; Marine on ship "Hero". Ent serv again 1781 in VA Militia **CEM:** Comer; GPS unk; Rt 662, Elk Creek; Grayson **GS:** U **SP:** Amy Epps **VI:** Son of Thomas R & Frances (Moore) Comer. Pensioned Grayson Co, 1832, where he had moved in 1782. R619 **P:** Y **BLW:** unk **RG:** unk **MK:** unk **PH:** unk **SS:** R 619; K Vol 1 pg 228; SAR P-136998 **BS:** JLARC 4.

COMPHER, John, Sr; b 16 Oct 1740, d 26 Mar 1815 **RU:** Patriot, Supported cause by paying supply tax included in his personal property tax in 1783 in Loudoun Co **CEM:** New Jerusalem Lutheran Church; GPS 39.25736, -77.63891 GS 39.25698, -77.63870; 12942 Lutheran Church Rd, Lovettsville; Loudoun **GS:** Yes **SP:** Maria Cathern (4 Feb 1755-14 Mar 1815) **VI:** No further data **P:** N **BLW:** N **RG:** Y **MK:** N **PH:** Y **SS:** DV 1783A image 05.pdf, Loudoun Co; SAR bio rpt sub Mar 2021 **BS:** 196; cem visit.

CONDE, Pierre; b unk; d 1781 **RU:** Soldier, Served in Soissonnais Bn; d Yorktown battle **CEM:** French Memorial; GPS 36.81944, -79.39933; Yorktown; York **GS:** U **SP:** No info **VI:** No further data **P:** unk **BLW:** unk **RG:** Y **MK:** unk **PH:** unk **SS:** J-Yorktown Historian; SAR P-137222 **BS:** JLARC 1v74.

CONN, William Young; b Mar 1753, Washington DC; d 15 Apr 1837 **RU:** Navy ship pilot, Ent serv Washington DC area 1776, later ent serv Alexandria as pilot for ships evading British fleet **CEM:** Sinking

RU=Rank/Unit	CEM=Cemetery	GS=Gravestone	SP=Spousal Information
VI=Other Veteran Info	P=Pension	BLW=Bounty/Land Warrant	RG=Registered Grave
MK=SAR/DAR Marker	PH=Photo	SS=Service Source	BS=Burial Source

93

Springs; GPS 36.71030, -81.98170, GS: 39.25698, -77.63870; 136 E Main St, Abingdon; Washington **GS:** U **SP:** Jane (-----) (4 May 1746-1 Apr 1832) **VI:** Pensioned Washington DC, 1833, age 78. R627 **P:** Y **BLW:** unk **RG:** Y **MK:** unk **PH:** unk **SS:** R 627; K Vol 1 pg 230-1; SAR P-137515 **BS:** JLARC 1, 2, 4, 34, 80.

CONNALY, Arthur Sr; b 1730; d 1805 **RU:** Patriot, Gave material aid to cause **CEM:** Augusta Stone Presbyterian; GPS 38.23926, -78.97356,GS 38.1407,-78.5815; 28 Old Stone Church Ln, Ft Defiance; Augusta **GS:** Y **SP:** Jean (-----) **VI:** Govt stone **P:** N **BLW:** N **RG:** Y **MK:** Y SAR plaque **PH:** unk **SS:** AL Ct Cert Augusta Co; SAR P-137517 **BS:** JLARC 1, 2, 8, 23, 62; 196.

CONNELL, William; b unk; d 27 Mar 1795 **RU:** Private, Served in Col Francis Marion's SC Regt Nov 1779 **CEM:** Old Christ Church Episcopal; GPS 38.80625, -77.04718; 118 N Washington St; Alexandria City **GS:** N **SP:** No info **VI:** Burial permit issued 27 Mar 1795 **P:** unk **BLW:** unk **RG:** Y **MK:** N **PH:** N **SS:** A pg 290 **BS:** 20 pg 146.

CONNER, James; b unk; d 1793 **RU:** Patriot, Signed Legislative Petition **CEM:** Old Christ Church Episcopal; GPS 38.80625, -77.04718; 118 N Washington St; Alexandria City **GS:** N **SP:** No info **VI:** Burial permit issued 7 Oct 1793 **P:** N **BLW:** N **RG:** N **MK:** N **PH:** N **SS:** BB **BS:** 20 pg 146.

CONNER (CONNOR), Patrick; b unk; d 1784 **RU:** Private, Served in 3rd, 5th, & 11th Cont Line **CEM:** Truro Parish; GPS unk; "On the middle ridge near Ox Road", the present site of Jerusalem Baptist Church off Rt 123; Fairfax **GS:** N **SP:** No info **VI:** No further data **P:** unk **BLW:** unk **RG:** N **MK:** N **PH:** N **SS:** E pg 172-3 **BS:** 110, pg 103-4.

CONNOR, Daniel; b unk; d unk **RU:** Private, Served in 2nd VA Brigade & 2nd, 6th Cont Lines. Also served in Col Daniel Morgan's Riflemen Regt **CEM:** Salem Cemetery; GPS 37.05014, -80.16004; Rt 221, Head of the River Church; Floyd **GS:** U **SP:** Mary (-----) **VI:** No further data **P:** unk **BLW:** unk **RG:** Y **MK:** unk **PH:** unk **SS:** E pg 174; SAR P-137605 **BS:** JLARC 29.

CONRAD, Henry; b 1759; d 1849 **RU:** Private, WPA report indicates service (not determined) **CEM:** Elk Run; GPS 38.41042, -78.61033; North St, Elkton; Rockingham **GS:** Y **SP:** Mar (1813 Rockingham Co) Sally Hansbarger **VI:** No further data **P:** unk **BLW:** unk **RG:** N **MK:** N **PH:** unk **SS:** AP Roll **BS:** 186.

CONRAD, John Peter; b 1745; d 1800 **RU:** Patriot, Gave material aid to the cause **CEM:** Old Peaked Mountain; GPS 38.37113, -78.73416; 9843 Town Hall Rd, McGaheysville; Rockingham **GS:** Y **SP:** Mary Nicholas, d/o Peter & (-----) Nicholas **VI:** No further data **P:** N **BLW:** N **RG:** N **MK:** V DAR plaque **PH:** unk **SS:** AL Ct Bk 1 pg 1 04 **BS:** 191 Peaked Mt 04.

CONRAD (CONROD), John Stephen Jr; b 26 Feb 1749, Tulpehocken, PA; d 28 Aug 1822 **RU:** Captain, Took oath for Lt, 7 Mar 1780 in Capt Jeremiah Beeslie's Co. Took Oath for Capt 23 Apr 1781 and commanded Co 15, Rockingham Militia until 1788 **CEM:** East Point; GPS unk; Rt 602 left fr Rt 33 E, Elkton; Rockingham **GS:** Y **SP:** Mary Margaret Moyer **VI:** No further data **P:** unk **BLW:** unk **RG:** Y SAR **MK:** Y **PH:** unk **SS:** AS; DAR A025142; SAR P-137674 **BS:** SAR regis.

CONRAD (CONROD/COONROD), Jacob; b Aug 1754 or 1747, PA; d 3 Jun 1824 or 1841 **RU:** Private, Enl Redstone Settlement, Monongahola River 1 Jan 1777. Served in Capt Benjamin Harrison's Co, Cols Russell's and John Gibson's VA Regts. Was in Battle of Brandywine and Germantown. Discharged 25 Jul 1783 **CEM:** East Point; GPS unk; Rt 602 left fr Rt 33 E, Elkton; Rockingham **GS:** N **SP:** No info **VI:** Pensioned Rockingham Co 1820 S.39361 **P:** Y **BLW:** unk **RG:** N **MK:** N **PH:** N **SS:** AH pg 146 **BS:** 142 Elk Run.

CONSTABLE, Thomas; b 1742; d 25 Apr 1805 **RU:** Ensign, Served in Baltimore MD Town Bn 23 May 1781 **CEM:** Cedar Grove; GPS 36.859056, -76.283160 238 E Princess Anne Rd; Norfolk City **GS:** Y **SP:** Marcy (----) (1748-1837) **VI:** A person by this name was head of household in Norfolk VA in 1810. **P:** unk **BLW:** unk **RG:** Y **MK:** N **PH:** unk **SS:** BF; SAR bio Rpt Jun 2020 cites CD ROM, MD & DL Rev War Pariots 1775-1783 Mil Rec; **BS:** 32 Tim Bonney.

COOK, Benjamin; b 1757; d 1830 **RU:** Private, Served in US Army, specific serv Lib VA, War files, vol 4, pg 151 **CEM:** Cook Family; GPS unk; Rt 630 nr Rt 890, nr Sago; Franklin **GS:** U **SP:** No info **VI:** No further data **P:** unk **BLW:** Y **RG:** Y **MK:** unk **PH:** unk **SS:** CU; CZ pg 110; SAR P-137846 **BS:** JLARC 2, 18.

RU=Rank/Unit	CEM=Cemetery	GS=Gravestone	SP=Spousal Information
VI=Other Veteran Info	P=Pension	BLW=Bounty/Land Warrant	RG=Registered Grave
MK=SAR/DAR Marker	PH=Photo	SS=Service Source	BS=Burial Source

COOK, David; b 1761; d Jan 1852 **RU**: Ensign Clarks Illinois Regt, VA State Troops **CEM**: Saint Matthews AKA Reformation; GPS 38.65131, -78.67121; end of Breckenridge Lane, behind church; Shenandoah **GS**: Y **SP**: Magdalene (-----) (____1842) **VI**: No further information **P**: No **BLW**: No **RG**: N **MK**: N **PH**: N **SS**: AP Serv Rec **BS**: 196.

COOK, Giles: b 1740; d 1839 **RU**: Cadet Capt Philip Taliaferro"s Co, 2nd VA State Regiment Mar-Apr 1778 **CEM**: Prospect Hill; GPS: 38.91310, -78.19690; 200 Prospect St, Front Royal; Warren **GS**: Y **SP**: No info **VI**: No further info **P**: No **BLW**: No **RG**: N **MK**: N **PH**: N **SS**: AP Serv Rec; E pg 176; Heitman Historical Register Officers Continental Army, Washington, DC 1914, vol 33, pg 386 **BS**: 196.

COOK, Henry; b 1761; d 13 Mar 1835 **RU**: Private, Served in 7th Cont Line **CEM**: Zion Lutheran; GPS 36.84110, -81.22310; 1417 Zion Church Rd, Crockett; Wythe **GS**: U **SP**: No info **VI**: No further data **P**: unk **BLW**: unk **RG**: N **MK**: unk **PH**: unk **SS**: E pg 176 **BS**: 196.

COOK (KOCH), Henry; b 1755, Frederick Co; d 14 Nov 1810 **RU**: Private, Capt William Nalle's Co Rockinghan Co Militia at battle of Pt Pleasant, Oct 1764 **CEM**: Cook-Dovel; GPS not determined; loc .5 mi W of East Pont Ch on Massanutten Mtn Rd, McGaheysville: Rockingham **GS**:N **SP**: Mary Magdalene Hudlow (2 Nov 1768, Frederick Co-1825), d/o Andrew Hudlow (1 Jun 1731, Ger-18 Mar 1785 & Mary Margaret Sehler (1740, PA-20 Jan 1807) **VI**: Son of Johannes Heinrich Koch (1734-1785) & (-----) **P**: N **BLW**: N **RG**: N **MK**: N **PH**: N **SS**: Z pg 113; DAR A025331 **BS**: 196.

COOK, Jacob; b unk; d 1789 **RU**: Patriot, Gave use of horse for six days **CEM**: Old Christ Church Episcopal; GPS 38.80625, -77.04718; 118 N Washington St; Alexandria City **GS**: N **SP**: No info **VI**: Burial permit issued 30 Oct 1789 **P**: N **BLW**: N **RG**: N **MK**: N **PH**: N **SS**: Z pg 61 **BS**: 20 pg 146.

COOKE, Dawson; b1757; d14 Nov 1829 **RU**: Entered service Dec 1775, Midshipman, Brig *Liberty*, 18 May to 30 Jul1776; acting midshipman *Gloucester*,30 Jul 1777 **CEM**: Cooke Family; GPS not determined; loc on his homesite in 1829; See county zoning property tax map for location; King & Queen; **SP**: Mar Dec 1775, Mildred Paschal (1758-14 Aug 1836) **VI**: His will 1829 describes property he owned and where loc; served as assistant county clerk and was elected sheriff of county. After wife died, his heirs rec'd pension # W4657 **P**: Y Heirs **BLW**: N **RG**: N **MK**: N **PH**: N **SS**: K vol 1, pg 237, L pg 172 AP pensions **BS**: 196.

COOLE, John M; b Oct 1745; d 8 Feb 1815 **RU**: Sergeant, Served in Capt Drury Ragsdale's Co, Col Chat Harrison's Regt **CEM**: Back Creek Quaker, aka Gainesboro United Methodist; GPS 39.27861, -78.25694; 166 Siler Ln, Gainesboro; Frederick **GS**: Y **SP**: Probably Nancy (-----) (___-4 May 1823), bur in cemetery listed **VI**: No further data **P**: unk **BLW**: unk **RG**: N **MK**: unk **PH**: unk **SS**: AP-Muster Roll **BS**: 196.

COOPER, James; b 1740; d 1798 **RU**: Patriot, Gave material aid to cause **CEM**: New Hope; GPS unk; Orange; Orange **GS**: U **SP**: Mary Quisenberry (1745-1810) **VI**: No further data **P**: N **BLW**: N **RG**: N **MK**: unk **PH**: unk **SS**: AL Ct Bk pg 6 **BS**: 196.

COOPER, John Jr; b 14 Jun 1766; d 27 Feb 1851 **RU**: Drummer, Enl Chester Co, in Capt Marshall's Co, PA Militia. Later served in VA in 1st, 3rd, 4th, 8th, 9th and 12th Cont Lines **CEM**: Cooper family; GPS unk; W side of Back Mtn Rd, 1 mi N of Mountain Falls; Frederick **GS**: U **SP**: Mar (23 Sep 1789) Catherine Secrist (1767-11 May 1849) d/o Henry & Anna Maria (-----) Secrist **VI**: Son of John Sr & (-----) Cooper. Pen filed Jun 1818 **P**: Y **BLW**: unk **RG**: N **MK**: unk **PH**: unk **SS**: E pg 177; CZ pg 64 **BS**: 196.

COOPER, Michael, Sr; b 20 Jun 1742, d 19 Feb 1815 **RU**: Patriot, Supported cause by paying supply tax included in his personal property tax in 1782 in Loudoun Co **CEM**: New Jerusalem Lutheran Church; GPS 39.25736, -77.63891, GS 39.25698, -77.63873; 12942 Lutheran Church Rd, Lovettsville; Loudoun **GS**: Yes **SP**: No data **VI**: No further data **P**: N **BLW**: N **RG** Y **MK**: N **PH**:Y **SS**: DV 1782B image 05.pdf, Loudoun Co; SAR bio rpt sub Mar 2021 **BS**: 222; cem visit.

COOPER, Robert; b 1738; d 20 Sep 1816 **RU**: Private, Served in Capt McCutchen's Co Augusta Co VA **CEM**: Old Providence; GPS 37.96151, -79.71000; 1005 Spottswood Rd, Spottswood; Augusta **GS**: Y **SP**: Susanna H. Blair, b 1742, d 5 Nov 1817 **VI**: Son of William Cooper. Elder of Old Providence & Timber Ridge 1776 **P**: unk **BLW**: unk **RG**: N **MK**: Y SAR plaque **PH**: Y **SS**: E pg 571 **BS**: 44 pg 57; 196.

RU=Rank/Unit	CEM=Cemetery	GS=Gravestone	SP=Spousal Information
VI=Other Veteran Info	P=Pension	BLW=Bounty/Land Warrant	RG=Registered Grave
MK=SAR/DAR Marker	PH=Photo	SS=Service Source	BS=Burial Source

COOPER, Samuel; b 1756, MA; d 19 Aug 1840 **RU:** Lieutenant, Made 2nd Lt, 3rd MA CL-Artillery as of 1 Feb 1777 and Regimental Quartermaster 14 May 1778-Jun 1783, Corps Artillery 17 Jun 1783. Was Adjutant of same to 20 June 1784. Fought at Bunker Hill, Trenton, Brandywine, Germantown, Monmouth **CEM:** Christ Church Episcopal; GPS 38.80216, -77.05689; Wilkes St & Hamilton Ln; Alexandria City **GS:** Y **SP:** Sarah Maria Mason and/or Mary Horton **VI:** Member Society of Cincinnati. Rank of Maj earned after war period. Died age 84 **P:** unk **BLW:** unk **RG:** Y **MK** Y SAR plaque **PH:** Y **SS:** A pg 417, 479; BT; SAR P-138621 **BS:** JLARC 1, 2, 25, 86; 20 pg 92; 196.

COOPER, Sterling; b 20 Jun 1760; d 9 Jan 1836 **RU:** Private, Served 18 mos in Capt Cunningham, 14th VA Regt at Valley Forge and Battle at Monmouth. Enl again 1780 for 3 mos under Capt Ship, and again under Capt Hayes. Was at Yorktown Battle **CEM:** Cooper Family; GPS unk; Snow Creek; Franklin **GS:** U **SP:** 1) Susannah Rainey Andrews (1756-1819), 2(Eleanor Willis (1804-1846) **VI:** Rec'd pen # S9206 **P:** Y **BLW:** unk **RG:** N **MK:** unk **PH:** unk **SS:** AP Pen Applic 1832; AZ pg 238 **BS:** 196.

COPELAND, James (Jas); b 1 Aug 1759, Ireland; d 15 Jun 1838, Loudoun Co **RU:** Private, Ent serv Loudoun Co 1778 in11th VA Regt, Cont Line. Served in Capt William George's Co, Loudoun Co Militia 1781 **CEM:** Ketoctin Baptist; GPS 39.15746, -77.74870; Ketoctin Church Rd, Purcellville; Loudoun **GS:** Y **SP:** Mar (26 Apr 1787) Sarah Akers of Shelburne Parish (Loudoun Co) (c1762-__) **VI:** Came to VA with parents at age 4. Pensioned Loudoun Co 1832. Widow penioned age 70 Loudoun Co in 1832. Resided there in 1843, age 73. W.6730. R650 **P:** Y **BLW:** unk **RG:** Y **MK:** SAR Plaque **PH:** unk **SS:** R 650; AK; E pg 178; K Vol 1 pg 242; SAR P-138696 **BS:** 04, JLARC 1, 2, 32.

COPELAND, John; b c1752, Londonderry, Ireland, d 11 Dec 1807 **RU:** Ensign, USA 1783 serving under Conl Line under General Morgan's 7th, 11th and 15th VA Regts **CEM:** Ketoctin Baptist Church; GPS: 39.15746, -77.74840; Ketoctin Church Rd, Rt 716, Purcellville; Loudoun **GS:** Yes **SP:** Rebecca (-----) **VI:** Son or brother of David Copeland. BS indicates Rev War soldier **P:** No **BLW:** No **RG:** N **MK:** SAR Plaque **PH:** N **SS:** CU; CZ **BS:** 196.

COPENHAVER, John Jacob; b 1758, d 10 Nov 1838 **RU:** Private, Capt Alexander Machir's Co, Strasburg's District, (Dunmore Co Lower District) **CEM:** Mt Hebron; GPS 39.10916, -78.09497; 305 E Boscawen St; Winchester City **GS:** Y **SP:** Mar 1 Jan 1788, Margaret Hofman (____-1834) **VI:** Buried in the German Lutheran Church portion of the cem. Service listed under Jacob **P:** N **BLW:** N **RG:** N **MK:** N **PH:** Y **SS:** C Sec IV, pg 606 **BS:** 196.

COPENHAVER (COPENHAVEN), Michal (Michael); b c1753; d 15 Sep 1823 **RU:** Patriot, Gave provisions to the cause **CEM:** Mt Hebron; GPS 39.10916, -78.09497; 305 E Boscawen St; Winchester City **GS:** Y **SP:** Mar (09 Mar 1786, Frederick Co by Rev Christian Streit) Margaret Price **VI:** No further data **P:** N **BLW:** N **RG:** N **MK:** Y SAR monument **PH:** Y **SS:** AL CT Bk 26 **BS:** 50 pg 46; 196.

COPLAND, Charles; b 1756; d 24 Nov 1836 **RU:** Private/Patriot, Signed Legislative Petition Hanover Co, 24 May 1782 **CEM:** St John's Episcopal; GPS 37.53183, -77.41958; 2401 E Broad St; Richmond City **GS:** Y **SP:** Rebecca (-----) (c1770-25 Jul 1800) **VI:** Member of the Diocese of VA and St John's Church **P:** unk **BLW:** unk **RG:** N **MK:** N **PH:** unk **SS:** CZ pg 112; E pg 179 **BS:** 28, pg 525.

CORBIN, Gawin Tayloe; b 15 Dec 1739; d 19 Jul 1779 **RU:** Patriot, Gave material aid to Army. Was member VA Council **CEM:** Christ Church; GPS 37.60968, -76.54643; Rt 33 2 mi E of Saluda; Middlesex **GS:** U **SP:** Martha (-----) (____-11 Jun 1839, King & Queen Co) **VI:** Son of Richard (____-1790) & Betty (Tayloe) (____-1781) Corbin of Mt Airy **P:** N **BLW:** N **RG:** Y **MK:** unk **PH:** unk **SS:** G pg 202; SAR Bio Rpt sent in Nov 2020 **BS:** 196.

CORBIN, George; b 1744; d 28 Sep 1793 **RU:** Colonel, Was in charge of Accomack Co Militia. Served as County Lt 31 Mar 1779 **CEM:** Scott Hall; GPS unk; Daugherty Rd, Onancock; Accomack **GS:** Y **SP:** Mar (17 Sep 1796 Accomack (bond) Nancy Sterling **VI:** No further data **P:** unk **BLW:** unk **RG:** N **MK:** N **PH:** unk **SS:** E pg 179; DAR Marker **BS:** 209; 196.

CORBIN, John; b 3 Jan 1747; d 16 Jun 1813 **RU:** Private?, Served in Capt Holmes Co **CEM:** Major-Corbin; GPS unk; Amissville; Rappahannock **GS:** Y **SP:** Frances (-----) (____-1 May 1814) **VI:** Son of William (1720-1796) & Sarah (Fant) (1726-____) Corbin. **P:** unk **BLW:** unk **RG:** Y **MK:** N **PH:** unk **SS:** E pg 179 **BS:** 04.

RU=Rank/Unit   CEM=Cemetery   GS=Gravestone   SP=Spousal Information
VI=Other Veteran Info   P=Pension   BLW=Bounty/Land Warrant   RG=Registered Grave
MK=SAR/DAR Marker   PH=Photo   SS=Service Source   BS=Burial Source

96

CORBIN, Richard; b c1714; d 20 May 1790 **RU**: Patriot, Gave 3805# of beef, 548 bushels corn & reimbursed for carting grain **CEM**: Christ Church; **GPS** 37.60968, -76.54643; Rt 33 2 mi E of Saluda; Middlesex **GS**: Y **SP**: Mar (1737) Elizabeth "Betty" Tayloe (1729-1784) **VI**: Son of Gawin (1659-1744) & 2nd wife Jane (Lane) Corbin. GS moved fr upper chapel **P**: N **BLW**: N **RG**: N **MK**: N **PH**: unk **SS**: AL Ct Bk pg 2; D Middlesex Co claims pg 2 May 1782 **BS**: 92 pg 6, 116.

CORBIN, William; b 1720; d 3 Dec 1796 **RU**: Patriot, Gave material aid to cause **CEM**: Major-Corbin; **GPS** 38.65282, -78.02353; Rt 642, Viewtown Rd nr jct with Ida Belle Ln; Rappahannock **GS**: U **SP**: Mar (1 Jan 1743) Sarah Jeenkins **VI**: Son of John (1697-1758, King George Co) & Elizabeth Jennings (1694-1754) Corbin **P**: N **BLW**: N **RG**: N **MK**: unk **PH**: unk **SS**: AL Ct Bk I pg 79 Culpeper Co **BS**: 196.

CORDER, John; b 1761, Fauquier Co; d 24 Jan 1849 **RU**: Private, Ent serv 1777, Fauquier Co in Col Gibson's Regt **CEM**: Corder-Pierce Family; **GPS** unk; Amissville; Rappahannock **GS**: N **SP**: 1) Hannah Way (?) 2) Mar (1845) Mary (-----) Maddox, his housekeeper and widow of Samuel Maddox. **VI**: Son of William (1703-___) & Alice (-----) Corder, Fauquier Co. Recd 200 acres fr Lord Fairfax. Brother James Corder also served in Rev War. Pensioned age 71 in 1832 and states sol blind when pen. Pen fr "near Fiery Run Meeting House" Fauquier Co 1836. R654 **P**: Y **BLW**: unk **RG**: Y **MK**: N **PH**: Y **SS**: K Vol 1 pg 245; DAR A025993; SAR P-138878 **BS**: 33.

CORLAIX, Jean; b unk; d 1781 **RU**: Seaman, Served on "Magnanime", d Yorktown battle **CEM**: French Memorial; **GPS** 36.81944, -79.39933; Yorktown; York **GS**: U **SP**: No info **VI**: No further data **P**: unk **BLW**: unk **RG**: Y **MK**: unk **PH**: unk **SS**: J-Yorktown; SAR P-138940 **BS**: JLARC 1, 74.

CORN, Jesse Sr; b 31 Oct 1753, Albemarle Co; d 5 May 1809 **RU**:2d Lieutenant, Ent serv Albemarle Co "early in the war"; Served later in Capt George Hairston's Co, Henry Co Militia and unit was sent to support General Greene **CEM**: Patrick Henry Allied Memorial; **GPS** unk; Fairy Stone State Park; Patrick **GS**: Y **Gov't SP**: Mar (1780 Fluvanna Co Bond 21 Feb 1780 signed by Benjamin Hancock, Fluvanna Co) Nancy Hancock (17 Feb 1780-17 Jun 1848 in TN), d/o John & (-----) Hancock **VI**: Pen in 1841, Franklin Co. Widow pen Franklin Co TN 1841. R655 **P**: Y **BLW**: unk **RG**: Y **MK**: Y SAR **PH**: unk **SS**: G pg 186; R 655; K Vol 1 pg 246; DAR A026108; SAR P-138980 **BS**: 125 pg 420.

CORNETT (CORNET), James Jr; b 1760; d April 1824 **RU**: Private, Served in Lt John McKinney or William Walling's Co **CEM**: Cornett Family; **GPS** 36.72401, -81.23889; Rt 662; Grayson **GS**: U **SP**: Mary (Molly) Vaughn **VI**: No further data **P**: unk **BLW**: unk **RG**: Y **MK**: N **PH**: unk **SS**: AK Apr 2007 DD: SAR P-139043 **BS**: 04, Apr 2007.

CORNICK, Lemuel, II; b 6 Feb 1749, d 1804 **RU**: Lieutenant/ Patriot, Commissioned a LT in Princess Anne Co; Gave material aid to cause, Princess Anne Co **CEM**: Atwood-Cornick; **GPS**: Not determined; Broad Bay Farm, Great Neck Rd; VA Beach **GS**: Yes **SP**: Not determined **VI**: Was first lightkeeper at Cape Henry lighthouse, later called Captain **P**: No **BLW**: No **RG**: N **MK**: N **PH**: N **SS**: AL Ct Book, pg 2; Comm Bk pgs 211, 212; Princess Anne Co **BS**: 196.

CORNISH, Daniel; b unk; d 1781 **RU**: Soldier, Served fr MA; d Yorktown battle **CEM**: Yorktown Victory Monument Tablet; **GPS** 38.28350, -78.54150; Yorktown; York **GS**: U **SP**: No info **VI**: No further data **P**: unk **BLW**: unk **RG**: Y **MK**: unk **PH**: unk **SS**: J-Yorktown Historian; SAR P-139057 **BS**: JLARC 74.

COSBY, Overton; b c1739; d 1806 **RU**: Patriot, Gave material aid to the cause **CEM**: Landsdowne House(AKA Arthur Lee Family); **GPS** 37.638569, -76.576164; on Rappahannock St vic jct Bonner St, Urbanna; Middlesex **GS**: Y **SP**: No info **VI**: No further data **P**: N **BLW**: N **RG**: N **MK**: N **PH**: unk **SS**: AL Ct Bk pg 9 **BS**: 92, pg 58; 196.

COSTAIL, Sidet; b unk; d 1781 **RU**: Soldier, Served in Touraine Bn; d Yorktown battle **CEM**: French Memorial; **GPS** 36.81944, -79.39933; Yorktown; York **GS**: U **SP**: No info **VI**: No further data **P**: unk **BLW**: unk **RG**: Y **MK**: unk **PH**: unk **SS**: J-Yorktown Historian; SAR P-139290 **BS**: JLARC 1, 74.

COSTE, Vidal; b unk; d 1781 **RU**: Soldier, Served in Touraine Bn; d Yorktown battle **CEM**: French Memorial; **GPS** 36.81944, -79.39933; Yorktown; York **GS**: U **SP**: No info **VI**: No further data **P**: unk **BLW**: unk **RG**: Y **MK**: unk **PH**: unk **SS**: J-Yorktown Historian; SAR P-139293 **BS**: JLARC 1, 74.

COUILLARD, Jacques; b unk; d 1781 **RU**: Seaman, Served on "Duc De Bourgogne"; d Yorktown battle **CEM**: French Memorial; **GPS** 36.81944, -79.39933; Yorktown; York **GS**: U **SP**: No info **VI**: No further

RU=Rank/Unit	CEM=Cemetery	GS=Gravestone	SP=Spousal Information
VI=Other Veteran Info	P=Pension	BLW=Bounty/Land Warrant	RG=Registered Grave
MK=SAR/DAR Marker	PH=Photo	SS=Service Source	BS=Burial Source

data **P:** unk **BLW:** unk **RG:** Y **MK:** unk **PH:** unk **SS:** J-Yorktown Historian; SAR P-139455 **BS:** JLARC 1, 74.

COUNTS (COUNCE)(KOONTZ), Peter Detrich, Sr; b 1735; d 1813 **RU:** Patriot, paid personal property tax, 1783, Rockingham Co, considered to be a supply tax for Rev War expenses **CEM:** Koontz Family; GPS not determined; loc N of dirt lane at end of Rt 806, Martz Rd, Lacey Spring; Rockingham **GS:** N **SP:** Christina Boyer (26 Aug 1732-12 Jan 1818), d/o Johann Adam Boyer (1701-1755) & Rosannah Schug (1711-1785) **VI:** Son of Johannes Cuntze (1706-1745) & Anna Catherine Stover(1710-1748) **P:** N **BLW:** N **RG:** N **MK:** N **PH:** N **SS:** DV image 22, 1783, Rockingham Co for Peter Counce **BS:** 196.

COURBET, Antoine; b unk; d 1781 **RU:** Soldier, Served in Touraine Bn; d Yorktown battle **CEM:** French Memorial; GPS 36.81944, -79.39933; Yorktown; York **GS:** U **SP:** No info **VI:** No further data **P:** unk **BLW:** unk **RG:** Y **MK:** unk **PH:** unk **SS:** J-Yorktown Historian; SAR P-139509 **BS:** JLARC 1, 74.

COURTNEY, John; b 1741; d 1824 **RU:** Patriot, Gave material aid to cause **CEM:** Hollywood; GPS 37.53560, -77.45720; 412 S Cherry St; Richmond City **GS:** U **SP:** No info **VI:** Memorial, not indiv GS **P:** N **BLW:** N **RG:** unk **MK:** unk **PH:** unk **SS:** D Stafford Co; SAR P-139527 **BS:** JLARC 99.

COURTNEY, William; b unk; d 1848 **RU:** Private, Served in Capt William Alexander's Co 1777, Col William Irvine's PA Regt **CEM:** Courtney Family; GPS unk; Nr N Bank Hamshill Creek; Page **GS:** N **SP:** No info **VI:** No further data **P:** unk **BLW:** unk **RG:** N **MK:** N **PH:** N **SS:** A pg 219 **BS:** 120.

COURTNEY (COURTNY), William; b unk; D aft Nov 1796 **RU:** Private/Patriot, Served in 3rd, 4th, 8th Cont lines. Gave material aid to cause **CEM:** Courtney Family; GPS unk; Hartwood Airfield; Fauquier **GS:** N **SP:** A man by this name mar (10 Jan 1786 (bond) Fauquier Co, John Smith security) Ann Smith **VI:** Filed petition in Stafford Co. Airport removed the GSs when building the runways **P:** unk **BLW:** unk **RG:** Y **MK:** N **PH:** N **SS:** CZ pg 114; D vol 1, pg 357 E pg 183; Fauquier Co Marriages pg 42; DAR A132116; SAR 330924 **BS:** 19 pg 47.

COURTOIS, Etienne; b unk; d 1781 **RU:** Soldier, Served in Bourbonnais Bn; d Yorktown battle **CEM:** French Memorial; GPS 36.81944, -79.39933; Yorktown; York **GS:** U **SP:** No info **VI:** No further data **P:** unk **BLW:** unk **RG:** Y **MK:** unk **PH:** unk **SS:** J-Yorktown Historian; SAR P-139533 **BS:** JLARC 1, 74.

COUSINS, Henry; b 22 Jul 1758; d 5 Jun 1824 **RU:** Matross/Patriot, Served in Lt Shockley's Co, VA Militia. Gave material aid to cause **CEM:** Fleetwood Plantation; GPS unk; 6630 Brills Rd, McKenney; Dinwiddie **GS:** Y **SP:** Margaret Boisseau **VI:** Newer Govt stone inscribed with service as a Matross **P:** N **BLW:** unk **RG:** Y **MK:** N **PH:** unk **SS:** D Amelia Co; DAR A026731; SAR P-139551 **BS:** JLARC 116; 196.

COUTEL, Guillaume; b unk; d 1781 **RU:** Soldier, Served in Santonge Bn; d Yorktown battle **CEM:** French Memorial; GPS 36.81944, -79.39933; Yorktown; York **GS:** U **SP:** No info **VI:** No further data **P:** unk **BLW:** unk **RG:** Y **MK:** unk **PH:** unk **SS:** J-Yorktown Historian; SAR P-139563 **BS:** JLARC 1, 74.

COVINGTON, Francis L; b 1754; d 21 Jul 1823 **RU:** Captain, Commanded Co in Culpeper Co Militia **CEM:** Covington Family; GPS unk; Nr Washington CH. This would put it in Rappahannock Co, not Culpeper Co; Culpeper **GS:** U **SP:** Lucy Strother **VI:** No further data **P:** unk **BLW:** unk **RG:** Y **MK:** N **PH:** unk **SS:** J- DAR Hatcher; CZ pg 114; DAR A026612; SAR P-139658 **BS:** JLARC 2.

COWHERD, Francis Kirtley; b 1753; d 25 Mar 1833 **RU:** Captain, Ent serv 1779. 2nd VA Regt (Heitman; Lt in 2nd Regt of Foot 1778 to spring 1779; Capt of Milita fr Caroline Co at Guilford CH, SC 15 Mar 1781 **CEM:** Cowherd Family, "Oak Hill"; GPS unk; Gordonsville; Orange **GS:** U **SP:** Mar (Aug 1787) Lucy Scott (1763-31 Jul 1847) **VI:** Pen 1828 Orange Co. Widow pen 1838, Orange Co **P:** Y **BLW:** unk **RG:** Y **MK:** Y SAR **PH:** unk **SS:** AK J-NSSAR 1993 Reg R 668; CE pg 37, 145; DAR A026867; SAR P-139794 **BS:** 04, JLARC 1.

COWLING, Josiah; b 1739, Suffolk City; d Dec 1799 or 1800 **RU:** Patriot, Gave material aid to the cause **CEM:** Cedar Hill; GPS 36.73640, -76.58000; 105 Mahan St, Suffolk; Suffolk City **GS:** Y **SP:** Urania Monro (1739-1799) **VI:** Died in Chuckatuck, Suffolk City. Originally grave was located on Cowling Farm bet Reid's Ferry and Chuckatuck, VA. Markers, but not remains relocated to Cedar Hill Cemetery, Suffolk, Co in 1957 **P:** N **BLW:** N **RG:** N **MK:** N **PH:** unk **SS:** AL CT Bk pg 13, 20 **BS:** 53 pg 99; 196.

RU=Rank/Unit	CEM=Cemetery	GS=Gravestone	SP=Spousal Information
VI=Other Veteran Info	P=Pension	BLW=Bounty/Land Warrant	RG=Registered Grave
MK=SAR/DAR Marker	PH=Photo	SS=Service Source	BS=Burial Source

98

COX, Charles; b 1755; d 1832 **RU:** Patriot, Paid supply tax 1780 **CEM:** Cox Family; **GPS** unk; Cox, nr Turkey Pen Branch & Smith River; Henry **GS:** N **SP:** Frances Kelly (c1760-aft 1820) **VI:** No further data **P:** N **BLW:** N **RG:** N **MK:** unk **PH:** unk **SS:** DAR A026979; DD cites County Deed books III, IV tax lists pg 22 **BS:** 196.

COX, Charles; b 1690, d 1790; **RU:**Patriot, Paid personal property tax, a supply tax for Rev War expenses, Henry Co in 1782 **CEM:** Cox Family; **GPS** unk; Cox, nr Turkey Pen Branch & Smith River; Henry **GS:** N **SP:** Ida Bennett (1692-1786) **VI:** They settled on Turkey Branch and Smith River in 1769 **P:** N **BLW:** N **RG:** N **MK:** N **PH:** N **SS:** DV, image 15 pdf Henry Co 1782 **BS:** 196.

COX, Charles II; b 1721; d 1816 **RU:** Patriot, Paid supply tax, Henry Co, 1780 **CEM:** Cox Family; **GPS** unk; Cox, nr Turkey Pen Branch & Smith River; Henry **GS:** U **SP:** Mar (1740) Eleanor Watts (1722-1810) **VI:** Son of Charles (1690-1790) & Ida (Bennett) (1692-1786) Cox. Recd Land Grant 1781 for Colonial War service by Thomas Jefferson **P:** N **BLW:** Y **RG:** N **MK:** unk **PH:** unk **SS:** EA pg 22 **BS:** 196.

COX, David; b 1737, Lancaster Co, PA; d 8 Jan 1818 **RU:** Lieutenant, Served in NC and VA. Ct order 5 April 1780 certifies military service under Preston (1755-6) on frontiers of Augusta. Served under brother Capt John Cox in battles of Point Pleasant & King's Mountain **CEM:** Cox Family Farm; **GPS** unk; Rt 629 W of Baywood; Grayson **GS:** Y **SP:** Mar (VA) Margaret Ann "Peggy" McGowan (1742-1811) **VI:** Son of Joshua "John" & Mary Katherine (Rankin) Cox. Owned land with brother John in "New River Settlement" with holdings across line to NC. Died in Brindle Creek, Grayson Co **P:** unk **BLW:** unk **RG:** Y **MK:** Y SAR **PH:** unk **SS:** AK; J-NASSR 2000 Reg; DAR A026986; SAR P-139929 **BS:** 04; JLARC 1, 2, 76.

COX, Enoch Sr; b 19 Jun 1757, Orange Co, NC; d 28 Mar 1840, Grayson Co **RU:** Private, Served in VA Battalion, 14th Regt 1776. Served 1st VA Regt in battles at Brandywine and Germantown **CEM:** Old Quaker; GPS 36.64067, -80.88620; Off Old Quaker Rd Rt 727, Pipers Gap; Carroll **GS:** Y **SP:** 1) Mar (9 Jan 1781) Mary Mackey 2) Mar (5 Feb 1831 Grayson Co) Sarah Stoneman **VI:** DAR marker **P:** unk **BLW:** unk **RG:** Y **MK:** Y SAR DAR **PH:** Y **SS:** NSDAR Patriot Index 2003; E pg 185; DAR A026996; SAR P-140068 **BS:** JLARC 1, 2,11, 43; 196.

COX, James; b 24 Feb1763, Fort Chisel, Botetourt Co (later Montgomery Co), d 17 Apr 1842 **RU:** Indian Spy; served in father Capt John Cox's Co, and Col Benjamin Cleveland's NC Militia. Taken prisoner **CEM:** James Cox Family; **GPS:** not determined; Bridle Creek; Grayson **GS:** Unk **SP:** Mar 1) Sarah Elizabeth Robertson (24 Feb 1753-1 Nov 1814), 2) 14 Jan 1815, widow Sarah (----) Fielder, She applied for pen age 75, in 1835 Independence, Grayson Co, but was rejected **VI:** Son of John Cox (25 Jul 1739-1818) and Margaret Davis (1736-1806) He applied for pen, Grayson Co which was rejected for proof of more than 6 mos svc **P:** No **BLW:** No **RG:** Y **MK:** N **PH:** N **SS:** K, Vol I, pgs 252, 253; DAR A027021, cites Kegley, "Militia of Montgomery Co, VA, pg 11; SAR P-330324; Application **BS:** 196.

COX, James, Sr; b 16 Mar 1745, Halifax Co, d 1833, Patrick Co **RU:** Private, served in Col Abraham Penn's Regt **CEM:** Billy Boyds (AKA-Moore Cox) **GPS:** Not determined; Rt 788, Endicott; Franklin **GS:** Unk **SP:** Mar 22 Jan 1799, Franklin County, Sarah Ross (1763-18 Sep 1854, Patrick Co) **VI:** Nothing further **P:** No **BLW:** No **RG:** N **MK:** N **PH:** N **SS:** K, Vol I, pg 253; DAR A209159; Cites Pedigo, "Hist of Patrick and Henry Co", pgs 72, 74 **BS:** 196

COX, Peter; b 10 Jul 1744; d 6 May 1792 **RU:** Patriot; Gave material aid to cause **CEM:** Cox Homestead; **GPS** unk; Cherry Point; Northumberland **GS:** Y **SP:** Mar (27 Mar 1771, License in Northumberland (fee books) Jane (Harding) Garner, widow of Parish Garner (22 Sep 1746-__) d/o William & Sarah (Ball) Harding **VI:** Son of Peter & Mary (-----) Cox **P:** N **BLW:** N **RG:** N **MK:** N **PH:** unk **SS:** AL Ct Bk pg 5 **BS:** 47; 105 pg 419.

COX, Philip; b 15 Nov 1763; d 30 Jan 1841 **RU:** Private, served in Capt Lewis Co Home Guards, Augusta Co Militia. Specific serv Lib VA, War files, vol 4, pg 143 **CEM:** New Providence Presbyterian; GPS 37.95130, -79.30250; 1208 New Providence Rd, Raphine; Rockbridge **GS:** Y **SP:** Ann Mary Wiseman **VI:** Recd BLW **P:** unk **BLW:** Y **RG:** unk **MK:** unk **PH:** unk **SS:** C sec II pg 231; AZ pg 239; CZ pg 115; SAR P-140012 **BS:** JLARC 62, 63, 79; 196

RU=Rank/Unit	CEM=Cemetery	GS=Gravestone	SP=Spousal Information
VI=Other Veteran Info	P=Pension	BLW=Bounty/Land Warrant	RG=Registered Grave
MK=SAR/DAR Marker	PH=Photo	SS=Service Source	BS=Burial Source

COX, Samuel: b 1755, Ireland, d 12 Jul 1828 **RU:** Private, Ent serv Fauquier Co 1776. Served in Capt Peyton Valentine's Co;, Lt Col William Heth's 3d VA Regt; later served in 4th & 7th Cont Line, totaling 3 years **CEM:** Cox Homestead; GPS: unk; Howellsville; Warren **GS:** Y **SP:** Elizabeth (___), b 1765 **VI:** Pen Fauquier Co 1818, age 62, moved to Frederick Co 1820 (now Warren Co). Recd BLW 100 acres Feb 1784 **P:** Y **BLW:** Y **RG:** Y **MK:** N **PH:** N **SS:** A pg 277; E pg 185; F pg 18: K, vol 1, pg 254; DAR A027081; SAR P-140028 **BS:** 196

COX, Solomon; b 1730, New Castle, DE; d 1812 **RU:** Soldier fought at Kings Mountain 1780 **CEM:** Glenwood Methodist; GPS 36.62769, -80.88667; .1 mile E of intersection of Rt 608 Coal Creek Rd & Rt 609 Peaks Mountain Rd; Carroll **GS:** Y **SP:** Naomi Hussey **VI:** Fought in Battle of Alamance 1771; D Ross Co, Ohio. Body probably in Ohio and only memorialized here **P:** unk **BLW:** unk **RG:** Y **MK:** N **PH:** unk **SS:** B; DAR A027084; SAR P-140033 **BS:** 199.

COX, Valentine; b c1750; d by 1812 **RU:** Patriot; Gave material aid to the cause **CEM:** Cox Family; GPS unk; Forest across fr Lake Vista; Bedford **GS:** Y **SP:** Nancy Cox (1756-1823) **VI:** Has DAR marker **P:** N **BLW:** N **RG:** Y **MK:** Y **PH:** unk **SS:** Al Ct Bk IV pg 283; SAR P-330612 **BS:** AK Sep 09.

COX, William (1765-1849) See Appendix G Addenda.

CRABTREE, Jacob; b c1760; d 9 May 1818 **RU:** Private, Ent serv Lee Co 1766,. served in Capt James Crabtree's Co; Col Arthur Cambell's Regt which was in Battle at King's Mountain **CEM:** Allison; GPS 36.91140, -81.75170; W of plaster mine on Locust Cove Rd on private property with closed gate, E of Saltville; Smyth **GS:** Y **SP:** Mar (4 Aug 1786 Russell Co) Mary Price (1768-22 Jul 1849) **VI:** Widow appl for pen which was approved after her death & distributed to heirs **P:** Y **BLW:** N **RG:** N **MK:** unk **PH:** N **SS:** K pg 255; CV pg 210; DAR A201522; SAR P-140126 **BS:** 97 pg 1; 196.

CRADDOCK, Robert; b 1751; d 15 Oct 1842 **RU:** First Lieutenant, Ent serv in VA 11th Cont Line 1777; 2nd Lt 10 Aug 1777; 1st Lt 4 Jul 1779; Prisoner at Charleston 12 May 1780; Parolled May 1783; Transferred to 4th Cont Line 1781 **CEM:** Craddock Family; GPS unk; off Darbytown Rd 5.6 mi SE of Richmond City; Henrico **GS:** Y **SP:** No info **VI:** BLW issued 15 Jul 1789. Awarded 3223 acres BLW. Pensioned at "The Hermitage" Warren Co KY, thus probably memorialized in VA cemetery. R674 **P:** Y **BLW:** Y **RG:** N **MK:** N **PH:** unk **SS:** E pg 186; K Vol 1 pg 256 **BS:** 114, pg 2-3; 196.

CRADDOCK, William Cross **See APPENDIX G**

CRAFFORD, Carter; b c1755; d 10 Nov 1800 **RU:** Patriot, Gave material aid to cause Surry Co **CEM:** Carter Crafford; GPS unk; Fort Eustis SW of golf course maintenance shop; York **GS:** U **SP:** Mar (25 May 1777) Sarah (-----) **VI:** No further data **P:** N **BLW:** N **RG:** N **MK:** unk **PH:** unk **SS:** D Surry Co **BS:** 41 pg 106; 45 pg 106.

CRAFFORD, Charles; b unk; d 10 Nov 1800 VA **RU:** Patriot; Gave material aid to the cause **CEM:** Carter Crafford; GPS unk; Fort Eustis SW of golf course maintenance shop; York **GS:** Y **SP:** Martha (-----). Second husband Charlews Moore **VI:** No further data **P:** N **BLW:** N **RG:** N **MK:** N **PH:** unk **SS:** AL Ct Bk pg 12 Surry Co; E pg 186 **BS:** 41 pg 106; 45 pg 106.

CRAGHEAD, John; b unk; d 1808 **RU:** Patriot; Gave material aid to the cause **CEM:** Graghead Family; GPS unk; Rt 1361 nr Radford; Franklin **GS:** Y **SP:** Mar (3 Apr 1789 Franklin Co) Elizabeth Hale **VI:** No further data **P:** N **BLW:** N **RG:** N **MK:** N **PH:** unk **SS:** AL O Ct Bk pg 7; SAR P-331724 **BS:** 82, pg 82.

CRAIG, Alexander; b 1757; d 30 Jun 1825 **RU:** Captain, Served in 2th PA Regt **CEM:** Old Lebanon; GPS 38.08090, -79.37545; Off Rt 42, Craigsville; Augusta **GS:** Y **SP:** Mar (c1780) Martha Crawford **VI:** SAR marker **P:** unk **BLW:** unk **RG:** Y **MK:** Y SAR **PH:** unk **SS:** AK; CI; SAR P-140207 **BS:** JLARC 62; 04; 196.

CRAIG, James; b c1762; d 8 Feb 1834 **RU:** Soldier, Served in Capt Pierce's Co 6 Apr 1781, Montgomery Co Militia **CEM:** Craig Family; GPS 37.13390, -80.39220; East Park Ln; Montgomery **GS:** Y **SP:** Anna Montgomery (___-2 Dec 1841) **VI:** No further data **P:** unk **BLW:** unk **RG:** Y **MK:** unk **PH:** Y **SS:** J- DAR Hatcher; G pg 241; DAR A027231; SAR P-140242 **BS:** JLARC 2, 80 vol 1, pg 212; 196.

CRAIG, James Jr; b 23 Jul 1745; d 22 Jun 1807 **RU:** Private; Ent serv 1777, Capt Given's Co, Augusta Co Militia **CEM:** Augusta Stone Presbyterian; GPS 38.23926, -78.97356, GS 38.1411,-78.5815; 28 Old Stone Church Ln, Ft Defiance; Augusta **GS:** Y **SP:** Jane Stuart **VI:** **same**s name mayhave served in a

RU=Rank/Unit	CEM=Cemetery	GS=Gravestone	SP=Spousal Information
VI=Other Veteran Info	P=Pension	BLW=Bounty/Land Warrant	RG=Registered Grave
MK=SAR/DAR Marker	PH=Photo	SS=Service Source	BS=Burial Source

100

Fincastle co commanded by Capt James Thompson, Point Pleasant in October 1774. Pensioned Augusta Co & drew BLW 5 Dec 1794. Govt stone does not show dates, but says he was in Capt Givens Co **P:** Y **BLW:** Y **RG:** N **MK:** Y SAR plaque **PH:** unk **SS:** JLARC report; B; K Vol 1 pg 257; AZ pg 158 **BS:** JLARC 1, 2, 62; 196.

CRAIG, James Sr; b 1715, Ireland; d 07 Feb 1791 **RU:** Patriot; Gave material aid to the cause **CEM:** Augusta Stone Presbyterian; GPS 38.23926, -78.97356, GS 38.1411,-78.5813; 28 Old Stone Church Ln, Ft Defiance; Augusta **GS:** Y **SP:** Mar (1742) Mary Laird (1715-20 Feb 1785) **VI:** Stone erected by descendant indicates Pprivate in Capt Given's Co VA Militia, Augusta Co; French & Indian War. Although he is listed on his GS as a private it was probably service before the Rev War as he would be over military age **P:** N **BLW:** N **RG:** N **MK:** Y SAR plaque **PH:** unk **SS:** J-NSSAR 1993 Reg, J- DAR Hatcher; AL Ct Bk Augusta Co pg 1 **BS:** JLARC 1, 2;.196.

CRAIG, John; b 1740; d 1803 **RU:** Patriot, Gave horse to cause **CEM:** West Augusta Cemetery; GPS 38.26670, -79.33330; Rt 716 W Augusta Rd, 8 mi N of Staunton; Augusta **GS:** N **SP:** No info **VI:** No further data **P:** N **BLW:** N **RG:** Y **MK:** N **PH:** N **SS:** Z pg 118; SAR P-140257 **BS:** 142.

CRAIG, John; b 1744; d 11 Jun 1811 **RU:** Private; this name may have served in a Fincastle Co Co under Capt James Thompson at Point Pleasant, Oct 1774; same name under Capt David Beatie at King's Mountain **CEM:** Old Stone Presbyterian; GPS 38.23926, -78.97356, GS 38.1413,-78.5818; 28 Old Stone Church Ln, Ft Defiance; Augusta **GS:** Y **SP:** No info **VI:** Newer Govt stone **P:** unk **BLW:** unk **RG:** Y **MK:** Y SAR plaque **PH:** unk **SS:** B; N pg 1241; AZ pg 158; SAR P-140258 **BS:** JLARC 1, 8, 23; 196.

CRAIG, Robert; b 1746; d 1834 or 4 Feb 1851 **RU:** Captain, Ent serv first in Lancaster PA; Capt in Washington Co Militia; Battle of Kings Mountain 1780 **CEM:** Sinking Springs; GPS 36.71030, -81.98170; 136 E Main St, Abingdon; Washington **GS:** U **SP:** Jean Denny **VI:** Widow appl for pension age 89, Washington Co. Not approved; service short of 6 mos. R677 **P:** N **BLW:** unk **RG:** N **MK:** Y SAR **PH:** unk **SS:** E pg 187; K Vol 1 pg 257 **BS:** JLARC 1,80; 196.

CRAIG, Samuel; b 1762; d Jan 1808 **RU:** Private, Served in MD Troops of Cont Line (Note not person of this name that was a Sgt at Battle of Point Pleasant as he would be too young or who served as a captain) **CEM:** Old Presbyterian Meeting House; GPS 38.48528, -77.23532; 323 S Fairfax St; Alexandria City **GS:** N **SP:** Joanna (-----) (c1756-21 Oct 1806) **VI:** Alexandria merchant. Bur 24 Jan 1808, age 45. Listed on an SAR plaque in cemetery **P:**N **BLW:** N **RG:** Y **MK:** Y SAR plaque **PH:** N **SS:** BF pg 100; SAR P-140218 **BS:** 23 pg 101; 196.

CRAIG, Samuel; b unk; d unk **RU:** Sergeant, Served in Capt Alexander McClanahan's Co of Augusta Co Militia in Battle at Point Pleasant **CEM:** John Sterrett Family; GPS unk; 1 mi W of Craigsville; Augusta **GS:** Y **SP:** No info **VI:** No further data **P:** unk **BLW:** unk **RG:** N **MK:** N **PH:** unk **SS:** Z pg 116 **BS:** 142 WPA.

CRAIG, William; b 18 Jan 1750; d 8 Sep 1829 **RU:** Private, Served in Capt Given's Co, Augusta Co Militia; perhaps is the person of this name that served in the VA 7th Cont Line in Capt Springer's Co; served three yrs+ **CEM:** Augusta Stone Presbyterian; GPS 38.23926, -78.97356, GS 38.1411,-78.5815; 28 Old Stone Church Ln, Ft Defiance; Augusta **GS:** Y **SP:** Jean/Jane Anderson (1744-1811) **VI:** D age 79 **P:** unk **BLW:** unk **RG:** Y **MK:** unk **PH:** unk **SS:** E pg 187; N pg 442; DAR A027284; SAR P-140317 **BS:** JLARC 1, 2, 8, 62, 63; 196.

CRAIK, James Dr; b 1727, Dumfries, Scotland; d 4 Feb 1814 **RU:** Surgeon, Physician, chief surgeon of Cont Army; Personal physician of George Washington **CEM:** Old Presbyterian Meeting House; GPS 38.48528, -77.23532; 323, GS 38.4806,-77.0237 S Fairfax St; Alexandria City **GS:** Y **SP:** Marianne Ewell (___VA-20 Apr 1815) **VI:** After war, Washington's personal physician; present when Washington d at Mt Vernon. Modern monument. Original table stone disappeared during the Civil War. Listed on an SAR plaque in cemetery **P:** unk **BLW:** Y **RG:** Y **MK:** Y SAR plaque **PH:** unk **SS:** AK; BY pg 378; DAR A027292; SAR P-140350 **BS:** JLARC 1, 86; 23 pg 101; 196.

CRAMWELL, John S; b 1740, d 21 Nov 1812 **RU:** Patriot, Supported cause by paying supply tax included in his personal property tax in 1783 in Loudoun Co **CEM:** Leesburg Presbyterian Church; GPS

RU=Rank/Unit	CEM=Cemetery	GS=Gravestone	SP=Spousal Information
VI=Other Veteran Info	P=Pension	BLW=Bounty/Land Warrant	RG=Registered Grave
MK=SAR/DAR Marker	PH=Photo	SS=Service Source	BS=Burial Source

39.11611,-77.56722; 207 W Market St, Leesburg; Loudoun **GS:** Yes **SP:** No spousal info **VI:** No further data **P:** N **BLW:** N **RG:** N **MK:** N **PH:** N **SS:** DV 1783A image 05.pdf, Loudoun Co **BS:** 196.

CRAVENS, Margaret Harrison; b 23 Jul 1724, Lews, Sussex Co, DL **RU:** Patriot, gave material aid to cause, Rockingham Co **CEM:** Old Unmarked Lacey Springs; GPS not determined; loc nr Lacey Springs; Rockingham **GS:** N **SP:** 1) Primrose (-----), 2) mar (23 Jul 1747) Zebulon Harrison of Augusta Co (1718-Jul 1792) **VI:** Daug of Robert Cravens (25 May 1696, Kent Acres, Kent Co, DL-18 May 1762, Arkton, Rockingham Co) & Mary Harrison (25 May 1696-27 Aug 1781) **P:** N **BLW:** N **RG:** N **MK:** N **PH:** N **SS:** AL Ct Bk II, pgs 22, 35 & Commission Bk V pg 112.

CRAVENS, Mary Harrison; b 25 May 1696, Oyster Bay. Nassau Co, NY; d 27 Aug 1781 **RU:** Patriot, gave material aid to cause, Rockingham Co **CEM:** Arkton Tunker Church; GPS 38.572320,-78.696250; Mountain Valley Rd Rt 620, Arkton; Rockingham **GS:** Unk **SP:** Capt Robert Cravens, Sr (25 May 1696, Kent Acres, Kent Co, DL-18 May 1762, Arkton, Rockingham Co), son of Joseph Cravens & Rachel (----) **VI:** Daug of Isaiah Harrison (1666-1738) & Elizabeth Wright (30 Mar 1668-1698) **P:** N **BLW:** N **RG:** N **MK:** N **PH:** N **SS:** AL Ct Bk II, pg 22 & cert Commisin BK V, pgs 112, 113; DAR A027561 **BS:** 196.

CRAVENS, Robert, Jr; b Apr 1733, Lewes, Sussex Co, DL; d 27 Mar 1784 **RU:** Patriot, Responsible for obtaining a list of tytheables and property Rockingham Co, 1783 and gave material aid to cause **CEM:** Arkton Tunker Church; GPS 38.572320, -78.696250; Mountain Valley Rd Rt 620, Arkton; Rockingham **GS:** Unk **SP:** Hester Harrison (1738, Linville Creek, Rockingham Co-27 Apr 1781), d/o Jeremiah Harrison & Catherine Adams **VI:** Son of Robert Cravens (25 May 1696, Kent Acres, Kent Co, DL-18 May 1762, Arkton, Rockingham Co) & Mary Harrison (25 May 1696-27 Aug 1781) **P:** N **BLW:** N **RG:** N **MK:** N **PH:** N **SS:** AL Ct Bk I, pg 2; DV 1783 personal property listing, Rockinham Co, image 18 pdf **BS:** 196.

CRAVENS, William; b 1730, Lewes, Sussex Co, DL; d Mar 1784 **RU:** Patriot, gave material aid to cause, Rockingham Co **CEM:** Arkton Tunker Church; GPS 38.572320,-78.696250; Mountain Valley Rd Rt 620, Arkton; Rockingham **GS:** Unk **SP:**Jane Harrison (1726-1762) **VI:** Son of Robert Cravens (25 May 1696, Kent Acres, Kent Co, DL-18 May 1762, Arkton, Rockingham Co) & Mary Harrison (25 May 1696-27 Aug 1781) **P:** N **BLW:** N **RG:** N **MK:** N **PH:** N **SS:** AL Ct Bk I, pgs 2, 8, Bk II, pg 17 & Comm Bk V pgs 111, 113; **BS:** 196.

CRAWFORD, Alexander; b 1751, Augusta Co; d 19 Jun 1830 **RU:** Private, Served in Capt Young's Co, Augusta Co Militia **CEM:** New Providence Presbyterian; GPS 37.95130, -79.30250; 1208 New Providence Rd, Raphine; Rockbridge **GS:** U **SP:** 1) (-----) 2) (-----) McClure **VI:** No further data **P:** unk **BLW:** unk **RG:** Y **MK:** unk **PH:** unk **SS:** E pg 189; SAR P-140754 **BS:** JLARC 63, 79.

CRAWFORD, Ann (Anderson); b 1708; d 1803 **RU:** Patriot; Gave material aid to cause in Amherst Co **CEM:** David Crawford Plantation; GPS unk; See property records for plantation location; Amherst **GS:** Y **SP:** David Crawford **VI:** Maiden name, Anderson **P:** N **BLW:** N **RG:** Y **MK:** N **PH:** unk **SS:** AL Ct Bk pg 11; SAR P-330082 **BS:** SAR regis.

CRAWFORD, George Jr; b 1748; d 1790 **RU:** Private, Served in Capt Rankin's Co Augusta Co **CEM:** Augusta Stone Presbyterian; GPS 38.23926, -78.97356; 28 Old Stone Church Ln, Ft Defiance; Augusta **GS:** Y **SP:** Florence Henderson d/o of Samuel & Jane (Henderson) Thompson. Mar (2) Christian Surface in 1799 **VI:** Govt stone indicates he d in 1791; will probated 21 Sep 1790 **P:** unk **BLW:** unk **RG:** Y **MK:** Y SAR plaque **PH:** unk **SS:** E pg 189; SAR P-140778 **BS:** JLARC 2, 62, 63; 196.

CRAWFORD, John; b 1741, Augusta Co, d 13 Jan 1832 **RU:** Captain/Patriot, Served in Lt Col Richard Campbell's 2d VA Regt; Captured at Charleston, Exchanged Jul 1781; Served to Jun 1783. Provided horse and flour to cause **CEM:** Hebron; GPS 38.14140, -79.15500; 423 Hebron Rd; Staunton City **GS:** Y **SP:** 1) Margaret "Peggy" Crawford d/o Patrick Crawford & Sally Wilson, 2) Mary Craig 3) Sarah Newman (1767-1850) **VI:** Son of Alexander Crawford & Mary McPheeters **P:** unk **BLW:** unk **RG:** Y **MK:** unk **PH:** unk **SS:** : D pg 67 Augusta Co; BS pg 32, 37, 56 DP pg 208; SAR P-140836 **BS:** 196.

CRAWFORD, John; b 1765; d 6 Apr 1845 **RU:** Private, Served in Capt Given's Co; Augusta Co Militia **CEM:** Bethel Presbyterian; GPS 38.04257, -79.17283; 563 Bethel Green Rd, Middlebrook; Augusta **GS:** N **SP:** No info **VI:** No further data **P:** unk **BLW:** unk **RG:** N **MK:** N **PH:** N **SS:** E pg 189 **BS:** 142 Bethel.

RU=Rank/Unit	CEM=Cemetery	GS=Gravestone	SP=Spousal Information
VI=Other Veteran Info	P=Pension	BLW=Bounty/Land Warrant	RG=Registered Grave
MK=SAR/DAR Marker	PH=Photo	SS=Service Source	BS=Burial Source

102

CRAWFORD, John; b 29 Mar 1761; d 17 Dec 1846 **RU:** Private/Ensign?, Served in Capt Given's Co, Augusta Co Militia; Ensign in militia before Oct 1783 in Capt Simpson's Co? **CEM:** Augusta Stone Presbyterian; **GPS** 38.23926, -78.97356, GS 38.1414,-78.5820; 28 Old Stone Church Ln, Ft Defiance; Augusta **GS:** Y **SP:** Rebecca Allen (22 Feb 1769-6 Jun 1851) **VI:** Son of Patrick (1723-1787) and Sally (Willson) (1726-1787) Crawford. Although the title "Maj" is styled on his GS, because of his age he would have probably obtained that rank after the war period ending Oct 1783 **P:** unk **BLW:** unk **RG:** Y **MK:** unk **PH:** unk **SS:** E pg 189; SAR P-140860 **BS:** JLARC 2, 8, 23, 63; 196.

CRAWFORD, Nathan; b 1750, Antrim, Ireland; d 1822 **RU:** Patriot, Furnished a substitute to serve **CEM:** Cleek; **GPS** 38.19310, -79.73220; Rt 220 Sam Snead Hwy, Warm Springs; Bath **GS:** Y **SP:** Jane/Jean Sitlington (____-1829) **VI:** Son of James & Mary (Gilbert) Crawford. Govt marker on grave **P:** N **BLW:** N **RG:** Y **MK:** N **PH:** Y **SS:** J-NSSAR 1993 Reg; SAR P-140869 B; DD **BS:** JLARC 1, 196.

CRAWFORD, Patrick; b 1723, Northern Ireland; d 18 Dec 1787 **RU:** Patriot; Gave material aid to cause **CEM:** Augusta Stone Presbyterian; **GPS** 38.23926, -78.97356, GS 38.1414,-78.5820; 28 Old Stone Church Ln, Ft Defiance; Augusta **GS:** Y **SP:** Mar (c1747) Sally Willson (1726 Northern Ireland-1787) **VI:** Son of William & Mary Ann (Douglas) Crawford of Scotland. Although the title "Maj" is styled on his GS, because of his age he would have probably obtained that rank other than in the war period ending in October 1783 **P:** N **BLW:** N **RG:** Y **MK:** unk **PH:** unk **SS:** B; AL Certificate Augusta Co; SAR P-140870 **BS:** JLARC 62; 196.

CRAWFORD, Thomas; b unk; d 1794 **RU:** Private, Served in Cont Line for three yrs **CEM:** Old Christ Church Episcopal; **GPS** 38.80625, -77.04718; 118 N Washington St; Alexandria City **GS:** N **SP:** No info **VI:** Drew pension in Frederick Co **P:** Y **BLW:** unk **RG:** N **MK:** N **PH:** N **SS:** E pg 189 **BS:** 110 pg 92.

CRAWFORD, William; b 1764; d 22 Feb 1832 **RU:** Lieutenant, Served in Monongalia Co Militia and is listed on payrolls of VA soldiers paid at Romney, IL **CEM:** Crawford Family #2; **GPS** unk; Rt 726, .6 mi fr jct with Rt 613 on Sam Brown property, Peaked Mountain; Rockingham **GS:** Y **SP:** Mar (1803) Nancy Smith (1783-25 Aug 1853) **VI:** Son of Patrick (1723 Ireland-1 Dec 1787) & Sally (Wilson) (1732-___) Crawford **P:** unk **BLW:** unk **RG:** N **MK:** unk **PH:** unk **SS:** E pg 189; CZ pg 117 fr MS at LVA **BS:** 51.

CREANCE, Guillaume; b unk; d 1781 **RU:** Seaman, Served on "Saint-Esprit"; d Yorktown battle **CEM:** French Memorial; **GPS** 36.81944, -79.39933; Yorktown; York **GS:** U **SP:** No info **VI:** No further data **P:** unk **BLW:** unk **RG:** Y **MK:** unk **PH:** unk **SS:** J-Yorktown Historian; SAR P-140940 **BS:** JLARC 1, 74.

CREASY, William; b unk; d 1828 **RU:** Patriot; Gave material aid to cause **CEM:** Creasy Family; **GPS** unk; nr jct Rts 615 and 648; Campbell **GS:** U **SP:** No info **VI:** No further data **P:** N **BLW:** N **RG:** Y **MK:** N **PH:** unk **SS:** D Campbell Co; SAR P-140946 **BS:** JLARC 36.

CREGER, George; b 1763; d 1838 **RU:** Private, Served in Montgomery Co Militia **CEM:** Browning's Mill; GPS unk; Old Stage Rd; Wythe **GS:** U **SP:** Elizabeth Catron **VI:** No further data **P:** unk **BLW:** unk **RG:** N **MK:** unk **PH:** unk **SS:** G pg 232 **BS:** JLARC 123.

CREIGHTON, Robert Dr; b c1735, Scotland; d 18 Nov 1801 **RU:** Physician; Served in Braddock's Army **CEM:** Old Presbyterian Meeting House; **GPS** 38.48528, -77.23532; 323 S Fairfax St; Alexandria City **GS:** Y **SP:** Left a widow, not named **VI:** Moved to Jamaica after Braddock's defeat for 40 yrs, returned to Alexandria for medical attention, and d of consumption age 66 (GS inscription) **P:** unk **BLW:** unk **RG:** N **MK:** N **PH:** unk **SS:** AK; AL Ct Bk lt pg 5, 6, 7; B **BS:** 04; 23 pg 101.

CREPEL, Pierre; b unk; d 1781 **RU:** Seaman, Served on "Languedoc"; d Yorktown battle **CEM:** French Memorial; **GPS** 36.81944, -79.39933; Yorktown; York **GS:** U **SP:** No info **VI:** No further data **P:** unk **BLW:** unk **RG:** Y **MK:** unk **PH:** unk **SS:** J-Yorktown Historian; SAR P-140995 **BS:** JLARC 1, 74.

CRESPOT, Francois; b unk; d 1781 **RU:** Seaman, Served on "Duc De Bourgogne"; d Yorktown battle **CEM:** French Memorial; **GPS** 36.81944, -79.39933; Yorktown; York **GS:** U **SP:** No info **VI:** No further data **P:** unk **BLW:** unk **RG:** Y **MK:** unk **PH:** unk **SS:** J-Yorktown Historian; SAR P-141014 **BS:** JLARC 1, 74.

CREWS, Joseph; b c1757; d 26 May 1843 **RU:** Private, Ent serv Amherst Co **CEM:** Crews Family; GPS unk; Nr Big Island; Bedford **GS:** Y **SP:** Mar (4 Jan 1822 Bedord Co (bond) Nancy Eubank/Newbank (c1790-___) She drew pension as blind person; cut off during Civil War until she signed oath of

RU=Rank/Unit	CEM=Cemetery	GS=Gravestone	SP=Spousal Information
VI=Other Veteran Info	P=Pension	BLW=Bounty/Land Warrant	RG=Registered Grave
MK=SAR/DAR Marker	PH=Photo	SS=Service Source	BS=Burial Source

103

allegiance to US Govt. Then granddaughter granted another BLW. **VI:** Pensioned age 75 in Bedford Co in 1832. Widow granded BLW 1855 age 65. R690 **P:** Y **BLW:** Y **RG:** N **MK:** N **PH:** unk **SS:** K Vol 1 pg 263; SAR P-141061 **BS:** 80 vol pg 217.

CRIM (KRIM/GRIM), Johann Peter; b 23 May 1749, Germany; d 6 Sept 1825 **RU:** Soldier, Served in Capt Exekiel Harrison's Co, East District **CEM:** Rader Lutheran; GPS 38.65073, -78.78055; 17072 Raders Church Rd, Timberville; Rockingham **GS:** Y **SP:** Anna Maria Sophia Mueller **VI:** No further data **P:** unk **BLW:** unk **RG:** Y **MK:** N **PH:** unk **SS:** E; I **BS:** Church records; JLARC 2.

CRIM, John; b 15 Oct 1755, Lancaster, PA, d 19 Apr 1840, Newton, Frederick Co **RU:** Private; Capt Rudolph Stroddler's Co; Col Boyd's NJ Regt; Capt Andrew Baer's Co; Col John Fierney's PA Regt **CEM:** Trinity Evangical Lutheran Church; GPS 39.082800, -78.216790; Newtown; Frederick **GS:** Yes with DAR marker **SP:** Mar 1) Julianna Mainzer (6 Jun 1762-12 May 1821), 2) Phoebe Drake **VI:** Recd pen and BLW of 160 acres in 1855 **P:** Yes # SW26182 **BLW:** Y #28508 **RG:** Y **MK:** DAR **PH:** N **SS:** DAR A027797; SAR P-141083 BS: SAR PRS.

CRITTENDEN, William; b c1729; d 27 Mar 1817 **RU:** Private; Served in VA State Line **CEM:** Schuler Place; GPS unk; Rt 705; Orange **GS:** Y **SP:** No info **VI:** No further data **P:** unk **BLW:** unk **RG:** N **MK:** N **PH:** unk **SS:** AK; AI app I pg 89 **BS:** 04; 22 pg 86.

CRITZ, Hamon Jr (Herman); b 1760; d 5 Aug 1828 **RU:** Captain, Ent serv Henry Co Militia 1777 **CEM:** Critz Baptist Church; GPS unk; 3294 Dogwood Rd, Critz; Patrick **GS:** U **SP:** Mar (1786) Nancy Dalton c1766-___). Resided as widow near Stokes Co NC line. **VI:** Widow pen 1841 Patrick Co. R692 **P:** Y **BLW:** unk **RG:** Y **MK:** unk **PH:** unk **SS:** K Vol 1 pg 265; DAR A027892; SAR P-141205 **BS:** JLARC 2, 4, 30.

CROCKETT, Hugh; b 1730 Lancaster, PA; d 1816 **RU:** Colonel; Specific serv Lib VA; War files; Auditors Acct XV, pg 401 **CEM:** White; GPS 37.15829, -80.25423; Rt 637, S of Shawsville; Montgomery **GS:** U **SP:** Mar (1773) Rebecca Larton (1749 Montgomery Co-1836 Crockett Springs) **VI:** No further data **P:** unk **BLW:** unk **RG:** N **MK:** unk **PH:** unk **SS:** J-NSSAR 1993 Reg, J- DAR Hatcher; CZ pg 119 **BS:** JLARC 1, 2; 196.

CROCKETT, John; b 1737, Orange Co; d Aft 14 Feb 1798 **RU:** 1st Lt; Served in Montgomery Co Militia; Promoted 3 Feb 1777 **CEM:** Crockett Family; GPS 37.01560, -81.05500; Off Rt 600, Crockett's Cove; Wythe **GS:** U **SP:** Elizabeth Betsey Montgomery **VI:** Son of Samuel (1694-1749) & Esther Thomson (Sayers) (1710-1770) Crockett; Juryman; Surveyor DAR marker **P:** unk **BLW:** unk **RG:** Y **MK:** Y **PH:** unk **SS:** E pg 193; DAR A027946; SAR P-141294 **BS:** JLARC 2, 101; 196.

CROCKETT, Joseph; b 1767; d 1853 **RU:** Captain/Patriot; Gave material aid to cause **CEM:** Crockett; GPS unk; SR 649, turn left to cross RR tracks to Suthers home; Wythe **GS:** U **SP:** Mar (1800) Catherine Montgomery (20 Jan 1772-18 Jan 1833) **VI:** No further data **P:** unk **BLW:** unk **RG:** Y **MK:** unk **PH:** unk **SS:** D Cumberland Co; SAR P-141302 **BS:** JLARC 76, 123.

CROPPER, John; b 23 Dec 1755; d 15 Jan 1821 **RU:** Colonel, Ent serv Accomac Co 1778; Served in 7th, 9th,11th Cont Line; Resigned 16 Aug 1779, Appointed Col of the militia to close of war **CEM:** Bowman's Folly; GPS unk; End of Rt 652, private lane, 2.4 mi NE of Accomac, Joynes Neck; Accomack **GS:** Y **SP:** 1) Mar (15 Aug 1776 Northampton Co) Margaret Pettit (___-Jun 1784, Occahannock, Northhampton Co) d/o William & Mary (-----) Pettit 2) Mar (18 Sep 1790 Hill's Farm, Accomack Co) Catharine Bayley (24 Jan 1772-24 Jan 1855) d/o Thomas & Ann (-----) Bayly. **VI:** Son of Sebastian & Sabra (-----) Cropper. Father was also a RW soldier. Member of General Assembly 1784. Styled "General" on his GS. Widow pensioned 1838 Accomack Co. Awarded BLW of 8,888 acres. R696 **P:** Y **BLW:** Y **RG:** Y **MK:** unk **PH:** unk **SS:** J-NSSAR 1993 Reg; K Vol 1 pg 267; DAR A028054; SAR P-141331 **BS:** JLARC 1.

CROPPER, Sebastian; b 1731; d 20 Mar 1776 **RU:** Captain, Served in Accomac Co Militia **CEM:** Bowman's Folly; GPS unk; End of Rt 652, private lane, 2.4 mi NE of Accomac, Joynes Neck; Accomack **GS:** Y **SP:** Sabra Corbin (___-2 Nov 1791) d/o Gen John & Sarah (-----) Corbin **VI:** D age 45. Son of Boman & Tabitha (-----) Cropper **P:** unk **BLW:** unk **RG:** Y **MK:** N **PH:** unk **SS:** AK; E pg 194; SAR P-141443 **BS:** 04; 37 pg 60.

RU=Rank/Unit · CEM=Cemetery · GS=Gravestone · SP=Spousal Information
VI=Other Veteran Info · P=Pension · BLW=Bounty/Land Warrant · RG=Registered Grave
MK=SAR/DAR Marker · PH=Photo · SS=Service Source · BS=Burial Source

104

CROSS, William; b 1760, Botetourt Co; d Mar 1820, **RU**: Private, served in 1st Light Dragoons, 1783 m**CEM**: Cranford United Methodist Church AKA Lewis Chapel; GPS 38.690563,-77.206405; loc off Old Colchester Rd N of jct with Gunston Rd, Lorton; Fairfax **GS**: Y Section H, lot Site 3 **SP**: Elizabeth Alderson (1818-1890) **VI**: Son of John Cross (1738-1811) & Mary Reid (___-1818) **P**: unk **BLW**: unk **RG**: N **MK**: N **PH**: unk **SS**: E pg 194 **BS**: 154.

CROSS, William; b 1748; d 1836 **RU**: Lieutenant; Under command of Maj James Crew, Monongalia Co Militia; Stationed at Ft Pitt in Oct 1777 **CEM**: High Bridge Presbyterian; GPS 37.62420, -79.58610; 67 High Bridge Rd, Natural Bridge; Rockbridge **GS**: Y **SP**: No info **VI**: No further data **P**: unk **BLW**: unk **RG**: Y **MK**: N **PH**: unk **SS**: E pg 680 **BS**: 154.

CROSS, William; b 1733, England; d 1798 **RU**: Patriot; Gave material aid to cause **CEM**: Cross Family Farm; GPS unk; Nr Roanoke; Botetourt **GS**: N **SP**: Elizabeth (-----) **VI**: No further data **P**: N **BLW**: N **RG**: N **MK**: unk **PH**: N **SS**: AL Ct Bk pg 6, 9, 13 **BS**: 196 Crumley.

CROUCHER, Thomas; b 1768, Dumfries, Scotland; d 22 May 1792 **RU**: Captain, In charge of taking prisoners fr Battle of Yorktown to Noland's Ferry on Potomac; Served 10th Cont Line **CEM**: Old Christ Church Episcopal; GPS 38.80625, -77.04718; 118 N Washington St; Alexandria City **GS**: Y **SP**: No info **VI**: D age 24; Place of birth on stone **P**: unk **BLW**: unk **RG**: Y **MK**: N **PH**: unk **SS**: AZ pg 169; **BS**: 110 pg 96; 20 pg 136; 196.

CROW, James; b unk, Spotsylvania Co; d 1798 **RU**: Patriot, Specific serv at Lib VA, War files, vol 4, pg 131 **CEM**: Nicholson Family; GPS unk; Syria; Madison **GS**: N **SP**: Elizabeth (-----) **VI**: No further data **P**: N **BLW**: N **RG**: Y **MK**: N **PH**: N **SS**: D pg 346; CZ pg 120; SAR P-141734 **BS**: 04.

CROW, Thomas, Sr; b unk, d 1811 **RU**: Private, Enlisted in C. Minnis's Co; Col Fleming's 1st VA Regt; Feb 1778; Served to Jan 1779 **CEM**: Scott; GPS 36.88110, -81.38720; Across I-81 from rest stop Phipps Rd, Atkins Smyth **GS**: N **SP**: No info **VI**: Son of Robert Crow and Mary (-----) **P**: unk **BLW**: unk **RG**: N **MK**: N **PH**: N **SS**: DP pg 209 **BS**: 196.

CROWE, Edward; b 1751; d 1830 **RU**: Soldier, Served 41 days Capt William Campbell's Co **CEM**: Royal Oak; GPS 36.84315, -81.49660; Behind Marion Baptist Church, Marion; Smyth **GS**: U **SP**: June Mackey **VI**: No further data **P**: unk **BLW**: unk **RG**: Y **MK**: Y **PH**: unk **SS**: SAR P-141774 **BS**: JLARC 114. **(CROXTON**, Carter See Appendix G)

CRUMLEY, William; b 1735, Chester Co, PA; d 30 Sep 1792 **RU**: Patriot; Gave material aid to cause **CEM**: Back Creek Quaker, aka Gainesboro United Methodist; GPS 39.27861, -78.25694; 166 Siler Ln, Gainesboro; Frederick **GS**: U **SP**: Mar (1763) Hannah Mercer (___-1774), mar 2) Sarah (___) **VI**: Son of James (1712-1764 & (-----) Crumley. **P**: N **BLW**: N **RG**: Y **MK**: unk **PH**: unk **SS**: AL three cert, Berkeley Co; DAR A028351; SAR P-141920 **BS**: 196.

CRUTCHFIELD, John; b 1756; d Aft 1820 **RU**: Private, Specific serv Lib VA, Report Sec of War (pensions); vol 2, pg 50 **CEM**: Belle Air Plantation; GPS 37.20490, -77.34000; Rt 5, New Hope; Charles City Co **GS**: U **SP**: No info **VI**: Grave near gate **P**: unk **BLW**: unk **RG**: N **MK**: N **PH**: unk **SS**: K Vol 1 Crutchfield; CZ pg 122 **BS**: 127 Crutchfield.

CRUTCHFIELD, Lewis; b unk; d unk **RU**: Soldier, Served in Charles City Co Militia **CEM**: Belle Air Plantation; GPS 37.20490, -77.34000; Rt 5, New Hope; Charles City Co **GS**: U **SP**: Mar (29 Oct 1779 Charles City Co) Mildred Jamison, spinster **VI**: Cem betw Belair house and gate, thereafter called "Soldiers' Burying Ground" **P**: unk **BLW**: unk **RG**: Y **MK**: unk **PH**: unk **SS**: CZ pg 122; SAR P-141961 **BS**: JLARC 110.

CRUTCHFIELD, Stapleton; b 4 Feb 1729, Middlesex Co, d 17 Jun 1788 **RU**: Private/Patriot; Served 3 yrs in 10th VA Regt, 2d VA Brigade and 1st Cont Line; Gave material aid to cause **CEM**: Spring Forest; GPS not determined; Snell, vic jcts Rts 606, 738 and 208 at Spring Forest Plantation house; Spotsylvania **GS**: Unk **SP**: Sarah Durrett (___-7 Aug 1792) **VI**: Enlisted age 47;Planter **P**: N **BLW**: N **RG**: Y **MK**: N **PH**: N **SS**: C pg 410; D Vol 3, pgs 256, 257, 863; E pg 151; F pg 16; DAR A203794; SAR P-141962; SAR application; **BS**: 196.

CULLEN (CULLINS), John; b 11 Mar 1748, Scotland; d 7 Aug 1827 **RU**: Sergeant, Served in 3rd VA Regt commanded by Col Thomas Marshall in Nov 1777 **CEM**: Bethleham Lutheran; GPS 38.05454,

RU=Rank/Unit	CEM=Cemetery	GS=Gravestone	SP=Spousal Information
VI=Other Veteran Info	P=Pension	BLW=Bounty/Land Warrant	RG=Registered Grave
MK=SAR/DAR Marker	PH=Photo	SS=Service Source	BS=Burial Source

-78.95222; 1148 Ladd Rd; Waynesboro City **GS:** Y **SP:** Nancy Foster (23-6 Feb 1758, England-24 Mar 1831) **VI:** Son of Dr William & (-----) Cullen **P:** unk **BLW:** unk **RG:** Y **MK:** N **PH:** unk **SS:** AP roll VA 3d Div; DAR A028453; SAR P-331216 **BS:** 142.

CULLER(CULLERS), Jacob and John see KULLERS,(KULLER), Jacob & John;

CULTON, Alexander; b unk, d 12 Sep 1824 **RU:** Patriot; Gave material aid to cause in Rockbridge Co **CEM**: Walkerland; GPS 37.94613, -79.38794; Rt 602 Walkers Creek Rd, S of jct with Rt 724, top of hill behind Maxwelton Camp Cabins; Rockbridge **GS:** Yes **SP:** Rebecca Woods (1760-12 Sep 1825) **VI:** No further information **P:** No **BLW:** No **RG:** N **MK:** N **PH:** N **SS:** AL Ct Bk pg 2, Comm Bk V, pg 71 Rockbridge Co **BS:** 196

CUMMINGS, Charles Rev; b 1731; d 1812 **RU:** Patriot; Member Fincastles Resolutions Committee of Safety 1775 **CEM**: Sinking Springs; GPS 36.71030, -81.98170; 136 E Main St, Abingdon; Washington **GS:** U **SP:** Mildred Carter (_____-_____Abingdon Washington Co) d/o John & (-----) Carter of Lancaster Co **VI:** No further data **P:** N **BLW:** N **RG:** Y **MK:** unk **PH:** unk **SS:** J-NSSAR 1993 Reg, J- DAR Hatcher; plaque in cemetery; DAR A028520; SAR P-142131 **BS:** JLARC 1, 2; 212 pg 73.

CURDINET, Francois; b unk; d 1781 **RU:** Soldier, Served in Gatinais Bn; D Yorktown battle **CEM**: French Memorial; GPS 36.81944, -79.39933; Yorktown; York **GS:** U **SP:** No info **VI:** No further data **P:** unk **BLW:** unk **RG:** unk **MK:** unk **PH:** unk **SS:** J-Yorktown Historian; SAR P-142351 **BS:** JLARC 74.

CURDON, Louis; b unk; d 1781 **RU:** Soldier, Served in Gatinais Bn D Yorktown battle **CEM**: French Memorial; GPS 36.81944, -79.39933; Yorktown; York **GS:** U **SP:** No info **VI:** No further data **P:** unk **BLW:** unk **RG:** Y **MK:** unk **PH:** unk **SS:** J-Yorktown Historian; SAR P-142352 **BS:** JLARC 74.

CURRIE, James; b 1744, Annandale, Scotland; d 23 Apr 1807 **RU:** Captain, Served in Cont Line. Specific serv Lib VA; MS Involved with arrangement of Cont Line pgs 10,16 **CEM**: St John's Episcopal; GPS 37.53183, -77.41958; 2401 E Broad St; Richmond City **GS:** Y **SP:** No info **VI:** Was a doctor in Richmond for 40 yrs **P:** unk **BLW:** unk **RG:** N **MK:** N **PH:** unk **SS:** CZ pg 124; E pg 201 **BS:** 28 pg 426.

CURRY, Robert; b 10 Nov 1717 Ulster, Ireland; d 5 Jan 1800 **RU:** Captain, Served in Homeguards **CEM**: Augusta Stone Presbyterian; GPS 38.23926, -78.97356, GS 38.1411,-78.5820; 28 Old Stone Church Ln, Ft Defiance; Augusta **GS:** Y **SP:** Anne (-----) (25 Sep 1727, Ulster, Ireland-15 May 1819) **VI:** Commanded Co in the Augusta Co Militia before war 16 August 1774. Elder of Augusta Church; Styled "Doctor" **P:** unk **BLW:** unk **RG:** Y **MK:** Y SAR plaque **PH:** Y **SS:** B; AH pg 7 DAR A028779; SAR P-142471 **BS:** JLARC 2, 8, 63; 196. **SEE APPENDIX G**

CURTIS, Charles; b unk; d 1 Apr 1778 **RU:** Private, Capt Thomas Triplett's Co, Col William Grayson' Regt Cont Line **CEM**: Rev War Court House Plaque; GPS not determined; 4110 Chain Bridge Rd; Fairfax **GS:** Memorialized on plaque 2017 by Geo Washington Chapter, VASSAR **SP** No info **VI:** Died in service **P:** N **BLW:** N **RG:** N **MK:** N **PH:** N **SS E pg 202**; EP sources: **BS:** None.

CURTIS, James; b 1763; d 6 Jan 1810 **RU:** Lieutenant/Patriot, Served US Navy on ship "Lancaster": Gave material aid to the cause **CEM**: Old Stone Methodist; GPS 39.11725, -77.56609; 168 W Cornwall St, Leesburg; Loudoun **GS:** Y **SP:** Unmarried **VI:** No further data **P:** unk **BLW:** unk **RG:** N **MK:** N **PH:** unk **SS:** L pg 177; AL Ct Booklet **BS:** 25 pg 73.

CURTIS, John; b 1735; d 1813 **RU:** Patriot; paid personal property tax 1783 Stafford Co; partially pay for Rev War expenses **CEM**: Broad Oak Farm; GPS not determined; Ferry Rd; Stafford **GS:** Plaque mounted on stone base **SP:** Elizabeth Porch (1759-1828 **VI:** Son of Richard & Sarah Jones Curtis **P:** N **BLW:** N **RG:** N **MK:** N **PH:** N **SS:** DV image 03 pdf; Stafford Co 1783 **BS:** 196.

CURTIS, John; b 1763; d 6 Jan 1810 **RU:** Corporal; Served in Capt Bullen's Co, Stafford Co Militia **CEM**: Jett Family #2; GPS unk; End Broad Oak Ln. See property records for homestead location; Stafford **GS:** Y **SP:** No info **VI:** No further data **P:** unk **BLW:** unk **RG:** N **MK:** N **PH:** unk **SS:** AP NARA fdr364 **BS:** 03 Addenump, 26.

CURTIS, (CUSTIS) John Parke; b unk; d 1781 **RU:** Soldier, Served fr VA; Aide to Washington; D battle Yorktown **CEM**: Yorktown Victory Monument Tablet; GPS 38.28350, -78.54150; Yorktown; York **GS:** U **SP:** No info **VI:** Actually buried in Eltham Plantation in York Co (GPS 37.269194, -76.662057);

RU=Rank/Unit	CEM=Cemetery	GS=Gravestone	SP=Spousal Information
VI=Other Veteran Info	P=Pension	BLW=Bounty/Land Warrant	RG=Registered Grave
MK=SAR/DAR Marker	PH=Photo	SS=Service Source	BS=Burial Source

106

memorialized on victory monument **P:** unk **BLW:** unk **RG:** Y **MK:** unk **PH:** unk **SS:** J-Yorktown Historian SAR P-142588 **BS:** JLARC 74.

CURTIS, William; b c1759; d 22 Apr 1808 **RU:** Ensign, Served in Middlesex Co Militia. Recommended as officer 28 Jul 1777; oath as Ens 24 Nov 1777 **CEM:** Highgate; GPS unk; Cash Post Office; Gloucester **GS:** Y **SP:** Ariana M Grymes (2nd husband Peter Kemp Jr.) **VI:** No further data **P:** unk **BLW:** unk **RG:** N **MK:** Y SAR **PH:** unk **SS:** AK; E pg 02 **BS:** 04; 48 pg 38.

CUSTER (CUSTARD), Paul; 1730; d 1820 **RU:** Patriot, paid personal property tax, 1782, Rockingham Co, considered to be a supply tax for Rev War expenses **CEM:** Custer Family; GPS 38.664260,-78.927229; Little Dry River Rd (Rt 818), Fulks Run; Rockingham **GS:** Unk **SP:** Lucinda Malone (1734-1811) **VI:** Son of Conrad Custer (1695-1772) & Susannah Adams (1695-1747) **P:** N **BLW:** N **RG:** Y **MK:** N **PH:** N **SS:** DV image 20 pdf; Rockingham Co, 1782; SAR P-142900 **BS:** 196.

CUSTER (CUSTARD), Richard Sr; b 1 Jun 1757, PA; d 14 Feb 1837 **RU:** Private, Ent serv Rockingham Co 1781; Served 3 mos-Capt George Huston's Co, Col Nall's Regt; Skirmishes at Wiliamsburg & Hot Water Creek 1781-served 3 mos Capt Anthony Rader's Co **CEM:** Custer Family; GPS 38.664260,-78.927229; Dry River S Rt 259, Fulks Run; Rockingham **GS:** Y **SP:** Mar (18 Mar 1790) Jane Humble (c1771-___) d/o Conrad & (-----) Humble. **VI:** Pensioned Rockingham Co 1832. Widow pen Rockingham Co 1841 age 70. R725. W6749 **P:** Y **BLW:** unk **RG:** Y **MK:** Y SAR **PH:** unk **SS:** K Vol 1 pg 278-9; O; AK; SAR P-142905 **BS:** 04, JLARC 4, 64.

CUSTIS, Henry; b 27 Jul 1743; d 28 Jul 1793 **RU:** Lieutenant Colonel, Oath-Maj 30 Jul 1777; Lt Col 30 Apr 1782 Accomack Co VA Militia **CEM:** Mt Custis; GPS unk; Off Rt 622 2.5 mi of Rt 13, Bayley's Neck; Accomack **GS:** Y **SP:** Mar (c1765) Matilda Hack **VI:** Son of Robinson Custis & Mary Parramore. Stone styles him Lt Col. DAR marker on gravesite **P:** unk **BLW:** unk **RG:** Y **MK:** Y SAR **PH:** unk **SS:** E pg 202; BT; SAR P-142906 **BS:** AS SAR reg; 196.

CUSTIS. John; b 23 Feb 1751, Northampton Co; d 3 Mar 1809 **RU:** Captain; 26 Nov 1777; Accomack Co Militia **CEM:** Custis Family Deep Creek Plantation; GPS unk; Mink Farm Rd, Onancock; Accomack **GS:** N **SP:** Mar 17 Dec 1772, Catherine Parker (30 Mar 1753-29 Oct 1839) **VI:** Son of Major Thomas W Custis (1721, Northampton Co-21 Dec 1810) and Casandra "Cassie" Elizabeth Wise (7 Apr 1728-26 Apr 1803) **P:** N **BLW:** N **RG:** N **MK:** Y **PH:** N **SS:** E pg 202; DAR A029137 **BS:** 80 vol 1, pg 225; 196.

CUSTIS, John Parke "Jacky;" b 27 Nov 1754, New Kent Co; d 5 Nov 1781, Eltham, New Kent Co **RU:** Aide/Patriot Aide-de-Camp, Gen Geo Washington, and gave material aid to cause **CEM:** Mount Vernon Estate; GPS 37.269194, -76.662057; burial grd, Mount Vernon; Fairfax **GS:** Y **SP:** Eleanor Calvert (1754-28 Sep 1811), d/o Benedict Swingate Calvart (1722-1788) & Elizabeth Calvert (1730-1798) **VI:** Son of Daniel Park Custis (1711-1757) & Martha Dandridge (1731-1802); died of camp fever, body taken to Mt Vernon **P:** N **BLW:** N **RG:** Y **MK:** Unk **PH:** N **SS:** DAR 029139; SAR P-142588 D vol !, pgs 340,345; EP sources **BS:** 196.

CUSTIS, Thomas; b 1721; d 21 Dec 1810 **RU:** Patriot; Gave material aid to the cause **CEM:** Deep Creek Plantation; GPS unk; Onancock; Accomack **GS:** N **SP:** No info **VI:** In 1792 Deep Creek House (at end of Mink Farm Rd) was built for him **P:** N **BLW:** N **RG:** N **MK:** unk **PH:** N **SS:** AI Cert Accomack Co **BS:** 196.

CUTLER, William; b c1762; d 17 May 1836 **RU:** Private, Specific serv Lib VA, Journal House of Delegates 1833-4, Doc 33 pg 11 **CEM:** Mt Pleasant; GPS unk; Rt 609; Dinwiddie **GS:** Y **SP:** 1) Mar (20 Jul 1790 Boston MA) Sally Henderson 2) Susan (-----) widow of Windfield Mason **VI:** Was called Dr fr Weston at time of marriage. After war owned a celebrated racing stable **P:** unk **BLW:** unk **RG:** N **MK:** N **PH:** unk **SS:** AJ Middlesex Co; CZ pg 125 **BS:** 70 pg 121.

DABNEY, Charles; b 1745, Montpelier, Hanover Co; d 15 Dec 1829 **RU:** Colonel, Marched fr Hanover Co with Patrick Henry to exhort public powder taken fr Williamsburg by Lord Dunmore, 1775. Organized Hanover District minutemen; Maj 3rd VA State Regt at Germantown & Princeton, 1777; Col of state Militia 1778-1781. Was Commander at York & Portsmouth Nov 1781. Served 1778 with Gen "Mad Anthony" Wayne at Stony Point, Lt Col of "Dabney's Legion." Joined Cont Line with 2nd VA State Line Regt at Valley Forge. Served under Lafayette; 1781, Yorktown and held confidence of the Marquis **CEM:** Aldingham; GPS unk; On Plantation this name. See property records for directions. Hanover **GS:**

RU=Rank/Unit	CEM=Cemetery	GS=Gravestone	SP=Spousal Information
VI=Other Veteran Info	P=Pension	BLW=Bounty/Land Warrant	RG=Registered Grave
MK=SAR/DAR Marker	PH=Photo	SS=Service Source	BS=Burial Source

N **SP:** No info **VI:** Son of William (1707-1773) & Anne (Barret) (1715-1779) Dabney. On 19 Oct 1781, Articles of Capitulation of Cornwallis given at dinner with Geo. Washington. Jan 1782 state line units consolidated to Charles Dabney's Virginia State Legion. Stopped mutiny Sep 1782. Legion disbanded Apr 1783. Charter member of The Society of the Cincinnati. D Montpelier, Hanover Co. Probably bur in cnr of garden of "Aldinham." BLW 6667 acres **P:** unk **BLW:** Y **RG:** N **MK:** unk **PH:** N **SS:** E pg 203 **BS:** 196.

DABNEY, Samuel; b 14 Apr 1752; d 1793 **RU:** Ensign, Promoted to Ens 9 Jun 1777, Louisa Co Militia **CEM:** Dabney Family; GPS unk; 4.3 mi NE of Orchid; Louisa **GS:** Y **SP:** Jane Meriwether (8 Apr 1757-1833) **VI:** No further data **P:** unk **BLW:** unk **RG:** N **MK:** N **PH:** unk **SS:** AZ pg 214 **BS:** 149 Dabney.

DADE, Baldwin, Sr; b13 Oct 1716, d aft 11 Aug 1782 **RU:** Patriot gave material aid to cause 1781 **CEM:** St Pauls Episcopal Ch; GPS 39.332222, -77.141666; 5486 St Pauls St, Owens; Stafford **GS:** Unk **SP:** 1) Sarah Alexander, 2) Verlinda (-----) **VI:** No further data **P:** N **BLW:** N **RG:** Y **MK:** N **PH:** N **SS:** D vol 2, pgs 562, 563; DAR A029281; SAR P-330658 **BS:** SAR PRS.

DADE, Francis L; b 1760; d 1791 **RU:** Captain, Served 3rd Cont Dragoons; Taken prisoner at Tappan 18 Sep 1778; Promoted Capt 1781; Retired 9 Nov 1782 **CEM:** Dade Family; GPS unk; Rose Hill; Orange **GS:** U **SP:** Mar (13 Mar 1782 Orange Co) Sarah Taliaferro d/o Lawrence & (-----) Taliaferro **VI:** BLW issued 7 Jul 1799. 4000 acres to minor children. R728 **P:** unk **BLW:** Y **RG:** unk **MK:** unk **PH:** unk **SS:** J- DAR Hatcher; E pg 203-4; F-S21153; K Vol II pg (__)*** ; SAR P-3364031*** **BS:** JLARC 2.

DAGGETT, Ebenezer; b unk; d 20 Nov 1781 **RU:** Ensign, Served in Capt Chapman's Co, CT Cont Troops; died on return fr siege at Yorktown **CEM:** Yorktown Victory Monument Tablet; GPS 38.28350, -78.54150; Yorktown; York **GS:** U **SP:** No info **VI:** Died in Head of Elk, MD **P:** unk **BLW:** unk **RG:** Y **MK:** unk **PH:** unk **SS:** J-Yorktown Historian; DY pg 328; SAR P-143122 **BS:** JLARC 74.

DAGONARD, Claude; b unk; d 1781 **RU:** Seaman, Served on "Caton"; D Yorktown battle **CEM:** French Memorial; GPS 36.81944, -79.39933; Yorktown; York **GS:** U **SP:** No info **VI:** No further data **P:** unk **BLW:** unk **RG:** Y **MK:** unk **PH:** unk **SS:** J-Yorktown Historian; SAR P-143176 **BS:** JLARC 1, 74.

DAILEY (DALEY), Thomas; b unk; d aft Sep 1777 **RU:** Private, Capt Thomas Arrell's Co, Col Thomas Marshall's 3d VA Regt; was wounded in battle of Brandywine,aqnd died fr wounds **CEM:**Rev War Court House Plaque;GPS;not determined; 4110 Chain Bridge Rd; Fairfax **GS:** Memorialized on plaque 2017 by Geo Washington Chapter, VASSAR **SP** No info **VI:** Died in service **P:** N **BLW:** Eligible **RG:** N **MK:** N **PH:** N **SS:**C sect II, pg 235 E pg 204; AP Fold3 muster rools: EP sources: **BS:** None.

DALTON, William; b 27 Apr 1740, Pittsylvania Co; d 14 Jan 1811 **RU:** Private, Served in Col William Nelson's Regt; 2 yrs in VA Line **CEM:** William Dalton Cem; GPS 36.79595, -80.64369; off Rt 221, Dugspur; Carroll **GS:** N **SP:** Elizabeth Sturman, probably also bur here **VI:** S 8295. NC 12202 **P:** Y **BLW:** unk **RG:** Y **MK:** N **PH:** N **SS:** VA Pen appl V26; DAR A029427; SAR P-143305 **BS:** JLARC 43; 68; 196.

DAME, George; b 1752 King & Queen Co; d Aft 16 Oct 1805 **RU:** Private/Patriot, GS indicates soldier, serv not identified; Gave material aid to cause **CEM:** Christ Church; GPS 37.60968, -76.54643; Rt 33 2 mi E of Saluda; Middlesex **GS:** U **SP:** Mary Green (1752 Culpeper Co-29 Jun 1832 Jones Co) d/o Nicholas & Elizabeth (Price) Green **VI:** Son of Solomon (1722-1780) & Martha (Brookings) (1712-1845) Dame **P:** unk **BLW:** unk **RG:** Y **MK:** unk **PH:** unk **SS:** J- DAR Hatcher; D Vol 2 pg 396; DAR A029430; SAR P-143322 **BS:** JLARC 2; 196.

DAMERON, John; b unk; d unk **RU:** Private, Specific service information not determined **CEM:** Dameron Family; GPS unk; 20 mi W of Covington; Covington City **GS:** U **SP:** No info **VI:** No further data **P:** unk **BLW:** unk **RG:** N **MK:** N **PH:** unk **SS:** E pg 205 **BS:** 160 Dameron.

DANDRIDGE, Francis West; 1754; d 1795 **RU:**Patriot, paid personal property tax, 1782, King William Co, a supply tax for Rev War expenses **CEM:** Huntington, aka Old Fox; GPS not determined; On Mattaponi River in King William Co adj New Kent Co; King William **GS:** U **SP:** Mar Goochland Co, Lucy Webb (1760, New Kent Co-1855), d/o Lewis Dandridge & Elizabeth (-----) **VI:** Son of William Dandridge (1734-May 1784, New Kent Co) & Unity West (1703-1753) **P:** N **BLW:** N **RG:** N **MK:** N **PH:** unk **SS:** DV 1782 King William Co, image 03.pdf BS: 196.

RU=Rank/Unit	CEM=Cemetery	GS=Gravestone	SP=Spousal Information
VI=Other Veteran Info	P=Pension	BLW=Bounty/Land Warrant	RG=Registered Grave
MK=SAR/DAR Marker	PH=Photo	SS=Service Source	BS=Burial Source

108

DANDRIDGE, Nathaniel West; b 7 Sep 1729 ,King & Queen Co, d 16 Jan 1786 **RU**: Patriot, gave material aid to cause, Hanover Co **CEM**: Dandridge/Underwood: GPS not determined; Rockville; Hanover **GS**: N **SP**: Mar 1733, Eng, Dorthea Spotswood **VI**: Son of Col William Dandridge of Elsing Green, King William Co & Unity West; after war period was member of Co Court and represented the County in the House of Burgesses, 1756-1758 & 1761-1764 **P**: N **BLW**: N **RG**: Y **MK**: N **PH**: N **SS**: D vol2, pgs 485, 493; DAR A029516; SAR P-143439 **BS**: 196.

DANDRIDGE, William; b 1734, King William Co; d May 1784 **RU**: Patriot; Gave material aid to cause **CEM**: Huntington, aka Old Fox; GPS unk; On Mattaponi River in King William Co adj New Kent Co; King William **GS**: U **SP**: Agnes West (1734-1759) d/o Francis & Susan (Littlepage) West **VI**: Son of William (1689-1744) & Unity (West) (1700-1753) Dandridge. D in New Kent Co **P**: N **BLW**: N **RG**: N **MK**: unk **PH**: unk **SS**: Al Comm Bk III pg 56; Henrico Co **BS**: 196.

DANIEL, Frances (Moncure); b c1745; d 1800 **RU**: Patriot; Gave 6 beeves, 65# bacon, and 172# beef Daughter of Rev John & Frances (Brown) Moncure **P**: N **BLW**: N **RG**: N **MK**: N **PH**: unk **SS**: AK; D pg 871, 874 **BS**: 04; 03 pg 186.

DANIEL, Marie; b unk; d 1781 **RU**: Seaman, Served on "Auguste"; D Yorktown battle **CEM**: French Memorial; GPS 36.81944, -79.39933; Yorktown; York **GS**: U **SP**: No info **VI**: No further data **P**: unk **BLW**: unk **RG**: Y **MK**: unk **PH**: unk **SS**: J-Yorktown Historian; SAR P-143574 **BS**: JLARC 1, 74.

DANIEL, Travers D Sr; b 16 Mar 1741, Mount Pleasant, Stafford Co; d 28 Jun 1824 **RU**: Soldier/Patriot, Served Stafford Resolutions Committee 1774; Gave musket, bayonet & beeves to cause **CEM**: Crows Nest; GPS unk; Crows Nest area; Stafford **GS**: Y **SP**: Mar (7 Oct 1762) Frances Moncure (1745-1800) d/o Rev John & Frances (Brown) Moncure. He received pension. **VI**: Son of Peter (1706-1789 & Sarah (Travers) (____-1788) Daniel. County Surveyor fr 1777 **P**: N **BLW**: N **RG**: Y **MK**: N **PH**: unk **SS**: AK; D pg 877. SAR Bios report submitted-No SAR #*** **BS**: 04; 03 pg 186.

DANIEL, William Sr; b 18 Jan 1762; d 15 May 1845 **RU**: First Lieutenant, Took 1st Lt oath; Cumberland Co Militia 23 Apr 1781 **CEM**: Old City; GPS 37.41472, -79.15667; 401 Taylor St; Lynchburg City **GS**: N **SP**: Ann Goode d/o Samuel & (-----) Goode **VI**: Pen 24 Jun 1833, Campbell Co R736 **P**: Y **BLW**: unk **RG**: N **MK**: Y SAR plaque **PH**: N **SS**: E pg 206; F-S3263; K Vol 2 pg 6-7; SAR Bio Rpt Submitted **BS**: 62 pg 103.

DANIK, Pierre; b unk; d 1781 **RU**: Seaman, Served on "Saint-Esprit"; D Yorktown battle **CEM**: French Memorial; GPS 36.81944, -79.39933; Yorktown; York **GS**: U **SP**: No info **VI**: No further data **P**: unk **BLW**: unk **RG**: Y **MK**: unk **PH**: unk **SS**: J-Yorktown Historian; SAR P-143680 **BS**: JLARC 1, 74.

DANNER (TANNER), Jacob; b 4 Dec 1763; d 17 Jun 1850 **RU**: Private, Entered serv 1775-76. Served in PA Line **CEM**: Mt Carmel; GPS 39.032048, -78.286455; 3rd & Commerce St, Middletown; Frederick **GS**: Y **SP**: Mar (25 Oct 1795 Frederick Co by Rev Simon Haar) Hannah Senseney (14 Aug 1775-12 Sep 1823) d/o Dr Peter & (-----) Sensensey, 2) Elizabeth Bechtel **VI**: His company manufactured compasses in Middleton. Also a clockmaker and jeweler. Pensioned 1818 Botetourt Co. Resident Botetourt Co in 1820 age 65 when wife as age 56 or 7. R739 **P**: Y **BLW**: unk **RG**: N **MK**: Y SAR Granite **PH**: unk **SS**: E pg 757 (for Tanner); F-S39411; K Vol 2 pg 7; SAR P-335942 **BS**: 59 pg 82.

DARAY, Bertrand; b unk; d 1781 **RU**: Soldier, Served in Gatinais Bn; D battle at Yorktown **CEM**: French Memorial; GPS 36.81944, -79.39933; Yorktown; York **GS**: U **SP**: No info **VI**: No further data **P**: unk **BLW**: unk **RG**: Y **MK**: unk **PH**: unk **SS**: J-Yorktown Historian; SAR P-143719 **BS**: JLARC 1, 74.

DARBY, John; b 1751; d 21 Sep 1789 **RU**: Lieutenant Colonel; Promoted in Co Militia; 14 May 1782; Became county Lt 14 Oct 1783 **CEM**: Darby's Wharf Farm; GPS unk; Nr Shields' Bridge, Belle Haven; Northampton **GS**: N **SP**: Mar (31 Dec 1777) Esther Harmanson (1 Oct 1762-12 Mar 1834) d/o John Sr. & (-----) Harmanson **VI**: D age 38. Styled "Col" on his wife's stone **P**: unk **BLW**: unk **RG**: Y **MK**: unk **PH**: N **SS**: E pg 207; SAR P-143737 **BS**: JLARC 4, 69; 42 pg 21.

DARBY, Nathaniel; b 15 Jun 1754; d 13 Nov 1811 **RU**: Lt; Ent serv VA 9th Cont Line 1776; Promoted to 2nd Lt, 7 Mar 1777; Germantown POW 4 Oct 1777. After release serv in 5th Cont Line until end of war **CEM**: Darby's Wharf Farm; GPS unk; Nr Shields Bridge, Belle Haven; Northampton **GS**: Y **SP**: No info **VI**: "As an officer he served his country with unsullied reputation, during her glorious contest with Great

RU=Rank/Unit	CEM=Cemetery	GS=Gravestone	SP=Spousal Information
VI=Other Veteran Info	P=Pension	BLW=Bounty/Land Warrant	RG=Registered Grave
MK=SAR/DAR Marker	PH=Photo	SS=Service Source	BS=Burial Source

109

Britain" (epitaph). BLW of 3480 acres issued 26 Jun 1789. R740 **P:** unk **BLW: Y RG: Y MK:** unk **PH:** unk **SS:** E pg 207, 220; K Vol II pg 8; F-BLW605; SAR P-143745. **BS:** JLARC 4, 69; 42 pg 21.

DARLINGTON, Gabriel; b 16 Aug 1767; d 30 Jul 1841 **RU:** Private (service info not determined fr BLW) **CEM:** Back Creek Quaker, aka Gainesboro United Methodist; GPS 39.27861, -78.25694; 166 Siler Ln, Gainesboro; Frederick **GS: N SP:** 1) Mar (19 Apr 1792 Frederick Co by Rev Christian Streit) Margaret Edwards (1777-c1841) 2) Mar (8 May 1798 Frederick Co (return) by Rev Alexander Balmain) Margaret Edwards 3) Mar (8 May 1798 Frederick Co) Martha Edwards **VI:** GS indicates 1844 d. Recd BLW **P:** unk **BLW: Y RG: N MK: N PH: N SS:** C pg 615; BY **BS:** 59 pg 82.

DARNALL, Jeremiah; b 1720; d 1795 **RU:** Patriot, Sold hay and mutton to militia **CEM:** Germantown Glebe; GPS unk; Rt 643 nr Licking Run, Midland; Fauquier **GS: Y SP:** 1) Catherine Holzclaw 2) Catherine (-----) **VI:** Died in Germantown **P: N BLW: N RG: N MK: N PH:** unk **SS:** AK; D Fauquier pg 30 **BS:** 04; 19 pg 66.

DARST, Benjamin; b 19 Jan 1760, Frederick Co; d 6 Oct 1835 **RU:** Patriot, paid for two days guard duty, 1778 Shenandoah Co **CEM:** Stonewall Jackson; GPS 37.78128, 79.44604; 314 Main St; Lexington City **GS: Y SP:** Mar 1781, Lucy Woodward (6 Oct 1758-1794) **VI:** Son of Abraham Derst (1725-1772). Grave stone description "Distinguished Citizen of Lexington" **P:** unk **BLW: Y RG: Y MK: Y SAR PH: N SS:** DAR A029881 cites Shenandoah Co Minute Bk, pg 56; SAR P-143917 **BS:** 196.

DARTER (TARTER), Nicholas; b 12 Mar 1746, Philadelphia; d 28 Apr 1821 **RU:** Soldier, Procure SAR application for service unit **CEM:** St John's Lutheran; GPS 36.96500, -81.10110; 405 W Main, Wytheville; Wythe **GS: Y SP:** Maria Parcell and Firwell Newbry Henderson **VI:** Son of Johann & Maria Elizabeth Kurtz (Darter) Anthon **P:** unk **BLW:** unk **RG: Y MK:** unk **PH:** unk **SS:** SAR applic; SAR P-143940 **BS:** JLARC 11, 23.

DAUCAN, Guillaume; b unk; d 1781 **RU:** Soldier, Served in Touraine Bn; D battle at Yorktown **CEM:** French Memorial; GPS 36.81944, -79.39933; Yorktown; York **GS: U SP:** No info **VI:** No further data **P:** unk **BLW:** unk **RG: Y MK:** unk **PH:** unk **SS:** J-Yorktown Historian; SAR P-143981 **BS:** JLARC 1, 74.

DAULIN, Jean; b unk; d 1781 **RU:** Seaman, Served on "Citoyen"; D Yorktown battle **CEM:** French Memorial; GPS 36.81944, -79.39933; Yorktown; York **GS: U SP:** No info **VI:** No further data **P:** unk **BLW:** unk **RG: Y MK:** unk **PH:** unk **SS:** J-Yorktown Historian; SAR P-143999 **BS:** JLARC 1, 74.

DAUSSENT, Pierre; b unk; d 1781 **RU:** Soldier, Served in Gatinais Bn; D Yorktown **CEM:** French Memorial; GPS 36.81944, -79.39933; Yorktown; York **GS: U SP:** No info **VI:** No further data **P:** unk **BLW:** unk **RG: Y MK:** unk **PH:** unk **SS:** J-Yorktown Historian; SAR P-144004 **BS:** JLARC 1, 74.

DAUVERGNE, Jacques; b unk; d 1781 **RU:** Soldier, Served in Soissonnais Bn; D Yorktown **CEM:** French Memorial; GPS 36.81944, -79.39933; Yorktown; York **GS: U SP:** No info **VI:** No further data **P:** unk **BLW:** unk **RG: Y MK:** unk **PH:** unk **SS:** J-Yorktown Historian; SAR P-144005 **BS:** JLARC 1, 74.

DAVENPORT, Bedford; b 21 Nov 1748, Halifax Co; d 16 Aug 1852 **RU:** 2nd Lt; Served in Capt Danile Parker's Co; Col John Crane's Regt 1778; 3rd & 4th Cont Line **CEM:** Davenport Family; GPS unk; Nr jct Rts 360 & 344, Scottsburg; Halifax **GS: N SP:** Annie Comer **VI:** No further data **P:** unk **BLW:** unk **RG: Y MK: N PH: N SS:** J-NASSR 2000 Reg; SAR P-144022 **BS:** JLARC 76.

DAVENPORT, Catrin (Catherine); b 1727; d Aft 29 Nov 1782 **RU:** Patriot; Gave material aid to cause **CEM:** Davenport Family; GPS unk; Nr jct Rts 360 & 344, Scottsburg; Halifax **GS: N SP:** James Davenport **VI:** No further data **P: N BLW: N RG: Y MK: N PH: N SS:** D Vol II pg 430; SAR P-144025 **BS:** 04.

DAVENPORT, David; b unk; d unk **RU:** Patriot; Gave material aid to cause **CEM:** Cherrydale; GPS unk; Rt 667; Hanover **GS: N SP:** No info **VI:** No further data **P: N BLW: N RG: N MK: N PH: N SS:** AL Ct Bk pg 8 **BS:** 31; vol 2 pg 80.

DAVID, Francois; b unk; d 1781 **RU:** Seaman, Served on "Victorie"; D Yorktown battle **CEM:** French Memorial; GPS 36.81944, -79.39933; Yorktown; York **GS: U SP:** No info **VI:** No further data **P:** unk **BLW:** unk **RG: Y MK:** unk **PH:** unk **SS:** J-Yorktown Historian; SAR P-144122 **BS:** JLARC 1, 74.

RU=Rank/Unit	CEM=Cemetery	GS=Gravestone	SP=Spousal Information
VI=Other Veteran Info	P=Pension	BLW=Bounty/Land Warrant	RG=Registered Grave
MK=SAR/DAR Marker	PH=Photo	SS=Service Source	BS=Burial Source

DAVID, Peter; b 8 Oct 1710, London,Eng; d 28 Nov 1785 **RU**: Patriot, paid personal property tax, 1783 Goochland Co, considered to be a supply tax for Rev War expenses **CEM**: Monacan (AKA Manakin) Farm; GPS not determined; Goochland **GS**: N **SP**: Elizabeth Morrisette (1 Mar 1721-2 Mar 1750), d/o Pierre Morisette (1690-1734) & Rhoda Ann Faure (1684-1750) **VI**:Son of Pierre David & Anne Deutterte, a Huguenot **P**: N **BLW**: N **RG**: Y **MK**: N **PH**: N **SS**: DAR A030042; SAR P-144141 **BS**: 196.

DAVID, Yves; b unk; d 1781 **RU**: Soldier, Served in Agenois Bn; D Yorktown **CEM**: French Memorial; GPS 36.81944, -79.39933; Yorktown; York **GS**: U **SP**: No info **VI**: No further data **P**: unk **BLW**: unk **RG**: Y **MK**: unk **PH**: unk **SS**: J-Yorktown Historian; SAR P-144149 **BS**: JLARC 1, 74.

DAVIDSON, Benjamin; b 1765, d1810 **RU**: Private; Hazen's Regt, Continental Line **CEM**: Bedford: GPS unk; McFalls Drive near jct Rts 746 & 122 Bedford City Bedford **GS**: Unk **SP**: Mar 30 Nov 1791, Campbell Co, Rebekah Newman (1770-1844), d/o Nimrod Newman (1750-1815) and Sarah Arthur **VI**: No further data **P** No **BLW** No **RG**: N **MK** No **PH**: No **SS**: Fold3 Serv Index Card **BS**: 196.

DAVIDSON, John Goolman; b 1 May 1720, Drumbo, County Down, Ireland; d 8 Mar 1793, Rocky Gap, Wythe Co (now Bland Co) **RU**: Private/Patriot, Capt James Moore's Co, Wythe Co Militia Also public service as Commissioner of the Peace and tax collector, Augusta Co **CEM**: John Goolman Davidson Plot; GPS unk; loc 2.5 fr I-77 exit. From Rt 52 go W on Rt 613 .7 miles, cem is on left, Rocky Gap; Bland **GS**: Y **SP**: Mar 1754, Ireland, Martha Draper (c1740 Montgomery Co-c 1791-1799) **VI**: Cooper by thade, Killed by Indians. A historical marker stands in Bluefield, West Virginia which reads: "Bluefield is on land which John Davidson patented in 1774. With Richard Bailey, he built a fort about 1777. Later he was killed by the Indians." **P**: N **BLW**: N **RG**: N **MK** Y **PH**: N **SS**: CD lists sources; CM: vol I pgs 202, 207, 211, 223: DAR A030103 **BS**: 196.

DAVIES, James II; b 1741; d unk **RU**: Sergeant; Served in 7th Cont Line; Served in VA unit in Illinois **CEM**: Davies Farm; GPS unk; See property records nr Abingdon; Washington **GS**: U **SP**: No info **VI**: No further data **P**: unk **BLW**: unk **RG**: Y **MK**: unk **PH**: unk **SS**: SAR P-144290; J-NSSAR 1993 Reg; E pg 209; CZ pg 129 **BS**: JLARC 1; 197.

DAVIES, Joseph Sr; b 1740; d 1781 **RU**: Soldier/Patriot; Gave material aid to cause **CEM**: Rural; GPS unk; Reed Creek; Montgomery **GS**: U **SP**: No info **VI**: No further data **P**: unk **BLW**: unk **RG**: Y **MK**: unk **PH**: unk **SS**: J-NSSAR 1993 Reg; D Montgomery Co **BS**: JLARC 1; 197.

DAVIS, Abraham; b 1750; d 1830 or 30 May 1839 **RU**: Private, Ent Serv 1775. 3rd VA Regt in Capt Thomas Cutleet's Co under Col Buford; Wounded at Buford's defeat near Hanging Rock, SC: Recd two wounds, left arm, suffered fr rupture lifting artillery pieces **CEM**: Tolersville Tavern burial ground; GPS 38.01321, -77.90345; Rt 677 nr Mineral Baptist Church, Mineral; Louisa **GS**: N **SP**: Mar (19 Feb 1818 Louisa Co) Mary or Polly Talley (c1790-___) **VI**: Given gratuity of £500 on 29 Nov 1780. Recd pen of £12 on 4 Mar 1789. Also on 1813 pen list. Pen in Louisa Co 1818. Widow pen Louisa Co 1853. B/d dates taken fr marker **P**: Y **BLW**: unk **RG**: N **MK**: Y **SAR PH**: N **SS**: E pg 210; BX pg 201; K Vol II pg 13 **BS**: 196.

DAVIS, Augustine; b 1752,Yorktown; d 2 Nov 1825 **RU**: Patriot; Gave material aid to the cause **CEM**: Shockoe Hill; GPS 37.55190, -77.43170; 4th & Hospital Sts; Richmond City **GS**: Y **SP**: No info **VI**: After war, Jun 1788, was appointed printer to the convention that considered the formation of the Federal Gov't. Later in 1786, started newspaper; Virginia Independent Chronicle; Later, publisher of The Virginia Gazette & Richmond Advertiser **P**: N **BLW**: N **RG**: N **MK**: N **PH**: unk **SS**: AL Ct Bk pg 3 **BS**: 57 pg 3.

DAVIS, Benjamin; b 1762; d 1836 **RU**: Private, Served in 4th, 8th, 12th Cont Line; ;erved in Capt John Green's Co, Col Edward Stevens Regt; Battle of Gilford CH, NC **CEM**: Davis Family; GPS unk; Cherrystone Plantation; Pittsylvania **GS**: U **SP**: Lydia Meadows (___-1848) **VI**: Son of William and (-----) Davis **P**: Y **BLW**: unk **RG**: Y **MK**: unk **PH**: unk **SS**: E pg 210; DAR A211612; SAR P-144378 **BS**: 196.

DAVIS, David; b 1749; d 1799 **RU**: Soldier/Patriot, Gave material aid to cause **CEM**: Pughtown; GPS unk; Gainesboro; Frederick **GS**: U **SP**: No info **VI**: No further data **P**: unk **BLW**: unk **RG**: Y **MK**: unk **PH**: unk **SS**: J- DAR Hatcher; D Frederick Co; SAR P-144434 **BS**: JLARC 2.

DAVIS, Hugh; b Nov 1758; d 26 Feb 1843 **RU**: Sergeant, Ent serv Prince William Co; 9th & 13th Cont Lines. Bullet through knee (crippled for life); Battle of Paulus Hook near Trenton, NJ **CEM**: Davis Family; GPS unk; Wolf Run Shoals Rd; Prince William **GS**: Y **SP**: Mar (1788) Jane (-----) (___-20 Sep 1796) **VI**:

RU=Rank/Unit	CEM=Cemetery	GS=Gravestone	SP=Spousal Information
VI=Other Veteran Info	P=Pension	BLW=Bounty/Land Warrant	RG=Registered Grave
MK=SAR/DAR Marker	PH=Photo	SS=Service Source	BS=Burial Source

111

Pen 1819, Prince William Co. Resided near Dumfries, VA 1829. S10136 **P:** Y **BLW:** unk **RG:** N **MK:** N **PH:** unk **SS:** K Vol 2 pg 15 **BS:** 94 pg 199.

DAVIS, Isaac; b 9 Jun 1754, Albemarle Co; d 8 Aug 1835 **RU:** Captain; Ent serv Albemarle Co; Served 6th, 10th, 11th Cont Lines; Capt 1781 **CEM:** Locust Grove; **GPS** unk; From Rt 623 take 641.4 mi to Locust Grove farm road, .35 mi; Greene **GS:** U **SP:** Elizabeth Kirtley (1 Apr 1766-1 Mar 1821) **VI:** After war moved to Orange Co in 1786 where he was pen 1833. Bur in Greene Co, which was formed fr Orange Co in 1838. S17916 **P:** Y **BLW:** unk **RG:** Y **MK:** unk **PH:** unk **SS:** K Vol II pg 15; SAR P-144536, P-144553 **BS:** JLARC 113; 196.

DAVIS, James; b 1745; d 1819 **RU:** Captain, Served in VA line **CEM:** Davis Family; **GPS** unk; Morefield; Russell **GS:** U **SP:** No info **VI:** Heirs recd BLW for 300 acres **P:** unk **BLW:** Y **RG:** N **MK:** N **PH:** unk **SS:** AS SAR applic; Gen Publ Co Baltimore MD 1975; SAR P-144601 **BS:** SAR Appl.

DAVIS, James; b c1761; d 1849 **RU:** Fifer, Ent serv Loudoun Co 1777 **CEM:** Sharon; **GPS** unk; Middleburg; Loudoun **GS:** Y **SP:** No info **VI:** Pen Loudoun Co 1832 S8288 **P:** unk **BLW:** unk **RG:** N **MK:** N **PH:** unk **SS:** E pg 211; K Vol II pg 15 **BS:** 25 pg 76.

DAVIS, Jesse; b 3 Feb 1756; d 1837 **RU:** Private; Ent serv 1776 Westmoreland Co; Served in 5th Cont line **CEM:** Davis Family; **GPS** unk; Edgehill; King George **GS:** U **SP:** m. 14 Dec 1789 (bond), Richmond Co, to Priscilla Downman, b. 3 Mar 1763, North Farnham Parish, Richmond Co, d/o James Downman & Lucy Sydnor, d. bef 4 May 1801 when her brother Traverse Downman wrote his will. Groom was of Northumberland Co at the time. **VI:** Resident of Northumberland Co when mar in 1789. Pen age 74 recd King George Co 1830 when he was Baptist minister. S8282 **P:** Y **BLW:** unk **RG:** unk **MK:** unk **PH:** unk **SS:** E pg 209; K Vol II pg 13; CZ pg 130; SAR P-144627; AR Vol 1 pg 238 **BS:** JLARC 2.

DAVIS, John A; b unk; d 14 Jan 1854 **RU:** Lt; Served in Navy **CEM:** Arlington National; **GPS** 38.88377, -77.06535; Jefferson Davis Hwy Rt 110; Arlington **GS:** Y lot 300 **SP:** No info **VI:** No further data **P:** unk **BLW:** unk **RG:** Y **MK:** unk **PH:** unk **SS:** J-NASSR 2000 Reg; SAR P-144724 **BS:** JLARC 76.

DAVIS, Joseph; b unk, Pittsylvania Co; d **RU:** 2nd Lt; Served Bedford Co Militia **CEM:** Davis Family; **GPS** unk; Cherrystone Plantation; Pittsylvania **GS:** U **SP:** Lucy McGehee Hodnett **VI:** Son of William (1729-1791) & (-----) (___-1789) Davis **P:** unk **BLW:** unk **RG:** N **MK:** unk **PH:** unk **SS:** E pg 212 **BS:** 196.

DAVIS, Samuel; b unk; d 1819 **RU:** Patriot; Gave material aid to the cause **CEM:** Cedar Grove; **GPS** 36.57204, -80.02599; 301 Fort Lane Rd; Portsmouth City **GS:** Y **SP:** No info **VI:** No further data **P:** N **BLW:** N **RG:** N **MK:** N **PH:** unk **SS:** AL Ct Bk pg 2 **BS:** 27 pg 108.

DAVIS, Samuel D: b 1745, d 6 Mar 1796 **RU:** Patriot; Gave material aid to cause **CEM:** Cedar Grove; **GPS** 36.57204, -80.02594; 301 Fort Lane, Rd; Portsmouth City **GS:** Y **SP:** No further info **VI:** Was Justice of Pease in Portsmouth, 1793 and was a sea captain fr Portsmouth and a merchant **P:** N **BLW:** N **RG:** Y **MK:** Y SAR **PH:** Y **SS:** E pg 859; AL Ct BK pgs 15, 25 Norfolk Co; SAR P-144953 **BS:** 196.

DAVIS, Thomas; b 1760, Orange Co; d 1811 **RU:** Patrio; Provided 300# beef to cause 2 Nov 1781 **CEM:** Mount Valley; **GPS** unk; Vic jct Rts 663 & 522; Orange **GS:** N **SP:** 1) Mar (24 Apr 1783) Elizabeth Early, d/o (-----) & Theodosia Early 2) Elizabeth Early Mar (10 Jan 1789 Orange Co) Elizabeth Pannill, d/o William & (-----) Pannill, Sr. **VI:** No further data **P:** N **BLW:** N **RG:** N **MK:** N **PH:** N **SS:** AK Jun 2007 **BS:** 04, Jun 2007.

DAVIS, Thomas; b 1760; d 1781 **RU:** Soldier, Served fr PA; D battle at Yorktown **CEM:** Yorktown Victory Monument Tablet; **GPS** 38.28350, -78.54150; Yorktown; York **GS:** U **SP:** No info **VI:** No further data **P:** unk **BLW:** unk **RG:** Y **MK:** unk **PH:** unk **SS:** J-Yorktown Historian; SAR P-145011 **BS:** JLARC 74.

DAVIS, Walter; b c1733, Ireland; d 20 Mar 1803 **RU:** Private, Serv in 6th & 10th Cont Line **CEM:** Tinkling Spring Presbyterian; **GPS** 38.08472, -78.98278; 30 Tinkling Spring Dr, Fishersville; Augusta **GS:** U **SP:** Martha Cunningham (1731 PA-12 Jan 1806) **VI:** No further data **P:** unk **BLW:** unk **RG:** N **MK:** unk **PH:** unk **SS:** C pg 165 **BS:** 196.

RU=Rank/Unit	CEM=Cemetery	GS=Gravestone	SP=Spousal Information
VI=Other Veteran Info	P=Pension	BLW=Bounty/Land Warrant	RG=Registered Grave
MK=SAR/DAR Marker	PH=Photo	SS=Service Source	BS=Burial Source

112

DAVIS, William; b 9 Aug 1729; d 4 Jun 1791 **RU:** Patriot; Gave material aid to cause **CEM:** Davis Family; GPS unk; Cherrystone Plantation; Pittsylvania **GS:** U **SP:** No info **VI:** No further data **P:** N **BLW:** N **RG:** N **MK:** unk **PH:** unk **SS:** AL Ct Bk pg 2, 12, 31 **BS:** 196.

DAVIS, William; b 13 Aut 1755, Louisa Co; d 1 Sep 1829 **RU:** Private, Served in 15th VA Regt **CEM:** South River Meeting House; GPS 37.37246, -79.19194; 5810 Fort Ave; Lynchburg City **GS:** Y **SP:** Judith (-----) (___-after 1787) **VI:** Widow recd pen in Louisa Co 1787 **P:** Y **BLW:** unk **RG:** N **MK:** N **PH:** N **SS:** G pg 718 **BS:** 196.

DAVIS, William; b c1750, d 1784 **RU:** Private/Patriot; Capt. Francis Taylor Co, Col. Alexander Spottswood's 2d VA Regt; Gave material aid to cause **CEM:** Edom United Methodist Church; GPS-38.5238100, -78.8607800; 5290 Jesse Bennett Way, Edom; Rockingham **GS:** Unk **SP:** Rachel (-----) **VI:** No further data **P:** N **BLW:** N **RG:** Y **MK:** N **PH:** N **ss:** D vol2 pg 835; CM-pg 490,499; SAR P-145081 **BS:** 196.

DAVIS, William D; b 12 Dec 1765; d 3 Feb 1852 **RU:** Private, Served in Capt Finley's Co, Augusta Co Militia **CEM:** Tinkling Spring Presbyterian; GPS 38.08472, -78.98278; 30 Tinkling Spring Dr, Fishersville; Augusta **GS:** Y **SP:** Mar (24 Jul 1789) Mary Howard **VI:** Was of Brunswick Co **P:** unk **BLW:** unk **RG:** N **MK:** N **PH:** unk **SS:** E pg 213 **BS:** 142 Tinkling Spr.

DAVIS (DAVIES), William; b 1745; d 1805 **RU:** Colonel/Patriot; Served Cont Line; Paid personal property tax Mecklenburg Co 1782 considered a supply tax for Rev War expenses **CEM:** Whittle and Davis Family; GPS unk; Left of old Whittle House off Hwy 636; Mecklenburg **GS:** N **SP:** No info **VI:** No further data **P:** unk **BLW:** unk **RG:** Y **MK:** unk **PH:** unk **SS:** CZ pg 129; DV 1782 image A03.pdf; SAR P-145077 **BS:** JLARC 2, 72; 80 vol 1, pg 241; 196.

DAWSON, Benjamin; b 1758 or 1760; d 4 Nov 1825 **RU:** Private; Ent Serv Fauquier Co **CEM:** Dawson Family; GPS unk; Culpeper; Culpeper **GS:** U **SP:** 1) (-----) 2) Ann Pope LeRoy **VI:** Pen Prince William Co 1818 age 60. S39405 **P:** Y **BLW:** unk **RG:** Y **MK:** N **PH:** unk **SS:** AS, DAR Report; K Vol II pg 24; SAR P-339121 **BS:** DAR Rpt.

DAWSON, Martin; b 1722; d 16 Mar 1812 **RU:** Patriot, Gave material aid to cause **CEM:** Valentine Cox; GPS unk; Forest; Bedford **GS:** Y **SP:** Mar (___ Amherst Co) Priscilla Sowell (c1719 James City Co-c1770 Amherst Co), 2) Elizabeth Carter **VI:** No further data **P:** N **BLW:** N **RG:** Y **MK:** unk **PH:** unk **SS:** DAR A030822; AL CT Bk Amherst Co pg 8, 12, 13, 31; SAR P-145273 **BS:** 196.

DAY, Benjamin; b 24 Sep 1752, London, England; d 16 Feb 1821 **RU:** Major, Was Adjutant, 2nd VA Regt; Aide de Camp to Gen Woodford **CEM:** Masonic Cemetery; GPS 38.30198, -77.46142; 900 Charles St; Fredericksburg City **GS:** Y **SP:** Mar (3 Nov 1804) (-----) d/o Ebenezer & (-----) (-----) **VI:** Twice Mayor of Fredericksburg; Grand Master, Grand Lodge of VA **P:** Y **BLW:** unk **RG:** Y **MK:** Y SAR plaque DAR **PH:** unk **SS:** J-NSSAR 1993 Reg; SAR P-145303; AR Vol 1 pg 242 **BS:** JLARC 1, 2.

DE BERTHELOT, Augustin; b unk; d 1781 **RU:** Soldier, Served in Gatinais Bn; D battle at Yorktown **CEM:** French Memorial; GPS 36.81944, -79.39933; Yorktown; York **GS:** U **SP:** No info **VI:** No further data **P:** unk **BLW:** unk **RG:** N **MK:** unk **PH:** unk **SS:** J-Yorktown Historian **BS:** JLARC 1, 74.

DEAN, Joseph; b 1763; d 21 Apr 1818 **RU:** Private, Served 3 yrs-Cont line, ending 20 Jun 1783 **CEM:** Presbyterian Church; GPS 38.80015, -77.05791; Wilkes St & Hamilton Ln; Alexandria City **GS:** Y **SP:** Hannah Boyd, b c1767, d 6 Feb 1843 **VI:** Received 100 acres bounty land; D notice in the Alexandria Gazette 23 Apr 1818 pg 3 **P:** unk **BLW:** Y **RG:** Y **MK:** Y SAR marker & plaque **PH:** unk **SS:** F pg 21; AK; SAR P-333951 **BS:** 04; 23 pg 25.

DEARING, John; b 24 Mar 1746, Orange Co, d 9 Sep 1822 **RU:** Captain; Lt Served in Louisa Co; Promoted Capt **CEM:** Dearing Family; GPS 38.760756,-78.127628; Caledonia Farm, 47 Dearing Rd, Flint Hill; Rappahannock **GS:** Y **SP:** Anna (Nancy) Jett (c1751-30 Jun 1823), d/o Francis & (-----) Jett **VI:** Built farm house "Fountain Hill" 1812 **P:** unk **BLW:** unk **RG:** Y **MK:** N **PH:** unk **SS:** AK; E pg 216; DAR A031294; SAR P-146191 **BS:** 04; 33.

DEARING/DEERING, James; b 1755; d 1811 **RU:** Captain/Patriot, Served in 2nd VA Regt; Gave material aid to cause **CEM:** Deering Family; GPS unk; At Otterburne, Old Deering Place on Otter River, Altavista/nr Evington; Campbell **GS:** U **SP:** Mar (3 Apr 1783 Campbell Co (bond) James Adams,

RU=Rank/Unit	CEM=Cemetery	GS=Gravestone	SP=Spousal Information
VI=Other Veteran Info	P=Pension	BLW=Bounty/Land Warrant	RG=Registered Grave
MK=SAR/DAR Marker	PH=Photo	SS=Service Source	BS=Burial Source

113

bondsman) Elizabeth Adams **VI:** No further data **P:** unk **BLW:** unk **RG:** Y **MK:** N **PH:** unk **SS:** D Louisa Co; SAR P-146190 **BS:** JLARC 1, 2, 4, 36, 66, 75.

DEBAPTIST (deBAPTIST, D. BAPTIST), John; b c1740, St Kitts, West Indies; d 3 Sep 1804 **RU:** Seaman; Served as crewman on "Dragon" fr Fredericksburg, Fall 1776 to end of war **CEM:** Union Church; GPS 38.32268, -77.46615; Carter St, Falmouth; Stafford **GS:** Y **SP:** Frances (-----) **VI:** Because of dark skin was considered a free black. Owned land in Fredericksburg area to include the wharf and ferry betw Fredericksburg and Falmouth. D Falmouth or Fredericksburg. SAR marker **P:** unk **BLW:** unk **RG:** N **MK:** Y SAR **PH:** Y **SS:** AK; Oscar H Darter, "Colonial Fredericksburg and Neighborhood in Perspective" New York 1957, pages 85-86, 247. **BS:** 04, JLARC, 48; CMM Chap 1998; GW Chap 2015.

DEBASE, Pierre; b unk; d 1781 **RU:** Seaman, Served on "Sceptre"; D Yorktown battle **CEM:** French Memorial; GPS 36.81944, -79.39933; Yorktown; York **GS:** U **SP:** No info **VI:** No further data **P:** unk **BLW:** unk **RG:** Y **MK:** unk **PH:** unk **SS:** J-Yorktown Historian; SAR P-146223 **BS:** JLARC 1 ,74.

DECOUNE, Louis; b unk; d 1781 **RU:** Soldier, Served in Gatinais Bn and died fr battle at Yorktown **CEM:** French Memorial; GPS 36.81944, -79.39933; Yorktown; York **GS:** U **SP:** No info **VI:** No further data **P:** unk **BLW:** unk **RG:** Y **MK:** unk **PH:** unk **SS:** J-Yorktown Historian; SAR P-146328 **BS:** JLARC 1, 74.

DEDERICK, Jacob; b 1752; d 28 Nov 1830 **RU:** Private; Served in PA Militia 14 Sep 1777 **CEM:** Neriah Baptist; GPS 37.78778, -79.36482; Jct Rts 631 & 706, South River; Rockbridge **GS:** Y **SP:** No info **VI:** No further data **P:** unk **BLW:** unk **RG:** N **MK:** N **PH:** unk **SS:** CI PA Archives **BS:** 154 Neriah.

DEEKINS, James; b unk; d 15 Mar 1778 **RU:** Private Capt Arrell's Co, 3rd VA Regt **CEM:**Rev War Court House Plaque; GPS not determined; 4110 Chain Bridge Rd; Fairfax **GS:** Memorialized on plaque 2017 by Geo Washington Chapter, VASSAR **SP** No info **VI:** Died in service **P:** N **BLW:** N **RG:** N **MK:** N **PH:** N **SS**; E pg 217;:EP sources: **BS:** None.

DEGRAFENREIDT, Tscharner; b 9 Feb 1752; d 1811 **RU:** Sergeant/Patriot; Wounded, Battle at Guilford CH; Gave material aid to cause **CEM:** DeGrafenreidt Family; GPS unk; See county property records; Lunenburg **GS:** U **SP:** Not mar **VI:** Son of Anthony & Mary (Baker) Degrafenreid. BLW recd 1810 of 400 acres **P:** N **BLW:** Y **RG:** N **MK:** unk **PH:** unk **SS:** J- DAR Hatcher; AL Ct Bk pg 17 Lunenburg Co **BS:** JLARC 2.

DEGRES, Michel; b unk; d 1781 **RU:** Soldier, Served in Santogne Bn; D battle at Yorktown **CEM:** French Memorial; GPS 36.81944, -79.39933; Yorktown; York **GS:** U **SP:** No info **VI:** No further data **P:** unk **BLW:** unk **RG:** Y **MK:** unk **PH:** unk **SS:** J-Yorktown Historian; SAR P-146429 **BS:** JLARC 1, 74.

DEHAVEN, Isaac; b 18 Feb 1750; d Bef 23 Dec 1835 **RU:** Corporal, Entered serv in Loudoun Co. Previously was private in 4th Bn, PA Militia and was Corporal in Capt Lee's Co, Col Blands Regt **CEM:** Back Creek Quaker, aka Gainesboro United Methodist; GPS 39.27861, -78.25694; 166 Siler Ln, Gainesboro; Frederick **GS:** Y **SP:** Mar (Frederick Co) Abigail Phillips **VI:** Pen 1832 Franklin Co. S8313 **P:** Y **BLW:** unk **RG:** Y **MK:** N **PH:** N **SS:** K Vol 2 pg 29; AK; DAR A031373; SAR P-331270 **BS:** 59 pg 87; 04.

DeHAVEN, Isaac; b 25 Apr 1765, Bucks Co, PA, d 26 Aug 1838 **RU:** Private; Served Capt Samuel Roberts Co; 4th Bn PA Militia; Cont Army unit; Battles at Brandywine, Paoli, Germantown, Monmouth and Sullivan Expedition **CEM:** Back Creek Quaker, AKA Gainesboro United Methodist Church; GPS 39.27861, -78.25694; Take Rt 522 fr Winchester, turn left Rt 600, .5 mi bef RR tracks on hill surrounded by rock wall; Frederick. **GS:** Yes **SP:** Mar 1784 Germantown, Montgomery Co, PA, Susannah Branaway. Perhaps mar 2) Abigaill Phillips (SS K) **VI:** Son of Peter DeHaven and Abigail West **P:** N **BLW:** N **RG:** Y **MK:** Y SAR granite **PH:** N **SS:** K vol 2, pg 29; AP PA Archives Series 6, vol VII, pg 114; SAR P-331270 **BS:** 196.

DEHAVEN, Peter, b 31 Jan 1741, Whitpan, Montgomery Co, PA; d 4 Jan 1822 **RU:** Private; Capt Alexander Quarrier's 4th Co; 4th Bn; Col Thomas Mifflin's Regt, PA Militia, 1776 **CEM:** Back Creek Quaker, AKA Gainesboro United Methodist Church; GPS 39.27861, -78.25694; Take Rt 522 fr Winchester, turn left Rt 600, .5 mi bef RR tracks on hill surrounded by rock wall; Frederick. **GS:** Yes **SP:** Abigail West **VI:** Son of William Dehaven (1714-1784) & Hannah Carter (1717-1786) Occupation-stone

RU=Rank/Unit	CEM=Cemetery	GS=Gravestone	SP=Spousal Information
VI=Other Veteran Info	P=Pension	BLW=Bounty/Land Warrant	RG=Registered Grave
MK=SAR/DAR Marker	PH=Photo	SS=Service Source	BS=Burial Source

mason **P**: N **BLW**: N **RG**: Y **MK**: Y SAR granite **PH**: N **SS**: AP PA Archives Quarrier, Alex, pg 24; Gravestone inscription; SAR P-145611 **BS**: 196.

DEJARNETTE, James Pemberton; b 9 Oct 1740, Caroline Co; d 9 Dec 1826 **RU**: Captain/Patriot; Commanded company in Halifax Co, Militia; Justice of Peace **CEM**: DeJarnette Family; GPS unk; Nathalie; Halifax **GS**: N **SP**: Mar 1) 1761, Caroline Co, Edna George (1740-1777), d/o John George & Mary Jordan, 2) Mary Walker (1740--___), 3) on 7 Sep 1791, Halifax Co, Elizabeth Pillow **VI**: Son of Joseph Latani Jarnette (1716-1791 and Jean Pemberton **P**: unk **BLW**: unk **RG**: Y **MK**: N **PH**: N **SS**: D vol 2, pg 448; SAR P-268038 cites Mary's Qtrtly.ser 2, vol 7, pg 60, Halifax Co **BS**: SAR PRS.

DEJARNETTE, Joseph Jr; b 9 Oct 1747; d Sep 1824 **RU**: 1st Lt; Served May 1781 under Capt James Sutton, McAllister's Militia **CEM**: DeJarnette Family; GPS unk; Rt 2, 5.5 mi fr Bowling Green; Caroline **GS**: U **SP**: Mary Hampton **VI**: No further data **P**: unk **BLW**: unk **RG**: Y **MK**: N **PH**: unk **SS**: AZ pg 194; SAR P-146483 **BS**: JLARC 15.

DELAGNEL, Julius Adolphus; b 31 Oct 1744; d 21 May 1840 **RU**: Captain of Ordinance in the US Army **CEM**: St Paul's Episcopal; GPS 38.79959, -77.05860; 228 S Pitt St; Alexandria City **GS**: Y **SP**: Harriet Sandford (1801-28 May 1891). After death, she moved to Alexandria with his children, sister and Rev James T. Johnson **VI**: His stone here may be a cenotaph; D New York; Widow moved Alexandria **P**: unk **BLW**: unk **RG**: Y **MK**: unk **PH**: unk **SS**: J-NSSAR 1993 Reg; SAR P-146494 **BS**: JLARC 1; 174 pg 392; 196.

DELAHAYE, Pierre; b unk; d 1781 **RU**: Seaman, Served on "Ville de Paris"; D Yorktown battle **CEM**: French Memorial; GPS 36.81944, -79.39933; Yorktown; York **GS**: U **SP**: No info **VI**: No further data **P**: unk **BLW**: unk **RG**: Y **MK**: unk **PH**: unk **SS**: J-Yorktown Historian; SAR P-146495 **BS**: JLARC 1,74.

DELANY, John; b 11 Jun 1740; d 5 Jan 1831 **RU**: Private, Ent serv 1776 in MD **CEM**: Old Stone Methodist; GPS 39.11725, -77.56609; 168 W Cornwall St, Leesburg; Loudoun **GS**: Y **SP**: No info **VI**: Pensioned age 88 in Fairfax Co in 1828. FS46Y38 recd 1780. S46438 **P**: Y **BLW**: unk **RG**: N **MK**: N **PH**: unk **SS**: K Vol 2 pg 29; AK **BS**: 04, 25 pg 78.

DELAPORT, Ubal; b unk; d 1781 **RU**: Seaman, Served on "Auguste"' D Yorktown battle **CEM**: French Memorial; GPS 36.81944, -79.39933; Yorktown; York **GS**: U **SP**: No info **VI**: No further data **P**: unk **BLW**: unk **RG**: unk **MK**: unk **PH**: unk **SS**: J-Yorktown Historian; SAR P-146586 **BS**: JLARC 1, 74.

DELLINGER, Christian Jr; b 13 Feb 1764, Swover Creek, Shenandoah Co; d 22 Sep 1856 **RU**: Private; Ent serv 1781 Shenandoah Co; Battle of Yorktown; Cornwallis death, Guard & marched prisoners to Fredericksburg **CEM**: Dellinger Family; GPS 38.5037, -78.4054; Madison District Conicville; Shenandoah **GS**: Y **SP**: Eva Mary Foltz **VI**: Appl for pension age 71 1836 and again in 1850 age 86. Both rejected. R2857. Died in Conicville, Shenandoah Co **P**: N **BLW**: unk **RG**: Y **MK**: N **PH**: unk **SS**: J-DAR Hatcher; BY; K Vol II pg 29; SAR P-146617 **BS**: 197; JLARC 2.

DELONG, John Nicholas; b 19 Jul 1756, Berks Co, PA; d 21 Feb 1823 **RU**: Private; Served 13th Cont Line **CEM**: Trinity Evangelical Lutheran; GPS 39.08280, -78.21679; Mulberry St, Stephens City; Frederick **GS**: Y **SP**: Mar (20 May 1794 by Rev Christian Streit) Mary Toomy **VI**: Son of Johannes (1730-1813) & Maria Katherina (Dussinger) (1725-1782) DeLang **P**: unk **BLW**: unk **RG**: Y **MK**: N **PH**: unk **SS**: E pg 218; SAR P-145705 **BS**: 59 pg 91; 196.

DELTRIEUX, Pierre; b unk; d 1781 **RU**: Seaman, Served on "Solitaire"; D Yorktown battle **CEM**: French Memorial; GPS 36.81944, -79.39933; Yorktown; York **GS**: U **SP**: No info **VI**: No further data **P**: unk **BLW**: unk **RG**: Y **MK**: unk **PH**: unk **SS**: J-Yorktown Historian; SAR P-146649 **BS**: JLARC 1, 74.

DEMARET, Nicolas; b unk; d 1781 **RU**: Soldier; Served in Gatinais Bn; D battle at Yorktown **CEM**: French Memorial; GPS 36.81944, -79.39933; Yorktown; York **GS**: U **SP**: No info **VI**: No further data **P**: unk **BLW**: unk **RG**: Y **MK**: unk **PH**: unk **SS**: J-Yorktown Historian; SAR P-146700 **BS**: JLARC 1, 74.

DEMBRE, Pierre; b unk; d 1781 **RU**: Seaman, Served on "Diademe"; D Yorktown battle **CEM**: French Memorial; GPS 36.81944, -79.39933; Yorktown; York **GS**: U **SP**: No info **VI**: No further data **P**: unk **BLW**: unk **RG**: Y **MK**: unk **PH**: unk **SS**: J-Yorktown Historian; SAR P-146705 **BS**: JLARC 1, 74.

RU=Rank/Unit	CEM=Cemetery	GS=Gravestone	SP=Spousal Information
VI=Other Veteran Info	P=Pension	BLW=Bounty/Land Warrant	RG=Registered Grave
MK=SAR/DAR Marker	PH=Photo	SS=Service Source	BS=Burial Source

DENNETT, John; b 1716; d 15 Jul 1787 **RU**: Patriot; Gave material support in Richmond Co **CEM**: St Peter's Episcopal; GPS unk; 8400 St Peters Ln, Quinton; New Kent **GS**: N **SP**: No info **VI**: No further data **P**: N **BLW**: N **RG**: N **MK**: N **PH**: N **SS**: G pg 317; SAR P-146950 **BS**: 85 pg 58.

DENSON, Jordan; b unk; d 1806 **RU**: Patriot; Gave material aid to the cause **CEM**: Jerico; GPS unk; Courtland; Southampton **GS**: Y **SP**: Ann Copeland **VI**: No further data **P**: N **BLW**: N **RG**: N **MK**: N **PH**: unk **SS**: AL Ct Bk pg 4 **BS**: 53 vol 5.

DENTY, Jonathan; b unk, d 1812 **RU**: Patriot; Supported cause by paying supply tax included in his personal property tax in 1782, Fairfax Co **CEM**: Pohick Episcopal Church; GPS: 38.70888, -77.19369; jct Rts 1 & 611, Lorton; Fairfax **GS**: Yes, **SP**: Sibel (___) **VI**: He may have been reinterred to Pohick cem fr his farm in Fairfax Co or just memorialized in the cem **P**: N **BLW**: N **RG**: N **MK**: N **PH**: N **SS**: DV **BS**: 196.

DEREUT, Pierre; b unk; d 1781 **RU**: Seaman; Served on "Citoyen"; D Yorktown battle **CEM**: French Memorial; GPS 36.81944, -79.39933; Yorktown; York **GS**: U **SP**: No info **VI**: No further data **P**: unk **BLW**: unk **RG**: Y **MK**: unk **PH**: unk **SS**: J-Yorktown Historian; SAR P-147218 **BS**: JLARC 1, 74.

DERINIER, Louis; b unk; d 1781 **RU**: Seaman, Served on "Palmier"; D Yorktown battle **CEM**: French Memorial; GPS 36.81944, -79.39933; Yorktown; York **GS**: U **SP**: No info **VI**: No further data **P**: unk **BLW**: unk **RG**: Y **MK**: unk **PH**: unk **SS**: J-Yorktown Historian; SAR P-147226 **BS**: JLARC 1, 74.

DESCHAMPS, Joseph; b unk; d 1781 **RU**: Soldier, Served in Gatinais Bn; D battle at Yorktown **CEM**: French Memorial; GPS 36.81944, -79.39933; Yorktown; York **GS**: U **SP**: No info **VI**: No further data **P**: unk **BLW**: unk **RG**: Y **MK**: unk **PH**: unk **SS**: J-Yorktown Historian; SAR P-147267 **BS**: JLARC 1, 74.

DESHAY, Francois; b unk; d 1781 **RU**: Soldier, Served in Gatinais Bn; D battle at Yorktown **CEM**: French Memorial; GPS 36.81944, -79.39933; Yorktown; York **GS**: U **SP**: No info **VI**: No further data **P**: unk **BLW**: unk **RG**: N **MK**: unk **PH**: unk **SS**: J-Yorktown Historian **BS**: JLARC 1, 74.

DESHAZO, William; b unk; d 24 or 27 Apr 1839 **RU**: Soldier; Enl Winter 1777; Capt Henry Dudley's Co for 3 yrs; Served 2nd VA State Regt, under Col Gregory Smith; Marched to Valley Forge and after to Brigade of Gen Muhlenburg; Battle of Monmouth-28 Jun 1778; Attack on Stoney Point on Paulus's Hook; Left service Spring 1780 at Williamsburg **CEM**: DeShazo; GPS unk; Leatherwood; Henry **GS**: U **SP**: Mar (Nov 1794, bond dated 5 Nov 1794) Person Co NC, Jane Cincy King (1770-__) **VI**: Recd pension 1832 age 73 Henry Co. Pension says he d 27 Apr. 1839. Widow pen Henry Co age 74 and was resident there 1855 age 85. W1832 & R801 **P**: Y **BLW**: Y **RG**: N **MK**: unk **PH**: unk **SS**: K Vol II pg 34; R Vol 2 pg 34 **BS**: 196.

DESMONT, Antoine; b unk; d 1781 **RU**: Soldier, Served in Bourbonnais Bn; D battle at Yorktown **CEM**: French Memorial; GPS 36.81944, -79.39933; Yorktown; York **GS**: U **SP**: No info **VI**: No further data **P**: unk **BLW**: unk **RG**: Y **MK**: unk **PH**: unk **SS**: J-Yorktown Historian; SAR P-147299 **BS**: JLARC 1, 74.

DESRIEU, Louis Sr; b unk; d 1781 **RU**: Seaman, Served on "Auguste"; D Yorktown battle **CEM**: French Memorial; GPS 36.81944, -79.39933; Yorktown; York **GS**: U **SP**: No info **VI**: No further data **P**: unk **BLW**: unk **RG**: Y **MK**: unk **PH**: unk **SS**: J-Yorktown Historian; SAR P-147302 **BS**: JLARC 1, 74.

DETERMINE, Nicolas; b unk; d 1781 **RU**: Soldier, Served in Santogne Bn and died fr battle at Yorktown **CEM**: French Memorial; GPS 36.81944, -79.39933; Yorktown; York **GS**: U **SP**: No info **VI**: No further data **P**: unk **BLW**: unk **RG**: Y **MK**: unk **PH**: unk **SS**: J-Yorktown Historian; SAR P-147309 **BS**: JLARC 1, 74.

DEVAISE, Joseph; b unk; d 1781 **RU**: Soldier; Served in Touraine Bn; D battle at Yorktown **CEM**: French Memorial; GPS 36.81944, -79.39933; Yorktown; York **GS**: U **SP**: No info **VI**: No further data **P**: unk **BLW**: unk **RG**: Y **MK**: unk **PH**: unk **SS**: J-Yorktown Historian; SAR P-147342 **BS**: JLARC 1, 74.

DEVIER, Hugh; b 1758, Augusta Co; d 1815 **RU**: Patriot, gave material aid to cause, Rockingham Co **CEM**: DeVier Family; GPS 38.405783, -79.038477; loc nr jct Nazarene Ch Rd & Rt 613, Spring Creek; Rockingham **GS**: Unk **SP**: Mar c1778, Dumfries, Pr Wm Co, Mary Pearlow, d/o Mason Pearlow & Mary Bennett **VI**: Son of Hugh E Devier (1728-1774) & Agnes Blain (1731-1790) **P**: N **BLW**: N **RG**: N **MK**: N **PH**: N **SS**: Al Ct Book II, pg 19, Rockingham Co **BS** 196.

RU=Rank/Unit	CEM=Cemetery	GS=Gravestone	SP=Spousal Information
VI=Other Veteran Info	P=Pension	BLW=Bounty/Land Warrant	RG=Registered Grave
MK=SAR/DAR Marker	PH=Photo	SS=Service Source	BS=Burial Source

116

DEVIER(DEVER), James E; b 1754, Augusta Co; d 1802 **RU**: Sergeant/ Patriot, Capt George Moffat's Co Augusta Co Oct 1774 in battle at Pt Pleasant and gave material aid to cause, Rockingham Co **CEM**: DeVier Family; GPS 38.405783, -79.038477; loc nr jct Nazarene Ch Rd & Rt 613, Spring Creek; Rockingham **GS**: Unk **SP**: Mar (c1779) Elizabeth Daniel, d/o Reuben Daniel & Elizabeth Penny **VI**: Son of Hugh E Devier (1728-1774) & Agnes Blain (1731-1790) **P**: N **BLW**: N **RG**: N **MK**: N **PH**: N **SS**: AL Ct Bk II, pgs 114,115,133; Z pg 117 **BS**: 196.

DEVERLE (DEYERLE), Peter; b c1734, Germany; d Jan 1813 **RU**: Patriot; Surveyor of Road, 1780 **CEM**: Deyerle Family; GPS unk; West part; Riverside Roanoke Co **GS**: U **SP**: Mar (c1763) Regina Ann Bowman (13 Jan 1743, Orange Co-May 1828, Montgomery Co) **VI**: D Montgomery Co **P**: N **BLW**: N **RG**: Y **MK**: N **PH**: unk **SS**: AR Vol 1 pg 254; AS DAR Report; DL pg 307; DAR A033362, SAR P-147641 **BS**: DAR Rpt.

DEVILLIERS, Gabriel; b unk; d 1781 **RU**: Soldier, Served in Bourbonnais Bn; D battle at Yorktown **CEM**: French Memorial; GPS 36.81944, -79.39933; Yorktown; York **GS**: U **SP**: No info **VI**: No further data **P**: unk **BLW**: unk **RG**: Y **MK**: unk **PH**: unk **SS**: J-Yorktown Historian; SAR P-147387 **BS**: JLARC 1, 74.

DEW, Thomas Roderick ; b 28 May 1763, MD; d 23 Apr 1849 **RU**: Private; Ent serv Caroline Co 1780; Serv King and Queen Co in Gen Steven's Bde; Battle of Camden, SC and at Battle at Guilford CH; Served Apr 1781 under Weeden's Bde & Marquis de Lafayette **CEM**: Dewsville plantation; GPS unk; Newtown; King & Queen **GS**: Y **SP**: Mar (07 Jan 1793) Lucy Gatewood (24 Mar 1776-17 Nov 1832) **VI**: Capt in War of 1812. Marker placed Nov 2012. Was President of William & Mary College 1836 to death. Appl for pension fr King & Queen Co 1842 age 78. Pension rejected due to less than six mos serv. R2909 & R803 **P**: No **BLW**: unk **RG**: Y **MK**: Y SAR bronze **PH**: Y **SS**: K Vol II pg 34; AK; DAR A031621; SAR P-147426 **BS**: JLARC 1, 4, 37.

DEZE, Andre; b unk; d 1781 **RU**: Soldier; Served in Gatinais Bn; D battle at Yorktown **CEM**: French Memorial; GPS 36.81944, -79.39933; Yorktown; York **GS**: U **SP**: No info **VI**: No further data **P**: unk **BLW**: unk **RG**: Y **MK**: unk **PH**: unk **SS**: J-Yorktown Historian; SAR P-147654 **BS**: JLARC 1, 74.

DIALE, Jean; b unk; d 1781 **RU**: Seaman, Served on "Sceptre"; D Yorktown battle **CEM**: French Memorial; GPS 36.81944, -79.39933; Yorktown; York **GS**: U **SP**: No info **VI**: No further data **P**: unk **BLW**: unk **RG**: Y **MK**: unk **PH**: unk **SS**: J-Yorktown Historian; SAR P-147664 **BS**: JLARC 1, 74.

DIAMOND, Moses; b unk; d 1781 **RU**: Private; Served Col Lewis Duboys 5th NY Regt; D battle at Yorktown **CEM**: Yorktown Victory Monument Tablet; GPS 38.28350, -78.54150; Yorktown; York **GS**: U **SP**: No info **VI**: No further data **P**: unk **BLW**: unk **RG** Y **MK**: unk **PH**: unk **SS**: J-Yorktown Historian; SAR P-147666. AX pg 56 **BS**: JLARC 74.

DICK, Archibald; b 1725; d 1811 **RU**: Patriot; Gave material aid to cause in Caroline Co **CEM**: Dick-Smith Family; GPS unk; Bullock's Rd; Caroline **GS**: Y **SP**: No info **VI**: Minister of St Margaret's Parish **P**: N **BLW**: N **RG**: N **MK**: N **PH**: unk **SS**: AL Ct Bk It II pg 24 **BS**: 02 pg 54.

DICK, Elisha Cullen Dr; b 15 Mar 1762, Chester Co, PA; d 22 Sep 1825 **RU**: Private 5th class; 5th Co. (Capt Jacob Martin, 4th Bn (Lt Col Paul Coxe) Philadelphia City, PA 1780/81; Private 7th Class, 8th Co (Capt Joh Cornish) 4th Battalion (Lt Col Paule Coxe, Philadelphia City Militia 1780/1; Listed as Doctor Dick **CEM**: Quaker Burial Ground; GPS 38.80749, -77.04676; 717 Queen St, Kate Walker Barrett Library; Alexandria City **GS**: N **SP**: Mar (Oct 1793 Chester Co, PA) to Hannah Harmon, (__-1843 Roanake, VA) **VI**: Recd medical degree fr Univ. PA in 1782. Studied w/ Dr. Benjamin Rush and Dr. William Shippen. Transcript of letter fr J.A. Pearce written 20 Aug 1885 shows he was b 15 Mar 1762, contrary to 1750 on 1937 plaque. D Cottage Farm, Fairfax Co. In 1937 Kate Waller Barrett Library was constructed on the burying ground. No GS found & marker moved **P**: unk **BLW**: unk **RG**: Y **MK**: Y SAR **PH**: N **SS**: www.digitalarchives.state.pa.us/archive.asp?view=ArchiveItems&ArchiveID=13&FL=D&FID=457214&LI D=457313 card 41&42. PA Mil records; AK Sep 2009; SAR P-335452 **BS**: 34 pg 63.

DICKENSON, Griffith; b 8 Aug 1757 Hanover Co; d 16 Oct 1843 **RU**: Corporal, Enl Oct 1776 under Capt Thomas Scott as musician. Discharged Nov 1779 after 3 mos as fifer and 33 mos as corporal **CEM**: Berger burial ground; GPS 36.92909, -79.25041; Rt 685, or Rt 927 E of Chalk Level, E fr Gretna 6

RU=Rank/Unit	CEM=Cemetery	GS=Gravestone	SP=Spousal Information
VI=Other Veteran Info	P=Pension	BLW=Bounty/Land Warrant	RG=Registered Grave
MK=SAR/DAR Marker	PH=Photo	SS=Service Source	BS=Burial Source

mi; Pittsylvania **GS:** Y **SP:** Susanna Shelton (1752 Christchurch, Middlesex Co-20 Oct 1747 Chalk Level, Pittsylvania Co) **VI:** Source 90 has second graveyard, says Baptist minister **P:** unk **BLW:** unk **RG:** Y **MK:** unk **PH:** unk **SS:** E pg 223; DAR A034156; SAR P-147751 **BS:** 174; JLARC 2, 90, 96.

DICKERSON, Elijah; b 1755, Halifax Co; d Aft 4 Sep 1834 **RU:** Private; Served Montgomery Co Militia, commanded by Col Christie **CEM:** Wright Family; GPS 36.97658, -80.21693; Pizarro off Rt 668; Floyd **GS:** U **SP:** Mar (23 May 1785, Montgomery Co) (-----) **VI:** Memorialized by DAR plaque in cem. Pen in 1835 list at age 79 **P:** Y **BLW:** unk **RG:** N **MK:** Y SAR **PH:** unk **SS:** DAR A034128; E pg 223 **BS:** 196 for John Mitchell.

DICKERSON, Joseph; b 11 Apr 1742; d 16 Sep 1818 **RU:** Patriot; Gave material aid to the cause **CEM:** Dickerson Family; GPS unk; Nr Moneta; Bedford **GS:** Y **SP:** Mar (5 Mar 1769) Elizabeth Wooldridge (11 Jan 1744, Buckingham Co-7 Nov 1818) **VI:** No further data **P:** N **BLW:** N **RG:** Y **MK:** N **PH:** unk **SS:** AL Ct Bk pg 11; SAR P-147792 **BS:** 80 vol 1 pg 255.

DICKERSON (DICKINSON)' Moses; b 1753, Lunenburg; d 23 Mar 1834 **RU:** Patriot; Took oath of allegiance in Henry Co 1776 **CEM:** Pine Creek Primitive Baptist; GPS 36.94622, -80.27357; Spangler Mill Rd Rt 682; Floyd **GS:** Y **SP:** Jemima (Jemina) Sullivan (1756-26 May 1846) **VI:** No further data **P:** N **BLW:** N **RG:** Y **MK:** unk **PH:** unk **SS:** DAR vol 1 pg 192; DAR A034296; SAR P-147796, SAR P-147937 **BS:** JLARC 29.

DICKINSON, James; b 1742; d 1828 **RU:** Private, Specific service may be found at the Lib of VA in Auditor's Acct Bk XVIII, pg 474 **CEM:** Belle Isle; GPS unk; Nr Frederick Hall; Louisa **GS:** U **SP:** Mary (Cole) Barclay **VI:** No further data **P:** unk **BLW:** unk **RG:** Y **MK:** unk **PH:** unk **SS:** J-NASSR 2000 Reg; CZ pg 137; SAR P-147910 **BS:** JLARC 76.

DICKINSON, John; b 1731; d 1799 **RU:** Captain, Served battle of Point Pleasant in Capt Charles Lewis's Co, Oct 1774 **CEM:** Augusta; GPS unk; See DAR Senate Doc year 1959; Bath **GS:** U **SP:** Mar (21 May 1767) Martha Usher (1745 Philadelphia-___) **VI:** SAR applic indicates cem name is Augusta **P:** unk **BLW:** unk **RG:** Y **MK:** unk **PH:** unk **SS:** SAR P-147922; SAR applic; AR Vol 1 pg 254; SAR P-147922 **BS:** JLARC 2.

DICKINSON, Thomas, b 1761, Amherst Co; d 7 Nov 1806, Henry Co **RU:** Corporal served in Capt Cabell's Company, Col Morgan's Regt, 6th Cont Line and was in battles at Trenton and Germantown in 1776 and 1777, serving long enough to qualify his widow for pension and BLW **CEM:** Dickinson Family; GPS not determined; loc on Deer Haven Drive, Turkey Fork, Pittsylvania **GS:** No **SP:** Mar 2 Oct 1783, Jemima Wells (25 Jul 1761, Prince George Co-3 Apr 1758, Henry Co), d/o Jonathan Wells (1732-1802) & Judith Morton-Walton (___ - 1819) She recd pen #W27891 for $88 yearly and BLW #14672 for 160 acres in 1855 **VI:** No further data **P:** Widow **BLW:** Widow **RG:** N **MK:** N **PH:** N **SS:** AP-Widows pen file **BS:** 196.

DICKINSON, Thomas Bowers; b c1751; d 25 Apr 1785 **RU:** Captain, Specific service may be found at the Lib of VA in War files vol 4 pg 167 **CEM:** Trinity Episcopal; GPS 36.83459, -76.30105; 500 Court St; Portsmouth City **GS:** N **SP:** No info **VI:** No further data **P:** unk **BLW:** unk **RG:** N **MK:** N **PH:** unk **SS:** B shows rank; CZ pg 137 **BS:** 92 stone 63.

DICKINSON (DICKSON), Henry; b 28 Oct 1747; Amelia d 6 Jul 1825 **RU:** Colonel, Served in 6th SC Regt Cont Line **CEM:** Dickinson Family; GPS unk; Nr Old Courthouse; Russell **GS:** U **SP:** Mar (3 Apr 1842) Mary Powell (1 Dec 1750-23 Apr 1842) **VI:** No further data **P:** Y **BLW:** unk **RG:** Y **MK:** unk **PH:** unk **SS:** J- DAR Hatcher; E pg 224; CI pen records of several soldiers; CZ pg 137; DD; DAR A034173; SAR P-332582 **BS:** JLARC 2.

DICKSON, Henry; b 1743 Hull, York, England; d 10 Dec 1810 **RU:** Captain, Probably had naval service, specifics not found **CEM:** Trinity Episcopal; GPS 36.83459, -76.30105; 500 Court St; Portsmouth City **GS:** Y **SP:** Janet Brown **VI:** Trustee Portsmouth 1796 & 1800 **P:** unk **BLW:** unk **RG:** Y **MK:** N **PH:** unk **SS:** B; H NC Service **BS:** 75 Portsmouth.

DIDIERRE, Nicolas; b unk; d 1781 **RU:** Soldier; Served in Touraine Bn; D battle at Yorktown **CEM:** French Memorial; GPS 36.81944, -79.39933; Yorktown; York **GS:** U **SP:** No info **VI:** No further data **P:** unk **BLW:** unk **RG:** Y **MK:** unk **PH:** unk **SS:** J Yorktown Historian; SAR P-148015 **BS:** JLARC 1, 74.

RU=Rank/Unit	CEM=Cemetery	GS=Gravestone	SP=Spousal Information
VI=Other Veteran Info	P=Pension	BLW=Bounty/Land Warrant	RG=Registered Grave
MK=SAR/DAR Marker	PH=Photo	SS=Service Source	BS=Burial Source

118

DIEHL, Abraham I; b 1741, Lancaster Co, PA; d 1825 **RU**: Private 6th Co,2d Battalion, PA State Militia **CEM**: Mill Creek Church; GPS 38.3375300, -78.820090; gravestone 38.337748, -78.820085; 7600 Port Republic Rd, Port Republic; Rockingham **GS**: Y w flat stone wRev War service **SP**: Mary Deardorf (1779-aft 1783), d/o Isaac Deardolf (18 Nov 1746-6 Sep 1823) & 1st or 2) Hannah Christina **VI**:Orig bur nr Cross Keys, Old Republic, moved to Mill Creek Church in 1980s **P**: Unk **BLW**: unk **RG**: Y **MK**:Y SAR Bronze **PH**: Y **SS**: B; AK; SAR P-148107 **BS**: 196.

DIGGES, Dudley Power; b 1728, Bellfield Plantation, York Co; d 3 May 1790, Yorktown **RU**: Patriot; Member Rev Conventions & Committee of Correspondence, and Committee of Safety, 1775 and member of VA Assembly; Captured by British during Charlottesville raid 4 Jun 1781; Lt Gov **CEM**: Abingdon Episcopal; GPS 37.33355, -76.51364; 4645 George Washington Mem Hwy Rt 17; Gloucester **GS**: U **SP**: 1) Mar (1745 Yorktown) Martha Burwell Armistead 2) Mar (1760 Yorktown) Elizabeth Wormeley, d/o Ralph & (-----) Wormeley of "Rosegill" **VI**: Son of Col Cole (1692-1744) & Elizabeth (Follott Power) (1697-___) Digges, Esq. Burgess fr York Co 1752-1776. Cenotaph. Orig bur Bluefield Cem, James City Co (source SAR) **P**: N **BLW**: N **RG**: Y **MK**: N **PH**: unk **SS**: AS DAR Report, CD; SAR P-148151 **BS**: DAR Rpt; 196.

DIGGES, Edward; b 22 Jan 1746; d 29 Oct 1818 **RU**: Captain, Commanded an Artillery Co in VA State Line, 2nd Bn, Fauquier Co Militia Nov 1777. Served in State Line for 3 yrs **CEM**: Diggs Family; GPS unk; Cliff Mill; Fauquier **GS**: N **SP**: 1) Mar (11 Jun 1775) Elizabeth Ann Gaskins (1756-___) 2) Mar (29 Mar 1798 Fauquier Co, Charles Marshal, security) Ann E. Gaskins, no stone **VI**: Son of Col Edward (1715-1769) & Anne (Harrison) (1720-1775) Digges. Justice of Peace Fauquier Co 1787. Recd BLW. Fieldstone only **P**: unk **BLW**: Y **RG**: Y **MK**: N **PH**: N **SS**: E pg 225; N; H; AK; CD; Fauquier Co Marriages pg 50; SAR P-148148 **BS**: 04;19 pg 212.

DIGGES (DIGGS), Dudley Jr; b 6 Apr 1766; d 4 Apr 1839 **RU**: Lt, Served in Calvary, VA line 1779-1783. Joined Southern Army 1780. Probably disabled in serv as authorized half pay **CEM**: Fork Episcopal Church; GPS 37.85340, -77.53100; 12566 Old Ridge Rd, Doswell; Hanover **GS**: Y **SP**: Alicy Grymes Page (___-1846) **VI**: Son of Dudley Power (1728-1790) & Elizabeth (Wormeley) Digges. Pensioned 8 Jan 1820, Louisa Co, $90 per annum and $100 immediate relief in lieu of half pay **P**: Y **BLW**: unk **RG**: N **MK**: N **PH**: unk **SS**: AH pg 219; M Vol 3 pg 514 **BS**: 109 pg 570.

DIGGS, Edward; b 1721; d 1810 **RU**: Colonel, Was Maj in 2d Bn Fauquier Co Militia 1777. Obtained rank of Colonel **CEM**: Denbigh United Presbyterian; GPS unk; 302 Denbigh Blvd; Newport News City **GS**: U **SP**: No info **VI**: No further data **P**: unk **BLW**: unk **RG**: N **MK**: unk **PH**: unk **SS**: SAR P-148155; E pg 225; AR Vol 1 pg 256 **BS**: JLARC 2.

DILLARD, George; b 1720, Williamsburg; d 3 Feb 1790 **RU**: Patriot; Gave material aid to cause **CEM**: St Mark's, aka Little Fork Church; GPS unk; See DAR Senate Doc 1956, serial #11999, vol 8; Culpeper **GS**: U **SP**: Priscilla Major (1716 New Kent Co-2 Mar 1790) **VI**: Son of Edward & (-----) Dillard. DAR indicates he d 20 Sep 1790 **P**: N **BLW**: N **RG**: Y **MK**: unk **PH**: unk **SS**: J- DAR Hatcher; D Vol 1 pg 263; DAR A036008; SAR P-148224 **BS**: JLARC 2; AR vol 1 pg 257.

DILLARD, James B; b 15 Oct 1727, James City Co; d 24 Aug 1794 **RU**: Patriot; Gave material aid to cause **CEM**: Mansion House; GPS unk; Buffalo Island; Amherst **GS**: U **SP**: Mar (8 Jul 1748) Mary Ann Hunt (28 Apr 1734-26 Aug 1787) **VI**: No further data **P**: N **BLW**: N **RG**: Y **MK**: unk **PH**: unk **SS**: AL Ct Bk pg 13 Amherst Co; DAR A036069; SAR P331345 **BS**: JLARC 115.

DILLARD, John; b 1751, Amherst Co; d 1 Dec 1822 **RU**: Captain/Patriot, Commanded a co, Henry Co Militia, 1780. Was wounded in Battle at Princeton **CEM**: Font Hill; GPS unk; Leatherwood Creek, Irisburg; Henry **GS**: U **SP**: Mar (23 Dec 1771) Sarah Stoval (c1758 Pittsylvania Co-aft 1800) **VI**: Son of James (1727-1794) & Mary (Hunt) (1748-1784) Dillard of Essex Co **P**: unk **BLW**: unk **RG**: Y **MK**: unk **PH**: unk **SS**: DAR #A036086; SAR P-329484; D Vol II pg 507, 510, 516; E pg 225; CZ **BS**: 196.

DILLARD, John; b unk; d 10 Jun 1808 **RU**: Patriot, Gave material aid to the cause **CEM**: Coons Family; GPS unk; vic Rixeyville Rt 640; Culpeper **GS**: Y **SP**: Ann Robertson, (1750-15 May 1815) also bur here **VI**: No further data **P**: N **BLW**: N **RG**: N **MK**: N **PH**: unk **SS**: ALCt bk I pg 47 **BS**: 75 Culpeper; 196.

DILLON, Henry; b 4 Dec 1732, Goochland Co; d I Nov 1806, Campbell Co **RU**: Patriot; Gave material aid to cause **CEM**: Hodges Family; GPS unk; nr Hodges Bicenntennial Farm; Rt 627 4.5 mi W of

---

RU=Rank/Unit	CEM=Cemetery	GS=Gravestone	SP=Spousal Information
VI=Other Veteran Info	P=Pension	BLW=Bounty/Land Warrant	RG=Registered Grave
MK=SAR/DAR Marker	PH=Photo	SS=Service Source	BS=Burial Source

119

Fieldale; Cumberland **GS**: Y **SP**: Mar 1751, Cumberland Co, Mary Byrn (___-1814) **VI**: Son of Thomas Dillon (1701-1744) & Mary LeBotille (1705-1748) **P**: N **BLW**: N **RG**: Y **MK**: N **PH**: N **SS**: D vol2, pg 434, Halifax Co; DAR A036143; SAR P-148274 **BS**: 196.

DILLON, Jesse; b unk; d 1833 **RU**: Bombardier, Served in Capt Thomas Baytop's Co, 1st Artillery at Valley Forge, Jun 1778 **CEM**: Dillon Family; GPS unk; Rt 900; Franklin **GS**: Y **SP**: Mar (18 Jan 1808 Franklin Co) Rebecca Plybon **VI**: No further data **P**: unk **BLW**: unk **RG**: N **MK**: N **PH**: unk **SS**: A pg 251 **BS**: 82 pg 95.

DILTZER, Jean; b unk; d 1781 **RU**: Soldier; Served in Royal Deaux Ponts Bn; D battle at Yorktown **CEM**: French Memorial; GPS 36.81944, -79.39933; Yorktown; York **GS**: U **SP**: No info **VI**: No further data **P**: unk **BLW**: unk **RG**: Y **MK**: unk **PH**: unk **SS**: J-Yorktown Historian; SAR P-148293 **BS**: JLARC 1, 74.

DIQUE-DOUNIER, Francois; b unk; d 1781 **RU**: Soldier; Served in Soissonnais Bn; D battle at Yorktown **CEM**: French Memorial; GPS 36.81944, -79.39933; Yorktown; York **GS**: U **SP**: No info **VI**: No further data **P**: unk **BLW**: unk **RG**: Y **MK**: unk **PH**: unk **SS**: J-Yorktown Historian; SAR P-148431 **BS**: JLARC 1, 74.

DIRONDELLES, Francois; b unk; d 1781 **RU**: Seaman; Served on "Citoyen"; D Yorktown battle **CEM**: French Memorial; GPS 36.81944, -79.39933; Yorktown; York **GS**: U **SP**: No info **VI**: No further data **P**: unk **BLW**: unk **RG**: Y **MK**: unk **PH**: unk **SS**: J-Yorktown Historian; SAR P-148435 **BS**: JLARC 1, 74.

DISHMAN, Samuel; b 26 Apr 1756, Westmoreland Co; d 14 May 1817 **RU**: Patriot, Gave material aid to the cause **CEM**: Dishman Family at Pine Hill; GPS unk; Off Rt 621, Shiloh; King George **GS**: Y **SP**: Mar (1830) Susanna Baker (1750 Tudex, King George Co) **VI**: No further data **P**: N **BLW**: N **RG**: Y **MK**: N **PH**: unk **SS**: ALCom Bk pg 334; DAR A032357; SAR P-148450 **BS**: 60 King George; 196.

DISHMAN, Sarah; b 1712; d 1782 **RU**: Patriot; Gave material aid to the cause **CEM**: Dishman Family; GPS unk; Pine Hill Hunt Club; Essex **GS**: Y **SP**: Peter Dishman **VI**: No further data **P**: N **BLW**: N **RG**: Y **MK**: N **PH**: unk **SS**: AL Ct Bk pg 7 Essex Co; AS; SAR applic; DAR A032358; SAR P-148453 **BS**: SAR Appl.

DISPANET(DISPANIT), Joseph; b 1743; d 1797, Frederick Co **RU**: Patriot, Paid personal property tax 1782, Rockingham Co, considered to be a supply tax for Rev War expenses **CEM**: Dispanet Family; GPS not determined; loc on Dispanet family property, vic Timberville; Rockingham **GS**: N **SP**: Mar 1) Elizabeth Shifflett (1743-1790), 2) Margaret Rust (1745-1802) **VI**: Son of Johann Jacob Dispanet (1717-1756) & Maria Euphrosina Barret (1718-1756). Rev War uniform in closet in house, but no service found **P**: N **BLW**: N **RG**: N **MK**: N **PH**: N **SS**: DV image 20, pdf, 1782 tax list, Rockingham Co **BS**: 196.

DIUGUID, George; b Oct 1762, Buckingham Co; d Aft 10 Sep 1832 **RU**: Private, Served in Capts Robert Hews', William Poor's, & David Patterson's Cos **CEM**: Diuguid; GPS unk; On Barry Jones Farm near Rt 460, on Co Rd 757, btw Concord & Lynchburg City; Campbell **GS**: U **SP**: Nancy Simpson **VI**: No further data **P**: unk **BLW**: unk **RG**: N **MK**: Y **SAR PH**: unk **SS**: DD **BS**: JLARC 1, 3, 4, 36.

DIUGUID, William, Jr; b 1746, d 1805 **RU**: Captain; Commanded company in the VA militia **CEM**: Christian Family; GPS not determined; Vera: Appomattox **GS**: Yes Govt **SP**: Mar 1773, Lucy Patteson (1752-1 Nov 1808) **VI**: Son of William Diuguid (1746-1805) & Ann Moss (1724-1805) **P**: N **BLW**: N **RG**: N **MK**: N **PH**: N **SS**: B.

DIVERS, George; b 1747; d 2 May 1830 **RU**: Paymaster/Patriot, Served in the 14th VA Regt, and resigned 28 Apr 1777. Paid Personal Property Tax Albemarle Co yrs 1782 and 1783 (considered as supply tax for Rev War expenses) **CEM**: Castle Hill; GPS 38.05683,-78.31828; 1625 Country Club Dr, can be seen 150 yds E of Wood Ln, Farmington; Albemarle **GS**: Y **SP**: Mar (1780) Martha Walker (2 May 1760, Albemarle Co-1829) d/o Thomas & Mildred (Thornton) Walker **VI**: No further data **P**: N **BLW**: N **RG**:Y **MK**: Y **SAR PH**: unk **SS**: E pg 227; SAR P-336919 **BS**: 196.

DIVERS, John b c1740, d aft 7 Jul 1800 **RU**: First Lieutenant/Patriot; 1st Lt Bedford Co Militia, 1781; Gave material aid to cause **CEM**: Divers Family; GPS unk; Burnt Chimneys; Franklin **GS**: Unk **SP**: Mary (___-aft Jul 1800) **VI**: No further data **P**: N **BLW**: N **RG**: Y **MK**: N **PH**: N **SS**: AL Bedford Co Ct Bk 6, pgs 292, 319; AZ pg 186; SAR P-148504 **BS**: 196.

RU=Rank/Unit	CEM=Cemetery	GS=Gravestone	SP=Spousal Information
VI=Other Veteran Info	P=Pension	BLW=Bounty/Land Warrant	RG=Registered Grave
MK=SAR/DAR Marker	PH=Photo	SS=Service Source	BS=Burial Source

DIVET, Henri; b unk; d 1781 **RU:** Seaman; Served on "Hector"; D Yorktown battle **CEM:** French Memorial; GPS 36.81944, -79.39933; Yorktown; York **GS:** U **SP:** No info **VI:** No further data **P:** unk **BLW:** unk **RG:** Y **MK:** unk **PH:** unk **SS:** J-Yorktown Historian; SAR P-148505 **BS:** JLARC 1, 74.

DIXON, James; b 1748 or 14 Feb 1749, Carlisle, Cumberland Co, PA; d 1786 **RU:** Captain, Served in Bedford Co Militia **CEM:** Dixon Family; GPS 37.18420, -79.59310; Off Rt 658, Concord quadrant, nr Rustburg; Campbell **GS:** U **SP:** 1) Elizabeth (-----) 2) Mar (18 Aug 1776 Bedford Co) Susanna Helm **VI:** Son of Thomas Dixon & Mary Ann Dinwiddie Bell **P:** unk **BLW:** unk **RG:** Y **MK:** N **PH:** unk **SS:** E pg 22; DAR A135154; SAR P-148548 **BS:** JLARC 36.

DIXON, John; b unk; d 1777 **RU:** Patriot; Gave material aid to the cause and was Sheriff Gloucester Co 1782-3 **CEM:** Trinity Episcopal (AKA Christ Church Kingston Parish); GPS 37.410692, -76.335776; Off Rt 614 nr jct Khyber Pass Trail; Mathews **GS:** U **SP:** No info **VI:** Son of John (of Bristol) & Lucy (Reade) (of Gloucester) Dixon **P:** N **BLW:** N **RG:** Y **MK:** N **PH:** unk **SS:** AL Ct Bk pg ii; ES pg 121; SAR bio rpt submitted Nov 2020 **BS:** 124 pg 117; 196.

DOAK, David, b 9 Dec 1740, d 1787 **RU:** Patriot; Gave use of horse for 22 days and hauled supplies for 6 days **CEM:** North Mountain; GPS unk; One mi N of Mt Tabor on Rt 620; Augusta **GS:** U **SP:** 1) Jennet Alexander, 2) Janet Davis **VI:** Son of Samuel Doak & Jane Mitchell. His name is on monument in cem with others at site of North Mountain Meeting House **P:** N **BLW:** N **RG:** N **MK:** unk **PH:** unk **SS:** DY pg 125; Al Ct Bk pg 15 and certificates **BS:** 73; 196.

DOAK, David D; b 1752; d 16 Jan 1829 **RU:** Patriot; Provided use of horses for 23 days; Collector of public tax 1782, 1783 **CEM:** Black Lick Rural Retreat; GPS 36.94435, -81.24377; 2390 Black Lick Rd; Wythe **GS:** U **SP:** Mary Hanna (Polly) (1753-19 Aug 1829) **VI:** No further data **P:** N **BLW:** N **RG:** N **MK:** unk **PH:** unk **SS:** CL pg 125; Public Service Claims; Augusta Co; pg 12 **BS:** 196.

DOAK, David Sr; b 1710; d 2 Oct 1787 **RU:** Patriot; Gave material aid to the cause in Augusta Co **CEM:** Black Lick Rural Retreat; GPS 36.94435, -81.24377; 2390 Black Lick Rd; Wythe **GS:** U **SP:** Mar (1745) Mary Breckinridge (1736-___) **VI:** DAR indicates he was also a soldier in the Montgomery Co Militia under Capt John Ward; doubtfull; too old **P:** N **BLW:** N **RG:** N **MK:** unk **PH:** unk **SS:** AL Ct Bk pg 15 Augusta Co **BS:** 196.

DOAK, Joseph; b unk; d unk **RU:** Second Lieutenant, Served in Montgomery Co Militia 6 Nov 1781 **CEM:** Black Lick Rural Retreat; GPS 36.94435, -81.24377; 2390 Black Lick Rd; Wythe **GS:** U **SP:** No info **VI:** No further data **P:** unk **BLW:** unk **RG:** N **MK:** Y SAR **PH:** unk **SS:** E pg 203 **BS:** JLARC 122.

DOAK, Robert; b 1751, Greenville, Augusta Co; d 12 Mar 1832 **RU:** Colonel, Capt of a Tazewell Co Co which fought at Battle of Point Pleasant Oct 1774 **CEM:** Bethel Presbyterian; GPS 38.04257, -79.17283, GS 38.0232,-79.1020; 563 Bethel Green Rd, Middlebrook; Augusta **GS:** Y **SP:** 1) Mar (28 Mar 1774 Augusta Co) Elizabeth Mitchell, (___-25 Dec 1824 Greenville, Augusta Co) 2) Mar (24 Aug 1826) Ann Tempelton McGuffin (c1780-1866 elsewhere) **VI:** Son of Samuel and Jane (Mitchell) Doak Sr. of Ireland. Source indicates served in Capt James Tate's Co of Militia 12 Mar 1832 on date of death, but doubtful. Bethel Presbyterian Church sign says was built by Elder Doak in 1779. Member VA House of Delegates 1812, raised troops 1813, high sheriff of Co. D Greenville, Augusta Co **P:** no **BLW:** no **RG:** Y **MK:** Y **PH:** Y **SS:** B; CD; Z pg 169; DAR A032611; SAR P-148617 **BS:** JLARC 2, 8, 62, 63; 196.

DOAK, Samuel; b 1746; d 1826 **RU:** Ensign, Served in Montgomery Co Militia 8 Sep 1779. **CEM:** Bethel Presbyterian; GPS 38.04257, -79.17283; 563 Bethel Green Rd, Middlebrook; Augusta **GS:** N **SP:** No info **VI:** No further data **P:** unk **BLW:** unk **RG:** Y **MK:** unk **PH:** N **SS:** E pg 227; SAR P-148622 **BS:** JLARC 62.

DOAK, William; b unk; d unk **RU:** Captain, Served in Montgomery Co Militia. Resigned 6 Nov 1781 **CEM:** Black Lick Rural Retreat; GPS 36.94435, -81.24377; 2390 Black Lick Rd; Wythe **GS:** U **SP:** No info **VI:** No further data **P:** unk **BLW:** unk **RG:** N **MK:** unk **PH:** unk **SS:** E pg 227 **BS:** JLARC 122.

DOBLER, Jacob; b 20 May 1764; d 7 Feb 1820 **RU:** Private, Served in Capt Robert Doad's Co of Militia, Jun 1774 **CEM:** Dobler Family; GPS unk; nr Kimbersville; Wythe **GS:** Y **SP:** No info **VI:** No further data **P:** unk **BLW:** unk **RG:** N **MK:** N **PH:** unk **SS:** Z pg 79-80 **BS:** 140 Doblerhome.

RU=Rank/Unit CEM=Cemetery GS=Gravestone SP=Spousal Information
VI=Other Veteran Info P=Pension BLW=Bounty/Land Warrant RG=Registered Grave
MK=SAR/DAR Marker PH=Photo SS=Service Source BS=Burial Source

121

DOGAN, Henry; b 23 Nov 1759; d 20 Dec 1823 **RU:** Soldier, Served Capt George Rice Co, Nov 1778. Served 7th, 11th & 15th Cont Lines **CEM:** Stonewall Memory Gardens; GPS 38.81530, -77.55170; 12004 Lee Hwy; Manassas City **GS:** U **SP:** Mar (11 Nov 1782) Mary Wheeler (4 Jul 1765-9 Jan 1832 Groveton, Prince William Co) d/o Drummond & (-----) Wheeler **VI:** DAR, SAR markers **P:** unk **BLW:** unk **RG:** Y **MK:** Y **PH:** Y **SS:** E pg 228; SAR P-149023 **BS:** JLARC 2, 3, 95; 196.

DOMINO, Jean; b unk; d 1781 **RU:** Soldier, Served in Gatinais Bn; D battle at Yorktown **CEM:** French Memorial; GPS 36.81944, -79.39933; Yorktown; York **GS:** U **SP:** No info **VI:** No further data **P:** unk **BLW:** unk **RG:** Y **MK:** unk **PH:** unk **SS:** J-Yorktown Historian **BS:** JLARC 1, 74.

DONALDSON, Robert: b 4 Mar 1764, Fayetteville, NC, d 1 Jul 1808 Brunswick Co **RU:** Private Capt Charles Polk's Co, NC Militia **CEM:** Blandford; GPS: 37.22433,-77.38604; 319 S Crater Rd; Petersburg City **GS:** Y **SP:** Margaret (___) (___-aft Feb 1853). Recd pen Feb 1853 **VI:** Had merchandise house in Petersburg; D enroute on business in Brunswick Co **P:** Widow **BLW:** N **RG:** Y **MK:** Y SAR monument **PH:** N **SS:** Fold3 Pen File of widow; DAR A033097; SAR P-334960 **BS:** 128 Donaldson; 213 pg 33; 196

DONOHOE, John V; b 16 May 1761; d 4 Dec 1821 **RU:** Corporal, Served in 8th Cont Line **CEM:** Mountain Chapel; GPS unk; Jct Rts 734 & 630; Loudoun **GS:** Y **SP:** Sarah Roszel (8 Aug 1775-23 Feb 1829) **VI:** No further data **P:** unk **BLW:** unk **RG:** N **MK:** N **PH:** unk **SS:** E pg 231 **BS:** 25 pg 83.

DORTON, William Jr; b 1750, Powhatan; d 1826 **RU:** Captain, Served in Washington Co Militia **CEM:** Dorton; GPS unk; Rt 71 near Dickensonville; Russell **GS:** U **SP:** Mary (-----) **VI:** No further data **P:** unk **BLW:** unk **RG:** Y **MK:** unk **PH:** unk **SS:** DL vol 2, pg 1098; DAR A200420; SAR P-149447 **BS:** JLARC 81.

DOUGHERTY (DOUGHTY), Edward; b c1750; d 6 Feb 1801 **RU:** Private, Served in Capt Robert Burns's Co, Col Moses Hazens's Regt, Jan 1779 **CEM:** Sanderson Home; GPS unk; Near NC line; Norfolk City **GS:** Y **SP:** No info **VI:** No further data **P:** N **BLW:** N **RG:** N **MK:** unk **PH:** unk **SS:** AP payroll Fold 3 **BS:** 75 pg 92.

DOUGLAS, William; b c1752; d 1803 **RU:** Seaman; Served on "Dragon" 22 Oct 1777-16 Dec 1777 **CEM:** St Paul's Episcopal; GPS 36.84733, -76.28554; 201 St Paul's Blvd; Norfolk City **GS:** Y **SP:** No info **VI:** No further data **P:** unk **BLW:** unk **RG:** N **MK:** N **PH:** unk **SS:** L pg 182 **BS:** 87 pg 26.

DOUGLAS (DOUGLASS), Hugh; b 1760; d 1815 **RU:** Captain, Served in Loudoun Co Militia May 1781 **CEM:** St James Episcopal, Old Cemetery; GPS 39.11555, -77.56250; Church St NE, Leesburg; Loudoun **GS:** U **SP:** No info **VI:** No further data **P:** unk **BLW:** unk **RG:** Y **MK:** unk **PH:** unk **SS:** E pg 233; SAR P-149666 **BS:** JLARC 1, 32.

DOUGLASS, Achilles; b 22 Feb 1752; d 5 Nov 1810 **RU:** Patriot, Gave material aid to cause **CEM:** South River Meeting House; GPS 37.37246, -79.19194; 5810 Fort Ave; Lynchburg City **GS:** U **SP:** No info **VI:** No further data **P:** N **BLW:** N **RG:** N **MK:** unk **PH:** unk **SS:** AL Ct Bk pg 18 Albemarle Co **BS:** 196.

DOUGLASS, Daniel; b 1768; d Sep 1803 **RU:** Private, Served in Harford Co, MD, Oct 1780 **CEM:** Old Presbyterian Meeting House; GPS 38.48528, -77.23532; 323 S Fairfax St; Alexandria City **GS:** N **SP:** No info **VI:** Died of bilious fever age 35, bur 7 Sep 1803 **P:** unk **BLW:** unk **RG:** N **MK:** N **PH:** N **SS:** AP roll **BS:** 23 pg 102.

DOUGLASS, John; b unk; d 1776 **RU:** Scout, Killed by Indians on way back fr Black's fort to warn settlement at Castle Woods of impending attack **CEM:** John Douglass; GPS unk; 100 yds N of John B Douglass Wayside Rt 19, 9 mi N of Abingdon; Washington **GS:** Y **SP:** No info **VI:** DAR monument erected 1929 **P:** unk **BLW:** unk **RG:** N **MK:** Y SAR **PH:** unk **SS:** AR Vol 1 pg 264 **BS:** 78 pg 142.

DOVE, Henry(Henrich Taube); b 1723 Germany; d Jan 1801 **RU:** Patriot, gave material aid to cause **CEM:** Old Dove; GPS not determined; Dovesville; Rockingham **GS:** N **SP:** Margaret Witmyer (1725 Germany-1801) **VI:** No further data **P:** N **BLW:** N **RG:** Y **MK:** N **PH:** N **SS:**D vol 3, pgs 828, 833, Rockingham DAR AO33888; SAR P-338347 **BS:** 196.

DOVE, William; b 27 Nov 1758, Charles Co, MD; d 20 Sep 1847 **RU:** Sergeant, Served in Capt Thomas Co, Col Rumley Regt, Alexandria. Marched to Gen Washington's headquarters, 1777. Enl Sep 1778-Jun 1779 as Marine on ship "Gen'l Washington" to France, Spain; enl again Mar 1780 same vessel to

---

RU=Rank/Unit	CEM=Cemetery	GS=Gravestone	SP=Spousal Information
VI=Other Veteran Info	P=Pension	BLW=Bounty/Land Warrant	RG=Registered Grave
MK=SAR/DAR Marker	PH=Photo	SS=Service Source	BS=Burial Source

Holland; again Jul 1781-Oct 1781 under Capt Powell **CEM:** George Family; GPS 36.58210,-79.19222; Gretna; Pittsylvania **GS:** Y **SP:** Mary Baker (1745 Culpeper Co-___) **VI:** Son of Joseph & Mary (-----) Dove. Moved to Fairfax Co as child. Moved to Pittsylvania Co after 1781 tour. Pen recd S-8336 **P:** Y **BLW:** unk **RG:** Y **MK:** unk **PH:** unk **SS:** E pg 234; G pg 263-5; DAR A033894; SAR P-149758 **BS:** 196.

DOVE, William: b unk; d bef Feb 1779 **RU:** Private Capt Arrell's Co, 3rd VA Regt **CEM:**Rev War Court House Plaque;GPS;not determined; 4110 Chain Bridge Rd; Fairfax **GS:** Memorialized on plaque 2017 by Geo Washington Chapter, VASSAR **SP** No info **VI:** Died in service **P:** N **BLW:** N **RG:** N **MK:** N **PH:** N **SS**; E pg 329; AP Fold3 muster roll:indicates dead, date not specified:EP sources: **BS:** None.

DOWNER, Ezra; b unk; d 1781 **RU:** Private, Served in CT Cont Line. Died fr battle at Yorktown **CEM:** Yorktown Victory Monument Tablet; GPS 38.28350, -78.54150; Yorktown; York **GS:** U **SP:** No info **VI:** No further data **P:** unk **BLW:** unk **RG:** Y **MK:** unk **PH:** unk **SS:** J-Yorktown Historian; SAR P-149918 DY pg 353 **BS:** JLARC 74.

DOWNMAN, Rawleigh; b c1719; d 18 Mar 1781 **RU:** Patriot, Gave material to cause for military certificates as will and inventory mentions several thousand dollars of Cont Certificates, left to his daughter Fanny Ball **CEM:** Morrattico House; GPS unk; Morattico House, Morattico; Lancaster **GS:** N **SP:** Fanny Ball d/o Joseph (1690-1760) & Frances (Ravenscroft) (1679-1762) Ball **VI:** Son of Rawleigh Downman (-- 1719) & Margaret Ball (1690-1758). His will bequeathed Continental certificates to be valued at £1000 specie to daughter Fanny Ball. His inventory listed £3894 in 17 Continental Certifcates. He and his wife Frances are bur in the orchard per the Downman family bible. Exact location is not known, but is vic Morattico House **P:** N **BLW:** N **RG:** Y **MK:** N **PH:** N **SS:** DT; SAR P-337542 **BS:** 214.

DRAKE, James Sr; b 8 May1725, Bertie, NC; d 1791 **RU:** Soldier/Patriot,Was POW. Gave material aid to cause **CEM:** St John's Episcopal; GPS 37.53183, -77.41958; 2401 E Broad St; Richmond City **GS:** N **SP:** 1) Sophia Valentine, 2) Hartwell Hodges Davis, rec'd pen W8676 **VI:** No further data **P:** Widow **BLW:** N **RG:** Y **MK:** N **PH:** N **SS:** AL Ct Bk pg 25 Powhatan Co; DAR A033347; SAR P-150156 **BS:** 80 vol 1 pg 266.

DRAKE, James; b 1740, d 3 Dec 1796 **RU:** 2d Lt, rec to this rank 21 Aug 1777, Capt Richard Crump's Co Powhatan Co Militia **CEM:** Peterville; GPS 37.564399, -77.964698; loc N of Anderson Rd by a pond 200 yds E of jct with Bell Rd; Powhatan **GS:** Unk **SP:** Mary "Molly" Taylor, d/o William Taylor (1696-___) & Mary Fleming (1714-___) **VI:** Son of Henry Drake (1720-___) & Sarah Dodd (1724, King George Co-1784, Westmoreland Co) **P:** N **BLW:** N **RG:** Y **MK:** N **PH:** N **SS:** AZ pg 221; DAR A033347; SAR P-150156 **BS:** 196.

DRAKE, James, Jr; b 1762, Cumberland, Co; d 1796 **RU:** Patriot, Paid personal property tax, 1783 at legal age 21, in Powhatan Co that is considered a tax to support Rev War expenses **CEM:** Peterville; GPS 37.564399, -77.964698; loc N of Anderson Rd by a pond 200 yds E of jct with Bell Rd; Powhatan **GS:** Unk **SP:** Tabitha Gentry (1764-___) **VI:** Son of James Drake (1740-3 Dec 1796) & Mary Taylor **P:** N **BLW:** N **RG:** N **MK:** N **PH:** N **SS:** ER Powhatan Co 1783 tax list **BS:** 196.

DRAKE, Thomas; b 13 Jul 1728, Piscataway, Middlesex Co, NJ; d 25 Jun 1811 **RU:** Soldier/Patriot, Served in Loudoun Co Militia. Gave material aid to the cause **CEM:** Unidentified; GPS unk; See DAR Senate report 1961, serial #12449, vol 6 for loc; Loudoun **GS:** U **SP:** Mar (4 Mar 1760) Eurah Humphrey **VI:** Son of Jonathan (1689-1754) & Mary (Clawson) (c1696,-1762) Drake. DAR report & AR vol 1, pg 267 show cem name as Loudoun **P:** N **BLW:** N **RG:** Y **MK:** N **PH:** unk **SS:** DAR A033363; SAR P-150159 AL Ct Bk pg 44 **BS:** 80 vol1 pg 267; 196.

DREUILHET, Dominique; b unk; d 1781 **RU:** Soldier, Served in Touraine Bn and died fr battle at Yorktown **CEM:** French Memorial; GPS 36.81944, -79.39933; Yorktown; York **GS:** U **SP:** No info **VI:** No further data **P:** unk **BLW:** unk **RG:** Y **MK:** unk **PH:** unk **SS:** J-Yorktown Historian; SAR P-150391 **BS:** JLARC 1, 74.

DRISKILL, Daniel; b c1740, Dublin, County Cork, Ire d 1813 **RU:** Patriot Paid supply tax for Rev War expenses 1783 Campbell Co **CEM:** Driskill; GPS unk; SE of Rt 40, Dog Creek; Campbell **GS:** U **SP:** Mar 1) Watkins, 2) Agnes Watkins **VI:** No further data **P:** unk **BLW:** unk **RG:** Y **MK:** N **PH:** unk **SS:** E pg 237; DAR A033792; SAR P-150469 **BS:** JLARC 36.

RU=Rank/Unit	CEM=Cemetery	GS=Gravestone	SP=Spousal Information
VI=Other Veteran Info	P=Pension	BLW=Bounty/Land Warrant	RG=Registered Grave
MK=SAR/DAR Marker	PH=Photo	SS=Service Source	BS=Burial Source

DRUMMOND, William; b c1765; d 1804 or 14 Oct 1809 **RU:** Patriot, Was town Alderman during war period **CEM:** Masonic Cemetery; GPS 38.30198, -77.46142; 900 Charles St; Fredericksburg City **GS:** Y **#45 SP:** Ann Fox (1759-22 Dec 1822) **VI:** Wine merchant and trustee of Fredericksburg Charity school **P:** N **BLW:** N **RG:** Y **MK:**Y SAR plaque **PH:** unk **SS:** 08 Vol 3 pg 42; SAR P-336975; Hodges, RA, *The Masonic Cem Fredericksburg, VA*1991 p9 **BS:** 08 vol 3 pg 421.

DRYDEN, James Jr; b 1730; d 1792 **RU:** Soldier/Patriot, Was in Battle at Kings Mountain 1780 in Col Campbell's Regt. Gave material aid to cause **CEM:** Dryden Family; GPS unk; See DAR Senate Doc 1958 serial 12259, vol 4; Rockbridge **GS:** U **SP:** No info **VI:** DAR source AR vol 1 pg 268 and SAR gives name of cem as Rockbridge **P:** unk **BLW:** unk **RG:** Y **MK:** unk **PH:** unk **SS:** DAR A033893; J-DAR Hatcher; AL Ct Bk pg 4 Rockbridge Co; SAR P-150559 **BS:** JLARC 2.

DRYDEN, James; d unk; d 7 Feb 1778 **RU:** Private, Capt Cleon Moore's Co, Col William Grayson's Regt, Cont Line **CEM:**Rev War Court House Plaque; GPS not determined; 4110 Chain Bridge Rd; Fairfax **GS:** Memorialized on plaque 2017 by Geo Washington Chapter, VASSAR **SP** No info **VI:**Son of William Dryden & Sally Broadwater; died in service **P:** N **BLW:** N **RG:** N **MK:** N **PH:** N **SS**; E pg 237; AP Fold3 muster roll::EP sources: **BS:** None.

DUBEAU, Pierre; b unk; d 1781 **RU:** Seaman, Served on "Auguste" and died from Yorktown battle **CEM:** French Memorial; GPS 36.81944, -79.39933; Yorktown; York **GS:** U **SP:** No info **VI:** No further data **P:** unk **BLW:** unk **RG:** Y **MK:** unk **PH:** unk **SS:** J-Yorktown Historian; SAR P-150654 **BS:** JLARC 1, 74.

DUBOURG, Nicolas; b unk; d 1781 **RU:** Soldier, Served in Soissonnais Bn and died fr battle at Yorktown **CEM:** French Memorial; GPS 36.81944, -79.39933; Yorktown; York **GS:** U **SP:** No info **VI:** No further data **P:** unk **BLW:** unk **RG:** Y **MK:** unk **PH:** unk **SS:** J-Yorktown Historian; SAR P-150688 **BS:** JLARC 1, 74.

DUCROS, Lue; b unk; d 1781 **RU:** Soldier, Served in Santonge Bn and died fr battle at Yorktown **CEM:** French Memorial; GPS 36.81944, -79.39933; Yorktown; York **GS:** U **SP:** No info **VI:** No further data **P:** unk **BLW:** unk **RG:** Y **MK:** unk **PH:** unk **SS:** J-Yorktown Historian; SAR P-150724 **BS:** JLARC 1, 74.

DUFF, Robert; b 23 Jun 1759, County Antrim, Northern Ireland; d 20 Jun 1820 **RU:** Private, Served in Capt David Clarks Co 138th PA Militia Regt **CEM:** Duff family; GPS unk; 3.2 mi E on Rt 612, fr jct Rts 58E and 421 E, Stickleyville; Lee **GS:** Y **SP:** Mary Powell Dickenson (15 Mar 1770-20 Dec 1859) **VI:** No further data **P:** unk **BLW:** unk **RG:** N **MK:** unk **PH:** unk **SS:** Cl PA Archives Vol X pg 109 **BS:** 196.

DUFF, Samuel, II; b 1750, Ireland; d 19 Jan 1825 **RU:** Private, Was in Kings Mountain Battle in Capt David Beatie's Co **CEM:** Green Spring Presbyterian; GPS 36.63670, -81.99560; 2007 Green Spring Ch Rd, Abingdon; Washington **GS:** Y **SP:** Mary Knox (1752-1799) **VI:** Son of Samuel Henry Duff (1720-1796) & Margaret (-----) (1722-1796) **P:** unk **BLW:** unk **RG:** Y **MK:** N **PH:** unk **SS:** J-DAR Hatcher; N pg 1241; DAR A034372; SAR P-150838 **BS:** JLARC 2; 80 vol1, pg 270; 196.

DUFF, Samuel Henry, Sr, b 1720, Scotland, d17 May 1796 RU: Patriot, had civil service as Juror in Washington Co in 1781 **CEM:** Green Spring Presbyterian; GPS 36.63670, -81.99560; 2007 Green Spring Ch Rd, Abingdon; Washington **GS:** Y **SP:** Margaret (-----) (1722-1796) VI: No further data **P:** unk **BLW:** unk **RG:** Y **MK:** unk **PH:** unk **SS: DL part 2, pg 10809; DAR A034371;** SAR P-150839 BS: 196.

DUFFEL, Edward; b 1754; d 1835 **RU:** Private, Was POW of British during RW **CEM:** Old City; GPS 37.41472, -79.15667; 401 Taylor St; Lynchburg City **GS:** U **SP:** No info **VI:** No further data **P:** unk **BLW:** unk **RG:** Y **MK:** Y SAR plaque **PH:** unk **SS:** BT Blue Ridge Chapter NS DAR; SAR P-150845 **BS:** JLARC 4; 196.

DUFFEL, James C; b 1761; d 1835 **RU:** Corporal, Served in 5th & 11th Cont Lines **CEM:** Old City; GPS 37.41472, -79.15667; 401 Taylor St; Lynchburg City **GS:** U **SP:** No info **VI:** No further data **P:** unk **BLW:** unk **RG:** N **MK:** Y SAR plaque **PH:** unk **SS:** AR Vol 1 pg 270 **BS:** JLARC 2; 80 vol 1, pg 270.

DUFOUR, Charles; b unk; d 1781 **RU:** Soldier, Served in Gatinais Bn and died fr battle at Yorktown **CEM:** French Memorial; GPS 36.81944, -79.39933; Yorktown; York **GS:** U **SP:** No info **VI:** No further data **P:** unk **BLW:** unk **RG:** Y **MK:** unk **PH:** unk **SS:** J-Yorktown Historian; SAR P-150867 **BS:** JLARC 1, 74.

RU=Rank/Unit	CEM=Cemetery	GS=Gravestone	SP=Spousal Information
VI=Other Veteran Info	P=Pension	BLW=Bounty/Land Warrant	RG=Registered Grave
MK=SAR/DAR Marker	PH=Photo	SS=Service Source	BS=Burial Source

124

DUFUT, Michel; b unk; d 1781 **RU**: Soldier, Served in Gatinais Bn and died fr battle at Yorktown **CEM**: French Memorial; GPS 36.81944, -79.39933; Yorktown; York **GS**: U **SP**: No info **VI**: No further data **P**: unk **BLW**: unk **RG**: Y **MK**: unk **PH**: unk **SS**: J-Yorktown Historian; SAR P-150871 **BS**: JLARC 1, 74.

DUGUE, Joseph; b unk; d 1781 **RU**: Seaman, Served on "Ville de Paris" and died from Yorktown battle **CEM**: French Memorial; GPS 36.81944, -79.39933; Yorktown; York **GS**: U **SP**: No info **VI**: No further data **P**: unk **BLW**: unk **RG**: Y **MK**: unk **PH**: unk **SS**: J-Yorktown Historian; SAR P-150898 **BS**: JLARC 1, 74.

DULAC, Jean; b unk; d 1781 **RU**: Seaman, Served on "Auguste" and died from Yorktown battle **CEM**: French Memorial; GPS 36.81944, -79.39933; Yorktown; York **GS**: U **SP**: No info **VI**: No further data **P**: unk **BLW**: unk **RG**: Y **MK**: unk **PH**: unk **SS**: J-Yorktown Historian; SAR P-150935 **BS**: JLARC 1, 74.

DULANEY, John; b 27 Jun 1747; d 1817 **RU**: Patriot, Gave material aid to cause **CEM**: Dulaney Family; GPS unk; See DAR Senate Doc1956, serial # 11999; vol 8; Fairfax **GS**: U **SP**: Mar (5 Mar 1773) Susannah Watts **VI**: Died in Culpeper Co **P**: N **BLW**: N **RG**: unk **MK**: N **PH**: unk **SS**: J- DAR Hatcher; AL Ct Bk I pg 45 Culpeper Co; AR pg 270; SAR P-150937 **BS**: JLARC 2.

DUMONT, Denis; b unk; d 1781 **RU**: Soldier, Served in Gatinais Bn and died fr battle at Yorktown **CEM**: French Memorial; GPS 36.81944, -79.39933; Yorktown; York **GS**: U **SP**: No info **VI**: No further data **P**: unk **BLW**: unk **RG**: Y **MK**: unk **PH**: unk **SS**: J-Yorktown Historian; SAR P-150981 **BS**: JLARC 1, 74.

DUNCAN, Andrew; b 1761; d Nov 1826 **RU**: Private, Served in Capt Edward's Co, Montgomery Co Militia **CEM**: Shockoe Hill; GPS 37.55190, -77.43170; 4th & Hospital Sts; Richmond City **GS**: Gov't **SP**: No info **VI**: Bur on 13 Nov 1826. Age at death: 85 **P**: N **BLW**: N **RG**: Y **MK**: Y SAR headstone marker **PH**: N **SS**: G pg 224; SAR P-335810 **BS**: **80 Vol 1 pg 270;** 196.

DUNCAN, Charles; b 1738, Strathblane Parish, Scotland; d 29 Jan 1808 **RU**: Patriot, Gave material aid to the cause **CEM**: Duncan Family; GPS unk; Roslyn Ave, 2 mi E of Town Hall, Chester; Chesterfield **GS**: Y **SP**: Elizabeth Peachy (__-09 Jun 1806) **VI**: Died in his 70th yr while visiting a daughter in London, England. Bur at church at Hampstead in Middlesex. Memorial stone **P**: N **BLW**: N **RG**: unk **MK**: N **PH**: unk **SS**: Al CT Bk Chesterfield Co pg 16, 55 **BS**: 196.

DUNCAN, Charles; b 1712, Perth and Kinross, Scotland; d 1780 **RU**: Patriot, Gave material aid to the cause **CEM**: Duncan; GPS 38.59068, -77.96277; Nr Oakshade; Culpeper **GS**: N **SP**: No info **VI**: Son of Henry (1664-1725) and Rebekkah Grace (Elson) (1684-1744) Duncan **P**: N **BLW**: N **RG**: N **MK**: unk **PH**: N **SS**: AL Ct Bk 1 Culpeper Co pg 13, 46, 47 **BS**: 196.

DUNCAN, George; b 1730, Scotland; d 1783 **RU**: Captain, Promoted to Capt, Fluvanna Co Militia in Sep 1777 **CEM**: Duncan Family; GPS unk; Nr Hardware River; Fluvanna **GS**: Y **SP**: Mar (1754) Ann Hall (1732-1783) **VI**: No further data **P**: unk **BLW**: unk **RG**: Y **MK**: N **PH**: unk **SS**: E pg 240; SAR P-151073, SAR P-151071 **BS**: 80 vol 1 pg 270.

DUNCAN, John; b 1741; d 1833 **RU**: Soldier, Specific service may be found at the Lib of VA in Auditor's Acct 1778-83 pg 106 **CEM**: Sumpter; GPS unk; Rt 619, Floyd; Floyd **GS**: U **SP**: Elizabeth (-----) **VI**: No further data **P**: unk **BLW**: unk **RG**: Y **MK**: unk **PH**: unk **SS**: CZ pg 146; SAR P-147026 & P-151102 **BS**: JLARC 4, 29.

DUNCAN, Robert; b 1760; d 1826 **RU**: Private served as a wagoner 1781-1782 Va Cont Line **CEM**: Duncan Family; GPS not determined; use property rec for exact loc nr So Anna River, Bumpass; Louisa **GS**: Unk **SP**: Rebecca Bacon (1785-1820), d/o Edmund Bacon & Elizabeth Edloe **VI**: No further data **P**: N **BLW**: N **RG**: Y **MK**:N **PH**: N **SS**: AP Fold3 Monthly QM rec 1781-1782; CZ; SAR P-151125 **BS**: 196.

DUNCANSON, James; b 11 Feb 1735, Scotland; d 1 Mar 1791 **RU**: Colonel/Patriot, Served in 2d VA Regt. Gave material aid to cause **CEM**: St George's Episcopal; GPS unk; 905 Princess Anne; Fredericksburg City **GS**: U **SP**: Mar (12 Jan 1766) Mary McCauley(3 Feb 1718-10 Oct 1790) **VI**: Arr in VA Jul 1752 **P**: unk **BLW**: unk **RG**: Y **MK**: unk **PH**: unk **SS**: J- DAR Hatcher; AL Ct Bk 1 pg 24, 47, 50 Culpeper Co; DD; SAR P-151147 **BS**: JLARC 2; 213 pg 577.

DUNGAN (DUNCAN), Elisha; b 1735, Bucks Co, PA; d 1 Dec 1808 **RU**: Patriot, Was member of Road Committee and Juror, Washington Co **CEM**: St Clair Bottom Primitive Baptist; GPS 36.76098, -

---

RU=Rank/Unit	CEM=Cemetery	GS=Gravestone	SP=Spousal Information
VI=Other Veteran Info	P=Pension	BLW=Bounty/Land Warrant	RG=Registered Grave
MK=SAR/DAR Marker	PH=Photo	SS=Service Source	BS=Burial Source

125

81.64556; Jct Rts 600 & 660, Chilhowie; Smyth **GS:** U **SP:** Mar (1760) Hannah Rogers (__-1800 Clair's Bottom) **VI:** Died in Washington Co **P:** N **BLW:** N **RG:** unk **MK:** N **PH:** unk **SS:** DL Part 2 pg 1053, 1058; DAR A034454; SAR P-151161 **BS:** JLARC 114.

DUNKIN, John Jr; b 25 Feb 1765; d 8 Apr 1832 **RU:** Sergeant, Served in 3rd & 4th Cont Lines **CEM:** Green Spring Presbyterian; GPS 36.63670, -81.99560; 2007 Green Spring Ch Rd, Abingdon; Washington **GS:** U **SP:** Mary Laughlin (20 Jul 1767 KY_22 Feb 1846, Lineville, VA) **VI:** Son of John Sr (1735-27 Oct 1740 Abingdon) & (-----) Dunkin. Died in Kentucky **P:** unk **BLW:** unk **RG:** Y **MK:** unk **PH:** unk **SS:** J- DAR Hatcher; E pg 241; SAR P-151310 **BS:** JLARC 2; 80 vol 1 pg 272.

DUNKIN, John Thomas; b 1743, Lancaster Co, PA; d 6 Aug 1818 **RU:** Captain, Promoted to Capt 1777 in Washington Co Militia. Was Sgt in 3rd & 4th Cont Lines **CEM:** Green Spring Presbyterian; GPS 36.63670, -81.99560; 2007 Green Spring Ch Rd, Abingdon; Washington **GS:** U **SP:** Eleanor Sharp **VI:** Son of (-----) & Elizabeth (Alexander) (1710-1814) Dunkin. POW in Quebec **P:** unk **BLW:** unk **RG:** N **MK:** Y SAR **PH:** Y **SS:** E pg 241; BT USDAR Gr Mkr **BS:** 80 vol 1 pg 272.

DUNLOP(DUNLAP), John; b 1756; d 1806 **RU:** Private, Served in Capt Durval Harrison Co, in 2nd VA Regt **CEM:** Old Presbyterian Meeting House; GPS 38.48528, -77.23532; 323 S Fairfax St; Alexandria City **GS:** N **SP:** No info **VI:** Died after a lingering illness age 50, bur 2 Nov 1806. Listed on an SAR plaque in cemetery **P:** unk **BLW:** unk **RG:** N **MK:** Y SAR plaque **PH:** N **SS:** J-NSSAR 1993 Reg; AP roll; AK **BS:** JLARC 1; 23 pg 102; 196.

DUNN, John; b 1750; d 11 Apr 1827 **RU:** Private, Served 3 yrs **CEM:** St James Episcopal, Old Cemetery; GPS 39.11555, -77.56250; Church St NE, Leesburg; Loudoun **GS:** Y **SP:** No info **VI:** Rector of St James Episcopal Church nearly 25 yrs. Was a Mason **P:** unk **BLW:** unk **RG:** N **MK:** N **PH:** unk **SS:** C Sec III pg 420 **BS:** 25 pg 87.

DUNN, William; b 1748; d 25 Dec 1787 **RU:** Corporal, Served in 9th & 13th Cont Line **CEM:** Old Christ Church Episcopal; GPS 38.80625, -77.04718; 118 N Washington St; Alexandria City **GS:** Y **SP:** No info **VI:** Died age 39 **P:** unk **BLW:** unk **RG:** N **MK:** unk **PH:** unk **SS:** J-NSSAR 1993 Reg; E pg 242; AP fold 3 serv rec **BS:** JLARC 1; 20 pg 137; 196.

DUPLAT, Michel; b unk; d 1781 **RU:** Seaman, Served on "Diademe" and died from Yorktown battle **CEM:** French Memorial; GPS 36.81944, -79.39933; Yorktown; York **GS:** U **SP:** No info **VI:** No further data **P:** unk **BLW:** unk **RG:** Y **MK:** unk **PH:** unk **SS:** J-Yorktown Historian; SAR P-151578 **BS:** JLARC 1, 74.

DUPREX, Joseph; b unk; d 1781 **RU:** Seaman, Served on "Hector" and died from Yorktown battle **CEM:** French Memorial; GPS 36.81944, -79.39933; Yorktown; York **GS:** U **SP:** No info **VI:** No further data **P:** unk **BLW:** unk **RG:** Y **MK:** unk **PH:** unk **SS:** J-Yorktown Historian; SAR P-151589 **BS:** JLARC 1, 74.

DUPUIS, Jean; b unk; d 1781 **RU:** Seaman, Served on "Diademe" and died from Yorktown battle **CEM:** French Memorial; GPS 36.81944, -79.39933; Yorktown; York **GS:** U **SP:** No info **VI:** No further data **P:** unk **BLW:** unk **RG:** Y **MK:** unk **PH:** unk **SS:** J-Yorktown Historian; SAR P-151592 **BS:** JLARC 1, 74.

DUPUY, James; b 1758; d 1823 **RU:** Patriot, Signed Legislative petition **CEM:** Dupuy; GPS unk; Jennings Ordinary, NW 647 for 1 mi to Carrington home; Nottoway **GS:** U **SP:** Mary Purnall **VI:** No further data **P:** N **BLW:** N **RG:** N **MK:** unk **PH:** unk **SS:** E pg 243 **BS:** JLARC 85.

DUPUY, John see Appendix G, Addenda

DURAND, Pierre; b unk; d 1781 **RU:** Seaman, Served on "Saint-Esprit" and died from Yorktown battle **CEM:** French Memorial; GPS 36.81944, -79.39933; Yorktown; York **GS:** U **SP:** No info **VI:** No further data **P:** unk **BLW:** unk **RG:** Y **MK:** unk **PH:** unk **SS:** J-Yorktown Historian; SAR P-151612 **BS:** JLARC 1, 74.

DURRETT, James; b 20 Apr 1762, d 20 Jan 1822 **RU:** Sergeant Gen George Rogers Clark"s Illinois Regt 1781 to end of war and eligible for BLW. On payroll of 1781 and Jan Feb 1782 **CEM:** Blue Ridge farm; GPS 37.7028608,-76.3789312; 1034 Ortman Road (Rt. 691). Afton; Albemarle **GS:** Y **SP:** Nancy (-----): C pg 176; E pg 243; G pg 697; AL Serv Rec; SAR P-151753 **BS:** 196.

RU=Rank/Unit	CEM=Cemetery	GS=Gravestone	SP=Spousal Information
VI=Other Veteran Info	P=Pension	BLW=Bounty/Land Warrant	RG=Registered Grave
MK=SAR/DAR Marker	PH=Photo	SS=Service Source	BS=Burial Source

DURRETT, Richard, Jr; b 13 Aug 1746, d 1 Nov 1820 **RU:** Lieutenant,Capt George Gilmer's Co, Albemarle Co Militia **CEM:** Wakefield; 38.1572770, -78.4652710; 975 Wakefield Farm Rd, Earlysville; Albermarle **GS:** Y **SP:** Elizabeth Davis (Nov 1753-15 Jul 1815 Richard Durrett (1721-15 Oct 1784) & Sarah Hampton (1720-___) **P:** N **BLW:** N **RG:** Y **MK:** N **PH:** N **SS:** AZ-175, 193; E pg 243; DAR A035454, cites "Woods, History of Albemarle Co; SAR P-151755 **BS:** 196.

DURRETT, Richard, Sr; b 14 Sep 1721, d 8 Oct 1784 **RU:** Patriot, gave material aid to cause **CEM:** Wakefield; 38.1572770, -78.4652710; 975 Wakefield Farm Rd, Earlysville; Albermarle **GS:** Y **SP:** Sarah Hampton (1720-___) **VI:** Son of John William Durrett (1675-1743) -___)**P:** N **BLW:** N **RG:** Y **MK:** N **PH:** N **SS:** D vol 1, pgs 9, 23; DAR A035452; SAR P-151754 **BS:** 196.

DUVAL, Philip Jr; b 1758; d 1817 **RU:** Patriot, Gave material aid to the cause **CEM:** Shockoe Hill; GPS 37.55190, -77.43170; 4th & Hospital Sts; Richmond City **GS:** Y **SP:** No info **VI:** No further data **P:** N **BLW:** N **RG:** N **MK:** N **PH:** unk **SS:** AL Ct Bk pg 26 **BS:** 179 pg 131.

DUVAL, Samuel; b 22 Jan 1714, Gloucester Co; d Feb 1784 **RU:** Patriot, Member House of Burgesses, 1775; First VA Convention, 1774; Committee of Safety, 1775; 2d VA Convention 1775; and Directorate for removing capital fr Richmond to Williamsburg, 1779 **CEM:** St Johns Episcopal Church: GPS 37.531830, -77.419580; 2401 East Broad St; Richond City **GS:** N **SP:** Lucie Claiborne (1725, New Kent Co-6 Mar 1810 Henrico Co), daug of William Claiborne (1696-1746) & Elizabeth Whitehead (1690-1746) **VI:** Son of Daniel DuVal (1675-___) **P:** N **BLW:** N **RG:** Y **MK:** N **PH:** N **SS:** CD; DAR A035704; SAR P-132467 **BS:** 196.

DUVAL, William, b 22 Jan 1714, Gloucester Co, d Feb 1784, Henrico Co **RU:** Patriot, member House of Burgesses, 1773 -1775; House of Burgesses, 1773 -1775, Committees of Safety and Correspondence Richmond and Henrico, 1775, Second Virginia Convention March 23, 1775, Directorate for removing Capital from Capitol from Williamsburg to Richmond, 1779-1784; and furnished supplies to LaFayette's Army **CEM:** St Johns Episcopal Church; GPS: 37.53183, -77.41958; 2401 E Broad St; Richmond City **GS:** N **SP:** Mar 1745, Lucie Claiborne,(1725-1810), d/o William Claiborne & Elizabeth Whitehead **VI:** Son of Daniel Duval (1675-___) **P:** N **BLW:** N **RG:** Y **MK:** N **PH:** unk **SS:** DAR A035704; SAR P-132467 **BS:** 196.

DYER, George; b 1753, Prince Georges Co, MD; d 1827 **RU:** Lieutenant, Served in Capt Daniel Hankins Co in the MD Cont Line. Also in Capt Charles Williamson's Co, Prince George's Co, MD **CEM:** Dyer Family; GPS 36.45261, -79.48125; Foxpipe Rd, Leatherwood; Henry **GS:** Y Gov't **SP:** Rachel Dalton 1759-1862) **VI:** Son of James & Eleanoer (Brown) Dyer. Will dated 15 Mar 1823 age 70 **P:** unk **BLW:** unk **RG:** Y **MK:** N **PH:** N **SS:** Archives of MD Vol 18 pg 328; AK; DAR A035154; SAR P-152075 **BS:** 04.

EALEY, John; b unk; d by 1826 **RU:** Private?, Served in 5th, 11th, 15th Cont lines **CEM:** Eastern State Hospital; GPS 37.25560 -76.71030; S Henry Street; Williamsburg City **GS:** N **SP:** No info **VI:** His name is on a plaque in the cemetery **P:** unk **BLW:** unk **RG:** N **MK:** N **PH:** unk **SS:** E pg 245-246 **BS:** 65 Williamsburg.

EARLY, James; b 1750; d 11 Oct 1822 **RU:** Ensign, Served in Capt Shackleford's Co, 27 Sep 1781, Orange Co Militia **CEM:** Wakefield Cemetery; GPS unk; Wakefield Farm Rd, Earlysville; Albemarle **GS:** U **SP:** Mar (1772) Elizabeth Thompson **VI:** No further data **P:** unk **BLW:** unk **RG:** Y **MK:** unk **PH:** unk **SS:** J- DAR Hatcher; E pg 246; DAR A035503; SAR P-152361 **BS:** JLARC 2.

EARLY, James Mattew; b 1752; d 1807 **RU:** Soldier, Served in 3rd, 4th & 9th Cont Line **CEM:** Fincastle Presbyterian; GPS 37.50017, -79.87558; 108 E Back St, Fincastle; Botetourt **GS:** N **SP:** Mar (c1780 in Albemarle Co) Jane Gatewood (1758-9 Mar 1832, Benton, Franklin Co., IL) d/o William & Ann (Ronsom) Gatewood of Albemarle Co **VI:** Name is on the SAR plaque at this cemetery. His cabin built ca 1796 serves today as loc of the Fincastle Museum **P:** unk **BLW:** unk **RG:** Y **MK:** Y SAR & plaque **PH:** N **SS:** AR Vol 2 pg 2; E pg 246, J-NSSAR 1993 Reg, J- DAR Hatcher; SAR P-152363 **BS:** 196; JLARC 1, 2.

EARLY, Jeremiah, Jr; b 1730; d 1779 **RU:** Colonel/Patriot, Commissioned Lt Col in Bedford Co Militia 23 Mar 1778, Col 28 Dec 1778. Gave material aid to cause **CEM:** Wyndholm, aka Early Family; GPS unk; Flat Creek nr Evington; Campbell **GS:** U **SP:** 1) Sarah (-----); 2) Mary (-----) **VI:** Son of Jeremiah Allen Early & Elizabeth Metstand Buford **P:** unk **BLW:** unk **RG:** Y **MK:** N **PH:** unk **SS:** D Campbell Co; SAR P-152367 **BS:** JLARC 2, 36; 196.(**EASLEY**, John See Appendix G)

RU=Rank/Unit	CEM=Cemetery	GS=Gravestone	SP=Spousal Information
VI=Other Veteran Info	P=Pension	BLW=Bounty/Land Warrant	RG=Registered Grave
MK=SAR/DAR Marker	PH=Photo	SS=Service Source	BS=Burial Source

EASLEY, Robert; b 2 May 1754, Cumberland Co; d 5 Dec 1814 **RU:** Soldier/Patriot, Served in 5th, 11th, 15th Cont Lines. Gave material aid to cause **CEM:** Oak Ridge; GPS 36.71912, -78.90321; Main St & Hamiliton St, South Boston; Halifax **GS:** Y **SP:** 1) Mar (1779) (-----) Jennings 2) Mar (1799) Ann Stephens **VI:** No further data **P:** unk **BLW:** unk **RG:** Y **MK:** unk **PH:** unk **SS:** D Halifax Co; DD; SAR P-152404 **BS:** JLARC 1, 2, 4.

EAST, Thomas; b 1740, Henrico Co; d Aft 17 Jul 1797 **RU:** Patriot, Took oath of Allegiance, Pittsylvania Co **CEM:** Alta Vista Plantation; GPS unk; Altavista; Pittsylvania **GS:** Y **SP:** Mar (1761) Obedience (-----) (__-19 Oct 1807) **VI:** No further data **P:** N **BLW:** N **RG:** N **MK:** N **PH:** unk **SS:** AR DAR report; BV Thomas Dillard's list; SAR P-152416 **BS:** 80 vol 2 pg 2.

EASTHAM, George; b unk; d 1 Jan 1841 **RU:** Patriot, Served as wagoner for Militia **CEM:** Eastman Family; GPS unk; Jct Rts 17 & 660; Fauquier **GS:** Y **SP:** No info **VI:** No further data **P:** N **BLW:** N **RG:** N **MK:** N **PH:** unk **SS:** D Fauquier pg 5 **BS:** 19 pg 50.

EASTON, William; b unk; d unk **RU:** Sergeant, Served in Capt William Motte Co in Col Francis Marion's SC Regt, 1 Nov 1779. Later promoted to Sgt in Hazen's Corps **CEM:** Eastin Family; GPS unk; Rt 601; Fluvanna **GS:** Y **SP:** No info **VI:** Recd BLW **P:** unk **BLW:** Y **RG:** N **MK:** N **PH:** unk **SS:** A pg 114 **BS:** 66 pg 26.

EDMON, Maurice; b unk; d 1781 **RU:** Soldier, Served in Touraine Bn and died fr battle at Yorktown **CEM:** French Memorial; GPS 36.81944, -79.39933; Yorktown; York **GS:** U **SP:** No info **VI:** No further data **P:** unk **BLW:** unk **RG:** Y **MK:** unk **PH:** unk **SS:** J-Yorktown Historian; SAR P-153159 **BS:** JLARC 1, 74.

EDMONDS, Elias Jr; b 1756; d 5 Dec 1800 **RU:** Captain, Served in Fauquier Co Militia 1776-1777 **CEM:** Oak Springs; GPS unk; 770 Fletcher Dr; Fauquier **GS:** N **SP:** A man of this name mar (11 Jan 1786 Fauquier Co, Simon Morgan security) Frances Edmonds **VI:** No further data **P:** unk **BLW:** unk **RG:** Y **MK:** N **PH:** N **SS:** AV; Fauquier Co Marriages pg 56; DAR A036275; SAR P-338595 **BS:** 83, Inv # NF-20.

EDMONDS, John; b 1737, Lancaster Co; d 1798 **RU:** Lieutenant/Captain, Served in 9th Cont Line **CEM:** Oak Springs; GPS unk; 770 Fletcher Dr; Fauquier **GS:** N **SP:** 1) Francis Jane Wildly (Wilder) 2) Helen Hack (nee Shepard, noted English actress) widow of Hack of Hacks Neck, VA. A John Edmonds Jr. mar (5 Jun 1793 (bond) Fauquier Co) Naomi Hicks d/o Kimble & (-----) Hicks **VI:** No further data **P:** unk **BLW:** unk **RG:** N **MK:** N **PH:** N **SS:** E pg 248; AK; AV; Fauquier Co Marriages pg 56 **BS:** 04; 83, Inv # NF-20.

EDMONDS, William; b 1734 or 1736, Lancaster Co; d 19 Feb 1816 **RU:** Colonel, Served in 1st Bn of Fauquier Co Militia. Was in 1st battle of Revolution fought on VA soil at Great Bridge, VA Dec 1775. Recd 24 Mar 1778 as Maj and as Lt Col Aug 1781. Served in 1st Bn Fauquier Co Militia. Resigned May 1783 **CEM:** Edmonds Family; GPS unk; Warrenton; Fauquier **GS:** Y **SP:** Mar (16 Mar 1764 Fauquier Co, William Blackwell security) Elizabeth Blackwell (1742-28 Feb 1817) **VI:** Also has a stone placed at Warrenton Cem by his daughter **P:** unk **BLW:** unk **RG:** Y **MK:** unk **PH:** unk **SS:** AK; Fauquier Co Marriages pg 56; SAR P-330967 **BS:** 04; JLARC 16.

EDWARDS, Ambrose   G pg 200 Vol #; b 17 Feb 1747, Albemarle Co; d 1812 **RU:** Patriot, Gave material aid to the cause **CEM:** Leatherwood Plantation; GPS 36.44534, -79.4558; Nr Martinsville; Henry **GS:** U **SP:** Mar (15 Mar 1774) Olive Martin (1754-1826) **VI:** No further data **P:** N **BLW:** N **RG:** unk **MK:** unk **PH:** unk **SS:** SAR P-153294; AR Vol 2 pg 7 **BS:** JLARC 2.

EDWARDS, Ambrose; b c1726, England; d Dec 1810 **RU:** Patriot, Gave material aid to the cause **CEM:** Edwards Family; GPS unk; Cherry Grove; King William **GS:** U **SP:** 1) Mar (1750) Wealthean Butler (__- 22 Dec 1800) 2) Barbara Finch **VI:** No further data **P:** N **BLW:** N **RG:** Y **MK:** N **PH:** unk **SS:** AL Ct Bk pg 20; SAR P-153291 **BS:** 86 pg 43.

EDWARDS, Ambrose, Jr; b 1757, d aft 1812 **RU:** Patriiot Gave material aid to the cause, King William Co **CEM:** Cherry Grove Farm; GPS not determined; loc vic servants quarters still standing on the farm, Rt 30, nr Aylett; King William **GS:** U **SP:** No spousal date; **VI:** Son of Ambrose Edwards, Sr **P:** N **BLW:** N **RG:** N **MK:** N **PH:** N **SS:** AL Ct Bk II, pgs 20.25 & Lists I pg 1, List II, pgs7,9 **BS:** 196.

RU=Rank/Unit	CEM=Cemetery	GS=Gravestone	SP=Spousal Information
VI=Other Veteran Info	P=Pension	BLW=Bounty/Land Warrant	RG=Registered Grave
MK=SAR/DAR Marker	PH=Photo	SS=Service Source	BS=Burial Source

128

EDWARDS, Benjamin; b c1758; d Aft 1835 **RU:** Private, Served in VA State Line for 3 yrs **CEM:** Wright Family; GPS 36.97658, -80.21693; Pizarro off Rt 668; Floyd **GS:** U **SP:** No info **VI:** Memorialized by DAR plaque in cem. Pensioned per 1835 list at age 77. BLW of 299 acres issued 1 May 1783 **P:** Y **BLW:** Y **RG:** N **MK:** Y **PH:** unk **SS:** E pg 250; F pg 25 **BS:** 196 for John Mitchell.

EDWARDS, Elias; b 1753; d 1830 **RU:** Lieutenant Colonel, Commanded 3rd VA Regt **CEM:** North End; GPS 36.77234, -80.73866; 101 Beaver Dam Rd, Hillsville; Carroll **GS:** U **SP:** No info **VI:** No further data **P:** unk **BLW:** unk **RG:** N **MK:** N **PH:** unk **SS:** E pg 255; CI pensions of soldiers **BS:** 123 pg 67.

EDWARDS, Isaac; b 25 Dec 1747; d 29 Jul 1825 **RU:** Private, Specific service may be found at the Lib of VA in Auditor's Acct Bk XXII, pg 19. **CEM:** North End; GPS 36.77234, -80.73866; 101 Beaver Dam Rd, Hillsville; Carroll **GS:** Y **SP:** Mar (27 Jan 1769, Rowan Co, NC) Catherine Rosanna Boone (1 Feb 1755 Guilford Co, NC-Feb 1835 Grayson Co) **VI:** Son of Thomas Hanuel (1706-1768) & Eleanor (Scaif) Edwards. Died in Grayson Co. Illegible stone has DAR marker mounted on it **P:** unk **BLW:** unk **RG:** Y **MK:** Y DAR **PH:** unk **SS:** E pg 250; CZ pg 137; SAR P-153339 **BS:** JLARC 43; 196.

EFFINGER, John Ignatius; b 4 Dec 1756, Mannheim, Germany; d 1 Sep 1839 **RU:** Sergeant, Served in Capt Bartholomew Von Heers Co of Dragoons, PA Line **CEM:** St Paul's Reformed Church; GPS 38.87780, -78.50663; Cnr S Church St & E South St, Woodstock; Shenandoah **GS:** U **SP:** 1) Ann Catherine Spatz 2) Barbara Cook **VI:** Pensioned in 1828. Died in Woodstock **P:** Y **BLW:** unk **RG:** Y **MK:** unk **PH:** unk **SS:** J-NSSAR 1993 Reg; DD; SAR P-153499 **BS:** JLARC 1; 196.

EGE, Jacob; b 13 Mar 1754; d 6 Oct 1795 **RU:** Patriot, Gave material aid to cause **CEM:** St John's Episcopal; GPS 37.53183, -77.41958; 2401 E Broad St; Richmond City **GS:** Y **SP:** Elizah W(-----) (14 Feb 1746-8 Jan 1829) **VI:** No further data **P:** N **BLW:** N **RG:** N **MK:** N **PH:** unk **SS:** D Vol II pg 499; AL Ct Bk pg 7 Henrico Co **BS:** 28 pg 439; 196.

EGE, Samuel; b 22 Jan 1742, Germany; d 11 Feb 1801 **RU:** Quartermaster, Served in Richmond E Co **CEM:** St John's Episcopal; GPS 37.53183, -77.41958; 2401 E Broad St; Richmond City **GS:** Y **SP:** Mar (1777) Elizabeth Walker (14 Jan 1746-8 Jan 1829) **VI:** Son of Johann Ege (1713-1795) & Maria Dorothea Scheerer **P:** unk **BLW:** unk **RG:** Y **MK:** Y SAR **PH:** unk **SS:** AK; E pg 251; D vol 2 pg 500, SAR Bio rpt submitted Aug 20 **BS:** 04; 28 pg 439.

EGGERS, Elijah; b unk; d 17 Dec 1781 **RU:** Private, Served in Capt Samuel Pell's 4th Co, Col Courtland's 2d NY Line Regt and died fr battle at Yorktown **CEM:** Yorktown Victory Monument Tablet; GPS 38.28350, -78.54150; Yorktown; York **GS:** U **SP:** No info **VI:** No further data **P:** unk **BLW:** unk **RG:** Y **MK:** unk **PH:** unk **SS:** J-Yorktown Historian; AX pg 190; SAR P-153521 **BS:** JLARC 74.

EGGLESTON, Joseph; b 24 Nov 1754; d 13 Feb 1811 **RU:** Major, Ent serv Amelia Co 1778 while student at W&M. Served as Cavalry major in Army. Prisoner at Elizabethtown, 25 Jan 1780 **CEM:** Grub Hill; GPS 37.39940, -77.97030, GS 37.2400,-77.5812; Grub Hill Church Rd Rt 609; Amelia **GS:** Y **SP:** 1) Mar (17 Oct 1776 (bond)) Judith Bentley, a widow; 2) Mar (7 May 1796 (bond) Amelia Co) Judith Cary (c1766-19 Feb 1859) **VI:** BLW #675 issued 10 Aug 1789 for 5,333 acres. Widow pen Amelia Co 1848 age 82. W8687. Maj in Lee's Legion during the War; member Virginia House of Delegates, 1785 to 1788 ;member Virginia Privy Council in 1787. In 1798, he was elected to Congress to fill the vacancy caused by the resignation of William B. Giles and reelected to the Sixth Congress, serving until 1801 **P:** Y **BLW:** Y **RG:** Y **MK:** Y **PH:** unk **SS:** E pg 251; K Vol II pg 74; SAR P-153452 **BS:** JLARC 4, 55; 196.

EGRE, Paul; b unk; d 1781 **RU:** Soldier, Served in Royal Deaux Ponts Bn and died fr battle at Yorktown **CEM:** French Memorial; GPS 36.81944, -79.39933; Yorktown; York **GS:** U **SP:** Mar (25 Feb 1788) Sally Meade **VI:** No further data **P:** unk **BLW:** unk **RG:** Y **MK:** unk **PH:** unk **SS:** J-Yorktown Historian; SAR P-153559 **BS:** JLARC 1, 74.

ELDRIDGE/ ELDREDGE, Rolfe, Sr; b 29 Dec 1745, Prince George Co; d 1831 **RU:** Patriot, Gave material aid to the cause **CEM:** Eldridge Family; GPS ; Fork of North & Slate Rivers; Buckingham **GS:** N **SP:** Mar (26 Nov 1773) Susanna Everard Walker (1744-1821), daug of George Walker (1720-1780) and Mary Meade (1735-___). **VI:** Son of Thomas Eldridge (1712-1754) and Martha Bolling (1713-1749). County Clerk of Buckingham Co **P:** N **BLW:** N **RG:** Y **MK:** N **PH:** unk **SS:** AL Ct Bk pg 7; DAR A037266; SAR Bio rpt submitted May 2020 **BS:** 173 Eldridge.

RU=Rank/Unit	CEM=Cemetery	GS=Gravestone	SP=Spousal Information
VI=Other Veteran Info	P=Pension	BLW=Bounty/Land Warrant	RG=Registered Grave
MK=SAR/DAR Marker	PH=Photo	SS=Service Source	BS=Burial Source

ELGIN, Francis Jr; b 1758, St Mary's Co, MD; d 6 Dec 1813 **RU:** Ensign, Took oath 9 Aug 1779 Loudoun Co Militia **CEM:** Elgin Family; GPS unk; Kingdom Farm on Evergreen Mill Rd, Sycolin, S of Leesburg; Loudoun **GS:** N **SP:** Mar 1783 at Port Tobacco, Charles Co MD, Jane Adams (1 Jul 1759-1834) d/o Andrew Adams (1732-1820) & Catherine (__)(1739-__) **VI:** Son of Francis Elgin, Sr (1728-1782) & Rebecca Cartwright (1732-1812).The gravestones removed to Union Cem in Leesburg aft 1945 **P:** unk **BLW:** unk **RG:** Y **MK:** unk **PH:** N **SS:** E pg 252; DAR A037286; SAR bio rpt submitted Jun 2020 **BS:** 196.

ELGIN, Gustavus; b 17 Sep 1754, St Mary's Co, MD; d 24 Jan 1834 **RU:** Captain, commanded a company in Loudoun Co Militia 1781 attached Col West's Regt at Gloucester. After Yorktown surrender escorted prisoners to Noland's ferry in Loudoun.Co **CEM:** Elgin Family; GPS unk; Kingdom Farm on Evergreen Mill Rd, Sycolin, S of Leesburg; Loudoun **GS:** N **SP:** Rebecca Thrift (24 Dec 1767 Fairfax Co-9 Oct 1822) d/o Charles & Rebekah (Hamilton) Thrift **VI:** Son of Francis Elgin, Sr. (1728-1782) and Rebecca Cartwright (1732-1812). After 1945, the stones were removed fr cem and dumped in a field.The stones w/o bodies were removed to Union Cemetery in Leesburg **P:** Y rec'd 1833 **BLW:** unk **RG:** Y **MK:** unk **PH:** N **SS:** E pg 252; DAR A037287; SAR P-153795 **BS:** 196.

ELGIN, Walter; b 12 Apr 1756, St Mary's Co, MD; d 9 Aug 1836 **RU:** Sergeant, Served in Loudoun Co Militia 1778. In July 1781 was the Orderly Sergeant for Captain Gustavus Elgin's Company, Colonel George West's Regt. After Cornwallis' surrender, aided in guarding prisoners. Was discharged November 1781. **CEM:** Elgin Family; GPS unk; Kingdom Farm on Evergreen Mill Rd, Sycolin, S of Leesburg; Loudoun **GS:** N **SP:** Diadama Pancoast (3 Apr 1768-29 Sep 1826) d/o Adin & Abigail (Boone) Pancoast **VI:** Son of Francis Sr. & Rebecca (Cartwright) Elgin. Grave stones were removed to Union Cemetery in Leesburg. No cemetery with burials now exist on Kingdom Farm **P:** Y **BLW:** N **RG:** Y **MK:** unk **PH:** N **SS:** E pg 252; SAR bio rpt submitted May 2020 **BS:** 196.

ELIE, Claude; b unk; d 1781 **RU:** Soldier, Served in Touraine Bn and died fr battle at Yorktown **CEM:** French Memorial; GPS 36.81944, -79.39933; Yorktown; York **GS:** U **SP:** No info **VI:** No further data **P:** unk **BLW:** unk **RG:** Y **MK:** unk **PH:** unk **SS:** J-Yorktown Historian; SAR P-153806 **BS:** JLARC 1, 74.

ELLIOTT, William; Greenleaf b 12 Jul 1699, County Galway, Ire, d 1795 **RU:** Patriot gave material aid to cause, Rockbridge Co **CEM:** Tinkling Springs Presbyterian Church ; GPS: 38.08472, -78.98278; 30 Tinkling Spring Drive, Fisherville; Staunton Elliott & Janet Young. Resided first in Cumberland, PA, Place of residence "Beverly Manor" **P:** unk **BLW:** unk **RG:** Y **MK:** unk **PH:** unk **SS:** AL Service source: AL Ct Bk pg 8 Certificate. Rockbridge Co, SAR bio rpt submitted Aug 20 **BS:** 196.

ELLIOTT, William; b 20 Oct 1754; d 23 Sep 1836 **RU:** Soldier, Ent serv age 16 1771, Accomack Co. Served again Capt William Polk's Co, Col Southey Simpson's Co at Melompkin Creek **CEM:** Bradford-Burton; GPS unk; Rt 182 and Rt 605, N fr Quinby at Bradfords Neck Road; Accomack **GS:** N **SP:** Mar (10 Dec 1781) Anzele Androse. Bradford (16 Sep 1757-aft 1851) **VI:** Son of Thomas Elliott (1705-1790) & Ann Westcott (1715-1795) Pen recd 1832. Widow recd pen 1851, W4668 **P:** Y **BLW:** unk **RG:** Y **MK:** unk **PH:** unk **SS:** JLARC app B; K Vol II pg 82; DAR A037628; SAR P-154032 **BS:** JLARC 4, 5; 196.

ELLIOTT (ELLIOT), Thomas; b 14 Feb 1744; d 19 Jul 1811 **RU:** Colonel, Served in 4th Cont Line. Commanded forces at Harnpton fr 23 Dec 1775-Jan 1776. Commanded 4th VA Regt of Foot 3 Sep 1776-28 Sep 1777, then resigned. Served in 4th Cont Line to 3 Sep 1776 to 28 Sep 1777 **CEM:** Shockoe Hill; GPS 37.55190, -77.43170; 4th & Hospital Sts; Richmond City **GS:** Y **SP:** Mary (-----) (c1751-12 Mar 1796) **VI:** Awarded 6666 acres BLW **P:** unk **BLW:** Y **RG:** Y **MK:** N **PH:** unk **SS:** E pg 253; CE pg 41; SAR P-154019 **BS:** 21 pg iv; 196.

ELLIS, Jacob; b unk; d 19 Dec 1781 **RU:** Private, Served in Capt Philip DeBevier's 4th Co, Col Lewis Dubois's 5th NY Line Regt. Died fr Yorktown battle **CEM:** Yorktown Victory Monument Tablet; GPS 38.28350, -78.54150; Yorktown; York **GS:** U **SP:** No info **VI:** No further data **P:** unk **BLW:** unk **RG:** Y **MK:** unk **PH:** unk **SS:** J-Yorktown Historian; AX pg 226; SAR P-154112 **BS:** JLARC 74.

ELLIS, Josiah B; b 27 Feb 1745, Henrico Co; d 29 Jun 1810 **RU:** Patriot, Gave material aid to cause; was head of a family, 1783, Amherst Co that paid personal property tax, a supply tax for Rev War expenses **CEM:** Shelton-Ellis-Watts; GPS 37.506680, -79.163774; Winesap Rd; Monroe;Amherst **GS:** Y **SP:** Jane Shelton(1 Sep 1747, Lousia Co-24 Aug 1800), d/o Richard Shelton (14 Aug 1728-5 Jan 1821) & Mary Wright (1728-3 Nov 1818) **VI:** Son of Charles Ellis (1719-1759) & Susannah Harding (1722-

RU=Rank/Unit	CEM=Cemetery	GS=Gravestone	SP=Spousal Information
VI=Other Veteran Info	P=Pension	BLW=Bounty/Land Warrant	RG=Registered Grave
MK=SAR/DAR Marker	PH=Photo	SS=Service Source	BS=Burial Source

130

1817); titled Major on GS **P:** N **BLW:** N **RG:** Y **MK:**N **PH:** N **SS:** AL Ct Bk pg 9, 39 Amherst Co; ER Amherst Co; SAR P-154153 **BS:** JLARC 115.

ELLIS, Richard; b unk; d Aft 1780 **RU:** Private, enlisted 15 Mar 1777, and served in Capt John Lynch's Co, 5th MD Regt of Foot, commanded by Col William Richardson. On 16 Aug 1780 was listed as missing after the battle at Camden **CEM:** Fairfax City; GPS 38.84690, -77.31330; Main St & Page Ave; Fairfax City **GS:** N **SP:** No info **VI:** No further data **P:** unk **BLW:** unk **RG:** Y **MK:** N **PH:** N **SS:** AP roll MD 5th R; SAR bio rpt submitted May 2020 **BS:** 61 vol III pg FX-153.

ELLZEY, William; b unk, Loudoun Co; d 30 Nov 1835 **RU:** Captain, Gave material aid to the cause **CEM:** Ellzey Family; GPS unk; Rt 621, Middleton; Loudoun **GS:** Y **SP:** Mar (4 Mar 1799) Frances Hill Westwood, (26 Jun 1780 Elizabeth City Co-16 Apr 1820) d/o William (1738 Elizabeth City Co-24 Jan 1782) & Anne (Stith) (1742-1780) Westwood **VI:** No further data **P:** unk **BLW:** unk **RG:** N **MK:** N **PH:** unk **SS:** AL Cert Issued; **BS:** 25 pg 90.

ELY, John; b 1755 ,Stafford Co, d Feb 1839 **RU:** Private, Enlisted Sep 1778, in Major John Webb's unit in 5th, 11th and 15th VA Regt commanded by Colonels Abraham Buford and William Russell for 3 year term **CEM:** John Ely Family; GPS: 36,42524,-83.14298; 7980 Sugar Run Rd, Jonesville; Lee **GS:** Yes **SP:** Mar 1783, Barbara Jane Fry (1755-30 Jun 1857) **VI:** Son of Thomas Ealy, Sr (1725-1782) & Elizabeth Jane Smith (1730-1796), d/o George Peter Fry (1725-1793) & Margaret Scott (c1729-1787) **P** No **BLW** No **RG:** Y; **MK** Y **PH:** Y **SS:** AP Serv Rec, Fold3; DAR A038230; SAR bio rpt submitted May 2020 **BS:** 32 Martin Station Chap Nov 2017; 196.

ELY, William; b 25 Mar 1748, PA or 1753; d 1850 **RU:** Private, Ent serv Bedford Co 1779.Served in Capt Thomas Helm's Co 15 Feb 1779. Served 18 mos Capt Hughes Woodson's & Capt Lawson's cos of Col Abraham Buford's command. Was in Battle of Hanging Rock, NC **CEM:** Russell Family; GPS unk; Rt 58 Rose Hill; Lee **GS:** Y **SP:** Rebecca Rawlings **VI:** Pensioned Lee Co 1820 age abt 80. S39493 **P:** Y **BLW:** unk **RG:** Y **MK:** Y SAR **PH:** unk **SS:** K Vol II pg 82; AK; AP; DAR A038291; SAR P-332517 **BS:** 04, Nov 06.

ENAUD, Antoine; b unk; d 1781 **RU:** Seaman, Served on "Languedoc" and died from Yorktown battle **CEM:** French Memorial; GPS 36.81944, -79.39933; Yorktown; York **GS:** U **SP:** No info **VI:** No further data **P:** unk **BLW:** unk **RG:** Y **MK:** unk **PH:** unk **SS:** J-Yorktown Historian; SAR P-154841 **BS:** JLARC 1, 74.

ENGLAND, John; b c1757 or 1 Apr 1767, Goochland Co; d 18 Mar 1840 **RU:** Private, Served in Capts Edward Smith & Joseph Leaks's Companies, Goochland Co in Cont Line **CEM:** England; GPS 36.60323, -82.94029; Looneys Gap #14; Scott **GS:** Y **SP:** Mar (22 Feb 1786 Amherst Co) Mary Parsons (c1765-after 1846) d/o John & (-----) Parsons **VI:** Son of William and (-----) England. Pen 1833 Scott Co age 76. Died in England Valley, Scott Co. Widow pen Hawkins Co, TN 1843 and was living there in 1846 age 81. Bronze marker ordered fr War Dept, placed 1983. W5270 **P:** Y **BLW:** unk **RG:** Y **MK:** Y SAR **PH:** unk **SS:** K Vol II pg 84; DAR A036752; SAR P-154871 **BS:** JLARC 4, 22.

ENGLISH, Stephen; b 1726, d 2 Jan 1783 **RU:** Patriot, gave material aid to cause Campbell Co **CEM:** Staunton Baptist Ch; GPS 37.0696983, -79.5813980; Jct Smith Mountain Lake Parkway & Braddock Ln; Huddleston; Bedford **GS:** N **SP:** Mar c1760, Dinah Haynes (c 1733, Caroline Co-5 Mar 1784) **VI:** Originally buried in Smith Mountain Gap Cem, moved 1960 **P** No **BLW** No **RG:** Y; **MK** N **PH:** Y **SS:** AL Ct Bk pg 20, Commissioner's Bk I, pg 287 Campbell Co; SAR P-154933 DAR A209243 **BS:** 196.

ENGLISH, William; b Bef 1765, Bedford Co; d 4 July 1816 **RU:** Private, Ent serv Bedford Co in Capt Jno Trigg's Co 1780-1781; Capt Peter Weller 1781; Capt Coleman or Clements at Siege of '96 **CEM:** English Family; GPS unk; Kemps Mill; Franklin **GS:** N **SP:** Mar (Oct or Nov 1793 - bond dated 4 Nov 1793 - while living on Blackwater River) Adria or Addria or Addry Kemp (Dudley) (1768 or 1771-___) of Franklin Co. - "former widow". **VI:** Widow pen Franklin Co age 74 in 1845 and pension increased there 1850 age 82. Grave now underwater beneath Smith Mountain Lake. W7970 **P:** Y **BLW:** unk **RG:** Y **MK:** N **PH:** N **SS:** K Vol II pg 85; AK; E pg 256; DAR A036845; SAR P-154938 **BS:** 04.

ENSORIEL, Espirit; b unk; d 1781 **RU:** Seaman, Served on "Diademe" and died from Yorktown battle **CEM:** French Memorial; GPS 36.81944, -79.39933; Yorktown; York **GS:** U **SP:** No info **VI:** No further

RU=Rank/Unit   CEM=Cemetery   GS=Gravestone   SP=Spousal Information
VI=Other Veteran Info   P=Pension   BLW=Bounty/Land Warrant   RG=Registered Grave
MK=SAR/DAR Marker   PH=Photo   SS=Service Source   BS=Burial Source

131

data **P:** unk **BLW:** unk **RG:** Y **MK:** unk **PH:** unk **SS:** J-Yorktown Historian; SAR P-155039 **BS:** JLARC 1, 74.

EPES (EPPES), Francis; b 1730, Amelia Co; d 1789 **RU:** Lieutenant Colonel, Was Capt of Guard, Charles City Co. Promoted to Lt Col 18 Mar 1776. Was wounded at Long Isand in 1st VA Regt of Foot 27 Aug 1776 **CEM:** The Old Place; GPS unk; 5 mi NW of Blackstone; Nottoway **GS:** N **SP:** Mar (c1754) Mary Williams (unk, Amelia Co-Mar 1795) **VI:** BLW of 6000 acres recd while residing in Dinwidde Co **P:** unk **BLW:** unk **RG:** Y **MK:** N **PH:** N **SS:** E pg 256; G pg 115; CE pg 29; SAR P-328655 **BS:** 151.

EPPERSON, David; b 22 Jun 1734, New Kent Co; d Btw 1776 & 1780; or Dec 1799 **RU:** Private, Served in14th Cont Line. Records indicate he died in service bet 1776 and 1780 **CEM:** Blue Ridge Farm; GPS unk; Rt 261, 2.1 mi off Rt 250 W, Greenwood; Albemarle **GS:** Y **SP:** Hannah Judith Thompson (1735-1814.) She moved to Estill Co, KY with her son after her husband d **VI:** Son of John Epperson, Sr. (1703-1737) & Elizabeth Michaux. Widow recd gratuity of 164 acres in Albemarle Co on 14 Dec 1780. His will is dated 2 Feb 1799 and probated Oct 1799. DAR marker **P:** unk **BLW:** Y **RG:** Y **MK:** Y DAR **PH:** Y **SS:** J- DAR Hatcher; E pg 256; BT; SAR P-155080 **BS:** JLARC 2; 67 vol 2 pg 291; 196.

EPPES, Peter; b 1759, Charles City Co; d 9 Dec 1828 **RU:** Sergeant, Served in 6th Regt. Ent serv Apr 1777. Discharged Mar 26 1778 **CEM:** Shockoe Hill; GPS 37.55190, -77.43170; 4th & Hospital Sts; Richmond City **GS:** Y **Gov't SP:** Mar (1796) Lucy Ballard (1764 Charles City Co-11 Dec 1844) **VI:** Pen 1832 Dinwiddie Co S8424 **P:** Y **BLW:** unk **RG:** Y **MK:** Y SAR, &monument, DAR, plaque **PH:** unk **SS:** E pg 257; K Vol II pg 86; SAR P-335071 **BS:** 57 pg 6.

ERVIN, William; b 1760, Rockingham Co, ; d Mar 1817 **RU:** Sergeant, Served in 1st, 8th,10th Cont Lines **CEM:** Mossy Creek Presbyterian; GPS 38.35331, -79.04914; 372 Kyles Mill Rd, Mt Solon; Augusta **GS:** Y **SP:** Margaret Robertson (1778-15 Mar 1797) d/o Col James & Margaret (Poage) Robertson **VI:** Son of Francis & Jane Curry (1712-1804) Ervin (1710-1791) **P:** unk **BLW:** unk **RG:** Y **MK:** N **PH:** unk **SS:** E pg 257; SAR bio rpt submitted May 2020 **BS:** 142; 196.

ESKRIDGE, Margaret (Mrs Kenner); b c1715; d 8 Oct 1801 **RU:** Patriot, Service in helping soldiers **CEM:** Kenner Family; GPS unk; 2452 Kenner Ln; Fauquier **GS:** Y **SP:** Mar (June 1732 Sandy Point) Howson Francis Kenner **VI:** d/o Col George & Rebecca (Bonum) Eskridge **P:** N **BLW:** N **RG:** Y **MK:** N **PH:** unk **SS:** AL Ct Bk pg 2, 19; DAR A064850; SAR P-155219 **BS:** AV Inv # 69.

ESOM (ESCOM), Hannah; b 1752; d 1843 **RU:** Patriot, Gave material aid to cause **CEM:** Esom Family; GPS unk; Nr Cave Spring; Roanoke Co **GS:** Y **SP:** No info **VI:** No further data **P:** N **BLW:** N **RG:** Y **MK:** N **PH:** unk **SS:** AR DAR report; SAR P-155225 **BS:** 80 vol 2 pg 16.

ESTES, Elisha; b 1749, Albemarle Co; d 1 Feb 1821 **RU:** Sergeant, Served in1st & 10th Cont Line, Maj Nocholas Co #5 **CEM:** Estes Family; GPS unk; Check property records for location, also in DAR 1959 Senate Doc serial #12260, vol 5; Nelson **GS:** U **SP:** Catherine Tompkins (1 Oct 1759-25 Apr 1804) **VI:** Son of Abraham Jr and Elizabeth (-----) Eases **P:** unk **BLW:** unk **RG:** Y **MK:** unk **PH:** unk **SS:** DAR A037271; A pg 273; SAR P-155307 E pg 246 **BS:** JLARC 2.

ESTES, George; b 3 Feb 1763 Amelia Co; d Jul 1859 **RU:** Private, Ent serv Halifax Co as substitute for father. Ent serv fr TN 1782.Served in 2nd, 6th, 10th Cont Lines **CEM:** Oak Ridge; GPS 36.71912, -78.90321; Main St & Hamiliton St, South Boston; Halifax **GS:** U **SP:** Mar 19Dec 1786, Mary Younger (1772-1850), d/o Marcus Younger (1725-1816) Sussanna Hart (1725-__) **VI:** Son of Moses Estes (1742-1813) & Luremia Susannah Combs (1747-1815). Moved "a family of people" in 1781 to NC and later TN by 1782. Recd pension 1833 Halifax Co. Granted BLW #26130 S18394 **P:** Y **BLW:** Y **RG:** Y **MK:** unk **PH:** unk **SS:** E pg 258; K Vol II pg 87. Bio rpt submitted May 2010 **BS:** 196.

ESTES, Richard; b 1758; d 5 Aug 1832 **RU:** Private, Served in Capt Cloyd's Co, Cont Line, 12 Sep 1777 **CEM:** Greenfield; GPS unk; Fawn Lake Pwy; Spotsylvania **GS:** Y **SP:** No info **VI:** Son of Abraham & Annie (Clark) Estes **P:** unk **BLW:** unk **RG:** Y **MK:** N **PH:** unk **SS:** E pg 258; SAR P-155316 **BS:** 07 pg 2, 3.

ESTES, William; b 1745; d 1827 **RU:** Corporal/Patriot, Served in Bedford Co Militia. Served in 2nd & 6th Cont Line. Gave material aid to cause **CEM:** Estes Family?; GPS unk; South/left side of Rt 648 after

RU=Rank/Unit	CEM=Cemetery	GS=Gravestone	SP=Spousal Information
VI=Other Veteran Info	P=Pension	BLW=Bounty/Land Warrant	RG=Registered Grave
MK=SAR/DAR Marker	PH=Photo	SS=Service Source	BS=Burial Source

crossing Buffalo River fr Rt 604; Greene **GS:** U **SP:** Frances Cox **VI:** Field stone "W.E. Dec ? 1827". RW service noted Greene Co Magazine **P:** unk **BLW:** unk **RG:** N **MK:** unk **PH:** unk **SS:** D Orange Co **BS:** JLARC 113.

ETTER, Daniel; b 28 Apr 1750, Lebanon Co, PA; d 5 Sep 1803 **RU:** Fife & Drummer, Served in PA **CEM:** St John's Lutheran; GPS 36.96500, -81.10110; 405 W Main, Wytheville; Wythe **GS:** U **SP:** 1) Elizabeth McMahon (1759-1781) 2) Mar (25 Apr 1781 in PA) Mary Magdalena Reihn (1749-1821) **VI:** Son of Gerhand (27 Jan 1718 Bern, Switzerland-26 Apr 1783) & Caterine (Banga) (26 Oct 1717 Bern, Switzerland-20 Apr 1788) Etter **P:** unk **BLW:** unk **RG:** Y **MK:** unk **PH:** unk **SS:** CD; SAR P-330091 **BS:** JLARC 123; 196.

EUBANK (EUBANKS), Richard; b 1758 Glouchester Co; d 1855 **RU:** Sergeant, Served in 1st, 10th, 14th Cont Lines. Served in Capt John Marks Co, Col Charles Lewis,14th Regt **CEM:** Forkquarter; GPS unk; Calno Rd Rt 601, Norment Ferry; King William **GS:** U **SP:** Mar (1797) Susan Gary (__-1857) **VI:** No further data **P:** unk **BLW:** unk **RG:** Y **MK:** unk **PH:** unk **SS:** J- DAR Hatcher; E pg 259; SAR P-155398 **BS:** JLARC 2.

EURACE, Josiah; b unk; d 1778 **RU:** Private, baggage guard, Capt Thomas Triplett's Co, Col William Grayson's Regt, Cont Line **CEM:** Rev War Court House Plaque; GPS not determined; 4110 Chain Bridge Rd; Fairfax **GS:** Memorialized on plaque 2017 by Geo Washington Chapter, VASSAR **SP** No info **VI:** Died in service **P:** N **BLW:** N **RG:** N **MK:** N **PH:** N **SS** E pg 259, marked dead 1778; AP Fold3 muster roll:EP sources: **BS:** None.

EVANS, Anthony, b 1741, Surry Co, d 17 Aug 1822 **RU:** Patriot, gave material sid to cause, Mecklenburg Co **CEM:** :Ephesus Baptist Church; GPS 36.6606730, -78.1894180; 1642 Smith Cross Road, South Hill; Mecklenburg **GS:** Y **SP:** Mary Davis (1745-1819) **VI:** No further data **P:** N **BLW:** N **RG*** RG:** Y **MK:** N **PH:** N **SS:** D vol 2, pgs 668-669, 673: E pg 260; SAR P-331658; DAR A101793 **BS:** 196.

EVANS, Daniel; b 22 Mar 1750, Wales; d 1 Jan 1829 **RU:** Soldier, Served in Chesterfield Co Militia and a VA unit in Illinois campaign **CEM:** Dixon Family; GPS 37.18420, -79.59310; Off Rt 658, Concord quadrant, nr Rustburg; Campbell **GS:** U **SP:** Mar (1781) Jane Davis (6 Aug 1751 PA-23 Sep 1819) **VI:** No further data **P:** unk **BLW:** unk **RG:** Y **MK:** N **PH:** unk **SS:** E pg 260; SAR P-155442 **BS:** JLARC 36.

EVANS George; b c1756, Chester Co, PA d 27 Jun 1822 **RU:** Surgeon; Col Baylor's Cont Dragoons, 20 May 1777, suffered severe wound Sep 1778 and was POW at Tappan, resigned fr service served 2 yrs, 9 mos **CEM:** Evans Family: GPS not deremined; loc "Oakland Plantation" along the Appomattox River; Chesterfield **GS:** N **SP:** Mar 1764 Mary Peyton (1758-1818), d/o William Peyton (1718-1792) and Sarah West Patterson (1711-1793). **VI** Son of Evan Rice Evans (1732-1794) & Margaret Nivin (1730-1807) William Peyton (1718-1792) & Sarah West Patterson (1711-1793). Awarded BLW #2450. 6000 acres 10 Feb 1784 **P:** N **BLW:** Y **RG:** Y **MK:** N **PH:** N **SS:** E pg 260; **C**; DAR A037521; SAR P-155488; Bio update May 2020 **BS:** SAR Bio Rpt cites *Richmond Enquirer* 5 Jul 1822 of him dying at his residence.

EVANS, John; b unk; d Feb 1790 **RU:** Seaman, Specific service may be found at the Lib of VA in Auditor's Acct Bk XXII, pg 441 and in War Files vol 5 pg 65 **CEM:** Old Christ Church Episcopal; GPS 38.80625, -77.04718; 118 N Washington St; Alexandria City **GS:** N **SP:** No info **VI:** Burial permit issued 23 Feb 1790 **P:** unk **BLW:** unk **RG:** N **MK:** N **PH:** N **SS:** L pg 186; CZ pg 156 **BS:** 20 pg 147.

EVANS, Reese; b unk; d unk **RU:** Ensign, Served in PA troops **CEM:** Dixon Family; GPS 37.18420, -79.59310; Off Rt 658, Concord quadrant, nr Rustburg; Campbell **GS:** U **SP:** Bridgett (-----) **VI:** No further data **P:** unk **BLW:** unk **RG:** Y **MK:** N **PH:** unk **SS:** SAR P-155599 **BS:** JLARC 36.

EVANS, Robert: b 1 Nov 1759, d 14 Dec 1810 **RU:** Private, Capt Richard Steven's Co, Col Edward Steven's 10th VA Regt, enlisting for 3 yrs 15 Dec 1776 **CEM:** Christ Church Episcopal; GPS 38.4822,-77.0251; 118 No Washington St, Alexandria City **GS:** No **SP:** No spousal info **VI:** Gravestone recorded in 1922 survey but not found 1992 **P** U **BLW** Y **RG** N **MK** N **PH:** N **SS:** E pg 260; AP Serv Rec, Fold3 **BS:** 196.

EVANS, William; b 8 Apr 1756; d 19 Sep 1839 **RU:** First Lieutenant, appointed 13 Jan 1778 Buckingham Miltia, Wounded at Brandywine battle 11 Sep 1777 **CEM:** Merionette; GPS unk; Nr Willis Mountain; Buckingham **GS:** U **SP:** Mary (-----) **VI:** Drew pen in Buckingham Co S250069 **P:** Y **BLW:** N **RG:** Y **MK:** N **PH:** unk **SS:** E pg 261; DAR A037742; SAR P-155641 **BS:** JLARC 4, 59.

RU=Rank/Unit	CEM=Cemetery	GS=Gravestone	SP=Spousal Information
VI=Other Veteran Info	P=Pension	BLW=Bounty/Land Warrant	RG=Registered Grave
MK=SAR/DAR Marker	PH=Photo	SS=Service Source	BS=Burial Source

133

EVERHART, Jacob, b 27 Nov 1765, Middletown, Frederick Co, MD d 24 Jan 1849 **RU:** Private, Capt George Mairs Company, 5th Bn, Washington County, PA Militia 19 Mar 1782 **CEM:** Green Hill (AKA Berryville); GPS: 39.1581,-77.9767 loc vic jct Mosby Blvd & S Buckmarsh St, Berrryville; Clarke **GS:** Yes plot M-131 **SP:** Mar 11 Mar 1794, Eleanor Kadle (1776-10 Oct 1820) **VI:** Son of Christain Everhart (1729-1807) & Marla Sybeilla Geyer (1731-1812) **P** No **BLW** No **RG:** Y; **MK** Y **PH:** Y **SS:** AP Fold3 PA Archives Series 6, vol II, 5th Bn; SAR bio rpt submitted May 2020 **BS:** 196.

EVERLET, Gaspard; b unk; d 1781 **RU:** Soldier, Served in Dillon Bn and died fr battle at Yorktown **CEM:** French Memorial; GPS 36.81944, -79.39933; Yorktown; York **GS:** U **SP:** No info **VI:** No further data **P:** unk **BLW:** unk **RG:** Y **MK:** unk **PH:** unk **SS:** J-Yorktown Historian; SAR P-155792 **BS:** JLARC 1, 74.

EVINS, William; b unk; d 1780 **RU:** Corporal, Served in 8th & 12th Cont Line **CEM:** Sinking Springs; GPS 36.71030, -81.98170; 136 E Main St, Abingdon; Washington **GS:** U **SP:** Ann Covill (1733-1790) **VI:** No further data **P:** N **BLW:** N **RG:** N **MK:** unk **PH:** N **SS:** E pg 262 **BS:** 212 pg 74.

EWELL, Jesse; b 24 Sep 1743, Bel Air, Prince William Co; d 30 Sep 1805 **RU:** Colonel/Patriot, Was a member of Prince William Co Committee of Safety,1775. Gave material aid to cause **CEM:** Ewell-Weems; GPS unk; Rt 640; Prince William **GS:** N **SP:** Mar (10 Oct 1767) Charlotte Ewell (14 Feb 1750-13 Apr 1823) d/o Bertrand & Frances (Kenner) Ewell **VI:** Son of Charles (1713-___) & Sarah (Ball) (1712-___) Ewell **P:** unk **BLW:** unk **RG:** Y **MK:** N **PH:** N **SS:** E pg 262; AL Ct Bk pg 5 Prince William Co; SAR P-155869 **BS:** 16 pg 180.

EWER (EWERS), John; b 27 Dec 1735, Bucks Co, PA; d 9 May 1815 **RU:** Private, Served in Capt David Marpole Co, Philadelphia Co PA Militia **CEM:** Unison; GPS unk; Unison; Loudoun **GS:** U **SP:** Sarah Gladny **VI:** No further data **P:** unk **BLW:** unk **RG:** Y **MK:** unk **PH:** unk **SS:** J-NSSAR 1993 Reg, J-DAR Hatcher; AP PA Archives 2nd series vol 13 pg 721 & 6th series Vol 1 pg 637, 649; SAR P-155878 **BS:** JLARC 1, 2.

EWING, James; b unk; d 16 Feb 1796 **RU:** Captain, Commanded a co in Augusta Co Militia, Mar 1776-17 Apr 1777 **CEM:** Glebe Burying Ground; GPS 38.10940, -79.22190; Glebe School Rd Rt 876, Swoopes; Augusta **GS:** Y **SP:** Martha (-----), named in his will **VI:** DAR marker (plaque) which styles him Capt. GS only gives date of death **P:** unk **BLW:** unk **RG:** Y **MK:** Y DAR **PH:** unk **SS:** E pg 262; BT; CZ pg 157; SAR P-155901 **BS:** JLARC 8, 62, 63; 196.

EWING, James; b 1740; d 14 Apr 1809 **RU:** Patriot, Gave material aid to the cause **CEM:** North Mountain; GPS unk; 7 mi S of Staunton on N side Rt 252; Augusta **GS:** Y **SP:** Jean Finley **VI:** No further data **P:** N **BLW:** N **RG:** N **MK:** Y SAR **PH:** unk **SS:** AL Com BK II pg 362 **BS:** 142; 196.

EWING, James; b 4 Mar 1762; d 26 Sep 1794 **RU:** Captain/Patriot, Served in Capt McCutchen's Co, Augusta Co Militia. Gave material aid to cause **CEM:** Glebe Burying Ground; GPS 38.10940, -79.22190; Glebe School Rd Rt 876, Swoopes; Augusta **GS:** Y **SP:** Martha (-----) (15 Feb 1741-2 Jul 1828) **VI:** Called Capt James Ewing on DAR plaque in cemetery **P:** unk **BLW:** unk **RG:** N **MK:** Y **PH:** unk **SS:** D pg 94; E pg 262 **BS:** 210 pg 394; 196.

EWING, Robert Sr; b 1718, County Londonderry, Ireland; d 1787 **RU:** Private/Patriot, Was in Battle of Point Pleasant, Oct 1774. Had civil service as Justice of the Peace, Bedford Co and gave material aid to the cause **CEM:** Ewing-Patterson Cem; GPS unk; Penick's Mill; Bedford **GS:** N **SP:** Mar (c1746) Mary Baker (1728 Prince Edward Co-___) **VI:** No further data **P:** unk **BLW:** unk **RG:** Y **MK:** N **PH:** N **SS:** J-NSSAR 1993 Reg, J- DAR Hatcher; AL Ct Bk pg 11, 12, 30 and cert listed as Capt military officer; SAR P-155945 **BS:** JLARC 1, 2.

EWING, Samuel; b unk, Fahan, Donegal, Ireland; d 24 Aug 1798 **RU:** unk, Specific service is at the Lib of VA, Auditors Acct vol XVIII pg 515 **CEM:** Ewing Family; GPS unk; Off Stickley Dr to Hayvenhurst Ct; Winchester City **GS:** U **SP:** Margaret McMichael (1773-___) **VI:** Son of John (1648-1745) & Jennet (Wilson) (1633-___) Ewing. Died in Stephen City, Frederick Co **P:** unk **BLW:** unk **RG:** Y **MK:** N **PH:** unk **SS:** J- DAR Hatcher; CZ pg 158; SAR P-155928 **BS:** JLARC 2; 196.

EWING, William; b Dec 1711, Fahan Co, Ire, d 27 Dec 1781 **RU:** Patriot, gave material aid to cause, Frederick Co **CEM:** Ewing Family; GPS 39.0691010,-78.2179300 GS 39.069339, -78.218007; 161

RU=Rank/Unit	CEM=Cemetery	GS=Gravestone	SP=Spousal Information
VI=Other Veteran Info	P=Pension	BLW=Bounty/Land Warrant	RG=Registered Grave
MK=SAR/DAR Marker	PH=Photo	SS=Service Source	BS=Burial Source

134

Havenhurst Ct, Stephens City; Frederick **GS**: Y **SP**: Elizabeth Tharp Buckley(1732-17 May1816) **VI**: Son of John Ewing (1648 Ire-23 Sep 1745) & Janette McElnancy (1652-1719) **P:**Y **BLW**: N **RG**: Y **MK**: Y granite **PH**: Y **SS**: D vol 2, pg 383; DAR A112527; SAR P-154959 **BS**: 196; Grave marking 10 Jul 2021.

EWING, William; b 9 May 1721; d 17 Jun 1794 **RU**: Patriot, Gave material aid to the cause **CEM**: Glebe Burying Ground; GPS 38.10940, -79.22190; Glebe School Rd Rt 876, Swoopes; Augusta **GS**: Y **SP**: No info **VI**: No further data **P**: N **BLW**: N **RG**: N **MK**: N **PH**: unk **SS**: AL Ct Bk pg 6 **BS**: 142; 196

EWING, William; b 1764; d 1852 **RU**: Sergeant, Served in VA Cont Line **CEM**: Ewing-McClure (aka Friendship Church); GPS unk; Jonesville; Lee **GS**: Y **SP**: 1) Elizabeth Saunders 2) Sarah Wynn (Hix) **VI**: No further data **P**: unk **BLW**: unk **RG**: Y **MK**: Y **PH**: unk **SS**: AK Dec 06; SAR P-155941 **BS**: 04, Dec 06.

FABRE, Paul; b unk; d 1781 **RU**: Soldier, Served in Touraine Bn and died fr battle at Yorktown **CEM**: French Memorial; GPS 36.81944, -79.39933; Yorktown; York **GS**: U **SP**: No info **VI**: No further data **P**: unk **BLW**: unk **RG**: Y **MK**: unk **PH**: unk **SS**: J-Yorktown Historian; SAR P-155988 **BS**: JLARC 1, 74.

FAIRFAX, Thomas; b 22 Oct 1693 Leeds Castle, Scotland; d 9 Dec 1781 **RU**: Patriot, Publically denounced British policies and urged neighbors to defend privileges. Helped stabilize currency by directing it be accepted for quit-rents. Helped with exchange of prisoners **CEM**: Christ Episcopal, Courtyard; GPS unk; 114 W Boscawen St; Winchester City **GS**: Y **SP**: No info **VI**: 6th Baron of Cameron. Gave provisions. Died in Frederick Co **P**: N **BLW**: N **RG**: Y **MK**: N **PH**: unk **SS**: AK; J-NSSAR 1993 Reg; P-156201 **BS**: 04 JLARC 1.

FAIRFAX, William; b 1720, Charles Co, MD; d 1793 **RU**: Patriot, Gave Oath of Allegiance 1778, MD. Also gave wheat to military Jul 1782 **CEM**: Bacon Race; GPS 38.69145, -77.46439; Davis Ford Rd & Bacon Race Rd; Prince William **GS**: Y **SP**: 1) Benedicta Blancett 2) Elizabeth Buckner **VI**: No further data **P**: N **BLW**: N **RG**: Y **MK**: Y SAR **PH**: Y **SS**: AK; DAR A038296; SAR P-156202 **BS**: 4.

FAISSANS, Maurice; b unk; d 1781 **RU**: Seaman, Served on "Saint-Esprit" and died from Yorktown battle **CEM**: French Memorial; GPS 36.81944, -79.39933; Yorktown; York **GS**: U **SP**: No info **VI**: No further data **P**: unk **BLW**: unk **RG**: Y **MK**: unk **PH**: unk **SS**: J-Yorktown Historian; SAR P-156241 **BS**: JLARC 1, 74.

FALL, George; b 1743, PA; d 1818 **RU**: Private, Served in 6th Bn, Berk's Co PA Militia. Served in Capt George Baxter's Co, Rockingham Co Militia as guard of prisoners going to Winchester Feb & Mar 1782 **CEM**: St James Methodist; GPS unk; 3777 Churchville Ave, Churchville; Augusta **GS**: Y **SP**: Catharine (-----) **VI**: Newer stone with engraved plaque of Pennsylvania **P**: unk **BLW**: unk **RG**: Y **MK**: N **PH**: unk **SS**: N pg 123; SAR P-156290 **BS**: JLARC 1 ,2, 62; 80, vol2, pg 22;196.

FAMBROUGH, Benjamin See Appendix G, ADDenda

FARIS, Martin; b 27 Nov 1763, Cumberland Co; d 15 Aug 1857 **RU**: Cpl, Ent Serv Sep 1779 Capt Thomas Young, Col Joseph Crockett, Regt, Gen Geoge Rogers Clark serving to Dec 1781 **CEM**: Fluvanna Heritage Trail; GPS 37.859720, -78.269160; end of Trailhead Dr, Palmyra; Fluvanna **GS**: Y **SP**: :Mar 1785, Rebecca Amos (1765-__) **VI**: Son of Benjamin Faris (1740-1763) & Nancy (-----); Rec'd pen # S8452 $80 per annum; BLW # 29747 160 acres 1855 **P**: Y **BLW**: Y **RG**: Y **PH**: N **SS**: E pg 764; G pg 758; K vol 2, pg 100; DAR A638577; SAR P-156390 **BS**: 196.

FARLEY, Thomas Jr; b 1760; d 11 Jun 1839 **RU**: Private, Ent serv 1776 Walker's Creek, Montgomery Co (Later Giles Co). Served in VA Line under Col Preston **CEM**: Sugar Run, Farmer Family; GPS unk; Staffordsville; Giles **GS**: U **SP**: Mar (8 May 1793 Montgomery Co) Patty/Patsey Lester/Lister (c1772-18 Nov 1853). QLF states he mar Martha V. Peck. **VI**: Sol appl pen 30 Jun 1834 Giles Co age 73 or 74. Widow appl 25 Sep 1848 Giles Co, age 76. W7244 **P**: Y **BLW**: unk **RG**: Y **MK**: unk **PH**: unk **SS**: J- DAR Hatcher. CG Vol 2 pg 1152; K Vol II pg 101; DAR A038646; SAR P-156440 **BS**: JLARC 2.

FARLEY, Thomas, Sr; b 1730, Henrico Co, d 1796 **RU**: Private/ Patriot as patriot erected Farley's Fort 1776; fought in campaign under General McIntosh 1778; was an Indian scout 1779 under Captain Patton **CEM**: Farley Family; GPS 37.22621, -80.69418; vic jct Rye Hollow and Bane Rds outside of Pearisburg on a small farm; Giles **GS**: Now gone destroyed by cattle or removed **SP**: Mar 7 Sep 1759 Chesterfield Co, Judith Clay (1737-aft 1806), d/o Mitchell Clay and Martha Lewis. She sold farm in 1806

RU=Rank/Unit VI=Other Veteran Info MK=SAR/DAR Marker | CEM=Cemetery P=Pension PH=Photo | GS=Gravestone BLW=Bounty/Land Warrant SS=Service Source | SP=Spousal Information RG=Registered Grave BS=Burial Source

VI: Son of Francis Marion Farley (1703-1791) USDAR chapters have erected a plaque listing service for him in 1944 at the Farley Wayside along Walker's Creek at jct with Rt 100 and Bane Rds **P** No **BLW** No **RG**: Y **MK** DAR plaque **PH**: N **SS**: BW; DAR Anc # A038649; SAR P-156436 **BS**: 196.

FARMER, James; b 1758; d 12 Aug 1838 **RU**: Private, Specific service is at the Lib of VA, Auditors Acct. vol XVIII pg 531 **CEM**: North End; GPS 36.77234, -80.73866; 101 Beaver Dam Rd, Hillsville; Carroll **GS**: Y **SP**: Susannah (-----) (1765-20 Sep 1850) **VI**: Son of Michael Farmer & Martha Latham **P**: unk **BLW**: unk **RG**: N **MK**: N **PH**: unk **SS**: E pg 264; CA pg 158 **BS**: 123 pg 67; 196.

FARRIS, Gideon; b 1748; d 1818 **RU**: Private/Patriot, Served in Washington Co Militia 1776, commanded by Col William Christian. Performed public service as Juror 19 Nov 1778 **CEM**: Rock Spring; GPS 37.78126, -79.44585; Jct Rt 803 & Liberty Hall Rd, Lodi; Washington **GS**: U **SP**: Sarah McSpadden (1745 Augusta Co-1820) d/o Thomas (1720-1765) & (-----) Spaden **VI**: Son of (------) & Deborah Faries **P**: unk **BLW**: unk **RG**: N **MK**: unk **PH**: unk **SS**: DD **BS**: 196.

FAULEY (FAWLEY), John; b Jan 1720, Loudoun Co; d 11 Jun 1803 **RU**: Private, Unit not identified but available at Lib of VA **CEM**: New Jerusalem Lutheran; GPS 39.25736, -77.63891; 12942 Lutheran Church Rd, Lovettsville; Loudoun **GS**: Y **SP**: Anna Maria Ault (1737-1803) **VI**: No further data **P**: unk **BLW**: unk **RG**: N **MK**: unk **PH**: Y **SS**: E pg 266 cites Eckenrode, Dr. H J Index to Rev War Records in VA State Archives **BS**: 196.

FAULKNER, Jacob; b 1744; d 24 Mar 1823 **RU**: Ensign, Served in Halifax Co Militia 1774-1777in Capt Moses Fortaine's and Capt Thomas Gaddis Co **CEM**: Faulkner Family; GPS unk; Nr Cherry Hill, 1 mi W of Hyco, nr Omega; Halifax **GS**: U **SP**: Mar (1770) Catherine Howerton (1750-__) **VI**: No further data **P**: unk **BLW**: unk **RG**: Y **MK**: unk **PH**: unk **SS**: J- DAR Hatcher; E pg 226; G pg 184; DAR A009952; SAR P-156895 **BS**: JLARC 1, 2.; 80 vol2, pg 25.

FAUNTLEROY, Moore; b unk; d 1791 **RU**: Major/Patriot, Served in 4th Regt of Dragoons Gave material aid to cause **CEM**: Farnham Episcopal; GPS unk; 231 N Farnham Church Rd, Farnham; Richmond Co **GS**: N **SP**: No info **VI**: BLW issued 21 Mar 1795. Records lost in Pension Office fire. F959 **P**: unk **BLW**: Y **RG**: N **MK**: N **PH**: N **SS**: AL Ct Bk pg 9 Richmond Co; K Vol II pg 105 **BS**: See SS BQ pg 7162.

FAUNTLEROY, Samuel Griffin; b 7 May 1759; d 8 Dec 1826 **RU**: Captain, Served in Richmond Co Militia 1781 **CEM**: Fauntleroy Family at Farmers Mt Plantation; GPS unk; Whitehall; King & Queen **GS**: Y **SP**: Sarah Lowry (25 Mar 1776-24 Nov 1840) **VI**: No further data **P**: unk **BLW**: unk **RG**: Y **MK**: N **PH**: unk **SS**: G pg 316; DAR A039353; SAR P-158920 **BS**: 129 pg 479.

FAW, Abraham; b 14 May 1747, (Bapt) Basel, Switzerland; d 26 Jun 1828 **RU**: Patriot, Member of Committee of Obervation; cared for prisoners in the "Poorhouse." Also loans Treasury of state of MD $1000 20 Jun 1780 **CEM**: Trinity United Methodist; GPS 38.802079,-77.057492 2911 Cameron Mills Rd; Alexandria City **GS**: Y **SP**: 1) Mar (16 Oct 1770) Juliana boyer Lowe 2) Mar (28 Mar 1790) Mary Ann Steiner (20 Nov 1760-19 Jan 1805) 3) Mar (20 Apr 1806) Sarah Moody (28 Mar 1764-28 Aug 1818) **VI**: Son of Jacob & Cathrine (Dyssly/Disslin) Pfau **P**: N **BLW**: N **RG**: Y **MK** Y SAR **PH**: Y **SS**: AK GW Chapter 2015; SAR P-334595 **BS**: 04.

FAWLEY, John; b Jan 1720, d 11 Jan 1803 **RU**: Patriot, Supported cause by paying supply tax included in his personal property tax in 1782, Loudoun Co **CEM: New Jerusalem Lutheran** Church; GPS 39.25736,-77.63891; 12942 Lutheran Church Rd, Lovettsville; Loudoun **GS**: Yes **SP**: Anna Maria Ault (1737-1803) **VI**: Son of Thomas Fawley (1681-1727) and Mary Frewell (1689-1736) **P**: N **BLW**: N **RG**: N **MK**: N **PH**: N **SS**: DV image 07. 1782, Loudoun Co **BS**: 196.

FELIX, (-----); b unk; d 1781 **RU**: Seaman, Served on "Solitaire" and died from Yorktown battle **CEM**: French Memorial; GPS 36.81944, -79.39933; Yorktown; York **GS**: U **SP**: No info **VI**: No further data **P**: unk **BLW**: unk **RG**: Y **MK**: unk **PH**: unk **SS**: J-Yorktown Historian; SAR P-157172 **BS**: JLARC 1, 74.

FENDALL, Philip Richard; b 24 Nov 1734; d Mar 1805 **RU**: Patriot, Public service claim **CEM**: Fendall Family; GPS unk; 614 N Washington St; Alexandria City **GS**: N **SP**: Mary Lee (__10 Nov 1827, Washington DC) sister of Henry "Lighthorse Harry" Lee **VI**: His 1799 will directed he be bur in the burying ground on his farm **P**: N **BLW**: N **RG**: N **MK**: N **PH**: N **SS**: AL Cert Issued **BS**: 20 pg 28.

RU=Rank/Unit	CEM=Cemetery	GS=Gravestone	SP=Spousal Information
VI=Other Veteran Info	P=Pension	BLW=Bounty/Land Warrant	RG=Registered Grave
MK=SAR/DAR Marker	PH=Photo	SS=Service Source	BS=Burial Source

136

FERET, Dominique; b unk; d 1781 **RU**: Soldier, Served in Gatinais Bn and died fr battle at Yorktown **CEM**: French Memorial; GPS 36.81944, -79.39933; Yorktown; York **GS**: U **SP**: No info **VI**: No further data **P**: unk **BLW**: unk **RG**: Y **MK**: unk **PH**: unk **SS**: J-Yorktown Historian; SAR P-157456 **BS**: JLARC 1, 74.

FERGUSON, Daniel; b 1752; d 3 Sep 1785 **RU**: Private, Served in Capt Francis Muir's 7th Co, Col Nathaniel Gist's VA Regt 1777 **CEM**: St Paul's Episcopal; GPS 36.84733, -76.28554; 201 St Paul's Blvd; Norfolk City **GS**: Y **SP**: No info **VI**: No further data **P**: unk **BLW**: unk **RG**: N **MK**: N **PH**: unk **SS**: A pg 287; G pg 253 **BS**: 87 pg 27; 196.

FERGUSON, Robert; b 30 Mar 1733; d 17 Sep 1796 **RU**: Soldier, Served in 1st Lt Dragoons **CEM**: Ferguson Family; GPS unk; 31356 Rochelle Swamp Rd, Vic Newsoms; Southampton **GS**: U **SP**: Sarah (-----) (1733-1800) **VI**: No further data **P**: unk **BLW**: unk **RG**: N **MK**: unk **PH**: unk **SS**: E pg 269 **BS**: 40 vol II pg 48; 196.

FERGUSSON (FARGUSSON FURGUSSON FURGUSON), Moses; b 1760; d 1851 **RU**: Captain, Served in Col Proctor's VA State 4th Regt of Artillery **CEM**: Farguson Family; GPS unk; 12951 Blue Stack Ct.; Chesterfield **GS**: U **SP**: No info **VI**: BLW 4 Jun 1789. Grave marked only by fieldstone **P**: unk **BLW**: Y **RG**: N **MK**: N **PH**: unk **SS**: CG pg 1294 **BS**: JLARC 4, 35.

FERRAND, Antoine; b unk; d 1781 **RU**: Seaman, Served on "Citoyen" and died from Yorktown battle **CEM**: French Memorial; GPS 36.81944, -79.39933; Yorktown; York **GS**: U **SP**: No info **VI**: No further data **P**: unk **BLW**: unk **RG**: Y **MK**: unk **PH**: unk **SS**: J-Yorktown Historian; SAR P-157614 **BS**: JLARC 1, 74.

FERRELL, William; b 1740, Russell Co, d 15 Jun 1778 **RU**: Private, in Capt William Nalle's Co, Rockingham Co Militia in the Point Pleasant battle, Oct 1774 **CEM**: Ferrell Family; GPS not determined; Horn Mountain, Whitewood; Buchanan **GS**: N **SP**: No spousal Info **VI**: No further data **P**: N **BLW**: N **RG**: N **MK**: N **PH**: N **SS**: Z pg 113 **BS**: 196.

FERRELL (FERRILL), William H; b 1752, Halifax Co; d 26 Nov 1826 **RU**: Private, Ent serv 1778 Halifax Co.in Capt Harry Ferrell's Co, 5th VA Regt; Served in SC & VA Lines **CEM**: Ferrell Family; GPS unk; Cherry Hill, W of Halifax; Halifax **GS**: U **SP**: Mar (16 Aug 1787) Frances Martin (unk Halifax Co-___) **VI**: Sol appl pen 28 Aug 1833 Halifax Co age 81. S13015 **P**: Y **BLW**: unk **RG**: Y **MK**: unk **PH**: unk **SS**: , J-DAR Hatcher; CG Vol 2 pg 1179; K Vol II pg 109; DAR A039430; SAR P-157655 **BS**: JLARC 1, 2.

FERREY, Claude; b unk; d 1781 **RU**: Soldier, Served in Auxonne Bn and died fr battle at Yorktown **CEM**: French Memorial; GPS 36.81944, -79.39933; Yorktown; York **GS**: U **SP**: No info **VI**: No further data **P**: unk **BLW**: unk **RG**: Y **MK**: unk **PH**: unk **SS**: J-Yorktown Historian; SAR P-157647 **BS**: JLARC 1, 74.

FIELDER, Dennis: b 21 Apr 1756, Goochland, d 3 May 1834 **RU**: Private, entered service Prince Edward Co in Grayson's Regt, VA Line serving under Capt John Clark for 6 mos under Col George Waller, May 1776 and again in 1781 under Capt Clark and Capt Holand under Col Holcombe, and was at Yorktown Oct 1781 **CEM**: Fielder Family; GPS 36.74338,-81.10123; Spring Valley Rd, Rt 805,past Rt 604, behind brick ranch house, Fallville, Grayson **GS**: Yes with DAR marker **SP**: Delilah Wheeler (5 Feb 1780, NC-27 May 1845) **VI**: Pen payment rec indicates died 30 May 1834. Applied for pen 24 Sep 1832, received shortly before death..S8476 **P** Y **BLW** N **RG**: Y; **MK** N **PH**: N **SS**: E pg 271; K vol II; AP Pen applic, Fold3 DAR A0399841; SAR P-157948 **BS**: 196.

FIELDER, Johnson (John); b c 1753, Prince Edward Co, d 1834 **RU**: Patriot, paid personal property tax, Botetourt Co 1783, considered to be a Rev War supply tax **CEM**: Fielder Family (AKA Knob Fork) GPS 36.743340,-81.101189; loc on right side of Spring Valley Rd, 4.5 mi past jct with Jerusalem Rd, 100 ft W of brick ranch house; Fallville; Grayson **GS**: Unk **SP**: Mar 27 Dec 1774, Prince Edward Co, Elizabeth Fielder (17 Feb 1777-Jul 1869, Grayson Co) **VI**: Son of Bartholomew Fielder & Anne Shoemaker **P**: N **BLW**: N **RG**: N **MK**: N **PH**: N **SS**: DV-image 06, 1783, Botetourt Co **BS**; 196.

FIELDS, Andrew; b c1751; d 1794 **RU**: Ensign, Served in Bedford Co or Campbell Co Militia in Capt Thomas Helm's Co. Was in Battle of Guilford CH **CEM**: Falling River Baptist; GPS 37.07531, -78.91543; 2874 Wickliffe Ave, Brookneal; Campbell **GS**: U **SP**: Margaret Galbraith (c1754 Northampton Co, PA-1835 Campbell Co) d/o Alexander & (-----) Galbreath **VI**: Son of John & Sarah (Milbert) Fields. JLARC

RU=Rank/Unit	CEM=Cemetery	GS=Gravestone	SP=Spousal Information
VI=Other Veteran Info	P=Pension	BLW=Bounty/Land Warrant	RG=Registered Grave
MK=SAR/DAR Marker	PH=Photo	SS=Service Source	BS=Burial Source

137

indicates location of cem is in Spring Mills which may not be location of the church by that name **P:** unk **BLW:** unk **RG:** Y **MK:** N **PH:** unk **SS:** SAR P-157994 **BS:** JLARC 36.

FINCOMB, Amos; b unk; d 25 Nov 1781 **RU:** Private, Served in Capt Dunscomb Co, Lewis Dubois's 5th NY Line Regt. Died fr the battle at Yorktown **CEM:** Yorktown Victory Monument Tablet; GPS 38.28350, -78.54150; Yorktown; York **GS:** U **SP:** No info **VI:** No further data **P:** unk **BLW:** unk **RG:** Y **MK:** unk **PH:** unk **SS:** J-Yorktown Historian; AX pg 220; SAR P-158201 **BS:** JLARC 74

FINLEY, James; b 10 Dec 1718, Nottingham, Chester Co, PA, d 1785 Staunton, Augusta Co **RU:** Patriot, Gave material aid to cause **CEM:** Tinkling Spring Presbyterian; GPS 38.08472, -78.98278; 30 Tinkling Spring Dr, Fishersville; Augusta **GS:** U **SP:** Mar Augusta Co, 1746, Agnes Morrison (___-1790) **VI:** No further data **P:** N **BLW:** N **RG:** N **MK:** N **PH:** N **SS:** AL Commissioners Bk IV pg 102, Ct Bk pgs 1, 9, Augusta Co **BS:** 196.

FINLEY, John; b 1706; d 1791 **RU:** Patriot, Gave material aid to cause **CEM:** Tinkling Spring Presbyterian; GPS 38.08472, -78.98278; 30 Tinkling Spring Dr, Fishersville; Augusta **GS:** U **SP:** Thankful Doak (___-after 1791) **VI:** No further data **P:** N **BLW:** N **RG:** N **MK:** unk **PH:** unk **SS:** AL Commissioners Bk II pg 358 Augusta Co **BS:** 196.

FINNELL, Reuben; b 1750, Orange Co, d 15 Oct 1823 **RU:** Private; Served in Virginia troops under Captain Taylor & Captain Mennis. Enlisted Aug 1776, discharged Aug 1779. Was at Valley Forge, Mar-May 1778 **CEM:** Finnell-Gardner; GPS: unk; loc on property of Conservation & Research Center of Smithsonian National Zoological Park (once "Cloverhill", Finnell Farm); Warren **GS:** No; **SP:** Mar 1775, 1) Henrietta Thorn 1775, 2) abt 1789, Sarah (Ashford) Mitchell (1758–Jul 1824, Shenandoah (now Warren) **VI:** Recd BLT #1910 **P** U **BLW** Y **RG:** Y; **MK** N **PH:** N **SS:** E pg 273; DAR A041195, SAR P-330739; **BS:** Cem records at Warren County Heritage Society Archives.

FINNIE, William; b c1739 d 15 Oct 1804 **RU:** Colonel, Quartermaster General, Southern Department appt 28 Mar 1776 serving to end of war **CEM:** St Pauls Episcopal Church; GPS 36.84733, -76.28554; 201 St Paul's Blvd; Norfolk **GS:** No **SP:** Elizabeth (___) (___-18 Aug 1795) **VI:** Virginia Argus newspaper indicates died in Norfolk age 65 and remains interred with Masonic honors. Was Mayor of Williamsburg, received half pay indicating disabled in service. Recd BLW 6,666 acres **P:** N **BLW:** Y **RG:** N **MK:** N **PH:** N **SS:** E pg 273; Fold3 file R.14.175 **BS:** 196.

FISHBACK, John Frederick; b 1716, Germanna Colony, Orange Co; d 20 Sep 1782 **RU:** Patriot, Gave material aid to cause **CEM:** Fleetwood; GPS unk; Fleetwood Ln off Rt 621, Jeffersonton; Culpeper **GS:** U **SP:** 1) Mar (abt 1740) Ann Elizabeth Holtzclaw 2) Mar (abt. 1757) Eve Mertain (Martin) **VI:** Son of Johannes & Agnes (Hager) Fishback **P:** N **BLW:** N **RG:** Y **MK:** unk **PH:** unk **SS:** AL Cert Fauquier Co; DAR A048812; SAR P-334013 **BS:** 196.

FISHBACK, Martin; b 12 Oct 1763; d 24 Jan 1842 **RU:** Private, Was in the battle of Yorktown **CEM:** Fleetwood; GPS unk; Fleetwood Ln off Rt 621, Jeffersonton; Culpeper **GS:** Y **SP:** Lucy Amiss (8 July 176_-12 Sep 1843) **VI:** Son of Johann Freidrich Fishback & Eve Martin. Born and d in the same room of "Fleetwood" the family home. SAR marker on Gr **P:** unk **BLW:** unk **RG:** N **MK:** Y SAR **PH:** unk **SS:** N pg 1109 **BS:** 04; 196.

FISHBURNE, Dietrick (Detrich); b 29 Jan 1760, PA; d Oct 1822 **RU:** Private, Served in Laird's Co of PA Militia **CEM:** Fishburne; GPS unk; At the end of Rt 847, behind Verona Methodist Church, Verona; Augusta **GS:** U **SP:** Mar (2 Mar 1784 Frederick, MD) Catharine/Catherine Burckardt **VI:** No further data **P:** unk **BLW:** unk **RG:** Y **MK:** unk **PH:** unk **SS:** CI PA Archives 5th Series Vol 7 pg 942, 944; SAR P-158492 **BS:** JLARC 8, 52, 62.

FISHER, John; b unk; d 1815 **RU:** Patriot, Gave material aid to the cause **CEM:** Back Creek Quaker, aka Gainesboro United Methodist; GPS 39.27861, -78.25694; 166 Siler Ln, Gainesboro; Frederick **GS:** N **SP:** No info **VI:** No further data **P:** N **BLW:** N **RG:** N **MK:** N **PH:** N **SS:** AL Cert Issued **BS:** 59 pg 110.

FISHER, William; b 1757, Essex Co, d 24 Nov 1843, Orange Co **RU:** Private, Enlisted in Essex and Orange Cos. Served 18 mos in Col Davis and Richard Campbell's 8th Regt VA Line and was in battles at Guilford CH and Camden. Enlisted again in 1781 serving 3 mos and was at siege at Yorktown **CEM:** Old Burying Ground at Cedar Grove; GPS: 38.22389,-77.81974; Turner Lane, Paytes; Spotsylvania **GS:** No **SP:** Mar 3 Jan 1826, Orange Co, Sarah Cox (1795-aft 1868). Resided Spotsylvania Co 1861, then later

---

RU=Rank/Unit	CEM=Cemetery	GS=Gravestone	SP=Spousal Information
VI=Other Veteran Info	P=Pension	BLW=Bounty/Land Warrant	RG=Registered Grave
MK=SAR/DAR Marker	PH=Photo	SS=Service Source	BS=Burial Source

resided P.O. Rapidan, Culpeper Co care of McDorman. Recd pen $96 per annum in Feb 1853 and BLW 160 acres in 1855 **VI:** Recd pen $70 per annum in1833. Perhaps only memorialized in cem on widows gr st as died in Orange Co **P** Both **BLW** Widow **RG:** N; **MK** N **PH:** N **SS:** E pg 274; AP Serv Rec, Comm ltr pen file Fold3 **BS:** 196.

FISSY, Antoine; b unk; d 1781 **RU:** Soldier, Served in Gatinais Bn and died fr battle at Yorktown **CEM:** French Memorial; GPS 36.81944, -79.39933; Yorktown; York **GS:** U **SP:** No info **VI:** No further data **P:** unk **BLW:** unk **RG:** Y **MK:** unk **PH:** unk **SS:** J-Yorktown Historian; SAR P-158827 **BS:** JLARC 1,74.

FITZ (FITTS), Robert Walker; b 1755 or 1756, Dinwiddie Co; d Sep 1840 **RU:** Soldier, Ent Serv Mecklenburg Co 1776 in Capt James Anderson Co. In 1779 was in Capt Reuben Vaughan's Co, at Battle of Stono. In 1781 was in Halifax Co, Capt Marmaduke Standfield's Co, and transferred at Cabin Point to Col Wm Dix, Jesse Conway's Co. In Apr or May 1781 was in Capt Edward King's Co, in Battle of Ninety-Six. Guarded prisoners to Halifax Old Town, Pittsylvania Co Aug 1781. Was in Capt Fleming Bates Co to Little York, and at surrender of Cornwallis **CEM:** Fitts; GPS 36.58428, -79.69962; Rt 621 off Rt 610, Aiken Summit; Pittsylvania **GS:** Y **SP:** Mar (16 May 1782) Susannah Pass (1762-21 Dec 1849 in TN) **VI:** Pen Mecklenburg Co 1832. Was residing in Pittsylvania Co in 1840. S8475 **P:** Y **BLW:** unk **RG:** Y **MK:** unk **PH:** unk **SS:** K Vol II pg 119; SAR P-158983 **BS:** 174, JLARC 4, 76, 96.

FITZGERALD, Edmund (Edmond); b 18 Mar 1745; d 6 Jun 1848 **RU:** First Lieutenant, Pittsylvania Co Militia 25 Nov 1778. 1st Lt 18 Apr 1781 **CEM:** Fitzgerald Family; GPS 36.80353, -79.24233; 1 mi E of Shockoe on Rt 832; Pittsylvania **GS:** Y **SP:** Mar (1774 Campbell Co) Mildred Payne (1752-12 Mar 1837) d/o Reuben & Agnes (Wade) Payne **VI:** Son of James & Mary (O'Brian) Fitzgerald of Ireland **P:** unk **BLW:** unk **RG:** Y **MK:** unk **PH:** unk **SS:** SAR P-158999; AR Vol 2 pg 37 **BS:** 174, JLARC 2, 90.

FITZGERALD, John; b unk, County Wiclow, Ireland; d 3 Dec 1799 **RU:** Lieutenant Colonel, Aide de Camp Gen Washington 1778. Wounded at Monmouth **CEM:** St Marys Catholic; GPS 38.79390, -77.04750; 310 S Royal St; Alexandria City **GS:** Y **SP:** Jane Digges (1754-__) d/o Charles & (-----) Digges **VI:** Awarded BLW of 4,666 acres **P:** unk **BLW:** Y **RG:** Y **MK:** unk **PH:** unk **SS:** SAR P-159007; E pg 275; SAR application **BS:** JLARC;196.

FITZHUGH, Thomas; b 15 Jun 1753, Bel Air, Stafford Co; d Oct 1829 **RU:** Patriot, Contributed Mar 1782 Prince William Co two beeves weighing 600 lbs & two cattle weighing 550 lbs **CEM:** Fitzhugh Plantation; GPS unk; Check property records for location of home; Prince William **GS:** U **SP:** Mar (1775) Lucinda Helm **VI:** Son of John & Alice Catlett (Thornton) Fitzhugh **P:** N **BLW:** N **RG:** N **MK:** unk **PH:** unk **SS:** CC Pr Wm Co Court Order Book 1778-1784 **BS:** 196.

FITZHUGH, William; b 13 Apr 1725, d 1791 **RU:** Patriot, Provided material aid to cause in King George Co **CEM:** Marmion; GPS: Not determined; loc jct Rt 3 & Rt 10; King George **GS:** Unk **SP:** c1741, Ursula Beverly (c1729, Blandfield, Essex Co-aft 1766) **VI:** Son of John Fitzhugh (c1692-31 Jan 1732/33, Stafford Co) & Ann Barbara McCarty (c1700, Surry Co-12Dec 1737, Stafford Co) **P:** N **BLW:** N **RG:** N **MK:** N **PH:** N **SS:** AL Ct Bk pgs 1, 2 **BS:** 196.

FITZHUGH, William; b 24 Aug 1741, Eagles Nest, King George Co; d 8 Jun 1809 **RU:** Patriot, Was Delegate 1st, 2nd, 3rd, 4th, 5th VA Conv; VA House of Delegates 1776-7 & 1780-1; Cont Congress 1779; VA State Senate 1782-3; signed Articles Non-importation 1775; Caroline [Military] District Comm 1776; Commissioner arms factory at Fredericksburg & Falmouth **CEM:** Pohick Episcopal; GPS 38.42546, -77.11598; 9301 Richmond Hwy, Lorton; Fairfax **GS:** Y **SP:** Ann Randolph **VI:** Died in Ravensworth, Fairfax Co **P:** Y **BLW:** N **RG:** Y **MK** Y SAR plaque **PH:** unk **SS:** I; D; SAR P-159031 **BS:** 01; 201.

FITZPATRICK (FITTZPATRICK), John; b 1740, Ireland; d 28 May 1801 **RU:** Patriot, Gave material aid to cause; also performed public service as member of Comm of Safety, Sheriff, and Justice of Peace **CEM:** Fitzpatrick Family; GPS unk; Nathalie; Halifax **GS:** U **SP:** Mar (9 Oct 1762) Behetherand Brent (c1740-27 Sep 1813) **VI:** Died in Pittsylvania Co **P:** unk **BLW:** unk **RG:** Y **MK:** unk **PH:** unk **SS:** ; AL Ct Bk pg 4, 10 Campbell Co; SAR P-159042 **BS:** JLARC 76.

FITZWATER, John; b 29 Jan 1726; d 1786 **RU:** Patriot gave material aid to cause,Rockingham Co **CEM:** Fitzswater Family; GPS not determined; from Rt 259 abt 1 mi fr Riverside United Methodist Ch turn on to concrete bridge to Ed Carter's house cem on right across creekbed in trees, Fulks Run;

RU=Rank/Unit　CEM=Cemetery　GS=Gravestone　SP=Spousal Information
VI=Other Veteran Info　P=Pension　BLW=Bounty/Land Warrant　RG=Registered Grave
MK=SAR/DAR Marker　PH=Photo　SS=Service Source　BS=Burial Source

139

Rockingham **GS**: N **SP**: Judith West (14 Mar 1728-__), d/o Thomas West & Christine Tossawa **VI**: Son of Thomas Foster Fitzwater (1701-1761) & Martha Reynolds (1703-1754); aft 1778 member 1st Co Ct **P**: N **BLW**: N **RG**: N **MK**: N **PH**: N **SS**: AL Ct Bk I pg 5 Ct Ck II, pg 15 Comm BK vol !, pg 120 **BS**: 196.

FIX, Phillip; b 2 Jun 1754, Schuykill river below Reading, Berks Co, PA; d 2 Dec 1834 **RU**: Private, Ent serv Loudoun Co and later Capt John Thomas's Company Augusta Co **CEM**: Old Monmouth Presbyterian; GPS 37.80810, -79.47280; Jct Rts 60 & 669; Lexington City **GS**: Y **SP**: Mar (15 Mar 1780 Augusta Co) Margaret Swink (c1762-__) **VI**: Sol appl 8 Aug 1833 Rockbridge Co age 79. Died in Rockbridge Co. Widow appl pen 26 Jan 1846 Rockbridge Co age 84. W7264 **P**: Y **BLW**: unk **RG**: Y **MK**: N **PH**: unk **SS**: E pg 226; K Vol II pg 121-2; CG Vol 2 pg 1207; DAR A040329; SAR P-159079 **BS**: 04.

FLAGLY (FLAGLEY), John; b unk; d 1781 **RU**: Private, Col John Lamb's 2d NY Artillery Regt. Killed in the battle at Yorktown **CEM**: Yorktown Victory Monument Tablet; GPS 38.28350, -78.54150; Yorktown; York **GS**: U **SP**: No info **VI**: No further data **P**: unk **BLW**: unk **RG**: Y **MK**: unk **PH**: unk **SS**: J-Yorktown Historian; AX pg 64; SAR P-159148 **BS**: JLARC 74.

FLEENOR, Michael; b c1757, Berks Co, PA; d 3 Aug 1837 **RU**: Soldier, Served in VA Line. Ent serv Washington Co 1777 as sub for brother (Jacob) **CEM**: Fleenor; GPS unk; North Fork, Holston; Washington **GS**: U **SP**: Mar (10 Dec 1781 Washington Co) Sally Lyndor (c1765-aft 1848) **VI**: Sol appl pen 26 Mar 1833 Washington Co age 76. Widow appl 21 Aug 1844 Washington Co age 79. W7288. Pensioned in 1833 **P**: Y **BLW**: unk **RG**: Y **MK**: unk **PH**: unk **SS**: CG Vol 2 pg 1210; K Vol II pg 123; DAR A040578; SAR P-159219 **BS**: JLARC 4, 34.

FLEET, William; b 1757; d 1833 **RU**: Lieutenant, Specific service is at the Lib of VA, Collection of Loose Manuscripts re pensions, vol 2 **CEM**: Private graveyard nr St Stephens Church; GPS unk; Goshen; Rockbridge **GS**: U **SP**: No info **VI**: No further data **P**: Y **BLW**: unk **RG**:N **MK**: unk **PH**: unk **SS**: J- DAR Hatcher; CZ pg 165 **BS**: JLARC 2.; 80, vol 2, pg 38

FLEET, William; b 18 Dec 1757, King & Queen Co; d 11 Apr 1833 **RU**: Lieutenant/Patriot, Served in King & Queen Co Militia and had other unidentified service to qualify him for a pension. Gave material aid to cause **CEM**: Goshen; GPS unk; Check property records for Fleet Family at "Goshen" also see Senate Document 1952,serial 11670, vol 3; King & Queen **GS**: Y **SP**: Mar (1 Oct 1795) Sarah Tomlin or Browne (1 Apr 1776 Essex Co-27Jan 1818) **VI**: This may or may not be the same person with same birth and death yrs that is buried in Rockbridge Co (see BS 80) **P**: Y **BLW**: unk **RG**: Y **MK**: N **PH**: unk **SS**: D King & Queen Co; E pg 277; AR Vol 2 pg 38; SAR P-159225 **BS**: 80, vol 2 pg 38; 129 pg 485.

FLEMING, Andrew; b 1759; d 6 Jan 1820 **RU**: Soldier, Specific service is at the Lib of VA, Journals House of Delegates, Dec 1824 pg 18 **CEM**: Presbyterian Church; GPS 38.80015, -77.05791; Wilkes St & Hamilton Ln; Alexandria City **GS**: Y **SP**: Prob mar Catherine (-----) (c1773-26 Mar 1846) also bur here **VI**: Died age 61 **P**: unk **BLW**: unk **RG**: Y **MK**: Y SAR plaque **PH**: unk **SS**: J-NASSAR 1993 Reg; CZ pg 165; SAR P-159233 **BS**: JLARC 1; 23 pg 32.

FLEMING, William; b 6 Jul 1736, Cumberland Co; d 15 Feb 1824 **RU**: Patriot, Delegate to 1775 & 1776 colonial conventions. Served in VA State House of Delegates fr 1776-1778. Cont Congress 1778-1779 **CEM**: Fleming Family; GPS unk; Midlothian; Chesterfield **GS**: U **SP**: No info **VI**: Judge of the General Ct. In 1789 was elected to Virginia's first Supreme Ct of Appeals to 1809 when he became presiding judge **P**: N **BLW**: N **RG**: N **MK**: unk **PH**: unk **SS**: CD **BS**: 196.

FLEMING, William; b 18 Feb 1729, Jedburgh, Scotland; d 24 Aug 1795 **RU**: Surgeon/Colonel, Gave orders as Co Lt to send troops to Fincastle Co who were being invaded by enemy. Wounded as Col at Battle of Point Pleasant in Oct 1774 **CEM**: Belmont; GPS unk; Frank Rd, Roanoke; Roanoke City **GS**: U **SP**: Mar (1763) Anne Christian (1744-1811) **VI**: Acting governor for 10 days in 1781 **P**: unk **BLW**: unk **RG**: Y **MK**: Y SAR **PH**: unk **SS**: C pg 589; Z pg 198; SAR P-159292 **BS**: JLARC 2, 41, 109.

FLINT, John; b 1763, Amherst Co; d 1818 **RU**: Private, Served in 4th Troop, 1st Battalion Light Dragoons, Jan 1783 **CEM**: Stonewall Jackson Memorial; GPS 37.78128, -79.44604; 314 S Main St; Lexington City **GS**: U **SP**: Mar (21 Oct 1784) Elizabeth Williams (1754 Rockbridge Co-1 Mar 1839) **VI**: Son of Richard (1739-1790) & Hannah (-----) (1742-1839) Flynt **P**: unk **BLW**: unk **RG**: Y **MK**: unk **PH**: unk **SS**: E pg 278; AP-Payroll; DAR A204534; SAR P-339134 **BS**: 196.

RU=Rank/Unit	CEM=Cemetery	GS=Gravestone	SP=Spousal Information
VI=Other Veteran Info	P=Pension	BLW=Bounty/Land Warrant	RG=Registered Grave
MK=SAR/DAR Marker	PH=Photo	SS=Service Source	BS=Burial Source

FLOHR, George Daniel; b 30 Aug 1762, d 30 Apr 1826 **RU:** Soldier Served in the French Royal Deux-Ponts Regiment supporting American cause **CEM:** St Johns Lutheran Church; GPS 36.96500,-81.10110; 405 W Main, Wytheville; Wythe **GS:** Y **SP:** Elizabeth (__) (19 Jun 1777-25 Jul 1858) **VI:** Served as Pastor of church from 1799 to death in 1826. His log cabin home about a mile away was dismantled and re-erected in cemetery. **P:** N **BLW:** N **RG:** N **MK:** N **PH:** N **SS:** Letter 26 Apr 2011, Wythe B Sharitz, President of the Church Cemetery Board. Correspondence from Historian Dr Robert Selig **BS:** 196.

FLOOD, Henry; b 1755; d 1827 **RU:** Soldier, Served in 2nd Regt Cont Line 1777-1780 **CEM:** Flood Family; GPS unk; Vera; Appomattox **GS:** Y **SP:** Mary Walker (1754- 24 Jul 1828) **VI:** No further data **P:** unk **BLW:** unk **RG:** Y **MK:** unk **PH:** unk **SS:** AP Muster roll; SAR P-159566 **BS:** 196.

FLOOD, Nicholas Dr; b Abt 1710; d 1776 **RU:** Patriot, His estate gave material aid to the cause **CEM:** North Farnham Episcopal; GPS unk; Farnham; Richmond Co **GS:** N **SP:** Eliabeth Peachey (18 Nov 1721, d. 1792 Richmond Co) d/o Samuel & Catherine (McCarty) Peachey **VI:** His will directed that he be bur next to his only daughter Catherine (Flood) McCall at North Farnham Church. His estate gave material aid to the cause. Only a fragment of the stone remains **P:** N **BLW:** N **RG:** Y **MK:** N **PH:** N **SS:** AL Ct Bk pg 1, 7; DU pg 111; SAR P-338330 **BS:** 196.

FLOOD, Noah; b unk; d 2 Oct 1818 **RU:** Soldier, Served in VA Line **CEM:** Flood Family, "Toga"; GPS unk; Rt 24; Buckingham **GS:** U **SP:** Mar (29 or 30 Nov 1785 in Buckingham Co) Sarah Fuqua (1763-aft 1841) **VI:** Widow appl pen 16 Oct 1841 Buckingham Co age 78- rejected. R3615 **P:** Y **BLW:** N **RG:** Y **MK:** N **PH:** unk **SS:** CG Vol 2 pg 1218; K Vol II pg 126; SAR P-159572 **BS:** JLARC 4, 10, 44, 59.

FLOOK (FLUCK), Henry (John Henry); b 2 Nov 1759, Middleton, MD; d 26 Sep 1841 **RU:** Private, Served in 33rd Bn MA Militia **CEM:** Bethel Cemetery; GPS 38.47592, -78.75641; 3061 Armentrout Path, Keezletown; Rockingham **GS:** Y **SP:** Elizabeth Rossel **VI:** No further data **P:** unk **BLW:** unk **RG:** Y **MK:** Y SAR **PH:** unk **SS:** SAR P-159577 **BS:** JLARC 3.

FLORI, Pierre; b unk; d 1781 **RU:** Seaman, Served on "Diademe" and died from Yorktown battle **CEM:** French Memorial; GPS 36.81944, -79.39933; Yorktown; York **GS:** U **SP:** No info **VI:** No further data **P:** unk **BLW:** unk **RG:** Y **MK:** unk **PH:** unk **SS:** J-Yorktown Historian; SAR P-159595 **BS:** JLARC 1, 74.

FLOURANCE, George Jr; b c1753, Prince William Co; d c1822 **RU:** Private, Served in 3rd VA Cont Line **CEM:** Flourance Family; GPS 38.71577, -77.46386; Lake Jackson; Prince William **GS:** Y **SP:** Eve (-----) (1778-__) **VI:** Son of George & (-----) Flourance Sr **P:** unk **BLW:** unk **RG:** Y **MK:** Y SAR **PH:** Y **SS:** 04; SAR P-159601 **BS:** 04.

FLOURANCE (FLORENCE, FLORANCE), William; b 7 Jan 1736, Prince William Co; d 14 Sep 1821 or 22 Oct 1822 **RU:** Lieutenant, Ent serv Col Buford's Brigade, Fauquier Co Militia **CEM:** Camp Glen Kirk; GPS 38.77367, -77.62360; Gainesville, Rt 29 N, Linter Hall Rd; Prince William **GS:** Y **SP:** 1) Mary Nash 2) Mar (21 Apr 1784 Prince William Co, bond dated 13 Apr 1784) Sarah Hutchison (c1759-__) **VI:** Widow pensioned Prince William Co 1838 age 79. F-W7291 R992, 7291 **P:** Y **BLW:** unk **RG:** Y **MK:** Y SAR **PH:** Y **SS:** K Vol II pg 127; SAR P-159600 **BS:** 04.

FLOYD, Matthew; b 7 Mar 1763; d 20 Aug 1844 **RU:** Soldier, VA Line. Enl St George Parrish, Accomack Co **CEM:** Morrison Hill; GPS unk; .8 mi S of Rt 622, W of Rt 600, Frogstool; Accomack **GS:** Y **SP:** 1) Elizabeth Custis 2) Lizzie Glenn (3 Feb 1789-1 Mar 1807) TS shared with husband Matthew Floyd. **VI:** Sol appl 1 Aug 1832 in St George Parish in Accomack Co. S184402. Was minister of gospel. Recd pen 1832. S2553. DAR marker on Gr **P:** Y **BLW:** unk **RG:** Y **MK:** unk **PH:** unk **SS:** CG Vol 2 pg 1219; K Vol II pg 129; BT; SAR P-159692 **BS:** JLARC 4, 5; 196.

FLYNN (FLIN) (FLINN), Daniel; b 30 Sep 1742 Fauquier Co, d 1836, Culpeper Co **RU:** Private, Enlisted Winchester City, 1766 for 3 yrs. Serv in Capt Stephen Ashby and Capt William Bayles Cos, James Woods 4th, 8th, 12th Regts VA & Cont lines. In battles at Germantown, Monmouth, and Brandywine where wounded in head **CEM:** Flynn Farm; GPS: unk; Marshall; Fauquier **GS:** Unk **SP;** Mary Howard (1755-17 Jan 1836) **VI:** Son of Valentine Flynn and Hannah (-----) CG, pg 1215; AP Serv & Pen Rec, Fold3 **BS:** 196

RU=Rank/Unit	CEM=Cemetery	GS=Gravestone	SP=Spousal Information
VI=Other Veteran Info	P=Pension	BLW=Bounty/Land Warrant	RG=Registered Grave
MK=SAR/DAR Marker	PH=Photo	SS=Service Source	BS=Burial Source

141

FLYNN (FLINN), John; b 1740, d 1793 **RU:** Patriot, Supported cause by paying supply tax included in his personal property tax in 1783, Fauquier Co **CEM:** Flynn Farm; GPS: not determined; see property records for specific location, Marshall; Fauquier **GS:** Unk **SP:** Mary (__) (1740-__) **VI:** Son of Valentine Flynn (1718-1793) and Hannah (-----)(1718-1813) **P:** N **BLW:** N **RG:** N **MK:** N **PH:** N **SS:** DV- Fauquier Co,1783 image 08.pdf **BS:** 196.

FLYNN, Valentine, Sr; b 1718, d 1793 **RU:** Patriot, Supported cause by paying supply tax included in his personal property tax in 1783, Fauquier Co **CEM:** Flynn Farm; GPS: not determined; see property records for specific location, Marshall; Fauquier **GS:** Unk **SP:** Hannah (-----) (1718-1813) **VI:** No further data **P:** N **BLW:** N **RG:** N **MK:** N **PH:** N **SS:** DV- Fauquier Co,1783 image 08.pdf **BS:** 196.

FOLE, Nicolas; b unk; d 1781 **RU:** Soldier, Served in Auxonne Bn and died fr battle at Yorktown **CEM:** French Memorial; GPS 36.81944, -79.39933; Yorktown; York **GS:** U **SP:** No info **VI:** No further data **P:** unk **BLW:** unk **RG:** Y **MK:** unk **PH:** unk **SS:** J-Yorktown Historian; SAR P-159836 **BS:** JLARC 1, 74.

FOLLIN, Catherine (Sandford); b 1765; d 1813 **RU:** Patriot, Service information not determined fr DAR **CEM:** Arlington National; GPS 38.88377, -77.06535; Jefferson Davis Hwy Rt 110; Arlington **GS:** Y **SP:** John Fallin, also bur here, shared stone **VI:** No further data **P:** N **BLW:** N **RG:** Y **MK:** N **PH:** unk **SS:** AR DAR repor; SAR P-159889 **BS:** 80 vol 2 pg 41; 196.

FOLLIN, John; b 5 Sept 1761, Fairfax Co; d 17 Apr 1841 **RU:** Seaman, US Navy, Ent serv Fairfax Co, age 17. Captured aboard the vessel "Neptune". Imprisoned for 3 yrs. Exchanged near close of the Revolution. Was Paymaster **CEM:** Arlington National; GPS 38.88377, -77.06535; Jefferson Davis Hwy Rt 110; Arlington **GS:** Y Sect 1, grave 295 VA **SP:** 1) Catherine Follin (1767-1813) 2) Mary Barker (1787-1863) **VI:** Died & bur Fairfax Co; reinterred at Arlington 23 May 1911. Shared stone with both wives **P:** unk **BLW:** unk **RG:** Y **MK:** Y **PH:** unk **SS:** B; DAR A040234; SAR P-159887 **BS:** JLARC 1, 27; 80 vol 2, pg 41; 196.

FONTAINE, William; b 1754; d 6 Oct 1810 **RU:** Lieutenant Colonel, Ent serv Amherst Co. Served in VA Line. At Yorktown, commanded 5th Co, 21 Oct 1775 of 2nd VA Regt of Foot. As Maj was in the Conventional Army Guard Regt 24 Dec 1779-15 June 1781 which transferred prisoners fr MA to VA. Was promoted to Lt Col Mar 1781 **CEM:** Beaver Dam; GPS unk; Rt 738; Hanover **GS:** U **SP:** Mar (27 Dec 1787 Hanover Co) Ann Morris (c1766-aft 1843) **VI:** Teacher in Amherst Co, 1773. Widow appl pen 20 Aug 1838 Hanover Co age 72. W7319, BLW #1949-450 issued to heirs 28 Jun 1833, also VA 1/2 pay **P:** Y **BLW:** Y **RG:** Y **MK:** unk **PH:** N **SS:** CE pg 36, 117, 118; CG Vol 2 pg 1224; K Vol II pg 130; DAR A040440; SAR P-160006 **BS:** JLARC 4, 71.

FONTENAY, Guillaume; b unk; d 1781 **RU:** Seaman, Served on "Diademe" and died from Yorktown battle **CEM:** French Memorial; GPS 36.81944, -79.39933; Yorktown; York **GS:** U **SP:** No info **VI:** No further data **P:** unk **BLW:** unk **RG:** Y **MK:** unk **PH:** N **SS:** J-Yorktown Historian; SAR P-160008 **BS:** JLARC 1, 74.

FORBES, Alexander; b 1763, Stafford Co; d 22 Feb 1838 **RU:** Soldier, Ent serv Buckingham Co 1780. Served in VA Line **CEM:** Loch Lomond; GPS unk; Check property records; Buckingham **GS:** U **SP:** 1) Mar (28 Jan 1787 Buckingham Co) Lucy Scruggs 2) Mar (27 Mar 1815 Buckingham Co) Judith Ammonette (c1778-aft 1855) **VI:** Sol appl pen 13 Aug 1832 Buckingham Co. Widow appl 20 Dec 1854 Buckingham Co age 76 and also 24 Mar 1855. W10998, BLW #26642-160-55 **P:** Y **BLW:** Y **RG:** Y **MK:** N **PH:** N **SS:** CG Vol 2 pg 1226; K Vol II pg 130; SAR P-160110 **BS:** 80; JLARC 2.

FORD, John; b 17 Jun 1755, Stafford Co; d Apr 1825 **RU:** Private, Served in 5th, Cont Line and in Capt Gillison's Co, Col Green's Regt, 6th Cont Line **CEM:** Ford Family; GPS unk; Nr Leon; Madison **GS:** Y **SP:** 1) Myrtle (-----) 2) Mar (4 Apr 1788) Rosanna Newmann **VI:** Son of John & Elizabeth (Thornton) Ford **P:** unk **BLW:** unk **RG:** Y **MK:** N **PH:** unk **SS:** E pg 281; DAR A040899; SAR P-160273; AP Fold 3 Muster/payrolls **BS:** 80 vol 2 pg 43.

FORD, John Thomas; b 17 Jun 1725, King George Co; d 19 Dec 1791 (WP 1792) **RU:** Lieutenant/Patriot, Served in 5th and 6th Cont line and Clark's Illinois Regt. Was entitled to 1/2 pay **CEM:** Ford Family; GPS unk; Merrimac; Culpeper **GS:** U **SP:** Elizabeth Myrtle Thornton (1733-1788) **VI:** No further data **P:** N **BLW:** N **RG:** Y **MK:** unk **PH:** N **SS:** A pg 419; AL Ct Bk I pg 19; EF pg 37; SAR P-160257 **BS:** 196.

RU=Rank/Unit	CEM=Cemetery	GS=Gravestone	SP=Spousal Information
VI=Other Veteran Info	P=Pension	BLW=Bounty/Land Warrant	RG=Registered Grave
MK=SAR/DAR Marker	PH=Photo	SS=Service Source	BS=Burial Source

FORD, William; b unk; d 1794 **RU:** Private, Served in Capt Ephraim Rucker's Co of Col Field's Regt at the Battle of Point Pleasant Oct 1784 **CEM:** Dumfries Public; GPS 38.34110, -77.19964; 17821 Mine Rd, Dumfries; Prince William **GS:** N **SP:** No info **VI:** SAR monument **P:** unk **BLW:** unk **RG:** Y SAR bio rpt submitted 2017 & May 2020 **MK** Y SAR monument **PH:** Y **SS:** Z pg 87 **BS:** 04; 96 pg 83.

FOREHAND, John Sr; b 29 Mar 1755, PA; d 27 Feb 1838 **RU:** Private, Served in Capts McGuire and Bell's Cos, 6th VA Regt **CEM:** Hattan Family; GPS unk; Rt 629, behind house on Frances Hostetter's property, Kerr's District; Rockbridge **GS:** Y **SP:** Rebecca Campbell (17 Mar 1754-29 Jan 1846) **VI:** Govt GS **P:** unk **BLW:** unk **RG:** Y **MK:** unk **PH:** unk **SS:** DAR A041018; SAR P-160379; B **BS:** 204.

FOREMAN, Robert; b 1740; d 4 Mar 1790 **RU:** Paymaster, 9th Cont Line in Apr 1777. Resigned 16 June 1778 **CEM:** Foreman Plot; GPS unk; NW of jct Rts 709 & 708, nr Miona; Accomack **GS:** Y **SP:** No info **VI:** Died age 50 **P:** unk **BLW:** unk **RG:** N **MK:** N **PH:** unk **SS:** E pg 281 **BS:** 38 pg 119.

FORREST, George; b c1747; d aft 1820 **RU:** Soldier, Ent serv 1776 in capt Charles Tompkies Co, 7th VA Regt for 2 yrs; enlisted again 1778, Capt Belfield's Co Troop of Horse, Col Theodorick Regt for 3 yrs **CEM:** St James Church; GPS unk; Mathews CH; Mathews **GS:** U **SP:** No info **VI:** Pen in Mathews Co in 1818. Resident there in 1820 when he was 73 Although USDAR & JLARC rpt indicate buried in St James Church nr CH in oounty, the burial and cemetery have not been found **P:** Y **BLW:** unk **RG:** unk **MK:** unk **PH:** N **SS:** Southern Campaigns Amer Rev Pen Statements & Rosters; J- DAR Hatcher; K Vol II pg 114; SAR P-160454 **BS:** JLARC 2; 80 vol 2, pg 44.

FORT, Lewis; b unk; d 1826 **RU:** Private, Probably served in Southampton Co Militia **CEM:** Mason Family; GPS unk; Rt 612 Fortsville Rd, 4 mi NW of Adam Grove; Southampton **GS:** Y **SP:** Elizabeth Harris Coleman (__-1823) **VI:** No further data **P:** unk **BLW:** unk **RG:** N **MK:** N **PH:** unk **SS:** AP roll **BS:** 144 Mason.

FORTUNE, Benjamin; b 1742; d 1784 **RU:** Private, Served in 10th Cont Line **CEM:** Fortune; GPS unk; Lovingston; Nelson **GS:** U **SP:** Sarah Eubank (1747-1824) d/o John & Hannah (-----) Eubank **VI:** Son of John & Lucey (-----) Fortune **P:** unk **BLW:** unk **RG:** N **MK:** unk **PH:** unk **SS:** E pg 283 **BS:** 196.

FORTUNE, John; b 1763,prob Amherst Co, d 10 Mar 1834 **RU:** Sergeant, VA Line, in Cavalry unit, entered serv Amherst Co **CEM:** Fortune family; GPS:37.78512, 78.89332; loc off Fortune Cove Lane (Rt 651)to E in field; Giles **GS:** Unk **SP:** Mar 1 Nov 1785, Albermale Co, Nancy Henderson, who she appl pen 17 Feb 1839, Kanawha Co, WVA at age 69 **VI:** Son of Thomas Fortune (1740-1804) and Elizabeth Eubank (1745-1821), Appl for pen Rockbridge Co, last payment 2d qtr 1834 **P:** N **BLW:** N **RG:** N **MK:** N **PH:** N **SS: AP Final Payment voucher and Serv Index card; CG; pg 1237** C Sec II, pg 237 Giles County Plaque listing Rev War soldiers **BS:** 196.

FORTUNE, Thomas; b 1740; d 1804 **RU:** Private, Served in Caroline Co Militia, 1781 **CEM:** Fortune; GPS unk; Lovingston; Nelson **GS:** U **SP:** Elizabeth Eubank (1745-1821) d/o John (1715-1789) & Hannah (-----) Eubank **VI:** Son of John (1711-1790) & Lucry (Fletcher) Fortune **P:** unk **BLW:** unk **RG:** N **MK:** unk **PH:** unk **SS:** CQ **BS:** 196.

FOSTER, Isaac; b c1750 Gloucester Co; d c1804 **RU:** Captain, Served in a VA unit in Illinois **CEM:** Foster; GPS unk; See property records for him and his wife in Mathews Co; Mathews **GS:** U **SP:** Mar (1776) Elizabeth Cayles Hodges (__Gloucester Co-aft 1810, Mathews Co) **VI:** DAR applic indicates he died in Gloucester County and his wife died in Mathews Co **P:** unk **BLW:** unk **RG:** Y **MK:** unk **PH:** unk **SS:** DAR A041568; NSSAR P-160760; CZ pg 168 **BS:** JLARC 68.

FOSTER, James; b Jun 1750, Prince William Co; d 10 Sep 1800 **RU:** Patriot, Gave material aid to the cause. Paid Supply Tax, Prince William Co in 1783 **CEM:** Whitewood; GPS unk; 2 mi N of The Plains; Fauquier **GS:** Y **SP:** Mar (15 May 1772) Elizabeth Grigsby (12 Jan 1755-20 May 1837) **VI:** Son of Robert & Sarah (Haley) Foster. Remains reinterred here fr Prince William Co where he died **P:** N **BLW:** N **RG:** N **MK:** N **PH:** unk **SS:** AL Ct Bk pg 5; DD **BS:** 95 Whitewood; 196.

FOSTER, Joseph; b c1757; d 1837 **RU:** Corporal, Served in 4th & 7th Cont lines **CEM:** Shockoe Hill; GPS 37.55190, -77.43170; 4th & Hospital Sts; Richmond City **GS:** Y **SP:** No info **VI:** No further data **P:** unk **BLW:** unk **RG:** N **MK:** N **PH:** unk **SS:** E pg 283 **BS:** 57 pg 14.

RU=Rank/Unit	CEM=Cemetery	GS=Gravestone	SP=Spousal Information
VI=Other Veteran Info	P=Pension	BLW=Bounty/Land Warrant	RG=Registered Grave
MK=SAR/DAR Marker	PH=Photo	SS=Service Source	BS=Burial Source

143

FOSTER, Peter G; b Mar 1756; d 31 Dec 1819 **RU**: Sergeant/Patriot, Served three years in the First VA Regt, serving three years; as a patriot paid personal property tax in 1782 in Gloucester Co, considered to be a supply tax for Rev War expenses **CEM**: Richard Foster; GPS unk; Rt 650, Hicks Wharf Rd, Rose Hill Plantation; Mathews **GS**: Y **SP**: Nancy Ann Hall (Sep 1756, Gloucester Co-Jan 1820) d/o Robert & Nancy (Johnston) Hall **VI**: Son of Richard (1723-1795) & (-----) Foster. Rec'd BLW 200 acres 28 Jul 1783. **P:**N **BLW:** Y # 1440 **RG: Y MK:** N **PH:** N **SS:** E pg 284; F pg 27; DV, Gloucester Co, 1782 , image 05.pdf; **SAR bio** report submitted Nov 2020, **BS:** 196.

FOSTER, Richard; b1723; d 1795 **RU**:Patriot, paid personal property tax, Gloucester Co, 1782, considered to be a supply tax for Rev War expenses **CEM**: Rose Hill Plantation; GPS not determined; Rt 650, Hicks Wharf Rd; Mathews **GS**:Unk **SP**: Priscilla Bailey Williams **VI**: No further data **P**: N **BLW**: Y **RG**: N **MK**: N **PH**: N **SS**: DV, Gloucester Co, 1782 , image 04.pdf **BS**: 196.

FOURNIER, Charles; b unk; d 1781 **RU**: Seaman, Served on "Sceptre" and died from Yorktown battle **CEM**: French Memorial; GPS 36.81944, -79.39933; Yorktown; York **GS**: U **SP**: No info **VI**: No further data **P**: unk **BLW**: unk **RG**: Y **MK**: unk **PH**: unk **SS**: J-Yorktown Historian; SAR P-161049 **BS**: JLARC 1, 74.

FOUSHEE, William; b 26 Oct 1749; d 21 Aug 1824 **RU**: Surgeon, Ent serv as army surgeon. Was Medical Director for VA **CEM**: Shockoe Hill; GPS 37.55190, -77.43170; 4th & Hospital Sts; Richmond City **GS**: Y **SP**: Elizabeth Harmondson **VI**: Recd pen R14223. Also VA 1/2 Pay (See N.A. Acc #874 #050068 1/2 Pay). Heirs recd BLW 28 Mar 1832. Was first mayor of Richmond **P**: Y **BLW**: Y **RG**: Y **MK**: Y SAR, Name on monument in cem **PH**: Y **SS**: AK; BY pg 277; CG Vol 2 pg 1246; K Vol II pg 139; DAR A040993; SAR P-161059 **BS**: 04, JLARC 4, 77, 104.

FOWLER, Samuel; b c1764, Salisbury, MA; d 31 Jul 1814 **RU**: Captain, Serv in Salisbury, MA fr 2 Dec 1780 to 24 Apr 1781. Was made capt by end of war **CEM**: Trinity Episcopal; GPS 36.83459, -76.30105; 500 Court St; Portsmouth City **GS**: Y **SP**: No info **VI**: No further data **P**: unk **BLW**: unk **RG**: N **MK**: N **PH**: unk **SS**: AJ MA Service **BS**: 57; 75 Portsmouth.

FOWLES, James; b unk; d 1781 **RU**: Private, Served in Col James Clinton's 3rd NY Line Regt. Killed in the battle at Yorktown **CEM**: Yorktown Victory Monument Tablet; GPS 38.28350, -78.54150; Yorktown; York **GS**: U **SP**: No info **VI**: No further data **P**: unk **BLW**: unk **RG**: Y **MK**: unk **PH**: unk **SS**: J-Yorktown Historian; AX pg 42; SAR P-161261 **BS**: JLARC 74.

FOWLKES, Henry Bass, Sr; b 1750, d 1808 **RU**: Lieutenant/Patriot, Served in Amelia Co, Militia. As patriot gave material aid to cause Amelia Co **CEM**: Fowlkes Family; GPS: 37.64862,-78.11087; 6808 W Court House Rd (Rt 625), on grounds of Hyde Park; Burkeville; Nottoway **GS**: Yes **SP**: Tabitha Bass **VI**: Son of John A Fowlkes (1722-1799) and Sarah Jennings (1730-1782) **P**: N **BLW**: N **RG**: Y **MK**: N **PH**: N **SS**: AL Lists pg 1; SAR P-334624 **BS**: 196.

FOWLKES, James; b 28 Sep 1760, Amelia Co; d Aug or Sep 1833, Pittsylvania Co **RU**: Sergeant, enlisted in Amelia Co and served in Capt Roland Ward's Co, Col Blunt's VA Regt and served sufficient time to qualify for a pension **CEM**: Fowlkes Family; GPS not determined; loc Hyde Park at 6808 West Courthouse Rd, Rt 625, Burkeville; Nottoway **GS**: Unk **SP**: Sally Foster (1758, Amelia Co-1785, Pittsylvania Co) d/o George Foster & Mary Forrest **VI**: Son of John A. Fowlkes (1722-1799) & Sarah Jennings Fowlkes (1730-1782). Drew pen # S8457 **P**: Y **BLW**: N **RG**; Y **MK**: N **PH**; N **SS**: E pg 285; CG: pg 1249; DAR A009190; SAR P-161264 **BS**: 196

FOWLKES, Jennings E; b 1744, d Oct 1802 **RU**: Patriot, Gave material aid to cause Amelia Co **CEM**: Fowlkes Family; GPS: 37.64862,-78.11087; 6808 W Court House Rd (Rt 625), on grounds of Hyde Park; Burkeville; Nottoway **GS**: Yes **SP**: Mar (1766, Amelia Co) Joyce Clark Motley (1745, Amelia Co-7 Jul 1825) **VI**: Son of John A Fowlkes (1722-1799) and Sarah Jennings (1730-1782) **P**: N **BLW**: N **RG**: Y **MK**: N **PH**: N **SS**: AL Ct Bk I, pgs 26, 27 CT Bk II, pg 20; DAR A041268; SAR P-161265 **BS**: 196

FOWLKES, John A; b 1722, Hanover Co, d 1799, Nottoway Co **RU**: Patriot, Gave material aid to cause, Amelia Co **CEM**: Fowlkes family; GPS: 37.64862,-78.11087; 6808 W Court House Rd, RT 625, on grds of Hyde Park; Nottoway **GS**:Y **SP**: 1) mar (1743, Hanover Co) Sarah Jennings (1730, Hanover Co-1782), d/o William Henry Jennings (1676-1775) & Mary Jane (Polly) Pulliam, (1704-1774), 2) mar (20 Aug 1787) Judith Penick (1747-1823) **VI**: Son of Gabriel Fowkles (1696-1823), VA Hist Rd sign "Hyde

---

RU=Rank/Unit	CEM=Cemetery	GS=Gravestone	SP=Spousal Information
VI=Other Veteran Info	P=Pension	BLW=Bounty/Land Warrant	RG=Registered Grave
MK=SAR/DAR Marker	PH=Photo	SS=Service Source	BS=Burial Source

144

Park" describes his home **P**: N **BLW**: N **RG**: Y **MK**: N **PH**: N **SS**: AL Ct Bk I, pgs 23,25 CT Bk II, pg 35; DAR A205436; SAR P161266 **BS**: 196.

FOWLKES, John Field; b 1745, d 1824, Amelia Co **RU**: Patriot, Gave material aid to cause Amelia Co **CEM**: Fowlkes Family; **GPS**: 37.64862,-78.11087; 6808 W Court House Rd (Rt 625), on grounds of Hyde Park; Burkeville; Nottoway **GS**: Yes **SP**: Mar 1) 1774, Dicey Hall (1744-___), d/o John Hall, Sr (1708-1799) & Elizabeth Botts, 2) mar (1799) Edith Jefferies (1784-1810), d/o Thomas Jeffries & Mary Jane Gunn **VI**: Son of John A Fowlkes (1722-1799) & Sarah Jennings (1730-1782) **P**: N **BLW**: N **RG**: N **MK**: N **PH**: N **SS**: AL Ct Bk I, pgs 51, 54 CT Bk II, pg 53 **BS**: 196.

FOWLKES, Joseph A; b 1724, d 3 Sep 1789, Nottoway Co **RU**: Patriot, Gave material aid to cause, Prince Edward Co **CEM**: Butterwood; **GPS**: 37.07220,-77.86060; vic jcts Rts 642 and 40, Darvills; Dinnwiddie **GS**: No **SP**: Mary Jane Jennings (Mar 3 1732-2 May 1822), d/o William Jennings (1676-1775) & Mary Jane Pulliam **VI**: Son of Gabriel Fowlkes (1696, Denbighshire, Wales-1775) & (-----). Grave re-interred fr Prince Edward Co cem, w/o gravestone **P**: N **BLW**: N **RG**: Y **MK**: N **PH**: N **SS**: AL Ct Bk pgs 10, Comm Bk V pg 44, Prince Edward Co; SAR P-161267 **BS**: 196.

FOX, John; b 29 Jun 1760, King William Co; d 29 Dec 1814 **RU**: Captain, Commanded a co in Louisa Co Militia Apr 178? **CEM**: Retreat; **GPS** unk; Aylett; King William **GS**: U **SP**: 1) Judith Turner (___-1780) 2) Frances Wyatt Woolfork (1762-1823) **VI**: No further data **P**: unk **BLW**: unk **RG**: N **MK**: N **PH**: unk **SS**: E pg 285 **BS**: 196.

FOX, Joseph; b 1748; d Jun 1782 **RU**: Private/ Patriot, served in Capt William Johnston's Co, 11th VA Regt commanded by Col Daniel Morgan, Jun 1777. As patriot gave material aid to cause **CEM**: Retreat (AKA Fox Family); **GPS** not determined; loc at "Retreat" house, Aylett; King William **GS**: N **SP**: No spousal data **VI** No further data **P**: N **BLW**: N **RG**: N **MK**: N **PH**: N **SS**: A Part II, pgs 258, 259; AL Comm Bk IV, pg 336, Lists I pg p9; AP Fold 3 serv rec **BS**: 196.

FOX, Samuel; b c1732, Bitton, Gloucestershire, England; d 13 Mar 1801 **RU**: Patriot, Gave material aid to cause **CEM**: St George's Episcopal; **GPS** unk; 905 Princess Anne; Fredericksburg City **GS**: Y **SP**: Elizabeth (-----) **VI**: No further data **P**: N **BLW**: N **RG**: N **MK**: N **PH**: unk **SS**: D pg 346 **BS**: 12 pg 105.

FRANCISCO, Peter; b 9 Jul 1760 1759; d 16 Jan 1831 **RU**: Private, Ent serv Prince Edward Co 1776. Served in 10th VA Regt, part of Cont Army in Dec '76. Was at Brandywine, Germantown, Ft Mifflin (at Valley Forge), Monmouth, Stony Pt; Camden, SC and saved Col Mayo's life. Was at Cowpens, and Guilford CH NC where severely wounded. Killed 3 Tarelton's Raiders near Ward's Tavern in Amelia Co **CEM**: Shockoe Hill; **GPS** 37.55190, -77.43170; 4th & Hospital Sts; Richmond City **GS**: Y **SP**: One or more?) (-----) 2) Mar (3 Jun 1823 Buckingham Co, later Appomattox Co) Mrs. Mary B West (soldier's last wife) **VI**: Was 6'6" 260-pound hero. Lifelong friend of Lafayette. Sergeant-at-Arms of house of Delegates. Bur with full military & Masonic honors. Also in War of 1812. Sol recd pen 1 Jan 1819 age 60. Widow appl pen 27 Feb 1854 Botetourt Co & for BLW 24 Mar 1855. W11021. BLW #8002-160-55 **P**: Y **BLW**: Y **RG**: Y **MK**: Y SAR & plaque, monument **PH**: unk **SS**: CG Vol 2 pg 1256; DAR A041640; SAR P-161532 **BS**: JLARC 1, 2, 4, 77.

FRANKLIN, James; b 1750; d 1813 **RU**: Corporal/Patriot, Served in 3rd, 4th, 5th Cont Line. Gave material aid to cause **CEM**: Franklin; **GPS** unk; Amherst; Amherst **GS**: U **SP**: Mar (15 Dec 1796 Amherst Co) Nancy Crews **VI**: No further data **P**: unk **BLW**: unk **RG**: Y **MK**: unk **PH**: unk **SS**: E pg 287; AL Ct Bk pg 9 Amherst Co; SAR P-161610 **BS**: JLARC 4.

FRANKLIN, John Sr; b 1763; d 1845 **RU**: Soldier/Patriot, Gave material aid to cause **CEM**: Franklin Family; **GPS** unk; Twp 50; Chesterfield **GS**: U **SP**: No info **VI**: Son of John (c1735-aft 1783 Chesterfield Co) & Ann (Hatcher(Franklin (c1738-1801 Chesterfield Co) **P**: unk **BLW**: unk **RG**: Y **MK**: N **PH**: unk **SS**: J- SAR P-161654; AI Ct Bk pg 22 **BS**: JLARC 76.

FRANKLIN, Lewis; b 1758, prob Orange Co; d 11 Apr 1842 **RU**: Private, Served in NC & VA Line. Ent serv Surry Co NC. Also Ent serv Orange Co 1779. Ent serv Henry Co 1780. Served in Orange Co Militia & guarded POWs at the Albemarle Barracks. While in Henry Co Militia, served against Tories in Western VA & served with Gen Greene during the "Race to the Dan" in 1781. Was wagon driver (QM dept) for 5 mos, 1781 **CEM**: Franklin Family; **GPS** 36.71597,-79.94299; Off US 57, btw Shadyview Rd SR 1404 and US 220 Bypass, behind "Old Franklin Home Place," nr community of Fieldale; Henry **GS**: Y **SP**: Milly Stone, d 1841 **VI**: Sol appl pen 13 Nov 1832 Henry Co age 74. S8519 Family records -

---

RU=Rank/Unit	CEM=Cemetery	GS=Gravestone	SP=Spousal Information
VI=Other Veteran Info	P=Pension	BLW=Bounty/Land Warrant	RG=Registered Grave
MK=SAR/DAR Marker	PH=Photo	SS=Service Source	BS=Burial Source

cemetery still owned by extended family member **P:** Y **BLW:** unk **RG:** Y **MK:** Y SAR **PH:** unk **SS:** Pension affidavit; CG Vol 2 pg 1259; K Vol II pg 144; SAR P-333037 **BS:** 196.

FRANKLIN, Thomas; b 8 Sep 1758, Bedford Co; d 23 Mar 1841 **RU:** Private, Ent serv Bedford Co. Served in VA Line and Campbell Co Militia **CEM:** Franklin Family; GPS 37.07200, -79.05100; SW Rt 646 3.2 mi N of Rt 615, Gladys quadrant; Campbell **GS:** N **SP:** Mar (29 Mar 1796) Letitia Evans (c1759-28-Jul 1862 Campbell Co) **VI:** Sol appl 2 Oct 1832 Campbell Co age 69. S8517. Widow pen Campbell Co 1850 age 81. BLW #26969 granted fr Campbell Co 1856. Her pen cut off during Civil War, then pen appl rejected. W1590. Survey at site of family in 1936 found one Gr (his). DAR marker on Gr **P:** Y **BLW:** Y **RG:** Y **MK:** Y SAR **PH:** N **SS:** E pg 287; CG Vol 2 pg 1259; K Vol II pg 144; SAR P-161647 & SAR P-161646 **BS:** JLARC 4, 36; 196.

FRANTZ, Christian; b 1740; d Feb 1824 **RU:** Private, Served in Capt John Anapach Co, Berks Co, PA **CEM:** Frantz Family; GPS unk; Check property records for location; Bedford **GS:** U **SP:** Mar (1763) Anna (-----) (__-1821) **VI:** Died in Botetourt Co. SAR database has correct burial county (Bedford), but wrong location of Fincastle which is in Botetourt Co. **P:** unk **BLW:** unk **RG:** Y **MK:** N **PH:** unk **SS:** J-NASSR 2000 Reg; CI, PA Archives Series 5 Vol 5 pg 18; SAR P-161672 **BS:** JLARC 76.

FRAY, Ephraim; b 1762; d 3 Feb 1846 **RU:** Private, Was placed on a draft list in Culpeper Co **CEM:** Hebron Lutheran; GPS 38.40676, -78.24808; 899 Blankenbaker Rd, Madison; Madison **GS:** Y **SP:** 1) Maria Huffman 2) Nancy Snyder (1781-22 Dec 1849) **VI:** No further data **P:** unk **BLW:** unk **RG:** N **MK:** N **PH:** unk **SS:** O; DJ Jan 1781 pg 25 **BS:** 04.

FRAYSER (FRAZIER), Jesse; b 27 Jul 1754 or 1764; d 28 Mar 1827 **RU:** Private, Served at Yorktown **CEM:** Glendale/Frayser Farm Family; GPS unk; 11 mi SE of Richmond City on Rt 5; Henrico **GS:** Y **SP:** Kesiah Hobson (12 May 1761-5 Dec 1854) **VI:** No further data **P:** unk **BLW:** unk **RG:** Y **MK:** unk **PH:** unk **SS:** J-NASSR 2000 Reg; SAR O-161707 B; DD **BS:** 114, JLARC 76.

FRAZIER, James; b 23 Dec 1758, Spotsylvania Co; d 20 Dec 1798 **RU:** Private, Served in Samuel Booker's Co, 11th VA Inf Regt and Capt Edwin Hull's Co, 15th VA Regt **CEM:** Bethel Presbyterian; GPS 38.04257, -79.17283, GS 38.0230,-79.1018; 563 Bethel Green Rd, Middlebrook; Augusta **GS:** Y **SP:** No info **VI:** Govt stone. Was a Capt of militia in 1794 **P:** unk **BLW:** unk **RG:** Y **MK:** Y SAR **PH:** Y **SS:** B; SAR P-161762 **BS:** JLARC 2, 8, 62, 63; 196.

FRAZIER, John; b 1750; d 1832 **RU:** Soldier, Served in 8th Cont Line **CEM:** New Providence Presbyterian; GPS 37.95130, -79.30250; 1208 New Providence Rd, Raphine; Rockbridge **GS:** U **SP:** No info **VI:** No further data **P:** unk **BLW:** unk **RG:** Y **MK:** unk **PH:** unk **SS:** E pg 287; SAR P-161761 **BS:** JLARC 63, 79.

FREEMAN, William; b 1754; d 2 Aug 1829 **RU:** Private, Ent serv 1775. Served in Cont & VA Lines. Served under many Capts in Col Henry Henderson's Regt **CEM:** Freeman Family; GPS unk; Rt778, Weber City; Scott **GS:** Y **SP:** Mar (1778) Hannah Epperson (1756-25 Nov 1836) **VI:** Sol appl pen 2 Jun 1818 Scott Co age 64. S39547 **P:** Y **BLW:** unk **RG:** Y **MK:** N **PH:** unk **SS:** O; CG Vol 2 pg 1269; K Vol II pg 147; SAR P-162027 **BS:** 04.

FRENCH, Matthew; b 2 Feb 1737, Westmoreland Co; d 1814 **RU:** Private, Served in Capt Cloyd's Co, Cont Line 12 Sep 1777 **CEM:** French (possibly same as Boyd); GPS unk; Wolf Creek near Curve; Giles **GS:** U **SP:** Sarah Paine **VI:** No further data **P:** unk **BLW:** unk **RG:** Y **MK:** unk **PH:** unk **SS:** G pg 215 Montgomery Co; BW pgs 58,59 ; DAR A042489; SAR P-162209 **BS:** JLARC 1, 2, 26, 63.

FRIES (FREIS, FREISE, FREIZE), Martin; b 1747, Berks CF, PA d 14 Jun1830 **RU:** Patriot, Gave material aid to cause **CEM:** Old Stone Church; GPS 39.30110, -78.16750; nr 461 Green Spring Rd, Green Spring; Frederick **GS:** Y **SP:** Mar (1817) Catherine Schaull (1750-1835), d/o Martin Fries (1747-1830) & Catherine Schaull (1750-1835) **VI:** No further data **P:** N **BLW:** N **RG:** N **MK:** Y **PH:** unk **SS:** AL Cert Issued **BS:** 59 pg 116.

FRIMIER, John; b unk; d 1781 **RU:** Private, Served in Col Van Cortlandt's 2d Regt, NY Line. Killed in the battle at Yorktown **CEM:** Yorktown Victory Monument Tablet; GPS 38.28350, -78.54150; Yorktown; York **GS:** U **SP:** No info **VI:** No further data **P:** unk **BLW:** unk **RG:** Y **MK:** unk **PH:** unk **SS:** J-Yorktown Historian; AX pg 33; SAR P-162383 **BS:** JLARC 74.

RU=Rank/Unit	CEM=Cemetery	GS=Gravestone	SP=Spousal Information
VI=Other Veteran Info	P=Pension	BLW=Bounty/Land Warrant	RG=Registered Grave
MK=SAR/DAR Marker	PH=Photo	SS=Service Source	BS=Burial Source

FRITTS, John; b c1762, Shenandoah Co; d c1847 **RU**: Private, Served in NC & VA Militias 1781-1782, in Capt John Lopp & then Capt Peter Faust Cos. Enl Rowan Co NC **CEM**: Fritts Family; GPS unk; Rumored to be next to federal prison, check property records of family; Lee **GS**: U **SP**: Mary Beaver **VI**: Son of Hans Ulrich & (-----) Fritts, also a Rev War veteran. Sol appl pen 27 May 1834 Hawkins Co TN age 72 S10701. Came back to Lee Co before death **P**: Y **BLW**: unk **RG**: N **MK**: N **PH**: N **SS**: K pg 14; CG Vol 2 pg 1277 **BS**: 4.

FROLEAUX, Julien; b unk; d 1781 **RU**: Seaman, Served on "Victorie" and died from Yorktown battle **CEM**: French Memorial; GPS 36.81944, -79.39933; Yorktown; York **GS**: U **SP**: No info **VI**: No further data **P**: unk **BLW**: unk **RG**: Y **MK**: unk **PH**: unk **SS**: J-Yorktown Historian; SAR P-162503 **BS**: JLARC 1, 74.

FROMENT, Pierre; b unk; d 1781 **RU**: Soldier, Served in Touraine Bn and died fr battle at Yorktown **CEM**: French Memorial; GPS 36.81944, -79.39933; Yorktown; York **GS**: U **SP**: No info **VI**: No further data **P**: unk **BLW**: unk **RG**: Y **MK**: unk **PH**: unk **SS**: J-Yorktown Historian; SAR P-162511 **BS**: JLARC 1, 74.

FROST, John; b 1756, Morristown, NJ; d 13 Jul 1834 **RU**: Corporal, Ent serv Morris Co, NJ, served in 4th NJ Regt. Ent serv Bedford Co Militia **CEM**: John Frost; GPS 36.71845, -80.89540; Roseberry Ln nr Hillsville; Carroll **GS**: Y Govt **SP**: Mar (8 Jul 1834 Rockingham Co, NC) Mary (-----) **VI**: Son of Ezekial Frost (1716-1762) & Alice Hopkins. Moved to NC after Rev War for 18 mos, then to Montgomery Co (later Grayson Co) 1784. Widow recd pen Grayson Co 1840 age 76. W7324 **P**: Y **BLW**: unk **RG**: Y **MK**: unk **PH**: N **SS**: K Vol II pg 149; SAR P-162568 **BS**: JLARC 4, 43; 196.

FROST, William; b unk; d unk **RU**: Captain/Patriot, Served in Frederick Co Militia 4 Aug 1779. Supplied hay, bushels of corn, 880# beef **CEM**: Frost; GPS unk; Vic Hopewell; Clarke **GS**: N **SP**: No info **VI**: "Middle Farm" owned by Mrs. Lorenzo Lewis in 1941; marked by a few trees. **P**: unk **BLW**: unk **RG**: Y **MK**: N **PH**: N **SS**: E pg 291; SAR P-162615 **BS**: JLARC 24.

FRY, Christopher; b c1728; d 10 May 1801 **RU**: Patriot, Provided waggonage to militia 1775 **CEM**: Mt Hebron; GPS 39.10916, -78.09497; 305 E Boscawen St; Winchester City **GS**: Y **SP**: No info **VI**: He served in the Colonial War in the Old VA Regt as an NCO in 1754 and on 08 Mar 1780 received bounty land of 200 acres for this service **P**: N **BLW**: N **RG**: N **MK**: Y SAR monument **PH**: N **SS**: Z pg 77; AH pg 311 **BS**: 196.

FRY, Henry; b 30 Oct 1738, Hanover d 6 Sep 1823 **RU**: Patriot, Was member of House of Burgess, and the VA Legislature **CEM**: Fry Family; GPS unk; Meander Plantation; Madison **GS**: Y **SP**: Susan Thorton Walker (1746-1808) **VI**: Son of Joshua (1700-1754) & Mary Hill (Micou) Fry (1716-1772). After overcoming severe alcoholism, became a Methodist minister and served 40 yrs. Was clerk of Albemarle Co for 8 yrs **P**: N **BLW**: N **RG**: N **MK**: N **PH**: Y **SS**: AK; AL Commissioner of Provisioners Law for Culpeper Co 1780/civil service; DAR A043026; SAR P-162661 **BS**: 196; 32 Oct 08.

FRYE, Benjamin; b 1754; d 8 Apr 1823 **RU**: Captain, Commissioned Capt 1779. Served in Christopher Lippett's Regt **CEM**: Frye Family; GPS unk; Wheatfield; Shenandoah **GS**: U **SP**: Mary Magdalena Secrist (__-__ Morgantown, WV) **VI**: No further data **P**: unk **BLW**: unk **RG**:N **MK**: unk **PH**: unk **SS**: C pg 155 **BS**: 196.

FUGENOT, Noel; b unk; d 1781 **RU**: Soldier, Served in Agenois Bn and died fr battle at Yorktown **CEM**: French Memorial; GPS 36.81944, -79.39933; Yorktown; York **GS**: U **SP**: No info **VI**: No further data **P**: unk **BLW**: unk **RG**: Y **MK**: unk **PH**: unk **SS**: J-Yorktown Historian; SAR P-162756 **BS**: JLARC 1, 74.

FULCHER, William; b c1762; d 30 May 1844 **RU**: Private?, Refer to pension or BLW records for service **CEM**: Longrow; GPS unk; Rt 658; Hanover **GS**: Y **SP**: No info **VI**: No further data **P**: Y **BLW**: Y **RG**:N **MK**: N **PH**: unk **SS**: E pg 291 **BS**: 31 vol 1 pg 8.

FULFERSON, Frederick; b 1739; d 1796 **RU**: Private, Served in Pittsylvania Co Militia **CEM**: Mayo Baptist Church; GPS unk; 85 Penn Store Rd, Spencer; Henry **GS**: Y **SP**: No info **VI**: Actual burial place on land owned by Frederick Fulkerson. SAR marker **P**: unk **BLW**: unk **RG**: N **MK**: Y **PH**: unk **SS**: AK correspondence **BS**: 32 Jun 2010; 196.

RU=Rank/Unit
VI=Other Veteran Info
MK=SAR/DAR Marker
CEM=Cemetery
P=Pension
PH=Photo
GS=Gravestone
BLW=Bounty/Land Warrant
SS=Service Source
SP=Spousal Information
RG=Registered Grave
BS=Burial Source

147

FULK, John; b 1741; d 1820 **RU**: Patriot, Paid personal property tax 1782 &1783, Rockingham Co, considered to be supply tax for Rev War expenses **CEM**: Farley-Fulk; **GPS** 38.661130, -78.913180; Blocks Gap Rd (Rt 629), .01 mi E of jct with Nash Hill Dr, Fulks Run; Rockingham **GS**: Y **SP**: Eva Biller (1749-1841) **VI**: Son of Mathew Fulk (1713-___) & Sedano Cornstalk (1715-___) **P**: N **BLW**: N **RG**: N **MK**: N **PH**: N **SS**: DV 1782 &1783 images 20 pdf & 13 pdf **BS**: 196.

FULKERSON, Abraham, b 3 May 1739, Somerset Co, NJ; d 20 Mar 1821 **RU**: Private/Patriot served in Washington Co Militia under Col William Campbell at Kings Mountain, NC battle, 7 Oct 1780. Was Juror during war period **CEM**: Fulkerson Family; **GPS** not determined; loc about 40 yards NW of Fulkerson-Hilton House, Hiltons; Scott **GS**: Unk **SP**: Mar 2 Jul 1766, Rowen County, NC, Sarah Elizabeth Gibson (1743-1835) **VI**: No further data **P**: N **BLW**: N **RG**: Y **MK**: N **PH**: N **SS**: DL, vol 2, pgs 1124,1149; DAR A043186; SAR P-162773 **BS**: 196.

FULKERSON, James (Jacobus); b 22 Jun 1737, NJ; d 22 Sep 1799 **RU**: Lieutenant, Served in Washington Co Militia, Col William Campbell"s Regt **CEM**:Burson Family, originally Fulkerson; **GPS** 36.66440, -82.17500; Nr Jct of Rt 633 & Spur Strap Rd, Burson's Cnr; Washington **GS**: N **SP**: Mary VanHook (19 Sep 1747-12 Jul 1830) **VI**: DAR marker **P**: unk **BLW**: unk **RG**: Y **MK**: Y DAR **PH**: N **SS**: E pg 291; AZ pg 233; SAR P-162776 **BS**: JLARC 1, 80; 78 pg 388; 196

FULLER, Arthur **See APPENDIX G Addenda**

FULTON, James; b 10 Aug 1755; d 14 Feb 1834 **RU**: Private/Patriot, Served in Capt John Tates Co, Augusta Co Militia. Gave material aid to cause **CEM**: Bethel Presbyterian; **GPS** 38.04256, -79.17283; 563 Bethel Green Rd, Middlebrook; Augusta **GS**: U **SP**: Mar (Sep 1809 or 1810) Elizabeth "Betsey" Mitchell (1 Mar 1776-11 Sep 1850) d/o Thomas & Elizabeth (McClahan) Mitchell **VI**: Son of John & Mary (Steele) Fulton **P**: unk **BLW**: unk **RG**: Y **MK**: unk **PH**: unk **SS**: JLARC 63; E pg 292; AL Cert Augusta Co 79; SAR P-163155 **BS**: 196.

FULWEIDER, Johannes; b 19 Apr 1756; d 30 Sep 1831 **RU**: Soldier, SAR registration did not specify service **CEM**: Hanger Family; **GPS** unk; Rt 670, near Greenville; Augusta **GS**: U **SP**: Catharinea Elizabeth (-----) (17 Dec 1757-8 Feb 1827) **VI**: No further data **P**: unk **BLW**: unk **RG**: Y **MK**: unk **PH**: unk **SS**: SAR P-163188 **BS**: JLARC 8.

FUNK, Jacob; b 16 Feb 1767; d 7 Jun 1847 **RU**: Private, Served in Capt Joseph Bowman's Co in the lower district of Dunmore Co (now Shenandoah Co) **CEM**: Funk Family; **GPS** unk; behind Travel Trailer Park, vic Strasburg; Shenandoah **GS**: N **SP**: No info **VI**: No further data **P**: unk **BLW**: unk **RG**: N **MK**: N **PH**: N **SS**: C pg 606 **BS**: 79 pg 120.

FUNKHOUSER, Abraham; b 1742; d 1796 **RU**: Private, Served in Capt Alexander Machir's Co, Strasburg District Militia **CEM**: Funkhouser Family; **GPS** unk; Vic Fishers Hill; Shenandoah **GS**: Y **SP**: Mary Magdalena Campbell **VI**: No further data **P**: unk **BLW**: unk **RG**: Y **MK**: N **PH**: unk **SS**: C pg 606; SAR P-163231 **BS**: 79 pg 121; 196.

FUNKHOUSER, Jacob Jr; b 1766; d 1846 **RU**: Private, Served in Capt Alexander Machir's Co, Strasburg District Militia **CEM**: Funkhouser Family; **GPS** 38.801981, -78.78390; Resort Dr Rt 835, Basye; Shenandoah **GS**: Y **SP**: No info **VI**: No further data **P**: unk **BLW**: unk **RG**: Y **MK**: Y SAR **PH**: unk **SS**: DAR A042663 C pg 606; SAR P-163233 **BS**: 155 Funkhouser.

FUNKHOUSER, Jacob Sr; b 1750, Shenandoah Co; d 27 Nov 1801 **RU**: Private/Patriot, Served in Capt Alexander Machir's Co. Gave to cause in Shenandoah Co **CEM**: Funkhouser Family; **GPS** unk; Mt Jackson; Shenandoah **GS**: Y **SP**: Mar (c1775) Dorothy Hottel (1755, Mt Olive-6 Oct 1802) **VI**: No further data **P**: unk **BLW**: unk **RG**: Y **MK**: Y **PH**: unk **SS**: T; SAR P-163233 **BS**: 04.

FUNKHOUSER, John III; b unk; d 11 Jun 1826 **RU**: Private, Served in Capt Alexander Machir's Co, Strasburg District Militia **CEM**: Funkhouser Family; **GPS** unk; Waxwing Ln on Shipe farm; Shenandoah **GS**: Y **SP**: No info **VI**: No further data **P**: unk **BLW**: unk **RG**: N **MK**: Y SAR **PH**: unk **SS**: C pg 606 **BS**: 79 pg 129; 196.

FUQUA, Joseph; b 4 May 1756; d 4 May 1829 **RU**: Private, Ent serv 1776 in 4th or 5th VA Regt. Fought at Cowpens and Brandywine **CEM**: Fuqua Family; **GPS** 37.33344, -79.48352; Orange Street; Bedford City **GS**: Y **SP**: Mar (13 Nov 1782 Bedford Co (bond)) Celia Bondurant (23 Dec 1762-28 Mar 1847) **VI**: Son of Ralph Fuqua (1693-1770) & Priscilla Owen (1702-1779). Donated 100 acres for the town of

RU=Rank/Unit	CEM=Cemetery	GS=Gravestone	SP=Spousal Information
VI=Other Veteran Info	P=Pension	BLW=Bounty/Land Warrant	RG=Registered Grave
MK=SAR/DAR Marker	PH=Photo	SS=Service Source	BS=Burial Source

148

Liberty. First Deacon of Meeting House (now Timber Ridge Baptist). Widow appl pen 27 Jan 1840 Bedford Co age 77. W734. Small Govt marker on grave **P**: Y **BLW**: unk **RG**: Y **MK**: N **PH**: unk **SS**: CG Vol 2 pg 1293; K Vol II pg 153; SAR P-163239 **BS**: JLARC 1, 56; 196.

FUQUA, Ralph Jr; b 1737, Lunenburg Co; d Feb 1777 **RU**: Soldier, Served in 5th VA Regt 1777 **CEM**: Fuqua Family; GPS 37.33344, -79.48352; Orange Street; Bedford **GS**: Y **SP**: Mar (17 May 1804) Fanny Minor, d/o William & (-----) Minor **VI**: Son of Ralph Fuqua (1693-1770) & Pricilia Owen (1702-1779). Small Govt marker denoting unit and death date (Feb 1777) **P**: unk **BLW**: unk **RG**: Y **MK**: N **PH**: unk **SS**: B; J-NSSAR 1993 Reg **BS**: JLARC 1; 196.

FURR, Enoch; b 1756, Fauquier Co; d 3 Apr 1845 **RU**: Soldier, Served in VA Line. Ent serv Loudoun Co **CEM**: Ebenezer Baptist; GPS 39.05824, -77.84142; 20421 Airmont Rd, Bluemont; Loudoun **GS**: U **SP**: Mar (Mar 1786) Sarah "Sally" Clawson (c1768-___) **VI**: Sol appl pen 9 May 1836 Loudoun Co, age 80. Widow appl pen 4 Feb 1846 Loudoun Co age 78. W11030 **P**: Y **BLW**: unk **RG**: Y **MK**: Y SAR plaque **PH**: unk **SS**: CG Vol 2 pg 1294; SAR P-163299 **BS**: JLARC 4, 32.

GAAR, Andrew; b 1750; d 1811; **RU**: Patriot, gave material aid to cause **CEM**: Gaar Mountain; GPS 38.43374,-78.29048; Mulatto Run nr Beamer Hill Rd; Madison **GS**: Y **SP**: Christina Wilhoite, d/o John & (-----) Wilhoite, also Eva Seidelmann **VI**: Brother of John **P**: N **BLW**: N **RG**: Y **MK**:Y SAR **PH**: N **SS**: AK; AL Ct Bk 1 pg3; DAR A133883; SAR P-163336 **BS**: 04.

GAAR, Johann (John) Adam aka Adam; b 24 Nov 1711, Illenschwang, Barvaria (Kingdom); d 11 Jan 1790 **RU**: Patriot, Performed public Service **CEM**: Mt Pisagah Church; GPS 38.39265, -78.30396; Rt 652 nr intersection of Ruth Rd; Madison **GS**: N **SP**: Elizabeth Kaffer (Kaffier) **VI**: Died at Gaar Mtn, Madison Co at his farm **P**: N **BLW**: N **RG**: Y **MK**: N **PH**: N **SS**: AK; SAR P-164322 **BS**: 04.

GAAR, John (Johannes); b 1744, Lorenz Gaar home at Gaar Mtn and Mulatto (Pass) Run, Madison Co; d 1809 **RU**: Militiaman, Served in a Culpeper Co, VA State Militia. Gave material aid to the cause **CEM**: Lorenz Gaar Family; GPS unk; Mulatto Run nr Beamer Hd Rd; Madison **GS**: Y **SP**: Margaritha Wilhoite (Margaretha Willheit) d/o John & (-----) Wilhoit **VI**: Brother of Andrew, mar sister of Andrew's wife. Died at Gaar Mountain, Madison **P**: unk **BLW**: unk **RG**: Y **MK**: Y SAR **PH**: unk **SS**: AK; AL Ct Bk 1 pg 44-6; DAR A042807; SAR P-163337 **BS**: 04; 32 Apr 09.

GABIANT, Benoit; b unk; d 1781 **RU**: Seaman, Served on "Hercule" and died from Yorktown battle **CEM**: French Memorial; GPS 36.81944, -79.39933; Yorktown; York **GS**: U **SP**: No info **VI**: No further data **P**: unk **BLW**: unk **RG**: Y **MK**: unk **PH**: unk **SS**: J-Yorktown Historian; SAR P-163355 **BS**: JLARC 1, 74.

GAGUEBEY, Bernard; b unk; d 1781 **RU**: Soldier, Served in Foix Bn and died fr battle at Yorktown **CEM**: French Memorial; GPS 36.81944, -79.39933; Yorktown; York **GS**: U **SP**: No info **VI**: No further data **P**: unk **BLW**: unk **RG**: Y **MK**: unk **PH**: unk **SS**: J-Yorktown Historian; SAR P-163463 **BS**: JLARC 1, 74.

GAINES, James; b 1710, King & Queen Co; d 1786 **RU**: Private/Patriot, Served in Capt Josiah Parker's VA Regt. Gave material aid to cause **CEM**: Gaines Family; GPS unk; See tax map for location; Madison **GS**: N **SP**: Mary Pendleton, b 1717, d 1803; d/o Henry Pendleton (1683-1721) & Mary Taylor (1688-1770) **VI**: Son of Richard (1686-1755) & (-----) Gaines. Died in Culpeper Co. VA. Widow pensioned commencing 08 May 1813 at $48 per yr **P**: Y **BLW**: N **RG**: N **MK**: unk **PH**: N **SS**: AG pg 264; AK Ct Bk #1 pg 19, 25 **BS**: 65 cites Notable Southern Families, Vol 1; 196.

GAINES, Richard; b 1726, King William Co; d 1801 **RU**: Sergeant, Enl 13 Feb 1778. Promoted to Sgt May 1778. Transferred fr Capt Reuben Lipscomb's Co, 7th VA Regt Nov 1778. Served in Lt Col Hold Richeson's 5th VA Regt. Discharged 16 Feb 1779 **CEM**: Cub Creek; GPS 37.03220, -78.75830; Rt 616 Cub Creek Church Rd, Brookneal; Charlotte **GS**: U **SP**: Mar (1747) Mildred Hollinger. She was mentioned in will. **VI**: BLW as Sgt **P**: unk **BLW**: Y **RG**: Y **MK**: unk **PH**: unk **SS**: C pg 239; E pg 294; SAR P-163506 **BS**: 196.

GAINES, Thomas; b 1738; d 1811 **RU**: Corporal, Served in 7th, 11th, 15th Cont line **CEM**: Fairview; GPS 38.48080,-78.00470; Sperryville Pike Rt 522, Culpeper; Culpeper **GS**: U **SP**: No info **VI**: No further data **P**: unk **BLW**: unk **RG**: N **MK**: unk **PH**: unk **SS**: J- DAR Hatcher; E pg 294 **BS**: JLARC 2.

RU=Rank/Unit	CEM=Cemetery	GS=Gravestone	SP=Spousal Information
VI=Other Veteran Info	P=Pension	BLW=Bounty/Land Warrant	RG=Registered Grave
MK=SAR/DAR Marker	PH=Photo	SS=Service Source	BS=Burial Source

GAINES, William C; b 1767, d 1850 **RU:** Private, Gen George Rogers Clarks Illinois Regt **CEM:** Gaines Family; GPS: unk; Jct Rts 617 and 619, Aspen; Charlotte **GS:** No **SP:** Mar 1) 16 Sep 1794, Mary Latine Jennings (Apr 1767-__), 2) Elizabeth Carter (1784-19 Sep 1864) **VI:** His plantation name was Oakland, now in ruins. Held rank of Major after war period **P:** N **BLW:** N **RG:** N **MK:** N **PH:** N **SS:** E pg 294; G pg 700 **BS:** 196.

GAINES, William Henry; b 3 Mar 1704, King and Queen Co, d 10 Jul 1796, Lagrange, Culpeper Co **RU:** Patriot, Paid 1783 Supply Tax **CEM:** Saint Stephens Episcopal Church; GPS unk; 115 N East St; Culpeper **GS:** No **SP:** 1)Mar (c 1730, Spotsylvania Co) Isabella Pendleton (1712, King & Queen Co-8 Feb 1790), d/o Henry Pendleton (1763-__) & Mary Bishop Taylor; 2) Maria Woods **VI:** Son of Richard Gaines (1686-1755). Soldier Colonial War 1753, again 1758. Member House of Burgesses **P:** N **BLW:** N **RG:** Y **MK:** N **PH:** N **SS:** DAR A043103; SAR P-163522; DV **BS:** 196.

GALBURE, Jean; b unk; d 1781 **RU:** Seaman, Served on "Magnanime" and died from Yorktown battle **CEM:** French Memorial; GPS 36.81944, -79.39933; Yorktown; York **GS:** U **SP:** No info **VI:** No further data **P:** unk **BLW:** unk **RG:** Y **MK:** unk **PH:** unk **SS:** J-Yorktown Historian; SAR P-163567 **BS:** JLARC 1, 74.

GALI (GALLIN) (GALING), Samuel; b 1763; d 1796 **RU:** Private, Capt Thomas Massie's Co, 6th VA Regt commanded by Col Simms, Oct 1777 **CEM:** Thomas Parker Family; GPS unk; Rt 180 nr Pungoteague; Accomack **GS:** Y **SP:** No info **VI:** No further data **P:** unk **BLW:** unk **RG:** N **MK:** N **PH:** unk **SS:** P 6th VA Regt **BS:** 178 Th. Parker.

GALLAGHER, Bernard; b c1749, Ireland; d 13 Oct 1821 **RU:** Seaman/Midshipman/Ships Master, Served first as a seaman, then as Acting Midshipman under John Paul Jones on sloop "Providence"; Mate on PA brigatine "Minerva"; Master of "St Patrick," "Bachelor" and others **CEM:** Dumfries Public; GPS 38.34110, -77.19964; 17821 Mine Rd, Dumfries; Prince William **GS:** Y **SP:** Mar (1785) Margaret Strother (1773-2 Feb 1834) **VI:** SAR monument **P:** Y **BLW:** unk **RG:** Y **MK:** Y SAR monument **PH:** unk **SS:** H; I; AK; SAR P-163638 **BS:** 16 pg 21.

GALOTET, Jean; b unk; d 1781 **RU:** Soldier, Served in Bourbonnais Bn and died fr battle at Yorktown **CEM:** French Memorial; GPS 36.81944, -79.39933; Yorktown; York **GS:** U **SP:** No info **VI:** No further data **P:** unk **BLW:** unk **RG:** Y **MK:** unk **PH:** unk **SS:** J-Yorktown Historian; SAR P-163745 **BS:** JLARC 1, 74.

GALT, John Minson; b 17 Oct 1744, Williamsburg; d 12 Jun 1808 **RU:** Surgeon, Served in 15th Cont Line, 1777. Taken prisoner at Germantown 4 Oct 1777. Was disabled due to service **CEM:** Bruton Parish Church; GPS 37.27127, -76.70248; 331 W Duke of Gloucester St; Williamsburg City **GS:** U **SP:** Mar (6 Apr 1769) Judith Craig (30 Aug 1749, Williamsburg-12 Jun 1808, Williamsburg) **VI:** Recd pen 1/2 pay 28 Mar 1849 indicating disabled during service. Recd BLW 6000 acres. Pension paid to James Lyon, Attorney for John M. Galt, administrator of soldier's estate R14353 **P:** Y **BLW:** Y **RG:**N **MK:** unk **PH:** unk **SS:** J-NSSAR 1993 Reg; E pg 258; K pg 158; CG pg 1302 **BS:** JLARC 1.

GALTIER, Jean; b unk; d 1781 **RU:** Soldier, Served in Bourbonnais Bn and died fr battle at Yorktown **CEM:** French Memorial; GPS 36.81944, -79.39933; Yorktown; York **GS:** U **SP:** No info **VI:** No further data **P:** unk **BLW:** unk **RG:** Y **MK:** unk **PH:** unk **SS:** J-Yorktown Historian; SAR P-163769 **BS:** JLARC 1,74.

GAMBLE, George; b 1755, Ireland; d 1836 **RU:** Soldier, Served in PA & VA Lines. Ent serv Lancaster Co PA. Also Ent serv Washington Co VA. Was in Battle of King's Mountain **CEM:** Glade Spring Presbyterian; GPS 36.76720, -81.78720; 33234 Lee Hwy, Glade Spring; Washington **GS:** U **SP:** Margaret (-----) (__-1847) **VI:** Sol appl pen 31 Mar 1834 Washington Co Age 79. S10720 **P:** Y **BLW:** unk **RG:** Y **MK:** unk **PH:** unk **SS:** CG Vol 2 pg 1303; SAR P-163801 **BS:** JLARC 4,34; 196.

GAMBLE, John; b 1760; d 14 Jan 1831 **RU:** Captain, Commanded cavalry troop in Augusta Co Militia 19 Nov 1782 **CEM:** Augusta Stone Presbyterian; GPS 38.23926, -78.97356, GS 38.1413,-78.5810; 28 Old Stone Church Ln, Ft Defiance; Augusta **GS:** Y **SP:** Rebecca McPheeters (27 Nov 1767-18 May 1832) d/o F Reverend William (1729-1807) & Rebecca Moore (__-1826) McPheeters **VI:** Govt stone, indicates Capt of VA Co of Troop **P:** unk **BLW:** unk **RG:** Y **MK:** Y SAR plaque **PH:** unk **SS:** B; E pg 296; SAR P-163807 **BS:** JLARC 1,2,8, 23 ,63; 196.

RU=Rank/Unit	CEM=Cemetery	GS=Gravestone	SP=Spousal Information
VI=Other Veteran Info	P=Pension	BLW=Bounty/Land Warrant	RG=Registered Grave
MK=SAR/DAR Marker	PH=Photo	SS=Service Source	BS=Burial Source

150

GAMBLE, Robert; b 3 Sep 1754, Augusta Co; d 12 Apr 1810 **RU:** Colonel, Served in VA Line and Augusta Co Militia. Fought at Yorktown **CEM:** St John's Episcopal; GPS 37.53183, -77.41958; 2401 E Broad St; Richmond City **GS:** Y **SP:** Catherine Grattan **VI:** Sol appl 3 Jun 1805 Richmond for BLW that was issued 18 Sep 1789 but not rec'd until soldier requested at Richmond in 1805 a survey of the bounty land. John G Gamble witness to the request BLW869 **P:** unk **BLW:** Y **RG:** Y **MK:** N **PH:** unk **SS:** K pg 158; J-NSSAR 1993 Reg; CG Vol 2 pg 1303; SAR P-163817 **BS:** JLARC 1.

GARDINER, Francis; b 1762; d 26 Jul 1842 **RU:** Private, Served in Capt Joseph Patterson's Co. Marched to Jamestown in Jan 1781 and was in skirmishes there **CEM:** Hebron Presbyterian; GPS 38.14140, -79.15500; 423 Hebron Rd; Staunton City **GS:** Y **SP:** Ann Bell **VI:** Died age 80 (stone) **P:** unk **BLW:** unk **RG:** N **MK:** N **PH:** unk **SS:** AZ pg 103 **BS:** JLARC 62, 63; 142 Hebron; 196.

GARDNER, James; b 26 Apr 1755, NY; d 21 April 1849 **RU:** Private, Ent serv 1777 Essex Co, NJ **CEM:** Gardner Family; GPS 36.76610, -80.72080; End of Lynhaven Rd, Hillsville; Carroll **GS:** Y **SP:** 1) ?Rachael Wilson? 2) Tabitha Martin (16 Dec 1780-7 Sep 1862) d/o William Martin & Delphia Walden **VI:** Son of Isaac Martin (1700-1774, Halifax C) & Phylis (-----) **P:** unk **BLW:** unk **RG:** Y **MK:** Y SAR **PH:** unk **SS:** Winchester Account Book 37; NSDAR; SAR P-164059 **BS:** JLARC 2, 4, 11, 43; 68; 196.

GARDNER, John; b 3 Jun 1760, Montgomery Co; d 15 Nov 1833 **RU:** Private, Served in Capt McCreevy's Co, Augusta Co Militia **CEM:** Sunset; GPS 37.12390, -80.40420; South Franklin near I-81, Christiansburg; Montgomery **GS:** U **SP:** Mar (20 Jan 1813 Montgomery Co) Betsy Page d/o John & (----) Page **VI:** No further data **P:** unk **BLW:** unk **RG:** N **MK:** unk **PH:** Y **SS:** E pg 297 **BS:** 196.

GARDNER, John; b 1750 Chester Co, PA; d 1807 **RU:** Sergeant, Served in 5th & 11th Cont Line **CEM:** Leesburg Presbyterian; GPS 39.11611, -77.56722; 207 W Market St, Leesburg; Loudoun **GS:** U **SP:** Mar (1782) Mary Douglas (___-10 Jul 1818) **VI:** DAR indicates he was a Colonel but perhaps too young to obtain this rank during the war period having been born in 1750. Recd BLW **P:** unk **BLW:** Y **RG:** N **MK:** unk **PH:** unk **SS:** J- DAR Hatcher; E pg 296 **BS:** JLARC 2.

GARDNER, Nathanial; b 1760; d 12 Dec 1832 **RU:** Private, Serv at Massey's Ferry in SC, then at Battle of Guilford CH **CEM:** Mill Meeting House; GPS unk; Nr Chatham; Pittsylvania **GS:** Y **SP:** No info **VI:** Perhaps son of Nathaniel (1739/40-Feb 1833) & Margaret (Heath) Gardner **P:** unk **BLW:** unk **RG:** N **MK:** N **PH:** unk **SS:** G, pg 287 **BS:** AW pg 2; 196.

GAREL, Julien; b unk; d 1781 **RU:** Seaman, Served on "Diademe" and died from Yorktown battle **CEM:** French Memorial; GPS 36.81944, -79.39933; Yorktown; York **GS:** U **SP:** No info **VI:** No further data **P:** unk **BLW:** unk **RG:** Y **MK:** unk **PH:** unk **SS:** J-Yorktown Historian; SAR P-164175 **BS:** JLARC 1, 74.

GARIQUE, Jacques; b unk; d 1781 **RU:** Seaman, Served on "Diademe" and died from Yorktown battle **CEM:** French Memorial; GPS 36.81944, -79.39933; Yorktown; York **GS:** U **SP:** No info **VI:** No further data **P:** unk **BLW:** unk **RG:** Y **MK:** unk **PH:** unk **SS:** J-Yorktown Historian; SAR P-164198 **BS:** JLARC 1, 74.

GARLAND, Nathaniel; b 1750; d 1793 **RU:** Lieutenant, Served in Albemarle Co Militia **CEM:** Garland Family; GPS unk; Refer to county property records for location; Albemarle **GS:** N **SP:** Mar (7 Dec 1772) Jane Rodes (c1754-1830) **VI:** Son of Rev War patriot James (c1722 Hanover Co-1812) & Mary (Rice) (c1732 Hanover Co-1812) Garland **P:** unk **BLW:** unk **RG:** Y **MK:** unk **PH:** N **SS:** J- DAR Hatcher; E pg 297; G pg 445; SAR P-164242 **BS:** JLARC 2.

GARNER, William, Sr; b 1740, Bertie Co, NC, d 1824, Northampton Co, NC **RU:** Patriot Gave material aid to cause in Brunswick Co **CEM:** Garner Family; GPS: unk; Garner's Mill; Greenville **GS:** Unk **SP:** Sarah Camp (1740-1815), d/o R S Thomas Camp and Sarah (-----) **VI:** Persons this name served as privates in Lee's Legion and Roger Clarks Illinois Regt but these regiments normally had privates born after year 1760 **P:** N **BLW:** N **RG:** N **MK:** N **PH:** N **SS:** E pg 298; AL Ct Bk pg 59, Brunswick Co; CG pg 1314 **BS:** 196

GARNETT, James Rev; b Nov 1743; d 16 Apr 1830 **RU:** Patriot, Gave material aid to cause **CEM:** Crooked Run Baptist Church; GPS unk; 7351 James Madison Hwy, Rapidan; Culpeper **GS:** N **SP:** (-----) Rowe **VI:** Baptist minister, was pastor of Crooked Run Church 55 yrs serving fr 1774-1830 **P:** N **BLW:** N **RG:** N **MK:** N **PH:** N **SS:** AL CT BK 1 pg 12, 44, 54 **BS:** 196.

RU=Rank/Unit	CEM=Cemetery	GS=Gravestone	SP=Spousal Information
VI=Other Veteran Info	P=Pension	BLW=Bounty/Land Warrant	RG=Registered Grave
MK=SAR/DAR Marker	PH=Photo	SS=Service Source	BS=Burial Source

GARNETT, Muscoe; b 17 Aug 1736; d Jan 1803 **RU:** Patriot, Gave material aid to cause **CEM:** Garnett Family; GPS unk; Elmwood, Loretto; Essex **GS:** U **SP:** Grace Fenton Mercer (20 Feb 1751 Stafford Co- 14 Jun 1814) d/o John (1704 Dublin, Ireland-__) & Ann (Roy) Mercer **VI:** Son of James (1691-1765) & Elizabeth (Muscoe) (1699-__) Garnett **P:** N **BLW:** N **RG:** N **MK:** unk **PH:** unk **SS:** AL Ct Bk pg 9, 10 Essex Co **BS:** 196.

GARNETT; Reuben; b 8 Oct 1749, d 18 Apr 1820 **RU**; Patriot, gave material aid to cause, Essex Co **CEM:** Liberty Hall; GPS not determined; loc nr line with King & Queen Co in Indian Neck, Farmers Fork; Essex **GS:** Unk **SP:** Mary Gaines Jameson (2 Mar 1760-27 Aug 1839) **VI:** No further data **P:** Unk **BLW:** Unk **RG:** N **MK:** N **PH:** N **SS:** AL ct Bk pg 10, Essex Co **BS** 196.

GARNETT, Reuben; b 27 Jul 1753; d 16 Jun 1839 **RU:** Second Lieutenant, Served in Essex Co Militia in Capt Hancock Lee's Co 21 Jul 1777, took oath as 2nd Lt 20 Apr 1779. **CEM:** Garnett Family; GPS unk; Rt 648, 10 mi off Rt 15; Culpeper **GS:** Y **SP:** Mary Twyman (7 Jul 1757-1841) **VI:** No further data **P:** unk **BLW:** unk **RG:** N **MK:** N **PH:** Y **SS:** E pg 298 **BS:** 167 Garnett; 196.

GARRETT, William; b 24 Dec 1752; d 11 Jul 1825 **RU:** Private, Served in Capt Everard Meade's Co & Capt William Taylor's Co; Col Alexander Spotswood & Col Christian Febiger's Regts **CEM:** Pitts Farm; GPS unk; Nr Slaydo; Essex **GS:** U **SP:** 1) Elizabeth (-----); 2) Mar (1803) Clara Favor (__-aft 15 Aug 1825) **VI:** No further data **P:** unk **BLW:** unk **RG:** Y **MK:** N **PH:** unk **SS:** AP roll #941; SAR P-164383 **BS:** JLARC 2, 76.

GARST, Frederick; b 24 Dec 1752; d 1842 **RU:** Private, Served fr PA **CEM:** Garst Family; GPS unk; Kesler Mill Rd up hill behind a business near RR tracks; Salem City **GS:** Y **SP:** Magdalena Rauch (1752-1845) **VI:** No further data **P:** unk **BLW:** unk **RG:** Y **MK:** N **PH:** unk **SS:** J-NASSAR 2000 Reg; SAR P-164462 **BS:** JLARC 76; 196.

GARY(GERY), James; b 1764; d 23 Apr 1831 **RU:** Private, Enl age 16, served in 1st VA State Regt **CEM:** Gary Family; GPS unk; Centreville; Fairfax **GS:** U **SP:** No info **VI:** Was a Private in the War of 1812, as member of Petersburg Volunteers **P:** unk **BLW:** unk **RG:** Y **MK:** N **PH:** unk **SS:** E pg 299; AS, SAR regis G pg 139; SAR P-164499 **BS:** SAR regis.

GASKINS, James; b 1761, d 1827 **RU:** Patriot and/or Private, As private, possible soldier of the Princess Anne County Militia and as a patriot preparing Rev War materials at the Gosport Naval Yard in Portsmouth. (Obituary indicates he served in the Rev War, but source not found) **CEM:** Cedar Grove; GPS 36.57204, -80.02599; 301 Fort Lane Rd; Portsmouth **GS:** Y **SP:** Mar 1st 1779, Nancy "Ann" Morris,(__-between 1797-1801), 2) Mary Hurt (1763-1851) **VI:** Son of Henry Gaskins (__-1765) and Ann Banister (__-1776); was first silversmith in Portsmouth Gravestone was moved to Cedar Grave fr a church cemetery **P:** N **BLW:** N **RG:** Y **MK:**Y SAR **PH:** N **SS:** BR-Obituary 1827; SAR P-336831 **BS:** 196.

GASKINS, John; b 13 July 1754; d 12 Mar 1838 **RU:** Private, Served in Capt Thomas Gaskin's Co, 5th VA Regt in 1777 **CEM:** Union Church; GPS 38.32268, -77.46615; Carter St, Falmouth; Stafford **GS:** Y **SP:** No info **VI:** No further data **P:** unk **BLW:** unk **RG:** N **MK:** N **PH:** unk **SS:** E pg 299; AP roll **BS:** 03 addendum.

GATES, Elijah; b 22 Jun 1744, Preston, New London, CT; d 11 Apr 1802 **RU:** Captain, Served in Vt in Col Olcott and Col Wait's Regts **CEM:** Wood; GPS unk; Wood; Scott **GS:** Y **SP:** Mar (23 Nov 1769, Norwich, VT) Eunice Hatch (16 Jun 1741 Preston, CT-__) **VI:** No further data **P:** unk **BLW:** unk **RG:** Y **MK:** N **PH:** unk **SS:** AS SAR applic; DD; SAR P-164631 **BS:** SAR Appl.

GATES, William; b 1760; d 9 Mar 1816 **RU:** Soldier, Served in VA Line **CEM:** Gates Family; GPS unk; Rt 614, .4 mi west on private road next to "Fairfield" Farm; Chesterfield **GS:** Y **SP:** Mar (May 1784) Lydia "Liddy" Granger **VI:** Widow appl pen 25 Feb 1840 Chesterfield Co age 80. W19485. Newer Govt stone **P:** Y **BLW:** unk **RG:** N **MK:** N **PH:** unk **SS:** K pg 165; CG Vol 2 pg 1324 **BS:** JLARC 4, 35; 196.

GATEWOOD, Phillip; b c1740, Essex Co, d 11 Jun 1793 **RU:** Patriot, was paid for wagon hire April 1776, Frederick Co. Perhaps gave material aid to cause as well **CEM:** Gatewood; GPS not determined; loc Warren Co two mi E of Strasburg on Rt 55; Warren **GS:** Unk **SP:** Susannah Wright (1740-20-Feb 1833) **VI:** No further data **P:** N **BLW:** N **RG:** Y **MK:** N **PH:** N **SS:** G pg 619; AL Ct Bk pg 31, Comm Bk II pg185; DAR Ancestor # A043602; SAR # P-164780 **BS:** 224.

RU=Rank/Unit	CEM=Cemetery	GS=Gravestone	SP=Spousal Information
VI=Other Veteran Info	P=Pension	BLW=Bounty/Land Warrant	RG=Registered Grave
MK=SAR/DAR Marker	PH=Photo	SS=Service Source	BS=Burial Source

GAUDARD, Jean; b unk; d 1781 **RU:** Soldier, Served in Gatinais Bn and died fr battle at Yorktown **CEM:** French Memorial; GPS 36.81944, -79.39933; Yorktown; York **GS:** U **SP:** No info **VI:** No further data **P:** unk **BLW:** unk **RG:** Y **MK:** unk **PH:** unk **SS:** J-Yorktown Historian; SAR P-164808 **BS:** JLARC 1, 74.

GAUSSE, Philippe; b unk; d 1781 **RU:** Soldier, Served in Soissonnais Bn and died fr battle at Yorktown **CEM:** French Memorial; GPS 36.81944, -79.39933; Yorktown; York **GS:** U **SP:** No info **VI:** No further data **P:** unk **BLW:** unk **RG:**N **MK:** unk **PH:** unk **SS:** J-Yorktown Historian **BS:** JLARC 1, 74.

GAUTIER, Jean; b unk; d 1781 **RU:** Seaman, Served on "Caton" and died from Yorktown battle **CEM:** French Memorial; GPS 36.81944, -79.39933; Yorktown; York **GS:** U **SP:** No info **VI:** No further data **P:** unk **BLW:** unk **RG:** Y **MK:** unk **PH:** unk **SS:** J-Yorktown Historian; SAR P-164859 **BS:** JLARC 1, 74.

GAVAUDANT, Michel; b unk; d 1781 **RU:** Soldier, Served in Soissonnais Bn and died fr battle at Yorktown **CEM:** French Memorial; GPS 36.81944, -79.39933; Yorktown; York **GS:** U **SP:** No info **VI:** No further data **P:** unk **BLW:** unk **RG:** Y **MK:** unk **PH:** unk **SS:** J-Yorktown Historian; SAR P-164861 **BS:** JLARC 1, 74.

GAY, William; b c1755; d 2 May 1815 **RU:** Captain, Commanded a co in Powhatan Co Militia until resignation 21 Aug 1777 **CEM:** Fairfield; GPS unk; 5.5 mi W of Goochland Rt 6, then S Rt 614 .4 mi; Goochland **GS:** Y **SP:** No info **VI:** No further data **P:** unk **BLW:** unk **RG:** N **MK:** unk **PH:** unk **SS:** G pg 288 G-VA Mil records pg 288; E pg 301 **BS:** 196; 46, pg 140.

GEDDES, Winston; b c1721; d 9 Jun 1781 **RU:** Patriot, Provided two beeves to cause **CEM:** St John's Episcopal; GPS 37.53183, -77.41958; 2401 E Broad St; Richmond City **GS:** Y **SP:** No info **VI:** No further data **P:** N **BLW:** N **RG:** N **MK:** N **PH:**Y **SS:** D Vol 2 pg 497; SAR Bios report sumitted **BS:** AK Dec 2006

GEE, Henry See Appendix G Addenda.

GELLY, Jacques; b unk; d 1781 **RU:** Seaman, Served on "Citoyen" and died from Yorktown battle **CEM:** French Memorial; GPS 36.81944, -79.39933; Yorktown; York **GS:** U **SP:** No info **VI:** No further data **P:** unk **BLW:** unk **RG:** Y **MK:** unk **PH:** unk **SS:** J-Yorktown Historian; SAR P-165186 **BS:** JLARC 1, 74.

GENIES, Joseph; b unk; d 1781 **RU:** Soldier, Served in Foix Bn and died fr battle at Yorktown **CEM:** French Memorial; GPS 36.81944, -79.39933; Yorktown; York **GS:** U **SP:** no info **VI:** No further data **P:** unk **BLW:** unk **RG:** Y **MK:** unk **PH:** unk **SS:** J-Yorktown Historian; SAR P-165197 **BS:** JLARC 1, 74.

GENTIL, Joseph; b unk; d 1781 **RU:** Seaman, Served on "Marseillais" and died from Yorktown battle **CEM:** French Memorial; GPS 36.81944, -79.39933; Yorktown; York **GS:** U **SP:** No info **VI:** No further data **P:** unk **BLW:** unk **RG:** Y **MK:** unk **PH:** unk **SS:** J-Yorktown Historian; SAR P-165205 **BS:** JLARC 1, 74.

GENTRY, James; b 1757, Hanover Co; d 22 Jun 1851 **RU:** Captain, Served in VA Cont Line. Ent serv Hanover Co **CEM:** Rockgate; GPS 38.06170, -78.70170; 981 Crozet Ave, Crozet; Albemarle **GS:** N **SP:** Mar (c1779) Mary Hicks (9 May 1763 Goochland Co-1835) d/o Stephen & Agnes (Hancock) Hicks **VI:** Son of George (c1732 Hanover Co-5 Nov 1810) & Elizabeth (___) (__-5 Nov 1810) Gentry. Sol appl pen 2 Oct 1832 Albemarle Co. S8555 **P:** Y **BLW:** unk **RG:** Y **MK:** unk **PH:** N **SS:** J- DAR Hatcher; K pg 168; CG Vol 2 pg 1332; SAR P-165214 **BS:** JLARC 2; 196.

GEOFFROY, Jean; b unk; d 1781 **RU:** Soldier, Served in Soissonnais Bn and died fr battle at Yorktown **CEM:** French Memorial; GPS 36.81944, -79.39933; Yorktown; York **GS:** U **SP:** No info **VI:** No further data **P:** unk **BLW:** unk **RG:** Y **MK:** unk **PH:** unk **SS:** J-Yorktown Historian; SAR P-165245 **BS:** JLARC 1, 74.

GEORGE, Benjamin; b c1740; d 5 Aug 1811 **RU:** Private, Served in 6th Cont Line **CEM:** George Family; GPS unk; Catlett; Fauquier **GS:** N **SP:** Mar (1768) Hannah (-----) (1749-1833) **VI:** Died in Prince William Co. GS destroyed by cattle **P:** unk **BLW:** unk **RG:** N **MK:** N **PH:** N **SS:** E pg 302 **BS:** 19, pg 64.

GEORGE, Byrd; b 17 May 1758; d 7 Dec 1836 **RU:** Private, Served in Capt Newell's Co, Montgomery Co Militia **CEM:** George Family; GPS unk; 9.7 mi E of Richmond City, on Rt 60, Briel's Farm Rd; Henrico **GS:** Y **SP:** Mary Crutchfield (20 May 1777-27 Sep 1807) **VI:** Also Maj in War of 1812, Henrico Co **P:** unk **BLW:** unk **RG:** N **MK:** unk **PH:** unk **SS:** G pg 238 **BS:** 114, Byrd Fam.

RU=Rank/Unit	CEM=Cemetery	GS=Gravestone	SP=Spousal Information
VI=Other Veteran Info	P=Pension	BLW=Bounty/Land Warrant	RG=Registered Grave
MK=SAR/DAR Marker	PH=Photo	SS=Service Source	BS=Burial Source

153

GEORGE, John, Sr; b 18 Aug 1704, Middlesex Co, d 1784 **RU**: Patriot, gave material aid to cause in Caroline Co **CEM**: Fairford; GPS not determined; loc Penola; Caroline **GS**: Unk **SP**: Mar 1) 1724, Mary Jordan (1704 King William Co-1750) 2) Ursula Dudley **VI**: Son of Robert George (1666-1733) & Sarah Elmore (1666-1734). He was a prosperous tobacconist, shipping it to Eng **P**: N **BLW**: N **RG**: Y **MK**: N **PH**: N **SS**: AL Ct Bk II, pg 13, Caroline Co; DAR A206327 SAR P-165281 **BS**:196.

GEORGE, Reuben; b unk; d 1834 **RU**: Private, Served 3 yrs in Cont Line **CEM**: Old City; GPS 37.41472, -79.15667; 401 Taylor St; Lynchburg City **GS**: Y **SP**: No info **VI**: Recd BLW 100 acres 14 Dec 1831 **P**: unk **BLW**: Y **RG**: N **MK**: Y SAR plaque **PH**: unk **SS**: N pg 112 **BS**: 62 pg 112.

GEORGE, Reuben; b 25 Nov 1734, d 12 Nov 1799 RU:Patriot, Paid personal property tax considered as a supply tax,Caoline Co, 1783 CEM: Fairford; GPS not determined; loc Penola; Caroline GS: Unk SP: Mildred Rogers (1732, King &Queen Co-1788) VI: Son of Robert George (1666-1733) & Sarah Elmore (1666-1734) P: N BLW: N RG: N MK: N PH: N SS: DV image 08 Caroline Co BS:196.

GEORGE, Reuben; b 25 Nov 1749; d 16 Jan 1832 **RU**: Sergeant, Ent serv Culpeper Co. Served in Capt John Gillison's Co, Col Edward Stephen's 10th VA Regt; also in Capt Peter Ward's Co. Was in Battles of Brandywine, Germantown & White Marsh **CEM**: Fairford; GPS unk; Nr Penola; Caroline **GS**: U **SP**: Mar (27 Dec 1780, NJ) Ailcy Frazy **VI**: Appl for pen 04 Dec 1818 **P**: Y **BLW**: unk **RG**: Y **MK**: unk **PH**: unk **SS**: CG pg 1334; SAR P-165306, DAR A044247 **BS**: 196.

GEORGE, William; b unk; d 11 Sep 27 **RU**: Captain, Served in VA Line **CEM**: Friendship Rest; GPS unk; Rt 623; Goochland **GS**: Y **SP**: Mar (21 Sep 1784) Miss Nancy Garthright, d/o William & (-----) Garthright of Henrico Co (__-21 Jun 1838) **VI**: R3977 **P**: Y **BLW**: unk **RG**: N **MK**: N **PH**: unk **SS**: E pg 303; K pg 169; CG Vol 2 pg 1334 **BS**: 46 pg 150.

GERAUD, Guillaume; b unk; d 1781 **RU**: Seaman, Served on "Languedoc" and died from Yorktown battle **CEM**: French Memorial; GPS 36.81944, -79.39933; Yorktown; York **GS**: U **SP**: No info **VI**: No further data **P**: unk **BLW**: unk **RG**: Y **MK**: unk **PH**: unk **SS**: J-Yorktown Historian; SAR P-165339 **BS**: JLARC 1, 74.

GERRY, Philippe; b unk; d 1781 **RU**: Seaman, Served on "Ville de Paris" and died from Yorktown battle **CEM**: French Memorial; GPS 36.81944, -79.39933; Yorktown; York **GS**: U **SP**: No info **VI**: No further data **P**: unk **BLW**: unk **RG**: Y **MK**: unk **PH**: unk **SS**: J-Yorktown Historian; SAR P-165442 **BS**: JLARC 1, 74.

GERTHIER, Francois; b unk; d 1781 **RU**: Soldier, Served in d'Auxonne Bn and died fr battle at Yorktown **CEM**: French Memorial; GPS 36.81944, -79.39933; Yorktown; York **GS**: U **SP**: No info **VI**: No further data **P**: unk **BLW**: unk **RG**: Y **MK**: unk **PH**: unk **SS**: J-Yorktown Historian; SAR P-165449 **BS**: JLARC 1, 74.

GIBBON, James; b 1759, PA; d 1 July 1835 **RU**: Captain, PA Line. "Hero of Stony Point." Aide de Camp to Brig Gen Irwin **CEM**: Shockoe Hill; GPS 37.55190, -77.43170;SAR monument 37.551247,-77.432429; gravestone 37.552380,-77.431386; 4th & Hospital Sts; Richmond City **GS**: U **SP**: Mar (17 Mar 1782) Ann Elizabeth Phyle (4 Jan 1762, Philadelphia, PA-25 Nov 1853) **VI**: Sol appl pen 8 Sep 1828 Richmond VA. S13138. BLW #1538-300. Was collector at Richmond port for 30 yrs **P**: Y **BLW**: Y **RG**: Y **MK**: Y monument **PH**: unk **SS**: K pg 170; CG Vol 2 pg 1336; DAR A044505; SAR P-165546 **BS**: JLARC 1, 77.

GIBBONS, Isaac; b 13 Mar 1757, Philadelphia, PA; d 22 Dec 1826 **RU**: Private, Served in PA Cont Line. Enl Easton PA and served in Capt John Craig's Co. 4th PA Dragoons **CEM**: Old Peaked Mountain; GPS 38.37113, -78.73416; 9843 Town Hall Rd, McGaheysville; Rockingham **GS**: U **SP**: Mar (28 Dec 1782 Allentown PA) Mary Gongwer (14 Nov 1760-1851) **VI**: Sol appl pen 25 May 1818 Shenandoah Co age 61. He d in Shenandoah Co. Widow appl pen 22 Oct 1839 Rockingham Co. Son appl BLW on 16 Mar 1840. W4204. BLW 22282-100 **P**: Y **BLW**: Y **RG**:Y **MK**: unk **PH**: unk **SS**: K pg 171; CG Vol 2 pg 1337; SAR P-165555 (P-165554 shows spouse, but dates are wrong; NSSAR should be corrected; Patriots are mixed) **BS**: JLARC 4, 76.

GIBBONS, John; b 1740; d 1812 **RU**: Private, Served in General Nelson's Corps **CEM**: Augusta Stone Presbyterian; GPS 38.23926, -78.97356; 28 Old Stone Church Ln, Ft Defiance; Augusta **GS**: U **SP**: No

RU=Rank/Unit	CEM=Cemetery	GS=Gravestone	SP=Spousal Information
VI=Other Veteran Info	P=Pension	BLW=Bounty/Land Warrant	RG=Registered Grave
MK=SAR/DAR Marker	PH=Photo	SS=Service Source	BS=Burial Source

154

info **VI**: No further data **P**: unk **BLW**: unk **RG**: N **MK**: Y SAR plaque k **PH**: unk **SS**: E pg 304; BY **BS**: JLARC 63.

GIBSON, George; b 9 Apr 1732 Cork Co, Ireland; d 23 Oct 1819 **RU**: Lt Colonel, Was at Point Pleasant 10 Oct 1774 as Lt in Capt James Ewing's Co fr Augusta Co. Was at Valley Forge during winter 1777-8 as Maj. Served 22 Mar 1777-5 Jun 1777. Later was Col of 1st VA Regt at Yorktown **CEM**: Gibson Family; GPS 36.6058,-88.6063; Chandler Drive, Gibson Station; Lee **GS**: Y **SP**: Elizabeth Smith **VI**: No further data **P**: unk **BLW**: unk **RG**: Y **MK**: Y SAR **PH**: unk **SS**: AK Nov 06; CF pg 42, 110, 184; SAR P-165683, DAR A044756 **BS**: 04, Nov 06.

GIBSON, John; b 1757, Fauquier Co; d 1826, Orange co **RU**: Private, member of the Culpeper Minute Men Battalion, 1776; afterwards became Sergeant in the 2d VA State Regt **CEM**: Gibson Family; GPS not determined; Burr Hill; Orange **GS**: Y **SP**: Ann (-----) **VI**: Son of Jonathan Gibson III (1729, Caroline Co-1791, Fauquier Co) & Susannah Harrison (1735-___), d/o Thomas Harrison (1704-1744) & Anne Grayson (1721-1774) **P**: Unk **BLW**: Unk **RG**: N **MK**: N **PH**: N **SS**: Culpeper Minute Men Battalion list (not published); E pg 305 **BS**: 196.

GIBSON, Joseph; b unk; d 1796 **RU**: Patriot, Gave material aid to the cause **CEM**: South Fork Meeting House; GPS 39.02640, -77.80220; Rt 630, Unison; Loudoun **GS**: Y **SP**: Prob Alice (-----) (1701-11 Apr 1796) **VI**: No further data **P**: unk **BLW**: unk **RG**: N **MK**: N **PH**: unk **SS**: AL Ct Booklet pg 4 **BS**: 25 pg 111.

GIBSON, William; b 1743, Louisa Co; d 1823 **RU**: Corporal, Enl 12 Jan 1776 Louisa Co in 9th, 10th, 13th Cont Lines **CEM**: Gibson Farm; GPS unk; Louisa; Louisa **GS**: U **SP**: Mary Napper (1740-1821) **VI**: Appl for pen 14 Aug 1832 age 72 **P**: Y **BLW**: unk **RG**:N **MK**: unk **PH**: unk **SS**: A pg 201; E pg 305; CG pg 1342 **BS**: 196.

GIDEON, Peter; b 22 Mar 1752, near Philadelphia PA; d 5 Feb 1844 **RU**: Soldier, Served in MD Line. Ent serv Taneytown MD **CEM**: Potts Family; GPS unk; Rts 716 & 714, Hillsboro; Loudoun **GS**: U **SP**: Catherine (-----) (12 Jan 1743-13 Aug 1836) **VI**: Sol appl pen 22 Mar 1752 Loudoun Co. S6887 **P**: Y **BLW**: unk **RG**: Y **MK**: unk **PH**: unk **SS**: CG Vol 2 pg 1342-3; SAR P-165825 **BS**: JLARC 4, 32.

GILBERT, Samuel; b 1761; d 1845 **RU**: Private, Served in VA Line. Ent serv Washington Co (later Russell Co), Capt James Crabree's Co under Col Aurthur Campbell. Served in militia commanded by Capt James Montgomery **CEM**: Tritt-Gilbert; GPS unk; Rt 642, Woodway; Lee **GS**: Y **SP**: Mary (-----) **VI**: Sol appl pen 18 Feb 1833 Lee Co age 72. S8569. He died in Lee Co at Thomas Gilbert's **P**: Y **BLW**: unk **RG**: Y **MK**: N **PH**: unk **SS**: 32 Pension list; CG Vol 2 pg 1347; SAR P-330680 **BS**: 04, Dec 06.

GILCHRIST, Robert; b c1721, Scotland; d 16 July 1790 **RU**: Patriot, Performed public service as Commissioner for specific taxes **CEM**: Townsfield Farm; GPS unk; Port Royal; Caroline **GS**: Y **SP**: Catherine (-----) (c1720-5 May 1789?) **VI**: No further data **P**: N **BLW**: N **RG**: N **MK**: N **PH**: unk **SS**: AL, CT Bk II pg 8 **BS**: 02 pg 75; 196.

GILES, Thomas; b 30 Nov 1763, Hartford Co, MD; d 21 Mar 1842 **RU**: Private, Served in VA troops, Northumberland Co **CEM**: Westview; GPS 37.23390, -80.40830; Blacksburg; Montgomery **GS**: U **SP**: Mar (10 May 1762) Anne Wheeler **VI**: No further data **P**: unk **BLW**: unk **RG**: Y **MK**: unk **PH**: unk **SS**: J-NSSAR 1993 Reg,; AR Vol 2 pg 73; SAR P-166148 **BS**: JLARC 1, 2.

GILES, William; b 1727; d unk **RU**: Colonel, Commissionary officer Amelia Co Militia, 22 Jan 1780 **CEM**: Jeter-Cadwell; GPS unk; Giles Rd Rt 636; Amelia **GS**: N **SP**: Ann Branch **VI**: Father of Governor William Branch Giles **P**: unk **BLW**: unk **RG**: N **MK**: unk **PH**: N **SS**: G pg 14 **BS**: 196.

GILES, William Branch; b 21 Aug 1762; d 4 Dec 1830 **RU**: Ensign, Served in Henrico Co Militia 1 Oct 1781 **CEM**: Wigwam Estate; GPS unk; Amelia CH; Amelia **GS**: Y **SP**: No info **VI**: US Rep 1790-98. US Senator 1804 & 1805-15. Governor 1827-30. Sponsored admission of TN as 18th state of Union 1809. Giles Co in TN named for him **P**: unk **BLW**: unk **RG**: N **MK**: unk **PH**: unk **SS**: E pg 306 **BS**: 196.

GILHAM, Peter, Sr; b 1747, England, d 1798 **RU**: Lieutenant Recommended for Lt 4 Aug 1779, took oath 2 May 1780, Frederick Co, Militia **CEM**: St Johns Lutheran Church; GPS: 39.15310, -78.36520; 3623; Back Mountain Rd, Rt 600 nr bridge over Furnace Run, Hayfield; Frederick **GS**: Unk **SP**: Mar 22

RU=Rank/Unit   CEM=Cemetery   GS=Gravestone   SP=Spousal Information
VI=Other Veteran Info   P=Pension   BLW=Bounty/Land Warrant   RG=Registered Grave
MK=SAR/DAR Marker   PH=Photo   SS=Service Source   BS=Burial Source

155

Jul 1792, Frederick Co, Mary Ann Kline, widow of Jacob Marker **VI**: Owned glebe land **P**: N **BLW**: N **RG**: Y **MK**: N **PH**: N **SS**: E pg 386; AZ pg 204; SAR P-166161 **BS**: 196.

GILKESON, Hugh; b 1744; d Feb 1806 **RU**: Private, Served in Capt Long's Co, Augusta Militia **CEM**: Tinkling Spring Presbyterian; GPS 38.08472, -78.98278; 30 Tinkling Spring Dr, Fishersville; Augusta **GS**: N **SP**: Elizabeth (-----) (1744-May 1830) **VI**: No further data **P**: unk **BLW**: unk **RG**:N **MK**: N **PH**: N **SS**: E pg 307 **BS**: 208 pg 468.

GILKESON, John; b c1749, PA; d 1 Jun 1793 **RU**: Major, Served as Capt 3rd Co 2nd VA Regt. Promoted to Maj **CEM**: Opequon Presbyterian; GPS 39.13938, -78.19494; 217 Opequon Church Ln; Winchester City **GS**: Y **SP**: Sarah Vance **VI**: No further data **P**: unk **BLW**: unk **RG**: Y **MK**: Y SAR; DAR plaque **PH**: unk **SS**: J-NASSR 2000 Reg; CE pg 33; SAR P-166162 **BS**: JLARC 76.

GILKESON, Samuel; b unk; d unk **RU**: Major, Promoted to Capt in Frederick Co Militia 4 Aug 1779. Promoted to Maj 2 May 1780 **CEM**: Opequon Presbyterian; GPS 39.13938, -78.19494; 217 Opequon Church Ln; Winchester City **GS**:Y **SP**: Mar (3 Jul 1777 Frederick Co (bond) John Peyton, security) Susannah Hayn **VI**: No further data **P**: unk **BLW**: unk **RG**: Y **MK**: Y SAR; DAR plaque **PH**: unk **SS**: J-NASSR 2000 Reg; E pg 307; SAR P-166163 **BS**: JLARC 76.

GILKESON, William; b 29 Aug 1750; d 3 Jul 1828 **RU**: Private, Served in Capt Robert McClannahan's Co, Dunmore's War of 1774 at Point Pleasant **CEM**: Bethel Presbyterian; GPS 38.04257, -79.17283, GS 38.0232,-79.1017; 563 Bethel Green Rd, Middlebrook; Augusta **GS**: Y **SP**: Sarah Love (29 Aug 1752-27 Jun 1826) **VI**: No further data **P**: unk **BLW**: unk **RG**:Y **MK**: unk **PH**:Y **SS**: CP Dunmore's War; SAR P-166164 **BS**: JLARC 62; 196.

GILL, Erasmus; b 15 Jul 1752; d 16 Mar 1807 **RU**: Captain, Served in 4th Cont Dragoons, Feb 1779 and taken prisoner at siege of Savannah 3 Oct 1779, and exchanged 22 Oct 1780, and served to close of war **CEM**: Blandford; GPS 37.22433, -77.38604; 319 S Crater Rd; Petersburg City **GS**: Y **SP**: Mar (8 Jun 1786, Dinnwiddie Co) Sarah Newsum (17 Aug 1765-16 Apr 1826) d/o Benjamin & Lucy (Jones) Newsum **VI**: Rank of Major perhaps made before Oct 1783. Recd BLW # 839-300-27, 27 Aug 1795 5,333 acres **P**: unk **BLW**: Y **RG**: Y **MK**: Y SAR monument **PH**: unk **SS**: E pg 307; CG pg 1350; SAR P-166185, DAR A044666 **BS**: 196; 217.(**GILL**, Jones See Appendix G Addenda)

GILLES, Pierre; b unk; d 1781 **RU**: Soldier, Served in Gatinais Bn and died fr battle at Yorktown **CEM**: French Memorial; GPS 36.81944, -79.39933; Yorktown; York **GS**: U **SP**: No info **VI**: No further data **P**: unk **BLW**: unk **RG**: Y **MK**: unk **PH**: unk **SS**: J-Yorktown Historian; SAR P-166253 **BS**: JLARC 1, 74.

GILLESPIE, John; b 10 Dec 1745; d 28 May 1801 **RU**:Corporal; Capt William Popham's Co, Col Moses Hazen's Regt. Muster roll, Jul 1779 **CEM**: Gillespie Family(AKA Hasher Farm) GPS:37.946200, -78.252800; loc S of N Boston Rd nrj ct w Troy Rd; Troy: Flivania **GS**: Y broken family stone **SP**: Mary Molly Pasley (1748, Goochland-1 Dec 1805) **VI**:Rec'd BLW # 13133 for 100 acres 2 Apr 1791 **P**: N **BLW**: Y **RG**: N **MK**: N **PH**: N **SS**: AP Fold 3 muster roll & serv rec; CG pg 1352 **BS**: 196.

GILLESPIE (GILLASPY), Thomas II; b 1760; d 1842 **RU**: Private, Served in Capt Alexander Breckenridge Co, Col Nathaniel Gist's Regt 1777 **CEM**: Sayer's Farm; GPS unk; Mouth of Thompson Valley, Foot of Clinch Mountain, Dry Fork; Tazewell **GS**: U **SP**: Mar (c1781 Washington Co) Margaret Bowen (c1760 Augusta Co-d1799) d/o Rees (c1737 Augusta Co-7 Oct 1780 Kings Mountain, SC) & Louisa (Smith c1740-16 Feb 1834) Bowen **VI**: No further data **P**: unk **BLW**: unk **RG**: Y **MK**: unk **PH**: unk **SS**: J- DAR Hatcher; A pg 285; SAR P-166292 **BS**: JLARC 2.

GILLET, Guillaume; b unk; d 1781 **RU**: Seaman, Served on "Diademe" and died from Yorktown battle **CEM**: French Memorial; GPS 36.81944, -79.39933; Yorktown; York **GS**: U **SP**: No info **VI**: No further data **P**: unk **BLW**: unk **RG**: N **MK**: unk **PH**: unk **SS**: J-Yorktown Historian **BS**: JLARC 1, 74.

GILLIES (GILLES), James Dr; b 1758; d 24 Aug 1807 **RU**: Soldier/Patriot, Mil serv info not determined. Paid the supply tax in Fairfax Co 1782 **CEM**: Old Presbyterian Meeting House; GPS 38.48528, -77.23532; 323 S Fairfax St; Alexandria City **GS**: N **SP**: No info **VI**: Died of decline age 49, bur 25 Aug 1807. Was Vice President of St Andrew's Society (Alexandria Gazette 7 Aug 1807). Listed on SAR plaque in cemetery **P**: unk **BLW**: unk **RG**: Y **MK**: Y SAR plaque **PH**: N **SS**: J-NSSAR 1993 Reg; AK; DV **BS**: JLARC 1; 23 pg 102; 196.

RU=Rank/Unit	CEM=Cemetery	GS=Gravestone	SP=Spousal Information
VI=Other Veteran Info	P=Pension	BLW=Bounty/Land Warrant	RG=Registered Grave
MK=SAR/DAR Marker	PH=Photo	SS=Service Source	BS=Burial Source

156

GILMER, George Dr; b 27 Nov 1742, Williamsburg; d 29 Nov 1795 **RU:** Lieutenant, Was Surgeon for 11th VA. Was Lt in Albemarle Co 1775. Was 1st Lt in an independent Co of Albemarle Co Apr to Jul 1775 **CEM:** Gilner Family; GPS 38.04851, -78.44964; Pen Park off Rio Rd; Charlottesville City **GS:** U **SP:** Mar (27 Aug 176_) first cousin Lucy Walker, d/o Dr. Thomas Walker **VI:** Son of George Gilmer (1700-1757) & Mary Peachey (1710-1745). Died in Pen Park, Charlottesvillle **P:** unk **BLW:** unk **RG:** Y **MK:** unk **PH:** unk **SS:** E pg 308; CE pg 10; SAR P-166565 **BS:** JLARC 2,3,58; 67 Vol 1 pg 234; 196.

GILMORE, James; b 1710; d 1782 **RU:** Captain, Commanded co Rockbridge Co Militia,1780 **CEM:** High Bridge Presbyterian; GPS 37.62420, -79.58610; 67 High Bridge Rd, Natural Bridge; Rockbridge **GS:** U **SP:** Martha Dennison (1738-17850 **VI:** Son of John (1692-1759) & Agnes (Anderson) (1702-1759) Gilmore **P:** unk **BLW:** unk **RG:** Y **MK:** unk **PH:** unk **SS:** J- DAR Hatcher; AL Ct Bk pg 3a Rockbridge Co; SAR P-166595 **BS:** JLARC 2; 196.

GILMORE (GILMOR, GILMER), Samuel; b 24 Mar 1760, Bucks Co, PA; d 25 Jan 1848 **RU:** Private, Severely wounded at Battle of Waxhaw, 1780 **CEM:** Gilmore Family; GPS unk; In woods in back of Briscoe's Grocery Store. (Rt 84). Mill Gap.; Highland **GS:** Y **SP:** Mar (Feb 1799) Eleanor Bailey McQuillen **VI:** Died in Back Creek, Highland Co. Stone found lying on ground, broken into three pieces **P:** unk **BLW:** unk **RG:** Y **MK:** N **PH:** unk **SS:** AR Vol 2 pg 76; SAR P-166615 **BS:** JLARC 2, 4,103.

GILMORE, Thomas; b 1762, Ireland ; d 1813 **RU:** Private served 3ys in PA militia **CEM:** Ralph Heatwole Place; GPS not determined; Hinton Rd (Rt 752), Hinton; Rockingham **GS:** N **SP:** Mar 1) 1784, Elizabeth (__) (1764-1800), who rec'd pen, # R4044, 2) 11 Jun 1801, Mary Grace **VI:** Son of James Gilmore **P:** Spouse # R 4044 **BLW:** unk **RG:** N **MK:** N **PH:** N **SS:** AP Fold 3 pen rec spouse, Elizabeth **BS:** 196.

GILPIN, George; b 4 Mar 1740; d 27 Dec 1813 **RU:** Major, Served in Fairfax Co.Militia 1776-78. Was 1/Lt in independent Co of Fairfax 1775. Gave material aid to cause **CEM:** Old Christ Church Episcopal; GPS 38.80625, -77.04718; 118 N Washington St; Alexandria City **GS:** N **SP:** 1) Catherine Peters 2) Jane Peters **VI:** Records of Ct Martial of Fairfax Co Militia of 29 Oct 1776 contain charges against 11 men in Capt George Gilpin's Co. At tiime of his death, at age 72, he was Postmaster and Magistrate for Fairfax Co and Alexandria, bur with Masonic orders (Alexandria Gazette, 28 Dec 1813) **P:** unk **BLW:** unk **RG:** Y **MK:** N **PH:** N **SS:** E pg 309; R pg 7, 12, 14; CE pg 10; SAR P-166650, DAR A045281 **BS:** 20 pg 97-8.

GINBERT, Julien; b unk; d 1781 **RU:** Seaman, Served on "Citoyen" and died from Yorktown battle **CEM:** French Memorial; GPS 36.81944, -79.39933; Yorktown; York **GS:** U **SP:** No info **VI:** No further data **P:** unk **BLW:** unk **RG:** Y **MK:** unk **PH:** unk **SS:** J-Yorktown Historian; SAR P-166695 **BS:** JLARC 1, 74.

GIRARD, Joseph; b unk; d 1781 **RU:** Seaman, Served on "Citoyen" and died from Yorktown battle **CEM:** French Memorial; GPS 36.81944, -79.39933; Yorktown; York **GS:** U **SP:** No info **VI:** No further data **P:** unk **BLW:** unk **RG:** Y **MK:** unk **PH:** unk **SS:** J-Yorktown Historian; SAR P-166722 **BS:** JLARC 74.

GIRAUD, Joseph; b unk; d 1781 **RU:** Soldier, Served in Gatinais Bn and died fr battle at Yorktown **CEM:** French Memorial; GPS 36.81944, -79.39933; Yorktown; York **GS:** U **SP:** No info **VI:** No further data **P:** unk **BLW:** unk **RG:** Y **MK:** unk **PH:** unk **SS:** J-Yorktown Historian; SAR P-166726 **BS:** JLARC 1, 74.

GISH, Jacob; b 5 Feb 1761; d 2 Aug 1836 **RU:** Private, Served in Lancaster Co, PA Militia **CEM:** Daleville; GPS 37.39869, -79.91069; Roanoke Rd Rt 220 nr Kroger store, Daleville; Botetourt **GS:** Y **SP:** Mar (PA) Ann Vineyard (2 Feb 1761 Botetourt Co-Dec 1830) **VI:** Son of Christain Sr & Sophia (Hook) Gish **P:** unk **BLW:** unk **RG:** N **MK:** unk **PH:** unk **SS:** CI PA Archives 5th series Vol 14 pg 323 **BS:** 123 pg 67; 196.

GIVEN, William; b 21 Mar 1740; d 29 Sep 1793 **RU:** Private/Patriot, Served in PA Militia. Signed petition to separate Bath Co fr Augusta Co in 1779 **CEM:** Cleek; GPS 38.19310, -79.73220; Rt 220 Sam Snead Hwy, Warm Springs; Bath **GS:** N **SP:** Mar (21 Mar 1764 Augusta Co) Nancy Bratton (17Apr 1747-22 Jul 1827) d/o Robert & Ann (McFarland) Bratton **VI:** Perhaps son of John & Margaret (Sitlington) Givens (This info fr Findagrave.com. It is expected that war service, spouse, & parents are incorrect on this site

RU=Rank/Unit	CEM=Cemetery	GS=Gravestone	SP=Spousal Information
VI=Other Veteran Info	P=Pension	BLW=Bounty/Land Warrant	RG=Registered Grave
MK=SAR/DAR Marker	PH=Photo	SS=Service Source	BS=Burial Source

with that of a William Givens, not William Given. His children have surname of Given, not Givens) **P:** unk **BLW:** unk **RG:** Y **MK:** N **PH:** N **SS:** BM Gleek; CD; SAR P-166779, DAR A045500 **BS:** 159 Cleek.

GIVENS, John; b May 1740; d 13 Apr 1812 **RU:** Captain, Commanded a company Augusta Co Militia 17 Feb 1778-October 1783 Marched his unit to near Jamestown in 1781 **CEM:** Augusta Stone Presbyterian; GPS 38.23926, -78.97356, GS 38.1407,-78.5814; 28 Old Stone Church Ln, Ft Defiance; Augusta **GS:** Y **SP:** Mary Margaret Sitlington **VI:** No further data **P:** unk **BLW:** unk **RG:** N **MK:** Y SAR plaque **PH:** unk **SS:** E pg 310; G pg 470; AZ pg 122, 182 **BS:** JLARC 1, 8, 23, 62, 63; 196.

GLANET, Louis; b unk; d 1781 **RU:** Soldier, Served in Santonge Bn and died fr battle at Yorktown **CEM:** French Memorial; GPS 36.81944, -79.39933; Yorktown; York **GS:** U **SP:** No info **VI:** No further data **P:** unk **BLW:** unk **RG:** Y **MK:** unk **PH:** unk **SS:** J-Yorktown Historian; SAR P-166823 **BS:** JLARC 1, 74.

GLASCOCK, Hezekiah; b 21 Jun 1746; d 1 Aug 1818 **RU:** Patriot, Gave material aid to cause **CEM:** Clascock "Glenmore"; GPS unk; Rectortown; Fauquier **GS:** U **SP:** Sarah (-----) (__-13 Oct 1815) **VI:** No further data **P:** N **BLW:** N **RG** N **MK:** unk **PH:** unk **SS:** AL Cert & List pg 1 Fauquier Co **BS:** 196.

GLASGOW, Arthur; b 1750, Rockbridge Co; d May 1822 **RU:** Soldier, DAR application does not specify service other than soldier **CEM:** Falling Springs Presbyterian; GPS 37.68494, -79.45105; 410 Falling Springs Rd, Glasgow; Rockbridge **GS:** Y **SP:** Mar (1782) Rebeckah McCorkle (1755-Jan 1818) **VI:** No further data **P:** N **BLW:** N **RG:** N **MK:** unk **PH:** unk **SS:** DAR Ancestor #A045298 **BS:** 204.

GLASS, John; b unk, d 21 Sep 1777 **RU:** Private, Capt Moore's Co, Col William Grayson's 1st VA Regt, Cont Line **CEM:** Rev War Court House Plaque; GPSnot determined; 4110 Chain Bridge Rd; Fairfax **GS:** Memorialized on plaque 2017 by Geo Washington Chapter, VASSAR **SP** No info **VI:** Died in service **P:** N **BLW:** N **RG:** N **MK:** N **PH:** N **SS:** E pg 214; AP Fold3 muster roll provides death date: EP sources: **BS:** None.

GLASS, Joseph; b 1722, Banbridge, Co Down, N Ire; d 12 Jun 1794 **RU:** Patriot, paid personal property tax, Frederick Co, 1782, considered to be a supply tax for Rev War expenses. **CEM:** Old Opequon; GPS 39.139381, -78.194939; 217 Opequon Church Ln, Kernstown; Frederick **GS:** Unk **SP:** Mar 1759, Elizabeth Wilson (18 Jun 1741-12 Jun 1824, Scott Co, KY) **VI:** No further data **P:** N **BLW:** N **RG:** N **MK:** N **PH:** N **SS:** ER, Frederick Co, 1782 tax list **BS:** 196.

GLASSBURN, David; b 1730, Germany; d 1834 **RU:** Private, Served in Capt Arbuckle's Co, Botetourt Co Militia **CEM:** Mallow Tract; GPS unk; nr Hot Springs; Bath **GS:** U **SP:** Mar (18 Mar 1778) Elizabeth Carpenter (1758-1837) **VI:** Died in Covington, Botetourt Co **P:** unk **BLW:** unk **RG:** Y **MK:** unk **PH:** unk **SS:** J- DAR Hatcher; DD; SAR P-166874 **BS:** JLARC 2.

GLASSCOCK (GLASCOCK), George; b 1741; d 4 Mar 1826 **RU:** Patriot, Gave material aid to cause, Richmond Co **CEM:** Rockburn; GPS unk; Rockburn Farm, 224 Crenshaw Rd, Rectortown; Fauquier **GS:** Y **SP:** Hannah Rector (1750-Sep 1816) **VI:** No further data **P:** N **BLW:** N **RG:** Y **MK:** N **PH:** unk **SS:** J-NSSAR 1993 Reg; NSSAR Ancestor # P-166878 **BS:** JLARC 1; 196.

GLASSCOCK, John; b 14 Jan 1699, Richmond; d 28 Jun 1784 **RU:** Patriot, Gave material aid to cause **CEM:** Rockburn (Rachburn); GPS unk; Nr Warrenton; Fauquier **GS:** Y **SP:** Margaret O'Rear **VI:** No further data **P:** N **BLW:** N **RG:** Y **MK:** N **PH:** unk **SS:** AL lists pg 6 Fauquier Co; SAR P-166882, DAR A045279 **BS:** SAR regis.

GLASSCOCK (GLASCOCK), Thomas; b 1731; d 1793 **RU:** Lieutenant/Patriot, Gave material aid to cause **CEM:** Glasscock Family Farm; GPS unk; Nr Marshall; Fauquier **GS:** U **SP:** 1) Catherine Rector and 2) Agatha Rector **VI:** No further data **P:** unk **BLW:** unk **RG:** Y **MK:** unk **PH:** unk **SS:** NSSAR Ancestor #P-166832; AR Vol 2 pg 77; AL Ct Bk pg 25 Fauquier Co **BS:** JLARC 2.

GLEAVES, Michael; b unk; d unk **RU:** Private, Capt James Newell's Co, Montgomery Co Militia, 5 Apr 1781 **CEM:** Gleaves Farm; GPS unk; Dunkley farm, Cripple Creek; Wythe **GS:** U **SP:** No info **VI:** No further data **P:** unk **BLW:** unk **RG:** Y **MK:** unk **PH:** unk **SS:** J-NASSR 2000 Reg; G pg 226 **BS:** JLARC 76.

GLEAVES, William Benjamin; b 1750; d 1820 **RU:** First Lieutenant, Capt James Newell's Co, Montgomery Co Militia, 5 Apr 1781 **CEM:** Gleaves Farm; GPS unk; Dunkley farm, Cripple Creek; Wythe

RU=Rank/Unit	CEM=Cemetery	GS=Gravestone	SP=Spousal Information
VI=Other Veteran Info	P=Pension	BLW=Bounty/Land Warrant	RG=Registered Grave
MK=SAR/DAR Marker	PH=Photo	SS=Service Source	BS=Burial Source

158

GS: U **SP:** Mar (3 May 1770) Elizabeth Turk (c1752-1840) **VI:** Son of Matthew & Esther (-----) Gleaves **P:** unk **BLW:** unk **RG:** unk **MK:** unk **PH:** unk **SS:** G pg 226 **BS:** JLARC 40; 196.

GLENN, George; b 1720, Germany; d Feb 1815 **RU:** Private, Served in Capt Reuben Harrison's & Capt Anderson's companies, Augusta Co Militia **CEM:** Augusta Stone Presbyterian; GPS 38.23925, -78.97356; 28 Old Stone Church Ln, Ft Defiance; Augusta **GS:** U **SP:** Mary Young **VI:** Came to VA fr PA **P:** unk **BLW:** unk **RG:** unk **MK:** Y SAR **PH:** Y **SS:** AK; SAR P-329550, DAR A045511 **BS:** 04; 196.

GLOVER, Anthony; b 15 Apr 1755; d 1838 **RU:** Patriot, Gave material aid to the cause **CEM:** Anthony Glover Cem; GPS unk; Dirt lane 1 mi S of Alcoma; Buckingham **GS:** N **SP:** Ann Tyndall (1770-27 May 1838) d/o Benjamin & Anne (Lewis) Tyndall **VI:** Son of Samuel & Judith (Benning) Glover **P:** N **BLW:** N **RG:** N **MK:** N **PH:** N **SS:** AL Ct bk pg 2, 49 **BS:** 52 pg 272.

GLOVER, Joseph; b c1767; d 1792 **RU:** Private, Served in Capt Williamson's Co, VA line. Was at siege of Yorktown Oct 1781 **CEM:** Tooker Family, Brandon Home; GPS unk; 5 mi NE of Burrowsville; Prince George **GS:** Y **SP:** No info **VI:** No further data **P:** Y **BLW:** unk **RG:** N **MK:** N **PH:** unk **SS:** AJ MA Service; Cl applic for pension **BS:** 111 Part 2 pg 43.

GLOVER, Samuel Jr; b 2 Jun 1759; d 7 Jun 1820 **RU:** Soldier, Served in VA Line **CEM:** Samuel Glover; GPS unk; Rt 742; Buckingham **GS:** N **SP:** Mar (16 Oct 1782 Buckingham) Mary Tindale, (__-11 Apr 1839) **VI:** Son of Samuel & Judith (Benning) Glover. R4074 **P:** Y **BLW:** N **RG:** Y **MK:** N **PH:** N **SS:** K pg 189; CG Vol 2 pg 1368; SAR P-167136 **BS:** JLARC 4, 10, 59; 196.

GODARD, Jean; b unk; d 1781 **RU:** Soldier, Served in Beaujolais Bn and died fr battle at Yorktown **CEM:** French Memorial; GPS 36.81944, -79.39933; Yorktown; York **GS:** U **SP:** No info **VI:** No further data **P:** unk **BLW:** unk **RG:** Y **MK:** unk **PH:** unk **SS:** J-Yorktown Historian; SAR P-167180 **BS:** JLARC 1, 74.

GODEAU, Nicolas; b unk; d 1781 **RU:** Seaman, Served on "Sceptre" and died from Yorktown battle **CEM:** French Memorial; GPS 36.81944, -79.39933; Yorktown; York **GS:** U **SP:** No info **VI:** No further data **P:** unk **BLW:** unk **RG:** Y **MK:** unk **PH:** unk **SS:** J-Yorktown Historian; SAR P-167228 **BS:** JLARC 1, 74.

GODSEY, Austin; b c1752, Chester, Chesterfield Co; d c1818 **RU:** Private, Served in VA Line. Enl serv Granville Co, NC **CEM:** Godsey Family; GPS unk; Rt 613, Nickelsville; Scott **GS:** Y **SP:** Mar (30 Dec 1782 Granville Co NC) Frances "Frankey" or "Franky" Hicks (__-18 Nov 1855) **VI:** Died in Russell Co (later Scott Co). Widow appl pen 30 July 1855 Lincoln Co GA age 90. R21991. Memorialized in Scott Co on widow's GS **P:** Y **BLW:** unk **RG:** Y **MK:** Y SAR **PH:** unk **SS:** K pg 191; AK Amherst Rec; CG Vol 2 pg 1371 SAR P-329257, DAR A045969 **BS:** 04, Nov 06.

GOGGIN, Stephen Jr; b 1752 Virginia; d 1802 **RU:** First Lieutenant, Served in Bedford Co Militia. Served in 1779 as 1st Lt, marched to Charlotte, NC & served under Gen Greene **CEM:** Quaker Baptist; GPS 37.20619, -79.51623; 4665 Chestnut Fork Rd, Chestnut Fork; Bedford **GS:** Y **SP:** Rachel Moorman (1754 Hanover Co-1835 Bedford Co) d/o Thomas (1705-1767) & Rachel (Clark) (1714-1792) Moorman. No stone **VI:** Govt marker inscribed "1st Lieut Bedford Cty Mil Rev War" **P:** unk **BLW:** unk **RG:** Y **MK:** N **PH:** unk **SS:** B; AZ pg 135; SAR P-167388 **BS:** 196.

GOLDMAN, David; b unk; d 31 Dec 1778 Capt Thomas Hamilton's Co Co, Lt Col William Heths, 1st[rd] VA Regt, 1 Mar 1778 **CEM:** Rev War Court House Plaque; GPS: not determined; 4110 Chain Bridge Rd; Fairfax **GS:** Memorialized on plaque 2017 by Geo Washington Chapter, VASSAR **SP** No info **VI:** Died in service **P:** N **BLW:** N **RG:** N **MK:** N **PH:** N **SS:** E pg 214; EP sources: **BS:** None.

GOLLADAY, David; b 15 Sep 1759, Gaithersburg, Montgomery Co, MD; d 23 Sep 1823 **RU:** Major, Served as staff officer in Shenandoah Co Militia **CEM:** Leland Brown Farm; GPS unk; Nr Weyers Cave; Augusta **GS:** Y **SP:** One son by Abigail Combs out of wedlock, who was Jacob Gallady (Aug 1785-__). Mar (24 Jun 1785) Rebecca Hockman (1764-1 Oct 1840 Montgomery Co) **VI:** Son of Jacob & Elinor (-----) Galladay. Govt stone. There is an image of a fine oil portrait of him on his memorial page at findagrave.com **P:** unk **BLW:** unk **RG** Y **MK:** unk **PH:** unk **SS:** NSSAR Ancestor #P-167485; B lists serv; SAR P-167485 **BS:** JLARC 62.

RU=Rank/Unit	CEM=Cemetery	GS=Gravestone	SP=Spousal Information
VI=Other Veteran Info	P=Pension	BLW=Bounty/Land Warrant	RG=Registered Grave
MK=SAR/DAR Marker	PH=Photo	SS=Service Source	BS=Burial Source

GOLLADAY (GOLLIDAY), Jacob; b 1735, Lancaster Co, PA; d 28 Feb 1795 **RU:** Lieutenant, Served in Shenandoah Co Militia **CEM:** Dry Run Church; GPS 38.85929, -78.40075; Rt 678, 8398 Fort Valley Rd nr jct with Dry Run Rd, Seven Fountains; Shenandoah **GS:** Y gov't **SP:** Elinor (-----)(__ Lancaster Co, PA-1774) **VI:** Son of Joseph (1703-1758) & Sybilla (Kneisley) (1709-1758) Golladay **P:** unk **BLW:** unk **RG:** Y **MK:** N **PH:** Y **SS:** B Govt; E pg 314; SAR P-167486 **BS:** 32 May 11; 196.

GOLLADAY (GOLLODAY), Joseph; b 1758; d Sep 1826 **RU:** Private, Enlisted as a Private in 1776 in the Company commanded by Captain Jonathan Clark of the 8th Virginia Regiment. Served until 1779, furloughed in Fredericksburg. Was in battles of Germantown, Brandywine and Monmouth. **CEM:** Dry Run Church #2; GPS 38.85929, -78.40075; Rt 678, 8398 Fort Valley Rd nr jct with Dry Run Rd, Fort Valley; Shenandoah **GS:** Y Govt **SP:** Mar (1784 NY State) Mary Huslander or Hulslander (22 Jan 1753-__), d/o Nicholas Holtzlander (1716-1788) & Anna Magdalene Genuigh (1724-1800) **VI:** Son of Jacob Golladay (1735-1795) & Maria Holtzlander (1753-1843); Sol appl pen 27 Oct 1819 Shenandoah Co age 61. Widow appl pen 16 Mar 1839 Shenandoah Co. W7555 **P:** Y **BLW:** unk **RG:** Y **MK:** N **PH:Y SS:** E pg 314; CG Vol 2 pg 1375 Bio form submitted 2020 **BS:** 32 May 11; 196.

GOODALL, Parke; b 1742; d 1816 **RU:** Ensign, Served in an Independent Co in Hanover Co, May-Jun 1775 **CEM:** Goodall's Tavern Property; GPS unk; .75 mi W of jct Rts 623 & 33; Hanover **GS:** N **SP:** Mary (-----) **VI:** No further data **P:** unk **BLW:** unk **RG:** YMK: unk **PH:** N **SS:** CE pg 11; SAR P-167573 **BS:** JLARC 71.

GOODE, Bennett, Jr; b 1744; d 1814 **RU:** Patriot gave material aid to cause in Powhatan Co **CEM:** Goode Family; GPS not determined; Michaux; Powhatan, **GS:** Unk **SP:** Mar 1) 1770, Isabella Lewis, 2) Rebecca Baugh (1784-_) **VI:** Son of Bennett Goode (1702, Henrico Co-1771) & Martha Jefferson (17 Mar 1705-20 Oct 1796) **P:** N **BLW:** N **RG:** Y **MK:** N **PH:** N **SS:** DAR A046307 cites Member of VA Conventions 1775-1776; AL Ct Bk pg 12, List IV pgs 2,10,16; SAR P-167584 **BS:** 196.

GOODE, Francis; b 1744; d 1795 **RU:** Colonel, Capt of Militia, Chesterfield Co, Nov 1775, later obtained rank of Col **CEM:** Skinquarter Baptist; GPS 37.40916, -77.792655; 6900 Moseley Rd, Moseley; Chesterfield **GS:** Y **SP:** No info **VI:** Marker. Bur at sea **P:** unk **BLW:** unk **RG:** Y **MK:** Y **SAR PH:** N **SS:** CF pg 13; SAR P-167589 **BS:** JLARC 4, 35.

GOODE, John; b 1743; d 1838 **RU:** Private/Patriot serv in Buckingham Co Militia; gave material aid to cause **CEM:** Goode Family ; GPS not determined; Michaux; Powhatan **GS:** Unk **SP:** Mar 31 Mar 1785. Martha Embry Simmons(1753, Chesterfield Co-__) **VI:** Son of Bennett Goode (1702, Henrico Co-1771) & Martha Jefferson (17 Mar 1705-20 Oct 1796): **P:** N **BLW:** N **RG:** Y **MK:** N **PH:** N **SS:** DAR A046329; AL Ct Bk pg 12, List IV pgs 2,3,14,19; SAR P-167593 **BS:** 196.

GOODE, John; b 1738 Henrico; d 1790 **RU:** Private/Patriot, Served in Buckingham Co Militia. Gave material aid to cause **CEM:** Skinquarter Baptist; GPS 37.40916, -77.792655; 6900 Moseley Rd, Moseley; Chesterfield **GS:** N **SP:** Sarah Brown (1745-1812), d/o George & (-----) Brown **VI:** Rev Son of Benjamin Goode (c1700-aft 1764) & Susanna (-----) of Henrico Co, VA Colony. Widow pensioned commencing 27 Aug 1814 at $48 per yr **P:** Y **BLW:** N **RG:** Y **MK:** N **PH:** N **SS:** J-NASSR 2000 Reg; E pg 315; G pg 559; AG pg 264; AL Ct Bk pg 24; SAR P-167611, DAR A046326 **BS:** JLARC 76; 196.

GOODE, Robert See Appendix G Addenda)

GOODE, Samuel; b 21 Mar 1756 Whitby; d 14 Nov 1822 **RU:** Lieutenant, Served in VA Dragoons 1776-1779 **CEM:** Invernay Family Center; GPS unk; Rt 138 at Invermay PO; Mecklenburg **GS:** U **SP:** Mar (28 Sep 1786) Mary Armistead Burwell d/o of Lewis Burwell **VI:** No further data **P:** unk **BLW:** unk **RG:** Y **MK:** unk **PH:** unk **SS:** J-NASSR 2000 Reg; E pg 315; SAR P-167601 **BS:** JLARC 76.

GOODRICH, David; b unk; d 1781 **RU:** Private, Served in Capt Chapman's Co, CT Cont line. Died fr battle at Yorktown **CEM:** Yorktown Victory Monument Tablet; GPS 38.28350, -78.54150; Yorktown; York **GS:** U **SP:** No info **VI:** No further data **P:** unk **BLW:** unk **RG:** YMK: unk **PH:** unk **SS:** J-Yorktown Historian; DY pg 352; SAR P-167776 **BS:** JLARC 74.

GOODSON, Thomas H II; b 18 Aug 1755, Frederick Co, MD; d 3 Sep 1837 **RU:** Lieutenant, Served in VA Line. Ent serv Botetourt Co. Promoted to 1st Lt in Isle of Wight Co Militia; served in 7th Cont Line **CEM:** Goodson Family; GPS unk; Pine Creek, near Turtle Rock; Floyd **GS:** U **SP:** Elizabeth Pogue or

RU=Rank/Unit	CEM=Cemetery	GS=Gravestone	SP=Spousal Information
VI=Other Veteran Info	P=Pension	BLW=Bounty/Land Warrant	RG=Registered Grave
MK=SAR/DAR Marker	PH=Photo	SS=Service Source	BS=Burial Source

Poague (__-5 Feb 1837) **VI**: Son of Thomas Sr (1735-14 Mar 1815 Montgomery Co) & (-----) Goodson. Moved to New River, Augusta Co with his father when he was five yrs old. Sol appl pen 17 Dec 1832 Floyd Co. S6901 **P**: Y **BLW**: unk **RG** Y **MK**: N **PH**: unk **SS**: G pg 192-4; K pg 196; CG Vol 2 pg 1382; SAR P-167907 **BS**: JLARC 2, 4, 29.

GOODSON, Thomas Washington I; b Aug 1735, Frederick Co MD; d 11 Mar 1815 **RU**: Major/Patriot, Gave material aid to cause. Also Juror 1780 **CEM**: Pine Creek Primitive Baptist; GPS 36.94622, -80.27357; Spangler Mill Rd Rt 682; Floyd **GS**: Y **SP**: Sarah Riddle Goodson (1740-1816). Mar also Keziah Harris. **VI**: Son of Thomas and 1) (-----) Goodson. Died in Montgomery Co (now Floyd Co) **P**: unk **BLW**: unk **RG**: Y **MK**: unk **PH**: Y **SS**: AN; AL Ct Bk pg 10 Isle of Wight Co; BC Part 1 pg 329-331; SAR P-167905 **BS**: 196.

GOODWYN, Joseph; b unk; d Aft 1781 **RU**: Soldier/Patriot, Served in VA and GA. Gave material aid to cause **CEM**: Sweden Plantation; GPS 37.15854, -77.54751; Nr jct Claiborne & White Oak rds, Sutherland; Dinwiddie **GS**: N **SP**: No info **VI**: Twin brother of Peterson Goodwyn **P**: N **BLW**: unk **RG**: unk **MK**: N **PH**: N **SS**: AL Cert Dinwiddie Co **BS**: JLARC 116.

GOODWYN, Peterson; b 1745; d 21 Feb 1818 **RU**: Colonel, Served in Goodwyn's Co. Commanded co at Great Bridge. Promoted fr Capt to Col for gallantry at Battle of Great Bridge **CEM**: Sweden Plantation; GPS 37.15854, -77.54751; Nr jct Claiborne & White Oak rds, Sutherland; Dinwiddie **GS**: Y **SP**: Elizabeth Peterson (1757-1818). Her inscription is on the back of her husband's V.A. marker. Daughter of Peter Peterson & Lucy Osborn **VI**: Was an attorney, House of Delegates 1789-1802; US Congress 1803-1818. Grave has a Vet Admin marker erected in the 1990s. Listed on cenotaph at Congressional Cemetery in Washington, DC **P**: N **BLW**: unk **RG**: Y **MK**: Y SAR **PH**: unk **SS**: CD; SAR P-168070 **BS**: JLARC 2, 4, 57,116; 196.

GOODWYN (GOODWIN), Robert; b 1739, York Co; d 12 May 1789 **RU**: Patriot, Gave material aid to cause **CEM**: Goodwyn house cem; GPS unk; Rt 16, 3.4 mi fr Louisa; Louisa **GS**: U **SP**: Jane Tulloch **VI**: No further data **P**: N **BLW**: N **RG**: Y **MK**: unk **PH**: unk **SS**: D Vol II pg 625, 633; BY; SAR P-168071 **BS**: JLARC 61.

GORDON, George; b unk; d 26 Feb 1778 RU: Sergeant, Capt David Arrell's Co, Col William Heth's 3rd VA Regt 1778 **CEM**: Rev War Court House Plaque; GPS; not determined; 4110 Chain Bridge Rd; Fairfax **GS**: Memorialized on plaque 2017 by Geo Washington Chapter, VASSAR **SP** No info **VI**: Died in service **P**: N **BLW**: N **RG**: Y **MK**: N **PH**: N **SS**: A pgs 277 E pg 317; AP Fold 3 Muster roll shows death date: EP sources; SAR P-168164 **BS**: None.

GORDON, James (Col); b 2 Aug 1750; d 29 Sep 1794 **RU**: Patriot, Had public service as Sheriff of Lancaster Co 17 Oct 1782 **CEM**: Old St John's Cemetery; GPS 37.68920, -76.38530; Off Rt 1066 (Harris Rd), abt .5 mi S of DMV Dr; Lancaster **GS**: N **SP**: Ann Payne, d/o John & (-----) Payne of Goochland Co **VI**: Son of Col James Gordon (1714 Newry Ireland-2 Jun 1768 Lancaster Co) & Mary (Harrison) ((1731-May 1771). **P**: N **BLW**: N **RG**: N **MK**: unk **PH**: N **SS**: DS pg 249 **BS**: 40 pg 128; 196.

GORDON, Nathaniel; b 28 Aug 1763, Lancaster Co; d -29160 **RU**: Patriot, Gave material aid to cause **CEM**: Maplewood; GPS 38.14640, -78.20060; Rt 33 W Gordonsville; Orange **GS**: U **SP**: Mar (20 Oct 1785) Mary Gordon, d/o John & Lucy (Churchill) Gordon **VI**: Son of James & Mary (Harrison) Gordon. Founder of Gordonsville 1787 **P**: N **BLW**: N **RG**: N **MK**: unk **PH**: unk **SS**: AL Ct Bk pg 3; Commissioner's Book III pg 273 **BS**: 196.

GORDON, Thomas; b 1752, Muddy Creek, Rockingham Co; d 2 Apr 1814 **RU**: Second Lieutenant/Patriot, Served in 6th Cont Line. Gave material aid to cause **CEM**: Salem Presbyterian; GPS unk; Cooks Creek; Rockingham **GS**: U **SP**: Catherine Davis **VI**: No further data **P**: unk **BLW**: unk **RG**: Y **MK**: unk **PH**: unk **SS**: J-NASSR 2000 Reg; D Rockbridge Co; SAR P-168233 **BS**: JLARC 76.

GORDON, William, b 4 Jul 1742, Fairfax Co; d 10 Apr 1783, SC **RU**: Captain, Commanded Troop of Dragoons, Col Brandon's 2d Spartan Regt, SC Militia **CEM**: Gordon's family; GPS not determined; Maybinton, Newberry, SC **GS**: Wooden cross with names, dates **SP** No info **VI**: Died in service. Memorialized on plaque at the Fairfax County Ct House in 2017 by Geo Washington Chapter, VASSAR: **P**: N **BLW**: N **RG**: Y **MK**: N **PH**: N **SS**: E pg 318; EP sources; SAR P-168241 **BS**: 196.

RU=Rank/Unit	CEM=Cemetery	GS=Gravestone	SP=Spousal Information
VI=Other Veteran Info	P=Pension	BLW=Bounty/Land Warrant	RG=Registered Grave
MK=SAR/DAR Marker	PH=Photo	SS=Service Source	BS=Burial Source

GORE, Joshua Sr; b 1752; d 1830 **RU:** Patriot, Gave material aid to cause **CEM:** Goose Creek; GPS 39.11250, -77.69527; Rt 722, Lincoln; Loudoun **GS:** Y **SP:** No info **VI:** No further data **P:** N **BLW:** N **RG:** Y **MK:** unk **PH:** Y **SS:** AL Ct Bk pg 19, 57; Comm Bk III pg 298; SAR bio rpt submitted 28 Feb 21 **BS:** 196.

GORRELIER, Pierre; b 1752; d 1781 **RU:** Soldier, Served in Beaujolais Bn and died fr battle at Yorktown **CEM:** French Memorial; GPS 36.81944, -79.39933; Yorktown; York **GS:** U **SP:** No info **VI:** No further data **P:** unk **BLW:** unk **RG:** N **MK:** unk **PH:** unk **SS:** J-Yorktown Historian **BS:** JLARC 1, 74.

GOSSAN, Jean; b 1752; d 1781 **RU:** Seaman, Served on "Sceptre" and died from Yorktown battle **CEM:** French Memorial; GPS 36.81944, -79.39933; Yorktown; York **GS:** U **SP:** No info **VI:** No further data **P:** unk **BLW:** unk **RG:** N **MK:** unk **PH:** unk **SS:** J-Yorktown Historian **BS:** JLARC 1, 74.

GOULD, William; b 1752; d 1781 **RU:** Soldier, Served fr MA and died as result of Yorktown battle **CEM:** Yorktown Victory Monument Tablet; GPS 38.28350, -78.54150; Yorktown; York **GS:** U **SP:** No info **VI:** No further data **P:** unk **BLW:** unk **RG:** N **MK:** unk **PH:** unk **SS:** J-Yorktown Historian **BS:** JLARC 74.

GOUYA, Antoine; b 1752; d 1781 **RU:** Soldier, Served in Gatinais Bn and died fr battle at Yorktown **CEM:** French Memorial; GPS 36.81944, -79.39933; Yorktown; York **GS:** U **SP:** No info **VI:** No further data **P:** unk **BLW:** unk **RG:** N **MK:** unk **PH:** unk **SS:** J-Yorktown Historian **BS:** JLARC 1, 74.

GOUZER, Albin; b 1752; d 1781 **RU:** Seaman, Served on "Citoyen" and died from Yorktown battle **CEM:** French Memorial; GPS 36.81944, -79.39933; Yorktown; York **GS:** U **SP:** No info **VI:** No further data **P:** unk **BLW:** unk **RG:** Y **MK:** unk **PH:** unk **SS:** J-Yorktown Historian; SAR P-168645 **BS:** JLARC 1, 4.

GRADY, James Sr; b 1747; d 9 Jan 1815 **RU:** Private, Served in 6th & 10th Va Cont Lines. Signed for clothing in 1779, perhaps for unit **CEM:** Ebenezer Baptist; GPS 39.05824, -77.84142; 20421 Airmont Rd, Bluemont; Loudoun **GS:** Y **SP:** Susanna Butcher (1754-26 Feb 1818) **VI:** Died in Bloomfield, Loudoun Co **P:** unk **BLW:** unk **RG:** Y **MK:** Y SAR plaque **PH:** unk **SS:** E pg 319; SAR P-336620 **BS:** 25 pg 116; 196.

GRAHAM, Andrew; b 1757; d 1823 **RU:** Private?, Served in 2d VA Regt Jan 1777 **CEM:** Old Lebanon; GPS 38.08090, -79.37545; Off Rt 42, Craigsville; Augusta **GS:** Y **SP:** Elizabeth (Warren) Cooper, widow of John Cooper **VI:** No further data **P:** unk **BLW:** unk **RG:** Y **MK:** Y SAR **PH:** unk **SS:** CI Numbered Record Book; SAR P-168809 **BS:** 04; 196.

GRAHAM, David; b 1758; d Oct 1803 **RU:** Soldier, Service information not determined **CEM:** Old Presbyterian Meeting House; GPS 38.48528, -77.23532; 323 S Fairfax St; Alexandria City **GS:** N **SP:** No info **VI:** Died of fever, bur 8 Oct 1803, age 45. Listed on SAR plaque in cemetery **P:** unk **BLW:** unk **RG:** Y **MK:** Y SAR plaque **PH:** N **SS:** J-NSSAR 1993 Reg; AK **BS:** JLARC 1; 23 pg 102; 196.

GRAHAM, Michael; b 6 Apr 1758, Lancaster Co, PA; d 18 May 1834 **RU:** Private, Served in PA & VA Line. Lived Paxton Twp, Lancaster Co, PA at enl. Moved to Rockbridge Co VA 1777 and Ent serv there again **CEM:** Longwood; GPS 37.34170, -79.51190; Nr jct Oakwood & Longwood Ave Rt 122; Bedford City **GS:** Y **SP:** Mar (Feb 1786 Rockbridge Co) Elizabeth Lyle **VI:** Sol appl pen 24 Dec 1832 Bedford Co. S8621. Was Bedford Co Magistrate 17 or 18 yrs, and High Sheriff of county. In 1832, was Escheator & Commissioner of Revenue **P:** unk **BLW:** unk **RG:** Y **MK:** N **PH:** unk **SS:** J- DAR Hatcher; K pg 202; CG Vol 2 pg 1400; SAR P-168885, DAR A046765 **BS:** JLARC 2.

GRAHAM, Robert; b 1750, Ireland; d 9 May 1811 **RU:** Private, LT, Served in Capt Baskin's Co, Augusta Co Militia **CEM:** Horseshoe Bend, Graham Family; GPS 36.94917, -80.90010; N side of Reed Creek on Formato Dr nr jct with E Lee Hwy; Wythe **GS:** U **SP:** 1) Mary Craig (1750 Ireland-26 Oct 1786) 2) Mary Cowen (17 Jun 1768-28 Dec 1819, Locust Hill, Wythe Co) **VI:** DAR marker **P:** unk **BLW:** unk **RG:** Y **MK:** Y SAR **PH:** unk **SS:** E pg 320; SAR P-168900, DAR A046787 **BS:** JLARC 123; 196.

GRAHAM, William; b 19 Dec 1746, PA; d 8 Jun 1799 **RU:** Captain, Led troops to Rockfish Gap in search of Tarleton. Later joined LaFayette **CEM:** Washington & Lee Univ Campus; GPS 36.60863, -81.01593; Nr Jefferson St; Lexington City **GS:** Y **SP:** No info **VI:** Was rector of Washington Academy in Rockbridge Co for 24 yrs. Rev Graham was 1st Rector of Liberty Hall, later to become Washington & Lee University. Died in Richmond. First bur at St John's Church, Richmond, but later reburied on

RU=Rank/Unit	CEM=Cemetery	GS=Gravestone	SP=Spousal Information
VI=Other Veteran Info	P=Pension	BLW=Bounty/Land Warrant	RG=Registered Grave
MK=SAR/DAR Marker	PH=Photo	SS=Service Source	BS=Burial Source

162

campus of Washington & Lee Univ **P:** unk **BLW:** unk **RG:** Y **MK:** Y SAR **PH:** unk **SS:** AD; SAR P-168926 **BS:** JLARC 1, 79.

GRAHAM, William; b 1746; d 1799 **RU:** Private, Served in Capt Benjamin Bartholaman's Co of Foot, 5th VA Regt, commanded by Col Thomas Johnson, July 1777 **CEM:** St John's Episcopal; GPS 37.53183, -77.41958; 2401 E Broad St; Richmond City **GS:** Y **SP:** No info **VI:** No further data **P:** unk **BLW:** unk **RG:** N **MK:** N **PH:** unk **SS:** AP **BS:** 28 pg 448.

GRANBON, Claude; b unk; d 1781 **RU:** Soldier, Served in Soissonnais Bn and died fr battle at Yorktown **CEM:** French Memorial; GPS 36.81944, -79.39933; Yorktown; York **GS:** U **SP:** No info **VI:** No further data **P:** unk **BLW:** unk **RG:** Y **MK:** unk **PH:** unk **SS:** J-Yorktown Historian; SAR P-168963 **BS:** JLARC 1, 74.

GRANDSTAFF (GRINSTAFF), George; b 8 Aug 1741, Lancaster Co, PA; d 15 May 1823 **RU:** Private/Patriot, Gave material aid to cause **CEM:** Grandstaff Family; GPS unk; Narrow Pass Creek; Shenandoah **GS:** Y **SP:** Magdalina Hough **VI:** No further data **P:** unk **BLW:** unk **RG:** Y **MK:** Y SAR **PH:** unk **SS:** E pg 330; AL Ct Bk pg 7, 12; SAR P-168970, DAR A046899 **BS:** 04.

GRANDY, James; b unk; d 1781 **RU:** Soldier, Served fr MA and died as result of Yorktown battle **CEM:** Yorktown Victory Monument Tablet; GPS 38.28350, -78.54150; Yorktown; York **GS:** U **SP:** No info **VI:** No further data **P:** unk **BLW:** unk **RG:** Y **MK:** unk **PH:** unk **SS:** J-Yorktown Historian; SAR P-168976 **BS:** JLARC 74.(**GRANT,** David See Appendix G Addenda **GRANT,** John See Appendix G Addenda)

GRAVELY, Joseph; b 10 Jan 1744, Hartfordshire, England; d 3 Oct 1844 **RU:** Private, Served in Capt James Tarrant's Co Henry Co Militia. Fought at Guilford CH **CEM:** Leatherwood Plantation; GPS 36.44534, -79.4558; Nr Martinsville; Henry **GS:** N **SP:** Eleanor Cox **VI:** Died in Leatherwood **P:** unk **BLW:** unk **RG:** Y**MK:** Y **PH:** N **SS:** G pg 181; J- DAR Hatcher; SAR P-169228, DAR A047172 **BS:** JLARC 2.

GRAVES, John; b 1760, Culpeper Co; d 1828 **RU:** Private, Served fr Orange Co. Was at Yorktown. Guarded prisoners that were taken **CEM:** Graves Family; GPS unk; Property records may reveal location within County; Madison **GS:** U **SP:** Mar (25 Nov 1788) Elizabeth Eddins (c1770, Culpeper Co-1828) d/o Joseph (c1745 Culpeper Co-Jun 1825 Orange Co) & Sarah (Blakey) (c1749 Middlesex Co-1790 Orange Co 1790) Eddins **VI:** No further data **P:** unk **BLW:** unk **RG:**Y **MK:** unk **PH:** unk **SS:** J- DAR Hatcher; DA pg 49 & 89; SAR P-169306 **BS:** JLARC 2.

GRAY, Daniel, b 1763; d 17 Jan 1844 **RU:** Private, ent serv Leesburg, 1779, Lee's Legion, VA Line, serving 3 yrs **CEM:** Union Church; GPS 38.746441, -78.642544; Main St, Mount Jackson; Shenandoah **GS:** Y **SP:** Polly (_) (1773-17 Sep 1837) **VI:** Rec'd BLW 8 Oct 1792 #12153 and pen # FS39621, R1113 **P:** N **BLW:** N **RG:** Y **MK:** Y DAR & SAR granite **PH:** N **SS:** G pg 650; K vol l2, pg 205; CG pg 1411; SAR P-169403 **BS:**196

GRAY, Francis; b 22 Oct 1759 Stafford; d 24 Apr 1827 **RU:** Lieutenant, Served in Cont & VA Lines. Enl serv Culpeper Co. Lost hearing fr sword wound at Battle of Lanneau's Ferry, SC **CEM:** Old City; GPS 37.41472, -79.15667; 401 Taylor St; Lynchburg City **GS:** U **SP:** Mar (23 Jun 1785 Culpeper Co) Eleanor Hening or Henning, d/o David & Mary (-----) Hening or Henning (1764-31 Aug 1839) **VI:** Widow appl pen 15 Aug 1838 Lynchburg City age 74. W7575. Recd BLW #873-200-24 Jun 1793. VA 1/2 Pay. In 1820 sol stated he was age 62 **P:** Y **BLW:** Y **RG:** Y **MK:** Y SAR plaque **PH:** unk **SS:** J-NSSAR 1993 Reg, J-DAR Hatcher; K pg 205; CG Vol 2 pg 1411; SAR P-169423 **BS:** JLARC 1, 2.

GRAY, James; b unk; d Dec 83 **RU:** Captain, Had sea serv as 2nd Lt on ship "Liberty" 27 Mar 1776. In 2nd overseas voyage in "Liberty" it was commanded by Capt J. Gray. Later he was Commander of "Cormorant" **CEM:** St John's Episcopal; GPS 37.53183, -77.41958; 2401 E Broad St; Richmond City **GS:** N **SP:** No info **VI:** R56 also VA 1/2 Pay (see Acc #837 VA State Navy, YS File VA 1/2 Pay). BLW #8026 for 4677 acres issued to heirs 16 Sep 1834. George W. Mallicote was estate admin and granted BLW 2026 for sailor's heirs 1846, who were granted 1/2 pay pension 1847 **P:** Y **BLW:** Y **RG:**N **MK:** Y SAR **PH:** N **SS:** AK; N pg 193; K pg 206; CG Vol 2 pg 1412 **BS:** 04; 28 pg 448.

GRAY(GREY), Daniel; b 1764; d 17 Jan 1844 **RU:** Private, Served in VA Line. Ent serv Leesburg VA. Served in Lee's Legion & 3rd Lt Dragoons. Served three yrs in Cont Line **CEM:** Union Church; GPS

RU=Rank/Unit	CEM=Cemetery	GS=Gravestone	SP=Spousal Information
VI=Other Veteran Info	P=Pension	BLW=Bounty/Land Warrant	RG=Registered Grave
MK=SAR/DAR Marker	PH=Photo	SS=Service Source	BS=Burial Source

38.44480, -78.38350; Mt Jackson nr jct Main St & Bridge St; Shenandoah **GS:** Y **SP:** Polly (-----) (c1766-__) **VI:** Sol appl 28 May 1818 Shenandoah Co age 56.S39621. Source 1 has burial at Mt Calvary Baptist Church Cem. Heirs recd bounty land in 1840. DAR Plaque by headstone **P:** Y **BLW:** Y **RG:** Y **MK:** Y SAR **PH:** unk **SS:** J-NSSAR 1993 Reg; J- DAR Hatcher; E pg 322; CG Vol 2 pg 1411; SAR P-169403 **BS:** JLARC 1, 2.

GRAY, Robert, b 1755, d 1826 Private, Capt Thomas Bowyer's Co, 8th VA Regt commanded by Col James Wood- muster roll of Jan 1777. Served 3 years including 4th and 12th Cont lines **CEM:** Mount Hebron; GPS 39.10916,-78.09497; 305 E Boscawen St; Winchester City; **GS:** unk **SP:** No spousal date **VI:** Awarded 100 acres BLW **P:** N **BLW:** Yes **RG:** N **MK:** N **PH:** N **SS:** C pg 436; E pg 322;F pg 32; O-Fold3 service index cards and Muster Roll; **BS:** 196

GRAYSON, Spencer; b 1734; d Dec 1792 **RU:** Chaplain, Served as Chaplain in Grayson's Regt May 1777 **CEM:** Grayson; GPS 38.64775, -77.27648; West Longview Dr, Woodbridge; Prince William **GS:** Y **SP:** No info **VI:** Son of Benjamin (1684-1757) & Susannah Monroe Tyler (Linton) (1695-1752) Grayson. SAR marker **P:** unk **BLW:** unk **RG:**Y **MK:** Y **PH:** Y **SS:** E pg 323; SAR bio rpt submitted May 2020 **BS:** JLARC 4.

GRAYSON, William; b 1736 Prince William Co.; d 12 Mar 1790 **RU:** Lieutenant Colonel, Was Capt of Independent Co of Cadets 1774-75 and Col of Prince William District Bn. Resigned 21 Mar 1776 **CEM:** Grayson; GPS 38.64775, -77.27648; West Longview Dr, Woodbridge; Prince William **GS:** Y **SP:** Eleanor Smallwood **VI:** Son of Benjamin (1684-1757) & Susannah (Monroe) Tyler Linton (1695-1752) Grayson. Assistant Secretary to Gen George Washington 21 Jun 1776. DAR plaque; He was one of the first two US senators fr VA **P:** unk **BLW:** Y **RG:** Y **MK:** Y SAR granite, DAR plaque **PH:** Y **SS:** CE pg 9, 22; SAR P-169634, DAR A047840 **BS:** JLARC 3.

GRAYSON, William; b 25 Nov 1732, Spotsylvania Co; d 17 May 1829 **RU:** Captain, Served in Cont Army & VA Militia. Was Capt in Albemarle Co Militia and Signer of Leedstown Resolutions fr Spotsylvania Co **CEM:** Carver; GPS 38.52735, -77.56054; Rt 610 vic jct with Rt 612; Prince William **GS:** Y **SP:** Elizabeth Smith **VI:** Son of Ambrose & Alice (Sharpe) Grayson. He died in Albemarle Co **P:** unk **BLW:** unk **RG:** N **MK:** unk **PH:** unk **SS:** E pg 323; BQ **BS:** 196.

GREEN, Abraham; b 1705, Charles City Co, d 1793 **RU:** Patriot, gave material aid to cause; Amelia Co **CEM:** Green Family; GPS not determined; Rt 622 on land he purchased from John Talley on 9 Oct 1733;Amelia **GS:** Unk **SP:** Elizabeth Aubyn Cowles **VI:** Son of Thomas Green (1635, Dinwiddie Co-1714) & Martha Elizabeth Filmer (1640-1714) **P:** N **BLW:** N **RG:** N **MK:** N **PH:** N **SS:** AL Ct Bk pgs 42,43,Amelia Co **BS:** 196

GREEN. Berryman; b 26 Jan 1754, Westmoreland Co, d 14 Sep 1825 **RU:** Captain; was this rank 1 Jan 1778 to 9 Apr 1779. Serving as Qtr Master and Paymaster, 31 Mar 1777, 1st Regt Light Dragoons, Cont Army, commanded by Col Theodore Bland **CEM:** Terry Family; GPS 36.749225,-78.848479; 1154 N Terrys Bridge Rd (Rt 613); Halifax **GS:** Y Gov't **SP:** Mar 25 May 1778, Anne Pritchard, 2) mar 16 Jan 1789, Nancy Terry (1758-14 Sep 1836), daug Col Nathaniel Terry & Sarah Royall (1731-1805) **VI:** Son of Thomas Green & Lucy Davis. Awarded in Nov 1808, 4000 acres BLW # 8210 **P:** N **BLW:** Y **RG:** N **MK:** N **PH:** N **SS:** C pg 98; E pg 323; G pgs 304, 404; DAR A046835 **BS:** 196

GREEN, Francis; b 1720, Bucks Co, PA, d 1788 **RU:** Patriot, Supported cause by paying a personal property tax in Rockingham Co in1783, considered a supply tax for Rev War expenses **CEM:** Coffman Farm; GPS 38.476359, -78.859336; 2985 Kratzer Rd (Rt 753); Harrisonburg City **GS:** Unk but FAG photo shows many dug up stones **SP:** Margaret (-----) (__-Sep 1743) **VI:** Son of James Green and a daug of Ellis Lewis, who was a widow with married name Large. He petitioned to build a mill on Brooks Creek in 1750 **P:** N **BLW:** N **RG:** Y **MK:** N **PH:** No **SS:** Lib VA Reel 304,1783; DAR # A210702; SAR P-337059 **BS:** 196

GREEN, Fortunatus; b 6 Apr 1754; d unk **RU:** Sergeant, Served in VA Line. Ent serv Hanover Co **CEM:** Green; GPS unk; Greenlands Farm, abt 4 mi N Ashland; Hanover **GS:** N **SP:** Sarah White (16 Jul 1760-27 Jan 1825) **VI:** Sol appl pen 7 Jun 1833 Hanover Co age 79. S15155 **P:** Y **BLW:** unk **RG:** Y **MK:** unk **PH:** N **SS:** CG Vol 2 pg 1419; SAR P-169754 **BS:** JLARC 4, 71; 196.

RU=Rank/Unit	CEM=Cemetery	GS=Gravestone	SP=Spousal Information
VI=Other Veteran Info	P=Pension	BLW=Bounty/Land Warrant	RG=Registered Grave
MK=SAR/DAR Marker	PH=Photo	SS=Service Source	BS=Burial Source

164

GREEN, John; b 1730, Liberty Hall; d 1793 **RU:** Colonel, Capt, Maj. LtCol 1st, 10th, 6th VA Regt 16 Sep 1775. Promoted to Maj 13 Aug 1776. Wounded at Mamaroneck 21 Oct 1776. Was Lt Col 1st VA, 22 Mar 1777 and Col 10th VA Regt 26 Jan 1778. Fought at Brandywine, Monmouth, Guilford CH. Retired 1783 **CEM:** Arlington National; GPS 38.88377, -77.06535; Jefferson Davis Hwy Rt 110; Arlington **GS:** Y Lot 503, Officer Sect **SP:** Susannah Blackwell (1739-1791) **VI:** BLW #866-500-20 Sep 1800. Died in Liberty Hall, Culpeper Co. Reinterred to Arlington National cem on 23 Apr 1931 in Sec 1, lot 503. He is one of eleven Rev War veterans bur there **P:** unk **BLW:** Y **RG:** Y **MK:** Y SAR **PH:** unk **SS:** J-NSSAR 1993 Reg, J- DAR Hatcher; CG Vol 2 pg 1422; SAR P-169840, DAR A047133 **BS:** JLARC 1, 2.

GREEN, John; b 1747, Amelia Co; d 22 Jan 1798 **RU:** Patriot, Gave material aid to cause **CEM:** Green Family; GPS unk; Rt 622; Amelia **GS:** N **SP:** Mar 5 Dec 1772 (bond) in Brunswick Co to Dolly Jones, b. c1754, d 14 Jun 1847 Lunenburg Co **VI:** Son of William (1705-1747) & Amey (Clay) (1708-1774) Green. Died in Brunswick Co **P:** N **BLW:** N **RG:** Y **MK:** unk **PH:** N **SS:** AL Ct Bk 1 pg 25, 59, II pg 34; SAR P-169846 **BS:** 196.

GREEN, John; b unk; d 1827 **RU:** Patriot, Gave material aid to the cause **CEM:** Goose Creek; GPS 39.11250, -77.69527; Rt 722, Lincoln; Loudoun **GS:** Y **SP:** No info **VI:** No further data **P:** N **BLW:** N **RG:** N **MK:** N **PH:** unk **SS:** AL Ct bk lt 46 **BS:** 25 pg 120.

GREEN, Joseph; b unk; d 1782 **RU:** Private, Served in 6th Cont Line **CEM:** Spears Family; GPS unk; N of Edom Rt 42 7.3 mi; Rockingham **GS:** Y **SP:** 1) Mar (1794 Rockingham Co) Amelia Matthews d/o Solloman & (-----) Matthews 2) Mar (1809 Rockingham Co) Mary Blain d/o Joseph & (-----) Blain **VI:** No further data **P:** unk **BLW:** unk **RG:**N **MK:** N **PH:** unk **SS:** AK; E pg 324 **BS:** 04; 191 Spears fam.

GREEN, Samuel; b unk; d 1822 **RU:** 2d Lt, Appointed 2nd Lt Amelia Co Militia 23 Apr 1778 **CEM:** Fairfax Meeting House; GPS 39.18557, -77.60589; Water St & Waterford Rd, Waterford; Loudoun **GS:** Y **SP:** No info **VI:** No further data **P:** unk **BLW:** unk **RG:** N **MK:** N **PH:** unk **SS:** AZ pg 178; E pg 324 **BS:** 25 pg 121.

GREEN, Thomas; b unk; d 30 Apr 1791 **RU:** Patriot, Gave material aid to cause **CEM:** Green Family; GPS unk; Rt 622; Amelia **GS:** N **SP:** No info **VI:** Son of William (1705-1747) & Amey (Clay) (1708-1774) Green **P:** N **BLW:** N **RG:** N **MK:** unk **PH:** N **SS:** AL Ct Bi II pg 10 **BS:** 196.

GREEN, William; b unk; d 1790 **RU:** Private/Patriot, Served in 1st, 4th, 5th, 11th, 14th & 15th Cont Lines. Gave material aid to cause **CEM:** Green Family; GPS unk; Rt 622; Amelia **GS:** N **SP:** Obedience Green (first cousin). She mar Richard Foster in 1793 after William Green's death. **VI:** Son of William Green (1705-1747) & Amey (Clay) (1708-1774) Green. Died in "Greenland." Widow recd pen commencing 8 Dec 1813 at $48 per yr **P:** Y **BLW:** N **RG:** N **MK:** unk **PH:** N **SS:** E pg 325; AG pg 264; AL Ct Bk 1, pg 6, 43, 48 Amelia Co **BS:** 196.

GREEN (GREENE), Berryman; b 26 Jan 1754, Westmoreland Co; d 14 Sep 1825 **RU:** Captain, As 1st Lt was Paymaster, 1st Cont Dragoons, 31 Mar 1777 Westmoreland Co. Appt Capt 31 Mar 1777; resigned 1779; Asst. Deputy QM 1781. Aide to Washington 1776. Deputy Sheriff Charlotte Co 1780 **CEM:** Terry Family; GPS unk; 1154 N Terry Rd, Halifax; Halifax **GS:** U **SP:** 1 Anne Pritchard, 2 Mar (6 Jan 1789) Nancy Terry (__ Halifax Co-20 Feb 1836, Green's Folly, Halifax Co) **VI:** Recd BLW 4000 acres **P:** N **BLW:** Y **RG:** Y **MK:** unk **PH:** N **SS:** J-NSSAR 1993 Reg; J- DAR Hatcher; E pg 323; BY; SAR P-170068, DAR A046835 **BS:** JLARC 1, 2; 196.

GREENHOW, John; b 12 Nov 1724, England; d 1787 **RU:** Patriot, Gave material aid to the cause **CEM:** Bruton Parish Church; GPS 37.27127, -76.70248; 331 W Duke of Gloucester St; Williamsburg City **GS:** Y **SP:** 1) Mar (29 Nov 1759, Williamsburg) Judith Davenport (1738-1765) 2) Elizabeth Tyler (1744-1781) **VI:** No further data **P:** unk **BLW:** unk **RG:** N **MK:** N **PH:** unk **SS:** AL Ct Bk pg 4, 8 **BS:** 26 pg 105.

GREENHOW, Robert; b 11 May 1761 Williamsburg; d Jun 1840 **RU:** Private?, In 1775 was in volunteer unit with other youth in Williamsburg under Capt Henry Nicholson to retrieve powder fr magazine that Dunmore was abt to take **CEM:** Shockoe Hill; GPS 37.55190, -77.43170; SAR monument 37.551247,-77.432429; gravestone 37.551798, -77.431931 4th & Hospital Sts; Richmond City **GS:** Y **SP:** Mar (1 Jul 1786, St John's Episcopal Church) Mary Ann Wills (4 May 1768, Fluvanna Co-26 Dec 1811, in the Richmond Theatre fire) d/o Elias & (-----) Wills of Richmond **VI:** No further data **P:** unk **BLW:** unk **RG:** Y **MK:** Y monument **PH:** Y **SS:** C pg 558; SAR P-250374 **BS:** 57 pg 20.

RU=Rank/Unit	CEM=Cemetery	GS=Gravestone	SP=Spousal Information
VI=Other Veteran Info	P=Pension	BLW=Bounty/Land Warrant	RG=Registered Grave
MK=SAR/DAR Marker	PH=Photo	SS=Service Source	BS=Burial Source

GREENWAY, James; b 1720, Cumbria, England; d 1797 **RU:** Patriot, Gave material aid to cause **CEM:** The Grove; GPS unk; Rt 662, 12 mi S of Dinwiddie; Dinwiddie **GS:** Y **SP:** Martha Dixon **VI:** Botanist, physician, surveyor, miller & planter. Came to Virginia c1758 where he is first found in Sussex Co records. Justice of Dinwiddie Co **P:** N **BLW:** N **RG:** N **MK:** N **PH:** unk **SS:** AL Ct Justice; Ct Bk pg 32 Dinwiddie Co **BS:** 70 pg 147; 166; 196.

GREER, Moses Sr; b 2 Jun 1744, Baltimore Co, MD; d 10 May 1834 Gogginsville (now Rocky Mount), Franklin Co **RU:** Ent serv Bedford Co (now Franklin Co); Commissioned Lt of Militia (1779) of Grayson Co; Lt of VA Troops (1780) & Captain of Bedford (Franklin) Co Militia (1781) by Gen. Thomas Jefferson. Served in VA Lines under William Leftwich & Charles Lynch Regts; **CEM:** Greer Family; GPS unk; .5 mi W of Rts 812 & 919; (Gogginsville) Rocky Mount **GS:** U **SP:** 1 Mar (1766) (Ann) Nancy Bailey **VI:** After Rev War, elected to State Legislature from Franklin Co (9 yrs); was presiding Judge of Franklin County Ct; Sol appl pen 12 Sep 1832, Bedford Co S 58609 **P:** Y **BLW:** unk **RG:** Y **MK:** unk **PH:** unk **SS:** K pg 213; CG Vol 2 1431; DAR A048070; SAR P-170337 **BS:** JLARC 4,2 0.

GREEVER (GREWER), Phillip Sr; b 2 Oct 1745 Holland; d 26 Mar 1830 **RU:** Soldier/Patriot, Served in VA Militia under Col Campbell. Fired 1st shot at Battle of Kings Mtn, 7 Oct 1780. Was Overseer of Roads Washington Co 1743 **CEM:** Old Grewer (Greever) Burial Ground; GPS 36.79250, -81.69860; W end of Skyview Dr, Chilhowie; Smyth **GS:** U **SP:** Mar (1773) Margaret Bosang (1758, Augusta Co-6 Mar 1831) **VI:** See entry, same name, Washington Co (memorial placed by descendants) **P:** unk **BLW:** unk **RG:** Y **MK:** unk **PH:** unk **SS:** B-Memorial stone; CV pg 204; SAR P-170547 **BS:** JLARC 2114; 78 pg 173; 196.

GREGG, John; b 16 Jan 1733, Chester Co, PA; d 9 Sep 1804 **RU:** Ensign, Served in Col McGaw's 6th Regt, PA Cont Line **CEM:** Goose Creek; GPS 39.11250, -77.69527; Rt 722, Lincoln; Loudoun **GS:** Y **SP:** Ruth Smith (6 Jun 1734 New Garden, PA-9 Sep 1804) **VI:** Son of Thomas (1703-1748) & Dinah (Harlan) (1707-1763) Gregg **P:** unk **BLW:** unk **RG:** N **MK:** unk **PH:** unk **SS:** Fold 3 Muster Roll **BS:** 196.

GREGG, John C; b 1756; d 1 Oct 1825 **RU:** Private, Served in Capt Francis Willis's Co, Col William Grayson's Regt, Jan 1777-Mar 1778 **CEM:** Goose Creek; GPS 39.11250, -77.69527; Rt 722, Lincoln; Loudoun **GS:** Y **SP:** No info **VI:** Son of John (1733-1804) & Ruth (Smith) (1734-1763) Gregg **P:** unk **BLW:** unk **RG:** N **MK:** unk **PH:** unk **SS:** Fold 3 Muster Roll **BS:** 196.

GREGORY, Roger; b 1 May 1729 King William Co; d 2 Oct 1803 **RU:** Patriot, Gave 550# beef for Cont use **CEM:** Gregory Family; GPS unk; Jct Rts 655 & 657; Mecklenburg **GS:** Y **SP:** Mar (31 Mar 1776) Fanny Garland Lory (__-30 Jun 1816) **VI:** No further data **P:** N **BLW:** N **RG:** N **MK:** N **PH:** unk **SS:** AL Ct Bk pg 6; DB pg 20 **BS:** 54 pg 255.

GRENON, Andre; b unk; d 1781 **RU:** Seaman, Served on "Duc De Bourgogne" and died from Yorktown battle **CEM:** French Memorial; GPS 36.81944, -79.39933; Yorktown; York **GS:** U **SP:** No info **VI:** No further data **P:** unk **BLW:** unk **RG:** Y **MK:** unk **PH:** unk **SS:** J-Yorktown Historian; SAR P-170519 **BS:** JLARC 1, 74.

GREROUA, Jean; b unk; d 1781 **RU:** Seaman, Served on "Diademe" and died from Yorktown battle **CEM:** French Memorial; GPS 36.81944, -79.39933; Yorktown; York **GS:** U **SP:** No info **VI:** No further data **P:** unk **BLW:** unk **RG:** Y **MK:** unk **PH:** unk **SS:** J-Yorktown Historian; SAR P-170520 **BS:** JLARC 1, 74.

GRICE, Joseph; b 1759; d 20 Aug 1820 **RU:** Private, Served in 5th VA Regt, Sep 1782 **CEM:** Trinity Episcopal; GPS 36.83459, -76.30105; 500 Court St; Portsmouth City **GS:** U **SP:** Mary (-----) (1757-2 Dec 1838) **VI:** No further data **P:** unk **BLW:** unk **RG:** Y **MK:** Y SAR plaque **PH:** unk **SS:** AP-roll; SAR P-170564, DAR A047967 **BS:** 57.

GRIFFIN, Cyrus; b 16 Jul 1748, Farnham, Richmond Co; d 14 Dec 1810 **RU:** Patriot, Gave material aid to cause. Was member VA House of Delegates 1777-78, 1786-87. Was member of Cont Congress 1787-88 and president Cont Congress 1788 **CEM:** Bruton Parish Church; GPS 37.27127, -76.70248; 331 W Duke of Gloucester St; Williamsburg City **GS:** U **SP:** Mar (c1779, Scotland) Lady Christina Stuart (1752, Scotland-8 Oct 1807, Williamsburg) **VI:** President of Ct of Admiralty. Commissioner to Creek nation. Judge of US District Ct of VA fr Dec 1789 until death. Died in Yorktown **P:** N **BLW:** N **RG:** N **MK:** unk **PH:** unk **SS:** DD **BS:** 201 pg 7389, 7390. **SEE APPENDIX G**

RU=Rank/Unit	CEM=Cemetery	GS=Gravestone	SP=Spousal Information
VI=Other Veteran Info	P=Pension	BLW=Bounty/Land Warrant	RG=Registered Grave
MK=SAR/DAR Marker	PH=Photo	SS=Service Source	BS=Burial Source

GRIFFIN, Henry; b unk; d 1812 **RU:** Captain, Service information not given in WPA report and not found **CEM:** Tapp & Griffin Families; **GPS** unk; Vic Amissville; Rappahannock **GS:** Y **SP:** No info **VI:** No further data **P:** unk **BLW:** unk **RG:** N **MK:** N **PH:** unk **SS:** BO WPA report **BS:** 163 Tapp.

GRIFFIN, Thomas; b unk; d 25 Oct 1843 **RU:** Private, Served in Capt Nicolas Cabell's Co, Albemarle Co Militia, Apr 1776 **CEM:** Shockoe Hill; **GPS** 37.55190, -77.43170; 4th & Hospital Sts; Richmond City **GS:** U **SP:** no info **VI:** GS indicates death date **P:** unk **BLW:** unk **RG:** Y **MK:** Y SAR headstone marker, name on monument **PH:Y SS:** DC pg 154 SAR P-35072 **BS:** 196.

GRIFFITH, Benjamin; b c1775(?), Bedford Co; d 26 Nov 1830 **RU:** Ensign/Patriot, Appt 23 Nov 1778, Franklin Co Militia. Paid supply tax in Franklin Co 1783 **CEM:** Overfelt; **GPS** 37.07377, -79.94785; Grassy Hill Rd, Helm; Franklin **GS:** U **SP:** Mar (c1774) Catherine (----) (1756-1829) **VI:** No further data **P:** unk **BLW:** unk **RG:** N **MK:** unk **PH:** unk **SS:** E pg 348 **BS:** 32, 196.

GRIGG, Abner; b 1720, Londonderry, Ireland; d 1795 **RU:** Private, Was an Artificer in an artillery unit of VA State Line **CEM:** Goshen Family; **GPS** unk; 8 mi S of Petersburg and W of Old Stage Rd on the "Goshen" site; Dinwiddie **GS:** U **SP:** Mar (1744) Mary Stokes (c1726-1782) **VI:** Recd BLW of 100 acres **P:** N **BLW:** Y **RG:** Y **MK:** N **PH:** unk **SS:** AR Vol 2 pg 96; C pg 203, 342; F pg 31; SAR P-170850 **BS:** JLARC 2.

GRIGG, Burwell; b 1741; d 1805 **RU:** First Lieutenant, Recommended 1st Lt Brunswick Co Militia 25 Oct 1779 **CEM:** Grigg Family; **GPS** unk; Jarratt; Greensville **GS:** Y **SP:** Sabra Elam **VI:** No further data **P:** unk **BLW:** unk **RG:** Y **MK:** unk **PH:** Y **SS:** G pg 78 SAR P-170851, DAR A048434 **BS:** 196.

GRIGG, William Sr; b 3 Dec 1745, Dinwiddie Co; d unk **RU:** unk, Specific service may be found at the Lib of VA, Auditors Acct XVIII pg 444 **CEM:** Goshen Family; **GPS** unk; 8 mi S of Petersburg and W of Old Stage Rd on the "Goshen" site; Dinwiddie **GS:** U **SP:** Mar (31 Jan 1767 Dinwiddie Co) Charlotte Williamson (1749-1800) **VI:** Son of Abner & Mary (Stokes) Grigg. Died in Bedford Co **P:** N **BLW:** unk **RG:** Y **MK:** N **PH:** unk **SS:** J- DAR Hatcher; CZ pg 192; SAR P-170859 **BS:** JLARC 2.

GRIGNON, Thomas; b unk; d 1781 **RU:** Seaman, Served on "Palmier" and died from Yorktown battle **CEM:** French Memorial; **GPS** 36.81944, -79.39933; Yorktown; York **GS:** U **SP:** No info **VI:** No further data **P:** unk **BLW:** unk **RG:** Y **MK:** unk **PH:** unk **SS:** J-Yorktown Historian; SAR P-170893 **BS:** JLARC 1, 74.

GRIGSBY, John; b 1720, Stafford Co; d 7 April 1794 **RU:** Private, Served in Capt William Nalle's Co of Rangers. Served in Rockingham Co Militia. Was in Battle of Point Pleasant Oct 1774. Served in 13th Regt of VA Line **CEM:** Falling Springs Presbyterian; **GPS** 37.68526, -79.44972; 410 Falling Springs Rd, Glasgow; Rockbridge **GS:** Y **SP:** 1) Mar (1745) Rosanna Etchison 2) Mar (1764) Elizabeth Porter (1734-1807) **VI:** First person bur in this cem **P:** unk **BLW:** unk **RG:** Y **MK:** Y SAR **PH:** Y **SS:** Z pg 113; SAR P-170899, DAR A048485 **BS:** JLARC 1, 2, 63, 79; 196.

GRIGSBY, John, b 1752, Rockingham Co, d 28 Sep 1826 Hawkins Co, TN **RU:** Private, Capt John Willis Co, Col Christian Febiger's. VA Regiment of Foot 2d Cont Line. Also served in Grayson's Regt **CEM:** Gray-Grigsby; **GPS** 36.7919,-82.5114; cem sign by road, nr Gray Branch, Fort Blackmore; Scott **GS:** Yes **SP:** Winifred Elizabeth Breeden (Breeding) (27 Aug 1757-1830) **VI:** No further data **P:** N **BLW:** N **RG:** N **MK:** N **PH:** N **SS:** E pg 329; O-Fold3 service index cards; **BS:** 196

GRIM, Charles; b c1755; d 13 Dec 1815 **RU:** Private, Marched under Morgan to Boston and was taken prisoner in the battle at Quebec in 1775 **CEM:** Mt Hebron; **GPS** 39.10916, -78.09497; 305 E Boscawen St; Winchester City **GS:** Y **SP:** No info **VI:** Stayed with militia after the war and earned rank of Capt. Bur in Centenary Reformed UCC portion of Mt Hebron Cemetery. Govt GS. **P:** N **BLW:** N **RG:** N **MK:** Y SAR & granite & SAR monument **PH:** Y **SS:** J-NSSAR reg;SAR P-170906, DAR A213803 **BS:** 196.

GRIM, John; b 15 Oct 1753, York, PA; d 19 Apr 1840 **RU:** Private, Served in Virginia militia. Ent serv in Winchester **CEM:** Mt Hebron; **GPS** 39.10916, -78.09497; 305 E Boscawen St; Winchester City **GS:** N **SP:** Mar (21 Mar 1821) Julianna Mainzer (__-21 May 1821) **VI:** Sol appl 5 Feb 1833 Winchester. S8628 **P:** Y **BLW:** unk **RG:** Y **MK:** Y SAR **PH:** N **SS:** J-NSSAR 1993 Reg; CG Vol 2 pg 1443; SAR P-170915 **BS:** JLARC 1; 196.

RU=Rank/Unit	CEM=Cemetery	GS=Gravestone	SP=Spousal Information
VI=Other Veteran Info	P=Pension	BLW=Bounty/Land Warrant	RG=Registered Grave
MK=SAR/DAR Marker	PH=Photo	SS=Service Source	BS=Burial Source

GRIMES, James S; b 25 Feb 1745; d 18 Jan 1804 **RU:** Private/Patriot, Served in Capt Powell's Co, 2nd Co, 3rd VA Regt 1778-1779. Also gave material to cause **CEM:** Dick Warren Farm; GPS unk; Lake Drummond; Norfolk City **GS:** Y **SP:** No info **VI:** No further data **P:** unk **BLW:** unk **RG:** N **MK:** N **PH:** unk **SS:** AL Ct Bk pg 11; AP payroll fr Fold 3 **BS:** 63 pg 169.

GRIMES, John; b unk; d May 1795 **RU:** Private, Served in Clarks Ill Regt at Ft Nelson, Portsmouth **CEM:** Old Christ Church Episcopal; GPS 38.80625, -77.04718; 118 N Washington St; Alexandria City **GS:** N **SP:** No info **VI:** Burial permit issued 3 May 1795 **P:** unk **BLW:** unk **RG:** Y **MK:** N **PH:** N **SS:** E pg 329, 332 **BS:** 20 pg 148.

GRIMES, Thomas; b 1738, Norfolk; d 8 May 1797 **RU:** Patriot, Gave material aid to cause in Norfolk **CEM:** Trinity Episcopal; GPS 36.83459, -76.30105; 500 Court St; Portsmouth City **GS:** Y **SP:** Chloe Grimes **VI:** Son of James & Mary (-----) Grimes. D in Edgecombe Co, NC. Memorialized on monument (stone # 117) in cemetery as one of the first vestrymen **P:** N **BLW:** N **RG:** N **MK:** unk **PH:** unk **SS:** D pg 105 **BS:** 00:00.0.

GRIMSLEY, John Parke; b unk; d 1 Mar 1778 **RU:** Private Capt Triplett's Co, Col William Grayson's 3rd VA Regt, Cont Line **CEM:** Rev War Court House Plaque; GPS; not determined; 4110 Chain Bridge Rd; Fairfax **GS:** Memorialized on plaque 2017 by Geo Washington Chapter, VASSAR **SP** No info **VI:** Died in service **P:** N **BLW:** Eligible **RG:** N **MK:** N **PH:** N **SS:** C Sect II. pg 240; E pg 329; AP Fold3 muster roll: EP sources: **BS:** None.

GRINNAN, Daniel Sr; b 1739, Accomack Co; d 25 Mar 1830 **RU:** Private, Served in Gen Edward Stevens unit. Was captured at Battle of Guilford CH but escaped on British officer's horse **CEM:** Masonic Cemetery; GPS 38.30198, -77.46142; 900 Charles St; Fredericksburg City **GS:** Y **SP:** Mar (31 Jul 1804) Eliza Richards Green (12 Jan 1787-7 Jul 1813) d/o Timothy & (-----) Green **VI:** Elder in 1st Presbyterian Church in Fredreickburg. Originally fr Madison Co **P:** unk **BLW:** unk **RG:** Y **MK:** Y SAR plaque **PH:** unk **SS:** D pg 267, 273; SAR P-170982 **BS:** 08 vol 1 pg 99.

GROOM, Jonathan; b 5 Feb 1756, London, England; d 1834 **RU:** Soldier, Ent serv Bedford Co in VA Line **CEM:** Groom Family; GPS unk; Nr Shady Grove Church; Bedford **GS:** N **SP:** Elizabeth Moon (1765-1835) **VI:** Sol appl pen 28 Jan 1833 Bedford Co. S19305 **P:** Y **BLW:** unk **RG:** Y **MK:** N **PH:** N **SS:** J- DAR Hatcher; CG Vol 2 pg 1448; SAR P-171222 **BS:** JLARC 2; 196.

GROSECLOSE, Peter Jr; b 20 May 1757, Lancaster Co, PA; d Dec 1805 **RU:** Private, Served in Capt Thomas Ingles Co of Militia 7 Apr 1781 **CEM:** Sharon Lutheran; GPS 37.05800, -81.20590; Rt 42 W of Ceres; Bland **GS:** Y **SP:** Mar (May 1782) Elizabeth Sluss (18 Mar 1766-12 Jul 1855, Smyth Co). Most of the Sluss family were massacred by Indians on 2 Aug 1774 during Lord Dunmore's War. She is bur at Kimberling Cemetery in Smyth Co. **VI:** Son of Peter Gloseclose Sr (1730-1803) & Mary Magdalena Ott (1732-1805). Widow appl pen fr Smyth Co 1853, age 87, rejected. R4354. Small Govt marker **P:** N **BLW:** unk **RG:** N **MK:** Y **PH:** unk **SS:** B; G pg 227; K pg 221 **BS:** 60 Bland Co; 196.

GROSECLOSE, Peter Sr; b 23 Feb 1730, Miesau, Rheinland-Pfalz; d 6 Dec 1803 **RU:** Private/Patriot, Serv not identified. Gave gun to cause Oct 1781 & two beeves Dec 1781 **CEM:** Sharon Lutheran; GPS 37.05800, -81.20590; Rt 42 W of Ceres; Bland **GS:** Y **SP:** Mar (abt 1755 PA) Mary Magdalena Ott (17 Aug 1732, Wila, Zurich, Switzerland-27 Oct 1805) **VI:** No further data **P:** unk **BLW:** unk **RG:** Y **MK:** N **PH:** unk **SS:** G pg 227; J-NASSR 2000 Reg; SAR P-171245 **BS:** JLARC 76; 196.

GROSNIER, Jacques; b unk; d 1781 **RU:** unk, Served on "Northumberland". Died fr battle at Yorktown **CEM:** French Memorial; GPS 36.81944, -79.39933; Yorktown; York **GS:** U **SP:** No info **VI:** No further data **P:** unk **BLW:** unk **RG:** Y **MK:** unk **PH:** unk **SS:** J-Yorktown Historian; SAR P-171249 **BS:** JLARC 1, 74.

GROSSETETE, Antoine; b unk; d 1781 **RU:** unk, Served in Auxonne Bn. Died fr battle at Yorktown **CEM:** French Memorial; GPS 36.81944, -79.39933; Yorktown; York **GS:** U **SP:** No info **VI:** No further data **P:** unk **BLW:** unk **RG:** Y **MK:** unk **PH:** unk **SS:** J-Yorktown Historian; SAR P-171294 **BS:** JLARC 1, 74.

GROULT, Jean; b unk; d 1781 **RU:** unk, Served on "Northumberland." Died fr battle at Yorktown **CEM:** French Memorial; GPS 36.81944, -79.39933; Yorktown; York **GS:** U **SP:** No info **VI:** No further data **P:** unk **BLW:** unk **RG:** Y **MK:** unk **PH:** unk **SS:** J-Yorktown Historian; SAR P-171328 **BS:** JLARC 1, 74.

RU=Rank/Unit	CEM=Cemetery	GS=Gravestone	SP=Spousal Information
VI=Other Veteran Info	P=Pension	BLW=Bounty/Land Warrant	RG=Registered Grave
MK=SAR/DAR Marker	PH=Photo	SS=Service Source	BS=Burial Source

168

GROVE, Marcus; b 1739, East Earl, Lancaster Co, PA; d 19 Sep 1808 **RU:** Private/Patriot, Served in Reader's VA Inf Co, Shenandoah Co Militia. Gave material aid to cause in Shenandoah Co **CEM:** Grove Family; GPS unk; Slade Farm on Rt 615 near Luray, Bixler's Ferry; Page **GS:** U **SP:** 1) Susan/Susannah Elizabeth Roades/Rhodes (massacred by Indians) 2) Mary Maria Strickler **VI:** Son of Rev Martin & (-----) Graff **P:** unk **BLW:** unk **RG** N **MK:** Y **SAR PH:** unk **SS:** C pg 602; D pg 106 **BS:** JLARC 67; 196.

GROVE (GROFF), Christian Sr (or Christley); b c1735, Lancaster PA; d 9 Jun 1786 **RU:** Private, Served in Michael Reader's Co 1786 **CEM:** Grove Family; GPS unk; Meadow Mills, off Rt 340, S fr Luray; Page **GS:** U **SP:** 1) Anna Rhodes 2) Esther Musselman **VI:** Died in Shenandoah Co **P:** unk **BLW:** unk **RG:** Y **MK:** unk **PH:** unk **SS:** 171388; SAR P-171388 **BS:** JLARC 1, 2, 67.

GRUBBS, Hensley (Henry); b 1754; d 1842 **RU:** Lieutenant, Served in VA Line Cont Army and wintered at Valley Forge **CEM:** Grubbs Family, aka called Spring Grove; GPS 37.43510, -77.36520; Spring Grove #2 Farm, nr Calvary Christian jct Rts 623 & 624; Hanover **GS:** U **SP:** (-----) in 1820 had wife age 54 **VI:** Sol appl pen 24 Jun 1818 Hanover Co. S37962, DAR marker 1997 **P:** Y **BLW:** unk **RG:** Y **MK:** unk **PH:** unk **SS:** CG Vol 2 pg 1453; B; SAR P-171482 **BS:** JLARC 4, 71.

GRUBBS (b VAN KRUPPS), William; b unk, New York City; d aft 1782 **RU:** unk, SAR registration did not specify service **CEM:** Grubbs Family, aka Spring Grove; GPS 37.43510, 77.36520; Spring Grove #2 Farm, nr Calvary Christian jct Rts 623 & 624; Hanover **GS:** Y **SP:** No info **VI:** Was a resident of Hanover Co in 1782 census **P:** unk **BLW:** unk **RG:** Y **MK:** unk **PH:** unk **SS:**; SAR P-171485 **BS:** JLARC 71.

GRYMES, Benjamin Jr; b 2 Jan 1756; d 13 Feb 1803 **RU:** Captain, Served in Clark's III Regt. Was at Ft Nelson 1782. Served in 1st Lt Dragoons, Col W Grayson Cont Line Regt **CEM:** Eagle's Nest; GPS unk; Rt 218 E to Rt 242 N to to Rt 682. Take immediate rt into cemetery. King George **GS:** Y **SP:** Ann Nicolas **VI:** Awarded 4000 acres BLW **P:** unk **BLW:** Y **RG:** Y **MK:** N **PH:** unk **SS:** E pg 331; BY; **SAR P-171510 BS:** 17 pg 37.

GRYMES, Philip Ludwell; b unk; d 1805 **RU:** Patriot, Gave material aid to cause **CEM:** Christ Church; GPS 37.60968, -76.54643; Rt 33 2 mi E of Saluda; Middlesex **GS:** U **SP:** Judith (-----) **VI:** No further data **P:** N **BLW:** N **RG:** N **MK:** N **PH:** unk **SS:** G pg 202; CT Bk pg iv, 6 Gloucester Co **BS:** 84 pg 198.

GUBIAUD, Benoist; b unk; d 1781 **RU:** Soldier, Served in Foix Bn and died fr battle at Yorktown **CEM:** French Memorial; GPS 36.81944, -79.39933; Yorktown; York **GS:** U **SP:** No info **VI:** No further data **P:** unk **BLW:** unk **RG:** Y **MK:** unk **PH:** unk **SS:** J-Yorktown Historian **BS:** JLARC 1, 74.

GUEGUEN, Joachim; b unk; d 1781 **RU:** Seaman, Served on "Magnanime" and died from Yorktown battle **CEM:** French Memorial; GPS 36.81944, -79.39933; Yorktown; York **GS:** U **SP:** No info **VI:** No further data **P:** unk **BLW:** unk **RG:** Y **MK:** unk **PH:** unk **SS:** J-Yorktown Historian; SAR P-171526 **BS:** JLARC 1, 74.

GUELIN, Nicolas; b unk; d 1781 **RU:** Soldier, Served in Gatinais Bn and died fr battle at Yorktown **CEM:** French Memorial; GPS 36.81944, -79.39933; Yorktown; York **GS:** U **SP:** No info **VI:** No further data **P:** unk **BLW:** unk **RG:** Y **MK:** unk **PH:** unk **SS:** J-Yorktown Historian; SAR P-171527 **BS:** JLARC 1, 74.

GUENARD, Pierre; b unk; d 1781 **RU:** Soldier, Served in Gatinals Bn and died fr battle at Yorktown **CEM:** French Memorial; GPS 36.81944, -79.39933; Yorktown; York **GS:** U **SP:** No info **VI:** No further data **P:** unk **BLW:** unk **RG:** Y **MK:** unk **PH:** unk **SS:** J-Yorktown Historian; SAR P-171528 **BS:** JLARC 1, 74.

GUIBOISEAU, Francois; b unk; d 1781 **RU:** Soldier, Served in Agenois Bn and died fr battle at Yorktown **CEM:** French Memorial; GPS 36.81944, -79.39933; Yorktown; York **GS:** U **SP:** No info **VI:** No further data **P:** unk **BLW:** unk **RG:** Y **MK:** unk **PH:** unk **SS:** J-Yorktown Historian; SAR P-171575 **BS:** JLARC 1, 74.

GUILIFORD, Allen; b unk; d 1815 **RU:** Patriot, Gave a horse to the army **CEM:** Fincastle Presbyterian; GPS 37.50017, -79.87558; 108 E Back St, Fincastle; Botetourt **GS:** N **SP:** No info **VI:** Name is on the SAR plaque at this cemetery **P:** N **BLW:** N **RG:** Y **MK:** Y SAR plaque **PH:** N **SS:** AR Vol 2 pg 100; Z pg 172; J-NSSAR 1993 Reg; J- DAR Hatcher **BS:** 196; JLARC 1, 2.

RU=Rank/Unit	CEM=Cemetery	GS=Gravestone	SP=Spousal Information
VI=Other Veteran Info	P=Pension	BLW=Bounty/Land Warrant	RG=Registered Grave
MK=SAR/DAR Marker	PH=Photo	SS=Service Source	BS=Burial Source

169

GUILLAUME, Joseph; b unk; d 1781 **RU:** Soldier, Served in Bourbonnais Bn and died fr battle at Yorktown **CEM:** French Memorial; GPS 36.81944, -79.39933; Yorktown; York **GS:** U **SP:** No info **VI:** No further data **P:** unk **BLW:** unk **RG:** Y **MK:** unk **PH:** unk **SS:** J-Yorktown Historian; SAR P-171634 **BS:** JLARC 1, 74.

GUILLERAUX, Joseph; b unk; d 1781 **RU:** Soldier, Served in Gatinais Bn and died fr battle at Yorktown **CEM:** French Memorial; GPS 36.81944, -79.39933; Yorktown; York **GS:** U **SP:** no info **VI:** No further data **P:** unk **BLW:** unk **RG:** Y **MK:** unk **PH:** unk **SS:** J-Yorktown Historian; SAR P-171639 **BS:** JLARC 1, 74.

GUILLON, Francois; b unk; d 1781 **RU:** Soldier, Served in Soissonnais Bn and died fr battle at Yorktown **CEM:** French Memorial; GPS 36.81944, -79.39933; Yorktown; York **GS:** U **SP:** No info **VI:** No further data **P:** unk **BLW:** unk **RG:** Y **MK:** unk **PH:** unk **SS:** J-Yorktown Historian; SAR P-171642 **BS:** JLARC 1, 74.

GUILLOT, Mathieu; b unk; d 1781 **RU:** Seaman, Served on "Languedoc" and died from Yorktown battle **CEM:** French Memorial; GPS 36.81944, -79.39933; Yorktown; York **GS:** U **SP:** No info **VI:** No further data **P:** unk **BLW:** unk **RG:** Y **MK:** unk **PH:** unk **SS:** J-Yorktown Historian; SAR P-171647 **BS:** JLARC 1, 74.

GUINELS, Francois; b unk; d 1781 **RU:** Seaman, Served on "Citoyen" and died from Yorktown battle **CEM:** French Memorial; GPS 36.81944, -79.39933; Yorktown; York **GS:** U **SP:** No info **VI:** No further data **P:** unk **BLW:** unk **RG:** Y **MK:** unk **PH:** unk **SS:** J-Yorktown Historian; SAR P-171650 **BS:** JLARC 1, 74.

GULLAMEBOURG, Antoine; b unk; d 1781 **RU:** Soldier, Served in Gatinais Bn and died fr battle at Yorktown **CEM:** French Memorial; GPS 36.81944, -79.39933; Yorktown; York **GS:** U **SP:** No info **VI:** No further data **P:** unk **BLW:** unk **RG:** Y **MK:** unk **PH:** unk **SS:** J-Yorktown Historian; SAR P-171684 **BS:** JLARC 1, 74.

GUM, Abraham; b 1755, Pendleton, Lousia Co; d 1804 Pendleton, Lousia Co **RU:** Corporal, Capt Westfall's Co 6th Cont Line & 13th VA Regt **CEM:** Gum Family; GPS not determined; Mill Gap; Highland **GS:** Y **SP:** Mar 20 Apr 1785, Priscilla Wade (27 Nov 1758-7 Jul 1842), d/o John Wade (1724-1815) & Sophia Howard (1727-1816) **VI:** No further data **P:** N **BLW:** Y **RG:** Y **MK:** N **PH:** N **SS:** C pg 241; E pg 333; DAR A048337; SAR P-329597 **BS:** 196

GUM, Isaac; b 1746; d Bef 7 Apr 1830 **RU:** Private, Served in Capt Peter Hull's Co, Augusta Co Militia **CEM:** Gum Family, aka Walker Wilfong Family; GPS unk; Hightown; Highland **GS:** Y **SP:** 1) Martha Jane McBride 2) Jane Erwin (__-12 May 1833) **VI:** No further data **P:** unk **BLW:** unk **RG:** Y **MK:** unk **PH:** unk **SS:** J-NSSAR 1993 Reg; E pg 333; SAR P-171706 **BS:** JLARC 1; 196.

GUM, Norton; b 15 Apr 1739, Sussex Co, DL; d 1789 **RU:** Patriot, paid personal property tax 1783, Rockingham Co, considered to be partially for Rev War expenses **CEM:** Broadway Presbyterian Church; GPS 38.618040,-78.795350; 107 Lee St, Broadway; Rockingham **GS:** Unk **SP:** Eleanor "Nelle" McElwain (29 Jun 1757, Palmer, Hampton Co, MA-1786, Ninville), d/o Thomas G McElwain & Nancy Rector **VI:** Son of Jacob Gum & Sarah Claypool, both of Sussex Co, DL **P:** N **BLW:** N **RG:** N **MK:** N **PH:** N **SS:** DV image 16.pdf, 1783 Rockingham Co **BS:** 196.

GUNNELL, Henry M; b 1705; d 20 Feb 1792 **RU:** Patriot, Gave material aid to cause **CEM:** Gunnell Family; GPS unk; 600 Innsbrook Ave, Great Falls; Fairfax **GS:** U **SP:** Catherine O'Daniel (1706-__) **VI:** No further data **P:** N **BLW:** N **RG:** N **MK:** N **PH:** unk **SS:** AL Certificate Fairfax **BS:** 196.

GUNNELL, John II; b 1763; d 1836 **RU:** Private/Patriot, Gave material aid to cause **CEM:** Gunnell Family; GPS unk; Buckner; Louisa **GS:** U **SP:** Mar (21 Aug 1807) Lucy Fleming (1790, Louisa Co-Aug 1856) **VI:** Son of John (1730, Hanover Co-13 Oct 1803) 7 Sarah Pons (Mountcastle) (1735-1735) Gunnell **P:** unk **BLW:** unk **RG:** Y **MK:** unk **PH:** unk **SS:** AL Ct Bk pg 2 Fairfax Co; SAR P-171776 **BS:** JLARC 2, 61.

GUNNELL, William R.; b 30 Jan 1750; d 1820 **RU:** Private, Served in 1st Light Dragoons **CEM:** Gunnell Family; GPS unk; 600 Innsbrook Ave, Great Falls; Fairfax **GS:** Y **SP:** 1) Sarah Coleman (1781-1812), 2) Martha Adkins **VI:** Son of Henry & Catherine (Daniel) Gunnell. Death yr is not part of stone, but was

RU=Rank/Unit	CEM=Cemetery	GS=Gravestone	SP=Spousal Information
VI=Other Veteran Info	P=Pension	BLW=Bounty/Land Warrant	RG=Registered Grave
MK=SAR/DAR Marker	PH=Photo	SS=Service Source	BS=Burial Source

170

entered by findagrave contributor **P:** unk **BLW:** unk **RG:** Y **MK:** N **PH:** unk **SS:** E pg 333; SAR P-171777 **BS:** 61 vol VI, pg MN-72; 196.

GUNNELL (GUNNILL), John Sr; b 1730, Louisa Co; d 13 Oct 1803 **RU:** Patriot, Gave material aid to the cause **CEM:** Gunnell Family; GPS unk; Buckner; Louisa **GS:** Y **SP:** Sarah Pons Mountcastle (__-6 Sep 1811) **VI:** BLW #12150 issued Mar 1794 **P:** N **BLW:** Y **RG:** Y **MK:** N **PH:** unk **SS:** K pg 255; AL Ct Bk pg 17; SAR P-171775 **BS:** 80 vol 2 pg 101.

GUTHRIE, John; b c1762; d 27 Jan 1845 **RU:** Private, Ent serv 1777, Capt Given's Co, Augusta Co Militia **CEM:** Tinkling Spring Presbyterian; GPS 38.08472, -78.98278; 30 Tinkling Spring Dr, Fishersville; Augusta **GS:** Y **SP:** 1) Ann (-----) (1772-27 Apr 1832) 2) Margaret Guthrie (c1762-7 Dec 1815) **VI:** No further data **P:** unk **BLW:** unk **RG:** N **MK:** unk **PH:** Y **SS:** E pg 333 **BS:** 196; 208.

GUY, Rene; b unk; d 1781 **RU:** Seaman, Served on "Ville de Paris" and died from Yorktown battle **CEM:** French Memorial; GPS 36.81944, -79.39933; Yorktown; York **GS:** U **SP:** No info **VI:** No further data **P:** unk **BLW:** unk **RG:** Y **MK:** unk **PH:** unk **SS:** J-Yorktown Historian; SAR P-171944 **BS:** JLARC 1, 74.

GWATHNEY, Joseph; b 1758; d 1824 **RU:** Private/Patriot, Gen Nelson's Corps, Lt Dragoons. As a patriot he paid the personal property supply tax 1783 in King William Co **CEM:** Burlington Plantation: GPS 37.845753,-77.143794; loc off West River Rd, 1 mi S of Smokey Rd, turn left on unamed lane approx .3 mi to farm house, cem behind storage bldg; King William **GS:** Y **SP:** No spousal info **VI:** No further data **P:** N **BLW:** Y **RG:** N **MK:** N **PH:** unk **SS:** E pg 324; DV 1783 Knig William Co, image 06 pdf **BS:** 196.

GWINN (GWIN), David; b c 1740-5, VA; d bef Jan 1822 **RU:** Captain/Patriot, Was in Battle of Guilford CH. Gave material aid to cause **CEM:** Clover Creek Church; GPS unk; Clover Creek Rt 678 S of McDowell, 7.7 mi, ri ght hand side; Highland **GS:** U **SP:** 1) Viola Jane Crawford 2) Jane Carlisle/Carlile **VI:** Also served in Colonial Wars in 1756 in Capt William Preston's Co of Rangers **P:** unk **BLW:** unk **RG:** Y **MK:** Y SAR **PH:** unk **SS:** D Augusta Co; SAR P-171979, DAR #A048697 **BS:** JLARC 2, 103.

GWIN, Jacob; b unk; d 26 Apr 1778 **RU:** Private, Capt Hamilton's Co, 1st VA State Regt **CEM:** Rev War Court House Plaque; GPS; not determined; 4110 Chain Bridge Rd; Fairfax **GS:** Memorialized on plaque 2017 by Geo Washington Chapter, VASSAR **SP** No info **VI:** Died in service **P:** N **BLW:** N **RG:** N **MK:** N **PH:** N **SS:** C Sect II, pg 214; E pg 234; AP Fold3 muster roll: EP sources: **BS:** None.

GWYNN, Thomas; b c1761,Co of Glanmorgan, South Wales, d 27 Jan 1788 **RU:** Private, Served in Volunteer Corps, Norfolk **CEM:** St Paul's Episcopal; GPS 36.84733, -76.28554; 201 St Paul's Blvd; Norfolk **GS:** Y **SP:** No info **VI:** Grave stone inscription indicates "A member of the Volunteer Corps" **P:** N **BLW:** N **RG:** N **MK:** N **PH:** No **SS:** The Alter Guild of St Paul's Church, "St. Paul's Church 1832 Originally The Borough Church, 1739, Elizabeth River Parish, Norfolk, VA", 1934 grave # 52 **BS:** 196.

HADEN (HADDEN), Anthony; b 26 Mar 1746; d 28 Apr 1828 **RU:** Captain, Served in VA Line and Albemarle Co Militia **CEM:** Haden family; GPS unk; Phillips Farm, Evington; Campbell **GS:** U **SP:** 3) Mar on 21 Dec 1787 Albemarle Co to Anna Dabney d 24 Dec 1824 **VI:** Recd pen R4418 **P:** Y **BLW:** unk **RG:** Y **MK:** N **PH:** unk **SS:** CG Vol 2 pg 1466-67; SAR P-172116 **BS:** JLARC 36.

HADEN, Benjamin; b 1762, Goochland Co; d 14 Aug 1837 **RU:** Soldier, Served in Albemarle Co Militia **CEM:** Haden family; GPS unk; Phillips Farm, Evington; Campbell **GS:** U **SP:** Mar (2 Dec 1780) Martha Moorman (__Bedford Co-__) **VI:** Son of John (1723-1817) & Jean (Moseley) (1 Oct 1723, Middlesex Co-1796) Haden **P:** unk **BLW:** unk **RG:** Y **MK:** N **PH:** unk **SS:** NSSAR Ancestor #P-172118 **BS:** JLARC 36.

HADEN, John Sr; b 10 May 1723 King William Co; d 1817 **RU:** Patriot, Gave material aid to cause **CEM:** Haden Family (AKA Old Phillips) ; GPS unk; Phillips Farm, Evington; Campbell **GS:** U **SP:** Jean Moseley (1 Oct 1723, Middlesex Co-1796) **VI:** Son of Anthony Haden (1694-_0 & Margaret Douglas ((_-1746) **P:** N **BLW:** N **RG:** Y **MK:** N **SS:** AL CT Bk pg 2 Fluvanna Co; SAR P-172120 **BS:** JLARC 36.; 196

HADEN, John Moseley; b 1749 Kents Store; d 1831 RU: First:Lieutenant, sworn in this rank 4 Sep 1777,Capt Levi Thompson, Fluvanna Co Militia, serving at Caben Point, VA **CEM:** Haden Family; GPS not determined; loc Elk Run Branch on land of John Haden 1759, gifted to Joseph Aug 1777 (see

RU=Rank/Unit	CEM=Cemetery	GS=Gravestone	SP=Spousal Information
VI=Other Veteran Info	P=Pension	BLW=Bounty/Land Warrant	RG=Registered Grave
MK=SAR/DAR Marker	PH=Photo	SS=Service Source	BS=Burial Source

property rec for specific loc); Fluvanna **GS**: Unk **SP**: Mar 1)1790, Anne(_), 2) Mary Ann, widow of Peter Hopkins **VI**: Son of John Haden (1723-1817) & Jeanie Mosley (1722-1796) **P**: N **BLW**: N **RG**: N **MK**: N **PH**: Nk **SS**: AZ pg 202; DAR A048977 **BS**: 196.

HADEN, Joseph; b 1751 Goochland Co, d 15 Oct 1820, Kents Store **RU**: Capt, took oath 2 Aug 1779, Fluvanna Co Militia; was under Col Charles Dabney at Yorktown, Oct 1781 **CEM**: Haden Family; GPS not determined; loc Elk Run Branch on land of John Haden 1759, gifted to Joseph Aug 1777 (see property rec for specific loc); Fluvanna **GS**: Unk **SP**: Mar 1) c 1772, Mary Peatross, d/o Matthew Peatross & Amey Bram(e), 2) Jane Turner **VI**: Son of John Haden (1723-1817) & Jeanie Mosley (1722-1796) **P**: N **BLW**: N **RG**: N **MK**: N **PH**: Nk **SS**: E pg 338; G pg 475; DAR A048979 **BS**: 196.

HAGAN, Francis Ignatius; b c1754, Fairfax Co; d 15 Dec 1830 **RU**: Private Corporal, Served in 3rd VA Cont line. Ent serv Hampton1775. Private under Capt David Arell 1777. Enl 7 Jan 1777 in Hagan's Corps **CEM**: St Mary's Catholic; GPS 38.79390, -77.04750; 310 S Royal St; Alexandria City **GS**: Y **SP**: Never mar **VI**: Sol appl 1 Apr 1818 Dist of Columbia. S36007. Died age 76 per death notice, funeral held fr home of Mrs. Sherfield's, upper end of King Street. He had entered service at the commencement of the war and served until its end (Alexandria Gazette, 17 Dec 1830) **P**: Y **BLW**: unk **RG**: Y **MK**: Plaque **PH**: Y **SS**:; E pg 336; K pg 231; AK Feb 2006; CG Vol 2 pg 1469; SAR P-334430 **BS**: 196.

HAGAN, Michael; b unk; d unk **RU**: Drummer, Served in 2d PA Regt **CEM**: Shockoe Hill; GPS 37.55190, -77.43170; 4th & Hospital Sts; Richmond City **GS**: Y **SP**: No info **VI**: No further data **P**: unk **BLW**: unk **RG**: N **MK**: N **PH**: unk **SS**: AP 2d PA Regt **BS**: 179 #939.

HAGERTY, Patrick; b unk; d Jul 1791 **RU**: Sergeant, Served in Capt Buller Clarborney Co, Col Alex Spotwood's 2nd VA Regt, 1777 **CEM**: Old Christ Church Episcopal; GPS 38.80625, -77.04718; 118 N Washington St; Alexandria City **GS**: N **SP**: No info **VI**: Burial permit issued 22 Jul 1791 **P**: unk **BLW**: unk **RG**: N **MK**: N **PH**: N **SS**: A pg 270 **BS**: 20 pg 148.

HAGUENEAU, Jerome; b unk; d 1781 **RU**: Soldier, Served in Beaujolais Bn and died fr battle at Yorktown **CEM**: French Memorial; GPS 36.81944, -79.39933; Yorktown; York **GS**: U **SP**: No info **VI**: No further data **P**: unk **BLW**: unk **RG**: Y **MK**: unk **PH**: unk **SS**: J-Yorktown Historian; SAR P-172301 **BS**: JLARC 1, 74.

HAINES, Casper; b unk; d unk **RU**: Lieutenant, Served in VA Militia in Capt Stephen Conrad's Co **CEM**: Old Peaked Mountain; GPS 38.37113, -78.73416; 9843 Town Hall Rd, McGaheysville; Rockingham **GS**: Y **SP**: No info **VI**: Name is on a plaque in cemetery of those that served in the Rev War **P**: unk **BLW**: unk **RG**: Y **MK**: Y SAR **PH**: unk **SS**:; SAR P-172386 **BS**: JLARC 76.

HAINES (HAYNES), Frederick; b unk; d Aft 1780 **RU**: Patriot, gave material to Frederick Co Militia, 2 Nov 1780 **CEM**: Old Peak Mountain; GPS 38. 37113, -78.73416; 9843 Town Hall Rd, McGaheysville; Rockingham GS: Y SP: Mar 1804, Rockingham Co, Barbara Pence **VI**: Name is on plaque in cem listing Rev War service **P**: N **BLW**: N **RG**: N **MK**: Y DAR plaque **PH**: unk **SS**: O pg 242 **BS**: 04.

HAINES, George; b unk; d unk **RU**: Private, Served in 6th Cont Line **CEM**: Old Peaked Mountain; GPS 38.37113, -78.73416; 9843 Town Hall Rd, McGaheysville; Rockingham **GS**: Y **SP**: No info **VI**: Name is on a plaque in cemetery of those that served in the Rev War. Recd BLW 4000 acres 27 Jun 1783 **P**: unk **BLW**: Y **RG**: Y **MK**: Y DAR plaque **PH**: unk **SS**: J-NASSR 2000 Reg; BY; SAR P-172392 **BS**: JLARC 76.

HAINES, John; b unk; d unk **RU**: Corporal, Enl 14 Mar 1777 and served in 4th & 11h Cont lines under Col Daniel Morgan 31 May 1777-30 Nov 1778 **CEM**: Old Peaked Mountain; GPS 38.37113, -78.73416; 9843 Town Hall Rd, McGaheysville; Rockingham **GS**: Y **SP**: Person this name mar (8 Dec 1791 Lunenburg Co) Martha Walker. Mar (1797 Rockingham Co) Dorothy Cash d/o Mathias & (-----) Cash **VI**: Name is on a plaque in cemetery of those that served in the Rev War **P**: unk **BLW**: unk **RG**: N **MK**: Y **PH**: unk **SS**: E pg 337 **BS**: 04.

HAINES, Jonas; b unk; d unk **RU**: Patriot, Gave material aid to cause **CEM**: Old Peaked Mountain; GPS 38.37113, -78.73416; 9843 Town Hall Rd, McGaheysville; Rockingham **GS**: Y **SP**: No info **VI**: Name is on a plaque in cemetery of those that served in the Rev War **P**: N **BLW**: N **RG**: Y **MK**: Y **PH**: unk **SS**: O pg 242; SAR P-172405 **BS**: 04.

RU=Rank/Unit	CEM=Cemetery	GS=Gravestone	SP=Spousal Information
VI=Other Veteran Info	P=Pension	BLW=Bounty/Land Warrant	RG=Registered Grave
MK=SAR/DAR Marker	PH=Photo	SS=Service Source	BS=Burial Source

172

HAINES, Joseph; b unk; d unk **RU:** Patriot, Gave material aid to cause **CEM:** Old Peaked Mountain; GPS 38.37113, -78.73416; 9843 Town Hall Rd, McGaheysville; Rockingham **GS:** Y **SP:** No info **VI:** Name is on a plaque in cemetery of those that served in the Rev War **P:** N **BLW:** N **RG:** Y **MK:** Y DAR plaque **PH:** unk **SS:** P pg 85; SAR P-172406 **BS:** 04.

HAINES (HAINS), Peter M; b c1754; d unk **RU:** Private, Served in VA Cont Line for 3 yrs **CEM:** Old Peaked Mountain; GPS 38.37113, -78.73416; 9843 Town Hall Rd, McGaheysville; Rockingham **GS:** Y **SP:** Mar (1775) Margaret Willis (1757-1831) **VI:** Sol appl 21 Apr 1818 Jefferson Co. Name is on a plaque in cemetery of those that served in the Rev War. S38008. Recd. BLW 100 acres 23 Jun 1787 **P:** Y **BLW:** Y **RG:** Y **MK:** Y DAR plaque **PH:** unk **SS:** E pg 337; BY; CG Vol 2 pg 1472; SAR P-172409 **BS:** 04.

HAINES (HAYNES), Frederick; b unk; d unk **RU:** Patriot, Gave 500# beef 2 Nov 1780 to Frederick Co Militia **CEM:** Old Peaked Mountain; GPS 38.37113, -78.73416; 9843 Town Hall Rd, McGaheysville; Rockingham **GS:** Y **SP:** Mar (1804 Rockingham Co) Barbara Pence **VI:** Name is on a plaque in cemetery of those that served in the Rev War **P:** N **BLW:** N **RG:** Y **MK:** Y **PH:** unk **SS:** O pg 242; SAR P-172391 **BS:** 04.

HAIRSTON, George; b 20 Sept 1750; d 5 Mar 1827 **RU:** Captain, Colonel, Commanded Co in the Henry Co Militia **CEM:** Hairston Family; GPS unk; SR 108, Beaver Creek, N of Martinsville; Henry **GS:** U **SP:** 1) Mar (1781) Elizabeth Perkins Letcher (1759-1819) **VI:** Mar William Letcher's widow. Became General in War of 1812 **P:** unk **BLW:** unk **RG:** Y **MK:** unk **PH:** unk **SS:** E pg 337; SAR P-172447, DAR A049162 **BS:** JLARC 2, 30.

HALE, Edward; b 1750, AugustaFranklin Co; d 1823 **RU:** Captain, Served in 13th Cont Line, Capt John Lucas Co of Militia, Montgomery Co **CEM:** Hale Farm; GPS unk; Wolf Creek nr Narrows; Giles **GS:** Y **SP:** Mar (26 Sep 1786) Martha Perdue (c1760-c1820) **VI:** Settled in Giles Co 1779 **P:** unk **BLW:** unk **RG:** Y **MK:** unk **PH:** unk **SS:** G pg 234; E pg 234; J-NSSAR 1993 Reg; J- DAR Hatcher; SAR P-172517 **BS:** 196; JLARC 1, 2.

HALE (HAIL), Lewis; b 2 Nov 1742; d 12 Mar 1802 **RU:** Private/Patriot, Served at Kings Mountain. Took oath of allegiance in Grayson Co **CEM:** Hale Family; GPS unk; Nr Elk Creek; Grayson **GS:** Y **SP:** Mary Burwell **VI:** No further data **P:** unk **BLW:** unk **RG:** Y **MK:** N **PH:** unk **SS:** AS SAR applic; CE Vol 9 pg 139; SAR P-172579, DAR A049270 **BS:** 80 vol 2 pg 106.

HALEY, James; b 4 May 1732; d 25 Aug 1827 **RU:** Sergeant, Served in 1st VA Regt **CEM:** Haley/Halley Family; GPS unk; 4422 San Carlos Rd, Fairfax; Fairfax **GS:** U **SP:** Mar (1767) Frances (-----) (19 May 1737 Fairfax-7 Oct 1824) **VI:** No further data **P:** unk **BLW:** Y **RG:** N **MK:** unk **PH:** unk **SS:** C pg 242; E pg 338 **BS:** JLARC 27, 14.

HALL, Asa Sr; b 1 Jun 1758, Westerly, Washington Co, RI; d 13 Feb 1841 **RU:** Private, enlisted 2 Mar 1776 in Dutchess Co NY in Capt Nathan Pearce Co, Col Richmore Regt, Gen Alexander, NY State Troops; in 1777 enl again in Capt John Salisbury's Co, 17th Regt, Albany, NY Militia; was at Saratoga and the surrender of Burgoyne **CEM:** Halls Methodist Church; GPS cem 37.238263'-80.268499; GS 37238359, -80.268949; loc at jct Flatwood Rd and North Fork Rd at Hall Cem sign, nr Ironto; Montgomery **GS:** Y Gov't **SP:** 1) Mar (c1779) Sarah Adams (1762-1801), 2) Mar (31 Jul 1803, Montgomery Co) Mary Vanover d/o Henry & (-----) Vanover **VI:** Was pensioned 1833 in Montgomery Co; moved to Montgomery Co in 1790. S6945. **P:** Y **BLW:** unk **RG:** Y **MK:** Y SAR bronze **PH:** Y **SS:** DAR A049416; K vol 2 pg 234; SAR P-172727 **BS:** 80 vol 2 pg 106;. JLARC 2, 196.

HALL, James; b Bef 1752; d Oct 1816 **RU:** Captain/Patriot, Served in Botetourt Co. Was Capt in Rockbridge Militia. Gave material aid to cause **CEM:** Oxford Presbyterian; GPS 37.75302, -79.56023; 18 Churchview Ln, Lexington; Lexington City **GS:** Y **SP:** Martha Gilmore **VI:** Died in Rockbridge Co **P:** unk **BLW:** unk **RG:** unk **MK:** N **PH:** unk **SS:** NSDAR #490826; D Rockbridge Co SAR P-172962 **BS:** JLARC 11, 26.

HALL, Jesse; b 22 Mar 1760, Charleston, Washington Co, RI; d 2 Oct 1848 **RU:** Private, Served in NY Line. Moved fr RI to Dutchess Co NY where he entered service in 1776. Was in Battle at White Plains, NY **CEM:** Barnett Family; GPS 36.80751, -80.15219; Alleghany Spring Rd, left side of Sisson Farm; Montgomery Co **GS:** Y **SP:** Mar (c1778 Dudley, MA) Phoebe Wilbur (13 Jul 1761, RI-aft 1830.

RU=Rank/Unit	CEM=Cemetery	GS=Gravestone	SP=Spousal Information
VI=Other Veteran Info	P=Pension	BLW=Bounty/Land Warrant	RG=Registered Grave
MK=SAR/DAR Marker	PH=Photo	SS=Service Source	BS=Burial Source

Montgomery Co) d/o Christopher & Sarah (Vaughn) Wilbur **VI**: Son of Benajah & Sarah (Crandall) Hall. Sol appl pen 7 Jan 1833 Montgomery Co. S8666. Pen 1837. Moved to Montgomery Co. 1789. SAR gr marker **P**: Y **BLW**: unk **RG**: N **MK**: Y SAR **PH**: Y **SS**: A part 2 pg 266; CG Vol 3 pg 1481 **BS**: 04; 196.

HALL, Patrick; b 1751, Ireland; d 23 Nov 1814 **RU**: Private, Served in Capt McCutchen's Co, Augusta Co Militia **CEM**: Old Providence; GPS 37.96151, -79.71000; 1005 Spottswood Rd, Spottswood; Augusta **GS**: Y **SP**: Mar (1773) Susanna McChesney (1749-19 Nov 1814). Both she and her husband d of yellow fever contracted by nursing their son William who had brought it back fr Norfolk during War of 1812 **VI**: Weaver by occupation, deeded land for Old Stone Church in 1794. Name also on SAR plaque at cemetery **P**: unk **BLW**: unk **RG**: Y **MK**: Y SAR plaque **PH**: unk **SS**: E pg 339; BT SAR P-173176 **BS**: JLARC 2, 8, 62, 63; 196.

HALL, Thomas Sr; b 1746; d 26 Jul 1804 **RU**: Private, Was in Battle at Point Pleasant in Capt Thomas Buford's Co of independents **CEM**: Hall Family; GPS unk; Rt 658 vic Winston; Culpeper **GS**: Y **SP**: No info **VI**: No further data **P**: unk **BLW**: unk **RG**: N **MK**: N **PH**: unk **SS**: Z pg 125 **BS**: 167 Hall.

HALL, William; b 1749; d 1814 **RU**: Captain, Commanded a co in Augusta Co Militia **CEM**: Old Providence; GPS 37.96151, -79.71000; 1005 Spottswood Rd, Spottswood; Augusta **GS**: Y **SP**: No info **VI**: Newer Govt stone. Name also is on SAR cemetery plaque **P**: unk **BLW**: unk **RG**: Y **MK**: Y SAR plaque **PH**: unk **SS**: B; G pg 632; BT SAR P-173309 **BS**: JLARC 2, 8, 62, 63; 196.

HALL, William Sr; b 1766; d 17 Oct 1844 **RU**: Private, Served in Capt William Campbell's Co against the Indians in 1782 in Montgomery Co **CEM**: North Mountain; GPS unk; 7 mi S of Staunton on N side Rt 252; Augusta **GS**: Y **SP**: No info **VI**: Died age 78 **P**: unk **BLW**: unk **RG**: N **MK**: N **PH**: unk **SS**: G pg 239 **BS**: 142; 196.

HALLER, Peter (Petter), b 7 Aug 1715, Mastall Alsace, France, d c1999 **RU**: Patriot, Gave material aid (beef) to cause in Shenandoah Co **CEM**: Haller Family, GPS: not determined; loc a few miles on family property fr Union Forge Methodist Church GPS 38.8372, -78.5897 where he is memorialized on monument with plaque; Edinburg, Shenandoah **GS**: Yes **SP**: Mar 1735, Berks, PA, Ann Dorothea (-----)(1722-20 Oct 1792) **VI**: Son of Heinrich Haller and Catherine (-----) fr Switzerland. Property was on 372 acres on both sides of Stoney Creek in 1761 including saw mill and grist mill **P**: N **BLW**: N **RG**: Y **MK**: N **PH**: N **SS**: D vol 3, pg 843; DAR Ancestor # A054355; SAR P-330812 **BS**: 32.

HALLEY, Henry Simpson; b 10 May 1762; d 28 Nov 1838 **RU**: Soldier, Served in VA Line. Ent serv Fairfax Co. Served in Capt Little's Co, Gen Weadon's Regt and under Marquis De Lafayette **CEM**: Haley/Halley Family; GPS unk; 4422 San Carlos Rd, Fairfax; Fairfax **GS**: U **SP**: Mar (8 Jun 1786) Elizabeth Hampton (21 Sep 1762, Fairfax Co-24 Sep 1824) **VI**: Pension applic rejected. Died with six children but no wife. R4493 **P**: Y **BLW**: unk **RG**: Y **MK**: unk **PH**: unk **SS**: K pg 239; CG Vol 2 pg 1489 SAR P-173432, DAR A049333 **BS**: JLARC 4, 28.

HALLEY, James Jr; b 4 Apr 1737; d 1795 **RU**: Sergeant/Patriot, Served in VA Inf unit. Gave material aid to cause **CEM**: Pleasant Green Farm-Popes Head Run; GPS unk; Nr Occoquan; Fairfax **GS**: U **SP**: Mar (1767) Frances Hampton (19 May 1737-25 Aug 1827) **VI**: No further data **P**: unk **BLW**: unk **RG**: Y **MK**: unk **PH**: unk **SS**: J- DAR Hatcher; AL Ct Bk pg 16 Fairfax Co SAR P-173435 **BS**: JLARC 2.

HALSTEAD (HOLSTEAD), Matt; b 26 Sep 1760; d 30 Mar 1829 **RU**: Private, Served in Capt William Crane's Troop of Horse, 20 Apr-20 May 1780 in NJ **CEM**: Halstead Family; GPS unk; Pond Lake; Chesapeake City **GS**: Y **SP**: Mary (-----) (29 Mar 1771-10 Jan 1832) **VI**: Listed with wife on monument **P**: N **BLW**: N **RG**: N **MK**: unk **PH**: unk **SS**: AP Payroll on Fold 3 **BS**: 63 pg 175.

HAMILTON, Alexander; b 1725; d 1781 **RU**: Captain, Commanded a company Botetourt Co Militia 1777 **CEM**: Fincastle Presbyterian; GPS 37.50017, -79.87558; 108 E Back St, Fincastle; Botetourt **GS**: N **SP**: No Info **VI**: Name is on VASSAR plaque at cemetery **P**: unk **BLW**: unk **RG**: Y **MK**: Y SAR plaque **PH**: N **SS**: E pg 341; J-NASSR 2000 Reg **SAR P-173687 BS**: 196; JLARC 76.

HAMILTON, Alexander; b Sep 1759, Augusta Co; d 1843 **RU**: Soldier, Ent Serv Augusta Co 1778, Capt Trembels's Co, Capt John McKittrick's Co, Capt Patrick Buchanan's Co. Served in VA Line. Brother James served with him and was severely wounded in Battle of Hot Water. Another brother John took his place **CEM**: Headstone states Cunninghams' Co., Bethel Presbyterian; GPS 38.04257, -79.17283; 563 Bethel Green Rd, Middlebrook; Augusta **GS**: Y Govt **SP**: Mary **VI**: Sol appl 29 Aug 1833 Augusta Co.

RU=Rank/Unit	CEM=Cemetery	GS=Gravestone	SP=Spousal Information
VI=Other Veteran Info	P=Pension	BLW=Bounty/Land Warrant	RG=Registered Grave
MK=SAR/DAR Marker	PH=Photo	SS=Service Source	BS=Burial Source

174

S9556.**P:** Y **BLW:** unk **RG:** Y **MK:** unk **PH:** N **SS:** K pg 240; AZ pg 111CG Vol 2 pg 1493 SAR P-173684, DAR A050061 **BS:** JLARC 2, 62, 63.

HAMILTON, Andrew; b abt 1740 Ireland, d 1823 **RU:** Captain, Served in Capt McClanahan's Co at Point Pleasant in 1774. Co Cmdr Botetourt Militia in 1777 **CEM:** Fincastle Presbyterian; GPS 37.50017, -79.87558; 108 E Back St, Fincastle; Botetourt **GS:** N **SP:** Mar (8 Nov 1800 Botetourt Co) Sarah C. Seldon **VI:** Name is on the SAR plaque at this cemetery **P:** unk **BLW:** unk **RG:** Y **MK:** Y SAR plaque **PH:** N **SS:** AR Vol 2 pg 100; Z pg 128; AZ pg 191; J-NSSAR 1993 Reg, J- DAR Hatcher SAR P-173697 **BS:** 196; JLARC 1, 2.

HAMILTON, David; b abt 1761; d 15 Mar 1828 **RU:** Soldier, Capt Cunningham's Co Augusta Co Militia **CEM:** Bethel Presbyterian; GPS 38.04257, -79.17283; 563 Bethel Green Rd, Middlebrook; Augusta **GS:** Y **SP:** No info **VI:** Died age 66 **P:** N **BLW:** N **RG:** Y **MK:** unk **PH:** unk **SS:** E pg 341 SAR P-173732 **BS:** JLARC 62, 63; 196.

HAMILTON, James; b 1739; d 1807 **RU:** Private, Served in Capt John Lewis's Co, Augusta Co Militia for 112 days **CEM:** Tinkling Spring Presbyterian; GPS 38.08472, -78.98278; 30 Tinkling Spring Dr, Fishersville; Augusta **GS:** N **SP:** No info **VI:** No further data **P:** unk **BLW:** unk **RG:** N **MK:** N **PH:** N **SS:** Z pg 116 **BS:** 142 Tinkling Spr.

HAMILTON, James; b c1714, Glen Carland, CountyTyrone, Ireland; d c1798 **RU:** Private, VA Line. Enl Berkeley Co **CEM:** Old Opequon Church; GPS 39.82237, -78.11412; 217 Opequon Church Ln, Kernstown; Frederick **GS:** Y **SP:** Mar (26 Dec 1793 near Bucks Co PA line) Rebecca (-----) **VI:** Sol appl pen 15 May 1818 Frederick Co age 60. Pen info says soldier d Apr 1830. Widow appl pen 14 May 1839 Loudoun Co age 68. W24403 **P:** Y **BLW:** unk **RG:** N **MK:** N **PH:** unk **SS:** E pg 341; CG Vol 2 pg 1494 **BS:** 112 Old Opeeq.

HAMILTON, James; b 2 Sep 1748, Tyrone Co, Ireland; d 19 Jan 1812 **RU:** Private, Served in Morgan's riflemen unit **CEM:** Opequon Presbyterian; GPS 39.13938, -78.19494; 217 Opequon Church Ln; Winchester City **GS:** Y **SP:** Jane Gilbreath **VI:** Recd pension in Frederick Co. Died in Botetourt Co **P:** unk **BLW:** unk **RG:** Y **MK:** Y SAR: DAR plaque **PH:** Y **SS:** E pg 341; DAR Index Patriot pg 1287; J-NSSAR 2000 Reg SAR P-173766 **BS:** JLARC 76.

HAMILTON, James; b 1755; d 29 Mar 1834 **RU:** Soldier, Served in Capt Patrick Buchanan's Co, Col Thomas Hugart's Regt in battle of Hot Water 1781 and was severely wounded **CEM:** Bethel Presbyterian; GPS 38.04257, -79.17283; 563 Bethel Green Rd, Middlebrook; Augusta **GS:** Y **SP:** Mar (26 Mar 1794) Belenah (-----) **VI:** Appl for disability pen 13 Nov 1786 Augusta Co VA age 30. Recd 18 Nov 1786. S25128. Increased under Act of 24 Apr 1816. Was still living 14 Sep 1822 Augusta Co. Papers burned in fire of 1800. Only dates on stone are death on March 29th (year not readable) **P:** Y **BLW:** unk **RG:** Y **MK:** unk **PH:** unk **SS:** AZ pg 111; CG Vol 2 pg 1494; SAR P-173772 **BS:** JLARC 62, 63; 196.

HAMILTON, John; b 1749; d Mar 1829 **RU:** Soldier, Nurse in 1781; was in Battle at Hot Water & replaced brother Alexander **CEM:** Bethel Presbyterian; GPS 38.04257, -79.17283; 563 Bethel Green Rd, Middlebrook; Augusta **GS:** Y **SP:** No info **VI:** D age 79 **P:** unk **BLW:** unk **RG:** Y **MK:** unk **PH:** unk **SS:** AZ pg 112; SAR P-173810 **BS:** JLARC 62, 63; 196.

HAMILTON, William; b 1748; d 1795 **RU:** Private, Served in Capt Johnston's Co, Augusta Co Militia and in1st Light Dragoons **CEM:** Tinkling Spring Presbyterian; GPS 38.08472, -78.98278; 30 Tinkling Spring Dr, Fishersville; Augusta **GS:** N **SP:** No info **VI:** No further data **P:** unk **BLW:** unk **RG:** Y **MK:** unk **PH:** N **SS:** E pg 342 SAR P-173895 **BS:** 208 pg 469; 196.

HAMILTON, William T; b unk; d 7 Jun 1810 **RU:** Patriot, Gave material aid to the cause **CEM:** Mt Zion Methodist; GPS 37.66596, -79.46615; Btw Buffalo & Tinkersville; Rockbridge **GS:** Y **SP:** No info **VI:** No further data **P:** N **BLW:** N **RG:** N **MK:** N **PH:** unk **SS:** AL Ct bk 3 **BS:** 154 Rockbridge.

HAMMER, Henry; b 26 Nov 1759, Winchester; d 5 Feb 1841 **RU:** Private, Served in VA Line. Ent serv Rockingham Co, May 1778. Served 3 mos/10 days in Capt Robert Craven's VA Co. Enl early 1781 and served 3 mos/8 days Capt Michael Coger's Co in Col Hall's VA Regt **CEM:** Elk Run; GPS 38.41042, -78.61033; North St, Elkton; Rockingham **GS:** Y **SP:** Mar (21 Jun 1786 Rockingham Co) Mary Davis d/o

---

RU=Rank/Unit	CEM=Cemetery	GS=Gravestone	SP=Spousal Information
VI=Other Veteran Info	P=Pension	BLW=Bounty/Land Warrant	RG=Registered Grave
MK=SAR/DAR Marker	PH=Photo	SS=Service Source	BS=Burial Source

Joseph & (-----) Davis of Rockingham Co **VI:** Moved as infant with father to Shenandoah Co for six yrs, then to Rockingham Co. Source 76 has Old Peaked Mountain Church Cem. Mem. Stone at Elk Run Cem. He was bur at Old Peake Mountain Church Cem in McGaheysville. At Old Peake Mountain, his name listed with other Rev soldiers bur there. SAR marker at that site. Death listed on pen 5 Feb 1841-- on stone is listed as 1842. Sol appl pen 29 Aug 1835 Rockingham Co. Widow appl pen 12 May 1843 Rockingham Co age 76. W7652 **P:** Y **BLW:** unk **RG:** Y**MK:** N **PH:** unk **SS:** K pg 243; CG Vol 2 pg 1498-99 SAR P-173988 **BS:** JLARC 4, 64, 76.

HAMMON, Edward; b 1764; d 1801 **RU:** Matross, Enlisted in Capt William Waters Co Jan 1777. Served in VA 1st Artillery and as Private in 14th VA Regt **CEM:** Blandford; GPS 37.22433, -77.38604; 319 S Crater Rd; Petersburg City **GS:** Y **SP:** No info **VI:** No further data **P:** unk **BLW:** unk **RG:** N **MK:** Y SAR monument **PH:** unk **SS:** E pg 342 **BS:** 188.

HAMMOND, Stephen; b unk; d bef 19 Oct 1781 **RU:** Soldier, Served fr MA, killed in the battle at Yorktown **CEM:** Yorktown Victory Monument Tablet; GPS 38.28350, -78.54150; Yorktown; York **GS:** U **SP:** No info **VI:** No further data **P:** unk **BLW:** unk **RG:** Y **MK:** unk **PH:** unk **SS:** J-Yorktown Historian **SAR P-174173 BS:** JLARC 74.

HAMNER, Nicholas; b 1742 Albemarle; d 13 June 1793 **RU:** Captain, Commanded Co Albemarle Co Militia 14 Apr 1781. **VI:** Source cites unindexed lot of Executive Papers at the VA State library containing recommendations for militia officers **CEM:** Hamner Family; GPS unk; Carter's Bridge, Keene; Albemarle **GS:** N **SP:** Mar (1768) Agnes Tompkins 9 (1751 Spotsylvania Co.-1825) d/o Giles (1719-1795) & Virginia (Chiles) Tomkins **VI:** No further data **P:** unk **BLW:** unk **RG:** Y **MK:** unk **PH:** N **SS:** J-NSSAR 1993 Reg; E pg 343 SAR P-174213 **BS:** JLARC 1.

HAMON, Guenole; b unk, France; d 1781 **RU:** Seaman, Served on "Saint-Esprit" and died from Yorktown battle **CEM:** French Memorial; GPS 36.81944, -79.39933; Yorktown; York **GS:** U **SP:** No info **VI:** No further data **P:** unk **BLW:** unk **RG:** Y **MK:** unk **PH:** unk **SS:** J-Yorktown Historian SAR P-174224 **BS:** JLARC 1, 74.

HAMON, Yves; b unk,France; d 1781 **RU:** Seaman, Served on "Auguste" and died from Yorktown battle **CEM:** French Memorial; GPS 36.81944, -79.39933; Yorktown; York **GS:** U **SP:** No info **VI:** No further data **P:** unk **BLW:** unk **RG:** Y **MK:** unk **PH:** unk **SS:** J-Yorktown Historian SAR P-174226 **BS:** JLARC 1, 74.

HAMPTON, Thomas; b 17 Oct 1728, Fairfax Co; d 17 Dec 1796 **RU:** Sergeant/Patriot, Gave material aid to cause **CEM:** Hampton Family; GPS unk; Cascade; Pittsylvania **GS:** U **SP:2)** Sarah Pattison Conyers (1728-1765) **VI:** Son of John II & Margaret (Wade) Hampton **P:** unk **BLW:** unk **RG:** Y **MK:** unk **PH:** unk **SS:** J- DAR Hatcher; AL Ct Bk pg 8 Pittsylvania Co SAR P-174264 **BS:** JLARC 2.

HANBY, Jonathan; b 9 Dec 1741, Patrick Co; d 26 Mar 1817 **RU:** Captain, Ent serv Henry Co Militia 1777 **CEM:** Creasey's Chapel; GPS unk; Stuart; Patrick **GS:** U **SP:** Mar (6 Apr 1769 on home of father on Mayo River, Guilford Co NC) Sarah Dalton **VI:** Justice of the Peace in Patrick Co. W4687 **P:** unk **BLW:** unk **RG:** Y **MK:** unk **PH:** unk **SS:** K pg 248; SAR P-174297 **BS:** JLARC 1, 4, 30.

HANCOCK, Austin; b 5 Oct 1760, Hanover Co; d 12 Nov 1849 **RU:** Sergeant, Lived in Hanover Co at enl. Served in Capt John White's Co, VA Line **CEM:** Little River Baptist; GPS unk; Bumpass; Louisa **GS:** Y **SP:** Mar (1781 Louisa Co) Anne Nuckolls (1762-___) d/o Charles N. & Sarah Keziah (Yancey) Nuckolls **VI:** Son of Benjamin & Mary (Beadles) Hancock. Govt Gr stone. Sol appl pen 14 Jan 1833 Louisa Co. S5499 **P:** Y **BLW:** unk **RG:** Y **MK:** unk **PH:** unk **SS:** J-NSSAR 1993 Reg, J- DAR Hatcher; CG Vol 2 pg 1503 SAR P-174315 **BS:** JLARC 1, 2.

HANCOCK, George; b 13 Jun 1754; d 18 Jul 1820 **RU:** Colonel, Served in VA Line. Was aide-de-camp to Gen Pulaski **CEM:** Fortheringay; GPS 37.19101, -80.23193; Nr Graham St, Shawsville; Montgomery **GS:** U **SP:** Mar (24 Aug 1781) Margaret Strother (16 Sep 1763-22 Oct 1834) d/o (-----) & Mary Kennerly (1746-1834) **VI:** US Congressman 1793 to 1797 **P:** unk **BLW:** unk **RG:** Y **MK:** unk **PH:** unk **SS:** J-NSSAR 1993 Reg, J- DAR Hatcher; SAR P-174328, DAR A050838 **BS:** JLARC 1, 2; 196.

HANCOCK, John (D?); b 1733, James Northern Parish, Goochland Co; d 10 Nov 1802 **RU:** Patriot, Gave material aid to the cause **CEM:** Liberty Primitive Baptist; GPS 36.69494, -80.16269; Patrick

RU=Rank/Unit	CEM=Cemetery	GS=Gravestone	SP=Spousal Information
VI=Other Veteran Info	P=Pension	BLW=Bounty/Land Warrant	RG=Registered Grave
MK=SAR/DAR Marker	PH=Photo	SS=Service Source	BS=Burial Source

176

Springs; Patrick **GS**: N **SP**: Mar (16 Oct 1755 Goochland Co) Elizabeth Maddox (1732-__) d/o John & Elizabeth (-----) Maddox of Goochland and Powhatan Cos. **VI**: Son of Benjamin & (-----) Hancock. Bur on the "NE slope of Bull Mountain." This cemetery seems to fit that description **P**: N **BLW**: N **RG**:Y **MK**: unk **PH**: N **SS**: AL Ct Bk pg 2 Fluvanna Co SAR P-174339, DAR A050862 **BS**: 196.

HANCOCK, Lewis John; b 25 Oct 1757, Albemarle Co, d 14 Mar 1828 **RU**: Patriot, Supported cause by signing a legislative petition, Fluvanna Co, 20 Oct 1778 **CEM**: Hancock Family; **GPS**: 36.97299,-79.68562; Novelty, Union Hall; Franklin **GS**: Unk **SP**: Mar 29 Dec 1778, Fluvanna Co, Celia Duncan (1754, Albemarle Co-1806) **VI**: Son of John D Hancock (1733-10 Nov 1802) and Elizabeth Maddox (1732-1805, IL) **P**: N **BLW**: N **RG**: N **MK**: N **PH**: N **SS**: DAR Anc # A050887, cites Lib of VA Legislative Petitions of Gen Assembly 1776-1785, possession box #36721, box 78, folder 2; **BS**: 196

HANDLEY, John; b c1760; d 1804 **RU**: Private?, Served in Clark's III Regt in 1781 **CEM**: North Fork Baptist; **GPS** 39.06014, -77.68509; 38130 North Folk Rd, North Fork; Loudoun **GS**: Y **SP**: Gwin (----) (__-17 Oct 1834) **VI**: No further data **P**: unk **BLW**: unk **RG**: N **MK**: N **PH**: unk **SS**: E pg 344 **BS**: 75 Loudoun; 196.

HANGER, Frederick Jr; b 1755; d 1812 **RU**: Ensign, Served in Capt Buchanan's Co, Augusta Co Militia fr 30 Mar 1780 to end of war **CEM**: St John's Reformed UCC; GPS 38.05081, -79.17761; 1515 Arbor Hill Rd, Middlebrook; Augusta **GS**: N **SP**: 1) Elizabeth Rush 2) Maria Hull Rush **VI**: Son of Frederick Sr. (17 Nov 1726 Germany-Jul 1799 VA) & Eva Margaretha (Mayer) Hanger **P**: unk **BLW**: unk **RG**: Y **MK**: N **PH**: N **SS**: E pg 345 SAR P-174502 **BS**: JLARC 9, 62; 196.

HANGER, Peter Sr.; b 15 Feb 1729, Germany; d 1802 **RU**: Private/Patriot, Served in Capt Thomas Smith's Co, Augusta Co Militia. Also gave 17 bushels of rye to cause 25 Apr 1782 & 26 Aug 1782 **CEM**: Trinity Episcopal; GPS 38.14917, -79.07521; 214 Beverley St; Staunton City **GS**: U **SP**: Hannah Gobbert (1724-1801) **VI**: Died in Staunton, Augusta Co **P**: unk **BLW**: unk **RG**: Y **MK**: unk **PH**: unk **SS**: E pg 345; CY pg 46, 92 SAR P-174503, DAR A051077 **BS**: 196.

HANGER, Peter; b 29 Jan 1761; d 23 Dec 1828 **RU**: Soldier, Served in Capt Thomas Smith's Co Augusta Co Militia **CEM**: Old Link; GPS unk; .5 mi W of Ft Defiance; Augusta **GS**: Y **SP**: Catherine Line/Link (1767-1837) d/o Matthias (1737-1815) & Anna Maria (Schmidt) (1746-1817) Link. **VI**: Son of Peter Sr (1729-1802) & (-----) Hangar **P**: unk **BLW**: unk **RG**: Y**MK**: unk **PH**: unk **SS**: E pg 345 SAR P-174504 **BS**: JLARC 8, 62; 196.

HANKS, Abraham; b 1745, Northern Neck of VA; d In 1790s **RU**: Private, Served in Lt Col Richard Taylor's 2nd VA Regt of Foot 1779-1781 **CEM**: Hat Creek Presbyterian; GPS 37.06570, -78.54240; 6442 Hat Creek Rd, Brookneal; Campbell **GS**: N **SP**: Sarah Harper Hanks (__ Prince William Co)-1790 Campbell Co), daughter of George & Elizabeth (Shipley) Harper **VI**: Farrier for the William Clark party which were going to meet Daniel Boone in KY. Met on the Rapidan River 14 Mar 1775 according to Clark's journal. Grandfather of Abraham Lincoln **P**: unk **BLW**: unk **RG**: N **MK**: N **PH**: N **SS**: E pg 345 **BS**: 196.

HANKS, Abraham; b 2 Apr 1759, Amelia Co; d 10 July 1833 **RU**: Soldier, Served in VA Line. Ent serv Bedford Co **CEM**: Harper Family; GPS unk; Nr Hat Creek Church, Brookneal; Campbell **GS**: N **SP**: 1) Sarah Harper; 2) mar (5 Apr 1788 Campbell Co) Lucy Jennings **VI**: Appl 16 Oct 1832 Lincoln TN. Widow appl 21 Dec 1840 Lincoln Co TN age 70. R4569. Died in Lincoln Co TN. Some say he was the grandfather of Abraham Lincoln **P**: Y **BLW**: unk **RG**: N **MK**: N **PH**: N **SS**: CG Vol 2 pg 1508 **BS**: 196.

HANKS, Joshua; b c1760, Amelia Co; d Feb 1854 **RU**: Private, Served in Capt Flower Swift's Co, Montgomery Co Militia **CEM**: Old Quaker; GPS 36.64067, -80.88620; Off Old Quaker Rd Rt 727, Pipers Gap; Carroll **GS**: Y **SP**: Ruth Bryant, b 1764 in NC, d 1840 Grayson Co **VI**: Recd land grant 15 Oct 178? Supposed to be bur next to wife **P**: unk **BLW**: Y **RG**: Y **MK**: N **PH**: unk **SS**: AK May 07; BW pg 41, 43; BY; SAR P-330876 **BS**: 04; 196.

HANNA, Joseph; b 1722 Scotland; d 27 Jul 1789 **RU**: Patriot, Operated a gunpowder mill and provided gunpowder for militia **CEM**: Hanna Family; GPS unk; Nr Grottoes; Augusta **GS**: Y **SP**: Anna (-----) **VI**: No further data **P**: N **BLW**: N **RG**: Y **MK**: N **PH**: unk **SS**:; D, Vol 3 pg 833; AS; SAR applic SAR P-174586, DAR A051192 **BS**: SAR Appl.

RU=Rank/Unit	CEM=Cemetery	GS=Gravestone	SP=Spousal Information
VI=Other Veteran Info	P=Pension	BLW=Bounty/Land Warrant	RG=Registered Grave
MK=SAR/DAR Marker	PH=Photo	SS=Service Source	BS=Burial Source

HANNA, Robert; b 1750; d 24 Mar 1824 **RU**: Private, Served in Capt Brent's Co, 4th VA Brigade **CEM**: Bethel Presbyterian; GPS 38.04257, -79.17283; 563 Bethel Green Rd, Middlebrook; Augusta **GS**: Y **SP**: Mary Ann Kilpatrick **VI**: Govt stone (cenotaph) **P**: unk **BLW**: unk **RG**: Y **MK**: unk **PH**: unk **SS**: NSSAR Ancestor # P-174593 SAR P-174593, DAR A051203 **BS**: JLARC 4, 62, 63; 196.

HANNAH, Alexander; b 1728 ; d Nov 1803 **RU**: Patriot, Gave material aid to cause **CEM**: Old Presbyterian Meeting House; GPS 38.48528, -77.23532; 323 S Fairfax St; Alexandria City **GS**: N **SP**: No info **VI**: Died of old age, bur 22 Nov 1803 age 74 **P**: N **BLW**: N **RG**: N **MK**: N **PH**: N **SS**: AL Cert Issued **BS**: 23 pg 103.

HANNAN, Esom; b 1752; d 20 Mar 1843 **RU**: Private, Served in Cont & VA Lines. Ent Botetourt Co **CEM**: Greenwood Family; GPS unk; Cave Springs; Roanoke Co **GS**: U **SP**: Mar (15 Sep 1783) Mary Greenlee d/o William & (-----) Greenlee of Botetourt Co **VI**: Sol appl pen 12 Nov 1833. Widow appl pen 11 Oct 1843 Roanoke Co. W7644 **P**: Y **BLW**: unk **RG**: N **MK**: unk **PH**: unk **SS**: J- DAR Hatcher; CG Vol 2 pg 1510 **BS**: JLARC 2.

HANSBROUGH (HANSBOROUGH), William; b 1755, Amherst Co; d 18 Jan 1816 **RU**: Private, Served in Capt William Fontaine's Co, VA Line **CEM**: Stevensburg Baptist; GPS unk; Stevensburg; Culpeper **GS**: Y **SP**: Mar (5 Nov 1786) Virginia Sarah Vaughn (c1767-23 Mar 1857) d/o William & (-----) Vaughn (father signed bond w/ sol 2 Nov 1786 in Culpeper Co) **VI**: Pen rec Jan 1816. Widow appl pen 18 Sep 1845 Culpeper Co age 77. W3808. Recd BLW #28518-160-55. Source 4 has esf 1775 and d in Stevensburg. Stone reads he d in 1815. **P**: Y **BLW**: Y **RG**: Y **MK**: Y SAR **PH**: unk **SS**: J-NSSAR 1993 Reg, J- DAR Hatcher; K pg 254; CG Vol 2 pg 1511 SAR P-174651, DAR A051225 **BS**: JLARC 1, 2; 196.

HANSFORD, Cary H; b unk; d 29 Oct 1801 **RU**: Surg Mate/Patriot, Served in VA Line and Navy. Served 3 yrs on galley, "Dragon".Was at siege of Yorktown. Took oath as a Common Councilman in 1782 **CEM**: St Paul's Episcopal; GPS 36.84733, -76.28554; 201 St Paul's Blvd; Norfolk City **GS**: Y **SP**: Maria T__ **VI**: Alderman and eminent physician, Mayor of Norfok in 1785, 1791-2. Half pay pen paid to wife and son. R14850 **P**: Y **BLW**: unk **RG**: N **MK**: Y SAR plaque **PH**: unk **SS**: CB K,Vol 2 pg 254; K pg 254; CG Vol 2 pg 1512 **BS**: 87 pg 27.

HARDING, Aesop; b unk; d 1781 **RU**: Soldier, Served fr MA, killed in the battle at Yorktown **CEM**: Yorktown Victory Monument Tablet; GPS 38.28350, -78.54150; Yorktown; York **GS**: U **SP**: No info **VI**: No further data **P**: unk **BLW**: unk **RG**: Y **MK**: unk **PH**: unk **SS**: J-Yorktown Historian SAR P-174931 **BS**: JLARC 74.

HARDING, Isaac; b 1736; d 1820 **RU**: Patriot, Gave 139 # of beef for guard of prisoners **CEM**: Old Hardin (Shirley) Property; GPS unk; Nr Greenwood; Albemarle **GS**: Y **SP**: No info **VI**: No further data **P**: N **BLW**: N **RG**: Y **MK**: N **PH**: unk **SS**: AL Ct Bk pg 22, 23; D Albemarle Co pg 25 SAR P- 174952 **BS**: 80 vol 2 pg 117.

HARDY, Joseph Austin; b 1761, Lunenburg Co; d 22 May 1831 **RU**: Soldier, Served in Harrison's Co, 2nd VA Regt, Cont Line **CEM**: Hardy Family; GPS 37.23460, -79.30230, GS37.2346,-79.3023; State Rts 122 & 640, Forbes Mill; Bedford **GS**: U **SP**: Mar (31 Aug 1788) Margaret Mackenzie (1768 Scotland-__) **VI**: Son of Thomas (4 May 1705-1791 KY) & Elizabeth (Austin) Hardy **P**: unk **BLW**: unk **RG**:Y **MK**: N **PH**: unk **SS**: J- DAR Hatcher; E pg 348 Govt marker shows service SAR P- 175056 **BS**: JLARC 2; App D;196.

HARDY, Joshua; b unk; d unk **RU**: Soldier, Served in Harrison's Co 2nd VA Regt, Cont Line **CEM**: Hardy Family; GPS unk; State Rts 122 & 640, Forbes Mill; Bedford **GS**: Y **SP**: No info **VI**: No further data **P**: unk **BLW**: unk **RG**: Y **MK**: N **PH**: unk **SS**: J-NSSAR 1993 Reg SAR P- 175057 **BS**: JLARC 1.

HARE, Joseph; b 1749, SC; d Sep 1855 **RU**: Scout, Served in militia **CEM**: Boyd, Wolf Creek; GPS unk; Wolf Creek Rd nr Narrows; Giles **GS**: U **SP**: 1) Nannie Clay 2) Phoebe Perdue **VI**: No further data **P**: unk **BLW**: unk **RG**: Y **MK**: unk **PH**: unk **SS**: J- DAR Hatcher; DD SAR P-175109 **BS**: JLARC 2.

HARKRADER (HARKRIDER), John; b 1 Oct 1750, Maxatawny Twp, Berks Co, PA; d 24 Nov 1837 **RU**: Captain, Served in PA Line. Ent serv Lancaster Co PA **CEM**: St John's Lutheran; GPS 36.96500, -81.10110; 405 W Main, Wytheville; Wythe **GS**: U **SP**: Barbara Sophia (-----) (7 Feb 1753-6 May 1802)

RU=Rank/Unit	CEM=Cemetery	GS=Gravestone	SP=Spousal Information
VI=Other Veteran Info	P=Pension	BLW=Bounty/Land Warrant	RG=Registered Grave
MK=SAR/DAR Marker	PH=Photo	SS=Service Source	BS=Burial Source

VI: Son of Johannes (1714, Germany-19 Dec 1773, Middletown, Frederick Co, MD) & Anna Dorthea (Manuschmidt) (1719-1753) Herrgereder. Sol appl pen 12 Nov 1832 Wythe Co. S13323 **P:** Y **BLW:** unk **RG:** Y **MK:** unk **PH:** unk **SS:** K pg 259; CG Vol 2 pg 1520 SAR P-175184 **BS:** JLARC 3, 4, 40; 196.

HARLESS, David Anthony; b 5 Jan 1745, Lancaster, Lancaster Co, PA; d 1817 **RU:** Private, Served in Capt John Taylor's Co, Montgomery Co Militia **CEM:** Harless Family; GPS 37.21331, -80.54910; Vic jct Rt 744 & Long Shop Rd, Blacksburg; Montgomery **GS:** U **SP:** Mar (20 Jan 1813 Montgomery Co) Polly Hill, surty - John Hill (This marriage could be for another same name) **VI:** Son of John Phillip (1716-1772) & Anna Margaretha (Price) (1713-1784) Harless. Born on what is now Rockbridge Co on Cow Pasture River 4 mi fr Natural Bridge **P:** unk **BLW:** unk **RG:** N **MK:** unk **PH:** unk **SS:** G pg 234-5 **BS:** 196.

HARLESS (HORLESS), Philip; b 1760, Augusta, Botetourt Co); d 22 Mar 1834 **RU: Indian** Spy. Served in VA Line. Ent serv Botetourt Co (now Montgomery) **CEM:** Harless Family; GPS 37.21331, -80.54910; Vic jct Rt 744 & Long Shop Rd, Blacksburg; Montgomery **GS:** U **SP:** Mar (7 Jun 1790 Montgomery Co) Molly Standley **VI:** Sol appl pen 22 Mar 1834 Giles Co age 73. R4613 **P:** Y **BLW:** unk **RG:** Y **MK:** unk **PH:** unk **SS:** J- DAR Hatcher; CG Vol 2 pg 1520 SAR P-175209, DAR A050704 **BS:** JLARC 2.

HARMAN, Daniel Conrad; b 26 Jan 1760 Rowan Co, NC; d 10 Jul 1791 **RU:** Patriot, Gave material aid to cause **CEM:** Henry Harmon; GPS unk; Fourway; Tazewell **GS:** Y **SP:** Phebey (Pheby) Davidson (1762 Rowan Co NC-1791 Tazewell Co) **VI:** Son of Henry Sr. (1726-1822) & Nancy Ann (Welburn/Wilburn) (1730-1808) Harman and brother of Daniel Harman. Was killed and scalped by an Indian a mile or two east of Five Oaks, in Tazewell Co. 1791 **P:** N **BLW:** N **RG:** N **MK:** N **PH:** N **SS:** AL Ct Bk pg 43 Montgomery Co **BS:** 196.

HARMAN, Henry ("Old Skygusta") Sr; b 30 Oct 1726, Isles of Man, Ireland; d 23 May or Jun 1822 **RU:** Patriot, Member of the Committee of Safety, Rowan Co, NC **CEM:** Holly Brook; GPS unk; Rt 606 off Hwy 42 adj Holly Brook Community Center; Bland **GS:** Y **SP: Anna** (Nancy) Wilburn (1734-1808) **VI:** Govt marker and another monument celebrating his and his two sons' victory over seven Black Hawk Indians in 1788. DAR Marker **P:** N **BLW:** N **RG:** Y **MK:** Y SAR **PH:** unk **SS:** J-NSSAR 1993 Reg; DD cites book by Saunders Colonial Records of NC Vol 9 pg 1073 SAR P-175279, DAR A050817 **BS:** JLARC 1; 196.

HARMAN, Mathias (Matthias); b c1736, Strausburg; d 2 Apr 1832 **RU:** Captain, Served in Cont Line **CEM: Dry Fork,** Sayer's Farm, or Harman; GPS unk; Rt 637, Dry Fork State marker nearby; Tazewell **GS:** U **SP:** Lydia Scaggs/Scraggs (1755-2 Oct 1814) d/o James & Rachel (Moredock) Skaggs **VI:** Son of Heinrich Adam (1700-1767) & Louisa Katrina (Martias) (1704-1749) Harman. He with others in a hunting party built a lodge in E KY in 1787 or 1789 which became a stockade called Harman Station which was later burned by Indians **P:** unk **BLW:** unk **RG:** Y **MK:** unk **PH:** unk **SS:** B Military Marker; SAR P-175290, DAR A050869 **BS:** JLARC 1, 2, 89; 196.

HARMAN, Michael; b 4 Nov 1766, Frederick Co, MD; d 11 Aug 1808 **RU:** Private, Served in German Bn Cont Troops. Also served in 4th PA Regt **CEM:** Trinity Episcopal; GPS 38.14917, -79.07521; 214 Beverley St; Staunton City **GS:** U **SP:** No info **VI:** No further data **P:** unk **BLW:** unk **RG:** N **MK:** unk **PH:** unk **SS:** CI **BS:** 196.

HARMAN (HARMON), Daniel; b 26 Jun 1760, Tazwell Co; d 10 Jul 1791 **RU:** Private, Served in Capt James Maxwell's Co Montgomery Co **CEM:** Wynn-Peery; GPS 37.12620, -81.4988; Campbell Ln, Tazewell; Tazewell **GS:** Y **SP:** No info **VI:** No further data **P:** unk **BLW:** unk **RG:** N **MK:** N **PH:** unk **SS:** G pg 237 **BS:** 135 vol 3 pg 52.

HARMON, Henry; b 1726, Isle of Mann, Scotland; d Aft 23 Jul 1822 **RU:** Private?, Served in the battle at Point Pleasant **CEM:** Old Peaked Mountain; GPS 38.37113, -78.73416; 9843 Town Hall Rd, McGaheysville; Rockingham **GS:** Y **SP:** Nancy Wilburn **VI:** A person this name is buried in Tazewell Co, who had civil service in Rowan Co, NC who married Anna Wilburn **P:** unk **BLW:** Y **RG:** Y **MK:** Y **PH:** unk **SS:** Q pg 70; CU Vol 9 pg 1073; SAR P-175326 **BS:** 04.

HARMON, Jacob Jr; b 2 Feb 1754; d 1792 **RU:** Private/Patriot, Served in Capt James Maxwell's Co, Montgomery Co. Signed Oath of Alligiance Sep 1777 Montgomery Co **CEM:** Old Peaked Mountain;

RU=Rank/Unit
VI=Other Veteran Info
MK=SAR/DAR Marker

CEM=Cemetery
P=Pension
PH=Photo

GS=Gravestone
BLW=Bounty/Land Warrant
SS=Service Source

SP=Spousal Information
RG=Registered Grave
BS=Burial Source

179

GPS 38.37113, -78.73416; 9843 Town Hall Rd, McGaheysville; Rockingham **GS:** N **SP:** No info **VI:** No further data **P:** unk **BLW:** unk **RG:** N **MK:** N **PH:** N **SS:** G pg 209, 237 **BS:** 116.

HARMON, Mathias; b Feb 1769; d 20 Dec 1802 **RU:** Soldier, Served in Capt James Maxwell's Co, Montgomery Co Militia **CEM:** Harmon Family; GPS 36.95470, -81.40080; Rt 610 Old Valley Rd, S of Hamon Creek nr Bland Co line; Smyth **GS:** Y **SP:** Mar (25 Jan 1791) Mary (-----) **VI:** SWS **P:** unk **BLW:** unk **RG:** N **MK:** unk **PH:** unk **SS:** G pg 237 **BS:** 97 pg 30.

HARNSBERGER, Adam; b 10 Jan 1751 Rockingham Co; d 1816 **RU:** Private/Patriot, Col. Wm. Noll's/Null's regt. Gave material aid to cause **CEM:** Elk Run; GPS 38.41042, -78.61033; North St, Elkton; Rockingham **GS:** U **SP:** Mar (9 Apr 1776) Catherine Null (b.1753) **VI:** No further data **P:** unk **BLW:** unk **RG:** Y **MK:** unk **PH:** unk **SS:** J- DAR Hatcher; D Vol 3 pg 828, 832 SAR P-175416 **BS:** JLARC 2.

HARNSBERGER, Robert; b 1761; d 7 Jun 1840 **RU:** Private, Served in Capt William Hall's Co **CEM:** Augusta Stone Presbyterian; GPS 38.23926, -78.97356; 28 Old Stone Church Ln, Ft Defiance; Augusta **GS:** N **SP:** Christina Miller **VI:** No further data **P:** unk **BLW:** unk **RG:**Y **MK:** Y SAR plaque **PH:** N **SS:** AP NARA Service Record, Pension rec Thomas Lewis & John Pence; AR Vol 2 pg 119 SAR P-175419, DAR A050978 **BS:** JLARC 2, 62.

HARPER, Edward; b 1763; d 4 Dec 1803 **RU:** Soldier, SAR registration did not specify service **CEM:** Old Presbyterian Meeting House; GPS 38.48528, -77.23532; 323 S Fairfax St; Alexandria City **GS:** N **SP:** No info **VI:** No further data **P:** unk **BLW:** unk **RG:** Y **MK:** unk **PH:** N **SS:** SAR P-175440 **BS:** JLARC 1; 5.

HARPER, John; b 3 Oct 1728, Philadelphia, PA; d 7 May 1804 **RU:** Captain/Patriot, Served in Navy. Was Councilman in Alexandria and took Oath of Allegiance 1780 Gave supplies At Fairfax Co. **CEM:** Old Presbyterian Meeting House; GPS 38.48528, -77.23532; 323 S Fairfax St; Alexandria City **GS:** Y **SP:** 1) Mary Reynolds Cunningham Mar 2) Sarah Wells(20 Oct 1750) **VI:** Died age 76. Bur 7 May 1704. Styled Capt on stone, which is mostly obscured by the church wall. Listed on SAR plaque in cemetery **P:** unk **BLW:** unk **RG:** Y **MK:** Y SAR plaque **PH:** unk **SS:** J-NSSAR 1993 Reg, J- DAR Hatcher; AK; CT Order Bk Vol 6 pg 2, 3 Alexandria SAR P-175461, DAR A051058 **BS:** JLARC 1 ,2; 23 pg 103; 196.

HARPER, Joseph; b 1751; d 31 Nov 1809 **RU:** Patriot, Signed a legislative petition **CEM:** Old Presbyterian Meeting House; GPS 38.48528, -77.23532; 323 S Fairfax St; Alexandria City **GS:** N **SP:** No info **VI**: Was rope maker. D of palsey age 58 (Alexandria Gazette, 1 Dec 1809), bur 1 Dec 1809 **P:** N **BLW:** N **RG:** N **MK:** N **PH:** N **SS:** BB **BS:** 23 pg 111.

HARPER, William; b 14 Mar 1761, Philadelphia; d 18 Apr 1829 **RU:** Captain, Served under Gen Washington at Princeton, Monmouth, Brandywine, & Valley Forge **CEM:** Presbyterian Church; GPS 38.80015, -77.05791; Wilkes St & Hamilton Ln; Alexandria City **GS:** Y **SP:** Mar (May 1763) Mary Scull, d/o William & (-----) Scull **VI:** Recd pen R4629 D age 69. Death notice in Alexandria Gazette 22 Apr 1829 **P:** unk **BLW:** unk **RG:** Y **MK:** Y SAR plaque **PH:** unk **SS:** K pg 263; AK GW 2015; SAR P-333953, DAR A051115 **BS:** 23 pg 39.

HARRIS, Benjamin; b 3 Jan 1754 Albemarle; d 25 Mar 1834 **RU:** Captain, Served in VA Line. Ent serv Albemarle Co **CEM:** Harris Family; GPS 37.81867, -78.66393; Irish Rd, Esmont; Albemarle **GS:** Y **SP:** Mar (27 Oct 1785 Albemarle Co) Mary Woods (c1767-15 Aug 1844) **VI:** Sol appl pen 8 Jan 1834 Albemarle Co. Widow appl pen 2 Oct 1841 Albemarle Co age 74. W7664 **P:** Y **BLW:** unk **RG:** Y **MK:** unk **PH:** unk **SS:** CG Vol 2 pg 1530 SAR P-175734 **BS:** JLARC 4; 196.

HARRIS, David; b c1761; d 1841 **RU:** Private, Served in 1st, 2nd, 7th, 11th, 15th Cont Lines **CEM:** Shockoe Hill; GPS 37.55190, -77.43170; 4th & Hospital Sts; Richmond City **GS:** Y **SP:** No info **VI:** Pensioned in Hanover Co. Recd BLW of 100 acres for 3 yrs service Jun 1786 **P:** Y **BLW:** Y **RG:** N **MK:** N **PH:** unk **SS:** E pg 352; F pg 39 **BS:** 57 pg 22.

HARRIS, Francis E; b unk; d 20 Oct 1820 **RU:** Patriot, Gave material aid to cause **CEM:** Patrick Harris Homesite; GPS unk; dirt rd off Rt 614 abt 3 mi; Powhatan **GS:** Y **SP:** Col Thomas Harris **VI:** No further data **P:** N **BLW:** N **RG:** N **MK:** unk **PH:** unk **SS:** AL Ct Bk pg 9 **BS:** 187; 196

RU=Rank/Unit	CEM=Cemetery	GS=Gravestone	SP=Spousal Information
VI=Other Veteran Info	P=Pension	BLW=Bounty/Land Warrant	RG=Registered Grave
MK=SAR/DAR Marker	PH=Photo	SS=Service Source	BS=Burial Source

180

HARRIS, James, Jr; b 22 May 1722 Albemarle Co; d 14 Apr 1792 **RU:** Patriot, Gave material aid to cause **CEM:** Stonewall Jackson Memorial/AKA Oak Grove/ Presbyterian; GPS 37.78128, -79.44604; 314 S Main St; Lexington City **GS:** Y **SP:** Mary Ann Harris (10 Feb 1730 Hanover Co-4 Jan 1819 Albemarle Co) **VI:** Son of Robert Overton Harris (1696-1765) & Mourning Gleason Glenn (1702-1775) Died in Albemarle Co **P:** N **BLW:** N **RG:** Y **MK:** N **PH:** N **SS:** AL Ct Bk V pg 72 Rockbridge Co SAR P-175835 **BS:** 196.

HARRIS, John; b unk; d bef 1826 **RU:** Patriot, Gave material aid to cause **CEM:** Eastern State Hospital; GPS 37.25560, -76.71030; S Henry Street; Williamsburg City **GS:** N **SP:** No info **VI:** No further data **P:** N **BLW:** N **RG:** Y **MK:** N **PH:** N **SS:** AL Ct bk pg 1 SAR P-175900 **BS:** 65 Williamsburg.

HARRIS, John C; b 24 Dec 1754, New Kent Co; d 1824 **RU:** Soldier, Ent Serv Lousia Co. Served in Lt Wm Harris Co **CEM:** Liberty Baptist; GPS 37.35181, -78.82862; 1709 Church St, Appomatox; Appomattox **GS:** N **SP:** Mary (-----) **VI:** Sol appl pen 26 Nov 1832 Nelson Co. S6953 **P:** Y **BLW:** unk **RG:** Y **MK:** unk **PH:** N **SS:** CG Vol 2 pg 1534 SAR P-175906 **BS:** JLARC 4, 59.

HARRIS, Jordan; b 20 May 1763, Goochland Co; d 7 Oct 1826 **RU:** Line Lieutenant, Served in Cont Army in VA Line **CEM:** Grubbs Family, aka Spring Grove; GPS 37.43510, 77.36520; Spring Grove #2 Farm, nr Calvary Christian jct Rts 623 & 624; Hanover **GS:** U **SP:** Mar (1789) Elizabeth Mosby Cannon (1771-1801) **VI:** BLW #1083-150-2 Apr 1796 to Joseph Fenwick. Record lost in 1814 fire **P:** unk **BLW:** Y **RG:** Y **MK:** unk **PH:** unk **SS:** K pg 267; CG Vol 2 pg 1534 SAR P-175912 **BS:** JLARC 71.

HARRIS, Nathan; b c1749, d 19 Mar 1827 **RU:** Lieutenant/ Patriot, Capt Nathaniel Massie's Co, Goochland County Militia. As a patriot gave material aid to cause in Louisa County **CEM:** Tolersville Tavern; GPS: 38.01321, -77.90345; 410 Old Tolersville Rd, Mineral; Louisa **GS:** Yes **SP:** Sarah Knight (1756-1826) **VI:** No further data **P:** N **BLW:** N **RG:** N **MK:** N **PH:** N **SS:** E pg 353; AL Ct Bk pg 18, Louisa Co **BS:** 196.

HARRIS, Robert; b unk; d 1805 **RU:** Second Lieutenant, Took oath 17 Sep 1777 as 2nd Lt in Capt Samuel McCutchen's Co, Augusta Co Militia **CEM:** New Providence Presbyterian; GPS 37.95170, -79.30250; 1208 New Providence Rd, Raphine; Rockbridge **GS:** U **SP:** No info **VI:** No further data **P:** unk **BLW:** unk **RG:** N **MK:** unk **PH:** unk **SS:** E pg 353 **BS:** 196.

HARRIS, Samuel; b 19 Jan 1724; d bef 21 Oct 1799 **RU:** Colonel/Patriot, Gave material aid to cause **CEM:** Harris Family; GPS unk; Rt 816 or Rt 703, 10 mi fr Chatham nr Chatham HS; Pittsylvania **GS:** U **SP:** Lucy Camp **VI:** Organizer of Baptists **P:** unk **BLW:** unk **RG:** Y **MK:** unk **PH:** unk **SS:** AL Ct Bk pg 30, 47, 53, 59 Pittsylvania Co SAR P-176003 **BS:** JLARC 76,96.

HARRIS, William; b 13 Jul 1749, Goochland Co (pen rec) or 1749; d 1815 **RU:** Major, Served in VA Line. Ent serv Amherst Co **CEM:** Rockfish Presbyterian; GPS unk; 5016 Rockfish Valley Hwy, Nellysford; Nelson **GS:** U **SP:** Elizabeth Wagstaff **VI:** Sol appl pen 22 Oct 1832 Nelson Co (formerly Amherst Co). S6956 **P:** Y **BLW:** unk **RG:** Y **MK:** unk **PH:** unk **SS:** CG Vol 2 pg 1537 SAR P-176077 **BS:** JLARC 83.

HARRIS, William Sr.; ca 1713; d bef 11 Dec 1788 **RU:** Patriot, Gave material aid to cause in Albemarle Co **CEM:** Harris Family; GPS 37.81867, -78.66393; Irish Rd, Esmont; Albemarle **GS:** Y **SP:** Mary Netherland (1719-1789) **VI:** No further data **P:** unk **BLW:** unk **RG:** Y **MK:** unk **PH:** Y **SS:** AL Ct Bk pg 7, 15; SAR P-329962 **BS:** 196.

HARRIS, William E; b 1752; d 1826 **RU:** Patriot, Gave material aid to the cause **CEM:** Spring Grove; GPS 39.10916, -78.09970; Rockville; Hanover **GS:** Y **SP:** Mar (20 Dec 1780 Hanover Co) Diana Goodwin **VI:** No further data **P:** N **BLW:** N **RG:** N **MK:** N **PH:** unk **SS:** AL Ct Bk lt I pg 24 **BS:** 31 vol I pg 104.

HARRIS, William, b 1748, d aft 1783 **RU:** Patriot Paid Personal Property Tax, Loudoun Co 1783 considered a supply tax for Rev War expenses **CEM:** Union; GPS: 39.12046, -77.56237; 323 No King St, Leesburg; Loudoun **GS:** No **SP:** No spousal info **VI:** Son of William Harris (1723-1766) and Hannah Moore (1723-1779) **P:** N **BLW:** N **RG:** N **MK:** N **PH:** No **SS:** DV Loudoun Co, 1783 BS: 196

HARRISON, Benjamin Jr.; b 1755 or 1757, Charles City Co; d 1799 **RU:** Captain, Commanded a co in Charles Co Militia, Dec 1776 **CEM:** Berkeley Plantation; GPS 37.31450, -77.17840; Rt 5, Harrison

RU=Rank/Unit	CEM=Cemetery	GS=Gravestone	SP=Spousal Information
VI=Other Veteran Info	P=Pension	BLW=Bounty/Land Warrant	RG=Registered Grave
MK=SAR/DAR Marker	PH=Photo	SS=Service Source	BS=Burial Source

Landing Rd; Charles City Co **GS:** U **SP:** Mar (15 Nov 1785) Anne Mercer (9 Sep 1760, Stafford Co-29 Jun 1822, Cabin Point, Surry Co) **VI:** Son of Benjamin (13 Dec 1730, Charles City Co-24 Apr 1791) & Elizabeth (Bassett) (13 Dec 1730, Eltham, VA-1792, Berkeley) Harrison. Rec'd BLW of 266.66 acres **P:** unk **BLW:** Y **RG:** N **MK:** unk **PH:** unk **SS:** A pg 534; G pg 116; N pg 1093; CZ **BS:** 196.

HARRISON, Benjamin; b 1741, Dayton, Rockingham Co; d 1819 **RU:** Colonel/Patriot, Was Capt in Battle of Point Pleasant 1774. Held rank of Col in VA Militia. Served under General LaFayette & General Andrew Lewis. Gave material aid to cause **CEM:** Dayton; GPS 38.42000, -78.94303; Bowman Rd, Dayton; Rockingham **GS:** Y **SP:** Mary McClure **VI:** NSSAR Graves database shows Benjamin's wife as Margaret Cravens. Benjamin is the son of Daniel Harrison and Margaret Cravens **P:** unk **BLW:** unk **RG:** Y **MK:** Y **SAR PH:** unk **SS:** J-NSSAR 1993 Reg; D Rockingham Co SAR P-176121 **BS:** JLARC 1.

HARRISON, Benjamin; b 1747; d 1807 **RU:** Lieutenant/Patriot, Gave material aid to cause **CEM:** Harrison Family; GPS unk; 5.5 mi NE of Burrowsville; Prince George **GS:** Y **SP:** Evelyn Taylor **VI:** No further data **P:** unk **BLW:** unk **RG:** Y **MK:** N **PH:** unk **SS:** E pg 354; AL Ct Bk pg 4 Prince George Co SAR P-176124 **BS:** 111 Part 5 pg 113.

HARRISON, Benjamin; b unk; d Aft 1781 **RU:** Lt Colonel/Patriot, Served in Rockingham Co Militia. Took oath as Lt Col 25 May 1778, and oath as Co Lt 1782.Gave material aid to cause in Rockingham Co adjacent to Shenandoah Co **CEM:** St Mathew's; GPS 36.65131, -78.67121; Breckenridge Ln, New Market; Shenandoah **GS:** U **SP:** No info **VI:** No further data **P:** unk **BLW:** unk **RG:** N **MK:** unk **PH:** unk **SS:** J- DAR Hatcher; AL Ct Bk II pg 36 **BS:** JLARC 2.

HARRISON, Benjamin Sr V.; b 5 Apr 1726; d 24 Apr 1791 **RU:** Patriot, VA Governor 1781-1784; Signer Declaration of Independence, member Cont Congress **CEM:** Berkeley Plantation; GPS 37.31450, -77.17840; Rt 5, 12602 Harrison Landing Rd; Charles City Co **GS:** U **SP:** Mar (1748) Elizabeth Bassett (13 Dec 1730, Eltham, VA-1792 Berkeley) **VI:** Presided over final debate of the Declaration of Independence **P:** N **BLW:** N **RG:** Y **MK:** Y **SAR Bronze PH:** unk **SS:** DD cites Dictionary of American Biography Vol 4 pg 330, 331 SAR P-176297, DAR A052117 **BS:** 196.

HARRISON, Carter Henry; b 1732, Barkley; d bef 22 Jan 1794 8 Oct 1793 **RU:** Captain/Patriot, Served at Ft Cumberland on 17 Sep 1775 in a VA Regt. Was on a committee of safety **CEM:** Clifton Cemetery; GPS 37.40752, -78.07579; Off Rt 690 N of Hamilton; Cumberland **GS:** Y **SP:** Mar (9 Nov 1760 Goochland Co) Susannah Randolph (25 Sep 1738, Goochland Co-___) d/o Isham Randolph (1685-1742) & Jane Lilburne Rogers (1692-1760) **VI:** Son of Benjamin Harrison (1694-1745) & Anne Carter (1704-1745). Was in Cumberland Co Committee of Safety,and author of Resolutions of Independence 22 Apr 1776; member House of Delegates 1782-1787 **P:** unk **BLW:** unk **RG:**Y **MK:** Y **SAR PH:** unk **SS:** G pg 357 **SAR P-176134, DAR A052132 BS:** 32 e-mail 01/07; 196.

HARRISON, Charles; b 30 Sep 1742, Berkeley, Charles City County; d 12 Dec 1793, Surry Co **RU:** Colonel 1st Artillery VA Regiment Sep 1778, Cont Line **CEM:** Huntington Quarter Plantation, GPS 36.5204,-77.1328; loc Huntington Quarter Rd S of jct with Poole Rd; Sussex **GS:** Y **SP:** Mar 1761, Mary Herbert Clairborne (19 Jan 1744, King William Co-25 Jul 1775), d/o Augustine Clairborne (1720-1787) **VI:** Son of Benjamin Harrison (1694-1745) & Sarah Anne Carter (1704-1745). Resigned his commission because of ill health **P:** unk **BLW:** Y **RG:** Y **MK:** N **PH:** N **SS:** DAR A052136; E pg 859; SAR 176138 **BS:** 196.

HARRISON, John Peyton; b 9 Mar 1748 Augusta Co; d Nov 1789 **RU:** Captain, Served in 2nd Cont Line May 1777 **CEM:** Lacey Springs; GPS 38.54475, -78.77072; Lacey Springs; Rockingham **GS:** U **SP:** Mar (c1772) Hannah Lincoln (9 Mar 1748, PA-Dec 1803) **VI:** Son of Zebulon (1718, Long Island, NY-Rockingham Co 1792) & Margaret (Cravens) (23 Jul 1724,Morristown, NJ-1800) Harrison. Recd BLW 4000 acres 4 May 1777 **P:** unk **BLW:** Y **RG:** N **MK:** unk **PH:** unk **SS:** E pg 355; **BS:** 196.

HARRISON, John Sr; b 1760; d 1844 **RU:** Private, Served in VA Line. Lived w/ father in King George Co at enl. Was age 15 at enl in 1776 **CEM:** Harrison Family; GPS 38.43373, -78.29048; Shelby; Madison **GS:** U **SP:** Jane Campbell **VI:** Sol appl pen 23 Aug 1832 Madison Co, age 72 where he lived for 42 yrs. S5471 **P:** Y **BLW:** unk **RG:** Y **MK:** unk **PH:** unk **SS:** J-NSSAR 2000 Reg; K pg 271; CG Vol 2 pg 1540 SAR P-176298 **BS:** JLARC 76.

RU=Rank/Unit	CEM=Cemetery	GS=Gravestone	SP=Spousal Information
VI=Other Veteran Info	P=Pension	BLW=Bounty/Land Warrant	RG=Registered Grave
MK=SAR/DAR Marker	PH=Photo	SS=Service Source	BS=Burial Source

HARRISON, Nathaniel; b 1703; d 1 Oct 1781 **RU**: Patriot, Gave material aid to cause. Was member of Prince George Co Committee of Safety & member of the State Senate, Oct 1779 **CEM**: Brandon Plantation; GPS 37.15271, -76.59362; Burrowsville; Prince George **GS**: Y **SP**: 1) Mary Digges d/o Cole & (-----) Digges of "Belfield" York Co 2) mar (bef 15 Feb 1748) Lucy Carter, d/o Robert & (-----) Carter of "Corotoman" **VI**: No further data **P**: unk **BLW**: unk **RG**: Y **MK**:Y **SAR PH**: unk **SS**: AS, DAR Report; AL Ct Bk I pg 5, 7 Prince George Co SAR P-176293 **BS**: 80 vol 2 pg 123; 213 pg 425.

HARRISON, Reuben; b 1731; d 1807 **RU**: Captain/Patriot, Took oath as Capt, 25 May 1778 and commanded a co in Rockingham Co Militia. Gave material aid to cause **CEM**: Harrison Family, Smith's Creek; GPS 38.4200, -78.94303; Nr Lacy Springs; Rockingham **GS**: U **SP**: 1) Lydia Harrison 2) Mary McDonald **VI**: Recd pen # W7689 **P**: Y **BLW**: unk **RG**: Y **MK**: unk **PH**: unk **SS**: J- DAR Hatcher; AL Ct Bk I pg 5, 7 Rockingham Co; SAR P-176231 **BS**: JLARC 2.

HARRISON, Reuben; b c1754 or 1757, Augusta Co, (later Rockingham Co); d 15 Aug 1840 **RU**: Private/Wagoneer, Served in VA Line. Ent serv Augusta Co (later became Rockingham). Served in Capt Robert Cravens Co Rockingham Militia at Tygarts Valley, Col Hamilton's, VA Regt. Also served under Gen Wayne at Jamestown **CEM**: Woodbine; GPS unk; Cnr of E Market St and Ott St, Harrisonburg; Rockingham **GS**: Y **SP**: Mar (27 Apr 1791) Mary Matthews or Mathews (3 Jul 1772-___) **VI**: Sol appl pen 22 May 1833 Augusta Co (later Rockingham) age abt 76. Widow appl pen 14 Jun 1843 Rockingham Co. She was there in 1848. W7689 **P**: Y **BLW**: unk **RG**: Y **MK**: N **PH**: unk **SS**: K pg 272; CG Vol 2 pg 1541 SAR P-176232 **BS**: JLARC 4.

HARRISON, Robert; b 11 Feb 1755 Prince George Co; d 8 Jul 1797 **RU**: Private, Served in Cont Line for 3 yrs **CEM**: Bicars; GPS unk; 75 yards behind house site on private road off Rt 641, Huntington; Prince George **GS**: N **SP**: Henrietta Maria Hardyman of Flower de Hundred **VI**: Recd 100 acres BLW **P**: N **BLW**: Y **RG**:Y **MK**: unk **PH**: N **SS**: J- DAR Hatcher; A pg 192; G pg 426 SAR P-176248 **BS**: JLARC 2; 111.

HARRISON, Thomas; b 1704, Smithtown, Suffolk Co, NY; d 1785 **RU**: Patriot, Gave material aid to cause **CEM**: Woodbine; GPS 38.44803, -78.86244; Jct Rt 33 & Reservoir St, Harrisonburg; Harrisonburg City **GS**: U **SP**: No info **VI**: Son of Isaiah (1666-1738) & Abigail (Herring) (1710-1780) Harrison. 23 names including his are listed on crypt moved to Woodbine fr another location **P**: N **BLW**: N **RG**: Y **MK**: unk **PH**: unk **SS**: AL Ct Bk I pg 2, 8, 11, 12 SAR P-176267 **BS**: 196.

HARRISON, Thomas; b 1750; d 1811 **RU**: Sergeant, Served in Col Gist's Regt **CEM**: Fairview; GPS unk; Chopawamic Creek; Stafford **GS**: Y **SP**: No info **VI**: Son of Thomas & Ann (Peyton) Harrioson. Was a reverend **P**: unk **BLW**: unk **RG**: N **MK**: N **PH**: unk **SS**: E pg 356 **BS**: 03 pg 198.

HARRISON, William; b c1730; d 20 Nov 1814 **RU**: Captain/Patriot, Commanded a Co in the Amelia Co Militia. Gave material aid to cause **CEM**: Blandford; GPS 37.22433, -77.38604; 319 S Crater Rd; Petersburg City **GS**: Y **SP**: Mar (1793) Anne Vaughn (1769-2 Jul 1829) **VI**: Was a reverend after the war **P**: unk **BLW**: unk **RG**:Y **MK**: Y SAR monument **PH**: Y **SS**: AL Ct Bk pg 30, 57 Brunswick Co; G pg 116; AZ pg 178; CD SAR P-335230, DAR A052321 **BS**: 47 vol 8 pg 179.

HARRISON, William H; b 1761; d 1817 **RU**: Sergeant, Served in Charles City Co Militia under Capt Benjamin Harrison fr 21 Nov 1776-11 Dec 1776. Was Sgt in Pulaski's Legion **CEM**: Harrison-Pinkards; GPS unk; 4.5 mi E Prince George, then N; Prince George **GS**: Y **SP**: No info **VI**: No further data **P**: unk **BLW**: unk **RG**: N **MK**: N **PH**: unk **SS**: E pg 356; G pg 116 **BS**: 111 pg 15.

HARRISON, William; b 1762; d 22 Jan 1849 **RU**: Drummer boy, Ent Serv Mecklenburg Co. Served in VA Line **CEM**: Grace Church; GPS unk; Manteo; Buckingham **GS**: U **SP**: Sina or Lina Wootton or Wooton (c1800-after 1868) **VI**: Sol appl pen 15 Aug 1832 Buckingham Co. W4481. Widow appl pen 9 May 1853 Buckingham Co age 53 & was still there 1868. Recd BLW #3977-160-55 **P**: Y **BLW**: Y **RG**: Y **MK**: N **PH**: unk **SS**: CG Vol 2 pg 1542 SAR P-176287 **BS**: JLARC 4 , 44, 59.

HARRISON, William; b 7 Dec 1762, d 30 Aug 1822 **RU**: Private or Musician, Served in 7th and 15th Cont Line as Private and possibly as Musician in 3rd, 7th, and 11th Cont Line **CEM**: Jerusalem Baptist Church; GPS: 38.80974,-77.32663; Ox Rd Rt 123, Fairfax Station; Fairfax Co **GS**: Yes **SP**: No spousal info **VI**: No further data **P**: N **BLW**: N **RG**: N **MK**: N **PH**: No **SS**: E pg 356 **BS**: 196.

RU=Rank/Unit	CEM=Cemetery	GS=Gravestone	SP=Spousal Information
VI=Other Veteran Info	P=Pension	BLW=Bounty/Land Warrant	RG=Registered Grave
MK=SAR/DAR Marker	PH=Photo	SS=Service Source	BS=Burial Source

HARRISON, Zebulon; b 1718, Oyster Bay, Nassau Co, NY; d Jul 1792 **RU:** Patriot, Gave material aid to cause **CEM:** Harrison Family; GPS 38.558720,-78.732220; loc 727 Mauzy Anthone Rd, Mauzy; Rockingham **GS:** Unk **SP:** Margaret Cravens (23 Jul 1724 Lewes, Sussex co, DL-1800) **VI:** Son of John Harrison (1691-1771) & Pheobe Harrison (1686-1783) **P:** N **BLW:** N **RG:** Y **MK:** N **PH:** N **SS:** AL Ct Bk I, pg 5, II, pgs1, 14 & Commission BK V pgs121,122, 124; DAR A052325; SAR P-176291 **BS:** 196.

HARSHBARGER, Christian Sr; b 20 Aug 1755, Lancaster Co, PA; d 29 Sep 1827 **RU:** Private/Patriot, Served in Lancaster Co PA in Capt Bradley's Co. Gave material aid to cause **CEM:** Old German; GPS unk; Roanoke; Roanoke City **GS:** U **SP:** Mar (Jun 1779) Barbara Ammen (19 Feb 1760, Lincoln Co, PA-9 Jan 1803) **VI:** Died in Mill Creek, Fincastle Co **P:** unk **BLW:** unk **RG:** Y **MK:** unk **PH:** unk **SS:** J-NSSAR 1993 Reg, J- DAR Hatcher; D Shenandoah Co; Cl SAR P-176342 **BS:** JLARC 1, 2.

HARTSHORNE, William; b Jun 1742, Burlington Co, NJ; d 13 Dec 1816 **RU:** Patriot, Signed legislative petition in Alexandria during RW period. Member of Fairfax Co Committee of Safety **CEM:** Quaker Burial Ground; GPS 38.80749, -77.04676; 717 Queen St, Kate Walker Barrett Library; Alexandria City **GS:** U **SP:** Mar (8 Oct 1767) Susannah Saunders (13 Jun 1745-1801) **VI:** Son of Hugh & Hannah (Pattison) Hartshorne. Alexandria Gazette says age75 yrs at death **P:** N **BLW:** N **RG:** N **MK:** unk **PH:** unk **SS:** S - Alexandria; DD cites DAR Mag (1916) Vol 49 pg 239 **BS:** 196.

HARVEY, John; b 1742; d 1807 **RU:** Captain, Served in 1776 or 1777 in US Navy. Taken prisoner for 12 to 18 mos. Served three yrs **CEM:** Harvey Family; GPS unk; Specific location not identified; Norfolk City **GS:** U **SP:** No info **VI:** Son of John (__-by 1749 (will proved) Northumberland Co) & Mary (-----) (__-aft 1749) Harvey. Fr Northumberland Co. Rank of Col on GS **P:** unk **BLW:** Y **RG:** N **MK:** unk **PH:** unk **SS:** B; E pg 357; L pg 199 **BS:** 196.

HARVEY, Mathew; b Mar 1760, Elkton, Cecil Co, MD; d 19 Sep 1825 **RU:** Private, Served in Cont Line (MD); under Capt Michael Rudolph, Lee's Legion, Ent serv Head of the Elk in MD at age 16. Was in the Battle at Guilford CH **CEM:** Fincastle Presbyterian; GPS 37.50017, -79.87558; 108 E Back St, Fincastle; Botetourt **GS:** Y **SP:** Mar (18 Aug 1788 at Catawba Creek, two mi fr Fincastle, at home of his brother Robert Harvey) Magdalen Hawkins (24 Jul 1775, Rockbridge Co-20 Apr 1845). Pensioned at age 67 in 1841. **VI:** Soldier at 16, with all three brothers, Robert, William, James, all of head of Elk River MD. William killed in Battle of Guilford CH (4). Widow appl pen 3 Apr 1841 Botetourt Co age 67. W19681. Recd BLW on 09 Apr 1796. No BLW number. Name is on the SAR plaque at this cemetery **P:** Y **BLW:** Y **RG:** N **MK:** Y SAR plaque **PH:** unk **SS:** K pg 276; AR Vol 2 pg 126; BY; CG Vol 2 pg 1550 **BS:** 196, JLARC 1,2,4.

HARVEY, Mungo; b unk; d 21 Mar 1794 **RU:** Patriot, Gave material aid to the cause **CEM:** St Paul's Episcopal; GPS 38.33200, -77.12500; 5486 St Paul's Rd off Rt 206; King George **GS:** N **SP:** Mar (18 Aug 1769 Lancaster Co (bond) Priscilla Glascock (18 Aug 1769-__), d/o William & Ester (Ball) Glascock of Richmond Co. Widow of Williamson Ball (__-1764 Westmoreland Co, bur King George Co)—she mar Ball 24 Mar 1763 Richmond Co bond. **VI:** No further data **P:** N **BLW:** N **RG:** N **MK:** N **PH:** N **SS:** D Lancaster Co; AL Ct Bk **BS:** 189 pg 59.

HARVEY, Robert; b 1756; d 1831 **RU:** Soldier, Served in Lee's Legion **CEM:** Fincastle Presbyterian; GPS 37.50017, -79.87558; 108 E Back St, Fincastle; Botetourt **GS:** N **SP:** 1) Martha Borden Hawkins 2) Nancy Moore **VI:** Name is on the SAR plaque at this cemetery, and the monument to Rev War soldiers **P:** unk **BLW:** unk **RG:** Y **MK:** Y SAR plaque **PH:** N **SS:** J-NSSAR 1993 Reg; J- DAR Hatcher; E pg 358 SAR P-176819 **BS:** JLARC 1, 2; 196.

HARVIE, John; b 1742, Albemarle Co; d 1807 **RU:** Colonel/Patriot, Commanded Albermarle Co Militia 1776-1781. Was Delegate fr VA to Cont Congress 1777-78 **CEM:** Hollywood; GPS 37.53560, -77.45720; 412 S Cherry St; Richmond City **GS:** Y **SP:** No info **VI:** Signer of the Articles of Confederation. Secretary of Commonwealth 1788. His estate became the location of the Hollywood Cemetery **P:** unk **BLW:** unk **RG:** Y **MK:** N **PH:** unk **SS:** E pg 358; SAR P-176858 **BS:** 130; 196.

HASH, John Sr; b 1724; d 13 Apr 1784 **RU:** Private, Served in Capt Enoch Osburn's Co and Draper's Co, Montgomery Co Militia **CEM:** Silas Ward Family; GPS unk; Bridle Creek; Grayson **GS:** Y **SP:** 1) Rebecca Anderson 2) Elizabeth Sturgill (1734, Orange Co-1785) d/o James (1700-1753) & (-----) Sturgill

RU=Rank/Unit	CEM=Cemetery	GS=Gravestone	SP=Spousal Information
VI=Other Veteran Info	P=Pension	BLW=Bounty/Land Warrant	RG=Registered Grave
MK=SAR/DAR Marker	PH=Photo	SS=Service Source	BS=Burial Source

VI: Govt Gr St **P:** unk **BLW:** unk **RG:** Y **MK:** unk **PH:** unk **SS:** G pg 212; SAR P-176967, DAR A052352 **BS:** 196.

HASH, William; b abt 1750 Montgomery; d abt 1818 **RU:** Private, Served in Capt Enoch Osburn Co, Montgomery Co Militia **CEM:** Silas Ward Family; GPS unk; Bridle Creek; Grayson **GS:** Y **SP:** Mar (1774) Ellender Osborne, (___, Rowan Co, NC-1820) **VI:** Son of John (___-1784) & Elizabeth (Stodgill) (1734-1785) Hash. Govt Gr St **P:** unk **BLW:** unk **RG:** Y **MK:** unk **PH:** unk **SS:** J-NSSAR 1993 Reg, J-DAR Hatcher; G pg 224; SAR P-176972, DAR A052349 **BS:** JLARC 1, 2.

HATCHER, Elijah Sr; b c1762, Bedford Co; d 10 Dec 1829 **RU:** Patriot, Gave material aid to cause **CEM:** Hatcher Family; GPS unk; Scruggs; Franklin **GS:** Y **SP:** Mar (c1782) Sarah Hall (c1764-1829) d/o Richard (1740-28 Jun 1784) & Elizabeth (-----) (___- c1797) Hale **VI:** SAR Gr marker **P:** N **BLW:** N **RG:** Y **MK:** Y SAR **PH:** unk **SS:** AE Vol 2 pg 84-6; SAR P-329082, DAR A134753 **BS:** 04.

HATCHER, James Sr; b 1732; d 1816 **RU:** Sergeant, Served in Capt Charles Thomas Co, 7th VA Regt 1777 **CEM:** Goose Creek; GPS 39.11250, -77.69527; Rt 722, Lincoln; Loudoun **GS:** N **SP:** No info **VI:** Son of William (1704-1780) & (-----) Hatcher **P:** unk **BLW:** unk **RG:** N **MK:** unk **PH:** N **SS:** CI NARA Muster Role **BS:** 196.

HATHAWAY, John; b 11 May 1733, Lancaster Co; d 19 Apr 1786 **RU:** Major/Patriot, Commanded a Co in Fauquier Co Militia Mar 1780. Promoted to Maj, resigned May 1783. Gave material aid to cause **CEM:** The Hatherage; GPS unk; Warrenton; Fauquier **GS:** U **SP:** Mar (26 Dec 1754) Sarah Timberlake (21 Apr 1739, Northumberland Co-1809) **VI:** No further data **P:** unk **BLW:** unk **RG:** Y **MK:** unk **PH:** unk **SS:** J- DAR Hatcher; E pg 359; AL Cert list pg 14 Fauquier Co; SAR P-177511, DAR A053031 **BS:** JLARC 2.

HAUTVILLE, Joseph; b unk; d 1781 **RU:** Soldier, Served in Agenais Bn and died fr battle at Yorktown **CEM:** French Memorial; GPS 36.81944, -79.39933; Yorktown; York **GS:** U **SP:** No info **VI:** No further data **P:** unk **BLW:** unk **RG:** Y **MK:** unk **PH:** unk **SS:** J-Yorktown Historian; SAR P-177636 **BS:** JLARC 1, 74.

HAWKINS, Issac; b unk; d 1781 **RU:** Private, Served in Capt Benjamin Hick's 4th Co, 1st Regt NY Line. Died fr the battle at Yorktown **CEM:** Yorktown Victory Monument Tablet; GPS 38.28350, -78.54150; Yorktown; York **GS:** U **SP:** No info **VI:** No further data **P:** unk **BLW:** unk **RG:** Y **MK:** unk **PH:** unk **SS:** J-Yorktown Historian; AX pg 179; SAR P-177801 **BS:** JLARC 74.

HAWKINS, John; b 1750,Charles Co, MD; d 1802 or 1805 **RU:** Captain, Served 3 yrs in 3rd VA Regt Cont Line 1776 and was 3rd Regt Adjutant 28 Dec 1776. On rolls to Feb 1781 **CEM:** Hawkins Family; GPS 38.77367, -77.62359; Buckland Farm, 6342 Pleasant Colony Ln, Warrenton; Fauquier **GS:** U **SP:** Alice Corbin Thompson, daughter of Dr. Adam & Lettice (Lee) Thompson **VI:** Possibly d in Alexandria. Recd BLW of 1333 acres 28 Apr 1785 **P:** unk **BLW:** Y **RG:** Y **MK:** Y SAR **PH:** Y **SS:** BX, pg 351, G, pg 405 & 626; E pg 361; BY; CE pg 41; SAR P-177822, DAR A053472 **BS:** 196; SAR Appl.

HAY, William; b, 10 Nov 1748, Kilsyth, Scotland; d 10 Nov 1825 **RU:** Soldier, Served in Capt Burgess Balls Co, Col Parker's VA Regt of Foot, Oct & Nov 1778 **CEM:** Old Chapel Episcopal; GPS 39.10677, -78.01470; Jct US 340 & Rt 255, Millwood; Clarke **GS:** U **SP:** 1) Elizabeth Cary; (2) (-----) Both mar in Richmond.) **VI:** Resided in Richmond. Died at home called "Farnley", Clarke Co **P:** unk **BLW:** unk **RG:** YMK: N **PH:** unk **SS:** E pg 362; AP Roll; SAR P-336563 **BS:** 206.

HAYLEY, James; b unk; d Aug 1789 **RU:** Sergeant, Served in 1st VA State Regt **CEM:** Old Christ Church Episcopal; GPS 38.80625, -77.04718; 118 N Washington St; Alexandria City **GS:** N **SP:** No info **VI:** Burial permit issued 15 Aug 1789 to Mr Carville **P:** unk **BLW:** unk **RG:** N **MK:** N **PH:** N **SS:** E pg 363 **BS:** 20 pg 149.

HAYNES, Benjamin; b 1738; d 1808 **RU:** Private, Served in Capt Joseph Hayne's Co, Rockingham Co that was in the Point Pleasant Battle **CEM:** Mountain View; GPS 37.81360, -79.81390; Clifton Forge; Alleghany **GS:** U **SP:** No info **VI:** No further data **P:** unk **BLW:** unk **RG:** Y **MK:** N **PH:** unk **SS:** J- DAR Hatcher; Z pg 107 SAR P-178260 **BS:** JLARC 2.

HAYNES, Joseph; b 3 Aug 1742, Augusta; d 3 Aug 1815 **RU:** Captain, Served in Co in Rockingham Co that was in the Point Pleasant Battle **CEM:** Mountain View; GPS 37.81360, -79.81390; Clifton Forge;

RU=Rank/Unit	CEM=Cemetery	GS=Gravestone	SP=Spousal Information
VI=Other Veteran Info	P=Pension	BLW=Bounty/Land Warrant	RG=Registered Grave
MK=SAR/DAR Marker	PH=Photo	SS=Service Source	BS=Burial Source

185

Alleghany **GS:** U **SP:** Jennette/Janet T. Young (16 Sep 1756, Ireland-Jun 1827) **VI:** No further data **P:** unk **BLW:** unk **RG:** Y **MK:** N **PH:** unk **SS:** J- DAR Hatcher; Z pg 107; SAR P-178306, DAR A053132 **BS:** JLARC 2; 196.

HAYNIE, Bridgar II; b 1 Jun 1739 Heathsville; d 13 Jun 1791 **RU:** Lieutenant/Patriot, Gave material aid to cause **CEM:** Haynie Family; GPS unk; Heathsville; Northumberland **GS:** U **SP:** Mar (16 Jun 1766 (bond) Lancaster Co) Sarah Shearman d/o Martin & Ann (Chinn) Shearman. Her brother owned "Pop Castle" in War of 1812. **VI:** No further data **P:** unk **BLW:** unk **RG:** Y **MK:** unk **PH:** unk **SS:** J-NASSR 2000 Reg; AL Ct Bk pg 12 Northumberland Co; SAR P-178354 **BS:** JLARC 76.

HAYS, John; b unk; d 1808 **RU:** Captain, Commanded a Co in Montgomery Co in Nov 1781 (Giles Co formed fr Montgomery Co in 1806) **CEM:** Indian Bottom Farm; GPS unk; Walkers Creek District Twp; Giles **GS:** U **SP:** No info **VI:** No further data **P:** unk **BLW:** unk **RG:** Y **MK:** unk **PH:** unk **SS:** J-NSSAR 1993 Reg; E pg 364; AL Cert lists pg 2, 7, 11 Botetourt Co; SAR P-178381 **BS:** JLARC 1.

HAYS, John; b 1739; d 1808 **RU:** Major, Served in 3rd VA Regt of Foot as Maj fr 23 Apr 1778-12 Feb 1781. Taken prisoner at Germantown Oct 1777 and remained captive until retirement **CEM:** Stone House Plantation; GPS unk; Hill behind Hays Creek, nr Staunton; Staunton City **GS:** U **SP:** 1) Campbell **VI:** Find-A Grave shows DAR plaque mounted on pile of stones in the Hays Cem at Rockbridge Baths; on Rt 602 Indian Bottom Farm, Rockbridge Co **P:** unk **BLW:** unk **RG:** Y **MK:**Y-DAR **PH:** unk **SS:** J-NSSAR 1993 Reg, J- DAR Hatcher; CE pg 39; SAR P-178386 **BS:** JLARC 1, 2.

HAYTER, Abraham M; b Dec 1735, Plumsteadville, Bucks Co, PA, d 22 Aug 1815 **RU:** Patriot, Paid Personal Property Tax, Washington Co 1783 considered a supply tax for Rev War expenses **CEM:** Hayter-Litton Family; GPS 36.844426,-81.926275; loc 7261 Hyters Gap Rd; Washington **GS:** Yes inscription indicates died age 80 **SP:** Susannah Anne Darrough (1728-1809) **VI:** Son of Abraham Hayter, Jr and Martha Rankin. Grave was surveyed in 1960 and data placed in a county cem book. **P:** N **BLW:** N **RG:** Y **MK:** N **PH:** N **SS:** DV Washington Co Pers Prop Tax, return 1783 of Capt Andrew Conan's District; SAR Bio & Graves Rpt submitted Oct 2019, patriot # pending **BS:** 196.

HAYTER, Israel; b 2 Oct 1754, Frederick Co, MD; d 11 Feb 1829 **RU:** Private, Served in Capt James Dysart's Co, Col William Campbell's VA Militia. Was wounded in thigh at Kings Mountain **CEM:** Hayter-Litton; GPS 36.84443, -81.92628; Nr the Litton Home, 7261 Hayter's Gap Rd; Washington **GS:** U **SP:** Mar (20 Apr 1781) Ann Crawford (19 Feb 1754-25 Apr 1843) **VI:** DAR plaque **P:** N **BLW:** N **RG:** Y **MK:** Y DAR plaque **PH:** N **SS:** AR pg 135; SAR P-178437 **BS:** JLARC 2,80; 196; 208 pg 49.

HAYWARD, James; b unk; d 1781 **RU:** Soldier, Served fr MA and died as result of Yorktown battle **CEM:** Yorktown Victory Monument Tablet; GPS 38.28350, -78.54150; Yorktown; York **GS:** U **SP:** No info **VI:** No further data **P:** unk **BLW:** unk **RG:** YMK: unk **PH:** unk **SS:** J-Yorktown Historian; SAR P-178468 **BS:** JLARC 74.

HEAD, Benjamin Sr; b 1731, Spotsylvania Co; d 19 Aug 1803 **RU:** Captain, Commanded a co of militia in Orange Co 1778-9 **CEM:** Westover United Methodist; GPS 38.28130, -78.38607; 2801 Fredericksburg Rd; Orange **GS:** Y **SP:** Mar (1754) Martha Sherman (c1734,-1803) d/o Robert & Lucy (-----) Sharman **VI:** Son of Henry (1695-1765) of Spotsylvania Co & Frances (Spence) Head. Cenotaph abt him in cem. SAR marker **P:** unk **BLW:** unk **RG:** Y **MK:** Y SAR **PH:** Y **SS:** AR Vol 2 pg 137; NSSAR Ancestor #P-178532; Orange Co Order Bk 2 pg 86-7; SAR P-178676 **BS:** JLARC 2.

HEADRICK, Charles; b unk; d unk **RU:** Patriot, Gave material aid to cause **CEM:** Old Peaked Mountain; GPS 38.37113, -78.73416; 9843 Town Hall Rd, McGaheysville; Rockingham **GS:** Y **SP:** No info **VI:** Listed on a plaque in the cemetery with others that had Rev War service **P:** unk **BLW:** unk **RG:** Y **MK:** Y DAR plaque **PH:** unk **SS:** O pg 143; AL Ct Bk pg 6 Rockingham Co; SAR P-178732 **BS:** 04.

HEALY, James; b 1756; d 1820 **RU:** Sergeant, Served in VA battalion, 1st VA Regt **CEM:** Clark's Neck; GPS unk; See property records for Clark's Neck & Healy family residence; Middlesex **GS:** U **SP:** Ruth Bristow **VI:** No further data **P:** unk **BLW:** unk **RG:** Y **MK:** unk **PH:** unk **SS:**; J-NSSAR 2000 Reg; E pg 365; SAR P-178802 **BS:** JLARC 76.

HEARD, John; b c1761, Albemarle Co; d Aft 1835 **RU:** Private, Served first under Capt Hairston. Served six tours of six weeks each **CEM:** Wright Family; GPS 36.97658, -80.21693; Pizarro off Rt 668; Floyd

---

RU=Rank/Unit	CEM=Cemetery	GS=Gravestone	SP=Spousal Information
VI=Other Veteran Info	P=Pension	BLW=Bounty/Land Warrant	RG=Registered Grave
MK=SAR/DAR Marker	PH=Photo	SS=Service Source	BS=Burial Source

GS: U **SP:** No info **VI:** #S8709 pen commenced 26 Aug 1833 age 74, annual amount of $23.33 **P:** Y **BLW:** unk **RG:** N **MK:** unk **PH:** unk **SS:** E pg 366; CG pg 1588 **BS:** 196 for John Mitchell.

HEATH, Henry; b 25 Oct 1755, Sussex Co; d 3 Apr 1797 **RU:** Captain, Served with Capt Bland's Co of Horse with his brother Howell, who was killed in battle **CEM:** Heath Family; GPS unk; See US Senate Doc 1938, serial 10448, vol 2; Prince George **GS:** U **SP:** (1779) Susanna Williams (c1753-1 Sep 1811) **VI:** Perhaps another person this name in rank of sergeant drew a pension and received a BLW. BLW indicates he d 1790, Prince George Co **P:** unk **BLW:** Y **RG:** Y **MK:** unk **PH:** unk **SS:** DAR Ancestor #A053934; BY pg 394, J- DAR Hatcher; SAR P-178914 **BS:** JLARC 2.

HEATH, Jesse; b 1765; d 1850 **RU:** Private, Enl 25 Apr 1777 for 3 yrs in Capt Amos Emerson's Co, Prince George Co Militia **CEM:** Blandford; GPS 37.22433, -77.38604; 319 S Crater Rd; Petersburg City **GS:** Y **SP:** Agnes Peebles **VI:** Son of William (1731-1771) of Surry Co and Margaret (Bonner) Heath. Plaque with his name is att to GS of Heartwell Peeples Heath; memorialized in the cemetery as bur elsewhere **P:** unk **BLW:** unk **RG:** N **MK:** SAR monument **PH:** unk **SS:** A pg 149; G pg 116 **BS:** 128 Heath; 196. **PH:** unk **SS:** A pg 149; G pg 116 **BS:** 128 Heath; 196.

HEATH / HAYTH, Thomas; b 1750, Bedford Co; d 1821 **RU:** First Lieutenant, Served in 6th VA Regt, Cont Line **CEM:** Jones Family; GPS unk; Gladys Twp; Campbell **GS:** U **SP:** Mar (25 Dec 1772) Martha Gilbert **VI:** No further data **P:** unk **BLW:** unk **RG:** Y **MK:** N **PH:** unk **SS:** J-NSSAR 1993 Reg; E pg 366 **BS:** JLARC 1.

HEATON, James; b 12 Jan 1759, Sussex Co NJ; d 14 Jul 1824 **RU:** Lieutenant Surgeon, Served in Frederick Co Militia 4 Aug 1779 **CEM:** Ketoctin Baptist; GPS 39.15746, -77.74870; Ketoctin Church Rd, Purcellville; Loudoun **GS:** Y **SP:** 1) Hannah Rachel Smith (1762-1784) 2) Lydia Osburn (1778-1839) **VI:** No further data **P:** unk **BLW:** unk **RG:** Y **MK:** SAR Monument **PH:** unk **SS:** E pg 366; SAR P179003 **BS:** JLARC 1, 32; 25 pg 137; 196.

HEDGES, John; b bef 1755; d bef 6 Apr 1804 **RU:** Captain/Patriot, Served in Prince William Co Militia. Gave material aid to cause **CEM:** Hedges Family; GPS unk; Quantico Marine Base; Stafford **GS:** U **SP:** Elizabeth Worsham **VI:** Elizabeth Eppes **P:** unk **BLW:** unk **RG:** YMK: unk **PH:** unk **SS:**; AL Ct Bk pg 7 Prince William Co; SAR P-179107, DAR A054114 **BS:** JLARC 48; 03 pg 243.

HEDGES, Joseph; b :c1739, WVA; d 1828 **RU:** Captain/ Patriot, commissionedcaptain 6 Mar 1776 militia and member of Committee of Safety Berkely Co **CEM:** Hedges Farm; GPS not determined; Edward Hedges farm, 1856, loc nr Timber Ridge Baptist Ch and Old Collin's PO; Cross Jct: Frederick **GS:** Unk **SP:** Mar (1774) Elizabeth Rawlings (1755-1824), d/o Stephen Rawlings (___-1783) & Mary Elizabeth Rawlings (1721-1795), d/o Stephen Rawlings (___-1783) & Mary Elizabeth Tyler (1721-1795) **VI:** Son of Jonas Hedge (1716-1804) & Agnes Powelson (1720-1800) **P:** N **BLW:** N **RG:** Y **MK:** N **PH:** N **SS:** CD; DAR A054129; SAR P-179110 **BS:** 196 (**HEDRICK,** Jacob **See Appendix G, Addenda)**

HEISKELL, Adam; b 1754, d 28 Jul 1822 **RU:** Private, Capt Daniel Morgan's Co, injuried at battle at Quebec, was part of Dutch Mess, after return to Winchester served in militia under Col John Smith **CEM:** Mt Hebron; GPS 39.4085,-78,75732; in Centenary Reformed UCC portion;305 E Boscawen St; Winchester City **GS:** No but SAR granite marker **SP:** Margaret UPP (1755-15 Feb 1812) VI: Achieving rank of Captain after war period **P:** N **BLW:** N **RG:** Y **MK:** Y SAR granite & Monument **PH:** Y **SS:** N pg 1427; CM vol 2, pgs 503-4; D; SAR P 1792256; DAR: A054294 **BS:** 04: 210.

HEISKELL (HISKILL), Peter; b 1760; d 4 Nov 1841 **RU:** Ensign, Served in Frederick Co Militia 4 Aug 1779 **CEM:** Trinity Episcopal; GPS 38.14917, -79.07521; 214 Beverley St; Staunton City **GS:** Y **SP:** 1) Susan Wetzel 2) Caroline Heiskell (___-1833) Later mar (-----) Brikenridge **VI:** No further data **P:** unk **BLW:** unk **RG:**Y **MK:** unk **PH:** Y **SS:** E pg 380; SAR P-179262 **BS:** JLARC 62; 196.

HELEH, Jean; b unk; d 1781 **RU:** Seaman, Served on "Ville de Paris" and died from Yorktown battle **CEM:** French Memorial; GPS 36.81944, -79.39933; Yorktown; York **GS:** U **SP:** No info **VI:** No further data **P:** unk **BLW:** unk **RG:** Y **MK:** unk **PH:** unk **SS:** J-Yorktown Historian **SAR P-179286 BS:** JLARC 1, 74.

HELM, John Steele; b 14 Aug 1741, Middlesex Co, NJ; d 20 Apr 1826 **RU:** Second Lieutenant, took oath this rank, 27 Mar 1780, Bedford Co Militia, March 1778 **CEM:** Old Concord Presbyterian Church; GPS 340017,-78.923862; 4909 Reedy Spring Rd (Rt 648), Sprout Spring; Appomattox **GS:** Unk **SP:**

RU=Rank/Unit	CEM=Cemetery	GS=Gravestone	SP=Spousal Information
VI=Other Veteran Info	P=Pension	BLW=Bounty/Land Warrant	RG=Registered Grave
MK=SAR/DAR Marker	PH=Photo	SS=Service Source	BS=Burial Source

187

Mary McAllister (Aug 1749-14 Sep 1824 **VI:** Son of Sarah Jameson (1711-19 Jan 1812) **P:** N **BLW:** N **RG:** Y **MK:** N **PH:** N **SS:** DAR A054382; E pg 367; SAR P-179327 **BS:** 196.

HELM, Meridith Jr; b 19 Nov 1753, Frederick Co; d 12 Oct 1804 **RU:** Captain, Daniels Morgan's Riflemen. Also furnished supplies to cause. Frederick Co Militia 1 Apr 1783 **CEM:** Milburn Chapel; GPS 39.22360, -78.11360; Milburn Rd Rt 622, Stephenson; Frederick **GS:** Y **SP:** Frances Sanford Fowler **VI:** Son of Major Meridith & Margaret Ann (Neill) Helm. Styled Col after the War. Lived and d at "Belleville Farm", 4 mi fr Winchester, Frederick Co. Granted land in Ohio. Memorial for him at Rest United Methodist Church Cemetery, Frederick Co. Original stone was at Milburn Chapel Cemetery in Frederick Co. Repaired, moved to another cem at Milburn **P:** unk **BLW:** unk **RG:** Y **MK:** N **PH:** unk **SS:** E pg 367; SAR P-179332, DAR A054387 **BS:** 59 pg 145; 196.

HELM, Meridith Sr; b c1724; d 12 Jun 1804 **RU:** Patriot, Gave material aid to the cause **CEM:** Goose Creek; GPS 39.11250, -77.69527; Rt 722, Lincoln; Loudoun **GS:** U **SP:** Mar (1745) Calmes (-----) **VI:** No further data **P:** N **BLW:** N **RG:** N **MK:** unk **PH:** unk **SS:** AL Ct Bk 8 **BS:** 196.

HELM, Meredith, b 19 Nov 1753; d 12 Oct 1804 **RU:**Lieutenant/ Patriot, was 2d Lt, Col George William Fairfax Company Frederick Co, Militia, and perhaps serv under Col, Daniel Morgan, US Army; as patriot paid personal property tax 1782, Frederick Co considered to be a supply tax for Rec War expenses **CEM:** Emmanuel United Methodist Church: GPS 39.233599,-78.113602; loc vic jct Milburn Rd & McCanns Rd, Stephenson: Frederick **GS:** Y Gov't **SP:**Frances Sanford Fowler (_-26 Jul 1820, KY) **VI:** Memorialized in cem as original burial is in unkept Milburn Chapel Cem in Frederick Co with broken GS, A Colonel Meredith Helm was in Frederick Co in 1775 in the Colonial War, perhaps his father **P:** N **BLW:** Y **RG:** Y **MK:** unk **PH:** unk **SS:** E pg 367; DAR A054387; SAR P-179332 **BS:** 196

HELM, William T; b 6 Apr 1736; d 11 Oct 1825 **RU:** Lieutenant, rec this rank 1 Apr 1783, Frederick Co Militia **CEM:** Helm Family; GPS not determined; loc original Helm property with cem sign, Berryville; Clarke **GS:** Unk **SP:** 1) mar (6 Mar 1764) Letticia Neville, d/o George Neville & Mary Gibbs, 2) mar (26 Aug 1784) Lucy Neville, Letticia's sister, 3) mar (17 Nov 1791) Ann Calmes, d/o Marquis Calmes & Winifred Waller **VI:** Made Captain rank after war period A colonel Meridith Helm was in Frederick Co in 1775 **P:** N **BLW:** N **RG:** Y **MK:** N **PH:** N **SS:** SAR P-179341 **BS:** 196.

HELPHENSTINE (HELVESTON, HELPHENSTIEN), Peter; b 17 Jun 1724, Koln, Germany; d 11 May 1779 **RU:** Major, Was Capt in General Mulenburg's 8th Cont Line. Appt Maj Dec 1775 in 8th VA Regt **CEM:** Mt Hebron; GPS 39.10916, -78.09497; 305 E Boscawen St; Winchester City **GS:** U **SP:** Mar (3 Jul 1750, Germany) Catherine Berger **VI:** Son of Pieter & Mary (Biedermann) Helfenstien. Took ill in SC, furlough, d at home (Source 112). Name listed on NSDAR plaque in cemetery **P:** unk **BLW:** Y **RG:** Y **MK:** Y SAR monument **PH:** unk **SS:** BY pg 350; J-NSSAR 1993 Reg; SAR P-330318 **BS:** JLARC 1; 112; 196.

HEMPENSTALL, Abraham; b 1740, NJ; d 1783 **RU:** Ensign, Served in Augusta Co Militia **CEM:** Doe Hill; GPS 38.25976, -79.26629; Across St fr Doe Hill Methodist Ch Rt 654; Highland **GS:** U **SP:** Mar (soon after Mar 1775) Mary Peter d/o of Capt (------) & Mary (Lewis) Peter (__-1789 Greenbriar Co) **VI:** No further data **P:** unk **BLW:** unk **RG:**N **MK:** unk **PH:** unk **SS:** CM Vol 1 pg 197 **BS:** JLARC 103.

HENDERSON, Alexander; b 2 Mar 1737, Glasglow, Scotland; d 22 Nov 1815 **RU:** Patriot, Was member of House of Burgesses & General Assembly of VA **CEM:** Henderson; GPS unk; Mountclair; Prince William **GS:** Y **SP:** Mar (19 Jan 1773, Fairfax Co) Sarah Moore (1752-Dec 1816) **VI:** Died in Dumfries. A plaque in cemetery with his story erected by the Montclair Bicentennial Commission 1976 **P:** N **BLW:** N **RG:** Y **MK:** Y SAR **PH:** unk **SS:** H; I; SAR P-179537 **BS:** 16 pg 17-8.

HENDERSON, David; b 1 Jun 1754 Kirkaldy, Scotland; d 22 Feb 1838 **RU:** Midshipman Sailor Patriot, Had VA Sea Serv. Ent serv 1777. Served on Warship "Dragon". Provided bolt of canvas to cause **CEM:** Masonic Cemetery; GPS 38.30198, -77.46142; 900 Charles St; Fredericksburg City **GS:** Y **SP:** Mildred XX **VI:** Sailor appl pen 12 Sep 1832 Spotsylvania Co age 78. Pen rec 28 Feb 1838. S5506 **P:** Y **BLW:** unk **RG:** Y **MK:** Y SAR memorial plaque **PH:** unk **SS:** C Vol 1 pg 11; K Vol 3 pg 292; CG Vol 2 pg 1600 SAR P-179085, DAR A208764 **BS:** 11 pg 57-8.

HENDERSON, Edward, b 1746 Cumberland Co, d 18 Mar 1833 **RU:** Private Served in Capt Rogers Co 1779 and Capt Moore's Co, 1781, Col Burwell's Militia Regt, Halifax Co as wagoner and serv VA Line

RU=Rank/Unit	CEM=Cemetery	GS=Gravestone	SP=Spousal Information
VI=Other Veteran Info	P=Pension	BLW=Bounty/Land Warrant	RG=Registered Grave
MK=SAR/DAR Marker	PH=Photo	SS=Service Source	BS=Burial Source

CEM: Oak Level Presbyterian Church; **GPS**: 36.7330,-79.10750; nr jct Rts 683/684, Vernon Hill; Halifax; **GS**: No but has family plot **SP**: Lydia Rice **VI**: Recd pen 1832 Halifax Co **P**: Y **BLW**: N **RG**: Y **MK**: N **PH**: No **SS**: AP pen rec; DAR Anc # A128265; SAR P-179545 **BS**: 196.

HENDERSON, James; b c1739, Scotland; d 8 Nov 1819 **RU**: Patriot, Carried arms fr Richmond for 24th Regt **CEM**: Blendon; GPS 37.14110, -78.08030; Rt F656 & Rt 460 Nottoway CH Rd; Nottaway **GS**: Y **SP**: No info **VI**: GS indicates member of county for 60 yrs, thus arrived c1759 Amelia Co of which portion became Nottoway 1789 **P**: N **BLW**: N **RG**: N **MK**: N **PH**: Y **SS**: G pg 96 **BS**: 196.

HENDERSON, James; b 1764; d 1818 **RU**: Private, Served in 9th & 15th Cont lines **CEM**: Bruton Parish Church; GPS 37.27127, -76.70248; 331 W Duke of Gloucester St; Williamsburg City **GS**: Y **SP**: Elizabeth (-----) **VI**: Was Reverend **P**: unk **BLW**: unk **RG**: N **MK**: unk **PH**: Y **SS**: E pg 368; CD **BS**: 196.

HENDERSON, John; b 1740, Montgomery Co; d Dec 1812 **RU**: Captain, Commanded a co in Montgomery Co Militia. Commissioned Capt 4 Mar 1778 **CEM**: Henderson; GPS unk; Catawba Rd Rt 785 Blacksburg; Montgomery **GS**: U **SP**: Mary Polly O'Brian Downard 1750-1834) **VI**: Son of George & Elizabeth (Moore) Henderson **P**: unk **BLW**: unk **RG**: Y **MK**: unk **PH**: unk **SS**: J- DAR Hatcher; E pg 368; SAR P-179574, DAR A054726 **BS**: JLARC 2, 196.

HENINGER (HENEGAR) (HENNINGAR), Jacob; b c1763; d 26 Mar 1830 **RU**: Soldier, Was in Battle at Kings Mountain **CEM**: Greever; GPS 36.79250, -81.69860; Rt 1019 off Rt 11, Chilhwie; Smyth **GS**: Y **SP**: No info **VI**: No further data **P**: unk **BLW**: unk **RG**: N **MK**: N **PH**: unk **SS**: CV pg 121 **BS**: 97 pg 29.

HENKEL, Paul Rev; b 15 Dec 1754, Rowan Co, NC; d 17 Nov 1825 **RU**: Soldier, Served in Capt John Skidmore's Co, Greenbrier Co at Ft Hinkle **CEM**: St Martin's Lutheran; GPS 38.64480, -78.67124; 2235 River Rd, New Market; Shenandoah **GS**: Y **SP**: Elizabeth Nagley (1757-1843) **VI**: Son of Jacob (1732-1779) & Mary Barbara (Teter) (1734-1814) Henkle, a traveling Baptist reverend **P**: unk **BLW**: unk **RG**: Y **MK**: unk **PH**: unk **SS**: J- DAR Hatcher; G pg 514; DD; SAR P-179761 **BS**: JLARC 2; 196.

HENLEY, James; b 19 Sep 1764; d 23 Jul 1832 **RU**: Private/Patriot, Served in 1st Cont Line and on a committee in Princess Anne County **CEM**: Cedar Grove; GPS 36.859549, -76.283752; 238 E Princess Anne Rd; Norfolk City **GS**: Y **SP**: Elizabeth (-----) (1781-1829) **VI**: Is listed as Capt on GS. Was not old enough to be capt in Rev War, therefore perhaps War of 1812 **P**: unk **BLW**: unk **RG**: Y **MK**: unk **PH**: unk **SS**: E pg 370; SAR Bio Rpt submitted Jun 2020 **BS**: 196.

HENLEY, Leonard; b 1748/49, James City Co; d 19 Nov 1798 **RU**: Sergeant/ Patriot, Was Quarter Master Sergeant, Capt John Belfield's Co, Col Theodoric Bland's 6th Troop, Light Dragoons. As patriot furnished two wagonloads wood and a gun to Kent Co Militia **CEM**: Cedar Grove; GPS 37.26140, -76.70720; Jct Rt 132 and Hunting Cove; Williamsburg City **GS**: U **SP**: Mar (31 Jan 1779) Elizabeth Dandridge (25 May 1749, New Kent Co-__) **VI**: No further data **P**: N **BLW**: N **RG**:Y **MK**: unk **PH**: unk **SS**: DAR Ancestor #A055043; G pg 472, 580; SAR P-179767 **BS**: AR pg 142.

HENNONE, Jean; b unk; d 1781 **RU**: Soldier, Served in Soissonnais Bn and died fr battle at Yorktown **CEM**: French Memorial; GPS 36.81944, -79.39933; Yorktown; York **GS**: U **SP**: No info **VI**: No further data **P**: unk **BLW**: unk **RG**: Y **MK**: unk **PH**: unk **SS**: J-Yorktown Historian; SAR P-179803 **BS**: JLARC 1, 74.

HENRY, Didier; b unk; d 1781 **RU**: Seaman, Served on "Duc De Bourgogne" and died from Yorktown battle **CEM**: French Memorial; GPS 36.81944, -79.39933; Yorktown; York **GS**: U **SP**: No info **VI**: No further data **P**: unk **BLW**: unk **RG**: Y **MK**: unk **PH**: unk **SS**: J-Yorktown Historian; SAR P-179829 **BS** JLARC 1, 74.

HENRY, Isaac; b 1738; d 1829 **RU**: Private, Served in VA unit in Illinois **CEM**: Pittsylvania (Carter); GPS 38.49711, -77.31305; Manassas National Battlefield Park; Manassas City **GS**: U **SP**: Judith Carter d/o Landon Jr. & (-----) Carter **VI**: He was a doctor. Some historians indicate he was a Navy officer **P**: unk **BLW**: unk **RG**: N **MK**: unk **PH**: unk **SS**: E pg 370 **BS**: 190 under cem name.

HENRY, James Jr; b 1762, Augusta Co; d 21 Mar 1828 **RU**: Private, Served in Capt Tate's Co, Augusta Co Militia **CEM**: New Providence Presbyterian; GPS 37.95130, -79.30250; 1208 New Providence Rd, Raphine; Rockbridge **GS**: U **SP**: Mar (13 Dec 1787 Augusta Co) Mary Berry (1862-1828) **VI**: Son of

---

RU=Rank/Unit	CEM=Cemetery	GS=Gravestone	SP=Spousal Information
VI=Other Veteran Info	P=Pension	BLW=Bounty/Land Warrant	RG=Registered Grave
MK=SAR/DAR Marker	PH=Photo	SS=Service Source	BS=Burial Source

James & Mary (-----) Henry **P:** unk **BLW:** unk **RG:**Y **MK:** unk **PH:** unk **SS:** E pg 370; SAR P-179941 **BS:** JLARC 62; 196.

HENRY, John; b 1757 Pine Slash, Hanover Co, d 1791 **RU:** Captain, Commanded a Co in Harrison's 1st VA Artillery Regt **CEM:** Leatherwood Plantation, GPS unk, Martinsville; Henry **GS:** N **SP:** Susannah Walker (1760-__) **VI:** Son of Patrick Henry (1736-1799) and Sarah Shelton (1738-1775). Buried in unmarked grave. Recd 100 acres at plantation fr father, 1778 **P:** N **BLW:** N **RG:** N **MK:** N **PH:** unk **SS:** E pg 859; DAR Ancestor # A053809 **BS:** 196.

HENRY. John; b 11 Nov 1761, Fairview, nr Castle Dawson, Ire; d 21 Aug 1801 **RU:** Private, served in Col Hazen's Regt **CEM:** Grace Episcopal Church,GPS 37.235600, -76.507500; 115 Church St, Yorktown; York **GS:** Y family plaque on top stone beside church **SP:** No spousal data **VI:** Re'cd BLW 13 Sep 1791 # 13177 for 100 acres **P:** Unk **BLW:** Y **RG:** N **MK:** N **PH:** unk **SS:** CG pg 1606 **BS:** 196.

HENRY, Patrick; b 29 May 1736, Hanover Co; d 6 Jun 1799 **RU:** Colonel/Patriot, Col in command of 1st VA Regt of Foot Jul 1775-13 Feb 1776. Commander in chief of VA forces. Resigned 28 Feb 1776 **CEM:** Henry Family; GPS unk; Red Hill Plantation, 1250 Red Hill Rd, Brookneal; Charlotte **GS:** Y **SP:** Mar (1) in 1754 at wife's family's house Rural Plains to Sarah Shelton, b 1738, d 1775; (2) on 25 Oct 1777 to Dorothea Spotswood Dandridge, b 175, d 1831 **VI:** Son of John Henry & Sarah Windson. Best known for his "Give me liberty or give me death" speech. Attorney. House of Burgesses 1764-1765, 1st & 2nd Continental Congress. First Governor of Virginia. Died in Campbell Co. Daug, Ms. Dorothea Spotswood Winsto, age 76 of Linestone AL appl 13 Dec 1853 Limestone Co AL age 76. Rej due to no record according to War Office. R4898 **P:** Y **BLW:** unk **RG:** Y **MK:** unk **PH:** unk **SS:** J-NSSAR 1993 Reg, J-DAR Hatcher; K Vol I pg 296; CG Vol 2 pg 1607; SAR P-179896, DAR A053828 **BS:** JLARC 1, 2; 196.

HENRY, William; b 1734, Hanover Co; d 1784 **RU:** Captain, Commanded a Co of minutemen. Wounded at Battle of Brandywine **CEM:** Winton Plantation; GPS unk; adj Winton Country Club, Clifford; Amherst **GS:** Y **SP:** 1) Lucy Taylor 2) Peggy McNair **VI:** Died in Fluvanna Co. Has a Vet Admin stone engraved "Lieutenant, Virginia Militia, Revolutionary War" **P:** unk **BLW:** unk **RG:** Y **MK:** unk **PH:** unk **SS:** B; Wm & Mary Qrtly, Vol 6 pg 189; SAR P-179931 **BS:** JLARC 1 ,4, 7, 46; 196.

HENSLEY, Samuel; b 19 Aug 1754 Culpeper, d 13 Feb 1841 **RU:** Soldier, Ent serv 1774 against Shawnee Indians. Ent serv again 1776 "on frontiers of VA" **CEM:** Hensley; GPS 36.64426, -82.71960; Sleepy Hollow Ln; Scott **GS:** U **SP:** 1) Eleanor Elliott 2) Margaret Crawford **VI:** Sol appl pen 20 Aug 1834 Washington Co. Formerly lived in Sullivan Co TN. S21278 **P:** Y **BLW:** unk **RG:** Y **MK:** unk **PH:** unk **SS:** J-NSSAR 2000; K Vol 3 pg 296; Reg CG Vol 2 pg 1608; SAR P-179979, DAR A053956 **BS:** JLARC 76.

HERBERT, Pascow (Pasco); b 1741; d 21 May 1801 **RU:** Lieutenant, Served in VA State Navy. Had sea service on ship "Liberty" **CEM:** Herbert; GPS 39.01475, -76.35013; Off Armstrong Ln; Hampton City **GS:** U **SP:** Mary Jones **VI:** R43, also VA 1/2 pay (see N.A. Acc #837 VA State Navy, file for Pascow Herbert). Died in Elizabeth City Co **P:** Y **BLW:** unk **RG:** Y **MK:** unk **PH:** unk **SS:** BY pg 202; J- DAR Hatcher; K Vol 3 pg 298; L pg 200; CG Vol 2 pg 1610; SAR P-180046 **BS:** JLARC 2, 196.

HERBERT, William; b 1746 Ireland; d 24 Feb 1819 **RU:** Private, Served in Capt William Rummey's Co, Fairfax Co. Militia, c1776-1779 **CEM:** Christ Church Episcopal; GPS 38.80216, -77.05689; Wilkes St & Hamilton Ln; Alexandria City **GS:** Y **SP:** Mar (c1776 Alexandria) Sarah Fairfax Carlyle (4 Jan 1757-Jul 1827) d/o John & (-----) Carlyle **VI:** Merchant. Moved to VA in 1773. Provided horse to unit under Gen Lafayette's command & 700 lbs beef. First of two Commissioners of Taxes for Alexandria 1780. Justice of Hustings Ct. Alexandria 1781-2. Mayor Alexandria 1781-2. City Council member 1783-8. Secretary, Masonic Lodge No. 39. President, Bank of Alexandria. Death notice in the Alexandria Gazette 27 Feb 1819, pg 3 **P:** unk **BLW:** unk **RG:** N **MK:** Y SAR **PH:** unk **SS:** I; R pg 2, 9 **BS:** 2 pg 99; 20 pg 99; 196.

HEREFORD, John E; b 1725 Alexandria; d 8 Apr 1793 **RU:** Sergeant/Patriot, Gave material aid to cause **CEM:** Old Stone Methodist; GPS 39.11725, -77.56609; 168 W Cornwall St, Leesburg; Loudoun **GS:** Y **SP:** 1) Elizabeth Barry 2) Margaret Ammon (1735 Loudoun Co-23 Oct 1809 Fauquier Co) **VI:** No further data **P:** unk **BLW:** unk **RG:** Y **MK:** N **PH:** unk **SS:** E pg 372; AL Ct Bk pg 30, 86 Loudoun Co; SAR P-180057, DAR A054066 **BS:** 25 pg 138.

RU=Rank/Unit	CEM=Cemetery	GS=Gravestone	SP=Spousal Information
VI=Other Veteran Info	P=Pension	BLW=Bounty/Land Warrant	RG=Registered Grave
MK=SAR/DAR Marker	PH=Photo	SS=Service Source	BS=Burial Source

HERMAIN, Jean; b unk; d 1781 **RU**: Soldier, Served in Touraine Bn and died fr battle at Yorktown **CEM**: French Memorial; GPS 36.81944, -79.39933; Yorktown; York **GS**: U **SP**: No info **VI**: No further data **P**: unk **BLW**: unk **RG**: Y **MK**: unk **PH**: unk **SS**: J-Yorktown Historian; SAR P-180091 **BS**: JLARC 1, 74.

HERNDON, Edward Jr; b 1761; d 10 or 12 Nov 1837 **RU**: Private, Ent service 1781, and served as Assistant Quartermaster of VA Troops **CEM**: Laurel Hill, Nywood Farm; GPS unk; Rt 210 3.3 mi east of courthouse; Spotsylvania **GS**: U **SP**: No info **VI**: Probably son of Edward (1730-1799) and Mary (Duerson) Herndon. Was wounded in service and drew half-pay for it. Wife not named as predeceased him. S30478 **P**: Y **BLW**: unk **RG**: Y **MK**: unk **PH**: unk **SS**: K Vol 3 pg 299; CG pg 1611; SAR P-180123 **BS**: JLARC 2, 91.

HERNDON, Edward Sr; b 5 Mar 1730, Spotsylvania Co; d 3 Sep 1799 **RU**: Patriot, Was member of County Committee of Safety **CEM**: Gordon Herndon; GPS 38.15467, -77.65341; Rt 656 S off Rt 208, Post Oak; Spotsylvania **GS**: Y **SP**: Mar (c1754/55) Mary Duerson **VI**: No further data **P**: N **BLW**: N **RG**:N **MK**: unk **PH**: unk **SS**: DD cites Force American Archives 4th series Vol 3 pg 1570 **BS**: 196.

HERNDON, William; b 1751; d 1823 **RU**: Private/Patriot, Served in VA 1st State Regt **CEM**: Belvoir House; GPS unk; Jct 608 E & 635; Spotsylvania **GS**: N **SP**: No info **VI**: No further data **P**: unk **BLW**: unk **RG**: N **MK**: N **PH**: N **SS**: D pg 260; E pg 372 **BS**: 08 vol 1 pg 90-5.

HERNSBERGER (HANSBERGER)(HARNSBERGER), Henry, b16 Oct 1752; d16 Jul 1834 **RU**: Patriot, paid personal property tax, Rockingham Co, 1783 that's considered a supply tax for Rev War expenses **CEM**: Hernsberger-Wynant Graveyard; GPS 38.366547, -78.963740; Waystation Rd (Rt 888) across rd fr airport bldg behind stonewall, Bridgewater; Rockingham **GS**: Yes, broken **SP**: Anna Maria Bear (Baer)(27 Mar 1757-27 Jun 1824), d/o Jacob Bear (1724-1783) & Anna Barbara Miller (1726-1791) **VI**: Son of Stephen Harnsberger (1716-aft 1782) & Ursula Scheitle (1722-1762) **P**: N **BLW**: N **RG**: N **MK**: N **PH**: N **SS**: DV image 10, 1783, Rockingham Co **BS**: 196.

HERON, James; b 1749; d 29 Sep 1801 **RU**: Captain, Served in Hazen's Regt in 1777 **CEM**: St John's Episcopal; GPS 37.53183, -77.41958; 2401 E Broad St; Richmond City **GS**: Y **SP**: Mar (11 Sep 1790) Sarah Taylor (25 Dec 1771-26 Dec 1811 in Richmond theatre fire). She also has headstone at St John's Church, Richmond. **VI**: No further data **P**: unk **BLW**: unk **RG**: N **MK**: N **PH**: unk **SS**: AP **BS**: 28 pg 454.

HERRING, Bethual (Bethuel Bethuard); b 1751, Sussex Co; d c1815 **RU**: Private/Patriot, Served in Capt William Herring's Co, Rockingham Co Militia. Gave material aid to cause **CEM**: Old Peaked Mountain; GPS 38.37113, -78.73416; 9843 Town Hall Rd, McGaheysville; Rockingham **GS**: U **SP**: Mar (16 Aug 1782) Mary Miller (__-c1800) **VI**: Son of Alexander (1708-1778) & Abigail (Harrison) (1710-1780) Herring. Name is on plaque in cemetery **P**: unk **BLW**: unk **RG**: Y **MK**: Y DAR plaque **PH**: unk **SS**: J-NSSAR 2000 Reg; AL Ct Bk II, pg 26, 37 Rockingham Co; DAR Chapter publication on Rev War soldiers in Rockingham Co pg 12; SAR P-180257 **BS**: JLARC 76.

HERRING, Leonard; b 1735; d 1805 **RU**: Patriot, Gave material aid to cause **CEM**: Old Peaked Mountain; GPS 38.37113, -78.73416; 9843 Town Hall Rd, McGaheysville; Rockingham **GS**: Y **SP**: Mar (1805 Rockingham Co) Anne Ervin d/o Benjamin & (-----) Ervin **VI**: Son of Alexander (1708-1778) & Abigail (Harrison) (1710-1780) Herring **P**: N **BLW**: N **RG**: Y **MK**: Y **PH**: unk **SS**: O pg 128; AL Ct Bk I pg 1, 7, 8 Rockbridge Co SAR P-180265 **BS**: 04; 196.

HERRING, William; b c1760; d 8 Oct 1812 **RU**: Captain, Served under Capt Cravens. Took oath as Capt in Militia. Served under Col Benjamin Harrison **CEM**: Old Peaked Mountain; GPS 38.37113, -78.73416; 9843 Town Hall Rd, McGaheysville; Rockingham **GS**: U **SP**: 1) Susannah Parham 2) Betsy T__) **VI**: No further data **P**: unk **BLW**: unk **RG**: Y **MK**: Y SAR **PH**: unk **SS**: Court minutes 23 Oct. 1780; J-NSSAR 2000 Reg SAR P-180274 **BS**: JLARC 76.

HERRINGTON, William; b unk; d 1781 **RU**: Soldier, Served fr MA, killed in the battle at Yorktown **CEM**: Yorktown Victory Monument Tablet; GPS 38.28350, -78.54150; Yorktown; York **GS**: U **SP**: No info **VI**: No further data **P**: unk **BLW**: unk **RG**: Y **MK**: unk **PH**: unk **SS**: J-Yorktown Historian SAR P-180297 **BS**: JLARC 74.

HERVE, Guillaume; b unk; d 1781 **RU**: Seaman, Served on "Saint-Esprit" and died from Yorktown battle **CEM**: French Memorial; GPS 36.81944, -79.39933; Yorktown; York **GS**: U **SP**: No info **VI**: No further

RU=Rank/Unit	CEM=Cemetery	GS=Gravestone	SP=Spousal Information
VI=Other Veteran Info	P=Pension	BLW=Bounty/Land Warrant	RG=Registered Grave
MK=SAR/DAR Marker	PH=Photo	SS=Service Source	BS=Burial Source

191

data **P:** unk **BLW:** unk **RG:** Y **MK:** unk **PH:** unk **SS:** J-Yorktown Historian SAR P-180404 **BS:** JLARC 1, 74.

HERVE, Jean; b unk; d 1781 **RU:** Seaman, Served on "Citoyen" and died from Yorktown battle **CEM:** French Memorial; GPS 36.81944, -79.39933; Yorktown; York **GS:** U **SP:** No info **VI:** No further data **P:** unk **BLW:** unk **RG:** Y **MK:** unk **PH:** unk **SS:** J-Yorktown Historian SAR P-180405 **BS:** JLARC 1, 74.

HERVE, Michel; b unk; d 1781 **RU:** Soldier, Served in Gatinais Bn and died fr battle at Yorktown **CEM:** French Memorial; GPS 36.81944, -79.39933; Yorktown; York **GS:** U **SP:** No info **VI:** No further data **P:** unk **BLW:** unk **RG:** Y **MK:** unk **PH:** unk **SS:** J-Yorktown Historian; SAR P-180406 **BS:** JLARC 1, 74.

HESS, Jacob; b unk; d Mar 1788 **RU:** Private, Served in Capt Driesback's Co, Col Armand's Command, 26 Feb 1777 **CEM:** Old Christ Church Episcopal; GPS 38.80625, -77.04718; 118 N Washington St; Alexandria City **GS:** N **SP:** No info **VI:** Burial permit issued 6 Mar 1788 to his estate **P:** unk **BLW:** unk **RG:** N **MK:** N **PH:** unk **SS:** A pg 219 **BS:** 20 pg 149.

HEYDE (HIDY), Johann Henrich (John); b 1751, Germany; d Aft 21 Mar 1823 **RU:** Asst Drill Master, Served in PA. Enl Philadelphia 25 Jan 1776, 3rd VA Regt. Was at Valley Forge and was Assistant Drill Master there. **CEM:** Heyde; GPS unk; Rt 644, Blue Grass; Highland **GS:** U **SP:** Mar (27 Feb 1781) Christian Ann Trexler (1763 Northumberland Co PA-1836) d/o Peter (1727-1764) & Maria (Albrecht) Trexler **VI:** Arrived in USA a Johann Heinrich Heyde. Changed name to John Hidy **P:** unk **BLW:** unk **RG:** Y **MK:** Y SAR **PH:** unk **SS:** J-NSSAR 1993 Reg; CD; CI, PA Archives, 5th series, 19 Feb Vol 2, pg 109, 947; SAR P-180630 **BS:** JLARC 1; 196.

HICKLE, Lewis; b 1751; d bef Jan 1808 **RU:** Soldier, Served in VA Line. Also Capt Robinson's Co, Frederick Co Militia **CEM:** Fincastle Presbyterian; GPS 37.50017, -79.87558; 108 E Back St, Fincastle; Botetourt **GS:** N **SP:** Elizabeth Huber **VI:** Son appl 30 Apr 1855 Grainger Co TN. R4947. Will dated of 21 Mar 1823. Name is on the SAR plaque at this cemetery and the monument to Rev War soldiers **P:** Y **BLW:** unk **RG:** Y **MK:** Y SAR plaque **PH:** N **SS:** J-NSSAR 1993 Reg, J- DAR Hatcher; AR Vol 2 pg 147; BW pg 479; CG Vol 2 pg 1622; SAR P- 180753, DAR A054788 **BS:** 196; JLARC 1, 2.

HICKMAN, Jacob; b 1765; d 24 Nov 1848 **RU:** Patriot, Gave material aid to the cause **CEM:** Mt Zion Methodist; GPS 37.66596, -79.46615; Btw Buffalo & Tinkersville; Rockbridge **GS:** Y **SP:** No info **VI:** No further data **P:** N **BLW:** N **RG:** N **MK:** N **PH:** unk **SS:** AL Certificate **BS:** 154 Rockbridge.

HICKOK, Ebenezer; b 02 Feb 1759, Stamford, CT; d Feb 1843 **RU:** Private, Served in CT Line. Ent ser 1775 in Fairfield, CT **CEM:** Fincastle Presbyterian; GPS 37.50017, -79.87558; 108 E Back St, Fincastle; Botetourt **GS:** Y **SP:** Mar (Amherst Co) widow Jane Linn (1760-1838) **VI:** He moved to Amherst Co in 1782. Appl 17 Oct 1832 Amherst Co. S5541. Name is on VASSAR plaque at cemetery **P:** Y **BLW:** unk **RG:** Y **MK:** Y SAR plaque **PH:** N **SS:** K Vol 2 pg 303; CG Vol 2 pg 1623; SAR P-333102 **BS:** 196.

HICKS, Kimble; b 1746; d 2 Feb 1837 **RU:** Patriot, Gave material aid to the cause **CEM:** Sherman-Hicks Family, aka Liberty Farm; GPS unk; Paris; Fauquier **GS:** Y **SP:** Matilda (-----) Hicks **VI:** Son of Charles & Mary (Kimble) Hicks of Bucks Co, PA **P:** N **BLW:** N **RG:** N **MK:** N **PH:** unk **SS:** AL Ct Bk II pg 239 **BS:** 95 Liberty farm.

HIELDEN, (------); b unk; d 1781 **RU:** Soldier, Served in Royal Deaux Ponts Bn and died fr battle at Yorktown **CEM:** French Memorial; GPS 36.81944, -79.39933; Yorktown; York **GS:** U **SP:** No info **VI:** No further data **P:** unk **BLW:** unk **RG:** N **MK:** unk **PH:** unk **SS:** J-Yorktown Historian **BS:** JLARC 1, 74.

HIGGINBOTHAM, James; b 25 Dec 1729; d 14 Mar 1813 **RU:** Colonel/Patriot, Was Maj in Amherst Co Militia. In 1778 promoted to Col in 9th VA Regt 1777-1780. Furnished part of clothing & beef for 16th Division **CEM:** Higginbotham Family; GPS 37.69140, -79.14280; Rt 617 N of jct with 761, Amherst; Amherst **GS:** N **SP:** Mar (30 May 1779) Rachel Campbell (1755-17 Apr 1805) **VI:** Son of Joseph Higginbotham. Widower at death. Surviving children appl pen which was rejected **P:** N **BLW:** unk **RG:** N **MK:** unk **PH:** N **SS:** E pg 376; G pg 72; K Vol 3 pg 306; Order bk pg 498 **BS:** 196.

HIGGINS, Thomas; b unk; d 1781 **RU:** Soldier, Served fr NY, killed in the battle at Yorktown **CEM:** Yorktown Victory Monument Tablet; GPS 38.28350, -78.54150; Yorktown; York **GS:** U **SP:** No info **VI:** No further data **P:** unk **BLW:** unk **RG:** Y **MK:** unk **PH:** unk **SS:** J-Yorktown Historian SAR P-181109 **BS:** JLARC 74.

RU=Rank/Unit	CEM=Cemetery	GS=Gravestone	SP=Spousal Information
VI=Other Veteran Info	P=Pension	BLW=Bounty/Land Warrant	RG=Registered Grave
MK=SAR/DAR Marker	PH=Photo	SS=Service Source	BS=Burial Source

HIGHT, George; b 3 Jul 1755, King & Queen Co; d 21 Aug 1837 **RU:** Private, Ent serv Botetourt Co, Jan 1776. Volunteered serv against Cherokees under Capt Bilmore Aug 1777. Served in Col George Baylors Regt of Light Dragoons and Cont VA Line **CEM:** Mt Zion Methodist; GPS 37.66596, -79.46615; Btw Buffalo & Tinkersville; Rockbridge **GS:** Y **SP:** Mar (24 May 1782) Lovia Lunsford (24 Jun 1760-3 Jun 1843) (Find A Grave says d. 1840) **VI:** Moved age 8 (1763) Albemarle Co, then Amherst (1767), then 1776 Botetourt. Sol appl pen 3 Dec 1832. W19769 Rockbridge Co. Died in Nelson Co. Widow appl pen 3 Jun 1843. Source 101 has Haines Chapel, South Mountain Cem **P:** Y **BLW:** unk **RG:** Y **MK:** unk **PH:** Y **SS:** K Vol 3 pg 307; CD; CG Vol 2 pg 1630; SAR P-181164 **BS:** JLARC 2, 79,101.

HIGIE, Richard; b unk, France; d 1781 **RU:** Seaman, Served on "Auguste" and died from Yorktown battle **CEM:** French Memorial; GPS 36.81944, -79.39933; Yorktown; York **GS:** U **SP:** No info **VI:** No further data **P:** unk **BLW:** unk **RG:** Y **MK:** unk **PH:** unk **SS:** J-Yorktown Historian **BS:** JLARC 1, 74.

HILL, Amos; b unk; d 1781 **RU:** Soldier, Service unit not determined. Died fr battle at Yorktown **CEM:** Yorktown Victory Monument Tablet; GPS 38.28350, -78.54150; Yorktown; York **GS:** U **SP:** No info **VI:** No further data **P:** unk **BLW:** unk **RG:** Y **MK:** unk **PH:** unk **SS:** J-Yorktown Historian; SAR P-181289 **BS:** JLARC 74.

HILL, Humphrey; b 2 Apr 1756; d 27 Jun 1841 **RU:** Soldier, Ent serv Middlesex Co. Served in VA Line **CEM:** Hill Family; GPS 37.93764, -77.55152; 5498 Mt Airy Dr, Mt Airy, Ruther Glen; Caroline **GS:** Y **SP:** 1) Mary Garlick (1771-1819) 2) Elizabeth Minor (1776-1833) **VI:** Sol appl pen 16 Jul 1832 Culpeper Co. S5530 **P:** Y **BLW:** N **RG:** N **MK:** N **PH:** Y **SS:** K pg 308; CG pg 1635; CI Serv Record; served VA Line **BS:** 196.

HILL, James; b c1759; d 1802 **RU:** Patriot, Gave material aid to cause **CEM:** Springfield; GPS unk; Abt 2 mi south of King William CH, on right side of Rt 621, leading fr Skyron to Palls; King William **GS:** N **SP:** Mildred Clopton **VI:** Formerly of "Porto Bello", located on Queens Creek, York Co VA. GS moved to Springfield abt 1771 **P:** N **BLW:** N **RG:** N **MK:** N **PH:** N **SS:** AL Ct Bk II pg 3, 9 York Co **BS:** 196.

HILL, James; b unk; d 1817 **RU:** Private, Served in Capt Thomas Hill's Co, Col Holt Richison's 7th VA Regt, Jun 1778 **CEM:** North End; GPS 36.77234, -80.73866; 101 Beaver Dam Rd, Hillsville; Carroll **GS:** N **SP:** Keziah (-----) (1761-3 Apr 1815) **VI:** No further data **P:** unk **BLW:** unk **RG:** N **MK:** N **PH:** N **SS:** E pg 377; CI Rev War Rolls **BS:** 123 pg 67; 196. **HILL,** James See Appendix G Addenda)

HILL, John Berry; b 1727; d 28 Dec 1817 **RU:** Patriot, Gave material aid to cause **CEM:** Stonewall Jackson Memorial; GPS 37.78128, -79.44604; 314 S Main St; Lexington City **GS:** U **SP:** Rachel Berry (___-28 Sep 1812) **VI:** No further data **P:** N **BLW:** N **RG:** N **MK:** unk **PH:** N **SS:** CI record book Officers & Men **BS:** 196.

HILL, Nathaniel; b 1740; d 1808 **RU:** Soldier, Served in VA unit in Illinois **CEM:** Hill Family; GPS unk; Cub Creek Rd Rt 789, Tyro; Nelson **GS:** U **SP:** Mar (3 Sep 1767) Nanny Parrish (c1745, Goochland Co-1808) **VI:** No further data **P:** unk **BLW:** unk **RG:** Y **MK:** unk **PH:** unk **SS:** E pg 377; SAR P-181518 **BS:** JLARC 83.

HILL, Robert; b 10 Sep 1713, Dublin, Ireland; d 17 Aug 1778 **RU:** Soldier, Served in Capt Thomas Buford's Co, Bedford Co, at the Battle of Point Pleasant 1774 **CEM:** Tanyard-Barnard-Hill; GPS unk; Rocky Mount; Franklin **GS:** U **SP:** mar (12 Sep 1741 Chester Co, PA) Violett Linnes (1725-1808) **VI:** Son of Sinfield & Mary (Wilson) Hill. Name on a DAR plaque in cemetery that shows his service **P:** unk **BLW:** unk **RG:** Y **MK:** unk **PH:** unk **SS:** Z pg 125; BT; SAR P-181553 **BS:** JLARC 20; 196.

HILL, Thomas; b 1745; d 5 Feb 1827 **RU:** Ensign, Ent serv 1779. Serv in 5th VA Regt 1778-9 **CEM:** Tanyard-Bernard-Hill; GPS unk; Rocky Mount; Franklin **GS:** U **SP:** Alianna Stranifer (c1756-15 Jun 1827) **VI:** Son of Robert (1713-1778) & Violet (Linus) (1725-1808) Hill. DAR plaque in cem. BLW issued 24 Aug 1789 #1429. Another BLW issued to brother James residing in Bedford Co on 6 Dec 1828 **P:** unk **BLW:** Y **RG:** Y **MK:** Y DAR plaque **PH:** unk **SS:** K pg 310; CG pg 1640; CI Rev War roll; SAR P-181608 **BS:** JLARC 1, 2,18; 196.

HILL, Thomas M or H; b 1758; d 29 Mar 1815 **RU:** Patriot, Was member of the trustees of the town of Portsmouth 1783 **CEM:** Trinity Episcopal; GPS 36.83459, -76.30105; 500 Court St; Portsmouth City **GS:**

RU=Rank/Unit
VI=Other Veteran Info
MK=SAR/DAR Marker
CEM=Cemetery
P=Pension
PH=Photo
GS=Gravestone
BLW=Bounty/Land Warrant
SS=Service Source
SP=Spousal Information
RG=Registered Grave
BS=Burial Source

193

Y **SP:** No info **VI:** No further data **P:** N **BLW:** N **RG:** N **MK:** N **PH:** unk **SS:** B gives service **BS:** 92 stone 64.

HILL, Violett (Linus); b 1710; d 1808 **RU:** Patriot, Gave material aid to the cause **CEM:** Tanyard-Bernard-Hill; GPS unk; Rocky Mount; Franklin **GS:** Y **SP:** Thomas Hill (1745-1827) **VI:** No further data **P:** N **BLW:** N **RG:** Y **MK:** N **PH:** unk **SS:** AL Ct Bk pg 33; SAR P-181628 **BS:** 80 vol 2 pg 151.

HILL, William; b unk; d 1800? **RU:** Private, Served in Capt Tate's Co, Augusta Co **CEM:** Hill Family; GPS unk; Cub Creek Rd Rt 789, Tyro; Nelson **GS:** U **SP:** Susanne Jacobs **VI:** No further data **P:** unk **BLW:** unk **RG:** Y **MK:** unk **PH:** unk **SS:** E pg 378; SAR P-181635 **BS:** JLARC 83.

HILLENBERG (HILLENBURG), Daniel; b 10 Sep 1752, Rohenfurth, Hesse-Kassel, Germany; d 19 Jun 1819 **RU:** unk, Serv listed in Wythe Co Historical Review, #18, Jul 1980, pub by Wythe Co Hist Soc **CEM:** Hillenberg; GPS unk; SW of Crockett?; Wythe **GS:** U **SP:** Mar (25 Mar 1787, Montgomery Co) Mary Barbara Shrader d/o John & Johannas (Christian) Shrader **VI:** Son of Christian & Anna Catherina (Sinninger) Hillenburg. Arrived Staten Island 24 Aug 1776. Was in British Army at Savannah; deserted with weapons and full pack. Family tradition is that he fought for American forces **P:** unk **BLW:** unk **RG:** N **MK:** unk **PH:** unk **SS:** JLARC Rpt App B-2 pg 71 **BS:** JLARC 122.

HILTON, Samuel; b 1759; d 1852 **RU:** Private, Served in 3rd MD Regt **CEM:** Trinity United Methodist; GPS 39.13600, -77.00610; 2911 Cameron Mills Rd; Alexandria City **GS:** N **SP:** No info **VI:** No further data **P:** unk **BLW:** unk **RG:** N **MK:** N **PH:** N **SS:** AP MD roll **BS:** 126 vol 2 pg 157.

HILTZENBERGER, Francois; b unk; d 1781 **RU:** Soldier, Served in Royal Deaux Ponts Bn and died fr battle at Yorktown **CEM:** French Memorial; GPS 36.81944, -79.39933; Yorktown; York **GS:** U **SP:** No info **VI:** No further data **P:** unk **BLW:** unk **RG:** Y **MK:** unk **PH:** unk **SS:** J-Yorktown Historian; SAR P-181911 **BS:** JLARC 1, 74.

HINKLE, Isaac; b 5 Dec 1754 Mocksville, Davie County, NC; d 1 Nov 1824 **RU:** Captain, Was corporal in WVA. Commanded a Co in Rockingham Co Militia 24 Sep 1781 **CEM:** Old Peaked Mountain; GPS 38.37113, -78.73416; 9843 Town Hall Rd, McGaheysville; Rockingham **GS:** U **SP:** Mar (13 Dec 1781) Mary Cunningham (1758, Chillicothe, Ross Co, Ohio-2 Mar 1819, Pendleton Co, WV) **VI:** Son of John Justus (1706-1778) & Maria Magdelena (Eschmann) (1710-1798) Hinkel. Died in Riverton, Pendleton Co, WV. Though bur in WV, memorialized on DAR plaque in cemetery **P:** unk **BLW:** unk **RG:** Y **MK:** Y DAR plaque **PH:** unk **SS:** J-NSSAR 2000 Reg; AZ pg 230; SAR P-182100, DAR A055284 **BS:** JLARC 76; 196.

HINKLE, Yost; b unk; d unk **RU:** Ensign, Served in Capt Isacc Hinkle's Co **CEM:** Old Peaked Mountain; GPS 38.37113, -78.73416; 9843 Town Hall Rd, McGaheysville; Rockingham **GS:** U **SP:** No info **VI:** Memorialized on DAR plaque in cemetery **P:** unk **BLW:** unk **RG:** Y **MK:** Y DAR plaque **PH:** unk **SS:** J-NSSAR 2000 Reg; SAR P-182116 **BS:** JLARC 76.

HINTON, Peter; b1761, d1813 **RU:** Patriot, paid personal property tax 1782 and 1783, Rockingham Co considered to be a supply tax for Rev War expenses **CEM:** Flook Armentrout; GPS not determined; end of Henton Mill Ln (Rt 934) on the left at knoll, Lacy Spring; Rockingham **GS:** Y **SP:** Mary Polly Scothorn (31 Aug 1762-7 Aug 1834) **VI:** Homeand Mill site bldg is shown on FAG **P:** N **BLW:** N **RG:** N **MK:** N **PH:** N **SS:** DV 1782 image 11, 1783 image 22, Rockingham Co **BS:** 196.

HIPKINS, John; b unk; d 1804 **RU:** Patriot, Gave material aid to the cause **CEM:** Emmanuel Episcopal; GPS unk; US 301, Port Conway; King George **GS:** N **SP:** Elizabeth Pratt (1754-1829) **VI:** His name is on a memorial plaque at the Port Royal Church at the Emmanuel Cemetery **P:** unk **BLW:** unk **RG:** N **MK:** N **PH:** N **SS:** AL Ct Bk I pg 5 **BS:** 64 pg 15. **P:** N **BLW:** N **RG:** N **MK:** N **PH:** N **SS:** AL Ct Bk I **BS:** 196

HITE, Isaac Jr.; b 7 Feb 1758, Frederick; d 30 Nov 1836 **RU:** Ensign, Served in VA Line. Ent Serv Frederick Co 1780 **CEM:** Old Hite Farm; GPS unk; Long Meadows, Middletown; Frederick **GS:** U **SP:** 1) Eleanor Madison 2) Ann Turnstall Maury, still living in 1844 **VI:** Sol appl pen 23 Jun 1828 Frederick Co. S8714. Recd BLW #189-200 **P:** Y **BLW:** Y **RG:** Y **MK:** Y SAR **PH:** unk **SS:** J-NSSAR 1993 Reg; BY; CG Vol 2 pg 1656; SAR P-182381, DAR A055678 **BS:** JLARC 1.

RU=Rank/Unit	CEM=Cemetery	GS=Gravestone	SP=Spousal Information
VI=Other Veteran Info	P=Pension	BLW=Bounty/Land Warrant	RG=Registered Grave
MK=SAR/DAR Marker	PH=Photo	SS=Service Source	BS=Burial Source

194

HITE, Isaac; b 12 May 1723, Perkiomen Creek, PA; d 18 Sep 1795 **RU:** Patriot, Approved 25 Oct 1775 in Frederick Co for reimbursement for provisions he provided. Performed public service as Justice of Frederick Co **CEM:** Hite Family; GPS unk; Middletown; Frederick **GS:** Y **SP:** Mar (12 Apr 1745) Eleanor Eltinge (29 Apr 1724, Kingston, NY-10 Nov 1792; Middletown, Frederick Co) **VI:** Son of Joseph (__-1761) & (-----) Hite **P:** N **BLW:** N **RG:** N **MK:** N **PH:** unk **SS:** Z pg 78; DD cites Norris History of the Lower Shenandoah Valley pg 136 **BS:** 113 (see Cem); 196.

HITE, Julius; b 10 Oct 1756, Sussex Co; d 2 Dec 1851 **RU:** Corporal, Served in Cont & VA Line. Lived in Sussex Co at enl. Served in Col Henry Lee's Legion in 1783 **CEM:** Hite Family; GPS unk; Forksville; Lunenburg **GS:** Y **SP:** Agnes Land of Sussex Co. **VI:** Wrote to Washington DC abt war penson. Walked all the way to Washington to collect pension in silver, then walked all the way back. Sol appl pen 4 Jul 1832 Lunenburg Co age 73, a res of Oak Grove. S18024. BLW #12223-130-8 May 1794 **P:** Y **BLW:** Y **RG:** Y **MK:** unk **PH:** unk **SS:** G pg 649-650; J- DAR Hatcher; CG Vol 2 pg 1656; SAR P-182374, DAR A055695 **BS:** 196; JLARC 2.

HITT, Nimrod (Nimrods); b 21 Jul 1765, Germantown, Fauquier Co; d 17 Sep 1825 **RU:** Soldier, Served in VA unit in Illinois **CEM:** Miller; GPS 38.734080, -78.171692 ; Rt 248 in Harris Hollow, Washington; Rappahannock **GS:** Y **SP:** Never mar **VI:** Died in Culpeper Co **P:** unk **BLW:** unk **RG:** N **MK:** N **PH:** unk **SS:** E pg 381 **BS:** 33.

HITT, Peter; b 1 Feb 1755; d 31 Aug 1802 **RU:** Private?, Served in VA Line. Ent serv Fauquier Co 1777 **CEM:** Hitt family; GPS 38.721407, -78.004989; 7535 Tapps Ford Rd, Amissville; Fauquier **GS:** Y **SP:** Mar (Apr 1783 Fauquier Co) Hannah (-----) (__-1846 Fauquier Co) **VI:** Son of John & Sarah (Pace) Hitt. Widow appl pen 7 Sep 1841 Fauquier Co age 78. F-W7732 R1291 **P:** Y **BLW:** unk **RG:** Y **MK:** N **PH:** Y **SS:** K pg 313; CG Vol 2 pg 1656; Germanna Record No 1; SAR P-182396, DAR A055721 **BS:** 19 pg 88.

HIX, James; b unk; d 1781 **RU:** Soldier, Served fr MA, killed in the battle at Yorktown **CEM:** Yorktown Victory Monument Tablet; GPS 38.28350, -78.54150; Yorktown; York **GS:** U **SP:** No info **VI:** No further data **P:** unk **BLW:** unk **RG:**Y **MK:** unk **PH:** unk **SS:** J-Yorktown Historian; SAR P-182410 **BS:** JLARC 74.

HIXON, Timothy; b 1730, Hunterdon Co, NJ; d 1812 **RU:** Captain, Took oath as Capt in Loudoun Co 13 Oct 1782. Rec to command a Co in 1st Battalion of Militia 10 Feb 1783 **CEM:** Hixon Family; GPS unk; Check property records for home place as burial site; Loudoun **GS:** Y **SP:** Mar (c1762) Rachel Lacey (1735 Essex, NJ- 1786 Leesburg) **VI:** Son of William (1647-1736) & Mary (Patterson) Hixon **P:** unk **BLW:** unk **RG:**Y **MK:** N **PH:** unk **SS:** E pg 381; DD; BY; SAR P-182426 **BS:** SAR Appl.

HOAGON, Cyprien; b unk France; d 1781 **RU:** Seaman, Served on "Saint-Esprit" and died from Yorktown battle **CEM:** French Memorial; GPS 36.81944, -79.39933; Yorktown; York **GS:** U **SP:** No info **VI:** No further data **P:** unk **BLW:** unk **RG:** Y **MK:** unk **PH:** unk **SS:** J-Yorktown Historian; SAR P-182476 **BS:** JLARC 1, 74.

HOBBS, Ezekiel; b abt 1762; d 13 Jun 1835 **RU:** Private, Served in VA Line. Ent serv Washington Co **CEM:** Hobbs; GPS unk; North Fork, Holston River; Washington **GS:** U **SP:** Elizabeth Lilly (a Hardy Lilley signed mar bond with sol 27 Jul 1803 Washington Co) (c1785-__) **VI:** Was Reverend. Sol appl pen 6 Oct 1834 Washington Co age 70. Widow appl pen 28 Jun 1853 & 24 Mar 1855 age 70. W8940. Recd BLW #26632-160-55. **P:** Y **BLW:** Y **RG:** Y **MK:** unk **PH:** unk **SS:** K Vol 3 pg 314; CG Vol 2 pg 1659; SAR P-182609 **BS:** JLARC 4,34,80; 80 cem #6.

HOBBS, Vincent; b 1735, Dorchester, Dorest, England; d 1804 **RU:** Private, Served in Dunsmore's War of 1774 at Point Pleasant fr Fincastle Co under Capt Joseph Cloyd **CEM:** Hobbs family, also called Debusk Family; GPS unk; Dryden; Lee **GS:** Y **SP:** No info **VI:** Plaque on GS, DAR marker **P:** unk **BLW:** unk **RG:** Y **MK:** Y DAR **PH:** unk **SS:** G pg 216; CP Dunmore's War SAR P-182605 **BS:** 196; Email Sep 09.

HOBSON (HOPSON), Joseph Calip/Caleb; b unk; d 1814 **RU:** First Lieutenant, Served in Capt Thomas Posey's Co, Col Morgan's picked riflemen. Promoted to 1st Lt 28 Nov 1776. Resigned 20 May 1778 **CEM:** Old Hobson; GPS unk; Blenheim, nr Balleville; Powhatan **GS:** Y **SP:** Pheobe Brackett **VI:** No further data **P:** unk **BLW:** unk **RG:** N **MK:** N **PH:** unk **SS:** E pg 381 **BS:** 187.

RU=Rank/Unit	CEM=Cemetery	GS=Gravestone	SP=Spousal Information
VI=Other Veteran Info	P=Pension	BLW=Bounty/Land Warrant	RG=Registered Grave
MK=SAR/DAR Marker	PH=Photo	SS=Service Source	BS=Burial Source

HODGES, John b 1708 Henrico Co, d 11 Oct 1805 **RU**: Patriot Gave material aid to cause Goochland Co **CEM**: Hodges-Thomas 1750 Family Farm Plot; GPS 37.3668, -78.3747; Raines Tavern; Cumberland **GS**: Yes **SP**: 1) Ann Johnson (8 Jun 1710, Prince George Co-1750), d/o William Johnson and Johannah (-----), 2) Judith DePriest Austin **VI**: Son of Thomas Hodges and Christian Woodson **P**: N **BLW**: N **RG**: N **MK**: N **PH**: N **SS**: AL Ct Bk, pg 21, Goochland Co **BS**: 196.

HOFF, Lewis; b c1738; d 29 May 1803 **RU**: Patriot, Filed claim 25 Oct 1775, Frederick Co, for gun carriage he gave to Dunmore Co Militia **CEM**: Mt Hebron; GPS 39.1183766, -78.160408; 305 E Boscawen St; Winchester City **GS**: Y **SP**: Susanna Catherine Fortney **VI**: No further data **P**: N **BLW**: N **RG**: Y **MK**: Y SAR monument **PH**: Y **SS**: Z pg 78 **BS**: 50 pg 53; 196.

HOFFMAN, Andre; b unk, France; d 1781 **RU**: Soldier, Served in Royal Deaux Ponts Bn and died fr battle at Yorktown **CEM**: French Memorial; GPS 36.81944, -79.39933; Yorktown; York **GS**: U **SP**: No info **VI**: No further data **P**: unk **BLW**: unk **RG**: Y **MK**: unk **PH**: unk **SS**: J-Yorktown Historian; SAR P-182910 **BS**: JLARC 1, 74.

HOGE, Edward; b unk; d 1782 **RU**: Patriot, Gave material aid to the cause **CEM**: Old Opequon Church; GPS 39.82237, -78.11412; 217 Opequon Church Ln, Kernstown; Frederick **GS**: Y **SP**: Elizabeth Brown (__ Ireland 1754-14 Apr 1844) **VI**: Son of James & Agnes (Crawford) Hoge **P**: N **BLW**: N **RG**: N **MK**: N **PH**: unk **SS**: AL Ct Bk, pg 8 **BS**: 59 pg 153; 196.

HOGE,(HOGG) James; b 22 Jan 1742; d 8 Apr 1812 **RU**: Private, Served in Capt Mayes Co, Montgomery Co Militia **CEM**: Sunnyside; GPS unk; Btw Radford and Dublin at Old Joseph Howe place, Back Creek; Pulaski **GS**: Y **SP**: Mar (21 Jan 1768) Elizabeth Howe (10 May 1750-1804) **VI**: No further data **P**: unk **BLW**: unk **RG**: N **MK**: unk **PH**: unk **SS**: DAR #A056515; G pg 238 **BS**: 196.

HOGE, William; b unk; d 1842 **RU**: Corporal, Served in 7th,11th & 15th Cont Lines **CEM**: Goose Creek; GPS 39.11250, -77.69527; Rt 722, Lincoln; Loudoun **GS**: Y **SP**: No info **VI**: No further data **P**: unk **BLW**: unk **RG** N **MK**: N **PH**: unk **SS**: C pg 243; E pg 38 **BS**: 25 pg 144.

HOGE, William; b c1727; d 1815 **RU**: Corporal/Patriot, Gave material aid to cause **CEM**: Back Creek Quaker, aka Gainesboro United Methodist; GPS 39.27861, -78.25694; 166 Siler Ln, Gainesboro; Frederick **GS**: Y **SP**: mar (16 Jun 1795 Frederick Co by Rev Alexander Balmain) Rachel Steel **VI**: No further data **P**: unk **BLW**: unk **RG**: N **MK**: N **PH**: unk **SS**: E pg 383; AL Ct Bk pg 10 Frederick Co **BS**: 59 pg 153.

HOGE (HOGG), James Sr; b 4 Jul 1706, PA; d 2 Jun 1795 **RU**: Patriot, Gave material aid to the cause **CEM**: Old Opequon Church; GPS 39.82237, -78.11412; 217 Opequon Church Ln, Kernstown; Frederick **GS**: Y **SP**: 1) Agnes Crawford (14 Apr 1700, Minnigaff, Kirkcudbright, Scotland-1743 VA) 2) Nancy Griffith **VI**: Son of William (1660-1749) & Barbara (Hume) (1670-1745) Hoge. Died in Winchester **P**: N **BLW**: N **RG**: Y **MK**: N **PH**: unk **SS**: AL Ct bk pg 5, 16; SAR P-183080 **BS**: AS DAR report; 196.

HOGSETT, James; b unk, d 18 Dec 1807 **RU**: Patriot, Gave beef and a wagon for two days for militia use **CEM**: Hogshead Family. GPS unk; Nr jct Rts 736/250 outside Parnassus, Jennings Gap; Augusta **GS**: U **SP**: No info **VI**: No further data **P**: N **BLW**: N **RG**: N **MK**: unk **PH**: unk **SS**: DY pg 29 **BS**: 142.

HOGSHEAD, David Jr; b c1761; d 1814 **RU**: Private/Patriot, Gave material aid to cause **CEM**: Hogshead Family; GPS unk; Off Rt 736 btw Rts 42 & 250, N of Jennings Gap; Augusta **GS**: Y **SP**: No info **VI**: No further data **P**: unk **BLW**: unk **RG**: Y **MK**: N **PH**: unk **SS**: E pg 384; AL Cert Aubusta Co; SAR P-331920 **BS**: 36 pg 73; 196.

HOGSHEAD, Michael; b unk; d 1818 **RU**: Patriot, Gave material aid to cause **CEM**: Hogshead Family; GPS unk; Off Rt 736 btw Rts 42 & 250, N of Jennings Gap; Augusta **GS**: Y **SP**: No info **VI**: No further data **P**: N **BLW**: N **RG**: N **MK**: N **PH**: unk **SS**: E pg 384; AL Cert Augusta Co **BS**: 36 pg 72-3; 196.

HOLKER, John; b 1743, England; d Jun 1820 **RU**: Patriot, Sent to USA during the Rev War c1778 by Govt of Louis XVI, or rather by Beaumarchais, to inquire into probability of the success of our armies against England. Favorable report and treaty made bet Louis and USA **CEM**: Stone Chapel Presbyterian; GPS 39.22610, -78.01060; Old Charles Town Rd, Berryville; Clarke **GS**: U **SP**: 1) (-----) 2) (-----) 3) Mrs. Nancy Davis (Stackpole) Stillman of Boston MA **VI**: Son of Jean and (-----) Holker of France. John Holker became Consul General of France & agent of Royal Marine. Brought letters fr

RU=Rank/Unit	CEM=Cemetery	GS=Gravestone	SP=Spousal Information
VI=Other Veteran Info	P=Pension	BLW=Bounty/Land Warrant	RG=Registered Grave
MK=SAR/DAR Marker	PH=Photo	SS=Service Source	BS=Burial Source

Benjamin Franklin to Robert Morris and Congress. Died in Springsberry, Clarke Co. Originally bur in holy ground in Winchester, but reinterred in Autumn 1904 to "Old Chapel" Clarke Co **P:** N **BLW:** N **RG:** N **MK**: N **PH:** unk **SS:** CD **BS:** 196.

HOLLADAY, Joseph; b c1726, Spotsylvania Co; d 24 Jul or 23 Sep 1785 **RU:** Patriot, Was inspector of tobacco and also gave material aid to cause in 1781 **CEM:** Elmwood; GPS unk; Rt 614; Spotsylvania **GS:** N **SP:** Elizabeth Lewis d/o Harry & (-----) Lewis **VI:** Son of John (__-Nov 1742) & Elizabeth (-----) Holladay of Spotsylvania Co. Will proved 4 Apr 1787 **P:** N **BLW:** N **RG:** Y **MK:** N **PH:** N **SS:** D pg 857; SAR P-183511 **BS:** 09 Part 2.

HOLLADAY, Joseph, Jr; b 30 Dec 1756, d Feb 1814 **RU:** Captain, served first as Sgt in Capt George Stubblefield's Co, 5th CL, then in 6th Continental Line, served from 1776 to 1783, promoted to captain 1780 **CEM:** Bellefonte; GPS: 38.09375, -77.737747; Rt 601, Bellefonte Rd, 3 mi W of Lewiston, Spotsylvania **GS:** Unk **SP:** Mar 1) Frances Johnson, 2) Mary Ann (__) (Will) **VI:** Son of Joseph Holladay (1718-1795) and Elizabeth Lewis (1724-1808) On 31 Mar 1836, heirs awarded BLW **P:** N **BLW:** Yes **RG:** N **MK:** N **PH:** N **SS:** E pg 386; N pg 913-4 **BS:** 196.

HOLLADAY, Lewis; b 1761; d 1837 **RU:** Lieutenant, Served through Rev War. Commissioned Lt of Spotsylvania Co Militia by the VA Committee of Safety, 5 Oct 1775. In 1785 & 1787 appointed Capt by Govrs Henry & Randolph, & Maj in 1793 by Governor Lee **CEM:** Holladay Family; GPS unk; Bellefont House; Fredericksburg City **GS:** Y **SP:** No info **VI:** Appointed Coroner in 1793, having previously been a Justice of Spotsylvania Co in 1790. Was Sheriff of the county, Justice and Overseer of the Poor, Farmer and planter **P:** unk **BLW:** unk **RG:** Y **MK:** unk **PH:** unk **SS:** AR vol 2 pg 161; J-NSSAR 2000 Reg; SAR P-183513 **BS:** 08 JLARC 76.

HOLLADAY, Lewis; b 22 May 1751, Spotsylvania Co; d 20 Oct 1820 **RU:** Major, Served in VA troops through Rev War. Appointed Maj 1793 by VA Gov Light Horse Harry Lee **CEM:** Bellefonte; GPS unk; Leiston; Spotsylvania **GS:** Y **SP:** Mar (15 Mar 1774) Elizabeth Lewis Littlepage (9 Oct 1732 Spotsylvania-1809) **VI:** Son of Capt Joseph & Ann Elizabeth (Lewis) Holladay. Sheriff of Spotsylvania Co **P:** unk **BLW:** unk **RG:** Y **MK:** Y SAR **PH:** unk **SS:** BZ; SAR P-183512 **BS:** 196.

HOLLAND, George; b unk; d Oct 1777 **RU:** Private Capt Moore's Co, Col William Grayson's 3rd VA Regt, Cont Troops, 1777 **CEM:** Rev War Court House Plaque; GPS not determined; 4110 Chain Bridge Rd; Fairfax **GS:** Memorialized on plaque 2017 by Geo Washington Chapter, VASSAR **SP** No info **VI:** Died in service **P:** N **BLW:** N **RG:** N **MK:** N **PH:** N **SS:** E pg 385; AP Fold3 muster roll; EP sources: **BS:** None.

HOLLAND, Nathaniel; b c1760; d 16 Jan 1838 **RU:** Soldier, Served in Northampton Co Militia **CEM:** Poplar Hill; GPS unk; Rt 631, Cherrystone; Northampton **GS:** Y **SP:** mar (20 Dec 1788) Susan Bryan (c1771-24 Dec 1843) d/o Henry & (-----) Bryan (__-1788) **VI:** Died age 78 **P:** unk **BLW:** unk **RG:** Y **MK**: N **PH:** unk **SS:** J-NSSAR 1993 Reg; E pg 385; SAR P-183564 **BS:** JLARC 1; 42 pg 40.

HOLLAND, Richard; b 1755, Prince Edward Co; d 1820 **RU:** Captain, Served in Capt Walker's Regt in battle of Guilford CH, NC 1779. Was Capt in Prince Edward Co Militia, Aug 1779, serving until end of war **CEM:** Old Walker Home; GPS unk; 5 mi N of Pamplin on Rt 600, then .4 mi W on Rt 627, then .4 mi NW on Rt 628; Appomattox **GS:** U **SP:** mar Capt Walker's widow at the end of the war after 2 yrs of courtship **VI:** No further data **P:** unk **BLW:** unk **RG:** Y **MK:** Y **PH:** unk **SS:** G pg 298; SAR P-183572 **BS:** JLARC 33; 196.

HOLLAND, Thomas; b 2 Feb 1764, Bedford Co; d 1 Jan 1816 or 1842 **RU:** Corporal, Served in 3rd, 4th, 5th Cont Line **CEM:** Holland Family; GPS unk; Rt 616 nr HancockCem; Franklin **GS:** Y **SP:** 1) Lydia Meador 2) Sally Gilbert **VI:** No further data **P:** unk **BLW:** unk **RG:** N **MK:** N **PH:** unk **SS:** E pg 385 **BS:** 82 pg 174.

HOLLANDSWORTH, Thomas Sr.; b abt 1745; d bef 1840 **RU:** Private/Patriot, Served in Capt John Cunningham's Co, Lt Col Abraham Penn's Regt. Took oath of allegiance Henry Co 1777 **CEM:** Blackberry Creek Private; GPS unk; Bassett; Henry **GS:** U **SP:** Susannah Mayze **VI:** No further data **P:** unk **BLW:** unk **RG:** Y **MK:** unk **PH:** unk **SS:** J-NSSAR 1993 Reg; DM pg 72-73; SAR P-183596, DAR A056468 **BS:** JLARC 1.

RU=Rank/Unit	CEM=Cemetery	GS=Gravestone	SP=Spousal Information
VI=Other Veteran Info	P=Pension	BLW=Bounty/Land Warrant	RG=Registered Grave
MK=SAR/DAR Marker	PH=Photo	SS=Service Source	BS=Burial Source

HOLLENBACH (HOLLENBECK), Daniel; b unk; d 11 Oct 1808 **RU:** Ensign/Patriot, Was acting wagonmaster for militia 27 Oct 1775 in Frederick Co. Served in 12th Cont Line in Dec 1776. Resigned as Ens Aug 1777. **CEM:** Mt Hebron; GPS 39.10916, -78.09497; 305 E Boscawen St; Winchester City **GS:** Y **SP:** No info **VI:** He was fr Harpers Ferry when he d in Winchester **P:** N **BLW:** N **RG:** N **MK:** Y SAR monument **PH:** N **SS:** E pg 386; Z pg 79 **BS:** 196.

HOLLIDAY, Israel Ellsworth; b 1750 or 1751, Simsbury Twp, Hartford Co, CT; d Aft 1832 **RU:** Soldier, Served in Cont & VT Line, also Green Mountain Boys. Ent serv Rutland Co, VT **CEM:** Dranesville United Methodist Church; GPS 39.00240, -77.35082; 11720 Sugarland Rd, Dranesville; Fairfax **GS:** U **SP:** Mar (1790) Ann Bennett (1768 Fairfax Co-__) **VI:** Sol appl pen 15 Oct 1832, Fairfax Co. S10856 **P:** Y **BLW:** unk **RG:** N **MK:** N **PH:** unk **SS:** K Vol 3 pg 320; CG Vol 2 pg 1681 **BS:** JLARC 4,14, 28.

HOLLOWAY, Daniel; b c1761; d 1824 **RU:** Patriot, On 25 Feb 1782 recd reimbursement for property impressed or taken for public use during war period **CEM:** Shockoe Hill; GPS 37.55190, -77.43170; 4th & Hospital Sts; Richmond City **GS:** Y **SP:** No info **VI:** No further data **P:** N **BLW:** N **RG:** N **MK:** N **PH:** unk **SS:** G pg 85; Brunswick Co Ct order Bk #13 **BS:** 57 pg 20.

HOLLOWAY, George; b 1760, England; d 1810 **RU:** Private, Served in Capt Steven's Co, 6th and 10th Regt Cont Lines for duration of War **CEM:** Holloway Family; GPS unk; Orange; Orange **GS:** U **SP:** 1) Mar (c1770) Martha Hall 2) Mar (1785) Frances Tiller (1762, Culpeper-1820, Clark Co, KY) **VI:** Elizabeth Holloway, heir in law recd BLW #3357 of 200 acres **P:** unk **BLW:** Y **RG:** Y **MK:** N **PH:** unk **SS:** N pg 1259; NSSAR Ancestor # P-183776; DAR P-183776 **BS:** AS DAR report.

HOLMAN, Henry; b 1760/1761, d 1830/1831 **RU:** Private/Patriot, Served in 5th Cont Line. Gave material aid to cause in Powhatan Co **CEM:** Holman Family; GPS-Not determined; loc on right of stable of Level Green Riding Academy; Powhatan **GS:** No **SP:** Descendant believes Elizabeth Barbara Branch (27 Mar 1766-1830/1831) **VI:** No further data **P:** N **BLW:** N **RG:** N **MK:** N **PH:** N **SS:** E pg 387; AL: Ct Bk, pg 7, Comm Bk IV, pg 235, Certificate, Powhatan Co; DAR Ancestor # A056944 **BS:** Vestry Bk St Luke's Church, recorded by Powhatan Historical Society

HOLMAN, John; b 21 Apr 1757; d 13 Jan 1852 **RU:** Private, Served in VA Line. Ent serv Cumberland Co **CEM:** Cotton Town; GPS 37.720206,-78.054889; Holman Square; Cumberland **GS:** U **SP:** Mar (1784) Anne Wright (1766-18 Feb 1833) **VI:** JP for Cumberland Co for several yrs. Sol appl 23 Feb 1850 Cumberland Co. S8738 **P:** Y **BLW:** unk **RG:** Y **MK:** N **PH:** unk **SS:** J- DAR Hatcher; CG Vol 2 pg 1686; SAR P-183838 **BS:** JLARC 2.

HOLMAN, Nathaniel; b 13 Mar 1735,Goochland Co, d 7 Feb 1804 **RU:** Patriot/First Lt; 33rd Regt Henrico County,VA Militia, and gave material aid to cause **CEM:** Old Holman Family; GPS not determined; loc Holman Plantation, Windsor; Henrico **GS:**U **SP:** Mar (1762, St Pauls Ch, Hanover) Ann Winn (1734, Henrico Co-1808), d/o John Quarles Winn & Mary Pledger VI; Son of Henry Holman & Mourning Bowles **P:** unk **BLW:** unk **RG:** Y **MK:** N **PH:** N **SS:** D vol 2, pg 501; E pg 306; AZ pg 208; DAR A056957; SAR P-333053 **BS:** 196.

HOLMAN, William Jr; b 1753; d 1776 **RU:** Ensign, Served in 9th Cont Line, 13 Mar 1776 **CEM:** Holman Family; GPS 37.720206, -78.054889, E of jct Cartersville Rd & Woody Ln at 5255 Bear Ct. Georges Tavern; Goochland **GS:** Y **SP:** No info **VI:** No further data **P:** unk **BLW:** unk **RG:** N **MK:** N **PH:** N **SS:** E pg 387 **BS:** 46 pg 167; 196.

HOLMAN, William Sr; b 1725; d 1796 **RU:** Patriot, Gave material aid to the cause **CEM:** Holman Family; GPS 37.720206, -78.054889, E of jct Cartersville Rd & Woody Ln at 5255 Bear Ct. Georges Tavern; Goochland **GS:** Y **SP:** 1) mar (by 30 Nov 1763) Jean Martin 2) 31 Aug 1766) Susannah Thompson 3) (1766) Becky Woodward. **VI:** No further data **P:** N **BLW:** N **RG:** N **MK:** N **PH:**N **SS:** AL Ct Bk lt pg 2, 6 **BS:** 46 pg 167; 196.

HOLMES, Hugh; b unk; d 1825 **RU:** Patriot, Performed public service as Judge **CEM:** Mt Hebron; GPS 39.10916, -78.09497; 305 E Boscawen St; Winchester City **GS:** Y **SP:** Mar (1797) Elizabeth Thomas **VI:** On chart of RW soldiers at Mt Hebron Cem **P:** N **BLW:** N **RG:** N **MK:** Y SAR monument **PH:** unk **SS:** BT: DAR Rev War chart I listing patriot burials in cemetery files **BS:** 119 chart.

RU=Rank/Unit	CEM=Cemetery	GS=Gravestone	SP=Spousal Information
VI=Other Veteran Info	P=Pension	BLW=Bounty/Land Warrant	RG=Registered Grave
MK=SAR/DAR Marker	PH=Photo	SS=Service Source	BS=Burial Source

HOLMES, William; b 23 Nov 1763, d 4 Nov 1842 **RU**: Private, Captain William Sanford's Company, 2d VA Regt under command of Col Alexander Spotswood, May 1777 **CEM**: Goose Creek: 39.11250,-77.69527; Rt 722, Lincoln; Loudoun **GS**: Yes **SP**: Mar (1784) Abigail Hughes (2 Sep 1770-23 Apr 1821), d/o Isaac Hughes (1740-1803) & Mary Warne (1743-1803) **VI**: No further data **P**: N **BLW**: N **RG**: N **MK**: N **PH**: N **SS**: A pg 275; Fold 3 **BS**: 196

HOLSINGER, Michael; b 1740, Germany; d Aug 1819 **RU**: Private, Served in Augusta Co 1776-78 under Capt Reuben Harrison. In 1778 served fr Rockingham Co under Capt Joseph (Josiah) Harrison. Was listed as "Vocher" **CEM**: Holsinger Family; GPS 38.61139, -78.76164; 2805 Holsinger Rd, Broadway; Rockingham **GS**: Y **SP**: Barbara (-----) **VI**: No further data **P**: unk **BLW**: unk **RG**: Y **MK**: N **PH**: unk **SS**: BC pg 46; AK Sep 09; BY; SAR P-184097, DAR A057163 **BS**: 4.

HOMAN (HOLMAN), John; b 1755, Germany; d 21 Jan 1824 **RU**: Private Capt Robert Beall's Co, Col Gibson's Regt & 13th VA Regt **CEM**: Holman Family; GPS not determined; fr Rt 259, turn R on Rt 1411, after crossing 2d bridge, turn left, then go .5 mi, cem loc top of hill on R, Broadway; Rockingham **GS**: Y **SP**: Mary "Polly" Robinson (28 Jan 1759-28 Jun 1825 **VI**: No further data Co **P**: N **BLW**: N **RG**: Y **MK**: N **PH**: N **SS**: E pg 389; AP: Serv Rec & Rolls; DAR A214241 **BS**: 196

HONAKER, Henry S Sr; b 10 Feb 1756, Philadelphia, PA; d 16 Sep 1830 **RU**: Private, Served in Capt Buck's Co, Dunmore Co Militia **CEM**: Honaker; GPS unk; Draper; Pulaski **GS**: U **SP**: 1) Mar (18 Jul 1785) Anna Baker 2) (Wythe Co) Edith Smith **VI**: Son of Hans Jacob & Maria (Goetz) Honaker. Died in Wythe Co **P**: unk **BLW**: unk **RG**: Y **MK**: unk **PH**: unk **SS**: E pg 389; J- DAR Hatcher; SAR P-184291 **BS**: 196; JLARC 2.

HONAKER, John; b 1755, Philadelphia, PA; d 1786 **RU**: Private, Served in Capt John Bright's Co, Col Nichols City Guard of Philadelphia, Feb 1777 **CEM**: Richardson Family; GPS 38.95750, -78.29610; 1.5 mi fr entrance to GW National Forest, Rt 678 nr Fortsmouth Vol Fire Dept; Warren **GS**: U **SP**: No info **VI**: Son of Hans Jacob (1718-1796) & Maria (Goetz/Gotz) Honaker **P**: unk **BLW**: unk **RG**: Y **MK**: unk **PH**: unk **SS**: AP Muster Roll PA Archives; SAR P-335886 **BS**: 196.

HONAKER, HONEGGER, Jacob; b 24 Jul 1718, Hinwil, outside Zurich, Switzerland; d before 10 May 1796 **RU**: Patriot, Gave material aid to cause **CEM**: Honaker; GPS unk; Draper; Pulaski **GS**: U **SP**: 2) Martha "Mary" Maria Gotz 2) Anna Bleyer (1726-1749) **VI**: Son of Hans Jacob & Elsbeth (Bosshart) Honegger. Carpenter. Indentured servant. Arrived HMS Crown in Phila. 30 Aug 1749. Freedom dues were horse and suit. Died in Wythe Co **P**: N **BLW**: N **RG**: Y **MK**: unk **PH**: unk **SS**: AL Ct bk pg 2,17 Shenandoah Co; SAR P-184290 **BS**: 196.

HONORE, Jean; b unk, France; d 1781 **RU**: Soldier, Served in Bourbonnais Bn and died fr battle at Yorktown **CEM**: French Memorial; GPS 36.81944, -79.39933; Yorktown; York **GS**: U **SP**: No info **VI**: No further data **P**: unk **BLW**: unk **RG**: Y **MK**: unk **PH**: unk **SS**: J Yorktown Historian; SAR P-184309 **BS**: JLARC 1, 74.

HOOE, Bernard; b 1740; d 1825 **RU**: Captain, Commanded a co in Prince William Co Militia 1777-1778 **CEM**: Hooe Family; GPS 38.80555, -77.53451; Chinn Ridge, Manassas National Battlefield Park; Manassas City **GS**: Y **SP**: Eleanor Buchanan Briscoe **VI**: Died in Prince William Co **P**: unk **BLW**: unk **RG**: Y **MK**: Y SAR **PH**: Y **SS**: E pg 369; G pg 473; SAR P-184357 **BS**: 16 pg 184; 196.

HOOE, Gerard (Garrard); b 14 Sep 1733; d 29 Sep 1785 **RU**: Patriot, Gave 1300 #, then 1000 # of beef to cause **CEM**: St Paul's Episcopal; GPS 38.33200, -77.12500; 5486 St Paul's Rd off Rt 206; King George **GS**: Y **SP**: 1) Ann 2) Sarah (-----) (20 Jul 1742-__) 3) mar (1 Jan 1761) (-----) 4) (-----) (__-8 May 1805) **VI**: Son of Capt Jonathan & Ann (-----) Hooe **P**: N **BLW**: N **RG**: Y **MK**: N **PH**: unk **SS**: D pg 563; E pg 242; SAR P-184357 **BS**: JLARC 48; 17 pg 632.

HOOE, Howson, b 1750, d 13 Oct 1833 **RU**: Patriot, Gave material aid to cause, Prince William Co **CEM**: Moor-Hooe; GPS 38.7076,-77.4957; 9850 Flint Rock Rd, Chevalle; Prince William **GS**: Unk **SP**: Jane Hewitt (1779-bef 1833 **VI**: Son of Howson Hooe (1726-1796) and Mary Elizabeth Dade (1727-1809) **P**: N **BLW**: N **RG**:Y **MK**: N **PH**: N **SS**: AL Ct Bk pg 6, Comm Bk IV pg199; SAR bio rpt submitted May 2020 **BS**: 196

RU=Rank/Unit	CEM=Cemetery	GS=Gravestone	SP=Spousal Information
VI=Other Veteran Info	P=Pension	BLW=Bounty/Land Warrant	RG=Registered Grave
MK=SAR/DAR Marker	PH=Photo	SS=Service Source	BS=Burial Source

199

HOOE, Robert Howson; b 1748; d 1833 **RU:** Lieutenant Captain, Served in Cont Line & Prince William Co Militia **CEM:** Mayfield Plantation; GPS 38.75290, -77.35571; Mayfield Park; Manassas City **GS:** Y **SP:** Mary Waugh **VI:** No further data **P:** unk **BLW:** unk **RG:** Y **MK:** Y SAR **PH:** Y **SS:** J-NSSAR 2000 Reg; SAR P-184359 **BS:** JLARC 76.

HOOE; Robert Townshend; b 3 Oct 1743, d 16 Mar 1809 **RU:** Patriot/Colonel; Lt Col in the 12th Bn, MD Militia, 1776, Colonel this unit in 1781; Delegate MD Convention 1774-1776; Mayor Alexandria,1774-1782 **CEM:** Saint Marys Catholic Church; GPS 38.793899, -778.047500; 310 Royal St; Alexandria City **GS:** Yes, Commemorative with plaque **SP:** Not determined **VI:** Deputy Surveyor Charles Co, MD 1774, Sheriff Fairfax Co, 1790, appointed by President John Adams, Justice of Peace, DC in 1801 **P:** N **BLW:** N **RG:** N **MK:** N **PH:** N **SS:** CD **BS:** 196.

HOOF, Lawrence; b. 1756; d 26 May 1834 **RU:** Patriot, Signed 1830, petition of Alexandria citizens to House of Delegates; for ferry across Potomac & representation in House of Delegates (Petition 1614-P). Signed petition to House of Delegates fr Fairfax Co on 27 May 1782 to reduce duties on commerce (Petition 1612-P); wason first vestry, St Pauls Ch; was pallbearer Washingtons funeral; house on Duke St still stands **CEM:** St Paul's Episcopal; GPS 38.799535, -77.056517; 228 S Pitt St; Alexandria City **GS:** Y **SP:** Ann Gretter (1760-8 Jun 1846) **VI:** Signed 3 petitions: 3 Dec 1778 Incorp Alexandria as town; 27 May 1782 Reduce VA import fees to that of MD; 21 Nov 1783 Parish elections. First Senior Warden of St Paul's Episcopal **P:** N **BLW:** N **RG:** Y **MK:** unk **PH:** unk **SS:** S #1612; SAR P-184360 **BS:** 04; 196.

HOOK, John; b 1745; d 1808 **RU:** Private, Served in Capt Charles Cameron's Co in 1781. Gave material aid, a rug to Capt Irvine for Cherokee Expedition **CEM:** Hook Family; GPS unk; Rt 122 nr US Cellular; Franklin **GS:** Y **SP:** No info **VI:** No further data **P:** unk **BLW:** unk **RG:** N **MK:** N **PH:** unk **SS:** E pg 389 **BS:** 82 pg 176.

HOOK, William; b 1750; d 1826 **RU:** Private/Patriot, Gave material aid to cause. Service as private not identified **CEM:** Augusta Stone Presbyterian; GPS 38.23926, -78.97356; 28 Old Stone Church Ln, Ft Defiance; Augusta **GS:** N **SP:** No info **VI:** No further data **P:** unk **BLW:** unk **RG:** N **MK:** Y SAR plaque **PH:** N **SS:** AL Ct Bk 1 pg 2, 23, 46 Buckingham Co **BS:** JLARC 62; 71 pg ??.

HOOKE (HOOK), Robert Sr; b 1712; d 1802 **RU:** Private/Patriot, A person with this name served in Capt Hewett's Co Augusta Co Militia, however would be above military age to have had this service. Served in Dunmore's War of 1774 at Point Pleasant fr Augusta Co under Sgt Joseph Dictorn. Gave material aid to cause **CEM:** Augusta Stone Presbyterian; GPS 38.23926, -78.97356, GS 38.1411,-78.5815; 28 Old Stone Church Ln, Ft Defiance; Augusta **GS:** Y **SP:** 1) Jean **VI:** Status verification: Source 76 has "furnished supplies." Memorial stone erected in 1958 states he was elected Capt of the Augusta militia on 13 Sep 1756 and had Rev War service **P:** unk **BLW:** unk **RG:** Y **MK:** Y SAR plaque **PH:** unk **SS:** CP Dunmore's War; J-NSSAR 2000 Reg; B; AL Comm Bk V pg 122; SAR P-184390 **BS:** JLARC 1, 2, 62, 76; 196.

HOOKE (HOOK), William Sr; b abt 1738,prob Ireland; d aft 25 Sep 1817 **RU:** Private, Served in Capt Hewett's Co, Augusta Co Militia **CEM:** Augusta Stone Presbyterian; GPS 38.23926, -78.97356, GS 38.1411,-78.5815; 28 Old Stone Church Ln, Ft Defiance; Augusta **GS:** Y **SP:** Mar (1772) Sarah Campbell (__-15 Apr 1790, Cross Keys, VA) **VI:** Memorial stone erected in 1958 says he had Rev War service, and that he was a private in the Augusta Co militia during the French and Indian War **P:** unk **BLW:** unk **RG:** Y **MK:** unk **PH:** unk **SS:** J-NSSAR 1993 Reg, J- DAR Hatcher; E pg 390; SAR P-184387 **BS:** JLARC 1, 2; 196.

HOOMES, John; b unk; d 14 Mar 1824 **RU:** Ensign, Appt ensign 10 Oct 1776 in Capt P. Johnson's Co of Caroline Co **CEM:** Old Mansion; GPS unk; S end of Main St, Bowling Green; Caroline **GS:** N **SP:** No info **VI:** Son of John Hoomes (1749-1805) & Judith Church Allen (1748-1822) **P:** unk **BLW:** unk **RG:** N **MK:** N **PH:** N **SS:** E pg 390 **BS:** 02 pg 87; 196.

HOOMES, John; b 1749; d Dec 1805 **RU:** Patriot, Gave material aid to cause **CEM:** Old Mansion; GPS unk; S end of Main St, Bowling Green; Caroline **GS:** N **SP:** Judith Churchill Allen b c1748, d 11 Aug 1822 **VI:** Richmond Enquirer gives death notice rank as Col. Was Ct Justice 1777 Caroline Co **P:** N **BLW:** N **RG:** N **MK:** N **PH:** N **SS:** G pg 105, 559; AL Ct Bk 1 pg 2 Caroline Co **BS:** 02 pg 87; 196.

RU=Rank/Unit   CEM=Cemetery   GS=Gravestone   SP=Spousal Information
VI=Other Veteran Info   P=Pension   BLW=Bounty/Land Warrant   RG=Registered Grave
MK=SAR/DAR Marker   PH=Photo   SS=Service Source   BS=Burial Source

200

HOOPER, George; b abt 1736. Great Britain; d aft Aug 1799 **RU:** Colonel/Patriot, Served in Buckingham Co Militia. Resigned 11 Jun 1781. Gave material aid to cause **CEM:** Hooper Family; GPS unk; Hooper's Mount, Arcanum; Buckingham **GS:** U **SP:** Mar (bef 1768 Cumberland Co) Elizabeth Cooke (174?-1818) **VI:** No further data **P:** N **BLW:** N **RG:** N **MK:** N **PH:** unk **SS:** E pg 369, 390; AL Ct Bk pg 2, 23, 46 Buckingham Co; CD; SAR P-184467, DAR A131322 **BS:** 32 e-mail 07; 196.

HOOVER, John; b c1764; d 1815 **RU:** Second Lieutenant, Appointed 2nd Lt 28 Feb 1782, Shenandoah Co **CEM:** Mt Hebron; GPS 39.10916, -78.09497; 305 E Boscawen St; Winchester City **GS:** Y **SP:** 1) Mar (20 Jun 1787 Frederick Co by John Montgomery) Elizabeth Erehart 2) Mar (28 Mar 1799 Frederick Co by Christian Streit) Mary Martin 3) mar (5 Feb 1800 Frederick Co by Alexander Balmain) Nancy McKeever d/o Paul & Rachel (Cheshire) McKeever **VI:** Died in Frederick Co **P:** no **BLW:** no **RG:** N **MK:** N Y SAR monument **PH:** Y **SS:** E pg 390 **BS:** 50 pg 48.

HOOVER, John Henry; b 05 Dec 1732; d 28 Mar 1815 **RU:** Private, Served in Capt Thomas Buck's Co of Volunteers, Dunmore Co, 1777 **CEM:** Mt Hebron; GPS 39.10916, -78.09497; 305 E Boscawen St; Winchester City **GS:** Y **SP:** Mar (5 Feb 1800 Frederick Co) Mary McKeever **VI:** No further data **P:** no **BLW:** no **RG:** N **MK:** Y SAR monument **PH:** Y **SS:** E pg 106, 390 **BS:** 50 pg 49; 196.

HOOVER, Michael; b 1761; d 12 Jun 1829 **RU:** Soldier, Served in Capt Hull's Co, Augusta Co Militia **CEM:** Hebron Presbyterian; GPS 38.14140, -79.15500; 423 Hebron Rd; Staunton City **GS:** Y **SP:** No info **VI:** Died age 68 (stone) **P:** unk **BLW:** unk **RG:** Y **MK:** unk **PH:** unk **SS:** E pg 390 **SAR P-184575 BS:** JLARC 62, 63; 196.

HOPE, Adam; b 1729; d 3 Aug 1802 **RU:** Patriot, Performed public service as Overseer of Roads, also gave material aid to cause **CEM:** Green Springs Presbyterian; GPS 36.63670, -81,99560; 2007 Gr Spr Ch Rd, Abingdon; Washington **GS:** U **SP:** Agnes Kincaid (1722-1804) **VI:** No further data **P:** N **BLW:** N **RG:** Y **MK:** unk **PH:** unk **SS:** DAR Ancestor #A135161; DD; SAR P-184583 **BS:** 200 pg 139.

HOPE, James; b 1754 PA; d 15 Oct 1811 **RU:** Private, Served in McFarland's Co **CEM:** Green Spring Presbyterian; GPS 36.63670, -81.99560; 2007 Green Spring Ch Rd, Abingdon; Washington **GS:** Y **SP:** Mar (21 Feb 1753 Washington Co) Margaret Dryden (25 Feb 1776 Augusta Co-5 May 1854) d/o Nathaniel & Mary (-----) Dryden **VI:** Son of Adam (1729-1802) & Agnes (Kincaid) (1722-1804) Hope **P:** unk **BLW:** unk **RG:** Y **MK:** unk **PH:** unk **SS:** J- DAR Hatcher; DL pg 1394; SAR P-184587 **BS:** JLARC 2.

HOPKIN, HOPKINS, Archibald; b abt 1737, Northern Ireland; d 8 May 1799 **RU:** Patriot, Personal service (specifics not given in SAR registry) **CEM:** Old Peaked Mountain; GPS 38.37113, -78.73416; 9843 Town Hall Rd, McGaheysville; Rockingham **GS:** Y **SP:** Jannet Love **VI:** No further data **P:** N **BLW:** N **RG:** Y **MK:** Y SAR **PH:** unk **SS:** SAR P- 184606 **BS:** 04.

HOPKIN, HOPKINS, John; b 1732, Goochland; d 25 Feb 1788 **RU:** Captain/Patriot, Was Private in David Stephens Co, Col Abraham Bowman's 8th Regt. Enl 21 Feb 1778 and served 3 yrs in Capt Croghan's Co 4th, 8th, 12th VA Regt commanded by Col James Wood 1778. Date promoted to Capt not determined. Gave material aid to cause **CEM:** Old Peaked Mountain; GPS 38.37113, -78.73416; 9843 Town Hall Rd, McGaheysville; Rockingham **GS:** U **SP:** Mar (12 Oct 1759, Augusta Co) Jean Jordon **VI:** No further data **P:** unk **BLW:** unk **RG:** Y **MK:** Y SAR **PH:** unk **SS:** J-NSSAR 2000 Reg; D Rockingham Co; SAR P-184607 **BS:** JLARC 76.

HOPKINS, Francis; b 27 Feb 1737, New Kent Co d 1804 **RU:** Patriot, Gave material aid to cause, Bedford Co **CEM:** Bedford County; GPS: unk; 1131 Park St; Bedford City **GS:** Unk **SP:** Jane Cox (1737, Cumberland Co-1815) **VI:** Son of William Hopkins (1685, Kent Co-1755) and Frances (_) (1687-1755) **P:** N **BLW:** N **RG:** N **MK:** N **PH:** N **SS:** AL Cert 2, Lists-pg 7, Bedford Co **BS:** 196

HOPKINS, James Sr.; b 22 Feb 1765; d 20 Jul 1844 **RU:** Private, Enl Amherst Co in Capt Azh Martin's Eighth Co of the 4th Regt of Line, 15 Jun-7 Sep 1780. Unit was at battle of Camden and Hillborough **CEM:** Hopkins; GPS unk; Behind Thomas Muse house near Franklin Co Line, Sago; Pittsylvania **GS:** Y **SP:** 1) Francis Carter 2) mar (15 Nov 1797 at home of her uncle Thomas Carter in Pittsylvania Co) Mary (-----) (c1761-31 May 1853) **VI:** Sol appl pen 17 Sep 1832 Pittsylvnia Co. Widow appl pen 2 Mar 1853 age 92. W3553. Sub for father (James, Sr). Cemetery moved when Quantico Marine Base took over a portion of Stafford Co **P:** Y **BLW:** unk **RG:** Y **MK:** unk **PH:** no **SS:** G pg 17; K Vol 3 pg 328; CG Vol 2 pg 1703; SAR P-184822 **BS:** JLARC 4, 90.

RU=Rank/Unit	CEM=Cemetery	GS=Gravestone	SP=Spousal Information
VI=Other Veteran Info	P=Pension	BLW=Bounty/Land Warrant	RG=Registered Grave
MK=SAR/DAR Marker	PH=Photo	SS=Service Source	BS=Burial Source

HOPKINS, Walter; b 1757; d 1800 **RU:** Captain, As Lt was Paymaster in Capt Ander's Co. Later was Capt in New Kent Co Militia 1775-6 **CEM:** Shockoe Hill; GPS 37.55190, -77.43170; 4th & Hospital Sts; Richmond City **GS:** U **SP:** Abigail Herbert Osborne (1762-1840) d/o Henry (1710-1778) & (-----) Herbert of Herbertsville, Norfolk Co. She later remarried. **VI:** No further data **P:** unk **BLW:** unk **RG:** N **MK:** unk **PH:** unk **SS:** E pg 391; G pg 624 **BS:** 196.

HOPPESS, John; b 1745; d 1836 **RU:** Soldier, Served in PA **CEM:** St Paul's Lutheran; GPS 36.91173, -81.23484; 330 St Pauls Church Rd, Rural Retreat; Wythe **GS:** U **SP:** No info **VI:** No further data **P:** unk **BLW:** unk **RG:** Y **MK:** unk **PH:** unk **SS:** JLARC pg 72; SAR P-184846 **BS:** JLARC 40, 123.

HORE, Elias; b 1747; d 16 Jul 1832 **RU:** Patriot, Gave material aid to the cause **CEM:** Cedar Run; GPS 38.36299, -77.33694; Quantico Marine Base; Stafford **GS:** U **SP:** No info **VI:** Remains moved there when base established. Burial source 95 says bur in Prince William Co **P:** N **BLW:** N **RG:** Y **MK:** N **PH:** Y **SS:** Al Ct Bk I pg 9, Bk II pg 6; SAR P-184884 **BS:** JLARC 48, 95; 3 pg 170; 95.

HORNER, Gustavus Brown; b 28 Feb 1761, Newport, Charles Co, MD; d 24 Jan 1815 **RU:** Surgeon's Mate, Served in Cont Army in MD commencing age 15, served 5 yrs **CEM:** Clermont; GPS 38.71262, -77.8003; Warrenton; Fauquier **GS:** Y **SP:** Mar (14 Apr 1786 Clermont) Frances Harrison Scott (1764-27 Nov 1837 Washington DC) d/o Capt James & Eliza (Harrison) Scott **VI:** Studied medicine in Alexandria VA. Finished training Philadelphia. Surgeon in War of 1812. Settled in Warrenton. Served VA Legislature & was presidential elector. Wife recd pen of 1/2 pay starting 4 Mar 1834 in MD **P:** Y **BLW:** unk **RG:** Y **MK:** unk **PH:** unk **SS:** BX pg 384; SAR P-184987 **BS:** 196.

HOSKINS, Robert; b c1755; d 1815 **RU:** Lieutenant, Promoted to Lt in Cont Army at Williamsburg. Served at Valley Forge, Monmouth, Middlebrook, Stony Point, and King's Ferry **CEM:** Bird-Boyd-Todd Family; GPS unk; Popular Grove Plantation, Stevensville; King & Queen **GS:** U **SP:** No info **VI:** No further data **P:** unk **BLW:** unk **RG:** Y **MK:** unk **PH:** unk **SS:** SAR Ancestor #P-185240; J-NSSAR 1993 Reg; CZ; SAR P-185240 **BS:** JLARC 1.

HOSKINS, Thomas Coleman; b 1752, Halifax Co; d 11 Feb 1833 **RU:** Corporal, Ent serv Lunenburg Co, 6th VA Regt **CEM:** Brightwood; GPS unk; Marilla Ln, Chatham; Pittsylvania **GS:** Y **SP:** Mar (19 Jul 1790 Campbell Co) Betsy Ellington **VI:** Son of William & Dorothy (-----) Hoskins. Appl pen 17 Sep 1827 age 75. S38044 **P:** Y **BLW:** N **RG:** N **MK:** N **PH:** Y **SS:** E pg 393 **BS:** 196 modified fr pension rec.

HOSTETTER, Ulrich; b 1749 Germany; d 26 Feb 1840 **RU:** Ensign, Served in PA Militia. Ent serv York Co PA 1776 **CEM:** Hostetter Family; GPS unk; Lexington; Lexington City **GS:** U **SP:** Elizabeth (-----) **VI:** Son of Ulrich Sr (1720 Switzerland-1785 York Co, PA) & Anna Marie (-----) Hostetter. Sol appl 7 Aug 1832 Rockbridge Co VA. S5563 **P:** Y **BLW:** unk **RG:** Y **MK:** N **PH:** unk **SS:** K Vol 3 pg 333; AG, pg 514; CG Vol 2 pg 1714; SAR P-185339, DAR A058853 **BS:** SAR report.

HOTELL, George; b 6 Dec 1728,Germany, d 8 Mar 1787 **RU:** Patriot, Gave material aid to cause and took oath at Ct in 1778 in Shenandoah Co **CEM:** Riverview; GPS 38.98420, -78.36140; on or near grounds of Strasburg HS; Shenandoah **GS:** unk **SP:** Elizabeth Pigot (1728-1787) **VI:** No further data **P:** N **BLW:** N **RG:** Y **MK:** N **PH:** N **SS:** AL Ct Bk pgs 1,2,5; Minute Bk A pg 51; SAR Ancestor # P185429 **BS:** 196.

HOTT (HOLT), George, Jr b 1738; d 1804 **RU Patriot:**, was on Col Holmes Tax list for Frederick Co 1782 **CEM:** George Hott, Sr; GPS unk; Rt 654 fr Nain 7 mi to Pleasant Valley Church, on right on top of hill, Gainesboro Frederick **GS:** Y **SP:** Eve Rebecca Steidley **VI:** Son of George Hott (1700-1797) & Magdalena Shantz(1710-1801 **P:** N **BLW:** N **RG:** N **MK:** N **PH:** N **SS:** **GS:** 196.

HOTT, George; b c1700; d 1797 **RU:** Patriot, Paid Personal Property Tax 1782, Frederick Co. Considered tax to support Rev war cause **CEM:** George Hott, Sr; GPS unk; Rt 654 fr Nain 7 mi to Pleasant Valley Church, on right on top of hill, Gainesboro Frederick **GS:** U **SP:** Magdalena Shantz (__-1801) d/o Jacob & (----) Shantz **VI:** No further data **P:** N **BLW:** N **RG:** N **MK:** unk **PH:** N **SS:** DV **BS:** 228.

HOTTEL, Johann; b 12 Apr 1722, Germany; d 28 Mar 1782 **RU:** Patriot, Gave material aid to cause **CEM:** Keller; GPS 38.56480, -78.46220; Tom's Brook nr Mt Olive; Shenandoah **GS:** U **SP:** No info **VI:** Died in Woodstock, Shenandoah Co **P:** N **BLW:** N **RG:**N **MK:** unk **PH:** unk **SS:** AL Cert Shenandoah Co **BS:** 196.

RU=Rank/Unit	CEM=Cemetery	GS=Gravestone	SP=Spousal Information
VI=Other Veteran Info	P=Pension	BLW=Bounty/Land Warrant	RG=Registered Grave
MK=SAR/DAR Marker	PH=Photo	SS=Service Source	BS=Burial Source

HOTTEL, John Jacob; b 20 Jan 1752, Frederick Co; d Aug 1820 **RU:** Private, Served in Capt Michael Reader and Capt Alexander Machir's Cos, Shenandoah Militia **CEM:** Keller; GPS 38.56480, -78.46220; Tom's Brook nr Mt Olive; Shenandoah **GS:** U **SP:** Mar (21 Jun 1774) Mary Dorothea Rinker (20 Jan 1755 York Co, PA-c1820) **VI:** No further data **P:** unk **BLW:** unk **RG:** Y **MK**: unk **PH:** unk **SS:** DAR Ancestor #A058954; J- DAR Hatcher; C pg 602-607; BY; SAR P-185431 **BS:** JLARC 2.

HOTTEL, Joseph; abt 1761, Frederick Co; d 1814 **RU:** Private, Served in VA line **CEM:** Keller; GPS 38.56480, -78.46220; Tom's Brook nr Mt Olive; Shenandoah **GS:** U **SP:** Barbara Dull **VI:** No further data **P:** unk **BLW:** unk **RG:**Y **MK**: unk **PH:** unk **SS:** J- DAR Hatcher; AP serv rec Muster roll; SAR P-185433 **BS:** JLARC 2.

HOTTENSTEIN, Jacob; b 1735, Barvaria; d After 7 Jun 1803 **RU:** Soldier, Cont Line **CEM:** Lutheran; GPS unk; Washington; Rappahannock **GS:** U **SP:** Catherine Widener **VI:** No further data **P:** unk **BLW:** unk **RG:** N **MK**: unk **PH:** unk **SS:** J- DAR Hatcher; BC part 2 pg 1394 **BS:** JLARC 2.

HOUBA, Remy; b unk; d 1781 **RU:** Soldier, Served in Gatinais Bn and died fr battle at Yorktown **CEM:** French Memorial; GPS 36.81944, -79.39933; Yorktown; York **GS:** U **SP:** No info **VI:** No further data **P:** unk **BLW:** unk **RG:** Y **MK**: unk **PH:** unk **SS:** J-Yorktown Historian; SAR P-185439 **BS:** JLARC 1, 74.

HOUCHOIS, Charles; b unk; d 1781 **RU:** Seaman, Served on "Duc De Bourgogne" and died from Yorktown battle **CEM:** French Memorial; GPS 36.81944, -79.39933; Yorktown; York **GS:** U **SP:** No info **VI:** No further data **P:** unk **BLW:** unk **RG:** Y **MK**: unk **PH:** unk **SS:** J-Yorktown Historian; SAR P-185442 **BS:** JLARC 1, 74.

HOUCK, George Michael; b 1757; d 13 Jan 1845 **RU:** Private, Served in Montgomery Co Militia **CEM:** St Paul's Lutheran; GPS 38.99140, -78.36250; 156 W Washington, Strasburg; Shenandoah **GS:** U **SP:** Margaretta Funk (Dec 1757-28 Jan 1841) **VI:** No further data **P:** unk **BLW:** unk **RG:** N **MK**: unk **PH:** unk **SS:** G pg 232 **BS:** 196.

HOUGH, Benjamin; b calc 31 Dec 1758, Orange; d 22 Sep 1816 **RU:** Private, Holman's Dunmore Co. Militia, See Bounty Land Warrant application for service units **CEM:** Fairfax Meeting House; GPS 39.18557, -77.60634; Water St & Waterford Rd, Waterford; Loudoun **GS:** Y **SP:** No info **VI:** Recd bounty land 1060 acres **P:** unk **BLW:** unk **RG:** Y **MK**: Y SAR granite **PH:** unk **SS:** C pg 610; SAR P-336054 **BS:** 25 pg 147.

HOUGH (HUFF), John; b 1763; d 1840 **RU:** Sergeant, Served in 2nd Cont Line **CEM:** Pigg River Primitive Baptist; GPS 36.96913, -80.07368; Rt 750 nr Callaway; Franklin **GS:** U **SP:** 1) (-----) 2) (-----) 3) Elizabeth **VI:** No further data **P:** unk **BLW:** unk **RG:** N **MK**: unk **PH:** unk **SS:** E pg 393 **BS:** JLARC 1,2,4,19.

HOUGH (HUFF), William; b 24 Nov 1744, Fairfax Co; d 18 Feb 1815 **RU:** Private, Served in VA Cont Line. Gave for cause 325# beef; 42 days wagon team and driver **CEM:** Fairfax Meeting House; GPS 39.185983, -77.606342; Water St & Waterford Rd, Waterford; Loudoun **GS:** Y **SP:** Eleanor Hite **VI:** US VA-style marker is intact and legible **P:** unk **BLW:** unk **RG:** Y **MK**: Y SAR granite **PH:** Y **SS:** J- DAR Hatcher; AK; D pg 6, 7; E pg 393; SAR P-185512 **BS:** JLARC 2; 04.

HOUNSHELL, John; b 5 Nov 1756, Lancaster, PA; d bef 12 Sept 1826 **RU:** Private, Served in Capt Daniel Trigg's Co, Montgomery Co Militia Sep 1777 **CEM:** St Paul's Lutheran; GPS 36.91173, -81.23484; 330 St Pauls Church Rd, Rural Retreat; Wythe **GS:** Y **SP:** Susannah (-----) (1766-1828) **VI:** Obtained rank of major probably after war period. DAR marker fr KY society **P:** unk **BLW:** unk **RG:** Y **MK**: Y SAR **PH:** unk **SS:** J-NSSAR 1993 Reg, J- DAR Hatcher; G pg 214; SAR P-332797, DAR A057431 **BS:** JLARC 1, 2; 196.

HOUPILLARD, Jacques; b unk; d 1781 **RU:** Soldier, Served in Santogne Bn and died fr battle at Yorktown **CEM:** French Memorial; GPS 36.81944, -79.39933; Yorktown; York **GS:** U **SP:** No info **VI:** No further data **P:** unk **BLW:** unk **RG:** Y **MK**: unk **PH:** unk **SS:** J-Yorktown Historian; SAR P-185597 **BS:** JLARC 1, 74.

HOUSE, James; b 1761 CT; d 17 Nov 1834 **RU:** Matross, Served in Capt Ragsdale's Co, 1st Battalion Artillery, Cont Line **CEM:** Arlington National; GPS 38.88377, -77.06535; Jefferson Davis Hwy Rt 110; Arlington **GS:** Y Lot 297A**SP:** No info **VI:** Died in DC. Originally bur at Old Presbyterian Church in

RU=Rank/Unit
VI=Other Veteran Info
MK=SAR/DAR Marker
CEM=Cemetery
P=Pension
PH=Photo
GS=Gravestone
BLW=Bounty/Land Warrant
SS=Service Source
SP=Spousal Information
RG=Registered Grave
BS=Burial Source

203

Georgetown, reinterred 12 May 1892. One of 11 Rev War soldiers bur at Arlington. Became General US Army after war period. **P:** unk **BLW:** unk **RG:** Y **MK:** Y SAR **PH:** unk **SS:** J-NSSAR 2000 Reg; NSSAR Ancestor #P-185624; SAR P-185624 **BS:** JLARC 76; 196.

HOUSE, Matthias; b abt 1738 8 Aug 1739; d bef 20 Oct 1829 **RU:** Patriot, Listed on the Culpeper Co Classes (recruiting list 1781) number 87 covering a portion of Madison Co **CEM:** House Hollow Farm; GPS unk; Slate Mills; Madison **GS:** N **SP:** Maria Margaretta Jaeckler (1743-1812) **VI:** No further data **P:** N **BLW:** N **RG:** Y **MK:** unk **PH:** unk **SS:** unk SAR P-330720, DAR A201191 **BS:** 229 Madison Co.

HOUSHOLDER, Adam. b 16 Sep 1746; d 27 Oct 1804; **RU:** Patriot, signed Oath of Fidelity and Support, 1778 in MD **CEM:** New Jerusalem Lutheran; GPS 39.25736, -77.63891; GS GPS 39.256925,-77.638641; 12942 Lutheran Church Rd, Lovettsville; Loudoun **GS:** Y **SP:** Mar 1) Catherine Bechtel, 2) Susannah Rickard **VI:** **P:** N **BLW:** N **RG:** Y **MK:** SAR granite **PH:** N **SS:** DAR A053148; EI pg 14; SAR P-343705 **BS:** 04.

HOUSTON, George; b unk; d 1819 **RU:** Captain, Served in Rockbri dge Co Militia & 9th Cont line **CEM:** New Providence Presbyterian; GPS 37.95130, -79.30250; 1208 New Providence Rd, Raphine; Rockbridge **GS:** U **SP:** No info **VI:** No further data **P:** unk **BLW:** unk **RG:** Y **MK:** unk **PH:** unk **SS:** E pg 394; SAR P-185702 **BS:** JLARC 63, 79.

HOUSTON, James; b 1745; d 1803 **RU:** Ensign, Was in Battle of Point Pleasant Oct 1774, in Capt Samuel McDowell's Co of Rockbridge Co. Was Ens Rockbridge Co Militia 2 Nov 1779 **CEM:** New Providence Presbyterian; GPS 37.95130, -79.30250; 1208 New Providence Rd, Raphine; Rockbridge **GS:** Y **SP:** No info **VI:** No further data **P:** unk **BLW:** unk **RG:** Y **MK:** unk **PH:** unk **SS:** Z pg 103; SAR P-185710 **BS:** JLARC 63, 79; 196.

HOUSTON, John Sr; b 1726, Ireland; d 1798 **RU:** Soldier/Patriot, Mil serv not identified. Gave material aid to cause **CEM:** Old Stone Presbyterian; GPS unk; 73 Sam Huston Way; Rockbridge **GS:** U **SP:** Sarah Todd **VI:** Son of John & Margaret (Cunningham) Houston **P:** unk **BLW:** unk **RG:** Y **MK:** unk **PH:** unk **SS:** SAR P-185776; AL Ct Bk pg 2, 5 Rockbridge Co; SAR P-185776 **BS:** JLARC 63.

HOUSTON, John III; b 1 Jan 1749; d 1809 **RU:**Private/Patriot served in Capt Isom's Co, Montgomery Co Militia, Jul 1778; gave material aid to cause **CEM:** Oxford Presbyterian; GPS: 37.753021,-79.560234; 18 Churchview Ln, Collierstown; Rockbridge **GS:** N **SP:** Anne Logan (__-1791) **VI:** Son of Sarah Todd (29 May 1727, PA-1795 TN) **P:** N **BLW:** N **RG:** N **MK:** N **PH:** N **SS:** G pgs 220, 221, cites Montgomery Co Ct rec; AL Ct Bk pg 2, Comm Bk V pg77, Rockbridge Co **BS:** 196.

HOUSTON, Samuel; b 1745; d 1807 **RU:** Captain/Patriot, Served in Morgan's Rifle Brigade. Gave material aid to cause **CEM:** High Bridge Presbyterian; GPS 37.62420, -79.58610; 67 High Bridge Rd, Natural Bridge; Rockbridge **GS:** U **SP:** Elizabeth Blair Paxton (1757-8 Sep 1831 Blount Co, TN) d/o John & Mary (Blair) Paxton **VI:** Son of Robert H. (1720-1760) & Margaret Dunlap (Davidson) (1720-__) Houston. Obtained rank of Maj after war period. Was VA Militia inspector. Died in Bath Co, KY in military duty after war. Body returned to VA **P:** unk **BLW:** unk **RG:** Y **MK:** unk **PH:** unk **SS:** J- DAR Hatcher; D Vol 3, pg 825, Bath Co; CD; SAR P-185749 **BS:** JLARC 2.

HOUSTON, Samuel; b 1737; d 18 Apr 1813 **RU:** Patriot, Gave material aid to cause **CEM:** North Mountain; GPS unk; 7 mi S of Staunton on N side Rt 252; Augusta **GS:** Y **SP:** No info **VI:** No further data **P:** N **BLW:** N **RG:** N **MK:** N **PH:** unk **SS:** AL Ct bk p5,8 **BS:** 75; 196.

HOUSTON, Samuel; b 1 Jan 1758, Hays Creek, now Rockbridge Co; d 20 Jan 1839 **RU:** Private, Served in Gen Stevens Brigade in Battle of Guildford CH, NC **CEM:** High Bridge Presbyterian; GPS 37.62420, -79.58610; 67 High Bridge Rd, Natural Bridge; Rockbridge **GS:** Y **SP:** Margaret (-----) **VI:** Cousin of General Sam Houston. Pastor of High Bridge Church for 43 yrs. Addition to church building is said to have been built over his grave **P:** unk **BLW:** unk **RG:** Y **MK:** Y SAR **PH:** Y **SS:** AR Vol 2 pg 171; NSSAR Ancestor #P-185752 **BS:** JLARC 1, 2, 79.

HOWARD, James; b 1763, Goochland Co; d c1841 **RU:** Private, Ent serv Bedford Co. Served in VA Line **CEM:** Howard Family; GPS unk; Nr Campbell Co CH, Rustburg; Campbell **GS:** Y **SP:** Mary (-----) **VI:** Appl for pension in Campbell Co 09 Sep 1833, #S9563 **P:** Y **BLW:** unk **RG:** Y **MK:** N **PH:** unk **SS:** AS DAR Report; CG pg 1727; SAR P-185998 **BS:** 80 vol 2 pg 173.

RU=Rank/Unit	CEM=Cemetery	GS=Gravestone	SP=Spousal Information
VI=Other Veteran Info	P=Pension	BLW=Bounty/Land Warrant	RG=Registered Grave
MK=SAR/DAR Marker	PH=Photo	SS=Service Source	BS=Burial Source

HOWARD, James; b 1752; d aft 1820 **RU:** Private, Served in VA battalion & 4th, 8th, 9th, & 12th Cont Lines. Served in Taylor's Regt. Was wounded at Guilford CH **CEM:** Union Baptist; GPS 37.94660, -77.65160; 16230 Union Church Rd, Beaverdam; Hanover **GS:** Y **SP:** No info **VI:** No family after 1820. Recd pen 1813 & appl again 27 May 18181 Hanover Co. S38045 **P:** Y **BLW:** unk **RG:** N **MK:** N **PH:** N **SS:** E pg 394-5; BX pg 388; CG pg 1721 **BS:** 196.

HOWARD, Peter Rev; b 4 Apr 1762, York County, England; d 9 May 1827 **RU:** Private, Served in 5th and 7th Regts in Co 10, Col Daniel's 11th & 15th Regts. Listed in Regt 10 Nov 1778 **CEM:** Pine Creek Primitive Baptist; GPS 36.94622, -80.27357; Spangler Mill Rd Rt 682; Floyd **GS:** Y **SP:** Sarah Jane Strickland (12 Mar 1761-23 Nov 1846) **VI:** X893 **P:** Y **BLW:** unk **RG:** Y **MK:** N **PH:** unk **SS:**; Pen Appl; SAR P-186150, DAR A058102 **BS:** JLARC 2, 29.

HOWARD, Robert; b c1757; d 1821 **RU:** Sergeant, Served in Regular Army Inf unit **CEM:** Pine Creek Primitive Baptist; GPS 36.94622, -80.27357; Spangler Mill Rd Rt 682; Floyd **GS:** Y **SP:** No info **VI:** BLW issued 1783 **P:** unk **BLW:** Y **RG:** N **MK:** N **PH:** unk **SS:** E pg 395; CU- VA BLW **BS:** 64 pg 122; 196.

HOWARD, Sir William; b 1732; d 1814 **RU:** Patriot, Gave material aid to cause **CEM:** Howard-Palmer; GPS 37.05575, -80.50448; 4165 Piney Woods Rd, behind House, Childress; Montgomery **GS:** Y **SP:** Hannah Psalter (1738-1810) **VI:** No further data **P:** N **BLW:** N **RG:** Y **MK:** N **PH:** unk **SS:** AS DAR Report; SAR P-186151 **BS:** 80 vol 2 pg 174; 196.

HOWARD, William Lawrence; b unk; d 1797 **RU:** Private?, Served in 13th Cont Line **CEM:** Pine Creek Primitive Baptist; GPS 36.94622, -80.27357; Spangler Mill Rd Rt 682; Floyd **GS:** Y **SP:** No info **VI:** No further data **P:** unk **BLW:** unk **RG:** N **MK:** N **PH:** unk **SS:** E pg 395 **BS:** 64 pg 122.

HOWE, Daniel; b c1758; d 1 Jan 1838 **RU:** Lieutenant, Major, Enl Montgomery Co 1776 and served until 1781. Was at surrender of Cornwallis **CEM:** Sunnyside; GPS unk; Btw Radford and Dublin at Old Joseph Howe place, Back Creek; Pulaski **GS:** U **SP:** Nancy Haven (3 Jan 1771-1 Mar 1830) **VI:** Appl pen 2 Oct 1832 Montgomery Co age 74. S5565. Died in Newbern, Montgomery Co **P:** Y **BLW:** unk **RG:** Y **MK:** unk **PH:** unk **SS:** J- DAR Hatcher; K Vol 3 pg 337; CG Vol 2 pg 1730; SAR P-SAR P-186181 **BS:** JLARC 2; 196.

HOWELL, Daniel Sr; b 1759, Philadelphia Co, PA; d 5 Mar 1836 **RU:** Private, Served in Capt Josuha Wilson's Co 1778. Served three tours. Was in Col Martin's and Crockett's Regts in the Cherokee Exposition **CEM:** Wright Family; GPS 36.97658, -80.21693; Pizarro off Rt 668; Floyd **GS:** U **SP:** Mar (c1784) Frances (-----) **VI:** Son of Benjamin & Maria Elizabeth (Beest) Howell. Memorialized by DAR plaque in cem. Pensioned 1835 age 75 making death date in 1840; #S 13413 **P:** Y **BLW:** unk **RG:** Y**MK:** Y SAR **PH:** unk **SS:** DAR A058496; E pg 395; SAR P-322667 **BS:** 196 for John Mitchell.

HOWELL, John F; b unk; d 1821 **RU:** Lieutenant/Patriot, Gave material aid to cause **CEM:** St Paul's Episcopal; GPS 36.84733, -76.28554; 201 St Paul's Blvd; Norfolk City **GS:** Y **SP:** No info **VI:** No further data **P:** unk **BLW:** unk **RG:** Y **MK:** N **PH:** unk **SS:** E pg 395; AL Ct Bk 1 pg 11 Nansemond Co **BS:** 87 pg 28.

HOWISON, Stephen; b 31 Jan 1736, St Mary's Co, MD; d 1 Feb 1815 **RU:** Second Lieutenant, Served in Prince William Co Militia, Patriotic Service **CEM:** Howison Family; GPS 38.63313, -77.38399; Minniville Rd; Prince William **GS:** Y **SP:** Mary Brooke (1752-14 Apr 1808) **VI:** No further data **P:** unk **BLW:** unk **RG:** Y **MK:** Y SAR & DAR plaque **PH:** Y **SS:** AK; AL Ct Bk pg 7; SAR P-186527, DAR A058763 **BS:** 04; 80 vol 2 pg 176.

HOYE (HOY), William; b Co Antrim, Ireland, d Jan 1800 **RU:** Private, Served in Capt McNitt's Co, (probably an Artillery company as after war was in Artillery Co in Alexandria), Webster's NY Regt **CEM:** Old Christ Church; GPS: 38.80625,-77.0704718; 118 N Washington St; Alexandria City; **GS:** Unk **SP:** Mar Prince George Co, MD 22 Apr 1786, Agnes Scott **VI:** Son of Richard Hoy (1732-1799). Member Masonic Lodge # 47 **P:** N **BLW:** N **RG:** N **MK:** N, **PH:** N **SS:** AX, pg 399 **BS:** 196.

HUBARD, William; b unk; d 1802 **RU:** Sergeant, Served in 1st & 10th Cont Lines **CEM:** St Luke's Church; GPS 36.93940, -76.58670; 14477 Benns Church Blvd, Smithfield; Isle of Wight **GS:** Y **SP:** No info **VI:** No further data **P:** N **BLW:** N **RG:** N **MK:** N **PH:** unk **SS:** E pg 396 **BS:** 117 pg 26.

RU=Rank/Unit	CEM=Cemetery	GS=Gravestone	SP=Spousal Information
VI=Other Veteran Info	P=Pension	BLW=Bounty/Land Warrant	RG=Registered Grave
MK=SAR/DAR Marker	PH=Photo	SS=Service Source	BS=Burial Source

205

HUBBLE (HUBBELL), Justus David; b 6 Aug 1732, Fairfield Co, CT, d 2 May 1796, Washington Co **RU**: Private, Col Levi Pawling's NY Line **CEM**: St Clair Bottom Primitive Baptist Church; GPS: 36.76098,-81.64556; jct Rts 600 & 660, Chilhowie; Smyth **GS**: Yes, Govt **SP**: Mar 18 Jun 1777, West Chester, NY, Waitstill Bishop **VI**: Son of David Hubbell (8 Aug 1705-1791) and Eunice Sanford, daug of Thomas Sanford and Hannah Stevens **P**: N **BLW**: N **RG**: Y **MK**: N **PH**: N **SS**: CD; SAR P-187093 **BS**: **196**

HUBERT, Jean; b unk; d 1781 **RU**: Seaman, Served on "Saint-Esprit"and died from Yorktown battle **CEM**: French Memorial; GPS 36.81944, -79.39933; Yorktown; York **GS**: U **SP**: No info **VI**: No further data **P**: unk **BLW**: unk **RG**: Y **MK**: unk **PH**: unk **SS**: J-Yorktown Historian; SAR P-187132 **BS**: JLARC 1, 74.

HUDNALL, John: b 22 Jun 1763, Goochland Co, d 19 Oct 1844 **RU**: Private; Served in Bedford co Militia under Maj Reid & Capts Trigg & Leftwich, VA Line **CEM**: Bedford City , GPS not determined; 1131 Park St, jct Walnut St and Longwood Ave; Bedford City **GS**: Unk **SP**: 1) Martha Ann Newman (1772-1809), d/o Nimrod Newman (1740-1815) & Sarah Arthur (1745-1818), 2) mar (7 Mar 1811, Bedford) Frances Miles McGhee (8 Feb 1789-aft 1855) She applied for pen and two BLW one 1853, one 1855 **VI** No further data **P**: Widow **BLW**: Widow **RG**: Y **MK**: N, **PH**: N **SS**: CG: vol 1 pg 1746; SAR P-187175 **BS**: 196.

HUDSON, Christopher; b 20 Jul 1758, Hanover Co; d 1 May 1825 **RU**: Private, Captain, Goochland Co Militia 1779. Was also serving as Capt in Louisa Co 1781-3 period **CEM**: Mt Air; GPS unk; Hardware River, Keene, NW of Scottsville; Albemarle **GS**: Y **SP**: Mar (19 Mar 1783 Hanover Co) Sarah Anderson (20 Jul 1758 Hanover Co-2 Apr 1807) d/o David Overton & Elizabeth (Mills) Anderson **VI**: Resided Louisa Co 1782. Moved to Albemarle Co in 1786 **P**: unk **BLW**: unk **RG**: Y **MK**: unk **PH**: unk **SS**: J- DAR Hatcher; E pg 398; AL Cert Louisa Co; SAR P-187183 **BS**: JLARC 2; 196.

HUDSON, James; b c1754; d 1820 **RU**: Private, Served in 5th Cont Line **CEM**: Hudson Family; GPS unk; Rt 721; Culpeper **GS**: Y **SP**: Sarah (-----) **VI**: Son of David Hudson (1727-14 Jan 1811) & Keziah Plunkett (1728-1807). Will proved 1820. Weathered chiseled limestone or fieldstone **P**: unk **BLW**: unk **RG**: N **MK**: N **PH**: unk **SS**: E pg 398; H pg 481; Research by CMK **BS**: 04.

HUDSON, John; b 1750, Albemarle; d bef 2 Feb 1801 **RU**: Captain/Patriot, Served in Albemarle Co Militia. Also gave material aid to cause **CEM**: Mt Air; GPS unk; Hardware River, Keene, NW of Scottsville; Albemarle **GS**: N **SP**: 1) Ann Barbour **VI**: No further data **P**: unk **BLW**: unk **RG**: Y **MK**: unk **PH**: N **SS**: AL Ct Bk pg 28; E pg 398; SAR P-187208 **BS**: JLARC 2, 76.

HUDSON, Thomas; b 20 Nov 1764; d 11 Mar 1843 **RU**: Private, Soldier, Ent serv Augusta Co in 2nd VA State Regt & 14th Cont Line **CEM**: Rinker; GPS unk; Conicville; Shenandoah **GS**: U **SP**: Mar (31 Aug 1784) Dorothy Helsley (c1756-__) **VI**: Sol appl pen 10 Sep 1832 Shenandoah Co. In 18 Aug 1837 Warren Co, sol made inquiry concerning BLW for services. Widow appl pen 30 Aug 1834 Shenandoah Co. W7832 **P**: Y **BLW**: unk **RG**: Y **MK**: unk **PH**: unk **SS**: E pg 398; CG Vol 2 pg 1749; SAR P-333633 **BS**: JLARC 3.

HUDSON, Vincent; b c1763, Essex Co; d 26 Nov1820 **RU**: Fifer, Joined 7th VA Regt Feb 1776. Discharged Valley Forge Feb 1778. Reenlisted 21st Gloucester Co Militia 1779. Was Fife Maj until 1781 **CEM**: Union Baptist; GPS 37.27882, -76.44331; 9524 Guinea Rd, Achilles; Gloucester **GS**: N **SP**: Mar (1794 at her father's, Gloucester Co) Mildred Shackelford (c1774-after 1851) **VI**: Also soldier in War of 1812. Sol appl pen 22 May 1818 Gloucester Co. He died in Saddler's Neck, Gloucester Co. Widow appl pen 27 Mar 1746 age 74. 6876. Widow's pension W7833 **P**: Y **BLW**: unk **RG**: Y **MK**: N **PH**: N **SS**: S #1274; K Vol 3 pg 343; SAR P-187239 **BS**: 04.

HUFF, Francis Jr; b 1758, Augusta Co; d 27 Aug 1832 **RU**: Private, Served in Capt John McKittrick's Co, Augusta Co Militia **CEM**: Trinity Episcopal; GPS 38.14917, -79.07521; 214 Beverley St; Staunton City **GS**: N **SP**: Sarah Salley (4 Mar 1764-13 Apr 1810) **VI**: Died in Augusta Co **P**: unk **BLW**: unk **RG**: N **MK**: unk **PH**: N **SS**: E pg 399 **BS**: 196.

HUFF, John; b Nov 1743; d 10 Feb 1804 **RU**: Patriot, Gave provisions to the cause **CEM**: Mt Hebron; GPS 39.10916, -78.09497; 305 E Boscawen St; Winchester City **GS**: Y **SP**: Mar Elizabeth (-----) (c1757-14 Jun 1838) **VI**: No further data **P**: N **BLW**: N **RG**: N **MK**: Y SAR monument **PH**: unk **SS**: AL Comm Bk II-211 **BS**: 01 pg 47; 09.

RU=Rank/Unit	CEM=Cemetery	GS=Gravestone	SP=Spousal Information
VI=Other Veteran Info	P=Pension	BLW=Bounty/Land Warrant	RG=Registered Grave
MK=SAR/DAR Marker	PH=Photo	SS=Service Source	BS=Burial Source

206

HUFF, John; b 1763, Pittsylvania Co; d 10 May 1840 **RU:** Private, Served in VA Line. Ent serv Henry Co **CEM:** Pigg River Primitive Baptist; GPS 36.96913, -80.07368; Rt 750 nr Callaway; Franklin **GS:** Y **SP:** 1) Mar (21 Nov 1784 Frederick Co by Alexander Balmain) Catherine Lemly 2) Mar (14 Jul 1786 Franklin Co) Mary (Polly) Gearhart 3) Mar (c 9 Feb 1837) Elizabeth Gulliams of Floyd Co. (Mar bond signed by James Ferguson 1 Feb 1837). Widow mar next Stephen A. Payne & moved to Athens Co, OH. **VI:** Sol appl pen 1 Jul 1833 Franklin Co. S5590, Recd BLW #87034-160-55 **P:** Y **BLW:** Y **RG:** Y **MK:** N **PH:** unk **SS:** E pg 399; CG Vol 2 pg 1750; SAR P-187295 **BS:** 82 pg 181.

HUFFER (HUFFORD)(HUFFERT), Jacob; b 6 Nov 1755, Lancaster Co, PA; d 1848 **RU:** Private, Served in PA Companies **CEM:** Emmanuel; GPS unk; Mt Solon; Augusta **GS:** N **SP:** Anna Schoenauer (1760 Berks Co, PA-__) **VI:** No further data **P:** unk **BLW:** unk **RG:** N **MK:** unk **PH:** N **SS:** JLARC Rpt App B-2 pg 9 **BS:** JLARC 125; 196.

HUFFMAN, Barnard; b unk; d 1826 **RU:** Private, Served at Ft Pitt (Pittsburgh PA) 1775 **CEM:** North End; GPS 36.77234, -80.73866; 101 Beaver Dam Rd, Hillsville; Carroll **GS:** N **SP:** No info **VI:** No further data **P:** unk **BLW:** unk **RG:** N **MK:** N **PH:** N **SS:** E pg 399 **BS:** 123 pg 67.

HUFFMAN, Daniel; b 22 Feb 1758; d Jun 1798 **RU:** Patriot; he paid the 1783 personal property tax in Shenandoah Co, considered to be a supply tax for Rev War expenses **CEM:** Friedens United Church of Christ; GPS 38.348480,-78.876530; GS GPS 38.348203, -78.876682; 3960 Friedens Church Rd, MT Crawford; Rockingham **GS:** Y broken stone has new one with birth & death dates **SP:VI: P:** N **BLW:** N **RG:** N **MK:** N **PH:** Y **SS:** Shenandoah Co pers prop tax list 1783 **BS:** 04.

HUFFMAN (HOOFMAN), Valentine (Valentin); b c1720-1730, Germany; d c1803 **RU:** Captain, Served in Chaplin, Berks Co PA Militia **CEM:** Friedens United Church of Christ; GPS 38.34848, -78.87653; 3960 Friedens Church Rd; Rockingham **GS:** Y **SP:** Ann Maria Franck **VI:** Son of John Jacob & (-----) Hoofman **P:** unk **BLW:** unk **RG:** Y **MK:** Y **SAR PH:** Y **SS:** J-NSSAR 2000 Reg **BS:** JLARC 76; 196.

HUGHART, Thomas; b 1725; d 23 May 1810 **RU:** Colonel/Patriot, Performed public and military service **CEM:** Rocky Spring Presbyterian; GPS 38.11470, -79.24250; 1 mi S of Deerfield; Augusta **GS:** Y **SP:** Rebecca Estill **VI:** Stone reads "A soldier of the Revolution in command of Augusta troops at the seige of Yorktown." Col rank fr Colonial war period **P:** unk **BLW:** unk **RG:** Y **MK:** N **PH:** unk **SS:** B; AL signature approval given Augusta Co 1781-3 period for public Claim; SAR P-187388 **BS:** JLARC 2, 62, 63; 196.

HUGHART, Thomas; b unk; d Aft 1781 **RU:** Patriot, Gave material aid to cause **CEM:** Trinity Episcopal; GPS 38.14917, -79.07521; 214 Beverley St; Staunton City **GS:** U **SP:** No info **VI:** May be duplicate of Thomas Hughart reported bur at Rock Spring Cem **P:** N **BLW:** N **RG:** N **MK:** unk **PH:** unk **SS:** J- DAR Hatcher; AL Cert Augusta Co **BS:** JLARC 2. **SEE APPENDIX G**

HUGHES, Archelaus; b 25 Sep 1747 Goochland; d 25 Dec 1796 **RU:** Colonel/Patriot, Was Appointed Apr 1780 as Henry Co Lt. Also Commissioner of Peace; Took Oath of Allegiance; Gave material aid to cause **CEM:** Hughesville; GPS unk; Hwy 631 nr Stuart; Patrick (died) Pittsylvania **GS:** U **SP:** Mary Dalton, d/o Samuel Dalton (1748-1841) & (----) **VI:** No further data **P:** unk **BLW:** unk **RG:** Y **MK:** unk **PH:** unk **SS:** AL Ct Bk pg 7a, 26, 30; SAR P-187392, DAR A059074 **BS:** JLARC 1,30, 102.

HUGHES, Isaac; b 15 Jun 1740, Bucks Co, PA; d 23 Mar 1803 **RU:** Private, Served in Col John Alexander's Regt **CEM:** Leesburg Presbyterian; GPS 39.11611, -77.56722; 207 W Market St, Leesburg; Loudoun **GS:** U **SP:** Mar (13 Mar 1764 Hunterdon Co NY) Mary Warne (25 Jul 1743 Cranbury, Middlesex Co NJ-1803) d/o George & Abigail (Warford) Warne **VI:** Son of Mathew & Elizabeth (Stevenson) Hughes **P:** unk **BLW:** unk **RG:** Y **MK:** unk **PH:** unk **SS:** J-NSSAR 1993 Reg, J- DAR Hatcher; CD; SAR P-187413 **BS:** JLARC 1, 2; 196.

HUGHES, James; b 1750; d 1801 **RU:** Soldier, Served in Capt Tate's Co, Augusta Co Militia **CEM:** Trinity Episcopal; GPS 38.14917, -79.07521; 214 Beverley St; Staunton City **GS:** U **SP:** Mar (1772) Cassandra Dunn (__ Jefferson Co-__) **VI:** Son of Felix (1723 Ireland-__) & Cynthia (Kaigan) (1723-1805) Hughes. Died in Waynesboro **P:** unk **BLW:** unk **RG:** unk **MK:** unk **PH:** unk **SS:** J- DAR Hatcher; E pg 400; SAR P-187416 **BS:** JLARC 2.

RU=Rank/Unit	CEM=Cemetery	GS=Gravestone	SP=Spousal Information
VI=Other Veteran Info	P=Pension	BLW=Bounty/Land Warrant	RG=Registered Grave
MK=SAR/DAR Marker	PH=Photo	SS=Service Source	BS=Burial Source

207

HUGHES, John W; b 4 Oct 1750, Bladensburg, MD; d 9 Feb 1851 **RU:** Private, Served in Capt Barton Lucas's 3rd Co, Smallwood's 1st MD Regt. Fought at Long Island & White Plains. Wounded and discharged at White Plains **CEM:** Neriah Baptist; GPS 37.78778, -79.36482; Jct Rts 631 & 706, South River; Rockbridge **GS:** Y **SP:** mar (c1778) Polly Rebecca Taylor (1753 Orange Co-26 Apr 1850 Fairfield, Rockbridge Co) **VI:** Appl pen 3 Sep 1832 Rockbridge Co. Died in Fairfield, Rockbridge Co. Widow recd pen #5594 **P:** Y **BLW:** unk **RG:** Y **MK:** Y **SAR PH:** Y **SS:** CG Vol 2 pg 1753; SAR P-187441, DAR A059168 **BS:** JLARC 1, 2, 79; 196.

HUGHES, Thomas A; b 10 Jan 1752, Bucks Co, PA; d 18 Jul 1822 **RU:** Soldier, Served in 3rd Cont Line **CEM:** Goose Creek; GPS 39.11250, -77.69527; Rt 722, Lincoln; Loudoun **GS:** U **SP:** mar (13 Jan 1779 at Fairfax Monthly Meeting, Loudoun Co) Sarah Schooley (31 Jan 1760 Waterford, Loudoun Co-5 Dec 1845 Franklin Co, IN) d/o of John (1727-1814) & Mary (Wright) Schooley. Moved to Franklin Co IN as widow. **VI:** Son of Matthew & Elizabeth (Stephenson) Hughes of Bucks Co, PA **P:** N **BLW:** N **RG:** N **MK:** unk **PH:** unk **SS:** E pg 400 **BS:** 196.

HUGUETT, Louis; b unk; d 1781 **RU:** Seaman, Served on "Auguste" and died from Yorktown battle **CEM:** French Memorial; GPS 36.81944, -79.39933; Yorktown; York **GS:** U **SP:** No info **VI:** No further data **P:** unk **BLW:** unk **RG:** Y **MK:** unk **PH:** unk **SS:** J-Yorktown Historian; SAR P-187517 **BS:** JLARC 1, 74.

HULING, Andrew, b 1761, Douglasville, PA; d 2 Apr 1844 **RU:** Private, Capts Robert Cravens & George Hutton's Companies, Rockingham Co Militia **CEM:** Huling Family; GPS not determined; Andrew Huling property, Lacey Spring; Rockingham **GS:** N **SP:** Mar 1790, Susannah Koontz (1770-1834), d/o Peter Detrich Counts (1735-1813) & Christina Boyer (1732-1818) **VI:** Son of Andrew Hulings, Sr (1726-1778) & Catherine Mansson (1730-1803) S13317 Recd pen # F-5584, R1362 **P:** Y **BLW:** N **RG:** Y **MK:** N **PH:** N **SS:** E pg 401; K vol 2, pg 350; DAR A050429 **BS:** 196.

HULL, George; b 15 Oct 1757, Rockingham Co; d 4 Sep 1849 **RU:** Private, Served in Capt Fraizer's Co Augusta Co, then VA Line **CEM:** Hull Family; GPS unk; Rt 640 to Rt 637, .9 mi to Elmer Ruckman farm; Highland **GS:** Y **SP:** Hannah Keister (1757 Brandywine, Pendleton Co WV-1837) d/o Frederick (1730-1815) & Hannah (Dyer) (1735-1811) Keister **VI:** Son of Peter Thomas (1706-1776) & Susanna Margetetha (Dieffenbach) (1725-1790) Hull. Resided in Augusta Co (part that became Pendleton Co), later moved to Bath Co. GS not readable, but there. Appl for pen 27 Aug 1832 age 74. S13317 **P:** Y **BLW:** N **RG:** Y **MK:** N **PH:** N **SS:** E pg 411; CG pg 1759; SAR P-187614 **BS:** 196.

HULL, Henry; b 27 Mar 1760, Lancaster Co, PA; d 16 Sep 1835 **RU:** Soldier, Served in Augusta Co Militia 1780-82 **CEM:** Peterstown; GPS 37.39470, -80.80140; Off Rt 219 btw Peterstown & Midway, on WV state line; Giles **GS:** N **SP:** 1) Elizabeth (-----) 2) mar (11 Sep 1821 Monroe Co VA/WVA) Elizabeth Hawkins **VI:** Son of Franz "Francis" Philip (1733-1808) and Maria "Mary" Agnes (Klingel) (1732-__) Hull. Recd pen for war service 1802. DAR plaque. Grave stone has been removed and probably stolen. Widow recd pen and BLW **P:** Y **BLW:** Y **RG** Y **MK:** unk **PH:** N **SS:** B; CG pg 1759; SAR P-187619 **BS:** 196.

HULL, Johiel; b unk; d 1781 **RU:** Soldier, Served fr NJ; killed in the battle at Yorktown **CEM:** Yorktown Victory Monument Tablet; GPS 38.28350, -78.54150; Yorktown; York **GS:** U **SP:** No info **VI:** No further data **P:** unk **BLW:** unk **RG:** Y **MK:** unk **PH:** unk **SS:** J-Yorktown Historian; SAR P-187637 **BS:** JLARC 74.

HULL, Peter; b 1733, Europe; d Jan 1818 **RU:** Captain, Served in Capt Hull's Co, 2nd Augusta Co Militia. Also commanded a troop of Calvary, Col John McCreey's Regt at Yorktown in Oct 1781 **CEM:** Hull Family; GPS unk; Rt 640 to Rt 637, .9 mi to Elmer Ruckman farm; Highland (DIED) Pendleton **GS:** U **SP:** Barbara Ann Keith Penniger **VI:** Son of Peter Thomas (1706-1776) & Susanna Margetetha (Dieffenbach) (1725-1790) Hull **P:** unk **BLW:** unk **RG:** Y **MK:** unk **PH:** unk **SS:** E pg 402; SAR P-187667, DAR A059545 **BS:** JLARC 103; 196.

HULVEY (HULVA)(HULVAH), Conrad; b 1715 Hessen, Ger; d Jul 1784, Shenandoah **RU:** Patriot, paid personal property tax, Rockingham Co 1783 considered a supply tax for Rev War expenses **CEM:** Columbia Furnace; GPS not determined; Columbia Furnace, Shenandoah Co **GS:** N **SP:** Anna Elizabeth

RU=Rank/Unit
VI=Other Veteran Info
MK=SAR/DAR Marker
CEM=Cemetery
P=Pension
PH=Photo
GS=Gravestone
BLW=Bounty/Land Warrant
SS=Service Source
SP=Spousal Information
RG=Registered Grave
BS=Burial Source

208

Keller (1720-1786), d/o Bastian & Elizaberth Hildebrandt **VI:** He worked in the Columbia and Liberty Iron furnaces **P:** N **BLW:** N **RG:** N **MK:** N **PH:** N **SS:** DV image04 Rockingham Co, 1783 **BS:** 196.

HUME, Francis; b abt 1730/31, Spotsylvania, Tridelphia, Spotsylvania Co; d 1813 **RU:** Captain/Patriot, Served in VA state troops and Culpeper Minutemen Bn. Served w/ Morgan and later Washington at Yorktown Oct 1781. Gave material aid to cause **CEM:** Hume; GPS unk; Rt 15 Business, nr SW side of River. Remington on James Madison St; Culpeper **GS:** Y **SP:** Mar (30 Aug 1763) Elizabeth Duncan (1728, Fauquier Co-__, Columbia, Boome Co, MO) **VI:** Original member Society of Cincinnati. Died in Walnut Plantation, Culpeper Co. SAR Marker **P:** unk **BLW:** unk **RG:** Y **MK:** Y SAR **PH:** Y **SS:** J-NSSAR 2000 Reg; D Vol 1 pg 264 Culpeper Co, SAR P- 187768, DAR A059648 **BS:** JLARC 76.

HUMES (HUME), William; b 1758; d 3 May 1808 **RU:** Private, Served in Fauquier Co Militia. Wounded near Williamsburg 1781 **CEM:** Mt Union; GPS 37.45133, -79.97055; 4614 Catawba Rd, Mt Union; Botetourt **GS:** Y **SP:** No info **VI:** Pen recd 19 Dec 1783. Was on 1785 pen list. Died age 50 **P:** Y **BLW:** unk **RG:** N **MK:** N **PH:** unk **SS:** A pg 402; BX pg 397 **BS:** 115 pg 41; 196.

HUMPHREY, Jesse; b 29 Sep 1766; d 1 Jan 1815 **RU:** Private, Ent serv Caroline Co **CEM:** Ebenezer Baptist; GPS 39.05824, -77.84142; 20421 Airmont Rd, Bluemont; Loudoun **GS:** Y **SP:** Winey (-----) **VI:** Died in Bloomfield, Loudoun Co **P:** unk **BLW:** unk **RG:** N **MK:** N **PH:** unk **SS:** E pg 402 **BS:** 25 pg 154.

HUMPHREY, William; b 1748; d 1827 **RU:** Private, Served in Capt Tates Co, Augusta Co Militia **CEM:** Humphries Lone Graves; GPS unk; 11 mi SW of Covington; Alleghany **GS:** N **SP:** Ruth (-----) **VI:** No further data **P:** unk **BLW:** unk **RG:** N **MK:** N **PH:** N **SS:** E pg 403 **BS:** 160 Humphrey.

HUMPHREY (HUMPHREYS), Abner; b 27 Oct 1763, Loudoun Co.; d 17 Dec 1824 **RU:** Private, Loudoun Co. Militia, Special service info is at the Lib VA in Auditors Accts XV pg 513 **CEM:** Ebenezer Baptist; GPS 39.05824, -77.84142; 20421 Airmont Rd, Bluemont; Loudoun **GS:** Y **SP:** Mary Van Hook Purcell (11 Sep 1758-11 Mar 1824) d/o Thomas (1720-1779) & Mary (Van Hook) (1723-1771) Purcell **VI:** No further data **P:** unk **BLW:** unk **RG:** Y SAR plaque **MK:** unk **PH:** unk **SS:** CZ pg 232; SAR P- 187824, DAR A059730 **BS:** JLARC 1, 2, 32; 196.

HUMPHREY (HUMPHREYS), Thomas; b 2 Jun 1742, PA; d 7 Jun 1824 **RU:** Captain, commanded a company in the Loudoun Co militia. Also served in the 2d VA Regt and the 11th and 15th Continental Line **CEM:** Ketoctin Baptist; GPS 39.15746, -77.74870; Ketoctin Church Rd, Purcellville; Loudoun **GS:** Y **SP:** 1) Mary Marks 2) Mary (-----) **VI:** Son of Thomas Humphrey , Sr and Hannah Yarborogh He was a blacksmith. The gravestone inscription shows his service **P:** unk **BLW:** unk **RG:** Y **MK:** SAR Plaque **PH:** unk **SS:** AK; E pg 403; AZ pg 211; SAR P- 187933, DAR A059966 **BS:** 04 JLARC 1, 2, 32.

HUMPHREYS (HUMPHRIES), David; b abt 1743, County Armagh, N. Ireland; d 15 Aug 1826 **RU:** Soldier/Patriot, Served in Capt Cunningham's Co, Augusta Co Regt, VA Militia. Also gave 365# beef to cause **CEM:** Bethel Presbyterian; GPS 38.04257, -79.17283 GS 38.0232,-79.1018; 563 Bethel Green Rd, Middlebrook; Augusta **GS:** Y **SP:** Margaret Finley (__-22 Sep 1849) **VI:** Died age 83 nr Greenville, Augusta Co **P:** unk **BLW:** unk **RG:** Y **MK:** Y SAR **PH:** unk **SS:** D pg 51 Augusta Co; DD; SAR P- 187963, DAR A131261 **BS:** JLARC 1, 62, 63; 196.

HUNDLEY, Josiah; b 1756; d 11 Aug 1827 **RU:** Private, Ent serv Amelia Co. Served in VA Line under Patrick Henry **CEM:** Bethel Baptist; GPS 37.50986, -77.71166; 1100 Huguenot Springs Rd, Midlothian; Chesterfield **GS:** Y **SP:** Mar (1758) Ann Holmes (13 May 1768-19 Jan 1852). **VI:** Newer stone says he was b in England, but this is doubtful as there were several Josias Hundleys long established in nearby Amelia Co. Sol appl pen age 62 on 27 Aug 1818 Mecklenburg Co without receipt. DAR plaque. Widow appl pen 8 July 1840 Mecklenburg Co. W7844 **P:** Y **BLW:** unk **RG:** Y **MK:** Y **PH:** unk **SS:** CG pg 1766; SAR P-188019 **BS:** JLARC 1, 2, 4,12, 35; 196.

HUNGATE, William; b unk; d Aft Jan 1833 **RU:** Lieutenant, Served in Montgomery Co Militia Aug 1775 **CEM:** Hungate Family; GPS unk; Rt 615 nr Little River; Floyd **GS:** U **SP:** No info **VI:** Will dated Jan 1833. Memorialized by DAR plaque in cem **P:** unk **BLW:** unk **RG:** Y **MK:** unk **PH:** unk **SS:** SAR Ancestor #P-188027; E pg 404; AZ pg 139 **BS:** JLARC 2, 29; 196 for John Mitchell.

HUNGERFORD, John Pratt; b 2 Jan 1761, Westmoreland Co; d 21 Dec 1833 **RU:** Captain, Served in Col. Taylor's VA State Regt in 1779 & 1780 **CEM:** Hungerford-Griffin; GPS unk; 373 Resolutions Rd,

RU=Rank/Unit	CEM=Cemetery	GS=Gravestone	SP=Spousal Information
VI=Other Veteran Info	P=Pension	BLW=Bounty/Land Warrant	RG=Registered Grave
MK=SAR/DAR Marker	PH=Photo	SS=Service Source	BS=Burial Source

209

Leedstown; Westmoreland **GS:** Y **SP:** no info **VI:** Rev War. VA House Delegates 1797-1801. VA Senate 1801-09. 12th Congress Member-elect 4 Mar-29 Nov 1811 but succeeded by John Taliaferro. US Rep 13th 14th Congress 1813-17. Brigadier Gen of militia in War of 1812. Sol appl pen Westmoreland Co. S5586. Died inTwiford, Westmoreland Co **P:** Y **BLW:** unk **RG:** Y **MK:** Y SAR plaque **PH:** unk **SS:** E pg 404; CG Vol 2 pg 1766; SAR P-336116 **BS:** 75 pg 1; 201 pg 7397.

HUNGERFORD, Thomas; b 4 Apr 1740, Westmoreland; d 3 May 1803 **RU:** Ens., First Lt., 2nd Lieutenant, Served in 3rd VA Regt VA Line; Capts John Thorton, Robert Powell, Reuben Briscoe, Col. Thomas Marshall, LCol Wm Heth, 3rd and 7th VA Regt; **CEM:** Hungerford-Griffin; GPS unk; 373 Resolutions Rd, Leedstown; Westmoreland **GS:** U **SP:** Anne Washington **VI:** Govt GS indicates service. Recd BLW #934-200-26 May 1789 (also recorded at #2476) **P:** unk **BLW:** Y **RG:** Y **MK:** Y SAR plaque **PH:** unk **SS:** J-NSSAR 1993 Reg; CG Vol 2 pg 1767; SAR P-188053, DAR A060051 **BS:** JLARC 1.

HUNSICKER, Peter; b 1761, Lancaster Co, PA; d 1816 **RU:** Patriot, Provided provisions to Cont Army, including 261# flour **CEM:** Stone Chapel Presbyterian; GPS 39.22610, -78.01060; Old Charles Town Rd, Berryville; Clarke **GS:** Y **SP:** Ann Eve Schmidt (c1761-30 Apr 1850) **VI:** Son of Daniel & Christina Hunsicke, natives of Wolfersheim, Germany. Had public service claims **P:** N **BLW:** N **RG:** N **MK:** N **PH:** Y **SS:** AL Cert Issued **BS:** 58 pg 90; 196.

HUNT, David; b 1745; d 1826 **RU:** Colonel/Patriot, In Aug 1781 marched fr Pittsylvania in Capt William Dix Co to Little York until surrender of Cornwallis. Marched with Capt Charles Williams to guard British prisoners at Noland's Ferry on Potomac. Gave material aid to cause **CEM:** Hunt; GPS 37.007097, -79.224135; Mt Airy Rt 640 near Renan; Pittsylvania **GS:** Y **SP:** No info **VI:** No further data **P:** unk **BLW:** unk **RG:** Y **MK:** unk **PH:** unk **SS:** D Pittsylvania Co; SAR P-188135 **BS:** 174; JLARC 76, 90, 96.

HUNT, James; b 1750; d 7 Nov 1820 **RU:** Private, Served in VA Line; entered serv 1776 **CEM:** Walnut Tree Farm; GPS unk; Btw Vienna & Oakton; Fairfax **GS:** Y **SP:** Mar (12 Jan 1792 in MD) Una Lovelace **VI:** Moved to Fairfax Co in 1814. Appl pen 29 May 1818 Prince William Co age 57. (however 24 May 1820 gave age as 70, living in Fairfax Co) S38062 **P:** Y **BLW:** unk **RG:** N **MK:** N **PH:** unk **SS:** KI Vol 2 pg 355; CG Vol 2 pg 1770 **BS:** 80 vol 2 pg 184.

HUNTER, Alexander; b 1706; d Jun 1798 **RU:** Patriot, Public service claim **CEM:** Old Presbyterian Meeting House; GPS 38.48528, -77.23532; 323 S Fairfax St; Alexandria City **GS:** N **SP:** No info **VI:** Bur 27 Jun 1798, age 82 **P:** N **BLW:** N **RG:** N **MK:** N **PH:** N **SS:** AL Comm Bk V **BS:** 110 pg 131.

HUNTER, Elizabeth (nee Chapman); b 13 Jun 1733, Charles Co., MD; d 1812 **RU:** Patriot, Provided driver and horses for 40 days (claim filed 1782 under Act of 1780) **CEM:** Pohick Episcopal; GPS 38.42546, -77.11598; 9301 Richmond Hwy, Lorton; Fairfax **GS:** Y **SP:** John Hunter MD **VI:** Interred at family cem at Summer Hill in Fairfax Co. **P:** N **BLW:** N **RG:** Y **MK:** Y SAR plaque **PH:** Y **SS:** R pg 2; SAR P-188498 **BS:** 04.

HUNTER, George; b 1742; d Feb 1798 **RU:** Patriot, Signed Legislative Petition at First Presbyterian Church, Alexandria **CEM:** Old Presbyterian Meeting House; GPS 38.48528, -77.23532; 323 S Fairfax St; Alexandria City **GS:** N **SP:** No info **VI:** Died of intemperance age 56, bur 15 Feb 1798 **P:** N **BLW:** N **RG:** N **MK:** unk **PH:** N **SS:** BB **BS:** 196; 23 pg 103.

HUNTER, George Dr; b 1753; d 1776 **RU:** Surgeon, Served in Revolutionary Navy, aboard the sloop "Congress" **CEM:** Pohick Episcopal; GPS 38.42546, -77.11598; 9301 Richmond Hwy, Lorton; Fairfax **GS:** Y **SP:** No info **VI:** Son of (-----) and Elizabeth (-----) Hunter. Died at sea. Grave moved fr Summer Hill Plantation. DAR plaque placed by Mount Vernon chapter.Memorialized on Rev War Court House Plaque;GPS;not determined; 4110 Chain, Bridge Rd; Fairfax in 2017by Geo Washington Chapter, VASSAR **P:** unk **BLW:** Y **RG:** Y **MK:** Y SAR plaque **PH:** Y **SS:** E pg 405; SAR P-188386 **BS:** JLARC 1, 14, 28, 51; 69 pg 83.

HUNTER, James; b 23 Oct 1721, Legenwood, Berwickshire Duns/Berwick Scotland; d 1784 **RU:** Patriot, Was owner of Hunter Ironworks, Falmouth. Made camp utensils, weapons, equipment for continental forces. Was not fully compensated-lost entire estate in debt **CEM:** Union Church; GPS 38.32268, -77.46615; Carter St, Falmouth; Stafford **GS:** Y **SP:** Margaret Shillinglaw **VI:** Son of James & Helen (Simson) Hunter of Duns Scotland. Gravesite has iron fence with his name. Iron Works in operation by 1761; by 1775 largest iron works in colonies. Sample musket was made standard. Will dated 18 Nov

RU=Rank/Unit	CEM=Cemetery	GS=Gravestone	SP=Spousal Information
VI=Other Veteran Info	P=Pension	BLW=Bounty/Land Warrant	RG=Registered Grave
MK=SAR/DAR Marker	PH=Photo	SS=Service Source	BS=Burial Source

210

1784 **P:** N **BLW:** N **RG:** Y **MK:** Y **SAR PH:** Y **SS:** D pg 883; SAR P-333998 **BS:** 30 pg 308-313; 04 1998.

HUNTER, John; b c1732 or earlier, d bef 6 Sep 1826 **RU:** Patriot, Gave material aid to the cause and paid supply tax in Fairfax County in 1782 **CEM:** Old Presbyterian Meeting House; GPS 38.48528, -77.23532; 323 S Fairfax St; Alexandria City **GS:** N **SP:** mar (1752) Elizabeth Chapman, d/o Nathaniel Chapman **VI:** Listed on SAR plaque in cemetery. For birth have assumed at least age 21 when married in 1752 **P:** N **BLW:** N **RG:** Y **MK:** Y **SAR plaque PH:** N **SS:** AL Ct BK pg 1; DV; Website 2017 Fairfax Co Gen Soc; SAR Ancestor #188416 (188438 is erroneous) **BS:** JLARC 1; 23 pg 103; 196.

HUNTER, John Jr; b 10 Jul 1760, Bedford Co, later Campbell Co; d unk **RU:** Soldier, Ent Serv Campbell Co. Served in VA Line **CEM:** Concord Presbyterian #2; GPS unk; .5 mi S of Hunter's Tavern; Campbell **GS:** U **SP:** Rachel (-----) **VI:** Son of John Hunter Sr. Lived in NC, TN, KY. Appl 14 Oct 1833 Campbell Co. S15897 **P:** Y **BLW:** unk **RG:** N **MK:** N **PH:** unk **SS:** CG Vol 2 pg 1775 **BS:** JLARC 36.

HUNTER, John Chapman. See Appendix G Addenda.

HUNTER, Nathaniel Chapman; b 1764, Alexandria; d 28 Apr 1812 **RU:** Private, Serv in VA Line for duration of war; recd wounds during serv **CEM:** Pohick Episcopal; GPS 38.42546, -77.11598; 9301 Richmond Hwy, Lorton; Fairfax **GS:** Y **SP:** Sarah Ann Tyler, d/o Charles & (-----) Tyler, Esq **VI:** Son of Dr. John & (__ Chapman) Hunter. Was a merchant in Dumfries, Prince William Co. In 1806 moved to Alexandria and was officer in a bank. Bur first in Summer Hill cem in Arlington moved to Pohick Church cem on 6 Apr 1940 **P:** unk **BLW:** unk **RG:** Y **MK:** Y **SAR plaque PH:** unk **SS:** AO Vol I pg 198; SAR P-335807, DAR A060548 **BS:** 69 pg 83, 83A.

HUNTER, Robert; b unk; d Aft 1781 **RU:** Patriot, Gave material aid to cause in Bedford Co **CEM:** Concord Presbyterian #3; GPS unk; 4909 Reedy Spring Rd, Sprout Springs; Campbell **GS:** U **SP:** Nancy (-----) **VI:** No further data **P:** N **BLW:** N **RG:** Y **MK:** N **PH:** unk **SS:** AL resided and gave in Bedford Co; SAR P-188460 **BS:** JLARC 36.

HUNTER, Samuel; b 1737; d 18 Apr 1813 **RU:** Patriot, Gave material aid to cause **CEM:** North Mountain; GPS unk; 7 mi S of Staunton on N side Rt 252; Augusta **GS:** Y **SP:** Susannah Alexander **VI:** Name also on cenotaph monument here **P:** N **BLW:** N **RG:** Y **MK:** N **PH:** unk **SS:** AL cert issued; BY; SAR P-188469 **BS:** 80 vol 2 pg 186;196.

HUNTER, William; b 1749; d Oct 1803 **RU:** Soldier/Patriot, Gave material aid to cause **CEM:** Old Presbyterian Meeting House; GPS 38.48528, -77.23532; 323 S Fairfax St; Alexandria City **GS:** N **SP:** No info **VI:** Bur 18 Oct 1803, age 54 **P:** unk **BLW:** unk **RG:** Y **MK:** Y **SAR plaque PH:** N **SS:** J-NSSAR 1993 Reg; AL Ct Bk pg 4 Fairfax Co **BS:** JLARC 1; 23 pg 104.

HUNTER, William Jr; b 20 Jan 1731, Galston, Scotland; d 19 Nov 1792 **RU:** Patriot, Gave material aid to cause. Signed a Legislative Petition in Alexandria **CEM:** Old Presbyterian Meeting House; GPS 38.48528, -77.23532; 323, GS 38.4806,-77.0238 S Fairfax St; Alexandria City **GS:** Y **SP:** No info **VI:** Mayor of Alexandria, and founder of St Andrew's Society in Alexandria. A slab in cemetery lists his RW service. Death notice in Alexandria Gazette, 22 Nov 1792 **P:** N **BLW:** N **RG:** Y **MK:** N **PH:** unk **SS:** AL Ct bk lt pg 4; AK; S-Alexandria; SAR P-188496 **BS:** 23 pg 103; 196.

HURDLE, Lawrence; b 1758, Prince Charles, MD; d 1 Dec 1848 **RU:** Private, Served in 7th Regt, MD Line 1776-1782. Was in battles at Harlan Height, NY & Camden, SC **CEM:** St Mary's Catholic; GPS 38.79390, -77.04750; 310 S Royal St; Alexandria City **GS:** Y **SP:** Mar (20 Oct 1792 Georgetown, MD) Nancy Wheeler, (__-13 Dec 1863) **VI:** He was wounded in battle. Sol appl pen 21 Aug 1818 Montgomery Co MD. Widow appl pen 30 Aug 1849 Alexandria Co. Widow appl for BLW 15 Mar 1855 Alexandria Co. W2157. BLW #1-60-55. Death notice in the Alexandria Gazette 2 Dec 1848, pg 3 says he died 1 Dec 1848 age 98 yrs. No dates on stone **P:** Y **BLW:** Y **RG:** Y **MK:** Y **SAR & plaque PH:** Y **SS:** SAR Ancestor #P-188773; M Vol 3 pg 514; CG pg 1781; SAR P-188773, DAR A060967 **BS:** 174 pg 164; 196.

HURSIN, Francois; b unk; d 1781 **RU:** Soldier, Served in Agenais Bn and died fr battle at Yorktown **CEM:** French Memorial; GPS 36.81944, -79.39933; Yorktown; York **GS:** U **SP:** No info **VI:** No further

RU=Rank/Unit VI=Other Veteran Info MK=SAR/DAR Marker
CEM=Cemetery P=Pension PH=Photo
GS=Gravestone BLW=Bounty/Land Warrant SS=Service Source
SP=Spousal Information RG=Registered Grave BS=Burial Source

211

data **P:** unk **BLW:** unk **RG:** Y **MK:** unk **PH:** unk **SS:** J-Yorktown Historian; SAR P-188856 **BS:** JLARC 74.

HURST, John; b 1713, Stafford Co; d 26 Apr 1789 **RU:** Patriot, Gave material aid to cause **CEM:** Summers; GPS 38.82121, -77.14098; Jct Rt 613 & Beaugard St, Lincolnia; Fairfax **GS:** U **SP:** Elizabeth Summers (1724-1781) d/o John (__-6 Dec 1747) & (-----) Hurst of Stafford Co **VI:** No further data **P:** N **BLW:** N **RG:** N **MK:** unk **PH:** unk **SS:** AL Ct Bk pg 10, 22 **BS:** 196.

HURT, Moses; b 1730; d 1806 **RU:** Lieutenant/Patriot, Gave material aid to cause **CEM:** Hurt Family; GPS unk; Nr Mobley's Creek; Bedford **GS:** N **SP:** Ruth Turner, d/o James Turner **VI:** No further data **P:** unk **BLW:** unk **RG:** Y **MK:** N **PH:** N **SS:** J- DAR Hatcher; AL Cert Bedford Co; SAR P-188880 **BS:** JLARC 2; 196.

HUTCHESON, Benjamin; b 3 Apr 1756; d 7 Sep 1823 **RU:** Patriot, Gave material aid to cause **CEM:** Hutchinson-Whaley; GPS unk; next to 4319 General Kearney Ct, Chantilly; Fairfax **GS:** Y **SP:** Elizabeth (----) (10 May 1756-30 Oct 1833) also bur here, "wife of B. Hutchinson" **VI:** No further data **P:** N **BLW:** N **RG:** N **MK:** N **PH:** unk **SS:** AL CT Bk pg 54 **BS:** 61 vol 4 pg CH-21.

HUTCHESON, William; b 1725; d 1779 **RU:** Private, Served in Capt Robert McClanahan's Co at Point Pleasant, Oct 1774 **CEM:** Old Hoges Chapel; GPS unk; Mount Lake Rd; Giles **GS:** U **SP:** No info **VI:** No further data **P:** unk **BLW:** unk **RG:** Y **MK:** unk **PH:** unk **SS:** E pg 407; Z pg 128-9; SAR P-188993 **BS:** 196.

HUTCHINGS, Moses; b 1 Mar 1754, Culpeper Co; d 2 Apr 1836 **RU:** Lieutenant, Ent serv Pittsylvania Co Mar 1777 in Capt John Donelson's Co. Marched to Long Island under Col Shelby against Cherokee & Chickamauga. Was Indian spy under Capt Thomas Dillard 1778. 1779, and Lt under Capt Armistead Shelton. In Feb 1781 harrassed British pickets with 9 others.Was in Capt Thomas Smith's Co Campbell's Regt at Battle of Guilford CH **CEM:** Hutchings, Jack Crane Farm; GPS 36.74674, -79.42226; Dry Fork Rt 718; Pittsylvania **GS:** Y **SP:** Lucy Parks **VI:** Son of Christopher and Elizabeth (-----) Hutchings. Pensioned in Pittsylvania 1832. S8742 **P:** Y **BLW:** unk **RG:** Y **MK:** Y SAR **PH:** unk **SS:** K Vol 3 pg 360; SAR P-189009, DAR A031219 **BS:** 174; JLARC 1, 2, 96.

HUTCHINS (HUTCHINGS), Christopher; b 1722, England; d 20 May 1807 **RU:** Patriot, Gave material aid to cause **CEM:** Rock Wall; GPS unk; Dry Fork; Pittsylvania **GS:** Y **SP:** Elizabeth Parks (1724-1807) d/o Thomas & Sarah (Miller) Parks **VI:** No further data **P:** N **BLW:** N **RG:** Y **MK:** N **PH:** unk **SS:** D Vol 3 pg 762, 769; AS; SAR regis **BS:** SAR regis.

INSKEEP, James; b 1734, Burlington, NJ; d 1802 **RU:** Patriot, Gave material aid to cause **CEM:** Fairview; GPS 38.48080,-78.00470; Sperryville Pike Rt 522, Culpeper; Culpeper **GS:** Y **SP:** Mar (1760) Hope Collins (1745 Burlington, NJ-1806) **VI:** No further data **P:** N **BLW:** N **RG:** Y **MK:** N **PH:** unk **SS:** AL Ct Bk pg 24; SAR P-189783 **BS:** 29 pg 27.(**IRBY**, William, See Appendix G Addenda)

IRELAND, James; b 3 Dec 1745, Edinburgh, Scotland; d 5 May 1806 **RU:** Patriot, DAR marker calls him a patriot. He was a Baptist minister imprisoned for proselytizing in early 1770s in Culpeper Co **CEM:** Berryville Baptist; GPS 39.94700, -77.53700; 114 Academy St, Berryville; Clarke **GS:** Y **SP:** 1) Mar (22 Apr 1771) Jane Burgess (c1750-Apr 1790, Page Co) 2) Ann Pollard **VI:** Imprisoned for proselytizing in early 1770s, Culpeper Co. Died in Crooked Run, Frederick Co. Buck Marsh Baptist Church location not known. Memorial stone at Berryville Baptist which says he was bur at Buck Marsh Baptist Church "near here." Served as pastor at Buck Mark Baptist 1778-1806 **P:** N **BLW:** N **RG:** Y **MK:** Y SAR **PH:** N **SS:** AR Vol 2 pg 195; BT; SAR P-189813 **BS:** JLARC 1, 2; 196.

IRONS, John; b 16 Dec 1825; d 1821 **RU:** Private, Served in Capt Lawson Smith's MD Rifle Co, Lt Col Moses Rawlings' Regt **CEM:** Royal Oak; GPS 36.84315, -81.49660; Behind Marion Baptist Church, Marion; Smyth **GS:** Y **SP:** No info **VI:** No further data **P:** unk **BLW:** unk **RG:** N **MK:** N **PH:** unk **SS:** A pg 240 **BS:** 97 vol I pg 139.

IRVINE, John Jr; b 1736, PA; d 15 Jan 1814 **RU:** Capt./Patriot, Served in Bedford Co. Militia; Gave material aid to cause **CEM:** Hat Creek Presbyterian; GPS 37.06570, -78.54240; 6442 Hat Creek Rd, Brookneal; Campbell **GS:** Y **SP:** Mar (4 Aug 1772, Amherst Co) Mary Anne Tucker (1752-1817) **VI:** Son of John (1700-1788) & Mary Margaret (Boyd) (1707-__) Irvine. Died in Hat Creek, Campbell Co. Newer

RU=Rank/Unit	CEM=Cemetery	GS=Gravestone	SP=Spousal Information
VI=Other Veteran Info	P=Pension	BLW=Bounty/Land Warrant	RG=Registered Grave
MK=SAR/DAR Marker	PH=Photo	SS=Service Source	BS=Burial Source

monument shared with his parents styles him "Maj"—achieved rank of Maj after RW **P:** N **BLW:** N **RG:**Y **MK:** N **PH:** Y **SS:** AL Ct Bk 3; SAR P-189910 **BS:** JLARC 36; 196.

IRVINE, John Sr; b 1700; d 1788 **RU:** 2nd Lieutenant/Patriot, Served in Militia. Gave to cause in Bedford Co **CEM:** Hat Creek Presbyterian; GPS 37.06570, -78.54240; 6442 Hat Creek Rd, Brookneal; Campbell **GS:** Y **SP:** Mary Margaret Boyd **VI:** Newer monument, shared with his son John Irvine Jr **P:** N **BLW:** N **RG:**Y **MK:** N **PH:** unk **SS:** AL Certificate J- DAR Hatcher; SAR P-189897 **BS:** JLARC 2; 196.

IRVINE, William; b unk; d unk **RU:** Soldier, Served in 1st, 10th, & 14th Cont Lines **CEM:** Stonewall Jackson Memorial; GPS 37.78128, -79.44604; 314 S Main St; Lexington City **GS:** U **SP:** No info **VI:** No further data **P:** unk **BLW:** unk **RG:** Y **MK:** unk **PH:** unk **SS:** E pg 410; SAR P-189903 **BS:** JLARC 63.

IRVINE (ERWIN, IRWIN), Edward; b 1740; d 1814 **RU:** Soldier/Patriot, Gave material aid to cause **CEM:** Mossy Creek Presbyterian; GPS 38.35331 -79.04914; 372 Kyles Mill Rd, Mt Solon; Augusta **GS:** Y **SP:** 1) Mary Curry; 2) Sarah Percy **VI:** Son of John and Jean (-----) Erwin **P:** unk **BLW:** unk **RG:** N **MK:** N **PH:** unk **SS:** AL List 1 pg 10 Augusta Co **BS:** JLARC 62, 63; 196.

IRWIN, James; b 1757, Belfast, Ireland; d 5 Sep 1822 **RU:** Private?, Served in 1st, 10th, 14th Cont Line **CEM:** Presbyterian Church; GPS 38.80015, -77.05791; Wilkes St & Hamilton Ln; Alexandria City **GS:** Y **SP:** No info **VI:** Guardian of John Adams, church elder. Died of fever age 64 **P:** unk **BLW:** unk **RG:** N **MK:** Y SAR plaque **PH:** unk **SS:** E pg 410 **BS:** 23 pg 44.

ISBELL, Benjamin; b 18 Mar 1763, Goochland Co; d 1851 Goochland **RU:** Private/Patriot, entered serv 1778 or 1779 as sub for brother LewisSigned Oath of Allegience **CEM:** Isbell Family; GPS 37.807210,-77.907870; 4675 E Grey Fox Circle Gum Springs; Louisa **GS:** U **SP:** Elizabeth Toler (1764- __) **VI:** Son of William Isbell (1722-1807) & Ann Dillard (1724-1829, Goochland); rec'd pen 1831 #F-S9358 R1395 **P:** Y **BLW:** N but eligible **RG:** N **MK:**N **PH:** NSS: E pg 410;K vol 3, pg 4 **BS:** 196.

ISBELL, Henry; 3 Oct 1761, Goochland; d 22 Apr 1847 Goochland Co **RU:** Private, Enlisted 13 Oct 1775 in 4th VA light Dragoons **CEM:** Isbell Family; GPS 37.807210, -77.907870; 4675 E Grey Fox Circle Gum Springss; Louisa **GS:** U **SP:** No spousal info **VI:** Son of William Isbell (1722-1807) & Ann Dillard (1724-1829, Goochland); rec'd pen 1831 #F-S9359 R1395 **P:** Y **BLW:** N but eligble **RG:** N **MK:**N **PH:** N **SS:** E pg 410K vol 3, pg 5 **BS:** 196.

ISBELL, Joseph; b 1747, Caroline Co; d 20 Jul 1823 **RU:** Patriot, Gave material aid to cause **CEM:** Isbell Family; GPS 37.807210, -77.907870; 4675 E Grey Fox Circle Gum Springs; Louisa **GS:** Y **SP:** No info **VI:** Son of William (1720-1807) & Ann (Dillard) (1724-1829) Isbell **P:** N **BLW:** N **RG:** N **MK:** unk **PH:** unk **SS:** AL Ct Bk pg 33 Louisa Co **BS:** 196.

ISBELL, William; b c1722; d 3 Oct 1807 **RU:** Patriot, Gave 11 pounds, 20 shillings to cause cause **CEM:** Isbell Family; GPS 37.807210, -77.907870; 4675 E Grey Fox Circle Gum Springs; Louisa **GS:** U **SP:** Mar (before 5 Mar 1757) Ann Dillard (1724-1829) **VI:** Lived in Lickinghold Twp, St James Parish, Goochland. No marker has been found **P:** N **BLW:** N **RG:** Y**MK:** unk **PH:** unk **SS:** AL Ct Bk pg 1, 13, 22; SAR P-189994, DAR A060653 **BS:** 196.

IVEY, John; b unk; d unk **RU:** Patriot, Gave material aid to the cause **CEM:** Ivey Family; GPS unk; Rt 611 5.5 mi W of Emporia; Greensville **GS:** Y **SP:** No info **VI:** No further data **P:** N **BLW:** N **RG:** N **MK:** N **PH:** unk **SS:** AL Ct bk pg 7 **BS:** 141 Ivey house.

JACKSON, Francis; b 1725, Henrico Co; d 1792 **RU:** Patriot, Gave material aid to cause and paid personal Property Tax Amelia Co 1782 (considered supply tax to support war) **CEM:** Jackson Family; GPS unk; 6101 Buckskin Rd, Rt 640, Jetersville; Amelia **GS:** U **SP:** Mar (1783) Mary Franklin (c1745-1790) **VI:** No further data **P:** N **BLW:** N **RG:** N **MK:** unk **PH:** unk **SS:** DAR Ancestor #A061251; Al Ct Bk II pg 15, 21, 75; DV **BS:** 196.

JACKSON, George; b 1764; d 18 Mar 1847 **RU:** Captain, Was in charge of Monongalia Co Militia; served in VA Line as volunteer. Was wounded in service **CEM:** Burnt Factory United Methodist Church; GPS 38,18490,-78.07550; 1943 Jordan Springs Rd Rt 664, Burnt Factory; Frederick **GS:** Y **SP:** Mar (18 May 1809 Jefferson Co, VA, now WV) Susan Goldsborough (__-14 Feb 1840) **VI:** Son of John (1715-1801 Clarksburg WVA) & (-----) Jackson. Recd pen R15396. Also recd 1/2 pay under Act of 5 Jul 1832

RU=Rank/Unit	CEM=Cemetery	GS=Gravestone	SP=Spousal Information
VI=Other Veteran Info	P=Pension	BLW=Bounty/Land Warrant	RG=Registered Grave
MK=SAR/DAR Marker	PH=Photo	SS=Service Source	BS=Burial Source

(disabled due to RW service) **P:** Y **BLW:** U **RG:** N **MK:** unk **PH:** Y **SS:** E pg 411; N pg 1228; CG pg 1810 **BS:** 196.

JACKSON, John; b unk; d 1795 **RU:** Patriot, Performed public service as Assistant Commissary officer, 24 Jun 1782 in Middlesex Co **CEM:** Christ Church; GPS 37.60968, -76.54643; Rt 33 2 mi E of Saluda; Middlesex **GS:** U **SP:** No info **VI:** No further data **P:** N **BLW:** N **RG:** N **MK:** N **PH:** unk **SS:** G pg 202-3 **BS:** 84, pg 198.

JACKSON, Josiah; b 5 Mar 1732, Chester Co, PA; d Apr 1794 **RU:** Patriot, Gave material aid to the cause **CEM:** Back Creek Quaker, aka Gainesboro United Methodist; GPS 39.27861, -78.25694; 166 Siler Ln, Gainesboro; Frederick **GS:** U **SP:** Mar (Lampeter M.M., Chester Co, PA) Ruth Steer (1747-1825) **VI:** No further data **P:** N **BLW:** N **RG:** N **MK:** unk **PH:** unk **SS:** AL Ct bk pg 7 **BS:** 196.

JACKSON, Richard; b 1750, PA, d 21 Oct 1820 **RU:** Private, Capt James Archer's Co, Washington Co, PA Militia **CEM:** Richard Jackson Family; GPS: not determined; Rosemont, Washington; Rappahannock **GS:** Unk **SP:** Mar aft Jun 1791, Washington Co, PA, Phebe Updike (1760-25 Mar 1833) d/o John Updike & Sarah Brown or Carker **VI:** Occupation-butcher **P:** N **BLW:** N **RG:** Y **MK:** N, **PH:** N **SS:** DAR Anc # A061227; SAR P-330197 **BS:** 196.

JACKSON, Thomas; b c1755; d Bef 15 Jul 1807 **RU:** Private, Served in Lousia Co Militia **CEM:** Jackson Family; GPS unk; Catalpa Hall, Rt 522; Louisa **GS:** U **SP:** No info **VI:** No further data **P:** unk **BLW:** unk **RG:** N **MK:** N **PH:** unk **SS:** AK May 2006 **BS:** 04, May 06.

JACKSON, Thomas; b 1740; d 14 Aug 1843 **RU:** Soldier, Served in Benjamin Brigg's and Uriah Springer's companies under Col Gibson, 9th VA Regt **CEM:** Green Hill; GPS 39.15810, -77.97690; Berryville; Clarke **GS:** Y **SP:** No info **VI:** Originally bur on "Cherry Hill" farm GS, but not body, moved to Green Hill Cemetery sometime after 1842, BLW 200 acres awarded 24 Jun 1783 **P:** unk **BLW:** Y **RG:**Y **MK:** N **PH:** Y **SS:** F pg 40; SAR P-223823 **BS:** JLARC 24.

JACKSON, William; b 1742 Louisa Co; d 13 Sep 1781 **RU:** Lieutenant, Sworn in 11 Aug 1777. Retired 1 Jun 1778 **CEM:** Jackson Family; GPS unk; Catalpa Hall, Rt 522; Louisa **GS:** U **SP:** Susanah Goodwin **VI:** No further data **P:** unk **BLW:** unk **RG:** Y **MK:** unk **PH:** unk **SS:** E pg 412; SAR P-331423 **BS:** 04, May 06.

JACKSON, William Sullivan; b 1759, Dorset Co, MD; d 22 Aug 1849 **RU:** Soldier, Served in MD Line. Ent serv 1777 **CEM:** Jackson Family; GPS unk; Rt 658, along Bear Creek; Grayson **GS:** U **SP:** Mar (8 Aug 1814) Jemima Burnet (c1787-__) **VI:** Sol appl pen12 Nov 1834 Grayson Co. Widow appl pen 3 Oct 1853 Carroll Co age 66. W7883 **P:** Y **BLW:** unk **RG:** Y **MK:** unk **PH:** unk **SS:** K Vol 3 pg 10; CG pg 1815; SAR P-223840 **BS:** JLARC 4.

JACOBS, George; b 1755; d 1840 **RU:** Private, Was paid at Romney in 1775 **CEM:** Cub Creek; GPS unk; Off Rt 789 Cub Creek Rd at Beech Grove Community; Nelson **GS:** U **SP:** No info **VI:** No further data **P:** unk **BLW:** unk **RG:** Y **MK:** unk **PH:** unk **SS:** E pg 412; SAR P-223883 **BS:** JLARC 83.

JACOBS, John; b 1740, Germany; d 24 Feb 1811 **RU:** Captain/Patriot, Gave material aid to cause **CEM:** Cub Creek; GPS unk; Off Rt 789 Cub Creek Rd at Beech Grove Community; Nelson **GS:** U **SP:** Mar (21 May 1740, Amherst Co) Sarah (Sally) Crawford (26 Sep 1740-1832, Nelson Co) d/o David & Ann (Anderson) Crawford **VI:** No further data **P:** unk **BLW:** unk **RG:**Y **MK:** unk **PH:** unk **SS:** AL Cert Amherst Co; SAR P-223894 **BS:** JLARC 83.

JACOBS, John; b unk; d 1781 **RU:** Corporal, Capt Van Rensselears 4th Co, Col James Livingston's Battalion, NY line Regt. Killed in the battle at Yorktown **CEM:** Yorktown Victory Monument Tablet; GPS 38.28350, -78.54150; Yorktown; York **GS:** U **SP:** No info **VI:** No further data **P:** unk **BLW:** unk **RG:** Y **MK:** unk **PH:** unk **SS:** J-Yorktown Historian; AX pg 237; SAR P-223888 **BS:** JLARC 74.

JACOBS, William H; b unk; d unk **RU:** Private, Served in Frederick Co Militia **CEM:** Trenary Farm; GPS unk; Bayard Post Office; Warren **GS:** Y **SP:** No info **VI:** No further data **P:** unk **BLW:** unk **RG:** N **MK:** N **PH:** unk **SS:** E pg 412 **BS:** 50 pg 24.

JACOBY, Nicolas; b unk; d 1781 **RU:** Soldier, Served in Soissonnais Bn and died fr battle at Yorktown **CEM:** French Memorial; GPS 36.81944, -79.39933; Yorktown; York **GS:** U **SP:** No info **VI:** No further

---

RU=Rank/Unit	CEM=Cemetery	GS=Gravestone	SP=Spousal Information
VI=Other Veteran Info	P=Pension	BLW=Bounty/Land Warrant	RG=Registered Grave
MK=SAR/DAR Marker	PH=Photo	SS=Service Source	BS=Burial Source

214

data **P:** unk **BLW:** unk **RG:** Y **MK:** unk **PH:** unk **SS:** J-Yorktown Historian; SAR P-223939 **BS:** JLARC 1, 74.

JAGOUS, Francois; b unk; d 1781 **RU:** Seaman, Served on "Saint-Esprit" and died from Yorktown battle **CEM:** French Memorial; GPS 36.81944, -79.39933; Yorktown; York **GS:** U **SP:** No info **VI:** No further data **P:** unk **BLW:** unk **RG:** Y **MK:** unk **PH:** unk **SS:** J-Yorktown Historian; SAR P-223961 **BS:** JLARC 1, 74.

JAMAIS, Sebastian; b unk; d 1781 **RU:** Soldier, Served in Touraine Bn and died fr battle at Yorktown **CEM:** French Memorial; GPS 36.81944, -79.39933; Yorktown; York **GS:** U **SP:** No info **VI:** No further data **P:** unk **BLW:** unk **RG:** Y **MK:** unk **PH:** unk **SS:** J-Yorktown Historian; SAR P-223964 **BS:** JLARC 1, 74.

JAMES, Edward; b unk; d Aft 1814 **RU:** USN Lieutenant, Was Lt on sloop "Scorpion" under Capt Westcott 20 Sep 1776 **CEM:** Red Mill Farm; GPS unk; Hedgelawn Rd; Virginia Beach City **GS:** Y **SP:** No info **VI:** No further data **P:** unk **BLW:** unk **RG:** N **MK:** N **PH:** unk **SS:** L pg 206 **BS:** 93 Red Mill Fm.

JAMES, John; b 16 Mar 1709, Stafford Co; d bef 25 May 1778 2 Jan 1778 **RU:** Patriot, He or son John James Jr gave use of wagon & beef to cause **CEM:** James Family; GPS unk; Midland; Hamilton/Fauquier **GS:** Y **SP:** Mar (before 16 Aug 1738 Stafford Co) Dinah Allen (1716 Stafford Co-16 May 1800), dau of Willam & (-----) Allen **VI:** Son of William & (-----) James **P:** N **BLW:** N **RG:** Y **MK:** N **PH:** unk **SS:** H; D Vol III pg 873, 879, 880; SAR P-223994, DAR A061587 **BS:** 19 pg 131.

JAMES, Thomas; b 1759; d 1828 **RU:** Patriot, Performed civil service as clerk of Kingston Parish **CEM:** James Family; GPS 37.35835, -76.33166; end of Bar Neck Rd, Susan; Mathews **GS:** Y **SP:** Betsy Davis, (1763-1830) **VI:** Son of Thomas James & Elizabeth Basye (Basey) **P:** Y **BLW:** N **RG:** Y **MK:** unk **PH:** unk **SS:** B; SAR bio report submitted **BS:** 196.

JAMES, Thomas; b unk; d 1833 **RU:** Private?, Served in 9th & 15th Cont Lines of VA **CEM:** Goose Creek; GPS 39.11250, -77.69527; Rt 722, Lincoln; Loudoun **GS:** Y **SP:** No info **VI:** No further data **P:** unk **BLW:** unk **RG:** Y **MK:** N **PH:** unk **SS:** E pg 413 **BS:** 25 pg 160.

JAMESON, David; b 19 Aug 1752, Orange Co; d 2 Oct 1839 **RU:** Lieutenant/Patriot, Served in VA Line. Lived in Culpeper Co at enl. Served as JP and Col of Militia. Served under Capt John Jameson **CEM:** Masonic Cemetery; GPS 38.48530, -77.99470; 950 N Main, Culpeper; Culpeper **GS:** Y **SP:** Mary Mennis **VI:** Source 4 has pensioned in 1832. Served 2 sessions in VA Assembly. Sol appl pen 16 Aug 1832 Culpeper Co. S5607. DAR plaque placed 14 May 1883 to him and Col John Jameson, both members of the Culpeper Minute Men Battalion in 1775 **P:** Y **BLW:** unk **RG:** Y **MK:** Y SAR granite & DAR plaque **PH:** unk **SS:** CG pg 1821; SAR P-224038, DAR A061624 **BS:** JLARC 3; 196.

JAMESON, John; b 1751; d 20 Nov 1810 **RU:** Lieutenant Colonel, Served as Lt Col in Cont & VA Line and First Cont Dragoons. Wounded at Valley Forge **CEM:** Masonic Cemetery; GPS 38.48530, -77.99470; 950 N Main, Culpeper; Culpeper **GS:** Y **SP:** No info **VI:** Recd pen R15404, also VA 1/2 pay. Recd BLW #1164-450-10 Aug 1789. Settlement made 20 Mar 1783 (See Hening's Statutes at Large, Vol 10 pg 462) Inquiry made 17 May 1751 Norfolk VA. DAR plaque placed 14 May 1883 to him and David Jameson, both members of the Culpeper Minute Men in 1775, that states under Col John's orders he became the captor and executioner of one "Andre" for being a spy on 2 Oct 1780. Member Society of Cincinnati **P:** Y **BLW:** Y **RG:** Y **MK:** Y SAR & DAR plaque **PH:** unk **SS:** CG pg 1821; SAR P-224044 **BS:** JLARC 3; 196.

JARRETT (JARRATT), Devereux; b 6 Jan 1733, New Kent Co; d 29 Jan 1801 **RU:** Patriot, Gave material aid to cause **CEM:** Old Saponey Church; GPS 36.97110, -77.63610; E of Rt 709 on Rt 692; Dinwiddie **GS:** U **SP:** Martha Claiborne (1744-9 Mar 1826) d/o Durnell & Hannah (Ravenscrott) Claiborne **VI:** Son of Robert II & Sarah (Bradley) Jarratt. A plate on wall of church is to him and his wife. They were first bur in Diamond Hill in Amelia Co and remains moved to under the church **P:** N **BLW:** N **RG:** N **MK:** unk **PH:** unk **SS:** AL Ct Bk pg 21 Dinwiddie Co **BS:** 213 pg 49, 196.

JARVIS, John Sr; b 1754, Gloucester Co; d 1822 **RU:** Patriot, Was approved for claim of loss by British troops in York Co in 1781 **CEM:** Cedar Grove; GPS 36.57204, -80.02599; 301 Fort Lane Rd;

RU=Rank/Unit	CEM=Cemetery	GS=Gravestone	SP=Spousal Information
VI=Other Veteran Info	P=Pension	BLW=Bounty/Land Warrant	RG=Registered Grave
MK=SAR/DAR Marker	PH=Photo	SS=Service Source	BS=Burial Source

215

Portsmouth City **GS:** Y **SP:** Married 23 Nov 1794 in Trinity Ch, spouse not identified **VI:** No further data **P:** N **BLW:** N **RG:** YMK: Y SAR **PH:** unk **SS:** G pg 330; SAR P-336832 **BS:** 27 pg 121.

JAUBERT, Jean; b unk; d 1781 **RU:** Soldier, Served in Beaujolais Bn and died fr battle at Yorktown **CEM:** French Memorial; GPS 36.81944, -79.39933; Yorktown; York **GS:** U **SP:** No info **VI:** No further data **P:** unk **BLW:** unk **RG:** Y **MK:** unk **PH:** unk **SS:** J-Yorktown Historian; SAR P-224242 **BS:** JLARC 1, 74.

JAUBERT, Joseph; b unk; d 1781 **RU:** Soldier, Served in Beaujolais Bn and died fr battle at Yorktown **CEM:** French Memorial; GPS 36.81944, -79.39933; Yorktown; York **GS:** U **SP:** No info **VI:** No further data **P:** unk **BLW:** unk **RG:** Y **MK:** unk **PH:** unk **SS:** J-Yorktown Historian; SAR P-224243 **BS:** JLARC 1, 74.

JAUNEAU, Julien; b unk; d 1781 **RU:** Seaman, Served on "Palmier" and died from Yorktown battle **CEM:** French Memorial; GPS 36.81944, -79.39933; Yorktown; York **GS:** U **SP:** No info **VI:** No further data **P:** unk **BLW:** unk **RG:** Y **MK:** unk **PH:** unk **SS:** J-Yorktown Historian; SAR P-224248 **BS:** JLARC 1, 74.

JAYNE, Henry; b 14 Mar 1754, Florida, Orange Co, NY; d 23 Jan 1828 **RU:** Private/Patriot, Served in NY Troops. Also on 8 Jun 1775 signed the revolutionary pledge at Goshen, NY **CEM:** St Clair Bottom Primitive Baptist; GPS 36.76098, -81.64556; Jct Rts 600 & 660, Chilhowie; Smyth **GS:** U **SP:** Abigail Wheeler (31 Jan 1751 Orang Co, NY-12 July 1824) d/o James & (-----) Wheeler **VI:** Son of Isaac (1715-1781) & Mary (Jones) (1718-1818) Jayne. Died in Washington Co **P:** unk **BLW:** unk **RG:** N **MK:** unk **PH:** unk **SS:** B; CD **BS:** 196.

JEAN, Jean; b unk; d 1781 **RU:** Seaman, Served on "Languedoc" and died from Yorktown battle **CEM:** French Memorial; GPS 36.81944, -79.39933; Yorktown; York **GS:** U **SP:** No info **VI:** No further data **P:** unk **BLW:** unk **RG:** Y **MK:** unk **PH:** unk **SS:** J-Yorktown Historian; SAR P-224274 **BS:** JLARC 1, 74.

JEAN, Pierre; b unk; d 1781 **RU:** Soldier, Served in Gatinais Bn and died fr battle at Yorktown **CEM:** French Memorial; GPS 36.81944, -79.39933; Yorktown; York **GS:** U **SP:** No info **VI:** No further data **P:** unk **BLW:** unk **RG:** Y **MK:** unk **PH:** unk **SS:** J-Yorktown Historian; SAR P-224275 **BS:** JLARC 1, 74.

JEFF, Henry; b May 1704; d 8 Jun 1784 **RU:** Patriot, Gave material aid to cause **CEM:** Neff-Kagey; GPS 38.69443, -78.65895; Rt 827, Old Bridge Rd, New Market; Shenandoah **GS:** U **SP:** No info **VI:** No further data **P:** unk **BLW:** unk **RG:** N **MK:** unk **PH:** unk **SS:** AL Certificate, Hampshire Co (now WV) **BS:** 196.

JEFFERS (JEFFRIES), John; b 1761; d 14 Nov 1795 **RU:** Private/Patriot, Served in Capt Jeffries Co, Pittsylvania Co Militia. Gave material aid to cause in Mecklenburg Co **CEM:** Blandford; GPS 37.22433, -77.38604; 319 S Crater Rd; Petersburg City **GS:** Y **SP:** Deliah (-----) **VI:** Soldier drew BLW. Widow drew pen W26158; BLW 26840-160-55 was received by spouse. After war Capt in the Pershing Troop of Horse. Was a Magistrate **P:** Y **BLW:** Y **RG:** N **MK:** Y SAR monument **PH:** unk **SS:** E pg 415; AL Ct Bk pg 4, 9, 10 Mecklenburg Co; AP service rec, pension rec & BLW rec; CG pg 1826 **BS:** 99 pg 44; 196.

JEFFERSON, Thomas; b 13 Apr 1743, Shadwell, Albemarle Co; d 4 Jul 1826 **RU:** Private/Patriot, Served in Albemarle Co, Independent Co 1775, Author of the Declaration of Independence, Governor of VA, member of the Continental Congress **CEM:** Monticello; GPS 38.00829, -78.45520; 931 Thomas Jefferson Pkwy; Charlottesville City, Monticello/Albemarle **GS:** Y **SP:** Mar (1722) Martha Wayles Skelton (30 Oct 1748 Charles City Co-6 Sep 1782) d/o John (1715-1773) & Martha (Epps) (1721-1748) Wayles **VI:** Son of Peter (1707-1757) & Jane (Randolph) (1720-1776) Jefferson. First Secretary of State under Washington, 1789-1793; third U.S. President 1881-1809 **P:** unk **BLW:** unk **RG:** Y **MK:** Y SAR **PH:** unk **SS:** E pg 415; AS SAR applic; SAR P-224313, DAR A061895 **BS:** 80 vol 2 pg 201.

JENKINS, Thomas; b unk; d 15 Jan 1778 **RU:** Private, Capt Arrell's Co, 3rd VA Regt, Cont Line **CEM:** Rev War Court House Plaque; GPS; not determined; 4110 Chain Bridge Rd; Fairfax **GS:** Memorialized on plaque 2017 by Geo Washington Chapter, VASSAR **SP:** No spousal info **VI:** Died in service **P:** N **BLW:** N **RG:** Y **MK:** N **PH:** N **SS** E pg 416; AP Fold3 EH: sources; SAR P-224475 **BS:** None

RU=Rank/Unit	CEM=Cemetery	GS=Gravestone	SP=Spousal Information
VI=Other Veteran Info	P=Pension	BLW=Bounty/Land Warrant	RG=Registered Grave
MK=SAR/DAR Marker	PH=Photo	SS=Service Source	BS=Burial Source

216

JENKINS, William; b unk; d 28 Dec 1794 **RU:** Patriot, Gave material aid to cause **CEM:** Masonic Cemetery; GPS 38.30198, -77.46142; 900 Charles St; Fredericksburg City **GS:** U **SP:** No info **VI:** Bur with Masonic honors **P:** N **BLW:** N **RG:** N **MK:** Y SAR plaque **PH:** unk **SS:** AL Ct Bk 1 pg 51 **BS:** 196.

JENNINGS, Charles; b 1749; d 1 Jan 1816 **RU:** unk, Specific service is in the Lib of VA, Auditor's Acct 1780-1781, pg 164 **CEM:** St John's Episcopal; GPS unk; 100 W Queen's Way; Hampton City **GS:** U **SP:** Jane (-----) (1759-15 Oct 1781) **VI:** No further data **P:** unk **BLW:** unk **RG:** N **MK:** Y SAR plaque cem wall **PH:** unk **SS:** CZ pg 240 **BS:** 89, pg 78.

JENNINGS, Lewis; b 1765; d Apr 1831 **RU:** First Lieutenant, Was Ens Fauquier Militia 1781, 1st Lt for 6 mos Jun 1780 under John Marshall **CEM:** Jennings-Foster Family; GPS unk; 11446 FreemansFord; Fauquier **GS:** N **SP:** 1) Mar (4 Oct 1786 Fauquier Co, William Churchhlll security) Lucinda Bradfird (c1770-before 1820) 2) Mar (23 Oct 1820 Fauquier Co, Alex L. Kelley security) Mrs. Margaret Franklin, a widow (1786-Dec 1842) **VI:** No further data **P:** unk **BLW:** unk **RG:** N **MK:** N **PH:** N **SS:** AV; Fauquier Co Marriages pg 108 **BS:** 83, Inv# 13.

JENNINGS, William; b 1750; d 10 Oct 1791 **RU:** Captain, Served in VA Line. Commissioned as an officer in 1777, rec pay as Lt and Capt **CEM:** St John's Episcopal; GPS unk; 100 W Queen's Way; Hampton City **GS:** U **SP:** No info **VI:** Appl pen 23 Aug 1832 Elizabeth City Co. S5615 **P:** Y **BLW:** unk **RG:** N **MK:** Y SAR plaque cem wall **PH:** unk **SS:** CG pg 1834 **BS:** JLARC 4; 89, pg 79.

JENNINGS, William; b 1758; d 21 Aug 1838 **RU:** Seaman, Had VA Sea Service. Ent serv 1777 on ship "Patriot" **CEM:** St John's Episcopal; GPS unk; 100 W Queen's Way; Hampton City **GS:** U **SP:** No info **VI:** Recd Pen 1838. R15422. Also VA 1/2 pay (See N.A. Acc #874 #050092 1/2 Pay also papers in N.A. Acc #837, VA State Navy, YS File) **P:** Y **BLW:** unk **RG:** N **MK:** Y SAR plaque cem wall **PH:** unk **SS:** K Vol 3 pg 20; CG pg 1834 **BS:** JLARC 4, 117.

JERDONE, Francis; b 9 Feb1756; **d 29 Apr** 1841 **RU:** Patriot, Gave material aid to cause **CEM:** Jerdone Castle AKA Pottie-Boxdley; GPS not determined; 4.4 mi NW of Buckner; Louisa **GS:** N **SP:** Sarah Macon (21 Feb 1731, New Kent Co-23 Oct 1818), d/o William Macon (1694-1773) & Mary Hartwell (1703-1770) **VI:** No further data **P:** N **BLW:** N **RG:** N **MK:** N **PH:** unk **SS:** AL Cert Issued **BS:** 102 pg 291; 196.

JERIFAFIN, Jean; b unk; d 1781 **RU:** Soldier, Served in Bourbonnais Bn and died fr battle at Yorktown **CEM:** French Memorial; GPS 36.81944, -79.39933; Yorktown; York **GS:** U **SP:** No info **VI:** No further data **P:** unk **BLW:** unk **RG:** Y **MK:** unk **PH:** unk **SS:** J-Yorktown Historian; SAR P-224641 **BS:** JLARC 1 ,74.

JETER, Henry; b 1744, Caroline Co; d 24 Sep1821 **RU:** First Lieutenant, Served in Bedford Co Militia 28 May 1780 **CEM:** Jeter Family; GPS unk; Btw Centerville & Otterville; Bedford **GS:** N **SP:** Elizabeth Betty/Betsy Bell (1747-1833) **VI:** Moved with his parents at an early age to Amelia Co, and upon their death moved to Bedford Co. Govt Gr stone **P:** unk **BLW:** unk **RG:** Y **MK:** N **PH:** N **SS:** J- DAR Hatcher; E pg 418; SAR P-224681 **BS:** JLARC 2.

JOBART, Joseph; b unk; d 1781 **RU:** Seaman, Served on "Citoyen" and died from Yorktown battle **CEM:** French Memorial; GPS 36.81944, -79.39933; Yorktown; York **GS:** U **SP:** No info **VI:** No further data **P:** unk **BLW:** unk **RG:** Y **MK:** unk **PH:** unk **SS:** J-Yorktown Historian; SAR P-224817 **BS:** JLARC 1, 74.

JOHNS, William; b 1765; d 1856 **RU:** Captain, Served in Buckingham Co Militia 1777 **CEM:** Indian Graveyard; GPS unk; Bear Mtn, Rt 643; Amherst **GS:** N **SP:** No info **VI:** No further data **P:** unk **BLW:** unk **RG:** N **MK:** N **PH:** N **SS:** E pg 419 **BS:** 01 pg 70.

JOHNSON, Andrew; b unk; d 1785 **RU:** Private/Patriot, Served in Clark's Illinois Regt, VA State Troops. Gave material aid to cause in Prince Edward Co **CEM:** Blandford; GPS 37.22433, -77.38604; 319 S Crater Rd; Petersburg City **GS:** Y **SP:** No info **VI:** No further data **P:** unk **BLW:** unk **RG:** N **MK:** Y SAR monument **PH:** unk **SS:** G ps 479, 480; AL Ct Bk ps 34, 37; AP record **BS:** JLARC 1; 188 #1359; 196.

JOHNSON(JOHNSTON), Dennis; b c1765; d 19 Jul 1811 **RU:** Soldier, Possibly the soldier fr ME that was in the Battle of Saratoga in 1777 **CEM:** Old Presbyterian Meeting House; GPS 38.48528, -

---

RU=Rank/Unit
VI=Other Veteran Info
MK=SAR/DAR Marker

CEM=Cemetery
P=Pension
PH=Photo

GS=Gravestone
BLW=Bounty/Land Warrant
SS=Service Source

SP=Spousal Information
RG=Registered Grave
BS=Burial Source

217

77.23532; 323 S Fairfax St; Alexandria City **GS:** N **SP:** No info **VI:** No further data **P:** Y **BLW:** unk **RG:** Y **MK:** Y SAR plaque **PH:** N **SS:** J-NSSAR 1993 Reg; SAR P-225025; CI pension files **BS:** JLARC 1; 5.

JOHNSON, Isaac; b 1755, d 1817 **RU:** Corporal, 9th Cont Line, performed duty of procurement of guns for Capt Thomas Tweats (Theats) Co **CEM:** Johnson #4; GPS not determined; 4124 Pace Rd, loc right front of dwelling, Hadensville; Goochland **GS:** Unk **SP:** No spousal data **VI:** No further Data **P:** N **BLW:** N **RG:** N **MK:** N **PH:** N **SS:** E pg 420, G pg 480 **BS:** 196.

JOHNSON, James; b 1727, Goochland Co d 1825 **RU:** Patriot, paid personal property tax, considered a supply tax for Rev War expenses, 1782 Goochland Co **CEM:** James Johnson Plantation; GPS not determined; loc on Rt 669, after one mi turn left at driveway,Kidds store; Fluvanna **GS:** N **SP:** Mildred Mims **VI:** Son of John Johnson **P:** N **BLW:** N **RG:** N **MK:** N **PH:** N **SS:** DV image 03.pdf Goochland Co, 1782 **BS:** 196.

JOHNSON, Thomas Jr; b 6 Mar 1736 Louisa, King William Co; d 12 Aug 1803 **RU:** Captain, Served as commander of 10th Co, 3rd VA Regt of Foot 21 Mar 1776-Jan 1777 fr Louisa Co **CEM:** Roundabout Castle; GPS unk; 3998 Yanceyville Rd; Louisa **GS:** U **SP:** Elizabeth Meriwether (3 Mar 1745-14 Sep 1812) d/o Thomas (1713-1757) and Elizabeth (Thornton) (1713-1774) Meriwether **VI:** No further data **P:** unk **BLW:** unk **RG:** Y **MK:** unk **PH:** unk **SS:** AR Vol 2 pg 208; CE pg 39; DAR A063768; SAR P-328744 **BS:** JLARC 2; 196.

JOHNSTON, David; b 1726 Ireland; d 1786 **RU:** Private, Served in Capt James Maxwell's Co, Montgomery Co Militia **CEM:** Phlegar Farm; GPS unk; Rt 626, Ripplemead; Giles, Montgomery **GS:** U **SP:** Annie Abbott (___-1813) **VI:** No further data **P:** unk **BLW:** unk **RG:** Y **MK:** unk **PH:** unk **SS:** J- DAR Hatcher; G pg 237; SAR P-225702 **BS:** JLARC 2; 196.

JOHNSTON, George; b unk; d 1 Oct 1777 **RU:** Lt Col, served 3 yrs, was aide to Gen Washington, 20 Jan 1777 to death 1 Oct 1777 **CEM:** Rev War Court House Plaque; GPS not determined; 4110 Chain, Bridge Rd; Fairfax **GS:** Memorialized on plaque 2017 by Geo Washington Chapter, VASSAR **SP:** No spousal info **VI:** Died in service **P:** N **BLW:** Y 6000 acres to heirs rec'd 20 Jul 1786 **RG:** N **MK:** N **PH:** N **SS** C sect II, pg 456; E pg 423: F pg 1370; EH: sources **BS:** None.

JOHNSTON, John; b 15 Nov 1761; d 8 Apr 1845 **RU:** Private, Served in Capt Rankins Co Augusta Co Militia **CEM:** West Hill; GPS 37.29313, -80.06753; Boon St; Salem City **GS:** Y **SP:** Mar (16 Sep 1794) Elizabeth Bell **VI:** Son of Zachariah (1742-1800) & Ann (Robertson) (1742-1818) Johnston. Died in Augusta Co **P:** unk **BLW:** unk **RG:** N **MK:** N **PH:** unk **SS:** E pg 424 **BS:** 122, pg 242.

JOHNSTON, William; b 1752, Fairfax Co; d 13 Apr 1815 **RU:** Captain, Served in VA Line. Served in 7th VA Cont Regt Nov 1779-May 1780. Commander of co in 3rd VA Regt. Was captured 1781 and POW to end of war **CEM:** Belle Vale; GPS unk; Belle Vale Manor, Doeg's Run; Fairfax **GS:** U **SP:** Mar (1785) Ann Simpson (1763, Fairfax Co-4 Mar 1815) **VI:** Recd BLW #1166-300-5 Jul 1799 **P:** unk **BLW:** Y **RG:** Y **MK:** N **PH:** unk **SS:** J- DAR Hatcher; CG pg 1865; CE pg 32, 41; SAR P-225837 **BS:** JLARC 2.

JOHNSTON, William Z; b 1742; d unk **RU:** Captain/Patriot, Gave material aid to cause **CEM:** Tinkling Spring Presbyterian; GPS 38.08472, -78.98278; 30 Tinkling Spring Dr, Fishersville; Augusta **GS:** N **SP:** No info **VI:** No further data **P:** unk **BLW:** unk **RG:** N **MK:** N **PH:** N **SS:** J- DAR Hatcher; AL Lists 1 pg 10 Augusta Co **BS:** JLARC 2.

JOHNSTON (JOHNSON), Peter; b unk; d 18 Dec 1831 **RU:** Officer, Served in Lee's Legion **CEM:** Johnston; GPS unk; 1 mi on ext of Valley St, Abingdon; Washington **GS:** U **SP:** 1) Mary (-----) 2) Mar (13 Dec 1831 home of Charles Copland Esq. Richmond VA) Ann or Anne Bernard (c1774-29 Jun 1865), d/o John & Henningham (Carrington) Bernard Esq. According to nephew who appl for pen, mentally incompetent when she wrote will. **VI:** Speaker of VA House of Delegates. Member Society of the Cincinatti. Was judge when he mar 2nd time. Grave at #130 in Source 80. Sol had recd pen under act of 15 May 1828. Widow appl BLW 4 May 1855 Richmond City. W27629. BLW #1171-200-9 Sep 1789 **P:** Y **BLW:** Y **RG:** N **MK:** unk **PH:** unk **SS:** K Vol 3 pg 34; CG pg 1864 **BS:** JLARC 4, 34, 80.

JOHNSTON (JOHNSON), Zachariah; b 1742, near Staunton, Augusta Co; d 7 Jan 1800 **RU:** Captain/Patriot, Served in VA Militia, Was in campaigns against Indians in west and Battle of Jamestown VA 1781. Was member of House of Delegates fr Augusta & Rockbridge. Was leader in passage of religious freedom. Was member of delegation to ratify constitution **CEM:** Stonewall Jackson

---

RU=Rank/Unit	CEM=Cemetery	GS=Gravestone	SP=Spousal Information
VI=Other Veteran Info	P=Pension	BLW=Bounty/Land Warrant	RG=Registered Grave
MK=SAR/DAR Marker	PH=Photo	SS=Service Source	BS=Burial Source

218

Memorial; GPS 37.78128, -79.44604; 314 S Main St; Lexington City **GS:** Y **SP:** Ann Robertson **VI:** Source 79 says he moved fr Augusta to Rockbridge in 1790. Died in Rockbridge Co **P:** unk **BLW:** unk **RG:** Y **MK:** N **PH:** unk **SS:** AD; SAR P-225848, DAR A064126 **BS:** JLARC 1, 2, 63, 79.

JOLIVET, Francois; b unk; d 1781 **RU:** Soldier, Served in Bourbonnais Bn and died fr battle at Yorktown **CEM:** French Memorial; GPS 36.81944, -79.39933; Yorktown; York **GS:** U **SP:** No info **VI:** No further data **P:** unk **BLW:** unk **RG:** Y **MK:** unk **PH:** unk **SS:** J-Yorktown Historian; SAR P-225873 **BS:** JLARC 1, 74.

JOLY (JOLLEY), (-----); b unk; d 1781 **RU:** Soldier, Service unit not determined. Died fr battle at Yorktown **CEM:** French Memorial; GPS 36.81944, -79.39933; Yorktown; York **GS:** U **SP:** No info **VI:** No further data **P:** unk **BLW:** unk **RG:** Y **MK:** unk **PH:** unk **SS:** J-NSSAR 1993 Reg; SAR P-225901 **BS:** JLARC 1.

JONES, Abraham; b 5 Mar 1761; d 2 Dec 1851 **RU:** Private Ent service 1779, Buckingham Co serving 3 years in Capt Thomas Company, Col Francis Taylor's VA Regt **CEM:** Abraham Jones Family; GPS 37.653993,-78.442092; loc Melita Rd (Rt 622), Arvonia; Buckingham **GS:** Y broken **SP:** Nancy or Margaret Garrett (28 Feb 1770-24 Jul 1836) **VI:** Rec'd pen # S46452 and in 1828 BLW #1893 in Buckingham Co **P:** Y **BLW:** Y **RG:** Y **MK:** N **PH:** N **SS:** G pg 452; K vol 3, pg 36; DAR A061772; SAR P-225915 **BS:** 196

JONES, Benjamin

JONES, Benjamin Dr; b 5 Feb 1752, Culpeper Co; d 22 Aug 1843 **RU:** Surgeon, Was Surgeon 3rd VA Regt. **CEM:** Oakwood; GPS 36.38690, -79.88000; 199 Cemetery St; Martinsville City, Henry **GS:** Y **SP:** Mar (7 Sep 1776 Prince William Co) Elizabeth de Remi (Reamey/Renii) (5 Feb 1756-22 Apr 1856) **VI:** Politician. Several times represented Henry Co in state legislature. Died in Henry Co. Govt Gr stone **P:** N **BLW:** N **RG:** Y **MK:** N **PH:** N **SS:** DD; SAR P-225974, DAR A061918 **BS:** JLARC 1, 2,102.

JONES, Charles; b unk; d 1810 **RU:** Seaman, Served in Navy. Had sea service until 1781 **CEM:** Cub Creek; GPS unk; Off Rt 789 Cub Creek Rd at Beech Grove Community; Nelson **GS:** U **SP:** Elizabeth (-----) **VI:** Administration granted to William Woodward of Norfolk for 1/2 pay pen. R50 **P:** Y **BLW:** unk **RG:** Y **MK:** unk **PH:** unk **SS:** K Vol 3 pg 37; SAR P-226002 **BS:** JLARC 83.

JONES, Charles G; b unk; d 1818 **RU:** Patriot, Gave material aid to cause **CEM:** St John's Episcopal; GPS 37.53183, -77.41958; 2401 E Broad St; Richmond City **GS:** Y **SP:** No info **VI:** No further data **P:** N **BLW:** N **RG:** N **MK:** N **PH:** unk **SS:** AL Lists I pg 2 **BS:** 28 pg 462.

JONES, Churchill; b 1748, Middlesex Co; d Sep 1822 **RU:** Major/Patriot, Provided 1655# beef to Lafayette Jun 1781 **CEM:** Ellwood Burial Ground; GPS unk; Wilderness Battlefield; Orange **GS:** N **SP:** 1) Judith Churchill 2) Mary Thornton Champe 3) Martha Selden Douglas **VI:** Lived at "Chatham" in Stafford Co. Appl pen 1806 fr "Chatham." BLW 304 issued 3 Jan 1807. Died at Woodville Plantation, Orange Co. QLF says he d in 1828 **P:** Y **BLW:** unk **RG:** Y **MK:** Y **SAR** **PH:** N **SS:** D Vol 2 pg 741; K Vol 3 pg 37; SAR P-226013 **BS:** 04.

JONES, Daniel; b 1748; d 16 Dec 1822 **RU:** Patriot, Furnished supplies to VA troops **CEM:** Jones-Nunn Family; GPS 37.21246, -76.47290; Farmville Ln, Norge; James City Co **GS:** Y **SP:** Mary Morris **VI:** No further data **P:** N **BLW:** N **RG:** N **MK:** N **PH:** unk **SS:** AL Ct Bk pg 10 **BS:** 32 Boelt; 04.

JONES, Edward; b 15 Dec 1754, New York; d 17 Sep 1829 **RU:** Private/Patriot, Treasury official under George Washington. Served in Capt Ackerson Co, Col Hays Regt, NY State **CEM:** Arlington National; GPS 38.88377, -77.06535; Jefferson Davis Hwy Rt 110; Arlington **GS:** Y Lot 278, officer sect **SP:** No info **VI:** Died age 78 yr 9 mos (Richmond Enquirer, 22 Sep 1829) **P:** unk **BLW:** N **RG** N **MK:** unk **PH:** unk **SS:** H; BS pg 405; SAR applic **BS:** JLARC 76; 196.

JONES, Gabriel Jr; b 1740, Essex; d bef 20 Oct 1777 **RU:** Captain, Served in VA State Line under Col George Gibson, joined the State Marines and died in service in 1777 **CEM:** Slaughter-Jones Family; GPS 38.45500, -77.84131; Stone's Mill Rd Rt 676, LaGrange; Culpeper **GS:** U **SP:** 1) Mary Waller 2) Martha Slaughter **VI:** Son of Gabriel Jones and Mary (Johnson) Edmondson. Created first Marine unit in Fredericksburg in 1775, which was abandoned and he joined the 1st VA Regiment. Govt stone styles

---

RU=Rank/Unit	CEM=Cemetery	GS=Gravestone	SP=Spousal Information
VI=Other Veteran Info	P=Pension	BLW=Bounty/Land Warrant	RG=Registered Grave
MK=SAR/DAR Marker	PH=Photo	SS=Service Source	BS=Burial Source

him Capt, Virginia State Navy **P:** unk **BLW:** Y **RG:** N **MK:** N **PH:** unk **SS:** SAR P-226121 **BS:** 29 pg 61; 196.

JONES, George; b 1763, MD; d 12 May 1843 **RU:** Private, with service in MD **CEM:** Old Jones Place; GPS unk; Rt 600 nr Troy; Fluvanna **GS:** Y **SP:** No info **VI:** No further data **P:** unk **BLW:** unk **RG:** N **MK:** N **PH:** unk **SS:** BJ pg 95 **BS:** 164 Old Jones.

JONES, Henry; b 1750, d 1807 **RU:** Private, Served in 9th VA Regt, Cont Line **CEM:** Jones Family; GPS unk; Left fr US 250 on Rt 614 traveling fr McDowell. Farm of Clay Botkins; Highland **GS:** U **SP:** 1) (-----) 2) Emily Jane Carlile **VI:** No further data **P:** unk **BLW:** unk **RG:** Y **MK:** unk **PH:** unk **SS:** SAR P-226145 **BS:** JLARC 62, 103.

JONES, Holmes; b 15 Jun 1758, Sussex Co; d 4 Oct 1810 **RU:** Sergeant, Served in Capt Edmunds Co, Lt Col Innes Regt, 15th Cont Line **CEM:** Jones Family; GPS unk; See US Senate Doc 1937 vol 1, serial 10173 DAR Report; Sussex **GS:** U **SP:** Mar (17 Oct 1783) Susanna Moss (4 Oct 1760, Sussex Co-aft 21 Jun 1816) **VI:** No further data **P:** unk **BLW:** unk **RG:** Y **MK:** unk **PH:** unk **SS:** DAR Ancestor #A062199; J- DAR Hatcher; E pg 426; DD; SAR P-226152 **BS:** JLARC 2.

JONES, Jacob; b unk; d 1781 **RU:** Soldier, Served fr MA, and died fr the battle at Yorktown **CEM:** Yorktown Victory Monument Tablet; GPS 38.28350, -78.54150; Yorktown; York **GS:** U **SP:** No info **VI:** No further data **P:** unk **BLW:** unk **RG:** Y **MK:** unk **PH:** unk **SS:** J-Yorktown Historian; SAR P-226176 **BS:** JLARC 74.

JONES, John; b 1760; d 18 May 1842 **RU:** Private, Capt Thomas Wagner's Co at Fort Holland; served long enough to receive pen **CEM:** St Pauls Episcopal Ch; GPS 37.829213, -76.968359; loc Rt 360 W at Mills Tavern jct with Minway Rd; Essex **GS:** Y **SP:** No spousal data **VI:** rec'd pen in Essex Co **P:** Y **BLW:** N **RG:** N **MK:** N **PH:** N **SS:** Epg 427; G pg 370 **BS:** 196

JONES, John; b 1752; d 1797 **RU:** Patriot, Gave material aid to the cause **CEM:** St John's Episcopal; GPS unk; 100 W Queen's Way; Hampton City **GS:** Y **SP:** No info **VI:** No further data **P:** N **BLW:** N **RG:** N **MK:** N **PH:** unk **SS:** AL Ct Bk pg 4,6 **BS:** 89 pg 81.

JONES, John; b 1738; d 1784 **RU:** Patriot, Gave material aid to the cause **CEM:** Jones Family; GPS unk; Rt 742 Nicholas St; Hanover **GS:** N **SP:** No info **VI:** No further data **P:** N **BLW:** N **RG:** N **MK:** N **PH:** N **SS:** AL Ct Bk lt l pg 34 **BS:** 31 vol 2 pg 75.

JONES, Joseph; b 23 Aug 1749 Cedar Grove, Petersburg; d 9 Feb 1824 **RU:** Captain/Patriot, Commanded a Co in Dinwiddie Co Militia, and was a Captain VA Line 1776-1779. As patriot had public service as a member of the Committee of Public Safety, 1775 **CEM:** Blandford; GPS 37.22433, -77.38604; 319 S Crater Rd; Petersburg City **GS:** Y **SP:** 1) Nanny Call 2) Jane Atkinson **VI:** Postmaster of Petersburg and Collector of Port 1821-24. Was Colonel of Militia 1783 and Major General 1802 **P:** unk **BLW:** unk **RG:** Y **MK:** Y SAR monument **PH:** Y **SS:** J-NSSAR 1993 Reg; G pg 479, 480; AL Ct Bk pg 34, 37; SAR P-226322, DAR A062398 **BS:** JLARC 1; 196.

JONES, Joseph; b 172***, King George Co; d 28 Oct 1805 **RU:** Commissary Officer/Patriot, Was commissary officer at Fredericksburg factory 1775-6. Gave material aid to cause. Elected 5th VA Convention 1775 **CEM:** Corporate Burial Ground GPS not determined, loc where Hurcamp Park is today Fredericksburg City **GS:** U **SP:** Mary Taliaferro d/o John & (-----) Taliaferro of Spotsylvania Co **VI:** Son of James & Hester (-----) Jones. Member of state convention in 1788 which ratified US Constitution **P:** unk **BLW:** unk **RG:** N **MK:** unk **PH:** unk **SS:** D Fredericksburg; E pg 427; CZ **BS:** 138 Joseph Jones, VA.

JONES, Michael; b unk; d 1821 **RU:** Private, Served in Mitchel's Co, 12th VA **CEM:** Jones; GPS unk; Rt 24, S of Togson, abt 2.5 mi then 1.5 mi on private road; Buckingham **GS:** U **SP:** No info **VI:** Has Govt GS **P:** N **BLW:** N **RG:** Y **MK:** N **PH:** unk **SS:** E pg 428; SAR P-226375 **BS:** JLARC 59.

JONES, Nicholas; b 3 Jul 1760; d 7 Apr 1831 or 1834 **RU:** Private, Ent serv Amherst Co in VA Line **CEM:** Neriah Baptist; GPS 37.78778, -79.36482; Jct Rts 631 & 706, South River; Rockbridge **GS:** U **SP:** Mar (3 Jul 1783 Rockbridge Co) Amarella (-----) (1765-aft 3 Apr 1838) **VI:** Stone Broken. Widow appl pen 3 Apr 1738 Rockbridge Co age 73. W7907 **P:** Y **BLW:** unk **RG:** N **MK:** unk **PH:** unk **SS:** CG pg 1878 **BS:** 196.

RU=Rank/Unit	CEM=Cemetery	GS=Gravestone	SP=Spousal Information
VI=Other Veteran Info	P=Pension	BLW=Bounty/Land Warrant	RG=Registered Grave
MK=SAR/DAR Marker	PH=Photo	SS=Service Source	BS=Burial Source

220

JONES, Peter; b 1751; d 7 Apr 1815 **RU:** Patriot, Gave material aid to the cause **CEM:** Locust Grove; GPS unk; Rt 66 abt 5 mi S of Victoria; Amelia **GS:** N **SP:** Mar (Lunenburg Co) Jane Stokes, d/o David & (-----) Stokes **VI:** No further data **P:** N **BLW:** N **RG:** Y **MK:** N **PH:** N **SS:** AL Ct Bk pg 64, 69; SAR P-226432 **BS:** 171 Locust Gr; 172.

JONES, Richard; b unk; d 1781 **RU:** Private, Was killed in the Battle of Green Spring near Williamsburg in 1781 **CEM:** Williamsburg Land Conservancy; GPS unk; 5000 New Point Rd; Williamsburg City **GS:** N **SP:** No info **VI:** No further data **P:** unk **BLW:** unk **RG:** N **MK:** N **PH:** N **SS:** AU, SAR study **BS:** 32.

JONES, Robert; b unk; d unk **RU:** Patriot, Gave material aid to cause **CEM:** Wade-Cox; GPS unk; Check property records, Floyd and Montgomery Co for loc of residence; Floyd **GS:** U **SP:** No info **VI:** Cem not listed with this name in Floyd Co Hist Soc listings **P:** N **BLW:** N **RG:** Y **MK:** unk **PH:** unk **SS:**; J- DAR Hatcher; AL Ct Bk pg 19 Henry Co; SAR P-226466 **BS:** JLARC 2; 80 vol 2 pg 212.

JONES, Robert Jr; b 1736; d 1820 **RU:** Patriot, Gave material aid to cause **CEM:** Ward Feazell; GPS unk; Ferrum; Franklin **GS:** U **SP:** Martha Riley (1736-___) **VI:** Son of Robert (1696-1775) & Margaret (Van Metre) (1706-1775) Jones **P:** unk **BLW:** unk **RG:** N **MK:** unk **PH:** unk **SS:** Al Ct Bk pg 19 Henry Co **BS:** 196.

JONES, Strother; b 1758; d 1790 **RU:** Captain, Served in VA Cont Line **CEM:** Jones Family; GPS unk; Vanchese; Frederick **GS:** U **SP:** Frances Thornton **VI:** Daughter Nancy Ann Jones appl pen 7 Nov 1855 Columbia Co, GA. BLW #2442-300 **P:** unk **BLW:** Y **RG:** Y **MK:** unk **PH:** unk **SS:** J- DAR Hatcher; CG pg 1882; SAR P-226542 **BS:** JLARC 2.

JONES, Thomas; b 6 Nov 1754, Bedford Co; d 1826 **RU:** Ensign/Patriot, Was Ensign 24 Apr 1781, Bedford Co Militia. Gave material aid to cause **CEM:** Blenheim; GPS 37.13150, -78.5700; Rt 648, Gladys; Campbell **GS:** N **SP:** Mar (1775) Betty Jones (09 Nov 1757, Bedford Co-13 Nov 1837) **VI:** No further data **P:** unk **BLW:** unk **RG:** Y **MK:** N **PH:** N **SS:** AL Ct Bk pg 3, 10 Campbell Co; AZ pg 187; SAR P-226596 **BS:** JLARC 36.

JONES, Thomas; b 21 May 1748, Frederick Co, MD; d 22 Mar 1830 **RU:** First Lieutenant, Served in Henry Co Militia 1780 **CEM:** Pigg River Primitive Baptist; GPS 36.96913, -80.07368; Rt 750 nr Callaway; Franklin **GS:** N **SP:** Mar (1770 Pittsylvania Co) Joanna Hill (24 Jan 1752 Lunenburg Co-2 Mar 1833 Callaway, Franklin Co). d/o Robert (1713-1778) & Violett (Linus) (1725-1808) Hill **VI:** Son of Robert (1696-1796) & Mary Marie Jansen (VanMeter) (1709-1796) Jones. Was a minister **P:** unk **BLW:** unk **RG:** N **MK:** N **PH:** N **SS:** E pg 429; AK cites DAR app **BS:** 04 cites DAR appl.

JONES, Thomas; b unk; d unk **RU:** Patriot, Gave material aid to cause **CEM:** Jones Family; GPS unk; Crooked Run; Culpeper **GS:** U **SP:** No info **VI:** No further data **P:** N **BLW:** N **RG:** Y **MK:** unk **PH:** unk **SS:** J-NSSAR 1993 Reg; AL Cert Culpeper Co **BS:** JLARC 1.

JONES, Thomas; b 1755; d 8 Jul 1835 **RU:** Orderly Sergeant, Served in VA Line. Ent serv Amherst Co that became Nelson. Enlisted US Army 1776, 10th Regt, VA Line later 6th Regt. Was in Battle of Brandywine and Germantown. Was wounded but served 3 yrs **CEM:** Jones-Clarkson; GPS 37.79438, -78.98530; Persimmon Hill Rd, Roseland; Nelson **GS:** N **SP:** Mar (17 Oct 1780) Catharine Clarkson (1 or 11 Jun 1760-1847) **VI:** Sol appl pen 8 Jul 1835 at Jonesboro in Nelson Co. Died in Jonesboro, Nelson Co. Widow appl pen 19 Oct 1838 Nelson Co. Recd BLW of 200 acres. W7905 **P:** Y **BLW:** Y **RG:** Y **MK:** unk **PH:** N **SS:** CG pg 1883; SAR P-226590 **BS:** JLARC 4, 83; 196.

JONES, Thomas C Sr; b 1736; d 15 Oct 1818 **RU:** Patriot, Gave material aid to cause **CEM:** South River Meeting House; GPS 37.37246, -79.19194; 5810 Fort Ave; Lynchburg City **GS:** U **SP:** Mar (abt 1765) Hannal Erwin (Irwin) (1747 Augusta Co-1826) **VI:** Cem records indicate b 1735, d 1815 with perhaps spouse Patsey, b 1743, d 1825 **P:** N **BLW:** N **RG:** N **MK:** unk **PH:** unk **SS:** AL Cert 1 Bedford Co **BS:** 196; 221..(**JONES,** Thomas V see Appendix G Addenda)

JONES, Thomas Sr; b c1746 Pittsylvania; d 1786 **RU:** First Lieutenant, Served in Pittsylvania Co Militia 27 Sep 1775 **CEM:** Jones Family; GPS 36.84300, -79.26227; Nr Mtn Top, 7 mi E Chatham; Pittsylvania **GS:** Y **SP:** Mar (12 May 1763) Mary (-----) (___-1798 Pittsylvania Co) **VI:** No further data **P:** unk **BLW:** unk **RG:** Y **MK:** N **PH:** unk **SS:** G pg 284; DD; SAR P-226692 **BS:** 174, 91

RU=Rank/Unit	CEM=Cemetery	GS=Gravestone	SP=Spousal Information
VI=Other Veteran Info	P=Pension	BLW=Bounty/Land Warrant	RG=Registered Grave
MK=SAR/DAR Marker	PH=Photo	SS=Service Source	BS=Burial Source

221

JONES, Walter; b 18 Dec 1745; d 31 Dec 1815 **RU:** Staff Officer/Physician General, Served in Hospital Middle Department 11 Apr-1 Jul 1777. **CEM:** Hayfield; GPS unk; Nr Callao; Northumberland, Westmoreland **GS:** U **SP:** Mar (c1773) Alice Flood **VI:** Rep in 5th Congress 1797-1799. VA House of Delegates 1802-03. US Congress 1803-1811 **P:** unk **BLW:** unk **RG:**Y **MK:** unk **PH:** unk **SS:** E pg 429; SAR P-226606, DAR A062760 **BS:** 201 pg 7397.

JONES, William; b 25 Oct 1734, Caroline Co; d Aft 1788 **RU:** Patriot, Gave material aid to cause **CEM:** Marlfield Plantation; GPS 37.44928, -76.62239; Rt 610 at 3780 Pebble Ln, Marlfield; Gloucester **GS:** U **SP:** Mar (1766) Lucy (Taliaferro) Carter, the widow of Charles Carter (1707-1764). D/o William & Anne (Walker) Talioferro. **VI:** Purchased Marlfield 1782 fr John Buckner, who built it 1732. Among first VA planters to use marl in agriculture **P:** N **BLW:** N **RG:** Y **MK:** unk **PH:** unk **SS:** AL Ct Bk IV pg 184 Caroline Co; SAR P-226618 **BS:** 196.

JONES, William; b 1730, Mecklenburg Co; d 15 Apr 1818 **RU:** Patriot, Gave material aid to the cause **CEM:** Dishman Family at Pine Hill; GPS unk; Off Rt 621, Shiloh; King George **GS:** U **SP:** Elizabeth Buckner **VI:** No further data **P:** N **BLW:** N **RG:** N **MK:** unk **PH:** unk **SS:** AL Ct Bk pg 3; Commissioner's Bk II pg 336 **BS:** 196.

JONES, William; b 1750, Middlesex Co; d 1845 **RU:** Patriot, Provided 700 lbs beef to Lafayette June 1781 **CEM:** Ellwood Burial Ground; GPS unk; Wilderness Battlefield; Orange **GS:** N **SP:** 1) Betty Churchill 2) Lucinda Gordon Jones Green **VI:** Died in Ellwood, Orange Co **P:** N **BLW:** N **RG:** Y **MK:** N **PH:** N **SS:** D Vol 2 pg 741; SAR P-226628 **BS:** 04.

JONES, William; b unk; d 12 Nov 1828 **RU:** Private, Served in VA Line **CEM:** Cross Road Baptist; GPS 36.62690, -79.04780; 1098 Flint Rock Rd, South Boston; Halifax **GS:** N **SP:** Mar (9 Oct 1776) Martha (-- ---) (1756-18 Aug 1843 Carroll Co TN) **VI:** Widow appl pen 25 Aug 1843 Carroll Co, TN R5724 **P:** Y **BLW:** N **RG:**Y **MK:** unk **PH:** N **SS:** CG pg 1886; SAR P-226626 **BS:** 196.

JONES, William; b unk; d 1781 **RU:** Private, Was killed in the Battle of Green Springs near Williamsburg in 1781 **CEM:** Williamsburg Land Conservancy; GPS unk; 5000 New Point Rd; Williamsburg City **GS:** N **SP:** Mar (Dec 1776 James City Co) Elizabeth Roberts **VI:** No further data **P:** unk **BLW:** unk **RG:** N **MK:** N **PH:** N **SS:** AU SAR study **BS:** 32 Willbg chap.

JONES, William (John) Paul; b 6 Jul 1747; d 18 Jul 1792 **RU:** Commodore, Cont Navy as 1st Lt 22 Dec 1775 on "Alfred." Capt on ship "Ranger" 14 Feb 1777. Capt on "Bonhomme Richard" 1779; later served as Commodore **CEM:** St George's Episcopal; GPS unk; 905 Princess Anne; Fredericksburg City **GS:** U **SP:** No info **VI:** Honorary GS in St Georges Cem in Fredericksburg erected by his brother. Died in Paris, France. Remains fr burial in Paris moved Apr 1906 to US Navy Academy Chapel, Annapolis MD **P:** unk **BLW:** unk **RG:** Y **MK:** unk **PH:** Y **SS:** J-NSSAR 2000 Reg; L pg 210; SAR P-226656 **BS:** JLARC 76.

JORDAN, Andrew; b 1760, d 8 Sep 1818 **RU:** Private Capt Peter Hull's Co, 2d Battalion, Augusta Co Militia in Yorktown campaign 1781 **CEM:** William Varner Family; GPS unk; Spring Run, Palo Alto; Highland **GS:** Yes **SP:** No spousal info **VI:** Serv inscribed on grave stone **P:** N **BLW:** N **RG:** N **MK:** N, **PH:** N **SS:** AZ pgs148, 149 **BS:** 196.

JORDAN, John; b 10 Apr 1757; d 1835 **RU:** Captain, Taken prisoner in Charleston SC in 2nd Cont Line 12 May 1780. Exchanged Apr 1781. Commanded a co 8 Sep 1781. Wounded in battle of Edge Hill **CEM:** Locust Bottom Church; GPS 37.74170, -79.8150; Eagle Rock; Botetourt **GS:** U **SP:** Catharine/Catherine Beale **VI:** Source 4 has Member of Society of Cincinnati. Pensioned 1811. Recd BLW 4666 acres **P:** Y **BLW:** Y **RG:**Y **MK:** N **PH:** unk **SS:** J- DAR Hatcher; E pg 430; CZ pg 248; BX pg 428; SAR P-226775 **BS:** JLARC 2.

JORDAN, John; b unk; d Feb 1795 **RU:** Private, Service information not determined **CEM:** Old Christ Church Episcopal; GPS 38.80625, -77.04718; 118 N Washington St; Alexandria City **GS:** N **SP:** No info **VI:** Burial permit issued 17 Feb 1795 **P:** unk **BLW:** unk **RG:** N **MK:** N **PH:** N **SS:** Z pg 36 **BS:** 20 pg 149.

JORDAN, Robert; b 17 May 1742, New London, Chester Co, PA, d 14 Aug 1835 **RU:** Private, enlisted Mar 1 1776 Morristown, NY in Capt Steele's Co, Col McDougall's NY Regt and was in battles of White Plains and Trenton. Discharged Mar 1 1778 **CEM:** Jordan Family; GPS Not determined; Old Jordan homestead loc SW of Smithfield on Rt 682; Isle of Wight **GS:** Unk **SP:** mar (1764) Margaret Gilmore

RU=Rank/Unit	CEM=Cemetery	GS=Gravestone	SP=Spousal Information
VI=Other Veteran Info	P=Pension	BLW=Bounty/Land Warrant	RG=Registered Grave
MK=SAR/DAR Marker	PH=Photo	SS=Service Source	BS=Burial Source

222

(1743-1799), d/o Robert Gilmore of Londonderry, NH **VI:** Pen Rec indicates he died 2 Mar 1835. Son of Joshua Josiah Jordan (1708-1785) and Mourning Ricks (1708-1792) **P:** Y **BLW:** N **RG:** N **MK:** N, **PH:** N **SS:** AP-Pen file Fold3 **BS:** 196.

JOSEPH, Jean; b unk; d 1781 **RU:** Seaman, Served on "Duc De Bourgogne" and died from Yorktown battle **CEM:** French Memorial; GPS 36.81944, -79.39933; Yorktown; York **GS:** U **SP:** No info **VI:** No further data **P:** unk **BLW:** unk **RG:** Y **MK:** unk **PH:** unk **SS:** J-Yorktown Historian; SAR P-226855 **BS:** JLARC 1, 74.

JOSSARD, Jean; b unk; d 1781 **RU:** Soldier, Served in Soissonnais Bn and died fr battle at Yorktown **CEM:** French Memorial; GPS 36.81944, -79.39933; Yorktown; York **GS:** U **SP:** No info **VI:** No further data **P:** unk **BLW:** unk **RG:** Y **MK:** unk **PH:** unk **SS:** J-Yorktown Historian; SAR P-226908 **BS:** JLARC 1, 74.

JOSSE, Jean; b unk; d 1781 **RU:** Seaman, Served on "Hercule" and died from Yorktown battle **CEM:** French Memorial; GPS 36.81944, -79.39933; Yorktown; York **GS:** U **SP:** No info **VI:** No further data **P:** unk **BLW:** unk **RG:** Y **MK:** unk **PH:** unk **SS:** J-Yorktown Historian; SAR P-226909 **BS:** JLARC 74.

JOSSE, Oliver; b unk; d 1781 **RU:** Seaman, Served on "Citoyen" and died from Yorktown battle **CEM:** French Memorial; GPS 36.81944, -79.39933; Yorktown; York **GS:** U **SP:** No info **VI:** No further data **P:** unk **BLW:** unk **RG:** Y **MK:** unk **PH:** unk **SS:** J-Yorktown Historian; SAR P-226910 **BS:** JLARC 1, 74.

JOUE, Jean; b unk; d 1781 **RU:** Seaman, Served on "Ville de Paris" and died from Yorktown battle **CEM:** French Memorial; GPS 36.81944, -79.39933; Yorktown; York **GS:** U **SP:** No info **VI:** No further data **P:** unk **BLW:** unk **RG:** Y **MK:** unk **PH:** unk **SS:** J-Yorktown Historian; SAR P-226928 **BS:** JLARC 1, 74.

JOULIN, Jean; b unk; d 1781 **RU:** Soldier, Served in Auxonne Bn and died fr battle at Yorktown **CEM:** French Memorial; GPS 36.81944, -79.39933; Yorktown; York **GS:** U **SP:** No info **VI:** No further data **P:** unk **BLW:** unk **RG:** Y **MK:** unk **PH:** unk **SS:** J-Yorktown Historian; SAR P-226934 **BS:** JLARC 1, 74.

JOYNES, Levin S; b 6 Jan 1753; d 16 Oct 1794 **RU:** Lieutenant Colonel, Served 7 yrs, 10 mos in VA Line of Cont Establishment. Comm Lt Col 11 Dec 1777. Wounded & taken prisoner at Germantown in Oct 1777 **CEM:** Joynes-Bayne; GPS unk; W end of Meadville Dr, Onancock; Accomack **GS:** Y **SP:** Anne (-----) (10 Jun 1756-16 Aug 1815) **VI:** Aft war member VA Senate.Recd BLW #63-500-24 Nov 1792 **P:** unk **BLW:** Y **RG:** Y **MK:** N **PH:** unk **SS:** CG pg 1892; SAR P-226996 **BS:** 37 pg 133; 196.

JULIAN, John; b 1748 or 1749; d 1785 or 1788 **RU:** Surgeon, Served in VA Cont Line **CEM:** Masonic Cemetery; GPS 38.30198, -77.46142; 900 Charles St; Fredericksburg City **GS:** Y **SP:** Mar (c1762) Margaret Isabella Lounds **VI:** Son of Charles & Phebe (Wilson) Julian. Was in practice with Hugh Mercer MD c1772. Was Vestryman at St George's Church. BLW file indicates he d before 1787 in Fredericksburg **P:** unk **BLW:** Y **RG:** N **MK:** Y SAR plaque **PH:** unk **SS:** BY pg 285; J- DAR Hatcher **BS:** JLARC 2; 196.

JULIEN, Claude; b unk; d 1781 **RU:** Soldier, Served in Gatinais Bn and died fr battle at Yorktown **CEM:** French Memorial; GPS 36.81944, -79.39933; Yorktown; York **GS:** U **SP:** No info **VI:** No further data **P:** unk **BLW:** unk **RG:** Y **MK:** unk **PH:** unk **SS:** J-Yorktown Historian; SAR P-227164 **BS:** JLARC 1, 74.

JUND, Francois; b unk; d 1781 **RU:** Soldier, Served in Auxonne Bn and died fr battle at Yorktown **CEM:** French Memorial; GPS 36.81944, -79.39933; Yorktown; York **GS:** U **SP:** No info **VI:** No further data **P:** unk **BLW:** unk **RG:** Y **MK:** unk **PH:** unk **SS:** J-Yorktown Historian; SAR P-227171 **BS:** JLARC 1, 74.

JUPIN, Laurent; b unk; d 1781 **RU:** Seaman, Served on "Diademe" and died from Yorktown battle **CEM:** French Memorial; GPS 36.81944, -79.39933; Yorktown; York **GS:** U **SP:** No info **VI:** No further data **P:** unk **BLW:** unk **RG:** Y **MK:** unk **PH:** unk **SS:** J-Yorktown Historian; SAR P-227190 **BS:** JLARC 1, 74.

JUVET, Barthelemy; b unk; d 1781 **RU:** Seaman, Served on "Hector" and died from Yorktown battle **CEM:** French Memorial; GPS 36.81944, -79.39933; Yorktown; York **GS:** U **SP:** No info **VI:** No further data **P:** unk **BLW:** unk **RG:** Y **MK:** unk **PH:** unk **SS:** J-Yorktown Historian; SAR P-227219 **BS:** JLARC 1, 74.

RU=Rank/Unit	CEM=Cemetery	GS=Gravestone	SP=Spousal Information
VI=Other Veteran Info	P=Pension	BLW=Bounty/Land Warrant	RG=Registered Grave
MK=SAR/DAR Marker	PH=Photo	SS=Service Source	BS=Burial Source

223

KABLER, Frederick; b 1695, Baden-Wurttemberg, Germany; d 1779 **RU:** Patriot, Gave material aid to cause **CEM:** Kabler Family; GPS unk; See property records for home place location; Chesterfield **GS:** U **SP:** Martha Miles (___-aft 7 Dec 1793) **VI:** Died in Culpeper Co **P:** N **BLW:** N **RG:** Y **MK:** unk **PH:** N **SS:** DAR A208552; Al Ct bk pg 30 **BS:** 196.

KAGEY, Abraham; b 1 Jul 1764, Conestoga, Lancaster Co, PA, d 15 Sep 1831 **RU:** Private, 4th Battalion, second Class, PA Militia **CEM:** Neff-Kagey; GPS: 38.69443-78.65895; Old Bridge Rd, New Market; Shenandoah **GS:** Yes **SP:** Ann Neff (1772-1828) **VI:** Son of Henry Kagy (1728-1783) and Barbara Stoner (1732-1813) **P:** N **BLW:** N **RG:** N **MK:** N **PH:** N **SS:** Cl: PA Archives, series 5, vol Vii **BS:** 196.

KAGEY, Henry; b 1728, PA, d 8 Oct 1783 **RU:** Private Patriot, Capt Jacob Holeman's Co, Dunmore County, Militia. As patriot paid personal property Tax, Shenandoah Co 1783, considered a supply tax for Rev War expenses **CEM:** Kagey Family; GPS: Undetermined; Mt Jackson; Shenandoah; **GS:** Yes; **SP:** Barbara Stoner (Dec 1732-Feb 1813) **VI:** Son of John Rudolph Kagey and Rebecca Patterson **P:** N **BLW:** N **RG:** Y **MK:** N **PH:** N **SS:** AY pgs 607, 608; DV: Image 11.pdf, DAR A122413; SAR P-227233 **BS:** 196.

KAGEY, John: b 7 Mar 1757,Lancaster Co, PA, d 11 Oct 1845 **RU:** Patriot, Patriot paid Personal Property Tax, Shenandoah Co 1783, considered a supply tax for Rev War expenses **CEM:** Neff-Kagey; Shenandoah GPS: 38.69443-78.65895; Old Bridge Rd, New Market **GS:** Yes **SP:** Elizabeth Brenneman (1758-1836) **VI:** Son of Henry Kagey (1728-1783) and Barbara Stoner (1732-1813), Minister German Baptist Church now Church of Brethren **P:** N **BLW:** N **RG:** N **MK:** N **PH:** N **SS:** DV: Image 11.pdf **BS:** 196

KAUFFMAN, David, b 5 Dec 1747 PA, d 15 Jul 1804 **RU:** Private, 8th Co, Lancaster co, PA **CEM:** Mauck-Coffman-Burner Families; GPS not determined; loc at Kauffman Mill Camp; Page **GS:** Unk **SP:** No spousal info **VI:** FindAGrave indicates born in VA but mil serv indicates born in PA **P:** N **BLW:** N **RG:** N **MK:** N **PH:** N **SS:** Cl: PA Archives, series 5, vol VII, pg 747 **BS:** 196.

KAUFMAN (KAUFFMAN) Samuel H; b 30 Oct 1752, Lancaster Co, PA, d 19 Aug 1828 **RU:** Private: 6th Class, 7th Co, 8th Bn, Lancaster Co, PA Militia **CEM:** Trissels Mennonite Church; GPS 38.60243,-78.84726;11246 Hisers Ln, Broadway; Rockingham **GS:** Yes **SP:** Findagrave indicates mar Barbara Brumbach (17 Aug 1762, Page Co-30 Jun 1829); DAR indicates mar instead 30 Sep 1783, Elizabeth Reist (21 Jan 1755-30 Sep 1783) This may be more accurate as one of their daughters had a middle name of Reist **VI:** Son of Michael Kaufman (1714-1788) **P:** N **BLW:** N **RG:** Y **MK:** N **PH:** N **SS:** Cl: PA Archives, series 5, vol VII, pg 860; DAR anc # A063702; SAR P-257783 **BS:** 196.

KAYLOR, Michael, b 1742, Hessen, Germany; d Apr 1807 **RU:** Patriot paid personal property tax 1783 Rockingham Co, considered to be a supply tax for Rev War expenses **CEM:** Old Peaked Mountain; GPS 38.371130,-78.734160; 9843 Town Hall Rd,beside Brown Memorial Community Ch, McGaheysville; Rokingham **GS:** Y **SP:** No spousal info **VI:** SAR has incorrect birth date of 1771 **P:** N **BLW:** N **RG:** Y **MK:** Y DAR plaque **PH:** N **SS:** DV image 22, Rockingham Co, 1783 for Michael Kallar(Kallor); SAR P-257807 **BS:** 196.

KAYSER / KEYSER, John J; b c1762; d 12 Sep 1823 **RU:** Private, Served in 8th Cont Line **CEM:** Locust Bottom; GPS unk; Jct Rts 622 & 696; Botetourt **GS:** N **SP:** No info **VI:** No further data **P:** unk **BLW:** unk **RG:** N **MK:** N **PH:** N **SS:** E pg 444 **BS:** 115 pg 12.

KEARFOOT (KERFOOT), William; b May 1749, Frederick Co; d 4 Feb 1811 **RU:** Sergeant/Patriot, Served full 8 yrs of war. Was1st Sergeant in Capt Stith's Co 4th VA Regt of Cont Line. He or father supplied mutton. Gave material aid to cause **CEM:** White Post aka Wheeler Family; GPS 39.71170, -78.5419; Nr White Post, nr Clarke-Frederick co line, Dearfield Farm; Frederick **GS:** U **SP:** 1) Mary Bryarly 2) Mar (27 Jan 1785 Frederick Co by Rev Alexander Balmain) Ann Peters **VI:** Son of William Sr (1724 Spotsylvania Co-7 Dec 1779) & Mary Margaret (Carter) Kerfoot **P:** unk **BLW:** unk **RG:** Y **MK:** N **PH:** Y **SS:** J- DAR Hatcher; AL Ct Bk pg 5; DD; SAR P-257834 **BS:** JLARC 2.

KEARNES, John; b 1753; d 1799 **RU:** Corporal, Served in 7th & 11th Cont Lines **CEM:** Trinity Episcopal; GPS 36.83459, -76.30105; 500 Court St; Portsmouth City **GS:** Y **SP:** No info **VI:** No further data **P:** unk **BLW:** unk **RG:** N **MK:** N **PH:** unk **SS:** E pg 434 **BS:** 92 stone 85.

RU=Rank/Unit	CEM=Cemetery	GS=Gravestone	SP=Spousal Information
VI=Other Veteran Info	P=Pension	BLW=Bounty/Land Warrant	RG=Registered Grave
MK=SAR/DAR Marker	PH=Photo	SS=Service Source	BS=Burial Source

KEATTS, William Sr; b unk, Lunenburg Co; d 22 Aug 1829 **RU**: Colonel/Patriot, Was in battle at Guilford Ct House. Had all the baggage fr the battle delivered to Halifax Co **CEM**: Keatts Family; GPS unk; Nr Mulberry Baptist Church, nr Pittsylvania; Halifax **GS**: U **SP**: Mary Lewis of Amelia Co **VI**: Son of Curtis & Tabitha (Dennis?) Keatts **P**: unk **BLW**: unk **RG**: Y **MK**: unk **PH**: unk **SS**: J-NSSAR 1993 Reg, J- DAR Hatcher; AL Ct Bk pg 13 Pittsylvania Co; SAR P-257861 **BS**: JLARC 1, 2; 196.

KEEBLE, Walter; b1729; d 1783 **RU**: Patriot, gave material aid to cause **CEM**: Keeble Family; GPS37.511470,-76.291975; Cherry Point Rd; Gwynn; Mathews **GS**: Yes, but no inscription, but family sign gives birth & death dates **SP**: Sarah Shewsbury **VI**:No further data **P**: N **BLW**: N **RG**: N **MK**: N **PH**: N **SS**: D vol1, pg 292 **BS**: 196

KEELING, Jacob; b 1750; d 20 Feb 1815 **RU**: Patriot, Gave material aid to the cause **CEM**: Keeling Family; GPS unk; Back of Laurel Manor; Virginia Beach City **GS**: Y **SP**: Mary (-----) (1749-7 Oct 1821) **VI**: No further data **P**: N **BLW**: N **RG**:N **MK**: unk **PH**: unk **SS**: AL CT BK pg S 4, 8 Princess Anne Co; AL Ct Bk pg 1 Norfolk Co **BS**: 212.

KEEN, Abraham (Abram); b c1762; d Aft 1847 **RU**: Private?, Served in VA Line. Ent serv Halifax Co 1777. Moved to Amelia in 1777 where ent serv 1781 **CEM**: Keen Family; GPS unk; Rt 92; Mecklenburg **GS**: Y **SP**: Mar (29 Dec 1790) Margaret Tabb **VI**: Moved to Mecklenburg 1785. Appl pen 31 May 1839 age 77. Mecklenburg Co. S11710; Edward L. Tabb, Security, pg 30 **P**: Y **BLW**: unk **RG**: N **MK**: N **PH**: unk **SS**: K Vol 3 pg 55; CG pg 1904 **BS**: 54, pg 235.

KEESEE (KEEZEE), Jeremiah; b 12 Oct 1751; d 2 Jan 1825 **RU**: Private, Served in Capt Abston's Co VA Militia **CEM**: Keesee Family; GPS 36.87683, -79.52109; Nr Green Pond; Pittsylvania **GS**: Y **SP**: 1) Mar (4 Sep 1793 Pittsylvania Co) Dorcas Perkins 2) Sarah Burch Else (4 Oct 1757-3 Dec 1813) **VI**: No further data **P**: unk **BLW**: unk **RG**: N **MK**: N **PH**: unk **SS**: BU **BS**: 174, 194.

KEESLING, Conrad; b 1744, Berks Co, PA; d Dec 1818 **RU**: Private, Served in Capt Jacob Baldy's Co. Served fr Berks Co PA **CEM**: Old Keesling; GPS unk; unk; Wythe **GS**: U **SP**: Mar (1794) Rebecca Ann Kegley (__-__Delaware Co, IN) **VI**: No further data **P**: unk **BLW**: unk **RG**: Y **MK**: unk **PH**: unk **SS**:; CI PA Archives 5th series Vol 5 pg 235; SAR P-258078 **BS**: JLARC 2, 40,123.

KEINADT/KOINER, Michael; b 29 Jan 1720, Winterlinger, Baden,Wuertemberg, Ger d 7 Nov 1796 **RU**: Patriot, paid supply tax, West Pennsborough, Cumberland Co, PA 1780 **CEM**: Trinity Lutheran Ch; GPS 38.1720100, -78.8682000; 2564 Rockfish Rd, Crimora; Augusta **GS**: Y Govt **SP**: Anna Margaret Diller (13 Aug 1734, New Holland, Lancaster Co, PA-18 Nov 1813, Waynesboro, Augusta Co) **VI**: Reportedly served as a private in PA Militia **P**: N **BLW**: N **RG**: Y **MK**: Y DAR **PH**: N **SS**: CI fold3 PA Archives, 3rd Series, vol 20, pgs 366,367; DAR A067254; SAR P-227687 **BS** 196.

KEITH, Alexander; b unk; d Dec 1788 **RU**: Patriot, Gave material aid to cause **CEM**: Old Christ Church Episcopal; GPS 38.80625, -77.04718; 118 N Washington St; Alexandria City **GS**: N **SP**: No info **VI**: Burial permit issued 3 Dec 1788 to the widow **P**: N **BLW**: N **RG**: N **MK**: N **PH**: N **SS**: E pg 435; AL Ct Bk pg 8 Prince William Co **BS**: 20 pg 149.

KEITH, Thomas Randolph; b 14 Mar 1736, Fauquier Co; d 1805 **RU**: Captain, Served in Fauquier Co Militia as 2nd Lt 24 Mar 1778. Listed as Capt in BLW records. Pen rec indicates was in VA Line **CEM**: Blackwell Family; GPS unk; The Meadows, E of Rt 628 at first farm past Bethel Methodist Ch, Bethel; Fauquier **GS**: N **SP**: Mar (25 May 1775) Judith Blackwell (1758-17 Apr 1837) **VI**: Son of James (1696-1758) & Mary Isham (Randolph) (1758-17 Apr 1837) Keith. Died on trip to GA in 1805 with son, but not known if body brought back. In some records, Thomas & Judith are bur in Blackwell Fam Cem in Fauquier Co. Wife appl pen 27 Dec 1836 Fauquier Co **P**: Y **BLW**: Y **RG**: Y **MK**: unk **PH**: N **SS**: E pg 436; CG pg 1907; DAR A064223; SAR P-227772 **BS**: 196.

KELL, Michel; b unk; d 1781 **RU**: Soldier, Served in Bourbonnais Bn and died fr battle at Yorktown **CEM**: French Memorial; GPS 36.81944, -79.39933; Yorktown; York **GS**: U **SP**: No info **VI**: No further data **P**: unk **BLW**: unk **RG**: Y **MK**: unk **PH**: unk **SS**: J-Yorktown Historian; SAR P-258231 **BS**: JLARC 1, 74.

KELLAR (KULLERS)(KOLLER), Jacob; b 1725 Germany; d 1805 **RU**: Patriot, paid personal property tax 1783, as Jacob Kellar in Shenandoah Co considered to be a suppy tax for Rev War expences **CEM**:

RU=Rank/Unit	CEM=Cemetery	GS=Gravestone	SP=Spousal Information
VI=Other Veteran Info	P=Pension	BLW=Bounty/Land Warrant	RG=Registered Grave
MK=SAR/DAR Marker	PH=Photo	SS=Service Source	BS=Burial Source

Dry Run Church; GPS 38.857689, -78.400195; 8398 Fort Valley Rd; Shenandoah **GS:** Y **SP:** Mar 1742, Germany, Mary Magdalene Abeline Cullers (1723, Germany-1775), however perhaps not true as was married to her instead in 1775, Frederick Co, MD **VI:** Grave stone inscription is Jacob Kullers **P:** unk **BLW:** unk **RG:** N **MK:**N **PH:** unk **SS**: DV, Shenandoah Co, 1783, image11 **BS:** 04; 196.

KELLER, Frederick Sr; b 1767, Augusta Co; d May 1839 **RU:** Patriot, Gave material aid to cause **CEM:** Keller Family; GPS unk; On Dr. Knopp's Farm, Churchville; Augusta **GS:** N **SP:** Barbara Baylor **VI:** No further data **P:** N **BLW:** N **RG:** unk **MK:** unk **PH:** N **SS:** AL Ct Bk pg 5 Augusta Co; DAR A132517; SAR P-258289 **BS:** JLARC 62.

KELLER, George; b 19 Apr 1758, nr Stovertown, Shenandoah Co; d 27 Jan 1844 **RU:** Ensign, Served in Augusta Co Militia & VA line **CEM:** Keller Family; GPS unk; On Dr. Knopp's Farm, Churchville; Augusta **GS:** U **SP:** Sophie Mowry (1776 PA-18 Oct 1759 West View, Augusta Co) **VI:** Son of George (1735-1818) & Anna Barbara (Hanger) (1766-1859) Keller. Appl pen in Monongolia Co 22 Aug 1832, S5649. Died in West View, Augusta Co **P:** Y **BLW:** N **RG:** Y **MK:** unk **PH:** unk **SS:** E pg 436; G pg 446; CG pg 1908; DAR A113286; SAR P-258259 **BS:** 196.

KELLER, George; b 1735, PA; d 1818 **RU:** Patriot, Gave material aid to cause **CEM:** Keller Family; GPS unk; On Dr Knopp's Farm, Churchville; Augusta **GS:** N **SP:** Anna Barbara Hanger (7 Nov 1736 Germany-___) **VI:** Son of George (1711-1782) & Barbara (Hottel) (1713-1798) Keller **P:** unk **BLW:** unk **RG:**N **MK:** unk **PH:** N **SS:** AL Ct Bk pg 5 Augusta Co **BS:** 196.

KELLER, George; b 17 May 1711; d 28 Mar 1783 **RU:** Patriot, Gave material aid to cause and was a member of the Committee of Safety, Dunmore Co, which Shanandoah became a part **CEM:** Keller Family; GPS 38.96580, -78.46220; Sand Ridge Rd, Mt Olive; Shenandoah **GS:** N **SP:** Barbara Hottel (1713-1798) **VI:** Son of Bastian & Elizabeth (Hildebrant) Keller, both German immigrants **P:** N **BLW:** N **RG:** Y **MK:** unk **PH:** N **SS:** AL Ct Bk pg 11 Shenandoah Co; SAR P-227822 **BS:** 196.

KELLER, George Jr; b 4 Mar 1731, Rotherfluh, Switzerland; d Jan 1788 **RU:** Patriot, Performed public service & gave material aid to cause **CEM:** Keller Family; GPS 38.49457, -78.25335; Burner Ln off Fort Valley Rd; Shenandoah **GS:** U **SP:** Mar (1760) Barbara Zimmerman **VI:** Was a doctor. Died in Ft Valley, Shenandoah Co. DAR marker **P:** N **BLW:** N **RG:** Y**MK:** Y DAR **PH:** unk **SS:** CA; DAR A128539; SAR P-227825; **BS:** 04.

KELLEY, James; b 1735; d 1795 **RU:** Patriot, Gave material aid to the cause **CEM:** Christ Church; GPS 37.61019, -76.54606; 420 Christ Church Rd, Weems; Lancaster **GS:** Y **SP:** No info **VI:** No further data **P:** N **BLW:** N **RG:** N **MK:** Y SAR & on plaque at church gate entrance **PH:** unk **SS:** AL Ct bk pg 20 **BS:** 40 pg 68.

KELLY, Edward; b c1752; d 17 Aug 1834 Russell Co **RU:** Private, Served in Capt Thomas Young in Western Bn commanded by Col Joseph Crockett in VA State service and Capt Edwin Hull in 15th VA Regt commanded by Lt Col Innes **CEM:** Kelly; GPS 36.95690, -82.09360; Just off Rt 621 on Sandy Ridge, nr home of Rev & Mrs Gonan Kelly; Russell **GS:** U **SP:** Mar (9 Apr 1774 Shenandoah Co) Bridget "Biddy" Nugent (c1752 Ireland-___ Russell Co) **VI:** Said to have preached sermon for Gen George Washington at Valley Forge. Moderator of Washington Baptist Assoc. (Regular Baptist) 1815, 1816, 1818, and a delegate fr Reed's Valley Church 1814-1822, 1826, 1827 **P:** unk **BLW:** unk **RG:**Y **MK:** unk **PH:** unk **SS:** E pg 437 indicates record at War Department at Nat Archives; DAR A064183; SAR P-228124 **BS:** 196.

KELLY, John; b 1747, County Donegal, Ireland; d 4 Dec 1822 **RU:** Soldier, Served 1780 in Cont Army at Battle of Kings Mountain. Served in 1st, 4th, 8th, 9th, 12th Cont Lines **CEM:** Ebbing Spring; GPS unk; N side of middle fork of Holstein River, vic Glade Spring; Washington **GS:** U **SP:** Jean Kirkham (___-bef 1822) Will specified husband to be bur next to her. **VI:** Honored 4 Jul 2001 when Black's Ft chapter of DAR put monument in Sinking Spring Cemetery in Abingdon to honor soldiers bur in Washington Co **P:** unk **BLW:** unk **RG:** N **MK:** Y **PH:** unk **SS:** E pg 436 **BS:** 196.

KELLO, Richard; bapt 24 Jun 1726, London, Eng, d 4 Jun 1789, Manry, Southampton Co **RU:** Colonel/Patriot; County Lieutenant 1777-1778, Commissioner 1777 **CEM:** Kello Family; GPS: not determined; vic jct Rts 605, 601 at edge of woods, Berlin; Southampton **GS:** Yes **SP:** Mar c1748, Mary (-----) (___-c1789) **VI:** Emigrated 1741 at age 16, Served as 1st Clerk VA Courts in Southampton, was

RU=Rank/Unit	CEM=Cemetery	GS=Gravestone	SP=Spousal Information
VI=Other Veteran Info	P=Pension	BLW=Bounty/Land Warrant	RG=Registered Grave
MK=SAR/DAR Marker	PH=Photo	SS=Service Source	BS=Burial Source

226

Major in Colonial War, Represented County in House of Delegates, 1777-1778 **P:** N **BLW:** N **RG:** N **MK:** N, **PH:** N **SS:** DAR A069312, CZ: pg 251 **BS:** 196.

KELSO, Robert; b 10 Apr 1761; d 21 Jul 1842 **RU:** Private, Served in Capt Edward Mumford's Co, Dec 1779 commanded by Col Willis & Col Mays Duval. Was in skirmish with British at Bland's Ordinary in Southampton Co. In 1780 or 1781 served in Capt Richard Crump's Co in Powhatan Co. **CEM:** Kelso Family; GPS unk; 1 mi N of Pamplin on Rt 600; Appomattox **GS:** Y **SP:** Susan Pollard (3 Aug 1773 Hanover Co-21 Nov 1848) d/o William & Mary (-----) Pollard **VI:** No further data **P:** unk **BLW:** unk **RG:** N **MK:** unk **PH:** unk **SS:** AP pension rec **BS:** 196; 201.

KEMPER (KAMPER), Charles Sr; b 27 Jun 1756; d 1 Dec 1841 **RU:** Private, Served in VA Line. Ent serv Fauquier Co 1777 **CEM:** Kemper Family; GPS unk; Rt 802 Nr Warrenton; Fauquier **GS:** Y **SP:** Mar (29 Nov 1774 or 1786 Fauquier Co) Susanna Mawzey by John Pickett, Baptist minister (c1766-__) **VI:** Sol appl pen 25 Jun 1833 Fauquier Co. Widow appl pen 4 May 1843 Fauquier Co. W20292 **P:** Y **BLW:** unk **RG:** N **MK:** N **PH:** unk **SS:** K Vol 3 pg 61; N pg 1258; CG pg 1919; Fauquier Co Marriages pg 112 **BS:** JLARC 4,16; 19 pg 132.

KENDALL, George; b 1759; d 24 Nov 1784 **RU:** Patriot, Gave material aid to cause **CEM:** Kendall Grove; GPS unk; Rt 674; Northampton **GS:** Y **SP:** No info **VI:** Died age 25. Stone erected by his friend George Parker **P:** N **BLW:** N **RG:** N **MK:** N **PH:** unk **SS:** G pg 483 **BS:** 42 pg 48.

KENDALL, William; b 1763; d 1807 **RU:** Private, Served in VA Battalion and was in Clark's Illinois Regt **CEM:** Hungerford-Griffin; GPS unk; 373 Resolutions Rd, Leedstown; Westmoreland **GS:** Y **SP:** No info **VI:** Received BLW **P:** unk **BLW:** Y **RG:** Y **MK:** Y SAR plaque **PH:** unk **SS:** E pg 439; AP rec; DAR A064592; SAR P-258902 **BS:** 189.

KENNAHORN, William Jr; b 20 Nov 1747; d 30 Nov 1840 **RU:** Soldier, Served in VA Line. Ent serv Accomack Co, 1776. Served in Capt Levin Jones Co for two yrs, discharged at Valley Forge, PA **CEM:** Kennahorn Family; GPS unk; N side of Rt 638, .4 mi E of 637, W fr Cashville; Accomack **GS:** Y **SP:** 1) unk 2) Mar (14 Jan 1824 Accomack) Delaney Butler (c1779-__) **VI:** Occupation cooper in 1829 age 82 & wife Delaney age 50. Sol appl pen 9 Jul 1818 Williamsburg. Pensioned Accomack Co 1818 age 70. Widow appl pen 28 Sep 1853 age 78 Accomack Co. Widow appl for BLW 3 Apr 1855. W26642, BLW #8175-160-55. DAR marker placed on the Gr of William Kennahorn, Sr **P:** Y **BLW:** Y **RG:** Y **MK:** Y SAR **PH:** unk **SS:** K Vol 3 pg 64; CG pg 1923; BT; SAR P-258968 **BS:** JLARC 4, 5; 209.

KENNAHORN, William Sr; b 20 Mar 1717; d 20 Nov 1810 **RU:** Soldier, Specific service not identified **CEM:** Kennahorn Family; GPS unk; N side of Rt 638, .4 mi E of 637, W fr Cashville; Accomack **GS:** Y **SP:** No info **VI:** GS reads "Soldier in the War of 1776", however over military age **P:** unk **BLW:** unk **RG:** N **MK:** unk **PH:** unk **SS:** BT **BS:** 209.

KENNEDY, James Dr; b c1753, Dumfrieshire, Scotland; d 6 Jan 1816 **RU:** Sergeant, Served 13th Cont Line as pvt; served 3rd, 5th, 7th, 11th Cont Line **CEM:** Presbyterian Church; GPS 38.80015, -77.05791; Wilkes St & Hamilton Ln; Alexandria City **GS:** Y **SP:** Mar (12 May 1780) Susannah (-----) (25 Jul 1766-30 May 1845) **VI:** Death notice in the Alexandria Gazette, 8 Jan 1816 **P:** unk **BLW:** unk **RG:** Y **MK:** Y SAR plaque **PH:** unk **SS:** E pg 439; SAR P-333955 **BS:** 23 pg 49.

KENNER, Howson Francis; b 10 Mar 1712, Northumberland Co; d 24 May 1778 **RU:** Midshipman, Navy service particulars not identified **CEM:** Kenner; GPS unk; Rt 616, Somerville; Fauquier **GS:** Y **SP:** Margaret Eskridge (19 May 1712 Westmoreland Co-8 Oct 1801 Warrenton, Fauquier Co) **VI:** Son of Francis (1675-1728) & Hannah (Howson) (1677-1712) Kenner. Recd BLW **P:** unk **BLW:** Y **RG:** Y **MK:** unk **PH:** unk **SS:** E pg 441; CZ pg 252; CU; SAR P-259095 & P-259096 **BS:** JLARC 16; 196.

KENNEY (KENNY, KINNEY), Robert; b 1743, PA; d 28 Nov 1806 **RU:** Captain, Commanded a Co in Augusta Co Militia after being commissioned as Capt 18 August 1778 **CEM:** Augusta Stone Presyterian; GPS 38.23926, -78.97356; 28 Old Stone Church Ln, Ft Defiance; Augusta **GS:** Y **SP:** Pheobe Huston (11 May 1788-23 Apr 1806) d/o James (1726 Baltimore-1818 Fayette Co, KY) & (-----) Huston **VI:** Gov't GS shows rank **P:** unk **BLW:** unk **RG:** Y **MK:** unk **PH:** unk **SS:** E pg 441; DAR A065339; SAR P-259126 **BS:** 196.

RU=Rank/Unit
VI=Other Veteran Info
MK=SAR/DAR Marker

CEM=Cemetery
P=Pension
PH=Photo

GS=Gravestone
BLW=Bounty/Land Warrant
SS=Service Source

SP=Spousal Information
RG=Registered Grave
BS=Burial Source

227

KENNEY (KENNY, KINNEY), Robert; b 1748; d unk **RU:** Private, Served in Dunmore's War 1774 at Point Pleasant fr Augusta Co under Capt George Matthews and later Capt Rankin's Co, Augusta Militia **CEM:** Augusta Stone Presbyterian; GPS 38.23926, -78.97356, GS 38.1413,-78.5812; 28 Old Stone Church Ln, Ft Defiance; Augusta **GS:** Y **SP:** No info **VI:** Stone erected in 1953 styles him a Capt of the Rev War **P:** unk **BLW:** unk **RG:** N **MK:** Y SAR plaque **PH:** unk **SS:** B; E pg 441; Z pg 105-6; CP Dunmore's War; J-NSSAR 2000 Reg **BS:** JLARC 1, 2, 8, 23 ,62, 76; 196.

KENNON, Richard; b 1759, Mecklenburg Co; d 4 Feb 1805 **RU:** Captain, Served in VA Line. Ent serv Mecklenburg Co **CEM:** Wimmer King; GPS unk; Copper Hill; Floyd **GS:** Y **SP:** Mar (16 May 1780) Elizabeth Beverley Munford (28 Mar 1762 Mecklenburg Co-1825) **VI:** Gov't gr st shows rank and service. BLW #2298-300 issued 22 Nov 1842 to heirs **P:** unk **BLW:** Y **RG:** Y **MK:** unk **PH:** unk **SS:** E pg 441; CG pg 1926; DD; SAR P-228714 **BS:** JLARC 2, 72; 80, vol 2,pg 224; 196.

KENNY, William; b c1764; d 1851 **RU:** Private?, Served in 3rd Cont Line **CEM:** Kenny Family; GPS unk; Vic jct Rts 802 & 709; Carroll **GS:** U **SP:** No info **VI:** No further data **P:** unk **BLW:** unk **RG:** N **MK:** N **PH:** unk **SS:** E pg 442 **BS:** 63 pg 384.

KENT, Luke; b c1762; d 28 Apr 1789 **RU:** Patriot, Supplied the militia with material aid **CEM:** Kent Family; GPS unk; Poplar Creek; Halifax **GS:** N **SP:** Mar (8Jan 1782 Bedford Co) Sarah Cocke (1767-Dec 1801) d/o George Sr (1725 Hanover Co- __) & Agnes (-----) (__-1785) Cocke **VI:** Died in Cumberland Co **P:** N **BLW:** N **RG:** Y **MK:** N **PH:** N **SS:** V bk 2 pg 279-280; DAR A131926; SAR P-259246 **BS:** 04.

KENT, Robert; b c1710-1715, Goochland Co; d 17 Jul 1783 **RU:** Patriot, Supplied the militia with material aid **CEM:** Kent Family; GPS unk; Poplar Creek; Halifax **GS:** N **SP:** Mary Easley (__-13 Oct 1782) **VI:** No further data **P:** N **BLW:** N **RG:** Y **MK:** N **PH:** N **SS:** DAR A065044; V bk 2 pg 279-280; SAR P-228797 **BS:** 04.

KEPLINGER, Christian; (Cristofiel) b 10 Mar 1750; d 28 Feb 1846 **RU:** Private/Patriot, served in German PA Bn, Cont Troops 1777-1780; paid personal property tax, a supply tax for Rev War expenses, Rockingham Co 1783 **EM:** Old Criders; GPS 38.750130, -79.006250; loc Dove Valley Ln, nr jct with Crider's Rd (Rt 826), Criders; Rockingham **GS:** N **SP:** Mary Anna Keifer (1749-1780) **VI:** Drew pen "S8776 **P:** Y **BLW:** N **RG:** Y **MK:** N **PH:** N **SS:** AP Fold3 serv index card; DV image 13, 1783 Rockingham Co; SAR P -331723 **BS:** 196.

KER, Edward; b unk; d 1790 **RU:** Patriot, Gave material aid to cause **CEM:** Melrose & Ker Family; GPS unk; Abt 2 mi SW Pungoteaque; Accomack **GS:** N **SP:** No info **VI:** No further data **P:** N **BLW:** N **RG:** N **MK:** N **PH:** N **SS:** G pg 483 **BS:** 145 Melrose Ker.

KER, John Shepard; b 1762; d Sep 1800 **RU:** Private, Served in Capt Stephenson's Co, 9th VA Regt, May 1776 **CEM:** Scott Hall, aka Edward Snead; GPS 37.71115; -75.75250; Nr River btw Mt Prospect Ave and South St, Onancock; Accomack **GS:** Y **SP:** Perhaps Agnes Drummond Corbin (Jan 1775-Feb 1814) as she has adjacent stone in cem **VI:** Son of Edward Jr & Margaret (Shepard) Ker **P:** N **BLW:** N **RG:** N **MK:** N **PH:** unk **SS:** AP Payroll 9th VA Regt **BS:** 145 Snead; 196.

KERFOOT (KEARFOOT), William; b c1719 or 1724, Castle Blaney, Monaghan, Ireland; d 1779 **RU:** Sergeant, Served in Capt John Stiths's Co 4th VA Regt. Served 3 yrs **CEM:** White Post aka Wheeler Family; GPS 39.71170, -78.5419; Nr White Post, nr Clarke-Frederick co line, Dearfield Farm; Frederick **GS:** U **SP:** Mar (1745) Mary Margaret Carter (1727 Frederick Co-1777) **VI:** Deed for 192 acres on Opequon Creek in 1763. Recd BLW **P:** unk **BLW:** Y **RG:**Y **MK:** unk **PH:** unk **SS:** C pg 459; E pg 443; BY; SAR P-259332 **BS:** 80 vol 2 pg 217.

KERR, James; b 1726, Lancaster Co, PA; d 5 Jan 1812 **RU:** Private, Served in Capt Rankin's Co, Augusta Co Militia. Augusta Co record of 16 Oct 1776 indicates "exempted fr military duty until he comes the use of his arm." He may be the person of this name that served in the 3rd, 5th, 7th, and 11th Cont Line and was at Valley Forge **CEM:** Augusta Stone Presbyterian; GPS 38.23926, -78.97356, GS 38.1411,-78.5813; 28 Old Stone Church Ln, Ft Defiance; Augusta **GS:** Y **SP:** Mar (c1755) Jane Robertson (1739-11 Feb 1824) **VI:** Stone reads b 1724 but other sources indicate 1734 and 1737. Also was at Valley Forge **P:** unk **BLW:** unk **RG:** Y **MK:** Y SAR plaque **PH:** unk **SS:** B; E pg 443; DAR A065164; SAR P-259374 **BS:** JLARC 63; 196.

RU=Rank/Unit	CEM=Cemetery	GS=Gravestone	SP=Spousal Information
VI=Other Veteran Info	P=Pension	BLW=Bounty/Land Warrant	RG=Registered Grave
MK=SAR/DAR Marker	PH=Photo	SS=Service Source	BS=Burial Source

KERR, John Jr; b unk; d 1794 **RU:** Soldier, Served in Capt Rankin's or Capt Kenny's Co, Augusta Co Militia, also in 1st VA Regt & Cont Line **CEM:** Augusta Stone Presbyterian; GPS 38.23926, -78.97356, GS 38.1411,-78.5813;; 28 Old Stone Church Ln, Ft Defiance; Augusta **GS:** Y **SP:** Christine Niswonger **VI:** Family stone erected in 1930, does not mention Rev War service, and gives no date of birth. A person this name recd BLW **P:** unk **BLW:** Y **RG:**N **MK:** Y SAR plaque **PH:** unk **SS:** C pg 249; E pg 443 **BS:** JLARC 63; 196.

KERR, John Sr; b unk; d 8 Jul 1830 **RU:** Private, Served in Capt Kenny's Co, Augusta Militia. He may be the person of this name that served in the 1st VA State Regt and the 4th, 7th, 8th, and 12th Cont Line **CEM:** Augusta Stone Presbyterian; GPS 38.23926, -78.97356 GS 38.1411,-78.5813;; 28 Old Stone Church Ln, Ft Defiance; Augusta **GS:** Y **SP:** Elizabeth Hogsettker (__-1842) **VI:** Family stone erected in 1930, does not mention Rev War service, and gives no date of birth **P:** unk **BLW:** unk **RG:** Y **MK:** unk **PH:** unk **SS:** E pg 443; SAR P-228982 **BS:** JLARC 1, 8, 23, 62; 196.

KERR, Joseph; b unk; d 1839 **RU:** Private?, Served in Capt Teater's Co, Augusta Co Militia **CEM:** Old Stone Presbyterian; GPS 38.23926, -78.97356; 28 Old Stone Church Ln, Ft Defiance; Augusta **GS:** Y **SP:** No info **VI:** No further data **P:** unk **BLW:** unk **RG:** N **MK:** Y SAR plaque **PH:** unk **SS:** E pg 443 **BS:** 71 pg 16.

KERR, William; b 1760, Fifeshare, Scotland; d 16 Jul 1828 **RU:** Private/Patriot, Served in VA & PA. Served in 3rd Co Rifleman, 5th Battalion, Washington Co, PA. Gave one bag of beef to cause **CEM:** Bethel Presbyterian; GPS 38.04257, -79.17283; 563 Bethel Green Rd, Middlebrook; Augusta **GS:** N **SP:** Mar (22 Dec 1796) Mary Ann Grove **VI:** No further data **P:** unk **BLW:** unk **RG:**Y **MK:** unk **PH:** N **SS:** D pg 45 Augusta Co; N; SAR P-259410 **BS:** JLARC 63.

KERSH. Mathias (Matthias); b 1735, Germany, d 19 Jan 1808 **RU:** Patriot, Gave material aid to cause in Rockingham County **CEM:** Kersh Family (AKA Cash Family); Rt 771 nr runway and entrance to Shenandoah Valley Airport, Weyers Cave; Augusta **GS:** Has been removed **SP:** Anna Margaret (__)(c1730-1808) **VI:** All gravestones removed by Airport to unk loc 1778 **P:** N **BLW:** N **RG:** N **MK:** N, **PH:** N **SS:**AL Ct Bk II, pg 19, Comm Bk V pg 134 Rockingham Co; DAR A065193, **BS:** 32.

KESSLAR, Jacob B; b22 Sep 1756, Montgomery Co, PA, d 20 Jul 1824, Troutville Botetourt Co **RU:** Private, PA 1st Regiment, POW 20 Feb 1782 **CEM:** Troutville; GPS: 37.42178,-79.87361; Rt 11, Lee Hwy, betw jct with Rts 757 & 670; Botetourt **GS:** Y **SP:** Elizabeth Shearer (20 Mar 1769-13 Aug 1844) **VI:** Son of Johannes Kesler (8 Mar 1727, Germany- 24 Mar 1823) and Eva Dorothea Leman (24 Jan 1734-24 Jul 1798). Moved fr PA to VA after war **P:** N **BLW:** N **RG:** N **MK:** N, **PH:** N **SS:** AP-PA 1st Regt Rev War Rolls, pg 53, Fold3 **BS:** 196.

KESSLER, John; b 8 Feb 1761; d 2 Jan 1847 **RU:** Private, Enl 28 Jan 1776 in 9th Co of Light Artillery **CEM:** Kessler Family; GPS unk; Nr Brick Union Ch; Botetourt **GS:** Y **SP:** Elizabeth (-----) (30 Sep 1822-c1883) **VI:** No further data **P:** unk **BLW:** unk **RG:**Y **MK:** N **PH:** unk **SS:** AP pension; DAR A020430; SAR P-229027 **BS:** 165.

KEY, John; b unk; d unk **RU:** Ensign, Served in 8th Cont Line.Was Ens 3 Feb 1777. Resigned 24 Apr 1778 **CEM:** Trinity Episcopal; GPS 36.83459, -76.30105; 500 Court St; Portsmouth City **GS:** Y **SP:** No info **VI:** Stone 86 B in W.B. Butt inventory. Govt marker **P:** unk **BLW:** unk **RG:** Y **MK:** Y SAR plaque **PH:** unk **SS:** E pg 444; SAR P-259539 **BS:** JLARC 105, 127; 196; 57.

KEYSER, Andrew Sr; b 16 Dec 1758,Shenandoah Co; d 23 Nov 1833 **RU:** Private/Major, Ent serv Shenandoah Co 1780 for 18 mos in Capt Conway Oldham's Co, Col Richard Campbell's VA Regt. Was in battles of Guilford, Camden, Ninety-Six, and Eutaw Springs **CEM:** Keyser Family; GPS 38.71675,-78.46305; Rt 684 at 2301 S Page Valley Rd; Page **GS:** N **SP:** 1) Sarah Margaret "Sally" Rinehart 2) Elizabeth Grove Strickler **VI:** Son of Carl Sebaastian Keyser (1726-1778) & Mary Elizabeth Kelly (1737-1776). Other writings show him as Major in the VA Troops which may have been for service after the Revolution. Sol appl pen 23 Jul 1832 Page Co. Died in Shenandoah Co, now Page Co. S5651 **P:** Y **BLW:** unk **RG:**Y **MK:** Y SAR granite **PH:** N **SS:** Pen Appl; CG pg 1937; DAR A065433; SAR P-259624 **BS:** JLARC 2, 4, 49; 120.

KEYSER, Charles Jr; b 1750; d Aft 12 Sep 1796 **RU:** Private, Served in Capt Michael Reader's Co, Shenandoah Militia **CEM:** Keyser Family; GPS unk; Rt 684, NW fr Luray 8 mi; Page **GS:** U **SP:**

RU=Rank/Unit	CEM=Cemetery	GS=Gravestone	SP=Spousal Information
VI=Other Veteran Info	P=Pension	BLW=Bounty/Land Warrant	RG=Registered Grave
MK=SAR/DAR Marker	PH=Photo	SS=Service Source	BS=Burial Source

Elizabeth Baker **VI:** No further data **P:** unk **BLW:** unk **RG:** Y **MK:** unk **PH:** unk **SS:** J- DAR Hatcher; C pg 602; DAR A065433; P-259624 **BS:** JLARC 2.

KEYSER/KISER, Michael; b 1735, Hessen, Germany, d 21 Sep 1792, Rockingham Co **RU:** Patriot, Paid Supply Tax Cumberland Twp, Berks Co, PA **CEM:** Christian Stroke Family; GPS: 38.56432,-78.65827; Pitt Spring Rd at Cub Run, Grove Hill; Page **GS:** Unk **SP:** Mar PA, Anna Maria (Mary) Eppert **VI:** Son of Valentin Kayser & Maria Magdalena Sommerlade **P:** N **BLW:** N **RG:** Y **MK:** N, **PH:** N **SS: DAR A 065478; SAR** P-261122 **BS:** 196

KEYSER (KEYSOR), William; b 1755; d 4 Dec 1837 **RU:** Private, Ent serv Gloucester Co in Capt Thomas Baytop's Co, 2d VA State Regt. Was at Valley Forge with Washington's Army, later Col Charles Dabney's Regt at Monmouth Battle & Battles at Sawmill River Bridge & Stoney Point **CEM:** Keyser Family; GPS 37.96885,-79.83694; nr Jct Rts 612 & 618, Warm Springs; Bath **GS:** N **SP:** Keziah Snead (1761 Hanover Co-1849 Alleghany Co) **VI:** Memorial GS placed at Healing Springs Baptist Church. Pen recd 9 Oct 1832; widow pen Bath Co W3427 **P:** Y **BLW:** unk **RG:** Y **MK:** unk **PH:** unk **SS:** G pg 723; CG pg 1937; DAR A065484; SAR P-229212 **BS:** 196.

KIBLER, Henry; b c1746, Germany; d 9 Sep 1796 **RU:** Patriot, Gave material aid to cause **CEM:** Robert T Kemp Farm; GPS unk; Luray; Page **GS:** U **SP:** Mary Amelia Pierce (__-1796) **VI:** No further data **P:** N **BLW:** N **RG:** Y **MK:** DAR **PH:** unk **SS:** J-NSSAR 2000 Reg; AL Ct Bk pg 12 Shenandoah Co; DAR A065527 SAR P-259690 **BS:** JLARC 76.

KIBLER, John; b 1765, Shenandoah Co; d Dec 1841 **RU:** Patriot, paid personal property tax, Shenandoah Co, 1783, considered a supply tax for Rev War expenses **CEM:** Martin Kibler Family; GPS not determined ; loc Rt 611 nr jct with Rt 658, Kimball; Page **GS:** Y **SP:**Mar 1793, Eve Pence (_-1845) **VI:** Son of Heinrich (Henry) Kibler (15 Aug 1746, Ger-9 Sep 1796) & Mary Amelia Pence(1744 Ger-1799, Shenandoah Co) **P:** N **BLW:** N **RG:** Y **MK:** DAR plaque **PH:** N **SS:** SAR Application; SAR bio rpt Mar 2021 **BS:** 196.

KIDD, James; b unk; d Nov 1795 **RU:** Private, Served in Capt Thomas Tebbe Co #4, 30 Apr 1777, 2nd Cont Line **CEM:** Old Christ Church Episcopal; GPS 38.80625, -77.04718; 118 N Washington St; Alexandria City **GS:** N **SP:** No info **VI:** Burial permit issued 4 Nov 1795 **P:** unk **BLW:** unk **RG:** Y **MK:** N **PH:** N **SS:** A pg 273; E pg 444 **BS:** 20 pg 149.

KILGORE, Robert b 1733, County Clare, Ireland d 31 Dec1783 **RU:** Private/Patriot was serving in 5th SC Regt 11 Jun 1776. Then served in VA militia in Capt Joseph Martins Co, Col Evan Shelby's Regt during May & Jun 1777. Was at battle of Kings Mountain. Paid peronal property tax Washington Co 1782 **CEM:** Hollowed Tree; GPS: not determined; Warrior's Camp, Pound; Wise **GS:** Unk **SP:** Winifred Clayton (1740-1815), d/o (-----) & Mary Denum (1705-1800) **VI:** Son of Thomas Kilgore & Lydia (-----). Scalped and killed by Indians that placed his body in hollowed out chestnut tree **P:** N **BLW:** RG: Y **MK:** N **PH:** N **SS:** DH; Washington Co Tax Rec 1782; DAR A203788; SAR P-229415; **BS:** 196.

KILGOUR (KILGORE), Charles J or (I); b unk d 29 Aug 1837 **RU:** Private/ Patriot, militiaman employed as guards, drivers, laborers building a road over Cumberland Mountain to KY ordered by county commissioners John Kinhead and William McBride in 1780 **CEM:** Mcilhany Family; GPS not determined; loc nr Hillsboro on E side Rt 690 btw Rts 90 & 611; Loudoun **GS:** Yes **SP:** Lousia Mcilhany **VI:** Serv fr a paper found in VA Land office. Commissioners entitled men to receive BLW for service. He recd 20 Jun1786 175 acres; 5 Dec 1798-60 acres and 6 Aug 1824 175 acres all in Washington Co, VA **P:** N **BLW:** Y **RG:** N **MK:** N, **PH:** N **SS:**N pg 1272; Lib VA Land Office Grants **BS:** 222.

KILGOUR (KILGORE) George; b 17 Mar 1739, d 16 Feb 1818 **RU:** Lieutenant, appointed this rank Jun 1779. Loudoun Co Militia **CEM:** Chestnut Grove; GPS 38.984441,-77.377892; 831 Dranesville Rd, Herndon; Fairfax **GS:** Yes new stone **SP:** Martina Bailey (1741-1815) **VI:** Memorialized in cem as first buried in Kilgour-Hummer burial grd loc on Old Kilmour Mill Rd near Broadrun, near Sterling, moved to current cem by VDOT in 2007 **P:** N **BLW:** N **RG:** Y **MK:** N, **PH:** N **SS:** G pg 22; SAR P-259837 **BS:** 196.

KILLINGER, George; b c1756, PA; d Bet 19 Aug 1841 - 23 Mar 1842 **RU:** Private, Served in PA Line. Ent serv Lancaster Co PA. Was in 4th class in Capt Patrick Hay's 2nd Co of 9th Battalion of Lancaster Co PA Militia under Col John Rogers **CEM:** Royal Oak; GPS 36.84315, -81.49660; Behind Marion Baptist Church, Marion; Smyth **GS:** Y **SP:** Mary Wampler **VI:** Appl pen 20 Mar 1841 Smyth Co. R5919.

RU=Rank/Unit	CEM=Cemetery	GS=Gravestone	SP=Spousal Information
VI=Other Veteran Info	P=Pension	BLW=Bounty/Land Warrant	RG=Registered Grave
MK=SAR/DAR Marker	PH=Photo	SS=Service Source	BS=Burial Source

Rejected **P:** N **BLW:** unk **RG:** Y **MK:** N **PH:** unk **SS:** J-NSSAR 1993 Reg; CG pg 1942; DAR A065830; SAR P-229458 **BS:** JLARC 1; 196.

KILPATRICK, Ann; b 1739; d 2 Aug 1815 **RU:** Patriot, Gave material aid to cause **CEM:** Hogshead Family; GPS unk; Off Rt 736 btw Rts 42 & 250, N of Jennings Gap; Augusta **GS:** U **SP:** Prob widow of David Hogshead, Sr; maiden name Kilpatrick **VI:** No further data **P:** N **BLW:** N **RG:** N **MK:** unk **PH:** unk **SS:** Al Cert, Augusta Co as Mrs Ann Hogstead **BS:** 36 pg 72-3; 196.

KIMBALL, Benjamin; b unk; d 1781 **RU:** Soldier, Served fr MA, and died fr the Battle at Yorktown **CEM:** Yorktown Victory Monument Tablet; GPS 38.28350, -78.54150; Yorktown; York **GS:** U **SP:** No info **VI:** No further data **P:** unk **BLW:** unk **RG:** YMK: unk **PH:** unk **SS:** J-Yorktown Historian; SAR P-259954 **BS:** JLARC 74.

KINCAID, John; b 1754, Ireland; d 30 Jan 1811 **RU:** Soldier, Served in VA unit in Illinois **CEM:** Presbyterian Church; GPS 38.80015, -77.05791; Wilkes St & Hamilton Ln; Alexandria City **GS:** Y **SP:** Lucy (-----), (1759-18 Apr 1842) **VI:** Died age 57 **P:** unk **BLW:** unk **RG:** Y **MK:** Y SAR plaque **PH:** unk **SS:** J-NSSAR 1993 Reg; E pg 446; SAR P-333956 **BS:** JLARC 1; 23 pg 49-50.

KINCAID, John; b 11 Jan 1758, Augusta Co; d 5 Aug 1835 **RU:** Private, Served in VA Line. Ent serv Botetourt Co in Hanley's Co of militia **CEM:** Falling Springs Presbyterian; GPS 37.68526, -79.44972; 410 Falling Springs Rd, Glasgow; Rockbridge **GS:** Y **SP:** Mar (25 Jul 1787) Alice "Alley" Dean (her marriage record says Alcy Elliott), (1767-25 Feb 1861) **VI:** Sol appl pen 19 Nov 1833 Alleghany Co. Widow appl pen 6 Jun 1842 Alleghany Co. W3428.Recd BLW #38513-160-55 **P:** Y **BLW:** Y **RG:** Y **MK:** unk **PH:** unk **SS:** CG pg 1947; SAR P-260232 **BS:** JLARC 2, 4, 53; 196.

KINCAID (KINKAID), William; b by 1762; d aft 1781 probably 1809 **RU:** Patriot/ 2d Lt, served as Adjutant 12th Cont Line, 18 mos fr 1 Jan 1777 to 21 Jul 1778; gave material aid to cause, Augusta Co **CEM:** Rocky Springs Presbyterian Ch; 38.11470, -79.24250; 1 mi S of Deerfield; Augusta **GS:** Y very difficult to read inscription, FAG has incorrect dates **SP:** No spousal data **VI:** No further data **P:** Unk **BLW:** Unk **RG:** Y **MK:** N **PH:** N **SS:** SAR P-260248; C pg 131; E pg 446; AL Ct Bk, pgs 3, 10, Comm Bk ii, pg 358 **BS:** JLARC, 62, 63

KING, Elisha; b 10 Apr 1756; d 13 May 1821 **RU:** Major, Served in VA Line and as 1st Lt 10th Cont Line. Later Maj in Dragoons **CEM:** Sweden Plantation; GPS 37.15854, -77.54751; nr jct Claiborne & White Oak rds, Sutherland; Dinwiddie **GS:** N **SP:** Mar (1789) Judith Brent (__-4 May 1807) **VI:** Recd BLW #324-200-14 Feb 1807. **P:** unk **BLW:** Y **RG:** N **MK:** N **PH:** N **SS:** DAR #A066428; E pg 447; K Vol 3 pg 76; CG pg 1951 **BS:** JLARC 116.

KING, George; b 1730, Brunswick Co; d 6 May 1806 **RU:** Private, Served in Gen George Rogers lll Regt and Joseph Crocketts Regt **CEM:** King; GPS unk; Leatherwood; Henry **GS:** U **SP:** Mar (1766) Mary Niblet (c1740-1848) **VI:** No further data **P:** unk **BLW:** unk **RG:** Y **MK:** unk **PH:** unk **SS:** DAR #A066468; G pg 701; SAR P-260365 **BS:** 196.

KING, John; b 1746; d 11 Sep 1810 **RU:** Ensign, Served in Capt William Doak's Co, Montgomery Co Militia **CEM:** King; GPS unk; W side of SR 625, S of jct with SR 667, Crockett; Wythe **GS:** U **SP:** Mar (1775) Savannah Sabine (c1757-12 Oct 1844) **VI:** Reported burial said to be on Claude Copernhaver farm. **P:** unk **BLW:** unk **RG:** N **MK:** unk **PH:** unk **SS:** DAR Ancestor #A012224; G pg 220; BW pg 1, 12, 13 **BS:** JLARC 40, 123.

KING, John; b 1760; d 1840 **RU:** Private, Probably the man by this name who served in Capt Campbell's Co, Augusta Co Militia **CEM:** Stull Family; GPS unk; 10 mi S of Lowmoor; Alleghany **GS:** Y **SP:** No info **VI:** No further data **P:** unk **BLW:** unk **RG:** Y **MK:** N **PH:** unk **SS:** E pg 447; SAR P-338364 **BS:** 160 Stull.

KING, John; b 1759, MD; d Mar 1843 **RU:** Private, Served in Capt Daniel Stull's Co, Col John Gunby, 7th MD Regt, MD Militia **CEM:** King; GPS unk; Nr MM 141 on Blue Ridge Pkwy; Floyd **GS:** U **SP:** Mar (4 Nov or Dec 1799) Sarah Addair (c1781-Mar 1843) **VI:** Recd VA pension in Floyd Co #S5553 **P:** Y **BLW:** unk **RG:** Y **MK:** unk **PH:** unk **SS:** DAR Ancestor #A066603; E pg 447; DD; SAR P-260468 **BS:** JLARC 4, 29; 196.

RU=Rank/Unit	CEM=Cemetery	GS=Gravestone	SP=Spousal Information
VI=Other Veteran Info	P=Pension	BLW=Bounty/Land Warrant	RG=Registered Grave
MK=SAR/DAR Marker	PH=Photo	SS=Service Source	BS=Burial Source

231

KING, John; b 1744; d 1802 **RU:** Private, Served in Capt Campbell's Co, Augusta Co Militia. Also in Capt George Moffat's Co at Point Pleasant Battle Oct 1774 **CEM:** Kring Salvage; GPS unk; Off John Deere Dr, behind Harman Machinery, Broadway; Rockingham **GS:** Y **SP:** No info **VI:** No further data **P:** unk **BLW:** unk **RG:** N **MK:** N **PH:** unk **SS:** E pg 447; Z pg 117-8 **BS:** 191 Salvage.

KING, John Sr; b 1758, Brunswick Co; d 1821 **RU:** Soldier, Served in Brunswick Co Militia Oct 1782 **CEM:** King; GPS unk; Leatherwood; Henry **GS:** U **SP:** 1) Mar (c1779) Mary Elizabeth Seward (1750-1760 Brunswick Co-Feb 1829) 2) Mary Love (1774-1847) **VI:** Son of George (1734-___) & Mary (Niblett) King. Pastor at Beaver Creek and Leatherwood Churches **P:** unk **BLW:** unk **RG:** Y **MK:** unk **PH:** unk **SS:** DAR Ancestor #A066681; G pg 90; SAR P-230001 **BS:** 196.

KING, Miles Sr; b 2 Nov 1746, Elizabeth City Co; d 9 Jun 1814 **RU:** Surg Mate Captain, Ent Serv Hampton in Elizabeth City Co. Commanded a co of Minutemen. Served when French arrived at Chesapeake and during siege of York **CEM:** St Paul's Episcopal; GPS 36.84733, -76.28554; 201 St Paul's Blvd; Norfolk City **GS:** Y **SP:** 1) Barbara Jones 2) Mar (27 Apr 1782 Elizabeth City Co) Martha Kirby (Nov 1765-29 Jan 1849 Norfolk) **VI:** One of first elected to VA legislature after Rev. Had 40+ yrs service to country, Burgoise representing Elizabeth City Co to Colonial assembly. Delegate & Justice of Peace Elizabeth City Co. In 1800 moved to Norfolk, as Alderman. Pen says he d in August. Widow appl pen Jan 1838 Norfolk. DAR marker 02 Dec 2012. W20342 **P:** unk **BLW:** Y **RG:** Y **MK:** Y DAR & SAR plaque **PH:** Y **SS:** CB; K Vol 3 pg 78; BY, pg 290; AK; CG pg 1955; DAR A064697; SAR P-260502 **BS:** 04.

KING, Robert; b 1765; d 1814 **RU:** Private, Served in 7th Cont Line **CEM:** King Family; GPS unk; Rt 658 Brent Point Rd; Stafford **GS:** Y **SP:** No info **VI:** No further data **P:** unk **BLW:** unk **RG:** N **MK:** N **PH:** unk **SS:** E pg 447 **BS:** 03 pg 262.

KING, Robert; b 1752; d 1821 **RU:** Soldier, Served in Capt John Smith's Co, Augusta Co **CEM:** West End; GPS 36.94140, -81.11670; off Rt 11, Wytheville; Wythe **GS:** U **SP:** No info **VI:** Remains moved fr Old West End Cemetery in 1959. Name listed on plaque in the cemetery **P:** unk **BLW:** unk **RG:** N **MK:** unk **PH:** unk **SS:** G pg 24 **BS:** 196.

KING, Stephen; b 2 Apr 1752; d 2 Apr 1836 **RU:** Soldier, Ent serv Henry Co 1780.Served in Capt James Shelton & Daniel Richardson's Co **CEM:** Ramsey-Stanley; GPS unk; Rt 764 nr Rt 606; Franklin **GS:** U **SP:** Mar (16 Dec 1785) Laurana Maupine (1750-1840) **VI:** Pen 1832 Franklin Co age 81. S5551 **P:** unk **BLW:** unk **RG:** Y **MK:** unk **PH:** unk **SS:** DAR #A064788; K Vol 3 pg 79; DD; SAR P-260557 **BS:** JLARC 4,19.

KING, William; b 1752; d 1810 **RU:** Private, Served in Christy's NC Regt **CEM:** Green Spring Presbyterian; GPS 36.63670, -81.99560; 2007 Green Spring Ch Rd, Abingdon; Washington **GS:** U **SP:** No info **VI:** Source 80 has d at age 88 **P:** unk **BLW:** unk **RG:** Y **MK:** unk **PH:** unk **SS:** NSSAR P-260583 **BS:** JLARC 2, 70, 80,101.

KING, William; b 8 Dec 1745, d 17 Mar 1817 **RU:** Soldier, Served in VA militia. Ent serv Bedford Co 1778. Assigned as guard at lead mines, Wythe Co in Capt Robert Adams Co **CEM:** King; GPS unk; W side of SR 625, S of jct with SR 667, Crockett; Wythe **GS:** U **SP:** Catherine Creger (9 Jun 1754-8 Feb 1841) d/o Michael & Catherine (-----) Creger **VI:** Cem reported in good condition in Oct 1998 **P:** unk **BLW:** unk **RG:** unk **MK:** unk **PH:** unk **SS:** AZ pg 134 **BS:** JLARC 40, 123.; 196

KING, William Sr; b unk; d unk **RU:** Private/Patriot, Ent serv Bedford Co 1778, then 2d VA State Regt and 3rd, 4th, 7th and 14th Cont Lines. Gave material aid to cause **CEM:** Trinity Episcopal; GPS 38.14917, -79.07521; 214 Beverley St; Staunton City **GS:** N **SP:** (-----) - she did receive a pension. **VI:** Son of Avra & (-----) King. Pen to widow commencing 2 Feb 1814 at $48 per yr **P:** Y **BLW:** N **RG:** N **MK:** N **PH:** N **SS:** E pg 448; AG pg 268; AL Ct Bk pg 43 Montgomery Co; AZ pg 134 **BS:** 142 Trinity.

KINHEAD (KINKEAD), Thomas; b 1757 Augusta Co; d 20 Nov 1841 **RU:** Private, Served in Capt Lockridge's Co, Augusta Co Militia **CEM:** Shinaberry; GPS unk; 3 mi N Hightown, Crabbottom; Highland **GS:** Y **SP:** Susan Hull (___-2 oct 1816) d/o Peter & Barbara (Penninger) Hull **VI:** Recd pension in Pendleton Co, WV **P:** unk **BLW:** unk **RG:** N **MK:** N **PH:** unk **SS:** E pg 448; CG pg 1980 **BS:** 181; 196.

RU=Rank/Unit	CEM=Cemetery	GS=Gravestone	SP=Spousal Information
VI=Other Veteran Info	P=Pension	BLW=Bounty/Land Warrant	RG=Registered Grave
MK=SAR/DAR Marker	PH=Photo	SS=Service Source	BS=Burial Source

232

KINSER (KENSOR), Michael; b 25 Feb 1762; d Dec 1822 **RU:** Private, Ent serv Wythe Co, 1st VA Regt. Wounded at Battle at Camden **CEM:** Broce-Kenser; GPS 37.23061, -80.45373; Boxwood Dr, Blacksburg; Montgomery **GS:** Y **SP:** Mar (4 Sep 1783 or 1784) Elizabeth (-----) **VI:** Pen disability commencing 1 Jan 1786. Widow appl pen 10 Jun 1844 in Wythe Co at 78 yrs, 11 mos, 21 days. Died (WP), Wythe Co. Pen records indicate death in Nov 1823. Will probated 10 Dec 1822, Wythe Co. W8001 **P:** Y **BLW:** unk **RG:** Y **MK:** N **PH:** N **SS:** E pg 719; K Vol 3 pg 81; CG pg 962; SAR P-260871 **BS:** 196.

KIPPS (KEPPS) (KIPS), Jacob; b 11 Nov 1760; d 20 Apr 1849 **RU:** Private, Served in VA Line **CEM:** Zirkle Family; GPS 38.65900, -78.69580; River Rd, New Market; Shenandoah **GS:** Y **SP:** Elizabeth Zirkle (19 May 1766-21 Jun 1857) d/o George Adam (1740-1800) & Elizabeth (Ridenour) (1752-1829) Zirkle **VI:** Son of George Michael & (-----) Kipps. Widow appl pen 1851.W7993. Also granted BLW 1855. BLW #35835 **P:** Y **BLW:** Y **RG:** Y Report sent but not up-dated **MK:** unk **PH:** unk **SS:** E pg 153; K Vol 3 pg 67; CG pg 1964 **BS:** 196.

KIRK, John II; b 10 Oct 1754, Fauquier Co; d 10 Dec 1850 **RU:** Soldier, Ent serv Fauquier Co 1776. Was at Valley Forge under command of Gen Washington **CEM:** Kirk Burial Grounds; GPS unk; Chapman-Straley Farm Rt 730, nr Eggleston Springs; Giles **GS:** Y **SP:** Elizabeth O'Bryant or O'Brien (1760-1829) **VI:** Appl for pension 27 Aug 1832 Giles Co S5558 **P:** Y **BLW:** unk **RG:** Y **MK:** unk **PH:** unk **SS:** E pg 449; K Vol 3 pg 82; CG pg 1965; SAR P-230544 **BS:** JLARC 1, 26; 196.

KIRKPATRICK, Robert; b 31 Dec 1764; d 12 Mar 1832 **RU:** Soldier, Served in 5th Cont line **CEM:** Alone Community, aka Bethany Lutheran; GPS unk; Rts 602 & 525, Kerrs Dist part 6; Rockbridge **GS:** U **SP:** Mar (5 Feb 1799) Anna Davidson (15 Dec 1780-18 Mar 1826) d/o Samuel (c1753-1799) & Elizabeth (Gilmore) Davidson **VI:** No further data **P:** N **BLW:** N **RG:** N **MK:** unk **PH:** unk **SS:** E pg 445 **BS:** 204.

KISER, Joseph, Sr; b 1756, d 1816 **RU:** Private Capt Michael Reader's Co, Shenandoah Co Militia **CEM:** Old Carbo; GPS: 36.92735,-82.19361; 100 yds N of E end Rt 664 bridge; Russell **GS:** Yes **SP:** Susannah Stacy (10 Jul 1754-23 Jul 1830) **VI:** Son of Charles Sebastian Keyser (16 Jan 1726, Germany-1778, Luray) and Mary Shelly (1737-1776) **P:** N **BLW:** N **RG:**Y **MK:** N, **PH:** N **SS:** C Sec IV, pg 602; DAR A204441; SAR P-331618 **BS;** 196

KISLING, George; b 1759, Berks Co, PA; d 19 Mar 1840 **RU:** Lieutenant, Served in Berks Co PA 1777-1780 **CEM:** Keesling; GPS unk; Rural Retreat; Wythe **GS:** Y **SP:** Catherine Gose (1766-1808) **VI:** Died in Speedwell, Wythe Co **P:** unk **BLW:** unk **RG** N **MK:** unk **PH:** Y **SS:** Cl PA Archives Series 3 Vol VI Stat of Accts pg Jacob Morgan **BS:** 196.

KISLING (KISSLING), Jacob; b 18 Jan 1760, Rockingham Co; d 1835 **RU:** Private, Ent serv Rockingham Co. Served in Capt Huston's Co, Maj Hamilton command at Wiliamsburg and at Yorktown 1781 in Capt Cowger's Co under Gen Muhlenburg & Washington **CEM:** Old Peaked Mountain; GPS 38.37113, -78.73416; 9843 Town Hall Rd, McGaheysville; Rockingham **GS:** Y **SP:** Mar (1782) Barbara Lingell (12 Mar 1742-14 Apr 1827) **VI:** Sol appl pen 15 Oct 1832 Rockingham Co S5554 **P:** Y **BLW:** unk **RG:**Y **MK:** Y DAR plaque **PH:** unk **SS:** J- DAR Hatcher, DAR #A065206; SAR P-261126 O pg 355; CG pg 1967 **BS:** JLARC 2.

KISSLING, Ditrick; b 12 Jan 1760; d 23 May 1785 **RU:** Private, Served 3 mos in Capt Knawl's VA Co. Enl fall 1780 for 3 mos in Capt John Rush's Co, Col Smith's VA Regt **CEM:** Old Peaked Mountain; GPS 38.37113, -78.73416; 9843 Town Hall Rd, McGaheysville; Rockingham **GS:** Y **SP:** No info **VI:** Common monument. Recd pen S16178 **P:** Y **BLW:** unk **RG:** Y **MK:** Y DAR plaque **PH:** unk **SS:** J-NSSAR 2000 Reg, B, C pg 38; P pg 383; SAR P-333539 **BS:** JLARC 76.

KISSLING, John; b unk; d unk **RU:** Patriot, Gave material aid to cause **CEM:** Old Peaked Mountain; GPS 38.37113, -78.73416; 9843 Town Hall Rd, McGaheysville; Rockingham **GS:** Y **SP:** No info **VI:** No further data **P:** N **BLW:** N **RG:** Y **MK:** Y DAR plaque **PH:** unk **SS:** P pg 353; SAR P-261146 **BS:** 04.

KISSLING (KISLING, KESLING), Hugh Conrad; b 1762, Berks Co, PA; d 12 May 1818 **RU:** Private, Served in PA Line. Enlisted Co Heisters Battalion. Served in Capt Baldys Co of Berks Co, PA Militia fr Aug-7 Sep 1780 **CEM:** Keesling; GPS unk; Grahams Forge; Wythe **GS:** Y **SP:** No info, has children **VI:** Son of Johann Georg (17 Feb 1734 Truchtelfinger, Baden-Wuerttemberg, Germany-3 Jun 1788 Wythe

RU=Rank/Unit	CEM=Cemetery	GS=Gravestone	SP=Spousal Information
VI=Other Veteran Info	P=Pension	BLW=Bounty/Land Warrant	RG=Registered Grave
MK=SAR/DAR Marker	PH=Photo	SS=Service Source	BS=Burial Source

233

Co) & (-----) Kissling. Died in Max Meadows, Wythe Co **P:** unk **BLW:** unk **RG:** Y **MK:** Y DAR plaque **PH:** Y **SS:** J-NSSAR 2000 Reg; P pg 353; P-261143 **BS:** JLARC 76; 47; 196.

KLEIN, George Jr; b 19 Dec 1740, Amwell, NJ; d 19 Aug 1798 **RU:** Private, Served in Armand's Legion, Capt Jacob Bauer's Co, in PA **CEM:** Kline Family; GPS 38.58118, -78.82895; Rt 1415 nr Broadway; Rockingham **GS:** Y **SP:** Elizabeth "Lizzie" Altaffer (1739-1825) **VI:** Son of Johannes George (1715-1783) & Dorothy (Rebman) (1714-1777) Klein **P:** unk **BLW:** unk **RG:** N **MK:** N **PH:** unk **SS:** AK; A pg 221 **BS:** 04; 191 Kline; 196.

KLINE, Jacob; b 23 Aug 1736; d 27 Aug 1816 **RU:** Private, Served in German Regt Cont Forces 1778, 1779 **CEM:** Trinity Evangelical Lutheran; GPS 39.08280, -78.21679; Mulberry St, Stephens City; Frederick **GS:** Y **SP:** Eva Dusong (6 Oct 1739 Germany-3 May 1815) **VI:** No further data **P:** unk **BLW:** unk **RG:** Y **MK:** N **PH:** unk **SS:** AP Service Roll; CI payroll; SAR P-230873 **BS:** 112 pg 2.

KOGER, Hans Jacob; b 24 Jul 1710, Baden Wurttemberg, Germany, d 13 Jul 1783 **RU:** Patriot, Gave material aid to cause in Henry Co **CEM:** Koger Family; GPS: not determined; Rt 698; Henry **GS:** Yes **SP:** Lucinda Crum (1710-1 Jan 1781) **VI:** No further data **P:** N **BLW:** N **RG :**N **MK:** N, **PH:** N **SS:** AL Certificate, Henry Co **BS**; 196.

KOGER, Henry, Sr; b 15 Oct 1742, Philadelphia Co, PA **RU:** Patriot, Paid Personal Property Tax, Henry Co 1783, considered a supply tax for Rev War expenses **CEM:** Koger Family; GPS: Not determined; Rt 698; Henry **GS:** Unk **SP:** Mar 1783, Henry Co, Mary King (1747-1845) **VI:** Son of Hans Jacob Koger (24 Jul 1710, Baden Wurttemberg, Germany-13 Jul 1783) and Lucinda Crum (1710-1 Jan 1781) **P:** N **BLW:** N **RG:** N **MK:** N, **PH:** N **SS:** DAR Ancestor A211536 cites Lib Va Pers Property Tax 1782-1830, Henry Co, reel 175 **BS**; 196

KOGER, John; b Jan 1745, Marrowbone Heights, Henry Co, d 18 Feb 1835 **RU:** Patriot, Gave material aid to cause **CEM:** Koger Family; GPS unk; E side Rt 626, just S jct with 703; Patrick **GS:** Yes **SP:** Mar 15 Sep 1807, Patrick Co, Mary Anderson (___-1 Aug 1845) **VI:** Son of Hans Jacob Koger (24 Jul Germany-13 Jul 1783) and Lucinda Crum (1710, PA-1 Jan 1781) **P:** N **BLW:** N **RG:** N **MK:** N, **PH:** N **SS:** AL Ct Bk pgs 15,30, Henry Co; DAR Ancestor A067202 **BS**; 196

KOINER, George Adam; b 7 Aug 1753, New Holland, Lancaster Co, PA; d 9 Dec 1830 **RU:** Private, Served in 2nd Bn, Col Samuel Lyon's Co **CEM:** Trinity Lutheran; GPS 38.17201, -78.86820; 2564 Rockfish Rd, Crimora; Augusta **GS:** Y **SP:** Barbara Smith **VI:** Son of Michael Keinadt (1720-1796) and Margaret Diller (1734-1813). DAR marker **P:** unk **BLW:** unk **RG:** Y **MK:** Y SAR **PH:** unk **SS:** BT; CD Cumberland Co, PA militia; SAR P-262080 **BS:** JLARC 1,3,8,62; 196.

KOINER, George Michael; b 1758, Lancaster Co, PA; d 10 Jun 1840 **RU:** Private, Served in PA Militia **CEM:** Trinity Lutheran; GPS 38.17201, -78.86820; 2564 Rockfish Rd, Crimora; Augusta **GS:** Y **SP:** Susanna Hawpe (1773-18 Dec 1848) d/o Rudolph (___-1802) & Catherine (Heilman) Hawpe **VI:** Son of Michael (1720-1796) & Margaret (Diller) (1734-1813) Keinadt. DAR marker **P:** unk **BLW:** unk **RG:** Y **MK:** Y **PH:** unk **SS:** AS SAR regis; AK cites DAR; BT; SAR P-262082 **BS:** JLARC 62, 63; 196.

KOINER, Kasper (Casper); b 25 Sep 1764 Millersville, Lancaster Co, PA; d 31 Oct 1856 **RU:** Private, Served in Capt John Stone Co, PA Militia 1781 **CEM:** Trinity Lutheran; GPS 38.17201, -78.86820; 2564 Rockfish Rd, Crimora; Augusta **GS:** Y **SP:** Anna Margaret Barger, d/o Jacob & (-----) Barger. "Eloped to Staunton" **VI:** Son of Michael Keinadt (1720-1796) and Margaret Diller (1734-1813). DAR marker **P:** unk **BLW:** unk **RG:** Y **MK:** Y **PH:** unk **SS:** AS; AK cites DAR; BT; CI PA Archives 5th Serv Vol 7 pg 137, 138; SAR P-262097 **BS:** 04 Aug 08; 80 vol 2 pg 240; JLARC 2, 8, 62; 196.

KOOGLER, George; b 3 Jan 1747, d 20 Apr 1819 **RU:** Patriot Paid personal property taxes in Rockingham County in1783 called supply tax to defray expenses of Rev War in Virginia **CEM:** Koogler Farm; GPS: unk; S side Rt 727 Airport Rd, Bridgewater; Rockingham **GS:** Yes but now gone as gravestones gathered in heap in field **SP:** mar (20 Jun 1806 (Bond)) Elizabeth Gilmore (___-aft Nov 1823), d/o Thomas & (-----) Gilmore **VI:** Cem loc on orig farm of ancestor **P:** N **BLW:** N **RG:** N **MK:** N, **PH:** N **SS:** DV **BS:** 191 Rockingham County Tombstones by Cemetery http://www.rootsweb.ancestry.com/~varockin/HRHS/cem/koogler.htm;

KREMER, KRAMER), Conrad; b 1748, Germany; d 29 May 1837 **RU:** Private, Served in PA Cont Line **CEM:** Mt Hebron; GPS 39.10916, -78.09497; 305 E Boscawen St; Winchester City **GS:** Y **SP:** Mar (before 1819) Catharine Helphenstine, (04 Jun 1761 Frederick Co-3 Jun 1825) d/o Major Peter & (-----)

RU=Rank/Unit	CEM=Cemetery	GS=Gravestone	SP=Spousal Information
VI=Other Veteran Info	P=Pension	BLW=Bounty/Land Warrant	RG=Registered Grave
MK=SAR/DAR Marker	PH=Photo	SS=Service Source	BS=Burial Source

234

Helphenstine. **VI**: He appl pen 2 Jun 1825 in Winchester, Frederick Co, age 77. S19372 **P**: Y **BLW**: N **RG**: Y **MK**: Y SAR monument **PH**: N **SS**: K Vol 3 pg 87; CG pg 1985; SAR P-262224 & SAR P-262168 **BS**: 196; JLARC 4, 47.

KRIDER, John, b c1754 PA, d 1814 **RU**: Private, Served in German Battalion. Continental Trps and/or Capt Jacob Brunner's Co, Lt Col Ludwick Wetbrier's PA Regt on payroll of Feb 1778 **CEM**: Trinity Evangelical Lutheran Church; GPS: 39.08280,-78.21679; Mulberry St, Stephens City; Frederick **GS**: Yes **SP**: Mary M (-----) (1781-1828) **VI**: No further data **P**: N **BLW**: N **RG**: N **MK**: N, **PH**: N **SS**: AP Fold3 Serv Index Card and Payrolls, pg 71 **BS**: 196.

KRIM (GRIM, CRIM), John; b Oct 1755/1756; d 19 Apr 1840 Frederick Co **RU**: Private, Ent serv Lancaster Co PA. Served in PA & NJ Lines. Fought at Trenton, Statton Island, Ft Washington **CEM**: Trinity Evangelical Lutheran; GPS 39.08280, -78.21679; Mulberry St, Stephens City; Frederick **GS**: Y **SP**: 1) Juliana Mainger 2) mar (2 Nov 1821) Phoebe (Coleman) Drake (c1776-__) **VI**: Sol appl pen 7 Nov 1832 Frederick Co. S26182. Widow appl pen 23 Nov 1853 Belmont Co OH; Widow appl BLW 3 Sep 1855, BLW 338508-160, NOTE: PRS has him buried in OH, perhaps memorialized there -55 **P**: Y **BLW**: Y **RG**: Y **MK**: Y **PH**: Y **SS**: B; CG pg 1986; SAR P-170915 **BS**: 04.

KRING, John; b 2 Sep 1744, Haiger, Germany; d 16 Dec 1802 **RU**: Sergeant, Served in 3rd, 5th, 7th, & 11th Cont Lines **CEM**: Kring Salvage; GPS unk; Off John Deere Dr, behind Harman Machinery, Broadway; Rockingham **GS**: N **SP**: Catherine Arnold (1746-1820) **VI**: Son of Johannes & Catherine (Arnold) (Kring) Jost of Lancaster, PA. Died at Linville Creek, Rockingham Co **P**: unk **BLW**: unk **RG**: N **MK**: N **PH**: N **SS**: AK; E pg 447 **BS**: 04; 191 Salvage.

KULLERS (CULLERS), Jacob; b 1725; d 1805 **RU**: Private?, For service, check DAR who installed grave marker **CEM**: Dry Run Church; GPS 38.85929, -78.40075; Rt 678, Fort Valley Rd nr jct with Dry Run Rd, Seven Fountains; Shenandoah **GS**: Y **SP**: Mar (1742 Germany) Mary Magdalena (-----) (1723-__) **VI**: No further data **P**: unk **BLW**: unk **RG**: N **MK**: N **PH**: unk **SS**: BT **BS**: 04; 196.

KULLERS (KULLER), Johannes, "John"; b 12 Dec 1748, Frederick Co, MD; d 13 Dec 1796 **RU**: Patriot, was member of Committee of Observation in MD **CEM**: Dry Run Church; GPS 38.857689, -78.400195; 8398 Fort Valley Rd; Shenandoah **GS**: Y **SP**: Mar (4 Apr 1775 Frederick Co MD) Anna Marie Muller (1750-1832) **VI**: Son of Jacob (1725-1805) Koeller & Mary Magdalene Abeline **P**: unk **BLW**: unk **RG**: Y **MK**:Y DAR plaque & SAR granite **PH**: unk **SS**: BT; DAR A028456 cites MD Hist Mag, Vol II, pgs 163,169 SAR P-142048 **BS**: 04.

KURTZ, Adam; b 1747, Germany; d 1815 **RU**: Private, Served in Gen Daniel Morgan's Riflemen fr Frederick Co. Was in Battle of Quebec, captured and was POW for 6 mos. Was member of Morgan's Dutch Mess **CEM**: Mt Hebron; GPS 39.10916, -78.09497; 305 E Boscawen St; Winchester City **GS**: Y **SP**: Mar (30 Dec 1813, Frederick Co) Elizabeth Bennett (Return) **VI**: Owned a boot and shoemakers shop in Winchester. Bur in the Centenary Reformed UCC portion of the Mt Hebron Cemetery. Marriage to Elizabeth may be for another member of his family **P**: unk **BLW**: unk **RG**: Y **MK**: Y SAR monument **PH**: Y **SS**: E pg 452; SAR P-262406 **BS**: J-NSSAR 1993 Reg.

KYGER, Christian; b 27 Nov 1748, Lancaster Co, PA; d Bef Jan 1830 **RU**: Lieutenant, Took oath 27 Aug 1781 **CEM**: Old Peaked Mountain; GPS 38.37113, -78.73416; 9843 Town Hall Rd, McGaheysville; Rockingham **GS**: U **SP**: Mar (c1762) Margaret Armentrout . 2) Caty Dundore **VI**: Son of Wilhelm & Eva Barbara (Stober) Geiger **P**: unk **BLW**: unk **RG**: Y **MK**: Y DAR plaque **PH**: unk **SS**: J-NSSAR 2000 Reg; SAR P-262438 **BS**: JLARC 76.

KYLE, David Sr; b 1757; d 25 Oct 1844 **RU**: Patriot, Gave material aid to cause **CEM**: Massanutten Cross Keys; GPS 38.35817, -78.84124; Rt 679 at Cross Keys, vic jct Rts 276 & 679; Rockingham **GS**: Y **SP**: Mar (period 1 Dec 1775-78 Buckingham Co) Elizabeth Chambers (__-1846) **VI**: No further data **P**: N **BLW**: N **RG**: N **MK**: N **PH**: Y **SS**: AL Ct Bk pg 33 **BS**: 191 Massan; 196.

KYLE, William; b 1736, Tyrone Co, Ireland; d 25 Jun 1832 **RU**: Private, Served in Botetourt Co Militia **CEM**: Fincastle Presbyterian; GPS 37.50017, -79.87558; 108 E Back St, Fincastle; Botetourt **GS**: Y **SP**: Mar (1750, Ireland) Sara Ann Stevens **VI**: Son of Robert Kyle & Betty Ann Campbell. Came to VA with his parents in 1759 first settling in Richmond Co. Pensioner. Name is on the SAR plaque at this

RU=Rank/Unit VI=Other Veteran Info MK=SAR/DAR Marker | CEM=Cemetery P=Pension PH=Photo | GS=Gravestone BLW=Bounty/Land Warrant SS=Service Source | SP=Spousal Information RG=Registered Grave BS=Burial Source

235

cemetery **P:** Y **BLW:** unk **RG:** Y **MK:** Y SAR plaque **PH:** unk **SS:** E pg 452; DAR A067652; SAR P-232018 **BS:** 196.

KYNION, William; b unk; d 1781 **RU:** Soldier, Served fr NY, killed in the battle at Yorktown **CEM:** Yorktown Victory Monument Tablet; GPS 38.28350, -78.54150; Yorktown; York **GS:** U **SP:** No info **VI:** No further data **P:** unk **BLW:** unk **RG:** unk **MK:** unk **PH:** unk **SS:** J-Yorktown Historian; SAR P-262458 **BS:** JLARC 74.

LABBE, Jean; b unk; d 1781 **RU:** Seaman, Served on "Caton" and died from Yorktown battle **CEM:** French Memorial; GPS 36.81944, -79.39933; Yorktown; York **GS:** U **SP:** No info **VI:** No further data **P:** unk **BLW:** unk **RG:** Y **MK:** unk **PH:** unk **SS:** J-Yorktown Historian; SAR P-232074 **BS:** JLARC 1, 74.

LACOSTE, Jean; b unk; d 1781 **RU:** Soldier, Served in Gatinais Bn and died fr battle at Yorktown **CEM:** French Memorial; GPS 36.81944, -79.39933; Yorktown; York **GS:** U **SP:** no info **VI:** No further data **P:** unk **BLW:** unk **RG:** Y **MK:** unk **PH:** unk **SS:** J-Yorktown Historian; SAR P-232130 **BS:** JLARC 1, 74.

LACROIX, Guillaume; b unk; d 1781 **RU:** Soldier, Served in Gatinais Bn and died fr battle at Yorktown **CEM:** French Memorial; GPS 36.81944, -79.39933; Yorktown; York **GS:** U **SP:** No info **VI:** No further data **P:** unk **BLW:** unk **RG:** Y **MK:** unk **PH:** unk **SS:** J-Yorktown Historian; SAR P-232135 **BS:** JLARC 1, 74.

LACROIX, Jean; b unk; d 1781 **RU:** Soldier, Served in Soissonnais Bn and died fr battle at Yorktown **CEM:** French Memorial; GPS 36.81944, -79.39933; Yorktown; York **GS:** U **SP:** No info **VI:** No further data **P:** unk **BLW:** unk **RG:** Y **MK:** unk **PH:** unk **SS:** J-Yorktown Historian; SAR P-232136 **BS:** JLARC 1, 74.

LACROIX, Pierre; b c1743; d 22 Sep 1830 **RU:** Private?, Check Geo Washington Chapter files for service **CEM:** St Mary's Catholic; GPS 38.79390, -77.04750; 310 S Royal St; Alexandria City **GS:** Y **SP:** No info **VI:** Served as drummer boy in the French & Indian War (for the French) and his death notice says he later served in the Revolution. Died at the home of Mr. Edward Smyth (Alexandria Gazette, 27 Sep 1831, pg 3) **P:** unk **BLW:** unk **RG:** Y **MK:** Y SAR plaque **PH:** Y **SS:** SAR P-334431; BP Obit **BS:** 174 pg 304;196.

LACY, Mathew; b Apr 1748, Hanover Co; d 7 Mar 1823 **RU:** Ensign Second Lieutenant/ Patriot, Ent serv Goochland Co 1779. Served in Capt Humphrey Parrish's Co, Taylors Regt, VA Troops **CEM:** Lacy Family; GPS 37.80571, -77.99405; Rt 615; Hadensville, Goochland **GS:** Y **SP:** Mar (8 Apr 1772) Susanna Rutherford (6 Apr 1750 Goochland Co-26 Jun 1839 Goochland Co) **VI:** Son of Stephen Lacy (1705-1772) & Sarah Johnson (1730-1794). Brother Charles Lacy also served fr Hanover Co. Widow appl pen 7 Mar 1838 age 88 Goochland Co. W8077 **P:** Y **BLW:** unk **RG:** Y **MK:** N **PH:** Y **SS:** D pg 143; E pg 453; K Vol 3 pg 88; CG pg 1990; SAR P-232146 **BS:** 46 pg 176; 196.

LADD, William; b 30 Dec 1736, Little Compton, RI; d 3 Dec 1800 **RU:** Captain, Served in Rhode Island **CEM:** Old Presbyterian Meeting House; GPS 38.48528, -77.23532; 323 S Fairfax St; Alexandria City **GS:** Y **SP:** Sarah Gardner (1725-30 Oct 1807) d/o Benoni & (-----) Gardner, Esq. of Newport, RI, "consort of William Ladd" **VI:** State legislator fr Rhode Island that ratified the US Constitution. Died visiting his children. Death notice in the Alexandria Gazette, 6 Dec 1800. Listed on SAR plaque in cemetery **P:** unk **BLW:** unk **RG:** Y **MK:** Y SAR plaque **PH:** unk **SS:** B; AK; SAR P-232221 **BS:** JLARC 1, 86; 23 pg 104; 196.

LAFAYETTE, James; b unk; d 9 Aug 1830 **RU:** Soldier, Served as a double agent and spy **CEM:** Afro-American aka East End; GPS 37.53640, -77.38640; Bulheller Rd; Henrico **GS:** U **SP:** No info **VI:** Black Soldier. Petitioned for pension in New Kent Co. He was the property of William Armistead. Emancipated by VA Legislature 1786 **P:** Y in Culpeper Co, at rate of $40 per year and was given $60 immediate relief **BLW:** unk **RG:** Y **MK:** unk **PH:** unk **SS:** J-NSSAR 1993 Reg;BX pg 457 SAR P-232235 **BS:** JLARC 1.

LAFOSSE, Antoine; b unk; d 1781 **RU:** Soldier, Served in Bourbonnais Bn and died fr battle at Yorktown **CEM:** French Memorial; GPS 36.81944, -79.39933; Yorktown; York **GS:** U **SP:** No info **VI:** No further data **P:** unk **BLW:** unk **RG:** Y **MK:** unk **PH:** unk **SS:** J-Yorktown Historian; SAR P-232267 **BS:** JLARC 1, 74.

RU=Rank/Unit
VI=Other Veteran Info
MK=SAR/DAR Marker

CEM=Cemetery
P=Pension
PH=Photo

GS=Gravestone
BLW=Bounty/Land Warrant
SS=Service Source

SP=Spousal Information
RG=Registered Grave
BS=Burial Source

236

LAFOSSE, Charles; b unk; d 1781 **RU:** Seaman, Served on "Duc De Bourgogne" and died from Yorktown battle **CEM:** French Memorial; GPS 36.81944, -79.39933; Yorktown; York **GS:** U **SP:** No info **VI:** No further data **P:** unk **BLW:** unk **RG:** Y **MK:** unk **PH:** unk **SS:** J-Yorktown Historian; SAR P-232268 **BS:** JLARC 1, 74.

LAFRANCE, Nicolas; b unk; d 1781 **RU:** Seaman, Served on "Diademe" and died from Yorktown battle **CEM:** French Memorial; GPS 36.81944, -79.39933; Yorktown; York **GS:** U **SP:** No info **VI:** No further data **P:** unk **BLW:** unk **RG:** Y **MK:** unk **PH:** unk **SS:** J-Yorktown Historian; SAR P-232270 **BS:** JLARC 1, 74.

LAGADENE, Jean; b unk; d 1781 **RU:** Seaman, Served on "Languedoc" and died from Yorktown battle **CEM:** French Memorial; GPS 36.81944, -79.39933; Yorktown; York **GS:** U **SP:** No info **VI:** No further data **P:** unk **BLW:** unk **RG:** Y **MK:** unk **PH:** unk **SS:** J-Yorktown Historian; SAR P-232271 **BS:** JLARC 1, 74.

LAGNEL, Louis; b unk; d 1781 **RU:** Seaman, Served on "Diademe" and died from Yorktown battle **CEM:** French Memorial; GPS 36.81944, -79.39933; Yorktown; York **GS:** U **SP:** No info **VI:** No further data **P:** unk **BLW:** unk **RG:** Y **MK:** unk **PH:** unk **SS:** J-Yorktown Historian; SAR P-232274 **BS:** JLARC 1, 74.

LAINE, Philippe; b unk; d 1781 **RU:** Solider, Served in Gatinais Bn and died fr battle at Yorktown **CEM:** French Memorial; GPS 36.81944, -79.39933; Yorktown; York **GS:** U **SP:** No info **VI:** No further data **P:** unk **BLW:** unk **RG:** Y **MK:** unk **PH:** unk **SS:** J-Yorktown Historian; SAR P-232289 **BS:** JLARC 1, 74.

LAINE, William; b 1760; d 1807 **RU:** Private, Served in 1st & 10th Cont Lines under Col William Christian, 1st Battalion, Cherokee Expedition Aug 1776 **CEM:** Laine Family; GPS unk; Amherst; Amherst **GS:** U **SP:** 1) (-----) 2) Mar (5 May 1794 Amherst Co) Rebeccah Berry, spinster **VI:** No further data **P:** unk **BLW:** unk **RG:** Y **MK:** N **PH:** unk **SS:** E pg 454; DL pgs 1419,1420; DN1884; DAR A068836; SAR P-232292 **BS:** SAR PRS.

LAIRD, James; b 1740; d 18 Nov 1827 **RU:** Private, Served in Capt Peachy Gilmore's Co, Augusta Co Militia **CEM:** Falling Springs Presbyterian; GPS 37.68494, -79.45105; 410 Falling Springs Rd, Glasgow; Rockbridge **GS:** Y **SP:** No info **VI:** No further data **P:** unk **BLW:** unk **RG:** N **MK:** unk **PH:** unk **SS:** E pg 454 **BS:** 196.

LALOGE, Pierre de; b unk; d 1781 **RU:** Soldier, Served in Auxonne Bn and died fr battle at Yorktown **CEM:** French Memorial; GPS 36.81944, -79.39933; Yorktown; York **GS:** U **SP:** No info **VI:** No further data **P:** unk **BLW:** unk **RG:** Y **MK:** unk **PH:** unk **SS:** J-Yorktown Historian; SAR P-232411 **BS:** JLARC 1, 74.

LAMBERT, Blaise; b unk; d 1781 **RU:** Soldier, Served in Touraine Bn and died fr battle at Yorktown **CEM:** French Memorial; GPS 36.81944, -79.39933; Yorktown; York **GS:** U **SP:** No info **VI:** No further data **P:** unk **BLW:** unk **RG:** Y **MK:** unk **PH:** unk **SS:** J-Yorktown Historian; SAR P-232503 **BS:** JLARC 1, 74.

LAMESSE, Etienne; b unk; d 1781 **RU:** Seaman, Served on "Marseillais" and died from Yorktown battle **CEM:** French Memorial; GPS 36.81944, -79.39933; Yorktown; York **GS:** U **SP:** No info **VI:** No further data **P:** unk **BLW:** unk **RG:** Y **MK:** unk **PH:** unk **SS:** J-Yorktown Historian; SAR P-232554 **BS:** JLARC 1, 74.

LAMM (LAMIE), John; b 1763; d 6 Mar 1830 **RU:** Private, Served in10th Cont Line **CEM:** Lamie Family; GPS unk; 2 mi E of Saltville; Smyth **GS:** N **SP:** Eleanor (-----) (__-1846) **VI:** Cemetery may have been destroyed by cattle. **P:** unk **BLW:** unk **RG:** N **MK:** N **PH:** unk **SS:** E pg 455 **BS:** 97 vol 1 pg 44.

LAMME, James; b 1732; d 3 Apr 1819 **RU:** Sergeant, Served in 8th Cont Line **CEM:** Lamie Family; GPS unk; 2 mi E of Saltville; Smyth **GS:** Y **SP:** No info **VI:** No further data **P:** unk **BLW:** unk **RG:** N **MK:** N **PH:** unk **SS:** E pg 455 **BS:** 97 vol 1 pg 44.

LAMY, Pierre; b unk; d 1781 **RU:** Seaman, Served on "Languedoc" and died from Yorktown battle **CEM:** French Memorial; GPS 36.81944, -79.39933; Yorktown; York **GS:** U **SP:** No info **VI:** No further data **P:** unk **BLW:** unk **RG:** Y **MK:** unk **PH:** unk **SS:** J-Yorktown Historian; SAR P-232647 **BS:** JLARC 1,74.

RU=Rank/Unit
VI=Other Veteran Info
MK=SAR/DAR Marker

CEM=Cemetery
P=Pension
PH=Photo

GS=Gravestone
BLW=Bounty/Land Warrant
SS=Service Source

SP=Spousal Information
RG=Registered Grave
BS=Burial Source

237

LANCASTER, John; b 3 Mar 1763, Goochland Co; d 28 Jan 1826 **RU**: Private, For service check special report by Department of Archives and History, Lib of VA **CEM**: Clover Forest; GPS unk; 3 mi W of Farmville nr Sandy Fork Bridge; Prince Edward **GS**: U **SP**: Drusilla Legrand (13 Apr 1769-14 Dec 1825) d/o Alexander (1728-1825) & Lucy (Walker) (1735-1825) Legrand **VI**: No further data **P**: unk **BLW**: unk **RG**: Y **MK**: unk **PH**: unk **SS**: E pg 455; CZ; SAR P-232656 **BS**: 196.

LAND, William See Appendix G Addenda

LANDES (LANDIS), John; b 1752, Windsor, York Co, PA; d Oct 1819 **RU**: Private, Served in Kaufflet's Co, PA Troops **CEM**: Landes   Family; GPS 38.30110, -78.97170; W fr Burketown 2 mi, near Weyers Cave; Augusta **GS**: Y **SP**: Catherine Miller (1749-May 1834) **VI**: Son of Christian Landes (1728-1782). Govt stone **P**: unk **BLW**: unk **RG**: N **MK**: unk **PH**: unk **SS**: B; Cl PA Archives 5th serv Vol 2 pg 443 **BS**: JLARC 2, 8, 62; 80 vol 3, pg 4; 196.

LANE, Anna Maria; b unk, prob NH; d 1810 **RU**: Soldier, Served when husband was wounded in 1776-1777 at Battle of Germantown by using his clothes. Was also wounded. Later served in Light Horse Harry Lee's Regt, in 2d siege of Augusta, GA, 22 May to 5 Jan 1781 **CEM**: Cem name unk; GPS 37.32337, -77.26132; Nr State Capitol; Richmond City **GS**: U **SP**: John Lane (1723-14 Jul 1823) **VI**: Only documented woman veteran of the Rev War to reside in Virginia. After war served in public guard in city and at military hospital. Rec'd $100 a yr effective 1808. Memorialized on Va Historical Road sign **P**: Y **BLW**: N **RG**: N **MK**: Y Y SAR **PH**: N **SS**: BX pg 460 **BS**: 196.

LANE, Corbin; b 1750, Baltimore MD; d 2 Sept 1816 or 8 Dec 1817 **RU**: Patriot, Provided support for NC Cont Line **CEM**: Pendleton; GPS 36.67145, -82.66248; Rt 664, Manville; Scott **GS**: Y **SP**: Frances "Fanny" Preck (possibly Brock, Prock, or Proctor) **VI**: Son of Samuel (1700-1799) & Mary Jane (Corbin) Lane (1708-1773) **P**: N **BLW**: N **RG**: Y **MK**: N **PH**: Y **SS**: O; H; DAR A113717; SAR P-232823 **BS**: 04.

LANE, John; b 1723; d 14 July 1823 **RU**: Private, Ent serv NH 1778. Was taken POW & released. Served in Capt Ambrose Madison's Co, Francis Taylor's VA Regt, & 3rd & 5th Cont Line **CEM**: Shockoe Hill; GPS 37.55190, -77.43170; 4th & Hospital Sts; Richmond City **GS**: Y **SP**: Ann Maria (-----) (1733-__). Wife also fought as man at Germantown and was seriously wounded and drew a pension in 1807, she being the only woman pensioned in VA for RW service. **VI**: Sol appl pen in Chesterfield Co 4 Dec 1819. S38129, R1520 **P**: Y **BLW**: unk **RG**: N **MK**: Name on monument **PH**: unk **SS**: E pg 456; G pg 1, 2; K Vol 3 pg 95; CG pg 2007 **BS**: 196.

LANE, Joseph; b 1750; d 12 Mar 1803 **RU**: Lieutenant Colonel/Patriot, Served in Westmoreland Co Militia. Was Commissioner of Provisional Law in 1780 **CEM**: Lane Family; GPS unk; Leithtown; Loudoun **GS**: Y **SP**: Mar (c1763) Katherine Newton (c1745-__) **VI**: No further data **P**: unk **BLW**: unk **RG** N **MK**: N **PH**: unk **SS**: E pg 456; J-Yorktown Historian **BS**: 25 pg 174.

LANE, William; b 30 Aug 1740; d 16 Mar 1808 **RU**: Captain, Served in Loudoun Co Militia. Promoted 9 Sep 1777 **CEM**: Lane Family; GPS 38.90658, -77.38822; 12700 Franklin Farm Rd, Centreville; Fairfax **GS**: U **SP**: 1) Katherine Eskridge 2) Sarah (Sally) Rowles Higgs (1760-1826) **VI**: Son of James L & Lydia (Hardage) Lane. Pen records indicate birthdate of 10 Mar 1754. Appl for pen 2 Mar 1824 Charlotte Co, VA **P**: Y **BLW**: unk **RG**: Y **MK**: unk **PH**: unk **SS**: E pg 456; CG pg 2010; SAR P-232993 & SAR P-334067 **BS**: 196.

LANGBORNE, William; b 1750; d 1814 **RU**: Major/Patriot, Was Ens 6th Cont Line 27 Apr 1777. Later was promoted to Maj. Recd Brevet Commission fr US Congress of Lt Col 6 Oct 1783. Also gave 2250# beef to cause **CEM**: Langborne Family; GPS unk; At Langborne on bank of Pamunkey River; King William **GS**: U **SP**: Elizabeth (-----) **VI**: Awarded 6224 acres BLW in 1824 as a major. Tomb reported in 1897 source: "A hero and patriot of the Revolution" **P**: unk **BLW**: Y **RG**: Y **MK**: unk **PH**: unk **SS**: D pg 17 King William Co; G pg 402; SAR P-233044 **BS**: JLARC 106.

LANGLOIS, Jacques; b 1750; d 1781 **RU**: Soldier, Served in Soissonnais Bn and died fr battle at Yorktown **CEM**: French Memorial; GPS 36.81944, -79.39933; Yorktown; York **GS**: U **SP**: No info **VI**: No further data **P**: unk **BLW**: unk **RG**: Y **MK**: unk **PH**: unk **SS**: J-Yorktown Historian; SAR P-233120 **BS**: JLARC 1, 74.

RU=Rank/Unit
VI=Other Veteran Info
MK=SAR/DAR Marker

CEM=Cemetery
P=Pension
PH=Photo

GS=Gravestone
BLW=Bounty/Land Warrant
SS=Service Source

SP=Spousal Information
RG=Registered Grave
BS=Burial Source

238

LANIER, Benjamin Bird; b 1711, Surry Co; d 12 Dec 1796 **RU**: Patriot, Signed Oath of Allegiance 10 Oct 1778. Gave money & supplies to aid the Revolution **CEM**: Lanier Family; GPS unk; Nr Smoky Ordinary & Poarch Store; Brunswick **GS**: N **SP**: 1) Mar (c1737 Surry Co) Elizabeth Warren (?) (1719-1775) 2) Mar (26 Nov 1776) Lucy (-----) Pennington (___-Dec 1781 or Jan 1782), a widow 3) Mar (28 Apr 1783 Brunswick Co) Ann (-----) Wilkinson, a widow **VI**: Son of John Lanier (1680-1727) DAR marker on Gr **P**: N **BLW**: N **RG**: Y **MK**: Y **DAR PH**: N **SS**: Al Ct Bk 1 pg 121; DAR A069061; SAR P-233153 **BS**: 196.

LANNOY, Jean de; b 1750; d 1781 **RU**: Soldier, Served in Gatinais Bn and died fr battle at Yorktown **CEM**: French Memorial; GPS 36.81944, -79.39933; Yorktown; York **GS**: U **SP**: No info **VI**: No further data **P**: unk **BLW**: unk **RG**: Y **MK**: unk **PH**: unk **SS**: J-Yorktown Historian; SAR P-233193 **BS**: JLARC 1, 74.

LANPHIER, Robert Going; b1765, d 1846 **RU**: Patriot, paid personal property tax, a Rev War supply tax, Fairfax Co 1782 & 1783 **CEM**: Trinity United Methodist; GPS 39.13600, -77.00610; 2911 Cameron Mills Rd; Alexandria City **GS**: Y **SP**: Elizabeth (-----)(8 Mar 1771-6 Jun 1853) **VI**: No further data **P**: N **BLW**: N **RG**: N **MK**: Y **PH**: N **SS**: DV Fairfax Co, 1782 & 1783 pdf images 10 & 16 **BS**: 196

LAROCHE, Etienne; b 1750; d 1781 **RU**: Soldier, Served in Soissonnais Bn and died fr battle at Yorktown **CEM**: French Memorial; GPS 36.81944, -79.39933; Yorktown; York **GS**: U **SP**: No info **VI**: No further data **P**: unk **BLW**: unk **RG**: Y **MK**: unk **PH**: unk **SS**: J-Yorktown Historian; SAR P-233330 **BS**: JLARC 1, 74.

LAROSE, Jean; b 1750; d 1781 **RU**: Seaman, Served on "Saint-Esprit" and died from Yorktown battle **CEM**: French Memorial; GPS 36.81944, -79.39933; Yorktown; York **GS**: U **SP**: No info **VI**: No further data **P**: unk **BLW**: unk **RG**: Y **MK**: unk **PH**: unk **SS**: J-Yorktown Historian; SAR P-233332 **BS**: JLARC 1, 74.

LARRICK, Casper; b c1730, France; d 1801 **RU**: Soldier/Patriot, Served in Ohio 1775-76. Gave material aid to cause **CEM**: Mt Olive; GPS 39.22610, -78.72000; 327 Mt Olive Rd, Hayfield; Frederick **GS**: Y **SP**: 1) (-----) 2) Mar (1772, Frederick Co) Elizabeth Sundown (c1750-23 Aug 1847) **VI**: Came to America abt 1755 with surname of La Roque, next revision was Laruck. DAR marker. **P**: unk **BLW**: unk **RG**: Y **MK**: Y **DAR PH**: unk **SS**: DAR A066852; AL cert issued; SAR P-233371 **BS**: 59 pg 185; 196.

LARUE, Isaac; b 11 Jan 1713, Hunterdon Co, NJ; d 20 Mar 1795 **RU**: Patriot, Gave 2419# beef, 1756# flour, over 150# bacon, pasturage for livestock **CEM**: Old Buck Marsh Meeting House; GPS 39.94730, -77.58370; nr Barryville Meeting House; Clarke **GS**: Y **SP**: Mar (1743) Phebe Carmen (4 Mar 1725, Cranbury, Middlesex Co, NJ-25 Jan 1804, Berryville, Clark Co) d/o James (1677-1756) & (-----) Carman **VI**: GS lost. Actually bur in field outside Berryville **P**: N **BLW**: N **RG**: Y **MK**: N **PH**: unk **SS**: DAR #A066874; AL Ct Bk pg 22, 23, 36 Frederick Co; SAR P-233384 **BS**: Serv Source AR vol 3 pg 1; DAR report; 80vol 3, pg 1; 196.

LATAUPE, Gilbert; b unk; d 1781 **RU**: Soldier, Served in Soissonnais Bn and died fr battle at Yorktown **CEM**: French Memorial; GPS 36.81944, -79.39933; Yorktown; York **GS**: U **SP**: No info **VI**: No further data **P**: unk **BLW**: unk **RG**: Y **MK**: unk **PH**: unk **SS**: J-Yorktown Historian; SAR P-233452 **BS**: JLARC 1.

LAUCK (LAUK), Peter; b 31 Dec 1753; d 2 Oct 1839 **RU**: Private, Served in Gen Daniel Morgan's Riflemen in Frederick Co. Ent serv 1775 in Winchester. Marched to Boston and was in the Battle at Quebec. Lost his hearing in the battle **CEM**: Mt Hebron; GPS 39.184016, -78.160553; 305 E Boscawen St; Winchester City **GS**: Y **SP**: Mar (27 Oct 1779) Emily (QLF says Amelia) Heiskell. (c1766-1840) **VI**: Built and ran the Red Lion Tavern in Winchester. Bur in the Centenary Reformed UCC portion of the Mt Hebron Cemetery. DAR marker. Sol appl pen 9 Aug 1832 Frederick Co. Widow appl pen 2 Apr 1840 Winchester VA. F-R6183, R1530 1832 Frederick Co. Her application rejected. **P**: Y **BLW**: unk **RG**: Y **MK**: Y **DAR & SAR** granite & monument **PH**: N **SS**: J-NSSAR 1993 Reg; K Vol 3 pg 102; CG pg 2024; DAR A071747; SAR P-233677 **BS**: 196; JLARC 1.

LAUCK, Simon; b 1760; d 1815 **RU**: Private, Participated in march to Boston under Morgan's riflemen **CEM**: Mt Hebron; GPS 39.18412, -78.16054; 305 E Boscawen St; Winchester City **GS**: Y **SP**: 1) Catherine Starr 2) Mar (26 Oct 1803 Frederick Co) Mary Sensency (Return) **VI**: He owned a gunsmith shop in Winchester and manufactured a rifle with his name. Bur in the Centenary Reformed UCC portion

RU=Rank/Unit	CEM=Cemetery	GS=Gravestone	SP=Spousal Information
VI=Other Veteran Info	P=Pension	BLW=Bounty/Land Warrant	RG=Registered Grave
MK=SAR/DAR Marker	PH=Photo	SS=Service Source	BS=Burial Source

of the Mt Hebron Cemetery. DAR marker. **P:** N **BLW:** N **RG:** Y **MK:** Y DAR & Y SAR granite & monument **PH:** N **SS:** CG pg 2024; J-NSSAR 1993 Reg; DAR A071749; SAR P-233640 **BS:** 196; JLARC 1.

LAUGHLIN, Alexander; b c1746; d 25 Nov 1806 **RU:** Patriot, Gave to cause in Montgomery Co **CEM:** Walnut Grove; GPS unk; Lee Hwy, Bristol; Washington **GS:** Y **SP:** Mar (9 Nov 1769 Hanover, York Co, PA) Ann Sharp (9 Nov 1751 Lancaster PA-18 Feb 1834) **VI:** No further data **P:** N **BLW:** N **RG:** N **MK:** N **PH:** unk **SS:** G pg 217-218 **BS:** 78 pg 375; 196.

LAURENCEAU, Jean; b unk; d 1781 **RU:** Soldier, Served in Gatinais Bn and died fr battle at Yorktown **CEM:** French Memorial; GPS 36.81944, -79.39933; Yorktown; York **GS:** U **SP:** No info **VI:** No further data **P:** unk **BLW:** unk **RG:** Y **MK:** unk **PH:** unk **SS:** J-Yorktown Historian; SAR P-233713 **BS:** JLARC 1, 74.

LAURENS, Jean; b unk; d 1781 **RU:** Soldier, Served on "Caton" and died from Yorktown battle **CEM:** French Memorial; GPS 36.81944, -79.39933; Yorktown; York **GS:** U **SP:** No info **VI:** No further data **P:** unk **BLW:** unk **RG:** Y **MK:** unk **PH:** unk **SS:** J-Yorktown Historian; SAR P-233716 **BS:** JLARC 1, 74.

LAURENT, Daniel; b unk; d 1781 **RU:** Soldier, Served in Touraine Bn and died fr battle at Yorktown **CEM:** French Memorial; GPS 36.81944, -79.39933; Yorktown; York **GS:** U **SP:** No info **VI:** No further data **P:** unk **BLW:** unk **RG:** Y **MK:** unk **PH:** unk **SS:** J-Yorktown Historian; SAR P-233718 **BS:** JLARC 1, 74.

LAURENT, Jacques; b unk; d 1781 **RU:** Soldier, Served in Gatinais Bn and died fr battle at Yorktown **CEM:** French Memorial; GPS 36.81944, -79.39933; Yorktown; York **GS:** U **SP:** No info **VI:** No further data **P:** unk **BLW:** unk **RG:** Y **MK:** unk **PH:** unk **SS:** J-Yorktown Historian; SAR P-233719 **BS:** JLARC 1, 74.

LAVERTY(LAFFERTY), Ralph; b 1715, Ireland; d Aft Jun 1792 **RU:** Patriot, Gave material aid to cause **CEM:** Laverty Farm; GPS unk; Cow pasture; Bath **GS:** U **SP:** 1) Elizabeth Stuart; 2) Jane Hicklin **VI:** No further data **P:** N **BLW:** N **RG:** Y **MK:** unk **PH:** unk **SS:** J-NSSAR 2000 Reg; CM Vol 1 pg 248; DAR A067034; SAR P-233739 **BS:** JLARC 76.

LAWRASON, James; b 2 Dec 1753, Sussex Co, NJ; d 18 Apr 1824 **RU:** Lieutenant/Patriot, Steward, Cont Army Hospital, Alexandria, 1777. Receiver for specific tax, Fairfax Co. Legislative petitions & civil positions in Alexandria. Was president of Bank of Alexandria **CEM:** Christ Church Episcopal; GPS 38.80216, -77.05689; Wilkes St & Hamilton Ln; Alexandria City **GS:** Y **SP:** Mar (23 Jun 1779 Loudoun Co) Alice Levering **VI:** GS records yr of death as 1823, but obit (20 Apr 1824) is taken to be more reliable. **P:** unk **BLW:** unk **RG:** Y **MK:** Y SAR **PH:** Y **SS:** J-NSSAR 1993 Reg; SAR P-233796 **BS:** JLARC 1; 20 pg 102; 196.

LAWRENCE, John; b c1734, Great Britain; d 25 Dec 1814 **RU:** Patriot, Served on Committee of Observation for the Borough of Norfolk in 1775. On 22 Aug 1774, was member of committee that recommended tea be sent back (refuse delivery fr Brigantine "Mary and Jane"). Gave material aid to the cause **CEM:** St Paul's Episcopal; GPS 36.84733, -76.28554; 201 St Paul's Blvd; Norfolk City **GS:** Y **SP:** No info **VI:** Served on the Committee of Observation for the Borough of Norfolk in 1775. Died Christmas day, 1814 at age of 80. **P:** N **BLW:** N **RG:** N **MK:** Y SAR plaque **PH:** unk **SS:** CB AL Ct Bk I pg 7, 17 **BS:** 87 pg 28.

LAWRENCE, John; b unk; d 4 Feb 1821 **RU:** Patriot, Gave material aid to cause **CEM:** St John's Episcopal; GPS 37.53183, -77.41958; 2401 E Broad St; Richmond City **GS:** Y **SP:** No info **VI:** Was delegate fr Isle of Wight Co to General Assembly after war in 1821. **P:** N **BLW:** N **RG:** N **MK:** N **PH:** unk **SS:** D Vol 2 pg 470; AL Ct Bk 1 pg 28 Hanover Co **BS:** 28 pg 469; 196.

LAWS, John; b 1764; d 1 Dec 1839 **RU:** Private, Served for 3 yrs **CEM:** Laws Family; GPS unk; Rt 13 nr Nelsonia; Accomack **GS:** Y **SP:** no info **VI:** Son of Robert W & Mary (Williams) Laws. Received 100 acres bounty land, 22 Nov 1784. **P:** unk **BLW:** Y **RG:** N **MK:** N **PH:** unk **SS:** F pg 46 **BS:** 178 Laws.

LAWSON, George; b 1735, d Dec 1786 Cornwale Parish **RU:** Patriot Paid personal property taxes in Charlotte County in1783 called supply tax to defray expenses of Rev War in Virginia **CEM:** Lawson Family; GPS: unk; Randolph; Charlotte **GS:** Unk **SP:** Mar about 1753, Jean (__) (__- aft 1802, bef 1818,

RU=Rank/Unit	CEM=Cemetery	GS=Gravestone	SP=Spousal Information
VI=Other Veteran Info	P=Pension	BLW=Bounty/Land Warrant	RG=Registered Grave
MK=SAR/DAR Marker	PH=Photo	SS=Service Source	BS=Burial Source

240

KY) **VI**: Will probated 1 Jan 1787. Had 5 sons that served in Rev War **P**: N **BLW**: N **RG**: N **MK**: N, **PH**: N **SS**: DV **BS**: 196.

LAWSON, Robert; b 23 Jan 1748, Yorkshire, England; d Apr 1805 **RU**: General, Served in 4th Regt Dec 1775-13 Feb 1776. As Col, was commander of 4th VA Regt of Foot 1 Apr 1777-17 Dec 1777. Later was Brigadier Gen of VA Militia **CEM**: St John's Episcopal; **GPS** 37.53183, -77.41958; 2401 E Broad St; Richmond City **GS**: Y **SP**: Mar (30 Nov 1769) Sarah Meriwether Pierce (1747, England-1809) **VI**: No further data **P**: unk **BLW**: unk **RG**: Y **MK**: Y SAR plaque **PH**: unk **SS**: DAR #A067381; SAR P-234028; E pg 462; N pg 1240; CE pg 41 **BS**: SAR regis.

LAWSON, William; b 1731; d Bef 1826 **RU**: Patriot, Gave material aid to the cause **CEM**: Eastern State Hospital; **GPS** 37.25560 -76.71030; S Henry Street; Williamsburg City **GS**: N **SP**: No info **VI**: No further data **P**: N **BLW**: N **RG**: Y **MK**: N **PH**: N **SS**: E pg 462; AL Ct Bk pg 23; SAR P-234046 **BS**: 65 Williamsburg.

LAWSON, William II; b Bef 1763, NC; d 30 Jan 1852 **RU**: Private, Ent serv Franklin Co, NC. Served in Capt Levary's Co. NC Militia **CEM**: Lawson Confederate Memorial; **GPS** 36.68728, -82.50114; Rt 71, Snowflake; Scott **GS**: Y **SP**: Nancy Baker **VI**: S10969, 12 Dec 1832 Scott Co **P**: Y **BLW**: unk **RG**: Y **MK**: Y **PH**: Y **SS**: O; CG pg 2031;; SAR P-234043 **BS**: 04.

LAWSON, William Sr; b 26 Jun 1731, Montrose, Scotland; d 18 Apr 1826 **RU**: Sergeant, Served in Capt Trigg's Co Montgomery Co Militia 13 Sept 1777 and was in Battle of Kings Mountain, SC 7 Oct 1780 **CEM**: Lawson Confederate Memorial; **GPS** 36.68728, -82.50114; Rt 71, Snowflake; Scott **GS**: Y **SP**: Rebecca (-----) (__-16 Jan 1827) **VI**: Son (also William) served too, and is believed bur in Wabash, Illinois **P**: unk **BLW**: unk **RG**:Y **MK**: Y SAR **PH**: unk **SS**: DAR #A067400; SAR P-234046; BW pg 47 **BS**: JLARC 22, 81.

LAYMAN, Benjamin; b 1723, PA; d 1787 **RU**: Patriot, Gave material aid to cause **CEM**: Clover Hill; **GPS** unk; Saumsville; Shenandoah **GS**: Y **SP**: Barbara Baughman (__PA-__) d/o John & (-----) Baughman of Lancaster Co, PA **VI**: No further data **P**: N **BLW**: N **RG**: N **MK**: unk **PH**: unk **SS**: AL Ct Bk pg 8 Shenandoah Co **BS**: 196.

LAYMAN, George; b 1760, Frderick Co MD; d 1854 **RU**: Private, Served in VA Line. Final pay received 11 April 1787 **CEM**: Laymantown; **GPS** 37.36278, -79.84909, GS 37.3245,-79.5056; Laymantown Rd, Laymantown; Botetourt **GS**: Y **SP**: Barbara Baumgartner **VI**: New monument placed by Willlium Preston Chapter DAR **P**: unk **BLW**: unk **RG**: Y **MK**: Y **PH**: unk **SS**: B; DAR A067530; SAR P-234099 **BS**: JLARC 1, 2, 124; 80, vol 3, pg11; 196.

LAYMAN, John; b 13 Mar 1763, Frederick Co, MD; d 25 Apr 1836 **RU**: Private?, Service used to support SAR grave marker not identified **CEM**: Bethel Cemetery; **GPS** 38.47592, -78.75641; 3061 Armentrout Path, Keezletown; Rockingham **GS**: U **SP**: Mar (23 Jan 1787 Frederick Co, MD) Maria Elizabeth Enhald (3 Feb 1762-21 Jul 1834) **VI**: SAR Gr Marker **P**: unk **BLW**: unk **RG**: N **MK**: Y **PH**: unk **SS**: CS **BS**: 196.

LEACH, John; b 1739, Ireland; d 1820 **RU**: Private, Cont Line **CEM**: Oxford Presbyterian; **GPS** 37.75302, -79.56023; 18 Churchview Ln, Lexington; Lexington City **GS**: U **SP**: Martha McComb **VI**: Recd Cont Line warrant. Reported as unmarked grave **P**: unk **BLW**: Y **RG**: N **MK**: unk **PH**: unk **SS**: C pg 465 **BS**: JLARC 126.

LEAKE, Josiah; b 19 Mar 1730; d 21 Sep 1795 **RU**: Captain, Commanded a co Goochland Co Militia. Resigned 16 May 1780 **CEM**: Rocky Spring Leake; **GPS** 37.709880, -77.958440; Jct Rts 6 & 600; Goochland **GS**: Y Govt **SP**: Mar (1 Jan 1759 Henrico Co) Ann Fenton by Rev William Douglas, 2) 1767, Anne Minter (__-1776), 3) Ann Foster. **VI**: Son of Walter Leake (1695-1757) & Judith Mask (1698-1758). Will recorded in Goochland Co in WB 16 pg 475 **P**: unk **BLW**: unk **RG**: Y **MK**: N **PH**: unk **SS**: E pg 463; DAR A067954; SAR P-234312 **BS**: 46 pg 224.

LEAKE (LEAK), Elisha; b 1739, Goochland Co; d 19 Oct 1806 **RU**: Captain, Commanded a co Goochland Co Militia, 1779-80 **CEM**: Woodlawn; **GPS** unk; Jct Rts 250 & 612; Goochland **GS**: Y **SP**: 1) (-----) 2) Mar (23 Mar 1791) Frances Curd (__-aft 1806) **VI**: No further data **P**: unk **BLW**: unk **RG**: N **MK**: N **PH**: unk **SS**: DAR #A067940; E pg 463; CZ Vol 1 pg 264; SAR P-234310 **BS**: 46 pg 251.

		GS=Gravestone	SP=Spousal Information
RU=Rank/Unit	CEM=Cemetery	BLW=Bounty/Land Warrant	RG=Registered Grave
VI=Other Veteran Info	P=Pension	SS=Service Source	BS=Burial Source
MK=SAR/DAR Marker	PH=Photo		

241

LEAKE, Mask(Mark); b 1735, d 1 Sep 1813 **RU**: Captain, commanded a company in Albemarle Co Militia **CEM**: Leake family; GPS not determined; loc off Appleberry Mountain Rd (Rt 631), North Garden; Albemarle **GS**: Y Gov't **SP**: Judith Ford Fauve (1732-1827), d/o James (Jacque) Fauve /Ford **VI**: Son of Walter Leake (1695-1757) & Judith Mask (1698-1758) **P**: N **BLW**: N **RG**: Y **MK**: N **PH**: N **SS**: E pg 463; G pg 446; SAR P-234313 **BS**: 196

LEBAIL, Guillaume; b unk; d 1781 **RU**: Seaman, Served on "Hector" and died from Yorktown battle **CEM**: French Memorial; GPS 36.81944, -79.39933; Yorktown; York **GS**: U **SP**: No info **VI**: No further data **P**: unk **BLW**: unk **RG**: Y **MK**: unk **PH**: unk **SS**: J-Yorktown Historia; SAR P-234541 **BS**: JLARC 1, 74.

LEBARS, Louis; b unk; d 1781 **RU**: Seaman, Served on "Languedoc" and died from Yorktown battle **CEM**: French Memorial; GPS 36.81944, -79.39933; Yorktown; York **GS**: U **SP**: No info **VI**: No further data **P**: unk **BLW**: unk **RG**: Y **MK**: unk **PH**: unk **SS**: J-Yorktown Historian; SAR P-234550 **BS**: JLARC 1, 74.

LEBERRE, Yves; b unk; d 1781 **RU**: Seaman, Served on "Ville de Paris" and died from Yorktown battle **CEM**: French Memorial; GPS 36.81944, -79.39933; Yorktown; York **GS**: U **SP**: No info **VI**: No further data **P**: unk **BLW**: unk **RG**: N **MK**: unk **PH**: unk **SS**: J-Yorktown Historian **BS**: JLARC 1, 74.

LEBIHAN, Isaac; b unk; d 1781 **RU**: Seaman, Served on "Palmier" and died from Yorktown battle **CEM**: French Memorial; GPS 36.81944, -79.39933; Yorktown; York **GS**: U **SP**: No info **VI**: No further data **P**: unk **BLW**: unk **RG**: Y **MK**: unk **PH**: unk **SS**: J-Yorktown Historian; SAR P-234557 **BS**: JLARC 1, 74.

LEBOURG, Jacques; b unk; d 1781 **RU**: Seaman, Served on "Languedoc" and died from Yorktown battle **CEM**: French Memorial; GPS 36.81944, -79.39933; Yorktown; York **GS**: U **SP**: No info **VI**: No further data **P**: unk **BLW**: unk **RG**: Y **MK**: unk **PH**: unk **SS**: J-Yorktown Historian; SAR P-234573 **BS**: JLARC 1, 74.

LEBREHEL, Pierre; b unk; d 1781 **RU**: Seaman, Served on "Victorie" and died from Yorktown battle **CEM**: French Memorial; GPS 36.81944, -79.39933; Yorktown; York **GS**: U **SP**: No info **VI**: No further data **P**: unk **BLW**: unk **RG**: Y **MK**: unk **PH**: unk **SS**: J-Yorktown Historian; SAR P-234575 **BS**: JLARC 1, 74.

LEBRUN, Edme; b unk; d 1781 **RU**: Soldier, Served in Touraine Bn and died fr battle at Yorktown **CEM**: French Memorial; GPS 36.81944, -79.39933; Yorktown; York **GS**: U **SP**: No info **VI**: No further data **P**: unk **BLW**: unk **RG**: Y **MK**: unk **PH**: unk **SS**: J-Yorktown Historian; SAR P-234578 **BS**: JLARC 1, 74.

LECAMUS, Francois; b unk; d 1781 **RU**: Seaman, Served on "Northumberland" and died from Yorktown battle **CEM**: French Memorial; GPS 36.81944, -79.39933; Yorktown; York **GS**: U **SP**: No info **VI**: No further data **P**: unk **BLW**: unk **RG**: Y **MK**: unk **PH**: unk **SS**: J-Yorktown Historian; SAR P-234580 **BS**: JLARC 1, 74.

LECLAIR, Francois; b unk; d 1781 **RU**: Seaman, Served on "Victorie" and died from Yorktown battle **CEM**: French Memorial; GPS 36.81944, -79.39933; Yorktown; York **GS**: U **SP**: No info **VI**: No further data **P**: unk **BLW**: unk **RG**: Y **MK**: unk **PH**: unk **SS**: J-Yorktown Historian; SAR P-234589 **BS**: JLARC 1, 74.

LECOEUR, Jean; b unk; d 1781 **RU**: Seaman, Served on "Hector" and died from Yorktown battle **CEM**: French Memorial; GPS 36.81944, -79.39933; Yorktown; York **GS**: U **SP**: No info **VI**: No further data **P**: unk **BLW**: unk **RG**: Y **MK**: unk **PH**: unk **SS**: J-Yorktown Historian; SAR P-234590 **BS**: JLARC 1, 74.

LECOMTE, Pierre; b unk; d 1781 **RU**: Soldier, Served in Soissonnais Bn and died fr battle at Yorktown **CEM**: French Memorial; GPS 36.81944, -79.39933; Yorktown; York **GS**: U **SP**: No info **VI**: No further data **P**: unk **BLW**: unk **RG**: Y **MK**: unk **PH**: unk **SS**: J-Yorktown Historian; SAR P-234594 **BS**: JLARC 1, 74.

LECOURTOIS, Philippe; b unk; d 1781 **RU**: Seaman, Served on "Languedoc" and died from Yorktown battle **CEM**: French Memorial; GPS 36.81944, -79.39933; Yorktown; York **GS**: U **SP**: No info **VI**: No further data **P**: unk **BLW**: unk **RG**: Y **MK**: unk **PH**: unk **SS**: J-Yorktown Historian; SAR P-234597 **BS**: JLARC 1, 74.

RU=Rank/Unit
VI=Other Veteran Info
MK=SAR/DAR Marker

CEM=Cemetery
P=Pension
PH=Photo

GS=Gravestone
BLW=Bounty/Land Warrant
SS=Service Source

SP=Spousal Information
RG=Registered Grave
BS=Burial Source

242

LECUNFF, Joseph; b unk; d 1781 **RU:** Seaman, Served on "Hector: and died from Yorktown battle **CEM:** French Memorial; GPS 36.81944, -79.39933; Yorktown; York **GS:** U **SP:** No info **VI:** No further data **P:** unk **BLW:** unk **RG:** Y **MK:** unk **PH:** unk **SS:** J-Yorktown Historian; SAR P-234601 **BS:** JLARC 1, 74.

LEDGERWOOD, James; b 1738, Ireland, d 14 Sep 1805, Botetourt Co **RU:** Private Served in 14th Cont Line in IL **CEM:** North Mountain; GPS unk; One mi N of Mt Tabor on Rt 620; Botetourt **GS:** U **SP:** No info **VI:** Son of William Ledgerwood (1700-1792) and Agness Mitchell **P:** N **BLW:** N **RG:** N **MK:** N **PH:** no **SS:** E pg 464 **BS:** 196

LEDGERWOOD, William; b 1700, Ireland, d 4 Dec 1792, **RU:** Private Served in IL **CEM:** North Mountain; GPS unk; One mi N of Mt Tabor on Rt 620; Botetourt **GS:** U **SP:** Agness Mitchell **VI:** Arrived with family in Augusta Co 1740. Served also in Colonial War **P:** N **BLW:** N **RG:** N **MK:** N **PH:** no **SS:** E pg 464 **BS:** 196

LEDUC, Jean; b unk; d 1781 **RU:** Seaman, Served on "Auguste" and died from Yorktown battle **CEM:** French Memorial; GPS 36.81944, -79.39933; Yorktown; York **GS:** U **SP:** No info **VI:** No further data **P:** unk **BLW:** unk **RG:** Y **MK:** unk **PH:** unk **SS:** J-Yorktown Historian; SAR P-234623 **BS:** JLARC 1, 74.

LEE, Arthur; b 20 Dec 1740, Westmoreland Co; d 12 Dec 1792 **RU:** Patriot, Was Commissioner to France 1776, Spain 1777. Was in VA House of Delegates & Cont Congress 1782-84. Also served on Treasury Board **CEM:** Landsdowne House (AKA Arthur Lee Family); GPS 37.638569, -76.576164; on Rappahannock St vic jct Bonner St, Urbanna; Middlesex **GS:** Y **SP:** Not married **VI:** Son of Thomas (1690-1750 Stradford) & Hannah Harrison (Ludwell) (1701-1749 Green Spring) Lee. Diplomat with Franklin and Adams to France. Graduated fr Edenburgh University in medicine; has Coat of Arms **P:** N **BLW:** N **RG:** Y **MK:** Lee Family plaque & VA Road sign **PH:** unk **SS:** AS; EO pg 52; VA historic road sign; SAR P-234649 **BS:** 92 pg 58; 201 pg 73, 90; 196 **SEE APPENDIX G**

LEE, Charles; b 1758; d 24 Jun 1815 **RU:** Patriot, Was Delegate to Cont Congress **CEM:** Warrenton; GPS unk; Chestnut St, Warrenton; Fauquier **GS:** Y **SP:** 1) Mar (11 Feb 1789) Anne Lee (1 Dec 1770-9 Sep 1804), d/o Richard Henry & Anne (Gaskins-Pinckard) Lee. 2) Mar (18 Jul 1809 Fauquier Co. Chandler Peyton, security) Margaret C. Peyton, widow of Yelverton Peyton, d/o Rev John & Elizabeth (Gordon) Scott **VI:** Brother of Light-Horse Harry Lee. Studied law with Jared Ingersoll in Philadelphia. Served in VA Assembly. Naval officer of Potomac District until 1795. Collector of customs at Alexandria. Appointed US Attorney General 10 Dec 1795-1801. Was offered Chief Justice of Supreme Ct by Jefferson, but declined **P:** N **BLW:** N **RG:** Y **MK:** N **PH:** unk **SS:** AT pg 541; SAR P-338580 **BS:** 18 pg 145.

LEE, David; b unk; d 19 Oct 1781 **RU:** Sergeant/Patriot, Was Sergeant in Capt Giles Meads co, 1st NJ Regt in 1780, and died fr the battle at Yorktown **CEM:** Yorktown Victory Monument Tablet; GPS 38.28350, -78.54150; Yorktown; York **GS:** Y **SP:** No info **VI:** No further data **P:** unk **BLW:** unk **RG:** unk **MK:** unk **PH:** unk **SS:** J-Yorktown Historian; AL Ct Bk pg 8 Prince William Co; SAR P-234670 **BS:** JLARC 74.

LEE, David; b 1740, Monmouth Co, NJ, d 17 Mar 1809 **RU:** Patriot, Gave material aid to cause, Prince William County **CEM:** Old Lee Family; GPS unk; Coverstone Rd behind Fast Tract Gas Station, off Rt 234, Manassas; Prince William **GS:** Has been removed **SP:** Margaret Perrine (1742, Middlesex Co, NJ-25 Apr 1817) **VI:** No further data **P:** N **BLW:** N **RG:** Y **MK:** N, **PH:** N **SS:** AL Ct Bk pg 6, Prince William Co; DAR Ancestor # A068511; SAR P-330590 **BS:**196

LEE, Edward; b 25 Dec 1760; d 16 Apr 1822 **RU:** Private, Served in Capt Hawkins Boone's Co of Riflemen, Col Daniel Morgan's Regt, Mar 1778 **CEM:** Blandford; GPS 37.22433, -77.38604; 319 S Crater Rd; Petersburg City **GS:** Y **SP:** 1) Nancy Price 2) Mary (-----) (__-Mar 1745) **VI:** Rec'd 26 Apr 1783, BLW 200 acres **P:** N **BLW:** Y **RG:**Y **MK:** Y SAR monument **PH:** unk **SS:** F pg 44; AP service record; DAR Newsletter Sep/Oct 2015 Vol 15 No 5 pg 417; SAR P-2234688 **BS:** 196.

LEE, Francis Lightfoot; b 14 Oct 1734, Stratford Hall, Westmoreland Co; d 11 Jan 1797 **RU:** Patriot, Served in Cont Congress 1775-79. Signed Leedstown Resolutions in 1766 in protest of Stamp Act. Signed Declaration of Independence with brother Richard Henry Lee. Was member VA House of Delegates, and VA Senate **CEM:** Tayloe Family; GPS 37.968329,-76.792284; Mt Airy, Rt 360, Warsaw;

RU=Rank/Unit	CEM=Cemetery	GS=Gravestone	SP=Spousal Information
VI=Other Veteran Info	P=Pension	BLW=Bounty/Land Warrant	RG=Registered Grave
MK=SAR/DAR Marker	PH=Photo	SS=Service Source	BS=Burial Source

Richmond Co **GS:** Y **SP:** 1) Rebecca Tayloe (1752-1797) 2) Reecca Plater Tayloe (1751-1797) **VI:** Son of Thomas (1690-1750) & Hannah (Ludwell) (1701-1750) Lee. Died in Menokin, Richmond Co **P:** N **BLW:** N **RG:** Y **MK:** Y Brass SAR emblem **PH:** unk **SS:** E pg 464; SAR P-234712 **BS:** 80 vol 3 pg 14; 201 pg 73, 90, 91.

LEE, George Fairfax; b 1754; d 1804 **RU:** Ensign, Served in Lee's Regt Cont troops. Was Ens in Capt John Rice's Westmoreland Co Militia **CEM:** Unidentified; GPS unk; Rt 675, nr Lee Creek, Hague; Westmoreland **GS:** N **SP:** No info **VI:** Son of George Lee (18 Aug 1714-19 Nov 1761) and Anne Fairfax (1728-14 Mar 1761) **P:** unk **BLW:** unk **RG:** N **MK:** N **PH:** N **SS:** AP rec; CN pg 85 **BS:** 189 pg 88.

LEE, Henry II; b 1729, Stratford Hall, Westmoreland Co; d 1787 **RU:** Lieutenant Colonel/Patriot, Was member of Convention 1774,75,76 and State Senator 1780. Also gave use of wagons, horses, hay shoes and other items to militia **CEM:** Leesylvania Plantation; GPS 38.35240, -77.15200; On a ridge overlooking Occoquan Bay, Woodbridge; Prince William **GS:** U **SP:** Lucy Grymes, d/o Charles & Frances (Jennings) Grymes **VI:** Resided at "Leesylvania" Prince William Co. Justice of Peace, Burgess before war. Will probated Oct 1787. Cem stone missing; replaced with bronze plaque. **P:** unk **BLW:** unk **RG:** Y **MK:** unk **PH:** unk **SS:** J-NSSAR 1993 Reg; D pg Prince William Co; DAR A068551; SAR P-234922 **BS:** JLARC 1

LEE, Henry III; b 29 Jan 1756, Prince William Co; d 25 Mar 1818 **RU:** Lieutenant Colonel, Was Lt Col in Lee's Legion. Served in Rev War. As "Lighthorse Harry". Served in VA House Delegate fr Westmoreland Co **CEM:** Washington & Lee Univ Campus; GPS 36.60863, -81.01593; Nr Jefferson St; Lexington City **GS:** U **SP:** Mar (1782) (-----) **VI:** Cont Congress 1787-88. Gov of VA 1791-94. US Rep 6th Congress 1799-1801. After Rev War became General. July 1812 severely hurt at Baltimore riots. Federalist. Support editor of Baltimore Federalist that editorialized against War of 1812. Gave George Washington eulogy: "first in war, first in peace, and first in the hearts of his countrymen." Father of Robert E. Lee. Died in Camden Co, GA. Reinterred to Lee Chapel Cem 1913. Recd BLW #1299-500-3 Jul 1789 **P:** unk **BLW:** Y **RG:** Y **MK:** unk **PH:** unk **SS:** J-NSSAR 1993 Reg; CG pg 2043; DAR A068555; SAR P-234926 **BS:** JLARC 1; 201 pg 7392.

LEE, John; b 1748; d 11 Jan 1819 **RU:** Captain, Served in the Marines **CEM:** Lee Family; GPS unk; Leesville; Campbell **GS:** Y **SP:** Sally(___) **VI:** Founder of Leesville, Campbell Co **P:** unk **BLW:** unk **RG:** Y **MK:** N **PH:** unk **SS:** J-NSSAR 1993 Reg; J- DAR Hatcher; G pg 783; SAR P-234757 **BS:** JLARC 1, 2; 80 vol 3 pg 14 196.

LEE, John; b 1750; d 1821 **RU:** Major, Served under Col Charles Dabney, Supernumerary Feb-Apr 1782 in rank of Maj **CEM:** Old Kiskiak; GPS unk; Nr Yorktown; York **GS:** U **SP:** No info **VI:** No further data **P:** unk **BLW:** unk **RG:** Y **MK:** unk **PH:** unk **SS:** J- DAR Hatcher; G pg 852; DAR A068634; SAR P-234768 **BS:** JLARC 2.

LEE, John; b 1757; d 19 Apr 1797 **RU:** Patriot, Submitted claim for losses suffered during burning of Norfolk **CEM:** St Paul's Episcopal; GPS 36.84733, -76.28554; 201 St Paul's Blvd; Norfolk City **GS:** Y **SP:** Mar (4 Dec 1769) Jane Brazill **VI:** No further data **P:** N **BLW:** N **RG;** N **MK:** Y SAR Plaque **PH:** unk **SS:** CB Friend Amer cause **BS:** 178 Jan 11.

LEE, Ludwell; b 13 Oct 1760, Westmoreland Co; d 25 Mar 1835 **RU:** Soldier? Served in VA Line. Lived in Westmoreland Co at enl. Was Aide-de-camp to General Lafayette, with unetermined rank **CEM:** St James Episcopal, Old Cemetery; GPS 39.11555, -77.56250; Church St NE, Leesburg; Loudoun **GS:** U **SP:** Flora Lee (Jun 1771, Stratford Hall, Westmoreland Co-1795, Fairfax Co) d/o Phillip Ludwell (1727-1775) & Elizabeth (Steptoe) (1743-1789), 2) Elizabeth Armistead **VI:** Son of Richard Henry (1732-1794) & (-----) Lee. Achieved rank of colonel after war. Appl pen 14 Jan 1833 Loudoun Co. S8829 **P:** Y **BLW:** unk **RG:** Y **MK:** unk **PH:** unk **SS:** CG pg 2045; SAR P-234801 **BS:** JLARC 1, 4, 32.

LEE, Nathaniel; b 1730; d 1820 **RU:** Patriot, Gave material aid to cause **CEM:** Nathaniel Lee Home; GPS unk; NE of Carson; Prince George **GS:** N **SP:** No info **VI:** No further data **P:** N **BLW:** N **RG:** N **MK:** N **PH:** N **SS:** E pg 465; AL Com Bk IV pg 363 Prince George Co **BS:** 148 Lee.

LEE, Philip Ludwell; b 1726; d 1775 **RU:** Patriot, Gave material aid to cause in Westmoreland Co **CEM:** Lee Family; GPS unk; Stratford Hall; Westmoreland **GS:** N **SP:** Elizabeth Steptoe **VI:** Son of Thomas Lee (1690-1750) and Hannah Ludwell **P:** N **BLW:** N **RG:** N **MK:** N **PH:** N **SS:** AL Ct Bk **BS:** 189 pg 88.

RU=Rank/Unit	CEM=Cemetery	GS=Gravestone	SP=Spousal Information
VI=Other Veteran Info	P=Pension	BLW=Bounty/Land Warrant	RG=Registered Grave
MK=SAR/DAR Marker	PH=Photo	SS=Service Source	BS=Burial Source

244

LEE, Richard Bland; b 20 Jan 1761, Leesylvania, Prince William Co; d 12 Mar 1827 **RU:** Matross/Patriot, Served in 1st Artillery. 1st congressman fr N. VA. State House of Delegates (1784-88) 1st, 2nd, 3rd Congresses (1789-95). Convinced Congress to locate nation's capital in Washington DC. Gave 223 pounds of beef to cause **CEM:** Sully Plantation; GPS unk; Sully Rd Rt 28, adj Dulles National Airport, Chantilly; Fairfax **GS:** Y **SP:** Elizabeth Collins (1770-1858) **VI:** Son of Henry Lee & Lucy Ludwell Grymes. Appointed by Madison as commissioner in 1816 to adjust claims of loss fr War of 1812. Judge in Orphans Ct in DC until death there. Originally interred at Congressional Cem, Washington DC. Monument erected by Lee Family Association **P:** unk **BLW:** unk **RG:** Y **MK:** Y **SAR PH:** Y **SS:** E pg 466; AL Ct Bk pg 43; SAR P-234826 **BS:** 61 vol IV pg CH 24; JLARC 14; 196.

LEE, Richard Henry; b 18 or 20 Jan 1732, Stratford Hall, Westmoreland Co; d 19 Jun 1794 **RU:** Patriot, Was member VA House of Burgesses 1758 -76. Believed in VA's resistance to Stamp & Townshend Acts. Was member 1774 of 1st Cont Congress. **CEM:** Burnt House Field; GPS unk; Hague; Westmoreland **GS:** Y **SP:** 1) Anne Aylette 2) Anne Pinckard **VI:** Son of Thomas & Hannah (Ludwell) Lee. Signer of the Declar. Independence fr VA; brother of Francis Lightfoot Lee who also signed. Brother of Gen "Lighthorse Harry" Lee, uncle of Civil War Conf Gen Robert E Lee. President of Congress (1784-1785) under Articles of Confederation, unofficially President of USA. Died in Chantilly **P:** N **BLW:** N **RG:** Y **MK:** N **PH:** unk **SS:** W pg 22-23; DAR A068703; SAR P-234823 **BS:** 189 pg 85; 201 pg 7392-93.

LEE, Thomas Ludwell; b 13 Dec 1730, Stratford Hall, Westmoreland Co; d 13 Apr 1778 **RU:** Patriot, Was active in VA Convention, Committee of Safety for Colony of VA. Served in House of Burgesses. Was judge of General Ct of VA **CEM:** Belleview Plantation; GPS unk; Rt 604; Stafford **GS:** N **SP:** Mary Aylett, daughter of William & (-----) Aylett **VI:** Known to have d at his plantation "Bellevue" and is thought to have been bur nearby. **P:** N **BLW:** N **RG:** Y **MK:** N **PH:** N **SS:** E pg 466; DAR A068794; SAR P-234863 **BS:** 04; 30 pg 230. **SEE APPENDIX G**

LEE, William, b 31 Aug 1739, Stratford Hall, Westmoreland Co, d 27 Jun 1795, Greenspring **RU:** Patriot, U.S Commissioner to France & Russia **CEM:** Jamestown Church; GPS: 37.12307,-76.46422; Jamestown; James City **GS:** Yes **SP:** Mar 7 Mar 1769, Hannah Phillppa Ludwell (21 Dec 1737-18 Aug 1784) **VI:** Son of Thomas Lee (1690-1750) and Hannah Ludwell (1701-1750). Had large mercantile business in London and was Alderman and Sheriff there **P:** N **BLW:** N **RG:** Y **MK:** N, **PH:** N **SS:** DAR # A068867; SAR P-234897 **BS:** 196.

LEE, William; b c1750; d Sep 1803 **RU:** Private/Patriot, Served in Capt Cobbs Co, Bedford Co Militia. Gave material aid to cause **CEM:** Lee Family; GPS unk; New London; Bedford **GS:** U **SP:** Ava Noel (1745-1820) **VI:** Son of Charles (c1720, Goochland Co-15 Mar 1799, Cumberland Co) & Ann (Dabbs) (c1722-1795) Lee. Source 2 has burial near Evington in Campbell Co. Source 66 has burial at Old Lee graveyard at the home of Mr. Edward Leftwick, bet Evington and New London **P:** unk **BLW:** unk **RG:** Y **MK:** N **PH:** unk **SS:** E pg 466; AL Ct Bk pg 13 Amherst Co; CZ; DAR A068876; SAR P-234894 **BS:** JLARC 1, 2, 4, 66, 75; 196.

LEE, William "Billy"; b 1750; d 1828 **RU:** Valet, Served as Washington's valet servant man **CEM:** Mt Vernon; GPS 38.42280, -77.05090; Mt Vernon Estate; Fairfax **GS:** N **SP:** Margaret Thomas Lee, a free black fr Philadelphia. It is not known if she ever moved to Mt Vernon **VI:** Emancipated in Washington's will for his service to him during the Rev War. Bur in the negro cemetery which only has a generic memorial stone for all the slaves as a group **P:** unk **BLW:** unk **RG:** Y **MK:** N **PH:** N **SS:** J-NSSAR 1993 Reg; SAR Ancestor #P-234885 **BS:** JLARC 1.

LEE, Zachariah Jr; b 1765; d 1854 **RU:** Soldier, Served in VA line **CEM:** Brickey-Lee; GPS unk; Rt 779, McAfees Knob; Botetourt **GS:** U **SP:** Mar (23 Dec 1813 Botetourt Co) Agnes Brickey d/o Peter & (-----) Brickey **VI:** Appl pen 12 May 1834 Botetourt Co. R6260 **P:** Y **BLW:** unk **RG:** Y **MK:** unk **PH:** unk **SS:** CG pg 2048; SAR P-234917 **BS:** JLARC 4, 60.

LEE, Zephaniah; b 1755; d unk **RU:** Private, Served in Capt Fraizer's Co, Augusta Co Militia **CEM:** Greenwood; GPS 38.38470, -78.97610; Vic Green St & North Grove St, Bridgewater; Rockingham **GS:** N **SP:** Mar (1781 Rockingham Co) Jean Bright **VI:** No further data **P:** unk **BLW:** unk **RG:** N **MK:** unk **PH:** N **SS:** E pg 466 **BS:** 196.

RU=Rank/Unit	CEM=Cemetery	GS=Gravestone	SP=Spousal Information
VI=Other Veteran Info	P=Pension	BLW=Bounty/Land Warrant	RG=Registered Grave
MK=SAR/DAR Marker	PH=Photo	SS=Service Source	BS=Burial Source

LEECH, John Sr; b 1739; d 1820 **RU:** Private, Served in 2nd PA Regt Jan 1781 to Jan 1782 **CEM:** Oxford Presbyterian; GPS 37.75302, -79.56023; 18 Churchview Ln, Lexington; Rockbridge **GS:** N **SP:** Mar (1761) Martha McComb **VI:** Moved to Rockbridge Co 1778 **P:** unk **BLW:** unk **RG:** N **MK:** N **PH:** N **SS:** AP **BS:** 32 Jan 2011.

LEFERME, Pierre; b unk; d 1781 **RU:** Soldier, Served in Gatinais Bn and died fr battle at Yorktown **CEM:** French Memorial; GPS 36.81944, -79.39933; Yorktown; York **GS:** U **SP:** No info **VI:** No further data **P:** unk **BLW:** unk **RG:** Y **MK:** unk **PH:** unk **SS:** J-Yorktown Historian; SAR P-235022 **BS:** JLARC 1, 74.

LEFEVRE, Jean; b unk; d 1781 **RU:** Seaman, Served on "Citoyen" and died from Yorktown battle **CEM:** French Memorial; GPS 36.81944, -79.39933; Yorktown; York **GS:** U **SP:** No info **VI:** No further data **P:** unk **BLW:** unk **RG:** Y **MK:** unk **PH:** unk **SS:** J-Yorktown Historian; SAR P-235036 **BS:** JLARC 1, 74.

LEFEVRE, Joseph; b unk; d 1781 **RU:** Soldier, Served in Touraine Bn and died fr battle at Yorktown **CEM:** French Memorial; GPS 36.81944, -79.39933; Yorktown; York **GS:** U **SP:** No info **VI:** No further data **P:** unk **BLW:** unk **RG:** Y **MK:** unk **PH:** unk **SS:** J-Yorktown Historian; SAR P-235038 **BS:** JLARC 1, 74.

LEFLOCH, Francois; b unk; d 1781 **RU:** Seaman, Served on "Northumberland" and died from Yorktown battle **CEM:** French Memorial; GPS 36.81944, -79.39933; Yorktown; York **GS:** U **SP:** No info **VI:** No further data **P:** unk **BLW:** unk **RG:** Y **MK:** unk **PH:** unk **SS:** J-Yorktown Historian; SAR P-235071 **BS:** JLARC 1, 74.

LEFTWICH, Augustine Jr; b 10 Sep 1744, Caroline Co; d unk **RU:** Lieutenant, Ent serv Bedford Co in VA Line **CEM:** Leftwich Family; GPS unk; Mt Airy, nr Leesville; Bedford **GS:** N **SP:** Mary (-----) **VI:** Sol appl pen 26 Oct 1833 Bedford Co. S11364 **P:** Y **BLW:** unk **RG:** Y **MK:** N **PH:** N **SS:** K Vol 3 pg 114; CG pg 2050; DAR A069028; SAR P-235076 **BS:** JLARC 1, 4, 36.

LEFTWICH, Augustine Sr; b 1712, New Kent Co; d 1795 **RU:** Soldier/Patriot, Served in Co F, 10th VA Militia. Gave material aid to cause **CEM:** Goose Creek; GPS unk; Lynch Station; Campbell **GS:** Y **SP:** 1) Mar (c1736) Mary Mosley (1720 Bedford Co-___) 2) Mar (c1777) Elizabeth (Fuqua) Stovall (1736 Bedford Co-24 Jun 1795), widow of John Stovall, d/o of Ralph & Priscilla (Owen) Fuqua **VI:** Also fought in French & Indian War. Died in Bedford Co. Govt stone says "Rev War Co. F, 10th VA Militia" **P:** unk **BLW:** unk **RG:** Y **MK:** N **PH:** unk **SS:** B; AL Lists pg 16, 18; DAR A068950; SAR P-235075 **BS:** 196.

LEFTWICH, Joel; b 17 Nov 1760, Caroline Co; d 20 Oct 1846 **RU:** Sergeant, Ent serv Bedford Co in VA Line. Ent serv again as Orderly Sergeant in Thomas Leftwich Co (no kinship given) **CEM:** Leftwich Family; GPS unk; Mt Airy, nr Leesville; Bedford **GS:** N **SP:** Mar (24 Dec 1781 Bedford Co) Nancy Turner **VI:** Son of Augustine Leftwich (1712-1795). Lived in Bedford Co after RW, then moved 1827 to Campbell Co where pen. Legislator & Justice of Peace after War. Commanded brigade as Brig Gen that marched to relieve Gen Harrison in Ohio, in 1812. Helped build Ft Meigs. Led brigade in Battle of Baltimore 1813. Sol appl pen 8 Oct 1832 Campbell Co. S8830. **P:** Y **BLW:** unk **RG:** Y **MK:** N **PH:** N **SS:** J- DAR Hatcher; K Vol 3 pg 114; CG pg 2050; SAR P-235079 **BS:** JLARC 2; 196.

LEFTWICH, Thomas; b 1740, Caroline Co; d 3 May 1816 **RU:** Colonel/Patriot, Served in Lunenburg & Bedford Co Militias 1758. Became Lt in Bedford Co Militia early part of Rev War, promoted to Capt & reassigned to Gen Edward Stevens Regt. At Battle of Camden, commanded rear-guard of Gen Gates' Division. Gave material aid to cause **CEM:** Leftwich Family; GPS unk; Mt Airy, nr Leesville; Bedford **GS:** N **SP:** 1) Mar (10 Dec 1764) Mary Challis (___-1777); 2) Mar (2 Apr 1771, prob Amherst Co) Bethunia Ellis (___-1780); 3) Mar (27 Oct 1783) Jane Gincey Stratton (1762-1806) **VI:** Son of Augustine (1712-1795). Soon after Rev War, served as Maj, Lt Col and Col, respectively, of 10th Regt of VA Militia **P:** unk **BLW:** unk **RG:** Y **MK:** N **PH:** N **SS:** D Bedford Co; SAR P-235087 **BS:** JLARC 1, 2, 36; 196.

LEFTWICH, Uriah; b 1748, Caroline Co; d 1838 **RU:** Second Lieutenant/Patriot, Served in Bedford Co Militia. Gave material aid to cause **CEM:** Leftwich Family; GPS unk; Mt Airy, nr Leesville; Bedford **GS:** N **SP:** Mar (c1769) Nancy Keith **VI:** Son of Augustine (1712-1795) & (-----) Leftwich. Appointed Ens 1779, Capt 1789 (Bedford Co). Pen recd by widow commencing 16 Sep 1812 at $12.50 per mo **P:** Y **BLW:** N **RG:** Y **MK:** N **PH:** N **SS:** E pg 467; AG pg 269; AK Sep 2007; AL Ct Bk pg 8, 18 Bedford Co; DAR A068899; SAR P-235089 **BS:** 04 Sep 07; 196.

RU=Rank/Unit	CEM=Cemetery	GS=Gravestone	SP=Spousal Information
VI=Other Veteran Info	P=Pension	BLW=Bounty/Land Warrant	RG=Registered Grave
MK=SAR/DAR Marker	PH=Photo	SS=Service Source	BS=Burial Source

LEFTWICH, William; b 1737; d 31 May 1820 **RU:** Lieutenant Colonel/Patriot, Gave material aid to cause **CEM:** Leftwich Family; GPS unk; Mt Airy, nr Leesville; Bedford **GS:** N **SP:** Elizabeth Haynes (1732-1780) **VI:** Capt of Militia 1772, Committee of Safety 1775, Justice 1777, Maj 1778, Lt Col 1780, Sheriff in 1796, Virginia Legislature 1786-87 **P:** unk **BLW:** unk **RG:** Y **MK:** N **PH:** N **SS:** AL Ct Bk pg 8, 9, 12, 32 Bedford Co; SAR P-235092 **BS:** JLARC 2, 36.

LEGG, John; b unk; d April 1799 **RU:** Private/Patriot, Served in VA Cont Line for 3 yrs. Also as patriot gave 26 gal rum to cause on Jul 1780 **CEM:** Masonic Cemetery; GPS 38.30198, -77.46142; 900 Charles St; Fredericksburg City **GS:** N **SP:** Lucy Lee (c1763 - 11 May 1787) **VI:** The Virginia Herald in April 1799 indicates he was a capt, but BLW indicates private thus rank obtained after war **P:** unk **BLW:** Y **RG:** N **MK:** Y SAR plaque **PH:** N **SS:** AK; F pg 44 **BS:** 04; 11 pg 68.

LEGOFF, Jean; b unk; d 1781 **RU:** Seaman, Served on "Saint-Esprit" and died from Yorktown battle **CEM:** French Memorial; GPS 36.81944, -79.39933; Yorktown; York **GS:** U **SP:** No info **VI:** No further data **P:** unk **BLW:** unk **RG:** Y **MK:** unk **PH:** unk **SS:** J-Yorktown Historian; SAR P-235129 **BS:** JLARC 1, 74.

LEGROSS, Pierre; b unk; d 1781 **RU:** Seaman, Served on "Duc De Bourgogne" and died from Yorktown battle **CEM:** French Memorial; GPS 36.81944, -79.39933; Yorktown; York **GS:** U **SP:** No info **VI:** No further data **P:** unk **BLW:** unk **RG:** Y **MK:** unk **PH:** unk **SS:** J-Yorktown Historian; SAR P-235137 **BS:** JLARC 1, 74.

LEGUEN, Louis; b unk; d 1781 **RU:** Seaman, Served on "Ville De Paris" and died from Yorktown battle **CEM:** French Memorial; GPS 36.81944, -79.39933; Yorktown; York **GS:** U **SP:** No info **VI:** No further data **P:** unk **BLW:** unk **RG:** Y **MK:** unk **PH:** unk **SS:** J-Yorktown Historian SAR P-235142 **BS:** JLARC 1, 74.

LEGUERN, Guillaume; b unk; d 1781 **RU:** Seaman, Served on "Hercule" and died from Yorktown battle **CEM:** French Memorial; GPS 36.81944, -79.39933; Yorktown; York **GS:** U **SP:** No info **VI:** No further data **P:** unk **BLW:** unk **RG:** Y **MK:** unk **PH:** unk **SS:** J-Yorktown Historian; SAR P-235143 **BS:** JLARC 1, 74.

LEGUILLOUX, Rene; b unk; d 1781 **RU:** Seaman, Served on "Marseillais" and died from Yorktown battle **CEM:** French Memorial; GPS 36.81944, -79.39933; Yorktown; York **GS:** U **SP:** No info **VI:** No further data **P:** unk **BLW:** unk **RG:** Y **MK:** unk **PH:** unk **SS:** J-Yorktown Historian; SAR P-235144 **BS:** JLARC 1, 74.

LEHMAN, Ludwick; b 1740, Philadelphia Co, PA; d 16 Mar 1820 **RU:** Private, Listed in 8th Class, 2nd Battalion, Lancaster Co PA Militia **CEM:** Bethel Cemetery; GPS 38.47592, -78.75641; 3061 Armentrout Path, Keezletown; Rockingham **GS:** Y **SP:** No info **VI:** Son of Christain K (__-1748) & Ann Margaret (-----) Lehman **P:** unk **BLW:** unk **RG:** Y**MK:** unk **PH:** unk **SS:** AP PA Archives Series 5 Vol VII pg 172; SAR P-329783 **BS:** 196.

LEHUP, Pierre; b unk; d 1781 **RU:** Soldier, Served in Soissonnais Bn and died fr battle at Yorktown **CEM:** French Memorial; GPS 36.81944, -79.39933; Yorktown; York **GS:** U **SP:** No info **VI:** No further data **P:** unk **BLW:** unk **RG:** Y **MK:** unk **PH:** unk **SS:** J-Yorktown Historian; SAR P-235164 **BS:** JLARC 1, 74.

LEIGH, John; b 1737, King William Co; d 14 Aug 1785 **RU:** Lieutenant, Served in 5th and 7th VA Regts. Was sick at end of service but received a certificate for full pay 14 Feb 1783 **CEM:** Leigh Family; GPS unk; Base of Leigh Mountain, Farmville; Prince Edward **GS:** U **SP:** Mar (21 Nov 1757) Virginia Greenhill (c1741 Amelia Co-9 Jul 1820 Madison Co) d/o David & Catherine (Clairborne) Greenhill **VI:** Son of Zacheriah (1704-1770) & Ellen (Jones) (1705-1745) Leigh. Recd BLW of 200 acres and another for 2487 acres, 5 Jan 1824 **P:** unk **BLW:** Y **RG:** unk **MK:** unk **PH:** unk **SS:** DAR ancestor #A069201; C pg 463; AP Ser Rec; SAR P-235199 **BS:** 196.

LEJORE, Jean; b unk; d 1781 **RU:** Soldier, Served in Gatinais Bn and died fr battle at Yorktown **CEM:** French Memorial; GPS 36.81944, -79.39933; Yorktown; York **GS:** U **SP:** No info **VI:** No further data **P:** unk **BLW:** unk **RG:** Y **MK:** unk **PH:** unk **SS:** J-Yorktown Historian; SAR P-235273 **BS:** JLARC 1, 74.

RU=Rank/Unit	CEM=Cemetery	GS=Gravestone	SP=Spousal Information
VI=Other Veteran Info	P=Pension	BLW=Bounty/Land Warrant	RG=Registered Grave
MK=SAR/DAR Marker	PH=Photo	SS=Service Source	BS=Burial Source

247

LELAND, John; b 14 May 1754, Grafton, Worchester Co, MA; d 14 Jan 1841, No Adams, Berkshire Co, MA **RU**: Patriot met with delegates to the conventions **CEM**; GPS; Leland Park;GPS not determined; loc vic jct Rt 628 & Rt 20 Constitution Rd; Orange Orange **GS**: Memorial tower **SP**: Mar 1776, Sarah (-----),(unk-1837) **VI**: A Baptist Preacher that met James Madison in Orange Co, VA to obtain assurances that he would incorporate "Freedom of Religion" in the Consttution. He is memorialized on a monument to him in Lelannd Park **P**: N **BLW**: N **RG**: N **MK**: Y monument **PH**: Y **SS**: Monument inscription **BS: 196**

LELAYER, Yves; b unk; d 1781 **RU**: Seaman, Served on "Ville de Paris" and died from Yorktown battle **CEM**: French Memorial; GPS 36.81944, -79.39933; Yorktown; York **GS**: U **SP**: No info **VI**: No further data **P**: unk **BLW**: unk **RG**: Y **MK**: unk **PH**: unk **SS**: J-Yorktown Historian; SAR P-235316 **BS**: JLARC 1, 74.

LEMAY, Jacques; b unk; d 1781 **RU**: Soldier, Served in Gatinais Bn and died fr battle at Yorktown **CEM**: French Memorial; GPS 36.81944, -79.39933; Yorktown; York **GS**: U **SP**: No info **VI**: No further data **P**: unk **BLW**: unk **RG**: Y **MK**: unk **PH**: unk **SS**: J-Yorktown Historian; SAR P-235335 **BS**: JLARC 1, 74.

LEMAY, Julien; b unk; d 1781 **RU**: Seaman, Served on "Diademe" and died from Yorktown battle **CEM**: French Memorial; GPS 36.81944, -79.39933; Yorktown; York **GS**: U **SP**: No info **VI**: No further data **P**: unk **BLW**: unk **RG**: Y **MK**: unk **PH**: unk **SS**: J-Yorktown Historian; SAR P-235336 **BS**: JLARC 1, 74.

LEMINGNON, Jean; b unk; d 1781 **RU**: Seaman, Served on "Magnanime" and died from Yorktown battle) **CEM**: French Memorial; GPS 36.81944, -79.39933; Yorktown; York **GS**: U **SP**: No info **VI**: No further data **P**: unk **BLW**: unk **RG**: Y **MK**: unk **PH**: unk **SS**: J-Yorktown Historian; SAR P-235344 **BS**: JLARC 1, 74.

LEMOING, Jean; b unk; d 1781 **RU**: Seaman, Served on "Hercule" and died from Yorktown battle **CEM**: French Memorial; GPS 36.81944, -79.39933; Yorktown; York **GS**: U **SP**: No info **VI**: No further data **P**:

LEPAGE, Pierre; b unk; d 1781 **RU**: Soldier, Served in Gatinais Bn and died fr battle at Yorktown **CEM**: French Memorial; GPS 36.81944, -79.39933; Yorktown; York **GS**: U **SP**: No info **VI**: No further data **P**: unk **BLW**: unk **RG**: Y **MK**: unk **PH**: unk **SS**: J-Yorktown Historian; SAR P-235641 **BS**: JLARC 1, 74.

LEPARC, Jean; b unk; d 1781 **RU**: Seaman, Served on "Citoyen" and died from Yorktown battle **CEM**: French Memorial; GPS 36.81944, -79.39933; Yorktown; York **GS**: U **SP**: No info **VI**: No further data **P**: unk **BLW**: unk **RG**: Y **MK**: unk **PH**: unk **SS**: J-Yorktown Historian; SAR P-235642 **BS**: JLARC 1, 74.

LEPELLE, Julien; b unk; d 1781 **RU**: Seaman, Served on "Auguste" and died from Yorktown battle **CEM**: French Memorial; GPS 36.81944, -79.39933; Yorktown; York **GS**: U **SP**: No info **VI**: No further data **P**: unk **BLW**: unk **RG**: Y **MK**: unk **PH**: unk **SS**: J-Yorktown Historian; SAR P-235644 **BS**: JLARC 1, 74.

LERICHE, Jacques; b unk; d 1781 **RU**: Soldier, Served in Auxonne Bn and died fr battle at Yorktown **CEM**: French Memorial; GPS 36.81944, -79.39933; Yorktown; York **GS**: U **SP**: No info **VI**: No further data **P**: unk **BLW**: unk **RG**: Y **MK**: unk **PH**: unk **SS**: J-Yorktown Historian; SAR P-235666 **BS**: JLARC 1, 74.

LEROUX, Etienne; b unk; d 1781 **RU**: Seaman, Served on "Magnanime" and died from Yorktown battle **CEM**: French Memorial; GPS 36.81944, -79.39933; Yorktown; York **GS**: U **SP**: No info **VI**: No further data **P**: unk **BLW**: unk **RG**: Y **MK**: unk **PH**: unk **SS**: J-Yorktown Historian; SAR P-235672 **BS**: JLARC 1, 74.

LEROUX, Jean; b unk; d 1781 **RU**: Soldier, Served in Touraine Bn and died fr battle at Yorktown **CEM**: French Memorial; GPS 36.81944, -79.39933; Yorktown; York **GS**: U **SP**: No info **VI**: No further data **P**: unk **BLW**: unk **RG**: Y **MK**: unk **PH**: unk **SS**: J-Yorktown Historian; SAR P-235674 **BS**: JLARC 1, 74.

LERSNE, Augustin; b unk; d 1781 **RU**: Soldier, Served in Touraine Bn and died fr battle at Yorktown **CEM**: French Memorial; GPS 36.81944, -79.39933; Yorktown; York **GS**: U **SP**: no info **VI**: No further data **P**: unk **BLW**: unk **RG**: Y **MK**: unk **PH**: unk **SS**: J-Yorktown Historian; SAR P-235678 **BS**: JLARC 1, 74.

RU=Rank/Unit	CEM=Cemetery	GS=Gravestone	SP=Spousal Information
VI=Other Veteran Info	P=Pension	BLW=Bounty/Land Warrant	RG=Registered Grave
MK=SAR/DAR Marker	PH=Photo	SS=Service Source	BS=Burial Source

248

LESAGNE, Pierre; b unk; d 1781 **RU:** Seaman, Served on "Magnanime" and died from Yorktown battle **CEM:** French Memorial; GPS 36.81944, -79.39933; Yorktown; York **GS:** U **SP:** No info **VI:** No further data **P:** unk **BLW:** unk **RG:** Y **MK:** unk **PH:** unk **SS:** J-Yorktown Historian; SAR P-235681 **BS:** JLARC 1, 74.

LESOURD, Sebastien; b unk; d 1781 **RU:** Seaman, Served on "Saint-Esprit" and died from Yorktown battle **CEM:** French Memorial; GPS 36.81944, -79.39933; Yorktown; York **GS:** U **SP:** No info **VI:** No further data **P:** unk **BLW:** unk **RG:** Y **MK:** unk **PH:** unk **SS:** J-Yorktown Historian; SAR P-235717 **BS:** JLARC 1, 74.

LESTER, John; b 1 Jan 1752, Bucks Co, PA; d 29 Jan 1825 **RU:** Private, Served in Capt David Trigg Co Montgomery Co Militia. Also in Capt Helvan's Co, 1st VA Regt, commanded by Col Green **CEM:** Lester; GPS 37.11698, -80.25156; S fr Riner; Montgomery **GS:** Y **SP:** Catherine Plick or Plickenstalver (1759 Bedford Co-15 Sep 1833 Montgomery Co) **VI:** No further data **P:** unk **BLW:** unk **RG:** Y **MK:** unk **PH:** unk **SS:** J-NSSAR 1993 Reg; J- DAR Hatcher; AP roll; DAR A069526; SAR P-235735 **BS:** JLARC 1, 2.

LESTER, John; b 1748, Sul, Suffolk Co, Great Britain; d 19 Dec 1804 **RU:** Sergeant, Served in 1st Cont Line **CEM:** St John's Episcopal; GPS 37.53183, -77.41958; 2401 E Broad St; Richmond City **GS:** Y **SP:** No info **VI:** Merchant of the city of Richmond. White marble slab on pedestals. **P:** unk **BLW:** unk **RG:** N **MK:** N **PH:** unk **SS:** E pg 469; AP **BS:** 28 pg 465; 196.

LESUEUR, Martel; b 6 Mar 1758, Manakin, Cumberland Co; d 10 Aug 1843 **RU:** Private, Ent serv Cumberland Co. Served in militia **CEM:** Prillman-Turner; GPS unk; Btw Ferrun & Philpott Res; Franklin **GS:** U **SP:** Mar (10 Jun 1781 Chesterfield Co) Elizabeth Bacon **VI:** Moved to Charlotte Co, then Henry Co, then Patrick Co, then Grayson Co, then Franklin Co where pen in 1832. Widow recd pension 1844 at age 79. F-W8035, R1552 **P:** Y **BLW:** unk **RG:** Y **MK:** N **PH:** Y **SS:** K Vol 3 pg 118; DAR A069552; SAR P-235757 **BS:** 04, Jul 07.

LETCHER, William; b 1741, Petersburg; d 7 Aug 1780 **RU:** Colonel/Patriot, Serv not identified. Was killed by a Tory, thus DAR considers him a patriot. **CEM:** Delionback Home; GPS 36.34040, -80.33240; End of Rt 749 on Ararat River; Patrick **GS:** U **SP:** Mar (20 Nov 1778) Elizabeth Perkins (May 1759-___) **VI:** Great-grandfather of J.E.B. Stuart. Was assasinated by a Tory. DAR marker **P:** unk **BLW:** unk **RG:** N **MK:** Y **PH:** unk **SS:** BT; DD DAR #A069559 **BS:** JLARC 30, 108; 196.

LETCHER, William; b unk; d 1781 **RU:** Private, Was killed at Battle of Green Springs, Williamsburg. Listed in the Lib of VA "Rev War Dead" Database as "Killed in Action" **CEM:** Williamsburg Land Conservancy; GPS unk; 5000 New Point Rd; Williamsburg City **GS:** N **SP:** No info **VI:** No further data **P:** unk **BLW:** unk **RG:** Y **MK:** N **PH:** N **SS:** AU SAR study; SAR P-235760 **BS:** 32.

LETOUX, Clement; b unk; d 1781 **RU:** Seaman, Served on "Saint-Esprit" and died from Yorktown battle **CEM:** French Memorial; GPS 36.81944, -79.39933; Yorktown; York **GS:** U **SP:** No info **VI:** No further data **P:** unk **BLW:** unk **RG:** Y **MK:** unk **PH:** unk **SS:** J-Yorktown Historian; SAR P-235765 **BS:** JLARC 1, 74.

LEVENT, Jean; b unk; d 1781 **RU:** Seaman, Served on "Northumberland" and died from Yorktown battle **CEM:** French Memorial; GPS 36.81944, -79.39933; Yorktown; York **GS:** U **SP:** No info **VI:** No further data **P:** unk **BLW:** unk **RG:** Y **MK:** unk **PH:** unk **SS:** J-Yorktown Historian; SAR P-235788 **BS:** JLARC 1, 74.

LEWIS, Andrew; b 9 Oct 1716 County Donegal, Ulster Ireland; d 26 Sep 1781 **RU:** General/Patriot, Served as Brig General in VA Line. Was in Battle of Point Pleasant. Promoted to Gen 1776. Resigned commission 1777. Performed patriotic service securing troops supporting Battle of Point Pleasant 1774 **CEM:** King; GPS unk; Bent Mountain, S fr Roanoke; Roanoke Co **GS:** U **SP:** Mar (1749) Elizabeth Givens **VI:** Monument to him at Point Pleasant. Died in Bedford Co. Was Brig Gen after war. Great-great-granddaughter Margaret W. Juny appl pen 17 Jun 1858 Christian Co, KY. Pen says d 1782. R6308. DAR Monument **P:** Y **BLW:** unk **RG:** Y **MK:** Y SAR **PH:** unk **SS:** J-NSSAR 1993 Reg; K Vol 3 pg 120; AZ various pages; CG pg 2066; DD; DAR A069714; SAR P-23583214 **BS:** JLARC 1, 4, 41.

RU=Rank/Unit	CEM=Cemetery	GS=Gravestone	SP=Spousal Information
VI=Other Veteran Info	P=Pension	BLW=Bounty/Land Warrant	RG=Registered Grave
MK=SAR/DAR Marker	PH=Photo	SS=Service Source	BS=Burial Source

249

LEWIS, Andrew Jr; b Oct 1758; d 25 Sep 1844 **RU**: Private, Served in VA Line. Ent serv Botetourt Co **CEM**: King; GPS unk; Bent Mountain, S fr Roanoke; Roanoke Co **GS**: U **SP**: Mar 1) Elizabeth Madison, 2)(10 Jun 1788) Margaret Briant (c1766 Botetourt Co.-__) **VI**: Sol appl pen 29 Apr 1833 Montgomery Co. Widow appl pen 22 Jan 1845 Montgomery Co. W3431 **P**: Y **BLW**: unk **RG**: unk **MK**: unk **PH**: unk **SS**: K Vol 3 pg 120; CG pg 2065; DAR A069714; SAR P-236229 **BS**: JLARC 2, 4,109.

LEWIS, Benjamin; b Nov 1763; d 25 Sep 1824 **RU**: Sergeant, Served in Illinois & Western Army under Gen George Rogers Clark 1778-1783 **CEM**: Lewis Family; GPS 38.80276, -77.96242; Woodstock Plantation, Meredithville; Brunswick **GS**: Y **SP**: Mar (8 Sep 1787 Brunswick Co (bond) by Rev Thomas Lundie) Elizabeth Edmunds, d/o John Flood & (-----) Edwards **VI**: Son of Zebulon and Sandal (Jackson) Lewis **P**: unk **BLW**: unk **RG**: Y **MK**: N **PH**: unk **SS**: G pg 697; SAR P-235856 **BS**: 196.

LEWIS, Benjamin; b unk; d 1781 **RU**: Soldier, Served fr NJ, and died fr the battle at Yorktown **CEM**: Yorktown Victory Monument Tablet; GPS 38.28350, -78.54150; Yorktown; York **GS**: U **SP**: No info **VI**: No further data **P**: unk **BLW**: unk **RG**: unk **MK**: unk **PH**: unk **SS**: J-Yorktown Historian; SAR P-235844 **BS**: JLARC 74.

LEWIS, Betty (Washington); b 20 Jun 1773, Westmoreland Co; d 31 Mar 1797 **RU**: Patriot, With husband's death as only heir she gave a warehouse in Fredericksburg for militia use **CEM**: Western View; GPS unk; 17434 Boldaker Ln; Culpeper **GS**: Y **SP**: Mar (7 May 1750 Fredericksburg) Fielding Lewis (7 Jul 1725 Warner Hall, Gloucester Co-7 Dec 1781 Fredericksburg) s/o John & Frances (Fielding) Lewis **VI**: Daughter of Augustine Washington (1694-1743) & Mary Ball (c1708-1789); DAR recognition; sister of President George Washington; died at home of her daughter at "Western View" Culpeper Co **P**: N **BLW**: N **RG**: Y but not recorded by NSSAR or USDAR **MK**: Y DAR **PH**:Y **SS**: D Vol 3 pg 866 **BS**: 32 Lyman; 196.

LEWIS, Charles; b 1730 or c1744; d 1779 **RU**: Colonel, Served in VA Cont Line. As Capt commanded an Infantry Co fr Albemarle Co Apr-Jun 1775. Commissioned Col of 2d Bn of Minutemen,10 May 1776. Serv as Col 14th Cont Line 12 Nov 1776. Killed by Shawnee Indians **CEM**: Berry Hill; GPS unk; 1.5 mi N of Sweet Briar College; Albemarle **GS**: Y **SP**: Mary Randolph **VI**: Awarded BLW of 6666 acres. Died in Canada **P**: unk **BLW**: Y **RG**: N **MK**: N **PH**: unk **SS**: BY pg 225; E pg 471; CE pg 10, 14; DAR A069807; SAR P-235860 **BS**: 161 Berry Hill.

LEWIS, Edward; b 1747; d 6 Jan 1800 **RU**: Private, VA service, specifics not identified **CEM**: Old Christ Church Episcopal; GPS 38.80625, -77.04718; 118 N Washington St; Alexandria City **GS**: Y **SP**: No info **VI**: Died age 53. Perhaps son of Patrick Lewis. Recd pen 1787 **P**: unk **BLW**: unk **RG**: N **MK**: N **PH**: unk **SS**: G pg 720, plus **BS**: 20 pg 138.

LEWIS, Edward; b Dec 1760; d 13 Oct 1828 **RU**: Soldier, Was incapacitated by his war service **CEM**: Lewis Family; GPS unk; 712 Heidleback School Rd, Dodson; Patrick **GS**: Y **SP**: Nancy Price (1759 Orange Co.-30 Dec 1835) d/o William (1726-1807) & Mary (Moore) Price **VI**: Son of Charles & Elizabeth (Parham) Lewis. Pen. Patrick Co, 27 Feb 1801 **P**: Y **BLW**: unk **RG**: Y **MK**: unk **PH**: unk **SS**: G pg 712;DAR A211090; SAR P-235885 **BS**: JLARC 30; 196.

LEWIS, Fielding; b 7 Jul 1725, Warner Hall, Gloucester Co; d Dec 1781 **RU**: Patriot, Was church leader, judge, County Lt, Chairman Committees of Correspondence and Safety, Director of Defense of the Rappahannock, Commissioner of Gun Manufactory **CEM**: St George's Episcopal; GPS 38.302678.-77.459859; 905 Princess Anne; Fredericksburg City **GS**: Y **SP**: 1) Mar (18 Oct 1748) Catharine Washington (11 Feb 1723/4-19 Feb 1749/50) d/o John & Catharine (Whiting) Washingto; 2) Mar (7 May 1750, Stafford Co) Elizabeth "Betty" Washington (20 Jun 1733 Wakefield, Westmoreland Co-31 Mar 1797 Western View, Culpeper Co) d/o Augustine & Mary (Ball) Washington. Bur in Culpeper Co. **VI**: Cenotaph. Son of John (1694-1754) & Frances (Fielding) (1701-1731) Lewis. Washington's brother-in-law. Not bur at St Georges Church in Fredericksburg. Bur in Clarke Co but memorialized at St Georges Cemetery in Fredericksburg. **P**: unk **BLW**: unk **RG**: Y **MK**: N **PH**: Y **SS**: D Spotsylvania Co & Fredericksburg; DAR A069909; SAR P-235901 **BS**: JLARC 1, 2, 91; 196.

LEWIS, George Washington; b 13 Mar 1757, Fredericksburg; d 13 Nov 1821 **RU**: Captain/Lieutenant, Served in 3rd Regt, Light Dragoons. On 12 Mar 1776, Gen Washington created the "Commander-in-Chief Guard" and appt Capt Caleb Gibbs as Commandant & George Lewis as 1st Lt as Second in

RU=Rank/Unit	CEM=Cemetery	GS=Gravestone	SP=Spousal Information
VI=Other Veteran Info	P=Pension	BLW=Bounty/Land Warrant	RG=Registered Grave
MK=SAR/DAR Marker	PH=Photo	SS=Service Source	BS=Burial Source

Command. (George Lewis was 19). Was in 2nd & 3rd Cont Dragoons. Resigned as Capt 1779 **CEM:** Willis Hill, Fredericksburg National Military Park; GPS unk; Marye Heights; Fredericksburg City **GS:** Y **SP:** Mar (15 Oct 1779) Catherine Daingerfield (1764-1820), d/o Col William & (-----) Daingerfield, Commander of 7th VA Regt of Cont Line. **VI:** Son of Col Fielding (1725-1781) & Betty (Washington) (1733-1797) Lewis. George Washington's nephew. Attended Princeton College. When Pres. Washington died, he gave George Lewis first choice of swords. Died at Kenmore Plantation, Fredericksburg. DAR marker **P:** unk **BLW:** unk **RG:** Y **MK:** Y DAR **PH:** unk **SS:** D Fredericksburg;DAR A069946 SAR P-235919 **BS:** JLARC 76, 91.

LEWIS, Jesse Pitman; b 13 May 1763. Albemarle Co; d 1849 **RU:** Soldier, Served in VA Line. Ent serv Albemarle Co **CEM:** Lewis Family, University Heights; GPS 38.02390, -78.31000; Jct 250 W and Colonnade Dr, nr Old Ivy Rd; Charlottesville City **GS:** U **SP:** Nancy (-----) **VI:** Sol appl pen 13 Oct 1832 Albemarle Co. S5680, DAR marker **P:** Y **BLW:** unk **RG:** Y **MK:** unk **PH:** unk **SS:** CG pg 2069 DAR A069999; SAR P-235971 **BS:** JLARC 2, 4.

LEWIS, John, b 8 Apr 1720, Goochland Co, d 21 Jul 1794, Pittsylvania Co **RU:** Patriot, Gave material aid to cause, Pittsylvania Co **CEM:** St Pauls Episcopal Church; GPS 37.76570,-77.37120; 8050 St Paul's Rd; Hanover **GS:** Unk **SP:** Mar, 1759,Jane Lewis Meriwether, (1727-1794) **VI:** Son of Col Charles Lewis and Mary Howell (1696-1779) **P:** N **BLW:** N **RG:** N **MK:** N **PH:** N **SS:** Al Ct Bk pgs 22, 54,; Commissioner's book V pgs 17,18 Pittsylvania Co **BS:** 196.

LEWIS, John; b 1749; d 1797 **RU:** Captain, Appt Capt 1 Nov 1777. Resigned 1780 **CEM:** Lewis Family; GPS unk; Nr Staunton; Augusta **GS:** N **SP:** No info **VI:** Awarded 5000 acres bounty land **P:** unk **BLW:** Y **RG:** N **MK:** N **PH:** N **SS:** E pg 471-2 **BS:** 80 vol 3 pg 21.

LEWIS, John T; b 1757 (per pen info, b 1761); d 1835 **RU:** Private?, Served in VA Line. Ent serv Mecklenberg Co **CEM:** Lewis Family; GPS unk; Rt 727; Mecklenburg **GS:** Y **SP:** No info **VI:** Sol appl pen 19 Aug 1835 Halifax Co, age 74. S10249 **P:** Y **BLW:** unk **RG:** N **MK:** N **PH:** unk **SS:** K Vol 3 pg 122; CG pg 2070 **BS:** 54 pg 366.

LEWIS, Mary; b 24 Jul 1742, Albemarle Co; d 9 Feb 1824 **RU:** Patriot, Gave material aid to the cause **CEM:** Riverview; GPS 38.02610, -78.45810; 1701 Chesapeake St; Charlottesville City **GS:** Y **SP:** Mar (2 Nov 1808, Charlottesville) Nicholas Lewis (19 Jan 1734, Henrico Co-8 Dec 1808 Charlottesville) **VI:** Daug of Dr Thomas & Mildred (Thornton) Walker **P:** unk **BLW:** unk **RG:** N **MK:** unk **PH:** unk **SS:** Al Ct Bk pg 28 Albemarle Co **BS:** 196.

LEWIS, Nicholas; b 19 Jan 1734; d 8 Dec 1808 **RU:** Colonel, Commanded a co of Militiamen in Albemarle Co 1776-7. Later became Col of Co Militia there in 1781 **CEM:** Lewis-Clarkson; GPS 38.04407, -78.51706; Collonade Dr; Charlottesville City **GS:** N **SP:** Mary Walker (24 Jul 1742-9 Feb 1824) d/o Dr Thomas (1715-1794) & Mildred (Thornton) (1734 1808) Walker **VI:** Son of Robert (1704-1765) & Jane Meriwether (1705-1757) Lewis. Stone is no longer visible **P:** unk **BLW:** unk **RG:** Y **MK:** unk **PH:** N **SS:** E pg 472; SAR P-236109 **BS:** 200 William & Mary Quarterly; JLARC 2; 196.

LEWIS, Taliaferro; b 4 Feb 1754; d 12 Jul 1810 **RU:** Corporal, Served in 9 VA Cav. Was at battle at Germantown, taken prisoner **CEM:** Lewis Family, University Heights; GPS 38.02390,-78.31000; Jct 250 W and Colonnade Dr, nr Old Ivy Rd; Charlottesville City **GS:** Y **SP:** No info **VI:** Son of John Terrell (1728-1784) & Sarah (Taliaferro) (1728-1789) Lewis. Govt issue marker and old stone. **P:** unk **BLW:** unk **RG:** Y **MK:** N **PH:** unk **SS:** E pg 472; SAR P-236165 **BS:** JLARC 2; 67 vol 1 pg 153.

LEWIS, Thomas; b 27 Apr 1718, County Donegal, Ulster, Ireland; d 31 Jan 1790 **RU:** Patriot, Was Delegate to 3rd, 4th, 5th VA Conventions 1775-1776 and voted for independence. Was Delegate to VA Contitutional Convention June 1778 and voted for US Constitution **CEM:** Lewis Family; GPS unk; Rt 708 & 340; Rockingham **GS:** Y **SP:** Mar (26 Jan 1749) Jane Strother (1732, Stafford Co-19 Sep 1820) **VI:** Died at Lynnwood, Rt 1, Port Republic **P:** N **BLW:** N **RG:** Y **MK:** Y SAR **PH:** Y **SS:** DAR #A070144; X; SAR P-236168 **BS:** 04.

LEWIS, Thomas; b 26 Jan 1760; d Aft 1832 **RU:** Private, Ent serv Augusta Co, that part that is now Rockingham. Served in VA Line **CEM:** Western State Hospital; GPS 38.14299, -79.06571; Village Dr; Staunton City **GS:** N **SP:** No info **VI:** Sol appl pen 20 Aug 1832. S7138 **P:** Y **BLW:** unk **RG:** N **MK:** N **PH:** N **SS:** E pg 472; CG pg 2073 **BS:** 80 vol 3 pg 22; 196.

RU=Rank/Unit VI=Other Veteran Info MK=SAR/DAR Marker CEM=Cemetery P=Pension PH=Photo GS=Gravestone BLW=Bounty/Land Warrant SS=Service Source SP=Spousal Information RG=Registered Grave BS=Burial Source

LEWIS, Thomas Walker; b 24 Jun 1763; d 7 Jun 1807 **RU:** Private, SAR registration did not provide service **CEM:** Lewis-Clarkson; GPS 38.04407, -78.51706; Collonade Dr; Charlottesville City **GS:** Y **SP:** Elizabeth Meriwether (24 Feb 1771 Albemarle Co-17 Apr 1855 Lincoln Co, Missouri) d/o Nicholas & Margaret (Douglas) Meriwether **VI:** Son of Nicolas (1734-1808) & Mary (Walker) (1742-1824) Lewis. Stone is no longer visible **P:** unk **BLW:** unk **RG:** YMK: unk **PH:** unk **SS:** AR Vol 3 pg 22; NSSAR P-236185 **BS:** JLARC 2; 196.

LEWIS, Warner II; b c1747; d 1791 **RU:** Captain/Patriot, Served as County Lt of Gloucester 1775 and was officer in Gloucester Co Militia **CEM:** Warner Hall; GPS 37.20403, -76.28539; 4750 Warner Hall Rd; Gloucester **GS:** Y **SP:** 1) Mary Criswell 2) Mary Fleming **VI:** No further data **P:** unk **BLW:** unk **RG:** Y **MK:** Y SAR granite **PH:** Y **SS:** E pg 473; SAR P-236193 **BS:** 32.

LEWIS, William; b 1748; d 14 Nov 1779 **RU:** Lieutenant, Served in 2d Battlion of Minutemen, Albemale Militia 1776 **CEM:** Clover Fields; GPS 38.0479170, -78.3395170; loc 46 Cloverfields Farm Rd, Keswick; Albermarle **GS:** Y **SP:** Lucy Meriweather,(4 Feb1752-8 Sep 1765) d/o Thomas Merweather & Elizabeth Thornton, She m 2) (-----) Marks; bur at Locust Hill, Ivy, Albemarle Co **VI:** Son of Robert Lewis (4 May 1704, Gloucester Co-10 Jan 1765) & Jane Meriwether (1705 New Kent Co-1 Sep 1757). Stone indicates "1740-1780" which was erected by the DAR. **P:** unk **BLW:** Y **RG:** Y **MK:** Y **PH:** unk **SS:** E pg 743; K Vol 3 pg 125; BY pg 317; CF pg 10; DAR A070178; SAR P-236209 **BS:** JLARC 2, 4, 58; 80, vol3, pg 22;196

LEWIS, William; b 1750; d 1824 or 1830 **RU:** Private, Probably served in Clark's Illinois Regt fr VA; possibly at Ft Nelson **CEM:** Lewis Family; GPS unk; Little Georgetown; Fauquier **GS:** Y **SP:** Ann Montgomery (3 Sep 1759 - __), daughter of Capt Wm & Catherine (Morris) Montgomery of Prince William Co **VI:** A Maj by this name served in 3rd VA Regt of Foot 12 Feb 1781-1 Jan 1783 as POW taken at Charleston, SC **P:** unk **BLW:** unk **RG:** Y **MK:** unk **PH:** unk **SS:** J-NSSAR 1993 Reg; AK; CE pg 39; SAR P-236211 **BS:** JLARC 1; 04; 18 pg 137.

LEWIS, William J; b 4 Jul 1766, Augusta Co; d 1 Nov 1828 **RU:** Private, Serv at Ft Nelson in Portsmouth in 1782 **CEM:** Mt Athos; GPS unk; Rt 460, Kelly; Campbell **GS:** N **SP:** Elizabeth Cabel (1773-1855) **VI:** Son of William (1724-1811) & Ann (Montgomery) (1737-1808) Lewis. US Congressman 1817-1819. VA House of Delegates. 1800 built "Mount Athos" above James River in Campbell Co **P:** unk **BLW:** unk **RG:** N **MK:** N **PH:** N **SS:** E pg 473 **BS:** 196.

LEWIS, William; b 8 Apr 1763, d 18 Jun 1851 **RU:** Private; Served in VA Line from Culpeper Co where enlisted at age 16. One source indicates he distinguished himself on a special mission by Washington. Was present at surrender at Yorktown **CEM:** Lewis Family Farm; GPS: not determined; Culpeper; Procure property records at death for specific location **GS:** Unk **SP:** Mar (1782) Mary Brown (1767-1828), d/o John Brown & Elizabeth (__) **VI:** Son of Henry Lewis (1724-1810) & Anna Buford (1738-__). Rec'd pen 1818, and 1832, R 1559, FS 8827 **P:** Y **BLW:** N **RG:** Y **MK:** N **PH:** N **SS:** K Vol #, pg 125; CG: pg 2074; SAR P-236218 **BS:** 196.

LIEBERT, Jean; b unk; d 1781 **RU:** Soldier, Served in Santogne Bn and died fr battle at Yorktown **CEM:** French Memorial; GPS 36.81944, -79.39933; Yorktown; York **GS:** U **SP:** No info **VI:** No further data **P:** unk **BLW:** unk **RG:** Y **MK:** unk **PH:** unk **SS:** J-Yorktown Historian; SAR P-236430 **BS:** JLARC 1, 74.

LIGHT, Peter; b unk; d 30 Nov 1813 **RU:** Patriot, Gave material aid to cause **CEM:** Back Creek Quaker, aka Gainesboro United Methodist; GPS 39.27861, -78.25694; 166 Siler Ln, Gainesboro; Frederick **GS:** Y **SP:** Catherine (-----) **VI:** No further data **P:** N **BLW:** N **RG:** N **MK:** unk **PH:** unk **SS:** AL Ct Bk 1 pg 25, 28 Berkeley Co, VA (now WVA) **BS:** 196.

LIGHTFOOT, Mildred Howell; b Feb 1752, Charles City Co; d 01 May 1799 **RU:** Patriot, Gave material aid to cause **CEM:** Coles-Carrington; GPS unk; Mildendo Plantation; Halifax **GS:** U **SP:** Walter Coles (14 Nov 1739-07 Nov 1780) **VI:** No further data **P:** N **BLW:** N **RG:** N **MK:** unk **PH:** unk **SS:** AL Ct Bk pg 58 Halifax Co **BS:** 196.

LIGHTFOOT, William; b 1758, James City Co; d 1809 **RU:** Lieutenant/Patriot, Gave material aid to cause **CEM:** Lightfoot Family; GPS unk; Teddington, Sandy Point; Charles City Co **GS:** Y **SP:** Mar (c1795) Lucy Armistead Digges (c1773, James City Co-__) d/o Cole (31 Dec 1748-__) Martha (Walker) Digges of Hampton **VI:** No further data **P:** unk **BLW:** unk **RG:** Y **MK:** unk **PH:** unk **SS:** J-NSSAR 1993 Reg; AL Ct Bk pg 13, 14, 18 Charles City Co; DAR A070314; SAR P-236470 **BS:** JLARC 1; 196.

RU=Rank/Unit	CEM=Cemetery	GS=Gravestone	SP=Spousal Information
VI=Other Veteran Info	P=Pension	BLW=Bounty/Land Warrant	RG=Registered Grave
MK=SAR/DAR Marker	PH=Photo	SS=Service Source	BS=Burial Source

LIGNOT, Pierre; b unk; d 1781 **RU:** Soldier, Served in Agenois Bn and died fr battle at Yorktown **CEM:** French Memorial; GPS 36.81944, -79.39933; Yorktown; York **GS:** U **SP:** No info **VI:** No further data **P:** unk **BLW:** unk **RG:** Y **MK:** unk **PH:** unk **SS:** J-Yorktown Historian; SAR P-236485 **BS:** JLARC 1, 74.

LILLARD, Benjamin; b c1740, Orange Co; d 26 Mar 1829 **RU:** Captain/Patriot, Commanded a co in Culpeper Co Militia. Furnished supplies to the Cont Army **CEM:** Hot Mountain; GPS unk; Nethers; Rappahannock **GS:** U **SP:** Mar (c1772) Frances Crow (__-26 Apr 1832, Madison Co) **VI:** Died in Madison Co **P:** unk **BLW:** unk **RG:** Y **MK:** unk **PH:** unk **SS:** J-NSSAR 2000 Reg; DD; DAR A070354; SAR P-236517 **BS:** JLARC 76.

LILLARD, James; b c1725 or c1735, Spotsylvania Co; d 1804 **RU:** Patriot, Gave material aid to cause **CEM:** Lillard Family; GPS unk; Nethers; Madison **GS:** N **SP:** Keziah Bradley **VI:** No further data **P:** N **BLW:** N **RG:** Y **MK:** Y SAR **PH:** N **SS:** AL Ct Bk 1 pg 14, 29 Culpeper Co; DAR A070355; SAR P-236520 **BS:** 04.

LINCOLN, Jacob; b 18 Nov 1751, Carnavon, PA; d 20 Feb 1822 **RU:** Lieutenant, Ent serv 1781. Served in Capt Abraham Lincoln's Co, Rockingham Co Militia, 26 Mar 1781 **CEM:** Lincoln Family; GPS 38.547650,-78.840280; 7884 Harpine Rd Rt 42, Linville, 3 mi S of Broadway on SR 42, N of Edom exit.; Rockingham **GS:** Y **SP:** Mar (Aug 1870) Dorcas Robertson (15 Mar 1822-25 Jan 1840) **VI:** SAR marker Widow R6347 **P:** Y **BLW:** unk **RG:** N **MK:** Y SAR **PH:** Y **SS:** E pg 475; K Vol 3 pg 128; DAR A070423; SAR P-236638 **BS:** JLARC 4, 64.

LINCOLN, John b 3 May 1716, Freehold, Monough Co, NJ; Nov 1788 **RU:** Patriot, paid personal property tax considered to be a supply tax for Rev War, Rockingham Co, 1782 & 1783 **CEM:** Lincoln Family; GPS 38.547650, -78.840280; 7884 Harpine Hwy, Linville; Rockingham Co **GS:** Y **SP:** Mar (1743) Rebekiah Flowers (1720-1806), d/o Enoch Flowers (1693-1730) & Rebecca Barnard (1693-1735) **VI:** VA historical roadsign on site indicating he moved to cemetery loc 1768 and he is grandfather of President Lincoln **P:** N **BLW:** N **RG:** N **MK:** Y a gravestone marker by Hist Soc and DAR chapter **PH:** N **SS:** DV image 09, 1782, image 16, 1783, Rockingham Co **BS:** 196.

LINDSAY, Reuben; b 15 Jan 1747, Caroline Co; d 7 Nov 1831 **RU:** Colonel/Patriot, Was commander of Caroline Co Militia. Gave material aid to cause **CEM:** Lidsay Family, Springfield Farm; GPS unk; W fr Gordonsville; Orange **GS:** U **SP:** Mar (1778) Sarah Walker (__Castle Hill, Albemarle Co- __), 2) Hanna Tidwell **VI:** No further data **P:** unk **BLW:** unk **RG:** Y **MK:** unk **PH:** unk **SS:** J-NSSAR 1993 Reg, J- DAR Hatcher; DAR #A070619; AL Ct Bk 1 pg 11 Albemarle Co; SAR P-236765 & SAR P -235766 **BS:** JLARC 1,2.

LINDSAY, Thomas; b 13 Nov 1750, "The Mount"; d 14 Sep 1830 **RU:** Patriot, Gave material aid to the cause **CEM:** The Mount; GPS unk; 2312 Col Lindsey Ct, Falls Church; Fairfax **GS:** Y **SP:** No info **VI:** No further data **P:** N **BLW:** N **RG:** N **MK:** N **PH:** unk **SS:** AL Ct Bk pg 4, 13 **BS:** 61 vol III pg FC-40.

LINDSAY, William; b 1742; d 15 Sep 1792 **RU:** Major, Recd as Maj 9 Nov 1780, Fairfax Co Militia. severely wounded at Guilford CH; Served in Taylor's Legion **CEM:** Lindsay Family; GPS 38.70958, -77.23767; Off Lorton Rd nr Laurel Golf Club, Lorton; Fairfax **GS:** Y **SP:** Mar (c1766) Ann Calvert (1751-1822) **VI:** Older Govt stone, does not give birth yr **P:** unk **BLW:** unk **RG:** Y **MK:** Y SAR **PH:** Y **SS:** E pg 476; Fpg 45 DAR A070640; SAR P-236766 **BS:** JLARC 1 ,2, 14, 27, 28; 196.

LINGAN, James McCubbin; b 13 May 1751, Hartford, MD; d 28 Jul 1812, Baltimore, MD **RU:** Bridgadier General, Capt MD Line. 2nd Lt of Stephenson's MD & VA Rifle Regt. Fought at Long Island, York Island, Ft Washington. Wounded & taken prisoner at Ft Washington Nov 1776 aboard British ship Jersey, exchanged Oct 1780; retired Jan 1781 **CEM:** Arlington National; GPS 38.88377, -77.06535; Jefferson Davis Hwy Rt 110; Arlington **GS:** Y lot 89A **SP:** Janet Henderson (2 Sep 1765-5 Jul 1832) **VI:** Collector of port of Georgetown. Free speech advocate who defended Alexander Hanson, publisher of the Federal Republican & Commercial Gazette, who criticized US for participation in War of 1812 and was killed by angry mob who stormed the publisher's offices. Died in Baltimore, MD. Originally bur Washington DC, reinterred 5 Nov 1908. BLW #1294-300-19 Mar 1792 **P:** unk **BLW:** Y **RG:** Y SAR **MK:** Y **PH:** unk **SS:** J-NSSAR 1993 Reg; CG pg 2087; SAR P-236901 **BS:** JLARC 1; 196.

LINK, Matthias(AKA John Matthias Link) b 11 Feb 1737, PA; d 8 Feb 1815 **RU:** Patriot, Gave material aid to cause **CEM:** Old Link; GPS unk; .5 mi W of Ft Defiance; Augusta **GS:** U **SP:** Mary Christiana

RU=Rank/Unit	CEM=Cemetery	GS=Gravestone	SP=Spousal Information
VI=Other Veteran Info	P=Pension	BLW=Bounty/Land Warrant	RG=Registered Grave
MK=SAR/DAR Marker	PH=Photo	SS=Service Source	BS=Burial Source

Schmidt (c1746 MD-12 Jun 1817) **VI:** Son of John Jacob Link (1692-1738) **P:** N **BLW:** N **RG:** N **MK:** unk **PH:** unk **SS:** DAR A132196; DD cites Augusta Co Ct Bk pg ? **BS:** 225.

LINN, William Sr; b unk; d 1808 **RU:** Patriot, Gave material aid to cause **CEM:** Linn Family Farm; GPS unk; Morgantown; Fauquier **GS:** U **SP:** No info **VI:** No further data **P:** N **BLW:** N **RG:** Y **MK:** unk **PH:** unk **SS:** J- DAR Hatcher; AL Lists pg 9 Fauquier Co; SAR P-236983 **BS:** JLARC 2; 80, vol 3, pg 25.

LINSEY, Stephen; b unk; d 1781 **RU:** Soldier, Served fr MA, and died fr the battle at Yorktown **CEM:** Yorktown Victory Monument Tablet; GPS 38.28350, -78.54150; Yorktown; York **GS:** U **SP:** No info **VI:** No further data **P:** unk **BLW:** unk **RG:** Y **MK:** unk **PH:** unk **SS:** J-Yorktown Historian; SAR P-237012 **BS:** JLARC 74.

LIPSCOMB, John; b 1756; d 28 Sep 1824 **RU:** Private, Served in VA Cont Line. Ent serv King William Co 1778 **CEM:** Meadow Hill Estate; GPS unk; Off Rt 613, 1.8 mi N of Luck's Store; Spotsylvania **GS:** Y **SP:** Mar (24 Dec 1783 King William Co) Elizabeth Lipscomb (c1761-__) d/o Ambrose & (-----) Lipscomb **VI:** Sol appl pen 27 May 1819 King William Co. age 67. Widow appl pen 25 Feb 1839 King William Co. W5323 **P:** Y **BLW:** unk **RG:** N **MK:** N **PH:** unk **SS:** B; K Vol 3 pg 132; CG pg 2091 **BS:** 09 grid 71.

LIPSCOMB, Thomas; b 1730, Albemarle Co; d 1799 **RU:** Captain, Served in 7th Cont Line as Ens 28 Oct 1776. Resigned 20 May 1778 **CEM:** Meadow Hill Estate; GPS unk; Off Rt 613, 1.8 mi N of Luck's Store; Spotsylvania **GS:** Y **SP:** Dorothy (-----) (__-aft 1799) as widow mar Thomas's brother Archibald Lipscomb. Another soldier same name (__-12 Jun 1825 Spotsylvania Co) mar Mary Smith (14 Dec 1733-__) relation not determined. **VI:** Son of Anderson & (-----) Lipscomb. Anderson was a delegate in the VA Assembly. Pen spouse Dorothy. BLW 2,666 acres **P:** Y **BLW:** Y **RG:** Y **MK:** N **PH:** unk **SS:** E pg 478; BG pg 2091; SAR P-237081 **BS:** 09 part 2.

LITTLEPAGE, Lewis; b 19 Dec 1762, Hanover Co; d 19 Jul 1802 **RU:** Soldier/Statesman, Was in VA & US Govt. Was one of William and Mary College students at Williamsburg that fought British raids spring 1779. Member Jay Commission to Spain. American volunteer in Monorcan Campaign 1781-82 which captured Minorca fr GB **CEM:** Masonic Cemetery; GPS 38.30198, -77.46142; 900 Charles St; Fredericksburg City **GS:** Y **SP:** No info **VI:** Son of Col James & Elizabeth (Lewis) (09 Oct 1732-1809) Littlepage **P:** unk **BLW:** unk **RG:** N **MK:** Y SAR plaque **PH:** Y **SS:** O **BS:** 13 Gr 183; 196.

LITTON, John Richard, Sr; b 4 Jul 1726, Prince George Co, MD, d l Jan 1804 **RU:** Private Washington County Militia. In Dunmore war, Oct 1774 but his unit was not in the battle at Pt Pleasant **CEM:** Soloman Litton Hollow; GPS 36.9453200,-82.0469650 loc off Rd 640 vic jct Rd 721; Russell **GS:** Y Govt incorrectly lists rank as PFC (Private First Class not used in Rev War period) **SP:** Sarah Ann Wilcoxen (26 Feb 1728-13 Jan 1808) **VI:** Son of Caleb Polleckfield Litton (1678-1763) and Mary Grace Hartlett Burton (1703-1791) **P:** N **BLW:** N **RG:** Y **MK:** Y DAR **PH:** N **SS:**DL pg 861; DAR A202089; SAR P-237354 (incorrectly lists rank as Lt) **BS:** 196.

LITTON, Martha (Duncan); b 22 Sep 1756, Lancaster Co, PA; d 21 Mar 1821 **RU:** Patriot, Was POW in Canada in 1780-1783 during Rev War **CEM:** Soloman Litton Hollow; GPS unk; nr Pinnacle Preserve; Russell **GS:** Y **SP:** Solomon Caleb Litton (1751-1814) **VI:** Daughter of Thomas & Elizabeth (Alexander) (1710-1814) Duncan. Died in Whitley Co, KY **P:** N **BLW:** N **RG:** Y **MK:** Y DAR **PH:** unk **SS:** AS, SAR regis; BT - DAR marker; SAR P-237357 **BS:** SAR regis; 196.

LITTON (LINTON), Burton Caleb (Caleb Burton) Sr; b 5 Aug 1763, Botetourt Co; d 5 May 1778 **RU:** Private, Served in Capt William Russell's Co, Russell Co Militia **CEM:** Soloman Litton Hollow; GPS unk; nr Pinnacle Preserve; Russell **GS:** Y Gov't **SP:** No info **VI:** Son of John Richard (1726-1804) & Sarah Ann (Wilcoxen) (1728-1808) Litton. Killed at Glade Hollow Ft, Washington Co by Indians. SAR Gr marker. Govt Gr stone lists service **P:** unk **BLW:** unk **RG:** Y **MK:** Y SAR **PH:** unk **SS:** J-NSSAR 2000 Reg; B; Z pg 152; DAR A132643; SAR P-237353 **BS:** JLARC 76; 196.

LITTON, Soloman Caleb, Jr; b 22 Dec 1751, Tinkers Creek, Augusta, Co, d 24 Feb 1844 **RU:** Ensign, Washington Co, Militia. Was POW **CEM:** Elliott; GPS: 36.925598,-82.000602; loc N of the US 19, (Trail of the Lonesome Pine) betw Rt 776 & Bethel Church, Barnett; Russell **GS:** Y Govt **SP:** Martha Duncan Sharp **VI:** No further data **P:** N **BLW:** N **RG:** Y **MK:**Y SAR **PH:** N **SS:** AZ pg 233; DL pgs 958, 1001, 1072 DAR A070738; SAR 237356 **BS:** SAR PRS.

RU=Rank/Unit	CEM=Cemetery	GS=Gravestone	SP=Spousal Information
VI=Other Veteran Info	P=Pension	BLW=Bounty/Land Warrant	RG=Registered Grave
MK=SAR/DAR Marker	PH=Photo	SS=Service Source	BS=Burial Source

LITTON (LINTON), Solomon Caleb Sr; b 1730; d 1843 **RU:** Ensign, Served in Washington Co Militia. Also in Dunmore's War 1774 **CEM:** Soloman Litton Hollow; GPS unk; nr Pinnacle Preserve; Russell **GS:** Y **Govt SP:** Martha Duncan **VI:** No further data **P:** unk **BLW:** unk **RG:** Y **MK:** Y **SAR PH:** unk **SS:** J-NSSAR 2000 Reg; E pg 479; Z pg 160; SAR P-237352 **BS:** JLARC 76.

LITTON (LITION), Thomas W; b 13 May 1754, Botetourt Co; d 11 June 1840 **RU:** Private, Served in Cont Line **CEM:** Soloman Litton Hollow; GPS unk; nr Pinnacle Preserve; Russell **GS:** Y **SP:** Carleen Dempsey (20 Feb 1760-16 Nov 1840) **VI:** Son of John Richard (1726-1804) & Sarah Ann (Wilcoxen) (1726-1808) Litton. Govt. Gr stone shows last name as "Lition" but suspect it is in error. SAR marker **P:** unk **BLW:** unk **RG:** Y **MK:** Y **SAR PH:** N **SS:** J-NSSAR 2000 Reg; B govt Gr stone; SAR P-237351 **BS:** JLARC 76; 196.

LIVERNOIS, Jacques; b unk; d 1781 **RU:** Soldier, Served in Gatinais Bn and died fr battle at Yorktown **CEM:** French Memorial; GPS 36.81944, -79.39933; Yorktown; York **GS:** U **SP:** No info **VI:** No further data **P:** unk **BLW:** unk **RG:** Y **MK:** unk **PH:** unk **SS:** J-Yorktown Historian; SAR P-237403 **BS:** JLARC 1, 74.

LIVINGSTON, Peter; b 1755, Russell Co; d 10 Jan1835 **RU:** Captain/ Patriot, Served in VA Militia. Drove cattle and horses for militia **CEM:** Livingston Family; GPS 36.67987, -82.35273; Rt 689, Mendota; Scott **GS:** Y **SP:** Mar 4 Mar 1783, Washington Co, Elizabeth Osborne Head(c1765, Montgomery Co-11 Feb 1783) **VI:** No furher data **P:** unk **BLW:** unk **RG:** Y **MK:** Y **PH:** unk **SS:** O;AZ pg DAR A070813; SAR P-237446 **BS:** 04.

LOCKETT, Edmund Sr; b 1755 (pen info says 3 Jun 1761); d 24 Jun 1834 **RU:** Captain, Served in VA Line. Ent serv 1780 Chesterfield Co **CEM:** Lockett Family; GPS unk; Brandermill, cnr of Long Gate & Huntgate; Chesterfield **GS:** U **SP:** Mar (8 Dec 1785 Powhatan Co) Sally Bryant (5 Nov 1762-___), d/o James & Jane (-----) Bryant **VI:** Son of Richard & Mary (-----) Lockett. JP and High Sheriff of Chesterfield Co. Sol appl pen 14 Aug 1832. Widow appl pen 27 Oct 1840 Chesterfield Co. W8064 **P:** Y **BLW:** unk **RG:** Y **MK:** N **PH:** unk **SS:** K Vol 3 pg 136; CG pg 2102; SAR P-237649 **BS:** JLARC 4, 12, 35.

LOCKHART, Patrick; b 1749, Scotland; d 1810 **RU:** Major, Appointed in militia to Major 12 Jul 1781,by Botetourt Co Court **CEM:** Fincastle Presbyterian; GPS 37.50017, -79.87558; 108 E Back St, Fincastle; Botetourt **GS:** N **SP:** Mary McDonald **VI:** Name is on the SAR plaque at this cemetery **P:** unk **BLW:** unk **RG:** Y **MK:** Y **SAR & plaque PH:** N **SS:** AZ pg 192, J-NSSAR 1993 Reg, J- DAR Hatcher; DAR A071023; SAR P-237656 **BS:** 80, Vol 3 pg 28 ; 196; JLARC 1, 2.

LOCKHART, Robert 1744, Scotland, d10 May 1817 **RU:**Sergeant, a member of the PA State Guard, Landcaster Co, PA, perhaps also as a Capt Robert Lockhart Co Commander in PA refers to him **CEM:** Lockhart-Phillips; GPS 39.264126; 78.329642; loc to the W of Sinking Spring Lane at jct with Gore Rd, Gore; Frederick **GS:** Y **SP:** Margary Wilson (Jul 1746-1837) **VI:** No further data **P:** N **BLW:** N **RG:**Y **MK:** N **PH:** N **SS** AP Serv rec & pen rec James Cupples shows him as Captain, DAR A071026; SAR P-340611 **BS:** 196.

LOCKRIDGE, Andrew; b 1755; d 1791 **RU:** Major, Served in 2nd Battalion, Rockbridge Co Militia 15 Sep 1788-Oct 1779 **CEM:** Rocky Spring Presbyterian; GPS 38.11470, -79.24250; 1 mi S of Deerfield; Augusta **GS:** N **SP:** Mar (6 Apr 1762) Jane Graham (1742 Augusta Co-1796) **VI:** No further data **P:** unk **BLW:** unk **RG:** Y**MK:** N **PH:** N **SS:** DAR #A071780; E pg 480; AZ pg 82, 93; 183; SAR P-237677 **BS:** JLARC 62, 103.

LOCKRIDGE, Andrew; b 10 Apr 1730, Spotsylvania Co, d bef 15 Mar 1791, Burnsville, Highland Co **RU:** Major As captain commanded a company 10 Oct 1774 in the battle at Point Pleasant and named Major of 2d Battalion, Augusta Co, 19 Aug 1778 **CEM:** Lockridge Family GPS: unk; on Burnsville Rd at jct with Bull Pasture Rd, McDowell; Highland **GS:** Yes Govt shows rank **SP:** Mar (7 Apr 1761 Rockbridge Co) Jean Graham (1742-1796), d/o John Graham & Elizabeth Elliott **VI:** No further data **P:**N; **BLW:** N **RG:** Y **MK:** Y **PH:** N **SS Z pg 102;** DAR A-071780; SAR P-237677 **BS:** 196

LOGAN, James; b 1733 Lurgan, Ireland; d 19 Jun 1825 **RU:** Patriot, Gave material aid to cause **CEM:** New Monmouth Presbyterian; GPS 37.83960, -79.48586; 2343 West Midland Rd; Lexington City **GS:** U **SP:** Mar (c1765) Hannah Erwin (Irwin) **VI:** Died in Rockbridge Co **P:** N **BLW:** N **RG:** Y **MK:** unk **PH:** unk **SS:** SAR P-237841 **BS:** JLARC 2

RU=Rank/Unit   CEM=Cemetery   GS=Gravestone   SP=Spousal Information
VI=Other Veteran Info   P=Pension   BLW=Bounty/Land Warrant   RG=Registered Grave
MK=SAR/DAR Marker   PH=Photo   SS=Service Source   BS=Burial Source

LOGAN, James; b 1755; d 1825 **RU:** Private, Served in 4th, 8th, & 12th Cont Lines **CEM:** New Monmouth Presbyterian; GPS 37.83960, -79.48586; 2343 West Midland Rd; Lexington City **GS:** U **SP:** No info **VI:** No further data **P:** unk **BLW:** unk **RG:** N **MK:** unk **PH:** unk **SS:** J- DAR Hatcher; E pg 481 **BS:** JLARC 2

LOGAN, John; b 26 Dec 1767; d 9 Jan 1837 **RU:** Private, Served in Capt McCutchen's Co, Augusta Co Militia **CEM:** Bethel Presbyterian; GPS 38.04257, -79.17283, GS 38.0230,-79.1020; 563 Bethel Green Rd, Middlebrook; Augusta **GS:** Y **SP:** Mar (30 Aug 179_ Augusta Co) Rachel McPheeters (28 Dec 1774-16 Dec 1849) d/o Rev William (1729-1807) and Rachel (Moore) (__-1826) McPheeters **VI:** Son of James (1733-1825) & Hannah (Irvine) (1747-1826) Logan **P:** unk **BLW:** unk **RG:** Y **MK:** unk **PH:** Y **SS:** E pg 481; SAR P-237857 **BS:** JLARC 62, 63; 196

LOGAN, Robert; b 1755; d 9 Oct 1828 **RU:** Drummer, Served in Capt Thomas Moultrie's 6th Co, Col Francis Marion's Regt Cont Line, Nov 1779 **CEM:** Fincastle Presbyterian; GPS 37.50017, -79.87558; 108 E Back St, Fincastle; Botetourt **GS:** Y **SP:** Margaret (-----) (c1781-10 May 1830) **VI:** Minister of church 30 yrs. Name is on the SAR plaque at this cemetery **P:** unk **BLW:** unk **RG:** N **MK:** Y SAR & plaque **PH:** unk **SS:** A pg 292 **BS:** 196.

LOGAN, William; b 1740; d 26 May 1812 **RU:** Private, Served in 8th and 12th Cont Line **CEM:** Logan Family; GPS unk; Off Rt 672, NE jct with Rt 666, .4 mi on private Rd; Halifax **GS:** Y **SP:** Nancy Sydnor (25 Sep 1764-2 Dec 1826) **VI:** Will indicated burial in cem at residence. BLW # 7761, 100 acres **P:** unk **BLW:** Y **RG:** N **MK:** unk **PH:** unk **SS:** C pg 318, 467; E pg 481 **BS:** 198.

LOGWOOD, Thomas; b 1740, Henrico Co; d 10 Sep 1821 **RU:** Major/Patriot, Commanded a company in Bedford Co Militia. Gave material aid to cause **CEM:** Logwood Family; GPS unk; Locust Hill; Bedford **GS:** U **SP:** Mar (c1775) Ann Aiken (__Chesterfield Co-1815 Bedford Co) **VI:** No further data **P:** unk **BLW:** unk **RG:** Y **MK:** N **PH:** unk **SS:** J-NSSAR 1993 Reg, J- DAR Hatcher; DAR #A071176; SAR P-237899 D Vol 1, pg 100, 102, 103, 112, 115; E pg 481 **BS:** JLARC 1, 2.; 80 vol 3, pg 29

LOHR, Johan Peter; b 25 Jan 1756, Codorus Furnace, York Co, PA; d 21 Sep 1841 **RU:** Soldier, Served in MD Line. Ent serv Hagerstown MD 1776. Was buried with military honors **CEM:** Trinity Episcopal; GPS 38.14917, -79.07521; 214 Beverley St; Staunton City **GS:** U **SP:** 1) Catherine Eyler 2) Elizabeth Satzer **VI:** Son of Johan George & Maria Margaretta (-----) Lohr. Moved to Maryland as a small child. Moved to Augusta Co VA c1790. Appl pen 24 Sep 1832. S5699 **P:** Y **BLW:** unk **RG:** Y **MK:** unk **PH:** unk **SS:** K Vol 3 pg 138; CG pg 2107; SAR P237904 **BS:** JLARC 2, 4 ,62.; 80,vol3 pg 29

LOMAX, Thomas; b 25 Jan1746, d 17 Oct 1811 **RU:** Major/Patriot, Served in Caroline Co, VA Militia **CEM:** Lomax-White; GPS unk; Rt 758, Port Tobago; Caroline **GS:** N **SP:** Ann Corbin Taylor (__-1835) **VI:** Son of Lunsford & Judith (-----) Lomax **P:** unk **BLW:** unk **RG:** Y **MK:** N **PH:** N **SS:** E pg 481; H; DAR A071187; SAR P-237913 **BS:** 02 pg 101. (**LONG**, Edward see Appendix, addenda)

LONG, Ellis, Sr; b 2 Aug 1758; d 12 Feb 1837 **RU:** Private, enlisted NJ in Capt Bonnel's Co, US Army:**CEM:** Old Town Cemetery; GPS not determined; lots 76 & 77, Mulberry St, Town of Stephensburg **GS:** Y **SP:** Elizabeth (-----) (28 Jan 1761-15 Jul 1844) **VI:** No further data **P:** N **BLW:** N **RG:** N **MK:** N **PH:** N **SS:** AP Fold3 Ser Rec **BS:** 196.

LONG, George; b 1746, d 1794 **RU:** Private/Patriot, Served in Lt Col John Cropper's Co, Col Morgan's Regt attached to Gen Woodford's Brigade, 30 Nov 1778. As patriot gave material aid to cause in Rockingham Co **CEM:** Long Family; GPS: unk; East Point; Rockingham **GS:** No **SP:** Catherine Anna Sprinkle (1737-1793) **VI:** Military service may apply to person this name that drew pension in TN **P:** N **BLW:** N **RG:** N **MK:** N, **PH:** N **SS:** A pg 268; AL Ct Bk II, pg 4 and Comm Bk V, pg 116 **BS:** 196

LONG, John; b 1742; d 14 Feb 1807 **RU:** Private, Served in Capt James McDaniel's Co, Montgomery Co Militia **CEM:** Thornrose; GPS 38,15120, -79.08460; 1041 W Beverly St; Staunton City **GS:** Y **SP:** No info **VI:** Son of James & Johanna (H-----) Long. **P:** N **BLW:** N **RG:** N **MK:** N **PH:** N **SS:** G pg 236 **BS:** 196.

LONG, Joseph Sr; b 8 Sep 1744 (bapt 16 Sep 1774); d 15 Jun 1829 **RU:** Captain, Commanded a company in Augusta Co Militia, Oct 1782. Served in Battle of Point Pleasant 1794 **CEM:** Tinkling Spring Presbyterian; GPS 38.08472, -78.98278; 30 Tinkling Spring Dr, Fishersville; Augusta **GS:** Y **SP:**

RU=Rank/Unit	CEM=Cemetery	GS=Gravestone	SP=Spousal Information
VI=Other Veteran Info	P=Pension	BLW=Bounty/Land Warrant	RG=Registered Grave
MK=SAR/DAR Marker	PH=Photo	SS=Service Source	BS=Burial Source

Catherine Thompson(16 Feb 1762-Nov 1836) **VI:** Son of William Long (1715-1781), DAR plaque **P:** unk **BLW:** unk **RG:** Y **MK**: Y DAR plaque **PH:** unk **SS:** E pg 482; SAR P-238050 **BS:** JLARC 1, 4, 62; Wilson, HM, *The Tinkling Spring Headwater of Freedom, the Church & Her People,* pub 1954 pg 185, 464; 196.

LONG, Mary; b c1755; d 10 Apr 1797 **RU:** Patriot, Gave material aid to cause **CEM:** Friedens United Church of Christ; GPS 38.34848, -78.87653; 3960 Friedens Church Rd; Rockingham **GS:** U **SP:** John Long **VI:** No further data **P:** N **BLW:** N **RG:** N **MK**: unk **PH:** unk **SS:** DAR Newsletter, Sep/Oct 2015 Vol 15 No 5 pg 417 **BS:** 196.

LONG, Philip; b 18 Dec 1742 d 5 Feb 1826 **RU:** Private, Served in Capt Michael Reader's Co, Shenandoah Co, and in Clark's Regt in Illinois **CEM:** Long Family Price Farm; GPS unk; Rt 616, Alma; Page **GS:** Y **SP:** 1) Katherine (-----) 2) Elizabeth Arey 3) Mary Hay **VI:** Son of Paul & Mary (Miller) Long. Died in Ft Long, Shenandoah, Rockingham Co. Common monument. **P:** unk **BLW:** unk **RG:** Y **MK**: Y SAR **PH:** unk **SS:** C pg 207, 602; E pg 482; DAR A071315; SAR P-238092 **BS:** JLARC 76, 94; 196.

LONGDEN, John; b c1754 or 1755; d 31 Mar 1830 **RU:** Corporal, Served in Cont & VA Line. Lived in Alexandria at enl. Served in the First Light Dragoons, Lee's Legion **CEM:** Trinity United Methodist; GPS 39.13600, -77.00610; 2911 Cameron Mills Rd; Alexandria City **GS:** Y **SP:** No info **VI:** Son of Ralph Longden. Died age 76. F-S 18033 R 15-81 BLW #423-100-28 19 Apr 1808. Death notice in the Alexandria Gazette 1 Apr 1830 **P:** Y **BLW:** Y **RG:** Y **MK**: N **PH:** unk **SS:** AK; E pg 483; K Vol 3 pg 142; CG pg 2112; SAR P-232684 **BS:** 04; 23 pg 130.

LORIVAT, Jean; b unk; d 1781 **RU:** Seaman, Served on "Solitaire" and died from Yorktown battle **CEM:** French Memorial; GPS 36.81944, -79.39933; Yorktown; York **GS:** U **SP:** No info **VI:** No further data **P:** unk **BLW:** unk **RG:** Y **MK**: unk **PH:** unk **SS:** J-Yorktown Historian; SAR P-238648 **BS:** JLARC 1, 74.

LORMIER, Augustin; b unk; d 1781 **RU:** Soldier, Served in Touraine Bn and died fr battle at Yorktown **CEM:** French Memorial; GPS 36.81944, -79.39933; Yorktown; York **GS:** U **SP:** No info **VI:** No further data **P:** unk **BLW:** unk **RG:** Y **MK**: unk **PH:** unk **SS:** J-Yorktown Historian; SAR P-238650 **BS:** JLARC 1, 74.

LORRAIN, Georges; b unk; d 1781 **RU:** Soldier, Served in Santogne Bn and died fr battle at Yorktown **CEM:** French Memorial; GPS 36.81944, -79.39933; Yorktown; York **GS:** U **SP:** No info **VI:** No further data **P:** unk **BLW:** unk **RG:** Y **MK**: unk **PH:** unk **SS:** J-Yorktown Historian; SAR P-238651 **BS:** JLARC 1, 74.

LOUIS, Jean; b unk; d 1781 **RU:** Seaman, Served on "Citoyen: and died from Yorktown battle **CEM:** French Memorial; GPS 36.81944, -79.39933; Yorktown; York **GS:** U **SP:** No info **VI:** No further data **P:** unk **BLW:** unk **RG:** Y **MK**: unk **PH:** unk **SS:** J-Yorktown Historian; SAR P-238765 **BS:** JLARC 1, 74.

LOVE, Charles; b 1748, Charles Co, MD; d 1792 **RU:** Private/Patriot, Served in MD Line. Enlisted 17 Apr 1782. Gave material aid to cause **CEM:** Love Family; GPS 38.43950, -77.40266; Buckland Farm, 6342 Pleasant Colony Ln, Warrenton; Fauquier **GS:** Y **SP:** Mar (c1734) Mary Harris (c1772 Charles City, MD-22 Jul 1757) **VI:** Died in Buckland, Prince William Co ("Buckland" is now in Fauquier Co). GS without data **P:** unk **BLW:** unk **RG:** Y **MK**: Y SAR **PH:** Y **SS:** DAR #A071808; D Vol 3 pg 806; Bk MD Settlers & Soldiers 1700-1800; SAR P-238798 **BS:** Buckland Farm rcds.

LOVE, James; b c1766; d 1846 **RU:** Private, Served in Cumberland Co PA Militia **CEM:** Goose Creek; GPS 39.11250, -77.69527; Rt 772, Lincoln; Loudoun **GS:** Y **SP:** Susanna (-----))1766-25 Jan 1847) **VI:** Stone illegible **P:** unk **BLW:** unk **RG:** N **MK**: unk **PH:** unk **SS:** Fold 3 Series 5 Vol VI pg 159 **BS:** 196.

LOVE, Samuel; b 1720, Charles Co, MD; d 24 Apr 1787 **RU:** Sergeant/Patriot, Served as Sgt in 3rd Cont Line. Gave beef, a very large amount of flour, meal, milk, cider and a 10-yr-old horse **CEM:** Love Family; GPS 38.43950, -77.40266; Buckland Farm, 6342 Pleasant Colony Ln, Warrenton; Fauquier **GS:** Y **SP:** Rebecca (-----) (__-1821) DAR/SAR show Mary Haw & Sarah (-----) **VI:** Died in Buckland, Prince William Co ("Buckland" is now in Fauquier Co). Stone broken & nearly illegible. Foot marker initials legible **P:** unk **BLW:** unk **RG:** Y **MK**: Y SAR **PH:** Y **SS:** E pg 484 public claims bk; DAR A071824; SAR P238643 **BS:** 94 Buckland Hall.

RU=Rank/Unit	CEM=Cemetery	GS=Gravestone	SP=Spousal Information
VI=Other Veteran Info	P=Pension	BLW=Bounty/Land Warrant	RG=Registered Grave
MK=SAR/DAR Marker	PH=Photo	SS=Service Source	BS=Burial Source

LOVELACE, Thomas; b 8 Feb 1739, Richmond Co; d 1792 **RU**: Patriot, Gave material aid to cause **CEM**: Lovelace Family; GPS unk; Off Rt 676, W of Asbury Church; Halifax **GS**: U **SP**: Tabitha Oldham d/o James & Tabitha (Haydon) Oldham **VI**: Son of Charles & Bridget (McLaughlin) Lovelace of North Farnham Parish **P**: N **BLW**: N **RG**: Y **MK**: unk **PH**: unk **SS**: AL Ct Bk pg 27,57; SAR P-238922 **BS**: 215.

LOVELL, Joseph; b c1765, Boston, MA; d 9 Oct 1784 **RU**: Private, Served in MA **CEM**: St John's Episcopal; GPS 37.53183, -77.41958; 2401 E Broad St; Richmond City **GS**: Y **SP**: No info **VI**: No further data **P**: unk **BLW**: unk **RG**: N **MK**: N **PH**: unk **SS**: AJ Vol 9 pg 1008 **BS**: 28 pg 467; 196.

LOVING, William; b 14 Feb 1740, Culpeper Co; d 30 Jan 1792 **RU**: Captain/Patriot, Co Commander in Amherst Co Militia. Gave material aid to cause **CEM**: Old Keys Church; GPS unk; Jct Rt 647 & 722; Amherst **GS**: N **SP**: Mar (21 Sep 1763) Elizabeth Hargrave (1750-1808) **VI**: No further data **P**: unk **BLW**: unk **RG**:Y **MK**: N **PH**: N **SS**: DAR #A071988; D Vol 1 pg 80, 81; AH pg 3; SAR P239068 **BS**: 01 pg 3.

LOVINGS (LOVING), John Jr; b 4 Oct 1739, Culpeper Co; d 10 May 1804 **RU**: Captain, Commanded a co in Amherst Co Militia 1780-1781. Was at Yorktown Oct 1781 **CEM**: Lovings Gap; GPS unk; Lovington; Nelson **GS**: U **SP**: Naomi "Amy" Seay (1741-1819) **VI**: Was sheriff of Amherst Co **P**: unk **BLW**: unk **RG**: Y **MK**: unk **PH**: N **SS**: E pg 485; SAR P-239068 **BS**: JLARC 115; 196.

LOYD, Henry; b 1756, Bucks, PA, d 4 May 1817 **RU**: Ensign, Served in Cont Navy **CEM**: Stiff Family; GPS unk; Union Church Rd 1 mi past Union Methodist, Thaxton; Bedford **GS**: Y **SP**: Rebecca Griffin **VI**: Govt stone with SAR marker attached indicates served as Ensign Cont Navy. DAR & SAR have erroneously used service in Loudoun Co Militia with no evidence he moved across VA to Bedford Co **P**: unk **BLW**: unk **RG**: Y **MK**: Y SAR **PH**: unk **SS**: AK Bedford Museum; DAR A070885; SAR P-239337 **BS**: 196.

LUCAS, Basil; b 20 Aug 1757, MD; d 6 Jul 1841 **RU**: Sergeant, Served in MD Line. Ent serv MD 1776 **CEM**: Mt Hebron; GPS 39.10916, -78.09497; 305 E Boscawen St; Winchester City **GS**: U **SP**: Mar (26 Feb 1786) Elizabeth (-----) **VI**: Sol appl pen 11 May 1833 Berkeley Co. In 1831 stated name was on MD pen roll. S18097. Died in Berkeley Co, WVA Memorialized in Cem **P**: Y **BLW**: unk **RG**: Y **MK**: Y SAR monument **PH**: unk **SS**: E pg 486; K Vol 3 pg 148; CG pg 2136; J-NSSAR 2000 Reg; SAR P-239354 **BS**: JLARC 76.

LUCAS (LUCASS), John; b 15 Jul 1749, Augusta Co; d 19 Apr 1836 **RU**: Captain, VA Line. Ent serv Montgomery Co 1778. Served under Col Preston to end of war **CEM**: Lucas Family (source 1), Old Cooper (source 2); GPS unk; S or E fr Riner; Montgomery **GS**: N **SP**: Mar (15 Feb 1777 Montgomery Co) Mary Polly Wilson (1 Jan 1758-17 May 1843) **VI**: Lucas family research & patriot ancestor war service produced DAR marker in Lucas fam cem indicates Capt John Lucas is bur in Old Cooper cem, 2-3 mi E of Calfees Mountain. Sol appl pen 8 Aug 1832 Montgomery Co. Widow appl pen 6 May 1839 Montgomery Co. W5468 **P**: Y **BLW**: unk **RG**: Y **MK**: Y SAR **PH**: N **SS**: J-NSSAR 1993 Reg, J- DAR Hatcher; K Vol 3 pg 149; CG pg 2137; DAR A072215; SAR P-239386 **BS**: JLARC 1, 2.

LUCAS, Parker; b 1756; d 27 Mar 1835 **RU**: Soldier, Ent serv Montgomery Co. Served in Capt John Lucas's Co, VA Line **CEM**: Cloverhollow; GPS 37.33470, -80.47580; Rt 715 Deerfield Ln before first sharp turn; Giles **GS**: U **SP**: Margaret (-----) **VI**: Sol appl pen 23 Sep 1832 Giles Co age 76. S8868 **P**: Y **BLW**: unk **RG**: Y **MK**: unk **PH**: unk **SS**: CG pg 2137; SAR P-239399 **BS**: JLARC 4, 26.

LUCKETT, John B; b 1747; d 10 Mar 1794 **RU**: Captain, Served in Loudoun Co Militia. Took oath as Capt 8 Jun 1778 **CEM**: Luckett; GPS unk; Nr Quantico Marine Base; Prince William **GS**: Y **SP**: No info **VI**: No further data **P**: unk **BLW**: unk **RG**: Y **MK**: N **PH**: unk **SS**: E pg 487; SAR bio rpt submitted May 2020 **BS**: 15 pg 195.

LUKE, Issac Sr; b 26 Nov 1729; d 31 Oct 1784 **RU**: Patriot, Gave 48 bushels of lime to the cause **CEM**: Trinity Episcopal; GPS 36.83459, -76.30105; 500 Court St; Portsmouth City **GS**: Y **SP**: Rachel Dale (11 Feb 1737-27 Jan 1775) **VI**: Resided at 436 Court St, Portsmouth **P**: N **BLW**: N **RG**: Y **MK**: Y SAR plaque **PH**: unk **SS**: G pg 485; DAR A072359; SAR P-239606 **BS**: 75 Portsmouth.

LUMSDEN, John; b 1738, Bedford Co; d 11 Mar 1788 **RU**: Corporal/Patriot, Served in 1st, 5th and 9th Cont Lines. Gave material aid to cause **CEM**: John Fisher Farm; GPS 37.03640, -79.72470; Rt 669;

RU=Rank/Unit   CEM=Cemetery   GS=Gravestone   SP=Spousal Information
VI=Other Veteran Info   P=Pension   BLW=Bounty/Land Warrant   RG=Registered Grave
MK=SAR/DAR Marker   PH=Photo   SS=Service Source   BS=Burial Source

258

Franklin **GS**: U **SP**: Mar (1752) Wilmouth Steele (1732-1788) **VI**: Rec'd BLW 1 Sep 1783, 409 acres in Franklin Co and on 31 March 1786, 440 acres **P**: unk **BLW**: Y **RG**: unk **MK**: unk **PH**: unk **SS**: E pg 488; AL Ct Bk pg 47 Henry Co; CD; DAR A072402; SAR P-239679 **BS**: JLARC 2,18; 196.

LUNDY, John; b 19 Nov 1751, Sussex Co, NJ; d 5 May 1831 **RU**: Private, Served in 6th PA Regt **CEM**: Nuckolls Family; GPS 36.63551, -80.95944; Beyond the end of Wild Turkey Ln, jct US-58 & Rt 94; Grayson **GS**: U **SP**: Mar (11 Dec 1777 NJ) Rebecca Silverthorn (8 May 1754 Morris Co, NJ-24 Dec 1839 Oldtown, Grayson Co) d/o Thomas & Johanna (Newman) Silverthorn **VI**: No further data **P**: unk **BLW**: unk **RG**: N **MK**: unk **PH**: unk **SS**: AP Service Rec **BS**: 196.

LYBROOK, John; b 20 Nov 1763, PA; d 18 Dec 1837 **RU**: Private, Ent serv Botetourt Co (now Giles). Served 6 mo under Capt Floyd in 1778, 1779 to 1782 and in Capt Lucas Co, VA Line **CEM**: Lybrook Family; GPS 37.33385, -80.61087; End Rt 65, Pembroke; Giles **GS**: Y **SP**: Anne L Chapman (1761, Culpeper Co-1831) d/o John C (1740-1813) & (-----) Chapman **VI**: Son of Balzar Palzer (1729-1804) & Catherine (Reihm) (1761-1831) Lybrook. Sol appl pen 19 Mar 1834 Giles Co. R6540 **P**: Y **BLW**: unk **RG**: Y **MK**: unk **PH**: unk **SS**: J- DAR Hatcher; K Vol 3 pg 153; CD; CG pg 2149; SAR P-239867 **BS**: JLARC 2; 196.

LYNCH, Anselm; b 8 Jun 1764; d 18 Feb 1826 **RU**: First Lieutenant, Served in Bedford Co Militia. Appointed 1st Lt 24 Sep 1781 **CEM**: Lynch Family; GPS 37.12946, -79.26853; Avoca Museum, 1514 Main St, Altavista; Campbell **GS**: Y **SP**: Susan Miller (___-1808) **VI**: Son of Charles Lynch (1736-1796) & Anne Terrell (d 1804) **P**: unk **BLW**: unk **RG**: Y **MK**: N **PH**: unk **SS**: E pg 489; SAR P-240006 **BS**: JLARC 36; 196.

LYNCH, Charles Sr; b 1736; d 29 Oct 1796 **RU**: Colonel, Bedford Militia. Appointed Col Bedford Co Militia 24 Feb 1778 **CEM**: Lynch Family; GPS 37.12946, -79.26853; Avoca Museum, 1514 Main St, Altavista; Campbell **GS**: Y **SP**: Anne Terrell (___-1804) **VI**: Connected with lead mines in county. Justice of Bedford Co and was disowned by the Quakers for taking the oath of office. House of Burgesses 1769-1778. At battle of Guilford CH. VA Senate 1784-1789 **P**: unk **BLW**: unk **RG**: Y **MK**: N **PH**: unk **SS**: E pg 489; DAR A072635; SAR P-240025 **BS**: JLARC 36, 66, 75; 196.

LYNCH, John; b 1740; d 13 Oct 1820 **RU**: PrivatePatriot, Served in 1st Cont Line, 2nd VA Regt. Served as ferry operator **CEM**: South River Meeting House; GPS 37.37246, -79.19194; 5810 Fort Ave; Lynchburg City **GS**: U **SP**: Mar (1 Aug 1769, Bedford Co) Mary Bowles (1752-5 Aug 1829) **VI**: Founder of Petersburg; petitioned VA Legislature 1784 to found city on land he possessed. City Council dedicated a plaque to him which is in cemetery **P**: unk **BLW**: unk **RG**: N **MK**: Y SAR **PH**: unk **SS**: DAR A072647; E pg 489 **BS**: 196; 221.

LYNCH, Patrick; b Ireland, d 7 May 1831 **RU**: Corporal, Served in MD and Bedford Co VA for 3 years. In Nov 1778 was in Capt James Gray's Co, Col Daniel Morgan's combined 11th & 15th VA Regt. Was in battles of Guilford Ct House and siege of 96th and at Yorktown Oct 1781 **CEM**: Patrick Lynch Home Place; GPS not determined; Bedford **GS**: N **SP**: Mar 1783, Martha "Patsy" Whorley (1748-9 Mar 1843) She recd widow's pen W8071 **VI**: Recd pen 4 Mar 1831 for $20 per annum **P**: Both **BLW**: Unk **RG**: Y **MK** N **PH**: N **SS**: A pgs 207, 256; C pg 461; CG: pg 2152; DAR A200405; SAR P-240020 **BS**: 196

LYNE, William; b 30 Jan 1734, Belfast Ireland; d 10 Sep 1808 **RU**: Colonel, Served as Ranger on frontier under Ens James Lynch, Westmoreland Co, PA. Was commander of King and Queen Co Militia. Was the County Lt in 1782 and was President of a Cts Marshall **CEM**: Lyne Family; GPS unk; See property records for location; King & Queen **GS**: U **SP**: Mar (1778) Lucy Foster Lyne (___ Granville Co, NC-aft 1799) d/o Henry & (-----) Lyne **VI**: Son of Willam of Bristol Co, NC & (-----) Lyne. DAR indicates burial in Richmond City **P**: unk **BLW**: unk **RG**: Y **MK**: N **PH**: unk **SS**: DAR A072676; E pg 490; CI: PA Archives 5th Series Vol 2 pg 675, 727, Vol 4, pg 597, 734, 747; SAR P-240042 **BS**: DAR report; 80 vol 3, pg 40.

LYONNOIS, Jean; b unk; d 1781 **RU**: Soldier, Served in Foix Bn and died fr battle at Yorktown **CEM**: French Memorial; GPS 36.81944, -79.39933; Yorktown; York **GS**: U **SP**: No info **VI**: No further data **P**: unk **BLW**: unk **RG**: Y **MK**: unk **PH**: unk **SS**: J-Yorktown Historian; SAR P-240265 **BS**: JLARC 1, 74.

LYONNOIS, Pierre; b unk; d 1781 **RU**: Seaman, Served in Soissonnais Bn and died fr battle at Yorktown **CEM**: French Memorial; GPS 36.81944, -79.39933; Yorktown; York **GS**: U **SP**: No info **VI**: No

RU=Rank/Unit	CEM=Cemetery	GS=Gravestone	SP=Spousal Information
VI=Other Veteran Info	P=Pension	BLW=Bounty/Land Warrant	RG=Registered Grave
MK=SAR/DAR Marker	PH=Photo	SS=Service Source	BS=Burial Source

259

further data **P:** unk **BLW:** unk **RG:** Y **MK:** unk **PH:** unk **SS:** J-Yorktown Historian; SAR P-240266 **BS:** JLARC 1, 74.

MACHAIN, Claude; b unk; d 1781 **RU:** Seaman, Served on "Magnanime" and died from Yorktown battle **CEM:** French Memorial; GPS 36.81944, -79.39933; Yorktown; York **GS:** U **SP:** No info **VI:** No further data **P:** unk **BLW:** unk **RG:** Y **MK:** unk **PH:** unk **SS:** J-Yorktown Historian; SAR P-240398 **BS:** JLARC 1, 74.

MACKEY, John Sr; b 1767; d 1818 **RU:** Private, Served in 11th Cont Line **CEM:** Lexington; GPS unk; Lexington; Lexington City **GS:** Y **SP:** No info **VI:** No further data **P:** unk **BLW:** unk **RG:** N **MK:** N **PH:** unk **SS:** AS **BS:** 80 vol 3 pg 43.

MACOMB, Alexander; b 27 Jul 1748, County Antrim, Ireland; d 19 Jan 1831 **RU:** Soldier, Probably served fr Detroit in the Navy **CEM:** Arlington National; GPS 38.88377, -77.06535; Jefferson Davis Hwy Rt 110; Arlington **GS:** Y **SP:** 1) Mar (4 May 1773 Detroit) Mary Catherine Navarre (__-17 Nov 1789, NYC) 2) Mar (11 Jul 1791 Trinity Church, NYC) Jane (Marshall) Rucker, widow of John Peter Rucker **VI:** Son of John Macomb and Jane Gordon, emigrated to Albany NY in 1755. Moved with his brother to Detroit where he mar in 1773. Moved to New York City in 1785 where he was a real estate speculator. He suffered ruinous financial setback and moved to his son's home in Georgetown in Washington DC where he died. He and his wife were reinterred fr Old Presbyterian Church in Georgetown to Arlington on 12 May 1892 **P:** unk **BLW:** unk **RG:** Y **MK:** unk **PH:** unk **SS:** J-NSSAR 2000 Reg; NSSAR Ancestor # P-240525 **BS:** JLARC 76; 196.

MACON, Mary; b 20 Jan1742, d aft 29 Dec 1781 **RU:** Patriot; Gave material aid to cause in King William Co **CEM:** Fairfield Plantation; GPS 37.7606970, -77.1027050; 806 East Mill Rd, Aylett; King William **GS:** U **SP:** 1) mar (1776) William Aylett (1743-1781), 2) Callohill Minnis **VI:** Daug of Col James & Elizabeth (Moore) Macon of Kennington (__-1787). Her heirs rec'd BLW on 6666 acres in 1809 **P:** N **BLW:** Y Hiers **RG:** Y **MK:** N **PH:** N **SS:** D vol 2, pgs 576, 581, 583, 589; BX pg 24; DAR A004153; SAR P-338521 **BS:** 196.

MACON, William; b 4 Jan 1725; d 25 Nov 1813 **RU:** Patriot, Gave provisions to the cause **CEM:** Fairfield; GPS unk; Sledd Run Sub Div; Hanover **GS:** Y in lot 303 **SP:** Lucy (-----) (9 Jun 1737-1 Dec 1802) **VI:** Burial is also listed in adjacent, New Kent Co in the St Peters Episcopal Ch. After war period he achieved Major General in US Army **P:** N **BLW:** N **RG:** N **MK:** N **PH:** unk **SS:** G pg 622 **BS:** 31 vol 1 pg 51.

MADDOX, Allison; b c1760, Charles County, MD; d 22 Jan 1843 **RU:** Private, Served in1st MD Line. Drafted fr the Charles Co Militia. Served fr mid-June to 1 Sep 1781 **CEM:** Maddox; GPS 38.620704,-77.376257; Hope Hill Crossing Subdivision, Hope Hill Rd; Prince William **GS:** Y **SP:** Ann Swann (1776-17 Feb 1857) **VI:** Died in Prince William or Fairfax Co **P:** N **BLW:** N **RG:** Y **MK:** Y SAR **PH:** Y **SS:** AK Oct 2015 Cites Archives of MD Vol 18; SAR P335845 **BS:** 31.

MADDOX, William; b c1750, d 21 May 1810, Fauquier **RU:** Sergeant Capt Hebard Smallwood's Co, Col William Grayson' Regt, VA Line, l Dec 1777 to 9 Sep 1778 **CEM:** Bacon Race Church AKA Oak Grove Church; GPS 38.6915665,-77.3630219; loc jct Bacon Race Rd & Davis Ford Rd; Prince William **GS:** Y but incorrectly has CSA marker and gravestone **SP:** Mar 1776, Peggy Wharton (1752-1791) **VI:** Rec'd one hundred acres BLW, Aug 1785 for 3 yrs service **P:** U **BLW:** Y **RG** Y **MK:** N **PH:** N **SS:** A pg 253; E pg 403; F pg 52: DAR A073044; SAR P- 240626 **BS:** 196.

MADEC, Jean; b unk; d 1781 **RU:** Seaman, Served on "Saint-Esprit" and died from Yorktown battle **CEM:** French Memorial; GPS 36.81944, -79.39933; Yorktown; York **GS:** U **SP:** No info **VI:** No further data **P:** unk **BLW:** unk **RG:** Y **MK:** unk **PH:** unk **SS:** J-Yorktown Historian; SAR P-240631 **BS:** JLARC 1, 74.

MADISON, Ambrose Sr; b 22 Jan 1755, Montpelier Station, Orange Co; d 3 Oct 1793 **RU:** Captain, Was Paymaster 2nd VA Regt 1777-78 and Capt of Regimental Convention Guards in 1779 **CEM:** Montpelier; GPS unk; 11407 Constitution Hwy, Montpelier Station; Orange **GS:** Y **SP:** Mar (11 Nov 1779 Fauquier Co) Mary Willis Lee (27 Jan 1757, Warrenton, Fauquier Co-14 Mar 1798 Montpelier Station, Orange Co) d/o Hancock & Mary (Willis) Lee **VI:** Son of Col James (1723-1801) & Eleanor "Nellie" Rose (Conway)

RU=Rank/Unit	CEM=Cemetery	GS=Gravestone	SP=Spousal Information
VI=Other Veteran Info	P=Pension	BLW=Bounty/Land Warrant	RG=Registered Grave
MK=SAR/DAR Marker	PH=Photo	SS=Service Source	BS=Burial Source

(1731-1829) Madison. Brother to President James Madison Jr. Requested BLW but not recd **P:** N **BLW:** N **RG:** N **MK:** unk **PH:** unk **SS:** E pg 493; AZ pg 101 **BS:** 196.

MADISON, James; b 16 Mar 1751, Port Conway, King George Co; d 28 Jun 1836 **RU:** Patriot, Served in 1st Gen Assembly VA 1776, and Exec. Council 1778. Was in Cont Congress 1780-83 **CEM:** Montpelier; GPS unk; 11407 Constitution Hwy, Montpelier Station; Orange **GS:** U **SP:** Dolley Payne Todd Madison **VI:** Secretary of State under Jefferson 1801-09. Fourth president of the US, 1809-1817 and president during War of 1812; Bronze plaque in Wrenn Hall, Williamsburg **P:** N **BLW:** N **RG:** Y **MK:** unk **PH:** unk **SS:** J-NSSAR 1993 Reg; SAR P-240647 **BS:** JLARC 1, 201 pg 1793.

MADISON, James; b 27 Aug 1749, Augusta Co, d 5 Mar 1812 **RU:** Lieutenant, 28 May1778, Orange Co Militia **CEM:** Chapel College William & Mary; 37.2707000, -76.7091000; Jamestown Rd; Williamsburg **GS:** Y in crypt under chapel **SP:** **Mar 1779,** Susan/Sarah Tait **VI:** Bishop. President of College of William and Mary fr 1777 until death. President first convention Episcopal Church VA in 1785. In 1790 was first bishop of VA **P:** N **BLW:** N **RG:** Y **MK:** Unk **PH:** N **SS:** AZ pg 220; DAR A073057; SAR P-240646 **BS:** 196.

MADISON, James, b 27 Mar 1723, Port Conway, King George, Co, d 27 Feb 1801 **RU:** Patriot, Member of Committee of Safety, Orange Co. Also he unofficially paid for a collection of arms, Orange Co, 24 Oct 1775 and was member of Committee of Safety, Orange Co **CEM:** Madison Family; GPS 38.2177730,-78.1748230; West Gate Rd, Montpelier; Orange **GS:** No **SP:** Mar 13 Sep1749, Fort Conway, King George Co, Eleanor "Nellie" Rose (9 Jan 1731-11 Feb 1829) **VI:** In an unmarked grave according to National Park Service. Son of Ambrose Madison (1696-1732) & Frances Taylor (1700-1761) **P:** N **BLW:** N **RG:** Y **MK:** Unk **PH:** N **SS:** E pg 493; DAR A073056; SAR P-240645 **BS:** 196.

MADISON, William Strother; b 1758; d 17 Mar 1782 **RU:** Patriot/Private, Was Justice & Sheriff of Botetourt Co & Surveyor of Washington Co. Served in Capt James Gray's Co, 15th VA Regt Jul 1778 **CEM:** Madison; GPS unk; Shawsville; Montgomery **GS:** Y **SP:** Elizabeth Preston (1763-1837) **VI:** Died of smallpox contracted in military service **P:** N **BLW:** N **RG:** N **MK:** unk **PH:** unk **SS:** Cl Muster Rol; **BS:** 196.

MADISON, William Taylor; b 5 May 1762 Montpelier, Orange Co; d 20 Jul 1843 **RU:** Lieutenant, Served in State Legion & Regt of Harrison's VA Artillery of VA Line 1781 **CEM:** Montpelier; GPS unk; 11407 Constitution Hwy, Montpelier Station; Orange **GS:** Y **SP:** 1) Mar (20 Dec 1783 Orange Co) Frances Throckmorton (24 Feb 1765-20 Aug 1832) 2) Mar (1834) Nancy Jarrell **VI:** Son of Col James (1723-1801) & Eleanor "Nellie" Rose (Conway) (1731-1829) Madison. Brother to President James Madison Jr. General in War of 1812. Heirs recd BLW on 29 Aug 1838 of 2666 acres **P:** Y **BLW:** Y **RG:** N **MK:** unk **PH:** unk **SS:** E pg 494;DAR A073065; SAR P-240655 **BS:** 196.

MAGILL, Charles; b 10 Jul 1760, Ireland; d 2 Apr 1827 **RU:** Major, Served in VA Line. Ent serv Winchester, Frederick Co 1777. Served on Gen Washington Staff as Maj of Calvary **CEM:** Mt Hebron; GPS 39.10916, -78.09497; 305 E Boscawen St; Winchester City **GS:** U **SP:** 1) Mar (29 Apr 1789, Spotsylvania Co) Elizabeth Dangerfield 2) Mar (24 May 1792 Frederick Co) May (Mary) Buckner Thurston, (27 Jul 1772-1850, DC **VI:** Widow appl pen 9 Aug 1838 Fauquier Co. W5336 **P:** Y **BLW:** unk **RG:** Y **MK:** Y SAR monument **PH:** unk **SS:** J-NSSAR 1993 Reg; CG pg 2165;DAR A073095; SAR P-240698 **BS:** JLARC 1.

MAGILL, James; b 1756; d 24 Aug 1840 **RU:** Private, Served in 12th VA Regt. Ent serv Rockingham Co **CEM:** Old Peaked Mountain; GPS 38.37113, -78.73416; 9843 Town Hall Rd, McGaheysville; Rockingham **GS:** Y **SP:** 1) Betsy Evans 2) Mar (10 Mar 1789 Greene Co, TN) Mary McMeans **VI:** Sol appl pen 4 Sep 1832 Green Co TN age 74 (Probably d and is bur there, not Rockingham Co VA). Widow appl pen 6 May 1844 Walker Co GA age 76 & rejected due to less than six mos service. Pen says he d 24 Aug 1839. Memorialized on common monument.Pen recd R-6827 **P:** Y **BLW:** unk **RG:** Y **MK:** Y DAR plaque **PH:** unk **SS:** K Vol 3 pg 159; N; CG pg 2165; SAR P-240701 **BS:** 196.

MAGILL, William; b 21 Apr 1748, Augusta Co, VA; d 1797 **RU:** Quartermaster/Patriot, Served in Rockingham Co Militia. Gave material aid to cause **CEM:** Old Peaked Mountain; GPS 38.37113, -78.73416; 9843 Town Hall Rd, McGaheysville; Rockingham **GS:** U **SP:** Mar (1770 Allegheny Co MD) Joan Fowler **VI:** Son of James & (-----) Magill Sr **P:** unk **BLW:** unk **RG:** N **MK:** Y DAR plaque **PH:** unk **SS:** J-NSSAR 2000 Reg; D Rockingham **BS:** JLARC 76.

RU=Rank/Unit	CEM=Cemetery	GS=Gravestone	SP=Spousal Information
VI=Other Veteran Info	P=Pension	BLW=Bounty/Land Warrant	RG=Registered Grave
MK=SAR/DAR Marker	PH=Photo	SS=Service Source	BS=Burial Source

261

MAGNAN, Francois; b unk; d 1781 **RU:** Soldier, Served in Touraine Bn and died fr battle at Yorktown **CEM:** French Memorial; GPS 36.81944, -79.39933; Yorktown; York **GS:** U **SP:** No info **VI:** No further data **P:** unk **BLW:** unk **RG:** Y **MK:** unk **PH:** unk **SS:** J-Yorktown Historian; SAR P-240706 **BS:** JLARC 1, 74.

MAGNAN, Jean; b unk; d 1781 **RU:** Seaman, Served on "Hercule" and died from Yorktown battle **CEM:** French Memorial; GPS 36.81944, -79.39933; Yorktown; York **GS:** U **SP:** No info **VI:** No further data **P:** unk **BLW:** unk **RG:** Y **MK:** unk **PH:** unk **SS:** J-Yorktown Historian;SAR P-240706 **BS:** JLARC 1, 74.

MAGNIEN, Bernard; b c1752, Luneville, France; d 4 Nov 1819 **RU:** Aide de Camp, Was Aide de Camp to Gen Lafayette. Came with Lafayette to serve in Rev **CEM:** Trinity Episcopal; GPS 36.83459, -76.30105; 500 Court St; Portsmouth City **GS:** Y **SP:** Margaret (-----) (__-5 Feb 1819) **VI:** Item 124 in W.B. Butt inventory. From Luneville, France, left to fight in Amer Rev. Was Lt Col in War of 1812. **P:** unk **BLW:** unk **RG:** Y **MK** Y SAR plaque **PH:** unk **SS:** CD; SAR P-336642 **BS:** JLARC 105127.

MAIDEN, James; b Bet 1750-1755, Augusta Co; d c1797 **RU:** Private, Enl in Rockingham Co 1777. Served in Capt David Laird's and Capt Nathan Lamb's Co 6th & 10th VA Lines **CEM:** Maiden Homestead; GPS unk; Bedor Rd Rt 628, .3 mi fr Rt 33 in Elkton; walk up hill abt .5 mi; Rockingham **GS:** N **SP:** Mar (Aug 1775 or 1776) Theodocia (Docia) Lee (c1753-__). She remar Bazil Hall (__-Aug 1839 Botetourt Co) **VI:** Theodosia was granted L 30 support in Rockingham Co 23 Nov 1779 while he was away in service. Widow appl pen 28 Dec 1843 Rockingham Co age 90. W5098 **P:** Y **BLW:** unk **RG:** Y **MK:** unk **PH:** N **SS:** DAR Ancestor #A072998; K Vol 3 pg 160; BX pg 534; CG pg 2167; DD; SAR 240792 **BS:** JLARC 4, 64; 51; http://www.heritagecenter.com/cemeteries/cem/cem388.htm.

MAILLET, Marcel; b unk; d 1781 **RU:** Seaman, Served on "Soliaire" and died from Yorktown battle **CEM:** French Memorial; GPS 36.81944, -79.39933; Yorktown; York **GS:** U **SP:** No info **VI:** No further data **P:** unk **BLW:** unk **RG:** Y **MK:** unk **PH:** unk **SS:** J-Yorktown Historian; SAR P-240794 **BS:** JLARC 1, 74.

MAINS, William; b unk; d 1815 **RU:** Private, Served in 3rd & 4th Cont Line **CEM:** Leesburg Presbyterian; GPS 39.11611, -77.56722; 207 W Market St, Leesburg; Loudoun **GS:** Y **SP:** Mary (-----) (__-12 Oct 1827) **VI:** No further data **P:** unk **BLW:** unk **RG:**N **MK:** N **PH:** unk **SS:** E pg 495 **BS:** 25 pg 190; 196.

MAIRE, Jacques; b unk; d 1781 **RU:** Seaman, Served on "Northumberland" and died from Yorktown battle **CEM:** French Memorial; GPS 36.81944, -79.39933; Yorktown; York **GS:** U **SP:** No info **VI:** No further data **P:** unk **BLW:** unk **RG:** Y **MK:** unk **PH:** unk **SS:** J-Yorktown Historian; SAR P-241405 **BS:** JLARC 1, 74.

MAISON, Jean; b unk; d 1781 **RU:** Soldier, Served in Foix Bn and died fr battle at Yorktown **CEM:** French Memorial; GPS 36.81944, -79.39933; Yorktown; York **GS:** U **SP:** No info **VI:** No further data **P:** unk **BLW:** unk **RG:** Y **MK:** unk **PH:** unk **SS:** J-Yorktown Historian; SAR P-240832 **BS:** JLARC 1, 74.

MAJOR, Richard; b c1722, Pennsbury, PA; d 3 Dec 1796 **RU:** Patriot, Gave material aid to the cause **CEM:** Hutchison-Major; GPS 38.90569, -77.47508; Pleasant Valley Rd & Lafayette Center Dr, Chantilly; Fairfax **GS:** Y **SP:** Sarah Major (1781-12 Apr 1801) **VI:** SAR Gr marker. Died age 74. He was instrumental in establishing several Baptist congregations in Fairfax and Loudoun counties during his ministry **P:** N **BLW:** N **RG:** Y **MK:** Y SAR **PH:** unk **SS:** G pg 81; SAR P-332076 **BS:** 61 vol IV, pg CH-20; 196.

MAJOR, William; b 4 Oct 1744; d 19 Mar 1847 **RU:** Private, Served in10th & 14th Cont Lines **CEM:** Major Family; GPS 38.65282, -78.02353; Rt 642, Viewtown Rd nr jct with Ida Belle Ln; Rappahannock **GS:** Y **SP:** Mar (13 Aug 1795) Elizabeth Thatcher Corbin (23 Dec 1779-16 Mar 1869) d/o John (1747-1813) & Frances (Thatcher) (1757-1814) Corbin **VI:** No further data **P:** unk **BLW:** unk **RG:** N **MK:** N **PH:** unk **SS:** E pg 496 **BS:** 163 Major; 196.

MALFROIS, Pierre; b unk; d 1781 **RU:** Seaman, Served on "Languedoc" and died from Yorktown battle **CEM:** French Memorial; GPS 36.81944, -79.39933; Yorktown; York **GS:** U **SP:** No info **VI:** No further data **P:** unk **BLW:** unk **RG:** Y **MK:** unk **PH:** unk **SS:** J-Yorktown Historian; SAR P-240882 **BS:** JLARC 1, 74.

RU=Rank/Unit	CEM=Cemetery	GS=Gravestone	SP=Spousal Information
VI=Other Veteran Info	P=Pension	BLW=Bounty/Land Warrant	RG=Registered Grave
MK=SAR/DAR Marker	PH=Photo	SS=Service Source	BS=Burial Source

262

MALLOW, George Sr; b 22 Dec 1727, Griesbach Alasce, France; d Aft 22 Nov 1789 **RU:** Patriot, Gave material aid to cause **CEM:** Mallow Family; GPS unk; McGaheysville; Rockingham **GS:** N **SP:** Mar (21 Apr 1750) France Anna Barbara Muller (26 Sep 1726, France-17 Jan 1797) **VI:** No further data **P:** N **BLW:** N **RG:** Y **MK:** N **PH:** N **SS:** DAR #A073275; O; AL Ct Bk II pg 11, 20, 24 Rockingham Co; DD: cites Levinson Rockingham Co, VA Minute Bk 1778-1786 pg 110, 121; SAR P-240952 **BS:** 04.

MALONE, Benjamin; b 1756; d 1824 **RU:** Lieutenant, Specific records are at Lib of VA, Auditor's Acct XXII pg 18. Took oath as Lt in Mecklenburg Militia 13 Sep 1779 **CEM:** Canaan Methodist Church; GPS 36.66848, -78.05323; Jct Blackridge Rd & Canaan Church Rd; Mecklenburg **GS:** Y **SP:** No info **VI:** No further data **P:** unk **BLW:** unk **RG:** N **MK:** N **PH:** unk **SS:** E pg 496; CZ pg 295; DB pg 102 **BS:** 54 pg 294.

MANADET, Bernard; b unk; d 1781 **RU:** Soldier, Served in Bourbonnais Bn and died fr battle at Yorktown **CEM:** French Memorial; GPS 36.81944, -79.39933; Yorktown; York **GS:** U **SP:** No info **VI:** No further data **P:** unk **BLW:** unk **RG:** Y **MK:** unk **PH:** unk **SS:** J-Yorktown Historian; SAR P-240987 **BS:** JLARC 1, 74.

MANN, Daniel; b unk; d unk **RU:** Private?, Served in 2nd & 5th Cont Lines **CEM:** Old City; GPS 37.41472, -79.15667; 401 Taylor St; Lynchburg City **GS:** N **SP:** No info **VI:** No further data **P:** unk **BLW:** unk **RG:** N **MK:** Y SAR plaque **PH:** N **SS:** E pg 497 **BS:** 62 pg 136.

MANN, Jacob; b unk; d 2 May 1824 **RU:** Private, Served in Capt William McBride's Co at Falls of Ohio in 1782 **CEM:** Back Creek Quaker, aka Gainesboro United Methodist; GPS 39.27861, -78.25694; 166 Siler Ln, Gainesboro; Frederick **GS:** Y **SP:** No info **VI:** No further data **P:** unk **BLW:** unk **RG:** N **MK:** unk **PH:** unk **SS:** N pg 1266 **BS:** 196.

MANNING, Samuel; b unk; d 1781 **RU:** Private, Served in Capt Chapman's Co, CT Cont line. Died fr the Battle at Yorktown **CEM:** Yorktown Victory Monument Tablet; GPS 38.28350, -78.54150; Yorktown; York **GS:** U **SP:** No info **VI:** BLW 1050-100 **P:** unk **BLW:** Y **RG:** Y **MK:** unk **PH:** unk **SS:** J-Yorktown Historian; DY pg 98, 351; SAR P241272 **BS:** JLARC 74.

MANSFIELD, Robert; b 19 Dec 1762, Albemarle Co; d 1 Oct 1833 **RU:** Soldier, Served in VA Line. Ent serv Albemarle Co 1779 **CEM:** Mansfield Family; GPS unk; Nr Barboursville; Orange **GS:** U **SP:** Mar (4 May 1785) Mourning Clark (27 Oct 1763, Albemarle Co-18 Mar 1831) d/o Micajah (27 Feb 1741-1774) & Mildred (Martin) (1741-1827) Clark **VI:** Appl pen 24 Sep 1832 Orange Co age 70. Occupation tailor when appl for pension. S7185 **P:** Y **BLW:** unk **RG:** Y **MK:** unk **PH:** unk **SS:** J- DAR Hatcher; K Vol 3 pg 167; CG pg 2182; SAR P-241335 **BS:** JLARC 2; 80, vol 3, pg 47.

MANSFIELD, Timothy; b unk; d 11 Oct 1781 **RU:** Private, Served in Col's Co, CT Cont troops and died fr battle at Yorktown **CEM:** Yorktown Victory Monument Tablet; GPS 38.28350, -78.54150; Yorktown; York **GS:** U **SP:** No info **VI:** No further data **P:** unk **BLW:** unk **RG:** unk **MK:** unk **PH:** unk **SS:** J-Yorktown Historian; DY; SAR P-241350 pg 213 **BS:** JLARC 74.

MARCHAND, Pierre; b unk; d 1781 **RU:** Seaman, Served on "Hector" and died from Yorktown battle **CEM:** French Memorial; GPS 36.81944, -79.39933; Yorktown; York **GS:** U **SP:** no info **VI:** No further data **P:** unk **BLW:** unk **RG:** Y **MK:** unk **PH:** unk **SS:** J-Yorktown Historian; SAR P-100946 **BS:** JLARC 1, 74.

MARCY NARCY, Jean; b unk; d 1781 **RU:** Seaman, Served on "Saint-Esprit" and died from Yorktown battle **CEM:** French Memorial; GPS 36.81944, -79.39933; Yorktown; York **GS:** U **SP:** No info **VI:** No further data **P:** unk **BLW:** unk **RG:** Y **MK:** unk **PH:** unk **SS:** J-Yorktown Historian; SAR P-100977 **BS:** JLARC 1, 74.

MARET, Nicolas; b unk; d 1781 **RU:** Soldier, Served in Agenois Bn and died fr battle at Yorktown **CEM:** French Memorial; GPS 36.81944, -79.39933; Yorktown; York **GS:** U **SP:** No info **VI:** No further data **P:** unk **BLW:** unk **RG:** Y **MK:** unk **PH:** unk **SS:** J-Yorktown Historian; SAR P-241396 **BS:** JLARC 1, 74.

MARGOT, Pierre; b unk; d 1781 **RU:** Seaman, Served on "Languedoc" and died from Yorktown battle **CEM:** French Memorial; GPS 36.81944, -79.39933; Yorktown; York **GS:** U **SP:** No info **VI:** No further data **P:** unk **BLW:** unk **RG:** Y **MK:** unk **PH:** unk **SS:** J-Yorktown Historian; SAR P-241401 **BS:** JLARC 1, 74.

RU=Rank/Unit	CEM=Cemetery	GS=Gravestone	SP=Spousal Information
VI=Other Veteran Info	P=Pension	BLW=Bounty/Land Warrant	RG=Registered Grave
MK=SAR/DAR Marker	PH=Photo	SS=Service Source	BS=Burial Source

MARIE, Jacques; b unk; d 1781 **RU:** Seaman, Served on "Ville de Paris" and died from Yorktown battle **CEM:** French Memorial; GPS 36.81944, -79.39933; Yorktown; York **GS:** U **SP:** No info **VI:** No further data **P:** unk **BLW:** unk **RG:** Y **MK:** unk **PH:** unk **SS:** J-Yorktown Historian; SAR P-241405 **BS:** JLARC 1, 74.

MARIN, Jean de; b unk; d 1781 **RU:** Soldier, Served in Soissonnais Bn and died fr battle at Yorktown **CEM:** French Memorial; GPS 36.81944, -79.39933; Yorktown; York **GS:** U **SP:** No info **VI:** No further data **P:** unk **BLW:** unk **RG:** Y **MK:** unk **PH:** unk **SS:** J-Yorktown Historian; SAR P-241407 **BS:** JLARC 1, 74.

MARION, Samuel; b 21 Sep 1756 (pen says Jan 1750) Goochland Co; d 30 Oct 1843 **RU:** Private, Served in VA Line. Ent serv Goochland Co 1776. Served in Capt Morris & Capt Lightfoot's Co **CEM:** Robert Clark, aka Thompson-Whitehead-Wilder; GPS unk; Rt 612 7 mi SW of Jonesville; Lee **GS:** Y **SP:** Tabitha Barnet (1762-1843) **VI:** Appl pen 27 May 1834 Lee Co, but also made application in Hawkins Co TN. S4180. Source 4 has pen 1834, and living in Lee Co 1843. Different birth dates on pension and stone **P:** Y **BLW:** unk **RG:**Y **MK:** Y **SAR PH:** Y **SS:** J- DAR Hatcher; B; K Vol 3 pg 169; CG pg 2188; DAR A073742; SAR P-241420 **BS:** JLARC 2; 80 vol3 pg 48;196.

MARIVAL, Francois; b unk; d 1781 **RU:** Soldier, Served in Agenois Bn and died fr battle at Yorktown **CEM:** French Memorial; GPS 36.81944, -79.39933; Yorktown; York **GS:** U **SP:** No info **VI:** No further data **P:** unk **BLW:** unk **RG:** Y **MK:** unk **PH:** unk **SS:** J-Yorktown Historian; SAR P-241430 **BS:** JLARC 1, 74.

MARKS, Abel; b 20 Mar 1760, Montgomery Co, PA; d 20 Mar 1817 **RU:** Soldier, Specific records are at Lib of VA, Auditor's Acct XXV, pg 513 **CEM:** Ketoctin Baptist; GPS 39.15746, -77.74870; Ketoctin Church Rd, Purcellville; Loudoun **GS:** Y **SP:** Mary Liddleton (__-1827) **VI:** Son of John & Uriah (Liddleton) Marks **P:** unk **BLW:** unk **RG:** Y **MK:** SAR Plaque **PH:** unk **SS:** E pg 499; CZ pg 297; SAR P-241494 **BS:** JLARC 1, 2, 32; 80, vol 3, pg 49; 196.

MARKS, George Elisha; b 26 Dec 1744, Loudoun Co; d 18 Oct 1805 **RU:** Corporal, Served in Col Moses Hazen's 2d Canadian Regt **CEM:** Ketoctin Baptist; GPS 39.15746, -77.74870; Ketoctin Church Rd, Purcellville; Loudoun **GS:** U **SP:** No info **VI:** Son of John (1716-1788) & (-----) Marks **P:** N **BLW:** N **RG:** N **MK:** SAR Plaque **PH:** unk **SS:** CI record book Officers & Men **BS:** 196.

MARKS, Isaiah; b 07 Apr 1754; d 20 Jan 1785 **RU:** Captain, Was 2nd Lt in 11th VA, 11 Nov 1776; 1st Lt 15 Mar 1777; wounded at Brandywine 11 Sep 1777; Regt designated 7th VA 14 Sep 1778; Capt 10 May 1779; transferred to 2nd VA 12 Feb 1781; served to 1 Jan 1783 **CEM:** Ketoctin Baptist; GPS 39.15746, -77.74870; Ketoctin Church Rd, Purcellville; Loudoun **GS:** Y **SP:** Never mar/no children **VI:** Brother Thomas appl for pen in 1834 fr Henderson Co, KY. BLW 1655, 300 acres issued 14 Jul 1830 to heirs. R116055 **P:** Y **BLW:** Y **RG:** Y **MK:** SAR Plaque **PH:** unk **SS:** K Vol 3 pg 170; AK; SAR P-241500 **BS:** 04; JLARC 1, 2, 32; 80 vol 3, pg 49; .

MARKS, John Jr; b c1716, Germany; d 3 Mar 1788 **RU:** Ensign/Patriot, Took Oath 11 Aug 1777 Loudoun Co Militia. As minister, peached patriotism and espoused Rev War causes **CEM:** Ketoctin Baptist; GPS 39.15746, -77.74870; Ketoctin Church Rd, Purcellville; Loudoun **GS:** Y **SP:** Mar (c1740) Uriah Ledyard (__-14 Apr 1788) **VI:** Died in Round Hill, Loudoun Co **P:** unk **BLW:** unk **RG:** Y **MK:** SAR Plaque **PH:** unk **SS:** DAR #A073929; E, pg 500; DD cites Nickols, Legends of Loudoun Valley pg 83, 84; SAR P-241505 **BS:** 25 pg 192; 80 vol 3 pg 49.

MARQUET, Francois; b unk; d 1781 **RU:** Seaman, Served on "Hercule" and died from Yorktown battle **CEM:** French Memorial; GPS 36.81944, -79.39933; Yorktown; York **GS:** U **SP:** No info **VI:** No further data **P:** unk **BLW:** unk **RG:** Y **MK:** unk **PH:** unk **SS:** J-Yorktown Historian; SAR P-241543 **BS:** JLARC 1, 74.

MARQUIS, William; b c1749; d 15 Jan 1815 **RU:** Patriot, Gave provisions to the cause and paid personal property tax 1782, Frederick Co **CEM:** Old Opequon Church; GPS 39.82237, -78.11412; 217 Opequon Church Ln, Kernstown; Frederick **GS:** Y **SP:** Elizabeth Vance (c1745/46 Winchester-c1780) **VI:** No further data **P:** N **BLW:** N **RG:**N **MK:** N **PH:** unk **SS:** DAR #A074002; AL Ct Bk pg 15, 17; ER Frederick Co tax list **BS:** 59 pg 209.

RU=Rank/Unit
VI=Other Veteran Info
MK=SAR/DAR Marker
CEM=Cemetery
P=Pension
PH=Photo
GS=Gravestone
BLW=Bounty/Land Warrant
SS=Service Source
SP=Spousal Information
RG=Registered Grave
BS=Burial Source

264

MARSH, Ephraim; b unk; d 1781 **RU**: Private, Served in Capt John Abbet's Co, Col John Knickerbacker's Albany, NY Militia Regt and died fr battle at Yorktown **CEM**: Yorktown Victory Monument Tablet; GPS 38.28350, -78.54150; Yorktown; York **GS**: U **SP**: No info **VI**: No further data **P**: unk **BLW**: unk **RG**: Y **MK**: unk **PH**: unk **SS**: J-Yorktown Historian; AX pg 127; SAR P-241626 **BS**: JLARC 74.

MARSHALL, James Markham; b 12 Mar 1764 Fauquier Co; d 26 Apr 1848 **RU**: Lieutenant, Served in VA Line in artillery co under Maj Nelson, Recd ½ pay indicating disabled in service **CEM**: Marshall Family; GPS;38.953626,-78.172861 Rt 55, Happy Creek Pl, 120 Mary's Shady Lane, Front Royal; Warren **GS**: Gov't **SP**: Mar (9 Apr 1795) Hester Morris (30 Jul 1774, Philadelphia-13 Apr 1816) and second, Elizabeth Hurst **VI**: Appl pen 23 May 1833 Frederick Co. S7173 also VA 1/2 pay (See N.A. Acc #874 #050109 1/2 Pay). Died in Frederick Co **P**: Y **BLW**: unk **RG**: Y **MK**: Y SAR Granite **PH**: unk **SS**: J-NSSAR 1993 Reg, J- DAR Hatcher; CG pg 2197; DD; DAR A073853 SAR P-241844 **BS**: JLARC 1 ,2.; 80 vol 3 pg 51.

MARSHALL, Jesse; b 1765; d 1840 **RU**: Midshipman, Served in VA State Navy **CEM**: Bethel Church; GPS unk; E Washington St; Suffolk City **GS**: N **SP**: No info **VI**: No further data **P**: unk **BLW**: unk **RG**: N **MK**: N **PH**: N **SS**: K pg 174; AR Vol 3 pg 51; BK pg 7; CZ **BS**: 32 e-mail.

MARSHALL, John Curtis; b Sept 24 1755, Westmoreland Co; d Jul 6 1835 **RU**: Captain/Patriot, Ent serv Fauquier Co. Was Lt in Fauquier Independent Co at outbreak of Rev in 1775. Served also in Capt William Pickett's Co. Served w/ father in Culpeper Minute Bn at battle of Great Bridge. Served in winter 1777-78 at Valley Forge w/ George Washington. Comm Lt 3rd Regt 30 Jul 1776. Was Deputy Judge-Advocate 20 Nov 1777. Became Capt 1 Jul 1778 serving in 7th Regt. Retired Feb 12 1781 **CEM**: Shockoe Hill; GPS 37.55190, -77.43170; 4th & Hospital Sts; Richmond City **GS**: U **SP**: Mary Willis Ambler (13 Mar 1776 Yorktown-25 Dec 1831 Richmond) d/o (-----) & Rebecca Burwell (1746-1806) **VI**: Son of Thomas & Mary (Keith) Marshall. 1780, George Wythe's law lectures at William and Mary in Williamsburg. Federalist. House of Rep. Sec of State to John Adams. Awarded BLW 4,000 acres as a capt. Chief Justice of US Supreme Ct in 1801 for 34 yrs, decisions form the basis of Constitutional Law. Sol appl 26 Jan 1833 Washington DC age 77, then living in Richmond. S5731. Died in Philadelphia **P**: Y **BLW**: Y **RG**: Y **MK**: Y monument & SAR Plaque at Gr Bridge park **PH**: Y **SS**: K Vol 3 pg 174; CG pg 2198; DAR A041640; SAR P-161532 **BS**: JLARC 1, 4, 77.

MARSHALL, Robert; b unk; d Aft 1783 **RU**: Sergeant, Served in Capt Thomas Craig's Co of Col St Clair's PA Bn 1776 of 4th Cont Line. Was appt Sgt 7 Jan 1776; discharged 18 Jul 1776 **CEM**: Bethel Church aka Old Lyle; GPS unk; Millboro Springs; Bath **GS**: N **SP**: Mar (1792) Jean Vance **VI**: No further data **P**: unk **BLW**: unk **RG**: N **MK**: N **PH**: unk **SS**: A pg 187 **BS**: 80 vol 3 pg 51; 196.

MARSHALL, Thomas; b Apr 2 1730, Westmoreland Co; d Jun 22 1802 **RU**: Colonel/Patriot, Organizer of Culpeper Minuteman. Was Maj at battle of Great Bridge with son John and in 3rd Regt 13 Feb 1776. Was Lt Col Aug 13 1776, Col, 21 Feb 1777. Appt Commander of State Artillery Regt until Feb 1782. Was captured at surrender of Charleston 1780. Gave material aid to the cause **CEM**: Marshall Family; GPS unk; Rt 55, Happy Creek Pl, Front Royal; Warren **GS**: Y **SP**: Mar (1754) Mary Randolph Keith (1737-1809) **VI**: Son of John & Elizabeth (Marham) Marshall. Childhood friend of Geo Washington. Surveyor to Lord Fairfax with help of Washington. Tax collector. High Sheriff. Lt in French & Indian War. Moved to KY after Rev. Died in Old Washington in Mason Co, KY. Memorialized in VA **P**: unk **BLW**: unk **RG**: N **MK**: Y SAR plaque at Gr Bridge Parl **PH**: unk **SS**: AL Ct Bk pg 15; CE pg 38 **BS**: 113.

MARSHALL, William; b 1753; d 16 May 1796 **RU**: Captain, Commanded a co in York Co Militia Oct 1775 **CEM**: Smyrna; GPS unk; Off Rt 604 Damney's Mill Rd, SE of Corinth Fork; King William **GS**: Y **SP**: No info **VI**: Became a doctor after RW. **P**: unk **BLW**: unk **RG**: N **MK**: N **PH**: unk **SS**: E pg 502 **BS**: 196.

MARSTELLER, Philip Balthasar or Phillip G; b 4 Jan 1741, Philadelphia Co, PA; d 1803 **RU**: Lieutenant Colonel, Served in PA. Maj, 2nd Battalion, Lancaster Co 1776; Lt Col, 1st Battalion Lancaster Co 1777; Assist Forage Master 1780; Paymaster, Lancaster Co Militia, 1777-1784 **CEM**: Old Christ Church Episcopal; GPS 38.80625, -77.04718; 118 N Washington St; Alexandria City **GS**: Y **SP**: Magdelena Reiss **VI**: Original table stone carried off during Civil War. Member (Lancaster Co) PA Constitutional Convention Jul 1776, Assistant Deputy Quartermaster General, PA Associators in 1777, Lt Col US

RU=Rank/Unit	CEM=Cemetery	GS=Gravestone	SP=Spousal Information
VI=Other Veteran Info	P=Pension	BLW=Bounty/Land Warrant	RG=Registered Grave
MK=SAR/DAR Marker	PH=Photo	SS=Service Source	BS=Burial Source

Army, 1st Batallion (plaque) **P:** unk **BLW:** unk **RG:** Y **MK:** Y SAR **PH:** unk **SS:** BT; DAR A073986; SAR P-241957 **BS:** JLARC 1, 25, 86; 20 pg 139; 196.

MARTIN, Alexis; b unk; d 1781 **RU:** Soldier, Served in Foix Bn and died fr battle at Yorktown **CEM:** French Memorial; GPS 36.81944, -79.39933; Yorktown; York **GS:** U **SP:** No info **VI:** No further data **P:** unk **BLW:** unk **RG:** Y **MK:** unk **PH:** unk **SS:** J-Yorktown Historian; SAR P-242003 **BS:** JLARC 1, 74.

MARTIN, Anthony; b 26 Sep 1737, Goochland Co; d 19 Jun 1805 **RU:** Patriot, Gave material aid to the cause **CEM:** Elioch Manor Family; GPS unk; Elioch Manor Dr, end of rd; Powhatan **GS:** Y **SP:** Mar (21 Dec 1758) Sarah Holman (__-aft 1805) **VI:** Son of Peter (1712-1742) & Mary Anne (Rapine) Martin **P:** N **BLW:** N **RG:** N **MK:** N **PH:** unk **SS:** DAR #A074079; D Vol 3 pg 774, 782-4; AL Ct bk pg 5 **BS:** 77, LVA website.

MARTIN, Antoine; b unk; d 1781 **RU:** Seaman, Served on "Marseillais"and died from Yorktown battle **CEM:** French Memorial; GPS 36.81944, -79.39933; Yorktown; York **GS:** U **SP:** No info **VI:** No further data **P:** unk **BLW:** unk **RG:**N **MK:** unk **PH:** unk **SS:** J-Yorktown Historian; SAR P-242010 **BS:** JLARC 1, 74.

MARTIN, Azariah; b 11 Jan 1742, Amherst Co; d 26 Jul 1824 **RU:** Captain, Commanded Co of militia in Amherst Co 1780 **CEM:** Martin Family; GPS unk; Check property records; Nelson **GS:** U **SP:** Mar (19 Mar 1772) Mary Rodes, (1758, Albemarle Co-1758, Nelson Co) d/o Charles (c1730, Hanover Co-17 Jun 1805, Amherst Co) & Lucy Rhodes **VI:** Son of James (25 Aug 1699-__) & Elizabeth (Crawford) Martin. Rank of Capt confirmed in pen appl by nephew of same name. Pen appl for Clay Co KY 1832 by nephew who served in his Co in Amherst Co. Pen appl by widow Lucy Rodes 28 Feb1840 in KY W554 **P:** Y **BLW:** unk **RG:** Y **MK:** unk **PH:** unk **SS:** J-NSSAR 1993 Reg; K Vol 3 pg 175; SAR P-242016 **BS:** JLARC 1.

MARTIN, Claude; b unk; d 1781 **RU:** Seaman, Served on "Languedoc" and died from Yorktown battle **CEM:** French Memorial; GPS 36.81944, -79.39933; Yorktown; York **GS:** U **SP:** No info **VI:** No further data **P:** unk **BLW:** unk **RG:** Y **MK:** unk **PH:** unk **SS:** J-Yorktown Historian; SAR P-242042 **BS:** JLARC 1,74.

MARTIN, Henry Andrew; b 1720 Germantown, Fauquier Co; d 1780 **RU:** Patriot, Gave material aid to cause **CEM:** Germantown Glebe; GPS unk; Rt 643 nr Licking Run, Midland; Fauquier **GS:** U **SP:** Mary Ann White (26 Nov 1720 Culpeper Co-1782) **VI:** Son of (-----) & Maria Katherina (Otterbach) (1699-1724) Martin **P:** N **BLW:** N **RG:** Y **MK:** unk **PH:** unk **SS:** AL Certificate Fauquier Co; SAR P-329976 **BS:** 196.

MARTIN, James; b 1749, d 1813 **RU:** Colonal/Patriot, paid personal property tax 1782 Albemarle Co, a supply tax for Rev War expenses **CEM:** Martin Family; GPS not determined; Edgefield: Albemarle **GS:** Unk **SP:** No spousal data **VI:** No further data **P:** N **BLW:** N **RG:** Y **MK:** N **PH:** N **SS:** DV image 05 pdf; SAR P-242360 **BS:** 80, vol 3, pg 52.

MARTIN, Jean; b unk; d 1781 **RU:** Seaman, Served on "Ville de Paris" and died from Yorktown battle **CEM:** French Memorial; GPS 36.81944, -79.39933; Yorktown; York **GS:** U **SP:** No info **VI:** No further data **P:** unk **BLW:** unk **RG:** Y **MK:** unk **PH:** unk **SS:** J-Yorktown Historian; SAR P-242367 **BS:** JLARC 1,74.

MARTIN, John; b c1735; d 1823 **RU:** Second Lieutenant/Patriot, Gave 180# beef to cause in 1781. Was 2nd Lt Jul 1779 in Capt Weavers' Co, Fauquier Co Militia **CEM:** Martin Family, Germantown; GPS unk; Rt 3 Germantown; Spotsylvania **GS:** N **SP:** 1) Catherine (-----) (__-after 1785 Germantown) 2) Margaret Elliot **VI:** Son of John Joseph & Catherine (-----) Martin. Died in Old Germantown Settlement, Fauquier Co **P:** unk **BLW:** unk **RG:** N **MK:** N **PH:** N **SS:** D pg 862 **BS:** 10 pg 52; 19 pg 65-66.

MARTIN, Joseph; b 18 Sep 1740, Goochland Co; d 18 Dec 1808 **RU:** Brig General/Patriot, Had military duty in the militia as general and public duty as VA agent to the Cherokee Nation in 1777 **CEM:** Martin Family; GPS 36.732611, -79.724556; Leatherwood Downs; Henry **GS:** U **SP:** 1) Susanna Graves (1758-1837) 2) Sarah Lucas (1754-1775) 3) Elizabeth Ward **VI:** Son of Joseph (1700-1761) & Susannah Page (Chiles) (1700-1754) Martin. Martinsville was named in his honor. **P:** unk **BLW:** unk **RG:** Y **MK:** unk **PH:** unk **SS:** E pg 503; CD; DAR A074375; SAR P-242445 **BS:** 196.

RU=Rank/Unit	CEM=Cemetery	GS=Gravestone	SP=Spousal Information
VI=Other Veteran Info	P=Pension	BLW=Bounty/Land Warrant	RG=Registered Grave
MK=SAR/DAR Marker	PH=Photo	SS=Service Source	BS=Burial Source

MARTIN, Joseph; b 1730, Germantown, Fauquier Co; d 1793 **RU**: Patriot, Gave material aid to cause **CEM**: Germantown Glebe; GPS unk; Rt 643 nr Licking Run, Midland; Fauquier **GS**: U **SP**: Catherine Holtclaw (1734 Germany-1807 Germantown) **VI**: Son of (-----) & Maria Katherina (Otterbach) (1699-1724) Martin **P**: N **BLW**: N **RG**: N **MK**: unk **PH**: unk **SS**: AL Ct Bk pg 2 Fauquier Co **BS**: 196.

MARTIN, Joseph; b c1755; d 14 Feb 1832 **RU**: Private, Enlisted Alexandria in 6th & 10th VA Cont Line **CEM**: Martin Family; GPS 36.732611, -79.724556; Leatherwood Downs; Henry **GS**: U **SP**: Mar (1 Mar 1782 Loudoun Co) Patsey Baily (1761-aft 1840 Patrick Co) **VI**: Pen both. He appl Henry Co 11 Nov 1811; she appl 26 Feb 1839 Rockingham Co NC **P**: Y **BLW**: unk **RG**: Y **MK**: unk **PH**: unk **SS**: J- DAR Hatcher; E pg 503; AL Ct Bk pg 21, 25 Henry Co; CG pg 2207; DAR A073374; SAR P-242448 **BS**: JLARC 2; AR pg 53.

MARTIN, Louis; b unk; d 1781 **RU**: Soldier, Served in Agenois Bn and died fr battle at Yorktown **CEM**: French Memorial; GPS 36.81944, -79.39933; Yorktown; York **GS**: U **SP**: No info **VI**: No further data **P**: unk **BLW**: unk **RG**: Y **MK**: unk **PH**: unk **SS**: J-Yorktown Historian; SAR P-242466 **BS**: JLARC 1, 74.

MARTIN, Nicolas; b unk; d 1781 **RU**: Seaman, Served on "Destin" and died from Yorktown battle **CEM**: French Memorial; GPS 36.81944, -79.39933; Yorktown; York **GS**: U **SP**: No info **VI**: No further data **P**: unk **BLW**: unk **RG**: Y **MK**: unk **PH**: unk **SS**: J-Yorktown Historian; SAR P-242506 **BS**: JLARC 1, 74.

MARTIN, Orson; b 1735, Goochland Co; d 24 Jul 1786 **RU**: Patriot, Gave material aid to cause **CEM**: Burnt Chimney; GPS unk; Cat Taile Branch; Cumberland **GS**: Y **SP**: Mar (c1763/4) Ann Foushee (07 Mar 1736-25 Aug 1800) **VI**: Son of Valentine Martin & Jane Bridgewater **P**: N **BLW**: N **RG**: Y **MK**: N **PH**: unk **SS**: DAR #A074456; AL Ct Bk pg 16, 28 Cumberland Co; AS; SAR P-242515 & 242513 **BS**: 80 vol 3 pg 53; 196.

MARTIN, Thomas; b 21 Oct 1759, Martins Cree, Northampton Co, PA; d 31 Mar 1856 **RU**: Lieutenant, Served in VA Line at Winchester VA, Jan-Mar 1783 **CEM**: New Providence Presbyterian; GPS 37.95170, -79.30250; 1208 New Providence Rd, Raphine; Rockbridge **GS**: Y **SP**: Letitia Ralston (1771-1861) **VI**: Son of James (1710-1767) & Ann (Miller) (1728-1799) Martin **P**: unk **BLW**: unk **RG**:Y **MK**: unk **PH**: unk **SS**: G pg 676; SAR P-242605 **BS**: JLARC 63,79; 196.

MARTIN, Thomas; b unk; d 1781 **RU**: Seaman, Served on "Hector" and died from Yorktown battle **CEM**: French Memorial; GPS 36.81944, -79.39933; Yorktown; York **GS**: U **SP**: No info **VI**: No further data **P**: unk **BLW**: unk **RG**: Y **MK**: unk **PH**: unk **SS**: J-Yorktown Historian; SAR P-242593 **BS**: JLARC 1, 74.

MARTIN, Thomas Bryan; b unk; d 4 Sep 1798 **RU**: Patriot, Supplied material goods, including horses, corn, 24, 244 lbs flour, 50 lbs beef, use of wagons, 121 gallons whiskey **CEM**: Greenway Court; GPS unk; Nr Lord Fairfax, White Post; Clarke **GS**: N **SP**: No info **VI**: 1879 letter said he was bur at Greenway Ct Cem. **P**: N **BLW**: N **RG**: N **MK**: N **PH**: N **SS**: AL Cert issued **BS**: 58 pg 10.

MARTIN, Vincent; b unk; d 1781 **RU**: Soldier, Served in Auxonne Bn and died fr battle at Yorktown **CEM**: French Memorial; GPS 36.81944, -79.39933; Yorktown; York **GS**: U **SP**: No info **VI**: No further data **P**: unk **BLW**: unk **RG**: Y **MK**: unk **PH**: unk **SS**: J-Yorktown Historian; SAR P-242607 **BS**: JLARC 1, 74.

MARTIN, William; b unk; d 1804 **RU**: Patriot, Gave material aid to cause **CEM**: Anglican Chapel; GPS unk; Court Street; Lynchburg City **GS**: U **SP**: No info **VI**: No further data **P**: N **BLW**: N **RG**:Y **MK**: unk **PH**: unk **SS**: AL Cert Bedford Co; SAR P-242614 **BS**: JLARC 36.

MARTIN, William; b 1742, Albemarle Co, NC, d 1809 **RU**: Captain/Patriot, Civil service as Committee of Safety 27 Sep 1775, then commanded a company in the Pittsylvania Co Militia. County records indicate he was in battles at Guilford C.H. and at Yorktown **CEM**: Hughesville; GPS unk; Rt 631 nr Stuart; Patrick **GS**: Yes **SP**: Rachel Dalton, d/o Samuel Dalton (1699-1802) of Mayo & (-----) **VI**: Son of Joseph Martin & Susanna Chiles. Before Rev was County LT **P**: N **BLW**: N **RG**: Y **MK**: N, **PH**: N **SS**: American Monthly Magazine, Jun 1912, pgs 225-229; DAR Anc # A059074; SAR P-242639 **BS**: 196 N.

MARTIN, William; b 1765; d 1809 **RU**: Private ent srev Pittsylvania Co, served in Col Davis Regt, 2d Cont Line1779-1783 **CEM**: Old Hickey-Martin; GPS 36.817191,-79.975069; loc E of original Henry Rd, Oak Level; Henry **GS**: N **SP**: Sarah Dodd (30 May 1767, Amelia Co-21 Feb 1851) as widow frew pension **VI**: Son of William Martin & Rachel (-----) **P**:Y widow **BLW**: Y # 1463 100 acres **RG**: N **MK**: N, **PH**: N **SS**: E pgs 504, 582; G pg 713 **BS**: 196.

RU=Rank/Unit	CEM=Cemetery	GS=Gravestone	SP=Spousal Information
VI=Other Veteran Info	P=Pension	BLW=Bounty/Land Warrant	RG=Registered Grave
MK=SAR/DAR Marker	PH=Photo	SS=Service Source	BS=Burial Source

MASON, George; b 1753; d 5 Dec 1796 **RU:** Captain/Patriot, Commanded a co in Fairfax Co Militia 1775-1776. Gave material aid to cause **CEM:** Gunston Hall; GPS 38.66862, -77.16823; Gunston Rd, Lorton; Fairfax **GS:** Y **SP:** Elizabeth Mary Ann Barnes Hooe (1768-28 May 1814, Lexington) d/o Gerard & Sarah Hooe. She m. 1) George Mason; 2) George Graham of Prince William Co. Memorial Stone **VI:** Son of George & Ann (-----) Mason. Died in his 44th yr in Lexington. Memorial stone **P:** unk **BLW:** unk **RG:** N **MK:** N **PH:** Y **SS:** AL Cert issued; CD **BS:** 61 vol V, pg MN-6; 196.

MASON, George Jr; b 1749; d 24 Mar 1796 **RU:** Captain, Served in Fairfax Co 1774-? commanded by Capt Geo. Washington as ensign. Was Capt in Reg Army 1775-76 **CEM:** Old Christ Church Episcopal; GPS 38.80625, -77.04718; 118 N Washington St; Alexandria City **GS:** Y **SP:** No info **VI:** Resigned Reg Army due to sickness & went to France. Died age 47 **P:** unk **BLW:** unk **RG:** Y **MK:** N **PH:** unk **SS:** E pg 505; H; SAR P-327475 **BS:** 20 pg 139; 196.

MASON, George Sr; b 1725; d 7 Oct 1792 **RU:** Patriot, Gave material aid to the cause **CEM:** Gunston Hall; GPS 38.66862, -77.16823; Gunston Rd, Lorton; Fairfax **GS:** Y **SP:** 1) Mar (1750) Anna Elbeck; 2) Mar (1780) Sarah Brent **VI:** Son of George & Ann (Thomson) Mason. Justice of Fairfax Co 1754-1759; VA House of Burgesses, 1765 opposed Stamp Act. 1774 Fairfax Resolves, 1775 VA Declaration of Rights. Helped write Constitution **P:** N **BLW:** N **RG:** Y **MK:** N **PH:** Y **SS:** AL Ct Bk pg 15; AJ;DAR A074817 SAR P-242293 **BS:** SAR regis; 196.

MASON, Stevens (Stephen) Thomson; b 29 Dec 1760; d 10 May 1803 **RU:** Private, Served in artillery fr Plymouth, MA **CEM:** Raspberry Plain; GPS unk; 16500 Agape Ln, Leesburg; Loudoun **GS:** U **SP:** No info **VI:** Served in US Senate fr 1794-1803 **P:** unk **BLW:** Y **RG:** N **MK:** unk **PH:** unk **SS:** C pg 617; BX pg 546 **BS:** 196.

MASON, Thomas; b unk; d 7 Oct 1781 **RU:** Drummer, Served in Capt Ten Eyck's Co, Col Van Cortlandt's 2d Regt, NY Line. Died fr the battle at Yorktown **CEM:** Yorktown Victory Monument Tablet; GPS 38.28350, -78.54150; Yorktown; York **GS:** U **SP:** No info **VI:** No further data **P:** unk **BLW:** unk **RG:** unk **MK:** unk **PH:** unk **SS:** J-Yorktown Historian; AX pg 191; SAR P-242774 **BS:** JLARC 74.

MASON, Thomson (Thompson); b 17 Aug 1733; d 26 Feb 1785 **RU:** Patriot, Gave material aid to cause **CEM:** Raspberry Plain; GPS unk; 16500 Agape Ln, Leesburg; Loudoun **GS:** N **SP:** Mary King Barnes (__-21 Oct 1771) **VI:** Son of George (1690-1735) & Ann (Thomson) (1699-1762) Mason. In 1778 was member of 1st Supreme Ct in VA **P:** N **BLW:** N **RG:** Y **MK:** N **PH:** N **SS:** AL Ct Bk pg 50; SAR P-242783 **BS:** 196.

MASSAL, Jean; b unk; d 1781 **RU:** unk, Served in Touraine Bn and died fr battle at Yorktown **CEM:** French Memorial; GPS 36.81944, -79.39933; Yorktown; York **GS:** U **SP:** No info **VI:** No further data **P:** unk **BLW:** unk **RG:** Y **MK:** unk **PH:** unk **SS:** J-Yorktown Historian; SAR P-242805 **BS:** JLARC 1, 74.

MASSEY, Lee; b 22 Sep 1732, probably Stafford Co; d 23 Sep 1814 **RU:** Patriot, Member, Fairfax Co Committee of Safety 1774. Member, committee to care for poor 1775. Provided 7000 lbs of hay to cause **CEM:** Pohick Episcopal; GPS 38.42546, -77.11598; 9301 Richmond Hwy, Lorton; Fairfax **GS:** Y **SP:** 1) (-----) 2 (-----) 3) Mar (after 1763) Elizabeth Bronaugh (Brunaugh) **VI:** Rector of Pohick Episcopal Church and thus for George Washington & George Mason. Removed fr burial ground at home "Bradley" on Belmot Bay. Lee rebur under pulpit; Elizabeth in church cem. **P:** N **BLW:** N **RG:** Y **MK:** Y SAR plaque **PH:** Y **SS:** D Fairfax Co; SAR P-242846 **BS:** 04.

MASSIE, Charles; b unk; d 1817 **RU:** Sergeant, Served in 5th Cont Line **CEM:** Johnson Family; GPS unk; Rt 658; Goochland **GS:** Y **SP:** No info **VI:** Erected by Jack Jouett Chapt. DAR 1948 **P:** unk **BLW:** unk **RG:** N **MK:** Y DAR **PH:** unk **SS:** E pg 506 **BS:** 46 pg 174.

MASSIE, Charles Sr; b 2 Aug 1727, Hanover Co; d 1817 **RU:** Captain/Patriot, Capt 6th VA Regt, 23 Mar 1776. Committee of Safety 1775-76. Gave material aid to cause **CEM:** Spring Valley (Massie Family); GPS 37.94277, -78.76863; 3808 Spring Valley Rd Batesville; Albemarle **GS:** Y **SP:** Mar (1755) Mary Davis (__-1817) **VI:** No further data **P:** unk **BLW:** unk **RG:** Y **MK:** Y DAR **PH:** unk **SS:** J- DAR Hatcher; DD cites Paid Supply Tax 1783 Albemarle Co; DAR A075085; SAR P-242947 **BS:** JLARC 2; 80, vol3, pg 55; 196.

RU=Rank/Unit	CEM=Cemetery	GS=Gravestone	SP=Spousal Information
VI=Other Veteran Info	P=Pension	BLW=Bounty/Land Warrant	RG=Registered Grave
MK=SAR/DAR Marker	PH=Photo	SS=Service Source	BS=Burial Source

268

MASSIE, John; b 3 Apr 1756, Albemarle Co, d 20 Oct 1800 **RU**: Ensign Amherst Co Militia serving long enough to apply for a pension **CEM**: Massie Family (AKA Spring Yalley); GPS not determined; loc in Spring Valley; Amherst **GS**: Unk **SP**: mar (1779) Susannah Wright, d/o Benjamin Wright and Elizabeth Jenkins **VI**: FindaGrave submitter "service is listed in the book (Amherst County, VA in the Revolution), including extracts from the Lost Order Book, 1773-1782 page 36)". Son of Captain Charles Massie (2 Aug 1727-1817) & Mary Davis (__-1817). Was a teacher in Piney River District **P**: Applied not accepted **BLW**: N **RG**: Y **MK**: N **PH**: N **SS**: Amherst Co Order Bk, 1773-1782, pg 36; SAR P-242850 **BS**: 196.

MASSIE, Thomas; b 11 or 22 Aug 1747, New Kent Co; d 2 Feb 1834 **RU**: Major, Was commissioned Capt 1775 in 6th VA Regt, recruiting soldiers fr New Kent Co. Was Aide to Gen Thomas Nelson. Was present at surrender of Cornwallis, Yorktown 1781. Served in 6th,11th Cont Lines. Appointed Maj 20 Feb 1778. Resigned 25 Jun 1779 **CEM**: Level Green; GPS unk; Massies Mill; Nelson **GS**: U **SP**: Mar (11 Apr 1781 Augusta Co) Sarah (Sally) Cocke (c1760-27 Apr 1838) **VI**: Son of William (__-1751) & (-----) Massie. Charter member, Society of the Cincinnati, established by officers of Rev to raise funds for widows & orphans of soldiers. One of first magistrates of Nelson Co when it was formed 1807. BLW of 5333 1/3 acres OH & KY. Sol appl 15 Feb 1833 Nelson Co. Widow appl pen 17 Jan 1837 Nelson Co age 77. W7403 also VA 1/2 Pay. **P**: Y **BLW**: Y **RG**:Y **MK**: Y SAR **PH**: unk **SS**: E pg 506; K Vol 3 pg 187; CG pg 2219; DAR A075129; SAR P-242857 **BS**: JLARC 4, 83.

MATHES (MATHEWS/MATTHEWS), Alexander/Alesander; b. abt 1722, Ulsyrt, Ireland; d. 1785 Shenandoah (now Warren) Co **RU**: Patriot, Had patriotic service & furnished supplies; **CEM**: Mathews Fam; GPS unk; loc Thompson Hollow Rd, Bentonville; Warren **GS**: Unk; **SP**: Mar (__) Grizzel? **VI**: DAR marker **P**:N; **BLW**: N **RG**: Y **MK**: Y **PH**: N **SS** DAR A010683; SAR P-242927; **BS** Cemetery records at Warren County Heritage Society Archives.

MATHEWS (MATTHEWS/MATHES), Benjamin; b. 1763, d. Apr 1797 **RU**: Lieutenant, 2nd Regiment of Virginia Troops, 11th Cont Line; **CEM**: Mathews Family; GPS unk; loc on Thompson Hollow Rd, Bentonville; Warren **GS**: Unk; **SP**: Mar 6 Aug 1783, Rachel Keller (1761-1840), d/o Abraham Keller & Elizabeth Painter **VI**: Son of Alexander & Grizzel Mathes, DAR marker **P**: N **BLW**: N **RG**: Y **MK**: Y, **PH**: N **SS**: E pgs 507, 508; SAR P-243087, DAR A075416; **BS**: Cemetery records at Warren County Heritage Society Archives.

MATHEWS, Thomas; b 1742, St Christopher's, aka St Kitts, British West Indies; d 20 Feb 1812 **RU**: Captain, Was Capt of Inf 8th Co, 5 Mar 1776-7 Nov 1777; Maj of VA State Artillery Regt in Col Thomas Marshall's Regt 15 Nov 1777; and Lt Col of State Line 8 Nov 1779-15 Apr 1780. Was captured at Charleston **CEM**: St Paul's Episcopal; GPS 36.84733, -76.28554; 201 St Paul's Blvd; Norfolk City **GS**: N **SP**: Mar (9 Jul 1773) Mary "Molly" Miller (c1752-8 Jul 1837) **VI**: Son of Samuel Augustus & Mary (Gacey) Mathews. Delegate in the General Assembly. Arrived in Norfolk by 1772. Wife permitted pen on applic in 1836. Widow appl 13 Sep 1836 Pasquotank Co NC. W17076 & R16019 also VA 1/2 Pay **P**: Y **BLW**: unk **RG**: Y **MK**: Y SAR plaque **PH**: N **SS**: J- DAR Hatcher; K Vol 3 pg 189; CB AS; CG pg 2219; CE pg 21, 43, 123, 124, 164; DAR report; DAR A075577; SAR P-242978 **BS**: JLARC 2; DAR report.

MATTHEWS, Richard; b 17 Nov 1761; d 8 Jun 1845 **RU**: Private, Served in Capt William Johnston's Co 11th VA Regt of Foot commanded by Col Morgan, Mar & Apr 1777 **CEM**: Bethel Church; GPS unk; Rt 610; Frederick **GS**: Y **SP**: Mar (c1797) Elizabeth Woolfkill (15 Feb 1777-6 Nov 1820) d/o John (Jun 1752, Germany-1 Jul 1839,Trunbull, OH) & Agnes (Conrad) (1747, PA-__) Woolfkill **VI**: No further data **P**: unk **BLW**: unk **RG**: N **MK**: N **PH**: unk **SS**: AP Service Rec **BS**: 59 pg 212.

MATTHEWS, Solomon; b 2 Feb 1745, PA, d 2 Apr 1834 **RU**: Lieutenant; Capt George Boocher's Co, Col Jacob Weaver's 5th Bn, Burks Co PA Militia **CEM**: Linville Creek Church of the Brethren; GPS: 38.60469,-78.79007; vic jct Rts 803 and Brethren Rd; Rockingham **GS**: Yes **SP**: Agnes Van Reid (23 Feb 1746-7 May 1828) **VI**: Son of Robert Matthews and Mary Coles Cherrington **P**: N **BLW**: Y **RG**: Y **MK**: N **PH**: N **SS**: DAR A075571; CT, vol V, pgs 213,216; SAR P-242975 **BS**: 196.

MAUBRUCHON, Yves; b unk; d 1781 **RU**: Seaman, Served on "Ville de Paris" and died from Yorktown battle **CEM**: French Memorial; GPS 36.81944, -79.39933; Yorktown; York **GS**: U **SP**: No info **VI**: No further data **P**: unk **BLW**: unk **RG**: Y **MK**: unk **PH**: unk **SS**: J-Yorktown Historian; SAR P-243237 **BS**: JLARC 1, 74.

MAUCHALIN, Yves (or Philibert); b unk; d 1781 **RU**: Soldier, Served in Gatinais Bn and died fr battle at Yorktown **CEM**: French Memorial; GPS 36.81944, -79.39933; Yorktown; York **GS**: U **SP**: No info **VI**: No

RU=Rank/Unit	CEM=Cemetery	GS=Gravestone	SP=Spousal Information
VI=Other Veteran Info	P=Pension	BLW=Bounty/Land Warrant	RG=Registered Grave
MK=SAR/DAR Marker	PH=Photo	SS=Service Source	BS=Burial Source

269

further data **P**: unk **BLW**: unk **RG**: Y **MK**: unk **PH**: unk **SS**: J-Yorktown Historian; SAR P-243238 **BS**: JLARC 1, 74.

MAUCK, Daniel; b 1736, Shenandoah Co, d Jan 1803 **RU**: Patriot, Gave material aid to cause, Shenandoah Co **CEM**: Mauck Meeting House; GPS not determined; 150 Hamburg Rd, Rt 766, Luray; Page **GS**: Unk **SP**: 1) Barbara Harnsbarger (1744-1777), d/o Stephen Harnsbarger (1716-19 Mar 1776, Rockingham Co) & Agnes Hoffman (24 Nov 1722-1750), 2) Rebecca Baker (1745, Eng-11 Mar 1805) **VI**: No further data **P**: N **BLW**: N **RG**: Y **MK**: N **PH**: N **SS**:AL Ct Bk pgs 2,9.11. & Comm Bk pgs 158-159; DAR A075673; SAR P-332300 **BS**: 196.

MAUGER, Pierre; b unk; d 1781 **RU**: Seaman, Served on "Auguste" and died from Yorktown battle **CEM**: French Memorial; GPS 36.81944, -79.39933; Yorktown; York **GS**: U **SP**: No info **VI**: No further data **P**: unk **BLW**: unk **RG**: Y **MK**: unk **PH**: unk **SS**: J-Yorktown Historian; SAR P-243242 **BS**: JLARC 1, 74.

MAUPIN, John; b 1725. Hanover Co, d 6 Sep 1806 **RU**: Patriot, Gave material aid to cause in Albemarle Co **CEM**: Sandridge; GPS: 38.12998, -78.69320; 3401 Cemetery Knoll, White Hall; Albemarle **GS**: Y **SP**: Frances Jennings Dabney (1731, Hanover Co-Jun 1806 Albemarle Co), d/o Cornelius Dabney & Sarah Jennings **VI**: Son of Daniel Maupin (1700, France-1788) & Margaret Via (1701-1789) **P**: N **BLW**: N **RG**: Y **MK**: N **PH**: N **SS**: AL Ct Bk pg 2, Albemarle Co; DAR A134342; SAR P-332480 **BS**: 196.

MAUPINE, Daniel; b 25 Mar 1700, France; d 20 Sep 1788 **RU**: Patriot, Gave 297# beef for Albemarle Barracks **CEM**: Maupin Family Farm; GPS unk; Morman's River; Albemarle **GS**: Y **SP**: Mar (1775) Margaret Via (c1701-9 Oct 1788) **VI**: No further data **P**: N **BLW**: N **RG**: Y **MK**: N **PH**: unk **SS**: DAR #A075691; AL Ct BK pg 3, 25; Albemarle Co; D vol 3 pg 3; SAR P-243260 **BS**: SAR Appl.

MAURE, Leon; b unk; d 1781 **RU**: Soldier, Served in Santogne Bn and died fr battle at Yorktown **CEM**: French Memorial; GPS 36.81944, -79.39933; Yorktown; York **GS**: U **SP**: No info **VI**: No further data **P**: unk **BLW**: unk **RG**: Y **MK**: unk **PH**: unk **SS**: J-Yorktown Historian; SAR P-243275 **BS**: JLARC 1, 74.

MAURY, Fontaine; b 3 Feb 1761 Spotsylvania Co; d 1 Jan 1814 **RU**: Private, Aide to Marquis de la Fayette in VA campaign **CEM**: Corporate Burial Ground; GPS unk; loc where Hurcamp Park is today Fredericksburg City **GS**: U **SP**: No info **VI**: Mayor of Fredericksburg Mar 1798 to Mar 1799. **P**: unk **BLW**: unk **RG**: Y **MK**: N **PH**: unk **SS**: AS; SAR regis; SAR P-243291 **BS**: SAR regis.

MAURY, Walker; b 20 Jul 1752 Albemarle Co; d 11 Oct 1788 **RU**: Patriot, Gave material aid to cause **CEM**: St Paul's Episcopal; GPS 36.84733, 76.28554; 201 St Paul's Blvd; Norfolk City **GS**: U **SP**: Mary Stith Grimes (25 Aug 1758-23 Sep 1839) d/o Ludwell (1733-1755) 7 Mary (Dawson) (__-1788) Grymes **VI**: Son of James (8 Apr 1717, Ireland,-9 Jun 1769) & (-----) Maury. Was Professor Wm & Mary College. Ordained priest. Died of Yellow Fever. **P**: N **BLW**: N **RG**:N **MK**: unk **PH**: unk **SS**: AL Ct Bk pg 17 Orange Co **BS**: 196.

MAUSSION, Charles; b unk; d 1781 **RU**: Seaman, Served on "Hector" and died from Yorktown battle **CEM**: French Memorial; GPS 36.81944, -79.39933; Yorktown; York **GS**: U **SP**: No info **VI**: No further data **P**: unk **BLW**: unk **RG**: Y **MK**: unk **PH**: unk **SS**: J-Yorktown Historian; SAR P-243299 **BS**: JLARC 1, 74.

MAXEY, Edward, Jr; b bef 1727, Henrico Co, d bef 1816, Buckingham Co **RU**: Patriot, signed a petition of the freeholders of Buckingham Co, VA to the Speaker and members of the House of Delegates 1778 **CEM**: Manakin Episcopal Church; GPS: 37.5655580,-77.7092300; 985 Huguenot Trail (Rt. 711); Powhatan, **GS**: Unk **SP**: Judith (-----) **VI**: Son of Edward Maxey (1660, Eng-1740) & Susannah Gates (1677-1743) **P**: N **BLW**: N **RG** Y **MK**: N **PH**: N **SS**: Legislative Petitions, Buckingham Co, VA, Box 4, Folder 7 (Church 627P) VA State Archives; SAR 243323 **BS**: 196.

MAXEY, Walter; b 1720, Goochland; d Sep 1791 **RU**: Patriot, Gave material aid to cause **CEM**: Mt Ivy; GPS unk; Scruggs; Franklin **GS**: Y **SP**: Mary Netherland (1720-1798) **VI**: Son of Edward (1660-1740) & (-----) Maxey **P**: N **BLW**: N **RG**: N **MK**: unk **PH**: unk **SS**: AL Ct Bk pg 8, 10, 11 **BS**: 196.

MAXWELL, David; b 1742; d 28 Jul 1794 **RU**: Private, Served in Illinois in Capt John Kennedy's Co, Col George Rogers Clark's Regt **CEM**: Maxwell Family; GPS unk; Abingdon; Washington **GS**: U **SP**: Elizabeth (-----) **VI**: No further data **P**: unk **BLW**: unk **RG**: Y **MK**: N **PH**: unk **SS**: DAR #A075911;SAR P-243385 E pg 510 **BS**: 80, vol 3, pg 58.

RU=Rank/Unit	CEM=Cemetery	GS=Gravestone	SP=Spousal Information
VI=Other Veteran Info	P=Pension	BLW=Bounty/Land Warrant	RG=Registered Grave
MK=SAR/DAR Marker	PH=Photo	SS=Service Source	BS=Burial Source

MAXWELL, James; b c1729, Northumberland, England; d 4 Oct 1791 **RU:** Captain, Appointed by Navy Board as "Superintendent General of the Shipyard" in Jan. 1777 to supervise construction and fitting of naval vessels. In Jun 1779, was Commissioner of the Navy under the Board of War Jul 1780. **CEM:** St Paul's Episcopal; GPS 36.84733, -76.28554; 201 St Paul's Blvd; Norfolk City **GS:** U **SP:** Helen (Calvert) Maxwell Read (1st husband) **VI:** Became Norfolk resident in 1767. Prominent in wife's memoirs. Wore "a cockade in his hat." Granted a special BLW fr VA Governor for naval service to state. William Maxwell appl for pen under his serv for the estate in 1845, which was granted. Recd 1/2 pay, thus probably disabled in service. Heirs also appl for 2nd BLW which was rejected as he already received one. R73 **P:** Y **BLW:** Y **RG** Y **MK:** Y SAR plaque **PH:** unk **SS:** K Vol 3 pg 195; CB, J- DAR Hatcher; CG pg 2231: DAR A075934; SAR P-243400 **BS:** JLARC 2; 80 vol 3, pg 58.

MAXWELL, Thomas; b 1740; d 1781 **RU:** Lieutenant, Served in Capt James Maxwell's Co, Montgomery Co Militia **CEM:** Rural; GPS unk; Maxwell Gap; Montgomery **GS:** U **SP:** No info **VI:** No further data **P:** unk **BLW:** unk **RG:** Y **MK:** unk **PH:** unk **SS:** J-NSSAR 2000 Reg; G pg 237; CZ; SAR P-243445 **BS:** JLARC 76.

MAY, George I; b 1 Oct 1758, Lancaster Co, PA; d 1815 **RU:** Private, Served in Capt Jonathan Hanby's Co, 3rd Cont Line **CEM:** May Family; GPS unk; May Creek Ln, Criders, Bergton; Rockingham **GS:** Y **SP:** Martha Magdalene (Houghman) **VI:** No further data **P:** unk **BLW:** unk **RG:** N **MK:** N **PH:** unk **SS:** E pg 510 **BS:** 191 May cem; 196.

MAYER, Jean; b unk; d 1781 **RU:** Seaman, Served on "Ville de Paris" and died from Yorktown battle **CEM:** French Memorial; GPS 36.81944, -79.39933; Yorktown; York **GS:** U **SP:** No info **VI:** No further data **P:** unk **BLW:** unk **RG:** Y **MK:** unk **PH:** unk **SS:** J-Yorktown Historian; SAR P-243569 **BS:** JLARC 1.

MAYO, Jacob; b 4 Aug 1744, Middlesex Co, d 29 Nov 1813 **RU:** Patriot, drove cattle and gave material aid to cause **CEM:** Grace Episcopal Church; GPS: 37.7164940, -78.2969490; loc 754 Bremo Bluff Rd; Fluvanna **GS:** N **SP:** mar (2 Jan 1768) Susannah Isbell (30 Sep 1749-6 Oct 1851) d/o William B Isbell & Ann Dillard **VI:** Son of James Mayo (11 Dec !711-13 Mar 1776) & Martha Williamson (21 Feb1718-27 Aug 1794) **P:** N **BLW:** N **RG:** Y **MK:** N **PH:** N **SS:** D vol2, pgs 623, 629:629; DAR A076242; SAR P-243694 **BS:** 196.

MAYO, John; b 21 Oct 1760, Deep Creek, Powhatan Co; d 28 May 1818 **RU:** Patriot, Gave material aid to cause **CEM:** St. Johns Episcopal Ch 37.5318300,-77.4195800; 2401 E. Broad St; Richmond City **GS:** U **SP:** Abigail Dellart (1 Mar 1761 Elizabeth Union, NJ-__) **VI:** Son of John (1736 Gloucester Co-__) & Mary (Tabb) (8 Jul 1733-__) Mayo. Rep Henrico Co General Assembly 1785, 1786, and 1791 to 1796. Was Lt Col in War of 1812 **P:** N **BLW:** N **RG:** N **MK:** unk **PH:** unk **SS:** Al Ct Bk **BS:** 32.

MAYO, John; b 17 Jul 1737, Henrico Co; d 17 Jan 1786 **RU:** Patriot, Gave material to the cause **CEM:** Hollywood; GPS 37.53560, -77.45720; 412 S Cherry St; Richmond City **GS:** Y **SP:** Mary Tabb (8 Jul 1733, Gloucester Co-17 Aug 1792) **VI:** Son of William (1685-1744) & Ann (Perratt) (1700-1773) Mayo. Died in Powhatan Co **P:** N **BLW:** N **RG:** Y **MK:** N **PH:** unk **SS:** E pg 511; D Vol I pg 254; DAR A076252; SAR P-243698 **BS:** 28 pg 198 Appdx.

MAYO, Joseph; b 1750, Goochland Co, d 1830 **RU:** 2d Lieutenant; 6 May 1779, in Capt D Tilman's Co, Fluvanna County Militia **CEM:** James Mayo Plantation; GPS not determined; across rd at 1807 Rolling Rd, Scottsdale, Palmyra; Fluvanna **GS:** N **SP:** Jean Richardson (1752-1830) **VI:** Son of James Mayo (1711-1776) & Martha Williamson (21 Feb 1718, Middlesex Co-27 Aug 1794) Was an attorney **P::** N **BLW:** N **RG:** Y **MK:** N **PH:** N **SS:** AZ pg 203; DAR A076259; SAR P-243710 **BS:** 196.

MAYO: William, b 7 Jan 1754, Cumberland Co, d 21 Oct 1804 **RU:** Patriot/ Captain Was a sea Captain; provided material aid to cause **CEM:** Hollywood; GPS 37.53560, -77.45720; 412 S Cherry St; Richmond City **GS:** Y Sec 5, lots 2 &3 **SP:** Mar 1772, Catherine Swann (__-1806) **VI:** Son of Daniel Mayo Sr (1733-1761) & Thirza Howard (1737-1784) **P:** N **BLW:** N **RG:** Y **MK:** N **PH:** N **SS:**; D vol3 pgs 779.781.784; E pg 511; DAR A076280; SAR P-243728 **BS:** 196.

MAYO, William; b 26 Sep 1757, Gloucester Co; d 12 Aug 1837 **RU:** Captain, commanded a company in Powhattan Co in Jan 1781 that marched to Sulffock Co **CEM:** Hollywood; GPS 37.53560, -77.45720; 412 S Cherry St; Richmond City **GS:** Y **GS:** Y **SP:** 1) Elizabeth Bland Poythress 2) Lucy Fitzhugh **VI:**

RU=Rank/Unit	CEM=Cemetery	GS=Gravestone	SP=Spousal Information
VI=Other Veteran Info	P=Pension	BLW=Bounty/Land Warrant	RG=Registered Grave
MK=SAR/DAR Marker	PH=Photo	SS=Service Source	BS=Burial Source

271

Son of John Mayo (1737-1786 & Marry Tabb (1733-1792) **P**: unk **BLW**: unk **RG**: Y **MK**: Y SAR **PH**: N **SS**: G, pg 288, 291; AZ pg 207 SAR P-243730 **BS**: 28 pg 198 Appdx; 196

MCALEXANDER, Alexander; b 1 May 1756, Albemarle Co, d 30 Jan 1840 **RU**: Sergeant, entered serv 1778, Amherst Co militia in Capt Higginbottom's Co, then VA Line serving at Saratoga, NY with last tour 1781 at Yorktown under Col Dabney **CEM**: Rockfish Presbyterian; GPS unk; 5016 Rockfish Valley Hwy, Nellysford; Nelson **GS**: Y memorial marker **SP**: Mar 2 Mar 1796, Amherst Co, Martha Brunett (1769-aft 1850) **VI**: Son of James McAlexander (1717-1798) **P**: Y both # SW5359 **BLW**: Unk **RG**: Y **MK**: N **PH**: N **SS**: CG pg 2238; AP pen application; DAR A074366; SAR P-243775 **BS**: 196.

MCALEXANDER, James Jr; b 1 May 1756; d 30 Jan 1840 **RU**: Lieutenant, Served as Private in Capt Nicholas Cabell's Co, Albemarle Co Militia Apr 1776. Became Lt before Oct 1781 in Amherst Co. **CEM**: Rockfish Presbyterian; GPS unk; 5016 Rockfish Valley Hwy, Nellysford; Nelson **GS**: Y **SP**: No info **VI**: Son of James Sr (17 Feb 1717-Jan 1798) & (-----) McAlexander. Family monument **P**: unk **BLW**: unk **RG**: N **MK**: unk **PH**: unk **SS**: E pg 512; DC pg 154 **BS**: 196.

MCALEXANDER, James Sr; b 17 Feb 1717, South Ayrshire, Scotland; d Jan 1798 **RU**: Patriot, Gave material aid to cause **CEM**: Rockfish Presbyterian; GPS unk; 5016 Rockfish Valley Hwy, Nellysford; Nelson **GS**: Y **SP**: No info **VI**: Died in Lovingston, Nelson Co. Family monument **P**: N **BLW**: N **RG**: N **MK**: unk **PH**: unk **SS**: AL Ct Bk pg 30 Amherst Co **BS**: 196.

MCALEXANDER, John; b 1750, Albemarle Co; d 1834 **RU**: Private, Served in Capt Nicholas Cabell's Co, Albemarle Co Militia Apr 1776 **CEM**: Thompson, Salmons, McAlexander; GPS unk; Rt 719 Woolwine; Patrick **GS**: Y **SP**: Mar (25 Mar 1780) Agnes (Nancy) Burnett (1763-1820) **VI**: Son of James Sr (17 Feb 1717-Jan 1798) & (-----) McAlexander **P**: N **BLW**: N **RG**: Y **MK**: unk **PH**: unk **SS**: DC pg 154; DAR A135058; SAR P-243776 **BS**: 196.

MCALEXANDER, William; b 13 Jan 1744, Albemarle Co, d 8 Mar 1822 **RU**: Patriot took oath of allegiance, Henry Co, 1777 and gave material aid to cause **CEM**: William McAlexander gravesite; GPS loc abt 1/2 mile W of Rd 710 on a ridge just S of Rockcastle Creek, on Carl Griffith farm, Woolvine; Patrick **GS**: N **SP**: Mar 1) 1765, Agnes Henderson, 2) 1776, Henry Co, Jane Jenny Ferguson, 3) 27 Dec 1798 Patrick Co, Taner Anna Boothe **VI**: Son of James S McAlexander(1717-1796) & Sarah Mary (__). Was in War of 1812 **P**: N **BLW**: N **RG**: Y **MK**: N **PH**: N **SS**:D vol 2, pg 511; DAR A074367; SAR P-243777 **BS**: 196.

MCALLISTER, James; b c1738, Spotsylvania Co; d 1798 **RU**: Private?, Served in Culpeper Militia 1781, and 7th Cont Line **CEM**: McAllister Family; GPS unk; Check property records for burial in or nr Syria; Madison **GS**: N **SP**: Eva (-----) **VI**: No further data **P**: unk **BLW**: unk **RG**: Y **MK**: N **PH**: N **SS**: E pg 512; SAR P-245358 **BS**: 04.

MCCALL, Thomas; b 22 Jul 1757; d 17 Aug 1818 **RU**: Soldier, Enl 29 Jan 1776. Served in Capt Willam Rippey's Co #4 Col Milliam Invenes PA Regt at Mount Independence 23 Nov 1776 **CEM**: Rock Spring; GPS 37.78126, -79.44585; Jct Rt 803 & Liberty Hall Rd, Lodi; Washington **GS**: U **SP**: Agnes Mongomery d/o John & (-----) Montgomery **VI**: Son of Thomas Sr. & (-----) McCall **P**: unk **BLW**: unk **RG**: N **MK**: unk **PH**: unk **SS**: A pg 209-210; CI Service rec cites PA 7th Regt **BS**: 196.

MCCARTER, James; b unk; d 1781 **RU**: Soldier, Served fr MA, and died fr the Battle at Yorktown **CEM**: Yorktown Victory Monument Tablet; GPS 38.28350, -78.54150; Yorktown; York **GS**: U **SP**: No info **VI**: No further data **P**: unk **BLW**: unk **RG**: Y **MK**: unk **PH**: unk **SS**: J-Yorktown Historian; SAR P-245480 **BS**: JLARC 74.

MCCARTHY (MCCARTY), Daniel; b 24 Aug 1757, Richmond Co; d 13 Mar 1801 **RU**: Lieutenant, Also listed as lieutenant (age 16!) at Brandywine and Germantown battles. Lt, Capt Thomas Triplett's Co, Col William Grayson's Additional Regt. 12 Jan - 1 Dec 1777 **CEM**: Pohick Episcopal; GPS 38.42546, -77.11598; 9301 Richmond Hwy, Lorton; Fairfax **GS**: Y **SP**: Mar (1778 Fairfax Co) Sarah Mason (1760-1823), d/o George, author of Bill of Rights & Ann (Elibeck) Mason **VI**: Son of Col Daniel (1727-1792) & Sinah (Ball) (1728-1798) McCarty of "Mt Air," Fairfax Co. After RW, became Vestryman at Pohick Church in Truro Parish. Bur at "Mt Air" (father's plantation), then moved to "Cedar Grove", then moved to Pohick Church 1991 **P**: Y **BLW**: unk **RG**: Y **MK**: Y SAR plaque **PH**: Y **SS**: E pg 514; AP rec; SAR P-245496 **BS**: JLARC 1, 2,13, 14, 27; 189 pg 91.

RU=Rank/Unit	CEM=Cemetery	GS=Gravestone	SP=Spousal Information
VI=Other Veteran Info	P=Pension	BLW=Bounty/Land Warrant	RG=Registered Grave
MK=SAR/DAR Marker	PH=Photo	SS=Service Source	BS=Burial Source

MCCARTY, Daniel; b 1727, Popes Creek, Westmoreland Co; d 1792 **RU:** Colonel/Patriot, Gave material aid to cause. Had civil service as Justice of Peace **CEM:** McCarty Family; GPS unk; Longwood, Horners Beach; Westmoreland **GS:** N **SP:** Mar (Jun 1748) Sinah Ball (14 Feb 1727-1798, Fairfax Co) **VI:** Died in Cedar Grove, Fairfax Co **P:** unk **BLW:** unk **RG:** Y **MK:** N **PH:** N **SS:** DAR #A074764; AL Ct Bk pg 2, 5 Westmoreland Co; BQ; DD cites Deed abstracts Fairfax Co; SAR P-243917 **BS:** 189 pg 91.

MCCARTY, Daniel; b 1743; d 1 Mar 1801 **RU:** Patriot, Gave material aid to the cause and paid personal property tax 1782, Frederick Co **CEM:** Old Opequon Church; GPS 39.82237, -78.11412; 217 Opequon Church Ln, Kernstown; Frederick **GS:** Y **SP:** No info **VI:** No further data **P:** N **BLW:** N **RG:** N **MK:** N **PH:** unk **SS:** AL Ct Bk pg 17; ER Frederick Co, tax list 1782 **BS:** 112 pg 6; 196.

MCCARTY, Daniel III see Appendix G, Addenda

MCCAULEY, Daniel; b 1743; d 4 Jul 1829 **RU:** Patriot, Gave material aid to cause **CEM:** Old Opequon Church; GPS 39.82237, -78.11412; 217 Opequon Church Ln, Kernstown; Frederick **GS:** Y **SP:** Elizabeth Marquis (1754 Frederick Co-29 Jul 1829) d/o Thomas & Mary (Colville) McCauley **VI:** No further data **P:** N **BLW:** N **RG:** Y **MK:** N **PH:** unk **SS:** AK; SAR P-243946 **BS:** 04; 112; 196.

MCCHESNEY, James; b 20 Jun 1735, Ireland; d Apr 1805 **RU:** Captain/Patriot, Gave material aid to cause **CEM:** Green Spring Presbyterian; GPS 36.63670, -81.99560; 2007 Green Spring Ch Rd, Abingdon; Washington **GS:** Y **SP:** No info **VI:** No further data **P:** unk **BLW:** unk **RG:** N **MK:** N **PH:** unk **SS:** E pg 515; AL Ct Bk 7 Augusta Co **BS:** 78 pg 275.

MCCHESNEY, James; b 1733, Ireland; d 1816 **RU:** Patriot, Gave material aid to cause. Also civil service as road surveyor, 1780 Augusta Co **CEM:** Old Providence; GPS 37.96151, -79.71000; 1005 Spottswood Rd, Spottswood; Augusta **GS:** Y **SP:** Mar (__Ireland) Mary Patterson (__-1781/2) **VI:** Elder of Church in 1776 and Trustee 1793. Newer Govt stone. Name also on SAR cemetery plaque **P:** N **BLW:** N **RG:** N **MK:** Y SAR plaque **PH:** unk **SS:** DAR #A074884; E pg 515; AL Ct Bk pg 7 Augusta Co **BS:** 196.

MCCHESNEY, John; b 1749, PA; d 22 Sep 1822 **RU:** Soldier, Served in PA Line and VA Militia. VA service, Capt William Hendrick's Co **CEM:** Old Providence; GPS 37.96151, -79.71000; 1005 Spottswood Rd, Spottswood; Augusta **GS:** Y **SP:** 1) Rebecca (-----) (1753-1813) **VI:** Recd disability pension in Augusta Co 10 Feb 1810. Newer Govt stone that incorrectly shows he d in 1795. Name also on SAR cemetery plaque **P:** Y **BLW:** unk **RG:** N **MK:** Y SAR plaque **PH:** unk **SS:** DAR #A074888; B; E pg 515; BT; CG pg 2245; DD **BS:** JLARC 62; 196.

MCCHESNEY, Samuel; b 22 Jun 1753, Ireland; d 4 Apr 1803 **RU:** Captain/Patriot, Commanded a co in Campbell Co Militia. Gave material aid to the cause **CEM:** Green Spring Presbyterian; GPS 36.63670, -81.99560; 2007 Green Spring Ch Rd, Abingdon; Washington **GS:** Y **SP:** Susannah Berry (2 Oct 1757-2 Oct 1822) **VI:** Son of James (1733-1818) & Sarah Mary (Patterson) (1733-__) McChesney **P:** unk **BLW:** unk **RG:** Y **MK:** N **PH:** unk **SS:** E pg 515; AL Comm Bk V pg 80 Rockbridge Co; DAR A074890; SAR P-245527 **BS:** 78 pg 274; 196.

MCCLANAHAN, Alexander; b 1743, near Staunton, Augusta Co, d 6 May 1797 **RU:** Was Capt Co Cmdr at Pt Pleasant, Oct 1774. Later Lt Col 7th VA Regt of Foot **CEM:** Tinkling Springs Presbyterian Church; GPS 38.087740, -78.982278; 30 Tinkling Springs Drive, Fisherville; Augusta **GS:** Unk **SP:** Eleanor Sallie Shelton (1743-1774), d/o John Shelton & Sarah Breckenridge **VI:** Brother Robert killed in Pt Pleasant battle. After war was County Clerk, Augusta Co **P:** Unk **BLW:** Unk **RG:** Y **MK:** N **PH:** N **SS:** Z pg 116; DAR A074896; SAR P-243964 **BS:** 196.

MCCLANAHAN (McCLENACHAN) Robert. Sr; b 1698 Antrim Co, Ireland, d 1791 **RU:** Patriot, Gave material aid to cause in Augusta Co **CEM:** Tinkling Springs Presbyterian Church; GPS 38.087740, -78.982278; 30 Tinkling Springs Drive, Fisherville; Augusta **GS** Unk **SP: Mar 1734,** Sarah Breckenridge (1718-1791) **VI:** Was sheriff of county 1765 **P:** N **BLW:** N **RG:** N **MK:** N **PH:** N **SS:** AL Comm Bk II pg 359, List III, pg 10 **BS:** 196.

MCCLINTIC, William Jr; b 30 Jun 1759, Ireland; d 13 Sep 1786 **RU:** Private, Drafted 28 Feb 1778 Bath Co. Joined army 17 May 1778 under Capt Andrew Wallace 8th VA Regt. VA Line. Ent serv Bath Co in 4th, 8th, 12th Cont Line. Discharged 16 Feb 1779. Volunteered Feb 1781 as rifleman under Capt John Bollar. Wounded at Guilford CH 15 Mar 1781 **CEM:** Warm Springs; GPS 38.05030, -79.78110; Rt 220

RU=Rank/Unit	CEM=Cemetery	GS=Gravestone	SP=Spousal Information
VI=Other Veteran Info	P=Pension	BLW=Bounty/Land Warrant	RG=Registered Grave
MK=SAR/DAR Marker	PH=Photo	SS=Service Source	BS=Burial Source

273

Sam Snead Hwy, Warm Springs; Bath **GS:** Y **SP:** Mar 4 Mar 1782, Alice Mann (c1762-__); she mar 2) (14 May 1804) Wm H. Cavendish (__-14 Aug 1818) **VI:** Son of William McClintic (b 1717 Tyrone, Ireland - c1801) & Nancy Shanklin (1723-c1809) Returned to Jackson's River in Bath Co, Mar 1782. The Botetourt Co Ct recommended him for pen but he d before receiving it fr effects of wound received at Battle of Guildford CH. Widow appl pen 21 Dec 1848 Bath Co VA age 86. Pension rejected. R1819 He appl for pension in 1785 or 1786? **P:** N **BLW:** unk **RG:** N **MK:** N **PH:** Y **SS:** E pg 517; K Vol 3 pg 207; CG pg 2248-49; **BS:** 159; 196.

MCCLINTIC (MCCLINTOCK), William Sr; b 1717, Tyrone, Ireland; d 1801 **RU:** Private/Patriot, Served in Battle of Point Pleasant. Gave material aid to cause **CEM:** McClintic Family; GPS unk; 12 mi W of Warm Springs; Bath **GS:** N **SP:** Nancy Shanklin (1723-1809) **VI:** No further data **P:** unk **BLW:** unk **RG:** Y **MK:** N **PH:** N **SS:** DAR #A075134; Al, Cert issued; DD cites Poffenbarger Battle of Point Pleasant pg 26; SAR P-244043 **BS:** 159.

MCCLOUGHRY, John; b unk; d 1781 **RU:** Lieutenant, Served fr NY killed in the battle at Yorktown **CEM:** Yorktown Victory Monument Tablet; GPS 38.28350, -78.54150; Yorktown; York **GS:** U **SP:** No info **VI:** No further data **P:** unk **BLW:** unk **RG:** Y **MK:** unk **PH:** unk **SS:** J-Yorktown Historian; SAR P-245645 **BS:** JLARC 74.

MCCLUER, John; b 1749, Augusta Co; d 4 Jul 1822 **RU:** Private, Served in VA unit in Illinois **CEM:** Falling Springs Presbyterian; GPS 37.68526 -79.44972; 410 Falling Springs Rd, Glasgow; Rockbridge **GS:** Y **SP:** Nancy Agnes Steele (2 Sep 1748-16 Sep 1839) **VI:** Son of John & Nancy (-----) McClurer. SAR marker **P:** unk **BLW:** unk **RG:** Y **MK:** Y SAR **PH:** unk **SS:** J-NSSAR 1993 Reg; CZ pg 282; SAR P-245646 **BS:** JLARC 1; 196.

MCCLUNG, Henry; b 1739, County Antrim, Ire, d 3 Feb 1784 **RU:** Patriot, Gave material aid to cause in Rockbridge Co **CEM:** Timber Ridge Presbyterian Churchyard; GPS: 37.84200,-79.35800; vic jct Rts 785 & 716, Timber Ridge; Rockbridge **GS:** Yes **SP**; Esther Caruthers (1744-27 Oct 1818), d/o William Caruthers & Margaret McCroskey **VI:** Son of James McClung (1790, Larne, Antrim, Ire-1799) & Mary McKy (1708, VA-1781) **P:** N **BLW:** N **RG:** N **MK:** N **PH:** N **SS:** AL Ct Bk pg 1, Rockbridge Co **BS:** 196.

MCCLUNG, John; b 1731, Ireland; d 1817 **RU:** First Lieutenant/Patriot, Was first LT on 4 Jul 1780 in Capt Lyle's Co, Rockbridge Militia Gave material aid to cause **CEM:** Timber Ridge Presbyterian; GPS 37.84200, -79.35800; Nr jct Rts 11 & 716, Timber Ridge; Rockbridge **GS:** U **SP:** Mar (1754) Elizabeth Alexander (28 Oct 1735-29 Oct 1802) d/o Archibald (4 Feb 1708-aft 1780) & Margaret (Parks) (__-Aug 1753) Alexander **VI:** No further data **P:** N **BLW:** N **RG:** N **MK:** unk **PH:** unk **SS:**E pg 517; G pg 120; AL Ct Bk pg 2, 16 Rockbridge Co; DAR A075170 **BS:** JLARC 63.

MCCLUNG, John Jr; b 1733, Ireland; d Sep 1832 **RU: Private/** Patriot,Was a private in Capt McCreerey's Co, Augusta Co Militia and in battle at Kings Mountain in Capt John Beatie's Co Gave material aid to cause **CEM:** McClung Family; GPS unk; nr Millboro; Bath **GS:** U **SP:** Mar (1793 Bath Co) Jane (-----) **VI:** Lived to be 99 **P:** N **BLW:** N **RG:** Y **MK:** unk **PH:** unk **SS:** N pg 1241; J-NSSAR 1993 Reg, J- DAR Hatcher; AL Cert Augusta Co; DAR A075175; SAR P-244065 **BS:** JLARC 1, 2.; 80 vol 3, pg 63.

MCCLUNG, William; b c1760, Rockbridge Co; d 1794 **RU:** Ensign, Served in VA Line. Ent serv Rockbridge Co 1780. Received rank of ensign 2 Nov 1779 in Capt James Gilmore's Co **CEM:** Timber Ridge Presbyterian; GPS 37.84200, -79.35800; Nr jct Rts 11 & 716, Timber Ridge; Rockbridge **GS:** Y **SP:** Jean Dun **VI:** Son of James (1700-1779) & Mary (McKy) (1708-1781) McClung. Appl pen 29 Mar 1836, Blount Co, TN. R6628 **P:** Y **BLW:** unk **RG:** N **MK:** unk **PH:** Y **SS:** K Vol 3 pg 207; AZ pg 228; CG pg 2250 **BS:** JLARC 2,63; 80,vol3, pg 63; 196.

MCCLUNG, William; b 1700, Ireland, d 20 Sep 1783 **RU:** Patriot With his son William they paid personal property tax 1782, Rockbridge Co, considered to be a supply tax for Rev War expenses **CEM:** Timber Ridge Presbyterian; GPS 37.84200, -79.35800; nr jct Rts 11 & 716, Timber Ridge; Rockbridge **GS:** U **SP:** Mar twice, names unk **VI** :Was Elder of Timber Ridge Presbyterian Church, 1753 **P:** Y **BLW:** N **RG:** Y **MK:** N **PH:** Y **SS:** DV 1782A image 13.pdf; SAR P-244074 **BS:** 80, vol 3, pg 63; 196.

MCCLURE, Alexander; b 1 Aug 1763, Rockbridge Co; d 6 Jul 1842 **RU:** Soldier, Enl Rockbridge Co in VA line **CEM:** Timber Ridge Presbyterian; GPS 37.84200, -79.35800; Nr jct Rts 11 & 716, Timber Ridge;

RU=Rank/Unit CEM=Cemetery GS=Gravestone SP=Spousal Information
VI=Other Veteran Info P=Pension BLW=Bounty/Land Warrant RG=Registered Grave
MK=SAR/DAR Marker PH=Photo SS=Service Source BS=Burial Source

274

Rockbridge **GS:** U **SP:** No info **VI:** Appl for pen Franklin Co, KY. Died in Franklin Co, KY, memorialized VA. S30575 **P:** Y **BLW:** unk **RG:** Y **MK:** unk **PH:** unk **SS:** K Vol 3 pg 207; SAR P-245663 **BS:** JLARC 63.

MCCLURE, Andrew; b Jun 1767; d 30 Oct 1847 **RU:** Lieutenant/Patriot, Served in battle of Guilford CH 1781. Gave flour and beef to cause **CEM:** Bethel Presbyterian; GPS 38.04257, -79.17283; 563 Bethel Green Rd, Middlebrook; Augusta **GS:** Y **SP:** Mary Mitchell **VI:** The birth date is probably incorrect. Died age 80 yrs 4 mos **P:** unk **BLW:** unk **RG:** Y **MK:** unk **PH:** Y **SS:** D pg 41 Augusta Co; CZ' SAR P-245667 **BS:** JLARC 62, 63; 196.

MCCLURE, Halbert; b unk; d unk **RU:** Patriot, Gave material aid to cause **CEM:** Timber Ridge Presbyterian; GPS 37.84200, -79.35800; Nr jct Rts 11 & 716, Timber Ridge; Rockbridge **GS:** U **SP:** No info **VI:** No further data **P:** N **BLW:** N **RG:** Y **MK:** unk **PH:** unk **SS:** AL Ct Bk II pg 36 Rockingham Co; SAR P-245677 **BS:** JLARC 63.

MCCLURE, John; b 1725, Ireland; d May 1779 **RU:** Private, Served in militia rolls listed in Virginia's Illinois Dept **CEM:** Fincastle Presbyterian; GPS 37.50017, -79.87558; 108 E Back St, Fincastle; Botetourt **GS:** U **SP:** Mary Allen (1741-1804) d/of Malcom (1712-1792) & Mary Margaret (Cunningham) (1720-1767) Allen **VI:** Son of Halbert Samuel (1684-1754) & Agnes (Steele) (1690-1750) McClure **P:** unk **BLW:** unk **RG:** Y **MK:** unk **PH:** unk **SS:** BY; DAR A075293; SAR P-318773 **BS:** 05 cites SAR application; 196.

MCCLURE, John; b 1 Nov 1749; d 4 Jul 1842 **RU:** Private, Served in VA unit in Illinois **CEM:** Stonewall Jackson Memorial; GPS 37.78128, -79.44604; 314 S Main St; Lexington City **GS:** Y **SP:** Mar (1775) Nancy Steele **VI:** Died in Rockbridge Co **P:** unk **BLW:** unk **RG:** N **MK:** Y SAR **PH:** Y **SS:** J- DAR Hatcher; E pg 517 **BS:** JLARC 2; 80, vol 3,pg 63.

MCCLURE, Robert; b unk; d unk **RU:** Patriot, Gave material aid to cause **CEM:** Falling Springs Presbyterian; GPS 37.68526 -79.44972; 410 Falling Springs Rd, Glasgow; Rockbridge **GS:** U **SP:** No info **VI:** No further data **P:** N **BLW:** N **RG:** Y **MK:** unk **PH:** unk **SS:** AL Ct Bk II pg 36 Rockingham Co; SAR P-245697 **BS:** JLARC 63.

MCCLURE, Robert A; b unk; d unk **RU:** Sergeant, Served in Capt Trimble's Co, Augusta Co Militia **CEM:** Timber Ridge Presbyterian; GPS 37.84200, -79.35800; Nr jct Rts 11 & 716, Timber Ridge; Rockbridge **GS:** U **SP:** No info **VI:** Recd BLW **P:** unk **BLW:** Y **RG:** N **MK:** unk **PH:** unk **SS:** C pg 207; E pg 517 **BS:** JLARC 63.

MCCLURE, Samuel; b 16 May 1748, Augusta Co (Wardell); d unk **RU:** Private/Patriot, served in Capt Johnston's Co, Augusta Co Militia. Gave material aid to cause **CEM:** Timber Ridge Presbyterian; GPS 37.84200, -79.35800; Nr jct Rt s 11 & 716, Timber Ridge; Rockbridge **GS:** U **SP:** Jane Hamilton **VI:** Pensioned Clark Co, IL 1833. S33079 **P:** Y **BLW:** N **RG:** Y **MK:** unk **PH:** unk **SS:** E pg 517; K Vol 3 pg 208; AL Ct Bk pg 2 Rockbridge Co;SAR P-245702 **BS:** JLARC 63.

MCCLURG, James; b 1747, Hampton; d 9 Jul 1823 **RU:** Surgeon, Was surgeon Jun 1776 until end of war. Was Superintendent & Inspector of Hospitals in VA **CEM:** St John's Episcopal; GPS 37.53183, -77.41958; 2401 E Broad St; Richmond City **GS:** Y **SP:** Mar (1779) Elizabeth Selden **VI:** Son of Dr. Walter & (-----) McClurg. Recd 6000 acre BLW 21 Oct. 1783. "No pension found for this officer "surgeon", see N.A. Acc #847 #050115 for VA 1/2 pay" (source CG) Was member of Constitutional Convention Philadelphia 1787and Privy Council 1786 & 87. Was Mayor of Richmond 1797, 1800, 1803 **P:** unk **BLW:** Y **RG:** N **MK:** N **PH:** unk **SS:** E pg 518; L pg 218; AK; CG pg 2251 **BS:** 28 pg 471; 04.

MCCOMB, James; b 8 Aug 1765; d 25 Oct 1846 **RU:** Private, Served in 3rd Cont Line **CEM:** Tinkling Spring Presbyterian; GPS 38.08472, -78.98278; 30 Tinkling Spring Dr, Fishersville; Augusta **GS:** Y **SP:** Susanah Henderson (31 Jul 176_-9 Jun 1848) **VI:** No further data **P:** unk **BLW:** unk **RG:** N **MK:** N **PH:** Y **SS:** E pg 518 **BS:** 142 Tinkling Spr; 208 pg 464; 196.

MCCONNEHEY, John; b 15 Apr 1752 Bucks Co, PA; d 1846 **RU:** Private, Entered service in Loudoun Co, 1780 in VA Line **CEM:** McConnehey-Updike; GPS 37.21162, -79.54527; 2730 Chestnut Fork Rd, Chestnut Fork; Bedford **GS:** Y **SP:** Mary Davis **VI:** Moved to Loudoun Co age 10. Moved to Bedford Co

RU=Rank/Unit VI=Other Veteran Info MK=SAR/DAR Marker CEM=Cemetery P=Pension PH=Photo GS=Gravestone BLW=Bounty/Land Warrant SS=Service Source SP=Spousal Information RG=Registered Grave BS=Burial Source

275

1801 or 1802. Pension appl for 25 Jan 1833 Bedford Co, but suspended for lack of 6 mos service, in Bedford 1836. S16953 **P:** N **BLW:** unk **RG:** N **MK:** N **PH:** unk **SS:** K Vol 3 pg 209 **BS:** 80 vol 3 pg 63.

MCCONNELL, Abram; b 1757; d 7 Aug 1830 **RU:** Private, Served in VA Line. **CEM:** Green Spring Presbyterian; GPS 36.63670, -81.99560; 2007 Green Spring Ch Rd, Abingdon; Washington **GS:** U **SP:** Mar (3 Mar 1780 Berkeley Co) Rosanna Fryatt (__-8 May 1846 Washington Co) **VI:** Son of James S. & (------) McConnell. An Abraham McConnell mar Margaret Touchstone in Frederick Co on 15 June 1809 by Alexander Balmain. Lived in Berkeley Co. Appl for pen 25 Feb 1856 Washington Co, R6643. DAR marker **P:** Y **BLW:** unk **RG:** Y **MK:** Y DAR **PH:** unk **SS:** CG pg 2253; SAR P-245764 **BS:** JLARC 2, 70, 80,101; 78 pg 275.

MCCORMICK, Martha (Sanderson); b 1747, Ulster, Ireland; d 1804 **RU:** Patriot, Gave material aid to the cause **CEM:** Old Providence; GPS 37.96151, -79.710; 1005 Spottswood Rd, Spottswood; Augusta **GS:** Y **SP:** Mar (1770) Robert McCormick (1738-12 Oct 1818); s/o Thomas & Elizabeth (Carruth) McCormick **VI:** Daug of George & Catherine (Ross) Sanderson of Scotland. Name also on SAR plaque at cemetery, and Gr has DAR marker **P:** N **BLW:** N **RG:** N **MK:** Y DAR & SAR plaque **PH:** unk **SS:** AS SAR regis **BS:** SAR regis; 196.

MCCORMICK, Robert; b 1738, Lancaster Co, PA; d 12 Oct 1818 **RU:** Private/Patriot, Gave material aid to the cause. Served several tours with Associators. Served in Jersey Campaign 1776 in VA Line and Southern Campaign of 1781. Was in Battle of Cowpens **CEM:** Old Providence; GPS 37.96151, -79.710; 1005 Spottswood Rd, Spottswood; Augusta **GS:** Y **SP:** Mar (1770) Martha Sanderson (1747-1804); d/o George & Catherine (Ross) Sanderson **VI:** Son of Thomas & Elizabeth (Carruth) McCormick of Ireland. Elder in Presbyterian Church. Name also on SAR plaque at cemetery **P:** unk **BLW:** unk **RG:** Y **MK:** Y SAR plaque **PH:** unk **SS:** BT; J-NSSAR 1993 Reg; K Vol 3 pg 209; DAR A075665; SAR P-245820 **BS:** JLARC 1; 196.

MCCOUGHRY, John; b unk; d 27 Oct 1781 **RU:** Lieutenant, Served in Capt James Rosekran's 1st Co, Lewis Dubois's 5th NY Line Regt, and died fr battle at Yorktown **CEM:** Yorktown Victory Monument Tablet; GPS 38.28350, -78.54150; Yorktown; York **GS:** U **SP:** No info **VI:** No futher data **P:** unk **BLW:** unk **RG:** N **MK:** unk **PH:** unk **SS:** J-Yorktown Historian; AX pg 220 **BS:** JLARC App B-5, 74.

MCCOWN, John; b 1720, Co Donegal, Ireland, d 1783 **RU:** Patriot, paid personal property tax 1782, Rockbridge Co, considered a tax to partially support paying for Rev War expenses **CEM:** McCown Family; GPS 37.8595400, -79.4270320; loc on Farmhouse Rd (Route 611) on McCown farm. Rockbridge Baths; Rockbridge **GS:** N **SP:** No spousal info **VI:** No further data **P:** N **BLW:** N **RG:** N **MK:** N **PH:** N **SS:** DV 1782B Rockbridge Co image 04.pdf **BS:** 196.

MCCOWN, Samuel; b unk; d 1853 **RU:** Private, Served in Capt Smith's Co, Dickerson's VA Regt **CEM:** Stonewall Jackson Memorial; GPS 37.78128, -79.44604; 314 S Main St; Lexington City **GS:** U **SP:** Elizabeth (-----) (18 Jun 1786-8 Jan 1835) **VI:** No further data **P:** unk **BLW:** unk **RG:** Y **MK:** unk **PH:** unk **SS:** B; SAR P-246378 **BS:** JLARC 63; 196.

MCCOY, John; b 1735; d 1796 **RU:** Captain, Commanded a Co in Augusta Co Militia 1777-1779 **CEM:** Doe Hill; GPS 38.25976, -79.26629; Across St fr Doe Hill Methodist Ch Rt 654; Highland **GS:** Y **SP:** Sarah Oliver **VI:** No further data **P:** unk **BLW:** unk **RG:** Y **MK:** Y SAR **PH:** unk **SS:** J- DAR Hatcher; E pg 520; SAR P-245862 **BS:** JLARC 2.

MCCUE, John; b 1715 Ireland; d Aft 27 Oct 1798 **RU:** Patriot, Civil service as Juror 1775, Amherst Co **CEM:** Tinkling Spring Presbyterian; GPS 38.08472, -78.98278; 30 Tinkling Spring Dr, Fishersville; Augusta **GS:** N **SP:** Mar (8 May 1753) Eleanor Mathews **VI:** No stone **P:** N **BLW:** N **RG:** Y **MK:** N **PH:** N **SS:** AS SAR applic; DD cites Sweeny, Amherst Co in the Revolution pg 73; DAR A075938; SAR P-245040 **BS:** SAR Appl; 208 pg 465.

MCCUE, John Rev; b 1752; d 20 Sep 1818 **RU:** Private, Served in Capt Anderson's Co Augusta Co Militia **CEM:** Tinkling Spring Presbyterian; GPS 38.08472, -78.98278; 30 Tinkling Spring Dr, Fishersville; Augusta **GS:** Y **SP:** No info **VI:** Tinkling Springs pastor for 27 yrs **P:** unk **BLW:** unk **RG:** N **MK:** N **PH:** Y **SS:** E pg 521; CD **BS:** 196.

MCCULLOUGH, Robert; b 2 May 1764; d 29 Aug 1849 **RU:** Private, Fought at Kings Mountain **CEM:** Dunn Family; GPS 36.62560, -81.72640; Abt 1 mi NW of Cherry Tree Gap off Rt 725; Washington **GS:**

RU=Rank/Unit	CEM=Cemetery	GS=Gravestone	SP=Spousal Information
VI=Other Veteran Info	P=Pension	BLW=Bounty/Land Warrant	RG=Registered Grave
MK=SAR/DAR Marker	PH=Photo	SS=Service Source	BS=Burial Source

276

U **SP:** Sarah Ann Clark (25 Nov 1775-25 Dec 1854) **VI:** Son of Thomas & Isabella (Patrick) McCulloch. **P:** unk **BLW:** unk **RG:** N **MK:** unk **PH:** unk **SS:** DAR Ancestor #A202096 **BS:** 196.

MCCUNE, John; b 20 Jan 1749; d 25 May 1812 **RU:** First Lieutenant/Patriot, Gave material aid to cause **CEM:** Tinkling Spring Presbyterian; GPS 38.08472, -78.98278; 30 Tinkling Spring Dr, Fishersville; Augusta **GS:** N **SP:** Mar (c1775) Margaret (-----) (__-17 Mar 1812) **VI:** No further data **P:** unk **BLW:** unk **RG:** Y **MK:** N **PH:** N **SS:** AL Cert Augusta Co; SAR P-245988 **BS:** JLARC 62.

MCCUTCHAN, Charles; b 1736; d 29 Jun 1814 **RU:** Soldier, SAR registration did not provide service **CEM:** Glebe Burying Ground; GPS 38.10940, -79.22190; Glebe School Rd Rt 876, Swoopes; Augusta **GS:** Y **SP:** No info **VI:** No further data **P:** unk **BLW:** unk **RG:** Y **MK:** N **PH:** unk **SS:** SAR P-246009; App D 210 pg 394 **BS:** JLARC 8.

MCCUTCHAN (MCCUTCHEN), Robert: b 1729,No Lanankshire Scotland, d 26 Jun 1800 **RU:** Private/Patriot, served in Capt John Wilson's Co Augusta Co Militia. As patriot paid personal property tax 1782 and 1783, Augusta Co, considered a tax to partially support paying for Rev War expenses **CEM:** North Mountain; GPS 38.0789160,-79.1779770; 7 mi S of Staunton on N side Rt 252;Craigsville; Augusta **GS:** Y monument **SP:** Mar 1776, Augusta Co, Margaret Callison (1730 Ireland-1790) **VI:** Son of John McCutchen **P:** unk **BLW:** unk **RG:** N **MK:** N **PH:** unk **SS:** G pg 67; DV 1782A & 1783 Augusta Co image 03.pdf & image 19.pdf BS: 196.

MCCUTCHAN, Samuel; b 1744 Ireland; d 2 Mar 1830 **RU:** Captain/Patriot, Commanded a company in Augusta Co Militia.His co was on W side of Ohio River in 1778 at Fort McIntosh, under Gen McIntosh. He gave material aid to cause and paid personal property supply tax in 1782 and 1783 **CEM:** North Mountain; GPS 38.0789160,-79.1779770; 7 mi S of Staunton on N side Rt 252; Augusta **GS:** Y **SP:** Mar 1) Betsy Blackwood; 2) Rebecca Downey (c1747-10 Jun 1820) d/o Samuel Downey (1722-1773) & Martha McPheeters (__-1801) **VI:** Govt marker **P:** unk **BLW:** unk **RG:** Y **MK:** N **PH:** unk **SS:** G pg 67; DAR #A076139; SAR P-246013; B; AL Comm Bk II pg 369, 360 Augusta Co; DV 1782B & 1783 Rockbridge Co image 03.pdf & image 08.pdf **BS:** 196.

MCCUTCHAN, William; b 17 or 27 Nov 1758; d 29 Jun 1848 **RU:** Sergeant, Served in VA Line. Enl Staunton in 1778. Enl Waynesboro in 1780. Served under Capt Samuel McCutcheon (called him "kin" in application) **CEM:** Bethel Presbyterian; GPS 38.04257, -79.17283; 563 Bethel Green Rd, Middlebrook; Augusta **GS:** N **SP:** Mar (20 May 1794 Augusta Co) Jean Finley or Finely (c1770-__), d/o Robert & (-----) Finley/Finely. **VI:** Appl pen 25 Jun 1833 Augusta Co. Widow appl pen 19 Nov 1849 Augusta Co age 79. W1888 **P:** Y **BLW:** unk **RG:**Y **MK:** unk **PH:** N **SS:** J- DAR Hatcher; SAR P-246015; K Vol 3 pg 214; AL Comm Bk II pg 361 Augusta Co; CG pg 2262-63 **BS:** JLARC 2, 4, 62, 63.

MCCUTCHAN (MCCUTCHEN), James; b unk; d unk **RU:** Soldier, Served in Capt James Beatie Co at Kings Mountain **CEM:** Bethel Presbyterian; GPS 38.04257, -79.17283; 563 Bethel Green Rd, Middlebrook; Augusta **GS:** N **SP:** No info **VI:** No further data **P:** unk **BLW:** unk **RG:** Y **MK:** unk **PH:** N **SS:** SAR P-246010; N pg 1241 **BS:** JLARC 62.

MCCUTCHEN, William, b 1722, Ireland, d 1786 **RU:** Lieutenant/Patriot, in Capt Alexander McClanahan's Co, Augusta Co Militia at Pt Pleasant, Ocy 1774. As patriot paid personal property tax 1782 and 1783, Augusta Co, considered a tax to partially support paying for Rev War expenses **CEM:** North Mountain; GPS 38.0789160, -79.1779770; 7 mi S of Staunton on N side Rt 252;Craigsville; Augusta **GS:** Y monument **SP:** Eleanor Fulton (1740-1800), d/o James Fulton (1690-1753) & Sarah Ann Lockhart (1694-1764) **VI:** Son of John McCutcheon (__-1755) & (-----) **P:** unk **BLW:** unk **RG:** N **MK:** N **PH:** unk **SS:** G pg 67; Z pg 116, AZ pg 125; DV 1782B & 1783 Augusta Co image 03.pdf & image 08.pdf **BS:** 196.

MCCUTCHEON, John; b 15 Nov 1758; d 29 Jun 1848 **RU:** Private, Served in Capt John Wilson's Co, Augusta Co Militia **CEM:** North Mountain; GPS 38.0789160, -79.1779770; 7 mi S of Staunton on N side Rt 252; Augusta **GS:** N **SP:** Jean Finley **VI:** Name is on a copper plate on a monument by DAR chapter listing Rev War soldiers bur in this Glebe **P:** unk **BLW:** unk **RG:** N **MK:** unk **PH:** N **SS:** G pg 26 **BS:** JLARC 63; 196. **SEE APPENDIX G**

MCDANIEL, George; b 17 May 1722, King William Co; d 22 Nov 1821 **RU:** Major, Served as Sergeant, Cont Line and as Maj in Bedford Co Militia **CEM:** McDaniel Family; GPS unk; Boonesboro Rd;

RU=Rank/Unit	CEM=Cemetery	GS=Gravestone	SP=Spousal Information
VI=Other Veteran Info	P=Pension	BLW=Bounty/Land Warrant	RG=Registered Grave
MK=SAR/DAR Marker	PH=Photo	SS=Service Source	BS=Burial Source

277

Lynchburg City **GS:** U **SP:** Mar (1748) Margaret Gough (c1728-1821) **VI:** No further data **P:** unk **BLW:** unk **RG:** Y **MK:** unk **PH:** unk **SS:** E pg 522; DAR A076177; SAR P-246031 **BS:** JLARC 36.

McDANIEL, James; b unk; d 4 Oct 1777, **RU:** Private, Capt Thomas Triplett's Co, Col William Grayson' VA Regt:, Cont Line **CEM:** Rev War Court House Plaque; GPS not determined; 4110 Chain Bridge Rd; Fairfax **GS:** Memorialized on plaque 2017 by Geo Washington Chapter, VASSAR **SP:** No spousal info **VI:** died in service **P:** N **BLW:** N **RG:** N **MK:** N **PH:** N **SS** E pg 522 shows killed with date: EH: sources **BS:** None.

MCDANIEL, Thomas; b unk; d 1807 **RU:** Private, Served in Clark's Illinois Regt, 11th Cont Line **CEM:** Back Creek Quaker, aka Gainesboro United Methodist; GPS 39.27861, -78.25694; 166 Siler Ln, Gainesboro; Frederick **GS:** Y **SP:** No info **VI:** No further data **P:** unk **BLW:** unk **RG:** N **MK:** N **PH:** unk **SS:** E pg 522 **BS:** 59 pg 214.

MCDONALD, Bryan; b 8 Jul 1732, New Castle, DE; d Jan 1777 **RU:** Private, Served in Capt John Taylor's Co, Montgomery Co Militia **CEM:** Glebe; GPS 37.45155, -79.96968; Vic jct Rts 779 and 630; Botetourt **GS:** U **SP:** Susanna Ogle (6 May 1728 New Castle, DE-1801) **VI:** Son of Bryan (1732-1777) & Susanna (Ogle) (1728-1801) McDonald **P:** unk **BLW:** unk **RG:** Y **MK:** unk **PH:** unk **SS:** G pg 234-5; SAR P-327638 **BS:** 196.

MCDONALD, Edward; b 3 Oct 1761; d 19 Apr 1855 **RU:** Private, Served in 7th, 9th, 13th Cont Lines **CEM:** Glebe; GPS 37.45155, -79.96968; Vic jct Rts 779 and 630; Botetourt **GS:** U **SP:** Mary Rowland (11 Mar 1764-11 Apr 1814) d/o of Jame & Margaret (Kyle) Rowland **VI:** Son of Bryan (1732-1777) & Susanna (Ogle) (1728-1801) McDonald **P:** unk **BLW:** unk **RG:** Y **MK:** unk **PH:** unk **SS:** E pg 523; SAR P-244487 **BS:** 196.

MCDONALD, James; b 18 Jan 1753; d Aug 1777 **RU:** Private, Served in Capt John Montgomery's Co, Montgomery Co Militia **CEM:** Glebe; GPS 37.45155, -79.96968; Vic jct Rts 779 and 630; Botetourt **GS:** N **SP:** No info **VI:** Son of Bryan (1732-1777) & Susanna (Ogle) (1728-1801) McDonald **P:** unk **BLW:** unk **RG:** N **MK:** unk **PH:** N **SS:** G pg 208 **BS:** 196.

McDONALD, Jane; b 1750; d 6 Jun 1810 **RU:** Patriot, gave material aid to cause **CEM:** Stony Hill (AKA Briggs-McDonald); GPS 38.439230, -77.581770; 99 Stony Hill Rd nr Curtis Lake, Hartwood; Stafford **GS:** Y with husband **SP:** David Briggs (9 May 1730-3 Dec 1815) **VI:** Name and service is on DAR plaque **P:** N **BLW:** N **RG:**N **MK:** Y DAR plaque **PH:** N **SS:** DAR A205207 **BS:** 196.

MCDONALD, Joseph; b 4 Apr 1722 Mill Creek New Castle Co, DL, d May 1809, Blacksburg, Montgomery Co **RU:** Private, served in Capt John Taylor's Company, Montgomery Co Militia **CEM:** McDonald Bane; GPS 37.2256040, -80.4839860 loc Walnut Springs Rd, Prices Fork; Montgomery **GS:** Y **SP:** Mar 17 Feb 1754, Elizabeth Ogle (18 Jun 1725-1795), d/o Thomas Ogle (1705-1771) & Elizabeth Arskin Graham **VI:** Son of Bryan McDonald (1686-1757) & Catherine Robinson (1698-1760) **P:** N **BLW:** N **RG:**Y **MK:** N **PH:** N **SS:** G PGS 234, 235; SAR P-244498 **BS:** 196.

MCDONALD, William; b 24 Sep 1756; d 13 Dec 1833 **RU:** Lieutenant, Served in 1st Lt Dragoons & 7th Cont Line **CEM:** Mt Union; GPS 37.45133, -79.97055; 4614 Catawba Rd, Mt Union; Botetourt **GS:** Y **SP:** Nancy Robinson **VI:** Son of Bryan (1732-1777) & Susanna (Ogle) (1728-1801) McDonald **P:** unk **BLW:** unk **RG:** Y **MK:** N **PH:** unk **SS:** E pg 523; SAR P-246118 **BS:** JLARC 21, 24;80, vol 3, pg 66; 196.

MCDORMENT (MCDORMAN), David; b 1758, Caroline Co; d 13 Oct 1835 **RU:** Private, Served in 3rd Co, VA line in Capt Field's Co, Col Gaskin's Regt **CEM:** Pine Cliff; GPS 38.28920, -77.64577; Vic jct Rts Jackson Trail Rd and Military Park Rd; Spotsylvania **GS:** Y **SP:** Anne "Nancy" Tiller **VI:** Veterans Admin GS installed 1935. Cemetery is located on private property and reportedly current owner does not allow visitors. Sol recd pension of $80 per annum starting 29 Jan 1829 through Richmond VA Agency. Claim adjudicated through Treasury Dept. No papers at pension bureau. BLW12404 issued 7 Jul 1792 **P:** Y **BLW:** Y **RG:** N **MK:** N **PH:** unk **SS:** DAR #A201568; K Vol 3 pg 218; AG pg 853; CG pg 2268; Applic for VA GS **BS:** 09 grid 19; 196.

MCDOWELL, William; b Bapt 9 Apr 1749, Augusta Co; d 25 Mar 1806 **RU:** Patriot, Was member of Committee of Peace 1777 **CEM:** Trinity Episcopal; GPS 38.14917, -79.07521; 214 Beverley St; Staunton City **GS:** Y **SP:** Mar (1772) Alice (-----) **VI:** No further data **P:** N **BLW:** N **RG:** N **MK:** N **PH:** unk **SS:** DAR #A113373; E pg 524; AL List l pg 2, 6 Augusta Co **BS:** 36 pg 203; 196.

RU=Rank/Unit	CEM=Cemetery	GS=Gravestone	SP=Spousal Information
VI=Other Veteran Info	P=Pension	BLW=Bounty/Land Warrant	RG=Registered Grave
MK=SAR/DAR Marker	PH=Photo	SS=Service Source	BS=Burial Source

MCFADEN (McFADDEN), James; b 1761; d Apr 1799 **RU**: Captain, Served in VA Cont Line **CEM**: Old Presbyterian Meeting House; GPS 38.48528, -77.23532; 323 S Fairfax St; Alexandria City **GS**: N **SP**: No info **VI**: Died of consumption age 38, bur 24 Apr 1799. Listed on an SAR plaque in cemetery **P**: unk **BLW**: Y **RG**: Y **MK**: Y SAR plaque **PH**: N **SS**: C pg 357; AK; SAR P-244615 **BS**: 23 pg 105; 196.

MCFARLAND, Robert, b Nov 1705, County Tyrone, IRE, d 25 Dec 1797 **RU**: Patriot Was witness in Rockbridge court, 1776 regards spy case. Paid personal property taxes in Rockbridge County in1783 called supply tax to defray expenses of Rev War in Virginia **CEM**: Falling Springs Presbyterian Church; GPS: 37.68494,-79.45105; 410 Falling Springs Rd, Glasgow; Rockbridge **GS**: Unk **SP**: Esther Huston (1726, IRE-1794) **VI**: Son of Robert McFarland and Jennet (-----) **P**: N **BLW**: N **RG**: Y **MK**: N **PH**: N **SS**: DAR A076832, cites our BS 210, vol 1, pg 567; DV; SAR P-244644 **BS**: 196

MCFARLAND, William; b 1732 Augusta Co, d 1801 **RU**: Lieutenant; Served in Gaddis's Command in Monongalia County, VA (now WVA) Militia Burial source 196 indicates he was wounded in eye at Pt Pleasant battle and was Captain of company in Indian raids **CEM**: Neel Family; GPS: not determined; Rt 61, abt 6 mi E of jct w Rt 722, on the left, Cove Creek; Tazewell **GS**: Yes field stone **SP**: Mar 1) 1772 Lucinda McFarland (__-1795, Wythe Co, 1850), 2) 1755 Augusta Co Elizabeth Gibson (1735, Augusta Co-1850), d/o Alexander Gibson & Mary Wilson **VI**: Son of Duncan McFarland (1700, Ire-1792, Augusta Co) & (__) **P**: N **BLW**: N **RG**: N **MK**: N **PH**: N **SS**: E pg 525 **BS**: 196.(**MCFARLIN**,John see Appendix G

MCFERRAN, Martin; b unk; d 1788 **RU**: Captain, Co Cmdr in Botetourt Co Militia in 1778 **CEM**: McFerran Family; GPS unk; Rt 220, 6 mi N of Fincastle; Botetourt **GS**: Y **SP**: No info **VI**: No further data **P**: unk **BLW**: unk **RG**: N **MK**: N **PH**: unk **SS**: E pg 526 **BS**: 115 pg 66.

MCGAVOCK, Hugh; b Sep 1761; d 2 Apr 1844 **RU**: Captain, Raised his own Regt 1779. Was Regt Quartermaster 1780 under Col Joseph Crockett, VA Line **CEM**: McGavock Family; GPS unk; NW of jct Rts 610 & 1012, W of Max Meadows; Wythe **GS**: Y **SP**: Nancy Kent (1763-1835) **VI**: Son of James. Appl pen 13 Aug 1834 Wythe Co. S16948 also VA 1/2 pay (See N.A. Acc #874 #050116 1/2 Pay) **P**: Y **BLW**: unk **RG**:Y **MK**: Y SAR **PH**: unk **SS**: K Vol 3 pg 221; CG pg 2275-76; SAR P-244676 & P-246312 **BS**: JLARC 2, 40,123; 196.

MCGAVOCK, James; b 1728, Antrim, Ireland; d 22 Mar 1812 **RU**: Patriot, Was Signer of Fincastle Declaration of Rights. Was Magistrate and Justice for Botetourt and Fincastle Cos **CEM**: McGavock Family; GPS unk; Peppers Ferry Rd, Ft Chiswell, off I-81 12 mi E of Wytheville; Wythe **GS**: Y **SP**: Mar (20 Jan 1760) Mary Cloyd **VI**: No further data **P**: N **BLW**: N **RG**: Y **MK**: Y SAR **PH**: unk **SS**: DAR patriotic index; SAR membership #45571; DAR A076914; SAR P-246313 **BS**: JLARC 2, 40, 101.

MCGOWAN, Samuel; b unk; d unk **RU**: Private, Served in Capt David Grier Co #6, Col Irvine William's Regt at Mount Independence, 28 Nov 1775 **CEM**: Stonewall Jackson Memorial; GPS 37.78128, -79.44604; 314 S Main St; Lexington City **GS**: U **SP**: No info **VI**: No further data **P**: unk **BLW**: unk **RG**: N **MK**: unk **PH**: unk **SS**: J-NSSAR 2000 Reg; A pg 212 **BS**: JLARC 76; 80, vol 3, pg 68.

MCGUFFIN, Thomas Sr; b unk; d 1823 **RU**: Private, Served in Montgomery Co Militia1781 **CEM**: New Providence Presbyterian; GPS 37.95170, -79.30250; 1208 New Providence Rd, Raphine; Rockbridge **GS**: U **SP**: No info **VI**: No further data **P**: unk **BLW**: unk **RG**: y **MK**: unk **PH**: unk **SS**: G pg 225; SAR P-246403 **BS**: JLARC 62.

MCILHANEY, James; b 1749; d 16 Sep 1804 **RU**: Captain, Served in Capts Andrew Russell and Lilliam Lae's companies of Fairfax Co in VA Cont Line **CEM**: McIlhaney Family; GPS unk; Nr Hillsboro E side Rt 690 btw Rts 90 & 611; Loudoun **GS**: U **SP**: Mar (25 Dec 1776 Loudoun Co, bond dated 21 Dec 1778) Margaret Williams, a widow (c1760-__). Both of Shelburn Parish when mar **VI**: Wid appl pen 20 Jul 1836 Loudoun Co VA age 76 at pen date R6734. BLW #7770-400 to heirs **P**: Y **BLW**: Y **RG**: N **MK**: unk **PH**: unk **SS**: K Vol 3 pg 225; BY pg 318; CG pg 2282 **BS**: JLARC 2, 32; 80, vol 3, pg 69.

MCINTURF (MCINTURFF), David; b 1729; d 1804 **RU**: Patriot, Gave material aid to cause. **CEM**: Dry Run Church; GPS 38.85929, -78.40075; Rt 678, Fort Valley Rd nr jct with Dry Run Rd, Seven Fountains; Shenandoah **GS**: Y **SP**: No info **VI**: No further data **P**: N **BLW**: N **RG**: N **MK**: N **PH**: unk **SS**: AL **BS**: 04.

McINTURFF/McKENTURF, Casper; b 1753 London Grove Township, Chester Co, PA; d 1808 **RU**: Patriot, paid personal property tax 1783 in Shenandoah Co, considerered to be a supply tax for Rev War

RU=Rank/Unit	CEM=Cemetery	GS=Gravestone	SP=Spousal Information
VI=Other Veteran Info	P=Pension	BLW=Bounty/Land Warrant	RG=Registered Grave
MK=SAR/DAR Marker	PH=Photo	SS=Service Source	BS=Burial Source

279

expenses **CEM**: Old John McInturff Farm; GPS not determined; Shenandoah Caverns; Shenandoah **GS**: N **SP**: No spousal info **VI**: Son of John McInturff (1729-1779) & Maria Rosina Kern(1735-1780) **P**: N **BLW**: N **RG**: N **MK**: N **PH**: N **SS**: ER; Shenandoah Co, VA GenWeb Project, pg 2 **BS**: 196

MCINTURFF, Frederick; b 1758, Chester Co, PA; d 1 Jul 1816 **RU**: Private, Served in Capt Joseph Bowman's Co, Shenandoah Co Militia **CEM**: Dry Run Church; GPS 38.85929, -78.40075; Rt 678, Fort Valley Rd nr jct with Dry Run Rd, Seven Fountains; Shenandoah **GS**: Y **SP**: Mar (25 Feb 1783) Susannah Carrier (c1768-3 Oct 1816) **VI**: Son of John McInturff (1729-1779) & Maria Rosina Kern (1735-1780) **P**: N **BLW**: N **RG**: Y **MK**: unk **PH**: N **SS**: DAR A077331; DD; SAR P-244822 **BS**: 196

.**McINTURFF/McKENTURF**, John, b 1729, Philadelphia; d-aft 1783 **RU**: Private/Patriot; Served as Private in Capt Joseph Bowman's Co, lower district of Dunmore Co during war period; as patriot paid personal property tax Shenandoah Co 1783 **CEM**: Old John McInturff Farm; GPS not determined; Shenandoah Caverns; Shenandoah **GS**: N **SP**: Maria Rosina Kern(1730, Baden-Wurttemberg, Ger-1780) **VI**: Son of Johannes MecKendorf (1703-1775) & Phronick Meckendorfer(1705-1742) **P**: N **BLW**: N **RG**:N **MK**: unk **PH**: N **SS**: C pg 605; ER; Shenandoah Co, VA GenWeb Project, pg 2 **BS**: 196.

MCIVER, Colin; b unk; d 1788 **RU**: Patriot, Gave material aid to cause **CEM**: Old Christ Church Episcopal; GPS 38.80625, -77.04718; 118 N Washington St; Alexandria City **GS**: N **SP**: No info **VI**: Burial permit issued 9 Jan 1788 **P**: N **BLW**: N **RG**: N **MK**: N **PH**: unk **SS**: AL cert issued **BS**: 20 pg 150.

MCKANN, Robert H; b unk; d 1804 **RU**: Private, Served in Capt Joseph Mitchell's Co at Battle of Point Pleasant, Oct 1774 **CEM**: Providence Burial Ground; GPS unk; Waterview; Middlesex **GS**: U **SP**: No info **VI**: No further data **P**: unk **BLW**: unk **RG**: N **MK**: N **PH**: unk **SS**: E pg 350; Z pg 54 **BS**: 88 pg 251.

MCKAY, Enos; b unk; d 1804 **RU**: Private, Served in Capt Jacob Springer's Co, VA Cont Line **CEM**: Spring Farm; GPS unk; 2 mi NE of Luray on Turnpike; Page **GS**: N **SP**: No info **VI**: WPA report says d in 1833. **P**: unk **BLW**: unk **RG**: N **MK**: N **PH**: N **SS**: N pg 442 **BS**: 120.

MCKEE, James; b 14 Mar 1752, PA; d 14 Aug 1832 **RU**: Ensign, Served in VA Militia. Lived in Rockbridge Co at enl. Served as sub for brother William McKee **CEM**: McKee, aka Big Springs; GPS unk; Clarence Hardy's farm, off Rt 60 on Rt 63, Kerrs Dist; Rockbridge **GS**: Y **SP**: 1) Jane Telford 2) Nancy (Leech) Scott (___-5 Feb 1835) **VI**: Moved with brother William to Rockbridge Co 1774, settling on Kerr's Creek). Pen granted 1835 to children that was due to their mother. S16954 **P**: Y **BLW**: unk **RG**: Y **MK**: Y SAR **PH**: Y **SS**: K Vol 3 pg 226; CG pg 2286; SAR P-246535 **BS**: JLARC 4, 76, 126.

MCKEE, Robert; b 18 Aug 1754 Ireland; d Jun 1841 **RU**: First Lieutenant, Took oath as 1st Lt in Rockbridge Co Militia 2 Dec 1778 **CEM**: New Providence Presbyterian; GPS 37.95170, -79.30250; 1208 New Providence Rd, Raphine; Rockbridge **GS**: U **SP**: 1) Margaret Mamilton, 2) Jane Jack (Jacque) **VI**: No further data **P**: unk **BLW**: unk **RG**: Y **MK**: unk **PH**: unk **SS**: E pg 530; DAR 077493; SAR P-248545 **BS**: JLARC 1, 63; 196.

MCKENZIE, Moredock (Mordicai Moredecai Mordock Morodock) Otis; b 1738, Glasgow, Scotland; d 1804 or 1812/13 **RU**: Private, Was in Battle of Pt. Peasant; 2nd Bn 15th VA Regt and Capt Daniel Smith's Co, Fincastle Co Militia **CEM**: Hare Family; GPS unk; Narrows; Giles **GS**: N **SP**: 1) Jemissa Chapman 2) Mar (1781) Abigail Marrs 3) Mar (1786) Sarah Huet **VI**: No further data **P**: unk **BLW**: unk **RG**: Y **MK**: N **PH**: N **SS**: E pg 531; SAR P-246603 **BS**: 04.

MCKIM, James; b 10 Jul 1754, Brandywine, New Castle Co, DE; d 1804 or 12 Sep 1820 **RU**: Private?, Served in 12th Cont Line in Clark's Illinois Regt **CEM**: McKim Family; GPS unk; Arcola; Loudoun **GS**: Y **SP**: Ruhamah Heath **VI**: Son of Alexander & Jeanette (-----) McKim **P**: unk **BLW**: unk **RG**:N **MK**: N **PH**: unk **SS**: E pg 200, 532 **BS**: 25 pg 200; 196.

MCKINNEY, James; b unk; d 1804 **RU**: Soldier, Served fr NY, and killed in the battle at Yorktown **CEM**: Yorktown Victory Monument Tablet; GPS 38.28350, -78.54150; Yorktown; York **GS**: U **SP**: No info **VI**: No further data **P**: unk **BLW**: unk **RG**: Y **MK**: unk **PH**: unk **SS**: J-Yorktown Historian; SAR P-246850 **BS**: JLARC 74.

MCKNIGHT, Charles; b unk; d 16 Nov 1791 **RU**: Surgeon, Service in NY. Wounded and entitled to half pay. As Capt served as commander of Alexandria Light Infantry Blues. **CEM**: Old Presbyterian Meeting House; GPS 38.48528, -77.23532; 323 S Fairfax St; Alexandria City **GS**: N **SP**: No info **VI**: Listed on an

---

RU=Rank/Unit	CEM=Cemetery	GS=Gravestone	SP=Spousal Information
VI=Other Veteran Info	P=Pension	BLW=Bounty/Land Warrant	RG=Registered Grave
MK=SAR/DAR Marker	PH=Photo	SS=Service Source	BS=Burial Source

SAR plaque in cemetery. **P:** unk **BLW:** unk **RG:** Y **MK:** Y SAR plaque **PH:** N **SS:** J-NSSAR 1993 Reg; A pg 427, 545; AK; SAR P-246692 **BS:** JLARC 1; 5.

MCKNIGHT, William; b c1733; d 25 Jul 1812 **RU:** Private/Patriot, Served in Capt Beatie's Co at Kings Mountain. Gave material aid to cause **CEM:** Presbyterian Church; GPS 38.80015, -77.05791; Wilkes St & Hamilton Ln; Alexandria City **GS:** Y Section 41, plot 20 **SP:** 1) Martha Bryan, (c1745-3 Jun 1775); 2) Susannah Evans (1746-10 Nov 1836) **VI:** Death notice in the Alexandria Gazette 27 Jul 1812 **P:** unk **BLW:** unk **RG:** Y **MK:** Y SAR **PH:** unk **SS:** N pg 1241; AL Ct Bk pg 88 Loudoun Co; SAR P-333957 **BS:** 23 pg 56; 196.

MCLAURINE, James; b 25 Nov 1758,. Cumberland Co; d 1848 **RU:** Private, Lived in Cumberland Co at enl. Ent service 1777, Cumberland Co in 7th VA Regt. Was in Capt Charles Fleming's Co, Col Crockett's 7th VA Regt **CEM:** Petersville; GPS 37.56440, -77.96470; Off Rt 60; Powhatan **GS:** N **SP:** Mar (9 Mar 1789) Catherine Steger (c1769,-aft 1809) **VI:** Appl for pen 26 Jun 1843 Cumberland Co age 84 not received as he had less than 6 mos service. R6780 **P:** N **BLW:** unk **RG:** Y **MK:** N **PH:** Y **SS:** DAR A077920; K Vol 3, pg 234; CG Vol 2295;DAR A077920; SAR P-245007 **BS:** SAR corres.

MCLEAN, James See Appendix G addenda

MCLINGAN, James; b unk; d unk **RU:** Soldier, SAR registration did not provide service **CEM:** Arlington National; GPS 38.88377, -77.06535; Jefferson Davis Hwy Rt 110; Arlington **GS:** N **SP:** No info **VI:** No further data **P:** unk **BLW:** unk **RG:** Y **MK:** unk **PH:** N **SS:** J-NSSAR 2000 Reg; SAR P-246804 **BS:** JLARC 76.

MCMAHON, Michael; b 1758; d 24 Mar 1786 **RU:** Soldier, Served in 3rd, 5th, 7th, & 11th Cont Lines **CEM:** Old Christ Church Episcopal; GPS 38.80625, -77.04718; 118 N Washington St; Alexandria City **GS:** Y **SP:** No info **VI:** Barber. D age 28. Death notice in the Alexandria Gazette 30 Mar 1786, pg 3 **P:** unk **BLW:** unk **RG:** N **MK:** unk **PH:** unk **SS:** J-NSSAR 1993 Reg; E pg 535 **BS:** JLARC 1; 20 pg 139.

MCNEIL, Jacob Sr; b Jun 1759; d 1841 **RU:** Indian Spy/Ranger, Served in VA Line. Lived on "Virginia frontier" at enl 1776 as Indian spy and ranger. Served with a Lt John McNeil **CEM:** McNeil Family; GPS unk; Rt 220 N, .1 mi E of MM 25, nr railroad tracks; Franklin **GS:** Y **SP:** Mar (2 Mar 1812 Franklin Co) Peggy Cool (This may be the wife of Jacob Jr.) **VI:** Govt GS says "Guard, Henderson's VA Co" Moved to Franklin Co after RW, where he was pensioned as Jacob, Sr. Sol appl pen 3 Sep 1832 Franklin Co. S5745 **P:** Y **BLW:** unk **RG:** Y **MK:** unk **PH:** Yes **SS:** K Vol 3 pg 238; CG pg 2305; SAR P-247006 & SAR P-245204 **BS:** JLARC 4, 20.

MCNUTT, Alexander; b 1725, prob Londonderry, Ireland; d 1811 **RU:** Captain, Served in MA & VA Militia **CEM:** Falling Springs Presbyterian; GPS 37.68526 -79.44972; 410 Falling Springs Rd, Glasgow; Rockbridge **GS:** Y **SP:** Never mar **VI:** Govt Gr stone **P:** unk **BLW:** unk **RG:** Y **MK:** Y SAR **PH:** Y **SS:** B; SAR P-247026 **BS:** JLARC 1, 63, 79.

MCNUTT, Alexander; b 10 Dec 1754; d 29 Mar 1812 **RU:** Ensign, Was Ens in Capt James Gilmore's Co of VA Militia under command of Gen Morgan in SC, 1780. Also served in Rockbridge Co Militia 1781 **CEM:** Stonewall Jackson Memorial; GPS 37.78128, -79.44604; 314 S Main St; Lexington City **GS:** Y **SP:** Rachel Grigsby (c1771 - 7 Jan 1840) **VI:** Son of John (1725-1781) & Katherine (Anderson) (__-1814) McNutt **P:** unk **BLW:** unk **RG:** Y **MK:** Y SAR plaque **PH:** unk **SS:** CD; SAR P-247027 **BS:** JLARC 2, 63; 80, vol3, pg 74; 196.

MCNUTT, James; b 1740; d 6 Sep 1811 **RU:** Ensign, Served in Capt Mathew Arbuckles Co, at Ft Pleasant 1774 **CEM:** Old Providence; GPS 37.96151, -79.71000; 1005 Spottswood Rd, Spottswood; Augusta **GS:** Y **SP:** Margaret McElroy (__-22 Sep 1820) **VI:** Son of Alexander and Jane (-----) McNutt. Name on SAR cemetery plaque **P:** unk **BLW:** unk **RG:** Y **MK:** Y SAR plaque **PH:** unk **SS:** BT; SAR P-247029 **BS:** JLARC 2, 8, 62, 63; 80, vol 3, pg 74 196; 213 pg 461.

MCNUTT, John; b 1726, Ulster North Ireland, d 1781 battle of Cowpens, Spartanburg, SC **RU:** Private/Patriot; A VA unit at the Battle of Cowpens. As patriot gave material aid to cause, Rockbridge Co **CEM:** Old Providence; GPS: 37.96151,-79,227; 1005 Spotswood Rd, Spotswood; Augusta **GS:** No **SP:** Mar (c1751) Katherine Rebecca Anderson (__-30 Jun 1814), prob d/o Robert Anderson & Catherine Graham **VI:** Known as "Scotch Johnny", memorialized in cemetery FindaGrave source of Rev War

RU=Rank/Unit	CEM=Cemetery	GS=Gravestone	SP=Spousal Information
VI=Other Veteran Info	P=Pension	BLW=Bounty/Land Warrant	RG=Registered Grave
MK=SAR/DAR Marker	PH=Photo	SS=Service Source	BS=Burial Source

281

service not found **P:** N **BLW:** N **RG:** N **MK:** N **PH:** N **SS:** AL Ct Bk pg 4 & Comm Bk V, pg 81, Rockbridge Co; CD Memorial 54057490 **BS:**196.

MCNUTT, John, Jr; b 1763, d 13 Jun 1818 **RU:** Private, Capt James Finley's Co, Montgomery County Militia **CEM:** Stonewall Jackson Memorial; GPS: 37.78128,-79.44604; 314 S Main St; Lexington City **GS:** Yes **SP:** Mar 13 Aug 1807, Rockbridge Co, Mary Laird **VI:** Son of John McNutt, Sr and Katherine Anderson. He was also a War of 1812 soldier in rank of Ensign **P:** N **BLW:** N **RG:** N **MK:** N **PH:** N **SS:** G pg 232; **BS:** 196.

MCNUTT, Robert; b unk; d 17 Jan 1781 **RU:** Soldier, Killed at battle of Cowpens, Spartanburg Co, SC **CEM:** Old Providence; GPS 37.96151, -79.71000; 1005 Spottswood Rd, Spottswood; Augusta **GS:** Y **SP:** No info **VI:** Died in Cowpens battle in SC. Newer Govt stone. Name also on SAR cemetery plaque **P:** unk **BLW:** unk **RG:** unk **MK:** Y SAR plaque **PH:** unk **SS:** B; BT; SAR P-247030 **BS:** JLARC 2, 63; 80, vol 3, pg 74; 196.

MCPHEETERS, William Jr; b 28 Sep 1729, PA; d 28 Oct 1807 **RU:** Soldier/Patriot, Gave material aid to cause **CEM:** Bethel Presbyterian; GPS 38.04257, -79.17283; 563 Bethel Green Rd, Middlebrook; Augusta **GS:** U **SP:** Rachel Moore (__-30 Jan 1826) d/o James (1711-1791) & Jane (Walker) (1712-1793) Moore **VI:** Son of William McPheeter (1690-1773) & Rebecca Thompson **P:** unk **BLW:** unk **RG:** Y **MK:** unk **PH:** unk **SS:** AL Comm Bk II pg 361 Augusta Co; SAR P-247038 **BS: SEE APPENDIX G**

MCPHERSON, Hugh; b 2 Mar 1756, Kippochan, County of Argyll and Bute, Scotland; d 20 Feb 1808 **RU:** Soldier, Enl 29 Jul 1782 in Col Moses Hazen's Regt, Cont Troops **CEM:** Trinity Episcopal; GPS 36.83459, -76.30105; 500 Court St; Portsmouth City **GS:** Y **SP:** Lilias Blair (1744 Scotland-3 Nov 1822 Norfolk) **VI:** Son of John & Effie (-----) McPherson. Presybyterian minister. D in Norfolk **P:** unk **BLW:** unk **RG:** Y **MK:** Y SAR plaque **PH:** Y **SS:** CI Service Rec; SAR P-336643 **BS:** 196.

MCREYNOLDS, James; b 1724, Ireland; d 25 Jun 1807 **RU:** Sergeant, Served in Bedford Militia **CEM:** McReynolds Family; GPS 37.17360, - 78.5334; Rt 623; Appomattox **GS:** U **SP:** Mar (1749) Mary Bell (27 Feb 1727-10 May 1799) **VI:** No further data **P:** unk **BLW:** unk **RG:** Y **MK:** unk **PH:** unk **SS:** E pg 539; DAR A076466; SAR P-247074 **BS:** JLARC 36.

MCREYNOLDS, John; b 1758; d 1796 **RU:** Captain, Served in Cont Line **CEM:** McReynolds Family; GPS unk; Off Rt 623; Campbell **GS:** U **SP:** 1) Mar (6 Dec 1788 (bond)) Jane Campbell d/o James & (-----) Campbell 2) Olivia (-----) **VI:** No further data **P:** unk **BLW:** unk **RG:** Y **MK:** N **PH:** unk **SS:** SAR P-247075 **BS:** JLARC 36.

MCREYNOLDS, Joseph; b 1755; d 1776 **RU:** Corporal, Served in 5th Cont line **CEM:** McReynolds Family; GPS 37.17360, - 78.5334; Rt 623; Appomattox **GS:** U **SP:** No info **VI:** No further data **P:** unk **BLW:** unk **RG:** Y **MK:** unk **PH:** unk **SS:** E pg 539; SAR P-247076 **BS:** JLARC 36.

MCROBERT, Archibald; b 1736, Scotland, d 1807 **RU:** Patriot, Gave material aid to cause **CEM:** Hampden-Sydney College Cem; GPS unk; Hampden-Sydney; Prince Edward **GS:** Y **SP:** Elizabeth Bland Munford, d/o Robert Munford & Ann Bland **VI:** Charter member of Hampton-Sidney College and Hampton-Sidney Presbyterian Church **P:** N **BLW:** N **RG:** Y **MK:** N **PH:** unk **SS:** AL Ct Bk pg 12, 17 Prince Edward Co; AS; SAR P-247079 **BS:** 80 vol 3 pg 74; 196.

MCROBERTS, Alexander; b 1755; d1805 **RU:** Private, Served in Col Clark's Illinois Regt **CEM:** Fincastle Presbyterian; GPS 37.50017, -79.87558; 108 E Back St, Fincastle; Botetourt **GS:** N **SP:** Mar (3 May 1784 Botetourt Co) Nancy Hillard **VI:** SAR plaque at this cemetery **P:** unk **BLW:** unk **RG:** Y **MK:** Y SAR plaque **PH:** N **SS:** E pg 539; SAR P-245273 & SAR P-247080 **& BS:** 196; JLARC 1.

MCROBERTS, John; b 1750; d Aft Aug 1793 **RU:** Soldier/Patriot, Gave material aid to cause **CEM:** Fincastle Presbyterian; GPS 37.50017, -79.87558; 108 E Back St, Fincastle; Botetourt **GS:** N **SP:** 1) Mar (12 Apr 1770 Botetourt Co) Sarah McClanahan d/o Francis & (-----) McClanahan 2) Mar (5 Aug 1793 Botetourt Co) Eunice Crawford **VI:** Name is on the SAR plaque at this cemetery **P:** unk **BLW:** unk **RG:** Y **MK:** Y SAR plaque **PH:** N **SS:** J-NSSAR 1993 Reg; AL Ct Bk pg 15 Augusta Co; SAR P-247086 **BS:** JLARC 1; 196.

MCROBERTS, Samuel; b 1725; d 1784 **RU:** Patriot, Gave material aid to cause **CEM:** Fincastle Presbyterian; GPS 37.50017, -79.87558; 108 E Back St, Fincastle; Botetourt **GS:** N **SP:** No info **VI:**

RU=Rank/Unit	CEM=Cemetery	GS=Gravestone	SP=Spousal Information
VI=Other Veteran Info	P=Pension	BLW=Bounty/Land Warrant	RG=Registered Grave
MK=SAR/DAR Marker	PH=Photo	SS=Service Source	BS=Burial Source

Name is on the SAR plaque at this cemetery **P:** N **BLW:** N **RG:** Y **MK:** Y SAR plaque **PH:** N **SS:** J-NSSAR 1993 Reg; AL Ct Bk pg 1, 11, 16, 19, 21 Botetourt Co; SAR P-247088 **BS:** JLARC 1; 196.

MCSPADDEN, Moses; b 1754, Rockbridge Co; d 24 Aug 1827 **RU:** Soldier, Served in Washington Co Militia **CEM:** Green Spring Presbyterian; GPS 36.63670, -81.99560; 2007 Green Spring Ch Rd, Abingdon; Washington **GS:** Y **SP:** Mar (1776 Rockbridge Co) Sarah Jane Whitesides (1754-1826) **VI:** Son of Thomas (c1720 Ireland-1765) & Dorothy (Edmiston) McSpadden. Farmer & miller near Abingdon VA **P:** unk **BLW:** unk **RG:** N **MK:** unk **PH:** unk **SS:** CD; CV pg 206, 208 **BS:** 196.

MCVEAGH (MCVAY), Jonathan; b 1 Sep 1743, Chester, PA; d 16 Sep 1824 **RU:** Soldier, Served in Capt Evan's Co, Col Thomas Bull's Regt, and 2d Bn Chester Co Militia **CEM:** McVeagh Family Plantation; GPS unk; Not identified by JLARC; Loudoun **GS:** U **SP:** Mar (10 Jan 1770) Elizabeth Bull (20 Aug 1746, PA-14 Dec 1831) **VI:** No further data **P:** unk **BLW:** unk **RG:** Y **MK:** unk **PH:** unk **SS:** J-NSSAR 2000 Reg; DD; AR Vol 3 pg 74 **BS:** JLARC 76.; 80,vol 3, pg 74.

MCWILLIAMS, William; b 1751; d 17 Apr 1801 **RU:** Lieutenant Colonel, Served in VA Line. Ent serv Fredericksburg. Commanded 7th Co, 3rd VA Regt of Foot Feb 1777-Jan 1777 Spotsylvania Co **CEM:** Masonic Cemetery; GPS 38.30198, -77.46142; 900 Charles St; Fredericksburg City **GS:** U **SP:** Mar (6 Apr 1782) Dorothea B. (-----) (c1765-c Aug 1839). She mar next to George Buckner (___-18 Nov 1828). **VI:** Widow appl pen10 Sep 1838 Caroline Co age 73. R1410 **P:** Y **BLW:** unk **RG:** Y **MK:** Y SAR plaque **PH:** unk **SS:** J- DAR Hatcher; CE pg 39; CG pg 2311; SAR P-247133 **BS:** JLARC 2; 80 vol 3, pg 75.

MEACHUM (MEACHAM), Ichabod; b 2 Feb 1759; d 3 Nov 1837 **RU:** Seaman, Served in 1775, MA Regt 1777 aboard "Trumbull" **CEM:** Meacham Family; GPS unk; Nr Christiansburg; Montgomery **GS:** Y **SP:** No info **VI:** Pen age 59 Montgomery Co 1818. F-S38204 R1702 **P:** Y **BLW:** unk **RG:** Y **MK:** N **PH:** unk **SS:** K Vol 3 pg 242; SAR P-247148 **BS:** SAR regis.

MEAD, Nicholas; b 16 Feb 1752, Bedford Co; d c1817 **RU:** Sergeant/Patriot, Was recruiting officer Bedford Co Militia. Gave material aid to cause **CEM:** Mead; GPS unk; Near Lowry on Norfolk/Western RR Lines; Bedford **GS:** U **SP:** Mar (18 Jan 1779) Mary Bates (c1753-12 Jan 1850) **VI:** No further data **P:** unk **BLW:** unk **RG:** Y **MK:** N **PH:** unk **SS:** DAR #A076767; J-NSSAR 2000 Reg; AL Ct Bk pg 20 Campbell Co; DD; SAR P-247282 **BS:** JLARC 76; 80 vol 3, pg 76.

MEAD, Samuel; b 1761; d unk **RU:** Soldier, Served in Bedford Co Militia **CEM:** Royal Forest; GPS unk; New London; Bedford **GS:** U **SP:** No info **VI:** No further data **P:** unk **BLW:** unk **RG:** Y **MK:** N **PH:** unk **SS:** SAR P-247292 **BS:** JLARC 36.

MEAD (MEADE), Everard Sr; b 1 Oct 1748; d Sep 1802 **RU:** Major/Patriot, Served in VA Line. Aide de Camp to Maj Gen Lincoln. Gave material aid to cause **CEM:** Meade Family; GPS unk; Nr Chula; Amelia **GS:** N **SP:** Mary Thornton. Her will dated 1 Sep 1830 **VI:** Son of David & Susannah (Everard) Meade. Sol will 13 Jan 1801 Amelia Co. BLW #2063-300 **P:** unk **BLW:** Y **RG:** Y **MK:** unk **PH:** N **SS:** AL Ct Bk I pg 14 Amelia Co; CG pg 2315; DAR A076672; SAR P-247338 **BS:** JLARC 1, 4, 55; 80 vol 3, pg 75; 196.

MEADE, Everard Jr; b unk; d 1834 **RU:** Lieutenant Colonel, Commissioned Capt 8 Mar 1776 in Woodsford's Brigade. Was Lt Col in 2nd VA State Legion 1781-83. Was Aide de Camp to Gen Washington **CEM:** H H Jones Property; GPS unk; Chula; Amelia **GS:** Y **SP:** No info **VI:** Became general after Rev War. Monument erected Sep 1834 by Hedijah Bayliss, fellow Aide de Camp to Gen Lincoln **P:** unk **BLW:** unk **RG:** Y **MK:** unk **PH:** unk **SS:** J-NSSAR 1993 Reg; CD pg 36, 134; SAR P-247337 **BS:** JLARC 1.

MEADE, Humberson; b unk; d unk **RU:** Colonel, Service information not listed in SAR Registry **CEM:** Meade Memorial Episcopal; GPS 39.05830, -78.10360; 192 White Post Rd, White Post; Clarke **GS:** U **SP:** No info **VI:** No further data **P:** unk **BLW:** unk **RG:**Y **MK:** N **PH:** unk **SS:** SAR P-247343; AR Vol 3 pg 76 **BS:** JLARC 2; 80 vol 3, pg 76.

MEADE, Richard Kidder; b 11 Jul 1746, Nansemond Co; d 9 Feb 1805 **RU:** Lieutenant Colonel, Served fr 24 Oct 1775 to end of Rev. Capt of 6th Co 2nd VA Regt of Foot 24 Oct 1775. As Lt Col was field officer in 14th VA Regt of Foot, 12 Nov 1776-12 Mar 1777. Capt 2nd VA Regt. Aide-de-Camp to Gen Washington (1777). Assist Gen von Steuben in VA until end of war **CEM:** Meade Memorial Episcopal;

RU=Rank/Unit	CEM=Cemetery	GS=Gravestone	SP=Spousal Information
VI=Other Veteran Info	P=Pension	BLW=Bounty/Land Warrant	RG=Registered Grave
MK=SAR/DAR Marker	PH=Photo	SS=Service Source	BS=Burial Source

GPS 39.05830, -78.10360; 192 White Post Rd, White Post; Clarke **GS:** Y **SP:** 1) 1765, Jane Randolph (__-1774), 2) 1780 Mary Grymes Randolph (__-1813) **VI:** Son of David Meade & Susannah Everard. Said to have been originally bur at plantation home "Lucky Hit" which was built after Rev and later moved to White Post **P:** unk **BLW:** unk **RG:** y **MK:**DAR **PH:** Y **SS:** CE pg 38, 70; DAR A076777; SAR P-247349 **BS:** JLARC 24; 196.

MEADOWS (MEDOWS), Francis; b 1759; d 20 Nov 1836 **RU:** Private, Ent serv Augusta Co, Feb 1777. Served in Capt David Laird's Co, Col Green's 10 VA Regt. Was taken prisoner at Charleston, SC. Also served in 6th Cont Line **CEM:** Peterstown; GPS 37.39470, -80.80140; Off Rt 219 btw Peterstown & Midway, on WV state line; Giles **GS:** Y **SP:** Mar (Fall 1790 or 91 Monroe Co Rockingham Co) Frances Bush (c1771-__) **VI:** Sol appl pen 16 Jun 1816 Monroe Co aged around 64. Died in Monroe Co. Widow appl pen 20 Sep 1841 age 70 in Monroe Co. W5367 **P:** Y **BLW:** unk **RG:** Y **MK:** N **PH:** unk **SS:** E pg 541 & AP; CG pg 2316; SAR P-247380; DAR A076867 **BS:** 60 Giles.

MEADOWS, James; b 10 Oct 1760, Orange Co; d Oct 1849 **RU:** Private, Ent serv Rockingham Co, May 1781. Served in Capt Garland Burnley's Co, Col Francis Taylor's VA Regt. Also served 3 months in Capt George Huston's Co, Col John Rush's VA Regt. Was in Battles of Burnt Chimneys and Hot Water. Was stationed at Albemarle Barracks. Discharged Apr 1781 **CEM:** James Meadows Sr. Family; GPS unk; 5130 Bear Foot Ln, Elkton; Rockingham **GS:** Y **SP:** Catherine Boswell (Bauswell) (___-1842) **VI:** Son of Francis Sr. (1717-1792) & Mary (-----) Meadows. GS says 1842, but gave 4 affidavits for Am Rev pensions 1843-1846. Birthdates in affidavits varied fr 1756-1762. Earliest affidavit gives birthdate as c1760. Sol appl pen 17 Sep 1832 Rockingham Co. S8895. Widow's pension S6783 or S6683 **P:** Y **BLW:** unk **RG:** Y **MK:** N **PH:** Y **SS:** CG pg 2316; DAR A076883; SAR P-247385 **BS:** JLARC 4, 64.

MEASE, Robert; b 1746; d 7 Mar 1803 **RU:** Patriot, Signed a legislative petition in Fairfax Co **CEM:** Old Presbyterian Meeting House; GPS 38.48528, -77.23532; 323 S Fairfax St; Alexandria City **GS:** N **SP:** No info **VI:** Died age 57 of decline (Alexandria Gazette, 9 Mar 1803, pg 3) **P:** N **BLW:** N **RG:** N **MK:** N **PH:** N **SS:** BB **BS:** 23 pg 105.

MEASON, Thomas; b 18 Nov 1726, Uniontown PA; d 10 Mar 1813 **RU:** Brigadier General, Served in Cont Army **CEM:** Arlington National; GPS 38.88377, -77.06535; Jefferson Davis Hwy Rt 110; Arlington **GS:** Y lot 297-B **SP:** No info **VI:** PA lawyer. Died in Washington DC. Originally bur in Old Presbyterian Cemetery in Washington DC. Moved to Arlington 12 May 1892. Oldest person bur there **P:** unk **BLW:** unk **RG:** Y **MK:** unk **PH:** unk **SS:** J-NSSAR 1993 Reg; SAR P-247455 **BS:** JLARC 1; 196.

MEEK, Samuel; b 1760; d 9 Jul 1812 **RU:** First Lieutenant, Served in Capt James Dysart's Co of Light Horse on tour of NC under command of Col William Campbell May 1781. Govt GS lists service **CEM:** Clark; GPS unk; Cedarville; Washington **GS:** U **SP:** Elizabeth (-----) (1761- 21 May 1831) **VI:** Daughter Mary M. Hopkins of Grainger Co TN appl pen 9 Oct 1856. R7094 **P:** Y **BLW:** unk **RG:**Y **MK:** unk **PH:** unk **SS:** K Vol 3 pg 249; N pg 1262-payroll; CG pg 2320; SAR P-247541 **BS:** JLARC 4, 34; N pg 184; 196.

MEINER, Francois; b unk; d 1781 **RU:** Soldier, Served in Gatinais Bn and died fr battle at Yorktown **CEM:** French Memorial; GPS 36.81944, -79.39933; Yorktown; York **GS:** U **SP:** No info **VI:** No further data **P:** unk **BLW:** unk **RG:** Y **MK:** unk **PH:** unk **SS:** J-Yorktown Historian; SAR P-247668 **BS:** JLARC 1, 74.

MELTON, Absolem; b 1735; d 23 Sep 1805, **RU:** Patriot, paid personal property tax 1783, Hanover Co determined to be a supply tax for Rev War expenses **CEM:** Signal Hill Memorial Park; GPS 37.743598,-77.357803; 12360 Hanover Courthouse Rd; Hanover **GS:** Unk **SP:** No info **VI:** Son of John Melton (1697-1750) & Mary Elizabeth Preston White (1700-1785) **P:** N **BLW:** N **RG:** N **MK:** N **PH:** N **SS: BS:** 196.

MELTON, James; b 1737, Hanover Co; d 15 Jul 1778 in service,at Valley Forge, PA **RU:** Private Maj Wallace's Co, Col Mason's Regt, Valley Forge Jun 1778 **CEM:** Signal Hill Memorial Park; GPS 37.743598,-77.357803; 12360 Hanover Courthouse Rd; Hanover **GS:** Unk **SP:** No info **VI:** Son of John Melton (1697-1750) & Mary Elizabeth Preston White (1700-1785) **P:** N **BLW:** N **RG:** N **MK:** N **PH:** N **SS:** AP Fold 3 muster & payrolls **BS:** 196.

RU=Rank/Unit	CEM=Cemetery	GS=Gravestone	SP=Spousal Information
VI=Other Veteran Info	P=Pension	BLW=Bounty/Land Warrant	RG=Registered Grave
MK=SAR/DAR Marker	PH=Photo	SS=Service Source	BS=Burial Source

MELVIN, James; b 1764; d 10 May 1826 **RU**: Private, Served 15th Cont Line **CEM**: Nelson Family; GPS unk; New Church; Accomack **GS**: Y **SP**: No info **VI**: Son of Smith & Alaney (-----) Melvin (stone) **P**: unk **BLW**: unk **RG**: N **MK**: N **PH**: unk **SS**: E pg 543 **BS**: 145; 196.

MELTON< James; b 1721, New Kent Co; d 9 Apr 1798 **RU**: Private served in 5th & 11th Cont Line until 14 Nov 1783 **CEM**: Hillcrest (AKA Town of Lousia);GPS 38.033599,-78.038299; loc jct Oak Leaf Dr & Louisa Rd; Lousia **GS**: UnK **SP**: Mar c1741, Hanover Co, Mary Preston **VI**: Son of John Melton (1697-1750) & Mary Elizabeth Preston White (1700-1785) **P**: N **BLW**: N **RG**: N **MK**: N **PH**: N **SS**: E pg 543 **BS**: 196.

MELTON, Joel; b 1727 New Kent Co; d 1783 **RU**: Private served in Capt Matthew Jonett's Co, Col Alexander McClenachan's 7th VA Regt, May & Jun 1777, last pay rec'd 10 Nov 1783; as patriot paid personal property tax 1783, Hanover Co **CEM**: Signal Hill Memorial Park; GPS 37.743598,-77.357803; 12360 Hanover Courthouse Rd; Hanover **GS**: Unk **SP**: No info **VI**: Son of John Melton (1697-1750) & Mary Elizabeth Preston White (1700-1785) **P**: N **BLW**: N **RG**: N **MK**: N **PH**: N **SS**: AP Fold 3 muster & payrolls **BS**: 196.

MELTON, John C; b 1740, Hanover Co; d 2 Apr 1795 (Will processed in Fluvanna Co) **RU**: Private/patriot, was part of Drum & Fife unit, Capt Jeremiaih Telbert's Co 8, Col William Irvine's PA Regt at Mount Independence 1776; also in Col Gibson's 6th VA Regt at Valley Forge, May/Jun 1778; was hospitalized Aug 1778 at Brunswick, NJ; in Capt John Stokes's Co, Col Febigov 2d VA Regt Nov 1779; as patriot gave material aid to cause; Fluvanna Co **CEM**: Signal Hill Memorial Park; GPS 37.743598,-77.357803; 12360 Hanover Courthouse Rd; Hanover **GS**: Unk **SP**: Mar 1763 Elizabeth Driver Wade **VI**: Son of John Melton (1697-1750) & Mary Elizabeth Preston White (1700-1785) **P**: N **BLW**: N **RG**: N **MK**: N **PH**: N **SS**: A sect III, pg 355; C part II, pg 214; AP Fold 3 serv rec, muster & payrolls **BS**: 196.

MELTON, Richard; b 1717 Hanover Co, d 1795 **RU**: Patriot, gave material aid to cause, Prince William Co **CEM**: Bedford Presbyterian Church; GPS not determined; 105 West Main St, Bedford; Bedford **GS**: Unk **SP**: No info **VI**: Son of John Melton (1697-1750) & Mary Elizabeth Preston White (1700-1785) **P**: N **BLW**: N **RG**: N **MK**: N **PH**: N **SS**:AL Comm Bk IV, pg 203 & Ct Bk, pg 10, PWC **BS**: 196.

MENAGER, Louis; b unk; d 1781 **RU**: Soldier, Served in Agenois Bn and died fr battle at Yorktown **CEM**: French Memorial; GPS 36.81944, -79.39933; Yorktown; York **GS**: U **SP**: No info **VI**: No further data **P**: unk **BLW**: unk **RG**: Y **MK**: unk **PH**: unk **SS**: J-Yorktown Historian; SAR P-247808 **BS**: JLARC 1, 74.

MENARDIER, Jean; b unk; d 1781 **RU**: Seaman, Served on "Saint-Esprit" and died from Yorktown battle **CEM**: French Memorial; GPS 36.81944, -79.39933; Yorktown; York **GS**: U **SP**: No info **VI**: No further data **P**: unk **BLW**: unk **RG**: Y **MK**: unk **PH**: unk **SS**: J-Yorktown Historian; SAR P-247811 **BS**: JLARC 1, 74.

MERCER, George; b 1711; d 1777 **RU**: Captain, Appointed Aide de Camp to Col Geo Washington, 17 Sep 1775 at Ft Cumberland. Killed in Battle at Princeton, 3 Jan 1777 **CEM**: St Stephen's Episcopal; GPS unk; 115 N East St, Culpeper; Culpeper **GS**: Y **SP**: No info **VI**: Son of General Hugh Mercer. Some confusion as to who was killed at Battle of Princeton. General Hugh Mercer certainly was killed there. His tombsone says he d age 66, son of Hugh Mercer "who fell at Princeton" **P**: unk **BLW**: unk **RG**: N **MK**: N **PH**: unk **SS**: G pg 357 **BS**: 167 St Stephens; 196.

MERCER, Hugh; b 27 Jan 1726, Roeharty, Scotland; d 12 Jan 1777 **RU**: Brigadier General, Commanded VA 34rd Regt of Foot Dec 1775-6 June 1782. Promoted to Brig Gen Mortally wounded at Princeton **CEM**: Corporate Burial Ground GPS not determined, loc where Hurcamp Park is today Fredericksburg City **GS**: U **SP**: No info **VI**: Died in Princeton NJ. Burial first in Philadelphia. Memorialized on monument on Washington Ave Fredericksburg **P**: unk **BLW**: unk **RG**: Y **MK**: unk **PH**: unk **SS**: CE pg 38; DAR A077458; SAR P-247878 **BS**: 32.

MERCER, James; b 26 Feb 1736, Marlborough, Stafford Co; d 31 Oct 1793 **RU**: Patriot, Was member VA House of Burgesses 1762-75 and 1st Cont Congress 1779 **CEM**: St John's Episcopal; GPS 37.53183, -77.41958; 2401 E Broad St; Richmond City **GS**: Y **SP**: Eleanor Dick **VI**: Judge of VA General Ct 1779-89. Judge of 1st VA Ct of Appeals 1789 until his death. **P**: N **BLW**: N **RG**: Y **MK**: N **PH**: unk **SS**: AQ; DAR A213427; SAR P-247882 **BS**: 04 Dec 06; 201 pg 7391.

RU=Rank/Unit	CEM=Cemetery	GS=Gravestone	SP=Spousal Information
VI=Other Veteran Info	P=Pension	BLW=Bounty/Land Warrant	RG=Registered Grave
MK=SAR/DAR Marker	PH=Photo	SS=Service Source	BS=Burial Source

MERCER, John; b 1736; d 1793 **RU:** Patriot, Gave material aid to cause **CEM:** St John's Episcopal; GPS 37.53183, -77.41958; 2401 E Broad St; Richmond City **GS:** Y **SP:** No info **VI:** No further data **P:** N **BLW:** N **RG: N MK:** N **PH:** unk **SS:** N pg 145; AL Ct Bk pg 10 Orange Co **BS:** 32 e-mail 3/06.

MERCIER, Andoche; b unk; d 1781 **RU:** Soldier, Served in Beaujolais Bn and died fr battle at Yorktown **CEM:** French Memorial; GPS 36.81944, -79.39933; Yorktown; York **GS:** U **SP:** No info **VI:** No further data **P:** unk **BLW:** unk **RG:** Y **MK:** unk **PH:** unk **SS:** J-Yorktown Historian; SAR P-247908 **BS:** JLARC 1, 74.

MEREDITH, Elijah; b 1756; d 1796 **RU:** Captain, Served in PA **CEM:** Meredith Family; GPS unk; Check property records; New Kent **GS:** U **SP:** Ann Layne Clopton **VI:** No further data **P:** unk **BLW:** unk **RG:** Y **MK:** unk **PH:** unk **SS:** J-NSSAR 1993 Reg; DAR 077571; SAR P-247916; Cl PA Archives **BS:** JLARC 1.Layne.

MEREDITH, James; b 8 Sep 1762; d 20 or 29 Mar 1840 **RU:** Private, Served in VA Line. Ent serv Chesterfield Co **CEM:** Dunham; GPS unk; Rt 630 Cold Harbor; Hanover **GS:** Y **SP:** Mar (27 Dec 1792) Mericha/Merica/Meecha/Megha Hooper (8 Aug 1775 - 5 July 1852) **VI:** Sol appl pen 27 Apr 1833 Hanover Co. Widow appl pen 24 Apr 1843 age 24 Apr 1843 Hanover Co age 68. W3849 **P:** Y **BLW:** unk **RG:** N **MK:** N **PH:** unk **SS:** E pg 544; K Vol 3 pg 249; CG pg 2327 **BS:** 31 vol 1 pg 35.

MEREDITH, Samuel Garland; b 1732; d 1808 **RU:** Colonel/Patriot, Col of 1st Bn of Minutemen in 1776 of the West Augusta District Bn. Member of Lee's Legion. Gave material aid to cause **CEM:** Winton Plantation; GPS unk; adj Winton Country Club, Clifford; Amherst **GS:** U **SP:** Jane Henry (Jun 1738-12 Aug 1819) d/o John (Aberdeen, Scotland) & Sarah (Winston) (___-1784) Henry **VI:** Brother-in-law of Patrick Henry. BLW #12354 **P:** unk **BLW:** Y **RG:** Y **MK:** unk **PH:** unk **SS:** K Vol 3 pg 250; AL List pg 2 Amherst Co; CE pg 23; DAR A077589; SAR P-247936 **BS:** JLARC 1, 4, 7, 101; 80 vol 3, pg 79.

MERIAN, Vincent; b unk; d 1781 **RU:** Seaman, Served on "Sceptre" and died from Yorktown battle **CEM:** French Memorial; GPS 36.81944, -79.39933; Yorktown; York **GS:** U **SP:** No info **VI:** No further data **P:** unk **BLW:** unk **RG:** Y **MK:** unk **PH:** unk **SS:** J-Yorktown Historian; SAR P-247961 **BS:** JLARC 1, 74.

MERIEL, Jean; b unk; d 1781 **RU:** Seaman, Served on "Diademe" and died from Yorktown battle **CEM:** French Memorial; GPS 36.81944, -79.39933; Yorktown; York **GS:** U **SP:** No info **VI:** No further data **P:** unk **BLW:** unk **RG:** Y **MK:** unk **PH:** unk **SS:** J-Yorktown Historian; SAR P-247963 **BS:** JLARC 1, 74.

MERIWETHER, William Douglas; b 2 Nov 1761; d 27 Jan 1845 **RU:** Sergeant, Served in Clark's Illinois Regt 1782 **CEM:** Clover Fields; GPS unk; Rt 22 NE off I-64, W of Charlottesville; Charlottesville City **GS:** N **SP:** Elizabeth Lewis (6 Jun 1769 Henrico Co-27 Mar 1841) d/o Nicholas (1734-1808) & Mary (Walker) (1742-1824) Lewis **VI:** Son of Nicholas Meriwether (1736-1772) & Margaret Douglas (1737-1812) **P:** unk **BLW:** unk **RG:** N **MK:** unk **PH:** N **SS:** E pg 545 **BS:** JLARC 58; 196.

MERKOT, Georges; b unk; d 1781 **RU:** Soldier, Served in Royal Deaux Ponts Bn and died fr battle at Yorktown **CEM:** French Memorial; GPS 36.81944, -79.39933; Yorktown; York **GS:** U **SP:** No info **VI:** No further data **P:** unk **BLW:** unk **RG:** Y **MK:** unk **PH:** unk **SS:** J-Yorktown Historian; SAR P-248008 **BS:** JLARC 1, 74.

MERRITT, Samuel; b c1758; d Aft 1820 **RU:** Soldier, Served in the 2nd VA Regt in1777 **CEM:** Fincastle Presbyterian; GPS 37.50017, -79.87558; 108 E Back St, Fincastle; Botetourt **GS:** N **SP:** Mar (30 Jul 1817 Botetourt Co) Mary Keith (___-Aft 1820) **VI:** Occupation: Laborer. Pensioned 1818 in Botetourt Co, residing there with family 1820. Appl for pen 14 May 1818. S38206. Name is on the SAR plaque at this cemetery **P:** Y **BLW:** unk **RG:** Y **MK:** Y SAR plaque **PH:** N **SS:** K Vol 3 pg 252; CG pg 2337; SAR P-248364 **BS:** 196; JLARC 1, 4, 60.

MERRYMAN, John; b 1763, MD; d 18 Aug 1849 **RU:** Private?, Served in 1st VA Regt **CEM:** Mt Hebron; GPS 39.10916, -78.09497; 305 E Boscawen St; Winchester City **GS:** Y **SP:** No info **VI:** No further data **P:** unk **BLW:** unk **RG:** N **MK:** Y SAR monument **PH:** unk **SS:** E pg 546 **BS:** 65 Winchester; 196.

MERY, Antoine; b unk; d 1781 **RU:** Soldier, Served in Bourbonnais Bn; Died battle at Yorktown **CEM:** French Memorial; GPS 36.81944, -79.39933; Yorktown; York **GS:** U **SP:** No info **VI:** No further data **P:** unk **BLW:** unk **RG:** Y **MK:** unk **PH:** unk **SS:** J-Yorktown Historian; SAR P-248462 **BS:** JLARC 1, 74.

RU=Rank/Unit	CEM=Cemetery	GS=Gravestone	SP=Spousal Information
VI=Other Veteran Info	P=Pension	BLW=Bounty/Land Warrant	RG=Registered Grave
MK=SAR/DAR Marker	PH=Photo	SS=Service Source	BS=Burial Source

286

MEYERS, John; b unk; d 1828 **RU:** Private, Served in Lee's Legion **CEM:** Mt Zion Church; GPS 36.83461, -81.59338; Old Ebenezer Rd, Marioin; Smyth **GS:** Y **SP:** No info **VI:** No further data **P:** unk **BLW:** unk **RG:** N **MK:** N **PH:** unk **SS:** A pg 115; G pg 650 **BS:** 97 pg 110.

MEYERS, Samuel; b 1748; d 22 Aug 1830 **RU:** Lieutenant, Served in Capt Crogham's Co, Nov 1778 **CEM:** Hebrew; GPS 33.55175, -77.42976; 300 Hospital St; Richmond City **GS:** Y **SP:** No info **VI:** No further data **P:** unk **BLW:** Y **RG:** N **MK:** N **PH:** unk **SS:** C pg 255; E pg 576; AP record; CI Muster Roll reel 119 pg 7 **BS:** 184.

MICHAUX, Jacob; b unk, Powhatan Co, d c1782 **RU:** Patriot, gave material aid to cause Powhatan Co **CEM:** Michaux Family; GPS-Not determined; east of Rt 522 just south of James River in sub-division Michaux Grant Farms; Powhatan **GS:** No **SP:** Sally Neville **VI:** Son of Jacob Michaux and Judith Woodson. His estate gave material aid to cause during period 1780-1783 as well as him just bef he died **P:** N **BLW:** N **RG:** N **MK:** N **PH:** N **SS:** AL Ct Bk pg 28 & Certificate **BS:** Powhatan Co Historical Society.

MICHELET, Jean; b unk; d 1781 **RU:** Soldier, Served in Soissonnais Bn and died fr battle at Yorktown **CEM:** French Memorial; GPS 36.81944, -79.39933; Yorktown; York **GS:** U **SP:** No info **VI:** No further data **P:** unk **BLW:** unk **RG:** Y **MK:** unk **PH:** unk **SS:** J-Yorktown Historian; SAR P-248738 **BS:** JLARC 1, 74.

MICKLE, Elijah Watson; b 26 Jul 1740, York Co, PA; d 26 May 1817 **RU:** Soldier, Served in Capt Jame's Elliot's Co in PA **CEM:** Rock Spring; GPS 37.78126, -79.44585; Jct Rt 803 & Liberty Hall Rd, Lodi; Washington **GS:** Y **SP:** Mary Cox (1740-1826) **VI:** No further data **P:** unk **BLW:** unk **RG:** N **MK:** unk **PH:** Y **SS:** CI PA Archives, CI PA Archives General Index Vol XXI pg 70, 339, 612 **BS:** 196.

MIDDLETON, William; b 1767; d 1832 **RU:** Drummer, Served also as a Coronet in Lee's Legion **CEM:** Old Opequon Church; GPS 39.82237, -78.11412; 217 Opequon Church Ln, Kernstown; Frederick **GS:** Y **SP:** No info **VI:** No further data **P:** unk **BLW:** unk **RG :** Y **MK:** unk **PH:** unk **SS:** J- DAR Hatcher; A pg 288; E pg 548; SAR P-248825 **BS:** JLARC 2; 80, vol 3, pg 83; 196.

MIFFORD, Jacob; b 1764; d 1798 **RU:** Private, Served at age 18 in Frederick Co, MD Regt in Mar 1782 **CEM:** Fincastle Presbyterian; GPS 37.50017, -79.87558; 108 E Back St, Fincastle; Botetourt **GS:** N **SP:** no info **VI:** Name is on the SAR plaque at this cemetery **P:** unk **BLW:** unk **RG:** Y **MK:** Y SAR plaque **PH:** N **SS:** AR Vol 3 pg 83; AP serv Record; J-NSSAR 1993 Reg, J- DAR Hatcher; SAR P-248845 **BS:** JLARC 1, 2; 80, vol 3, pg 83 196.

MILLAN, Thomas; b 01 Mar 1750, Millstone, Somerset Co, NJ; d 27 Apr 1828 **RU:** Ensign/ Patriot, Served in Loudoun Co Militia in Capt William Lane's Co, 1779-1781. He donated time as waggoner and gave 1100# beef, 50 bu of rye and cash payments of L900 sterling **CEM:** Fairfax City; GPS 38.84690, -77.31330; Main St & Page Ave; Fairfax City **GS:** Y **SP:** 1) Mar (c1774) Elizabeth Shedd (1750-1791); 2) Susannah Summers **VI:** Son of William & Elizabeth (Lyle) Millan of Scotland. Older Govt stone marks his grave **P:** N **BLW:** N **RG:** Y SAR **MK:** Y **PH:** Y **SS:** AK; AZ pg 213, CD; DAR A978915; SAR P-248892 **BS:** JLARC 1, 2, 14, 27; 04; 80, vol 3, pg 83; 196.

MILLAN, William; b 1765; d 28 Jul 1813 **RU:** Patriot, Gave material aid to the cause **CEM:** Millan/Potter Family; GPS unk; 7925 Telegraph Rd; Fairfax **GS:** Y **SP:** No info **VI:** No further data **P:** N **BLW:** N **RG:** N **MK:** N **PH:** unk **SS:** AL Ct Bk pg 26 **BS:** 60 Fairfax Co; 61 vol V pg FB-17.

MILLAN, William; b unk; d 1810 **RU:** Patriot, Gave material aid to cause **CEM:** Fairfax City; GPS 38.84690, -77.31330; Main St & Page Ave; Fairfax City **GS:** N **SP:** No info **VI:** No further data **P:** N **BLW:** N **RG:** Y **MK:** N **PH:** N **SS:** J-NSSAR 2000 Reg; D Loudoun Co; SAR P-248983 **BS:** JLARC 76.

MILLER, Christian; b 1744, near Woodstock, Shenandoah Co; d 26 Apr 1836 **RU:** Sergeant, Served in Shenandoah Co Militia where ent serv **CEM:** Miller Family; GPS unk; Woodstock; Shenandoah **GS:** U **SP:** Mar (1770) Catharine Wisman (__-2 Feb 1839) **VI:** Sol appl pen 10 Sep 1832 Shenandoah Co age 88. Widow appl 28 Jul 1837 Shenandoah Co. W18515 **P:** Y **BLW:** unk **RG:** Y **MK:** N **PH:** unk **SS:** E pg 549; CG pg 2349; SAR P-249103 **BS:** DAR report. 80, vol 3, pg 84.

MILLER, Henry; b unk, d 1815 **RU:** Private Capt Joseph Bowman's Co, Shenandoah County, Col William Crawford's Regt 1774-1775 for 156 days; Served later in Dunmore County Militia which became Shenandoah County 1778 **CEM:** Shenandoah Farm; GPS ; 38.9345640, -78.4414930; loc Tea Berry

RU=Rank/Unit	CEM=Cemetery	GS=Gravestone	SP=Spousal Information
VI=Other Veteran Info	P=Pension	BLW=Bounty/Land Warrant	RG=Registered Grave
MK=SAR/DAR Marker	PH=Photo	SS=Service Source	BS=Burial Source

Rd, E in field adjacent to power line, Maurerton; Shenandoah **GS**: Unk **SP**: No info **VI**: No further data **P**: Unk **BLW**: Unk **RG**: N **MK**: N **PH**: unk **SS**: C pg 605; E pg 549 **BS**: 196.

MILLER, Henry; b unk; d 1812 **RU**: Captain, Served in Fraizer's Co, Augusta Co Militia **CEM**: Miller Family; GPS unk; 4998 Scenic Hwy, Bridgewater; Augusta **GS**: Y **SP**: No info **VI**: GS lying flat--needs resetting **P**: unk **BLW**: unk **RG**: N **MK**: unk **PH**: Y **SS**: E pg 549 **BS**: 196.

MILLER, Henry; b 1726; d 1798 **RU**: Patriot, Gave material aid to cause in Rockbridge Co **CEM**: Miller-Irwin; GPS 37.65116, -79.52014; Dry Well Rd Rt 813, on left at Charles Ln; Lexington City **GS**: Y **SP**: Rebecca Beggs/Boggs (1736-1816) **VI**: Moved fr Lancaster Co to Botetourt (now Rockbridge). Recd BLW 400 acres in Greenlee Grant. Died in Farquier Co. Will proved Oct 1797. New memorial monument **P**: N **BLW**: Y **RG**: N **MK**: unk **PH**: Y **SS**: AL Ct Bk 4 & 16 **BS**: 196.

MILLER, Henry; b 14 Jul 1761 or 1764, Rockingham Co, d 18 Sep 1850 **RU**: Private Entered serv 1781, served in Capt Joseph Bowmans Co at Romney, OH, less than 6 mos serv. Also under Col Nalle and his uncle Capt Michael Coger **CEM**: Elk Run; GPS: 38.4102,-78.61033; off Rt 623 to E, vic jct with E Spotswood Ave; Rockingham **GS**: Y **SP**: Mar 1787, Mary Price (12 May 1765-__), d/o Augustine Price (31 May 1722-16 Oct 1802) & Anna Elizabeth Scherp **VI**: Sol appl pen 21 Aug 1832 Rockingham Co, pen #FR7196, and R 1725. Obit shows rank of Captain **P**: Y **BLW**: N **RG**: N **MK**: N **PH**: N **SS**: K vol 3, pg 260; N pg 1251; AK; E pg 549; CG pg 2354; DAR A078931 **BS**: 196.

MILLER, Henry II; b 4 Jan 1759; d 7 Jan 1833 **RU**: Private?, Served in Col Morgan's Rifle Regt **CEM**: Masonic Cemetery; GPS unk; Rt 522, Washington; Rappahannock **GS**: Y **SP**: Mar (14 May 1782, Winchester) Achsah Margaret Warner (1762-23 Feb 1833) **VI**: Son of Henry (1727 Germany-1796 Madison Co) & Susannah (Sibler) (2 Feb 1730, Germany-1796) Miller **P**: unk **BLW**: unk **RG**: N **MK**: N **PH**: unk **SS**: E pg 549 **BS**: 33.

MILLER, Jacob; b 2 Oct 1748, Washington Co, MD; d 11 Jul 1815 **RU**: Patriot, Gave material aid to the cause **CEM**: Garber Family; GPS unk; Vic Moores Store; Shenandoah **GS**: Y **SP**: Anna Martha Wine (1753 Lancaster Co, PA-1795) d/o Locowich (1724-1792) & Barbara Ann (-----) Miller **VI**: No further data **P**: N **BLW**: N **RG**: N **MK**: N **PH**: unk **SS**: AL ct Bk pg 18 **BS**: 79 pg 24.

MILLER, John; b 1753, d aft will signed 19 May1811 **RU**: Private Illinois Regt VA State Line **CEM**: Old Fairfield Baptist Church; GPS 37.90305, -7636295, loc at jct Rts 640 and 646, Edwardsville; Northumberland **GS**: Unk **SP**: No info **VI**: Heirs recd BLW # 8352 for 100 acres 3 Aug 1835 **P**: N **BLW**: Y **RG**: Y **MK**: N **PH**: N **SS**: E pg 550; N pgs 1051-1053; SAR P-249441 **BS**: 196.

MILLER, John; b 5 Feb 1762, Philadelphia, PA; d 3 Aug 1841 **RU**: Captain, Probably served in Morgan's Co in Grayson's Regt or in Capt Maybury's Co in May 1778. Served fr July 1775 to Jan 1783. **CEM**: Miller at Mountain Green; GPS 38.734112, -78.171700; Rt 248, Harris Hollow, Washington; Rappahannock **GS**: Y **SP**: Nancy Hitt (14 Jun 1774 - 22 Sep 1859) **VI**: Son of Henry Miller (1727-1801) & Susannah Sibler (1731-__). Grave moved fr Kinloch farm. An original member of Society of Cincinnati **P**: unk **BLW**: unk **RG**: N **MK**: N **PH**: Y **SS**: E pg 550 **BS**: 33; 163; 210 pg 353; 196.

MILLER, John; b 1709 Northern Ireland, d 1784 **RU**: Patriot, paid personal property tax 1782 Augusta Co, considered applied toward Rev War expenses **CEM**: Miller Family; GPS not determined; loc top of hill at 4998 Iron Works Road (Rt. 42); Augusta **GS**: Unk **SP**: Mar c1735, Ireland, Martha Blankenship (1712, Ireland-__) **VI**: Son of William Miller. Was militiamen in Captain John Smith's Company in 1742, and fought in the French and Indian War as members of Captain George Wilson's Company in 1756 **P**: N **BLW**: N **RG**: N **MK**: N **PH**: N **SS**: DV 1782B image 08.pdf, Augusta Co **BS**: 196.

MILLER, John; b 6 May 1760, Shenandoah Co, d 1826 **RU**: Patriot, paid personal property tax, Shenandoah Co, 1783 considered a partial payment for Rev War expenses **CEM**: First Trinity Lutheran Church; GPS not determined; loc Ida; Page **GS**: Unk **SP**: No spousal data **VI**: No further data 1756 **P**: N **BLW**: N **RG**: N **MK**: N **PH**: N **SS**: DV 1783 image.13.pdf, Shenandoah Co **BS**: 196.

MILLER, Mathias; b 18 Oct 1743, Berks City, PA; d Dec 1805 **RU**: Private, Served in 3rd PA Regt **CEM**: Rader Lutheran; GPS 38.65073, -78.78055; 17072 Raders Church Rd, Timberville; Rockingham **GS**: Y **SP**: 1) Susanna C. Mueller 2) Catherine Aulenbach 3) (-----) 4) Anna Mariea Moyer Schaeffer **VI**: Moved to VA in 1794-5 **P**: unk **BLW**: unk **RG**: Y **MK**: Y SAR **PH**: Y **SS**: J-NSSAR 1993 Reg; P pg 386; CI Serv Rec Muster Roll; SAR P-249544 **BS**: JLARC 1.

RU=Rank/Unit	CEM=Cemetery	GS=Gravestone	SP=Spousal Information
VI=Other Veteran Info	P=Pension	BLW=Bounty/Land Warrant	RG=Registered Grave
MK=SAR/DAR Marker	PH=Photo	SS=Service Source	BS=Burial Source

MILLER, Michael; b 1765 York Co PA; d 17 Sep 1817 **RU**: Private, Served in VA unit in Illinois in Capt James Taylor's Co, Col Wayne's PA Bn 1776 **CEM**: Old Weaver Church; GPS 38.44868, -78.90463; Harrisonville; Rockingham **GS**: Y **SP**: Elizabeth Breneman (22 Feb 1773-Mar 1815) D/o Abaham (1744-1815) & Maria (Reiff) (1746-1788) Breneman **VI**: No further data **P**: unk **BLW**: unk **RG**: Y **MK**: N **PH**: unk **SS**: E pg 550; SAR P-249553 **BS**: 191 Shank; 196.

MILLER, Peter; b 1741 PA; d 15 Nov. 1819 **RU**: Patriot, Gave material aid to cause **CEM**: Old Peaked Mountain; GPS 38.37113, -78.73416; 9843 Town Hall Rd, McGaheysville; Rockingham **GS**: Y **SP**: 1) Martha Kropp 2) Rachel Ramsey **VI**: Common DAR monument **P**: N **BLW**: N **RG**: Y **MK**: Y DAR plaque **PH**: unk **SS**: J-NSSAR 2000 Reg; AL Ct Bk II pg 10, 11 Rockingham Co; DAR A079529; SAR P-249609 **BS**: JLARC 76.

MILLER, Robert; b 5 May 1734 Albemarle Co, d 24 Oct 1806 **RU**: Captain, took oath 27 May 1779, Orange Co Militia **CEM**: Miller Family; GPS Unk; 4899 So River Rd, Stanardsville; Greene **GS**: Yes **SP**: Mar 1763, White Hall, Albemarle Co, Margaret Maupin (1735 Albemarle Co-26 Jan 1827) **VI**: Son of Robert Miller (1707, Ireland-18 Oct 1781) and Ann Lynn (1710, Orange Co-1750 Albemarle Co), He drew a pension in Orange Co **P**: Y **BLW**: N **RG**: Y **MK**: Y **PH**: N **SS**: E pg 550; AZ pg 220; DAR A079576; SAR application; SAR P-248638 **BS**: 196.

MILLER, Samuel; b 1738, Lancaster, PA; d 1789 **RU**: Private, Served in Capt Henry Mathias Co, Col Smyser's Regt, PA Militia. **CEM**: Miller Family; GPS unk; Harrisonburg; Harrisonburg City **GS**: Y **SP**: Mar (c1760) Magdalena Wiley (__ York Co, PA-aft 8 Aug 1768) **VI**: No further data **P**: unk **BLW**: unk **RG**:Y **MK**: N **PH**: unk **SS**: DAR A079600; E pg 550; AS SAR applic; CI: PA Archives 6th Series Vol 2 pg 481, 482; SAR P-249662 **BS**: SAR Appl.

MILLER, Samuel; b 1 Mar 1760, Lancaster Co, PA; d 26 Apr 1846 **RU**: Private, Served in Capt Reuben Harrison's Co, Augusta Co Militia **CEM**: Miller-Irwin; GPS 37.65116, -79.52014; Dry Well Rd Rt 813, on left at Charles Ln; Lexington City **GS**: U **SP**: Mar (1 Jan 1787) Margaret Lackey (c1767-1854) d/o Thomas & Agnes (Leech) Lackey **VI**: Son of Henry (1726-1798) & Rebecca (Boggs) (1736-1816) Miller. Died in Rockbridge Co **P**: unk **BLW**: unk **RG**: N **MK**: unk **PH**: unk **SS**: E pg 550 **BS**: 196.

MILLER, William; b unk; d 1793 **RU**: Captain/Patriot, Served in1st Cont artillery. Gave material aid to cause. **CEM**: Vauter's Episcopal; GPS unk; Rt 368 off Rt 17, Loretto; Essex **GS**: U **SP**: Susanna Neale **VI**: Grave moved fr family plot **P**: unk **BLW**: unk **RG**: Y **MK**: N **PH**: unk **SS**: D Caroline Co; SAR P-249723 **BS**: JLARC 1, 65.

MILLER, William; b 1 Mar 1757, Lancaster, PA; d 7 Nov 1840 **RU**: Private, Ent serv 1780. Served in Capt Gaines Gilmore Co Rockbridge Co Militia **CEM**: Broad Creek-Miller; GPS unk; Buffalo Dist; Rockbridge **GS**: Y **SP**: Elizabeth Lackey **VI**: Moved to Rockbridge Co c1767. **P**: unk **BLW**: unk **RG**: Y **MK**: N **PH**: unk **SS**: J-NSSAR 1993 Reg; K Vol 3 pg 264; DAR A079698; SAR P-249737 **BS**: JLARC 1.

MILLERT, Michel; b unk; d 1781 **RU**: Soldier, Served in Metz Bn and died fr battle at Yorktown **CEM**: French Memorial; GPS 36.81944, -79.39933; Yorktown; York **GS**: U **SP**: No info **VI**: No further data **P**: unk **BLW**: unk **RG**: Y **MK**: unk **PH**: unk **SS**: J-Yorktown Historian; SAR P-249776 **BS**: JLARC 1, 74.

MILLIOT, Gaspard; b unk; d 1781 **RU**: Soldier, Served in Gatinais Bn; D battle at Yorktown **CEM**: French Memorial; GPS 36.81944, -79.39933; Yorktown; York **GS**: U **SP**: No info **VI**: No further data **P**: unk **BLW**: unk **RG**: Y **MK**: unk **PH**: unk **SS**: J-Yorktown Historian; SAR P-249863 **BS**: JLARC 1, 74.

MILLS, John; b c1760, nr Dromore, County Down, Ireland; d 14 Jun 1800 **RU**: Private, Served in Capt Trimble's & Capt Campbell's companies, Augusta Co; Served in the 12th and 13th Cont Line long enough to receive a pension for service **CEM**: Augusta Stone Presbyterian; GPS 38.23926, -78.97356, GS38.1414,-78.5820; 28 Old Stone Church Ln, Ft Defiance; Augusta **GS**: Y **SP**: Frances Hall, d/o John & Elizabeth Hall, d Aug 1843 **VI**: Recd pension in Augusta Co. Memorial stone erected in 1926 says he settled on Middle River abt 1780, gives no date of birth **P**: Y **BLW**: unk **RG**: Y **MK**: Y SAR plaque k **PH**: unk **SS**: E pg 551; DAR A079975; SAR 249949 **BS**: JLARC 1, 2, 8, 23, 62; 196.

MILLS, Robert; b c1760, nr Dromore, County Down, Ireland; d Sep 1785 **RU**: Sergeant, Served in 6th & 11th Cont line. Served as Sgt in Capt Charles Gallahue's Co,12th Cont line, May 1777 **CEM**: Augusta Stone Presbyterian; GPS 38.23926, -78.97356 GS38.1414,-78.5820; 28 Old Stone Church Ln, Ft Defiance; Augusta **GS**: Y **SP**: Susannah (------) (__-1799) **VI**: Memorial stone erected in 1926 says he

RU=Rank/Unit	CEM=Cemetery	GS=Gravestone	SP=Spousal Information
VI=Other Veteran Info	P=Pension	BLW=Bounty/Land Warrant	RG=Registered Grave
MK=SAR/DAR Marker	PH=Photo	SS=Service Source	BS=Burial Source

settled on Middle River before 1780. Gives no date of birth **P:** unk **BLW:** unk **RG:** Y **MK** Y SAR plaque **PH:** unk **SS:** A pg 257; E pg 552; SAR P-250009 **BS:** JLARC 2, 8; 196.

MILLS, William; b 1760; d 22 Aug 1798 **RU:** Captain, Signed oath as Capt 18 Sep 1777, Spotsylvania Co Miitia. Possibly also served in 6th & 8th Cont Lines **CEM:** Brawner; GPS unk; Rt 1 at Potomac HS; Prince William **GS:** Y **SP:** Peggy Swift **VI:** No further data **P:** unk **BLW:** unk **RG:** N **MK:** N **PH:** unk **SS:** E pg 552; H **BS:** 15 pg 226.

MILLS, William; b 1740, Hanover Co; d bef will proven date 14 Nov 1831, Henry Co **RU:** Patriot, gave material aid to cause, Hanover Co, during 1781-1782 period **CEM:** Mills Family; GPS not determined; loc on land owned by his son, Francis Mills called "Mills Order,"adjacent to land of John Fontaine on Matrimony Creek; Henry **GS:** N **SP:** Elizabeth Fontaine (1747-1804), d/o Rev Peter Fontaine (1691-1757) & Elizabeth Ware (1720-1784) **VI:** No further data **P:** unk **BLW:** unk **RG:** N **MK:** N **PH:** N **SS:** AL Ct Bk1 pg 25, Comm List III, pg 191, Hanover Co **BS:** 196.

MILLS, William; b 1760; d unk **RU:** Private, Served in 6th & 8th Cont Line **CEM:** Mills' Family; GPS unk; Standardsville; Greene **GS:** N **SP:** No info **VI:** No further data **P:** unk **BLW:** unk **RG:** N **MK:** N **PH:** N **SS:** E pg 552 **BS:** 192.

MILNER, Thomas; b 1760; d By 1826 **RU:** Private?/Patriot, Served in 4th Cont line. Gave to cause in Isle of Wight Co **CEM:** Eastern State Hospital; GPS 37.25560, -76.71030; S Henry Street; Williamsburg City **GS:** N **SP:** No info **VI:** No further data **P:** unk **BLW:** unk **RG:** N **MK:** N **PH:** N **SS:** E pg 552; AL Ct Bk pg 12 **BS:** 65 Williamsburg.

MIMS, David; b 1 Jan 1701, d Oct 1781 **RU:** Patriot, Gave material aid to cause **CEM:** Mims Family; GPS unk; Manakin; Goochland **GS:** U **SP:** Mar (1721 Goochland Co) Agnes Weldy (1705-1May 1777) **VI:** Son of Thomas & Amelia Anne (Martin) Mims **P:** N **BLW:** N **RG:** N **MK:** unk **PH:** unk **SS:** AL Ct Bk pg 4 **BS:** 196.

MIMS, David Jr; b 1748, Goochland Co; d 16 Oct 1786 **RU:** Patriot, Gave material aid to cause **CEM:** Mims Family; GPS unk; Licking Hole Creek Farm; Richmond Co **GS:** Y **SP:** Mar (5 Oct 1773) Martha Duiguid (20 Mar 1756-aft 1786) **VI:** No further data **P:** N **BLW:** N **RG:**Y **MK:** N **PH:** unk **SS:** DAR A080131; AL Certificate, Goochland Co; AS; SAR P-250122 **BS:** 80 vol 3; pg 90.

MINGE, David; b c1746, Charles City Co; d Aft 16 May 1779 **RU:** Captain/Patriot, Was Co Cmdr in May 1779 in Charles City Co Militia. Civil service on County Committee **CEM:** Weyanoke; GPS 37.17300, -77.35600; Rt 619 off Rt 5; Charles City Co **GS:** U **SP:** Mar (1765) Christiana Shields (25 Dec 1745, York Co-aft 1790) **VI:** No further data **P:** unk **BLW:** unk **RG:** Y **MK:** N **PH:** unk **SS:** DAR A080314; SAR P-250191; E pg 552 **BS:** 127 Minge.

MINIO, Antoine; b unk; d 1781 **RU:** Seaman, Served on "Saint-Esprit"; D Yorktown battle **CEM:** French Memorial; GPS 36.81944, -79.39933; Yorktown; York **GS:** U **SP:** No info **VI:** No further data **P:** unk **BLW:** unk **RG:** Y **MK:** unk **PH:** unk **SS:** J-Yorktown Historian; SAR P-250206 **BS:** JLARC 1, 74.

MINOR, Garritt (Garit/Garett); b 11 Mar 1744; d 25 Jun 1799 **RU:** Major; Capt, commanded a co of Louisa Co Militia, Oct 1776; Later achieved rank of Major **CEM:** Sunning Hill Plantation; GPS not determined; Louisa; Louisa **GS:** Y **SP:** mar (18 May 1769) Mary Overton Terrill (22 May 1760, Louisa Co-30 Oct 1830, Louisa Co) **VI:** Son of John Minor (1707-1755) & Sarah Dabney (1719-1791) **P:** unk **BLW:** unk **RG:** Y **MK:** unk **PH:** unk **SS:** CE pg 19; SAR 250272 **BS:** JLARC 2, 76; 80, vol 3, pg 90; 196.

MINOR, James Carr; b 18 Jul 1745, d 9 Jun 1791 **RU:** Patriot; Commissioner of Provision Law and Justice during war period, Albemarle Co; Gave material aid to cause **CEM:** Gale Hill; GPS: unk; 2438 Quarles Rd, Proffit, Albemarle **GS:** Yes **SP:** Mary Carr (14 Sep 1756, Louisa Co-7 Jul 1797), d/o John Carr (1706-1778) & Barbara Overton (1720-1794) **VI:** Married his first cousin **P:** N **BLW:** N **RG:** N **MK:** N **PH:** N **SS:** AL Ct Bk pgs l, 10, 11, 16, 17, 29, 32, Albemarle Co; **BS:** 196

MINOR, John Jr; b 13 May 1761, Topping Forest, Caroline Co; d 8 Jun 1816 **RU:** Soldier/Patriot, Specific service not determined. Gave material aid to cause **CEM:** Masonic Cemetery; GPS 38.30198, -77.46142; 900 Charles St; Fredericksburg City **GS:** Y **SP:** 1) Mary Berkeley of Hanover Co (d mos after wedding) 2) Lucy Landon Carter (29 Apr 1776 - 26 Dec 1855) d/o Landon C. & (-----) Carter of "Cleve", King George Co. **VI:** Member VA House of Delegates; Attorney; Presidential Elector for James Monroe;

RU=Rank/Unit	CEM=Cemetery	GS=Gravestone	SP=Spousal Information
VI=Other Veteran Info	P=Pension	BLW=Bounty/Land Warrant	RG=Registered Grave
MK=SAR/DAR Marker	PH=Photo	SS=Service Source	BS=Burial Source

290

Introduced first bill to emancipate slaves and colonize them elsewhere, which was soundly defeated; General in War of 1812. Moved to Masonic Cem fr Hazel Hill in Fredericksburg in 1855. D Richmond **P:** unk **BLW:** unk **RG:** Y **MK:** Y SAR plaque & Marker **PH:** Y **SS:** D Caroline Co SAR P-250249 **BS:** JLARC 2, 4, 76, 91; 80, vol 3, pg 90; 196.

MINOR, Thomas; b 17 Dec 1751; d 21 Jul 1834 **RU:** Captain/Patriot, Ent serv 1777 in VA Regt. Was commander of Spotsylvania Co 1775. Was also Aide-de-Camp to General Edward Stevens,1781 at the siege of Yorktown. Gave beef to cause Jun 1781. **CEM:** Minor Family; GPS unk; Rt 633, nr Locust Grove homestead; Spotsylvania **GS:** Y **SP:** Mar (1780, probably Caroline Co) Elizabeth Taylor (__-7 Dec 1836) d/o Col James & (-----) Taylor of Caroline Co **VI:** Recd BLW #5374 & #1679-300 & Pension and VA Half Pay See N.A. Account #874 & #050117 1/2 pay. Filed 15 May 1828 Spottsylvania Co. Widow and surviving children granted pen W5374 **P:** Y **BLW:** Y **RG:** Y **MK:** Y SAR **PH:** unk **SS:** H; K Vol 3 pg 270; CG pg 2374-75; CE pg 15; SAR P-250264 **BS:** 09 Part 2.

MINOR, Vivion; b 4 Nov 1750; d 29 Sep 1791 **RU:** Captain, Ent serv 1775 Caroline Co. Served in 3rd VA Regt. Was Capt of Caroline Co Militia 1776 **CEM:** Jericho; GPS unk; North Anna River; Caroline **GS:** U **SP:** 1) Mar (11 Feb 1752) Barbara Crosby (11 Feb 1752-21 Sep 1778) d/o David & Mary (-----) Crosby; 2) Mar (31 Mar 1780 at her father's in Caroline Co) Elizabeth Dick (12 Jan 1760-1 Apr 1846) d/o Rev Archibald Dick **VI:** Son of John & Sarah (-----) Minor. Recd pen W-23992, filed 26 Nov 1838 Caroline Co. **P:** Y **BLW:** unk **RG:** Y **MK:** N **PH:** unk **SS:** K Vol 3 pg 270; CG pg 2375; CE pg 15; SAR P-250269 **BS:** JLARC 4, 15.

MINTER, Anthony; b 1739; d 1808 **RU:** Patriot, Gave material aid to cause **CEM:** Rural; GPS unk; Powhatan; Powhatan **GS:** N **SP:** Mar (19 Dec 1777) Catherine Brownley **VI:** No further data **P:** N **BLW:** N **RG:** Y **MK:** N **PH:** N **SS:** AL Ct Bk pg 24 Powhatan Co; AS SAR regis; SAR P-250300 **BS:** SAR regis.

MINTER, John Silas; b 1750, Powhatan Co; d 1833 **RU:** Patriot, gave material aid to cause, Henry Co **CEM:** Silas Minter Sr; GPS unk; loc on hill above 596 Ravenscroft Rd, Martinsville, Leatherwood; Henry **GS:** Yes new **SP:** Susannah Williams (1756, Powhatan Co-1853) d/o John Williams (1722-1772) & Elizabeth Weaver **VI:** Son of Anthony Morgan Minter, Jr & Elizabeth Jane Harris **P:** N **BLW:** N **RG:** Y **MK:** N **PH:** N **SS:** D, vol 2, pgs 507, 519; DAR A133334; SAR P-250308 **BS:** 196.

MION, Pierre; b unk; d 1781 **RU:** Soldier, Served in Touraine Bn; D battle at Yorktown **CEM:** French Memorial; GPS 36.81944, -79.39933; Yorktown; York **GS:** U **SP:** No info **VI:** No further data **P:** unk **BLW:** unk **RG:** Y **MK:** unk **PH:** unk **SS:** J-Yorktown Historian SAR P-250324 **BS:** JLARC 1, 74.

MIOT, Pierre; b unk; d 1781 **RU:** Soldier, Served in Touraine Bn; D battle at Yorktown **CEM:** French Memorial; GPS 36.81944, -79.39933; Yorktown; York **GS:** U **SP:** No info **VI:** No further data **P:** unk **BLW:** unk **RG:** Y **MK:** unk **PH:** unk **SS:** J-Yorktown Historian; SAR P-250327 **BS:** JLARC 1, 74.

MITCHELL, James; b 1750, Glascow, Scotland; d 19 Jun 1787 **RU:** Corporal, Enlisted 25 Jan 1776, served entire war in Cont Line **CEM:** Old Presbyterian Meeting House; GPS 38.48528, -77.23532; 323 S Fairfax St; Alexandria City **GS:** N **SP:** No info **VI:** Recd 400 acres BLW Apr 1785 for 3 yrs service; died age 37; death notice in the Alexandria Gazette 21 Jun 1793 **P:** unk **BLW:** Y **RG:** Y **MK:** Y SAR plaque **PH:** N **SS:** C pg 474; F pg 48; SAR P-250436. **BS:** 23 pg 105; 196.

MITCHELL, James; b 1740; d 1806 **RU:** Lieutenant, Served in Lt Tate's Co VA Inf **CEM:** Bethel Presbyterian; GPS 38.04257, -79.17283, GS 38.0232,-79.1020; 563 Bethel Green Rd, Middlebrook; Augusta **GS:** Y **SP:** Elizabeth Beard **VI:** Govt stone gives yr of death only, thus birth yr is only an estimate. DAR marker placed here. **P:** unk **BLW:** unk **RG:** Y **MK:** Y DAR **PH:** Y **SS:** E pg 554; B; BT; DAR A080545; SAR P-250431 **BS:** JLARC 2, 9, 62, 63; 80 vol3, pg 91; 196.

MITCHELL, James; b 1750; d 1795 **RU:** Lieutenant/Patriot, Gave material aid to cause **CEM:** Mitchell Family; GPS unk; Chatham; Pittsylvania **GS:** U **SP:** No info **VI:** According to 76, one mile E of Callands PO **P:** unk **BLW:** unk **RG:** Y **MK:** unk **PH:** unk **SS:** AL Ct Bk pg 3, 14 Pittsylvania Co; DAR A080540; SAR P-250424 **BS:** JLARC 2, 76; 80 vol3, pg 91; 196.

MITCHELL, John; b 4 May 1763, Amelia Co; d 6 May 1836 **RU:** Fife Major, Enl Amelia Co 1776 in Capt Roland Ward's Co **CEM:** Wright Family; GPS 36.97658, -80.21693; Pizarro, off Rt 668; Floyd **GS:** U **SP:** Obedience Vaughn (27 Sep 1767 Amelia Co-6 May 1836, Floyd Co) d/o James (1763-1803) & (-----)

RU=Rank/Unit VI=Other Veteran Info MK=SAR/DAR Marker / CEM=Cemetery P=Pension PH=Photo / GS=Gravestone BLW=Bounty/Land Warrant SS=Service Source / SP=Spousal Information RG=Registered Grave BS=Burial Source

291

Vaughan **VI:** Name is on DAR plaque in Cem. Filed for pension Sep 1832, age 72 **P:** Y **BLW:** unk **RG:** N **MK:** unk **PH:** unk **SS:** E pg 554; DZ pg 64 **BS:** 196.

MITCHELL, Robert; b 1750; d 29 Apr 1834 **RU:** Ensign, Served in Capt James Kelly's Co, Richmond Co Militia 1776 **CEM:** Bethel Presbyterian; GPS 38.04257, -79.17283, GS 38.0232,-79.1020;; 563 Bethel Green Rd, Middlebrook; Augusta **GS:** Y **SP:** No info **VI:** Age at death on stone illegible, yr of birth, estimate **P:** unk **BLW:** unk **RG:** Y **MK:** unk **PH:** Y **SS:** B; E pg 555; SAR P-250539 **BS:** JLARC 62, 63; 196.

MITCHELL, Robert II; b 1748; d 1827 **RU:** Second Lieutenant, Served in Capt Thomas Belfield's Co, Richmond Co, 3 Nov 1777 **CEM:** Opequon Presbyterian; GPS 39.13938 -78.19494; 217 Opequon Church Ln; Winchester City **GS:** U **SP:** No info **VI:** No further data **P:** unk **BLW:** unk **RG:** N **MK:** unk **PH:** unk **SS:** J- DAR Hatcher; G pg 314 **BS:** JLARC 2.; 80, vol 3, pg 92; 196.

MITCHELL, Stephen; b 1754; d 21 Mar 1807 **RU:** Sergeant, Served in Col Charles Lewis, 14th Regt **CEM:** Mitchell Family; GPS unk; Off Rt 764, 1 mi S of Rt 765, Sylvatus; Carroll **GS:** Y **SP:** Mar (13 Mar 1783) Kitturah/Keturah Wade (1768-1834) **VI:** Son of Robert Mitchell (1714-1799) & Mary Enos (1718-1800). D Grayson Co; Small Govt marker with rank of Sergeant **P:** unk **BLW:** unk **RG:** Y **MK:** Y **PH:** unk **SS:** AP roll #1082; DAR A080682; SAR **250584** **BS:** JLARC 2, 11, 43; 80, vol 3, pg 92; 196.

MITCHELL, Thomas; b 1732; d 30 Dec 1806 **RU:** Private, Served in Porterfield's Co, 11th VA Inf and in Capt Tate's Co, Augusta Co Militia **CEM:** Bethel Presbyterian; GPS 38.04257, -79.17283, GS 38.0232,-79.1020;; 563 Bethel Green Rd, Middlebrook; Augusta **GS:** Y **SP:** 1) Elizabeth McClanahan Moore; 2) Elizabeth Wales **VI:** Govt stone. No date of birth on stone **P:** unk **BLW:** unk **RG:** Y **MK:** unk **PH:** unk **SS:** B **BS:** JLARC 2,9,62, 63; 80, vol 3, pg 92 196.

MITCHELL, William; b 1750; d Dec 1802 **RU:** Captain, Specific service in Lib of VA Council Journals, 1776-7, pgs 45, 64 **CEM:** Old Presbyterian Meeting House; GPS 38.48528, -77.23532; 323 S Fairfax St; Alexandria City **GS:** N **SP:** No info **VI:** Styled Capt in his burial record; Bur 28 Dec 1802 age 42. SAR plaque in cemetery **P:** unk **BLW:** unk **RG:** Y **MK:** Y SAR plaque **PH:** N **SS:** J-NSSAR 1993 Reg; AK; CZ pg 313; SAR P-250589 **BS:** JLARC 1; 23 pg 105; 196.

MITCHELL, William; b 1745 Kilmarnock, East Ayrshire, Scotland; d 10 Feb 1805 **RU:** Captain, Served in Marines as Quartermaster at York. On 12 Jul 1776 supplied Co of Marines with 52 muskets & bayonets **CEM:** St John's Episcopal; GPS 37.53183, -77.41958; 2401 E Broad St; Richmond City **GS:** Y **SP:** Mary Miller **VI:** Burial date on GS **P:** unk **BLW:** unk **RG:** N **MK:** Y SAR **PH:** unk **SS:** E pg 668; N pg 668 **BS:** 28 pg 481; 196.

MITCHELL, William; b 1793, Augusta Co; d 13 Feb 1834 **RU:** Drummer, Served in Smith's Co, Gist's Cont Troops **CEM:** Bethel Presbyterian; GPS 38.04257, -79.17283; 563 Bethel Green Rd, Middlebrook; Augusta **GS:** Y **SP:** Mar (16 Feb 1826) Sarah Newton (1807 Rockbridge Co-3 Nov 1857) **VI:** Son of James (__Augusta Co-17 Jul 1816) & Susannah (Brownlee) Mitchell; Govt stone, no dates **P:** unk **BLW:** unk **RG:** Y **MK:** unk **PH:** unk **SS:** B; SAR P-250594 **BS:** JLARC 9, 62, 63; 196.

MOFFATT, William Sr; b 1755; d 8 Apr 1839 **RU:** Captain USN 1780 & Mate on Brig Neptune **CEM:** Cedar Grove; GPS 36.57204, -80.02599; 301 Fort Lane Rd; Portsmouth City **GS:** U **SP:** No info **VI:** No further data **P:** unk **BLW:** unk **RG:** Y **MK:** Y SAR **PH:** unk **SS:** Fold3 BLW Application; SAR P-250745; AR Vol 3 pg 93 **BS:** JLARC 2, 3980, vol 3, pg 93.

MOFFETT, George; b 1735; d 26 Aug 1811 **RU:** Colonel/Patriot, Commanded a co in 1776 in the Augusta Co Militia. On 16 Jun 1778 took oath as colonel and served to end of war effectively using the militia to protect the citizens of the county fr the Indians. Gave material aid to cause **CEM:** Augusta Stone Presbyterian; GPS 38.23926, -78.97356, GS 38.1411,-78.5815; 28 Old Stone Church Ln, Ft Defiance; Augusta **GS:** Y **SP:** Sarah McDowell **VI:** Govt stone erected in 1935 styles him Col and indicates Augusta Co Militia **P:** unk **BLW:** unk **RG:** Y **MK** Y SAR plaque **PH:** unk **SS:** B; E pg 556; AL Cert Augusta Co; SAR P-250748 **BS:** JLARC 1 ,2, 8, 23, 62, 63; 80, vol 3, pg 93; 196.

MOFFETT, James; b 30 Aug 1764; d 5 Jul 1826 **RU:** Private, Served in Capt James Ball's Co, Augusta Co Militia **CEM:** Bethel Presbyterian; GPS 38.04257, -79.17283; 563 Bethel Green Rd, Middlebrook; Augusta **GS:** Y **SP:** Mar (29 Dec 1789, Augusta Co) Mary Stewart (19 Dec 1765-15 Sep 1826) d/o of

RU=Rank/Unit	CEM=Cemetery	GS=Gravestone	SP=Spousal Information
VI=Other Veteran Info	P=Pension	BLW=Bounty/Land Warrant	RG=Registered Grave
MK=SAR/DAR Marker	PH=Photo	SS=Service Source	BS=Burial Source

292

Thomas Steward (1727-1788) and Elizabeth Moore (1725-1805) **VI:** Son of John Moffett (1731-1805) and Jane Ledgerwood (1734-1821. Lived on Christian Creek. D Staunton **P:** unk **BLW:** unk **RG:** N **MK:** N **PH:** unk **SS:** E pg 556 **BS:** 142 Bethel; 196.

MOFFETT, Jesse; b 2 Mar 1759; d 6 Dec 1836 or 31 Aug 1852 **RU:** Soldier, Served in VA Line. Served under Capt Harrison 1777 **CEM:** Moffett; GPS unk; Nr Marshall; Fauquier **GS:** Y **SP:** 1) Mar (27 Dec 1782) Hannah (-----) (c1760-__) 2) Mar (27 Dec 1782 Fauquier Co) Elizabeth (-----) **VI:** Sol appl pen 31 Aug 1832 Fauquier Co. Pen says he d 6 Dec 1836. Widow Elizabeth appl pen 30 May 1839 Fauquier Co. W3446 **P:** Y **BLW:** unk **RG:** Y **MK:** unk **PH:** unk **SS:** J-NSSAR 1993 Reg; CG pg 2386; K Vol 3 pg 278; SAR P-250751 **BS:** JLARC 1.

MOFFETT, John; b 31 Jan 1731; d 10 Oct 1805 **RU:** Private/Patriot, Served in Capt James Trimble's Co. Was Commissioner of the Provision Law for Publick Claims in 1780. Gave material aid to the cause **CEM:** Bethel Presbyterian; GPS 38.04257, -79.17283; 563 Bethel Green Rd, Middlebrook; Augusta **GS:** Y **SP:** 1) Esther Moody d/o James Moody & Rebecca Wilson; 2) Mar (8 May 1760) Jane Ledgerwood (1725-1821) d/o William & Agnes (-----) Ledgerwood **VI:** Son of James Moffett and father of James Moffett, also bur here. Newer marker. D age 89, "Soldier in Indian Wars" **P:** unk **BLW:** unk **RG:**Y**MK:** N **PH:** unk **SS:** AS SAR code dj SAR P-246293 **BS:** JLARC 62; 196.

MOFFETT, William; b 20 Feb 1761; d 20 Jun 1828 **RU:** Captain (Navy) and in 1780 was a Mate for the brig "Neptune" **CEM:** Bethel Presbyterian; GPS 38.04257, -79.17283; 563 Bethel Green Rd, Middlebrook; Augusta **GS:** Y **SP:** 1) Mar (28 Jun 1785 Augusta Co) Elizabeth Gamble, (1761-31 Mar 1790) 2) (11 May 1791 Augusta Co) Mary McClanachan (__-1829) **VI:** Son of John (1731-1805) & Jane (Ledgerwood) (1734-1821) Moffett. Recd pen with Mary as his widow **P:** Y **BLW:** unk **RG:** Y **MK:** unk **PH:** unk **SS:** A pg 278; E pg 556; CG pg 2386; SAR P-250759 **BS:** JLARC 62, 63; 196.

MOFFETT, William Mead; b unk; d 31 Jul 1838 **RU:** Private, Served in Capt Valentine Payton's Co, Mar 1778. Cont Line VA **CEM:** Fairfax Meeting House; GPS 39.18557, -77.60589; Water St & Waterford Rd, Waterford; Loudoun **GS:** Y **SP:** Ellen Mead (-----) (__-13 Jan 1842) **VI:** No further data **P:** unk **BLW:** unk **RG:** N **MK:** N **PH:** unk **SS:** E pg 556 **BS:** 25 pg 209.

MOINET, Laurent; b unk; d 1781 **RU:** Seaman, Served on "Ville de Paris"; D Yorktown battle **CEM:** French Memorial; GPS 36.81944, -79.39933; Yorktown; York **GS:** U **SP:** No info **VI:** No further data **P:** unk **BLW:** unk **RG:** Y **MK:** unk **PH:** unk **SS:** J-Yorktown Historian; SAR P-250792 **BS:** JLARC 1, 74.

MOLES, Jeremiah; b 1747, Rockingham Co; d 1825 **RU:** Private, Enlisted 1775, Capt Joseph Crocket, 7th VA Regt, Commanded by Col Dangerfield. Had service at Guinn's Island. Service was fr neighboring Patrick Co **CEM:** Moses Martin; GPS unk; Bassett; Henry **GS:** U **SP:** Mar (18 Jul 1776) Lydia Smith (1750-1819) **VI:** D Patrick Co **P:** unk **BLW:** unk **RG:** Y **MK:** unk **PH:** unk **SS:** E pg 506; SAR P-250801 **BS:** 196.

MOLIN, Jean; b unk; d 1781 **RU:** Soldier, Served in Beaujolais Bn; D battle at Yorktown **CEM:** French Memorial; GPS 36.81944, -79.39933; Yorktown; York **GS:** U **SP:** No info **VI:** No further data **P:** unk **BLW:** unk **RG:** Y **MK:** unk **PH:** unk **SS:** J-Yorktown Historian; SAR P-250803 **BS:** JLARC 1, 74.

MOLLIERE, Antoine; b unk; d 1781 **RU:** Seaman, Served on "Caton"; D Yorktown battle **CEM:** French Memorial; GPS 36.81944, -79.39933; Yorktown; York **GS:** U **SP:** No info **VI:** No further data **P:** unk **BLW:** unk **RG:** Y **MK:** unk **PH:** unk **SS:** J-Yorktown Historian; SAR P-250808 **BS:** JLARC 1, 74.

MOLTON, Caesar; b unk; d 1781 **RU:** Soldier, Served fr MA; D battle Yorktown **CEM:** Yorktown Victory Monument Tablet; GPS 38.28350, -78.54150; Yorktown; York **GS:** U **SP:** No info **VI:** No further data **P:** unk **BLW:** unk **RG:** Y **MK:** unk **PH:** unk **SS:** J-Yorktown Historian; SAR P-250812 **BS:** JLARC 74.

MONART, Nicolas; b unk; d 1781 **RU:** Soldier, Served in Touraine Bn D battle Yorktown **CEM:** French Memorial; GPS 36.81944, -79.39933; Yorktown; York **GS:** U **SP:** No info **VI:** No further data **P:** unk **BLW:** unk **RG:** Y **MK:** unk **PH:** unk **SS:** J-Yorktown Historian; SAR P-250817 **BS:** JLARC 1, 74.

MONCURE, John II; b 22 Jan 1747, Clermont, Stafford Co; d 1784 **RU:** Patriot, Gave 400# beef Nov 1781 **CEM:** Aquia Episcopal; GPS 38.46466, -77.40325; 2938 Jeff Davis Hwy, Aquia; Stafford **GS:** U **SP:** Anne Conway (c1750-__) d/o George & Anne (Heath) Conway **VI:** Son of John I (__ Scotland-10

RU=Rank/Unit   CEM=Cemetery   GS=Gravestone   SP=Spousal Information
VI=Other Veteran Info   P=Pension   BLW=Bounty/Land Warrant   RG=Registered Grave
MK=SAR/DAR Marker   PH=Photo   SS=Service Source   BS=Burial Source

293

Mar 1764 VA) & Frances (Brown) Moncure of Charles City, MD. Bur in the Chancel. Originally bur at "Dipple" Cem in Stafford Co. **P:** N **BLW:** N **RG:** N **MK:** unk **PH:** unk **SS:** D Stafford Co pg 874 **BS:** 196.

MONDAY, Evan; b Unk; d Feb 1778 **RU:** Private, Capt Moore'sCo, Col William Grayson' VA Regt, Cont Line: **CEM:** Rev War Court House Plaque; GPS not determined; 4110 Chain Bridge Rd; Fairfax **GS:** Memorialized on plaque 2017 by Geo Washington Chapter, VASSAR **SP:** No spousal info **VI:** died in service **P:** N **BLW:** N **RG:** N **MK:** N **PH:** N **SS:**E pg 557; AP Fold3 muster rolls **BS:** None.

MONDRE, Pierre; b unk; d 1781 **RU:** Seaman, Served on "Diademe"; D Yorktown battle **CEM:** French Memorial; GPS 36.81944, -79.39933; Yorktown; York **GS:** U **SP:** No info **VI:** No further data **P:** unk **BLW:** unk **RG:** Y **MK:** unk **PH:** unk **SS:** J-Yorktown Historian; SAR P-250826 **BS:** JLARC 1, 74.

MONET, Jean; b unk; d 1781 **RU:** Soldier, Served in Soissonnais Bn and died fr battle at Yorktown **CEM:** French Memorial; GPS 36.81944, -79.39933; Yorktown; York **GS:** U **SP:** No info **VI:** No further data **P:** unk **BLW:** unk **RG:** Y **MK:** unk **PH:** unk **SS:** J-Yorktown Historian; SAR P-250833 **BS:** JLARC 1, 74.

MONGER, Henry; b unk; d Aft 1802 **RU:** Patriot, Gave material aid to cause **CEM:** Old Peaked Mountain; GPS 38.37113, -78.73416; 9843 Town Hall Rd, McGaheysville; Rockingham **GS:** Y **SP:** Mar (1802 Rockingham Co) Catherine Fultz d/o George & (-----) Fultz **VI:** No further data **P:** N **BLW:** N **RG:** Y **MK:** Y SAR **PH:** unk **SS:** O pg 120; AL Ct Bk II pg 19 Rockingham Co; SAR P-250842 **BS:** 04.

MONGIN, Jean; b unk; d 1781 **RU:** Soldier, Served in Touraine Bn and died fr battle at Yorktown **CEM:** French Memorial; GPS 36.81944, -79.39933; Yorktown; York **GS:** U **SP:** No info **VI:** No further data **P:** unk **BLW:** unk **RG:** Y **MK:** unk **PH:** unk **SS:** J-Yorktown Historian; SAR P-250844 **BS:** JLARC 1, 74.

MONNIER, Nicolas; b unk; d 1781 **RU:** Seaman, Served on "Auguste" and died from Yorktown battle **CEM:** French Memorial; GPS 36.81944, -79.39933; Yorktown; York **GS:** U **SP:** No info **VI:** No further data **P:** unk **BLW:** unk **RG:** Y **MK:** unk **PH:** unk **SS:** J-Yorktown Historian; SAR P-250875 **BS:** JLARC 1, 74.

MONROE, James; b 28 Apr 1758, Westmoreland Co; d 1831 **RU:** Major/Patriot, Served in 3rd VA Regt. Ent serv 1775. Was wounded at Battle of Harlem Heights. Was in Cont Congress 1783 **CEM:** Hollywood; GPS 37.53560, -77.45720; 412 S Cherry St; Richmond City **GS:** U **SP:** Mar (16 Feb 1786 New York City) Elizabeth Kortright (1768-1830) d/o Laurence & Hannah (Aspinwall) Kortright **VI:** US Senator 1790-94. Minister to France 1794-96 & 1803 and England 1803-07. Was Gov VA 1799-1802, Sec of State under President Madison 1811-17. Sec of War 1814-15. Fifth president of the US 1817-25. President of 2nd Const Conv of VA 1829. Remains moved fr NY to Richmond in 1858. Pen recd by widow's children, Maria H. Governeur & Eliza K. Hay. W26271 **P:** Y **BLW:** unk **RG:** Y **MK:** unk **PH:** unk **SS:** K Vol 3 pg 280; DAR A081100; SAR P250894 **BS:** JLARC 1, 4, 76; 201 pg 73, 93, 94.

MONROE, William; b c1760, Westmoreland Co; d 1 Jan 1848 **RU:** Private, Ent serv 1777 Capt James Quarles Co, 2d VA Regt,and was at Yorktown 1781 **CEM:** North Fork Baptist; GPS 39.06014, -77.68509; 38130 North Folk Rd, North Fork; Loudoun **GS:** Y **SP:** Ann (-----) **VI:** Lived in Westmoreland until age 17. Pen age 72 in 1832 Frederick Co. S5784 **P:** Y **BLW:** unk **RG:** Y **MK:** N **PH:** unk **SS:** K Vol 3 pg 281; CG pg 2388; DAR A118112; SAR P-250926 **BS:** 25 pg 210.

MONTAGUE, Thomas; b c1754, Cumberland Co; d 1839 **RU:** Soldier, Served in VA Line. Lived in Cumberland Co at enl 1775. **CEM:** Olnorary; GPS unk; Old quarry on Old Stage Rd fr CH (see source 4). Behind Cumberland & Cartersville; Cumberland **GS:** U **SP:** No spousal data **VI:** Sol appl pen 27 Aug 1832 Cumberland Co age 78. Widow granted pen due arrears in 1841. S5775 **P:** Y **BLW:** unk **RG:** unk **MK:** N **PH:** unk **SS:** K Vol 3 pg 282; CG pg 2389 **BS:** JLARC 2, 4; 04; 196.

MONTAGUE, Thomas II; b 20 Feb 1719. Christchurch, Middlesex Co, d Jun 1778 **RU:** Private Capt Alexander Parker's Co, 2d VA Regt, Cont Line served until 1777 or 8, when he died in camp of small pox. **CEM:** Montague (AKA Olnorary) GPS; not determined; loc old quarry on old stage road from courthouse, abt 5 mi fr Cartersville: Cumberland **GS:** Unk **SP:** Jane Daniel (18 Aug 1733-1812), d/o Charles Daniel & Jane (-----) **VI:** Son of Thomas Montague (1694-1756) & Grace Nicholson (1699-1725) **P:** N **BLW:** N **RG:** N **MK:** N **PH:** N **SS:**K pg 282 **BS**: 196.

MONTCHALEN, Antoine; b unk; d 1781 **RU:** Seaman, Served on "Ville de Paris" and died from Yorktown battle **CEM:** French Memorial; GPS 36.81944, -79.39933; Yorktown; York **GS:** U **SP:** no info

RU=Rank/Unit	CEM=Cemetery	GS=Gravestone	SP=Spousal Information
VI=Other Veteran Info	P=Pension	BLW=Bounty/Land Warrant	RG=Registered Grave
MK=SAR/DAR Marker	PH=Photo	SS=Service Source	BS=Burial Source

VI: No further data **P:** unk **BLW:** unk **RG:** N **MK:** unk **PH:** unk **SS:** J-Yorktown Historian **BS:** JLARC 1, 74.

MONTGOMERY, Francis; b 17 Jan 1761; d 1825 **RU:** Patriot, paid personal property taxes in Prince William Co in 1782 and 1783, considered to be a supply tax for Rev War expenses **CEM:** Lewis-Montgomery Families (AKA Manassas Presbyterian Church); GPS 38.780256, -77.513690; 8201 Ashton Ave behind church; Manassas City **GS:** Y **SP:** No info **VI:** Son of William Montgomery (1732-1803) & Katherine Mars (1742-1800) **P:** Y **BLW:** N **RG:** Y **MK:** Y SAR **PH:** Y **SS:** EN; SAR bio submitted Nov 2020 **BS:** 04; 190 by cem name.

MONTGOMERY, Humphrey Jr; b 1750, PA; d 1798 **RU:** Private, Served in Capt Samuel Lapsley's 2nd Co, Col Nathaniel Gist's VA Regt in 1777 **CEM:** Oxford Presbyterian; GPS 37.75302, -79.56023; 18 Churchview Ln, Lexington; Lexington City **GS:** U **SP:** Jean Gay **VI:** Reported as unmarked grave. Bur in area inside iron railing **P:** unk **BLW:** unk **RG** Y **MK:** unk **PH:** unk **SS:** A pg 285; C pg 257; SAR P-251044 **BS:** JLARC 126.

MONTGOMERY, John; b 1724, Ireland, d 1795 **RU:** Patriot, gave material aid to cause **CEM:** New Providence Presbyterian Ch; GPS 37.9516983, 79.3024979; loc 1208 New Providence Rd near jct with Brownsburg Turnpike; Rapine; Rockbridge **GS:** Unk **SP:** Ester Houston c1724-___) **VI:** Son of James Montgomery and Mary McCullough **P:** N **BLW:** N **RG:** Y **MK:** N **PH:** N **SS:** D, vol1, pg 80; SAR P_251066 **BS:** 196.

MONTGOMERY, John; b unk; d aft 1800 **RU:** Patriot, Gave material aid to cause **CEM:** Montgomery Family; GPS unk; Vic Christianburg; Montgomery **GS:** Y **SP:** No info **VI:** Held title of Colonel **P:** N **BLW:** N **RG:** Y **MK:** N **PH:** unk **SS:** AL Comm Bk IV; SAR P-251057 **BS:** 80 vol 3 pg 94.

MONTGOMERY, John; b 1717; d 1802 **RU:** Patriot, Was a member of the Safety Committee for Fincastle Co 1775-1776; Sheriff; and Justice, Montgomery Co **CEM:** Montgomery family; GPS unk; Nr Ft Chiswell in field abt .75 mi behind Ft Chiswell Mansion; Wythe **GS:** U **SP:** Ann Agnes Crocket **VI:** Cem in disrepair, became property of DAR chapter **P:** N **BLW:** N **RG:** Y **MK:** unk **PH:** unk **SS:** G pg 207; DL pgs 647, 673-675, 680, 699; DAR A079040; SAR P-251068 **BS:** JLARC 76, 123.

MONTGOMERY, John Rev; b Dec 1752; d 10 Feb 1818 **RU:** Lieutenant / Patriot, Served in VA State Line for 3 yrs. 21 days in Augusta Co. As patriot purchased cattle for army **CEM:** Rocky Spring Presbyterian; GPS 38.11470, -79.24250; 1 mi S of Deerfield; Augusta **GS:** Y **SP:** Agnes Hughart (24 Jan 176_-8 Feb 1824) **VI:** Pastor of Ricky Spring, Lebanon and Windy Grove churches. Trustee and teacher of Liberty Hall Academy. Recd BLW 6000 acres 3 Mar 1784 **P:** unk **BLW:** Y **RG:** N **MK:** N **PH:** unk **SS:** F pg 51; Z pg 93 **BS:** 142 RockySpr; 196.

MONTGOMERY, Joseph; b 1760; d 1842 **RU:** Captain, Served in VA Militia **CEM:** Montgomery Family; GPS unk; Nellysford, near Wintergreen; Nelson **GS:** U **SP:** Jane Woods daughter of Samuel & (-----) Woods, Albemarle Co. **VI:** No further data **P:** unk **BLW:** unk **RG:** Y **MK:** Y SAR **PH:** unk **SS:** J-NSSAR 1993 Reg; SAR P-251092 **BS:** JLARC 1.

MONTGOMERY, Richard; b 1755, York Co, PA; d 8 Feb 1840 **RU:** Soldier, Ent serv York Co PA Line **CEM:** Rocky Spring Presbyterian; GPS 38.11470, -79.24250; 1 mi S of Deerfield; Augusta **GS:** N **SP:** Mar (1787, York Co PA) Elizabeth McCall (__-1855). Became "insane" in widowhood; son appointed her guardian & appl for her **VI:** Moved to Washington Co 1793. Sol appl pen 28 Jan 1833 Washington Co VA age 75. Son Richard Montgomery Jr. appl pen for widow 28 May 1853 Washington Co. BLW appl for 30 Mar 1855 Washington Co. W7485, BLW #26383-160-55 **P:** Y **BLW:** Y **RG:** Y **MK:** N **PH:** N **SS:** JLARC 62, 63, 79; K Vol 3 pg 283; CG pg 2391; SAR P-251100 **BS:** JLARC 4, 34, 62, 63.

MONTGOMERY, William; b 20 Jan 1732, Rosemount, County Down, Ireland; d 1803 **RU:** Patriot, Gave material aid to cause in Prince William Co **CEM:** Lewis-Montgomery Families (also Manassas Presbyterian Church); GPS 38.78089, -77.5133656; 8201 Ashton Ave; Manassas City **GS:** Y **SP:** Mar (8 Nov 1758) Katherina Mars (20 Mar 1742 Aberdeen, Scotland-1800) **VI:** Son of Francis & Elizabeth (-----) Montgomery of London, England **P:** unk **BLW:** unk **RG:** Y **MK:** Y SAR **PH:** Y **SS:** Al Ct Bk pg 10; DAR A079103; SAR P-340461 **BS:** 190 by cem name.

MONTGOMERY, William; b c1762 (year wife born); d 22 Sep 18?3 (GS inscription) **RU:** Private, Clark's Illinois Regt **CEM:** St John's Episcopal; GPS unk; 100 W Queen's Way; Hampton City **GS:** Y **SP:** Mary

RU=Rank/Unit	CEM=Cemetery	GS=Gravestone	SP=Spousal Information
VI=Other Veteran Info	P=Pension	BLW=Bounty/Land Warrant	RG=Registered Grave
MK=SAR/DAR Marker	PH=Photo	SS=Service Source	BS=Burial Source

295

(-----) (15 May 1762-3 Jan 1832) **VI:** No further data **P:** N **BLW:** N **RG:** N **MK:** N **PH:** N **SS:** G pg 702 **BS:** 89 pg 110.(MOODY, Edward See Appendix G Addenda)

MOODY, John; b 1735; d 1804 **RU:** Private, Served in 3rd, 5th, 7th Cont Line **CEM:** Staunton Baptist; GPS 37.06970, -79.58140; 15267 Smith Mountain Lake Pkwy, Huddleston; Bedford **GS:** N **SP:** Susanna Amoss (1750-1829) **VI:** Son of Edward (1707-1775) & (-----) Moody. SAR plaque **P:** N **BLW:** N **RG:** Y **MK:** Y SAR plaque **PH:** N **SS:** E pg 559; SAR P-251219 **BS:** 196.

MOORE, Alexander; b unk; d Jul 1786 **RU:** Captain/Patriot, Served in William Edmiston's Co fr Washington Co at Battle of Point Pleasant, Oct 1774. Gave material aid to cause **CEM:** Moore Family; GPS 37.22110, -81.40170; Adj to RR track E of Tiptop abt halfway to jct Rts 650 & 656; Tazewell **GS:** N **SP:** no info **VI:** Son of Capt James (__-1786) & Martha (Poage) (__-1786) Moore. Killed by Shawnee Indians who attacked family home **P:** N **BLW:** N **RG:** N **MK:** unk **PH:** N **SS:** Z pg 166; AL Ct Bk pg 1, 5 Rockbridge Co **BS:** 196.

MOORE, Alexander Spotswood; b 1763; d 1799 **RU:** Corporal, Served in 7th & 8th Cont Line **CEM:** Fairfield Plantation; GPS unk; Aylett; King William **GS:** N **SP:** Mar (17 Jul 1787) Elizabeth Aylett (1769-__), said to have mar a Judge Hamilton & moved to Chucky Bend, TN **VI:** Son of Col Bernard & Ann Catherine (Spotswood) Moore. Great uncle of Gen Robert E. Lee. BIL of John Robinson, speaker of House of Burgesses/treasurer of Colony **P:** unk **BLW:** unk **RG:** Y **MK:** unk **PH:** N **SS:** E pg 560; DAR A131292; SAR P-251347 **BS:** 196.

MOORE, Amos Lad; b 13 May 1747, Albemarle Co; d 7 Mar 1836 **RU:** Private?, Served in VA Line. Ent serv Goochland Co **CEM:** Moore Family; GPS unk; Cardwell Rd; Goochland **GS:** Y **SP:** Mar (21 Dec 1775 Albemarle Co) Ann Rogers (c1756-__ of St James Northern Parish) **VI:** Sol appl pen 17 Sep 1832 Goochland Co age 85. Widow appl pen 10 Nov 1841 Goochland Co age 85. W5145 **P:** Y **BLW:** unk **RG:** N **MK:** N **PH:** unk **SS:** E pg 560; K Vol 3 pg 287; CG pg 2397 **BS:** 46 pg 191.

MOORE, Andrew; b 1750; d 10 Aug 1791 **RU:** Captain, Served in VA Militia. Served on Courts Martial in Augusta Co 1776. Served in Rockbridge Co Co at Great Bridge area 1781. Appt Capt 6 May 1778 **CEM:** Old Providence; GPS 37.96151, -79.71000; 1005 Spottswood Rd, Spottswood; Augusta **GS:** Y **SP:** Martha (-----) (176_-1839) **VI:** Name also on SAR plaque at cemetery **P:** unk **BLW:** unk **RG:** Y **MK:** Y SAR plaque **PH:** Y **SS:** E pg 560; SAR P-251355 **BS:** JLARC 62, 63, 79; 196.

MOORE, Andrew; b Jan 1752 "Cannicello" Rockbridge Co; d 14 Apr 1821 **RU:** Major General, Was a Lt in Capt Samuel McDowell's Co of Rockbridge Co that served at Pt Pleasant 1774. Ent serv Augusta Co (now Rockbridge). Led 9th Va Regt Cont Army under Gen Gates at Battle of Saratoga. Became Maj Gen VA Militia. **CEM:** Stonewall Jackson Memorial; GPS 37.78128, -79.44604; 314 S Main St; Lexington City **GS:** Y **SP:** Mar (31 Mar 1795 Rockbridge Co) Sarah "Sally" Reid (c1777-after 16 Feb 1856), d/o Andrew & (-----) Reid of Rockbridge Co. **VI:** Was member VA House of Delegates 1780-1800; member VA Privy Council 1788; delegate to VA convention which ratified Constitution 1788; served At-Large in US House 1789-1797; US Congressman fr VA 1-4th, 8th Congresses; VA Senate 1800-01; and US Senate 1804-09. Was US Marshall and Trustee Washington & Lee University 1782-1821. Was US Congressman, US Senator. Wid appl pen 4 Sep 1848 Rockbridge Co age 71. W1454, BLW #38539-160-55 **P:** Y **BLW:** Y **RG:** Y **MK:** N **PH:** Y **SS:** K pg 287; Z pg 103; CG pg 2397; SAR P-251356 **BS:** JLARC 1, 63.

MOORE, Charles; b c1753; d 1790 **RU:** Seaman, Served in VA State Navy **CEM:** St John's Episcopal; GPS 37.53183, -77.41958; 2401 E Broad St; Richmond City **GS:** Y **SP:** No info **VI:** No further data **P:** unk **BLW:** unk **RG:** N **MK:** N **PH:** unk **SS:** E pg 560; L pg 227 **BS:** 04, Dec 06.

MOORE, James; b 1711, County Down, Ireland d 7 Jan 1791 **RU:** Patriot; Gave material aid to cause, Botetourt Co **CEM:** Walkerland, Maxwelton Farm; **GPS:** 37.94613,-79.38794; vic jct Rts 602 & 724, behind Maxwelton Cabins; Rockbridge **GS:** Unk **SP:** Mar Chester Co, PA Apr 1734, Jane Walker (1712-1793) **VI:** No further data **P:** N **BLW:** N **RG:** N **MK:** N **PH:** N **SS:** AL Ct Bk pg 5, Botetourt Co **BS:** 196

MOORE, James; b 1734, Augusta Co; d 14 Jul 1786 **RU:** Captain, Commanded a co at battles of Cowpens, Guilford CH, Kings Mtn **CEM:** Moore Family; GPS unk; Abb's Valley; Tazewell **GS:** Y **SP:** Martha Poage, massacred by raiding Shawnee Indians **VI:** On obelisk, "Capt James Moore, killed by the Indians 1786." Memorialized on Moore Monument. Abbs Valley in the cemetery **P:** unk **BLW:** unk **RG:** Y

RU=Rank/Unit	CEM=Cemetery	GS=Gravestone	SP=Spousal Information
VI=Other Veteran Info	P=Pension	BLW=Bounty/Land Warrant	RG=Registered Grave
MK=SAR/DAR Marker	PH=Photo	SS=Service Source	BS=Burial Source

MK: unk **PH**: Y **SS**: J-NSSAR 2000 Reg; D; pg 689; DAR A079520; SAR P-251537 **BS**: JLARC 76.; 196.

MOORE, James; b 1756, Chester Co, PA; d 20 May 1813 **RU**: Lieutenant Colonel, Served in PA line 2 Sept 1778 in the rank of Maj. Was in Battles of Brandywine, Germantown, Monmouth, Charleston, Savannah, and Yorktown **CEM**: Northumberland House; GPS 37.967183,-76.436608; Rt 631,Clarktown Rd off of Rt 360 to Clark Lane, cem loc N of house; Northumberland **GS**: Y **SP**: Mar (18 Oct 1787) Sarah Delaney (c1767-1 Dec 1814) probably PA, d/o Sharp & (-----) Delaney of Philadelphia **VI**: Son of James & Elizabeth (Whitehall) Moore. Was a wine and liquor merchant **P**: N **BLW**: unk **RG**:.Y **MK**: Y-DAR & SAR **PH**: Y **SS**: AP; AK; SAR P-251565; DAR A079504 **BS**: JLARC 2, 93; 200; 04; 47; 196.

MOORE, James; b 20 Sep 1759, Rockbridge Co; d 21 May 1828 **RU**: Private, Capt Cunningham's Co, Augusta Co Militia **CEM**: Stonewall Jackson Memorial; GPS 37.78128, -79.44604; 314 S Main St; Lexington City **GS**: Y White 2A7 **SP**: Hannah Barclay (1 Aug 1768-6 Nov 1839) d/o Hugh (1729-1806) & Mary (Culbertson) Barclay **VI**: No further data **P**: unk **BLW**: unk **RG**: Y **MK**: unk **PH**: unk **SS**: E pg 561; SAR P-251569 **BS**: JLARC 63; 196.

MOORE, Jeremiah Rev; b 7 Jun 1746, Stafford Co; d 23 Feb 1815 **RU**: Corporal, Served in Prince William & Fairfax Co Militia. Was Baptist preacher, challenged preeminence of Episcopal Church and preached contrary to British enforcement of religious freedom laws **CEM**: Moore-Hunter Family; GPS 38.88600, -77.27336; 1001 Tapawingo Rd SW, Vienna; Fairfax **GS**: Y **SP**: Lydia French Reno (1745-8 Oct 1835) d/o Francis (1713-1797) & Elizabeth (Bayliss) (___-1764) Reno **VI**: Owned "Moorefield" where this graveyard is located **P**: N **BLW**: unk **RG**: Y **MK**: Y **PH**: Y **SS**: AK; 47, 1933, 1917; SAR P-251587 **BS**: JLARC 1, 2, 14, 27, 28; 196.

MOORE, John; b 1749; d 1833 **RU**: Patriot, Gave provisions to cause **CEM**: Fincastle Presbyterian; GPS 37.50017, -79.87558; 108 E Back St, Fincastle; Botetourt **GS**: Y **SP**: Mary S. Bright (c1758-Sep 1837) **VI**: Name is on the SAR plaque at this cemetery **P**: N **BLW**: N **RG**: N **MK**: Y SAR plaque **PH**: unk **SS**: Z pg 131 **BS**: 196.

MOORE, John; b 1717, Spotsylvania Co; d 1 Jan 1795 **RU**: Patriot, Gave material aid to cause **CEM**: Beaver Dam Baptist Church; GPS 37.98377, -78.29179; Richmond Rd, Paynes Mill; Fluvanna **GS**: U **SP**: No info **VI**: No further data **P**: N **BLW**: N **RG**: Y **MK**: unk **PH**: unk **SS**: AL Ct Bk pg 3; SAR P-251604 **BS**: 196.

MOORE, John; b 1754; d Apr 1838 **RU**: Private, Served in Capt Stewart's Co, Augusta Co Militia **CEM**: Fincastle Presbyterian; GPS 37.50017, -79.87558; 108 E Back St, Fincastle; Botetourt **GS**: Y **SP**: Mary S Bright (1765-Sep 1837) **VI**: Died age 84. Name is on VASSAR plaque at cemetery **P**: unk **BLW**: unk **RG**: N **MK**: Y SAR plaque **PH**: unk **SS**: E pg 561; J-NSSAR 1993 Reg **BS**: 196; 115 pg 16; JLARC 1.

MOORE, John; b 12 Jan 1760, d 2 Sep 1841; **RU**: Private served in The First Independent Company of Dunmore Co which became Shenandoah Co in 1778 **CEM**: Moore Family; GPS 38.5867400,-78.7075350; loc in field S of Moore's Mill Road (796) and W of Stultz Mill Lane, approx 400 ft NW of the point where War Branch flows into Smith Creek, Tenth Legion; Rockingham **GS**: Y **SP**: Sarah Bird, (2 Jun 1758,Shenandoah Co-3 Mar 1833) **VI**: Son of Thomas Moore (1728-1797) & Phebe Harrison (1728-1807) **P**: N **BLW**: Unk **RG**: N **MK**: Y- **PH**: Y **SS**: G pg 143 **BS**: 196.

MOORE, Merritt; b Before 1758, York Co; d 1793 **RU**: Patriot, In Apr 1783, gave 4 oxen, a horse, and other items to cause **CEM**: St Luke's Church; GPS 36.93940, -76.58670; 14477 Benns Church Blvd, Smithfield; Iasle of Wight **GS**: Y **SP**: Anne Robinson **VI**: Son of Augustine & Mary (Wooley) Moore. Died in York Co **P**: N **BLW**: N **RG**: N **MK**: N **PH**: unk **SS**: G pg 334 **BS**: 117 pg 6.

MOORE, Reuben; b 10 Jun 1755, Augusta Co or Rockingham Co; d 6 Aug 1803 **RU**: Captain, Served in Rockingham Co Militia under Col Benjamin Harrison. In 1781, was in expedition to North Fork of Potomac against band of Tories. Became Capt 26 Mar 1781 **CEM**: Moore Family; GPS unk; Timberville; Rockingham **GS**: Y **SP**: Mar (1779) Phoebe Harrison (1764-27 Aug 1821) **VI**: No further data **P**: unk **BLW**: unk **RG**: Y **MK**: Y SAR **PH**: unk **SS**: DD cites Levinson Rockingham Co VA Minute Book 1778-1792 Part 1 1778-1786 pg 2, 12, 81, 146, 219; SAR P-251740 **BS**: JLARC 76.

MOORE, Stephen; b 1751; d 1835 **RU**: Soldier, 1st VA Regt & 9th Cont line **CEM**: Moore Family; GPS 37.97113, -78.63598; 2393 Taylor's Gap Rd, North Garden; Albemarle **GS**: Y **SP**: Elizabeth Royster

RU=Rank/Unit	CEM=Cemetery	GS=Gravestone	SP=Spousal Information
VI=Other Veteran Info	P=Pension	BLW=Bounty/Land Warrant	RG=Registered Grave
MK=SAR/DAR Marker	PH=Photo	SS=Service Source	BS=Burial Source

297

(1764-1844) **VI:** No further data **P:** unk **BLW:** unk **RG:** Y **MK:** unk **PH:** unk **SS:** E pg 562; SAR P-251809 **BS:** JLARC 58; 196.

MOORE, Thomas, Jr; b 20 Feb 1763, d 31 Aug 1829 **RU:** Private, Capt Edmund Worthington's Co of Cav, Col George Rogers Clark's Illinois Regt Aug 1778 to Mar 1779 **CEM:** Moore Family; GPS 38.5867400, -78.7075350; loc in field S of Moore's Mill Road (796) and W of Stultz Mill Lane, approx 400 ft NW of the point where War Branch flows into Smith Creek, Tenth Legion; Rockingham **GS:** Y **SP:** Mary "Polly" Hughes Coffman (__-24 Jun 1853, Shenandoah Co) **VI:** Son of Thomas Moore (1728-1797) & Phebe Harrison (1728-1807) **P:** N **BLW:** Unk **RG:** N **MK:** Y **PH:** Y **SS:** G pg 708 **BS:** 196.

MOORE, Thomas; b 1728, Frederick Co, MD, d 1797 **RU:** Patriot, paid personal property tax Rockingham County 1782 considered to be partial payment for Rev War expenses **CEM:** Moore Family; GPS 38.5867400, -78.7075350; loc in field S of Moore's Mill Road (796) and W of Stultz Mill Lane, approx 400 ft NW of the point where War Branch flows into Smith Creek, Tenth Legion; Rockingham **GS:** Y **SP:** Mar (after 1750) Phebe Harrison (1728, Oyster Bay, Nassau Co, NY-1807), d/o John Harrison (1691-1771) & Phebe (-----). She previously mar to Daniel Davidson (1717-1750) **VI:** No further data **P:** N **BLW:** N **RG:** N **MK:** Y- **PH:** Y **SS:** DV 1782 image.11.pdf, Rockingham Co **BS:** 196.

MOORE, William; b 1749, Rockbridge Co; d 1840 or 27 Dec 1842 **RU:** Captain, VA Militia. Lived in Rockbridge Co at enl. Served under Capt Andrew Moore. Served under Gen Lewis at Battle of Point Pleasant. Served under Col John Bowyer. Guarded prisoners fr Battle of Yorktown after Cornwallis surrender **CEM:** Stonewall Jackson Memorial; GPS 37.78128, -79.44604; 314 S Main St; Lexington City **GS:** Y **SP:** Nancy McClung **VI:** Sol appl pen 7 Aug 1832 Rockbridge Co. S5787. Died in Rockbridge Co **P:** Y **BLW:** unk **RG:** Y **MK:** Y **PH:** unk **SS:** J-NSSAR 1993 Reg; CG pg 2409; DAR A080067; SAR P-251880 **BS:** JLARC 1; JLARC 2, 63.

MOORE, William; b unk; d 14 Jul 1786 **RU:** Patriot, Gave material aid to cause **CEM:** Moore Family; GPS 37.22110, -81.40170; Adj to RR track E of Tiptop abt halfway to jct Rts 650 & 656; Tazewell **GS:** U **SP:** No info **VI:** Son of James & Martha (Poage) Moore. Killed by Indians **P:** N **BLW:** N **RG:** N **MK:** unk **PH:** N **SS:** Al Ct Bk pg 2, 25 Montgomery Co **BS:** 196.

MOORE, William; b 1741; d 2 Jan 1827 **RU:** Soldier, Severely wounded and lost leg at Battle of Kings Mountain **CEM:** Rock Spring; GPS 37.78126, -79.44585; Jct Rt 803 & Liberty Hall Rd, Lodi; Washington **GS:** Y **SP:** Elizabeth (-----) (__-11 Oct 18?8 age 76) **VI:** Recd disability pen of $5 per mo. Later increased to $8. DAR Marker. S25312 **P:** Y **BLW:** unk **RG:** Y **MK:** Y **PH:** N **SS:** CG pg 2409; SAR P251864 **BS:** JLARC 4, 34.

MOORMAN, Micajah; b 28 Jun 1735 Louisa Co; d 25 Nov 1806 **RU:** Patriot, Performed public service **CEM:** South River Meeting House; GPS 37.37246, -79.19194; 5810 Fort Ave; Lynchburg City **GS:** N **SP:** Mar (13 Oct 1754) Susannah Chiles **VI:** Died in Campbell Co **P:** N **BLW:** N **RG:** Y **MK:** N **PH:** unk **SS:** 04 BY; DAR A080087; SAR P-251969 **BS:** 04; 137.

MOORMAN, Zachariah; b 2 Feb 1732, Hanover or Henrico Co, d 1789 Campbell Co **RU:** Patriot, gave material to cause **CEM:** Liberty Univ (AKA Moorman); GPS ; Lynchburg City **GS:** Y **SP:** Elizabeth Ann "Betty" Terrell (7 Sep 1738, Caroline Co-26 Jul 1773- Bedford Co) **VI:** Son of Thomas Moorman (1705-1767) & Rachel Clark (1714-1792 **P:** N **BLW:** N **RG:** Y **MK:** N **PH:** N **SS:** D, vol 1, pg 177; DAR A080097; SAR P-336099 **BS:** 196.

MORET, Barthelemy; b unk; d 1781 **RU:** Seaman, Served on "Saint-Esprit" and died from Yorktown battle **CEM:** French Memorial; GPS 36.81944, -79.39933; Yorktown; York **GS:** U **SP:** No info **VI:** No further data **P:** unk **BLW:** unk **RG:** Y **MK:** unk **PH:** unk **SS:** J-Yorktown Historian; SAR P-252103 **BS:** JLARC 1, 74.

MORGAN, Daniel; b 1736, County Derry, Ireland or Winter 1736, Hunterdon Co, NJ; d 6 Jul 1802 **RU:** General, Was Capt of VA Riflemen July 1775; prisoner at Quebec 31 Dec 1775; Col 11 CL Nov 12 1776; became Brigadier Gen 13 Oct 1780. Served to close of war **CEM:** Mt Hebron; GPS 39.10916, -78.09497; 305 E Boscawen St; Winchester City **GS:** Y **SP:** Abigail Bailey **VI:** Supposedly came to America in early days with father. Served in Craddock's campaign in 1755. Awarded 11,666 acres BLW #1496-850-25 Aug 1789, also BLW Reg #336254-55. Originally buried near Old Stone Presbyterian Church, Winchester **P:** unk **BLW:** Y **RG:** Y **MK:** Y SAR monument **PH:** Y **SS:** J-NSSAR 1993 Reg E pg 563; CG pg 2415; DAR A080333; SAR P-252178 **BS:** JLARC 1.

RU=Rank/Unit	CEM=Cemetery	GS=Gravestone	SP=Spousal Information
VI=Other Veteran Info	P=Pension	BLW=Bounty/Land Warrant	RG=Registered Grave
MK=SAR/DAR Marker	PH=Photo	SS=Service Source	BS=Burial Source

MORGAN, Hayes (Haynes); b unk; d 1795 **RU:** Colonel, Served in VA State Line. Commanded 1st State Regt, 5 Jun 1777-1 Jul 1777 **CEM:** Morgan Family; GPS unk; Nr White Falls, Banister River; Pittsylvania **GS:** Y **SP:** Mary Thompson (c1750-___), d/o William & (-----) Thompson of Halifax Co. **VI:** Granted BLW 1784. Widow pen in Davis Co, NC, 1837 age 87 **P:** Y **BLW:** Y **RG:** N **MK:** N **PH:** unk **SS:** BY pg 178; G pg 850-1 **BS:** 91 pg 2.

MORGAN, Zackwell; b 1739, Orange Co; d 1 Jan 1795 **RU:** Colonel/Patriot, County Lt Monongalia Co 1777. Also service listed Lib of VA, Auditor's Accts XV, pg 309. Gave material aid to cause **CEM:** Morgantown; GPS unk; Morgantown; Fauquier **GS:** U **SP:** Drucilla Springer (9 May 1745, Burlington-1795 Morgantown, Monongalia Co, WV) **VI:** JLARC indicates town of Morgantown is in Fauquier Co, but not found **P:** unk **BLW:** unk **RG:** Y **MK:** unk **PH:** unk **SS:** DAR #A080660; J- DAR Hatcher; D Vol 2 pg 682; E pg 564; CZ pg 318; SAR P-252341 **BS:** JLARC 2. DELETED NOT BURIED IN VA BUT WVA.

MORIN, Jean; b unk; d 1781 **RU:** Seaman, Served on "Diademe" and died from Yorktown battle **CEM:** French Memorial; GPS 36.81944, -79.39933; Yorktown; York **GS:** U **SP:** No info **VI:** No further data **P:** unk **BLW:** unk **RG:** Y **MK:** unk **PH:** unk **SS:** J-Yorktown Historian; SAR P-252359 **BS:** JLARC 1, 74.

MORRIS, John; b 1762, King and Queen Co, d 27 Dec 1834 **RU:** Private, Served in Captain Robert Barrett's Company, Colonel Francis Taylor's Continental Army Guard **CEM:** Morris-Payne; GPS: Not determined; Columbia Rd, vic jct with Rts 615 & 617, 600 yds into woods, Zion; Louisa **GS:** Y Gov't **SP:** mar 3 Mar 1791, Lucy Walker (1766-14 Sep 1840) **VI:** Rec'd pension **P:** Y **BLW:** N **RG:** N **MK:** N **PH:** N **SS:** DAR A200041 **BS:** 196

MORRIS, Nathaniel; b 1744; d 21 Jan 1813 **RU:** Private, Served in 3rd, 4th, 5th, & 9th Cont Lines **CEM:** Morris Family; GPS unk; Rt 609 at Vassars; Buckingham **GS:** U **SP:** Nancy Ann Jeffries **VI:** No further data **P:** N **BLW:** N **RG:** Y **MK:** N **PH:** unk **SS:** E pg 565; SAR P-252537 **BS:** JLARC 2, 33, 59.

MORRIS, Samuel Coleman; b 3 Aug 1740, Goochland, d 1826 **RU:** Patriot, Gave material aid to cause, Henry Co **CEM:** Morris; GPS: Not determined; jct Windfield Orchard Rd and Skyview Trail, Henry **GS:** Memorialized on family monument which indicates was buried in Old Morris Cemetery off Rt 698 **SP:** Susannah Wade (1744, Goochland-1828) **VI:** Moved to Henry Co fr Goochland Co c1776 **P:** N **BLW:** N **RG:**Y **MK:** N **PH:** N **SS:** AL Ct Bk pg 2a & Comm Bk III, pg 147, Henry Co; DAR A101324; SAR P-252548 **BS:** 196.

MORRIS, William; b 6 Feb 1736; d 25 Apr 1820 **RU:** Private/Patriot, Was in Illinois Regt Co #8, 30 Nov 1778, and discharged Apr 1779. Signed a petition in Hanover Co **CEM:** Morris at Taylor's Creek; GPS unk; Bethany Ch Rd; Hanover **GS:** N **SP:** No info **VI:** No further data **P:** unk **BLW:** unk **RG:** N **MK:** N **PH:** N **SS:** C pg 263; E pg 566 **BS:** 31 vol 2 pg 103.

MORRISON, John; b 1 May 1765, Orange Co, d 20 Aug 1849 **RU:**Sergeant; Enlisted Orange Co in VA line serving under Captans James Hawkins and George Waugh; was Sergeant 28 Nov 1776 at Mt Independence in Capt James A Wilson's Co, Col William Ervine's PA Regt **CEM:** Tolersville Tavern; GPS: 38.01321,-77.90345; 410 Old Tolersville Rd; Mineral; Louisa **GS:** No **SP:** 1) mar (7 Feb 1789) Ann Davis (1769-1836), d/o Rev William Davis & (-----), 2) mar (18 Jan 1839) Polly Thomason (1773-Sep 1853), d/o Fleming Thomason & Ann Smith. She applied for pen 6 May 1853, age 71 a few months before she died **VI:** Lived in Orange Co many years, moving to Goochland Co, then Louisa Co to marry Polly. Recd pen # SR7424, on pen list of 1835, age 69 **P:** Y **BLW:** N **RG:** Y **MK:** N **PH:** N **SS:** A pg 282, 284; E pg 556; CG: pg 2428; DAR A081148; SAR P-252663 **BS:** 196.

MORRISOT, Jacques; b unk; d 1781 **RU:** Seaman, Served on "Diademe" and died from Yorktown battle **CEM:** French Memorial; GPS 36.81944, -79.39933; Yorktown; York **GS:** U **SP:** No info **VI:** No further data **P:** unk **BLW:** unk **RG:** unk **MK:** unk **PH:** unk **SS:** J Yorktown Historian **BS:** JLARC 2, 33, 59, 74.

MORSON, Arthur; b 11 Feb 1734, Scotland; d 30 May 1798 **RU:** Patriot, Gave material aid to cause **CEM:** Hartwood Presbyterian; GPS 38.401883, -77.567450; 50 Hartwood Ch Rd, Fredericksburg; Stafford **GS:** Y **SP:** Marion Andrew (c1734-1808) **VI:** Son of Barton Morson and Sarah Stone. Was a merchant in Falmouth **P:** N **BLW:** N **RG:** Y **MK:** N **PH:** Y **SS:** D pg 259, 877; AL Ct Bk I pg 27, 28 Stafford Co; SAR P-333997 **BS:** 03 pg 240.

MORTON, George; b c1746, Orange Co; d 1787 **RU:** Patriot, Provided wagon w/ team of horses for Orange Co Militia. Also gave grain to barracks 20 Dec 1780 **CEM:** Soldier's Rest Plantation; GPS unk;

RU=Rank/Unit	CEM=Cemetery	GS=Gravestone	SP=Spousal Information
VI=Other Veteran Info	P=Pension	BLW=Bounty/Land Warrant	RG=Registered Grave
MK=SAR/DAR Marker	PH=Photo	SS=Service Source	BS=Burial Source

299

Rt 620; Orange **GS**: Y **SP**: Jane (-----) (c1756-1802) **VI**: He was a doctor **P**: N **BLW**: N **RG** N **MK**: N **PH**: unk **SS**: DAR #A081759; D **BS**: 22 pg 89.

MORTON, James; b 1756; d 21 Jan 1847 **RU**: Captain, Served in VA Line. Was Commander of co in 4th VA Regt **CEM**: High Hill; GPS unk; See homeplace property loc; Cumberland **GS**: Y **SP**: No info **VI**: Member Board of Trustees Hampton Sidney Colleges and a civil magistrate. Appl 18 Jul 1828 Prince Edward Co. S9035, BLW #1514-200-26 Apr 1798 **P**: Y **BLW**: Y **RG**: N **MK**: N **PH**: unk **SS**: N pg 408; CG pg 2415 **BS**: 157.

MORTON, John; b 20 Nov 1733, Henrico Co, d 1797 **RU**: Lt Colonel/Patriot, appointed Captain 4th Virginia Regt, Cont Line, 19 Feb 1776, resigned 12 Mar 1777 and appointed Lt. Col on 23 Feb 1778. **CEM**: Morton Family; GPS not determined; loc at Sandy River on estate of Lt. Col Morton: Pittsylvania **GS**: Unk **SP**: Mar 1) 1732, Pittsylvania Co, Amy Johnson (1733, Brunswick Co- 17 Jun 1776), 2) 27 Sep 1777, Lucy Blakely (8 Oct 1760, Lunenburg Co-26 Sep1839 in KY) **VI**: Son of Joseph Morton (1693, Henrico Co-22 Mar 1735, Halifax Co). Rec'd 400 acres BLW by VA **P**:N **BLW**: Y **RG**: Y **MK**: N, **PH**: N **SS**: A pg 393; E pg 567; DAR A081827 cites White, Mil Rec Pittsylvania Co; VA 1767-1783, pg 9; SAR P-253073 **BS**: 196.

MORTON, William; b c1750; d 5 Sep 1835 **RU**: Patriot, Provided wagon and team of three horses for militia fr Aug to 31 Oct 1781 that were not returned **CEM**: Oak Green Farm #1; GPS unk; Rt 663 nr Palmyra Church; Orange **GS**: Y **SP**: No info **VI**: No further data **P**: N **BLW**: N **RG**: N **MK**: N **PH**: unk **SS**: Al App II pg 101 **BS**: 22 pg 77; 196. (**MORTON,** William see Appendix G, Addenda)

MOSBY, Littleberry Jr; b 1757 or 28 Jan 1758; d 1 Oct 1821 **RU**: Captain/Patriot, Served in VA & GA Lines. Was in Cont Line as Lt & Capt and was at Siege of Savannah. Was captured at Charleston or Savannah and later furloughed home to VA. Was in House of Delegates fr Powhatan **CEM**: Mosby Family; GPS unk; Powhatan; Powhatan **GS**: U **SP**: No info **VI**: Son of Benjamin & Mary (Poindexter) Mosby. After Revolution became Col and later General in state militia. BLW #64-300, 4000 acres was awarded **P**: unk **BLW**: Y **RG**: Y **MK**: N **PH**: unk **SS**: E pg 568; K pg 310; CG pg 2436; SAR P-253136 **BS**: SAR regis.

MOSELEY, Arthur; b 1752, Powhatan Co; d 1803 **RU**: Lieutenant, Drafted 1780 in Capt Robert Hughes Co while crossing Roanoke at Peyton's Ferry. Was in battle at Guilford CH. Promoted to 2nd Lt 29 Jun 1779. Served in Capt John Torbett's Co. Marched to Yorktown 1781 **CEM**: Fincastle Presbyterian; GPS 37.50017, -79.87558; 108 E Back St, Fincastle; Botetourt **GS**: N **SP**: 1) Nancy Trigg, 2) Pamelia Thorp Crump **VI**: Pen recd 15 Aug 1832. Name is on the SAR plaque at this cemetery **P**: Y **BLW**: unk **RG**: Y **MK**: Y **PH**: N **SS**: AZ pg 78; J-NSSAR 1993 Reg, J- DAR Hatcher; SAR P-253147 **BS**: 80, vol 3,pg 106; 196, JLARC 1, 2.

MOSELEY, Arthur; b 9 Nov 1760, Chesterfield Co; d 31 Aug 1829 **RU**: Lieutenant, Served in VA Line. Ent serv Buckingham Co. Was Orderly Sgt in Capt Joh Moseley's Co. Was 2/Lt in VA Militia. Was in Battle of Guilford CH & at Yorktown **CEM**: Moseley Family; GPS unk; "Wheatlands", 10 mi E of Courthouse on Rt 647; Buckingham **GS**: U **SP**: mar (Dec 1788 Buckingham Co) Sally Perkins (c1722-aft 1855) **VI**: Son of Robert Peter Moseley (1732-1804) & Magdalen Guerrant (1740-1826). Widow appl pen 26 Jan 1848 Buckingham Co & appl there again 20 Mar 1855 for BLW. W7481, BLW #26542-160-55 **P**: Y **BLW**: Y **RG**: Y **MK** Y SAR plaque **PH**: unk **SS**: CG pg 2436; SAR P-253210 **BS**: JLARC 4, 10, 59, 90; 196.

MOSELEY, Benjamin; b 6 Dec 1755; d 25 Jul 1799 **RU**: First Lieutenant, Served in Cont Artillery **CEM**: Rolfton; GPS unk; Hwy 749; Buckingham **GS**: U **SP**: Mar (25 Dec 1783 Chesterfield Co, bond signed by Peter Branch) Mary Branch (1764-1848) d/o Mr. & Mrs. Ridley Branch **VI**: Sol recd 2666 2/3 acres of BL fr State of VA on VA State BLW $1468. Widow appl pen 11 Feb 1839 Buckingham Co. W5387 Name on memorial stone. BLW #2436-300 **P**: Y **BLW**: Y **RG**: Y **MK**: N **PH**: unk **SS**: CG pg 2436; SAR P-253153 **BS**: JLARC 4, 10, 59.

MOSELEY, Edward; b 4 May 1718; d 1808 **RU**: Patriot, Clerk of Princess Anne Co Ct, Jul 1775 **CEM**: Moseley Family; GPS unk; Nr Buffalo Creek; Charlotte **GS**: U **SP**: Amey Green **VI**: Son of Arthur (__-1736) & Martha Branch (Cocke) (1688-__) Moseley. Rank of Capt obtained before Rev War **P**: N **BLW**: N **RG**: Y **MK**: unk **PH**: unk **SS**: J- DAR Hatcher; CO pg 46; DAR A081969; SAR P-253164 **BS**: JLARC 2;.80, vol 3, pg 106.

RU=Rank/Unit	CEM=Cemetery	GS=Gravestone	SP=Spousal Information
VI=Other Veteran Info	P=Pension	BLW=Bounty/Land Warrant	RG=Registered Grave
MK=SAR/DAR Marker	PH=Photo	SS=Service Source	BS=Burial Source

300

MOSELEY, Edward Hack Jr; b 1740; d 1811 or 1814 **RU:** Colonel/Patriot, Commanded Princess Anne Co Militia 1779. Also gave to cause **CEM:** Old Donation Episcopal; GPS 36.86730, -76.12860; 4449 N Witchduck Rd; Virginia Beach City **GS:** U **SP:** 1) Mar (18 Nov 1862) Ann Lovett (1745- by 1774). Charles Gaskin was guardian in 1761 and gave consent for marriage. 2) mar (May 1774) Martha (Patsey) Westwood (1747-1824) **VI:** Son of Edward Hack (1717-1782) & Amey (Green) Moseley. Served on the House of Burgess. Clerk of Princess Anne Co. Vestryman at Old Donation. Father was loyalist. Plaque placed by broken GS by Princess Anne Co NSDAR Bicentennial Project 1977 **P:** unk **BLW:** unk **RG:** Y **MK:** Y SAR plaque **PH:** unk **SS:** E pg 568; AL Ct Bk pg 4 Princess Anne Co; SAR P-253165 **BS:** JLARC 1, 78.

MOSELEY, James; b unk; d 1843 **RU:** Sergeant, Served in Bedford Co Militia **CEM:** Old City; GPS 37.41472, -79.15667; 401 Taylor St; Lynchburg City **GS:** Y **SP:** No info **VI:** No further data **P:** unk **BLW:** unk **RG:** N **MK:** Y SAR plaque **PH:** unk **SS:** E pg 568 **BS:** 62 pg 60.

MOSELEY, Robert Peter; b 14 Feb 1732, Powhaten Co; d 30 Jan 1804 **RU:** Lieutenant/Patriot, Served in VA Colonial Troops. Gave material aid to cause **CEM:** Moseley Family; GPS unk; Willowlake, Rt 56; Buckingham **GS:** U **SP:** 1) Mary Magdalene Guerrant (31 Aug 1740, Goochland Co-3 Apr 1826) d/o Pierre Sr & Magdalene (Trabue) Guerant 2) Martha Povall, d/o Richard & Tabitha (Hudspeth) Povall **VI:** Son of Robert Ligon & Sarah Rachel (Taylor) Moseley **P:** unk **BLW:** unk **RG:** Y **MK:** N **PH:** unk **SS:** AL ct Ck Bk pg 6, 4; SAR P-2532077 **BS:** JLARC 59.

MOSELY, Hildarh (Hillary); b c1760, "prob Princess Anne Co"; d April 1813 **RU:** Patriot, Provided supplies in Norfolk and Princess Anne counties. Filed "Publick Claim" for 260 pounds of beef given to cause.Took oath to the Commonwealth in 1783 as a Common Councilman **CEM:** St Paul's Episcopal; GPS 36.84733, -76.28554; 201 St Paul's Blvd; Norfolk City **GS:** Y **SP:** No info **VI:** "The Order Book and Related Papers of the Common Hall of the Borough of Norfolk Virginia, 1736-1798" lists his public service there **P:** N **BLW:** N **RG** N **MK:** Y SAR plaque **PH:** unk **SS:** CB Counciman 1783 **BS:** 178 Jan 11.

MOSHER, William; b unk; d 1781 **RU:** Soldier, Served fr MA, and killed in the battle at Yorktown **CEM:** Yorktown Victory Monument Tablet; GPS 38.28350, -78.54150; Yorktown; York **GS:** U **SP:** No info **VI:** No further data **P:** unk **BLW:** unk **RG:** Y **MK:** unk **PH:** unk **SS:** J-Yorktown Historian; SAR P-253326 **BS:** JLARC 74.

MOSS, Ann; b 30 Sep 1724, New Kent Co, d 1805 Powhatan **RU:** Patriot; Gave material aid to cause **CEM:** Christian Family; GPS: not determined; loc Vera; Appomattox **GS:** Y **SP:** Mar 25 Nov 1745, William Diuguid (1717-1764) **VI:** d/o Alexander Moss (1680-1772) & Elizabeth Clopton (1682-1745) **P:** N **BLW:** N **RG:** Y **MK:** N **PH:** N **SS:** D vol 3, pgs 774,784, 785; DAR A207031; SAR P-334079 **BS:** 196.

MOSS, John; b c1750, York Co; d 11 Dec 1813 **RU:** Captain, Was clothier for VA Cont Line and 1st VA Regt **CEM:** St John's Episcopal; GPS 37.53183, -77.41958; 2401 E Broad St; Richmond City **GS:** Y **SP:** Sarah Gibbons (c1749-19 Oct 1813) **VI:** No further data **P:** unk **BLW:** unk **RG:** unk **MK:** N **PH:** Y **SS:** J-NSSAR 2000 Reg; SAR P-253367 **BS:** JLARC 76; 196.

MOSS, Joshua; b 5 Aug 1744, Surry Co; d 5 Feb 1829 **RU:** Sergeant/Patriot, Gave material aid to cause **CEM:** Moss Family; GPS unk; See property records; Sussex **GS:** U **SP:** Mar (15 Jun 1769 Sussex Co) Sarah Pennington (c1752-5 Feb 1829) **VI:** No further data **P:** unk **BLW:** unk **RG:** Y **MK:** unk **PH:** unk **SS:** DAR A081478; J-DAR Hatcher; AL Ct Bk pg 6, 10 Mecklenberg Co; SAR P-253371 **BS:** JLARC 2.

MOSS, Nathaniel; b 1730; d 1807 **RU:** Chaplain/Patriot, Gave material aid to cause **CEM:** Moss Meeting House; GPS unk; N fr Upperville; Fauquier **GS:** U **SP:** No info **VI:** No further data **P:** unk **BLW:** unk **RG:** Y **MK:** unk **PH:** unk **SS:** J-NSSAR 1993 Reg; AL Ct Bk pg 36 Frederick Co; SAR P-253378 **BS:** JLARC 1.

MOTLEY, Joseph; b 1720, Gloucester Co; d Aft 15 Dec 1806 **RU:** Patriot, Gave material aid to cause. Performed civil service as member of Grand Jury, Pittsylvania Co **CEM:** Motley Family; GPS unk; Nr Chatham; Pittsylvania **GS:** Y **SP:** (c1750) Martha Ellington (c1730-1780) **VI:** Son of Joseph (1695-1777) & Elizabeth (Forrest) (1700-___) Motley. Fought with Geo Washington in French & Indian Wars and battle

RU=Rank/Unit	CEM=Cemetery	GS=Gravestone	SP=Spousal Information
VI=Other Veteran Info	P=Pension	BLW=Bounty/Land Warrant	RG=Registered Grave
MK=SAR/DAR Marker	PH=Photo	SS=Service Source	BS=Burial Source

of Braddocks Defeat. Will dated 15 Dec 1806 **P:** N **BLW:** N **RG:** Y **MK:** N **PH:** unk **SS:** DAR #A082205; SAR P-253441 AL Ct Bk pg 14,57; **DD BS:** 80, vol 3, pg 107; 196.

MOUGAL, Nicolas; b unk; d 1781 **RU:** Soldier, Served in Touraine Bn and died fr battle at Yorktown **CEM:** French Memorial; GPS 36.81944, -79.39933; Yorktown; York **GS:** U **SP:** No info **VI:** No further data **P:** unk **BLW:** unk **RG:** Y **MK:** unk **PH:** unk **SS:** J-Yorktown Historian; SAR P-**253493 BS:** JLARC 1, 74.

MOULINS, Antoine; b unk; d 1781 **RU:** Soldier, Served in Touraine Bn and died fr battle at Yorktown **CEM:** French Memorial; GPS 36.81944, -79.39933; Yorktown; York **GS:** U **SP:** No info **VI:** No further data **P:** unk **BLW:** unk **RG:** Y **MK:** unk **PH:** unk **SS:** J-Yorktown Historian; SAR P-253507 **BS:** JLARC 1, 74.

MOUNT, Ezekiel; b 22 Nov 1758, Anwell Twp, NJ; d Aft Aug 1833 **RU:** Soldier, Served in NJ & VA Line. Ent Serv Amwell Twp, NJ **CEM:** Mount Family; GPS unk; Mountville off Rts 733 & 734; Loudoun **GS:** U **SP:** No info **VI:** His family established the town. Appl for pen 13 Aug 1833 Loudoun Co. S11117 **P:** Y **BLW:** unk **RG:** Y **MK:** unk **PH:** unk **SS:** CG pg 2444; SAR P-253606 **BS:** JLARC 4.

MOUNTJOY, William; b 17 Apr 1711; d 27 Sep 1777 **RU:** Patriot, Gave material aid to the cause **CEM:** St Paul's Episcopal; GPS 38.33200, -77.12500; 5486 St Paul's Rd off Rt 206; King George **GS:** Y **SP:** No info **VI:** Carried rank of Capt fr Colonial war service. Was originally bur at St Paul's Parrish of Stafford Co **P:** N **BLW:** N **RG:** Y **MK:** unk **PH:** N **SS:** AL Ct Bk 1 pg 5 ll pg 2 Cert; SAR P-253628 **BS:** 03 pg 347.

MOUTEL, Liberal; b unk; d 1781 **RU:** Soldier, Served in Foix Bn and died fr battle at Yorktown **CEM:** French Memorial; GPS 36.81944, -79.39933; Yorktown; York **GS:** U **SP:** No info **VI:** No further data **P:** unk **BLW:** unk **RG:** Y **MK:** unk **PH:** unk **SS:** J-Yorktown Historian; SAR P-253640 **BS:** JLARC 1, 74.

MOWRY (MOWREY), Henry; b 19 Jun 1752, Philadelphia, PA; d 1833 **RU:** Private, Served in Capt Joseph Bell's Co & Capt David Bell's Co, Augusta Co Militia **CEM:** Trinity Episcopal; GPS 38.14917, -79.07521; 214 Beverley St; Staunton City **GS:** Y **SP:** Mar (10 Jun 1791) Mary Gibson **VI:** Son of Johann Peter & Anna Sophia (Germann) Maurer. Gr St shows war service **P:** unk **BLW:** unk **RG:** Y **MK:** unk **PH:** Y **SS:** B; E pg 570; SAR P-263679 **BS:** JLARC 62; 196.

MOYER, Micheal (William); b 27 Sep 1745 Northampton Co, PA; d 7 Apr 1834 **RU:** Private, Drafted Rockingham Co for 4 mos under Capt Jacob Lincoln, McIntosh Campaign. After Cornwallis's surrender,1781 drafted as Militiaman under Capt Baker. Transferred to Capt Baxter's Co. Sent to Winchester to guard British prisoners **CEM:** Moyer Family; GPS 38.48315,-78.55285; Crab Run Rd, nr Bergton; Rockingham **GS:** Y **SP:** Elizabeth (-----) **VI:** Appl for pen 1 Nov 1833. S18107 **P:** Y **BLW:** unk **RG:** N **MK:** N **PH:** Y **SS:** K Vol 3 pg 316; CG pg 2447 **BS:** 32 Hutchens 08.

MOYERS, Casper (Gasper) Jr, b 1755, d Oct 1814 **RU:** Private/ Patriot Capt Sheppard's Co, VA line was paid for serv 24 Oct 1783. As patriot paid supply tax, 1783 Frederick Co. **CEM:** Meyers Family (AKA Old Linville Creek Baptist Ch); Williamsburg Road (Rt. 782), 1.2 mi fr jct Rt 42; Singers Glen; Rockingham **GS:** N **SP:** Nancy Anna Hammock (1763-9 Aug 1842) mar 2d Jacob Weller **VI:** Son of Casper Moyers (1730-Oct 1792, Frederick Co), d/o Rudolph Hammock (1735-1787) & (-----) **P:** N **BLW:** N **RG:** Y **MK:** N **PH:** N **SS:** DAR A202461; SAR P-253733 **BS:** 196.

MOYERS, Michael, b 1747, d aft 1783, **RU:** Patriot, paid personal property tax considered to be a supply tax for Rev War, Rockingham Co, 1782 & 1783 **CEM:** Meyers Family(AKA Old Linville Creek); GPS not determined; fr Rt 42 on Williamsburg Rd (Rt 782) go 1.2 mi, cem on R; Rockingham **GS:** N **SP:** Mary Elizabeth "Polly" Showwalter (1744-1776), d/o Jacob Mathias Showalter (1702, Switzerland-27 Apr 1773, PA) & Maria Saunders (1706-10 May 1778) **VI:** Son of (-----) & Mary Elizabeth Sager (1722-1761) **P:** N **BLW:** N **RG:** N **MK** N **SS:** DV image 13, 1783, Rockingham Co **BS:** 196.

MUIR, James Rev; b 1750, Scotland; d 8 Aug 1820 **RU:** Soldier/Patriot, Signed a Legislative Petition in Alexandria **CEM:** Old Presbyterian Meeting House; GPS 38.48528, -77.23532; 323 S Fairfax St; Alexandria City **GS:** Y **SP:** No info **VI:** Death notice in the *Alexandria Gazette* 9 Aug 1820 **P:** unk **BLW:** unk **RG:** N **MK:** unk **PH:** unk **SS:** J-NSSAR 1993 Reg; S- Alexandria **BS:** JLARC 1; 23 pg 106.

RU=Rank/Unit	CEM=Cemetery	GS=Gravestone	SP=Spousal Information
VI=Other Veteran Info	P=Pension	BLW=Bounty/Land Warrant	RG=Registered Grave
MK=SAR/DAR Marker	PH=Photo	SS=Service Source	BS=Burial Source

MUIR, John; b 1732; d 29 Mar 1791 **RU:** Midshipman, Served in VA State Navy for 3 yrs **CEM:** Old Christ Church Episcopal; GPS 38.80625, -77.04718; 118 N Washington St; Alexandria City **GS:** Y **SP:** No info **VI:** "Here lieth the body of John Muir, late merchant of Alexandria, eldest son of Hugh Muir merchant of Dumfries in Scotland, who departed this life March 20th A.D. 1791 in the 60th yr of his Age". Recd BLW of 2667 acres March 1784 **P:** unk **BLW:** Y **RG:** N **MK:** N **PH:** unk **SS:** E pg 571 **BS:** 20 pg 139; 196.

MUIR, Robert; b 1748; d 21 Dec 1786 **RU:** Captain, Served in 1779-80, unit not determined **CEM:** Old Christ Church Episcopal; GPS 38.80625, -77.04718; 118 N Washington St; Alexandria City **GS:** Y **SP:** No info **VI:** "Here lieth the body of Robert Muir, son of Hugh Muir, Merchant of Dumfries, Scotland, who departed this life December 21, 1786, aged abt 38 yrs." Vestry minutes indicate grave was moved inside churchyard on 28 Mar 1791. Death notice in the Alexandria Gazette 21 Dec 1786, pg 3 **P:** unk **BLW:** unk **RG:** Y **MK:** N **PH:** unk **SS:** E pg 571; SAR P-253795 **BS:** 20 pg 140; 196.

MULL, David; b 5 May 1731, Germany; d 27 Dec 1794 **RU:** Patriot, Gave material aid to the cause **CEM:** St James Reformed; GPS 39.27027, -77.62968; Lovettsville Rd, Lovettsville; Loudoun **GS:** Y **SP:** Eva Margaret Boothe (9 Sep 1731-20 Apr 1801) **VI:** No further data **P:** N **BLW:** N **RG:** N **MK:** N **PH:** unk **SS:** AL Ct Bk lt pg 11 **BS:** 25 pg 215; 196.

MULLER, Nicolas; b unk; d 1781 **RU:** Soldier, Served in Royal Deaux Ponts Bn and died fr battle at Yorktown **CEM:** French Memorial; GPS 36.81944, -79.39933; Yorktown; York **GS:** U **SP:** No info **VI:** No further data **P:** unk **BLW:** unk **RG:**Y **MK:** unk **PH:** unk **SS:** J-Yorktown Historian; SAR P-253885 **BS:** JLARC 1, 74.

MULLINS, David; b 11 May 1758, Goochland Co; d 1829 **RU:** Captain, Served in Marks' Co, 14th VA, with Gen Greene. Held rank of Sergeant in 1st, 10th, 14th Cont Lines. Served in Goochland Co Militia. Appt rank of Capt 16 Jun 1783 **CEM:** Single burial; GPS unk; Off Rt 758, 100 yards off Price Rd, nr Horsepasture, Donnybrook Rd, Ridgeway; Henry **GS:** Y **SP:** 1) Mar (30 Aug 1781, Goochland Co.) Susannah Herndon 2) Mary Alexander Burgess **VI:** Son of John & (-----) Mullins. Named one of his sons after Gen Greene. Recd BLW of 100 acres **P:** unk **BLW:** Y **RG:**Y **MK:** unk **PH:** unk **SS:** E pg 571; BY; SAR P-253910 **BS:** JLARC 2, 4, 38.

MULLINS, John; b unk; d 1849 **RU:** Soldier, Served in Over Mountain Men and fought at Kings Mountain **CEM:** John Powers Plantation; GPS unk; Hwy 83, Clintwood; Dickenson **GS:** Y **SP:** Nancy (-----) **VI:** Info taken fr roadside plaque. Widow drew pen and BLW **P:** Y **BLW:** Y **RG:** Y **MK:** Y SAR **PH:** Y **SS:** CG pg 2450; DAR A082733; SAR P-253920 **BS:** JLARC 81.

MULLINS, Matthew; b 1720; d 1785 **RU:** Sergeant, As Sgt (perhaps QM Sgt) obtained materials to aid the cause in Culpeper Co **CEM:** Mullins; GPS unk; Nr Fife; Goochland **GS:** U **SP:** Mary Maupin **VI:** No further data **P:** unk **BLW:** unk **RG:** Y **MK:** unk **PH:** unk **SS:** J-NSSAR 2000 Reg; AL Ct Bk 1 pg 25; DAR A082734; SAR P-253928 **BS:** JLARC 76.

MUNFORT (MUNFORD, MONFORT, MONFORD), Robert; b unk; d Aft 1781 **RU:** Colonel/Patriot, Commanded militia at battle of Guilford CH. Was recruiting officer for VA troops. Gave material aid to cause **CEM:** Munfort-Lockett Family; GPS unk; Directions to cem in Source 72. Nr Boydton; Mecklenburg **GS:** U **SP:** No info **VI:** No further data **P:** unk **BLW:** unk **RG:** Y **MK:** unk **PH:** unk **SS:** AL Comm Bk IV pg 67, 70 Mecklenburg Co; DB pg 108; SAR P-253995 **BS:** JLARC 72.

MURPHY, Francis; b c1763, County of Queens, Ireland; d 30 Jun 1837 **RU:** Private, Served in Capt John Bankson's PA Militia Regt, 9 Sep 1777 **CEM:** St Mary's Catholic; GPS 38.79390, -77.04750; 310 S Royal St; Alexandria City **GS:** Y **SP:** No info **VI:** Place of birth fr GS, d in his 75th yr **P:** unk **BLW:** unk **RG:** N **MK:** Y SAR Plaque **PH:** Y **SS:** SAR P-334432; AP Muster roll **BS:** 174 pg 111; 196.

MURPHY, John, b 1756 Ayr, So Ayrshire, Scotland, d 18 Jan 1835 **RU:** Private. Capt John Roger's Co in VA from 1 Oct 1781 to 14 Feb 1782 **CEM:** Ayrfield; GPS not determined; loc behind family dwelling in woody area; Kinsale; Westmoreland **GS:** Unk **SP:** No info **VI:** No further data **P:** N **BLW:** N **RG:** N **MK:** N **PH:** N **SS:** G pg 706 **BS:** 196

MURPHY, Timothy; b 1745; d 1837 **RU:** Private, Served in Capt William Alexander's Co. Col William Irvine's PA Regt Nov 1777, part of VA 9th Regt **CEM:** Murphy Family; GPS 36.59220, -80.93800; Rt

RU=Rank/Unit	CEM=Cemetery	GS=Gravestone	SP=Spousal Information
VI=Other Veteran Info	P=Pension	BLW=Bounty/Land Warrant	RG=Registered Grave
MK=SAR/DAR Marker	PH=Photo	SS=Service Source	BS=Burial Source

303

607; Grayson **GS**: U **SP**: No info **VI**: No further data **P**: unk **BLW**: unk **RG**: N **MK**: unk **PH**: unk **SS**: A pg 215-9 **BS**: 04, Apr 2007.

MURRAY, George; b unk; d Feb 1789 **RU**: Private, Served in VA State Artillery **CEM**: Old Christ Church Episcopal; GPS 38.80625, -77.04718; 118 N Washington St; Alexandria City **GS**: N **SP**: No info **VI**: Burial permit issued 10 Feb 1789, "a poor man" **P**: unk **BLW**: unk **RG**: N **MK**: N **PH**: N **SS**: A pg 355 **BS**: 20 pg 151.

MURRAY, James; b 1765, Novum, Madison Co, d Mar 1813 **RU**: Private Capt Reuben Briscoe's Co, Lt Col William Heth's 3rd VA Regt 1778, 3rd Cont Line also serv 4th & 8th Cont Line completing 4 yrs serv **CEM**: Murray Family: GPS not determined; loc .5 mi fr old Novum P.O. Virginia, on Rt 606, at 2d gate; Madison **GS**: N **SP**: Susannah Aylor (1761 Orange CO-1841), d/o Georg Heinrich (Henry) Ochler (Aylor) (1718-1806) & Anna Margaret Thomas (1718-1807). She rec'd pen # R7526 **VI**: SAR indicates rank as LT, perhaps after fall 1783. Paid taxes in Culpeper as James Murry. Recd BLW 200 acres in 1784 **P**: Spouse and heir **BLW** Y **RG**; Y **MK**: N **PH**: N **SS**: C pgs 276, 279; E pg 574; F pg 50; SAR P-254412 **BS**: 196.

MURRAY, James; b unk; d Jun 1795 **RU**: Private, Served in Capt Reuben Briscoe Co, 3rd Cont Line, commanded by Col Thomas Marshall, Sep 1777-Apr 1778 **CEM**: Old Christ Church Episcopal; GPS 38.80625, -77.04718; 118 N Washington St; Alexandria City **GS**: N **SP**: No info **VI**: Burial permit issued 18 Jun 1795 **P**: unk **BLW**: unk **RG**: N **MK**: N **PH**: N **SS**: A pg 279 **BS**: 20 pg 151.

MURRAY, Reuben; b 1761; d 1845 **RU**: Sergeant, Served 1781 in Capt Turner Morehead's Co at Williamsburg, and on next tour was at Yorktown in Capt James Winn & Capt Linn Sharps Co. Awarded Sgt on this tour. Guarded prisoners on way to Winchester **CEM**: Marshall; GPS 38.86919, -77.83445; Marshall; Fauquier **GS**: Y **SP**: Mar (23 Sep 1795 (bond) Fauquier Co, Thomas Glascock security, Marriage return by John Monroe, minister 24 Sept 1795) Cathrine Chinn Glascock. Called Catherine Glascock on the bond and Catherine Chinn (Glascock) by Gott. **VI**: Claim was rejected for pen 1833. In 1838 he was living in Fauquier Co, where papers were returned. R7524 **P**: N **BLW**: unk **RG**: Y   **MK**: unk **PH**: unk **SS**: AZ pg 171-172; CG pg 2461; Fauquier Co Marriages pg 145; SAR P-254461 **BS**: JLARC 4,16; 196.

MURRAY/MURREY Samuel; b unk; d 2 Nov 1808 **RU**: Corporal, Served in Capt Thomas Moultries 5th Co, Col Francis Marion's SC Regt in Nov 1779 **CEM**: Old Stone Methodist; GPS 39.11725, -77.56609; 168 W Cornwall St, Leesburg; Loudoun **GS**: Y **SP**: Mary (-----) (_-13 Dec 1799) **VI**: Son of Samuel Murrey & Betsey (-----) Justice of Peace in Loudoun Co, VA Sep 1809 **P**: unk **BLW**: unk **RG**:N **MK**: N **PH**: unk **SS**: A pg 290-292 **BS**: 25 pg 216.

MURREY, Samuel M; b 1774, probably DL, d 10 Sep 1821 **RU**: Private Haslet's Regt, DL Militia **CEM**: Old Stone Church (AKA Old Methodist Church); GPS: 39.11725,-77.65509; 168 Cornwell St, NW Leesburg; Loudoun **GS**: Yes **SP**: Elizabeth "Betsey" Donohoe (22 Jun 1765-21 Oct 1831), d/o Cornelius Kirkley Donohoe (_-1799) & Mary McDowell (1733-1815) **VI**: No further data **P**: N **BLW**: N **RG**: N **MK**: N **PH**: N **SS**: Fold 3 Serv Index Card **BS**: 196.

MURSON, Arthur; b 1734, Greenook, Scotland; d 30 May 1798 **RU**: Patriot, Gave to cause 10 pairs of shoes, wood, fodder, corn, beef, other items 1775. Was trustee for Falmouth VA **CEM**: Hartwood Presbyterian; GPS 38.40188, -77.56745; 50 Hartwood Ch Rd, Fredericksburg; Stafford **GS**: Y **SP**: No info **VI**: Died in Hartwood, Stafford Co. Pierce found his grave is physically located in Jefferson Co WV. However this is not true as compiler has been to his gr site in Hartwood cem. **P**: N **BLW**: N **RG**: N **MK**: N **PH**: Y **SS**: D Vol II pg 817 Vol 1 pg 754 **BS**: 03 pg 240. 34 pg 211.

MUSE, Battaile; b c1755; d 1805 **RU**: Patriot, Gave material aid to the cause **CEM**: Muse-Lewis "The Moorings"; GPS unk; Lewis Farm nr WV; Clarke **GS**: Y **SP**: No info **VI**: No further data **P**: N **BLW**: N **RG**: Y **MK**: N **PH**: unk **SS**: AL Ct Bk pg 18; SAR P-254500 **BS**: 58 pg 13.

MUSE, Daniel Sr; b 1715, Washington Parish, Westmoreland Co; d 6 Dec 1784 **RU**: Patriot, Gave material aid to cause **CEM**: Muse Family; GPS unk; See property records; Richmond Co **GS**: U **SP**: mar (1739, Lunenburg Parish, Richmond Co) Hannah Dozier (bef 1720, Westmoreland Co-__) **VI**: Son of Thomas (1665-__) & Elizabeth (Sturman) (abt 1680-__) Muse. Died in Lunenburg Parish, Richmond Co

RU=Rank/Unit	CEM=Cemetery	GS=Gravestone	SP=Spousal Information
VI=Other Veteran Info	P=Pension	BLW=Bounty/Land Warrant	RG=Registered Grave
MK=SAR/DAR Marker	PH=Photo	SS=Service Source	BS=Burial Source

304

P: N **BLW:** N **RG:** Y **MK:** unk **PH:** unk **SS:** AL Ct Bk pg 14 Richmond Co; SAR P-254514 **BS:** JLARC 76.

MUSTAIN (MUSTEIN), Avery; b 26 Feb 1756, Pittsylvania Co; d 31 Aug 1833 **RU:** Private, In 1776 served in Capt Thomas Dillard Co. Marched to Gwynns Island against Lord Dunmore. Was in Capt Jesse Heard Co to Holston River against Cherokees. In 1780 was in Capt Isaac Clement's Co in Battle of Camden. In Feb 1781 was in Capt Gabriel Shelton/Capt Thomas Smith Cos. In Aug 1781 was in Capt William Dix/Capt Charles Williams's Cos, in Siege of York. After Cornwallis, surrendered was guard of prisoners on march to Noland's Ferry on Potomac **CEM:** Mustain Barn; GPS 36.56637, -79.18520; Btw Gretna & Mt Airy, private property behind barn; Pittsylvania **GS:** Y **SP:** Mar (Mar 1783) Mary Barber **VI:** Sol appl pen 1832. Widow appl pen1839 Pittsylvania Co **P:** Y **BLW:** unk **RG:** N **MK:** N **PH:** unk **SS:** K Vol 3 pg 330-1; AS; AX; DAR A083621; SAR P-254562 **BS:** 174.(MUSTAIN, Jesse see Appendix G)

MUSTOE, Anthony; b 1748 Tongue Yard, London, England; d 1807 **RU:** Sergeant, Served in Augusta Co Militia as well as 3rd, 5th, 7th, 12th Cont Lines **CEM:** Mustoe Family; GPS unk; 5 mi S of Healing Springs; Bath **GS:** U **SP:** 1) Mary Wright 2) Mar (13 Mar 1780) Dorothy Silor (6 Feb 1760 Frederick Co MD-25 Jul 1831), d/o Jacob & Dorothy (-----) Silor **VI:** Came to America 1772. Sherriff of Augusta Co. Postmaster in Warm Springs 1796-Oct 1807 **P:** unk **BLW:** unk **RG:** N **MK:** N **PH:** unk **SS:** E pg 576; SAR P-254566 **BS:** 159 Mustoe.

MYERS, Lewis; b 1764, Leichtenburg, Ger d 24 Feb 1800 **RU:** Private, Capt James Bell's Company, Augusta Co Militia **CEM:** St Johns Episcopal; GPS: 37.53183,-77.41598; 401 E. Broad St; Richmond City **GS:** Yes **SP:** No spousal data; **VI:** No further data **P:** N **BLW:** N **RG:** N **MK:** N **PH:** N **SS:** E pg 576 **BS:** 196.

MYERS, Samuel; b 1748; d 1830 **RU:** Private, Served in VA Line **CEM:** Hebrew; GPS 33.55175, -77.42976; 300 Hospital St; Richmond City **GS:** Y **SP:** No info **VI:** No further data **P:** unk **BLW:** unk **RG:** N **MK:** N **PH:** unk **SS:** E pg 576 **BS:** 168 Hebrew.

MYERS / MYRES, John C; b 1761; d 17 Mar 1802 **RU:** Private, Served in 1st VA Regt of Foot, Mar 1777 **CEM:** Old Christ Church Episcopal; GPS 36.83407, -81.59338; Old Ebenezer Rd Rt 659; Alexandria City **GS:** Y **SP:** Mar (14 Nov 1799) Mrs. Margaret Bowyer, relict of Mr. Henry Bowyer, dec'd **VI:** Died age 41 after along and painful illness **P:** unk **BLW:** unk **RG:**N **MK:** N **PH:** unk **SS:** AP RW Roll **BS:** 110 pg 95; 196.

MYTINGER, Daniel; b 14 Dec 1760, Lancaster, PA; d 23 Mar 1836 **RU:** Captain, Specific service not found; Gr St indicates rank **CEM:** German Reformed Church; GPS 39.08150, -78.21840; Mulberry St, Stephen City; Frederick **GS:** Y **SP:** Catherine Elizabeth Campbell (8 Jul 1768-21 Nov 1843) **VI:** Son of George Ludwig & Maria Margaretha (Engelhardt) Meittinger **P:** unk **BLW:** unk **RG:** N **MK:** unk **PH:** unk **SS:** B **BS:** 112.

NAFUERN, Francois; b unk; d 1781 **RU:** Seaman, Served on "Hextor" and died from Yorktown battle **CEM:** French Memorial; GPS 36.81944, -79.39933; Yorktown; York **GS:** U **SP:** No info **VI:** No further data **P:** unk **BLW:** unk **RG:** Y **MK:** unk **PH:** unk **SS:** J-Yorktown Historian; SAR P-254756 **BS:** JLARC 1, 74.

NALFIN, Remy; b unk; d 1781 **RU:** Soldier, Served in Santogne Bn and died fr battle at Yorktown **CEM:** French Memorial; GPS 36.81944, -79.39933; Yorktown; York **GS:** U **SP:** No info **VI:** No further data **P:** unk **BLW:** unk **RG:** Y **MK:** unk **PH:** unk **SS:** J-Yorktown Historian; SAR P-254797 **BS:** JLARC 1, 74.

NALLE, Martin II; b 1707 Tappahannock, Essex Co; d 15 Sep 1788 **RU:** Captain, Served in 3rd VA Regt **CEM:** Devils Run Farm; GPS unk; Use tax records for location; Culpeper **GS:** U **SP:** Isabelle (-----) (1710-1788) **VI:** Son of Martin (1675 England-1728 Essex Co) & Mary (Aldin) (1681-1734) Nalle **P:** unk **BLW:** unk **RG:** Y **MK:** unk **PH:** unk **SS:** Al Ct Bk I pg 12; DAR A081440; SAR P-254803 **BS:** 196.

NANCE, Reuben; b 8 Jul 1745; d 13 Jan 1812 **RU:** Ensign/Patriot, Served in Henry Co Militia Oct 1777. Gave material aid to cause **CEM:** Nance Plantation Home; GPS unk; Rt 58, 2 mi E of Martinsville; Henry **GS:** U **SP:** 1) Amy Williamson 2) Nancy Brown **VI:** Son of William and Ann (Epps) Nance Jr **P:** unk **BLW:** unk **RG:** Y **MK:** unk **PH:** unk **SS:** E pg 577; AL Ct Bk pg 4 Henry Co; DAR A081461; SAR P-254807 **BS:** 196.

RU=Rank/Unit	CEM=Cemetery	GS=Gravestone	SP=Spousal Information
VI=Other Veteran Info	P=Pension	BLW=Bounty/Land Warrant	RG=Registered Grave
MK=SAR/DAR Marker	PH=Photo	SS=Service Source	BS=Burial Source

NEBLE, Georges; b unk; d 1781 **RU**: Soldier, Served in Royal Deaux Ponts Bn and died fr battle at Yorktown **CEM**: French Memorial; **GPS** 36.81944, -79.39933; Yorktown; York **GS**: U **SP**: No info **VI**: No further data **P**: unk **BLW**: unk **RG**: Y **MK**: unk **PH**: unk **SS**: J-Yorktown Historian; SAR P-255075 **BS**: JLARC 1, 74.

NEBLETT, Sterling; 23 Oct 1753,Surry Co, d 1832 **RU**: Patriot; Provided stores for the Continental Army **CEM**: Neblett; **GPS**; 36.86750,-78.08420; Rt 138, S of jct with Rt 619, Lunenburg **GS**: No **SP**: 1) mar (1744) Mary Chappell (c1756, Sussex Co-1792), d/o James Chappell & Elizabeth Briggs, 2) mar (bond Lunenburg Co, 23 Sep 1797) Mrs Betsey Coleman **VI**: No further data **P**: N **BLW**: N **RG**: N **MK**: N **PH**: N **SS**: CD, Memorial # 141652981 **BS**: 196.

NEEL, William; b 1761, Lancaster, PA; d 11 Feb 1841 **RU**: Private, Enlisted Augusta Co 1777-8. Served in VA Line **CEM**: Sifford; **GPS** unk; White Gate; Giles **GS**: U **SP**: mar (1792 or 93) Rhoda Harman (__-16 Jan 1846 Giles Co) **VI**: Had lived in Giles Co since 1794. Pen appl for 29 Oct 1832 Giles Co age 71. S15945 **P**: Y **BLW**: unk **RG**: Y **MK**: unk **PH**: unk **SS**: K Vol 4 pg 6; CG Vol 3 pg 2475; DAR A081829; SAR P-255114 **BS**: JLARC 3.

NEFF, Abraham; b c1760; d unk **RU**: Private?, Served in Capt Jacob Holeman's Co, Dunmore Co Militia **CEM**: Neff Family; **GPS** unk; Vic Stonewall Jackson HS; Shenandoah **GS**: N **SP**: No info **VI**: No further data **P**: unk **BLW**: unk **RG**: N **MK**: N **PH**: N **SS**: C Sec IV pg 608 **BS**: 79 pg 22.

NEFF, Christian; b 1754, Augusta Co; d 21 May 1814 **RU**: Private, Served in Capt Jacob Holeman's Co, Dunmore Co Militia **CEM**: Neff-Kagey; **GPS** 38.69443, -78.65895; Rt 827, Old Bridge Rd, New Market; Shenandoah **GS**: U **SP**: Maria Grabill (1751-24 Jan 1813) **VI**: Son of John Henry (1705-1784) & Ann (-----) (1714-1796) Neff **P**: unk **BLW**: unk **RG**: N **MK**: unk **PH**: unk **SS**: C pg 607-608 **BS**: 196.

NEFF, Francis "Frantz"; b 1740, Conestoga, Lancaster Co, PA, d 3 Oct 1812, Mt Jackson, Shenandoah Co **RU**: Patriot Gave material aid to cause **CEM**: Neff-Kagey; **GPS**: 38.69443,-78.86895; E of Rt 827 loop, New Market, Shenandoah **GS**: Yes **SP**: Elizabeth (-----) (1743-1804) **VI**: Son of John Henry Neff (1705-1784) & Ann (-----) (1714 -1796) **P**: N **BLW**: N **RG**: N **MK**: N **PH**: N **SS**: AL Ct Bk pgs 4,16 Shenandoad Co **BS**: 196.

NEFF, Jacob; b 1742, Frederick Co; d 5 Aug 1820 **RU**: Patriot, Paid personal property supply tax, Shenandoah Co, 1782 **CEM**: Neff-Kagey; **GPS** 38.69443, -78.65895; Rt 827, Old Bridge Rd, New Market; Shenandoah **GS**: Y **SP**: Mar (3 Dec 1765) Barbara Grabill (1742-1804); 2) Mandy Burkholder **VI**: Son of John Henry (1705-1784) & Ann (-----) (1714-1796) Neff. Was a doctor **P**: unk **BLW**: unk **RG**: Y **MK**: N **PH**: unk **SS**: DV; SAR P-255164 **BS**: 79 pg 56; 196.

NEFF, John Henry; b 1705, Germany, d 8 Jun 1784 **RU**: Patriot, Paid personal property tax 1783, Shenandoah Co considered a payment to support cause **CEM**: Neff-Kagey; **GPS**: 38.69443,-78.86895;; E of Rt 827 loop, New Market; Shenandoah **GS**: Yes **SP**: mar c1734, Lancaster Co, PA, Ann (-----) (1714 Germany-14 Apr 1796) **VI**: Son of Hans Heinrich Neff **P**: N **BLW**: N **RG**: N **MK**: N **PH**: N **SS**: CD, Memorial # 72557806; DV: image 14.pdf **BS**: 196

NEFF, Michael; b 15 May 1756, Lancaster Co, PA; d 22 Jan 1825 **RU**: Private, Served in Capt Duck's Co, 1st Co, 3rd Bn, Lancaster Co PA Militia **CEM**: Neff Family; **GPS** unk; E of Fairview Church on Charles Roberts property, Rural Retreat; Wythe **GS**: U **SP**: Christina Kapp (1746-1830) **VI**: Son of John George & Elizabeth (Stupp) Neff. Death date only on original stone. DAR Plaque **P**: unk **BLW**: unk **RG**: Y **MK**: Y DAR plaque **PH**: unk **SS**: CD; DAR A081995; SAR P-255169 **BS**: JLARC 1,2,40,123; 80, vol 3, pg 116; 196.

NEHS, Jacob; b 1738, PA; d 1823 **RU**: Private/ Patriot, Served in PA. Took Oath of allegiance in PA **CEM**: Mt Solomon's Lutheran; **GPS** 38.44180, -78.44201; Solomon Church Rd & Rt 42, Forestville; Shenandoah **GS**: Y **SP**: Anna Marie Dettamore **VI**: SAR marker **P**: N **BLW**: N **RG**: Y **MK**: Y SAR Granite **PH**: N **SS**: AK - Col James Wood II Nov 2014; DAR A081962; SAR P-330733 **BS**: 04.

NEILL, William; b 20 Oct 1753, Baltimore MD; d 14 May 1824 **RU**: Captain, Commanded a co in William Campbell's Regt **CEM**: Cem Name unk; **GPS** unk; Rt 58,west ofJonesville; Lee **GS**: Y **SP**: Bathsheba Harrison **VI**: No further data **P**: unk **BLW**: unk **RG**: N **MK**: N **PH**: unk **SS**: 32 Dec 06 **BS**: 4.

RU=Rank/Unit	CEM=Cemetery	GS=Gravestone	SP=Spousal Information
VI=Other Veteran Info	P=Pension	BLW=Bounty/Land Warrant	RG=Registered Grave
MK=SAR/DAR Marker	PH=Photo	SS=Service Source	BS=Burial Source

NELSON, Alexander; b 14 Jan 1749; d 2 Jan 1834 **RU:** Private, Enlisted 24 Jan 1776; served in Capt James's Taylor's Co, Col Wayne's PA Battalion until 26 Nov 1776. **CEM:** Augusta Stone Presbyterian; GPS 38.23926, -78.97356, GS 38.1415,-78.5821; 28 Old Stone Church Ln, Ft Defiance; Augusta **GS:** Y **SP:** Mar (29 Jan 1784) Anne Mathews (17 Jul 1763-9 Jan 1829) d/of Sampson (1737 Ireland-__) & Mary (Lockhart) (__-1781) Mathews **VI:** Died age "nearly 85 yrs" **P:** unk **BLW:** unk **RG:** Y **MK:** Y SAR plaque **PH:** unk **SS:** A pg 200-2; E pg 580; JLARC Repor: SAR P-255263 **BS:** JLARC 1, 2, 8, 23, 62; 2 pg 21; 196.

NELSON, Alexander; b 1750; d 12 Sep 1828 **RU:** Private, Enlisted in Army autumn 1780 in Staunton and served in Capt Lapsley's Co, 1st VA Regt **CEM:** Augusta Stone Presbyterian; GPS 38.23926, -78.97356; 28 Old Stone Church Ln, Ft Defiance; Augusta **GS:** Y **SP:** Nancy Mathews (1763-19 Jan 1829) **VI:** Appl pen 23 Aug 1825 Augusta Co. **P:** Y **BLW:** unk **RG:** Y **MK:** Y SAR plaque **PH:** unk **SS:** G pg 60-1; JLARC Report; SAR P-255262 **BS:** JLARC 8, 23.; 80 vol 3, pg 117

NELSON, Alexander; b unk; d unk **RU:** Soldier, SAR graves Registry does not provide military or patriotic service **CEM:** New Providence Presbyterian; GPS 37.95130, -79.30250; 1208 New Providence Rd, Raphine; Rockbridge **GS:** U **SP:** No info **VI:** No further data **P:** unk **BLW:** unk **RG:** Y **MK:** unk **PH:** unk **SS:** SAR P-255261; SAR application **BS:** JLARC 63, 79.

NELSON, Hugh; b 1750; d 3 Oct 1800 **RU:** Patriot, Gave material aid to cause **CEM:** Grace Episcopal; GPS 37.23560, -76.50750; 115 Church St, Yorktown; York **GS:** U **SP:** Judith Page (7 Mar 1753-19 Mar 1827) d/o John Williamson (1724-1774) & Jane (Byrd) (1729-1774) Page **VI:** Son of William (1711-1772) & Elizabeth (Burwell) (1718-1798) Nelson **P:** N **BLW:** N **RG:** Y **MK:** unk **PH:** unk **SS:** AL Ct Bk II pg 3a; SAR P-255298 **BS:** 196.

NELSON, John; b 1753 or 1756; d 18 Feb 1827 **RU:** Soldier, Served in Cont & VA Lines **CEM:** Bethel Presbyterian; GPS 38.04257, -79.17283, GS38.0230,-79.1018; 563 Bethel Green Rd, Middlebrook; Augusta **GS:** Y row 17 **SP:** Mar (25 Jul 1781, Wm & Mary College chapel) Nancy "Ann" Carter of Williamsburg **VI:** Widow appl pen 13 Nov 1837 Mecklenburg Co age 74. W5414 & VA 1/2 Pay (see N.A. Acc #874 #050124 1/2 Pay). Son of "Secretary Nelson of York" **P:** Y **BLW:** unk **RG:** Y **MK:** unk **PH:** N **SS:** CG Vol 3 pg 2478; SAR P-255326 **BS:** JLARC 62, 63.

NELSON, Lucy Grymes; b 24 Aug 1743, Brandon, Middlesex Co; d 14 Sep 1830 **RU:** Patriot, Patriotic information not determined, See DAR Senate Document year 1975 for pacifics **CEM:** Fork Episcopal Church; GPS 37.85340, -77.53100; 12566 Old Ridge Rd, Doswell; Hanover **GS:** Y **SP:** Thomas Nelson, Jr (18 Dec 1738 York (later Yorktown)-2 Jan 1789 Hanover Co) **VI:** Daug of Philip & Mary (Randolph) Grymes **P:** N **BLW:** N **RG:** Y **MK:** N **PH:** unk **SS:** AR Vol 3 pg 117; SAR P-255400 **BS:** 80 vol 3 pg 117.

NELSON, Thomas, b 1716; d 1782 **RU:** Patriot; Served as Secretary of Colnial Council of VA Journal. 1775 **CEM:** Grace Episcopal Church: GPS 37.235600,-76.507500; 115 Church St, Yorktown;York **GS:** N but rec indicate burial there **SP:** Mar c1745, Lucy Armistead **VI:** Son of Thomas Nelson, (1677-1745) & Margaret Reade (1681-__) **P:** N **BLW:** N **RG:** Y **MK:**N **PH:** N **SS:** DAR A082255 cites *Journal of Colonial VA*, vol I, pg 86 **BS:** 196.

NELSON, Thomas Jr; b 18 Dec 1738, York (later Yorktown); d 2 Jan 1789 **RU:** General/Patriot, At Yorktown seige. Was Signer Declaration of Independence and Wartime Gov of VA. Commander of VA forces during Rev War **CEM:** Grace Episcopal; GPS 37.23560, -76.50750; 115 Church St, Yorktown; York **GS:** Y **SP:** mar (29 Jul 1762 York Co) Lucy Grymes (24 Aug 1743 Brandon, Middlesex Co-14 Sep 1830 Hanover Co), d/o Philip & Mary (Randolph) Grymes **VI:** Signed Declaration of Independence. Died in Hanover Co **P:** unk **BLW:** unk **RG:** Y **MK:** Y SAR **PH:** unk **SS:** J-NSSAR 1993 Reg, AR Vol 3 p118; DAR A082824; SAR P-255377 **BS:** JLARC 1,2; Nelson-Page fam archives.; 80, vol3, pg 118.

NELSON, Thomas; b 9 Aug 1763; d 8 Jan 1801 **RU:** Lieutenant, rec'd as Co Lt, 20 Aug 1782 **CEM** Grace Episcopal Church; GPS 37.235600, -76.507500; 115 Church St, Yorktown; York **GS:** N but rec indicate burial there **SP:** mar c1790, Sally Burwell Page, d/o John Page & Frances Burwell **VI:** Son of Thomas Nelson, Jr (18 Dec 1738-2 Jan 1789) & Lucy Grimes (24 Aug 1743-14 Sep 1830) **P:** N **BLW:** N **RG:** N **MK:** N **PH:** unk **SS:** E pgs 580, 581 **BS:** 196.

NELSON, Willaim; b 1754; d 1813 **RU:** Patriot, Gave material aid to cause. Captured by British at Castle Hill, Albemarle Co **CEM:** Grace Episcopal; GPS 37.23560, -76.50750; 115 Church St, Yorktown; York

RU=Rank/Unit	CEM=Cemetery	GS=Gravestone	SP=Spousal Information
VI=Other Veteran Info	P=Pension	BLW=Bounty/Land Warrant	RG=Registered Grave
MK=SAR/DAR Marker	PH=Photo	SS=Service Source	BS=Burial Source

307

GS: U **SP:** 1) Mary Taliaferro (1760 James City Co-1786) d/o Richard (1732-1789) & Rebecca (Cocke) (1725-1818) Taliaferro 2) Abby Byrd d/o Willliam E. & Mary (Willing) Byrd **VI:** Son of William (1711-1772) & Elizabeth (Burwell) (1718-1798) Nelson. Judge of District Ct **P:** N **BLW:** N **RG:** N **MK:** unk **PH:** unk **SS:** AL Ct Bk Albemarle Co **BS:** 196.

NELSON, William; b unk; d 1854 **RU:** Captain, Served in Fairfax Co Militia 25 Jan 1777 to 21 Jun 1781 **CEM:** Adams-Nelson-Sewell Family; GPS unk; 1443 Layman St, McLean; Fairfax **GS:** Y **SP:** No info **VI:** Died age 76 in 1854 **P:** unk **BLW:** unk **RG:** Y **MK:** N **PH:** unk **SS:** A pg 389; SAR P-255313 **BS:** 61 vol VI, pg MI 90.

NELSON, William; b 11 Apr 1754; d 30 Jun 1831 **RU:** Colonel, Served in 7th VA Regt as Lt in Co. Oct 1776-Oct 1777; as Capt commanded Co militia fr Westmoreland Co Sep 1779; was promoted to Col, 8th VA Regt **CEM:** Nelson Fam at Wingfield; GPS unk; Coatesville; Hanover **GS:** Y **SP:** Mildred (-----) (21 Jul1758-3 Jun 1806) **VI:** No further data **P:** unk **BLW:** unk **RG:** Y **MK:** N **PH:** unk **SS:** E pg 581;SAR P-255313; **BS:** 31 vol 1 pg 7; 196.

NELSON, William; b 17 Jun 1746, Yorktown; d 24 Nov 1807 **RU:** Lit Colonel, Served as a Private in a VA Co 1775. Promoted to Maj in 7th Cont Line 29 Feb 1776; to Lt Col 7 Oct 1776; resigned 25 Oct 1777 **CEM:** Forkquarter; GPS unk; Calno Rd Rt 601, Norment Ferry; King William **GS:** U **SP:** Mar (24 Nov 1770) Lucy Chiswell (1752- 4 Apr 1811) d/o Col John & Elizabeth (Randolph) Chiswell. Also bur here **VI:** Son of Thomas (1716-1782) and Lucy (Amistead) Nelson **P:** unk **BLW:** unk **RG:**Y **MK:** unk **PH:** unk **SS:** E pg 581; SAR P- 255392 **BS:** 196.

NELSON, William; b unk; d 1823 **RU:** Major, Served in 7th VA Regt 29 Feb to 7 Oct 1776 **CEM:** Tinkling Spring Presbyterian; GPS 38.08472, -78.98278; 30 Tinkling Spring Dr, Fishersville; Augusta **GS:** N **SP:** No info **VI:** Only stone for William Nelson was b 1785 **P:** unk **BLW:** unk **RG:** N **MK:** N **PH:** N **SS:** G pg 832 **BS:** 142 Tingling Spr.

NELSON, William; b 9 Aug 1763, Yorktown; d 8 Jan 1801 **RU:** Navy Enlisted Man, Served on Brig "Jefferson," Dec 1779, 20 Jan 1780 **CEM:** Grace Episcopal; GPS 37.23560, -76.50750; 115 Church St, Yorktown; York **GS:** N **SP:** Mar (1790) Sally Burwell Page, d/o Gov John & Frances (Burwell) Page **VI:** No further data **P:** unk **BLW:** unk **RG:** N **MK:** unk **PH:** N **SS:** L pg 230 **BS:** 196.

NESTEL (NESTELL, NESTLE, NISTELL), Peter; b 1750, Albany, NY; d 30 Apr 1817 **RU:** Major, Served in 6th Co, 2nd NY Artillery. Obit records indicate Rev War services at the period of Arnold's defection [as] particularly conspicuous and procured him a prominent place in the favor of Gen Washington, who afterwards gave him many evidences of his esteem and approbation, and to the hour of his death, spoke of him as one of his most faithful co-operators **CEM:** St Paul's Episcopal; GPS 36.84733, -76.28554; 201 St Paul's Blvd; Norfolk City **GS:** N **SP:** 1) Lucy (Nistell) 2) Mary (-----) **VI:** Member of Society of the Cincinnati. Cenotaph marked beside first wife's grave. Educated in Germany **P:** unk **BLW:** unk **RG:** Y **MK:** Y SAR plaque **PH:** N **SS:** CB; G pg 902; SAR P-255447 **BS:** 32 Jul 2010.

NEUVEU, Edme; b unk; d 1781 **RU:** Soldier, Served in Touraine Bn and died fr battle at Yorktown **CEM:** French Memorial; GPS 36.81944, -79.39933; Yorktown; York **GS:** U **SP:** No info **VI:** No further data **P:** unk **BLW:** unk **RG:** Y **MK:** unk **PH:** unk **SS:** J-Yorktown Historian; SAR P-255493 **BS:** JLARC 1, 74.

NEUVILLE, Jean; b unk; d 1781 **RU:** Seaman, Served on "Magnanime" and died from Yorktown battle **CEM:** French Memorial; GPS 36.81944, -79.39933; Yorktown; York **GS:** U **SP:** No info **VI:** No further data **P:** unk **BLW:** unk **RG:** Y **MK:** unk **PH:** unk **SS:** J-Yorktown Historian; SAR P-255494 **BS:** JLARC 1, 74.

NEW, Pierre; b unk; d 1781 **RU:** Soldier, Served in Royal Deaux Ponts Bn and died fr battle at Yorktown **CEM:** French Memorial; GPS 36.81944, -79.39933; Yorktown; York **GS:** U **SP:** No info **VI:** No further data **P:** unk **BLW:** unk **RG:** unk **MK:** unk **PH:** unk **SS:** J-Yorktown Historian; SAR P-255565 **BS:** JLARC 1, 74.

NEWELL, James Sr; b 29 Sep 1749, Augusta Co; d 2 Mar 1823 **RU:** Captain/Patriot, Commanded a co in Montgomery Co Militia. Gave material aid to cause **CEM:** Newell-Trigg-Sanders; GPS unk; N side of 619 abt .5 mile W of jct with 636, Austinville; Wythe **GS:** U **SP:** Mar (23 Jan 1771) Sarah Wood (3 Mar 1752-23 Mar 1831) d/o William & Martha (Drake) Wood **VI:** Cemetery in grove of trees, enclosed by

RU=Rank/Unit
VI=Other Veteran Info
MK=SAR/DAR Marker

CEM=Cemetery
P=Pension
PH=Photo

GS=Gravestone
BLW=Bounty/Land Warrant
SS=Service Source

SP=Spousal Information
RG=Registered Grave
BS=Burial Source

308

fence. DAR plaque in cemetery **P:** unk **BLW:** unk **RG:** Y **MK:** unk **PH:** unk **SS:** AL Ct Bk pg 4 Henry Co; SAR P-255700 **BS:** JLARC 2, 40,123 ; 80 vol 3, pg 119; 196.

NEWELL, John; b 29 Sep 1743; d 16 Apr 1833 **RU:** Captain, Commanded a company of frontier troops **CEM:** Beeler; GPS unk; Cedar Creek; Frederick **GS:** Y **SP:** 1) Mar (1768) Margaret Ware) 2) Mar (1804) Elizabeth Wright **VI:** No further data **P:** unk **BLW:** unk **RG:** N **MK:** N **PH:** unk **SS:** DAR #A45210; G pg 595 **BS:** 50 pg 75.

NEWLAND, John; b 29 Sep1743; d 1833 **RU:** Patriot, Gave material aid to cause **CEM:** Newland; GPS unk; 1 mi W on Rt 692 fr jct with Rt 749, on hill on right, Cedar Springs; Wythe **GS:** Y **SP:** Savina Waggoner (1751-1801) **VI:** Bur on property owned in 1981 by Leroy Sloper **P:** N **BLW:** N **RG:** N **MK:** unk **PH:** unk **SS:** AL Ct Bk pg 25 Montgomrey Co **BS:** JLARC 123.; 196.

NEWMAN, John; b unk; d unk **RU:** Captain, Served in 13th VA Militia Regt **CEM:** David Kagy Farm; GPS unk; Nr New Market; Shenandoah **GS:** U **SP:** No info **VI:** No further data **P:** unk **BLW:** unk **RG:** Y **MK:** unk **PH:** unk **SS:** AR Vol 3 p120; SAR P- 255894 **BS:** JLARC 2; 80, vol 3; pg 120.

NEWMAN, Walter; b 1742, Augusta Co; d 29 Jul1815 **RU:** Private/Patriot, Gave material aid to cause **CEM:** Arthur Hirsh Family; GPS unk; Nr New Market; Shenandoah **GS:** U **SP:** Mar (c1766) Catherine Lair (5 Nov 1747-1 Feb 1815) d/o Mathias (1714, Palatinate, Germany-25 jun 1787 Rockingham Co) & Catherine Margaretha (Moyer) (__ Germany-1804) Lair **VI:** No further data **P:** unk **BLW:** unk **RG:** Y **MK:** unk **PH:** unk **SS:** J-NSSAR 1993 Reg, J- DAR Hatcher; AL Ct Bk pg 1 Shenandoah Co; SAR P-255931 **BS:** JLARC 1, 2; 80, vol 3; pg 121.

NEWTON, Solomon; b unk; d 1781 **RU:** Soldier, Served fr MA, and died fr the Battle at Yorktown **CEM:** Yorktown Victory Monument Tablet; GPS 38.28350, -78.54150; Yorktown; York **GS:** U **SP:** No info **VI:** No further data **P:** unk **BLW:** unk **RG:** Y **MK:** unk **PH:** unk **SS:** J-Yorktown Historian; SAR P-256051 **BS:** JLARC 74.

NEWTON, William; b c1762; d 26 Dec 1814 **RU:** Soldier, Served in Western Bn of State troops **CEM:** Presbyterian Church; GPS 38.80015, -77.05791; Wilkes St & Hamilton Ln; Alexandria City **GS:** Y **SP:** Jane Barr Stuart (c1777-25 Feb 1815) **VI:** Died age 51 (stone.) Death notice in the *Alexandria Gazette* 29 Dec 1814, pg 3 give death date as 25 Dec. GS reads 26 Dec **P:** unk **BLW:** unk **RG:** Y **MK:** Y SAR plaque **PH:** unk **SS:** J-NSSAR 1993 Reg; SAR P-256062 **BS:** JLARC 1; 174, pg 60; 23 pg 60.

NEWTON, Willoughby II; b 27 Dec 1761, d bef 22 Jun 1812 **RU:** Patriot, Gave material aid to cause, Westmoreland Co **CEM:** Newton Family; GPS 38.0673141,-76.6496277; loc Linden Farm, (Rt 202), Hague; Westmoreland Co **GS:** Unk, name on spouse's plaque **SP:** Sally Bland (Poythress) Lee (1767, Prince George Co, MD- 1828 Lee Hall, Westmoreland Co) **VI:** Son of Willoughby Newton I **P:** N **BLW:** N **RG:** Y **MK:** N **PH:** N **SS:** AL Westmoreland Co Ct Bk pg 3, Comm Bk V pg 222; ; SAR P-256063 **BS:** 196

NICHOLAS, Jacob; b 15 Jul 1724,, Germany (or VA); d 26 Mar 1781 **RU:** Patriot, His estate filed claim for impressed material **CEM:** Old Peaked Mountain; GPS 38.37113, -78.73416; 9843 Town Hall Rd, McGaheysville; Rockingham **GS:** Y **SP:** Barbara Zellers (Sellers) **VI:** Common Monument. Son of John & Margaret (Lorentz) Nicholas **P:** N **BLW:** N **RG:** Y **MK:** Y DAR plaque **PH:** unk **SS:** J-NSSAR 2000 Reg AL pg 38; SAR P-256103 **BS:** JLARC 76.

NICHOLAS, Jean; b unk; d 1781 **RU:** Seaman, Served on "Ville de Paris" and died from Yorktown battle **CEM:** French Memorial; GPS 36.81944, -79.39933; Yorktown; York **GS:** U **SP:** No info **VI:** No further data **P:** unk **BLW:** unk **RG:** Y **MK:** unk **PH:** unk **SS:** J-Yorktown Historian; SAR P-256106 **BS:** JLARC 1, 74.

NICHOLAS, Lewis; b 1718; d 9 Aug1807 **RU:** Brigadier General, Served in US Army **CEM:** Old Presbyterian Meeting House; GPS 38.48528, -77.23532; 323 S Fairfax St; Alexandria City **GS:** N **SP:** No info **VI:** Died age 90 (*Alexandria Gazette*, 7 Aug 1807, pg 3). Listed on SAR plaque in cemetery **P:** unk **BLW:** unk **RG:** N **MK:** Y SAR plaque **PH:** N **SS:** AK **BS:** JLARC 1, 2, 25, 86; 23 pg 106; 196.

NICHOLAS, Lewis; b unk; d Aft 1783 **RU:** Captain & Patriot, Commanded an Independent Co in Albemarle Co according to pension record of Benjamin Harris and James Lewis **CEM:** Fincastle Presbyterian; GPS 37.50017, -79.87558; 108 E Back St, Fincastle; Botetourt **GS:** N **SP:** No info **VI:**

RU=Rank/Unit	CEM=Cemetery	GS=Gravestone	SP=Spousal Information
VI=Other Veteran Info	P=Pension	BLW=Bounty/Land Warrant	RG=Registered Grave
MK=SAR/DAR Marker	PH=Photo	SS=Service Source	BS=Burial Source

309

Name is on VASSAR plaque at cemetery **P**: unk **BLW**: unk **RG**: N **MK**: Y SAR plaque **PH**: N **SS**: AS Vol 3 pg 121 **BS**: 80 vol 3 pg 117.

NICHOLAS, Peter; b 5 Apr 1762; d 10 Jul 1852 **RU**: Private, Served in Capt Peachey Gilmer's Co, Augusta Co Militia **CEM**: Old Peaked Mountain; GPS 38.37113, -78.73416; 9843 Town Hall Rd, McGaheysville; Rockingham **GS**: Y **SP**: 1) Mar (1786 Rockingham Co) Euly Boshang d/o Jacob & (-----) Boshang 2) Mar (1782 Rockingham Co) Elizabeth (-----) Sellers, widow of Henry Sellers **VI**: No further data **P**: unk **BLW**: unk **RG**: Y **MK**: Y DAR plaque **PH**: unk **SS**: E pg 584; SAR P-256114 **BS**: 04.

NICHOLAS, Robert Carter; b 18 Jan 1728, d 8 Sep 1780 **RU**: Patriot, he was a member VA Gen Assembly fr 1776 to 1778 and in 1779 was appointed to the high court of chancery, consequently he became a member of the first Court of Appeals, predecessor of the Supreme Court of Virginia **CEM**: Mount Brilliant; GPS not determined; Farrington; Hanover **GS**: Unk **SP**: 1) Ann Cary (1735 Hampton City-5 Dec 1786, *Newport News*) **VI**: Son of George Nicholas (1685, Manston, Dorset Eng-1734, Williamsburg) & Elizabeth Carter (May 1692, Lancaster Co-Mar 1734, Hayes, Gloucester Co) **P**: N **BLW**: N **RG**: Y **MK**: N **PH**: N **SS**: DAR A083350; SAR P-256116; CD **BS**: 196.

NICHOLAS, Wilson Cary; b 31 Jan 1761, Williamsburg; d 11 Oct 1820 **RU**: Lieutenant, Commanded a Co in Lt Col George Meade's Legion 1781 **CEM**: Monticello; GPS 38.00829, -78.4552; 931 Thomas Jefferson Pkwy; Charlottesville City **GS**: Y **SP**: Margaret Smith **VI**: No further data **P**: unk **BLW**: unk **RG**: Y **MK**: unk **PH**: unk **SS**: J- DAR Hatcher; DD; DAR A206763; SAR P-256120 **BS**: JLARC 2; 196.

NICHOLS, Daniel; b unk; d 1847 **RU**: Private?, Served in 3rd, 4th, 8th, 12th VA Cont Lines **CEM**: Goose Creek; GPS 39.11250, -77.69527; Rt 722, Lincoln; Loudoun **GS**: Y **SP**: No info **VI**: No further data **P**: unk **BLW**: unk **RG**: N **MK**: N **PH**: unk **SS**: E pg 585 **BS**: 25, pg 221.

NICHOLS, Isaac; b 1720, Chester Co PA; d 9 May 1803 **RU**: Patriot, Paid the Rev War supply and state tax in County of Philadelphia, PA for yrs of 1781, 1782, & 1783. **CEM**: Goose Creek; GPS 39.11250, -77.69527; Rt 722, Lincoln; Loudoun **GS**: U **SP**: mar (26 Mar 1742, New Castle Co, DE) Margary Cox (1724 PA-1806 Loudoun Co) **VI**: Son of Thomas & Mary (Ludford) Nichols **P**: N **BLW**: N **RG**: N **MK**: unk **PH**: unk **SS**: Fold 3 PA Archives, series 3 Vol XVI pg 331 **BS**: 196.

NICHOLSON, Henry; b unk, d 14 Nov 1821 **RU**: Patriot, Service not identified however listed on SAR PRS **CEM**: Presbyterian Church; GPS 38.80028300, -77.05784700 loc jct Hamilton Ave & Wilkes St; Alexandria City **GS**: Yes Section 41 Plot 32 **SP**: Precious Talbert (1768-15 Oct 1802) **VI**: FindaGrave 115512580 has no service listed **P**: N **BLW**: N **RG**: Y **MK**: SAR memorial plaque **PH**: Y **SS**: SAR P-333958 **BS**: 196.

NICHOLSON, Jesse or Jessee; b 1759; d 26 Sep 1834 **RU**: Captain, Enl 1776, and served throughout the war. Served fr Brunswick Co, under Lt Binns Jones, 15th VA Regt, Cont line for 3 yrs **CEM**: Cedar Grove; GPS 36.57204, -80.02599; 301 Fort Lane Rd; Portsmouth City **GS**: Y **SP**: Lucy (-----) **VI**: Moved to Portsmouth after Rev War and was Postmaster there. Minister after war. Marker moved 1929 fr Monumental graveyard. Pension recd 16 Jul 1832 Norfolk Co. S5832, BLW #4134-100-22 Mar 1732 through Richmond Land Office. Also BLW #6015, 200 acres for War of 1812 **P**: Y **BLW**: Y **RG**: Y **MK**: Y SAR **PH**: unk **SS**: N pg 915; AP Serv Rec; CG Vol 3 pg 2499; SAR P-256342 **BS**: JLARC 3,105; 178 Jan 2011.

NICHOLSON, John; b c1750 d Aug 1810 **RU**: Corporal, Served in Capt John Mercer's Co, 3rd VA Regt Cont Line Feb 1778. Had 3 yrs service **CEM**: Nicholson Family; GPS unk; Syria; Madison **GS**: U **SP**: Ann Wiggins **VI**: No further data **P**: unk **BLW**: unk **RG**: Y **MK**: unk **PH**: unk **SS**: A pg 276; SAR P-338610 **BS**: 196; SAR PRS

NICHOLSON, Robert; b 1725, York Co; d 15 Aug 1798 **RU**: Surgeon, Served in VA Line **CEM**: St John's Episcopal; GPS 37.53183, -77.41958; 2401 E Broad St; Richmond City **GS**: Y **SP**: mar (21 Apr 1784 James City Co) Elizabeth Digges (c1762-__) **VI**: Died in York Co where he lived for 15 yrs. Prior to that he lived in Williamsburg. Widow pensioned 22 Nov 1838 Gloucester Co age 76 in May 1838. W5422; also VA 1/2 Pay (See N.A. Acc #874 #050127 1/2 Pay) Widow lived in Gloucester Co age 84 when BLW #7774 issued to children 2 Jun 1844 **P**: Y **BLW**: Y **RG**: N **MK**: N **PH**: unk **SS**: E pg 586; K Vol 4 pg 20; CG Vol 3 pg 2499 **BS**: 39 pg 99.

NICOLAS, Pierre; b unk; d 1781 **RU**: Seaman, Served on "Northumberland" and died from Yorktown battle **CEM**: French Memorial; GPS 36.81944, -79.39933; Yorktown; York **GS**: U **SP**: No info **VI**: No

---

RU=Rank/Unit	CEM=Cemetery	GS=Gravestone	SP=Spousal Information
VI=Other Veteran Info	P=Pension	BLW=Bounty/Land Warrant	RG=Registered Grave
MK=SAR/DAR Marker	PH=Photo	SS=Service Source	BS=Burial Source

310

further data **P:** unk **BLW:** unk **RG:** Y **MK:** unk **PH:** unk **SS:** J-Yorktown Historian; SAR P-256430 **BS:** JLARC 1, 74.

NICOLE, Jean; b unk; d 1781 **RU:** Soldier, Served in Gatinais Bn and died fr battle at Yorktown **CEM:** French Memorial; GPS 36.81944, -79.39933; Yorktown; York **GS:** U **SP:** No info **VI:** No further data **P:** unk **BLW:** unk **RG:** N **MK:** unk **PH:** unk **SS:** J-Yorktown Historian **BS:** JLARC 1, 74.

NICOLSON, Thomas; b c1750; d 10 Nov 1808 **RU:** Private, Served in 8th Cont Line **CEM:** St John's Episcopal; GPS 37.53183, -77.41958; 2401 E Broad St; Richmond City **GS:** Y **SP:** No info **VI:** No further data **P:** unk **BLW:** unk **RG:** N **MK:** N **PH:** Y **SS:** E pg 586 **BS:** 04, Dec 2006.

NIEL, Antoine; b unk; d 1781 **RU:** Seaman, Served on "Duc De Bourgogne" and died from Yorktown battle **CEM:** French Memorial; GPS 36.81944, -79.39933; Yorktown; York **GS:** U **SP:** No info **VI:** No further data **P:** unk **BLW:** unk **RG:** Y **MK:**   unk **PH:** unk **SS:** J-Yorktown Historian; SAR P-256436 **BS:** JLARC 1, 74.

NIXON, George; b 25 Feb 1730, Ireland; d 27 Nov 1800 **RU:** Patriot, Gave material aid to the cause **CEM:** Nixon Family; GPS unk; 19010 Woodburn Rd; Loudoun **GS:** Y **SP:** Mary Combs (1729, Ireland-29 Oct 1804) **VI:** No further data **P:** N **BLW:** N **RG:** N **MK:** N **PH:** unk **SS:** AL Ct Bk pg 31, 58; **BS:** 60 Loudoun; 196.

NIXON, George; b 30 Sep 1751, Loudoun Co; d 17 Nov 1818 **RU:** Private, Served in VA Line **CEM:** Nixon Family; GPS unk; 19010 Woodburn Rd; Loudoun **GS:** Y **SP:** Anna Craven(1778, Loudoun Co-23 Feb 1829) **VI:** Son of George (25 Feb 1730, Ireland-27 Nov 1800) & Mary (Combs) 1729, Ireland-29 Oct 1804) Nixon. Recd BLW **P:** unk **BLW:** Y **RG:** N **MK:** N **PH:** unk **SS:** C pg 258 **BS:** 60 Loudoun; 196.

NIXON, John; b 21 Mar 1755, Ireland; d 27 Aug 1815 **RU:** Private/Patriot, Served in 1st, 10th, 14th Cont Line. Gave material aid to cause **CEM:** Nixon Family; GPS unk; 19010 Woodburn Rd; Loudoun **GS:** Y **SP:** Mar (1778) Rebecca Todd (c1757, MD-__) **VI:** Son of George IV (25 Feb 1730 Ireland-27 Nov 1800) & Mary (Combs) (1729-1804) Nixon **P:** unk **BLW:** unk **RG:** N **MK:** N **PH:** unk **SS:** DAR #A083895; D Vol 2 pg 599; E pg 587 **BS:** 25 pg 225; 196.

NOBLE, Joseph; b 1742; d bef 23 Feb 1826, Amelia Co **RU:** Ensign; recommended rank Ensign 22 Jun 1780 in Capt Edmund's Co, Amelia Co **CEM:** Bunker Hill; GPS not determined; loc Stevensville; King & Queen Co **GS:** Y **SP:** Mary Wheeler (21 Jan 1745-25 Oct 1818, Amelia Co) **VI:** No further data **P:** Unk **BLW:** Unk **RG:** N **MK:** N **PH:** N **SS:** DAR #A083990; G pg 14 **BS:** 196

NOEL, Jean; b unk; d 1781 **RU:** Soldier, Served in Bourbonnais Bn and died fr battle at Yorktown **CEM:** French Memorial; GPS 36.81944, -79.39933; Yorktown; York **GS:** U **SP:** No info **VI:** No further data **P:** unk **BLW:** unk **RG:** Y **MK:** unk **PH:** unk **SS:** J-Yorktown Historian; SAR P-256701 **BS:** JLARC 1, 74.

NOLLY, Laurent; b unk; d 1781 **RU:** Soldier, Served in Agenois Bn and died fr battle at Yorktown **CEM:** French Memorial; GPS 36.81944, -79.39933; Yorktown; York **GS:** U **SP:** No info **VI:** No further data **P:** unk **BLW:** unk **RG:** Y **MK:** unk **PH:** unk **SS:** J-Yorktown Historian; SAR P-256740 **BS:** JLARC 1, 74.

NORMAN, Courtney,Jr; b 1730; d 1783 **RU:** Soldier, Served in Culpeper Co Militia **CEM:** Fairview; GPS 38.48080,-78.00470; Sperryville Pike Rt 522, Culpeper; Culpeper **GS:** U **SP:** Frances (-----) **VI:** No further data **P:** unk **BLW:** unk **RG:** Y **MK:** unk **PH:** unk **SS:** DAR A084301; SAR P-256791; DD **BS:** JLARC 76.

NORMAN, George; b Jun 1743, Stafford Co; d Jun 1807 **RU:** Patriot, Gave wagonage to the cause **CEM:** Norman Family # 2; GPS unk; Hope Point Rd; Stafford **GS:** Y **SP:** Elizabeth Waller (c1749 - cNov 1822) **VI:** No further data **P:** N **BLW:** N **RG:** Y **MK:** N **PH:** Y **SS:** D pg 874, 882; SAR P-256778 **BS:** 03 pg 296.

NORMAN, Thomas, Sr; b 1711-1712 Prob. Stafford Co; d 2 Mar 1785 **RU:** Patriot, Gave for cause beef and 52 lbs bacon **CEM:** Norman Family #1; GPS unk; Quarry Rd; Stafford **GS:** Y **SP:** Elizabeth Duncan (c1714-20 Jun 1771) **VI:** No further data **P:** N **BLW:** N **RG:** Y **MK:** N **PH:** Y **SS:** D pg 881; SAR P-256784 **BS:** 03 pg 295.

NORMAN, William; b 22 Sep 1763, d 1 Jul 1841, McMinn Co, TN **RU:** Private, entered serv,Oct 1780, Capt Richard Yancey Co in Carolinas;.2d tour under Capt. James Brown, Col John Green's Regt

RU=Rank/Unit	CEM=Cemetery	GS=Gravestone	SP=Spousal Information
VI=Other Veteran Info	P=Pension	BLW=Bounty/Land Warrant	RG=Registered Grave
MK=SAR/DAR Marker	PH=Photo	SS=Service Source	BS=Burial Source

311

Culpeper militia in battles at Petersburg; 3rd tour drove wagon for Major Strode; 4th tour in battle of Yorktown Oct 1781 under Capt William Green, VA Line **CEM**: Oakwood; GPS 36.6869011,-79.8799973 ;loc 107 Cem St, Martinsville; Martinsville City **GS**: Unk **SP**: 1) mar (1787) Elizabeth Lane (22 Sep 1822, Henry Co), d/o Reverend Dutton Lane, Sr & Elizabeth Oakes, 2) mar (11 Oct 1823, Henry Co) Hannah Oakes (c1794-1857, TX). She rec'd pen W26583 & BLW # 33772 for 160 acres in 1855 **VI**: Son of John C. Norman (1732-1787) & Ann Pence (1741-1765). Perhaps memorialized in cem if Gr Stone exists as died in TN **P**: Widow **BLW**: Widow **RG**: Y **MK**: N **PH**: N **SS**: SAR P-256790; CG pgs 2508, 2509 **BS**: 195.

NORRELL, Henry Holdcraft (Hallcraft); b Jan 1759 VA; d 29 Dec 1846 **RU**: Sergeant, Ent serv 1775 in1st VA Regt, later in 10th Cont Line **CEM**: Old City; GPS 37.41472, -79.15667; 401 Taylor St; Lynchburg City **GS**: Y **SP**: Mary (-----) (Oct 1789-__) **VI**: Pen 1818 Campbell Co. BLW #1796 issued 12 Jun 1783. Died in Campbell Co **P**: Y **BLW**: Y **RG**: N **MK**: Y SAR plaque **PH**: unk **SS**: E pg 589; K Vol 4 pg 28 **BS**: 35 pg 3.

NORTH, Roger; b unk; d 17 Oct 1776 **RU**: Patriot, Gave material aid to the Augusta Co Militia for the Battle of Point Pleasant in 1774 **CEM**: Trinity Episcopal; GPS 38.14917, -79.07521; 214 Beverley St; Staunton City **GS**: Y **SP**: No info **VI**: No further data **P**: N **BLW**: N **RG**: N **MK**: N **PH**: unk **SS**: Z pg 93 **BS**: 142 Trinity; 196.

NORTHEN, Peter S.; b 23 Aug 1750, Farnham, Richmond Co, d 8 Sep 1811 **RU**: Patriot/Captain, Received as Ensign in Capt Brockenbrough's Co, Richmond County Militia, 4 Jun 1781, took oath 1 Oct 1781, promoted to Captain before war ended in Continental Line. Claim for providing material aid to cause Richmond Co, 3 Apr 1782. **CEM**: Peter Northen Family; GPS 37.941115, -76.742656; BS; loc back corner of Al Pugh Distribution Ctr at 13548 Historyland Hwy (Rt-3), Richmond Co **GS** Y **SP**: mar Jan 1744, Jane Alderson (22 Sep 1756-30 Sep 1811) **VI**: Son of William Northen & Abigail Minty **P**: N **BLW**: N **RG**: Y **MK**: Y SAR bronze on GS **PH**: Y **SS**: B; E pg 598; G pg 317; SAR P-327826; DAR # A084593 **BS**: 196.

NORTON, Henry; b unk; d 1 Dec 1781 **RU**: Soldier, Served in 1st NY Regt and died fr Yorktown battle **CEM**: Yorktown Victory Monument Tablet; GPS 38.28350, -78.54150; Yorktown; York **GS**: U **SP**: No info **VI**: No further data **P**: unk **BLW**: unk **RG**: Y **MK**: unk **PH**: unk **SS**: J-Yorktown Historian;SAR P-257089 AX pg 548 **BS**: JLARC 74.

NORVELL(NORWELL), Henry Holdcraft; b Jan 1759; d 29 Dec 1846, Campbell Co) **RU**: Sergeant, ent serv 1775, Campbell Co, 1st VA Regt serving at least 3 years **CEM**: Old City; GPS 37.414719,-79.156670, 401 Taylor St; Lynchburg City **GS**: Y Gov't **SP**: Mary "Polly" (_)(Oct 1769-1831) **VI**: Son of Hugh Norvell (1725-unk). Rec'd BLW1796 and pen 1818 Campbell Co # F-S8441, R 1831 **P**: Y **BLW**: Y **RG**: N **MK**: Y SAR individual plaque 1977**PH**: N **SS**: K vol IV, pg 28 BS: 196.

NORWELL (NORVALL), Aquilla; b 1745; d 1795 **RU**: Surgeon, Served for 3 yrs **CEM**: Norvall Family; GPS unk; Nr Dumfries; Prince William **GS**: U **SP**: No info **VI**: No further data **P**: unk **BLW**: unk **RG**: N **MK**: N **PH**: unk **SS**: C pg 481; AS, SAR P-257210; DAR A084090 **BS**: DAR report.

NUCKOLLS, Charles; b 1745 Louisa Co; d 12 Aug 1820 **RU**: Major, Contact SAR Fincastle Resolution's chapter for service **CEM**: Nuckolls Family; GPS 36.63551, -80.95944; Beyond the end of Wild Turkey Ln, jct US 58 & Rt 94; Grayson **GS**: Y **SP**: Mar (1764) Mary Black (17 Jul 1741 Albemarle Co-21 Jun 1824) **VI**: Son of James (c1720, Hanover Co-17 Mar 1810 Louisa Co) & Mary (Henderson) Nuckolls **P**: unk **BLW**: unk **RG**: N **MK**: N **PH**: unk **SS**: AK Apr 2007 **BS**: 04 Apr 2007; 196.

NUCKOLLS, John Nathaniel; b 12 Jul 1755; d 1835 **RU**: Patriot, paid personal property tax 1782, Louisa Co, a supply tax for Rev War expenses **CEM**: Nuckolls Family, (AKA Hamilton Family); GPS 38.056987, -77.825121; 8736 Kentucky Springs Rd;(Rt 652): Louisa **GS**: Y **SP**: Mary Garland (20 Mar 1755-__), d/o Robert Garland & Mary Elizabeth Bullock **VI**: Son of James Nuckolls (1720-1810) & Mary Henderson (1726-1810) **P**: N **BLW**: N **RG**: Y **MK**: N **PH**: N **SS**: DV-1782, Louisa Co, image 09 pdf; SAR P-340606 **BS**: 196

NUSTER, Claudius; b unk; d unk **RU**: Soldier?, See DAR Senate Report series 10094, vol 5, 1936 for service details **CEM**: Trinity Episcopal; GPS 38.14917, -79.07521; 214 Beverley St; Staunton City **GS**: U **SP**: No info **VI**: No further data **P**: unk **BLW**: unk **RG**: Y **MK**: unk **PH**:Y **SS**: J-DAR Hatcher; SAR P-257469 **BS**: JLARC 2; 80 vol 3 pg 129.

RU=Rank/Unit	CEM=Cemetery	GS=Gravestone	SP=Spousal Information
VI=Other Veteran Info	P=Pension	BLW=Bounty/Land Warrant	RG=Registered Grave
MK=SAR/DAR Marker	PH=Photo	SS=Service Source	BS=Burial Source

312

NUTTER, Zadock (Zadok); b 20 Apr 1759, Somerse,t MD; d 1839 **RU:** Soldier, Served in Capt John Woodgate Co, Col Samuel Patterson's Regt, Delaware. Also in Flying Camp **CEM:** Nutter Property; GPS unk; Pott's Creek; Craig **GS:** U **SP:** Mar (Apr 1794) Catherine Lynn (1765-1846, Botetourt Co) **VI:** No further data **P:** unk **BLW:** unk **RG:** unk **MK:** unk **PH:** unk **SS:** J-DAR Hatcher; DD; SAR P-257516 **BS:** JLARC 2; 80 vol 3 pg 129.

O'BANNON, John; b 1735; d Apr 1797 **RU:** Captain, Served in Fauquier Co Militia, possibly promoted to Maj **CEM:** O'Bannon; GPS unk; Warrenton; Fauquier **GS:** Y **SP:** Lydia Duncan (Stampe) (c1742, Prince William Co-aft 1807) **VI:** Son of Joseph (c1720, Orange Co-Sep 1793) & Lydia (-----) (c1773-1797 Fauquier Co) Duncan **P:** unk **BLW:** unk **RG:** N **MK:** N **PH:** unk **SS:** DAR #A085506; H **BS:** 19 pg 154,151,152, 242.

OBANNON (OBANON), William; b 1730; d 19 Oct 1807 **RU:** Patriot, Gave material aid to cause **CEM:** Obannon-Lawrence; GPS unk; Marshall; Fauquier **GS:** Y **SP:** Mar (1752) Anne Neville (1734 Hampshire Co-___) **VI:** No further data **P:** N **BLW:** N **RG:** N **MK:** unk **PH:** unk **SS:** DAR #A085510; AL Ct Bk pg 2, 15 Fauquier Co **BS:** 196.

O'BRYANT, Thomas; b 1721, Ireland; d 23 Jan 1793 **RU:** Private, Served in 2nd Cont Line **CEM:** Spears Family; GPS unk; N of Edom Rt 42 7.3 mi; Rockingham **GS:** N **SP:** No info **VI:** No further data **P:** unk **BLW:** unk **RG:** N **MK:** N **PH:** N **SS:** E pg 592 **BS:** 32.

OGLESBY, Daniel; b c1763; d 1859 **RU:** Soldier, Served in militia **CEM:** Old City; GPS 37.41472, -79.15667; 401 Taylor St; Lynchburg City **GS:** U **SP:** No info **VI:** Son of Richard & Susan (-----) Oglesby. Died in Bedford Co **P:** unk **BLW:** unk **RG:** Y **MK:** Y SAR plaque **PH:** unk **SS:** SAR P-262807 **BS:** JLARC 36.

OLIVER, Benjamin; b 2 July 1766; d 9 Sep 1820 **RU:** Private, Served probably in Hanover Co Militia **CEM:** Retreat Farm; GPS unk; Pamunkey River near old church; Hanover **GS:** Y **SP:** No info **VI:** Rank of Capt obtained after war **P:** unk **BLW:** unk **RG:** N **MK:** N **PH:** unk **SS:** E pg 595 **BS:** 31 vol 1 pg 28.

OLIVER, James; b 1756; d 1827 **RU:** Corporal, Served in VA Line in the Artillery, 6th, 8th, 14th Cont Lines **CEM:** Mt Hebron; GPS 39.18170, -78.15720; 305 E Boscawen St, Winchester; Frederick **GS:** Y **SP:** No info **VI:** Appl pen Frederick Co 11 Jun 1818 #S38269 **P:** Y **BLW:** Y **RG:** N **MK:** unk **PH:** unk **SS:** C pg 260; E pg 595; CG pg 2536 **BS:** 196.

OLIVER, William; b 10 Apr 1754; d 15 Mar 1842 **RU:** Corporal, Served in 2nd VA State Regt and 3rd Cont Line **CEM:** Old Glade Creek; GPS 37.35989, -79.81828; Grace Hollow Rd, Blue Ridge; Botetourt **GS:** Y **SP:** No info **VI:** No further data **P:** unk **BLW:** unk **RG:** Y **MK:** N **PH:** unk **SS:** K Vol 4 pg 40; SAR P-263051 **BS:** 74 pg 3; 196.

OLLINGER (OLIFER), John Christopher Sr; b 18 Feb 1737, Germany; d 20 Feb 1827 **RU:** Private, Served in Capt James Ewing's Co fr Augusta Co. Served in Bates Co and had service in the 2nd Regt PA Line under Col Seylock and in Col Smith's and Col Lewis's Regt of VA **CEM:** Slemp Memorial; GPS unk; Turkey Cove; Lee **GS:** Y **SP:** Eve Margaret Siler (2 Aug 1754-1 Jun 1854 Lee Co) D/o Jacob Sr & Dorothy (Blubaugh) Siler **VI:** Son of Philip Johann & Juliana (Umberger) Olinger **P:** unk **BLW:** unk **RG:** N **MK:** Y SAR **PH:** unk **SS:** CA; Z pg 108 **BS:** 196.

OLLIVIER, Paul; b unk; d 1781 **RU:** Seaman, Served on "Duc De Bourgogne" and died from Yorktown battle **CEM:** French Memorial; GPS 36.81944, -79.39933; Yorktown; York **GS:** U **SP:** No info **VI:** No further data **P:** unk **BLW:** unk **RG:** N **MK:** unk **PH:** unk **SS:** J-Yorktown Historian **BS:** JLARC 1, 74.

OMOHUNDRO, Richard; b 1733, Westmoreland Co; d 1811 **RU:** Ensign/Patriot, Gave material aid to cause **CEM:** Omohundro Family; GPS 37.742344,-78-286631; 400 yds E of Rt 15, 1 mi S of Fork Union, Nr Fork Union 1 mi; Fluvanna **GS:** N **SP:** Mar (1763) Elizabeth Muse (1750-1809) **VI:** Son of Richard Omohundro (1709-___) & Mary Browning (___-1745) **P:** unk **BLW:** unk **RG:** N **MK:** unk **PH:** N **SS:** AL Ct Bk pg 8, 21 Fluvanna Co **BS:** JLARC 2, 46,100; 80 vol3 pg 134; 196.

ORGAIN, William Derby; b unk; d 20 Dec 1824 **RU:** Patriot, Gave material aid to the cause **CEM:** Orgain Family; GPS 36.86010, -77.94002; Jct Rts 644 & Rt 648, Alberta; Brunswick **GS:** Y **SP:** Elizabeth Neblett, (23 Nov 1746 - 27 May 1815). She is said by legend to haunt this property **VI:** New stone erected 1984 **P:** N **BLW:** N **RG:** N **MK:** N **PH:** unk **SS:** AL Ct Bk pg 22 Brunswick co **BS:** 196.

RU=Rank/Unit	CEM=Cemetery	GS=Gravestone	SP=Spousal Information
VI=Other Veteran Info	P=Pension	BLW=Bounty/Land Warrant	RG=Registered Grave
MK=SAR/DAR Marker	PH=Photo	SS=Service Source	BS=Burial Source

ORGAN, unk; b unk; d 1781 **RU:** Soldier, Served fr PA, and died fr the battle at Yorktown **CEM:** Yorktown Victory Monument Tablet; GPS 38.28350, -78.54150; Yorktown; York **GS:** U **SP:** No info **VI:** No further data **P:** unk **BLW:** unk **RG:** N **MK:** unk **PH:** unk **SS:** J-Yorktown Historian **BS:** JLARC 74.

ORIEUX, Francois; b unk; d 1781 **RU:** Seaman, Served on "Magnanime" and died from Yorktown battle **CEM:** French Memorial; GPS 36.81944, -79.39933; Yorktown; York **GS:** U **SP:** No info **VI:** No further data **P:** unk **BLW:** unk **RG:** Y **MK:** unk **PH:** unk **SS:** J-Yorktown Historian; SAR P-263378 **BS:** JLARC 1, 74.

ORKENSUDE, Erasmus; b unk; d 1781 **RU:** Soldier, Served in Royal Deaux Ponts Bn and died fr battle at Yorktown **CEM:** French Memorial; GPS 36.81944, -79.39933; Yorktown; York **GS:** U **SP:** No info **VI:** No further data **P:** unk **BLW:** unk **RG:** Y **MK:** unk **PH:** unk **SS:** J-Yorktown Historian; SAR P-263382 **BS:** JLARC 1,74.

ORR, John; b c1728, Muirkirk, Scotland; d 20 Jul 1795, Loudoun Co **RU:** Patriot, Gave 800# of beef "for public use" in 1780, Loudoun Co **CEM:** St John's Episcopal; GPS 38.84217, -77.42716; 5649 Mt Gilead Rd; Fairfax **GS:** Y **SP:** Susannah Grayson **VI:** "Waterside" was home. Died in Cub Run, Loudoun Co. SAR memorial. GS was moved to St John's Episcopal. He is bur at the Orr family cemetery next to 6709 Jade Post Ln **P:** N **BLW:** N **RG:**Y **MK:** Y SAR plaque **PH:** Y **SS:** AL Ct Bk pg 18; SAR P-322077 **BS:** 61 vol IV pg CN-23.

ORVAULT, Dupe d'; b unk; d 1781 **RU:** Seaman, Served on "Auguste" and died from Yorktown battle **CEM:** French Memorial; GPS 36.81944, -79.39933; Yorktown; York **GS:** U **SP:** No info **VI:** No further data **P:** unk **BLW:** unk **RG:** Y **MK:** unk **PH:** unk **SS:** J-Yorktown Historian; SAR P-263513 **BS:** JLARC 1, 74.

OSBORN (OSBORNE), Enoch; b 1741, Yadkin, Rowan Co, NC; d Sep 1818 **RU:** Captain/Patriot, Commanded a Co in Montgomery Co miltia. Took Oath of Fidelity, Montgomery Co in 1777 **CEM:** Osborn-Cox; GPS unk; Rt 711, Independence; Grayson **GS:** U **SP:** Jane Hash **VI:** No further data **P:** unk **BLW:** unk **RG:** N **MK:** unk **PH:** unk **SS:** J-NSSAR 1993 Reg, J- DAR Hatcher; B; DD **BS:** JLARC 1, 2; 196.

OSBORNE, Reps; 1723, Henrico Co, d bef 6 Jun 1808 **RU:** Patriot, Gave material aid to cause by providing flour and oxen with cart **CEM:** Union; GPS 37.0732994, -78.6260986; Union Cem Rd (Rt 709), Charlotte Ct House; Charlotte **GS:** Unk **SP:** mar (1749, Amelia Co) Ann Turpin (1729-1805), d/o Phillip Turpin & Elizabeth Jones **VI:** Son of Thomas Osborne & Ann Worsham (1696, Henrico Co-1739) **P:** N **BLW:** N **RG:** Y **MK:** N **PH:** N **SS:** D vol 1, pg 226; DAR A131550; SAR P-263608 **BS:** 196.

OSBORNE, Samuel, b 1759, d Sep 1815 **RU:** Private enlisted 1776 and served in VA 7th Cont Line and 13th VA Regt, commanded by Col John Gibson for war period. Capt Uriah Springer was last commanding officer in 1783 that certified his service **CEM:** Union; GPS 37.0732994, -78.6260986; Union Cem Rd (Rt 709),Charlotte Ct House; Charlotte **GS:** Unk **SP:** Elizabeth Goode (1767-___) **VI:** Son of Reps Osborne (1723, Henrico Co-bef 6 Jun 1808) & Ann Turpin (1729-1805), d/o Phillip Turpin & Elizabeth Jones. Rec'd pen # S40227 & BLW # 12442 issued 24 Jun 1789 for 100 acres **P:** Y **BLW:** Y **RG:** N **MK:** N **PH:** N **SS:** N pg 442; AP pen records Fold3; CG pg 2552 **BS:** 196.

OSBURN, Richard; b 1739, d 2 Jun 1795 **RU:**Patriot, Paid personal property tax in 1782 and 1783, Loudoun Co considered a payment to support cause **CEM:** Ketoctin Baptist Church; GPS 39.157931 -77.49377; Ketoctin Church Rd, Purcellville; Loudoun **GS:** Yes **SP:** Hannah Purcell (1740-13 Jul 1819), d/o Thomas Purcell (9 Apr 1720, Readington, NJ-1779) & Mary Van Hook (9 Aug 1723, Albany, NY-1771) **VI:** Son of John Osburn (1712, Chester, PA-Dec 1786) and Sarah Morris (1719-1804) **P:** N **BLW:** N **RG :**Y **MK:** SAR monument **PH:** N **SS:** DV: 1782C; image 17; 1783c image 10 pdf; SAR P-340167 **BS:** 196.

OSBURN, William; b 1750; d 13 Dec 1805 **RU:** Private, Served in PA Regt commanded by Col Lewis Nicola in Apr 1783 **CEM:** Ketoctin Baptist; GPS 39.15746, -77.74870; Ketoctin Church Rd, Purcellville; Loudoun **GS:** Y **SP:** Hannah Gore (1755-1810) **VI:** Son of John (___-1786) and Sarah (Morris) (___-1804) Osburn **P:** unk **BLW:** unk **RG:** Y **MK:** SAR monument **PH:** unk **SS:** A pg 222-224; SAR P-263686 **BS:** 196.

RU=Rank/Unit	CEM=Cemetery	GS=Gravestone	SP=Spousal Information
VI=Other Veteran Info	P=Pension	BLW=Bounty/Land Warrant	RG=Registered Grave
MK=SAR/DAR Marker	PH=Photo	SS=Service Source	BS=Burial Source

314

OSPELL, Mathieu; b unk; d 1781 **RU**: Soldier, Served in Gatinais Bn and died fr battle at Yorktown **CEM**: French Memorial; GPS 36.81944, -79.39933; Yorktown; York **GS**: U **SP**: No info **VI**: No further data **P**: unk **BLW**: unk **RG**: Y **MK**: unk **PH**: unk **SS**: J-Yorktown Historian; SAR P-263782 **BS**: JLARC 1, 74.

OTEY, James Walter, Sr; b 1 Jul 1754, New Kent Co, d 10 Jun 1807 **RU**: Patriot, gave material aid to cause, James City Co **CEM**: Otey St; GPS 37.3316994, -79.5216980; loc vic jct with E Franklin St, Bedford; Bedford **GS**: Unk **SP**: Frances Mary Graves (6 Feb 1755, New Kent Co-__) **VI**: He resided in adjcent James City Co during Rev War period **P**: N **BLW**: N **RG**: Y **MK**: N **PH**: N **SS**: AL Ct Bk pgs 8, 35 James City Co; DAR #: A084781; SAR P-263835 **BS**: 196.

OTEY, John Armistead; b 1713 or 1735; d 1817 **RU**: Captain/Patriot, Gave material aid to cause **CEM**: Otey Street; GPS 37.33170, -79.52170; W Franklin St jct with Otey; Bedford **GS**: Y **SP**: Mary F Hopkins (1764-__) d/o John (1791-__) & Jean (Gordon) Hopkins **VI**: No further data **P**: unk **BLW**: unk **RG**: Y **MK**: N **PH**: unk **SS**: J-NSSAR 1993 Reg, J- DAR Hatcher; AL Ct Bk pg 6, 8, 9 Bedford Co; SAR P-263839 **BS**: JLARC 1, 2; 80 vol 3 pg 137; 196.

OUDOT, Claude; b unk; d 1781 **RU**: Soldier, Served in Gatinais Bn and died fr battle at Yorktown **CEM**: French Memorial; GPS 36.81944, -79.39933; Yorktown; York **GS**: U **SP**: No info **VI**: No further data **P**: unk **BLW**: unk **RG**: Y **MK**: unk **PH**: unk **SS**: J-Yorktown Historian; SAR P-263941 **BS**: JLARC 1, 74.

OUIN, Jean; b unk; d 1781 **RU**: Seaman, Served on "Saint-Esprit" and died from Yorktown battle **CEM**: French Memorial; GPS 36.81944, -79.39933; Yorktown; York **GS**: U **SP**: No info **VI**: No further data **P**: unk **BLW**: unk **RG**: Y **MK**: unk **PH**: unk **SS**: J-Yorktown Historian; SAR P-263944 **BS**: JLARC 1, 74.

OUVENANT, Rene; b unk; d 1781 **RU**: Seaman, Served on "Hercule" and died from Yorktown battle **CEM**: French Memorial; GPS 36.81944, -79.39933; Yorktown; York **GS**: U **SP**: No info **VI**: No further data **P**: unk **BLW**: unk **RG**: Y **MK**: unk **PH**: unk **SS**: J-Yorktown Historian; SAR P-263973 **BS**: JLARC 1, 74.

OVERACRE (OVERAKER, OBERAKER, OBERACKER), George; b 15 May 1738 or 15 Apr 1733, Germany; d 15 Oct 1809 **RU**: Private/Patriot, Served in MD and VA. Served in Capt Adam Ott's Co of Select Militia, Washington Co, MD. Provided 870 lbs of beef for Cont Use, Frederick Co, VA **CEM**: Mt Hebron; GPS 39.10916, -78.09497; 305 E Boscawen St; Winchester City **GS**: Y **SP**: Margaret (-----) (9 Jan 1733-16 Jun 1804) **VI**: Died in Frederick Co. Recd BLW **P**: N **BLW**: Y **RG**: Y **MK**: Y SAR bronze & monument **PH**: Y **SS**: AF pg 238; AL CT Bk 17; SAR P-327766 **BS**: 04; 50 pg 47.

OVERBEY, Peter Z; b 1759; d 13 Jun 1824 **RU**: Patriot, Gave 475# beef to Cont Army **CEM**: Overby & Holt Families; GPS unk; Rt 602 W; Mecklenburg **GS**: Y **SP**: Anne Yancey, d/o Robert & (-----) Yancey **VI**: No further data **P**: N **BLW**: N **RG**: N **MK**: N **PH**: unk **SS**: AL Ct Bk pg 16; DB pg 112 **BS**: 54 pg 223.

OVERBOKER (OFFENBACHER), Frederick; b c1735; d 27 Jun 1831 **RU**: Private, Served in Capt Michael Reader's Co, Dunmore Co Militia **CEM**: Offenbacher; GPS unk; Nr Stanley; Page **GS**: U **SP**: Mar (1796) Elizabeth (-----) (c1745-aft 1796) **VI**: No further data **P**: unk **BLW**: unk **RG**: Y **MK**: unk **PH**: unk **SS**: DAR #A085000; SAR P-263989; J- DAR Hatcher; C pg 603 **BS**: JLARC 2.; 80 vol 3, pg 138.

OWEN, James; b 1754, Campbell Co; d 26 Nov 1827 **RU**: Private, Served in 6th and 14th Cont Line **CEM**: Staunton Baptist; GPS 37.06970, -79.58140; 15267 Smith Mountain Lake Pkwy, Huddleston; Bedford **GS**: Y Crude grave 31 **SP**: Mar (23 Oct 1776) Elizabeth Russell (1754 Campbell Co-26 Nov 1827) **VI**: No further data **P**: unk **BLW**: unk **RG**: N **MK**: unk **PH**: unk **SS**: E pg 599 **BS**: 196.

OWEN, Owen; b 1750, New Castle, Lawrence Co, PA; d 3 Jun 1819 **RU**: Private, Served in Capt Moor's Co, Col Francis' 5th PA Regt **CEM**: Old City; GPS 37.41472, -79.15667; 401 Taylor St; Lynchburg City **GS**: Y **SP**: Jane Hughes (1760, Bedford Co-1835) **VI**: No further data **P**: N **BLW**: N **RG**: N **MK**: Y SAR plaque **OWINGS**, Richard; b 13 Nov 1738, Baltimore Co, MD; d 7 Oct 1786 **RU**: Patriot, Performed public service on the Baltimore Circuit Ct in 1775 **CEM**: Old Stone Methodist; GPS 39.11725, -77.56609; 168 W Cornwall St, Leesburg; Loudoun **GS**: U **SP**: Mar (1759, Baltimore) Rachael (-----) (4 Nov 1737, Baltimore-aft Aug 1812, KY) **VI**: Son of Joshua (5 Apr 1704-11 Apr 1785) & Mary (Cockey) (10 Dec 1736-10 Dec 1768) Owings **P**: unk **BLW**: unk **RG**: N **MK**: unk **PH**: unk **SS**: B plaque in cemetery **BS**: 196.

RU=Rank/Unit	CEM=Cemetery	GS=Gravestone	SP=Spousal Information
VI=Other Veteran Info	P=Pension	BLW=Bounty/Land Warrant	RG=Registered Grave
MK=SAR/DAR Marker	PH=Photo	SS=Service Source	BS=Burial Source

OXLEY, Henry; b 24 Nov 1746, NJ, d 1799 **RU**: Patriot, Paid personal property tax in 1782 and 1783, Loudoun Co considered a payment to support cause **CEM** Oxley Family; GPS: not determined; near Lucketts on the western part of the farm now owned by Mr. Dyer Gum; beside new cut Rd to Stumptown by parallel Rd to the Point of Rocks Loudoun **GS**: No **SP**: Catherine (-----), (14 Sep 1743-Jun 1780) **VI**: Son of Henry Oxley, Sr (14 May 1699-17 Mar 1777 and Mary Everitt **P**: N **BLW**: N **RG**: N **MK**: N **PH**: N **SS**: DV:1782B image 11.pdf; 1782C; image 11; 1783A image 10 pdf **BS**: 196.

OZANNE, Pierre; b unk; d 1781 **RU**: Soldier, Served in Gatinais Bn and died fr battle at Yorktown **CEM**: French Memorial; GPS 36.81944, -79.39933; Yorktown; York **GS**: U **SP**: No info **VI**: No further data **P**: unk **BLW**: unk **RG**: Y **MK**: unk **PH**: unk **SS**: J-Yorktown Historian; SAR P-264235 **BS**: JLARC 1, 74.

OZOU, Jean; b unk; d 1781 **RU**: Seaman, Served on "Hercule" and died from Yorktown battle **CEM**: French Memorial; GPS 36.81944, -79.39933; Yorktown; York **GS**: U **SP**: No info **VI**: No further data **P**: unk **BLW**: unk **RG**: Y **MK**: unk **PH**: unk **SS**: J-Yorktown Historian; SAR P-264244 **BS**: JLARC 1, 74.

PABST, Christian; b unk; d 1781 **RU**: Soldier, Served in Royal Deaux Ponts Bn and died fr battle at Yorktown **CEM**: French Memorial; GPS 36.81944, -79.39933; Yorktown; York **GS**: U **SP**: No info **VI**: No further data **P**: unk **BLW**: unk **RG**: Y **MK**: unk **PH**: unk **SS**: J-Yorktown Historian; SAR P-264246 **BS**: JLARC 1, 74.

PACE, John; b 28 May 1751; d 12 Apr 1822 **RU**: Patriot, Took oath of Allegiance 1778 in Henry Co **CEM**: Pace Family; GPS unk; Pace Airport Rd abt .5 mi past airport, Ridgeway; Henry **GS**: U **SP**: Mar (10 Sep 1772) Elizabeth Nunn **VI**: Title of Capt, thus probably served in militia during war period **P**: unk **BLW**: unk **RG**: N **MK**: unk **PH**: unk **SS**: DAR Ancestor #A085511; DD cites *VA Historical Mag* Vol 9 pg 142 **BS**: 196.

PACE, William; b 11 Oct 1745, Goochland Co; d Bef 21 Oct 1815 **RU**: Sergeant, Served in VA Militia and as lifeguard for Gen George Washington **CEM**: Jones Family; GPS 36.61690, -82.68580; Rt 635, Yuma, across RR and E of Cowan Branch Baptist Ch; Scott **GS**: Y **SP**: Mary Winiger **VI**: Son of John H (14 Mar 172, Middlesex Co-20 Sep 1790) & Susannah (Houchin) (1723-1809) Pace **P**: unk **BLW**: unk **RG**: Y **MK**: Y SAR **PH**: Y **SS**: H; O; AK; SAR P-264268; DAR A085538 **BS**: 04;196.

PACET, Etienne; b unk; d 1781 **RU**: Seaman, Served on "Sceptre" and died from Yorktown battle **CEM**: French Memorial; GPS 36.81944, -79.39933; Yorktown; York **GS**: U **SP**: No info **VI**: No further data **P**: unk **BLW**: unk **RG**: Y **MK**: unk **PH**: unk **SS**: J-Yorktown Historian; SAR P-264273 **BS**: JLARC 1,74.

PACKETT(PACKETTE), William; b 4 Apr 1736, Westmoreland Co, d Sep 1792 **RU**: Private/Patriot served in an artillery unit not identified (NARA Service Index Card) as patriot, supported cause by paying supply tax included in his personal property tax in 1783, Richmond Co **CEM**: Sabine Hall; GPS; not determined; 226 Main St, Warsaw; Richmond County **GS**: N **SP**:Mar 1) Mary Harford, 2) Anne Cooper **VI**: No further data **P**: N **BLW**: N **RG**: N **MK**: N **PH**: N **SS**: DAR A085686; AP-Serv Index Card indicates recd balance of pay 13 May 1783; DV: image 20,pdf **BS**: 196.

PACKWOOD, Samuel; b 1750; d 15 Aug 1824 **RU**: Private, Served in Capt John Cunningham's Co, Henry Co Militia 1781 **CEM**: Prillaman; GPS 37.01080, -80.06080; Foothills Rd Rt 642 W of Highland United Methodist, Callaway; Franklin **GS**: U **SP**: Mar (c1769) Elizabeth Turner (1747, Amelia Co-2 Aug 1845) d/o Shadrack & Ann (Pollard) Turner of Pittsylvania Co **VI**: Son of Samuel & Penelope (Stout) Packwood **P**: unk **BLW**: unk **RG**:Y **MK**: unk **PH**: unk **SS**: J- DAR Hatcher; G pg 186; SAR P-264367; DAR A085705 **BS**: JLARC 2; 80 vol3, pg 141;196.

PADGETT, Frederick; b 1753 or 1754, Essex Co; d 22 Sep 1846 **RU**: Soldier, Ent Serv Amherst Co in VA Line **CEM**: Millner Estate; GPS unk; See property records; Bedford **GS**: U **SP**: Mar (30 Apr 1787 Amherst Co) Lucia Magan **VI**: Son of Edmund & Mary (-----) Padgett. Pension application 22 Jul 1833 Bedford Co. S8930, possibly pensioned in Bedford in 1828 **P**: Y **BLW**: unk **RG**: Y **MK**: N **PH**: unk **SS**: J-DAR Hatcher; CG Vol 3 pg 2571; SAR P-264431 **BS**: JLARC 2; 80 vol3, pg 141.

PAGE, Carter; b c1758; d 9 Apr 1825 **RU**: Captain, Served in Capt 3rd Continental Dragoons and Aide-de-Camp to Gen Nelson, and later Lafayette **CEM**: Page Family, "The Fork"; GPS unk; See Source 101; Cumberland **GS**: N **SP**: 1) (-----) 2) mar (14 Dec 1799 Yorktown) Lucy Nelson (c1777-___) d/o General

RU=Rank/Unit · CEM=Cemetery · GS=Gravestone · SP=Spousal Information
VI=Other Veteran Info · P=Pension · BLW=Bounty/Land Warrant · RG=Registered Grave
MK=SAR/DAR Marker · PH=Photo · SS=Service Source · BS=Burial Source

316

Thomas & (-----) Nelson **VI:** Widow pensioned 11 Jun 1849 Cumberland Co age 72 **P:** Y **BLW:** unk **RG:** N **MK:** N **PH:** N **SS:** CG Vol 3 pg 2568; SAR P-264456 **BS:** JLARC 4,101.

PAGE, John; b 17 Apr 1743, "Rosewell" Gloucester Co; d 11 Oct 1808 **RU:** Colonel/Patriot, Was Delegate to VA Const Convention 1776 and Counselor of State by appt by Gov Patrick Henry 5 July 1776. Became Lt Gov VA 76-79. Raised Regt of troops for Gloucestor Co Milita. Was member State House of delegates 1781-83 **CEM:** St John's Episcopal; GPS 37.53183, -77.41958; 2401 E Broad St; Richmond City **GS:** Y **SP:** 1) Frances Burwell 2) Margaret Lowther **VI:** Son of (-----) & Alice Grymes (1724-1813). US Rep fr VA 1789-97. Governor of VA 1802-05. Was serving as US Commissioner of Loans for VA at time of death **P:** unk **BLW:** unk **RG:** Y **MK:** N **PH:** unk **SS:** G pg 777; DAR A085866; SAR P-335231 **BS:** 28 pg 493.

PAGE, John; b 1720; d 1780 **RU:** Patriot, Was member Committee of Safety Mathews Co **CEM:** Page home; GPS unk; North portion of Co; Mathews **GS:** U **SP:** Jane Byrd **VI:** No further data **P:** N **BLW:** N **RG:** Y **MK:** N **PH:** unk **SS:** AS SAR applic; SAR P-334365; DARA085867 **BS:** SAR Appl.

PAGE, John; b 29 Jun 1760, Hanover Co; d 17 Sep 1838 **RU:** Private, Served in 5th, 7th and 9th Cont Line **CEM:** Old Chapel Episcopal; GPS 39.10670, -78.01470; Jct US 340 & Rt 255, Millwood; Clarke **GS:** U **SP:** Mar (27 May 1784) Maria Horsemanden Byrd (26 Nov 1761, Philadelphia-__) d/o William (6 Sep 1728-1 Jan 1777) & Mary (-----) (10 Sep 1740-Mar 1814) Byrd **VI:** No further data **P:** unk **BLW:** unk **RG:** N **MK:** unk **PH:** unk **SS:** E pg 601; **BS:** 196.

PAGE, Mann III; b 1749, Gloucester Co; d 1781 **RU:** Colonel/Patriot, Commissioned Col 16 Aug 1781. Elected to Cont Congress 1777 **CEM:** Page Family; GPS unk; Mansfield Hall; Spotsylvania **GS:** Y **SP:** 1) Alice Grymes, 2) Mary Tayloe (28 Oct 1759-26 Jan 1835) d/o Hon. Joen & (-----) Tayloe of Mt Airy **VI:** Son of Mann (1716-1764) and Ann Corbin (Tayloe) Page (1723-__). Graduate of William & Mary, lawyer. House of Burgesses **P:** unk **BLW:** unk **RG:** Y **MK:** N **PH:** unk **SS:** Cont Congress 77; E pg 601; DAR A085881; SAR P-264545 **BS:** 130 Gloucester; 196.

PAGE, Mann II; b 8 Dec 1716; d 7 Nov 1780 **RU:** Patriot; public service as a member of the VA General Assembly 1777, and member of the Committee of Safety **CEM:** Page Family; GPS 37.327901 -76.576214 loc at the end of Rosewell Plantation Rd (Rt 644) on right in tree area; Gloucester **GS:** N grave stones were moved in 1969 to Abington Episcopal Church but bodies were not moved **SP:** Mar 31 Dec 1741, Alice Grymes (10 Aug 1724-11 Jan 1746), d/o John Grymes (1691-1748) & Jucy Ludwell (1698-1748) **VI:** Son of Mann Page (1691-24 Jan 1730) & Judith Carter (1695-1750). SAR & DAR have incorrect burial location **P:** unk **BLW:** unk **RG:** N **MK:** Unk **PH:** Unk **SS:** Lib of VA Misc Reel 5372: ltr dated 20 May 1777; DAR A085881; SAR P-264545 **BS:** 196.

PAGE, Matthew; b 4 Mar 1762, Broadneck, Hanover Co; d 5 Oct 1826 **RU:** Patriot Gave material aid to cause, Frederick Co **CEM:** Old Chapel; GPS 39.10670, -78.01470; loc jct US 340 & Rt 255, Millwood; Clarke **GS:** Y **SP:** Anne Randolph Meade (3 Dec 1781-28 Mar 1838), d/o Richard K Meade (1746-1805) & Mary Fitzhugh Grymes (1753-1819) **VI:** Son of Robert Page & Sarah Walker 1801 **P:** N **BLW:** N **RG:** N **MK:** unk **PH:** unk **SS:** AL Ct Bk pg 4, Comm Bk II, pg 205 **BS:** 196.

PAGE, Robert; b 4 Feb 1765, Mathews Co; d 8 Dec 1840 **RU:** Captain, Served in Frederick Co Militia **CEM:** Old Chapel Episcopal; GPS 39.10670, -78.01470; Jct US 340 & Rt 255, Millwood; Clarke **GS:** Y **SP:** mar (1788) Sarah N. Page (16 Feb 1766 Hanover Co-4 Apr 1843) **VI:** Attended College of William & Mary. Served VA House of Delegates and US Congress 1799-1801 **P:** N **BLW:** N **RG:** unk **MK:** unk **PH:** unk **SS:** DAR A985888; SAR P-335855; E pg 601 **BS:** 196.

PAILLARD, Jean; b unk; d 1781 **RU:** Seaman, Served on "Auguste" and died from Yorktown battle **CEM:** French Memorial; GPS 36.81944, -79.39933; Yorktown; York **GS:** U **SP:** No info **VI:** No further data **P:** unk **BLW:** unk **RG:** Y **MK:** unk **PH:** unk **SS:** J-Yorktown Historian; SAR P-264624 **BS:** JLARC 1, 74.

PAINE, Joseph; b 28 Feb 1758, Goochland Co, d 5 Apr 1826 **RU:** Lieutenant, serv Capt Woodson's and Capt Snead's Companies; Col Flemings Regt **CEM:** Windy Cove Presbyterian Church; GPS not determined; Warm Springs; Bath **GS:** Unk **SP:** Mar 30 Dec 1779, Long Island, Ann Van Clief (1761-14 Feb 1761) **VI:** Rec'd pen # S*W 18693 **P:** Both **BLW:** N **RG:** Y **MK:** N **PH:** N **SS:** DAR #: A086055; cites

RU=Rank/Unit	CEM=Cemetery	GS=Gravestone	SP=Spousal Information
VI=Other Veteran Info	P=Pension	BLW=Bounty/Land Warrant	RG=Registered Grave
MK=SAR/DAR Marker	PH=Photo	SS=Service Source	BS=Burial Source

317

"Marked Graves of Revolutionary Soldiers and Patriots, *DAR Mag* "SAR P-264698 **BS**: 80 vol3, pg 143 196

PAINE, Tarleton see Payne, Tarleton

PAINE, Thomas; b c1739, Spotsylvania Co; d Bef 5 Sep 1815 **RU**: Patriot, Gave material aid to cause **CEM**: Unidentified; GPS unk; Gordonsville; Orange **GS**: Y **SP**: Mar (18 Nov 1773) Elizabeth (-----) **VI**: Son of John (1705-1770) & Frances (Coleman) (1710-1783) Paine. Will probated 5 Sep 1815 **P**: N **BLW**: N **RG**: N **MK**: unk **PH**: unk **SS**: *DAR Newsletter*, Sep/Oct 2015 Vol 15 No 5 pg 417 **BS**:196.

PALIS, Paul; b unk; d 1781 **RU**: Seaman, Served in Gatinais Bn and died fr battle at Yorktown **CEM**: French Memorial; GPS 36.81944, -79.39933; Yorktown; York **GS**: U **SP**: No info **VI**: No further data **P**: unk **BLW**: unk **RG**: Y **MK**: unk **PH**: unk **SS**: J-Yorktown Historian; SAR P-264796 **BS**: JLARC 1, 74.

PALMER, Job; b c1759; d 1820 **RU**: Corporal, Served in a RI Regt and was on a prison ship in NY harbor on 18 May 1781 **CEM**: St Paul's Episcopal; GPS 36.84733, -76.28554; 201 St Paul's Blvd; Norfolk City **GS**: Y **SP**: No info **VI**: No further data **P**: unk **BLW**: unk **RG**: N **MK**: N **PH**: unk **SS**: AP RI roll **BS**: 139.

PALUT, Louis; b unk; d 1781 **RU**: Seaman, Served on "Ville de Paris" and died from Yorktown battle **CEM**: French Memorial; GPS 36.81944, -79.39933; Yorktown; York **GS**: U **SP**: No info **VI**: No further data **P**: unk **BLW**: unk **RG**: Y **MK**: unk **PH**: unk **SS**: J-Yorktown Historian; SAR P-265058 **BS**: JLARC 1, 74.

PALY, B; b unk; d 1781 **RU**: Soldier, Served in Gatinais Bn and died fr battle at Yorktown **CEM**: French Memorial; GPS 36.81944, -79.39933; Yorktown; York **GS**: U **SP**: No info **VI**: No further data **P**: unk **BLW**: unk **RG**: Y **MK**: unk **PH**: unk **SS**: J-Yorktown Historian; SAR P-265059 **BS**: JLARC 1, 74.

PANGLE, Henry, b 1755, Germantown, Philadelphia Co; d Sep 1822 **RU**: Private, enlisted as a drummer 10 Sep 1777, Capt Thomas Buck's Co, 8th VA Regt **CEM**: Pangle Fam; GPS not determined; Middletown: Frederick **GS**: Unk **SP** mar 21 Mar 1773, Dunmore Co, Susannah Keller **VI**: Son of John Henry Pangle (1725, Hessen, Ger-1781, Shenandoah Co) & Anna Catherina Koehler (19 Sep 1732-1810) **P**: N **BLW**: N **RG**: N **MK**: N **PH**: N **SS**: E pg 602, DAR A 086857 **BS**: 196.

PANIOLET, Jean; b unk; d 1781 **RU**: Soldier, Served in Bourbonnais Bn and died fr battle at Yorktown **CEM**: French Memorial; GPS 36.81944, -79.39933; Yorktown; York **GS**: U **SP**: No info **VI**: No further data **P**: unk **BLW**: unk **RG**: Y **MK**: unk **PH**: unk **SS**: J-Yorktown Historian; SAR P-265079 **BS**: JLARC 1, 74.

PANKEY, John; b 1736, Goochland Co; d 1810 **RU**: Patriot, Gave material aid to cause **CEM**: Pankey Family; GPS unk; Tower Hill, Appomattox; Appomattox **GS**: U **SP**: Keziah Chambers (c1762-8 Jul 1832) **VI**: Died in Buckingham Co **P**: N **BLW**: N **RG**: Y **MK**: unk **PH**: unk **SS**: AL Ct Bk pg 4, 31; SAR P-265080 **BS**: 196.

PANNILL, William; b 30 Oct 1738; d 22 Sep 1806 **RU**: Patriot, Donated food to cause **CEM**: Green-Level Family; GPS unk; Rt 663 so of True Blue Corners; Orange **GS**: N **SP**: Ann Morton d/o Jeremiah & Sarah (Mallory) Morton **VI**: Son of William & Sarah (Baily) Pannill of Urbanna, Middlesex Co. Was Sheriff of Orange Co. Burial in family plot known as Green Level **P**: N **BLW**: N **RG**: Y **MK**: N **PH**: N **SS**: D; SAR P-265090 **BS**: 04, Sep 07; 196.

PAON, Jean; b unk; d 1781 **RU**: Seaman, Served on "Saint-Esprit" and died from Yorktown battle **CEM**: French Memorial; GPS 36.81944, -79.39933; Yorktown; York **GS**: U **SP**: No info **VI**: No further data **P**: unk **BLW**: unk **RG**: Y **MK**: unk **PH**: unk **SS**: J-Yorktown Historian; SAR P-265092 **BS**: JLARC 1, 74.

PAPELARD, Jacques; b unk; d 1781 **RU**: Soldier, Served in Agenois Bn and died fr battle at Yorktown **CEM**: French Memorial; GPS 36.81944, -79.39933; Yorktown; York **GS**: U **SP**: No info **VI**: No further data **P**: unk **BLW**: unk **RG**: Y **MK**: unk **PH**: unk **SS**: J-Yorktown Historian; SAR P-265093 **BS**: JLARC 1, 74.

PAPON, Louis; b unk; d 1781 **RU**: Seaman, Served on "Sceptre" and died from Yorktown battle **CEM**: French Memorial; GPS 36.81944, -79.39933; Yorktown; York **GS**: U **SP**: No info **VI**: No further data **P**: unk **BLW**: unk **RG**: Y **MK**: unk **PH**: unk **SS**: J-Yorktown Historian; SAR P-265094 **BS**: JLARC 1, 74.

RU=Rank/Unit	CEM=Cemetery	GS=Gravestone	SP=Spousal Information
VI=Other Veteran Info	P=Pension	BLW=Bounty/Land Warrant	RG=Registered Grave
MK=SAR/DAR Marker	PH=Photo	SS=Service Source	BS=Burial Source

PARIEL, Leonard; b unk; d 1781 **RU:** Soldier, Served in Touraine Bn and died fr battle at Yorktown **CEM:** French Memorial; GPS 36.81944, -79.39933; Yorktown; York **GS:** U **SP:** No info **VI:** No further data **P:** unk **BLW:** unk **RG:** Y **MK:** unk **PH:** unk **SS:** J-Yorktown Historian; SAR P-265159 **BS:** JLARC 1, 74.

PARIS, Claude; b unk; d 1781 **RU:** Soldier, Served in Auxonne Bn and died fr battle at Yorktown **CEM:** French Memorial; GPS 36.81944, -79.39933; Yorktown; York **GS:** U **SP:** No info **VI:** No further data **P:** unk **BLW:** unk **RG:** Y **MK:** unk **PH:** unk **SS:** J-Yorktown Historian; SAR P-265161 **BS:** JLARC 1, 74.

PARIS, Gabriel; b unk; d 1781 **RU:** Soldier, Served in Santogne Bn and died fr battle at Yorktown **CEM:** French Memorial; GPS 36.81944, -79.39933; Yorktown; York **GS:** U **SP:** No info **VI:** No further data **P:** unk **BLW:** unk **RG:** Y **MK:** unk **PH:** unk **SS:** J-Yorktown Historian; SAR P 265162**BS:** JLARC 1, 74.

PARIS, Jacques de; b unk; d 1781 **RU:** Soldier, Served in Brie Bn and died fr battle at Yorktown **CEM:** French Memorial; GPS 36.81944, -79.39933; Yorktown; York **GS:** U **SP:** No info **VI:** No further data **P:** unk **BLW:** unk **RG:** Y **MK:** unk **PH:** unk **SS:** J-Yorktown Historian; SAR P-265163 **BS:** JLARC 1, 74.

PARKER, Ebenezer; b 1749, Westford MA; d 29 Dec 1831 **RU:** Private, Served in Capt Jonathan Minot's Co, Col Prescott's MA Regt in Lexington Alarm **CEM:** St John's Episcopal; GPS 37.53183 - 77.41958; 2401 E Broad St; Richmond City **GS:** U **SP:** Mar (1777) Experience Keep Hildreth (1752-1817), 2) Roxanna (__) **VI:** No further data **P:** unk **BLW:** unk **RG:** Y **MK:** unk **PH:** unk **SS:** DD; SAR P-265386 **BS:** JLARC 1, 76.

PARKER, Elias; b 3 Jun 1760, Boston, MA; d 8 Dec 1799 **RU:** Lieutenant, Served in Col Joseph Vose's 1st MA Regt **CEM:** Blandford; GPS 37.22433, -77.38604; 319 S Crater St; Petersburg City **GS:** Y **SP:** mar (29 Sep 1790, Trinity Church, Boston) Mary Brown Parker **VI:** Son of Daniel & Margaret (-----) Parker. Mayor of Petersburg 1796 to 1797. DAR marker. Spouse awarded pen 4 Mar 1843 of $400 a yr **P:** Y **BLW:** unk **RG:** N **MK:** Y **PH:** unk **SS:** BT **BS:** 196.

PARKER, George; b 28 Oct 1735; d 3 Sep 1784 **RU:** Patriot, Gave material aid to the cause **CEM:** Poplar Cove Wharf; GPS unk; Nr end of Rt 653, Onancock; Accomack **GS:** Y **SP:** Adah Bagwell (12 Sep 1734-26 Aug 1766) **VI:** No further data **P:** N **BLW:** N **RG:** N **MK:** N **PH:** unk **SS:** E pg 603; AL Comm Bk 1 pg 30 **BS:** 37 pg 193.

PARKER, Joseph; by 1721, d 23 Nov 1793 **RU:** Patriot, Patriot, Paid personal property tax 1782, Loudoun Co considered a payment to support cause **CEM:** Goose Creek; GPS 39.11250, -77.60589; Rt 722, Lincoln; Loudoun **GS:** Unk **SP:** No spousal info **VI:** No further data **P:** N **BLW:** N **RG:** N **MK:** N **PH:** N **SS:**; DV Loudoun Co list 1782C image 17 pdf **BS:** 222.

PARKER, Josiah; b 11 May 1751 Macclesfield, Isle of Wight; d 10 Mar 1810 **RU:** Colonel/Patriot, Served in VA Regt at Trenton. Recd British sword of surrender at Trenton. Fought at Princeton & Brandywine. Was commander of VA Militia south of James 1781. Commanded the unit that defeated Tarleton at Scotts Old Field (1781). Was Nominal Commander at Yorktown. Served in VA House of Delegates (1779-1783). **CEM:** Parker Family; GPS 36.58569, -76.32136; 3.5 mi E of Rescue, Macclesfield; Isle of Wight **GS:** Y **SP:** Mary Pierce Bridger **VI:** Son of Nicolas & Ann (Copeland) Parker. Served as Naval officer in Portsmouth, VA in 1786. Elected to first six US Congresses, serving 1789-1801. Exact location of grave.has been discovered Cedar Grove Cem in Portsmouth rec'd his gravrstone fr Ct St Baptist which no longer had a burial ground, thus memorialized there VS12VA **P:** Y SAR **BLW:** unk **RG:** Y **MK:** Y SAR **PH:** unk **SS:** AK; SAR P-265557 **BS:** 04.

PARKER, Nicholas; b 31 Oct 1722, Macclesfield, Isle of Wight; d 1789 **RU:** Patriot, Gave material aid to cause **CEM:** Parker Family; GPS 36.58569, -76.32136; 3.5 mi E of Rescue, Macclesfield; Isle of Wight **GS:** N **SP:** Ann Copeland **VI:** Earned rank of Lt Col before Rev War, probably in county militia. Commemorative marker exists **P:** N **BLW:** N **RG:** N **MK:** N **PH:** N **SS:** AK Ct Bk pg 14; AP Roll, SAR Applic **BS:** 04; 153 macclesfield.

PARKER, Thomas; b 1757; d Dec 1819 **RU:** Captain, Served in VA Line fr 1775 to end of war. Was prisoner at Germantown and confined on British ship **CEM:** Poplar Grove; GPS 36.58569, -76.32133; Off Rt 180, Pungoteague, Hack's Neck; Accomack **GS:** Y **SP:** No info **VI:** Recd BLW **P:** unk **BLW:** Y **RG:** N **MK:** N **PH:** unk **SS:** G pg 770; N pg 1028; BY pg 79; CG pg 2596 **BS:** 37 pg 193,194.

RU=Rank/Unit
VI=Other Veteran Info
MK=SAR/DAR Marker
CEM=Cemetery
P=Pension
PH=Photo
GS=Gravestone
BLW=Bounty/Land Warrant
SS=Service Source
SP=Spousal Information
RG=Registered Grave
BS=Burial Source

319

PARKER, Thomas; b 1753; d 24 Jan 1820 **RU**: Captain, Served 23 Apr 1778, 5th Cont Line 12 Feb 1781 and 1st Cont Line Jan 1783 **CEM**: St James Episcopal, Old Cemetery; GPS 39.11555, -77.56250; Church St NE, Leesburg; Loudoun **GS**: U **SP**: Sallie Opie **VI**: Son of Richard Parker & Elizabeth Beale; was Brig Gen War of 1812 **P**: unk **BLW**: Y **RG**: N **MK**: unk **PH**: unk **SS**: E pg 604 **BS**: 196.

PARKER, Timothy; b unk; d 14 Oct 1781 **RU**: Private, Served in Ct Troops Cont line. Died fr the battle at Yorktown **CEM**: Yorktown Victory Monument Tablet; GPS 38.28350, -78.54150; Yorktown; York **GS**: U **SP**: No info **VI**: BLW 259-100 **P**: unk **BLW**: Y **RG**: Y **MK**: unk **PH**: unk **SS**: J-Yorktown Historian; SAR P-265698; DY 342 **BS**: JLARC 74.(**PARKER**, William Alexander See Appendix G Addenda)

PARKER, William Harwar; b 1759; d 1815 **RU**: Captain, Served in VA Navy on "Tempest." Was wounded **CEM**: McIlhaney Family; GPS unk; Nr Hillsboro E side Rt 690 btw Rts 90 & 611; Loudoun **GS**: U **SP**: Mary Sturman **VI**: BLW of 2667 acre as Lt for 3 yrs serv was awarded 23 Jun 1783 **P**: unk **BLW**: Y **RG**: Y **MK**: unk **PH**: unk **SS**: E pg 604; G pg 778; L pg 102; DAR A087818; SAR P-265732 **BS**: JLARC 4,32.

PARKINS, Isaac; b Nov 1746, Frederick Co; d 15 Feb 1829 **RU**: Patriot, Gave material aid to the cause in Frederick Co **CEM**: Hollingsworth-Parkins; GPS 39.16600, -78.17490; W Jubal Early Dr; Frederick **GS**: Y **SP**: Mary Steer (1752-1842) **VI**: Son of Isaac Parkins, Sr (1697-1773) & Mary Grace Booth (1706-1762). He died in Winchester, Frederick Co **P**: N **BLW**: N **RG**: Y **MK**: unk **PH**: Y **SS**: AL Ct Bk pg 20, 40; SAR P-335902 **BS**: 196.

PARKINSON, Joseph Christian; b unk; d 1845 **RU**: Patriot, Gave material aid to cause **CEM**: St John's Episcopal; GPS 37.53183, -77.41958; 2401 E Broad St; Richmond City **GS**: N **SP**: Mar (25 Jan 1842, Richmond) Ann Elizabeth Quarles **VI**: No further data **P**: N **BLW**: N **RG**: N **MK**: N **PH**: N **SS**: D Vol 3 pg 712; AL Ct Bk pg 17 New Kent Co **BS**: 28, pg 351; 196.

PARKS, John; b 1713; d Jul 1793 **RU**: Patriot, Gave material aid to cause **CEM**: McDowell; GPS 37.86860, -79.31080; Nr jct Rts 11 and 712, Fairfield; Rockbridge **GS**: Y **SP**: No info **VI**: No further data **P**: N **BLW**: N **RG**: N **MK**: unk **PH**: unk **SS**: Al Ct Bk pg 9 Rockbridge Co; **BS**: 196.

PARKS, Joseph; b unk; d 21 Aug 1810 **RU**: Private, Served as Private in Illinois Regt **CEM**: Tinkling Spring Presbyterian; GPS 38.08472, -78.98278; 30 Tinkling Spring Dr, Fishersville; Augusta **GS**: Y **SP**: Rebekah (-----) (1734-Dec 1794) **VI**: Stone nearly illegible and wedged bet tree trunks **P**: unk **BLW**: unk **RG**: N **MK**: N **PH**: unk **SS**: E pg 605 **BS**: 208 pg 466; 196.

PARMENTER, James; b unk; d 1781 **RU**: Soldier, Served fr MA and died as result of Yorktown battle **CEM**: Yorktown Victory Monument Tablet; GPS 38.28350, -78.54150; Yorktown; York **GS**: U **SP**: No info **VI**: No further data **P**: unk **BLW**: unk **RG**: Y **MK**: unk **PH**: unk **SS**: J-Yorktown Historian; SAR P-265984 **BS**: JLARC 74.

PARRAMORE, Thomas; b 24 Dec 1764; d 18 May 1832 **RU**: Captain, commanded 9th Co, 9th VA Regt, Cont Line 4 Jul 1776 with service in Accomack Co **CEM**: Parramore; GPS not determined; Onley, Accomack **GS**: Unk **SP**: Not determined **VI**: Son of William Parramore (27 Dec 1741-4 Jun 1816) & Rose (-----) **P**: unk **BLW**: unk **RG**: Y **MK**: unk **PH**: unk **SS**: CE pg 60 **BS**: 196.

PARRAMORE, William; b 27 Dec 1741; d 4 Jun 1816 **RU**: Colonel, Promoted to Col, Accomack Co Militia on 30 Apr 1782 **CEM**: Belle Vue; GPS unk; Off Rt 646, 7 mi E of Locustville; Accomack **GS**: Y **SP**: Sarah Seymour (c1739-25 Apr 1802 age 63) d/o Digby & Rose Seymore of Northampton Co **VI**: Son of Thomas & Joannah (-----) Parramore **P**: unk **BLW**: unk **RG**: Y **MK**: N **PH**: unk **SS**: E pg 605; SAR P-266024 **BS**: 37 pg 201.

PARRE, Pierre; b unk; d 1781 **RU**: Seaman, Served on "Duc De Bourgogne" and died from Yorktown battle **CEM**: French Memorial; GPS 36.81944, -79.39933; Yorktown; York **GS**: U **SP**: No info **VI**: No further data **P**: unk **BLW**: unk **RG**: Y **MK**: unk **PH**: unk **SS**: J-Yorktown Historian; SAR P-266028 **BS**: JLARC 1, 74.

PASCON (PASCOW, PASCHO), Herbert; b c1741; d 3 Apr or 21 May 1801 **RU**: Lieutenant, Served in VA Navy on Boat "Liberty" 1777 to late 1781 **CEM**: Herbert; GPS 39.01475, -76.35013; Off Armstrong Ln; Hampton City **GS**: N **SP**: Mary (-----) **VI**: Recd BLW of 2666 acres **P**: unk **BLW**: Y **RG**: N **MK**: unk **PH**: N **SS**: C pg 52; BY **BS**: 202 WPA Hampton City.

RU=Rank/Unit	CEM=Cemetery	GS=Gravestone	SP=Spousal Information
VI=Other Veteran Info	P=Pension	BLW=Bounty/Land Warrant	RG=Registered Grave
MK=SAR/DAR Marker	PH=Photo	SS=Service Source	BS=Burial Source

PATALIER, Joseph; b unk; d 1781 **RU**: Soldier, Served in Santogne Bn and died fr battle at Yorktown **CEM**: French Memorial; GPS 36.81944, -79.39933; Yorktown; York **GS**: U **SP**: No info **VI**: No further data **P**: unk **BLW**: unk **RG**: Y **MK**: unk **PH**: unk **SS**: J-Yorktown Historian; SAR P-266391 **BS**: JLARC 1, 74.

PATRICK, John; b 1732, PA; d 1809 **RU**: Patriot, Gave material aid to cause **CEM**: Patrick family; GPS unk; Locust Isle, Rt 865 N fr Waynesboro; Waynesboro City **GS**: Y **SP**: Janet McPheeters (1739-Jun 1820) **VI**: Son of Robert & Rachel (-----) Patrick **P**: N **BLW**: N **RG**: Y **MK**: U **PH**: unk **SS**: AL Ct Bk pg 8 Augusta Co; DAR A206507; SAR P-266497 **BS**: JLARC 62; 196.

PATRICK, William; b 21 Jan 1763; d 1835 **RU**: Soldier, Ent serv Augusta Co. Served in VA Line **CEM**: Patrick Family; GPS unk; Locust Isle, Rt 865 N fr Waynesboro; Waynesboro City **GS**: U **SP**: No info **VI**: Pension appl 25 Sep 1832 age 69. S5882 **P**: Y **BLW**: unk **RG**:Y **MK**: U **PH**: unk **SS**: K Vol 4 pg 72; CG Vol 3 pg 2616; SAR P-266523 **BS**: JLARC 4, 8, 62.

PATTERSON, John; b 1760, Caroline Co; d 22 Nov 1811 (FAG) **RU**: Mid-Shipman; US Navy, served as clerk, 16 Jan 1783 **CEM**: Poplar Grove Plantation; GPS 37.399444,-76.333055; 265 Poplar Grove Ln, Williams; Mathews **GS**:   Unk **SP**: mar 1) unk, 2) mar 3 Dec 1790, Elizabeth Todd (31 Jul 1760-24 Nov 1824) **VI**: Son of Col John Patterson & Elizabeth Smith Tabb. DAR indicates he died 1 Aug 1824 **P**: N **BLW**: Unk **RG**: N **MK**: U **PH**: Unk **SS**: DAR A086418; BE pg 67, rolls pg 235 **BS**: 196.

PATTERSON, Samuel; b unk; d 26 Mar 1797 **RU**: First Lieutenant, Promoted 1st Lt 01 Sep 1778 **CEM**: Fincastle Presbyterian; GPS 37.50017, -79.87558; 108 E Back St, Fincastle; Botetourt **GS**: Y **SP**: No info **VI**: Name is on the plaque as a 1st Lt **P**: unk **BLW**: unk **RG**: N **MK**: Y SAR plaque **PH**: unk **SS**: AZ pg 228 **BS**: 196.

PATTERSON, William; b 1752; d 16 Feb 1816 **RU**: Sergeant, Served in Capt John Hay's Co, 9th VA Regt Jun 1777 **CEM**: Trinity United Methodist; GPS 39.13600, -77.00610; 2911 Cameron Mills Rd; Alexandria City **GS**: Y **SP**: Mary (-----) **VI**: No further data **P**: unk **BLW**: unk **RG**: Y **MK**: N **PH**: unk **SS**: AP roll; SAR P-266782 **BS**: 23 pg 135.

PATTERSON, William; b 1760, Augusta Co; d 25 Jan 1825 **RU**: Soldier?/Patriot, Gave material aid to cause. He perhaps is the man this name that was a private in the 11th Cont Line or the one who was in General John Clark's Illinois Regt **CEM**: Old Crockett; GPS 37.04161, -80.97662; Rt 600, Crockett's Creek Rd, Wytheville; Wythe **GS**: Y **SP**: Agnes Patton (1765 Botetourt Co-1843 Giles Co) d/o John J. (1689-1757) & Agness (Snodgrass) (1715-__) Patton **VI**: No further data **P**: N **BLW**: N **RG**: Yk **MK**: unk **PH**: unk **SS**: AL Ct Bk pg 45 Montgomery Co; DAR A086545; SAR P-266786 **BS**: 196.

PATTESON, David; b 30 Aug 1746, Chesterfield Co; d 2 May 1821 **RU**: First Lieutenant, Served in Chesterfield Militia.Took oath as Lt 30 Oct 1777 **CEM**: Patteson Family; GPS unk; Laurel Meadows; Richmond City **GS**: U **SP**: Eliza Ann Jordan **VI**: Died in Chesterfield Co **P**: unk **BLW**: unk **RG**: Y **MK**: N **PH**: unk **SS**: AC; SAR P-266797 **BS**: 04.

PATTESON, David; b 15 Aug 1758; d 22 Oct 1846 **RU**: Major, Was a Cadet in 1776 **CEM**: Patteson Family; GPS unk; Mt Pleasant; Buckingham **GS**: N **SP**: Judith Dibrel **VI**: Son of Thomas (1735-1790) & (-----) Paterson (Patteson?). No GS but on memorial stone **P**: unk **BLW**: unk **RG**:Y **MK**: N **PH**: N **SS**: E pg 609; SAR P-266798 **BS**: JLARC 59; 52 pg 443; 196.

PATTESON, Thomas; b 1735; d 1790 **RU**: Captain, Ent serv Buckingham Co. Served in 6th VA Militia **CEM**: Patteson Family; GPS unk; Mt Pleasant; Buckingham **GS**: N **SP**: No info **VI**: Pension appl 24 Jul 1832 Davidson Co, TN. S2011 **P**: Y **BLW**: unk **RG**: Y **MK**: N **PH**: unk **SS**: CG Vol 3 pg 2621; SAR P-266801 **BS**: JLARC 59.

PATTON, George, Gordon; b 17 Jan 1757, d 14 Oct 1813 **RU**: Sergeant, Enlisted Falmouth, Stafford Co, 1777 in Capt William Wallace's Company, Col Fowler's Regt; 3rd Cont line; was at battle of Brandywine **CEM**: Hartwood Baptist Meeting House; GPS 38.4031590,-77.5633220; 24 Shackleford Rd; Stafford **GS**: N **SP**: mar 24 Dec 1784, Sarah Stringfellow (1 Nov 1766-11 Jul 1848), d/o James Madison Stringfellow (1734-1805) & Susannah Smith (1725-1777). She rec'd pen # W4049 in1840 in Fayette Co, OH **VI**: Son of James Patton (1722-1768) & Eleanor(Helen) Gordon **P**: Widow **BLW**:N **RG**: Y **MK**: N **PH**: Y **SS**: E pg 309; K vol 4, pg 75; CG pg 2621; DAR A088808; SAR P-266827 **BS**: 196.

RU=Rank/Unit	CEM=Cemetery	GS=Gravestone	SP=Spousal Information
VI=Other Veteran Info	P=Pension	BLW=Bounty/Land Warrant	RG=Registered Grave
MK=SAR/DAR Marker	PH=Photo	SS=Service Source	BS=Burial Source

PATTON, Henry; b unk; d Aft 1779 **RU:** Captain, Commanded a co in Montgomery Co Militia 7 Sep 1779 **CEM:** Patton Family; GPS unk; nr Dublin; Pulaski **GS:** U **SP:** No info **VI:** No further data **P:** unk **BLW:** unk **RG:** N **MK:** N **PH:** unk **SS:** E pg 609 **BS:** 80 vol 3 pg 155.

PAUL, Nicholas; b 1728 or 1729, PA or Germany; d 1817 **RU:** Second Lieutenant, Was 2nd Lt in 3rd Co, 5th Bn, Northhampton Co, PA Militia 1777. Served in Capt George Noff's 7th Co, 3rd Bn, PA Militia **CEM:** Dayton; GPS 38.42000, -78.94303; Bowman Rd, Dayton; Rockingham **GS:** Y **SP:** 1) Catharine (-----) 2) Barbara Hess. Order unk. **VI:** No further data **P:** unk **BLW:** unk **RG:** Y **MK:** Y **SAR PH:** Y **SS:** J-NSSAR 1993 Reg; SAR P266934; DAR A086620 **BS:** JLARC 1.

PAUL, Peter; b 1759 or 1760; d 16 Feb 1844 **RU:** Ensign, Served in Flying Camp of militia in PA. Was Prisoner of War and exchanged 15 Aug 1778 **CEM:** Dayton; GPS 38.42000, -78.94303; Bowman Rd, Dayton; Rockingham **GS:** Y **SP:** Catharine Swope **VI:** No further data **P:** unk **BLW:** unk **RG:** Y **MK:** Y **SAR PH:** Y **SS:** J-NSSAR 1993 Reg; SAR P-266937 **BS:** JLARC 1.

PAULARD, Jean; b unk; d 1781 **RU:** Soldier, Served in Gatinais Bn and died fr battle at Yorktown **CEM:** French Memorial; GPS 36.81944, -79.39933; Yorktown; York **GS:** U **SP:** No info **VI:** No further data **P:** unk **BLW:** unk **RG:** Y **MK:** unk **PH:** unk **SS:** J-Yorktown Historian; SAR P-266948 **BS:** JLARC 1, 74.

PAXTON, John; b 1747, Augusta Co; d 8 Aug 1832 **RU:** Captain/Patriot, Commanded co in Rockbridge Co Militia. Served at Point Pleasant in 1777. Gave material aid to cause **CEM:** Glasgow Cemetery; GPS 37.60320, -79.45914; 13th St & Fitzlee, Glasgow; Rockbridge **GS:** Y **SP:** Mar (c1772) Sarah Walker (20 Jun 1750, Augusta Co-24 Nov 1839) **VI:** No further data **P:** unk **BLW:** unk **RG:** Y **MK:** unk **PH:** unk **SS:** DAR #A086701; AL Ct Bk pg 3, 7 Rockbridge Co; AZ pg 42; SAR P-267012 **BS:** JLARC 79; 196.

PAXTON, John Sr; b 1716, PA; d 13 Feb 1787 **RU:** Patriot, Gave material aid to cause **CEM:** Timber Grove; GPS unk; Buffalo Dist, Timber Ridge; Rockbridge **GS:** N **SP:** Mar (1742 Lancaster, PA) Mary Martha Blair (1726 Ireland-12 Aug 1821) d/o Samuel (1667-1754) & Martha Campbell (Lye) Blair **VI:** No further data **P:** N **BLW:** N **RG:** N **MK:** unk **PH:** N **SS:** D Vol 3 pg 822, 826 **BS:** 196.

PAXTON, Thomas; b c1719; d 27 Sep 1788 **RU:** Patriot, Gave material aid to cause **CEM:** Paxton Family; GPS 37.71666, -79.40271; Forge Rd, Mechanicsville; Rockbridge **GS:** Y **SP:** 1) Elizabeth McClung (1724-1773) 2) Mary Barclay **VI:** No further data **P:** N **BLW:** N **RG:** N **MK:** unk **PH:** unk **SS:** DAR Newsletter, Sep/Oct 2015 Vol 15 No 5 pg 417 **BS:** 196.

PAXTON, William; b 7 Apr 1757, Rockbridge Co; d 27 Dec 1838 **RU:** Captain, Commanded a co in Rockbridge Co Militia 5 May 1778 to 1781 **CEM:** Falling Springs Presbyterian; GPS 37.68526 -79.44972; 410 Falling Springs Rd, Glasgow; Rockbridge **GS:** Y **SP:** Mar (Jun 1787) Jane Grigsby, d/o John & (-----) Grigsby **VI:** Pension appl 17 Aug 1832 Rockbridge Co. S5873. Source 2 has him bur on McCormick Farm, Served 3 mos in Whiskey Insurrection in PA in 1794 **P:** Y **BLW:** unk **RG:** Y **MK:** Y **SAR PH:** Y **SS:** CG Vol 3 pg 2625; E pg 610; SAR P-267031 **BS:** JLARC 1, 2, 63.

PAXTON, William; b unk; d Aft 1781 **RU:** Major/Patriot, Gave material aid to cause **CEM:** Old Graveyard nr Wesley Chapel; GPS unk; Glasgow; Rockbridge **GS:** U **SP:** No info **VI:** No further data **P:** unk **BLW:** unk **RG:** unk **MK:** unk **PH:** unk **SS:** SAR P-267028; AL Ct Bk pg 3 Rockbridge Co **BS:** JLARC 79.

PAXTON, William Sr; b 1732; d 30 Sep 1795 **RU:** Captain/Patriot, Appointed Capt 5 May 1778 in Rockbridge Co Militia and served to 1781. Gave material aid to the cause **CEM:** Mt Zion Methodist; GPS 37.66596, -79.46615; Btw Buffalo & Tinkersville; Rockbridge **GS:** Y **SP:** Elanor (-----) (c1741-13 Aug 1815) **VI:** No further data **P:** unk **BLW:** unk **RG:** N **MK:** N **PH:** unk **SS:** E pg 610; AL Ct Bk pg 3; CZ pg 343 **BS:** JLARC 79; 193; 154 Rockbridge.

PAYNE, Augustine; b 11 Dec 1761; d 16 Mar 1844 **RU:** Private, Ent serv Fauquier Co. Served in John O'Bannon's Co, Fauquier Co Militia, wounded in service **CEM:** Orlean; GPS unk; Nr Orlean; Fauquier **GS:** Y **SP:** A man by this name mar (1787 Fauquier Co, bond dated 14 Jan 1789) Catharine "Caty" Young (12 Jul 1769-___) d/o Harmon & (-----) Young **VI:** Pension appl 31 Aug 1832 Fauquier Co. Moved to Parke Co, IN in 1835 and d there in Raccoon Twp. Widow appl pen 19 Dec 1844 Parke Co, IN. W10850 **P:** Y **BLW:** unk **RG:** Y **MK:** N **PH:** unk **SS:** K Vol 4 pg 78; CG Vol 3 pg 2625; Fauquier Co Marriages pg 154; DAR A085943; SAR P-267042 **BS:** JLARC 1.

RU=Rank/Unit	CEM=Cemetery	GS=Gravestone	SP=Spousal Information
VI=Other Veteran Info	P=Pension	BLW=Bounty/Land Warrant	RG=Registered Grave
MK=SAR/DAR Marker	PH=Photo	SS=Service Source	BS=Burial Source

322

PAYNE, Daniel; b 15 Sep 1728; d 12 Apr 1796 **RU**: Patriot, In 1777 was named a trustee for Falmouth in Stafford Co. Also was Treasurer. He paid resonal property tax in 1782 in Stafford Co. **CEM**: Payne Family, aka Cedar Hill; **GPS** 38.13357, -76.97069; Red house, Horners, 2 mi NE of Leedstown; Westmoreland **GS**: U **SP**: Never mar **VI**: Son of John Monroe & Mary (___). One of three to inventory James Hunter's estate in 1785 owner of Hunter Iron Works that provided weapons and equipment during Rev War **P**: N **BLW**: N **RG**: Y **MK**: N **PH**: unk **SS**: J pg 211 Pub serv; SAR P-332475 **BS**: 34 pg 211; 196.

PAYNE, Francis; b 1743, King George Co; d 1816 **RU**: Ensign, Served in Fauquier Co Militia; oath for ensign Feb 1799 **CEM**: Orlean; **GPS** unk; Nr Orlean; Fauquier **GS**: Y **SP**: Susannah Jett; A man by this name mar (bond 4 Nov 1807, John Nelson security) Patsy Withers **VI**: No further data **P**: unk **BLW**: unk **RG**: Y **MK**: N **PH**: unk **SS**: J-NSSAR 1993 Reg; Fauquier Co Marriages pg 154; DAR A085994; SAR P-267057 **BS**: JLARC 1.

PAYNE, George; b 1743; d 1831 **RU**: Lieutenant Colonel, Appointed Lt Col of Goochland Co Militia, 20 Aug 1781 **CEM**: Grace Episcopal; **GPS** 37.68321, -77.88765; 2955 River Rd West, Goochland CH; Goochland **GS**: Y **SP**: Mar (31 Dec 1765) Betty McCartey-Morton by Rev William Douglas **VI**: No further data **P**: unk **BLW**: unk **RG**: N **MK**: N **PH**: unk **SS**: E pg 610 **BS**: 46 pg 156.

PAYNE, George, Jr; b 21 Nov 1707, Henrico Co, d 15 Mar 1784 **RU**: Patriot, gave material aid to cause Goochland Co **CEM**: Payne Family; **GPS** 37.847801, -78.071899; Payne Rd, Goochland; Goochland **GS**: N **SP**: mar 23 Mar 1745, Judith Burton (1710-1748) **VI**: Son of George Payne, Sr (1670-1744) & Mary Jane Woodson (1678-1743) **P**: N **BLW**: N **RG**: N **MK**: N **PH**: N **SS**: DAR A086006; AL Ct Bk pgs 13 ,25, Comm Bk III, pg 78, IV pg 315 **BS**: 196.

PAYNE, John; b 4 Dec 1713, Goochland Co; d 28 Jul 1784 **RU**: Lieutenant Colonel/Patriot, Was member of House of Burgesses 1752-88. Was Lt Col of Militia and member of Goochland Co Committee of Safety. Gave material aid to cause **CEM**: Payne Family; **GPS** 37.84780, -78.07190; Rt 681 S of Rt 605; Goochland **GS**: U **SP**: 1) Dorothea Spotswood d/o Alexander (1676-1740) Spotswood & Elizabeth Butler (Brayne) Spotwood Thompson (1698-1751) 2) mar (23 Jun 1757) Jane Smith **VI**: Son of George (1680-1744) and Mary (Woodson) (1670-__) Payne. Died in Campbell Co **P**: unk **BLW**: unk **RG**: Y **MK**: unk **PH**: unk **SS**: J- DAR Hatcher; AL Ct Bk pg 1 Goochland Co; DAR A086043; SAR P-267070 **BS**: JLARC 2; 196.

PAYNE, John; b 1753 Baynesville, Westmoreland Co; d 21 May 1824 **RU**: Private, Served in 5th & 6th Cont Lines **CEM**: Payne Family, aka Cedar Hill; **GPS** 38.13357, -76.97069; Red house, Horners, 2 mi NE of Leedstown; Westmoreland **GS**: N **SP**: No info **VI**: No further data **P**: Y **BLW**: unk **RG**: N **MK**: N **PH**: N **SS**: E pg 610; AP rec; Application 631 **BS**: 189 pg 110; 196.

PAYNE, John Jr; b unk; d July 1787 or 1788 **RU**: Sailing Master, Served in VA State Navy. Died at Siege of York of smallpox. Master of pilot boat "Hiram" **CEM**: St John's Episcopal; **GPS** unk; 100 W Queen's Way; Hampton City **GS**: U **SP**: No info **VI**: Son of Thomas and (-----) Payne **P**: unk **BLW**: Y **RG**: N **MK**: unk **PH**: unk **SS**: BY pg 176 **BS**: 32.

PAYNE, Joseph; b 1758; d 5 Apr 1826 **RU**: Ensign, Ent Serv Goochland Co 1776. Served in 8th VA Regt **CEM**: Windy Cove Presbyterian; **GPS** unk; 102 Windy Cove Rd, Millboro; Bath **GS**: N **SP**: Mar (30 Oct or 30 Dec 1779 while prisoner on Long Island) Ann (-----) (c1761-4 Feb 1847) **VI**: Moved to Bath Co in 1807 where appl for pen 12 May 1818 age 59. Widow appl pen 12 Sep 1837 age 76 W18693. DAR plaque on church wall **P**: Y **BLW**: unk **RG**: N **MK**: Y DAR plaque **PH**: N **SS**: E pg 611; K Vol 4 pg 79; CG Vol 3 pg 2626 **BS**: 159 Windy Cove; 196.

PAYNE, Josiah; b 1705; d 1785 **RU**: Patriot, Gave material aid to cause in Goochland Co **CEM**: Robert Payne Plantation; **GPS** unk; Dix Ferry Rd nr Dan River; Danville City **GS**: Y **SP**: No info **VI**: Served in VA House of Delegates 1761-1765 **P**: N **BLW**: N **RG**: N **MK**: N **PH**: unk **SS**: AL Cert Issued **BS**: 81 chart.

PAYNE (PAINE), Phillip; b 29 Mar 1760, Goochland Co; d 7 Jul 1840 **RU**: Private/Patriot, Served in Goochland Co Militia. As patriot, was hired to build road to KY during war period **CEM**: Payne Family; **GPS** unk; "Oak Grove," Rt 659, Altavista; Campbell **GS**: Y **SP**: Elizabeth Dandridge, d/o Nathaniel West & Dorothea (Spotswood) Dandridge (19 Sep 1764 Hanover Co-26 Apr 1833) **VI**: Son of John Payne

RU=Rank/Unit
VI=Other Veteran Info
MK=SAR/DAR Marker

CEM=Cemetery
P=Pension
PH=Photo

GS=Gravestone
BLW=Bounty/Land Warrant
SS=Service Source

SP=Spousal Information
RG=Registered Grave
BS=Burial Source

323

(1713-1784) & Jane Smith (1736-181). Only the stones are here. Bodies are bur at "Airy Mont" near Gladys **P:** unk **BLW:** unk **RG:** unk **MK:** N **PH:** unk **SS:** N Vol 3 pg 1272; DAR A086094; SAR P-267095 **BS:** JLARC 36; 196.

PAYNE, Reuben; b c1756; d 1840 **RU:** Captain, Served in Pittsylvania Co Militia **CEM:** Watkins; **GPS** unk; Axton; Henry **GS:** U **SP:** Mar (1 Oct 1781 Henry Co) Ann (Nancy) Ray (Rae) **VI:** Operated an Ordinary, Was bur at Payne Cemetery, but was moved to Watkins Cem **P:** unk **BLW:** unk **RG:**N **MK:** unk **PH:** unk **SS:** G pg 284 **BS:** 196.

PAYNE, Richard; b 18 Jun 1763, Baynesville, Westmoreland Co; d 31 Mar 1843 **RU:** Second Lieutenant, served first as a Private in Capt Muse's Co, Col Hungerford Regt, Westmoreland Co. Served in Capt Johnson's Co, Orange Co Militia 24 Mar 1780. Ent serv Westmoreland 1781 under Cols Mercer and Washington **CEM:** Fairview; GPS 38.48080,-78.00470; Sperryville Pike Rt 522, Culpeper; Culpeper **GS:** Y **SP:** 1) Susannah Kelly, 2) Mary Major (1780-1840) **VI:** Appl for pension 15 Aug 1836 Culpeper Co. S8929. Last payment of pension was in 1840. Recd BLW of 777.5 acres. Stone was moved fr near Atlantus where it was found on the WPA Survey **P:** Y **BLW:** Y **RG:** Y **MK:** N **PH:** unk **SS:** E pg 611; K Vol 4 pg 80; CG Vol 3 pg 2626; DAR A086125; SAR P-267097 **BS:** 75 Culpeper; 196.

PAYNE /PAINE, Robert, b 1738 Goochland Co, d 1791 **RU:** Captain/ Patriot, In 1775 was a Captain in the Pittsylvania Co Militia. As patriot was member of Commission of Peace in the county 1777 **CEM:** Payne Family; GPS 37.8478012, -78.0718994; loc Payne Rd, SE of Tabscott East: Goochland **GS:** No **SP:** Anne Burton (12 Aug 1742-1819), d/o Robert Burton(1718-1775) & Christain (-----) **VI:** Son of Josias Payne (1705-1785) & Mary Anna Fleming (1710-1794) **P:** N **BLW:** N **RG:** Y **MK:** N **PH:** N **SS:** G pg 284 cites Deed Bk 4 listing officers of militia in 1775; SAR P-339590; DAR A086137, cites Clement's "History of Pittsylvania Co", pgs 159, 160 **BS:** SAR PRS; 196.

PAYNE (PAINE), Tarleton; b 21 Feb 1758; d 1812 **RU:** Captain, Served in VA Line. Commanded a co 18 Nov 1777 in 1st VA Regt of Foot, Cont Line. Was taken prisoner at Charleston,12 May 1780, after release 12 Feb 1781, transferred to 7th Cont Line. Resigned Jan 1783 **CEM:** Payne Family, Hickory Hill; GPS unk; Rts 609 & 603, Goochland; Goochland **GS:** Y **SP:** Mar (before 28 Jun 1784) Elizabeth Winston **VI:** Son of Joseph & Elizabeth (Fleming) Payne BLW #1737-300 26 Mar 1792, later more totalling 5444 acres. Will probated in 1817 **P:** unk **BLW:** Y **RG:** Y **MK:** N **PH:** unk **SS:** J-NSSAR 1993 Reg; J- DAR Hatcher C pg 109; E pg 611; N pg 391; CG Vol 3 pg 2626; CE pg 31; SAR P-264740 **BS:** JLARC 1, 2; 46 pg 164; 80 vol3, pg 143.

PAYNE, William; b 31 Mar 1755, Baynesville, Westmoreland Co; d 19 Sep 1837 **RU:** Captain, Served in VA Line. Ent serv first in 1776 Stafford Co. Moved to Westmoreland in 1780 where he again ent service **CEM:** Payne Farm, Clifton Farm; GPS unk; 5 mi NW of Warrentown; Fauquier **GS:** U **SP:** 1) Elizabeth Susannah Richards, 2) Marion Andrew Morson (11 Feb 1765, Falmouth-21 Nov 1840) d/o Arthur (1735-1798) & Marion (Andrew) (__-1808) Morson **VI:** After RW, lived in Fredericksburg, then moved to Fauquier Co where pensioned. SAR & DAR markers. Pension application 31 Aug 1832 Stafford Co S8938 **P:** Y **BLW:** unk **RG:** Y **MK:** Y **PH:** unk **SS:** J-NSSAR 1993 Reg; CG Vol 3 pg 2626; K Vol 4 pg 80; DAR A086213; SAR P-267119 **BS:** JLARC 1; 196.

PAYNE, William; b 1762; d 1815 **RU:** Patriot, Gave material aid to cause **CEM:** Payne Family; GPS unk; Chesterbrook; Fairfax **GS:** U **SP:** Elizabeth Adams **VI:** Son of Annias & (-----) Payne **P:** N **BLW:** N **RG:** N **MK:** unk **PH:** unk **SS:** AL CT Bk, pg 7, 22 Fairfax Co **BS:** 196.

PAYNE, William; b 1758; d Aft 1832 **RU:** Private/Sergeant, Ent serv 1775 Fauquier Co Culpeper Minute Men Bn in Cpt William Pickett's Co. Paid 8 Nov 1775-2 Apr 1776 as Sgt in Capt Hezekiah Turner's Co Fauquier Militia; in 1780 & 81 served as Sgt in Capt John O'Bannon's Co **CEM:** Oak Springs; GPS unk; 770 Fletcher Dr.; Fauquier **GS:** N **SP:** No info **VI:** Pension appl 29 Nov 1832 Fauquier Co S8938.5 **P:** Y **BLW:** unk **RG:** N **MK:** N **PH:** N **SS:** K Vol 4 pg 80; AV; CG Vol 3 pg 2626; Fauquier Co Marriages pg 156 **BS:** 83 Inv # NF-20.

PAYNE, William; b 10 Feb 1732, Goochland Co, d 2 Mar 1822 **RU:** Patriot, Gave material aid to cause, Fluvania Co **CEM:** Payne Family; GPS: not determined; at end of Little Mtn Rd, Rt 682 W of Carybrook, go further.9 mi SE to cem in woods; Fluvania **GS:** Yes **SP:** Mar 1) Mary Thompson (1732-bef 1755), mar 2) mar 1755, Mary Barrett (1739-1822) **VI:** Son of Josias Payne (30 Oct 1705-5 Mar 1785) & Mary

RU=Rank/Unit	CEM=Cemetery	GS=Gravestone	SP=Spousal Information
VI=Other Veteran Info	P=Pension	BLW=Bounty/Land Warrant	RG=Registered Grave
MK=SAR/DAR Marker	PH=Photo	SS=Service Source	BS=Burial Source

Anna Fleming (1710, New Kent Co-6 May 1794) **P**: N **BLW**: N **RG**: Y **MK**: N **PH**: N **SS**: AL Ct Bk pgs 2, 12, Comm Bk 2, pg 362; DAR A086212; SAR P-267115 **BS**: 196.

PEACHY, Thomas G Jr; b 1760; d 1781 **RU**: Patriot, Gave material aid to cause **CEM**: Cedar Grove; GPS 37.26140, -76.70720; Jct Rt 132 and Hunting Cove; Williamsburg City **GS**: Y **SP**: No info **VI**: Son of Thomas (23 Dec 1734-6 Mar 1810) & Elizabeth (Gilliam) (1741-1781) Peachy. Name and family members on monument originally bur behind Randolph home Colonial Williamsburg **P**: N **BLW**: N **RG**: N **MK**: unk **PH**: unk **SS**: AL Ct Bk I pg 42 Amelia Co **BS**: 196.

PEACHY, Thomas G Sr; b 23 Dec 1734, Richmond Co; d 6 Mar 1810 **RU**: Patriot, Gave material aid to cause also did public service as Clerk of Amelia Co Ct Jul 1776 **CEM**: Cedar Grove; GPS 37.26140, -76.70720; Jct Rt 132 and Hunting Cove; Williamsburg City **GS**: Y **SP**: Elizabeth Gilliam (26 Mar 1741 Farnham Richmond Co-27 May 1781 Farnham, Richmond Co) **VI**: Son of Samuel (1699-1750) & Winnifred Judith (Griffin) (1709-1739) Peachy. Name and family members on monument originally bur behind Randolph home Colonial Williamsburg **P**: N **BLW**: N **RG**: N **MK**: unk **PH**: unk **SS**: AL Cert Amelia Co; G pg 4 **BS**: 196.

PEAKE, Humphrey Sr; b 13 Jan 1731, Prince William Co; d 11 Jan 1785 **RU**: Patriot, Gave material aid (125 lbs beef) to the cause in Fairfax Co **CEM**: Peake Family; GPS 38.73686, -77.08430; Within Martin Luther King Jr Park, 8115 Fordson Rd, path past pool & tennis courts to black metal fencing; Alexandria City **GS**: Y **SP**: Mar (c1755) Mary Stonestreet (1738 Prince George's, MD - 21 Nov 1805, Fairfax Co), d/o Butler & Frances (Tolson) Stonestreet. **VI**: Son of William Peake (bef 1688 Prince William Co bet 11 Jan-17 Feb, 1761, Bradley, Fairfax) & Sarah Jean Hereford. **P**: N **BLW**: N **RG**: Y **MK**: N **PH**: Y **SS**: AL Ct Bk pg 19; DAR A086893; SAR P-327879 **BS**: 89 vol 5 pg SA 103.

PEAKE, Thomas; b unk; d 27 Dec 1777, **RU**: Private, Capt Peter Grant's Co, Col William Grayson's VA Regt: **CEM**: Rev War Court House Plaque; GPS not determined; 4110 Chain Bridge Rd; Fairfax **GS**: Memorialized on plaque 2017 by Geo Washington Chapter, VASSAR **SP**: Mar Kinston Parriah, Dorothy Hudgin **VI**: died in service **P**: N **BLW**: Eligible **RG**: Y **MK**: N **PH**: N **SS**:C Sec II, pg 262; N pg 225; AP Fold3 muster rolls shows death date: SAR P -267229: **BS**: None.

PEAKE, William; b 1761; d 19 Sep 1793 **RU**: Quartermaster Sergeant, Served in 5th Troop, 1st Lt Dragoons. Was wounded in war and taken prisoner 19 Jan 1778 **CEM**: Peake Family; GPS 38.73686, -77.08430; Within Martin Luther King Jr Park, 8115 Fordson Rd, path past pool & tennis cts to black metal fencing, Alexandria City **GS**: Y **SP**: Mar 1791, Elizabeth Shockley **VI**: Son of Humphrey Peake & Mary Stonestreet. Pension records indicate he d 16 Aug 1816. Appl pen 11 Aug 1788. Recd VA BLW 1796 of 440 acres **P**: Y **BLW**: Y **RG**: Y **MK**: N **PH**: Y **SS**: E pg 612; BX pg 623; CU; DAR A086914; SAR P-333981 **BS**: 61 Vol. V, pg SA 104; 196.

PEARIS, George; b 16 Feb 1746, Pearis Island, SC; d 4 Nov 1810 **RU**: First Lieutenant, Commissioned in Montgomery Co Militia, 3 Mar 1779 **CEM**: Pearis Family; GPS unk; Bluff City; Giles **GS**: Y **SP**: 1) Eleanor Howe 2) Rebecca Clay **VI**: No further data **P**: unk **BLW**: unk **RG**: Y **MK**: Y SAR **PH**: unk **SS**: E pg 613; SAR P-267291 **BS**: JLARC 2, 26; 80 vol 3, pg 157.

PEARSON, Thomas; b 1751; d 1835 **RU**: Lieutenant, Served May 1780, in Cont Line under Col Abraham Buford. Rec'd arm & head sword wounds at Battle of Waxhaws (SC) against British Lt Col Banastre Talerton **CEM**: Pearson Memorial Park; GPS 36.84000, -79.95030; S off Henry Rd Rt 605; Franklin **GS**: Y **SP**: Mar (3 Aug 1806) Elizabeth Palmer **VI**: Family tradition says was b in Yorkshire, England. Pensioned first in Henrico Co 12 Feb 1813 receiving $60 per annum. Penson continued in Bedford & Franklin Co. Govt grave stone **P**: Y **BLW**: unk **RG**: Y **MK**: unk **PH**: Y **SS**: Rev war service Pen Applic: http://revwarapps.org/va6.pdf; BX pg 624; DAR A087212; SAR P-267392 **BS**: 80 vol 3, pg 157. 196.

PEARSON, William. See Appendix G Addenda

PECK, Benjamin; b 1761; d 1 Jun 1827 **RU**: Drummer/Patriot, Served in 2nd Regt of Artillery Mar 1780 **CEM**: Fincastle Presbyterian; GPS 37.50017, -79.87558; 108 E Back St, Fincastle; Botetourt **GS**: N **SP**: Mar (1769) Margaret Carper (27 Dec 1751, MD-1820) **VI**: Name is on the SAR plaque at this cemetery **P**: unk **BLW**: unk **RG**: N **MK**: Y SAR plaque **PH**: N **SS**: AP Muster Roll; BT; DL pg 336, 378; AS; DAR report; DAR A087443; SAR P-267560 **BS**: DAR report.

RU=Rank/Unit	CEM=Cemetery	GS=Gravestone	SP=Spousal Information
VI=Other Veteran Info	P=Pension	BLW=Bounty/Land Warrant	RG=Registered Grave
MK=SAR/DAR Marker	PH=Photo	SS=Service Source	BS=Burial Source

325

PECK, Benjamin; b 1744, Frederick Co, MD; d 1 Jun 1824 **RU:** Patriot, Performed public service as Surveyor of Roads and Juror in Botetourt Co **CEM:** Miller; **GPS** unk; Rt 42, Midway; Craig **GS:** U **SP:** Mar (1769) Margaret Carper (27 Dec 1751, Botetourt Co-after 1824) **VI:** DAR indicates he was b in Sharpsburg, Washington Co, MD **P:** N **BLW:** N **RG:** Y **MK:** unk **PH:** unk **SS:** DAR #A087443; J- DAR Hatcher; SAR P-267559 **BS:** JLARC 2; 80 vol 3, pg 158.

PECK, Jacob; b 7 Jul 1723; d 1801 **RU:** Private/Patriot, Served in Capt Thomas Smith's Co, Augusta Militia. As patriot paid suppy tax, Botetourt Co, 1783. **CEM:** Fincastle Presbyterian; **GPS** 37.50017, -79.87558; 108 E Back St, Fincastle; Botetourt **GS:** Y **SP:** Lydia Borden, b 1723, d 1800. **VI:** Name is on the SAR plaque at this cemetery **P:** unk **BLW:** unk **RG:** Y **MK:** Y SAR plaque **PH:** unk **SS:** E pg 613; DAR A087522; SAR P-267625 **BS:** 04; 80 vol 3, pg 159; 196.

PECK, Jacob Sr; b 14 Oct 1739, Frederick Co, MD; d 23 Sep 1827 **RU:** Soldie, Served Capt Thomas Smith's Co, Augusta Co. Militia. Gave 88 pairs men's shoes & 30 pairs boots 20 Apr 1782 **CEM:** Trinity Episcopal; **GPS** 38.14917, -79.07521; 214 Beverley St; Staunton City **GS:** Y **SP:** 1) mar (1778 Orange Co) Mary Coursey 2) mar (9 Mar 1789 Augusta Co) Elizabeth Butt 3) mar (after 1803 Staunton, Augusta Co) Catherin Fackler Schnebly **VI:** Son of Johann Jacob (1723-1821) & Lydia (Borden) (1728-1800) Peck **P:** unk **BLW:** unk **RG:** Y **MK:** unk **PH:** Y **SS:** E pg 613; CY pg 37; SAR P-267801 **BS:** JLARC 62, 63; 196.

PECK, John; b 1750; d 1820 **RU:** Ensign/Patriot, Gave material aid to the cause **CEM:** Fincastle Presbyterian; **GPS** 37.50017, -79.87558; 108 E Back St, Fincastle; Botetourt **GS:** N **SP:** No info **VI:** Name is on the SAR plaque at this cemetery **P:** unk **BLW:** unk **RG:** Y **MK:** Y SAR plaque **PH:** N **SS:** J-NSSAR 1993 Reg, J- DAR Hatcher, AR Vol 3, pg159; AL Ct Bk pg26; DAR A087566; SAR P-267664 **BS:** JLARC 1, 2; 80 vol 3, pg 159 196.

PECK (PEAKE), John; b 1760, d 1794 **RU:** Patriot, Gave material aid to cause in King George Co **CEM:** Bladensfield; **GPS:** 37.98481, -76.71679; On Rt 203 at VA American Water, go S on unmarked rd to end; Richmond County **GS:** Yes **SP:** Mar c1775, Ann Tasker Carter (17 Jan 1762-7 Mar 1798),his pupil, d/o Robert Carter of Nomini & Francis Ann Tasker **VI:** Some records show name as Peck, others as Peake. Plantation conveyed to him 1790 **P:** N **BLW:** N **RG:** N **MK:** N **PH:** N **SS:** AL Ct Bk pg 10, King George Co **BS:** 196.

PECK, Joseph; b 1757; d 1842 **RU:** Patriot; Gave material aid to cause, Botetourt Co **CEM:** Fincastle Presbyterian; **GPS** 37.50017, -79.87558; 108 E Back St, Fincastle; Botetourt **GS:** N **SP:** Mar (29 Aug 1792 Botetourt Co) Susanna Franklin **VI:** **P:** N **BLW:** unk **RG:** Y **MK:** Y SAR plaque **PH:** N **SS:** J-NSSAR 1993 Reg; D vol 1, pg137; DAR A119234; SAR P-267677 **BS:** JLARC 1, 2; 80 vol 3, pg 159196.

PEEBLES, Fred; b 1736; d aft 1780 **RU:** Patriot, Gave material aid to cause **CEM:** Peebles Family; **GPS** unk; Brink; Greensville **GS:** Y **SP:** No info **VI:** No further data **P:** N **BLW:** N **RG:** N **MK:** unk **PH:** unk **SS:** AL Ct Bk pg 25 Greenville Co **BS:** 196.

PEIRCE/PIERCE; David; b 8 Apr 1756, Chester Co, PA d 28 Oct 1833 **RU:** Private, served in Capt Joseph Luckie's Co, Lt Col John Hannum's Bn, Chester Co, PA Militia **CEM:** Peirce Family AKA Chaffin; **GPS:** 36.8491070, -80.8625680; loc Lead Mine Rd, vic jct interstate hwy; Bethany; Wythe **GS:** Y **SP:** mar 24 Apr 1798, Mary Bell (1777, Montgomery Co, VA-26 Jul 1858, Poplar Camp, Wythe Co) **VI:** No further data **P:** N **BLW:** N **RG:** N **MK:** Y DAR Plaque **PH:** N **SS:**CI; PA Archives 5th ser, vol 5 pgs 569,573,792; DAR A091248 **BS:** 196

PEIRCE, John see PIERCE, John

PEIRCE, Joseph; b unk; d Aft 1788 **RU:** Captain/Patriot, Gave material aid to cause, Botetourt Co **CEM:** Level Green; **GPS** unk; Kinsale; Westmoreland **GS:** N **SP:** No info **VI:** Was Justice of Peace in Westmoreland Co in 1788 **P:** unk **BLW:** unk **RG:** N **MK:** N **PH:** N **SS:** AL Ct Bk pg 2, 3, 4 Westmoreland Co, AS, DAR report **BS:** DAR report 80 vol 3, pg 160.

PEIRCE (PIERCE), Joseph; b 1728; d 5 Jun 1798 **RU:** Captain/Patriot, Gave material aid to the cause **CEM:** Old Pierce Homestead; **GPS** unk; Level Green; Westmoreland **GS:** Y **SP:** Sarah E. Pierce (__-20 Sep 1783) **VI:** Son of William Pierce & (-----) of Westmoreland. Magistrate and Deacon. Liberated a

RU=Rank/Unit	CEM=Cemetery	GS=Gravestone	SP=Spousal Information
VI=Other Veteran Info	P=Pension	BLW=Bounty/Land Warrant	RG=Registered Grave
MK=SAR/DAR Marker	PH=Photo	SS=Service Source	BS=Burial Source

326

large number of slaves in will. Honorably mentioned in Semples History of Virginia Baptists **P:** unk **BLW:** unk **RG:** Y **MK:** Y SAR **PH:** unk **SS:** AL Cert Issued; SAR P-270374 **BS:** 107 pg 550, 551.

PEIRCE, Solomon; b 1742; d 1821 **RU:** Private, Served in Capt Hugh Maxwell's Co,1st MA Battalion commanded by Col John Bailey, 9 Sep 1778. Served total of three years **CEM:** Old Burying Ground; GPS unk; Directions in Senate Doc DAR annual report 1955 vol 4 serial 11912; Arlington **GS:** N **SP:** No info **VI:** No further data **P:** unk **BLW:** unk **RG:** N **MK:** unk **PH:** N **SS:** J- DAR Hatcher; AP Roll **BS:** JLARC 2; 80 vol 3, pg 160.

PELHAM, Peter; b 9 Dec 1721, London, Eng; d 28 Apr 1805 **RU:** Patriot, Performed public service as keeper of the jail, Williamsburg, 1775-1780 **CEM:** Bruton Parish Church; GPS 37.27127, -76.70248; 331 W Duke of Gloucester St; Williamsburg City **GS:** U **SP:** Ann Creese (1721-1778) **VI:** Son of Peter (1696-1751) & (-----) Pelham **P:** N **BLW:** N **RG:** N **MK:** unk **PH:** unk **SS:** Wilkipedia.org **BS:** 196.

PELITIER, Jacques; b unk; d 1781 **RU:** Soldier, Served in Auxonne Bn and died fr battle at Yorktown **CEM:** French Memorial; GPS 36.81944, -79.39933; Yorktown; York **GS:** U **SP:** No info **VI:** No further data **P:** unk **BLW:** unk **RG:** Y **MK:** unk **PH:** unk **SS:** J-Yorktown Historian; SAR P-267978 **BS:** JLARC 1, 74.

PELLETAN, Jean; b unk; d 1781 **RU:** Seaman, Served on "Sceptre" and died from Yorktown battle **CEM:** French Memorial; GPS 36.81944, -79.39933; Yorktown; York **GS:** U **SP:** No info **VI:** No further data **P:** unk **BLW:** unk **RG:** Y **MK:** unk **PH:** unk **SS:** J-Yorktown Historian;SAR P-267990 **BS:** JLARC 1, 74.

PELLETIER, Joseph; b unk; d 1781 **RU:** Seaman, Served on "Citoyen" and died from Yorktown battle **CEM:** French Memorial; GPS 36.81944, -79.39933; Yorktown; York **GS:** U **SP:** No info **VI:** No further data **P:** unk **BLW:** unk **RG:** Y **MK:** unk **PH:** unk **SS:** J-Yorktown Historian; SAR P-267992 **BS:** JLARC 1, 74.

PENCE, George; b 1750; d 1818 **RU:** Captain, Commanded a co Aug 1777 Augusta Co Militia **CEM:** Old Peaked Mountain; GPS 38.37113, -78.73416; 9843 Town Hall Rd, McGaheysville; Rockingham **GS:** U **SP:** Jane Carpenter **VI:** No further data **P:** unk **BLW:** unk **RG:** Y **MK:** Y DAR plaque **PH:** unk **SS:** J-NSSAR 2000 Reg; E pg 615; SAR P-268052 **BS:** JLARC 76.

PENCE, Henry; b 1739; d 1824 **RU:** Patriot, Gave material aid to cause **CEM:** Old Peaked Mountain; GPS 38.37113, -78.73416; 9843 Town Hall Rd, McGaheysville; Rockingham **GS:** Y **SP:** 1) mar (1799 Rockingham Co) Cathy Munger d/o Henry Munger 2) mar (1800 Rockingham Co) Rebecca Dundore d/o Jonathan & (-----) Dundore **VI:** No further data **P:** N **BLW:** N **RG:** Y **MK:** Y DAR plaque **PH:** unk **SS:** O pg 113; AL Ct Bk II pg 13 Rockingham Co; SAR P-268054 **BS:** 04.

PENCE, Jacob; b 20 Dec 1730, Frankfort, Germany; d Feb 1800 **RU:** Private, Served in Capt William Nall's Co, Augusta Co Regt **CEM:** Old Peaked Mountain; GPS 38.37113, -78.73416; 9843 Town Hall Rd, McGaheysville; Rockingham **GS:** U **SP:** Catherine Persinger (1750, Botetourt Co-__) **VI:** Son of Jacob & Catherine (-----) Pence. Died at Cub Run, Rockingham Co **P:** unk **BLW:** unk **RG:** Y **MK:** unk **PH:** unk **SS:** J-NSSAR 2000 Reg; SAR P-268057 **BS:** JLARC 76.

PENCE, Jacob; b c1760; d bef 1783 **RU:** Private/Patriot, Served in Capt Micheal Reader's Co, Shenandoah Co Militia; paid personal property tax 1782 Rockingham Co **CEM:** Old Bethel; GPS 38.79113, -78.58904; off Old Bethel Rd (Rt 700), Edinburg; Shenandoah **GS:** Y **SP:** ?) Barbara Harsburger (_-aft 1782) **VI:** No further data **P:** unk **BLW:** unk **RG:** N **MK:** N **PH:** unk **SS:** C pg 603; AL Comm Bk Cert 1782; SAR application **BS:** 79 pg 92.

PENCE, James; b unk; d unk **RU:** Corporal, Rank achieved 1777 in Rockingham Co Militia **CEM:** Old Peaked Mountain; GPS 38.37113, -78.73416; 9843 Town Hall Rd, McGaheysville; Rockingham **GS:** U **SP:** No info **VI:** No further data **P:** unk **BLW:** unk **RG:** Y **MK:** Y DAR plaque **PH:** unk **SS:** J-NSSAR 2000 Reg; AZ pg 230; SAR P-268058 **BS:** JLARC 76.

PENCE, John; b 23 Nov 1755, Augusta Co (now Rockingham); d 10 Jan 1834 **RU:** Soldier, Served in Rockingham Co Militia & VA Regt. Served in Capt William Nall's Co 1778 and in Capt John Rush's Co under Col Sampson Matthews in 1781 **CEM:** Old Peaked Mountain; GPS 38.37113, -78.73416; 9843 Town Hall Rd, McGaheysville; Rockingham **GS:** U **SP:** mar (6 May 1793, same day as marriage bond)

RU=Rank/Unit	CEM=Cemetery	GS=Gravestone	SP=Spousal Information
VI=Other Veteran Info	P=Pension	BLW=Bounty/Land Warrant	RG=Registered Grave
MK=SAR/DAR Marker	PH=Photo	SS=Service Source	BS=Burial Source

327

Nancy Swisher (Swesher) (c1774-15 Mar 1834) d/o John & (-----) Swisher **VI:** Son of Valentine & Anna Maria Catherine (Oberlin) Pence. Appl for pension Rockingham Co, 20 Aug 1832. Widow appl pen 19 Aug 1839 age 65. W5511, R1906 **P:** Y **BLW:** unk **RG:** unk **MK:** Y DAR plaque **PH:** unk **SS:** K Vol 4 pg 89; CG Vol 3 pg 2650; SAR P-268059 **BS:** JLARC 4, 64.

PENCE, William; b 1745, Lancaster Co, PA; d 21 May 1820 **RU:** Private, Served in Capt Peachey Gilman's Co, Augusta Co Militia in 1776 **CEM:** Old Peaked Mountain; GPS 38.37113, -78.73416; 9843 Town Hall Rd, McGaheysville; Rockingham **GS:** U **SP:** Elizabeth Price **VI:** Son of Jacob & Catherine (-----) Pence **P:** unk **BLW:** unk **RG:** Y **MK:** Y DAR plaque **PH:** unk **SS:** J-NSSAR 2000 Reg; E pg 615; SAR P-268063 **BS:** JLARC 76.

PENDEL (PENDALL), Thomas; b Ireland, d 13 Nov 1793 (burial) **RU:** Patriot, Gave funds to the cause accumulated from the Hudson Bay Fur Co in Alexandria **CEM:** Old Christ Church; GPS: 38.80625,-77.0704718; 118 N Washington St; Alexandria City; **GS:** Unk **SP:** No spousal info **VI:** No further data **P:** N **BLW:** N **RG:** N **MK:** N **PH:** N **SS:** E pg 615 cites Eckenrode War Dept Fairfax Co **BS:** 196.

PENDLETON, Edmund; b 9 Sep 1721; d 23 Oct 1803 **RU:** Patriot, Was member Comm of Safety for Colony of VA and author of resolutions offered in VA House of Burgesses, 15 May 1776. Was President of Convention 1775 and President VA Ct of Appeals. Was elected to Congress, 1788; President of Convention of VA which met to consider adoption of Federal Constitution; member of Committee that drafted law establishing "Religious Freedom in Virginia" **CEM:** Bruton Parish Church; GPS 37.27127, -76.70248; 331 W Duke of Gloucester St; Williamsburg City **GS:** Y **SP:** 1) Elizabeth Roy (___-17 Nov 1742) 2) Sarah Pollard (4 May 1725-1815) **VI:** Son of Henry & Mary Bishop (Taylor) Pendleton. Was member of House of Representatives for 25 yrs. He and wives were bur first in the Pendleton family cemetery in Caroline Co. Was elected to Congress,1788 and President of Convention of VA which met to consider adoption of Federal Constitution. Was member of Committee that drafted law establishing "Religious Freedom in Virginia" **P:** N **BLW:** N **RG:** Y **MK:** N **PH:** unk **SS:** E pg 615; SAR P-268098 **BS:** 02 pg 116; 26 pg 143; 196.

PENDLETON, Micajah; b 1758 Buckingham Co, d 24 Feb 1844 **RU:** Private, served 3 mos under Capt William Duiguid, Col Taylor's command, VA Line and in 1781 in Capt Charles Patteson's Co and aft Jun 1781 in Capt Robert Cary's Co **CEM:** Woodland; GPS 37.7098636,-78.9275227; loc 4434 Thomas Nelson Hwy (Rt. 29) Arrington; Nelson **GS:** Unk **SP:**1) Mar 16 Dec 1779, (-----) Breckenburg, 2) Mary Horsely **VI:** Son of Philip Pendleton (1728-1778) & Spicey Freeland (1730-1804). Pen # S8951 approved 26 Aug 1833 **P:** Y **BLW:** N **RG:** Y **MK:** N **PH:** N **SS:** CG pg 2651; AP Fold3 pen files; DAR A088367; SAR P-268126 **BS:** 196.

PENDLETON, Nathaniel Sr; b 1715 or 1716; d Aug 1794 or 1795 **RU:** Patriot, Chairman of the Committee of Safety and Correspondence **CEM:** Redwood Plantation; GPS unk; Rt 522 N; Culpeper **GS:** N **SP:** Mar (14 Oct 1744) Elizabeth Clayton (1714-1771) d/o Major Samuel (1685-1735) & Elizabeth (Pendleton) (1684-1761) Clayton. Widow of Joseph Anderson. **VI:** Son of Henry (1683-1721) & Mary Bishop Taylor (1688-1770) Pendleton. Chief magistrate and High Sheriff of Culpeper Co 1765. Author & signer of first protest against the Stamp Act 1765. One of the founders of Fairfax. The family cemetery here was in ruins with no stones in 2008 **P:** N **BLW:** N **RG:** Y **MK:** N **PH:** N **SS:** AL Ct Bk, pg 3, 20; K Vol 4 pg 90; CE pg 41; CF pg 33; SAR5 P-268128 **BS:** 80 vol 3 pg 161; 196.

PENDLETON, William; b 1720; d 1780 **RU:** Private, Served in Capt Richard Yancey's Co fr Culpeper Co. Was in Point Pleasant Battle Oct 1774 **CEM:** Old Pendleton; GPS unk; Monroe; Amherst **GS:** U **SP:** Elizabeth Tinsley (1727 New Kent Co-1783) **VI:** Son of John P (1691-1775) & Mary (Tinsley) (1727-1783) Pendleton **P:** N **BLW:** N **RG:**N **MK:** unk **PH:** unk **SS:** Z pg 87 **BS:** 196.

PENN, Abram or Abraham; b 27 Dec 1743, Drysdale Parrish, Caroline Co; d 26 Jun 1801 **RU:** Colonel, Was Commander of Minute Men Battalion,1776. Served in Henry Co Militia 1780-81. Led Patrick Co troops in Battle at Guilford CH **CEM:** Poplar Grove; GPS unk; W on Rt 626 off Rt 627 Co Line Rd, nr Critz; Patrick **GS:** U **SP:** Ruth Stovall **VI:** DAR Col Abram Penn Chapter is named for him **P:** unk **BLW:** unk **RG:** Y **MK:** unk **PH:** unk **SS:** AZ pg 209; E pg 616; DAR A088474; SAR P-268188 **BS:** JLARC 2, 4, 30.

PENN, Gabriel; b 17 Jul 1741, Drysdale Parrish, Caroline Co; d Jul 1798 **RU:** Lieutenant/Patriot, Served in Amherst Co Militia. Paymaster Buckingham Co Militia, 1775-6. Gave material aid to cause **CEM:**

RU=Rank/Unit	CEM=Cemetery	GS=Gravestone	SP=Spousal Information
VI=Other Veteran Info	P=Pension	BLW=Bounty/Land Warrant	RG=Registered Grave
MK=SAR/DAR Marker	PH=Photo	SS=Service Source	BS=Burial Source

328

Penn Family; GPS unk; Rt 151, Clifford; Amherst **GS:** U **SP:** Sarah "Betsy" Calloway **VI:** No further data **P:** unk **BLW:** unk **RG:** Y **MK:** N **PH:** unk **SS:** E pg 616, G appendix pg 501; AL Cert 2 Amherst Co; SAR P-268197 **BS:** 04.

PENN, George; b 12 Dec 1737, Drysdale Parish, Caroline Co; d 5 Feb 1790 **RU:** Ensign/Patriot, Served in Amherst Co Militia. Gave material aid to cause **CEM:** Penn Family; GPS unk; Rt 151, Clifford; Amherst **GS:** U **SP:** 1) Sara Lea (Lee) 2) mar (29 May 1783 Amherst Co) Mary Walden, widow **VI:** Family tradition is bur with family at the Gabriel Penn Graveyard **P:** unk **BLW:** unk **RG:** Y **MK:** N **PH:** unk **SS:** G pg 15; AL Cert 1 Amherst Co; SAR P-331425 **BS:** 04.

PENN, John; b 1736; d 1818 **RU:** Cook/Patriot, Served in the USN on the ship "Manley" in 1779. Gave material aid to cause **CEM:** Miller Family; GPS unk; Rt 690; Amherst **GS:** Y **SP:** No info **VI:** No further data **P:** unk **BLW:** unk **RG:** N **MK:** N **PH:** unk **SS:** E pg 616; AL Ct Bk pg 33 Amherst Co **BS:** 01 pg 146.

PENN, William; b 9 Apr 1746, Caroline Co; d 15 Mar 1777 **RU:** Lieutenant/CPT Dragoons, Died fr small pox while serving in Trenton, NJ **CEM:** Penn Family; GPS unk; Rt 151, Clifford; Amherst **GS:** U **SP:** Martha Smith **VI:** Died in Trenton, NJ, and body may not have been carried to cemetery **P:** unk **BLW:** Y **RG:** N **MK:** N **PH:** unk **SS:** C pg 364 **BS:** 04, May 06.

PENNYWEIGHT (PENNYWITT), Jacob; b 30 Jul 1751; d 27 Jan 1813 **RU:** Captain, Took oath as Capt 31 Aug 1780 Shenandoah Co Militia **CEM:** St Mary Pine Lutheran; GPS 38.74470, -78.68390; 7103 S Middle Rd, Mt Jackson; Shenandoah **GS:** Y **SP:** mar (30 Mar 1782) Margaret Harpine, (__-15 May 1835) d/o Philip Harpine & Mary Catherine (-----) **VI:** Son of John Pennywitt & Rosina Yieser **P:** unk **BLW:** unk **RG:** N **MK:** N **PH:** unk **SS:** E pg 616, pg 540; SAR P-335816 **BS:** 155 Old Pine Church.

PERCHE, Louis; b unk; d 1781 **RU:** Soldier, Served in Soissonnais Bn and died fr battle at Yorktown **CEM:** French Memorial; GPS 36.81944, -79.39933; Yorktown; York **GS:** U **SP:** No info **VI:** No further data **P:** unk **BLW:** unk **RG:** Y **MK:** unk **PH:** unk **SS:** J-Yorktown Historian; SAR P-268340 **BS:** JLARC 1, 74.

PERDUE, Meshack; b 1755 or 1756, Chesterfield Co; d 30 Dec 1837 **RU:** Patriot, Performed patriotic service. Signed Oath of Allegiance Montgomery Co **CEM:** Mark Perdue Farm/Crossroads Burnt Chimney; GPS unk; Rt 672 vic Foxfire Nursery; Franklin **GS:** Y **SP:** Eleanor Dillon **VI:** No further data **P:** N **BLW:** N **RG:** Y **MK:** Y **SAR PH:** unk **SS:** AK Sep 2009; DAR A092290; SAR P-268363 **BS:** AK Sep 09.

PERKINS, Constantine; b unk; d 1790 **RU:** Major/Patriot, Gave material aid to cause **CEM:** Nicholas Perkins 2d Home; GPS unk; S of Dan River, Danville; Danville City **GS:** U **SP:** No info **VI:** No further data **P:** unk **BLW:** unk **RG:** N **MK:** N **PH:** unk **SS:** 17 81 Militia; AL Ct Bk pg 6, 34, 51, 60 Pittsylvania Co **BS:** 81 chart.

PERKINS, John Watkins; b 31 May 1752; d 17 Mar 1803 **RU:** Lieutenant, Appointed Lt Goochland Co Militia 18 Sep 1777, took oath 16 Feb 1778 **CEM:** Perkins/Hall; GPS unk; Hwy 56; Buckingham **GS:** U **SP:** Elizabeth Bondurant **VI:** No further data **P:** unk **BLW:** unk **RG:** Y **MK:** N **PH:** unk **SS:** E pg 617; H; DAR A088844; SAR P-268528 **BS:** 29 pg 453.

PERKINS, Stephen; b unk; d 1821 **RU:** Patriot, Gave material aid to cause in Buckingham Co **CEM:** Perkins family; GPS unk; Vic Rts 600 & 633; Fluvanna **GS:** Y **SP:** No info **VI:** No further data **P:** N **BLW:** N **RG:** N **MK:** N **PH:** unk **SS:** AL Comm Bk I pg 203 **BS:** 66 pg 75.

PERNOT, Nicolas; b unk; d 1781 **RU:** Soldier, Served in Soissonnais Bn and died fr battle at Yorktown **CEM:** French Memorial; GPS 36.81944, -79.39933; Yorktown; York **GS:** U **SP:** No info **VI:** No further data **P:** unk **BLW:** unk **RG:** Y **MK:** unk **PH:** unk **SS:** J-Yorktown Historian; SAR P-268694 **BS:** JLARC 1, 74.

PEROT, Milan; b unk; d 1781 **RU:** Seaman, Served on "Citoyen" and died from Yorktown battle **CEM:** French Memorial; GPS 36.81944, -79.39933; Yorktown; York **GS:** U **SP:** No info **VI:** No further data **P:** unk **BLW:** unk **RG:** Y **MK:** unk **PH:** unk **SS:** J-Yorktown Historian; SAR P-268697 **BS:** JLARC 1, 74.

RU=Rank/Unit	CEM=Cemetery	GS=Gravestone	SP=Spousal Information
VI=Other Veteran Info	P=Pension	BLW=Bounty/Land Warrant	RG=Registered Grave
MK=SAR/DAR Marker	PH=Photo	SS=Service Source	BS=Burial Source

329

PEROTIN, Julien; b unk; d 1781 **RU:** Seaman, Served on "Auguste" and died from Yorktown battle **CEM:** French Memorial; GPS 36.81944, -79.39933; Yorktown; York **GS:** U **SP:** No info **VI:** No further data **P:** unk **BLW:** unk **RG:** Y **MK:** unk **PH:** unk **SS:** J-Yorktown Historian **BS:** JLARC 1, 74.

PEROY, Louis; b unk; d 1781 **RU:** Seaman, Served on "Auguste" and died from Yorktown battle **CEM:** French Memorial; GPS 36.81944, -79.39933; Yorktown; York **GS:** U **SP:** No info **VI:** No further data **P:** unk **BLW:** unk **RG:** Y **MK:** unk **PH:** unk **SS:** J-Yorktown Historian; SAR P268699 **BS:** JLARC 1, 74.

PERPETTE, Antoine; b unk; d 1781 **RU:** Seaman, Served on "Palmier" and died from Yorktown battle **CEM:** French Memorial; GPS 36.81944, -79.39933; Yorktown; York **GS:** U **SP:** No info **VI:** No further data **P:** unk **BLW:** unk **RG:** Y **MK:** unk **PH:** unk **SS:** J-Yorktown Historian; SAR P-268700 **BS:** JLARC 1, 74.

PERRIER, Joseph; b unk; d 1781 **RU:** Soldier, Served in Bourbonnais Bn and died fr battle at Yorktown **CEM:** French Memorial; GPS 36.81944, -79.39933; Yorktown; York **GS:** U **SP:** No info **VI:** No further data **P:** unk **BLW:** unk **RG:** Y **MK:** unk **PH:** unk **SS:** J-Yorktown Historian; SAR P-268704 **BS:** JLARC 1, 74.

PERSINGER, Jacob; b 19 Jan 1749, nr Pittsburg, PA; d 3 Jul 1840 **RU:** Corporal, Ent serv Botetourt Co (now Allegheny) 1775. Was in Battle of Point Pleasant 1774. Served in Capt Matthew Arbuckle's Co 1775 to 1 Nov 1776 **CEM:** Persinger Memorial; GPS unk; 3707 Llama Dr; Covington City **GS:** Y Gov't **SP:** Mary Kimoerils **VI:** Appl for pension 18 Nov 1833 fr Alleghany Co "where resided since RW". S30019 **P:** Y **BLW:** unk **RG:** Y **MK:** Y DAR **PH:** Y **SS:** K Vol 4 pg 97; CG Vol 3 pg 2667; DAR A089554; SAR P-268993 **BS:** JLARC 1, 4, 51.

PETERS, John; b 1761, d 7 Oct 1796 **RU:** Patriot, Gave material aid to cause in Sussex County. Was a sail maker in Chesapeake perhaps during war period, thus patriotic duty **CEM:** Massenburg; GPS 36.74344, -76.26115; loc behind Southgate Shopping Ctr on Bainbridge Blvd between parking lot and Oscar Smith Middle School; Chesapeake **GS:** No as cem destroyed during Civil War a monument marks cem loc **SP:** No spousal data **VI:** Service source BR shows obit data and occupation as sailmaker in Chesapeake **P:** N **BLW:** N **RG:** N **MK:** N **PH:** N **SS:** BR-Tuesday 11 Oct 1796 pg 3, c 3 **BS:** 196.

PETERS, John, Sr; b 17 Oct 1755, d 6 Feb 1836 **RU:** Ensign, enlisted Rockingham Co, 1779 and served two tours of 3 mos each, was in Capt John Rust's Co, Col Noll's Regt, 2d and 6th Cont Line Served also in Capt Raegan's Co, discharged aft battle of Green Springs nr Williamsburg in 1781 **CEM:** Fairview: GPS 37.3383,-80.8075; on Riverside Ave, Narrows; Giles **GS:** No **SP:** Mar 1776, Frances Simms (1758, Giles,-bef 1836) **VI:** Son of Jacob Peters; received pen F-S55897, R1917 **P:** Y **BLW:** N **RG:** Y **MK:** N **PH:** N **SS:** Fold3 Serv Index Card pen rec & last payment voucher; K pg 98; DAR A089627; SAR P-269071 **BS:** 196.

PETTETT, John; b unk; d unk **RU:** Private, Served in Fairfax Co Militia **CEM:** Fairfax City; GPS 38.84690, -77.31330; Main St & Page Ave; Fairfax City **GS:** N **SP:** No info **VI:** No further data **P:** unk **BLW:** unk **RG:** N **MK:** N **PH:** N **SS:** E pg 620 **BS:** 61 vol III pg FX-153.

PETTIES (PETTES, PETTUS), Samuel Overton; b 11 Mar 1751, Lunenburg Co; d 12 Feb 1819 **RU:** Lieutenant, Served in Cont Line in an artillery unit **CEM:** Petties Family; GPS unk; Chase City; Mecklenburg **GS:** Y **SP:** Mar 1) Jane Freeman, 2) 1783, Hannah Minor (Mar 1755-1829) **VI:** Recd BLW **P:** unk **BLW:** Y **RG:** Y **MK:** N **PH:** unk **SS:** C pg 135; DB pg 115-6 cites TN USDAR Roster pg 127; AS; CU;SAR P-269217 **BS:** 80 vol 3 pg 167.

PETTITT, William; b 1751; d 11 Nov 1783 **RU:** Private, Served in VA & Cont Lines **CEM:** Bowman's Folly; GPS unk; End of Rt 652, private lane, 2.4 mi NE of Accomac, Joynes Neck; Accomack **GS:** Y **SP:** No info **VI:** Son of William of Northampton Co & Mary (-----) Pettitt **P:** unk **BLW:** unk **RG:** N **MK:** N **PH:** unk **SS:** AP Cont Line VA **BS:** 209; 196.

PETTYPOOL, William; b 1732; d Mar 1813 **RU:** Ensign/Patriot, Served in Capt Richard Jone's Co, Halifax Co Militia. Gave material aid to cause **CEM:** Halifax Town; GPS 36.76403, -78.92668; Check property records; Halifax **GS:** U **SP:** Mar 09 Apr 1772 Sarah Tynes **VI:** No further data **P:** unk **BLW:** unk **RG:** Y **MK:** unk **PH:** unk **SS:** J- DAR Hatcher; AL Ct Bk pg 24 Lunenburg Co; DAR A089881; SAR P-269314 **BS:** JLARC 2; 80 vol 3, pg 167.

RU=Rank/Unit	CEM=Cemetery	GS=Gravestone	SP=Spousal Information
VI=Other Veteran Info	P=Pension	BLW=Bounty/Land Warrant	RG=Registered Grave
MK=SAR/DAR Marker	PH=Photo	SS=Service Source	BS=Burial Source

330

PEYLLARD, Jacques; b unk; d 1781 **RU:** Soldier, Served in Beaujolais Bn and died fr battle at Yorktown **CEM:** French Memorial; GPS 36.81944, -79.39933; Yorktown; York **GS:** U **SP:** No info **VI:** No further data **P:** unk **BLW:** unk **RG:** Y **MK:** unk **PH:** unk **SS:** J-Yorktown Historian; SAR P-269329 **BS:** JLARC 1, 74.

PEYTON, Francis; b 1764; d 26 Aug 1836 **RU:** Lieutenant, Paymaster, Prince William District Bn 1775-76 **CEM:** St Paul's Episcopal; GPS 38.79959, -77.05860; 228 S Pitt St; Alexandria City **GS:** Y **SP:** Sarah West (1776-22 Jun 1849) d/o Hugh & Elizabeth (Minor) West. mar 2) 1789,Sarah Foushee (1776-1849) **VI:** Mayor of Alexandria, VA. 1797-98, 1799-1800 with title of Colonel. Death notice in the Alexandria Gazette 30 Aug 1836 pg 3. (Too young for service above but may have had service in county militia in 1781-1783 age 17 to 19 or perhaps birthdate is incorrect) **P:** unk **BLW:** unk **RG:** Y **MK:** Y DAR **PH:** unk **SS:** CE pg 22; DAR A089983; SAR P-269337 & SAR P-269335 indicates b 1752 **BS:** JLARC 1, 2, 25; 196; 80 vol 3, pg 167.

PEYTON, Henry; b 1744; d 1814, The Plains **RU:** First Lieutenant/Patriot, Farquier Militia. 1st Lt Oct 1719. Gave material aid to cause **CEM:** Gordonsdale; GPS unk; The Plains; Fauquier **GS:** Y **SP:** A man by this name mar (bond 19 Nov 1796 Fauquier Co) Ann Brent, d/o William Jr. & (-----) Brent **VI:** No further data **P:** unk **BLW:** unk **RG:** Y **MK:** N **PH:** unk **SS:** E pg 621; H; AL Ct Bk pg 3 Fauquier Co; Fauquier Co Marriages pg 158; SAR P-269340 **BS:** 19 pg 68.

PHARES (PHARIS, FERRIS, FARRIS, FARES), Amariah (Emaria Emeriah Araziah Emerica Amaziah); b 23 May 1778, Middlesex, NJ; d 1 Jan 1824, Montgomery Co **RU:** Private, Ent serv 1778 in NJ, Mar 1777-1778 in 2nd Regt, Middlesex NJ Militia under Capts Williamson & Gulick. Served in NJ Cont Line 23 May 1778 - 23 Feb 1779. Also served in Capt Longstreet's Co, 1st Regt **CEM:** Eastview; GPS unk; Rome; Floyd **GS:** N **SP:** 1) mar (19 Jun 1780) Sarah Van Zandt, 2) mar (13 Jan 1791 Franklin Co) Elizabeth BeHeler,who rec'd pension W5541 aft applying 26 Dec 1840 Floyd Co VA age 71 **VI:** Certificate 1542 for Cont pay in Middlesex. **P:** Y **BLW:** unk **RG:** Y **MK:** N **PH:** N **SS:** K Vol 4 pg 103; CG Vol 3 pg 2676, 04; DAR A204840; SAR P-269370 **BS:** 04.

PHILIPEAU, Gabriel; b unk; d 1781 **RU:** Seaman, Served on "Languedoc" and died from Yorktown battle **CEM:** French Memorial; GPS 36.81944, -79.39933; Yorktown; York **GS:** U **SP:** No info **VI:** No further data **P:** unk **BLW:** unk **RG:** Y **MK:** unk **PH:** unk **SS:** J-Yorktown Historian; SAR P-269701 **BS:** JLARC 1, 74.

PHILIPPE, Pierre; b unk; d 1781 **RU:** Seaman, Served on "Saint-Esprit" and died from Yorktown battle **CEM:** French Memorial; GPS 36.81944, -79.39933; Yorktown; York **GS:** U **SP:** No info **VI:** No further data **P:** unk **BLW:** unk **RG:** Y **MK:** unk **PH:** unk **SS:** J-Yorktown Historian; SAR P-269702 **BS:** JLARC 1, 74.

PHILLIPS, John; b 1749; d 1828 **RU:** Private, Served in Capt John Cropper's Co, Col Dan Morgan's 11th & 15th VA Regt 30 Nov 1788 **CEM:** Old Phillips; GPS unk; Rt 696 NS Troublesome Creek, Evington; Campbell **GS:** U **SP:** 1) Sarah (-----) 2) Margaret (-----) **VI:** No further data **P:** unk **BLW:** unk **RG:** Y **MK:** N **PH:** unk **SS:** A pg 267; SAR P-269882 **BS:** JLARC 4,36.

PHILLIPS, John; b 1765, Amherst Co; d 22 Nov 1822 **RU:** Private, Served in 6th Cont Line 3 yrs **CEM:** Old Phillips; GPS unk; Rt 696 N side of Troublesome Creek, Evington; Campbell **GS:** N **SP:** Mar (12 Dec 1808, Campbell Co) Margaret Weber (1780-Dec 1833) d/o John & Elizabeth Margaret (-----) Weber **VI:** Recd 100 acres BLW 10 Dec 1785 **P:** unk **BLW:** Y **RG:** N **MK:** N **PH:** N **SS:** E pg 623; F pg 82; BY **BS:** 196.

PHILLIPS, John M; b c1759; d 1834 **RU:** Patriot, Gave material aid to the cause **CEM:** Shockoe Hill; GPS 37.55190, -77.43170; 4th & Hospital Sts; Richmond City **GS:** Y **SP:** No info **VI:** No further data **P:** N **BLW:** N **RG:** N **MK:** N **PH:** unk **SS:** AL Ct Bk pg 55 **BS:** 57 pg 13.

PHILLIPS, Thomas Fretwell; b Bridgetown, Barbadoes; d 1808 Celays Elizabeth City Co **RU:** Patriot, Gave material aid to the cause **CEM:** St John's Episcopal; GPS unk; 100 W Queen's Way; Hampton City **GS:** Y **SP:** No info **VI:** No further data **P:** N **BLW:** N **RG:** N **MK:** Y SAR plaque cem wall **PH:** unk **SS:** AL Ct Bk 2 pg 3a **BS:** 89 pg 121.

RU=Rank/Unit	CEM=Cemetery	GS=Gravestone	SP=Spousal Information
VI=Other Veteran Info	P=Pension	BLW=Bounty/Land Warrant	RG=Registered Grave
MK=SAR/DAR Marker	PH=Photo	SS=Service Source	BS=Burial Source

331

PHILLIPS, Tobias; b 25 Jan 1750, No Farnham, Richmond Co d 12 Feb 1808, Grayson Co **RU:** Soldier/Patriot, Served in Capt Jonathan Isom's Co, Montgomery Co Militia & gave material aid to cause **CEM:** Tobias Phillips; GPS unk; Rt 619 nr Rt 757; Carroll **GS:** U **SP: Margaret** Peggy Jennings (__-12 Feb 1806) **VI:** No further data **P:** unk **BLW:** unk **RG:** Y **MK:** unk **PH:** unk **SS:** D vol 46 pg 346, vol 47, pg 37; G pg 221; DAR A090772; SAR P-269729 **BS:** JLARC 43; 196.

PHILLIPS, William; b 1 Nov 1744; d 30 Dec 1797 **RU:** Lieutenant Colonel/Patriot, Served in Stafford Co Militia. Gave beef & gun to cause **CEM:** Phillips Family; GPS 38.50238, -77.29626; Rt 610, Quantico Marine Base; Stafford **GS:** Y **SP:** Mar (7 Jul 1774) Elizabeth Fowke (__-c1830) **VI:** Sheriff Stafford Co 1792-4, SAR marker **P:** unk **BLW:** unk **RG:** Y **MK:** Y SAR **PH:** Y **SS:** D pg 872; E pg 623; DAR A090824; SAR P-333979 **BS:** 03 pg 300.

PHILLIPS, William; b 12 Nov 1760, Shenandoah Co; d 17 May 1837 **RU:** Soldier, Served in 5th & 8th Cont Line **CEM:** Philllips; GPS unk; Edinburg; Shenandoah **GS:** U **SP:** Christiana Foltz (1768-1837) **VI:** No further data **P:** unk **BLW:** unk **RG:** N **MK:** unk **PH:** unk **SS:** E pg 623 **BS:** 196.

PHIPPS, William Sr; b 1759; d Aug 1818 **RU:** Private, Served in Capt James Fenley's Co, Montgomery Co Militia **CEM:** Phipps Family; GPS unk; Wytheville; Wythe **GS:** N **SP:** (-----), have children **VI:** Family tradition is bur on his farm. Cemetery is lost **P:** unk **BLW:** unk **RG:** N **MK:** N **PH:** N **SS:** G pg 232 **BS:** 196.

PHIPPS (PHIPS), Benjamin; b 1761 or 1762, Guilford Co, NC; d 3 May 1838 **RU:** Private, Served in SC & in Capt James Cox's and Enoch Osbornes Companies, Grayson Co Militia **CEM:** Benjamin-Phipps; GPS unk; Saddle Creek Rt 681; Grayson **GS:** U **SP:** mar (5 July 1782) Jean Hash **VI:** Appl for pen 24 Sep 1832, Montomery Co, NC (Now Grayson Co) W5539. Widow appl 5 Jul 1844 Grayson Co, VA **P:** Y **BLW:** unk **RG:** Y **MK:** unk **PH:** unk **SS:** J-NSSAR 1993 Reg, J- DAR Hatcher; CG Vol 3 pg 2691; DAR A090895; SAR P-270083 **BS:** JLARC 1, 2; .80 vol 3, pg 171.

PHIPPS (PHIPS), John; b 1761; d 1838 **RU:** Private, Served in 10th Cont Line **CEM:** Phipps Family; GPS unk; Saddle Creek; Grayson **GS:** U **SP:** No info **VI:** No further data **P:** unk **BLW:** unk **RG:** N **MK:** unk **PH:** unk **SS:** J-NSSAR 1993 Reg; E pg 624 **BS:** JLARC 1.

PICHON, Noel; b unk; d 1781 **RU:** Seaman, Served on "Citoyen" and died from Yorktown battle **CEM:** French Memorial; GPS 36.81944, -79.39933; Yorktown; York **GS:** U **SP:** No info **VI:** No further data **P:** unk **BLW:** unk **RG:** Y **MK:** unk **PH:** unk **SS:** J-Yorktown Historian; SAR P-270114 **BS:** JLARC 1, 74.

PICHON, Pierre; b unk; d 1781 **RU:** Seaman, Served on "Hextor" and died from Yorktown battle **CEM:** French Memorial; GPS 36.81944, -79.39933; Yorktown; York **GS:** U **SP:** No info **VI:** No further data **P:** unk **BLW:** unk **RG:** Y **MK:** unk **PH:** unk **SS:** J-Yorktown Historian; SAR P-270115 **BS:** JLARC 1, 74.

PIELEE, Gilbert; b c1740, Holland; d 22 Feb 1790 **RU:** Patriot, Gave material aid to the cause **CEM:** Tavern Lot; GPS unk; Center of Accomac; Accomack **GS:** Y **SP:** No info **VI:** Native of Holland, d age 40 **P:** N **BLW:** N **RG:** N **MK:** N **PH:** unk **SS:** AL Com Bk I pg 30 **BS:** 37 pg 205.

PIERCE(PEIRCE), John; b 1750 or 1760, Westmoreland Co; d 1833 **RU:** Private, Midshipman **CEM:** Pierce Family; GPS 38.688886,-78.025927; Rt 211, Amissville; Rappahannock **GS:** Y **SP:** 1) Petunia Hune (1769-1808), 2) Betsy Muse Moxley **VI:** No further data **P:** unk **BLW:** unk **RG:** Y **MK:** N **PH:** Y **SS:** E pg 625; SAR P-334906 **BS:** 33; 163.

PIERCE (PEIRCE), Joseph; b 1728; See PEIRCE , Joseph

PIERCY, Henry; b unk; d 17 Jun 1809 **RU:** Captain, Served in 2nd PA Regt until end of war **CEM:** Christ Church Episcopal; GPS 38.80216, -77.05689; Wilkes St & Hamilton Ln; Alexandria City **GS:** N **SP:** Nancy (-----) **VI:** Member of Society of Cinncinatti. Bur with military, Masonic, civil honors (Alexandria Gazette, 20 Jun 1809, pg 3). Entitled to 200 acres bounty land which was issued 1794 to Paul Bentalow. Widow appl pen 1810 and was denied and was advised to take legal action **P:** unk **BLW:** Y **RG:** Y **MK:** N **PH:** N **SS:** E pg 625; BX pg 637; SAR P-270308 **BS:** 20 pg 110.

PIERROT, Nicholas; b unk; d 1781 **RU:** Seaman, Served on "Diademe" and died from Yorktown battle **CEM:** French Memorial; GPS 36.81944, -79.39933; Yorktown; York **GS:** U **SP:** No info **VI:** No further

RU=Rank/Unit	CEM=Cemetery	GS=Gravestone	SP=Spousal Information
VI=Other Veteran Info	P=Pension	BLW=Bounty/Land Warrant	RG=Registered Grave
MK=SAR/DAR Marker	PH=Photo	SS=Service Source	BS=Burial Source

332

data **P:** unk **BLW:** unk **RG:** Y **MK**: unk **PH:** unk **SS:** J-Yorktown Historian; SAR P-270506 **BS:** JLARC 1, 74.

PIERSON, Charles; b unk; d 1781 **RU:** Soldier, Served in Gatinais Bn and died fr battle at Yorktown **CEM:** French Memorial; GPS 36.81944, -79.39933; Yorktown; York **GS:** U **SP:** No info **VI:** No further data **P:** unk **BLW:** unk **RG:** Y **MK**: unk **PH:** unk **SS:** J-Yorktown Historian; SAR P-270528 **BS:** JLARC 1, 74.

PIGG, Hezekiah Ford; b 1742, Jones Mill, Pittsylvania Co; d 21 Nov 1785 **RU:** Patriot, Gave material aid to the cause in Pittsylvania Co **CEM:** Pigg Mill Farm; GPS 36.77373, -79.46067; Rt 703, Jones Mill; Pittsylvania **GS:** Y **SP:** 1) Elizabeth Nash 2) Mary Clement 3) Agnes Owen **VI:** Son of Capt John Ghent (1716-1785) & Ann (Clement) Pigg **P:** N **BLW:** N **RG:** N **MK:** N **PH:** unk **SS:** D pg 197; AL CT BK pg 18 **BS:** 82 pg 283; 196.

PIGG, John; b c1720, Amelia Co; d 21 Feb 1785 **RU:** Artillery Captain/Patriot, Provided corn, bacon, flour, brandy for state and continental troops. Was Capt of Militia & VA Artillery **CEM:** Pigg Mill Farm; GPS 36.77373, -79.46067; Rt 703, Jones Mill; Pittsylvania **GS:** Y **SP:** Ann Clement (mar in Amelia) **VI:** Son of Paul and (-----) Pigg **P:** unk **BLW:** unk **RG:** Y **MK**: unk **PH:** unk **SS:** D vol 3,pg 768 Pittsylvania Co; DAR A088978; SAR P-270600 **BS:** 174, JLARC 20.

PIGGOTT, William; b unk; d 1846 **RU:** Sergeant, Served in VA First Artillery **CEM:** Goose Creek; GPS 39.11250, -77.69527, GS 39.11321,-77.69594; Rt 722, Lincoln; Loudoun **GS:** Y **SP:** No info **VI:** No further data **P:** unk **BLW:** unk **RG:** Y **MK:** N **PH:** Y **SS:** E pg 625; SAR bio rpt submitted 28 Feb 21 **BS:** 25 pg 243.

PIGIBIT, Jean; b unk; d 1781 **RU:** Soldier, Served in Soissonnais Bn and died fr battle at Yorktown **CEM:** French Memorial; GPS 36.81944, -79.39933; Yorktown; York **GS:** U **SP:** No info **VI:** No further data **P:** unk **BLW:** unk **RG:** Y **MK**: unk **PH:** unk **SS:** J-Yorktown Historian; SAR P-270605 **BS:** JLARC 1, 74.

PILAU, Jean; b unk; d 1781 **RU:** Soldier, Served in Gatinais Bn and died fr battle at Yorktown **CEM:** French Memorial; GPS 36.81944, -79.39933; Yorktown; York **GS:** U **SP:** no info **VI:** No further data **P:** unk **BLW:** unk **RG:** Y **MK**: unk **PH:** unk **SS:** J-Yorktown Historian; SAR P-270673 **BS:** JLARC 1, 74.

PINCERON, Francois; b unk; d 1781 **RU:** Seaman, Served on "Duc De Bourgogne" and died from Yorktown battle **CEM:** French Memorial; GPS 36.81944, -79.39933; Yorktown; York **GS:** U **SP:** No info **VI:** No further data **P:** unk **BLW:** unk **RG:** Y **MK**: unk **PH:** unk **SS:** J-Yorktown Historian; SAR P-270726 **BS:** JLARC 1, 74.

PINET, Jean; b unk; d 1781 **RU:** Soldier, Served in Touraine Bn and died fr battle at Yorktown **CEM:** French Memorial; GPS 36.81944, -79.39933; Yorktown; York **GS:** U **SP:** No info **VI:** No further data **P:** unk **BLW:** unk **RG:** Y **MK**: unk **PH:** unk **SS:** J-Yorktown Historian; SAR P-270760 **BS:** JLARC 1, 74.

PINNELL, Thomas; b Nov 1740, Amherst Co; d 12 Nov 1812 **RU:** Private, Served in 2nd Cont Line. Served in Capt Peyton's Co, Col Alexander's Regt and in Col Spotswood's 2d Regt of Foot **CEM:** Amherst; GPS 37.59640, -79.03670; Bus Rt 29, Amherst; Amherst **GS:** U **SP:** Mar (15 Jun 1765) Sarah Clopton (3 Mar 1742, Amherst Co-___) **VI:** No further data **P:** unk **BLW:** unk **RG:** Y **MK**: unk **PH:** unk **SS:** DAR #A089190; SAR P-270819; J-NSSAR 2000 Reg; E pg 627; DD **BS:** JLARC 76.

PIPER, James; b 11 Feb 1737; d 20 Sep 1825 **RU:** Soldier, Fought at Kings Mountain **CEM:** Sinking Springs; GPS 36.71030, -81.98170; 136 E Main St, Abingdon; Washington **GS:** U **SP:** Margaret Vance (22 Apr 1744-28 Dec 1831) d/o Samuel & Sarah (Colvill) Vance. She mar William Lusk 2nd as widow. **VI:** No further data **P:** unk **BLW:** unk **RG:** Y **MK**: Y DAR **PH:** unk **SS:** AR Vol 3 pg 176; SAR P-270881 **BS:** JLARC 1, 2, 80; 212 pg 76; 196.

PITMAN (PITTMAN), Andrew; b 1760; d 22 Sep 1838 **RU:** Private, Served in Frederick Co Militia. Served also in VA Line **CEM:** German Reformed Church; GPS 39.08150, -78.21840; Mulberry St, Stephen City; Frederick **GS:** Y **SP:** Mar (08 Sep 1829, Frederick Co) Margaret Lefevre (1796-___) her 2d mar to John Minnix **VI:** Former widow appl pen 2 Jan 1860 # W9998; he appl pen 7 Nov 1832, no evidence of receiving **P:** Y **BLW:** unk **RG:** N **MK:** N **PH:** unk **SS:** E pg 628; CG pg 2707-8 **BS:** 112. GerReform.

RU=Rank/Unit	CEM=Cemetery	GS=Gravestone	SP=Spousal Information
VI=Other Veteran Info	P=Pension	BLW=Bounty/Land Warrant	RG=Registered Grave
MK=SAR/DAR Marker	PH=Photo	SS=Service Source	BS=Burial Source

PITMAN, Anthony; b 1740; d 10 Mar 1805 **RU**: Patriot, gave material aid to cause, Frederick Co **CEM**: :Old Town Cemetery; GPS not determined; lots 76 & 77, Mulberry St, Town of Stephensburg **GS**: Y but broken **SP**: Catherine (-----) **VI**: No further data **P**: N **BLW**: N **RG**: N **MK**: N **PH**: N **SS**: AL Ct Bk pg 37, Commission Bk IV pg 308 **BS**: 196.

PITMAN, Nicholas, b 1735, Germany, d 1797 Strasburg **RU**: Private/ Patriot, Captain Machir's Company, Strasburg VA District Militia. As patriot was Overseer of Roads, 1774-1780 Shenandoah Co **CEM**: Kern: GPS 38.957119, -78.376433; Deer Papids Rd (Rt on 601), formally Pitman Farm; Strasburg; Shenandoah **GS**: No **SP**: Catherine Snapp (1734 Frederick Co-1797), d/o Johannes Schnepp & Barbara Dutt **VI**: Son of Andreas Pitman & (-----) **P**: N **BLW**: N **RG**: Y **MK**: N **PH**: N **SS**: C pg 606; SAR P-270975; DAR # A089377; **BS**: 196; James Wood Chap VASSAR Rpt Dec 2018.

PITMAN (PITTMAN), Phillip; b unk; d 1820 **RU**: Private, Served in Capt Alexander Machir's Co in the Strasburg District of the Militia **CEM**: Hockmans; GPS unk; vic Lebanon Church; Frederick **GS**: Y **SP**: No info **VI**: No further data **P**: unk **BLW**: unk **RG**: N **MK**: N **PH**: unk **SS**: C pg 606 **BS**: 50 pg 76.

PITOZZEAU, N; b unk; d 1781 **RU**: Seaman, Served on the "Destin" and died from Yorktown battle **CEM**: French Memorial; GPS 36.81944, -79.39933; Yorktown; York **GS**: U **SP**: No info **VI**: No further data **P**: unk **BLW**: unk **RG**: Y **MK**: unk **PH**: unk **SS**: J Yorktown Historian; SAR P-270984 **BS**: JLARC 1, 74.

PITTS, Hezekiah; b 19 Oct 1745; d 1 Oct 1823 **RU**: Captain/Patriot, Served in Northampton Co Militia. Took oath as Capt 14 May 1782. Gave material aid to cause **CEM**: Long Point Farm; GPS unk; Rt 711; Northampton **GS**: Y **SP**: Mar (10 Jun 1773) Mildred Scarburg (26 Feb 1754-29 Jun 1819) **VI**: No further data **P**: unk **BLW**: unk **RG**: Y **MK**: N **PH**: unk **SS**: E pg 628; AL Ct Bk pg 4 Northampton Co; SAR P-271020 **BS**: 42 pg 64.

PITTS, Major; b 25 Nov 1755; d 15 Oct 1839 **RU**: Sergeant, Served in VA Line. Ent serv 1775 Northampton Co **CEM**: Wescott Farm; GPS unk; Rt 606 NW of Nassawadox; Northampton **GS**: Y **SP**: No info **VI**: Lived in Northhampton Co. Pen appl for 10 Sep 1832 at age 78. S5931 **P**: Y **BLW**: unk **RG**: Y **MK**: N **PH**: unk **SS**: E pg 628; K Vol 4 pg 116; CG Vol 3 2709; SAR P-271029 **BS**: JLARC 4, 69, 42, pg 64.

PLACET, Claude; b unk; d 1781 **RU**: Seaman, Served on "Hextor" and died from Yorktown battle **CEM**: French Memorial; GPS 36.81944, -79.39933; Yorktown; York **GS**: U **SP**: No info **VI**: No further data **P**: unk **BLW**: unk **RG**: Y **MK**: unk **PH**: unk **SS**: J-Yorktown Historian; SAR P-271079 **BS**: JLARC 1, 74.

PLAGNOLET, Jean; b unk; d 1781 **RU**: Soldier, Served in Soissonnais Bn and died fr battle at Yorktown **CEM**: French Memorial; GPS 36.81944, -79.39933; Yorktown; York **GS**: U **SP**: No info **VI**: No further data **P**: unk **BLW**: unk **RG**: Y **MK**: unk **PH**: unk **SS**: J-Yorktown Historian; SAR P-271080 **BS**: JLARC 1, 74.

PLANTO, Jean; b unk; d 1781 **RU**: Seaman, Served on "Languedoc" and died from Yorktown battle **CEM**: French Memorial; GPS 36.81944, -79.39933; Yorktown; York **GS**: U **SP**: No info **VI**: No further data **P**: unk **BLW**: unk **RG**: Y **MK**: unk **PH**: unk **SS**: J-Yorktown Historian; SAR P-271099 **BS**: JLARC 1, 74.

PLASTER. Henry, Sr; b 9 Feb 1760, New Garden, Chester Co PA, d 12 Oct 1852 **RU**: See SAR application of Cory Alan Plaster ACN 214527 dated 1992 **CEM**: Ebenezer Baptist Church; GPS 39.058237, -77.811423; loc 20421 Airmont Rd. Bluemont; Loudoun **GS**: Y **SP**: Mar 20 Apr 1783, Susannah Burson (19 Dec 1757, Fairfax Co-13 Mar 1821), d/o James Burson (17 Apr 1733, Providence TWP, Philidelphia-9 Oct 1815) & Mary Kregan (21 Jul 1736-5 Feb 1814) **VI**: No further data **P**: Unk **BLW**: Unk **RG**: Y **MK**: N **PH**: N **SS**: DAR A089562; SAR P-271108 **BS**: 196.

PLASTER, Michael; b c1724, Germany; d 14 Jun 1803 **RU**: Private?, Took oath of Allegiance He also paid personal property tax in 1782 in Henry Co from which Franklin Co was formed **CEM**: Green Hill Primitive Baptist; GPS unk; Patrick Springs; Patrick **GS**: Y **SP**: 1) (-----) 2) Mar (c1770) Tamer Houston (__-1804) **VI**: Died in Franklin Co **P**: unk **BLW**: unk **RG**: N **MK**: N **PH**: unk **SS**: DAR #A089562; B; BE Vol 9 pg 141; *VA Mag Hist & Bio* Vol 9 pg 141; DV Henry Co, 1782 image 10 pdf **BS**: 125 pg 383.

RU=Rank/Unit	CEM=Cemetery	GS=Gravestone	SP=Spousal Information
VI=Other Veteran Info	P=Pension	BLW=Bounty/Land Warrant	RG=Registered Grave
MK=SAR/DAR Marker	PH=Photo	SS=Service Source	BS=Burial Source

334

PLISSON, Jean; b unk; d 1781 **RU**: Seaman, Served on "Sceptre" and died from Yorktown battle **CEM**: French Memorial; GPS 36.81944, -79.39933; Yorktown; York **GS**: U **SP**: No info **VI**: No further data **P**: unk **BLW**: unk **RG**: Y **MK**: unk **PH**: unk **SS**: J-Yorktown Historian; SAR P-271220 **BS**: JLARC 1, 74.

PLUMMER, William; b 1748, Gloucester Co, d aft 1785 Gloucester Co **RU**: Sergeant, was serving 27 May 1778 of 3 yr tour as Sergeant in Capt John Belfield's Co, Col Theodorick Bland's 1st Cont Dragoons **CEM**: Bruton Parish; GPS 37,27127,-76.70248; 331 W Duke of Gloucester St; Williamsburg City **GS**: Unk **SP**: Mary Hayes **VI**: No further data **P**: N **BLW**: N **RG**: Y **MK**: N **PH**: N **SS**: C Sec III, pg 486; Fold3 Serv Index Card & Rev War Rolls; SAR P-271310; DAR A087837 **BS**: 196

POAGE, James; b 1750, d 9 Sep 1814 **RU**: Lieutenant, Served as Ensign in Capt Joseph Patterson's Company, Augusta Co Militia. Was stationed in Dismal Swamp 1781. Promoted to Lt 20 Mar 1782 in Capt Bell's Augusta Co Militia **CEM**: Old Providence ARP Church (AKA Stonewalled Cem); GPS 37.9615097, -79.2271042; Old Providence Rd (Rt 919), Spotswood; Augusta **GS**: Yes row 1, #19 **SP**: No info **VI**: No further data **P**: N **BLW**: N **RG**: Y **MK**: Y SAR plaque **PH**: Unk **SS**: E pg 629; AZ pg 184; SAR P-271328 **BS**: 80 vol 3, pg179; 196

POAGE (POAGUE), James; b 1747; d 9 Sep 1811 **RU**: Patriot, Gave material aid to cause **CEM**: Old Providence; GPS 37.96151, -79.71000; 1005 Spottswood Rd, Spotswood; Augusta **GS**: N **SP**: No info **VI**: Name is on SAR plaque at cemetery May be the same person b 1750-d 1814 **P**: N **BLW**: N **RG**: Y **MK**: Y SAR plaque **PH**: N **SS**: AL Lists pg 10 Augusta Co; BT, SAR P-271328 **BS**: JLARC 2, 62; 80 vol 3, pg 179 213 pg 460.

POAGE (POAGUE), John; b unk; d 1810 **RU**: Captain, Commanded co in Augusta Co Militia **CEM**: Locust Bottom; GPS unk; Jct Rts 622 & 696; Botetourt **GS**: Y **SP**: No info **VI**: No further data **P**: unk **BLW**: unk **RG**: N **MK**: N **PH**: unk **SS**: E pg 629 **BS**: 80 vol 3, pg 179; 115 pg 12.

POAGE (POAGUE), John Jr; b 1757; d 10 Apr 1827 **RU**: Ensign, Served in Capt Anderson's Co, Augusta Co Militia. Took oath as ensign 18 Sep 1781 **CEM**: Augusta Stone Presbyterian; GPS 38.23926, -78.97356, GS 38.1411,-78.5815; 28 Old Stone Church Ln, Ft Defiance; Augusta **GS**: U **SP**: 1) Mar (16 Nov 1802 Botetourt Co) Jane Kyle d/o William & (-----) Kyle 2) Mar (20 Jun 1807 Botetourt Co) Catherine Sheets **VI**: Son of John (1726-1789) & (-----) Poague. Govt stone **P**: unk **BLW**: unk **RG**: Y **MK**: Y SAR plaque **PH**: unk **SS**: E pg 629; AZ pg 328; SAR P-271339; DAR A089875 **BS**: JLARC 1, 2, 8, 23, 62, 63; 80 vol 3, pg 179; 196.

POAGE, Robert; b 1760; d 1836 **RU**: Second Lieutenant, Served in Rockbridge Co Militia 7 Jul 1778 **CEM**: Augusta Stone Presbyterian; GPS 38.23926, -78.97356; 28 Old Stone Church Ln, Ft Defiance; Augusta **GS**: Y **SP**: No info **VI**: Govt stone **P**: unk **BLW**: unk **RG**: Y **MK**: Y SAR plaque **PH**: unk **SS**: AZ pg 228; SAR P-271334 **BS**: JLARC 1, 2, 8, 23, 62, 63; 196.

POAGE, Robert Preston; b 15 Apr 1730, Ireland, d 1787, Botetourt Co **RU**: Patriot, Justice of Peace, Botetourt Co **CEM**: Augusta Stone Presbyterian; GPS 38.23926, -78.97356, GS 38.1411,-78.5815;; 28 Old Stone Church Ln, Ft Defiance; Augusta **GS**: Y Govt **SP**:Mar 1756,Abemarle Co Jean Wallace (6 Jun 1738 Charlottesville-1821) **VI**: Son of Robert Poage (1702, Ireland-1774-1774, Staunton) & Elizabeth Preston (__Ireland-1760, Augusta Co) **P**: N **BLW**: N **RG**: Y **MK**: Plaque **PH**: Unk **SS**:DL vol 1, pgs 272,281; DAR A089888; SAR P-271333; **BS**: 80 vol 3, pg179;196.

POAGE, Thomas; b 1740; d 1803 **RU**: Private/Patriot, Served in Capt Anderson's Co, Augusta Co Militia. Gave material aid to cause **CEM**: Augusta Stone Presbyterian; GPS 38.23926, -78.97356; 28 Old Stone Church Ln, Ft Defiance; Augusta **GS**: Y **SP**: Agnes "Polly" McClanahan (1744-__) **VI**: Govt stone says he was in Capt Anderson's Co. Died in Staunton **P**: unk **BLW**: unk **RG**: Y **MK**: Y SAR plaque **PH**: unk **SS**: B; E pg 629; AL Com Bk II pg 361 Augusta Co; SAR P-271336 **BS**: JLARC 1, 2, 8, 23, 62; 196.

POAGE, William; b 1759; d 23 Sep 1834 **RU**: Private, Served in VA Line. Ent serv 1777 Botetourt Co **CEM**: Poage's Mill; GPS 37.19800, -80.05600; Rt 221, Bent Mountain Rd, village of Poages Mill; Roanoke Co **GS**: U **SP**: Mar (23 Dec 1806 Botetourt Co) Elizabeth Franklin (c1785-10 or 11 Jul 1867) d/o Nathan & (-----) Franklin **VI**: Pension appl for 12 Nov 1832 age 73 Botecourt Co. Widow appl pen 28 Jul 1853 age 68 Roanoke Co. W8502 **P**: Y **BLW**: unk **RG**:Y **MK**: unk **PH**: unk **SS**: J- DAR Hatcher, K Vol 4 pg 117; CG Vol 3 pg 2716; SAR P-271338 **BS**: JLARC 2; 80 vol 3, pg 179.

RU=Rank/Unit	CEM=Cemetery	GS=Gravestone	SP=Spousal Information
VI=Other Veteran Info	P=Pension	BLW=Bounty/Land Warrant	RG=Registered Grave
MK=SAR/DAR Marker	PH=Photo	SS=Service Source	BS=Burial Source

335

POHEAGUE, Josias; b unk; d 16 Oct 1781 **RU:** Private, Served in Capt Eldridge Co, CT Cont Line, and died fr battle at Yorktown **CEM:** Yorktown Victory Monument Tablet; GPS 38.28350, -78.54150; Yorktown; York **GS:** U **SP:** No info **VI:** No further data **P:** unk **BLW:** unk **RG:** Y **MK:** unk **PH:** unk **SS:** J-Yorktown Historian; DY; SAR P-271381 pg 152 **BS:** JLARC 74.

POIGNARD, Jean or Hector; b unk; d 1781 **RU:** Seaman, Served on "Languedoc" and died from Yorktown battle **CEM:** French Memorial; GPS 36.81944, -79.39933; Yorktown; York **GS:** U **SP:** No info **VI:** No further data **P:** unk **BLW:** unk **RG:** Y **MK:** unk **PH:** unk **SS:** J-Yorktown Historian; SAR P-271382 **BS:** JLARC 1, 74.

POINDEXTER, John Sr; b 1765, Meclenburg Co; d 1817 **RU:** Private, Served in VA Calvary unit in Illinois **CEM:** Poindexter Family; GPS unk; Jct Rts 655 & 834; Franklin **GS:** Y **SP:** Mar (11 Oct 1792 Lunenburg Co) Nancy Neal **VI:** Son of Phillip (c1707-__) & Sarah (Grymes) (20 Aug 1744-__) Poindexter **P:** unk **BLW:** unk **RG:** N **MK:** N **PH:** unk **SS:** E pg 629 **BS:** 82 pg 286; 196.

POINDEXTER, Joseph; b 1736;Hanover Co, d 29 Jun 1826 **RU:** Captain, Commanded Co in Bedford Co Militia, oath taken 28 Sep 1778 **CEM:** Whipping Creek; GPS 37.03430, -79.00180; Rt 633 Epsons Rd nr Long Island; Campbell **GS:** N **SP:** (Order of marriages unk) Elizabeth Kennerly mar (19 May 1800 Campbell Co (bond)); Frances I. Harrison **VI:** No further data **P:** unk **BLW:** unk **RG:** Y **MK:** N **PH:** N **SS:** E pg 630; DAR a089950; SAR P-271391 **BS:** JLARC 2, 3, 4, 36; 196.

POINDEXTER, Thomas; b 25 May 1760, Elk's Creek, Loudoun Co; d 10 Apr 1843 **RU:** Soldier/Patriot, Ent serv Louisa Co in VA Line. Gave material aid to cause **CEM:** Valetta; GPS unk; Nr Green Springs; Louisa **GS:** U **SP:** Mar (18 or 28 Mar 1790) Sarah Ragland (c1769-__) **VI:** Lived in KY after RW for short time, then came back to Loudoun. Appl for pension 15 Jun 1837 W5556. Recd BLW #26961-160-55. Widow appl pen 3 Nov 1846 age 77 W5556 **P:** Y **BLW:** Y **RG:** Y **MK:** unk **PH:** unk **SS:** K Vol 4 pg 129; AL Ct Bk pg 20 Louisa Co; CG Vol 3 pg 2717; SAR P-271395 **BS:** JLARC 4, 61.

POLLARD, Joseph; b 18 Mar 1758; d 6 Sep 1836 **RU:** Sergeant, Ent serv c1779 Goochland Co in a VA regt. Served in 2nd Cont Line in Capt Everard Meades Co in Mar 1777. Brother Robert was discharged fr RW service 1781, went to grandfather's house in Goochland Co, & took supplies to Joseph "who was then serving on retreat of General Lafayette May 1781" **CEM:** Mattaponi Church; GPS unk; Nr Cumnor; King & Queen **GS:** U **SP:** Mar (17 Mar 1791 Hanover Co) Catharine Robinson (__-22 May 1843) **VI:** Pension appl for 10 Dec 1832 age 74 King and Queen Co. Widow appl pen 9 Nov 1840 in King & Queen Co age 71 W5555 **P:** Y **BLW:** unk **RG:** Y **MK:** unk **PH:** unk **SS:** J-NSSAR 1993 Reg; K Vol 4 pg 120; CG Vol 3 pg 2720; DAR A 090229; SAR P-271509 **BS:** 196; JLARC 1; E pg 660.

POLLARD, Robert; b 3 Jul 1756, Culpeper Co; d 10 Oct 1847 **RU:** Captain, Served in VA line. Ent serv Culpeper Co 1777 **CEM:** Shockoe Hill; GPS 37.55190, -77.43170; SAR monument 37.551247,-77.432429; gravestone 37.552178, -77.431631; 4th & Hospital Sts; Richmond City **GS:** Y **SP:** Jael Underwood **VI:** Moved Richmond City c1784. Pension appl for 30 Jul 1832 Richmond age 76, S5944 **P:** Y **BLW:** unk **RG:** Y **MK:** Y monument **PH:** Y **SS:** K Vol 4 pg 120; AK; CG Vol 3 pg 2720; DAR A203386; SAR P-271514 **BS:** 04.

POLLARD, Robert; b 1758; d 30 Apr 1819 **RU:**Lieutenant, served on the Norfolk *Revenge* NBJ *8 May* 1777 **CEM:** North Bank Plantation; GPS not determined; loc in Newtown at the plantation site. Obtain county property records for directions; King & Queen **GS:** N **SP:** Prob mar as person this name, probably son, was clerk of King & Queen Co 1820-1835 **VI:** No further data **P:** N **BLW:** N **RG:**N **MK:** N **PH:** N **SS:** BE pg 237 **BS:** 196

POLLARD, William; b c1732; d 1792 **RU:** Patriot, Served as Clerk of Ct, Hanover Co, 1775-1781 **CEM:** Mattaponi Baptist; GPS unk; Vic King & Queen CH; King & Queen **GS:** N **SP:** Mary Anderson **VI:** Son of Joseph (1701-26 Dec 1791) & Priscilla (Holmes) (1701 Caroline Co-26 Jul 1795) Pollard **P:** N **BLW:** N **RG:**Y **MK:** unk **PH:** unk **SS:** DAR A090267; CD; SAR P-338385 **BS:** 196.

POLLET, Denis; b unk; d 1781 **RU:** Seaman, Served on "Duc De Bourgogne" and died from Yorktown battle **CEM:** French Memorial; GPS 36.81944, -79.39933; Yorktown; York **GS:** U **SP:** No info **VI:** No further data **P:** unk **BLW:** unk **RG:** Y **MK:** unk **PH:** unk **SS:** J-Yorktown Historian; SAR P-271542 **BS:** JLARC 1, 74.

RU=Rank/Unit	CEM=Cemetery	GS=Gravestone	SP=Spousal Information
VI=Other Veteran Info	P=Pension	BLW=Bounty/Land Warrant	RG=Registered Grave
MK=SAR/DAR Marker	PH=Photo	SS=Service Source	BS=Burial Source

336

POLLOCKFIELD, John Richard Sr; b 4 Jul 1726, Prince George Co, MD; d 1 Jan 1804 **RU:** Private, Served in Lt William Edmiston's Co, Washington Co Militia in Dunmore's War **CEM:** Soloman Litton Hollow; GPS unk; nr Pinnacle Preserve; Russell **GS:** U **SP:** Sarah Ann Wilcoxen (1728-1808) **VI:** Son of Caleb Pollockfield (1678-1763) & Mary Grace Burton (Willett) (1703-1791) Litton. SAR Grave marker. Govt Grave stone lists service **P:** unk **BLW:** unk **RG:** N **MK:** Y SAR **PH:** unk **SS:** J-NSSAR 2000 Reg; Z pg 152 **BS:** JLARC 76; 196.

POPE, Nathaniel; b 1761, Chilton, Montpelier, Hanover Co; d 13 Mar 1809 **RU:** Private served in the calalry during the war **CEM:** Chilton Family; GPS not determined; Montpelier; Hanover **GS:** Unk **SP:** Mar 1784, Mary "Polly" Duval, d/o Samuel Duval (1713-1764) & Lucy Claiborne (1725-1810) **VI:** Son of Nathaniel Pope (1729, Hanover Co- 21 Nov 1806, Powhatan Co) & Lucy Smith Fox (15 Aug 1732, Hanover Co-21 Jul 1789) Was an attorney; was killed in a duel **P:** N **BLW:** Y **RG:** N **MK:** N **PH:** N **SS:** E pg 632; AP fold3 muster roll; DAR A 090771**; BS:** 196.

POPE, Nathaniel; b 1729, Hanover Co; d 21 Nov 1806, Powhatan Co **RU:** Patriot Gave material aid to cause in Powhatan Co **CEM:** Fox Family; GPS 37.896327,-77.860170; loc 3731 Gardner's Rd (Rt 648); Louisa **GS:** Y **SP:** Lucy Smith Fox (15 Aug 1732, Hanover Co-21 Jul 1789 **VI:** Son of John Pope (1695, Westmoreland Co-1735) & his cousin Elizabeth Pope.He was listed as a Captain in his obituary **P:** N **BLW:** Y **RG:** N **MK:** N **PH:** N **SS:** D vol 2, pg 630; DAR A090773 **BS:** 196.

POPE, William; b 23 Oct 1762, Louisa Co; d 19 Jul 1852 **RU:** Private, Served in Brig Gen Armand's Command 15 Nov 1783 **CEM:** Dabney at Montpelier; GPS unk; Maiden's Rd, abt 2 mi N of Anderson Hwy, E side of rd, N of Montpelier Plantation; Powhatan **GS:** Y **SP:** Mar (14 Jun 1774 Henrico Co) Ann Woodson (1774-28 Oct 1823) d/o Charles & Nancy (Trotter) Woodson Jr. **VI:** The Commonwelth Attorney of Powhatan Co; also Capt in the War of 1812. Recd 100 acres BLW fr VA, and 100 acres fr US **P:** N **BLW:** Y **RG:** Y **MK:** unk **PH:** unk **SS:** N pg 1253; SAR P-271941 **BS:** 196.

PORTER, Patrick; b 1 May 1737, Ireland; d 28 Apr 1798 **RU:** Sergeant/Patriot, Served in Capt Joseph Martin's Militia Co; furnished supplies **CEM:** Porter Family; GPS unk; Rt 682 Dungannon; Scott **GS:** Y **SP:** Susannah Walker **VI:** VA historical road sign indicates he had a mill in1774 and built a fort to protect residents fr Indian attacks. DAR plaque **P:** unk **BLW:** unk **RG:** Y **MK:** Y DAR plaque **PH:** Y **SS:** AK Payrolls; SAR P-272164; DAR A091277 **BS:** 04, Oct 06; 196.

PORTER, Samuel; b 1764; d 1814 **RU:** Captain, Served in VA unit in Illinois. His Co was with Daniel Boone in KY in the defense of Boonesborough, KY, 1778 **CEM:** Trinity Episcopal; GPS 36.83459, -76.30105; 500 Court St; Portsmouth City **GS:** Y **SP:** No info **VI:** No further data **P:** unk **BLW:** unk **RG:** N **MK:** N **PH:** unk **SS:** B indicates Capt; CZ pg 356; VA Historical Road sign inscription # K18 **BS:** 147 Trinity Ch.

PORTER, Thomas; b 1756, Fauquier Co; d bef 1 May 1840 burial date **RU:** Sergeant, Served in Col Christian Febiger's 2nd Regt **CEM:** Old Presbyterian Meeting House; GPS 38.48528, -77.23532; loc Wolke St nr jct with S Fairfax St; Alexandria City **GS:** N **SP:** Susannah "Sukey" Nancy (-----) **VI:** Died in Trevilians, Louisa Co. Death notice in Alexandria Gazette 1 May 1800, pg 3. Listed on SAR plaque in cemetery **P:** unk **BLW:** unk **RG:** Y **MK:** Y SAR plaque **PH:** N **SS:** J-NSSAR 1993 Reg; AK; DD; SAR P-272199 **BS:** JLARC 1; 196.

PORTER, William; b c1749-50, Norfolk Co; d 20 Jun 1807 **RU:** Lieutenant, Ent serv Norfolk Co in Capt Ballard's Co,12th VA Regt until end of war serving over 7 yrs. Was one of oldest Lts **CEM:** Glasgow Street Park; GPS 36.8373030, -76.3018600; 425 Glasgow St; Portsmouth City **GS:** Y **SP:** Mar (31 Oct 1782 Norfolk Co) Elizabeth Luke d/o Isaac & (-----) Luke **VI:** Son of William & Patience (-----) Porter. Stepfather Joshua Nicholson. Marker moved 1929 fr Monumental graveyard. Ancestor of John Luke Porter; designer of Merrimack; Founding member of Monumental UMC in 1772. Widow appl pen $320/yr 1838 as resident Portsmouth W5159 **P:** Y **BLW:** unk **RG:** Y **MK:** Y SAR Granite; DAR Plaque **PH:** Y **SS:** K Vol 4 pg 128; Z; DAR A091354; SAR P-272827 **BS:** JLARC 2, 4, 39, 105.

PORTERFIELD, Josiah; b 1737 Chester Co, PA, d 1828 **RU:** Private, Enlisted 24 Apr 1778, Capt John McKee's New London Company, Col Charles Evans Regt, PA Militia **CEM:** Porterfield family; GPS 37,32455, -80.52869; sml fenced cem on Portersfield Ln, off Rt 765 Mount Lake Rd; Giles **GS:** Unk **SP:**

RU=Rank/Unit	CEM=Cemetery	GS=Gravestone	SP=Spousal Information
VI=Other Veteran Info	P=Pension	BLW=Bounty/Land Warrant	RG=Registered Grave
MK=SAR/DAR Marker	PH=Photo	SS=Service Source	BS=Burial Source

337

Mar 1781, Jean McDowell (1747-1824) **VI**: No further data **P**: N **BLW**: N **RG**: N **MK**: N **PH**: N **SS**: PA Archives series 5, Vol 5 Muster rolls; DAR A091364 **BS**: 196.

PORTERFIELD, Robert; b 22 Feb 1752, Frederick Co; d 13 Feb 1843 **RU**: Captain, Commissioned 2nd Lt in Cont Army 12 Dec 1776 and assigned 11th VA Militia. Promoted 1st Lt 1 Jun 1777. Transferred to 7th VA Regt 14 Sep 1778. Promoted to Capt 16 Aug 1779. Taken as POW at surrender of Charleston SC and kept on prison ship to end of war **CEM**: Thornrose; **GPS** 38,15120, -79.08460; 1041 W Beverly St; Staunton City **GS**: Y **SP**: 1) Mary Margaret Heth 2) Rebecca Farrar **VI**: Appl pen 16 Jun 1828 Augusta Co. S8965. BLW rec'd 18 Sep 1789, #1738-300. He was re-interred **P**: Y **BLW**: Y **RG**:Y **MK**: N **PH**: Y **SS**: AP Natl Service Records; K Vol 4 pg 129; CG Vol 3 pg 2727; DAR A091366; SAR P-272253 **BS**: JLARC 2, 4, 62, 63.

POSTON, William King, b 6 Oct 1760, MD, d 1 Jun 1823 **RU**: Private, VA State Troops in Clark's ILL Regt. Also served in 9th VA Cont Line **CEM**: Littrell; **GPS** 36.9094,-81.71; on George Debusk's farm E of farmhouse in field, farm rd is off Cedar Branch Rd, Saltville; Smyth **GS**: Yes **SP**: Sarah Hammill (1767-11 Apr 1841) **VI**: Son of William John Poston (1721, Charles Co, MD-9 Mar 1777, Charles Co, MD), & Priscilla (___) **P**: N **BLW**: N **RG**: N **MK**: N **PH**: N **SS**: C Sec II, pg 209; E pg 634; Fold3 Serv Index Cards **BS**: 196.

POTTEN, John; b 1763; d 30 Sep 1835 **RU**: Private, Served in Capt Andrew Fitch's Co, 4th Battalion of CT forces **CEM**: Trinity United Methodist; **GPS** 39.13600, -77.00610; 2911 Cameron Mills Rd; Alexandria City **GS**: Y **SP**: Sarah (-----) (1775-7 Sep 1829) **VI**: Death notice in Alexandria Gazette 1 Oct 1835, pg 3 **P**: unk **BLW**: unk **RG**:Y **MK**: N **PH**: unk **SS**: AP roll ; SAR P-266461 **BS**: 23 pg 136.

POTTER, Charles, b Unk; d 9 Apr 1778 **RU**: Private, Capt Thomas West's Co, 10th VA Regt, Cont Line,1778: **CEM**: Rev War Court House Plaque; **GPS** not determined; 4110 Chain Bridge Rd; Fairfax **GS**: Memorialized on plaque 2017 by Geo Washington Chapter, VASSAR **SP** No info **VI**: died in service **P**: N **BLW**: N **RG**: Y **MK**: N **PH**: N **SS**: E pg 634; AP Fold3 muster rolls; EP sources; SAR P 272413 **BS**: None.

POTTER, Ebenezer; b Apr 1764; d 7 Oct 1807 **RU**: Private, Served in Illinois Regt & Western Army under Gen George Clark **CEM**: Leesburg Presbyterian; **GPS** 39.11611, -77.56722; 207 W Market St, Leesburg; Loudoun **GS**: Y **SP**: Elizabeth (-----) (1776-18 Feb 1844) **VI**: No further data **P**: unk **BLW**: unk **RG**: N **MK**: N **PH**: unk **SS**: G pg 702-3 **BS**: 25 pg 245.

POTTS, Ezekiel; b 8 Jan 1743, Fairfax Co; d 16 Jan 1809 **RU**: Private?/Patriot, Served in Capt Burgess Ball's Co 5th Cont Line. Gave material aid to cause **CEM**: Potts Family; **GPS** 39.19455, -77.76157; Rts 716 & 714, Hillsboro; Loudoun **GS**: Y **SP**: Mar (29 Nov 1769) Elizabeth Mead (6 Oct 1745-22 Jan 1825 Hillsboro) **VI**: No further data **P**: unk **BLW**: unk **RG**: Y **MK**: N **PH**: unk **SS**: E pg 634; AL Ct Bk pg 11 Loudoun Co; DARA091836; SAR P-338453 **BS**: 25 pg 246.

POTTS, John; 1756 d 15 Jun 1830 (burial 16 Jun 1830); **RU**: Corporal, Served in the 7th VA Regt **CEM**: Shockoe Hill; **GPS** 37.55190, -77.43170; SAR monument 37.551247,-77.432429; gravestone 37.551778, -77.431892 4th & Hospital Sts; Richmond City **GS**: Y Govt, Range12, sec 11 **SP**: No info **VI**: No further data **P**: unk **BLW**: unk **RG**: Y **MK**: Monument lists name **PH**: unk **SS**: SAR P-189753; AP Fold3 serv index card **BS**: 57 pg 8; 196.

POTTS, Jonas; b 22 Aug 1779; d 26 Sep 1828 **RU**: Private, Served on "Romney" in 1775, then joined the Army of the Revolution in Capt Hugh Stephenson's Co **CEM**: Potts Family; **GPS** 39.19455, -77.76157; Rts 716 & 714, Hillsboro; Loudoun **GS**: Y **SP**: Martha Dowling (28 Dec 1782-15 Mar 1852) **VI**: Son of Ezekiel (1743-1809) & Elizabeth (Mead) (1821-1825) Potts **P**: unk **BLW**: unk **RG**: N **MK**: N **PH**: unk **SS**: E pg 634 **BS**: 25 pg 247; 196.

POTTS, Nathaniel; b unk; d 1830 **RU**: Patriot, Gave material aid to cause **CEM**: Ketoctin Baptist; **GPS** 39.15746, -77.74870; Ketoctin Church Rd, Purcellville; Loudoun **GS**: Y **SP**: No info **VI**: No further data **P**: N **BLW**: N **RG**: N **MK**: N **PH**: unk **SS**: D Vol 2 pg 599; AL Ct Bk pg 11 Loudoun Co **BS**: 25 pg 247.

POULAIN, Charles; b unk; d 1781 **RU**: Soldier, Served in Soissonnais Bn and died fr battle at Yorktown **CEM**: French Memorial; **GPS** 36.81944, -79.39933; Yorktown; York **GS**: U **SP**: No info **VI**: No further data **P**: unk **BLW**: unk **RG**: Y **MK**: unk **PH**: unk **SS**: J-Yorktown Historian; SAR P-272666 **BS**: JLARC 1, 74.

RU=Rank/Unit	CEM=Cemetery	GS=Gravestone	SP=Spousal Information
VI=Other Veteran Info	P=Pension	BLW=Bounty/Land Warrant	RG=Registered Grave
MK=SAR/DAR Marker	PH=Photo	SS=Service Source	BS=Burial Source

338

POULAIN, Jean; b unk; d 1781 **RU:** Seaman, Served on "Citoyen" and died from Yorktown battle **CEM:** French Memorial; GPS 36.81944, -79.39933; Yorktown; York **GS:** U **SP:** No info **VI:** No further data **P:** unk **BLW:** unk **RG:** Y **MK:** unk **PH:** unk **SS:** J-Yorktown Historian; SAR P-272667 **BS:** JLARC 1, 74.

POULSON, George B; b unk; d 1801 **RU:** Ensign/Patriot, Was paid for work on Ft Matompkin **CEM:** Ketoctin Baptist; GPS 39.15746, -77.74870; Ketoctin Church Rd, Purcellville; Loudoun **GS:** U **SP:** No info **VI:** No further data **P:** unk **BLW:** unk **RG:** Y **MK:** SAR Plaque **PH:** unk **SS:** G pg 501; SAR P-272669 **BS:** JLARC 1, 2, 32.; 80 vol3 pg 185

POUPON, Francois; b unk; d 1781 **RU:** Soldier, Served in Gatinais Bn and died fr battle at Yorktown **CEM:** French Memorial; GPS 36.81944, -79.39933; Yorktown; York **GS:** U **SP:** No info **VI:** No further data **P:** unk **BLW:** unk **RG:** Y **MK:** unk **PH:** unk **SS:** J-Yorktown Historian; SAR P-272686 **BS:** JLARC 1, 74.

POUVEREAU, Jean; b unk; d 1781 **RU:** Soldier, Served in Santogne Bn and died fr battle at Yorktown **CEM:** French Memorial; GPS 36.81944, -79.39933; Yorktown; York **GS:** U **SP:** No info **VI:** No further data **P:** unk **BLW:** unk **RG:** Y **MK:** unk **PH:** unk **SS:** J-Yorktown Historian; SAR P-272689 **BS:** JLARC 1, 74.

POWELL, John; b 1746; d unk **RU:** Doctor/Captain, Served in Col Meriweathers' Militia 1781, and died fr battle at Yorktown **CEM:** Unidentified; GPS unk; Yorktown; York **GS:** U **SP:** No info **VI:** No further data **P:** unk **BLW:** unk **RG:** Y **MK:** N **PH:** unk **SS:** AS DAR report; AZ pg 143; SAR P-272746 **BS:** 80 vol3, pg 185 (**POWELL**, Joshua See Appendix G, Addenda)

POWELL, Lucas; b 1722; d 1811 **RU:** Patriot, Gave material aid to the cause; also had public service as Juror and member of Committee of Safety **CEM:** Powell Family; GPS unk; Amherst; Amherst **GS:** Y **SP:** Mar (1752) Elizabeth Edwards **VI:** No further data **P:** N **BLW:** N **RG:** Y **MK:** N **PH:** unk **SS:** AL CT BK pg 10; AS; SAR Appl; DD; DAR A092099; SAR P-272781 **BS:** SAR Appl.

POWELL, Ptolemy; b c1766 or 1767, King William Co; d 1840 **RU:** Private, Served at age15 fr 1777-1783 **CEM:** Green Level; GPS unk; Rt 652; Spotsylvania **GS:** Y **SP:** Sidney Daniel (1768-1843) Widow of James Leavette **VI:** No further data **P:** unk **BLW:** unk **RG:** Y **MK:** Y **PH:** unk **SS:** 08 Vol 1 pg 417-8; SAR P-272803 **BS:** 09 Part 2.

POWELL, William; b 1758; d 1829 **RU:** Lieutenant, Served in Co 3, Col Danial Morgan's Regt Jun 1777 **CEM:** Shady Grove Methodist; GPS unk; 11007 W Catharpin, Shady Grove Corner; Spotsylvania **GS:** U **SP:** No info **VI:** Blw 2666 Acres rec'd 08 Mar 1833 **P:** unk **BLW:** Y **RG:** N **MK:** unk **PH:** unk **SS:** E pg 635 **BS:** 196.

PRADHOUT, Jean; b unk; d 1781 **RU:** Soldier, Served in Touraine Bn and died fr battle at Yorktown **CEM:** French Memorial; GPS 36.81944, -79.39933; Yorktown; York **GS:** U **SP:** No info **VI:** No further data **P:** unk **BLW:** unk **RG:** Y **MK:** unk **PH:** unk **SS:** J-Yorktown Historian; SAR P-272970 **BS:** JLARC 1, 74.

PRATT, Anne Birkett; b 26 Oct 1718; d 8 May 1800 **RU:** Patriot, Provided one day 5 hands to ferry cattle to camp across Rappahannock River and pasturage for 80 cattle for 3 days, plus a beef and two bushels of corn **CEM:** Hungerford-Griffin; GPS; 38.105994 -76.9855706; 373 Resolutions Rd, Leedstown; Westmoreland **GS:** Y **SP:** Thomas Hungerford (1740-1803) **VI:** d/o John (__-1724) & Margaret (Birkett) (__-1749) Pratt **P:** N **BLW:** N **RG:** Y **MK:** Y SAR plaque **PH:** Y **SS:** D pg 2, 9: AL Ct bk pg 1, 4 & Comm Bk V pg 220; SAR P-336117 **BS:** 196.

PRATT, John Birkett; b 4 Sep 1761; d 15 Jan 1843 **RU:** Corporal, Served in 3rd, 4th, 5th, & 8th Cont Lines for 3 yrs **CEM:** Pratt Family; GPS unk; Rt 686 Camden Rd; Caroline **GS:** U **SP:** Alice Fitzhugh (1789-1845) **VI:** No further data **P:** unk **BLW:** unk **RG:** N **MK:** N **PH:** unk **SS:** E pg 636; C pg 488 **BS:** 02 pg 117,118; 196.

PRENTIS, Joseph; b 24 Jan 1754, York Co; d 19 Jun 1809 **RU:** Patriot, Was member of VA Convention1775, and Judge of Court of Admiralty during Revolution, and a member of VA House of Delegates 1777-78. Was Speaker of the House 1778, and member of Privy Council under Gov Patrick Henry 1779-81 **CEM:** Green Hill; GPS unk; Nassau St; Williamsburg City **GS:** N **SP:** Mar (16 Dec 1778)

RU=Rank/Unit	CEM=Cemetery	GS=Gravestone	SP=Spousal Information
VI=Other Veteran Info	P=Pension	BLW=Bounty/Land Warrant	RG=Registered Grave
MK=SAR/DAR Marker	PH=Photo	SS=Service Source	BS=Burial Source

339

Margaret Bowden (27 Nov 1758-27 Aug 1801) **VI:** No further data **P:** N **BLW:** N **RG:** Y **MK:** N **PH:** N **SS:** G pg 546, 47 Vol 6 No 3 pg 190, 199; SAR P-273372 **BS:** 32.

PRESTON, Francis; b 2 Aug 1765, Botetourt Co; d 26 May 1835, Columbia SC **RU:** Private/Patriot, Served in Botetourt Co Militia.Had civil service as a VA senator in 1783 **CEM:** Aspenvale; GPS 36.81420, -81.64000; Rts 641 & 642, Seven Mile Ford; Smyth **GS:** Y **SP:** Sarah Buchanan Campbell (1778-1846) d/o Gen William Campbell **VI:** Son of William Preston (1729-1823) & Susanna (Smith) (1740-1823), d/o Francis Smith (1705-1775) & Elizabeth Waddy (1708-1799). He was Brig Gen in War of 1812 and US Congressman 1793-1797. He was elected a member of the Virginia State House of Delegates, serving 1812-14, 1816-1820. He died in Columbia SC **P:** unk **BLW:** N **RG:** Y **MK:** Y DAR plaque **PH:** Unk **SS:** J-NSSAR 1993 Reg; C pg 617; CD; SAR P-273527 **BS:** JLARC 1; 97 pg 8; 196.

PRESTON, John; b May 1762; d Mar 1787 **RU:** Captain, Served in Montgomery Co Militia **CEM:** Weaver's; GPS unk; Not identified; Bristol City **GS:** U **SP:** 1) Mary Radford 2) Msr (1811) Elizabeth Ann Carrington of Richmond **VI:** Held rank after war Lt Col and Maj General. Treasurer of VA 1808-1819 **P:** unk **BLW:** unk **RG:** N **MK:** N **PH:** unk **SS:** J-NSSAR 1993 Reg; AZ pg 131; **BS:** JLARC 1.

PRESTON, John; b 2 May 1764; d 27 Mar 1827 **RU:** Private, Served in Capt James Bryne's Co in 1781 **CEM:** Greenfield; GPS 37.43750, -79.91420; Off International Pkwy, W of Rt 220, Amsterdam; Botetourt **GS:** U **SP:** No info **VI:** Maj General in War of 1812. Treasurer of VA. Prestonburg, KY named for him **P:** unk **BLW:** unk **RG:** N **MK:** N **PH:** unk **SS:** G pg 241 **BS:** 115 pg 77; 196.

PRESTON, John; b 24 Feb 1750 Buckingham, Bucks Co PA; d 24 Jun 1820 or 1829 **RU:** Private, Served in Capt John Thomas, 2nd Co, 4th Bn, Bucks Co PA **CEM:** South River Meeting House (aka Quaker Memorial Presbyterian); GPS 37.37246, -79.19194; 5810 Fort Ave; Lynchburg City **GS:** Y **SP:** Rebecca Vickers (1753-1834) **VI:** Son of John (1699-1785) & Elizabeth (Tucker) (1728-1752) Preston. Died in Campbell Co. DAR plaque **P:** unk **BLW:** unk **RG:** Y **MK:** Y DAR plaque **PH:** N **SS:** CD cites PA service; SAR P-273541 **BS:** JLARC 2, 4, 36; 80, vol3,pg 189; 196.

PRESTON, Robert; b 1750, Ireland; d 16 Dec 1833 **RU:** Private, Served in Capt Thomas Tebb's Co, Col Alexander Spotswood's 2nd VA Regt Jan-Jun 1777. Fought at Point Pleasant and Kings Mountain **CEM:** Walnut Grove; GPS unk; 3012 Lee Hwy Rt 11; Bristol City **GS:** Y **SP:** Margaret Rhea (1757-4 Jun 1822) **VI:** DAR marker **P:** unk **BLW:** unk **RG:** Y **MK:** Y SAR **PH:** unk **SS:** A pg 277; SAR P-273577 **BS:** JLARC 2, 4, 34, 80; 78 pg 376; 80 vol 3 pg 190; 196.

PRESTON, William; b 25 Dec 1729, Lima Vaddy, Ireland; d 1783 **RU:** Colonel/Patriot, Performed civil service as County Lt and a member of Committee of Safety and Justice of Peace **CEM:** Smithfield Plantation; GPS unk; VMI Campus, Blacksburg; Montgomery **GS:** U **SP:** Mar (17 Jul 1761) Susanna Smith (4 Jan 1739-19 Jun 1823) **VI:** No further data **P:** unk **BLW:** unk **RG:** Y **MK:** unk **PH:** unk **SS:** DAR #A092996; J-NSSAR 1993 Reg, AL Ct Bk pg 11 Loudoun Co; CZ pg 258 **BS:** JLARC 1, 2; 80 vol 3 pg 190.

PRESTON, William; b 1745; d 1781 **RU:** General, Was hero of Kings Mountain. Died near Richmond serving under Gen LaFayette **CEM:** Aspenvale; GPS 36.81420, -81.64000; Rts 641 & 642, Seven Mile Ford; Smyth **GS:** U **SP:** No info **VI:** Remains were brought to Aspenville Cemetery in 1932 **P:** unk **BLW:** unk **RG:** unk **MK:** unk **PH:** unk **SS:** E pg 637; SAR P-273597 **BS:** JLARC 97; 97 Vol 1 pg 8.

PREVOST, Charles; b unk; d 1781 **RU:** Soldier, Served in Santogne Bn and died fr battle at Yorktown **CEM:** French Memorial; GPS 36.81944, -79.39933; Yorktown; York **GS:** U **SP:** No info **VI:** No further data **P:** unk **BLW:** unk **RG:** Y **MK:** unk **PH:** unk **SS:** J-Yorktown Historian; SAR P-273610 **BS:** JLARC 1, 74.

PRIBBLE (PREBBLE), John; b 1760, MD; d 14 Oct 1850 **RU:** Soldier, Ent Serv 1777 Bedford Co. Militia, VA Line. Served in Capts Charles Watkins, Robert Adams in Cols Calloway and Boones Regts **CEM:** Pribble - Dunn; GPS 37.30800, -79.24700; Castle Craig Quadrant, Evington; Campbell **GS:** U **SP:** Mar (1779, Campbell Co) Elizabeth Mason (1759 Henrico Co-__) **VI:** Lived on Otter River (later Campbell Co). Pensioned Campbell Co age 73 S5951 **P:** Y **BLW:** unk **RG:** Y **MK:** N **PH:** unk **SS:** K Vol 4 pg 143; CG Vol 3 pg 2768; DD; DAR A093028; SAR P-273627 **BS:** JLARC 4, 36.

RU=Rank/Unit	CEM=Cemetery	GS=Gravestone	SP=Spousal Information
VI=Other Veteran Info	P=Pension	BLW=Bounty/Land Warrant	RG=Registered Grave
MK=SAR/DAR Marker	PH=Photo	SS=Service Source	BS=Burial Source

340

PRICE, Augustine; b 24 Dec 1754; d 8 Feb 1820 **RU:** Teamster/Patriot, Gave material aid to cause **CEM:** Old Peaked Mountain; **GPS** 38.37113, -78.73416; 9843 Town Hall Rd, McGaheysville; Rockingham **GS:** U **SP:** Margaret Margaret Miller **VI:** Son of Augustice & Anna Elizabeth (Scherp) Preisch. Died in Ohio **P:** unk **BLW:** unk **RG:** Y **MK:** Y SAR **PH:** unk **SS:** J-NSSAR 2000 Reg; AL Ct Bk II pg 25 Rockingham Co; BT plaque; SAR P-273632 **BS:** JLARC 76; 196.

PRICE, Barrett (Barret); b 17 Apr 1749, Henrico Co; d 4 Sep 1794 **RU:** Captain/Patriot, Gave material aid to cause **CEM:** Hollywood; **GPS** 37.53560, -77.45720; 412 S Cherry St; Richmond City **GS:** U **SP:** Mar (25 Aug 1771) Sarah Graves (1755, Goochland Co-Jul 1852) **VI:** No further data **P:** unk **BLW:** unk **RG:** Y **MK:** unk **PH:** unk **SS:** DAR #A093021; J-NSSAR 1993 Reg; AL Ct Bk pg 9 Henrico Co; DD; SAR P-273634 **BS:** JLARC 1.

PRICE, John Michael, Sr; b 9 Oct 1719, Germany, d 1802 **RU:** Patriot, had civil service, Montgomery Co **CEM:** Wall Family; **GPS** 37.2117500, -80.4708000; loc edge of field on Brunswick Dr; Montgomery **GS:** Y **SP:** Margaret Killian (1726, Germany-1810) **VI:** No further data **P:** N **BLW:** N **RG:** Y **MK:** DAR **PH:** N **SS:** SAR P-273679 cites Summers, Annals of SW VA, part 1, pg 749; DAR A093008 **BS:** 196 memorial # 9086434

PRICE, Joseph; b 1753; d 1828 **RU:** Patriot, Gave material aid to cause **CEM:** Price Family; GPS unk; Nr Cattail Branch & Willis River; Cumberland **GS:** Y **SP:** No info **VI:** DAR Bur Source 80 doesn't agree with DAR A092995 with PA burial **P:** N **BLW:** N **RG:** Y **MK:** N **PH:** unk **SS:** AL Ct Bk pg 3, 14, 31 Cumberland Co; AS; DAR A092995; SAR P-273685 **BS:** 80 vol 3 pg 190.

PRICE, Joseph; b 1712; d 28 Apr 1783 **RU:** Patriot, Gave material aid to cause **CEM:** Joseph Shores Price Family; GPS unk; Rt 817 or Dillions Mill; Franklin **GS:** U **SP:** Ann Shores (1713-28 Feb 1791) d/o Richard (1700-1750) & Susanna (------) Shores **VI:** No further data **P:** N **BLW:** N **RG:** Y **MK:** unk **PH:** unk **SS:** AL Ct Bk pg 5a, 30 Henry Co; DAR A092997; SAR P-273682 **BS:** 80 vol3 pg 190; 196.

PRICE, Joseph Shores; b 17 Jul 1734, New Kent Co; d 20 Oct 1801 **RU:** Patriot, Gave material aid to cause **CEM:** Joseph Shores Price Family; GPS unk; Rt 817 or Dillions Mill; Franklin **GS:** U **SP:** Carity Bagby (1735-6 Feb 1803) d/o James M & Marietta (McNail) Bagby **VI:** Son of Joseph (1712-28 Apr 1783) & Ann (Shores) (1713-28 Feb 1791) Price. Died in Buckingham Co **P:** N **BLW:** N **RG:** Y **MK:** unk **PH:** unk **SS:** AL Ct Bk III pg 149; DAR A093001; SAR P-273688 **BS:** 196.

PRICE, Michael I; Jr; b 15 Jan 1748, New River, Montgomery Co d 24 Jun 1839 **RU:** Private, served in Capt John Taylor's Co, Montgomery Co Militia. **CEM:** Wall Family; **GPS** 37.2117500,-80.4708000; loc edge of field on Brunswick Dr; Montgomery **GS:** Y **SP:** Mar 1782, Ester Francisco (1749, Toms Creek, Montgomery Co-16 Apr 1854, Augusta Co) **VI:** No further data **P:** N **BLW:** N **RG:** N **MK:** DAR **PH:** N **SS:** G pg 235 **BS:** 196

PRICE, Richard; b 1756; d unk **RU:** Sergeant, Served in Capt William Russell's Co, Russell Co Militia **CEM:** Elk Garden; GPS unk; On Red Wine Plantation, Elk Garden; Russell **GS:** N **SP:** Priscilla Crabtree (1757, Salt Lick-__) Elk Garden) **VI:** Became a famous preacher **P:** N **BLW:** N **RG:** Y **MK:** N **PH:** N **SS:** Z pg 154; SAR P-327029 **BS:** 196.

PRICE, Thomas Sr; b 29 Aug 1754, "Forks of Hanover," Hanover Co; d 21 or 22 Dec 1836 **RU:** Captain, Ent serv Hanover Co 25 Sept 1832. Served in VA Line **CEM:** Fork Episcopal Church; **GPS** 37.85340, -77.53100; 12566 Old Ridge Rd, Doswell; Hanover **GS:** Y **SP:** Barbara Winston (__-21 May 1831) **VI:** DAR marker. Pensioned Hanover Co 1832. S5954 **P:** Y **BLW:** Y **RG:** Y **MK:** unk **PH:** N **SS:** J-NSSAR 1993 Reg, J- DAR Hatcher; K Vol 4 pg 146; CG Vol 3 pg 2771; SAR P-273755 **BS:** JLARC 1, 2; 80 vol3 pg 190; 196; 213 pg 586.

PRICE, William; b 16 Sep 1759; Henrico Co, d 27 Jun 1830 **RU:** Major, Served in 1st Va Regt, 1776. Discharged 1783 at Point of Fork **CEM:** Shockoe Hill; **GPS** 37.55190, -77.43170; 4th & Hospital Sts; Richmond City **GS:** Y **SP:** Sarah Lewis (8 Apr 1772 Goochland Co-26 Jan 1837) d/o Richard & (-----) Lewis of Goochland **VI:** Was register of VA land office for many yrs. Recd BLW of 2666 acres 22 Mar 1783 #1440. Pen fr Richmond City by special Act of Congress, #199. Widow pensioned 1833 by special Act of Congress, no file number **P:** Y **BLW:** Y **RG:** Y **MK:** Y SAR monument **PH:** unk **SS:** A pg 388; SAR P-339624 **BS:** 57 pg 8.

RU=Rank/Unit	CEM=Cemetery	GS=Gravestone	SP=Spousal Information
VI=Other Veteran Info	P=Pension	BLW=Bounty/Land Warrant	RG=Registered Grave
MK=SAR/DAR Marker	PH=Photo	SS=Service Source	BS=Burial Source

341

PRICE, William; b 22 Jan 1725, Orange Co; d 15 Sep 1807 **RU**: Patriot, Gave material aid to cause **CEM**: Edward Lewis; GPS unk; Nr Heidleback School, Rt 712 Dodson; Patrick **GS**: U **SP**: Mar (1752) Mary Morton (12 Nov 1733, Goochland Co-1815, Prince Edward Co) d/o Joseph (27 Dec 1709 Henrico Co-28 Jun 1782, Charlotte Co) & Mary (Goode) (c1712-1734) Morton **VI**: No further data **P**: N **BLW**: N **RG**: N **MK**: unk **PH**: unk **SS**: AL Ct Bk pg 28 Pittsylvania Co **BS**: 196.

PRIDE, John, III; b 1741, d 1794 **RU**: Patriot, served as VA House of Delegates from Amelia Co 1778 to 1782, also gave material aid to cause **CEM**: Pride Family GPS not determined; Pridesville Rd, property of Wayne Keene, 1949 (Deed Bk 99, pg 298); Amelia **GS**: Unk **SP**: No spousal info **VI**: Son of John Pride Jr (__-1773) and Frances Rowlett(1717-1785). A VA Senator 1782-1793 **P**: N **BLW**: N **RG**: N **MK**: N **PH**: N **SS**: AL Ct Bk I, pgs 29,40 Bk II, pgs 8,49 **BS**: 196.

PRIDE, William; b 1740, d 1777 **RU**; Quarter Master, Field and Staff, 5th VA Regt **CEM**: Pride Family; GPS: not determined; Pridesville Rd; Amelia **GS**: Unk **SP**: Mar 31 Aug 1764, Amelia Co, Mary (Molly) Townes (1742-__) **VI**: Will probated in Charlotte Co 4 Aug 1777 **P**: N **BLW**: N **RG**: N **MK**: N **PH**: N **SS**: Fold3 Serv Index Cards **BS**: 196.

PRILLAMAN (PRILLMAN), Jacob Sr; b 1721; d Aft Sep 1796 **RU**: Patriot, Gave material aid to cause **CEM**: Prillaman; GPS 37.01080, -80.06080; Foothills Rd Rt 642 W of Highland United Methodist, Callaway; Franklin **GS**: U **SP**: Mar (c1750) Walburga Helm (c1723-22 Mar 1799) **VI**: No further data **P**: N **BLW**: N **RG**:Y **MK**: unk **PH**: unk **SS**: DAR #A093217; AL Ct Bk pg 37 Henry Co; SAR P-273846 **BS**: JLARC 3.

PRINTZ, George; b cNov1741, Duerhren/Baden, Germany; d 8 May 1834 **RU**: Captain, Was aide to Washington. Also commanded a co in Nelson's Corps of Lt Dragoons **CEM**: Printz or Prince Family; GPS unk; Rt 651 nr Ida; Page **GS**: U **SP**: mar (1764) Elizabeth Henry, 2) Mary Magdalene Shaffer **VI**: No further data **P**: unk **BLW**: unk **RG**: Y **MK**: unk **PH**: unk **SS**: SAR P-273929; DAR #A093238 **BS**: JLARC 1, 2, 94; 80 vol 3, pg 191.

PRINTZ (PRINCE), Gottlieb (Cutlip); b 20 Sep 1752 York Co; d 15 Dec 1806 **RU**: Private, Served in Capt Joseph Bowman's Co fr Shenandoah Co, Lt Col William Crawford's Regt, Frederick Co. Was at Point Pleasant 1774. Served at Romney, PA 2 Nov 1775 **CEM**: Printz or Prince Family; GPS unk; Rt 651 nr Ida; Page **GS**: U **SP**: Magdeline Crumm **VI**: No further data **P**: unk **BLW**: unk **RG**: Y **MK**: unk **PH**: unk **SS**: J-NSSAR 1993 Reg, J- DAR Hatcher; N pg 1251; Z pg 51; SAR P-273930 **BS**: JLARC 1, 2; 80 vol3, pg 191.

PRINTZ (PRINCE), Philip; b 1747; d 1806 **RU**: Private, Served in Michael Reader's Co, Shenandoah Co **CEM**: Printz or Prince Family; GPS unk; Rt 651 nr Ida; Page **GS**: U **SP**: No info **VI**: No further data **P**: unk **BLW**: unk **RG**: Y **MK**: unk **PH**: unk **SS**: SAR P-273932; J-NSSAR 1993 Reg; C pg 603 **BS**: JLARC 1.

PRIOUX, Gilles; b unk; d 1781 **RU**: Seaman, Served on "Ville de Paris" and died from Yorktown battle **CEM**: French Memorial; GPS 36.81944, -79.39933; Yorktown; York **GS**: U **SP**: No info **VI**: No further data **P**: unk **BLW**: unk **RG**: Y **MK**: unk **PH**: unk **SS**: J-Yorktown Historian; SAR P-273945 **BS**: JLARC 1, 74.

PRITCHARD, Stephen Cornelius; b 1745; d 1819 **RU**: Private/Patriot, a person this name served in the 1st SC Regt; as patriot paid personal property tax 1782 in Frederick Co considered to be used to pay Rev War expenses **CEM**: Pritchard Family; GPS 39.145290, -78.196410; loc 150 yds W of Kerrnstown Ct in field; Kernstown, Frederick **GS**: Y **SP**:No spousal data **VI**: Son of Reese Pritchard, Jr (1710-1760) **P**: N **BLW**: N **RG**: N **MK**: N **PH**: N **SS**: Fold3 Serv Index Cards; ER Frederick Co tax list 1782 **BS**: 196.

PROFIT(PROFFIT)(PROFFITT), David, b 1730; d 6 May 1803, Amherst Co; **RU**: Patriot, paid personal propery tax as head of family in Amherst Co 1783, considered to be a supply tax for Rev War expenses **CEM**: Proffitt; GPS not determined; loc on property of Sylvester Proffitt, Goochland: Goochland **GS**: Unk **SP**: Mar 7 Apr 1757 in St James Parrish, Goochland, Elizabeth Smith **VI**: Son of Sylvester Proffitt (1698, Scotland-1767) & Alice Pleasants(1698-1771) **P**: N **BLW**: N **RG**: N **MK**: N **PH**: N **SS**: ER Amherst Co head of property list 1783 **BS**: 196.

PROU, Joseph; b unk; d 1781 **RU**: Soldier, Served in Bourbonnais Bn and died fr battle at Yorktown **CEM**: French Memorial; GPS 36.81944, -79.39933; Yorktown; York **GS**: U **SP**: No info **VI**: No further

RU=Rank/Unit	CEM=Cemetery	GS=Gravestone	SP=Spousal Information
VI=Other Veteran Info	P=Pension	BLW=Bounty/Land Warrant	RG=Registered Grave
MK=SAR/DAR Marker	PH=Photo	SS=Service Source	BS=Burial Source

data **P:** unk **BLW:** unk **RG:** Y **MK:** unk **PH:** unk **SS:** J-Yorktown Historian; SAR P-274066 **BS:** JLARC 1, 74.

PROUX, Pierre; b unk; d 1781 **RU:** Soldier, Served in Bourbonnais Bn and died fr battle at Yorktown **CEM:** French Memorial; GPS 36.81944, -79.39933; Yorktown; York **GS:** U **SP:** No info **VI:** No further data **P:** unk **BLW:** unk **RG:** Y **MK:** unk **PH:** unk **SS:** J-Yorktown Historian; SAR P-274096 **BS:** JLARC 1, 74.

PROVOL, Charles; b unk; d 1781 **RU:** Soldier, Served in Soissonnais Bn and died fr battle at Yorktown **CEM:** French Memorial; GPS 36.81944, -79.39933; Yorktown; York **GS:** U **SP:** No info **VI:** No further data **P:** unk **BLW:** unk **RG:** Y **MK:** unk **PH:** unk **SS:** J-Yorktown Historian; SAR P-274103 **BS:** JLARC 1, 74.

PRUNTZIGER, Jean; b unk; d 1781 **RU:** Seaman, Served on "Northumberland" and died from Yorktown battle **CEM:** French Memorial; GPS 36.81944, -79.39933; Yorktown; York **GS:** U **SP:** No info **VI:** No further data **P:** unk **BLW:** unk **RG:** Y **MK:** unk **PH:** unk **SS:** J-Yorktown Historian; SAR P-274149 **BS:** JLARC 1, 74.

PRYOR, John; b c1748; d 19 Mar 1823 **RU:** Major, Ent serv 1777 in Cont Artillery. Was Aide-de-Camp to Gen Alexander, 9 Jun 1779. Retired 14 Jan 1783 **CEM:** Shockoe Hill; GPS 37.55190, -77.43170; 4th & Hospital Sts; Richmond City **GS:** Y **SP:** 1) (-----) daughter of Thomas & (-----) Whiting of Gloucester Co, VA 2) mar (22 Feb 1815 Richmond City) Elizabeth Quarles Graves **VI:** BLW issued 10 Aug 1789. W12064, #1750-20-10 for 4555 acres **P:** Y **BLW:** Y **RG:** Y **MK:**Y DAR & SAR, monument **PH:** Y **SS:** E pg 641; K Vol 4 pg 154; CG Vol 3 pg 2782; CD; SAR P-335067 **BS:** 57 pg 1.

PUCKETT, Nathaniel; b 6 Jun 1733, Chesterfield Co, d 1842 **RU:** Private, Entered service 1775 as minuteman in Chesterfield Co under Capt Thomas Goode and Col Joseph Jones. Then enlisted as volunteer under Colonel Thomas Goode and served many other tours thereafter to include Col Boyce's Regt under General Lafayette **CEM:** Shockoe Hill; GPS 37.55190, -77.43170; SAR monument 37.551247,-77.432429; gravestone 37.552387,-77.430884 4th & Hospital Sts; Richmond City **GS:** Unk **SP:** No spousal data **VI:** Rec'd pen 5 Aug 1832 with last payment made in 1841 #S5958 data **P:** Y **BLW:** N **RG:** Y **MK:** Y SAR monument **PH:** N **SS:** G pg 134; K vol 4, pgs 155,156;AP Pension file; CG pg 2782; SAR P-339622 **BS:** 196.

PUGH, Job; b 4 Jul 1737, Prince George Co; d 1809 **RU:** Patriot, Gave material aid to cause **CEM:** Back Creek Quaker, aka Gainesboro United Methodist; GPS 39.27861,-78.25694;166 Siler Ln, Gainesboro; Frederick **GS:** Y **SP:** Ruch John (24 Aug 1741 Chester Co, PA-1804 Frederick Co) **VI:** Son of Jessie & Alice (Malin) Pugh/Peugh, both fr Chester Co, PA **P:** N **BLW:** N **RG:** N **MK:** unk **PH:** unk **SS:** AL Ct Bk pg 18, Shenandoah Co **BS:** 196.

PUGH, Joseph; b c1713; d Aft 7 Jan 1778 **RU:** Patriot, Gave material aid to cause. Also performed public service as High Sheriff, Dunmore Co 1776-1777 **CEM:** Back Creek Quaker, aka Gainesboro United Methodist; GPS 39.27861, -78.25694; 166 Siler Ln, Gainesboro; Frederick **GS:** Y **SP:** Mar (c1750 prob Lancaster Co, PA) Mary Postlethwaite (c1714-aft 28 Dec 1793, Washington Co) **VI:** Bur with other Pughs in cemetery. GS not readable **P:** N **BLW:** N **RG:** N **MK:** unk **PH:** unk **SS:** DAR #A208784; AL Ct Bk pg 9, 18 Shenandoah Co; DD cites Painter, Shenandoah Co & Its Courthouse pg 12, 13 **BS:** 196.

PUISSANT, Etiene; b unk; d 1781 **RU:** Soldier, Served in Soissonnais Bn and died fr battle at Yorktown **CEM:** French Memorial; GPS 36.81944, -79.39933; Yorktown; York **GS:** U **SP:** No info **VI:** No further data **P:** unk **BLW:** unk **RG:** Y **MK:** unk **PH:** unk **SS:** J-Yorktown Historian; SAR P-274226 **BS:** JLARC 1, 74.

PULLER, John; b 27 Aug 1744; d 5 Mar 1818 **RU:** Patriot, Gave material aid to the cause **CEM:** Puller Family; GPS unk; 1 mi E of Amissville; Culpeper **GS:** Y **SP:** mar (23 Apr 1772) Ann (-----) (c1749-21 Apr 1829) **VI:** No further data **P:** N **BLW:** N **RG:** N **MK:** N **PH:** unk **SS:** AL Cert **BS:** 167 Puller.

PULLIN, John; b 1763; d 1828 **RU:** Private?, Specific serv may be found at the Lib of VA, Auditors Accts Vol XVIII pg 681 **CEM:** Court Street Baptist Church; GPS unk; 447 Court St; Portsmouth City **GS:** Y **SP:** Margaret Powell (c1775-1849) **VI:** No further data **P:** unk **BLW:** unk **RG:** N **MK:** N **PH:** unk **SS:** E pg 642; CZ pg 361 **BS:** 27 pg 122.

RU=Rank/Unit	CEM=Cemetery	GS=Gravestone	SP=Spousal Information
VI=Other Veteran Info	P=Pension	BLW=Bounty/Land Warrant	RG=Registered Grave
MK=SAR/DAR Marker	PH=Photo	SS=Service Source	BS=Burial Source

343

PULLIN, Loftus, b c1720, d aft 2 May 1801, Bull Pasture, Bath Co **RU**: Patriot, gave military aid in Augusta Co **CEM**: Shumate-Vance *(AKA Pullin)*; GPS not determined; loc Kermit Sloan farm, Rt 678, McDowell, Highland **GS**: N **SP**: Nancy Ann Jane (Usher) **VI**: Was private in Colonial War and rec'd BLW 50 acres **P**: N **BLW**: N **RG**: Y **MK**: N **PH**: N **SS**: D vol 1 pg 87; DAR A092084; SAR P-274269 **BS**: 196.

PULLIN, Samuel, b 1761, Augusta Co, d Sep 1850 **RU**: Private Served in 2d Bn Augusta Co Militia in Capt Davis Gwin's Co at the battle at Gilford Ct House. A Samuel Pullen (probably him) served as a Pvt in Hazen's Regt, **CEM**: Shumate-Vance *(AKA Pullin)*; GPS not determined; loc Kermit Sloan farm, Rt 678, McDowell; Highland **GS**: Y Gov't **SP**: Mar (bond) 20 Jan 1793, Rockingham Co, Sarah Nancy Henry (1770, Rockingham Co-___) Bath Co), d/o Henry Henry & Mary Chestnuts **VI**: Son of Loftus Pullin (c1720-2 May 1801) & Nancy Ann Jane "Jenny" Usher. Rec'd BLW of 100 acres Jul 1789 # 13600-100-16 **P**: N **BLW**: Y **RG**: Y **MK**: N **PH**: N **SS**: CG pg 2784; DAR A001460; SAR P-274274 **BS**: 196.

PURCELL, John; b 1762; d 15 Aug 1838 **RU**: Private?, Ent serv Prince William Co. Served in Lee's Legion and 1st VA Cont Line. Taken prisoner 10 Sep 1778 **CEM**: Upper Ridge; GPS unk; Rt 739; Frederick **GS**: Y **SP**: 1) (-----) 2) mar (1816) Elizabeth Carter (___-1850) **VI**: Awarded BLW 18 Apr 1794 of 100 acres. Widow appl pen 16 Nov 1846 Washington DC **P**: Y **BLW**: Y **RG**: N **MK**: N **PH**: unk **SS**: E pg 642; CG pg 2786 **BS**: 59 pg 264.

PURCELL, Thomas Sr; b Bapt 9 Apr 1720, Hunterdon Co, NJ; d Aft 17 Apr 1779 **RU**: Patriot, Gave material aid to the cause **CEM**: Petts Family; GPS unk; Purcellville; Loudoun **GS**: Y **SP**: Mary Van Hook (1723-___) **VI**: No further data **P**: N **BLW**: N **RG**: N **MK**: N **PH**: unk **SS**: DAR #A092227; SAR P-274323 AL Ct Bk pg 75 **BS**: 80 vol3 pg 193; SAR Appl.

PURDIE, George; b by 1758; d Aft 1820 **RU**: Patriot, Gave use of wagon and sundry items for the Nansemond Militia. Also furnished sulfer for public use. On 5 Oct 1780 appt by court to arrange for repair of court house damaged by the enemy **CEM**: St Luke's Church; GPS 36.93940, -76.58670; 14477 Benns Church Blvd, Smithfield; Isle of Wight **GS**: Y **SP**: Mar (1784 Isle of Wight Co) Mary Robinson **VI**: No further data **P**: N **BLW**: N **RG**: N **MK**: N **PH**: unk **SS**: G pg 193 **BS**: 117 pg 6.

PURSEL, Samuel; b 1760, d13 May 1828 **RU**: Patriot, Supported cause by paying supply tax included in his personal property tax in 1783, Loudoun Co **CEM**: Old Potts; GPS 39.19455,-77.76157; loc vic Shannondale Rd and Edgegrove Rd, Hillsboro; Loudoun **GS**: Yes **SP**: Margaret (-----) (26 Feb 1769-17 Jun 1849) **VI**: No further data **P**: N **BLW**: N **RG**: N **MK**: N **PH**: N **SS**: DV 1783 Loudoun Co, part 1783A, image 11 pdf **BS**: 196.

QUARLES, John; b 1745, King William Co; d 7 Jan 1798 **RU**: Colonel, Served in Prince William District Bn Mar 1776. May have given to cause. Gr Stone inscription shows was Capt of Artillery Co **CEM**: Quarles Family; GPS unk; SE fr Bedford; Bedford **GS**: Y Gov't **SP**: Mar (c1774) Sarah Winston (9 Feb 1747 Hanover Co.-28 Jan 1822) **VI**: No further data **P**: unk **BLW**: unk **RG**: Y **MK**: N **PH**: N **SS**: J- DAR Hatcher; CE pg 22; SAR P-274708 **BS**: JLARC 2;80 vol 3 pg 196; 196.

QUARLES, John; b unk; d 1844 **RU**: Patriot, Gave material aid to cause **CEM**: St John's Episcopal; GPS 37.53183, -77.41958; 2401 E Broad St; Richmond City **GS**: Y **SP**: No info **VI**: No further data **P**: N **BLW**: N **RG**: N **MK**: N **PH**: unk **SS**: D Vol 2 pg 581; AL Ct Bk pg 11 New Kent Co **BS**: 28 pg 351.

QUARLES, Minor; b 1762; d 1831 **RU**: Patriot, Gave material aid to cause **CEM**: Carmel Baptist; GPS unk; 24230 Jefferson Davis Pkwy, Ruther Glen; Caroline **GS**: Y **SP**: Sarah Nelson **VI**: Son of William & Merry (Terry) Quarles. Grave reinterred fr homes on the North Anna River. Has newer memorial stone **P**: N **BLW**: N **RG**: N **MK**: N **PH**: unk **SS**: AL Ct Bk lt II pg 22 **BS**: 14 pg 22; 196.

QUARLES, William; b 1735; d 1817 **RU**: Patriot, Gave material aid to Capt Parker's Militia Co **CEM**: Carmel Baptist; GPS unk; 24230 Jefferson Davis Pkwy, Ruther Glen; Caroline **GS**: Y **SP**: Merry Terry **VI**: Has newer memorial stone **P**: N **BLW**: N **RG**: Y **MK**: N **PH**: N **SS**: D pg 857, 862, 880; DAR A132368; SAR P-274714 **BS**: 14 pg 22; 196.

QUENARD, Pierre; b unk; d 1781 **RU**: Soldier, Served in Gatinais Bn and died fr battle at Yorktown **CEM**: French Memorial; GPS 36.81944, -79.39933; Yorktown; York **GS**: U **SP**: No info **VI**: No further data **P**: unk **BLW**: unk **RG**: Y **MK**: unk **PH**: unk **SS**: J-Yorktown Historian; SAR P-274739 **BS**: JLARC 1,74.

RU=Rank/Unit	CEM=Cemetery	GS=Gravestone	SP=Spousal Information
VI=Other Veteran Info	P=Pension	BLW=Bounty/Land Warrant	RG=Registered Grave
MK=SAR/DAR Marker	PH=Photo	SS=Service Source	BS=Burial Source

344

QUERJEAN, Herve; b unk; d 1781 **RU:** Seaman, Served on "Hextor" and died from Yorktown battle **CEM:** French Memorial; GPS 36.81944, -79.39933; Yorktown; York **GS:** U **SP:** No info **VI:** No further data **P:** unk **BLW:** unk **RG:** Y **MK:** unk **PH:** unk **SS:** J-Yorktown Historian; SAR P-274741 **BS:** JLARC 1,74.

RADER (RIDER), Adam; b 4 Feb 1761, Germany; d 28 Nov 1817 **RU:** Soldier, Served in 11th Cont Line **CEM:** Rader Family; GPS unk; Past Motts Hill Ln on right, take left on Radar Barn Rd, N of Troutville on Rt 11; Botetourt **GS:** N **SP:** mar (14 Jan 1789) Mary Hotzenpeller (7 May 1769, Frederick Co-11 Mar 1853) d/o Peter (__-1782) & Anna (-----) Hotzenpeller **VI:** Immigrant Ancestor of Radars in Botetourt Co **P:** unk **BLW:** unk **RG:** Y **MK:** N **PH:** N **SS:** DAR #A093349; E pg 686; BY SAR applic; SAR P-274927 **BS:** JLARC 60, 124.

RADFORD, Richard; b unk; d 19 Nov 1843 **RU:** Patriot, Gave material aid to cause **CEM:** St John's Episcopal; GPS 37.53183, -77.41958; 2401 E Broad St; Richmond City **GS:** N **SP:** No info **VI:** No further data **P:** N **BLW:** N **RG:** N **MK:** N **PH:** N **SS:** D Vol 3 pg 775 **BS:** 28 pg 350.

RAGLAND, John; b 1751; d 2 Jun 1831 **RU:** Private, Served in 10th & 14th Cont Line. Served Capt Winston's Co 14th VA Regt, Cont Line **CEM:** St John's Episcopal; GPS unk; 197 Mountain Rd, Halifax; Halifax **GS:** U **SP:** mar (1780) Elizabeth Pettus (__ Lunenburg Co-1834 Halifax Co) **VI:** No further data **P:** unk **BLW:** unk **RG:** Y **MK:** unk **PH:** unk **SS:** DAR A093390; J- DAR Hatcher; E pg 646; G pg 770; SAR P-274970 **BS:** JLARC 2; 80 vol 3 pg 199..

RAGLAND, John Dudley; b 1761, Hanover Co; d 17 Jun 1832, Goochland Co **RU:** Lieutenant, Ent serv Henrico Co, 1777. Served in 1st VA Regt as Lt **CEM:** Charlie Londeree; GPS unk; DAR and SAR burial sources do not provide location; Buckingham **GS:** U **SP:** Mar (23 Oct 1788, Hanover Co) Margaret S. Thompson (__ Goochland Co-18 Nov 1844, Goochland Co) **VI:** Son of John Jr (1721-__) & Ann (Dudley) (4 Jul 1737-__) Ragland, both of Hanover Co. DAR plaque. Pension appl for 15 Sep 1832, Buckingham Co, S5974. Widow also recd pension # W5662 **P:** Y **BLW:** N **RG:** Y **MK:** Y DAR plaque **PH:** unk **SS:** DAR A093392; K Vol 4 pg 172; CG Vol 3 pg 2800; SAR P-274971 **BS:** JLARC 4, 44, 59.

RAGLAND, Reuben; b c1740, Hanover Co; d Aft 26 Dec 1806 **RU:** Lieutenant/Patriot, Served in Capt James Hill's Co Halifax Co Militia. Gave material aid to cause **CEM:** Ragland Family; GPS unk; Check property records for location. Also see DAR Senate Doc 93, vol 54; Halifax **GS:** U **SP:** Ann (-----) (__ Hanover Co-Dec 1806, Halifax Co) **VI:** No further data **P:** unk **BLW:** unk **RG:** Y **MK:** unk **PH:** unk **SS:** DAR A093395; AR Vol 3 pg 199; AL Ct Bk pg 11, 30 Halifax Co; DD cites Halifax Co Order Book 9 pg 261 Jun 1779; SAR P-274974 **BS:** JLARC 2; 80, vol 3, pg 199.

RAGLAND, William, Jr; b 1759, d 1789 **RU:** Private, served n 6th Cont Line **CEM:** Mc Donough; GPS not determined; loc McDonough; Henry **GS:** N **SP:** No info **VI:** No further data **P:** unk **BLW:** unk **RG:** Y **MK:** N **PH:** N **SS:** E pg 647; SAR P-274981 **BS:**; 80 vol 3 pg 199 Henry **GS:** N **SP:** No info **VI:** No further data **P:** unk **BLW:** unk **RG:** Y **MK:** N **PH:** N **SS:** E pg 647; SAR P-274961 **BS:** DAR report; 80 vol 3 pg 199.

RAINEY (RAINY), Williamson; b 2 Nov 1760, Mecklenburg Co; d 1847 **RU:** Private, Ent serv Mecklenburg Co 1776-77. Served in VA Line **CEM:** Rainey Family; GPS unk; Rt 627; Mecklenburg **GS:** U **SP:** Mar (23 Nov 1779) Edith Morgan. Francis Rainey, security, note fr Reuben Morgan. **VI:** Pension appl for 23 Oct 1841 Mecklenburg Co R8563 **P:** Y **BLW:** unk **RG:** Y **MK:** unk **PH:** unk **SS:** J- DAR Hatcher; K Vol 4 pg 173; CG Vol 3 pg 2801; SAR P-275048 **BS:** JLARC 2.

RALSTONE/ ROLSTONE (ROLSTON/RALSTON), David see Rolstone

RAMEY, Sanford; b 2 Jan 1759; d 25 Jul 1828 **RU:** Patriot, Gave material aid to cause **CEM:** Catoctin Free Church; GPS 39.16274, -77.64527; Charlestown Pike Rt 9, Paeonian Springs; Loudoun **GS:** Y **SP:** Lydia Wilson (30 Mar 1767-30 Jun 1845) **VI:** No further data **P:** N **BLW:** N **RG:** N **MK:** N **PH:** unk **SS:** D Vol 2 pg 606 **BS:** 25 pg 253; 196.

RAMSAY, Dennis; b 1756; d 1 Sep 1810 **RU:** Colonel, Capt in an Alexandria Regt in Aug 1777. Was capt at battle at Germantown. Later in war may have achieved rank of Col **CEM:** Presbyterian Church; GPS 38.80015, -77.05791; Wilkes St & Hamilton Ln; Alexandria City **GS:** Y **SP:** Jane Allen Taylor (c1768-24 Nov 1848) death notice in Alexandria Gazette 25 Nov 1814, p. 3 **VI:** Son of William (1716-

RU=Rank/Unit	CEM=Cemetery	GS=Gravestone	SP=Spousal Information
VI=Other Veteran Info	P=Pension	BLW=Bounty/Land Warrant	RG=Registered Grave
MK=SAR/DAR Marker	PH=Photo	SS=Service Source	BS=Burial Source

345

1785) & (-----) Ramsay of Galway Scotland who resided in Alexandria as early as 1744. He possibly made rank of Col after the RW. Death notice in Alexandria Gazette 1 Sep 1840, pg 3 **P:** unk **BLW:** unk **RG:** Y **MK:** Y- SAR Marker **PH:** unk **SS:** G pg 263; AK GW Chapter 2015; DAR A093766; SAR P-275133 **BS:** JLARC 86; 23 pg 65; 196.

RAMSAY, Dennis; b c1741, Cumberland Co, NJ; d 25 Nov 1813 **RU:** Officer, Served in NJ Line **CEM:** First Presbyterian Church; GPS 38.79992, -77.05799; 601 Hamilton Ln; Alexandria City **GS:** U **SP:** Jane Allen Taylor **VI:** No further data **P:** unk **BLW:** unk **RG:** N **MK:** Y SAR Plaque **PH:** unk **SS:** AK GW Chap - 2014 **BS:** 04.

RAMSAY, William; b 1716, Scotland; d 10 Feb 1785 **RU:** Surgeon/Patriot, Justice of Fairfax Co, Public Service as Surgeon. Was a capt of Independent Co of Fairfax Co in 1774. Gave material aid to cause **CEM:** Old Christ Church Episcopal; GPS 38.80625, -77.04718; 118 N Washington St; Alexandria City **GS:** N **SP:** Ann McCarthy (c1730-2 Apr 1785) **VI:** Son of Dr. William & (-----) Ramsey. Justice of Fairfax Co, overseer of Alex Academy, Postmaster 1772. Resided at SE cnr of King & Fairfax Sts, "oldest house in Alexandria" **P:** unk **BLW:** Y **RG:** Y **MK:** N **PH:** N **SS:** 20, pg 141; E pg 649; H; AL Ct Bk pg 20 Fairfax Co; BY pg 356; CE pg 10; DAR A093867; SAR P-275139 **BS:** 20 pg 141.

RAMSEY, Anthony; b unk; d 18 Sep 1814 **RU:** Soldier, SAR Ancester service not identified **CEM:** Presbyterian Church; GPS 38.80015, -77.05791; Wilkes St & Hamilton Ln; Alexandria City **GS:** N **SP:** Mary (-----) **VI:** No further data **P:** unk **BLW:** unk **RG:** Y **MK:** unk **PH:** N **SS:** J-NSSAR 1993 Reg;SAR P-275187 **BS:** JLARC 1.

RAMSEY, James Dr; b 1 Apr 1756; d 1815 **RU:** Private, Served in Capt Andrew Wagner's Co, 12th VA Regt **CEM:** Old Lebanon; GPS 38.08090, -79.37545; Off Rt 42, Craigsville; Augusta **GS:** Y **SP:** Mar (178?) Jane Lyle (1758 Rockingham Co-1836) d/o Samuel & Sarah (McClung) Lyle, both of Antrim Co., Ireland **VI:** Newer stone; marker placed 28 Jul 2003 **P:** unk **BLW:** unk **RG:** Y **MK:** Y SAR **PH:** unk **SS:** B; BT; AD; SAR P-275207 **BS:** 04; 196.

RAMSEY, John b c1730, d bef 13 Jul 1782 (will processed) **RU:** Patriot, A person this name was paid by Francis Peyton for wagon hire in Mar 1776, also paid personal property tax, 1782, Henry Co **CEM:** John Ramsey; GPS not determined; loc on his property vic Chestnut Crk, Rocky Mount; Franklin **GS:** Unk **SP:** 1) Elizabeth Stovall McBride, 2) Mary (-----)(___-aft 1781) **VI:** Will signed 3 Nov 1781. Personal property tax may have been paid by his son John that is mentioned in his will, thus obtain SAR application for approved service **P:** N **BLW:** N **RG:** Y **MK:** N **PH:** N **SS:** G pg 608; CD; SAR P-275215; **BS:** 196 # 169738540

RAMSEY/RAMSAY, Thomas Fancis. b 1760, Henry Co, d 24 Oct 1844 **RU:** Private, Capt Samuel Hewes's 8th Company, Col Alexander Spotswood's, 2d VA Regt, 2d Cont Line, Jan to Jun 1777: **CEM:** Ramsey Family; GPS: Not determined; Penhook, Franklin **GS:** N **SP:** Name determined, died bef soldier **VI:** A person this name took the Oath of Allegiance in Pittsylvania County, if him it would before he entered service. He rec'd pensions F8572 and R-1996 **P:** Y **BLW:** Unk **RG:** Y **MK:** N **PH:** N **SS:** A pg 275; K vol 3, pg 177; CG pg 2805; DAR A093848; SAR P-275253 **BS:** SAR PRS;196.

RANAUD, Francois; b unk; d 1781 **RU:** Seaman, Served on "Sceptre" and died from Yorktown battle **CEM:** French Memorial; GPS 36.81944, -79.39933; Yorktown; York **GS:** U **SP:** No info **VI:** No further data **P:** unk **BLW:** unk **RG:** Y **MK:** unk **PH:** unk **SS:** J-Yorktown Historian; SAR P-275278 **BS:** JLARC 1, 74.

RANDLE, Henry; b unk; d 16 Oct 1781 **RU:** Private, Served in Capt Elias Van Bunscoten 1st Co, Col Peter Gansevoort's 3rd NY Regt, Died fr battle at Yorktown **CEM:** Yorktown Victory Monument Tablet; GPS 38.28350, -78.54150; Yorktown; York **GS:** U **SP:** No info **VI:** No further data **P:** unk **BLW:** unk **RG:** Y **MK:** unk **PH:** unk **SS:** J-Yorktown Historian;SAR P-275460 AX pg 198 **BS:** JLARC 74.

RANDOLPH, Beverley; b 1754; d 2 Feb 1797 **RU:** Colonel, Ent serv 1775 Cumberland Co where was col commanding VA unit while also student at William & Mary College. Commanded Cumberland Co Militia until resignation 22 Jan 1781 **CEM:** Westview; GPS unk; Farmville; Prince Edward **GS:** Y **SP:** Mar (14 Feb 1775 York Co) Martha "Patty" Cocke, (2 Jun 1753 Henrico Co-21 Sep 1838) d/o James & Ann (Brown) Cocke. **VI:** Son of Peter (1717-1767) and Lucy (Bolling) (1719-__) Randolph. Eighth Governor of Virginia 1788-1791. Died in Green Creek, Cumberland Co. Widow pen 1837 fr Warren Co,

RU=Rank/Unit CEM=Cemetery GS=Gravestone SP=Spousal Information
VI=Other Veteran Info P=Pension BLW=Bounty/Land Warrant RG=Registered Grave
MK=SAR/DAR Marker PH=Photo SS=Service Source BS=Burial Source

346

while living at Happy Creek Manor. W4774 **P:** Y **BLW:** unk **RG:** N **MK:** N **PH:** unk **SS:** E pg 649; K Vol 4 pg 179-80 **BS:** 130.

RANDOLPH, David Meade; b 1758; d 27 Sep 1830 **RU:** Captain/Patriot, Was Lt in Capt Carter Page's Co Theodorick Bland's 1st Regt, Lt Dragoons. Later was Captain. Gave material aid to cause **CEM:** Bruton Parish Church; GPS 37.27127, -76.70248; 331 W Duke of Gloucester St; Williamsburg City **GS:** U **SP:** Mary Randolph (9 Aug 1762-28 Jan 1828) d/o Thomas Mann & Anne (Cary) (1745-1789) Randolph. **VI:** Son of Richard (1716-1786) and Ann (Cary) Randolph of Curles of Henrico Co. Assigned duties in DC by President Washington after War. Death reported in Whig newspaper 5 Oct 1830. First person bur on grounds that later became Arlington National Cemetery. Not sure which cem contains body **P:** Y #S36252 **BLW:** unk **RG:** Y **MK:** Y **SAR PH:** unk **SS:** J-NSSAR 1993 Reg; AL Ct Bk pg 40 Chesterfield Co; DAR A094162; SAR P-275478 **BS:** JLARC 1; 196.

RANDOLPH, Edmund Jennings; b 10 Aug 1753, Tazewell Hall, Williamsburg; d 13 Sep 1813 **RU:** Colonel/Patriot, Served as Aide-de-Camp to General Washington after Bunker Hill 1775; first VA Attorney General in 1775; Cont Congress 1779. Signed VA Declaration of Rights **CEM:** Old Chapel Episcopal; GPS 39.10677, -78.01470; Jct US 340 & Rt 255, Millwood; Clarke **GS:** Y **SP:** Elizabeth Carter Nicolas (1753-1810) **VI:** Son of John & (-----) Randolph. Was Governor of Virginia 1786, member of Continental Congress 1779. Was Grand Master of Masons in VA 1786. Attended Constitutional Convention 1787, was First Attorney General of US 1789. Served as Secretary of State 1794. Died at Carter Hall at Millwood **P:** unk **BLW:** unk **RG:** Y **MK:** Y SAR granite **PH:** Y **SS:** E pg 649; DD; SAR P-275480 **BS:** JLARC 1, 24; 196.

RANDOLPH, Henry; b 7 Oct 1758, Dursley, Eng, d 9 Feb 1804 **RU:** Private/ Patriot, in1781 was in Capt Robert Bolling's Troop of Cavalry. As patriot gave material aid to cause **CEM:** Randolph Family; GPS not determined; Warwick; Chesterfield **GS:** Unk **SP:** 1) Mary Peterson Poythress, 2) Lucy Ward (c1760-1818 Campbell Co) **VI:** Son of Brett Randolph (4 Sep 1732 Curles, Henrico Co-4 Sep 1759; Dursey, Eng) & Mary Scott of London, Eng **P:** N **BLW:** N **RG:** Y **MK:** N **PH:** N **SS:** D vol1, pg 249; G pg 646; AZ pg 130; DAR A094237; SAR P-275489 **BS:** SAR PRS.

RANDOLPH, John; b 29 Jun 1742; d 28 Oct 1775 **RU:** Patriot, Gave material aid to cause **CEM:** Matoax, Randolph Family; GPS unk; Matoaca; Chesterfield **GS:** U **SP:** Mar (9 Mar 1769) Frances Bland (24 Sep 1752-18 Jan 1788) d/o Theodorick & Frances (Bolling) Bland **VI:** No further data **P:** N **BLW:** N **RG:** Y **MK:** unk **PH:** unk **SS:** AL Cert Chesterfield Co; SAR P-275498 **BS:** 80, vol3, pg201; 196.

RANDOLPH, Peyton; b Sep 1721, Williamsburg; d 22 Oct 1775 **RU:** Patriot, Was President of Conventions 1774, Mar 1775, & Jul 1775 **CEM:** Wren Chapel, College of William & Mary; GPS 37.27070, -76.70910; Sir Christopher Wren Building, W&M campus; Williamsburg City **GS:** Y **SP:** Elizabeth Harrison (__-1783) d/o Benjamin (1694-1745) & Anne (Carter) (1704-1745) Harrison **VI:** Son of Sir John (1693-1737) & Lady Susanna (Beverly) (1692-1754) Randolph. King's Attorney for the Commonwealth in 1745. Member House of Burgesses 1764-1774 & Speaker 1766, President of VA conventions 1774 & 75. President of 1st & 2nd Continental Congresses at time of death. Was Grand Master of Masons 1786 and member Constitutional Convention 1787; Was First US Attorney General 1789 and US Secretary of State 1794. Died in Philadelphia Randolph City, PA **P:** N **BLW:** N **RG:**Y **MK:** Y SAR **PH:** Y **SS:** N pg 495; AK; SAR P-275514 **BS:** 130.

RANDOLPH, Richard III; b 1757, Nansemond, Suffolk City, d 16 Mar 1799 **RU:** Colonel/Patriot, was 1/Sgt General Nelson's Corps Lt Dragoons and given Colonel rank in 1782. As patriot provided flour for Pr Edward County Militia **CEM:** Bruton Parish Episcopal Church; GPS 37.2712708,-76.7024765; loc on E Duke of Gloucester St nr jct with N Nassau St; Williamsburg City **GS:** Y **SP:** Maria Beverley (15 Dec 1764, Essex Co-2 Oct 1625), d/o Robert Beverley (1740-1800) & Maria Carter (1745-1817) **VI:** Son of Richard Randolph II (1715-1786) **P:** N **BLW:** N **RG:** N **MK:** N **PH:** N **SS:** E pg 649; G pg 505 **BS:** 196.

RANDOLPH, .Richard II; b 11 Jan 1715, d 6 Jun 1786 **RU:** Patriot, was member of Convention, 1775 **CEM:** Curles Neck Farm; GPS not determined; loc 18 mi E of Richmond off Rt 5, Randolph Ridge; Henrico **GS:** Y **SP:** Anne "Nancy" (1731 Flushing Queens Co, NY-9 Dec 1814) **VI:** Son of Richard Randolph I (1686-17 Dec 1748) & Jane Bolling (1698-4 Mar 1766) **P:** N **BLW:** N **RG:** N **MK:** N **PH:** N **SS:** DAR A094301 **BS:** 196.

RU=Rank/Unit	CEM=Cemetery	GS=Gravestone	SP=Spousal Information
VI=Other Veteran Info	P=Pension	BLW=Bounty/Land Warrant	RG=Registered Grave
MK=SAR/DAR Marker	PH=Photo	SS=Service Source	BS=Burial Source

RANDOLPH, Robert; b 1760, Henrico Co; d 12 Sep 1825 **RU:** Captain, Served in 3rd Lt Dragoons, Cont Line **CEM:** Randolph Family at Eastern View; GPS unk; Nr Casanova; Fauquier **GS:** Y **SP:** Elizabeth Hill Carter (1764-1832), d/o Charles Carter (1732-1806) & Mary Walker (1736-1770) **VI:** BLW received for 4000 acres **P:** unk **BLW:** Y **RG:** Y **MK:** unk **PH:** unk **SS:** E pg 649; SAR P-275520 **BS:** JLARC 16.; 196.

RANDOLPH, Thomas Mann; b 1741; d 20 Nov 1793 **RU:** Colonel/Patriot, Served in Goochland Co Militia prior to 20 Sep 1779, when replaced. Gave material aid to cause **CEM:** Tuckahoe Plantation; GPS unk; 12601 River Rd Rt 650, W of Richmond near Manakin; Goochland **GS:** Y **SP:** Anne Cary (1745-6 Mar 1789 Tuckahoe) **VI:** Son of William (1712-1745) and Maria/Mary Judith (Page) (1715-1742) Randolph. Perhaps first person bur on grounds that would later become Arlington National Cem **P:** unk **BLW:** unk **RG:** Y **MK:** N **PH:** unk **SS:** E pg 649; AL Cert 1 Albemarle Co; DAR A094314; SAR P-275526 **BS:** 46 pg 244; 196.

RANDOLPH, William; b 1737, Elizabeth City Co; d 1795 **RU:** Pilot, Served in 5th & 9th Cont Line **CEM:** Hampton; GPS unk; DAR and SAR burial sources do not provide location; Hampton City **GS:** U **SP:** Mar (c1763) Sarah Minson (c1767-aft 1796) **VI:** No further data **P:** unk **BLW:** unk **RG:** Y **MK:** unk **PH:** unk **SS:** DAR A094332; J-NSSAR 2000 Reg;SAR P-275528; AR Vol 3 pg 201; E pg 650 **BS:** JLARC 76; 80 vol3 pg 201.

RAUSCH (ROUSH), John Adam; b 1711, Palatinate, Germany; d 19 Oct 1786 **RU:** Patriot, Gave material aid to cause **CEM:** Old St Mary's; GPS unk; Mt Jackson; Shenandoah **GS:** U **SP:** Susannah Sehler **VI:** No further data **P:** N **BLW:** N **RG:** Y **MK:** Y **SAR PH:** unk **SS:** DAR A098982; J-NSSAR 1993 Reg; SAR P-275828; AL Cert Shenandoah Co **BS:** JLARC 1.

RAUSCH (RAUCH), Nicholas; b 1748, Germany; d 31 Oct 1813 **RU:** Private, Served in Capt Esterly's Co, Col Bradford's Regt, Philadelphia PA Militia **CEM:** St Mary Pine Lutheran; GPS 38.74470, -78.68390; 7103 S Middle Rd, Mt Jackson; Shenandoah **GS:** U **SP:** Dorothea Reinefeld **VI:** Died in Martinsburg, Berkeley Co WV **P:** unk **BLW:** unk **RG:** Y **MK:**Unk **PH:** unk **SS:** J-NSSAR 1993 Reg; SAR P-275833; DD **BS:** JLARC 1.

RAUTZ, Francois; b unk; d 1781 **RU:** Seaman, Served on "Duc De Bourgogne" and died from Yorktown battle **CEM:** French Memorial; GPS 36.81944, -79.39933; Yorktown; York **GS:** U **SP:** No info **VI:** No further data **P:** unk **BLW:** unk **RG:** Y **MK:** unk **PH:** unk **SS:** J-Yorktown Historian; SAR P-275841 **BS:** JLARC 1, 74.

RAVAN, Jean; b unk; d 1781 **RU:** Seaman, Served on "Sceptre" and died from Yorktown battle **CEM:** French Memorial; GPS 36.81944, -79.39933; Yorktown; York **GS:** U **SP:** No info **VI:** No further data **P:** unk **BLW:** unk **RG:** Y **MK:** unk **PH:** unk **SS:** J-Yorktown Historian; SAR P-275842 **BS:** JLARC 1, 74.

RAY, Benjamin; b 1756; d 28 Jan 1841 **RU:** Private, Served in NC Line. Ent serv Surry Co NC 1775. Taken POW and remained so for14 mos **CEM:** Whitt Family; GPS unk; Rt 646, W fr Honaker; Russell **GS:** U **SP:** 1) (-----) (c1770-__) 2) mar (31 Jan 1830) Nancy Wilson or Sutherland (a widow) **VI:** Moved fr Surry NC to Russell Co VA 1798. Pension appl for 5 May 1818 Russell Co age 62. BLW issued to widow. Widow appl pen Russell Co 27 Apr 1854 age 72. She appl for BLW 31 Dec 1857. W26355. BLW #79035-160-55 **P:** Y **BLW:** Y **RG:** Y **MK:** unk **PH:** unk **SS:** J-NSSAR 1993 Reg, J- DAR Hatcher; K Vol 4 pg 185; CG Vol 3 pg 2819; SAR P-275927 **BS:** JLARC 1, 2; 80 vol3, pg 203.

RAY/WRAY, William b 1764; d 30 May 1842 **RU:** Private Serv in 5th & 6th Cont Line and/or Capt Page Co 9th VA Regt **CEM:** Cedar Grove; GPS 36.57204, - 80.02594; 301 Fort Lane, Rd; Portsmouth City **GS:** N **SP:** No spousal data **VI:** No further data **P:** N **BLW:** N **RG:** N **MK:**N **PH:** N **SS:**A part 2,pg 196; E pgs 129, 899 **BS:** Norfolk DAR Chapter.

RAYBLET, Philippe; b unk; d 1781 **RU:** Seaman, Served on "Saint-Esprit" and died from Yorktown battle **CEM:** French Memorial; GPS 36.81944, -79.39933; Yorktown; York **GS:** U **SP:** No info **VI:** No further data **P:** unk **BLW:** unk **RG:** Y **MK:** Richmond, age 62. S38324 **P:** Y **BLW:** unk **RG:** N **MK:** Y-SAR, DAR **PH:** Y **SS:** E pg 652; K Vol 4 pg 187; CG Vol 3 pg 2822 **BS:** 57 pg 6. unk **PH:** unk **SS:** J-Yorktown Historian; SAR P-276010 **BS:** JLARC 1, 74.

RU=Rank/Unit	CEM=Cemetery	GS=Gravestone	SP=Spousal Information
VI=Other Veteran Info	P=Pension	BLW=Bounty/Land Warrant	RG=Registered Grave
MK=SAR/DAR Marker	PH=Photo	SS=Service Source	BS=Burial Source

348

RAYBURN (RAYBORNE, RAYBORN, RAYBURN, RAIBORNE), George; b c1755; d 22 Nov 1828 **RU:** Fifer/Musician, Ent serv Chesterfield Co 1778. Was Fifer in 5th VA Regt and in 3rd and 4th VA Regts. Was captured by British at siege of Charlestown, taken POW and released at end of war **CEM:** Shockoe Hill; GPS 37.55190, -77.43170; 4th & Hospital Sts; Richmond City **GS:** Y **SP:** Had wife age 45. (-----) (c1780-__) **VI:** Pen appl for 6 Jun 1818 Richmond, age 62. S38324 **P:** Y **BLW:** unk **RG:** N **MK:** Y SAR granite; name on monument **PH:** Y **SS:** E pg 652; K Vol 4 pg 187; CG Vol 3 pg 2822 **BS:** 57 pg 6.

REA, John; b 1763; d 1826 **RU:** Private, Served in Henry Co Militia in Capt Tarrant's Co **CEM:** Mayo Baptist Church; GPS unk; 85 Penn Store Rd, Spencer; Henry **GS:** Y **SP:** No info **VI:** Memorial dedicated by SAR George Waller Chapter 13 Jun 2010 **P:** unk **BLW:** unk **RG:** N **MK:** Y SAR **PH:** unk **SS:** AK correspondence; G pg 187 **BS:** 32 Jun 2010; 196.

REA, William; b 1735; d 1812 **RU:** Private, served first in Capt Andrew Wallace's Co 8th VA Regt, then served in Capt Page's Co, Col Benjamin Tupper's Regt, 11th Cont Line in battle of King's Mtn **CEM:** Cedar Grove; GPS 36.57204, -80.02599; 301 Fort Lane Rd; Portsmouth City **GS:** Y **SP:** No info **VI:** No further data **P:** unk **BLW:** unk **RG:** Y **MK:** Y SAR **PH:** unk **SS:** A pg 129; SAR P-338454 **BS:** 147.

READ, Edmund (Edmond); b c1756; d 23 Dec 1836 **RU:** Soldier, Ent serv c1772 age 16, Accomack Co, served in VA Regt **CEM:** Chestnut Vale; GPS unk; .6 mi N of Rt 605, W of Rt 789, nr Locustville; Accomack **GS:** N **SP:** No info **VI:** Pensioned Accomack Co 1832 age 76. S18564 **P:** unk **BLW:** unk **RG:** Y **MK:** unk **PH:** unk **SS:** K Vol 4 pg 188; CG pg 2826; SAR P-276194 **BS:** JLARC 4, 5.

READ, John; b unk; d Aft 1781 **RU:** Patriot, Gave material aid to cause **CEM:** Robson Farm; GPS unk; Location ot identified in JLARC report; Culpeper **GS:** U **SP:** No info **VI:** No further data **P:** N **BLW:** N **RG:** Y **MK:** unk **PH:** unk **SS:** AL Ct Bk pg 4, 35 Culpeper Co; SAR P-276217 **BS:** JLARC 63.

READ, John; b c 1759; d 14 Dec 1827 or 12 Mar 1831 **RU:** Private/Patriot, Served in Capt William Lowther Co at Nutter's Ft for six mos, 1777. Served again 6 mos in same Co,1780. Volunteered to serve in Capt John D. DeVall at Blockhouse as spy, town of Harrison,1781. Gave material aid to cause **CEM:** Rock Spring; GPS 37.78126, -79.44585; Jct Rt 803 & Liberty Hall Rd, Lodi; Washington **GS:** Y **SP:** Elizabeth Read (1757-14 Dec 1827) **VI:** Rev War pension **P:** Y **BLW:** unk **RG:** N **MK:** N **PH:** Y **SS:** AL Com Bk IV pg 270; CI - RW Pen **BS:** 78 pg 210; 196.

READ, John K; b c1746, Philadelphia 1758; d 10 Feb 1805 **RU:** Surgeon, Served in1st Battalion of Minutemen **CEM:** St Paul's Episcopal; GPS 36.84733, -76.28554; 201 St Paul's Blvd; Norfolk City **GS:** Y **SP:** Helen (Calvert) Maxwell Read - 2nd husband **VI:** Moved to Borough of Norfolk c1796. Mayor of Norfolk 1799 **P:** unk **BLW:** unk **RG:** N **MK:** Y SAR plaque **PH:** unk **SS:** CB; G pg 502 **BS:** 87 pg 29.

READ, Jonathan; b 6 Dec 1752, Lunenburg Co, d 5 Nov 1801 **RU:** First Lieutenant, received this rank Nov 1779 in Charlotte Co Militia **CEM:** Bushy Forest; GPS not determined; loc vic Charlotte Co Ct House; Charlotte **GS:** Unk **SP:** mar Nov 1776, Jane Lewis (1760-__) **VI:** Son of Col Clement Read (1707-1763) & Mary Hill (1711-1786). After war period in Oct 1785 became a Captain in the militia **P:** N **BLW:** N **RG:** Y **MK:** N **PH:** N **SS:** AZ pg 196; DAR A094532; SAR P-276231 **BS:** 196

READ, Samuel; b 31 Mar 1767; d 25 Jan 1831 **RU:** Private, Served in Capt John Robert's Co, Bedford Co Militia **CEM:** Callaway-Steptoe; GPS 37.30560, -79.29470 GS37.1820,-79.1742; Rt 460, New London; Bedford **GS:** Y **SP:** Elizabeth (-----) **VI:** Severely weathered stone. Source of service derived fr Campbell Co Historical Society correspondence to JLARC Committee is obviously incorrect. If he was b in 1767, he could not have achieved Capt rank by 1783 at age 16. Perhaps he was in War of 1812 or perhaps birth date incorrect **P:** unk **BLW:** unk **RG:** Y **MK:** N **PH:** unk **SS:** E pg 653; SAR P-276256 **BS:** JLARC 36; 196.

READ, Thomas; b 21 Nov 1742, Lunenburg Co; d 1817 **RU:** Colonel/Patriot, Was Burgess, member of State Conventions of 1774-76. Committee of Safety for Charlotte Co 1775-76. During RW, served as County Lt. Marched to Petersburg himself. Supplied quotas of that county in men and means to state of VA and Cont Lines. Col of Charlotte Co Millitia 1781 **CEM:** Ingleside, Thomas Read Family; GPS unk; Charlotte CH; Charlotte **GS:** U **SP:** Elizabeth Nash (__-1790), sister of Col Thomas Nash & Mary Nash Read. **VI:** Son of Clement & (-----) Read. Deputy clerk for father in Lunenburg Co, then deputy clerk in Charlotte Co. Clerk in 1770, which office he held until his death in 1817. Member of Constitutional Convention of 1788 **P:** unk **BLW:** unk **RG:** N **MK:** unk **PH:** unk **SS:** E pg 653 **BS:** 196.

RU=Rank/Unit	CEM=Cemetery	GS=Gravestone	SP=Spousal Information
VI=Other Veteran Info	P=Pension	BLW=Bounty/Land Warrant	RG=Registered Grave
MK=SAR/DAR Marker	PH=Photo	SS=Service Source	BS=Burial Source

READ, William; b 1720; d 1798 **RU:** Corporal, Served in a VA battalion **CEM:** Read; GPS 37.18220, -79.18510; New London, nr jct Rts 460 & 811; Bedford **GS:** U **SP:** Johanna (-----) **VI:** JLARC site visit could only find stone for his son **P:** unk **BLW:** unk **RG:** N **MK:** N **PH:** unk **SS:** J-NSSAR 1993 Reg; E pg 653 **BS:** JLARC 1.

REBOUL, Pierre; b unk; d 1781 **RU:** Seaman, Served on "Saint-Esprit" and died from Yorktown battle **CEM:** French Memorial; GPS 36.81944, -79.39933; Yorktown; York **GS:** U **SP:** No info **VI:** No further data **P:** unk **BLW:** unk **RG:** Y **MK:** unk **PH:** unk **SS:** J-Yorktown Historian; SAR P-276385 **BS:** JLARC 1, 74.

RECTOR, Henry, b 1715, Germanna, Essex Co, d 30 Jun 1799 **RU:** Patriot, Paid personal property tax, Fauquier Co, 1783 and gave material aid to cause **CEM:** Rectortown; GPS 38.9201290, -77.8622970; loc betw jct Maidstone Rd & Rectortown Rd; Fauquier **GS:** Unk **SP:** mar 1) Anne Nancy Robinson (__-1803), 2) Anne Spencer (__-1804) **VI:** Son of Hans Jacob Richter (1674-1729) & Anna Elsbeth Fischbach) (1685-1773) **P:** N **BLW:** N **RG:** Y **MK:** N **PH:** N **SS:** D vol 1, pgs 346, 348; DV image 19.pdf, Fauquier Co 1783; DAR A094029; SAR P-276414 **BS:** 196.

RECTOR, Jacob John; b 23 Aug 1724. Fauquier Co, d 31 Jul 1810 **RU:** Paid personal property tax Fauquier Co, 1783 **CEM:** Linton Family; GPS 36.5886880, -80.9901280; loc Greenwich Rd (Rt 623), Delhart; Grayson **GS:** Unk **SP:** Mary Hitt, (1723, Fauquier Co- 16 Nov 1813), d/o Peter Hitt (1683-1772) & Elizabeth Otterbach (1689-1772) **VI:** Son of Hans Jacob Rector & Anna Elizabeth Fischbach. **P:** N **BLW:** N **RG:** N **MK:** N **PH:** N **SS:** DV image 19.pdf, Fauquier Co 1783 **BS:** 196.

REDCROSS, John; b c1760; d bef 16 Reb 1800 **RU:** Private, Served in Amherst Co Militia under Lt Col John Pope, Jr 3 Jun 1781 and in 2nd VA State Regt **CEM:** Indian Graveyard; GPS unk; Bear Mtn, Rt 643; Amherst **GS:** N **SP:** No info **VI:** Recd BLW #4748 **P:** unk **BLW:** Y **RG:** N **MK:** N **PH:** N **SS:** E pg 655; CZ pg 368; DAR A205122; SAR P-336210 **BS:** 01 pg 70.

REDD, John Franklin; b 25 Oct 1755, Orange Co; d 11 Aug 1850 **RU:** Second Lieutenant, Walked fr Albemarle Co to Henry Co at age 17 to enlist. Served under Gen Joesph Martin. Apted 2nd Lt Apr 1780 in Henry Co. Was at Yorktown 1781 **CEM:** Redd; GPS unk; Fontaine; Henry **GS:** Y **SP:** Mar (24 Aug 1782 Henry Co) Mary Winston Carr Waller (26 Oct 1765 Stafford Co-17 Jul 1828 Henry Co), daughter of Col George (1734-1814) & Ann Winston (Carr) (1735-1839) Waller (1765-1828) **VI:** Son of George (1735-1755) of Orange Co. & Lucy (Franklin) (1737-(-----) Albemarle Co.) Redd. Also served in Indian Wars. Rec'd rank of Maj after RW. Member of court in Henry Co for 40 yrs. Pen Henry Co 1833 **P:** Y **BLW:** unk **RG:** Y **MK:** Y **PH:** unk **SS:** E pg 645; K Vol 4 pg 195; DAR A094070; SAR P-276426 **BS:** JLARC 2, 4, 38,102; 80 vol 3 pg 205; 196.

REDIN, John; b 1752, England; d 5 Aug 1832 **RU:** Private?, Served in 6th Cont Line **CEM:** Southern-Shreve; GPS unk; 5300 N 10th St; Arlington **GS:** Y **SP:** Mary (-----) b 1764 England, d 1874 **VI:** No further data **P:** unk **BLW:** unk **RG:** Y **MK:** N **PH:** unk **SS:** E pg 655; SAR P-274944 **BS:** 69 pg 73; 196.

REDMAN, Henry; b unk; d Dec 1790 **RU:** Private, Served in 3rd, 4th, & 8th Cont Lines **CEM:** Old Christ Church Episcopal; GPS 38.80625, -77.04718; 118 N Washington St; Alexandria City **GS:** N **SP:** No info **VI:** Burial permit for "Mr. Redman" issued 15 Dec 1790 to son Thomas Redman **P:** unk **BLW:** unk **RG:** N **MK:** N **PH:** N **SS:** E pg 655 **BS:** 20 pg 152.

REECE, Josiah; b Unk; d 1 Sep 1777 **RU:** Private, Capt Thomas Triplett's Co, Col William Grayson's 3rd VA Regt Sep 1777 **CEM:** Rev War Court House Plaque;GPS;not determined; 4110 Chain Bridge Rd; Fairfax **GS:** Memorialized on plaque 2017 by Geo Washington Chapter, VASSAR **SP** No info **VI:** died in service **P:** N **BLW:** N **RG:** N **MK:** N **PH:** N **SS:**E pg 691; AP Fold3 muster roll Oct 1777::EP sources: **BS:** None.

REED, William; b c1762, Dunmore (now Shenandoah) Co; d 11 Sep 1839 **RU:** First Sergeant, Ent serv 1778 in Dunmore Co 8th Va Regt. Served in Capt Thomas Bucks Co (Buck's Minute Men), Dunmore Co Militia **CEM:** Stone Chapel Presbyterian; GPS 39.22610, -78.01060; Old Charles Town Rd, Berryville; Clarke **GS:** Y **SP:** Susan (-----) **VI:** Sergeant during French & Indian War and accompanied George Rogers Clarke on his Illinois/Indiana campaign **P:** unk **BLW:** unk **RG:**N **MK:** N **PH:** Y **SS:** E pg 656 **BS:** 50 pg 39.

RU=Rank/Unit	CEM=Cemetery	GS=Gravestone	SP=Spousal Information
VI=Other Veteran Info	P=Pension	BLW=Bounty/Land Warrant	RG=Registered Grave
MK=SAR/DAR Marker	PH=Photo	SS=Service Source	BS=Burial Source

REEDY, George Peter; b c1749, Goshenhoppen, Montgomery Co, PA; d c1837 **RU**: Sergeant, Served in 7th Co, 6th Bn, Northampton Co PA Militia **CEM**: Reedy; GPS 39.13594, -78.00630; Reedy Groves, Grossy Creek; Grayson **GS**: U **SP**: Mary (Sisk?) (__-after 1840) **VI**: Sol appl BLW Montgomery Co, 25 Jan 1782 (rejected). Purchased 200 acres in Grayson Co **P**: unk **BLW**: N **RG**: N **MK**: unk **PH**: unk **SS**: PA Archives, Series 5 Vol 8 pg 469, 525 **BS**: 32.

REESE, John; b 1737; d 13 Nov 1794; **RU**: Patriot, gave material aid to cause, Southampton Co **CEM**: Old Adams Grove; GPS not determined; loc L of jct U.S. 58 & Adams Grove Rd (Rt 651) **GS**: Unk **SP**: Mary Thorpe (24 Jun 1735-15 Oct 1798), d/o John Thorpe (1698-1772) & Mary Mathewes (1713-1772) **VI**: No further data **P**: N **BLW**: N **RG**: N **MK**:N **PH**:N **SS**: DAR A210778;D vol 3, pg 851 **BS**: 196.

REEVES, George Sr; b 1735, Drewry's Bluff, Chesterfield Co; d 15 Nov 1811 **RU**: Lieutenant, Served in Capt James McDonald's Co, Montgomery Co Militia **CEM**: Reeves Farm; GPS unk; Rt 700, SE of Independence; Grayson **GS**: Y **SP**: Mar (1765) Jane Burton (1745-1811 Independence, VA); 2) Mary Fordham **VI**: Son of Thomas (1700-1760) & (-----) Reeves. DAR plaque **P**: unk **BLW**: unk **RG**: Y **MK**: Y DAR plaque **PH**: unk **SS**: DAR A095020; J-NSSAR 1993 Reg, J- DAR Hatcher; E pg 656; CE pg 23; DD; DL pg 766; SAR P-277089 **BS**: JLARC 1, 2.; 80 vol 3, pg 209.

REIBAUD, Antoine; b unk; d 1781 **RU**: Seaman, Served on "Victorie" and died from Yorktown battle **CEM**: French Memorial; GPS 36.81944, -79.39933; Yorktown; York **GS**: U **SP**: No info **VI**: No further data **P**: unk **BLW**: unk **RG**: Y **MK**: unk **PH**: unk **SS**: J-Yorktown Historian; SAR P-277113 **BS**: JLARC 1, 74.

REID, Andrew; b 2 Feb 1751 VA; d 1837 **RU**: Patriot, Was Justice of Rockbridge Co Ct and Clerk 7 Apr 1778 **CEM**: Stonewall Jackson Memorial; GPS 37.78128, -79.44604; 314 S Main St; Lexington City **GS**: Y **SP**: Magdalene McDowell (1755-1838) **VI**: Son of Andrew Jr & Sarah (-----) Reid. Died in Rockbridge Co **P**: N **BLW**: N **RG**: Y **MK**: unk **PH**: Y **SS**: G pg 320; SAR P-277134 **BS**: JLARC 63.

REID, Francis; b 1752; d 1827 **RU**: First Midshipman, Served on "Henry" Galley **CEM**: Reid Family; GPS unk; 9 mi NE of Eagle Rock; Botetourt **GS**: Y **SP**: No info **VI**: Was fr Gloucester Co **P**: unk **BLW**: unk **RG**: N **MK**: N **PH**: unk **SS**: E pg 657; L pg 240 **BS**: 165 Reid.

REID, James; b 1755; d 20 Jul 1821 **RU**: First Lieutenant, Served in 3rd VA Regt Cont Line. Promoted to 1st Lt 01 Mar 1777 **CEM**: Dumfries Public; GPS 38.34110, -77.19964; 17821 Mine Rd, Dumfries; Prince William **GS**: Y **SP**: No info **VI**: SAR monument **P**: unk **BLW**: unk **RG**: Y **MK**: Y SAR monument **PH**: unk **SS**: AP 3rd VA Reg; SAR P-335847 **BS**: 94 pg 18.

REID, John; b 1762; d 31 Mar 1837 **RU**: Soldier, Ent serv Fairfax Co in 1780. Served in VA Regt **CEM**: Fairfax City; GPS 38.84690, -77.31330; Main St & Page Ave; Fairfax City **GS**: N **SP**: No info **VI**: Pen fr Fairfax Co 1836. Unnamed child granted his pension in arrears S10254 **P**: Y **BLW**: unk **RG**: Y **MK**: N **PH**: N **SS**: K Vol 4 pg 201; SAR P-277158 **BS**: JLARC 4,14, 27, 28.

REID, Nathan; b 1753; d 1830 **RU**: Captain, Was Capt of 7th Co 28 Jan 1777 in 14th VA Regt of Foot. Later was Capt of 1st Co 1781-2 in Col Thomas Posey's VA Bn. As capt commanded 3rd Co, 1st VA Regt of Foot, Jun-Nov 1779, then 2nd Co 1st VA Regt Jan 1783 **CEM**: Reid Estate "Poplar Grove"; GPS unk; New London; Bedford **GS**: U **SP**: No info **VI**: WPA survey says bur in the old garden, then at Reeves Lemon's home **P**: unk **BLW**: unk **RG**: Y **MK**: N **PH**: unk **SS**: CE pg 32, 33, 71, 92; SAR P-277165 **BS**: JLARC 1, 2, 36; 75; 80 vol 3, pg 209.

REIFF (REIFH), John; b 1724; d 1778 **RU**: Patriot, paid personal property tax, Rockingham Co, 1782 that was used to pay Rev War expenses **CEM**: Driver-Rife; GPS 38.647310,-78.752090; 16092 Evergreen Lalley Rd, Timberville: Rockingham **GS**: N **SP**: Anna Gerber (1725-1782), d/o Nicholas Gerber & Elizabeth (-----) **VI**: Son of Hans Jacob Reiff (__-4 Jan 1756) & Elizabeth Kaufman **P**: N **BLW**: N **RG**: N **MK**:N **PH**:N **SS**: DV 1782 Rockingham Co, image 05 pdf **BS**: 196.

REMAIN, Jacques; b unk; d 1781 **RU**: Seaman, Served on "Northumberland" and died from Yorktown battle **CEM**: French Memorial; GPS 36.81944, -79.39933; Yorktown; York **GS**: U **SP**: No info **VI**: No further data **P**: unk **BLW**: unk **RG**: Y **MK**: unk **PH**: unk **SS**: J-Yorktown Historian; SAR P-277302 **BS**: JLARC 1, 74.

RU=Rank/Unit	CEM=Cemetery	GS=Gravestone	SP=Spousal Information
VI=Other Veteran Info	P=Pension	BLW=Bounty/Land Warrant	RG=Registered Grave
MK=SAR/DAR Marker	PH=Photo	SS=Service Source	BS=Burial Source

351

REMONT, Charles; b unk; d 1781 **RU:** Soldier, Served in Gatinais Bn and died fr battle at Yorktown **CEM:** French Memorial; GPS 36.81944, -79.39933; Yorktown; York **GS:** U **SP:** No info **VI:** No further data **P:** unk **BLW:** unk **RG:** Y **MK:** unk **PH:** unk **SS:** J-Yorktown Historian; SAR P-277368 **BS:** JLARC 1, 74.

RENARD, Jean; b unk; d 1781 **RU:** Seaman, Served on "Hextor" and died from Yorktown battle **CEM:** French Memorial; GPS 36.81944, -79.39933; Yorktown; York **GS:** U **SP:** No info **VI:** No further data **P:** unk **BLW:** unk **RG:** Y **MK:** unk **PH:** unk **SS:** J-Yorktown Historian; SAR P-277388 **BS:** JLARC 1, 74.

RENNOLDS, Sthreshley, b 14 Apr 1759, d 25 Jul 1822 **RU:** Captain 6th VMR Received as captain 20 Mar 1780 Essex County Militia **CEM:** Rockland; GPS 37.9455,-76.96935; loc N side Rt627, opposite Frog Loop; Rexburg; Essex **GS:** Unk **SP:** Maria D Beale (7 Feb 1775-17 Nov 1832) **VI:** Son of John Rennolds and (__- Sthreshley), d/o Thomas Sthresheley.He was a gentleman Sheriff and Justice, Essex County and a Presidential Elector for VA **P:** N **BLW:** N **RG:** Y **MK:** N **PH:** N **SS:** E pg 658; SAR P-277431; DAR # A095859 **BS:** 196; Old Homes of Essex Co, compiled by Women's Club, Essex Co,1957.

RENOUARD, Jean; b unk; d 1781 **RU:** Seaman, Served on "Hercule" and died from Yorktown battle **CEM:** French Memorial; GPS 36.81944, -79.39933; Yorktown; York **GS:** U **SP:** No info **VI:** No further data **P:** unk **BLW:** unk **RG:** Y **MK:** unk **PH:** unk **SS:** J-Yorktown Historian; SAR P-277443 **BS:** JLARC 1, 74.

REVEL, Gaspard; b unk; d 1781 **RU:** Seaman, Served on "Caton" and died from Yorktown battle **CEM:** French Memorial; GPS 36.81944, -79.39933; Yorktown; York **GS:** U **SP:** No info **VI:** No further data **P:** unk **BLW:** unk **RG:** Y **MK:** unk **PH:** unk **SS:** J-Yorktown Historian; SAR P-277504; **BS:** JLARC 1, 74.

REYNOLDS, Bernard; b 1763, Caroline Co; d 23 Jan 1833 **RU:** Private, Served in Va Line. Ent serv 1779 Caroline Co **CEM:** Reynolds Family; GPS unk; Hammonville; Russell **GS:** U **SP:** Mar (1 Feb 1787) Lucy Johnston (c1764-__) **VI:** Lived in Henrico Co 1810, then Russell Co 1828. Pension appl for 7 Aug 1832 age 69. She appl pen 26 Dec 1840 age 76 W188904 **P:** Y **BLW:** unk **RG:** Y **MK:** unk **PH:** unk **SS:** J-DAR Hatcher; K Vol 4 pg 205; CG Vol 3 pg 2853; SAR P-277576 **BS:** JLARC 2.

REYNOLDS, William; b 1757; d 22 Aug 1830 **RU:** Private, Served in Capt Peter Bernard's Co, York Garrison; 2nd VA State Regt Mar & Apr 1778 **CEM:** Old Presbyterian Meeting House; GPS 38.48528, -77.23532; 323 S Fairfax St; Alexandria City **GS:** Y sect 41, plot 26 **SP:** Sarah (1774-15 Nov 1811)**VI:** Died age 73 **P:** unk **BLW:** unk **RG** Y **MK:** N **PH:** unk **SS:** AP; SAR P-277565 **BS:** 23 pg 67; 196.

RHODES (ROTH), Bishop "Henry" B; b 2 Nov 1747, or 11 Feb 1748, Germany; d 18 Mar 1827 **RU:** Corporal, Served in VA Navy **CEM:** Rhodes (Roth) Family; GPS unk; Vic Broadway Rt 42; Rockingham **GS:** Y **SP:** Elizabeth (-----) **VI:** Son of Anthony Rhodes & Magdalena Ettinger (1730-19 Jul 1799) **P:** unk **BLW:** unk **RG:** N **MK:** N **PH:** unk **SS:** AK; E pg 660 **BS:** 04; 191 Rhodes; 196.

RHODES, John see RODES, John

RHODES, Michael; b 1 May 1749; d 11 Oct 1819 **RU:** Private, Served in Michael Reader's Co, VA Cont Line **CEM:** Coffman's Rivermont Farm, Rhodes Family; GPS 38.91623, -78.41480; Fisher Rd Rt 649 to end of state maintenance; Shenandoah **GS:** U **SP:** Anna (Nancy) Stricker **VI:** Son of John (1712-1764) & Eve Catherine (Albright) (1723-1764) Roads **P:** unk **BLW:** Y **RG:** Y **MK:** unk **PH:** unk **SS:** BY pg 306; J-NSSAR 1993 Reg J- DAR Hatcher; SAR P-277869; DAR A096034 **BS:** JLARC 1, 2; 80 vol3 pg 212; 196.

RIAU, Joseph; b unk; d 1781 **RU:** Seaman, Served on "Saint-Esprit" and died from Yorktown battle **CEM:** French Memorial; GPS 36.81944, -79.39933; Yorktown; York **GS:** U **SP:** No info **VI:** No further data **P:** unk **BLW:** unk **RG:** Y **MK:** unk **PH:** unk **SS:** J-Yorktown Historian; SAR P-277916 **BS:** JLARC 1, 74.

RICE, John Sr; b 1720, Culpeper Co; d 1804 **RU:** Patriot, Gave material aid to the cause **CEM:** Fishback Family; GPS unk; Dayton; Rockingham **GS:** N **SP:** Mar (Shenandoah Valley) Mary Finney (1723-1808), d/o James & Elizabeth (Turner) Finney. **VI:** Son of William (1686-1780) of Hanover Co & Sarah (Nelms or Helms) (1713-1780) of Hampshire Co, WV, Rice **P:** N **BLW:** N **RG:** unk **MK:** unk **PH:** N **SS:** AL CT BK II pg 16 Rockingham Co; CD **BS:** 196.

RU=Rank/Unit	CEM=Cemetery	GS=Gravestone	SP=Spousal Information
VI=Other Veteran Info	P=Pension	BLW=Bounty/Land Warrant	RG=Registered Grave
MK=SAR/DAR Marker	PH=Photo	SS=Service Source	BS=Burial Source

352

RICE, Thomas; b 18 Aug 1764; d 3 Dec 1819 **RU**: Private, Served in Capt Robert Powell's Co, 3rd VA Regt under Lt Col Heth. **CEM**: Rice Fam; GPS unk; Rt 743 W of Dayton; Rockingham **GS**: Y **SP**: No info **VI**: No further data **P**: unk **BLW**: unk **RG**: N **MK**: N **PH**: unk **SS**: AK; A pg 278 **BS**: 04; 191 Rice.

RICHARD, John; b 9 Dec 1762; London d 27 Oct 1824 **RU**: Purser, Was in VA Navy on sloop "Scorpian" **CEM**: Shockoe Hill; GPS 37.55190, -77.43170; 4th & Hospital Sts; Richmond City **GS**: Y **SP**: No info **VI**: No further data **P**: unk **BLW**: unk **RG**: N **MK**: N **PH**: Y **SS**: L pg 241 **BS**: 57 pg viii; 32.

RICHARD, Pierre; b unk; d 1781 **RU**: Seaman, Served on "Languedoc" and died from Yorktown battle **CEM**: French Memorial; GPS 36.81944, -79.39933; Yorktown; York **GS**: U **SP**: No info **VI**: No further data **P**: unk **BLW**: unk **RG**: Y **MK**: unk **PH**: unk **SS**: J-Yorktown Historian; SAR P-278270 **BS**: JLARC 1, 74.

RICHARDS, Christian; b 1748; d 18 Aug 1818 **RU**: Private, Served in Capt Jacob Colman's Co, Dunmore Co Militia **CEM**: Red Oak Grove; GPS 36.98184, -80.28639; Off Red Oak Grove Rd Rt 684; Floyd **GS**: U **SP**: Catherine (-----) (1751-1825) **VI**: No further data **P**: unk **BLW**: unk **RG**: Y **MK**: unk **PH**: unk **SS**: C pg 608; SAR P-278300 **BS**: JLARC 29; 196.

RICHARDS, Edward; b 25 Jun 1731, Baltimore Co, MD; d 16 Apr 1812 **RU**: Private/Patriot, served as a drummer in Capt Thomas Bower's Co, under Maj Jonathan Clark, Col James Wood's 4th, 8th & 12th Regts. Gave material aid to cause **CEM**: Richards Family; GPS unk; 2.5 mi SW of Callaway off Foothills Rd; Franklin **GS**: U **SP**: Elizabeth Henley Stewart (1742-1812) d/o James & (-----) Stuart **VI**: Son of Benjamin (1710-__) & Ann (Meryman) (1711-__) Richards. Applied for pen1820, Rockbridge Co recd # S39042 **P**: Y **BLW**: N **RG**: Y **MK**: unk **PH**: unk **SS**: AL Ct Bk pg 25 Henry Co; AP Muster roll # 1051; CG pg 2870; DAR A095838; SAR P-339255 **BS**: 196.

RICHARDS, George; b unk; d Jul 1789 **RU**: Patriot, Signed Fairfax Co legislative petition during war period **CEM**: Old Christ Church Episcopal; GPS 38.80625, -77.04718; 118 N Washington St; Alexandria City **GS**: N **SP**: No info **VI**: Burial permit issued 4 Jul 1789 **P**: N **BLW**: N **RG**: N **MK**: N **PH**: N **SS**: BB **BS**: 20 pg 152.

RICHARD(S), Henry; b 14 Nov 1753; d 25 Feb 1847 **RU**: Sergeant/Patriot, served in the Cont Line. Gave material aid to the cause **CEM**: Mountain View Methodist; GPS 39.11410, -78.40920; Richards Ln, Mountain Falls; Frederick **GS**: Y **SP**: Catherine Elizabeth Rudolph Keckley (15 Aug 1758, Gadernheim, Germany-21 Apr 1828) d/o Johann (1720-1788) & Margretha (Weimer) (c1732-1788) Rudolph **VI**: Burial site has DAR marker **P**: N **BLW**: N **RG**: N **MK**: Y **PH**: unk **SS**: E pg 661; AL CT Bk pg 12; CD **BS**: 59 pg 271; 196.

RICHARDS, John; b 30 Nov 1754; d 22 Jun 1843 **RU**: Soldier, Ent serv 1778 and enlisted in VA Regt **CEM**: Lacy Family; GPS 37.80571, -77.99405; Rt 615; Goochland **GS**: Y **SP**: mar (before 2 Jul 1781) Ursula Rutherford **VI**: Appl pen 17 Sep 1832, Goochland Co. S15967 **P**: Y **BLW**: unk **RG**: Y **MK**: N **PH**: unk **SS**: E pg 661; CG Vol 3 pg 2871; SAR P-278357 **BS**: 46 pg 176.

RICHARDS, John; b unk; d 1781 **RU**: Soldier, Served fr MA and died as result of Yorktown battle **CEM**: Yorktown Victory Monument Tablet; GPS 38.28350, -78.54150; Yorktown; York **GS**: U **SP**: No info **VI**: No further data **P**: unk **BLW**: unk **RG**: Y **MK**: unk **PH**: unk **SS**: J-Yorktown Historian; SAR P-278351 **BS**: JLARC 74.

RICHARDS, John; b unk; d 6 Apr 1806 **RU**: Patriot, Gave material aid to the cause, King & Queen Co **CEM**: Williams Family; GPS 37.412750, -76.338500;.loc 100yds along coast fr 62 Williamsdale Ln; Mathews **GS**: Y **SP**: No info **VI**: No further data **P**: N **BLW**: N **RG**: Y **MK**: N **PH**: N **SS**: AL Ct Bk lt pg 15; SAR P-342340, **BS**: 43 pg 155; 48 pg 142; 196. **SEE Appendix G, Errata**

RICHARDSON, George W; b unk; d after 1781 **RU**: Patriot, Gave material aid to the cause **CEM**: Boscobel; GPS unk; Vic Rt 621 Manakin; Goochland **GS**: Y **SP**: mar (1766) Elizabeth Miller of St James Northern Parish **VI**: No further data **P**: N **BLW**: N **RG**: Y**MK**: N **PH**: unk **SS**: AL Ct Bk lt pg 2; SAR P-278530 **BS**: 46 pg 104.

RICHARDSON, John Sr; b 1 May 1751, Philadelphia Co, PA; d 22 Oct 1837 **RU**: Captain, Served in PA Line. Ent serv 1776 in PA Regt, then moved to Shenandoah Co VA and was made Capt there 28 Feb 1782 **CEM**: Falling Springs Presbyterian; GPS unk; 115 Spring Church Rd, Covington; Covington City

RU=Rank/Unit	CEM=Cemetery	GS=Gravestone	SP=Spousal Information
VI=Other Veteran Info	P=Pension	BLW=Bounty/Land Warrant	RG=Registered Grave
MK=SAR/DAR Marker	PH=Photo	SS=Service Source	BS=Burial Source

GS: Y **SP:** Nancy Mossman **VI:** Moved to MD, then Frederick Co VA, then Rockingham Co, then to Botetourt (later Allegheny). Appl pen Alleghany Co 17 Mar 1834. Pension in arrears granted to 3 of 6 children (not named). S18177 **P:** Y **BLW:** unk **RG:** N **MK:** N **PH:** unk **SS:** K Vol 4 pg 216; CG Vol 3 pg 2876 **BS:** 72 vol 2 pg 67.

RICHARDSON, Nightingale; b unk; d 1833 **RU:** Private, Served in PA Line. Served also in Capt Joseph Smith's Co, Col Nathaniel Gist's VA Regt 1777 **CEM:** Goose Creek; GPS 39.11250, -77.69527; Rt 722, Lincoln; Loudoun **GS:** Y **SP:** No info **VI:** BLW #10302-100-11 Jun 1793 **P:** unk **BLW:** Y **RG:** N **MK:** N **PH:** unk **SS:** E pg 622; CG Vol 3 pg 2878 **BS:** 25 pg 259.

RICHARDSON, Samuel; b 1741; d 1794 **RU:** Captain/Patriot, Commanded a co 18 May 1778, Goochland Co Militia. Signed Oath of Allegiance in Goochland Co 1777 **CEM:** The Oaks; GPS unk; 1.4 mi SE of Tapscott on Rt 603; Goochland **GS:** U **SP:** No info **VI:** No further data **P:** unk **BLW:** unk **RG:** Y **MK:** unk **PH:** unk **SS:** AZ pg 207; DU; SAR P-278683 **BS:** 218.

RICHARDSON, Samuel Marquis; b 1 Feb 1760 ,Frederick Co, MD; d 18 Jan 1831 **RU:** Private, Served in Capt William Rieley Co, Col Hazen's Regt **CEM:** Richardson Family; GPS 38.95750, -78.29610; 1.5 mi fr entrance to GW National Forest, Rt 678 nr Fortsmouth Vol Fire Dept; Warren **GS:** Y **SP:** Mar (3 Jan 1784) Catherine Bainbridge Hal (3 Feb 1760-19 Aug 1837) **VI:** Son of (-----) & Isabell (-----) Calmes (1729-1796). Died in Front Royal **P:** unk **BLW:** unk **RG:** N **MK:** unk **PH:** unk **SS:** DAR Ancestor #A095733 **BS:** 196.

RICHARDSON, William; b 22 Dec 1750, Stafford Co; d 6 Jul 1821 **RU:** First Lieutenant, Served in Greensville Co Militia Sep 1782 **CEM:** Buck Family; GPS unk; 1 mi W of Buckton Station, Waterlick; Warren **GS:** Y **SP:** 1) Elizabeth Philand 2) Polly Webb (__-1799) **VI:** Son of (-----) and Isabella (Calmes) (__-1796) Richardson **P:** unk **BLW:** unk **RG:** N **MK:** N **PH:** Y **SS:** DAR Ancestor # A097564; AP Serv Rec; DD cites Brown's Sketches of Greensville Co VA 1650-1967 pg 365 **BS:** 113.

RICHARDSON, William Sr; b 1 Sep 1748, Surry Co, NC; d Aug 1835 **RU:** Private, Enl 3 Apr 1777 in Capt Jason Watts' Co. Served 3 yrs. Fought in battle of Kings Mountain 7 Oct 1780 & battle of Point Pleasant 1774 **CEM:** Richardson; GPS 36.93250, 81.53360; Rt 610 Valley Rd; Smyth **GS:** U **SP:** Mar (1764 Washington Co) Rebecca Hays, d/o John & Elizabeth (Bass) Hays (1750-1810) **VI:** Parents unk. Warrant of 100 acres of land 10 Feb 1784, "Rich Valley" Smyth Co **P:** unk **BLW:** Y **RG:** Y **MK:** unk **PH:** unk **SS:** F pg 64; N pg 1430; A pg 145; SAR P-278734 **BS:** 196.

RICKMAN, William Dr; b 1731, England; d 1 Dec 1784 **RU:** Colonel, Served as Col in Cont Line **CEM:** Rickman Family; GPS 37.30529, -77.04826; Kittiewan Plantation, 12104 Weyanoke Rd, Charles City; Charles City Co **GS:** Y **SP:** 1) mar (1754) Sarah Van Meter 2) Elizabeth Harrison **VI:** Both a newer monument and newer Govt stone mark his grave. His origins in England and the identity of his wife have recently been asserted by the Kittiewan Plantation historian, reflected here. Served as Director of Hospital in VA; Widow Awarded BLW 6,666 acres. Signed Charles City Co petition **P:** unk **BLW:** Y **RG:** N **MK:** unk **PH:** unk **SS:** E pg663 **BS:** JLARC 110; 196.

RIDDICK, Josiah; b 5 Sep 1748; d 1795 **RU:** Colonel/Patriot, Ent serv during Gen Matthew's invasion. Was captured and sent to New York. Was Commander of Nansemond Co Militia. Gave material aid to cause **CEM:** Riddick Cemetery; GPS 36.68140, -76.55860; Off White Marsh Rd; Suffolk City **GS:** Y **SP:** 1) Elizabeth Godwin, d/o Willis & Mary (Folke) Riddick 2) Anne (-----) (28 Aug 1752-__) **VI:** Son of Mills (1721-1764) & Margaret (Barradall) (__-1764) Riddick. Was granted gratuitiy of 5000 # tobacco 25 Mar 1782 **P:** unk **BLW:** unk **RG:** N **MK:** N **PH:** unk **SS:** E pg 663; AL Ct Bk II pg 9 Nansemond Co; BX pg 674 **BS:** 53 vol I pg 31.

RIDDICK, Mills; b unk; d 1812 **RU:** Lieutenant, Served 3 yrs, units not identified **CEM:** Soldiers Hope; GPS unk; Rt 642, 3.5 mi S of Suffolk; Suffolk City **GS:** Y **SP:** Mary (-----) **VI:** Recd BLW #5921 **P:** unk **BLW:** Y **RG:** N **MK:** N **PH:** unk **SS:** C pg 494 **BS:** 143 Sold Hope.

RIDDLE, Joshua; b unk; d unk **RU:** Soldier, SAR Ancester service not identified **CEM:** Old Presbyterian Meeting House; GPS 38.48528, -77.23532; 323 S Fairfax St; Alexandria City **GS:** N **SP:** No info **VI:** No further data **P:** unk **BLW:** unk **RG:** Y **MK:** unk **PH:** N **SS:** J-NSSAR 1993 Reg; SAR P-278993 **BS:** JLARC 1; 5.

RU=Rank/Unit	CEM=Cemetery	GS=Gravestone	SP=Spousal Information
VI=Other Veteran Info	P=Pension	BLW=Bounty/Land Warrant	RG=Registered Grave
MK=SAR/DAR Marker	PH=Photo	SS=Service Source	BS=Burial Source

354

RIEBARD, Francois; b unk; d 1781 **RU:** Seaman, Served on "Saint-Esprit" and died from Yorktown battle **CEM:** French Memorial; GPS 36.81944, -79.39933; Yorktown; York **GS:** U **SP:** No info **VI:** No further data **P:** unk **BLW:** unk **RG:** Y **MK:** unk **PH:** unk **SS:** J-Yorktown Historian; SAR P-279131 **BS:** JLARC 1, 74.

RILEY, John; b c1756; d 22 Dec 1825 **RU:** Lieutenant, Received as Lt 25 Nov 1777 In Accomac Co Militia **CEM:** Riley Family; GPS unk; Rt 684, .5 mi W of Rt 658; Accomack **GS:** Y **SP:** Susannah Fletcher, d/o John Fletcher; d 22 Dec 1830 age 75y 10m 26d **VI:** Died age 69 yrs **P:** unk **BLW:** unk **RG:** N **MK:** N **PH:** unk **SS:** E pg 665 **BS:** 38 pg 234. 80 vol 3, pg 220.

RINKER, Casper, b 25 Dec 1727, Nuerensdorf, Canton Zurich Switszerland, d 11 Feb 1804 **RU:** Captain/Patriot, Commanded a compay in Frederick Co, Militia. Also gave material aid to cause **CEM:** Back Creek Quaker, AKA Gainesboro United Methodist Church; GPS 39.27861,-78.25694; Take Rt 522 fr Winchester, turn left Rt 600, .5 mi bef RR tracks on hill surounded by rock wall; Winchester. **GS:** Yes **SP:** mar (11 Apr 1757, Germantown, PA} Maria Schultz **VI:** Son of Jakob Ringger and Barbara Moriff. Large property owner. **P:** N **BLW:** N **RG:** Y **MK:** N **PH:** N **SS:** CM; vol2, pg 504; D pg 384; E pg 666; DAR A 097035; SAR P-279376 **BS:** 196

RINKER, Edward; b c1764; d 15 May 1847 **RU:** Sergeant, Served 3 yrs in various units to include Col Grayson's 16th Regt **CEM:** Waterford Union of Churches; GPS 39.18557, -77.60802; Fairfax St, Waterford; Loudoun **GS:** Y **SP:** Sarah Wagley/Waigley was furnished assistance in Loudoun Co in Apr 1778 **VI:** No further data **P:** unk **BLW:** unk **RG:** Y **MK:** N **PH:** unk **SS:** E pg 666; BX pg 674; DAR A097042; SAR P-279377 **BS:** 25 pg 260.

RINKER, Hans Casper; b 25 Dec 1727, Zurich, Switzerland; d 11 Feb 1804 **RU:** Captain, Commanded a co in Frederick Co Militia 1 Apr 1777 **CEM:** Back Creek Quaker, aka Gainesboro United Methodist; GPS 39.27861, -78.25694; 166 Siler Ln, Gainesboro; Frederick **GS:** Y **SP:** Mar (11 Apr 1757 Germantown, PA) Mary Anna Schultz (28 May 1730, Switzerland-28 Jan 1826) d/o Jacob & Margreth (Huber) Schultz **VI:** No further data **P:** unk **BLW:** unk **RG:**N **MK:** N **PH:** unk **SS:** E pg 666 **BS:** 59 pg 275; 196.

RINKER, Jacob; b 28 Mar 1749, Lancaster Co, PA; d 18 Jan 1827 **RU:** Colonel, Appt Col Shenandoah Militia 28 Jun 1781. Took oath 28 Jun 1782, Shenandoah Co Militia **CEM:** Conicville School; GPS 38.8938, -78.69532; Off Rt 703, SW of Conicville nr Swover Creek; Shenandoah **GS:** Y **SP:** Mary Keller (c1753-15 May 1806) **VI:** Marker placed 12 May 2001 **P:** unk **BLW:** unk **RG:** Y **MK:** Y **PH:** unk **SS:** E pg 666; SAR P-279381 **BS:** JLARC 1, 2, 3.

RINKER, Jacob; b 1723; d 26 Aug 1797 **RU:** Patriot, Gave to the cause **CEM:** Conicville School; GPS 38.8938, -78.69532; Off Rt 703, SW of Conicville nr Swover Creek; Shenandoah **GS:** Y **SP:** Catherine (-----) (c1710-15 Mar 1799) **VI:** GS says he was a "true Republican" **P:** N **BLW:** N **RG:** N **MK:** N **PH:** unk **SS:** AL Ct Bk pg 2, 12 **BS:** 155 Conicville; 80 vol 3, pg 220.

RIORDAN, John; b Feb 1763; d 10 Oct 1803 **RU:** Private, Served in Capt Joseph Anderson's Co, 3rd NJ Regt, Jun 1778 **CEM:** St Mary's Catholic; GPS 38.79390, -77.04750; 310 S Royal St; Alexandria City **GS:** Y **SP:** No info **VI:** Was bur with daughter Mary, age 14. Died age 40 yrs, 6 mos **P:** unk **BLW:** unk **RG:** Y **MK:** Y SAR plaque **PH:** Y **SS:** SAR P-33433; AP Roll **BS:** 174 pg 127; 196.

RIOTTE, Pierre; b unk; d 1781 **RU:** Soldier, Served in Gatinais Bn and died fr battle at Yorktown **CEM:** French Memorial; GPS 36.81944, -79.39933; Yorktown; York **GS:** U **SP:** No info **VI:** No further data **P:** unk **BLW:** unk **RG:** Y **MK:** unk **PH:** unk **SS:** J-Yorktown Historian; SAR P-279383 **BS:** JLARC 1, 74.

RIPTON, John; b unk; d 1781 **RU:** Soldier, Served fr PA, killed in the battle at Yorktown **CEM:** Yorktown Victory Monument Tablet; GPS 38.28350, -78.54150; Yorktown; York **GS:** U **SP:** No info **VI:** No further data **P:** unk **BLW:** unk **RG:** Y **MK:** unk **PH:** unk **SS:** J-Yorktown Historian; SAR P-279447 **BS:** JLARC 74.

RITCHEY, David; b unk; d Mar 1807 **RU:** Patriot, Gave material aid to cause **CEM:** Hogshead Family; GPS unk; Off Rt 736 btw Rts 42 & 250, N of Jennings Gap; Augusta **GS:** Y **SP:** No info **VI:** No further data **P:** N **BLW:** N **RG:** N **MK:** N **PH:** unk **SS:** AL Cert **BS:** 142.

RU=Rank/Unit VI=Other Veteran Info MK=SAR/DAR Marker CEM=Cemetery P=Pension PH=Photo GS=Gravestone BLW=Bounty/Land Warrant SS=Service Source SP=Spousal Information RG=Registered Grave BS=Burial Source

355

RITCHIE, Archibald; b unk, Scotland; d By 20 Apr 1784 **RU**: Patriot, Gave material aid to cause **CEM**: Ritchie Family; GPS unk; Burial vault on lot 18 or 22, Tappahannock; Essex **GS**: U **SP**: Mary Roane (__-1803) **VI**: Was merchant in Tappahannock, by 1766. His vault was opened and coffin contents mutilated by British War of 1812 **P**: N **BLW**: N **RG**: N **MK**: unk **PH**: unk **SS**: Al Ct bk pg 5 and 6 **BS**: 223 pg 154.

RITCHIE, Jacob; b 1762; d 1850 **RU**:Patriot, paid personal property tax 1783 Rockingham Co, a supply tax for Rev War expenses **CEM**: Ritchie Family; GPS 38.636870, -78.936600; loc Forest Creek Ln, Fulks Run; Rockingham **GS**: Unk **SP**: Maria Turner (1764, Abingdon, Harford Co, MD-1859), d/o James Turner (1732-1800) & Zetty Maria (-----) **VI**: Son of Isaac Ritchie (1735-1824) & Maria Catharina Wolfe (1738-1787) **P**: N **BLW**: N **RG**: N **MK**: N **PH**: N **SS**: **BS**: 196.

RITCHIE, William; b 1750s; d Fall 1797 **RU**: Private, Served in VA Cont line for 3 yrs **CEM**: Ritchie Family; GPS unk; Burial vault on lot 18 or 22, Tappahannock; Essex **GS**: U **SP**: No info **VI**: Son of Archibald & Mary (Roane) Ritchie (__-1803). this vault was opened and coffin contents mutilated by British War of 1812. BLW issued 20 Jan 1785 100 acres **P**: unk **BLW**: Y **RG**: N **MK**: unk **PH**: unk **SS**: F pg 65 **BS**: 223 pg 154.

ROADCAP, Peter, Sr; b 1739; d 1824 **RU**: Private, Captain Reader's Co 1775-1777 **CEM**: Roadcap Family; GPS 38.649730, -78.936510; 3rd Hill Rd, Rt 817, Fulks Run; Rockingham **GS**: N **SP**: Mar 1785, Hannah (__)(10 Jul 1760, Page Co-7 Aug 1818) **VI**: No further data **P**: N **BLW**: N **RG**: Y **MK**: N **PH**: N **SS**: DAR A096568; SAR P -279639 **BS**: 196.

ROANE, John Jr; b 9 Feb 1766, "Uppowac" King William Co; d 15 Nov 1838 **RU**: Private/Patriot, Served in Reg Army appeared on Army Register. Served in VA House of Delegates and was a Delegate to State Constitutional Convention 1788 **CEM**: Uppowac; GPS unk; Rumford; King William **GS**: U **SP**: No info **VI**: Elected Democratic-Republican to Congress 1809-1815. Was Jacksonian Democrat 1827-1831 and Democrat 1835-1837. Son was also Congressman fr VA **P**: unk **BLW**: unk **RG**: N **MK**: unk **PH**: unk **SS**: C pg 210; E pg 667 **BS**: 196.

ROBERDEAU (ROBERDEAN), Daniel; b 1727, St Christopher; West Indies d 5 Jan 1795 **RU**: Brigadier General/Patriot, In Jun 1775 elected Col 2nd Bn of Associators & President of Board of Officers and a Board of Privates, governing Associators. In May 1776 provided provisions for 10,000 men for 3 mos. On 10 Jun 1775 was member PA Council of Safety. Was elected Brig Gen 4 July 1776 Lancaster PA. Advanced $18,000 for Commisioners, never reimbursed. Was member 5 Feb 1777 of Cont Congress **CEM**: Mt Hebron; GPS 39.10916, -78.09497; 305 E Boscawen St; Winchester City **GS**: U **SP**: 1) mar (3 Oct 1761) Mary Bostwick, d/o Rev Mr. David & Mary (Hinman) Bostwick, (1741_15 Feb 1777 Lancaster PA) 2) mar (2 Dec 1778 Philadelphia PA) Jane Milligan, prob d/o James & (-----) Milligan (__-3 Sep 1835) **VI**: Son of Isaac & Mary (Cunyngham) Roberdeau **P**: unk **BLW**: unk **RG**: Y **MK**: Y SAR monument **PH:Y SS**: J-NSSAR 1993 Reg, SAR P-279849; DAR #A096869 **BS**: JLARC 1, 2; 80 vol 3, pg 222.

ROBERTS, Jacob; b 1743, d bef 21 Oct 1821 **RU**: Ensign/ Patriot, was Ensign, 25 May 1780 in Capt Craddock's Co, Amelia Co Militia. As patriot gave material aid to cause **CEM**: Roberts Family; GPS not determined; Folkes Bridge Rd (Rt 644), Paineville; Amelia **GS**: N **SP**: mar 22 Nov 1791, Magdain Hudson (c1760-1823), d/o Nicholas Hudson & Sarah Burton **VI**: No further data **P**: unk **BLW**: N **RG**: Y **MK**: unk **PH**: N **SS**: D vol 1, pg 30; G pg 13; AZ pg 179; DAR A200051; SAR P-331419 **BS**: 196.

ROBERTS, Stephen; b 29 Apr 1762; d 15 Jun 1842 **RU**: Sergeant, Enl 2nd SC Regt 1 May 1777. Appt Corporal 6 May 1777 in Grenadier Co. Absent without leave 4 Nov 1777. Promoted to Sergeant 27 June 1778 in Moultrie's Co. Transferred to 1st Vacant Co commanded by Lt Richard Bohun Baker 13 Jul 1778. Reenlisted 1 Nov 1779 under Capt Thomas Moultrie's 6th Co, Col Francis Marion's SC Regt, Nov 1779. Was at siege of Savannah **CEM**: Arnold Grove Episcopal Church; GPS 39.19796, -77.71557; Rt 9, vic jct with Rt 690, Hillsboro; Loudoun **GS**: Y **SP**: Debra Williams (26 Jun 1764-22 Nov 1842) **VI**: No further data **P**: unk **BLW**: unk **RG**: Y **MK**: Y SAR **PH**: Y **SS**: E pg 669; Unwanted Patience and Fortitude: Frances Marion's Orderly Book - Patrick O'Kelley; SAR P-335940 **BS**: 25 pg 262; 196.

ROBERTS, Thomas, b 14 Dec 1748, d 16 Dec 1784, York Co **RU**: Private, Capt William Johnston's Co, 7th, 11th, 15th, Cont Line **CEM**: Smith; GPS 37.1286565,-76.4387762; loc 515 Pleasant Dale Ln; York

RU=Rank/Unit	CEM=Cemetery	GS=Gravestone	SP=Spousal Information
VI=Other Veteran Info	P=Pension	BLW=Bounty/Land Warrant	RG=Registered Grave
MK=SAR/DAR Marker	PH=Photo	SS=Service Source	BS=Burial Source

356

GS: N **SP:**:Lucy Powell (1750-___) **VI:** Will processed York Co 1785 **P:** Unk **BLW:** Unk **RG:** N **MK:** N **PH:** N **SS:** A pg 258; E pg 669 **BS:** 196

ROBERTSON, Alexander; b 1753, Augusta Co; d 22 Apr 1801 **RU:** Ensign, Made ensign 16 Dec 1777 in Capt Alexander Robertson's Co in the Augusta Co Militia and then served in Capt Kenny's & Capt Rankin's Cos **CEM:** Augusta Stone Presbyterian; GPS 38.23926, -78.97356; 28 Old Stone Church Ln, Ft Defiance; Augusta **GS:** Y **SP:** Mar (10 Apr 1786) Jean/Jane Cord (c1753-25 Nov 1825) **VI:** Son of William (___Ireland-26 Oct 1812, Augusta Co) & Lettice (-----) (___-1809) Robertson. Died age 48 **P:** unk **BLW:** unk **RG:** Y **MK:** Y SAR plaque **PH:** unk **SS:** E pg 670; AZ pg 184; SAR P-280144 **BS:** JLARC 2 ,8, 23, 62; 196.

ROBERTSON, Alexander; b 1 Mar 1744; d 25 Nov 1816 **RU:** Major/Patriot, Received rank of Maj 21 Oct 1778 in the Augusta Co Militia and served to the end of the war in the 2d Battalion. Was Commissioner of the Provisions Law, Augusta Co 1781 **CEM:** Augusta Stone Presbyterian; GPS 38.23926, -78.97356, GS 38.1407,-78.5815; 28 Old Stone Church Ln, Ft Defiance; Augusta **GS:** U **SP:** Elizabeth (-----) **VI:** After the war he was promoted to the Lt Col rank **P:** unk **BLW:** unk **RG:** Y **MK:** Y SAR plaque **PH:** unk **SS:** E pg 670; AZ pg 184; AL Cert; SAR P-280142 **BS:** JLARC 2, 8, 23, 62, 63.

ROBERTSON, David; b unk; d 1815 **RU:** Private, Served in Capt John Morton's Co, 4th VA Regt, Jun & Jul 1776 **CEM:** John Conner Family; GPS unk; 200 yds W of jct Rts 616 & 826; Patrick **GS:** Y **SP:** 20 Aug 1796 Patrick Co) Mary Henry d/o John Sr. & (-----) Henry **VI:** No further data **P:** unk **BLW:** unk **RG:** N **MK:** N **PH:** unk **SS:** G pg 679 **BS:** 125 pg 219.

ROBERTSON, Edward; b 1755, Amelia Co; d 1826 **RU:** Private, Served in VA unit paid at Ft Pitt, PA **CEM:** Robertson Family; GPS unk; Dry Fork; Pittsylvania **GS:** Y **SP:** Mar (2 Feb 1782) Mary Ann Jennings **VI:** A Jr and Sr of this same name were in the same unit. Whether he was Jr or Sr not determined **P:** unk **BLW:** unk **RG:** Y **MK:** unk **PH:** unk **SS:** E pg 670; CZ pg 49;SAR P- 280160 **BS:** JLARC 76; 196.

ROBERTSON, James; b 16 Nov 1751, Augusta Co; d 1811 **RU:** Private, Ent serv 1777 Augusta Co in VA Regt. Served in Capt Rankin's Co, Augusta Co Militia **CEM:** Trinity Episcopal; GPS 38.14917, -79.07521; 214 Beverley St; Staunton City **GS:** N **SP:** Mar (12 Feb 1789 Augusta Co) Mary Russell **VI:** Pensioned Augusta Co 28 Aug 1833 **P:** Y **BLW:** unk **RG:** Y**MK:** N **PH:** N **SS:** E pg 670; K Vol 4 pg 239; CG pg 2913; SAR P-280177 **BS:** 142 trinity.

ROBERTSON, James Sr; b c1744; d 29 Nov 1819 **RU:** Patriot, Gave material aid to cause **CEM:** Robertson Family; GPS unk; Off Rt 641 nr Appomattox CH; Appomattox **GS:** N **SP:** Mar (3 Nov 1763) Rachel Phair (c1749-27 Mar 1822) **VI:** Died in Lynchburg, Campbell Co **P:** N **BLW:** N **RG:** Y **MK:** unk **PH:** N **SS:** DAR A092250; D Vol 1, pg 181-182; AL Ct Bk pg 22 Campbell Co; SAR P-280247 **BS:** JLARC 36.

ROBERTSON, Jeffrey Jr; b 1709; d 16 Dec 1784 **RU:** Patriot, Gave material aid to cause **CEM:** Robertson Farm; GPS 37.367321, -77.607786; Vic jct Robbie Rd & Christina Rd; Chesterfield **GS:** U **SP:** Mar (1734/5) Judith Tanner Mills (c1710-aft 1784 Chesterfield Co) **VI:** No further data **P:** N **BLW:** N **RG:** Y **MK:** N **PH:** unk **SS:** DAR A097253; D Vol 1, pg 248; J-NSSAR 1993 Reg; AL Ct Bk pg 38, 40 Chesterfield Co; SAR P-280244 **BS:** JLARC 1.

ROBERTSON, John; b 1730, PA; d 8 Aug 1828 **RU:** First Lieutenant/Patriot, Served in PA. Appraised beef for the commissioners approving public service claims **CEM:** Shockoe Hill; GPS 37.55190, - 77.43170; 4th & Hospital Sts; Richmond City **GS:** Y **SP:** No info **VI:** Was cashier of US Bank in Richmond. **P:** unk **BLW:** unk **RG:** Y **MK:** N **PH:** unk **SS:** E pg 670; AL Cert Chesterfield Co; SAR P-280191 **BS:** 57 pg 6; 196.

ROBERTSON, John Jr; b 1763; d 1814 **RU:** First Lieutenant, was appointed Lt, 6 Aug 1779 Chesterfield Co Militia. Serv in 2nd Cont Line **CEM:** Robertson Family; GPS unk; Off Rt 641 nr Appomattox CH; Appomattox **GS:** Y **SP:** No info **VI:** No further data **P:** unk **BLW:** unk **RG:** N **MK:** N **PH:** unk **SS:** E pg 671 **BS:** 76 Robertson.

ROBERTSON, John; b 6 Feb 1750, Scotland, d 17 May 1818; **RU:** Patriot, gave material aid to cause, Rockbridge Co **CEM:** Robertson Family; GPS not determined; loc on Rt 645, 2.4 mi up mtn fr jct with

RU=Rank/Unit	CEM=Cemetery	GS=Gravestone	SP=Spousal Information
VI=Other Veteran Info	P=Pension	BLW=Bounty/Land Warrant	RG=Registered Grave
MK=SAR/DAR Marker	PH=Photo	SS=Service Source	BS=Burial Source

357

Glade Rd; Nelson **GS:** Unk **SP:** No spousal data VI: No further data **P:** N **BLW:** N **RG:** N **MK:** N **PH:** N **SS:** **BS:** 196.

ROBERTSON, John; b 1755, d Mar 1826 **RU:** First Lt, Appointed 6 Aug 1779, Chesterfield Co Militia **CEM:** Royall; GPS not determined; loc off Promise Land Rd, Rt 661, Amelia C H; Amelia **GS:** Unk **SP:** Mar Jul 1776, Sarah Jennings **VI:** No further data **P:** N **BLW:** N **RG** Y **MK:** N **PH:** N **SS:** SAR P-280196 **BS:** 196.

ROBERTSON, William; b Dec 1748, Colerain, County Antrim, Ireland; d 12 Nov 1831 **RU:** Captain, Promoted to Capt on 16 Mar 1779, 9th Regt VA Militia. Served as officer fr 1775 until end of war **CEM:** Augusta Stone Presbyterian; GPS 38.23926, -78.97356; 28 Old Stone Church Ln, Ft Defiance; Augusta **GS:** U **SP:** 1) mar (3 Jun 1788, Augusta Co) Ann Crawford (c1767-10 Dec 1815); 2) Letitice Kerr (12 Jan 1790-18 Dec 1836). Both wives have stones. **VI:** Son of Mathew & Mary (Paxton) Robertson. Recd BLW #1860-200-21 Jan 1790. After the war he served as the county Magistrate. Recd pension of $320 per annum under act of 22 Oct 1828 on Cert #731 while living in Augusta Co **P:** Y **BLW:** Y **RG:** Y **MK:** Y SAR granite & plaque **PH:** unk **SS:** E pg 671; K Vol 4 pg 242; AZ pg 184; CG Vol 3 pg 2915; DAR A097178; SAR P-280230 **BS:** JLARC 1, 8, 23, 62; 196.

ROBERTSON, William; b unk; d 1831 **RU:** Patriot, Gave material aid to cause **CEM:** Stonewall Jackson Memorial; GPS 37.78128, -79.44604; 314 S Main St; Lexington City **GS:** U **SP:** No info **VI:** No further data **P:** N **BLW:** N **RG:** N **MK:** unk **PH:** unk **SS:** AL Comm Bk II pg 360 Augusta Co **BS:** JLARC 63.

ROBERTSON, William; b 12 Nov 1748, Charles Co, MD; d 19 Aug 1828 **RU:** Private/Patriot, Served in Capt Belain Posey,Co 3rd MD Militia of the fying Camp Gave material aid to cause **CEM:** Rileyville; GPS 38.766337, -78.387365; At end Cemetery Rd on the right, Luray; Page **GS:** U **SP:** Mar (1779, MD) Mary Timms (1760-1812), d/o William Timms (1730-1803) & Mary Ross (1730-unk) **VI:** Son of William Robertson II (1721-1773) & Rebecca Chatham (1725-unk) **P:** unk **BLW:** unk **RG:** Y **MK:**Y SAR granite **PH:** unk **SS:** J- DAR Hatcher; AL Ct Bk pg 18 Shenandoah Co; DD cites MD Archives Vol 18 pg 12; DAR A097171; SAR P-280235 **BS:** JLARC 2; 196.

ROBERTSON, William; b 1750, Prince George Co, d 10 Dec 1829 **RU:** Second Lieutenant, Served in Capt Ogelby's Co Chesterfield Co Militia **CEM:** Cobbs Family; GPS unk; Bolling Family property, Enon; Chesterfield **GS:** Y **SP:** Elizabeth Bolling **VI:** Son of William & (-----) Robertson Jr. One son Wyndham Robertson became Gov of VA. Another son, Thomas Bolling Robertson became Gov of LA. Family memorial stone-not contemporary. Stones destroyed during Civil War **P:** unk **BLW:** unk **RG:** Y **MK:** N **PH:** unk **SS:** G pg 13; DAR A097179; SAR P-280236 **BS:** 56 pg; 196.

ROBERTSON, William; b 7 Feb 1720, Ire; d 17 Oct 1812 Captain As private served in the battle at Point Pleasant in Capt James Kirtley's Co,Oct 1774; on Mar 1778 he qualified as Captain in the Augusta Co Militia **CEM:** Augusta Stone Presbyterian; GPS 38.23926, -78.97356; 28 Old Stone Church Ln, Ft Defiance; Augusta **GS:** U **SP** Lettice Kerr (7 Jan 1724, Fiherville, Augusta Co-14 Jul 1775) d/o James Kerr & Martha Ball **VI:** Son of James Robertson & Rebecca Royston **P:** Unk **BLW:** Unk **RG:** Y **MK:** N **PH:** unk **SS:** DAR A097178; Z pg 88 SAR P-280230 **BS:** 196.

ROBICHON, Ferdinand; b unk; d 1781 **RU:** Soldier, Served in Royal Deaux Ponts Bn and died fr battle at Yorktown **CEM:** French Memorial; GPS 36.81944, -79.39933; Yorktown; York **GS:** U **SP:** No info **VI:** No further data **P:** unk **BLW:** unk **RG:** Y **MK:** unk **PH:** unk **SS:** J-Yorktown Historian; SAR P-280272 **BS:** JLARC 1, 74.

ROBINS, Thomas; b 11 Feb 1745; d 8 Nov 1808 **RU:** Private?, Served in 5th Cont Line **CEM:** Robins Family; GPS not determined; Point Lookout, Robin's Neck; Gloucester **GS:** Y **SP:** Frances Stubbs(14 Feb 1745-18 Jul 1800) **VI:** Son of William & Elizabeth (-----) Robins **P:** unk **BLW:** unk **RG:** Y **MK:** N **PH:** unk **SS:** E pg 672; SAR P-280305 **BS:** 48 pg 53; 196; 213 pg 78.

ROBINSON, Braxton; b c1724; d 1799 **RU:** Ensign, Appt Ensign in Greensville Co Militia 23 May 1782 **CEM:** Emporia Tree; GPS unk; Emporia; Emporia City **GS:** Y **SP:** Mar (20 Nov 1789) Frances Walton **VI:** Son of Littleberry & Susanna (-----) Robinson. After war on 27 Jan 1791, promoted to Capt **P:** unk **BLW:** unk **RG:** Y **MK:** N **PH:** unk **SS:** G pg 170; SAR P-280341 **BS:** 80 vol 3 pg 224.

ROBINSON, Isaac; b 8 Oct 1765, Botetourt Co; d 21 Sep 1835 **RU:** Second Lieutenant, Appointed 12 Jul 1781 to 2nd Lt in Botetourt Co Militia **CEM:** North Mountain; GPS unk; 7 mi S of Staunton on N side

RU=Rank/Unit	CEM=Cemetery	GS=Gravestone	SP=Spousal Information
VI=Other Veteran Info	P=Pension	BLW=Bounty/Land Warrant	RG=Registered Grave
MK=SAR/DAR Marker	PH=Photo	SS=Service Source	BS=Burial Source

358

Rt 252; Augusta **GS:** U **SP:** Mar (6 Sep 1804 Botetourt Co) Eleanor Moffett (20 Mar 1773-3 Sep 1856) d/o John & Jane (Ledgerwood) Moffett **VI:** Cenotaph momument has different dates of 1761-1830 **P:** unk **BLW:** unk **RG:** N **MK:** N **PH:** unk **SS:** E pg 672 **BS:** 75 No. Mtn; 196.

ROBINSON, James; b 1757, Brunswick Co; d Bef Oct 1801 **RU:** Captain, Commanded a co in Greensville Co Militia **CEM:** Robinson Family; GPS unk; Emporia; Emporia City **GS:** U **SP:** Winnifred Fox **VI:** No further data **P:** unk **BLW:** unk **RG:** Y **MK:** unk **PH:** unk **SS:** J- DAR Hatcher; DD cites Wm & Mary Quarterly Series 1 Vol 27 pg 96; SAR P-280451 **BS:** JLARC 2.

ROBINSON, John; b 22 Dec 1750; d 1832 **RU:** Lieutenant, Served in VA militia and Cont Line **CEM:** Crossroads Primitive Baptist; GPS 36.60868, -81.01592; Nr Baywood Elem Sch, Rt 624, Baywood; Grayson **GS:** U **SP:** 1) Elizabeth Pyland 2) Polly Webb **VI:** By tradition, Maj Robinson and his wife are bur in unmarked graves in the Robinson-Fields Cemetery. Obtained rank of Maj after RW. Received 2,666 acres BLW **P:** unk **BLW:** Y **RG:** N **MK:** N **PH:** Y **SS:** E pg 672; AK, Apr 2007 **BS:** 04, Apr 2007; 196.

ROBINSON, John; b 1754 Ireland; d 26 Jun 1826 **RU:** Soldier/Patriot, Gave material aid to cause **CEM:** Washington & Lee Univ Campus; GPS 36.60863, -81.01593; Nr Jefferson St; Lexington City **GS:** U **SP:** No info **VI:** No further data **P:** unk **BLW:** unk **RG:** YMK: unk **PH:** unk **SS:** G pg 770; AL Ct Bk pg 7; SAR P-280524 **BS:** JLARC 2, 79.

ROBINSON, John; b 1720; d 1795 **RU:** Captain, Service information not given in SAR registry **CEM:** Robinson Family; GPS unk; Emporia; Emporia City **GS:** U **SP:** No info **VI:** No further data **P:** unk **BLW:** unk **RG:** Y **MK:** unk **PH:** unk **SS:** SAR P-280500; AR Vol 3 pg 225 **BS:** JLARC 2.

ROBINSON, John; b Unk; d 30 Jun 1778 **RU:** Corporal Capt Moore's Co, Col William Grayson's 3rd VA Regt, Cont Line, Jun 1778 **CEM:** Rev War Court House Plaque; GPS not determined; 4110 Chain Bridge Rd; Fairfax **GS:** Memorialized on plaque 2017 by Geo Washington Chapter, VASSAR **SP** No info **VI:** died in service **P:** N **BLW:** N **RG:** N **MK:** N **PH:** N **SS:** E pg 691; AP Fold3 muster roll: EP sources: **BS:** None.

ROBINSON, Littlebury; b 1715; d 1792 **RU:** Captain/Patriot, Gave material aid to cause **CEM:** Robinson Family; GPS unk; Emporia; Emporia City **GS:** U **SP:** No info **VI:** No further data **P:** unk **BLW:** unk **RG:** N **MK:** unk **PH:** unk **SS:** J- DAR Hatcher; AL Ct Bk pg 5 Greenville Co **BS:** JLARC 2.

ROBINSON, Robert; b 1764; d 1808 **RU:** Private, Served in 3rd Artillery Regt, Cont Troops **CEM:** Blandford; GPS 37.22433, -77.38604; 319 S Crater Rd; Petersburg City **GS:** Y **SP:** No info **VI:** No further data **P:** unk **BLW:** unk **RG:** N **MK:** Y SAR monument **PH:** unk **SS:** AP service rec **BS:** 99 pg 33.IIii.

ROBINSON, William; b unk, d aft 1781 **RU:** Lieutenant Colonel, commanded Botetourt Co Militia until 12 Apr 1781 when he resigned **CEM:** Mt Pleasant; GPS unk; 6 mi NE of Covington; Covington City **GS:** U **SP:** No info **VI:** No further data **P:** unk **BLW:** unk **RG:** N **MK:** N **PH:** unk **SS:** E pg 673 **BS:** 160 Mt Pleasant.

ROBINSON, William, b 1760, d 17 Oct 1831 **RU:** Private served in Clarks Illinois Regt 1781-1783 **CEM:** Rock Spring; GPS 36.7094710, -81.7849770; Rock Springs Rd, Rt 803, Lodi, Glade Spring; Washington **GS:** N **SP:** No Info **VI:** No further data **P:** N **BLW:** N **RG:** N **MK:** N **PH:** N **SS:** E pg 673 **BS:** 196.

ROCHE, Jean; b unk; d 1781 **RU:** Soldier, Served in Soissonnais Bn and died fr battle at Yorktown **CEM:** French Memorial; GPS 36.81944, -79.39933; Yorktown; York **GS:** U **SP:** No info **VI:** No further data **P:** unk **BLW:** unk **RG:** unk **MK:** unk **PH:** unk **SS:** J-Yorktown Historian; SAR P-280774 **BS:** JLARC 1, 74.

ROCHE, Pierre de; b unk; d 1781 **RU:** Soldier, Served in Soissonnais Bn and died fr battle at Yorktown **CEM:** French Memorial; GPS 36.81944, -79.39933; Yorktown; York **GS:** U **SP:** No info **VI:** No further data **P:** unk **BLW:** unk **RG:** Y **MK:** unk **PH:** unk **SS:** J-Yorktown Historian; SAR P-280776 **BS:** JLARC 1, 74.

ROCHEFORT, Jean; b unk; d 1781 **RU:** Seaman, Served on "Auguste" and died from Yorktown battle **CEM:** French Memorial; GPS 36.81944, -79.39933; Yorktown; York **GS:** U **SP:** No info **VI:** No further

RU=Rank/Unit	CEM=Cemetery	GS=Gravestone	SP=Spousal Information
VI=Other Veteran Info	P=Pension	BLW=Bounty/Land Warrant	RG=Registered Grave
MK=SAR/DAR Marker	PH=Photo	SS=Service Source	BS=Burial Source

359

data **P:** unk **BLW:** unk **RG:** Y **MK:** unk **PH:** unk **SS:** J-Yorktown Historian;SAR P- 280776 **BS:** JLARC 1, 74.

ROCHELLE, John; b 1746; d unk **RU:** Captain, Was Commissary Officer, VA Troops **CEM:** Rochelle Family, Hermitage Plantation; GPS unk; Hwy 671 nr Hansom, Franklin; Franklin City **GS:** Y **SP:** No info **VI:** Son of John & Mary (-----) Rochelle. Govt grave stone, DAR marker **P:** unk **BLW:** unk **RG:** Y **MK:** Y DAR plaque **PH:** unk **SS:** B; **SAR P-280779 BS:** JLARC 76; 196.

ROCHESTER, John Jr; b 1746, Westmoreland Co; d 1794 **RU:** Captain, Served in Westmoreland Co Militia July 1777 **CEM:** Rochester Family; GPS unk; Probably old homestead at Lydell's Store, jct Rts 3 & 202; Westmoreland **GS:** U **SP:** 1) Mar (before Jan 1776) Ann Jordan, d/o Robert & (-----) Jordan 2) Anne (-----) McClanahan, widow of William McClanahan **VI:** Son of John (1708-1754) and Hester (Thrift) Rochester **P:** unk **BLW:** unk **RG:** unk **MK:** unk **PH:** unk **SS:** E pg 673; CN pg 85 Westmoreland Co Order Bk; SAR P-280783 **BS:** 80 vol 3 pg 227; 196.

RODES, Charles; b c1730, Hanover Co; d 17 Jun 1805 **RU:** Patriot, Had Civil service as Juror and gave material aid to cause **CEM:** Rodes family; GPS unk; See county property records for homeplace; Amherst **GS:** N **SP:** mar (c1751) Amy Duke (c1733 Hanover Co-13 Nov 1812). SAR applicant indicates also mar Elizabeth Stowe. **VI:** Son of John (6 Nov 1697-aft Feb 1774) & Mary (Crawford) (Mar 1703-__) Rodes. Will dated 19 Mar 1805, Amherst Co **P:** N **BLW:** N **RG:** Y **MK:** N **PH:** N **SS:** DAR A095948; SAR P-280908; D Vol 1 pg 71, 78; AS, SAR applic **BS:** SAR Appl.

RODES (RHODES), John; b 1729; d 1810 **RU:** Fifer/Patriot, Served in Cont Line. Gave material aid to cause **CEM:** Rodes family at Midway Plantation; GPS unk; E of Whitehall; Albemarle **GS:** U **SP:** Mar (24 May 1757) Sarah Harris (1735-1803) **VI:** Son of Charles & Amy (Duke) Rodes **P:** unk **BLW:** unk **RG:** Y **MK:** Y DAR **PH:** unk **SS:** J-NSSAR 1993 Reg; AL Ct Bk pg 14 Albemarle Co; SAR P-280914 **BS:** JLARC 1; 80 vol3, pg 212; 196

RODGERS, Robert; b 29 Jun 1753; d 14 Dec 1827 **RU:** Private, Served in 9th Cont Line **CEM:** Rodgers Plot; GPS unk; Rt 180 off Rt 178, .9 mi W of Pungoteague, Hacks Neck; Accomack **GS:** Y **SP:** Mar (31 Oct 1775 (bond) Accomack Co) Tabitha Bundick (22 Jan 1755-28 Nov 1824) d/o Justice Bundick **VI:** Son of Abel & Rosey (-----) Rodgers **P:** unk **BLW:** unk **RG:** N **MK:** Y **PH:** unk **SS:** E pg 674 **BS:** 37 pg 218.

ROEBUCK, William; b unk; d 1781 **RU:** Soldier, Served fr VA, killed in the battle at Yorktown **CEM:** Yorktown Victory Monument Tablet; GPS 38.28350, -78.54150; Yorktown; York **GS:** U **SP:** No info **VI:** No further data **P:** unk **BLW:** unk **RG:** N **MK:** unk **PH:** unk **SS:** J-Yorktown Historian **BS:** JLARC 74.

ROGERS, Hamilton; b unk; d 10 Jul 1820 **RU:** Private/Patriot, Served in Capt Henry McCabes Co fr Loudoun Co. Gave material aid to cause **CEM:** North Fork Baptist; GPS 39.06014, -77.68509; 38130 North Folk Rd, North Fork; Loudoun **GS:** Y **SP:** No info **VI:** No further data **P:** unk **BLW:** unk **RG:** N **MK:** N **PH:** unk **SS:** N pg 1267; AL Ct Bk pg 37, 47 Loudoun Co **BS:** 25 pg 263.

ROGERS, James; b unk; d 1804 **RU:** Private?, 9th Cont Line **CEM:** Back Creek Quaker, aka Gainesboro United Methodist; GPS 39.27861, -78.25694; 166 Siler Ln, Gainesboro; Frederick **GS:** Y **SP:** no info **VI:** No further data **P:** unk **BLW:** unk **RG:** N **MK:** N **PH:** unk **SS:** E pg 675 **BS:** 59 pg 283.

ROGERS, John; b 31 Oct 1750, Frederick Co; d 6 Oct 1826 **RU:** Corporal, Serv in Capt John Mercer's Co Feb 1778 of the 3rd VA Regt commanded by Lt Col Heth **CEM:** Back Creek Quaker, aka Gainesboro United Methodist; GPS 39.27861, -78.25694; 166 Siler Ln, Gainesboro; Frederick **GS:** Y **SP:** Mar (30 Oct 1787 Frederick Co. by Christian Streit) Mary Olleman **VI:** No further data **P:** unk **BLW:** unk **RG:** N **MK:** N **PH:** unk **SS:** A pg 276 **BS:** 59 pg 283.

ROGERS, Samual; b unk; d 1781 **RU:** Lieutenant, Served fr MA, and died fr the battle at Yorktown **CEM:** Yorktown Victory Monument Tablet; GPS 38.28350, -78.54150; Yorktown; York **GS:** U **SP:** No info **VI:** No further data **P:** unk **BLW:** unk **RG:** Y **MK:** unk **PH:** unk **SS:** J-Yorktown Historian; SAR P- 281284 **BS:** JLARC 74.

ROITOUX, Pierre; b unk; d 1781 **RU:** Soldier, Served in Soissonnais Bn and died fr battle at Yorktown **CEM:** French Memorial; GPS 36.81944, -79.39933; Yorktown; York **GS:** U **SP:** No info **VI:** No further

---

RU=Rank/Unit   CEM=Cemetery   GS=Gravestone   SP=Spousal Information
VI=Other Veteran Info   P=Pension   BLW=Bounty/Land Warrant   RG=Registered Grave
MK=SAR/DAR Marker   PH=Photo   SS=Service Source   BS=Burial Source

360

data **P**: unk **BLW**: unk **RG**: Y **MK**: unk **PH**: unk **SS**: J-Yorktown Historian; SAR P-281403 **BS**: JLARC 1, 74.

ROLLER, Conrad; b 3 Mar 1752, Bucks Co, PA; d Oct 1824 **RU**: Soldier, Ent serv 1781 in VA Line **CEM**: New Jerusalem Lutheran; GPS 39.25736, -77.63891; GS GPS 39.25699,-77.63889, 12942 Lutheran Church Rd, Lovettsville; Loudoun **GS**: Y **SP**: mar (21 Mar 1779 Loudoun Co by Rev Charles Wildahne, German Lutheran Church) Elizabeth Slates(1761-1845) d/o Frederick & (-----) Slates of Pine Run Hundred, Frederick Co. **VI**: Son of Johannes Andreas David Roller (1730-1802). Was fr Loudoun Co. Widow appl pen 28 Apr 1840 Loudoun Co age 79. Rec'd BLW. W4325 **P**: Y **BLW**: Y **RG**:Y **MK**: Y SAR granite **PH**: Y **SS**: C pg 265; K Vol 4 pg 253; CG Vol 3 pg 2941 **BS**: JLARC 4, 32; SAR P-343721 **BS**: 196, cem visit.

ROLLER(ROLER); Peter, Sr: b 1 Apr 1763; d 17 Aug 1836: **RU**: Patriot. Paid personal property tax, 1782 in Rockingham Co which was a supply tax for Rev War expenses **CEM**: Friedens United Church of Christ GPS 38.348480, -78.876530; GPS GS 38.347888, -78.877228; 3960 Friedens Church Rd, Mt Crawford; Rockingham **GS**:Y-new stone gives b & d dates **SP**: No spousal data **VI**: No further data **P**: N **BLW**: N **RG**: N **MK**: N **PH**: Y **SS**: AK **BS**: 04; 196.

ROLSTONE (ROLSTON/RALSTON), David; b 20 Oct 1760, Rockingham Co; d 5 Jun 1849 **RU**: Private, Served in Capts Hopkins and John Rice Cos 1776; Capt Robert Craven's Co under Col Stubblefield 1780; Capt Richard Ragan's Co under Maj Long 1781. Was at the siege of Yorktown. Discharged 20 Oct 1781 **CEM**: Cooks Creek Presbyterian; GPS 38.47472, -78.92997; 4222 Mt Clinton Pike; Harrisonburg City **GS**: Y **SP**: Mar (18 Jan 1783. Rockingham Co) Sarah Hinton (__ Shenandoah Co-10 Mar 1804) **VI**: Died in Rockingham Co **P**: unk **BLW**: unk **RG**: Y **MK**: Y SAR **PH**: unk **SS**: E pg 676; DAR A093673; AP Fold3 pen files; SAR P-281508 **BS**: JLARC 7.; 80 vol 3, pg 199.

ROSBUCK, William; b unk; d 1781 **RU**: Private, Service unit not identified. Died fr Yorktown battle **CEM**: Yorktown Victory Monument Tablet; GPS 38.28350, -78.54150; Yorktown; York **GS**: Y **SP**: No info **VI**: No further data **P**: unk **BLW**: unk **RG**: Y **MK**: N **PH**: unk **SS**: AS; SAR P-281737 **BS**: SAR report.

ROSE, Alexander; b Britain; d 28 Nov 1800 **RU**: Major/ Captain, Retired as Maj 14 Sep 1778 **CEM**: St George's Episcopal; GPS unk; 905 Princess Anne; Fredericksburg City **GS**: Y **SP**: 1) Mildred Washington 2) Sarah Fontaine **VI**: Recd 5111 acres BLW #1863-300-3 Mar 1791 **P**: unk **BLW**: Y **RG**:N **MK**: N **PH**: unk **SS**: E pg 677; CG Vol 3 pg 294 **BS**: 12 pg 113.

ROSE, Henry; b unk; d 4 Feb 1810 **RU**: Soldier, SAR Ancester service not identified **CEM**: Presbyterian Church; GPS 38.80015, -77.05791; Wilkes St & Hamilton Ln; Alexandria City **GS**: N **SP**: No info **VI**: Death notice in Alexandria Gazette 6 Feb 1810, pg 3 **P**: unk **BLW**: unk **RG**: Y **MK**: Y SAR plaque **PH**: N **SS**: J-NSSAR 1993 Reg; SAR P-281761 **BS**: JLARC 1.

ROSE, John; b 3 Sep 1761; d 4 Feb 1844 **RU**: Captain, Served in John Clark's III Regt. Was a sea capt in 1780 and was captured by the British **CEM**: Old Stone Methodist; GPS 39.11725, -77.56609; 168 W Cornwall St, Leesburg; Loudoun **GS**: Y **SP**: Anna Beall (3 Feb 1762-22 Jan 1840) d/o George (1729-1807) & (-----) Beale **VI**: Son of Isaac (1729-1805) & Rachel (Grigsby) (1737-1805) Rose. First mayor of Leesburg. Sheriff of Loudoun Co 11 Nov 1822 to 8 Nov 1824 **P**: unk **BLW**: unk **RG**; N **MK**: N **PH**: unk **SS**: E, pg 677 **BS**: 25, pg 265; 196.

ROSS, Alexander; b 9 Feb 1741; d unk **RU**: Private/Patriot, Service as private in undetermined unit. As a patriot in Frederick Co he furnished the militia paint and iron **CEM**: Augusta Stone Presbyterian; GPS 38.23926, -78.97356; 28 Old Stone Church Ln, Ft Defiance; Augusta **GS**: U **SP**: No info **VI**: No further data **P**: unk **BLW**: unk **RG**: Y **MK**: Y SAR plaque **PH**: unk **SS**: Z pg 77; JLARC report; SAR P-281885 **BS**: JLARC 23; 71; 196.

ROSS, Daniel Sr; b 1740; d 1823 **RU**: Second Lieutenant/Patriot, Appt 2nd Lt Jun 1780, Henry Co Militia. Gave material aid to cause **CEM**: Ross Harbour Methodist; GPS unk; 6260 Elamsville Rd, Stuart; Patrick **GS**: U **SP**: Mar (24 Jul 1798) Nancy Ingram d/o James & (-----) Ingram **VI**: Died in and was probably bur in Missouri. Cemetery has stone memorial to him **P**: unk **BLW**: unk **RG**: Y **MK**: unk **PH**: unk **SS**: AL Comm Bk II pg 153 Henry Co; DAR A098289; SAR P-281897 **BS**: JLARC 30,108.

RU=Rank/Unit   CEM=Cemetery   GS=Gravestone   SP=Spousal Information
VI=Other Veteran Info   P=Pension   BLW=Bounty/Land Warrant   RG=Registered Grave
MK=SAR/DAR Marker   PH=Photo   SS=Service Source   BS=Burial Source

361

ROSS, John, Sr; b 21 Oct 1756,Scotland, d 24 Jul 1838 **RU:** Sergeant, served in an undetetrmined cavalry unit **CEM:** Ebenezer Baptist Church; GPS 39.05824,-77.81142; 20421 Airmount Rd, Bluemont; Loudoun **GS:** Unk **SP:** Agness Miller (17 Feb 1763-12 Dec 1843) **VI:** Rec'd 200 acres bounty land, eligible for 200 more **P:** N **BLW:** Yes **RG:** Y **MK:** Y SAR plaque **PH:** N **SS:** C Sec II, pgs178, 210; E pg 678; SAR P-336621 **BS:** 196

ROSS, Peter; b unk; d 1818 **RU:** Private/Patriot, Served in Capt Burnam's Co, 8th VA Regt, for 15 mos, 18 days. Also gave to cause in Fluvanna Co **CEM:** Ross Family; GPS unk; Vic Rts 600 & 633; Fluvanna **GS:** Y **SP:** No info **VI:** No further data **P:** unk **BLW:** unk **RG:** N **MK:** N **PH:** unk **SS:** A, pg 126; AL Comm Bk 1, pg 364 Fluvanna Co **BS:** 66 pg 80.

ROSSIGNOL, Francois; b unk; d 1781 **RU:** Soldier, Served in Bourbonnais Bn and died fr battle at Yorktown **CEM:** French Memorial; GPS 36.81944, -79.39933; Yorktown; York **GS:** U **SP:** No info **VI:** No further data **P:** unk **BLW:** unk **RG:** Y **MK:** unk **PH:** unk **SS:** J Yorktown Historian; SAR P-282060 **BS:** JLARC 1, 74.

ROSSON, Reuben; b 8 Sep 1752; d unk **RU:** Soldier, Ent serv Culpeper 1777. Served in VA Line **CEM:** Farm; GPS unk; Behind Culpeper & Racoon Ford; Culpeper **GS:** U **SP:** Nancy Lovelace **VI:** Pensioned Culpeper Co 1832 age 80. Son Edmund gave Power of Attny in Culpeper 1853 to apply for pension in arrears due father S6016 **P:** Y **BLW:** unk **RG:** Y **MK:** unk **PH:** unk **SS:** J-NSSAR 1993 Reg; K Vol 4 pg 264; DAR A132054; SAR P-282077 **BS:** JLARC 1.

ROSZEL (ROSZELL), Stephen George; b 1739; d 1792 **RU:** Patriot, Gave material aid to cause **CEM:** Mountain Chapel; GPS unk; Jct Rts 734 & 630; Loudoun **GS:** Y **SP:** Sarah Chilton **VI:** No further data **P:** N **BLW:** N **RG:** N **MK:** N **PH:** unk **SS:** D Vol 2 pg 607; AL Ct Bk pg 47 Loudoun Co **BS:** 25 pg 266.

ROUAY, Charles; b unk; d 1781 **RU:** Soldier, Served in Gatinais Bn and died fr battle at Yorktown **CEM:** French Memorial; GPS 36.81944, -79.39933; Yorktown; York **GS:** U **SP:** No info **VI:** No further data **P:** unk **BLW:** unk **RG:** Y **MK:** unk **PH:** unk **SS:** J-Yorktown Historian; SAR P-282117 **BS:** JLARC 1, 74.

ROUFFE, Gottfried; b unk; d 1781 **RU:** Soldier, Served in Royal Deaux Ponts Bn and died fr battle at Yorktown **CEM:** French Memorial; GPS 36.81944, -79.39933; Yorktown; York **GS:** U **SP:** No info **VI:** No further data **P:** unk **BLW:** unk **RG:** Y **MK:** unk **PH:** unk **SS:** J-Yorktown Historian; SAR P-282120 **BS:** JLARC 1, 74.

ROUSH (ROUSCH), Balser (Balster); b 1745, Shenandoah Co; d 1845 **RU:** Private, Was in battle at Point Pleasant **CEM:** St Mary Pine Lutheran; GPS 38.74470, -78.68390; 7103 S Middle Rd, Mt Jackson; Shenandoah **GS:** U **SP:** No info **VI:** Son of John Adam (__Germany-__) & Susannah (Schlern) Roush. Listed as Palster Rouse in militia **P:** unk **BLW:** unk **RG:** Y **MK:** unk **PH:** unk **SS:** J-NSSAR 1993 Reg; Z pg 162; SAR P-282204 **BS:** JLARC 1.

ROUSH (ROUCH), Daniel; b 1754, Shenandoah Co; d Dec 1832 **RU:** Private, Served in Capt Andrew Waggoner's Co, Col James Wood's 12th VA Regt Cont Line **CEM:** St Mary Pine Lutheran; GPS 38.74470, -78.68390; 7103 S Middle Rd, Mt Jackson; Shenandoah **GS:** **GS:** Y family stone erected 1935 indicating he served his country in the cause of independence **SP:** No info **VI:** Son of John Adam (__Germany-__) & Susannah (Schlern) Roush; **P:** unk **BLW:** unk **RG:** Y **MK:** unk **PH:** unk **SS:** J-NSSAR 1993 Reg; E pg 679; AP Fold 3; SAR P-282205 **BS:** JLARC 1; 221.

ROUSH (ROUSK), George; b Jul 1761; d 1845, Meigs Co, OH **RU:** Private, served in brother, Capt John Roush's Co, VA Line CEM: Old Pine Church; GPS not determined; loc 1mi S of Pinkerton east of rd on land of Milton Funkhouser 1936; Shenandoah **GS:**Y memorialized on family memorial in cem 1936 **SP:** No further data **VI:** Son of John Adam (__Germany-__) & Susannah (Schlern) Roush; moved to OH 1802 and applied for pen there1 Oct 1833, rec'd 1835 #S18579 at age 73 **PEN:** Y # 1701 **BLW:** Y by heirs S1815 for 160 acres in 1855 **RG:** N **MK:** N **PH:** N **SS:** E pg 679; AP Fold3, Pen BLW rec; CG vol III, pg 2063 **BS:** 221.

ROUSH (ROUSE), Henry b 1742; d 1831 **RU:**Patriot gave axes and other material aid to cause, 1776 **CEM:** Old Pine Church; GPS not determined; loc 1mi S of Pinkerton east of rd on land of Milton Funkhouser 1936; Shenandoah **GS:** Y family stone erected 1935 indicating he served his country in the cause of independence **SP:** No spousat data **VI:** Son of John Adam Roush (1711-1786) & Susanne

---

RU=Rank/Unit	CEM=Cemetery	GS=Gravestone	SP=Spousal Information
VI=Other Veteran Info	P=Pension	BLW=Bounty/Land Warrant	RG=Registered Grave
MK=SAR/DAR Marker	PH=Photo	SS=Service Source	BS=Burial Source

362

(-----) (1713-1796), He was in colonial war being paid at Rommy **1775 P**: N **BLW**: N **RG**: N **MK**: N **PH**: N **SS**: EQ Old Pine Church Cem Survey rpt 1936; Z pg 84 indicates cert iassued 7 Jan 1776 **BS**: 221.

ROUSH (ROUSCH), Jacob; b 1746, Frederick Co; d 16 Jan 1830 **RU**: Private/Patriot, Was in Battle at Point Pleasant in Capt John Tipton's Co, Shenandoah Co Militia;also served in 3rd Pa militia; gave material aid to cause **CEM**: St Mary Pine Lutheran; GPS 38.74470, -78.68390; 7103 S Middle Rd, Mt Jackson; Shenandoah **GS**: Y family stone erected 1935 indicating he served his country in the cause of independence **SP**: mar 1) (21 Feb 1776, New Market) Catherine Fox (c1746-   ); 2) Anna (-----) who rec'd pen # W8558 **VI**: Son of John Adam (Germany-   ) & Susannah (Schlern) Roush **P**: Y spouse **BLW**: N **RG**: Y **MK**: unk **PH**: unk **SS**: J-NSSAR 1993 Reg; AL Ct bk pg 1 Shenandoah Co; AP Fold3 pen rec Z pg 54; SAR P-282237 **BS**: JLARC 1.

ROUSH, Jonas; b Sep 1763, Holman's Fort ; d 1850 Meig's Co, OH **RU**: Served as a substistute for brother Henry Rouse (Roush) in VA Cont Line, also was in Mason's Co serving 3 yrs **CEM**: Old Pine Church; GPS not determined; loc 1mi S of Pinkerton east of rd on land of Milton Funkhouser 1936; Shenandoah **GS**:Y memorialized on family memorial in cem 1936 **SP**: Unk name who died Jun 1837 **VI**: Son of John Adam Roush (1711-1786) & Susanne (-----)(1713-1796); moved to Mason Co, WVA 1798, and applied for pen, 6 Nov 1832, and rec'd # S4788; moved to Meigs Co, OH 1848 **P**: Y **BLW**: N **RG**: N **MK**: N **PH**: N **SS**:CG: vol III, pg 2961; AP Fold3 serv and pen rec **BS**: 221.

ROUSCH (ROUSH), John; b 1742, PA; d 1816 **RU**: Captain/Patriot, Served in Shenandoah Co Militia 1779-1780; gave material aid to cause **CEM**: St Mary Pine Lutheran; GPS 38.74470, -78.68390; 7103 S Middle Rd, Mt Jackson; Shenandoah **GS**: Y family stone erected 1935 indicating he served his country in the cause of independence **SP**: No info **VI**: Son of John Adam (Germany-   ) & Susannah (Schlern) Roush **P**: unk **BLW**: unk **RG**: Y **MK**: unk **PH**: unk **SS**: J-NSSAR 1993 Reg; E pg 679; AL Cert 1 Shenandoah Co; SAR P-282239 **BS**: JLARC 1; 221.

ROUSCH (ROUSH), Philip; b 18 Mar 1739, Northampton Co, PA; d 1 Mar 1820 **RU**: Private, Service information not stated in SAR registry **CEM**: St Mary Pine Lutheran; GPS 38.74470, -78.68390; 7103 S Middle Rd, Mt Jackson; Shenandoah **GS**: Y family stone erected 1935 indicating he served his country in the cause of independence **SP**: No info **VI**: Son of John Adam (Germany-   ) & Susannah (Schlern) Roush **P**: unk **BLW**: unk **RG**: N **MK**: unk **PH**: unk **SS**: J-NSSAR 1993 Reg, J- DAR Hatcher; Z pg 162 **BS**: JLARC 1,2; 221.

ROUSH, John Adam; b 1711, Germany; d 19 Oct 1786 **RU**: Patriot, Gave material aid to cause **CEM**: St Mary Pine Lutheran; GPS 38.74470, -78.68390; 7103 S Middle Rd, Mt Jackson; Shenandoah **GS**: Y family stone erected 1935 indicating he served his country in the cause of independence and had nine sons in Rev War **SP**: Mar 1739, Philadelphia, Susanne Schlem/Sehler (1713-1796) **VI**: Emigrant fr Dermstandt, Germany 1736, Early settler of the Shenandoah Valley **P**: N **BLW**: N **RG**:Y **MK**:SAR bronze **PH**: unk **SS**: AL Cert; DAR A098982; SAR P282241 **BS**: 80 vol3, pg 234; 155, 221.

ROUSH, Susannah (Schlem); b 1713, Germany; d 1796 **RU**: Patriot, Gave material aid to cause **CEM**: St Mary Pine Lutheran; GPS 38.74470, -78.68390; 7103 S Middle Rd, Mt Jackson; Shenandoah **GS**: Y **SP**: Mar (c1739/40) Johannes Roush (1711 Germany-19 Oct 1786) **VI**: No further data **P**: N **BLW**: N **RG**: Y **MK**: N **PH**: unk **SS**: AS, SAR regis; SAR P-282249 **BS**: SAR regis.

ROUSSE, Antoine; b unk; d 1781 **RU**: Seaman, Served on "Hercule" and died from Yorktown battle **CEM**: French Memorial; GPS 36.81944, -79.39933; Yorktown; York **GS**: U **SP**: No info **VI**: No further data **P**: unk **BLW**: unk **RG**: Y **MK**: unk **PH**: unk **SS**: J-Yorktown Historian; SAR P-282250 **BS**: JLARC 1, 74.

ROUSSEAU, Pierre; b unk; d 1781 **RU**: Seaman, Served on "Diademe" and died from Yorktown battle **CEM**: French Memorial; GPS 36.81944, -79.39933; Yorktown; York **GS**: U **SP**: No info **VI**: No further data **P**: unk **BLW**: unk **RG**: Y **MK**: unk **PH**: unk **SS**: J-Yorktown Historian; SAR P-282255 **BS**: JLARC 1, 74.

ROUSSEL, Jean; b unk; d 1781 **RU**: Soldier, Served in Bourbonnais Bn and died fr battle at Yorktown **CEM**: French Memorial; GPS 36.81944, -79.39933; Yorktown; York **GS**: U **SP**: No info **VI**: No further data **P**: unk **BLW**: unk **RG**: Y **MK**: unk **PH**: unk **SS**: J-Yorktown Historian; SAR P-282258 **BS**: JLARC 1, 74.

RU=Rank/Unit	CEM=Cemetery	GS=Gravestone	SP=Spousal Information
VI=Other Veteran Info	P=Pension	BLW=Bounty/Land Warrant	RG=Registered Grave
MK=SAR/DAR Marker	PH=Photo	SS=Service Source	BS=Burial Source

363

ROUSSEL, Vincent; b unk; d 1781 **RU:** Seaman, Served on "Hextor" and died from Yorktown battle **CEM:** French Memorial; GPS 36.81944, -79.39933; Yorktown; York **GS:** U **SP:** No info **VI:** No further data **P:** unk **BLW:** unk **RG:** Y **MK:** unk **PH:** unk **SS:** J-Yorktown Historian; SAR P-282259 **BS:** JLARC 1, 74.

ROUX, Jean; b unk; d 1781 **RU:** Seaman, Served on "Auguste" and died from Yorktown battle **CEM:** French Memorial; GPS 36.81944, -79.39933; Yorktown; York **GS:** U **SP:** No info **VI:** No further data **P:** unk **BLW:** unk **RG:** Y **MK:** unk **PH:** unk **SS:** J-Yorktown Historian; SAR P-282270 **BS:** JLARC 1, 74.

ROUX, Jean; b unk; d 1781 **RU:** Seaman, Served on "Victorie" and died from Yorktown battle **CEM:** French Memorial; GPS 36.81944, -79.39933; Yorktown; York **GS:** U **SP:** No info **VI:** No further data **P:** unk **BLW:** unk **RG:** Y **MK:** unk **PH:** unk **SS:** J-Yorktown Historian; SAR P-282271 **BS:** JLARC 1, 74.

ROWLAND, John; b c1765; d 1834 **RU:** Private, Served in PA Regt commanded by Col Lewis Nicola Apr 1783. Also served in 6th and 13th Cont Lines **CEM:** Shockoe Hill; GPS 37.55190, -77.43170; 4th & Hospital Sts; Richmond City **GS:** Y **SP:** No info **VI:** Served in War of 1812 **P:** unk **BLW:** unk **RG:** N **MK:** N **PH:** unk **SS:** A pg 223 **BS:** 57 pg 13.

ROWLES, William; b c1759; d 1846 **RU:** Private, Served in MD & VA. Entered service 1777, MD State Regt. Served in VA Cont Line Regts 3rd, 5th, & 9th **CEM:** Rowles Family; GPS unk; Markham; Fauquier **GS:** N **SP:** No info **VI:** Pension appl for 28 Nov 1832 Fauquier Co age 73. FS6687RZ094 S6687 **P:** Y **BLW:** unk **RG:** Y **MK:** N **PH:** N **SS:** K Vol 4 pg 268; CG Vol 3 pg 2968; SAR P-282454 **BS:** 19 og 179.

ROY, Wily; b 12 Jan 1747; d 11 Jan 1816 **RU:** Captain/Patriot, Was Quartermaster Fauquier Co Militia,1781. Also gave supplies to cause **CEM:** Roy Family; GPS unk; Clover Hill Dr; Stafford **GS:** Y **SP:** Sarah (-----) **VI:** No further data **P:** unk **BLW:** unk **RG:** N **MK:** N **PH:** unk **SS:** D pg 874 **BS:** 03 pg 341.

ROYALL, John; b c1743; d Aft Aug 1777 **RU:** Second Lieutenant/Patriot, Served in 19th Co of the Amelia Co Militia, May 1764. Gave material aid to cause **CEM:** Royall; GPS unk; Off Promise Land Rd Rt 661, Amelia CH; Amelia **GS:** U **SP:** Mar ; SAR(May 1764 Amelia Co) Elizabeth Townes **VI:** No further data **P:** unk **BLW:** N **RG:** Y **MK:** unk **PH:** N **SS:** G pg 6; AL Ct Bk I pg 54 Amelia Co; DAR A099369; SAR 282528 **BS:** 196.

ROYALL, Littleberry; b 1742; d 1827 **RU:** Lieutenant, Served in Amelia Co Militia 22 Jun 1780 **CEM:** Royall; GPS unk; Off Promise Land Rd Rt 661, Amelia CH; Amelia **GS:** U **SP:** Mar (25 May 1780 Amelia Co) Elizabeth Jones (__-Sep 1786) **VI:** Son of Littleberry & Mary (Eppes) Royall **P:** unk **BLW:** unk **RG:** N **MK:** unk **PH:** unk **SS:** G pg 14 **BS:** 196.

ROYALL, Sarah See Appendix G Adenda

ROYER, Jean; b unk; d 1781 **RU:** Seaman, Served on "Reflechi" and died from Yorktown battle **CEM:** French Memorial; GPS 36.81944, -79.39933; Yorktown; York **GS:** U **SP:** No info **VI:** No further data **P:** unk **BLW:** unk **RG:** Y **MK:** unk **PH:** unk **SS:** J-Yorktown Historian; SAR P-282569 **BS:** JLARC 1, 74.

ROYSTON (ROYSTAN), James; b 1756; d 1800 **RU:** Corporal, Served in MD line **CEM:** City Cemetery; GPS 38.30112, -77.46628; 1000 Washington Ave; Fredericksburg City **GS:** U **SP:** No info **VI:** Drew BLW 5 Sep 1789 **P:** U **BLW:** Y **RG:** Y **MK:** unk **PH:** unk **SS:** CG pg 2970; SAR P-282587 **BS:** JLARC 2.

ROYSTON (ROYSTAN), James; b 1756; d 1800 **RU:** Corporal, Served in MD line **CEM:** Corporate Burial Ground; GPS not determined; loc where Hurcamp Park is today; Fredericksburg City **GS:** U **SP:** No info **VI:** Drew BLW 5 Sep 1789 **P:** unk **BLW:** Y **RG:** Y **MK:** unk **PH:** unk **SS:** CG pg 2970; SAR P-282587 **BS:** JLARC 2.

RUBEL (RUBLE), George; b unk; d 20 May 1814 **RU:** Patriot, Gave material aid to the cause **CEM:** Back Creek Quaker, aka Gainesboro United Methodist; GPS 39.27861, -78.25694; 166 Siler Ln, Gainesboro; Frederick **GS:** Y **SP:** Mar (12 Apr 1805 Frederick Co, James Wall, minister) Jane Gobin **VI:** No further data **P:** N **BLW:** N **RG:**N **MK:** N **PH:** Y **SS:** AL Ct Bk pg 13 **BS:** 59 pg 285.

RUCKER, Ambrose; b 20 Jan 1724, Orange Co; d 14 Dec 1807 **RU:** Lt Colonel/Patriot, Served in Va Militia as Captain 1778 to 1779, then promoted to Lt Col; appointed and served as Sheriff of Amherst Co. In 1781-82 was in VA Legislature in House of Delegates representing Amherst Co. Gave material aid to cause **CEM:** Rucker Family; GPS 37.54062, -77.18508; Shepherd Farm Ln off Rt 653 Ambrose

RU=Rank/Unit	CEM=Cemetery	GS=Gravestone	SP=Spousal Information
VI=Other Veteran Info	P=Pension	BLW=Bounty/Land Warrant	RG=Registered Grave
MK=SAR/DAR Marker	PH=Photo	SS=Service Source	BS=Burial Source

364

Rucker Rd; Amherst **GS**: N **SP**: 1) Mary Clifton Headley 2) Mar (c1760) Mary Tinsley (1738-26 Jul 1818) d/o Edward (1700-1782) & Margaret (Taylor) (1705-1782) Tinsley **VI**: Son of John Rucker (c1700-c1741) & Susannah Phillips. Founded Rucker's Chapel in Amherst Co. (then known as Harris Creek Church, later St Matthew's Chapel) by 1751. In 1791 active in process to establish Warminster Academy in Amherst Co. Findagrave.com entry incorrectly gives his place of birth as Norfolk City. HIs will reserved a half acre of land to be used in perpetuity for the family graveyard, and this could be the Graham Cove site. **P**: unk **BLW**: unk **RG**:Y **MK**: unk **PH**: N **SS**: E pg 681; D Amherst Co; AZ pgs 17,112; SAR application 352, 374; DAR 620A099452; SAR P-282620 **BS**: JLARC 2, 4,115; 196.

RUCKER, Angus; b 1753; d 2 Sep 1836 **RU**: Captain, enlisted 1775,Culpeper commissioned Capt Jul 1777. Served in VA Line. Was superintendant of the Chesterfield Hospital 1781-1783 **CEM**: Rucker, Blakey, Hoffman, Rose; GPS 38.34745, -78.32997; Nr Wolftown; Madison **GS**: U **SP**: No info **VI**: Son of Ephraim Rucker (1715-1796) & Margaret VawTer (1720-1811) Rec'd S19068 BLW #1695-300. (Also N.A. Acc #874 #050151 1/2 pay). Pen appl for 26 Feb 1830 Madison Co age 77 **P**: Y **BLW**: Y **RG**: Y **MK**: Y SAR & DAR plaque **PH**: unk **SS**: BY pg 87 J-NSSAR 1993 Reg; CG Vol 3 pg 2971; DAR A099462; SAR P-282622 **BS**: JLARC 1.

RUCKER, Anthony Jr; b 1740; d 27 Jan 1821 **RU**: Captain/Patriot, commanded a company guarding prisoners from Yorktown at Albemarle Barracks in 1781; gave material aid to cause and was a Commissioner **CEM**: Rucker Family; GPS 37.54062, -77.18508; Shepherd Farm Ln off Rt 653 (Ambrose Rucker Rd); Amherst **GS**: N **SP**: Rebecca Burgess **VI**: Son of John Rucker (c1700-c1741) & Susannah Phillips. Original inventory w/ brother of James River Batteau **P**: unk **BLW**: unk **RG**: Y **MK**: unk **PH**: N **SS**: AL Ct Bk pg 6 Amherst Co; AZ pgs 92; DAR A099464; SAR P-331899 **BS**: JLARC 115.

RUCKER, Isaac; b Bef 1740; d aft 1798 **RU**: Lieutenant Colonel/Patriot, Served in Amherst Co Militia. Lt Col of Co Militia. Ordered to join Gen Lafayette. Gave material aid to cause **CEM**: Rucker Family; GPS 37.54062, -77.18508; Shepherd Farm Ln off Rt 653 (Ambrose Rucker Rd); Amherst **GS**: N **SP**: Mar (28 Jan 1793 Amherst Co as bachelor) Mary Higginbotham, spinster, d/o John & (-----) Higginbotham, 2) Mrs Mildred Plunkett **VI**: Son of John Rucker (c1700-c1741) & Susannah Phillips. Original inventory w/ brother of James River Batteau **P**: unk **BLW**: unk **RG**: Y **MK**: unk **PH**: N **SS**: JALARC App B pg 4; AL Ct Bk pg 5, 31, 32 Amherst Co; SAR P-282631 **BS**: JLARC 115.

RUCKER, John Sr; b 1720, Orange Co; d Aft 04 Sep 1780 **RU**: Ensign/Patriot, commissioned Ensign 1780, Amherst Co Militia. Civil service as road viewer Amherst Co, 1778 **CEM**: Rucker Family; GPS 37.54062, -77.18508; Shepherd Farm Ln off Rt 653 (Ambrose Rucker Rd); Amherst **GS**: U **SP**: Mar (1747) Eleanor Mildred Warren **VI**: No further data **P**: N **BLW**: N **RG**: Y **MK**: unk **PH**: unk **SS**: DAR A099485; SAR P-282634; SAR application; DD cites Amherst Co Order Book 1773-1782 pg 325, 336 **BS**: 197.

RUCKMAN, David; b 1747, Summerset, NJ; d 11 Jul 1822 **RU**: Sergeant, Served in Somerset Co, NJ Militia as teamster **CEM**: Ruckman; GPS unk; Little Egypt Rd, US 220 fr Mill Gap to Rt 604, turn left. 2-3 miles grave on right side; Highland **GS**: Y **SP**: Mar (NJ) Susannah Little (1757-1843) **VI**: Son of Samuel (1643-___) & (-----) Ruckman **P**: unk **BLW**: unk **RG**: Y **MK**: unk **PH**: Y **SS**: B; CA; DAR A099499; SAR P-282647 DD **BS**: JLARC 103; 196.

RUFFIN, Edmund Jr; b 2 Jan 1744; d 1807 **RU**: Captain/Patriot, As patriot performed public service as member of House of Delegates **CEM**: Ruffin family, Tar Bay House; GPS unk; 4 mi E of Hopewell; Prince George **GS**: Y **SP**: Mar (c1764) Jane Skipwith (1746-after 1807) **VI**: No further data **P**: unk **BLW**: unk **RG**: Y **MK**: N **PH**: unk **SS**: T; G pg 84; AL Cert 1 Dinwiddie Co; AZ pg 47; DAR A099662; DD; SAR P-282752 **BS**: 111 Part 3 pg 28.

RUFFIN, Edmund Sr; b 1713; d 1790 **RU**: Patriot, Gave material aid to cause **CEM**: Ruffin family, Tar Bay House; GPS unk; 4 mi E of Hopewell; Prince George **GS**: Y **SP**: No info **VI**: No further data **P**: N **BLW**: N **RG**: N **MK**: N **PH**: unk **SS**: G pg 83-4; AL Cert I Prince George Co **BS**: 111 Part 3 pg 28.

RUFFNER, Peter Sr; b c1715; d c1781 **RU**: Patriot, Gave material aid to the cause **CEM**: Ruffner Family; GPS unk; Rt 211, Luray; Page **GS**: N **SP**: No info **VI**: No further data **P**: N **BLW**: N **RG**: N **MK**: N **PH**: N **SS**: AL Ct Bk pg 5,12 **BS**: 79 pg 177,178.

RU=Rank/Unit	CEM=Cemetery	GS=Gravestone	SP=Spousal Information
VI=Other Veteran Info	P=Pension	BLW=Bounty/Land Warrant	RG=Registered Grave
MK=SAR/DAR Marker	PH=Photo	SS=Service Source	BS=Burial Source

365

RULLINS, William; b unk; d 1781 **RU:** Soldier, Served fr NY, and died fr the Battle at Yorktown **CEM:** Yorktown Victory Monument Tablet; GPS 38.28350, -78.54150; Yorktown; York **GS:** U **SP:** No info **VI:** No further data **P:** unk **BLW:** unk **RG:** Y **MK:** unk **PH:** unk **SS:** J-Yorktown Historian; SAR P-282849 **BS:** JLARC 74.

RUSH, Charles; b c1730, Germany; d 4 Apr 1806 **RU:** Patriot, Gave material aid to cause **CEM:** Old Peaked Mountain; GPS 38.37113, -78.73416; 9843 Town Hall Rd, McGaheysville; Rockingham **GS:** U **SP:** (Anna) Elizabeth Suess **VI:** No further data **P:** N **BLW:** N **RG:** Y **MK:** Y DAR plaque **PH:** unk **SS:** J-NSSAR 2000 Reg; AL Ct Bk II pg 26, 27, 35 Rockingham Co; DAR A100016; SAR P-282999 **BS:** JLARC 76.

RUSH, John; b 6 Dec 1753, Rockingham (was Augusta Co); d 26 Jun 1835 **RU:** Captain, Served in Capt George Huston's Co and in Col Benjamin Harrison's VA Regt, **CEM:** Old Peaked Mountain; GPS 38.37113, -78.73416; 9843 Town Hall Rd, McGaheysville; Rockingham **GS:** N **SP:** Anna Maria Nicholas **VI:** Son of John Jacob & Anna Barbara (Zeller) Nicholas. App Rockingham Co 23 Nov 1832. R9090. Died in Cub Run, Rockingham Co **P:** Y **BLW:** unk **RG:** N **MK:** Y DAR plaque **PH:** N **SS:** E pg 683; CG Vol 3 pg 2981 **BS:** 116 Monument.

RUSSELL, Andrew; b 1716 Ireland; d 20 Nov 1780 **RU:** Patriot, Gave material aid to cause **CEM:** Tinkling Spring Presbyterian; GPS 38.08472, -78.98278; 30 Tinkling Spring Dr, Fisherville; Augusta **GS:** U **SP:** Florence Henderson (1718 Scotland-20 Jul 1764) **VI:** No further data **P:** N **BLW:** N **RG:** N **MK:** unk **PH:** unk **SS:** AL Commissioners Bk II pg 360 **BS:** 196.

RUSSELL, James; b 1754, PA, d 12 Dec 1831; **RU:** Sergeant/ Patriot, he joined Cont Army age 19 and served 7 yrs. He was at the siege and fall of Yorktown and surrender of Cornwallis, and was in the battle of Guilford. CH in an artillery company in Col William Russell's 13th VA Regt until 20 Jun 1783. He also paid personal property tax in 1783, Loudoun Co **CEM:** Loudoun Heights; GPS not determined; loc Harpers Ferry Rd (Rt 671) on left 0.6 mi fr jct US 340, Loudoun Heights; Loudoun; **GS:** Y broken **SP:** mar 1) 18 Apr 1775, Sarah "Sallie" Osburn (c1755-1795), d/o Nicholas Osburn & Margaret Conard/Cunnard, 2) 27Jun 1803, Ann Nancy Heath who applied for pen 1 Jun 1854 in Loudoun Co **VI** Rec'd pen #R9097 and 200 acres BLW **P:** Both **BLW:** Y **RG:** Y **MK:** N **PH:** N **SS:** F pg 63; CG pg 2984; DAR A098375; SAR P-283146 **BS:** 196.

RUSSELL, Joshua; b 1738, Augusta Co; d Bef 15 Oct 1793 **RU:** Private, Served in Capt Johnston's Co, Augusta Co Militia **CEM:** Tinkling Spring Presbyterian; GPS 38.08472, -78.98278; 30 Tinkling Spring Dr, Fisherville; Augusta **GS:** N **SP:** Jane (-----) (1741-__) **VI:** Son of Andrew (1716-1780) & Florence (Henderson) (1718-1764) Russell **P:** N **BLW:** N **RG:** N **MK:** unk **PH:** N **SS:** E pg 684 **BS:** 196.

RUSSELL, Robert; b 24 Apr 1753, d 28 Jun 1827 **RU:** Ensign, commissioned in Loudoun Co Militia 1780 **CEM:** Ebenezer Baptist; GPS 39.05824,-77.81142; 20421 Airmount Rd, Bluemont; Loudoun **GS:** Unk **SP:** No spousal data **VI:** Son of Samuel Russell (_-8 Sep 1806) and Sarah Hatcher (_-1780) **P:** N **BLW:** N **RG:** Y **MK:** Y SAR plaque **PH:** N **SS:** AZ pg 213; SAR P-336669 **BS:** 196.

RUSSELL, Samuel; b unk; d Bef 23 Feb 1784 **RU:** Sergeant, Served in 9th Cont line for 3 yrs **CEM:** Truro Parish; GPS unk; "On the middle ridge near Ox Road", the present site of Jerusalem Baptist Church off Rt 123; Fairfax **GS:** N **SP:** Sarah (-----) recd aid while he was in service in Loudoun Co in Nov 1780 **VI:** Vestry Minutes Truro Parish 23 Feb 1784 indicate Silvester Gardiner was paid for maintaining him for 13 mos, and for a coffin and burying him **P:** unk **BLW:** unk **RG:** N **MK:** Y SAR plaque **PH:** N **SS:** C pg 493; E pg 685; BX pg 697 **BS:** 110 pg 104.

RUSSELL, Samuel; b c1725, d 8 Sep 1806 **RU:** Patriot, Supported cause by paying supply tax included in his personal property tax in 1782, Loudoun Co **CEM:** Ebenezer Baptist; GPS 39.05824,-77.81142; 20421 Airmount Rd, Bluemont; Loudoun **GS:** Yes **SP:** Sarah Hatcher (__-1780) **VI:** FindaGrave indicates he served in the Loudoun Co Militia but can not find source and he would not be of military age to do so **P:** N **BLW:** N **RG:** Y **MK:** N **PH:** N **SS:** DV 1782 Personal Property Tax List 1782C, image 19.pdf; SAR P-336670 **BS:** 196.

RUSSELL, William; b 1735, Orange Co; d 14 Jan 1793 **RU:** Brigadier General, Capt, Co commander fr Fincastle Co at Battle of Point Pleasant. Commanded substantial forces at Battle of Kings Mountain in 13th & 5th/11th VA Regts. Was Col 13th VA Regt 19 Dec 1776 and 5th VA Regt 14 Sep 1778; taken

RU=Rank/Unit	CEM=Cemetery	GS=Gravestone	SP=Spousal Information
VI=Other Veteran Info	P=Pension	BLW=Bounty/Land Warrant	RG=Registered Grave
MK=SAR/DAR Marker	PH=Photo	SS=Service Source	BS=Burial Source

366

prisoner Charleston SC 12 May 1780; exchanged Nov 1780; served until 3 Nov 1783. Brevet Brig Gen by act of Cont Congress 3 Nov 1783 **CEM:** Arlington National; GPS 38.88377, -77.06535; Jefferson Davis Hwy Rt 110; Arlington **GS:** Y 314A **SP:** 1) Tabitha Adams (1738-1776) 2) Elizabeth (Henry) Campbell (1749-1825, Chilhowie, Smyth Co) d/o John & Sarah (Winston) Henry. Widow of Gen William Campbell and sister of Patrick Henry **VI:** After War, produced salt in Saltville and served in VA State Senate. Died in Shenandoah Co **P:** unk **BLW:** unk **RG:** Y **MK:** Y **SAR PH:** unk **SS:** AK; DAR A098535; SAR P-283287 **BS:** 04; JLARC 1, 2, 114; 80 vol3, pg 239; 196.

RUST, Benjamin; b 1749, Prince William Co; d 21 Jun 1834 **RU:** Private/Patriot, Served in Capt Scott's Co, Fauquier Co Militia. Gave material aid to cause **CEM:** Rust Family; GPS 38.52878, -77.04540; Rt 619, Upperville; Fauquier **GS:** Y **SP:** Hannah (-----) (1757-Jul 1824) **VI:** No further data **P:** unk **BLW:** unk **RG:** N **MK:** N **PH:** unk **SS:** DAR Ancestor #098798; D Fauquier pg 1; AL Cert Fauquier Co **BS:** 19 pg 180.

RUST, Peter; b 1762; d 1828 **RU:** Captain/Patriot, As Sgt, was in the 9th & 10th Cont Lines. Was Signer of Leedstown Resolutions fr Spotsylvania Co **CEM:** Mt Hebron; GPS 39.10916, -78.09497; 305 E Boscawen St; Winchester City **GS:** U **SP:** Mar (9 Jan 1816, Frederick Co) Elizabeth Rust **VI:** Appl for pen 10 Dec 1823 Loudoun Co. S25415 **P:** unk **BLW:** unk **RG:** Y **MK:** Y **SAR** monument **PH:** unk **SS:** J-NSSAR 2000; Reg; E pg 685; BQ; CG pg 2988; SAR P-283346 **BS:** JLARC 76.

RUTROUGH, John; b 1756, Chester Co, PA; d 12 Dec 1824 **RU:** Private, Floyd CH Chapter DAR has his specific service **CEM:** Zion Lutheran; GPS 37.13507, -80.41662; Rts 693 & 615, Wades Ln; Floyd **GS:** Y **SP:** Mary Anne Krank (15 May 1755-28 Jan 1839) **VI:** No further data **P:** unk **BLW:** unk **RG:** Y **MK:** unk **PH:** unk **SS:** SAR P-283460 **BS:** JLARC 17, 29; 196.

RYMER, George; b 1755, England; d 30 Nov 1845 **RU:** Private,. enlisted in Augusta Co,1781.He served in Capt James Bell's Co, Col George Moffett's Regt, and Capt Patrick Buchannon's Co, Col Samuel Vance's Regt, VA Line. He was in the battle at Guilford Ct House, and later escorted prisoners fr Yorktown battle to Winchester **CEM:** Rymer Family; GPS 38.26022, -79.3072; Rt 624. left through wooden gate to pasture, up over ridge and slightly to right side of mountain (rec 4 wheel dr veh) N fr McDowell; Highland **GS:** Y Govt 1936 **SP:** 1) Eleanor Blanch Murphy (b Eng1755-1825, Pendleton, WVA), 2) mar (6 Jan 1829, Pendleton Co, WVA) Delila Davis(1810, Pendletpn Co, WVA-aft 1860) **VI:** Came to America 1772. Penson appl for 2 Oct 1833, Pendleton Co, WVA # S9469 & R2107. **P:** Y **BLW:** N **RG:** Y **MK:** N **PH:** Y **SS:** K vol 4, pg 287; AP pen rec Fold3; CG Vol 3 pg 2993; DAR A098873; SAR P-283553 **BS:** 196.

SABE, Jean; b unk; d 1781 **RU:** Seaman, Served on "Hercule" and died from Yorktown battle **CEM:** French Memorial; GPS 36.81944, -79.39933; Yorktown; York **GS:** U **SP:** No info **VI:** No further data **P:** unk **BLW:** unk **RG:** Y **MK:** unk **PH:** unk **SS:** J-Yorktown Historian SAR P-283576 **BS:** JLARC 1, 74.

SAFFROY, Jean; b unk; d 1781 **RU:** Soldier, Served in Bourbonnais Bn and died fr battle at Yorktown **CEM:** French Memorial; GPS 36.81944, -79.39933; Yorktown; York **GS:** U **SP:** No info **VI:** No further data **P:** unk **BLW:** unk **RG:** Y **MK:** unk **PH:** unk **SS:** J-Yorktown Historian; SAR P-283722 **BS:** JLARC 1, 74.

SAGE, James; b 26 Aug 1754, England; d 14 Mar 1820 **RU:** Private, Served in VA Line **CEM:** Sawyers -Elk Creek Community; GPS 36.72960000, 81.17756000 Victory Lane (Rt. 791) Elk Creek, Hwy 668, Independence; Grayson **GS:** U **SP:** Mar (25 Dec 1780, Montgomery Co) Lovice (Lovise) Ott (Utt) (___-28 Aug 1854 Grayson Co) **VI:** Was baker in London before moving to America. Recd pen #R9140 **P:** Y **BLW:** unk **RG:** Y **MK:** unk **PH:** unk **SS:** J-NSSAR 1993 Reg; J- DAR Hatcher; CG Vol 3 pg 2997; DAR A099114; SAR P-283751 **BS:** JLARC 1, 2.

SALAUN, Francois; b unk; d 1781 **RU:** Seaman, Served on "Citoyen" and died from Yorktown battle **CEM:** French Memorial; GPS 36.81944, -79.39933; Yorktown; York **GS:** U **SP:** No info **VI:** No further data **P:** unk **BLW:** unk **RG:** Y **MK:** unk **PH:** unk **SS:** J-Yorktown Historian; SAR P-283798 **BS:** JLARC 1, 74.

SALE, Bertrand; b unk; d 1781 **RU:** Seaman, Served on "Hercule" and died from Yorktown battle **CEM:** French Memorial; GPS 36.81944, -79.39933; Yorktown; York **GS:** U **SP:** No info **VI:** No further data **P:** unk **BLW:** unk **RG:** Y **MK:** unk **PH:** unk **SS:** J-Yorktown Historian; SAR P-283800 **BS:** JLARC 1, 74.

RU=Rank/Unit   CEM=Cemetery   GS=Gravestone   SP=Spousal Information
VI=Other Veteran Info   P=Pension   BLW=Bounty/Land Warrant   RG=Registered Grave
MK=SAR/DAR Marker   PH=Photo   SS=Service Source   BS=Burial Source

367

SALE, John; b 30 Sep 1729, Essex Co, d 30 Mar 1815, d unk **RU:** Captain Amherst Co Militia, under Col Christian's Brigage,1776 and guarded prizoners at Alemarle Barracks, 1779 **CEM:** Fairmont; GPS 37.3280983, -79.5049973; loc E Main St,at jct with Independence Blvd; Bedford City **GS** Y no dates **SP:** Mar 1) Frances Saunders/Sanders, 2) Louise (__) **VI:** No further data **P:** Unk **BLW:** Unk **RG:** Y **MK:** N **PH:** N **SS:** E pg 688, AZ pg 61; CZ:vol 1, pg 387; DAR A099275; SAR 283801 **BS:** 196.

SALLEMON, Antoine; b unk; d 1781 **RU:** Soldier, Served in Gatinais Bn and died fr battle at Yorktown **CEM:** French Memorial; GPS 36.81944, -79.39933; Yorktown; York **GS:** U **SP:** No info **VI:** No further data **P:** unk **BLW:** unk **RG:** Y **MK:** unk **PH:** unk **SS:** J-Yorktown Historian; SAR P-283862 **BS:** JLARC 1, 74.

SALLES, Jean; b unk; d 1781 **RU:** Soldier, Served in Gatinais Bn and died fr battle at Yorktown **CEM:** French Memorial; GPS 36.81944, -79.39933; Yorktown; York **GS:** U **SP:** No info **VI:** No further data **P:** unk **BLW:** unk **RG:** Y **MK:** unk **PH:** unk **SS:** J-Yorktown Historian; SAR P-283864 **BS:** JLARC 1, 74.

SALMON, Guillaume; b unk; d 1781 **RU:** Seaman, Served on "Solitaire" and died from Yorktown battle **CEM:** French Memorial; GPS 36.81944, -79.39933; Yorktown; York **GS:** U **SP:** No info **VI:** No further data **P:** unk **BLW:** unk **RG:** Y **MK:** unk **PH:** unk **SS:** J-Yorktown Historian; SAR P-283879 **BS:** JLARC 1, 74.

SALMON, John; b 1735; d 24 Jan 1791 **RU:** Captain/Patriot, Commanded a Co in Henry Co Militia in Jun 1780. Had civil service as First Sheriff Henry Co 1776 and Commissioner of Peace of VA, 1777 **CEM:** Salmon Family; GPS unk; See property records; Bedford **GS:** U **SP:** Mar (c1758) Naomi Depriest (c1735, Goochland Co-aft 1791) d/o William & Judith (-----) DePriest **VI:** Son of John (c1700-c1741) (-----) Salmon. Will proves death date **P:** unk **BLW:** unk **RG:** Y **MK:** N **PH:** unk **SS:** DAR A099376; SAR P283885 J-NSSAR 1993 Reg; E pg 688 **BS:** JLARC 1.

SALMON, Philibert; b unk; d 1781 **RU:** Soldier, Served in Auxonne Bn and died fr battle at Yorktown **CEM:** French Memorial; GPS 36.81944, -79.39933; Yorktown; York **GS:** U **SP:** No info **VI:** No further data **P:** unk **BLW:** unk **RG:** Y **MK:** unk **PH:** unk **SS:** J-Yorktown Historian; SAR P-283891 **BS:** JLARC 1, 74.

SAMPSON, Seth; b unk; d 1781 **RU:** Soldier, Served fr MA, and killed in the battle at Yorktown **CEM:** Yorktown Victory Monument Tablet; GPS 38.28350, -78.54150; Yorktown; York **GS:** U **SP:** No info **VI:** No further data **P:** unk **BLW:** unk **RG:** unk **MK:** unk **PH:** unk **SS:** J-Yorktown Historian; SAR P-284023 **BS:** JLARC 74.

SAMSEL, Nicholas; b 2 May 1749, Bicks co, PA, d 4 Nov 1817 **RU:** Private, Served in 7th Co, 2d Battalion, Northampton Co, Militia, PA **CEM:** Trinity Evangelical Lutheran Church; 39.08280,-78.21679; Mulberry St, Stephens City: Frederick **GS:** Yes **SP:** Mar 26 Aug 1770, Lehigh Co, PA, Anna Elizabeth Ott (1750-1827) **VI:** Son of Johann Paul Samsel & Catherine Born **P:** N **BLW:** N **RG:** N **MK:** N **PH:** N **SS:** AP Fold3 PA Archives Series 5, Vol VIII; DAR A0996754 **BS:** 04 Reg Form James Wood 11 Chapter Dec 2018; 196.

SAMUEL, Vance; b 1749; d 1838 **RU:** Lieutenant, Served in Capt John Lewis Militia Co, Was wounded at the battle of Point Pleasant Oct 1774 **CEM:** Sinking Springs; GPS 36.71030, -81.98170; 136 E Main St, Abingdon; Washington **GS:** Y **SP:** No info **VI:** Militia listed him as Samuel Vance instead of Vance Samuel **P:** unk **BLW:** unk **RG:** Y **MK:** N **PH:** unk **SS:** AS DAR Report; Z pg 114; SAR P-284085 **BS:** 80 vol 4 pg 4.

SANDERS, Robert; b 22 Jan 1748; d 20 Oct 1815 **RU:** Patriot, Gave material aid to cause **CEM:** Trigg; GPS unk; Wytheville, N side of Rt 619, abt .5 mi W of jct Rts 619 & 636; Wythe **GS:** U **SP:** Catherine Gannaway (1749-1808) **VI:** Son of Thomas (1699-1772 & Anna (Adams) Sanders (__-1769) **P:** N **BLW:** N **RG:**Y **MK:** Y SAR **PH:** Y **SS:** AL Ct Bk pg 33 Montgomery Co; SAR P-284288 **BS:** JLARC 123.

SANDERS (SAUNDERS), Stephen; b 10 May 1747; d 1830 **RU:** Captain/Patriot, Served in Cont Line. Gave material aid to cause **CEM:** Harris; GPS unk; SR651, nr SW cnr of jct with SR 690, Cripple Creek; Wythe **GS:** Y **SP:** 1) Miss Adams 2) Isabella Campbell **VI:** Son of Thomas (16 Oct 1699-7 Apr 1772) & Anne (Adams) (__-18 Mar 1769) Sanders. Orig stone not legible, but marker placed 1982 **P:** unk **BLW:**

RU=Rank/Unit	CEM=Cemetery	GS=Gravestone	SP=Spousal Information
VI=Other Veteran Info	P=Pension	BLW=Bounty/Land Warrant	RG=Registered Grave
MK=SAR/DAR Marker	PH=Photo	SS=Service Source	BS=Burial Source

368

unk **RG:** Y **MK:** Y SAR **PH:** unk **SS:** AL Ct Bk pg 24 Montgomery Co; SAR P-284295 **BS:** JLARC 40,123.

SANFORD, Joseph; b 1744, Westmoreland Co; d 1828 **RU:** Sergeant, Served in Fauntleroy's Co of 5th VA Regt **CEM:** Sanford Family #1; GPS unk; Rt 654 to 656, follow 656 S for 3.2 mi; Stafford **GS:** U **SP:** Mar (8 May 1766) Jane Bunbury (12 Nov 1741, King George Co-1818) **VI:** No further data **P:** unk **BLW:** unk **RG:** Y **MK:** unk **PH:** unk **SS:** E pg 690; DAR A099882; SAR P-284430 **BS:** JLARC 1, 48, 73.

SANFORD, Lawrence; b unk; d unk **RU:** Soldier, SAR Ancestor service not identified **CEM:** Old Presbyterian Meeting House; GPS 38.48528, -77.23532; 323 S Fairfax St; Alexandria City **GS:** N **SP:** Lavinia Edgerton **VI:** No further data **P:** unk **BLW:** unk **RG:** Y **MK:** unk **PH:** N **SS:** J-NSSAR 1993 Reg; SAR P-284436 **BS:** JLARC 1; 5.

SANFORD, Robert; b 12 Mar 1745; d 18 Mar 1792 **RU:** Patriot, Signed a legislative petition in Fairfax Co. Prisoner on ship "Jersey" **CEM:** Old Christ Church Episcopal; GPS 38.80625, -77.04718; 118 N Washington St; Alexandria City **GS:** N **SP:** Mar (26 Apr 1768) Jean Sanders (22 Oct 1748-9 Jan 1792) **VI:** Burial permit issued 19 Mar 1792 **P:** N **BLW:** N **RG:** N **MK:** N **PH:** N **SS:** DAR A100086; BB; DD **BS:** 20 pg 152; 196.

SANFORD, Thomas; b unk; d unk **RU:** Second Lieutenant, Served in 2nd VA State Regt 1777-1778 **CEM:** Old Presbyterian Meeting House; GPS 38.48528, -77.23532; 323 S Fairfax St; Alexandria City **GS:** N **SP:** no info **VI:** Also could be person this name that was Matross, 1st Artilley **P:** unk **BLW:** unk **RG:** Y **MK:** unk **PH:** N **SS:** J-NSSAR 1993 Reg; E pg 691; SAR P-284465 **BS:** JLARC 1; 5.

SANFORD, William; b Unk; d bef Feb 1779 **RU:** Private, Capt Powell's Co Co, 3rd VA Regt, wounded in battle at Brandywine **CEM:**Rev War Court House Plaque;GPS;not determined; 4110 Chain Bridge Rd; Fairfax **GS:** Memorialized on plaque 2017 by Geo Washington Chapter, VASSAR **SP** No info **VI:** died in service **P:** N **BLW:** N **RG:** N **MK:** N **PH:** N **SS:**E pg 691; AP Fold3 muster rolls::EP sources: **BS:** None.

SANSFACON, Jean; b unk; d 1781 **RU:** Soldier, Served in Picardie Bn and died fr battle at Yorktown **CEM:** French Memorial; GPS 36.81944, -79.39933; Yorktown; York **GS:** U **SP:** No info **VI:** No further data **P:** unk **BLW:** unk **RG:** Y **MK:** unk **PH:** unk **SS:** J-Yorktown Historian; SAR P-284504 **BS:** JLARC 1, 74.

SANTO, Pierre; b unk; d 1781 **RU:** Seaman, Served on "Auguste" and died from Yorktown battle **CEM:** French Memorial; GPS 36.81944, -79.39933; Yorktown; York **GS:** U **SP:** No info **VI:** No further data **P:** unk **BLW:** unk **RG:** Y **MK:** unk **PH:** unk **SS:** J-Yorktown Historian; SAR P-284515 **BS:** JLARC 1, 74.

SARGEANT, Nathaniel; b unk; d 1781 **RU:** Soldier, Served fr MA, and died fr the battle at Yorktown **CEM:** Yorktown Victory Monument Tablet; GPS 38.28350, -78.54150; Yorktown; York **GS:** U **SP:** No info **VI:** No further data **P:** unk **BLW:** unk **RG:** Y **MK:** unk **PH:** unk **SS:** J-Yorktown Historian; SAR P-284569 **BS:** JLARC 74.

SATUR, de; b unk; d 1781 **RU:** Soldier, Served in Picardie Bn and died fr battle at Yorktown **CEM:** French Memorial; GPS 36.81944, -79.39933; Yorktown; York **GS:** U **SP:** No info **VI:** No further data **P:** unk **BLW:** unk **RG:** Y **MK:** unk **PH:** unk **SS:** J-Yorktown Historian; SAR P-284735 **BS:** JLARC 1, 74.

SAUFLEY(SEFTLEY)(SEFLY) Valentine; b 1728, Osteim, Bayern, Ger; d 16 Feb 1802 **RU:** Patriot. Paid personal property tax, 1782 in Rockingham Co which was a supply tax for Rev War expenses **CEM:** Friedens United Church of Christ GPS 38.348480, -78.876530;GPS GS 38.347851, -78.877085; 3960 Friedens Church Rd, Mt Crawford; Rockingham **GS:**Y-new stone gives b & d dates **SP:** no spousal data **VI:** Emigrated 27 Sep 1747 **P:** N **BLW:** N **RG:** N **MK:** N **PH:** Y **SS:** AK **BS:** 04; 196.

SAUNDERS, Aaron; b 24 Dec 1757; d 28 Dec 1828 **RU:** Captain/Patriot, Gave material aid to cause **CEM:** Saunders Family; GPS unk; Leithtown; Loudoun **GS:** Y **SP:** Susan C(1771- 26 May 1846)- **VI:** Son of James (1719-1778) & Sarah (Gunnell) (1710-1793) Saunders **P:** unk **BLW:** unk **RG:** N **MK:** N **PH:** unk **SS:** B **BS:** 25 pg 271; 196.

SAUNDERS, David; b Feb 1761, Hanover Co; d 29 Sep 1845 **RU:** Sergeant, Ent Serv Hanover Co 1780. Served as Sergeant of Inf in VA Cont Line **CEM:** Saunders Family; GPS 37.31808, -79.43264; Jct Rt 460 & Krantz's Corner Rd; Bedford **GS:** Y **SP:** Mar (4 Sep 1788 Bedford Co) Lockey Leftwich (1 Jan 1767 Bedford Co-29 Nov 1853, Bedford) d/o Maj Augustine, Jr & Mary Ann (Turner) Leftwich **VI:** Lived

RU=Rank/Unit	CEM=Cemetery	GS=Gravestone	SP=Spousal Information
VI=Other Veteran Info	P=Pension	BLW=Bounty/Land Warrant	RG=Registered Grave
MK=SAR/DAR Marker	PH=Photo	SS=Service Source	BS=Burial Source

369

in Charlotte Co during Revolution. Appl pension 21 Aug 1832 Bedford Co. Widow appl pen there 28 Aug 1843 age 70. W3872; Served as Lt Col War of 1812 **P:** Y **BLW:** unk **RG:** Y **MK:** N **PH:** unk **SS:** J- DAR Hatcher, CG Vol 3 pg 3021; 112; SAR P-284762 **BS:** JLARC 2; 80 vol 4, pg 2;196.

SAUNDERS, John; b unk, d 18 May 1790 **RU:** Patriot, public service as he signed a legislative petition, City of Alexandria in 1778 for two new streets and certaiin lots to become town lands **CEM:** Quaker Burial Ground; GPS 38.80749, -77.04676; 717 Queen St, Kate Walker Barrett Library; Alexandria City **GS:** Unk **SP:** Mary Pancoast (1752-1846) **VI:** No further data **P:** N **BLW:** N **RG:** Y **MK:** N **PH:** N **SS:** BB,-Alexandria; SAR P-284753 **BS:** 196.

SAUNDERS, Robert Hyde; b c1757; d Oct 1833 **RU:** Lieutenant, Served in VA State Regt VA Line. Appointed Lt 18 Sep 1777. Resigned Feb 1778 **CEM:** Bruton Parish Church; GPS 37.27127, -76.70248; 331 W Duke of Gloucester St; Williamsburg City **GS:** Y **SP:** No info **VI:** Appl for pen Henrico Co age 74. S6046. Recd BLW of 266 acres **P:** Y **BLW:** Y **RG:** N **MK:** N **PH:** unk **SS:** N pg 461; BG pg 3022; SAR application 71, 119, 140 **BS:** 65, Bruton Par.

SAUNDERS, William; b 1755, King George Co; d 11 May 1819 **RU:** Private, Capt Henry Young's Co, Col Alexander McClannahan's 5th & &7th VA Regts **CEM:** Saunders Family; GPS unk; See property records for location; King George **GS:** U **SP:** 1) Mar (c1790) Sarah Jones (c1770-11 Nov 1827) 2) Nancy Cunningham **VI:** No further data **P:** unk **BLW:** unk **RG:** Y **MK:** unk **PH:** unk **SS:** DAR Ancestor #A100578; BY pg 22; AP rolls #102 & 104; AR Vol 4 pg 8; SAR P-284808 **BS:** JLARC 2.

SAVAGE, Francis; b c1740; d 20 Sep 1823 **RU:** Lieutenant, Served in Accomack Co Militia. Took oath as Lt 30 Jul 1777 **CEM:** Coal Kiln; GPS unk; 1 mi S jct Rts 607 & 600, R off Rt 600; Accomack **GS:** Y **SP:** Mar (1781, Accomack Co) Leah Custis (1763-31 Aug 1823) **VI:** Died age 73. Styled Capt on his GS **P:** unk **BLW:** unk **RG:** N **MK:** N **PH:** unk **SS:** DAR A100594; E pg 692 **BS:** 37 pg 224.

SAVAGE, Lyttleton; b 1740; d 9 Jan 1805 **RU:** Patriot, Gave material aid to the cause. Took oath as Court Officer on 13 Aug 1776 **CEM:** Cherry Grove; GPS unk; Rt 634; Northampton **GS:** Y **SP:** 1) mar (14 Jan 1768) Margaret Burton (1747-6 Dec 1772) d/o William & (-----) Burton 2) mar (11 Dec 1792) Elizabeth Jacob 3) Leah (-----) (1751-5 Jun 1795) **VI:** Styled "Col" on his GS **P:** N **BLW:** N **RG:** N **MK:** N **PH:** unk **SS:** AL Ct bk pg 6,7 **BS:** 42 pg 72.

SAVAGE, Thomas Lytllteton; b 8 Jun 1760; d 20 Jun 1815 **RU:** Private?, Served in 3rd, 5th, 7th Cont Lines **CEM:** Cugley; GPS unk; Rt 634; Northampton **GS:** Y **SP:** 1) Mar (21 May 1789) Mary Burton Savage, d/o Lylleton & (-----) Savage 2) Margaret Teackle (28 Feb 1778-28 Sep 1846) d/o Thomas & (-----) Teackle of Accomack Co. **VI:** A charter member of Phi Beta Kappa in 1779 (Cugley historic landmark plaque) **P:** unk **BLW:** unk **RG:** N **MK:** N **PH:** unk **SS:** E pg 693 **BS:** 42 pg 73; 209.

SAVAGE, William; b 1764; d 15 Nov 1815 **RU:** Private, 4th Cont Line **CEM:** Savage Family; GPS unk; Rt 180, Pungoteaque; Accomack **GS:** Y **SP:** No info **VI:** No further data **P:** unk **BLW:** unk **RG:** N **MK:** N **PH:** unk **SS:** E pg 693; CD **BS:** 145 Savage.

SAVEQUET, Dominique; b unk; d 1781 **RU:** Soldier, Service unit or ship not identified **CEM:** French Memorial; GPS 36.81944, -79.39933; Yorktown; York **GS:** U **SP:** No info **VI:** No further data **P:** unk **BLW:** unk **RG:** Y **MK:** unk **PH:** unk **SS:** J-Yorktown Historian; SAR P-284893 **BS:** JLARC 1, 74.

SAVILLE, Abram (Abraham); b 26 Dec 1763, Chester Co, PA; d 19 Jun 1841 **RU:** Private, Served in Capt Jame Huston's Co, Chester Co PA Militia 1781-1783 **CEM:** Old Anderson farm; GPS unk; W Buffalo Rd; Rockbridge **GS:** N **SP:** Martha Keeble (1765-1841) **VI:** Son of Samuel & Ann (Booth) Saville **P:** unk **BLW:** unk **RG** N **MK:** N **PH:** N **SS:** AK; CD **BS:** 04 Oct 06; 196.

SAVOIX, Martiel; b unk; d 1781 **RU:** Soldier, Served in Touraine Bn and died fr battle at Yorktown **CEM:** French Memorial; GPS 36.81944, -79.39933; Yorktown; York **GS:** U **SP:** No info **VI:** No further data **P:** unk **BLW:** unk **RG:** Y **MK:** unk **PH:** unk **SS:** J-Yorktown Historian; SAR P-284910 **BS:** JLARC 1, 74.

SAYERS, Robert; b 29 Oct 1754; d 17Apr 1826 **RU:** Ensign, Served in Montgomery Co Militia 6 Nov 1781 **CEM:** Crockett Family; GPS 37.01560, -81.05500; Off Rt 600, Crockett's Cove; Wythe **GS:** U **SP:** No info **VI:** Obtained rank of Col after RW. Single stone across fr burying ground **P:** unk **BLW:** unk **RG:** Y **MK:** unk **PH:** unk **SS:** E pg 693; SAR P-285167 **BS:** JLARC 1, 40, 123; 196.

RU=Rank/Unit	CEM=Cemetery	GS=Gravestone	SP=Spousal Information
VI=Other Veteran Info	P=Pension	BLW=Bounty/Land Warrant	RG=Registered Grave
MK=SAR/DAR Marker	PH=Photo	SS=Service Source	BS=Burial Source

370

SAYERS, William; b 19 Oct 1728, PA, d 23 Jan 1781, Montgomery Co **RU**: Patriot, Performed public service as a member of the Fincastle Co Committee of Safety 1775-76 **CEM**: Oglesby Sayers; GPS 36.96440, -80.83030; Rt 701, Draper's Valley; Wythe **GS**: U **SP**: 1) Esther Thompson Crocket, 2) Elizabeth Draket **VI**: Rank of Ensign dates fr before Rev War period **P**: N **BLW**: N **RG**: Y **MK**: unk **PH**: unk **SS**: J-NSSAR 1993 Reg; G pg 207; DAR A100421; SAR P-285169 **BS**: JLARC 1.

SAYERS (SAYRES), John Thompson; b 19 Jul 1758; d 20 Mar 1816 **RU**: Lieutenant Colonel, As Maj served in 4th VA Regt of Foot 13 Aug 1776-30 Jan 1777. Promoted to Lt Col in 9th VA Regt serving fr 30 Jan 1777-4 Oct 1777 **CEM**: Oglesby Sayers; GPS 36.96440, -80.83030; Rt 701, Draper's Valley; Wythe **GS**: U **SP**: Susan/Susanna Crockett (26/29 Sep 1764 Wythe Co-14/16 Oct 1828 Wythe Co) **VI**: Report fr 1986 indicated lower sec of cem "overgrown" **P**: unk **BLW**: unk **RG**: Y **MK**: unk **PH**: unk **SS**: DAR A100399; CE pg 18,30,42,58; SAR P-285163 **BS**: JLARC 1, 40,123; 196.

SCAMMELL, Alexander; b NH; d 1781 **RU**: Colonel, Served fr NH, as Adjutant General, d died fr the battle at Yorktown **CEM**: Governor's Palace; GPS unk; Williamsburg; Williamsburg City **GS**: U **SP**: No info **VI**: The Governor's Palace was used as a hospital for soldiers wounded in the Yorktown battle. Those that d were bur in a mass grave there **P**: unk **BLW**: unk **RG**: Y **MK**: unk **PH**: unk **SS**: J-Yorktown Historian; SAR P-285236 **BS**: JLARC 74.

SCARA, Michel; b unk; d 1781 **RU**: Seaman, Served on "Marseillais" and died from Yorktown battle **CEM**: French Memorial; GPS 36.81944, -79.39933; Yorktown; York **GS**: U **SP**: No info **VI**: No further data **P**: unk **BLW**: unk **RG**: Y **MK**: unk **PH**: unk **SS**: J-Yorktown Historian; SAR P-285244 **BS**: JLARC 1, 74.

SCARBURGH (SCARBOROUGH), John; b unk; d 1794 **RU**: Lieutenant, Served in 9th Cont Line **CEM**: Scarburgh Farm; GPS unk; Opposite jct Rts 601 & 683, across field to old house "Scarborough"; Northampton **GS**: U **SP**: 1) Mar (26 Jun 1759) Ann Kendall, d/o John & (-----) Kendall 2) Mary (Polly) Jacob, a widow **VI**: Widow Mary appl pen & recd BLW 10 Feb 1823 in OH **P**: Y **BLW**: Y **RG**: Y **MK**: unk **PH**: unk **SS**: J-NSSAR 2000 Reg; E pg 694; CG pg 3033; SAR P-285264 **BS**: JLARC 76.

SCHENCK, Jacob; b 1815 **RU**: Patriot. Paid personal property tax, 1780 in York Co, PA which was a supply tax for Rev War expenses **CEM**: Friedens United Church of Christ GPS 38.348480,-78.876530; GPS GS 38.347930, -78.877012; 3960 Friedens Church Rd, Mt Crawford; Rockingham **GS**:Y only a portion of inscription above ground, with new stone giving no birth or death dates **SP**:No spousal data **VI**: No further data **P**: N **BLW**: N **RG**: N **MK**: N **PH**: N **SS**: AK shows tax payment in PA **BS**: 04; 196

SCHLOSSER, George Ernst; b 18 Jan 1721; d 28 Feb 1815 **RU**: Patriot. Paid personal property tax, 1780 in Philadelphia Co, PA which was a supply tax for Rev War expenses **CEM**: Friedens United Church of Christ GPS 38.348480, -78.876530; 3960 Friedens Church Rd, Mt Crawford; Rockingham **GS**:Y with new stone giving birth and death dates **SP**:No spousal data **VI**: No further data **P**: N **BLW**: N **RG**: N **MK**: N **PH**: N **SS**: AK shows tax payment in PA **BS**: 04

SCHOLDER, Francois; b unk; d 1781 **RU**: Soldier, Served in Royal Deaux Ponts Bn and died fr battle at Yorktown **CEM**: French Memorial; GPS 36.81944, -79.39933; Yorktown; York **GS**: U **SP**: No info **VI**: No further data **P**: unk **BLW**: unk **RG**: Y **MK**: unk **PH**: unk **SS**: J-Yorktown Historian; SAR P-285642 **BS**: JLARC 1, 74.

SCHOLFIELD, Thomas; b 1763, Bucks Co PA; d 1810 **RU**: Private, Served in PA units **CEM**: Goose Creek; GPS 39.11250, -77.69527; Rt 722, Lincoln; Loudoun **GS**: N **SP**: Eleanor Flood (1763-1836) **VI**: Recd 400 acres BLW in Northumberland Co, PA **P**: unk **BLW**: Y **RG**: N **MK**: unk **PH**: N **SS**: CI: PA Archives series 3 Vol XXV pg 320 **BS**: 196.

SCHOLT, Sebastian; b unk; d 1781 **RU**: Soldier, Served in Royal Deaux Ponts Bn and died fr battle at Yorktown **CEM**: French Memorial; GPS 36.81944, -79.39933; Yorktown; York **GS**: U **SP**: No info **VI**: No further data **P**: unk **BLW**: unk **RG**: Y **MK**: unk **PH**: unk **SS**: J-Yorktown Historian; SAR P-285658 **BS**: JLARC 1, 74.

SCHOOLFIELD, John; b 1 Feb 1766, PA; d 8 Dec 1831 **RU**: Midshipman, Served on Frigate "Virginia" 28 Oct 1781 **CEM**: Old City; GPS 37.41472, -79.15667; 401 Taylor St; Lynchburg City **GS**: Y **SP**: No

RU=Rank/Unit	CEM=Cemetery	GS=Gravestone	SP=Spousal Information
VI=Other Veteran Info	P=Pension	BLW=Bounty/Land Warrant	RG=Registered Grave
MK=SAR/DAR Marker	PH=Photo	SS=Service Source	BS=Burial Source

371

info **VI**: No further data **P**: unk **BLW**: unk **RG**: N **MK**: Y SAR plaque **PH**: unk **SS**: M pg 125 **BS**: 172, City Lynch.

SCHOOLEY, Samuel; b 16 Apr 1743, Hunterdon Co, NJ, d Apr 1832AT Ocala **RU**: Captain In fall of 1778 commanded a company in the Sussex Co Militia, 1st Regt under Col Jacob West **CEM**: Quaker-Nester (AKA Fruit Hill); GPS 36.8021200, -80.5758760; loc Rt 624 (Nester School Rd) at sharp turn: Carroll **GS**: Unk **SP**: mar 1) (Sep 1770) Margaret Brown (1744-1767), 2) Elizabeth Willson (1751-__) **VI**: Son of Samuel Schooly (1699-1761) & Avis Holloway (1707-1785) **P**: N **BLW**: N **RG**: Y **MK**: N **PH**: N **SS**: DAR A101053; SAR P-285669 **BS**: 196.

SCHULTZ, John; b 3 Dec 1753, PA; d 5 Nov1840) **RU**: Private, Served in Gen Daniel Morgan's Rifle Co. Was member of Morgan's Dutch mess. Was POW at Siege of Quebec **CEM**: Mt Hebron; GPS 38.184120, -78.160698; 305 E Boscawen St; Winchester City **GS**: Y **SP**: mar (8 Mar 1791, Frederick Co) Catherine Harr (Return) **VI**: Appl for pen 9 Aug 1832 Winchester in Frederick Co. 56066 **P**: Y **BLW**: unk **RG**: Y **MK**: Y SAR granite & __ monument **PH**: Y **SS**: J-NSSAR 1993 Reg; CG Vol 3 pg 3039; SAR P-285778 **BS**: JLARC 1.

SCOTT, Andrew; b 18 Jul 1734; d 4 Mar 1821 **RU**: Private, Served in Capt Lyles Co, Augusta Co **CEM**: McDowell Family; GPS 39.18410, -78.16278; 10 mi N Lexington on Rt 11; Rockbridge **GS**: Y **SP**: No info **VI**: Moved to Rockbridge Co **P**: unk **BLW**: unk **RG**: N **MK**: N **PH**: unk **SS**: E pg 695 **BS**: 154 Rockledge.

SCOTT, George; b 30 Nov 1755; d 13 May 1826 **RU**: Private, Served in Culpeper Co Militia **CEM**: The "Hilton"; GPS unk; vic Rt 15 Madison Mills; Madison **GS**: Y **SP**: Betsey (-----) (27 Oct 1768-26 Jun 1849) **VI**: No further data **P**: unk **BLW**: unk **RG**: N **MK**: N **PH**: N **SS**: AW Class 103 **BS**: 90 vol 62 pg 211; 213 pg 294.

SCOTT, George, b c1754, d 1814 **RU**: Patriot, Gave material aid to cause, Amelia Co **CEM**: Scott Family; GPS not determined; his 307 acres was on the Amelia/Nottoway county border. Will book 8, pg 204 gives description and approximate location; Amelia **GS**: Unk **SP**: Elizabeth (----- (__ aft 1814) **VI**: A son born 1774 indicates approximate age of 1754 or earlier **P**: N **BLW**: N **RG**: N **MK**: N **PH**: N **SS**: AL Ct Bk I, pg 29, Bk II, pg 8, Comm Bk pgs 85, 94 **BS**: 196.

SCOTT, Gustavus; b 1753, Prince William Co; d 23 Dec 1800, Rock Hill, DC **RU**: Patriot, Performed public service as delegate to MD Convention and as member of MD Council of Safety **CEM**: Fairfax City; GPS 38.84690, -77.31330; Main St & Page Ave; Fairfax City **GS**: Y **SP**: Margaret Hall Caile (1759-__) **VI**: Reinterred Oct 1967 fr family cemetery Strawberry Vale, vic jct VA 123 & I-495. SAR & DAR marker **P**: N **BLW**: N **RG**: Y **MK**: Y SAR & DAR **PH**: Y **SS**: AS SAR regis; DAR A101477; SAR P-286015 **BS**: SAR regis; 04.

SCOTT, James; b 1715, Dipple Parish, Morayshire, Scotland; d Sep 1782 **RU**: Patriot, Gave use of property and 300# beef in Fauquier Co & 3 beeves Prince William Co **CEM**: Aquia Episcopal; GPS 38.46466, -77.40325; 2938 Jeff Davis Hwy, Aquia; Stafford **GS**: Y **SP**: Sarah Brown **VI**: Was a reverend after Rev War. Died in Prince William Co. Originally bur in Scott Family cemetery ("Dipple"). Reinterred to Aquia Cemetery 1942. SAR monument **P**: N **BLW**: N **RG**: Y **MK**: Y SAR plaque **PH**: Y **SS**: D Prince Wm Co; DAR A207177; SAR P-286053 **BS**: Fairfax Resolves 2014; 196.

SCOTT, James I; b 12 Aug 1736, Ireland; d 18 Nov 1817 **RU**: Private/ Patriot, served in Montgomery Co Militia and as patriot gave material aid to cause **CEM**: Scott; GPS unk; Blue Springs; Smyth **GS**: N **SP**: Rachel Holmes (1753-1833) **VI**: Died in Wythe Co **P**: N **BLW**: N **RG**: Y **MK**: unk **PH**: N **SS**: AL Ct Bk pg 6; BW pg 55; DAR A101546; SAR P-286034 **BS**: JLARC 114; 196.

SCOTT, John; b 1733, Scotland; d 7 Oct 1799 **RU**: Private, Served in10th VA Regt Jul 1778 **CEM**: Scott Family; GPS unk; Across fr 15000 Conference Center Dr, Washington Technology Park, Chantilly; Fairfax **GS**: Y **SP**: Mary (-----) (c1735-12 Mar 1795 "after a violent illness") **VI**: Died age 66 "after an illness of one hour" **P**: unk **BLW**: unk **RG**: N **MK**: N **PH**: unk **SS**: AP roll **BS**: 61 vol IV pg CH-36.

SCOTT, John; b unk; d 1781 **RU**: Private, Served in 4th NY Regt. Drowned on march to Yorktown **CEM**: Yorktown Victory Monument Tablet; GPS 38.28350, -78.54150; Yorktown; York **GS**: U **SP**: No info **VI**:

RU=Rank/Unit
VI=Other Veteran Info
MK=SAR/DAR Marker

CEM=Cemetery
P=Pension
PH=Photo

GS=Gravestone
BLW=Bounty/Land Warrant
SS=Service Source

SP=Spousal Information
RG=Registered Grave
BS=Burial Source

372

No further data **P:** unk **BLW:** unk **RG:** Y **MK:** unk **PH:** unk **SS:** J-Yorktown Historian; AX pg 212; SAR P-286067 **BS:** JLARC 74.

SCOTT, John Baytop; b 26 Sep 1761, Prince Edward Co; d 1 Feb 1814 **RU:** Lieutenant, Served in 1st Light Dragoons, Lee's Legion in 1780. Probably disabled fr wounds **CEM:** Scott Home Site; GPS unk; Off Rt 724, NW fr Scottsburg; Halifax **GS:** Y **SP:** 1) mar (22 Oct 1782 Halifax Co) Elizabeth Coleman (__-27 Mar 1783 Halifax Co) 2) mar (29 Sep 1785) Martha "Patsy" Thompson (1769-1817) (2nd cousin to Elizabeth) **VI:** Son of Thomas (21 Mar 1727-__Glouchester Co) & Catherine (Tompkins) (1733-__ VA). Attended Hampden-Sydney College. After Rev, William & Mary College, grad Law degree.Had 2000 acre farm and saw & grist mills on Difficult Creek. Was Lt of Lee's Legion, and Capt in War of 1812,and General of Militia. Was Vice Pres VA Society of the Cincinatti. Headstone was set by Berryman Green Chapter DAR. Recd1/2 pay pension & BLW **P:** Y **BLW:** Y **RG:** unk **MK:** Y SAR **PH:** unk **SS:** J- DAR Hatcher; BG pg 3046; DAR A101648; SAR P-286090 **BS:** JLARC 2; 80, vol4, pg 14; 215.

SCOTT, John E; b unk; d Aft 1805 **RU:** Lieutenant/Patriot, Gave material aid to cause **CEM:** Scott Family; GPS 37.45250, -78.18890; VES Rd; Lynchburg City **GS:** N **SP:** No info **VI:** BLW awarded 18 Nov 1811 **P:** unk **BLW:** Y **RG:** N **MK:** N **PH:** N **SS:** N pg 1361; AL Ct Bk pg 41 Amherst Co **BS:** 131 Scott.

SCOTT, Johnny (Jonny); b 1718, Orange Co; d 1778 **RU:** Captain/Patriot, Served as Commissary in Orange Co Militia. Resigned prior to 23 July 1778. Gave material aid to cause **CEM:** Scott Family; GPS unk; Madison Run; Orange **GS:** U **SP:** mar (c1750) Mary Hackett (1721-5 Nov 1811) **VI:** No further data **P:** unk **BLW:** unk **RG:** Y **MK:** unk **PH:** unk **SS:** DAR A101609; E pg 696; AL Ct Bk pg 4, 22 Orange Co; SAR P-286101 **BS:** JLARC 76; 80, vol4, pg 14.

SCOTT, Joseph; b 1757; d 15 Oct 1833 **RU:** Private, Served in VA and Cont Lines **CEM:** Scott; GPS unk; Rich Valley; Washington **GS:** U **SP:** mar (1783) Mary Talbot (__-10 May 1840) **VI:** Son Obediah Scott. Appl for pension 16 May 1853 Washington Co. S9474 **P:** Y **BLW:** unk **RG** N **MK:** unk **PH:** unk **SS:** CG Vol 3 pg 3046 **BS:** JLARC 1, 4.

SCOTT, Mathew; b 1751, Ireland; d Feb 1815 **RU:** Sergeant, Served in 4th, 8th, 12th Cont Lines. Perhaps acquired rank as ensign **CEM:** Salem Cemetery; GPS 37.05014, -80.16004; Rt 221, Head of the River Church; Floyd **GS:** U **SP:** Lucretia Ogle (6 Mar 1759-Jun 1836) **VI:** No further data **P:** unk **BLW:** unk **RG:** N **MK:** unk **PH:** unk **SS:** DAR A101690; E pg 696 **BS:** JLARC 29.

SCOTT, Samuel; b 14 Mar 1754, Caroline Co; d 20 Jun 1822 **RU:** Major, Enl as lieutenant in VA Calvary. In 1777 was Capt in GA Cavalry. Was in battles of Savannah, Guilford CH. Held rank of Major in VA troops. **CEM:** Maj Samuel Scott Family; GPS 37.41330, -79.20304; 2627 Old Forest Rd; Lynchburg City **GS:** Y **SP:** mar (17 Jun 1794, Spotsylvania Co) Ann Roy (28 Feb 1762-1 Apr 1846) d/o John & Ann (Waller) Roy **VI:** Son of Thomas Scott & Martha Williams. Owned "Locust Thicket" **P:** unk **BLW:** Y **RG:** Y **MK:** Y SAR **PH:** Y **SS:** BY pg 240; AK wid pension; DAR A101807; SAR P-286184 **BS:** JLARC 1, 2, 3, 6, 84, 90; 04 Sep 07; 80, vol4, pg 14; 196.

SCOTT, Samuel; b 7 Dec 1761, Peach Bottom, Lancaster Co, PA; d 1 Aor 1811 **RU:** Private, Served in Capt Cloyd's Co, Montgomery Co Militia 12 Sep 1777 **CEM:** Glade Spring Presbyterian; GPS 36.76720, -81.78720; 33234 Lee Hwy, Glade Spring; Washington **GS:** U **SP:** mar (1783) Jane Hutton (1765, Morristown, PA-Sep 1844, Cole Co, OH) d/o (-----) & Sarah Dixon (__-17 Aug 1815) **VI:** No further data **P:** N **BLW:** N **RG:** N **MK:** N **PH:** N **SS:** G pg 215 **BS:** 196.

SCOTT, Stephen; b unk; d 1824 **RU:** Private?, Served in 1st, 10th, & 14th Cont Lines **CEM:** Fairfax Meeting House; GPS 39.18557, -77.60589; Water St & Waterford Rd, Waterford; Loudoun **GS:** Y **SP:** No info **VI:** No further data **P:** unk **BLW:** unk **RG:** N **MK:** N **PH:** unk **SS:** E pg 696 **BS:** 25 pg 275.

SCOTT, Thomas; b 21 Mar 1727, Gloucester Point, d 29 Nov 1804 **RU:** Patriot, Performed public service as: member of Prince Edward Co Committee, 1775; signed petition there 1776; and served as Commissioner there 1782 **CEM:** Scott Family; GPS not determined; at home place called "Union Grove, adjacent to Belena," at Briery Creek, Briery; Prince Edward **GS:** Unk **SP:** 1) mar (6 Apr 1754) Catherine Tomkies (10 Jun 1733, Gloucester Co-2 Jan 1766), d/o Charles Tomkies and Ann Alexander, 2) Sarah Barford, 3) mar (16 Jul 1790) Ruth Billups **VI:** Son of Thomas Scott, (1676, Cumberland, Eng-__) &

RU=Rank/Unit	CEM=Cemetery	GS=Gravestone	SP=Spousal Information
VI=Other Veteran Info	P=Pension	BLW=Bounty/Land Warrant	RG=Registered Grave
MK=SAR/DAR Marker	PH=Photo	SS=Service Source	BS=Burial Source

373

Anne Baytop (c1707, Springfield, Gloucester Co-___); Trustee Hampton Sydney College, 1783; Magistrate in county 1785 **P:** N **BLW:** N **RG:** Y **MK:** N **PH:** N **SS:** CD; DAR A101849; SAR P-286197 **BS:** 196.

SCOTT, Thomas Hugh; b 28 Feb 1749, Caroline Co; d Jul 1799; **RU:** Private, served in either Capt John Harvey or Capt John Venable's Company, Charlotte Co Militia **CEM:** Saint Andrews Episcopal Ch; GPS 36.759490, -77.850443; 400 Windsor Ave, Lawrenceville; Brunswick **GS:** Unk **SP:** mar (11 Jan 1781) Sarah Embrey Read (1747, Brunswick Co-Oct 1802), d/o Henry Emery (1700-1758) & Priscilla Wilkinson (1720-1798) **VI:** Son of Thomas Killin & Ann Baytop **P:** N **BLW:** N **RG:** N **MK:** N **PH:** N **SS:** G pg 133 **BS:**

SCOTT, William; b 1766; d 4 Nov 1844 **RU:** Patriot, Gave material aid to the cause **CEM:** Penny Hill; GPS 38.79861, -77.05559; S Payne & Franklin Sts; Alexandria City **GS:** N **SP:** Emma Redman **VI:** Son of Robert Scott & Mary Edwards. Died at Alexandria Hospital **P:** N **BLW:** N **RG:** N **MK:** N **PH:** N **SS:** AL Ct bk pg 17,22 **BS:** 20 pg 45.

SCOTT, William; b c1751, Prince William Co; d 18 Oct 1787 **RU:** Patriot, Gave 545# beef & two horses for five days **CEM:** Aquia Episcopal; GPS 38.46466, -77.40325; 2938 Jeff Davis Hwy, Aquia; Stafford **GS:** Y **SP:** No info **VI:** Died in Fairfax Co. Originally bur 1787 in Scott Family cemetery. Reinterred to Aquia Cemetery 1942 **P:** N **BLW:** N **RG:** N **MK:** Y SAR **PH:** Y **SS:** D Prince Wm Co; SAR application 886 **BS:** Fairfax Resolves 2014.

SCOTT, William; b unk; d 1798 **RU:** Private/Patriot, Gave material aid to the cause. Wife given allowance for support while he was away in service **CEM:** Dumfries Public; GPS 38.34110, -77.19964; 17821 Mine Rd, Dumfries; Prince William **GS:** N **SP:** No info **VI:** No further data **P:** unk **BLW:** unk **RG:** Y **MK:** Y SAR monument **PH:** N **SS:** D Prince William Co; AL Ct Bk pg 13, 14; SAR P-340460 **BS:** 96 pg 91.

SCOTT, William E; b 30 Jan 1744, Chesterfield Co; d 1 Jan 1797 **RU:** Lieutenant, Served in Bedford Co Militia **CEM:** Scott Family; GPS unk; Episcopal School Rd 200 yds fr school; Bedford **GS:** N **SP:** Mar (20 May 1784) Elizabeth Wade (c1764-20 May 1814) **VI:** No further data **P:** unk **BLW:** unk **RG:** N **MK:** unk **PH:** unk **SS:** DAR A101890 **BS:** 131.

SCOTT, William W; b 15 Dec 1756, Caroline Co; d 16 Oct 1817, Campbell Co **RU:** Captain, Ent serv 1776 as 1st Lt under brother Capt Thomas Scott, Prince Edward Co & Charlotte Co. Later served in Col Critten's 3rd Regt of GA Line at battles of Sunbury & Savannah **CEM:** Scott Family; GPS 37.45250, -78.18890; VES Rd; Lynchburg City **GS:** U **SP:** mar (1 Mar 1781) Ann "Nancy" Jones (13 Mar 1763, Spotsylvania Co-1846, Campbell Co) d/oGabriel (c1740-1777) & Mary Anne (Waller) Jones **VI:** No further data **P:** unk **BLW:** Y **RG:** Y **MK:** unk **PH:** unk **SS:** BY pg 224; DAR A101887; SAR P-286228 **BS:** JLARC 4, 36.

SCRUGGS, Drury; b 1725; d 26 Aug 1782 **RU:** Patriot, Gave material aid to the cause **CEM:** Scruggs Family; GPS unk; Head of Huddy Ck; Cumberland **GS:** Y **SP:** mar (c1747) Mary (-----) (1720,-24 Jul 1804) **VI:** No further data **P:** N **BLW:** N **RG:** Y **MK:** N **PH:** unk **SS:** DAR A100805; SAR P-286350 AL Com Bk pg 233 **BS:** 80 vol 4 pg 15.

SCRUGGS, Samuel; b 1765; d 20 Mar 1814 **RU:** Private, Served three yrs **CEM:** Old City; GPS 37.41472, -79.15667; 401 Taylor St; Lynchburg City **GS:** Y **SP:** Jane (-----) Had wife in 1828 **VI:** Sol appl pen 1826, Nelson Co age 70. S38357 **P:** Y **BLW:** unk **RG:** N **MK:** Y SAR plaque **PH:** unk **SS:** C pg 506; CG pg 3053 **BS:** 162 Methodist.

SCULL, William; b Jun 1739, Philadelphia; d 6 Feb 1813 **RU:** Captain, Was Capt in 11th VA Regt, commanded by Col Richard Hampton, May 1777 **CEM:** Old Presbyterian Meeting House; GPS 38.48528, -77.23532; 323 S Fairfax St; Alexandria City **GS:** N **SP:** Mar (25 Oct 1763, Philadelphia) Jane Lodge **VI:** Died age 75 (Alexandria Gazette, 9 Feb 1813, pg 3) **P:** unk **BLW:** unk **RG:** N **MK:** N **PH:** N **SS:** DAR A205576; AP **BS:** 23 pg 112.

SEABROOK, Nicholas B; b c1733; d 29 Jun 1790 **RU:** Patriot, Gave material aid to cause **CEM:** St John's Episcopal; GPS 37.53183, -77.41958; 2401 E Broad St; Richmond City **GS:** Y **SP:** No info **VI:** No further data **P:** N **BLW:** N **RG:** N **MK:** N **PH:** unk **SS:** D Vol 2 pg 466; AL Cert Henrico Co **BS:** 28 pg 504; 196.

RU=Rank/Unit   CEM=Cemetery   GS=Gravestone   SP=Spousal Information
VI=Other Veteran Info   P=Pension   BLW=Bounty/Land Warrant   RG=Registered Grave
MK=SAR/DAR Marker   PH=Photo   SS=Service Source   BS=Burial Source

374

SEAUCE, Jacques; b unk; d 1781 **RU:** Seaman, Served on "Ville de Paris" and died from Yorktown battle **CEM:** French Memorial; GPS 36.81944, -79.39933; Yorktown; York **GS:** U **SP:** No info **VI:** No further data **P:** unk **BLW:** unk **RG:** Y **MK:** unk **PH:** unk **SS:** J-Yorktown Historian; SAR P-286642 **BS:** JLARC 1,74.

SEAY, Austin Sr; b 25 Dec 1759, Albemarle Co (later Fluvanna); d 1 Feb 1834 **RU:** Sergeant, Ent serv Albemarle Co and served in VA Line **CEM:** Fork Union Military Academy; GPS unk; 4744 James Madison Hwy, Fork Union; Fluvanna **GS:** U **SP:** mar (1780 or early 1781 in Fluvanna or Goochland Co) Elizabeth Weaver (c1754-c1 Jan 1844) **VI:** Appl pen 24 Jun 1833 age 75, Fluvanna Co. Widow appl pen 4 Oct 1841 age 87. W19341. Source 100 shows dates of 1758-1836 **P:** Y **BLW:** unk **RG:** Y **MK:** Y SAR **PH:** unk **SS:** CG Vol 3 pg 3061; DAR A101231; SAR 286702 **BS:** JLARC 3,46, 100; 80, Vol 4, pg 17; 196.

SEBIRE, Martin; b unk; d 1781 **RU:** Seaman, Served on "Ville de Paris" and died from Yorktown battle **CEM:** French Memorial; GPS 36.81944, -79.39933; Yorktown; York **GS:** U **SP:** No info **VI:** No further data **P:** unk **BLW:** unk **RG:** Y **MK:** unk **PH:** unk **SS:** J-Yorktown Historian; SAR P-286713 **BS:** JLARC 1, 74.

SEIGLE, Frederick; b unk; d unk **RU:** Surgeon, Served in Cont Line **CEM:** Mt Hebron; GPS 39.10916, -78.09497; 305 E Boscawen St; Winchester City **GS:** U **SP:** No info **VI:** Recd BLW of 6000 acres, Jul 1797 **P:** unk **BLW:** unk **RG:** Y **MK:** Y SAR monument **PH:** unk **SS:** J-NSSAR 2000 Reg; SAR P-286957 **BS:** JLARC 76.

SELDEN, Wilson Cary; b 1762; d 1835 **RU:** Surgeon, Served in VA State Line as surgeon's mate & full surgeon **CEM:** St James Episcopal, Old Cemetery; GPS 39.11555, -77.56250; Church St NE, Leesburg; Loudoun **GS:** U **SP:** 1) (-----) 2) Mary Mason Page (c1749-17 Sep 1787) **VI:** Pen appl for 13 Jun 1832 in Washington DC age 70. S4815, also VA 1/2 Pay (See N>A. Acc #874 #050159 1/2 pay) Surgeon **P:** Y **BLW:** Y **RG:** Y **MK:** unk **PH:** unk **SS:** BY pg 232; CG Vol 3 pg 3066; SAR P-287008 **BS:** JLARC 4, 32.

SELIGNET, Jean; b unk; d 1781 **RU:** Soldier, Served in Bourbonnais Bn and died fr battle at Yorktown **CEM:** French Memorial; GPS 36.81944, -79.39933; Yorktown; York **GS:** U **SP:** No info **VI:** No further data **P:** unk **BLW:** unk **RG:** Y **MK:** unk **PH:** unk **SS:** J-Yorktown Historian; SAR P-287023 **BS:** JLARC 1, 74.

SELIQUET, Jean; b unk; d 1781 **RU:** Soldier, Served in Bourbonnais Bn and died fr battle at Yorktown **CEM:** French Memorial; GPS 36.81944, -79.39933; Yorktown; York **GS:** U **SP:** No info **VI:** No further data **P:** unk **BLW:** unk **RG:** unk **MK:** unk **PH:** unk **SS:** J-Yorktown Historian; SAR P-287023 **BS:** JLARC 74.

SELLERS, John; b 1742; d 1821 **RU:** Private/Patriot, served in Capt Cuthbert Harrison's 1st Regt Light Dragoons, Cont Troops, commanded by Col Theoderick Bland, Nov 1777 to Oct 1778 and was in the battle at Trenton. He gave material aid to cause in Rockingham Co and paid personal property tax there in 1783 which was a supply tax for Rev War expenses **CEM:** Old Peaked Mountain; GPS 38.37113, -78.73416; 9843 Town Hall Rd, McGaheysville; Rockingham **GS:** U **SP:** mar (1792 Rockingham Co) Eve Fifer, prob d/o Adam & (----) Fifer **VI:** Listed on memorial at Peaked Mountain Cemetery as "potentially having been bur there with Capt Cuthbert; memorialized on DAR plaque in the cemetery as John Adam Sellers. **P:** Unk **BLW:** Unk **RG:** Y **MK:** Y DAR plaque **PH:** Unk **SS:** E pg 700; AL Ct Bk I pg 4, II pg 6 & Comm Bk V pgs 131,136 Rockingham Co; AP Fold 3 serv rec; DV image 1783 pdf 09; SAR P-287067 **BS:** 196.

SELLERS, Henry; b 1720; d 1804 **RU:** Patriot, **RU:** Patriot, paid personal property tax Rockingham Co in 1783 which was a supply tax for Rev War expenses **CEM:** Old Peaked Mountain; GPS 38.37113, -78.73416; 9843 Town Hall Rd, McGaheysville; Rockingham **GS:** U **SP:** Not determined **VI:** memorialized on DAR plaque in the cemetery as John Henry Sellers **P:** Unk **BLW:** Unk **RG:** N **MK:** Y DAR plaque **PH:** Unk **SS;** DV image 1783 pdf 08 **BS:** DAR plaque.

SELLERS, Peter b Unk; d aft 1783 **RU:** Patriot, gave material aid to cause in Rockingham Co and paid personal property tax there in 1783 which was a supply tax for Rev War expenses **CEM:** Old Peaked Mountain; GPS 38.37113, -78.73416; 9843 Town Hall Rd, McGaheysville; Rockingham **GS:** U **SP:** No information **VI:** memorialized on DAR plaque in the cemetery as John Peter Sellers **P:** Unk **BLW:** Unk

RU=Rank/Unit	CEM=Cemetery	GS=Gravestone	SP=Spousal Information
VI=Other Veteran Info	P=Pension	BLW=Bounty/Land Warrant	RG=Registered Grave
MK=SAR/DAR Marker	PH=Photo	SS=Service Source	BS=Burial Source

375

RG: Y **MK:** Y DAR plaque **PH:** Unk **SS:** AL Ct Bk I pg 4, II pg 6 & Comm Bk V pgs 131,136 Rockingham Co DV image 1783 pdf 09; SAR P-331260 **BS:** DAR plaque; SAR PRS.

SEPEDRE, Antoine; b unk; d 1781 **RU:** Soldier, Served in Soissonnais Bn and died fr battle at Yorktown **CEM:** French Memorial; GPS 36.81944, -79.39933; Yorktown; York **GS:** U **SP:** No info **VI:** No further data **P:** unk **BLW:** unk **RG:** Y **MK:** unk **PH:** unk **SS:** J-Yorktown Historian; SAR P-287168 **BS:** JLARC 1, 74.

SERREE, Jacques; b unk; d 1781 **RU:** Soldier, Served in Santogne Bn and died fr battle at Yorktown **CEM:** French Memorial; GPS 36.81944, -79.39933; Yorktown; York **GS:** U **SP:** No info **VI:** No further data **P:** unk **BLW:** unk **RG:** Y **MK:** unk **PH:** unk **SS:** J-Yorktown Historian; 287194 **BS:** JLARC 1, 74.

SERVE, Antoine; b unk; d 1781 **RU:** Soldier, Served in Gatinais Bn and died fr battle at Yorktown **CEM:** French Memorial; GPS 36.81944, -79.39933; Yorktown; York **GS:** U **SP:** No info **VI:** No further data **P:** unk **BLW:** unk **RG:** Y **MK:** unk **PH:** unk **SS:** J-Yorktown Historian; SAR P-287197 **BS:** JLARC 1, 74.

SEYBERT, Christian; b 1744, Montgomery Co; d 1838 **RU:** Soldier, Served in VA Line. Enl in Montgomery Co, in Capt Issac Taylor's Co, Col John Montgomery's Regt **CEM:** Seybert Family; GPS unk; Gunton Park; Wythe **GS:** U **SP:** mar (1780) Mary (-----) (1750 Holland-c1830) **VI:** Appl pen 8 Oct 1832 Wythe Co, age 88. S7475. Source 76 has a Christian Scybert bur in Wythe, no city or fam cem. Stones now illegible **P:** Y **BLW:** unk **RG:** Y **MK:** unk **PH:** unk **SS:** DAR A102283; CG Vol 3 pg 3075; SAR P-286406; **BS:** JLARC 4, 40, 76.

SEYBERT, Henry; b unk; d 1830 **RU:** Private, Served in Capt Weiser's Co Germ Bn, Cont Troops **CEM:** Seybert Hills Farm; GPS unk; US 200 N fr Monterery to Rt 629, then 1.8 mi; Highland **GS:** U **SP:** No info **VI:** Son of Johan (1717-1758) & Maria Elisabeth (Theiss) (1721-1758) Seybert **P:** unk **BLW:** unk **RG:** Y **MK:** unk **PH:** unk **SS:** SAR P-287400; Gov't Gr st gives service **BS:** JLARC 103; 196.

SEYBERT, Nicholas; b 1741, Berks Co, PA; d 1813 **RU:** Captain, Served 7th MD Bn **CEM:** Seybert Chapel; GPS unk; Nr jct Rt 629 Strait Creek and Rt 631, Monterey; Highland **GS:** Y **SP:** No info **VI:** No further data **P:** unk **BLW:** unk **RG:** Y **MK:** N **PH:** unk **SS:** E pg 701; SAR P-287402 **BS:** JLARC 103; 181.(SHACKELFORD, William See Appendix G, Addenda)

SHAKLETT (SHACKLETT), Edward; b 1752; d 23 Apr 1826 **RU:** Sergeant, Served in Cont Line. Entered service Surry Co. Served as Sgt in Col Charles Harrison's Regt of Artillery. Discharged Morristown 10 Jan 1780 **CEM:** Cool Spring Church; GPS 38.899955 -77.926749 .5 mi S of Delaplane; Fauquier **GS:** Y **SP:** Mar (10 May 1782 Farquier Co, bond dated 4 May 1782 Hezekiah Shacklett security) Elizabeth "Betsy" Rector (c1766-24 Oct 1839) **VI:** Widow appl pen 25 Jul 1838 Fauquier Co age 72 W6037 **P:** Y **BLW:** unk **RG:** Y **MK:** Y SAR **PH:** Y **SS:** E pg 702; K pg 44; CG Vol 3 pg 3077; Fauquier Co Marriages pg 178; DAR A102512; SAR P-287521 **BS:** 95, Cool Spring; JLARC 2, 4,16; 80, vol 4, pg 22.

SHANNON, John; b 1759; d 18 Dec 1832 **RU:** Soldier, Served in VA Line in Capt Robert McFarland's Co, Col William Campbell's Expedition to Ransom's Mill, Rutherford, TN **CEM:** Old Shannon Place; GPS 38.53999, -77.55610; Head of Long Hollow, Rich Valley; Smyth **GS:** U **SP:** Mar (10 Jan 1788 Washington Co) Ann (Nancy) Marshall (c1770-___) **VI:** Widow appl pen 22 Jul 1845 Smyth Co age 75. R9419. Wounded in hip. GSs destroyed **P:** Y **BLW:** unk **RG:** Y **MK:** unk **PH:** unk **SS:** CG Vol 3 pg 3081; SAR P-287718 **BS:** JLARC 4, 114.

SHANNON, Thomas Reid; b 25 Mar 1753, Albemarle Co; d 12 Nov 1841 **RU:** Captain, Commanded Middle New River Co, Montgomery Co Troops. Also served in Capt Patton's Co, Montgomery Co Militia **CEM:** Shannon-King; GPS 37.21810, -80.74170; Nr Jct Rts 42 & 100, Poplar Hill nr Walker's Creek; Giles **GS:** Y **SP:** Agnes Crowe (17 Jun 1760-16 Oct 1823) **VI:** Son of Samuel (1727 Sadsbury Meeting House, Lancaster Co, PA-1811 Whites Creek, Davidson Co, TN) & Jean (Reid) Shannon.Was a sheriff of Montgomery Co & a state legislator. Name listed on bronze plaque in the cemetery **P:** unk **BLW:** unk **RG:** Y **MK:** unk **PH:** unk **SS:** J- DAR Hatcher; G pg 223; DAR A102846; SAR P-287732 **BS:** JLARC 2; 80, vol 4, pg 22; 196.

SHARP, John; b 1727; d 18 Oct 1816 **RU:** Soldier, Served in Capt Cunningham's Co, Augusta Co Militia **CEM:** North Mountain; GPS unk; 7 mi S of Staunton on N side Rt 252; Augusta **GS:** Y **SP:** 1) Mar (30

RU=Rank/Unit	CEM=Cemetery	GS=Gravestone	SP=Spousal Information
VI=Other Veteran Info	P=Pension	BLW=Bounty/Land Warrant	RG=Registered Grave
MK=SAR/DAR Marker	PH=Photo	SS=Service Source	BS=Burial Source

376

Sep 1797 Augusta Co) Elizabeth Curry; (2) Ann (-----) **VI:** Name inscribed on newer family stone **P:** unk **BLW:** unk **RG:** Y **MK:** N **PH:** unk **SS:** JLARC 62, 63; E pg 703; SAR P-287793 **BS:** JLARC 62, 63; 196.

SHARP, John; b 1763, PA, d 25 Jul 1866 **RU:** Private, served in Capt Cunningham's Company, Augusta County Militia **CEM:** Sharp Family; GPS not determined; loc Big Valley Rd on "Sharps Hill" at Trimble on restricted private property; Highland.**GS:** Y **SP:** Elizabeth Curry (1763, Ireland-25 Dec 1859), d/o Richard Curry **VI:** Lived to age 103, death reported by neighbor. Highland Co was formed from Bath Co that was formed from Augusta Co, thus service applies **P:** Unk **BLW:** Unk **RG:** N **MK:** N **PH:** N **SS:** E pg 703 **BS:** 196.

SHARP, John Anderson; b 30 Aug1745, PA; d 1 Dec 1823 **RU:** Ensign, Served in NC Rangers **CEM:** Green Spring Presbyterian; GPS 36.63670, -81.99560; 2007 Green Spring Ch Rd, Abingdon; Washington **GS:** Y **SP:** Elizabeth Laughlin (1748 PA-5 Jan 1825) **VI:** Gov't Gr St shows service SAR PRS shows burial in TN **P:** unk **BLW:** unk **RG:** Y **MK:** unk **PH:** unk **SS:** AR Vol 4 pg 22; DAR A102957; SAR P-287798 **BS:** JLARC 2, 70, 80,101; 78 pg 276; 80, vol 4, pg 22; 196.

SHARP, Joseph; b 1753; d Oct 1828 **RU:** Soldier, Served in 10th Cont Line **CEM:** Bethel Presbyterian; GPS 38.04257, -79.17283, GS 38.0232,-79.1019; 563 Bethel Green Rd, Middlebrook; Augusta **GS:** Y **SP:** mar (30 Sep 1797 Augusta Co) Julianna Scott **VI:** Lower half of stone now missing **P:** unk **BLW:** unk **RG:** Y **MK:** unk **PH:** unk **SS:** E pg 703; SAR P-287805 **BS:** JLARC 62; 196.

SHARP, Thomas; b 24 Aug 1761; d 24 Jan 1826 **RU:** Lieutenant, Private in Capt Thomas Church's Co, Col Wayne's PA Bn, 1776 and also Hazen's Regt. Was Corporal in 3rd Cont Line. May be person this name promoted to Lt in 1780 **CEM:** Bethel Presbyterian; GPS 38.04257, -79.17283, GS 38.0232,-79.1020;; 563 Bethel Green Rd, Middlebrook; Augusta **GS:** Y **SP:** 1) Jean Wilson 2) Mary Ann Reed (marriages are fr JLARC) **VI:** Recd BLW 8 Nov 1791; served in War of 1812 **P:** unk **BLW:** Y **RG:** Y **MK:** unk **PH:** Y **SS:** C pg 507; E pg 703; CG pg 3082; SAR P-287828 **BS:** JLARC 62, 63; 196.

SHAW, James; b unk; d Mar 1793 **RU:** Private, Served as orderly in hospital. Was in consolidated 4th, 8th, 12th VA Regts **CEM:** Old Christ Church Episcopal; GPS 38.80625, -77.04718; 118 N Washington St; Alexandria City **GS:** N **SP:** No info **VI:** Burial permit issued 18 Mar 1793 **P:** unk **BLW:** unk **RG:** N **MK:** N **PH:** N **SS:** AP roll **BS:** 20 pg 152.

SHEETS, Jacob; b unk; d Aft 1781 **RU:** Private/Patriot, Served in Capt Anderson, Augusta Co. Gave material aid to cause **CEM:** Sheets Family; GPS unk; W of Rt 220, Bessemer area; Botetourt **GS:** Y **SP:** No info **VI:** No further data **P:** unk **BLW:** unk **RG:** Y **MK:** N **PH:** unk **SS:** E pg 705; AL Cert 1 Augusta Co; SAR P-333767 **BS:** 115 pg 82.

SHEETS, Samuel; b unk; d 27 May 1782 **RU:** Patriot, Gave material aid to cause **CEM:** Keezletown; GPS unk; Keezletown; Rockingham **GS:** U **SP:** Elizabeth (-----) (__-1807) **VI:** No further data **P:** N **BLW:** N **RG:**N **MK:** unk **PH:** unk **SS:** AL Ct Bk pg 28 Albemarle Co **BS:** 96.

SHELBY, Elvan; b 1754; d 1813 **RU:** Patriot, Service information in DAR Senate Document 113, 1973 and 1993 **CEM:** East Hill; GPS 36.59438, -82.17233; E State St on line btw VA and TN; Bristol City **GS:** Y **SP:** No info **VI:** No further data **P:** N **BLW:** N **RG:**Y **MK:** N **PH:** unk **SS:** AR Vol 4 pg 26; AS DAR Report; SAR P-288383 **BS:** 80 vol 4, pg 26

SHELBY, Evan; b 1754; d 18 Jan 1793 **RU:** General, Was Brig Gen of VA Milita. As Capt commanded an Independent co Sep-Dec 1774. As Maj was in charge of expedition against Indians 1776 and commander of militia unit at Battle of Kings Mountain Oct 1780 **CEM:** East Hill, Sec 1; GPS unk; West of Circles (Source 80 Cem #279A); Washington **GS:** Y **SP:** No info **VI:** Killed by Indians at age 74 after Rev War. First bur where the First Presbyterian Church now stands, and was later removed to this cemetery. Coffin-sized iron mounted over grave **P:** unk **BLW:** unk **RG:** unk **MK:** unk **PH:** unk **SS:** E pg 705; CE pg 24, 141 **BS:** ; 80, vol 4, pg 26; 183; JLARC 80.

SHELBY, Isaac; b 11 Dec 1750, Hagerstown, MD; d 18 Jul 1826 **RU:** Colonel/Patriot, Was in battle at Point Pleasant and was hero at Kings Mountain. Gave material aid to cause **CEM:** East Hill; GPS 36.59438, -82.17233; E State St on line btw VA and TN; Bristol City **GS:** U **SP:** Susanna Hart **VI:** After war became general. Was first governor of Kentucky. Was Secretary of War on Monroe's cabinet. Died in Traveller's Rest, Lincoln Co, KY. Memorialized in the cemetery at the burial site of his father Evan

RU=Rank/Unit
VI=Other Veteran Info
MK=SAR/DAR Marker

CEM=Cemetery
P=Pension
PH=Photo

GS=Gravestone
BLW=Bounty/Land Warrant
SS=Service Source

SP=Spousal Information
RG=Registered Grave
BS=Burial Source

377

Shelby & Letitia Cox **P:** unk **BLW:** unk **RG:** Y **MK:** N **PH:** unk **SS:** J- DAR Hatcher; Z pg 154; AL Ct Bk pg 1 Montgomery Co; BY; DAR A102449; SAR P-288390 **BS:** JLARC 2.;80, vol 4, pg 26.

SHELDON, Parker; b 1755; d 1825 **RU:** Soldier, See DAR Senate Document 1930 serial 9337, vol 5 for service **CEM:** Newport; GPS unk; Newport; Giles **GS:** U **SP:** No info **VI:** No further data **P:** unk **BLW:** unk **RG:** Y **MK:** unk **PH:** unk **SS:** J-NSSAR 2000 Reg; SAR P-288485; AR Vol 4 pg 27 **BS:** JLARC 76.

SHELOR, Daniel; b 3 Mar 1750, MD; d 13 Dec 1847 **RU:** Captain, Served in MD Cont Line **CEM:** Pine Creek Primitive Baptist; GPS 36.94622, -80.27357; Spangler Mill Rd Rt 682; Floyd **GS:** Y **SP:** Mar (1784) Mary Wickham (1756 Frederick Co, MD-4 Oct 1834) **VI:** Son of Lawrence & (-----) Shelor. Recd pen S6079 **P:** Y **BLW:** unk **RG:** Y **MK:** N **PH:** Y **SS:** NSDAR Patriot Index 2002; Rev War Survivor's Pens Appl File: M804 Roll 2168; JLARC 1, 2, 9; SAR P-268573 **BS:** JLARC 1, 29; 196.

SHELTON, Daniel; b 17 May 1729, Mecklenburg Co, d 18 Sep 1809 **RU:** Major, was appointed a captain of Pittsylvania Co Militia, 21 Sep 1775, and major of militia in 1778 **CEM:** Brightwood Memorial Park; GPS 36.8277780, -79.3795560; loc end of Marilla Ln, Chatham; Pittsylvania **GS:** Y Gov't **SP:** mar (c1750 Amelia Co) Lettice Young **VI:** Son of Ralph Shelton (1685-1733) & Mary Jane Crispen Buford (1688-1750) **P:** N **BLW:** N **RG:** Y **MK:** N **PH:** N **SS:** G pg 284; CD; SAR P-288573 **BS:** 196.

SHELTON, Eliphaz; b 1741; d 16 Feb 1826 **RU:** Captain/Patriot, Appt Capt Mar 1779 and commanded a co in Henry Co Militia serving until 1781. Gave material aid to cause **CEM:** Eliphaz Shelton-Pilson Family; GPS unk; At foot of Main St, Stuart; Patrick **GS:** U **SP:** Ann (Nancy) (-----) **VI:** Son of Ralph (1709-1789) & Susannah Mary (Daniel) (1713-1787) Shelton. Plaque to him on Patrick CH wall indicates he gave land to build it on **P:** unk **BLW:** unk **RG:** Y **MK:** unk **PH:** unk **SS:** E pg 706; AL Ct Bk pg 22 Henry Co; DAR A102770; SAR P-288580 **BS:** JLARC 30; 196.

SHELTON, James; b 1759; d Aft 14 Nov 1840 **RU:** Sergeant, Served in VA Line fr Louisa Co. **CEM:** Woodland; GPS unk; Jackson District; Louisa **GS:** U **SP:** Mar (7 Jun 1798) Elizabeth Thompson (c1774-Jun 1814) **VI:** Was substitute for his brother John. Appl pen Louisa Co 7 May 1836. S10257 **P:** Y **BLW:** unk **RG:** Y **MK:** unk **PH:** unk **SS:** DAR A102788; SAR P-288586; CG pg 3100 **BS:** JLARC 4, 61.

SHELTON, John "Jack", b 19 Nov 1758, d 20 Nov 1853 **RU:**Private served in 2d Cont Line commanded by Col Alexander Spotswood, Jul 1777 **CEM:** Shelton/Ellis/Watts; GPS 37.30459, -79.09698; loc Winesap Rd (Rt 675) at house # 1559, then W on dirt Ln 400 ft; Monroe; Amherst **GS:** Y **SP:** Nancy Poindexter (13 Feb 1764-1 Feb 1824) **VI:** Son of Richard Shelton (1728-1821) & Mary Wright (1728-1818) **P:** N **BLW:** N **RG:** N **MK:** N **PH:** N **SS:** E pg 706; AP Fold3 Rev War Rolls **BS:** 196.

SHELTON, Lemuel; b c1765; d 1848 **RU:** Soldier, Served in VA Line **CEM:** Pine Creek; GPS unk; SAR registration did not give directions; Pittsylvania **GS:** U **SP:** Mar (Aug 1796) Lettis Weeks (__-1815 Pittsylvania Co) **VI:** Son of Gabriel (1740-20 Jun 1803) and Elizabeth (Sheppherd) Shelton. Son Hubbard C. Shelton appl pen 1 Feb 1853 Todd Co KY age 47 R9474 **P:** Y **BLW:** unk **RG:** Y **MK:** unk **PH:** unk **SS:** SAR P-288594; CG Vol 3 pg 3100 **BS:** JLARC 4.

SHELTON, Ralph II, b 23 Oct 1709, Middlesex Co, d Mar 1789 **RU:** Patriot. Paid personal property taxes, Henry co, 1782 considered to offset Rev War expenses **CEM:** Eliphaz Shelton-Pilson Family; GPS unk; at foot of Main St, Stuart; Patrick **GS:** U **SP:** mar (10 Jun 1731) Mary Daniel (1713-1787) **VI:** Son of Ralph Shelton (1685-1733) & Mary Jane Crispen Buford (1688-1750) **P:** N **BLW:** N **RG:** Y **MK:** N **PH:** N **SS:** DV Henry Co 1782 personal property tax image 07 pdf; SAR P-288598 **BS:** 196.

SHELTON, Richard; b 14 Aug 1728, d 5 Jan 1821 **RU:** Patriot, gave material aid to cause and provided civil service **CEM:** Shelton/Ellis/Watts; GPS 37.30459, -79.09698; loc Winesap Rd (Rt 675) at house # 1559, then W on dirt Ln 400 ft; Monroe; Amherst **GS:** Y **SP:** Mary Wright (1728-3 Nov 1818) **VI:** Son of Ralph Shelton & Mary Pollard of King and Queen Co. He was a Vestryman of Lexington Parish, Commissioner of Peace and one of several appointed to administer the Oath of Allegiance. In 1775 he petitioned for a ferry between Amherst and Bedford Counties, believed to be the site for a tavern run by the Shelton family. **P:** N **BLW:** N **RG:**N **MK:** N **PH:** N **SS;** D vol1, pgs 74,76; DAR A102811 cites Sweeny, "Amherst Co VA in the Rev," pgs 78, 80 **BS:**196.

SHELTON, Thomas; b 1738, Old Town, Louisa Co; d 10 Jul 1826 **RU:** Patriot, Gave material aid to cause **CEM:** Roseneath; GPS unk; Jackson District; Louisa **GS:** U **SP:** Mar (12 Mar 1809) Sallie Farrar

RU=Rank/Unit	CEM=Cemetery	GS=Gravestone	SP=Spousal Information
VI=Other Veteran Info	P=Pension	BLW=Bounty/Land Warrant	RG=Registered Grave
MK=SAR/DAR Marker	PH=Photo	SS=Service Source	BS=Burial Source

378

(c1763 Goochland Co-1 Jul 1823) d/o Mathew (29 Oct 1760 Louisa Co-1844) & Martha (Murrell) (c1763-aft 1827) Farrar **VI:** No further data **P:** N **BLW:** N **RG:** Y **MK:** unk **PH:** unk **SS:** DAR A102823; SAR P-288609; AL Ct Bk pg 21, 24, 30 Lousia Co **BS:** JLARC 61.

SHEPARD, William; b 1740; d 16 Feb 1813 **RU:** Private, Served in Henrico Co Militia **CEM:** Shockoe Hill; GPS 37.55190, -77.43170; 4th & Hospital Sts; Richmond City **GS:** U **SP:** No info **VI:** No further data **P:** unk **BLW:** unk **RG:** N **MK:** unk **PH:** unk **SS:** E pg 707 **BS:** 196.

SHEPHERD, David; 9 Jun 1760; d 20 Mar 1823 **RU:** Lieutenant, Served in VA Cont Line **CEM:** Shepherd family; GPS 37.897059, -78.110683; Laughton Ln vic Rts 623 & 659; Fluvanna **GS:** Y **SP:** Mary Rosetta Baskett (1770-1843) **VI:** Rec'd BLW 100 acres 31 Jan 1784 **P:** unk **BLW:** Y **RG:** N **MK:** N **PH:** unk **SS:** F pg 68; CZ pg 398 cites Council Journals Lib VA 1777-8 pg 30 **BS:** 66 pg 86.

SHEPHERD, John; b 1738; d 1796 **RU:** Private/Patriot. Served in Capt John Moore's Co of Militia of Kanawha Co (now WV). Wounded in his hand and thigh; gave material aid to cause **CEM:** Parrish Family; GPS unk; Vic Rts 619 & 660; E side of Kents Store Rd (Rt 659) 0.6 mi N jct Perkin's Rd; Fluvanna **GS:** N **SP:** Mary Ann Lilly (1737-1838) **VI:** Appl & recd pen of $40 per annum, 22 Jan 1798 **P:** Y **BLW:** unk **RG:** Y **MK:** N **PH:** N **SS:** D vol1, pg 364; AN Kanawha Co; CZ pg 398 cites War Files #4 pg 362, 363 Lib VA;DAR A103013; SAR P-338873 **BS:** 66 pg 68.

SHEPHERD, Richard; b Unk; d 15 Jaqn 1778, **RU:**Private, Capt Arrell's Co, 3rd VA Regt **CEM:**Rev War Albemarle Court House Plaque; GPS not determined; 4110 Chain Bridge Rd; Fairfax **GS:** Memorialized on plaque 2017 by Geo Washington Chapter, VASSAR **SP** No info **VI:** died in service **P:** N **BLW:** N **RG:** N **MK:** N **PH:** N **SS:**E pg 707; AP Fold3 Serv Rec; EP sources: **BS:** None.

SHIELDS, James, III; b 1750 Rockbridge Co; d Apr 1809 **RU:** Private, enlisted Augusta Co, served in Capt Thomas Bell's 5th Co, Col Nathaniel Gist's VA Regt, Cont Line 1777, serving 3 yrs **CEM:** Oak Grove AKA Stonewall Jackson Memorial; GPS 37.780830, -79.445060; 314 S Main St; Lexington City **GS:** Y **SP:** mar (10 Mar 1788, Augusta Co) Rachel Anderson (1762, Augusta Co-aft Oct 1845) who appl 1 Oct 1845, age 82 & rec'd pen W6027 **VI:** Son of James Shields II & Anne Moore **P:** Spouse **BLW:** N **RG:**N **MK:** N **PH:** N **SS:** A pgs 269, 286; E pg 708, CG pg 3114 **BS:** 196.

SHIELDS, Alexander, See Aoppendix G Addenda

SHIELDS, William; b unk; d unk **RU:** Fife Major, Served in 2nd VA Regt **CEM:** Cub Creek; GPS unk; Off Rt 789 Cub Creek Rd at Beech Grove Community; Nelson **GS:** U **SP:** No info **VI:** No further data **P:** unk **BLW:** unk **RG:** Y **MK:** unk **PH:** unk **SS:** SAR P-289160 **BS:** JLARC 83.

SHIPMAN, Benjamin; b Bapt 30 Apr 1749, Morristown, NJ; d 30 Dec 1825 **RU:** Lieutenant, Specific service at Lib of VA, Auditor's Accts, XV, pg 527 **CEM:** Mossy Creek Presbyterian; GPS 38.35331, -79.04914; 372 Kyles Mill Rd, Mt Solon; Augusta **GS:** N **SP:** mar (c1767) Augusta Mary Osburn (c1747 NJ-28 Sep 1786 Frederick Co) **VI:** No further data **P:** unk **BLW:** unk **RG:** Y **MK:** N **PH:** N **SS:** DAR Ancestor #A132451; SAR P-289226; DD **BS:** JLARC 62, 63; 196.

SHIPMAN, Jonathan; b 1759; d 19 May 1848 **RU:** Private, Served in Capt John Hopkin's Co, Rockingham Co Militia **CEM:** Mossy Creek Presbyterian; GPS 38.35331, -79.04914; 372 Kyles Mill Rd, Mt Solon; Augusta **GS:** N **SP:** Abigail Fox **VI:** No further data **P:** unk **BLW:** unk **RG:**Y **MK:** N **PH:** N **SS:** Z pg 100; CZ cites Auditors Acct XXXI pg 356 Lib VA SAR P-289249 **BS:** JLARC 62, 63; 196.

SHIRKEY, Nicholas; b 1752; d 2 Jul 1830 **RU:** Soldier, Served in VA Line **CEM:** Shirkey-Far; GPS unk; Across James River fr Gala; Botetourt **GS:** U **SP:** Mar (3 Dec 1777) Sarah (-----) (c1761-__) **VI:** Widow appl pen 5 Feb 1844 Botetourt Co age 83. Reappl 2 Sep 1848. W6049 **P:** Y **BLW:** unk **RG:** Y **MK:** N **PH:** unk **SS:** CG Vol 3 pg 3177; SAR P-289296 **BS:** JLARC 4, 60, 124.

SHIRLEY, Michael; b 1755; d 1842 **RU:** Soldier, Served in 4th & 7th Cont Lines **CEM:** St Peter's Lutheran; GPS 38.22569, -79.16125; 3795 Churchville Ave, Churchville; Augusta **GS:** N **SP:** Submit Bogle **VI:** No further data **P:** unk **BLW:** unk **RG:** Y **MK:** N **PH:** N **SS:** SAR P-289308; E pg 709 **BS:** JLARC 62.

SHOCKLEY, Richard Esau, Jr; b 5 Mar 1732 Marion, Somerset Co, MD, d 31 Jan 1798 **RU:** Private, served in Capt James Robertson's company at Kings Mountain Oct 1774. **CEM:** Richard Shockley; GPS loc Rt 962 (Water Plant Rd), 1.5 miles from jct SR 58, grave is Interred in the Lawn of Elwood Reynolds

RU=Rank/Unit	CEM=Cemetery	GS=Gravestone	SP=Spousal Information
VI=Other Veteran Info	P=Pension	BLW=Bounty/Land Warrant	RG=Registered Grave
MK=SAR/DAR Marker	PH=Photo	SS=Service Source	BS=Burial Source

Home; Carroll **GS**: Unk **SP**: mar (1754, Halifax Co) Elizabeth Meredith Adkins,(1734, Goochland Co-aft 1795), d/o William Adkins (1721-1784) & Lydia Owens(1724-1782) **VI**: Son of Richard Shockley & Elizabeth Paynter. Rec'd BLW of 500 acres **P**: N **BLW** Y **RG**: Y **MK**; N **PH**: N **SS**: Z pg 168; BW pgs 44-45; SAR P-289363 **BS**: 196.

SHOEMAKER, George A; b 1730, d 1796 **RU**: Patriot, Gave material aid to cause **CEM**: Reedy/Shoemaker; GPS not determined; Hopkins Gap Rd, Genoa nr Oak Grove Brethan Ch; Fulks Run: Rockingham **GS**: N **SP**: Elizabeth Hawn (1730-1796) **VI**: No further data **P**: N **BLW** N **RG**: N **MK**; N **PH**: N **SS**: AL Ct Bk I, pg 95, Comm Bk V pg 131 **BS**: 196.:

SHOMO, Anthony; b 29 Dec 1756, Berks Co, PA; d 14 Apr 1812 **RU**: Ensign, Served in PA 4th Bn 8th Co Berks Co Militia **CEM**: St Mathew's; GPS 36.65131, -78.67121; Breckenridge Ln, New Market; Shenandoah **GS**: Y **SP**: Elizabeth Obold Shomo (__-1842) **VI**: No further data **P**: unk **BLW**: unk **RG**: Y **MK**: Y SAR **PH**: unk **SS**: B CD; SAR P-289444 **BS**: 196; 32.

SHORE, Thomas; b1753, Hanover Co; d 18 Oct 1800 Chesterfield Co; **RU**: Captain, perhaps he was the indivdual this name that was in the Loudoun Co militia; as patriot he paid personal property taxes 1783 in Chesterfield Co considered to be a supply tax for Rev War expenses **CEM**: Violet Bank; GPS 37.241875, -77.405085; 303 VA Ave; Colonial Heights **GS**: Yes **SP**: Jane Gray Wall (1768-22 May 1831) **VI**: Son of John Shore (__-1796) & Elizabeth Smith **P**: N **BLW** N **RG**: N **MK**; N **PH**: N **SS**: AL Lib VA Capt Mililia Officer public Claims; ER Chesterfield Co **BS**: 196.

SHORES, Thomas Jr; b 1753; d 15 Oct 1841 **RU**: Private, Enlisted Feb 1776. Capt Matthew Joulett's Co, Col Lewis & Alexander's Regts. Discharged Mar 1778. Also Served in Capt George Rice's Co #9 30 Nov 1778 **CEM**: Shores & Tutwiler Families; GPS 37.74641, -78.38259; Seven Islands; Fluvanna **GS**: N **SP**: Mar (May 1778) Susanna Bugg (Jul 1760 New Kent Co.-5 Aug 1827) d/o William (1711-1796) & Mary (Bacon) (1713-1770) Bugg **VI**: Pensioned Fluvanna Co **P**: Y **BLW**: unk **RG**: Y **MK**: unk **PH**: N **SS**: A pg 264; E pg 710; SAR P-289466 **BS**: 196.

SHOWALTER, Christain Jr; b 1768 Cherry Grove, Pendleton, WVA; d Aft 1841 **RU**: Private, Listed in 8th Recruiting Class, 9th Bn, Lancaster Co Militia **CEM**: Trissel's Mennonite Ch; GPS unk; Rt 752, Harrisonburg; Harrisonburg City **GS**: N **SP**: Catherine Roadcap **VI**: No further data **P**: unk **BLW**: unk **RG**: N **MK**: N **PH**: N **SS**: CI PA Archives series V Vol VII; SAR P-289542 **BS**: 04.

SHOWLATER, Daniel; b 20 Jun 1738, Europe; d May 1822 **RU**: Patriot, paid personal property tax 1779, PA; considered to be a supply tax for Rev War expenses **CEM**: Trissels Mennonite Church; GPS 38.602811, -78.846787; 112 Hisers Lane, Broadway; Rockingham **GS**: Y **SP**: Margaret Saunders **VI**: Nothing further **P**: N **BLW** N **RG**: N **MK**; N **PH**: N **SS**: DAR A213457; AP PA Archives, 3d Ser, vol 12, pg 151 **BS**: 04.

SHREVE, Benjamin Jr; b 7 Oct 1747, Burlington Co, NJ; d 18 Nov 1801 **RU**: Patriot, Signed Legislative Petition City of Alexandria Nov 1778 **CEM**: Quaker Burial Ground; GPS 38.80749, -77.04676; 717 Queen St, Kate Walker Barrett Library; Alexandria City **GS**: U **SP**: 1)Hannah Vail, 2) Susannah Wood **VI**: Son of Benjamin & Sarah (Areson) Shreve. Alexandria merchant. Alexandria Gazette notes burial was in Quaker Cemetery **P**: N **BLW**: N **RG**: Y **MK**: unk **PH**: unk **SS**: BB; SAR P-289559 **BS**: 196.

SHREVE, Samuel; b 25 Jan 1750, Burlington Co, NJ; d 24 Apr 1815 **RU**: Lieutenant Colonel, Capt, 1st Battalion, Gloucester Co; Was Lt Col, in Bn, NJ Militia, Cont Line 5 Feb 1777; resigned 2 Oct 1778 **CEM**: Oakwood; GPS unk; N Roosevelt St; Falls Church City **GS**: Y **SP**: Mira Trout **VI**: Came to Arlington abt 1780 fr New Jersey. Died in Fairfax Co. Sign with info abt him in cemetery nr Fairfax Dr & North Harrison St. Grave moved fr N. Abingdon St **P**: unk **BLW**: unk **RG**: Y **MK**: Y-DAR **PH**: unk **SS**: AK; DAR A104423; SAR P-289568 **BS**: 04; 69 pg 74, 74A; JLARC 2,14, 28; 80 vol 4, pg 32.

SHUEY, John Ludwig "Lewis"; b 6 May 1755, Lebanon Co, PA; d 22 Jan 1839 **RU**: Private, Served in the 3rd Co, 2nd Bn, Lancaster Co, PA Militia **CEM**: Glebe Burying Ground; GPS 38.10940, -79.22190; Glebe School Rd Rt 876, Swoopes; Augusta **GS**: Y **SP**: Mar (18 Mar 1780) Anna Maria Loesch (12 Apr 1760-12 Mar 1822) d/o of Johann Balthasar (1734-1804) & Anna Christina (Heyl) (1740-1816) Loesch **VI**: DAR marker **P**: unk **BLW**: unk **RG**: Y **MK**: Y DAR **PH**: unk **SS**: AR Vol 4 pg 32; BT; DAR A103143; SAR P-289635 **BS**: JLARC 2, 4, 62; 80 vol 4, pg 32I; 196.

SHULTZ, John; b c1753; d 03 Nov 1840 **RU**: Private, Served in PA **CEM**: Mt Hebron; GPS 39.184120, -78.160697; 305 E Boscawen St; Winchester City **GS**: Y **SP**: 1) mar (12 Aug 1788 Frederick Co by

RU=Rank/Unit	CEM=Cemetery	GS=Gravestone	SP=Spousal Information
VI=Other Veteran Info	P=Pension	BLW=Bounty/Land Warrant	RG=Registered Grave
MK=SAR/DAR Marker	PH=Photo	SS=Service Source	BS=Burial Source

Alexander Balmain) Catherine Otto (c1764-21 Mar 1839) 2) (8 Mar 1791 Frederick Co by Christian Streit) Catherine Haar (Gaar?) **VI:** Was pensioned while residing in Frederick Co **P:** N **BLW:** N **RG:** Y **MK:** Y SAR granite & monument **PH:** N **SS:** E pg 694; SAR P-285778 **BS:** 196.

SHUMAKER (SCHUMACHER), George; b 26 Oct 1763; d 30 Dec 1834 **RU:** Soldier/Patriot, Served in Capt John Cope's Co of Militia, Frankkoney Twp, Philadelphia, PA **CEM:** Old Presbyterian; GPS 39.27343, -77.69341; Behind Primitive Baptist on S Church St, Lovettsville; Loudoun **GS:** Y **SP:** Mar (7 Jan 1789 Loudoun Co) Magdalena "Mary" Frantz (1773-aft Aug 1839) **VI:** Spouse appl pen 13 Aug 1839, W6004 **P:** Y **BLW:** unk **RG:** N **MK:** N **PH:** unk **SS:** D Vol 2 pg 599; AP Muster Roll PA Archives series 6 Vol 1; CG pg 3039 **BS:** 25 pg 282.

SHUMATE, Daniel III; b 14 Jun 1751, Fauquier Co; d 19 Jul 1826 **RU:** Second Lieutenant, Served in Fauquier Co Militia. Was Ens Aug 1777, and 2nd Lt 24 Mar 1778. Resigned May 1781 **CEM:** Sunrise Memorial Gardens; GPS unk; Rich Creek; Giles **GS:** Y **SP:** Millicent "Millie" Callison (5 Oct 1758-22 May 1841 Mercer Co, WVA) d/o Isaac & (-----) Callison **VI: P:** unk **BLW:** unk **RG:** Y **MK:** N **PH:** unk **SS:** JLARC App B-2 pg 37; E pg 711; AZ pg 202; SAR P-289677; DAR A103305 **BS:** JLARC 1, 26; 196.

SHUMATE, Daniel; b 14 Jun 1734, Prince William Co, 21 Feb 1806 **RU:** Patriot. Paid personal property taxes, Fauquier Co, 1783 considered to offset Rev War expenses **CEM:** Bell-Shumate; GPS 38.6638160, -77.7985140; loc on a knoll W of Route 29 on Licking Run. Cemetery is actually three different burial groupings with the Shumate portion wihin the fence, Warrennton; Fauquier **GS:** Unk **SP:** 1) mar (1778) Sarah Ann Bowley (1726-Unk), 2) Sarah Ann James (1738-1841) **VI:** SAR DAR indicate burial is in Monroe CO, WVA and is only memorialized in cem. There appears to be six additional graves north of the Shumate fenced area that one may be his. Will of Daniel Shumate Leeds Parish, Fauquier County dated 29 January 1806 **P:** N **BLW** N **RG:** Y **MK;** N **PH:** N **SS:** DV Fauquier Co 1783 personal property tax image 19 pdf; SAR P-289675; **BS:** 196.

SIDEBOTTOM (SIDEBOTHOM), Joseph; b 1761; d 10 Nov 1848 **RU:** Private, Served in 3rd VA Regt **CEM:** Robinson-Sidebottoms-Hawkins; GPS unk; nr Round Hill; Frederick **GS:** U **SP:** No info **VI:** No further data **P:** unk **BLW:** unk **RG:** N **MK:** unk **PH:** unk **SS:** E pg 754; CZ pg 400, cites W.F. Boogher's Gleanings of Virginia History Washington DC 1903 pg 177 **BS:** 196.

SIEG, Paul; b 14 Nov 1753; d 22 Sep 1817 **RU:** Soldier, Served in PA Militia **CEM:** St Peter's Lutheran; GPS 38.22569, -79.16125; 3795 Churchville Ave, Churchville; Augusta **GS:** Y **SP:** Susannah Fauber **VI:** Rev War service marker "Private, PA Militia" **P:** unk **BLW:** unk **RG:** Y **MK:** Y SAR **PH:** unk **SS:** B; SAR P-289850 **BS:** JLARC 62; 196.

SIGLER, Michael; b 4 Jan 1754, Berks Co, PA; d 6 Feb 1833 **RU:** Soldier, Served in PA **CEM:** Union Church; GPS 38.44480, -78.38350; Mt Jackson nr jct Main St & Bridge St; Shenandoah **GS:** Y **SP:** Mary Pennywitt (1777-1849) **VI:** No further data **P:** unk **BLW:** unk **RG:** N **MK:** unk **PH:** Y **SS:** I 519 555; II pg 487; CI PA Archives 6th services Index pg 303 **BS:** 196.

SIMM (SIMMS), James; b 17 Jul 1754; d 2 Dec 1793 **RU:** Private, Served in Capt John Webb's Co of the 5th & 11th Cont Line combined segments Oct 1779 **CEM:** St John's Episcopal; GPS 37.53183, -77.41958; 2401 E Broad St; Richmond City **GS:** Y **SP:** No info **VI:** No further data **P:** unk **BLW:** unk **RG:** N **MK:** N **PH:** unk **SS:** AP **BS:** 28 pg 504; 196.

SIMMERMAN, Christopher (Christian); b 1746; d 1813 **RU:** Soldier, enl Montgomery Co in Capt Findlay and Capt James Kent Cos **CEM:** St John's Lutheran; GPS 36.96500, -81.10110; 405 W Main, Wytheville; Wythe **GS:** Y **SP:** Margaret Reinhardikin (1743-3 Jun 1821) **VI:** Gave 90 acres to establish the town of Evansham, later known as Wytheville in Wythe Co. DAR plaque at home location **P:** N **BLW:** N **RG:** Y **MK:** unk **PH:** unk **SS:** B; SAR P-290030 **BS:** JLARC 3, 40,123; 196.

SIMMERMAN, Earhart (Arehart); b 1762; d 31 Aug 1827 **RU:** Private, Served in Capt James Fenley's Co, Montgomery Co Militia **CEM:** Simmerman, aka Cedar Hill; GPS unk; Off I-81 N, open field abt .25 mi east of gravel plant on SR 649; Wythe **GS:** U **SP:** Mary (-----) (c1764-28 Nov 1834) **VI:** No further data **P:** unk **BLW:** unk **RG:** N **MK:** unk **PH:** unk **SS:** G pg 233 **BS:** JLARC 123.

SIMMERMAN, Stophel (Staphel); b 1759, Montgomery Co; d 4 Feb 1813 **RU:** Private, Served in Capt James Fenley's Co, Montgomery Co Militia **CEM:** Simmerman, aka Cedar Hill; GPS unk; Off I-81 N,

RU=Rank/Unit   CEM=Cemetery   GS=Gravestone   SP=Spousal Information
VI=Other Veteran Info   P=Pension   BLW=Bounty/Land Warrant   RG=Registered Grave
MK=SAR/DAR Marker   PH=Photo   SS=Service Source   BS=Burial Source

381

open field abt .25 mi east of gravel plant on SR 649; Wythe **GS:** Y **SP:** Mar (1774) Anna Margaret Reinhardin (1743 Montgomery Co-3 Jun 1821) **VI:** No further data **P:** unk **BLW:** unk **RG:** Y **MK:** N **PH:** unk **SS:** G pg 233; SAR P-290031 **BS:** 140 Mason B.

SIMMONS, Joshua; b unk; d c1800 **RU:** Private, Served in Chesterfield Co Militia **CEM:** Kirkham Family; GPS unk; 1.2 mi N of Disputana; Prince George **GS:** Y **SP:** No info **VI:** No further data **P:** unk **BLW:** unk **RG:** N **MK:** N **PH:** unk **SS:** E pg 712; CZ pg 401 cites supplement to Chesterfield Co Militia pg 68 **BS:** 111 Part 5 pg 79.

SIMMS, Charles; b 1755, Prince William Co; d 30 Aug 1819 **RU:** Colonel, Served as Maj, 12th Virginia Regt, 12 Nov 1776; Lt Col 6th VA Regt, 29 Sep 1777; transferred to 2nd VA Regt, 14 Sep 1778; resigned 7 Dec 1779 **CEM:** Old Christ Church Episcopal; GPS 38.80625, -77.04718; 118 N Washington St; Alexandria City **GS:** Y **SP:** Nancy Ann Douglas **VI:** Inscription on a newer stone: "SACRED to the memory of COL. CHARLES SIMMS, An officer in the Army of Independence and for many yrs an honored Citizen of Alexandria & Mayor of that City in 1811." He d in the yr 1819. He was a member of the Society of the Cincinnati & a friend of General Washington. Original stone is lost. Was also collector at the port of Alexandria **P:** Y **BLW:** N **RG:** Y **MK:** Y **SAR PH:** Y **SS:** AK; SAR P-290157 **BS:** JLARC 1, 25, 87; 20 pg 141-2; 196.

SIMMS, Joseph; b 1741; d 1790 **RU:** Private, Enl 29 Aug 1777. Served in Maj Lewis Winder's MD Regt of Foot, Mar 1780 **CEM:** Cloverhill Farm; GPS 38.737282, -77.476585; 9750 Wellington Rd; Manassas City **GS:** Y **SP:** No info **VI:** SAR marker **P:** unk **BLW:** unk **RG** N **MK:** Y **SAR PH:** unk **SS:** AY pg 31 **BS:** 94 appendix pg 3; 196.

SIMMS, Thomas; b 1762; d 5 Apr 1808 **RU:** Sergeant, Served in Grayson's Regt **CEM:** Old Presbyterian Meeting House; GPS 38.48528, -77.23532; 323 S Fairfax St; Alexandria City **GS:** N **SP:** Margaret (-----) d 28 Dec 1797 in childbirth **VI:** Died age 46. Listed on SAR plaque in cemetery **P:** unk **BLW:** unk **RG:** Y **MK:** Y **SAR plaque PH:** N **SS:** E pg 713; AK; SAR P-290416 **BS:** 23 pg 107; 196.

SIMPSON, Jeremiah; b 23 Aug 1749; d 25 Feb 1822 **RU:** Sergeant/Patriot, Served three yrs. Signer of Oath of Allegiance. Provided corn to State Troops **CEM:** St Mary's Catholic; GPS 38.79390, -77.04750; 310 S Royal St; Alexandria City **GS:** Y **SP:** Rachel (-----) (14 Feb 1752-8 Dec 1806) **VI:** A person this name with similar birth and death dates had patriotic service and d in Pittsylvania Co, thus may be memorialized at this location **P:** unk **BLW:** Y **RG:** Y **MK:** unk **PH:** unk **SS:** DAR A104143; C pg 499; SAR P-290307 **BS:** 174.

SIMPSON, John, b unk, England, d 14 Jul 1786 **RU:** Private Capts Edwards and John Adam's companies, Montgomery Co Militia 24 Mar 1781. May be person this name that also served in 4th, 7th, 8th, 10th, 11th 12th and 15th Cont Line that received a BLW **CEM:** Moore; GPS 37.2211,-81.4017; Bailey Switch Rd, Bailey; Tazewell **GS:** Yes **SP:** No further data **VI:** Was shot by Indians while in bed at home of James Moore **P:** N **BLW:** ? **RG:** N **MK:** N **PH:** N **SS:** E pg 714; G pgs 224, 240 **BS:** 196

SIMPSON, John; b 1740, Prince William Co; d 18 Feb 1800 **RU:** Private/Patriot, Served in 4th, 7th, 8th, 10th, 12th, and 15th Cont Lines, Supported cause by paying supply tax included in his personal property tax in 1782, Prince William Co **CEM:** Simpson Family; GPS unk; On original family homeplace, check property records for location; Henry **GS:** U **SP:** Mar (before 1755, Prince William Co) Hannah Roberts (1733-1800) **VI:** No further data **P:** unk **BLW:** unk **RG:** N **MK:** unk **PH:** unk **SS:** E pg 714; DV 1782 Personal Property Tax List image 09.pdf **BS:** 196.

SIMPSON, Thomas; b c1752; d 1824 **RU:** Private, Served in a VA unit in Illinois **CEM:** Grove Baptist Church; GPS 36.63750, -79.24924; NW edge of Goldvein; Fauquier **GS:** Y **SP:** A man by this name mar (12 Sep 1799 by Ephraim Abell (Baptist) returned 17 Sep 1799) Hannah Blackwell **VI:** No further data **P:** unk **BLW:** unk **RG:** N **MK:** N **PH:** unk **SS:** E pg 714; CZ pg 402; Fauquier Co Marriages pg 182 **BS:** 95 Grove B. Ch.

SIMRALL, Alexander; b Sep 1763, Chester Co, PA; d 19 Jul 1802 **RU:** Private probably served in Capt Alexander Simrall's Militia at Winchester Barracks May 1882(Note militia not paid by federal gov't have no serv rec/rolls at NARA, thus local militia lists needed to confirm) **CEM:** Old Opequon; GPS 39.139381, -78.194939; 217 Opequon Church Ln, Kernstown; Frederick **GS:** Y needs cleaning to view

RU=Rank/Unit	CEM=Cemetery	GS=Gravestone	SP=Spousal Information
VI=Other Veteran Info	P=Pension	BLW=Bounty/Land Warrant	RG=Registered Grave
MK=SAR/DAR Marker	PH=Photo	SS=Service Source	BS=Burial Source

inscription **SP** Mar 4 Dec 1797, Sallie Donalson **VI**: Son of Capt James Simrall & Sarah Ferguson **P**: N **BLW**: N **RG**: N **MK**: N **PH**: N **SS**: See Frederick Co militia rolls **BS**: 196.

SIMRALL (SIMRELL), James Jr; b 3 Feb 1740, PA; d 1 Jul 1798 **RU**: Captain, Commanded a co in Frederick Co Militia **CEM**: Opequon Presbyterian; GPS 39.13938, -78.19494; 217 Opequon Church Ln; Winchester City **GS**: Y **SP**: Mar (18 Mar 1762) Sarah Ferguson (1740-1814 Shelby, KY) **VI**: Died in Kernstown **P**: unk **BLW**: unk **RG**: Y **MK**: Y SAR; DAR plaque **PH**: Y **SS**: DAR A104262; J-NSSAR 2000 Reg; E pg 714; SAR P-290379 **BS**: JLARC 76.

SINCLAIR, John; b 14 Mar 1755, Hampton; d 1819 or 1820 **RU**: Navy Captain/Patriot, Was Privateer. Commanded "Nicholson", a small boat. In 1781 hired as pilot to guide French fleet to Chesapeake **CEM**: Sinclair at "Sherwood"; GPS 37.08370, -78.11672; Selden Post Office; Gloucester **GS**: Y **SP**: 1) Ann Wilson 2) Mary Mackie Lanson **VI**: Died in "Land's End" Gloucester Co. Memorial stone to Capt John Sinclair erected c1937 **P**: unk **BLW**: unk **RG**: Y **MK**: N **PH**: unk **SS**: L pg 247; SAR P-290455 **BS**: 48 pg 60.

SINCLAIR, Samuel; b 1762; d 27 May 1806 **RU**: Patriot, Gave material aid to cause **CEM**: New Valley Baptist; GPS 39.21918, -77.54746; Bald Hill Rd Rt 673, Lucketts; Loudoun **GS**: Y **SP**: No info **VI**: No further data **P**: N **BLW**: N **RG**: N **MK**: N **PH**: unk **SS**: D Vol 2 pg 612 **BS**: 25 pg 287.

SINCLAIR, Thomas; b 1752; d aft 1778 **RU**: Sailor, was on NBJ 20 Mar 1778 **CEM**:Petsworth Parish Episcopal Ch (AKA Poplar Spring) GPS not determined; loc by original church foundation; Popular Spring; Gloucester **GS**: N all grave stones removed **SP**: No information **VI**: Son of Henry Sinclair (___-1819) & Martha Brock (___-aft 1752) **P**: N **BLW**: N **RG**: N **MK**: N **PH**: Unk **SS**: L pg 247, roster **BS**: 196.

SINGLETON, Daniel; b 1720, d 27 Oct 1794 **RU**: Sergeant/ Patriot, served 12th VA Regt of Foot and 1st, 10th, 12th Cont line and was under Gen Van Steubien at Valley Forge assisting training with new manuel **CEM**: Old Orange Co Courthouse; GPS not determined; loc vic old courthose area; Orange **GS**: Unk **SP**: Susannah (-----) (Eng-10 Nov 1792) **VI**: No further data **P**: N **BLW**: N **RG**: Y **MK**: N **PH**: unk **SS** D vol 2 pgs 744, 749, vol 3, pg 756; E pg 715; AP Rev War Rolls #930; DAR A104456 SAR P-290496 **BS**: 196.

SINGLETON, John; b unk; d unk **RU**: Brigadier General/Patriot, Raised and commanded a body of calvary in 1781. Performed public service as member of Committee of Safety 1775-6 **CEM**: Mt Hebron; GPS 39.10916, -78.09497; 305 E Boscawen St; Winchester City **GS**: U **SP**: No info **VI**: No further data **P**: unk **BLW**: unk **RG**: Y **MK**: Y SAR monument **PH**: unk **SS**: SAR P-290500; CZ pg 402 **BS**: JLARC 76.

SINGLETON, John; b 1758; d Jun 8, 1825 **RU**: Private, Served in Capt John Gregory's Co under Daniel Morgan 1778. Served in other regiments of VA Line until discharge in Philadelphia at end of war **CEM**: St Paul's Episcopal; GPS 36.84733, -76.28554; 201 St Paul's Blvd; Norfolk City **GS**: Y **SP**: Sarah Dyson **VI**: Son of Henry Singleton & Mary Ann Waldron (Reynolds) Singleton **P**: unk **BLW**: unk **RG**: Y **MK**: Y SAR plaque **PH**: unk **SS**: C pg 266-7; SAR P-290506 **BS**: 178 Jan 11.

SINK, Stephen; b 17 Sep 1758, Chester Co, PA; d 11 Sep 1835 **RU**: Soldier, Enrolled 12 Aug 1780 in 4th Co, 2nd Bn, Chester Co PA Militia **CEM**: Stephen Sink Family; GPS 37.08092, -79.79286; Rt 670 behind house at 956 Three Oaks Rd; Franklin **GS**: U **SP**: Susan Plybon (1752-1843) **VI**: No further data **P**: unk **BLW**: unk **RG**: Yk **MK**: unk **PH**: unk **SS**: CD; SAR P-290530 **BS**: JLARC 19; 196.

SIREUIL, Jean de; b unk; d 1781 **RU**: Soldier, Served in Gatinais Bn and died fr battle at Yorktown **CEM**: French Memorial; GPS 36.81944, -79.39933; Yorktown; York **GS**: U **SP**: No info **VI**: No further data **P**: unk **BLW**: unk **RG**: Y **MK**: unk **PH**: unk **SS**: J-Yorktown Historian; SAR P-290567 **BS**: JLARC 1, 74.

SITLINGTON, Robert; b Nov 1748; d 15 Sep 1833 **RU**: Private, Served in VA Cont Line, Ent serv Augusta Co 1776 as subsitute for Nathan Crawford **CEM**: Sitlington Family; GPS unk; 8.5 mi S of Millboro Springs; Bath **GS**: Y **SP**: No info **VI**: Appl pen 26 Sept 1832 Bath Co. S7517 **P**: Y **BLW**: unk **RG**: N **MK**: Y **PH**: unk **SS**: E pg 715; K Vol 5 pg 80; CG pg 3149 **BS**: 159.

RU=Rank/Unit	CEM=Cemetery	GS=Gravestone	SP=Spousal Information
VI=Other Veteran Info	P=Pension	BLW=Bounty/Land Warrant	RG=Registered Grave
MK=SAR/DAR Marker	PH=Photo	SS=Service Source	BS=Burial Source

383

SKINKER, Thomas; b unk; d 1803 **RU:** Patriot, Gave material aid to the cause **CEM:** Grove Baptist Church; GPS 36.63750, -79.24924; NW edge of Goldvein; Fauquier **GS:** Y **SP:** No info **VI:** No further data **P:** N **BLW:** N **RG:** N **MK:** N **PH:** unk **SS:** AL Ct Bk pg 3,13 **BS:** 95 Grove B Ch.

SKINNER, Cornelius, b 27 Feb 1757, Woodbridge, Middlesex Co, NJ, d 21 Mar 1814 **RU:** Private, enlisted US Army, October 1775 in Regt of VA Line under Capt. Charles West, and was discharged early at White Plains, NY **CEM:**Skinner Family; GPS 38.9742400, -77.6366200; loc Rt 50, .5 mi NW of jct with New Mountain Rd, Addie; Loudoun **GS:** Unk **SP:** mar (9 Mar 1786) Sarah McMakin (8 Nov 1767-29 Dec 1847, Warren Co, OH), d/o Alexander McMakin, an officer in the 3rd Battalion of Loudoun Co. Militia 1777 and Elizabeth Corsen **VI:** Son of Richard Alexander (1740-29-Jun 1811) a soldier in the Revolution 1777-1779 & Adaline Van Deventer (1740-1810) **P:** N **BLW:** N **RG:** N **MK:** N **PH:** N **SS:** DAR A104868; AP Fold3 Roll #968, 976 **BS:** 196.

SKINNER, Frederick; b unk; d unk **RU:** Lieutenant, Served in MD Flying Camp in 1776 under Col Charles Griffith's 2nd Bn. By 1758, was in Capt John Brooks Co, MD **CEM:** Fairfax City; GPS 38.84690, -77.31330; Main St & Page Ave; Fairfax City **GS:** N **SP:** Mar (1778 MD) Betty Johns **VI:** No further data **P:** unk **BLW:** unk **RG:** N **MK:** N **PH:** N **SS:** A pg 239 **BS:** 61 vol III pg FX-153.

SKINNER, Henry; b 16 Jan 1760; d Aft Jan 1845 **RU:** Lieutenant, Served in VA Line. Ent serv 1779 in 7th & 8th Cont Lines in 1779. Served in Capt's Reddick and Knott's companies, Col Matthew's Regt **CEM:** Cypress Chapel; GPS 36.61799, -76.59148; 1891 Cypress Chapel Rd; Suffolk City **GS:** Y **SP:** Sarah Augusta Lassiter **VI:** Appl for BLW #2014-100 (BLW claim was indicated as fraudulent). Sol appl for pen 8 Jul 1833 in Nansemond Co age 74. S7521; had War of 1812 service **P:** Y **BLW:** N **RG:** N **MK:** N **PH:** unk **SS:** DAR A104814; E pg 716; K Vol 5 pg 82; CG Vol 3 pg 3153 **BS:** 144 Henry Skin.

SKINNER, Richard Alexander, b 1746, NJ, d 29 Jun 1811 **RU:** Private served in Capts Mathews, Cherry, Walls and Steed under Cols Elliott, Lawson, Wood and Nevill **CEM:**Skinner Family; GPS 38.9742400, -77.6366200; loc Rt 50, .5 mi NW of jct with New Mountain Rd, Addie; Loudoun **GS:** Y **SP:** Adaline Van Deventer (1740, NJ-1810), d/o Jan Van Deventer & Ann Wynant. **VI:** Son of Cornelius and Sarah (-----) Skinner. Rec'd BLW Jun 1783 for 100 acres **P:** N **BLW:** Y **RG:** Y **MK:** N **PH:** N **SS:** A pg 497; E pg 716; F pg 67; DAR A104868; AP Fold3 Roll #968, 976; SAR: P290803 **BS:** 196

SKIPWITH, Peyton; b BD unk, Mecklenburg Co; d 11 Oct 1824 **RU:** Lieutenant Colonel, Commanded a Regt in Lawson's Brigade **CEM:** Fincastle Presbyterian; GPS 37.50017, -79.87558; 108 E Back St, Fincastle; Botetourt **GS:** Y **SP:** No info **VI:** Son of Humberston & Lelia (-----) Skipworth of Prestwould, Mecklenburg Co. Name is on the SAR plaque at this cemetery **P:** unk **BLW:** unk **RG:** N **MK:** Y SAR plaque **PH:** unk **SS:** Unit Named in Pension Record **BS:** 196.

SKIPWITH, Peyton Sr; b 11 Dec 1740; d 9 Oct 1805 **RU:** Patriot, Gave material aid to the cause. Performed public service as member of Committee of Safety 8 May 1775, Justice 13 Nov 1775, Sherriff 10 Mar 1777 **CEM:** Prestwould; GPS unk; Clarksville; Mecklenburg **GS:** Y **SP:** Jean (-----) (__-19 May 1826) **VI:** No further data **P:** N **BLW:** N **RG:** Y**MK:** N **PH:** unk **SS:** AL Ct Bk pg 2, 18; DB pg 129; SAR P-290828 **BS:** 54 pg 106; 213 pg 335.

SLACK, Abraham; b 26 Dec 1755 Bucks Co, PA; d 1833 **RU:** Private, Served in Capt Henry Vanhorn's Co, Lt Col Joseph Kirkbride Regt, Buck Co, PA Militia **CEM:** Slack Family, aka Chattin Family; GPS unk; On hillside of Chattin farm, nr Chamblissburg; Bedford **GS:** Y **SP:** Mary Patterson (1743 Bucks Co, PA-1825 Bedford Co) widow of Abraham Huddleston **VI:** No further data **P:** unk **BLW:** unk **RG:** Y **MK:** N **PH:** Y **SS:** J- DAR Hatcher; Cl PA Archives 2d series Vol 14 pg 175; DD; DAR A104920; SAR P-290835 & SAR P-290837 **BS:** JLARC 2; 80, vol 4, pg 38; 196.

SLADE, William; b unk; d Jul 1800 **RU:** Private, Served at Baltimore, May - Sep 1781 **CEM:** Old Christ Church Episcopal; GPS 38.80625, -77.04718; 118 N Washington St; Alexandria City **GS:** N **SP:** No info **VI:** No further data **P:** unk **BLW:** unk **RG:** N **MK:** N **PH:** N **SS:** AP RW Roll MD **BS:** 20 pg 142.

SLAGLE, George; b c1761, PA; d 21 Apr 1820 **RU:** Drummer, Served in Forman's Troops, York Co, PA **CEM:** Trinity Lutheran; GPS 38.17201, -78.86820; 2564 Rockfish Rd, Crimora; Augusta **GS:** Y **SP:** Catharine Koiner (1766-1855) d/o Michael (1720-1796) & Margaret (Diller) Keinadt (1734-1813) **VI:** Served in War of 1812 **P:** unk **BLW:** unk **RG:** Y **MK:** Y SAR **PH:** unk **SS:** BT; SAR P-290896 **BS:** JLARC 1 ,52, 62; 196.

RU=Rank/Unit
VI=Other Veteran Info
MK=SAR/DAR Marker

CEM=Cemetery
P=Pension
PH=Photo

GS=Gravestone
BLW=Bounty/Land Warrant
SS=Service Source

SP=Spousal Information
RG=Registered Grave
BS=Burial Source

384

SLATER, John: b 14 Nov 1763, Montgomery Co, PA, d 15 Jan 1824 **RU**: Private, Served in a calvary unit in the 6th Cont Line **CEM**: New Jerusalem Lutheran Church; GPS 39.25736,-77.63891; 12942 Lutheran Church Rd, Lovettsville; Loudoun **GS**: Yes **SP**: Catherine Souder (25 Apr 1772-York Co, PA-6 Sep 1807) **VI**: Son of Jacob Slater (1729-1815) and Anna Habicht (1729-1807) Served in War of 1812 **P**: N **BLW**: Y **RG**: N **MK**: N **PH**: N **SS**: C pg 267; E pg 717 **BS**: 196.

SLAUGHTER, Augustin(e) Augustus; b c1752-1758; d Bet 23 Nov-27 Dec 1814 **RU**: Surgeon, Served in 7th VA Regt, VA Line, Apr 1776 to Feb. 1777 as supernumerary surgeon **CEM**: St Paul's Episcopal; GPS 36.84733, -76.28554; 201 St Paul's Blvd; Norfolk City **GS**: Y **SP**: No info **VI**: Recd BLW #2168-400 & 2198. Longtime resident of the borough of Norfolk. Was a surgeon **P**: unk **BLW**: Y **RG**: Y **MK**: Y SAR plaque **PH**: unk **SS**: CB, J-NSSAR 1993 Reg; K Vol 5 pg 84; CG Vol 3 pg 3158; SAR application 252, 529; SAR P-290940 **BS**: JLARC 1.

SLAUGHTER, John Suggart (Suggate); b 2 Nov 1759, Culpeper Co; d 16 Jan 1830 **RU**: Lieutenant Colonel, Enlisted c1776 age 17, and was Lt and Capt Cont Army, Gen Daniel Morgan's Riflemen. Was in battles at Princeton, Trenton, and Saratoga. Was at Valley Forge **CEM**: Slaughter Family "Clover Hill"; GPS unk; Woodville, Hawthorne; Rappahannock **GS**: Y **SP**: Mar (Oct/Nov 1779) Susanna (Susan) Brown **VI**: Mar while stationed in barracks **P**: unk **BLW**: Y **RG**: Y **MK**: N **PH**: unk **SS**: BY pg 57; J-NSSAR 1993 Reg; SAR P-290972; DAR A105046 **BS**: JLARC 1; 196.

SLAUGHTER, Philip; b 2 Dec 1758, (pension) or 4 Dec 1748, (TS) Catalpa, Culpeper Co; d 26 Apr or Dec 1849 **RU**: Captain, Served in PA Line. Was Pvt Culpeper Minute Men 1775 and in Col Jameson's Troop of Calvary Spring 1776. Served as Lt in Capt Gabriel Long's Rifle Co 1776 and in 11th Cont Regt 1777. Promoted to Capt 1778 in 7th VA Regt and fought at Brandywine, Germantown, Monmouth, and Stoney Pt. Wintered at Valley Forge **CEM**: Shockoe Hill; GPS 37.55190, -77.43170; 4th & Hospital Sts; Richmond City **GS**: Y **SP**: 1) Margaret French Strother (1759-1835) 2) Elizabeth Towles **VI**: Son of James (1732-1799) & Susannah (Clayton) (1740-1818) Slaughter. Recd BLW #1653-300 8 Jul 1830. Sol had appl BLW Culpeper Co where sol lived during rev. Recd pension 1830 Culpeper Co. W29886. Dau. Ann Mercer Slaughter blind & helpless, pensioned by special act of Congress 8 Feb 1893 **P**: Y **BLW**: Y **RG**: Y **MK**: Y SAR, DAR, SAR monument **PH**: unk **SS**: BY pg 283; K Vol 5 pg 85; CG Vol 3 pg 3159; DAR A105070; SAR P-290980 **BS**: JLARC 1, 2, 77; 80, vol 4, pg 38.

SLAUGHTER, Robert; b 1748; d 2 Jan 1832 **RU**: Second Lieutenant/Patriot, Served in 3rd Cont Line. Became 2nd Lt 20 Jun 1776, and resigned 18 Dec 1777. Gave material aid to cause **CEM**: Hamilton Family; GPS unk; Rt 636; Spotsylvania **GS**: Y **SP**: mar (2 Dec 1772) Sarah (-----) (__-17 Nov 1834) **VI**: No further data **P**: unk **BLW**: unk **RG**: Y **MK**: N **PH**: unk **SS**: E pg 718; AL Ct Bk II pg 9 Culpeper Co; DAR A105076; SAR P-290986 **BS**: 06 pg 83.

SLOAN, John; b Mar 1758; d 26 Feb 1815 **RU**: Private, Served in 8th Cont Line **CEM**: Trinity United Methodist; GPS 39.13600, -77.00610; 2911 Cameron Mills Rd; Alexandria City **GS**: Y **SP**: Ann Rebecca (-----) (3 Sep 1756-26 Feb 1815) **VI**: No further data **P**: unk **BLW**: unk **RG**: Y **MK**: N **PH**: unk **SS**: E pg 718; SAR P-329188 **BS**: 23 pg 139.

SLUTE, James; b unk; d 1823 **RU**: Ensign, Served in Augusta Co Militia. (Refer to Augusta Co Order books for Militia Co assigned) **CEM**: Old Providence; GPS 37.96151, -79.71000; 1005 Spottswood Rd, Spottswood; Augusta **GS**: N **SP**: No info **VI**: No further data **P**: unk **BLW**: unk **RG**: Y **MK**: unk **PH**: N **SS**: SAR P-291228 **BS**: JLARC 63.

SMITH, Abraham; b c1722, Ulster Province, Ireland; d c1783 **RU**: Colonel/Patriot, Was in 1776 Col of Militia. In 1778 was one of the Justices of Rockingham Co and was County Lt, 27 Apr 1778 **CEM**: Smith Family; GPS unk; Rt 727; Rockingham **GS**: Y **SP**: 1) Martha McDowell Reed 2) Charlotte Gamble 3) Sarah Caldwell **VI**: Son of Capt John & (-----) Smith. Capt of Militia Augusta 1756 in French & Indian War. In 1757 prisoner French dominions. In 1758 court marshalled, and acquitted. Died at Egypt Plantation, Rockingham Co **P**: unk **BLW**: unk **RG**: Y **MK**: Y SAR **PH**: Y **SS**: O; SAR P-291423 **BS**: 04.

SMITH, Abraham; b 1752; d 1808 **RU**: Colonel, took oath, 25 May 1778 as Augusta County Lt **CEM**: Early Family; GPS 38.395360, -78.904650; 2588 Early Rd: Rockingham **GS**: N **SP**; Maria (-----) (__-Jul 1797) **VI**: Son of Abraham Smith (c1722, Ireland-c1783) & Sarah Caldwell **P**: N **BLW**: N **RG**: N **MK**:N **PH**: N **SS**: E pg 719 **BS**: 196.

RU=Rank/Unit	CEM=Cemetery	GS=Gravestone	SP=Spousal Information
VI=Other Veteran Info	P=Pension	BLW=Bounty/Land Warrant	RG=Registered Grave
MK=SAR/DAR Marker	PH=Photo	SS=Service Source	BS=Burial Source

385

SMITH, Andrew; b c1756; d 1822 **RU:** Sergeant, Appt Sergeant 9 Feb 1776. Served in Capt John Nelson's Co, PA Regt, commanded by Col John De Haas **CEM:** Shockoe Hill; GPS 37.55190, -77.43170; 4th & Hospital Sts; Richmond City **GS:** Y **SP:** No info **VI:** Pen # SS254 indicates served in VA artilery **P:** Y **BLW:** N **RG:** Y **MK:** Y SAR headstone marker; monument **PH:** unk **SS:** A pg 181; SAR P-335799 **BS:** 57 pg 1.

SMITH, Armistead; b 01 Jan 1737 or 1757, Mathews Co; d 12 Sep 1817 **RU:** Patriot, Gave material aid to cause **CEM:** Ware Episcopal; GPS 37.42275, -76.50789; 7825 John Clayton Mem Hwy; Gloucester **GS:** Y **SP:** Martha Tabb (21 Oct 1757-16 Sep 1821) d/o Edward & Lucy (-----) Tabb **VI:** GS moved fr Toddsbury Plantation on North River in July 1924. He was the 8th Rector of Ware Church 1792-1817. Epitaph recorded 1959 **P:** N **BLW:** N **RG:** Y **MK:** Y SAR **PH:** Y **SS:** AL Ct Bk lt pg iii, 2, 17 Gloucester Co; AK; SAR P-336115 **BS:** 48 pg 80; 207.

SMITH, B Egbert; b unk; d 1781 **RU:** Soldier, Served fr NY, killed in the battle at Yorktown **CEM:** Yorktown Victory Monument Tablet; GPS 38.28350, -78.54150; Yorktown; York **GS:** U **SP:** No info **VI:** No further data **P:** unk **BLW:** unk **RG:** unk **MK:** unk **PH:** unk **SS:** J-Yorktown Historian; SAR P-291518 **BS:** JLARC 74.

SMITH, Byrd; b c1762; d 23 Jul 1827 **RU:** Private, Served in Cumberland Co Militia **CEM:** Moses Smith Place; GPS 37.49639, -78.24486; Jct Rt 60 and Stoney Point Rd; Cumberland **GS:** U **SP:** Gillea Arnold (__-bef 1822) **VI:** Son of Robert (1725-1776) & Elizabeth (-----) (__-1804) Smith **P:** unk **BLW:** unk **RG:** Y **MK:** N **PH:** unk **SS:** E pg 720; CZ; SAR P-291565 **BS:** 60 Cumberland; 196.

SMITH, Caleb Jr; b 1765; d 14 Jul 1803 **RU:** Private, 2 VA bde, 5th, 7th, 11th, 14th Cont Lines. Also in Col Morgan's Rifleman Regt **CEM:** Old Christ Church Episcopal; GPS 38.80625, -77.04718; 118 N Washington St; Alexandria City **GS:** Y **SP:** No info **VI:** Died age 38 **P:** unk **BLW:** unk **RG:**N **MK:** N **PH:** unk **SS:** E pg 720 **BS:** 20 pg 142; 196.

SMITH, Edward; b 10 Jun 1752; d 17 Dec 1826 **RU:** Patriot, Gave two guns to Dunmore Co Militia, 1775 **CEM:** Mt Hebron; GPS 39.10916, -78.09497; 305 E Boscawen St; Winchester City **GS:** Y **SP:** Elizabeth (-----) (11 Aug 1761-7 Nov 1832) **VI:** Died in Frederick Co **P:** N **BLW:** N **RG:** N **MK:** Y SAR monument **PH:** no **SS:** AL CT Bk pg 26, 30; Z pg 80 **BS:** 50 pg 51, 52.

SMITH, Francis, b 1761, Eng, d 18 Jul 1830 **RU:** Private, had MD service **CEM:** Cedar Grove; GPS 36.858754, -76.283445; loc 238 E Prinsess Anne Rd, Norfolk City **GS:** Y block, 2d AW, lot 28, space 14 **SP:** Anne Marsden (15 Jul 1778-3 Jun 1857) **VI:** *Portsmouth Herald* provides death date and that he was a merchant in Norfolk and he arr fr Eng bef Rev War and he resided in Baltimore & Northern Neck of VA bef moving to Norfolk abt 1795 **P:** Y **BLW:** N **RG:** N **MK:** N **PH:** N **SS: EL BS:** 196.

SMITH, Fred; b 1717; d 1794 **RU:** Major, Served in Bedford Co Militia **CEM:** Hat Creek Presbyterian; GPS 37.06570, -78.54240; 6442 Hat Creek Rd, Brookneal; Campbell **GS:** U **SP:** Susanna (-----) **VI:** No further data **P:** unk **BLW:** unk **RG:** Y **MK:** N **PH:** unk **SS:** SAR P-291940 **BS:** JLARC 36.

SMITH, George; b unk, d 29 Mar 1794 **RU:** Patriot as patriot supported cause by paying supply tax included in his personal property tax in 1782, and 1783, Loudoun Co and gave material aid to cause **CEM** Goose Creek; GPS 39.11250, -77.60589; Rt 722, Lincoln; Loudoun **GS:** Unk **SP:** No spousal info **VI:** No further data **P:** N **BLW:** N **RG:** N **MK:** N **PH:** N **SS:** AL Ct Bk pg 88; DV Loudoun Co list 1782B, image 18 pdf, 1783A image 12 pdf **BS:** 222.

SMITH, George; b 19 Aug 1765; d 30 Aug 1822 or 1828 **RU:** Private, Served in Capt John Hodge's Troop of Light Dragoons 1 Oct 1781 to 14 Feb 1782 **CEM:** Dumfries Public; GPS 38.34110, -77.19964; 17821 Mine Rd, Dumfries; Prince William **GS:** Y **SP:** No info **VI:** SAR Monument (monument is a marker, as well) **P:** N **BLW:** N **RG:** N **MK:** Y SAR monument **PH:** Y **SS:** G pg 706 **BS:** 94 pg 18.

SMITH, George W; b unk; d 1833 **RU:** Patriot, Gave material aid to cause **CEM:** Fairfax Meeting House; GPS 39.18557, -77.60589; Water St & Waterford Rd, Waterford; Loudoun **GS:** Y **SP:** No info **VI:** No further data **P:** unk **BLW:** unk **RG:** N **MK:** N **PH:** unk **SS:** D Vol 1 pg 344 **BS:** 25 pg 291.

SMITH, George William; b 1762, Bathurst, Essex Co; d 26 Dec 1811 **RU:** Private, Served in John Marshall's Co, Fauquier Co Militia **CEM:** Monumental Church; GPS unk; 1224 E Broad St; Richmond City **GS:** U **SP:** 1) Sara Adams 2) Lucy Franklin Read (1733-1845) d/o John Royall & (-----) Read **VI:**

RU=Rank/Unit	CEM=Cemetery	GS=Gravestone	SP=Spousal Information
VI=Other Veteran Info	P=Pension	BLW=Bounty/Land Warrant	RG=Registered Grave
MK=SAR/DAR Marker	PH=Photo	SS=Service Source	BS=Burial Source

386

Son of Meriwether (1730-1790) & Elizabeth (Daingerfield) Smith. Was VA Governor 1811. Died in theater fire in Richmond **P:** unk **BLW:** unk **RG:** N **MK:** unk **PH:** unk **SS:** DQ Chapter 1 **BS:** 196.

SMITH, Henry; b 1758; d 1831 **RU:** Private, Capt Tate's Co, Augusta Co Militia **CEM:** Smith Family AKI Shaw Farm; GPS 38.392970, -78.061034; loc Sangersville Rd (Rt 727), Spring Creek; Rockingham **GS:** N **SP:** Margaret Cravens (1771-1833), d/o Robert Cravens & Hester Harrison **VI:** Son of Abraham Smith (c1722, Ireland-c1783) & Sarah Caldwell **P:** N **BLW:** N **RG:** N **MK:**N **PH:** N **SS:** E pg 721 **BS:** 196.

SMITH, Henry II; b 5 Feb 1741,Stafford Co, d 17 Feb 1801 **RU:** Patriot,was given a certificate for items given to support the cause in Washington Co **CEM:** Smith Family: GPS 37.0315100, -81.8367000; loc N side Rt 640, Clifton; Russell **GS:** Y **SP:** 1) Mary J James Strother (28 Dec 1736, Fredericksburg-19 Feb 1822), 2) ElizabethTaylor (1738-Mar 1820), **VI:** He could be the Capt of the Washington Co Militia in 1776 and/or the Capt of the Botetourt Co Militia in 1778. This is likely as FAG indicates rank of Colonel perhaps achieved after the war period. **P:** N **BLW:** N **RG:**Y **MK:** N **PH:** N **SS**; E pg 721; AL-Washington Co Commission BK, IV pg 271 SAR P-292015 **BS:** 196

SMITH, Humphrey (Humphreys); b Sep 1760, Botetourt Co; d Jun 1847 **RU:** Private, Served in 1st Cont Line **CEM:** Smith Chapel; GPS 37.03873, -80.20393; Directions not identified; Floyd **GS:** N **SP:** mar (5 Jul 1785 Botetourt Co) Eleanor McElhaney (c1740-30 May 1842) d/o Robert (1740-aft Jul 1785) & May (-----) (__-1784) McElhaney **VI:** No further data **P:** unk **BLW:** unk **RG:** Y **MK:** unk **PH:** N **SS:** E pg 721; SAR P-292038 **BS:** JLARC 29.

SMITH, Isaac; b 4 Nov 1734, Accomack Co; d 23 Mar 1813 **RU:** Paymaster, Served in the Navy **CEM:** Selma; GPS unk; E of Bus Rt 13, .4 mi N of Rt 631 Eastville; Northampton **GS:** Y **SP:** 1) Mar (c1755) Elizabeth Custis Teakle d/o Thomas & Elizabeth (Custis) Teackle 2) Mar (8 May 1790) Elizabeth Goffigon **VI:** Son of Isaac Sr. & Sarah (West) Smith **P:** unk **BLW:** unk **RG:** N **MK:** N **PH:** unk **SS:** E pg 721 **BS:** 42 pg 77; 196.

SMITH, Isaac Watt Sr; b 1760; d 1845 **RU:** Sergeant, Served in 1st, 2d, 3rd and 10th Cont Lines **CEM:** Locust Grove; GPS unk; Locust Grove nr Red Hill Boys Home; Charlotte **GS:** U **SP:** Sarah Hancock (__-1812) **VI:** On pension list of 1835 age 74. Rec'd 200 acres BLW 19 Mar 1784 **P:** Y **BLW:** Y **RG:** Y **MK:** unk **PH:** unk **SS:** E pg 721; F pg 69; SAR P-292054 **BS:** 226.

SMITH, Jacob; b 1756; d 19 Aug 1836 **RU:** Private, Served in VA Line. Ent serv in Rockingham Co. Served in Capt Burbank's Co,12th Regt. Was taken prisoner 7 Jul 1777 **CEM:** Jollett United Methodist Ch; GPS unk; Rt 609 N of Jollett A 2067 Jollett Rd; Page **GS:** Y **SP:** Mar (1782 Rockingham Co) Winna (-----) **VI:** Appl pen Rockingham Co 18 Sep 1818 age 59. Widow appl pen 23 Oct 1939 Page Co age 75. W19052 **P:** Y **BLW:** unk **RG:** Y **MK:** Y SAR **PH:** unk **SS:** A pg 130-1; CG Vol 3 pg 3192; DAR A203177; SAR P-292085 **BS:** 120 Hartman.

SMITH, James; b c1761; d 11 Jan 1815 **RU:** Patriot, Paid personal property Tax 1782 (considered supply tax for paying Rev War expenses) **CEM:** Smith Family; GPS unk; Mantua Farm Rd; Northumberland **GS:** Y **SP:** No info **VI:** No further data **P:** N **BLW:** N **RG:** N **MK:** unk **PH:** unk **SS:** EB pg 21 **BS:** 227 pg 124. **SEE APPENDIX G**

SMITH, James; b 1752; d 1833 **RU:** Soldier, Served in Cont Line **CEM:** Blue Spring; GPS 36.65967, -82.41181; Hiltons Area; Scott **GS:** U **SP:** No info **VI:** No further data **P:** unk **BLW:** unk **RG:** N **MK:** unk **PH:** unk **SS:** E pg 721 **BS:** 196.

SMITH, Jeremiah; b 1711 NJ; d 4 Sep 1787 **RU:** Captain/Patriot, Gave material aid to cause **CEM:** Smith; GPS not determined; loc just off Knobb Rd nr Gore; Frederick **GS:** Y **SP:** Mar 13 Oct 1750 (Lic), PA, Martha McCrachen (__-Nov 1769) **VI:** Cem sign indicates property was granted to him in 1762 **P:** unk **BLW:** unk **RG:** Y **MK:**N **PH:** unk **SS:** J-NSSAR 1993 Reg, J- DAR Hatcher; AL Ct Bk pg 36 Frederick Co; SAR P-292211; DAR A105752 **BS:** JLARC 1, 2; 196.

SMITH, Jesse; b 1730; d 12 Jun 1821 **RU:** Corporal/Patriot, Served in VA Line. Enl Henry Co 1778 in 3rd VA Regt of VA Light Dragoons. Served in Capt Scott's Co, 3rd Cont Line 1779. Gave material aid to cause **CEM:** Smith family; GPS unk; 1 mi W of Skipwith Rd, 1.5 N of Three Chopt; Henrico **GS:** Y **SP:** 1) mar (10 Nov 1787, Chesterfield Co) Martha Keys (__-29 Mar 1805 - two days before marrying 2d wife) 2) mar (31 Mar 1805) Mrs. Lucy Cooke/Cocke (1773-__), wid of Robert Cocke. (Elisha Price signed mar

RU=Rank/Unit	CEM=Cemetery	GS=Gravestone	SP=Spousal Information
VI=Other Veteran Info	P=Pension	BLW=Bounty/Land Warrant	RG=Registered Grave
MK=SAR/DAR Marker	PH=Photo	SS=Service Source	BS=Burial Source

387

bond with him on 29 Mar 1805 Henrico Co) **VI:** Widow appl pen Jan 1855 Henrico Co age 82. R9789 **P:** Y **BLW:** unk **RG:** N **MK:** N **PH:** unk **SS:** E pg 721; K Vol 5 pg 100; AL Ct Bk pg 9 Henrico Co; CG Vol 3 pg 3196 **BS:** 114; 168 Smith Bur.

SMITH, John; b 07 May 1750, Middlesex Co; d 4 Mar 1836 **RU:** Colonel, Ent serv 1776 Frederick Co as Col of VA Militia. Ent serv Frederick Co in 3rd Div of VA Miltia **CEM:** Mt Hebron; GPS 39.10916, -78.09497; 305 E Boscawen St; Winchester City **GS:** U **SP:** Mar (1782) Animus Anna Bull (1760 PA-15 Sep 1831) **VI:** After RW, obtained rank of Maj General of 3rd Div of Militia in War of 1812. Appl for pen 4 Mar 1833. Lived at "Hackwood". Widower recd pen S6114. Was 15 term member of Congress, VA State Legislature 1779, Senator 1792. Died in Frederick Co **P:** Y **BLW:** unk **RG:** Y **MK:** Y SAR monument **PH:** unk **SS:** DAR A105975; SAR P-292359; CG Vol 3 pg 3204-5 **BS:** JLARC 4, 47; 196.

SMITH, John; b c1745, d bef 19 Aug 1816 **RU:** Pvt in Capt John Morton's Grp, Prince Edward Co, Militia **CEM:** Smith Family; GPS not determined; loc 2586 Vellano Ln, Edmond; Prince Edward **GS:** Unk **SP:** Susannah Watson **VI:** No Further data **P:** Unk **BLW:** Unk **RG:** Y **MK:** Unk **PH:** N **SS:** DAR A105997; SAR P-292342 **BS:** SAR PRS.

SMITH, John; b c1745; d 1811 **RU:** Patriot, Gave 3 complete pairs of horse harnesses to cause **CEM:** Smith Family; GPS unk; Rt 688, Orlean; Fauquier **GS:** Y **SP:** No info **VI:** No further data **P:** N **BLW:** N **RG:** N **MK:** N **PH:** unk **SS:** D Fauquier Co pg 18 **BS:** 18 pg 79.

SMITH, John; b c1757; d 1785 **RU:** Patriot, Gave material aid to the cause **CEM:** St Paul's Episcopal; GPS 36.84733, -76.28554; 201 St Paul's Blvd; Norfolk City **GS:** Y **SP:** No info **VI:** No further data **P:** N **BLW:** N **RG:** N **MK:** N **PH:** unk **SS:** AL Ct Bk I pg 7, 18 **BS:** 87 pg 30; 196

SMITH, John; b 26 Aug 1753, PA; d 1851 **RU:** Private, Served first in1775 in a PA artillery unit and served one yr fighting Indians. Later served in Capt McCutchen's Co Augusta Co Militia **CEM:** Old Stone Presbyterian; GPS 38.23926, -78.97356; 28 Old Stone Church Ln, Ft Defiance; Augusta **GS:** U **SP:** Mar (13 Sep 1791 Albemarle Co) Martha Wallace (1774-1821) **VI:** He received a pension in 1818 while residing in Ft Defiance. He also resided after the war in Albemarle and Goochland Cos **P:** Y **BLW:** unk **RG:** Y **MK:** Y SAR plaque **PH:** unk **SS:** DAR A105935; SAR P-292393; J- DAR Hatcher; E pg 722; K Vol 5 pg 101 **BS:** JLARC 2; 80 vol 4 pg 48; 196.

SMITH, John; b c1761, Frederick Co; d 29 Oct 1812 **RU:** Private, Served in Capt Peter Byron Bruin's Co, 11th VA Regt, commanded by Co Daniel Morgan **CEM:** Stone Chapel Presbyterian; GPS 39.22610, -78.01060; Old Charles Town Rd, Berryville; Clarke **GS:** Y **SP:** Elizabeth (-----) - wife or consort **VI:** No further data **P:** unk **BLW:** unk **RG:** N **MK:** Y SAR **PH:** Y **SS:** E pg 722 **BS:** 58 pg 95.

SMITH, John; b 1755, England; d Oct 1802 **RU:** Private/Patriot, Served in VA State Militia. Gave material aid to cause **CEM:** Smith Family; GPS unk; Mt Pleasant Farm, now Fentress Naval Auxiliary Airfield; Chesapeake City **GS:** Y **SP:** mar (__, Norfolk Co) Julia Phillips (__-18 Oct 1802) **VI:** Govt grave stone **P:** unk **BLW:** unk **RG:** unk **MK:** unk **PH:** unk **SS:** DAR A106003; B; D Vol 2, pg 719, 723, 726 **BS:** JLARC 116; 196.

SMITH, John "Dutch"; b Mar 1760, Burke Co, NC; d 1815 **RU:** Private, Served in Capt Mordelia Clarke's Co. Was in Battle of Cowpens, SC. Discharged Mar 1781. Also served 6 mos NC Militia. Served again Apr 1781 & Sep 1781 in NC for total of 12 mos service **CEM:** Spurrier Family; GPS unk; Rt 691, Hiltons; Scott **GS:** Y **SP:** No info **VI:** Recd pen 81931 **P:** Y **BLW:** unk **RG:** Y **MK:** Y SAR Granite & DAR plaque **PH:** unk **SS:** AK pension rec; SAR P-292405 **BS:** 4-Nov-06.

SMITH, John; b unk, d 14 Nov 1786 **RU:** Lieutenant/Patriot obtained rank of LT 4 Feb 1777 Frederick Co. As patriot supported cause by paying supply tax included in his personal property tax in 1782, Loudoun Co **CEM** Goose Creek; GPS 39.11250,-77.60589; Rt 722, Lincoln; Loudoun **GS:** Unk **SP:** No spousal info **VI:** No further data **P:** N **BLW:** N **RG:** N **MK:** N **PH:** N **SS:** AZ pg 205; DV Loudoun Co list 1782A, image 18 pdf **BS:** 222 NO SAR #.

SMITH, John; b unk. d 11 Apr 1811 **RU:** Patriot, Chief Clerk, War Department **CEM:** Arlington National; GPS38,88377, -77.06535; Jefferson Davis Hwy, Rt 110 **GS:** Yes betw graves #5221 & 5221-A; Arlington **SP**; No spousal info **VI:** Reinterred from Holmead Cemetery, MD 28 May 1875 **P:** N **BLW:** N **RG:** Y **MK:** N **PH:** N **SS:** See BS 223; SAR P-292303 **BS:** 223.

RU=Rank/Unit	CEM=Cemetery	GS=Gravestone	SP=Spousal Information
VI=Other Veteran Info	P=Pension	BLW=Bounty/Land Warrant	RG=Registered Grave
MK=SAR/DAR Marker	PH=Photo	SS=Service Source	BS=Burial Source

SMITH, Joseph; b 14 Feb 1761, Berkeley Co; d 20 Jul 1846 **RU:** Private, Served in Col Jehu Eyre Regt, Philadelphia Militia. Was POW **CEM:** Trinity United Methodist; GPS 39.13600, -77.00610; 2911 Cameron Mills Rd; Alexandria City **GS:** Y **SP:** Mary Donahue (Apr 1767-20 Mar 1847) **VI:** Died age 85 yrs 5 mos. Recd pen **P:** Y **BLW:** unk **RG:** N **MK:** N **PH:** unk **SS:** E pg 722; AP Gen Morgan R; CI PA Archive 6th series Vol 1 pg 474-475, 484 Fairfax pension **BS:** 23 pg 140.

SMITH, Joseph; b 1763, MD; d 9 Jul 1842 **RU:** Private, Ent serv Halifax Co. Enl as substitute for Harmon Miller. Ent serv later as substitute for father James Smith. Served in Capt Charles Wall's Co Jan 1781. In Apr 1781 was under Capt Wm Clark. Discharged 28 Jul 1781 by Col Priddy **CEM:** GSA Camp Shawnee; GPS unk; Ringgold; Pittsylvania **GS:** Y **SP:** Mar (5 Jun 1793 Pittsylvania Co) Barsha Humphrey (c1770-__) d/o James & (-----) Humphrey **VI:** Son of James & (-----) Smith. Sol appl pen 17 Sep 1832 Pittsylvania Co. Widow appl pen 26 Aug 1847 Pittsylvania Co age 77. W3725, Recd BLW #13900-160-55. Discharge preserved in pension application **P:** Y **BLW:** Y **RG:** Y **MK:** unk **PH:** unk **SS:** J-NSSAR 2000 Reg; K Vol 5 pg 107; CG Vol 3 pg 3207; SAR P-292550 **BS:** 174 JLARC 76.

SMITH, Joseph T; b 1722, King George Co; d 6 Jan 1793 **RU:** Lieutenant/Patriot, Appointed as Lt 27 Aug 1781. Gave material aid to cause **CEM:** Mt Eccentric; GPS unk; 2 mi S of The Plains; Fauquier **GS:** N **SP:** Margaret Rowley (__-1793) **VI:** No further data **P:** unk **BLW:** unk **RG:** Y **MK:** N **PH:** N **SS:** DAR A106282; SAR P-292509 AL Ct Bk pg 3, 6 Fauquier Co; AZ pg 201 **BS:** 95 Mt Eccentric.

SMITH, Matthew; b 1745, Edenburg, Scotland; d 1795 **RU:** Private, Served in Lt Col Edward Hand's 1st Regt of Cont Troops, PA **CEM:** White Oak Crossroads; GPS unk; Nr Charlottesville; Charlottesville City **GS:** U **SP:** Mar (1763) Permelia Greene (1746/7-1803) **VI:** No further data **P:** unk **BLW:** unk **RG:** Y**MK:** unk **PH:** unk **SS:** DAR A106441; J- DAR Hatcher; SAR P-292647 DD **BS:** JLARC 2; 80, vol 4 pg 50.

SMITH, Meriwether; b 1730; d 25 Jan 1794 **RU:** Colonel/Patriot, Served as Col of Essex Co Militia. Gave material aid to cause Was member House of Burgesses 1774-75, and delegate to Rev War Conventions 1775-76, and member Continental Congress 1778-79 & 1781. **CEM:** Bathhurst Plantation; GPS 37.88976, -76.82628; Nr Dunnsville; Essex **GS:** N **SP:** 1) mar (c1760) Alice Lee 2) mar (c1769) Elizabeth Daingerfield **VI:** Born and bur at "Bathurst" nr Dunnsville.Essex Co. Was on Committee of Safety in 1774 and signer of Leedstown Resolves in 1766. Was member House of Delegates 1781-1782, 1785, 1788 **P:** unk **BLW:** N **RG:** Y **MK:** N **PH:** N **SS:** AL Ct Bk pg 2 Essex Co; BQ pg 7155; SAR P-292670; DAR A106455 **BS:** JLARC 65;196.

SMITH, Ralph; b 1753; d 28 Feb 1827 **RU:** Patriot, Gave material aid to cause **CEM:** Mt Hermon United Methodist; GPS 37.14500, -79.31170; Rt 712, Lynch Station; Campbell **GS:** Y **SP:** No info **VI:** Founder of Mt Herman Methodist Church 1825 **P:** N **BLW:** N **RG:** N **MK:** unk **PH:** N **SS:** AL Ct Bk pg 3 Pittsylvania Co **BS:** 196. **SEE APPENDIX G**

SMITH, Samuel; b unk; d 1841 **RU:** Lieutenant, Received as Lt 1782, Loudoun Co Militia **CEM:** Goose Creek; GPS 39.11250, -77.69527; Rt 722, Lincoln; Loudoun **GS:** Y **SP:** No info **VI:** No further data **P:** unk **BLW:** unk **RG:** N **MK:** N **PH:** unk **SS:** E pg 724 **BS:** 25 pg 293.

SMITH, Samuel; b unk, d 25 Aug 1784 **RU:** Lieutenant, recd as LT Aug 1782, Loudoun Co **CEM:** Goose Creek; GPS 39.11250,-77.60589; Rt 722, Lincoln; Loudoun **GS:** Unk **SP:** No spousal info **VI:** No further data **P:** N **BLW:** N **RG:** N **MK:** N **PH:** YN **SS:** E pg 724 Loudoun Co Records **BS:** 222

SMITH, Thomas; b unk; d Aft Jan 1787 **RU:** Captain/Patriot, Appointed Capt Isle of Wight Co Militia, 14 Jul 1782. Gave material aid to cause **CEM:** St Luke's Church; GPS 36.93940, -76.58670; 14477 Benns Church Blvd, Smithfield; Isle of Wight **GS:** Y **SP:** Mar (9 Jan 1787, Isle of Wight Co) Ann Edwards **VI:** No further data **P:** unk **BLW:** unk **RG:** N **MK:** unk **PH:** unk **SS:** G pg 194; AL Ct Bk pg 16 Isle of Wight Co **BS:** 117 pg 6.

SMITH, Thomas; b 29 Dec 1719, d 25 Sep 1786, Henrico Co **RU:** Patriot, Gave material aid to cause **CEM:** Manakin (AKA Manakin Episcopal Church; GPS 37.565617, -77.709313; 985 Huguenot Trail (Rt 711); Powhatan **GS:** U **SP:** Frances Martha Stovall **VI:** Son of Joseph Smith (1696, Kent, ENG-1748, Goochland Co) & Sarah Bodfish (1700 Barnstable, MS-2 Jan 1749 MA) **P:** N **BLW:** N **RG:** N **MK:** unk **PH:** unk **SS:** Al Ct Bk pg 33 Cumberland Co **BS:** 196.

SMITH, Thomas; b 1739; d 20 May 1789 **RU:** Patriot, Was presiding officer over First and Second Committee of Safety 1775, Westmoreland Co **CEM:** Glebe; GPS unk; In garden area of Glebe Parish

RU=Rank/Unit	CEM=Cemetery	GS=Gravestone	SP=Spousal Information
VI=Other Veteran Info	P=Pension	BLW=Bounty/Land Warrant	RG=Registered Grave
MK=SAR/DAR Marker	PH=Photo	SS=Service Source	BS=Burial Source

389

House, Glebe Creek, Cople Parish; Westmoreland **GS:** U **SP:** Mar (7 Dec 1765) Mary Smith (___-14 Dec 1791) d/o John & Mary (Jacquelin) Smith **VI:** Son of Gregory & Lucy (Cooke) Smith. Rector of Cople Parish 1764 – 1789 **P:** N **BLW:** N **RG:** N **MK:** unk **PH:** unk **SS:** EC pg 6473 **BS:** 189 pg 57.

SMITH, Thomas; b 1738; d 1789 **RU:** Patriot, Gave material aid to cause **CEM:** Glebe; GPS unk; In garden area of Glebe Parish House, Glebe Creek, Cople Parish; Westmoreland **GS:** N **SP:** mar (1756 Northumberland Co) Elizabeth Garlington **VI:** No further data **P:** N **BLW:** N **RG:** N **MK:** N **PH:** N **SS:** AL Comm Bk **BS:** 189 pg 56.

SMITH, William; b 5 Feb 1741, Prince William Co; d 22 Feb 1803 **RU:** Ensign, Was in Fauquier Co Militia in 1778 and 1779 **CEM:** Mt Eccentric; GPS unk; 2 mi S of The Plains; Fauquier **GS:** N **SP:** Mar (1773) Elizabeth Doniplan (12 Apr 1744,-15 jan 1809 Fauquier Co) **VI:** No further data **P:** unk **BLW:** unk **RG:** N **MK:** N **PH:** N **SS:** DAR Ancestor #A106143; E pg 725 **BS:** 95 Mt Eccentric.

SMITH, William; b 25 May 1746, prob Gloucester England; d 7 Oct 1802 **RU:** Patriot, Was on Committee for Articles of Confederation 1774. Gave beef to cause and use of stable 1781 **CEM:** St George's Episcopal; GPS unk; 905 Princess Anne; Fredericksburg City **GS:** Y **SP:** Mary (-----) (20 Mar 1750-8 Jul 1822) **VI:** Processioner & vestryman of church. Son Jr was in War of 1812 **P:** N **BLW:** N **RG:** N **MK:** N **PH:** unk **SS:** D pg 857-8,860 **BS:** 12 pg 114.

SMITH, William; b 1755; d 1835 **RU:** Private, Service information not obtained from pension records **CEM:** Smith Family; GPS unk; 7 mi N of Covington; Alleghany **GS:** N **SP:** No info **VI:** Rec'd pen Alleghany Co **P:** Y **BLW:** unk **RG:** N **MK:** N **PH:** N **SS:** E pg 725 **BS:** 160 Smith.

SMITH, William; b 19 Mar 1743, Farnham Parish, Richmond Co; d 4 Feb 1836 **RU:** Spy-Scout, Entered service 1775 in VA Regt. Began serving as spy at time of Point Pleasant and remained same throughout war **CEM:** Smith Cemetery; GPS 37.86140, -79.98970; Rt 687, Mt Pleasant; Alleghany **GS:** Y **SP:** 1) (-----) 2) Mar (10 Aug 1780) Mary Wright (14 Jun 1759, Botetourt Co-6 Oct 1858) **VI:** Son of David Smith and Mary Bryant. Sol appl pen 17 Nov 1832. Widow appl pen Jun 1842 Alleghany Co. W6094, 16897. Vet Admin monument, reads "Continental Line." Mary Wright's name inscribed on this stone as well **P:** Y **BLW:** unk **RG:** Y **MK:** N **PH:** Y **SS:** K pg 119; K Vol 5 pg 119; CG Vol 3 pg 3235; B; DAR A200193; SAR P-333038 **BS:** 196.

SMITH, William (1756-1823) See Appendix G Addenda

SMITH, William Henry; b unk; d 1808 **RU:** Soldier, Contact George Washington SAR Chapter for service for men listed on their cemetery plaque **CEM:** Old Presbyterian Meeting House; GPS 38.48528, -77.23532; 323 S Fairfax St; Alexandria City **GS:** Y **SP:** No info **VI:** Listed on SAR plaque in cemetery **P:** unk **BLW:** unk **RG:** Y **MK:** Y SAR plaque **PH:** unk **SS:** J-NSSAR 1993 Reg; AK; SAR P-293377 **BS:** JLARC 1; 23 pg 108; 196.

SMITH (SMYTH), Adam B; b 1720; d 1785 **RU:** Chaplain, Served in Botetourt Co Militia 1777 **CEM:** Fincastle Presbyterian; GPS 37.50017, -79.87558; 108 E Back St, Fincastle; Botetourt **GS:** N **SP:** No info **VI:** Name is on the SAR plaque in cemetery **P:** unk **BLW:** unk **RG:** N **MK:** Y SAR plaque **PH:** N **SS:** E pg 749; AR Vol 4 pg 41 **BS:** JLARC 2, 76.

SNAPP, Lawrence Sr; b 1723, Mulhausen, Departement du Bas Rhin, Alsace, France; d May 1782 **RU:** Captain, Served in Dunmore (Shenandoah) Co Militia in Capt Alexander Machir's Co, Strasburg District. Later commanded a co there **CEM:** St Paul's Lutheran; GPS 38.99140, -78.36250; 156 W Washington, Strasburg; Shenandoah **GS:** U **SP:** Mar (1746 Frederick Co) Margaret Stephens (1724/25 Rhineland, Germany-Jun 1801 Shenandoah Co), d/o Hans Peter & Maria Christina (-----) Stephens **VI:** Member of Frederick Co Militia on 24 July 1758 in French and Indian War. Vestryman of Beckford Parish in St Paul's Lutheran Church in Strasburg, Shenandoah Co. Probably bur there or on family farm, long since disappeared **P:** unk **BLW:** unk **RG:** Y **MK:** unk **PH:** unk **SS:** C pg 606; DAR A826163; SAR P-293551 **BS:** 196.

SNEAD, Robert; b 23 May 1762 "within 9 mi of Hanover Court House"; d 19 Jan 1841 **RU:** Private, Ent serv 1778 as substitute for brother John, later brother Richer, later brother-in-law Elijah Pridee. Was at Battle of Yorktown Oct 1781 **CEM:** Snead Family; GPS unk; Rt 624 nr Hylas, nr main road; Hanover **GS:** U **SP:** Mar (1 Mar 1792) Sophia (-----) (28 Jun 1777-12 Mar 1844) **VI:** DAR marker placed at grave

RU=Rank/Unit	CEM=Cemetery	GS=Gravestone	SP=Spousal Information
VI=Other Veteran Info	P=Pension	BLW=Bounty/Land Warrant	RG=Registered Grave
MK=SAR/DAR Marker	PH=Photo	SS=Service Source	BS=Burial Source

390

1978. Pensioned 1832 Hanover Co, when living nr Ground Squirrel. Widow appl pen 1843 fr Hanover, Co age 65. Pension rejected - no reason given. R9891 **P:** N **BLW:** unk **RG:** Y **MK:** Y SAR **PH:** unk **SS:** K Vol 5 pg 124; DAR A106358; SAR P-293562 **BS:** JLARC 1, 2, 71; ; 80 vol 4 pg 55.

SNIDOW, Christian; b 15 Mar 1760, Lancaster, Pa; d Oct 1836 **RU:** Lieutenant, Ent serv Montgomery Co 1776. Served in Giles Co Militia **CEM:** Horseshoe; **GPS** unk; Pembroke; Giles **GS:** Y **SP:** Mar (24 Aug 1784 Montgomery, Kanawha Co, WVA) Mary Burk (22 Jan 1762-3 May 1825) d/o Thomas (1741-1808) & Clara (Frazer) (1742-1811) Burke **VI:** Son of John Jacob & Mary Elizabeth (Helm) Snidow. Sol appl pen 26 May 1834 Giles Co. S17112. Represented Giles Co in VA House of Delegates. Gov't Gr st; DAR plaque. A Lt Col in War of 1812 **P:** Y **BLW:** unk **RG:** Y **MK:** Y SAR **PH:** unk **SS:** K Vol 5 pg 127; CG Vol 3 pg 3241; SAR P-293647 **BS:** JLARC 1,2,26; 80 vol 4 pg 56; 196.

SNIDOW, Jacob; b 15 Nov 1763, Lancaster Co, PA; d 1847 **RU:** Soldier, Ent serv Montgomery (later Giles) Co. Enlisted 1780, 81, 82 "to fight Indians". Also served in VA Line under Capt John Lucas & John Floyd **CEM:** Snidow Farm, "Sugar Maple"; **GPS** unk; Rt 460 on Lilly Hill, Pembroke; Giles **GS:** U **SP:** 1) Clara Burke, 2) Sara Pickelsimer, 3) Mary Ann Hankey **VI:** Sol appl pen 23 Nov 1835. R9903. Pension denied, prob because not part of regularly constituted military unit **P:** Y #R99003V **BLW:** unk **RG:** Y **MK:** unk **PH:** unk **SS:** K Vol 5 pg 127; CG Vol 3 pg 3241; DAR A106501; SAR P-293649 **BS:** JLARC 2,4,26; 80 vol 4 pg 56.

SNIDOW, Philip; b 1756, Lancaster Co, PA; d 28 Oct 1792 **RU:** Private, Served in Capt John Lucas's Co, Montgomery Co Militia **CEM:** Snidow Farm, "Sugar Maple"; **GPS** unk; Rt 460 on Lilly Hill, Pembroke; Giles **GS:** U **SP:** Mar (14 Feb 1782 Henry Co) Barbara (Prillarman) Martin (1764-1848) **VI:** Son of John Jacob & Mary Elizabeth (Helm) Snidow. DAR plaque **P:** unk **BLW:** unk **RG:** Y **MK:** Y DAR plaque **PH:** Y **SS:** J- DAR Hatcher; B; G pg 234; DAR A105502; SAR P-293651 **BS:** JLARC 2; ; 80 vol 4 pg 56; 196.

SNODGRASS, David; b 1725, Washington Co; d 18 Oct 1814 **RU:** Patriot, Gave beef to cause 1776 **CEM:** Glade Spring Presbyterian; **GPS** 36.76720, -81.78720; 33234 Lee Hwy, Glade Spring; Washington **GS:** U **SP:** Margaret Glenn (1740-1816) **VI:** Son of William (1697-1766) & Catherine (Patterson) (1705-1783) Snodgrass **P:** N **BLW:** N **RG:** Y **MK:** unk **PH:** unk **SS:** DD cites Draper Papers, VA MSS, 5225, reel 121; SAR P-293676 **BS:** 196.

SNODGRASS, James; b 31 Oct 1762; d 3 Jul 1828 **RU:** Lieutenant, Was at King's Mountain under Campbell **CEM:** Rock Spring; **GPS** 37.78126, -79.44585; Jct Rt 803 & Liberty Hall Rd, Lodi; Washington **GS:** U **SP:** Ann Long (23 May 1766-14 Oct 1845) **VI:** Son of David (1725-1814) & Margaret Ann (Glenn) (1740-1816) Snodgrass **P:** Y **BLW:** unk **RG:** Y **MK:** unk **PH:** unk **SS:** Cl Rev War pen VA; DAR A106543; SAR P-293 683: **BS:** 196.

SNODGRASS, John Jr; b 1746 or 1747, Jones Springs, Berkeley Co, WV; d 1796 **RU:** Patriot, Gave material aid to cause **CEM:** Glade Spring Presbyterian; **GPS** 36.76720, -81.78720; 33234 Lee Hwy, Glade Spring; Washington **GS:** U **SP:** Mary Miller (1747-1838) **VI:** Son of John (1726-1788) & Elizabeth (-----) (1726-1787) Snodgrass. Wrote will 8 Jun 1795 **P:** N **BLW:** N **RG:** Y **MK:** unk **PH:** unk **SS:** AL Cert Berkeley Co WV; SAR P-293684 **BS:** 196.

SNODGRASS, William; b 10 May 1760 Frederick Co (later Berkeley Co); d 18 Sep 1849 **RU:** Soldier, Lived in Washington Co at enl 1775 & 1776. Served in VA Line **CEM:** Snodgrass; **GPS** unk; Bristol (or Blountsville, TN); Bristol City **GS:** U **SP:** No info **VI:** Sol appl pen 22 Aug 1832, Sullivan Co, TN **P:** Y **BLW:** unk **RG:** Y **MK:** unk **PH:** unk **SS:** J- DAR Hatcher; K Vol 5 pg 127; CG Vol 3 pg 3242; SAR P-293699 **BS:** JLARC 2; 80 vol4 pg 56; 196.

SNOW, Edward; b unk; d 1781 **RU:** Soldier, Served fr MA, and killed in the battle at Yorktown **CEM:** Yorktown Victory Monument Tablet; **GPS** 38.28350, -78.54150; Yorktown; York **GS:** U **SP:** No info **VI:** No further data **P:** unk **BLW:** unk **RG:** Y **MK:** unk **PH:** unk **SS:** J-Yorktown Historian; SAR P-293729 **BS:** JLARC 74.

SNOW, Richard; b Jun 1753; d Aft 28 Sep 1833 **RU:** Private, Served in Albemarle Co Militia commencing spring 1777 for 20 mos on several re-enlistments. Was at seige of Yorktown Oct 1781 in Capt John Harris's Co, VA Cont Line **CEM:** Snow Johnson Family; **GPS** unk; S base Buck Mountain, approx .5 mi behind house; Albemarle **GS:** N **SP:** Lorana Davis (c1765-__) **VI:** No GS, thus no specific

RU=Rank/Unit   CEM=Cemetery   GS=Gravestone   SP=Spousal Information
VI=Other Veteran Info   P=Pension   BLW=Bounty/Land Warrant   RG=Registered Grave
MK=SAR/DAR Marker   PH=Photo   SS=Service Source   BS=Burial Source

391

burial proof. Son or eldest grandson of John Snow. Pen recd 1832 #514540 **P:** unk **BLW:** unk **RG:** Y **MK:** unk **PH:** N **SS:** DAR A201695; SAR P-340223 G pg 755; AP pen rec; CG pg 3244 **BS:** 32 Sheap Mar 2015.

SOLNE, Andre; b unk; d 1781 **RU:** Soldier, Served in Gatinais Bn and died fr battle at Yorktown **CEM:** French Memorial; GPS 36.81944, -79.39933; Yorktown; York **GS:** U **SP:** No info **VI:** No further data **P:** unk **BLW:** unk **RG:** Y **MK:** unk **PH:** unk **SS:** J-Yorktown Historian; SAR P-294009 **BS:** JLARC 1,74.

SOLOMAN, Richard; b unk; d 25 Dec 1777 **RU:** Private; Capt Thomas Triplett's Co, Col William Grayson's VA Regt, Cont Line Dec 1777 **CEM:** Rev War Court House Plaque; GPS not determined; 4110 Chain Bridge Rd; Fairfax **GS:** Memorialized on plaque 2017 by Geo Washington Chapter, VASSAR **SP** No info **VI:** died in service **P:** N **BLW:** N **RG:** N **MK:** N **PH:** N **SS:** E pg 728; AP Fold3 Serv Rec & rools: EP sources: **BS:** None.

SOMERVILLE, James; b 25 Feb 1742, Glascow, Scotland; d 4 Apr 1798 **RU:** Patriot, Gave use of warehouse Dec 1779-Apr 1781. Alderman in Fredericksburg 1782 **CEM:** Masonic Cemetery; GPS 38.30198, -77.46142; 900 Charles St; Fredericksburg City **GS:** Y **SP:** No info **VI:** Died in Port Royal **P:** N **BLW:** N **RG:** N **MK:** Y SAR plaque **PH:** unk **SS:** D pg 867 **BS:** 11 pg 107-9.

SOMMERS, Simon;SEE SUMMERS, Simon

SONNER, John; b 4 Dec 1763, d 7 Jun 1850 **RU:** Private. Served in Thomas Buck's Co, Dunmore County Militia **CEM:** Fairview; GPS: 38.985649, -78.361924; E Alden St, Strasburg; Shenandoah **GS:** Yes, Gov't, behind memorial wall of American Legion building **SP:** 1) Margaret Didiwick, 2) Anna Bowman, d/o Jacob Bowman (1724-1778) & Elizabeth Stover (1758-1795) **VI:** Originally buried on Sonner farm. Son of Johann Phillip Sonner (1730-1806) and Anna Elizabeth Windel (Windell) (1738-1825) **P:** N **BLW:** Y **RG:** Y **MK:** Y SAR granite **PH:** Yes **SS:** E pg 728; SAR P-336168 **BS:** 04; 196.

SORBETZ, Barthelemy; b unk; d 1781 **RU:** Soldier, Served in Gatinais Bn and died fr battle at Yorktown **CEM:** French Memorial; GPS 36.81944, -79.39933; Yorktown; York **GS:** U **SP:** No info **VI:** No further data **P:** unk **BLW:** unk **RG:** Y **MK:** unk **PH:** unk **SS:** J-Yorktown Historian; SAR P-294107 **BS:** JLARC 1, 74.

SORIN, Pierre; b unk; d 1781 **RU:** Seaman, Served on "Victorie" and died from Yorktown battle **CEM:** French Memorial; GPS 36.81944, -79.39933; Yorktown; York **GS:** U **SP:** No info **VI:** No further data **P:** unk **BLW:** unk **RG:** Y **MK:** unk **PH:** unk **SS:** J-Yorktown Historian; SAR P-294112 **BS:** JLARC 1, 74.

SOUDER, Philip, Sr; b 10 Apr 1760, d 24Sep 1821 **RU:** Patriot Supported cause by paying supply tax included in his personal property tax in 1782, Prince William Co **CEM:** Saint James Reformed: GPS 39.27627, -77.62968; Lovettsville; Loudoun **GS:** Yes row 17 site 177 **SP:** Susana Boger (26 Apr 1760-28 Mar 1836) d/o Michael Joseph Boger (1723-1783) & (-----) **VI:** Son of Anthony Souder (c1730-18 Dec 1803) & Margaret (-----) **P:** N **BLW:** N **RG:** N **MK:** N **PH:** N **SS:** DV Loudoun Co, list 1782B, image 14 pdf **BS:** 196.

SOULIGNAC, Mathieu; b unk; d 1781 **RU:** Soldier, Served in Beaujolais Bn and died fr battle at Yorktown **CEM:** French Memorial; GPS 36.81944, -79.39933; Yorktown; York **GS:** U **SP:** No info **VI:** No further data **P:** unk **BLW:** unk **RG:** Y **MK:** unk **PH:** unk **SS:** J-Yorktown Historian; SAR P-294198 **BS:** JLARC 1, 74.

SOURSON, Jean; b unk; d 1781 **RU:** Soldier, Served in Soissonnais Bn and died fr battle at Yorktown **CEM:** French Memorial; GPS 36.81944, -79.39933; Yorktown; York **GS:** U **SP:** No info **VI:** No further data **P:** unk **BLW:** unk **RG:** Y **MK:** unk **PH:** unk **SS:** J-Yorktown Historian; SAR P-294203 **BS:** JLARC 1, 74.

SOUTHER, Micheal; b c1754, Culpeper Co; d 1813 **RU:** Patriot, Furnished supplies to the Cont Army & performed public service **CEM:** John Robertson Property; GPS unk; Ruth; Madison **GS:** N **SP:** Mary Fisher **VI:** No further data **P:** N **BLW:** N **RG:** Y **MK:** N **PH:** N **SS:** D Vol I pg 26, 33; SAR P-294240 **BS:** 04.

SOWDER/SOUDER, Jacob; b 1734, PA; d May 1819 **RU:** Private, Served in Capt John Smith's Co, Col Wood's & Nevill's 4th VA Regt, Gen Scott's Bde, and in the 8th, & 12th Cont lines **CEM:** Mt Pleasant Church; GPS 37.13289, -80.30640; 1024 Mt Pleasant Rd, Shawsville; Montgomery **GS:** N **SP:** 1)

RU=Rank/Unit CEM=Cemetery GS=Gravestone SP=Spousal Information
VI=Other Veteran Info P=Pension BLW=Bounty/Land Warrant RG=Registered Grave
MK=SAR/DAR Marker PH=Photo SS=Service Source BS=Burial Source

392

Elizabeth Story (1738, Frederick Co, MD-1785), 2) Anna Prillaman **VI:** No further data **P:** N **BLW:** N **RG:** Y **MK:** unk **PH:** N **SS:** E pg 729; DAR A107136; SAR P-294311 **BS:** JLARC 29; 196.

SOWERS, Jacob; b c1742; d 29 Aug 1822 **RU:** Patriot, Provided material aid to cause **CEM:** Mt Hebron; GPS 39.10916, -78.09497; 305 E Boscawen St; Winchester City **GS:** Y **SP:** No info **VI:** Bur in the Centenary Reformed UCC portion of the Mt Hebron Cemetery **P:** N **BLW:** N **RG:** N **MK:** Y SAR monument **PH:** N **SS:** AL Ct Bk pg 18 **BS:** 196.

SOWERS, George; b 1750, York Co, PA; d 18 Mar 1834 **RU:** Private, Served in Capt Andrew Forman, York Co, PA Militia **CEM:** Zion Lutheran; GPS 37.13507, -80.41662; Rts 693 & 615, Wades Ln; Floyd **GS:** Y **SP:** Elizabeth Spangler (1764 MD-Nov 1857 Floyd Co) **VI:** Govt grave stone **P:** unk **BLW:** unk **RG:** Y **MK:** unk **PH:** Y **SS:** B Rev War Marker; DAR A107454; Cl: Fold3 Pa Archives, 6th series,vol 2, pgs 642,643; SAR P-294320 **BS:** JLARC 17, 29; 196.

SPANGLER, Daniel; b c1753; d 1823 **RU:** Patriot, Gave material aid to the cause **CEM:** Pine Creek Primitive Baptist; GPS 36.94622, -80.27357; Spangler Mill Rd Rt 682; Floyd **GS:** Y **SP:** Mary Nofsinger **VI:** Son of Daniel (1716-1787) & Mary (Noffsinger) (1720-1820) Spangler. Died in Franklin Co **P:** N **BLW:** N **RG:** N **MK:** N **PH:** unk **SS:** AL Ct Bk **BS:** 64 pg 120; 196.

SPANGLER, Daniel; b 1716; d 3 Nov 1787 **RU:** Patriot, Gave material aid to cause **CEM:** Pigg River Primitive Baptist; GPS 36.96913, -80.07368; Rt 750 nr Callaway; Franklin **GS:** U **SP:** No info **VI:** No further data **P:** N **BLW:** N **RG:** N **MK:** N **PH:** unk **SS:** AK; AL Ct Bk pg 30 Henry Co **BS:** 04, Oct 06.

SPANGLER, Jacob; b 3 Apr 1756; d 14 Jan 1827 **RU:** Private, Served in Capt Thomas Ingles Co, Montgomery Co Militia, Apr 1781 **CEM:** Sharon Lutheran; GPS 37.05800, -81.20590; Rt 42 W of Ceres; Bland **GS:** Y **SP:** Margaret Groseclose (1760 Lancaster Co, PA-11 Aug 1838 Wythe Co), d/o Peter Sr (1730-1803) & Mary Magdalena (Ott) (1732-1805) Gloseclose **VI:** No further data **P:** unk **BLW:** unk **RG:** N **MK:** N **PH:** unk **SS:** E pg 729 **BS:** 60 Bland Co; 196.

SPANGLER, Peter Jr; b 1742, Berks Co, PA; d 1833 **RU:** Private, Served in Capt Thomas Ingles Co, 7 Apr 1781, Montgomery Co Militia **CEM:** Zion Lutheran; GPS 36.84110, -81.22310; 1417 Zion Church Rd, Crockett; Wythe **GS:** U **SP:** Mar (22 Sep 1773 Shenandoah Co) Elizabeth (Pheiffer, Piper, or Pfeiferin) Huddle **VI:** Generally believed to have d in Wythe Co, though one source says he d in Ohio **P:** unk **BLW:** unk **RG:** N **MK:** unk **PH:** unk **SS:** G pg 227 **BS:** 196.

SPANGLER (SPENGER), Daniel; b c1747, PA; d 14 Feb 1823 **RU:** Patriot, Performed public service Henry Co **CEM:** Pine Creek Primitive Baptist; GPS 36.94622, -80.27357; Spangler Mill Rd Rt 682; Floyd **GS:** Y **SP:** Sarah Bolt (1753, 8 May 1823 age 80+) **VI:** Son of Daniel Spangler (1716-1787) and Mary Noftsinger (1720-1839) **P:** N **BLW:** N **RG:** N **MK:** N **PH:** unk **SS:** AL Ct Bk **BS:** 196.

SPEAR (SPEARS), James; b 30 Jul 1759; d 29 Oct 1836 **RU:** Soldier, Served in 2nd Bn under Col Moses McClean **CEM:** Rock Spring; GPS 37.78126, -79.44585; Jct Rt 803 & Liberty Hall Rd, Lodi; Washington **GS:** U **SP:** No info **VI:** Pensioned Washington Co, as Vet Admin Ltr 13 April 1835 lists him as recd pension certificate **P:** Y **BLW:** unk **RG:** N **MK:** unk **PH:** unk **SS:** Cl; **BS:** 196.

SPEARS, John; b 12 Feb 1759; d 4 Oct 1842 **RU:** Soldier, Served in VA Line. Ent serv Chesterfield Co 1778 **CEM:** Bethel Baptist; GPS 37.50986, -77.71166; 1100 Huguenot Springs Rd, Midlothian; Chesterfield **GS:** U **SP:** Mar (12 Apr 1804, Chesterfield Co) Susannah (Sussanah) Womack (c1779-__) **VI:** Sol appl pen 26 Jan 1833 Chesterfield Co. Widow appl pen there 30 Apr 1853 age 74 & BLW 17 Apr 1855 there. W2363, BLW #26915-160-55. DAR marker **P:** Y **BLW:** Y **RG:** Y **MK:** Y DAR plaque **PH:** unk **SS:** K Vol 5 pg 134; CG Vol 3 pg 3261; SAR P-294732 **BS:** JLARC 2, 4,12, 35; 80,vol4, pg 62; 196.

SPEED, John; b 1754, NC, d 1806 NC **RU:** Lt Colonel, commanded Richmond County, NC Militia. As Capt was wounded at the battle of Stono Ferry, SC 20 Jun 1779 **CEM:** First Presbyterian Church Memorial; GPS 37.5635150, -77.5033150; loc 4602 Cary St Rd; Richmond City **GS:** No **SP:** mar (1774) Catherine Stewart **VI:** Son of William Terrell Speed (1716-1781 Charleston Co, SC) & (-----).Obituary is in the Raleigh Register. The reasoning of the Findagrave memorial writer for him being buried in Richmond, VA instead of Richmond Co, NC is not known **P:** N **BLW:** N **RG:** N **MK:** N **PH:** N **SS:** CD cites; "Return of the Killed, Wounded, and Missing in the Action of Stono Ferry, 20th June 1779,"NC Archives **BS** 196.

RU=Rank/Unit	CEM=Cemetery	GS=Gravestone	SP=Spousal Information
VI=Other Veteran Info	P=Pension	BLW=Bounty/Land Warrant	RG=Registered Grave
MK=SAR/DAR Marker	PH=Photo	SS=Service Source	BS=Burial Source

SPEED, Joseph; b 27 May 1750, Mecklenburg Co; d 23 Apr 1806 **RU:** Patriot, Was in May 1776 in VA Convention **CEM:** Speed Family; GPS unk; Check property records for family land; Mecklenburg **GS:** Y **SP:** Mar (3 Dec 1782 in NC) Ann Bignall **VI:** Son of John & Mary (Taylor-Mintry) Speed Obituary in The Raleigh Register **P:** N **BLW:** N **RG:**Y **MK:** N **PH:** unk **SS:** AR Vol 4 pg 62; AT Vol 1 pg 153; SAR P-294755 **BS:** 80,vol 4, pg 62.

SPENCE, John; b 11 Jul 1766 1766, Scotland; d 18 May 1829 **RU:** Private, Served in Capt Samuel Booker's Co Nov 1778. Served in 5th, 11th, and 15th Cont Lines **CEM:** Tebbsdale Plantation; GPS unk; Rt 633 off US 1 Dumfries; Prince William **GS:** Y **SP:** Mary Fushee Tebbs **VI:** Was a physician. SAR marker **P:** unk **BLW:** unk **RG:** N **MK:** Y SAR **PH:** unk **SS:** E pg 730 **BS:** 94 pg 471; 196.

SPENGLER, Philip; b 17 Mar 1761, York, York Co PA; d 1823 **RU:** Private, Served in PA Line **CEM:** Mt Zion United Methodist; GPS unk; 399 W Queens St, Strasburg; Shenandoah **GS:** Y **SP:** Regina Stover, d/o Peter & (-----) Stover **VI:** Son of Phillip Sr. & Anna Margaret Salome (Dinkel) Spengler. Was Lt Col, 6th VA Milita Regt War of 1812 **P:** unk **BLW:** unk **RG:**Y **MK:** unk **PH:** Y **SS:** B; SAR P-295018 **BS:** 196.

SPERRY, Jacob; b 26 Jan 1751; d 3 Apr 1808 **RU:** Captain, Served in VA Line. Ent serv 1775 in Winchester. Was prisoner of war in Quebec **CEM:** Mt Hebron; GPS 39.10916, -78.09497; 305 E Boscawen St; Winchester City **GS:** U **SP:** mar (23 Aug 1790, Winchester) Elizabeth Lauck (c1766 or c1779-___) **VI:** Son of Peter Spirri (1711-1773) & Catherine Elizabeth Wolff (1715-1798) Widow appl pen 3 Nov 1838, Winchester, age 59. Widow appl for BLW in 1855 age 89. W3470, BLW #26042-160-55 **P:** Y **BLW:** Y **RG:**Y **MK:** Y SAR granite & monument **PH:** unk **SS:** K Vol 5 pg 141; CG Vol 3 pg 3271; SAR P-295039 **BS:** JLARC 4, 47.

SPERRY, John; b 10 Nov 1757, Frederick Co; d 14 Nov 1842 **RU:** Soldier, Ent serv 1775 Frederick Co for 2 yrs in 8th VA Regt serving part of time for Capt Charles M Thurston **CEM:** Mt Hebron; GPS 39.10916, -78.09497; 305 E Boscawen St; Winchester City **GS:** Y **SP:** mar (29 Sep 1779) Sarah Maria Orrbetter (___-3 Mar 1836 Winchester), d/o Valentine & Catherine (Foltz or Stoltz) Urlettig **VI:** Originally bur in Presbyterian Cemetery next to German Reformed Church Cem in Mt Hebron. Remains removed to Presbyterian reburial site along with 71 others in 1912. Sol never appl for pen however heirs appl pen. R9992 **P:** Y **BLW:** unk **RG:** Y **MK:** Y SAR monument **PH:** unk **SS:** NARA M804; K Vol 5 pg 141; CG Vol 3 pg 3271-2; SAR P-295044 **BS:** JLARC 1, 2, 4, 47; 80,vol4, pg 63.

SPILMAN, James; b c1725, Germantown, Fauquier Co; d 20 Sep 1790 **RU:** Patriot, Gave material aid to cause **CEM:** Campbell, also Roy Neff Farm; GPS 38.46970, -77.99190; N of Jeffersonville, Rt 45 on left; Fauquier **GS:** U **SP:** 1) Martha (-----) (__, Jeffersonton, Culpeper Co-7 Sep 1771) 2) Alice Huffman **VI:** No further data **P:** N **BLW:** N **RG:** Y **MK:** unk **PH:** unk **SS:** AL Cert Culpeper Co; DAR Newsletter Sep/Oct 2015, Vol 15 #5 pg 418; SAR P-295105 **BS:** 196.

SPITLER, Abraham; b Jul 1746, Augusta Co; d 26 Mar 1830 **RU:** Private Capt Michael Reader's Co, Dunmore Co (now Page Co) Militia **CEM:** Spitler Family; GPS: unk; Luray, Page **GS:** Y **SP:** Mary Strickler (20 Feb-2 Jul 1825), d/o Isaac Strickler & (-----) **VI:** Son of John Spitler, (1720 Switzerland, 19 Dec 1752) & Mary Elizabeth (-----), GS mounted on small block building with cover. Was Baptist Minister **P:** N **BLW:** N **RG:** Y **MK:** N **PH:** N **SS:** C pg 603; DAR A107290; SAR P-295133 **BS:** SAR Application; 196.

SPITLER, Jacob; b 1766; d 1840 **RU:** Private, Served in Capt Michael Reader's Co, Shenandoah Co Militia **CEM:** Union Presbyterian; GPS 39.10916, -78.09497; Churchville; Augusta **GS:** N **SP:** Mar (21 Sep 1800, Augusta Co) Elizabeth Crist **VI:** No further data **P:** unk **BLW:** unk **RG:** N **MK:** N **PH:** N **SS:** C pg 603 **BS:** 142.

SPOONER, Charles; b 1741; d 15 Oct 1800 **RU:** Captain, Contact George Washington SAR Chapter for service for men listed on their cemetery plaque **CEM:** Old Presbyterian Meeting House; GPS 38.48528, -77.23532; 323 S Fairfax St; Alexandria City **GS:** N **SP:** No info **VI:** Called "Capt Spooner" in burial record, without first name. Bur 27 Apr 1798 age 40. Died of dropsey. Listed on SAR plaque in cemetery **P:** unk **BLW:** unk **RG:** Y **MK:** Y SAR plaque **PH:** N **SS:** SAR P-295200; J-NSSAR 1993 Reg; AK **BS:** JLARC 1; 23 pg 108; 196.

SPRAGINS (SPRAGANS), Thomas; b Bef 1755; d 17 Dec 1793 **RU:** Patriot, Gave material aid to cause **CEM:** Clarkton; GPS unk; Rt 632, Clarkton; Halifax **GS:** N **SP:** Maacah Abney (___-21 Sep 1794) d/o

RU=Rank/Unit	CEM=Cemetery	GS=Gravestone	SP=Spousal Information
VI=Other Veteran Info	P=Pension	BLW=Bounty/Land Warrant	RG=Registered Grave
MK=SAR/DAR Marker	PH=Photo	SS=Service Source	BS=Burial Source

394

Danney & (-----) Abney **VI:** Son of William (__-1755) & Martha (Abney) (1705-__) Spragins **P:** N **BLW:** N **RG:** N **MK:** unk **PH:** N **SS:** AL Ct Bk pg 40 **BS:** 196.

SPRAKER (SPRECHER), John Christopher; b 11 Jun 1738, Linn, Fayette Co, PA; d 11 May 1830 **RU:** unk, Probably served in Montgomery Co Militia, specific service at the Kegley Room, Wytheville Community College **CEM:** Zion Lutheran; GPS 36.84110, -81.22310; 1417 Zion Church Rd, Crockett; Wythe **GS:** Y **SP:** Catherina Reichart (11 Jun 1738 Linn, Fayette Co, PA-11 May 1830) **VI:** Son of Johan Christopher & Maria Ernestine (Beck) Sprecher. Died in Cripple Creek, Wythe Co **P:** unk **BLW:** unk **RG:** N **MK:** unk **PH:** unk **SS:** JLARC 123 **BS:** JLARC 123; 196.

SPROUL, William; b c1731 Ireland; d 1806 **RU:** Patriot, Gave material aid to cause **CEM:** Airy Knoll; GPS unk; E of Rt 252 abt .4 mi N of Rt 620, S of Newport; Augusta **GS:** Y **SP:** 1) mar (1757 Augusta Co) Jane (-----) 2) mar (1773 Augusta Co) Susannah Ewing **VI:** Was in Colonial War **P:** N **BLW:** N **RG:** unk **MK:** unk **PH:** unk **SS:** AL Cert Augusta Co; SAR P-331512 **BS:** 32 e-mail 28 Sep 2011.

ST CLARE, Robert; b 1755; d 1817 **RU:** Private, Served in VA Militia at Ft Pitt, PA 1775 **CEM:** St Clare Family; GPS unk; Appomattox; Appomattox **GS:** U **SP:** No info **VI:** No further data **P:** unk **BLW:** unk **RG:** Y **MK:** unk **PH:** unk **SS:** NSSAR P-295647; E pg 734 **BS:** JLARC 2; 80 vol 4 pg 66.

STAFFORD, Ralph Sr; b 1757,Staffordshire, Eng; d 17 Aug1794, Montgomery Co **RU:** Private/Patriot, Served in Cont Line. Rec'd wounds at Yorktown which caused death. Paid Supply tax 1779, Cumberland Co **CEM:** Staffville; GPS unk; Hillsville; Giles **GS:** Y **SP:** mar (Ireland 1777) Jane Kane (1758-1800) **VI:** No further data **P:** unk **BLW:** unk **RG:** Y **MK:** N **PH:** unk **SS:** E pg 754; Fold3 PA Archives, 3rd series, vol 20,pg 240; DAR A654028; SAR P-295795 **BS:** 55 pg 165; 196.

STALLARD, Samuel, William; b c1745, Essex Co; d Aft 28 Oct 1815 **RU:** Patriot, Gave material aid to cause **CEM:** Stallard-Moore; GPS 36.81155, -82.46172; Nr jct Rts 780 & 671 nr Nickelsville, Dungannon; Scott **GS:** Y **SP:** Jael Ellen Duncan (1751, Culpeper-1851) d/o Raleigh & (-----) Duncan **VI:** Son of Walter (1720-1807) & Elizabeth (Williams) (1720-1748) Stallard A plaque at gravesite4 shows family erected by descendants in 1936 **P:** N **BLW:** N **RG:** N **MK:** unk **PH:** unk **SS:** DAR Newsletter Sep/Oct 2015 Vol 15 #5 pg 418 **BS:** 196.

STANARD, Larkin; b May 1760, Spotsylvania Co; d Aft 1833 **RU:** Captain/Patriot, Served in VA Line 1776 in 6th VA Regt. Ent serv Spotsylvania Co. Was Cadet in Col Mordecei, Buckner's Regt. Was member House of Delegates **CEM:** Stanard (Stanfield) Family; GPS unk; Rt 646; Spotsylvania **GS:** N **SP:** Elizabeth Parrot Chew, d/o Robert & (-----) Chew **VI:** Appl pen 6 Aug 1833, Spotsylvania Co. S7807 **P:** Y **BLW:** unk **RG:** N **MK:** N **PH:** N **SS:** H; K Vol 5 pg 149; CG Vol 3 pg 3290 **BS:** 09 part 2.

STANFIELD, Thomas; b 1747; d 1796 **RU:** Lieutenant/Patriot, Gave material aid to cause **CEM:** Stanfield Family, Boyd Farm; GPS unk; Rt 658, 2 mi S of Turbeville; Halifax **GS:** U **SP:** No info **VI:** Gr St indicates was Lt **P:** unk **BLW:** unk **RG:** Y **MK:** unk **PH:** unk **SS:** J-NSSAR 1993 Reg, J- DAR Hatcher; AL Ct Bk pg 13 Halifax Co; SAR P-295959 **BS:** JLARC 1,2; 215.

STANDLEY, John; bapt 11 Nov 1691, New Kent Co; d 17 Jul 1783 **RU:** Patriot, gave material aid to cause, 1782 Hanover Co **CEM:** Cedar Creek Quaker; GPS not determined; loc 3mi E of Cedar Grove Meeting House, Montpelier; Hanover **GS:** N **SP:** 1) mar (1714 Northumberland Co) Elizabeth Hall (1695-1726), 2) mar (1726, New Kent Co) Alice Ballard (1697-1742), 3) Martha Hutchuns (1709-1789) **VI:** Son of Thomas Stanley (1670-1714) & Mary Holmes (1666-1728) **P:** N **BLW:** N **RG:** Y **MK:** N **PH:** N **SS:** DAR A204584; D vol 2, pgs 470, 472; SAR P-125176 **BS:** 196.

STAPLES, Samuel; b 23 Mar 1762, Buckingham Co; d 23 Mar 1825 **RU:** Major, Served in 6th Cont Line. Also served as private in Capt Nicolas Cabell's Co, Albemarle Co Militia, Apr 1776. Was at siege at Yorktown and for gallantry there was promoted to Maj Oct 1781 **CEM:** Stuart Town; GPS unk; Chestnut St, Stuart; Patrick **GS:** Y **SP:** Lucinda Penn (1771-1850) **VI:** Son of John & Keziah (Norman) Staples. GS moved fr home cemetery **P:** unk **BLW:** unk **RG:** Y **MK:** N **PH:** unk **SS:** E, pg 735; CD; DC pg 154; SAR P-296152 **BS:** JLARC 30; 60 Patrick; 196.

STARK, William; b 1757; d 1 Aug 1844 **RU:** Second Lieutenant, Enl serv in Dinwiddie Co 1776. Served in 6th VA Regt, VA Line. Was severely wounded at Battle of Brandywine and resigned fr Army 1778 **CEM:** Cedar Grove; GPS 36.858780, -76.283520; 238 E Princess Anne Rd; Norfolk City **GS:** N **SP:** Mar

RU=Rank/Unit   CEM=Cemetery   GS=Gravestone   SP=Spousal Information
VI=Other Veteran Info   P=Pension   BLW=Bounty/Land Warrant   RG=Registered Grave
MK=SAR/DAR Marker   PH=Photo   SS=Service Source   BS=Burial Source

395

during RW period **VI**: Sol appl pen 23 Jul 1832 Norfolk age 75. S7592 **P**: Y **BLW**: unk **RG**: Y **MK**: N **PH**: Y **SS**: K Vol pg 151; BR 1827; CG Vol 3 pg 3300; SAR P-341118 **BS**: 176.

STARK (STARKE), William; b 14 Dec 1754; d 29 Dec 1838 **RU**: Sergeant, VA Line. Ent serv Stafford Co 1781 serving under Capts Harding & Ballard, under Cols Philips & Darke **CEM**: Stark-Payne; GPS unk; On Quantico Marine Base opposite Ruby fire station; Stafford **GS**: U **SP**: mar (16 Feb 1786) Mary Kendall (1770-__) d/o John & (-----) Kendall **VI**: Widow appl pen 18 Aug 1852 age 92 & appl for BLW 3 Dec 1855. Pen #R10059 **P**: Y **BLW**: Y **RG**: Y **MK**: unk **PH**: unk **SS**: K Vol 5 pg 152; CG pg 3300; DAR A108990; SAR P-296235 **BS**: JLARC 48, 63; 3 pg 365.

STARKES, William Harrison; b 1762; d 1849 **RU**: Private, served as Drummer in Cont Line **CEM**: Starkes-Gunter; GPS not determined; loc Rt 601 or 655) Manteo Rd; Buckingham **GS**: Yes, govt lists service **SP**: Not determined **VI**: Nothing further **P**: Unk **BLW**: Unk **RG**: N **MK**: N **PH**: N **SS**: B **BS**: 196.

STATLER, John; b 1759, d 30 Jun 1856 **RU**: Patriot Supported cause by paying supply tax included in his personal property tax in 1782, Loudoun Co **CEM**: New Jerusalem Lutheran Church; GPS 39.25736, -77.63891, GS 39.25723, -77.63663; 12942 Lutheran Church Rd, Lovettsville; Loudoun **GS**: Yes **SP**: Priscilla Vencil (__28 Feb 1852) **VI**: No further data **P**: N **BLW**: N **RG**: Y **MK**: N **PH**: N **SS**: DV Loudoun Co, list 1782B, image 14 pdf; SAR bio rpt swub Mar 2021 **BS**: 196; cem visit.

STAUTZER, Jacob; b unk; d 1781 **RU**: Soldier, Served in Royal Deaux Ponts Bn and died fr battle at Yorktown **CEM**: French Memorial; GPS 36.81944, -79.39933; Yorktown; York **GS**: U **SP**: No info **VI**: No further data **P**: unk **BLW**: unk **RG**: Y **MK**: unk **PH**: unk **SS**: J-Yorktown Historian; SAR P-296403 **BS**: JLARC 1, 74.

STEELE, Alexander; b c1735, Brunswick Co; d 25 Jun 1808 **RU**: First Lieutenant, Private in Capt John Peyton's Co 3rd VA Regt, commanded by Col George Weedon, Oct 1776 to 1 Jan 1777 **CEM**: Second Concord Presbyterian; GPS 37.34209, -78.96585; Phoebe Pond Rd Rt 609 E of Concord; Appomattox **GS**: Y **SP**: Mar (15 May 1758 (probably) Bedford Co) Elizabeth Carson Helm **VI**: No further data **P**: unk **BLW**: unk **RG**: Y **MK**: unk **PH**: unk **SS**: AP; SAR P-296667 **BS**: JLARC 36; 196.

STEELE, Andrew; b 1743; d 13 Feb 1800 **RU**: Soldier, Served in Bedford Militia **CEM**: Old Providence; GPS 37.96151, -79.71000; 1005 Spottswood Rd, Spottswood; Augusta **GS**: Y **SP**: Mary Ramsey **VI**: Newer Govt stone. Name also on SAR cemetery plaque **P**: unk **BLW**: unk **RG**: N **MK**: Y SAR plaque **PH**: unk **SS**: B; BT **BS**: JLARC 62; 196.

STEELE, David; b 1756; d 1840 **RU**: Private/Rifleman, Served in VA Cont Line and Lee's Regt VA Vol. Severely wounded by numerous saber cuts at Guilford CH and taken as prisoner **CEM**: Old Providence; GPS 37.96151, -79.71000; 1005 Spottswood Rd, Spottswood; Augusta **GS**: Y **SP**: No info **VI**: Invalid pen 4 Sep 1790. Increased under act of 16 Apr 1816. S7605. Has Govt stone with no dates. Name in on SAR plaque at cemetery **P**: Y **BLW**: unk **RG**: Y **MK**: Y SAR plaque **PH**: unk **SS**: B; K pg 155; CG Vol 3 pg 3310; SAR P-296678 **BS**: JLARC 2, 8, 9, 62, 63; 80 vol4, pg 71.

STEELE, James Wendle; b 1752; d 10 Jan 1823 **RU**: Lieutenant, Served in Capt Tate's Co, Augusta Co **CEM**: Old Providence; GPS 37.96151, -79.71000; 1005 Spottswood Rd, Spottswood; Augusta **GS**: Y **SP**: Mar (17 May 1781) Margaret "Maggie" Parks (1765-1848), d/o John & (-----) Parks **VI**: One of 12 Augusta Co Justices. Newer Govt stone. Name also on SAR cemetery plaque **P**: unk **BLW**: unk **RG**: Y **MK**: Y SAR plaque **PH**: Y **SS**: B; BT; K pg 213; SAR P-296707 **BS**: JLARC 2 ,8, 62; ; 80 vol4, pg 71; 196.

STEELE, John; b unk; d 1814 **RU**: Lieutenant, Served in Augusta Co Militia and 8th & 9th VA Regt **CEM**: Tinkling Spring Presbyterian; GPS 38.08472, -78.98278; 30 Tinkling Spring Dr, Fishersville; Augusta **GS**: N **SP**: No info **VI**: Person same name and death yr has Gov't Grave stone in the Old Providence cemetery in Augusta Co, thus perhaps only memorialized there or in this cemetery, Perhaps was promoted to Capt before Oct 1783. Rec'd 2667 acres BLW 20 May 1783 for 3 yrs service and on 12 Feb 1808, 387 acres for an additional 7 mos service **P**: unk **BLW**: Y **RG**: Y **MK**: unk **PH**: N **SS**: SAR P-296718; C pg 113; N pg 44 **BS**: JLARC 62, 63.

RU=Rank/Unit	CEM=Cemetery	GS=Gravestone	SP=Spousal Information
VI=Other Veteran Info	P=Pension	BLW=Bounty/Land Warrant	RG=Registered Grave
MK=SAR/DAR Marker	PH=Photo	SS=Service Source	BS=Burial Source

STEELE, John; b unk; d 1804 **RU:** Soldier/Patriot, Gave use of horse for 29 days **CEM:** Tinkling Spring Presbyterian; GPS 38.08472, -78.98278; 30 Tinkling Spring Dr, Fishersville; Augusta **GS:** N **SP:** No info **VI:** No further data **P:** unk **BLW:** unk **RG:** N **MK:** N **PH:** N **SS:** D pg 66 Augusta Co **BS:** JLARC 62; 196.

STEELE, John Jr; b unk; d 1814 **RU:** Private, Served in Capt Tate's Co, Augusta Co Militia **CEM:** Old Providence; GPS 37.96151, -79.71000; 1005 Spottswood Rd, Spottswood; Augusta **GS:** Y **SP:** No info **VI:** Newer Govt stone. Name also on SAR cemetery plaque. Person same name and death yr bur in Tinkling Springs cemetery but believed not to be him **P:** unk **BLW:** unk **RG** N **MK:** Y SAR plaque **PH:** unk **SS:** B; BT **BS:** 196.

STEELE, John Sr; b 1755; d 1804 **RU:** Private, Served in Capt Tate's Co, Augusta Militia **CEM:** Old Providence; GPS 37.96151, -79.71000; 1005 Spottswood Rd, Spottswood; Augusta **GS:** Y **SP:** No info **VI:** Newer Govt stone. Name also on SAR cemetery plaque **P:** unk **BLW:** unk **RG:**Y **MK:** Y SAR plaque **PH:** unk **SS:** B; BT; E pg 737; SAR P-296717 **BS:** 44;196.

STEELE, Nathaniel; b 1722; d 30 May 1796 **RU:** Soldier/ Patriot, Gave material aid to cause **CEM:** Old Providence; GPS 37.96151, -79.71000; 1005 Spottswood Rd, Spottswood; Augusta **GS:** Y **SP:** 1) Lydia Pratt 2) Rosannah (-----) (__-1808) **VI:** Son of David & Janet (-----) Steele. Stone nearly destroyed. Name on SAR plaque at cemetery **P:** unk **BLW:** unk **RG:** Y**MK:** Y SAR plaque **PH:** unk **SS:** SAR P-296737; BT **BS:** JLARC 8; 196.

STEELE, Robert; b 1730 or 1733; d 10 Apr 1800 **RU:** Private, Served in Capt Campbell's Co, Augusta Co Militia **CEM:** Old Providence; GPS 37.96151, -79.71000; 1005 Spottswood Rd, Spottswood; Augusta **GS:** U **SP:** Elizabeth Wendel **VI:** No further data **P:** unk **BLW:** unk **RG:** N **MK:** unk **PH:** unk **SS:** E pg 738 **BS:** 196.

STEELE, Robert; b 1750; d 11 Jun 1821 **RU:** Soldier, Served in Capt John Adam's Co, Montgomery Co Militia **CEM:** Steele Family; GPS unk; nr Bland; Wythe **GS:** U **SP:** 1) Mary Keeling 2) Rebecca Oury **VI:** No further data **P:** unk **BLW:** unk **RG:** Y **MK:** unk **PH:** unk **SS:** J-NSSAR 2000 Reg; DD cites VA Mag Hist & Blog Vol 47 2nd series pg 160; SAR P-296745; DAR A108285 **BS:** JLARC 76.

STEELE, Samuel Jr; b 1747; d 8 Jun 1837 **RU:** Captain, Commanded a company of Rockbridge Militia, 5 May 1778. Resigned commission on 5 May 1779 **CEM:** Old Providence; GPS 37.96151, -79.71000; 1005 Spottswood Rd, Spottswood; Augusta **GS:** Y **SP:** Margret Campbell **VI:** Son of Samuel Steele, Sr & Margaret Fulton **P:** unk **BLW:** unk **RG:** N **MK:** Y SAR plaque **PH:** unk **SS:** BT **BS:** JLARC 2, 8, 62, 63; 196.

STEELE, Samuel Jr; b 1762; d 1823 **RU:** Private, Served in a VA Regt and Capt Smith's Co, Augusta Co Militia **CEM:** Old Providence; GPS 37.96151, -79.71000; 1005 Spottswood Rd, Spottswood; Augusta **GS:** Y **SP:** No info **VI:** Govt grave stone **P:** N **BLW:** N **RG:**Y **MK:** N **PH:** N **SS:** E pg 738; SAR P-296755 **BS:** 196.

STEELE, Samuel Sr; b 1707; d 16 Feb 1790 **RU:** Patriot, Gave material aid to cause **CEM:** Old Providence; GPS 37.96151, -79.71000; 1005 Spottswood Rd, Spottswood; Augusta **GS:** Y **SP:** 1) Sarah Campbell (1720-1748) 2) Margraret Fulton 3) Martha Fulton, sister of Margaret **VI:** No further data **P:** N **BLW:** N **RG:** Y **MK:** Y SAR plaque **PH:** unk **SS:** AL Ct Bk pg 7 Augusta Co; SAR P-296782 **BS:** JLARC 8 ,9, 62, 63; ;80 vol4, pg 72. 196.

STEELE, Thomas; b 1750; d 1834 **RU:** Private, 3rd Regt, 3rd Cont Line **CEM:** Old Methodist Church; GPS 39.08620, -78.21670; 5291 Main St, Stephens City; Frederick **GS:** Y **SP:** Possible marriage (24 Feb 1816 Frederick Co by George M. Frye) Sarah Carver **VI:** No further data **P:** unk **BLW:** unk **RG:** N **MK:** N **PH:** unk **SS:** E pg 738; AP roll 3rd Regt **BS:** 112; 196.

STEELE, Thomas; b 3 Jun 1747; d 4 Jul 1799 **RU:** Soldier, Ent serv Rockbridge Co on 2 Nov 1779 **CEM:** Old Providence; GPS 37.96151, -79.71000; 1005 Spottswood Rd, Spottswood; Augusta **GS:** Y **SP:** Jane Moore (1750-2 Jan 1826) **VI:** Son of David & Janet (-----) Steele. Name is on SAR plaque at cemetery **P:** unk **BLW:** unk **RG:**Y **MK:** Y SAR plaque **PH:** unk **SS:** BT; SAR P-296761 **BS:** JLARC 62, 63; 196.

STEELE, William; b unk; d 1818 **RU:** Private, Served in Capt Tate's Co, Augusta Co Militia **CEM:** Old Providence; GPS 37.96151, -79.71000; 1005 Spottswood Rd, Spottswood; Augusta **GS:** Y **SP:** No info

RU=Rank/Unit	CEM=Cemetery	GS=Gravestone	SP=Spousal Information
VI=Other Veteran Info	P=Pension	BLW=Bounty/Land Warrant	RG=Registered Grave
MK=SAR/DAR Marker	PH=Photo	SS=Service Source	BS=Burial Source

VI: Newer Govt stone. Name is on SAR cemetery plaque **P**: unk **BLW**: unk **RG**: Y **MK**: Y SAR plaque **PH**: unk **SS**: B; E pg 738; BT; SAR P-296767 **BS**: JLARC 63; 196.

STEERS, Isaac; b 1757; d 1824 **RU**: Patriot, Gave material aid to cause **CEM**: Fairfax Meeting House; GPS 39.18557, -77.60589; Water St & Waterford Rd, Waterford; Loudoun **GS**: Y **SP**: No info **VI**: No further data **P**: N **BLW**: N **RG**: N **MK**: N **PH**: unk **SS**: D Vol 2 pg 602; AL Ct Bk pg 2, 21 Loudoun Co **BS**: 25 pg 298.

STEFFEY, John; b 21 Dec 1745, Lancaster Co, PA; d 6 Jun 1836 **RU**: Private, Ent serv Lancaster Co PA in PA Line. Served in Capt Farnstsler's Co PA Militia **CEM**: St Paul's Lutheran; GPS 36.91173, -81.23484; 330 St Pauls Church Rd, Rural Retreat; Wythe **GS**: U **SP**: 1) (-----) 2) Mar (10 Jan 1813 Wythe Co VA while in service War of 1812) Rosanna (Rosena) Philippy (c1780-__) **VI**: Also had War of 1812 service. Sol appl pen 26 May 1834 Wythe Co. Widow appl pen 24 Jan 1854 Wythe Co VA age 74. W7205, Recd BLW #26543-160-55 **P**: Y **BLW**: Y **RG**: Y **MK**: unk **PH**: unk **SS**: K Vol 5 pg 157; CG Vol 3 pg 3314; SAR P-296843 **BS**: JLARC 4, 40,123.

STEIN, Jean; b unk; d 1781 **RU**: Soldier, Served in Royal Deaux Ponts Bn and died fr battle at Yorktown **CEM**: French Memorial; GPS 36.81944, -79.39933; Yorktown; York **GS**: U **SP**: No info **VI**: No further data **P**: unk **BLW**: unk **RG**: Y **MK**: unk **PH**: unk **SS**: J-Yorktown Historian; SAR P-296857 **BS**: JLARC 1, 74.

STEPHAN, Guillaume; b unk; d 1781 **RU**: Seaman, Served on "Auguste" and died from Yorktown battle **CEM**: French Memorial; GPS 36.81944, -79.39933; Yorktown; York **GS**: U **SP**: No info **VI**: No further data **P**: unk **BLW**: unk **RG**: Y **MK**: unk **PH**: unk **SS**: J-Yorktown Historian; SAR P-296898 **BS**: JLARC 1, 74.

STEPHENS, Lawrence; b 1755, Frederick Co; d 1847 **RU**: Corporal, Served in VA Line 1st VA Regt. Lived in Fincastle Co (later Montgomery) at enl 1775 in Frederick Co **CEM**: Stephens aka Hurst; GPS unk; SR 100 S to SR 607 E to Jett farm, Wytheville, nr Carroll Co line; Wythe **GS**: U **SP**: Joanna (-----) **VI**: Sol appl pen10 Dec 1832 Wythe Co. S7639 **P**: Y **BLW**: unk **RG**: Y **MK**: unk **PH**: unk **SS**: K Vol 5 pg 159; CG Vol 3 pg 3315; SAR P-296973 **BS**: JLARC 2, 4, 40, 43,123; 80 vol4, pg 71..

STEPHENS, Lewis, Sr; b 1714, Germantown, Philadelphia, PA; d 22 Jul 1802 **RU**: Patriot, Gave material aid to cause, Frederick Co **CEM**: :Old Town Cemetery; GPS not determined; lots 76 & 77, Mulberry St, Town of Stephensburg **GS**: Unk **SP**: mar (1743, Frederick Co) Mary Rittenhouse (1715 PA-Apr 1798), d/o Peter Rittenhouse (1690-1782) & Maria Christina (-----) **VI**: Son of Peter Stephens (3 Mar 1687-Nov 1757) & Maria Christina (-----) **P**: N **BLW**: N **RG**: N **MK**: N **PH**: N **SS**: D, vol 2, pgs 377, 387; DAR A109042 **BS**: 196.

STEPHENS, Lewis, Jr; b 1746; d 1822 **RU**: Private, 8th VA Regt **CEM**: :Old Town Cemetery; GPS not determined; lots 76 & 77, Mulberry St, Town of Stephensburg **GS**: Unk **SP**: mar (1770) Mary Henning (1748-1832) d/o Samuel Henning & Eleanor(-----) **VI**: Son of Lewis Stephens (1714 PA-22 Jul 1802) & Mary Rittenhouse (1715 PA-Apr 1798) **P**: N **BLW**: N **RG**: N **MK**: N **PH**: N **SS**: AP Fold3 serv rec **BS**: 196.

STEPHENS, Lewis; b 1747; d 25 Nov 1817 **RU**: Patriot, gave material aid to the cause **CEM**: Old Stephens Family; GPS 38.527625, -78.747620; 1844 Maryz Rd, Lacey Springs; Rockingham **GS**: Y **SP**: (-----) Woolf (Wolf), d/o Valentine & (-----) Woolf (1721-3 Jun 1808) **VI**: No further data **P**: N **BLW**: N **RG**: N **MK**: N **PH**: N **SS**: Al Ct bk pgs 9, 40, Frederick Co **BS**: 196.

STEPHENSON, John; b 1710; d 23 Nov 1778 **RU**: Patriot, Paid for recruiting doctor in Western Augusta Co, Mar 1776 and gave 120# flour 26 Aug 1782 **CEM**: Cross Keys; GPS unk; Cross Keys; Rockingham **GS**: U **SP**: 1) Sarah Waite d/o James & Catherine (Rothgab) Waite. 2) Esther (Waite) Taylor, widow of John Taylor & d/o James & Catherine (Rothgab) Waite (Sarah's sister) **VI**: Signed the Orange Co Importation books in 1740 with wife Mary & daughter Sarah **P**: N **BLW**: N **RG**: N **MK**: unk **PH**: unk **SS**: E pg 739; CY pg 100 **BS**: 196.

STEPTOE, James Jr; b 16 Jul 1750, Westmoreland Co; d 9 Feb 1826 **RU**: Patriot, Had civil service as Clerk of Bedford Co **CEM**: Callaway-Steptoe; GPS 37.30560, -79.29470; Rt 460, New London; Bedford

RU=Rank/Unit	CEM=Cemetery	GS=Gravestone	SP=Spousal Information
VI=Other Veteran Info	P=Pension	BLW=Bounty/Land Warrant	RG=Registered Grave
MK=SAR/DAR Marker	PH=Photo	SS=Service Source	BS=Burial Source

GS: Y **SP**: No info **VI**: Clerk of Bedford Co Ct 54 yrs. Died in Campbell Co **P**: N **BLW**: N **RG**: N **MK**: unk **PH**: unk **SS**: DAR A108749; DD **BS**: 196.

STERRETT, William; b c1757; d Apr 1818 **RU**: Private, Served in Capt Bell's Co, Augusta Co Militia **CEM**: Hebron Presbyterian; GPS 38.14140, -79.15500; 423 Hebron Rd; Staunton City **GS**: Y **SP**: No info **VI**: No further data **P**: unk **BLW**: unk **RG**: N **MK**: N **PH**: unk **SS**: E pg 740 **BS**: 36 pg 67; 196.

STEVENS, Edward; b 1745, Culpeper Co; d 17 Aug 1820 **RU**: Colonel/Patriot, Was Lt Col in Culpeper District Bn 1775. Served in battles at Great Bridge, Brandywine, Camden, Guilford CH, and siege of Yorktown. As public servant signed Culpeper Co petitions **CEM**: Masonic Cemetery; GPS 38.484502, -77.994604; 950 N Main, Culpeper; Culpeper **GS**: U **SP**: Gilly Coleman, d/o Robert Esq & (-----) Coleman **VI**: Name is on VA Historical Road sign; SAR marker **P**: unk **BLW**: Y **RG**: Y **MK**: Y SAR granite & DAR plaque **PH**: Y **SS**: J-NSSAR 1993 Reg; AL Ct Bk I pg 1, 52 Culpeper Co; CE pg 16; CZ pg 417; SAR P-297265 **BS**: JLARC 1; 196.

STEVENS, John; b 1746; d Sep 1831 **RU**: Private, Served in Capt Daniel Trigg's Co, Montgomery Co Militia **CEM**: Northern Methodist; GPS 38.35777, -78.94344; Rt 867 Old Bridgewater Rd, Mt Crawford; Rockingham **GS**: N **SP**: No info **VI**: No further data **P**: N **BLW**: N **RG**: N **MK**: unk **PH**: N **SS**: G pg 221 **BS**: 196.

STEVENS, John (1764-1820) See Appendix G Addenda

STEVENSON, James; b 1740; d Jun 1809 **RU**: Patriot, Paid the personal property tax which included Rev War supply tax, Culpeper Co, 1783 **CEM**: Masonic Cemetery; GPS 38.30198, -77.46142; 900 Charles St; Fredericksburg City **GS**: U **SP**: Mar (1759) Francis Littlepage **VI**: Listed as a Reverend on Culpeper Co tax lists. Died in Culpeper Co **P**: unk **BLW**: unk **RG**: Y **MK**: Y SAR plaque **PH**: unk **SS**: DAR Ancestor #A109240; SAR P-297556; DV Culpeper Co 1783 **BS**: JLARC 2; 80 vol4, pg 76.

STEVENSON (STEPHENSON), William Jr; b unk; d 1805 **RU**: Lieutenant/Patriot, Had Recruiting duty 13 Feb 1777. Later served in Col Charles Harrison's Regt of Artillery in York Co, serving until 1783. Gave material aid to cause **CEM**: Stephenson Family; GPS unk; Clayton Rd; Southampton **GS**: N **SP**: No info **VI**: Recd BLW 2666 acres **P**: unk **BLW**: Y **RG**: N **MK**: N **PH**: N **SS**: N pg 454; AL Ct Bk pg 12 Southampton Co; CZ pg 419 **BS**: 53 vol I pg 37.

STEWART, Charles; b c1730, Norfolk; d Feb 1801 **RU**: Second Lieutenant, Served 28 Jun 1777 in 15th VA Regt which later became the 11th Regt, serving 3 yrs. Stone says served in "11 Va. Mil. Inf" **CEM**: Stewart Family; GPS unk; Beechwood Plantation on Dismal Swamp Trail; Chesapeake City **GS**: N **SP**: Martha Foreman **VI**: Recd BLW 2666 acres **P**: unk **BLW**: Y **RG**: N **MK**: N **PH**: N **SS**: N pg 1211; DAR A109390; SAR P-297667 **BS**: DAR Rpt, JLARC 88; 63 pg 101.

STEWART, John; b 1746; d Sep 1800 **RU**: Captain, Served as Marine officer US Navy and appointed Capt 24 Aug 1776 **CEM**: Old Presbyterian Meeting House; GPS 38.48528, -77.23532; 323 S Fairfax St; Alexandria City **GS**: N **SP**: No info **VI**: Bur 12 Sep 1800, age 54. Listed on SAR plaque in cemetery **P**: unk **BLW**: unk **RG**: Y **MK**: Y SAR plaque **PH**: N **SS**: J-NSSAR 1993 Reg; AK; CI General Navy Register; SAR P-297803 **BS**: JLARC 1; 23 pg 108; 196.

STEWART, William; b 1757,Halifax Co, d 10 Sep 1850 **RU**:Private, NC service in Capts George Maxwell, Benjamin Hern in Cols Isaac Shelby's and William Campbell's Regt in battle at Kings Mountain **CEM**: Joseph Carter; GPS 36.7116930, -82.6977830; loc Johnson Rd nr Rye Cove; Scott **GS**: Unk **SP**: mar (c1789 Russell Co) Jemima Carter (1772, King George Co-1843) **VI**: Son of John Stewart & Susanna Fulkerson. Rec'd pen # S11472: **P**: Y **BLW**: Unk **RG**: Y **MK**: N **PH** N **SS**: DAR A109724; SAR P-297896 **BS**: 196.

STEWART, William; b c1749; d 14 Nov 1824 **RU**: Private, Served in Capt Pierce's Co, Montgomery Co, 6 Apr 1781 **CEM**: Glade Spring Presbyterian; GPS 36.76720, -81.78720; 33234 Lee Hwy, Glade Spring; Washington **GS**: Y **SP**: Susan (-----) (9 Sep 1760-1821) **VI**: No further data **P**: N **BLW**: N **RG**: N **MK**: N **PH**: unk **SS**: E pg 472; G pg 241 **BS**: 78, pg 188; 196.

STICKLEY, Benjamin; b c1750; d c1796 **RU**: Lieutenant/Patriot, Was Lt 31 May 1782, Shenandoah Co Militia. Gave material aid to cause **CEM**: Stickley Family; GPS unk; Strasburg; Shenandoah **GS**: U **SP**:

RU=Rank/Unit VI=Other Veteran Info MK=SAR/DAR Marker CEM=Cemetery P=Pension PH=Photo GS=Gravestone BLW=Bounty/Land Warrant SS=Service Source SP=Spousal Information RG=Registered Grave BS=Burial Source

399

Mar (1772) Ann Stover (__, Strasburg-aft 1796) **VI:** No further data **P:** unk **BLW:** unk **RG:** Y **MK:** U **PH:** unk **SS:** DAR A109762; D Vol 3 pg 841; E pg 742; SAR P-297935 **BS:** 04.

STIFF, James; b 1757, Cumberland Co; d 19 May 1837 **RU:** Private, Ent Serv Bedford Co Militia 1775 in 5th VA Regt in Capt Thomas Leftwich Co **CEM:** Stiff Family; GPS unk; Union Church Rd 1 mi past Union Methodist, Thaxton; Bedford **GS:** Y **SP:** Mar (1 Sep 1779) Mary "Molly" Lewis (bc1760-24 May 1841) **VI:** Appl pen 12 Feb 1833, Russell Parish, Bedford Co, age 76. Widow appl pen 20 Jun 1839 Bedford Co age 79. W4344 Stone reads "Jas. Stiff, Fowler's Co. 5 VA Regt. Rev War". **P:** Y **BLW:** unk **RG:** Y **MK:** N **PH:** unk **SS:** B; K Vol 5 pg 169-70; CG Vol 3 pg 3341; SAR P-298014; DAR A090999 **BS:** JLARC 2; 80 vol4, pg 78; 196.

STIGLEMAN (STICKLEMAN, STIGGLEMAN, STRICKLEMAN, STEICHELMAN), Philip (Phillip); b c1758, Germany; d Bef 1841 **RU:** Private, Served in Capt Alexander Martin & Col Peter Grub's cos of Lancaster Co, PA Militia. Destined for "Camp in ye Jerseys" 13 Aug 1776 **CEM:** Goodykoontz; GPS unk; Rt 729; Floyd **GS:** N **SP:** Margaret Weaver d/o Peter & (-----) Weaver **VI:** Died in Floyd/Montgomery Co. Widow moved to Wayne Co IN & bur there **P:** unk **BLW:** unk **RG:** Y **MK:** N **PH:** N **SS:** CI: Fold3 PA Archives, 3rd Serv, vol23, pg 429,430; SAR P-298023; DAR A109867 **BS:** JLARC 29.

STIMSON, Jeremiah, Jr See Appendix G Addenda

STITH, Buckner; b 1722, Rockspring, Brunswick Co; d Jul 1791 **RU:** Captain, Appointed Capt in Brunswick Co Militia Jan 1782 **CEM:** Mt Vernon Unitarian; GPS unk; 1909 Winhill Ln; Alexandria City **GS:** N **SP:** Susanna Munford **VI:** No further data **P:** unk **BLW:** unk **RG:** Y **MK:** N **PH:** N **SS:** SAR P-298268; DAR A110256; G pg 80 **BS:** 61 FX 298.

STITH, Griffin; b 24 Aug 1753, Northampton Co; d 18 Jun 1794 **RU:** Patriot, Was Clerk of Northampton Co 13 Mar 1777. Was paid for moving prisoners fr Eastern Shore **CEM:** Kings Creek; GPS unk; Cape Charles; Northampton **GS:** U **SP:** Ann Stratton (Sep 1757-1779) **VI:** Son of Griffin (1720-1784) & Mary (Blaikley) (1726-1784) Stith **P:** N **BLW:** N **RG:** N **MK:** unk **PH:** unk **SS:** N pg 538; G pg 563 **BS:** 196.

STITH, John Buckner; b 24 Mar 1755, d 10 Feb 1810 **RU:** Major 4th VA Regt. Was in battles of Trenton, Princeton, Brandywine, Germanton and Monmooth, **CEM:** Mount Vernon Estate; GPS 38.7068560, -77.0887230 loc on Stith field on the estate **GS:** Lost **SP:** Mar 11 Dec 1783 St Pauls Parish, King George Co, Ann Washington (1764-1823), d/o Lawrence Washington IV of Chotank (March 31, 1727-1804) & Elizabeth Dade **VI:** Son of Buckner Stith & Susannah Field. Rec'd BLW 300 acres **P:** N **BLW:** Y **RG:** Y **MK:** N **PH:** N **SS** DAR A110259; SAR P-298270 **BS:** 196

STOBO, Jacob; b c1760; d 30 Jan 1794 **RU:** Captain, Taken prisoner when US Sloop "Washington" was captured 29 May 1781 in NY. Was sent to Old Mill Prison in England **CEM:** Trinity Episcopal; GPS 36.83459, -76.30105; 500 Court St; Portsmouth City **GS:** Y **SP:** Mar (12 Oct 1783 Baltimore MD) Sarah Hughes **VI:** Resided in Philadelphia PA before coming to VA. Died in Gosport, Portsmouth **P:** unk **BLW:** unk **RG:** Y **MK:** Y SAR plaque **PH:** unk **SS:** B gives rank; CI Revolution Navy & Privateer Records; SAR P-336644 **BS:** 92 stone 15; 196.

STOHER, Balthazar; b unk; d 1781 **RU:** Soldier, Served in Royal Deaux Ponts Bn and died fr battle at Yorktown **CEM:** French Memorial; GPS 36.81944, -79.39933; Yorktown; York **GS:** U **SP:** No info **VI:** No further data **P:** unk **BLW:** unk **RG:** Y **MK:** unk **PH:** unk **SS:** J-Yorktown Historian; SAR P-296491 **BS:** JLARC 1, 74.

STONE, Hawkin/Hawkins/Hawken; b 1735 Charles Co MD; d 10 Mar 1810 **RU:** Patriot, Provided 5 beeves one time and 3 another time to cause **CEM:** Aquia Episcopal; GPS 38.46466, -77.40325; 2938 Jeff Davis Hwy, Aquia; Stafford **GS:** Y **SP:** 1) (-----) 2) Jemima Smith 3) Elizabeth (Burroughs) **VI:** Originally bur in Scott Family cem at Dipple. Reinterred to Aquia Cemetery in 1942. Son of Barton Stone and Sarah (-----) **P:** N **BLW:** N **RG:** Y **MK:** Y SAR **PH:** Y **SS:** D Vol 3 pg 876; DAR A206843; SAR P-333980 **BS:** 03 pg 129.

STONE, Jeremiah; b 1742; d 1827 **RU:** Private, Served in Capt Love's Co, Montgomery Co Militia **CEM:** Stone Family; GPS unk; Elk Creek; Grayson **GS:** U **SP:** Susannah Hurt (1744-18 Sep 1809) **VI:** Son of Barton & Sarah (-----) Stone **P:** unk **BLW:** unk **RG:** Y **MK:** unk **PH:** unk **SS:** D Fr Wm Co; G pg 233; AK Fairfax Resolves 2014; DAR A110037; SAR P-298605 **BS:** JLARC 1, 3; 94; 196.

RU=Rank/Unit	CEM=Cemetery	GS=Gravestone	SP=Spousal Information
VI=Other Veteran Info	P=Pension	BLW=Bounty/Land Warrant	RG=Registered Grave
MK=SAR/DAR Marker	PH=Photo	SS=Service Source	BS=Burial Source

400

STONE, John; b 25 Nov 1754, Richmond Co; d 10 Jul 1824 **RU**: Private/Patriot, Served in Cont Line. Received money for services as soldier in infantry, Nov 1782 **CEM**: Hubbard-Stone; **GPS** unk; Rt 650 Hermosa; Pittsylvania **GS**: Y **SP**: Dollie Hoskins (10 Nov 1761-4 Apr 1862) **VI**: Son of Joshua & Dolly (Hoskins) Stone **P**: unk **BLW**: unk **RG**: Y **MK**: U **PH**: unk **SS**: J-NSSAR 2000 Reg; SAR P-298626; DAR A110087 **BS**: JLARC 76; 196.

STONE, Joshua; b 1744; d 20 Oct 1821 **RU**: Captain, Was 2nd Lt 23 Oct 1777 in Capt Joseph Farris Co and 1st Lt 20 Jun 1780 Capt John Buckley Co. Later Capt of militia himself **CEM**: Stone Family; **GPS** unk; Nr Mulberry Church; Pittsylvania **GS**: Y **SP**: Mary Hoskins **VI**: Son of Josiah & Wilmoth (Bryant) Stone **P**: unk **BLW**: unk **RG**: Y **MK**: N **PH**: unk **SS**: G pg 269; SAR P-298660 **BS**: 174 AS, AW.

STONE, William; b c1765; d 23 May 1827 **RU**: Private, Ent serv 1777 in 1st VA Regt & 8th, 10th, 14th Cont Lines **CEM**: City Cemetery; **GPS** 38.30112, -77.46628; 1000 Washington Ave; Fredericksburg City **GS**: Y **SP**: Mar (1781) Mary McGuire (c1751 or c1761-__) **VI**: Sol appl pen 8 May 1818 Stafford Co age 59. Pen rec 1829 or 1830, Stafford Co. Widow appl pen 7 Dec 1838 Harrison Co KY age 77. However in 1839 she gave age as abt 88. W8752 **P**: Y **BLW**: unk **RG**: N **MK**: N **PH**: unk **SS**: A pg 195; E pg 744; CG Vol 3 pg 3358 **BS**: 06 pg 29.

STONE, William B; b 8 Sep 1757; d 15 Oct 1793 **RU**: unk, Served in 1st VA State Regt and 8th, 10th 14th Cont Lines **CEM**: Edrington Family; **GPS** 38.44378, -77.38064; End of Rt 692, Quarry Rd, across fr 34 Edrington Court; Stafford **GS**: Y **SP**: No info **VI**: Son of Barton & Sarah (-----) Stone. Recd pen in Stafford Co **P**: Y **BLW**: unk **RG**: Y **MK**: N **PH**: Y **SS**: E pg 744; SAR P-334408 **BS**: 03 pg 196.

STONEBRIDGE, John; b unk; d 1805 **RU**: Patriot, Gave material aid to the cause **CEM**: Back Creek Quaker, aka Gainesboro United Methodist; **GPS** 39.27861, -78.25694; 166 Siler Ln, Gainesboro; Frederick **GS**: Y **SP**: No info **VI**: No further data **P**: N **BLW**: N **RG**: N **MK**: N **PH**: unk **SS**: AL Ct Bk pg 40 **BS**: 59 pg 319.

STORKE, William; b c1753; d 27 Aug 1822 **RU**: Patriot, Gave beef to cause, King George Co, 1781 **CEM**: Masonic Cemetery; **GPS** 38.30198, -77.46142; 900 Charles St; Fredericksburg City **GS**: Y **SP**: 1) Anna Rosetta Bryson 2) Elizabeth Washington **VI**: Vestryman St George Church. Son of John & Frances (-----) Storke **P**: N **BLW**: N **RG**: N **MK**: Y SAR plaque **PH**: unk **SS**: D pg 568 **BS**: 11 pg 114-5.

STOUDERT, Claude; b unk; d 1781 **RU**: Soldier, Served in Gatinais Bn and died fr battle at Yorktown **CEM**: French Memorial; **GPS** 36.81944, -79.39933; Yorktown; York **GS**: U **SP**: No info **VI**: No further data **P**: unk **BLW**: unk **RG**: Y **MK**: unk **PH**: unk **SS**: J-Yorktown Historian; SAR P-298989 **BS**: JLARC 1, 74.

STOUTSENBERGER (STOUSEBERGER), John; b 1762; d 3 Mar 1837 **RU**: Drum major, Ent serv 1778. Was Drum Major PA Artillery Regt **CEM**: New Jerusalem Lutheran; GS 39.257280, -77.639123; 12942 Lutheran Church Rd, Lovettsville; Loudoun **GS**: U **SP**: Maria Margaretha Kitchinden (c1762-c1847). Also Elizabeth Conklin (SAR) **VI**: Widow pen 1838 Loudoun Co. 3 children appl pen, 1854, W6207 **P**: Y **BLW**: unk **RG**: Y **MK**: SAR granite **PH**: unk **SS**: K Vol 5 pg 179; SAR P-299102 **BS**: JLARC 4, 32.

STOVER, Peter; b 1715; d 1799 **RU**: Patriot, Gave material aid to cause **CEM**: Riverview; **GPS** 38.98420, -78.36140; Grounds of Riverview HS, Strasburg; Shenandoah **GS**: Y **SP**: Frances Funk (1723-1796) **VI**: No further data **P**: N **BLW**: N **RG**: N **MK**: unk **PH**: unk **SS**: Al Ct Bk pg 2-4, 8-10, 12, 13, 20 **BS**: 196.

STOVER, Peter; b 1763; d 1814 **RU**: Private, Served in Capt Alexander Machir's Co, Strasburg District, Shenandoah Co. **CEM**: Mt Zion United Methodist; **GPS** unk; 399 W Queens St, Strasburg; Shenandoah **GS**: Y **SP**: No info **VI**: No further data **P**: unk **BLW**: unk **RG**: N **MK**: N **PH**: unk **SS**: C pg 607 **BS**: 65 Strasburg.

STRANGE, John Alloway; b 15 Jan 1727, Goochland Co; d 1 Sep 1811 **RU**: Patriot, Gave material aid to cause **CEM**: Oak Hill; **GPS** 37.70690, -78.25360; Rt 655; Fluvanna **GS**: N **SP**: mar (22 Sep 1756, New Kent Co) Ann Mildred Mitchell (3 Jan 1727-29 Apr 1782) **VI**: No further data **P**: N **BLW**: N **RG**: N **MK**: unk **PH**: N **SS**: DAR A202286; AL Ct bk pg 5, Fluvanna Co **BS**: 196.

RU=Rank/Unit	CEM=Cemetery	GS=Gravestone	SP=Spousal Information
VI=Other Veteran Info	P=Pension	BLW=Bounty/Land Warrant	RG=Registered Grave
MK=SAR/DAR Marker	PH=Photo	SS=Service Source	BS=Burial Source

401

STRATTON, Henry; b 1735, Dale Parish, Chesterfield Co; d 1799 **RU:** Lieutenant/Patriot, Took oath as Lt 14 Sep 1766, Bedford Co Militia. Gave material aid to cause **CEM:** Stratton Family; GPS unk; Jct Rts 122 & 736; Bedford **GS:** N **SP:** Sarah Hampton **VI:** No further data **P:** unk **BLW:** unk **RG:** Y **MK:** N **PH:** N **SS:** AL Ct Bk pg 7, 19 Bedford Co; AK Bedford Mus; DAR A111122; SAR P-299339. **BS:** 04 Sep 07.

STRATTON, John Handley; b 1745, Chesterfield Co; d 6 Apr 1805 **RU:** Trooper/Patriot, Served in First Lt Dragoons, 25th VA Regt Cont Line. Gave material aid to cause **CEM:** Stratton Family; GPS unk; New Canton; Buckingham **GS:** U **SP:** Susan Ann Douglass **VI:** No further data **P:** unk **BLW:** unk **RG:** Y **MK:** N **PH:** unk **SS:** AL Ct Bk pg 18 Amherst Co; AS SAR Report; SAR P-299349; DAR #A111137 **BS:** unk.

STREET, Anthony, b 1710 King William Co; d 7 Jun 1790 **RU:** Patriot, gave material aid to cause, Amherst Co **CEM:** Anthony Street; GPS 37.505203, -79.166647; loc to the West off Winesap Rd at Old Anthony Street Plantation, beside Graham Creek & Pedler Madison Heights; Amherst **GS:** Y **SP:** Elizabeth Brockman (1715-1793) **VI:** No further data **P:** N **BLW:** N **RG:** Y **MK:** N **PH:** N **SS:** DAR A133723; AL Ct Bk, pg 13, Amherst Co SAR P-299422 **BS:** 196.

STREIT (STRAIGHT), Christian; b 07 Jun 1749, NJ; d 15 Mar 1812 **RU:** Chaplain, Served in 8th Cont Line, 1 Aug 1776-Jul 1777 **CEM:** Mt Hebron; GPS 39.10916, -78.09497; 305 E Boscawen St; Winchester City **GS:** Y **SP:** Mar (15 Oct 1789, Frederick Co) Susannah Barr, (Return) **VI:** No further data **P:** unk **BLW:** unk **RG:** Y **MK:** Y SAR monument **PH:** Y **SS:** J-NSSAR 1993 Reg. E, pg 745-746 NARA M246; SAR P-299455 **BS:** 50 pg 50; JLARC 1.

STRICKLER, Benjamin; b 21 Jan 1726, W. Hempfield Twp, Lancaster Co, PA; d 11 Apr 1791 **RU:** Patriot, Gave material aid to cause **CEM:** Beaver-Brubaker (Mauck's Mill); GPS 39.18343, -78.16278; Rt 615, vic Luray; Page **GS:** N **SP:** Mary Baidler **VI:** Tradition states that Benjamin Strickler is bur at Strickler Cemetery on Massanutten Tract, where Isaac Strickler is bur. More likely bur with wife & children and memorialized there **P:** N **BLW:** N **RG:** Y **MK:** N **PH:** unk **SS:** C pg 603; SAR P-332298 **BS:** 79 pg 174-6.

STRICKLER, Daniel, b 16 Oct 1745, Page Co, d 6 Nov 1827 **RU:** Patriot, Gave material aid to cause Shenandoah Co **CEM:** Strickler Springs; GPS: 37.923864,-79.425273; loc on top of steep hill on Rt 39W, past jct Rt 623 on left, Rockbridge Baths; Rockbridge **GS:** No **SP:** Barbara Lehman (27 Mar 1747, PA-11 Oct 1825) **VI:** A Reverend assigned to VA Circuit. He owned the land where this cemetery is, thus likely buried here **P:** N **BLW:** N **RG:** N **MK:** N **PH:** N **SS:** AL Ct Bk pgs 4,5 and Comm Bk V pgs 160,164, Shenandoah Co **BS:** 196.

STRICKLER, Isaac; b 15 Aug 1749, Egypt Bend, Page Co; d 1 May 1817 **RU:** Private, Served in Michael Reader's Co, Shenandoah Co Militia **CEM:** Strickler Monument; GPS unk; SW side of Rts 615 & Rt 211, Ft Egypt; Page **GS:** N **SP:** 1) mar (24 Dec 1779 Linville, Rockingham Co) Susanna Brubaker (15 Jul 1759 Lancaster Co PA-8 Aug 1805 Massanutten Heights, Shenandoah Co) d/o Abraham & Barbara (Long) Brubaker 2) mar (11 Jul 1807, Luray, Shenandoah Co) Catherine Mauck Beaver (widow of Christian Beaver) (29 Jan 1764 Shenandoah Co-29 May 1829) d/o Daniel & Barbara (Harnsbarger) Mauck **VI:** Son of Isaac & Magdalena (Neff) Strickler. Died in Egypt Bend, Page Co **P:** unk **BLW:** unk **RG:** Y **MK:** N **PH:** N **SS:** C pg 603; SAR P-332007 **BS:** 79 pg 174-6.

STRICKLER, Jacob; b 9 Dec 1728, W. Hempfield Co, Lancaster Co, PA; d 29 Jan 1784 **RU:** Patriot, Gave material aid to cause **CEM:** Strickler Monument; GPS unk; SW side of St Rt 615, Rt 211, Ft Egypt; Page **GS:** N **SP:** 1) Nancy Kauffman 2) Magdalena Moomaw **VI:** Died in Fortt Egypt, Page Co **P:** N **BLW:** N **RG:** Y **MK:** N **PH:** N **SS:** D vol3, pgs 842,844,845; H; DAR A111389; SAR P-299496; Al Ct bk pg 141, Shenandoah Co **BS:** 79 pg 235, 236; 196.

STRICKLER, Joseph; b 1 Sep 1731, W. Hempfield Twp, Lancaster Co PA; d 30 Aug 1795 **RU:** Patriot, Gave material aid to cause **CEM:** Strickler Monument; GPS unk; SW side of St Rt 615, Rt 211, Ft Egypt; Page **GS:** N **SP:** 1) Mar (1 Feb 1755 Shenandoah Co) Elizabeth Stoeckli (Stickley) d/o Johannes & Barbara (Morgan) Stoeckli (25 Jan 1733 PA-21 Jan 1773 Egypt Bend, Dunmore Co) 2) Mar (21 Jun 1774 Shenandoah Co) Barbara Harnish d/o Christian & Barbara (Hiestand) Hamish Jr (c1753-aft Aug 1807) **VI:** Son of Abraham & Anna Maria (Ruffner) Strickler. Died in Egypt Plantation, Page Co **P:** N **BLW:** N **RG:** Y **MK:** N **PH:** N **SS:** C, pg 603; SAR P-332006 **BS:** 79, pg 197.

STROBIA, John; b 1742; d 10 Mar 1809 **RU:** Patriot, Was Legislative Petitioner for Rev War supplies furnished western counties **CEM:** St John's Episcopal; GPS 37.53183, -77.41958; 2401 E Broad St; Richmond City **GS:** U **SP:** Mary P-----) (1762-1795) **VI:** No further data **P:** N **BLW:** N **RG:** N **MK:** unk **PH:** unk **SS:** S VA Legislative Petitions **BS:** 196.

STRODE, John; b 1734 PA, Chester Co; d c1820 **RU:** Patriot, Ran an ironworks during war and gave much material to the cause **CEM:** Fairview; GPS 38.48080,-78.00470; Sperryville Pike Rt 522, Culpeper; Culpeper **GS:** Y **SP:** Anne (-----) **VI:** Originally bured at "Fleetwood" in Culpeper Co. He may have d in North Carolina **P:** N **BLW:** N **RG:** N **MK:** N **PH:** Y **SS:** 34 pg 114-5 **BS:** 34 pg 114, 115.

STROME (STROM), Henry A; b unk d aft 1779 **RU:** Private, Capt William Heyier's Co, Col Arend's German Regt, discharged 17 Jul 1779 at a Muster of MD Troops; was POW fr 14th SC Regt **CEM:** Old Christ Church; GPS: 38.80625, -77.04718; 118 N Washington St; Alexandria City **GS:**Yes listed on GS with others **SP:** No spousal info **VI:** Died in a federal hospital. Disinterred from Alexandria Soldiers Cemetery. Reinterred in Old Christ Church Cemetery 27 Dec 1879 **P:** N **BLW:** N **RG:** N **MK:** N **PH:** N **SS:** Fold3 Serv Index Cards; EI: added to App C Family Archives *MD Settlers and Soldiers*, Record of MD Troops with Cont Serv, Vol 2, pg 250 **BS:** 196.

STROTHER, French; b 1733; d 3 Jun 1800 **RU:** Colonel/Patriot, Served in VA militia as he received pension. Member of VA Constitution Conventions 1776 and 1788. As patriot gave to the cause in Culpeper Co **CEM:** St George's Episcopal; GPS unk; 905 Princess Anne; Fredericksburg City **GS:** Y **SP:** Lucy Coleman daughter of Gilly C & (-----) Coleman. Also Ann (-----) **VI:** Son of James (__-1761 Culpeper Co.) & Margaret (French) Strother. Represented Culpeper Co in General Assembly for 25 yrs. Served as County Justice and County Lt. **P:** Y **BLW:** unk **RG:** Y **MK:** N **PH:** unk **SS:** H; SAR P-299754 **BS:** 12 pg 114.

STROTHER, John; b 1758; d 1790 **RU:** Captain, Commanded a co 24 Oct 1776 in Culpeper Co Militia **CEM:** Strother-Jones; GPS unk; Stephens City; Frederick **GS:** Y **SP:** Hellen Piper (1768-after 1840) **VI:** No further data **P:** unk **BLW:** unk **RG:** N **MK:** N **PH:** unk **SS:** E pg 747 **BS:** 59 pg 322.

STROTHER, John Dabney Sr; b 31 Dec 1721; d Apr 1795 **RU:** Patriot, Member of Committee of Safety for Culpeper 1775. Gave material aid to cause Culpeper Co **CEM:** Wadefield, Strother Family; GPS unk; Nr Washington; Rappahannock **GS:** U **SP:** Mar (1741) Mary Wade **VI:** Son of Francis & Suzanne (Dabney) Strother. Father was Lt in Colonial militia. Was Capt in French and Indian War. One of 16 Culpeper justices who signed the 1765 Stamp Act Protest. Was Justice and Sheriff of Co **P:** unk **BLW:** unk **RG:** Y **MK:** unk **PH:** unk **SS:** J- DAR Hatcher; D pg 238; AL Ct Bk I pg 5 Culpeper Co; DAR A111748; SAR P-299764 **BS:** JLARC 2; 80 vol4, pg 86; 196.

STROUD, Thomas A; b 1765; d 1838 **RU:** Private, Served in Capt Felix Warley's Co, 3rd Carolina Regt of Cont Line Jul 1779 **CEM:** Blandford; GPS 37.22433, -77.38604; 319 S Crater Rd; Petersburg City **GS:** Y **SP:** Susanna (Susan) Bacon Bishop (15 Aug 1770 Woodstock, Windham Co, CT-19 Jul 1847, Petersburg) **VI:** No further data **P:** unk **BLW:** unk **RG:** N **MK:** Y SAR monument **PH:** unk **SS:** AP roll SC Cont Line **BS:** 128 pg 1; 196.

STUART, Archibald; b 19 Mar 1757; d 11 Jul 1832 **RU:** Private, Served in Augusta & Rockbridge Co Militias, Was at the Battle of Guilford CH in NC, Mar 1781 **CEM:** Trinity Episcopal; GPS 38.14917, -79.07521; 214 Beverley St; Staunton City **GS:** Y **SP:** Eleanor Briscoe (1768-1858) **VI:** Son of Alexander (1734-1822) & (-----) Stuart. Attended College of William and Mary fr 1777-1780. A lawyer and judge. Read law under Thomas Jefferson. Member of VA federal convention of 1788. Favored ratification of US Constitution **P:** unk **BLW:** unk **RG:** Y **MK:** unk **PH:** Y **SS:** B; SAR P-299866 **BS:** JLARC 62, 63; 196.

STUART, Benjamin; b 1736, PA; d 12 Dec 1808 **RU:** Private/Patriot, Served as private in First Light Dragoons. Gave material aid to cause **CEM:** Tinkling Spring Presbyterian; GPS 38.08472, -78.98278; 30 Tinkling Spring Dr, Fishersville; Augusta **GS:** N **SP:** Eleanor Tate **VI:** Son of Archibald Stuart (1696-1761) & Janet Brown **P:** unk **BLW:** unk **RG:**Y **MK:** N **PH:** N **SS:** E pg 747; AL Comm Bk II pg 360 Augusta Co; SAR P-299867 **BS:** JLARC 62, 63; 196; 208 pg 467.

STUART, John: b 10 May 1728, d 31 Oct 1787 **RU:** Patriot, he gave material aid to cause in King George Co period !781-1783 **CEM:** Stuart & Grymes Family, GPS 38.3360100, -77.1340700; loc on Dahlgren Railroad Heritage Trail nr jct w Caledon Rd; King George **GS:** Unk **SP:** Frances Alexander (5

RU=Rank/Unit	CEM=Cemetery	GS=Gravestone	SP=Spousal Information
VI=Other Veteran Info	P=Pension	BLW=Bounty/Land Warrant	RG=Registered Grave
MK=SAR/DAR Marker	PH=Photo	SS=Service Source	BS=Burial Source

403

Oct 1728, Stafford Co-1777, Stafford Co d/o Philip Alexander (1704-1753) & Sarah Hooe (1704-1758) **VI**: P: N **BLW**: N **RG**: N **MK**: N **PH**: N **SS**: AL Ct Bk pg 2, Comm Bk II, pg 338 **BS**: 196.

STUART, John; b 1756, Glasgow Scotland; d 1 Feb 1814 **RU**: Private, Served in Capt Robert Powell's Co, 3rd VA Regt of Foot, commanded by Col William Heath Feb 1779. Also served in 15th VA Regt **CEM**: Blandford; GPS 37.22433, -77.38604; 319 S Crater Rd; Petersburg City **GS**: Y **SP**: No info **VI**: Merchant in Petersburg **P**: unk **BLW**: unk **RG**: Y **MK**: Y SAR monument **PH**: unk **SS**: E pg 747; AP Payroll and service rec; SAR P-335466 **BS**: 188 # 1358; 196.

STUART, John Ainsworth; b unk, Belfast Ireland; d unk **RU**: Soldier, SAR registry did not provide service **CEM**: Old Presbyterian Meeting House; GPS 38.48528, -77.23532; 323 S Fairfax St; Alexandria City **GS**: N **SP**: No info **VI**: No further data **P**: unk **BLW**: unk **RG**: Y **MK**: unk **PH**: N **SS**: J-NSSAR 1993 Reg; SAR P-299893 **BS**: JLARC 1; 5.

STUART, Robert; b 1759; d 28 Oct 1827 **RU**: Sergeant, Served in 8th Cont Line **CEM**: Stuart Family; GPS unk; Rt 727, Blackwells property; Rockbridge **GS**: Y **SP**: No info **VI**: Son of Alexander Sr (27 Aug 1734 Chester PA-1822) & (-----) Stuart **P**: unk **BLW**: unk **RG**: N **MK**: unk **PH**: unk **SS**: E pg 747 **BS**: 196.

STUART, William David; b 13 Dec 1723 Stafford Co; d 1799 **RU**: Patriot, Performed public service as member of Committee of Safety **CEM**: Stuart-Grymes Family; GPS 38.33601, -77.13407; Rt 218 on Cedar Grove Farm; King George **GS**: Y **SP**: Mar (26 Nov 1750) Sarah Foote (29 Jun 1732 Cedar Grove, Stafford Co-aft 1799 St Paul's Parish) **VI**: Son of William (1723-1799) & Sarah (Foote) (1732-___) Stuart. Was a reverend **P**: N **BLW**: N **RG**: N **MK**: unk **PH**: unk **SS**: DAR A109740; AL Ct Bk pg 4 King George Co **BS**: 196.

STUBERT, Adam; b unk; d 1781 **RU**: Soldier, Served in Royal Deaux Ponts Bn and died fr battle at Yorktown **CEM**: French Memorial; GPS 36.81944, -79.39933; Yorktown; York **GS**: U **SP**: No info **VI**: No further data **P**: unk **BLW**: unk **RG**: Y **MK**: unk **PH**: unk **SS**: J-Yorktown Historian; SAR P-299946 **BS**: JLARC 1, 74.

SUMMERS, Francis; b 3 Mar 1732; d 10 Sep 1800 **RU**: Soldier/Patriot, Overseer of the Poor for Fairfax Co 1776. VA, donated 750 lbs of beef **CEM**: Summers Family; GPS 38.49150, -770828; Lincolnia, nr Deming Avenue and Rt 613; Fairfax **GS**: Y **SP**: Jane Watkins Charlton (1736-22 Aug 1814) **VI**: Son of John & (-----) Summers. DAR marker by Thomas Lee Chapter **P**: unk **BLW**: unk **RG**: Y **MK**: Y **PH**: unk **SS**: DAR #A032424; SAR P-300284 AK; BT **BS**: JLARC 1, 3,14, 25, 27, 28; 04; 47 pg 55.2; 196.

SUMMERS, Horsey; b 1762, Somerset Co, MD; d 25 Feb 1852 **RU**: Soldier, MD Line. Lived in Somerset Co, MD at enl. Was age 15 at time **CEM**: Parksley; GPS unk; .5 mi N of Rt 176, W of Rt 678, NE fr Parksley; Accomack **GS**: N **SP**: Mar (Accomac Co) (-----) **VI**: Appl pen 12 Sep 1851, Accomac Co, age 89. Children granted pen in arrears. S7664 **P**: Y **BLW**: unk **RG**: Y **MK**: unk **PH**: N **SS**: K Vol 5 pg 192; CG Vol 3 pg 3389; DAR A110906; SAR P-300292 **BS**: JLARC 4 , 5.

SUMMERS, John; b 14 Nov 1687, Middlesex Co; d 4 Dec 1790 **RU**: Patriot, Gave material aid to the cause **CEM**: Summers Family; GPS 38.49150, -770828; Demming Ave & Lincolnia Rd; Alexandria City **GS**: N **SP**: Elizabeth Blake **VI**: Son of John & Elizabeth (-----) Summers. Died at 103 yrs old in "Summers Grove" nr Annanndale, Alexandria, Fairfax Co **P**: N **BLW**: N **RG**: Y **MK**: N **PH**: N **SS**: AL Ct Bk lt, pg 2, 6; SAR P-300317 **BS**: 20 pg 194.

SUMMERS, John; b 13 Dec 1746; d 28 Jan 1806 **RU**: Soldier/Patriot, Served in Capt McCuthen's Co, Augusta Co Militia. Gave material aid to cause **CEM**: St John's Reformed UCC; GPS 38.05081, -79.17761; 1515 Arbor Hill Rd, Middlebrook; Augusta **GS**: Y **SP**: Mar (1770) Elizabeth Reidenauer (Ridenour) (28 Jan 1752-28 Dec 1812) **VI**: Eroded stone. Son of Johan George & Maria Margaretha (-----) Summers **P**: unk **BLW**: unk **RG**: Y **MK**: unk **PH**: Y **SS**: DAR A110926; SAR P-340280; D Vol 1 pg 98; E pg 750; CD **BS**: JLARC 62; 196.

SUMMERS, William J; b unk; d 3 Jun 1805 **RU**: Bombardier, Appointed bombardier Dec 1776, in Capt John Canter's Co of Artillery at Valley Forge **CEM**: Sharon; GPS unk; Middleburg; Loudoun **GS**: Y **SP**: No info **VI**: No further data **P**: unk **BLW**: unk **RG**: N **MK**: N **PH**: unk **SS**: E pg 750 **BS**: 25 pg 302.

RU=Rank/Unit	CEM=Cemetery	GS=Gravestone	SP=Spousal Information
VI=Other Veteran Info	P=Pension	BLW=Bounty/Land Warrant	RG=Registered Grave
MK=SAR/DAR Marker	PH=Photo	SS=Service Source	BS=Burial Source

404

SUMMERS (SOMMERS), Simon; b 23 Nov 1747, Fairfax Co; d 2 Dec 1836 **RU:** Major or Adjutant/Patriot, Served as the Adjutant, 6th VA Regt fr 21 Mar 1776 to end of campaign in 1781. Also donated "waggon and team 13 days hawling public stores." - Fairfax Co. Ct claim Feb 1782 **CEM:** Falls Church Episcopal; GPS 38.88077, -77.17166; 115 E Fairfax St; Falls Church City **GS:** Y **SP:** Elizabeth Ferguson **VI:** Died in Fairfax Co VA. Find a Grave indicates he d in 1806. Govt Grave Stone. Rec pen S905 and BLW 1480-200; Appl pen 28 Dec 1828 Alexandria Co (then DC but now in VA) W9705, Recd 4000 acres bounty land. BLW #1480-200. Died in Alexandria **P:** Y **BLW:** Y **RG:** Y **MK:** Y **SAR PH:** unk **SS:** AK M805 Roll 758; BY; AL Ct Bk; A pg 507; CD; F pg 70; K Vol 4 pg 129; CG Vol 3 pg 3248; DAR A110950; SAR P-294053 **BS:** 04; JLARC 1, 2,14, 27, 28, 45; 80 vol 4 pg 58.

SWAN, Caleb; b 2 Jul 1758, Fryeburg, York Co, MA (now Oxford Co, ME); d 29 Nov 1809 **RU:** Ensign, Served as Corporal and Sergeant 9th MA Regt, 1 Feb 1777; appointed Ensign 26 Nov 1779; transferred to 8th MA 1 Jan 1781; transferred to 3rd MA 12 Jun 1783; retained in Jackson's Cont Regt Nov 1783 **CEM:** Arlington National; GPS 38.88377, -77.06535; Jefferson Davis Hwy Rt 110; Arlington **GS:** Y **SP:** No info **VI:** Died in DC. Bur at Old Presbyterian Cem in DC. Reinterred 12 May 1892. Fryeburg was located in York Co. MA prior to 1804 (formation of Oxford Co.). Area of MA became ME in 1820. He became Paymaster General, US Army **P:** unk **BLW:** unk **RG:** Y **MK:** N **PH:** unk **SS:** J-NSSAR 1993 Reg, J- DAR Hatcher; SAR P-300655 **BS:** JLARC 1, 2; 80 vol4, pg 91; 196.

SWEENEY, Moses; b 11 Aug 1756, Amherst Co; d 15 Mar 1833, Buckingham Co **RU:** Private, enlisted Buckingham Co 1776 in Capt Patterson's Col Buckners 7th VA Regt and 6th VA Regt, Cont Line serving 18 months, injured and was medically discharged **CEM:** Sweeney Family; GPS not determined; 1 mi NE Appomattox Ct House on Richmond/Lynchburg Stage Rd; Appomattox **GS:** Y Govt **SP:** Mar 4 Sep 1826, Bedford Co, Martha Buress **VI:** Pensioned 1832, Buckingham Co #F-S6180, R2329 **P:** Y **BLW:** N **RG:** Y **MK:** N **PH:** Y **SS:** K vol 6, pg 200; DAR A207983; SAR P-300909 **BS:** 196.

SWIFT, Thomas; b 1765; d 28 May 1804 **RU:** Marine, Served in shipyard at Portsmouth **CEM:** Trinity Episcopal; GPS 36.83459, -76.30105; 500 Court St; Portsmouth City **GS:** U **SP:** No info **VI:** GS indicates rank of capt probably obtained after war period **P:** unk **BLW:** unk **RG:** N **MK:** unk **PH:** unk **SS:** See burial source 57 **BS:** 57.

SYDNOR, Joseph; b 17 Oct 1740, Lancaster Co; d 1787 **RU:** Patriot, Gave material aid to cause **CEM:** Sydnor - Young Family; GPS unk; Petersburg National Battlefield; Dinwiddie **GS:** N **SP:** Ann Chowning (1751-__) **VI:** Son of Anthony Sydnor (1711-1779) and Elizabeth Taylor (1722-1785) **P:** N **BLW:** N **RG:** Y **MK:** Y **SAR PH:** N **SS:** Comm Bk V pg 239 Dinwiddie Co; DAR A112169; SAR P-301235 **BS:** 192; 196.

SYDNOR, William; b c1734; d Jun 1794 **RU:** Patriot, Signer of Leedstown Resolutions 1766. Served on Lancaster Co Committee of Safety during war period **CEM:** St Mary's Whitechapel Episcopal; GPS 37.44782, -76.33181; 5940 White Chapel Rd, Lively; Lancaster **GS:** N **SP:** Mar (12 Oct 1763 (bond) Richmond Co) Ellen Fauntleroy (__-14 Dec 1807 Fairfax Co) d/o Capt Moore & Ann (Heale) Fauntleroy **VI:** Son of William & Cathrine (-----) Sydnor **P:** N **BLW:** N **RG:** N **MK:** N **PH:** N **SS:** BQ pg 7157 **BS:** Serv Source BQ pg 7158.

SYME (SIMS, SYMES), John II; b 25 Dec 1729; d 25 Nov 1805 **RU:** Colonel/Patriot, Gave material aid to cause **CEM:** Syme; GPS unk; Rts 6763 & 703 nr Rockville, Rocky Mills; Hanover **GS:** N **SP:** 1) Mildred Thornton Meriwether (1739-1760) 2) Sarah Hoops (1747-1810) **VI:** Son of John (1690-1732) & Sarah (Winston) (1710-1784) Syme **P:** unk **BLW:** unk **RG:** Y **MK:** unk **PH:** N **SS:** AL Ct Bk I pg 22-26, 38 Hanover Co; DAR A112257; SAR P-301270 **BS:** JLARC 71; 196

SYME, John III; b 1755, Rockville, Hanover Co, d 10 Feb !793 **RU:** Colonel/Patriot member VA Assembly & VA Conventions 1775 &1776. Was Capt in Cont Line 3 Dec 1776, resigned 3 Jan 1778, was Col in militia 1780 and County LT Hanover Co 1779-1782 **CEM:** Rocky Mills; GPS 37.755560, -77.648890; loc vic Newcastle, Hanover **GS:** N **SP:** mar (May 1779) Sallie Overton, d/o William Overton & Jeminia Harris **VI:** Son of John Syne (1729-1805) & Mildred Thornton Meriwether (1739-1760) **P:** N **BLW:** N **RG:** Y **MK:** N **PH:** N **SS:**E pg 1754; DAR A112261; SAR P-301271 **BS:** SAR PRS.

TABB, Edward; b 03 Feb 1719; d 21 Dec 1782 **RU:** Patriot, Gave material aid to cause In Gloucester Co **CEM:** Ware Episcopal; GPS 37.42275, -76.50789; 7825 John Clayton Mem Hwy; Gloucester **GS:** Y **SP:** Lucy Todd (20 Nov 1721-18 Feb 1791) d/o Christopher (1690-1743) & (-----) Todd **VI:** Son of John

RU=Rank/Unit	CEM=Cemetery	GS=Gravestone	SP=Spousal Information
VI=Other Veteran Info	P=Pension	BLW=Bounty/Land Warrant	RG=Registered Grave
MK=SAR/DAR Marker	PH=Photo	SS=Service Source	BS=Burial Source

405

& Martha (-----) Tabb. Stone moved fr Toddsbury on North River in August 1924. Epitaph recorded 1959 **P:** N **BLW:** N **RG:** Y **MK:** Y **SAR PH:** Y **SS:** AL Ct Bk pg iii,15; SAR P-336113 **BS:** 48 pg 81; 196; 207.

TABB, Philip (Phillip); b 6 Nov 1750; d 25 Feb 1822 **RU:** Captain/patriot, Served in Capt Gloucester Co Militia, 25 Jul 1775 to 1776. Appointed Lt 13 Sep 1775. Also gave material aid to cause **CEM:** Ware Episcopal; GPS 37.42275, -76.50789; 7825 John Clayton Mem Hwy; Gloucester **GS:** Y **SP:** Mary Mason Wythe (7 Sep 1751-22 Sep 1814) d/o Nathaniel & Elizabeth (-----) Wythe. **VI:** Son of Edward and Lucy (-----) Tabb. Died in "Toddsbury" Gloucester Co. Stone moved fr Toddsbury on North River in August 1924. Epitaph recorded 1959 **P:** N **BLW:** N **RG:** Y **MK:** Y **SAR PH:** Y **SS:** E pg 755; AK; AL Ct Bk pg iii, 12; SAR P-336114 **BS:** 48 pg 83; 207.

TABB, Thomas; b 1755, Seaford, Gloucester Co; d 1818/1819 **RU:** Ensign/Patriot, Served in Gloucester Co Militia 1775. Performed recruiting services in Amelia & Lunenburg Co in 1776. Delegate fr Lunenburg Co to VA Legislature 1775 **CEM:** Toddsbury Plantation; GPS unk; Elmington; Mathews **GS:** U **SP:** Elizabeth H.Teakle, d 04 Dec 1824, **VI:** Death date determined by Mathews Co tax record **P:** unk **BLW:** unk **RG:** Y **MK:** unk **PH:** unk **SS:** E pg 755; SAR P- 301321 **BS:** 196.

TAFT, Nathan; b unk; d 1781 **RU:** Soldier, Served fr MA and died fr Yorktown battle **CEM:** Yorktown Victory Monument Tablet; GPS 38.28350, -78.54150; Yorktown; York **GS:** U **SP:** No info **VI:** No further data **P:** unk **BLW:** unk **RG:** Y **MK:** unk **PH:** unk **SS:** J-Yorktown Historian; SAR P-301416 **BS:** JLARC 74.

TALBOTT, Samuel G; b 1726; d 30 Dec 1777 **RU:** Captain, Served in 2nd PA Regt; died at Valley Forge Dec 1777 **CEM:** Falls Church Episcopal; GPS 38.88077, -77.17166; 115 E Fairfax St; Falls Church City **GS:** U **SP:** Mary Magdalene Demoville (___-2 Jul 1791) d/o Samuel & Rose (Neale) Demoville **VI:** Son of Benjamin & Hannah Elizabeth (Neale) Talbott. He died fr exposure and his fam awarded half pay. Was member Society Cincinnati; memorialized on a plaque at the Fairfax Co Court House **P:** Y **BLW:** unk **RG:** N **MK:** unk **PH:** unk **SS:** A pg 434, 488 **BS:** 196.

TALIAFERRO, Lawrence; b 9 Dec 1734; d 8 Apr 1798 **RU:** Colonel, Appointed Lt Col 28 May 1778. Col Commandant of the Minute Men raised in Orange, Culpeper, Fauquier Co **CEM:** Rose Hill; GPS unk; Rapidan; Orange **GS:** Y **SP:** 1) Mar (1758) Mary Jackson 2) mar (3 Feb 1774) Sarah Dade **VI:** Son of Francis & Elizabeth (Hay) Taliaferro, of "Epson". Gov't and SAR markers **P:** unk **BLW:** unk **RG:** Y **MK:** Y **SAR PH:** unk **SS:** DAR A112546; SAR Ancestor #P-301602; J-NSSAR 2000 Reg **BS:** JLARC 76; 196.

TALIAFERRO, Walker; b unk; d Bef 13 Mar 1826 **RU:** Colonel/Patriot, Served in Caroline Co Militia. Col rank given 14 Aug 1777. Member House of Burgesses **CEM:** Taliaferro Family; GPS unk; Rt 654; Caroline **GS:** N **SP:** Sallie Turner d/o Thomas Turner, Jr. & Sallie (-----) **VI:** Member of Masonic Lodge **P:** unk **BLW:** unk **RG:** Y **MK:** N **PH:** unk **SS:** E pg 756; H; SAR P-301613; **BS:** 02 pg 143.

TALLEY (TALLY), Nathaniel (Nathan); b unk; d c1823 **RU:** Sergeant, Served in Capt Timberlake's Co,Taylor's VA Regt **CEM:** Cowlands Site; GPS unk; Rt 613; Spotsylvania **GS:** U **SP:** Mollie (-----), also Julianna Harris **VI:** Was also a patriot as he gave material aid to cause **P:** unk **BLW:** unk **RG:** Y **MK:** N **PH:** unk **SS:** E pg 757; SAR application 454; DAR A112566; SAR P-301632 **BS:** 09 grid 32.

TANKARD, John Dr; b 1752; d 24 Apr 1836 **RU:** Colonel, Enl serv nr Williamsburg as surgeon in 1778 for the Flying Hospital and was deputy director for VA hospitals at time he enlisted. Surgeon for the VA State troops, stationed at Williamsburg. Also was with LaFayette when he retreated to mountains in Orange Co **CEM:** Tankard's Rest; GPS unk; Exmore; Northampton **GS:** U **SP:** 1) Zillah (-----) 2) Mar (12 Feb 1778) Sarah (-----) Andrews, widow of Southy Andrews **VI:** Was Surgeon. Pen 1834 Northampton Co. S48512. DAR Grave marker says he was in the 8th VMR, LaFayette's Division **P:** Y **BLW:** Y **RG:** Y **MK:** unk **PH:** unk **SS:** K Vol 5 pg 207; CG Vol 3 pg 3418; BT; SAR P-301722 **BS:** JLARC 2, 4, 69; 42 pg 82; 80 Vol4,pg 97; 209.

TANNER, Abraham; b Feb 1759, Culpeper Co; d 1844 **RU:** Private, Ent serv Culpeper Co (later Madison Co) 1779-80. Served in Culpeper Militia 1781 **CEM:** Tanner Family; GPS unk; Hebron Valley; Madison **GS:** N **SP:** Elizabeth (-----) **VI:** Son of Christopher Sr. (___-1792) & Elizabeth Aylor Tanner. Appl pen 23 Aug 1832 Madison Co. S6190 **P:** Y **BLW:** unk **RG:** Y **MK:** N **PH:** N **SS:** E pg 757; K Vol 5 pg 208; CG Vol 3 pg 3418; DAR A112698; SAR P-301741 **BS:** 04.

RU=Rank/Unit	CEM=Cemetery	GS=Gravestone	SP=Spousal Information
VI=Other Veteran Info	P=Pension	BLW=Bounty/Land Warrant	RG=Registered Grave
MK=SAR/DAR Marker	PH=Photo	SS=Service Source	BS=Burial Source

TANNER, Christopher; b c1751; d 1781 **RU**: Sergeant, Was listed in Culpeper recruiting classes. Died in service 1781 **CEM**: Williamsburg Land Conservancy; GPS unk; 5000 New Point Rd; Williamsburg City **GS**: N **SP**: Mary Cook (14 Dec 1753-___) d/o George & Mary Sarah (Reiner) Cook. **VI**: Son of Christopher Sr. (___-1792) & Elizabeth Aylor Tanner. Memorialized at Yorktown Victory Monument Tablet **P**: unk **BLW**: unk **RG**: Y **MK**: N **PH**: N **SS**: AU Will Chap; J-Yorktown Historian; DAR A112708; SAR P-301745 **BS**: JLARC 74.

TANNER, Jacob; b c1743, d 20 Oct 1781 **RU**: Private Served under Ensign John Hume, Capt Kirkpatrick's Co, from Madison Co, VA State line. Died in service at Williamsburg. **CEM**: Williamsburg Governors Palace Rev War Cem; GPS 37.262500, -76.699722; 300 Palace Green St; Williamsburg City **GS**: N Mass grave **SP**: Dorothy Zimmerman (c1782 Orange Co-c1807 Culpeper), d/o John Zimmerman & Ursula Blankenbaker. LNR Shenandoah 1807. She rec'd pen, Madison Co 26 Oct 1793 and a relief payment 18 Dec 1794 **VI**: Was in the Culpeper Classes Jan 1781 **P**: Widow **BLW**: N **RG** Y **MK** N **PH**: N **SS**: AJ; DJ; DAR A112717; SAR P-331318 **BS**: 196

TAPP (TOPP), Vincent; b 1757; d Mar 1824 **RU**: Sergeant-Major, Served in VA Line. Ent serv Wheeling, OH 1776 **CEM**: Trinity Episcopal; GPS 38.14917, -79.07521; 214 Beverley St; Staunton City **GS**: U **SP**: Mar (Charlottesville, VA) Susanna Gamble (___-Apr 1835) **VI**: Prob son of Vincent Tapp (___-1757 Frederick Co, MD). His grandfather was William Tatico (___-1719) of Northumberland Co, last King of Wicomico Indians. Disability pen fr 16 Jul 1811 for severe wound to arm at Battle of Brandywine. Granted regular pension fr Augusta Co in 1820, age 63, as resident of Staunton. Reapplied 19 Jan 1820, Staunton VA age 63. S41231. Moved to Albemarle Co after RW. After Rev taught school nr Charlottesville. Clerk of the Ct of Hustings at Staunton **P**: Y **BLW**: unk **RG**: Y **MK**: unk **PH**: unk **SS**: K Vol 5 pg 210; CG Vol 3 pg 3420; DAR A112784; SAR P-301811 **BS**: JLARC 1, 4, 62, 63.

TATE, John; b 1725, Hanover Co; d 1794 **RU**: Private, Served in Capt Tate's Co, Augusta Militia **CEM**: Tinkling Spring Presbyterian; GPS 38.08472, -78.98278; 30 Tinkling Spring Dr, Fishersville; Augusta **GS**: N **SP**: No info **VI**: No further data **P**: unk **BLW**: unk **RG**: N **MK**: N **PH**: N **SS**: E pg 758; J- DAR Hatcher **BS**: 80 Vol4, pg 98; 196; JLARC 2.

TATE, John; b 6 Aug 1761 (1731 per GS), Augusta Co; d end of Aug 1836 **RU**: Soldier, Served in VA Line. Lived in Augusta Co at enl in 1777. Served under James Tate (relative). Moved with father to Botetourt Co where enl again 1781 **CEM**: Bethel Presbyterian; GPS 38.04257, -79.17283; 563 Bethel Green Rd, Middlebrook; Augusta **GS**: U **SP**: No info **VI**: Appl pen 7 Sep 1832, Botetourt Co. S6191 This is not the same John Tate bur at Bethel with Govt stone, dates 1739-1802, with RW service **P**: Y **BLW**: unk **RG**: Y **MK**: unk **PH**: unk **SS**: E pg 758; K Vol 5 pg 212; CG Vol 3 pg 3423; SAR P-301950 **BS**: JLARC 62,63.

TATE, John; b 25 Feb 1749 (baptized); d 13 Dec 1802 **RU**: Soldier, Served in brother James Tate's Co, Augusta Co Militia & in Capt May's Co Botetourt Co. Was in Battle at Kings Mountain in Yorktown **CEM**: Old Providence; GPS 37.96151, -79.710; 1005 Spottswood Rd, Spottswood; Augusta **GS**: Y **SP**: mar (1774) Jane Steele (___-1834) **VI**: Son of John & Mary (Doak) Tate. Trustee of Saunton Academy 1792, VA Legislator 1798. Newer Govt stone. Name also on SAR cemetery plaque **P**: unk **BLW**: unk **RG**: Y **MK**: Y SAR plaque **PH**: unk **SS**: B; BT;DAR A112151; SAR P-301968 **BS**: JLARC 1, 2, 8, 62, 63; 196.

TATE, John; b 1743, Augusta Co; d 15 Dec 1828 **RU**: Soldier, Served in Oct 1780 Washington Co, Militia. In 1776 built Tate's Fort. Was in Battle of Kings Mountain, SC **CEM**: Tate-Burdine; GPS unk; Lebanon; Russell **GS**: Y **SP**: Mar (c1766 VA) Mary Bracken (1742-1817), d/o John & Martha (Green) Bracken. **VI**: Son of Robert & Mary (-----) Tate. Moved to Moccasin Valley in Russell Co, Nov 1772. In 1789 was Capt in 72nd Regt of VA Militia. In 1795, was Maj in 2nd Bn 72nd Regt VA Militia. In 1801-3 was Sheriff & Collector of Revenue for Russell Co. In 1802 was Lt Col Commandant 72 Regt, 3rd Div VA Militia by appt of Gov (later President) James Monroe. In 1826-8 again became Sheriff & Collector **P**: N **BLW**: N **RG**:Y **MK**: unk **PH**: Y **SS**: CD; SAR P-301946 **BS**: 196.

TATE, Robert; b Mar 1753; d 8 or 20 Jul 1832 **RU**: Private, Served in Co commanded by his brother, James Tate and in William Tate's Co, Augusta Co Militia **CEM**: Bethel Presbyterian; GPS 38.04257, -79.17283, GS 38.0230,-79.1018;; 563 Bethel Green Rd, Middlebrook; Augusta **GS**: Y **SP**: Margaret Alexander McClug (5 Oct 1755 Greenville, Augusta Co-23 Sep 1839) d/o John & Elizabeth (Alexander)

RU=Rank/Unit	CEM=Cemetery	GS=Gravestone	SP=Spousal Information
VI=Other Veteran Info	P=Pension	BLW=Bounty/Land Warrant	RG=Registered Grave
MK=SAR/DAR Marker	PH=Photo	SS=Service Source	BS=Burial Source

407

McClung **VI**: Birth & death data fr 11 Aug 1936 WPA survey of cemetery by Scioto M. Herndon, available at Library of VA; **P**: unk **BLW**: unk **RG**: Y **MK**: unk **PH**: Y **SS**: G pg 772; DAR A112166; SAR P-301956 **BS**: JLARC 62, 63; 196.

TATE, Thomas; b 1740; d Aft 1781 **RU**: Private/Patriot, Gave material aid to cause **CEM**: Tinkling Spring Presbyterian; GPS 38.08472, -78.98278; 30 Tinkling Spring Dr, Fishersville; Augusta **GS**: N **SP**: Elizabeth Caldwell **VI**: No further data **P**: unk **BLW**: unk **RG**: unk **MK**: N **PH**: N **SS**: SAR P-301961; AL Cert Augusta Co **BS**: JLARC 2, 63; 80 Vol 4 pg 98

TATE, William; b 20 Nov 1753, Augusta Co; d 11 Feb 1830 **RU**: Captain, Took oath as Capt in Augusta Co Miltia 21 Aug 1781. Served to end of war **CEM**: Tate Family, nr Buchanan House; GPS unk; Broadford; Smyth **GS**: N **SP**: Dorcas Mitchell **VI**: No further data **P**: unk **BLW**: unk **RG**: Y **MK**: unk **PH**: N **SS**: DAR A112194; E pg 758; SAR P-301967 **BS**: JLARC 11, 14.

TATE, William; b 1747; d 15 Sep 1803 **RU**: Lieutenant Colonel, Served in Washington Co Militia 1776 **CEM**: Glenwood; GPS unk; Clarksville; Washington **GS**: U **SP**: Elizabeth (-----) (1755-1840) **VI**: No further data **P**: unk **BLW**: unk **RG**: N **MK**: unk **PH**: unk **SS**: E pg 758 **BS**: 196.

TATSAPAUGH, Peter See Appendix G addenda

TAVINER (TAVENNER), Ritchard (Richard); b unk; d 1844 **RU**: Private, Served in Capt Samuel Noland's Co, Loudoun Co Militia **CEM**: Goose Creek; GPS 39.11250, -77.69527; Rt 722, Lincoln; Loudoun **GS**: Y **SP**: No info **VI**: No further data **P**: unk **BLW**: unk **RG**:Y **MK**: N **PH**: Y**SS**: N pg 1254; SAR bio rpt submitted 28 Feb 21 **BS**: 25 pg 306.

TAYLOE, John; b 28 May 1721, Richmond Co; d 12 Apr 1779 **RU**: Patriot, Had public serv as member of First Council of State under Gov Patrick Henry. Resigned 9 Oct 1776. Gave tools to the cause Nov 1778 **CEM**: Tayloe Family; GPS 37.58200, -76.4729; Mt Airy, Rt 360, Warsaw; Richmond Co **GS**: U **SP**: Mar (11 Jul 1747) Rebecca Plater (8 Aug 1731-22 Jan 1787) **VI**: No further data **P**: N **BLW**: N **RG**: Y **MK**: unk **PH**: unk **SS**: DAR A112260; G pg 518; DD cites VA Hist Mag Vol 1 pg 64; SAR P-302012 **BS**: 196.

TAYLOR, Alexander; b 1737; d 1801 **RU**: Patriot, Gave material aid to cause, Prince George Co **CEM**: Blandford; GPS 37.22433, -77.38604; 319 S Crater Rd; Petersburg City **GS**: Y **SP**: No info **VI**: No further data **P**: N **BLW**: N **RG**: Y **MK**: Y SAR monument **PH**: unk **SS**: AL Comm Bk IV 364 Prince George Co; SAR P-335466 **BS**: 99 pg 30.

TAYLOR, Charles; b 3 Jan 1755, Orange Co; d 27 Jan 1821 **RU**: Surgeon, Was Surgeon of the Regt of Convention, Cont Line.and the Surgeon of Albemarle Barracks **CEM**: **Dr** Charles Taylor Residence 1821;GPS not determined; Rapidan; Orange **GS**: N **SP**: Mar (11 May 1777) Sarah Conway **VI**: Son of George & Rachel (Gibson) Taylor. Heirs recd BLW 1845 of 400 acres. Family Physician of President Madison. Last will and testiment 1821 indicates died at his residence, thus assume buried there. Son Charles born in Rapidan thus assume residence is there. (See Cem listed <u>FindaGrave</u> for James Taylor III on the Taylor-Quarles Plantation in Rapidan) **P**: N **BLW**: Y heirs **RG**: Y **MK**: Y SAR **PH**: N **SS**: E pg 759; AK; SAR P-302058; DAR anc# A112332 **BS**: JLARC 2; 200; 04; 196.

TAYLOR, Edmund; b 16 Aug 1741; d 28 Jan 1822 **RU**: Patriot, Gave material aid to cause **CEM**: Taylor Family; GPS 37.40850, -76.25405; VAQ 738 Old Ridge Rd; Hanover **GS**: Y **SP**: Mar (16 May 1771) Ann Day (18 Mar 1753 Hanover Co-12 Jul 1835) **VI**: No further data **P**: N **BLW**: N **RG**: Y **MK**: unk **PH**: Y **SS**: DAR Ancestor #A112406; J-NSSAR 2000 Reg; AL Ct Bk I pg 30 Hanover Co; SAR P-302111 **BS**: JLARC 76.

TAYLOR, Erasmus; b 5 Sep 1715, Rapidan, Culpeper Co; d 18 Dec 1794 **RU**: Patriot, Gave material aid to cause **CEM**: Greenfields Family; GPS 38.25335, -78.10039; Rt 2021, back of cem on Madex Dr; Orange **GS**: Y **SP**: I) Debrah Otis, 2), Jane Moore (22 Dec 1728-19 Sep 1812) d/o John & Rebecca (Catlett) Moore **VI**: Son of James (1675-1729) & Martha (Thompson) (1679-1762) Taylor **P**: N **BLW**: N **RG**: Y **MK**: N **PH**: unk **SS**: Al Comm Bk IV, pg 188 Orange Co; SAR P-302148 **BS**: 22 pg 64; 196.

TAYLOR, George; b 1745 Wales; d 12 Apr 1824 **RU**: First Lieutenant, Served in Capt Dillard's Co Henry Co Militia. Perhaps the George Taylor, who served as 1st Lt, Henry Co Militia **CEM**: Taylor; GPS unk; George Taylor Hwy; Henry **GS**: Y **SP**: Mar (1767) Elizabeth Anyon of Wales (__-aft 1823) **VI**: Died

RU=Rank/Unit	CEM=Cemetery	GS=Gravestone	SP=Spousal Information
VI=Other Veteran Info	P=Pension	BLW=Bounty/Land Warrant	RG=Registered Grave
MK=SAR/DAR Marker	PH=Photo	SS=Service Source	BS=Burial Source

408

in Mayo, Henry Co **P**: unk **BLW**: unk **RG**: Y **MK**: Y **PH**: unk **SS**: DAR A112488; Z pg 210, 230; AZ pg 210; SAR P-302159 **BS**: JLARC 102.

TAYLOR, George; b 11 Feb 1711, King & Queen Co; d 4 Nov 1792 **RU**: Patriot, Gave material aid to the cause in Orange Co. Served as Clerk of Ct 1776 **CEM**: Greenfield; GPS unk; Rapidan; Culpeper **GS**: N **SP**: Mar (28 Feb 1738) Rachel Gibson (4 May 1717-16 Feb 1761) **VI**: Son of James & Martha (Thompson) Taylor. Was not a Col in the Revolution but held the rank of Sgt. Was Col in the French & Indian War and was with Washington at Braddock's defeat. Died in Orange Co **P**: unk **BLW**: unk **RG**: Y **MK**: N **PH**: N **SS**: DAR A112475; AL recd Cert Orange Co; DD cites Joyner First Settlers of Orange Co VA; SAR P-302154 pg 242 **BS**: 196.

TAYLOR, James; b 1742, d 12 Sep 1808 **RU**: Patriot, Supported cause by paying supply tax included in his personal property tax in 1782, Mechlenburg Co **CEM**: Taylor Family; GPS 36.7190910, -78.1305770; loc jct Brook Ave & 3rd St, South Hill; Mechlenburg **GS**: N **SP**: Rebecca Davis (1746-23 Jun 1780) **VI**: No further data 1 **P**: N **BLW**: N **RG**: N **MK**: N **PH**: N **SS**: DV Binns Gen Mecklenburg Co Pers Prop Tax list 1782 image11.pdf **BS**: 196.

TAYLOR, James III; b 20 Mar 1703, Essex Co, d 1 Mar 1784 **RU**: Patriot, performed public service as was on a Committee of Public Safety during war period in Orange Co **CEM**: Taylor-Quarles Families; GPS 38.2562940, -78.0539430; loc Bloomsbury Rd on plantation property on right of Taylor-Quarles plantation house from driveway entrance in section without gate, Rapidan; Orange **GS**: N **SP**: Alice Thornton Catlett **VI**: Son of James Taylor & Martha Thompson **P**: N **BLW**: N **RG**: Y **MK**: unk **PH**: N **SS**: DAR A112609, quotes Scott, History of Orange Co, pg 65; SAR P-302225 **BS**: 196.

TAYLOR, James; b 2 Mar 1739, Ireland; d 23 Feb 1801 **RU**: Corporal, Served in Capt Joseph Smith's Co, Col Nathaniel Gist's Regt **CEM**: Taylor Family; GPS unk; Short Hill Mountain; Rockbridge **GS**: U **SP**: Mar (20 Jun 1775) Anna Paul (30 Aug 1753, Botetourt Co-15 Dec 1828) **VI**: No further data **P**: unk **BLW**: unk **RG**: Y **MK**: unk **PH**: unk **SS**: DAR A112628; E pg 760; AP roll 72; D; SAR P-302232 **BS**: 196.

TAYLOR, James; b cAug 1737; d 13 Nov 1814 **RU**: Patriot, Was Mayor of Norfolk during War (1778, 1780, 1782). Submitted claims for losses incurred during burning of Norfolk **CEM**: St Paul's Episcopal; GPS 36.84733, -76.28554; 201 St Paul's Blvd; Norfolk City **GS**: Y **SP**: No info **VI**: "The Order Book and Related Papers of the Common Hall of the Borough of Norfolk, Virginia 1736-1798" shows public service. Mayor of Norfolk after war in 1790 **P**: N **BLW**: N **RG**: N **MK**: Y SAR plaque **PH**: unk **SS**: CB; AL Ct Bk pg 2 **BS**: 87 pg 30.

TAYLOR, James; b 27 Dec 1732, Caroline Co; d 12 Mar 1814 **RU**: Patriot/Colonel, Commander Caroline Co Militia. Gave material aid to cause **CEM**: Taylor-Quarles Family; GPS 38.25629, -78.05394; End of Bloomsbury Rd; Caroline **GS**: U **SP**: 1) Nancy Ann Owen, 2), mar (Jun 1758) Ann Berry Hubbard (26 Mar 1738-27 May 1789) **VI**: Son of James (1703-1784) & Alice (Thornton) (1708-1739) Taylor **P**: unk **BLW**: unk **RG**: Y **MK**: unk **PH**: unk **SS**: E pg 760: AL List II pg 1 Caroline Co; SAR P-302228 & 336705 **BS**: 196.

TAYLOR, Jesse; b unk; d 24 Dec 1787 **RU**: Patriot, Signed legislative petition Alexandria **CEM**: Old Christ Church Episcopal; GPS 38.80625, -77.04718; 118 N Washington St; Alexandria City **GS**: U **SP**: No info **VI**: No further data **P**: N **BLW**: N **RG**: N **MK**: unk **PH**: unk **SS**: BB **BS**: 110 pg 91.

TAYLOR, Jesse; b 1741; d Oct 1800 **RU**: Patriot, Gave material aid to cause **CEM**: Old Presbyterian Meeting House; GPS 38.48528, -77.23532; 323 S Fairfax St; Alexandria City **GS**: N **SP**: No info **VI**: Died of biious fever, bur 15 Oct 1800, age 49. Listed on SAR plaque in cemetery **P**: N **BLW**: N **RG**: Y **MK**: Y SAR plaque **PH**: N **SS**: J-NSSAR 1993 Reg; AL Ct Bk pg 7, 14 Fairfax Co; AK; D; SAR P-302259 **BS**: JLARC 1; 23 pg 108; 196.

TAYLOR, John; b 19 Dec 1753; d 21 Aug 1824 **RU**: Lieutenant Colonel & Paymaster, Paymaster, Caroline Co Bn 1775-6. Commander, Caroline & Militia 1780 **CEM**: Hazelwood; GPS 38.18667, -77.22639; Hazelwood Ln at Rt 674, Port Royal; Caroline **GS**: Y **SP**: Mar (4 Dec 1783) Lucy Penn (17 Oct 1766 Mt Airy, Caroline Co- Aug 1831 Hazelwood, Port Royal) d/o John (2 Sep 1741 Caroline Co-14 Sep 1788, NC) & Susannah (Lyme) (c1745 Caroline Co-1 Mar 1784, NC) Penn **VI**: US Senator fr VA 1792-94. In Jun 1803, appointed to fill vacancy caused by death of Stevens T. Mason & served until Dec

RU=Rank/Unit	CEM=Cemetery	GS=Gravestone	SP=Spousal Information
VI=Other Veteran Info	P=Pension	BLW=Bounty/Land Warrant	RG=Registered Grave
MK=SAR/DAR Marker	PH=Photo	SS=Service Source	BS=Burial Source

409

1803. Served again fr 1822 until death 1824 **P:** unk **BLW:** unk **RG:** N **MK:** N **PH:** unk **SS:** E pg 761 **BS:** 60.

TAYLOR, John; b unk, d 28 Jun 1848 **RU:** Lieutenant, appointed Feb 1781 in Loudoun Co mititia **CEM:** Goose Creek; GPS 39.11250, -77.69527; Rt 722, Lincoln; Loudoun **GS:** Unk **SP:** No spousal info **VI:** No further data **P:** N **BLW:** N **RG:** N **MK:** N **PH:** N **SS:** E pg 761; **BS:** Loudoun Co Cemetery database cites microfilm burial records NO SAR # https://www.leesburgva.gov/government/departments/thomas-balch-library/loudoun-county-cemetery-database.

TAYLOR, John, Sr; b c1747 NC, d aft 21 Jul 1807, Ashe Co, NC **RU:** Private Capt Enoch Osborne's Co, NC Militia **CEM:** Bethany Community Cemetery GPS 36.571126, -81.170454; loc jct Shady Hill Rd & Starling Ln Independence; Grayson **GS:** Unk **SP:** Mar (24 Sep 1768, New Garden, NC) Mary "Polly" Lewis (1750-1830), d/o Gideon Lewis, Sr & (-----) **VI:** Son of Simeon Taylor (1704-1774) & Esther Dicks/Dix (1710 Birmingham, Chester, PA - Oct 8, 1794 Guilford Co.NC). Cem is on VA/NC line. He ran a grist mill on Elk Creek, NC; will probated Aug 1807, Ashe Co, NC **P:** N **BLW:** N **RG:** N **MK:** N **PH:** N **SS:** CD **BS:** 196.

TAYLOR, John; b 1751, Cumberland Co; d aft Aug 1777 **RU:** Patriot, Signed an Oath of Allegience Powhattan Co, 1777 **CEM:** Taylor Family; GPS not determined; 5609 Old Buckingham Rd; Powhatan **GS:** Unk **SP:** Lavina Drake (1769, Cumberland Co-__), d/o James Drake (1740-1796) & Mary Taylor (1744-1828) **VI:** Son of James Taylor (1724-1773) & Elizabeth Hughes (1730-1805). He sold property Aug 1777 in Powhattan Co **P:** N **BLW:** N **RG:** N **MK:** N **PH:** N **SS:** Oaths of Allegience Powhattan Co **BS:** 196.

TAYLOR, Nimrod; b 1756, Fauquier Co; d 16 Jul 1834 **RU:** Private, Ent serv 1780 Fauquier Co in Col Edmonds' Regt of Militia. Served in Capt Balls Co for 23 days **CEM:** Carter Family; GPS unk; Rt 649, Rye Cove; Scott **GS:** Y **SP:** Mar (1777) Mary Lutz (__-7 Sep 1840 Scott Co) **VI:** Appl for pension 12 Dec 1832 Scott Co. R10422 **P:** Y **BLW:** unk **RG:** Y **MK:** Y SAR **PH:** Y **SS:** H pg 3436; K Vol 5 pg 223; N pg 1347-8; DAR A112783; SAR P-302428 **BS:** JLARC 2, 22.

TAYLOR, Peter; b c1752; d 30 May 1823 **RU:** Soldier, Enl Accomack Co, and served in 3rd, 4th, 8th, and 12th Cont Lines **CEM:** Lincoln Memorial; GPS 36.80830, -76.32810; Jct Kirby St and Deep Creek Blvd; Portsmouth City **GS:** N **SP:** Mar (Jul 1783 Accomack Co) Elizabeth Kelly (1766-1 Sep 1855) **VI:** Obit indicates soldier in the Revolution. He appl for pen 25 Oct 1818 in Norfolk. Spouse appl pen 21 Aug 1843 at Portsmouth **P:** Y **BLW:** Y **RG:** N **MK:** unk **PH:** unk **SS:** C pg 273; E pg 761; CG pg 3436 **BS:** 196.

TAYLOR, Robert; b 1744; d 24 Apr 1825 **RU:**Patriot/Corporal, in Capt James Baytop's Co,5th VA Regt commanded by Col Daniel Morgan shown on payroll 1 Dec 1776 to Feb 1779; also served in 3rd and 7th Regts totaling 3 yrs; signed oath of allegence 1777 and paid personal property tax 1783 **CEM:** Peterville; GPS 37.564399, -77.964698; loc N of Anderson Rd by a pond 200 yds E of jct with Bell Rd; Powhatan **GS:** Unk **SP:** No spousal info **VI:** Son of William Taylor (1696-__) & Mary Fleming (1714-__); rec'd BLW 100 acres, 6 May 1785 # S3854 **P:** Unk **BLW:** Y **RG:** N **MK:** N **PH:** N **SS:** E pg 761; Lib of VA call # 24760, author Ann Waller Reddy oath list **BS:** 196

TAYLOR, Robert; b 8 May 1749; d 10 Oct 1826 **RU:** Patriot, Publicly toasted "the Congress, General Washington, success to the American Arms, etc" Was Mayor of Norfolk during War (1778, 1780, 1782). Submitted claims for losses incurred during burning of Norfolk. Gave material aid to the cause **CEM:** St Paul's Episcopal; GPS 36.84733, -76.28554; 201 St Paul's Blvd; Norfolk City **GS:** Y **SP:** "Sally Curle Barraud" likely "Sarah Crull Taylor" fr St Paul's Churchyard **VI:** Was Mayor of Norfolk 1784, 1789, 1793 **P:** N **BLW:** N **RG:** N **MK:** Y SAR plaque **PH:** unk **SS:** CB; AL Ct Bk pg 12 **BS:** 87 pg 30.

TAYLOR, Robert; b 29 Apr 1763, Orange Co; d 3 Jul 1845 **RU:** Sergeant, Served at Yorktown in Alcock's Regt Oct 1781 **CEM:** Taylor Family, Meadow Farm; GPS 38.22898, -78.07895; 16823 Monrovia Rd; Orange **GS:** Y **SP:** Mar (7 Jul 1784) Frances Pendleton (1767-1831) **VI:** Son of Erasmus (1715-1794) & (-----) Taylor. Served in VA State Senate 1804-1812. Served US Legislature 1825-1827 **P:** unk **BLW:** unk **RG:** N **MK:** N **PH:** N **SS:** C pg 576 **BS:** 22 pg 91; 196.

TAYLOR, Robert Square; b 1732, New Kent Co; d Oct 1806 **RU:**Corporal 5th Regt **CEM:** Ferry Farm; GPS 37.765735, -77.328597; loc off Etna Mills Rd just W of Norman's Bridge in field; King William **GS:**

RU=Rank/Unit	CEM=Cemetery	GS=Gravestone	SP=Spousal Information
VI=Other Veteran Info	P=Pension	BLW=Bounty/Land Warrant	RG=Registered Grave
MK=SAR/DAR Marker	PH=Photo	SS=Service Source	BS=Burial Source

410

N **SP**: Ann Meade Meux (15 Mar 1736-16 Oct 1802) **VI**: Son of M Daniel Taylor (1704-1742) & Allice Littlepage (1708-1787) **P**: N **BLW**: N **RG**:N **MK**:N **PH**: SS AP serv Rec **BS**: 196.

TAYLOR, Sarah Crull (Croel (Curle Barraud) Huitt); b c1755; d Jan. 15, 1787, Norfolk **RU**: Patriot, Submitted claim for losses suffered during the burning of Norfolk **CEM**: St Paul's Episcopal; GPS 36.84733, -76.28554; 201 St Paul's Blvd; Norfolk City **GS**: Y **SP**: Probably mar to Mayor Robert Taylor **VI**: No further data **P**: N **BLW**: N **RG**:N **MK**: Y SAR plaque **PH**: unk **SS**: CB Friend Amer Cause **BS**: 178 Jan 11.

TAYLOR, Stacy; b 28 Feb 1757, Bucks Co, PA; d 1836 **RU**: Private, Served in Capt Jacob Bennet's Light Dragoons fr Bucks Co, PA **CEM**: Goose Creek; GPS 39.11250, -77.69527; Rt 722, Lincoln; Loudoun **GS**: Y **SP**: Ruth Beans (1775-1846) **VI**: Son of Timothy & Letitia (Kirkbride) Taylor **P**: unk **BLW**: unk **RG**: Y **MK**: N **PH**: unk **SS**: Cl PA Archives pg 208; D; SAR P-302526 **BS**: 196.

TAYLOR, Thomas; b c1751; d 31 Dec 1802 **RU**: Private, Served in Capt Samuel Noland's Co, Loudoun Co Militia **CEM**: Level Green Farm; GPS unk; 6275 Old Centerville Rd, Chantilly; Fairfax **GS**: Y **SP**: No info **VI**: No further data **P**: unk **BLW**: unk **RG**: N **MK**: N **PH**: unk **SS**: N pg 1254 **BS**: 61 Vol IV pg CN-22.

TAYLOR, Thomas: b 1761; d 11 Jan 1815 **RU**: Private Capt Joseph Smith's Co, Col Nathaniel Gist's Regt, Cont Troops **CEM**: Mantua-Smith Family; loc GPS 37.957330, -76.471840; loc end of Mantua Rd, Heathsville; Northumberland **GS**: Unk **SP**: Charlotte McAdam(1751-c1836), d/o Joseph Mc Adam (28 May 1719, Scotland-__) & Sarah Ann Gaskins (1720-1788): **VI**: No further data **P**: N **BLW**: N **RG**: N **MK**: N **PH**: unk **SS**: E pg 762; AP Fold3 Serv Index Card **BS**: 196.

TAYLOR, Timothy II; b 11 Jan 1761, Newtown, Bucks Co, PA; d 8 Jun 1838 **RU**: Private, Served in 12th VA Regt, Cont Line **CEM**: Goose Creek; GPS 39.11250, -77.69527; Rt 722, Lincoln; Loudoun **GS**: Y **SP**: Mar (Feb 1780 Bucks Co, PA) Achrah (-----) (5 Feb 1759-16 May 1826) **VI**: Commissioned Lt Col 25 May 1810 in War of 1812 and commanded 56th VA Regt **P**: unk **BLW**: unk **RG**: Y **MK**: N **PH**: unk **SS**: E pg 762; Serv Record Card; SAR P-302575 **BS**: 196.

TAYLOR, William; b c1738; d 11 Sep 1820 **RU**: Patriot, Was a county clerk during war period. Gave material aid to the cause **CEM**: Taylor Family; GPS unk; 18 mi S of Kenbridge; Lunenburg **GS**: Y **SP**: Mar 15 Mar 1757, Martha Waller (28 Nov 1747 James City Co-11 Mar 1828) **VI**: Son of M. Daniel (1704-1742) & Alice (Littlepage) (1708-1787) Taylor **P**: N **BLW**: N **RG**:Y **MK**: Y DAR **PH**: unk **SS**: Al Ct Bk pg 14, 17; BN WPA report; DAR A113153; SAR P-302591; **BS**: 196; 172 The Taylor.

TAYMAN (LAYMAN, LAYMON), George; b 1760, Frederick, Frederick Co, MD; d 15 Jul 1854 **RU**: Private/Patriot, Military service not determined. As patriot gave material aid to cause under name Laymon **CEM**: Temontown; GPS unk; Laymantown; Botetourt **GS**: U **SP**: Mar (1785 MD) Barbara Baumgardner (Sep 1763-Mar 1852) **VI**: Son of George Hans & Salome (-----) Lehman **P**: unk **BLW**: unk **RG**: unk **MK**: N **PH**: unk **SS**: DAR Ancestor #A067530; AL cert Botetourt Co under name Lymon; AR DAR Application; AR pg 102; BY; SAR P-302658 **BS**: JLARC 2.

TEACKLE, Arthur; b 28 Feb 1755; d 31 Jan 1791 **RU**: First Lieutenant, Served in 9th Cont Line for 7 yrs. Was 1st Lt 26 Jul 1776. **CEM**: Teackle House; GPS unk; Rt 1709 & Brooklyn St, Wachapreague; Accomack **GS**: Y **SP**: Elizabeth Read (27 Feb 1760-10 May 1815) **VI**: Recd BLW of 3111 acres for 7 yrs service **P**: unk **BLW**: Y **RG**: N **MK**: N **PH**: unk **SS**: C pg 118; E pg 762 **BS**: 37 pg 252.

TEACKLE (TEAKLE), Levin; b 1717; d 28 Sep 1794 **RU**: Patriot, Gave material aid to the cause **CEM**: Teackle House; GPS unk; Rt 1709 & Brooklyn St, Wachapreague; Accomack **GS**: Y **SP**: Joyce (-----) (Feb 1735-Dec 1760) **VI**: Son of John & (-----) Teackle. Died age 70 **P**: N **BLW**: N **RG**: N **MK**: N **PH**: unk **SS**: AL Com Bk 1 pg 32 **BS**: 37 pg 252.

TEBBS; Foushee, b 1723 Westmoreland Co, d 20 Oct 1784 **RU**: Patriot, performed public service as Sheriff Prince William Co, 1777; Committee of Safety, 1776; and paid personal property tax (a portion was a supply tax for Rev War expenses) in Prince William Co in 1782 and 1783 **CEM**: Tebbsdale; GPS 38.33324, -77.17953; Possum Point Rd, behind sub-division, Dumfries; Prince William **GS**: Yes-VA stone installed and dedicated Oct 2019 **SP**: Mar (1752) Mary Innis Baxter, d/o John Baxter & (-----) **VI**: Son of Daniel Tebbs (__-1742) & Charlotte Foushee; was captain in Prince William Co militia, 1761 and represented county in House of Burgesses 1765-1774 **P**: N **BLW**: N **RG**: Y **MK**: Y SAR **PH**: Y **SS**:

RU=Rank/Unit	CEM=Cemetery	GS=Gravestone	SP=Spousal Information
VI=Other Veteran Info	P=Pension	BLW=Bounty/Land Warrant	RG=Registered Grave
MK=SAR/DAR Marker	PH=Photo	SS=Service Source	BS=Burial Source

411

Prince Wm Co Reliquary Apr 2005, #2 pg 25; Rev VA The Road to Independence, vol VII; pg 42 ; Pr Wm Co Personal Prop Tax lists; SAR P-337741; DAR Anc # A129768; AK **BS:** 04.

TEBBS, Willoughby; b 1759, prob Dumfries, Prince William Co; d 22 Oct 1803 **RU:** Lieutenant, Served 1 Mar 1777-21 Sep 1778, Grayson's Cont Regt. Was Regt QM Jul 1778 and 2nd Lt 8 Jun 1777. Resigned 21 Sep 1778 **CEM:** Tebbsdale Plantation; GPS unk; Rt 633 off US 1 Dumfries; Prince William **GS:** Y **SP:** Mar (16 Oct 1771, however, pen info says 1787 Dumfries) Betsey Carr (c1780-18 Mar 1858) d/o of William & (-----) Carr. (Wm Carr signed mar bond with sol on 30 Aug 1786 in Prince William Co). **VI:** Practiced law in Dumfries VA. Later after War, Col of Prince William Co. Militia. Son of Foushee & Mary (Baxter) Tebbs. W6284. Widow pen 1840 Loudoun Co age 60. BLW #4946 issued to brother John Tebbs then to heirs **P:** Y **BLW:** Y **RG:** Y **MK:** Y SAR & stone plaque **PH:** Y **SS:** K Vol 5 pg 231; CG Vol 3 pg 3423; SAR Patriot Index CD; SAR P-302719 **BS:** JLARC 4, 31.

TEBBS, Willoughby William; b c1750; d 1832 **RU:** Captain, Gave material aid to the cause **CEM:** Tebbsdale Plantation; GPS unk; Rt 633 off US 1 Dumfries; Prince William **GS:** Y **SP:** No info **VI:** No further data **P:** unk **BLW:** unk **RG:** N **MK:** N **PH:** unk **SS:** AL,Ct Bk pg 14 as Capt **BS:** 94 pg 471.

TEE William; b 1758,St Marys Co, MD, d 14 Oct 1849 **RU:** Naval Pilot, guided the French fleet to Yorktown, Oct 1781 **CEM:** Cedar Grove; GPS 36.57204, - 80.02594; 301 Fort Lane, Rd; Portsmouth City **GS:** Y lot 370 **SP:** No spousal data **VI:** After war named captain of Craney Island Lightship and performed this duty for 30 years. Was in the War of 1812 as a Naval pilot and was injured by a fall **P:** N **BLW:** N **RG:** N **MK:** N **PH:** N **SS:** Historian, Margaret Windley, of Portsmouth cites books *Heritage of Portsmouth*, *The Elizabeth River* and The Hendley Index **BS:** 196.

TEETER, John; b 1753 Rhine Valley, Germany; d 6 Aug 1818 **RU:** Patriot, Served as juryman and constable Washington Co 1777-1783 **CEM:** Teeter Family; GPS 36.66470, -82.12080; Vic Clear Creek Dam; Washington **GS:** Y **SP:** Mar (20 May 1769) Eve Turner/Tournai (1753-aft 6 May 1818) **VI:** No further data **P:** N **BLW:** N **RG:** Y **MK:** N **SS:** I; AR Vol 4 pg 102; DD; SAR P-302770 **BS:** 78 pg 382.

TEPHANY, Remy; b unk; d 1781 **RU:** Seaman, Served on "Pluton" and died from Yorktown battle **CEM:** French Memorial; GPS 36.81944, -79.39933; Yorktown; York **GS:** U **SP:** No info **VI:** No further data **P:** unk **BLW:** unk **RG:** Y **MK:** unk **PH:** unk **SS:** J-Yorktown Historian; SAR P-303008 **BS:** JLARC 1, 74.

TERRELL, David Jr; b 10 Jun 1829; d 14 Feb 1805 **RU:** Patriot, Gave material aid to cause **CEM:** South River Meeting House; GPS 37.37246, -79.19194; 5810 Fort Ave; Lynchburg City **GS:** Y **SP:** Jane Johnson (30 May 1762-2 Jun 1850) Note PRS indicates married Sarah Johnson **VI:** No further data **P:** N **BLW:** N **RG:**Y **MK:** unk **PH:** N **SS:** AL Cert Caroline Co; SAR P-303050 **BS:** 196; 221.

TERRELL, Samuel; b By 1766; d unk **RU:** Patriot, Provided material support to the cause fr Louisa Co **CEM:** Golansville Meeting House; GPS unk; Golansville on US1; Caroline **GS:** N **SP:** Mar (7 May 1800) Elizabeth Harris **VI:** Son of Pleasant & (-----) Terrell **P:** N **BLW:** N **RG:** N **MK:** N **PH:** unk **SS:** Al Ct Bk pg 42 Louisa Co **BS:** 14 pg 44.

TERRY, Champness; b 1695, New Kent Co; d 1782 **RU:** Patriot, his spouse paid the personal property tax in Louisa Co, the year he died. SAR indicates he was a patriot but source not provided **CEM:** Terry Homestead; GPS not determined; only Fredericksville Parish, thus use property rec to detertmine location; Louisa **GS:** N **SP:** Christian Bibb **VI:** SAR applicant has incorrect birth date of 1777 **P:** N **BLW:** N **RG:** Y **MK:** N **PH:** unk **SS:** SAR P-303107; **BS:** 196.

TERRY, Joseph; b 1749, d 22 Sep 1817 **RU:** Lieutenant, Sep 1775 appointed LT in Pittsylvania Co Militia. Drove cattle to SC forces in spring of 1780, thus more than four years service **CEM:** Sycamore Hill; GPS not determined; loc on Rt 614, South Boston; Halifax **GS:** Unk **SP:** Mar (21 Nov 1783) Sarah Coleman Williams (6 Aug 1758-30 Mar 1820 **VI:** No further data **P:** Unk **BLW:** Unk **RG:** N **MK:** N **PH:** N **SS:** G pg 284 **BS:** 196.

TERRY, Nathaniel Sr; b 1724; d 21 Apr 1780 **RU:** Patriot, Was member of the House of Burgesses **CEM:** Terry Family; GPS unk; 1154 N Terry Rd, Halifax; Halifax **GS:** Y **SP:** 1) Lucy Hatcher 2) mar (1746) Sarah Royale (3 feb 1715-16 Jun 1778) **VI:** DAR marker & VA Historical Rd sign **P:** N **BLW:** N **RG:** Y **MK:** Y DAR plaque **PH:** Y **SS:** DAR Ancestor #A113709; J-NSSAR 1993 Reg; AR Vol 4 pg 105; DD cites VA Mag Hist & Bio Vol 37 No 1 pg 27; SAR P-303194 **BS:** JLARC 1, 2; 80 pg 105.

RU=Rank/Unit	CEM=Cemetery	GS=Gravestone	SP=Spousal Information
VI=Other Veteran Info	P=Pension	BLW=Bounty/Land Warrant	RG=Registered Grave
MK=SAR/DAR Marker	PH=Photo	SS=Service Source	BS=Burial Source

412

TERRY, Royal; b 1754; d 1825 **RU**: Private, Service information not listed in SAR registry **CEM**: Terry Family; GPS unk; 1154 N Terry Rd, Halifax; Halifax **GS**: U **SP**: No info **VI**: No further data **P**: unk **BLW**: unk **RG**: Y **MK**: unk **PH**: unk **SS**: J-NSSAR 2000 Reg; NSSAR Ancestor #P-303163 **BS**: JLARC 76.

TERRY, William; b 1752, Cumberland Co; d 1814 **RU**: Captain, Commanded a company in Bedford Co Militia. Took oath as capt 28 May 1781 **CEM**: Terry Family; GPS unk; Oakwood; Bedford **GS**: N **SP**: Susan Turner (1755 Bedford Co-1814) **VI**: No further data **P**: unk **BLW**: unk **RG**: unk **MK**: N **PH**: N **SS**: J- DAR Hatcher; E pg 765; SAR P-303185 **BS**: JLARC 2; 80 vol 4 pg 105.

TERRY, William E; b unk; d 1845 **RU**: Patriot, Gave material aid to cause **CEM**: St John's Episcopal; GPS 37.53183, -77.41958; 2401 E Broad St; Richmond City **GS**: N **SP**: No info **VI**: No further data **P**: N **BLW**: N **RG**: N **MK**: N **PH**: N **SS**: D Vol 2, pg 572 **BS**: 28 pg 351.

TERVILLE, Andre; b unk; d 1781 **RU**: Soldier, Served in Bourbonnais Bn and died fr battle at Yorktown **CEM**: French Memorial; GPS 36.81944, -79.39933; Yorktown; York **GS**: U **SP**: No info **VI**: No further data **P**: unk **BLW**: unk **RG**: unk **MK**: unk **PH**: unk **SS**: J-Yorktown Historian; SAR P-303196 **BS**: JLARC 74.

TESTELIN, Louis; b unk; d 1781 **RU**: Soldier, Served in Bourbonnais Bn and died fr battle at Yorktown **CEM**: French Memorial; GPS 36.81944, -79.39933; Yorktown; York **GS**: U **SP**: No info **VI**: No further data **P**: unk **BLW**: unk **RG**: Y **MK**: unk **PH**: unk **SS**: J-Yorktown Historian; SAR P-303214 **BS**: JLARC 1,74.

TETER (TETOR), Paul; b c1730, PA; d 27 Nov 1784 **RU**: Corporal/Patriot, Gave material aid to cause **CEM**: Old Peaked Mountain; GPS 38.37113, -78.73416; 9843 Town Hall Rd, McGaheysville; Rockingham **GS**: N **SP**: Mar (c1760) Rebecca Hinkle (5 Oct 1736-aft 29 Mar 1797 S Clair, IL) d/o Justus (10 Feb 1706 Germany; 24 Aug 1778 German Valley, VA) & Mary Margareta (Eshman) Hinkle **VI**: No further data **P**: unk **BLW**: unk **RG**: Y **MK**: Y DAR plaque **PH**: N **SS**: AL Ct Bk I pg 7,14 Rockingham Co; AZ pg 184; SAR P-303219 **BS**: 116 Monument.

TEYO, Rene; b unk; d 1781 **RU**: Seaman, Served on "Palmier" and died from Yorktown battle **CEM**: French Memorial; GPS 36.81944, -79.39933; Yorktown; York **GS**: U **SP**: No info **VI**: No further data **P**: unk **BLW**: unk **RG**: Y **MK**: unk **PH**: unk **SS**: J-Yorktown Historian; SAR P-303257 **BS**: JLARC 1, 74.

THATCHER, Stephen; b 2 Dec 1765; d 2 May 1845 **RU**: Private, Served in Capt Samuel Noland's Co, Loudoun Co Militia **CEM**: Ebenezer Baptist; GPS 39.05824, -77.84142; 20421 Airmont Rd, Bluemont; Loudoun **GS**: Y **SP**: Alcy Chew (5 Nov 1744-5 Apr 1829) d/o James & (-----) Chew **VI**: Son of Richard & (-----) Thatcher. Died in Bloomfield or Bluemont, Loudoun Co **P**: unk **BLW**: unk **RG**: Y **MK**: Y SAR plaque **PH**: unk **SS**: N pg 1254; SAR P-336645 **BS**: 25 pg 310; 196.

THEVENIN, Louis; b unk; d 1781 **RU**: Soldier, Served in Agenois Bn and died fr battle at Yorktown **CEM**: French Memorial; GPS 36.81944, -79.39933; Yorktown; York **GS**: U **SP**: No info **VI**: No further data **P**: unk **BLW**: unk **RG**: Y **MK**: unk **PH**: unk **SS**: J-Yorktown Historian; SAR P-303479 **BS**: JLARC 1, 74.

THOMAS, Evan; b 10 Feb 1753, Chester Co, PA; d Jul 1820 **RU**: Private, Capt Reuben Briscoe's Co, 3rd VA Regt commmanded by Lt Col William Heath Apr 1778, serving long enough to rec pen. Paid for wagonage, 1781 **CEM**: Coffman Family; GPS not determined: 2985 Kratzer Rd (Rt 753); Rockingham **GS**: Unk **SP**: Mar (1764) Rebecca Green (21 Sep 1743, PA-1835), d/o Francis Green & Margaret (-----) **P**: Y **BLW**: VI: Son of Rees Thomas (1690-1759). Applied for pen 30 Nov 1833 age **81** (Recd # S16002) **RG**: Y **MK**: unk **PH**: unk **SS**: A pg 273; C pg 279; E pg 726; CG pg 2463; DAR A114238; SAR P-303610 **BS**: 196.

THOMAS, Francis; b 23 Mar 1743; d 27 Jun 1835 **RU**: Private, Served in Bn of VA forces commanded by Col James Hendricks May 1777 **CEM**: Fincastle Presbyterian; GPS 37.50017, -79.87558; 108 E Back St, Fincastle; Botetourt **GS**: Y **SP**: Grace Metcalfe (14 Mar 1741-6 Sep 1829) **VI**: Name is on SAR plaque in cemetery **P**: unk **BLW**: unk **RG**: Y **MK**: Y SAR plaque **PH**: unk **SS**: J-NSSAR 1993 Reg, J-DAR Hatcher, AR Vol 4 pg 108; AP Serv Record; SAR P-303618 **BS**: JLARC 1, 2;80 Pg 108; 196.

THOMAS, Giles; b 30 Nov 1763, Harford Co, MD; d 21 Mar 1842 **RU**: Private, Served in MD Cont Line. Served under General Nathaniel Greene in battles at Guilford, Camden, and Ninety Six **CEM**: Westview;

RU=Rank/Unit	CEM=Cemetery	GS=Gravestone	SP=Spousal Information
VI=Other Veteran Info	P=Pension	BLW=Bounty/Land Warrant	RG=Registered Grave
MK=SAR/DAR Marker	PH=Photo	SS=Service Source	BS=Burial Source

413

GPS 37.23390, -80.40830; Blacksburg; Montgomery **GS:** Y **SP:** Mar (4 Jun 1786, Blacksburg) Nancy Anne Wheeler (10 May 1762-12 Jun 1845) d/o Benjamin & Mary (Neale) Wheeler **VI:** Son of David & Hannah (Greene) Thomas. Gov't Gr Stone. Appl for pen Aug 1832. Recd BLW # 1747 **P:** Y **BLW:** Y **RG:** Y **MK:** unk **PH:** unk **SS:** SAR Ancestor #P-303628; SAR applic **BS:** 196.

THOMAS, Harrison; b 1760; d 1809 **RU:** Sergeant, Served in the 10th Regt. Perhaps also served as Capt **CEM:** Old Thomas Farm; GPS unk; N of Rt 617, NW of Weirwood; Northampton **GS:** Y **SP:** 1) (-----) 2) Elizabeth Downing **VI:** No further data **P:** unk **BLW:** unk **RG:** Y **MK:** N **PH:** unk **SS:** NSSAR Ancestor #P-303630 **BS:** JLARC 2, 69; 42 pg 83, 80 pg 108.

THOMAS, John; b 8 Apr 1757, Buckingham Co; d 13 Sep 1849 **RU:** Captain, Ent serv 1779 as Ensign in VA Line. Lived Albemarle Co 1778 at enl. Served in the Regt of Guards at the Albemarle Barracks under Col Francis Taylor **CEM:** Martin Marietta's Land; GPS unk; Nr Red Hill; Albemarle **GS:** U **SP:** No info **VI:** Sol appl pen 6 May 1833 Albemarle Co. Rejected due to less than six mos service. R10502. Recd BLW that indicates he d c1849 Buckingham Co **P:** N **BLW:** Y **RG:** Y **MK:** unk **PH:** unk **SS:** DAR Ancestor #A113057; SAR Ancestor #P-303742; K Vol 5 pg 245; BY pg 373; J- DAR Hatcher; CG Vol 3 pg 3565 **BS:** JLARC 2.

THOMAS, John; b 1764; d 1850 **RU:** Ensign, Served in Albemarle Co Militia **CEM:** Thomas Family; GPS unk; Nr Red Hill; Albemarle **GS:** U **SP:** No info **VI:** No further data **P:** unk **BLW:** unk **RG:** N **MK:** unk **PH:** unk **SS:** E pg 767 **BS:** JLARC 2.

THOMAS, John; b 16 Oct 1733, Southampton Co; d 9 Jul 1821 **RU:** Private, Served in Capt Faunteroy's Co 5th & 9th VA Regts 1778 **CEM:** St Clair Bottom Primitive Baptist; GPS 36.76098, -81.64556; Jct Rts 600 & 660, Chilhowie; Smyth **GS:** Y **SP:** Mary Robinette (1740 Southampton Co-9 Jul 1821) **VI:** No further data **P:** unk **BLW:** unk **RG:** N **MK:** unk **PH:** unk **SS:** AP payroll **BS:** 196.

THOMAS, John Sr; b 1760, Montgomery Co, PA; d 1829 **RU:** Private, Served in Capt B Raug's Co, 1st PA Militia Regt **CEM:** Ebenezer Baptist; GPS 39.05824, -77.84142; 20421 Airmont Rd, Bluemont; Loudoun **GS:** U **SP:** Mar (c1790) Leah Jones **VI:** Son of Japhet & Mary (Drake) Thomas. Arr in Loudoun Co 1794 **P:** unk **BLW:** unk **RG:** Y **MK:** Y SAR plaque **PH:** unk **SS:** AP; SAR P-336645 **BS:** 196.

THOMAS, Joseph (Japhet); b 1735, PA, d 1811 **RU"** Patriot Gave material aid to cause and paid his personal property tax in 1782 that was partially used to support the cause **CEM:** Ebenezer Baptist; GPS 39.05824, -77.84142; 20421 Airmont Rd, Bluemont; Loudoun **GS:** U **SP:** Mar (20 Jul 1761, Montgomery Co, PA) Mary Drake, d/o George & (-----) Drake **VI:** Given name on marriage liecense and property records was Japhet **P:** N **BLW:** N **RG:** Y **MK:** Y SAR plaque **PH:** N **SS:** AL Ct Bk pg 62 and Comm Bk III, pg 330; DV 1782 Personal Property Tax List 1782, image 14.pdf; SAR P-336624 **BS:** 196.

THOMAS, Richard; b 29 Aug 1764; d 25 Feb 1840 **RU:** Private, Served in 11th Cont Line **CEM:** Thomas Family; GPS unk; nr Timberville; Rockingham **GS:** Y **SP:** Elizabeth (-----) (1769-1840) **VI:** No further data **P:** unk **BLW:** unk **RG:** N **MK:** N **PH:** unk **SS:** AK; E pg 767 **BS:** 04; 191 ThomasFam.

THOMAS, William; b 1752; d 1834 **RU:** Patriot, Gave material aid to cause **CEM:** Thomas-Lowry Farm; GPS unk; E fr Bedford; Bedford **GS:** U **SP:** Elizabeth (-----) (__-26 Sep 1836) **VI:** No further data **P:** N **BLW:** N **RG:** Y **MK:** N **PH:** unk **SS:** DAR Ancestor #A133859; J- DAR Hatcher; AL Ct Bk pg 8, 27.

THOMPSON, Alexander; b 1732; d 5 May 1824 **RU:** Lieutenant Colonel, In charge of Augusta Co Militia 1776 & 1777 **CEM:** Tinkling Spring Presbyterian; GPS 38.08472, -78.98278; 30 Tinkling Spring Dr, Fishersville; Augusta **GS:** N **SP:** No info **VI:** No further data **P:** unk **BLW:** unk **RG:** N **MK:** N **PH:** N **SS:** E pg 768; CZ pg 434 **BS:** 142 Tinkling Spr; 208 pg 467.

THOMPSON, Amos Rev; b 7 Aug 1731 New Haven CT; d 8 Sep 1804 **RU:** Chaplain, Appointed Chaplain 23 Jul 1776 in Bn commanded by Col Hugh Stevenson **CEM:** Leesburg Presbyterian; GPS 39.11611, -77.56722; 207 W Market St, Leesburg; Loudoun **GS:** Y **SP:** Jane Evans of MD **VI:** Son of Amos Thompson (1702-1795) & Sarah Alling (1702-1787). Baptized in New Haven, CT on 31 Oct 1731. Died shortly after Leesburg Presbyterian was organized **P:** unk **BLW:** unk **RG:** Y **MK:** unk **PH:** unk **SS:** Journal Congress 9/7/1776 pg 585; SAR P-303972 **BS:** JLARC 1, 2, 32; 196.

THOMPSON, Andrew; b 1750, Ireland; d 1840 **RU:** Ensign/Patriot, Served in Capt Thomas Ingles Co, Montgomery Co Militia 7 Apr 1781. Also served in Battle of Pt Pleasant Oct 1774. Had public service as Justice of Peace, Montgomery Co **CEM:** Bird; GPS unk; Rt 42 2.5 mi E of Bland village; Bland **GS:** U

RU=Rank/Unit	CEM=Cemetery	GS=Gravestone	SP=Spousal Information
VI=Other Veteran Info	P=Pension	BLW=Bounty/Land Warrant	RG=Registered Grave
MK=SAR/DAR Marker	PH=Photo	SS=Service Source	BS=Burial Source

414

SP: Ann (-----) (1755-1840) **VI:** DAR marker **P:** unk **BLW:** unk **RG:** Y **MK:** Y DAR plaque **PH:** unk **SS:** SAR Ancestor #P-303981; DAR Ancestor #A113833; J- DAR Hatcher; G pg 227 **BS:** JLARC 2; 196.

THOMPSON, Archibald; b 10 Jun 1764; d 4 Aug 1846 **RU:** Private, Served in Capt Daniel Trigg's Co, Montgomery Co Militia 7 Apr 1781 **CEM:** Thompson Family; GPS unk; Thompson Valley; Tazewell **GS:** U **SP:** Mar (29 Mar 1796) Rebecca Perry (Jul 1778-12 Nov 1836) **VI:** No further data **P:** unk **BLW:** unk **RG:** Y **MK:** unk **PH:** unk **SS:** SAR Ancestor #P-303992; DAR Ancestor #A113848; J-NSSAR 2000 Reg; G pg 227 **BS:** JLARC 76; 196.

THOMPSON, Daniel; b 1755; d c1835 **RU:** Private, Served in 1st VA State Regt for 3 yrs. Served under Capt Thomas Ewell, Col George Gibson Regt 1775-1778 **CEM:** Thompson Family; GPS 38.87201, -77.26178; Vic jct Rt 29 & Nutley St; Fairfax **GS:** N **SP:** Mar (1782) Sarah Blundon (1759, Fairfax Co-1785) **VI:** Son of Samuel Pierce (__-1705) & Nanie (Ballinger) Thompson. Recd 100 acres BLW **P:** unk **BLW:** Y **RG:** N **MK:** N **PH:** N **SS:** DAR Ancestor #A113923; C pg 377; E pg 768; F pg 73 **BS:** 60 Fairfax Cem.

THOMPSON, Hugh; b unk; d 25 Dec 1823 **RU:** Sergeant, Served in Capt Jeremiah Talbott's Co, 30 Nov 1777. Served also in a VA unit in the IL Department **CEM:** Potts Family; GPS unk; Rts 716 & 714, Hillsboro; Loudoun **GS:** Y **SP:** No info **VI:** No further data **P:** unk **BLW:** unk **RG:** N **MK:** N **PH:** unk **SS:** A pg 217; CZ pg 436 **BS:** 25 pg 313.

THOMPSON, James; b 1732; d 1824 **RU:** Colonel, Service information not listed in SAR registry **CEM:** Tinkling Spring Presbyterian; GPS 38.08472, -78.98278; 30 Tinkling Spring Dr, Fishersville; Augusta **GS:** N **SP:** No info **VI:** No further data **P:** unk **BLW:** unk **RG:** Y **MK:** N **PH:** N **SS:** NSSAR Ancestor #P-304136 **BS:** JLARC 62,63.

THOMPSON, James; b c1750; d 1831 **RU:** Private/Patriot, Gave material aid to cause **CEM:** Thompson-Ford Family; GPS unk; Green Branch Farm; Fauquier **GS:** N **SP:** No info **VI:** No further data **P:** unk **BLW:** unk **RG:** N **MK:** N **PH:** N **SS:** E pg 768; AL Ct Bk pg 26 Fauquier Co **BS:** 83 e-mail 07.

THOMPSON, James Paxton; b 1 Sep 1736, Spotsylvania Co; d 1814 **RU:** Captain, Service information not determined. See DAR Senate Doc for year 1950 ser 11507, vol 6 for unit **CEM:** Thompson Family; GPS unk; Not identified; Tazewell **GS:** U **SP:** 1) Rebecca Gray 2) Elizabeth Shantafer **VI:** No further data **P:** unk **BLW:** unk **RG:** Y **MK:** unk **PH:** unk **SS:** DAR Ancestor #A115416; SAR Ancestor #P-304169; J-NSSAR 2000 Reg **BS:** JLARC 76; 80 VOL 4 PG 110.

THOMPSON, John; b 27 Feb 1764, Augusta Co; d 16 Jul 1850 **RU:** Captain, Served in VA Line. Ent serv 1780 Montgomery Co **CEM:** Thompson Family; GPS unk; Thompson Valley; Tazewell **GS:** U **SP:** Mar (1789) Louisa Bowen (c1767-1812) d/o Rees (1737, MD-7 Oct 1780 Kings Mountain, NC) & Louisa (Smith) (c1741, Augusta Co-16 Feb 1830) Bowen **VI:** Appl pen 31 Mar 1834 Tazewell Co, age 70. Pension rejected R10540 **P:** N **BLW:** unk **RG:** Y **MK:** unk **PH:** unk **SS:** J- DAR Hatcher; K Vol 5 pg 253-4; CG Vol 3 pg 3478; SAR P-304234 **BS:** JLARC 2.

THOMPSON, John; b 1760, d 15 Feb 1815 **RU:** Private Served in Gen Armand's Command for 3 years ending in 1783 **CEM:** Christ Church Episcopal; GPS 38.8021584, -77.0568924; Wilkes St; Alexandria; **GS:** Y **SP:** No spousal info **VI:** No further data **P:** N **BLW:** Eligible **RG:** N **MK:** N **PH:** N **SS:** C pgs 115,116; E pg 769; **BS:** 80 pg 111; 196.

THOMPSON,(AKA THOMASSON) John; b 1753, d 1840 **RU:** 1ST Lieutenant, was 2nd LT in Captain Samuel Tribble's Co, Dec 1777, promoted to 1/LT in Caroline Co Militia Dec 9 Nov 1780. He also was a patriot as he gave material aid to the cause **CEM:** Little River Baptist Church; GPS of Ch 37,945166, -77.800052; loc N side Rt 609, Buckner Rd; Louisa **GS:** Y Gov't **SP:** Grizel Ellis **VI:** PRS indicates data fr DAR mag **P:** N **BLW:** N **RG:** Y **MK:** N **PH:** N **SS:** E pg 769; G pg 105; J- DAR Hatcher; AL Ct Bk pg 21 Louisa Co; CD serv on Gr St as Drummer; SAR P-304215 and 304453 **BS:** JLARC 2; JLARC 1, 2, 4, 61; 80 pg 111.

THOMPSON, Robert; b unk; d 1847 **RU:** Captain, Commanded a company 1776-1780 in Augusta Co Militia. Resigned 21 Mar 1780 **CEM:** Tinkling Spring Presbyterian; GPS 38.08472, -78.98278; 30 Tinkling Spring Dr, Fishersville; Augusta **GS:** N **SP:** No info **VI:** No further data **P:** unk **BLW:** unk **RG:** Y **MK:** N **PH:** N **SS:** E pg 769; SAR P-304338 **BS:** JLARC 62, 63.

RU=Rank/Unit	CEM=Cemetery	GS=Gravestone	SP=Spousal Information
VI=Other Veteran Info	P=Pension	BLW=Bounty/Land Warrant	RG=Registered Grave
MK=SAR/DAR Marker	PH=Photo	SS=Service Source	BS=Burial Source

THOMPSON, Samuel; b 1705; d unk **RU:** Patriot, Signed Legislative petition **CEM:** Thompson Family; GPS 38.87201, -77.26178; Vic jct Rt 29 & Nutley St; Fairfax **GS:** Y **SP:** No info **VI:** No further data **P:** N **BLW:** N **RG:** N **MK:** N **PH:** unk **SS:** BB Legislative Pet **BS:** 60 Fairfax Co.

THOMPSON, Samuel Yancey, b 24 Dec 1728, Spotsylvania Co, d 11 Sep 1779, Amelia Co **RU:** Captain, Virginia Militia 1778-1779 **CEM:** George W Thompson Family; GPS not determined; loc on plantation nr Chrestnut Level; Pittsylvania **GS:** Yes-Cenotaph indicates buried in Amelia Co **SP:** Mar (1752 Amelia Co) Anne "Nancy" Jennings (1736-1811 Pittsylvania Co), d/o British officer William Jennings & (-----) **VI:** Son of Rev Samuel S Thompson & Mary McDonald. He is memorialized in the cemetery **P:** N **BLW:** N **RG:** Y **MK:** N **PH:** N **SS:** E pg 769; DAR A114551, SAR P-304366 **BS:** 196

THOMPSON, Smith; b 1748; d 1840 **RU:** Soldier, Served in VA Line in 16th VA Regt. Lived in Augusta Co at enl 1777. **CEM:** Trinity Episcopal; GPS 38.14917, -79.07521; 214 Beverley St; Staunton City **GS:** U **SP:** Nancy McCullock **VI:** Occupation weaver. Sol appl pen 26 Jul 1819 Augusta Co. S38438. Widow made inquiry 11 Dec 1840 fr Staunton VA **P:** unk **BLW:** unk **RG:** Y **MK:** unk **PH:** unk **SS:** K Vol 5 pg 255; SAR P-304390 **BS:** JLARC 2, 62.

THOMPSON, William; b 1762 d 11 Sep 1831 **RU:** Corporal, Served in John Clark's Illinois Regt 1782 **CEM:** Potts Family; GPS unk; Rts 716 & 714, Hillsboro; Loudoun **GS:** Y **SP:** No info **VI:** No further data **P:** unk **BLW:** unk **RG:** Y **MK:** N **PH:** unk **SS:** E pg 770; SAR P-304494 **BS:** 25 pg 313.

THOMPSON, William; b 1722, Ireland; d 9 Jul 1798 **RU:** Lieutenant/Patriot, Signed Oath of Allegiance Montgomery Co **CEM:** Thompson Family; GPS unk; Thompson Valley; Tazewell **GS:** U **SP:** 1) Margaret (-----) 2) Lydia Ward (c1743-12 Oct 1830) **VI:** No further data **P:** unk **BLW:** unk **RG:** Y **MK:** unk **PH:** unk **SS:** DAR A114675; SAR P-304454 J-NSSAR 2000 Reg **BS:** JLARC 76.

THOMPSON, William; b 12 Sep 1742, Augusta Co; d 26 Jun 1815 **RU:** Soldier/Patriot, Gave material aid to cause **CEM:** Bethel Presbyterian; GPS 38.04257, -79.17283; 563 Bethel Green Rd, Middlebrook; Augusta **GS:** N **SP:** Mar (16 Jun 1771) Rachel Allen (19 Oct 1740, Augusta Co-__) d/of James (__-18 Oct 1791) & Mary (-----) Allen **VI:** No further data **P:** unk **BLW:** unk **RG:** N **MK:** unk **PH:** N **SS:** SAR P-304453, 304454; J-Hatcher; Al Cert pg 2, Augusta Co **BS:** JLARC 2.

THOMASON (THOMASSON), George; b 10 Nov 1703, King William Co, d 22 Aug 1783 **RU:** Patriot Gave beef to cause in Louisa Co **CEM:** Thomasson; GPS not determined; loc on plantation at the beginning of Thomasson Court House Rd leading to court house; Louisa **GS:** N **SP:** Mar (22 Feb 1735 Hanover Co) Mary Pollard, d/o Richard Pollard & Martha Fleming **VI:** Son of Thomas Thomasson & Genia Reeves (1648-1720) **P:** N **BLW:** N **RG:** N **MK:** N **PH:** unk **SS:** D vol 2, pgs 621,624; DAR A132536; SAR P-329068 **BS:** 196; SAR PRS.

THOMPSON (THOMASSON), John; b 1753; d 1840 **RU:** Drummer/Patriot, served in Capt Johnson's Company, Lousia Co Militia and gave material aid to cause **CEM:** Little River Baptist; GPS not determined; Bumpass; Lousia **GS:** Y Gov't **SP:** Grizel Ellis **VI:** Nothing further **P** N **BLW:** N **RG:** Y **MK:** unk **PH:** N **SS:** CD: serv on GS; SAR P-304215 & 304453; J-Hatcher; Al Ct Bk pg 21, Lousia Co **BS:**

THOMPSON (THOMASSON), William; b 1734; d 23 Nov 1800 **RU:** Private/Patriot, Served in Capt Given's Co, Augusta Co Militia. Gave material aid to cause **CEM:** Falling Springs Presbyterian; GPS 37.68494, -79.45105; 410 Falling Springs Rd, Glasgow; Rockbridge **GS:** Y **SP:** Margaret (-----) (1743-5 Oct 1815) **VI:** FindA Grave shows him buried on his Leatherwood Plantation in Henry Co **P:** N **BLW:** N **RG:** N **MK:** unk **PH:** unk **SS:** E pg 770 **BS:** 204.

THOMASSON, George Jr; b 18 Feb 1742; d aft 1782 **RU:** Private/ Patriot, Capt Robert McDowell's Co, Col Thomas Marshall's 3rd VA Regt, Cont Line. As patriot paid pers property tax 1782, Louisa Co 1782 **CEM:** Thomasson; GPS not determined; loc on plantation at the beginning of Thomasson Court House Rd leading to court house; Louisa **GS:** N **SP:** Elizabeth Timberlake: **VI:** Son of George Thomasson (10 Nov 1703, King William Co- 22 Aug 1783) & Mary Pollard (6 Nov 1706-1783 **P:** N **BLW:** N but eligible **RG:** N **MK:** N **PH:** unk **SS:** C Sec II, pg 271; E pg 768; AP Fold3 Muster Roll; DV 1782 Louisa Co, image 12 pdf **BS:** 196.

THOMSON, Daniel; b unk; d 1781 **RU:** Soldier, Served fr MA and died fr Yorktown battle **CEM:** Yorktown Victory Monument Tablet; GPS 38.28350, -78.54150; Yorktown; York **GS:** U **SP:** No info **VI:**

RU=Rank/Unit
VI=Other Veteran Info
MK=SAR/DAR Marker

CEM=Cemetery
P=Pension
PH=Photo

GS=Gravestone
BLW=Bounty/Land Warrant
SS=Service Source

SP=Spousal Information
RG=Registered Grave
BS=Burial Source

416

No further data **P:** unk **BLW:** unk **RG:**Y **MK:** unk **PH:** unk **SS:** J-Yorktown Historian; SAR P-304520 **BS:** JLARC 74.

THOMSON, James; b Jan 1739, Glasgow, Scotland; d Feb 1812 **RU:** Chaplain/Patriot, Served in a VA unit in Illinois. Gave material aid to cause and performed public service as member of Committee of Safety 1775-6 **CEM:** Globe Farm; GPS unk; Nr The Plains; Fauquier **GS:** U **SP:** Mar (1769) Mary Ann Farrow **VI:** No further data **P:** unk **BLW:** unk **RG:** Y **MK:** unk **PH:** unk **SS:** DAR A114174; J- DAR Hatcher; D Vol 1 pg 357; E pg 770; AR pg 112; CZ pg 436; SAR P-304529 **BS:** JLARC 2.

THORNHILL, Jesse; b 13 Oct 1763, Buckingham Co; d 5 Jun 1837 **RU:** Soldier, Ent Serv Buckingham Co. Served in VA Line **CEM:** Thornhill Family; GPS unk; Off Rt 656, Rustburg; Campbell **GS:** N **SP:** Elizabeth Stevens (7 May 1766-12 Jun 1845) **VI:** Sol appl pen 14 Aug 1832, Campbell Co. S14679 **P:** Y **BLW:** unk **RG:** Y **MK:** N **PH:** N **SS:** CG Vol 3 pg 3487; SAR P-304619 **BS:** JLARC 4, 21 ,36; 196.

THORNTON, Anthony; b 15 Nov 1727, Ormesby, Caroline Co; d 1782 **RU:** Lieutenant Colonel/Patriot, Was County Lt in 1781, according to a letter fr him to Governor Thomas Nelson in 1781. Had public service as Chairman of Committee of Safety. Gave material aid to cause,1775 **CEM:** Thornton Family; GPS unk; Ormsby; Caroline **GS:** Y **SP:** Mar (31 Dec 1746) Sarah Taliaferro (17 May 1728-c1760) **VI:** No further data **P:** unk **BLW:** unk **RG:** Y **MK:** N **PH:** unk **SS:** DAR A200971; D Vol 1 pg 193; G pg 105; CZ pg 436 cites Calendar of VA State papers pg 439; SAR P-304622 **BS:** 80 vol 4 pg 113.

THORNTON, Francis See Appendix G, Addenda

THORNTON, George; b 18 Nov 1752, Guinea's Bridge, Caroline Co; d 30 Aug 1853 **RU:** Lieutenant, Served in VA Line. Ent serv 1775 Caroline Co in brother Capt Anthony Thornton's Co. Ent serv again 1781 as 1st Lt in that Co **CEM:** Thornton; GPS unk; Haney property, E side of Rt 619, btw South River Bridge & Dundee Graveyard; Greene **GS:** U **SP:** Mar (9 Jan 1774) Margaret (-----) (20 Jun 1758-29 Jan 1823) **VI:** Sol appl pen 14 Jun 1845, Greene Co. S7709 **P:** Y **BLW:** unk **RG:** Y **MK:** unk **PH:** unk **SS:** K Vol 5 pg 258; CG Vol 3 pg 3487; SAR P-335250 **BS:** JLARC 113.

THOROUGHGOOD, Adam; b 1750; d c1785 **RU:** Colonel, Served under Gen Washington during Battle of Yorktown 1781. Was one of 56 wounded **CEM:** Old Donation Episcopal; GPS 36.86730, -76.12860; 4449 N Witchduck Rd; Virginia Beach City **GS:** U **SP:** No info **VI:** No further data **P:** unk **BLW:** unk **RG:** N **MK:** Y SAR plaque **PH:** unk **SS:** Amy Waters Yarsinske, Virginia Beach: "A History of Virginia's Golden Shore" pg 78 **BS:** Church Historian.

THRIFT, Jeremiah; b 24 Dec 1719, North Farnham Parish, Richmond Co; d 10 Feb 1806 **RU:** Patriot, Gave material aid to the cause **CEM:** Old Ball Burying Ground; GPS unk; 3427 Washington Blvd, behind American Legion Bldg; Arlington **GS:** U **SP:** Ann Trammel **VI:** Son of Nathaniel & Elizabeth (Parsons) Thrift. Name is on monument **P:** N **BLW:** N **RG:** N **MK:** unk **PH:** unk **SS:** AL Ct Bk TBA **BS:** 196.

THROCKMORTON, William; b 1755; d 1812 **RU:** Private, Served in 6th Troop, 1st Regt Lt Dragoons **CEM:** Ware Episcopal; GPS 37.42275, -76.50789; 7825 John Clayton Mem Hwy; Gloucester **GS:** U **SP:** Mary Dixon (1762-__), Also Sarah Gillet **VI:** Son of John & Rebecca (Richardson) Throckmorton **P:** unk **BLW:** unk **RG:** unk **MK:** unk **PH:** unk **SS:** J- DAR Hatcher; C pg 511; SAR P-304784 **BS:** JLARC 2; 196.

THURMAN, Richard Sr; b 18 Dec 1743, Lynchburg; d 14 Aug 1830 **RU:** Captain, Served in VA Regt under LaFayette. Was capt in Cont Line in Col Holcombe's Regt **CEM:** Old City; GPS 37.41472, -79.15667; 401 Taylor St; Lynchburg City **GS:** Y **SP:** Mar (1762) Ann Brown (5 Apr 1745-7 Jun 1790) **VI:** GS indicates patriot was interred with honors **P:** unk **BLW:** unk **RG:** Y **MK:** Y SAR plaque **PH:** Y **SS:** DAR A115121; C pg 525; DD cites newspaper article Richmond Enquirer 29 Oct 1824; SAR P-304859 **BS:** 35 pg 4.

THURMAN, Robert; b 1753; d 19 Oct 1817 **RU:** Patriot, Signed Legislative Petition 14 Oct 1779 to move county court house. As patriot paid personal Property Tax (Rev War Supply tax) 1783, Prince William Co **CEM:** Thurman Family; GPS 38.741289, -77.502166; Glen-Gery Brick Co, 9905 Godwin Dr; Manassas City **GS:** Y **SP:** No info **VI:** No further data **P:** N **BLW:** N **RG:** Y **MK:**Y SAR **PH:** unk **SS:** DV; SAR P-336579 **BS:** 190 cem name.

RU=Rank/Unit	CEM=Cemetery	GS=Gravestone	SP=Spousal Information
VI=Other Veteran Info	P=Pension	BLW=Bounty/Land Warrant	RG=Registered Grave
MK=SAR/DAR Marker	PH=Photo	SS=Service Source	BS=Burial Source

TIBBS, Thomas; b Unk; d bef 4 May 1778 **RU**: Captain, commanded co in VA 2d Bn Cont Line , total serv 3 yrs **CEM**:Rev War Court House Plaque; GPS not determined; 4110 Chain Bridge Rd; Fairfax **GS**: Memorialized on plaque 2017 by Geo Washington Chapter, VASSAR **SP** No info **VI**: died in service **P**: N **BLW**: Y, rec'd # 1330 by heir John Tibbs, 5 Jul 1793 for 4000 acres **RG**: N **MK**: N **PH**: N **SS**: A sec II, pgs 117, 380; E pg 773; G pg 407; AP Fold3 Serv rec:& muster roll: EP sources: **BS**: None.

TILDEN, John Bell; b 9 Dec 1762, Philadelphia, PA; d 21 Jul 1838 **RU**: Lieutenant, Served as an officer in the PA Line and was at Yorktown. Was a Lt of the 2nd PA Regt at the close of war **CEM**: Stephens City United Methodist; GPS 39.08620, -78.21670; 5291 Main St, Stephens City; Frederick **GS**: Y **SP**: Jane (-----) (18 Dec 1766-26 May 1827) **VI**: Son of (-----) and Anna (-----) Bell. Sol appl pen 22 Jul 1828, Frederick Co. S42497. Recd BLW #2200-300-10 Oct 1796. Also recd PA State BLW **P**: Y **BLW**: Y **RG**: Y **MK**: N **PH**: unk **SS**: A, pg 434, CG Vol 3 pg 3499; SAR P-305124 **BS**: 59 pg 329.

TILFORD, David; b Bef 1765; d after 1783 **RU**: Soldier, Rank & serv unk, but Co Hist Soc indicates soldier bur in county cem **CEM**: Tilford Cub Creek; GPS unk; Cub Creek Rd Rt 789, Tyro; Nelson **GS**: U **SP**: No info **VI**: No further data **P**: unk **BLW**: unk **RG**: Y **MK**: unk **PH**: unk **SS**: G pg 538; SAR P-305148 **BS**: JLARC 83 Nelson Co Hist Soc.

TILFORD, James; b Aft 1739, Ireland; d 4 Jun 1787 **RU**: Patriot, Gave rifle to the cause 7 Nov 1775 **CEM**: Tilford Cub Creek; GPS unk; Cub Creek Rd Rt 789, Tyro; Nelson **GS**: U **SP**: Elizabeth (-----) **VI**: No further data **P**: N **BLW**: N **RG**: Y **MK**: unk **PH**: unk **SS**: DAR Ancestor #A115441; G pg 538; DD cites VA Mag of Hist & Biog Vol 26, #1 pg 58, 66, 68; SAR P-305149 **BS**: JLARC 83 Nelson Co Hist Soc.

TILQUAZ, Nicolas; b unk; d 1781 **RU**: Soldier, Served in Soissonnais Bn and died fr battle at Yorktown **CEM**: French Memorial; GPS 36.81944, -79.39933; Yorktown; York **GS**: U **SP**: No info **VI**: No further data **P**: unk **BLW**: unk **RG**: Y **MK**: unk **PH**: unk **SS**: J-Yorktown Historian; SAR P-305247 **BS**: JLARC 1, 74.

TINCELIN, Jean; b unk; d 1781 **RU**: Soldier, Served in Gatinais Bn and died fr battle at Yorktown **CEM**: French Memorial; GPS 36.81944, -79.39933; Yorktown; York **GS**: U **SP**: No info **VI**: No further data **P**: unk **BLW**: unk **RG**: Y **MK**: unk **PH**: unk **SS**: J-Yorktown Historian; SAR P-305356 **BS**: JLARC 1, 74.

TINIER, Joseph; b unk; d 1781 **RU**: Soldier, Served in Gatinais Bn and died fr battle at Yorktown **CEM**: French Memorial; GPS 36.81944, -79.39933; Yorktown; York **GS**: U **SP**: No info **VI**: No further data **P**: unk **BLW**: unk **RG**: Y **MK**: unk **PH**: unk **SS**: J-Yorktown Historian; SAR P-305391 **BS**: JLARC 1, 74.

TINSLEY, Parker; b unk; d aft 1813 **RU**: unk, Service not listed in SAR registry **CEM**: Spring Grove; GPS 39.10916, -78.09970; Rockville; Hanover **GS**: U **SP**: No info **VI**: JLARC site visit reveals govt grave stone indicates service after Rev War. (See Report, App D pg 12) He had 1812 service **P**: unk **BLW**: unk **RG**: Y **MK**: unk **PH**: unk **SS**:; JLARC 71; SAR P-305452 **BS**: JLARC 71.

TINSLEY, Thomas; b 4 Sep 1755; d 17 Dec 1822 **RU**: Captain/Patriot, Was Capt 1782/83 Hanover Co Militia. Gave material aid to cause **CEM**: Spring Grove; GPS 39.10916, -78.09970; Rockville; Hanover **GS**: Y **SP**: Susanna Thomson (5 Dec 1765-29 Jul 1844) d/o John & Ann (Garland) Thompson **VI**: No further data **P**: unk **BLW**: unk **RG**: Y **MK**: unk **PH**: unk **SS**: SAR P-305455; AL Ct Bk II pg 13 Hanover Co **BS**: JLARC 71; 196.

TINSLEY, William; b 1762; d 15 Jul 1836 **RU**: Fifer, Enlisted Cumberland Co. Served in VA Bn, Taylor's Regt **CEM**: Spring Grove; GPS 39.10916, -78.09970; Rockville; Hanover **GS**: Y **SP**: Deliah (-----) (__-after 1837) **VI**: After RW, became capt of Co A, 2nd Bn, Hanover Grenadiers in 74th VA Line, 1789. Appl pen 26 Jun 1818. S41255 **P**: Y **BLW**: Y **RG**: N **MK**: unk **PH**: unk **SS**: E pg 774; CG pg 3506; CZ pg 438 **BS**: 196.

TISSIER, Jacques; b unk; d 1781 **RU**: Seaman, Served on "Citoyen" and died from Yorktown battle **CEM**: French Memorial; GPS 36.81944, -79.39933; Yorktown; York **GS**: U **SP**: No info **VI**: No further data **P**: unk **BLW**: unk **RG**: Y **MK**: unk **PH**: unk **SS**: J-Yorktown Historian; SAR P-305546 **BS**: JLARC 1, 74.

RU=Rank/Unit	CEM=Cemetery	GS=Gravestone	SP=Spousal Information
VI=Other Veteran Info	P=Pension	BLW=Bounty/Land Warrant	RG=Registered Grave
MK=SAR/DAR Marker	PH=Photo	SS=Service Source	BS=Burial Source

TOBLER (DOBLER), Jacob Sr; b 14 May 1764; d 7 Feb 1820 **RU**: Private, Served in James Cox Co, Montgomery Co Militia **CEM**: Kimberling; GPS 36.91750, -81.30440; Rt 617, Rural Retreat; Wythe **GS**: U **SP**: Maria Magdalene Roush **VI**: Son of Jacob & Anna (Hough) Tobler. Name on stone spelled Dobler **P**: unk **BLW**: unk **RG**: Y **MK**: unk **PH**: unk **SS**: DAR A116115; BW pg 9; SAR P-305666 **BS**: JLARC 123; 196.

TODD, Charles; b unk; d 1817 **RU**: Captain/Patriot, Commanded a Co Caroline Co Militia May 1782. Gave material aid to cause **CEM**: Hickory Grove; GPS unk; Hickory Grove Plantation; Caroline **GS**: N **SP**: Mary (-----) (__-1821) **VI**: Son of Dr George (1711-1790) & (----) Todd **P**: unk **BLW**: unk **RG**: N **MK**: N **PH**: N **SS**: E pg 1775; AL Ct Bk II pg 9, 30 Caroline Co; CD **BS**: 196.

TODD, George Dr; b 1711; d 10 Mar 1790 **RU**: Patriot/Physician, Gave material aid to cause. Treated soldiers during Rev **CEM**: Hickory Grove; GPS unk; Hickory Grove Plantation; Caroline **GS**: N **SP**: No info **VI**: Deputy Sheriff in Co 1737-1747. Physician **P**: unk **BLW**: unk **RG**: N **MK**: N **PH**: N **SS**: AL Ct Bk I pg. 268,269; CD **BS**: 196.

TODD, Mallory; b 1 Jan 1742 Battery Park; d 4 Nov 1817 **RU**: Patriot, Gave material aid to cause **CEM**: Wrenn's Cemetery; GPS unk; Rt 10, 5 mi N of Smithfield; Isle of Wight **GS**: Y **SP**: Ann (-----) (8 Feb 1761-6 Sep 1832) **VI**: Cured first Smithfield ham **P**: N **BLW**: N **RG**: N **MK**: N **PH**: N **SS**: AL Ct Bk pg 20; AK **BS**: 153 Wrenn's Ch.

TOLON, Francois; b unk; d 1781 **RU**: Seaman, Served on "Languedoc" and died from Yorktown battle **CEM**: French Memorial; GPS 36.81944, -79.39933; Yorktown; York **GS**: U **SP**: No info **VI**: No further data **P**: unk **BLW**: unk **RG**: Y **MK**: unk **PH**: unk **SS**: J-Yorktown Historian; SAR P-305851 **BS**: JLARC 1, 74.

TOMPKINS, Benjamin; b 19 Sep 1732, Mathews Co; d 23 Jul 1811 **RU**: Patriot, gave material aid to cause in Caroline Co **CEM**: Tomkins Family; GPS not determined; loc on patriots land in 1811 See tax map for location; Fluvanna **GS**: Unk **SP**: Mar (11 Nov 1758) Elizabeth Goodloe (28 May 1738-25 Apr 1808), d/o George Goodloe (1701-1741) & Diana Minor (1710-__) **VI**: Son of Christopher (1705-1779) & Joyce Reade (1701-1771) **P**: N **BLW**: N **RG**: N **MK**: unk **PH**: N **SS**: AL, Ct Bk 2, pg 28, lists II pgs 11,12,20,28,31 **BS**: 196.

TOMPKINS, Christopher; b 27 Oct 1740, Chilesburg, Caroline Co; d 5 Apr 1823 **RU**: Colonel, Served in Cont Army, and participant in siege of Yorktown. Commanded a Co as Captain in King William Co Militia 1775-1776 **CEM**: Fleet Street, Plantation Grounds; GPS 37.78166, -77.25359; Rt 604 S of Webb Creek, Etna Mills, on Rt 4 1 mi fr Jct Rt 30; King William **GS**: U **SP**: Mar (25 Nov 1774) Ann Temple Fleet (23 Nov 1752, King & Queen Co-21 Oct 1822) d/o William (1726-1773) & Ann (Temple) (1726-1754) Fleet **VI**: Son of Christopher (1705-1779) & Joyce (Reade) (1701-1771). Died in Etna Mills, Enfield, King William Co **P**: N **BLW**: N **RG**: Y **MK**: unk **PH**: N **SS**: E pg 776-7; CZ; SAR P-305946 **BS**: 196.

TOMPKINS, Christopher; b 17 Oct 1705, Gloucester Co; d 16 Mar 1779 **RU**: Patriot, Gave material aid to cause **CEM**: Maple Swamp; GPS unk; Chilesburg; Caroline **GS**: U **SP**: Joyce Reade (6 Mar 1701, Gloucester Co-8 Aug 1771) d/o Thomas (1649-1716) & Lucy (Gwynne) (1651-1731) Reade **VI**: Son of Christopher (1662-__) & Lucy (Gwynne) (1670-1750) Tompkins **P**: N **BLW**: N **RG**: N **MK**: unk **PH**: unk **SS**: Ak Ct Bk Pgs 8, 29 **BS**: 196.

TOMPKINS, Harry; b 1777; d 17 Apr 1829 **RU**: Patriot, Was Clerk of Henrico Co and Committee of Safety 1775-6 **CEM**: Shockoe Hill; GPS 37.55190, -77.43170; 4th & Hospital Sts; Richmond City **GS**: N **SP**: Fanny Taylorson **VI**: Son of William Overton & Mary (Michie) Tompkins. Member #1219 Clan of Tomkyns, vol 1, bur 18 Apr 1829 age 52 **P**: N **BLW**: N **RG**: unk **MK**: unk **PH**: unk **SS**: E pg 777; CZ pg 440 **BS**: 196.

TONEY, Archibald; b unk; d 24 Mar 1811 **RU**: Private?, Served in 1st, 10th, 14th Cont Lines fr Goochland Co **CEM**: St John's Episcopal; GPS 37.53183, -77.41958; 2401 E Broad St; Richmond City **GS**: Y **SP**: No info **VI**: No further data **P**: unk **BLW**: unk **RG**: N **MK**: N **PH**: unk **SS**: E pg 777 **BS**: 28 pg 512.

TONEY, John; b 1758; d 1832 **RU**: Private, Served in 7th Cont Line 7 Apr 1781 **CEM**: Toney Family; GPS unk; Glen Lyn; Giles **GS**: U **SP**: Mary Toney (c1765-unk, Giles Co) **VI**: He or the John Toney fr

RU=Rank/Unit
VI=Other Veteran Info
MK=SAR/DAR Marker
CEM=Cemetery
P=Pension
PH=Photo
GS=Gravestone
BLW=Bounty/Land Warrant
SS=Service Source
SP=Spousal Information
RG=Registered Grave
BS=Burial Source

419

Powhatan Co drew a BLW **P:** unk **BLW:** Y **RG:** Y **MK:** unk **PH:** unk **SS:** SAR Ancestor #P-306019; J-DAR Hatcher; A pg 258; C pg 221; E pg 777; AZ pg 179 **BS:** JLARC 2.

TONEY, William; b 28 Jan 1737, New Kent Co, d 30 Dec 1804 Dillons Mill, Franklin Co **RU:** Patriot, Gave material aid to cause in Bedford Co **CEM:** Toney; GPS: 37.0719141,-79.6268002; off Rt 1325 on R side of Park Place Drive; Franklin **GS:** Yes **SP:** Mar as 3rd wife c1755, Margaret Sutherland (1731-1812) **VI:** No further data **P:** N **BLW:** N **RG:** Y **MK:** N **PH:** N **SS:** AL Ct Bk pg 8; DAR A113331; SAR P-306020 **BS:** 196.

TOTTEN, John; b unk; d 1823 **RU:** Private, Served in Capt Thomas Ingles Co, Montgomery Co Militia 7 Apr 1781 **CEM:** Totten Family; GPS unk; Vic jct Rts 610 & 687; Smyth **GS:** Y **SP:** No info **VI:** No further data **P:** unk **BLW:** unk **RG:** N **MK:** N **PH:** unk **SS:** G pg 227 **BS:** 97 pg 183.

TOUGARE, Francis; b unk; d 1781 **RU:** Seaman, Served on "Diademe" and died from Yorktown battle **CEM:** French Memorial; GPS 36.81944, -79.39933; Yorktown; York **GS:** U **SP:** No info **VI:** No further data **P:** unk **BLW:** unk **RG:** Y **MK:** unk **PH:** unk **SS:** J-Yorktown Historian; SAR P-306195 **BS:** JLARC 1, 74.

TOURNIS, Jacques; b unk; d 1781 **RU:** Soldier, Served in Angoumois Bn and died fr battle at Yorktown **CEM:** French Memorial; GPS 36.81944, -79.39933; Yorktown; York **GS:** U **SP:** No info **VI:** No further data **P:** unk **BLW:** unk **RG:** Y **MK:** unk **PH:** unk **SS:** J-Yorktown Historian' SAR P-306204 **BS:** JLARC 1, 74.

TOUSSET, Jean; b unk; d 1781 **RU:** Soldier, Served in Gatinais Bn and died fr battle at Yorktown **CEM:** French Memorial; GPS 36.81944, -79.39933; Yorktown; York **GS:** U **SP:** No info **VI:** No further data **P:** unk **BLW:** unk **RG:** Y **MK:** unk **PH:** unk **SS:** J-Yorktown Historian; SAR P-306224 **BS:** JLARC 1, 74.

TOUTIN, Eustache; b unk; d 1781 **RU:** Seaman, Served on "Saint-Esprit" and died from Yorktown battle **CEM:** French Memorial; GPS 36.81944, -79.39933; Yorktown; York **GS:** U **SP:** No info **VI:** No further data **P:** unk **BLW:** unk **RG:** Y **MK:** unk **PH:** unk **SS:** J-Yorktown Historian; SAR P-306227 **BS:** JLARC 1, 74.

TOWLER, Joseph; b 1743; d 1843 **RU:** Private, Served in Cont line, commanded by Col Fowler **CEM:** Towler Family; GPS unk; Nr Anthony's Ford; Pittsylvania **GS:** U **SP:** Francis Dixon **VI:** No further data **P:** unk **BLW:** unk **RG:** Y **MK:** unk **PH:** unk **SS:** J-NSSAR 2000 Reg; E pg 778; SAR P-306331 **BS:** JLARC 76.

TOWLES, Oliver; b c1741; d 18 Nov 1821 **RU:** Colonel, Served in VA Line. Was Capt of Spotsylvania Co Miltia 1775, Maj of 6th Regt of Foot 15 Aug 1777. Was in Battle of Germantown 4 Oct 1777. Taken prisoner Germantown Dec 1777 to fall 1780, promoted to Col 5th VA Regt 12 Feb 1781. Present at surrender Yorktown **CEM:** Towles Family; GPS unk; See DAR Senate Report 1954, serial 11831, vol 4 for loc; Lynchburg City **GS:** Y **SP:** Mar (bef 1770) Mary Chew d/o Larkin & Mary (Beverly) Chew **VI:** Son of Oliver Towles (c1710-1770) & Mary (-----) Gilleson, a widow, of Caroline and Spotsylvania Cos. Attorney. Recd BLW #2213-450-7 Dec 1791, records lost in DC fire 1814. Moved to Lynchburg **P:** unk **BLW:** Y **RG:** Y **MK:** N **PH:** unk **SS:** K Vol 5 pg 276; CG Vol 3 pg 3522; CE pg 15, 48, 49; SAR P-306336 **BS:** DAR Rpt.

TOWN, Asce; b unk; d 1781 **RU:** Soldier, Served fr MA, and died fr the Battle at Yorktown **CEM:** Yorktown Victory Monument Tablet; GPS 38.28350, -78.54150; Yorktown; York **GS:** U **SP:** No info **VI:** No further data **P:** unk **BLW:** unk **RG:** Y **MK:** unk **PH:** unk **SS:** J-Yorktown Historian; SAR P-306341 **BS:** JLARC 74.

TOWNES, John; b 1761; d 1845 **RU:** Ensign, Served in Amelia Co Militia. Appt Ensign 25 May 1780 in Capt William Johnston's Co, Col Morgan's VA Regt 1777. In 1778 taken prisoner Charleston **CEM:** Townes; GPS unk; Rt 38 at Level Mount Estates, Amelia CH; Amelia **GS:** U **SP:** Mar (1780) Elizabeth Leigh (1760 Farmville-1795) d/o John (1737-1785) & Elizabeth (Greenhill) (1740-1820) Leigh **VI:** Recd BLW 2,666 acres **P:** unk **BLW:** Y **RG:** Y **MK:** unk **PH:** unk **SS:** G pg 13; SAR P-306423 **BS:** 196.

TOWNSEND, Henry; b 1765; d 5 Jul 1831 **RU:** Private, Served in 2nd VA Regt **CEM:** Royal Oak; GPS unk; Behind Marion Baptist Church; Washington **GS:** Y **SP:** Mar (1785) Catherine (-----) (__-7 Jun 1835)

RU=Rank/Unit	CEM=Cemetery	GS=Gravestone	SP=Spousal Information
VI=Other Veteran Info	P=Pension	BLW=Bounty/Land Warrant	RG=Registered Grave
MK=SAR/DAR Marker	PH=Photo	SS=Service Source	BS=Burial Source

420

VI: Sol appl 4 Mar 1830, Washington Co. R10658. Died in Marion **P:** Y **BLW:** unk **RG:** N **MK:** N **PH:** unk **SS:** K pg 277; CG Vol 3 pg 3525 **BS:** 97 vol 1 pg 140.

TRAIL, Thomas; b c1746, Frederick Co, MD; d Aft 1835 **RU:** Private, Ent serv in Amherst Co in Capt John Loving's Co, then to Capt Baret's Co, Gen Nelson's Command. Was at the surrender of Cornwallis in Oct 1781 **CEM:** Wright Family; GPS 36.97658, -80.21693; Pizarro off Rt 668; Floyd **GS:** U **SP:** No info **VI:** Memorialized by DAR plaque in cem. Age 86 on 17 Sep 1832 on pension listing, # S7748 **P:** Y **BLW:** unk **RG:** N **MK:** Y DAR plaque **PH:** unk **SS:** E pg 780 **BS:** 196 for John Mitchell.

TREASURE, Richard; b unk; d 1781 **RU:** Soldier, Served fr DE, killed in the battle at Yorktown **CEM:** Yorktown Victory Monument Tablet; GPS 38.28350, -78.54150; Yorktown; York **GS:** U **SP:** No info **VI:** No further data **P:** unk **BLW:** unk **RG:** unk **MK:** unk **PH:** unk **SS:** J-Yorktown Historian; SAR P-306862 **BS:** JLARC 74.

TREMPER, Laurence (Lawrence); b 1753; d 15 Jan 1841 **RU:** Lieutenant, Served in NY Line. Ent serv Rhineback NY where resided. Was Lt in NY Militia. Moved to VA nr end of war where ent serv again **CEM:** Trinity Episcopal; GPS 38.14917, -79.07521; 214 Beverley St; Staunton City **GS:** U **SP:** Unmarried **VI:** Lived at Rhinebeck in Dutchess Co, NY during Rev War. Moved soon after the war to Staunton, Augusta Co where he was postmaster for many yrs. S7754 **P:** Y **BLW:** unk **RG:** Y **MK:** unk **PH:** unk **SS:** K Vol 5 pg 281; CG Vol 3 pg 3536; SAR P-306947 **BS:** JLARC 2, 4 62.

TRENT, Thomas; b 6 Feb 1757, Prince Edward Co; d 28 Jun 1820 **RU:** Sergeant, Served in 15th VA Regt for three yrs. Wounded at Momnough Battle **CEM:** Old Trent Mill Farm; GPS unk; Rt 631; Appomattox **GS:** U **SP:** Elizabeth (-----) **VI:** Awarded gratuity of L250 in addition to pay on 2 Nov 1779 for loss of both arms in battle at Monmouth **P:** Y **BLW:** Y **RG:** Y **MK:** unk **PH:** unk **SS:** DAR A115007; SAR P-306963; C pg 510; BX pg 812; CZ pg 442 **BS:** JLARC 33.

TRIBBLE, Andrew; b 1740; d 1822 **RU:** Chaplain/Patriot, Gave material aid to cause **CEM:** Tribble Family, Shirley Durbin Farm; GPS unk; 2 mi S jct Rts 25 & 75; Madison **GS:** U **SP:** Sarah Ann **VI:** No further data **P:** unk **BLW:** unk **RG:** Y **MK:** unk **PH:** unk **SS:** AL Ct Bk pg 15 Albemarle Co; SAR P-307015 **BS:** JLARC 99.

TRIGG, Daniel; b 14 Aug 1749, Bedford Co; d 3 Apr 1819 **RU:** Captain/Patriot, Was Capt in Montgomery Co Militia. Gave material aid to cause **CEM:** Trigg Family; GPS unk; Abingdon; Washington **GS:** Y **SP:** Helen Hancock Dillinger **VI:** After war in 1788 was Col of Militia in Montgomery Co. Became practicing physician in Johnson City TN **P:** unk **BLW:** unk **RG:** Y **MK:** N **PH:** unk **SS:** N pg 1245; AL Ct Bk pg 46 Montgomery Co; SAR P-307039 **BS:** SAR regis.

TRIGG, John (Johns); b 28 Jun 1748, New London, Caroline Co; d 28 Jun 1804 **RU:** Captain, Recommended rank of capt 24 Feb 1778 Bedford Co Militia **CEM:** Trigg Family (aka Old Liberty Plantation); GPS unk; Nr Liberty; Bedford **GS:** U **SP:** Dinah (Dianna) Ayers (1757-1809) **VI:** Was a VA State Representative **P:** unk **BLW:** unk **RG:** Y **MK:** N **PH:** unk **SS:** J- DAR Hatcher; E pg 781; AZ pg 189; SAR P-307046 **BS:** JLARC 2; 196.

TRIMBLE, James; b Bef 1730, Armagh, Ireland; d 9 Apr 1776 **RU:** Captain/Patriot, Commanded co Augusta Co Militia. Gave material aid to cause **CEM:** Old Monmouth Presbyterian; GPS 37.80810, -79.47280; Jct Rts 60 & 669; Lexington City **GS:** U **SP:** Mar (c1745) Sarah Kersey (c 1727-aft 7 Dec 1787) **VI:** No further data **P:** unk **BLW:** unk **RG:** Y **MK:** unk **PH:** unk **SS:** AL Ct Bk pg 7 Bedford Co; CZ pg 443 cites Lib VA Auditors Accts, Vol XV pg 103; SAR P-307068 **BS:** JLARC 63.

TRIMBLE, John; b 1742; d 22 Apr 1824 **RU:** Private, Served in Capt James Bell's Co **CEM:** Glebe Burying Ground; GPS 38.10940, -79.22190; Glebe School Rd Rt 876, Swoopes; Augusta **GS:** Y **SP:** 1) (probably) Mary (-----) (__-18 Feb 1770) 2) (probably) Clarissa Sidney Claypoole **VI:** Died aged abt 82 yrs **P:** unk **BLW:** unk **RG:** Y **MK:** unk **PH:** unk **SS:** SAR Ancestor #P-307072; E pg 781 **BS:** JLARC 8; 210 pg 395; 196.

TRIMBLE, Sarah (nee Kersey); b c 1727; d Aft 7 Dec 1787 **RU:** Patriot, Gave material aid to cause **CEM:** Old Monmouth Presbyterian; GPS 37.80810, -79.47280; Jct Rts 60 & 669; Lexington City **GS:** U **SP:** Mar (c1745) James Trimble (bef 1730-1776) **VI:** No further data **P:** N **BLW:** N **RG:** N **MK:** unk **PH:** unk **SS:** DAR A203233; D Vol 3 pg 824 **BS:** 196.

RU=Rank/Unit	CEM=Cemetery	GS=Gravestone	SP=Spousal Information
VI=Other Veteran Info	P=Pension	BLW=Bounty/Land Warrant	RG=Registered Grave
MK=SAR/DAR Marker	PH=Photo	SS=Service Source	BS=Burial Source

TRIPLETT, Simon; b 1740, King George Co; d 14 May 1810 **RU**: Colonel/Patriot, Served as Capt in Prince William District Bn fr Loudoun Co, Mar 1776. Later became Colonel and performed public service as member Committee of Safety 1775-6. Gave material aid to cause **CEM**: Rock Quarry on Goose Creek; **GPS** unk; Mt Pleasant; Loudoun **GS**: U **SP**: Mar (aft 20 Apr 1764) Martha Lane (__ Truro Parish-aft 1810) **VI**: No further data **P**: unk **BLW**: unk **RG**: Y **MK**: unk **PH**: unk **SS**: DAR A116621; J-NSSAR 1993 Reg; AL Ct Bk pg 51 Loudoun Co; CE pg 22; SAR P-307108 **BS**: JLARC 1.

TRIPLETT, Thomas, Jr; b 1732; d 24 Oct 1780 **RU**: Patriot, member of Fairfax Co Committee of Safety and gave material aid to cause **CEM**: Triplett Family; GPS38.742367, -77.143067; loc on grounds of Humphrey's Engineer Center at John J. Kingman Rd nr the gate to the Army Geospatial Center at Fort Belvoir; Fairfax **GS**: Uuk **SP**: Mar Sarah Dade **VI**: Son of Thomas Triplett & Sarah Harrison; memorialized on plaque at Fairfax Co Ct House **P**: N **BLW**: N **RG**: N **MK**: N **PH**: N **SS**: :EH sources except those citing military serv **BS** 196.

TRIPLETT, William; b 1730; d 1803 **RU**: Lieutenant/Patriot, Served as Ens, 1 Nov 1777, Lt 10 May 1778, Paymaster 10 Jan 1779, in Grayson's Additional Regt. Transferred to Capt Thomas Bell's Co, Gist's Regt 22 Apr 1779. Was Lt & Adjutant, Capt John Steed's Co, 2nd VA Brigade (Col Christian Febiger) Dec 1779-Mar 1780. Retired 1 Jan 1781. Provided 550# beef 26 Apr 1781 **CEM**: Triplett Family; GPS 38.74246, -77.14318; On grounds of Humphrey's Engineer Center at John J. Kingman Rd nr the gate to the Army Geospatial Center at Fort Belvoir; Fairfax **GS**: Y **SP**: Mar (c1762) Sarah Massey **VI**: Both SAR & DAR markers on gravesite **P**: unk **BLW**: unk **RG**: Y **MK**: Y SAR & DAR **PH**: Y **SS**: 47 Vol 21 pg 115; SAR P-307113 **BS**: JLARC 1,13,14, 27, 28.

TROTTER, John; b unk; d Aft 1781 **RU**: Patriot, Gave material aid to cause **CEM**: Trinity Episcopal; GPS 38.14917, -79.07521; 214 Beverley St; Staunton City **GS**: U **SP**: No info **VI**: No further data **P**: N **BLW**: N **RG**: Y **MK**: unk **PH**: unk **SS**: J- DAR Hatcher; AL Ct Bk pg 6 Augusta Co; SAR P-307175 **BS**: JLARC 2.

TROUP, Jacob; b 26 Jun 1749, Philadelphia, PA, d 19 Oct 1781 **RU**: Private, served in Capt Owen Ruble's Co, Henry Co Militia, Col Skipwith's Regt at Yorktown. Killed 19 Oct 1781 **CEM**: Mass Burial site: GPS 37.274365,-76.70164; behind Governor's Palace, Colonial Williamsburg; Williamsburg City **GS**: No **SP**: Mar prob prior to 1769, MD, Mary (__-by 1803, Henry Co) **VI**: No further data **P**: N **BLW**: N **RG**: Y **MK**: N **PH**: N **SS**: CZ, Lib VA Audit Acct Vol XV, pg 196; DAR A116172; SAR P-330893 **BS**: 196.

TROUT (TROUTT), (George) Michael; b 1740 Augusta Co; d 1822 **RU**: Ensign, Served in Capt Laird's Co, Augusta Co Militia **CEM**: Trout or Kline family; GPS unk; 5180 Trissels Rd, Broadway; Rockingham **GS**: Y **SP**: Elizabeth Bear (Baer) **VI**: 1999 SAR marker shows two George Michael Trouts, one b in VA, one b in PA Both b 1750 mar to Eliz. Baer **P**: unk **BLW**: unk **RG**: Y **MK**: N **PH**: Y **SS**: E pg 783, AK Jan 209; SAR P-307200 **BS**: 04, Jan 2009.

TROUTWINE (TROUTVINE), George Jacob; b c1739, Prussia; d 8 Oct 1783 **RU**: Surgeon's Mate, Served in 11th Cont Line 13 Nov 1776. Resigned 22 Nov 1777 **CEM**: Mt Hebron; GPS 39.10916, -78.09497; 305 E Boscawen St; Winchester City **GS**: U **SP**: Lucy Martin **VI**: No further data **P**: unk **BLW**: unk **RG**: Y **MK**: Y SAR monument **PH**: unk **SS**: DAR A132357; J-NSSAR 2000 Reg; SAR P-307226 **BS**: JLARC 76.

TROWBRIDGE, Samuel; b c1746, Morristown, Morris Co, NJ; d 8 Nov 1822 **RU**: Patriot, Gave material aid to the cause **CEM**: Little Mountain United Methodist; GPS 39.27280, -78.18910; 259 Little Mountain Church Rd, Cedar Grove; Frederick **GS**: Y **SP**: 1) Mar (1768 Winchester) Jane Ruble 2) Mar (1786) Christianna Dumire **VI**: No further data **P**: N **BLW**: N **RG**: N **MK**: N **PH**: unk **SS**: AL Ct Bk pg 18 **BS**: 59 pg 331.

TUCKER, Daniel; b 1755; d 1800 **RU**: Private, Served in 4th Cont line **CEM**: Tucker; GPS 37.71440, -79.08610; Rt 621, Indian Creek; Amherst **GS**: N **SP**: Mar (15 Sep 1792 Amherst Co as bachelor) Judith Coleman, widow **VI**: Son of Drury (1719-1801) & Susanna Douglass (1722-1765) Tucker. Likely at Tucker Cemetery historic graveyard adjacent to old Tucker homeplace in Amherst VA **P**: unk **BLW**: unk **RG**: N **MK**: unk **PH**: N **SS**: E pg 783 **BS**: 196.

TUCKER, St George; b 10 Jul 1752, Southampton Parish, Bermuda; d 20 Nov 1827 **RU**: Lieutenant Colonel, Was Secretary & Aide de Camp to Gen Nelson 1779. Served in VA Militia 1780-81. Wounded

RU=Rank/Unit	CEM=Cemetery	GS=Gravestone	SP=Spousal Information
VI=Other Veteran Info	P=Pension	BLW=Bounty/Land Warrant	RG=Registered Grave
MK=SAR/DAR Marker	PH=Photo	SS=Service Source	BS=Burial Source

422

in Gilford CH battle 15 Mar 1781 **CEM:** Cabell Family; GPS unk; Edgewood, 3008 Warminster Dr, Wingina; Nelson **GS:** Y **SP:** 1) Frances Bland Randolph, 2) Lelia Skipwith Carter **VI:** Son of Bermuda & (-----) Tucker. Professor of Law, College Wm & Mary 1790-1804. Justice of VA Court of Appeals 1803-1811. Judge US District Court 1813-1825. Died in Warminster, Albemarle Co **P:** unk **BLW:** unk **RG:** Y **MK:** Y SAR **PH:** N **SS:** E pg 784; SAR P-307713 **BS:** 32 email Oct. 2013.

TULLOSS (TULLOS), Rodham Jr; b unk; d Dec 1815 **RU:** Ensign, Served in Fauquier Co Militia, recorded as ensign 24 Mar 1778 **CEM:** Tulloss Family; GPS unk; Somerville; Fauquier **GS:** N **SP:** Mar (bond 21 Aug 1764, Peter Grant security) Ann Finnie **VI:** No further data **P:** unk **BLW:** unk **RG:** Y **MK:** N **PH:** N **SS:** 19 pg 243; Fauquier Co Marriages pg 202; SAR P-307828 **BS:** 19 pg 243.

TUMELIN, Nicolas; b unk; d 1781 **RU:** Soldier, Served in Bourbonnais Bn and died fr battle at Yorktown **CEM:** French Memorial; GPS 36.81944, -79.39933; Yorktown; York **GS:** U **SP:** No info **VI:** No further data **P:** unk **BLW:** unk **RG:** Y **MK:** unk **PH:** unk **SS:** J-Yorktown Historian; SAR P-307833 **BS:** JLARC 1,74.

TURBERVILLE, George; b 1742, d 20 Oct 1792 **RU:** Patriot, Gave material aid to cause, Westmoreland Co **CEM:** Peckatone; GPS of town 38.072222, -76.651111 ; Hague; Westmoreland **GS:** Unk **SP:** Martha "Patty" Corbin (1749-20 Nov 1809), d/o Gawin Corbin (1725-1760) & Hannah Ludwell Lee (1728-1782) **VI:** Son of George Turberville (1694-30 Mar 1742) & Martha Lee (1716, England-12 Nov 1751) **P:** N **BLW:** N **RG:** N **MK:** N **PH:** N **SS:** AL Ct Bk pgs 2, 3,5 and Comm Bk V pgs 225-6 **BS see Appendix G**

TURBERVILLE, George Lee; b 7 Sep 1760, Hague, Westmoreland Co; d 26 Mar 1798 **RU:** Major, Served 6 yrs, 11 mos in Cont Line. Was Capt in VA Line **CEM:** Hickory Hill, aka Epping; GPS unk; Hague; Westmoreland **GS:** U **SP:** Elizabeth "Betty" Tayloe Corbin (1764-1798) d/o Gawin & Johanna (Tucker) Corbin **VI:** Son of John (1737-1799) & Martha (Corbin) (1738-1792) Turberville. Member VA House of Delegates 1785-87 and Sheriff of Richmond Co 1798. Held rank as Col at end of life. BLW of 4611 acres awarded to daughters.BLW 2153 & 2508 issued 15 Jul 1789 **P:** unk **BLW:** Y **RG:** N **MK:** unk **PH:** unk **SS:** G pg 904; DAR Ancestor # A116986; K Vol 5 pg 296 **BS:** 196.

TURBERVILLE, John; b 14 Sep 1737, Hickory Hill, Hague, Westmoreland Co; d 10 Jul 1799 **RU:** Second Lieutenant/Patriot. Was member Committee of Safety fr Westmoreland Co along with brother George Richard Turberville, 31 Jan 1775. Was 2/Lt in Capt John Rice's Co, Westmoreland Co Militia Aug 1777 **CEM:** Hickory Hill, aka Epping; GPS unk; Hague; Westmoreland **GS:** U **SP:** 1) Martha Corbin (1738-1792), d/o Hon. Col John & Lettice (Lee) Corbin 2) Anne Ballentine **VI:** Son of Maj George & Martha (Lee) Turberville. Listed as Major. A stipulation of burial was that he be next to first wife Martha Corbin, with whom he had 10 children. Court action was needed to divide property even though he had will **P:** unk **BLW:** unk **RG:** N **MK:** unk **PH:** unk **SS:** CN pg 85 **BS:** 196.

TURNER, Francis; b 1740 Buckingham Co, d 1803 **RU:** Private, entered service Apr 1777, 3rd VA Regt Cont Line until 23 Dec 1777 when he enlisted in Light Horse Henry Lee's Cav,of Lee's Legion. He was in battles at Brandywine and Germantown and wintered at Valley Forge, serving 3 yrs **CEM:** Francis Turner; GPS not determined; loc at the Nolen Dalton Place, Rt 40: Patrick **GS:** Unk **SP:** Elizabeth Gilley(1744-1817), d/o Francis Gilley and Elizabeth (-----) **VI:** Son of James Turner (1710-1793) & Mary Admire (1738-1818). Drew BLW of 100 acres 9 Sep 1783 **P:** N **BLW:** Y **RG:** Y **MK:** N **PH:** N **SS:** F pg 74; DAR A117052; SAR P-307967 **BS:** 196.

TURNER, Hezekiah; b 23 Jul 1739, Charles Co, MD; d c1817 **RU:** Captain/Patriot, Was Paymaster, 3rd VA Regt, Sep 1777-May 1778. Performed public service as Justice of the Commission of Peace, Fauquier Co **CEM:** Turner Family; GPS unk; Delaplane; Fauquier **GS:** N **SP:** Mar (29 Apr 1764) Henrietta Chunn (1736 Charles Co, MD-aft 1817 Culpeper Co) **VI:** No further data **P:** unk **BLW:** unk **RG:** N **MK:** N **PH:** N **SS:** DAR A117060; A pg 276; C pg 139; CG pg 3558 **BS:** 19 pg 343

TURNER, James; b 7 May 1759; d 8 Jan 1828 **RU:** Patriot, Gave material aid to cause **CEM:** Longwood; GPS 37.34170, -79.51190; Nr jct Oakwood & Longwood Ave Rt 122; Bedford City **GS:** Y **SP:** Sarah Frances "Sally" Leftwich (20 Jan 1762-27 Nov 1834) d/o William (1737-1820) & Elizabeth "Betsey" (Haynes) (1737-1820) Leftwich **VI:** Son of Richard (1730-1769) & Ann Nancy (Johns) (1732-1822) Turner **P:** N **BLW:** N **RG:** N **MK:** unk **PH:** unk **SS:** AL Ct Bk pg 10,17 Bedford Co **BS:** 196.

RU=Rank/Unit	CEM=Cemetery	GS=Gravestone	SP=Spousal Information
VI=Other Veteran Info	P=Pension	BLW=Bounty/Land Warrant	RG=Registered Grave
MK=SAR/DAR Marker	PH=Photo	SS=Service Source	BS=Burial Source

TURNER, John; b c1751; d 1781 **RU:** Patriot, Gave material aid to the cause **CEM:** Moore House; GPS unk; Rt 238, Yorktown; York **GS:** Y **SP:** No info **VI:** No further data **P:** N **BLW:** N **RG:** N **MK:** N **PH:** unk **SS:** AL Ct Bk pg 10 **BS:** 65 Yorktown.

TURNER, John L; b 13 Jul 1755, Mathews Co; d 16 Jul 1820, Mathews Co **RU:** Private, Served in Capt George Armstrong's 3rd MD Regt. Enlisted Middlebrook MD 14 Jan 1778,and trained at Camp Charlotte. Served 3 yrs Cont Army **CEM:** Turner Family; GPS 37.368520, -76.317220; Rt 14, W end Horn Branch; Mathews **GS:** Y **SP:** Elizabeth (-----) (__-14 Oct 1817) **VI:** Pen recd 1818 Mathews Co. S41273 **P:** Y **BLW:** unk **RG:** N **MK:** N **PH:** Y **SS:** K Vol 5 pg 298 **BS:** 43 pg 190; 196.

TURNER, Mattocks; b unk; d 1781 **RU:** Soldier, Served fr DE, and killed in the battle at Yorktown **CEM:** Yorktown Victory Monument Tablet; GPS 38.28350, -78.54150; Yorktown; York **GS:** U **SP:** No info **VI:** No further data **P:** unk **BLW:** unk **RG:** Y **MK:** unk **PH:** unk **SS:** J-Yorktown Historian; SAR P-308049 **BS:** JLARC 74.

TURNER, Nathaniel; b c1739; d 27 Apr 1795 **RU:** Patriot, Gave material aid to cause **CEM:** Turner Family; GPS unk; Eastern View; Hanover **GS:** Y **SP:** No info **VI:** He is listed in the War files # 4, Lib VA so may have had service **P:** unk **BLW:** unk **RG:** N **MK:** N **PH:** unk **SS:** E pg 786; AL Ct Bk II pg 15 Hanover Co; CZ pg 446 **BS:** 31 vol 1 pg 30.

TURNER, Shadrock; b 1720, King William Co (now Caroline Co), d aft 22 Jul 1784 **RU:** Patriot. Gave horse and material aid to Capt Robel's Co, Henry Co **CEM:** Shadrack Turner; GPS not determined; Henry Rd, Butram Town Creek; Henry **GS:** Unk **SP:** Mar (1746 or 1747) Ann Pollard (1724-1811) **VI:** Home still stands **P:** N **BLW:** N **RG:** Y **MK:** N **PH:** N **SS:** D vol 2, pgs 506, 522; DAR A117212; SAR P-308090 **BS:** 196.

TURPIN, Thomas; b1747, Henrico Co, d 1826 **RU:** Ensign, in 15th Cont Line 28 Aug 1777 to 11 Mar 1778 **CEM:** Turpin Family; GPS 37.474999, -79.452220; loc Flitstone Mountain Rd nr jct with Big Island Hwy; Bedford **GS:** Unk **SP:** Mar 9 Aug 1779, Bedford Co, Rachel Cheatwood (1758, Chesterfield Co-13 Dec 1825), d/o William Cheatwood, Sr & Jean Flournoy **VI:** Son of Phillip Turpin (1692-1763) & Elizabeth Burton (1704-1767) data **P:** N **BLW:** N **RG:** N **MK:** N **PH:** Unk **SS:** E pg 786 **BS:**196.

TUTWILER, Leonard; b 10 Jan 1739 Switzerland; d 25 Jan 1804 **RU:** Private, Served in Dunmore Co's Independent Co, and Capt George Baxter's Co, Col Harrison's Regt, Rockingham, Co and was in battle of Cowpens **CEM:** Friedens United Church of Christ; GPS 38.34848, -78.87653; 3960 Friedens Church Rd; Rockingham **GS:** Y **SP:** Catherine (-----) **VI:** No further data **P:** unk **BLW:** unk **RG:** N **MK:** unk **PH:** unk **SS:** DAR Ancestor #A117496; G pg 144 **BS:** 196.

TYLER, Charles Nelson; b 1730; d Mar 1795 **RU:** Patriot; provided civil service as road surveyor and patriotc service by providing beef & pork to militia in Amherst Co **CEM:** Tyler-Davies; GPS 37.502494, -79.215558; loc off of Monacan Park Rd, S of Salt Peter Rd (Rt 652), Elon; Amherst **GS:** Yes inscribed Amherst Co Patriot **SP:** Ann A Lewis **VI:** Find A Grave lists him as Nelson Charles Tyler **P:** N **BLW:** N **RG:** Y **MK:** N **PH:** N **SS:** County Order Bk 6 Aug 1782, pg 2; SAR P-308559 **BS:** 196.

TYLER, John; b 28 Feb 1747, York Co; d 6 Jan 1813 **RU:** Captain, Commanded co in Charles Co Militia Co Sep 1775 **CEM:** Greenway; GPS 37.20190, -77.05200; Rt 5, Charles City CH; Charles City Co **GS:** Y **SP:** 1) Anne Blackington, 2) Mary Armistead (1761-1777) **VI:** Son of John Tyler (1714-1773) & Anne Contesse. Was an attorney; member VA House of Delegates 1778-86; was Speaker fr 1781-85; Judge VA Admiralty Ct 1776 & 1786-88; Judge of State Supreme Ct 1788; Vice President of state conv called to ratify US Constitution; 1788-1808 Chief Judge of VA General Ct; VA Governor 1808-11. In 1812 appointed by President Madison as VA US District Ct Judge. Tyler Co WV named for him. Father of US President John Tyler **P:** unk **BLW:** unk **RG:** Y **MK:** N **PH:** unk **SS:** E pg 787; SAR P-308635 **BS:** JLARC 110; SAR Appl; 196.

TYLER, John; b 15 Jun 1761, Prince William, Co; d 19 Aug 1830 **RU:** First Lieutenant, Served in Capt Scott Co as private and as 1st Lt in 3rd VA Regt **CEM:** Davies; GPS unk; Nr Elon; Amherst **GS:** Y **SP:** Mar (bond dated 2 Feb 1780, Amherst Co) Elizabeth "Betsey" Dillard (__-5 Feb 1849) d/o William & (-----) Dillard **VI:** Vet Admin GS, does not give date of birth, inscribed "Served at Charlottesville, The Surrender at Yorkstown, and Winchester." Widow appl pen 21 Apr 1845. W6328 **P:** Y **BLW:** unk **RG:** Y **MK:** unk **PH:** unk **SS:** AP; CG pg 3568; SAR P-308559 **BS:** 196.

RU=Rank/Unit	CEM=Cemetery	GS=Gravestone	SP=Spousal Information
VI=Other Veteran Info	P=Pension	BLW=Bounty/Land Warrant	RG=Registered Grave
MK=SAR/DAR Marker	PH=Photo	SS=Service Source	BS=Burial Source

424

TYLER, John; b c1749; d 1809 **RU:** Major, Served as 1st Lt 3rd VA Regt, Major serv not determined. Gave material aid to cause **CEM:** Sharon; GPS unk; Middleburg; Loudoun **GS:** Y **SP:** Mar (2 Feb 1789 Amherst Co as bachelor) Elizabeth Dillard, spinster d/o William & (-----) Dillard. Buried lot 53 **VI:** Son of Charles & (-----) Tyler. **P:** unk **BLW:** unk **RG:** N **MK:** N **PH:** unk **SS:** AL Cert Issued; **AP BS:** 65 pg 87.

UMBERGER (UMBARGER), Henry; b 1752, Lebanon TWP, Lancaster Co, PA; d bef 23 Mar 1837 **RU:** Lieutenant Colonel, Served in Capt John Harkerader's Co, Lancaster Co, PA Militia. Also took Oath of Allegiance **CEM:** Rose Hill; GPS unk; Kegley farm 840 Rose Hill Rd, Wytheville; Wythe **GS:** U **SP:** 1) Ann Margaret Baurin 2) Catherine Neff **VI:** No further data **P:** unk **BLW:** unk **RG:**Y **MK:** unk **PH:** unk **SS:** AP PA Archives 2d Ser, Vol 13 pg 403-4 Muster roll; AR Vol 4 pg 135 DAR applic; BY-SAR applic; SAR P-308735 **BS:** JLARC 2, 40.

UPDIKE, Amon; b 25 Feb 1749, Bordertown, Burlington Co, NJ, d 3 Jun 1828 **RU:** Patriot, Supported cause by paying supply tax included in his personal property tax in 1782, Bedford County **CEM:** Amon Updike Family Burial Ground; GPS 37.20291,-79.42952; loc Leesville Rd just S of jct with Lone Oak Crossing, Huddleston; Bedford **GS:** Y **SP:** Mar Loudoun Co, Hannah Harris (1793-__) **VI:** Son of John Updike (1718-1801) and Sarah Farnsworth (1717-1749) **P:** N **BLW:** N **RG:** N **MK:** N **PH:** N **SS:** DV Bedford Co 1782 image 13 pdf **BS:** 196

UPSHUR, Arthur IV; b 1726, Warwick, Accomack Co; d 15 Jan 1784 **RU:** Lieutenant/Patriot, Public service as member of Committee of Safety **CEM:** Warwick House; GPS unk; Rt 605 1 mi S of Quinby, Upshur Bay; Accomack **GS:** Y **SP:** Mar (c1755) Leah Custis (1728-24 Apr 1792) **VI:** No further data **P:** unk **BLW:** unk **RG:** N **MK:** N **PH:** unk **SS:** DAR #A118083; AL Comm Bk I pg 13 Accomack Co; BG pg 200 **BS:** 145 Quimby.

UPSHUR, Caleb; b 1744; d 17 Oct 1778 **RU:** Patriot, Specific service not identified **CEM:** Warwick House; GPS unk; Rt 605 1 mi S of Quinby, Upshur Bay; Accomack **GS:** Y **SP:** No info **VI:** No further data **P:** N **BLW:** N **RG:** N **MK:** N **PH:** unk **SS:** BH Upshur pg 4 **BS:** 145 Quimby.

UPSHUR, John; b 1741, Northampton Co; d 5 Sep 1799 **RU:** Patriot, Justice of Peace and Justice of Ct of Oyer & Terminor 1778 and Commissioner of Grain Tax 1781 **CEM:** Quimby; GPS unk; Painter; Accomack **GS:** U **SP:** 1) Ann Emmerson (1745-1775) 2) Mar (17 Mar 1781) Margaret Downing (1753-1789) **VI:** Son of Abel (1702-1753) & Rachael (Revell) (1702-1749) Upshur **P:** N **BLW:** N **RG:** Y **MK:** unk **PH:** unk **SS:** DAR A118099; DD cites Northampton Co Minute Book 1777-1778 pg 44 and Calendar VA State Papers Vol 2 pg 454; SAR P-308885 **BS:** 196.

UPSHUR, Thomas; b 2 Jul 1739; d 19 Dec 1792 **RU:** Captain, Commanded Inf Co in VA State Troops **CEM:** Brownsville Family; GPS unk; .25 mi N on Rt 600 fr Exmore; Northampton **GS:** U **SP:** Mar (29 Jan 1761) Anne Stockley **VI:** Mar 1761, Anne Stockley (1739-1817) **P:** unk **BLW:** Y **RG:** N **MK:** unk **PH:** unk **SS:** C pg 537 **BS:** 42 pg 87; 196

URVOY, Jean; b unk; d 1781 **RU:** Seaman, Served on "Soliaire" and died from Yorktown battle **CEM:** French Memorial; GPS 36.81944, -79.39933; Yorktown; York **GS:** U **SP:** No info **VI:** No further data **P:** unk **BLW:** unk **RG:** Y **MK:** unk **PH:** unk **SS:** J-Yorktown Historian; SAR P-308953 **BS:** JLARC 1, 74.

VACHERE, Andre; b unk; d 1781 **RU:** Soldier, Served in Gatinais Bn and died fr battle at Yorktown **CEM:** French Memorial; GPS 36.81944, -79.39933; Yorktown; York **GS:** U **SP:** No info **VI:** No further data **P:** unk **BLW:** unk **RG:** Y **MK:** unk **PH:** unk **SS:** J-Yorktown Historian; SAR P-309005 **BS:** JLARC 74.

VADEN, Burwell; b 2 Sep 1733, Henrico Co; d c1824 **RU:** Private/Patriot, Signed the Oath of Allegiance. In 1777 served in Capt Reuben Payne's Co. Also served on Grand Jury of Inquest in 1781 **CEM:** Chatham; GPS 36.81900, -79.39900; Ennis Dr, Chatham; Pittsylvania **GS:** Y **SP:** Mar (1758) Sarah (-----) (1742-6 Feb 1824) **VI:** No further data **P:** unk **BLW:** unk **RG:** Y **MK:** N **PH:** Y **SS:** DAR A116714; Y Bk 4 pg 387; AW; SAR P-309007 **BS:** 174; 04.

VAISSE, Jean; b unk; d 1781 **RU:** Seaman, Served on "Magnanime" and died from Yorktown battle **CEM:** French Memorial; GPS 36.81944, -79.39933; Yorktown; York **GS:** U **SP:** No info **VI:** No further data **P:** unk **BLW:** unk **RG:** Y **MK:** unk **PH:** unk **SS:** J-Yorktown Historian; SAR P-309056 **BS:** JLARC 74.

RU=Rank/Unit	CEM=Cemetery	GS=Gravestone	SP=Spousal Information
VI=Other Veteran Info	P=Pension	BLW=Bounty/Land Warrant	RG=Registered Grave
MK=SAR/DAR Marker	PH=Photo	SS=Service Source	BS=Burial Source

VALENTINE, Batchelder; b 1750; d 1807 **RU**: Patriot, Gave material aid to cause **CEM**: Hollywood; GPS 37.53560, -77.45720; 412 S Cherry St; Richmond City **GS**: Y **SP**: Ann Satterwhite (1752-1829) d/o Mann (of York Co) & Ann (Palmer) Satterwhite **VI**: Listed on obelisk with other family members **P**: N **BLW**: N **RG**: N **MK**: unk **PH**: unk **SS**: AL Ct Bk pg 20 King William Co **BS**: 196.

VALENTINE, Edward; b 1763; d 1832 **RU**: Captain, Served in artillery unit in Cont Line. Was wounded **CEM**: Trinity Episcopal; GPS 38.14917, -79.07521; 214 Beverley St; Staunton City **GS**: U **SP**: no info **VI**: Restitution for back pay to his estate 29 Nov 1850 of $3952.50 was made. R18626. Recd 1/2 pay NARA Acct #874 and #050179 **P**: Y **BLW**: unk **RG**: Y **MK**: unk **PH**: unk **SS**: SAR P-309065; C pg 585, 3578 **BS**: JLARC 8, 51, 62, 63.

VALEOT, Jean; b unk; d 1781 **RU**: Seaman, Served on "Languedoc" and died from Yorktown battle **CEM**: French Memorial; GPS 36.81944, -79.39933; Yorktown; York **GS**: U **SP**: No info **VI**: No further data **P**: unk **BLW**: unk **RG**: Y **MK**: unk **PH**: unk **SS**: J-Yorktown Historian; SAR P-309082 **BS**: JLARC 74.

VALLANCE, William; b unk; d 1781 **RU**: Soldier, Served fr NY, killed in the battle at Yorktown **CEM**: Yorktown Victory Monument Tablet; GPS 38.28350, -78.54150; Yorktown; York **GS**: U **SP**: No info **VI**: No further data **P**: unk **BLW**: unk **RG**: Y **MK**: unk **PH**: unk **SS**: J-Yorktown Historian; SAR P-309091 **BS**: JLARC 74.

VALLE, Jean; b unk; d 1781 **RU**: Seaman, Served on "Hercule" and died from Yorktown battle **CEM**: French Memorial; GPS 36.81944, -79.39933; Yorktown; York **GS**: U **SP**: No info **VI**: No further data **P**: unk **BLW**: unk **RG**: Y **MK**: unk **PH**: unk **SS**: J-Yorktown Historian; SAR P-309097 **BS**: JLARC 74.

VALLEE, Pierre; b unk; d 1781 **RU**: Seaman, Served on "Ville de Paris" and died from Yorktown battle **CEM**: French Memorial; GPS 36.81944, -79.39933; Yorktown; York **GS**: U **SP**: No info **VI**: No further data **P**: unk **BLW**: unk **RG**: Y **MK**: unk **PH**: unk **SS**: J-Yorktown Historian; SAR P-309098 **BS**: JLARC 74.

VALLEE, Vincent; b unk; d 1781 **RU**: Seaman, Served on "Citoyen" and died from Yorktown battle **CEM**: French Memorial; GPS 36.81944, -79.39933; Yorktown; York **GS**: U **SP**: No info **VI**: No further data **P**: unk **BLW**: unk **RG**: Y **MK**: unk **PH**: unk **SS**: J-Yorktown Historian; SAR P-309099 **BS**: JLARC 74.

VAN BUSKIRK, Abraham; b 1753, d 2 Jul 1813 **RU**: Patriot, Gave material aid to cause, Frederick Co **CEM**: Old Besthesda Methodist; GPS 39.02822,-77.78938 S of Union nr stream, Union: Loudoun **GS**: Yes **SP**: Ann V Cochran (1749-16 Dec 1839 **VI**: No further data **P** N **BLW**: N **RG**: N **MK**: N **PH**: N **SS**: AL Ct Bk pg 31, Comm Bk pg 215 **BS**: 196

VANCE, James D; b 1752, Orange Co; d 21 Dec 1816 **RU**: Private,/Patriot Served in 4th, 8th, 12th Cont Lines, and paid personal property tax, Frederick Co, 1782 **CEM**: Opequon Presbyterian; GPS 39.13938, -78.19494; 217 Opequon Church Ln; Winchester City **GS**: Y **SP**: No info **VI**: Died in Frederick Co **P**: unk **BLW**: unk **RG**: N **MK**: N **PH**: unk **SS**: E pg 79; ER Frederick Co Tax List 1782 **BS**: 59 pg 333; 196.

VANCE, John; b 12 Feb 1736; d 28 Aug 1823 **RU**: Lieutenant, Served in Capt James Dysart's Co of Light Horse on tour of NC under command of Col William Campbell. Was listed on payroll of 21 May 1781 **CEM**: Vance Family; GPS unk; Rt 695; Washington **GS**: Y **SP**: Jane (-----) (12 Feb 1741-2 Feb 1824) **VI**: No further data **P**: N **BLW**: N **RG**: Y **MK**: unk **PH**: N **SS**: N pg 1262-payroll; CI Muster Roll; SAR P-310126 **BS**: 212 pg 108.

VANCE, Robert; b 1728; d 18 Aug 1818 **RU**: Patriot, Was Commissioner in 1780-81, Berkeley Co **CEM**: Montour; GPS unk; Not identified by SAR source; Winchester City **GS**: U **SP**: Jean White (1747 Culpeper-__) **VI**: Son of Samuel & Sarah (Covllie) Vance **P**: N **BLW**: N **RG**: Y **MK**: unk **PH**: unk **SS**: DAR A117359; SAR P-310142; J- DAR Hatcher; AL Ct Bk I pg 9 **BS**: JLARC 2.

VANCE, Samuel; b 1734, Ireland; d 1807 **RU**: Captain/Patriot, Served in 8th Cont Line. Gave material aid to cause **CEM**: Opequon Presbyterian; GPS 39.13938, -78.19494; 217 Opequon Church Ln; Winchester City **GS**: U **SP**: Sarah Byrd **VI**: No further data **P**: unk **BLW**: unk **RG**: Y **MK**: Y SAR **PH**: unk **SS**: J-NSSAR 2000 Reg; AL Cert 1 Frederick C; SAR P-310149 **BS**: JLARC 76.

RU=Rank/Unit	CEM=Cemetery	GS=Gravestone	SP=Spousal Information
VI=Other Veteran Info	P=Pension	BLW=Bounty/Land Warrant	RG=Registered Grave
MK=SAR/DAR Marker	PH=Photo	SS=Service Source	BS=Burial Source

426

VANCE, Samuel; b 1749; d 8 Dec 1838 **RU:** Soldier, Was in battles at Point Pleasant & Kings Mountain **CEM:** Sinking Springs; GPS 36.71030, -81.98170; 136 E Main St, Abingdon; Washington **GS:** U **SP:** Margaret Laughlin **VI:** No further data **P:** unk **BLW:** unk **RG:** Y **MK:** Y SAR **PH:** unk **SS:** SAR P-310151 **BS:** JLARC 2, 80.

VANCE, William; b 1741; d Oct 1792 **RU:** Captain, Served in 8th VA Regt Frederick Co Militia. Took oath as ensign 4 Aug 1779 **CEM:** Old Opequon Church; GPS 39.82237, -78.11412; 217 Opequon Church Ln, Kernstown; Frederick **GS:** Y **SP:** 1) Nancy Gilkeson 2) Mary Colville 3) Ann Glass **VI:** No inscription on GS. No record of pension **P:** unk **BLW:** unk **RG:** Y **MK:** Y SAR; DAR plaque **PH:** Y **SS:** J-NSSAR 2000 Reg; E pg 790; SAR P-310156 **BS:** JLARC 76.

VANDEVANTER (VANDEVINDER, VAN DEVENTER, VANDEVENTER), Isaac; b 8 Feb 1747, Hunterdon Co, NJ; d 12 Jul 1803 **RU:** Second Lieutenant/Patriot, Served in Loudoun Co Militia, and took oath as 2nd Lt, 15 Sep 1778. Also gave 335# beef to cause **CEM:** Fairfax Meeting House; GPS 39.18557, -77.60589; Water St & Waterford Rd, Waterford; Loudoun **GS:** Y **SP:** Elizabeth McGeath **VI:** No further data **P:** unk **BLW:** unk **RG:** Y **MK:** N **PH:** unk **SS:** D pg 2; E pg 191; AZ pg 212; AL Ct BK pg 3 Loudoun Co; DAR A118666; SAR P-309421 **BS:** 25 pg 323.

VAN LEAR (VANLEAR), Jacob; b unk; d 1822 **RU:** Private, Served in Capt Long's Co, Augusta Co Militia **CEM:** Tinkling Spring Presbyterian; GPS 38.08472, -78.98278; 30 Tinkling Spring Dr, Fishersville; Augusta **GS:** N **SP:** Jane (-----) **VI:** No further data **P:** unk **BLW:** unk **RG:** Y **MK:** N **PH:** N **SS:** E pg 791 SAR P-309859 **BS:** JLARC 6; 196

VAN METER, Henry Jr; b 12 May 1754, Frederick Co; d 17 May 1830 **RU:** Private/Patriot, Served in militia. Gave to cause in Berkeley Co **CEM:** Miller Family; GPS unk; Mountain View Farm, vic Front Royal; Warren **GS:** Y **SP:** Elizabeth Miller (19 Nov 1755-24 Jan 1808) **VI:** No further data **P:** unk **BLW:** unk **RG:** N **MK:** N **PH:** unk **SS:** E pg 791; AL Ct Bk pg 6 **BS:** 01 pg 36; 196.

VANPELT, Peter; b unk; d 4 Apr 1831 **RU:** Private, Ent serv Amherst Co. In fall of 1777, served 3 mos in Capt Robert Cravens Co at Tygart's Valley VA. Enlisted April 1778, and served 18 mos in Capts David Stephenson's and John Steed's Cos, Col Neville's VA Regt. Was at Battle of Monmouth **CEM:** Frank Harman Place; GPS unk; Rt 42 N, Harrisonburg; Harrisonburg City **GS:** N **SP:** Mar (13 Mar 1778) Agnes (Agness) (c1761-25 Aug 1840) **VI:** Died in Rockingham Co. Widow appl pen 17 Apr 1837 Buckingham Co, age 76. W18198 **P:** Y **BLW:** unk **RG:** N **MK:** N **PH:** N **SS:** E pg 791; AK; CG Vol 3 pg 3599 **BS:** 04; 191 Fr Harman.

VAN PELT, Tunis; b unk; d 1840 **RU:** Patriot, Gave material aid to cause **CEM:** Frank Harman Place; GPS unk; Rt 42 N, Harrisonburg; Harrisonburg City **GS:** Y **SP:** No info **VI:** No further data **P:** N **BLW:** N **RG:** N **MK:** unk **PH:** unk **SS:** AL Cert Berkeley Co **BS:** 219.

VAN SICKLER, Ferdinand (Fernandus); b 11 May 1738, NJ; d 1818 **RU:** Private, Probably served in Loudoun Co Militia **CEM:** North Fork Baptist; GPS 39.06014, -77.68509; 38130 North Folk Rd, North Fork; Loudoun **GS:** U **SP:** Mar (10 Jun 1757) Eleanor WinKoop, d/o Philip & Margaret (Conover) Wynkoop **VI:** No further data **P:** unk **BLW:** unk **RG:** Y **MK:** unk **PH:** unk **SS:** BY cites DAR Mag; SAR P-309894 **BS:** JLARC 32.

VAN VOST, Christian; b unk; d 1781 **RU:** Private, Served in 1st Regt NY Line. Killed in the battle at Yorktown **CEM:** Yorktown Victory Monument Tablet; GPS 38.28350, -78.54150; Yorktown; York **GS:** U **SP:** No info **VI:** No further data **P:** unk **BLW:** unk **RG:** Y **MK:** unk **PH:** unk **SS:** J-Yorktown Historian; AX pg 348; SAR P-310020 **BS:** JLARC 74.

VAQUIER, Francois; b unk; d 1781 **RU:** Seaman, Served on "Diademe" and died from Yorktown battle **CEM:** French Memorial; GPS 36.81944, -79.39933; Yorktown; York **GS:** U **SP:** No info **VI:** No further data **P:** unk **BLW:** unk **RG:** Y **MK:** unk **PH:** unk **SS:** J-Yorktown Historian; SAR P-310387 **BS:** JLARC 74.

VARNER, Joseph; b 1758; d 1848 **RU:** Soldier, Served in Cont & VA Lines. Ent serv Charlotte Co **CEM:** Varner Family; GPS unk; Nr jct of Rts 696 & 626, btw Critz & Salem Church, Locust Grove; Patrick **GS:** N **SP:** Mar (7 Oct 1790) Polly (Molly) Kinney (c1772-_) **VI:** Also served in the War of 1812. Listed as a pensioner in 1840. Sol appl pen Apr 1820 Halifax Co age 56. Widow appl pen 4 Mar 1850 Patrick Co

RU=Rank/Unit	CEM=Cemetery	GS=Gravestone	SP=Spousal Information
VI=Other Veteran Info	P=Pension	BLW=Bounty/Land Warrant	RG=Registered Grave
MK=SAR/DAR Marker	PH=Photo	SS=Service Source	BS=Burial Source

427

age 78 and BLW 11 Apr 1855 age 85 Patrick Co. W1762, BLW #12641-100 & BLW #139-60-55. Unmarked grave **P:** Y **BLW:** Y **RG:**Y **MK:** unk **PH:** N **SS:** CG Vol 3 pg 3608; SAR P-310412 **BS:** JLARC 4, 30.

VARNER (WERNER), Phillip; b 1746, Alsace, Germany; d 1830 **RU:** Patriot, Gave material aid to the cause **CEM:** James Varner Family; GPS unk; SE of Luray; Page **GS:** Y **SP:** Barbara Hottel **VI:** No further data **P:** N **BLW:** N **RG:** N **MK:** N **PH:** unk **SS:** AL Ct Bk pg 6, 120; **BS:** 120 Hartman.

VARRENNES, Jean; b unk; d 1781 **RU:** Soldier, Served in Beaujolais Bn and died fr battle at Yorktown **CEM:** French Memorial; GPS 36.81944, -79.39933; Yorktown; York **GS:** U **SP:** No info **VI:** No further data **P:** unk **BLW:** unk **RG:** Y **MK:** unk **PH:** unk **SS:** J-Yorktown Historian; SAR P-310439 **BS:** JLARC 74.

VAUGHAN, James; b c1738-1741; d 1803 **RU:** Sergeant, Rank obtained 1778. Serv in 3rd & 4th Cont Line **CEM:** Vaughan Family; GPS unk; Not identified; Amelia **GS:** Y **SP:** 1) Mar (c1771) Ann Hill (__-1782) d/o James & (-----) Hill, 2) Mar (bef 14 Mar 1783) Lucy Jeter d/o Thomas & (-----) Jeter **VI:** Son of Robert (c1705, Prince George Co-1779) & Martha (-----) Vaughan **P:** unk **BLW:** Y **RG:** Y **MK:** N **PH:** unk **SS:** DAR A118308; E pg 793; SAR 310464 **BS:** 80 vol 4 pg 144.

VAUGHAN, William; b 3 Feb 1720, Christchurch, Middlesex Co, d 1806 **RU:** Patriot, paid Personal Property Tax 1783, Washington Co, Capt Andrew Cowan's return. A portion of this tax partially paid for Rev War expenses **CEM:** Mark Jones Family; GPS not determined; loc vic Elk Creek; Grayson **GS:** No **SP:** Mary Ann Napier (1724-1800), d/o Booth Napier & Sarah LaForce **VI:** Son of William Vaughan (1684-__) & Mary Ann Wake (1688-__) **P:** N **BLW:** N **RG:** N **MK:** N **PH:** N **SS:** DV Personal Property Tax 1783, Washington Co, Capt Andrew Cowan's return, image 05.pdf **BS** 196.

VAUGHAN (VAUGHN), William Jr; b 18 Nov 1760, Hanover Co; d 22 Mar 1841 **RU:** Sergeant, Ent serv Bedford Co 1780. Served in Webber's VA Co, 4th Cont Line and wounded at siege of 96 **CEM:** Vaughan Family; GPS 36.44200, -81.41660; Fries, Spring Valley Community; Grayson **GS:** Y **SP:** Mar (8 May 1794) Elizabeth "Betsey" Fielder (17 Feb 1777-__) d/o John & (-----) Fielder **VI:** Son of William & Mary (-----) Vaughan. Sol appl pen 24 Sep 1832 Grayson Co. Widow appl pen 27 Jan 1851, and for BLW 19 Apr 1855 both in Grayson Co. W2708 in 1851. BLW 29019-160 (55) **P:** Y **BLW:** Y **RG:** N **MK:** Y SAR **PH:** unk **SS:** J- DAR Hatcher; E pg 173, 793; CG Vol 3 pg 3611 **BS:** 199, JLARC 2.

VAUGHN, James; b c1756; d 14 Dec 1830 **RU:** Sergeant, Promoted in 1778 and served in 3rd & 4th Cont Lines **CEM:** Shockoe Hill; GPS 37.55190, -77.43170; 4th & Hospital Sts; Richmond City **GS:** Y-Gov't **SP:** No info **VI:** No further data **P:** unk **BLW:** unk **RG:**N **MK:** Y monument **PH:** unk **SS:** E pg 793 **BS:** 57 pg 9.

VAUGHN, William; b unk; d unk **RU:** Sergeant, Served in Spencer's Regt, Cont Troops **CEM:** Fairmont Baptist; GPS unk; 3948 Findlay Gap Dr, Shipley; Nelson **GS:** Y **SP:** No info **VI:** No further data **P:** unk **BLW:** unk **RG:** N **MK:** N **PH:** unk **SS:** AP roll **BS:** 182.

VAWTER, Benjamin; b unk; d 1830 **RU:** Private, Served in 2nd VA State Regt **CEM:** Old City; GPS 37.41472, -79.15667; 401 Taylor St; Lynchburg City **GS:** N **SP:** No info **VI:** No further data **P:** unk **BLW:** unk **RG:** N **MK:** Y SAR plaque **PH:** N **SS:** E pg 793 **BS:** 62 pg 173.

VAWTER, John; b unk; d 1834 **RU:** Private?, Served 3 yrs in VA Cont Line **CEM:** Old City; GPS 37.41472, -79.15667; 401 Taylor St; Lynchburg City **GS:** Y **SP:** No info **VI:** Heir, Beverly Vawter recd BLW of 100 acres for his service **P:** unk **BLW:** Y **RG:** N **MK:** Y SAR plaque **PH:** unk **SS:** C pg 213; E pg 793; F pg 77 **BS:** 62 pg 173.

VBEL, Geroges; b unk; d 1781 **RU:** Soldier, Served in Royal Deux Ponts Bn and died fr battle at Yorktown **CEM:** French Memorial; GPS 36.81944, -79.39933; Yorktown; York **GS:** U **SP:** No info **VI:** No further data **P:** unk **BLW:** unk **RG:** Y **MK:** unk **PH:** unk **SS:** J-Yorktown Historian; SAR P-310550 **BS:** JLARC 74.

VEALE, Thomas; b 1725, Norfolk Co; d 16 Dec 1793 **RU:** Patriot, Gave material aid to cause in Norfolk **CEM:** Trinity Episcopal; GPS 36.83459, -76.30105; 500 Court St; Portsmouth City **GS:** Y **SP:** Mar (15 Nov 1763. Norfolk) Bethiah Edwards **VI:** Capt in Colonial War. Was Burgess fr Norfolk Co 1762-1765. One of the Trustees of Portsmouth **P:** N **BLW:** N **RG:** N **MK:** unk **PH:** unk **SS:** D pg 255 **BS:** 75.

RU=Rank/Unit	CEM=Cemetery	GS=Gravestone	SP=Spousal Information
VI=Other Veteran Info	P=Pension	BLW=Bounty/Land Warrant	RG=Registered Grave
MK=SAR/DAR Marker	PH=Photo	SS=Service Source	BS=Burial Source

VEINTEFFER, JH; b unk; d 1781 **RU:** Seaman, Served on "Auguste" and died from Yorktown battle **CEM:** French Memorial; GPS 36.81944, -79.39933; Yorktown; York **GS:** U **SP:** No info **VI:** No further data **P:** unk **BLW:** unk **RG:** Yk **MK:** unk **PH:** unk **SS:** J-Yorktown Historian; SAR P-310635 **BS:** JLARC 74.

VENABLE, Abraham Bedford Jr; b 20 Nov 1758; d 28 Dec 1811 **RU:** Patriot, Gave material aid to cause **CEM:** Monumental Church; GPS unk; 1224 E Broad St; Richmond City **GS:** Y **SP:** No info **VI:** Son of Nathaniel (1733-1804) & Elizabeth Michaux (Woodson) (1740-1791) Venable. Was US Congressman & US Senator and elected to represent VA's 6th & 7th Districts & at-Large in US House of Representatives, 1791-99. Was US Senator fr VA fr 1803-4. Died in theater fire in Richmond 26 Dec 1811 **P:** N **BLW:** N **RG:** N **MK:** unk **PH:** unk **SS:** AL Ct Bk pg 30 Prince Edward Co **BS:** 196.

VENABLE, Charles See Appendix G, Addenda)

VENABLE, Joseph Morton, b 28 Jun 1761, Charlotte Co, d 23 Jul 1833 **RU:** Aide to General Lawson and carried dispatches to General Lafayette 1781 **CEM:** Watkins Family; GPS:37.093105,-78.029729; Poplar Hill Plantation (owned by Hamden-Sydney College); Prince Edward **GS:** Unk **SP:** Mar Jan 1791, Elizabeth Watkins (6 Dec 1769-Apr 1832, KY) **VI:** Son of James Venable and Judith Morton. Graduated 1783, Hampden-Sydney College and later Princeton, NJ. Was Commonwealth Attorney for Charlotte and Prince Edward Counties bef 1810 **P** N **BLW:** N **RG:** N **MK:** N **PH:** N **SS:** CD **BS:** 196.

VENABLE, Nathaniel; b 1 Nov 1733, Lousia Co; d 26 Dec 1804 **RU:** Patriot, Gave material aid to cause **CEM:** Venable-Slate Hill Plantation; GPS unk; Worsham; Prince Edward **GS:** Y **SP:** Elizabeth Michaux Woodson (6 Jun 1740-29 Sep 1791) d/o Richard & Anne Madeline (Michaux) Woodson. **VI:** Son of Abraham (II) & Martha (Davis) Venable. Was member of House of Burgesses; VA House of Delegates 1766, 1769, 1776; and a State Senator fr P.E. Co fr 1780-85. One of founders of Hampden-Sydney College **P:** N **BLW:** N **RG:** Y **MK:** unk **PH:** unk **SS:** AL Ct Bk pg 29, 37 Prince Edward Co; SAR P-310646 **BS:** 196.

VENABLE, Richard Nathaniel, b 16 Jan 1763, d 17 Jan 1838 **RU:** Lieutenant, Prince Edward Co Militia, 8th Co. Filed petition for pension with supportng affidavid of service as Ensign in Pr Edward Co Ct in Jun 1785. Service as Lt may have been after war officially ended in Sep 1783 **CEM:** Venable Slate Hill Plantation; GPS not determined; loc 2 mi S of Worsham; Prince Edward **GS:** Unk **SP:** Mar 35 Mar 1797, Pr Edw Co, Mary Morton (29 Aug 1780-1839) **VI:** Son of Nathaniel Venable (1 Nov 1733, Lousia Co-26 Dec 1804) and Elizabeth Michaux Woodson (6 Jun 1740-29 Sep 1791). Was Trustee and contributor to Hampden-Sydney College 1792-1838, and Senator and member of Convention of 1829 **P:** Applied **BLW:** N **RG:** N **MK:** N **PH:** N **SS:** G pg 304; **BS:** 196.

VERDAVOIR, Oger; b unk; d 1781 **RU:** Soldier, Served in Agenois Bn and died fr battle at Yorktown **CEM:** French Memorial; GPS 36.81944, -79.39933; Yorktown; York **GS:** U **SP:** No info **VI:** No further data **P:** unk **BLW:** unk **RG:**Y **MK:** unk **PH:** unk **SS:** J-Yorktown Historian; SAR P-310662 **BS:** JLARC 74.

VERDIER, Jacques; b unk; d 1781 **RU:** Seaman, Served on "Marseillais" and died from Yorktown battle **CEM:** French Memorial; GPS 36.81944, -79.39933; Yorktown; York **GS:** U **SP:** No info **VI:** No further data **P:** unk **BLW:** unk **RG:** Y **MK:** unk **PH:** unk **SS:** J-Yorktown Historian; SAR P-310664 **BS:** JLARC 74.

VERRIER, Joseph; b unk; d 1781 **RU:** Soldier, Served in Bourbonnais Bn and died fr battle at Yorktown **CEM:** French Memorial; GPS 36.81944, -79.39933; Yorktown; York **GS:** U **SP:** No info **VI:** No further data **P:** unk **BLW:** unk **RG:** Y **MK:** unk **PH:** unk **SS:** J-Yorktown Historian; SAR P-310726 **BS:** JLARC 74.

VERSIN, Pierre; b unk; d 1781 **RU:** Seaman, Served on "Hextor" and died from Yorktown battle **CEM:** French Memorial; GPS 36.81944, -79.39933; Yorktown; York **GS:** U **SP:** No info **VI:** No further data **P:** unk **BLW:** unk **RG:** Y **MK:** unk **PH:** unk **SS:** J-Yorktown Historian; SAR P-310731 **BS:** JLARC 74.

VEXLIN, Emanuel; b unk; d 1781 **RU:** Seaman, Served on "Soliaire" and died from Yorktown battle **CEM:** French Memorial; GPS 36.81944, -79.39933; Yorktown; York **GS:** U **SP:** No info **VI:** No further

RU=Rank/Unit	CEM=Cemetery	GS=Gravestone	SP=Spousal Information
VI=Other Veteran Info	P=Pension	BLW=Bounty/Land Warrant	RG=Registered Grave
MK=SAR/DAR Marker	PH=Photo	SS=Service Source	BS=Burial Source

429

data **P:** unk **BLW:** unk **RG:** Y **MK:** unk **PH:** unk **SS:** J-Yorktown Historian; SAR P-310752 **BS:** JLARC 74.

VEXTAIN, Emanuel; b unk; d 1781 **RU:** Soldier, Served in Gatinais Bn and died fr battle at Yorktown **CEM:** French Memorial; GPS 36.81944, -79.39933; Yorktown; York **GS:** U **SP:** No info **VI:** No further data **P:** unk **BLW:** unk **RG:** Y **MK:** unk **PH:** unk **SS:** J-Yorktown Historian; SAR P-310753 **BS:** JLARC 74.

VIA /VIER/VIAH, John B; b Dec 1759, Buckingham Co, d 7 Mar 1834 **RU:** Sergeant,enlisted Amherst Co served in Capts Jesse Allen, Holman Rice, and James Burton Cos, Col Francis Taylor Regt, VA Line long enough to be pension eligble **CEM:** John Via Family' GPS vic Endicott 36.8876339, -80.1672758; loc Endicott, Franklin **GS:** N **SP:** Mar (4 Mar 1784, Buckingham Co) Sarah Wright (1761-1851) who recd pen W3896, in Franklin Co **VI:** Son of Gideon Via & Isabel Horsley. Applied for pen 24 Jan 1834, recd # R 2459 **P:**Yes both **BLW:** eligible but not recd **RG:** Y **MK:** unk **PH:** unk **SS:** C pg 274; E pg 794; K vol 6, pg 23; CG pg 3618; DAR A118749; SAR P-310757 **BS** 196.

VIA, William; b 1761; d 27 Jun 1836 **RU:** Private, Served in VA Line Bn **CEM:** Via Family; GPS unk; Brown's Cove; Albemarle **GS:** U **SP:** Mar (7 Dec 1781) Mary Craig **VI:** Appl pen 7 Dec 1828 and recd same in Albemarle Co age 67. Widow appl pen 5 Aug 1829 **P:** Y **BLW:** unk **RG:** Y **MK:** unk **PH:** unk **SS:** J- DAR Hatcher; E pg 794; CG pg 3616; SAR P-310759 **BS:** JLARC 2.

VIAL, Pierre; b unk; d 1781 **RU:** Soldier, Served in Soissonnais Bn and died fr battle at Yorktown **CEM:** French Memorial; GPS 36.81944, -79.39933; Yorktown; York **GS:** U **SP:** No info **VI:** No further data **P:** unk **BLW:** unk **RG:** Y **MK:** unk **PH:** unk **SS:** J-Yorktown Historian; SAR P-310763 **BS:** JLARC 74.

VICARS, Robert, b 8 Nov 1747, Eng, d 13 Mar 1821 **RU:** Private, Captain William Russell's Co at Point Pleasant Oct 1774. Also Capt Baird's Co, Botetourt Co Militia **CEM:** Old Vicars; GPS: 36.7858, -82.3094; Grassy Creek; Russell **GS:** Yes **SP:** Lydia Jackson (Norfolk, VA 1752-1795) **VI:** No further data **P:** N **BLW:** N **RG:** Y **MK:** Y SAR **PH:** N **SS:** DAR A118678; SAR P 310788 Z **BS:** SAR PRS; 196

VIGOUREUX, Francois; b unk; d 1781 **RU:** Soldier, Served in Gatinais Bn and died fr battle at Yorktown **CEM:** French Memorial; GPS 36.81944, -79.39933; Yorktown; York **GS:** U **SP:** No info **VI:** No further data **P:** unk **BLW:** unk **RG:** N **MK:** unk **PH:** unk **SS:** J-Yorktown Historian **BS:** JLARC 74.

VILATON, Jean; b unk; d 1781 **RU:** Soldier, Served in Santogne Bn and died fr battle at Yorktown **CEM:** French Memorial; GPS 36.81944, -79.39933; Yorktown; York **GS:** U **SP:** No info **VI:** No further data **P:** unk **BLW:** unk **RG:** Y **MK:** unk **PH:** unk **SS:** J-Yorktown Historian; SAR P-310849 **BS:** JLARC 74.

VILLARET, Joseph; b unk; d 1781 **RU:** Soldier, Served in Bourbonnais Bn and died fr battle at Yorktown **CEM:** French Memorial; GPS 36.81944, -79.39933; Yorktown; York **GS:** U **SP:** No info **VI:** No further data **P:** unk **BLW:** unk **RG N MK:** unk **PH:** unk **SS:** J-Yorktown Historian **BS:** JLARC 74.

VILLEDIEU, Jean; b unk; d 1781 **RU:** Seaman, Served on Caton and died from Yorktown battle **CEM:** French Memorial; GPS 36.81944, -79.39933; Yorktown; York **GS:** U **SP:** no info **VI:** No further data **P:** unk **BLW:** unk **RG:** Y **MK:** unk **PH:** unk **SS:** J-Yorktown Historian; SAR P-310862 **BS:** JLARC 74.

VILLEON, de la; b unk; d 1781 **RU:** Seaman, Served on "Diademe" and died from Yorktown battle **CEM:** French Memorial; GPS 36.81944, -79.39933; Yorktown; York **GS:** U **SP:** No info **VI:** No further data **P:** unk **BLW:** unk **RG:** N **MK:** unk **PH:** unk **SS:** J-Yorktown Historian **BS:** JLARC 74.

VINCE, Joseph; b unk; d 1781 **RU:** Seaman, Served on "Ville de Paris" and died from Yorktown battle **CEM:** French Memorial; GPS 36.81944, -79.39933; Yorktown; York **GS:** U **SP:** No info **VI:** No further data **P:** unk **BLW:** unk **RG:** Y **MK:** unk **PH:** unk **SS:** J-Yorktown Historian; SAR P-310871 **BS:** JLARC 74.

VINCENT, Nicolas; b unk; d 1781 **RU:** Seaman, Served on "Solitaire" and died from Yorktown battle **CEM:** French Memorial; GPS 36.81944, -79.39933; Yorktown; York **GS:** U **SP:** No info **VI:** No further data **P:** unk **BLW:** unk **RG:** Y **MK:** unk **PH:** unk **SS:** J-Yorktown Historian; SAR P-310899 **BS:** JLARC 74.

VINEYARD, George; b 21 Jun 1759; d 5 Oct 1852 **RU:** Private, Served in VA Line. Ent serv Rockbridge Co Militia **CEM:** Vineyard; GPS unk; loc vic jct Red Hill Rd & Red Bluff Rd Gate City; Scott **GS:** Y **SP:**

RU=Rank/Unit	CEM=Cemetery	GS=Gravestone	SP=Spousal Information
VI=Other Veteran Info	P=Pension	BLW=Bounty/Land Warrant	RG=Registered Grave
MK=SAR/DAR Marker	PH=Photo	SS=Service Source	BS=Burial Source

430

Mar (Nov 1790, Rockbridge Co) Mary Campbell (1769-1815) **VI:** Sol appl 13 Feb 1844 Scott Co age 84. S7794 **P:** Y **BLW:** unk **RG:** Y **MK:** DAR Plaque **PH:** unk **SS:** CG Vol 3 pg 3619; DAR A118926; SAR P-310911 **BS:** JLARC 4; 196.

VINYARD, Christain; b unk, Palatinate, Germany; d 27 Feb 1798 **RU:** Patriot, Performed patriotic service to VA Militia. Furnished supplies 11 Apr 1782 **CEM:** Vinyard Family; GPS unk; Lauderale Ave; Roanoke Co **GS:** Y **SP:** Mar (1772) Chritiania Tabler **VI:** No further data **P:** N **BLW:** N **RG:** Y **MK:** N **PH:** unk **SS:** D Roanoke area; SAR P-310957 **BS:** 04.

VINYARD, Christian; b unk; d 1837 **RU:** Patriot, Gave material aid to the cause **CEM:** Vinyard Family; GPS unk; Vinton; Roanoke Co **GS:** U **SP:** No info **VI:** No further data **P:** N **BLW:** N **RG:** Y **MK:** N **PH:** unk **SS:** AL Ct Bk pg 25; SAR P-310958 **BS:** DAR report.

VITRE, Jean; b unk; d 1781 **RU:** Soldier, Served in Gatinais Bn and died fr battle at Yorktown **CEM:** French Memorial; GPS 36.81944, -79.39933; Yorktown; York **GS:** U **SP:** No info **VI:** No further data **P:** unk **BLW:** unk **RG:** Y **MK:** unk **PH:** unk **SS:** J-Yorktown Historian; SAR P-310987 **BS:** JLARC 74.

VITRIER, Andre; b unk; d 1781 **RU:** Soldier, Served in Gatinais Bn and died fr battle at Yorktown **CEM:** French Memorial; GPS 36.81944, -79.39933; Yorktown; York **GS:** U **SP:** No info **VI:** No further data **P:** unk **BLW:** unk **RG:** Y **MK:** unk **PH:** unk **SS:** J-Yorktown Historian; SAR P[-310988 **BS:** JLARC 74.

VIVANSON, Bernard; b unk; d 1781 **RU:** Soldier, Served in Touraine Bn and died fr battle at Yorktown **CEM:** French Memorial; GPS 36.81944, -79.39933; Yorktown; York **GS:** U **SP:** No info **VI:** No further data **P:** unk **BLW:** unk **RG:** Y **MK:** unk **PH:** unk **SS:** J-Yorktown Historian; SAR P-310990 **BS:** JLARC 74.

VIRTZS (WIRTZ) (WERTS) Peter Phillip (Phillip Peter) b 14 Jun 1737 Germany, d 22 May 1798 **RU:** Private/Patriot (New grave stone shows variation of spelling as Phillip Peter Wirtz and service as Continental Line, Revolutionary War. DAR indicates service as Patriot Servant) **CEM:** New Jerusalem Lutheran Church; GPS 39.257087, -77.638844; 12942 Lutheran Church Rd, Lovettsville; Loudoun **GS:** Yes Row KK, stone 3 **SP:** Christina Everhart (18 Jan 1737-20 Jun 1813) **VI:** Son of William Wurtz (1703-1782) and Anna Catherine (-----) (1706-1791) **P:** N **BLW:** N **RG:** Y **MK:** Y SAR granite **PH:** N **SS:** B; DAR Patiot Index, Vol 3, pg 3155; SAR P-328888 & SAR P-341256 **BS:** 04; 196.

VIZET, Joseph; b unk; d 1781 **RU:** Seaman, Served on "Diademe" and died from Yorktown battle **CEM:** French Memorial; GPS 36.81944, -79.39933; Yorktown; York **GS:** U **SP:** No info **VI:** No further data **P:** unk **BLW:** unk **RG:** Y **MK:** unk **PH:** unk **SS:** J-Yorktown Historian; SAR P-311001 **BS:** JLARC 74.

VON EFFINGER, John; b unk; d unk **RU:** Corporal, Served in Voneffinge's unitr **CEM:** Woodstock; GPS unk; Woodstock; Shenandoah **GS:** U **SP:** no info **VI:** No further data **P:** unk **BLW:** unk **RG:** Y **MK:** unk **PH:** unk **SS:** J-NSSAR 2000 Reg; AR Vol 4 pg 147; SAR P-311039 **BS:** JLARC 76.

VORRIOT, Pierre; b unk; d 1781 **RU:** Seaman, Served on "Hextor" and died from Yorktown battle **CEM:** French Memorial; GPS 36.81944, -79.39933; Yorktown; York **GS:** U **SP:** No info **VI:** No further data **P:** unk **BLW:** unk **RG:** Y **MK:** unk **PH:** unk **SS:** J-Yorktown Historian; SAR P-311125 **BS:** JLARC 74.

VOWELL, John G; b unk; d 1806 **RU:** Soldier, Served in 6th Cont Line **CEM:** Old Presbyterian Meeting House; GPS 38.48528, -77.23532; 323 S Fairfax St; Alexandria City **GS:** N **SP:** No info **VI:** No further data **P:** unk **BLW:** unk **RG:** Y **MK:** unk **PH:** N **SS:** J-NSSAR 2000 Reg; SAR P-311198; E pg 796 **BS:** JLARC 1; 5.

WACKER, John(Johannes) Michael; b 23 Jul 1731 prob PA; d 22 Jan 1799 **RU** Patriot, served for one year as a bateauman, laborer or fatiqueman under Col Patterson's Regt, Cont Trps **CEM:** Old Pine Church: GPS 38.742677, -78.683408; loc 1mi S of Pinkerton, east of rd on land of Milton Funkhouser 1936 **GS:** No but name on memorial marker **SP:** Mar 19 Dec 1752, Old Goshenhoppen, Montgomery Co, PA, Margaret Fischback(1733-unk) **VI:** No further data **P:** N **BLW:** N **RG:** N **MK:** N **PH:** Y **SS:** AP Fold3 service index card **BS:** 196.

WADDELL, James; b Jul 1739, Ireland; d 17 Sep 1805 **RU** Patriot worked as a spy for the cause as a blind preacher **CEM:** Waddell Memorial Presbyterian Church; GPS 38.308330, -78.062700; 7133 Rapidan Rd, Rapidan, Culpeper **GS** Y **SP:** Mary Gordon (17 Jul 1752-21 Feb 1813) **VI:** An article by

RU=Rank/Unit	CEM=Cemetery	GS=Gravestone	SP=Spousal Information
VI=Other Veteran Info	P=Pension	BLW=Bounty/Land Warrant	RG=Registered Grave
MK=SAR/DAR Marker	PH=Photo	SS=Service Source	BS=Burial Source

431

William Wirt provides details **P:** N **BLW:** N **RG:** N **MK:** Y SAR **PH:** N **SS:** DAR A119638 has some personal data but wrong death place and service **BS:** 196.

WADDELL, D James; b 2 Jul 1752, Lancaster Co; d 21 Feb 1813 **RU:** Soldier/Patriot, Served in Capt Thomas Massie's Co of Foot, 6th Cont line, commanded by Col James Hendrick. Also gave 330# of beef, (5 quarters) 20 Apr 1782 **CEM:** Trinity Episcopal; GPS 38.14917, -79.07521; 214 Beverley St; Staunton City **GS:** Y **SP:** Mary Gordon (__-1813) **VI:** No further data **P:** unk **BLW:** unk **RG:** N **MK:** unk **PH:** Y **SS:** Cl Muster Roll Fold 3 CY pg 33 **BS:** 196.(**WADE**, Edward See Appendix G, Addenda)

WADE, Isaac Sr; b c1758; d 9 Aug 1823 **RU:** Private, Ent ser 1777 in Bedford Co Militia and was in 14th VA Regt. Served at battles of Brandywine and Germantown. Ent serv again 1781 Bedford Co. Wounded at Yorktown **CEM:** Woodford/Wade; GPS unk; 11477 Falling Creek Rd; Bedford **GS:** N **SP:** Mar (11 Feb 1779 Bedford Co) Polly Gibbs, widow of Thomas Stevens. Source CG says marriage date is 11 Feb 1779. **VI:** Son of Isaac listed in records as War of 1812 veteran also bur here. Widow appl pen 1 May 1839 Bedford Co, age 78. W6389 **P:** Y **BLW:** unk **RG:** Y **MK:** N **PH:** N **SS:** AK, Bedford Mus; E pg 797; K Vol 6 pg 27; CG Vol 3 pg 3628; SAR P-311312 **BS:** 04, Sep 07.

WADE, Robert; b 17 Feb 1761, Fairfax Co, d 4 Sep 1834 **RU:** Sergeant, in 1777 as Private in Capt Taylor's Co, Col West's Regt Loudoun Co Militia. As Sergeant in Capt Thomas Humphrey's and Capt Moffett's Companies with service in battles at Williamsburg and Yorktown and then with duty escorting prisoners back to Loudoun Co in fall of 1781 **CEM:** Wade-Barret; GPS not determined; nr Leesburg; Loudoun Co **GS:** Yes **SP:** No spousal info **VI** Was elder of Leesburg Presbyterian Church. Drew pen 1782 paid $50.52 # F-S6325 and R 2466 **P:** Y **BLW:** N **RG:**-N **MK:** N **PH:** N **SS:** K pg 29; AP Fold3 pen rec **BS:** 196.

WADE, Stephen; b unk; d 12 Oct 1781 **RU:** Private, Served in Ct Cont line and died fr battle at Yorktown **CEM:** Yorktown Victory Monument Tablet; GPS 38.28350, -78.54150; Yorktown; York **GS:** U **SP:** No info **VI:** No further data **P:** unk **BLW:** unk **RG:** Y **MK:** unk **PH:** unk **SS:** J-Yorktown Historian; DY pg 340; SAR P-311364 **BS:** JLARC 74.

WAFORD, George; b 1737; d Jan 1810 **RU:** Soldier, Served in Capt Thomas Hill's Co, Col McClanahan's 7th Regt, 7th Cont line, Nov 1776-Jan 1777. Also was in Lt Thomas Buckmerson's Co at Morristown **CEM:** Trinity Episcopal; GPS 38.14917, -79.07521; 214 Beverley St; Staunton City **GS:** Y **SP:** No info **VI:** No further data **P:** unk **BLW:** unk **RG:** N **MK:** unk **PH:** Y **SS:** E pg 7, 98; Cl **BS:** 196.

WAGENER (WEGENER), Peter; b 1730 or 10 Oct 1744, Prince William Co; d 1797/98 **RU:** Colonel/Patriot, Appointed 4 July 1777 to Col, Fairfax Co Militia. He imported cannon fr Annapolis, MD to Alexandria. Was clerk of the county **CEM:** Pohick Episcopal; GPS 38.42546, -77.11598; 9301 Richmond Hwy, Lorton; Fairfax **GS:** Y **SP:** Mar (14 Apr 1774 Fairfax Co) Sarah McCarty **VI:** Succeeded father as clerk, Fairfax Co fr 1744 through war. Was Associate, Fairfax Co, VA 1770; Still listed as County Lt 22 Jul 1783. Memorial marker Pohick Church Cem, Alexandria **P:** unk **BLW:** unk **RG:**Y **MK:** Y SAR plaque & DAR plaque **PH:** Y **SS:** SAR P-311506 **BS:** JLARC 2, 4,14, 27, 28, 45.

WAITE, William; b 1 Jan 1700 England; d 11 Oct 1782 **RU:** Patriot, Gave material aid to cause **CEM:** Waite Family; GPS 38.42539, -77.11615; Bristerburg; Fauquier **GS:** Y **SP:** No info **VI:** No further data **P:** N **BLW:** N **RG:** N **MK:** N **PH:** unk **SS:** D Vol 1 pg 360 Vol 2 pg 251 **BS:** 19 pg 205.

WALES, Andrew; b 1737; d Nov 1799 **RU:** Patriot, Gave material aid to cause **CEM:** Old Presbyterian Meeting House; GPS 38.48528, -77.23532; 323 S Fairfax St; Alexandria City **GS:** N **SP:** Margaret (-----), b c1737, bur 3 Mar 1798 **VI:** Died age 57, bur 23 Nov 1799 **P:** N **BLW:** N **RG:** N **MK:** N **PH:** N **SS:** AL pg 232 Ct Bk It pg 5 **BS:** 23 pg 110.

WALKE, Anthony II; b 3 Jan 1725; d 2 Oct 1779 **RU:** Patriot, Performed public service and gave to cause **CEM:** Greenwich; GPS unk; Euclid Station; Virginia Beach City **GS:** U **SP:** 1) Jane Bolling Randolph (1729-1756) 2) Mary Mosely **VI:** Son of Col Anthony I & (-----) Walke. Member of VA House of Burgesses. United with Patrick Henry, Mason, Madison, Marshall, Jefferson, & other patriots resisting British oppression **P:** N **BLW:** N **RG:**Y **MK:** unk **PH:** unk **SS:** AL Cert Princess Anne Co; SAR P-311990 **BS:** 220.

RU=Rank/Unit	CEM=Cemetery	GS=Gravestone	SP=Spousal Information
VI=Other Veteran Info	P=Pension	BLW=Bounty/Land Warrant	RG=Registered Grave
MK=SAR/DAR Marker	PH=Photo	SS=Service Source	BS=Burial Source

WALKE, Thomas IV; b 1760, Richmond; d 1797 **RU:** Captain, Commissioned Capt 1780 Princess Anne Co Militia **CEM:** Old Donation Episcopal; **GPS** 36.86730, -76.12860; 4449 N Witchduck Rd; Virginia Beach City **GS:** U **SP:** Elizabeth (-----) (1797-1815) no children **VI:** Son of Thomas III & (-----) Walke. One of 2 representatives to the VA Convention. Helped VA ratify US Constitution by narrow margin. Was Vestryman & Warden of Lynnhaven Parish. Helped design & build Eastern Shore Chapel **P:** Y **BLW:** unk **RG:** N **MK:** Y SAR plaque **PH:** unk **SS:** Fold 3 Rev war pen files **BS:** Church Historian.

WALKER, Alexander; b 19 May 1716, Londonderry, Newry, Down, N Ireland; d 1784 **RU:** Patriot, Provided equipment & supplies **CEM:** Walker Creek; **GPS** unk; Walker Creek; Rockbridge **GS:** Y **SP:** Mar (8 Jan 1747 Augusta Co) Jane Hammer **VI:** Son of John and Catherine (Rutherford) Walker **P:** N **BLW:** N **RG:** Y **MK:** N **PH:** unk **SS:** E pg 799; AL Ct Bk Rockbridge Co pg 3, 5; SAR P-312004 **BS:** SAR Appl.

WALKER, Alexander; b 1718, Scotland; d 1820 **RU:** Soldier, Served in Capt Samuel Mc'Dowell's Co, Augusta Co Militia. Also served in VA unit at Point Pleasant Oct 1774, and wounded in battle there **CEM:** Augusta Stone Presbyterian; **GPS** 38.23926, -78.97356, GS 38.1410,-78.6812; 28 Old Stone Church Ln, Ft Defiance; Augusta **GS:** Y **SP:** Mar (Sep 1777 Augusta Co) Jane Stuart (__-13 Dec 1843(d/o Alexander & (-----) Stuart **VI:** Private in the French & Indian war, Capt James Allen's Co 1756-1758 (Gov't GS) Ran Little Run Plantation. Death date given in SAR and DAR Ancestor files are incorrect as pension records give date of 1820 a more accurate source. Widow Jane recd pen #R11040 **P:** Y **BLW:** unk **RG:** Y **MK:** Y SAR plaque **PH:** unk **SS:** Z pg 199; CG pg 3642; SAR P-312005 **BS:** JLARC 1, 8, 23, 62; 196.

WALKER, Charles, b 1745, Orange Co, d aft 1780 **RU:** Patriot, Gave material aid to cause, Orange Co **CEM:** Fairview: GPS 37.3383, `-80.8075; on Riverside Ave, Narrows; Giles **GS:** N **SP:** Mar (Orange Co) Margaret Peters, d/o Johann Jacob Peters & (-----) **VI:** Son of Thomas Walker & Elizabeth Taylor **P:** N **BLW:** N **RG:** Y **MK:** N **PH:** N **SS:** AL Comm Bk IV, pgs 179,189, pg 334, Ct Bk pg 29,Orange Co; SAR P-312045 **BS:** 196.

WALKER, Francis; b 22 Jun 1764, Castle Hill, Albemarle Co; d Mar 1806 **RU:** Soldier, Probably served in county militia **CEM:** Castle Hill; GPS 38.05683, -78.31828; 1625 Country Club Dr, can be seen 150 yds E of Wood Ln, Farmington; Albemarle **GS:** Y **SP:** Jane Byrd Nelson (May 1775-Jun 1808) **VI:** No further data **P:** unk **BLW:** unk **RG:** Y **MK:** unk **PH:** unk **SS:** SAR P-312087 **BS:** JLARC 58; 196.

WALKER, George; b 1753, Germany; d 29 Dec 1839 **RU:** Fifer, Served as Fifer in Capt Thomas B. Bowen's Co 9, Oct 1777. Fought with Bedford Co, PA Militia **CEM:** Leffel; GPS 37.48080, -80.13970; Off Cumberland Gap Rd, Meadow Creek; Craig **GS:** U **SP:** Mar (1780, Hagerstown, MD) Margaret Heefner (c1763-1830) **VI:** Known as Col George Walker. Emigrated to the Colonies fr Germany 1765-70. Moved fr PA to MD where he met and mar Margaret Heefner. Around 1798 moved to Botetourt Co, Walker homestead on Craigs Creek, and to Valley of Sinking Creek, Botetourt Co, at New Castle, VA. This portion of Botetourt Co is now Craig Co. Received BLW **P:** unk **BLW:** Y **RG:** N **MK:** N **PH:** unk **SS:** AP payroll; CU Vol 5 pg 96-103; CV Vol 23 pg 236 **BS:** 196.

WALKER, George Reynolds; b 3 Apr 1760, Princess Anne Co; d 4 Mar 1822 **RU:** Lieutenant, Served in VA Line. Was Ensign in VA Troops 1777. and commissioned Lt 1778 in VA Co **CEM:** Walker Farm; GPS 37.25327, -79.49419; 1972 Montevido Rd, Rt 667; Bedford **GS:** U **SP:** 1) Mar (7 Aug 1782, Princess Anne Co) Judith Haynes (1765-20 Jul 1787) d/o Maj Erasmus & (-----) Haynes; 2) Mar (26 Jan 1788, Blunt Point, Warwick Co) Lucy West (c1770-Apr 1849 Johnson Co, KY) d/o Col John & (-----) West of Blunt Point, Warwick Co **VI:** Son of Thomas (__-28 Jan 1788) & Sarah (Reynolds) (__-1792) Walker. Buried on his farm in Bedford Co. Widow appl pen 13 Jul 1844 Johnson Co KY age 75. She had moved to Floyd Co, KY to live with son but was living in Johnson Co, KY when applying. R11046 **P:** Y **BLW:** unk **RG:** Y **MK:** N **PH:** unk **SS:** K Vol 6 pg 38; CG Vol 3 pg 3644; SAR P-3121102 **BS:** JLARC 4.

WALKER, Henry; b 1760; d Jun 1803 **RU:** Major, Served in 6th & 10th Cont Lines. Was at Valley Forge 1777-79 **CEM:** Walker Family; GPS unk; Covington; Covington City **GS:** N **SP:** Martha Woods (22 Dec 1761 Albemarle Co-13 Dec 1834 Fincastle, Botetourt Co) d/o Andrew (1722-1781) & Martha (Poage) (1728-1818) Woods. **VI:** Son of William (1725-1810) & Mary Levenia (Bartley) (1732-1808) Walker **P:** unk **BLW:** unk **RG:** Y **MK:** unk **PH:** N **SS:** E pg 800; SAR P-32114 **BS:** 196.

RU=Rank/Unit	CEM=Cemetery	GS=Gravestone	SP=Spousal Information
VI=Other Veteran Info	P=Pension	BLW=Bounty/Land Warrant	RG=Registered Grave
MK=SAR/DAR Marker	PH=Photo	SS=Service Source	BS=Burial Source

433

WALKER, James; b 5 Apr 1726, King & Queen Co; d 18 Dec 1801 **RU:** Patriot, Was member of Committee of Safety, Orange Co, VA 1775 **CEM:** Walker United Methodist; GPS 38.29328, -78.16756; Nr Bent Tree; Madison **GS:** Y **SP:** Sarah Jane Ware (1740-1819) **VI:** Member VA House of Burgesses 1761-1771. Died in Orange Co **P:** N **BLW:** N **RG:** Y **MK:** N **PH:** unk **SS:** J-NSSAR 2000 Reg; SAR P-312151 **BS:** JLARC 76.

WALKER, John; b 13 Feb 1744, Cobham, Albemarle Co; d 2 Dec 1809 **RU:** Colonel/Patriot, Aide to Gen George Washington, 1777. Gave 107 cords of wood furnished for officers of Convention troops **CEM:** Belvoir; GPS unk; 5172 Stony Point Pass, Cismont; Albemarle **GS:** Y **SP:** Mar (c1764) Elizabeth Moore (21 Oct 1746, King William Co-10 Sep 1809, Belvoir, Cismont, Albemarle Co) d/o Col Bernard & Ann Catherine (Spotswood) Moore of King William Co **VI:** Graduated College of William & Mary in 1764. Was delegate to Continental Congress 1780. Was attorney, and planter. Was appointed to fill a vacant US Senate seat, Mar 1790, serving there until Nov 1790. Died in Madison Run, Orange Co **P:** unk **BLW:** unk **RG:** Y **MK:** Y SAR **PH:** unk **SS:** SAR P-312151; DAR A119424 **BS:** JLARC 1, 2; 196.

WALKER, John Sr; b 1714 Scotland; d 1797 **RU:** Patriot, Gave material aid to cause, Also paid personal property tax 1782 Rockbridge Co, considered to be partial payment for Rev War expenses, **CEM:** Walkerland; GPS 37.94613, -79.38794; Vic jct Rts 602 & 724, behind Maxwelton Cabins; Rockbridge **GS:** Y **SP:** Mary Culton (1717-___) **VI:** Known as Gunstalker **P:** N **BLW:** N **RG:**N **MK:** unk **PH:** unk **SS:** AL Ct Bk pg 2; DV Rockbridge Oo 1782A, image 22.pdf **BS:** 196.

WALKER, Joseph; b c1748, Lancaster Co, PA; d Aft 1815 **RU:** Patriot, Paid supply tax Rockbridge Co, 1783 **CEM:** Falling Springs Presbyterian; GPS 37.68494, -79.45105; 410 Falling Springs Rd, Glasgow; Rockbridge **GS:** Y **SP:** Mar (1772 PA) Jane Moore (c1749 Chester Co, PA-aft 18 Feb 1818) **VI:** No further data **P:** N **BLW:** N **RG:** unk **MK:** unk **PH:** unk **SS:** DAR A119491; DD; SAR P-312256 **BS:** BY.

WALKER, Martha; b 2 May 1760; d 1829 **RU:** Patriot, Provided housing and food for Jack Jouett and assistants enroute to warn Thomas Jefferson of the coming of the British **CEM:** Castle Hill; GPS 38.05683,-78.31828; 1625 Country Club Dr, can be seen 150 yds E of Wood Ln, Farmington; Albemarle **GS:** Y **SP:** Mar (1780) George Divers (1747-2 May 1830) **VI:** Daug of Thomas (1715-1794) & Mildred (Thornton) (1721-1778) Walker **P:** N **BLW:** N **RG:** N **MK:** unk **PH:** unk **SS:** BT- DAR is marking her grave as patriot 2016 **BS:** 196.

WALKER, Thomas; b 15 Jan 1715, Walkerton, King and Queen Co; d 9 Nov 1794 **RU:** Patriot, Gave material aid to cause **CEM:** Castle Hill; GPS 38.05683, -78.31828; 1625 Country Club Dr, can be seen 150 yds E of Wood Ln, Farmington; Albemarle **GS:** Y **SP:** 1) Mar (1741) Midred (Thornton) Meriweather (1721-1778), widow of Nicholas Meriweather & cousin to George Washington; 2) mar (c1781) Elizabeth Mary Gregory **VI:** Son of Col Thomas (1650-1734) & Susannah (Peachy) (1688-1736) Walker. Named Cumberland Gap. Built 1st KY log cabin, 1750. Was a Surgeon. Served VA House of Burgesses three times. Was Commissary to VA troops French & Indian War. Was guardian to young Thomas Jefferson. Signed peace treaties w/ Indians VA & Ohio. Was delegate fr Albemarle Co to VA House of Delegates along w/ Jefferson. Died in Cismont, Albemarle Co **P:** N **BLW:** N **RG:** Y **MK:** N **PH:** unk **SS:** AL Ct Bk pg 4, 5, 12, 38;DAR A119663; SAR P-312402 **BS:** 67 vol 2 pg 282; 196.

WALKER, William; b 26 Feb 1757, Cumberland Co; d 1840 **RU:** Sergeant, Ent serv 1778 Cumberland Co, serving in 4th VA Regt. Was at Battle of Trenton, Iron Hill, Brandywine, White Horse, Germantown, Yorktown **CEM:** Walker Family; GPS unk; Farmville; Cumberland **GS:** U **SP:** Mary Ann Smith **VI:**; Capt in Cumberland Militia after the war. Lived within one mi of Airygreen when he appl for pen,14 Jul 1832 "where he had always lived." Pen last paid in 1839. **P:** Y **BLW:** unk **RG:** Y **MK:** N **PH:** unk **SS:** J-NSSAR 1993 Reg; K Vol 6 pg 44; CG Vol 3 pg 3651;DAR A119737; SAR P-312481 **BS:** JLARC 1.

WALKER, William; b 19 Dec 1725, Lancaster Co, PA; d 17 Aug 1810 **RU:** Patriot, Gave material aid to cause **CEM:** Caldwell family; GPS unk; End of Rt 611 across Craig Creek fr Camp Easter Seals; Botetourt **GS:** Y **SP:** Mary Levenia Bartley (19 Jan 1732-1810) **VI:** No further data **P:** N **BLW:** N **RG:** N **MK:** unk **PH:** N **SS:** AK Ct Bk pg 8, 24 **BS:** 196.

WALKER, William; b unk; d 1848 **RU:** Patriot, Gave material aid to the cause **CEM:** St John's Episcopal; GPS 37.53183, -77.41958; 2401 E Broad St; Richmond City **GS:** U **SP:** No info **VI:** No further data **P:** N **BLW:** N **RG:** N **MK:** N **PH:** unk **SS:** AL, Ct Bk pg 7,8 **BS:** 28 pg 351.

RU=Rank/Unit
VI=Other Veteran Info
MK=SAR/DAR Marker
CEM=Cemetery
P=Pension
PH=Photo
GS=Gravestone
BLW=Bounty/Land Warrant
SS=Service Source
SP=Spousal Information
RG=Registered Grave
BS=Burial Source

434

WALKER, William; b 1758; d 17 Apr 1837 **RU**: Private, Served in Capt Holcomb's Co, 4th VA Regt, Nov 1777 **CEM**: Walkerland, Maxwelton Farm; GPS 37.94613, -79.38794; Vic jct Rts 602 & 724, behind Maxwelton Cabins; Rockbridge **GS**: U **SP**: No info **VI**: No further data **P**: unk **BLW**: unk **RG**: N **MK**: unk **PH**: unk **SS**: AP Payroll **BS**: 196.

WALKER, William; b 1757, Dinwiddie Co; d 10 Oct 1850 **RU**: Soldier, Served in Bedford Co Militia **CEM**: Walker Family; GPS 37.28481, -79.51186; Rt 723, Boxwood Hill, Five Forks; Bedford **GS**: Y **SP**: Elizabeth Rice (1784-__) d/o Benjamin (1735-1827) & (-----) Rice **VI**: Styled Capt on his GS, died age 92 yrs **P**: unk **BLW**: unk **RG**: Y **MK**: N **PH**: unk **SS**: J- DAR Hatcher; E pg 801; SAR P-312450 **BS**: JLARC 2; 196.

WALL, Conrad; b 1721 Germany, d 1787 Augusta Co **RU**: Private, Served in Capt James Cox's and Capt John Taylor's Companies, Montgomery Co Militia **CEM**: Wall Family; GPS GPS 37.2117500,-80.4708000; loc edge of field on Brunswick Dr; Montgomery **GS**: N **SP**: Catherine Christina (Caty) Hermann **VI**: Son of Hans George "John" Wall (27 May 1679 Hessen Germany-1761, Augusta Co) & (-----) **P**: N **BLW**: N **RG**: N **MK**: N **PH**: N **SS**: G pgs 230,234, 235 **BS**: 196 # 199059150.

WALL, John C; b 1758; d Aft 1815 or c1840 **RU**: Private, Volunteered 1776. Enlisted 1 Apr 1777 and served in co of Regulars commanded by Capt John Washington, in 4th VA Regt commanded by Col Thomas Elliott. Enlisted again in 1780, fought in Battle of Guilford CH in March 1781, marched fr there to Ramsey's Mills in Deep River, then to Yorktown. After surrender guarded prisoners to Winchester. **CEM**: Mt Hebron; GPS 39.10916, -78.09497; 305 E Boscawen St; Winchester City **GS**: Y **SP**: Mary (-----) (c1806-16 Jun 1849) **VI**: Appl for pension,but was rejected Also served in War of 1812 **P**: unk **BLW**: unk **RG**: N **MK**: Y SAR monument **PH**: Y **SS**: B Volunteer 1776; E pg 801 **BS**: 50 pg 47.

WALL, John Jr; b 1745, d 1827 Montgomery Co **RU**: Soldier/Patriot, guarded lead mines with two wagon loads of lead for the use of the southern army after General Gates defeat, by order of Col. Preston and as patriot gave a horse for Army use **CEM**: Wall Family; GPS 37.2117500, -80.4708000; loc edge of field on Brunswick Dr; Montgomery **GS**: N **SP**: Sarah (-----) **VI**: Son of John Wall Sr. (c1726-1761) and Margaret (-----) **P**: N **BLW**: N **RG**: N **MK**: N **PH**: N **SS**: CD cites Kegley, Early Adventures on the Western Waters Vol 1, page 278; DL pg 774; **BS**: 196 # 195028963.

WALL, Peter; b 1754, Dinwiddie Co; d 19 Jul 1848 **RU**: Private, Served in VA Line. Ent Serv Dinwiddie Co 1781 in VA Regt **CEM**: Wall Family; GPS 39.18335, -78.16268; Vic Danville; Danville City **GS**: U **SP**: Mar (Dec 1825) Elizabeth Daly (or Dailey) **VI**: Moved to Brunswick Co, then Mecklenburg Co, then to Rockingham Co, NC, then to Pittsylvania Co. Died in Pittsylvania Co. Widow appl pen 18 Aug 1855 age 80. W25857. Recd BLW 35678-160-55 **P**: Y **BLW**: Y **RG**: Y **MK**: N **PH**: unk **SS**: K Vol 4 pg 46; CG Vol 3 pg 3652; AS; SAR P-312523 **BS**: VASSAR Roster 2007.

WALLACE, Gustavus Brown; b 9 Nov 1751, Ellerslie Pt, King George Co; d 17 Aug 1802 **RU**: Lieutenant Colonel, Served as Capt of 5th Co, 3rd VA Regt of Foot 20 Feb 1776-Jan 1777 in King George Co. Served in 2nd VA Regt of Foot, 12 Feb 1781-1 Jan 1783. Was captured at Charleston SC May 1780 **CEM**: Masonic Cemetery; GPS 38.30198, -77.46142; 900 Charles St; Fredericksburg City **GS**: U **SP**: No info **VI**: BLW #24122-450-13, Dec 1791 awarded to Francis Greaves **P**: unk **BLW**: Y **RG**: Y **MK**: Y SAR plaque **PH**: unk **SS**: DAR A119888; K Vol 6 pg 46; CE pg 39; CG Vol 3 pg 3653; SAR P-312567 **BS**: JLARC 1, 2, 48, 91.

WALLACE, John; b 19 Jan 1761; d 4 May 1829 **RU**: Private, Served in Capts William Payne's and Charles Ewell's Companies, Col George Gibson's 1st VA Regt **CEM**: Liberty Hall; GPS unk; Rt 652 abt 1.4 mi fr jct Rt 653, and .5 mi N, nr Wallace farm rd; Stafford **GS**: U **SP**: Mar (1792) Elizabeth Hooe (c1766-3 Sep 1850) d/of Howson (c1725-5 Sep 1796) & Mary (Dade) Hooe **VI**: No further data **P**: unk **BLW**: unk **RG**: Y **MK**: unk **PH**: unk **SS**: DAR A119926; E pg 802; AP-roll #918; SAR P-312620 **BS**: JLARC 48.

WALLACE, John D; b 1754, Scotland; d 29 Jan 1829 **RU**: Private, Served in 1st or 9th Cont line. Served in Capt James Dysart's Co of Light Horse on tour of NC under command of Col William Campbell, 21 May 1781 **CEM**: Wallace; GPS 38.15972, -77.79558; 8630 Peppertree Rd, Wilderness Corner; Spotsylvania **GS**: Y **SP**: Anne Hammond **VI**: Died in Chancellorsville, Spotsylvania Co **P**: N **BLW**: unk **RG**: N **MK**: N **PH**: Y **SS**: E pg 802; **BS**: 09 part 2, 196.

RU=Rank/Unit	CEM=Cemetery	GS=Gravestone	SP=Spousal Information
VI=Other Veteran Info	P=Pension	BLW=Bounty/Land Warrant	RG=Registered Grave
MK=SAR/DAR Marker	PH=Photo	SS=Service Source	BS=Burial Source

435

WALLACE, Robert; b 1744, Botetourt Co; d Feb 1812 **RU**: Private, Was in Battle at Point Pleasant 1774 in Capt John Murray's Co of Rockbridge Co **CEM**: Old Lebanon; GPS 38.08090 -79.37545; Off Rt 42, Craigsville; Augusta **GS**: Y **SP**: Esther Boyd (1750-1824) d/o Robert & Eleanor (Porterfield) Boyd **VI**: Son of Samuel & Elizabeth Jane (Archer) Wallace **P**: unk **BLW**: unk **RG**: Y **MK**: Y SAR **PH**: Y **SS**: Z pg103; SAR P-312663 **BS**: 04; 196.

WALLACE, Stephen; b Unk; d by 7 May 1778 **RU**:Private,Capt Moore's Co, Col William Grayson's Regt 1778 at Valley Forge, PA Apr 1778 **CEM**: Rev War Court House Plaque; GPS not determined; 4110 Chain Bridge Rd; Fairfax **GS**: Memorialized on plaque 2017 by Geo Washington Chapter, VASSAR **SP**: No info **VI**: Died in service **P**: N **BLW**: N **RG**: Y **MK**: N **PH**: N **SS**: E pg 802; AP Fold 3 Muster Roll indicates Hospital Apr 1778, died by 7 May 1778 EP sources; SAR P-312622 **BS**: None.

WALLACE, William; b unk; d 1831 **RU**: Soldier, Was Lt in Capt Samuel McDowell's Co of Rockbridge Co. Served in 1st VA State Regt. Then served in 3rd, 4th, 10th, & 14th Cont Lines **CEM**: Stonewall Jackson Memorial; GPS 37.78128, -79.44604; 314 S Main St; Lexington City **GS**: U **SP**: No info **VI**: No further data **P**: unk **BLW**: unk **RG**: Y **MK**: unk **PH**: unk **SS**: E pg 802; SAR P-312688 **BS**: JLARC 63.

WALLER, Benjamin; b 1 Oct 1716, d 1 May 1786 **RU**: Patriot, was on the Committee of Safety; as a judge he read the "Declaration of Independence" from the courthouse steps in Williamsburg, 25 Jul 1776; was presiding Judge 1777 of the "Court of Admiralty" in Williamsburg; gave material aid to the cause in James City Co **CEM**: Buckingham House & Lodge; GPS not determined; loc at Church Point at end of Rt 693, on La Grange Creek nr Corbin Hall; Middlesex **GS**: N gravestones have been removed without bodies **SP**: Mar (1746) Martha Hall (1728-1780) **VI**: Son of John Waller (1673-1754) & Dorothy King (1675-1758) **P**: N **BLW**: N **RG**: N **MK**: N **PH**: N **SS**: AL Ct Bk, pg 12 **BS**: 196.

WALLER, George; b 1731, Spotsylvania Co; d 18 Nov 1814 **RU**: Major/Patriot, Served as Adjutant to Col Abram Penn. Gave material aid to cause **CEM**: Oakwood; GPS 39.68690, -78.88000; 199 Cemetery St; Martinsville City **GS**: Y **SP**: Ann Winston Carr, dates on cenotagph say b. 1735, d 1839 **VI**: SAR/DAR markers on stone **P**: unk **BLW**: unk **RG**: Y **MK**: Y SAR & DAR **PH**: unk **SS**: AL Ct bk pg 7a, 9, 38 Henry Co; DAR A120035; SAR P-312723 **BS**: JLARC 1, 2, 4, 38; 196.

WALLER, Pomfret; b 20 Jan 1747, d 20 Jun 1799 **RU**: Patriot, Gave material aid to cause, Spotsylvania Co **CEM**: Martin Family; GPS: 36.7410, -79.7464; nr jct Rts 57 & 710, Leatherwood; Henry **GS**: Yes; **SP**: Martha Martin (1747-1813) **VI**: Son of John Waller (1701-1776) and Agnes Carr (1712-1779) **P**: N **BLW**: N **RG**: N **MK**: N **PH**: N **SS**: AL Ct Bk pg 8, Spotsylvania Co **BS**: 196.

WALLER, Thomas Carr; b 1732; d 1787 **RU**: Patriot, Gave material aid to cause **CEM**: Meadowbrook Memorial Gardens; GPS 36.82940, -76.46640; 4569 Shoulders Hill Rd; Suffolk City **GS**: U **SP**: Sarah (-----) d/o John & Ann (Harris) (-----) **VI**: Son of John & Agnes (Carr) Waller **P**: N **BLW**: N **RG**: Y **MK**: unk **PH**: unk **SS**: AL Ct Bk pg 5, 6, 24 Spotsylvania Co; SAR P-312741 **BS**: 196.

WALLER, William Edmund; b 1747, Newport, Spotsylvania Co; d 11 Aug 1830 **RU**: Private, Served in Lt Walker Scott's Co & Capt Thomas Minor's Co, Col Gregory Smith's 2nd VA State Regt. Also served in 1st VA State Regt & Cont Line for 3 yrs **CEM**: Prospect Hill; GPS unk; Waller Rd, nr Forest Green, Partlow; Spotsylvania **GS**: U **SP**: Mildred Smith (1755-1804) d/o Stephen & Phoebe (Hawkins) Smith **VI**: Son of Edmund (1718-1771) & Mary (Pendleton) (1720-1808) Waller. Baptist Minister. Moved to KY & later returned where to Louisa Co. Recd 447,200 acres BLW **P**: unk **BLW**: Y **RG**: Y **MK**: unk **PH**: unk **SS**: DAR A120071; N pg 1433, 1056, 1057; SAR P-312746 **BS**: 196.

WALLER, William Jr; b 1766; d 1815 **RU**: Private, Served in 1st VA Regt. Was at Charlestown 26 May 1783. Discharged 11 July 1783 **CEM**: Olde Concord Road; GPS unk; Rt 721; Stafford **GS**: Y **SP**: No info **VI**: Was a Baptist clergyman fighting for religious freedom **P**: unk **BLW**: unk **RG**: N **MK**: N **PH**: unk **SS**: N pg 1057; Archives Lib of VA **BS**: 03 pg 183; 196.

WALLER, William Sr; b 26 Nov 1740, Stafford Co; d 4 Aug 1817 **RU**: Corporal/Patriot, Served in 11th and 15th Cont Lines and Capt George Rice's Co # 9, VA Battalion. As patriot gave 425 pounds of beef to cause and was a tobacco inspector **CEM**: Waller Family; GPS 38.43891, -77.38353; Rt 721; Stafford **GS**: Y **SP**: 1) Elizabeth Allen (1746-1768) 2) Margaret (-----) (1744-1772)) 3) Ursula Withers (1750-1815) **VI**: Son of Edward Waller 91703-1753) & Ann Tandy (c1721-1748 of Essex Co. Cemetery

RU=Rank/Unit	CEM=Cemetery	GS=Gravestone	SP=Spousal Information
VI=Other Veteran Info	P=Pension	BLW=Bounty/Land Warrant	RG=Registered Grave
MK=SAR/DAR Marker	PH=Photo	SS=Service Source	BS=Burial Source

436

originally listed as Concord **P**: unk **BLW**: unk **RG**: Y **MK**: N **PH**: Y **SS**: A pg 264; D pg 855,884; E pg 803; EJ-pg 4; SAR P-312748 **BS**: 196; 30 pg 55:2.

WALLIS, Colley; b unk; d 1781 **RU**: Soldier, Served fr MA, killed in the battle at Yorktown **CEM**: Yorktown Victory Monument Tablet; GPS 38.28350, -78.54150; Yorktown; York **GS**: U **SP**: No info **VI**: No further data **P**: unk **BLW**: unk **RG**: Y **MK**: unk **PH**: unk **SS**: J-Yorktown Historian; SAR P-312781 **BS**: JLARC 74.

WALTERS, Michael; b c1750, Germany; d Aug 1798 **RU**: Private, Served in Doack's VA Militia **CEM**: Browning's Mill; GPS unk; Old Stage Rd; Wythe **GS**: Y **SP**: Mar (as 2nd husband) Catherine Creger/Krieger (9 Jun 1754-8 Feb 1841) **VI**: Gov't Gr St shows service **P**: unk **BLW**: unk **RG**: unk **MK**: unk **PH**: unk **SS**: DAR #A120169; SAR P-312919; **BS**: JLARC 40,123; 196.

WALTON, Jesse; b 10 Nov 1739, Hanover Co; d 30 April 1821 or 1822 **RU**: Lieutenant, Was on War Dept supernumary list as Lt, 16 Sep 1777. Also provided material aid to cause **CEM**: Walton Family; GPS unk; probably "Whitmel"; Pittsylvania **GS**: Y **SP**: Mar (c1764/1765) Ann Pleasant **VI**: Son of William & (-----) Walton **P**: unk **BLW**: unk **RG**: Y **MK**: N **PH**: unk **SS**: E pg 804; SAR P-312980 **BS**: SAR application

WALTON, Joel; b 20 Sep 1759, Hanover Co; d 13 Apr 1840 **RU**: Soldier, Lived Louisa Co at enl, 1780 in 2nd VA Regt. Served in Battle of Camden SC in VA Line **CEM**: Spring Valley; GPS unk; Cuckoo District; Louisa **GS**: U **SP**: Sarah Sims (__-10 Mar 1840) **VI**: Son of John (1 Apr 1738-23 Sep 1793) & Mary (Baker) (5 Dec 1739-1812) Walton. Moved to Louisa Co as child. Appl pen 11 Feb 1833. S3627 **P**: Y **BLW**: unk **RG**: Y **MK**: unk **PH**: unk **SS**: K Vol 6 pg 54; CG Vol 3 pg 3664; SAR P-312983 **BS**: JLARC 4, 61.

WALTON, John B; b 1758; d 27 Mar 1836 **RU**: Private/Patriot, Gave material aid to cause **CEM**: Walton Family; GPS unk; Nr Ft Lewis; Salem City **GS**: Y **SP**: Mary L (-----) (1758-21 Aug 1824) **VI**: No further data **P**: unk **BLW**: unk **RG**: unk **MK**: unk **PH**: unk **SS**: J- DAR Hatcher; D Bedford Co; SAR P-312992 **BS**: JLARC 2; 123 pg 68; 196.

WALTON, William; b 1751; d 1836 **RU**: Lieutenant, Specific service in DAR 1973 in Senate Document serial #93, -Doc 113 **CEM**: Walton Family; GPS unk; Nr Ft Lewis; Salem City **GS**: U **SP**: No info **VI**: No further data **P**: unk **BLW**: unk **RG**: Y **MK**: unk **PH**: unk **SS**: AR Vol 4 pg 157; SAR P-313030 **BS**: JLARC 2.

WALTON, William Sr; b 25 Oct 1749; GA; d 29 Jan 1845 **RU**: Second Lieutenant/Patriot, Served in Capt John Lewis Co, Botetourt Co. As patriot was Commissioner of Peace **CEM**: Walton Family; GPS unk; Nr Ft Lewis; Salem City **GS**: Y **SP**: Mary Leftwich (1758-1824) **VI**: No further data **P**: unk **BLW**: unk **RG**: Y **MK**: unk **PH**: Y **SS**: J- DAR Hatcher; DL part 1 pg 295, 297, 34; SAR P-313028 **BS**: JLARC 2; 123 pg 68.

WAMPLER, Hans George Michael; b 19 Nov 1724, Hinsingen, Alsace, France; d Dec 1789 **RU**: Soldier, Served in PA Militia **CEM**: St John's Lutheran; GPS 36.96500, -81.10110; 405 W Main, Wytheville; Wythe **GS**: U **SP**: Mar (1746) Anna Elizabeth Steffey (__-1807) **VI**: Son of Hans Peter Sr. (1701-1749) & Veronica (Lung) (1703-1743) Wampler. Lived in Lebanon Twp, Lancaster Co, PA and moved by 1771 to Fincastle Co, of which Montgomery Co was formed. Was on William Crockett's list of tithables in 1771. He served in Lord Dunsmore's War in 1774. He was an Elder in his Church in 1782 **P**: unk **BLW**: unk **RG**: Y **MK**: unk **PH**: unk **SS**: SAR P-313064; DAR A120379 **BS**: JLARC 123; 196.

WANGER, Henry; b 1753 PA; d 9 Aug 1819 **RU**: Private, Served in Capt Alexander Milvain's Co, 5th Battalion, Lancaster Co PA Militia **CEM**: Early; GPS 38.39536, -78.90465; 3588 Early Rd, Pleasant Valley; Rockingham **GS**: U **SP**: No info **VI**: No further data **P**: unk **BLW**: unk **RG**: N **MK**: unk **PH**: unk **SS**: PA Archives Series 5, Vol VII, pg 520 **BS**: 196.

WAPLES, Samuel; b 19 Jun1755, Sussex, DL; d 11 Aug 1834 **RU**: Lieutenant, Served in VA Line. Lived Accomack Co at enl. Ent serv 1776 as Lt 9th VA Regt and was in battles of Brandywine & Germantown where taken prisoner but escaped. Was also Lt in 1777 **CEM**: Onancock; GPS unk; Rts 718 & 638, Onancock; Accomack **GS**: Y **SP**: Mar (20 Aug 1822 Accomack) Sabra P. Townsend (3 May 1791-24 Dec 1856) d/o Henry & Sally (-----) Townsend [TS] PRS show wives Ann Curtis & Mrs Sabra

RU=Rank/Unit	CEM=Cemetery	GS=Gravestone	SP=Spousal Information
VI=Other Veteran Info	P=Pension	BLW=Bounty/Land Warrant	RG=Registered Grave
MK=SAR/DAR Marker	PH=Photo	SS=Service Source	BS=Burial Source

437

Scarbouough **VI:** Styled "Capt" on his GS which reads "of the Revolution." Sol appl pen 17 Jun 1828 Accomack Co age 70. Widow appl pen 25 Apr 1853 Accomack Co, age 62 & appl BLW 7 Apr 1855. W6427. BLW #1733-200 & BLW #14529-160-55 **P:** Y Sabra W6427 **BLW:** Y **RG:** Y **MK:** unk **PH:** unk **SS:** K Vol 6 pg 57; CG Vol 3 pg 3666; BT; SAR P-313105 **BS:** JLARC 1, 4, 5; 209.

WARD, Charles; b Unk ; d 18 Jul 1778 **RU:** Fifer; in Col William Grayson's Regt until died serving18 jul 1778 **CEM:** Rev War Court House Plaque; GPS not determined; 4110 Chain Bridge Rd; Fairfax **GS:** Memorialized on plaque 2017 by Geo Washington Chapter, VASSAR **SP** No info **VI:** died in service **P:** N **BLW:** N **RG:** N **MK:** N **PH:** N **SS:**E pg 805; AP Fold3 Serv Rec; EP sources: **BS:** None

WARD, Henry; b 5 Apr 1751, Bedford Co; d 12 Apr 1823 **RU:** Major/Commissary/Patriot, QM in Bedford Co Militia. As patriot was Co Sheriff **CEM:** Adams-Ward; GPS 37.13210, -79.24073; Mansion Bridge Rd Rt 640, Altavista; Campbell **GS:** Y **SP:** Mar (1781) Martha Barber/Barbour (__-1851) **VI:** Son of John Waed (1708-1816) & Ann Chiles (1729-1765) **P:** unk **BLW:** unk **RG:** Y **MK:** N **PH:** unk **SS:** DD; SAR P-313187 **BS:** JLARC 36; 196.

WARD, Henry "Hal", Jr. b 1747, d aft 1787, Charlotte Co **RU:** Patriot Gave material aid to cause, Mecklenburg, Co **CEM:** Henry Ward Homestead; GPS not determined; find loc of homestead; Amelia **GS:** Unk **SP:** No spousal info **VI:** Son of Henry Ward Sr (12 Aug 1720-1765) & Prudence Jones, d/o Richard & (-----) Jones **P:** N **BLW:** N **RG:** N **MK:** N **PH:** N **SS:** AL Ct Bk pg 3-4, Mecklenburg Co **BS:** 196.

WARD, John; b 1716; d 1816 **RU:** Major, Served in Bedford Co Militia **CEM:** Adams-Ward; GPS 37.13210, -79.24073; Mansion Bridge Rd Rt 640, Altavista; Campbell **GS:** Y **SP:** 1) Ann Harrelson Chiles, (__-1765); 2) Sarah (Clark) Lynch (1716-20 Jan 1792) d/o Christopher Clark and widow of Charles Lynch **VI:** No further data **P:** unk **BLW:** unk **RG:** Y **MK:** N **PH:** unk **SS:** SAR P-313227 **BS:** JLARC 36; 196.

WARD, William; b 30 May 1753; d 21 Dec 1817 **RU:** Captain, Served in Montgomery Co Militia 6 Nov 1781 **CEM:** Black Lick Rural Retreat; GPS 36.94435, -81.24377; 2390 Black Lick Rd; Wythe **GS:** Y **SP:** Mar (1775) Jean Watson (2 Mar 1758-12 Apr 1836) **VI:** Grave stone not found in 1997 **P:** unk **BLW:** unk **RG:** Y **MK:** unk **PH:** unk **SS:** DAR A120748; SAR P-313363; E pg 805; DL Vol 1 pg 754 **BS:** JLARC 1123.

WARD, William; b 1725, Ireland; d 1795 **RU:** Lieutenant Colonel/ Patriot, In charge of Montgomery Co Militia, 15 Feb 1782. Was Commissioner of Land Tax 15 Feb 1782 **CEM:** Ward's Cove; GPS unk; Thompson Valley; Tazewell **GS:** Y **SP:** No info **VI:** Sergeant in Co of Rangers 1756 and 1757 **P:** unk **BLW:** unk **RG:** N **MK:** N **PH:** unk **SS:** C pg 274; E pg 805; AR Vol 4 pg 158 **BS:** SAR application.

WARDLOW (WARDLAW), William; b Jun 1745, Augusta Co; d 7 Feb 1819 **RU:** Patriot, Gave material aid to cause. Was also a justice during war period **CEM:** New Providence Presbyterian; GPS 37.95130, -79.30250; 1208 New Providence Rd, Raphine; Rockbridge **GS:** U **SP:** Mary Coalter (__-15 May 1808) **VI:** No further data **P:** N **BLW:** N **RG:** Y **MK:** unk **PH:** unk **SS:** DAR A206516; SAR P-313404; AL Ct Bk pg 5 Rockbridge Co **BS:** JLARC 79.

WARE, John; b 12 Dec 1736, Gloucester Co; d 17 Jun 1816 **RU:** Captain/Patriot, Commanded a co in Albemarle Co Militia, Sep 1775. Gave material aid to cause **CEM:** Ben Glade; GPS unk; Rock Castle; Goochland **GS:** Y **SP:** 1) mar (27 May 1756 Caroline Co "on the Byrd in this County") Ann Harrison 2) mar (6 Apr 1762 Maniken Town, Henrico Co) Mary Watson **VI:** No further data **P:** unk **BLW:** unk **RG:** Y **MK:** N **PH:** unk **SS:** J- DAR Hatcher; CE pg 14; AL Ct Bk pg 3, 41 Goochland Co; SAR P-313451 **BS:** JLARC 2; 196.

WARE, Malachi (Malickic) b 1750; d Jun 1795 **RU:** Patriot, paid personal property tax 1783, Louisa Co, considered to be a supply tax for Rev War expenses **CEM:** Ware-Waller; GPS 38.082904, -77.856280; loc on New Bridge Rd halfway betw jcts with Cutalong Way and Kentucky Springs Rd; Louisa **GS:** N **SP:** Elizabeth Brown (1762-1818) **VI:** No further data **P:** N **BLW:** N **RG:** N **MK:** N **PH:** N **SS:** DV 1783, Louisa Co image 18pdf **BS:** 196.

WARREN, Jesse; b 1751 Surry Co; d June 1832 **RU:** Patriot, Gave material aid to cause **CEM:** Lawn's Creek Parish Church; GPS unk; Hog Island (no public access); Surry **GS:** Y **SP:** Martha Phillips (1788-

RU=Rank/Unit	CEM=Cemetery	GS=Gravestone	SP=Spousal Information
VI=Other Veteran Info	P=Pension	BLW=Bounty/Land Warrant	RG=Registered Grave
MK=SAR/DAR Marker	PH=Photo	SS=Service Source	BS=Burial Source

438

15 Dec 1863) **VI**: No further data **P**: N **BLW**: N **RG**: Y **MK**: N **PH**: Y **SS**: Al Ct Bk pg 4; SAR P-313899 **BS**: 196; 133.

WARWICK, Jacob; b 1743, Augusta Co; d 11 Jan 1826 **RU**: Captain, Commanded a company Augusta Co Milita after 1779. Rank of Capt 20 Mar 1777 **CEM**: Fort Dinwiddie; GPS 38.09228, -79.83140; NE of jct of Dinwiddie Trail & River Rd, Warm Springs; Bath **GS**: Y **SP**: Mar (1765) Mary Vance (1743-11 Jan 1823) **VI**: Styled "Maj" on GS **P**: unk **BLW**: unk **RG**: Y **MK**: N **PH**: unk **SS**: DAR A121754; E pg 807; AZ pg 185; SAR P-314060 **BS**: SAR regis.

WASHINGTON, Bushrod; b 5 Jun 1762; d 26 Nov 1829 **RU**: Private, Enl in Cont Army nr end of Rev War. Present at surrender of Cornwallis at Yorktown **CEM**: Mt Vernon; GPS 38.42280, -77.05090; Mt Vernon Estate; Fairfax **GS**: U **SP**: Anna Blackburn (8 Dec 1768 Woodbridge, Prince William Co-28 Nov 1829 Darby, Delaware Co, PA) **VI**: Son of John Augustine Washington (1736-1787) & Hanna (Bushrod) (1738-1801) Washington. Elected to VA House of Delegates. Served as delegate to VA Convention, ratified the Constitution in 1788. President John Adams nominated him to Supreme Ct for 30 yrs, until his death at age 67 in Philadelphia, PA. Memorialized in cemetery at Mt Vernon **P**: unk **BLW**: unk **RG**: N **MK**: unk **PH**: unk **SS**: CD **BS**: 196.

WASHINGTON, Edward; b c1712, Westmoreland Co; d Bef 18 Sep 1792 **RU**: Patriot, Gave equipment and/or supplies **CEM**: Huntington; GPS unk; 3 mi fr Pohick Church; Fairfax **GS**: Y **SP**: Mary (Stone) Barry/Barre (c1718-___) d/o Edward & (-----) Barre of France **VI**: Son of Edward (c1693 Prince George Co, MD-__) & (-----) Washington. Collected taxes as sub sheriff in Prince William Co, 1730. Will probated 18 Sep 1792 in Truro Parish **P**: N **BLW**: N **RG**: Y **MK**: N **PH**: unk **SS**:; AL Ct Bk pg 21 BY; SAR P-314186 **BS**: 8 vol 4 pg 163.

WASHINGTON, George; b 22 Feb 1732, Pope's Creek Plantation, Westmoreland Co; d 14 Dec 1799 **RU**: General, Commander in Chief of VA forces 1755; VA House of Burgesses 1758-74; 1st, 2nd Cont Congress. Commander in chief of all forces raised or to be raised 1775 **CEM**: Mt Vernon; GPS 38.42280, -77.0509; Mt Vernon Estate; Fairfax **GS**: U **SP**: Mar (8 Jan 1755) Martha (Dandridge) Custis (2 Jun 1731-22 May 1802) d/o John (1700-1756) & Frances (Jones) (1710-1785) Dandridge and widow of Daniel Parke Custis (1711-1757). **VI**: Son of Augustine (1694-1743) & Mary (Ball) (c1708-1789) Washington. Family moved to "Ferry Farm" in Stafford Co when he was a young boy. Had service in French & Indian War. Inaugurated as President 30 Apr 1789 & 1792 **P**: unk **BLW**: unk **RG**: Y **MK**: unk **PH**: unk **SS**: SAR P-314188; DAR #A121962 **BS**: JLARC 1,13, 23; 201 pg 7391-7392.

WASHINGTON, George Augustine; b 1758; d 15 Jun 1793 **RU**: Second Lieutenant, Aide-de-camp to General Lafayette **CEM**: Mt Vernon; GPS 38.42280, -77.0509; Mt Vernon Estate; Fairfax **GS**: U **SP**: Mar (15 Oct 1785. Mount Vernon) Frances Bassett (19 Dec 1767-1796) **VI**: Son of Charles (21 May 1738, Westmoreland Co-1800) & Mildred (Thornton) (__Spotsylvania Co-__) Washington. Bur in Washington family vault **P**: unk **BLW**: unk **RG**: Y **MK**: unk **PH**: unk **SS**: SAR Ancestor # P-314189 **BS**: JLARC 14; 196.

WASHINGTON, John A; b 1734, Leedstown (FAG- Stafford Co); d 26 Jun 1787 **RU**: Colonel/Patriot, Gave beef to the Army **CEM**: Bushfield Family; GPS 38.80, -76,4251; Mount Holly, Nomini River; Westmoreland **GS**: U **SP**: 1) mar (1755, Stafford Co) Sarah Sanborn, 2) mar (1759, Westmoreland Co) Nancy Constance Terrett; **VI**: Son of Robert Washington (3 Sep 1700, Stafford Co-13 May 1765) & Sarah Fossaker (6 Nov 1701, Stafford Co-25 Nov 1761, Westmoreland Co). Will dated 3 Jul 1785 provided other information **P**: unk **BLW**: unk **RG**: N **MK**: unk **PH**: unk **SS**: J- DAR Hatcher; AL Certificate Westmoreland Co **BS**: JLARC 2, 196.

WASHINGTON, John Augustine; b 13 Jan 1736, Stafford Co; d 10 Jan 1797 **RU**: Colonel/Patriot, Served in VA Militia, and was member VA Conventions 1775-6. Gave material aid to cause **CEM**: Pohick Episcopal; GPS 38.42546, -77.11598; 9301 Richmond Hwy, Lorton, Mt Holly; Fairfax **GS**: U **SP**: Mar (14 Apr 1756 Westmoreland Co) Hannah Bushrod (1738-1801) d/o John & Hannah (Corbin) Bushrod. **VI**: Son of Augustine (1694-1743) & Mary (Ball) (c1708-1789) Washington. Will dated 31 Jul 1787. Died in Mount Holly, Westmoreland Co **P**: unk **BLW**: unk **RG**: Y **MK**: Y SAR plaque **PH**: unk **SS**: AL Ct Bk pg 1, 4 Westmoreland Co; DAR A121967; SAR P-314201 **BS**: JLARC 14, 28; 196.

RU=Rank/Unit	CEM=Cemetery	GS=Gravestone	SP=Spousal Information
VI=Other Veteran Info	P=Pension	BLW=Bounty/Land Warrant	RG=Registered Grave
MK=SAR/DAR Marker	PH=Photo	SS=Service Source	BS=Burial Source

WASHINGTON, John H; b unk; d 1830 **RU:** Patriot, Gave material aid to the cause **CEM:** Washingon Family; GPS unk; Potomac View; King George **GS:** Y **SP:** No info **VI:** No further data **P:** N **BLW:** N **RG:** N **MK:** N **PH:** unk **SS:** AL Ct Bk pg 2 **BS:** 17 pg 63.

WASHINGTON, John; b 1735, d 14 Mar 1777 **RU:** Captain commissioned Apr 1776, 4th VA Regt, commanded co to his death this unit 14 Mar 1777 **CEM:** Rev War Court House Plaque; GPS not determined; 4110 Chain Bridge Rd; Fairfax **GS:** Memorialized on plaque 2017 by Geo Washington Chapter, VASSAR **SP** No info **VI:** died in service **P:** N **BLW:** N **RG:** Y **MK:** N **PH:** N **SS:** AP Fold3 Serv Rec; EP sources: SAR -314196: **BS:** None.

WASHINGTON, Martha (Dandridge); b 21 Jul 1732, New Kent Co; d 22 May 1802 **RU:** Patriot, Wife of George Washington. Spearheaded relief efforts for soldiers, giving them soup, medicine, and clothes while in the field with her husband **CEM:** Mt Vernon; GPS 38.42280, -77.0509; Mt Vernon Estate; Fairfax **GS:** Y **SP:** 1) Mar (15 May 1750, New Kent Co) Daniel Parke Custis (1700-1756); 2) Mar (6 Jan 1759, New Kent Co) George Washington (11 Feb 1732 Pope's Creek, Westmoreland Co-14 Dec 1799, Mt Vernon) son of Augustine (1694-1743) & Mary (Ball) (c1708-1789) Washington **VI:** d/o John Dandridge (1700-1756) & Frances Jones **P:** N **BLW:** N **RG:** Y **MK:** unk **PH:** unk **SS:** AS SAR regist; SAR P-314224 **BS:** 196.

WASHINGTON, Mary (Ball); b c1708; d 25 Aug 1789 **RU:** Patriot, As patriot knitted socks for Militia and furnished supplies **CEM:** Kenmore Plantation; GPS unk; 1500 Washington Ave; Fredericksburg City **GS:** Y **SP:** mar (6 Mar 1731 per bible) to Augustine Washington (12 Nov 1694- 12 Apr 1743, Ferry Farm, King George (now Stafford) Co) **VI:** d/o Joseph Ball (24 May 1649-1711, Lancaster Co) & Mary (-----) Johnson Ball Hews (__-1721 Cherry Point, Northumberland Co). Mother of Gen George Washington. Her exact burial location is not known, but monument erected at "Mediation Rock" where she is said to have gone to contemplate. The monument was begun in the 1830s, the project abandoned, the land sold and offered for auction in 1889, which was halted by court order and public outrage, and the monument finally completed **P:** N **BLW:** N **RG:** Y **MK:** N **PH:** unk **SS:** D Vol 3 pg 869; SAR P-314225 **BS:** 196; Historical site.

WASHINGTON, William Augustine; b 25 Nov 1757; d 2 Oct 1810 **RU:** Lieutenant Colonel, Served in VA Line. Was Capt of 6th Co 3rd VA Regt of Foot, 26 Feb 1776-Sep 1778, fr Westmoreland Co. Later was Lt Col in VA 3rd Regt of Light Dragoons 20 Nov 1778-9 Nov 1782. This unit served in Carolinas in 1779. He later commanded the combined 1st & 3rd Regts at Charleston **CEM:** Mt Vernon; GPS 38.42280, -77.0509; Mt Vernon Estate; Fairfax **GS:** U **SP:** 1) mar (25 Sep 1777) Jane "Jenny" Washington (1764-1795), cousin 2) mar (10 Jul 1792) Mary Lee (1775-1791) 3) mar (11 May 1799) Sarah "Sally" Tayloe (1765-1834) **VI:** Son of Augustine II (1720-1762) & Anne (Aylett) (1724-1774) Washington & nephew of George Washington. Bur in vault at Mt Vernon 4 Oct 1810 & removed to new vault 1824. Recd BLW #2421-450-7 Mar 1798 **P:** unk **BLW:** Y **RG:** Y **MK:** unk **PH:** unk **SS:** CE pg 39, 104, 105, 181; CG Vol 3 pg 3690;DAR A122016; SAR P-314222 **BS:** JLARC 14.

WASSON, James; b unk; d 1781 **RU:** Private, Served in Lt Inf fr CT Cont Line. Killed in the battle at Yorktown **CEM:** Yorktown Victory Monument Tablet; GPS 38.28350, -78.54150; Yorktown; York **GS:** U **SP:** (-----) Ames **VI:** Widow recd BLW #152-60-55 **P:** unk **BLW:** Y **RG:**Y **MK:** unk **PH:** unk **SS:** J-Yorktown Historian; DY pg 121, 156, 351; SAR P-314237 **BS:** JLARC 74.

WATKINS, John; b 1732; d 10 Mar 1785 **RU:** Patriot, Gave equipment and/or supplies **CEM:** Littlepage; GPS unk; Nr Pamunkey R, Cumberland; New Kent **GS:** Y **SP:** Betty Clairbourne, d/o Philip Whitehead & (-----) Claiborne Esq. of King William Co. **VI:** No further data **P:** N **BLW:** N **RG:** N **MK:** N **PH:** unk **SS:** AL Ct Bk pg 17,18,20 **BS:** 104 pg 359.

WATKINS, Samuel; b 21 Jan 1748, MD; d 1830 **RU:** Private, Served in Capts John Gerault's & Edward Worthington's companies, VA Illinois Regt **CEM:** Petersville; GPS 37.56440, -77.96470; Off Rt 60; Powhatan **GS:** U **SP:** Mary McClure **VI:** No further data **P:** unk **BLW:** unk **RG:** Y **MK:** unk **PH:** unk **SS:** cites Geo Rogers Clark papers, 1781-1783 VA Series; E pg 810; SAR P-314527 **BS:** 80 vol 4, pg 165.

WATKINS, Samuel; b 26 Apr 1750, Cumberland Co; d Jan 1795 **RU:** Second Lieutenant/Patriot, Served in Amelia Co Militia. Recd rank 23 Nov 1780. Gave material aid to cause **CEM:** Petersville; GPS 37.56440, -77.96470; Off Rt 60; Powhatan **GS:** U **SP:** Mar (26 Jul 1773) Elizabeth Goode (1 Jan 1760-

RU=Rank/Unit	CEM=Cemetery	GS=Gravestone	SP=Spousal Information
VI=Other Veteran Info	P=Pension	BLW=Bounty/Land Warrant	RG=Registered Grave
MK=SAR/DAR Marker	PH=Photo	SS=Service Source	BS=Burial Source

440

Jan 1792) **VI**: No further data **P**: unk **BLW**: unk **RG**: N **MK**: unk **PH**: unk **SS**: DAR A122393; J- DAR Hatcher; E pg 810; AL Ct Bk I pg 17 Amelia Co **BS**: JLARC 2.

WATKINS, Thomas J; b unk; d 19 Nov 1821 **RU**: Patriot, Gave material aid to cause **CEM**: Ben Lomond; GPS unk; Off Rt 600 on Rt 627; Goochland **GS**: Y **SP**: Ruth Hail (__-16 Nov 1821) **VI**: No further data **P**: N **BLW**: N **RG**: Y **MK**: N **PH**: unk **SS**: AL Ct Bk II, pg 23 **BS**: 46 pg 100.

WATKINS, William J; b unk; d 1838 **RU**: Patriot, Gave material aid to cause **CEM**: Ben Lomond; GPS unk; Off Rt 600 on Rt 627; Goochland **GS**: Y **SP**: No info **VI**: No further data **P**: N **BLW**: N **RG**: N **MK**: N **PH**: unk **SS**: AL Cert Issued **BS**: 46 pg 100.

WATLINGTON (WADLINGTON), John; b 1756; d 6 Feb 1812 **RU**: Captain, Served in VA Line. Ent serve Halifax Co 1777, Served as Lt of Artillery and later as Capt of Artillery. Served in Battles of Camden and Guilford CH as well as Gate's defeat **CEM**: Watlington Family; GPS unk; Halifax town; Halifax **GS**: Y **SP**: 1) Elizabeth Allen 2) Mar (6 Sep 1792, Caswell Co NC) Elizabeth "Betsey" Donohu d/o Thomas & Keisiah (-----) Donohu **VI**: Son of Col Armistead & (-----) Watlington, Esf 1777 Halifax Co, where resided. Widow recd pen W4097, also VA 1/2 pay (see N.A. Acc #874 #050186 1/2 pay) **P**: Y **BLW**: Y **RG**: Y **MK**: N **PH**: unk **SS**: K Vol 6 pg 73; AK Vol 4, pg 73-4; CG Vol 3 pg 3700; SAR -314557 **BS**: DAR Rpt.

WATSON, Benjamin; b 1767; d 10 Mar 1838 **RU**: Private, Served in 3rd Cont Line **CEM**: Colonna Family aka Wakefield Farm; GPS unk; 1 mi east of Pennyville, Hacks Neck; Accomack **GS**: Y **SP**: Susan (-----) (1775-11 Apr 1837). TS "wife of Benjamin Watson" **VI**: No further data **P**: unk **BLW**: unk **RG**: N **MK**: N **PH**: unk **SS**: E pg 810 **BS**: 145 Colonna; 196.

WATSON, John, Sr; b 1737, England; d 1824 **RU**: Private, Served in Mathews Co Militia and VA Line **CEM**: Trinity Episcopal; GPS 37.41069, -76.33578; Off Rt 614 nr jct Khyber Pass Trail; Mathews **GS**: U **SP**: Mar (Feb 1776) Hannah Tabor (1749-__) **VI**: Pen recd by spouse, #W18258, at $40 per annum **P**: Y **BLW**: unk **RG**: Y **MK**: unk **PH**: unk **SS**: CG pg 3702; SAR bio submitted Nov 2020 **BS**: 196.

WATSON, Joseph; b c1758; d 8 Apr 1828 **RU**: Corporal/Patriot, Served in Capt Harris Co 19-21 Sep 1781 at Williamsburg. Also gave material aid to cause **CEM**: Shockoe Hill; GPS 37.55190, -77.43170; 4th & Hospital Sts; Richmond City **GS**: Y **SP**: No info **VI**: No further data **P**: unk **BLW**: unk **RG**: N **MK**: N **PH**: unk **SS**: AL Ct Bk I pg 3; N pg 1246-7 **BS**: 57 pg 6.

WATSON, Robert; b unk; d unk **RU**: Corporal, Served in 5th & 11th VA Cont Lines **CEM**: Watson Family; GPS unk; Vic Rts 678 & 625; Fluvanna **GS**: Y **SP**: Belle (-----) **VI**: No further data **P**: unk **BLW**: unk **RG**: N **MK**: N **PH**: unk **SS**: E pg 811 **BS**: 66 pg 96.

WATSON, William; b 1755; d 25 Aug 1844 **RU**: Private/Patriot, Served in VA Line. Ent serv Powhatan Co in Capts Robert Hughes & Richard Crump's Cos, Powhatan Co Militia. Also gave material aid to cause **CEM**: Watson-Perrow; GPS unk; Gunter Mountain; Buckingham **GS**: Y **SP**: 1) Christiana Clelland 2) Fannie Wilkerson (1759-1840) **VI**: Sol appl 13 Aug 1832 Buckingham Co age 77. R11211. Newer Govt stone **P**: Y **BLW**: unk **RG**: Y **MK**: N **PH**: unk **SS**: DAR A003855; D Vol 3 pg 784, 785; E pg 811; CG Vol 3 pg 3704; SAR P-314744 **BS**: JLARC 4, 59; 196.

WATSON, William, b 1751,Amelia Co, d aft1801 **RU**: Captain/Patriot, Captain Amelia Co Militia 1777 and had public serv as Justice, Amelia Co. **CEM**: Glenmore; GPS not determined; loc 3 mi N of Burkeville on old Rd betw Burkeville and Jennings Ordinary; Nottoway **GS**: N **SP**: Nancy Ann Randolph (1759-1795) **VI**: Son of William Watson (1719-1751) & Amy Jones (c1719-4 Oct 1780) **P**: N **BLW**: N **RG**: N **MK**: N **PH**: N **SS**: E pg 811; AZ pg 180 **BS**: 196.

WATSON, William J; b unk; d 27 Oct 1838 **RU**: Soldier, Ent serv Powhatan Co 1777. Later ent serv in "Virginia Regt" and served at Battle of Guilford CH. Gave material aid to cause **CEM**: Ben Lomond; GPS unk; Off Rt 600 on Rt 627; Goochland **GS**: U **SP**: Mar (17 Dec 1767) Martha Pleasants, surety Richard Pleasants **VI**: Pen rejected because service less than six mos **P**: N **BLW**: unk **RG**: N **MK**: unk **PH**: unk **SS**: AL **BS**: 46 pg 100.

WATTERS, William; b 16 Oct 1751; d 29 Mar 1827 **RU**: Patriot, he signed an oath of alligence at Mayberry's Chapel, in Va in 1777 **CEM**: Watters-Adams Family; GPS GS 38.925614, -77.163081; 6430 Linway Terr, McLean, Fairfax **GS**: Y **SP**: Sarah Adams **VI**: Stone erected by Virginia Conference of the

RU=Rank/Unit	CEM=Cemetery	GS=Gravestone	SP=Spousal Information
VI=Other Veteran Info	P=Pension	BLW=Bounty/Land Warrant	RG=Registered Grave
MK=SAR/DAR Marker	PH=Photo	SS=Service Source	BS=Burial Source

441

Methodist Episcopal Church. Epitaph- "He was a pioneer, leading the way for the vast army of American Methodist Itinerates having the Everlasting Gospel to preach." This is also considered patriotic service **P:** unk **BLW:** unk **RG:** Y **MK:** Y DAR Plaque **PH:** unk **SS:** E pg 811; AR vol 4 pg 166; SAR P-314760 **BS:** 61 vol I pg ML-43; 196.

WATTERSON, Henry; b 1744, Augusta Co; d 1791 **RU:** Captain/Patriot, Commanded a co in Botetourt Co Militia. Gave material aid to cause **CEM:** Watterson Family; GPS unk; Christiansburg; Montgomery **GS:** Y **SP:** mar (1764) Agnes Reaburn (__-4 Feb 1817) **VI:** SAR applic indicates rank of Capt **P:** unk **BLW:** unk **RG:** Y **MK:** N **PH:** unk **SS:** DAR A122674; AS SAR applic; DF pg 123, 126, 130, 134; SAR P-314763 **BS:** 80 vol 4 pg 166.

WATTS, Jacob; b 19 Jul 1730, Scotland, d 22 Jul 1821, Orange Co **RU:** Patriot, Was a 38.1572770, -78.4652710; 975 Wakefield Farm Rd, Earlysville; Albermarle **GS:** N **SP:**Elizabeth Durrett **P:** N **BLW:** N **RG:** Y **MK:** N **PH:** N **SS:** DAR A124222, cites Albemarle Co Order Bk 1783-1785, pg 154; SAR P-314795 **BS:** SAR PRS; 196.

WATTS, John; b 1752, Dinwiddie Co; d 8 Jun 1830 **RU:** Captain, Ent serv Bedford Co. Served as Capt 1st VA Regt of Dragoons. Wounded at Eutaw Springs, nr Savannah, GA **CEM:** Gravelly Hill; GPS unk; Town of Gravelly Hill; Bedford **GS:** U **SP:** No info **VI:** After war served rank of Lt Col US Army Light Dragoons 8 Jan 1799. Pen in Bedford Co.Recd BLW #243 of 4,944 acres issued 27 Aug 1795. Records lost in DC fire of 1800 **P:** Y **BLW:** Y **RG:** Y **MK:** N **PH:** unk **SS:** SAR P-314802; J-NSSAR 1993 Reg; K Vol 6 pg 80; CG pg 3706 **BS:** JLARC 1.

WAX, Henry Sr; b 1744, Baden-Wurtenburg, Germany; d 6 Nov 1796 **RU:** Sergeant, Sgt in Capt Daniel DeTurcks' Co of Berks Co PA 1776-1778 and promoted to Capt after the War period on 5 Jan 1784 **CEM:** Fincastle Presbyterian; GPS 37.50017, -79.87558; 108 E Back St, Fincastle; Botetourt **GS:** Y **SP:** 1) Mar (11 May 1767 Alace, Berks Co, PA) Margaret Geshwind (1750 Berks Co, PA-10 Feb 1791) 2) Mar (1 May 1791) Catherine Kerns Keyser **VI:** Son of Johann Philippus Wachs. Moved to VA in 1786 **P:** unk **BLW:** unk **RG:** Y **MK:** Y SAR plaque **PH:** unk **SS:** J-NSSAR 1993 Reg; J- DAR Hatcher; AR Vol 4 pg 166;DAR A122951; SAR P-314866 **BS:** JLARC 1, 2; 196.

WAYLAND, John; b 1725, Spotsylvania Co; d 1804 **RU:** Patriot/ Soldier, Gave material aid to cause, also listed in the Culpeper Classes 1781, thus ready for call-up **CEM:** Hebron Lutheran; GPS 38.40676, -78.24808; 899 Blankenbaker Rd, Madison; Madison **GS:** N **SP:** Cayherine Broyles (1730-1830) d/o Hans Jacob (1705-1763) & Maria Catherine (Fleishman) (1705-1710) Broyles **VI:** A member of the church when he died with burial there likely but not proved **P:** N **BLW:** N **RG:** Y **MK:** unk **PH:** N **SS:** ALCt Bk 1 pg 33, 35; DJ vol 213, pg 25; DAR A122983; SAR P-314911 **BS:** 196.

WEATHERFORD, John William; b 4 May 1747, Charlotte Co; d 23 Jan 1833 **RU:** Chaplain or Soldier, Served in VA Line. Ent serv 1779 Henry Co in VA Regt to fight Indians. Moved to Pittsylvania Co & enl there again **CEM:** Shockoe Baptist; GPS 36.80960, -79.26590; Rt 640, Chatham; Pittsylvania **GS:** U **SP:** Martha Patsy Sublette (1752, Charlotte Co-Nov 1829) d/o William (__-1751) & Susannah (Allen) (__-1803) Sublett **VI:** Appl pen 20 Feb 1845 Bartholomew Co at age 97 on 5 May 1844. R11231. Baptist preacher for 70 yrs. Early advocate for religious liberty. Jailed five mos in 1773 for preaching. Release secured by Patrick Henry. Memorialized at burial site in VA **P:** Y **BLW:** unk **RG:** Y **MK:** Y SAR **PH:** Y **SS:** K Vol 6 pg 84-5; CG Vol 3 pg 3710; SAR P-314970 **BS:** JLARC 96,99; 196.

WEAVER, John Peter; b 1745; d 1815 **RU:** Private, Served in Capt Tate's Co of Miliitia, Augusta Co **CEM:** St John's Reformed UCC; GPS 38.05081, -79.17761; 1515 Arbor Hill Rd, Middlebrook; Augusta **GS:** Y **SP:** Elizabeth (-----) (1746-1814) **VI:** No further data **P:** unk **BLW:** unk **RG:** Y **MK:** N **PH:** unk **SS:** DAR A123365; E pg 813; SAR P-315094 **BS:** JLARC 9, 62; 196.

WEAVER, Peter; b c1736, Orange Co; d 1817 **RU:** Private/Patriot, Served in Culpeper Co Militia 1781. Gave material aid to cause **CEM:** Hebron Valley; GPS unk; Hebron Valley; Madison **GS:** N **SP:** Mary Barbara Huffman **VI:** Son of German immigrant John & (-----) Weaver of Culpeper Co (later Madison Co). **P:** unk **BLW:** unk **RG:** Y **MK:** N **PH:** N **SS:** D; AS SAR appl; AM pg 30. SAR P-3125092 **BS:** 04, Feb 1994.

WEAVER, Tilman Jr; b c1745, Germantown, Prince William Co (later Fauquier Co); d 1809 **RU:** Captain, Served in Fauquier Co Militia, obtained Capt rank 24 Mar 1778 **CEM:** Germantown Glebe; GPS unk; Rt 643 nr Licking Run, Midland; Fauquier **GS:** Y **SP:** Elizabeth (-----) (__-bef 1809,

---

RU=Rank/Unit	CEM=Cemetery	GS=Gravestone	SP=Spousal Information
VI=Other Veteran Info	P=Pension	BLW=Bounty/Land Warrant	RG=Registered Grave
MK=SAR/DAR Marker	PH=Photo	SS=Service Source	BS=Burial Source

442

Germantown) **VI**: Son of Tilman Sr. (1703-1760) & Ann Elizabeth (Cuntze) (1708 Germany-__) Weaver **P**: unk **BLW**: unk **RG**: N **MK**: U **PH**: unk **SS**: E pg 813 **BS**: 19 pg 66.

WEBB, Henry "Hal"; b c1750, Franklin Co; d c1845 **RU**: Private, Served in VA Militia under Capt Jonathan Isom **CEM**: Thompson-Bolt; GPS 36.81040, -80.55030; Off Bannon Rd Rt 625, Willis; Carroll **GS**: Y **SP**: Susannah Cocke **VI**: Son of Jacob Webb & Mary Austin. Died in Grayson Co **P**: unk **BLW**: unk **RG**: Y **MK**: N **PH**: Y **SS**: DAR A123781; SAR P-315165; G pg 221; DD cites VA Mag of Hist & Biog Vol 46 #4 pg 345-6 **BS**: 196; 04; 196.

WEBB, James b 1764, d 19 Feb 1832, at his home "Smithfield" **RU**: Patriot, paid the supply tax portion of the personal property tax in Essex Co, 1783 **CEM**: Fleet Family, GPS Not determined; loc on the estate site of Alexander Fleet, Obtain county property tax records for directions in Newtown; King & Queen **GS**: Y **SP**: Mar 22 Jul 1790, Essex Co, Dorothy Throckmorton (1769-7 Jan 1829) d/o Capt Gabriel Throckmorton & Judith Edmondson **VI**: Son of James Webb & Mary Smith. He was an attorney in Essex Co **P**: N **BLW**: N **RG**: N **MK**: N **PH**: N **SS**: DV Essex Co 1783A Personal Prperty Tax image 2 **BS**: 196.

WEBB, John; b 1750, Frederick Co, MD; d 1803 **RU**: Private, Served in MD Line. Ent serv Frederick Co, MD 1776. Was in Battle at Trenton, NJ in Capt Neely's Co and in his father-in-law, Capt William Duvall's Co **CEM**: Hebron United Methodist; GPS unk; Rt 606 jct Bobcat Ln; Craig **GS**: U **SP**: Mar (15 or 16 Jun 1775 Frederick Co MA) Susannah Duvall (1757-__) **VI**: Died in Botetourt Co. Widow appl pen 1 Apr 1848 Belmont Co OH & BLW 15 Mar 1855 Belmont Co. W4384. BLW #530-160-55 **P**: Y **BLW**: Y **RG**: Y **MK**: unk **PH**: unk **SS**: SAR P-315198; CG Vol 3 pg 3717 **BS**: JLARC 4, 60.

WEBB, Tapley (Tarpley); b 1763, Richmond City; d 2 Mar 1836 **RU**: Seaman, Served in VA State Navy. Served in Thomas Gaskin's Company, 2d (later 5th) VA Regt **CEM**: Cedar Grove; GPS 36.838136, -76.307112; 301 Fort Lane Rd; Portsmouth City **GS**: U **SP**: Mar (16 Dec 1809 Portsmouth) Elizabeth W. Poiner (1787-1836) **VI**: He rec'd rank of Lt Colonel, under MG Josiah Parker. Vet's daughter Mrs. Ann P. Young appl pen 4 Sep 1856 Norfolk Co. She was issued BLW 9776 13 Oct 1856. S36113 **P**: Y. **BLW**: Y **RG**: Y **MK**: Y SAR **PH**: unk **SS**: K Vol 6 pg 90; BY pg 240; CG Vol 3 pg 3719; SAR P-315255 **BS**: JLARC 4; 196.

WEBB, Thomas T; b 1745; d 1796 **RU**: Corporal, Capt Thomas Posey's Co, 7th VA Regt **CEM**: Old Christ Church Episcopal; GPS 38.80625, -77.04718; 118 N Washington St; Alexandria City **GS**: N **SP**: No info **VI**: No further data **P**: unk **BLW**: unk **RG**: N **MK**: N **PH**: N **SS**: A -7th VA Regt **BS**: 110 pg 96.

WEBB, William; b unk; d 26 Apr 1805 **RU**: Captain/Patriot, Mil serv not identified. Gave material aid to cause **CEM**: St John's Episcopal; GPS 37.53183, -77.41958; 2401 E Broad St; Richmond City **GS**: Y **SP**: No info **VI**: No further data **P**: unk **BLW**: unk **RG**: N **MK**: unk **PH**: unk **SS**: AL Ct Bk lt pg 13 **BS**: 28; 196.

WEBB, William; b unk; d 1796 **RU**: Patriot, Gave material aid to the cause **CEM**: St John's Episcopal; GPS 37.53183, -77.41958; 2401 E Broad St; Richmond City **GS**: Y **SP**: N o info **VI**: No further data **P**: N **BLW**: N **RG**: N **MK**: N **PH**: unk **SS**: AL Ct Bk lt pg 13 **BS**: 28 pg 517.

WEBB, William "Will"; b 2 Jan 1729, Leicestershire, Eng, d 19 Mar 1818 **RU**: Gave material aid to cause in Botetout Co. Also public service as Juror **CEM**: Boyd Family; GPS 36.9383011, -81.9428024; loc off Rt 603 Mountain Rd, Elk Garden; Russell **GS**: N **SP**: Mary Oney (__-1816) **VI**: No further data **P**: N **BLW**: N **RG**: N **MK**: N **PH**: N **SS**: D Vol 1, pg 342; DL-pg 342; DAR A124222 **BS**: 28 pg 517.

WEBB, William Warren; b 1699, Isle of Wight Co; d Aft 28 Aug 1783 **RU**: Patriot, Gave material aid to cause **CEM**: Blue Run Baptist; GPS unk; Rt 20 N of jct with Rt 655, Barboursville; Orange **GS**: N **SP**: Mar (c1727) Mary Jane Elizabeth Crittenden (1702, Spotsylvania Co-__) **VI**: Son of John & Martha (Riggens) Webb **P**: N **BLW**: N **RG**: N **MK**: unk **PH**: N **SS**: DAR A201743; AL Ct Bk pg 27, 29 Orange **BS**: Church records.

WEBBER, William; b 15 Aug 1747, Goochland Co; d 28 Feb 1808 **RU**: Soldier/Patriot, Served in VA infantry during RW. Gave material aid to cause **CEM**: Webber Family; GPS unk; W Rt 6 fr Richmond 9.2 mi, right Rt 621 3.5 mi; Goochland **GS**: U **SP**: Mar (23 Jan 1773) Mary Woolfolk (21 Oct 1752, Spotsylvania Co-c1833) d/o John (6 Nov 1727, Spotsylvania Co-18 Jan 1816) & Elizabeth

---

RU=Rank/Unit	CEM=Cemetery	GS=Gravestone	SP=Spousal Information
VI=Other Veteran Info	P=Pension	BLW=Bounty/Land Warrant	RG=Registered Grave
MK=SAR/DAR Marker	PH=Photo	SS=Service Source	BS=Burial Source

443

(Wigglesworth) (17 Mar 1732-10 Aug 1791) Woolfolk Note SAR PRS indicates wives were 1) Isabel, 2) Alice Richie **VI**: Baptist minister. Recd BLW **P**: unk **BLW**: Y **RG**: Y **MK**: unk **PH**: unk **SS**: DAR A134528; C pg 274; AL Ct Bk pg 16 Goochland Co; DD; SAR P-315323 **BS**: JLARC 99.

WEBSTER, George; b unk; d 1796 **RU**: Soldier, Served fr MA, and died fr the Battle at Yorktown **CEM**: Yorktown Victory Monument Tablet; GPS 38.28350, -78.54150; Yorktown; York **GS**: U **SP**: No info **VI**: No further data **P**: unk **BLW**: unk **RG**: Y **MK**: unk **PH**: unk **SS**: J-Yorktown Historian; SAR P-315401 **BS**: JLARC 74.

WEDDLE (WADDELL, WODLE, WEDEL), Benjamin; b 1751, Lancaster Co, PA; d 1807 **RU**: Private, Served in Capt James Byrn's Co, Montgomery Co. Also served in Capt John Lucas Co, Col William Preston's Regt **CEM**: Weddle Family; GPS unk; Bent Mountain; Roanoke Co **GS**: N **SP**: Mar (__ Lancaster Co, PA) Annie Mary Eiler (1751-1834) **VI**: Died in Montgomery Co on return trip fr Richmond with wagonload of supplies. Monument in Weddle Family Cem. Indicates he is bur on Bent Mountain in Roanoke Co in unk location **P**: unk **BLW**: unk **RG**: Y **MK**: N **PH**: N **SS**: DAR A119631; SAR P-315551; Montgomery Cthse; G pg 241; DD cites VA Mag of Hist & Biog Vol 47 pg 154 **BS**: 04; 196.

WEEDON, George; b 1734 or 1735; d 1793 or 1796 **RU**: Brig General, Was in charge of Stafford Co & Fredericksburg Militia, Cont Line 3 yrs. Commanded VA 3rd Regt of Foot 13 Aug 1776 to 21 Feb 1777. Was Brigade Commander as well Oct 1776 at Trenton **CEM**: Masonic Cemetery; GPS 38.30198, -77.46142; 900 Charles St; Fredericksburg City **GS**: Y **SP**: Mar (Fredericksburg) Catherine Gordon (__-1797) **VI**: Owned and operated tavern in Fredericksburg until 1776 and again after war. Mayor of Fredericksburg after war. Recd 10,000 acres BLW #2418-850-3 May 1791. Records lost in 1800 DC fire **P**: unk **BLW**: Y **RG**: Y **MK**: Y SAR plaque **PH**: Y **SS**: F pg 77; K Vol 6 pg 91; CE pg 38, 39; CG Vol 3 pg 3727; SAR P-315641 **BS**: 13 pg 18.

WEIR, Hugh; b 1746; d 16 Jul 1822 **RU**: Captain, Commanded a co in Rockbridge Co Militia 7 Aug 1781 **CEM**: McKee, aka Big Springs; GPS unk; Clarence Hardy's farm, off Rt 60 on Rt 63, Kerrs Dist; Rockbridge **GS**: U **SP**: Mary McKee (1746-2 Aug 1822) **VI**: No further data **P**: N **BLW**: N **RG**: N **MK**: unk **PH**: unk **SS**: E pg 815 **BS**: 204.

WEISER, Henry; b 15 Apr 1755, Pulaski Co; d 12 Jan 1844 **RU**: Private, Served in Capts Berry, Bell, Long & Knox's Cos, Col Bowman's Regt, 8th Cont Line under General Morgan **CEM**: Bell Farm; GPS unk; Dublin; Pulaski **GS**: U **SP**: Mar (1778) Barbara Ann Ripseed (14 Feb 1758-10 May 1837) **VI**: Recd Pen #S7854 **P**: Y **BLW**: unk **RG**: Y **MK**: unk **PH**: unk **SS**: DAR A121737; E pg 815; DD cites pension rec as serv source; SAR P-315835 **BS**: JLARC 2.

WEISS, Matthias; b 12 Mar 1752, Bethlehem Twp, Northampton Co, PA; d 5 May 1831 **RU**: Private, Served in Capt Jacob Weidman's Co, Lt Col Robert Knox Regt, Philadelphia Militia **CEM**: Weiss Family; GPS unk; Rt 637 or 736, Independence; Grayson **GS**: U **SP**: Rachel Bonham Ball **VI**: No further data **P**: unk **BLW**: unk **RG**: Y **MK**: unk **PH**: unk **SS**: J-NSSAR 1993 Reg, J- DAR Hatcher; AP Muster Roll PA Archives 6th series Vol 1 pg 401-2; SAR P-315852 **BS**: JLARC 1, 2.

WELBURN (WELBOURNE), William Sr; b 11 Oct 1762; d 11 Oct 1839 **RU**: Captain, Served in VA Line. Ent serv Accomack Co 1777-8. Capt Thomas Marshall's Co. Later was Capain in Accomack Co Militia **CEM**: Welburn or Welbourne Family; GPS unk; Rts 709 & 679, Horntown; Accomack **GS**: Y **SP**: Mar (5 Feb 1784 Accomac Co (bond) Coleburn Lang, security) Sabra Corbin (__-bef 11 Oct 1839) **VI**: Appl pen 1 Aug 1832 Accomack Co age 70. S7856 **P**: Y **BLW**: unk **RG**: Y **MK**: unk **PH**: N **SS**: K Vol 6 pg 93; CG Vol 3 pg 3731; SAR P-315874 **BS**: JLARC 4, 6.

WELCH, Nathaniel, b 17 Jan 1755, d 20 Nov 1815 **RU**: Captain, 2d VA Regt VA Line commanded by Col William Brent, under Gen George Rogers Clark 1777-1780 **CEM**: Locust Dale; GPS: 38.3451140, -78.1237920; vic jct Rts Oak Park Rd & James Madison Hwy; Madison **GS**: N **SP**: 1) Elizabeth Terrill, 2) Mary(-----); **VI**: Heirs rec'd bounty land of 789 acres, 7 Dec 1832. **P**: N **BLW**: Heirs **RG**: Y **MK**: N **PH**: N **SS**: G pg 648; N pg 755; SAR P-315932 **VI**: **BS**: 196.

WELCH, Sylvester Sr; b 15 Mar 1764; d 19 Apr 1834 **RU**: Soldier, Served in Cont Line. Ent Serv Northumberland Co 1777. Served in 1st VA Regt **CEM**: Marshall; GPS 38.86919, -77.83445; Marshall; Fauquier **GS**: Y **SP**: A man by this name mar (bond 25 Nov 1793, Joseph Jackson security) Sarah Jackson **VI**: Sol appl pen 1 Dec 1832 in Fauquier Co age 77. S6342 **P**: Y **BLW**: unk **RG**: Y **MK**: Y SAR

RU=Rank/Unit   CEM=Cemetery   GS=Gravestone   SP=Spousal Information
VI=Other Veteran Info   P=Pension   BLW=Bounty/Land Warrant   RG=Registered Grave
MK=SAR/DAR Marker   PH=Photo   SS=Service Source   BS=Burial Source

444

PH: Y **SS:** K Vol 6 pg 95; CG Vol 3 pg 3735; Fauquier Co Marriages pg 210; SAR P-315940 **BS:** JLARC 1,16; 196.

WELCH, Thomas; b 1 Feb 1753, Orange Co; d 10 Jul 1821 **RU:** Private, Served in Col Daniel Morgan's 11th & 15th VA Regts. 7th Cont Line **CEM:** Falling Springs Presbyterian; GPS 37.68494, -79.45105; 410 Falling Spring Rd, Glasgow; Rockbridge **GS:** Y **SP:** Sarah Grigsby, d/o John & (-----) Grigsby **VI:** Son of Thomas & (-----) Welch Sr **P:** unk **BLW:** unk **RG:** Y **MK:** Y SAR **PH:** unk **SS:** J-NSSAR 1993 Reg; E pg 80; SAR P-3159413 **BS:** JLARC 1; 196.

WELLFORD, Robert; b 12 Apr 1753, Ware, Hertfordshire, England; d 24 Apr 1823 **RU:** Patriot, Was British surgeon, treated American soldiers due to poor treatment by British captors, gave horse & beef to cause. Resigned fr British Army **CEM:** Willis Hill, Fredericksburg National Military Park; GPS unk; Marye Heights; Fredericksburg City **GS:** Y **SP:** Catherine Randolph Yates (24 Mar 1760-11 Feb 1831) **VI:** Son of William (1726-1790) & Jane (Brasenar) (1724-1783) Welford. Came to colonies with First Royal Grenadiers. Friend of Col Spotswood during RW and later accompanied Gen Washington, who gave letters of introduction to friends in Fredericksburg. During Whiskey Rebellion (1794), became Surgeon General of Army raised to surpress uprising **P:** N **BLW:** N **RG:** Y **MK:** N **PH:** Y **SS:** D pg 873,861; SAR P-316067 **BS:** 06 pg 95, 96; 196.

WELLS, David, Sr; b 1730 d 1799 **RU:** Patriot, paid 1783 Lunenburg Co supply tax considered a partial payment of Rev War expenses **CEM:** Old Wells Family; GPS not determined; loc behind Horeb Baptist Ch, 10077 Old Coxs Rd;Chase City; Mecklenburg; **GS:** N; **SP:** Susanna (-----) **VI:** Cem sign lists patriot and family data and depicts general loc of cem at family farm. Heirs gave farmland to church **P:** N **BLW:** N **RG:** Y **MK:** N **PH:** N **SS:** SAR P-337054 **BS:**196.

WELLS, Zachariah; b 1739; d Oct 1813 **RU:** Private, Served in VA Line. Ent serv Loudoun Co 1776. Was in Battles of Brandywine & Germantown. Ent serv again 1778 in VA Cavalry unit on KY frontier **CEM:** Wells Family; GPS 36.84640, -82.81720; Rt 739 abt 1 mi S of jct with 605; Wise **GS:** U **SP:** Rebecca (-----) (_-before 1813) **VI:** Son of Zachariah (__-1781) & (-----) Wells though DNA evidence shows his parents may be George & Susannah (Ward) Wells. Wells & Ward families together in MD. Appl pen 29 Mar 1825 Sullivan Co TN age 80 S39119. Died in Sullivan Co, TN or Wilkes Co, NC. BLW recd 1784 **P:** Y **BLW:** Y **RG:** Y **MK:** unk **PH:** unk **SS:** J- DAR Hatcher; K Vol 6 pg 100; CG Vol 3 pg 3745; SAR P-316385 **BS:** JLARC 2; 196.

WENDREWECK, Armand; b unk; d 1796 **RU:** Soldier, Served in Gatinais Bn and died fr battle at Yorktown **CEM:** French Memorial; GPS 36.81944, -79.39933; Yorktown; York **GS:** U **SP:** No info **VI:** No further data **P:** unk **BLW:** unk **RG:** Y **MK:** Y **PH:** unk **SS:** J-Yorktown Historian; SAR P-316474 **BS:** JLARC 1,74.

WENGER, Henry; b 15 Aug 1753, Lancaster Co, PA; d 9 Aug 1819 **RU:** Private, Served in10th PA Regt **CEM:** Early; GPS 38.39536, -78.90465; 3588 Early Rd, Pleasant Valley; Rockingham **GS:** Y **SP:** Anna Huber (1758 Lancaster Co, PA-20 Jun 1824) **VI:** No further data **P:** unk **BLW:** unk **RG:** N **MK:** unk **PH:** unk **SS:** AP Serv Record N ARA M881 Roll 0832 **BS:** 196.

WENGER, Joseph Grabill; b 8 Aug 1747, Lancaster Co, PA, d May 1812 **RU:** Lieutenant, Served in Capt Wright's Co, PA Militia **CEM:** Lindale Mennonite Church; GPS: 38.53581, -78.84925; 6225 Jesse Bennett Hwy, Linville; Rockingham **GS:** Yes **SP:** Barbara Huber (1747, New Holland, PA-Jul 1792) **VI:** Son of Christian Wenger (1698-1772) and Anna Graybill (1764-1847) **P:** N **BLW:** N **RG:**Y **MK:** N **PH:** N **SS:** CI-PA Archives, series 3, vol VI, pg 433; SAR P-316483 **BS:** 196.

WERTS see VIRTZS

WESCOTT, John; b c1741, Cumberland Co, NJ; d 25 Nov 1813 **RU:** Captain/ Patriot, Served as Cumberland Co NJ Board of Freeholders, 1775; and on a Deerfield Twp Committee on Observation & Correspondence, 17 Sep 1775, Served in rank of Lt in 1st Western Co of Artillery, NJ State Troops, 1 May 1776, and as Capt Oct. 1776 and 1777 **CEM:** Old Presbyterian Meeting House; GPS 38.48528, -77.23532; 323 S Fairfax St; Alexandria City **GS:** Y **SP:** Annie (-----) of Cumberland Co., NJ; 2) Sarah Diament **VI:** No further data **P:** unk **BLW:** unk **RG:**Y **MK:** Y SAR & plaque **PH:** unk **SS:** AS; BT; SAR P-316853 **BS:** JLARC 86; 23 pg 84.

RU=Rank/Unit	CEM=Cemetery	GS=Gravestone	SP=Spousal Information
VI=Other Veteran Info	P=Pension	BLW=Bounty/Land Warrant	RG=Registered Grave
MK=SAR/DAR Marker	PH=Photo	SS=Service Source	BS=Burial Source

WEST, Abel; b 30 May 1734; d 30 May 1816 **RU**: Lieutenant, Oath as Lt Accomack Militia 30 Sep 1777 **CEM**: Old West Place, aka Cedar View; GPS unk; N of Craddockville off Rt 616; Accomack **GS**: Y **SP**: Nanney (-----) (23 Oct 173_ -20 Dec 1805) **VI**: No further data **P**: unk **BLW**: unk **RG**: N **MK**: N **PH**: unk **SS**: E pg 817 **BS**: 37 pg 274.

WEST, Anthony Jr; b 24 Aug 1760; d 2 Feb 1795 **RU**: Patriot, Provided equipment and/or supplies **CEM**: West Family; GPS unk; Deep Creek; Accomack **GS**: Y **SP**: No info **VI**: Son of Anthony & Eleanor (-----) West Sr **P**: N **BLW**: N **RG**: N **MK**: N **PH**: unk **SS**: AL cert issued **BS**: 106 pg 538; 47 Vol 3 pg. 259.

WEST, George; b c1725, d 1786 **RU**: Colonel/Patriot Selected as Major 11 May 1788, Loudoun Co Militia. Gave material aid to cause as Colonel Loudoun Co **CEM**: Pohick Episcopal Church; GPS: 38.70888,-77.19369; jct Rts 1 & 611, Lorton; Fairfax **GS**: Yes, name listed on plaque **SP**; Not determined **VI**: Son of Hugh West (1705-1787) and Sybil Harrison (1705-1787) **P**: N **BLW**: N **RG**: N **MK**: Y SAR plaque **PH**: N **SS**: AL Comm Bk III, pg 334, Ct Bk pg 5, Loudoun Co; AZ pg 213 **BS**: 196.

WEST, John; b 7 Nov 1753; d 17 Dec 1835 **RU**: Soldier, Ent serv 1776 in Philadelphia PA **CEM**: Goose Creek; GPS 39.11250, -77.69527; Rt 722, Lincoln; Loudoun **GS**: U **SP**: Mar (24 Oct 1791) Hannah (-----) **VI**: Pensioned Loudoun Co 1833 W6453 **P**: Y **BLW**: unk **RG**: unk **MK**: unk **PH**: unk **SS**: K Vol 6 pg 102; SAR P-316737 **BS**: JLARC 4, 32.

WEST, John IV; b 1710, d 1777 **RU**: Colonel/Patriot Performed public service as Burgess and member of VA Assembly, 1776, Fairfax Co **CEM**: Pohick Episcopal Church; GPS: 38.70888,-77.19369; jct Rts 1 & 611, Lorton; Fairfax **GS**: Yes **SP**: Mar 1) Mary Harris 2) Margaret Pearson (1720-1797) **VI**: Son of John West (1657-1716) & Elizabeth Semmes (1672-1753). His Bush Plantation home, now called Watson House, still exists. **P**: N **BLW**: N **RG**: N **MK**: Y SAR plaque **PH**: N **SS**: CD **BS**: 196.

WEST, Joseph; b 1 Jan 1719, Chadds Ford, Delaware Co, PA; d 12 Sep 1802 **RU**: Patriot, Gave material aid to cause **CEM**: West Plantation; GPS unk; Straightstone; Pittsylvania **GS**: U **SP**: 1) Elizabeth Hazard 2) mar (6 Mar 1740 Chester Co PA) Jane Owen (1720-1791), d/o John & Hannah (Maris) Owen **VI**: Son of John (1690-1776) & Sarah (Pearson) West **P**: N **BLW**: N **RG**: unk **MK**: unk **PH**: unk **SS**: J- DAR Hatcher; NSSAR Ancestor # P-316746 **BS**: JLARC 2.

WEST, Sybil Harrison; b 1705, d 1787 **RU**: Patriot, Supported cause by paying supply tax included in her personal property tax in 1782, Fairfax Co **CEM**: Pohick Episcopal Church; GPS: 38.70888, -77.19369; jct Rts 1 & 611, Lorton; Fairfax **GS**: Yes, name listed on plaque; **SP**: Hugh West (1705-1754)) **VI**: No further information **P**: N **BLW**: N **RG**: N **MK**: Y SAR plaque **PH**: N **SS**: DV **BS**: 196.

WEST, Thomas; b 1730, d 1785 KY **RU**: Private Capt Thomas Hamilton's Co, 1st VA Regt, VA State Line. In Col Peter Muhlenberg's Brigade 1777. Was at siege of Yorktown **CEM**: Fairfax-Buckley; GPS: 38.728958, -77.357581; Wolf Run Shoals Rd, Fountainhead Regional Park, Clifton; Fairfax Co **GS**: Y **SP**: Mar c1755, Fairfax Co, Sarah Trammell **VI**: Son of Thomas West and Sarah (-----). Buried in KY, but memorialized with GS in VA. Family tradition was killed by Indians while searching for BLT tract in KY. Recd BLW 100 acres 1855 **P**: N **BLW**: Y **RG**: Y **MK**: Y- SAR **PH**: Y **SS**: F pg 81; SAR P-316781 **BS**: 196.

WEST, Thomas Wade; b 1745; d 28 Jul 1799 **RU**: Patriot, Performed public service **CEM**: Old Christ Church Episcopal; GPS 38.80625, -77.04718; 118 N Washington St; Alexandria City **GS**: N **SP**: No info **VI**: Manager of the Virginia & South Carolina Companies of Comedians, killed when he fell fr the upper story to the stage in his new Alexandria theater, age 54 (Alexandria Gazette, 29 Jul 1799 pg 3) **P**: N **BLW**: N **RG**: N **MK**: N **PH**: N **SS**: BB Legislative Pet. **BS**: 20 pg 143.

WEST, William; b 1762; d 1815 **RU**: Patriot, Gave material aid to cause **CEM**: Good Hope United Methodist; GPS 36.6305321, 76.2755421; 1633 Benefit Rd; Chesapeake City **GS**: Y **SP**: No info **VI**: No further data **P**: N **BLW**: N **RG**: N **MK**: unk **PH**: unk **SS**: Al Ct Bk pg 6 Princess Anne Co **BS**: 20 pg 153.

WEST, William; b unk; d 1790 **RU**: Patriot, Gave material aid to the cause **CEM**: Dumfries Public; GPS 38.34110, -77.19964; 17821 Mine Rd, Dumfries; Prince William **GS**: N **SP**: No info **VI**: Name on SAR monument **P**: N **BLW**: N **RG**: N **MK**:Y SAR monument **PH**: N **SS**: AL Ct Bk I pg 18; SAR Bio submitted 2020 **BS**: 96 pg 74.

RU=Rank/Unit   CEM=Cemetery   GS=Gravestone   SP=Spousal Information
VI=Other Veteran Info   P=Pension   BLW=Bounty/Land Warrant   RG=Registered Grave
MK=SAR/DAR Marker   PH=Photo   SS=Service Source   BS=Burial Source

446

WESTON, Lewis; b unk; d Jul 1795 **RU:** Patriot, Signed a Legislative Petition in Alexandria **CEM:** Old Christ Church Episcopal; GPS 38.80625, -77.04718; 118 N Washington St; Alexandria City **GS:** N **SP:** no info **VI:** Burial permit issued 13 Jul 1792 **P:** N **BLW:** N **RG:** N **MK:** N **PH:** N **SS:** BB; S-Alexandria **BS:** 20 pg 153.

WETHERBEE, James; b unk; d 1781 **RU:** Soldier, Served fr MA, and died fr the Battle at Yorktown **CEM:** Yorktown Victory Monument Tablet; GPS 38.28350, -78.54150; Yorktown; York **GS:** U **SP:** No info **VI:** No further data **P:** unk **BLW:** unk **RG:** N **MK:** unk **PH:** unk **SS:** J-Yorktown Historian; SAR P-317025 **BS:** JLARC 74.

WHALEY, Zedekaih (Zadock); b unk; d 30 Nov 1782 **RU:** Commodore, US Navy, MD, was killed in Naval "Battle of the Barges" **CEM:** Scott Hall; GPS unk; Daugherty Rd, Onancock; Accomack **GS:** Y **SP:** no info **VI:** Son of William & Mary (Radcliffe) Whaley **P:** Y **BLW:** unk **RG:**N **MK:** Y SAR **PH:** unk **SS:** B DAR marker **BS:** 37 pg 276.

WHARTON, John Esq; b 25 Nov 1762; d 25 Feb 1811 **RU:** Private, Capt Wallace's Co, 3rd VA Regt, commanded by Col Geo Weeden, 8 Oct -7 Dec 1776 **CEM:** Wharton Family; GPS unk; Assawoman Creek; Accomack **GS:** Y **SP:** Mar (10 Jun 1784) Elizabeth Williams (24 May 1746-13 Nov 1831) d/o William & Margaret (-----) Williams **VI:** Died in Philadelphia and body moved to cem here **P:** unk **BLW:** unk **RG:** N **MK:** N **PH:** unk **SS:** AP roll **BS:** 145 Wharton; 196.

WHARTON, Samuel; b 27 Jul 1761; d 10 Dec 1841 **RU:** Soldier, Ent serv Spotsylvania Co 1777. Severely wounded by cannonball at siege of Yorktown **CEM:** Whartons; GPS 38.104730,-77.889537; ; Christopher Run; Louisa **GS:** U **SP:** Mar (8 Mar 1786 Spotsylvania Co) Letitia "Letty" Hutcherson d/o William & Sarah (-----) Hutcherson **VI:** Widow appl pen 16 Jun 1842 Louisa Co. age abt 74, and for increase in 1849 Louisa Co. She appl for BLW 1855. W6488. BLW #38832-160-55 **P:** Y **BLW:** Y **RG:** Y **MK:** unk **PH:** unk **SS:** K Vol 6 pg 106; CG Vol 3 pg 3764; SAR P-317181 **BS:** JLARC 4, 61; 196

WHEELER, Drummond; b 1727, Truro, Fairfax Co; d 1804 **RU:** Patriot, Paid personal Property Tax (Rev War Supply Tax) 1782 and 1783, Fairfax Co **CEM:** Wheeler-Greenville Family; GPS 38.795916, -77.502166; 7300 Old Compton Rd; Prince William **GS:** Y **SP:** Mar (5 Jun 1750 Fairfax Co) Jean Wesley (c1725-May 1799) **VI:** Son of Richard & Rebecca (Frizzell) Wheeler **P:** unk **BLW:** unk **RG:** Y **MK:** Y SAR bronze **PH:** unk **SS:** DV; SAR P-336355 **BS:** 190 by cem name.

WHEELER, John Sr; b c1746; d 3 May 1819 **RU:** Private, Served in Capt John Brent, Col Lawson Regt, Cont Line **CEM:** Wheeler-Pugh-Jennings; GPS unk; Off Rt 663 nr Bear Creek, down little dirt rd; Charlotte **GS:** U **SP:** Mar (aft 1765) Mary Trisdale (c1745-1804) **VI:** No further data **P:** unk **BLW:** unk **RG:** N **MK:** unk **PH:** unk **SS:** DAR A064914; JLARC Rpt App B-2 pg 27; C pg 278; CU 1806 **BS:** JLARC 118.

WHEELER, William; b unk; d Aug 1796 **RU:** Surgeon, Served as surgeon in Col Ebenezer's Regt of NY Artillery. Commissioned 4 Sep 1777, resigned 8 Jan 1779 **CEM:** Old Christ Church Episcopal; GPS 38.80625, -77.04718; 118 N Washington St; Alexandria City **GS:** N **SP:** No info **VI:** Burial permit issued 15 Aug 1796 **P:** unk **BLW:** unk **RG:** N **MK:** N **PH:** N **SS:** A pg 155 **BS:** 20 pg 153.

WHETSELL(WHETZEL)(WETZEL), Henry; b May 1758, Shenandoah Co; d 16 Apr 1839 **RU:** Private, Entered service Rockingham Co in Capt Isaac Lincoln's Co, Benjamin Harrison's VA Regt, served in battles at Williamsburg & Hot Water **CEM:** Whetzel Fam; GPS 38.613060, -78.799171; jct S Main St & Broadway Ave, Brocks Gap, Broadway; Rockingham **GS:** N **SP:** Mar (28 Dec 1773, Shenandoah Co) Elizabeth Rubleson **VI:** Son of George Henry Whetzel (1735-1816) & Sarah Catherine Wheatherholz (1730-1794); rec'd pen, 1832 # F-S7873 & R2547 **P:** Y **BLW:** N **RG:** Y **MK:** unk **PH:** N **SS:** K Vol 6 pg 110; DAR A123597; SAR P-317083 **BS:** 196.

WHETZEL, George "Henry", b 1735, Chester, Delaware Co, PA; d 1816, Fulks Run **RU:** Patriot, paid personal property tax, Rockingham Co, 1783 considered a supply tax for Rev War expenses **CEM:** Whetzel Fam; GPS 38.613060, -78.799171; jct S Main St & Broadway Ave, Brocks Gap, Broadway; Rockingham **GS:** N **SP:** Sarah Catherine Wheatherholz (1730-1794) **VI:** No further data **P:** N **BLW:** N **RG:** N **MK:** N **PH:** N **SS:** DV image 13 pdf, Rockingham Co 1783; **BS:** 19.

RU=Rank/Unit	CEM=Cemetery	GS=Gravestone	SP=Spousal Information
VI=Other Veteran Info	P=Pension	BLW=Bounty/Land Warrant	RG=Registered Grave
MK=SAR/DAR Marker	PH=Photo	SS=Service Source	BS=Burial Source

447

WHETZEL (WHITZEL), Martin; b 1708; d 1794 **RU**: Patriot, paid personal property tax, Rockingham Co, 1783 considered a supply tax for Rev War expenses **CEM**: Whetzel Fam; GPS 38.613060, -78.799171; jct S Main St & Broadway Ave, Brocks Gap, Broadway; Rockingham **GS**: N **SP**: Elizabeth Crommerston (1712-1807) **VI**: Son of Elias Whetzel (1683-1760) & Margaret Emrich (1693-1763) **P**: N **BLW**: N **RG**: N **MK**: N **PH**: N **SS**: DV image 13 pdf, Rockingham Co 1783; **BS**: 19.

WHIDDON, John; b 19 Sep 1730; d 14 May 1796 **RU**: Patriot, Gave material aid to cause **CEM**: Old Massenburgh; GPS unk; South Norfolk; Norfolk City **GS**: Y **SP**: Mary (-----) (c1740-13 Jan 1818) **VI**: No further data **P**: N **BLW**: N **RG**: N **MK**: N **PH**: unk **SS**: AL Ct Bk pg 10 **BS**: 63 pg 110.

WHITACRE, John III; b 1737, Makefield, Bucks Co, PA; d 1785 **RU**: Private, Served in 8th & 9th Cont Lines **CEM**: Goose Creek; GPS 39.11250, -77.69527; Rt 722, Lincoln; Loudoun **GS**: U **SP**: Mar (c1758 NJ) Keziah Taylor (1738-__) **VI**: Son of John II (1704-1768) & Naomi (Hulme) (1713-1789) Taylor. Moved with parents to VA 1761 **P**: unk **BLW**: unk **RG**: N **MK**: unk **PH**: unk **SS**: C pg 275; E pg 820 **BS**: 196.

WHITACRE (WHITAKER), George; b 1745 Bucks Co, PA; d 12 Sep 1785 **RU**: Patriot, Gave material aid to cause **CEM**: Goose Creek; GPS 39.11250, -77.69527; Rt 722, Lincoln; Loudoun **GS**: N **SP**: Mar (c1765) Ruth (-----) (1749-__) **VI**: No further data **P**: N **BLW**: N **RG**: Y **MK**: unk **PH**: N **SS**: DAR A124215; SAR P-317785 AL Ct Bk pg 5 **BS**: 196.

WHITAKER, James; b 1753, Buckingham Co; d 4 May 1842 **RU**: Private, Ent serv Buckingham Co and served in VA Line in Capts Winston's, Miller's and Moseley's Cos, Col Charles Fleming's Regt. Served at Siege of Yorktown **CEM**: Whitaker Family Farm; GPS unk; Not identified; Campbell **GS**: U **SP**: Mar (10 Mar 1791 Buckingham Co by Rev William Flowers) Susannah Beckham **VI**: Sol appl pen 14 Aug 1832 Campbell Co age 69. Widow appl pen 2 Jun 1843 Campbell Co age 74. W3482 **P**: Y **BLW**: unk **RG**: Y **MK**: N **PH**: unk **SS**: DAR A124219; J-NSSAR 2000 Reg; K Vol 6 pg 112; CG Vol 3 pg 3780; SAR P-317810 **BS**: JLARC 76.

WHITAKER, John; b unk; d Oct 14 1781 **RU**: Private, Served in Capt Aaron Ogden's Co, Lt Col Francis Barber's Battalion, NJ Cont Line. Died fr service at Yorktown **CEM**: Yorktown Victory Monument Tablet; GPS 38.28350, -78.54150; Yorktown; York **GS**: U **SP**: No info **VI**: No further data **P**: unk **BLW**: unk **RG**: Y **MK**: unk **PH**: unk **SS**: J-Yorktown Historian; DX pg 24; SAR P-317812 **BS**: JLARC 74.

WHITE, Alexander; b 1738; d 9 Oct 1804 **RU**: Patriot, Gave material aid to cause. Member of House of Delegates 1782-83 **CEM**: Woodville Estate; GPS unk; Winchester; Frederick **GS**: U **SP**: No info **VI**: Son of Robert (1689-1755) & Margaret (Hoge) (1700-1752) White. Delegate to state convention that considered adoption of US Constitution. President Washington appointed White to commission that laid out Washington DC and oversaw construction of first public buildings. Member of VA House of Delegates again 1799-1801 **P**: N **BLW**: N **RG**: N **MK**: unk **PH**: unk **SS**: AL Ct Bk pg 8, 17 Frederick Co **BS**: 196.

WHITE, Ambrose; b 1754, Caroline Co; d 2 Jun 1823 **RU**: First Lieutenant, Served in Caroline Co Militia **CEM**: Greenlawn; GPS 38.07030, -77.33830; Lakewood Rd, Bowling Green; Caroline **GS**: Y **SP**: Mar (Jan 1776) Ann Jones (1754 Caroline Co-22 Jun 1827) **VI**: New monument with DAR insignia was placed in 1971,that gives rank as Lieutenant of Militia **P**: unk **BLW**: unk **RG**: Y **MK**: Y DAR plaque **PH**: unk **SS**: DAR A124572; J-NSSAR 2000 Reg; SAR P-317987 **BS**: JLARC 76; 196.

WHITE, Benjamin; b 14 May 1760, Loudoun Co; d 1837 **RU**: Private, Served in Clark's Illinois Regt & possibly 13th & 15th Cont Lines **CEM**: Goose Creek; GPS 39.11250, -77.69527; GS 39.11294,-77.69588 Rt 722, Lincoln; Loudoun **GS**: Y **SP**: Mary (-----) **VI**: Son of Richard & Rebekah (Canthron) White **P**: unk **BLW**: unk **RG**: Y **MK**: N **PH**: Y **SS**: E pg 821; SAR bio rpt submitted 28 Feb 21 **BS**: 196.

WHITE, Isaac; b PA; d 1781 **RU**: Soldier, Served fr PA, and died fr the Battle at Yorktown **CEM**: Yorktown Victory Monument Tablet; GPS 38.28350, -78.54150; Yorktown; York **GS**: U **SP**: 1)Margaret Allison, 2) Charlotte Weitzel **VI**: No further data **P**: unk **BLW**: unk **RG**: Y **MK**: unk **PH**: unk **SS**: J-Yorktown Historian; SAR P-318191 **BS**: JLARC 74

WHITE, Jacob; b 1765; d 2 Jun 1832 **RU**: Captain, Ent serv 1778 in VA Line. Ent serv again 1781 in "VA Co" and served in Battle of Guilford CH **CEM**: White Family; GPS 37.28400, -79.24130, GS

RU=Rank/Unit	CEM=Cemetery	GS=Gravestone	SP=Spousal Information
VI=Other Veteran Info	P=Pension	BLW=Bounty/Land Warrant	RG=Registered Grave
MK=SAR/DAR Marker	PH=Photo	SS=Service Source	BS=Burial Source

448

37.2840,-79.2413; Nr Charlemont, jct 638 & 637; Bedford **GS:** Y **SP:** Mar (1775) Mary Allen (__-14 Dec 1840). Widow mar 2nd to John Lafoy/Lafo/Lafoe in 1804 or 1805 **VI:** Served in Siege of '96 (District, SC). Widow granted pen 1849 W8076 **P:** Y **BLW:** unk **RG:** Y **MK:** unk **PH:** Yes **SS:** J- DAR Hatcher; K Vol 6 pg 115; CG Vol 3 pg 3789; SAR P-318212 **BS:** JLARC 2.

WHITE, James; b 16 Sep 1765, d 20 Sep 1826 **RU:** Corporal, served Lees Legion for 3 yrs **CEM:** Ketoctin Baptist Church; GPS 39.15746, -77.74870; Ketoctin Church Rd, Purcellville; Loudoun **GS** Unk **SP:** Mary Potts (__-1819) **VI:** Recd BLW of 100 acres for Frankfort KY but no evidence he moved there Records burned in DC fire 1800 **P:** Yes **BLW:** Yes **RG:** Y **MK:** SAR monument **PH:** N **SS:** C Part IV, pg 114; E pg 821; Fold3 Ltr fr Commisioner; CG pg 3789; SAR P-318215 **BS** 242; 196.

WHITE, John; b Mar 1756, Kingston Parish, Gloucester Co; d 12 Jun 1834 **RU:** 2nd LT, Enl serv 1776 VA Line. Was in Gloucester Co Militia. Served a six month tour at Gwynn's Island when Lord Dunmore invaded; was involved in ousting Dunmore fr VA in 1776. In 1781 served under Capt Hungerford & Col Mercer. Was in Cont Army at Battle of Sewell's Old Field, nr Tyndall's Point (now Gloucester Point). Left service after Siege of Yorktown in Oct 1781, however commissioned 2nd Lt May 1782 in Capt Edmund Jones Co **CEM:** White Family (Whitehaven); GPS unk; 160 Pine View Dr; Mathews **GS:** U **SP:** Mar (26 Mar 1791 Norfolk by Minister James McBride, Church of England) Elizabeth Davenport (27 Nov 1771 Norfolk-1843) d/o Capt William (20 Sep 1746-5 July 1787) & Mary (Hunley) (1752-1843) Davenport. **VI:** Son of William & Elizabeth (Bartlett) White. Sol appl pen 13 Aug 1832 Mathews Co. Widow appl there 13 Aug 1838 age 66. W6476 **P:** Y **BLW:** unk **RG:Y MK:** unk **PH:** unk **SS:** E pg 822; K Vol 6 pg SAR P-318258 **BS.**

WHITE, Joseph; b 1755, Amelia Co; d 26 Mar 1844 **RU:** Private, Served in Capt Thomas Buford's Co at Battle of Point Pleasant, Oct 1774; also later in Capts John Trigg's Co, Bedford Co Militia **CEM:** White Family; GPS unk; Stewartsville; Bedford **GS:** U **SP:** Mar (14 Mar 1826, Bedford Co) Penalope Angel (1771-aft 1866) **VI:** He appl pen 11 Sep 1822 and d in Otterville, Bedford Co. She appl pen 18 Jun 1853 #W11809; Widow appl BLW 3 Apr 1855 # 26168-160-55 **P:** Y **BLW:** Y **RG:** Y **MK:** unk **PH:** unk **SS:** DAR A125221; CG pg 3793; DD; Z pg 125; SAR P-318367 **BS:** 196.

WHITE, Josiah (Josias); b 1 Feb 1760; d 7 Sep 1820 **RU:** Patriot, VA, gave material to cause **CEM:** Ketoctin Baptist; GPS 39.15746, -77.74870; Ketoctin Church Rd, Purcellville; Loudoun **GS:** Y **SP:** No info **VI:** No further data **P:** N **BLW:** N **RG:Y MK:** SAR Monument **PH:** unk **SS:** D, Vol 2, pg 612; SAR P-340174 **BS:** 25, pg 338.

WHITE, Michael; b 1750; d 2 Apr 1832 **RU:** Sergeant/Patriot, 6th & 10th VA Regts; served at Valley Forge, PA. Paid supply tax 1783 **CEM:** St John's Lutheran; GPS 39.15310, -78.36520; 3623 Buck Mountain Rd, Hayfield; Frederick **GS:** Y **SP:** Mar (9 Sep 1783) Elizabeth Fry (1765-1817) **VI:** Son of Michael & Catherine (-----) White. DAR plaque on grave site **P:** unk **BLW:** unk **RG:** Y **MK:** Y DAR plaque **PH:** unk **SS:** DAR A208022; SAR P-335841; E pg 822; DD **BS:** 196.

WHITE, Robert; b c1734; d 5 Aug 1815 **RU:** Lieutenant, Served in 2nd, 5th, 6th, 9th, 11th, 15th Cont Lines **CEM:** White Family; GPS unk; Rt 615; Frederick **GS:** Y **SP:** Mar (9 Sep 1783 Frederick Co by John Montgomery) Elizabeth Fry **VI:** Drew pension Frederick Co **P:** Y **BLW:** unk **RG:** N **MK:** N **PH:** unk **SS:** E pg 822-3 **BS:** 59 pg 350.

WHITE, Robert; b c1759; d 2 Nov 1831 **RU:** Lieutenant Colonel, Served in VA Line. Ent serv 20 Jan 1775 for one yr under Hugh Stephenson. Promoted to Lt in Capt Joseph Mitchell's Co, 12th VA Regt 1776. Severely wounded Jun 1777 which disqualified him fr further service. Promoted to Lt Col 4 Aug 1779, Frederick Co Militia **CEM:** Mt Hebron; GPS 39.10916, -78.09497; 305 E Boscawen St; Winchester City **GS:** Y **SP:** unk **VI:** Recd BLW #1678-300. Was judge after war. Pensioned 1828 Frederick Co #S7893. Died in Frederick Co abt age 72. Originally bur in Presbyterian cem next to German Reformed Cem in Mt Hebron. Moved to present location 1912 with 71 other people. S. 7,893 **P:** Y **BLW:** Y **RG:** Y **MK** Y SAR monument **PH:** Y **SS:** A pg 551; E pg 822; K Vol 6 pg 120-1; CG Vol 3 pg 3795; SAR P-318462 **BS:** JLARC 1, 4, 47.

WHITE, Thomas; b 20 May 1760; d 21 Mar or 23 Apr 1825 **RU:** Captain, Ent serv Fauquier Co 1776 in 1st VA Regt at age 17 Was at Seige of Yorktown, **CEM:** Spring Grove; GPS 39.10916, -78.09970; Rockville; Hanover **GS:** N **SP:** 1) Elizabeth Cross 2) mar (Feb 1783) Elizabeth Blackwell (c1763-1842)

RU=Rank/Unit	CEM=Cemetery	GS=Gravestone	SP=Spousal Information
VI=Other Veteran Info	P=Pension	BLW=Bounty/Land Warrant	RG=Registered Grave
MK=SAR/DAR Marker	PH=Photo	SS=Service Source	BS=Burial Source

449

VI: Member of House of Delegates and magistrate for many yrs. Later held rank of Brigadier-General. Justice of Peace. Obit in Richmond Enquirer 23 Apr 1825 pg 3 says "died at his seat, Spring Grove, Hanover Co, on 21st…" Died at "Spring Grove" Hanover Co. Widow pensioned 1840 age 77 but rejected due to insufficient proof of service. R11409 **P:** N **BLW:** unk **RG:** N **MK:** N **PH:** N **SS:** G pg 774; K Vol 6 pg 122 **BS:** 31 vol 1 pg 21.

WHITE, William; b 1 Jun 1762, Caroline Co; d Oct 1781 **RU:** Captain, Served in VA Line. Ent serv 1775 as Sgt, later promoted to Lt, 1st VA Regt. A person this name died fr battle at Yorktown believed to be him **CEM:** Yorktown Victory Monument Tablet; GPS 38.28350, -78.54150; Yorktown; York **GS:** U **SP:** Agnes Cardwell **VI:** Widow age 71 appl pen 19 Jan 1838 Hanover Co & appl BLW 24 Mar 1855. W4099. BLW #3190-160-55 to widow, BLW #2213-200 to heirs **P:** Y **BLW:** Y **RG:** Y **MK:** unk **PH:** unk **SS:** J-Yorktown Historian; K Vol 6 pg 124; CG Vol 3 pg 3801; SAR P-318566 **BS:** JLARC 74.

WHITING, James; b unk; d 1781 **RU:** Soldier, Served fr MA, and died fr the Battle at Yorktown **CEM:** Yorktown Victory Monument Tablet; GPS 38.28350, -78.54150; Yorktown; York **GS:** U **SP:** No info **VI:** No further data **P:** unk **BLW:** unk **RG:** Y **MK:** unk **PH:** unk **SS:** J-Yorktown Historian; SAR P-318832 **BS:** JLARC 74.

WHITNEY, Silas; b unk; d 1781 **RU:** Soldier, Served fr MA, and died fr the Battle at Yorktown **CEM:** Yorktown Victory Monument Tablet; GPS 38.28350, -78.54150; Yorktown; York **GS:** U **SP:** No info **VI:** No further data **P:** unk **BLW:** unk **RG:** Y **MK:** unk **PH:** unk **SS:** J-Yorktown Historian; SAR P-319209 **BS:** JLARC 74.

WHITTEN, Thomas, Jr; b 7 Jan 1759, Fredericktown, Prince George Co, MD, d 15 Mar 1830 **RU:** Scout,Capt James Maxwell's & James Robertson's Cos, Augusta Co, Militian **CEM:** Whitten family; GPS; Not determined; Paintick; Tazewell **GS:** Unk **SP:** Rebecca Cecil **VI:** (See Thomas Witten, Jr with similar burial data with different birth and death dates & same service source, thus perhaps same person) **P:** N **BLW:** N **RG:** Y **MK:** N **PH:** N **SS:** BW-pgs 27,56; DAR A125451; SAR P-323120 **BS:** PRS.

WHITTEN, Thomas Sr; b 10 Sep 1719, Prince George Co, MD; d 1794 **RU:** Patriot, Signed Oath of Allegiance 30 Sep 1777. Also was Commissioner for Supply Distribution, Montgomery Co **CEM:** Maplewood; GPS 37.12803, -81.52104; nr Jct Rts 19, 460, & 16 Tazewell Ave; Tazewell **GS:** U **SP:** Mar (1742 MD) Elizabeth Cecil (15 Mar 1720-__) **VI:** No further data **P:** N **BLW:** N **RG:** N **MK:** unk **PH:** unk **SS:** DAR A125475; D Vol 2 pg 609; G pg 209 **BS:** 196.

WHITWORTH, Thomas; b 26 Jun 1726, King William Co; d 4 Jul 1801 **RU:** Patriot, Gave material aid to cause **CEM:** Whitworth; GPS unk; Paineville; Amelia **GS:** N **SP:** Elizabeth Southerland (1726-1819) **VI:** Died in Lunenburg Co **P:** N **BLW:** N **RG:** N **MK:** unk **PH:** N **SS:** AL Ct Bk 1 pg 10 in Amelia Co **BS:** 196.

WIATT, John E.; b 1740, Gloucester Co; d Mar 1827 **RU:** Colonel/Patriot, served in 3rd & 4th VA Regt, was in Battle of Guilford CH; gave material aid to cause **CEM:** Wiatt-Norvell; GPS unk; City Farm Quadrant; Campbell **GS:** U **SP:** Mar (c1794 Buckingham Co) Wilhelmina Jordan (1750, Buckingham Co-1836 Lynchburg) d/o Samuel & Judith (Scott) Jordan **VI:** Find a Grave.com indicates he is bur in the Radchiffe cem in Lynchburg City & source DD indicates he was b 1750 in Spotsylvania Co and d in Lynchburg **P:** unk **BLW:** unk **RG:** Y **MK:** N **PH:** unk **SS:** AL Cert Amherst Co; AP Fold3 Serv card; SAR P-319426 **BS:** JLARC 36; 196.

WIATT, John; b 1732; d 5 Jan 1805 **RU:** Patriot, paid personal property tax Gloucester Co, considered to be a supply tax for Rev War expenses **CEM:** Toddsbury Plantation; GPS not determined; on North River, Elmington; Gloucester **GS:** N gravestone moved to undetermind loc **SP:** Mary Todd (5 Feb 1725-9 Nov 1794), d/o Cristopher Todd & Elizabeth Mason **VI:** No further data **P:** N **BLW:** N **RG:** N **MK:** N **PH:** N **SS:** DV1783B, image 06, pdf **BS:** 196.

WIATT, Thomas; b unk; d 1828 **RU:** Captain, Commanded a Co King & Queen Co Militia **CEM:** Avoca; GPS unk; Altavista; Campbell **GS:** U **SP:** Mary (18 May 1793 Campbell Co (bond)) Sarah/Sally Miller d/o John & (-----) Miller **VI:** No further data **P:** unk **BLW:** unk **RG:** Y **MK:** N **PH:** unk **SS:** SAR P-319429 **BS:** JLARC 36.

WIATT, William; b c1752, poss Liverpool. Eng; d 16 Apr 1800 **RU:** Patriot, Gave the use of a stable for the cause **CEM:** Masonic Cemetery; GPS 38.30198, -77.46142; 900 Charles St; Fredericksburg City

---

RU=Rank/Unit
VI=Other Veteran Info
MK=SAR/DAR Marker

CEM=Cemetery
P=Pension
PH=Photo

GS=Gravestone
BLW=Bounty/Land Warrant
SS=Service Source

SP=Spousal Information
RG=Registered Grave
BS=Burial Source

450

GS: Y **SP:** Mar Fredericksburg, 11 Jan 1776, Catherine Julian (c1736-27 May 1792), d/o Charles & Phoebe Julian **VI:** Was postmaster Fredericksburg **P:** N **BLW:** N **RG:** N **MK:** Y SAR plaque **PH:** unk **SS:** D pg 861 **BS:** 08 vol 3 pg 299.

WILBERGER, Mathias; b MD, d 10 Jun 1818 **RU:** Private, Served in undetermined unit in MD perhaps under surname of Weberger or Wheelberger **CEM:** Friedens Church; GPS: 38.3484604,-78.8761376; 3960 Friedens Church Rd, Mt Crawford; Rockingham **GS:** Yes **SP:** Margaretha (-----) **VI:** No further data **P:** N **BLW:** N **RG:** N **MK:** N **PH:** N **SS:** SAR member application **BS:** 32.

WICKLIFF(E) (WYCLIFFE), Arrington (Aaron); b c1750; d 1820 **RU:** Private, Served in 2nd VA Regt 3 yrs under Capt Davis & Lt Tyler in 8th Regt at Baltimore. Was in Battles of Brandywine, Germantown, Monmouth. Believed to have served under Gen Daniel Morgan in 1776 with brothers **CEM:** Wickliff Family; GPS 38.46243, -77.24409; Behind 13220 Yates Ford Rd, Clifton; Fairfax **GS:** Y **SP:** Catherine Davis **VI:** DAR gr marker in Cem and Gov't Gr Stone **P:** unk **BLW:** unk **RG:** Y **MK:** Y DAR **PH:** unk **SS:** AK; SAR P-319478 **BS:** JLARC 1, 2, 13, 14, 27.

WICKLIFF(E) (WYCLIFFE), Moses; b unk; d 13 Feb 1796 **RU:** Private, Served in 2nd VA Regt 3 yrs under Capt Davis & Lt Tyler in 8th Regt at Baltimore. Was in Battles of Brandywine, Germantown, Monmouth. Believed to have served under Gen Daniel Morgan in 1776 with brothers **CEM:** Wickliff Family; GPS 38.46243, -77.24409; Behind 13220 Yates Ford Rd, Clifton; Fairfax **GS:** Y **SP:** No info **VI:** DAR gr marker in cem and Gov't gr stone **P:** unk **BLW:** unk **RG:** Y **MK:** Y DAR **PH:** Y **SS:** AK' SAR P-319479 **BS:** JLARC 1,2,13, 14, 27.

WIDENER, Michael; b 1 Jun 1758, Germany, Rockingham Co; d 12 Apr 1843 **RU:** Private, Served in Capt Craven's & Capt Lincoln's companies VA militia & VA Line **CEM:** Pleasant View; GPS 36.68670, -81.74970; Vic jct Rts 801 & 605, Glade Spring; Washington **GS:** U **SP:** Mar (13 Jan 1823-1825, Washington Co) Elizabeth Callahan **VI:** Son of John & Elizabeth (Worrell) Widner. Soldier appl pen 26 Nov 1832, widow appl pen 28 Jun 1853 W8303. Widow appl BLW in 1855 # 26617-160-55 **P:** Y **BLW:** Y **RG:** Y**MK:** Y SAR granite & DAR **PH:** unk **SS:** VA Bulletin fall 2000; CG pg 3821; DAR A202077 SAR P-319508 **BS:** 196.

WIDENER, Samuel; b unk; d 1833 **RU:** Sergeant, Served in Capt Thomas Church Co, Col Wayne's PA Battalion 1776 **CEM:** Widener's Valley; GPS unk; Cem #239 in Source 80; Washington **GS:** U **SP:** No info **VI:** DAR marker placed by Ft Chiswell Chapt at foot of crude native stone **P:** unk **BLW:** unk **RG:** Y **MK:** Y **PH:** unk **SS:** SAR P-319509; A pg 196 **BS:** JLARC 80.

WIGGINTON, John; b c1758, Prince William Co; d 19 Aug 1843 **RU:** Private, Served in Cont Line in Capt George Hardy's Co, Lee's Partison Legion. Ent serv again Prince William Co 1780 **CEM:** Wigginton Family; GPS unk; Off Rt 7, Huddleston; Bedford **GS:** Y **SP:** Mar (6 Sep 1787 Bedford Co) Margaret McGeorge (c1764 Hanover Co-17 Oct 1851) **VI:** Sol appl pen 14 Jun 1828 Bedford Co. Widow appl pen 29 Nov 1843 Bedford Co. Patriot Pensioned 14 Jul 1828. Widow recd pension of $100 per yr. W6547. He perhaps is the person this name that drew BLW # 12673-100-14, 14 Jul 1792 **P:** Y **BLW:** unk **RG:** Y **MK:** N **PH:** unk **SS:** DAR Ancestor #A126013; SAR Ancestor #P-319589; J-NSSAR 2000 Reg; K Vol 6 pg 135; CG Vol 3 pg 3823, 3825; SAR P-319589 **BS:** JLARC 4, 36, 76.

WIGGINTON, John Sr; b 1741; d 27 Apr 1825 **RU:** Patriot, Gave material aid to cause. Served as Tax Assessor 1783 **CEM:** Wigginton; GPS unk; Rt 29, Lakota; Culpeper **GS:** Y **SP:** Elizabeth Botts (__-15 Jul 1824) **VI:** No further data **P:** N **BLW:** N **RG:** Y **MK:** N **PH:** unk **SS:** D Vol 1 pg 267; E pg 826; SAR P-319588 **BS:** 29, pg 28; 33.

WILCOX, John; b unk; d 1781 **RU:** Soldier, Served fr NY, and killed in the battle at Yorktown **CEM:** Yorktown Victory Monument Tablet; GPS 38.28350, -78.54150; Yorktown; York **GS:** U **SP:** No info **VI:** No further data **P:** unk **BLW:** unk **RG:**Y **MK:** unk **PH:** unk **SS:** J-Yorktown Historian; SAR P-319811 **BS:** JLARC 74.

WILHOITE (WILHOIT), Daniel W;; b c1744, Orange Co; d 1797 **RU:** Private?, Listed in Culpeper Classes 1781, VA Militia **CEM:** Wilhoite Family; GPS unk; Hebron Valley; Madison **GS:** N **SP:** Mary Blankenbeckler (c1747-__) d/o Michael & Elizabeth Barbara (Gaar) Blankenbaker **VI:** Son of John & Margaret (Weaver) Wilhoit **P:** unk **BLW:** unk **RG:** Y **MK:** N **PH:** N **SS:** See BS 04; SAR P-320112 **BS:** 04.

RU=Rank/Unit	CEM=Cemetery	GS=Gravestone	SP=Spousal Information
VI=Other Veteran Info	P=Pension	BLW=Bounty/Land Warrant	RG=Registered Grave
MK=SAR/DAR Marker	PH=Photo	SS=Service Source	BS=Burial Source

451

WILHOITE (WILHOIT), John; b c1745, Orange Co; d 1820 **RU:** Private, Listed in Culpeper Classes 1781, VA Militia **CEM:** Wilhoite Family; GPS unk; Hebron Valley; Madison **GS:** N **SP:** Mary Fishback (___-1838 Madison Co) d/o Harman & Kathrina (-----) Fishback **VI:** Son of John & Margaret (Weaver) Wilhoit **P:** unk **BLW:** unk **RG:** N **MK:** N **PH:** N **SS:** See BS 29 pg 41 **BS:** 04.

WILKES, Burwell, b 4 Jun 1757, d 31 Mar 1815 **RU:** Sergeant, in 11th VA Regt Cont Line, in Hillsborough, NC in Nov 1779. As Corporal was in Capt James Mason's Co, Major Gustavius B Wallace's 15th Regt Cont Line payroll of March 1778 **CEM:** Wilkes Family; GPS 36.755721,-77.924678.; loc on Grandy Rd (Rt 644) nr Charlie Hope; Brunswick **GS:** Yes **SP:** Mar 3 Dec 1787, Elizabeth Gunn (bef1774-1846) as widow mar Major Philip Claiborne **VI:** No further data **P:** N **BLW:** N **RG:** N **MK:** N **PH:** N **SS:** Cl: Payroll record **BS:** http://www.brunswickcemeteries.org/html/Wilkes.htm#1.

WILKES, James; b Unk; d 15 Apr 1778 **RU:** Private Capt David Arrell's Co, Lt Col William Heths, 3rd VA Regt, 1 Mar 1778 **CEM:** Rev War Court House Plaque; GPS not determined; 4110 Chain Bridge Rd; Fairfax **GS:** Memorialized on plaque 2017 by Geo Washington Chapter, VASSAR **SP** No info **VI:** died in service **P:** N **BLW:** N **RG:** N **MK:** N **PH:** N **SS:** A pgs 277, 278; E pg 828; EP sources: **BS:** None.

WILKES, Minor, Jr; b Jul 1761, d Jul 1801 **RU:** Private, Militia, Lunenburg Co **CEM:** Wilkes Family Farm; GPS Not determined; loc about 2 miles east of Victoria, on a 500 acre tract of land in the south fork of Big Hounds Creek; Lunenburg **GS:** N **SP:**mar 1) Margaret White (c1786-1790), d/o Carter White & Margaret Wynne 2) mar (13 Jan 1791) Phoebe White, d/o Carter White & Margaret Wynne **VI:** Son of Reverand Minor Wilkes (1737, New Kent Co-1811) & Phebe Yancey Stone **P:** N **BLW:** N **RG:** N **MK:** N **PH:** N **SS:**DAR A125505 cites Lib of VA Audited Account 1783-1784 pg 606 Militia list; SAR P-320149 **BS:** 196.

WILKES, Minor, Sr; b 1737, New Kent Co, d Victoria, Lunenburg Co **RU:** Patriot Paid personal Property Tax (Rev War Supply Tax) 1782, Lunenburg Co **CEM:** Wilkes Family Farm; GPS Not determined; loc about 2 miles east of Victoria, on a 500 acre tract of land in the south fork of Big Hounds Creek; Lunenburg **GS:** N **SP:** 1) mar (1758, Lunenburg Co) Phoebe Yancy Stone (___-1785), d/o Richard Stone & Mary Yancey of Cumberland Co Parish, 2) mar (5 May 1786) Susannah Hazelwood (___-c1790), d/o John Hazelwood & Nancy Cole. 3) 3 Dec 1796, Nancy Ann Tisdale **VI:** No further data **P:** N **BLW:** N **RG:** N **MK:** N **PH:** N **SS:** DV 1782 Per Property Tax #12 pdf.

WILKINS, Willis; b 1 Feb 1757; d 4 Apr 1815 **RU:** Patriot, Gave material aid to cause **CEM:** Deer Crossing; GPS unk; Adjacent to 2017 Coral Ivy Ln; Chesapeake City **GS:** Y **SP:** No info **VI:** Was Capt of the Sliver Greys fr Deep Creek during War of 1812 **P:** N **BLW:** N **RG:** Y **MK:** N **PH:** N **SS:** H Public Servant; SAR P-320230 **BS:** 75 Portsmouth; 196.

WILKINSON, John; b 8 Feb 1757, Sussex Co; d 23 Jan 1823 **RU:** Private, Served in 4th Co, 3rd VA Regt, Baylor's Dragoons **CEM:** Salem Methodist; GPS unk; 19312 Templeton Rd; Prince George **GS:** Y **SP:** Martha "Patsey" Rives (1767 Sussex Co-1829) **VI:** Gov't Gr Stone **P:** N **BLW:** unk **RG:** N **MK:** N **PH:** unk **SS:** JLARC 116 **BS:** JLARC 116; 196.

WILKINSON, John; b 22 Mar 1761(Albemarle Parish birth registry), d 3 Jan 1823 **RU:** Private, Served in an artillery unit, VA Cont Line. A person this name,'perhaps him, was a Boatswain on the "Tartar" and also in the 4th Co, 3rd VA Regt Baylor's Dragoons **CEM:** Wilkinson Farm; GPS: 36.9483903, -77.4076197, vic jct Rts 40 & 618; Sussex **GS:** No **SP:** Martha "Patsy" Rives (22 Feb 1767-1829), d/o George & Sarah (Eldridge) of Sussex.**VI:** Son of William Wilkinson & Elizabeth (-----). Rec'd 200 acres bountyland,12 Dec 1785 **P:** N **BLW:** Y **RG:** N **MK:** N **PH:** N **SS:** A pg 278; E pg 829; F pg 82; **BS:** 196.

WILKINSON, Thomas; b unk; d Jun 1790 **RU:** Private, Served in15th VA Regt **CEM:** Old Christ Church Episcopal; GPS 38.80625, -77.04718; 118 N Washington St; Alexandria City **GS:** N **SP:** Sarah (-----);**VI:** Burial permit issued 4 Jun 1790. Widow pensioned file # not determined **P:** Y **BLW:** unk **RG:** N **MK:** N **PH:** N **SS:** G pg 722 **BS:** 20 pg 154.

WILKINSON, William; b 1745; d 1823 **RU:** Private, Served in VA Line, 6th VA Regt. Ent serv Greensville Co. Served in Illinois **CEM:** Wilkinson Family; GPS unk; Rt 610, Gold Hill; Buckingham **GS:** Y **SP:** No info **VI:** Plaque on remnants of old stone **P:** unk **BLW:** unk **RG:** Y **MK:** Y SAR plaque **PH:** unk **SS:** B; E pg 829; CG Vol 3 pg 3841; SAR P-320287; BY **BS:** JLARC 59; 196.

WILKISON, William Sr; b Jun 1766; d 11 Mar 1857 **RU:** Private?, Served in a VA unit in Illinois. Also in MD militia between 1 Aug 1780 to 1 Jan 1782 **CEM:** North Fork Baptist; GPS 39.06014, -77.68509;

RU=Rank/Unit	CEM=Cemetery	GS=Gravestone	SP=Spousal Information
VI=Other Veteran Info	P=Pension	BLW=Bounty/Land Warrant	RG=Registered Grave
MK=SAR/DAR Marker	PH=Photo	SS=Service Source	BS=Burial Source

452

38130 North Folk Rd, North Fork; Loudoun **GS**: Y **SP**: Sarah Fox **VI**: The MD service may be for a person named Wilkerson buried in this cemetery **P**: unk **BLW**: unk **RG**: Y **MK**: N **PH**: unk **SS**: E pg 829; DAR A125494; SAR P-331413 **BS**: 25, pg 341.

WILKS, Samuel; b 24 Oct 1761, Loudoun Co; d 1 Jul 1837 **RU**: Soldier, Ent Serv Bedford Co 1780-1781 in VA Line **CEM**: Wilks Family; GPS unk; Nr Leftwich Church; Bedford City **GS**: U **SP**: 1) Elizabeth (-----) 2) Mar (11 Oct 1826 Bedford Co by Rev William Leftwich) Margaret Witt (c1785 or c1789-before 1 Nov 1858) **VI**: Sol appl pen 28 Mar 1833 Bedford Co. Widow appl pen 21 Jan 1854 age 65 (in 1857 said she was 72.) R11553 **P**: Y **BLW**: unk **RG**: Y **MK**: N **PH**: unk **SS**: SAR P-320297; K Vol 6 pg 139; CG Vol 3 pg 3841 **BS**: JLARC 4, 36.

WILLIAMS, David, Sr; b 1730 PA, d Mar 1789 **RU**: Patriot, Gave material aid to cause, Loudoun Co **CEM**: Old Potts; GPS 39.19455,-77.76157; loc vic Shannondale Rd and Edgegrove Rd, Hillsboro; Loudoun **GS**: Unk **SP**: Anne (__) (1730, PA-1805) **VI**: Likely son of William Williams, Sr of Frederick Co **P**: N **BLW**: N **RG**: N **MK**: N **PH**: N **SS**: AL Comm Bk III, pg 334, Ct Bk pg 11, Loudoun Co **BS**: 196

WILLIAMS, Edward, b Unk; d 1 Dec 1777 **RU**: Sergeant, Col William Grayson's Regt 1778 **CEM**: Rev War Court House Plaque; GPS not determined; 4110 Chain Bridge Rd; Fairfax **GS**: Memorialized on plaque 2017 by Geo Washington Chapter, VASSAR **SP**: No info **VI**: Died in service **P**: N **BLW**: N **RG**: N **MK**: N **PH**: N **SS**: E pg 830 **BS**: None.

WILLIAMS, James; b 1758, "Cedar Farm" Culpeper Co; d 22 Mar 1822 **RU**: Captain, Was 2nd Lt 10th VA Regt Dec 1776; 1st Lt 18 Mar 1777; and Capt 2 Jan 1778, Regt 6th VA. Appointed Capt 19 Sep 1778 & served to close of war. Served also in 8th and 10th VA Regt **CEM**: Williams Family, "Soldier's Rest Farm"; GPS unk; Rt 620; Orange **GS**: Y **SP**: 1) Eleanor Green 2) Elizabeth Bruce (4 Feb 1777 "Soldier's Rest" Orange Co-1823 Orange Co) d/o Charles & Frances (Stubblefield) Bruce. She mar (3 Jun 1795) James Williams as his second wife. She is bur at Soldiers Rest Plantation Grounds, Orange Co. **VI**: Son of William & Lucy (Clayton) Williams. Was an original member of the Society of the Cincinatti. Served as a Maj General of Miltia in War of 1812. Recd BLW 2 Oct 1807 of 5054 acres. Died at "Soldier's Rest" Orange Co **P**: unk **BLW**: Y **RG**: Y **MK**: unk **PH**: unk **SS**: E pg 83; CG Vol 3 pg 3857; SAR P-320777 **BS**: JLARC 1, 98.

WILLIAMS, James; b 3 May 1763, Augusta Co d 21 Jul 1818 **RU**: Captain/Patriot, Served in Cont Line over 7 years; Gave material aid to cause **CEM**: Blandford; GPS 37.22433, -77.38604; 319 S Crater Rd; Petersburg City **GS**: Y **SP**: Kiziah Wilson **VI**: Member VA Society of Cincinnati as Captain **P**: Y **BLW**: Y **RG**: Y **MK**: Y SAR monument **PH**: Y **SS**: E pg 831; G pg 407, 676, 714, 879, 904; N pg 776 AL Comm Bk IV pg 256 Prince George Co; SAR P-335467 **BS**: 196.

WILLIAMS, James; b unk; d 1781 **RU**: Sergeant, Served fr MA, and died fr the Battle at Yorktown **CEM**: Yorktown Victory Monument Tablet; GPS 38.28350, -78.54150; Yorktown; York **GS**: U **SP**: No info **VI**: No further data **P**: unk **BLW**: unk **RG**: Y **MK**: unk **PH**: unk **SS**: J-Yorktown Historian; SAR P-320780 **BS**: JLARC 74.

WILLIAMS, James Mastin; b 23 Sept 1763, Pittsylvania Co (then Hallifax); d 12 Jan 1838 **RU**: Private, Ent serv PA 1781 for brother John Williams. Served at Battle of Guilford CH, Feb 1781. Discharged Rockingham Co, NC. Reinlisted for brother in Capt William Dix's Co, under Col Nathaniel Cocke, Gen Stephens Brigade. Discharged Mar 1781 at Ramsey's Mill, Deep River. Guarded British prisoners under Capt Morton **CEM**: Williams Family; GPS unk; SR 698 Cliff Hetzel Farm, Pickway; Pittsylvania **GS**: Y **SP**: Mar (2 Dec 1784) Wilmouth or Wilmoth (-----), d/o (-----) & Catharine Walker (Oct 1768-__) She was living in PA in 1845 & 1849. **VI**: Sol appl pen 6 Sep 1832, Pittsylvania Co. Widow appl pen 14 Oct 1840 Pittsylvania Co. W6505 **P**: Y **BLW**: unk **RG**: Y **MK**: unk **PH**: unk **SS**: J-NSSAR 2000 Reg; K Vol 6 pg 146; CG Vol 3 pg 3857; SAR P-320808 **BS**: 174; JLARC 76.

WILLIAMS, John; b 1747 Studley, Hanover Co; d 30 Apr 1795 **RU**: Patriot, Gave material aid to cause **CEM**: Williams-Knight Family; GPS unk; Vic jct Rt 623 & Eubanks Rd; Lunenberg **GS**: U **SP**: Mar (4 Jan 1768 Charlotte Co) Frances Hughes **VI**: Son of Joseph (1720-1792) & Henrietta (Jouett) Williams (1727-1778). One of earliest Baptist ministers of Lunenberg, Charlotte and Mecklenberg. He and father founded Meherrin Baptist Church when no other Baptist church existed in these counties. Died at Ft Mitchell, Lunenberg Co **P**: N **BLW**: N **RG**: Y **MK**: unk **PH**: unk **SS**: AK Ct Bk pg 25 Lunenburg Co; SAR P-320863 **BS**: 19. **(WILLIAMS**, John See Appendix G Addenda)

RU=Rank/Unit	CEM=Cemetery	GS=Gravestone	SP=Spousal Information
VI=Other Veteran Info	P=Pension	BLW=Bounty/Land Warrant	RG=Registered Grave
MK=SAR/DAR Marker	PH=Photo	SS=Service Source	BS=Burial Source

453

WILLIAMS, John; b 24 Aug 1763, Stafford County, d 29 Sep 1812, Camp New Hope, FL **RU:** Navy Pilot, also served as Landsman **CEM:** Arlington National Cem; GPS 38.88377, -778.96535; Arlington City; Arlington **GS:** Yes Section 1, site 158 **SP:** No spousal data **VI:** Stone inscription indicates was killed as Captain in Marine Corps while serving gallantly on a patrol against Indians in Florida during War of 1812 **P:** N **BLW:** N **RG:** N **MK:** N **PH:** N **SS:** BE pg 75; Fold3 Naval serv index card **BS:** 196.

WILLIAMS, Joseph Adams b 1748; d Aft 29 Jun 1829 **RU:** Patriot, Gave beef to cause **CEM:** Morgan Family; GPS 36.76690, -81.43750; 1.5 mi fr Teas on private rd beyond Rt 601; Smyth **GS:** Y **SP:** Catherine Edwards (1751-1823) **VI:** No further data **P:** N **BLW:** N **RG:** Y **MK:** N **PH:** unk **SS:** AS SAR regis; D Vol 2 pg 599; DAR A126274; SAR P-320932 **BS:** SAR PRS; 196.

WILLIAMS, Richard; b 1730, Bucks Co, PA; d Aft 9 May 1797 **RU:** Patriot, Gave material aid to cause **CEM:** Morgan; GPS unk; Rye Valley; Smyth **GS:** U **SP:** Mar (3rd 12 Dec 1772, Northampton Co) Margaret Nottingham (c1752-1 Oct 1810, Mathews Co) **VI:** Appears widow moved body fr Gloucester Co to her cemetery in Mathews Co or he is memorialized there **P:** N **BLW:** N **RG:** Y **MK:** unk **PH:** unk **SS:** DAR Ancestor #A13400; NSSAR Ancestor #P-321027 **BS:** JLARC 114.

WILLIAMS, Richard, b 1717, Bucks Co, PA, d 8 May 1797 **RU:** Patriot, Gave material aid to cause, Loudoun Co **CEM:** Williams/Brown; GPS of cem not determined, loc of town 39.216095,-77.534352; Lucketts, Loudoun; **GS:** Yes **SP:** Margaret Jones (1720, Chester Co, PA-21 Oct 1795) **VI:** Son of Robert Williams (1647, Merrion, Pembrokeshire, Wales-12 Oct 1734, Goshenville, Chester Co, PA) and Gwen Cadwallader (1720, Chester Co, PA-21 Oct 1795) **P:** N **BLW:** N **RG:** N **MK:** N **PH:** N **SS:** AL Comm Bk III, pg 332, Ct Bk pg 98, Loudoun Co; **BS:** 196.

WILLIAMS, Samuel; b 25 Nov 1725 d 19 May 1789 Gloucester Co **RU:** Patriot, Gave material aid in Gloucester Co **CEM:** Williams Family; GPS 37.412750, -76.338500; loc 100 yds along coast fr 62 Williamsdale Ln; Mathews **GS:** Y **SP:** 1) mar (7 Nov 1753) Sarah Haggoman (__-1763), d/o John Haggomam & Sarah Powell, 2) mar (2 Dec 1764) Sarah Dunton, d/o Levin & (-----) Dunton, 3) Margaret Nottingham, d/o Thomas Nottingham & (-----) Scarbrough **VI:** Son of John & (-----) Williams whose will was probated 27 Dec 1760 **P:** N **BLW:** N **RG:** N **MK:** N **PH:** unk **SS:** AL Ct Bk pg iii,9 **BS:** 48 pg 141; 196. **SEE APPENDIX G**

WILLIAMS, Sarah; b c1741; d 13 Jul 1812 **RU:** Patriot, Gave a beef and contributed material support to the cause **CEM:** Dumfries Public; GPS 38.34110, -77.19964; 17821 Mine Rd, Dumfries; Prince William **GS:** Y **SP:** No info **VI:** SAR monument **P:** N **BLW:** N **RG:** Y **MK:** Y SAR monument **PH:** Y **SS:** D Vol 3 pg 808; SAR P-335846 **BS:** 04.

WILLIAMS, Thomas; b 1745; d Bef Oct 1784 **RU:** Major, Gave material aid to cause. Served as Grand Juror and Overseer of Roads **CEM:** Williams Family; GPS 38.56808, -77.33511; See 1938 DAR Senate doc 10448, vol 2; Nottoway **GS:** U **SP:** Alice (-----) **VI:** No further data **P:** unk **BLW:** unk **RG:** Y **MK:** unk **PH:** unk **SS:** J- DAR Hatcher; DN pg 409, 411; SAR P-321118 **BS:** JLARC 2. **SEE APPENDIX G**

WILLIAMS, Thomas; b 4 May 1762, Gloucester Co; d 30 Sep 1823 **RU:** Private/Patriot, Served in Capt John Billup's Co, Gloucester Co Militia; as patriot gave material aid to cause, Gloucester Co as well as paying personal property tax in the county in 1783 **CEM:** Williams Family; GPS 37.412750, -76.338500; loc 100 yds along coast fr 62 Williamsdale Ln; Mathews **GS:** Y **SP:** 1) mar (15 Jun 1793) Susannah Billups (__-1804), 2) mar (18 Oct 1804) Mary Lilly Billup (21 Jan 1785, Gloucester Co-23 Jun 1857), d/o Joseph Billups & Joice Repress **VI:** Son of Samuel Williams & Sarah Haggman **P:** N **BLW:** N **RG:** Y **MK:** N **PH:** N **SS:** E pg 833; AL Ct Bk iii, pg 30; SAR P-342397 **BS:** 196. **SEE APPENDIX G**

WILLIAMS, William; b 9 Apr 1759, d 28 Sep 1801 **RU:** Private, Capt John Billup's Co, Gloucester Co Militia, 2 Aug to 8 Oct 1776 **CEM:** Williams Family; GPS 37.412750, -76.338500; loc 100 yds along coast fr 62 Williamsdale Ln; Mathews **GS** Y **SP:** 1) Mary Nottingham (29 May 1786- __), 2) Leah Goffigon (3 Aug 1795- __) **VI:** Son of Samuel Williams (25 Nov 1725-19 May 1789) & Sarah Haggoman (1732-1760) **P:** N **BLW:** N **RG:** Y **MK:** N **PH:** N **SS:**N pg 1264 fr Archives Dept State Library; SAR P-324398 **BS:** 196. **SEE APPENDIX G**

WILLIAMSON, James; b; d 15 Feb 1778 **RU:** Private Capt Hamilton's Co,Col George Gibson's 1st VA Regt of Fairfax Co **CEM:** Rev War Court House Plaque; GPS not determined; 4110 Chain Bridge Rd; Fairfax **GS:** Memorialized on plaque 2017 by Geo Washington Chapter, VASSAR **SP:** 1) Hannah Brock, 2) Martha Baldwin **VI;** Died in service at Valley Forge **P:** N **BLW:** N **RG:** Y **MK:** N **PH:** N **SS:** E pg 823; **AP:** Muster roll **EP** sources: SAR P321274 **BS:** None.

RU=Rank/Unit	CEM=Cemetery	GS=Gravestone	SP=Spousal Information
VI=Other Veteran Info	P=Pension	BLW=Bounty/Land Warrant	RG=Registered Grave
MK=SAR/DAR Marker	PH=Photo	SS=Service Source	BS=Burial Source

WILLIAMSON, Martha; b 21 Feb 1718, Middlesex Co; d 27 Aug 1784 **RU**: Patriot, Paid personal property supply tax Fluvanna Co 1783 **CEM**: James Mayo Plantation; GPS not determined; loc Haislip Ln, Cunningham: Fluvanna **GS**: Y field stone **SP**: Mar (1735) James Mayo (11 Dec 1711, Middlesex Co-13 Mar 1776, Palmyra, Fluvanna Co) **VI**: Daug of Robert Williamson (1695-1789) **P**: N **BLW**: N **RG**: N **MK**: N **PH**: N **SS** DAR A214014 **BS**: 196.

WILLIAMSON; William; b Unk; d aft Mar 1778, Valley Forge, Chester, PA **RU**: Private, enlisted Feb 1776 with Dr McCrae, in Capt Watson's Co, Col Arthur Sinclair's Bn, then in Capt David Arrell's Co, Lt Col William Heath's 3rd VA Regt in Mar 1778, dying later at Valley Forge **CEM**: Rev War Court House Plaque; GPS not determined; 4110 Chain Bridge Rd; Fairfax **GS**: Memorialized on plaque 2017 by Geo Washington Chapter, VASSAR **SP** Rosa (-----)(___-aft 1855) rec'd pen # W3637, BLW 1855 #26667 for 160 acres **P**: Y-S **BLW**: Y-S **RG**: Y **MK**: N **PH**: N **SS**: A pg 185, 277; C Sec II, pg 214; E pg 833; EP sources; SAR P-321311 **BS**: None.

WILLIS, Lewis; b 11 Nov 1734; d 15 Jan 1813 **RU**: Lt Col, Served as staff officer; 10th Cont Line in Gen Weedon's Brigade on 13 Nov 1776; Resigned 1 Mar 1778 **CEM**: Willis Hill; GPS not determined; loc Maryes Heights on Lafayette Blvd on grounds of Fredericksburg National Battlefield; Fredericksburg City **GS**: Unk **SP**: 1) Ann Byrd Carter (1740-1812), 2) Elizabeth Stevenson (1760-1810), 3) Mary Champe (1735-___) **VI**: Son of Henry Willis (1696-1740) & Mildred Washington (1696-1747) **P**: N **BLW**: N **RG**: Y **MK**: N **PH**: N **SS**: G pg 840; SAR P-321430 **BS**: 196. **SEE APPENDIX G**

WILLOUGHBY, William; b 1758; d 14 Jun 1800 **RU**: Ensign/Patriot, Signer of Leedstown Resolutions in 1766. Served in Capt James Dysart's Co of Light Horse, Col William Campbells Regt May 1781 **CEM**: St Paul's Episcopal; GPS 36.84733, -76.28554; 201 St Paul's Blvd; Norfolk City **GS**: Y **SP**: Margaret (-----) (1766-11 Jan 1827) **VI**: No further data **P**: unk **BLW**: unk **RG**: N **MK**: N **PH**: unk **SS**: N pg 1252 **BS**: 87 pg 31; 196.

WILLSON, John Sr; b c1749; d 12 Jul 1826 **RU**: Corporal, Served in 9th Cont Line **CEM**: Second Concord Presbyterian; GPS 37.34209, -78.96585; Phoebe Pond Rd Rt 609 E of Concord; Appomattox **GS**: Y **SP**: Elizabeth (-----) (c1748-22 Nov 1814) **VI**: Died age 77 **P**: unk **BLW**: unk **RG**: N **MK**: unk Y SAR **PH**: unk **SS**: E pg 835 **BS**: 196; 199.

WILLSON, Matthew; b Augusta Co; d 1825 **RU**: Captain/Patriot, Gave material aid to cause **CEM**: Bethel Presbyterian; GPS 38.04257, -79.17283; 563 Bethel Green Rd, Middlebrook; Augusta **GS**: U **SP**: No info **VI**: Son of James & Rebecca (-----) Willson **P**: N **BLW**: N **RG**: N **MK**: unk **PH**: unk **SS**: AL Comm Bk II pg 360 Augusta Co; **BS**: 196.

WILLSON, Moses; b 1754; d 4 Mar 1826 **RU**: Private?/Patriot, Capt Charles Campbell's Co, Augusta Co Militia. Patriot service as Constable, Augusta Co 1 Jul 1778 **CEM**: New Providence Presbyterian; GPS 37.95170, -79.30250; 1208 New Providence Rd, Raphine; Rockbridge **GS**: Y **SP**: Elizabeth (-----) (___-1837) **VI**: Son of James (1717-1801) & Rebeccal (-----) (1728-1820) Willson **P**: unk **BLW**: unk **RG**: N **MK**: unk **PH**: unk **SS**: E pg 836 **BS**: 196.

WILLSON, William; b 6 Nov 1745; d 13 Dec 1832 **RU**: Major, Ent serv Augusta Co 1774 & served at Battle of Point Pleasant. Ent serv again Augusta Co 1776 & served in siege of Jamestown **CEM**: Willson Family; GPS 38.07283, -79.12096; Rt 697 White Oak Gap Rd, W of Rt 11, Mint Spring; Augusta **GS**: U **SP**: Margaret Kerr Shields **VI**: Was pensioned 1832 Augusta Co where he had always lived. S6393 **P**: Y **BLW**: unk **RG**: Y **MK**: N **PH**: unk **SS**: K Vol 6 pg 164; SAR P-321575 **BS**: JLARC 62; 196.

WILLSON (WILSON), John; b 1753, PA; d 19 Jun 1826 **RU**: Major, Was 2nd Lt Rockbridge Co Militia, 4 Aug 1778 and was Maj Augusta Co Militia in 2nd Bn 20 Mar 1781 **CEM**: New Providence Presbyterian; GPS 37.95170, -79.30250; 1208 New Providence Rd, Raphine; Rockbridge **GS**: Y **SP**: Rachel Downey **VI**: Delegate to VA Legislature 1797. Sheriff 1811; Justice 1795-1801 **P**: unk **BLW**: unk **RG**: Y **MK**: Y **PH**: unk **SS**: SAR P-321925 **BS**: 196.

WILMER, William Holland; b 9 Mar 1734 Chester Towne, MD; d 24 Jul 1827 **RU**: Private, Served in MD Militia **CEM**: Bruton Parish Church; GPS 37.27127, -76.70248; 331 W Duke of Gloucester St; Williamsburg City **GS**: Y **SP**: Marion Hannah Cox (1796-15 Sep 1821 Alexandria) **VI**: Was President of William & Mary College; Rector of Bruton Parish Church **P**: unk **BLW**: unk **RG**: N **MK**: N **PH**: unk **SS**: BJ pg 106 **BS**: 170 Bruton; 196.

RU=Rank/Unit	CEM=Cemetery	GS=Gravestone	SP=Spousal Information
VI=Other Veteran Info	P=Pension	BLW=Bounty/Land Warrant	RG=Registered Grave
MK=SAR/DAR Marker	PH=Photo	SS=Service Source	BS=Burial Source

455

WILSON, Abraham Sr; b King & Queen Co; d Apr 1793 **RU:** Private, Served in Spotsylvania Co Militia **CEM:** Clark-Jayne; GPS unk; Jonesville; Lee **GS:** U **SP:** Mar (c1768 Botetourt Co) Catherine Livingston (1760-1815) **VI:** Died in Smyth Co **P:** unk **BLW:** unk **RG:** N **MK:** unk **PH:** unk **SS:** E pg 836 **BS:** 196.

WILSON, Daniel; b 1735; d 1807 **RU:** Ensign, In Jan 1781 served in Capt Charles Wall's Co at Cabin Point and then at Portsmouth under General Mullenberg **CEM:** Old Monmouth Presbyterian; GPS 37.80810, -79.47280; Jct Rts 60 & 669; Lexington City **GS:** Y **SP:** No info **VI:** No further data **P:** unk **BLW:** unk **RG:** N **MK:** N **PH:** unk **SS:** AZ pg 161-2 **BS:** 154 Rockbridge.

WILSON, David; b c1740; d 4 Feb 1820 **RU:** Sergeant, Capt William Henshaw's Co, Col Wm Craford's Regt fr Frederick Co in Oct 1774 at Ft Charlotte **CEM:** Long-Stephens; GPS unk; Stephens City; Frederick **GS:** Y **SP:** Mar (11 March 1783 Frederick Co by Rev John Montgomery) Mary Henning (4 Aug 1766-14 Apr 1843) **VI:** Oldest graveyard in Stevens City. Cemetery also known as Long-Stephens **P:** unk **BLW:** unk **RG:** Y **MK:** N **PH:** unk **SS:** Z pg 53; SAR P-321700 **BS:** 122; 59, pg 355.

WILSON, Elibabb (Eli); b c1755, Augusta Co; d 11 Nov 1845 **RU:** Soldier, Ent serv Pendleton Co 1776 & 1781 at Bull Pasture **CEM:** Unidentified; GPS 37.96151, -79.71000; Nr Doe Hill; Highland **GS:** U **SP:** No info **VI:** Pen 1832 Pendleton Co age 77. Bur in Highland Co which was formed in 1842 fr Pendleton & Bath Cos **P:** Y **BLW:** unk **RG:** Y **MK:** unk **PH:** unk **SS:** K Vol 6 pg 167; SAR P-321724 **BS:** JLARC 76.

WILSON, Harris; b c1730, Halifax Co, d Jan 1808 **RU:** Patriot, Gave material aid to cause, Henry Co **CEM:** Wilson/Abner; GPS 37.0571500, -81.9065800; loc Rt 633, Clarks Valley Rd, Swords Creek; Russell **GS:**Y **SP:** Sarah (-----) **VI:** Son of Richard Wilson & Micha Floyd **P:** Unk **BLW:** Unk **RG:** N **MK:** N **PH:** N **SS:** AL Ct Bk pg 17, Comm Bk III, pg 161, Henry Co **BS:** 196.

WILSON, Hugh; b 1740; d 1809 **RU:** Lieutenant, Was commissioned Lt 1 Apr 1783. Served in Capt Samuel McDowell's Co of Rockbridge Co and also in Frederick Co Militia, **CEM:** Old Monmouth Presbyterian; GPS 37.80810, -79.47280; Jct Rts 60 & 669; Lexington City **GS:** Y **SP:** No info **VI:** No further data **P:** unk **BLW:** unk **RG:** N **MK:** N **PH:** unk **SS:** E pg 836 **BS:** 154 Rockbridge.

WILSON, James; b 22 Dec 1739; d 6 Aug 1824 **RU:** Patriot, Gave material aid to the cause **CEM:** Sharon Lutheran; GPS 37.05800, -81.20590; Rt 42 W of Ceres; Bland **GS:** Y **SP:** Elizabeth Poage (1739-12 May 1824) **VI:** No further data **P:** N **BLW:** N **RG:** N **MK:** N **PH:** unk **SS:** AL Ct Bk pg 10 **BS:** 60, Bland Co; 196. **SEE APPENDIX G**

WILSON, James; b unk; d 1799 **RU:** Patriot, Gave material aid to the cause **CEM:** St Paul's Episcopal; GPS 36.84733, -76.28554; 201 St Paul's Blvd; Norfolk City **GS:** Y **SP:** No info **VI:** No further data **P:** N **BLW:** N **RG:** N **MK:** N **PH:** unk **SS:** AL Ct Bk pg 3, 28 **BS:** 87 pg 31.

WILSON, James; b 1760; d 1818 **RU:** Sergeant, Served Oct 1779 in 6th VA Regt **CEM:** St John's Episcopal; GPS 37.53183, -77.41958; 2401 E Broad St; Richmond City **GS:** Y **SP:** No info **VI:** No further data **P:** unk **BLW:** unk **RG:** N **MK:** N **PH:** unk **SS:** AP **BS:** 28 pg 516.

WILSON, James; b 1767; d 9 Jul 1805 **RU:** Soldier, SAR registry did not provide service **CEM:** Old Presbyterian Meeting House; GPS 38.48528, -77.23532; 323 S Fairfax St; Alexandria City **GS:** N **SP:** Eliza John Taylor, d/o Jesse & (-----) Taylor **VI:** Died of fever age 38 (Alexandria Gazette, 10 Jul 1805, pg 2). Merchant of Alexandria. Listed on SAR plaque in cemetery **P:** unk **BLW:** unk **RG:** N **MK:** Y SAR plaque **PH:** N **SS:** J-NSSAR 1993 Reg; AK **BS:** JLARC 1; 23 pg 110; 196.

WILSON, James R; b unk; d 17 Aug 1819 **RU:** US Navy,Purser **CEM:** Arlington National; GPS 38.88377, -77.06535; Jefferson Davis Hwy Rt 110; Arlington **GS:** N **SP:** No info **VI:** Findagrave indicates he was in the US Navy but lists no birth year or gravestone, thus could be War of 1812 veteran not Rev War veteran **P:** unk **BLW:** unk **RG:** Y **MK:** unk **PH:** N **SS:** J-NSSAR 2000 Reg; SAR P-321856 **BS:** JLARC 76; 196. (**WILSON**, James Eli See Appendix G, Addenda)

WILSON, John; b 1740, Pittsylvania Co; d 21 May 1820 **RU:** Colonel/Patriot, Served in Pittsylvania Co Militia 1777-78. Gave material aid to cause **CEM:** Dan's Hill; GPS unk; Danville at Wilson's ferry; Danville City **GS:** Y **SP:** Mar (2 Apr 1767) Mary Lumpkin (1749 King & Queen Co-4 Jan 1827) **VI:** Son of Peter of the Ferry Farm. Was County Lt (in charge of all military affairs for the county) fr 1779 until end of Rev War. In 1783 was member of Constitutional Convention. Died in Pittsylvania Co **P:** unk **BLW:** unk **RG:** N **MK:** N **PH:** unk **SS:** E pg 836; AL Ct Bk pg 18, 60 Pittsylvania Co **BS:** 81 Chart.

RU=Rank/Unit	CEM=Cemetery	GS=Gravestone	SP=Spousal Information
VI=Other Veteran Info	P=Pension	BLW=Bounty/Land Warrant	RG=Registered Grave
MK=SAR/DAR Marker	PH=Photo	SS=Service Source	BS=Burial Source

WILSON, John; b Dec 1732,, Chester Co, PA; d 21 Jan 1820 **RU**: Major, Took oath as Maj 20 Mar 1781 Augusta Co Militia, 2d Bn and was Major at Yorktown with men from Highland Co **CEM**: Stony Run; GPS 38.22920, -79.7003; US Rt 220, N of jct with 607; Highland **GS**: Y Govt 1929 **SP**: 1) Isabella Seawright, 2) Mar (1785) Sally Alexander **VI**: Son of William & Barbara (McKane) Wilson of Dublin, Ireland. Note Highland Co formed from Bath Co & Bath from Augusta Co in 1791, therefore Augusta Co service. A John Wilson Sr also served as Major from Augusta Co **P**: unk **BLW**: unk **RG**: N **MK**: unk **PH**: unk **SS**: E pg 837; AZ pg 185 **BS**: 196.

WILSON, John; b 1748; d 1826 **RU**: Soldier, Served in Cont Line **CEM**: Old Concord Presbyterian; GPS unk; Rt 648, Concord; Campbell **GS**: N **SP**: Mar (18 Mar 1793 Pittsylvania Co) Sarah Lynch **VI**: No further data **P**: Unk **BLW**: Unk **RG**: Y **MK**: N **PH**: N **SS**: NSSAR Ancestor # P-321917 **BS**: JLARC 36.

WILSON, John; b 1759, Henry Co, d 1851 **RU**: Ensign, Washington County Militia **CEM**: Wilson/Abner; GPS 37.0571500, -81.9065800; loc Rt 633, Clarks Valley Rd, Swords Creek; Russell **GS**: Unk **SP**: Rhoda Lawson **VI**: Son of Harris Wilson, Sr (1730 Halifax Co-Jan 1808) & Sarah (-----) **P**: Unk **BLW**: Unk **RG**: N **MK**: N **PH**: N **SS**: E pg 837; AZ pg 233 **BS**: 196.

WILSON, John Sr; b 1753, Staunton; d 23 Sep 1799 **RU**: Colonel/Patriot, Perhaps took oath as Maj in Militia 20 Mar 1781. Gave material aid to cause **CEM**: Glebe Burying Ground; GPS 38.10940, -79.22190; Glebe School Rd Rt 876, Swoopes; Augusta **GS**: U **SP**: Mar (25 Oct 1775) Druscilla Swearington (1755-1826 KY) **VI**: Son of George (1728 Scotland-Feb 1777 NJ) & Elizabeth Crawford (McCreavy) (__Scotland-__) Wilson **P**: unk **BLW**: unk **RG**: Y **MK**: N **PH**: unk **SS**: E pg 837; AL Cert 3 Augusta Co; SAR P-321924 **BS**: 80 vol 4 pg 203; AR.

WILSON, Nathaniel; b 1764; d 5 Apr 1803 **RU**: Patriot, Mended uniforms for Capt John Edmonds Co at Norfolk **CEM**: Wilson Family; GPS 36.61178,-76.18304; 701 Saunderson Rd, City Prison Farms,Mc Brides Correction Ctr, St Brides Plantation; Chesapeake City **GS**: U **SP**: Margaret Bartee (1 Dec 1768-6 Jan 1816) d/o Thomas & Ann (Keeling) Bartee **VI**: Son of Malichi & Lidia (-----) Wilson **P**: N **BLW**: N **RG**: N **MK**: N **PH**: N **SS**: G pg 521 **BS**: 63 pg 97; 196.

WILSON, Richard; b Dec 1762, Caroline Co; d 1836 **RU**: Orderly Sergeant, Ent serv Caroline Co 1779. Served in VA Line as Orderly Sgt **CEM**: Wilson Family, R.L. Bowling Property; GPS unk; Rt 659; Amherst **GS**: U **SP**: No info **VI**: Moved to Amherst Co in 1796. Appl pen 23 Aug 1832 Amherst Co. S6416 **P**: Y **BLW**: unk **RG**: Y **MK**: unk **PH**: unk **SS**: K Vol 6 pg 173; CG Vol 3 pg 3894; SAR P-322038 **BS**: JLARC 4, 7.

WILSON, Robert; b unk; d unk **RU**: Colonel/Patriot, Gave material aid to cause **CEM**: Wilson; GPS unk; Dans Hill; Danville City **GS**: U **SP**: 1) Ruth Hairston 2) Catherine Ann Pannill **VI**: Son of John (1740-1820) & Mary (Lumpkin) Wilson. Died in Pittsylvania Co **P**: unk **BLW**: unk **RG**: N **MK**: unk **PH**: unk **SS**: AL Ct Bk pg 11 Henry Co **BS**: 196.

WILSON, Samuel; b 16 Apr 1750; d 6 Apr 1826 **RU**: Captain, Commanded a company in Augusta Co Militia,and served at Battle of Point Pleasant Oct 1774 **CEM**: Old Providence; GPS 37.96151, -79.71000; 1005 Spottswood Rd, Spottswood; Augusta **GS**: Y **SP**: Mary Wilson (1759-23 Jul 1819). Shared stone with husband **VI**: Name on SAR plaque at cemetery **P**: unk **BLW**: unk **RG**: N **MK**: Y SAR plaque **PH**: unk **SS**: Z pg 101; BT **BS**: JLARC 2, 8 ,62, 63, 79; 196.

WILSON, Samuel; b 1735, Northern Ireland; d Nov 1807 **RU**: Soldier, Served in Capt Adam Clemson's Co, Bedford Co Militia **CEM**: Old Monmouth Presbyterian; GPS 37.80810, -79.47280; Jct Rts 60 & 669; Rockbridge **GS**: U **SP**: Mar (1788) Mary Mackey (1737-1820) **VI**: Will veriies death year and place **P**: unk **BLW**: unk **RG**: N **MK**: unk **PH**: unk **SS**: E pg 837 **BS**: 196.

WILSON, Thomas; b 1750; d 1830 **RU**: Corporal, Served in Col Daniel Morgan's Regt **CEM**: Goose Creek; GPS 39.11250, -77.69527; Rt 722, Lincoln; Loudoun **GS**: Y **SP**: No info **VI**: No further data **P**: N **BLW**: N **RG**: unk **MK**: unk **PH**: unk **SS**: E pg 837; SAR P-322116 **BS**: 196.

WILSON, Thomas; b 1727; d 6 Apr 1800 **RU**: Lt Col/Patriot, commanded Amelia Co, Militia, ss patriot, gave material aid to the cause **CEM**: Old Monmouth Presbyterian; GPS 37.80810, -79.47280; Jct Rts 60 & 669; Lexington City **GS**: Y **SP**: Mar 2 Dec 1774, Judith Friend (__)Charlottesvile-__) **VI**: No further

RU=Rank/Unit	CEM=Cemetery	GS=Gravestone	SP=Spousal Information
VI=Other Veteran Info	P=Pension	BLW=Bounty/Land Warrant	RG=Registered Grave
MK=SAR/DAR Marker	PH=Photo	SS=Service Source	BS=Burial Source

457

data **P**: N **BLW**: N **RG**: N **MK**: N **PH**: unk **SS**: AL Ct Bk pg 2, 4; DAR A184964 **BS**: 154 Old Mon'th; 196.

WILSON, Wallis; b c1755; d Jul 1846 **RU**: Private, Served in VA Line. Ent serv Halifax Co in VA Regt 1781. Served at Siege of Yorktown. Served in Capts Standfield, Wall, Powell, Gains, and Faulkner's Cos, Col Peter Rodger's Regt **CEM**: Wallis Wilson Family; GPS unk; By Rt 737, 4 mi fr Mecklenburg line; Halifax **GS**: Y **SP**: 1) Mar (c1785) Rebecca Wall (__-1812) 2) Mar (12 Jun 1812) Sarah Wade (1775-__) **VI**: Appl pen 19 Dec 1832 age 76 or 77. S6418 **P**: Y **BLW**: unk **RG**: Y **MK**: N **PH**: Y **SS**; K Vol 4 pg 175; CG Vol 3 pg 3897; DAR A127866; SAR P-322129 **BS**: SAR regis; 196.

WILSON, William; b 1 Aug 1751; d 1 Dec 1835 **RU**: Captain, Commanded a company Augusta Co Militia 15 Apr 1783 **CEM**: Augusta Stone Presbyterian; GPS 38.23926, -78.97356; 28 Old Stone Church Ln, Ft Defiance; Augusta **GS**: U **SP**: 1) Isabella Larrabee 2) Mar (14 Jun 1786) Elizabeth Poage (c1768-1 Dec 1835) d/o Thomas (1740-24 Dec 1803) & Agnes (McClanahan) (__-19 Sep 1792) Poage **VI**: Obtained the rank of major after the war period. Second pastor of Presbyterian Stone Church fr 1780-1810. Appl pen 25 Sep 1832 Augusta Co. S6393. On plaque to pastors on Augusta Stone Church. Discrepency on birth date and yr **P**: Y **BLW**: unk **RG**: Y **MK**: Y SAR plaque **PH**: unk **SS**: SAR P-322165; E pg 837; CG Vol 3 pg 3883 **BS**: JLARC 8;196.

WILSON, William, Jr; b 1760, or 6 Dec 1761, Norfolk Co; d 19 Jul 1838 **RU**: Captain, Served in the Norfolk Co Militia at battle at Great Bridge. Served also in 11th Regt VA Line. Was taken prisoner 7 Jul 1777 **CEM**: Cedar Grove; GPS 36.57204, -80.02599; 301 Fort Lane Rd; Portsmouth City **GS**: Y **SP**: Nancy Wormington (1765-26 Jan 1840) **VI**: Son of John & (-----) Wilson. Sol appl pen 19 May 1834 in Portsmouth, Norfolk Co. R11686. Govt grave stone. Was Trustee City of Portsmouth **P**: Y **BLW**: unk **RG**: Y **MK**: Y SAR **PH**: Y **SS**: C Sec 2 pg 214; CG Vol 3 pg 3899; SAR P-322149 **BS**: 27 pg 29; 196.

WILSON, William; b 1760; d 1824 **RU**: Private, Served in Capt Hugh Caperton's Co, New River Valley Men, Indian Wars (this would be in Rev War timeframe considering his age). Also probably the man of this name who served in Capt John Lewis's Co of Rangers **CEM**: Peterstown; GPS 37.39470, -80.80140; Off Rt 219 btw Peterstown & Midway, on WV state line; Giles **GS**: Y **SP**: Mar (23 Mar 1793) Mary Doak **VI**: Govt grave stone. **P**: N **BLW**: N **RG**: N **MK**: unk **PH**: Y **SS**: Z pg 129 **BS**: 195.

WILSON, Willis; b 1748; d 1798 **RU**: Colonel, Had VA sea serv. Was Capt of the galley "Caswell." Served also in 5th Regt of Artillery **CEM**: Trinity Episcopal; GPS 36.83459, -76.30105; 500 Court St; Portsmouth City **GS**: U **SP**: No info **VI**: Pen granted 1845 to his son William of Norfolk. R109. Also VA 1/2 pay (see N.A. Acct #837 Va State Navy-YS File VA 1/2 Pay) Stone 57 in W.B. Butt inventory **P**: Y **BLW**: unk **RG**: Y **MK**: Y SAR plaque **PH**: unk **SS**: K Vol 6 pg 176; CG Vol 3 pg 3899; SAR P-336628 **BS**: JLARC 127.

WILSON, Willis; b 1757; d 10 Feb 1822 **RU**: Lieutenant, Served in Cumberland Co Militia.; wounded at Buford's Defeat **CEM**: Bonbrook House; GPS unk; 7.5 mi N of Cumberland; Cumberland **GS**: Y **SP**: No info **VI**: No further data **P**: Y, 19 Jun 1788 **BLW**: unk **RG**: Y **MK**: N **PH**: unk **SS**: E pg 838; BX pg 883; SAR P-322183 **BS**: 157 Bonbrook. **SEE APPENDIX G**

WILSON (WILLSON), John; b 1753; d 19 Jun 1826 **RU**: Second Lieutenant, Served in Rockbridge Co Militia, 4 Aug 1778 **CEM**: New Providence Presbyterian; GPS 37.95130, -79.30250; 1208 New Providence Rd, Raphine; Rockbridge **GS**: U **SP**: Rachel Downey **VI**: Delegate to VA Legislature 1797 **P**: unk **BLW**: unk **RG**: Y **MK**: unk **PH**: unk **SS**: SAR P-321925; E pg 835 **BS**: JLARC 1, 63.

WINE, Jacob; b 6 Oct 1757, Germany, d 11 Oct 1823 **RU**: Private, 1st VA Regt and Rawlings Regt, Cont Troops. Reported to be a prisoner and was disabled in service **CEM**: New Jerusalem Lutheran Church; GPS 39.25736,-77.63891; 12942 Lutheran Church Rd, Lovettsville; Loudoun **GS**: Yes **SP**: Catherine Hough (24 Man 1755-25 Aug 1826) **VI**: Awarded 18 pounds to commence from I Jan 1786. Recd BLW **P**: Yes **BLW**: Yes **RG**: N **MK**: N **PH**: N **SS**: A pg 275; E pg 838; **G pgs** 714, 716, 722; AP Fold3 Serv Index Card **BS**: 196.

WINGFIELD, Charles; b 3 Dec 1728, Hanover Co; d 5 Dec 1803 **RU**: Patriot, Was signer of Albemarle Co Declaration of Independence 1779. Also gave material aid to cause **CEM**: Wingfield Family; GPS unk; 531 Woodlands Rd; Charlottesville City **GS**: U **SP**: Mar (27 Feb 1750, Hanover Co) Rachel Joyner (1728-__) **VI**: Son of John (c1695 New Kent Co-1700) & Martha (Hudson) (1704-1779) Wingfield **P**: N

RU=Rank/Unit
VI=Other Veteran Info
MK=SAR/DAR Marker

CEM=Cemetery
P=Pension
PH=Photo

GS=Gravestone
BLW=Bounty/Land Warrant
SS=Service Source

SP=Spousal Information
RG=Registered Grave
BS=Burial Source

BLW: N **RG**: Y **MK**: unk **PH**: unk **SS**: DAR A128457; AL Cert Albemarle Co; CD; SAR P-322503 **BS**: 196.

WINGFIELD, John; b 13 Feb 1742; d 7 Feb 1814 **RU**: Private/Patriot, Served in 10th Cont Line and Capt John Winston's Co, 14th Cont Line. Signed Albemarle Co Declaration of Independence **CEM**: Wingfield Family; GPS unk; Shepard Property, Slaughter Pen Creek; Charlottesville City **GS**: U **SP**: Mar (7 Mar 1764) Robina Langford (1747 Albemarle Co-1817) **VI**: No further data **P**: unk **BLW**: unk **RG**: Y **MK**: unk **PH**: unk **SS**: DAR A128478; SAR P-322508; E pg 839 **BS**: JLARC 58.

WINGFIELD, John M; b 6 May 1765; d 26 July 1849 **RU**: Private, Enl in Goochland Co **CEM**: Shepherd Family; GPS unk; Batesville; Albemarle **GS**: U **SP**: No info **VI**: Sol appl pen 22 May1845, Hanover Co # R11715 **P**: Y **BLW**: unk **RG**:Y **MK**: unk **PH**: unk **SS**: SAR P-322509 **BS**: JLARC 58; 196.

WINGFIELD, Thomas Jr; b 1750; d 1825 **RU**: Captain, Commanded a co in Hanover Co Militia **CEM**: Marl Ridge; GPS unk; Rt 54, Ashland; Hanover **GS**: Y **SP**: Rhoda Davis (1760-1830) **VI**: Son of John & Mary (Hudson) Winfield. One large stone with many names inscribed **P**: unk **BLW**: unk **RG**: N **MK**: N **PH**: unk **SS**: E pg 839 **BS**: 31 vol 1 pg 91.

WINGFIELD, Thomas Sr; b 1740, Walnut Shade, Hanover Co; d 1830 **RU**: Patriot, Gave material aid to cause and signed a legislative petition **CEM**: Walnut Shade; GPS unk; Walnut Shade Ln off Rt 54; Hanover **GS**: U **SP**: Ann Davis (1754-1831) **VI**: Son of John (c1695) New Kent Co & Martha Hudson (1704-1779) Wingfield. Rev War service may pertain to individual with same name b 1750 in the county **P**: unk **BLW**: unk **RG**: Y **MK**: unk **PH**: unk **SS**: E pg 839; AL Cert 2 Hanover Co; SAR P-322514 **BS**:

WINN, Minor Jr; b 1730; d 25 Oct 1813 **RU**: First Lieutenant, Served in Fauquier Co Militia as 1st Lt Oct 1779 and took oath on Mar 1780 **CEM**: Winn Family; GPS unk; Probably at Rock Hill Rt 626 nr Halfway; Fauquier **GS**: N **SP**: Mar (bond 7 Oct 1766, James Withers, security) Elizabeth "Betty" Withers (c1748-c1803) d/o Thomas (15 Feb 1723 Stafford Co-12 Nov 1794) & Elizabeth (Williams) (__-27 Mar 1783) Withers **VI**: Son of Minor, Sr (1704 Westmoreland Co-1788) & Margaret (Connor) Winn. Cemetery has vanished **P**: unk **BLW**: unk **RG**: Y **MK**: N **PH**: N **SS**: Fauquier Co Marriages pg 216; SAR P-322575 **BS**: 19 pg 243.

WINN, Richard; b 1753; d 1816 **RU**: Sergeant, Served in 5th & 9th Cont Line **CEM**: White-Yancey-Jones Family; GPS unk; Rt 49 S fr Chase City, left on 697 at Reese's old store, 2.5 mi on right at old homeplace; Mecklenburg **GS**: U **SP**: Priscilla McKinney **VI**: No further data **P**: unk **BLW**: unk **RG**: Y **MK**: unk **PH**: unk **SS**: SAR P-322585; E pg 829; AZ pg 180 **BS**: JLARC 72.

WINN, Thomas; b 27 Dec 1753, Hanover Co; d 16 Nov 1824 **RU**: First Lieutenant, Served in Fluvanna Co Militia 8 Apr 1782. (DAR plaque at GS shows service fr 1776 to 1783) **CEM**: Winnsville; GPS unk; Rts 612 and 671, Fork Union; Fluvanna **GS**: Y **SP**: Elizabeth Dabney Anderson (17 Dec 1753-30 Nov 1819) **VI**: No further data **P**: unk **BLW**: unk **RG**: Y **MK**: Y DAR plaque **PH**: unk **SS**: DAR A128769; E pg 829; SAR P-322588 **BS**: JLARC 1, 3, 18, 46; 196.

WINNIFORD, David; b 1750; d 26 Apr 1794 **RU**: Sergeant, Served in VA Line. Ent serv Powhatan Co "in VA unit" (no yr), then entered serv Cumberland Co as Sergeant 1779. Served at Battle of Brandywine where wounded **CEM**: Winniford Family; GPS 37.71653, -78.16861; Fork of Willis Baptist Church, jct Rts 660 & 713; Cumberland **GS**: U **SP**: Mar (16 Nov 1780 Cumberland Co) Judith (-----) (c1763-__). She was living in Adair Co KY with her daughter in 1852. **VI**: Widow moved to KY in 1800 where pen 14 Aug 1840, Adair Co, KY age 77, living 12 mi fr Columbia. W9021 **P**: Y **BLW**: unk **RG**: Y **MK**: N **PH**: unk **SS**: J-NSSAR 1993 Reg; K Vol 6 pg 182-3; CG Vol 3 pg 3908; SAR P-322608 **BS**: JLARC 1.

WINSTON, Geddes; b 1724, Hanover Co; d 6 Jun 1784 **RU**: Private/Patriot, Mil serv not determined. Was Sheriff, Hanover Co 1782 **CEM**: St John's Episcopal; GPS 37.53183, -77.41958; 2401 E Broad St; Richmond City **GS**: Y **SP**: Mary Jordan (c1742-9 Dec 1811 Richmond) **VI**: Recd pen Hanover Co **P**: Y **BLW**: unk **RG**: Y **MK**: N **PH**: unk **SS**: DAR A128885; E pg 840; AL Ct Bk I pg 50 Hanover Co; SAR P-322733 **BS**: 39, pg 100.

WINSTON, William Overton; b 1747; d 1815 **RU**: Captain, Commanded a co in Hanover Co Militia, May 1779 **CEM**: Blenheim-Winston; GPS unk; Rt 646, Hanover; Hanover **GS**: Y **SP**: Mar (1 Dec 1770)

RU=Rank/Unit	CEM=Cemetery	GS=Gravestone	SP=Spousal Information
VI=Other Veteran Info	P=Pension	BLW=Bounty/Land Warrant	RG=Registered Grave
MK=SAR/DAR Marker	PH=Photo	SS=Service Source	BS=Burial Source

459

Joanna Robinson (1755-1794) **VI:** Son of John (1724-1772) & Alice (Bickerton) (1730-1773) Winston **P:** unk **BLW:** unk **RG:** Y **MK:** N **PH:** unk **SS:** E pg 840; SAR P-322749 **BS:** 31 vol 1 pg 55; 196.

WIRE, William; b c1753; d 27 Feb 1840 **RU:** Private, Served in Capt J Lewis in 7th Co, VA Regt fr Frederick Co, VA **CEM:** St James Reformed; GPS 39.27027, -77.62968; Lovettsville Rd, Lovettsville; Loudoun **GS:** Y **SP:** No info **VI:** No further data **P:** unk **BLW:** unk **RG:**N **MK:** N **PH:** unk **SS:** G pg 373 **BS:** 25 pg 344; 196.

WISE, John; b c1765; d 30 Mar 1812 **RU:** Corporal, Served in 9th Cont Line **CEM:** Wise Family; GPS unk; Chesconessex; Accomack **GS:** Y **SP:** Mar (18 Apr 1799) Sarah Corbin Cropper (21 Mar 1777 Bowman's Folly, Accomack Co-21 Jan 1813) d/o John Jr (23 Dec 1755-15 Jan 1821) & Margaret Douglas (Pettitt) (12 Apr 1755-3 Jun 1784) Cropper **VI:** Son of John & Margaret (Douglas) Wise. GS inscription indicates he had rank of Maj and was Speaker of House and Clerk of County Ct (Major rank perhaps obtained after war period) **P:** unk **BLW:** unk **RG:** Y **MK:** N **PH:** unk **SS:** E pg 840; SAR P-322845 **BS:** 37 pg 284; 196.

WITCHER, William Jr; b 1739; d 1820 **RU:** Major, Raised a co of militia in 1775. Promoted 16 Nov 1779 to Maj in Pittsylvania Co Militia. Resigned 19 Sep 1780 **CEM:** Witcher Family; GPS unk; nr Sandy Level Post Office; Pittsylvania **GS:** Y **SP:** Mar (1 Apr 1782 Pittsylvania Co) Molly or Polly Dalton **VI:** Was vestryman of Camden District Parish 1763 **P:** unk **BLW:** unk **RG:** Y **MK:** N **PH:** unk **SS:** N pg 1228;AS; AW; SAR P-336554 **BS:** 174.

WITCHER, William Sr; b 1724, England; d 8 Jun 1808. Chatham; **RU:** Major/Patriot, Served in VA Militia. Provided equipment and/or supplies and was Justice of Peace **CEM:** Witcher family; GPS 36.57047, -79.35798; Penhook; Pittsylvania **GS:** Y **SP:** Rachel Ann Majors **VI:** Was Justice, Franklin Co **P:** unk **BLW:** unk **RG:** Y **MK:** N **PH:** unk **SS:** AL Ct Bk pg I, 56; DAR A126994; SAR P-332956 **BS:** SAR Application; SAR PRS.

WITHAM, William; b NY; d 1781 **RU:** Private, Served in Col Peter Gansevort's 3rd NY Regt. Died fr the battle at Yorktown **CEM:** Yorktown Victory Monument Tablet; GPS 38.28350, -78.54150; Yorktown; York **GS:** U **SP:** No info **VI:** No further data **P:** unk **BLW:** unk **RG:** Y **MK:** unk **PH:** unk **SS:** J-Yorktown Historian; AX pg 46; SAR P-322974 **BS:** JLARC 74.

WITHERS, Enoch Keene; b 14 Oct 1760, d 26 Jul 1813 **RU:** Ensign, became this rank on 1 Nov 1777 in Captain Peter Grayson's Co, Col William Grayson's Regt, Cont Line. Served as recruiting officer and as Adjutant to Col Richard Campbell. He saw action at battle of Eutaw Springs, SC, 8 Sep 1781 and was at Cowpen's battle under Major Triplett. He resigned 13 Mar 1778 **CEM:** Warrenton; GPS: 38.7126236, -77.8000336; 110 West Lee St, Warrenton; Fauquier **GS:** Unk **SP:** Sarah Gaskins **VI:** Heirs claim for pension was rejected 3 Feb 1842 because he resigned during war period **PEN:** N **BLW:** N **RG:** Y **MK:** N **PH:** N **SS:** BW pg 887; DAR: A127084; SAR P-323000 **BS:** 196.

WITHERS, Lewis; b 1758; d 4 May 1821 **RU:** Private, Served in Winn's Co, Fauquier Co Militia 1781 and wounded at Battle of Cowpens **CEM:** Withers-Nelson family; GPS unk; 9337 James Madison Hwy; Fauquier **GS:** Y **SP:** Katherine Potts **VI:** No further data **P:** unk **BLW:** unk **RG:** N **MK:** N **PH:** Y **SS:** AV **BS:** 83 Inv # 58.

WITHERS, William; b 6 Apr 1726; d 5 Jan 1804 **RU:** Sergeant, Served in Grayson's Regt, Cont Line **CEM:** Withers-Nelson family; GPS unk; 9337 James Madison Hwy; Fauquier **GS:** Y **SP:** Mar (15 Dec 1756 or 1777 Fauquier Co) Elizabeth Hord Barbey or Barbee (22 Sep 1732-17 Oct 1871) d/o Andrew & Jane Lacey (Dulaney) Barbee **VI:** Son of Capt James & Elizabeth (Keene) Withers, Sr **P:** unk **BLW:** unk **RG:** N **MK:** Y SAR **PH:** Y **SS:** E pg 841; AV; Fauquier Co Marriages pg 217 **BS:** 83 Inv # 58.

WITTEN/WHITTEN, James; b 7 Jan 1759, MD; d 15 Mar 1830 **RU:** Private, Served in Capt James Maxwell's Co, Montgomery Co Militia as a scout **CEM:** Wilkerson Witten Family; GPS unk; Plum Creek nr his cabin, on County Road 634 loc N about 350 feet from the end of the paved road and across from the old Col. Wilkerson Witten's homestead, Pisgah; Tazewell **GS:** U **SP:** Mar (1783) Rebecca Cecil (1765 MD-1840) **VI:** No further data **P:** unk **BLW:** unk **RG:** Y **MK:** unk **PH:** unk **SS:** DAR A125451; SAR P-323120; J- DAR Hatcher; E pg 237; BW pg 27, 56 **BS:** JLARC 2.

WITTEN, Thomas Jr; b 23 Jan 1753, Prince George Co, MD; d 6 Oct 1841 **RU:** Ensign, Served in VA Line. Ent serv Tazewell Co 1776 as Ens and served in Capt James Maxwell's Co Montgomery Co.

RU=Rank/Unit	CEM=Cemetery	GS=Gravestone	SP=Spousal Information
VI=Other Veteran Info	P=Pension	BLW=Bounty/Land Warrant	RG=Registered Grave
MK=SAR/DAR Marker	PH=Photo	SS=Service Source	BS=Burial Source

Fought in Battle of King's Mountain under Lt Rees Bowen and Tazwell Comar, 29 Mar 1774, Fincastle Co **CEM**: W. A. Leece Family; GPS unk; Off Rt 91 south of Rt 460, Fort Witten, Paintlick; Tazewell **GS**: U **SP**: Mar (29 Mar 1774 Augusta, Fincastle Co) Eleanor "Nellie" Cecil (1755-1836) **VI**: Son of Thomas (1719-1794) & Elizabeth Bean (Cecil) Witten. Rec pen for protecting frontier settlements fr Indians. He and David Ward were first representatives fr Tazewell Co elected to VA legislature 1801, 02, 03. Appl pen 15 Oct 1832 Tazewell Co. S6407. Source 89 has death in 1844 for Thomas Witten Jr **P**: Y **BLW**: unk **RG**: Y **MK**: unk **PH**: unk **SS**: E pg 825; G pg 237; K Vol 6 pg 190; CG Vol 3 pg 3920; SAR P-323123 **BS**: JLARC 4, 89; 196.

WLOVASSE, Jean; b unk; d 1781 **RU**: Seaman, Served on "Ville de Paris" and died from Yorktown battle **CEM**: French Memorial; GPS 36.81944, -79.39933; Yorktown; York **GS**: U **SP**: No info **VI**: No further data **P**: unk **BLW**: unk **RG**: N **MK**: unk **PH**: unk **SS**: J-Yorktown Historian **BS**: JLARC 1, 74.

WONEYCUTT, Edward; b unk; d 1 Jun 1811 **RU**: Captain, Was 1st Lt & Capt 1777-78 on "Greyhound" and "Hornet" **CEM**: Cedar Grove; GPS 36.57204, -80.02599; 301 Fort Lane Rd; Portsmouth City **GS**: U **SP**: No info **VI**: Pen granted to heirs 1849. Also recd 1/2 pay for being disabled or wounded. R110 **P**: Y **BLW**: unk **RG**: Y **MK**: Y SAR **PH**: unk **SS**: K Vol 6 pg 191; CG Vol 3 pg 3924; SAR P-323370 **BS**: JLARC 4, 39.

WOOD, Benjamin; b 15 Mar 1761; d 29 Apr 1829 **RU**: Soldier, Served in 1st VA Regt **CEM**: Wood-Conn; GPS unk; Rileyville, 9 mi Luray; Page **GS**: Y **SP**: 1) Mar (25 Jan 1792) Sarah Fallis/Follice (1766-1822) 2) Mar (18 Jun 1823) Elizabeth Pasquette Abbott (1789-1871) **VI**: Son of Nehemiah (1731-1816) & Abigale (Grigsby) Wood **P**: unk **BLW**: unk **RG**: Y **MK**: Y SAR **PH**: Y **SS**: E pg 842; SAR P-323414 **BS**: JLARC 76.

WOOD, James; b 28 Jan 1741, Winchester City; d 16 Jun or 16 Jul 1813 **RU**: Brig General, Commander 12th VA Regt as Col, 12 Nov 1776. Served until 1 Jan 1783, afterwards commanded 1st VA Regt to end of war **CEM**: St John's Episcopal; GPS 37.53183, -77.41958; 2401 E Broad St; Richmond City **GS**: Y **SP**: Jean Moncure **VI**: Governor of Virginia 1796-1799. BLW awarded 14 Feb 1792 for 7,777 acres. No GS, however plaque inside church indicates burial **P**: unk **BLW**: Y **RG**: N **MK**: Y SAR plaque **PH**: unk **SS**: E pg 843; N pg 293; CE pg 33 **BS**: 32 e-mail 06.

WOOD, Nehemiah; b 1731, Prince William Co; d 3 Oct 1816 **RU**: Private/Patriot, Served in 8th Cont Line. Gave material aid to cause **CEM**: Fairview; GPS unk; Rileyville, 7 mi fr Luray; Page **GS**: Y **SP**: Mar (c1755) Abigale Grigsby (c1735-28 Jul 1800), 2) mar (1816) Dinah Wood (1732-1829) **VI**: DAR plaque on gravestone **P**: N **BLW**: unk **RG**: Y **MK**: Y SAR **PH**: unk **SS**: D Vol 3 pg 841; E pg 843; DAR A128108; SAR P-323688 **BS**: JLARC 76.

WOOD, Robert; b 27 Jul 1747, Winchester; d 1801 **RU**: Patriot, Furnished equipment and/or supplies. Was Commissioner of Peace, Frederick Co **CEM**: Wood Family; GPS unk; Glen Burnie nr Winchester; Frederick **GS**: Y **SP**: 1) Mar (2 Apr 1774) Comfort Welsh (1751-c1840) 2) Abigail Rudd **VI**: No further data **P**: N **BLW**: N **RG**: Y **MK**: N **PH**: unk **SS**: DAR A128143; SAR P-323714; AL Ct Bk pg 18, 48 **BS**: 80 vol 4 pg 212.

WOOD, Thomas (1700-1777). See Appendix G Addenda.

WOOD, Thomas; b unk; d 1817 **RU**: Patriot, Gave material aid to cause **CEM**: Wood family; GPS unk; Vic jct Rts 659 & 610; Fluvanna **GS**: Y **SP**: Mary Hope (__-1823) **VI**: No further data **P**: N **BLW**: N **RG**: N **MK**: N **PH**: unk **SS**: AL Ct Bk pg 1,45 **BS**: 66 pg 102.

WOOD, Thomas; b 1753, Lunenburg Co; d 26 Jan 1824 **RU**: Private, Served in VA Line. Ent Serv Lunenburg Co 1780 where then living. Served in Battles of Camden, Guilford CH, and Siege of Yorktown **CEM**: Old Wood Family; GPS 36.50000, -79.46520; Rodgers Chapel Rd btw Rts 605 & 608, Clover; Halifax **GS**: U **SP**: Mar (1774 or 1775 Lunenburg Co by Rev Craig, Episcopal) Mary Moore (c1759-__) **VI**: Widow appl pen 30 Jan 1839 Halifax Co age 80. W6568, Govt Gr Stone **P**: Y **BLW**: unk **RG**: Y **MK**: unk **PH**: unk **SS**: ; J-NSSAR 1993 Reg; K Vol 6 pg 198; CG Vol 3 pg 3957; DAR A128234; SAR P-323784 **BS**: JLARC 1 App D pg 12. (**WOOD**, William Crane See Appendix G, Addenda)

WOOD, William Sr; b unk; d 1811 **RU**: Second Lieutenant, Served in Capt Anderson's Militia Co 1778 **CEM**: Wood; GPS unk; Rt 620 nr Rt 616, Rodophil; Amelia **GS**: N **SP**: Ann Crane (4 Dec1733,

RU=Rank/Unit VI=Other Veteran Info MK=SAR/DAR Marker | CEM=Cemetery P=Pension PH=Photo | GS=Gravestone BLW=Bounty/Land Warrant SS=Service Source | SP=Spousal Information RG=Registered Grave BS=Burial Source

461

Spotsylvania Co-1770) **VI:** He made his will 28 Nov 1809. Son of William Wood Jr. Lived at Ingleside in Amelia Co. **P:** unk **BLW:** unk **RG:** N **MK:** unk **PH:** N **SS:** AZ pg 180 **BS:** 196.

WOODARD, William; b 1710, Dublin, County Dublin, Ireland; d 1818 **RU:** Patriot, Gave material aid to cause in Princess Anne Co before moving to Rappahannock Co **CEM:** Woodard; GPS unk; James Woodard Farm, off Co Rd 600 in field N of "Caboose Pond"; Rappahannock **GS:** U **SP:** Olive Butt **VI:** Ran away fr home & came to VA as indentured servant on plantation in East VA for seven yrs. Then moved to Piedmont area. Died in Sperryville, Rappahannock Co **P:** N **BLW:** N **RG:** N **MK:** unk **PH:** unk **SS:** JLARC 116; AL Comm Bk IV Princess Anne Co **BS:** JLARC 116.

WOODDELL, Thomas; b c1730; d 1785 **RU:** Patriot, Gave material aid to cause **CEM:** Mossy Creek Presbyterian; GPS 38.35331, -79.04914; 372 Kyles Mill Rd, Mt Solon; Augusta **GS:** Y **SP:** Mar (c1752) PA Alise (-----) (__-1818 Bath Co) **VI:** No further data **P:** N **BLW:** N **RG:** Y **MK:** N **PH:** unk **SS:** SAR P-323972; AS SAR regist **BS:** 80 vol 4 pg 213; 196.

WOODFIN, Samuel; b 21 Sep 1752; d 13 Jan 1832 **RU:** Patriot, Gave material aid to cause **CEM:** Muddy Creek Baptist; GPS unk; 3470 Rt 629, Powhatan; Powhatan **GS:** N **SP:** Obedience Gaithright (7 Nov 1753-15 Dec 1827) **VI:** No further data **P:** N **BLW:** N **RG:** Y **MK:** unk **PH:** N **SS:** AL Ct Bk pg 24 Powhatan Co; SAR P-329442 **BS:** 196.

WOODFORD, William; b 1734; d 30 Nov 1780 **RU:** Brig General, Promoted to Brig Gen 21 Feb 1777, 1st VA Brigade comprised 2nd, 3rd, 6th, 11th, 15th Regts in 1779. After White Plains rearrangements, Regts were 2nd, 3rd, 4th, 5th, 7th, 8th, 9th. Taken prisoner at Charleston. Died as prisoner in NY in Nov 1780 **CEM:** White Hall; GPS unk; 2.4 mi N of Woodford; Caroline **GS:** N **SP:** Mary (__), recd pen **VI:** Died in Charleston SC. Contrary to statement that Gen Woodford was bur in Trinity Churchyard, NYC, is the tradition that he is bur in graveyard in "White Hall" **P:** SP Yes **BLW:** unk **RG:** Y **MK:** N **PH:** N **SS:** G pg 401, 792; CE pg 34; BX pg 892; SAR P-323995 **BS:** 98 Caroline.

WOODHOUSE, William; b 1750; d 1783 **RU:** Captain/Patriot, Gave material aid to cause. Commanded a co in Princess Anne Co, Militia 1777 **CEM:** Old Donation Episcopal; GPS 36.86984, -76.13316; 4449 N Witchduck Rd; Virginia Beach City **GS:** U **SP:** Mar (c1774) Susan Pallett (__-1820) **VI:** No further data **P:** unk **BLW:** unk **RG:** Y **MK:** unk **PH:** unk **SS:** DAR A128492; J- DAR Hatcher; E pg 844; AL Comm Bk IV pg 228 Princess Anne Co; DD cites VA Mag Hist & Biog Vol 15, Oct 1907, pg 188; SAR P-324005 **BS:** JLARC 2.

WOODRUFF, David Jr; b c1762; d 14 Nov 1814 **RU:** Captain, Served in Amherst Co Militia **CEM:** Monument Hill; GPS 37.55115, -79.09496; Nr jct Rt 663 on Stable Ln, Sweet Briar College; Amherst **GS:** Y **SP:** Judith McDaniel (c1786-3 Jun 1844) **VI:** Son of David Sr & Clary (Powell) Woodruff **P:** unk **BLW:** unk **RG:** N **MK:** N **PH:** unk **SS:** E pg 844; AL cert issued **BS:** 01 pg 167.

WOODS, Andrew Sr; b 1722; d 10 Apr 1781 **RU:** Private/Patriot, Served in Capt Daniel Smith's Co, Fincastle Co Militia in Lord Dunmore's war at Point Pleasant. Also was in Capt James Robertson's Co. Was Sheriff of Botetourt Co. Gave material aid to cause **CEM:** Buchanan; GPS unk; Buchanan; Botetourt **GS:** U **SP:** Mar (31 Jan 1747 Staunton) Martha Poage (1728 Augusta Co-15 Apr 1818) **VI:** High Sheriff **P:** unk **BLW:** unk **RG:** Y **MK:** unk **PH:** unk **SS:** DAR A128819; AL Ct Bk pg 4,10,28 Botetourt Co; DF pg 456; SAR P-324310 **BS:** JLARC 76.

WOODS, Samuel; b 17 May 1727, Ireland; d 10 Jan 1781 **RU:** Sergeant, Enl 25 Jan 1776 in Co 2, Col Wm Irvine's PA Regt. Served in Canada Campaign. Captured 10 Jun 1776 at Three Rivers on St Lawrence River **CEM:** Woods Family; GPS unk; Rockfish Presbyterian Church S of Afton; Nelson **GS:** Y **SP:** Mar (1760) Mary (-----) (1742-20 Apr 1779) **VI:** Died in Albemarle Co **P:** unk **BLW:** unk **RG:** N **MK:** N **PH:** unk **SS:** A pg 202 **BS:** 01 pg 191.

WOODS, William; b 31 Dec 1744; d 4 May 1837 **RU:** Ensign, Appt ensign in Albemarle Co Militia 8 Mar 1781 **CEM:** Woods Family; GPS unk; .5 mi S of Mechum River; Fluvanna **GS:** Y **SP:** No info **VI:** No further data **P:** unk **BLW:** unk **RG:** N **MK:** N **PH:** unk **SS:** E pg 845 **BS:** 164 Woods.

WOODS, William; b 2 Nov 1715, Dunshaughlin, County Meath, Ireland; d 12 Apr 1783 **RU:** Lieutenant Colonel, Probably served in Albemarle Co Militia **CEM:** St Paul's; GPS 38.05830, -78.59580; 851 Owensville Rd, Ivy; Albemarle **GS:** U **SP:** Mar (1 Oct 1735 Augusta Co VA) Susannah Wallace d/o

RU=Rank/Unit	CEM=Cemetery	GS=Gravestone	SP=Spousal Information
VI=Other Veteran Info	P=Pension	BLW=Bounty/Land Warrant	RG=Registered Grave
MK=SAR/DAR Marker	PH=Photo	SS=Service Source	BS=Burial Source

462

Peter & Elizabeth (Woods) Wallace **VI:** Son of Michael Marion (1684-1762) & Mary Catherine (Campbell) (1690-1742) Woods. Was a Minister. Plaque in cem lists his descendants **P:** unk **BLW:** unk **RG:** Y **MK:** unk **PH:** unk **SS:** CD; SAR P-324307 **BS:** 196.

WOODSON, Elizabeth Michaux; b 6 Jun 1740, Amelia Co, d 29 Sep 1791 **RU:** Patriot, Gave material aid to Army in Oct 1781 in Prince Edward Co **CEM:** Venable Slate Hill Plantation; GPS 37.223611,-78.442500; loc Farmville Rd., (US 15), abt.7 miles south of intersection with County Rd., 665, Farmville; Prince Edward **GS:** Name on plaque **SP:** Nathaniel Venable (1 Nov 1733, Louisa Co-26 Dec 1804, son of Abraham Venable and Martha Davis **VI:** Daug of Richard Woodson & Anne Madeline Michaux **P:** N **BLW:** N **RG** Y **MK:** N **PH:** N **SS:** D; SAR P-330479 **BS:** 196

WOODSON, Jacob; b 11 May 1748; d 5 Dec 1838 **RU:** Captain, Commanded a co Prince Edward Co Militia in 1780 **CEM:** Woodson Family; GPS unk; Farmville; Prince Edward **GS:** U **SP:** Elizabeth Morton (28 Nov 1754-12 Feb 1845) d/o Capt John Morton **VI:** Was a justice & magistrate. Signed the Statute for Religious Freedom written by Thomas Jefferson. **P:** unk **BLW:** unk **RG:** N **MK:** unk **PH:** unk **SS:** E pg 845 **BS:** 196.

WOODSON, John; b 28 Feb 1763, Goochland Co; d Aft 23 Oct 1832 **RU:** Ensign, Served in Capts Miller, Curd, Pleasants, & Duke companies **CEM:** Deanery Family; GPS unk; Cartersville on James River; Cumberland **GS:** Y **SP:** Mar (30 Mar 1786 Hanover Co) Mary Lightfoot Anderson (c1760, Louisa Co-__ Hanover Co) **VI:** Appl pen 23 Oct 1832 #S6434 **P:** Y **BLW:** unk **RG:** Y **MK:** N **PH:** unk **SS:** E pg 845; CG pg 3950; DAR A205266; SAR P-324343 **BS:** 157 Deanery.

WOODSON, Tarleton; b 22 Mar 1758, Goochland Co; d 1795 **RU:** Major, served in Colonel Hazen's Regt, Was prisoner 22 Aug 1777. Served at Norfolk, Trenton, Yorktown and Trenton. **CEM:** Woodson; GPS unk; Directions not identified; Albemarle **GS:** N **SP:** Annis Shepard (__-aft 1830) **VI:** Son of John & Elizabeth (Bailey) Woodson, both of Goochland Co, His son Charles rec as heir a pen by Congress 21 Feb 1846 **P:** unk **BLW:** Y **RG:** Y **MK:** unk **PH:** N **SS:** DAR A129220, SAR P-324342; J- DAR Hatcher; BY pg 344; BX pg 893 **BS:** JLARC 2.

WOODWARD, James; b unk; d Mar 1788 **RU:** Captain, Served in 1st VA Regt **CEM:** Old Christ Church Episcopal; GPS 38.80625, -77.04718; 118 N Washington St; Alexandria City **GS:** N **SP:** No info **VI:** Burial permit for Capt James Woodward issued 19 Mar 1788 to Capt Joseph Greenway **P:** unk **BLW:** Y **RG:** N **MK:** N **PH:** N **SS:** E pg 846 **BS:** 20 pg 154.

WOODWARD, Thomas; b 1729 Fairfax Co; d 12 May 1779. Fairfield Co, SC **RU:** Captain; raised a company of Militia in SC which he commanded, was in the battle at Sullivan's Island and killed by Tories at Little Dutchman's Creek, SC **CEM:** Thomas Woodward: GPS not determined; loc Rockton, Fairfield Co, SC **GS:** Y **SP:** Mar (1747) Jeminia Collins **VI:** memorialized on a plaque at the Fairfax Co Court House **P:** N **BLW:** N **RG:** Y **MK:** Unk **PH:** N **SS:** EH; DAR A130051; SAR P-324468 **BS:** 196.

WOODWARD, William; b 1746, Rappahannock Co; d during or after war **RU:** Private, Served in 6th VA Regt **CEM:** Smith Family; GPS 36.69923, -76.11877; Mt Pleasant Farm, now Fentress Naval Auxiliary Airfield; Chesapeake City **GS:** Y **SP:** No info **VI:** Govt GS shows service **P:** unk **BLW:** unk **RG:** N **MK:** unk **PH:** unk **SS:** E pg 844 **BS:** 196.

WOODY, Martin; b 31 Mar 1758, Goochland Co; d 6 Dec 1846 **RU:** Soldier, Enlisted 1777-78 Amherst Co where he then lived, then enlisted 1781 Bedford Co Militia **CEM:** Woody Family; GPS unk; Plantation Rd, Rocky Mount; Franklin **GS:** U **SP:** Mar (27 Oct 1785 Henry Co by Rev Robert Jones) Susanna Roberson (1765 Franklin Co-15 Jul 1852 Franklin Co) **VI:** Son of Henry & (-----) Woody. Soldier appl pen 6 May 1833 in Franklin Co age 75. Widow appl pen 3 May 1847 age 76. W3912 **P:** Y **BLW:** unk **RG:** Y **MK:** unk **PH:** unk **SS:** K Vol 6 pg 206; CG Vol III; SAR P-324545 **BS:** JLARC 4,19; 196.

WOOLDRIDGE, William; b 1756; d Feb 1830 **RU:** Private in Capt McCreery's Co Augusta Co Militia **CEM:** Wooldridge Family; GPS 37.496567, -77.646347; loc by traffic circle in iron fence; cem in the 13700 block of Grove Hill Rd, Midlotham, Chesterfield **GS:** Unk **SP:** Mildred Logwood (1757-1830) **VI:** No further data **P:** N **BLW:** N **RG:** N **MK:** Unk **PH:** N **SS:** E pg 846 **BS:** 196.

WOOLF (WOLF), Valentine; b 1721; d 3 Jun 1808 **RU:** Patriot, paid personal property tax, 1783, Rockingham Co considered to be a supply tax for Rev War expenses **CEM:** Old Stephens Family; GPS 38.527625, -78.747620; 1844 Maryz Rd, Lacey Springs; Rockingham **GS:** Y partial unreadable **SP:** Not

RU=Rank/Unit	CEM=Cemetery	GS=Gravestone	SP=Spousal Information
VI=Other Veteran Info	P=Pension	BLW=Bounty/Land Warrant	RG=Registered Grave
MK=SAR/DAR Marker	PH=Photo	SS=Service Source	BS=Burial Source

463

derermined **VI**: No further data **P**: N **BLW**: N **RG**: N **MK**: N **PH**: N **SS**: DV image 20 pdf, Rockingham Co, 1793 **BS**: 196.

WOOLFOLK, John George; b 1750; d 1819 **RU**: Second Lieutenant, Took oath 13 Jan 1779 in Caroline Co Militia **CEM**: Woolfolk Family; GPS unk; Rt 721 Sparta Rd, DeJarnette; Caroline **GS**: U **SP**: Elizabeth Powers Boadnax **VI**: No further data **P**: unk **BLW**: unk **RG**: Y **MK**: N **PH**: unk **SS**: E pg 847; SAR P-324584 **BS**: JLARC 76.

WOOLSLEY, Thomas; b 1719, Weschester Co, NY; d 26 Feb 1794 **RU**: Private, Served in 1st Light Dragoons of VA **CEM**: Riverbend; GPS unk; Vic jct Rts 650 & 660; Smyth **GS**: Y **SP**: 1) Mar (1739 Bedford NY) Elizabeth Waters 2) Mar (1782 Radford VA) Sarah Pierce (__-1794) d/o John & Sarah (-----) Pierce **VI**: Son of Richard & Sarah (Fowler) Woolsey. Was pioneer and Baptist Minister. Recd 100 acres BLW **P**: unk **BLW**: Y **RG**: N **MK**: N **PH**: unk **SS**: E pg 847 **BS**: 97 vol 1 pg 120; 196.

WORMELEY, Ralph IV; b 5 Oct 1715; d 19 Aug 1790 **RU**: Gave material aid to Army,1782 **CEM**: Rosegill Orchard; GPS 37.3739, -76.3357; loc off Rt 227, E of Urbanna; Middlesex **GS**: N **SP**: Mar (4 Nov 1736) Sarah Berkeley (9 Feb 1713-__), d/o Edmund Berkeley & Lucy Mann Burwell (1683-1716) **VI**; Son of Ralph Wormeley III; died at Rosegill, thus very likely buried there **P**: N **BLW**: N **RG**: N **MK**: N **PH**: N **SS**:G pgs 291, 292, Military Claims, Middlesex Co 1782 **BS**: 196.

WORMELEY, Ralph V; b c1744; d 19 Jan 1806 **RU**: Patriot, Furnished equipment and supplies to cause **CEM**: Tayloe Family; GPS 37.58200, -76.47290; Mt Airy, Rt 360, Warsaw; Richmond Co **GS**: Y **SP**: Eleanor Tayloe (16 Oct 1756-25 Feb 1815) d/o John II & Rececca Plater (Addison) Tayloe **VI**: Son of Ralph IV & Jane (Boles) Wormeley. Served several times as a member of the House of Delegates and in the Virginia Convention of 1788. Died in Middlesex Co. He and his wife have a gravetone in the Christ Church Cemetery in Saluda, Middlesex Co, thus perhaps only memorialized at Mt Airy **P**: N **BLW**: N **RG**: N **MK**: N **PH**: unk **SS**: AL Ct Bk pg 6 **BS**: 84 pg 98; 196.

WORRELL, James; b 1752, Chester Co, PA; d 31 Jan 1802 **RU**: Private, Served in 6th Battalion of PA Militia Capt John Quin's Co under Col Caleb Davis **CEM**: Worrell Family; GPS 36.78290, -80.66173; Off Pils Trail Rt 673, .6 mi S of Rt 221, Eona; Carroll **GS**: Y **SP**: 1) Barbary Pennicic 2) Elizabeth Crandell **VI**: Son of Peter Worrell & Mary Trego. DAR plaque on small stone **P**: unk **BLW**: unk **RG**: Y **MK**: Y DAR plaque **PH**: unk **SS**: DAR A130538; SAR P-324814 **BS**: JLARC 2, 4, 43; 68; 196.

WORSHAM, Essex; b 1758, Amelia Co; d Aft 1832 **RU**: Private, Ent serv Amelia Co 1778 as substitute for brother Henry Worsham. Ent serv again in 1781 as substitute for brother Cannon Worsham. Served in Capt William Finner & Creed Haskinns's Cos **CEM**: Worsham Family; GPS unk; Check county property rec for loc; Pittsylvania **GS**: Y **SP**: Mar (28 Dec 1786) Elizabeth Dunnavant, d/o Hodges & (-----) Dunnavant **VI**: Lived in Amelia for 10 yrs after RW, then moved to Prince Edward where he lived 15 yrs, then Pittsylvania Co. Appl pen 17 Nov 1832 in Pittsylvania Co. S6447 **P**: Y **BLW**: unk **RG**: Y **MK**: N **PH**: unk **SS**: K Vol 6 pg 211; CG Vol 3 pg 3962-3; DAR A130555; SAR P-324820 **BS**: DAR Rpt.

WORSHAM, George; b c1757; d Oct 1822 **RU**: Patriot, Gave material aid to cause **CEM**: Shockoe Hill; GPS 37.55190, -77.43170; 4th & Hospital Sts; Richmond City **GS**: Y **SP**: No info **VI**: No further data **P**: N **BLW**: N **RG**: N **MK**: N **PH**: unk **SS**: AL Ct Bk pg 44 **BS**: 57 pg 1.

WORSHAM, William; b 16 Jun 1752, Chesterfield Co; d 27 Aug 1836 **RU**: Captain/Patriot, As QM Sgt, served under Joseph Scott, 1st Cont Dragoons Jan 1777. Was taken prisoner 15 mos later. Was Capt of Prince Edward Co Militia. Gave material aid to cause **CEM**: Worsham Family Square; GPS 37.32163, -78.44328; Vic Rts 665 & 15 Farmville Rd, Worsham; Prince Edward **GS**: N **SP**: Margaret Jones (1758-1827) **VI**: Pen rec'd by son Richard. Also rec'd BLW 2666 acres **P**: Y **BLW**: Y **RG**: N **MK**: unk **PH**: N **SS**: E pg 848; AL Ct Bk pg 52 Chesterfield Co; CG pg 3963 **BS**: 196.

WORTHINGTON, William; b unk; d 29 May 1825 **RU**: Matross, Served in Co #6, John Dandridge Co at Valley Forge in Jun 1778 **CEM**: Ketoctin Baptist; GPS 39.15746, -77.74870; Ketoctin Church Rd, Purcellville; Loudoun **GS**: Y **SP**: No info **VI**: The GS inscription can be read as dying in the 14th yr of his age however it is believed to be in error and should read 74th yr of his age **P**: unk **BLW**: unk **RG**: N **MK**: N **PH**: unk **SS**: A pg 248 **BS**: 25 pg 347.

RU=Rank/Unit	CEM=Cemetery	GS=Gravestone	SP=Spousal Information
VI=Other Veteran Info	P=Pension	BLW=Bounty/Land Warrant	RG=Registered Grave
MK=SAR/DAR Marker	PH=Photo	SS=Service Source	BS=Burial Source

WRAY/RAY, Benjamin Oat; b 28 May 1757, James River, d 16 Apr 1849 **RU**: Private, entered service Bedford County, Capt Davis, militia and Capt Richardson, company of rifleman, 4th VA Regt, Cont Line **CEM**: Wray Family; GPS: 37.656, -79.5714; Boones Mill, Rt 607, 10 mi S Rocky Mount; Franklin **GS**: N **SP**: 1) Mar (1778) Susannah Poteet (1767, Bedford Co-1805), 2) Patsy Goode, 3) Mar (9 May 1832) Frances Hartwell (1795-1878) who rec'd pen Franklin Co # S5657, R2005 and BLW 26263 for 150 acres in 1855, She resided 1866 Rocky Mount, Franklin Co **VI**: Son of Moses Wray (1727-1802) & Mary Morris (1701 Henrico Co-1780 Amherst Co): **P**: Y 3d spouse **BLW**: Y 3rd spouse **RG**: Y **MK**: N **PH**: N **SS** E pg 652; K vol 4, pg 186; DAR A093559; SAR P-331048CG: pg 3965; **BS**: SAR PRS; 196.

WRAY, David; b 1751, Brunswick Co; d 3 Sep 1833 **RU**: Private, Ent serv Apr or May 1778 then again in 1780. Was in expedition against Indians in western part of VA called New River in Capt John Donlison's Co. In 1780 volunteered in Henry Co under Capt Wm Witcher and sent to NC, then SC. Then guarded prisoners fr Battle of Cowpens. Also was in Battle of Guilford CH **CEM**: Wray Family; GPS unk; Check Co property rec for loc; Pittsylvania **GS**: Y **SP**: Mar (11 Feb 1797 Botetourt Co) Elizabeth (28 May 1757, James River- 16 Apr 18, Carvin) **VI**: Appl for pen 17 Sep 1832 age 81 Henry Co (now Pittsylvania Co). S7973 **P**: Y **BLW**: unk **RG**: Y **MK**: N **PH**: unk **SS**: E pg 848; K Vol 6 pg 212; CG Vol 3; SAR P-324931 **BS**: DAR Rpt.

WRAY, Moses, Jr; b 1727, Henrico Co, d Oct 1802 (will) Maggodee Creek **RU**: Patriot, paid personal property tax 1782, Bedford Co considered a partial tax for Rev War expenses **CEM**: Wray Family: GPS: 37.656, -79.5714; Boones Mill, Rt 607, 10 mi S Rocky Mount; Franklin **GS**: N **SP**: Elizabeth Morris, d/o Daniel Morris & Tabitha (-----) **VI**: Son of Moses Wray (1701 Henrico Co-1780 Amherst Co) & (-----) **P**: N **BLW**: N **RG**: N **MK**: N **PH**: N **SS**: DV Bedford Co Personal Prop tax 1782 image 14 pdf **BS**: 196.

WREN, James; b c1728, Fairfax Co; d bef 21 Nov 1815 **RU**: Colonel/Patriot, Commanded the Fairfax Co Militia. Performed public service as Justice of Peace and County Sherriff, Gave material aid to cause **CEM**: Wren Family; GPS 38.884197, -77.212530; Hillsman Dr and Mahala Ln; Falls Church City **GS**: U **SP**: 1) Mar (27 Mar 1753) Catherine Brent (13 Jan 1729, Stafford Co-c1770 Fairfax Co) 2) Sarah Jones **VI**: His manor house was built in 1770 and still stands. He designed Falls Church and Pohick Church **P**: Y **BLW**: Y **RG**: Y **MK**: Y SAR **PH**: unk **SS**: DAR A130667; D Vol 2 pg 346; AL Ct Bk pg 27 Fairfax Co; DD cites pen of Samuel Barker Davis as source; SAR P-324936 **BS**: JLARC 14; 196 Son of Thomas Ren & Jean (-----).

WREN, William; b 1747; d bef 29 May 1777 **RU**: Private/Patriot, serv as Drummer in 1st VA Regt, as patriot signed a legislative petition Fairfax Co, dated 29 May 1777 **CEM**: Rev War Court House Plaque; GPS not determined; 4110 Chain Bridge Rd; Fairfax **GS**: Memorialized on plaque 2017 by Geo Washington Chapter, VASSAR **SP**: No spousal info **VI**: War Claim filed, thus injuried in serv **P**: N **BLW**: Unk **RG**: N **MK**: N **PH**: N **SS**: AP Fold3 Serv Rec; EP source indicates soldier filed war claim, Fairfax Co **BS**: None

WRIGHT, John; b 1707 (FAG 1712), Westmoreland Co, d 27 Feb 1792 his estate called Pine View **RU**: Patriot, gave material aid to cause, Fauquier Co **CEM**: Pine View Estate Family Cem; GPS Liberty 38.3600, -77.4618; nr unincorporated town of Liberty; Fauquier **GS**: Unk **SP**: 1) Mar (1729) Elizabeth Darnall (__-1 Jun 1784), 2) Elizabeth Bronaugh (1699-1792) **VI**: Public Career began in Dumfries Pr Wm Co as vestryman and in Fauquier Co as Justice and Sheriff & was a Judge before 1743 **P**: N **BLW**: N **RG**: Y **MK**: N **PH**: N **SS**: D vol 1 pg 355; DAR A130893; SAR P-325148 **BS**: 196.

WRIGHT, John; b 8 Aug 1767; d Bef 23 Jun 1851 **RU**: Private, Served in Col Daniel Gaines Regt, Amherst Co Militia **CEM**: Moore; GPS unk; Fort Edmiston; Washington **GS**: U **SP**: Mar (1792, Washington Co) Mary Kincannon (10 Sep 1774, Washington Co-aft 1840) d/o Francis (21 Mar 1750 York Co, PA-__ Hardin Co, TN) & Martha (Snodgrass) (__-26 Aug 1817, Maury Co, TN) Kincannon **VI**: No further data **P**: unk **BLW**: unk **RG**: Y **MK**: unk **PH**: unk **SS**: DN pg 409, 411; SAR P-325194 **BS**: JLARC 2. (**WRIGHT**, John see Appendix G Addenda)

WRIGHT, Joseph; b 1752; d 8 Oct 1826 **RU**: Private, Served in Capt Trimble's Augusta Co Militia **CEM**: Hebron Presbyterian; GPS 38.14140, -79.15500; 423 Hebron Rd; Staunton City **GS**: Y **SP**: Ruth Evans **VI**: Died age 74 (stone) **P**: unk **BLW**: unk **RG**: N **MK**: unk **PH**: unk **SS**: E pg 850 **BS**: JLARC 62, 63; 196. **SEE APPENDIX G**

RU=Rank/Unit	CEM=Cemetery	GS=Gravestone	SP=Spousal Information
VI=Other Veteran Info	P=Pension	BLW=Bounty/Land Warrant	RG=Registered Grave
MK=SAR/DAR Marker	PH=Photo	SS=Service Source	BS=Burial Source

WRIGHT, Robert Mosley Sr; b 1766; d 20 Jan 1838 **RU:** Soldier, Ent serv Caroline Co **CEM:** Elmwood; GPS unk; Rt 651, 5.3 mi S of DeJarnette; Caroline **GS:** N **SP:** Margaret Hawkins Boutwell, d/o William Boutwell (1773-29 Oct 1855) **VI:** Son of Robert & Mary Catherine (Bell) Wright. Appl for pen Caroline Co 8 Oct 1832 age 69 **P:** Y **BLW:** unk **RG:** N **MK:** N **PH:** N **SS:** CG Vol 3 pg 3975 **BS:** 196.

WRIGHT, Stephen; b 24 Dec 1763, Craney Island, Norfolk Co; d Aft 1852 **RU:** Colonel, Ent Sea Service at Craney Island where he lived as Ens, VA Militia. Served on small navy cruiser with his guardian, Capt W Westcott. Captured by British and held on prison ship until 1783. Obtained rank of Colonel **CEM:** Cedar Grove; GPS 36.859096, -76.283081; 238 E Princess Anne Rd; Norfolk City **GS:** Y **SP:** Mar (12 Jun 1795, Norfolk Co) Abigail O'Conner **VI:** Son of Steven & Anne (Phripp) Wright. Was in Legislature fr county for abt 50 yrs. Was County Justice. Appl for pen 4 Aug 1849 Norfolk where he then lived and was known as "Col" and was presiding Magistrate "for many yrs." Pen applic rejected due to insufficient proof. R11907. He was living in 1852 **P:** N **BLW:** unk **RG:** Y **MK:** N **PH:** Y **SS:** K Vol 6 pg 222; BR; CG Vol 3; see Burial source 136; SAR Bio rpt submitted Jul 2020 **BS:** 136 2009 newsltr.

WRIGHT, William; b 18 Nov 1740, York Co; d 29 Aug 1806 **RU:** Sergeant/Patriot, Served in Fauquier Co Militia. Gave material aid to cause **CEM:** Dermonte Burying Ground; GPS unk; Liberty; Fauquier **GS:** U **SP:** Mar (25 Dec 1768 New York Co, VA) Elizabeth Lloyd (7 Nov 1750 York Co-25 Jul 1830 Fauquier Co) d/o William & Sarah (Chowning) Lloyd **VI:** Son of John & Ann (-----) Wright **P:** unk **BLW:** unk **RG:** Y **MK:** unk **PH:** unk **SS:** J- DAR Hatcher, E pg 850; AL Ct Bk pg 26 Fairfax Co; SAR P-325364 **BS:** JLARC 2; 196. (**WYATT**, Edward see Appendix G, Addenda)

WYATT, John; b c1740, Stafford Co; d 1808 **RU:** Soldier, Served 3 yrs in VA Cont Lines 3rd, 4th, 8th, 12th, & 2nd VA State Regt **CEM:** Wyatt; GPS unk; Rt 601, 3.6 mi S of South Boston; Halifax **GS:** U **SP:** Mar (25 Jan 1790 Halifax Co) Leah Younger d/o William & Patience (-----) Younger **VI:** Son of William Edward & Lettice (-----) Wyatt. John's will in Hallifax Co, drawn 24 Feb 1801, proved 22 Feb 1808. VA Recd BLW of 100 acres, 30 May 1783 **P:** unk **BLW:** Y **RG:** N **MK:** unk **PH:** unk **SS:** E pg 851; F pg 78 **BS:** 196. (**WYATT**, William, Jr See Appendix G Addenda)

WYCKLIFFE (WICKLIFF), Aaron; b unk; d unk **RU:** Private, Served in 11th VA Regt **CEM:** Wickliff Family; GPS 38.46243, -77.24409; Behind 13220 Yates Ford Rd, Clifton; Fairfax **GS:** Y **SP:** No info **VI:** DAR Marker **P:** unk **BLW:** unk **RG:** Y **MK:** Y DAR **PH:** unk **SS:** AS DAR Report; SAR P-325475 **BS:** DAR report.

WYCKLIFFE (WICKLIFF), Moses; b unk; d unk **RU:** Private, Served in 11th VA Regt **CEM:** Wickliff Family; GPS 38.46243, -77.24409; Behind 13220 Yates Ford Rd, Clifton; Fairfax **GS:** Y **SP:** No info **VI:** DAR Marker **P:** unk **BLW:** unk **RG:** Y **MK:** Y **PH:** unk **SS:** AS DAR Report; SAR P-325476 **BS:** DAR report.

WYLIE, Samuel; b unk; d 1781 **RU:** Private, Killed in Battle of Green Springs nr Williamsburg **CEM:** Williamsburg Land Conservancy; GPS unk; 5000 New Point Rd; Williamsburg City **GS:** N **SP:** No info **VI:** Name is on the monument erected in Williamsburg **P:** unk **BLW:** unk **RG:** N **MK:** N **PH:** N **SS:** AU Will Chap **BS:** 32.

WYNNE, Edmund; b 26 Mar 1744; d 6 May 1763 **RU:** Patriot, Gave material aid to cause **CEM:** Essex Lodge, aka Washington's Lodge; GPS unk; See property records for loc; York **GS:** N **SP:** Mary Llewellyn (19 Jan 1750-21 Mar 1809) **VI:** Son of John & Lucy (Hill) Wynne **P:** N **BLW:** N **RG:** N **MK:** unk **PH:** N **SS:** AL Ct Bk II pg 1, 7 Warwick Co **BS:** 32 Frederick W Bolt, Historian York Co Dec 2004.

WYNNE, Thomas; b c1742; d Jan 1794 **RU:** Patriot, Gave material aid to cause **CEM:** Essex Lodge, aka Washington's Lodge; GPS unk; See property records; York **GS:** N **SP:** Frances Harwood (c1732-aft 1792) **VI:** Son of John & Lucy (Hill) Wynne **P:** N **BLW:** N **RG:** N **MK:** unk **PH:** N **SS:** AL Ct Bk II pg 1, 7 Warwick Co **BS:** 32 Frederick W Bolt, Historian York Co Dec 2004.

WYNNE, Thomas H; b c1720; d bet 1826-1860 **RU:** Patriot, Provided equipment & supplies **CEM:** St John's Episcopal; GPS 37.53183, -77.41958; 2401 E Broad St; Richmond City **GS:** Y **SP:** No info **VI:** No further data **P:** N **BLW:** N **RG:** N **MK:** N **PH:** unk **SS:** AL Ct Bk 1 pg 1, 7 **BS:** 28 pg 349.

WYNNE (WYNN), William Jr; b 25 Feb 1762, Pittsylvania Co; d 1835 **RU:** Private, Served in Capt Thomas Mastin's Co of Militia stationed at Wynn's Garrison fort fr 1779 to end of war in 1783 **CEM:**

RU=Rank/Unit   CEM=Cemetery   GS=Gravestone   SP=Spousal Information
VI=Other Veteran Info   P=Pension   BLW=Bounty/Land Warrant   RG=Registered Grave
MK=SAR/DAR Marker   PH=Photo   SS=Service Source   BS=Burial Source

466

Wynn-Peery; GPS 37.12620, -81.4988; Campbell Ln, Tazewell; Tazewell **GS:** Y **SP:** No info **VI:** Son of William Sr. & Cynthia (Harmon) Wynn (1735 Montgomery Co-___). Appl pen 4 Apr 1834 R11920 **P:** Y **BLW:** unk **RG:** N **MK:** unk **PH:** unk **SS:** CG pg 3983 **BS:** 196.

WYNNE (WYNN), William Sr; b 10 Aug 1729; d 8 Jul 1808 **RU:** Patriot, Gave material aid to cause **CEM:** Wynn-Peery; GPS 37.12620, -81.4988; Campbell Ln, Tazewell; Tazewell **GS:** Y **SP:** 1) Cynthia Harmon (1735 NC-17 Jul 1776) 2) Mar (1 Jan 1782, Montgomery Co) Phyllis Marrs (20 Sep 1763-12 Jan 1855) **VI:** Son of William (1699-26 Nov 1778, Pittsylvania Co) & Francis (Reade) Wynne **P:** unk **BLW:** unk **RG:** Y **MK:** N **PH:** unk **SS:** AL Ct Bk pg 43, 44, 45 Montgomery Co; AS SAR applic; SAR P-325693 **BS:** 80 vol 4 pg 221; 196.

WYSONG, Feidt (Fyette); b 1754 or 1759, York PA; d 1837 **RU:** Soldier, Drafted and served under Capt Josiah Swearington in Col Morrison's Regt for abt 5 mos. Marched to Ft McIntosh to the Muskingum and was discharged there. In Jul 1781, drafted and marched under Capt Looney to Bottom's Bridge below Richmond then to Yorktown and was at the siege. **CEM:** Fincastle Presbyterian; GPS 37.50017, -79.87558; 108 E Back St, Fincastle; Botetourt **GS:** N **SP:** Mar (27 May 1814 Botetourt Co) Susanna Coffman d/o Henry & (-----) Coffman **VI:** Name is on SAR plaque at this cemetery. Pensioned 3 Sep 1832 **P:** N **BLW:** N **RG:** Y **MK:** Y SAR plaque **PH:** N **SS:** AZ pg 127; DAR A129329; SAR P-325697 **BS:** JLARC 1; 196.

WYSOR (WEYSOR, WEIZER), Henry; b 1756; d 12 Jan 1844 **RU:** Sergeant, Served in Frederick Co, Feb 1776 in Capt Berry's Co, Col Muhlenburg's 8th VA Cont Line. Was at Charleston at Ft Moultrie attack. Later with Gen Morgan, at Saratoga at surrender of Burgoyne, and at Valley Forge. In 1781 rejoined and was at siege at Yorktown. Had 5 tours serving 28 mos **CEM:** Wysor; GPS unk; Dublin; Pulaski **GS:** U **SP:** Mar (31 May 1811 Montgomery Co) Cynthia Charlton (3 Nov 1787-14 Jan 1866) **VI:** He moved to Montgomery Co after the war and was a Lt in War of 1812. Appl for pension 3 Sep 1832 age 78. His 1833 address was at Christiansburg. S7854 **P:** Y **BLW:** unk **RG:** N **MK:** unk **PH:** unk **SS:** E pg 851; K Vol 6 pg 228; AZ pg 164; CG Vol III **BS:** 196.

WYTHE, George; b 1726; Elizabeth City Co, d 8 Jun 1806 **RU:** Patriot, Was Signer of Declaration of Independence. Provided supplies to Maj Nelson's Troops of Horse & Gen Steven's Brigade **CEM:** St John's Episcopal; GPS 37.53183, -77.41958; 2401 E Broad St; Richmond City **GS:** U **SP:** 1) Ann Lewis, 2) Elizabeth Eggleston Taliaferro (1739 Williamsburg-Aug 1787, James City Co) d/o Richard & (-----) Taliaferro **VI:** No further data **P:** N **BLW:** N **RG:** Y **MK:** N **PH:** Y **SS:** E pg 851; SAR P-325703 **BS:** 28 pg 349.

YAGER, John Sr; b 15 Sep 1732, Madison Co; d 17 Aug 1826 **RU:** Patriot, Gave material aid to cause **CEM:** Hebron Lutheran; GPS 38.40676, -78.24808; 899 Blankenbaker Rd, Madison; Madison **GS:** U **SP:** Mar (c1757 Madison Co) Mary Margaret Wilhoit, d/o John Christian & Walburga (Weaver) Wilhoit (1737-1800) **VI:** Son of Adam Sr (1708-1794) & Susanna (Kobler) Yager (1710-___). Known as "Blind" John Yeager in old age **P:** unk **BLW:** unk **RG:** Y **MK:** unk **PH:** unk **SS:** AL Ct Bk 1 pg 43 Culpeper Co; SAR P-325712 **BS:** 196.

YANCEY, Charles; b 10 May 1741; d 9 Jan 1814 **RU:** Captain, Commanded a Co in the Louisa Co Militia 1781-1782 **CEM:** Yancey/Crawford Family; GPS unk; Yanceyville; Louisa **GS:** N **SP:** Mary Crawford (8 Aug 1742-1841) **VI:** Son of Robert (___-1746) & Temperance (Dumas) Yancey **P:** N **BLW:** N **RG:** N **MK:** N **PH:** N **SS:** CZ pg 486 **BS:** 196.

YANCEY, Charles Sr; b 1732; d 15 Apr 1805 **RU:** Patriot, Gave material aid to the cause **CEM:** Yancey Family; GPS 38.51709, -77.95532; Off Rt 685 Auburn Rd, 3.5 mi WNW of Brandy Station; Culpeper **GS:** Y **SP:** Mar (1740) Caroline Powers **VI:** No further data **P:** N **BLW:** N **RG:** Y **MK:** N **PH:** unk **SS:** DAR A108720; AL Ct Bk I pg 16; SAR P-338206 **BS:** 167 Yancey; 196.

YANCEY, Lewis Davis; b 1689; d 1784 **RU:** Patriot, Provided beef and cattle to the army and paid peronal property tax in 1783. **CEM:** Yancey Family; GPS 38.51709, -77.95532; Off Rt 685 Auburn Rd, 3.5 mi WNW of Brandy Station; Culpeper **GS:** Y **SP:** Mar (c1710) Mildred Winifred Cavenaugh (1710-1780) **VI:** No further data **P:** N **BLW:** N **RG:** Y **MK:** N **PH:** unk **SS:** AK; SAR P-325751 **BS:** 29 pg 28; 196.

RU=Rank/Unit	CEM=Cemetery	GS=Gravestone	SP=Spousal Information
VI=Other Veteran Info	P=Pension	BLW=Bounty/Land Warrant	RG=Registered Grave
MK=SAR/DAR Marker	PH=Photo	SS=Service Source	BS=Burial Source

467

YANCEY, Mary; b 8 Aug 1742; d 1841 **RU:** Patriot, Gave material aid to cause **CEM:** Yancey/Crawford Family; **GPS** unk; Yanceyville; Lousia **GS:** U **SP:** Charles Yancey (10 May 1741-9 Jan 1814 **VI:** No further data **P:** N **BLW:** N **RG:** N **MK:** unk **PH:** unk **SS:** AL Ct Bk pg 16, 24 Lousia Co **BS:** 196.

YANCEY, Robert; b 1 Jan 1742, Hanover Co; d 20 Jul 1818 **RU:** Patriot, Performed public service by viewing, making report on alterations on Gillis Rd as ordered by Mecklenburg Co Ct on 13 May 1776 **CEM:** Yancey Family; **GPS** unk; Hwy 736 S fr 602 abt 2.5 mi, Averett; Mecklenburg **GS:** Y **SP:** Mar (aft 5 Mar 1765) Philadelphia Jones (c1754- aft 1818) d/o John (c1715, Mecklenburg Co-1791) & (-----) Jones **VI:** Cem in wooded area with periwinkle **P:** N **BLW:** N **RG:** Y **MK:** unk **PH:** unk **SS:** Mecklenburg Co Order Book #4 (1773-79) pg 337; DAR Patriot Index Vol 3 pg 3047; SAR P-325756 **BS:** 196.

YANCEY, William Layton (Leighton); b 1754, Lousia or Rockingham Co; d 4 Apr 1813 **RU:** Lieutenant, Served in 1st Regt of Light Dragoons under Col Theodrick Bland. Taken prisoner at Charleston 12 May 1780 and was prisoner on parole to end of war. Perhaps became a Capt before war ended **CEM:** Hilltop-Yancey Farm; **GPS** unk; Elkton; Rockingham **GS:** Y **SP:** Fanny Lynn Lewis (17 May 1763-30 Aug 1845) d/o Thomas (1718-1790) & Jane (Strother) (1732-1820) Lewis **VI:** Recd pen W7380. Awarded 4000 acres BLW #4894, 22 May 1799 & 1333 acres and # 2921 for 2667 acres. **P:** Y **BLW:** Y **RG:** Y **MK:** Y SAR **PH:** unk **SS:** SAR P-325761 **BS:** JLARC 2, 4, 64, 76; 196.

YATES, Charles; b 20 Apr 1727, Whitehaven, England; d 11 Jan 1809 **RU:** Patriot, Was member Committee of Correspondence for Fredericksburg Jun 1774 **CEM:** Masonic Cemetery; **GPS** 38.30198, -77.46142; 900 Charles St; Fredericksburg City **GS:** Y **SP:** No info **VI:** Son of Rev Francis & Anne (Offeur) Yates **P:** N **BLW:** N **RG:** Y **MK:** Y SAR & SAR plaque **PH:** Y **SS:** D pg 870; SAR P-325811 **BS:** 11 pg 124-7; 196.

YATES, Enoch; b 1761; d 27 Jan 1852 **RU:** Soldier, Served in Augusta Co Militia. **CEM:** Bell; **GPS** 38.26140, -78.95560; Rt 11, Mt Sidney; Augusta **GS:** Y **SP:** Mar (20 Jan 1803) Sally Wilson **VI:** Listed in "Burials in Augusta Co Cemeteries" pub by the county historical society 1979 and 1985 **P:** unk **BLW:** unk **RG:** Y **MK:** N **PH:** unk **SS:** SAR P-325818 **BS:** JLARC 8; 196.

YATES, John III; b 1715, New Kent Co; d 25 Oct 1777 **RU:** Patriot, Gave material aid to cause **CEM:** Richardson-Yates Family; **GPS** unk; Ringhold; Pittsylvania **GS:** U **SP:** Elizabeth Kilgore (1720 Orange Co. NC-3 Sep 1793 Pittsylvania Co.) **VI:** No further data **P:** N **BLW:** N **RG:** N **MK:** unk **PH:** unk **SS:** AL Ct Bk pg 16 New Kent Co **BS:** 196.

YATES, William; b 1744; d 2 Dec 1789 **RU:** Lieutenant Colonel, Served on Washington's staff. Also in VA Cont Line **CEM:** Abingdon Episcopal; **GPS** 37.33355, -76.51364; 4645 George Washington Mem Hwy Rt 17; Gloucester **GS:** U **SP:** 1) Mar (22 Jun 1777) Ann Isham Poythress (___-24 Jun 1764) 2) Mar (21 Sep 1785) Elizabeth Booth **VI:** Son of Bartholomew (24 Aug 1676-__) & Elizabeth (Randolph) Yates. Graduated William & Mary College 1764 and later was Justice, Amelia Co **P:** unk **BLW:** Y **RG:** N **MK:** unk **PH:** unk **SS:** N pg 415CZ pg 486 **BS:** 196.

YEARY, Benedict; b 1732, Scotland; d 1802 **RU:** Patriot, Supplied horse for 14 days **CEM:** Benedict Yeary; **GPS** unk; Nr Rocky Station Fort; Lee **GS:** N **SP:** Mary (-----) (__-1799) **VI:** No further data **P:** N **BLW:** N **RG:** Y **MK:** unk **PH:** N **SS:** CD;DAR #A877910; SAR P-332466 **BS:** 196.

YEARY, Henry Jr; b 1765, Fairfax Co VA; d 11 Jul 1840 **RU:** Private, Served in Gen William Campbell's Regt fr Abingdon as waterboy to Battle of Kings Mountain, 7 Oct 1780 **CEM:** Yeary Family; **GPS** unk; W fr Ewing; Lee **GS:** Y **SP:** Martha Ball **VI:** Son of Henry David (1730, Fairfax Co-1799, Boones Path, Lee Co) & (-----) Yeary **P:** unk **BLW:** unk **RG:** Y **MK:** Y SAR **PH:** Y **SS:** J-NSSAR 1993 Reg; SAR #P-325874; J- DAR Hatcher **BS:** JLARC 1, 2.

YEARY, Henry Sr; b c1725 or 1730; d 1799 **RU:** Private/Patriot, USDAR records indicate service, details unk. Allowed 15# for a horse lost in service **CEM:** Ball Family; **GPS** unk; Rt 684 vic Ewing; Lee **GS:** Y **SP:** Mar (1760 Washington Co) Elizabeth Croxall (Croxtall) (1729 MD-1805) **VI:** No further data **P:** unk **BLW:** unk **RG:** Y **MK:** N **PH:** unk **SS:** DAR A133186; AK Nov 06; SAR P-325872 **BS:** 04, Nov 06.

YEATMAN, Thomas Muse; b 1762; d 14 Sep 1812 **RU:** Lieutenant/patriot, Served in Capt James Muse's Co Westmoreland Co Militia. Appt Lt 1777 and commanded Co. Also gave a beef to cause in

RU=Rank/Unit	CEM=Cemetery	GS=Gravestone	SP=Spousal Information
VI=Other Veteran Info	P=Pension	BLW=Bounty/Land Warrant	RG=Registered Grave
MK=SAR/DAR Marker	PH=Photo	SS=Service Source	BS=Burial Source

468

Westmoreland Co **CEM:** Ware Episcopal; GPS 37.42275, -76.50789; 7825 John Clayton Mem Hwy; Gloucester **GS:** Y **SP:** Mary Tompkins (1765-Oct 1796) d/o John & (-----) Tomkins **VI:** Stone moved fr Yeatman Plantation in Mathews Co to Ware Episcopal Church cemetery **P:** N **BLW:** N **RG:** Y **MK:** Y SAR **PH:** unk **SS:** E pg 853; DAR #A129539; SAR P-325886 **BS:** 48 pg 143; 196; 207.

YOST, Jacob: b 16 Sep 1744, Germany; d 27 Apr 1801 **RU:** Patriot. Paid personal property tax, 1783 in Shenandoah Co which was a supply tax for Rev War expenses **CEM:** Friedens United Church of Christ GPS 38.348480, -78.876530;GPS GS 38.347888, -78.877228; 3960 Friedens Church Rd, Mt Crawford; Rockingham **GS:** N **SP:** Maria Hoover (b 4 Sep 1744, Germany-21 Mar 1815) **VI:** No further data **P:** N **BLW:** N **RG:** N **MK:** N **PH:** N **SS:** AK **BS:** 04; 196.

YOUEL, William; b 1734, Sterling, Scotland; d 1 Sep 1834 **RU:** Soldier, Served in Capt James Gilmore's Co at Battle of Cowpens in Gilmore Rifles **CEM:** Youel Family, Meadow Lawn Farm; GPS unk; Rt 601, Goshen; Rockbridge **GS:** U **SP:** Mar (8 Aug 1774) Elizabeth Nelson (1736 Scotland-aft 9 Jan 1834) **VI:** No further data **P:** unk **BLW:** unk **RG:** Y **MK:** Y SAR **PH:** unk **SS:** DAR A129687; J-NSSAR 1993 Reg; SAR P-326076; J- DAR Hatcher; N pg 1249 **BS:** JLARC 1,2.

YOUNG, Ezekiel; b Bef 1736, England; d Jun 1800 **RU:** First Lieutenant/ Patriot. As Private served in James MaCorkle Co, Montgomery Co, 5 Dec 1777. Serves as 1/LT in Capt Enoxch Osborn's Co, Montgomery Co Militia. As patriot held position as collector of fines **CEM:** Young Family; GPS unk; Nr jct Rts 711 & 680; Grayson **GS:** U **SP:** Ruth Whitehead **VI:** No further data **P:** unk **BLW:** unk **RG:** Y **MK:** N **PH:** unk **SS:** A pg 212; BW pgs 32,33,34,51; H Apr 07; DAR A129778; SAR P-326146 **BS:** 4-Apr-07.

YOUNG, Henry; b 1741 Essex Co VA; d 15 Nov 1817 **RU:** Quartermaster General, Entered Conl Army as Lt in 1776, promoted to Capt 28 Dec 1776. Was appt Quartermaster of VA 1781 by Gov Digges. Served in 5th Regt, Cont Line **CEM:** Young Family; GPS unk; Walkerton; King & Queen **GS:** Y **SP:** No info **VI:** Son of Henry & Rachel (Smith) Young. Member of King and Queen Co court. Records lost in DC fire of 1800. Recd BLW #32466 on 3 Jun 1695 of 6666 acres. R18332 **P:** Y **BLW:** Y **RG:** N **MK:** unk **PH:** unk **SS:** K Vol 6 pg 236; N pg 412 **BS:** 196 (**YOUNG**, James See Appendix G, Addenda)

YOUNG, James; b unk. Ireland; d 1790 **RU:** Second Lieutenant, Served in Lt Young's Co. Appt in Augusta Co militia rank of 2nd Lt, 20 Oct 1778 in Capt Patterson's Co. Served also in Capt John Young's Co **CEM:** Augusta Stone Presbyterian; GPS 38.23926, -78.97356, GS 38.1411,-78.5815; 28 Old Stone Church Ln, Ft Defiance; Augusta **GS:** Y **SP:** Mary McComb **VI:** Govt stone **P:** unk **BLW:** unk **RG:** Y **MK:** Y SAR plaque plaque **PH:** Y **SS:** E pg 854; SAR P-326204 **BS:** JLARC 1, 2, 8, 23, 62; 196.

YOUNG, John; b 25 Mar 1737, Ireland d 25 Dec 1824 **RU:** Captain/Patriot, Listed in Augusta Co militia. As patriot gave material aid to cause **CEM:** Glebe Burying Ground; GPS 38.10940, -79.22190; Glebe School Rd Rt 876, Swoopes; Augusta **GS:** Y **SP:** 1) Mar (13 Sep 1763) Mary Elizabeth White (1746-2 Apr 1779) d/o Isaac White 2) Mar (23 Jan 1781) Mary Sitlington (15 Sep 1759-25 Jul 1838) **VI:** Son of Hugh Young (1699-1756) & Agnes Sitlington. VA DAR plaque styles him Capt **P:** unk **BLW:** unk **RG:** Y **MK:** Y **PH:** unk **SS:** DAR A130075; SAR P-326247 **BS:** JLARC 8, 62, 63; 196.

YOUNG, John; b 1760; d 1792 **RU:** Private, Served in Capt Simpson's Co, Augusta Co Militia **CEM:** Trinity Episcopal; GPS 38.14917, -79.07521; 214 Beverley St; Staunton City **GS:** U **SP:** No info **VI:** No further data **P:** unk **BLW:** unk **RG:** Y **MK:** unk **PH:** unk **SS:** E pg 854; SAR P-326265 **BS:** JLARC 2, 8.

YOUNG, John; b 1760, Paris, Fauquier Co; d 24 May 1813 **RU:** Soldier, SAR registry did not provide service **CEM:** Old Presbyterian Meeting House; GPS 38.48528, -77.23532; 323 S Fairfax St; Alexandria City **GS:** Y Sec 41, plot 18 **SP:** Euphemia Humphrey (1770, Loudoun Co-16 Apr 1822) d/o Thomas (2 Jun 1742 PA-6 Jun 1823) & Mary (Marks) (12 Jul 1742,-5 Sep 1811) Humphrey **VI:** No further data **P:** unk **BLW:** U **RG:** Y **MK:** Y SAR plaque **PH:** N **SS:** NSSAR 1993 Reg; SAR P-326234 **BS:** JLARC 1; 5.

YOUNG, Robert; b 27 Dec 1768 (Gr St inscription) , died 17 Oct 1824; Lsted erroneously on SAR plaque as too young for Rev War sevice (Would be age 15 in 1783); Presbyterian Cem Alexandria. Was general in War of 1812 **MK:** Y SAR plaque.

YOUNG, Thomas; b 6 Apr 1766; d 16 Apr 1840 **RU:** Soldier, Served in VA or Continental Line long enough to be a warranty for bounty land **CEM:** Glebe Burying Ground; GPS 38.10940, -79.22190; Glebe School Rd Rt 876, Swoopes; Augusta **GS:** Y **SP:** Mary (-----) (27 May 1759-10 Mar 1831) (Gr st says

RU=Rank/Unit	CEM=Cemetery	GS=Gravestone	SP=Spousal Information
VI=Other Veteran Info	P=Pension	BLW=Bounty/Land Warrant	RG=Registered Grave
MK=SAR/DAR Marker	PH=Photo	SS=Service Source	BS=Burial Source

wife of Thomas Young) **VI:** Son of John Young (1737-1824) & Mary Elizabeth White (1744-1779) His name is on a DAR plaque as Rev war soldier. **P:** unk **BLW:** unk **RG:** Y **MK:** Y DAR plaque **PH:** unk **SS:** C pg 386; SAR P-326403 **BS:** JLARC 62, 63; 210 pg 394; 196 indicates there was a cemetery inventory taken in 1902 and a W.P.A. inventory taken in 1936.

YOUNG, William; b 2 May 1740; d c1810 **RU:** Patriot, Gave material aid to cause **CEM:** Young Family; GPS unk; Ruther Glen; Caroline **GS:** U **SP:** Jane Mickelborough (15 Jan 1752 Middlesex Co-9 Nov 1835) d/o Henry (10 Feb 1705 Middslesex Co-1783) & Susanna (Daniel) Mickleborough **VI:** Died in Middlesex Co **P:** N **BLW:** N **RG:** N **MK:** unk **PH:** unk **SS:** AL Ct Bk II pg 33 **BS:** 196.

YOUNG, William; b unk; d unk **RU:** Private/Patriot, Served in Capt Trimble's Co, Augusta Co Militia, Gave material aid to cause **CEM:** Glebe Burying Ground; GPS 38.10940, -79.22190; Glebe School Rd Rt 876, Swoopes; Augusta **GS:** N **SP:** No info **VI:** Name is on DAR plaque **P:** unk **BLW:** unk **RG:** N **MK:** N **PH:** N **SS:** E pg 855; AL Comm Bk II pg 30 Augusta Co **BS:** 36 pg 28, 32; King, W.W. Mrs "Glebe Burial Ground, 1749, Augusta Co,.VA", pub 1934, 12 pages.

YOUNT, Jacob; b c1755, PA; d 7 Oct 1821 **RU:** Soldier, Served in York Co PA in 1778. Served in Capt Adam Serfoos' Co 1781 **CEM:** Yount Family; GPS unk; Rts 253 & 278, 2.8 mi E; Rockingham **GS:** N **SP:** Catherine Dagen **VI:** No further data **P:** unk **BLW:** unk **RG:** N **MK:** N **PH:** N **SS:** AK **BS:** 4.

YOWELL (YOWEL), William; b 1 May 1763, Culpeper Co; d 6 Mar 1845 **RU:** Private, Ent serv 1779 Culpeper Co. Served at battle of Petersburg & Siege of Yorktown **CEM:** Yowell Family; GPS 38.19420, -78.49120; Syria; Madison **GS:** N **SP:** Mar (Jul 1782, nr Slate Mills, Culpeper Co) Nellie (Nelly) Crane (15 Apr 1763-__) **VI:** He was pen Madison Co 1832. Widow appl pen 19 Jun 1847 Madison Co, Recd BLW 16 Mar 1855. W5551. BLW 26208-160-55 **P:** Y **BLW:** Y **RG:** Y **MK:** N **PH:** N **SS:** K Vol 6 pg 242; AK; CG Vol 3 pg 4055; SAR P-326519 **BS:** 4.

YVES, Andre; b unk; d 1781 **RU:** Seaman, Served on "Ville de Paris" and died from Yorktown battle **CEM:** French Memorial; GPS 36.81944, -79.39933; Yorktown; York **GS:** U **SP:** No info **VI:** No further data **P:** unk **BLW:** unk **RG:** Y **MK:** unk **PH:** unk **SS:** J-Yorktown Historian; SAR P-3236530 **BS:** JLARC 1, 74.

ZANE, Isaac II; b 24 Apr 1743, Philadelphia PA; d 10 Aug 1795 **RU:** Brigadier General/Patriot, Was in 1773 in House of Burgesses. During War his Marlboro Iron Works produced four and six pound ordnance, shot, kettles, salt pans, camp stoves, and cannons. In 1794 was Brig Gen of Frederick Co VA Militia. Gave material aid to cause **CEM:** Mt Pleasant Meeting House; GPS 39.12080, -78.30440; Rt 622, Mt Pleasant; Frederick **GS:** U **SP:** With mistress Elizabeth McFarland (c1762-10 Oct 1831) had a child **VI:** Son of Isaac & Sarah (Elfreth) Zane **P:** N **BLW:** N **RG:** Y **MK:** unk **PH:** unk **SS:** AL Ct Bk pg 5 & 10 Shenandoah Co; SAR P-335849 **BS:** 196.

ZEA, Martin; b c1756 or 1760, Lancaster Co, PA; d 3 Nov 1838 **RU:** Soldier, Served in VA Line **CEM:** St Pauls Lutheran; GPS 38.99140, -78.36250; 156 W Washington, Strasburg; Shenandoah **GS:** Y **SP:** Mar (30 Jan 1787) Ann Stockshlager (3 Feb 1766-10 Jul 1842 Strasburg, Shenandoah Co) **VI:** Moved to Shenandoah Co with parents before RW. Appl for pen Shenandoah Co 7 Oct 1833. Wife's pen rejected because she was not a widow at date of the act **P:** Y **BLW:** unk **RG:** N **MK:** unk **PH:** Y **SS:** E pg 544; CG Vol 3 pg 4005 **BS:** 196.

ZELL, John; b unk; d 1781 **RU:** unk, Was killed in the Battle at Yorktown **CEM:** Yorktown Victory Monument Tablet; GPS 38.28350, -78.54150; Yorktown; York **GS:** U **SP:** No info **VI:** No further data **P:** unk **BLW:** unk **RG:** Y **MK:** unk **PH:** unk **SS:** J-Yorktown Historian; SAR P-326610 **BS:** JLARC 74.

ZIMMERMAN, Christopher; b 1719, Spotsylvania Co; d 1781 **RU:** Patriot, Gave material aid to cause **CEM:** Hebron Lutheran; GPS 38.40676, -78.24808; 899 Blankenbaker Rd, Madison; Madison **GS:** U **SP:** No info **VI:** Son of Johann (1692-1748) & Anna (Albrecht) (1687-1757) Zimmerman. Died in Culpeper Co **P:** N **BLW:** N **RG:** N **MK:** unk **PH:** unk **SS:** AL Ct Bk I pg 24, 27 **BS:** 196.

ZIMMERMAN, Henry; b 1755; d 16 Nov 1806 **RU:** Ensign, Served in PA **CEM:** Old Christ Church Episcopal; GPS 38.80625, -77.04718; 118 N Washington St; Alexandria City **GS:** N **SP:** Mar (1803) Elizabeth Fairhurst (__ Loudoun Co-1850) d/o Jeremiah & Ann (Slaughter) Fairhurst **VI:** GS indicates he d 16 Nov 1806, age 51 **P:** unk **BLW:** unk **RG:** N **MK:** N **PH:** N **SS:** A pg 543; A pg 144 **BS:** 20 pg 144.

RU=Rank/Unit	CEM=Cemetery	GS=Gravestone	SP=Spousal Information
VI=Other Veteran Info	P=Pension	BLW=Bounty/Land Warrant	RG=Registered Grave
MK=SAR/DAR Marker	PH=Photo	SS=Service Source	BS=Burial Source

470

ZIMMERMAN, John; b 1737, Orange Co; d 1819 **RU:** Patriot, Gave material aid to cause **CEM:** Hebron Lutheran; **GPS** 38.40676, -78.24808; 899 Blankenbaker Rd, Madison; Madison **GS:** U **SP:** No info **VI:** Son of Johann (1692-1748) & Anna (Albrecht) (1687-1757) Zimmerman **P:** N **BLW:** N **RG:** N **MK:** unk **PH:** unk **SS:** AL Ct Bk I pg 24,27 **BS:** 196.

ZIRKLE, Andrew; b 1737, Telford, Montgomery Co, PA; d 1816 **RU:** Private/Patriot, served Capt Jacob Holeman's Co, Dunmore Co, Militia; gave beef and a wagon for use by Shenandoah County Militia **CEM:** Rader Lutheran Church; **GPS** 38.650733-78.780550; Radars Church Rd, Timberville; Rockingham **GS:** Y **SP:** Mary Catherine(___) **VI:** Son of Johann Ludwick Zircle (1705-1747) & Maria Eva Bear (1709-1771) **P:** N **BLW:** N **RG:** Y **MK:** N **PH:** N **SS:** C pg 607; D vol 3, pgs 843, 845; DAR A131097; SAR P 326735 **BS:** 196

ZIRKLE, George Adam; b Sep 1738, Telford, Montgomery Co, MD; d 8 Sep 1800 **RU:** Patriot/Private, Served in MD. Took the oath of Fidelity **CEM:** Zirkle Family; **GPS** 38.65900, -78.69580; River Rd, New Market; Shenandoah **GS:** Y **SP:** Elizabeth Rettenour/Reidenauer (1752-1829) **VI:** Son of Johan Ludwig (1705-1747) & Maria Eva (Bear) (1709-1771) Zirkle. SAR marker **P:** N **BLW:** N **RG:** Y **MK:** Y SAR Granite **PH:** N **SS:** DAR # A2109621 cites Brumbaugh & Hodges, Rev war Rec of MD, pg 19; AK -Col James Wood II Nov 2014; SAR P-328914 **BS:** 04; 196; SAR PRS.

ZIRKLE, Lewis; b 1740, PA, d 22 Jan 1815, Rockingham Co **RU:** Patriot, Gave material aid to cause Rockingham Co **CEM:** Saint Mathews (AKA Reformation) Church; **GPS:** 38.651311,-78.671207: loc North Congress St, New Market; Shenandoah **GS:** Y **SP:** Mar 1764/1765, Mary Magdalene Raush (27 Nov 1746, Rinkerton, Shenandoah Co-22 Jan 1746) **VI:** Son of Johann Ludwig "Lewis" Zirkle (9 Oct 1705, Baden Wurttem, Germany-10 Mar 1747, Franconia, Montgomery Co, PA) & Maria Eva Bear (1709, Telford, Montgomery Co, PA-1771, Forestville, Shenandoah Co} **PEN:** N **BLW:** N **RG:** Y **MK:** N **PH:** N **SS:** D, vol 3, pgs 830,834; DAR A131098; SAR P-326736 **BS:** 196; SAR PRS.

ZIRKLE, Michael; b 29 Jun 1735, Montgomery Co, PA, d 2 Oct 1811, Forestville, Shenandoah, Co **RU:** Private, Patriot, serv in Capt Jacob Holeman's Company 1776, Dunmore Co Militia. Also gave some beef to the cause. **CEM:** Zerchel-Nehs Family; **GPS** not determined; loc on east bank of Holman's Creek northeast of Forestville; Shenandoah **GS:** Y **SP:** Mar c1762, Catharina (-----) (12 Jul 1747-16 Nov 1830) **VI:** Son of Ludwig Zirkle & Eve (-----) **PEN:** N **BLW:** N **RG:** Y **MK:** N **PH:** N **SS:** C pg 607; D, vol 3, pgs 840; "Dunmore County, Papers 1775-1776" (21127), 65-2550, Virginia State Library); DAR A131099; SAR P-326737 **BS:** 196; SAR PRS **BS:** 196; SAR PRS.

ZIRKLE(CIRCLE), Peter; b ca1740, Telford, Montgomery Co, PA, d Sep 1818, Alleghany Co **RU:** Private, served in Capt Jacob Holman's Co, Dunmore County Militia, 1776 **CEM** Locust Bottom; **GPS** 37.741485, -79.814564; nr Jct Locuct Bottom Rd & Prices Bluff Rd; Botetourt **GS:** Unk **SP:** Mar (c1773) Fern "Fannie" Meyer of Moyer **VI:** Son of Johann Ludwig Zirlke (1705-1747) & Maria Eva Bear (1709-1771) **P:** N **BLW:** N **RG:** Y **MK:** Y DAR **PH:** N **SS:** C pg 607; DAR A131100; SAR P-133075 **BS:** 196

RU=Rank/Unit	CEM=Cemetery	GS=Gravestone	SP=Spousal Information
VI=Other Veteran Info	P=Pension	BLW=Bounty/Land Warrant	RG=Registered Grave
MK=SAR/DAR Marker	PH=Photo	SS=Service Source	BS=Burial Source

REVOLUTIONARY WAR VETERANS & PATRIOTS BURIED IN THIS CEMETERY

PATRIOT ROBERT ANDERSON	PRIVATE LEWIS HICKLE	SECOND LT ARTHUR MOSLEY
PRIVATE WILLIAM ANDERSON	PRIVATE EBENEZER HICKOK	CAPTAIN LEWIS NICHOLAS
CAPTAIN THOMAS BOWYER	PRIVATE WILLIAM KYLE	FIRST LT SAMUEL PATTERSON
MAJOR NATHANIEL BURWELL	MAJOR PATRICK LOCKHART	PATRIOT BENJAMIN PECK
PATRIOT JACOB CARPER	DRUMMER ROBERT LOGAN	PRIVATE JACOB PECK
PRIVATE NICHOLAS CARPER	PRIVATE ALEXANDER MCROBERTS	ENSIGN JOHN PECK
PRIVATE JAMES EARLY	SECOND LT JOHN MCROBERTS	PRIVATE JOSEPH PECK
PATRIOT ALLEN GULLIFORD	PRIVATE SAMUEL MCROBERTS	LT COL PEYTON SKIPWITH
CAPTAIN ALEXANDER HAMILTON	PRIVATE SAMUEL MERRITT	CHAPLAIN ADAM SMYTH
CAPTAIN ANDREW HAMILTON	PRIVATE JACOB MIFFORD	PRIVATE FRANCIS THOMAS
PRIVATE MATTHEW HARVEY	PRIVATE JOHN MOORE	SERGEANT HENRY WAX, SR
PATRIOT ROBERT HARVEY	PATRIOT JOHN D MOORE	PRIVATE FEIDT WYSONG

DEDICATED JUNE 30, 2012

THE VIRGINIA SOCIETY SONS OF THE AMERICAN REVOLUTION

Plaque at Fincastle Presbyterian Church, Botetourt County

REVOLUTIONARY WAR PATRIOTS AND WAR OF 1812 VETERANS BURIED IN THIS CEMETERY

REVOLUTIONARY WAR

PRIVATE SAMUEL CARSON
PRIVATE ROBERT COOPER
CAPTAIN PATRICK HALL
CAPTAIN WILLIAM HALL
PRIVATE JAMES MCCHESNEY
PRIVATE JOHN MCCHESNEY
PATRIOT MARTHA MCCORMICK
PRIVATE ROBERT MCCORMICK

ENSIGN JAMES MCNUTT
PRIVATE ROBERT MCNUTT
CAPTAIN ANDREW MOORE
PRIVATE JAMES POAGE
PRIVATE ANDREW STEELE
PRIVATE DAVID STEELE
ENSIGN JAMES W. STEELE
PRIVATE JOHN STEELE, JR.

PRIVATE JOHN STEELE, SR.
PRIVATE NATHANIEL STEELE
CAPTAIN SAMUEL STEELE
PRIVATE SAMUEL STEELE, JR.
PRIVATE THOMAS STEELE
PRIVATE WILLIAM STEELE
PRIVATE JOHN TATE
CAPTAIN SAMUEL WILSON

WAR OF 1812

SERGEANT DAVID CARSON
PRIVATE ELIJAH CARSON
PRIVATE JOHN CARSON
LIEUTENANT SAMUEL CARSON, SR.
PRIVATE JOHN COOPER
PRIVATE RICHARD GIBBS

PRIVATE ROBERT HALL
PRIVATE WILLIAM HALL
PRIVATE THOMAS JACKSON
PRIVATE WILLIAM LUSK
SERGEANT WILLIAM MCCHESNEY
CORPORAL WILLIAM MCCORMICK
PRIVATE ROBERT MCNUTT

PRIVATE WILLIAM MOORE
PRIVATE WILLIAM MOORE
PRIVATE JAMES E. POAGUE
PRIVATE JOHN POAGUE
PRIVATE WILLIAM STEELE
PRIVATE JOHN M. WILSON

FUNDED BY THE NATIONAL SOCIETY SONS OF THE AMERICAN REVOLUTION (SAR) GEORGE WASHINGTON ENDOWMENT FUND, VIRGINIA SOCIETY SAR KNIGHT-PATTY TRUST FUND AND THE SOCIETY OF THE WAR OF 1812 IN THE COMMONWEALTH OF VIRGINIA.
DEDICATED MAY 15, 2010

Plaque at Old Providence Presbyterian Church Cemetery, Augusta County

473

BURIALS OF REVOLUTIONARY WAR PATRIOTS IN THIS
HISTORICAL CEMETERY

SERGEANT DANIEL ANDERSON
PRIVATE DAVID ANDERSON
LT COLONEL JOHN BANISTER
CAPTAIN ROBERT BOLLING
SERGEANT JOHN CAMERON
PRIVATE ROBERT DONALDSON
MATROSS EDWARD HAMMON
CAPTAIN WILLIAM HARRISON
PRIVATE JESSE HEATH
CAPTAIN JOHN JEFFERS
PRIVATE ANDREW JOHNSON
GENERAL JOSEPH JONES
PRIVATE EDWARD LEE
PRIVATE ROBERT ROBINSON
PRIVATE THOMAS STROUD
PRIVATE JOHN STUART
PATRIOT ALEXANDER TAYLOR
MAJOR JAMES WILLIAMS
CAPTAIN ERASMUS GILL
DEDICATED BY THE VIRGINIA SOCIETY SONS
OF THE AMERICAN REVOLUTION

Monument at Blandford Cemetery, Petersburg City

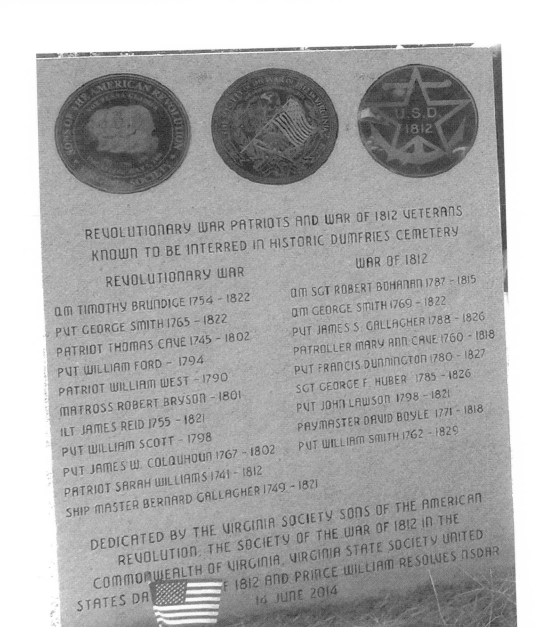

Monument at Dumfries, Prince William County

REVOLUTIONARY WAR PATRIOTS MEMORIALIZED IN THIS HISTORIC CEMETERY

PRIVATE JAMES ALLEN
CAPTAIN ANDREW ANDERSON
CAPTAIN DAVID BELL
CAPTAIN JOSEPH BELL, JR
PRIVATE JOSEPH BELL, SR
PRIVATE JOSEPH BELL
PRIVATE WILLIAM BELL
PATRIOT ARTHUR CONNALY, SR
PRIVATE JAMES CRAIG, JR
PRIVATE JAMES CRAIG, SR
PRIVATE JOHN CRAIG
PRIVATE WILLIAM CRAIG
PRIVATE GEORGE CRAWFORD, JR
MAJOR JOHN CRAWFORD
PATRIOT PATRICK CRAWFORD
CAPTAIN ROBERT CURRY
CAPTAIN JOHN GAMBLE
PRIVATE JOHN GIBBONS
CAPTAIN JOHN GIVENS
PRIVATE ROBERT HARNSBERGER
PRIVATE WILLIAM HOOK
PRIVATE WILLIAM HOOKE, SR
PRIVATE ROBERT HOOK(HOOKE), SR

PRIVATE ROBERT KENNY
PRIVATE JAMES KERR
PRIVATE JOHN KERR, JR
PRIVATE JOHN KERR, SR
PRIVATE JOSEPH KERR
CAPTAIN ROBERT KENNEY
PRIVATE JOHN MILLS
SERGEANT ROBERT MILLS
COLONEL GEORGE MOFFETT
PRIVATE ALEXANDER NELSON
PRIVATE ALEXANDER NELSON
ENSIGN JOHN POAGE, JR
2D LIEUTENANT ROBERT POAGE
PRIVATE THOMAS POAGE
ENSIGN ALEXANDER ROBERTSON
LT COL ALEXANDER ROBERTSON, SR
LIEUTENANT WILLIAM ROBERTSON
PRIVATE ALEXANDER ROSS
PRIVATE JOHN SMITH
PATRIOT ALEXANDER WALKER
MAJOR WILLIAM WILSON
LIEUTENANT JAMES YOUNG

DEDICATED JULY 25, 2015

BY THE VIRGINIA SOCIETY
SONS OF THE AMERICAN
REVOLUTION

Plaque at Old Stone Church Cemetery, Fort Defiance, Augusta County

476

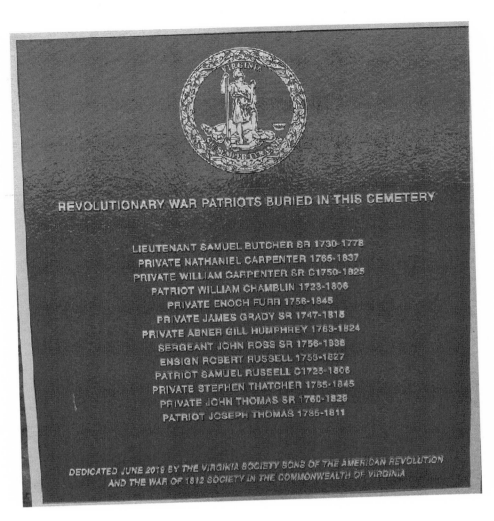

REVOLUTIONARY WAR PATRIOTS BURIED IN THIS CEMETERY

LIEUTENANT SAMUEL BUTCHER SR 1730-1778
PRIVATE NATHANIEL CARPENTER 1765-1837
PRIVATE WILLIAM CARPENTER SR C1750-1825
PATRIOT WILLIAM CHAMBLIN 1723-1806
PRIVATE ENOCH FURR 1756-1845
PRIVATE JAMES GRADY SR 1747-1818
PRIVATE ABNER GILL HUMPHREY 1763-1824
SERGEANT JOHN ROSS SR 1756-1938
ENSIGN ROBERT RUSSELL 1756-1827
PATRIOT SAMUEL RUSSELL C1723-1806
PRIVATE STEPHEN THATCHER 1765-1845
PRIVATE JOHN THOMAS SR 1760-1828
PATRIOT JOSEPH THOMAS 1765-1811

DEDICATED JUNE 2019 BY THE VIRGINIA SOCIETY SONS OF THE AMERICAN REVOLUTION
AND THE WAR OF 1812 SOCIETY IN THE COMMONWEALTH OF VIRGINIA

Plaque at Ebenezer Baptist Church, Loudoun County

THIS MONUMENT IS DEDICATED TO THE REVOLUTIONARY
WAR PATRIOTS BURIED HERE. SOME NAMED BELOW,
AND OTHERS KNOWN BUT TO GOD

FREDERICK ARMENTROUT	GEORGE ARMENTROUT	HENRY ARMENTROUT	JOHN ARMENTROUT
AUGUSTINE BERRY	BENJAMIN BERRY	JOHN BERRY	JOHN PETER CONRAD
ISAAC GIBBONS	CASPER HAINES	FREDERICK HAINES	GEORGE HAINES
JOHN HAINES	JONAS HAINES	JOSEPH HAINES	PETER HAINES
HENRY HAMMER	JACOB HARMON	CHARLES HEADRICK	MICHAEL HERRING
LEONARD HERRING	WILLIAM HERRING	ISAAC HINKLE	YOST HINKLE
ARCHIBALD HOPKINS	JOHN HOPKINS	MICHAEL KAYTOR	CONRAD KISSLING
DITRICH KISSLING	JACOB KISSLING	JOHN KISSLING	CHRISTIAN KYSER
PHILIP LONG	JAMES MAGILL	WILLIAM MAGILL	PETER MILLER
HENRY MONGER	JACOB NICHOLAS	PETER NICHOLAS	GEORGE PENCE
HENRY PENCE	JACOB PENCE	JAMES PENCE	JOHN PENCE
WILLIAM PENCE	AUGUSTINE PRICE	CHARLES RUSH	JOHN RUSH
JOHN ADAM SELLERS	JOHN HENRY SELLERS	JOHN PETER SELLERS	PAUL TETER

Plaque at Fairfax Co Court House, Fairfax County

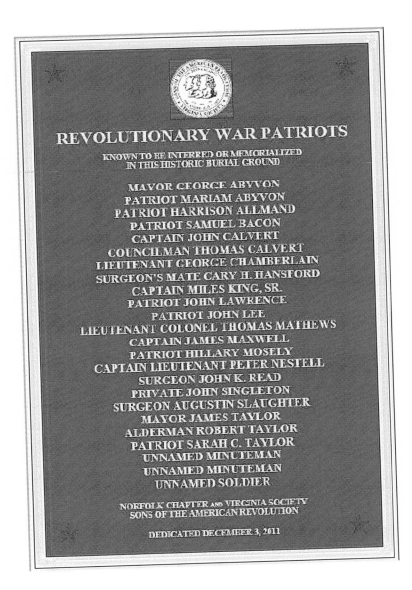

REVOLUTIONARY WAR PATRIOTS

KNOWN TO BE INTERRED OR MEMORIALIZED IN THIS HISTORIC BURIAL GROUND

MAYOR GEORGE ABYVON
PATRIOT MARIAM ABYVON
PATRIOT HARRISON ALLMAND
PATRIOT SAMUEL BACON
CAPTAIN JOHN CALVERT
COUNCILMAN THOMAS CALVERT
LIEUTENANT GEORGE CHAMBERLAIN
SURGEON'S MATE CARY H. HANSFORD
CAPTAIN MILES KING, SR.
PATRIOT JOHN LAWRENCE
PATRIOT JOHN LEE
LIEUTENANT COLONEL THOMAS MATHEWS
CAPTAIN JAMES MAXWELL
PATRIOT HILLARY MOSELY
CAPTAIN LIEUTENANT PETER NESTELL
SURGEON JOHN K. READ
PRIVATE JOHN SINGLETON
SURGEON AUGUSTIN SLAUGHTER
MAYOR JAMES TAYLOR
ALDERMAN ROBERT TAYLOR
PATRIOT SARAH C. TAYLOR
UNNAMED MINUTEMAN
UNNAMED MINUTEMAN
UNNAMED SOLDIER

NORFOLK CHAPTER AND VIRGINIA SOCIETY
SONS OF THE AMERICAN REVOLUTION

DEDICATED DECEMBER 3, 2011

Plaque at St. Paul's Episcopal Church, Norfolk City

Monuments Shockoe Hill Cemetery, Richmond City

Plaque at Masonic Cemetery, Fredericksburg City

REVOLUTIONARY WAR PATRIOTS BURIED IN THIS CEMETERY

LIEUTENANT SAMUEL BUTCHER SR 1730-1778
PRIVATE NATHANIEL CARPENTER 1785-1837
PRIVATE WILLIAM CARPENTER SR C1750-1825
PATRIOT WILLIAM CHAMBLIN 1723-1806
PRIVATE ENOCH FURR 1758-1845
PRIVATE JAMES GRADY SR 1747-1815
PRIVATE ABNER GILL HUMPHREY 1783-1824
SERGEANT JOHN ROSS SR 1758-1838
ENSIGN ROBERT RUSSELL 1753-1827
PATRIOT SAMUEL RUSSELL C1725-1808
PRIVATE STEPHEN THATCHER 1785-1845
PRIVATE JOHN THOMAS SR 1760-1829
PATRIOT JOSEPH THOMAS 1735-1811

DEDICATED JUNE 2019 BY THE VIRGINIA SOCIETY SONS OF THE AMERICAN REVOLUTION

Plaque at Ketoctin Church Cemetery, Loudoun County

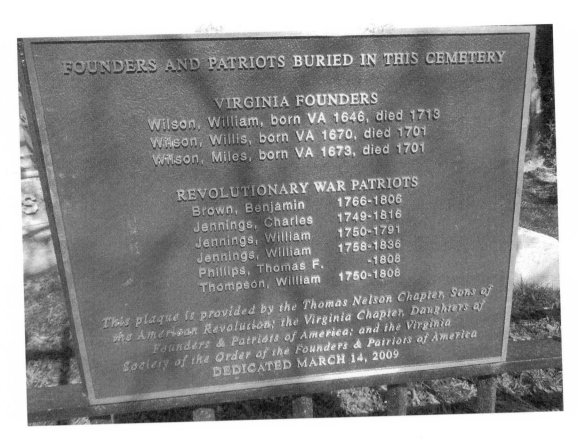

Plaque at St Johns Church, Hampton City

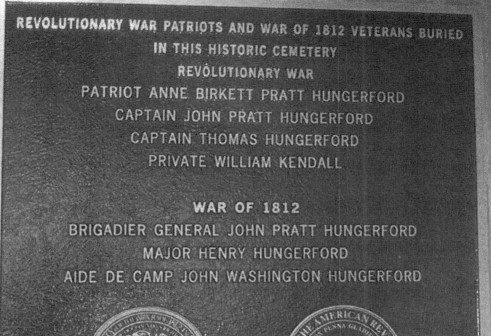

REVOLUTIONARY WAR PATRIOTS AND WAR OF 1812 VETERANS BURIED
IN THIS HISTORIC CEMETERY
REVOLUTIONARY WAR
PATRIOT ANNE BIRKETT PRATT HUNGERFORD
CAPTAIN JOHN PRATT HUNGERFORD
CAPTAIN THOMAS HUNGERFORD
PRIVATE WILLIAM KENDALL

WAR OF 1812
BRIGADIER GENERAL JOHN PRATT HUNGERFORD
MAJOR HENRY HUNGERFORD
AIDE DE CAMP JOHN WASHINGTON HUNGERFORD

Dedicated by the James Monroe Chapter,
Virginia Society Sons of the American Revolution
and the Society War of 1812 in the Commonwealth of Virginia

Plaque at Hungerford-Pratt Cemetery, Westmoreland County

REVOLUTIONARY WAR PATRIOTS
KNOWN TO BE INTERRED OR MEMORIALIZED IN
THE HISTORIC BURIAL GROUND

PRIVATE HENRY BAKER	PRIVATE JOHN MERRYMAN
PATRIOT MICHAEL COPENHAVER	PRIVATE JOHN SCHULTZ
PATRIOT LEWIS HOFF	PRIVATE GEORGE SNAPP
PATRIOT JOHN HUFF	SURGEONS MATE JACOB TROUTVINE
SERGEANT BASIL LUCAS	CAPTAIN WILLIAM BALL
BRIGADIER GENERAL DANIEL ROBERDEAU	PRIVATE JOHN GRIM
PATRIOT EDWARD SMITH	2D LIEUTENANT JOHN HOOVER
PRIVATE JOHN SPERRY	PRIVATE PETER LAUCK
PRIVATE WILLIAM H. BAKER	BRIGADIER GENERAL DANIEL MORGAN
PATRIOT CHRISTOPHER FRY	SURGEON FREDERICK SEIGLE
ENSIGN DANIEL HOLLENBACH	PATRIOT JACOB SOWERS
PRIVATE CONRAD KREMER	PRIVATE JOHN C WALL
MAJOR CHARLES MAGILL	PRIVATE HENRY BEATTY
PRIVATE PETER RUST	MAJOR PETER HELPHENSTINE
MAJOR GENERAL JOHN SMITH	PRIVATE JOHN H. HOOVER
CHAPLAIN CHRISTIAN STREIT	PRIVATE SIMON LAUCK
SURGEON CORNELIUS BALDWIN	PRIVATE GEORGE OVERACRE
PRIVATE CHARLES GRIM	BRIGADIER GENERAL JOHN SINGLETON
PATRIOT HUGH HOLMES	CAPTAIN JACOB SPERRY
PRIVATE ADAM KURTZ	LT COLONEL ROBERT WHITE

DEDICATED BY THE VIRGINIA SOCIETY SONS OF THE
AMERICAN REVOLUTION
AUGUST 24. 2013

Monument at Mount Hebron Cemetery, Winchester City

THIS MARKER HONORS THE SERVICE OF THE REVOLUTIONARY WAR PATRIOTS AND WAR OF 1812 VETERANS BURIED OR MEMORIALIZED ON THE GROUNDS OF HISTORIC POHICK CHURCH

REVOLUTIONARY WAR PATRIOTS

Patriot Charles Alexander, Sr
Patriot Susanna Pearson Alexander
Surgeon William Brown
Patriot George Chapman
Patriot William Fitzhugh
Patriot Elizabeth Hunter
Private Nathaniel C Hunter

Patriot Lee Massey
Lieutenant Daniel McCarty
Colonel Peter Wagener (Wegener)
Colonel John A Washington
Colonel George West
Patriot Colonel John West IV
Patriot Sybil Harrison West

WAR OF 1812 VETERANS

Private Richard B. Alexander
Private George Chapman, Jr
Private William H Fitzhugh
Adjutant Alexander Hunter
Major George W Hunter

Major John C Hunter
Private William Nevitt
Private John E Robertson
Private William T Swann

DEDICATED JULY 29, 2017 BY THE VIRGINIA SONS OF THE AMERICAN REVOLUTION AND THE SOCIETY OF THE WAR OF 1812 IN THE COMMONWEALTH OF VIRGINIA

Plaque at Pohick Church, Lorton, Fairfax County

D.A.R plaque at Glebe Cemetery, Augusta County

SAINT MARY'S CATHOLIC CEMETERY

SAINT MARY'S CATHOLIC CHURCH WAS ESTABLISHED IN 1795 AND IS THE OLDEST CATHOLIC PARISH IN THE COMMONWEALTH OF VIRGINIA. SAINT MARY'S CEMETERY IS LIKEWISE THE OLDEST PUBLIC CATHOLIC CEMETERY IN VIRGINIA AND THE OLDEST ACTIVE CEMETERY IN ALEXANDRIA. THE CEMETERY DATES TO 1795, AND PARISH RECORDS INDICATE THAT WILLIAM THORTON ALEXANDER DEEDED THE LAND TO SAINT MARY'S IN 1803. CONSTRUCTION OF SAINT MARY'S CHURCH, ORIGINALLY A CHAPEL LOCATED WITHIN THE EXISTING CEMETERY, WAS FUNDED THROUGH A SUBSCRIPTION UNDERTAKEN BY COLONEL JOHN FITZGERALD. COLONEL FITZGERALD EMIGRATED FROM IRELAND AND ACHIEVED PROMINENCE AT A TIME WHEN CATHOLICISM WAS NEITHER PREVALENT NOR WIDELY REGARDED IN THE COMMONWEALTH, MANAGING A MERCANTILE BUSINESS IN ALEXANDRIA AND BECOMING A MAJOR IN THE 3RD VIRGINIA REGIMENT IN 1776 DURING THE AMERICAN REVOLUTION. HE JOINED GENERAL GEORGE WASHINGTON'S STAFF AS AIDE DE CAMP IN NOVEMBER 1776, WAS ON THE BATTLEFIELD AT PRINCETON, NEW JERSEY, ON JANUARY 3, 1777, WHEN AMERICAN FORCES DEFEATED THE BRITISH ARMY, ENCAMPED AT VALLEY FORGE, PENNSYLVANIA, IN DECEMBER 1777, AND WAS WOUNDED IN THE BATTLE OF MONMOUTH COURTHOUSE, NEW JERSEY, ON JUNE 28, 1778. HE THEREAFTER RETIRED FROM THE MILITARY AND RETURNED TO ALEXANDRIA, BECOMING MAYOR IN 1783. COLONEL FITZGERALD'S FRIENDSHIP WITH GENERAL WASHINGTON CONTINUED AFTER THE REVOLUTION AND, UPON COLONEL FITZGERALD'S TAKING UP THE SUBSCRIPTION FOR SAINT MARY'S, GENERAL WASHINGTON MADE THE FIRST DONATION. THE PRECISE LOCATION OF COLONEL FITZGERALD'S GRAVE IS UNKNOWN AND IT MAY BE HERE IN SAINT MARY'S CEMETERY OR ACROSS THE POTOMAC RIVER IN MARYLAND ON LAND HE OWNED THERE.

IN THIS CEMETERY REST THE EARTHLY REMAINS OF PATRIOTS IN THE REVOLUTIONARY WAR WHO FOUGHT FOR THE CAUSE OF LIBERTY.

FRANCIS IGNATIUS HAGEN, 3D VIRGINIA REGIMENT; ENLISTED 1777; BORN ABOUT1754; DIED DECEMBER 15, 1830
LAWRENCE HURDLE, PRIVATE, MARYLAND LINE; SERVED 1776-1782; BORN ABOUT 1750, DIED DECEMBER 1, 1848
PIERRE LA CROIX, SERVED IN FRENCH AND INDIAN WAR AND AMERICAN REVOLUTION; BORN ABOUT 1742; DIED SEPTEMBER 22, 1830
FRANCIS MURPHY, PENNSYLVANIA MILITIA; ENLISTED 1777; BORN ABOUT 1763; DIED JUNE 30, 1837
JOHN RIORDAN, 3D NEW JERSEY REGIMENT; ENLISTED 1778; BORN ABOUT 1763; DIED OCTOBER 10, 1803

SAINT MARY'S CATHOLIC CHURCH AND THE STUDENTS OF SAINT MARY'S CATHOLIC SCHOOL
AND
THE GEORGE WASHINGTON CHAPTER, VIRGINIA SOCIETY SONS OF THE AMERICAN REVOLUTION
DEDICATE THIS MARKER AS A MEMORIAL TO THESE PATRIOTS.

2015

Plaque at St Mary's Catholic Church, Alexandria City

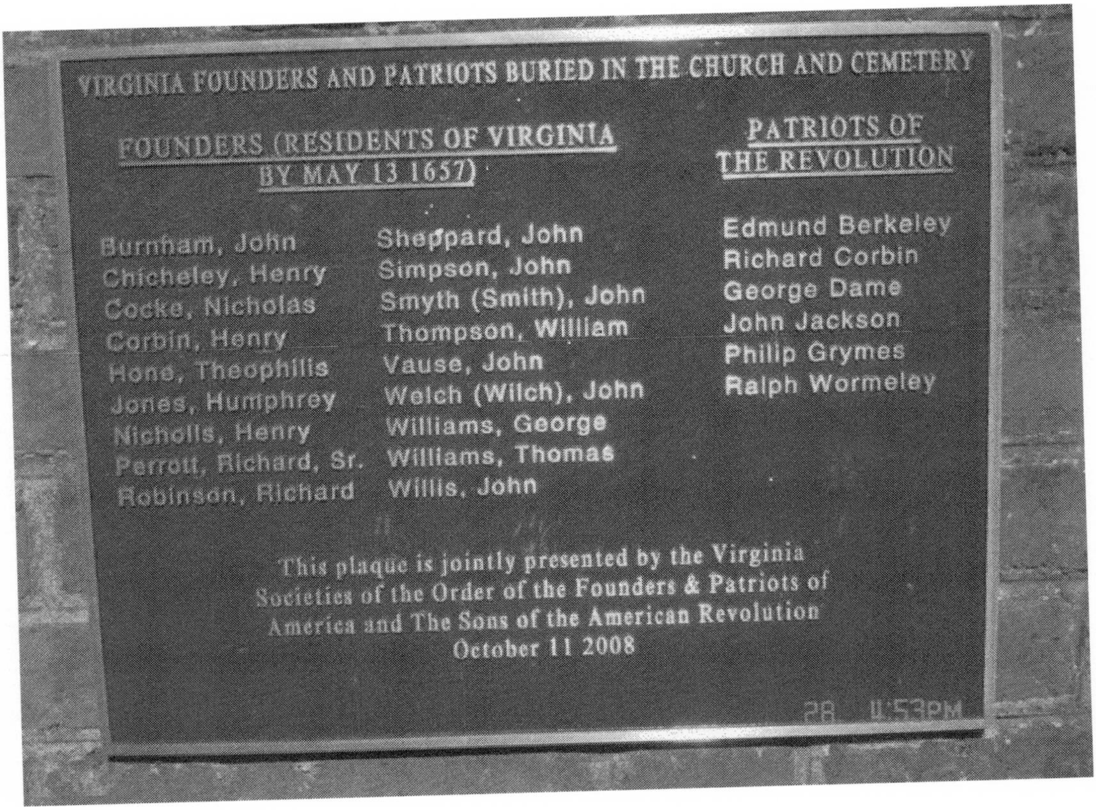

Plaque at Christ Church, Middlesex County

D.A.R plaque Peaked Mountain Cemetery, Rockingham County

FREDERICK ARMENTROUT	GEORGE ARMENTROUT
AUGUSTINE BERRY	BENJAMIN BERRY
ISAAC GIBBONS	CASPER HAINES
JOHN HAINES	JONAS HAINES
HENRY HAMMER	JACOB HARMON
LEONARD HERRING	WILLIAM HERRING
ARCHIBALD HOPKINS	JOHN HOPKINS
DITRICH KISSLING	JACOB KISSLING
PHILIP LONG	JAMES MAGILL
HENRY MONGER	JACOB NICHOLAS
HENRY PENCE	JACOB PENCE
WILLIAM PENCE	AUGUSTINE PRICE
JOHN ADAM SELLERS	JOHN HENRY SELLERS

Plaque at Trinity Episcopal Church, Portsmouth City

FOUNDERS & VETERANS OF LYNNHAVEN PARISH CHURCH
INTERRED IN THIS CEMETERY AND SURROUNDING AREA

CAPT ADAM THOROWGOOD (1604-1640) FOUNDER
COL THOMAS WALKE I (1642-1694) COLONIAL WAR
COL EDWARD MOSELEY (1661-1736) COLONIAL WAR
COL ANTHONY WALKE I (1692-1768) COLONIAL WAR
COL EDWARD HACK MOSELEY (1717-1783) COLONIAL WAR
LT COL EDWARD HACK MOSELEY JR (1740-1814) REVOLUTIONARY WAR
CPT JONATHAN SAUNDERS (1726-1765) COLONIAL WAR
COL ANTHONY WALKE II (1726-1779) COLONIAL WAR
COL ADAM THOROUGHGOOD (1750's-1780's) REVOLUTIONARY WAR
CAPT THOMAS WALKE IV (1760-1797) REVOLUTIONARY WAR
PVT JOHN HENDERSON (1769-1825) WAR OF 1812
PVT ANTHONY WALKE (1778-1820) WAR OF 1812
SGT JOHN BROWNLEY (1780-1853) WAR OF 1812

DEDICATED MAY 17, 2014 BY VA. SOCIETY ORDER OF FOUNDERS & PATRIOTS
OF AMERICA; VA. SOCIETY COLONIAL WARS; LYNNHAVEN PARISH CHAPTER, NSDAR;
NORFOLK CHAPTER, SONS OF THE AMERICAN REVOLUTION; COLONIAL DAMES
XVIIC SUFFOLK CHAPTER; FT. NORFOLK CHAPTER US DAUGHTER'S WAR OF 1812;
SOCIETY OF THE WAR OF 1812 IN THE COMMONWEALTH OF VA.

Plaque at Lynnhaven Parish Church Cemetery, Virginia Beach, City

Plaque at the Lynchburg City Cemetery, Lynchburg City

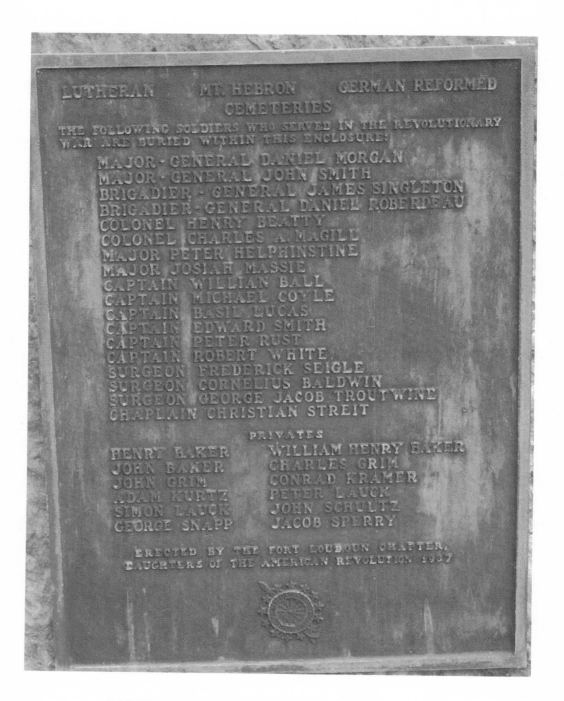

LUTHERAN   MT. HEBRON   GERMAN REFORMED
CEMETERIES
THE FOLLOWING SOLDIERS WHO SERVED IN THE REVOLUTIONARY
WAR ARE BURIED WITHIN THIS ENCLOSURE:

MAJOR - GENERAL DANIEL MORGAN
MAJOR - GENERAL JOHN SMITH
BRIGADIER - GENERAL JAMES SINGLETON
BRIGADIER - GENERAL DANIEL ROBERDEAU
COLONEL HENRY BEATTY
COLONEL CHARLES A. MAGILL
MAJOR PETER HELPHINSTINE
MAJOR JOSIAH MASSIE
CAPTAIN WILLIAM BALL
CAPTAIN MICHAEL COYLE
CAPTAIN BASIL LUCAS
CAPTAIN EDWARD SMITH
CAPTAIN PETER RUST
CAPTAIN ROBERT WHITE
SURGEON FREDERICK SEIGLE
SURGEON CORNELIUS BALDWIN
SURGEON GEORGE JACOB TROUTWINE
CHAPLAIN CHRISTIAN STREIT

PRIVATES
HENRY BAKER   WILLIAM HENRY BAKER
JOHN BAKER   CHARLES GRIM
JOHN GRIM   CONRAD KRAMER
ADAM KURTZ   PETER LAUCK
SIMON LAUCK   JOHN SCHULTZ
GEORGE SNAPP   JACOB SPERRY

ERECTED BY THE FORT LOUDOUN CHAPTER,
DAUGHTERS OF THE AMERICAN REVOLUTION 1937

DAR Plaque in the Mt. Hebron Cemetery, Winchester City

OLD PRESBYTERIAN MEETING HOUSE BURIAL GROUND

IN THIS CEMETERY REST THE EARTHLY REMAINS OF PATRIOTS IN THE REVOLUTIONARY WAR,
MANY OF WHOM WERE OF SCOTTISH ANCESTRY.
THESE PATRIOTS, ALONG WITH MANY PRESBYTERIANS FROM ALEXANDRIA, FOUGHT FOR
THE CAUSE OF LIBERTY AND ASSISTED THE SOLDIERS OF WASHINGTON'S ARMIES.
THE OLD PRESBYTERIAN MEETING HOUSE ALSO ADMINISTERS THE PRESBYTERIAN CEMETERY ON
HAMILTON LANE IN ALEXANDRIA WHERE MANY OTHER PATRIOTS REST.

ROBERT ALLISON	JOHN HARPER	THOMAS SIMMS
DAVID ARELL	JOHN HUNTER	WILLIAM HENRY SMITH
SAMUEL ARELL	WILLIAM HUNTER	CHARLES SPOONER
ROBERT BAILIE	WILLIAM LADD	JOHN STEWART
JOHN CARLYLE	JAMES McFADDEN	JESSE TAYLOR
SAMUEL CRAIG	CHARLES McKNIGHT	JAMES WILSON
JAMES CRAIK	JAMES MITCHELL	
JOHN DUNLAP	WILLIAM MITCHELL	
JAMES GILLES	LEWIS NICHOLAS (ALSO "NICHOLA")	A SOLDIER
DAVID GRAHAM	THOMAS PORTER	KNOWN BUT TO GOD

THE GEORGE WASHINGTON CHAPTER, VIRGINIA SOCIETY SONS OF THE AMERICAN REVOLUTION
AND
THE SAINT ANDREW'S SOCIETY OF WASHINGTON, D.C.
DEDICATE THIS MARKER AS A MEMORIAL TO THESE PATRIOTS

2006

Plaque at Old Presbyterian Meeting House Cemetery, Alexandria City

D.A.R Monument at Pine Creek Baptist Church Cemetery, Floyd County

THIS MONUMENT IS DEDICATED
TO THOSE FROM HALIFAX COUNTY
WHO DIED IN AMERICAN WARS

REVOLUTIONARY WAR
1775-1783

William Ashlock
John Easley
Benjamin Fambrough
John Fambrough
Henry Gee
David Grant
John Grant
James Hill
Anthony Irby, Jr.

Elkanah Lacy, Sr.
William Land
John McFarlin
Edward Moody
Joshua Powell
William Shackleford
Thomas Tunks
John Walrond
Edward Wade

Monument at the Halifax Center, Halifax County

Plaque at St John's Episcopal Church Cemetery, Richmond City

APPENDIX A – VETERAN LIST BY COUNTY / INDEPENDENT CITY

About Virginia Counties and Independent Cities:

In 1634, the Virginia Colony was divided into eight "shires" later renamed counties. Today the Commonwealth of Virginia has 95 Counties and 38 Independent Cities. Unlike in most states, Virginia's cities are not part of counties. Incorporated cities are independent jurisdictions with their own political and administrative systems and are equal to counties as governmental subdivisions of the state. They have their own court systems, and with a few exceptions, their own record repositories. Confusion can occur because some cities and counties are named the same, yet may or may not be geographically contiguous. Also, a county's seat (courthouse) is sometimes located within the boundaries of a city. For example, Fairfax County surrounds the City of Fairfax City and its county seat is located there. However, Richmond County and the City of Richmond are in different parts of the state, as are Franklin County and the City of Franklin. Also, the names of James City County and Charles City can be misleading. Two of the originial shires, they have always been counties and never incorporated cities.
Research sources for county/city information in this section include *The Hornbook of Virginia History* published by the Library of Virginia and *Encyclopedia Virginia* published online by the Virginia Foundation for the Humanities.

ACCOMACK COUNTY. Original 1634 shire of Accawmack or Accomac County comprised Virginia's Eastern Shore. Name changed to Northampton County in 1643. Split into the present Accomack and Northampton Counties in 1663. County seat is Accomac (23301).

ANDREWS, Robert	GALI (GALLIN, GALING), Samuel	SAVAGE, Francis
ANDREWS, William	JOYNES, Levin S	SAVAGE, William
BAGWELL, Isaiah	KENNAHORN, William Jr	SUMMERS, Horsey
BENSON, James Sr	KENNAHORN, William Sr	TEACKLE, Arthur
BRADFORD, Thomas A	KER, Edward	TEACKLE (TEAKLE), Levin
BURTON, Thomas	KER, John Shepard	UPSHUR, Arthur IV
CAMPBELL, Archibald	LAWS, John	UPSHUR, Caleb
CHAPMAN, John	MELVIN, James	UPSHUR, John
COLONNA, Benjamin	PARKER, George	WAPLES, Samuel
CORBIN, George	PARKER, Thomas	WATSON, Benjamin
CROPPER, John	PARRAMORE, Thomas	WELBURN (WELBOURNE), William Sr
CROPPER, Sebastian	PARRAMORE, William	WEST, Abel
CUSTIS, Henry	PETTITT, William	WEST, Anthony Jr
CUSTIS, John	PIELEE, Gilbert	WHALEY, Zedekaih (Zadock)
CUSTIS, Thomas	READ, Edmund (Edmond)	WHARTON, John Esq
ELLIOTT, William	RILEY, John	WISE, John
FLOYD, Matthew	RODGERS, Robert	
FOREMAN, Robert		

ALBEMARLE COUNTY. Formed in 1744 from Goochland County. County seat is Charlottesville (22902). **See also CHARLOTTESVILLE CITY.**

ANDERSON, Edmund	HAMNER, Nicholas	THOMAS, John
ARTHUR, William	HARDING, Isaac	THOMAS, John
BOWEN, Ephraim	HARRIS, Benjamin	VIA, William
BOWEN, Micajah	HARRIS, William Sr.	WALKER, Francis
BROCKMAN, William Sr	HUDSON, Christopher	WALKER, John
BROWN, Bernis	HUDSON, John	WALKER, Martha
BROWN, Brightberry	LEAKE, Mask (Mark)	WALKER, Thomas
CHILDRESS, Benjamin	LEWIS, Charles	WATTS, Jacob
COLES, John	MARTIN, James	WINGFIELD, John M
DIVERS, George	MASSIE, Charles Sr	WOOD, John
DURRETT, James	MAUPIN, John	WOODS, William
DURRETT, Richard, Jr	MAUPINE, Daniel	WOODSON, Tarleton
DURRETT, Richard, Sr	MINOR, James Carr	
EARLY, James	MOORE, Stephen	
EPPERSON, David	RODES (RHODES), John	
GARLAND, Nathaniel	SNOW, Richard	
GENTRY, James		

ALEXANDRIA CITY (22314). Incorporated as a town in 1779 in portion of Fairfax County which became part of District of Columbia, then Alexandria County, then Arlington County. Achieved Independent City status from Arlington County in 1852. Court records begin in 1780. **See also ARLINGTON COUNTY and FAIRFAX COUNTY.**

ALLISON, Robert
ANDERSON, James
ARELL, David
ARELL, H (Henry)
ARELL, Samuel
AYRES, William
BAILLIE,(BAILIE), Robert
BARTLEMAN, William
BENNETT, Charles
BIRD, William
BLACK, Benjamin
BLACK, David
BLUNT, Washer
BOYAR (BOYARS), John
BOYER, Henry
BRAWNER, William Henry
BROOKS, John Turpin
BURNES (BURNS), John
BUTCHER, John
CALLENDER, John
CAMPBELL, James
CARLYLE, John
CHAPIN, Benjamin
CHEW, Rodger
CONNELL, William
CONNER, James
COOK, Jacob
COOPER, Samuel
CRAIG, Samuel
CRAIK, James Dr
CRAWFORD, Thomas
CREIGHTON, Robert Dr
CROUCHER, Thomas
DEAN, Joseph
DELAGNEL, Julius Adolphus
DICK, Elisha Cullen Dr
DOUGLASS, Daniel
DUNLOP, John
DUNN, William
EVANS, John
EVANS, Robert
FAW, Abraham
FENDALL, Philip Richard
FITZGERALD, John
FLEMING, Andrew
GILLIES (GILLES), James Dr
GILPIN, George
GRAHAM, David
GRIMES, John
HAGAN, Francis Ignatius
HAGERTY, Patrick
HANNAH, Alexander
HARPER, Edward
HARPER, John

HARPER, Joseph
HARPER, William
HARTSHORNE, William
HAYLEY, James
HERBERT, William
HESS, Jacob
HILTON, Samuel
HOOE; Robert Townshend
HOOF, Lawrence
HOYE (HOY), William
HUNTER, Alexander
HUNTER, George
HUNTER, John
HUNTER, William
HUNTER, William Jr
HURDLE, Lawrence
IRWIN, James
JANNEY, Abel
JOHNSON, Dennis
JORDAN, John
KEITH, Alexander
KENNEDY, James Dr
KIDD, James
KINCAID, John
LACROIX, Pierre
LADD, William
LAWRASON, James
LEWIS, Edward
LONGDEN, John
MARSTELLER, Philip
    Balthasar or Phillip G
MASON, George Jr
MCFADEN (McFADDEN),
    James
MCIVER, Colin
MCKNIGHT, Charles
MCKNIGHT, William
MCMAHON, Michael
MEASE, Robert
MITCHELL, James
MITCHELL, William
MUIR, James Rev
MUIR, John
MUIR, Robert
MURPHY, Francis
MURRAY, George
MURRAY, James
MYERS (MYRES), John C
NEWTON, William
NICHOLAS, Lewis
NICHOLSON, Henry
PATTERSON, William
PEAKE, Humphrey Sr
PEAKE, William

PENDEL (PENALL), Thomas
PEYTON, Francis
PIERCY, Henry
PORTER, Thomas
POTTEN, John
RAMSAY, Dennis
RAMSAY, Dennis
RAMSAY, William
RAMSEY, Anthony
REDMAN, Henry
REYNOLDS, William
RICHARDS, George
RIDDLE, Joshua
RIORDAN, John
ROSE, Henry
ROYAL, Thomas T.
SANFORD, Lawrence
SANFORD, Robert
SANFORD, Thomas
SAUNDERS, John
SCOTT, William
SCULL, William
SHAW, James
SHREVE, Benjamin Jr
SIMMS, Charles
SIMMS, Thomas
SIMPSON, Jeremiah
SLADE, William
SLOAN, John
SMITH, Caleb Jr
SMITH, Joseph
SMITH, William Henry
SPOONER, Charles
STEWART, John
STITH, Buckner
STROME (STROM), Henry A.
STUART, John Ainsworth
SUMMERS, John
TATSAPAUGH, Peter
TAYLOR, Jesse
TAYLOR, Jesse
THOMPSON, John
VOWELL, John G
WALES, Andrew
WEBB, Thomas T
WESCOTT, John
WEST, Thomas Wade
WESTON, Lewis
WHEELER, William
WILKINSON, Thomas
WILSON, James
WOODWARD, James
YOUNG, John
ZIMMERMAN, Henry

ALEXANDRIA COUNTY. Renamed in 1920. **See ARLINGTON COU**

ALLEGHANY COUNTY. Formed in 1822 from Bath County and Botetourt County. Includes the former independent city of Clifton Forge (1906) which reverted in 2001 to a town within the County. County seat is Covington (24426). **See also COVINGTON CITY.**

ARMENTROUT, Frederick	HUMPHREY, William	SMITH, William
HAYNES, Benjamin	KING, John	
HAYNES, Joseph	SMITH, William	

AMELIA COUNTY. Formed in 1735 from Brunswick County and Prince George County. County seat is Amelia (23002).

ARCHER, John	GREEN, Abraham	ROYALL, John
AVARY, Wiliam	GREEN, John	ROYALL, Littleberry
BOOKER, Edmund	GREEN, Thomas	SCOTT, George
BOOKER, Edmund	GREEN, William	THOMPSON, Samuel Yancey
BOOKER, George	JACKSON, Francis	TOWNES, John
BOOKER, Richardson	JONES, Peter	VAUGHAN, James
(Richerson)	MEAD(E), Everard Sr	WARD, Henry "Hal", Jr.
BOOTH, William	MEADE, Everard Jr	WHITWORTH, Thomas
CHAPPELL, John Sr	PRIDE, John, III	WOOD, William Sr
EGGLESTON, Joseph	PRIDE, William	WOOD, William C
GILES, William	ROBERTS, Jacob	
GILES, William Branch	ROBERTSON, John	

AMHERST COUNTY. Formed in 1761 from Albemarle County. County seat is Amherst (24521).

BICKLEY, John James	JOHNS, William	RODES, Charles
BURTON, Samuel	LAINE, William	RUCKER, Ambrose
CABELL, William Jr	LOVING, William	RUCKER, Anthony Jr
CLEMENTS, William	MASSIE, John	RUCKER, Isaac
CLEMENTS, William Right	MEREDITH, Samuel Garland	RUCKER, John Sr
(Wright)	PENDLETON, William	SHELTON, John "Jack"
CRAWFORD, Ann (Anderson)	PENN, Gabriel	SHELTON, Richard
DILLARD, James B	PENN, George	STREET, Anthony
ELLIS, Josiah B	PENN, John	TUCKER, Daniel
FRANKLIN, James	PENN, William	TYLER, Charles N
HENRY, William	PINNELL, Thomas	TYLER, John
HIGGINBOTHAM, James	POWELL, Lucas	WILSON, Richard
GILL, Jones	REDCROSS, John	WOODRUFF, David Jr

APPOMATTOX COUNTY. Formed in 1845 from parts of Buckingham, Campbell, Charlotte, and Prince Edward Counties. A fired destroyed all county records in 1892. County seat is Appomattox (24552).

AKERS, William	HOLLAND, Richard	ROBERTSON, John Jr
CARSON, James	KELSO, Robert	ST CLARE, Robert
DIUGUID, William Jr	MCREYNOLDS, James	STEELE, Alexander
FLOOD, Henry	MCREYNOLDS, Joseph	SWEENEY, Moses
GOODE, Robert	MOSS, Ann	TRENT, Thomas
HARRIS, John C	PANKEY, John	WILLSON, John Sr
HELM, John S	ROBERTSON, James Sr	

ARLINGTON COUNTY. Formed from a portion of Fairfax County, including the town of Alexandria, that was ceded by Virginia to the federal government in 1789. Became part of the District of Columbia in 1801 and named

ALEXANDRIA COUNTY by Congress. Returned to Viriginia jurisdiction in 1847. Name changed to Arlington County in 1920. County seat is Arlington (22210). **See also ALEXANDRIA CITY.**

ADAMS, William
AULD, Hugh Sr
BALL, John
BALL, Moses
BURROWS, William Ward
CARLETON, Joseph
CARLIN, William
CASSIN, John
CHARLES, Pierre l"EnFant
DAVIS, John A

FOLLIN, Catherine (Sandford)
FOLLIN, John
GREEN, John
HOUSE, James
JONES, Edward
L'ENFANT, Pierre Charles
LINGAN, James McCubbin
MACOMB, Alexander
MCLINGAN, James
MEASON, Thomas

PEIRCE, Solomon
PEYTON, Francis
REDIN, John
RUSSELL, William
SWAN, Caleb
THRIFT, Jeremiah
WILLIAMS, John
WILSON, James R

AUGUSTA COUNTY. Created in 1738 from Orange County. County government formed in 1745. County seat is Staunton (24401). **See also STAUNTON CITY and WAYNESBORO CITY.**

ABNEY, John
ALLEN, James
ALEXANDER, Archibald
ALEXANDER, Gabriel
ALLEN, James
ANDERSON, Alexander
ANDERSON, Andrew
ANDERSON, George
ANDERSON, George
ANDERSON, John
ANDERSON, William
ARMSTRONG, William
BALSLEY (BALSEY),
    Christian
BARGER, Jacob
BASKIN, Charles
BELL, David
BELL, David
BELL, James
BELL, John
BELL, Joseph
BELL, Joseph Jr
BELL, Joseph Sr
BELL, Samuel
BELL, William
BELL, William
BERRY, John
BLACK, John
BLAIR, William
BRATTON, Robert
BREEDEN, George
BUCHANAN, Andrew
BUMGARDNER, Christian
BUMGARDNER, Jacob
BURNSIDE, John
CALLISON, James
CARSON, Samuel
CHRISTIAN (CHRISTAIN),
    John
CLAYTON, John
COCHRAN, James
COCHRAN, William

CONNALY, Arthur Sr
COOPER, Robert
CRAIG, Alexander
CRAIG, James Jr
CRAIG, James Sr
CRAIG, John
CRAIG, John
CRAIG, Samuel
CRAIG, William
CRAWFORD, George Jr
CRAWFORD, John
CRAWFORD, John
CRAWFORD, Patrick
CURRY, Robert
DAVIS, Walter
DAVIS, William D
DOAK, David
DOAK, Robert
DOAK, Samuel
DOAK (DOACK),
DavidERVIN, William
EWING, James
EWING, James
EWING, James
EWING, William
FALL, George
FINLEY, James
FINLEY, John
FISHBURNE, Dietrick
    (Detrich)
FRAZIER, James
FULTON, James
FULWEIDER, Johannes
GAMBLE, John
GIBBONS, John
GILKESON, Hugh
GILKESON, William
GIVENS, John
GLENN, George
GOLLADAY, David
GRAHAM, Andrew
GUTHRIE, John

HALL, Patrick
HALL, William
HALL, William Sr
HAMILTON, Alexander
HAMILTON, David
HAMILTON, James
HAMILTON, James
HAMILTON, John
HAMILTON, William
HANGER, Frederick Jr
HANGER, Peter
HANNA, Joseph
HANNA, Robert
HARNSBERGER, Robert
HOGSETT, James
HOGSHEAD, David Jr
HOGSHEAD, Michael
HOOK, William
HOOK(E), Robert Sr
HOOK(E), William Sr
HOUSTON, Samuel
HUFFER (HUFFORD,
    HUFFERT), Jacob
HUGHART, Thomas
HUMPHREYS (HUMPHRIES),
    David
HUNTER, Samuel
IRVINE (ERWIN, IRWIN),
    Edward
JOHNSTON, William Z
KEINADT/KOINER, Michael
KELLER, Frederick Sr
KELLER, George
KELLER, George
KENNEY (KENNY, KINNEY),
    RobertKENNEY (KENNY,
KINNEY),
    Robert
KERR, James
KERR, John Jr
KERR, John Sr
KERR, Joseph

KERR, William
KILPATRICK, Ann
KINCAID/KINKAID, William
KOINER, George Adam
KOINER, George Michael
KOINER, Kasper
LANDES, John
LEWIS, John
LINK, Matthias
LOCKRIDGE, Andrew
LOGAN, John
LONG, Joseph Sr
MCCHESNEY, James
MCCHESNEY, John
MCCLANAHAN, Alexander
MCCLANAHAN
(MCCLENACHAN), Robert,
Sr.
MCCLURE, Andrew
MCCOMB, James
MCCORMICK, Martha
(Sanderson)
MCCORMICK, Robert
MCCUE, John
MCCUE, John Rev
MCCUNE, John
MCCUTCHAN, Charles
MCCUTCHAN, James
MCCUTCHAN(McCUTCHEN),
Robert
MCCUTCHEN, William
MCCUTCHAN, Samuel
MCCUTCHAN, William
MCCUTCHEON, John
MCNUTT, James
MCNUTT, John)
MCNUTT, James
MCNUTT, John
MCNUTT, Robert
MCPHEETERS, William Jr
MILLER, Henry
MILLS, John
MILLER, John
MILLS, RobertMITCHELL,
James

MITCHELL, Robert
MITCHELL, Thomas
MITCHELL, William
MOFFETT, George
MOFFETT, James
MOFFETT, John
MOFFETT, William
MONTGOMERY, John Rev
MONTGOMERY, Richard
MOORE, Andrew
NELSON, Alexander
NELSON, Alexander
NELSON, John
NELSON, William
PARKS, Joseph
POAGE, James
POAGE, Robert
POAGE, Robert Preston
POAGE, Thomas
POAGUE (POAGE), James
POAGUE (POAGE), John
  Jr
RAMSEY, James Dr
RITCHEY, David
ROBERTSON, Alexander
ROBERTSON, Alexander
ROBERTSON, William
ROBERTSON, William
ROBINSON, Isaac
ROSS, Alexander
RUSSELL, Andrew
RUSSELL, Joshua
SHARP, John
SHARP, Joseph
SHARP, Thomas
SHIRLEY, Michael
SHIPMAN, Benjamin
SHIPMAN, Jonathan
SHUEY, John Ludwig "Lewis"
SIEG, Paul
SLAGLE, George
SLUTE, James
SMITH, John
SPITLER, Jacob
SPROUL, William

STEELE, Andrew
STEELE, David
STEELE, James Wendle
STEELE, John
STEELE, John
STEELE, John Jr
STEELE, John Sr
STEELE, Nathaniel
STEELE, Robert
STEELE, Samuel Jr
STEELE, Samuel Jr
STEELE, Samuel Sr
STEELE, Thomas
STEELE, William
STUART, Benjamin
SUMMERS, John
TATE, John
TATE, John
TATE, John
TATE, Robert
TATE, Thomas
THOMPSON, Alexander
THOMPSON, James
THOMPSON, Robert
THOMPSON, William
TRIMBLE, John
VAN LEAR (VANLEAR),
  Jacob
WALKER, Alexander
WALLACE, Robert
WEAVER, John Peter
WILLSON, Matthew
WILLSON, William
WILSON, John Sr
WILSON, Samuel
WILSON, William
WOODDELL, Thomas
YATES, Enoch
YOUNG, James
YOUNG, John
YOUNG, Thomas
YOUNG, Willi

BATH COUNTY. Formed in 1791 from Augusta County, Bedford County and Greenbriar County (WV). County Seat is Warm Springs (24484).

ARBUCKLE, Mathew
BOLAR, John
BRADLEY, William
BRATTON, James
CAMERON, Charles
CRAWFORD, Nathan
DICKINSON, John

GIVEN, William
GLASSBURN, David
KEYSER (KEYSOR), William
LAVERTY, Ralph
MARSHALL, Robert
MCCLINTIC, William Jr
MCCLINTIC (MCCLINTOCK),

William Sr
MCCLUNG, John Jr
MUSTOE, Anthony
PAINE, Joseph
PAYNE, Joseph
SITLINGTON, Robert
WARWICK, Jacob

BEDFORD [CITY] (24523). Achieved Independent City status in 1968, then in 2013 reverted to a town within Bedford County in 2013. **See also BEDFORD COUNTY.**

FUQUA, Joseph	HOPKINS, Francis	TURNER, James
GRAHAM, Michael	HUDNALL, John	WILKS, Samue
	MELTON, Richard	

BEDFORD COUNTY. Formed in 1754 from Lunenburg County. Part of Albemarle County was added in 1755. County seat is town of Bedford (2452

ANDERSON, Nelson	FRANTZ, Christian	READ, William
ANDREWS, Thomas	FUQUA, Ralph J	REID, Nathan
ARTHUR, Thomas Sr	FUQUA, Joseph	SALE, John
AYERS, John	GOGGIN, Stephen Jr	SALMON, John
BUFORD, Henry	GROOM, Jonathan	SAUNDERS, David
BARTON, Elisha	HARDY, Joshua	SCOTT, William E
BLANKENSHIP, Abraham Sr	HARDY, Joseph Austin	SLACK, Abraham
BROWN, Henry	HURT, Moses	STEPTOE, James Jr
BURNETT, Williamson	JETER, Henry	STiFF, James
CALLAWAY (CALLOWAY), William	LEE, William	STRATTON, Henry
	LEFTWICH, Augustine Jr	TERRY, William
CALLAWAY (CALLOWAY), William Jr	LEFTWICH, Joel	THOMAS, William
	LEFTWICH, Thomas	TRIGG, John (Johns)
CAMPBELL, Thomas	LEFTWICH, Uriah	TURPIN, Thomas
CHAPMAN, Nathan	LYNCH, Patrick	UPDIKE, Amon
CLAY, Charles Green	McCONNEHEY, John	WADE, Isaac Sr.
COBBS, John L	MEAD, Nicholas	WALKER, George Reynolds
COFER, George	MEAD, Samuel	WALKER, William
COX, Valentine	MOODY, John	WATTS, John
CREWS, Joseph	OTEY, James Walter	WHITE, Jacob
DAVIDSON, Benjamin	OTEY, John Armistead	WHITE, Joseph
DAWSON, Martin	OWEN, James	WIGGINTON, John
DICKERSON, Joseph	PADGETT, Frederick	WOOD, Jeremiah
ENGLISH, Stephen	QUARLES, John	
EWING, Robert Sr	READ, Samuel	

BLAND COUNTY. Formed in 1861 from Giles County, Tazewell County, and Wythe County. County seat is Bland (24315).

DAVIDSON, John Goodman	HARMAN, Henry Sr	WILSON, James
GROSECLOSE, Peter Jr	SPANGLER, Jacob	
GROSECLOSE, Peter Sr	THOMPSON, Andrew	

BOTETOURT COUNTY. Formed 1770 from Augusta County. County seat is Fincastle (24090).

ABENDSCHON (OBENSHAIN), Samuel	BRUGH, Hermanus	HUME(S), William
	BURWELL, Nathaniel T	JORDAN, John
ALLEN, Hugh	CAHOON, Charles	KAYSER (KEYSER), John J
ALLEN, James	CARLOCK, Hanchrist	KESSLAR, Jacob
ALLEN, John	CARPER, Jacob	KESSLER, John
ALLEN, Malcolm	CARPER, Nicholas	KYLE, William
ALLEN, Robert	CARTER, Nicholas	LAYMAN, George
ANDERSON, Robert	CROSS, William	LEDGERWOOD, James
ANDERSON, William	EARLY, James Matten	LEE, Zachariah Jr
BAKER, Henry Sr	GISH, Jacob	LEMON, George
BELL, James	GUILIFORD, Allen	LEMON (LEMAN), Frederick J
BOWYER, Henry	HAMILTON, Alexander	LEMON, Jacob
BOYER (BOWYER), Thomas	HAMILTON, Andrew	LOCKHART, Patrick
BRECKENRIDGE, James	HARVEY, Matthew	LOGAN, Robert
BRICKEY, Peter	HARVEY, Robert	MCCLURE, John
BROUGH, Daniel	HICKLE, Lewis	MCDONALD, Bryan
BRUGH, Daniel Sr	HICKOK, Ebenezer	MCDONALD, Edward

MCDONALD, James
MCDONALD, William
MCFERRAN, Martin
MCROBERTS, Alexander
MCROBERTS, John
MCROBERTS, Samuel
MERRITT, Samuel
MIFFORD, Jacob
MOORE, John
MOORE, John
MOSELEY, Arthur
NICHOLAS, Lewis

OLIVER, William
PATTERSON, Samuel
PECK, Benjamin
PECK, Jacob
PECK, John
PECK, Joseph
POAGUE (POAGE), John
PRESTON, John
RADER (RIDER), Adam
REID, Francis
SHEETS, Jacob
SHIRKEY, Nicholas

SKIPWITH, Peyton
SMITH (SMYTH), Adam B
TAYMAN (LAYMAN, LAYMON), George
THOMAS, Francis
WALKER, William
WAX, Henry Sr
WOODS, Andrew Sr
WYSONG, Feidt (Fyette)
ZIRKLE(CIRCLE), Peter

BRISTOL CITY (24201). Achieved Independent City status in 1890. City boundaries include part of Tennessee. **See also WASHINGTON COUNTY.**

PRESTON, John
PRESTON, Robert

SHELBY, Elvan
SHELBY, Isaac

SNODGRASS, Willia

BRUNSWICK COUNTY. Formed in 1720 from Prince George County. County government formed in 1732. County seat is Lawrenceville (23868).

ABERNATHY, John D Jr
ABERNATHY, John Sr
BISHOP, John
BISHOP, Mathew

CLAIBORNE, Thomas
LANIER, Benjamin Bird
LEWIS, Benjamin
ORGAIN, William Derby

SCOTT, Thomas H
WILKES, Burwell

BUCHANAN COUNTY. Formed in 1858 from Russell County and Tazewell County. County seat is Grundy (24614).

FERRELL, William

BUCKINGHAM COUNTY. Formed in 1761 from Albemarle County. County seat is Buckingham (23921).

AGEE, Jacob
AGEE, James
BOATWRIGHT, Reuben
BRANCH, Olive
BROWN, Benjamin
CABELL, John
CHAMBERS, John
COLEMAN, Julius
COLEMAN, Robert
ELDRIDGE, Rolfe
EVANS, William

FLOOD, Noah
FORBES, Alexander
GLOVER, Anthony
GLOVER, Samuel Jr
HARRISON (later STARKS), William
HOOPER, George
JONES, Abraham
JONES, Michael
MORRIS, Nathaniel
MOSELEY, Arthur

MOSELEY, Benjamin
MOSELEY, Robert Peter
PATTESON, David
PATTESON, Thomas
PERKINS, John W
RAGLAND, John Dudley
STARKES. William H
STRATTON, John Handley
WATSON, William
WILKINSON, William

BUENA VISTA CITY. Achieved Independent City status in 1892. **See also ROCKBRIDGE County.**

No known veteran burials.

CAMPBELL COUNTY. Formed in 1782 from Bedford County. County seat is Rustburg (25688). **See also LYNCHBURG CITY.**

ADAMS, Robert "Old Robin"
ALEXANDER, Robert
ANTHONY, John
BLANKENSHIP, Hudson
BROWN, Henry
BROWN, John
BROWN, John
CALLAWAY (CALLOWAY), John

CARDWELL, Robert
CARWILE(S), Jacob Sr
CLARK, John
CLEMENT, Adam Sr
COBBS, Charles
COBBS, Jesse
COBBS, John Sr
COBBS, Robert
CREASY, William

DEARING (DEERING), James
DIUGUID, George
DIXON, James
DRISKILL, Daniel
EARLY, Jeremiah
EVANS, Daniel
EVANS, Reese
FIELDS, Andrew
FRANKLIN, Thomas

HADEN, Anthony
HADEN, Benjamin
HADEN, John Sr
HANKS, Abraham
HANKS, Abraham
HEATH (HAYTH), Thomas
HOWARD, James
HUNTER, John Jr
HUNTER, Robert
IRVINE, John Jr
IRVINE, John Sr

JONES, Thomas
LEE, John
LEFTWICH, Augustine Sr
LEWIS, William J
LYNCH, Anselm
LYNCH, Charles Sr
MCREYNOLDS, John
PAYNE (PAINE), Phillip
PHILLIPS, John
PHILLIPS, John
POINDEXTER, Joseph

PRIBBLE (PREBBLE), John
SMITH, Fred
SMITH, Ralph
THORNHILL, Jesse
WARD, Henry
WARD, John
WHITAKER, James
WIATT, John
WIATT, Thomas
WILSON, John

CAROLINE COUNTY. Formed in 1728 from Essex County, King and Queen County, and King William County. County seat is Bowling Green (22427). Many older records are housed at the Central Rappahannock Heritage Center in Fredericksburg.

BAYLOR, George
BAYLOR, John
BAYLOR, Walker
BAYNHAM, Richard
BOULWARE, Mark
BOUTWELL, John T
BOUTWELL, William
BOWIE: John
BRIDGES, Richard
BUCKNER, George
BURKE, Thomas
CARR, John
CHEWNING, Samuel

DEJARNETTE, Joseph Jr
DICK, Archibald
GEORGE, Reuben
GILCHRIST, Robert
HILL, Humphrey
HOOMES, John
HOOMES, John
LOMAX, Thomas
MINOR, Vivion
PRATT, John Birkett
QUARLES, Minor
QUARLES, William
TALIAFERRO, Walker

TAYLOR, James
TAYLOR, John
TERRELL, Samuel
THORNTON, Anthony
TODD, Charles
TODD, George Dr
TOMPKINS, Christopher
WHITE, Ambrose
WOODFORD, William
WOOLFOLK, John George
WRIGHT, Robert Mosley Sr
YOUNG, William

CARROLL COUNTY. Formed in 1842 from Grayson County. County seat is Hillsville (24343).

BLAIR, Thomas
BOBBITT, John
BOBBITT, Robert
BOBBITT, William Sr
BOWMAN, Robert
CLOUD, William
COLLIER, Aaron
COX, Enoch Sr
COX, Solomon

DALTON, William
EDWARDS, Elias
EDWARDS, Isaac
FARMER, James
FROST, John
GARDNER, James
HANKS, Joshua
HILL, James
HUFFMAN, Barnard

KENNY, William
MITCHELL, Stephen
PHILLIPS, Tobias
SCHOOLEY, Samuel
SHOCKLEY, Richard E
WEBB, Henry "Hal"
WORRELL, James

CHARLES CITY COUNTY. An original 1634 shire. County seat is Charles City (23030).

BISHOP, Billy
BROWN, Isaac
CARTER, Charles
CARTER, Edward
CHRISTIAN, James
CHRISTIAN, Joseph

CRUTCHFIELD, John
CRUTCHFIELD, Lewis
HARRISON, Benjamin Jr.
HARRISON, Benjamin Sr.
LIGHTFOOT, William
MINGE, David

RICKMAN, William Dr
TYLER, John

CHARLOTTE COUNTY. Formed in 1765 from Lunenburg County. County seat is Charlotte Court House (23923).

BEDFORD, Thomas Sr
BOULDIN, Thomas Sr
BOULDIN, Wood
BOULDIN (BOUDLIN), Thomas
CALDWELL, John F
CARRINGTON, Clement
CARRINGTON, Paul

GAINES, Richard
GAINES, William
HENRY, Patrick
LAWSON, George
MOSELEY, Edward
OSBORNE, Reps
OSBORNE, Samuel
READ, Jonathan

READ, Thomas
SMITH, Isaac Watt Sr
WHEELER, John Sr

CHARLOTTESVILLE CITY. Achieved Independent City status in 1888. **See also ALBEMARLE COUNTY.**

BROWN, Bazael (Bazel)	LEWIS, Jesse Pitman	MERIWETHER, William Douglas
BRYAN, John Patterson	LEWIS, Mary	NICHOLAS, Wilson Cary
CARR, Dabney Jr	LEWIS, Nicholas	SMITH, Matthew
CARR, John	LEWIS, Taliaferro	WINGFIELD, Charles
GILMER, George Dr	LEWIS, Thomas Walker	WINGFIELD, John
JEFFERSON, Thomas	LEWIS, William	

CHESAPEAKE CITY (23320). Formed in 1963 by the consolidation of Norfolk County (created in 1691) and South Norfolk City (created in 1921), which both then became extinct.

BUTT, Epaphroditus	PETERS, John	WILKINS, Willis
FINNIE, William	SMITH, John	WILSON, Nathaniel
GWYNN, Thomas	STEWART, Charles	WOODWARD, William
HALSTEAD (HOLSTEAD), Matt	WEST, William	

CHESTERFIELD COUNTY. Formed in 1749 from Henrico County. County seat is Chesterfield Court House (23823).

ANDREWS, Isham	FURGUS(S)ON), Moses	LOCKETT, Edmund Sr
BAILEY, Benjamin	FLEMING, William	RANDOLPH, Henry
BOLLING, Thomas	FRANKLIN, John Sr	RANDOLPH, John
BROOKS, Elias	GATES, William	ROBERTSON, Jeffrey Jr
CLARKE, William	GOODE, Francis	ROBERTSON, William
CLAY, Eleazer	GOODE, John	SPEARS, John
DUNCAN, Charles	HUNDLEY, Josiah	WOOLDRIDGE, William
FERGUSSON (FARGUSSON	KABLER, Frederick	

CLARKE COUNTY. Formed in 1836 from Frederick County. Part of Warren County added in 1860. County seat is Berryville (22611).

ANDERSON, Joseph Edward Sr	EVERHART, Jacob	MEADE, Humberson
	FROST, William	MEADE, Richard Kidder
BARNETT, Ambrose	HAY, William	MUSE, Battaile
BERRY, Benjamin	HELM, William T	PAGE, John
BLAKEMORE, George	HOLKER, John	PAGE, Matthew
BLAKEMORE, Thomas Sr	HUNSICKER, Peter	PAGE, Robert
BURWELL, Nathaniel	IRELAND, James	RANDOLPH, Edmund Jennings
BUTLER, Lawrence (Lance)	JACKSON, Thomas	
BYRD, Thomas Taylor	LARUE, Isaac	REED, William
CHANDLER, Carter	MARTIN, Thomas Bryan	SMITH, John

COLONIAL HEIGHTS CITY (23834). Achieved Independent City status in 1948. **See also CHESTERFIELD COUNTY.**

SHORE, Thomas

COVINGTON CITY (24426). Achieved Independent City status in 1952. **See also ALLEGHANY COUNTY.**

BROWN, James	PERSINGER, Jacob	ROBINSON, William
DAMERON, John	RICHARDSON, John Sr	WALKER, Henry

CRAIG COUNTY. Formed in 1851 from Botetourt County, Giles County, Roanoke County, and part of Monroe County (WV). County seat is New Castle (24127).

ALLEN, Moses	PECK, Benjamin	WEBB, John
NUTTER, Zadock (Zadok)	WALKER, George	

CULPEPER COUNTY. Formed in 1749 from Orange County. County seat is Culpeper (22701).

BROWN, Daniel	GARNETT, James Rev	NORMAN, Courtney
CLARKE, William	GARNETT, Reuben	PAYNE, Richard
CLAYTON, Phillip	HALL, Thomas Sr	PENDLETON, Nathaniel Sr
COLVIN, Daniel	HANSB(O)ROUGH, William	PULLER, John
COVINGTON, Francis L	HUDSON, James	READ, John
DAWSON, Benjamin	HUME, Francis	ROSSON, Reuben
DILLARD, George	INSKEEP, James	STEVENS, Edward
DILLARD, John	IRELAND, James	STEVENS. John
DUNCAN, Charles	JAMESON, David	STRODE, John
FISHBACK, John Frederick	JAMESON, John	TAYLOR, George
FISHBACK, Martin	JONES, Gabriel Jr	YANCEY, Charles Sr
FORD, John Thomas	JONES, Thomas	YANCEY, Lewis Davis
GAINES, Thomas	LEWIS, Betty (Washington)	WIGGINTON, John
GAINES, William Henry	MERCER, George	WILLIAMS, John
	NALLE, Martin II	

CUMBERLAND COUNTY. Formed in 1749 from Goochland County. County seat is Cumberland (23040).

ALLEN, Benjamin	DILLON, Henry	PAGE, Carter
ANDERSON, James	HARRISON, Carter Henry	PRICE, Joseph
ANDERSON, Samuel	HODGES, John	SCRUGGS, Drury
ANDERSON, Thomas	HOLMAN, John	SMITH, Byrd
BOATWRIGHT, Daniel	MARTIN, Orson	WALKER, William
BOOKER, E Nash	MONTAGUE, Thomas	WILSON, Willis
BOOKER, Edward	MONTAGUE, Thomas II	WINNIFORD, David
CARRINGTON, George Jr	MORTON, James	WOODSON, John

DANVILLE CITY. Achieved Independent City status in 1890. **See also PITTSYLVANIA COUNTY.**

CLAY, Matthew	PERKINS, Constantine	WILSON, John
PAYNE, Josiah	WALL, Peter	WILSON, Robert

DICKENSON COUNTY. Formed in 1880 from Buchanan County, Russell County, and Wise County. County seat is Clintwood (24228).

MULLINS, John

DINWIDDIE COUNTY. Formed in 1752 from Prince George County. County seat is Dinwiddie (23841).

BASS, Joseph	GOODWYN, Peterson	SYDNOR, Joseph
BISHOP, James	GREENWAY, James	WYATT, Edward
BISHOP, Jeremiah	GRIGG, Abner	
COUSINS, Henry	GRIGG, William Sr	
CUTLER, William	JARRETT (JARRATT),	
FOWLKES, Joseph A	Devereux	
GOODWYN, Joseph	KING, Elisha	

DUNMORE COUNTY. Renamed in 1778. **See SHENANDOAH COUNTY.**

ELIZABETH CITY COUNTY (extinct). See HAMPTON CITY. An original 1634 shire, consolidated in 1952 with Hampton.

EMPORIA CITY. Achieved Independent City status in 1967. **See also GREENSVILLE COUNTY.**

ROBINSON, Braxton	ROBINSON, John
ROBINSON, James	ROBINSON, Littlebury

ESSEX COUNTY. Formed in 1692 from [Old] Rappahannock County which formed from Lancaster County. County seat is Tappahannock (22560).

BOOKER, Lewis	CROXTON, Carter	GARNETT, Muscoe
CAMPBELL, Hugh	DISHMAN, Sarah	GARRETT, William

JONES, John
MILLER, William

RENNOLDS, Sthreshley
RITCHIE, Archibald

RITCHIE, William
SMITH, Meriwether
WOOD, Thomas

FAIRFAX CITY (22030). Achieved Independent City status in 1961. **See also FAIRFAX COUNTY.**

BOWIE, William S Sr
CHAPMAN, Thomas
ELLIS, Richard

MILLAN, Thomas
MILLAN, William
PETTETT, John

REID, John
SCOTT, Gustavus
SKINNER, Frederick

FAIRFAX COUNTY. Formed in 1742 from Prince William County. County seat is Fairfax (22030). **See also FAIRFAX CITY.**

ADDISON, John
ALEXANDER, Charles Sr
ALEXANDER, Georg D
ALEXANDER< Susanna
 Pearson
ASHFORD, George
ATHEY, Benjamin
BARKER, Nathaniel
BENTER, William
BROADWATER, Charles
BROADWATER, Charles
 Lewis
BROWN, William
BRYANT, William
CARLYLE, George W
CHAPMAN, Elizabeth
CHAPMAN, George
CHICHESTER, Richard "Hard"
CLARK, Thomas
COCKBURN, Martin
COFFER, Thomas W
CONNER (CONNOR), Patrick
CROSS, William
CURTIS, Charles
CUSTIS, John P
DAILEY(DALEY), Thomas
DEEKINS, James
DENTY, Jonathan
DOVE, William
DULANEY, John
DRYDEN, James
EURACE, Josiah
FITZHUGH, William
GARY (GERY), James
GLASS, John
GOLDMAN, David
GORDON, George
GORDON, William
GRIMSLEY, John P
GUNNELL, Henry M
GUNNELL, William R.
GWIN, Jacob
HALEY, James
HALLEY, Henry Simpson
HALLEY, James Jr

HARRISON, William
HOLLAND, George
HOLLIDAY, Israel Ellsworth
HUNT, James
HUNTER, Elizabeth
 (Chapman)
HUNTER, George Dr
HUNTER, John Chapman
HUNTER, Nathaniel Chapman
HURST, John
HUTCHESON, Benjamin
JENKINS, Thomas
JOHNSTON, William
JONES, Benjamin
KILGOUR, George
LANE, William
LEE, Richard Bland
LEE, William "Billy"
LINDSAY, Thomas
LINDSAY, William
LINDSAY, William
MAJOR, Richard Rev
MASON, George
MASON, George Sr
MASSEY, Lee
MCCARTY (MCCARTHY)
 Daniel
MCDANIEL, James
MILLAN, William
MONDAY, Evan
MOORE, Jeremiah Rev
NELSON, William
ORR, John
PAYNE, William
PEAKE, Thomas
POTTER, Charles
REECE, Josiah
ROBINSON, John
RUSSELL, Samuel
SANFORD, William
SCOTT, John
SHEPHERD, Richard
SOMMERS, Simon
SOLOMAN, Richard
STITH, John B

SUMMERS, Francis
TALBOT, Thomas
TAYLOR, Thomas
THOMPSON, Daniel
THOMPSON, Samuel
TIBBS, Thomas
TRIPLETT, Thomas
TRIPLETT, William
WAGENER (WEGENER),
 Peter
WALLACE;,Stephen
WARD, Charles
WASHINGTON, Bushrod
WASHINGTON, Edward
WASHINGTON, George
WASHINGTON, George
 Augustine
WASHINGTON, John
WASHINGTON, John
 Augustine
WASHINGTON, Martha
 (Dandridge)
WASHINGTON, William
 Augustine
WATTERS, William
WEST, George
WEST, John IV
WEST, Sybil Harrison
WEST, Thomas
WICKLIFF(E) (WYCLIFFE),
 Arrington (Aaron)
WICKLIFF(E) (WYCLIFFE),
 Moses
WILKES, James
WOODWARD, Thomas
WREN, William
WILLIAMS, Edward
WILLIAMSON, James
WILLIAMSON, William
WYCKLIFFE (WICKLIFF),
 Aaron
WYCKLIFFE (WICKLIFF),
 Moses

FALLS CHURCH CITY (22046). Achieved Independent City status in 1948. **See also FAIRFAX COUNTY.**

BOWIE, James	SUMMERS (SOMMERS),	TALBOTT, Samuel
SHREVE, Samuel	Simon	WREN, James

FAUQUIER COUNTY. Formed in 1759 from Prince William County. County seat is Warrenton (22186).

ASBURY (ASHBURY), Joseph	George	PAYNE, William
ASH, Francis	GLASSCOCK (GLASCOCK),	RECTOR, Henry
ASH, George	Thomas	PEYTON, Henry
ASHBY, John	HATHAWAY, John	RANDOLPH, Robert
BALL, John	HAWKINS, John	ROWLES, William
BALL, William	HICKS, Kimble	RUST, Benjamin
BLACKWELL, John Gard	HITT, Peter	SHAKLETT (SHACKLETT),
BLACKWELL, Joseph Jr	HORNER, Gustavus Brown	Edward
BLACKWELL, Joseph Sr	JAMES, John	SHUMATE, Daniel
BRONOUGH, Thomas	JENNINGS, Lewis	SKINKER, Thomas
BURKE, William	KEITH, Thomas Randolph	SIMPSON, Thomas
CHILTON, John	KEMPER (KAMPER),	SMITH, John
CHUNN, John Thomas	Charles Sr	SMITH, Joseph T
COMBS, Robert	KENNER, Howson Francis	SMITH, William
COURTN(E)Y, William	LEE, Charles	SPILMAN, James
DARNALL, Jeremiah	LEWIS, William	THOMPSON, James
DIGGES, Edward	LINN, William Sr	THOMSON, James
EASTHAM, George	LOVE, Charles	TULLOS(S), Rodham Jr
EDMONDS, Elias Jr	LOVE, Samuel	TURNER, Hezekiah
EDMONDS, John	MARTIN, Henry Andrew	WAITE, William
EDMONDS, William	MARTIN, Joseph	WEAVER, Tilman Jr
ESKRIDGE, Margaret	MOFFETT, Jesse	WELCH, Sylvester Sr
(Mrs Kenner)	MORGAN, Zackwell	WINN, Minor Jr
FLYNN (FLIN) (FLINN), Daniel	MOSS, Nathaniel	WITHERS, Enoch Keene
FLYNN (FLINN), John	MURRAY, Reuben	WITHERS, Lewis
FLYNN, Valentine, Sr	O'BANNON, John	WITHERS, William
FOSTER, James	OBANNON (OBANON),	WRIGHT, John
GEORGE, Benjamin	William	WRIGHT, John 2
GLASCOCK, Hezekiah	PAYNE, Augustine	WRIGHT, William
GLASSCOCK, John	PAYNE, Francis	
GLASSCOCK (GLASCOCK),	PAYNE, William	

FINCASTLE COUNTY (extinct). Formed in 1772 from Botetourt County. Became extinct in 1776 when divided to form Montgomery County, Washington County, and Kentucky County (now the state of Kentucky). **See MONTGOMERY COUNTY and WASHINGTON COUNTY.**

FLOYD COUNTY. Formed in 1831 from Montgomery County. County seat is Floyd (24091).

BANKS, John		SCOTT, Mathew
BISHOP, Henry	HOWARD, William Lawrence	
BOOTH, George	HOWELL, Daniel Sr	SHELOR, Daniel
CONNOR, Daniel	HUNGATE, William	SMITH, Humphrey
DICKERSON, Elijah	JONES, Robert	(Humphreys)
DICKERSON, Moses	KENNON, Richard	SOWERS, George
DUNCAN, John	KING, John	SPANGLER, Daniel
EDWARDS, Benjamin	MITCHELL, John	SPANGLER (SPENGER),
GOODSON, Thomas H II	PHARES (PHARIS, FERRIS,	Daniel
GOODSON, Thomas	FARRIS, FARES), Amariah	STIGLEMAN (STICKLEMAN,
Washington I	(Emaria(h), Araziah,	STIGGLEMAN,
HEARD, John	Emerica, Amaziah)	STRICKLEMAN,
HOWARD, Peter Rev	RICHARDS, Christian	STEICHELMAN), Philip
HOWARD, Robert	RUTROUGH, John	(Phillip)

TRAIL, Thomas

FLUVANNA COUNTY. Formed in 1777 from Albemarle County. County seat is Palmyra (22963).

ADAMS, James Sr
ALLEGRE, Daniel
ASHLIN, John
BASKETT, William
BLACK, Jonathan
BOWLES, Knight
BURGESS, John
BYBEE, Pleasant
CARY, Wilson Miles
DUNCAN, George
EASTON, William
FARIS, Martin
GILLESPIE, John
HADEN, Joseph
HADEN, John M
JONES, George
MAYO, Jacob
MAYO, Joseph
MOORE, John
OMOHUNDRO, Richard
PAYNE, William
PERKINS, Stephen
ROSS, Peter
SEAY, Austin Sr
SHEPHERD, David
SHEPHERD, John
SHORES, Thomas Jr
STRANGE, John Alloway
TOMPKINS, Benjamin
WATSON, Robert
WILLIAMSON, Martha
WINN, Thomas
WOOD, Thomas
WOODS, William

FRANKLIN CITY (23851). Achieved Independent City status in 1961. **See also SOUTHAMPTON COUNTY.**

ROCHELLE, John

FRANKLIN COUNTY. Formed in 1786 from Bedford County and Henry County. County seat is Rocky Mount (24151).

ABSHIRE, Abraham
ANGLE (ANGELL), Peter
BERNARD, Walter
BOOTH, John
BRIZENDINE, William Sr
CANNADAY, James
COOK, Benjamin
COOPER, Sterling
COX, James, Sr
CRAGHEAD, John
DILLON, Jesse
DIVERS, John
ENGLISH, William
EVANS, George
GREER, Moses Sr
GRIFFITH, Benjamin
HANCOCK, Lewis John
HATCHER, Elijah SrHILL, Robert
HILL, Thomas
HILL, Violet (Linus)
HOLLAND, Thomas
HOOK, John
HOUGH (HUFF), John
HUFF, John
JONES, Robert Jr
JONES, Thomas
KING, StephenLESUEUR, Martel
LUMSDEN, John
MAXEY, Walter
MCNEIL, Jacob Sr
PACKWOOD, Samuel
PEARSON, Thomas
PERDUE, MeshackPOINDEXTER, John Sr
PRICE, Joseph
PRICE, Joseph Shores
PRILLAMAN (PRILLMAN), Jacob Sr
RAMSEY, John
RAMSEY(RAMSAY), Thomas F.
RICHARDS, Edward
SINK, Stephen
SPANGLER, Daniel
TONEY, William
WINGFIELD, Willam
WITCHER, William Sr
WOODY, Martin
WRAY/RAY, Benjamin
WRAY, Moses, Jr.

FREDERICK COUNTY. Formed in 1738 from Orange County. County seat is Winchester (22601). **See also WINCHESTER CITY.**

ADAMS, William
ALLEMONG, (ALLAMONG) Jacob
ARCHER, Benjamin
BAKER, Joseph
BRAITHWAITE, William, Sr
BROWNLEY, John Jr
BRYARLY (BRYERLY), Thomas
BUCHER, Philip Peter
BUCK, Thomas
CAPPER< John
CARTNELL (CARTMELL, CARTMILL), Nathaniel
CATHER, Jasper
CHRISMAN, Henry
COOLE, John M
COOPER, John Jr
CRIM, John
CRIM, Joseph
CRUMLEY, William
DANNER (TANNER), Jacob
DARLINGTON, Gabriel
DAVIS, David
DEHAVEN, Isaac
DeHAVEN, Isaac
DEHAVEN, Peter
DELONG, John Nicholas
EWING, William
FISHER, John
FRIEZ (FREIS, FREISE, FREIZE), Martin
GILHAM, Peter, Sr
GLASS, Joseph
HAMILTON, James
HEDGES, Joseph
HELM, Meredith
HELM, William T
HITE, Isaac Jr.
HITE, Isaac
HOGE, Edward
HOGE, James

HOGE, William
HOGE (HOGG), James Sr
HOTT HOLT, George, Jr
HOTT, George, Sr
JACKSON, George
JACKSON, Josiah
JONES, Strother
KEARFOOT (KERFOOT),
   William
KERFOOT (KEARFOOT),
   William
KLINE, Jacob
KRIDER, John
KRIM (GRIM, CRIM), John
LARRICK, Casper
LIGHT, Pete
LOCKHART, Robert
LONG, Ellis, Sr
MANN, Jacob
MARQUIS, William
MATTHEWS, Richard

MCCARTY, Daniel
MCCAULEY, Daniel
MCDANIEL, Thomas
MIDDLETON, William
MYTINGER, Daniel
NEWELL, John
OLIVER, James
PANGLE, Henry
PARKINS, Isaac
PIT(T)MAN, Andrew
PITMAN, Anthony
PIT(T)MAN, Phillip
PRITCHARD, Stephen C
PUGH, Job
PUGH, Joseph
PURCELL, John
RICHARD(S), Henry
RINKER, Hans Casper
ROGERS, James
ROGERS, John
RUBEL (RUBLE), George

SAMSEL, Nicholas
SIDEBOTTOM
(SIDEBOTHOM), Joseph
SIMRALL, Alexander
SMITH, Jeremiah
STEELE, Thomas
STEPHENS, Lewis, Sr
STEPHENS, Lewis, Jr
STONEBRIDGE, John
STROTHER, John
TILDEN, John Bell
TROWBRIDGE, Samuel
VANCE, William
WHITE, Alexander
WHITE, Michael
WHITE, Robert
WILSON, David
WOOD, Robert
ZANE, Isaac I

FREDERICKSBURG CITY (22401). Achieved Independent City status in 1879. **See also SPOTSYLVANIA COUNTY.**

BARTON, Seth
BROOKE, Robert
BRUCE, Charles
CALLENDER, Eleazer
CARTER, Charles
CHEW, John Jr
CHEW, Robert Beverly
DAY, Benjamin
DRUMMOND, William
EVANS, Daniel
DUNCANSON, James
FOX, Samuel
GRINNAN, Daniel Sr
HENDERSON, David
HOLLADAY, Lewis
JENKINS, William

JONES, Joseph
JONES, William (John) Paul
JULIAN, John
LEGG, John
LEWIS, Fielding
LEWIS, George Washington
LITTLEPAGE, Lewis
MAURY, Fontaine
MCWILLIAMS, William
MERCER, Hugh
MINOR, Garritt
MINOR, John Jr
PEARSON, William
ROSE, Alexander
ROYSTON (ROYSTAN),
   James

SMITH, William
SOMERVILLE, James
STEVENSON, James
STONE, William
STORKE, William
STROTHER, French
THORNTON, Francis
WAITT, William
WALLACE, Gustavus Brown
WASHINGTON, Mary (Ball)
WEEDON, George
WELLFORD, Robert
WILLIS, Lewis
YATES, Charles
YOUNG, James

GALAX CITY (24333). Achieved Independent City status in 1954. **See also CARROLL COUNTY and GRAYSON COUNTY**

No known veteran burials.

GILES COUNTY. Formed in 1806 from Montgomery County, Tazewell County, and Monroe County (WV). County seat is Pearisburg (24134).

ALBERT, Jacob Allen
BURK (BURKE), Thomas
BURKE, Thomas
CARTER, William
CHAPMAN, Isaac
CHAPMAN, John
CLAY, Mitchell
CLAY, William M Sr
FARLEY, Thomas Jr
FARLEY, Thomas, Sr
FORTUNE, John

FRENCH, Matthew
HALE, Edward
HARE, Joseph
HAYS, John
HULL, Henry
HUTCHESON, William
JOHNSTON, David
KIRK, John II
LUCAS, Parker
LYBROOK, John
MCKENZIE, Moredock

(Mordicai, Moredecai,
   Mordock, Morodock) Otis
ME(A)DOWS, Francis
NEEL, William
PEARIS, George
PETERS, John Sr.
PORTERFIELD, Josiah
SHANNON, Thomas Reid
SHELDON, Parker
SHUMATE, Daniel III
SNIDOW, Christian

SNIDOW, Jacob
SNIDOW, Philip

STAFFORD, Ralph Sr
TONEY, John

WALKER, Charles
WILSON, William

GLOUCESTER COUNTY. Formed in 1651 from York County. County seat is Gloucester (23061).

ANDERSON, Matthew
(Mathew)
BOOTH, George W
BUCKNER, Baldwin M
BURWELL, Lewis, Jr
CAFFEE, William
CLARK, James
COBB, William B, Jr

CURTIS, William
DIGGES, Dudley Power
HUDSON, Vincent
JONES, William
LEWIS, Warner II
PAGE, Mann II
ROBINS, Thomas
SINCLAIR, John

SINCLAIR, Thomas
SMITH, Armistead
TABB, Edward
TABB, Philip (Phillip)
THROCKMORTON, William
WIATT, John
YATES, William
YEATMAN, Thomas Muse

GOOCHLAND COUNTY. Formed in 1728 from Henrico County. County seat is Goochland (22063).

GAY, William
GEORGE, William
HOLMAN, William Jr
HOLMAN, William Sr
JOHNSON, Isaac
LACY, Mathew
LEAKE, Josiah
LEAKE (LEAK), Elisha
MASSIE, Charles

MIMS, David
MOORE, Amos Lad
MULLINS, Matthew
PAYNE, George
PAYNE, George Sr
PAYNE, John
PAYNE, Tarleton
PAYNE/PAINE, Robert
PROFFITT, David

RANDOLPH, Thomas Mann
RICHARDS, John
RICHARDSON, George W
RICHARDSON, Samuel
WARE, John
WATKINS, Thomas J
WATKINS, William J
WATSON, William J
WEBBER, William

GRAYSON COUNTY. Formed in 1793 from Wythe County. County seat is Independence (24348).

ANDERSON, Jacob
BOURNE, William, Sr
BREWER, Lewis
BROWN, John
BYRD, William
CAMPBELL, John
COMER, John
CORNET(T), James Jr
COX, David
COX, James
FIELDER, Dennis
FELDIER, Johnson

HALE, Lewis
HASH, John Sr
HASH, William
JACKSON, William Sullivan
LUNDY, John
MURPHY, Timothy
NUCKOLLS, Charles
OSBORN (OSBORNE), Enoch
PHIPPS (PHIPS), Benjamin
PHIPPS (PHIPS), John
RECTOR, Jacob John

REEDY, George Peter
REEVES, George Sr
ROBINSON, John
SAGE, James
STONE, Jeremiah
TAYLOR, John Sr.
VAUGHAN, William
VAUGHAN (VAUGHN),
William Jr
WEISS, Matthias
YOUNG, Ezekiel

GREENE COUNTY. Formed in 1838 from Orange County. Count seat is Stanardsville (22973).

THORNTON, George

BEADLES, John
BURTON, May Jr
DAVIS, Isaac

ESTES, William
MILLER, Robert
MILLS, William

GREENSVILLE COUNTY. Formed in 1781 from Brunswick County. County seat is Emporia (23847).
See also EMPORIA CITY.

GARNER, William, Sr
GRIGG, Burwell

IVEY, John
PEEBLES, Fred

HALIFAX COUNTY. Formed in 1752 from Lunenburg County. Includes the former independent city of South Boston (1960) which reverted in 1995 to a town within the County. County seat is Halifax (24558).

ADAMS, Nipper (Napier)
BARKSDALE, Beverly
BARKSDALE, Peter
BETTS, Spencer
BROOKS, John
BRUCE, James

CARRINGTON, George
CARRINGTON, Paul
CLARK, John
CLARK, Thomas
COLE, William
COLE, William

COLES, Walter
DAVENPORT, Bedford
DAVENPORT, Catrin
(Catherine)
DEJARNETTE, James
Pemberton

EASLEY, John
EASLEY, Robert
ESTES, George
FAMBROUGH, Benjamin
FAULKNER, Jacob
FERRELL (FERRILL),
    William H
FIT(T)ZPATRICK, John
GEE, Henry
GRANT, David
GRANT, John
GREEN(E), Berryman
HENDERSON, Edward
HILL, James
JONES, William

KEATTS, William Sr
KENT, Luke
KENT, Robert
LAND, William
LIGHTFOOT, Mildred Howell
LOGAN, William
LOVELACE, Thomas
McFARLIN, John
MOODY, Edward
PETTYPOOL, William
POWELL, Joshua
RAGLAND, John
RAGLAND, Reuben
ROYALL, Sarah
SCOTT, John Baytop

SHACKLEFORD, William
SPRAGINS (SPRAGANS),
    Thomas
STANFIELD, Thomas
TERRY, Joseph
TERRY, Nathaniel Sr
TERRY, Royal
WADE, Edward
WATLINGTON
    (WADLINGTON), John
WILSON, Wallis
WOOD, Thomas
WYATT, John

HAMPTON CITY (23669). Achieved Independent City status in 1908 when separated from Elizabeth City County, but remained the county seat and shared many services with the county. In 1952, Hampton City and Elizabeth City County reunited and consolidated, along with town of Phoebus, into an enlarged independent Hampton City.

BARRON, James:
BOOKER, George
BOOKER, John
BROWN, Benjamin
HERBERT, Pascow (Pasco)

JENNINGS, Charles
JENNINGS, William
JENNINGS, William
JONES, John
MONTGOMERY, William

PASCON (PASCOW,
    PASCHO), Herbert
PAYNE, John Jr
PHILLIPS, Thomas
RANDOLPH, William

HANOVER COUNTY. Formed in 1721 from New Kent County. County seat is Hanover (23069).

ALEXANDER, John
ANDERSON, Thomas, Sr
ANDERSON, Robert
BELL, George
BERKELEY, Nelson
BLACKWELL, David
BOWLES, Thomas
BOWLES, Thomas Philip
BOWLES (BOLLS), William
BRADFORD, John
BROCK, John P
BROWN, Isaac
BUMPASS, Samuel
CARTER, Robert
CHRYSTIE, Thomas
DABNEY, Charles
DANDRIDGE, Nathaniel
DAVENPORT, David
DIGGES (DIGGS), Dudley Jr
FONTAINE, William

FULCHER, William
GOODALL, Parke
GREEN, Fortunatus
GRUBBS, Hensley (Henry)
GRUBBS (VAN KRUPPS),
    William
HARRIS, Jordan
HARRIS, William E
HOWARD, James
JONES, John
LEWIS, John
MACON, William
MELTON, Absolem
MELTON, James
MELTON, Joel
MELTON, John C
MEREDITH, James
MORRIS, William
NELSON, Lucy Grymes
NELSON, William

NICHOLAS, Robert Carter
OLIVER, Benjamin
POPE, Nathaniel
PRICE, Thomas Sr
SNEAD, Robert
STANLEY, John
SYME(S) (SIMS), John II
TAYLOR, Edmund
TINSLEY, Parker
TINSLEY, Thomas
TINSLEY, William
TURNER, Nathaniel
WHITE, Thomas
WINGFIELD, Thomas Jr
WINGFIELD, Thomas Sr
WINN, Jesse Durrett
WINSTON, William Overton
SYME, John III

HARRISONBURG CITY (22801). Achieved Independent City status in 1916. **See also ROCKINGHAM COUNTY.**

CHRISMAN, George
GREEN, Francis
HARRISON, Thomas
MILLER, Samuel

ROLSTONE (ROLSTON,
    RALSTON), David
SHOWALTER, Christain Jr
VANPELT, Peter

VANPELT, Tunis

HENRICO COUNTY. An original 1634 shire. County seat was Varina until 1752, then Richmond until 1974, and now Henrico (23228).

ANDREWS, Benjamin

ANDREWS, Bullard

BRACKETT, John I

CRADDOCK, Robert
FRAYSER (FRAZIER), Jesse
GEORGE, Byrd

HOLMAN, Nathaniel
LAFAYETTE, James
MAYO, John

RANDOLPH, Richard II
SMITH, Jesse

HENRY COUNTY. Formed in 1776 from Pittsylvania County. County seat is Martinsville (24112). **See also MARTINSVILLE CITY.**

ANGLIN, Philip II or Jr
BARKSDALE, Thomas Henry
BOULDIN, Thomas Jr
BURRUS (BURRIS)
(BURRUSS), Jacob
COX, Charles
COX, Charles II
DESHAZO, William
DILLARD, John
DYER, George
EDWARDS, Ambrose
FRANKLIN, Lewis
FULFERSON, Frederick
GRAVELY, Joseph

HAIRSTON, George
HENRY, John
HOLLANDSWORTH, Thomas
JONES, Benjamin Dr.
KING, George
KING, John Sr
KOGER, Hans Jacob
KOGER, Henry Sr.
MARTIN, Joseph
MARTIN, Joseph
MARTIN, William
MILLS, William
MINTER, John Silas
MOLES, Jeremiah

MORRIS, Samuel Coleman
MULLINS, David
NANCE, Reuben
PACE, John
PAYNE, Reuben
RAGLAND, William
REA, John
REDD, John Franklin
SIMPSON, John
TAYLOR, George
TURNER, Shadrock
WALLER, Pomfret
WINN, Francis

HIGHLAND COUNTY. Formed in 1847 from Bath County and Pendleton County (WV). County seat is Monterey (24465).

ARBOGAST, Michael
ARMSTRONG, John
ARMSTRONG, John
BIRD, John
CARLISLE (CARLILE,
CARLYLE), James
GILMOR(E) (GILMER),
Samuel
GUM, Abraham
GUM, Isaac
GWIN(N), David

HEMPENSTALL, Abraham
HEYDE (HIDY), Johann
Henrich (John)
HULL, George
HULL, Peter
JONES, Henry
JORAN, Andrew
KINHEAD (KINKEAD),
Thomas
LOCKRIDGE, Andrew
MCCOY, John

PULLIN, Loftus
PULLIN, Samuel
RUCKMAN, David
RYMER, George
SEYBERT, Henry
SEYBERT, Nicholas
SHARP, John
WILSON, Elibabb (Eli)
WILSON, James
WILSON, John

HOPEWELL CITY (23860). Originally known as City Point. Achieved Independent City status in 1916. **See also PRINCE GEORGE COUNTY.**

No known veteran burials.

ISLE OF WIGHT COUNTY. An original 1634 shire as Warrosquyoake County. Renamed in 1637. County seat is Isle of Wight (23397).

BARLOW, Jesse
BENN, George
HUBARD, William
JORDAN, Robert

MOORE, Merritt
PARKER, Josiah
PARKER, Nicholas
PURDIE, George

SMITH, Thomas
TODD, Mallory

JAMES CITY COUNTY. An original 1634 shire. County seat is Williamsburg (23185). **See also WILLIAMSBURG CITY.**

CARY, Mary

JONES, Daniel

LEE, William

KING AND QUEEN COUNTY. Formed in 1691 from New Kent County. County seat is King and Queen Court House (23085).

BAGBY, Richard
CAMPBELL, Whittaker,
COLLIN, Thomas
COOKE, Dawson
DEW, Thomas

FAUNTLEROY, Samuel Griffin
FLEET, William
HOSKINS, Robert
LYNE, William
NOBLE, Joseph

POLLARD, Joseph
POLLARD, Robert
POLLARD, William
WEBB, James
YOUNG, Henry

KING GEORGE COUNTY. Formed in 1721 from Richmond County. Count seat is King George (22485).

ALEXANDER, Robert	DISHMAN, Samuel	MOUNTJOY, William
ARNOLD, William	GRYMES, Benjamin Jr	SAUNDERS, William
ASHTON, Henry Alexander	HARVEY, Mungo	STUART; John
BRAXTON, Carter	HIPKINS, John	STUART, William David
DAVIS, Jesse	HOOE, Gerard (Garrard)	WASHINGTON, John H
DAVIS (DAVIES), Jesse	JONES, William	

KING WILLIAM COUNTY. Formed in 1702 from King and Queen County. County seat is King William (23086).

AYLETT, William	EDWARDS, Ambrose, Jr	MARSHALL, William
BROWNE, William Burrnett	EUBANK(S), Richard	MOORE, Alexander
BURWELL, Nathaniel	FOX, John	Spotswood
CLAIBORNE, Thomas	FOX, Joseph	NELSON, William
CLAIBORNE, William	GWATHNEY, Joseph	ROANE, John Jr
DANDRIDGE, Francis W	HILL, James	TAYLOR, Robert S
DANDRIDGE, William	LANGBORNE, William	TOMPKINS, Christopher
EDWARDS, Ambrose	MACON, Mary	

LANCASTER COUNTY. Formed in 1651 from Northumberland County and York County. The portion from York County (south of the Rappahannock River) became Middlesex County in 1669. County seat is Lancaster (22503).

BALL, James	DOWNMAN, Rawleigh	SYDNOR, William
BALL, James	GORDON, James (Colonel)	TAYLOR, Charles
CHOWNING, William	KELLEY, James	

LEE COUNTY. Formed in 1793 from Russell County. County seat is Jonesville (24263).

BAKER, Andrew II	EWING, William	Christopher Sr
BALES, Jonathan	FRITTS, John	WILSON, Abraham Sr
BALL, George	GIBSON, George	YEARY, Benedict
BALL, John	GILBERT, Samuel	YEARY, Henry Jr
CAMPBELL, James	HOBBS, Vincent	YEARY, Henry Sr
CARMACK, William	MARION, Samuel	
DUFF, Robert	NEILL, William	
EALY (ELY), John	OLLINGER (OLIFER), John	
ELY, William		

LEXINGTON CITY (24450). Achieved Independent City status in 1966. **See also ROCKBRIDGE COUNTY.**

ALEXANDER, Andrew	HOSTETTER, Ulrich	MONTGOMERY, Humphrey Jr
ALEXANDER, John	IRVINE, William	MOORE, Andrew
ALEXANDER, William	JOHNSTON (JOHNSON),	MOORE, James
ANDERSON, Thomas	Zachariah	MOORE, William
BERRYHILL, John	LEACH, John	REID, Andrew
BOWYER, Henry	LEE, Henry III	ROBERTSON, William
BOWYER, John	LOGAN, James	ROBINSON, John
BRADLEY, William	LOGAN, James	SHIELDS, Alexander
CAMPBELL, Alexander	MACKEY, John Sr	SHIELDS, James
DARST, Benjamin	MCCLURE, John	TRIMBLE, James
FIX, Phillip	MCCOWN, Samuel	TRIMBLE, Sarah (Kersey)
FLINT, John	MCGOWAN, Samuel	WALLACE, William
GRAHAM, William	MCNUTT, Alexander	WILSON, Daniel
HALL, James	MCNUTT, John, Jr.	WILSON, Hugh
HARRIS, James	MILLER, Henry	WILSON, Thomas
HILL, John Berry	MILLER, Samuel	

LOUDOUN COUNTY. Formed in 1747 from Fairfax County. County seat is Leesburg (22075).

ADAMS, James
ALDRIDGE, John
ANDERSON, Andrew
ANSLEY, William
AXLINE, John
BALL, Burgess
BAYLY, Pierce, Sr
BEANS, William
BELSE, Frederic
BENEDUM, Peter
BERRY, David
BINNS, Charles
BOGER (BOGAR), Michael
BROWN, Isaacher
BROWN, John
BURSON, Benjamin
BURSON, Joseph
BUTCHER, Samuel, Sr
CAMPBELL, Aeneas
CARPENTER, Nathaniel
CARPENTER, William, Sr
CARR, John
CARR, John
CARR, Peter
CARR, Thomas Sr
CARTER, Edward
CARTER, James
CARTER, Richard
CHAMBLIN, William
CHEW, John
CHEW, John Sr
CLAPHAM, Josias
COCHRAN, Samuel R
COMBS, John
COMPHER, John, Sr;
COOPER, Michael, Sr
COPELAND, James (Jas)
COPELAND, John
CRAMWELL, John S
CURTIS, James
DAVIS, James
DELANY, John
DONOHOE, John V
DOUGLAS(S), Hugh
DRAKE, Thomas
DUNN, John
ELGIN, Francis Jr
ELGIN, Gustavus
ELGIN, Walter
ELLZEY, William
EWER (EWERS), John
FAULEY (FAWLEY), John
FURR, Enoch
GARDNER, John
GIBSON, Joseph
GIDEON, Peter
GORE, Joshua Sr
GRADY, James Sr

GREEN, John
GREEN, Samuel
GREGG, John
GREGG, John C
HANDLEY, John
HARRIS, William
HATCHER, James Sr
HEATON, James
HELM, Meridith Sr
HEREFORD, John E
HIXON, Timothy
HOGE, William
HOLMES, William
HOUGH, Benjamin
HOUGH (HUFF), William
HOUSHOLDER, Adam
HUGHES, Isaac
HUGHES, Thomas A
HUMPHREY, Jesse
HUMPHREY(S), Abner
HUMPHREY(S), Thomas
JAMES, Thomas
KLGOUR (KILGORE), Charles J or I
LANE, Joseph
LEE, Ludwell
LOVE, James
MAINS, William
MARKS, Abel
MARKS, George Elisha
MARKS, Isaiah
MARKS, John Jr
MASON, Stevens (Stephen) Thomson
MASON, Thomson (Thompson)
MCILHANEY, James
MCKIM, James
MCVEAGH (MCVAY), Jonathan
MOCK, John Harrison
MOFFETT, William Mead
MONROE, William
MOUNT, Ezekiel
MULL, David
MURRAY (MURREY), Samuel
MURREY, Samuel
NICHOLS, Daniel
NICHOLS, Isaac
NICHOLS, Nathaniel
NIXON, George
NIXON, George
NIXON, John
OSBURN, Richard
OSBURN, William
OWINGS, Richard
OXLEY, Henry

PARKER. Joseph
PARKER, Thomas
PARKER, William Harwar
PIGGOTT, William
PLASTER, Henry
POTTER, Ebenezer
POTTS, Ezekiel
POTTS, Jonas
POTTS, Nathaniel
POULSON, George B
PURCELL, Thomas Sr
PURSEL, Samuel
RAMEY, Sanford
RICHARDSON, Nightingale
RINKER, Edward
ROBERTS, Stephen
ROGERS, Hamilton
ROLLER, Conrad
ROSE, John
ROSS, John Sr.
ROSZEL(L), Stephen G
RUSSELL, James
RUSSELL, Robert
RUSSELL, Samuel
SAUNDERS, Aaron
SCHOLFIELD, Thomas
SCOTT, Stephen
SELDEN, Wilson Cary
SHUMAKER (SCHUMACHER), George
SINCLAIR, Samuel
SKINNER, Cornelius
SKINNER, Richard A
SLATER, John
SMITH, George
SMITH, George W
SMITH, John
SMITH, Samuel
SMITH, Samuel
SOUDER, Philip, Sr.
STATLER, John
STEERS, Isaac
STOUTSENBERGER (STOUSEBERGER), John
SUMMERS, William J
TAVINER (TAVENNER), Ritchard (Richard)
TAYLOR, John
TAYLOR, Stacy
TAYLOR, Timothy II
THATCHER, Stephen
THOMAS, John Sr
THOMAS, Joseph
THOMPSON, Amos Rev
THOMPSON, Hugh
THOMPSON, William
TRIPLETT, Simon

TYLER, John
VAN BUSKIRK, Abraham
VANDEVANTER
   (VANDEVINDER,
   VANDEVENTER), Isaac
VANSICKLER, Ferdinand
   (Fernandus)
VIRTZS (WIRTZ),Peter Phillip

(Phillip Peter)
WADE, Robert
WEST, John
WHITACRE, John III
WHITACRE (WHITAKER),
   George
WHITE, Benjamin
WHITE, James

WHITE, Josiah (Josias)
WILKISON, William Sr
WILLIAMS, David Sr.
WILLIAMS, Richard
WILSON, Thomas
WINE, Jacob
WIRE, William
WORTHINGTON, William

LOUISA COUNTY. Formed in 1742 from Hanover County. County seat is Louisa (23093).

ANDERSON, David Jr
ANDERSON, Matthew
BAGBY, John
BARRAT (BARRET), John
BOXLEY, Joseph I Sr
BULLOCK, David
CAMPBELL, Francis Lee
DABNEY, Samuel
DAVIS, Abraham
DICKINSON, James
DUNCAN, Robert
GIBSON, William
GOODWYN (GOODWIN),
   Robert
GUNNELL, John II

GUNNELL (GUNNILL),
   John Sr
HANCOCK, Austin
HARRIS, Nathan
ISBELL, Benjamin
ISBELL, Henry
ISBELL, Joseph
ISBELL, William
JACKSON, Thomas
JACKSON, William
JERDONE, Francis
JOHNSON, Thomas Jr
MELTON, James
MORRIS, John
MORRISON, John

NUCKOLLS, James
NUCKOLLS, John
POINDEXTER, Thomas
SHELTON, James
SHELTON, Thomas
TERRY, Champress
THOMASSON, George, Jr
THOMPSON (THOMASSON),
   John
WALTON, Joel
WARE, Malickic
WHARTON, Samuel
YANCEY, Charles
YANCEY, Mary
WILLIAMS, John Rev

LUNENBURG COUNTY. Formed in 1746 from Brunswick County. County seat is Lunenburg (23952).

BOSWELL, John Iverson
CLARK, John Shadrock
   (Shadrick)
DEGRAFENREIDT, Tscharner

HITE, Julius
NEBLETT, Sterlin
TAYLOR, William
WILLIAMS, John Rev

WILKES, Minor, Jr.
WILKES, Minor, Sr.

LYNCHBURG CITY (24505). Achieved Independent City status in 1852. See also CAMPBELL COUNTY.

BAILEY, John
BALLARD, Barclay
BALLARD, William Jr
BECK, Jesse
BURKE, Richard H
CHILTON (CHELTON),
   Richard Sr
DANIEL, William Sr
DAVIS, William
DOUGLASS, Achilles
DUFFEL, Edward
DUFFEL, James C
GEORGE, Reuben

GRAY, Francis
JONES, Thomas C Sr
LYNCH, John
MANN, Daniel
MARTIN, William
MCDANIEL, George
MOORMAN, Micajah
MOORMAN, Zachariah
MOSELEY, James
NORRELL, Henry Holdcraft
   (Hallcraft)
OGLESBY, Daniel
OWEN, Owen

PRESTON, John
SCHOOLFIELD, John
SCOTT, John E
SCOTT, Samuel
SCOTT, William W
SCRUGGS, Samuel
TERRELL, David Jr
THURMAN, Richard Sr
TOWLES, Oliver
VAWTER, Benjamin
VAWTER, John

MADISON COUNTY. Formed in 1793 from Culpeper County. County seat is Madison (22727).

AYLOR, Abraham
AYLOR, Henry
AYLOR, Jacob
BEALE, Reuben
BLANKENBAKER, Michael
CAMPBELL, Cammuel
   Elias Sr
CAMPBELL, Elias
CAMPBELL, John

CARPENTER, Samuel
CLORE, John Peter
CROW, James
FORD, John
FRAY, Ephraim
FRY, Henry
GAAR, Andrew
GAAR, Johann (John) Adam
GAAR, John (Johannes)

GAINES, James
GRAVES, John
HARRISON, John Sr
HOUSE, Matthias
LILLARD, James
MCALLISTER, James
MOORMAN, Zachariah
NICHOLSON, John
RUCKER, Angus

SCOTT, George
SOUTHER, Micheal
TANNER, Abraham
TRIBBLE, Andrew
WALKER, James

WAYLAND, John
WEAVER, Peter
WELCH, Nathaniel
WILHOITE (WILHOIT), Daniel
WILHOITE (WILHOIT), John

YAGER, John Sr
YOWELL (YOWEL), William
ZIMMERMAN, Christopher
ZIMMERMAN, John

MANASSAS CITY (22110). Achieved Independent City status in 1975. **See also PRINCE WILLIAM COUNTY.**

ALEXANDER, William
BALL, Spencer
CARTER, Landon Jr
DOGAN, Henry

HENRY, Isaac
HOOE, Bernard
HOOE, Robert Howson
HOUSE, Matthias

MONTGOMERY, Francis
MONTGOMERY, William
SIMMS, Joseph
THURMAN, Robert

MANASSAS PARK CITY (20111). Achieved Independent City status in 1975. **See also PRINCE WILLIAM COUNTY.**

No known veteran burials.

MARTINSVILLE CITY (24112). Achieved Independent City status in 1928. **See also HENRY COUNTY.**

JONES, Benjamin
NORMAN, William

WALLER, George
WINN, James

MATHEWS COUNTY. Formed in 1791 from Gloucester County. County seat is Mathews (23109).

BILLUPS, Joseph
BILLUPS, Joseph Jr
DIXON, John
FORREST, George
FOSTER, Isaac
FOSTER, Peter G

JAMES, Thomas
PAGE, John
PATTERSON, John
RICHARDSON, John
TABB, Thomas
TURNER, John L

WATSON, John
WHITE, John
WILLIAMS, Samuel
WILLIAMS, Thomas S
WILLIAMS, William M

MECKLENBURG COUNTY. Formed in 1765 from Lunenburg County. County seat is Boydton (23917).

ANDREWS, Benjamin
ANDREWS, Varney Sr
ANDREWS, William A
BASKERVILLE, William
BENNETT, Jordan
BOYD, Alexander
BOYD, Francis
BOYD, Robert
BRAME, John
BRAME, Richens
BROOKS, Robert

BURWELL, Lewis
DAVIS (DAVIES), William
EVANS, Anthony
GOODE, Samuel
GREGORY, Roger
KEEN, Abraham (Abram)
LEWIS, John T
MALONE, Benjamin
MUNFORT (MUNFORD,
    MONFORT, MONFORD),
    Robert

OVERBEY, Peter Z
PETTIES (PETTES,
    PETTUS), Samuel Overton
RAINEY (RAINY), Williamson
SKIPWITH, Peyton Sr
SPEED, Joseph
TAYLOR, James
WELLS, David
WINN, Richard
YANCEY, Robert

MIDDLESEX COUNTY. Formed in 1669 from the portion of Lancaster County south of the Rappahannock River that had formed from York County in 1651. County seat is Saluda (23149).

BERKELEY, Edmund
CORBIN, Gawin Tayloe
CORBIN, Richard
COSBY, Overton

DAME, George
GRYMES, Philip Ludwell
HEALY, James
JACKSON, John

LEE, Arthur
MCKANN, Robert H
WALLER, Benjamin
WOWMELEY, Ralph IV

MONTGOMERY COUNTY. Formed in 1776 from Fincastle County, which became extinct at that time. County seat is Christianburg (24073).

ALTIZER (ALTHAUSEN),
    Emery (Emera)
BARGER, Philip
BLACK, John
BOOTHE, George
BOWEN, Arthur
BRATTON, James

BROWN, John
CRAIG, James
CROCKETT, Hugh
DAVIES, Joseph Sr
GARDNER, John
GILES, Thomas
HALL, Asa Sr

HALL, Jesse
HANCOCK, George
HARLESS, David Anthony
HARLESS (HORLESS), Philip
HENDERSON, John
HOWARD, Sir William
JOHNSTON, David

KINSER (KENSOR), Michael
LESTER, John
LUCAS(S), John
MADISON, William Strother
MAXWELL, Thomas
MCDONALD, Joseph

MEACHUM (MEACHAM), Ichabod
MONTGOMERY, John
PRESTON, William
PRICE, John Michael Sr
PRICE, Michael I

SOWDER, Jacob
THOMAS, Giles
WaLL, Conrad
WALL, John Jr
WATTERSON, Henry

NANSEMOND COUNTY (extinct). See SUFFOLK CITY. Formed in 1637 as Upper Norfolk County from New Norfolk County, which formed from Elizabeth City County (an original 1634 shire). Renamed Nansemond County in 1646. Suffolk was the county seat from 1750 to 1972. County became the City of Nansemond in 1972, then merged with the City of Suffolk in 1974. A good deal of Nansemond County historical records are housed at the David R. Rubenstein Rare Books and Manuscript Library at Duke University, Durham, NC.

NELSON COUNTY. Formed in 1808 from Amherst County. County seat is Lovingston (22949).

BALLARD, Proctor
CABELL, Nicholas
CABELL, Samuel Jordan
CABELL, William Sr
CLARKE, Christopher
CLARKSON, James
COFFEY (COFFEE), Edmund
COLEMAN, Hawes
ESTES, Elisha
FORTUNE, Benjamin
FORTUNE, Thomas

HARRIS, William
HILL, Nathaniel
HILL, William
JACOBS, George
JACOBS, John
JONES, Charles
JONES, Thomas
LOVINGS (LOVING), John Jr
MARTIN, Azariah
MASSIE (MASSIE), Thomas
MCALEXANDER, Alexander

MCALEXANDER, James Jr
MCALEXANDER, James Sr
MONTGOMERY, Joseph
PENDLETON, Micajah
ROBERTSON, John
SHIELDS, William
TILFORD, David
TILFORD, James
TUCKER, St George
VAUGHN, William
WOODS, Samuel

NEW KENT COUNTY. Formed in 1654 from York County. County seat is New Kent (23124).

BASSETT, Burwell Col
BASSETT, Burwell
BUGGS, Sherwood

CLOPTON, John
CLOPTON, William
DENNETT, John

MEREDITH, Elijah
WATKINS, John

NEWPORT NEWS CITY (23607). Achieved Independent City status in 1896 from Warwick County. Enlarged in 1958 when it reconsolidated with Warwick City which was the former Warwick County.

CARY, John
CARY, Richard

CARY, Richard Jr
CARY, Thomas Jr

DIGGS, Edward

NORFOLK CITY (23510). Created as the Borough of Norfolk by royal charter in 1736 in Norfolk County. Achieved Independent City status in 1845.

ABYVON, George
ABYVON (ABYNON), Marrim
 (Miriam, Manim, Meriam, Marsam)
ALLMAND, Harrison
ASHLEY, Warren
BACON, Samuel
BURT, John M
CALVERT, Christopher
CALVERT, John Salvage
CALVERT, Thomas
CHAMBERLAIN(E), George
CONSTABLE, Thomas
DOUGHERTY (DOUGHTY), Edward
DOUGLAS, William

FERGUSON, Daniel
GRIMES, James S
HANSFORD, Cary H
HARVEY, John
HENLEY, James
HOWELL, John F
KING, Miles Sr
LAWRENCE, John
LEE, John
MATHEWS, Thomas
MAURY, Walker
MAXWELL, James
MOSELY, Hildarh (Hillary)
NESTEL (NESTELL, NESTLE, NISTELL), Peter
PALMER, Job

READ, John K
SINGLETON, John
SLAUGHTER, Augustin(e)
 (Augustus)
SMITH, Francis
SMITH, John
STARK, William
TAYLOR, James
TAYLOR, Robert
TAYLOR, Sarah Crull (Croel, Curle) Barraud Huitt
WHIDDON, John
WILLOUGHBY, William
WILSON, James
WRIGHT, Stephen

NORFOLK COUNTY (extinct). See CHESAPEAKE CITY. Formed in 1691 from Lower Norfolk County, which formed from New Norfolk County, which formed from Elizabeth City County (an original 1634 shire). County seat was Portsmouth. Over time, the county was reduced as several cities split off. In 1963, the remaining county consolidated with South Norfolk city as the new City of Chesapeake.

NORTHAMPTON COUNTY. Original 1634 shire of Accawmack or Accomac County comprised Virginia's Eastern Shore. Name changed to Northampton County in 1643. Split into the present Accomack and Northampton Counties in 1663. County seat is Eastville (23347).

BAIN, William	PITTS, Hezekiah	STITH, Griffin
BELL, George	PITTS, Major	TANKARD, John Dr
BELL, William	SAVAGE, Lyttleton	TAYLOR, Margaret
DARBY, John	SAVAGE, Thomas Lytllteton	THOMAS, Harrison
DARBY, Nathaniel	SCARBURGH	UPSHUR, Thomas
HOLLAND, Nathaniel	(SCARBOROUGH), John	
KENDALL, George	SMITH, Isaac	

NORTHUMBERLAND COUNTY. Formed in 1649 from the Chickacoan (Indian) District, the early 17th-century name for the region between the Potomac and Rappahannock Rivers. "Mother County" of the Northern Neck. County seat is Heathsville (22473).

BALL, David	HAYNIE, Bridgar II	MOORE, James
BLACKWELL, William	JONES, Walter Dr	SMITH, James
COX, Peter	MILLER, John	TAYLOR, Thomas

NORTON CITY (24273). Achieved Independent City status in 1954. **See also WISE COUNTY.**

No known veteran burials.

NOTTOWAY COUNTY. Formed in 1789 from Amelia County. County seat is Nottoway (23955).

ALLEN, Charles	FOWLKES, James	HENDERSON, James
DUPUY, James	FOWLKES, John A	IRBY, William
EPES (EPPES), Francis	FOWLKES, Jennings E	WILLIAMS, Thomas
FOWLKES, Henry Bass	FOWLKES, John Field	

ORANGE COUNTY. Formed in 1735 from Spotsylvania County. County seat is Orange (22960).

BROCKMAN, Samuel Jr	JONES, Churchill	PANNILL, William
BRUCE, Charles	JONES, William	SCOTT, Johnny (Jonny)
CAMPBELL, William	LINDSAY, Reuben	SINGLETON, Daniel
COOPER, James	MADISON, Ambrose Sr	TALIAFERRO, Lawrence
COWHERD, Francis Kirtley	MADISON, James	TAYLOR, Charles
CRITTENDEN, William	MADISON, James	TAYLOR, Erasmus
DADE, Francis L	MADISON, William Taylor	TAYLOR, James III
DAVIS, Thomas	MANSFIELD, Robert	TAYLOR, Robert
GIBSON, John	MORTON, George	WEBB, William Warren
GORDON, Nathaniel	MORTON, William	WILLIAMS, James
HEAD, Benjamin Sr	MORTON, William 2	
HOLLOWAY, George	PAINE, Thomas	

PAGE COUNTY. Formed in 1831 from Rockingham County and Shenandoah County. County seat is Luray (22835).

ALESHIRE, John Conrad	MCKAY, Enos	
COURTNEY, William	MILLER, John	STRICKLER, Benjamin
GROVE, Marcus	OVERBOKER	STRICKLER, Isaac
GROVE (GROFF), Christian	(OFFENBACHER),	STRICKLER, Jacob
Sr (Christley)	Frederick	STRICKLER, Joseph
KAUFMAN, David	PRINTZ, George	VARNER (WERNER), Phillip
KEYSER, Andrew Sr	PRINTZ (PRINCE), Gottlieb	WOOD, Benjamin
KEYSER, Charles Jr	(Cutlip)	WOOD, John
KEYSER (KISER), Michael	PRINTZ (PRINCE), Philip	WOOD, Nehemiah
KIBLER, Henry	ROBERTSON, William	
KIBLER, John	RUFFNER, Peter Sr	
LONG, Philip	SMITH, Jacob	
MAUCK, Daniel	SPITLER, Abraham	

PATRICK COUNTY. Formed in 1791 from Henry County. County seat is Stuart (24171).

ADAMS, Jacob	LETCHER, William	ROBERTSON, David
BRYANT, William	LEWIS, Edward	ROSS, Daniel Sr
CORN, Jesse Sr	MARTIN, William	SHELTON, Eliphaz
CRITZ, Hamon Jr (Herman)	MCALEXANDER, John	SHELTON, Ralph II
HANBY, Jonathan	MCALEXANDER, William	SHELTON, Richard
HANCOCK, John	PENN, Abram or Abraham	STAPLES, Samuel
HUGHES, Archelaus	PLASTER, Michael	TURNER, Francis
KOGER, John	PRICE, William	VARNER, Joseph

PETERSBURG CITY (23803). Achieved Independent City status in 1850. Formed from parts of Chesterfield County, Dinwiddie County, and Prince George County. Records begin in 1784.

ALEXANDER, David	CAMERON,	PARKER, Elias
ANDERSON, Daniel	JohnDONALDSON,	ROBINSON, Robert
ANDERSON, David	RobertGILL, Erasmus	STROUD, Thomas ASTUART,
BANISTER (BANNISTER),	HAMMON, Edward	John
John Monroe	HARRISON, William	TAYLOR, Alexander
BASS, William	HEATH, Jesse	WILLIAMS, James
BOLLING, Robert	JEFFERS (JEFFRIES), John	
BOLLING, Robert, Sr	JOHNSON, Andrew	
BURK, John Daly	JONES, JosephLEE, Edward	

PITTSYLVANIA COUNTY. Formed in 1767 from Halifax County. County seat is Chatham (24531). **See also CITY OF DANVILLE.**

AARON, Abraham Sr	DAVIS, Benjamin	MORTON, John
ADAMS, Robert Jr	DAVIS, Joseph	MOTLEY, Joseph
ADKINS, William	DAVIS, William	MUSTAIN (MUSTEIN), Avery
BENNETT, John	DICKENSON, Griffith	MUSTAIN, Jesse
BERGER, Jacob	DICKINSON, Thomas	PARKER, William A
BLAIR, William E	DOVE, William	PIGG, Hezekiah Ford
BOAZ, Thomas	EAST, Thomas	PIGG, John
BRUCE, John	FITZ (FITTS), Robert Walker	ROBERTSON, Edward
BUCKLEY, James Jr	FITZGERALD, Edmund	SHELTON, Daniel
BUCKLEY, James Sr	(Edmond)	SHELTON, Lemuel
BUCKLEY, John	FULLER, Arthur	SMITH, Joseph
BULLINGTON, Robert	GARDNER, Nathanial	SMITH, Ralph
CALLAND(S), Samuel	HAMPTON, Thomas	STIMSON, Jeremiah
CALLAWAY (CALLOWAY),	HARRIS, Samuel	STONE, John
Charles	HEDRICK, Jacob, Sr	STONE, Joshua
CARTER, Thomas	HOPKINS, James Sr.	TOWLER, Joseph
CHENEY (CHANEY),	HOSKINS, Thomas Coleman	VADEN, Burwell
Abram (Abraham)	HUGHES, Archelaus	WALTON, Jesse
CHENEY (CHANEY), Jacob	HUNT, David	WEATHERFORD, John
CIRCLE (CIRKLE), Peter	HUTCHINGS, Moses	William
CLARK, William	HUTCHINS (HUTCHINGS),	WEST, Joseph
CLEMENT(S), Benjamin	Christopher	WILLIAMS, James Mastin
CLOPTON, Robert	JONES, Thomas Sr	WITCHER, William Jr
COLEMAN, Daniel	JONES, Thomas V	WITCHER, William Sr.
COLEMAN, Isaac	KEESEE (KEEZEE), Jeremiah	WORSHAM, Essex
COLEMAN, Stephen	LONG, Edward	WRAY, David
COLES, Isaac Sr	MITCHELL, James	YATES, John III
CRADDOCK, William	MORGAN, Hayes (Haynes)	

POQUOSON CITY. Achieved Independent City status in 1975. **See also YORK COUNTY.**

No known veteran burials.

PORTSMOUTH CITY (23704). Established as a town in 1752 in Norfolk County. Achieved Independent City status in 1858, but remained the county seat until 1963.

BALLARD, Edward
BARRON, James
BENSON, Robert
BILISOLY, Antonio S
BLOW, Richard
BRAIDFOOT, John
BROWN, Henry
DAVIS, Samuel
DAVIS, Samuel D
DICKINSON, Thomas Bowers
DICKSON, Henry
FOWLER, Samuel
GASKINS, James
GRICE, Joseph
GRIMES, Thomas
HILL, Thomas M or H
JARVIS, John Sr
KEARNES, John
KEY, John
LUKE, Issac Sr
MAGNIEN, Bernard
MCPHERSON, Hugh
MOFFATT, William Sr
NICHOLSON, Jesse(e)
PORTER, Samuel
PORTER, William
PULLIN, John
REA, William
STOBO, Jacob
STOKES, Christopher C
SWIFT, Thomas
TAYLOR, Peter
TEE, William
VEALE, Thomas
WEBB, Tapley (Tarpley)
WILSON, William Jr.
WILSON, Willis
WONEYCUTT, Edward

POWHATAN COUNTY. Formed in 1777 from Cumberland County. County seat is Powhatan (23139).

CLARKE, John
DRAKE, James, Sr
DRAKE, James, Jr
GOODE, Bennett, Jr
GOODE, John
HARRIS, Francis E
HOBSON (HOPSON), Joseph
HOLMAN, Henry
MARTIN, Anthony
MAXEY, Edward, Jr.
MCLAURINE, James
MICHAUX, Jacob
MINTER, Anthony
MOSBY, Littleberry Jr
POPE, Nathaniel
POPE, William
SMITH, Thomas
TAYLOR, John
TAYLOR, Robert
WATKINS, Samuel
WATKINS, Samuel
WOODFIN, Samuel

PRINCE EDWARD COUNTY. Formed in 1754 from Amelia County. County seat is Farmville (23901).

ALLEN, Charles
ALLEN, James Jr
ALLEN, James Anderson
DUPUY, John
LANCASTER, John
LEIGH, John
McROBERT, Archibald
RANDOLPH, Beverley
SCOTT, Thomas
SMITH, John
VENABLE, Charles
VENABLE, Joseph Morthon
VENABLE, Nathaniel
VENABLE, Richard Nathaniel
WOODAON, Elizabeth
Michaux
WOODSON, Jacob
WORSHAM, William

PRINCE GEORGE COUNTY. Formed in 1703 from Charles City County. County seat is Prince George (23875).

ALDRIDGE, James
AVERY, William
BIRCHETT, Drury
BLAND; Edward
BLAND, John Jr
BLAND, Richard III
BLAND. Richard, IV
BLAND, Richard Jr
BLAND, Theoderick
EPPES, Francis
FITZHUGH, William
GLOVER, Joseph
HARRISON, Benjamin
HARRISON, Nathaniel
HARRISON, Robert
HARRISON, William H
HEATH, Henry
LEE, Nathaniel
RUFFIN, Edmund Jr
RUFFIN, Edmund Sr
SIMMONS, Joshua
WILKINSON, John

PRINCE WILLIAM COUNTY. Formed in 1731 from King George County and Stafford County. County seat is Manassas (22110). **See also MANASSAS CITY.**

ALEXANDER, William
ASHMORE, William
ATKINSON, George
BEAVER(S), John Sr
BLACKBURN, Thomas
BRUNDIGE, Timothy
BRYSON, Robert
CAVE, Thomas
CLARKE, Christopher
COLQUHOUN, James W
DAVIS, Hugh
EWELL, Jesse
FAIRFAX, William
FITZHUGH, Thomas
FLOURANCE, George Jr
FLOURANCE (FLORENCE, FLORANCE), William
FORD, William
GALLAGHER, Bernard
GRAYSON, Spencer
GRAYSON, William
GRAYSON, William
HENDERSON, Alexander
HOOE, Howson
HOWISON, Stephen
LEE, David
LEE, Henry II
LUCKETT, John B
MADDOX, Allison
MADDOX, William

MILLS, William
NORWELL (NORVALL), Aquilla
REID, James
SCOTT, William

SMITH, George
SPENCE, John
TEBBS, Foushee
TEBBS, Willoughby
TEBBS, Willoughby William

WEST, William
WHEELER, Drummond
WILLIAMS, Sarah
WYATT, William, Jr

PRINCESS ANNE COUNTY (extinct). See VIRGINIA BEACH CITY. Formed in 1691 from Lower Norfolk County, which formed from New Norfolk County, which formed from Elizabeth City County (an original 1634 shire). Consolidated in 1963 with the City of Virginia Beach.

PULASKI COUNTY. Formed in 1839 from Montgomery County and Wythe County. County seat is Pulaski (24301).

BELL, Robert
BROOK, Edmund (Edmond)
CADDELL, Samuel
CECIL, John
CECIL, Samuel Witten Sr
CLOYD, Josep

HOGE, James
HOGG (HOGE), James Jr
HONAKER (HONEGGER), Hans Jacob
HONAKER, Henry S Sr
HOWE, Daniel

WYSOR (WEYSOR, WEIZER), Henry
PATTON, Henry
WEISER,HenryWYSOR

RADFORD CITY. Achieved Independent City status in 1892. See also MONTGOMERY COUNTY.

No known veteran burials.

RAPPAHANNOCK COUNTY. Formed in 1833 from Culpeper County. County seat is Washington (22747).

AMIS(S), Joseph
AMIS(S), Levi
ANDERSON, Elijah
BROWNING, John
COLVIN, Mason
CORBIN, John
CORBIN, William
CORDER, John

DEARING, John
GRIFFIN, Henry
HITT, Nimrod(s)
HOTTENSTEIN, Jacob
JACKSON, Richard
LILLARD, Benjamin
MAJOR, William
MILLER, Henry II

MILLER, John
PIERCE, John
SLAUGHTER, John Suggart (Suggate)
STROTHER, John Dabney Sr
WOODARD, William

[OLD] RAPPAHANNOCK COUNTY (extinct). Formed in 1656 from Lancaster County. Became extinct in 1692 when it was divided to form Essex County and Richmond County.

RICHMOND CITY (23219). Founded in 1742, became capital in 1780. Incorporated as a town in 1782 in Henrico County, but called a city. Achieved Independent City status in 1842. Includes the former independent city of Manchester (1874) which was consolidated in 1910.

ABBOTT, Joseph
ADAMS, Richard Jr.
ADAMS, Richard Sr.
ADAMS, Thomas Bowler
ALLEGREE, William
AMBLER, John Esq
AMES, Isaac
ANDREE, John G
BAILEY, Ansel Anselm Ansolem Anselem
BAKER, Hilary (Hillary) Jr
BALL, David
BARKER, William (Deleted)
BARTON, Richard
BEALE, John
BELL, Nathaniel Nathan
BELL, Robert
BLAIR, John

BLANKENSHIP, James W
BROACH, Charles
BROWN, Richard
BROWN, William
BURTON, John P
BUTLER, James F
CALL, Daniel
CARRINGTON, Edward
CARRINGTON, George
CARTER, William
CARTER, William
CHAMBERLAYNE, William
CLAIBORNE, William
COLQUITT, John
COPLAND, Charles
COURTNEY, John
CURRIE, James
DAVIS, Augustine

DRAKE, James Sr
DUNCAN, Andrew
DUVAL, Plilip Jr
DUVAL, William
EGE, Jacob
EGE, Samuel
ELLIOTT (ELLIOT), Thomas
EPPES, Peter
FOSTER, Joseph
FOUSHEE, William
FRANCISCO, Peter
GAMBLE, Robert
GEDDES, Winston
GEORGE, Byrd
GIBBON, James
GRAHAM, William
GRAY, James
GREENHOW, Robert

GRIFFIN, Thomas
HAGAN, Michael
HARRIS, David
HARVIE, John
HERON, James
HOLLOWAY, Daniel
HOPKINS, Walter
JONES, Charles G
LANE, Anna Maria
LANE, John
LAWRENCE, John
LAWSON, Robert
LESTER, John
LOVELL, Joseph
MARSHALL, John Curtis
MAYO, John
MAYO, William
McCLURG, James
MERCER, James
MERCER, John
MEYERS, Samuel
MITCHELL, William
MONROE, James
MOORE, Charles
MOSS, John

MYERS, Lewis
MYERS, Samuel
NICHOLSON, Robert
NICOLSON, Thomas
PAGE, John
PARKER, Ebenezer
PARKINSON, Joseph Christian
PATTESON, David
PHILLIPS, John M
POLLARD, Robert
POTTS, John
PRICE, Barrett (Barret)
PRICE, William
PRYOR, John
PUCKETT, Nathaniel
QUARLES, John
RADFORD, Richard
RAYBURN(E) (RAYBORN(E), RAIBORNE), George
RICHARD, John
ROBERTSON, John
ROWLAND, John
SEABROOK, Nicholas B
SHEPARD, William

SIMM(S), James
SLAUGHTER, Philip
SMITH, Andrew
SMITH, George William
SPEED, John
STROBIA, John
TERRY, William E
TOMPKINS, Harry
TONEY, Archibald
VALENTINE, Batchelder
VAUGHN, James
VENABLE, Abraham Bedford Jr
WALKER, William
WATSON, Joseph
WEBB, William
WEBB, William
WILSON, James
WINSTON, Geddes
WOOD, James
WORSHAM, George
WYNNE, Thomas H
WYTHE, George

RICHMOND COUNTY. Formed in 1692 from [Old] Rappahannock County which formed from Lancaster County. County seat is Warsaw (22572).

BEALE, Robert
BEALE, Richard
BEALE, William Jr
BELFIELD, John
BELFIELD, Sydnor
BELFIELD, Thomas Wright
BROCKENBROUGH, John
BROCKENBROUGH, William

CARTER, Landon
CARTER, Landon
CARTER, Robert Wormley
FAUNTLEROY, Moore
FLOOD, Nicholas Dr
LEE, Francis Lightfoot
MIMS, David Jr
MUSE, Daniel Sr

NORTHERN, Peter
PACKET(PACKETTE), Williams
PECK (PEAKE), John
RICHARD, John
TAYLOE, John
WORMELEY, Ralph V

ROANOKE CITY (24101). Achieved Independent City status in 1884. **See also ROANOKE COUNTY.**

COLLINS, Benjamin

FLEMING, William

HARSHBARGER, Christian Sr

ROANOKE COUNTY. Formed in 1838 from Botetourt County. County seat is Salem (24153).

DEVERLE (DEYERLE), Peter
ESOM (ESCOM), Hannah
HANNAN, Esom
LEWIS, Andrew

LEWIS, Andrew Jr
POAGE, William
VINYARD, Christain
VINYARD, Christian

WEDDLE (WADDELL, WODLE, WEDEL), Benjamin

ROCKBRIDGE COUNTY. Formed in 1778 from Augusta County and Botetourt County. County seat is Lexington (24450). **See also LEXINGTON CITY.**

ADAMS, John
ALBRIGHT, Frederick
ALEXANDER, Archibald
BARCLAY, Hugh
BENNINGTON, Job
BERRY, Charles
CAMPBELL, Alexander
CAMPBELL, Charles
CAMPBELL, Charles
CLOYD, David

COINER, Conrad
COX, Philip
CRAWFORD, Alexander
CROSS, William
CULTON, Alexander
DEDERICK, Jacob
DRYDEN, James Jr
FLEET, William
FOREHAND, John Sr
FRAZIER, John

GILMORE, James
GLASGOW, Arthur
GRIGSBY, John
HAMILTON, William T
HARRIS, Robert
HENRY, James Jr
HICKMAN, Jacob
HIGHT, George
HOUSTON, George
HOUSTON, James

HOUSTON, John Sr
HOUSTON, John III
HOUSTON, Samuel
HOUSTON, Samuel
HUGHES, John W
JONES, Nicholas
KINCAID, John
KIRKPATRICK, Robert
LAIRD, James
LEECH, John Sr
MARTIN, Thomas
MCCLUER, John
MCCLUNG, Henry
MCCLUNG, John
MCCLUNG, William
MCCLUNG, William
MCCLURE, Alexander
MCCLURE, Halbert
MCCLURE, Robert

MCCLURE, Robert A
MCCLURE, Samuel
MCCOWN, John
MCGUFFIN, Thomas Sr
MCKEE, James
MCKEE, Robert
MCNUTT, Alexander
MILLER, William
MONTGOMERY, John
MOORE, James
NELSON, Alexander
PARKS, John
PAXTON, John
PAXTON, John Sr
PAXTON, Thomas
PAXTON, William
PAXTON, William
PAXTON, William Sr
SAVILLE, Abram (Abraham)

SCOTT, Andrew
STRICKLER Daniel
STUART, Robert
TAYLOR, James
THOMPSON, William
WALKER, Alexander
WALKER, John Sr
WALKER, Joseph
WALKER, William
WARDLOW (WARDLAW),
  William
WEIR, Hugh
WELCH, Thomas
WILLSON, Moses
WILLSON (WILSON), John
WILSON, Samuel
WILSON (WILLSON), John
YOUEL, William

ROCKINGHAM COUNTY. Formed in 1778 from Augusta County. County seat is Harrisonburg (22801). See also HARRISONBURG CITY.

ANDES, Andrew
ARMENTROUT, Frederick
ARMENTROUT, George
ARMENTROUT, Henry
ARMENTROUT, John Henry
ARMENTROUT, Peter
ARMENTROUT
  (ERMENTRAUDT), Philip
BAKER, John Sr
BAKER, Martin
BAKER, Michael
BAR(BAER), John
BEAR (BAER), Jacob Jr
BEARD, James
BEERY, Abraham
BEERY, Abraham
BERRY, Benjamin
BERRY, John
BERRY (BEERY), Abraham
BIBLE, Adam Jr
BIBLE, Johann Adam
BOWMAN, Benjamin
BOWMAN, Jacob
BOWMAN, John
BOWMAN, Peter
BRENEMAN, Abraham
BRIGHT, John
BROCK, John Sr
BRYAN, Thomas
BYRD, Andrew V
COFFMAN, Jacob, Sr;
CONRAD, Henry
CONRAD, John Peter
CONRAD (CONROD), John
  Stephen Jr
CONRAD (CONROD,

COONROD), Jacob
COOK(KOCH), Henry
COUNTS(COUNCE)
  (KOONTZ), Peter D
CRAVENS, Margaret
CRAVENS, Mary Harrison
CRAVENS, Robert, Jr
CRAVENS, William
CRAWFORD, William
CRIM (KRIM, GRIM), Johann
  Peter
CUSTER (CUSTARD),
  Richard Sr
CUSTER(CUSTARD), Paul
DAVIS, William
DEVIER DEVER), Hugh
DEVIER(DEVER), James E
DIEHL, Abraham
DISPANET, Joseph
DOVE, Henry
FITZSWATER, John
FLOOK (FLUCK), Henry (John
  Henry)
FULK, John
GIBBONS, Isaac
GILMORE, Thomas
GORDON, Thomas
GREEN, Joseph
GUM, Norton
HAINES, Casper
HAINES, George
HAINES, John
HAINES, Jonas
HAINES, Joseph
HAINES (HAINS), Peter M
HAINES (HAYNES), Frederick

HAMMER, Henry
HARMON, Henry
HARMON, Jacob Jr
HARNSBERGER, Adam
HARNSBERGER, Philip
HARRISON, Benjamin
HARRISON, John Peyton
HARRISON, Reuben
HARRISON, Reuben
HEADRICK, Charles
HERNSBERGER, Henry
HERRING, Bethual (Bethuel
  Bethuard)
HERRING, Leonard
HERRING, William
HINKLE, Isaac
HINKLE, Yost
HINTON, Peter
HOLSINGER, Micheal
HOMAN, John
HOPKIN(S), Archibald
HOPKIN(S), John
(HUFFMAN, Daniel
HUFFMAN (HOOFMAN),
  Valentine (Valentin)
HULING, Andrew
KAYLOR, Micheal
KAUFMAN, Samuel H.
KEPLINGER, Christian
KING, John
KISLING (KISSLING), Jacob
KISSLING, Ditrick
KISSLING, John
KLEIN, George Jr
KOOGLER, George
KRING, John

KYGER, Christian
KYLE, David Sr
LAYMAN, John
LEE, Zephaniah
LEHMAN, Ludwick
LEWIS, Thomas
LINCOLN, Jacob
LINCOLN, John
LONG, George
LONG, Mary
MAGILL, James
MAGILL, William
MAIDEN, James
MALLOW, George Sr
MATTHEWS, Solomon
MAY, George I
MCFARLAND, Williams
MEADOWS, James
MILLER, Henry
MILLER, Henry B Sr
MILLER, Mathias
MILLER, Michael
MILLER, Peter
MONGER, Henry
MOORE, John
MOORE, Reuben
MOORE, Thomas Jr
MOORE, Thomas
MOYER, Micheal (William)

MOYERS, Casper (Gasper) Jr
MOYERS, Michael
NICHOLAS, Jacob
NICHOLAS, Peter
O'BRYANT, Thomas
PAUL, Nicholas
PAUL, Peter
PENCE, George
PENCE, Henry
PENCE, Jacob
PENCE, James
PENCE, John
PENCE, William
PRICE, Augustine
REIFF, John
RHODES (ROTH), Henry B
RICE, John Sr
RICE, Thomas
RITCHIE, Jacob
ROADCAP, Peter, Sr
ROLLER(ROLER); Peter, Sr
RUSH, Charles
RUSH, John
SAUFLEY(SEFTLEY)(SEFLY) Valentine
SCHENCK, Jacob
SCHLOSSER, George
SELLERS, John
SELLERS, Henry

SELLERS, Peter
SHEETS, Samuel
SHOWLATER, Daniel
SHOEMAKER, George A
SMITH, Abraham
SMITH, Abraham
SMITH, Henry
STEPHENSON, John
STEPHENS, Lewis
STEVENS, John
TETER (TETOR), Paul
THOMAS, Evan
THOMAS, Richard
TROUT(T), (George) Michael
TUTWILER, Leonard
WANGER, Henry
WENGER, Henry
WENGER, Joseph Grabil
WETZEL George "Henry"
WETZEL(WHETZEL), Henry
WETZEL, Martin
WILBERGER. Mathias
WOOLF, Valentine
YANCEY, William Layton (Leighton)
YOST, Jacob
YOUNT, Jacob

RUSSELL COUNTY. Formed in 1786 from Washington County. County seat is Lebanon (24266).

BANNER, John
BICKLEY, Charles William
BICKLEY, John
BICKLEY, Sebastian
BROWNING, Francis
DAVIS, James
DICKINSON (DICKSON), Henry
DORTON, William Jr
KELLY, Edward

KISER, Joseph, Sr.
LITTON, John Richard, Sr.
LITTON, Martha (Duncan)
LITTON, Solomon Caleb, Jr.
LITTON (LINTON), Burton Caleb Sr
LITTON (LINTON), Solomon Caleb Sr
LITTON (LITION), Thomas W
POLLOCKFIELD, John

Richard Sr
PRICE, Richard
RAY, Benjamin
REYNOLDS, Bernard
SMITH, Henry II
TATE, John
VICARS, RRobert
WEBB, William "Will"

SALEM CITY (24153). Achieved Independent City status in 1968. **See also ROANOKE COUNTY.**

BRYAN, William Jr
GARST, Frederick

JOHNSTON, John
WALTON, John B

WALTON, William
WALTON, William Sr

SCOTT COUNTY. Formed in 1814 from Lee County, Russell County, and Washington County. County seat is Gate City (24251).

BROWN, William
CARTER, Joseph
CARTER, Thomas
COCKE, David
ENGLAND, John
FREEMAN, William
FULKERSON, Abraham
GATES, Elijah

GODSEY, Austin
GRIGSBY, John
HENSLEY, Samuel
LANE, Corbin
LAWSON, William II
LAWSON, William Sr
LIVINGSTON, Peter
PACE, William

PORTER, Patrick
SMITH, James
SMITH, John "Dutch"
STALLARD, Samuel
STEWART, William
TAYLOR, Nimrod
VINEYARD, George
WOOD, Jonathan Sr

SHENANDOAH COUNTY. Originally named Dunmore County when formed in 1772 from Frederick County. Renamed in 1778. County seat is Woodstock (22664).

BAKER, Philip Peter	HULVEY, Conrad	PHILLIPS, William
BRANNER, Casper	JEFF, Henry	RAUSCH (RAUCH), Nicholas
BRANNER, John	KAGEY, Abraham	RAUSCH (ROUSH), John
BLY, John	KAGEY, Henry	Adam
BOWERS, Christian Phillip	KAGEY, John	RHODES, Michael
BOWMAN, Isaac Hite	KELLAR, Jacob	RINKER, Jacob
BUCK, Charles Jr	KELLER, George	RINKER, Jacob
CLEM (KLEIM), John D	KELLER, George Jr	ROUSCH (ROUSH), Balser
COOK, David	KIPPS (KEPPS, KIPS), Jacob	(Balster)
DELLINGER, Christian Jr	KULLERS (CULLERS), Jacob	ROUSCH (ROUSH), Daniel
EFFINGER, John Ignatius	KULLERS (KULLER,	ROUSH, George
FRYE, Benjamin	CULLERS), John	ROUSH, Henry
FUNK, Jacob	LAYMAN, Benjamin	ROUSH, Jacob
FUNKHOUSER, Abraham	McINTURF(McKENTURF),	ROUSCH (ROUSH),, Jonas
FUNKHOUSER, Jacob Jr	Casper	ROUSCH (ROUSH), John
FUNKHOUSER, Jacob Sr	MCINTURF (MCINTURFF),	ROUSCH (ROUSH), Philip
FUNKHOUSER, John III	David	ROUSH, John Adam
GOLLADAY (GOLLIDAY),	McINTURF(McKENTURF),	ROUSH, Susannah (Schlem)
Jacob	John	SHOMO, Anthony
GOLLADAY (GOLLODAY),	MCINTURFF, Frederick	SIGLER, Michael
Joseph	MILLER, Christian	SNAPP, Lawrence Sr
GRANDSTAFF (GRINSTAFF),	MILLER, Henry	SONNER, John
George	MILLER, Jacob	SPENGLER, Philip
GRAY (GREY), Daniel	NEFF, Abraham	STICKLEY, Benjamin
HALLER, Peter (Petter)	NEFF, Christian	STOVER, Peter
HARRISON, Benjamin	NEFF, Francis "Frantz"	STOVER, Peter
HENKEL, Paul Rev	NEFF, Jacob	VON EFFINGER, John
HOTELL, George	NEHS, Jacob	WACKER, John
HOTTEL, Johann	NEWMAN, John	ZEA, Martin
HOTTEL, John Jacob	NEWMAN, Walter	ZIRKLE, George Adam
HOTTEL, Joseph	PENCE, Jacob	ZIRKLE, Lewis
HOUCK, George Michael	PENNYWEIGHT	ZIRKLE, Michael
HUDSON, Thomas	(PENNYWITT), Jacob	

SMYTH COUNTY. Formed in 1832 from Washington County and Wythe County. County seat is Marion (24354).

BISHOP, John	CRABTREE, Jacob	LAMME, James
BISHOP, Levi	CROW, Thomas, Sr	MEYERS, John
BLANKENBECKLER	CROWE, Edward	POSTON, William King
(BLANKENBAKER),	DUNGAN (DUNCAN), Elisha	PRESTON, Francis
Zachariah Jr	GREEVER (GREWER),	PRESTON, William
BOWEN, Arthur	Phillip Sr	RICHARDSON, William Sr
BRODY, John	HARMON, Mathias	SCOTT, James I
BUCHANAN, Alexander	HENINGER (HENEGAR)	SHANNON, John
BUCHANAN, John	(HENNINGAR), Jacob	TATE, William
CAMPBELL, John	HUBBLE (HUBBELL), Justus	THOMAS, John
CAMPBELL, William	David	TOTTEN, John
COLE, Hugh	IRONS, John	WILLIAMS, Joseph Adams
COLE, Joseph Jr	JAYNE, Henry	WILLIAMS, Richard
COLE, Joseph L, Sr	KILLINGER, George	WOOLSLEY, Thomas
COX, William	LAMM (LAMIE), John	

SOUTHAMPTON COUNTY. Formed in 1749 from Isle of Wight County. County seat is Courtland (23837).

ADAMS, Thomas	DENSON, Jordan	REESE, John
BOYKIN, Simon	FERGUSON, Robert	STEVENSON (STEPHENSON),
BOYKIN, Simon	FORT, Lewis	William Jr
CARY, George	KELLO, Richard	

SPOTSYLVANIA COUNTY. Formed in 1721 from Essex County, King and Queen County, and King William County. County seat is Spotsylvania (22552).

ALSOP, Benjamin	HERNDON, William	PAGE, Mann III
BALLARD, James	HOLLADAY, Joseph	POWELL, Ptolemy
BROOKE, Francis Taliaferro	HOLLADAY, Joseph, Jr	POWELL, William
CHANCELLOR, John	HOLLADAY, Lewis	SLAUGHTER, Robert
COLSON, Thomas	LIPSCOMB, John	STANARD, Larkin
CRUTCHFIELD, Stapleton	LIPSCOMB, Thomas	TALLEY (TALLY), Nathaniel
ESTES, Richard	MARTIN, John	(Nathan)
FISHER, William	MCDORMENT	WALLACE, John D
HERNDON, Edward Jr	(MCDORMAN), David	WALLER, William Edmund
HERNDON, Edward Sr	MINOR, Thomas	

STAFFORD COUNTY. Formed in 1664 from Westmoreland County. County seat is Stafford (22554).

BENSON, William (Willis) Lee	GASKINS, John	PATTON, George Gordon
BOLES, William	HARRISON, Thomas	PHILLIPS, William
BOWEN, John Pratt	HEDGES, John	ROY, Wily
BRENT, Richard	HORE, Elias	SANFORD, Joseph
BRIGGS, David	HUNTER, James	SCOTT, James
CURTIS, John	KING, Robert	SCOTT, William
CURTIS, John	LEE, Thomas Ludwell	STARK (STARKE), William
DADE, Baldwin Sr.	MONCURE, John II	STONE, Hawkin(s) (Hawken)
DANIEL, Frances (Moncure)	MORSON, Arthur	STONE, William B
DANIEL, Travers D Sr	MURSON, Arthur	WALLACE, John
DEBAPTIST (deBAPTIST,	NORMAN, George	WALLER, William Jr
D. BAPTIST), John	NORMAN, Thomas	WALLER, William Sr

STAUNTON CITY. Achieved Independent City status in 1871. **See also AUGUSTA COUNTY.**

ARGENBRIGHT	HAYS, John	PORTERFIELD, Robert
(ARGENTINE), Augustus	HEISKELL (HISKILL), Peter	ROBERTSON, James
(Augustine)	HOOVER, Michael	STERRETT, William
BELL, Samuel	HUFF, Francis Jr	STUART, Archibald
BLACKBURN, Samuel	HUGHART, Thomas	TAPP (TOPP), Vincent
BROWN, John	HUGHES, James	THOMPSON, Smith
BUMGARDNER, Jacob	KING, William Sr	TREMPER, Laurence
BUSTER, Claudius	LEWIS, Thomas	(Lawrence)
CLARK, James	LOHR, Johan Peter	TROTTER, John
CLARKE, James	LONG, John	VALENTINE, Edward
CRAWFORD, John	MCDOWELL, William	WADDELL, D James
ELLIOTT, William	MOWRY (MOWREY), Henry	WAFORD, George
GARDINER, Francis	NORTH, Roger	WRIGHT, Joseph
HANGER, Peter	NUSTER, Claudius	YOUNG, John
HARMAN, Michael	PECK, Jacob Sr	

SUFFOLK CITY (23434). Founded in 1742 as a town in Nansemond County and became county seat in 1750. Achieved Independent City status in 1910, but remained the county seat until 1972 when Nansemond County changed to a city. In 1974, the cities of Suffolk and Nansemond consolidated as an enlarged City of Suffolk.

COWLING, Josiah	RIDDICK, Josiah	SKINNER, Henry
MARSHALL, Jesse	RIDDICK, Mills	WALLER, Thomas Carr

SURRY COUNTY. Formed circa 1652 from James City County. County seat is Surry (23883).

BOOTH, Beverly	COCKE, John Hartwell
BROWNE, William	WARREN, Jesse

SUSSEX COUNTY. Formed in 1754 from Surry County. County seat is Sussex (22884).

BOBBITT, John	JONES, Holmes
CLAIBORNE, Augustine	MOSS, Joshua
HARRISON, Charles	WILKINSON, John

TAZEWELL COUNTY. Formed in 1800 from Russell County and Wythe County. County seat is Tazewell (24651).

BAILEY, Richard	HARMAN, Mathias (Matthias)	THOMPSON, William
BOWEN, Rees	HARMAN (HARMON), Daniel	WARD, William
BOWLING/BOLLING/BOLING, Jarrett	MOORE, Alexander	WHITTEN, Thomas Jr.
BROOKS, William	MOORE, James	WHITTEN, Thomas Sr
BROWN, Low (Lowe)	MOORE, William	WITTEN/WHITTEN, James
GILLESPIE (GILLASPY), Thomas II	SIMPSON, John	WITTEN, James
HARMAN, Daniel Conrad	THOMPSON, Archibald	WITTEN, Thomas Jr
	THOMPSON, James Paxton	WYNN(E), William Jr
	THOMPSON, John	WYNN(E), William Sr

VIRGINIA BEACH CITY (23456). Oceanside resort incorporated as a town in 1906 in Princess Anne County. Achieved Independent City status in 1952. Enlarged in 1963 by reconsolidation with Princess Anne County, which became extinct at that time.

BOUSH, William Sr	CORNICK, Lemuel II	THOROUGHGOOD, Adam
ACKISS, John	JAMES, Edward	WALKE, Anthony II
ACKISS, John	KEELING, Jacob	WALKE, Thomas IV
BOUSH, William Sr	MOSELEY, Edward Hack Jr	WOODHOUSE, William

WARREN COUNTY. Formed in 1836 from Frederick County and Shenandoah County. County seat is Front Royal (22630).

ALLEN, Thomas	JACOBS, William H	RICHARDSON, Samuel Marquis
CLOUD, Daniel	MARSHALL, James Markham	
COX, Samuel	MARSHALL, Thomas	RICHARDSON, William
FINNELL, Reuben	MATHES(MATHEWS)(MATT HEWS), Alex(s)ander	VANMETER, Henry Jr
GATEWOOD, Phillip		
HONAKER, John		

WARWICK COUNTY AND WARWICK CITY (extinct). See NEWPORT NEWS CITY. An original 1634 shire as Warwick River County; renamed in 1643. County became an independent city in 1952, then consolidated with Newport News City in 1958.

WASHINGTON COUNTY. Formed in 1776 from Fincastle County which became extinct at that time. County seat is Abingdon (24210).

BAKER, Isaac	CARMACK, John	DUFF, Samuel II
BARKER, Charles	CARSON, Charles	DUFF, Samuel Henry
BARKER, John	CARSON, David	DUNKIN, John Jr
BARKER, Edward	CLAPP, Earl B	DUNKIN, John Thomas
BEATIE, David	CLARK, James	EVINS, William
BEATTY (BEATTIE), William	CLARK, Peter	FARRIS, Gideon
BERRY, John	CONN, William Young	FLEENOR, Michael
BRADLEY, John	COOK, Giles	FULKERSON, James (Jacobus)
BUCHANAN, John	CRAIG, Robert	
BUCHANAN, John	CUMMINGS, Charles Rev	GAMBLE, George
CAMPBELL, James	DAVIES, James II	HAYTER, Abraham M
CAMPBELL, John	DOUGLASS, John	HAYTER, Israel

HOBBS, Ezekiel
HOPE, Adam
HOPE, James
JOHNSTON (JOHNSON), Peter
KELLY, John
KING, William
LAUGHLIN, Alexander
LEONARD, Frederick
MAXWELL, David
MCCALL, Thomas
MCCHESNEY, James
MCCHESNEY, Samuel
MCCONNELL, Abram

MCCULLOUGH, Robert
MCSPADDEN, Moses
MEEK, Samuel
MICKLE, Elijah Watson
MOORE, William
PIPER, James
READ, John
SAMUEL, Vance
SCOTT, Joseph
SCOTT, Samuel
SHARP, John Anderson
SHELBY, Evan
SNODGRASS, David
SNODGRASS, James

SNODGRASS, John Jr
SPEAR(S), James
STEWART, William
TATE, William
TEETER, John
TOWNSEND, Henry
TRIGG, Daniel
VANCE, John
VANCE, Samuel
WIDENER, Michael
WIDENER, Samuel
WRIGHT, John

WAYNESBORO CITY. Achieved Independent City status in 1948. **See also AUGUSTA COUNTY.**

ALLEN, Robert
CULLEN (CULLINS), John

PATRICK, John
PATRICK, William

WESTMORELAND COUNTY. Formed in 1653 from Northumberland County. County seat is Montross (22520).

BANKHEAD, James
CARTER, Robert III
HUNGERFORD, John Pratt
HUNGERFORD, Thomas
JONES, Walter
KENDALL, William
LEE, George Fairfax
LEE, Philip Ludwell
LEE, Richard Henry

MCCARTY, Daniel
MCCARTY, Daniel III
MURPHY, John
NEWTON, Willoughby II
PAYNE, Daniel
PAYNE, John
PEIRCE, Joseph
PIERCE (PEIRCE), Joseph
PRATT, Anne Birket

ROCHESTER, John Jr
SMITH, Thomas
SMITH, Thomas
TURBERVILLE, George
TURBERVILLE, George Lee
TURBERVILLE, John
WASHINGTON, John A

WILLIAMSBURG CITY (23185). Founded as Middle Plantation in James City County and York County in 1633. Established as Williamsburg when the capital move there in 1699. Capital of Virginia from 1699 to 1780. Granted a royal charter in 1722 as a borough, but called a city. Achieved Independent City status in 1884. **See also JAMES CITY COUNTY.**

AMBLER, Jacquelin
ANDERSON, James
ASLIN, Samuel
BLAIR, John Jr
BRICKEY, Peter
BURWELL, Thomas H N
CABEL, Joseph
EALEY, John
GALT, John Minson
GREENHOW, John
GRIFFIN, Cyrus
HARRIS, John

HENDERSON, James
HENLEY, Leonard
JONES, Richard
JONES, William
LAWSON, William
LETCHER, William
MADISON, James
MILNER, Thomas
PEACHY, Thomas G Jr
PEACHY, Thomas G Sr
PELHAM, Peter
PENDLETON, Edmund

PLUMMER, Williams
PRENTIS, Joseph
RANDOLPH, David Meade
RANDOLPH, Peyton
RANDOLPH, Richard III
SAUNDERS, Robert Hyde
SCAMMELL, Alexander
TANNER, Christopher
TANNER, Jacob
TROUP, Jacob
WILMER, William Holland
WYLIE, Samuel

WINCHESTER CITY (22601). Achieved Independent City Status in 1874. **Also see FREDERICK COUNTY.**

ALLEN, John
ALLEN, Robert
ALLEN, Robert
ANDERSON, Nathaniel
BAKER, Henry
BAKER, William Henry
BALDWIN, Cornelius Dr
BALL, William

BEATTY, Henry
BUSH, Philip
CHIPLEY, William
COPENHAVER, John Jacob
COPENHAVER (COPENHAVEN), Michal (Michael)
EWING, Samuel

FAIRFAX, Thomas
FRY, Christopher
GILKESON, John
GILKESON, Samuel
GRAY, Robert
GRIM, Charles
GRIM, John
HAMILTON, James

HEISKELL, Adam
HELPHENSTINE
(HELVESTON,
HELPHENSTIEN),
PeterHOFF, Lewis
HOLLENBACH
(HOLLENBECK), Daniel
HOLMES, Hugh
HOOVER, John
HOOVER, John Henry
HUFF, John
KREMER (KRAMER), Conrad
KURTZ, Adam
LAUCK, Simon
LAUCK (LAUK), Peter

LUCAS, Basil
MAGILL, Charles
MERRYMAN, John
MITCHELL, Robert II
MORGAN, Daniel
OVERACRE (OVERAKER,
OBERAKER,
OBERACKER), George
ROBERDEAU
(ROBERDEAN), Daniel
RUST, Peter
SCHULTZ, John
SEIGLE, Frederick
SHULTZ, John
SIMRALL, James Jr

SINGLETON, John
SMITH, Edward
SMITH, John
SOWERS,Jacob
SPERRY, Jacob
SPERRY, JohnSTREIT
(STRAIGHT),
Christian
TROUTWINE (TROUTVINE),
George Jacob
VANCE, James D
VANCE, Robert
VANCE, Samuel
WALL, John C
WHITE, Robert

WISE COUNTY. Formed in 1856 from Lee County, Russell County, and Scott County. County seat is Wise (24293).

BOWLING, James | KILGORE, Robert | WELLS, Zachariah

WYTHE COUNTY. Formed in 1790 from Montgomery County. Count seat is Wytheville (24382).

BEAN, Mordecai
BROWN, Christopher Sr
BUSTER, William
CASSELL, Michael
COOK, Henry
CREGER, George
CROCKETT, John
CROCKETT, Joseph
DARTER (TARTER), Nicholas
DOAK, David D
DOAK, David Sr
DOAK, Joseph
DOAK, William
DOBLER, Jacob
ETTER, Daniel
FLOHR, George Daniel
GLEAVES, Michael
GLEAVES, William Benjamin
GRAHAM, Robert
HARKRADER (HARKRIDER),
John
HILLENBERG
(HILLENBURG), Daniel

HOPPESS, John
HOUNSHELL, John
KEESLING, Conrad
KING, John
KING, Robert
KING, William
KISLING, George
KISSLING (KISLING,
KESLING), Hugh Conrad
MCGAVOCK, Hugh
MCGAVOCK, James
MONTGOMERY, John
NEFF, Michael
NEWELL, James Sr
NEWLAND, John
PATTERSON, William
PEIRCE (PIERCE), David
PHIPPS, William Sr
SANDERS, Robert
SANDERS (SAUNDERS),
Stephen
SAYERS, Robert
SAYERS, William

SAYERS (SAYRES), John
Thompson
SEYBERT, Christian
SIMMERMAN, Christopher
SIMMERMAN, Earhart
(Arehart)
SIMMERMAN, Stophel
(Staphel)
SPANGLER, Peter Jr
SPRAKER (SPRECHER),
John Christopher
STEELE, Robert
STEFFEY, John
STEPHENS, Lawrence
TOBLER (DOBLER), Jacob Sr
UMBERGER (UMBARGER),
Henry
WALTERS, Michael
WAMPLER, Hans George
Michael
WARD, William

YORK COUNTY. An original 1634 shire as Charles River County; renamed in 1643. County seat is Yorktown (23490).

ADAM, Paul
ADAMS, Jesse
AGNES, Jean
AIMONT, Jean
ALAIN, Georges
ALARDIOT, Antoine
ALLARD, Andre
ALLEN, Joseph
AMIRAUD, Philippe
ANDRE, Jean
ANDREW, Seth

ANDUTEAU, Jacques
ANGEVAISE, Nicolas
ANGIBAUD, Joseph
ANIBEL, William
ANIEER, William
ARISMENDY, Jean
ARTEAU, Andre
ASSELIN, Claude
ATHEAN, Claude
AUBIN, Jean
AUDIGER, Henri

AUDIOT, Jean
AUGE, Jean
AUGER, Etienne
AUGER, Pierre
AUVRAY, Louis
BAGGAGE, Jean
BAGOUS, Michel
BAORTON, Robert
BARBARAN, Francois
BARBATON, Joseph
BARCY, (-----)

BARDOU, Michel
BARNUM, Zeanas
BARON, Bernard
BARRETT, John
BARTHELEMY, Louis
BATTEZ, Pierre
BATTLES, James
BEAUJEARD, Francois
BEAUMARTIN, Jean
BEDEL, Etienne
BEDEL, Jacques
BEDEL, Jean
BEDESQUE, Vincent
BEGA, Nicolas
BEGAIN, Francois
BEHER, Pierre
BELANGER, Vincent
BELLEDENT, Pierre
BENNETT, William
BENTON, Calab
BERGER, Jacques
BERNAN, Julien
BERTHELOT, Francois
BERTIN, Jean
BESARD, Jean
BESCOND, Jean
BESSARD, Claude
BEVEL, Abel
BEZE, Antoine
BIDEAU, Ange
BIDOT, Jean
BILLEBOUX, Oliver
BIS, Georges
BLANCHET, Louis
BLANDELET, Jean
BLEUTAU, Henri
BLEVEL, Guillaume
BLEVENET, Paul
BLONDEL, Pierre
BLONDELLE, Nicolas
BOCQ, Jean
BODEVER, Bernard
BOHEU, Chretian
BOISSARD, Michel
BOISSEAU, Pierre
BONET, Guillaume
BONGAR, Francois
BONNET, Jean
BOUCAULT, Mathieu
BOUILLOT, Benoist
BOULAIRE, Julien
BOULANGER, Nicolas
BOUQUET, Marcel
BOURDER, Jean
BOURDIN, Nicolas
BOURGAIN, Jean
BOURHIS, Francois
BOURHIS, Gregoire

BOURIGEOT, Francois
BRASSON, Jean
BRIAN, Louis
BROSTMAN, Jean
BROWN, Jonas
BRULON, Francois
BRUN, Jean
BRUNET, Jean
BUIS, Louis
BULLE, Jean
BURCK, Justus
BURNLEY, Joel Terrell
BURT, John
BURWELL, Nathaniel B
CABANNES, Jean
CABARE, Francois
CABON, Yves
CAILLET, Jean
CAIN, Abel
CALAGHAN, John
CALLINAN, Guillaume
CAMBERNON, Antoine
CAMPBELL, William
CANNELLE, Jean
CANTON, Antoine
CANYS, Pierre
CARBONEL, Louis
CARPIER, Gilles
CARRE, Rene
CATEL, Jean
CAVALIER, Francois
CHABRIER, Fleury
CHAMOIS, Claude
CHANPEAU, Francois
CHARET, Gilbert
CHARLES, Jean
CHASE, Jonathan
CHATILLON, Jacques
CHATTE, Pierre
CHAUNIET, Guillaume
CHAUVIN, Julien
CHAVAILLARD, Thomas
CHEMITTE, Jean
CHERET, Andre
CHEROT, Jean
CHEVALIER, Joseph
CHEVALIER, Paul
CHRISTOL, Jacques
CHUMARD, Thomas
CLEACH, Jean
CLOARET, Jean
COCQ, Antoine
COFFEY, Jean
COLAR, Andre
COLERAN, Jean
COLUE, Andre
COMBOT, Bernard
COMBRUN, Jean

CONDE, Pierre
CORLAIX, Jean
CORNISH, Daniel
COSTAIL, Sidet
COSTE, Vidal
COUILLARD, Jacques
COURBET, Antoine
COURTOIS, Etienne
COUTEL, Guillaume
CRAFFORD, Carter
CRAFFORD, Charles
CREANCE, Guillaume
CREPEL, Pierre
CRESPOT, Francois
CURDINET, Francois
CURDON, Louis
CURTIS, John Parke
DAGGETT, Ebenezer
DAGONARD, Claude
DANIEL, Marie
DANIK, Pierre
DARAY, Bertrand
DAUCAN, Guillaume
DAULIN, Jean
DAUSSENT, Pierre
DAUVERGNE, Jacques
DAVID, Francois
DAVID, Yves
DAVIS, Thomas
DE BERTHELOT, Augustin
DEBASE, Pierre
DECOUNE, Louis
DEGRES, Michel
DELAHAYE, Pierre
DELAPORT, Ubal
DELTRIEUX, Pierre
DEMARET, Nicolas
DEMBRE, Pierre
DEREUT, Pierre
DERINIER, Louis
DESCHAMPS, Joseph
DESHAY, Francois
DESMONT, Antoine
DESRIEU, Louis Sr
DETERMINE, Nicolas
DEVAISE, Joseph
DEVILLIERS, Gabriel
DEZE, Andre
DIALE, Jean
DIAMOND, Moses
DIDIERRE, Nicolas
DILTZER, Jean
DIQUE-DOUNIER, Francois
DIRONDELLES, Francois
DIVET, Henri
DOMINO, Jean
DOWNER, Ezra
DREUILHET, Dominique

DUBEAU, Pierre
DUBOURG, Nicolas
DUCROS, Lue
DUFOUR, Charles
DUFUT, Michel
DUGUE, Joseph
DULAC, Jean
DUMONT, Denis
DUPLAT, Michel
DUPREX, Joseph
DUPUIS, Jean
DURAND, Pierre
EDMON, Maurice
EGGERS, Elijah
EGRE, Paul
ELIE, Claude
ELLIS, Jacob
ENAUD, Antoine
ENSORIEL, Espirit
EVERLET, Gaspard
FABRE, Paul
FAISSANS, Maurice
FELIX, (-----)
FERET, Dominique
FERRAND, Antoine
FERREY, Claude
FINCOMB, Amos
FISSY, Antoine
FLAGLY (FLAGLEY), John
FLORI, Pierre
FOLE, Nicolas
FONTENAY, Guillaume
FOURNIER, Charles
FOWLES, James
FRIMIER, John
FROLEAUX, Julien
FROMENT, Pierre
FUGENOT, Noel
GABIANT, Benoit
GAGUEBEY, Bernard
GALBURE, Jean
GALOTET, Jean
GALTIER, Jean
GAREL, Julien
GARIQUE, Jacques
GAUDARD, Jean
GAUSSE, Philippe
GAUTIER, Jean
GAVAUDANT, Michel
GELLY, Jacques
GENIES, Joseph
GENTIL, Joseph
GEOFFROY, Jean
GERAUD, Guillaume
GERRY, Philippe
GERTHIER, Francois
GILLES, Pierre
GILLET, Guillaume

GINBERT, Julien
GIRARD, Joseph
GIRAUD, Joseph
GLANET, Louis
GODARD, Jean
GODEAU, Nicolas
GOODRICH, David
GORRELIER, Pierre
GOSSAN, Jean
GOULD, William
GOUYA, Antoine
GOUZER, Albin
GRANBON, Claude
GRANDY, James
GRANT, John
GRENON, Andre
GREROUA, Jean
GRIGNON, Thomas
GROSNIER, Jacques
GROSSETETE, Antoine
GROULT, Jean
GUBIAUD, Benoist
GUEGUEN, Joachim
GUELIN, Nicolas
GUENARD, Pierre
GUIBOISEAU, Francois
GUILLAUME, Joseph
GUILLERAUX, Joseph
GUILLON, Francois
GUILLOT, Mathieu
GUINELS, Francois
GULLAMEBOURG, Antoine
GUY, Rene
HAGUENEAU, Jerome
HAMMOND, Stephen
HAMON, Guenole
HAMON, Yves
HARDING, Aesop
HAUTVILLE, Joseph
HAWKINS, Issac
HAYWARD, James
HELEH, Jean
HENNONE, Jean
HENRY, Didier
HENRY, John
HERMAIN, Jean
HERRINGTON, William
HERVE, Guillaume
HERVE, Jean
HERVE, Michel
HIELDEN, (------)
HIGGINS, Thomas
HIGIE, Richard
HILL, Amos
HILTZENBERGER, Francois
HIX, James
HOAGON, Cyprien
HOFFMAN, Andre

HONORE, Jean
HOUBA, Remy
HOUCHOIS, Charles
HOUPILLARD, Jacques
HUBERT, Jean
HUGUETT, Louis
HULL, Johiel
HURSIN, Francois
JACOBS, John
JACOBY, Nicolas
JAGOUS, Francois
JAMAIS, Sebastian
JAUBERT, Jean
JAUBERT, Joseph
JAUNEAU, Julien
JEAN, Jean
JEAN, Pierre
JERIFAFIN, Jean
JOBART, Joseph
JOLIVET, Francois
JOLY (JOLLEY), (-----)
JONES, Jacob
JOSEPH, Jean
JOSSARD, Jean
JOSSE, Jean
JOSSE, Oliver
JOUE, Jean
JOULIN, Jean
JULIEN, Claude
JUND, Francois
JUPIN, Laurent
JUVET, Barthelemy
KELL, Michel
KIMBALL, Benjamin
KYNION, William
LABBE, Jean
LACOSTE, Jean
LACROIX, Guillaume
LACROIX, Jean
LAFOSSE, Antoine
LAFOSSE, Charles
LAFRANCE, Nicolas
LAGADENE, Jean
LAGNEL, Louis
LAINE, Philippe
LALOGE, Pierre de
LAMBERT, Blaise
LAMESSE, Etienne
LAMY, Pierre
LANGLOIS, Jacques
LANNOY, Jean de
LAROCHE, Etienne
LAROSE, Jean
LATAUPE, Gilbert
LAURENCEAU, Jean
LAURENS, Jean
LAURENT, Daniel
LAURENT, Jacques

LEBAIL, Guillaume
LEBARS, Louis
LEBERRE, Yves
LEBIHAN, Isaac
LEBOURG, Jacques
LEBREHEL, Pierre
LEBRUN, Edme
LECAMUS, Francois
LECLAIR, Francois
LECOEUR, Jean
LECOMTE, Pierre
LECOURTOIS, Philippe
LECUNFF, Joseph
LEDUC, Jean
LEDUC, Jean
LEE, David
LEE, John
LEFERME, Pierre
LEFEVRE, Jean
LEFEVRE, Joseph
LEFLOCH, Francois
LEGOFF, Jean
LEGROSS, Pierre
LEGUEN, Louis
LEGUERN, Guillaume
LEGUILLOUX, Rene
LEHUP, Pierre
LEJORE, Jean
LELAYER, Yves
LEMAY, Jacques
LEMAY, Julien
LEMINGNON, Jean
LEMOING, Jean
LENOIR, Rene
LEPAGE, Pierre
LEPARC, Jean
LEPELLE, Julien
LERICHE, Jacques
LEROUX, Etienne
LEROUX, Jean
LERSNE, Augustin
LESAGNE, Pierre
LESOURD, Sebastien
LETOUX, Clement
LEVENT, Jean
LEWIS, Benjamin
LIEBERT, Jean
LIGNOT, Pierre
LINSEY, Stephen
LIVERNOIS, Jacques
LORIVAT, Jean
LORMIER, Augustin
LORRAIN, Georges
LOUIS, Jean
LYONNOIS, Jean
LYONNOIS, Pierre
MACHAIN, Claude
MADEC, Jean

MAGNAN, Francois
MAGNAN, Jean
MAILLET, Marcel
MAIRE, Jacques
MAISON, Jean
MALFROIS, Pierre
MANADET, Bernard
MANNING, Samuel
MANSFIELD, Timothy
MARCHAND, Pierre
MARCY (NARCY), Jean
MARET, Nicolas
MARGOT, Pierre
MARIE, Jacques
MARIN, Jean de
MARIVAL, Francois
MARQUET, Francois
MARSH, Ephraim
MARTIN, Alexis
MARTIN, Antoine
MARTIN, Claude
MARTIN, Jean
MARTIN, Louis
MARTIN, Nicolas
MARTIN, Thomas
MARTIN, Vincent
MASON, Thomas
MASSAL, Jean
MAUBRUCHON, Yves
MAUCHALIN, Yves
  (or Philibert)
MAUGER, Pierre
MAURE, Leon
MAUSSION, Charles
MAYER, Jean
MCCARTER, James
MCCLOUGHRY, John
MCCOUGHRY, John
MCKINNEY, James
MCLEAN, James
MEINER, Francois
MENAGER, Louis
MENARDIER, Jean
MERCIER, Andoche
MERIAN, Vincent
MERIEL, Jean
MERKOT, Georges
MERY, Antoine
MICHELET, Jean
MILLERT, Michel
MILLIOT, Gaspard
MINIO, Antoine
MION, Pierre
MIOT, Pierre
MOINET, Laurent
MOLIN, Jean
MOLLIERE, Antoine
MOLTON, Caesar

MONART, Nicolas
MONDRE, Pierre
MONET, Jean
MONGIN, Jean
MONNIER, Nicolas
MONTCHALEN, Antoine
MORET, Barthelemy
MORIN, Jean
MORRISOT, Jacques
MOSHER, William
MOUGAL, Nicolas
MOULINS, Antoine
MOUTEL, Liberal
MULLER, Nicolas
NAFUERN, Francois
NALFIN, Remy
NEBLE, Georges
NELSON, Hugh
NELSON, Thomas, Sr
NELSON, Thomas Jr
NELSON. Thomas (b1782)
NELSON, Willaim
NELSON, William
NEUVEU, Edme
NEUVILLE, Jean
NEW, Pierre
NEWTON, Solomon
NICHOLAS, Jean
NICOLAS, Pierre
NICOLE, Jean
NIEL, Antoine
NOEL, Jean
NOLLY, Laurent
NORTON, Henry
OLLIVIER, Paul
ORGAN, unk
ORIEUX, Francois
ORKENSUDE, Erasmus
ORVAULT, Dupe d'
OSPELL, Mathieu
OUDOT, Claude
OUIN, Jean
OUVENANT, Rene
OZANNE, Pierre
OZOU, Jean
PABST, Christian
PACET, Etienne
PAILLARD, Jean
PALIS, Paul
PALUT, Louis
PALY, B
PANIOLET, Jean
PAON, Jean
PAPELARD, Jacques
PAPON, Louis
PARIEL, Leonard
PARIS, Claude
PARIS, Gabriel

PARIS, Jacques de
PARKER, Timothy
PARMENTER, James
PARRE, Pierre
PATALIER, Joseph
PAULARD, Jean
PELITIER, Jacques
PELLETAN, Jean
PELLETIER, Joseph
PERCHE, Louis
PERNOT, Nicolas
PEROT, Milan
PEROTIN, Julien
PEROY, Louis
PERPETTE, Antoine
PERRIER, Joseph
PEYLLARD, Jacques
PHILIPEAU, Gabriel
PHILIPPE, Pierre
PICHON, Noel
PICHON, Pierre
PIERROT, Nicholas
PIERSON, Charles
PIGIBIT, Jean
PILAU, Jean
PINCERON, Francois
PINET, Jean
PITOZZEAU, N
PLACET, Claude
PLAGNOLET, Jean
PLANTO, Jean
PLISSON, Jean
POHEAGUE, Josias
POIGNARD, Jean or Hector
POLLET, Denis
POULAIN, Charles
POULAIN, Jean
POUPON, Francois
POUVEREAU, Jean
POWELL, John
PRADHOUT, Jean
PREVOST, Charles
PRIOUX, Gilles
PROU, Joseph
PROUX, Pierre
PROVOL, Charles
PRUNTZIGER, Jean
PUISSANT, Etiene
QUENARD, Pierre
QUERJEAN, Herve
RANAUD, Francois
RANDLE, Henry
RAUTZ, Francois
RAVAN, Jean
RAYBLET, Philippe
REBOUL, Pierre
REIBAUD, Antoine
REMAIN, Jacques

REMONT, Charles
RENARD, Jean
RENOUARD, Jean
REVEL, Gaspard
RIAU, Joseph
RICHARD, Pierre
RICHARDS, John
RIEBARD, Francois
RIOTTE, Pierre
RIPTON, John
ROBERTS, Thomas
ROBICHON, Ferdinand
ROCHE, Jean
ROCHE, Pierre de
ROCHEFORT, Jean
ROEBUCK, William
ROGERS, Samual
ROITOUX, Pierre
ROSBUCK, William
ROSSIGNOL, Francois
ROUAY, Charles
ROUFFE, Gottfried
ROUSSE, Antoine
ROUSSEAU, Pierre
ROUSSEL, Jean
ROUSSEL, Vincent
ROUX, Jean
ROUX, Jean
ROYER, Jean
RULLINS, William
SABE, Jean
SAFFROY, Jean
SALAUN, Francois
SALE, Bertrand
SALLEMON, Antoine
SALLES, Jean
SALMON, Guillaume
SALMON, Philibert
SAMPSON, Seth
SANSFACON, Jean
SANTO, Pierre
SARGEANT, Nathaniel
SATUR, de
SAVEQUET, Dominique
SAVOIX, Martiel
SCARA, Michel
SCHOLDER, Francois
SCHOLT, Sebastian
SCOTT, John
SEAUCE, Jacques
SEBIRE, Martin
SELIGNET, Jean
SELIQUET, Jean
SEPEDRE, Antoine
SERREE, Jacques
SERVE, Antoine
SIREUIL, Jean de
SMITH, B Egbert

SNOW, Edward
SOLNE, Andre
SORBETZ, Barthelemy
SORIN, Pierre
SOULIGNAC, Mathieu
SOURSON, Jean
STAUTZER, Jacob
STEIN, Jean
STEPHAN, Guillaume
STOHER, Balthazar
STOUDERT, Claude
STUBERT, Adam
TAFT, Nathan
TEPHANY, Remy
TERVILLE, Andre
TESTELIN, Louis
TEYO, Rene
THEVENIN, Louis
THOMSON, Daniel
TILQUAZ, Nicolas
TINCELIN, Jean
TINIER, Joseph
TISSIER, Jacques
TISSIER, Jacques
TOLON, Francois
TOUGARE, Francis
TOURNIS, Jacques
TOUSSET, Jean
TOUTIN, Eustache
TOWN, Asce
TREASURE, Richard
TUMELIN, Nicolas
TURNER, John
TURNER, Mattocks
URVOY, Jean
VACHERE, Andre
VAISSE, Jean
VALEOT, Jean
VALLANCE, William
VALLE, Jean
VALLEE, Pierre
VALLEE, Vincent
VAN VOST, Christian
VAQUIER, Francois
VARRENNES, Jean
VBEL, Geroges
VEINTEFFER, JH
VERDAVOIR, Oger
VERDIER, Jacques
VERRIER, Joseph
VERSIN, Pierre
VEXLIN, Emmanuel
VEXTAIN, Emmanuel
ViA/VIER/VIAH, John B.
VIA, WilliamVIAL, Pierre
VIGOUREUX, Francois
VILATON, Jean
VILLARET, Joseph

VILLEDIEU, Jean
VILLEON, de la
VINCE, Joseph
VINCENT, Nicolas
VITRE, JeanVITRIER, Andre
VIVANSON, Bernard
VIZET, Joseph
VORRIOT, Pierre
WADE, Stephen
WALLIS, Colley
WASSON, James
WEBSTER, George
WENDREWECK, Armand
WETHERBEE, James
WHITAKER, John
WHITE, Isaac
WHITE, William

WHITING, James
WHITNEY, Silas
WILCOX, John
WILLIAMS, James
WITHAM, William
WLOVASSE, Jean
WYNNE, Edmund
WYNNE, Thomas
YVES, Andre
ZELL, John

APPENDIX B – CEMETERY LIST BY COUNTY / INDEPENDENT CITY

Cemetery Name	GPS Coordinates	Location Directions
ACCOMACK COUNTY		
Belle Vue	unk	Off Rt 646, 7 mi E of Locustville
Benson Family	37.8771570,-75.6217830	Nr Jct Cattail Rd Rt 690 & Whites Crossing Rd Rt 690
Bowman's Folly	unk	End of Rt 652, private lane, 2.4 mi NE of Accomac, Joynes Neck
Bradford-Burton	37.5563800,-75.7313900	Rt 182 and Rt 605, N fr Quinby
Burton Private	unk	Wachapreague
Chestnut Vale	unk	.6 mi N of Rt 605, W of Rt 789, nr Locustville
Coal Kiln	unk	1 mi S jct Rts 607 & 600, R off Rt 600
Colonna Family, aka Wakefield Farm	unk	1 mi east of Pennyville, Hacks Neck
Deep Creek Plantation	unk	Mink Farm Rd., Onancock
Foreman Plot	unk	NW of jct Rts 709 & 708, nr Miona
Joynes-Bayne	unk	W end of Meadville Dr, Onancock
Kennahorn Family	unk	N side of Rt 638, .4 mi E of 637, W fr Cashville
Laws Family	unk	Rt 13 nr Nelsonia
Melrose & Ker Family	unk	Abt 2 mi SW Pungoteague
Morrison Hill	unk	.8 mi S of Rt 622, W of Rt 600, Frogstool
Mt Custis	unk	Off Rt 622 2.5 mi of Rt 13, Bayley's Neck
Mt Holly	37.7045681,-75.7414503	Hill St, Onancock
Nelson Family	unk	New Church
Old West Place, aka Cedar View	unk	N of Craddockville off Rt 616
Onancock	37.6998600,-75.7465500	Rts 718 & 638, Onancock
Parramore	unk	Onley
Parksley	unk	.5 mi N of Rt 176, W of Rt 678, NE fr Parksley
Poplar Cove Wharf	unk	Nr end of Rt 653, Onancock
Poplar Grove	36.5856900,-76.3213300	Off Rt 180, Pungoteague, Hack's Neck
Quimby	unk	Painter
Riley Family	unk	Rt 684, .5 mi W of Rt 658
Rodgers Plot	unk	Rt 180 off Rt 178, .9 mi W of Pungoteague, Hacks Neck
Savage Family	unk	Rt 180, Pungoteague
Scott Hall	unk	Daugherty Rd, Onancock
Scott Hall, aka Edward Snead	37.7111500,-75.7525000	Nr River btw Mt Prospect Ave and South St, Onancock
Tavern Lot	unk	Center of Accomac
Teackle House	37.6069120,-75.6885630	Rt 1709 & Brooklyn St, Wachapreague
Thomas Parker Family	unk	Rt 180 nr Pungoteague
Warwick House	unk	Rt 605 1 mi S of Quinby, Upshur Bay
Waterfield Farm	unk	1.4 mi N of Rt 614, W of Rt 617, SE fr Pennyville
Welburn or Welbourne Family	37.9697490,-75.4631410	Rts 709 & Rt 679, Horntown
West Family	unk	Deep Creek
Wharton Family	unk	Assawoman Creek
Wise Family	unk	Chesconessex

ALBERMARLE COUNTY (See also Charlottesville City)

Belvoir	37.6283490,-76.3134230	5172 Stony Point Pass, Cismont
Berry Hill	unk	1.5 mi N of Sweet Briar College
Blue Ridge Farm	37.7028608,-76.3789312	Rt 261, 2.1 mi off Rt 250 W, Greenwood
Bowen Farm	unk	Red Hill
Brightberry Brown Family	38.2070645,-78.6715356	5525 Brown's Gap Turnpike, Brown's Cove
Brockman-Mitchell	unk	Petty's Creek Annex, Stony Point
Brown Family #2	unk	Rt 810, Brown's Cove
Castle Hill	38.0568300,-78.3182800	1625 Country Club Dr, can be seen 150 yds E of Wood Ln, Farmington
Enniscorthy	37.8738000,-78.5852000	loc Green Mountain Rd, Keene
Findowire	38.0330590,-78.3111310	728 Campbell Rd (Rt 600
Garland Family	unk	Check property records
Hamner Family	unk	Carter's Bridge, Keene
Harris Family	37.8186700,-78.6639300	Irish Rd, Esmont
Locust Hill	unk	Off Rt 676 N of Rt 250, Ivy
Martin Marietta's Land	unk	Nr Red Hill
Maupin Family Farm	unk	Morman's River
Moore Family	37.9711300,-78.6359800	2393 Taylor's Gap Rd, North Garden
Mt Air	unk	Hardware River, Keene, NW of Scottsville
Mt Zion Methodist	37.8022000,-78.5914000	Rt 170 off Portress Rd Rt 627, Esmont
Old Hardin (Shirley) Property	unk	Nr Greenwood
Rockgate	38.0617000,-78.7017000	981 Crozet Ave, Crozet
Rodes Family,	unk	E of Whitehall
Midway Plantation		
Shepherd Family	unk	Batesville
Snow Johnson Family	unk	S base Buck Mtn, abt .5 mi behind house
Spring Valley, Massie Family	37.9427700,-78.7686300	3808 Spring Valley Rd, Batesville
St Paul's Church	38.0583000,-78.5958000	851 Owensville Rd, Ivy
Thomas Family	unk	Nr Red Hill
Via Family	unk	Brown's Cove
Wakefield Cemetery	38.1572770,-78.4652710	975 Wakefield Farm Rd, Earlysville
Wood Family	38.2027900,-78.5323800	Off Markwood Rd Rt 664, Earlysville
Woodson	unk	Not identified

ALEXANDRIA CITY (See also Arlington County)

Christ Church Episcopal	38.8021600,-77.0568900	Wilkes St & Hamilton Ln
Fendall Family	38.8113612,-77.0459896	614 N Washington St
First Presbyterian	38.7999200,-77.0579900	601 Hamilton Ln
Mt Vernon Unitarian	38.7551800,-77.0634100	1909 Winhill Ln
Old Christ Church Episcopal	36.8340700,-81.5933800	Old Ebenezer Rd Rt 659
Old Christ Church Episcopal	38.8062500,-77.0471800	118 N Washington St
Old Presbyterian Meeting House	38.4852800,-77.2353200	323 S Fairfax St
Peake Family	38.7368600,-77.0843000	M L King Jr Park, 8115 Fordson Rd, past pool & tennis cts to black metal fence
Penny Hill	38.7986100,-77.0555900	S Payne & Franklin Sts
Presbyterian Church	38.8001500,-77.0579100	Wilkes St & Hamilton Ln
Quaker Burial Ground	38.8074900,-77.0467600	717 Queen St, Kate Walker Barrett Library
St Marys Catholic Church	38.7939000,-77.0475000	310 S Royal St
St Paul's Episcopal	38.7995900,-77.0586000	228 S Pitt St
Summers Family	38.4915000,-77.0828000	Demming Ave & Lincolnia Rd
Trinity United Methodist	39.1360000,-77.0061000	2911 Cameron Mills Rd

ALLEGHANY COUNTY (See also Covington City)

Humphries Lone Grave	unk	11 mi SW of Covington
Mountain View	37.8136000,-79.8139000	Clifton Forge
Smith Cemetery	37.8614000,-79.9897000	Rt 687, Mt Pleasant
Smith Family	unk	7 mi N of Covington
Stull Family	unk	10 mi S of Lowmoor

AMELIA COUNTY

Archer, Red Lodge	unk	Red Lodge Rd
Avary Family	unk	Avary Church Rd
Booker	unk	Rt 612
Booker Family	unk	Grub Hill Church Rd, check property records for location of plantation
Booth Family	unk	loc on land where Manassas Hill Baptist Church now stands nr Sheathouse Creek
Chappell	unk	Fowlkes Bridge Rd, Paineville
Green Family	unk	Rt 622
Grub Hill	37.3994000,-77.9703000	Grub Hill Church Rd Rt 609
H H Jones Property	unk	Chula
Jackson Family	37.2901190,-78.0469548	6101 Buckskin Creek Rd, Rt 640, Jetersville
Jeter-Cadwell	37.4736900,-77.9842220	Giles Rd Rt 637
Locust Grove	unk	Rt 66 abt 5 mi S of Victoria
Meade Family	unk	Nr Chula
Royall	unk	Off Promise Land Rd Rt 661, Amelia CH
Townes	unk	Rt 38 at Level Mount Estates, Amelia CH
Vaughan Family	unk	Not identified
Whitworth	unk	Paineville
Wigwam Estate	unk	Amelia CH
Wood lc off Rt 60	unk	Rt 620 nr Rt 616, Rodophil

AMHERST COUNTY

Amherst	37.5964000,-79.0367000	Bus Rt 29, Amherst
Anthony Street	37.5052030,-79.1666470	loc to the West off Winesap Rd at Old Anthony Street Plantation, beside Graham Creek & Pedler Madison Heights
Burton Family	unk	1 mi SW jct Genitoe and Brick Church Ln, property of Roger Epperson in a .5 acre lot
Clements Family	unk	loc off Rt 60 on Mount Horeb Rd for 1.4 mi, Willow
David Crawford Plantation	unk	Check property records for plantation location
Davies	unk	Nr Elon
Franklin	unk	Amherst
Gill Family	37.730845,-79.100752	Loc Page Mountain Way (Rt 746) Indian Creek; ;Amherst
Higginbotham Family	37.6914000,-79.1428000	Rt 617 N of jct with 761, Amherst
Indian Graveyard	unk	Bear Mtn, Rt 643
Laine Family	unk	Amherst
Mansion House	unk	Buffalo Island
Miller Family	unk	Rt 690
Monument Hill	37.5511500,-79.0949600	Stable Ln nr jct Rt 663, Sweet Briar College
Old Keys Church	37.6916510,-78.8156559	Jct Rts 647 & 722
Old Pendleton	unk	Monroe
Penn Family	unk	Rt 151, Clifford
Powell Family	unk	Amherst
Rodes family	unk	Check property records
Rucker Family	37.5406200,-77.1850800	Shepherd Farm Ln off Rt 653 Ambrose Rucker Rd
Shelton-Ellis-Watts	unk	Winesap Rd
Tucker	37.7144000,-79.0861000	Rt 621, Indian Creek
Tyler-Davies	37.5024940,-79.2155580	loc off of Monacan Park Rd, S of Salt Peter Rd (Rt 652), Elon;
Wilson Family, R.L. Bowling Property	unk	Rt 659

| Winton Plantation | unk | adj Winton Country Club, Clifford |

APPOMATTOX COUNTY

First Concord Presbyterian	unk	Hwy 460 E fr Lynchburg City.
Flood Family	unk	Vera
Goode Fam	unk	Loc 4.5 mi from Appomatox River
Kelso Family	unk	1 mi N of Pamplin on Rt 600
Liberty Baptist	37.3518100,-78.8286200	1709 Church St, Appomatox
McReynolds Family	37.1736000,-78.5334000	Rt 623
Old Concord Presbyterian Ch	37.3403705,-78.9232109	4909 Reedy Spring Rd (Rt 648), Sprout Spring
Old Trent Mill Farm	unk	Rt 631
Old Walker Home	unk	5 mi N of Pamplin on Rt 600, then .4 mi W on Rt 627, then .4 mi NW on Rt 628
Pankey Family	unk	Tower Hill, Appomattox
Robertson Family	unk	Off Rt 641 nr Appomattox CH
Second Concord Presbyterian	37.3420900,-78.9658500	Phoebe Pond Rd Rt 609 E of Concord
St Clare Family	unk	Appomattox
Sweeney Family	unk	1 mi NE Appomattox Ct House on Richmond/Lynchburg Stage Rd;

ARLINGTON COUNTY (See also Alexandria City)

Arlington National	38.8837700,-77.0653500	Jefferson Davis Hwy Rt 110
Ball-Carlin Family	38.8636192,-77.1258875	300 S Kensington St
Old Ball Burying Ground	unk	3427 Washington Blvd, behind American Legion Bldg
Old Burying Ground	unk	See Senate Doc DAR annual report 1955 vol 4 serial 11912
Southern-Shreve	38.8814000,-77.1269400	5300 N 10th St

AUGUSTA COUNTY (See also Staunton City and Waynesboro City)

Abney Family	unk	Springfield Ln., Fisherville
Airy Knoll	unk	E of Rt 252 abt .4 mi N of 620, just to S of Newport
Augusta Stone Presbyterian	38.2392500,-78.9735600	28 Old Stone Church Ln, Ft Defiance
Bell	38.2614000,-78.9556000	Rt 11, Mt Sidney
Bethel Presbyterian	38.0425600,-79.1728300	563 Bethel Green Rd, Middlebrook
Bratton Family	unk	Nr Goshen
Buchanan Family	unk	Nr Rockbridge Co line, possibly on Ben Jacobs' land, btw Rts 602 & 681
Emmanuel	unk	Mt Solon
Fishburne	unk	End of Rt 847, behind Verona Methodist Church, Verona
Glebe Burying Ground	38.1094000,-79.2219000	Glebe School Rd Rt 876, Swoopes
Hanger Family	unk	Rt 670, near Greenville
Hanna Family	unk	Nr Grottoes
Hogshead Family	unk	Off Rt 736 btw Rts 42 & 250, N of Jennings Gap
John Sterrett Family	unk	1 mi W of Craigsville
Jones-Van Lear	unk	Rt 613, .3 mi S jct with Rt 742, farm of Alfred Ryder
Keller Family	unk	Dr Knopp's Farm, Churchville
Landes Family	38.3011000,-78.9717000	W fr Burketown 2 mi, near Weyers Cave
Leland Brown Farm	unk	Nr Weyers Cave
Lewis Family	unk	Nr Staunton
Miller Family	38.3562900,-79.0314900	4998 Scenic Hwy, Bridgewater
Mossy Creek Presbyterian	38.3533100,-79.0491400	372 Kyles Mill Rd, Mt Solon
North Mountain	unk	7 mi S of Staunton on N side Rt 252

Old Lebanon	38.0809000,-79.3754500	Off Rt 42, Craigsville
Old Link	unk	.5 mi W of Ft Defiance
Old Providence	37.9610053,-79.2248048	1005 Spottswood Rd, Spottswood
Old Stone Presbyterian	38.2383087,-78.9757954	28 Old Stone Church Ln, Ft Defiance
Rocky Spring Presbyterian	38.1147000,-79.2425000	1 mi S of Deerfield
Samuel Bell Family	38.2277000,-78.8908500	Nr NW jct Craigshop Rd & Rt 608 toward Middle River
Schutterle Community	38.2203000,-79.1047000	Off Rt 728 SE of Rt 732, Franks Mill
Shenandoah Methodist	38.9816000,-78.9577300	1919 Howardsville Turnpike, Sherando
St James Methodist	38.2095781,-79.1291465	3777 Churchville Ave, Churchville
St John's Reformed UCC	38.0508100,-79.1776100	1515 Arbor Hill Rd, Middlebrook
St Peter's Lutheran	38.2256900,-79.1612500	3795 Churchville Ave, Churchville
Tinkling Spring Presbyterian	38.0847200,-78.9827800	30 Tinkling Spring Dr, Fishersville
Trinity Lutheran	38.1720100,-78.8682000	2564 Rockfish Rd, Crimora
Union Presbyterian	39.1091600,-78.0949700	1471 Union Church Rd, Churchville
West Augusta Cemetery	38.2667000,-79.3333000	Rt 716 W Augusta Rd, 8 mi N of Staunton
Willson Family	38.0728300,-79.1209600	Rt 697 White Oak Gap Rd, W of Rt 11, Mint Spring

BATH COUNTY

Augusta	unk	See DAR Senate Doc year 1959
Bethel Church aka Old Lyle	unk	Millboro Springs
Bratton	37.9975000,-79.5617000	Rts 39 & 42 Mountain Valley Rd 4 mi E of Millboro Springs
Fort Dinwiddie	38.0922800,-79.8314000	NE of jct of Dinwiddie Trail & River Rd, Warm Springs
George Revercomb Property	unk	McClintic by Jackson River
Cleek	38.1931000,-79.7322000	Rt 220 Sam Snead Hwy, Warm Springs
Keyser Family	37.9688500,-79.8369400	Nr Jct Rts 612 & 618, Warm Springs
Laverty Farm	unk	Cow pasture
Mallow Tract	unk	Nr Hot Springs
McClintic Family	unk	12 mi W of Warm Springs
McClung Family	unk	Nr Millboro
Mustoe Family	unk	5 mi S of Healing Springs
Sitlington Family	unk	8.5 mi S of Millboro Springs
Warm Springs	38.0503000,-79.7811000	Rt 220 Sam Snead Hwy, Warm Springs
Windy Cove Presbyterian	38.0021208,-79.6328848	102 Windy Cove Rd, Millboro

BEDFORD COUNTY AND BEDFORD CITY

Anderson Family	37.3897000,-79.3904500	2370 Cifax Rd, Goode
Andrews Family	unk	Evington
Ayers-Wingert-Wilson	unk	loc on Byrd Farm Rt 608, 2 mi E of jct Rt 737, Moneta
Bedford Presbyterian Church	37.3343346,-79.5239420	105 West Main St, Bedford City
Blankenship Family	unk	Nr Montvale
Brown Family	unk	Off New London Rd Rt 709, Forest
Callaway-Steptoe	37.3056000,-79.2947000	Rt 460, New London
Campbell Family	unk	Nr Irving
Chapman Family	unk	Goodview
Cox Family	unk	Forest across fr Lake Vista
Crews Family	unk	Nr Big Island
Dickerson Family	unk	Nr Moneta
Ewing-Patterson	unk	Penick's Mill
Frantz Family	unk	Check property records
Fuqua Family	37.3334400,-79.4835200	Orange Street
Gravelly Hill	unk	Town of Gravelly Hill
Groom Family	unk	Nr Shady Grove Church
Hardy Family	37.2346000,-79.3023000	State Rts 122 & 640, Forbes Mill
Harkin (Heathering) Hill	unk	Peaks of Otter

Name	Coordinates	Location
Hurt Family	unk	Nr Mobley's Creek
Jeter Family	unk	Btw Centerville & Otterville
Lee Family	unk	New London
Leftwich Family	unk	Mt Airy, nr Leesville
Locust Level	37.2318000,-79.4342000	Rt 460, nr Montvale
Logwood Family	unk	Locust Hill
Longwood	37.3417000,-79.5119000	Nr jct Oakwood & Longwood Ave Rt 122
McConnehey-Updike	37.2116200,-79.5452700	2730 Chestnut Fork Rd, Chestnut Fork
McManaway Family	unk	Chamblissburg
Mead	unk	Near Lowry on Norfolk/Western RR Lines
Millner Estate	unk	Check property records
Otey Street	37.3317000,-79.5217000	W Franklin St jct with Otey
Quaker Baptist	37.2061900,-79.5162300	4665 Chestnut Fork Rd, Chestnut Fork
Quarles Family	unk	SE fr Bedford
Read	37.1822000,-79.1851000	New London, nr jct Rts 460 & 811
Reid Estate, "Poplar Grove"	unk	New London
Royal Forest	unk	New London
Rural	unk	Check property records
Salmon Family	unk	Check property records
Saunders Family	37.3180800,-79.4326400	Jct Rt 460 & Krantz's Corner Rd
Scott Family	unk	Episcopal School Rd 200 yds fr school
Slack Family, aka Chattin Family	unk	On hillside of Chattin farm, nr Chamblissburg
St Stephen's Episcopal	37.3773277,-79.3086314	1694 Perrowville Rd, Forest
St Steven's Episcopal	unk	Jct Rts 663 and 221
Staunton Baptist	37.0701317,-79.5801222	15267 Smith Mountain Lake Pkwy, Huddleston
Stiff Family	unk	Union Church Rd 1 mi past Union Methodist, Thaxton
Stratton Family	37.2619230,-79.5510330	Jct Rts 122 & 736
Terry Family	unk	Oakwood
Thomas-Lowry Farm	unk	E fr Bedford
Trigg Family, aka Old Liberty Plantation	unk	Nr Liberty
Turpin Family	37.4749990,-79.4522200	on Flitstone Mountain Rd nr jct with Big Island Hwy
Valentine Cox	unk	Forest
Walker Family	37.2848100,-79.5118600	Rt 723, Boxwood Hill, Five Forks
Walker Farm	37.2532700,-79.4941900	1972 Montevido Rd, Rt 667
White Family	37.2840000,-79.2413000	Nr Charlemont, jct 638 & 637
White Family	unk	Stewartsville
Wigginton Family	unk	Rt 7, Huddleston
Wilks Family	unk	Nr Leftwich Church
Woodford-Wade	37.2315945,-79.4310272	11477 Falling Creek Rd

BLAND COUNTY

Name	Coordinates	Location
Bird	unk	Rt 42 2.5 mi E of Bland village
Holly Brook	unk	Rt 606 off Hwy 42 adj Holly Brook Community Center
Sharon Lutheran	37.0580000,-81.2059000	Rt 42 W of Ceres

BOTETOURT COUNTY

Name	Coordinates	Location
Abendschon Family	unk	Nr Mill Creek Baptist
Allen Family	unk	5.5 mi S of Buchanan
Allen-Carper	unk	Rt 43 nr Eagle Rock
Allen-Lauderdale	unk	Fincastle
Baker-Ferry Family	unk	East of Rt 779, Daleville

Breckenridge Family	unk	Grove Hill Farm, Rt 606 1 mi NW of Fincastle
Brickey Family	unk	Check property records
Brickey-Lee	unk	Rt 779, McAfees Knob
Buchanan	unk	Buchanan
Cahoon Family	unk	Glade Creek nr Bedford Co line
Caldwell family	unk	End of Rt 611 across Craig Creek fr Camp Easter Seals
Carlock Family	unk	Lick Run
Cross Family Farm	unk	Nr Roanoke
Daleville	37.3986900,-79.9106900	Roanoke Rd Rt 220 nr Kroger store, Daleville
Fincastle Presbyterian	37.5001700,-79.8755800	108 E Back St, Fincastle
Glebe	37.4515500,-79.9696800	Vic jct Rts 779 and 630
Greenfield	37.4375000,-79.9142000	Off International Pkwy, W of Rt 220, Amsterdam
Kessler Family	unk	Nr Brick Union Ch
Laymantown	37.3627800,-79.8490900	Laymontown Rd, Laymantown
Lemon Family	37.7712600,-79.7816000	Nr jct Rts 220 & 698 Lick Run Rd, Lick Run
Locust Bottom	37.7414850,-79.8145640	Nr Jct Locust Bottom Rd & Prices Bluff Rd
Locust Bottom Church	37.7417109,-79.8147145	4084 Prices Bluff Rd, Eagle Rock
McFerran Family	unk	Rt 220, 6 mi N of Fincastle
Mt Union	37.4513300,-79.9705500	4614 Catawba Rd, Mt Union
Old Dutch	unk	W side of Rt 11 at Mill Creek, 9 mi S of Buchanan
Old Glade Creek	37.3598900,-79.8182800	Grace Hollow Rd, Blue Ridge
Rader Family	unk	Past Motts Hill Ln on right, take left on Radar Barn Rd, N of Troutville on Rt 11
Reid Family	unk	9 mi NE of Eagle Rock
Sheets Family	unk	W of Rt 220, Bessemer area
Shirkey-Far	unk	Across James River fr Gala
Simmons-Brugh	unk	Nr Mill Creek Baptist Church
Temontown	unk	Laymantown

BRISTOL CITY (See also Washington County)

East Hill	36.5943800,-82.1723300	E State St on line btw VA and TN
Snodgrass	unk	Bristol (or Blountsville, TN)
Walnut Grove	36.6335722,-82.1294130	3012 Lee Hwy Rt 11
Weaver's	unk	Not identified

BRUNSWICK COUNTY

Abernathy Family	36.5042000,-77.8804700	400 yds W of Preswood Rd, Rt 646, 1.2 mi N of Linerty Rd, Rt 634
Bishop Family	36.6264000,-77.9558000	Rt 644, Brunswick
Claiborne Family	unk	Nr jct Rts 713 & 715, Lawrenceville
Flournoy	unk	Rt 58
Lanier Family	unk	Nr Smoky Ordinary & Poarch Store
Lewis Family	38.8027600,-77.9624200	Woodstock Plantation, Meredithville
Orgain Family	36.8601000,-77.9400200	Jct Rts 644 & Rt 648, Alberta
St Andrews Episcopal Ch	36.7594900,-77.8504430	400 Windsor Ave, Lawrenceville

BUCKINGHAM COUNTY

Abraham Jones Family	37.6539930,-78.4420920	Melita Rd (Rt 622), Arvonia
Agee Family	unk	Nr Dillwyn
Anthony Glover Cem	unk	Dirt lane 1 mi S of Alcoma
Boatwright Family	unk	Nr Mt Zion Church, 6277 Cartersville Rd, New Canton
Branch	37.5825000,-78.4900000	Rt 631, Manteo

Cemetery	Coordinates	Location
Chambers Family	unk	Rt 659, 2.75 mi W of Ransons
Charlie Londeree	unk	Not identified by DAR and SAR sources
Coleman Family	unk	Nr Salem Methodist Church
Coleman Family	unk	Bent Creek
Eldridge Family	unk	Fork of North & Slate Rivers
Flood Family, "Toga"	unk	Rt 24
Grace Church	unk	Manteo
Greenfield	unk	On Rocky Creek nr Penlan
Greenhill	unk	James River State Park
Hooper Family	unk	Hooper's Mount, Arcanum
Jones	unk	Rt 24, S of Togson, abt 2.5 mi then 1.5 mi on private road
Loch Lomond	unk	Check property records
Merionette	unk	Nr Willis Mountain
Morris Family	unk	Rt 609 at Vassars
Moseley Family	unk	Willowlake, Rt 56
Moseley Family	unk	"Wheatlands", Rt 647 10 mi E of CH
Patteson Family	unk	Mt Pleasant
Perkins-Hall	unk	Hwy 56
Physics Springs	unk	Buckingham
Rolfton	unk	Hwy 749
Samuel Glover	unk	Rt 742
Starkes-Gunter	unk	loc Rt 601 or 655, Manteo Rd
Stratton Family	unk	New Canton
Watson-Perrow	unk	Gunter Mountain
Wilkinson Family	unk	Rt 610, Gold Hill

CAMPBELL COUNTY (See also Lynchburg City)

Cemetery	Coordinates	Location
Adams-Ward	37.1321000,-79.2407300	Mansion Bridge Rd Rt 640, Altavista
Alexander-Adams	unk	Rt 652, Gladys
Avoca	unk	Altavista
Blankenship-Oldham	unk	Winfall
Blenheim	37.1315000,-78.5700000	Rt 648, Gladys
Browns #207	unk	loc Old E Ferry Rd, off Rt 705 in woods on property of a Mining Co, Rustburg
Brown Family-Thompson Valley	unk	New London
Carwile	37.0847000,-78.5802000	Rt 708 Seamster Rd, go to end, abt 1 mi walk, Noruna
Clark Family	37.2956300,-79.2108600	Cnr Lawyer's Rd and Missionary Manor Plain Dealing, Naruna
Cobbs Family	unk	Nr Rt 643, Brookneal
Cobbs Hall	unk	.5 mi S of Hunter's Tavern
Concord Presbyterian #2	unk	4909 Reedy Spring Rd, Sprout Spring
Concord Presbyterian #3	37.3403705,-78.9232109	Nr jct Rts 615 and 648
Creasy Family	unk	At Otterburne, Old Deering Place on Otter River, Altavista nr Evington
Deering Family	unk	On Barry Jones Farm near Rt 460, on Co Rd 757 btwn Concord & Lynchburg City
Diuguid	unk	Off Rt 658, Concord quadrant, nr Rustburg
Dixon Family	37.1842000,-79.5931000	SE of Rt 40, Dog Creek
Driskill	unk	2874 Wickliffe Ave, Brookneal
Falling River Baptist	37.0753100,-78.9154300	SW Rt 646 3.2 mi N of Rt 615, Gladys quadrant
Franklin Family	37.0720000,-79.0510000	Lynch Station
Goose Creek	unk	Phillips Farm, Evington
Haden family	unk	Nr Hat Creek Church, Brookneal
Harper Family	unk	6442 Hat Creek Rd, Brookneal
Hat Creek Presbyterian	37.0657000,-78.5424000	Nr Campbell Co CH, Rustburg
Howard Family	unk	

Jones Family	unk	Gladys Twp
Lee Family	unk	Leesville
Lynch Family	37.1294600,-79.2685300	Avoca Museum, 1514 Main St, Altavista
McReynolds Family	unk	Off Rt 623
Mt Athos	unk	Rt 460, Kelly
Mt Zion United Methodist	37.2152987,-79.0377775	5662 Red House Rd, Rustburg
Mt Hermon United Methodist	37.1450000,-79.3117000	Rt 712, Lynch Station
Oakdale	37.1707600,-79.0476800	Mollies Creek Rd, Gladys
Old Concord Presbyterian	unk	Rt 648, Concord
Old Phillips	unk	Rt 696 N side of Troublesome Creek, Evington
Otter Oaks	unk	Nr Evington
Payne Family	unk	"Oak Grove," Rt 659, Altavista
Pribble - Dunn	37.3080000,-79.2470000	Castle Craig Quadrant, Evington
Thornhill Family	unk	Off Rt 656, Rustburg
Walnut Hill	unk	Anthony home on Otter River, Evington
Whipping Creek	37.0343000,-79.0018000	Rt 633 Epsons Rd nr Long Island
Whitaker Family Farm	unk	Not identified
Wiatt-Norvell	unk	City Farm Quadrant
Wyndholm, aka Early Family	unk	Flat Creek nr Evington

CAROLINE COUNTY

Baylor Family	unk	Newmarket, Rt 2, 6 mi S of Bowling Green
Baynham Family	unk	Rt 653, Ruther Glen
Boutwell-Smith Family	unk	Rt 17, 3.1 mi S of Port Royal
Buckner-Washington-Burke	unk	Off Rt 2, W on Rt 626 Woodford Rd for 4 mi to gate of "Braynefield"
Burke Family	unk	1 mile N of Burke's Bridge, on Burke's Bridge Rd Rt 654, Bowling Green
Carmel Baptist	37.9345080,-77.4808062	24230 Jefferson Davis Pkwy, Ruther Glen
Cool Spring Farm	38.1291260,-77.4083440	10065 Rozell Rd, Woodford
DeJarnette Family	unk	Rt 2, 5.5 mi fr Bowling Green
Dick-Smith Family	unk	Bullock's Rd
Elmwood	unk	Rt 651, 5.3 mi S of DeJarnette
Fairford	unk	Nr Penola
Golansville Meeting House	unk	Golansville on US1
Greenlawn	38.0703000,-77.3383000	Lakewood Rd, Bowling Green
Hazelwood	38.1866700,-77.2263900	Hazelwood Ln at Rt 674, Port Royal
Hickory Grove	unk	Hickory Grove Plantation
Hill Family	37.9376400,-77.5515200	5498 MtAiry Dr, Mt Airy, Ruther Glen
Jericho	unk	North Anna River
Lomax-White	unk	Rt 758, Port Tobago
Maple Swamp	unk	Chilesburg
Old Mansion	unk	S end of Main St, Bowling Green
Pratt Family	unk	Rt 686 Camden Rd
Samuel Chewning Estate	unk	See tax map for location
Taliaferro Family	unk	Rt 654
Taylor-Quarles Family	38.2562900,-78.0539400	End of Bloomsbury Rd
Thornton Family	unk	Ormsby
Townsfield Farm	unk	Port Royal
White Hall	unk	2.4 mi N of Woodford
Woolfolk Family	unk	Rt 721 Sparta Rd, DeJarnette
Young Family	unk	Ruther Glen

CARROLL COUNTY

Blair	unk	Cliffview
Bobbitt Family	36.4784100,-80.4055400	Rt 682 E of Rt 52, Hillsville

Bowman-Fariss Family	36.6654100,-80.6654100	Blue Ridge Pkwy MM 194, Volunteer Rd W side btw Alpine Court Rd & Boundary Rd
Collier Family	36.7816000,-80.5983000	Jct Rts 628 & 624, Dugspur
Gardner Family	36.7661000,-80.7208000	End of Lynhaven Rd, Hillsville
Glenwood Methodist	36.6276900,-80.8866700	.1 mile E of jct Rt 608 Coal Creek Rd and Rt 609 Peaks Mountain Rd
John Frost	36.7184500,-80.8954000	Roseberry Ln nr Hillsville
Kenny Family	unk	Vic jct Rts 802 & 709
Mitchell Family	unk	Off Rt 764, 1 mi S of Rt 765, Sylvatus
North End	36.7723400,-80.7386600	101 Beaver Dam Rd, Hillsville
Old Quaker	36.6406700,-80.8862000	Off Old Quaker Rd Rt 727, Pipers Gap
Thompson-Bolt	36.8104000,-80.5503000	Off Bannon Rd Rt 625, Willis
Tobias Phillips	unk	Rt 619 nr Rt 757
William Dalton	36.7959500,-80.6436900	Off Rt 221, Dugspur
Worrell Family	36.7829000,-80.6617300	Off Pils Trail Rt 673, .6 mi S of Rt 221, Eona

CHARLES CITY COUNTY

Belle Air Plantation	37.2049000,-77.3400000	Rt 5, New Hope
Berkeley Plantation	37.3145000,-77.1784000	Rt 5, Harrison Landing Rd
Greenway	37.2019000,-77.0520000	Rt 5, Charles City CH
Lightfoot Family	unk	Teddington, Sandy Point
Rickman Family	37.3052900,-77.0482600	Kittiewan Plantation, 12104 Weyanoke Rd
Shirley Plantation	unk	Rt 5 SE of Richmond
Soldier's Rest	unk	Blanks Crossroads
Weyanoke	37.1730000,-77.3560000	Rt 619 off Rt 5

CHARLOTTE COUNTY

Cub Creek	37.0322000,-78.7583000	Rt 616 Cub Creek Church Rd, Brookneal
Edgehill Plantation (AKA Mulberry Hill)	36.8862900,-78.7035300	1035 Fort Hill Trail, Randolph
Golden Hills Estate	unk	Drakes Branch
Henry Family	37.0319449,-78.8979580	Red Hill Plantation, 1250 Red Hill Rd, Brookneal
Ingleside, Thomas Read Family	unk	Charlotte CH
Locust Grove	unk	Drakes Branch
Locust Grove	unk	Locust Grove nr Red Hill Boys Home
Moseley Family	unk	Nr Buffalo Creek
Mulberry Hill	36.8862900,-78.7035300	Staunton River Battlefield State Park, 1035 Fort Hill Trail, Randolph
Wheeler-Pugh-Jennings	unk	Off Rt 663 nr Bear Creek, down dirt rd

CHARLOTTESVILLE CITY (See also Albermarle County)

Brown Family #1	unk	Mt Fair nr Charlottesville
Bryan Family	unk	Farmington Country Club, 10th tee
Carr Family	unk	Stoney Pt Rd Rt 20 nr Charlottsville
Clover Fields	unk	Rt 22 NE off I-64, W of Charlottesville
Gilner Family	38.0485100,-78.4496400	Pen Park off Rio Rd
Lewis Family, University Heights	38.0239000,-78.3100000	Jct 250 W and Colonnade Dr, nr Old Ivy Rd
Lewis-Clarkson	38.0440700,-78.5170600	Collonade Dr
Monticello	38.0082900,-78.4552000	931 Thomas Jefferson Pkwy
Riverview	38.0261000,-78.4581000	1701 Chesapeake St
White Oak Crossroads	unk	Nr Charlottesville
Wingfield Family	38.1060467,-78.5005182	531 Woodlands Rd
Wingfield Family	unk	Shepard Property, Slaughter Pen Creek

CHESAPEAKE CITY

Butt Family	unk	Old Brooks Farm, St Julian Creek
Deer Crossing	unk	Adj to 2017 Coral Ivy Ln

Good Hope United Methodist	36.6302292,-76.2747487	1633 Benefit Rd
Halstead Family	unk	Pond Lake
Smith Family	36.6992300,-76.1187700	Mount Pleasant Farm, now Fentress Naval Auxiliary Airfield
Stewart Family	unk	Beechwood Plantation, Dismal Swamp Trail
Wilson Family	36.61178,-76.18304	701 Saunderson Rd, City Prison Farms, St Brides Correctional Center

CHESTERFIELD COUNTY

Andrews Family	37.2700200,-77.4665000	loc S of Matoaca Rd nr jct with Woodpecker rd, Matoaca
Bailey Family	37.3707500,-77.7763500	Matoaca
Bethel Baptist	37.5094783,-77.7113605	1100 Huguenot Springs Rd, Midlothian
Brooks Family	unk	North of Walmsley Blvd. Btw Angus and Shackleford roads
Clarke Family	37.2435400,-77.4465500	Ravensbourne Dr, Ettrick
Clay Family	unk	At his homeplace, check property records
Cobbs Family	unk	Bolling Family property, Enon
Duncan Family	unk	Roslyn Ave, 2 mi E of Town Hall, Chester
Farguson Family	37.3715674,-77.6286656	12951 Blue Stack Ct.
Fleming Family	unk	Midlothian
Franklin Family	unk	Twp 50
Gates Family	unk	Rt 614, .4 mi west on private road next to "Fairfield" Farm
Kabler Family	unk	Check property records for homeplace
Lockett Family	unk	Brandermill, cnr of Long Gate & Huntgate
Matoax, Randolph Family	unk	Matoaca
Robertson Farm	37.3673210,-77.6077860	Vic jct Robbie Rd & Christina Rd
Skinquarter Baptist	37.4074363,-77.7926483	6900 Moseley Rd, Moseley
Wooldridge Family	37.4965670,-77.6463470	loc by traffic circle in iron fence cem in the 13700 block of Grove Hill Rd, Midlotham

CLARKE COUNT

Anderson Family	39.8516000,-77.5235000	"Springfield Farm," Rt 608 nr Morgan Spring Run, Webbtown
Berryville Baptist	39.1535278,-77.9827649	114 Academy St, Berryville
Blakemore Family	39.1021600,-77.5924600	Byrd Farm vic Rt 7, Moreland
Blakemore Family	39.1724500,-77.9900800	Blakemore Ln, off Rt 7, Berryville
Butler Family	39.5368000,-78.6385000	Family farm in SE part of Co, named as Dearmont Farm by one source
Chandler Family	39.1121000,-78.0300000	Helvestine Farm, Rt 7 vic Rt 633
Frost	unk	Vic Hopewell
Grace Episcopal	39.1521289,-77.9795307	110 N Church St, Berryville
Green Hill	39.1581000,-77.9769000	Berryville
Greenway Court	unk	Nr Lord Fairfax, White Post
Helm Family	unk	loc original Helm property with cem sign, Berryville
Meade Memorial Episcopal	39.0580302,-78.1037656	192 White Post Rd, White Post
Muse-Lewis, "The Moorings"	unk	Lewis Farm nr WV
Old Buck Marsh Meeting House	39.9473000,-77.5837000	nr Barryville Meeting House
Old Chapel Episcopal	39.1067000,-78.0147000	Jct US 340 & Rt 255, Millwood
Stone Chapel Presbyterian	39.2261000,-78.0106000	Old Charles Town Rd, Berryville

COLONIAL HEIGHTS

Violet Bank Mansion	37.2418750,-77.4050850	305 VA Ave

COVINGTON CITY (See also Alleghany County)

Dameron Family	unk	20 mi W of Covington
Falling Springs Presbyterian	unk	115 Spring Church Rd
Mt Pleasant	unk	6 mi NE of Covington

Persinger Memorial	37.7178704,-80.0509819	3707 Llama Dr
Samuel Brown Family	unk	9 mi W of Covington
Walker Family	unk	Covington

CRAIG COUNTY

Allen Family	unk	Off Craig Creek, nr Oriskany
Hebron United Methodist	unk	Rt 606 jct Bobcat Ln
Leffel	37.4808000,-80.1397000	Off Cumberland Gap Rd, Meadow Creek
Miller	unk	Rt 42, Midway
Nutter Property	unk	Pott's Creek

CULPEPER COUNTY

Brown	unk	Rt 636 1 mi NW of Reva, 2 mi NW to gate
Catalpa Plantation	unk	His homeplace on mountain nr town, check property records
Coons Family	unk	vic Rixeyville Rt 640
Covington Family	unk	Reported nr Washington CH but that would place it in Rappahannock Co, not Culpeper. Not in findagrave. Check JLARC report
Crooked Run Baptist	38.3620305,-78.1080877	7351 James Madison Hwy, Rapidan
Culpeper National	38.469700,-77.991898	loc N of E Chandler St vic US Ave
Dawson Family	unk	Culpeper
Devils Run Farm	unk	Check tax records for location
Duncan	38.5906800,-77.9627700	Nr Oakshade
Fairview	38.4808000,-78.0047000	Sperryville Pike Rt 522, Culpeper
Farm	unk	Behind Culpeper & Racoon Ford
Fleetwood	unk	Fleetwood Ln off Rt 621, Jeffersonton
Ford Family	unk	Merrimac
Garnett Family	unk	Rt 648, 10 mi off Rt 15
Greenfield	unk	Rapidan
Hall Family	unk	Rt 658 vic Winston
Hudson Family	unk	Rt 721
Hume	unk	Nr Remington on James Madison St
Jones Family	unk	Crooked Run
Madden Family		23512 Madden's Tavern Rd, Elkwood
Masonic Cemetery	38.4839820,-77.9929353	950 N Main, Culpeper
Puller Family	unk	1 mi E of Amissville
Redwood Plantation	unk	Rt 522 N
Robson Farm	unk	Not identified, not in findagrave
Slaughter-Jones Family	38.4550000,-77.8413100	Stone's Mill Rd Rt 676, LaGrange
St Mark's, aka Little Fork Church	unk	See DAR Senate Doc 1956, serial 11999 vol 8
St Stephen's Episcopal	38.473444,-77.99380500	115 N East St, Culpeper
Stevensburg Baptist	unk	Stevensburg
Western View	38.4596930,-77.9360491	17434 Oldaker Ln
Wigginton	unk	Rt 29, Lakota
Yancey Family	38.5170900,-77.9553200	Off Rt 685 Auburn Rd, 3.5 mi WNW of Brandy Station

CUMBERLAND COUNTY

Allen Family	37.4307760,-78.2762810	On unnamed rd off Putney Rd 3 mi NW of jct with Norwood Ln, Allendale Farm
Bonbrook House	unk	7.5 mi N of Cumberland
Booker Family	unk	Rt 641 outside Cumberland CH
Boston Hill Plantation	unk	Cartersville
Burnt Chimney	unk	Cat Taile Branch
Clifton	37.4075200,-78.0757900	Off Rt 690 N of Hamilton
Cotton Town	unk	Holman Square
Deanery Family	unk	Cartersville on James River

High Hill	unk	Check property records for homeplace
James Anderson Fam	37.327850,-78.422020	loc E of Anderson Trail, Farmville
Moses Smith Place	37.4963900,-78.2448600	Jct Rt 60 and Stoney Point Rd
Olnorary	unk	Old quarry on Old Stage Rd fr CH. Behind Cumberland & Cartersville
Page Family, "The Fork"	unk	Check Source 101
Price Family	unk	Nr Cattail Branch & Willis River
Scruggs Family	unk	Head of Huddy Ck
Walker Family	unk	Farmville
Winniford Family	37.7165300,-78.1686100	Fork of Willis Baptist Ch, jct Rts 660 & 713

DANVILLE CITY (See also Pittsylvania County)

Clay Family	unk	Danville
Dan's Hill	unk	Danville at Wilson's ferry
Nicholas Perkins, 2nd Home	unk	S of Dan River, Danville
Robert Payne Plantation	unk	Dix Ferry Rd nr Dan River
Wall Family	39.1833500,-78.1626800	Vic Danville
Wilson	unk	Dans Hill

DICKENSON COUNTY

John Powers Plantation	unk	Hwy 83, Clintwood

DINWIDDIE COUNTY

Carraway	36.917198,-77.566399	loc S of Bolster's Rd, E of pond in field
Fleetwood Plantation	unk	6630 Brills Rd, McKenney
French Green(AKA Bourdon Fam	unk	24920 Cutback Rd, Mc Kenney
Goshen Family	unk	8 mi S of Petersburg and W of Old Stage Rd on the "Goshen" site
Mt Pleasant	unk	Rt 609
Old Saponey Church	36.9711000,-77.6361000	E of Rt 709 on Rt 692
Sweden Plantation	37.1585400,-77.5475100	Nr jct Claiborne & White Oak rds, Sutherland
Sydnor-Young Family	unk	Petersburg National Battlefield
The Grove	unk	Rt 662, 12 mi S of Dinwiddie

EMPORIA CITY (See also Greensville County)

Emporia Tree	unk	Emporia
Robinson Family	unk	Emporia

ESSEX COUNTY

Bathhurst Plantation	37.8897600,-76.8262800	Nr Dunnsville
Campbell Family	unk	Lot 44, Tappahannock
Cherry Walk	unk	Fenced cem, Millers Tavern
Dishman Family	unk	Pine Hill Hunt Club
Garnett Family	unk	Elmwood, Loretto
Pitts Farm	unk	Nr Slaydo
Ritchie Family	unk	Burial vault on lot 18 or 22, Tappahannock
St Paul's Episcopal	37.8292100,-76.9683600	7924 Richmond-Tappahannock Hwy, Millers Tavern
Vauter's Episcopal	unk	Rt 368 off Rt 17, Loretto

FAIRFAX COUNTY, FAIRFAX CITY, AND FALLS CHURCH CITY

Adams-Nelson-Sewell Family	unk	1443 Layman St, McLean
Addison Family	unk	Homeplace Oxen Hill on the Potomac River opposite Mt Vernon
Belle Vale	unk	Belle Vale Manor, Doeg's Run

Broadwater Family	38.8894000,-77.2610000	Cnr of Tapawingo Rd and Frederick St SW, Vienna
Cockburn Family	unk	"Springfield," Gunston Rd Rt 242, W of Gunston Hall, Mason Neck
Court House Plaque	38.8456280,-77.3072640	4110 Chain Bridge Rd
Cranford United Methodist Ch	38.6905630,-77.2064050	loc off Old Colchester Rd N of jct with Gunston Rd, Lorton
Dranesville United Methodist	39.0024000,-77.3508200	11720 Sugarland Rd, Dranesville
Dulaney Family	unk	See DAR Senate Doc 1956, serial 11999 vol 8
Fairfax City	38.8469000,-77.3133000	Main St & Page Ave, Fairfax
Falls Church Episcopal	38.8809604,-77.1710285	115 E Fairfax St, Falls Church
Flint Hill	38.8819000,-77.2939000	Chain Bridge Rd, Oakton
Frying Pan Meeting House	38.9399884,-77.4131556	2615 Centreville Rd, Herndon
Gary Family	unk	Centreville
Gunnell Family	39.0035946,-77.2848271	600 Innsbrook Ave, Great Falls
Gunston Hall	38.6686200,-77.1682300	Gunston Rd, Lorton
Haley/Halley Family	38.8407966,-77.3305355	4422 San Carlos Rd, Fairfax
Huntington	unk	3 mi fr Pohick Church
Hutchinson-Whaley	38.9015760,-77.4738496	Next to 4319 General Kearney Ct, Chantilly
Hutchison-Major	38.9056900,-77.4750800	Pleasant Valley Rd & Lafayette Center Dr, Chantilly
Lane Family	38.9065800,-77.3882200	12700 Franklin Farm Rd, Centreville
Laurel Hill	38.7096100,-77.2346400	Former Lorton Reformatory grounds, Lorton
Level Green Farm	unk	6275 Old Centerville Rd, Chantilly
Lindsay Family	38.7095800,-77.2376700	Off Lorton Rd nr Laurel Golf Club, Lorton
Millan-Potter Family	38.7455740,-77.1477800	7925 Telegraph Rd
Moore-Hunter Family	38.8853409,-77.2713120	1001 Tapawingo Rd SW, Vienna
Mt Air	38.7334000,-77.1753300	Newington Rd, Newington
Mt Vernon	38.4228000,-77.0509000	Mt Vernon Estate
Oakwood	unk	N Roosevelt St, Falls Church
Payne Family	unk	Chesterbrook
Pleasant Green Farm, Popes Head Run	unk	Nr Occoquan
Pohick Episcopal	38.7089868,-77.1939408	9301 Richmond Hwy, Lorton
Scott Family	unk	Across fr 15000 Conference Center Dr, Washington Technology Park, Chantilly
Sommers Family	38.8809604,-77.1710285	115 E Fairfax St, Falls Church
St John's Episcopal	38.8417251,-77.4263147	5649 Mt Gilead Rd
Sully Plantation	unk	Sully Rd Rt 28, adj Dulles National Airport, Chantilly
Summers	38.8212100,-77.1409800	Jct Rt 613 & Beaugard St, Lincolnia
Summers Family	38.4915000,-77.0828000	Lincolnia, nr Deming Avenue and Rt 613
The Mount	38.8963078,-77.2034413	2312 Col Lindsey Ct, Falls Church
Thompson Family	38.8720100,-77.2617800	Vic jct Rt 29 & Nutley St
Triplett Family	38.7424600,-77.1431800	On grounds of Humphrey's Engineer Center at John J. Kingman Rd nr the gate to the Army Geospatial Center at Fort Belvoir
Truro Parish	unk	"On the middle ridge near Ox Road", the present site of Jerusalem Baptist Church off Rt 123
Walnut Tree Farm	unk	Btw Vienna & Oakton
Watters-Adams Family	38.9253830,-77.1633211	6444 Linway Terr, McLean
Wickliff Family	38.4624300,-77.2440900	Behind 13220 Yates Ford Rd, Clifton
Wren Family	unk	Hillsman Dr and Mahala Ln, Falls Church

FAUQUIER COUNTY

Ash-Blackmore	unk	Delaplane

Ashby Family, Belmont	unk	Greenland Farm, nr Rt 724, Delaplane
Ball-Shumate	38.6638200,-77.7985100	On a knoll W & slightly S of Rts 15, 29, & 17 where it crosses Licking Run Stream
Blackwell Family	unk	The Meadows, E of Rt 628 at the first farm past Bethel United Methodist Church
Bronough Family	unk	Blue Ridge
Burke-Shaw	unk	Rt 688
Campbell, also Roy Neff Farm	38.4697000,-77.9919000	N of Jeffersonville on Rt 45 on left
Chunn Family	unk	Behind Mt Independence on Rt 17, N of Delaplane
Clascock, "Glenmore"	unk	Rectortown
Clermont	unk	Warrenton
Combs Family	unk	Hopewell
Cool Spring Church	unk	.5 mi S of Delaplane
Courtney Family	unk	Hartwood Airfield
Dermonte Burying Ground	unk	Liberty
Diggs Family	unk	Cliff Mill
Eastman Family	unk	Jct Rts 17 & 660
Edmonds Family	unk	Warrenton
George Family	unk	Catlett
Germantown Glebe	unk	Rt 643 nr Licking Run, Midland
Glasscock Family Farm	unk	Nr Marshall
Globe Farm	unk	Nr The Plains
Gordonsdale	unk	The Plains
Grove Baptist Church	36.6375000,-79.2492400	NW edge of Goldvein
Hawkins Family	38.7736700,-77.6235900	Buckland Farm, 6342 Pleasant Colony Ln, Warrenton
Hitt Family	38.7214070,-78.0049890	7535 Tapps Ford Rd, Amissvile
James Family	unk	Midland
Jennings-Foster Family	38.5644890,-77.8544826	11446 Freemans Ford, Remington
Kemper Family	unk	Rt 802 Nr Warrenton
Kenner	unk	Rt 616, Somerville
Kenner Family	38.5344610,-77.6153285	2452 Kenner Ln, Midland
Lewis Family	unk	Little Georgetown
Linn Family Farm	unk	Morgantown
Love Family	38.4395000,-77.4026600	Buckland Farm, 6342 Pleasant Colony Ln, Warrenton
Marshall	38.8691900,-77.8344500	Marshall
Moffett	unk	Nr Marshall
Morgantown	unk	Morgantown
Moss Meeting House	unk	N fr Upperville
Mt Eccentric	unk	2 mi S of The Plains
Oak Springs	38.7324274,-77.7961166	770 Fletcher Dr, Warrenton
O'Bannon	unk	Warrenton
Obannon-Lawrence	unk	Marshall
Orlean	unk	Nr Orlean
Paris Community	unk	Paris
Payne Farm, Clifton Farm	unk	5 mi NW of Warrentown
Pine View Estate Family Cem	38.3600, -77.4618	nr unincorporated town of Liberty
Randolph Family, Eastern View	unk	Nr Casanova
Rockburn	unk	Rockburn Farm, 224 Crenshaw Rd, Rectortown
Rockburn (Rachburn)	unk	Nr Warrenton
Rockspring	unk	Check property records
Rowles Family	unk	Markham
Rust Family	38.52878, -77.04540	Rt 619, Upperville
Sherman-Hicks Family, aka Liberty Farm	unk	Paris

Smith Family	unk	Rt 688, Orlean
The Hatherage	unk	Warrenton
Thompson-Ford Family	unk	Green Branch Farm
Tulloss Family	unk	Somerville
Turner Family	unk	Delaplane
Waite Family	38.42539, -77.11615	Bristerburg
Warrenton	38.7126236, -77.8000336	110 West Lee St., Warrenton
Whitewood	unk	2 mi N of The Plains
Winn Family	unk	Probably at Rock Hill Rt 626 nr Halfway
Withers-Nelson family	unk	9337 James Madison Hwy
Wright-James	38.504946,-77.760893	6200 Liberty Rd, Bealton

FLOYD COUNTY

Eastview	unk	Rome
Goodson Family	unk	Pine Creek, near Turtle Rock
Goodykoontz	unk	Rt 729
Hungate Family	unk	Rt 615 nr Little River
King	unk	Nr MM 141 on Blue Ridge Pkwy
Pine Creek Primitive Baptist	36.9462200,-80.2735700	Spangler Mill Rd Rt 682
Red Oak Grove	36.9818400,-80.2863900	Off Red Oak Grove Rd Rt 684
Salem Cemetery	37.0501400,-80.1600400	Rt 221, Head of the River Church
Smith Chapel	37.0387300, 80.2039300	Not identified
Sumpter	unk	Rt 619, Floyd
Wade-Cox	unk	Check property records
Wimmer King	unk	Copper Hill
Wright Family	36.9765800,-80.2169300	Pizarro off Rt 668
Zion Lutheran Church	37.1350700,-80.4166200	Rts 693 & 615, Wades Ln

FLUVANNA COUNTY

Adams	unk	Bybee
Allegre Tavern	37.9866060,-78.3152630	860 White Hall Rd, Keswick
Ashlin Family	unk	End Rt 606
Baskett Family;	unk	loc Rt 631(Dogwood Drive) across East Fork Kent Branch stream on logging rd on top of knoll 400 ft fr rd , Wilmington
Beaver Dam Baptist	37.9837700,-78.2917900	Richmond Rd, Paynes Mill
Bybee Family	unk	Nr Rt 633, Troy Neighborhood
Cary Family	unk	Carysbrook
Duncan Family	unk	Nr Hardware River
Eastin Family	unk	Rt 601
Fluvanna Heritage Trail	37.8597200,-78.2691600	End of Trailhead Dr, Palmyra
Fork Union Military Academy	unk	4744 James Madison Hwy, Fork Union
Gillespie Family(Hasher Farm)	37.9462000,-78.2528000	loc S of N Boston Rd nr jct w Troy Rd; Troy
Haden Family	unk	loc Elk Run Branch on land of John Haden 1759, gifted to Joseph Aug 1777 (see property rec for specific loc)
James Mayo Plantation	ubk	loc Haislip Ln, Cunningham
Lyles Church	37.8479300,-78.2033700	Palmyra
Norcross-Parrish	37.8743780,-78.3366830	4514 Ruritan Lake Rd, Cunningham
Oak Hill	37.7069000,-78.2536000	Rt 655 n
Old Jones Place	unk	Rt 600 nr Troy
Omohundro Family	unk	400 yds E of Rt 15, 1 mi S of Fork Union
Parrish Family	unk	Vic Rts 619 & 660
Perkins family	unk	Vic Rts 600 & 633
Ross Family	unk	Vic Rts 600 & 633
Shepherd family	37.8970590,-78.1106830	Laughton Ln vic Rts 623 & 659 Kents store
Shores & Tutwiler Families	37.7464100,-78.3825900	Seven Islands
Tomkins Family	unk	loc on patriots land in 1811

Unmarked Grave	unk	Overlooking Hardware River N of Rt 6.
Watson Family	unk	Vic Rts 678 & 625
Winnsville	37.3648699,-78.2924215	Rts 612 and 671, Fork Union
Wood family	unk	Vic jct Rts 659 & 610
Woods Family	unk	.5 mi S of Mechum River

FRANKLIN CITY (See also Southampton County)

Rochelle Family, Hermitage Plantation	unk	Hwy 671, nr Hansom

FRANKLIN COUNTY

Abshire	unk	Boones Mill
Angle Family	37.0694000,-79.8631000	Rt 699
Booth Family	unk	Rt 666 nr Smith Mountain Lake
Cook Family	unk	Rt 630 nr Rt 890, nr Sago
Cooper Family	unk	Snow Creek
Dillon Family	unk	Rt 900
Elsie Jones	unk	Nr Endicott Assembly of God Ch, Rt 793
English Family	unk	Kemps Mill
Graghead Family	unk	Rt 1361 nr Radford
Greer Family	unk	.5 mi W of Rts 812 & 919
Hatcher Family	unk	Scruggs
Holland Family	unk	Rt 616 nr HancockCem
Hook Family	unk	Rt 122 nr US Cellular
John Fisher Farm	37.0364000,-79.7247000	Rt 669
John Via Family	36.8876339, -80.1672758	loc vic Endicott
Joseph Shores Price Family	unk	Rt 817 or Dillions Mill
Mark Perdue Farm,	unk	Rt 672 vic Foxfire Nursery Crossroads Burnt Chimney
McNeil Family	unk	Rt 220 N, .1 mi E of MM 25, nr RR tracks
Mt Ivy	unk	Scruggs
Overfelt	37.0737700,-79.9478500	Grassy Hill Rd, Helm
Pearson Memorial Park	36.8400000,-79.9503000	S off Henry Rd Rt 605
Pigg River Primitive Baptist	36.9691300,-80.0736800	Rt 750 nr Callaway
Poindexter Family	37.0320564,-79.7598965	Jct Rts 655 & 834
Prillaman	37.0108000,-80.0608000	Foothills Rd Rt 642 W of Highland United Methodist, Callaway
Prillman-Turner	unk	Btw Ferrun & Philpott Res
Private	unk	Nr Glade Hill
Ramsey Family	unk	Penhook
Ramsey-Stanley	unk	Rt 764 nr Rt 606
Richards Family	unk	2.5 mi SW of Callaway off Foothills Rd
Stephen Sink Family	37.0809200,-79.7928600	Rt 670 behind house at 956 Three Oaks Rd
Tanyard-Barnard-Hill	unk	Rocky Mount
Ward Feazell	unk	Ferrum
Wingfield Family	36.8483800,-79.7848200	Off Bonfield Dr Rt 890
Witcher Family	36.5704700,-79.3579800	Penhook
Woody Family	unk	Plantation Rd, Rocky Mount
Wray Family	37.6560000,-79.5714000	Boones Mill, Rt 607, 10 mi S Rocky Mount

FREDERICK COUNTY (See also Winchester City)

Back Creek Quaker, aka Gainesboro United Methodist	39.2786100, -78.2569400	166 Siler Ln, Gainesboro
Baker Tomb	unk	Albin
Beeler	unk	Cedar Creek
Bethel Church	unk	Rt 610
Bucher	unk	Mountain Falls

Burnt Factory United Methodist	38,1849000,-78.0755000	1943 Jordan Springs Rd Rt 664, Burnt Factory
Buckton Graveyard	unk	Not identified
Castleman's Farm	unk	Berryville
Capper Family	unk	fence of cem loc on WVA line, Rock Even Springs, High View:
Cooper Family	unk	W side of Back Mtn Rd, 1 mi N of Mountain Falls
Emmanuel United Methodist Ch	39.2335990,-78.1136020	loc vic jct Milburn Rd & McCanns Rd, Stephenson
George Hott	unk	Rt 654 fr Nain 7 mi to Pleasant Valley Church, on right on top of hill
German Reformed Church	39.0815000,-78.2184000	Mulberry St, Stephens City
Hedges Farm	unk	Edward Hedges farm, 1856, loc nr Timber Ridge Baptist Ch and Old Collin's PO; Cross Jct
Hite Family	unk	Middletown
Hockmans	unk	Vic Lebanon Church
Hollingsworth-Parkins	39.1660000,-78.1749000	W Jubal Early Dr
Jones Family	unk	Vanchese
Little Mountain United Methodist	39.2728000,-78.1891000	259 Little Mountain Ch Rd, Cedar Grove
Lockhart-Phillips	39.2641260,-78.3296420	loc to the W of Sinking Spring Lane at jct with Gore Rd, Gore
Long-Stephens	unk	Stephens City
Milburn Chapel	39.2236000,-78.1136000	Milburn Rd Rt 622, Stephenson
Mountain View Methodist	39.1141000,-78.4092000	Richards Ln, Mountain Falls
Mt Carmel	39.0317000,-78.2872000	3rd & Commerce St, Middletown
Mt Hebron	39.1817000,-78.1572000	305 E Boscawen St, Winchester
Mt Olive	39.2261000,-78.7200000	327 Mt Olive Rd, Hayfield
Mt Pleasant Meeting House	39.1208000,-78.3044000	Rt 622, Mt Pleasant
Old Cemetery	unk	lots 76 & 77, Town of Stephensburg
Old Hite Farm	unk	Long-Meadows, Middletown
Old Methodist Church	39.0862000,-78.2167000	5291 Main St, Stephens City
Old Opequon Church	39.8223700,-78.1141200	217 Opequon Church Ln, Kernstown
Old Stone Church	39.3011000,-78.1675000	Nr 461 Green Spring Rd, Green Spring
Pangle Fam	unk	Middletown
Pughtown	unk	Gainesboro
Pritchard Family	39.145290,-78.196410	loc 150 yds W of Kerrnstown Ct in field; Kernstown
Robinson-Sidebottoms-Hawkins	unk	Nr Round Hill
Smith	unk	loc just off Knobb Rd nr Gore
St John's Lutheran	39.1531000,-78.3652000	3623 Buck Mountain Rd, Hayfield
Stephens City United Methodist	39.0862000,-78.2167000	5291 Main St, Stephens City
Strother-Jones	unk	Stephens City
Trinity Evangelical Lutheran	39.0828000,-78.2167900	Mulberry St Stephens City
Upper Ridge	unk	Rt 739
Walnut Grove Plantation	unk	White Post
White Family	unk	Rt 615
White Post, aka Wheeler Family	39.7117000,-78.5419000	Nr White Post, nr Clarke-Frederick co line, Dearfield Farm
Wood Family	unk	Glen Burnie nr Winchester
Woodville Estate	unk	Winchester

FREDERICKSBURG CITY (See also Spotsylvania County)

City Cemetery	38.3011200,-77.4662800	1000 Washington Ave
Holladay Family	unk	Bellefont House
Kenmore Plantation	unk	1500 Washington Ave
Masonic Cemetery	38.3019800,-77.4614200	900 Charles St

St George's Episcopal	38.3026780,-77.4598590	905 Princess Anne
Fredericksburg Natl Military Park	unk	Willis Hill, Marye Heights
Thornton/Forbes/Washington	38.314274,-77.468399	loc vic jct Hunter St & Princess Anne St

GILES COUNTY

Birchlawn Burial Park	39.3261000,-80.7108000	Wenonah Ave Rt 460, Pearisburg
Boyd, Wolf Creek	unk	Wolf Creek Rd nr Narrows
Cloverhollow	37.3347000,-80.4758000	Rt 715 Deerfield Ln before first sharp turn
Doe Mountain Farm	unk	Nr Pembroke
French (possibly same as Boyd)	unk	Wolf Creek nr Curve
Hale Farm	unk	Wolf Creek nr Narrows
Hare Family	unk	Narrows
Horseshoe	unk	Pembroke
Indian Bottom Farm	unk	Walkers Creek District Twp
Kirk Burial Grounds	unk	Chapman-Straley Farm Rt 730, nr Eggleston Springs
Lybrook Family	37.3338500,-80.6108700	End Rt 65, Pembroke
Mt Prospect	unk	Rt 634, Old Strother Farm, Ripplemeade
Newport	unk	Newport
Old Hoges Chapel	unk	Mount Lake Rd
Pearis Family	unk	Bluff City
Peterstown	37.3947000,-80.8014000	Off Rt 219 btw Peterstown & Midway, on WV state line
Phlegar Farm	unk	Rt 626, Ripplemead
Private Grave	unk	Nr Celanese, Pearisburg
Shannon-King	37.2181000,-80.7417000	Nr Jct Rts 42 & 100, Poplar Hill nr Walker's Creek
Sifford	unk	White Gate
Snidow Farm, "Sugar Maple"	unk	Rt 460 on Lilly Hill, Pembroke
Staffville	unk	Hillsville
Sugar Run, Farmer Family	unk	Staffordsville
Sunrise Memorial Gardens	unk	Rich Creek
Toney Family	unk	Glen Lyn

GLOUCESTER COUNTY

Abingdon Episcopal	37.3335500,-76.5136400	4645 George Washington Mem Hwy Rt 17
Bellamy Methodist Church	37.4014900,-76.5888300	4870 Chestut Fork Rd
Colonial Era Farm Memorial	37.5299450,-76.6276020	loc on Waste Mgt Memorial Hwy, nr jct with G W Memorial Hwy, Owl Trap
Fairfield Family	unk	Wicomico
First United Baptist Church	37.3713300,-76.5344900	6188 George Washington Mem Hwy Rt 17
Highgate	unk	Cash Post Office
Marlfield Plantation	37.4492800,-76.6223900	Rt 610 at 3780 Pebble Ln, Marlfield
Page Family	37.3279010,-76.5762140	loc at the end of Rosewell Plantation Rd (Rt 644) on right in tree area
Petsworth Parish Epis Ch	unk	loc by original church foundation; Popular Spring
Robins Family	unk	Robin's Neck
Sinclair, "Sherwood"	37.0837000,-78.1167200	Selden Post Office
Toddbury Plantation	unk	Elmington, on North River
Union Baptist	37.2788200,-76.4433100	9524 Guinea Rd, Achilles
Ware Episcopal	37.4227500,-76.5078900	7825 John Clayton Mem Hwy
Warner Hall	37.2040300,-76.2853900	4750 Warner Hall Rd

GOOCHLAND COUNTY

Ben Glade	unk	Rock Castle
Ben Lomond	unk	Rt 627 off Rt 600
Boscobel	unk	Vic Rt 621 Manakin

Fairfield	unk	5.5 mi W of Goochland Rt 6 to Rt 614 .4 mi
Friendship Rest	unk	Rt 623
Grace Episcopal	37.6832100,-77.8876500	2955 River Rd West, Goochland CH
Holman Family	37.7202060,-78.0548890	E of jct Cartersville Rd & Woody Ln at 5255 Bear Ct. Georges Tavern
Johnson Family	unk	Rt 658
Johnson Family # 4	unk	4124 Pace Rd, loc right front of dwelling, Hadensville
Lacy Family	37.8057100,-77.9940500	Rt 615
Mims Family	unk	Manakin
Moore Family	unk	Cardwell Rd
Mullins	unk	Nr Fife
Payne Family	37.8478000,-78.0719000	Rt 681 S of Rt 605 Payne Rd, Goochland
Payne Family, Hickory Hill	37.8288040,-78.0480050	Rts 609 & 603, Goochland
Proffitt Family	unk	loc on property of Sylvester Proffitt, Goochland
Rocky Spring Leake	37.7058151,-77.9465564	Jct Rts 6 & 600
The Oaks	unk	1.4 mi SE of Tapscott on Rt 603
Tuckahoe Plantation	37.5699764,-77.6527703	12601 River Rd Rt 650, W of Richmond near Manakin
Webber Family	unk	W Rt 6 fr Richmond 9.2 mi, right on Rt 621 3.5 mi
Woodlawn	37.6854905,-77.7387483	Jct Rts 250 & 612

GRAYSON COUNTY

Anderson-Hash	36.6659300,-81.3311000	Flatridge & Old Bridle Creek Rd
Benjamin-Phipps	unk	Saddle Creek Rt 681
Brown-Osborne	unk	1168 White Pine Rd
Comer	unk	Rt 662, Elk Creek
Cornett Family	36.7240100,-81.2388900	Rt 662
Cox Family Farm	unk	Rt 629 W of Baywood
Crossroads Primitive Baptist	36.6086800,-81.0159200	Nr Baywood Elem Sch, Rt 624, Baywood
Fielder Family (AKA Knob Fork)	36.7433400,-81.1011890	loc on right side of Spring Valley Rd, 4.5 mi past jct with Jerusalem Rd, 100 ft W of brick ranch house; Fallvile
Hale Family	unk	Nr Elk Creek
Jackson Family	unk	Rt 658, along Bear Creek
Mark Johnes Family	unk	loc vic Elk Creek, Grayson
Murphy Family	36.5922000,-80.9380000	Rt 607
Nuckolls Family	36.6355100,-80.9594400	Beyond the end of Wild Turkey Ln, jct US 58 & Rt 94
Osborn-Cox	unk	Rt 711, Independence
Phipps Family	unk	Saddle Creek
Reedy	39.1359400,-78.0063000	Reedy Groves, Grossy Creek
Reeves Farm	unk	Rt 700, SE of Independence
Rudy	unk	Rt 660 near Elk Creek, Independence
Samuel Byrd Family	unk	Old Colonial Rd
Sauger	unk	Elk Creek
Sawyers-Elk Creek Community	unk	Hwy 668, Independence
Silas Ward Family	unk	Bridle Creek
Stone Family	unk	Elk Creek
Vaughan Family	36.4420000,-81.4166000	Fries, Spring Valley Community
Weiss Family	unk	Rt 637 or 736, Independence
Young Family	unk	Nr jct Rts 711 & 680

GREENE COUNTY

Beadles Family	unk	Btw Green Acres Rd & N side of Green Acres Lake, Greene Hills

Burton Graveyard	38.1624000,-78.2057000	NE cnr of Rt 29 N and Rt 609 E
Locust Grove	unk	From Rt 623 take 641 .4 mi to Locust Grove farm rd, .35 mi
Mill's Family	unk	Standardsville
Thornton	unk	Haney property, E side of Rt 619, btw South River Bridge & Dundee Graveyard
Unidentified	unk	South/left side Rt 648 after crossing Buffalo River fr Rt 604

GREENSVILLE COUNTY (See also Emporia City)

Grigg Family	unk	Jarratt
Ivey Family	unk	Rt 611 5.5 mi W of Emporia
Peebles Family	unk	Brink

HALIFAX COUNTY

Adams Family	unk	Check property records
Barksdale Family	unk	End of Rt 689 at Depot, Cedar View, South Boston
Betts Family, Snow Hill	36.3546500,-78.5731100	2091 Snow Hill Rd, Cluster Springs
Brooks Private	unk	Rt 681 West of Halifax, Cluster Springs
Carrington Family	unk	Bruce Estate "Berry Hill" W of South Boston, off Rt 659, on the "River Rd" E of the house
Clark Family	unk	Bannister Lodge
Clark Plantation	unk	Strawberry Br
Clarkton	unk	Rt 632, Clarkton
Cole Family	unk	Off Rt 672, NW of Asbury Church nr Halifax
Coles-Carrington	unk	Mildendo Plantation
Cross Road Baptist	36.6269000,-79.0478000	1098 Flint Rock Rd, South Boston
Davenport Family	unk	Nr jct Rts 360 & 344, Scottsburg
Faulkner Family	unk	Nr Cherry Hill, 1 mi W of Hyco, nr Omega
Ferrell Family	unk	Cherry Hill, W of Halifax
Fitzpatrick Family	unk	Nathalie
Halifax Memorial War Monument	unk	Loc jct Mountain Rd & Rt 501, Halifax
Keatts Family	unk	Nr Mulberry Baptist Church, nr Pittsylvania
Kent Family	unk	Poplar Creek
Logan Family	unk	Off Rt 672, NE jct with Rt 666, .4 mi on private Rd
Lovelace Family	unk	Off Rt 676, W of Asbury Church
Oak Hill	unk	South Boston
Oak Ridge	36.7191200,-78.9032100	Main St & Hamilton St, South Boston
Old Wood Family	36.5000000,-79.4652000	Rodgers Chapel Rd btw Rts 605 & 608, Clover
Ragland Family	unk	Check property records and DAR Senate doc 93, vol 54
Scott Home Site	unk	Off Rt 724, NW fr Scottsburg
St John's Episcopal	36.7671555,-78.9324263	197 Mountain Rd, Halifax
Stanfield Family, Boyd Farm	unk	Rt 658, 2 mi S of Turbeville
Terry Family	36.750630,-78.851800	1154 N Terry Rd, Halifax
Wallis Wilson Family	unk	By Rt 737, 4 mi fr Mecklenburg line
Watlington family	unk	Halifax town
Wyatt	unk	Rt 601, 3.6 mi S of South Boston

HAMPTON CITY

Herbert	39.0147500,-76.3501300	Off Armstrong Ln
Sherwood Cemetery	37.0738400,-76.3497300	Langley Air Force Base
St John's Episcopal	unk	100 W Queen's Way

HANOVER COUNTY

Airwell	unk	Rt 738
Aldingham	unk	Check property records
Anderson Family	unk	loc on his property "Laurel Branch" along Little River nr Caroline Co line
Beaver Dam	unk	Rt 738
Blackwell Family	unk	Spring Grove
Blenheim-Winston	unk	Rt 646, Hanover
Bowles Family	unk	Waterloo, Chickahominy Point
Brock Spring	unk	Old Telegraph Rd
Brown Family	unk	New Castle
Cherrydale	unk	Rt 667
Cedar Creek Quaker	unk	loc 3mi E of Cedar Grove Meeting House Montpelier
Chilton Family	unk	Montpelier
Dunham	unk	Rt 630 Cold Harbor
Dandridge/Underwood:	unk	Rockville
Fairfield	unk	Sledd Run Sub Div
Fork Episcopal	37.8534000,-77.5310000	12566 Old Ridge Rd, Doswell
Goldmine farm	unk	Rt 271, Rockville
Goodall's Tavern Property	unk	.75 mi W of jct Rts 623 & 33
Green	unk	Greenlands Farm, abt 4 mi N Ashland
Grubbs Family, aka Spring Grove	37.4351000,-77.3652000	Spring Grove #2 Farm, nr Calvary Christian jct Rts 623 & 624
Jones Family	unk	Rt 742 Nicholas St
Longrow	unk	Rt 658
Marl Ridge	unk	Rt 54, Ashland
Mills Family	unk	Loc on land owned by his son, Francis Mills called "Mills Order,"adjacent to land of John Fontaine on Matrimony Creek
Morris at Taylor's Creek	unk	Bethany Ch Rd
Nelson Fam at Wingfield	unk	Coatesville
Pleasant Valley	unk	Mechanicsville
Retreat Farm	unk	Pamunkey River near old church
Signal Hill Memorial Park	37.7435980,-77.3578030	12360 Hanover Courthouse Rd
Snead Family	unk	Rt 624 nr Hylas, nr main road
Spring Grove	39.1091600,-78.0997000	Rockville
St Paul's Episcopal	37.7657000,-77.3712000	8050 St Paul's Rd, Hanover
Still House Spring	unk	Rt 669
Studley	37.4010000,-77.1727000	Studley Farm Rd, under tree in front yard of Mr. J.A. Francieni, Jr residence (as of 1978)
Syme	unk	Rts 6763 & 703 nr Rockville, Rocky Mills
Taylor Family	37.4085000,-76.2540500	VAQ 738 Old Ridge Rd
Turner Family	unk	Eastern View
Union Baptist	37.9466000,-77.6516000	16230 Union Church Rd, Beaverdam
Walnut Shade	unk	Walnut Shade Ln off Rt 54

HARRISONBURG CITY (See also Rockingham County)

Cooks Creek Presbyterian	38.4747200,-78.9299700	4222 Mt Clinton Pike
Frank Harman Place	unk	Rt 42 N
Miller Family	unk	Harrisonburg
Trissel's Mennonite	unk	Rt 752
Woodbine	38.4480300,-78.8624400	Jct Rt 33 & Reservoir St

HENRICO COUNTY

Afro-American, aka East End	37.5364000,-77.3864000	Bulheller Rd
Andrews Family	unk	Thomas Andrews Plantation, Appomattox River
Belleville Estate	unk	Check property records

Craddock Family	unk	Off Darbytown Rd 5.6 mi SE of Richmond
George Family	unk	Rt 60, Briel's Farm Rd 9.7 mi E of Richmond
Glendale/Frayser Farm Family	unk	Rt 5, 11 mi SE of Richmond
Old Holman Family	unk	Holman Plantation, Windsor
Rural	unk	Check property records for plantation
Smith family	unk	1 mi W of Skipwith Rd, 1.5 mi N of Three Chopt Rd

HENRY COUNTY (See also Martinsville City)

Anglin Plantation	unk	Nr Patrick Co line
Barksdale Family	unk	Camden Parish
Blackberry Creek Private	unk	Bassett
Cox Family	unk	Cox, nr Turkey Pen Branch & Smith River
DeShazo	unk	Leatherwood
Dyer Family	36.4526100,-79.4812500	Foxpipe Rd, Leatherwood
Font Hill	unk	Leatherwood Creek, Irisburg
Franklin Family	36.7159700,-79.9429900	Off US 57 btw Shadyview Rd Rt 1404 & US 220 Bypass, behind "Old Franklin Home Place," nr community of Fieldale
Grassy Creek	36.6471600,-79.9194300	Nr Horsepasture, Rt 829, Drakes Branch
Hairston Family	unk	SR 208, Beaver Creek, N of Martinsville
King	unk	Leatherwood
Leatherwood Plantation	36.4453400,-79.4558000	Nr Martinsville
Martin Family	unk	Leatherwood Downs
Mayo Baptist Church	36.5719511,-80.0257648	85 Penn Store Rd, Spencer
Moses Martin	unk	Bassett
Nance Plantation Home	unk	Rt 58 2 mi E of Martinsville
Oakwood	36.6870544,-79.8881364	107 Cemetery St., Martinsville
Old Hickey-Martin	36.8171910,-79.9750690	loc E of original Henry Rd, Oak Level
Pace Family	unk	Pace Airport Rd abt .5 mi past airport, Ridgeway
Ragland Family	unk	McDonough
Redd	unk	Fontaine
Shadrack Turner	unk	Henry Rd. Butram Town Creek, Henry
Simpson Family	unk	Family homeplace, check property records
Single burial	unk	Off Rt 758, 100 yards off Price Rd, nr Horsepasture, Donnybrook Rd, Ridgeway
Taylor	unk	George Taylor Hwy
Watkins	unk	Axton

HIGHLAND COUNTY

Arbogast Family	unk	Wimer Mountain Rd, Blue Grass
Armstrong Family	unk	N of McDowell
Armstrong Family	unk	Stonewall District
Clover Creek Church	unk	Clover Creek Rt 678 S of McDowell, 7.7 mi, right side
Doe Hill	38.2597600,-79.2662900	Rt 654, across from Doe Hill Methodist
Gilmore Family	unk	In woods in back of Briscoe's Grocery Store Rt 84, Mill Gap
Gum Family	unk	Mill Gap
Gum Family, aka Walker Wilfong Family	unk	Hightown
Heyde	unk	Rt 644, Blue Grass
Hull Family	unk	Rt 640 to Rt 637, .9 mi to Elmer Ruckman farm
Jones Family	unk	Farm of Clay Botkins, left fr US 250 on Rt 614 traveling fr McDowell

Ruckman	unk	Little Egypt Rd, US 220 fr Mill Gap to Rt 604, turn left, 2 to 3 miles grave on right
Rymer Family	unk	Rt 624 N fr McDowell. Left through wooden gate to pasture, up over ridge and slightly to right side of mountain.
Seybert Chapel	unk	Nr jct Rt 629 Strait Creek & Rt 631, Monterey
Seybert Hills Farm	unk	US 200 N fr Monterery to Rt 629, 1.8 mi
Shinaberry	unk	3 mi N Hightown, Crabbottom
Stony Run	38.2292000,-79.7003000	US Rt 220, N of jct with 607
Unidentified	37.9615100,-79.7100000	Nr Doe Hill

ISLE OF WIGHT COUNTY

Benns United Methodist	36.5617000,-76.3510000	1457 Benns Church Blvd, Smithfield
Parker Family	36.5856900,-76.3213600	3.5 mi E of Rescue, Macclesfield
St Luke's Church	36.9394000,-76.5867000	14477 Benns Church Blvd, Smithfield
Wrenn's Cemetery	unk	Rt 10, 5 mi N of Smithfield

JAMES CITY COUNTY

Jones-Nunn Family	37.2124600,-76.4729000	Farmville Ln, Norge

KING AND QUEEN COUNTY

Bird-Boyd-Todd Family	unk	Popular Grove Plantation, Stevensville
Bunker Hill	unk	Stevensville
Campbell Family	unk	loc1/3 mi S Bruington Comm College
Collins Family	unk	Check property tax records
Cooke Family	unk	Check property tax records
Dewsville plantation	unk	Newtown
Fauntleroy Family, Farmers Mount Plantation	unk	Whitehall
Fleet Family	unk	Newtown
Goshen	unk	Check property records and Senate Doc 1952, serial 11670 vol 3
Lyne Family	unk	Check property records
Mattaponi Baptist	unk	Vic King & Queen CH
Mattaponi Church	unk	Nr Cumnor
North Bank Plantation	unk	North Bank Plantation , Newtown
Society Hill	unk	Stevensville
Young Family	unk	Walkerton

KING GEORGE COUNTY

Alexander Family	38.3372970,-77.1329490	12181 Caledon Rd on Cedar Grove farm
Braxton Estate	unk	Chericoke
Davis Family	unk	Edgehill
Dishman Family, Pine Hill	unk	Off Rt 621, Shiloh
Eagle's Nest	unk	Rt 218 E to Rt 242 N to Rt 682
Emmanuel Episcopal	unk	US 301, Port Conway
Mt Mariah Plantation	unk	Rt 619, 10 mi NE of King George
Saunders Family	unk	Check property records
St Paul's Episcopal	38.3320000,-77.1250000	5486 St Paul's Rd off Rt 206
Stuart-Grymes Family	38.3360100,-77.1340700	Rt 218 on Cedar Grove Farm
Unidentified, Private	unk	Edgehill
Washingon Family	unk	Potomac View
Willow Hill	unk	Jct Kennedy Dr and Van Buren Dr, Presidential Lake subdiv

KING WILLIAM COUNTY

Burlington Plantation:	37.8457530,-77.1437940	loc off West River Rd, 1 mi S of Smokey Rd.
Cherry Grove Farm	unk	loc vic servants quarters still standing on the farm, Rt 30, nr Aylett
Claiborne Family	unk	Sweet Hall, Rocky Mount
Edwards Family	unk	Cherry Grove
Elsing Green Plantation	37.6160800,-77.0407300	Off Mt Olive Cohoke Rd Rt 632
Fairfield Plantation	37.7606970,-77.1027050	Aylett
Ferry Farm	37.7657350,-77.3285970	loc off Etna Mills Rd just W of Norman's Bridge in field
Fleet Street, Plantation Grounds	37.7816600,-77.2535900	Rt 604 S of Webb Creek, Etna Mills, on Rt 4 1 mi fr Jct Rt 30
Forkquarter	unk	Calno Rd Rt 601, Norment Ferry
Huntington, aka Old Fox	unk	On Mattaponi River
Langborne Family	unk	At Langborne on bank of Pamunkey River
Retreat	unk	Aylett
Smyrna	unk	Off Rt 604 Damney's Mill Rd, SE of Corinth Fork
Springfield	unk	Abt 2 mi S of King William CH, on right side of Rt 621, leading fr Skyron to Palls
St. John's Episcopal	37.5318300,-77.4195800	24011 E Broad St., Richmond
Uppowac	unk	Rumford
Vermont Plantation	unk	W River Rd Rt 600, .5 mi E of Dorrel Rd Rt 628, River Hill

LANCASTER COUNTY

Chowning Ferry Farm	unk	Chownings Ferry Rd
Christ Church	37.6101900,-76.5460600	420 Christ Church Rd, Weems
Morrattico House	unk	Morattico
Old St John's Cemetery	37.6892000,-76.3853000	Off Rt 1066 Harris Rd abt .5 mi S of DMV Dr
St Mary's Whitechapel Episcopal	37.4478200,-76.3318100	5940 White Chapel Rd, Lively

LEE COUNTY

Ball Family	unk	Rt 684 vic Ewing
Benedict Yeary	unk	Nr Rocky Station Fort
Brooks	36.6116000,-83.4880000	Ewing on Kesterson Rd Rt 690, 3 mi fr town
Campbell-Hobbs	unk	Rt 682, vic Ewing
Clark-Jayne	unk	Jonesville
Clifton Neff Farm	unk	Ewing
Duff family	unk	3.2 mi E on Rt 612, fr jct Rts 58E and 421 E, Stickleyville
Ewing-McClure, aka Friendship Church	unk	Jonesville
Fritts Family	unk	Maybe adj to federal prison, check property records
Gibson Family	36.6058000,-88.6063000	Chandler Dr., Gibson Station
Hobbs family, aka Debusk Family	unk	Dryden
Jonathan Bales Family	unk	Rt 682 vic Ewing
Robert Clark, aka Thompson-Whitehead-Wilder	unk	Rt 612 7 mi SW of Jonesville
Russell Family	unk	Rt 58, Rose Hill
Slemp Memorial	unk	Turkey Cove
Tritt-Gilbert	unk	Rt 642, Woodway
Yeary Family	unk	W fr Ewing
Unidentified	unk	Rt 58, W of Jonesville

LEXINGTON CITY (See also Rockbridge County)

Hostetter Family	unk	Lexington
Lexington	unk	Lexington
Miller-Irwin	37.6511600,-79.5201400	Dry Well Rd Rt 813, on left at Charles Ln
New Monmouth Presbyterian	37.8396000,-79.4858600	2343 West Midland Rd
Old Monmouth Presbyterian	37.8081000,-79.4728000	Jct Rts 60 & 669
Oxford Presbyterian	37.7530200,-79.5602300	18 Churchview Ln, Lexington
Stonewall Jackson Memorial	37.7808300,-79.4450600	314 S Main St (AKA Oak Grove)
Washington & Lee Univ Campus	36.6086300,-81.0159300	Nr Jefferson St

LOUDOUN COUNTY

Arnold Grove Episcopal Church	39.1979600,-77.7155700	Rt 9, vic jct with Rt 690, Hillsboro
Ball Burial Ground	39.1440400,-77.5469000	Off Rt 15 nr N Spring Behavioral Healthcare
Benedum Family	unk	Leesburg
Campbell-Belt Estate	unk	Rock Hill, Leesburg
Carter Family	unk	Nr Middleburg
Catoctin Free Church	39.1627400,-77.6452700	Charlestown Pike Rt 9, Paeonian Springs
Ebenezer Baptist	39.0582400,-77.8414200	20421 Airmont Rd, Bluemont
Elgin Family	unk	Kingdom Farm, Evergreen Mill Rd, Sycolin, S of Leesburg
Ellzey Family	unk	Rt 621, Middleton
Fairfax Meeting House	39.1855700,-77.6058900	Water St & Waterford Rd, Waterford
Fox Family	unk	Waterford S on Hwy 62, Paeonian Springs
Goose Creek	39.1125000,-77.6952700	Rt 722, Lincoln
Hixon Family	unk	Check property records
Ketoctin Baptist	39.1574600,-77.7487000	Ketoctin Church Rd, Purcellville
Lane Family	unk	Leithtown
Leesburg Presbyterian	39.1161100,-77.5672200	207 W Market St, Leesburg
McIlhaney Family	unk	Nr Hillsboro E side Rt 690 btw Rts 90 & 611
McKim Family	unk	Arcola
McVeagh Family Plantation	unk	Not identified by JLARC
Mount Family	unk	Mountville off Rts 733 & 734
Mountain Chapel	unk	Jct Rts 734 & 630
New Jerusalem Lutheran	39.2573600,-77.6389100	12942 Lutheran Church Rd, Lovettsville
New Valley Baptist	39.2191800,-77.5474600	Bald Hill Rd Rt 673, Lucketts
Nixon Family	39.0906779,-77.6179692	19010 Woodburn Rd, Leesburg
North Fork Baptist	39.0601400,-77.6850900	38130 North Folk Rd, North Fork
Old Presbyterian	39.2734300,-77.6934100	Behind Primitive Baptist, S Church St, Lovettsville
Old Stone Methodist	39.1172500,-77.5660900	168 W Cornwall St, Leesburg
Petts Family	unk	Purcellville
Potts Family	39.1945500,-77.7615700	Rts 716 & 714, Hillsboro
Raspberry Plain	39.1593382,-77.5483367	16500 Agape Ln, Leesburg
Richard Carter Property	unk	Nr Leesburg
Rock Quarry, Goose Creek	unk	Mt Pleasant
Rokeby	unk	Nr Leesburg
Saunders Family	unk	Leithtown
Sharon	38.9692000,-77.7308000	loc vic jct E Federal and S Jay Sts., Middleburg
South Fork Meeting House	39.0264000,-77.8022000	Rt 630, Unison
St James Episcopal, Old Cemetery Lot	39.1155500,-77.5625000	Church St NE, Leesburg
St James Reformed	39.2702700,-77.6296800	Lovettsville Rd, Lovettsville
Union Cemetery	39.1204600,-77.5623900	323 N King St, Leesburg
Unison	unk	Unison
Upperville Methodist	unk	11134 Delaplane Grade Rd, Upperville
Waterford Union of Churches	39.1855700,-77.6080200	Fairfax St, Waterford

LOUISA COUNTY

Anderson	unk	Nr South Anna River, Rt 642
Anderson Family	unk	loc off Crewsville Rd (Rt 661) .2 mi S on private rd; Inez
Belle Isle	unk	Nr Frederick Hall
Bullock Family	unk	Rt 758, Walnut Hill
Clover Hill	unk	S Anna River, Rt 647
Dabney Family	unk	4.3 mi NE of Orchid
Duncan Family	unk	use property rec for exact loc nr So Anna River, Bumpass
Fox Family	37.8963270,-77.8601700	loc 3731 Gardner's Rd (Rt 648)
Gibson Farm	unk	Louisa
Goodwyn house cem	unk	Rt 16, 3.4 mi fr Louisa
Gunnell Family	unk	Buckner
Hermitage	unk	Cedar Hill Rd, Pendleton
Hillcrest (AKA Town of Lousia)	38.0335990,-78.0382990	loc jct Oak Leaf Dr & Louisa Rd
Isbell Family	37.8072100,-77.9078700	4675 E Grey Fox Circle Gum Springs
Jackson Family	unk	Catalpa Hall, Rt 522
Jerdone Castle	unk	4.4 mi NW of Buckner
Little River Baptist	unk	Bumpass
Mt Air/Pleasant View	unk	Overton Fork, Rt 723 Bohannon Rd nr Lake Anna
Nuckolls Family, (AKA Hamilton)	38.0569870,-77.8251210	8736 Kentucky Springs Rd;(Rt 652)
Roseneath	unk	Jackson District
Roundabout Castle	unk	3998 Yanceyville Rd
Spring Valley	unk	Cuckoo District
Terry Homestead	unk	Fredericksville Parish
Tolersville Tavern Burial Ground	38.0132100,-77.9034500	Rt 677 nr Mineral Baptist, Mineral
Thomasson	unk	loc on plantation at the beginning of Thomasson Court House Rd leading to court house
Valetta	unk	Nr Green Springs
Ware-Waller	38.0829040,-77.8562800	loc on New Bridge Rd halfway betw jcts with Cutalong Way and Kentucky Springs Rd
Whartons	unk	Christopher Run
Woodland	unk	Jackson District
Yancey-Crawford Family	unk	Yanceyville
Williams-Knight Family	unk	Vic jct Rt 623 & Eubanks Rd

LUNENBURG COUNTY

Boswell Family	unk	Off Rt 634, SE of Rebobeth
DeGrafenreidt Family	unk	Check property records
Hite Family	unk	Forksville
Taylor Family	unk	18 mi S of Kenbridge
Wilkes Family Farm	unk	loc abt 2 mi east of Victoria on a 500 acre tract of land in the south fork of Big Hounds Creek, Lunenburg

LYNCHBURG CITY (See also Campbell County)

Anglican Chapel	unk	Court Street
Chilton-Moorman	unk	Off Rt 221
Maj Samuel Scott Family	37.4133000,-79.2030400	2627 Old Forest Rd
McDaniel Family	unk	Boonesboro Rd
Old City	37.4147200,-79.1566700	401 Taylor St
Presbyterian Church	37.4020600,-79.1384800	2020 Grace St
Scott Family	37.4525000,-78.1889000	VES Rd
South River Meeting House, aka Quaker Memorial Presbyterian	37.3724600,-79.1919400	5810 Fort Ave

| Towles Family | unk | See DAR Senate Report 1954, serial 11831, vol 4 |

MADISON COUNTY

Cemetery	Coordinates	Location
Aylor Family	unk	.75 mi N of Novum Post Office
Carpenter Family	unk	on first patent land complied 1940, VA346
Ford Family	unk	Nr Leon
Fry Family	unk	Meander Plantation
Gaar Mountain	38.4337400,-78.2904800	Mulatto Run nr Beamer Hd Rd
Gaines Family	unk	Check tax map for location
Graves Family	unk	Check property records
Harrison Family	38.4337300,-78.2904800	Shelby
Hebron Lutheran	38.4067600,-78.2480800	899 Blankenbaker Rd, Madison
Hebron Valley	unk	Hebron Valley
Henry Aylor	38.4835080,-78.2035440	2012 Novum Rd., Novum
House Hollow Farm	unk	Slate Mills
Jillard-Weakley	unk	Rt 600 Syria
John Robertson Property	unk	Ruth
Lillard Family	unk	Nethers
Lillard Family	unk	Syria
Locust Dale	38.3451140,-78.1237920	vic jct Rts Oak Park Rd & James Madison Hwy, Madison
Lorenz Gaar Family	unk	Mulatto Run nr Beamer Hd Rd
McAllister Family	unk	Check property records near Syria
Mt Pisgah Church	38.3926500,-78.3039600	Rt 652 nr intersection of Ruth Rd
Nicholson Family	unk	Syria
Repton Family	unk	Vic Pratts Post Office
Rucker, Blakey, Hoffman, Rose	38.3474500,-78.3299700	Nr Wolftown
Tanner Family	unk	Hebron Valley
The "Hilton"	unk	vic Rt 15 Madison Mills
Tribble Family, Shirley Durbin Farm	unk	2 mi S jct Rts 25 & 75
Walker United Methodist	38.2932800,-78.1675600	Nr Bent Tree
Wilhoite Family	unk	Hebron Valley
Yowell Family	38.1942000,-78.4912000	Syria

MANASSAS CITY (See also Prince William County)

Cemetery	Coordinates	Location
Ball Family	38.8094500,-77.5089500	Manassas Battlefield, off Vandor Ln across fr Strayer University
Bethel Luthern	36.4685600,-77.3082300	8712 Plantation Ln
Cloverhill	unk	Hastings Dr
Hooe Family	38.8055500,-77.5345100	Chinn Ridge, Manassas National Battlefield Park
Lewis-Montgomery Families, Manassas Presbyterian	38.4685600,-77.3082300	8201 Ashton Ave
Mayfield Plantation	38.7529000,-77.3557100	Mayfield Park
Pittsylvania (Carter)	38.4971100,-77.3130500	Manassas National Battlefield Park
Stonewall Memory Gardens	38.8153000,-77.5517000	12004 Lee Hwy
Thurman Family	38.7581517,-77.4995621	Glen-Gery Brick Co, 9905 Godwin Dr

MARTINSVILLE CITY (See also Henry County)

Cemetery	Coordinates	Location
Oakwood	36.3869000,-79.8800000	199 Cemetery St

MATHEWS COUNTY

Cemetery	Coordinates	Location
Foster	unk	Check property records
James Family	37.3583500,-76.3316600	End of Bar Neck Rd, Susan
Old Billups	unk	Rt 643, Moon
Page Home	unk	North portion of Co
Poplar Grove Plantation	37.3994440,-76.3330550	265 Poplar Grove Ln, Williams;

Richard Foster	unk	Rt 650, Hicks Wharf Rd, Rose Hill Plantation
St James Church	unk	Mathews CH
Toddsbury Plantation	unk	Elmington
Trinity Episcopal	37.4106900,-76.3357800	Off Rt 614 nr jct Khyber Pass Trail
Turner Family	unk	Rt 14, W end Horn Branch
White Family (Whitehaven)	37.3742579,-76.3525981	160 Pine View Dr, Foster
Williams Family	37.4127500,-76.3385000	loc at Williams Wharf at end of Williams Ln, N of Rt 614

MECKLENBURG COUNTY

Andrews Family	36.7889400,-78.1349400	Whittles Mill Rd, South Hill
Bennett Family	unk	Check property records
Boyd Family	unk	Behind Health Dept Bldg, Boyton
Boyd Family	unk	Hwy 895, end of Rt 875
Boydton Presbyterian	36.4010100,-78.2312700	Boydton
Burwell Family	unk	Stoneland
Canaan Methodist	36.6684800,-78.0532300	Jct Blackridge Rd & Canaan Church Rd
Gregory Family	unk	Jct Rts 655 & 657
Invernay Family Center	unk	Rt 138 at Invernay Post Office
Keen Family	unk	Rt 92
Lewis Family	unk	Rt 727
Munfort-Lockett Family	unk	Nr Boydton, see Source 72
Old Wells Family	unk	loc behind Horeb Baptist Ch. 10077 Old Coxs Rd., Chase City
Overby-Holt Family	unk	Rt 602 W
Petties Family	unk	Chase City
Prestwould	unk	Clarksville
Rainey Family	unk	Rt 627
Speed Family	unk	Check property records
St James Episcopal	36.6662600,-78.3868300	Boydton
Taylor Family	36.7190910,-78.1305770	loc jct Brook Ave & 3rd St, South Hill
White-Yancey-Jones Family	unk	Rt 49 S fr Chase City, left on 697 at Reese's old store, 2.5 mi on right at old homeplace
Whittle-Davis Family	unk	Left of old Whittle House off Hwy 636
William A. Andrews 1400 acres	36.7889400,-78.1349400	South Hill
Yancey Family	unk	Hwy 736 S fr 602 abt 2.5 mi, Averett
Young-Brame Family	unk	5 mi E of Boydton, 1 mi S of Antlers

MIDDLESEX COUNTY

Buckingham House & Lodge Grange Creek nr Corbin Hall	unk	loc at Church Point at end of Rt 693, on La
Christ Church	37.6096800,-76.5464300	Rt 33 2 mi E of Saluda
Clark's Neck	unk	Check property records
Arthur Lee Family	37.6385690,-76.5761640	on Rappahannock St vic jct Bonner St, Urbanna
Providence Burial Ground	unk	Waterview
Rosegill Orchard	37.3739000,-76.3357000	loc off Rt 227, E of Urbanna

MONTGOMERY COUNTY

Barger Family	unk	Blacksburg
Barnett Family	36.8075100,-80.1521900	Alleghany Spring Rd, Sisson Farm
Blacksburg	unk	Nr Blacksburg
Boothe Family	unk	Little River, Christiansburg
Broce-Kenser	37.2306100,-80.4537300	Boxwood Dr, Blacksburg
Brown Family	37.272130,-80.306460	loc Catawba Rd, Blacksburg;
Craig	unk	Christiansburg
Craig Family	37.1339000,-80.3922000	East Park Ln

Fortheringay	37.1910100,-80.2319300	Nr Graham St, Shawsville
Halls Methodist Church	37.2383590,-80.2689490	loc at jct Flatwood Rd and North Fork Rd at Hall Cem sign, nr Ironto
Harless Family	37.2133100,-80.5491000	Vic jct Rt 744 & Long Shop Rd, Blacksburg
Henderson	unk	Catawba Rd Rt 785 Blacksburg
Howard-Palmer	37.0557500,-80.5044800	4165 Piney Woods Rd, behind House, Childress
Lester	37.1169800,-80.2515600	S fr Riner
Lucas Family or Old Cooper	unk	S or E fr Riner
Madison	unk	Shawsville
Meacham Family	unk	Nr Christiansburg
Montgomery Family	unk	Vic Christianburg
Mt Pleasant Church	37.1328900,-80.3064000	1024 Mt Pleasant Rd, Shawsville
Oakley-Altizer	unk	Chestnut Ridge, Riner
Rural	unk	Maxwell Gap
Rural	unk	Reed Creek
Smithfield Plantation	unk	VMI Campus, Blacksburg
Sunset	37.1239000,-80.4042000	South Franklin near 1-81, Christiansburg
Watterson Family	unk	Christiansburg
Westview	37.2339000,-80.4083000	Blacksburg
White	37.1582900,-80.2542300	Rt 637, S of Shawsville

NELSON COUNTY

Cabell Family	unk	Edgewood, 3008 Warminster Dr, Wingina
Cabell Family	unk	Norwood
Clarkson-Meeks, aka Clarkson #2	unk	5 mi N of Massies Mill cross Tye River Bridge
Coffey Family	unk	Cub Creek Rd Rt 789, Tyro
Cub Creek	unk	Off Cub Creek Rd Rt 789 at Beech Grove Community
Estes Family	unk	Check property records and DAR 1959 Senate Doc serial 12260 vol 5
Fairmont Baptist	37.6696537,-78.7995393	3948 Findlay Gap Dr, Wingina
Fortune	unk	Lovingston
Hill Family	unk	Cub Creek Rd Rt 789, Tyro
Jones-Clarkson	37.7943800, 78.9853000	Persimmon Hill Rd, Roseland
Level Green	unk	Massies Mill
Lovings Gap	unk	Lovington
Martin Family	unk	Check property records
Montgomery Family	unk	Nellysford, near Wintergreen
Old Bardstown City	unk	Bardstown
Rockfish Presbyterian	37.9113929,-78.8445190	5016 Rockfish Valley Hwy, Nellysford
Soldier's Joy	unk	Wingina
Tilford Cub Creek	unk	Cub Creek Rd Rt 789, Tyro
Tompkins Family	unk	Shipman at Burk Homestead
Warminster	37.6836000,-78.6942000	Warminster, Norwood
Wintergreen	unk	Rt 151 beyond Nellysford
Woods Family	unk	Rockfish Presbyterian S of Afton

NEW KENT COUNTY

Eltham Plantation house	unk	loc vic Eltham burned house in Eltham
Littlepage	unk	Nr Pamunkey R, Cumberland
Meredith Family	unk	Check property records
St Peter's Episcopal	37.3224000,-77.0324000	8400 St Peters Ln, Quinton

NEWPORT NEWS CITY (formerly Warwick County)

Denbigh United Presbyterian	37.1244522,-76.5464298	302 Denbigh Blvd
Peartree Hall	37.1189400,-76.5378630	Nr Warwick Hall CH and Tabbs Ln

Windmill Point	unk	N of jct Warwick River and Lucas Creek and S of Rt 173

NORFOLK CITY

Cedar Grove	36.8586000,-76.2831000	238 E Princess Anne Rd
Dick Warren Farm	unk	Lake Drummond
Harvey Family	unk	Not identified
Old Massenburgh	unk	South Norfolk
Sanderson Home	unk	Near NC line
St Paul's Episcopal	36.8473300,-76.2855400	201 St Paul's Blvd

NORTHAMPTON COUNTY

Brownsville Family	unk	.25 mi N on Rt 600 fr Exmore
Cherry Grove	unk	Rt 634
Cugley	unk	Rt 634
Darby's Wharf Farm	unk	Nr Shields Bridge, Belle Haven
Eyre Hall	37.313824,-75.981967	3215 Eyre Hill Drive, Cheriton
Fatherly Farm	unk	Wierwood
Kendall Grove	unk	Rt 674
Kings Creek	unk	Cape Charles
Long Point Farm	unk	Rt 711
Maria Robins House	unk	1 mi N of center of Eastville
Old Thomas Farm	unk	N of Rt 617, NW of Weirwood
Poplar Hill	unk	Rt 631, Cherrystone
Red Bank Church	unk	Jct Rts 600 & 617
Scarburgh Farm	unk	Opposite jct Rts 601 & 683,across field to old house "Scarborough"
Selma	unk	E of Bus Rt 13, .4 mi N of Rt 631 Eastville
Tankard's Rest	unk	Exmore
Wescott Farm	unk	Rt 606 NW of Nassawadox

NORTHUMBERLAND COUNTY

Ball Family	37.4591200,-76.1953600	Cress Field, Bay View on Balls Neck
Cox Homestead	unk	Cherry Point
Hayfield	unk	Nr Callao
Haynie Family	unk	Heathsville
Mantua-Smith Family	37.9573300,-76.4718400	loc end of Mantua Rd, Heathsville
Northumberland House	37.5031000,-76.2619400	Cod's Creek, off of Rt 360
Roseland	37.5113100,-76.1657600	Reedville
Smith Family	unk	Mantua Farm Rd

NOTTOWAY COUNTY

Blendon	37.1411000,-78.0803000	Rt F656 & Rt 460 Nottoway Court House Rd
Dupuy	unk	Jennings Ordinary, NW 647 for 1 mi to Carrington home
Glenmmore	unk	loc 3 mi N of Burkeville on old d betw Burkeville and Jennings Ordinary
Lakeview	37.0709100,-78.0114300	8th St, Blackstone
Pleasant Hill	unk	Loc in walled cem at jct with Jordan Bridge, Blackstone
The Old Place	unk	5 mi NW of Blackstone
Wards Chapel	unk	Crewe
Williams Family	38.5680800,-77.3351100	See 1938 DAR Senate doc 10448, vol 2

ORANGE COUNTY

Blue Run Baptist	unk	Rt 20 N of jct with Rt 655, Barboursville
Brockman Family	unk	Greenway, Monrovia

Campbell Family	unk	Campbellton near Barboursville
Cowherd Family, "Oak Hill"	unk	Gordonsville
Dade Family	unk	Rose Hill
Ellwood Burial Ground	unk	Wilderness Battlefield
Gibson Family	unk	Burr Hill
Greenfields Family	38.2533500,-78.1003900	Rt 2021, back of cem on Madex Dr
Green-Level Family	unk	Rt 663 S of True Blue Corners
Holloway Family	unk	Orange
Lidsay Family, Springfield Farm	unk	W fr Gordonsville
Mansfield Family	unk	Nr Barboursville
Maplewood	38.1464000,-78.2006000	Rt 33 W Gordonsville
Montpelier	38.2297064,-78.1765383	11407 Constitution Hwy, Montpelier Station
Mount Valley	unk	Vic jct Rts 663 & 522
Morton Hall		Rhoadesville
New Hope	unk	Orange
Oak Green Farm #1	unk	Rt 663 nr Palmyra Church
Orane CH area	unk	loc vic Old Courthouse
Rose Hill	unk	Rapidan
Schuler Place	unk	Rt 705
Scott Family	unk	Madison Run
Soldier's Rest Plantation	unk	Rt 620
Taylor Family, Meadow Farm	38.2289800,-78.0789500	16823 Monrovia Rd
Taylor-Quarles Families	38.2562940, -78.0539430	loc Bloomsbury Rd on plantation propery on right of Taylor-Quarles plantation house from driveway entrance in section without gate, Rapidan
Unidentified	unk	Gordonsville
Westover United Methodist	38.2813000,-78.3860700	2801 Fredericksburg Rd
Williams Family, "Soldier's Rest Farm"	unk	Rt 620

PAGE COUNTY

Aleshire Family	unk	E of Rt 616, 8 mi S of Luray, in back of canning factory
Beaver-Brubaker, Mauck's Mill	39.1834300,-78.1627800	Rt 615, vic Luray
Courtney Family	unk	Nr N Bank Hamshill Creek
Fairview	unk	Rileyville, 7 mi fr Luray
Grove Family	unk	Meadow Mills off Rt 340, S fr Luray
Grove Family	unk	Slade Farm Rt 615 near Luray, Bixler's Ferry
James Varner Family	unk	SE of Luray
Jollett	unk	Rt 609 N of Jollett
Keyser Family	unk	Rt 684 NW fr Luray 8 mi
Long Family Price Farm	unk	Rt 616, Alma
Martin Kibler	unk	loc Rt 611 nr jct w Rt 658, Kimball
Offenbacher	unk	Nr Stanley
Printz or Prince Family	unk	Rt 651 nr Ida
Rileyville	38.7661000,-78.3861000	At end of Cemetery Rd, Luray
Robert T Kemp Farm	unk	Luray
Ruffner Family	unk	Rt 211, Luray
Spring Farm	unk	2 mi NE of Luray on Turnpike
Strickler Monument	unk	SW side of Rts 615 & 211, Ft Egypt
Wood-Conn	unk	Rileyville, 9 mi from Luray

PATRICK COUNTY

Adams-Graves-Pilson Families	unk	.5 mi south of Rt 717, N side of Goblintown Creek nr Fairystone Park
Bryant Family	unk	Charity, behind Heidelbach School

Creasey's Chapel	unk	Stuart
Critz Baptist Church	36.6303791,-80.1505268	3294 Dogwood Rd, Critz
Delionback Home	36.3404000,-80.3324000	End of Rt 749 on Ararat River
Edward Lewis	unk	Nr Heidleback School, Rt 712 Dodson
Eliphaz Shelton-Pilson Family	unk	Main St, Stuart
Francis turner	unk	loc at theNolen Dalton Place, Rt. 40, Patrick
Green Hill Primitive Baptist	unk	Patrick Springs
Hughesville	unk	Hwy 631 nr Stuart
John Conner Family	unk	200 yds W of jct Rts 616 & 826
Lewis Family	36.8122924,-80.1410788	712 Heidleback School Rd, Dodson
Liberty Primitive Baptist	36.6949400,-80.1626900	Patrick Springs
Patrick Henry Allied Memorial	unk	Fairy Stone State Park
Poplar Grove	unk	W on Rt 626 off Rt 627 Co Line Rd, nr Critz
Ross Harbour Methodist	36.7548187,-801977278	6260 Elamsville Rd, Stuart
Stuart Town	unk	Chestnut St, Stuart
Thompson-Salmons-McAlexander	unk	Rt 719 Woolwine
Varner Family	unk	Nr jct Rts 696 & 626, btw Critz & Salem Church, Locust Grove

PETERSBURG CITY

Bass Family	unk	Bass St, Appomattox River at Exeter Mills
Blandford	37.2243300,-77.3860400	319 S Crater Rd

PITTSYLVANIA COUNTY (See also Danville City)

Atkins-Owens (AKA Adkins-Lunsford)	unk	loc on his plantation nr Chatham
Alta Vista Plantation	unk	Altavista
Berger Burial Ground	36.9290900,-79.2504100	Rt 685, or plot on Rt 927 E of Chalk Level, E fr Gretna 6 mi
Bergers	36.9574800,-79.4840800	Nr Siloan Church nr Rt 605
Blair-Stamps	36.621933,-79.278270	loc W side Hillside Rd, Ringgold
Boaze Family	36.7105500,-79.5500300	1148 Couny Rd 945, Dry Fork
Brightwood	unk	Marilla Ln, Chatham
Buckley Family	36.9550600,-79.1414500	Rt 40, Mt Airy
Bullington Family	unk	Nr Sandy River
Callands Family	36.8558700,-79.6254900	NE of Callands
Chatham	36.8190000,-79.3990000	Ennis Dr, Chatham
Cheney Burial Grounds AKA Chaney-Farson-Reeves	unk	lc on Reeves Rd., Keeling
Cheney Family	unk	Nr Keeling
Clark Family	36.8482300,-79.3219800	Pineville nr Chatham
Clement Hill	37.1005800,-79.3001700	Rt 29 N, btw Chatham & Hurt
Clopton Family	unk	Slatesville Rd, N of jct US Rt 360
Coleman Family	unk	Nr Riceville
Coleman Family	unk	Off Yeats Store Rd, Java
Coles	36.5472200,-79.1647000	8 mi NE of Chatham. Off Rt 690 (Source 76) or Rt 685 at Chalk Level, Java (Source 101)
Craddock at Piney Fork	36.933770,-79.432860	loc on W side of Piney Rd just N of jct w Old Mine Rd; Gretna
Davis Family	unk	Cherrystone Plantation
Dews Family	unk	13 mi SE of Gretna Rt 677
Easley Family	unk	Callands
Edward Long Family		loc vic forks of Strawberry Creek, Danville;
Fitts	36.5842800,-79.6996200	Rt 621 off Rt 610, Aiken Summit
Fitzgerald Family	36.8035300,-79.2423300	1 mi E of Shockoe on Rt 832
George Family	unk	Gretna
George W. Tompson Family	unk	loc on plantation nr Chestnut Level

Glenrock	36.8006000,-79.4454800	E of Rt 824, .5 mi S of Greenbuck Branch
GSA Camp Shawnee	unk	Ringgold
Hampton Family	unk	Cascade
Harris Family	unk	SR 816 or on Rt 703,10 mi fr Chatham nr Chatham HS
Hopkins	unk	Behind Thomas Muse house near Franklin Co Line, Sago
Hubbard-Stone	unk	Rt 650 Hermosa
Hunt	37.0070900,-79.2241300	Rt 640 Mount Airy nr Renan
Hutchings, Jack Crane Farm	36.7467400,-79.4222600	Rt 718 Dry Fork
Jacob Hedrick, Jr Family		loc Toshes on family land
Jeremiah Stimson Family		Ringgold
Jones Family	36.8430000,-79.2622700	Nr Mtn Top, 7 mi E of Chatham
Jones Family Farm	36.797310,-79.354630	loc on Fairview Rd nr jct w Catawba Drive, Jonesboro;
Keesee Family	36.8768300,-79.5210900	Nr Green Pond
Lawrence		Callands
Locust Bottom	37.7414800,-79.8145600	Jct Rts 633 & 696
Mill Meeting House	unk	Nr Chatham
Mitchell Family	unk	Chatham
Morgan Family	unk	Nr White Falls, Banister River
Motley Family	unk	Nr Chatham
Mustain Barn	36.5663700,-79.1852000	Btw Gretna & Mt Airy, private property behind barn
Parker Family	37.039675,-79.473309	loc E of Reservoir View Terris nr jct w Reservoir View Rd, Toshes
Pigg Mill Farm	36.7737300,-79.4606700	Rt 703, Jones Mill
Pine Creek	unk	Not identified in SAR registration
Richardson-Yates Family	unk	Ringhold
Robertson Family	unk	Dry Fork
Rock Wall	unk	Dry Fork
Shockoe Baptist	36.8096000,-79.2659000	Rt 640, Chatham
Stone Family	unk	Nr Mulberry Church
Towler Family	unk	Nr Anthony's Ford
Walton Family	unk	probably "Whitmel"
Ward	37.0549200,-79.4363700	Hurt
West Plantation	unk	Straightstone
William Atkins Family	unk	Rt 649 nr Cooper's Store, Callands
Williams Family	unk	SR 698 Cliff Hetzel Farm, Pickway
Witcher Family	unk	Nr Sandy Level Post Office
Worsham Family	unk	Check property records
Wray Family	unk	Check property records

PORTSMOUTH CITY

Cedar Grove	36.5720400,-80.0259900	301 Fort Lane Rd
Cedar Grove	36.8386000,-76.3081000	Salter St
Court Street Baptist	36.8357334,-76.3008732	447 Court St
Glasgow Street Park	36.8376400,-76.3019800	425 Glasgow St
Lincoln Memorial	36.8083000,-76.3281000	Jct Kirby St and Deep Creek Blvd
Trinity Episcopal	36.8345900,-76.3010500	500 Court St

POWHATAN COUNTY

Dabney, Montpelier	unk	Maiden's Rd, abt 2 mi N of Anderson Hwy, E side of rd, N of Montpelier Plantation
Elioch Manor Family	unk	Elioch Manor Dr, end of rd
Goode Family	unk	Michaux
Manakin	37.5656000,-77.7100000	Rt 711 vic jct Rt 635
Mosby Family	unk	Powhatan

Muddy Creek Baptist	unk	3470 Rt 629, Powhatan
Old Hobson	unk	Blenheim, nr Balleville
Patrick Harris Homesite	unk	Dirt Rd off Rt 614 abt 3 mi
Peterville	37.5643990,-77.9646980	loc N of Anderson Rd by a pond 200yds E of jct with Bell Rd
Rural	unk	Powhatan
Taylor Family	37.4938957,-78.0450821	5609 Old Buckingham Rd

PRINCE EDWARD COUNTY

Allen-Watkins Family	unk	Farmville
Clover Forest	unk	3 mi W of Farmville nr Sandy Fork Bridge
Col Charles Allen Family	unk	Farmville:
Dupuy Famil	unk	loc nr Abilene, Rice
Hampden-Sydney College	unk	Hampden-Sydney campus
Leigh Family	unk	Base of Leigh Mountain, Farmville
Venable-Slate Hill Plantation	unk	Worsham
Westview	unk	Farmville
Woodson Family	unk	Farmville
Worsham Family Square	37.3216300,-78.4432800	Vic Rts 665 & 15 Farmville Rd, Worsham

PRINCE GEORGE COUNTY

Aldridge Family	unk	Off Rt 607, 2 mi E of Rt 654
Bicars	unk	75 yds behind house on private road off Rt 641, Huntington
Bland Family	unk	2 mi E of Hopewell on Rt 10, 1.2 mi N on Rt 36, then 10 ft E
Brandon Plantation	37.1527100,-76.5936200	Burrowsville
Eppes Family	unk	Off Rt 616, 3.9 mi SE of jct with Rt 37
Harrison Family	unk	5.5 mi NE Burrowsville
Harrison-Pinkards	unk	4.5 mi E Prince George, then N
Heath Family	unk	See Senate Doc 1938 serial 10448 vol 2
Jordan Point Plantation	37.303925,-77.223250	Waters Edge Rd, Jordan Pt Manor
Kirkham Family	unk	1.2 mi N of Disputana
Martins Brandon Episcopal Ch	37.215380,-77.074508	18706 James River Dr (Rt 10), Burrowsville
Nathaniel Lee Home	unk	NE of Carson
Ruffin Family, Tar Bay House	unk	4 mi E of Hopewell
Salem Methodist Church	37.0448039,-77.3453864	19312 Templeton Rd, Carson
Tooker Family, Brandon Home	unk	5 mi NE of Burrowsville

PRINCE WILLIAM COUNTY (See also Manassas City)

Bacon Race	38.6914500,-77.4643900	Davis Ford Rd & Bacon Race Rd
Beaver Family	38.6611800,-77.4732400	13380 Bristol Rd, Nokesville
Blackburn-Atkinson	38.3687800,-77.1668500	Rippon Lodge off Rt 638, Woodbridge
Brawner	unk	Rt 1 at Potomac HS
Camp Glen Kirk	38.7736700,-77.6236000	Gainesville, Rt 29 N, Linter Hall Rd
Carver	38.5273500,-77.5605400	Rt 610 vic jct with Rt 612
Clarke Family	unk	Nr Woodbridge PO, Woodbridge
Davis Family	unk	Wolf Run Shoals Rd
Dumfries Public	38.3411000,-77.1996400	17821 Mine Rd, Dumfries
Effingham Plantation	38.3839300,-77.3129000	1 mi E of Adan, 14325 Trotter's Ridge Place, Nokesville
Ewell-Weems	unk	Rt 640
Fitzhugh Plantation	unk	Check property records
Flourance Family	38.7157700,-77.4638600	Lake Jackson
Grayson	38.6477500,-77.2764800	West Longview Dr, Woodbridge
Henderson	unk	Mountclair
Howison Family	38.6331300,-77.3839900	Minniville Rd
Lane Family	unk	Cement Rd

Leesylvania Plantation	38.3524000,-77.1520000	On a ridge overlooking Occoquan Bay, Woodbridge
Luckett	unk	Nr Quantico Marine Base
Maddox	unk	Hope Hill Crossing Subdiv, Hope Hill Rd
Norvall Family	unk	Nr Dumfries
Tebbsdale Plantation	unk	Rt 633 off US 1 Dumfries
Wheeler-Greenville Family	38.4775500,-77.3245800	7300 Old Compton Rd

PULASKI COUNTY

Bell Family, Dunkards Bottom	37.0570200,-80.6208700	Claytor Lake State Park, Dublin
Bell Farm	unk	Dublin
Caddall	unk	Thornspring Farm
Cecil Family	unk	Nr Radford and Dublin
Cecil Family Farm #2	unk	Neck's Creek, Belspring
Cloyd	37.1616600,-80.7058300	Rt 100 Cleyburne Blvd N of Dublin
Honaker	unk	Draper
Patton Family	unk	nr Dublin
Sunnyside	unk	Btw Radford and Dublin at Old Joseph Howe place, Back Creek
Unidentified	unk	Snowville
Wysor	unk	Dublin

RAPPAHANNOCK COUNTY

Browning Family	unk	Nr Salem Baptist Ch
Corder-Pierce Family	unk	Amissville
Dearing Family	38.7607560,-78.1276280	Caledonia Farm, 47 Dearing Rd, Flint Hill
Elijah Anderson	38.4538000,-77.5833000	27 Shurgen Ln, Amissvile
Hot Mountain	unk	Nethers
Lutheran	unk	Washington
Major-Corbin	38.6528200,-78.0235300	Rt 642 Viewtown Rd nr jct with Ida Belle Ln, Amissville
Masonic Cemetery	unk	Rt 522, Washington
Miller	38.7340800,-78.1716920	Rt 248, Harris Hollow, Washington
Miller, Mountain Green	unk	Washington
Pierce Family	38.6888860,-78.0250970	Rt 211, Amissville
Slate Mills	unk	Vic Woodville
Slaughter Family, "Clover Hill"	unk	Woodville, Hawthorne
Tapp-Griffin Families	unk	Vic Amissville
Unidentified	unk	Amissville
Wadefield-Strother Family	unk	Nr Washington
Woodard	unk	James Woodard Farm, off Co Rd 600 in field N of "Caboose Pond"

RICHMOND CITY

Hebrew	33.5517500,-77.4297600	300 Hospital St
Hollywood	37.5356000,-77.4572000	412 S Cherry St
Monumental Church	unk	1224 E Broad St
Patteson Family	unk	Laurel Meadows
Shockoe Hill	37.5519000,-77.4317000	4th & Hospital Sts
St John's Episcopal	37.5318300,-77.4195800	2401 E Broad St
Unidentified	37.3233700,-77.2613200	Nr State Capitol

RICHMOND COUNTY

Beale Family	unk	Chestnut Hill, E of Ethel
Belfield Family	38.0395513,-76.8164301	2804 County Bridge Rd, Warsaw
Doctor's Hall	unk	Nr jct Rappahannock River & Creek
Farnham Episcopal	unk	231 N Farnham Church Rd, Farnham
Lower Lunenburg Parish	37.9606600,-76.7692000	Off N side Rt 360, Warsaw
Mims Family	unk	Licking Hole Creek Farm

Muse Family	unk	Check property records
North Farnham Episcopal	unk	Farnham
Tayloe Family	37.5820000,-76.4729000	Mt Airy, Rt 360, Warsaw

ROANOKE CITY (See also Roanoke County)

Belmont	unk	Frank Rd, Roanoke
Old German	unk	Roanoke
Old Lick, aka First Baptist	37.2825000,-79.9369000	Hart Ave btw 2nd & 4th St

ROANOKE COUNTY (See also Roanoke City and Salem City)

Deyerle Family	unk	W part of Co
Esom Family	unk	Nr Cave Spring
Greenwood Family	unk	Cave Springs
King	unk	Bent Mtn, S fr Roanoke
Old German	unk	Roanoke
Old Lick, aka First Baptist	37.28250, -79.93690	Hart Ave btw 2nd & 4th St, Roanoke
Poage's Mill	37.19800, -80.05600	Rt 221, Bent Mtn Rd, Poages Mill village
Vinyard Family	unk	Lauderale Ave
Vinyard Family	unk	Vinton
Weddle Family	unk	Bent Mtn

ROCKBRIDGE COUNTY (See also Lexington County)

Alone Community, aka Bethany Lutheran	unk	Rts 602 & 525, Kerrs Dist part 6
Bennington-Gaylor	unk	Waterloo Rd
Broad Creek-Miller	unk	Buffalo Dist
Dryden Family	unk	See DAR Senate Doc 1958 serial 12259, vol 4
Falling Springs Presbyterian	37.6849400,-79.4510500	410 Falling Springs Rd, Glasgow
Glasgow Cemetery	37.6032000,-79.4591400	13th St & Fitzlee, Glasgow
Hattan Family	unk	Rt 629, behind house on Frances Hostetters property, Kerrs Dist
High Bridge Presbyterian	37.6242000,-79.5861000	67 High Bridge Rd, Natural Bridge
McDowell	37.8686000,-79.3108000	Nr jct Rts 11 & 712, Fairfield
McDowell Family	39.1841000,-78.1627800	10 mi N Lexington on Rt 11
McKee, aka Big Springs	unk	Clarence Hardy's farm, off Rt 60, on Rt 631, Kerrs Distr
Mt Zion Methodist	37.6659600,-79.4661500	Btw Buffalo & Tinkersville
Muse, aka Irvine Family, Timber Grove, or Timber Ridge Presbyterian	37.8427452,-79.3578033	9 mi N of Lexington off Rt 11, SW of jct Rts 11 & 716, 73 Sam Huston Way, Buffalo Dist
Neriah Baptist	37.7877800,-79.3648200	Jct Rts 631 & 706, South River
New Providence Presbyterian	37.9513000,-79.3025000	1208 New Providence Rd, Raphine
Old Anderson farm	unk	W Buffalo Rd
Old Monmouth Presbyterian	37.8081000,-79.4728000	Jct Rts 60 & 669
Old Stone Presbyterian	37.8427452,-79.3578033	73 Sam Huston Way
Oxford Presbyterian	37.7530200,-79.5602300	18 Churchview Ln,Collierstown
Paxton Family	37.7166600,-79.4027100	Forge Rd, Mechanicsville
Stuart Family	unk	Rt 727, Blackwells property
Taylor Family	unk	Short Hill Mountain
Timber Grove	unk	Buffalo Dist, Timber Ridge
Timber Ridge Presbyterian	37.8420000,-79.3580000	Nr jct Rts 11 & 716, Timber Ridge
Unidentified, Old Graveyard	unk	Nr Wesley Chapel, Glasgow
Unidentified, Private Graveyard	unk	Nr St Stephens Church, Goshen
Walker Creek	unk	Walker Creek
Walkerland, Maxwelton Farm	37.9461300,-79.3879400	Vic jct Rts 602 & 724, behind Maxwelton Cabins
Youel Family,	unk	Rt 601, Goshen

Meadow Lawn Farm

ROCKINGHAM COUNTY

Arkton Tunker Church	38.5723200,-78.6962500	Mountain Valley Rd Rt 620, Arkton
Baker-Smith Thompson Familes	38.5160800,-78.7243900	War Spring Ln nr jct with Mountain Valley Rd, Oakwood
Bear Family	38.4347700,-78.6181600	2145 East Side Hwy (Rt 340); Elktonr
Bethel Cemetery	38.4759200,-78.7564100	3061 Armentrout Path, Keezletown
Bible Family	38.8972000,-78.1444000	Dull Hunt Rd at Fulks Run
Bowman Family	unk	War Branch, Peaked Mountain Rt 726 abt 1 mi fr jct with Rt 613 on private rd
Brenneman Mennonite	38.6262000,-78.8758800	Brenneman Church Rd
Broadway Presbyterian Church	38.6180400,-78.7953500	107 Lee St, Broadway
Brock Family	36.7105500,-79.5500300	2401 Indian Trail Rd, Keezletown 22832
Byrd Family	38.6154310,-78.6750890	Craney Island Rd,.25 mi NW jct with Smith Creek Rd Tenth Legion
Coffman Family	unk	2985 Kratzer Rd (Rt 753);
Crawford Family #2	unk	Rt 726 .6 mi fr jct with Rt 613 on Sam Brown property, Peaked Mountain
Cook-Dovel	unk	loc .5 mi W of East Pont Ch on Massanutten Mtn Rd, McGaheysville
Cross Keys	unk	Cross Keys
Custer Family	38.6642600,-78.9272290	Dry River S of Rt 259, Fulks Run
Dayton	38.4200000,-78.9430300	Bowman Rd, Dayton
DeVier Family	38.4057830,-79.0384770	loc nr jct Nazarene Ch Rd & Rt 613, Spring Creek
Dispanet Family	unk	loc on Dispanet family property, vic Timberville
Driver-Rife;	38.6473100,-78.7520900	16092 Evergreen Valley Rd, Timberville
Early	38.3953600,-78.9046500	3588 Early Rd, Pleasant Valley
East Point	unk	Rt 602 left fr Rt 33 E, Elkton
Elk Run	38.4104200,-78.6103300	North St, Elkton
Farley-Fulk	38.6611300,-78.9131800	Blocks Gap Rd (Rt 629),.01 mi E of jct with Nash Hill Dr, Fulks Run
Fishback Family	unk	Dayton
Fitzswater Family	unk	from Rt 259 abt 1 mi fr Riverside United Methodist Ch turn on to concrete bridge to Ed Carter's house, cem on right across creekbed in trees, Fulks Run
Flook Armentrout	unk	end of Henton Mill Ln (Rt 934) on the left at knoll, Lacy Spring
Friedens United Church of Christ	38.3484800,-78.8765300	3960 Friedens Church Rd
Greenmount	38.5184560,-78.9014170	loc Rt 722
Greenwood	38.3847000,-78.9761000	Vic Green St & North Grove St, Bridgewater
Harley Good Farm	unk	Brock's Gap, SW side of SR 259
Harrison Family, Smith's Creek	38.4200000,-78.9430300	Nr Lacey Springs
Hernsberger-Wynant Graveyard	38.3665470,-78.9637400	Waystation Rd (Rt 888) across rd fr airport bldg behind stonewall, Bridgewater
Hilltop-Yancey Farm	unk	Elkton
Holman Family	unk	fr Rt 259, turn R on Rt 1411, after crossing 2d bridge, turn left, then go .5 mi, cem loc top of hill on R, Broadway
Holsinger Family	38.6113900,-78.7616400	2805 Holsinger Rd, Broadway
Huling Family	unk	Andrew Huling property, Lacey Spring
Jacob Bowman Farm	unk	loc Jacob Baumann (Bowmann) farm, Linville
James Meadows Sr. Family	38.4060318,-78.5343491	5130 Bear Foot Ln, Elkton
Keezletown	unk	Keezletown

Kline Family	38.5811800,-78.8289500	Rt 1415 nr Broadway
Koontz Family	unk	loc N of dirt lane at end of Rt 806, Martz Rd, Lacey Spring
Kring Salvage	unk	Off John Deere Dr, behind Harman Machinery, Broadway
Lacey Springs	38.5447500,-78.7707200	Lacey Springs
Lewis Family	unk	Rts 708 & 340
Lincoln Family	38.5476500,-78.8402800	7884 Harpine Rd Rt 42, Linville, 3 mi S of Broadway on SR 42, N of Edom exit
Lindale Mennonite	unk	Jesse Bennett Way, Linville
Maiden Homestead	unk	Bedor Rd Rt 628, .3 mi fr Rt 33 in Elkton, walk up hill abt .5 mi
Mallow Family	unk	McGaheysville
Massanutten Cross Keys	38.3581700,-78.8412400	Rt 679 at Cross Keys, vic jct Rts 276 & 679
May Family	unk	May Creek Ln, Criders, Bergton
Mill Creek Church	38.3375300,-78.8200900	7600 Port Republic Rd, Port Republic
Moore Family	unk	Timberville
Moyer Family	38.4831500,-78.5528500	Crab Run Rd, nr Bergton
Meyers Family (aka Old Linville Creek)	unk	fr Rt 42 on Williamsburg Rd (Rt 782) go 1.2 mi, cem on R
Mt Olivet Church of Brethren	unk	2977 Pineville Rd, McGayesville
Northern Methodist	38.3577700,-78.9434400	Rt 867 Old Bridgewater Rd, Mt Crawford
Old Criders	38.7501300,-79.0062500	loc Dove Valley Ln, nr jct with Crider's Rd (Rt 826), Criders
Old Dove	unk	Dovesville
Old Unmarked Lacey Springs	unk	Nr Lacey Springs
Old Peaked Mountain	38.3711300,-78.7341600	9843 Town Hall Rd, McGaheysville
Old Weaver Church	38.4486800,-78.9046300	Harrisonville
Rader Lutheran	38.6507300,-78.7805500	17072 Raders Church Rd, Timberville
Ralph Heatwole Place	unk	Hinton Rd (Rt 752), Hinton
Reedy/Shoemaker	unk	Hopkins Gap Rd, Genoa nr Oak Grove Brethan Ch; Fulks Run
Rhodes (Roth) Family	unk	Vic Broadway Rt 42
Rice Fam	unk	Rt 743 W of Dayton
Ritchie Family	38.6368700,-78.9366000	loc Forest Creek Ln, Fulks Run
Roadcap Family	38.6497300,-78.9365100	3rd Hill Rd, Rt 817, Fulks Run
Salem Presbyterian	unk	Cooks Creek
Smith Family AKI Shaw Farm	38.3929700,-78.0610340	loc Sangersville Rd (Rt 727), Spring Creek
Spears Family	unk	N of Edom Rt 42 7.3 mi
Stephens Family	38.5276250,-78.7476200	1844 Maryz Rd, Lacey Springs
Thomas Family	unk	Nr Timberville
Trissels Mennonite Church	38.6028110,-78.8467870	112 Hisers Lane, Broadway
Trout or Kline family	38.5834693,-78.8311472	5180 Trissels Rd, Broadway
Union Church	unk	Rt 679 Battlefield Rd
Whetzel Family	38.6130600,-78.7991710	jct S Main St & Broadway Ave, Brocks Gap, Broadway
Woodbine	unk	Cnr of E Market St and Ott St, Harrisonburg
Yount Family	unk	Rts 253 & 278, 2.8 mi E

RUSSELL COUNTY

Bickley Family	36.8853000,-82.2778000	Rt 615 across fr Rt 640, Castlewood
Boyd Family	36.9383011,-81.9428024	loc off Rt 603 Mountain Rd., Elk Garden
Dickinson Family	unk	Nr Old Courthouse
Dorton	unk	Rt 71 near Dickensonville
Elk Garden	unk	Red Wine Plantation, Elk Garden
Kelly	36.9569000,-82.0936000	Off Rt 621 on Sandy Ridge, nr home of Rev & Mrs Gonan Kelly
Reynolds Family	unk	Hammonville

Soloman Litton Hollow	unk	nr Pinnacle Preserve
Tate-Burdine	unk	Lebanon
Thomas Family	unk	Poor Farm Rd, Lebanon
Unidentified	unk	Morefield
Whitt Family	unk	Rt 646, W fr Honaker

SALEM CITY (See also Roanoke County)

Garst Family	unk	Kesler Mill Rd up hill near RR tracks
Walton Family	unk	Nr Ft Lewis
West Hill	37.2931300,-80.0675300	Boon St

SCOTT COUNTY

Blue Spring	36.6596700,-82.4118100	Hiltons Area
Brown Family	unk	Eagle hills
Carter Family	unk	Rt 649, Rye Cove
Cocke Family	unk	Ft Blackmore
England	36.6032300,-82.9402900	Looneys Gap #14
Freeman Family	unk	Rt 778, Weber City
Godsey Family	unk	Rt 613, Nickelsville
Hensley	36.6442600,-82.7196000	Sleepy Hollow Ln
Jones Family	36.6169000,-82.6858000	Rt 635, Yuma, across RR and E of Cowan Branch Baptist Ch
Lawson Confederate Memorial	36.6872800,-82.5011400	Rt 71, Snowflake
Livingston Family	36.6798700,-82.3527300	Rt 689, Mendota
Pendleton	36.6714500,-82.6624800	Rt 664, Manville
Porter Family	unk	Rt 682 Dungannon
Spurrier Family	unk	Rt 691, Hiltons
Stallard-Moore	36.8115500,-82.4617200	Nr jct Rts 780 & 671 nr Nickelsville, Dungannon
Vineyard	unk	loc vic jct Red Hill Rd & Red Bluff Rd., Gate City
Wood	36.7172000,-82.3694000	Rt 613

SHENANDOAH COUNTY

Arthur Hirsh Family	unk	Nr New Market
Boehm	unk	Nr Clary
Buckton Family	unk	1 mi W of Buckton Station
Clover Hill	unk	Saumsvill
Coffman's Rivermont Farm,	38.9162300,-78.4148000	Fisher Rd Rt 649 to end of state Maintenance
Columbia Furnace	unk	Columbia Furnance
Conicville School	38.8938000,-78.6953200	Off Rt 703, SW of Conicville nr Swover Crk
David Kagy Farm	unk	Nr New Market
Dellinger Family	38.5037000,-78.4054000	Madison Dist, Conicville
Dry Run Church	38.8592900,-78.4007500	Rt 678, Ft Valley Rd nr jct with Dry Run Rd, Seven Fountains
Frye Family	unk	Wheatfield
Funk Family	unk	behind Travel Trailer Park, vic Strasburg
Funkhouser Family	38.8019810,-78.7839000	Resort Dr Rt 835, Basye
Funkhouser Family	unk	Mt Jackson
Funkhouser Family	unk	Vic Fishers Hill
Funkhouser Family	unk	Waxwing Ln on Shipe farm
Garber Family	unk	Vic Moores Store
Grandstaff Family	unk	Narrow Pass Creek
Keller	38.5648000,-78.4622000	Tom's Brook, nr Mt Olive
Keller Family	38.4945700,-78.2533500	Burner Ln off Fort Valley Rd
Keller Family	38.9658000,-78.4622000	Sand Ridge Rd, Mt Olive
Miller Family	unk	Woodstock

Mt Solomon's Lutheran	38.4418000,-78.4420100	Solomon Church Rd & Rt 42, Forestville
Mt Zion United Methodist	38.9889600,-78.3670700	399 W Queens St, Strasburg
Neff Family	unk	Vic Stonewall Jackson HS
Neff-Kagey	38.6944300,-78.6589500	Rt 827, Old Bridge Rd, New Market
Old Bethel	38.7911300,-78.5890400	Off Old Bethel Rd Rt 700, Edinburg
Old John McInturff Farm	unk	Shenandoah Caverns
Old Pine Church	unk	loc 1mi S of Pinkerton east of rd on land of Milton Funkhouser 1936
Old St Mary's	unk	Mt Jackson
Philllips	unk	Edinburg
Rinker	unk	Conicville
Riverview	38.9842000,-78.3614000	Grounds of Riverview HS, Strasburg
Soloman's Lutheran Ch	38.7446400,-78.6426500	Solomans Church Rd, Forestville
St Martin's Lutheran	38.6448000,-78.6712400	2235 River Rd, New Market
St Mary Pine Lutheran	38.7447000,-78.6839000	7103 S Middle Rd, Mt Jackson
St Mathew's	36.6513100,-78.6712100	Breckenridge Ln, New Market
St Paul's Lutheran	38.9914000,-78.3625000	156 W Washington, Strasburg
St Paul's Reformed Church	38.8778000,-78.5066300	Cnr S Church Sr & E South St, Woodstock
Stickley Family	unk	Strasburg
Union Church	38.4448000,-78.3835000	Mt Jackson nr jct Main St & Bridge St
Woodstock	unk	Woodstock
Zirkle Family	38.6590000,-78.6958000	River Rd, New Market
Zerchel-Nehs Family	unk	loc on east bank of Holmaan's Creek northeast of Forestville

SMYTH COUNTY

Allison	36.9114000,-81.7517000	W of plaster mine, Locust Cove Rd private property with closed gate, E of Saltville
Aspenvale	36.8142000,-81.6400000	Rts 641 & 642, Seven Mile Ford
Bowen Family	36.8142000,-81.6400000	Aspenvale
Brody Family	unk	Saltville
Buchanan Family	36.9561000,-81.5447000	New Cove, E of Saltville
Greever	36.7925000,-81.6986000	Rt 1019 off Rt 11, Chilhowie
Harmon Family	36.9547000,-81.4008000	Rt 610 Old Valley Rd, S of Hamon Creek nr Bland Co line
Lamie Family	unk	2 mi E of Saltville
Locust Grove	unk	W fr Chatham Hill
Morgan	unk	Rye Valley
Morgan Family	36.7669000,-81.4375000	1.5 mi fr Teas on private rd beyond Rt 601
Mt Zion Church	36.8346100,-81.5933800	Old Ebenezer Rd, Marioin
Old Grewer (Greever) Burial Ground	36.7925000,-81.6986000	W end of Skyview Dr, Chilhowie
Old Shannon Place	38.5399900,-77.5561000	Head of Long Hollow, Rich Valley
Rich Valley Presbyterian	36.9024800,-81.6249000	3811 Valley Rd, Saltville
Richardson	36.9325000,-81.5336000	Rt 610 Valley Rd
Riverbend	unk	Vic jct Rts 650 & 660
Royal Oak	36.8431500,-81.4966000	Behind Marion Baptist Church, Marion
Scott	unk	Blue Springs
St Clair Bottom Primitive Baptist	36.7609800,-81.6455600	Jct Rts 600 & 660, Chilhowie
Tate Family	unk	Nr Buchanan House, Broadford
Totten Family	unk	Vic jct Rts 610 & 687

SOUTHAMPTON COUNTY (See also Franklin City)

Boykin Family	unk	Rt 460, across river fr Zuni
Ferguson Family	36.5883611,-77.1100902	31356 Rochelle Swamp Rd, Vic Newsoms
George Cary Family	unk	4.5 mi W of Courtland
Jerico	unk	Courtland

Mason Family	unk	Rt 612 Fortsville Rd, 4 mi NW of Adam Grove
Old Adams Grove	unk	left side of U.S. 58 East in a field nr jct with Rt 651, Adams Grove
Stephenson Family	unk	Clayton Rd

SPOTSYLVANIA COUNTY

Alsop	unk	Lake View Estates subdivision in small grove, Snow Hill
Ballard Family	unk	Nr Catherine Furnace, see property records
Bellefonte	unk	Leiston
Belvoir House	38.2247855,-77.4527172	Jct Rts 608 E & 635
Brooke Family	unk	Rt 2, 6 mi N Fredericksburg, E side of St Julian house
Cowlands Site	unk	Rt 613
Elmwood	unk	Rt 614
Fairview	unk	Rt 3
Gordon Herndon	38.1546700,-77.6534100	Rt 656 S off Rt 208, Post Oak
Green Level	unk	Rt 652
Greenfield	unk	Fawn Lake Pwy
Hamilton Family	unk	Rt 636
Laurel Hill, Nywood Farm	unk	Rt 210 3.3 mi E of CH
Martin Family, Germantown	unk	Rt 3 Germantown
Meadow Hill Estate	unk	Off Rt 613, 1.8 mi N of Luck's Store
Minor Family	unk	Rt 633, nr Locust Grove homeplace
Page Family	unk	Mansfield Hall
Pine Cliff	38.2892000,-77.6457700	Vic jct Jackson Trail Rd and Military Park Rd
Prospect Hill	unk	Waller Rd nr Forest Green, Partlow
Shady Grove Methodist	unk	11007 W Catharpin, Shady Grove Cnr
Stanard (Stanfield) Family	unk	Rt 646
Vauxhall Site	unk	Rt 607
Wallace	38.1597200,-77.7955800	8630 Peppertree Rd, Wilderness Cnr

STAFFORD COUNTY

Aquia Episcopal	38.4646600,-77.4032500	2938 Jeff Davis Hwy, Aquia
Belleview Plantation	unk	Rt 604
Broad Oak Farm	unk	Ferry Rd., Stafford
Cedar Run	38.3629900,-77.3369400	Quantico Marine Base
Crows Nest	unk	Crows Nest area
Edrington Family	38.4437800,-77.3806400	End of Rt 692, Quarry Rd, aross fr 34 Edrington Court
Fairview	unk	Chopawamic Creek
Hartwood Presbyterian	38.4018800,-77.5674500	50 Hartwood Ch Rd, jct rts 705 & 612
Hedges Family	unk	Quantico Marine Base
Jett Family #2	unk	End of Broad Oak Ln, see property records
King Family	unk	Rt 658 Brent Point Rd
Liberty Hall	unk	Rt 652 abt 1.4 mi fr jct Rt 653 and .5 mi N nr Wallace farm rd
Norman Family #1	unk	Quarry Rd
Norman Family #2	unk	Hope Point Rd
Olde Concord Road	unk	Rt 721
Phillips Family	38.5023800,-77.2962600	Rt 610, Quantico Marine Base
Pratt Family, aka Glebe	38.2993400,-77.3445000	1374 White Oak
Richland, aka Brent Family	unk	Rt 637, Aquia
Roy Family	unk	Clover Hill Dr
Sanford Family	unk	#1 Rocky Pen area
Sanford family #1	unk	Rt 654 to 656, follow 656 S for 3.2 mi
Stark-Payne	unk	Quantico Marine Base opp Ruby fire station

Stony Hill(aka Briggs-McDonald)	38.4392300,-77.5817700	99 Stony Hill Rd nr Curtis Lake, Hartwood
Union Church	38.3226800,-77.4661500	Carter St, Falmouth
Waller Family	38.4389100,-77.3835300	Rt 721

STAUNTON CITY (See also Augusta County)

Hebron Presbyterian	38.1414000,-79.1550000	423 Hebron Rd
Stone House Plantation	unk	Hill behind Hays Creek, nr Staunton
Thornrose	38,1512000,-79.0846000	1041 W Beverly St
Trinity Episcopal	38.1491700,-79.0752100	214 Beverley St
Western State Hospital	38.1429900,-79.0657100	Village Dr

SUFFOLK CITY (formerly Nansemond County)

Bethel Church	unk	E Washington St
Cedar Hill	36.7364000,-76.5800000	105 Mahan St
Cypress Chapel	36.6179900,-76.5914800	1891 Cypress Chapel Rd
Meadowbrook Mem Gardens	36.8294000,-76.4664000	4569 Shoulders Hill Rd
Riddick Cemetery	36.6814000,-76.5586000	Off White Marsh Rd
Soldiers Hope	unk	Rt 642, 3.5 mi S of Suffolk

SURRY COUNTY

Cocke Family	unk	Mount Pleasant
Four Mile Tree	unk	Off Swan's Point Rd
Lawn's Creek Parish Church	unk	Hog Island, no public access
Rogers Family	unk	Off Rt 40

SUSSEX COUNTY

Claiborne Family	unk	Check property records
Huntington Quarter Plantation	36.5204000,-77.1328000	loc Huntington Quarter Rd S of jct with Poole Rd
Jones Family	unk	See DAR Senate 1937 serial 10173 vol 1
Moss Family	unk	Check property records
Wilkinson Farm	36. 9483903,-77.4076197	loc vic jct Rts 40 & 618, Sussex

TAZEWELL COUNTY

Bowen Family	unk	Cove Creek
Brooks	unk	Rt 604, .2 mi fr grocery behind silo, Thompson Valley
Dry Fork, Sayer's Farm, or Harman	unk	Rt 637, Dry Fork, State Marker nearby
Henry Harmon	unk	Fourway
Hezekiah Harman	unk	In front of HS off Rtst 460 & 19, Tazewell
Leatherwood Farm	unk	Rt 460, Bluefield
Maplewood	37.1280300,-81.5210400	Nr Jct Rts 19, 460, & 16 Tazewell Ave
Moore	37.2211000,-81.4017000	Adj to RR track E of Tiptop abt halfway to jct Rts 650 & 656
Moore Family	unk	Abb's Valley
Sayer's Farm	unk	Mouth of Thompson Valley, foot of Clinch Mountain, Dry Fork
Thompson Family	unk	Not identified
Thompson Family	unk	Thompson Valley
W. A. Leece Family	unk	Off Rt 91 S of Rt 460, Fort Witten, Paintlick
Ward's Cove	unk	Thompson Valley
Whitten Family	unk	Patrick
Wilkerson Witten Family	unk	loc nr his cabin on Country Rd 634 loc N about 350 feet from end of paved road and across from the old Col. Wilkerson Witten's homestead, Pisgah

Witten Family	unk	Plum Creek nr his cabin
Wynn-Peery	37.1262000,-81.4988000	Campbell Ln, Tazewell

VIRGINIA BEACH CITY (formerly Princess Anne County)

Greenwich	unk	Euclid Station
Old Baptist Meeting House	36.6100100,-76.0349400	Vic 664 Princess Anne Rd, Creeds
Old Donation Episcopal	36.8673000,-76.1286000	4449 N Witchduck Rd
Keeling Family	unk	Back of Laurel Manor
Lynhaven House	unk	Shore Dr
Red Mill Farm	unk	Hedgelawn Rd
Kempsville Skirmish Monument	unk	Pleasant Hall

WARREN COUNTY

Buck Family	38.9749020,-78.2740690	1 mi W of Buckton Station, Waterlick
Cloud Family	unk	1.5 mi West Front Royal
Marshall Family	38.9536260,-78.1728610	Rt 55, Happy Creek Pl, Front Royal
Millar Family	unk	W Main St, Front Royal
Miller Family	unk	Mountain View Farm, vic Front Royal
Prospect Hill	38.9133030,-78.1983320	200 W Prospect St, Front Royal
Richardson Family	38.9575000,-78.2961000	1.5 mi fr entrance to GW National Forest, Rt 678 nr Fortsmouth Vol Fire Dept
Trenary Farm	unk	Bayard Post Office

WASHINGTON COUNTY (See also Bristol City)

Baker Family, aka Spring Creek	unk	N Jct with 647 Bristol-Abingdon Rd
Buchanan Family	36.8416300,-81.7519900	Rt 696, S of Saltville
Burson Family, orig Fulkerson	36.6644000,-82.1750000	Nr Jct of Rt 633 & Spur Strap Rd, Burson's Corner
Carmack	unk	Nr Bristol
Clark	unk	Cedarville
Davies Farm	unk	Check property records nr Abingdon
Dunn Family	36.6256000,-81.7264000	Abt 1 mi NW of Cherry Tree Gap off Rt 725
East Hill, Sec 1	unk	West of Circles, see Source 80 Cem #279A
Ebbing Spring	unk	N side of middle fork of Holstein River, vic Glade Spring
Fleenor	unk	North Fork, Holston
Glade Spring Presbyterian	36.7672000,-81.7872000	33234 Lee Hwy, Glade Spring
Glenwood	unk	Clarksville
Green Spring Presbyterian	36.6367000,-81.9956000	2007 Green Spring Ch Rd, Abingdon
Hayter-Litton	36.8444300,-81.9262800	Nr the Litton Home, 7261 Hayter's Gap Rd
Hobbs	unk	North Fork, Holston River
Jackson Lewis	unk	Taylors Valley
John Douglass	unk	100 yds N of John B Douglass Wayside Rt 19, 9 mi N of Abingdon
Johnston	unk	1 mi on ext of Valley St, Abingdon
Malone Family	unk	Three Springs
Maxwell Family	unk	Abingdon
Moore	36.6514015,-82.1905975	20585 Haskell Station Road, Bristol
Pleasant View	36.6867000,-81.7497000	Vic jct Rts 801 & 605, Glade Spring
Rock Spring	37.7812600,-79.4458500	Jct Rt 803 & Liberty Hall Rd, Lodi
Royal Oak	unk	Behind Marion Baptist Church
Scott	unk	Rich Valley
Sinking Springs	36.7103000,-81.9817000	136 E Main St, Abingdon
Teeter family	36.6647000,-82.1208000	Vic Clear Creek Dam
Trigg Family	unk	Abingdon
Vance Family	unk	Rt 695
Walnut Grove	unk	Lee Hwy, Bristol
Widener's Valley	unk	See Source 80, Cem #239

WAYNESBORO CITY (See also Augusta County)

Allen Marker	unk	E Waynesboro at Winchester Heights, lot 4, Elkin Ave
Bethleham Lutheran	38.0545400,-78.9522200	1148 Ladd Rd
Patrick Family	unk	Locust Isle, Rt 865 N fr Waynesboro

WESTMORELAND COUNTY

Burnt House Field	unk	Hague
Bushfield Family	38.8000000,-76.4252000	Mount Holly,Nomini River, Westmoreland
Dishman Family	unk	Forest Glen
Glebe	unk	In garden area of Glebe Parish House, Glebe Creek, Cople Parish
Hickory Hill, aka Epping	unk	Hague
Hungerford-Griffin	38.1059940,-76.9855700	373 Resolutions Rd, Leedstown
Lee Family	unk	Stratford Hall
Level Green	unk	Kinsale
McCarty Family	unk	Longwood, Horners Beach
Nomini Hall Graveyard	unk	Hague
Old Pierce Homestead	unk	Level Green
Payne Family, aka Cedar Hill	38.1335700,-76.9706900	Redhouse Horners, 2 mi NE of Leedstown
Rochester Family	unk	Probably old homestead at Lydell's Store, jct Rts 3 & 202
Unidentified	unk	Rt 675, nr Lee Creek, Hague

WILLIAMSBURG CITY

Bruton Parish Church	37.2712700,-76.7024800	331 W Duke of Gloucester St
Cedar Grove	37.2614000,-76.7072000	Jct Rt 132 and Hunting Cove
Eastern State Hospital	37.2556000,-76.7103000	S Henry Street
Governor's Palace Rev War	37.2625000,-76.6997220	300 Palace Green St
Green Hill	unk	Nassau St
Jamestown Church	37.2695297,-76.7563595	3827 Ironbound Rd, Williamsburg
Williamsburg Land Conservancy	37.3092769,-76.7526116	5000 New Point Rd
Wren Chapel, William & Mary	37.2707000,-76.7091000	College of William & Mary, nr jct Jamestown Rd and Richmond Rd

WINCHESTER CITY (See also Frederick County)

Christ Episcopal, Courtyard	38.1846977,-78.1675545	114 W Boscawen St
Ewing Family	unk	Off Stickley Dr to Hayvenhurst Ct
Montour	unk	Not identified by SAR source
Mt Hebron	39.1091600,-78.0949700	305 E Boscawen St
Opequon Presbyterian	39.1393800,-78.1949400	217 Opequon Church Ln

WISE COUNTY

Benjamin Bolling	37.0772100,-82.7054300	Sulpher Springs Dr., Flat Gap
Wells Family	36.8464000,-82.8172000	Rt 739 abt 1 mi S of jct with Rt 605

WYTHE COUNTY

Black Lick Rural Retreat	36.9443500,-81.2437700	2390 Black Lick Rd
Browning's Mill	unk	Old Stage Rd
Crockett	unk	SR 649, turn left to cross RR tracks, to Suthers home
Crockett Family	37.0156000,-81.0550000	Off Rt 600, Crockett's Cove
Dobler Family	unk	nr Kimbersville
Gleaves Farm	unk	Dunkley farm, Cripple Creek
Harris	unk	SR 651, near the SW cnr of jct with SR 690, Cripple Creek
Hillenberg	unk	Maybe SW of Crockett

Horseshoe Bend, Graham Family	36.9491700,-80.9001000	N side of Reed Creek on Formato Dr near jct with E Lee Hwy
Keesling	unk	Grahams Forge
Keesling	unk	Rural Retreat
Kimberling	36.9175000,-81.3044000	Rt 617, Rural Retreat
King	unk	W side Rt 625, S of jct with Rt 667, Crockett
McGavock Family	unk	NW of jct of Rts 610 & 1012, W of Max Meadows
McGavock Family	unk	Peppers Ferry Rd, Ft Chiswell, off I-81, 12 mi E of Wytheville
Montgomery family	unk	Nr Ft Chiswell, in field abt .75 mi behind Ft Chiswell Mansion
Neff Family	unk	E of Fairview Church on Charles Roberts property, Rural Retreat
Newell-Trigg-Sanders	unk	N side of Rt 619 abt .5 mi W of jct with Rt 636, Austinville
Newland	unk	1 mi W on 692 fr jct with SR 749, on hill on right, Cedar Springs
Oglesby Sayers	36.9644000,-80.8303000	Rt 701, Draper's Valley
Old Crockett	37.0416100,-80.9766200	Rt 600, Crockett's Creek Rd, Wytheville
Old Keesling	unk	unk
Peirce Family, aka Chaffin	unk	On hill overlooking SR 69 at jct with I-77 in Poplar Camp
Phipps Family	unk	Wytheville
Rose Hill	unk	Kegley farm 840 Rose Hill Rd, Wytheville
Seybert Family	unk	Gunton Park
Simmerman, aka Cedar Hill	unk	Off I-81 N, open field abt .25 mi E of gravel plant on SR 649
St John's Lutheran	36.9650000,-81.1011000	405 W Main, Wytheville
St Paul's Lutheran	36.9117300,-81.2348400	330 St Pauls Church Rd, Rural Retreat
Steele Family	unk	nr Bland
Stephens, aka Hurst	unk	SR 100 S to SR 607 E to Jett farm, Wytheville, nr Carroll Co line
Trigg	unk	Wytheville, N side of Rt 619, abt .5 mi W of jct Rts 619 & 636
West End	36.9414000,-81.1167000	Off Rt 11, Wytheville
Zion Lutheran	36.8411000,-81.2231000	1417 Zion Church Rd, Crockett

YORK COUNTY

Carter Crafford	unk	Fort Eustis SW of golf course maint shop
Cheatham Cemetery Annex	37.2822000,-76.5911000	loc adjacent to a tee on the golf course, Naval Weapons Station, Yorktown
Eltham Plantation	37.2691940,-76.6620570	Yorktown
Essex Lodge, aka Washington's Lodge	unk	Check property records
French Memorial	36.8194400,-79.3993300	Yorktown
Grace Episcopal	37.2356000,-76.5075000	115 Church St, Yorktown
Moore House	unk	Rt 238, Yorktown
Old Kiskiak	unk	Nr Yorktown
Yorktown Victory Monument	38.2835000,-78.5415000	Yorktown

APPENDIX C - CODE TO & BIBLIOGRAPHY OF SERVICE SOURCES

(Note: volume, issue, type, pages, etc. for many of these sources are listed in the main patriot text)

A Saffell, W.T.R. *Records of the Revolutionary War.* 1894. Reprint, Bowie, MD: Clearfield Co., Inc., 1996.

B Gravestone Inscriptions.

C Brumbaugh, Gaius Marcus. *Revolutionary War Records, Volume I, Virginia.* 1936. Reprint, Baltimore: Genealogical Publishing Company, 1967.

D Abercrombie, Janice L. & Richard Slatten. *Virginia Revolutionary Publick Claims.* Athens, GA: Iberian Publishing Company, 1992. This source includes authors *Index to Virginia Revolutionary War Publick Claims.*

E Gwathmey, J.H. *Historical Register of Virginians in the Revolution 1775-1783.* Richmond, VA: The Dietz Press, 1938.

F Wilson, Samuel M., *Catologue of Revolutionary Soldiers and Sailors of the Commonwealth of Virginia to Whom Land Bounty Warrants Were Granted by Virginia for Military Services in the War for Independence.* 1953. Reprint, Baltimore: Southern Book Company, 2002.

G *Virginia Military Records.* Baltimore: Clearfield Publishing, 2002. Arranged by county. Compiled articles originally published in *The Virginia Magazine of History and Biography*, vthe *William and Mary College Quarterly*, and *Tyler's Quarterly.*

H SAR Patriot Index, Edition III, 2000.

I SAR Revolutionary War Graves Register, NASSAR, edition 2000

J Eby Jerri Lyn. *Laying the Hoe: A Century of Iron Manufacturing, Stafford County, Virginia, With Genealogical Notes on Over 300 Families.* Westminster, MD: Willowbend Books, 2003.

K Wardell, Patrick G. *Virginia/West Virginia Genealogical Data from Revolutionary War Pension and Bounty Land Warrant Records.* 6 volumes. Bowie, MD: Heritage Books, Inc., 1988-1998.

L Stewart, Robert Armistead. *The History of Virginia's Navy in the Revolution.* Richmond: Mitchell & Hoskiss Printers, 1933.

M United States War Department. *The Pension Rolls of 1835.* 4 volumes. 1835. Reprint, Baltimore: Genealogical Publishing Co., Inc., 2002.

N Burgess, Louis A. *Virginia Soldiers of 1776.* 3 volumes. 1927. Reprint, Baltimore: Clearfield Company, 1994.

O Rockingham County, Virginia. Minute Book 1, 1778-1786. County Records, microfilm reel 25. Richmond: Library of Virginia.

P Wayland, John W. *Virginia Valley Records, Genealogical and Historical Materials of Rockingham County, Virginia.* Baltimore: Genealogical Publishing Company, 1965.

Q Thwaite, Reuben Gold and Louis Phelps Kellogg. *Documentary History Lord Dunmore's War 1774.* 1905. Reprint, Harrisonburg, VA: Wisconsin Historical Society, 1974.

R Virginia. Fairfax County Court Booklet 1782.

S NASSAR Graves Registry Patriot & Graves Index http://patriot.sar.org/fmi/iwp/cgi?-db=Grave%20Registry&-loadframes (this site reflects latest up-dates and should be used rather than source BY. Also it provides the NASSAR assigned patriot number.)

T Funkhouser, Jacob. *A Historical Sketch of the Funkhouser Family.* Harrisonburg, VA: Rockingham Register Press, 1902.

U Wayland, John Walter. *Men of Mark and Representative Citizens of Harrisonburg and Rockingham County, Virginia; Portraits and Biographies of Men and Women.* Staunton, VA: McClure Co., 1943.

V Halifax County Commissioner's Book.

W Handbook Stratford Hall Plantation & Lees of Virginia, pub 2004.

X Grigsby, Hugh Blair. "Thomas Lewis." *The History of the Virginia Federal Convention of 1788.* Vol. II. 1890. Abridged, New York: DeCapo Press, 1969.

Y Pittsylvania County Court Book

Z Skidmore, Warren with Donna Kaminsky. *Lord Dunmore's Little War of 1774.* Bowie, MD: Heritage Books, Inc., 2002.

AA Montgomery County Revolutionary War Records. *Southern Campaign American Revolution Pension Statements & Rosters* pertains to Montgomery County, VA http://www.rootsweb.ancestry.com/~vamontgo/southerncampaignamericanrevolutionpensionstatements.

AB Wayland, John Walter. *A History of Rockingham County, Virginia.* Dayton, VA: Ruebush-Elkins Co., 1912.

AC Cabell, James Branch. *The Majors and Their Marriages.* Richmond, VA: Hill Printing Co., 1915.

AD Waddell, Joseph Addison. *Annals of Augusta County, Virginia, From 1726 to 1871.* 2d Ed, Staunton, Va : Caldwell, 1902,c1901

AE *Virginia Genealogy Society Quarterly*, volume 2 (Richmond, VA: Virginia Genealogical Society, 1964.

AF Clements, S. Eugene and F. Edward Wright. *The Maryland Militia in the Revolutionary War.* Silver Spring, MD: Family Line Publications, 1987.

AG Family Tree Maker CD #145, *Military Records: Revolutionary War Pension Lists*

AH Bockstruck, Lloyd D. *Virginia's Colonial Soldiers.* Baltimore: Genealogical Publishing Co., Inc., 1988.

AI Scott, W. W. *A History of Orange County, Virginia.* Richmond, VA: Everett Waddey Company, 1907.

AJ Office of the Secretary of State. *Massachusetts Soldiers and Sailors of the Revolutionary War: A Compilation from the Archives.* Boston: Wright & Potter Printing Company, State Printers, 1896-1898.

AK VASSAR Graves Registration Submissions

AL *Revolutionary War Public Service Claims.* "On-line Catalog: Images and Indexes." Library of Virginia. Searchable by name only, giving County and citation to the County Court Booklet and State Auditor's Commissioners Book. Original images are on microfilm. http://www.lva.virginia.gov/ : 2015.

AM McIlwaine, Henry Read, *Executive Journals of the Council of Colonial Virginia,* Vol II, VA State Library, 1864-1934, pub 1925.

AN *Virginia Revolutionary War State Pensions.* "Images and Indexes." Library of Virginia. Not to be confused with federal pensions at the National Archives. Original images are on microfilm. http://www.lva.virginia.gov/ : 2015.

AO Lineage Books, NSDAR, Vol I & II, Ancestors Index.

AP   National Archives Records Administration, Washington, D.C. Revolutionary War Compiled Military Service Record and/or Pension File. File numbers given in the text.

AQ   *Biographical Directory of the United States Congress 1774 to Present.* Washington, DC: U.S. Government Printing Office. On line http://bioguide.congress.gov : 2015.

AR   Hatcher, Patricia Law. *Abstract of Graves of Revolutionary Patriots*. 4 volumes. Dallas, TX: Pioneer Heritage Press, 1987. Also available at ancestry.com (subscription service).

AS   Rev War Graves Committee, NSSAR *Master Roster of Patriots of Rev War,* Jan 2007.

AT   *Virginia Genealogies and Biographies 1500's-1900's.* Genealogy.com. Novato, UT: Brøderbund Software, 2000. This 2-CD bundle is a compilation of 22 Genealogical Publishing Company volumes. Applies to: see text for patriot.

AU   Williamsburg Chapter VASSAR, "Study of Burials from Green Springs Battle", Ltr Feb 2007.

AV   CMM SAR Chapter *CMM Battalion Roster,* prepared 2005, revised 2007.

AW   Hurt, Frances Hallum. *An Intimate History of the American Revolution in Pittsylvania County, Virginia.* Danville, VA: Womack Press, 1976.

AX   *New York in the Revolution and the War of 1812.* CD-ROM. Family Tree Maker. Novato, UT: Brøderbund Software, 2000.

AY   Brumbaugh, Gaius Marcus. *Genealogical Records: Maryland Settlers & Soldiers 1700s-1800s.* CD-ROM. Novato, CA: Genealogy.com, 2000. Muster rolls and other records of service.

AZ   McAllister, Joseph Thompson. *Virginia Militia in the Revolutionary War.* Hot Springs, VA: McAllister Publishing Company, 1913.

BA   Virginia Historical Inventory. WPA Survey Reports of Burials in Prince George County, Library of Virginia, Richmond.

BB   Fairfax Resolves Chapter, VASSAR *Legislative Petitions Alexandria & Fairfax County, VA* 2009.

BC   Lewis Preston et al. *Annals of Southwest Virginia, 1769-1800.* Vol. I. 1929. Reprint, Baltimore: Genealogical Publishing Co., Inc., 1996.

BD   Berg, Fred Anderson. *Encyclopedia of Continental Army Units—Battalions, Regiments and Independent Corps.* Harrisburg, PA: Stackpole Books, 1992.

BE   Stewart, Robert Armistead, *Virginia Navy in the Revolution,* Virginia Magazine of History and Biography. Richmond: Virginia Historical Society. Also at Ancestry.com. *Virginia Navy in the Revolution* [database on-line]. Provo, UT, USA: Ancestry.com Operations Inc., 1998.

BF   *Maryland and Delaware Revolutionary Patriots 1775-1783, Military Records.* CD-ROM. Genealogy.com. Novato, UT: Brøderbund Software, 2001.

BG   Boddie, John Bennett. *Historical Southern Families,* volume X. (For page numbers see text for patriot).

BH   *Southern Genealogies 1600-1800. (*For volume and page numbers see text for patriot).

BI   Dixon, Joan M. *National Intelligencer Newspaper Abstracts 1814-1817.* Westminster, MD: Heritage Books, 2006.

BJ   Newman, Harry Wright. *Maryland Revolutionary Records.*1938. Reprint, Baltimore: Genealogical Publishing Co., Inc, 2002.

BK   Virginia Historical Inventory. WPA Survey Reports of Burials in Russell County, Library of Virginia, Richmond.

BL   Stryker, William S. *Official Register of the Officers and Men of New Jersey in the Revolutionary War*. New   Jersey Historical Records Project, Adjutant-Generals Office. Trenton, NJ: W. T. Nicholson & Co., 1872.

BM   Virginia Historical Inventory. WPA Survey Reports of Burials in Bath County, Library of Virginia, Richmond.

BN   Virginia Historical Inventory. WPA Survey Reports of Burials in Lunenburg County, Library of Virginia, Richmond.

BO   Virginia Historical Inventory. WPA Survey Reports of Burials in Rappahannock County, Library of Virginia, Richmond.

BP   Henley, B. J. *Obituaries from VA Newspapers,* on Microfilm Lib of VA. (For name of reel; Reel #, etc. see text for patriot).

BQ   Charles R. Sydnor, Jr. "Northern Neck of Virginia Historical Society, February 27, 2009, Annual   Commemoration of the Leedstown Resolutions." Text of Mr. Sydnor's address reprinted in the   *Northern Neck of Virginia   Historical Magazine* LIX (December 2009), 7153-7163. (Contains biographical   information on some of the signers).

BR   *American Beacon & Norfolk Daily Advertizer (*Obituaries.*or Death Notices?)* Microfilm# Reel # see text for patriot.

BS   Bushman, Katherine Gentry. *Augusta County, Virginia Court of Claims, 1782-1785.* Staunton, VA: Virginia Daughters of the American Revolution, Col. Thomas Hughart Chapter, 1970.

BT   Daughters of the American Revolution grave markers.

BU   Hanks, Chris W. "Patriots' Graves in Pittsylvania County." *Pittsylvania County History.com*. http://pittsylvaniacountyhistory.com/patriots/: 1 March 2015. Email: cwhanks@gmail.com.

BV   Chiarito, Marian Dodson, "Oaths of Allegiance - 1777 Pittsylvania County, VA." *Magazine of Virginia Genealogy* 23 (February, 1985). Retyped and digitized by Cynthia Hubbard Headen at rootsweb.ancestry.com under the same title at http://www.rootsweb.ancestry.com/~vapittsy/Oaths.html : 2015.

BW   Kegley, Mary B. *Militia of Montgomery County, Virginia, 1777-1790.* 1970. Reprint, Dublin, VA: private printing, 1997.

BX   Bockstruck, Lloyd Dewitt. *Revolutionary War Pensions Awarded By State Governments 1775-1884, The   General and Federal Governments Prior to 1814, and by Private Acts of Congress Prior to 1905.* Baltimore: Genealogical Publishing Co, Inc., 2011.

BY   "Patriot Grave Search." *National Society of the Sons of the American Revolution.* https://memberinfo.sar.org/patriotsearch/search.aspx : 2015.

BZ   DAR Records 56th-77th Annual Reports DAR. Senate documents (United States Congress, Senate). Government Printing Office: Washington, DC.

CA   National Society of the Sons of the American Revolution. Louisville, KY. Approved membership applications.

CB   Hogandobler, Matt. "Service for Veterans & Patriots Buried at St Paul's Church, Norfolk, VA, Dec 2011." Unpublished copy for compiler.

CC   Prince William County, Virginia. Order Book 1778-1784. Prince William County Records, microfilm reel 88. Richmond: Library of Virginia.

CD   Find A Grave. www.findagrave.com. Memorials giving biographical information that include documented service in the Revolutionary War.

CE   Sanchez-Saavedra, E. M. *A Guide to Virginia Military Organizations in the American Revolution, 1774-1787*. Richmond: Virginia State Library, 1978.

CF   Arlington National Cemetery Interment Cards. "U.S., Burial Registers, Military Posts and National Cemeteries Internment Cards, and National Cemeteries, 1862-1960." *Ancestry.com*. http://search.ancestry.com/search/db.aspx?dbid=3135 : 2015. Under an agreement reached in 2002 between the Veterans Administration and Ancestry.com, all burial records for national cemeteries were merged into a single database. Users must enter the name of the deceased veteran and the name of the cemetery to narrow the search to a specific person and cemetery.

CG   White, Virgil D. *Genealogical Abstracts of Revolutionary War Pension Files*. 3 vols. Waynesboro, TN: National Historical Publishing Co., 1990-1992.

CH   Hay, Gertrude May (Sloan). *Roster of Soldiers from North Carolina in the American Revolution, with an appendix containing a collection of miscellaneous records*. Durham, NC: private printing, 1932.

CI   "Revolutionary War." *Fold3.com*. Online index and images. Fold3.com by ancestry.com. There are 21 sources, (For particular source with volumes, pages, etc., see text for patriot).

CJ   Adam, Robert. "Naval Office on the Potomac." *William & Mary Quarterly* 2, 2nd Series (October 1922): 292-295.

CK   Cartmell, T.K. *Shenandoah Valley Pioneers & Their Descendants: A History of Frederick County, Virginia from Its Formation in 1738 to 1908*. Berryville, VA: Chesapeake Book Co., 1963.

CL   Hamilton, Clay and Marti Hiatt. *Claims Presented to the Court of Augusta: 21 March 1782 to March 1785*. Richmond: Virginia Genealogical Society, 2005.

CM   Chalkley, Lyman. *Chronicles of the Scottish-Irish Settlement in Virginia 1745-1800; Extracted from the Original Court Records of Augusta County*. 3 vols. 1912. Reprint, Baltimore: Genealogical Publishing Co, Inc., 1965. (For vol # and page # see text for patriot).

CN: Crozier, William Armstrong. *Virginia County Records: Westmoreland County*. New Series, Vol. I. 1913. Reprint, Baltimore: Genealogical Publishing Co., Inc., 2008.

CO   James, Edward Wilson. *The Lower Norfolk County, Virginia Antiquary,* pub. 1895. Richmond: Whittet & Shepperson, 1895-1906. (For volume # and name of article see text for patriot).

CP   *Dunmore's War (Virginia Payrolls/Public Service Claims, 1775)*. "Online Catalog: Images & Indexes." The Library of Virginia. http://lva1.hosted.exlibrisgroup.com/F/YY5IQP14B3S4JQNSF2DBRNC5QYRNVVV2NQ XR4MLUVCH   YQ8GM9E-22624?func=file&file_name=find-b-clas36&local_base=CLAS36: 2015. Part of Record Group 1. Online database and images contains the names of Virginia citizens or soldiers from the counties of Augusta, Bedford, Botetourt, Culpeper, Dunmore (now Shenandoah), Fincastle and Kentucky who were compensated in 1775 for supplies or service during Dunmore's Expedition against the Delaware, Mingo and Shawnee tribes in 1774. Entries in the volume typically include names, county of residence, name of commander, length of service or item being compensated for, and the amount of compensation.

CQ   Hadfield, Kathleen Halverson, ed. *Historical Notes on Amelia County, Virginia*. Amelia, VA: Amelia County Historical Committee, 1982.

CR   Egle, William Henry. *Some Pennsylvania Women During the War of the Revolution,* Harrisburg, PA: Harrisburn Publishing Co., 1898.

CS   SAR grave marker or cemetery plaque.

CT   Egle, William Henry, ed. *Provincial Papers: Supply, and State Tax Lists of the City and County of Philadelphia for the Years 1781, 1782 and 1783.* Pennsylvania Archives, Third Series, volume XVI. Philadelphia: Secretary of the Commonwealth by W. S. Ray, state printer, 1898.

CU   *Revolutionary War Bounty Warrants.* "On-Line Catalog: Images & Indexes." The Library of Virginia: http://lva1.hosted.exlibrisgroup.com/F/H4BCGKCX18A5AF7IDJLE2FM4KP24SN2CYCV1 IG7JJS3N2KY6VF-26256?func=file&file_name=find-b-clas39&local_base=CLAS39: 2015

CV   Palmer, William Pitt, ed. *Calendar of Virginia State Papers & Other Manuscripts.* Volumes 1 & 2 (1652-1781). 1875-1878. Reprint, New York: Kraus Reprint Corp., 1968.

CW   Liles, Frankie. "Washington County Militia at Kings Mountain." *Magazine of Virginia Genealogy* 52 (Feb 2014), 78-82.

CX   Harman, John Newton. *Annals of Tazewell County, Virginia, 1800-1922.* Richmond: W. C. Hill Printing, 1923. [Original was one volume. Followed up with another author with two volumes, and a later version by Nellie Schreiner-Yantis] (See text for patriot).

CY   Saunders, William L, ed. *The Colonial Records of North Carolina, 1662-1776.* 10 Vols. Raleigh, NC: Trustees of the Public Libraries, pub by State of NC, 1886-1890.

CZ   Eckenrode, James Hamilton, archivist. Virginia State Library, Archives Division. *List of Revolutionary Soldiers of Virginia: Special Report of the Department of Archives and History for 1911.* Richmond: D. Bottom, Superintendent of Public Printing, 1912.

DA   Thomas, William H. B. *Patriots of the Upcountry: Orange County, Virginia in the Revolution.* Orange, VA: Orange County Bicentennial Commission, 1976.

DB   Elliott, Katherine B. *Revolutionary Records, Mecklenburg County, Virginia.* South Hill, VA: private printing by Prestwood Chapter, US Daughters of the American Revolution, 1964.

DC   Little, Barbara Vines. "Amherst County Minute Men, 1776." *Magazine of Virginia Genealogy,* 52 (May 2014), 153-154.

DD   Daughters of the American Revolution. "Ancestor Search." On line database. Index to approved applications. http://services.dar.org/public/dar_research/search/?Tab_ID=1 : 2015.

DE   Rockingham County Minute Books. (See text for patriot for specific record and page numbers).

DF   Stoner, Robert Douthat. *A Seed Bed of the Republic: A Study of the Pioneers in the Upper (Southern) Valley of Virginia.* Roanoke, VA: Roanoke County Historical Society, 1962.

DG   Hill, Judith Parks America. *A history of Henry County, Virginia: With Biographical Sketches of its Most Prominent Citizens and Genealogical Histories of Half a Hundred of its Oldest Families.* 1925. Reprint, Baltimore: Regional Publishing Co., 1962.

DH   Draper, Lyman C. *Kings Mountain and Its Heroes: History of the Battle of Kings Mountain, October 7th 1780 and the Events that Led to It.* Cincinnati: Peter G. Thompson Publishers, 1881.

DI   PA Historical Museum Commission http://phmc.info/historicpreservation.

DJ   *Culpeper County Classes, 1781.* "On-Line Catalog: Images & Indexes." The Library of Virginia. http://www.lva.virginia.gov/ : 2015. Index only, made from a typed transcript from a Photostat copy of the original, which contains errors. Original manuscript is on Revolutionary War Public Service Claims, microfilm reel 7. For an accurate and complete transcript, see: John V. Blankenbaker, *The Culpeper Classes in Culpeper County for January 1781 for Recruiting this State's Quota of Troops to serve in the Continental Army.* Chad's Ford, PA: private printing, 1999 for a complete transcript.

DK   Brumbaugh, Gaius Marcus. *Maryland Settlers & Soldiers 1700s-1800s*. Family Archives CD. *Baltimore:* Genealogical Publishing Co, Inc., 2000.

DL   Summers, Lewis Preston et al. *Annals of Southwest Virginia, 1769-1800.* Vol. II. Johnson City, TN: Overmountain Press, 1929. Has undergone several reprints. (See text for patriot for specifics).

DM   Pedigo, Virginia G. and Lewis Gravely Pedigo, *History of Patrick and Henry Counties, Virginia*. 1933. Reprint, Baltimore: Clearfield Co., 2002.

DN   Evans, James. *Historical and Geographical Encyclopedia, Illustrated*. Chicago: H. H. Hardesty, 1883.   Includes Amherst County, VA families and history.

DO   Ancestry.com. *Partial list of early settlers, Revolutionary soldiers and the graves of Augusta County soldiers located to date* [database on-line]. Provo, UT: Ancestry.com Operations Inc., 2005. Original data: King, Fannie Bayly, *Partial List of Early Settlers, Revolutionary Soldiers and the Graves of Augusta County Soldiers located to date.* Staunton, Va.: private printing, 1935. Ancestry.com. http://search.ancestry.com/search/db.aspx?dbid=10553 : 2015.

DP   Minnis, M. Lee. *The First Regiment of Foot 1775-1783*. [Continental Line, Virginia.] Westminster, MD: Willow Bend Books, 1998.

DQ   Bell, John W. *Memoirs of Governor William Smith, of Virginia. His Political, Military, and Personal History*. New York: The Moss Engraving Co., 1891.

DR   Rager, Susan Godman. "Leedstown Resolves: 1766." *Northern Neck of Virginia Law Page*. Online transcript. http://www.ragerlaw.com/leedstownresolutionspage.htm : Accessed September 2015.

DS   Rev. Horace Edwin Hayden. *Virginia Genealogies*. 1885. Reprint, Baltimore: Southern Book Co., 1959.

DT   Will of Rawleigh Downman, signed 10 March 1781, proved 19 April 1791. Will Book 20, p. 188a-189, Circuit Clerk's Office, Lancaster County Court House, Lancaster, VA.

DU   Reid, R. J., *Oaths of Allegiance, Goochland Co, VA,* Papers,1777-1870, Accession 22032, Personal Papers Collection, The Library of VA.

DV   Binns Genealogy, *1782 and 1783 Personal Property and land Tax Lists for Virginia cities and counties.,* These taxes were used to support cost of Rev War expenses proving patriotic service. Substitute the Virginia county or city and the year 1782 or 1783 and the image pdf number from the service source code "SS" in the patriot paragraph in the site below that shows Fairfax http://www.binnsgenealogy.com/MembersOnlyArea/pdfs/Fairfax/1782Personal/06.pdf

DW   See source AD.

DX   Styker, William Scudder, *New Jersey Continental Line in the Virginia Campaign of 1781,* Jan 20, 2012.

DY   Family Archives CD, *New York in the Revolution as a Colony & State,* vol I the Militia.

DZ   Worrell, Anne Lowry, *Over Mountain Men Their Early Court Records in Southwest Virginia,* Genealogy Publishing Co, Inc., Baltimore, 1976.

EA   Lela C. Adams, Compiler, "1778-1780 Tax Lists of Henry County, Virginia," (Bassett, VA: privately published, 1973).

EB   The Bulletin of the Northumberland County Historical Society, vol 9, 1972, *Northumberland County Tax List, 1782.*

EC: Lohrenz, Otto, *Reverend Thomas Smith of Revolutionary Virginia: A case Study in Social Rank,* Northern Neck of Virginia Historical Magazine, 2004, pgs 6458-6475.

ED: Bryant, William C., Jr, *Packett Family Graveyard-Sabine Hall,* Northern Neck of Virginia Historical Magazine, 2006, pgs 6734-675.

EE: Hopkins, William Lindsay, *Virginia Revolutionary War Land Grant Claims 1783-1850 (Rejected),* Privately printed Richmond, VA 1988.

EF   Jones, Mary Stephens, Complier, Editor, "*18th Century Perspective: Culpeper County,* Culpeper County Historical Society, 1976.

EG   Lillard, Dewey, *Culpeper Classes for 1781: An In Depth Study*, Sep 2001, unpublished, lists classes pertaining to Madison County inhabitants.

EH   Transcribed by Clay Hamilton and Marty Hiatt, *Book of Claims Presented to the Court of Augusta County 1782-1785,* Virginia Genealogical Society, 2005.

EI   Genealogical Publications & Family Archives, CD Rom *Maryland Settlers & Soldiers,* 2000

EJ   Eby, Jerrilyn, *45th Regiment of Virginia Militia, Stafford County 1781-1856 With Biographical Notes on Over 1600 Militia,* Heritage Books, 2011

EK   Wise, Donald ArlingtonCo, VA *Some Eighteenth Century Family Profiles, Part I, Issue 1977 Arlington Hisorical So0ciety Magazine*

EL   Family Archives CD Rom *MD Settlers & Solders,* Gen Publ Co, Inc

EM   VASSAR website, Doc View *Tax list for VA Counties*

EN: Ruth E. Lloyd Information Center (RELIC), Bull Run Regional Library, Manassas, VA *"Prince William County People, 1701-1865" Tithables*

EO   Louise L. Gray & Richard A. Genders, *Historic Buildings in Middlesex Co, VA 1650-1875,* Delmar Printing Co, Charlotte, NC; 1978

EP   Calender, Jamie, *Fairfax'County Men Who Served and Died Advancing The Cause of American Independence 1775-1783,* provided his research and service sources to compiler for a plaque placed at the Fairfax Co Court House 2017 by George Washington SAR Chapter

EQ   Library of Virginia Digital Collections of WPA Survey Reports accessed at http://www.usgwarchives.net

ER   USGenweb Archives Project (List county) Virginia contains county tax lists 1782, 1783 cemeteries, military officers and pensions and other Revolutionary lists/topics

ES: *Epitaphs of Gloucester and Mathews Co in Tidewater VA, Through 1865,* VA State Library, 1959

APPENDIX D – CODE TO & BIBLIOGRAPHY OF BURIAL SOURCES

JLARC, "Special Report: Preservation of Revolutionary War Veteran Gravesites." Virginia. Joint Legislative and Audit Review Commission of the Virginia General Assembly. House Document 42. Also available as a downloadable pdf file at *JLARC*. http://jlarc.virginia.gov/reports/Rpt264.pdf : January 2001. This report used 127 sources, which are numbered in Appendix B of the report. For example, a burial in this book reading JLARC 4, 154 means that sources #4 and #154 were used for that individual.

01　Moxley, J. M. *Gravestone Inscriptions in Amherst County, VA. 1985. Gravestone Inscriptions in Amherst County, Virginia*. Amherst, VA: Amherst County Museum and Historical Society, 1999.

　　This has since been supplemented with: "Gravestone Inscriptions in Amherst County—Gravestones 2." *Amherst County Museum and Historical Society*. Online database. http://www.amherstcountymuseum.org/gravestones.html : 2015. With GPS coordinates. Users will need the original book to use this web site. From the website: "The digital edition contains cemeteries not found in the 1999 edition, corrections to the 1999 edition, and in some instances a cemetery has been re-surveyed. The digital edition will be revised periodically as corrections are noted and new cemeteries and burials are recorded. For this reason, instead of citing by page numbers (which may change as revisions occur), references are to　the cemetery number."

02　Collins, Herbert Ridgeway. *Cemeteries of Caroline County, Volume 2, Private Cemeteries*. Westminster, MD: Family Line Publishers, 1995. (Now published by Colonial Roots, Lewes, DE)

03　Musselman, Homer D. *Stafford County, Virginia Veterans and Cemeteries*. Fredericksburg, VA: Bookcrafters, 1994. Source also includes data from an unpublished addendum by the author in May 2002.

04　SAR Rev War Graves Register Completed Forms, VASSAR.

05　SAR Rev War Graves Register. NASSAR, 2000 Edition.

06　Klein, Margaret C. *Tombstone Inscriptions of Spotsylvania County, Virginia*. Palm Coast, FL: private printing, 1983.

07　Bowers, D. "Pillars of the Past." Fredericksburg (VA) *Free Lance Star*, Nov. 4, 2000, p. 2-3.

08　Virginia Historical Inventory. WPA Cemetery Survey Reports, Spotsylvania County. Library of Virginia, Richmond. See Service Code 75.

09　Durrett, Virginia Wright and Sonya V. Harvison. *Handbook of Historic Sites in Spotsylvania County, Virginia*. Spotsylvania, VA: Spotsylvania Historical Association, 1987.

10　Holtzclaw, B. C. and W. B. Hackley. *Germantown Revisited*. Germanna Record, No. 2, 1962 . Reprint: Locust Grove, VA: Memorial Foundation of the Germanna Colonies, 1980.

11　Jett, Dora Chinn. *Minor Sketches of Major Folk and Where They Sleep: The Old Masonic Burying Ground, Fredericksburg, Virginia*. Richmond: Old Dominion Press, 1928.

12　Quenzel, Carol H. *The History and Background of St, George's Episcopal Church, Fredericksburg, Virginia*. Richmond: for the Vestry, 1951.

13　Hodges, Robert Allen. *The Masonic Cemetery of Fredericksburg, Virginia*. Fredericksburg, VA: private printing, 1991—original entry here said published 1951.

14　Collins, Herbert Ridgeway. *Cemeteries of Caroline County, Virginia*. Vol. 1, Public Cemeteries. Westminster, MD: Family Line Publications, 1994. Currently published by Colonial Roots, Lewes, Delaware.

15   Turner, Ronald R. *Prince William County, Virginia Burial index 1800-2001.* Manassas, VA: private printing, 2001.

16   Conners, E.R., III. *One Hundred Old Cemeteries of Prince William County, Virginia.* Manassas, VA: private printing, 1981.

17   Klein, Margaret C. *Tombstone Inscriptions of King George County, Virginia.* Baltimore: Genealogical Publishing Co., Inc., 1979.

18   Baird, Nancy Chappalear, Carol Jordan and Joseph Scherer. *Fauquier County, Virginia Tombstone Inscriptions.* Vol. I. Bowie, MD: Heritage Books, 2000.

19   Baird, Nancy Chappalear, Carol Jordan and Joseph Scherer. *Fauquier County, Virginia Tombstone Inscriptions.* Vol. II. Bowie, MD: Heritage Books, 2000.

20   Pippenger, Wesley E. *Tombstone Inscriptions of Alexandria, Virginia.* Vol. III. Westminster, MD: Family Line Publications, 1992.

21   Rudd, Alice B. *Shockoe Cemetery, Richmond, Virginia: Register of Internments, April 10 1822 –December 31, 1950.* 2 volumes. Washington, DC: private printing, 1960.

22   Klein, Margaret C. *Tombstone Inscriptions of Orange County, Virginia.* 1979. Reprint, Baltimore: Clearfield Publishing Co., Inc., 2001.

23   Pippenger, Wesley E. *Tombstone Inscriptions of Alexandria, Virginia.* Vol, I. Westminster, MD: Family Line Publications, 2000.

24   Pearson, Virginia Drewry McGeorge. "Family and Cemetery Records." *Northern Neck of Virginia Historical Magazine,* XX (1970), xxxx. Used for Wellford Family Cemetery at Sabine Hall" in Warsaw, Richmond County.

25   Thomas Balch Library. *Loudoun County, Virginia Cemeteries: A Preliminary Index.* Lovettsville, VA: Willow Bend Books, 1996.

26   Goodwin, William Arthur Rutherford. *Bruton Parish Church Restored & Its Historic Environment.* Petersburg, VA: The Franklin Press, 1907. *Historical Sketch of Bruton Church, Williamsburg, VA,* pub 1903.

27   Matthews, Bettie Jo. *Cedar Grove Cemetery, Portsmouth, Virginia Plot Book 1 and Book 2.* Bowie, M: Heritage Books, 1992.

28   Moore, J. Staunton and L. W. Burton. The *Annals and History of Henrico Parish, Diocese of Virginia, and St. John's Church P.E. Church.* 1904. Reprint, Baltimore: Genealogical Publishing Co., Inc., 1997.

29   Jones, Mary Stevens. *An 18th Century Perspective: Culpeper County.* Culpeper, VA: Culpeper Historical Society, 1976.

30   Eby, Jerrilyn. *They Called Stafford Home: The Development of Stafford County, Virginia from 1600 until 1865.* Bowie, MD: Heritage Books, Inc., 1997.

31   Yates, Helen Kay and W. E. Winfrey. *Family Graveyards in Hanover County, Virginia.* 2 volumes. Hanover, VA: Hanover County Historical Society, 1995, 2000.

32   Letters and e-mail correspondence from submitters. Compiler's files.

33   Cemetery Files. Rappahannock County Historical Society, 328 Gay St., Washington, VA.

34   Eby, Jerrilyn. *Laying the Hoe: A Century of Iron Manufacturing, Stafford County, Virginia, With Genealogical Notes on Over 300 Families.* Westminster, MD: Willowbend Books, 2003.

35   Delaney, T. *Veteran Burials in Old City Cemetery, Lynchburg, VA,* revised list of 2005.

36   *Burials in Augusta County, Virginia Cemeteries*. Staunton, VA: Augusta County Historical Society, 1985. Original entry was: Hamrick, R. M. Jr., *Burials in Augusta County, VA Cemeteries, Part I*.

37   Mihalyka, Jean Merritt and Faye Downing Wilson. *Graven Stones of Lower Accomack County, Virginia*. Pub 1986.

38   Cary, Mary Frances with Moody K. Miles III and Barry W. Miles. *Tombstone Inscriptions of Upper Accomack County, Virginia*. Bowie, MD: Heritage Books, 1995.

39   Wright, F. Edward. *Quaker Records of Henrico Monthly Meeting, And Other Church Records of Henrico, New Kent and Charles City Counties, Virginia*. Lewes, MD: Colonial Roots, 2002.

40   Hill, Margaret Lester and Clyde H. Ratcliffe. *In Remembrance: Gravestone Inscriptions and Burials of Lancaster County, Virginia*. White Stone, VA: private printing, 2002.

41   Miles, Barry W. with James H. Mero and Joseph A. Atkins. *Cemeteries City of Hampton, VA, Formally Elizabeth County*. Bowie, MD: Heritage Books, 1999.

42   Mihalyka, Jean Merrit. *Gravestone Inscriptions in Northampton County, Virginia*. Richmond: Virginia State Library, 1984.

43   Sheridan, Christine L. and Elsie W. Ernst. *Tombstones of Mathews County, Virginia, 1711-1986*. Mathew, VA: Mathews County Historical Society, 1988.

44   Augusta County Historical Society. *Burials in Augusta County, Virginia Cemeteries*. Staunton, VA: The Society, 1985.Original entry was: Hamrick, R.M. Jr., *Burials in Augusta County, VA Cemeteries, Part II*.

45   Miles, Barry W. & Gertrude Stead. *Cemeteries of the City of Newport News, Formerly Warwick County, Virginia*. Bowie, MD: Heritage Books, 1999.

46   Hamner, Ann K. *Grave Sites and Cemeteries in Goochland County, Virginia*. Goochland, VA: private printing, 1990.

47   *William & Mary Quarterly*. See text for patriot for volume, pages, etc.

48   Branch, Joseph Bryan. Association for the Preservation of Virginia Antiquities. *Epitaphs of Gloucester and Mathews Counties, Virginia, Through 1865*. Richmond: Virginia State Library, 1959.

49   Murphy, W.A., Mrs. & Fanny Bayly King. *Glebe Burying Ground, 1749*. [Augusta County.] Staunton, VA: Col. Thomas Hughart Chapter, Virginia Daughters of the American Revolution, 1934.

50   Winchester-Frederick Co Historical Society. *2200 Gravestone Inscriptions from Winchester and Frederick County, Virginia*, also *Gravestone Inscriptions from 61 Graveyards in Frederick Co. Both were published by Winchester-Frederick County Historical Society in 1960.*

51   Not used.

52   Hull, Janice J. R. *Buckingham Burials, A Survey Cemeteries in Buckingham County, Virginia*. Vol. I. Alexandria, VA: Hearthside Press, 1997.

53   "Southampton County Historical Society Cemetery Project." *Southampton County Historical Society—Rootsweb*. http://www.rootsweb.ancestry.com/~vaschs/cemetery.htm : 2015.

54   Moore, Munsey Adams. *Cemetery and Tombstone Records of Mecklenburg County, Virginia*. 2 vols. Chase City, VA: Munsey Moore pub., 1982-1987.

55   Research Committee, Giles County Historical Society. *Giles County, Virginia, History—Families*. No place: Giles County Historical Society, 1982.

56   Lipowicz, Rachel Baker. *Gone But Not Forgotten, Gravestone Inscriptions and Burials of Chesterfield County, Virginia.* Chesterfield, VA: Chesterfield County Historical Society Cemetery Committee, 1998.

57   Not used.

58   Royston, Donald R and Mary L. Royston. *Cemeteries of Clarke County, Virginia.* Athens, GA: New Papyrus Publishing, 2005.

59   Delaney-Painter, Nancy and Susan L. McCabe. *Index to Burials in Frederick County, Virginia.* Westminster, MD: Willow Bend Books, 2004.

60   "Virginia Cemetery Records." On-line database, searchable by county / independent city. *Interment.net.* http://interment.net/us/va/index.htm : 2015.

61   Fairfax Genealogical Society. *Fairfax County, Virginia Gravestones.* 6 volumes. Merrifield, VA: The Society, 1994-1998.

62   Baber, Lucy H. M. *Behind the Old Brick Wall: A Cemetery Story.* Lynchburg Committee of the Colonial Dames of America in the Commonwealth of Virginia, 1968. Whittet & Shepperson printers, Richmond.

63   *Tombstone Inscriptions of Norfolk, County, Virginia.* Norfolk, VA: Norfolk County Historical Society of Chesapeake, Virginia and National Society of the Daughters of the American Revolution (Norfolk, VA), 1979.

64   *Cemeteries King George County.* Vol. 1, Church Cemeteries. King George, VA: King George County Historical Society, 2000.

65   Rootsweb, VA Tombstone Photo Project Index

66   *Family Cemeteries in Fluvanna County, Virginia.* Palmyra, VA: Fluvanna County Historical Society and US Daughters of the American Revolution, Point of Fork Chapter (Fort Union), by Seven Islands Publishing, 1996.

67   Early, Mrs. John E. and Mrs. Gordon F. Harris. *Records of Cemeteries in Albemarle County, Virginia, including Charlottesville.* 12 volumes. Charlottesville, VA: US Daughters of the American Revolution, Jack Jouett Chapter (Charlottesville), 1971-72.

68   Burow, Suzanne. Carroll County Historical Society. *Cemetery Records of Carroll County, Virginia.* Baltimore: Gateway Press, 1990.

69   Arlington Genealogy Club. *Graveyards of Arlington County, Virginia.* Arlington, VA: National Genealogical Society, 1985.

70   US Daughters of the American Revolution, Frances Bland Chapter (Petersburg). *Dinwiddie County, Virginia Graveyard Records.* Petersburg, VA: The Society, 1945.

71   Rudolph, Mrs. C. F. *Record Tombstone Inscriptions in the Old Fort Defiance Cemetery, Fort Defiance, Augusta County, Virginia.* No place: private printing, 1952.

72   Alleghany Highlands Genealogical Society. *Survey of Various Cemeteries of Alleghany County. Virginia.* 3 volumes. Covington, VA: The Society, 1995-97.

73   McNeely, Mike. "The Brugh Cemetery, Botetourt County, Virginia." Text file. *The Tombstone Transcription Project, Virginia, Botetourt County. USGenWeb Archives.* http://files.usgwarchives.net/va/botetourt/cemeteries/brugh.txt : 2015

74   Ayers, Charles Linard and Ruth G. Hale. "Old Glade Creek Cemetery Additions—Botetourt County." Text file. *The Tombstone Transcription Project, Virginia, Botetourt County. USGenWeb Archives.* http://files.usgwarchives.net/va/botetourt/cemeteries/oldglade02.txt : 2015.

75   Virginia Historical Inventory. WPA Cemetery Survey Reports. Library of Virginia, Richmond. Available at Library of Virginia>online Catalog> Indexes and Images>Virginia

Historical Inventory, search word "cemeteries." Alphabetical listing by county. http://www.lva.virginia.gov/

76   Early, Ruth Hairston. *Campbell Chronicles & Family Sketches, 1782-1926.* 1927, Reprint. Baltimore: Regional Publishing Company, 1978.

77   Nowery, Catherine Lynn. *Tombstone Inscriptions of Powhatan County, Virginia.* 2 volumes. Rock Hill, SC: privately printed, 1996-97.

78   McConnell, Catherine S. *High on A Windy Hill.* Bristol, TN: The King Printing Company, 1968. Washington County Historical Society. High on A Windy Hill: Cemeteries of Washington County, Vol. II, 2002? Or the 1968 book plus addendum which is: Niemann, John P. and Rubinette Miller Neimann. *High on A Windy Hill: Index and Addendum, Washington County, Virginia Cemeteries.* Abingdon, VA: Washington County Historical Society, 1989. Original entry read: *High on a Windy Hill (Cem Washington, Co, VA),* pub 1968, additions 1999 [not 1989].

79   Borden, Duane Lyle. *Tombstone Inscriptions of Shenandoah & Page Counties, Virginia.* Ozark, MO: Yates Publishing Co., 1984.

80   Hatcher, Patricia Law. *Abstract of Graves Revolutionary Patriots.* 4 volumes. Westminster, MD: Willow Bend Books, 2001. Citations in the book refer to volume and page number. These volumes are consolidations of annual reports made by the DAR to the U.S. Senate from 1900 to 1974.

81   Ricketts, R. D. "Danny". *Dan River Plantations, Danville & Pittsylvania Co, VA.* He also has a blog site called Ricketts.com

82   Franklin County Heritage Society. *Cemeteries of Franklin County, Va.* Henry, VA: B & C Publishing Co., 1998.

83   Payne, L. C. & L. W. *Fauquier family Cemeteries of Rev War,* Mar 2007.

84   The National Society of the Colonial Dames of America in the State of Virginia. *The Parish Register of Christ Church, Middlesex County, Va. from 1653 to 1812.* 1897. Reprint with revised index, Easley, SC: Southern Historical Press, 1988.

85   The National Society of the Colonial Dames of America in the State of Virginia. *Parish Register of St Peter's Parish, New Kent County, Virginia 1680-1787.* Richmond: Wm. Ellis Jones, Book and Job Printer, 1904.

86   Clarke, Peyton Neale. *Old King William Homes & Families: An Account of Some of the Old Homesteads and Families of King William County, From Its Earliest Settlement.* 1897. Reprint, Baltimore: Regional Publishing Company, 1964.

87   "St. Paul's Church." *The Key* (December 1984). Norfolk Genealogical Society.

88   Gray, Louise E., Richard H. Genders et al. Middlesex County Board of Supervisors. *Historic Buildings in Middlesex County, Virginia 1650-1875.* Charlotte, NC: Delmar Printing Co., 1978.

89   The Hugh S. Watson, Jr. Genealogical Society of Tidewater, Virginia. *Gravestone Inscriptions From the Cemetery of St Johns Episcopal Church, Hampton, Virginia. Hampton, VA: Thomas Nelson Community College, 1975.*

90   *Tombstone Inscriptions from the Family Cemetery at 'Hilton,' Madison County, Virginia.* Virginia Magazine of History and Biography 62 (April 1954), 211-212.

91   Pittsylvania Historical Society. "Gravestones in Pittsylvania County." *The Quill Pen.* This is a quarterly journal started in 1982, now called the *Pittsylvania Packet.* Name changed in August 1991.

92   Butt, Marshall W. and Dean Burgess, D. *Surviving Gravestones at Trinity Church, Portsmouth, Virginia.* Portsmouth, VA: private printing, 2000.

93   "Cemetery Records." Photos and transcripts of inscriptions of tombstones, often annotated with   additional biographical data. Listed in alphabetical order by cemetery name. *Carol's House.* http://carolshouse.com/cemeteryrecords/ : 2015.

94   Virginia Historical Inventory. WPA Cemetery Survey Reports, Prince William County. Library of Virginia, Richmond. See Service Code 75.

95   Virginia Historical Inventory. WPA Cemetery Survey Reports, Fauquier County. Library of Virginia, Richmond. See Service Code 75.

96   *Records of Dettingen Parish, Prince William County, Virginia 1745-1802.* Dumfries, VA: Historic Dumfries, 1976.

97   Sturgill, Mack Howard and Kenneth Lee. *Smyth County Virginia Cemeteries.* 4 vols. No place: private printing, 1993-1994.

98   Virginia Historical Inventory. WPA Cemetery Survey Reports, Caroline County. Library of Virginia, Richmond. See Service Code 75.

99   *Virginia Vital Records, Compiled from Virginia Magazine of History & Biography, William & Mary Quarterly and Tyler's Quarterly.* Baltimore: Clearfield Publishing, 2007. From:C. G. Chamberlayne. "Old Blandford Tombstones," *William and Mary Quarterly* 5, 1st Series (April 1897), 230-240.

100   *Virginia Vital Records.* From: Lyon G. Tyler. "Inscriptions on Old Tombs in Gloucester Co.,Virginia," *William and Mary Quarterly* 3, 1st Series (July 1894), 28-43.

101   *Virginia Vital Records.* Taken from: Rev. S. O. Southall. "Tombstones. New Castle, Hanover County." Tyler's Quarterly 3 (1921), 69.

102   *Virginia Vital Records.* From: George H. S. King. "Tombstone Inscriptions From the Family   Cemetery at 'Jerdone Castle,' Louisa County, Virginia*." Virginia Magazine of History and Biography* 62 (Apr 1954), 208-209.

103   *Virginia Vital Records.* From: Lenora Higginbotham Sweeney. "Epitaphs Copied from the Family   Cemetery at Soldier's Joy, Nelson County, Virginia." *Virginia Magazine of History and Biography* 64 (Apr 1956), 208-209.

104   *Virginia Vital Records.* From: Lyon G. Tyler. *"Old Tombstones in New Kent County." William and Mary Quarterly* 5, 1st Series (1896), 77-81.

105   *Virginia Vital Records.* From: "Early Tombstones in Northumberland, County." *William and Mary Quarterly* 8, 1st Series (Jul 1899), 42-47.

106   *Virginia Vital Records.* From: "Old Tombstones in Northampton & Accomac Counties, Va." *William and Mary Quarterly* 3, 1st Series (Apr 1895), 256-262.

107   *Virginia Vital Records.* From: G. W. Beale. "Inscriptions on Old Tombstones in Westmorelandand Northumberland Counties." *William and Mary Quarterly* 9 (Jul 1990), 25-31.

108   *Virginia Vital Records.* From: G.W. Beale. "Early Tombs in Westmoreland, Richmond and Northumberland Counties." *William and Mary Quarterly* 11, 1st Series (Oct 1902), 123-130; (Jan 1903), 191-195.

109   *Virginia Vital Records*, Appendix A. From: "Inscriptions From Tombstones in King & Queen, Westmoreland, Hanover and Albemarle Counties." *William and Mary Quarterly* 9, 1st Series (Jan 1901), 25-31.

110   Wright, F. Edward, and Wesley E. Pippenger. *Early Church Records of Alexandria City and Fairfax County, Virginia.* Westminster, MD: Family Line Publications, 1996.

111   Virginia Historical Inventory. WPA Cemetery Survey Reports, Prince George County. Library of Virginia, Richmond. See Service Code 75.

112   Virginia Historical Inventory. WPA Cemetery Survey Reports, Frederick County. Library of Virginia, Richmond. See Service Code 75.

113   Virginia Historical Inventory. WPA Cemetery Survey Reports, Warren County. Library of Virginia, Richmond. See Service Code 75.

114   Virginia Historical Inventory. WPA Cemetery Survey Reports, Henrico County. Library of Virginia, Richmond. See Service Code 75.

115   Botetourt County American Bi-Centennial Commission. *Botetourt County History Before 1900 Through County Cemetery Records.* Fincastle, VA: Publications Committee, 1978.

116   Revolutionary War Monument, Peaked Mountain Cemetery, McGaheysville, Rockingham County, Virginia. Bronze plaque commemorating patriots known to be buried here. Erected by the Massanutton Chapter NSDAR on 12 Oct 1981. Original stones are not extant.

117   "Old St. Luke's Church Cemetery" Benn's Church Blvd, Gravestone Study Task Force, Isle of Wight County Historical Society, 2006.

118   Fitzgerald, Magdalene V. *Cole's Burial Ground, Pittsylvania County,* VA (Publisher not determined).

119   Chart of Revolutionary War Soldiers Buried in Mt Hebron Cemetery, Winchester, VA http://www.historicalmarkerproject.com/markers/HMHU6_revolutionary-war-soldiers-in-mt-hebron-cemetery_Winchester-VA.html

120   Virginia Historical Inventory. WPA Cemetery Survey Reports, Page County. Library of Virginia, Richmond. See Service Code 75.

121   Levy, Andrew. *The Great Emancipator: The Forgotten Story of Robert Carter III, The Founding Father Who Freed his Slaves.* New York: Random House, 2005.

122   Roanoke Valley Historical Society. *Roanoke County Graveyards Through 1920.* Roanoke, VA: The Society, 1986.

123   Worrell, Anne Lowry, comp. *Over The Mountain Men: Their Early Court Records in Southwest Virginia.* Baltimore: Genealogical Publishing Co., Inc., 1976.

124   Matheny, Emma R. & Helen K. Yates. *Kingston Parish Register, Gloucester and Matthews Counties, 1749-1827.* Richmond: the authors, 1963.

125   Pilson, O. E. *Tombstone Inscriptions of the Cemeteries in Patrick County, Virginia.* Baltimore:Gateway Press, 1984.

126   Pippenger, Wesley E. *Tombstone Inscriptions of Alexandria, Virginia.* Vol. 2. Westminster, MD: Family Line Publications, 1992.

127   Charles City County Revolutionary War Roster http://www.charlescity.org/rwr/rwr-search.php?button=go&page=1

128   Morrison, Carol A. *Miscellaneous Headstone Inscriptions, Old Blandford Cemetery, Petersburg, Virginia.* Online document: http://vagenweb.petersburghistory.com/old/cemetery/blandfd2.htm. Email: camorrison@ibm.net. June, 2015.

129   Harris, Malcomb H. *Old New Kent County, Virginia: Some Account of the Planters and Plantations in King William County, Virginia.* Vol. I. West Point, VA: private printing, 1977.

130   Virginia county websites, *Burials of Virginia Politicians* http://politicalgraveyard.com/geo/VA

131   "Bedford County Cemetery Listings." On-line database. *USGENWEB Tombstone Transcription Project.* http://www.usgwtombstones.org/virginia/bedford.html - June 2015.

132 Fairfax Resolves Chapter, VASSAR *Virginia Legislative Petitions for Alexandria and Fairfax County.*

133 "Surry County, VA, Cemeteries." *Rootsweb.ancestry.com.* Online database. http://www.rootsweb.ancestry.com/~vaschsm/cemetery.html - June 2105. Compiled by Surry County Historical Society, Surry, VA.

134 Princess Anne Chapter USDAR. *Old Tombstone Records Mathews County, VA,* 1970.

135 Wilson, Thurman Robert & Ruth Boyd Wilson. *Tazewell County Cemeteries.* 3 Vols. No place: private printing, 1992-1994.

136 Friends of Norfolk Historic cemeteries, *Cedar Grove Cemetery Rev War Veterans* 2009 newsletter. For name of newsletter, publication data (issue/volume, number, page number, etc. place published See text for patriot).

137 Letter Jun 2001, Historian Poquoson Presbyterian church.

138 Not used.

139 Virginia Historical Inventory. WPA Cemetery Survey Reports, City of Norfolk. Library of Virginia, Richmond. See Service Code 75.

140 Virginia Historical Inventory. WPA Cemetery Survey Reports, Wythe County. Library of Virginia, Richmond. See Service Code 75.

141 Virginia Historical Inventory. WPA Cemetery Survey Reports, Greenville County. Library of Virginia, Richmond. See Service Code 75.

142 Virginia Historical Inventory. WPA Cemetery Survey Reports, Augusta County. Library of Virginia, Richmond. See Service Code 75.

143 Virginia Historical Inventory. WPA Cemetery Survey Reports, Suffolk County. Library of Virginia, Richmond. See Service Code 75.

144 Virginia Historical Inventory. WPA Cemetery Survey Reports, Southampton County. Library of Virginia, Richmond. See Service Code 75.

145 Virginia Historical Inventory. WPA Cemetery Survey Reports, Accomack County. Library of Virginia, Richmond. See Service Code 75.

146 Dixon, Joan M. *National Intelligencer Newspaper Abstracts 1814-1817.* Bowie, MD: Heritage Books, 2006.

147 Virginia Historical Inventory. WPA Cemetery Survey Reports, City of Portsmouth. Library of Virginia, Richmond. See Service Code 75.

148 Virginia Historical Inventory. WPA Cemetery Survey Reports, Prince Edward County. Library of Virginia, Richmond. See Service Code 75.

149 Virginia Historical Inventory. WPA Cemetery Survey Reports, Louisa County. Library of Virginia, Richmond. See Service Code 75.

150 Virginia Historical Inventory. WPA Cemetery Survey Reports, Floyd County. Library of Virginia, Richmond. See Service Code 75.

151 Virginia Historical Inventory. WPA Cemetery Survey Reports, Nottoway County. Library of Virginia, Richmond. See Service Code 75.

152 Virginia Historical Inventory. WPA Cemetery Survey Reports, Orange County. Library of Virginia, Richmond. See Service Code 75.

153 Virginia Historical Inventory. WPA Cemetery Survey Reports, Isle of Wight County. Library of Virginia, Richmond. See Service Code 75.

154   Virginia Historical Inventory. WPA Cemetery Survey Reports, Rockbridge County. Library of Virginia, Richmond. See Service Code 75.

155   Virginia Historical Inventory. WPA Cemetery Survey Reports, Shenandoah County. Library of Virginia, Richmond. See Service Code 75.

156   Virginia Historical Inventory. WPA Cemetery Survey Reports, Pittsylvania County. Library of Virginia, Richmond. See Service Code 75.

157   Virginia Historical Inventory. WPA Cemetery Survey Reports, Cumberland County. Library of Virginia, Richmond. See Service Code 75.

158   Virginia Historical Inventory. WPA Cemetery Survey Reports, Russell County. Library of Virginia, Richmond. See Service Code 75.

159   Virginia Historical Inventory. WPA Cemetery Survey Reports, Bath County. Library of Virginia, Richmond. See Service Code 75.

160   Virginia Historical Inventory. WPA Cemetery Survey Reports, Alleghany County. Library of Virginia, Richmond. See Service Code 75.

161   Virginia Historical Inventory. WPA Cemetery Survey Reports, Amherst County. Library of Virginia, Richmond. See Service Code 75.

162   Virginia Historical Inventory. WPA Cemetery Survey Reports, City of Lynchburg. Library of Virginia, Richmond. See Service Code 75.

163   Virginia Historical Inventory. WPA Cemetery Survey Reports, Rappahannock County. Library of Virginia, Richmond. See Service Code 75.

164   Virginia Historical Inventory. WPA Cemetery Survey Reports, Fluvanna County. Library of Virginia, Richmond. See Service Code 75.

165   Virginia Historical Inventory. WPA Cemetery Survey Reports, Botetourt County. Library of Virginia, Richmond. See Service Code 75.

166   Virginia Historical Inventory. WPA Cemetery Survey Reports, Dinwiddie County. Library of Virginia, Richmond. See Service Code 75.

167   Virginia Historical Inventory. WPA Cemetery Survey Reports, Culpeper County. Library of Virginia, Richmond. See Service Code 75.

168   Virginia Historical Inventory. WPA Cemetery Survey Reports, City of Richmond. Library of Virginia, Richmond. See Service Code 75.

169   Virginia Historical Inventory. WPA Cemetery Survey Reports, Madison County. Library of Virginia, Richmond. See Service Code 75.

170   Virginia Historical Inventory. WPA Cemetery Survey Reports, City of Williamsburg. Library of Virginia, Richmond. See Service Code 75.

171   Virginia Historical Inventory. WPA Cemetery Survey Reports, Amelia County. Library of Virginia, Richmond. See Service Code 75.

172   Virginia Historical Inventory. WPA Cemetery Survey Reports, Lunenburg County. Library of Virginia, Richmond. See Service Code 75.

173   Virginia Historical Inventory. WPA Cemetery Survey Reports, Buckingham County. Library of Virginia, Richmond. See Service Code 75.

174   Pippenger, Wesley E. *Tombstones of Alexandria Virginia.* Vol V. Bowie, MD: Heritage Books,   2005. Used for St. Mary's Catholic Church.

175   Burial Register St Mary's Catholic Church, Alexandria, VA. http://www.alexandriagazette.com/news/2015/dec/09/column-founding-father-st-marys-catholic-church-an/

176   "Cedar Grove Cemetery." Norfolk Bureau of Cemeteries' [sic] Interment Database. From Cedar Grove Cemetery web page, City of Norfolk web site http://www.norfolk.gov/Facilities/Facility/Details/46 : "The Norfolk Bureau of Cemeteries' interment database is now available online via WebCemeteries.com. [Not searchable by cemetery.] The Bureau's database does not include obituaries or monument photographs. USGenWeb Archives, a cooperative network of volunteers that provides genealogical information on the internet, provides many of these in its interment catalog of Cedar Grove Cemetery." http://www.usgwarchives.net/va/norfolkcity/cemeteries/elmwoodcedargrove/elmcg08-a-bap.html -: June 2015.

177.   Obituaries in American Commercial Beacon & Portsmouth Advertiser http://ldsgenealogy.com/cgi-bin/News-VA.cgi?43036_American_Beacon_and_Norfolk_and_Portsmouth_Daily_Advertiser. (Norfolk, Va.) 1827-1851.

178   VASSAR Burial Committee for St Paul's Church Graveyard (Compiler a member).

179.   Virginia Historical Inventory. WPA Cemetery Survey Reports, Shockoe Hill Cemetery, City of Richmond. Library of Virginia, Richmond. See Service Code 75.

180.   Burial Cards Hollywood Cemetery, City of Richmond. Burial cards on microfilm. Business Records from 1847-2012 (includes interments). On Misc. Reels 626-628, 1015-1024, 1025-1027, 1130-1131, 1829, 4656, 4657, 5403, 6146. (23 reels total). http://lva1.hosted.exlibrisgroup.com/F/AYNNF89VD3EVPVLLD3SLN92BBV1V7TYG877 CFVSYBG5CMSDJ1L-38154?func=full-set-set&set_number=003537&set_entry=000042&format=999

181   Virginia Historical Inventory. WPA Cemetery Survey Reports, Highland County. Library of Virginia, Richmond. See Service Code 75.

182   Virginia Historical Inventory. WPA Cemetery Survey Reports, Nelson County. Library of Virginia, Richmond. See Service Code 75.

183   Virginia Historical Inventory. WPA Cemetery Survey Reports, Bristol Cemetery, Washington County. Library of Virginia, Richmond. See Service Code 75.

184   Virginia Historical Inventory. WPA Cemetery Survey Reports, Hebrew Cemetery, City of Richmond. Library of Virginia, Richmond. See Service Code 75.

185   Virginia Historical Inventory. WPA Cemetery Survey Reports, Roanoke County. Library of Virginia, Richmond. See Service Code 75.

186   Virginia Historical Inventory. WPA Cemetery Survey Reports, Rockingham County. Library of Virginia, Richmond. See Service Code 75.

187   Virginia Historical Inventory. WPA Cemetery Survey Reports, Powhatan County. Library of Virginia, Richmond. See Service Code 75.

188   Virginia Historical Inventory. WPA Cemetery Survey Reports, Blandford County. Library of Virginia, Richmond. See Service Code 75.

189   Mallory, Dalton W. *Westmoreland County, Virginia Cemeteries, Vol. 1*. Athens, GA: New Papyrus Publishing, 2009.

190   Prince William County cemetery website. *http://www.historicprincewilliam.org/cemeteries.html*

191   Rockingham County Historical Society 2011 rootsweb.ancestry.com

192   Norfolk/Portsmouth Obituaries Journal *https://www.genealogybank.com/explore/newspapers/historical-obituaries/usa/virginia/norfolk*

193   *Death Notices from Richmond, Virginia Newspapers 1821-1840.* Special Publication No. 9. Richmond: Virginia Genealogical Society, 1987.

194   Chris Hanks. *Pittsylvania County History.* http://www.PittsylvaniaCountyHistory.com

195   Wikipedia, the free encyclopedia. *https://en.wikipedia.org/wiki/Home_page*

196   Find A Grave. http://findagrave.com/index.html

197   NSSAR Patriot Grave Search https://memberinfo.sar.org/patriotsearch/search.aspx

198   Not used.

199   http://usgwtombstone.org/virginia/virginia.html VA tombstone Transcription Project (WPA Reports).

200   William & Mary Quarterly. See text for patriot for specifics.

201   Virginia Historical Inventory. WPA Cemetery Survey Reports, Appomattox County. Library of Virginia, Richmond. See Code 75.

202   Virginia Historical Inventory. WPA Cemetery Survey Reports, Hampton [City]. Library of Virginia, Richmond. See Code 75.

203   Arlington National Cemetery Interment Cards. "U.S., Burial Registers, Military Posts and National Cemeteries Internment Cards, and National   Cemeteries, 1862-1960." *Ancestry.com.*   http://search.ancestry.com/search/db.aspx?dbid=3135 : 2015. Under an agreement reached in 2002 between the Veterans Administration and Ancestry.com, all burial records for national cemeteries were merged into a single database. Users must enter the name of the deceased veteran and the name of the cemetery to narrow the search to a specific person and cemetery.

204   Not used.

205   Mt Hebron Cemetery, Winchester, VA website Internment Records http://mthebroncemetery.org

206   Charles Randolph Hughes, *Gravestone Records from Old Chapel Cemetery, Located at Berryville, Clarke Co., Virginia,* Berryville, VA printed by Blue Ridge Press, 1906.

207   *Gravestones in the Cemetery, Ware Episcopal Church* [Gloucester County]. Alphabetical listing by name, with plot numbers. http://warechurch.org - June 2015.

208   Wilson, Howard McKnight. *The Tinkling Spring, Headwater of Freedom: The Study of a Church and Her People 1732-1952.* Fisherville, VA: private printing, 1954.

209   Stith, Wayne. "Cemetery Documentation Project—Gravestones of the Eastern Shore of Virginia." *Easternshore.com.* Accomack County. *http://easternshorestuff.com/cemeteryproject/acccems.htm*

210   Chalkley, Lyman. *Chronicles of the Scotch-Irish Settlement in Virginia.* Vol. II. 1912. Reprint, Baltimore: Genealogical Publishing Co., Inc., 1965.

211   Frain, Elizabeth R. *Union Cemetery, Leesburg, Loudoun County, Virginia: Plats A & B 1784-1995.* Lovettsville, VA: 1995

212   Green, Laurie Boush & Virginia Bonney West. *Old Churches, Their Cemeteries and Family Graveyards of Princes Anne County, Virginia.* Virginia Beach: the authors, 1985.

213   Mary R. Miller. *Place Names of the Northern Neck.* Richmond: Virginia State Library, 1983.

214   Downman Family Bible. Photostat of original. Mary Ball Washington Museum & Library, Lancaster, VA.

215   Dew, Allen, *Halifax County, VA Cemeteries.* Website
        http://cemeterycensus.com/va/halif/index.htm

216   Culpeper Co, VA Genealogy Family Search; Tombstone Transcription Project
        https://familysearch.org/learn/wiki/en/Culpeper_County,_Virginia_Genealogy#Cemeteries

217   Chamberlayne, C. G., *Burials in Old Blandford Church Graveyard,* 1896, transcribed by
        K. Torp *http//genealogytrails.com/vir/Dinwiddie/cem_oldblandfordchurch.html;* (Reprinted
        William & Mary Quarterly, 2 volumes, Vol 5, No 4, (Apr 1897) and Vol 6, No1 (Jul 1897)

218   Tombstone Transcription Project, Goochland Co, VA
        http://usgwtombstones.org/virginia/goochland.html

219   *http://www.heritagecenter.com/cemeteries/*

220   *www.genealogy.com/forum/surnames/topics*

221   U.S Genealogical Web Archives for Virginia. *http://www.usgwarchives.net* provides
        Library of Virginia Digital Collections -WPA Survey Reports for all of Virginia 15 pages
        containing 249 surveys 1936-1938

APPENDIX E – GENERAL BIBLIOGRAPHY OF OTHER SOURCES

Note: Books by the same author are denoted with "-----" after the first entry

Adams, Lela C. *Marriages of Patrick County, Virginia 1791-1850*. Bassett, VA: Private printing, 1972.

Ashby, Bernice M. *Shenandoah County Virginia Marriage Bonds 1772-1850*. Berryville, VA: Virginia Book Company, 1967. Marriages are arranged in chronological order.

Baber, Lucy Harrison Miller and Hazel Letts Williamson. *Marriages of Campbell County, Virginia 1782-1810*. Lynchburg, VA: Private printing, 1971.

Biographical Directory of the American Congress 1774-Present. Alexandria, VA: Congressional Quarterly Staff. Biographies of the members of the Continental Congress from September 5, 1774 to October 21, 1788 and the United States Congress from March 4, 1789 to the present. Available on line at:
<http://bioguide.congress.gov/biosearch/biosearch.asp> Active as of June 2012.

Chalkley, Lyman. *Chronicles of the Scotch-Irish Settlement in Virginia, Extracted from the Original Court Records of Augusta County 1745-1800*. 3 Vols. 1912, Reprint. Baltimore: Genealogical Publishing Company, Inc., 1965.

Chamberlayne, Churchill Gibson. *The Vestry Book and Register of Bristol Parish, Virginia 1720-1789*. 1898, Reprint. Greensville, SC: Southern Historical Press, Inc., 1994.

Chapman, Blanche Adams. *Marriages of Isle of Wight County, Virginia, 1628-1800*. 1933, Reprint with Revised Index by Anita Comois. Baltimore: Genealogical Publishing Co., Inc., 1976.

Chiarito, Marian Dodson and James Headley Prendergast. *Marriages of Halifax County Virginia 1801-1831*. Nathalie, VA: The Clarkton Press, 1985.

Davis, Eliza Timberlake. *Frederick County, Virginia, Marriages 1771-1825*. Baltimore: Genealogical Publishing Co., Inc., 1975.

Dennis, Earl S. and Jane E. Smith. *Marriage Bonds of Bedford County, Virginia 1755-1800*. 1933, Reprint with Index to Wills from 1754 to 1830 by Rowland D. Buford. Baltimore: Genealogical Publishing Co., Inc., 1981. Marriages are arranged alphabetically by first letter of last name and thereafter in no discernable order.

Dodd, Virginia Anderson. *Henry County Marriage Bonds 1778-1849*. Richmond, VA: Private printing, 1953.

Elliott, Katherine B. *Marriage Records 1749-1840 Cumberland County Virginia*. South Hill, VA: Private printing, 1969.

First Marriage Record of Augusta County, VA. 1785-1813. Verona, VA: McClure Press for the Col. Thomas Hughart Chapter, D.A.R., 1970. Marriages are arranged chronologically, with an every name index.

Fisher, Theresa A. *Marriage Records of the City of Fredericksburg, and of Orange, Spotsylvania Counties, Virginia 1722-1850*. Bowie, MD: Heritage Books, Inc., 1990.

------. *Marriages of Caroline County, Virginia, 1777-1853*. Bowie, MD: Heritage Books, Inc., 1998.

Fothergill, Augusta B. *Marriage Records of Brunswick County, Virginia 1730-1852*. 1953, Revised. Baltimore: Genealogical Publishing Co., Inc., 1976

Hill, Margaret Lester. *Ball Families of Virginia's Northern Neck: An Outline*. Private printing, 1990.

Hopkins, William Lindsay. *Caroline County Court Records and Marriages, 1787-1810*. Richmond, VA: Private printing, 1987.

Hodge, Robert A. *The Church Register of Rev. Silas M. Bruce for 1832-1881*. Locust Grove, VA: Germania Community College, 1975, Transcript of marriages. Index omits many names.

Jewell, Mrs. Walter Towner. *Loudoun County, Virginia Marriage Bonds 1762-1850*. Berryville, VA: Chesapeake Book Company, 1962.

Kiblinger, William H. and Janice L. Abercrombie. *Marriages of Louisa County, Virginia 1815-1861*. Orange, VA: Central Virginia Newspapers, Inc., 1969. Entries in this book are arranged in chronological order by only. Indexed.

Kilby, Craig M. "The Kelley Brothers and the American Colonization Society: From Northumberland to Liberia." *The Bulletin of the Northumberland County Historical Society*, 45 (2008), 34-53.

Kilby, Craig M. and Jane Langloh. "Lancaster County Estates 1835-1865." Lancaster, VA: Mary Ball Washington Museum & Library. On line at: http://mbwm.org/estates.asp Active as of June 2012.

King, George Harrison Sanford. *Marriages of Richmond County, Virginia 1668-1853*. Fredericksburg, VA: Private Printing, 1964.

Knorr, Catherine L. *Marriages of Brunswick County Virginia 1750-1810*. Pine Bluff, AR: The Perdue Company, 1953.

-----. *Marriages of Charlotte County Virginia 1764-1815*. Pine Bluff, AR: The Perdue Company, 1951.

-----. *Marriages of Halifax County Virginia 1753-1800*. Pine Bluff, AR: The Perdue Company, 1957.

-----. *Marriages of Chesterfield County, Virginia 1771-1815*, Pine Bluff, AR: The Perdue Company, 1958.

-----. *Marriages of Fredericksburg Virginia 1782-1850*. Pine Bluff, AR: Private printing, 1954.

-----. *Marriages of Halifax County Virginia 1753-1800*. Pine Bluff, AR: The Perdue Company, 1957.

-----. *Marriages of Orange County Virginia 1747-1810*. Pine Bluff, AR: The Perdue Company, 1959.

-----. *Marriages of Pittsylvania County Virginia 1767-1805*. Pine Bluff, AR: The Perdue Company, 1956.

-----. *Marriages of Powhatan County Virginia 1777-1830*. Pine Bluff, AR: The Perdue Company, 1957.

-----. *Marriages of Prince Edward County Virginia 1754-1810*. Pine Bluff, AR: The Perdue Company, 1950.

-----. *Marriages of Southampton County Virginia 1750-1810*. Pine Bluff, AR: The Perdue Company, 1955.

-----. *Marriages of Surry County Virginia 1768-1825*. Pine Bluff, AR: The Perdue Company, 1960.

Lee, Elizabeth Nuckolls, *King George County Virginia Marriages, Vol. I, Marriages Book 1, 1786-1850 (including ministers' returns)*. Athens, GA: Iberian Publishing Company, 1995. Arranged alphabetically by first letter of groom's surname, then chronologically. Indexed.

------. *King George County Virginia, Vol. II, Implied Marriages*. Athens, GA: Iberian Publishing Company, 1995.

Lewis, James F. "Westmoreland County, Virginia, Marriages." *The Virginia Genealogist*, Vol. 10, No. 1, 24-56 (January-March, 1966). This article supplements *Westmoreland County Marriages* published by Stratton Nottingham in 1928

Lindsay, Joyce H. *Marriages of Henrico County Virginia 1680-1808*. Richmond, VA: Private printing, 1960.

Marriage Notices from Richmond, Virginia Newspapers 1821-1840. Special Publication No. 10. Richmond, VA: Virginia Genealogical Society, 1988.

Marriages and Deaths from Lynchburg, Virginia Newspapers 1794-1836. Baltimore: Genealogical Publishing Co., Inc., for the Randall Holt Chapter, National Society Daughters of the American Colonists, 1993.

Marriages and Deaths from Richmond, Virginia Newspapers 1780-1820. Special Publication No. 8. Richmond, VA: Virginia Genealogical Society, 1983. Deaths comprise pages 1-175. Marriages comprise pages 176-266. Index to brides comprises pages 267-285. There is no comprehensive index.

Marriage Records 1811-1853, Mecklenburg County Virginia. South Hill, VA: Preswould Chapter of Daughters of the American Revolution, 1962.

Marriages of Middlesex County, Virginia 1740-1852, Special Publication No. 3. Richmond, VA: Virginia Genealogical Society, 1965. The information for this book comes from the Marriage Register compiled from original bonds by the WPA in the 1930s, which is known to contain errors.

Matheny, Emma R. and Helen K. Yates. *Marriages of Lunenburg County Virginia 1746-1853*. Richmond, VA: Private printing, 1967.
McCarty, William M. and Kathleen Much. *McCartys of the Northern Neck, 350 Years of a Virginia Family*. 2005. Revised. Baltimore: Otter Bay Books, 2010.

McGinnis, Carol. *Virginia Genealogy, Sources & Resources*. Baltimore: Genealogical Publishing Co., Inc., 1993.

McIlwaine, H. R. *Index to Obituary Notices in the Richmond Enquirer from May 9, 1804 through 1828 and the Richmond Whig from January, 1824, through 1838*. 1921, Reprint. Baltimore: Genealogical Publishing Co., Inc., 1974. Originally published in the Bulletin of the Virginia State Library Vol. XIV, No. 4, October 1921.

Mihalyka, Jean M. *MARRIAGES Northampton County, Virginia 1660-1854*. 1991, Revised. Bowie, MD: Heritage books, Inc., 2000. This book –itself revised--is a major revision of the work of Stratton Nottingham in 1929.

Morten, Oren F. *A History of Rockbridge County Virginia*. Staunton, VA: The McClure Co., Inc., 1920.

Nance, Joanne Lovelace. *Charlotte County, Virginia 1816-1850, Marriage Bonds and Ministers' Returns (with additions to marriages 1764-1815)*. Charlottesville, VA: The N. W. Lapin Press, 1987.

Nottingham, Stratton. *The Marriage License Bonds of Lancaster County, Virginia from 1701 to 1848*. 1927, Reprint. Baltimore: Clearfield Publishing Company, Inc., 2002.

-----. *The Marriage License Bonds of Mecklenburg County, Virginia from 1765-1810*. Onancock, VA: Private printing,1926.

-----. *The Marriage License Bonds of Northampton County, Virginia from 1706 to 1854*. 1929, Reprint. Baltimore: Genealogical Publishing Company, Inc., 1974. This work was considerably enhanced and revised by Jean M. Mihalyka, see above. Mihalyka' s book is considered the superior source.

-----. *The Marriage License Bonds of Northumberland County, Virginia, from 1783 to 1850*. 1929, Reprint. Baltimore: Genealogical Publishing Co., Inc., 1976.

-----. *The Marriage License Bonds of Westmoreland County 1786-1850*. Onancock, VA: Private printing, 1929. This work was supplemented by James F. Lewis in 1966 (see above.)

Pippenger, Wesley E. *Death Notices from Richmond, Virginia Newspapers 1841-1853.* Richmond: Virginia Genealogical Society, 2002.

-----. *Index to Virginia Estates 1800-1865*. Ten vols. Richmond, VA: Virginia Genealogical Society, 2001-2010.

Pollock, Michael E. *Marriage Bonds of Henrico County, Virginia 1782-1853*. Baltimore: Genealogical Publishing Co., Inc., 1984.

Reddy, Anne Waller and Andrew Lewis Riffe. *Virginia Marriage Bonds Richmond City,* Vol 1. Staunton, VA: The McClure Co., Inc., 1939. Covers years 1797-1853. Entries are in chronological order. Indexed.

Second Marriage Record of Augusta County, VA. 1813-1850. Verona, VA: McClure Press for the Col. Thomas Hughart Chapter, D.A.R., 1972. The entries in the book are in chronological order only.

Strickler, Harry M. *Old Tenth Legion Marriages. Marriages in Rockingham County, Virginia From 1778 to 1816, Taken from the marriage bonds*. Dayton, VA: Joseph K. Ruebush Co., 1928.

Sweeny, Lenora Higginbotham. *Marriage Records of Amherst County, Virginia 1815-1821 And Subscription for Building St. Mark's Church Amherst County, Virginia*. Lynchburg, VA: J. P. Bell Company, Inc., 1961.

Sweeny, William Montgomery. *Marriage Bonds and Other Marriage Records of Amherst County, Virginia 1763-1800*. 1937, Reprint. Baltimore: Genealogical Publishing Company, Inc., 1973.

Turman, Nora Miller. *Marriage Records of Accomack County, Virginia 1776-1854, Recorded in Bonds, Licenses and Ministers' Returns*. Bowie, MD: Heritage Books, Inc., 1994.

Tyler, Lyon G., ed. *Encyclopedia of Virginia Biography*. 4 vols. NY: Lewis Historical Publishing Co., 1915.

Virginia: A Guide to the Old Dominion. Federal Writers' Project. 1941. Reprint. Richmond: Library of Virginia, 1991. Also on line in hypertext format and searchable as *The WPA Guide to the Old Dominion*, University of Virginia, American Studies Program (1999) at: <http://xroads.virginia.edu/~hyper/VAGuide/frame.html> Active as of June 2012.

"Virginia, Marriages, 1785-1946." Salt Lake City, UT: Genealogical Society of Utah. Index based on data collected by the Genealogical Society of Utah. Sources in this collection are varied and noted in the batch number of each entry. It is searchable online at: <https://familysearch.org/search/collection/show#uri=http://familysearch.org/searchapi/search/collection/1708698> Active as of June 21012.

Vogt, John and T. William Kethley, Jr. *Albemarle County Marriages 1780-1853*. 3 vols. Athens, GA: Iberian Publishing Co., 1991.

-----. *Virginia Historic Marriage Register: Clarke County Marriages, 1836-1850*. Athens, GA: Iberian Press, 1983. Clarke County was formed in 1836 from Frederick County.

-----. *Culpeper County Marriages, 1780-1853*. Athens, GA: Iberian Publishing Company, 1986.

-----. *Virginia Historic Marriage Register: Fluvanna County Marriages 1781-1849*. Athens, GA: Iberian Press, 1984.

-----. *Virginia Historic Marriage Register: Frederick County Marriages 1738-1850*. 1984, Revised. Athens, GA: Iberian Press, 1987.

-----. *Virginia Historic Marriage Register: Greene County Marriages 1838-1850*. Athens, GA: Iberian Press, 1984.

-----. *Virginia Historic Marriage Register: Madison County Marriages 1792-1850*. Athens, GA: Iberian Press, 1983.

-----. *Virginia Historic Marriage Register: Nelson County Marriages, 1808-1850*. Athens, GA: Iberian Publishing Company, 1985.

-----. *Virginia Historic Marriage Register: Orange County Marriages, 1747-1850*. Athens, GA: Iberian Press, 1984.

-----. *Virginia Historic Marriage Register: Rappahannock County Marriages, 1833-1850*. Athens, GA: Iberian Press, 1984.

-----. *Virginia Historic Marriage Register: Roanoke County Marriages, 1838-1850*. Athens, GA, Iberian Press, 1984.

-----. *Virginia Historic Marriage Register: Smyth County Marriages, 1832-1850*. Athens, GA, Iberian Press, 1984. Smyth County was formed in 1832 from Washington and Wythe Counties.

-----. *Virginia Historical Marriage Register: Warren County Marriages, 1836-1850*. Athens, GA: Iberian Press, 1983. Warren County was formed from Shenandoah County in 1836. Negative research.

-----. *Virginia Historical Marriage Register: York County Virginia Marriages, volume 1, Bond & Ministers' Returns 1769-1853*. Athens, GA: Iberian Publishing Company, 1994.

Wertz, Mary Alice. *Marriages of Loudoun County, Virginia 1757-1853*. Baltimore: Genealogical Publishing Co., Inc., 1985.

Wingo, Elizabeth B. *Marriages of Norfolk County, Va. (Now City of Chesapeake), 1788, 1793-1817*. Norfolk, VA: Private printing, 1963.

-----. *Marriages of Princess Anne County Virginia 1749-1821*. Norfolk, VA: Private printing, 1961. Princess Anne County became extinct in 1963 and became part of Virginia Beach.

Williams, Kathleen Booth. *Marriages of Amelia County, Virginia 1735-1815*. Private printing, 1961.

-----. *Marriages of Goochland County Virginia 1733-1815*. Private printing, 1960.

-----. *Marriages of Louisa County Virginia 1766-1815*. Alexandria, VA: Private printing, 1959.

-----. *Marriages of Orange County Virginia 1747-1810*. Private printing, 1959.

-----. *Marriages of Pittsylvania County Virginia 1767-1805*. Private printing, 1956.

-----. *Marriages of Pittsylvania County Virginia 1806-1830*. Private printing, 1965.

Wingfield, Marshall. *A History of Caroline County Virginia*. Baltimore: Regional Publishing Co., 1969.

Worrell, Anne Lowry. *A Brief of Wills and Marriages in Montgomery and Fincastle Counties, Virginia 1773-1831*. 1932, Reprint. Berryville, VA: Virginia Book Company, no date

-----. *Early Marriages, Wills, and Some Revolutionary War Records, Botetourt County, Virginia*. Baltimore: Genealogical Publishing Co., Inc., 1975. Marriages generally go no later than 1812.

Yates, William A. "Wythe County, Virginia Marriages, 1790-1800." The Ridge Runners, Vol. 4, No. 1, 58-61 (May 1975).

APPENDIX F –
LISTING OF PARENTS & SPOUSES (FOR SPOUSES LISTING IS BY MAIDEN NAME IF KNOWN, IF NOT KNOWN BY MARRIED NAME)

Abbott, Annie 218
Abbott, Elizabeth Pasquette 461
Abbott, Sallie 80
Abeline, Mary Magdalene 235
Abernathy, Lucy 1
Abernathy, Robert A III 1
Abney, Damney 394
Abney, Maacah 394
Abney, Martha 394
Abney, Mary 34
Abney, Paul 1
Abyvon, George 1
Abyvon, Mariam 1
Accinelli, Marie Adelaide 36
Adams, Abigail 2
Adams, Alice 75
Adams, Andrew 129
Adams, Ann 16
Adams, Anna 368
Adams, Anne 3
Adams, Catherine 102
Adams, Ebenezer 2
Adams, Elizabeth 113
Adams, Elizabeth 324
Adams, Jane 129
Adams, John 16
Adams, John 2
Adams, Judith 85
Adams, Mary 2
Adams, Richard 3
Adams, Richard Sr 2
Adams, Robert Sr 2
Adams, Sara 386
Adams, Sarah 173
Adams, Sarah 441
Adams, Susannah 107
Adams, Tabitha 367
Adams, Thomas Sr 3
Addair, Sarah 231
Addison, Rebecca Plater 464
Adkins, Elizabeth Meredith 380
Adkins, Martha 170
Adkins, William 3
Adkins, William 380
Admire, Mary 423
Aiken, Ann 256
Akers, Sarah 96
Albrecht, Anna 470, 471
Albrecht, Maria 192
Albright, Eve Catherine 352

Alderson, Elizabeth 105
Alderson, Jane 312
Aldin, Mary 305
Aldridge, Jacob 4
Alexander, Archibald 274
Alexander, Archibald 6
Alexander, Elizabeth 126, 254, 274, 407
Alexander, Frances 403
Alexander, Henry 17
Alexander, Jane 17, 38
Alexander, John 5
Alexander, Nancy 4
Alexander, Philip 403
Alexander, Phillip M 6
Alexander, Robert 5
Alexander, Sally 457
Alexander, Sarah 108
Alexander, Susannah 211
Alexander, William 4
Allegre, Giles 6
Alleman, Johann 6
Allen, Dinah 215
Allen, Elizabeth 436
Allen, Elizabeth 441
Allen, Elizabeth 6
Allen, James 416
Allen, James 6
Allen, James 7
Allen, Judith Church 200
Allen, Lydia 7
Allen, Malcolm 275
Allen, Margaret 32
Allen, Martha 7, 8
Allen, Martha Hunt 79
Allen, Mary 7, 275, 416, 449
Allen, Rachel 416
Allen, Rebecca 103
Allen, Robert 7, 8
Allen, Susannah 442
Allen, William 7, 215
Alley, James 651
Alley, Jane 651
Alling, Sarah 414
Allison, Margaret 448
Allison, Mary 29
Allmand, Aaron 8
Allmand, Ann 8
Altaffer, Elizabeth 233
Amber, Jacquelin 75
Ambler, Edward 8, 78

Ambler, Lucy Nelson 68
Ambler, Mary Willis 265
Amiss, Lucy 138
Ammen, Barbara 184
Ammon, Margaret 13, 190
Ammonette, Judith 142
Amonet, Magdelaine 86
Amos, Rebecca 135
Amoss, Susanna 296
Anderson, Agnes 157
Anderson, Ann 214
Anderson, Anne 6
Anderson, Bartholomew 10
Anderson, David Overton 206
Anderson, Edith Cobb 44
Anderson, Elizabeh Dabney 459
Anderson, Elizabeth 50
Anderson, Fanny 88
Anderson, Frances 88
Anderson, James 9, 11, 653
Anderson, Jane 6, 7, 101
Anderson, Jean 101
Anderson, John 7, 651
Anderson, Katherine 281, 282
Anderson, Katherine Rebecca 281
Anderson, Margaret 7
Anderson, Mary 10, 11, 234, 336
Anderson, Mary Lightfoot 463
Anderson, Miriam 9
Anderson, Phebe 10
Anderson, Rachel 379
Anderson, Rebecca 184
Anderson, Robert, 281, 651
Anderson, Sarah 68, 206
Anderson, Sarah Weldon 11
Anderson, Thomas 10
Anderson, William 9
Andrew, Marion 299, 324
Andrews, Abraham 12
Andrews, Benjamin 12
Andrews, Mark 12
Andrews, Sally 12
Andrews, Sarah 406
Andrews, Southy 406
Andrews, Susannah Rainey 96
Andrews, Thomas 12
Andrews, William A 13
Angel, Penalope 449

Appendix F -- Listing of Parents & Spouces (For Spouces Listing is by Maiden Name If Known, If Not Known By Married Name)

Bartee, Margaret 457
Bartee, Thomas 457
Bartleman, Margaret 26
Bartlett, Ann 22
Bartlett, Elizabeth 449
Bartley, Mary Levenia 433, 434
Baskerville, George 26
Baskett, Mary Rosetta 379
Bass, Elizabeth 354
Bass, Joseph 654
Bass, Tabitha 144
Bassett, Elizabeth 182
Bassett, Frances 439
Bassett, William 27
Bates, Mary 283
Baugh, Rebecca 160
Baughman, Barbara 241
Baughman, John 241
Baumann, Johann Jakob 49
Baumgardner, Barbara 411
Baumgartner, Barbara 241
Baurin, Ann Margaret 425
Bauswell, Catherine 284
Baxter, John 411
Baxter, Mary 412
Baxter, Mary Innis 411
Bayley, Ann 104
Bayley, Catharine 104
Bayley, Thomas 104
Bayliss, Elizabeth 297
Baylor, Barbara 225
Baylor, Hannah 77
Baylor, John W 27
Baylor, Lucy 65
Baytop, Ann 374
Beach, Elizabeth 92
Beach, Reuben 92
Beadles, Elizabeth 28
Beadles, Mary 176
Beadles, Robert 28
Beale, Ann Harwar 30
Beale, Catharine 222
Beale, Elizabeth 76
Beale, George 361
Beale, Maria D 352
Beale, Thomas 651
Beale, William 28, 77, 651
Beale, Winifred Travers 77, 651
Beall, Anna 361
Bean, Barbara 42
Bean, Sarah 78
Beans, Ruth 411
Bear, Anna Maria 191
Bear, Barbara 11
Bear, Elizabeth 422

Bear, Jacob 191
Bear, Maria Eva 52, 471
Beard, Elizabeth 291
Beard, Ester 5
Beauford, John 62
Beaver, Catherine Mauck 402
Beaver, Christian 402
Beaver, Mary 146
Bechtel Catherine 204
Bechtel, Elizabeth 109
Beck, Maria Ernestine 395
Beckham, Susannah 448
Bedford, Druscilla 29
Beery, Abraham 30
Beest, Maria Elizabeh 205
Beggs, Rebecca 288
BeHeler, Elizabeth 331
Belcher, Phoebe 87
Belfield, John 30
Belfield, Mary Meriwether 30
Bell, Ann 151
Bell, Anna 418
Bell, Betsey 30
Bell, Elizabeth 218
Bell, Elizabeth 31, 32
Bell, Elizabeth Betty 217
Bell, Esther 31
Bell, James 31
Bell, Jane 32
Bell, John 30
Bell, Margaret 32
Bell, Mary 282, 326
Bell, Mary Catherine 465
Bell, Robert 32
Bell, Sarah 31
Bell, William 32
Belt, Elizabeth Liza Ann 70
Benger, Dorothea Brayne 61
Benger, John 61
Bennett, Ann 198
Bennett, Elizabeth 235
Bennett, Ida 99
Bennett, Mary 116
Benning, Judith 159
Bennington, Henry 651
Bentley, Judith 129
Berger, Catherine 188
Berkeley, Edmund 464
Berkeley, Mary 290
Berkeley, Sarah 464
Bernard, Ann 218
Bernard, Anne 218
Bernard, John 218
Bernard, Margaret 75
Bernard, Mary Anne 2

Berry, Charles 34
Berry, Johanna 34
Berry, Mary 189
Berry, Rachel 193
Berry, Rebeccah 237
Berry, Susannah 273
Berryhill, John 35
Bertrand, Mary 652
Beverley, Elizabeth 227
Beverley, Maria 347
Beverley, Robert 347
Beverly, Judith 25
Beverly, Mary 420
Beverly, Ursula 139
Bibb, Christian 412
Bickerton, Alice 460
Bickley, John James 36
Biedermann, Mary 188
Bignall, Ann 394
Bill, Sarah 83
Biller, Eva 147
Billup, Mary Lilly 454, 653
Billups, Joseph 36, 454, 653
Billups, Ruth 373
Billups, Susannah 454, 653
Binns, Charles Sr 37
Binns, Hannah 37
Birchett, Catherine 37
Bird, Andrew 66
Bird, Sarah 297
Birkett, Margaret 339
Bishop, Joseph 37
Bishop, Martha 38
Bishop, Mathnay 38
Bishop, Rachel 37
Bishop, Rhoda 38
Bishop, Sarah 90
Bishop, Stephen 37
Bishop, Susan Bacon 403
Bishop, Susanna Bacon 403
Bishop, Waitstill 205
Black, Jane 5
Black, Mary 312
Black, Samuel 38
Blackburn, Anna 439
Blackburn, Benjamin 38
Blackburn, Elizabeth 62
Blackburn, Mary 38
Blackburn, Mildred 62
Blackburn, William 62
Blackington, Anne 424
Blackwell, Elizabeth 128, 449
Blackwell, Hannah 382
Blackwell, Joseph 39
Blackwell, Judith 225

Blackwell, Leticia 83
Blackwell, Lucy Steptoe 39
Blackwell, Margery 651
Blackwell, Samuel 651
Blackwell, Susannah 165
Blackwood, Betsy 277
Blaikley, Mary 400
Blain, Agnes 116
Blain, Joseph 165
Blain, Mary 165
Blair, Alexander 39, 651
Blair, Anne 23
Blair, Christian 65
Blair, John 39
Blair, John 78
Blair, Lilias 282
Blair, Mary 204
Blair, Mary Elizabeth 43
Blair, Mary Martha 322
Blair, Samuel 322
Blair, Sarah 78
Blair, Susanna H 95
Blake, Elizabeth 404
Blakely, Lucy 300
Blakemore, Thomas Sr 40
Blakey, Sarah 163
Blancett, Benedicta 135
Blanchecil, Ann 85
Bland, Ann 282
Bland, Frances 347
Bland, Mary Elizabeth 40
Bland, Richard 40, 654
Bland, Theodorick 347
Blank, Elizabeth 40
Blankenbaker, Margaret 73
Blankenbaker, Michael 451
Blankenbaker, Ursula 407
Blankenbaker, Zachariah 41
Blankenbeckler, Mary 451
Blankenship, John 41
Blankenship, Martha 828
Bledsoe, Ann 27
Blevins, Sarah 48
Bleyer, Anna 199
Blubaugh, Dorothy 313
Blue, Hannah D 10
Blundon, Sarah 415
Boadnax, Elizabeth Powers 464
Boaz, Thomas 42
Bodby, Isabella 1
Bodfish, Sarah 389
Boger, Susana 392
Boger,Michael Joseph 392
Boggs, Rebecca 288
Boggs, Rebecca 289

Bogle, Submit 379
Boisseau, Margaret 98
Boles, Jane 464
Bolling, Elizabeth 358, 654
Bolling, Frances 347
Bolling, Jane 347
Bolling, John 43
Bolling, John Kennon 40
Bolling, Lucy 346
Bolling, Martha 129
Bolling, Mary 40
Bolling, Mary Agnes 19
Bolling, Robert 43
Bolt, Sarah 393
Bond, Mary 63
Bond, Thomas 63
Bondurant, Celia 148
Bondurant, Elizabeth 329
Bonner, Margaret 187
Bonum, Rebecca 132
Booker, Edmund 44
Booker, Richard 44
Boone, Abigail 130
Boone, Catherine Rosanna 129
Boone, Martha 89
Booth, Ann 370
Booth, Elizabeth 468
Booth, Frances 45
Booth, Mary Grace 320
Booth, Phoebe 654
Booth, Robert 44
Both, William 654
Boothe, Eva Margaret 303
Boothe, Taner Anna 272
Borden, Magdalene Woods McDowell 49
Bordon, Lydia 326
Born, Catherine 368
Bosang, Margaret 166
Boshang, Euly 310
Boshang, Jacob 310
Bosshart, Elsbeth 199
Bostwick, David 356
Bostwick, Mary 356
Boswell, Catherine 284
Boswell, Frances 8
Boswell, Joseph Colgate 45
Botts, Elizabeth 145
Botts, Elizabeth 451
Boughton, Sarah 37, 38
Bouldin, Thomas 46
Boulware, Milly 46
Bourne, Hannah 47
Bourne, Stephen 47
Bourne, William 47

Boush, Mary 47
Boush, Peggy 69
Boutwell, Margaret Hawkins 465
Boutwell, William 465
Bowden, Margaret 340
Bowen, Ann 47
Bowen, Elizabeth 47
Bowen, Ephraim 47
Bowen, Fannie 47
Bowen, John 47
Bowen, Louisa 156, 415
Bowen, Margaret 156
Bowen, Rees 415
Bowen, Robert 47
Bowker, Anna 69
Bowles, John 48
Bowles, Mary 259
Bowles, Mourning 198
Bowley, Sarah Ann 381
Bowling, Benjamin 48
Bowling, Simon 48
Bowman, Anna 392
Bowman, Jacob 392
Bowman, Johann Jakob 49
Bowman, Regina Ann 116
Bowyer, Henry 305
Bowyer, Margaret 305
Bowyer, Mary 49
Bowyer, Michael 49
Boxley, George 49
Boyd, Alexander 50
Boyd, Esther 436
Boyd, Hannah 113
Boyd, Mary Margaret 212
Boyd, Robert 436
Boyd, Robert 50
Boyer, Christina 208
Boyer, Christina 98
Boyer, Johann Adam 98
Boyer, Margaret 50
Boykin, Simon 50
Boykin, William 50
Bracken, John 407
Bracken, Mary 407
Brackett, Elizabeth 50
Brackett, Pheobe 195
Brackett, Thomas 50
Bradford, Anzele Androse 130
Bradford, Lucinda 217
Bradley, Elizabeth Susan 51
Bradley, Keziah 253
Bradley, Sarah 215
Bram, Amey 172
Brambly, Abigail 55

Dandridge William 109
Dandridge, Anna Marie 27
Dandridge, Dorothea Spotswood 190
Dandridge, Elizabeth 108, 189, 323
Dandridge, John 27, 439
Dandridge, Lewis 108
Dandridge, Martha 107, 439
Dandridge, Nathaniel West 323
Dandridge, William 108
Dangerfield, Elizabeth 261
Daniel, Catherine 170
Daniel, Charles 294
Daniel, Elizabeth 116
Daniel, Jane 294
Daniel, Mary 378
Daniel, Peter 109
Daniel, Reuben 116
Daniel, Sarah Travers 2
Daniel, Sidney 339
Daniel, Susanna 470
Daniel, Susannah Mary 378
Daniel, Travers 2
Darnall, Catherine 110
Darnall, Elizabeth 465
Darrough, Susannah Anne 186
Darter, Maria Elizabeth Kurtz 110
Davenport, Elizabeth 449
Davenport, James 110
Davenport, Judith 165
Davenport, William 449
David, Pierre 110
Davidson, Anna 233
Davidson, Jane 58
Davidson, John Goolman 58
Davidson, Margaret Dunlap 204
Davidson, Phebey 179
Davidson, Pheby 179
Davidson, Samuel 233
Davies, Edith Landon 86
Davies, Henrian 67
Davies, Henry Landon 86
Davis, Agness 42
Davis, Ann 299, 459
Davis, Betsy 215
Davis, Catherine 161, 451
Davis, Delila 367
Davis, Elizabeth 126
Davis, Hartwell Hodges 123
Davis, Jane 111, 133
Davis, Janet 121
Davis, Joseph 176

Davis, Judith 112
Davis, Lorana 391
Davis, Lucy 42, 164
Davis, Mar 275
Davis, Margaret 99
Davis, Martha 429, 463
Davis, Mary 133
Davis, Mary 175, 268
Davis, Rachel 113
Davis, Rebecca 409
Davis, Rhoda 459
Davis, William 111, 112, 299
Dawson, Frances 90
Dawson, Mary 270
Dawson, Rebecca 78
Day, Ann 408
de Reamey, Elizabeth 219
de Remi, Elizabeth 219
Dean, Alice 231
Deardorf, Hannah Christina 118
Deardorf, Isaac 118
Deardorf, Mary 118
Debaptist, Frances 113
Degrafenreid, Anthony 114
DeHaven, Peter 114
Delaney, Sarah 297
Delaney, Sharp 297
DeLang, Johannes 115
Dellart, Abigail 271
Demoville, Mary Magdalene 406
Demoville, Samuel 406
Dempsey, Carleen 254
Dennis, Tabitha 224
Dennison, Martha 157
Denny, Jean 101
Dent, Mary 16
Denty, Sibel 115
Denum, Mary 230
DePriest, Judith 368
DePriest, Naomi 368
DePriest, William 368
Derst, Abraham 110
Dettamore, Anna Marie 306
Deutterte, Anne 110
Devier, Hugh E 116
Dibrel, Judith 321
Dick, Archibald 291
Dick, Eleanor 285
Dick, Elizabeth 291
Dickenson, Mary Powell 124
Dickerson, Mourning 25
Dicks, Esther 410
Didwick, Margaret 392

Dieffenbach, Susanna Margaretha 208
Digges, Charles 139
Digges, Cole 119, 183
Digges, Dudley Power 119
Digges, Dudley Powers 65
Digges, Edward 119
Digges, Elizabeth 310
Digges, Jane 139
Digges, Lucy Armistead 252
Digges, Martha Armistead 65
Digges, Mary 182
Dillard, Ann 213, 271
Dillard, Edward 119
Dillard, Elizabeth 424, 425
Dillard, James 119
Dillard, William 424, 425
Diller, Anna Margaret 225
Diller, Margaret 234, 384
Dillinger, Helen Hancock 421
Dillon, Eleanor 329
Dillon, Thomas 119
Dinkel, Anna Margaret Salome 394
Dishman, Peter 120
Dispanet, Johann Jacob 120
Disslin, Cathrine 136
Diuguid, William 120, 301
Divers, Mary 120
Dix, Esther 410
Dixon, Elizabeth 120
Dixon, John 121
Dixon, Martha 166
Dixon, Mary 417
Dixon, Sally 16
Dixon, Sarah 373
Doak, Mary 407, 458
Doak, Mary Hanna 121
Doak, Samuel 121
Doak, Samuel Sr 121
Doak, Thankful 138
Docia, Theodocia 262
Dodd, Elizabeth (Betsy) 12
Dodd, Sarah 123, 267
Donahue, Mary 389
Donaldson, Margaret 122
Donalson, Nancy 82
Donalson, Sallie 382
Doniplan, Elizabeth 390
Donnelson, Nancy 651
Donohoe, Cornelius Kirkley 304
Donohoe, Elizabeth 304
Donohu, Elizabeth 441
Donohu, Keisiah 441
Donohu, Thomas 441

Dorton, Mary 122
Dortzbach, George Adam 652, 657
Doss, Lucy 59
Doss, Lucy 59
Douglas, Margaret 171, 286, 460
Douglas, Martha Selden 219
Douglas, Mary 151
Douglas, Mary Ann 103
Douglas, Nancy Ann 382
Douglass, Susan Ann 402
Douglass, Susanna 422
Dove, Joseph 122
Dove, Mary 122
Dowell, Charity 22
Dowling, Martha 338
Downer, Mary Elizabeth 74
Downey, Elizabeth 651
Downey, Mary Ann 70
Downey, Rachel 455, 458
Downey, Rebecca 277
Downey, Samuel 277
Downing, Elizabeth 414
Downing, Margaret 425
Downman, Fanny 21
Downman, James 112
Downman, Priscilla 112
Downman, Rawleigh 123
Downman, Traverse 112
Dozier, Hannah 304
Drake, George 414
Drake, Henry 123
Drake, James 123, 410
Drake, Lavinia 410
Drake, Martha 308
Drake, Mary 414
Drake, Phoebe 104, 235
Draket, Elizabeth 371
Draper, Martha 111
Dryden, Margaret 201
Dryden, Mary 201
Dryden, Nathaniel 201
Dryden, William 124
Dudley, Adria Kemp 131
Dudley, Ann 345
Dudley, Armistead 57
Dudley, Judith 44
Dudley, Phillis 57
Dudley, Ursula 154
Duerson, Mary 191
Duff, Margaret 124
Duff, Samuel Henry 124
Duiguid, Martha 290
Duke, Amy 360

Dulaney, Jane Lacey 460
Dull, Barbara 203
Dumas, Temperance 467
Dumire, Christianna 422
Dun, Jean 274
Dunbarrow, Elizabeth 39
Duncan, Celia 177
Duncan, Elizabeth 125, 208
Duncan, Elizabeth 311
Duncan, Henry 125
Duncan, Jael Ellen 395
Duncan, Joseph 313
Duncan, Lydia 313
Duncan, Martha 254
Duncan, Raleigh 395
Duncan, Thomas 254
Dundore, Jonathan 327
Dundore, Rebecca 327
Dunkin, John Sr 126
Dunlap, Anne McFarland 52
Dunn, Cassandra 207
Dunn, Elizabeth 53
Dunnavant, Elizabeth 464
Dunnavant, Hodges 464
Dunton Levin 454, 653
Dunton, Sarah 454, 653
Dunton, Sukey 19
Dunton, Susanna 19
Dupree, Mary 53
Durrett, Elizabeth 442
Durrett, John William 127
Durrett, Nancy 126
Durrett, Richard 16
Durrett, Sarah 105
Dusong, Eva 234
Dussinger, Maria Katherina 115
Dutt, Barbara 334
Duval, Daniel 127
Duval, Mary 337
Duval, Samuel 337
Duvall, Susannah 443
Dyer, Hannah 208
Dyer, James 127
Dysart, Elizabeth 76
Dysart, James 76
Dyson, Sarah 383
Dyssly, Cathrine 136
Ealy, Thomas Sr 131
Early, Elizabeth 68, 112
Early, Jeremiah 68
Early, Jeremiah Allen 127
Early, Judith 62
Early, Mary 127
Early, Sarah 127

Early, Theodosia 112
Eases, Abraham Jr 132
Eases, Elizabeth 132
Easley, Mary 228
East, Obedience 128
Eaton, Mary 26
Eblin, Hannah 76
Eddins, Elizabeth 163
Eddins, Joseph 163
Edgerton, Lavinia 369
Edloe, Elizabeth 88, 125
Edmiston, Dorothy 283
Edmonds, Frances 128
Edmonds, John Jr 128
Edmondson, Gabriel Jones 219
Edmondson, Judith 443
Edmunds, Elizabeth 250
Edwards, Ambrose Sr 128
Edwards, Ann 389
Edwards, Bethiah 428
Edwards, Catherine 454
Edwards, Elizabeth 80, 339
Edwards, John Flood 250
Edwards, Margaret 110
Edwards, Martha 110
Edwards, Mary 16, 374
Edwards, Sarah 58
Edwards, Thomas Hanuel 129
Ege, Elizah W 129
Ege, Johann 129
Eggleston, Elizabeth 14
Eiler, Annie Mary 444
Elam, Sabra 167
Elbeck, Anna 268
Eldridge, Sarah 452
Eldridge, Thomas 129
Elfreth, Sarah 470
Elgin, Catherine 129
Elgin, Francis Sr 129, 130
Elibeck, Ann 272
Ellington, Betsy 202
Ellington, Martha 301
Elliott, Alcy 231
Elliott, Eleanor 190
Elliott, Elizabeth 255
Elliott, Elizabeth 45
Elliott, Mary 130
Elliott, Thomas 130
Ellis, Bethunia 246
Ellis, Charles 130
Ellis, Grizel 415, 416
Ellis, Joseph 657
Ellis, Susannah 657
Ellis, Susannah Harding 36
Ellzey, Letitia 24

Elmore, Sarah 154
Else, Sarah Burch 225
Elsey, Letitia 24
Elsey, Letty 24
Elson, Rebekah Grace 125
Eltinge, Eleanor 195
Elzey, Letitia 24
Embrey, Henry 374
Emmerson, Ann 425
Emrich, Margaret 448
Engelhardt, Maria Margaretha 305
England, William 131
Enhald, Maria Elizabeth 241
Enos, Mary 292
Epperson, Hannah 146
Epperson, John Sr 132
Eppert, Anna Maria 229
Eppes, Elizabeth 187
Eppes, Mary 364
Epps, Amy 93
Epps, Ann 305
Epps, Martha 216
Erehart, Elizabeth 201
Ergebrecht, Catherine 15
Ervin, Anne 191
Ervin, Benjamin 191
Ervin, Francis 132
Ervin, Jane Curry 132
Ervine, Agnes 15
Erwin, Agnes 15
Erwin, Hannah 221, 255
Erwin, Jane 170
Erwin, Jean 213
Erwin, John 213
Eschmann, Maria Magdelena 194
Eshman, Mary Margareta 413
Eskridge, George 132
Eskridge, Katherine 238
Eskridge, Margaret 227
Estes, Abraham 132
Estes, Moses 132
Estill, Rebecca 207, 652
Etchison, Rosanna 167
Etheridge, Sophia 66
Etter, Gerhand 133
Ettinger, Magdalena 352
Eubank, Elizabeth 143
Eubank, Hannah 143
Eubank, John 143
Eubank, Nancy 103
Eubank, Sarah 143
Eustace, Agatha 39
Eustace, Elizabeth 39

Eustace, Isaac 39
Evans, Ann 25
Evans, Betsy 261
Evans, Bridgett 133
Evans, Evan Rice 133
Evans, Jane 414
Evans, Letitia 146
Evans, Mary 133
Evans, Ruth 465, 653
Evans, Susanna 9
Evans, Susannah 281
Everard, Susannah 283
Everhart, Christian 133
Everhart, Christina 431
Everitt, Mary 316
Ewell, Bertrand 134
Ewell, Charlotte 134
Ewell, Marianne 101
Ewing, Susannah 395
Ewing, John 134
Ewing, Margaret Eleanor 68
Ewing, Martha 134
Eyler, Catherine 256
Eyre, Severn 657
Fairfax, Anne 244
Fairhurst, Elizabeth 470
Fairhurst, Jeremiah 470
Falkner, Sarah 55
Fall, Catharine 135
Fallin, John 142
Fallis, Sarah 461
Fant, Sarah 96
Faries, Deborah 136
Faris, Benjamin 135
Faris, Nancy 135
Farley, Francis Marion 135
Farmer, Keziah 31
Farmer, Michael 136
Farmer, Susannah 136
Farnsworth, Sarah 425
Farrar, Mathew 379
Farrar, Rebecca 338
Farrar, Sallie 378
Farrow, Mary Ann 417
Fauber, Susannah 381
Faunteler, Elizabeth Embree 54
Fauntleroy, Elizabeth 54
Fauntleroy, Ellen 405
Fauntleroy, Judith 77
Fauntleroy, Moore 54, 405
Faure, Rhoda Ann 110
Fauve, Jacque 241
Fauve, James 241
Fauve, Judith Ford 241
Favor, Clara 152

Fawcett, Alice 72
Fawcett, Ann 53
Fawcett, Joseph 72
Fawley, Thomas 136
Fenton, Ann 241
Fenwick, Joseph 181
Fergusn, Jane Jenny 272
Ferguson, Elizabeth 404
Ferguson, Sarah 137, 382, 383
Field, Susannah 400
Fieldeer, Sarah 99
Fielder, Bartholomew 137
Fielder, Elizabeth 137, 428
Fielder, John 428
Fielding, Frances 250
Fields, John 137
Fifer, Adam 375
Fifer, Eve 375
Filmer, Martha Elizabeth 164
Finch, Barbara 128
Finely, Jean 277
Finely, Robert 277
Fink, Mary Ann Elizabeth 20
Finley, Jean 134, 277, 652
Finley, Margaret 209
Finley, Robert 277
Finney, James 352
Finney, Mary 352
Finnie, Ann 423
Finnie, Elizabeth 138
Fischbach, Anna Elizabeth 350
Fischbach, Anna Elsbeth 350
Fischback, Margaret 431
Fishback, Harman 452
Fishback, Johann Freidrich 138
Fishback, Kathrina 452
Fishback, Mary 452
Fisher, Mary 392
Fitzgerald, James 139
Fitzhugh, Alice 339
Fitzhugh, John 139
Fitzhugh, Lucy 271
Fitzwater, Thomas Foster 139
Flauntleroy, Margaret 54
Fleet, Ann Temple 419
Fleet, William 419
Fleishman, Maria Catherine 442
Fleming, Catherine 140
Fleming, Elizabeth 324
Fleming, Lucy 170
Fleming, Martha 416
Fleming, Mary 123, 252, 410
Fleming, Mary Anna 324, 325
Fletcher, John 355

Jennings, Sarah 144, 145, 270, 358
Jennings, William 145
Jennings, William Henry 144
Jerrell, Nancy 261
Jeteer, Thomas 428
Jeter, Lucy 428
Jett, Anna 113
Jett, Francis 113
Jett, Nancy 113
Jett, Susannah 323
Johann Ludwick 471
John, Ruch 343
Johns, Ann Nancy 423
Johns, Betty 384
Johnson, Agnes 87
Johnson, Amy 300
Johnson, Ann 196
Johnson, Anne Key 83
Johnson, Elizabeth 61
Johnson, Frances 67, 197
Johnson, James T 115
Johnson, Jane 412
Johnson, Johannah 196
Johnson, Mary 219
Johnson, Sarah 236
Johnson, William 196
Johnston, Lucy 352
Johnston, Mary 218
Johnston, Nancy 144
Johnston, Zachariah 218
Jones Elizabeth 66
Jones, Amarella 220
Jones, Amy 441
Jones, Ann 54, 65, 374, 448
Jones, Barbara 232
Jones, Betty 221
Jones, Constant 9
Jones, Dolly 165
Jones, Eaven 66
Jones, Elizabeth 38, 219, 314, 364
Jones, Elizabeth L 56
Jones, Ellen 247
Jones, Frances 27, 439
Jones, Frances Harrod 10, 11
Jones, Gabriel 374
Jones, Hester 220
Jones, Jane Sallie 656
Jones, John 38, 468
Jones, Leah 414
Jones, Lucy 156
Jones, Margaret 454, 464
Jones, Martha 222
Jones, Mary 190, 216, 221

Jones, Nancy 374
Jones, Nancy Ann 66, 221
Jones, Philadelphia 468
Jones, Prudence 438
Jones, Richard 438
Jones, Robert 221
Jones, Rosamond 47
Jones, Sarah 370, 465
Jones, Sarah Anderson 50
Jones, Thomas 656
Jones, Tignal 50
Jordan, Ann 360
Jordan, Eliza Ann 321
Jordan, Jean 201
Jordan, Joshua Josiah 222
Jordan, Margaret Meredith 67
Jordan, Mary 114, 154, 459
Jordan, Samuel 450
Jordan, Wilhelmina 450
Jouett, Henrietta 453
Joyner, Rachel 458
Joynes, Anne 223
Julian, Catherine 451
Julian, Charles 223, 451
Julian, Phoebe 451
Juny, Margaret W 249
Kadle, Eleanor 133
Kaffer, Elizabeth 149
Kaffier, Elizabeth 149
Kagey, Henry 224
Kagey, John Rudolph 224
Kagy, Henry 223
Kaigan, Cynthia 207
Kane, Jane 395
Kapp, Christina 306
Karger, Anna Juliana 56
Kauffman, Nancy 402
Kaufman, Michael 224
Kayser, Valentin 229
Keatts, Curtis 224
Keckley, Catherine Elizabeth Rudolph 353
Keeble, Martha 370
Keele, Louisa 8
Keeling, Ann 457
Keeling, Mary 225, 397
Keen, Amelia 73
Keene, Elizabeth 460
Keersh, Anna Margaret 229
Kegley, Rebecca Ann 225
Keifer, Mary Anna 228
Keinadt, Ann Elizageth 23
Keinadt, Michael 234, 384
Keister, Frederick 208
Keister, Hannah 208

Keith, James 225
Keith, Mary 265, 286
Keith, Mary Randolph 265
Keith, Nancy 246
Keller, Abraham 269
Keller, Anna Elizabeth 208
Keller, Bastian 226
Keller, Esther 42
Keller, George 226
Keller, Mary 355
Keller, Rachel 269
Keller, Susannah 318
Kello, Mary 226
Kelly, Elizabeth 410
Kelly, Frances 99
Kelly, Mary Elizabeth 229
Kelly, Susannah 324
Kemp, Peter Jr 107
Kendall, Ann 371
Kendall, John 371, 396
Kendall, Mary 396
Kennedy, Susannah 227
Kenner, Frances 134, 227
Kenner, Howson Francis 132
Kennerly, Elizabeth 336
Kennerly, Mary 176
Kennon, Elizabeth 89
Kent, Nancy 279
Ker, Edward Jr 228
Kerfoot, William Sr 224
Kern, Maria Rosina 279, 280
Kerr, James 358
Kerr, John 55
Kerr, Lettice 358
Kerr, Peggy 55
Kerr, Sarah 55
Kersey, Sarah 421
Kesler, Johannes 229
Kessler, Elizabeth 229
Key, Agnes Witt 34
Key, John W 34
Keyser, Carl Sebastian 229
Keyser, Catherine Kerns 442
Keyser, Charles Sebastian 233
Kibler, Heinrich 230
Kilgore, Elizabeth 468
Kilgore, Lydia 230
Kilgore, Thomas 230
Killian, Margaret 341
Killin, Thomas 374
Kilpatrick, Mary Ann 178
Kimble, Mary 192
Kimoerils, Mary 330
Kincaid, Agnes 201
Kincaid, Lucy 231

Norris, Judith 76, 77
Northen, William 312
Norton, Catherine Bush 8
Norton, Frances 27
Norvell, Hugh 312
Norvell, Mary 312
Nottingham, Margaret 454, 653
Nottingham, Mary 454, 653
Nottingham, Thomas 454, 653
Nowlin, Catey 33
Nuckolls, Anne 176
Nuckolls, Charles N 176
Nuckolls, James 312
Nugent, Bridget 226
Null, Catherine 180
Nunn, Elizabeth 316
Nunnally, Patience 655
Nutter, Elizabeth 73
Nutter, Zadock 73
Oakes, Elizabeth 312
Oakes, Hannah 312
Oberlin, Anna Maria Catherine 328
O'Brian, Mary 139
O'Brian, Mary Polly 189
O'Brien, Elizabeth 233
O'Bryant, Elizabeth 233
Ochler, Georg Heinrich 304
O'Conner, Abigail 466
O'Daniel, Catherine 170
Oehler, Georg Henry 18
Offeur, Anne 468
Ogle, Elizabeth 278
Ogle, Lucretia 373
Ogle, Susanna 278
Ogle, Thomas 278
Oglesby, Richard 313
Oglesby, Susan 313
Oldham, James 257
Oldham, Tabitha 257
Olinger, Philip Johann 313
Oliver, Sarah 276
Olleman, Mary 360
Omohundro, Richard 313
Oney, Mary 443
O'Rear, Margaret 158
Orrbetter, Sarah Maria 394
Osborn, Lucy 161
Osborne, Abigail Herbert 201
Osborne, Ellendeer 185
Osborne, Reps 314
Osborne, Thomas 314
Osburn, Augusta Mary 379
Osburn, John 314

Osburn, Lydia 187
Osburn, Nicholas 366
Osburn, Sarah 366
Otis, Deborah 408
Ott, Anna Elizabeth 368
Ott, Lovice 367
Ott, Mary Magdalena 168
Ott, Mary Magdalena 393
Otterbach, Elizabeth 350
Otterbach, Maria Katherina 266
Otto, Catherine 380
Oury, Rebecca 397
Overaker, Margaret 315
Overboker, Elizabeth 315
Overton, Barbara 74, 290
Overton, Mary Elizabeth 651
Overton, Sallie 405
Overton, William 405
Owen, Agnes 333
Owen, Joshua 315
Owen, Nancy Ann 409
Owen, Priscilla 148, 149, 246
Owen, Rachael 315
Owens, Lydia 380
Owens, Lydia Lunsford 3
Owens, Sarah 22
Oxley, Catherine 316
Oxley, Henry 316
Pace, John H 316
Pace, John L 26
Pace, Mary 26
Pace, Sarah 195
Packwood, Samuel 316
Padgett, Edmund 316
Padgett, Mary 316
Page, Alicy Grymes 119
Page, Betsy 151
Page, John 151, 307, 308
Page, John Williamson 307
Page, Judith 64, 307
Page, Lucy 27, 65
Page, Mann 27, 64, 317
Page, Maria Judith 33
Page, Mari3 Judith 348
Page, Mary Judith 348
Page, Mary Mason 375
Page, Robert 317
Page, Sally Burwell 307, 308
Page, Sally Burwell 308
Paine, Elizabeth 318
Paine, John 318
Paine, Sarah 146
Painter, Elizabeth 269
Pallett, Susan 462

Palmer, Ann 426
Palmer, Elizabeth 60, 325
Palzer, Balzar 259
Pancoast, Adin 130
Pancoast, Diadama 130
Pancoast, Mary 370
Pangle, John Henry 318
Pannill, Catherine Ann 457
Pannill, Elizabth 112
Pannill, William 318
Pannill, William Sr 112
Parcell, Maria 110
Parham, Susannah 191
Parker, Catherine 107
Parker, Daniel 319
Parker, Elizabeth 3
Parker, Margaret 319
Parker, Mary Brown 319
Parker, Nicolas 319
Parker, Roxanna 319
Parker, William Henry 656
Parkins, Isaac Sr 320
Parks, Elizabeth 212
Parks, John 396
Parks, Lucy 212
Parks, Margaret 4, 274, 396
Parks, Rebekah 320
Parks, Thomas 212
Parramore, Joannah 320
Parramore, Mary 107
Parramore, Thomas 320
Parramore, William 320
Parrish, Nanny 193
Parsons, Elizabeth 417
Parsons, John 131
Parsons, Mary 131
Paschal, Mildred 95
Pascon, Mary 320
Pasley, Mary Molly 156
Pass, Susannah 139
Paterson, Thomas 321
Patrick, Isabella 276
Patrick, Rachel 321
Patsey, Martha 301
Patterson, Catherine 391
Patterson, Elizabeth 654
Patterson, John 321
Patterson, Mary 195, 273, 321, 384
Patterson, Rebecca 224
Patterson, Sarah Mary 273
Patterson, Sarah West 133
Patteson, Lucy 120
Patteson, Thomas 321
Pattison, Hannah 184

Poague, Rebecca 7
Pogue, Elizabeth 160
Poindeter, Mary 300
Poindexter, Ann Gizzage 89
Poindexter, Nancy 378
Poindexter, Phillip 336
Poiner, Elizabeth W 443
Pollard, Ann 212, 316, 424
Pollard, Joseph 336
Pollard, Mary 226, 378, 416
Pollard, Richard 416
Pollard, Sarah 328
Pollard, Susan 226
Pollard, William 226
Pollock, Ann 7
Pollock, Thomas 7
pollockfield, Caleb 337
Ponder, Ann B 83
Pope, Elizabeth 337
Pope, John 337
Pope, Nathaniel 337
Porch, Elizabeth 106
Porter, Elizabeth 167
Porter, John Luke 337
Porter, Patience 337
Porter, Susannah Nancy 337
Porter, William 337
Porterfield, Eleanor 436
Postlethwaite, Mary 343
Poston, Priscilla 338
Poston, William John 338
Poteet, Susannah 464
Potten, Sarah 338
Potter, Elizabeth 338
Potts, Ezekiel 338
Potts, Katherine 460
Potts, Mary 449
Povall, Martha 301
Povall, Richard 301
Polvell, Sarah 656
Powell, Clary 462
Powell, Lucy 357
Powell, Margaret 343
Powell, Mary 118
Powell, Sarah 454, 653
Powelson, Agnes 187
Power, Elizabeth Follott 119
Powers, Caroline 467
Poythress, Ann Isham 468
Poythress, Anne 40, 654
Poythress, Elizabeth Bland 271
Poythress, Mary Peterson 347
Poythress, Sally Bland 309
Poythress, Susannah 40
Pratt, Elizabeth 194

Pratt, John 339
Pratt, Lydia 397
Preck, Frances 238
Preisch, Augustice 341
Presberry, Jane 10
Presley, Elizabeth 76
Preston, Elizabeth 261
Preston, Elizabeth 335
Preston, John 340
Preston, Mary 284
Preston, William 340
Price, Anna Margaretha 179
Price, Augustine 288
Price, Elisha 387
Price, Elizabeth 108, 328
Price, Joseph 341
Price, Margaret 96
Price, Mary 100, 288
Price, Nancy 243, 250
Price, Polly 61
Price, William 250
Priddy, Mildred 66
Pride, John Jr 342
Pride, Mary 44
Priest, Mary 9
Prillaman, Anna 393
Prillarman, Barbara 391
Pritchard, Anne 164, 165
Pritchard, Reese Jr 342
Pritchard, Susan 21
Prock, Frances 238
Proctor, Frances 238
Proffitt, Sylvester 342
Psalter, Hannah 205
Pugh, Jessie 343
Puller, Ann 343
Pulliam, Mary Jane 144, 145
Pullin, Loftus 344
Purcell, Hannah 314
Purcell, Mary Van Hook 209
Purcell, Thomas 314
Purnall, Mary 126
Pursel, Margaret 344
Pyland, Elizabeth 359
Quarles, Ann Elizabeth 320
Quarles, William 344
Quisenberry, Mary 95
Radcliffe, Mary 447
Radford, Mary 340
Rae, Ann 324
Rae, Nancy 324
Ragland, Ann 345
Ragland, John Jr 345
Ragland, Sarah 336
Raikes, Elizabeth 72

Rainey, Francis 345
Ralston, Letitia 267
Ramsay, William 345, 346
Ramsey, Mary 346
Ramsey, Mary 396
Ramsey, Rachel 289
Ramsey, William 346
Randolh, Frances Bland 422
Randolph, Ann 139
Randolph, Anne 347
Randolph, Brett 347
Randolph, Elizabeth 308, 468, 654
Randolph, Elizabeth Southall 2
Randolph, Isham 182
Randolph, Jane 216, 283
Randolph, Jane Bollin 432
Randolph, John 347
Randolph, Judith 33
Randolph, Mary 65, 250, 307, 347
Randolph, Mary Grymes 283
Randolph, Mary Isham 225
Randolph, Nancy Ann 441
Randolph, Peter 346
Randolph, Peter Skipsworth 2
Randolph, Richard 347
Randolph, Richard I 347
Randolph, Richard II 347
Randolph, Susannah 182
Randolph, William 33, 348
Rankin, Martha 186
Rankin, Mary Katherine 99
Rapine, Mary Anne 266
Rauch, Magdalena 152
Raush, Mary Magdalene 471
Ravenscroft, Frances 123
Ravenscroft, Hannah 215
Rawlings, Elizabeth 187
Rawlings, Mary Elizabeth 187
Rawlings, Rebecca 131
Rawlings, Stephen 187
Ray, Ann 324
Ray, Nancy 324
Raymer, Sally 73
Reaburn, Agnes 442
Read, Clement 349
Read, Elizabeth 349, 411
Read, Helen Maxell 349
Read, Johanna 350
Read, John Royall 386
Read, Lucy Franklin 386
Read, Margaret 75
Read, Maxwell 349
Read, Sarah Embrey 374

Appendix F -- Listing of Parents & Spouces (For Spouces Listing is by Maiden Name If Known, If Not Known By Married Name)

Smith, Robert 386
Smith, Ruth 166
Smith, Sarah 31
Smith, Stephen 436
Smith, Susan 658
Smith, Susanna 340, 386
Smith, Susannah 34, 321
Smith, Winna 387
Snapp, Catherine 334
Snead, Keziah 230
Snead, Martha 24
Snead, Sophia 390
Snidow, John Jacob 391
Snodgrass, Agnes 321
Snodgrass, David 391
Snodgrass, Elizabeth 391
Snodgrass, John 391
Snodgrass, Martha 465
Snodgrass, William 391
Snoe, Elizabeth 6
Snow, John 39158
Snyder, Nancy 146
Sonner, Phillip 392
Sorrell, Letitia 61
Souder, Anthony 392
Souder, Catherine 385
Souder, Margaret 392
Southerland, Elizabeth 450
Spangler, Daniel 393
Spangler, Elizabeth 393
Sparks, Frances 18
Spatz, Ann Catherine 129
Speed, John 394
Speed, William Terrell 393
Spencer, Anne 350
Spengler, Phillip Sr 394
Spiller, Catherine 49
Spilman, Martha 394
Spirri,, Peter 394
Spitler, John 394
Spitler, Mary Elizabeth 394
Spotswood, Alex 64
Spotswood, Ann 64
Spotswood, Ann Catherine 434
Spotswood, Dorothea 323
Spotswood, Dorthea 108
Spotswood, Mary Randolph 55
Spragins, William 394
Sprecher, Johan Christopher 395
Springer, Drucilla 299
Sprinkle, Catherine Anna 256
Sproul, Jane 395
Stackpole, Nancy Davis 196
Stacy Susannah 233

Stallard, Walter 395
Stampe, Lydia Duncan 313
Standley, Molly 179
Stanley, Thomas 395
Staples, John 395
Steel, Rachel 196
Steele, Agnes 275
Steele, David 397
Steele, Jane 7, 407
Steele, Janet 397
Steele, Mary 148
Steele, Nancy 275
Steele, Nancy Agnes 274
Steele, Rosannah 397
Steele, Samuel SR 397
Steele, Wilmouth 258
Steer, Mary 320
Steer, Ruth 214
Steffey, Anna Elizabeth 437
Steger, Catherine 281
Steidley, Eve Rebecca 202
Steiner, Mary Ann 136
Stephens, Ann 127
Stephens, Hans Peter 390
Stephens, Joanna 398
Stephens, Lewis 398
Stephens, Margaret 390
Stephens, Maria Christina 390
Stephens, Peter 398
Stephenson, Elizabeth 208
Steptoe, Elizabeth 244
Steptoe, John 39
Steptoe, Judith 21
Steptoe, Lucy 39, 651
Sterling, Nancy 96
Stevens, Elizabeth 417
Stevens, Hannah 205
Stevens, Sara Ann 235
Stevens, Thomas 432
Stevenson, Elizabeth 297, 455, 653
Stevenson, Judith 19
Steward, Thomas 292
Stewart, Ann 36
Stewart, Catherine 393
Stewart, Elizabeth Henley 353
Stewart, John 399
Stewart, Mary 6, 292
Stewart, Susan 399
Sthreshley, Thomas 352
Stickley, Elizabeth 402
Stimson, Jeremiah 657
Stimson, Rachel 657
Stith, Anne 131
Stith, Buckner 400

Stith, Catharine 43
Stith, Griffin 400
Stober, Eva Barbara 235
Stockley, Anne 425
Stockshlager, Ann 470
Stoddard, Marianne 5
Stodgill, Elizabeth 185
Stoeckli, Elizabeth 402
Stoeckli, Johannes 402
Stokes, David 220
Stokes, Jane 220
Stokes, Mary 167
Stoltz, Catherine 394
Stone, Alaney 284
Stone, Barton 400, 401
Stone, Joshua 400, 401
Stone, Josiah 401
Stone, Mary 439
Stone, Milly 145
Stone, Phebe Yancey 452
Stone, Richard 452
Stone, Sarah 299
Stone, Sarah 400, 401
Stoneman, Sarah 99
Stoner, Barbara 223
Stoner, Barbara 224
Stonestreet, Butler 325
Stonestreet, Mary 325
Stonestreet, Mary 325
Story, Elizabeth 393
Stout, Penelope 316
Stoval, Sarah 119
Stovall, Elizabeth 246
Stovall, Frances Martha 389
Stovall, John 246
Stovall, Ruth 328
Stover, Ann 399
Stover, Anna Catherine 98
Stover, Elizabeth 392
Stover, Peter 394
Stover, Regina 394
Stowe, Elizabeth 360
Strachan, Mary 25
Strachan, Peter 25
Stranifer, Alianna 193
Stratton, Ann 400
Stratton, Jane Gincey 246
Streit, Christian 79
Strep, Anna Margaretha 37
Stricker, Anna 352
Strickland, Sarah Jane 205
Strickler, Abraham 402
Strickler, Benjamin 402
Strickler, Elizabeth Grove 229
Strickler, Isaac 394, 402

Wimercast, Elizabeth 58
Windell, Anna Elizabeth 392
Windson, Sarah 190
Windston, Dorothea Spotswood 190
Wine, Anna Martha 288
Wingfield, John 458, 459
Wingfield, Martha Hudson 459
Winiger, Mary 316
Winkoop, Eleanor 427
Winn, Ann 198
Winn, John Quarles 198
Winn, Minor Sr 459
Winniford, Judith 459
Winston, Barbara 341
Winston, Elizabeth 324
Winston, John 460
Winston, Mary 39
Winston, Mary Ann 91
Winston, Sarah 286, 344, 367, 405
Wintrow, Anna Margaret Sussanna 37
Wise, Casandra Elizabeth 107
Wise, John 460
Wiseman, Ann Mary 99
Wisman, Catharine 287
Withers, Elizabeth 459
Withers, James 459, 460
Withers, Patsy 323
Withers, Thomas 459
Withers, Ursula 436
Witmer, Susan 73
Witmyer, Margaret 122
Witt, Margaret 453
Witten, Keziah 79
Witten, Thomas 461
Witten, Thomas Jr 450
Wolf, Margaret 15
Wolfe, Margreta 15
Wolfe, Maria Catharina 356
Wolff, Catherine Elizabeth 394
Womack, Charles 25
Womack, Judith 25
Womack, Susannah 393
Wood, Dinah 461
Wood, Martha 48
Wood, Nehemiah 461
Wood, Sarah 308
Wood, Susannah 380
Wood, William 308, 657
Wood, William Jr 461
Wooddell, Alise 462
Woodford, Mary 462
Woodruff, David Sr 462

Woods, Andrew 433
Woods, Elizabeth 88, 462
Woods, Jane 66, 295
Woods, Maria 150
Woods, Martha 433
Woods, Mary 180, 462
Woods, Michael Marion 462
Woods, Rebecca 106
Woods, Samuel 295
Woodson, Ann 337
Woodson, Charles Jr 337
Woodson, Christian 196
Woodson, Elizabeth Michaux 429
Woodson, John 463
Woodson, Judith 287
Woodson, Mary Jane 323
Woodson, Richard 429, 463
Woodward, Becky 198
Woodward, James 463
Woodward, Lucy 110
Woody, Henry 463
Wooldridge, Elizabeth 118
Wooley, Mary 297
Woolfkill, John 269
Woolfkill, Elizabeth 269
Woolfolk, John 443
Woolfolk, Mary 443
Woolford, Mary 54
Woolfork, Frances Wyatt 145
Woolsey, Richard 464
Wootton, Lina 183
Wootton, Sina 183
Wormeley, Elizabeth 119
Wormeley, Elizabeth 76
Wormeley, Ralph 119
Wormeley, Ralph III 464
Wormeley, Ralph IV 464
Wormington, Nancy 458
Wormley, Elizabeth 33, 77, 651
Worrell, Elizabeth 451
Worrell, Peter 464
Worrell, Rebecca 31
Worsham, Ann 314
Worsham, Elizabeth 187
Worsham, Richard 464
Wray, Elizabeth 465
Wray, Moses 465
Wright, Ann 466
Wright, Anne 198
Wright, Benjamin 268
Wright, Elizabeth 102, 309
Wright, Frances Phripp 41
Wright, John 466
Wright, Mar 130

Wright, Mary 208, 305, 378, 390
Wright, Robert 465
Wright, Sarah 430
Wright, Steven 466
Wright, Susannah 49, 268
Wright, Thomas 30
Wurtz, Anna Catherine 431
Wurtz, William 431
Wyatt, Lettice 466
Wyatt, William 658
Wyatt, William Edward 466
Wynant, Ann 384
Wynkoop, Philip 427
Wynne, John 466
Wynne, Margaret 452
Wynne, William 467
Wynn, William Sr 466
Wythe, Elizabeth 406
Wythe, Mary Mason 405, 406
Wythe, Nathaniel 406
Yager, Adam Sr 467
Yager, John 467
Yancey, Anne 315
Yancey, Charles 467
Yancey, Mary 452
Yancey, Robert 315, 467
Yancey, Sarah Keziah 176
Yantis, Catherine 32
Yarborough, Hannah 209
Yates, Bartholomew 468
Yates, Catherine Randolph 445
Yates, Clara 654
Yates, Francis 468
Yeary, Henry David 468
Yeary, Mary 468
Yeary, Mary Polly 22, 73
Yieser, Rosina 329
Young, Ann 30
Young, Catharine 322
Young, Elliott 130
Young, Hannah 64
Young, Harmon 322
Young, Henry 469
Young, Hugh 469
Young, Janet 130
Young, Janet T 185
Young, Jennette T 185
Young, John 469
Young, Lettice 378
Young, Mary 159, 469
Young, Thomas 469
Young, William 30
Younger, Leah 466
Younger, Marcus 132

APPENDIX G
ERRATA-ADDENDA

ANDERSON, Andrew; b 1748; d 6 Jun 1783 **RU:** Captain, Co Commander Augusta Co Militia 1783 **CEM:** Augusta Stone Presbyterian; GPS 38.23926, -78.97356; 28 Old Stone Church Ln, Ft Defiance; Augusta **GS:** N **SP:** 1) (-----) 2) Martha Crawford **VI:** Son of John Anderson (1707-1786) **P:** unk **BLW:** unk **RG:** N **MK:** Y SAR plaque **PH:** N **SS:** E pg 14 **BS:** JLARC 62; 196

ANDERSON, Robert; b 1 Jan 1712; d 19 Dec 1792 **RU:** Patriot, Gave material aid to cause **CEM:** Goldmine farm; GPS unk; Rt 271, Rockville; Hanover **GS:** Y **SP:** Elizabeth Clough (1722-1779) **VI:** Son of Robert Penn Anderson (1663-1716) & Mary Elizabeth Overton (1673-1735) **P:** N **BLW:** N **RG:** N **MK:** N **PH:** unk **SS:** AL Cert Issued **BS:** 31 pg 3; 196.

BARKER, William. Deleted as born 1785.

BEALE, William Jr; b 31 Aug 1710; d 26 Jun 1778 **RU:** Patriot, Signer of Leedstown Resolutions **CEM:** Beale Family; GPS unk; Chestnut Hill, E of Ethel; Richmond Co **GS:** U **SP:** Mar 1729, Ann Harwar (1710-1766) **VI:** Son of Thomas Beale (1675-1729) & Anne Hamilton (1711-1784); called Captain **P:** N **BLW:** N **RG:** Y **MK:** N **PH:** N **SS:** DR; SAR P-336279 **BS:** 213 pg 26; 196.

BELL, Joseph Jr; b Feb 1755; d 13 Sep 1833 **RU:** Captain, Drafted in 1776; served under Capt John Lyle, Col Russell's Regt in battle against Cherokees. Drafted again in 1777, and served under Capts Thomas Smith & Long, part, VA Troops of General Lafayette's Army at Yorktown. Took oath as Capt 15 Aug 1780- 18 Sep 1781, Augusta Co Militia **CEM:** Augusta Stone Presbyterian; GPS 38.23926, -78.97356; 28 Old Stone Church Ln, Ft Defiance; Augusta **GS:** Y **SP:** Elizabeth Betsey Henderson **VI:** Still lived on farm where he was b at time of pen application. Appl pen 30 Aug 1832 Augusta Co S6608; R207; Govt stone reads 1755-1833 **P:** Y **BLW:** unk **RG:** Y **MK:** Y SAR plaque **PH:** unk **SS:** B; E pg 56; K Vol 1 pg 66; AZ pg 104-5, 18; SAR P-112659 **BS:** JLARC 8, 23.

BENNINGTON, Job; b 13 Feb 1758, Harford Co, MD; d 24Jul 1823 **RU:** Matross, Served in PA Cont Line. Enl in PA 1777 **CEM:** Bennington-Gaylor; GPS unk; Waterloo Rd; Rockbridge **GS:** N **SP:** Sarah Agnes Morris (1835-1860) **VI:** Son of Henry Bennington(1727-__) & Elizabeth Barnes (1735-__); Appl pen 5 May 1823 Rockbridge Co. S37753. R221 **P:** Y **BLW:** unk **RG:** Y **MK:** N **PH:** N **SS:** DAR A009338; M pg 734; CG pg 240; K Vol 1 pg 68; SAR P-113469 **BS:** 04, May 06.

BLACKWELL, Joseph Sr; b 9 Jul 1715, Northumberland Co; d 30 May 1787 **RU:** Patriot, Gave material aid to cause Fauquier Co; signed the Leedstown Reslutions 27 Feb 1766 **CEM:** Blackwell Family; GPS unk; The Meadows, E of Rt 628 at the first farm past Bethel United Methodist Church; Fauquier **GS:** U **SP:** Mar (Jun 1745) Lucy Steptoe (1720-26 Apr 1787) **VI:** Son of Samuel & Margery (Downing Hudnall) Blackwell **P:** N **BLW:** N **RG:** Y **MK:** unk **PH:** unk **SS:** Leedstown Resolutions 1766; AL Ct Bk pg 1, 21; SAR P-115701 **BS:** 196.

BLAIR, William; b 5 Jul 1741; d aft 1798 **RU:** Private, Served in Capt Cunningham's Co, Augusta Co Militia **CEM:** Bethel Presbyterian; GPS 38.04257, -79.17283; 563 Bethel Green Rd, Middlebrook; Augusta **GS:** N **SP:** 1) Mary Logan 2) Elizabeth Downey (1756-1836) **VI:** Son of Alexander Blair & Jane Preston Scott. Another FindaGrave memorial indicates he is buried in the Glebe Cemetery GPS 38.109402,-79.22110, los on Glebe School Rd (Rt 876), Swoop in Augusta Co **P:** unk **BLW:** unk **RG:** Y **MK:** unk **PH:** N **SS:** E pg 68: SAR P -115811 **BS:** 196.

BYRD William; b 1752; d 31 May 1829 **RU:** Private, Entered serv 1776 in Prince Edward Co Militia **CEM:** Samuel Byrd Family; GPS unk; Old Colonial Rd; Grayson **GS:** N **SP:** Jane Alley (1766-1821), daug of James Alley(1728-1799) & Azby Christian (1730-1799)) **VI:** Son of John Byrd (1725-1775) & Sarah (__); pen Grayson Co age 65 in 1818, R444 **P:** unk **BLW:** unk **RG:** N **MK:** N **PH:** N **SS:** K pg 149; **BS:** 04, Apr 2007; 196

CARTER, Robert Wormley; b 7 Jun 1734, d 6 Jun 1797 **RU:** Colonel ; signed the Leedstown Resolutions 27 Feb 1766. Appointed Richmond County Lieutenant 8 Oct 1776, recd as Col 2 Jun 1777 **CEM:** Lower Nunenburg Parish Church, ruins removed, thus no longer exists; GPS 37.940132, -76.781693; loc in town of Warsaw by water tower on Rt 360; Richmond Co **GS:** N **SP:** Mar 9 Mar 1776, Winifred Travers Beale (1733-1794), d/o William Beale & Ann Harwar **VI:** Son of Landon Carter (7 Jun

1709-10 Aug 1778) & Elizabeth Wormley (1714, Middlesex Co-1740) **P:** NBLW: N **RG:** N **MK:** N **PH:** N **SS:** Leedstown Resolutions 1766; E pg 135 **BS:** 196.

CHANEY, Abraham; b 1758, Halifax Co; d 25 Dec 1848 **RU:** Private Capt J0hn Donalson, Jr Co 9 Mar 1776 to Jul 1776;vol this unit again 7 Apr 1778 until 12 Aug 1778; next tour winter 1781 Capt Clements Co discharged sick in Hillsborough, NC **CEM:** Chaney Family; GPS 36.707015,-79.195524; loc on Reeves Mill Rd (Rt 660), Keeling; Pittsylvanis **GS:** Yes gov't **SP:** Mar 1) Mary Ann Cheatham (1767-1810), 2) Nancy Donnelson (1776-1855) who rec'd pen act of 1853, cert 3788 & BLW 28653 for 160 acres issued Jun 1856; **VI:** Son of Jacob Chaney (1715-1801) & Sarah Midkiff (1727-1801)) **P: Y** Spouse **BLW:** Y spouse **RG:** Y **MK:**N **PH:** N **SS:** DAR A021307; AZ pg 160-161; CD; SAR P-131281 **BS:** 196

CURRY, Robert; b 10 Nov 1717 Ulster, Ireland; d 5 Jan 1800 **RU:** Captain, Served in Homeguards; was appointed road overseer, Auguste Co, Mar 1783 **CEM:** Augusta Stone Presbyterian; GPS 38.23926, -78.97356; 28 Old Stone Church Ln, Ft Defiance; Augusta **GS:** Y **SP:** Anne (-----) (25 Sep 1727, Ulster, Ireland-15 May 1819) **VI:** Commanded Co in the Augusta Co Militia before war 16 August 1774. Elder of Augusta Church; Styled "Doctor" **P:** unk **BLW:** unk **RG:** Y **MK:** Y SAR plaque **PH:** Y **SS:** B; AH pg 7 DAR A028779; Augusta Co Ct Rec March 1783; SAR P-142471 **BS:** JLARC 2, 8, 63; 196.

GRIFFIN, Cyrus; b 16 Jul 1748, Farnham, Richmond Co; d 14 Dec 1810 **RU:** Patriot, Gave material aid to cause. Was member VA House of Delegates 1777-78, 1786-87. Was member of Cont Congress 1787-88 and president Cont Congress 1788 **CEM:** Bruton Parish Church; GPS 37.27127, -76.70248; 331 W Duke of Gloucester St; Williamsburg City **GS:** U **SP:** Mar (c1779, Scotland) Lady Christina Stuart (1752, Scotland-8 Oct 1807, Williamsburg) **VI:** Son of Leroy Griffin (1711-1750) & Mary Bertrand (c1717-1770); Pres of Ct of Admiralty. Commissioner to Creek nation. Judge of US District Ct of VA fr Dec 1789 until death. Died in Yorktown **P:** N **BLW:** N **RG:** N **MK:** unk **PH:** unk **SS:** DD **BS:** 201 pg 7389, 7390.

HARRISON, Benjamin bur Berkley Plantation-add **MK:** SAR Bronze

HUGHART, Thomas; b unk; d May 1810 **RU:Colonel/** Patriot, commanded 2d Bn, Augusta Co, Militia effective 19 sep 1780, was in battle at Williamsburg,and Yorktown 1781; gave material aid to cause **CEM:** Trinity Episcopal; GPS 38.14917, -79.07521; 214 Beverley St; Staunton City **GS:** Y **SP:** Rebecca Estill (1739-1824) **VI:** May be duplicate of Thomas Hughart reported bur at Rock Spring Cem **P:** N **BLW:** N **RG:** N **MK:** unk **PH:** unk **SS:** J- DAR Hatcher; AL Cert Augusta Co; AZ pgs 139, 182 **BS:** JLARC 2; 196

LEE, Arthur; b 20 Dec 1740, Westmoreland Co; d 12 Dec 1792 **RU:** Patriot, signed the Leedstown Resolutions, 27 Feb 1766; was Commissioner to France 1776, Spain 1777; was in VA House of Delegates & Cont Congress 1782-84; also served on Treasury Board **CEM:** Landsdowne House(AKA Arthur Lee Family); GPS 37.638569,-76.576164;on Rappahannock St vic jct Bonner St, Urbanna; Middlesex **GS:** Y **SP:** Not married **VI:** Son of Thomas Lee (1690-1750 Stradford) & Hannah Harrison (Ludwell) (1701-1749 Green Spring); Diplomat with Franklin and Adams to France. Graduated fr Edenburgh University in medicine; has Coat of Arms **P:** N **BLW:** N **RG:** Y **MK:** Lee Family plaque & VA Road sign **PH:** unk **SS:** Leedstown Resolutions, 27 Feb 1766; AS; EO pg 52; VA historic road sign; SAR P-234649 **BS:** 92 pg 58; 201 pg 73, 90; 196

LEE, Thomas Ludwell; b 13 Dec 1730, Stratford Hall, Westmoreland Co; d 13 Apr 1778 **RU:** Patriot, signed the Leedstown Resolutions of 1766; was active in VA Convention, Committee of Safety for Colony of VA. Served in House of Burgesses. Was judge of General Ct of VA **CEM:** Belleview Plantation; GPS unk; Rt 604; Stafford **GS:** N **SP:** Mary Aylett, daughter of William & (-----) Aylett **VI:** Son of Thomas Lee (1690-1750) & Hannah Harrison (1701-1750); known to have d at his plantation "Bellevue" and is thought to have been bur nearby. **P:** N **BLW:** N **RG:** Y **MK:** N **PH:** N **SS:** E pg 466; DAR A068794; Leedstown Resolutions of 1766 SAR P-234863 **BS:** 04; 30 pg 230.

MCCUTCHEON/McCUTCHAN John; b 15 Nov 1758; d 29 Jun 1848 **RU:** Private, Served in Capt John Wilson's Co, Augusta Co Militia; then enl in VA line serving long enough to qualify for pen **CEM:** North Mountain; GPS 38.0789160,-79.1779770; 7 mi S of Staunton on N side Rt 252; Augusta **GS:** N **SP:** Jean Finley **VI:** Name is on a copper plate on a monument by DAR chapter listing Rev War soldiers bur in this Glebe; appl & rec'd pen #S13886 26 Oct 1832 **P:** Y **BLW:** unk **RG:** N **MK:** unk **PH:** N **SS:** G pg 26; CG pg 2262 **BS:** JLARC 63; 196.

MCPHEETERS, William Jr; b 28 Sep 1729, PA; d 28 Oct 1807 **RU:** Soldier/Patriot, took tithables 20 Mar 1783 in Capts McCutchen's and Bell's Companies, Augusta Co Militia; Gave material aid to cause **CEM:** Bethel Presbyterian; GPS 38.04257, -79.17283; 563 Bethel Green Rd, Middlebrook; Augusta **GS:** U **SP:** Rachel Moore (__-30 Jan 1826) d/o James (1711-1791) & Jane (Walker) (1712-1793) Moore **VI:** Son of William McPheeter (1690-1773) & Rebecca Thompson; was a Reverend **P:** unk **BLW:** unk **RG:** Y **MK:** unk **PH:** unk **SS:** AL Comm Bk II pg 361 Augusta Co; Augusta Co Order Bk, 1783; SAR P-247038 **BS:** JLARC 62; 196.

RICHARDS, John; b bef 1735. Gloucester Co; d 6 Apr 1806 **RU:** Patriot gave material aid to the cause in King & Queen Co **CEM:** Williams Family; GPS 37.412750,-76.338500;.loc 100yds along coast fr 62 Williamsdale Ln;; Mathews **GS:** Y **SP:** No info **VI:** Probably son of John Richards (c1689, Kent, Eng-12 Nov 1725 Gloucester Co & Amy (__) (c1785-23 Nov 1735) **P:** N **BLW:** N **RG:** Y **MK:** N **PH:** N **SS:** AL Ct Bk t pg 15; SAR P-342340, **BS:** 32; 43 pg 155; 48 pg 142; 196

SKINNER, Charles W. DELETED, too young.

SMITH, James M; b c1761; d 8 Feb 1825 **RU:** Capt/Patriot, commanded a company Oct 1779 in Col Nathaniel Gist's 4th VA Regt of Cont Troops; paid personal property tax 1782 (considered supply tax for paying Rev War expenses) **CEM:** Smith Family; GPS unk; loc end of Mantua Farm Rd; Northumberland **GS:** Y **SP:** No info **VI:** No further data **P:** N **BLW:** N **RG:** N **MK:** unk **PH:** unk **SS:** E pg 721; N pgs 441,442; AP serv; EB pg 21 **BS:** 227 pg 124; 196

SMITH, Ralph; b 1753; d 28 Feb 1827 **RU:** Patriot, Gave material aid to cause **CEM:** Mt Hermon United Methodist; GPS 37.14500, -79.31170; Rt 712, Lynch Station; Campbell **GS:** Y **SP:** No info **VI:** Founder of Mt Herman Methodist Church 1825; Another Findagrave memorial indicates buried w/o GS instead in Pocket Cem; GPS 37.131407,-79.338974; loc Heartstone Ln, Hurt; Pittsylvania **P:** N **BLW:** N **RG:** N **MK:** unk **PH:** N **SS:** AL Ct Bk pg 3 Pittsylvania Co **BS:** 196.

TURBERVILLE, George; b 1742, d 20 Oct 1792 **RU:** Patriot, a signer of the Leedstown Resolutions 27 Feb 1766; and gave material aid to cause, Westmoreland Co **CEM:** Peckatone; GPS of town 38.072222, -76.651111 ; Hague; Westmoreland **GS:** Unk **SP:** Martha "Patty" Corbin (1749-20 Nov 1809), daug of Gawin Corbin (1725-1760) & Hannah Ludwell Lee (1728-1782) **VI:** Son of George Turberville (1694-30 Mar 1742) & Martha Lee (1716, England-12 Nov 1751) **P:** N **BLW:** N **RG:** N **MK:** N **PH:** N **SS:** Leedstown Resolutions of 1766; AL Ct Bk pgs 2, 3,5 and Comm Bk V pgs225-6 **BS** 196

WILLIS, Lewis; b 11 Nov 1734; d 15 Jan 1813 **RU:** Lt Col, a signer of the Leedstown Resolutions 27 Feb 1766; served as staff officer;10th Cont Line in Gen Weedon's Brigade on 13 Nov 1776; resigned 1 Mar 1778 **CEM:** Willis Hill; GPS not determined; loc Maryes Heights on Lafayette Blvd on grounds of Fredericksburg National Battlefield; Fredericksburg City **GS:** Unk **SP:** Mar 1) Ann Byrd Carter (1740-1812), 2) Elizabeth Stevenson (1760-1810), 3) Mary Champe (1735-_) **VI:** Son of Henry Willis (1696-1740) & Mildred Washington (1696-1747) **P:** N **BLW:** N **RG:** Y **MK:** N **PH:** N **SS:** Leedstown Resolutions of 1766; G pg 840; SAR P-321430 **BS:** 196.

WILLIAMS, Samuel; b 25 Nov 1725, Somerset Co, MD; d 19 May 1789 Mathews Co **RU:** Patriot, Gave material aid to cause in Gloucester Co **CEM:** Williams Family; GPS 37.412750,-76.338500;.loc 100 yds along coastline fr 62 Williamsdale Ln; Mathews **GS:** Y **SP:** Mar 1) 7 Nov 1753, Sarah Haggoman (__-1763), daug of John Haggomam & Sarah Powell, 2) 2 Dec 1764, Sarah Dunton,(__-4 Dec 1772), daug of Levin Dunton, 3) Margaret Nottingham,(c1752-1 Oct 1810). daug of Thomas Nottingham & (__) Scarbrough **VI:** Son of John Williams whose will was probated 27 Dec 1760 **P:** N **BLW:** N **RG:** N **MK:** N **PH:** unk **SS:** DAR A134001; AL Ct Bk pg iii,9 **BS:** 48 pg 141; 196

WILLIAMS, Thomas; b 1745; d bef Oct 1784 **RU:** Major/Patriot, Gave material aid to cause; served as Grand Juror and Overseer of Roads **CEM:** Williams Family; GPS not determined; loc nr Crewe, See 1938 DAR Senate doc 10448, vol 2; Nottoway **GS:** U **SP:** Alice (__) **VI:** No further data **P:** unk **BLW:** unk **RG:** Y **MK:** unk **PH:** unk **SS:** J- DAR Hatcher; DN pg 409, 411; SAR P-321118 **BS:** JLARC 2, 196

WILLIAMS, Thomas; b 4 May 1762, Gloucester Co; d 30 Sep 1823 **RU:** Patriot, gave material aid to cause, Gloucester Co as well as paying personal property tax in the county in 1783 **CEM:** Williams Family; GPS 37.412750,-76.338500;.loc 100 yds along coast fr 62 Williamsdale Ln; Mathews **GS:** Y **SP:** Mar 1) 15 Jun 1793, Susannah Billups(__-1804), 2) 18 Oct 1804, Mary Lilly Billup (21 Jan 1785, Gloucester Co-23 Jun 1857), daug of Joseph Billups & Joice Repress **VI:** Son of Samuel Williams & Sarah Haggman; Another person this name in the county may have given material to the cause and not him, however doubtful if another person paid taxes in 1783, as the other person had more family members and blacks then he would have had unmarried at age 21 **P:** N **BLW:** N **RG:** Y **MK:** N **PH:** N **SS:** E pg 833; AL Ct Bk iii, pg 30; ER Kingston Parish, Mathews Co; SAR P-342397 **BS:** 196.

WILLIAMS, William; b 9 Apr 1759, d 28 Sep 1801 **RU:** Private, Capt John Billup's Co, Gloucester Co Militia,serving at age 17 fr 2 Aug to 8 Oct 1776 **CEM:** Williams Family; GPS 37.412750,-76.338500;.loc 100 yds along coast fr 62 Williamsdale Ln; Mathews **GS** Y **SP:** Mar 1) Mary Nottingham (29 May 1786-__), 2) Leah Goffigon (3 Aug 1795- __) **VI:** Son of Samuel Williams (25 Nov 1725-19 May 1789) & Sarah Haggoman (1732-1760); Another person this name in Gloucester Co,could have served in Capt John Billup's Co; however the payroll listing William Williams was named "For the Invasion" meaning the British forces occupation of Gynn's Island nearby in 1776, and this William would have been age 17 and a private, while the other William is a person born in the1740s or earlier and would probably not have been a private but would have a higher rank in the company **P:** N **BLW:** N **RG:** Y **MK:** N **PH:** N **SS:**N pg 1264 payroll fr Archives Dept State Library; SAR P-324398 **BS:** 196

WILSON, James; b 22 Dec 1739, Augusta Co; d 6 Aug 1824 **RU:** Patriot, Gave material aid to the cause **CEM:** Sharon Lutheran; GPS 37.05800, -81.20590; Rt 42 W of Ceres; Bland **GS:** Y **SP:** Elizabeth Poage (1739-12 May 1824) **VI:** Son of John Burgess Willson (1702-1774) & Martha Crouchman (1695-1755) **P:** N **BLW:** N **RG:** N **MK:** N **PH:** unk **SS:** AL Ct Bk pg 10 **BS:** 60, Bland Co; 196.

WILSON, Willis; b 1758; d 10 Feb 1822 **RU:** Lieutenant, serv in 11th VA regt; was at Buford's Defeat at Waxsaw, SC, rec'd eight wounds right arm and hand, others on his head and bayonet wound **CEM:** Bonbrook house; GPS 37.545547,-78.235081; loc off Bonbrook Creek Rd, nr dam; Cumberland **GS:** Y **SP:** Elizabeth Trent **VI:** rec'd pen19 Jun 1788, paid fr 1783-1788 and was on 1813 pen list **P:** Y **BLW:** N **RG:** Y **MK:** N **PH:** N **SS:** DAR A127921; E pg 838; BX pg 883; SAR P 322183 BS:157, Bonbrook; 196

WRIGHT, Joseph; b 1752; d 8 Oct 1826 **RU:** Private, Served in Capt Trimble's Augusta Co Militia **CEM:** Hebron Presbyterian; GPS 38.14140, -79.15500; 423 Hebron Rd; Staunton City **GS:** Y **SP:** Ruth Evans (2 Oct 1756-21 Apr 1834) **VI:** Died age 74 (stone) **P:** unk **BLW:** unk **RG:** N **MK:** unk **PH:** unk **SS:** E pg 850 **BS:** JLARC 62, 63; 196.

ADDENDA: (New patriots)

ALLEN, James; b 1716, Ireland; d bef 28 May 1810 **RU:** Lieutenant, was in battle at Point Pleasant 10 Oct 1774 in Capt George Mathew's Co **CEM:** Old Stone Presbyterian; 38.2383087,-78.9757954; 28 Old Stone Church Ln, Ft Defiance; Augusta **GS:** Y Govt **SP:** Margaret Anderson, daug of John Anderson **VI:** Son of William Allen; was Elder of the Church **P:** N **BLW: N RG:** Y **MK:** N **PH:** N **SS: DAR** A01614; Z pgs 105-6; SAR P-100747 **BS:** 196

ANDERSON, Samuel b 25 Jun 1757; d 4 Apr 1826 **RU:** Sergeant in Capt John Morton's Co, Prince Edward Co Militia, 28 Jun 1781 **CEM:** James Anderson Fam; GPS37.327850,-78.422020; loc E of Anderson Trail, Farmville; Cumberland **GS:** U **SP:** Mar 29 Mar 1781, Ann Dabney (10 Feb 1759-18 Jun 1831) **VI:** Son of James Anderson (1714-1782) & Elizabeth Baker (1737-1792) **P:** N **BLW: N RG:** Y **MK:** N **PH:** N **SS:** DAR A002507; E pg 16; Az pg 226; SAR P-103640 **BS:** 196

AVERY, William Haley "Billey"; b 1740; d 20 Apr 1802 RU: Major in VA militia; entered serv as First Lt, 1 Jan 1776; promoted 4 Jan 1777 to Captain; he commanded a company May 1778, in the 6th VA Regt commanded by Gen Nathaniel Greene, serving at Valley Forge, crossed Deleware River as advanced Bridgehead unit for George Washington; resigned 28 Jun 1778 **CEM:** Martins Brandon Episcopal Ch; GPS 37.215380,-77.074508; 18706 James River Dr (Rt 10), Burrowsville; Prince George **GS:** Unk **SP:** Betty Symonds **VI:** Was after war period a Col in VA militia and Sherriff of Pr Geoge Co **P:** N **BLW:** Y 4000 acres **RG:** Y **MK:** N **PH:** N **SS:** DAR A004034; E pg 28; SAR P-105838 **BS:** 196

BASS, Joseph; 30 Nov 1759, Chesterfield **Co**; d 30 Mar 1844 **RU:** Ensign, appointed by Chesterfield Co Ct, 6 Apr 1781; served in Capt Benjamin Branch's Co Chesterfield Co Militia **CEM:** French Green(AKA Bourdon Family); GPS not determined; 24920 Cutback Rd, Mc Kenney; Dinwiddie **GS:** N **SP:** Mar 1) 5 Dec 1790. Mary Robertson (__-8 May 1790), 2) Jane Manlove (8 Oct 1772-17 Jan 1852), daug of Christopher Manlove & Elizabeth Bolling **VI:** Son of Col Joseph Bass & Elizabeth Royall Co **C**

BEALE, Richard; b 1720, Chestnut Hill, Dauphin Co, PA; d 1797, Southampton Co; **RU:** Patriot, gave material aid to cause **CEM:** Beale Family; GPS unk; Chestnut Hill, E of Ethel; Richmond Co **GS:** U **SP:**

No data **VI**: No further data **P**: N **BLW**: N **RG**: N **MK**: N **PH**: N **SS**: AL Ct Bk pg 2 Southampton Co **BS**: 196

BECK, Jesse; b Sep 1758, Albemarle Co; d 4 May 1841, Amherst Co **RU**:Sergeant,1781, Capt Benjamin Harrison's Co, Col Thomas Posey VA Regt; was in battlte at Yorktown Oct 1781 **CEM**: Old City; GPS 37.414718,-79.156669; 401 Taylor St; Lynchburg City **GS**: U **SP**: Mar 4 Dec 1786, Ann Hughes (1766-25 Jul 1846); recd pen # W5805 **VI**: Son of Lucy Eugenia Clark (1733-1827) **P**: Y both **BLW**: U eligible **RG**: N **MK**: N **PH**: N **SS**: DAR A008280; C pg 225; E pg53; N pg 1023; AP Fold3 pen rec **BS** 196

BELL, William; b 1764; d 22 Aug 1833 **RU**: Private, served in Capt Joseph Belll's Co Augusta Co Militia in 1781 **CEM**: Augusta Stone Presbyterian; GPS 38.23926, -78.97356, GS 38.1411,-78.5819; 28 Old Stone Church Ln, Ft Defiance; Augusta **GS**: Y **SP**: Margaret Allen (1767-1844) **VI**: Son of Joseph Bell (1742-1823)& Elizabeth Henderson (1746-1833); was a Major in War of 1812 **P**: N **BLW**: N **RG**: N **MK**: N **PH**: N **SS**: E pg 56 **BS**: 196

BLAIR, William E; b 1750, Moneymore, Londonderry,Ulster IRE; d 1789 **RU**: Private, enl 28 Feb 1776, Samuel Hay's Co, 6th Bn, Col William Irvin's Regt, York Co, PA Militia; captured by British 8 Jun 1776, Trois Rivers, Quebec; paroled 6 Aug 1776 **CEM**: Blair-Stamps; GPS 36.621933,-79.278270; loc W side Hillside Rd, Ringgold, Pittsylvania **GS**: Y **SP**: Sarah Sutter **VI**: No further data **P**: N **BLW**: N **RG**: Y **MK**:N **PH**: N **SS**: AP PA Achives 5th Ser vol 2, pg 206 & 6th serv vol 2, pgs 549-551; DAR A010890; SAR P-115814 **BS**: 196

BLAND, John, Jr; b 19 Oct 1739; d Apr 1777, Amelia Co **RU**: Patriot, signed the Leedstown Resolution, 7 Feb 1766 **CEM**: Jordan Point Plantation; GPS: 37.303925,-77.223250; Waters Edge Rd, Jordan Pt Manor; Prince George **GS**:Y **SP**: Clara Yates(1743-Aug 1832, Brunswick Co), daug of William Yates(1720-1764) & Elizabeth Randolph (1724-1783) **VI**: Son of Richard Bland (1710-1776) & Anne Poythress (1712-1758); attended William & Mary College1756-1758 **P**: N **BLW**: N **RG**: N **MK**: Y plaque **PH**: N **SS**: Leedstown Resolutions 1766; **BS**: 196

BOOTH, William; b 1722; d 1783 **RU**: Patriot, signed the Leedstown Resolutions, 7 Feb 1766 **CEM**: Booth Family; GPS not determined; loc on land where Mannass Hill Baptist Church now stands, nr Sheathouse Creek; Amelia **GS**: N **SP**: Phoebe Booth (1740-1795) **VI**: Son of William Booth Sr as he purchased land as Jr **P**: N **BLW**: N **RG**: N **MK**:N **PH**: N **SS**: Leedstown Resolutions 1766; **BS**: 196

BROWN, John; b 1749, Augusta Co,; d 3 Feb 1830 **RU**: Captain, commanded a company in the Augusta Co Militia 15 May 1781; was taken prisoner at the battle at Jamestown **CEM**: Brown Family; GPS 37.272130,-80.306460; loc Catawba Rd, Blacksburg; Montgomery **GS**: Y descendents have placed a new one **SP**: No spousal info **VI**: No further data **P**: N **BLW**: N **RG**: N **MK**: N **PH**: N **SS**: AZ pgs 20, 181 **BS**: 196

BURNSIDE, John; b c1726, Ire; d 1809, Bath Co **RU**: Patriot gave material aid to cause Augusta Co **CEM**: Augusta Stone Presbyterian; GPS: 38.23925o,-78.973556; loc 28 Old Stone Church Ln, Ft Defiance; Augusta **GS**: Y **SP**: Mary Walker (1754-15 Jun 1815), daug of Alexander Walker & Elizabeth Patterson **VI**: Son of Robert Burnside (__-c1726) & Esther Mayse(__-1756) **P**: N **BLW**: N **RG**: Y **MK**: N **PH**: N **SS** DAR A018670; D vol 1, pg 43; Al Ct Bk lists; SAR P-125689 **BS**: 196

CARTER, William; b 21 Apr 1760, Albemarle Co; d Dec 1845 **RU**: Private ent serv Sep 1778; was in Kings Mountain battle; served three years **CEM**: Peterstown; GPS 37.394699,-80.801379; Peterstown Cem Rd, Rich Creek; Giles **GS**: U **SP**: Ann French **VI**: Rec'd pen Monroe Co WVA 1833; BLW # 1317 or #3055 for 100 acres **P**: Y **BLW**: Y **RG**: N **MK**: N **PH**: N **SS**: E pg 135; F pgs 16,18 **BS**: 196

CLARKE, William; b c1758; York Co; d 8 Dec 1827 **RU**; Private, enlisted 1775 or 1776 under Capt Thomas Wells, 15th VA Regt, Colonels Mason, Wallace, William Heth, John Jameson, Jones and Edwards, Virginia Troops; was in battles of Germantown and Monmouth and served to end of war **CEM**: Madden Family; GPS not determined; loc 23512 Madden's Tavern Rd, Elkwood; Culpeper **GS**: N **SP**: Mar 19 Mar 1785, Stafford Co, Hannah Peters (c1758-aft 18 Aug 1838 application date), rec'd pen # W6687 **VI**: Recd pension 6 Apr 1818 in Culpeper Co. and BLW # 2259, 21 Jan 1784 for 100 acres **P**: Y both **BLW**: Y **RG**: Y **MK**:N **PH**: N **SS**: E pg 155; F pg 17; AP Fold3 pen rec Comm Ltr; SAR P-134217 **BS**: 04

COX, William; b 19 Sep 1765, d 1949 **RU**: Private, Capt Abraham Trigg's Co, Montgomery Co, Apr 1781 **CEM**: Cox Fam; Smyth Co **GS** U **SP**: No spousal data VI: Served in War of 1812 **P**: N **BLW**: N **RG**: N **MK**: N **PH**: N **SS; G pg 225 BS**: 196

CRADDOCK, William Cross; b 1735, Amelia Co, d 23 Jul 1795 **RU**: Captain/Patriot, sworn in as Captain 22 Jun 1778, commanded a company Amelia Co Militia that was in battle in Camden,SC Jul 1781; as patriot gave aid to the cause and was Justice of Peace 1782 and census taker **CEM**: Craddock at Piney Fork; GPS 36.933770,-79.432860; on W side of Piney Rd just N of jct w Old Mine Rd; Gretna; Pittsylvania **GS**: U **SP**: Obedience Hill (1744-1816) **VI**: Was deputy sheriff 1767 and Justice of Peace 1785-1794 and trustee of Nottoway Parish 1788, Amelia Co **P**: N **BLW**: Y 1500 acres **RG**: Y **MK**: N **PH**: 8N **SS**: DAR A027149; SAR P 140137; E pg 186; G pg 14; AZ pgs 138, 177 **BS**: 196

CROXTON, Carter; b 16 mar 1761; d 29 Apr 1845 **RU**: Sergeant, Entered serv 1778 wounded at Cowpen's battle; serv 2d tour in Capt Turner Allen's Co, Col Allen Porterfield's VA Regt; was at Yorktown battle **CEM**: Cherry Walk; GPS not determined; fenced cem, Miller's Tavern; Essex; **GS**: U **SP**: Mar 24 Nov 1825, Frances Paulooner (__-2 Nov 1849) **VI**: Rec'd pen # S59259 18 Feb 1833; rec'd BLW # 7635 for 200 acres **P**: Y **BLW**: Y **RG**: N **MK**: N **PH**: N **SS**: AZ pg 238,AP Fold3 pen rec **BS**: 196

DUPUY, John; b 20 Jun 1776, Amelia Co; d 1 Oct 1832; **RU**: Lieutenant, comm 1778, Prince Edward Co Militia; was in battle at Gilford C.H. **CEM**: Dupuy Family; GPS not determined; loc nr Abilene, Rice: Prince Edward **GS**: U **SP**: Mar 31 Dec 1783, Charlotte Co, Mary Watkins (30 Oct 1776-4 Aug 1840)' daug Joel Watkins & Agnes Morton **VI**: Recd pen 1732 **P**: Y **BLW**: Y **RG**: N **MK**: N **PH**: N **SS**:K vol 2, pg 62; AZ pgs 64, 224; AP Fold3 pen rec **BS**: 196

EASLEY, John; b 1757; d 17 Jan 1782 **RU** Private/Patriot served as Juror, Halifax Co 1779 and gave a gun to Capt Thomas Ballow, 2d Minute Bn, Halifax Co. Military service not determined **CEM**:Halifax Co memorial War monument; loc jct Mountain Rd & Rt 501, Halifax; Halifax **GS**: N **SP**: Married Mar 1779, Sallie Mann (__-1732) **VI**: Memorialized as died in mil unit while serving **P**: N **BLW**: N **RG**: N **MK**: N **PH**: N **SS**; DAR A035594; G pg 464 **BS**; Halifax Co War Memorial

FAMBROUGH, Benjamin; b unk; d 24 Jan 1788 in unit **RU**: Private, Capt William Moseley's Co, Col Alexander McClenachan's Regt May 1777 to Jan 24 1778 **CEM**:Halifax Co memorial War monument; loc jct Mountain Rd & Rt 501, Halifax; Halifax **GS**: N **SP**:No spousal info **VI**: Memorialized as died in mil unit while serving **P**: N **BLW**: N **RG**: N **MK**: N **PH**: N **SS**: AP Fold3 Serv index card **BS**; Halifax Co War Memorial

FULLER, Arthur, b 1717, Isle of Wight Co; d 4 Oct 1797 **RU**: Patriot signed Oath of Allegience 1777,Pittsylvania Co; and paid personal property tax on 150 acres 1782 **CEM**: Lawrence; GPS not determined; Callands; Pittsylvania **GS**:U **SP**: Sarah Littleton (1725-1797) **VI**: Son of Ezekiel Fuller (1675-1723); DAR indicates he was born in Brunswick Co **P**: N **BLW**: N **RG**: Y **MK**:N **PH**: N **SS**: DAR A042106; ER Pittsylvania Land Tax List 1782 & Oath of Allegience List 1777; SAR P-162814 **BS**: 196

GEE, Henry b1732 Sussex Co; d 6 Jul 1778 **RU**: Private, Capt Thomas Thweatt's Co, 14th VA Regt Cont Line commanded by Col Charles Lewis **CEM**:Halifax Co memorial War monument; loc jct Mountain Rd & Rt 501, Halifax; Halifax **GS**: N **SP**:No spousal info **VI**: Son of Henry Gee and Broyce Scott; memorialized as died 6 Jul 1778 in serv unit with no gravesite found **P**: N **BLW**: N **RG**: N **MK**: N **PH**: N **SS**: AP Fold3 serv rec; CZ pg 121 **BS**; Halifax Co War Memorial

GILL, Jones; b 1764, Charles City Co; d 26 Nov 1844 **RU**: Private, Capt Seth Stubblefields Co, Col Thomas Nelson 1780-1781, VA line serving long enough to qualify for pen **CEM**: Gill Family; GPS 37.730845,-79.100752; loc Page Mountain Way (Rt 746) Indian Creek; ;Amherst; Amherst **GS**:U **SP**: Patience Nunnally (1770-1830) **VI**: Applied for pen 19 Jun 1834, rec'd # S10185 **P**: Y **BLW**: N **RG**: Y **MK**: N **PH**: N **SS**: DAR A027149; CG pg 1350; SAR P 166204; **BS**: 196

GOODE, Robert; b 1746, Brunswick Co; d 17 Aug 1804 **RU**: 2nd Lieutenant, Prince Edward Co Militia **CEM**: Goode Fam; GPS not determined; loc 4.5 mi from Appomatox River; Appomatox **GS**: N **SP**: Sarah Collier (1749-1811) **VI**: Son of Samuel Goode (1700-1797) & Susannah Burwell (1704-__); became a Judge **P**: N **BLW**: N **RG**: N **MK**: N **PH**: N **SS**: DAR A044704; AZ pg 224 **BS**: 196

GRANT, David; b c1747, Dinwiddie Co; d Sep 1781 **RU**: Private Capt John Mark's Co 10th VA Regt, and in Major Cabell's Co, 14th VA Regt'later commanded by Col Charles Lewis serving 3 yrs 1777-1780 **CEM**:Halifax Co memorial War monument; loc jct Mountain Rd & Rt 501, Halifax; Halifax **GS**: N

SP:Faith was granted support in Halifax Co 17 Jun 1779 & 19 Oct 1780 **VI:** Memorialized as died in Halifax Co after serving in 1781 with no gravesite found **P:** N **BLW:** N **RG:** Y **MK:** N **PH:** N **SS:** DAR A047007; AP Fold3 Serv index card & rolls; BX pg 312; CZ pg 127 SAR P -169063 **BS;** Halifax Co War Memorial

GRANT, John; b unk, d by 1783 **RU:** Was serving in Capt John Mark's Co, 10th VA Regt commanded by Col William Davis Nov 1779 as they traveled southward **CEM:**Halifax Co memorial War monument; loc jct Mountain Rd & Rt 501, Halifax; Halifax **GS:** N **SP:**No spousal data **VI:** Memorialized as died in service unit by Oct 1783 with no gravesite found **P:** N **BLW:** N **RG:** N **MK:** N **PH:** N **SS:** AP Fold3 Serv index card & rolls; CZ pg 127 **BS;** Halifax Co War Memorial

GRANT, John; b 1720; d1799 **RU:** Patriot, Gave material aid to cause in Dinwiddie Co **CEM:** Yorktown National; GPS 37.225333,-76.505645; loc jct Cook Rd (704) & Union Rd, Yorktown; York; **GS:** Y plat 1421 **SP:** No spousal data **VI:** No further data) **P:** N **BLW:** N **RG:** N **MK:** N **PH:** N **SS;** AL Ct Bk pg 9, Comm Bk pg 329 **BS:** 196

HEDRICK:, Jacob, Sr; b 1735, Germany; d 1822 **RU:** Private, serv in Capt Buchanan's Co, Montgomery Co Militia and is on a list of militia that was discharged at Romney in 1775 **CEM:** Jacob Hedrick, Jr Family; GPS not determined; loc Toshes on family land; Pittsylvanis **GS:** U **SP:** Mar 1760, Berks Co, PA to unk **VI:** Had son John listed in county land and tax records as John Hendrick **P:** N **BLW:** N **RG:** Y **MK:** N **PH:** N **SS** :E pg 369; G pg 230; SAR P-179133 **BS:** 196

HILL, James, Sr; b Jan 1750; d 1781 **RU:** Captain, Haifax Co Militia als a Sergeant, 1st VA state Regt, and a Corporal in the 7th Cont Line **CEM:**Halifax Co memorial War monument; loc jct Mountain Rd & Rt 501, Halifax; Halifax **GS:** N **SP:**Marrried 16 Mar 1775, Sarah Williams **VI:** Memorialized as died in Halifax Co after serving in 1781 with no gravesite found **P:** N **BLW:** N **RG:** N **MK:** N **PH:** N **SS:** DAR A055802; E pg 377; CZ pg 149 **BS;** Halifax Co War Memorial

HUNTER. John Chapman; b c1762; d 14 Feb 1849, Fairfax Co **RU:** Private 5th VA Regt **CEM:** Flint Hill Cem; GPS 38.88.2353,-77.2912; loc10 yrds W of Church of Bretheran Oakton; Fairfax **GS:** Y **SP:** Mar Sarah Dade Triplett,(1768-1845) **VI:** Son of John Hunter (1721-1764) & Elizabeth Chapman Triplet, actually bur in fam cem named "Contemplation" in Vienna, Fairfax Co; GS only moved to Flint cem in 1999; commissioned Major 15 Jan 1807; was Major in War of 1812, after war became Brig Gen **P:** N **BLW:** N **RG:** N **MK:** N **PH:** Y **SS:** E pg405,406; **SAR** P-183438 **BS** 196

IRBY, William, b 29 Oct 1752, Sussex Co; d 5 Dec 1811 **RU:** Private, served in 1st and 10th Cont Lines for 3 yrs **CEM:** Pleasant Hill; GPS not determined; loc in walled cem at jct with Jordan Bridge, Blackstone; Nottoway **GS:** U **SP:** Mar 21 Jan 1792, Elizabeth Williams (1771-_); **VI:** Rec'd BLW # 4292 for 100 acres 1 May 1785 **P:** N **BLW:** Y **RG:** Y **MK:** N **PH:** N **SS** :DAR A060359; C pg 456; E pg 409; SAR P-189803 **BS:** 196

JONES, Thomas V; b 1720-1785 **RU:** Ensign, 24 Apr 1781 in Capt William Johnston's Co, Col Daniel Morgan's Regt that was enroute to NC **CEM:** Jones Family Farm; GPS 36.797310,-79.354630; loc on Fairview Rd nr jct w Catawba Drive, Jonesboro; Pittsylvania **GS:** U **SP:** not determined **VI:**Son of Thomas Jones (1684-1755) & Mary Wharton (1685-1755); family farm initially called "Crooked Run Estate", later "Jonesboro" (FAG cites Encyclopedia of VA, vol V) **P:** N **BLW:** N **RG:** Y **MK:** N **PH:** N **SS:** CD; SAR P-226559 **BS:** 196

LAND, William; b unk; d cOct 1777 **RU:** Private, Capt Thomas Thweatt's Co, 14th VA Regt commanded by Col Charles Lewis, May 1777 to Oct 1777, discharges fr being blind from smallpox **CEM:**Halifax Co memorial War monument; loc jct Mountain Rd & Rt 501, Halifax; Halifax **GS:** N **SP:**No spousal info **VI:** Memorialized as died in serv unit or Halifax Co after serving in Oct 1777 with no gravesite found **P:** N **BLW:** N **RG:** N **MK:** N **PH:** N **SS:** E pg 455; CZ pg 179 **BS;** Halifax Co War Memorial

LONG, Edward; b 1737 PA, d 16 Aug 1806 **RU:** Private/Patriot, served in Capt Chrystie's Co, PA 3rd Regt commanded by Col Thomas Craig's Co, 1777; as patriot paid personal property tax 1783, Pittslvania Co, a supply tax for Rev War expenses **CEM:** Edward Long's Family; GPS not determined; loc vic forks of Strawberry Creek, Danville; Pittsylvania **GS:** U **SP:** Jane Sallie Jones (1743-1821) **VI:** Recd head wound **P:** N **BLW:** N **RG:** Y **MK:** N **PH:** N **SS:** DAR A210666; AP pg 112, Rev War Rolls; SAR P 236892 **BS:** 196

MCCARTY, Daniel III; b 1732, d 1795 **RU:** Patriot, signer of the Leedstown Resolutions, 27 Feb 1766 **CEM:** McCarty Burial Vault Longwood Plantation: GPS not determined; Longwood, Horners Beach; Westmoreland **GS:** N **SP:** Mar 1) Mary Mercer (1740-1764), 2) 1765 Winifred Thornton (1748-1791) **VI:**

Son of Daniel McCarty (__-1744) & Elizabeth Smith **P:** N **BLW:** N **RG:** N **MK:** N **PH:** N **SS:** Leedstown Resolutions 1766; **BS:** 196

McFARLIN, John; b unk; d 21 Mar 1778 **RU:** Private, Capt Thomas Thweatt's Co, 14th VA Regt commanded by Col Abraham Buford Jan-Mar 1778 **CEM:**Halifax Co memorial War monument; loc jct Mountain Rd & Rt 501, Halifax; Halifax **GS:** N **SP:**No spousal info **VI:** Memorialized as died Mar 1778 in serv unit while serving in 1778 with no gravesite found **P:** N **BLW:** N **RG:** N **MK:** N **PH:** N **SS:** E pg 525; AP Fold3 serv rec **BS;** Halifax Co War Memorial

McLEAN, James; b 1749; d 1791 **RU:** Sergeant; QM Sgt in Capt Cleon Moore's Co, Col William Grayson's Regt of Foot, 1 Jul 1777 to 11 Aug 1777 when transferred to hospital in Philadelphia **CEM:** Grace Episcopal; GPS 37.23560, -76.50750; 115 Church St, Yorktown; York **GS:** Y broken **SP:** None identified **VI:** No further data **P:** N **BLW:** N **RG:** N **MK:** N **PH:** N **SS:** E pg 534; AP Fold3 serv rec **BS:** 196

MOODY, Edward; b unk; d Feb 1781 **RU:** Captain, VA Arty Co, Jun 1777, commanded by Col Edmond, serving 7 yrs **CEM:**Halifax Co memorial War monument; loc jct Mountain Rd & Rt 501, Halifax; Halifax **GS:** N **SP:**Elizabeth(__) who rec'd BLW # 4637 of 100 acres 10 Dec 1782 **VI:** Memorialized as died Feb 1781 perhaps in unit, with no gravesite found **P:** N **BLW:** Y Spouse **RG:** N **MK:** N **PH:** N **SS:** E pg 559;; F pg 48**BS;** Halifax Co War Memorial

MORTON, William; b 1748; d 1833 **RU:** QM Sgt, procured wagon hire and drums for Orange Co Militia **CEM:** Morton Hall Cem; GPS not determined; Rhoadesville: Orange **GS:** U **SP:**No spousal info **VI:** He also may be memorialized in the Davis Cem in Unionville, Orange Co **P:** N **BLW:** N **RG:** N **MK:** N **PH:** N **SS:** E pg 567; G pg s 491, 603 **BS:** 196

MUSTAIN, Jesse, b Jun 1750; d 16 Jun 1794 **RU**; Patriot signed Oath of Allegience, Pittsylvania Co 1777 **CEM:** Mustain Barn; GPS 36.56637, -79.18520; Btw Gretna & Mt Airy, private property behind barn; Pittsylvania **GS:** U **SP:** Mar c1776 Jenny(__) (1755-1792) V!: Son of Thomas Mustain & Mary Avery **P:** N **BLW:** N **RG:** N **MK:** N **PH:** N **SS:** ER: Oath Listing of Crispin Shelton, Pittsylvania Co 1777 **BS:** 174, 196

PARKER, William Alexander, b 1735 MD; d 1805 **RU:** Patriot, paid personal property tax, Pittsylvania Co 1782, a supply tax for Rev War expenses **CEM:** Parker Family; GPS 37.039675,-79.473309; loc E of Reservoir View Terris nr jct w ReservoirView Rd, Toshes; Pittsylvania **GS:** Unk **SP:**Henrietta Hyde (1740, Fauquier Co-1830) **VI:** Son of William Henry Parker (1707-1790) & Elizabeth Clark (1705-__); moved fr Fauquier Co 1768 **P:** N **BLW:** N **RG:** N **MK:** N **PH:** N **SS:** ER Pittsylvania Co tax list 1782 **BS:** JLARC 74; 196.

PEARSON, William; b 1761; d 28 Mar 1824 **RU:** Corporal/Patriot was in the 11th & 15th Cont Line; as patriot gave leather & shoes for public use **CEM:** St George's Episcopal; Fredericksburg; 905 Princess Anne St **GS:** Y **SP:** No spouse information **VI:** Died in his 64th year; was in the War of 1812 **P:** N **BLW:** Eligible **RG** N **MK** N **PH:** N **SS:** C pg 261; E pg 613; G pgs 575, 584; CZ pg 236 **BS:** 37 pg 110; 245 **BS:** 196

POWELL, Joshua; b 172o; d 17 May 1781 RU: Captain/Patriot commanded a company in the Halifax Co Militia 1774-1777and paid for supplies for his company,1778 **CEM:**Halifax Co memorial War monument; loc jct Mountain Rd & Rt 501, Halifax; Halifax **GS:** N **SP:**Mary (__) ((__-17 May 1781) **VI:** Memorialized as died 17 May 1781 with no gravesite found **P:** N **BLW:** N **RG:** Y **MK:** N **PH:** N **SS:** DAR A092040; D vol 2 pg 437; G pg 184; SAR P-272767 **BS:** Halifax Co War Memorial

ROYALL, Sarah; b 3 Feb 1715, 21 Nov 1805 **RU:** Patriot; as a widow and head of household,she paid personal property taxes in Halifax Co in 1782 which was a supply tax for Rev War expenses: **CEM:** Terry Family; GPS 36.749225,-78.848479; 1154 N Terrys Bridge Rd (Rt 613); Halifax **GS:** Y **SP:** Nathaniel Terry (1724-21 Apr 1780) **VI:** Daug of William Royall and Sarah Povell **P:** N **BLW:** N **RG:** N **MK:** N **PH:** N **SS:** ER Halifax Co 1782 tax list **BS:** 196

SHACKELFORD, William; b 1728, Hanover Co; d 23 Nov 1777 **RU:** Second Lieutenant, Capt Thomas Thweatt's Co, 14th VA Regt,Cont Line commanded by Col Charles Lewis; was killed in the Battle of Germantown, PA **CEM:**Halifax Co memorial War monument; loc jct Mountain Rd & Rt 501, Halifax; Halifax **GS:** N **SP:**Rebecca Cook, **VI:** Memorialized as died 23 Nov 1777 on battlefield with no gravesite found; assignee representative for receiving BLW of 100 acres 13 Apr 1784 was William Reynolds **P:** N **BLW:** Y **RG:** Y **MK:** N **PH:** N **SS:** DAR A102502; E pg 702; F pg 69; SAR P-287504 **BS:** Halifax Co War Memorial

SHIELDS, Alexander; b 1760; d 1832 **RU:** Private, served in Captian John Willson's Co, Augusta Co Militia **CEM:** Stonewall Jackson Memoria/AKA Oak Grove; **GPS** 37.780830, -79.445060; Lexington; S Main St **GS:** Y **SP:** Mar 1796, Pheobe Caruthers **VI:** Had tavern license in 1802 & 1820 in Lexington; served in War of 1812 as a First Sergeant **P:** N **BLW:** N **RG:** N **MK:** N **PH:** N **SS:** E pg 708 **BS:** SAR member submission

SMITH, William; b Jan 1756; d 12 Feb 1823 **RU** Private serv in Illinois Regt under Gen George Rogers Clark **CEM:** Dumfries Public; **GPS** 38.568729,-77.333938; 17821 Mine Rd, Dumfries; Prince William **GS:** Y **SP:** Margaret (__)(__-21 Oct 1821) **VI:** Perhaps the person this name rec'd BLW #12531-100-7 Jul 1792, assignee Robert Means **P:** N **BLW:** Y **RG:** N **MK:** N **PH:** Y **SS:** G pgs 697, 703 **BS:** 196

STEVENS, John; b 1764; d 8 Feb 1820 **RU:** Corporal, served in 1St VA State Regt & 2d, 6th & 7th Cont Line **CEM:** Masonic; **GPS** 38.4839820,-77.9929353; 950 N Main St; Culpeper **GS:** Y **SP:** Mar 8 Dec 1789, Mary Williams (c1765-11 May 1828) **VI:** Son of Gen Edward Stevens & Gilly Coleman (1746-1820); served in War of 1812 **P:** N **BLW:** N **RG:** N **MK:** N **PH:** N **SS:** E pg 740 **BS:** 245

STIMSON, Jeremiah, Jr; b 23 Aug 1749, Prince George Co, MD; d 25 Feb 1822 **RU:** Patriot, signed Oath of Allegence 1777, and paid personal property tax, 1782, Pittsylvania Co **CEM:** Jeremiah Stimson Family; **GPS** not determined; Ringgold; Pittsylvania **GS:** Y **SP:** Rachel (__) (14 Feb 1752-Dec 1806) **VI:** Son of Jeremiah Stimson, Sr & Rachel Ringgold **P:** N **BLW:** N **RG:** N **PH:** N **SS:** ER Pittsylvania Land Tax List 1782 & Oath of Allegience List 1777 **BS:** 196

TAYLOR, Margaret; b 20 Mar 1739; Norfolk; d 2 Mar 1812 **RU:** Patriot, gave material aid to cause, Northampton Co **CEM:** Eyre Hall; **GPS** 37.313824,-75.981967; 3215 Eyre Hill Drive, Cheriton; Northampton **GS:** Y **SP:** Severn Eyre (1735-25 Jan 1773, Norfolk) **VI:** nothing further **P:** N **BLW:** N **RG:** N **MK:** N **PH:** N **SS:** AL Ct Bk Lists Northampton Co **BS:** 196

TATSAPAUGH, Peter; b 1752 Lancaster Co, PA, d 5 Oct 1818 **RU:** Sergeant, Capt Peter Mantz's Company of Infantry, MD Militia serving Sep 1775-Oct 1776 **CEM:** Saint Paul's Episcopal Ch; **GPS** 38.799534,-77.056517; loc Sect 4, site 170, Wilkes St, Alexandria City **GS:** Y Gov't **SP:** Mar 1) Margaret Hooff, 2) Susanna V Tatsapaugh(1763-10 Jul 1830) **VI:** Son of George Adam Dortzbach (23 Apr 1722, Ger-7 Apr1780 Frederick MD); alternate surname spelling Tertesebaugh & Tatsebaugh; appears to have accepted his mother's maiden name **P:** N **BLW:** N **RG:** Y **MK:** SAR bronze **PH:** Y **SS:** B; SAR P-329280 cites MD Historical Mag (190), pg 50 **BS:** 196

THORNTON, Francis, b 1737 Spotsylvania Co; d 1795 **RU:** Patriot, signer of the Leedstown Resolutions, 27 Feb 1766 **CEM:**Thornton/Forbes/Washington; **GPS** 38.314274,-77.468399' loc vic jct Hunter St & Princess Anne St; Fredericksburg **GS:** N **SP:** Ann Thompson (1744-1815), daug of John Thompson(1702-1772) & Ann Brayne (1685-1758) **VI:** Son of Francis Thornton, III (1712-1749) & Frances Gregory(1718-1790) **P:** N **BLW:** N **RG:** N **MK:** N **PH:** N **SS:** Leedstown Resolutions 1766; **BS:** 196

VENABLE, Charles; b 12 Apr 1730, Hanover Co; d 31 Oct 1815 **RU:** Captain, commanded a company, Prince Edward Co 1778 **CEM:** Hamden-Sydney **GPS** not determined; loc Old Stable Hill Plantation, Old Slade Hill Rd; Prince Edward **GS:** U **SP:** Elixabeth Ann Smith (1733, Port Royal, King George Co-1793) **VI:** Nothing further data **P:** N **BLW:** N **RG:** Y **MK:** N **PH:** N **SS:** DAR A168417; AZ pg 224 SAR P-310641 **BS:** 196

WADE, Edward; b c1750; d 26 Apr 1776 **RU:** First Lt, commissioned 7 Mar 1776, 7th VA Regt Cont Line; died while serving in unit **CEM:**Halifax Co memorial War monument; loc jct Mountain Rd & Rt 501, Halifax; Halifax **GS:** N **SP:** Mar 15 Oct 1768, Charlotte Co,:Letty Martin (25 Sep 1747___) **VI:** Memorialized as died 26 Apr 1776 on battlefield with no gravesite found; assignee son William Shackleford receiving BLW # 9476 for 3330 acres and #9777 of 150 acres 1 Jan 1838 **P:** N **BLW:** Y heir **RG:** Y **MK:** N **PH:** N **SS:** DAR A119682; C pg 524; E pg 797; N pg 884; AP Fold 3 serv index cards; SAR P-311295 **BS:** Halifax Co War Memorial

WILLIAMS, John; b 1734, Spotsylvania Co, d 1777, Orange Co **RU:** Patriot, signer of the Leedstown Resolutions, 27 Feb 1766; perhaps served as a Culpeper minuteman in Orange Co **CEM:** Culpeper National; **GPS** 38.469700,-77.991898; loc N of E Chandler St vic US Ave; Culpeper **GS:** U **SP:** Susannah Ellis, daug of Joseph Ellis & Elizabeth Perkins of Goochland Co **VI:** No further data **P:** N **BLW:** N **RG:** N **MK:** N **PH:** N **SS:** Leedstown Resolutions 1766; **BS:** 196

WILSON, James Eli; b 8 Mar 1758, Rockingham Co; d 6 Dec 1810 **RU:**Private Capt Trimble's Co, Augusta Co Militia **CEM:** Doe Hill; **GPS** 38.432802,-79.443299; 7617 Doe Hill Rd (Rt 654), Doe Hill; Highland **GS:** U **SP:**Mar 29 Mar 1785, Elizabeth Hempenstall (1755-1833) **VI:** No further data **P:** U

BLW: U **RG:** N **MK:**N **PH:** N **SS:** E pg 836 **BS:** 196

WOOD, Thomas; b 1700, Middlesex Co; d 13 Feb 1777 **RU:** Patriot,was Deputy Commissioner, Auditor of Public Accounts Essex Co **CEM:**Good Hope Baptist Church; GPS 37.856559,-76.826658; 342 Johnsonville Rd, Dunnsville; Essex **GS:** Y no dates **SP:** No info **VI:** Son of John Wood (1664-1740) & Mary Church (1666-1748) **P:** N **BLW:** N **RG:** N **MK:** N **PH:** N **SS:**AL Ct Bk Essex Co, list **BS:** 196

WOOD; William Crane, Jr; b 1753, Albemarle Co; d 5 May 1820 **RU:** 2/LT, sworn in 22 Jan 1778, in Capt Paulin Anderson Co, Amelia Co Militia **CEM:** Wood; GPS unk; Rt 620 nr Rt 616, Rodophil; Amelia **GS:** N **SP:** 1) Martha Glen, 2) Elizabeth Burke (1765-1817) **VI:** Son of William Wood (__-1811) & Anne Crane (1733-1770) **P:** N **BLW:** N **RG:** Y **MK:** N **PH:** N **SS:** DAR A128273;E pg 843; AZ pg 180; P-323820 **BS:** 196

WRIGHT, John; b 30 Oct 1728; d 1791 **RU:** Captain, Fauquier Co Militia impressed items listed in public claims **CEM:** Wright-James; GPS 38.504946,-77.760893; 6200 Liberty Rd, Bealton: Fauquier **GS:** N **SP:** No spousal data **VI:** Nothing further **P:** U **BLW:** U **RG:** N **MK:**N **PH:** N **SS** Lib VA Public Claims Fauquier Co llst him as Captain impressing items **BS:** 196

WYATT, Edward, b 1759; d Mar 1831 **RU:** Private, Capt Thomas Miner's Co, 2d VA State Regt, Oct 1778 seving long enough to receive BLW **CEM:** Carraway; GPS 36.917198,-77.566399; loc S of Bolster's Rd, E of pond in field; Dinwiddie **GS:** Y **SP:** No spousal data **VI:** No further data **P:** N **BLW:** Y rec'd by son William **RG:** Y **MK:** N **PH:** N **SS:** C pg 384; E pg 851; N pg 811; AP ser rec & roll ; SAR P-325435 **BS:** 196

WYATT, William, Jr; b 22 Jan 1742; d 28 Feb 1815 **RU:** Private, enl 13 Feb 1778 Capt Henry Faunteroy's Co in 5th VA Regt; after served in 3rd,4th, 6th, 9th, 11[th.], 15th VA Regts **CEM:** Dumtries Public; GPS 38.34110, -77.19964; 17821 Mine Rd, Dumfrries; Prince William; **GS :** N **SP:** 1) Franses Newton, (2 Nov 1747-15 Jun 1783), daug of William Newton & Mary Holloway, 2) Elizabeth Snoe **VI:** Son of William Wyatt (1707-1774) & Lettice Nichols (1706-1776) Cenotath monument memorializes him in the Greenville Presbyterian Ch in SC; rec'd BLW 100 acres 6 Jun 1783 **P:** U **BLW:** Y **RG:** N **MK:** N **PH:** N **SS:** C pg 517; E pg 851; F pg 78; CZ pg 333 **BS:** 196

YOUNG, James; b 1758; d 1831 **RU:** Served in Capt Moses White's and/or William Satterly's Co, Col Hazen's, Cont Trps 1777-1779 **CEM:** St George's Episcopal; GPS 38.302678,-77.459859; 905 Princess Anne St **GS:** N listed on Parish Register as unmarked grave **SP:** Susan Smith (1784-1836) **VI:** No further data **P:** U **BLW:** U **RG:** N **MK:**N **PH:** N **SS:** E pg 854; AP Fold3 serv index cards; CZ pg 334 **BS:** 196

Made in the USA
Middletown, DE
15 May 2023

30589152R00404